The Encyclopedia of **British Film**

Also by Brian McFarlane

Lance Comfort

The Companion to Australian Film (*with Geoff Mayer and Ina Bertrand*)

An Autobiography of British Cinema

Novel to Film: An Introduction to the Theory of Adaptation

Sixty Voices: Celebrities Recall the Golden Age of British Cinema

New Australian Cinema: Sources and Parallels in American and British Film (*with Geoff Mayer*)

Australian Cinema 1970-1985

Cross-Country: An Anthology of Australian Poetry (*co-ed, with John Barnes*)

Words and Images: Australian Novels into Film

Martin Boyd's 'Langton' Novels

The Encyclopedia of
British Film

Edited by **BRIAN McFARLANE**

Associate Editor **Anthony Slide**

Foreword by **PHILIP FRENCH**

Methuen

For my wife Geraldine, with love

First published by Methuen in 2003

Copyright © 2003 Brian McFarlane, Anthony Slide
Foreword © 2003 Philip French

Methuen Publishing Limited
215 Vauxhall Bridge Road, London, SW1V 1EJ

Methuen Publishing Ltd Reg. No. 3543167

A CIP catalogue record for this book is available
from the British Library

ISBN 0 413 77301 9

Designed by Bryony Newhouse

Printed and bound in Great Britain by The Bath Press

Typeset by SX Composing DTP, Rayleigh, Essex

CONTENTS

FOREWORD

This is a book I've been waiting for all my life, though inevitably it's bigger and better than it could have been when I first needed it. Let me explain why.

Mid-20th century, when as a provincial (or 'regional', the preferred BBC term that long preceded standard PC) grammar school sixth-former I was beginning to take a serious interest in film, my school library owned three books on the cinema. They were Paul Rotha's *The Film Till Now*, Raymond Spottiswoode's *A Grammar of Film* and Béla Balasz's *Theory of Film*. My local public library didn't need more than half a shelf to contain its complete cinematic collection in a section devoted to Theatre, Music and the Arts. I owned two or three books about the movies, all Penguin paperbacks by Roger Manvell – his seminal *Film*, first published in 1945, and a couple of editions of his short-lived *Penguin Film Review* – which had to be bought because they were not available for public borrowing back then when libraries were strictly forbidden to put hardcovers on paperbacks. In the 1960s I worked quite often with Manvell on the air. I also corresponded with, but never met, Paul Rotha, who became violently involved with the one-time British starlet Constance Smith. After her success as the Irish servant at Windsor Castle, stealing scenes from Irene Dunne and Alec Guinness in *The Mudlark* (1950), Smith was signed up by 20th Century-Fox and went to Hollywood with her husband Bryan Forbes. Their marriage soon broke up and Forbes returned to Britain to establish one of the most significant careers in British cinema. Smith was dropped by Fox and came home to engage in her sad publicised affair with Rotha.

Manvell, a decent, jolly, earnest man, more educationist than critic, had grave reservations about British cinema. The pictorial section of *Film* included twice as many illustrations from the Odessa Steps sequence of *Battleship Potemkin* than from the whole history of British feature films, though he put in 40 stills from British documentaries. Like many of his profesional circle (John Grierson, Basil Wright, Edgar Anstey, Athur Elton), he was forever fighting to have cinema accepted as a legitimate art form. Manvell was embarrassed by popular entertainment and looked with suspicion on film as an industry, though in fact the documentaries he admired were with few exceptions subsidised by private or public enterprise organisations. In the 1950 edition of *Film*, Manvell managed to list 30 films of high quality made by the British film industry between 1946 and 1949 (e.g. Ealing at its zenith, Lean's Dickens movies, Carol Reed at his peak, Powell and Pressburger in full flower). One would be pushed to name another list as good in the theatre or fiction of the time. Nevertheless he felt obliged to proclaim that this had been 'a period in which the flag was lowered to half-mast in the public interest'. In comparison with the films of Rossellini, he went on, 'How many of them do not appear like faded leaves painted in exquisite detail by a lady in Cornwall?'. We were not encouraged to like British cinema as an institution. Indeed we were urged to disparage it as socially and artistically inauthentic – contaminated by theatre and literature, as well as by patronising middle-class attitudes.

Meanwhile, the indefatigable Manvell played a part in initiating *The History of the British Cinema* by Rachael Low, the first volume of which, covering the years 1896 to 1906, appeared in 1948. It attracted from C.A. Lejeune, the *Observer*'s film critic, the backhanded compliment 'although some of the earlier records make amusing reading to modern eyes, the book has the coolly impersonal authority of a Government White Paper'. Many of us were to grow up and grow old with Low's unfinished, seemingly unfinishable history. When the first volume appeared I was officially too young to get into an 'A' certificate film; when her seventh and last (bringing the story up to 1939) appeared in 1985, I had turned fifty. By then, starting in the late 60s, books on the movies were being published in abundance both by trade publishers and university presses.

But it took some time for the British cinema to benefit from this, largely because the French New Wave, as critics and directors, were as cool towards Britain as they were enthusiastic about Hollywood, and engendered this attitude in their admirers in the English-speaking world. This was rather odd considering that François Truffaut, the most quotably contemptuous of the group, included those archetypal Londoners, Chaplin and Hitchcock, in his personal pantheon. In the BFI's trail-blazing series of monographs, Cinema One, which began in 1965, only two of the 28 books it published were devoted to British cinema – the inevitable *Studies in Documentary* and Kevin Brownlow's account of the making of *It Happened Here*, the independent feature he co-directed with Andrew Mollo. Brownlow made his considerable reputation as an historian of American silent cinema and a restorer of silent pictures, mostly American. Not until the 1990s did he turn his attentions to British cinema with his authorised biography of David Lean.

Things at last began to change significantly in the mid-1970s, and if one were looking for a milestone it would be Charles Barr's *Ealing Studios*, a seminal work, still the best book about the British cinema. Rejected as too serious (probably because insufficiently anecdotal) by the publishing house that commissioned it, *Ealing Studios* appeared in 1977 under the auspices of the small company of Cameron and Tayleur. It was edited and designed by its co-publisher Ian Cameron, using the style made familiar by the influential auteur-orientated *Movie*, that had been launched by Cameron, V.F. Perkins, Mark Shivas, Paul Mayersberg and others in 1962. This editorial group were as hostile to the torpor – as they saw it – of British cinema as Gavin Lambert, Lindsay Anderson, Karel Reisz and their fellow members of the editorial board of *Sequence* had been a dozen years or so before. Broadly speaking, what united these two generations was their dislike of what A. Alvarez, writing at the time as the influential poetry editor of the *Observer*, called 'the gentility principle'. What divided them were their different attitudes towards realism and the continuing post-war debate over political and social commitment. All the *Movie* collective admired Robert Hamer and Alexander Mackendrick, and most of them embraced the gifted, short-lived Seth Holt. Gavin Millar came to the defence of Karel Reisz and Lindsay Anderson in *Movie*; and Raymond Durgnat made a vigorous case there for the reappraisal of Michael Powell. Anyway, Cameron brought out Barr's book, and I managed to write about it in both the *Observer* and the *Times Literary Supplement*, as well as having it discussed on my BBC arts programme, *Critics' Forum*.

My enthusiasm for Barr's book received extra fuel from my embarrassment at having reluctantly withdrawn in 1973 (as a result of commitments at the BBC) from writing an authorised history of Ealing, drawing on Sir Michael Balcon's archives.

I'd come to know Sir Michael, one of the toughest, most charming and principled men I've ever met, as a colleague on the BFI's Production Board, and I'm glad he lived to read Barr's book which honoured him, as I had hoped to.

Barr had been involved in various forms of film education before teaching movie studies at university. His *Ealing Studios* created academic waves, which attracted the Australian editor of this *Encyclopedia* to graduate studies under Barr at East Anglia. Film studies had been established in the Department of English and American Studies there since the early 1970s. Barr's work and that of his colleagues and former followers have gone some way to tempering my hostility to media studies in higher education, something I advocated and sponsored but have at times come to have certain doubts about, even to regret. Still, one way or another, serious attention has been given to British cinema these past 25 years, much of it coming from academe, whether out of true enthusiasm or the searching for virgin territory. Apart from Barr one thinks especially of Jeffrey Richards, Anthony Aldgate and Robert Murphy on campus; of Roy Armes, Alexander Walker, Geoffrey Macnab, Charles Drazin and George Perry in the outside world.

So with the 20th century ended and the 21st getting on its way, British cinema is at last getting the attention it deserves; monographs on unfashionable directors from Manchester University; studies of individual films in a new series published by I.B. Tauris; articles in magazines like the *Journal of Popular British Cinema*. Forty years ago volumes of Rachael Lowe's magnum opus and Charles Oakley's *Where We Came In: The Story of the British Cinematograph Industry* (1963) were almost alone on my shelves. There are now several dozen, most from Britain but some from the States, and several in French. Bertrand Tavernier, Philippe Pilard and the editors of *Positif* have done wonders in introducing British cinema to France, helping to establish the annual Festival du Film Britannique at Dinard (it began in 1990) and culminating in the magnificent season of British movies at the Beaubourg Centre in 1999. It was Pilard who began his revisionary 1989 book *Le Nouveau Cinéma Britannique* with the lapidary words: '*Il y a un fantôme qui hante le cinéma britannique. Il est français. Il se nomme François Truffaut.*'

We now know that Truffaut was wrong. The British cinema may have been in a state of crisis from World War One onwards, but it is in fact a rich and fascinating story, an essential thread in world cinema and a central part of the social and cultural history of 20th-century Britain. It has also been the better, rather than the worse, for involving the theatre and literature to such an extent. Not insignificantly, one of the greatest British novelists, Graham Greene, has been more involved as critic, screenwriter, student of film technique and source of adapted material, than any other writer of comparable status the world over. By a nice irony, Greene made his only screen appearance in a Truffaut film, *La nuit américaine*, albeit under a pseudonym, playing an English accountant preparing to pull the plug on a French film.

This massive tome is the culmination of a quarter of a century of enthusiasm, diligent research and scholarship by McFarlane and his associates. The books that working cinéphiles have beside their desks – Leslie Halliwell, Ephraim Katz, David Thomson and others – have rarely been fair to British cinema. They've done scant justice to what they include, and constantly irritate the user by what they ignore. More significantly, for us living in the British Isles, they haven't boldly gone, as we say on *Star Trek*'s USS Enterprise, to definitively record the individual contributions of artists small and large, on screen and behind the cameras, metropolitan and regional. We need our own reference work, to consult or browse in, and McFarlane and his team have produced a book that does this in detail, from the Brighton School to Jamie Bell, from the Sheffield Photo Company to Ealing.

This book is packed with extraordinary revelations. I had no idea, for instance, that Marianne Stone, most famous now as the silent Vivienne Darkbloom in Kubrick's *Lolita*, had appeared in more movies than any other British actress. I knew her principally as the wife of Peter Noble, who had abandoned a serious critical career (as author of *The Negro in Film* and the first biography of Orson Welles) to be the sweet-natured, sybaritic showbiz writer for trade magazines. McFarlane's *Encyclopedia of British Film* will take its place beside the late Denis Gifford's labour of love, *The British Film Catalogue*. His *Encyclopedia* is an essential work that will grow over the years as its readers send in their emendations or suggestions, and as more movies get made.

Philip French
April 2003

INTRODUCTION

The purpose of this book is to fill a gap. There have been various books which cover, for example, stars, directors and studios relevant to British cinema history, as well as a heartening growth of critical and theoretical works from many points of view. To date, however, there has been no comprehensive reference book which might act as, in the words of one of its contributors, 'the first port of call' for anyone wanting to pursue an interest in British cinema.

In large international reference works, British cinema is apt to be, if not exactly marginalised, skimpily treated at best, with even key figures in its history, whether before or behind the camera, quite frequently omitted. In one well-known work, for instance, Phyllis Calvert is missing whereas Joanne Dru's career is generously canvassed, and this is only one graphic example of the way in which the (in many ways deserved) dominance of Hollywood has been allowed to overshadow achievement in other cinemas.

What is a British film?

Whereas the answer to this question might have seemed simple in the 1940s – a British film was made in British studios and/or locations, with predominantly British personnel involved – this has clearly not been the case since the last two decades of the 20th century. (And one might note in passing, the idea of 'Britishness' in those earlier decades also tended to embrace first the 'Empire', then the 'Commonwealth'; some consideration is given to this, but the emphasis is, of course, on the film industry centred in the UK.) One could apply an arbitrary rule relating to where the finance has come from or where the film was made or who the film's makers were, but no hard and fast categorisation of this kind seems satisfactory. The aim of this book has, in this respect, been to tend towards inclusiveness. In listing at the end of entries the OTHER BRITISH FILMS in which individual film-makers have been involved, if there is some ascertainable British involvement the abbreviation UK will follow the film's title or year, then in alphabetic order, abbreviations indicating the other countries that had some substantial involvement. UK is listed first, not because its contribution is necessarily the most important but because without its contribution the film would not be listed at all. It is not possible in a work such as this to distinguish the extent of contributions made by several countries in every film: the mere listing of the relevant countries, though, conforms to the 'first port of call' approach. For example, anyone making a special study of the film *Sunshine* will find it listed among Ralph Fiennes's OTHER BRITISH FILMS as follows: *Sunshine* (2000, UK/Austria/Can/Ger/Hung) and take more detailed researches

from there. A film such as *Batman* (1989) was substantially shot at Pinewood, yet it will scarcely seem to most people to qualify as a British film. *Nicholas and Alexandra* (1971), designated US in some places, UK in others, was filmed mainly in Spain and Britain, with almost entirely British cast and crew. There seems no point in excluding a film on arbitrary grounds if its inclusion will help to give a fuller picture of the career involved.

In the *BFI Film and Television Handbook 1999*, one finds six 'UK Film Categories' and the list is worth repeating here:

- **Category A** Films where the cultural and financial impetus is from the UK and the majority of the personnel are British

- **Category B** Majority UK Co-Productions. Films in which, though there are foreign partners, there is a UK cultural content and a significant amount of British finance and personnel

- **Category C** Minority UK Co-Productions. Foreign (non-US) films in which there is a small UK involvement in finance or personnel

- **Category D** American films with a UK creative and/or minor financial involvement

- **Category D1** American financed or part financed films made in the UK. Most films have a British cultural content

- **Category D2** American films with some UK financial involvement.

The list is repeated partly to suggest the complexity of the matter and partly because it has been used as an unofficial guideline in the present book. In April 2002, however, the definition of 'British' was tightened in a parliamentary Budget statement aimed at curtailing abuse of tax breaks originally designed to encourage British film-makers but which had been used by producers describing as British films which in all important ways are foreign.

For the purpose of deciding whether an individual might be included in this encyclopedia, the number of UK or part-UK films in which he/she was involved has been taken into account, and, in the case of co-productions, the number would be arrived at along lines suggested above. Where film-makers have had substantial careers in countries other than Britain, this will normally be noted in the descriptive paragraphs preceding the British filmography at the end of the entry. For major figures every attempt has been made to list all OTHER BRITISH FILMS; for others, that phrase is followed by the word INCLUDE.

Some emerging patterns

It is not possible to have been so intensely engaged in a project of this size without a sense of recurring patterns. In most cases, these patterns do not represent especially new insights so much as the reinforcing, through the accumulation of evidence as distinct from generalised feeling, of what one had previously suspected.

It was striking, in writing the several thousand biographical entries, how few wholly *film* careers there have been in British cinema. In the first half of the 20th century, there was a remarkable reliance on stage background, especially among performers but also to some extent among directors, writers and designers. This connection between British cinema and British theatre remains to this day, but it is less pronouncedly a matter of the theatre's being the likeliest path into film. Nor is there so strong a sense of personnel moonlighting in cinema while carving out their serious careers on stage. There is no doubt that this was previously the case for many, and when one reads obituaries of actors and actresses in particular it is quite common to find their film careers compressed into an unobtrusive paragraph. It was of course always geographically feasible for British actors to maintain careers in each medium because of the proximity of the film studios to the West End, but there was in addition a strong sense of cultural hierarchy involved.

From the 60s on, while the theatre connection remains, if less tenaciously, the links are more likely to be with television and the shift is not coincidental. Before the ascendancy of television, though, radio was a hugely popular entertainment form, and many film personnel either began in or continued to work in radio. However, as television ownership increased, the nature of the film-going habit, and those who practised it, changed both in numbers and in demographic terms. As television performers and programmes became popular, there would be a good deal of crossover to the cinema whose production output declined as television increasingly satisfied the appetite for moving images. These are large and complex questions and this is not the place to do more than allude to them.

What became a recurring refrain in the compilation of this encyclopedia was the sentence that said something like ' . . . but his first allegiance remained the stage' or ' . . . but television has persistently offered her more interesting work'. And this is not just a matter of performers, but of writers and directors and other personnel as well. Except perhaps for a brief shining hour in the 40s, cinema has always had to fight for its place in the sun of British cultural life, under serious pressure from competing media. While this book is essentially concerned with cinema, it seemed important to indicate where careers were at least partly, and sometimes predominantly, spent in these other media.

It is not just the performance media that have exerted a strong influence on British cinema, but what emerges as well are the very strong links with literature. Astonishing numbers of British films, at every period, were derived from novels, plays and short stories, and the British cinema's adaptations, so the conventional wisdom went, were much more respectful, more faithful than their Hollywood counterparts, where a famous work was acquired, gutted and reshaped to box-office success. Now, the Hollywood adaptors (including expat Brits) are more likely to be praised for their bolder response to their literary antecedents, but it was not always so. A good many authors and playwrights are included in this book, partly because their

works have been so much adapted and also because, in some cases, of their connections with the cinema (one thinks of Terence Rattigan, Graham Greene, Edgar Wallace and Hanif Kureishi, to pluck but four from the air). But apart from these obvious links with literature, one is struck by the prominence of the 'literary' in periods of highest distinction in British cinema. There is a strong reliance on the verbal, on the literary virtues of detailed characterisation and setting, and the well-made play's stress on structure, as well as on the predominance of literary sources in such productive periods as the mid 40s and the late 50s/early 60s.

Indeed, this matter of 'productive periods' asserts itself again and again. The encyclopedia, if read (improbably) from cover to cover would most likely reflect the rediscovery of British silent cinema, the quota-driven prolificacy of the 30s, the wonderful efflorescence of wartime and immediately postwar film-making, the 'New Wave' rejuvenation of the late 50s until the mid 60s, then no more than rather fitful starts until the 90s when production at least stepped up, even if quality and commercial success were variable. These periods of notable achievement have characteristically seen the emergence of new talents or of talents finally being given their heads, but they also need to be seen in terms of the industrial shifts that have helped to produce them. To this end, the entries on matters such as studio structures, legislation, finance and film-associated organisations are important. They have helped to highlight and sometimes to reconceptualise crucial shifts in British cinema history.

British cinema was often criticised in the past for being too resolutely middle-class in its orientation: it tended to espouse implicitly the values of middle-class decency and sobriety and to neglect especially not merely the values but the *value* of working-class life. This was never a wholly true proposition but it took account of certain tendencies. It was very instructive in writing the biographical entries for this book to note how many personnel had educational backgrounds involving major public schools and Oxbridge. This information has been included, not because one is in awe of it, but because it perhaps helps to explain the prevailing class attitudes of so much British cinema. Even when it has very clearly set out to explore other kinds of living, as the 30s documentarists or the New Wave film-makers did, it was often from precisely this kind of educational background. This is not to say that the mores implanted by the latter were uncritically endorsed but that this kind of background was so common in the industry that it needs to be taken into account in understanding its ideological cast. Again, with people now entering the industry from television or from the film schools, as they once routinely did from the famous acting schools, some change of perspectives might be expected.

That reference to the acting schools draws attention to another aspect of British cinema: the precariousness of its star system. It may be that those trained in the ensemble arts of the theatre and subsequently finding the theatre to be more clearly an actor's medium than the film were less likely than Hollywood players to be interested in pursuing star careers in film. It may be that they resisted the studios' attempts to build them into stars, or that the studios were less competent in doing so than their US counterparts. There were certainly popular domestic stars but only occasionally did they become international phenomena of the kind on which sturdy commercial industries are built. Again and again one was aware of the actors' preference for the stage and then by contrast the comparatively few of whom it could be said 'This was essentially a *film* star'. By a further contrast it was impossible not to be aware of the extraordinary richness of British film's character acting, and this refers not merely to those one-scene delights who could briefly vivify the most mundane enterprise but also to remarkable actors who never aspired to conventional stardom but often grabbed the chance to draw richly detailed character performances. Hence, the reader will find entries on the one hand for Sam Kydd and, on the other, for Mona Washbourne. One of the book's aims is to do justice to precisely such people: the stars, the major directors, the other key players, are written about everywhere, but the character people have very rarely been given the credit they deserve for their way of embedding often flimsy structures in recognisable reality.

Stars were characteristically a product of a studio system, most potently exemplified by Hollywood but emulated by the British industry from the later 20s to the 60s; emulated, that is, but not really rivalled. All the major studios (and production companies) and quite a number of the minor ones receive separate entries, and certainly some sense of their difference emerges. Rank and Associated British may seem confusable but on closer inspection their individuality is felt, and no one will confuse Ealing and Hammer, but none, it has to be acknowledged, ever quite assumed the aura of the Hollywood giants. This does not mean that their histories, or those of Tempean or Independent Artists or a number of others, are not worth pursuing; some of them knew exactly what they were doing and did it with great proficiency.

Reference to Ealing and Hammer inevitably invokes the genres of comedy and horror, not that the output of either studio was so narrowly circumscribed. The critically privileged modes of British cinema have been the realist and the literary but other genres have always been there vying for audience – if not always critical – favour. The various guises of melodrama, most famously typified in Gainsborough's costume melodrama, the long and changing history of the comedy genre from silent screen favourites to international successes such as *Notting Hill* (1999), the history of horror with its apotheosis in Hammer's output, the war film, the biopic, science-fiction and others: these all required separate entries because, despite the long-held official line, they have always been part of the texture of British cinema.

And running through all the research was the idea of Hollywood. Very often it beckoned with a siren song to British practitioners; sometimes it had its eye on how to make the most of British markets; sometimes its faded grandeur (stars and others) would be invoked to imbue the local industry with a touch of glamour – and to help with US distribution; almost always British film-makers have had to contend with the supremacy of Hollywood films at British box-offices. Some expatriate British fell in love with Hollywood and virtually never came back; others tried it and couldn't get back fast enough. One way or other, Hollywood is an unignorable motif in the tapestry of British cinema and it is highlighted constantly in the appraisals of individual careers.

The encyclopedia has been compiled out of enormous affection for and pleasure in British cinema. This has been the *sine qua non* of its inception and production. This does not imply, however, that it was put together with no regard for critical edge, though it does mean to avoid the merely idiosyncratic – as well as the merely blandly consensual.

Criteria for inclusion

The first task in preparing this encyclopedia was to establish the rules of selection. No work of this kind can ever be truly exhaustive, but my aim was to go well beyond the expected names. Because a book will always have some word limitation, the initial decision had to be whether to opt for 'less about more' or 'more about less'. In settling for the former, the aim was to ensure the inclusion of entries which might not usually be found in such a reference work. Obviously big names and companies, recurring genres and motifs have been allocated space commensurate with their importance, but among more than 5,800 entries are a good many that would not normally be found: these include hundreds of character actors, cinematographers, producers, editors, costume and production designers, special effects technicians, sound recordists and continuity personnel. Whereas the major figures are widely discussed in books and articles, many others who have also made their contributions to the history of British cinema have been persistently overlooked. There are dangers in opting for this approach; if this minor figure is included, then why not that one? Up to a point, this will always be unanswerable, but a part-answer lies in the idea of representativeness. Further, in choosing to acknowledge those often omitted, there is the chance of reducing the substance of other entries. The 'first port of call' perspective is perhaps an answer to this: the book is predicated on the notion that anyone wanting to do detailed research on, say, any person or company might see this as the starting point for that study.

For those whose careers were conducted largely in the decades from the 30s to the 80s, it was comparatively easy to decide inclusions: the scope of the film-maker's work would settle this. However, the silent period presented more problems: the period is now receiving much more attention than was the case a decade or so back and interesting careers, once overlooked, are being brought to light, some of which may be represented here for the first time in a reference book. At the other end of the century and into the new one, there is inevitably an element of clairvoyance involved. Again, the general rule favouring inclusiveness has been followed: new film-makers whose output, in some cases, is still small have been included where signs of real interest and promise have been discerned.

Non-biographical entries also present problems of selection. Companies and studios are comparatively easy but even with these, at the lesser end, there will be discriminations to be made. In relation to British silent cinema, in particular, recent scholarship has suggested there is more that is worthy of notice than has often – dismissively – been allowed. Thematic entries will always be contentious. Some will wonder at the inclusion of this concept and not of that other; some will exclaim at the omission, in such entries, of certain film titles. This is inevitable and the contention, one hopes, may provide matter for fruitful debate. One of the charms of an encyclopedia may also be the occasional surprising inclusion: we all tend to know what we would include, but it can sometimes be stimulating to find the unexpected. Film titles as such are not included as entries, partly because they would have made the book unwieldy and partly because there are plenty of places where information on individual films is available.

Sources of information are so numerous as to defy comprehensive listing. The characteristic procedure was to start by using works of international reference on the understanding that any British person or company listed here was sure to be necessary in this encyclopedia. Then it was a matter of working one's way down through works of increasing specialism in deciding which – say – cinematographers to include. In general, if there was doubt in a particular case I have settled for inclusion. I acknowledge all those earlier, more and less specialised works which helped establish the 'headwords' that form the basis of the present encyclopedia, and this includes many popular as well as scholarly sources.

As well as sifting written and electronic sources of information, more and less reliable, I must acknowledge gratefully those – perhaps two hundred – participants in British cinema, or their relatives, who provided data not otherwise readily available. One of the problems in compiling such a book is that some kinds of misinformation get handed down from one reference work to another. Not merely dates and places of birth and death, though there are plenty of mistakes about those, but matters of supposition which congeal into received wisdom. One example: obituaries for director Leslie Arliss suggested that he had developed his love of cinema while in Hollywood in the 1920s with his famous actor father George Arliss. There seemed reason to doubt this lineage and, indeed, the purchase of the birth and death certificates of Leslie Arliss established that his father was 'Collector to Gas Company' and that his real name was Arliss, whereas George Arliss's real name was Andrews. There are probably many other instances of the perpetuation of such errors: this one is quoted merely to suggest the extreme care that needs to be taken in accepting such information.

It is not of course possible to check birth and/or death certificates for about 4,500 biographical entries but wherever there has seemed room for doubt this has been done. The truth is simply elusive in some cases, and it is not, after all, the most important information relating to individuals. Where I have had to use a source that seems less than wholly reliable or less than exact (e.g., an interview with a '35-year-old director'), I have used the formula b c 1967, to indicate that, at very least, it is not clear which of two possible years might be accurate.

Sources

The sources enlisted in compiling the encyclopedia are too numerous to list in full, but some of the main ones are given below. All were useful but one learns to rely on no particular source for infallible information:

- International encyclopedias of film
- Reference works devoted to specific aspects of British film or dealing with it selectively (see Bibliography)
- The British Film Institute's SIFT Database and the *Film Index International* CD-Rom derived from it
- The *BFI Film and Television Handbook* (published annually from 1983)
- Denis Gifford's *The British Film Catalogue 1895–1970* (3rd edition): Volume 1: *Fiction Film, 1894–1994*; Volume 2: *Non-Fiction Film, 1888–1994*
- Old 'Who's Who' or similar volumes relating to cinema from the 1930s, 1940s and 1950s
- *Who's Who in the Theatre* (various editions)
- *International Who's Who* and *Who Was Who* (various editions)
- *British Television*, Oxford, 1996
- *Encyclopedia Britannica*

- Peter Noble's *British Film Yearbook*s and, later, *British Film and Television Handbook*s (various editions between the late 1940s and the early 1980s)
- Rachael Low's *The History of the British Film*, seven volumes, London, 1949–85
- Family Records Centre, London
- Principal Probate of the Family Division, London
- Obituaries in many newspapers, including *The Times*, *Independent*, *Guardian*, *Daily Telegraph*, *Variety*
- Journals and magazines, including *The Monthly Film Bulletin*, *Sight and Sound*, *Films and Filming*, *Picture Show*, *Picturegoer*
- Innumerable memoirs, biographies and autobiographies
- *Stage Deaths: A Biographical Guide to International Theatrical Obituaries* (1991)
- Interviews in newspapers and journals
- Individual testimony, oral and written, in answer to hundreds of letters and telephone calls
- Internet databases, including *Internet Movie Database* and *All-Movie Guide*, and many more specialised web sites devoted to British film and theatre
- The *International Motion Picture Almanac* (various years) and the *International Television Almanac* (various years)
- André Siscot's *Les gens du cinéma* [*Cinema's People*], Paris 1998.

Notes to the reader

The encyclopedia is obviously organised on alphabetic lines, whether the headwords indicate individuals, companies, studios, institutions or thematic entries. Within entries, words appearing in small capitals indicate a cross-reference to other entries, though some discretion has been exercised with regard to these. For instance, the word 'comedy' is not always highlighted if it is simply used in passing; the general rule is that the word is highlighted in such cases only if the reference is of a kind to suggest that it may be useful to follow up such a term in a thematic reference. All proper names, whether of individuals, companies, studios or institutions, are cross-referenced. Sometimes capitals are used even if the wording isn't exactly the same – e.g., DOCUMENTARY, DOCUMENTARY FILMS, DOCUMENTARY MOVEMENT, etc – but if it nevertheless seems worth making the cross-reference. Names given in **bold** in the text of an entry indicate that this person will not have a separate entry, though the actual name may be listed alphabetically when this is thought to be helpful.

Individual biographical entries begin with dates and places of birth, and where relevant, death. Where it may reasonably be assumed that a person is dead but the details of place and date have resisted research a question mark is used. If only a town name is given for either birth or death place, this means

- that it is in England and is the only town or village of that name (according to the AA 'Milemaster' CD), or
- that it is so much the better known of two possibilities as to be able to stand alone: for example, Brighton, standing alone clearly refers to the city in Sussex, as distinct from the village in Cambridgeshire; the much less well known village would be followed by its county name, or
- that it is so well known (e.g. Chicago) as not to need the country's name.

If only county or country is given, this means that no further reliable information could be found.

These biographical entries are followed by a list of either all, or a selection of, other British films, listed according to release dates. The dates in these lists come at the end of all the films in any given year, and any information following such dates is applicable to all the films in that year. Where information may be applicable to only some of the films of that year, it will be given after each film. If a person's credits all derive from the performance of one function (e.g., he/she was always a designer), then what follows OTHER BRITISH FILMS (INCLUDE) will be just titles and dates; when he/she performs other functions, this will be noted in ways that will make clear which was relevant to which film, either by breaking up the list into chief functions, or by a parenthetical abbreviation after the particular film. OTHER of course means 'not referred to in the preceding descriptive paragraph(s)'.

Some examples:

(1) the last part of the OTHER BRITISH FILMS list for James Mason reads:

> *Great Expectations, Inside Out, The Water Babies* (UK/Pol) (1975), *Voyage of the Damned* (1976), *Cross of Iron* (1977, UK/Ger), *Murder by Decree* (UK/Can), *The Passage* (1978), *North Sea Hijack* (1979), *Evil Under the Sun* (1981), *Group Madness* (1983, doc).

Where no gloss follows the date, it may be assumed that all the films preceding that date are UK unless otherwise noted, as in the cases of *The Water Babies* and *Murder by Decree*, and that the first three films were all released in the UK in 1975.

(2) in the John Mills entry, the filmography is introduced thus:

OTHER BRITISH FILMS: (a, unless noted)

and the 'other' films from 1947 to 1949 are listed as follows:

> *So Well Remembered* (1947), *Three Days* (d, short), *The History of Mr. Polly* (+ p) (1948), *Friend of the Family* (short, narr), *The Rocking Horse Winner* (+ p) (1949).

In the one film listed for 1947, he only acted; of the two films for 1949, he only directed the former (a short film) and produced as well as acted in the latter. The + sign always indicates additional to the main function.

In many cases, the filmography will be followed by BIBLIOG (to a maximum of three) and giving (auto)biographical works and/or key critical texts. Unless these have some further relevance, they will not be listed again in the SELECT BIBLIOGRAPHY at the end of the book.

As to film dates, release dates have been based largely on the British Film Institute's CD-Rom, *Film Index International*, and on Denis Gifford's *The British Film Catalogue, 1895–1970*. On rare occasions when there is a serious gap between dates of production and of release this has been noted.

All entries bear either (a) the signature of the contributor; (b) the letters AS (Anthony Slide), who had the major responsibility for silent screen contributions; or (3) no signature, which indicates that the entry was written by the book's compiler/editor.

Abbreviations

The following abbreviations have been used:

a	actor, actress
AA	(American) Academy Award (Oscar)
AAn	(American) Academy Award nomination
add dial	additional dialogue
adpt	adapter
adptn	adaptation
anim	animation
art d	art director
ass	assistant
assoc	associate
BAA	British Academy Award
BAAn	British Academy Award nomination
c	cinematographer, director of cinematography/photography
cam op	camera operator
co-(d) (p) (sc)	co-(director) (producer) (screenwriter), etc
comm	commentator
commy	commentary
comp	composer
cond	conductor
cont	continuity
cos des	costume design
d	director
des	(production) design
DOP	director of photography (only used anecdotally)
doc	documentary
e	editor
ex	executive
fx	special effects
m	music
m d	music director
narr	narrator
orch	orchestration
p	producer
ph	photography
prod man	production manager
RN:	real name
sc	screenplay, scriptwriter
sd	sound
st	story
sup	supervising/supervisor
supp a	supporting actor/actress
2uc	second unit
unc	uncredited
w	writer (i.e. other than scriptwriter)

Examples of use:

In the entry for Robert S. Baker the last part of his filmography reads as follows:

> OTHER BRITISH FILMS: (p, unless noted): [. . .] *The High Terrace* (1956), *Hour of Decision, Stranger in Town, Professor Tim** (+ sc) (1957), *Stormy Crossing, The Trollenberg Terror, Sally's Irish Rogue**, *Blind Spot* (+ co-st), *Blood of the Vampire, Jack the Ripper* (+ d, co-c) (1958), *Home is the Hero**, *The Flesh and the Fiends* (1959), *Boyd's Shop**, *The Hellfire Club* (+ d), *The Treasure of Monte Cristo* (+ d) (1960), *What a Carve Up!* (1961), *Crossplot* (1969). *=Made in Dublin.

Acronyms and other abbreviations commonly used include:

ACT/ACTT	Association of Cine-Technicians/of Cinema and Television Technicians
ABPC	Associated British Picture Corporation
Aust	Australia/n (Austria, comparatively rare, is given in full)
BFI	British Film Institute
CBE	Commander of the British Empire
CH	Companion of Honour
G-B	Gaumont-British
LSO	London Symphony Orchestra
LSE	London School of Economics
MGM	Metro-Goldwyn-Mayer
MOI	Ministry of Information
NFTS	National Film and Television School
NZ	New Zealand
OBE	Officer of the British Empire
OM	Order of Merit
OUDS	Oxford University Dramatic Society
POW	Prisoner of War
RCM	Royal College of Music
S Af	South Africa
UK	United Kingdom
US	United States
WW1/2	World War One/Two

Abbreviations for countries involved in co-productions are self-explanatory.

Drama schools/theatres:

- Central School — Central School of Speech and Drama
- RADA — Royal Academy of Dramatic Art
- RSC — Royal Shakespeare Company
- LAMDA — London Academy of Music and Dramatic Art
- Webber-Douglas — Webber-Douglas School of Singing and Dramatic Art
- Guildhall — Guildhall School of Music and Drama
- National — National Theatre London
- Stratford — Memorial Theatre, Stratford-upon-Avon (as distinct from Stratford, East London and Stratford, Ontario)

Some very long titles abbreviated:

Can Hieronymus Merkin Ever Forget . . . for *Can Hieronymus Merkin Ever Forget Mercy Humppe and Find True Happiness?* (1969)

Decline and Fall . . . for *Decline and Fall of a Bird Watcher* (1968)

Dr Strangelove . . . for *Dr Strangelove; or How I Learned to Stop Worrying and Love the Bomb* (1963)

The Englishman Who Went Up . . . for *The Englishman Who Went Up a Hill but Came Down a Mountain* (1995)

Greystoke . . . for *Greystoke: The Legend of Tarzan, Lord of the Apes* (1984)

Marat/Sade . . . for *The Persecution and Assassination of Jean-Paul Marat . . .* (1966)

Rob Roy . . . for *Rob Roy, the Highland Rogue* (1953)

The Story of Robin Hood . . . for *The Story of Robin Hood and His Merrie Men* (1953)

Those Magnificent Men . . . for *Those Magnificent Men in Their Flying Machines . . .* (1965)

When *Carry On* films appear in a series, the first two words are replaced with . . . ; similarly with the *Confessions of . . .* series, when there is no possibility of confusion.

Acknowledgements

It is hard to imagine a more collaborative exercise than the assembling of an encyclopedia – except perhaps making a film. In this case, so many people and institutions have been involved in ways great and small, all of them valuable, that it is hard to know where to begin and it is impossible to name them all.

First, though, I must thank the Australian Government's Research Council without whose extremely generous grant I doubt if I could have undertaken the project. This grant, supplemented by follow-up grants from the Monash University Arts Faculty and its School of Literary, Visual and Performance Studies, made possible the employment of a research assistant for three years and a research trip to London in 2000.

Without my research assistant Melinda Hildebrandt the whole process would have taken at least twice as long. I thank her for her patience, good humour, diligence and willingness to exercise initiative. She set up valuable research practices that made the whole project much more manageable than it could otherwise have been, had a happy knack of seeing what needed to be done, and the skill and imagination to ensure that it was.

Special thanks are due to Anthony Slide who accepted my invitation to handle the silent cinema entries and did so with the sort of efficiency that made him a pleasure to work with. He also did more than this: he volunteered many further entries and he read the entire manuscript, making many helpful suggestions.

There are almost 120 contributors to this book's 5,800 entries and it is clear that they require special thanks. Many of them volunteered to do extra entries and put me in touch with others who were interested in contributing. For their patience in dealing with editorial suggestions and taking up more of their time than they had anticipated I am greatly indebted.

I have an enormous debt of gratitude to the three 'vetters', Allan Eyles, Luke McKernan and Jeffrey Richards, who also read the entire manuscript with scrupulous and critical eyes and whose contribution was invaluable. Luke McKernan also performed many other advisory and practical services beyond the demands of this particular role. In Australia, Thelma Gellie and Ian Britain also read everything and were punctilious in their suggestions for amendments. Others who read parts of the manuscript and whom I thank for their insights are Clyde Jeavons, Vincent Porter and Andrew Spicer (UK), Brenda Niall and Tom Ryan (Australia). It is difficult to say how much I owe to the care and encouragement of all these people. It is certainly the case that any remaining errors are mine.

There are several groups of people at the British Film Institute to whom I am especially beholden. In the endless checking of dates and places and honorifics and other awards, Janice Healey exercised an unwearying patience and pertinacity that filled many gaps that would otherwise have been difficult for me to deal with from Australia. She has my heartfelt thanks. In the National Film and Television Archive, I was treated with great courtesy and kindness during the two months I spent there doing the kinds of research that could not have been done anywhere else. I thank all the staff of this department, with special mention of John Oliver who has continued to be a valuable source of information, checking all kinds of esoteric 'facts'. In the BFI National Library, David Sharp was particularly helpful and Markku Salmi cleared up several problems. My thanks to both.

Other institutions to which I must record my thanks include: the Australian Film Institute, Melbourne, and especially to Aysen Mustafa for her unfailing help; the BECTU History Project group, London, who have given me a great deal of support over a number of years, with particular thanks to Roy Fowler who put me in touch with several people who became contributors; the British Society of Cinematographers, whose secretary, Frances Russell, went to endless trouble to find and check information about her members; the Producers' Alliance for Cinema and Television, with thanks to David Mills; and the Film Studies staff at De Montfort University, Leicester, who organised a useful seminar for the exchange of ideas about the book's organisation.

To Monash University, I owe major thanks for the continued use of office and computer facilities, for the support of many members of the School of Literary, Visual and Performance studies, especially to Clive Probyn and Chris Worth, successive heads of School, to Terry Burke for providing me with valuable video assistance, to Carlin Payne who administered my grant; and for a great deal of help from the Computer Centre, which treated me very generously with computer access and advice in dealing with the problems inevitably encountered by one who can use a computer without really understanding how it works. In this latter respect, my thanks are also due to Tim Roman and my son Duncan McFarlane.

There are also numerous individuals connected with British cinema who responded to requests for information and advice. These include: Michael Craig, Bryan Forbes, Martyn Friend, Peter Handford, Julie Harris, the late Sir Anthony Havelock-Allan, Jean Kent, Nicolas Roeg, Dinah Sheridan, Sylvia Syms and especially Sir Sydney Samuelson, helpful on many occasions, and the nearly two hundred other actors, directors, cinematographers, producers, production and costume designers and other personnel who responded with courtesy and precision to what must sometimes have seemed impertinent or tedious requests, by letter, email and telephone, for the giving or clarifying of biographical information that had proved elusive. They made the project seem worth the effort. And I thank those busy agents who passed on either letters or telephone enquiries.

Other individuals who should be gratefully named include: Roger Mellor, for researching awards won by British film personnel; Cathy Surowiec who very generously made available the fruits of her own still-to-be-published research on production and costume designers, and especially in relation to birth and death dates and places; Geoff Brown, who cleared up several matters of fact; David Burnand, of the Royal College of Music, for fielding many queries about British film music; Geoff Mayer, for the loan of many tapes of British films; Monica Maughan, who gave me very useful answers to queries; my daughters Susannah McFarlane and Sophie Scully and my daughter-in-law Meredith McFarlane, for their various kinds of assistance.

In regard to the processes involved in putting this book together, I must thank an invariably courteous, helpful and painstaking team at Methuen. Also, in relation to the British Film Institute's share in the publishing, I am grateful to publisher Andrew Lockett for his continuing interest in the project over several years and to Sophie Contento for her help with illustrations.

Finally, my main thanks, with my love, go to my wife Geraldine, who has had far more exposure to British cinema than she ever bargained for, and has borne heroically with more than three years of necessary, if enjoyable, monomania.

Brian McFarlane
Melbourne, April 2003

Email: britishfilm@arts.monash.edu.au

CONTRIBUTORS

EDITOR **Brian McFarlane**, Honorary Associate Professor, Monash University, Melbourne, lectured in film and literature for many years. He has published widely in Britain, Australia and the US, his recent books including *Novel to Film: An Introduction to the Theory of Adaptation*, *An Autobiography of British Cinema*, *The Oxford Companion to Australian Film* (co-editor) and *Lance Comfort*.

ASSOCIATE EDITOR **Anthony Slide** is the author of over sixty books on the history of popular entertainment and editor of over ninety volumes in the 'Filmmakers' series. He was former resident film historian of the Motion Picture Arts and Sciences, and was described by Lillian Gish as 'our pre-eminent historian of the silent film'.

Ian Aitken is Senior Research Fellow at De Montfort University, Leicester, and is the author of *The Documentary Film Movement: an Anthology*, *Strange Realism: the Cinema of Alberto Cavalcanti* and *European Cinema and Film Theory: Realism and Modernism*.

Tony Aldgate is Reader in Film and History at The Open University of the United Kingdom. He has published extensively on British cinema history and is Course Director of the Oxford University Diploma in Film Studies

John Aldred was a production sound, music and dubbing mixer in major British studios for 50 years. His many credits include *Lawrence of Arabia*, *Guns of Navarone*, *Anne of a Thousand Days*.

Robert (Bob) Allen, founder member and fellow of the Association of Motion Picture Sound, was production sound mixer on over 50 films, made in several countries. Is now researching the origins of motion picture sound.

Robert Angell joined Technicolor (1946), then Crown Film Unit. His company, Film Partnership (1952), produced documentaries and TV. He wrote *Getting into Films and Television*; for 14 years was Chairman of BAFTA Short Film Jury.

Justine Ashby is Lecturer in Film Studies at the University of East Anglia. She is co-editor of *British Cinema, Past and Present* and is currently writing a book about Muriel and Betty Box.

Bruce Babington is Professor of Film at the University of Newcastle upon Tyne. Among his books are *British Stars and Stardom* and *Launder and Gilliat*.

Iola Baines co-founded and directed the Wales Film and TV Archive before it became, in 2001, The National Screen and Sound Archive of Wales. She currently heads Collection Development for NSSAW.

Charles Barr is Professor of Film at the University of East Anglia. His books include *Ealing Studios* and *English Hitchcock*, and he co-wrote Stephen Frears's film *Typically British: a Personal History of British Cinema*.

Tim Bergfelder is Lecturer in Film Studies at the University of Southampton. He has published several articles on Anglo-German and European film relations and is the co-editor of *The German Cinema Book* (BFI, 2000).

Anne Bittner wrote her doctoral thesis on the relationship between vaudeville and film in the 1920s, when entertainment at the cinema often consisted of live performance and film.

Stephen Bourne is the author of *Brief Encounter: Lesbians and Gays in British Cinema 1930–71* and *Black in the British Frame: Black People in British Film and Television 1896–1996*.

Ian Britain has lectured in history, film and literature. He has published several books, including *Fabianism and Culture*, and is currently the editor of *Meanjin* magazine, Melbourne.

Geoff Brown writes film and music criticism for *The Times*. Studies of British cinema include books on Walter Forde, Launder and Gilliat, and John Baxter, and contributions to *The Unknown 1930s* and *British Cinema of the 90s*.

Simon Brown is the Archival Footage Sales Officer for the British Film Institute. He has lectured extensively on early cinema, and is currently researching a PhD on the Hepworth Manufacturing Company 1904–1911.

Stephen Brown is an Anglican priest, freelance writer for radio, press and books, co-founder of Faith & Film. His background is adult education, film festivals (juries, programming) and television.

Kevin Brownlow is a documentary and feature film-maker and film historian. He is the author of many works on cinema, including *The Parade's Gone By* and *David Lean: A Biography*.

David Burnand is Head of the Centre for Screen Music at the Royal College of Music. He composes film and electroacoustic music, and is currently researching the narrative and dramatic functions of music for the screen.

Elaine Burrows has been a member of staff at the National Film and Television Archive since the mid-60s, in the Cataloguing Department, as head of the Archive's Viewing Service, and latterly as the Archive's Special Projects Manager.

Alan Burton, Senior Lecturer in Media Studies at De Montfort University, Leicester, has co-edited studies of Basil Dearden and the Boulting brothers, and is compiling a reference guide to British film directors for the British Film Institute.

Edward Buscombe was formerly Head of Publishing at the British Film Institute and Visiting Professor at Southampton Institute. Recent publications are *The Searchers* (BFI Film Classics) and *Cinema Today*, a history of world cinema since 1970.

Matthew Caterson has written film reviews for numerous Australian newspapers, and contributed to *Worth Watching: Thirty Film Reviewers on Review*.

Simon Caterson is a freelance writer and reviewer who was educated in Ireland and is based in Melbourne.

John Caughie is Professor of Film and Television Studies at the University of Glasgow. His most recent book is *Television Drama: Realism, Modernism and British Culture*. He is an editor of *Screen*.

James Chapman is Lecturer in Film and Television History at The Open University. His publications include *The British at War: Cinema, State and Propaganda, 1939–1945* and *Licence To Thrill: A Cultural History of the James Bond Films*.

Steve Chibnall is Co-ordinator of the British Cinema and Television Research Group, De Montfort University, Leicester, UK. He has published books on British crime and horror films, and on the directors J. Lee Thompson and Pete Walker.

Ian Christie has researched many aspects of Russian and British cinema. He is a regular broadcaster, an associate editor of the *New Dictionary of National Biography* and Professor of Film and Media History at Birkbeck College, University of London.

Fiona Clark completed a Master of Arts at Monash University, Melbourne, examining costume design in British cinema in the 1960s.

Andrew Clay teaches Media Technology at De Montfort University. He is the author of several articles on the British crime film and is currently researching moving image culture on the Internet.

Ian Conrich is Senior Lecturer in Film Studies at University of Surrey, Roehampton, and an editor of the *Journal of Popular British Cinema*. He has contributed to *Sight and Sound*, to *The British Cinema Book* and *British Horror Cinema*.

John Cook lectures in Media at Glasgow Caledonian University, Scotland. The author of *Dennis Potter: A Life on Screen*, he is co-writing a study of director Peter Watkins.

Pam Cook is Professor of European Film and Media at the University of Southampton. She is the author of *Fashioning the Nation: Costume and Identity in British Cinema* and editor of *Gainsborough Pictures*.

Barbara Creed is Head of the Cinema Studies Program at Melbourne University. She is the author of *The Monstrous-Feminine: Film, Feminism, Psychoanalysis* and *Pandora's Box: Media, Sexuality and the Global Self*.

David Curtis is Senior Research Fellow at Central St Martins (London Institute). He was Film Officer at the Arts Council of England 1977–2000; his publications include *Experimental Cinema*.

Richard Dacre writes and lectures on British cinema and is the author of *Trouble In Store: Norman Wisdom a Career in Comedy*. He also runs Flashbacks Memorabilia shop and archive.

Teddy Darvas entered film cutting-rooms in 1948, was successively second assistant, assembly cutter and sound editor, and worked with David Lean, the Boultings and many others. Also edited for television.

Margaret Dickinson is a film-maker and writer, whose books include *Cinema and State* (co-authored) and *Rogue Reels*. She is currently co-ordinating a network in Europe and India, encouraging co-operation in the field of social video.

Wheeler Winston Dixon, Professor of Film Studies at the University of Nebraska, Lincoln, is Editor-in-Chief of the *Quarterly Review of Film and Video*. Books include *The Second Century of Cinema* and *Collected Interviews: Voices from 20th Century Cinema*.

Kevin J. Donnelly lectures at Staffordshire University. Once a professional musician, he has written *Pop Music in British Cinema* and edited *Film Music: Critical Approaches*.

Charles Drazin is an editor and freelance writer, based in London. His books include *The Finest Years: British Cinema of the 1940s*, *In Search of The Third Man* and *Korda: Britain's Only Movie Mogul*.

Raymond Durgnat's many books included the seminal *A Mirror for England* and the studies: *WR – Mysteries of the Organism* and *A Long Hard Look at Psycho*. He was Visiting Professor to the University of East London.

Sarah Easen is a cataloguer on the Newsreel Scripts project at the British Universities Film & Video Council. She has also catalogued films at the Imperial War Museum and the National Film and Television Archive.

Jan Epstein is a Melbourne film critic and broadcaster. She has published widely in newspapers, magazines and books, and in 2000 co-produced *Australians at Cannes* for ABC TV.

Peter William Evans is Professor of Hispanic Studies at Queen Mary, University of London. He has written books on European and Hollywood cinema. He is currently writing a book on Carol Reed.

Wendy Everett teaches Cinema Studies at the University of Bath. She publishes extensively on European cinema, and is a member of the *Literature/Film Quarterly* board.

Allen Eyles is a freelance film historian with a specialist interest in cinema buildings. His most recent book is *Odeon Cinemas 1: Oscar Deutsch Entertains Our Nation* and he is working on the sequel about the J. Arthur Rank years.

Dick Fiddy is a TV consultant currently under contract to the British Film Institute. He is the author of *Missing, Believed Wiped*, a study and listing of lost British TV material.

Eugene Finn formerly worked at the National Film and TV Archive (BFI) and is currently Collections Archivist at the Irish Film Archive. He collaborated on *Still Irish: A Century of the Irish in Film*.

Gwendolyn Foster is Associate Professor of English, University of Nebraska, Lincoln, and Editor-in-Chief of *Quarterly Review of Film and Video*. Books include *Captive Bodies: Postcolonial Subjectivity in Cinema* and *The Films of Chantal Akerman*.

Kevin Foster was born in Manchester. He teaches in the School of Literary, Visual and Performance Studies at Monash University, Melbourne, and is the author of *Fighting Fictions: War, Narrative and National Identity*.

Roy Fowler founded the ACTT/BECTU History Project, has produced and directed films and television, has published several books, and serves on the management board of the Bill Douglas Centre at the University of Exeter.

Rodney Giesler is a scriptwriter, director, producer and film historian. He has made over one hundred documentaries for industry and television in all parts of the world, including many award-winners.

Ben Gibson, Director of the London Film School, was Head of Production at the British Film Institute, 1988–98, partner in The Other Cinema and Metro Pictures during the '80s, and has worked as freelance producer and film journalist.

Christine Geraghty is Professor of Film and Television Studies at University of Glasgow. She is the author of *Women and Soap Opera* and *British Cinema in the Fifties* and co-editor of *The Television Studies Book*.

Mark Glancy is Lecturer in Film and History at Queen Mary and Westfield College (University of London). He is the author of *When Hollywood Loved Britain*.

Christine Gledhill is Professor of Cinema Studies at Staffordshire University. She has written widely on feminist film criticism, melodrama and British cinema. She is currently completing *Reframing British Cinema: 1918–1928*.

Kevin Gough-Yates taught for many years at the University of Westminster and now works for Channel 4. His latest books are on German-speaking exiles in 1930s/1940s Britain and the films of Michael Powell and Emeric Pressburger.

Richard Gregson was an agent operating an independent agency for British cinema during the 60s, and went to Los Angeles to head London International there in 1968. He represented actors, directors and writers.

Stephen Guy is a freelance writer, editor and designer. He has taught film and history at Queen Mary College, London, and is the author of several articles on British film history.

Sue Harper is Professor of Film History at the University of Portsmouth. Her books include *Picturing the Past, Women in British Cinema*, and (co-author) *The Decline of Deference: British Cinema in the 1950s*.

Andrew Higson, Professor of Film Studies at University of East Anglia, has published widely on British cinema, including *Waving the Flag* and *English Heritage, English Cinema: The Costume Drama in the 1980s and 1990s*.

Melinda Hildebrandt, research assistant on the *Encyclopedia of British Film*, is completing a doctoral thesis on patterns of realism in British cinema.

John Hill is Professor of Media Studies at the University of Ulster. He is the author of *Sex, Class and Realism: British Cinema 1956–63* and *British Cinema in the 1980s*, and co-author of *Cinema and Ireland*.

Paul Howson is Director of Film & Television at the British Council, London, and the UK representative of European Film Promotion. He is also a trustee of the UK's National Film and Television School.

I.Q. Hunter is Senior Lecturer in Film Studies at De Montfort University, Leicester. He is the editor of *British Science Fiction Cinema* (Routledge, 1999).

Peter Hutchings is Senior Lecturer in Film Studies at Northumbria University and has published widely on British cinema. His books include *Hammer and Beyond: The British Horror Film* and *Terence Fisher*.

Clyde Jeavons is a film archivist, programmer and historian. He was formerly Curator of the National Film and Television Archive (British Film Institute) and has written books on the Western, war films and sex in the movies.

Glen Jones is a lecturer in film studies at Staffordshire University and with the Open University. His research interests include the British film industry and its relationship with New Labour, the sports film and film censorship.

Marcia Landy is Distinguished Service Professor of English and Film Studies at the University of Pittsburgh. Her publications include *Fascism in Film: The Italian Commercial Cinema, 1930–1943*, and *British Genres, 1930–1960* and numerous articles.

Roy Lansford entered show business as a big band singer and in the 1950s became a recording and radio artiste. He appeared in *Murder by Decree* (1978), has published short stories and worked as a composer/lyricist.

Alan Lovell, now retired, taught film at Staffordshire University. He has both written film criticism and worked in independent cinema. His publications include *Anarchist Cinema, Studies in Documentary, Don Siegel-Hollywood Cinema* and *Screen Acting*.

Geoffrey Macnab is a London author who has written widely on British cinema and whose books include *J. Arthur Rank and the British Film Industry* and *Searching for Stars*.

Race Mathews is a Senior Research Fellow in the International Centre for Management in Government at Monash University, a former federal MP, state MP and minister and municipal councillor.

Geoff Mayer is Chair of Cinema Studies at LaTrobe University, Melbourne. He is co-editor of *The Oxford Companion to Australian Film* and is the author of the forthcoming *Guide to British Cinema*.

David McGillivray has written widely on British cinema and is the author of *Doing Rude Things: The History of the British Sex Film, 1957–1981*.

Kara McKechnie is a lecturer in dramaturgy at Leeds University, UK, and granddaughter of the actor James McKechnie. She has published articles on British historical films and Alan Bennett.

Luke Mckernan is the author of *Topical Budget* (1992) and *Who's Who of Victorian Cinema* (1996), and is researching the life of Charles Urban. He is Head of Information at the British Universities Film & Video Council.

Andy Medhurst teaches film at the University of Sussex, has written widely on British cinema and is a frequent contributor to *Sight and Sound*.

David Meeker, MBE, has been with the British Film Institute since 1961. He is the author of *Jazz in the Movies*, and *Missing Believed Lost: the Great British Film Search*.

Roger Philip Mellor, retired drama lecturer and university Media Studies librarian, is now researching the representation of popular culture in British film for a book on British musical movies.

Robert Murphy is Professor in Film Studies at De Montfort University. His books include: *Realism and Tinsel, Sixties British Cinema, British Cinema and the Second World War, British Cinema of the 90s* and *The British Cinema Book*.

Steve Norris entered the film industry in 1977, subsequently joining Warner Bros. in California. In the UK in 1988 he reformed Enigma Productions. In January 1998, he became British Film Commissioner.

Dan North is currently writing his doctoral thesis on special effects at the University of Exeter.

John Oliver, with an MA (East Anglia) in Film Archiving, is a cataloguer at the National Film and Television Archive, London, and programmes British cinema at the National Film Theatre.

Tim O'Sullivan is Head of Department of Media & Cultural Production at De Montfort University, Leicester. He is currently completing a study of British television and the home 1945–60.

Julian Petley teaches Media and Communications studies at Brunel University, chairs the editorial board of the *Journal of British Cinema*, and is co-editor of *Ill Effects: the Media Violence Debate* and of *British Horror Cinema*.

Duncan Petrie is Reader in Film and Director of the Bill Douglas Centre for the History of Cinema and Popular Culture at the University of Exeter. His books include *The British Cinematographer* and *Screening Scotland*.

Vincent Porter is Professor of Mass Communication at the University of Westminster. He is author of *On Cinema* and co-editor of *British Cinema History*, and is currently co-authoring a history of 1950s British cinema.

Tim Pulleine is on the editorial staff of the *Guardian* (London) and has written on the cinema for that newspaper and for sundry other journals and publications, including the Aurum film encyclopedias.

Paul Quinn, an MA in Film Studies, is now working towards a doctorate entitled, *The British B Thriller in the 1950s*.

Philip Reed wrote his doctoral thesis on Britten's incidental music for film, theatre and radio. He has published studies of Britten's *Peter Grimes*, *Billy Budd* and *War Requiem*, and co-edited Britten's *Selected Letters and Diaries*.

Jeffrey Richards is Professor of Cultural History at Lancaster University. Among his many books on British cinema are *Films and British National Identity* and *The Unknown 1930s: An Alternative History of the British Cinema 1929–1939*.

John Riley is a speaker, writer, film programmer and broadcaster, particularly on music and on Russian and Soviet culture. He has contributed to forthcoming books from Greenwood Press and Routledge, and his work on Shostakovitch's cinema career will be published in 2003. He works for the British Universities Film & Video Council..

James C. Robertson, a retired history teacher, is the author of two books and several articles on British film censorship. He has also published a study of Hollywood director, Michael Curtiz.

David Robinson, film critic and historian, is currently director of the Pordenone Silent Film Festival. Formerly film critic of *The Financial Times* and *The Times*, he has published widely on the cinema and directed several documentary films.

Tim Roman is a Melbourne-based writer who has a research interest in British film music.

Frances Russell started in the industry at Rank Film Labs, Denham, in 1970, later moving to Technicolor, and took over the administrative and financial affairs of the British Society of Cinematographers in 1982.

Tom Ryall is Professor in Film Studies at Sheffield Hallam University and is author of *Alfred Hitchcock and the British Cinema*, *Blackmail*, and *Britain and the American Cinema*.

Tom Ryan is film critic for *The Sunday Age*, Melbourne. A long-time contributor to *Cinema Papers*, he has also written for numerous local and international journals and lectured on film in Australian and British universities.

Elaine Schreyeck was a continuity 'girl' in British films of the 40s and 50s and subsequently a script supervisor. She worked for many British and American directors.

Stephen Shafer is Assistant Dean and Professor of Cinema Studies at the University of Illinois where he has taught film history for nearly thirty years. His publications include *British Popular Film, 1929–39: The Cinema of Reassurance*.

Neil Sinyard is Senior Lecturer in Film Studies at Hull University. He has authored many books on the cinema, including studies of Jack Clayton, Richard Lester and Nicolas Roeg.

Roger Smither is Keeper of the Film and Video Archive at the Imperial War Museum, London and Secretary General of the International Federation of Film Archives (FIAF).

Andrew Spicer teaches at the University of the West of England. He has written numerous articles on British cinema, and a book *Typical Men: the Representation of Masculinity in Popular British Cinema*.

Martin Stockham is a television producer and media consultant. He has been involved in documentaries on *Alexander Korda* and *Sabu: The Elephant Boy* as well as numerous other factual programmes.

Sarah Street is Reader in the Department of Drama at the University of Bristol. Her books include *British National Cinema*, *British Cinema in Documents* and *Transatlantic Crossings: British Feature Films in the USA*.

Catherine A. Surowiec, film historian and editor, has worked for the Museum of Modern Art, NY, and British Film Institute, London. Publications include *Accent on Design: Four European Art Directors* and *This Film Is Dangerous* (FIAF nitrate anthology).

Olwen Terris is Chief Cataloguer with the National Film and Television Archive, British Film Institute.

Anne-Marie Thomas has worked in academic publishing for the past ten years. She is also a musician and writer and is currently working on her first book.

Estella Tincknell is Senior Lecturer in Media and Cultural Studies at Nottingham Trent University. She is co-editor of a forthcoming collection of essays about the post-classical film musical.

Tom Vallance is a London-based arts journalist who writes regularly for the *Independent* and is the author of *The American Musical*.

Patricia Warren is a British film historian and consultant whose books include *Elstree: The British Hollywood, The British Film Collection* and *British Film Studios: An Illustrated History*.

Paul Wells is Head of the Media Portfolio at the University of Teeside. His many publications in the field of animation include *Understanding Animation, Animation and America* and *Animation: Genre and Authorship*.

Deane Williams is Senior Lecturer in the School of Literary, Visual and Performance Studies, Monash University, Melbourne. He has published widely on documentary and is currently writing the biography of documentary filmmaker John Heyer.

Tony Williams is Professor and Area Head of Film Studies in Southern Illinois University at Carbondale. He is the author of *Structures of Desire: British Cinema 1939–1955* and numerous articles on British Cinema.

Linda Wood is a freelance writer and researcher whose publications include *Maurice Elvey* and *British Films 1927–1939;* she edits the London Film Festival Official Programme, and is coordinating of an oral history project on Elstree Studios.

Orly Yadin trained at the Israel Film Archive, became a film researcher in the UK on major historical TV documentaries, and now directs and produces archival documentaries and animation films.

Andrew Youdell is a film historian and long-time employee of the British Film Institute in London. He is passionate about transport in films, especially railways, presenting special archive programmes around Britain.

Aardman Animation Founded in 1972 by Peter Lord (*b c* 1953) and David Sproxton (*b c* 1954), Aardman specialised in BBC children's animation, creating 'Morph', a playful plasticine character, who featured in *Take Hart*. It was their quasi-documentary approach in the anthologies *Animated Conversations* (1978) and *Conversation Pieces* (1983), however, which ensured them international recognition. Using unscripted live soundtracks and clay figures engaged in closely observed, highly gestured performances, Aardman created everyday stories including *Sales Pitch* (1983), *Babylon* (1985) and the Oscar winners, *Creature Comforts* (1990), *The Wrong Trousers* (1993) and *A Close Shave* (1995), all by Nick PARK. Park's now-famous leading characters, Wallace and Gromit, appear in the latter two, having first been seen in *A Grand Day Out* (1993). The studio has produced work by Barry Purves, Richard Goleszowski and Darren Walsh, and continued groundbreaking with the full-length model-animation feature, *Chicken Run* (2000, UK/US), the first in a multiple picture deal with Dreamworks SKG. Aardman also makes commercials and rock videos.
OTHER BRITISH FILMS INCLUDE: *Next, Going Equipped* (1989), *Adam* (1991), *Pib and Pog* (1994), *Pop, Wat's Pig* (1996), *Stagefright* (1997), *Rex the Runt, Angry Kid* (1998). Paul Wells.

Abady, Temple (*b* 1903 – *d* 1970). Composer. First worked in the theatre, and came into film-making via DOCUMENTARIES for the CROWN FILM UNIT, and was with GAINSBOROUGH post-war. Married Anna DUSE, costume designer.
OTHER BRITISH FILMS INCLUDE: (shorts) *Railways, Hausa Village* (1946), *The Three A's, Boy Builders* (1947); (features) *Miranda, Easy Money* (1948), *Dear Mr Prohack* (1949), *Folly to be Wise* (1952), *Street Corner* (1953).

Abbey, Eleanor Costume designer. Often worked as assistant to Oliver MESSEL and also to Cecil BEATON on *My Fair Lady* (1964, US), sometimes as designer in her own right.
OTHER BRITISH FILMS INCLUDE: *Hungry Hill* (1947), *The Mark of Cain* (1948), *Cardboard Cavalier* (1949), *The Romantic Age* (1949), *Tony Draws a Horse* (1950), *Jacqueline* (1956), *Dangerous Exile* (1957), *The 3 Worlds of Gulliver* (1960, UK/Sp/US).

Abbott, John (*b* London, 1906 – *d* Los Angeles, 1996). Actor. Distinctively large-eyed purveyor of frightened and devious men, in Hollywood from 1941 where he often played in British-set films, such as *Jane Eyre* (1943) and *The Woman in White* (1948).
BRITISH FILMS: *Return of the Scarlet Pimpernel, Mademoiselle Docteur* (1937), *Ten Days in Paris, This Man is News, The Saint in London* (1939), *The Conquest of the Air* (1940).

Academy Cinema, London Exhibitor Eric Hakim opened the Academy Cinema in Oxford Street, London, in 1931, as a venue for foreign-language and other films of specialist interest, including revivals of famous films. Under the management of Elsie Cohen, it began with a season of French films, and went on to provide public access to the sort of fare that had hitherto been largely restricted to the FILM SOCIETIES which had begun their flourishing life in the 20s. The Academy, which lasted until 1986, was a cinema devoted to the idea of film as an art, and other such ART-HOUSE CINEMAS, as they came to be called to distinguish them from the popular mainstream houses, sprang up in the 30s, including the EVERYMAN, Hampstead (1933), the Curzon (1934) and Studios One and Two (1936). The Academy was important in the growing acceptance of the practice of subtitling foreign-language films, and its importance in the growth of a film culture that went beyond Hollywood and RANK is considerable. It was not, however, to be confused with those cinema chains (e.g. Gala) which concentrated on risqué continental fare. The Academy was heavily bombed during the war, but was restored to enjoy several further decades of enlightened exhibition, under the management of George HOELLERING (1939–80).

Academy of Motion Picture Arts and Sciences *see* **awards**

Acheson, James (aka Jim) (*b* Leicester, 1946). Costume designer. Worked on a range of high-profile films since 1980, including the surrealities of *Time Bandits* (1981), *Monty Python's The Meaning of Life* (1983) and *Brazil* (1985) and international period pieces such as *The Last Emperor* (1987, Ch/It) and *Dangerous Liaisons* (1988, US), winning Oscars for both, *Mary Shelley's Frankenstein* (1994, UK/US) and *The Man in the Iron Mask* (1998, US).
OTHER BRITISH FILMS INCLUDE: (cos des, unless noted) *Sir Henry at Rawlinson End* (1980, art d), *Bullshot* (1983), *Water* (1985), *Highlander* (1986), *Biggles* (1986), *The Sheltering Sky* (1990), *Little Buddha* (1993), *The Wind in the Willows* (1996, + des).

Ackland, Joss (*b* London, 1928). Actor. In his 50-year career, tall, burly Ackland (trained at Central School) made his name in the theatre, including a major season at the Old Vic, and appeared in a good deal of TV before becoming a fixture as a character actor in British cinema from the early 70s. He has also appeared in American films such as *The Hunt for Red October* (1990) and *Miracle on 34th Street* (1994). With mellifluous voice (he has been much in demand for voice-overs) and imposing presence, he can register equally persuasively as dangerous or benign. He has continued to work in all the acting media: he was a formidable Hook in the RSC's *Peter Pan*, and scored one of his biggest successes as C.S. Lewis in the stage and TV version of *Shadowlands* (1985). Awarded CBE in 2001.

OTHER BRITISH FILMS INCLUDE: *Seven Days to Noon* (1950), *Crescendo* (1969), *Villain* (1971), *England Made Me* (1972, UK/Yug), *Hitler: The Last Ten Days* (1973, UK/It), *Great Expectations* (1975, as Joe Gargery), *Watership Down* (1978, anim, voice only), *A Zed & Two Noughts* (1985, UK/Neth), *Lady Jane* (1985), *White Mischief* (1987), *The Object of Beauty* (1991, UK/US), *Mad Dogs and Englishmen* (1994), *Amy Foster* (1997, UK/Fr/US), *Mumbo Jumbo* (2001).

Ackland, Rodney (*b* London, 1908 – *d* Richmond, Surrey, 1991). Screenwriter. RN: Bernstein. In 1995 Rodney Ackland's name came to the fore after many years when his 1952 play, *The Pink Room*, was revived at London's National Theatre under the title of *Absolute Hell* with Judi DENCH in the lead. Trained as actor at Central School and made stage debut in 1924, but by the 30s his career was set firmly in the direction of writing, particularly the ADAPTATION of novels to the stage, and then as a screenwriter. He was the author or co-author of the screenplays for such films as Carol REED's *Bank Holiday* (1938) and Anthony ASQUITH's *Uncensored* (1942), he streamlined A.J. Cronin's remorselessly depressing *Hatter's Castle* for Lance COMFORT's fine film version (1941), and director Thorold DICKINSON acknowledged gratefully the 'un-British' quality of his work on *The Queen of Spades* (1948), on which Ackland began as director and over which he fought a successful court case about his inadequate credit as the film's writer. He also appeared in small roles in several films such as *The Skin Game* (1931), *The Case of Gabriel Perry* (1935) and *Alibi* (1942), and, for a couple of decades, was an interesting figure hovering around the performing arts in Britain.

OTHER BRITISH FILMS INCLUDE (SC): *Number Seventeen* (1932), *The Silent Battle* (1939), *49th Parallel* (1941, co-sc), *Thursday's Child* (1943, + d), *Love Story* (1944), *Wanted for Murder* (1946), *Temptation Harbour* (1947).

BIBLIOG: Autobiography, *Celluloid Mistress*, 1954.

Ackroyd, Barry (*b* Oldham, Lancs, 1954). Cinematographer. Significant 90s figure, responsible for shooting all Ken LOACH's films of the decade from *Riff-Raff* (1991), Ackroyd's feature debut, to *My Name is Joe* (1998, UK/Fr/Ger); for several other darkly realist films such as *Stella Does Tricks* (1996) and *Under the Skin* (1997); and for Chris MENGES' thriller, *The Lost Son* (1999, UK/Fr/US), to which he gave a stylish *noir* patina. Trained at Portsmouth Polytechnic, he first worked as camera assistant (1976–80), then photographed several DOCUMENTARIES – *The Leader, His Driver and the Driver's Wife* (1991), *Aileen Wuornos: The Selling of a Serial Killer* (1992), *Tracking Down Maggie* (1994), *Anne Frank Remembered* (1995) – and some television, including *Hillsborough* (1996), and directed the short film, *The Butterfly Man* (1996).

OTHER BRITISH FILMS INCLUDE: *Raining Stones* (1993), *Ladybird Ladybird* (1994), *Land and Freedom* (UK/Ger/Sp), *Life After Life* (1995), *Carla's Song* (1996, UK/Ger/Sp), *Beautiful People* (1999), *Bread and Roses* (2001, UK/Fr/Ger/Sp/Switz).

Acres, Birt (*b* Richmond, Virginia, *c* 1854 – *d* London, 1918). Pioneer. To Acres belongs a number of cinema 'firsts'. As early as February 1895, he photographed a motion picture, as cameraman for Robert W. PAUL, and on 27 May 1895, was granted a patent for a 'kinetic camera'. On 29 May 1895, he filmed the Derby, and, on 22 June 1895, he filmed the opening of Germany's Kiel Canal. On 10 January 1896, he gave a film show to the Lyonsdown Photographic Club, and, on 14 January, he demonstrated motion pictures, filmed with his camera, to the Royal Photographic Society. On 27 June 1896, he was first to film a member of the royal family, the Prince of Wales (later Edward

VII) at Cardiff, and on 21 July 1896, he was the first to screen a film of a member of the royal family to that august body, assembled at Marlborough House. Acres came to the UK in the 1880s as a photographer, and became an associate of Paul, with whom he broke up in June 1895. As historian John BARNES has written, 'Paul supplied the technical knowledge and Acres the photographic expertise and together they produced England's first films.' Acres produced more than 30 SHORTS through December 1896, but unlike Paul, he was not a businessman and had no understanding of the commercial potential of the motion picture, although he did invent (in 1898) and market a combined camera/projector for home use, called the Birtac and utilizing 17.5 mm film. He ceased film-making in 1900 and continued with a film-developing and -printing business until his bankruptcy in 1909. AS.

ACT/ACTT/BECTU In 1933 any benefits from the incipient boom in production remained unshared by British film technicians, whose hours were long, whose pay was low, and who felt threatened by an influx of émigrés. Talk of a union, mostly centring on the GAUMONT–BRITISH studio in SHEPHERD'S BUSH, led to a first General Meeting in May, and in June the Association of Cine-Technicians was registered as a trade union. (It is worth noting that the **ACT** was preceded by the Kine Cameraman's Society, a 'social organisation', not a union as such, founded in 1918.) Initially the membership of around 1,200, entrance fee 2/6d (12½p), looked promising, but it quickly collapsed in the absence of discernible benefits. By the time George ELVIN was appointed General Secretary in January 1934, less than a quarter of the 80-odd remaining members were fully paid-up and three months' rent was owed for the office. Although the situation remained precarious, this was a turning point. In May 1935, a journal, the *Cine-Technician* (later the *Film & Television Technician*, then *Stage Screen & Radio*), was being published, while in December 1936 the union affiliated with the TUC and the first industrial agreement was made with GAUMONT–BRITISH. However, the industry was largely ramshackle. In the absence of employers' federations elusive, fly-by-night producers had to be tackled individually but the Laboratory Branch (1936) increasingly provided industrial clout with the threat of strike.

May 1937 saw Anthony ASQUITH elected as President, an office he held until his death in 1968. Elvin, Asquith (assisted by his mother, the redoubtable Margot) and the membership at large ran a magnificent campaign to influence the 1938 Cinematograph Films Act, replacing the infamous 1927 'QUOTA QUICKIES' legislation and introducing a fair wages clause. After the outbreak of war in 1939, ACT found its standing hugely improved. It was influential in persuading the government that film work was vital to the war effort, and was made the vetting body for 'reserved' technicians (leading not surprisingly to a membership boom). The arrival of peace led to a brief period of full employment, but by 1949 the industry's decline saw an increasing casualisation of labour, which has continued to this day.

Commercial television was introduced into England in 1955. After initial opposition, the union became, in March 1956, the Association of Cinematograph Television & Allied Technicians. The following year agreement was reached with the Programme Contractors Association and for the next thirty years Independent Television membership supplied considerable industrial and financial strength as the film industry measurably shrank.

By the end of the 80s reducing membership (at its peak about

30,000), financial weakness, anti-union legislation, the loss of the closed shop, technological change, Luddite tendencies, industry fragmentation and hostile management were all threatening ACTT's position. Survival required a broader base and in January 1991 the Broadcasting Entertainment Cinematograph & Theatre Union (BECTU) was formed by amalgamation with the Broadcasting & Entertainment Trades Alliance (BETA), itself derived from the Association of Broadcasting Staff (ABS) and the National Association of Theatrical Television and Kine Employees (NATTKE, whose origin dated back to 1890). This successor union represents diverse workers (half of whom are now freelance) in most areas of the cinema, television, video, theatre and leisure activity industries. Roy Fowler.

ACT Films This was the name of the film production company set up at a meeting of the General Council of the ASSOCIATION OF CINE-TECHNICIANS (ACT) to provide employment for its members, many of whom were unemployed as a result of the crisis in the British film industry in the late 40s. Director Anthony ASQUITH, a life-long champion of the ACT, was elected chairman of the board of ACT Films and the first production, *Green Grow the Rushes*, starring Richard BURTON and Honor BLACKMAN, was released in 1951. Sidney COLE, Ealing producer-editor and member of ACT Films board, recalled in 1995 that, 'Apart from buying a few hundred pounds of shares, the union did not have anything directly to do with the running of the company, though its board of directors included some members of the executive committee'. This unique and laudable enterprise made chiefly low-budget second features, though some, including *Private Information* (1952) and *Room in the House* (1955) were above average in quality. Probably the most ambitious films produced by the company were Asquith's *The Final Test* (1953), Don CHAFFEY's *The Man Upstairs* (1958), starring Richard ATTENBOROUGH, and James HILL's *The Kitchen* (1961), which Cole produced. The company's affairs ended somewhat messily with a large debt which the Union had to settle.

OTHER TITLES INCLUDED: *Night Was Our Friend* (1951), *Circumstantial Evidence* (1952), *House of Blackmail* (1953), *Final Appointment* (1954), *Stolen Assignment* (1955), *The Last Man to Hang?* (1956), *Diplomatic Corpse* (1958), *Don't Panic Chaps* (1959), *The Piper's Tune* (1961).

acting styles in British silent cinema. The first actors on screen in both the UK and the US came either from the THEATRE or from the ranks of the non-professional. In many ways, there is little to differentiate the professional and the amateur. Actors from the theatre, whether the legitimate stage or the MUSIC HALL, made little effort to refine their technique for the screen, and the British propensity for filmed MELODRAMA did not encourage REALISM in performance.

The low pay of British film players may have deterred some stage actors who might have had the ability to embrace the craft of acting for the screen. With a leading producer like Cecil HEPWORTH, who saw no difference between a good actor and a good electrician and determinedly kept pay low, there was little incentive for a good actor to embark on a film career. It was Hepworth who thought make-up restricted emotion and so barred it from his productions, unaware perhaps that emotion is within an actor regardless of greasepaint.

A general lack of any creative direction in the 1910s and earlier obviously had its effect on the acting fraternity. It took an American, Florence TURNER, to show her British sisters how to emote for the camera. In the 1910s, Ivy CLOSE and Gladys

COOPER brought beauty to the screen, if not much else. Whatever daring or adventure leading men such as Percy MORAN attempted to display was subjugated to a wooden acting style that was positively amateurish when compared with the American heroics of a Douglas Fairbanks or a Tom Mix. Fred EVANS as 'Pimple' represented popular British COMEDY, but the emphasis was on the grotesque, and it was not until the 20s that Walter FORDE developed a comedic performance with a degree of sophistication, albeit far removed from the American philosophy of screen comedy. Only the character actors – exemplified by Donald CALTHROP and Frank STANMORE – seemed at ease on screen. Overacting was the norm, but surprisingly when Chrissie WHITE and Henry EDWARDS did it for comic effect in the 1918 wartime short, *The Poet's Windfall*, the audience realised hidden depths in these two British performers. Personality could, and did, shine through in the 20s, and when combined with talent, as with Betty BALFOUR, Estelle BRODY (UK-based, American) and Mabel POULTON, proved British performers could be a match for their American counterparts. The male support was generally limp-wristed, aged or totally lacking in sex appeal, although several leading men, notably Edwards, Stewart ROME and John STUART, were always reliable.

If nothing else, British silent cinema did break through the ubiquitous British CLASS system. Without the regional accents being heard, all actors on screen were equal. But unfortunately, more often than not, equally mediocre. AS.

acting styles in British sound cinema Stylistic confusion reigned as soon as films started talking. Britain's first completed talking picture, HITCHCOCK's *Blackmail* (1929), is characteristic: the main roles were taken by a foreign star, Anny ONDRA, dubbed by Joan BARRY into ladylike English, a silent player, John LONGDEN, with a ponderous vocal delivery, and a recruit from the stage, Donald CALTHROP. The crisp delivery of stage actors remained an enduring feature of film production. The 30s also saw a talent invasion from musical comedy and MUSIC HALL, including Jack HULBERT, Will HAY and Max MILLER: performers ideally equipped to play themselves, less equipped to mould themselves to fit specific characters. Film scripts encouraged caricatures across the social scale, from aristocrats to Gordon HARKER's cheerful Cockneys. As the British film industry gathered momentum, attempts were made to build certain actors into STARS, such as the dancer and singer Jessie MATTHEWS, her London vowels ironed out through elocution lessons, Charles LAUGHTON, a great character star, and Robert DONAT, the decade's epitome of the debonair gentleman. Films in the 30s followed clear CLASS divisions; acting followed suit.

From this welter of voices, something like a distinctive British acting style began to emerge during WW2. Films saluting heroic endeavours in battle or at home encouraged a quiet, unboastful manner, well displayed in the Everyman figures played by John MILLS. Regional accents began to be heard among the troops. In the middle-class romance of *Brief Encounter* (1945), Trevor HOWARD and Celia JOHNSON demonstrated the stiff upper lip trembling under emotional pressure. At the same time, a more robust tradition developed in GAINSBOROUGH's historical melodramas or the urban CRIME FILMS of the late 40s, with James MASON acting the brute and Jean KENT and Diana DORS perfecting their images as bad girls.

By the 50s, the biggest male stars of the previous decade –

Mason, Stewart GRANGER – had been lost to Hollywood. The RANK ORGANISATION attempted to manufacture replacements like Anthony STEEL, but the players audiences took most to their hearts were Kenneth MORE, ever cheerful, raffish round the edges, and Dirk BOGARDE, pushed into a whirlwind of comedies and dramas. The undemonstrative styles of John Mills and Jack HAWKINS flourished in films revisiting WW2, but, by the end of the decade, a new brand of REALISM entered from the theatre with actors like Tom COURTENAY and Albert FINNEY signalling a decisive shift in speech and subject-matter from polite southern England to the rougher lands further north. British cinema's gentility and professional sheen held sway no longer: actors learned to don fangs and scream in HAMMER horrors, or appear in support to pop stars like Cliff RICHARD.

The range of acting styles continued to widen in the 60s. The old brigade lingered, playing authority figures, but the decade belonged to unorthodox, regional youth, like Rita TUSHING-HAM. Cockney Michael CAINE came into his own in *Alfie* (1966). Malcolm McDOWELL and, briefly, Nicol WILLIAMSON showed us rebellious modern man. When the film production bubble burst at the beginning of the 70s, actors found work in TV, the stage, or, for the fortunate, Hollywood. It took until the boom of the mid 90s for another new wave of actors to appear, headlined by Ewan McGREGOR, who achieved pin-up status in *Trainspotting* (1996).

As with the previous New Wave, the 90s intake spoke with marked regional accents (particularly Scots). In *Trainspotting* and jaunty crime films like *Lock, Stock and Two Smoking Barrels* (1998), their characters' behaviour brought British screen acting closer than ever to life on the streets, the dialogue spattered with four-letter words and substance abuse. In another sphere, Hugh GRANT's yuppie ditherer in *Four Weddings and a Funeral* (1994) behaved like a bumbling Ian CARMICHAEL, transported to a different era. The more traditional virtues of British acting – careful timing, the ability to delineate characters quickly and be convincing in period clothes – flourished in films of literary pedigree, like *Howards End* (1992) and *Sense and Sensibility* (1995, UK/US).

Such skills have always made British actors in demand abroad. A fashion rose in the 90s for casting them as Hollywood villains. Anthony HOPKINS, the perfect screen chameleon, dominated *The Silence of the Lambs* (1991, US). The decade was also marked by actors moving into direction: Tim ROTH in *The War Zone* (1999, UK/It), Gary OLDMAN in *Nil by Mouth* (1997). In the latter film, Ray WINSTONE's alcoholic-fuelled rages took British screen acting into new territory, the beast within lashing out in a way even James Mason could never have imagined. Geoff Brown.

action/adventure films George ORWELL thought it symptomatic of characteristic British self-deprecation that the most famous battle poem in the language was about a company that charged in the wrong direction. Something of that same modesty occurs in British cinema, where some of its most memorable adventures – Charles FREND's *Scott of the Antarctic* (1948), Basil DEARDEN's *Khartoum* (1966), Tony RICHARDSON's *The Charge of the Light Brigade* (1968) – commemorate missions that ended in defeat and even ignominy. Swagger does not come easily to the British temperament. Even in a stirring tale like *Campbell's Kingdom* (1957), the most extrovert element in the performances of Dirk BOGARDE and Stanley BAKER is the colour of their shirts. Yet the British are not short of tales that

lend themselves to stirring cinematic treatment – tales of Empire (as in *The Four Feathers*, 1939, 1978, 2003, or *North West Frontier*, 1959), Arthurian legend (as in John BOORMAN's *Excalibur*, 1981, UK/US) or the deeds of legendary heroes, like ROBIN HOOD (most memorably incarnated by Sean CONNERY in Richard LESTER's *Robin and Marian*, 1976, UK/US) and James BOND. And let us not forget those British directors with reckless and fantastical ideas, from Michael POWELL to US-born, UK-based Terry GILLIAM. Neil Sinyard.

Actors' Equity *see* **British Actors' Equity Association**

actualities The term is used to describe films of actual events (no matter how mundane), and these were the first productions of fledgling film-makers throughout the world. All were less than ten minutes in length and most ran only for one or two minutes. The events and happenings depicted were sometimes real and sometimes staged and were often of a commonplace variety, devoid of celebrity or historical importance. Emphasis was on movement, be it the *Royal Henley Regatta* (filmed by Haydon & Urry in 1897), the *Portsmouth Express* (G.A. SMITH, 1898) or *Waves Breaking on the Sea Shore* (C. Goodwin Norton, 1898). One of the earliest actualities was the 1896 film of *Workers Leaving the Lumière Factory*, and it was commonplace activities such as these that appealed to cinema's first audiences.

Actualities formed the basis for the first screenings of films at MUSIC HALLS and as bioscope shows at fairgrounds supplemented by the occasional comedy or dramatic short. Foreign actualities were as popular with audiences as those from Britain. By the turn of the century, interest in the actuality faded as audiences demanded storylines rather than scenics; there was a limit to how many times the viewer wanted to watch waves breaking on the shore or trains rushing into stations. However, actuality survived in such new formats as NEWSREELS and cinéma vérité DOCUMENTARIES. AS.

Adair, Janice (*b* Morpeth, 1904 – *d* Gerrards Cross, 1996). Actress. RN: Beatrice Duffy. Pretty, diminutive actress who appeared in about 15 early talkies before retiring to marry editor Alfred ROOME.
BRITISH FILMS INCLUDE: *To What Red Hell*, *The Informer* (1929), *Contraband Love* (1931), *Lucky Ladies* (1932), *Nine Forty-Five*, *Flood Tide* (1934).

Adair, Robert (*b* San Francisco, 1900 – *d* London, 1954). Actor. American-born, English (Harrow)-educated, Adair made his film debut in Hollywood in *Raffles* (1925), also appearing there in *Journey's End* (1930, UK/US). In 1937 he returned to Britain where he spent the rest of his film career in supporting roles, often as blustering types like the jury foreman in *Eight O'Clock Walk* (1954) or the bibulous Italian barman in *The Intruder* (1953).
OTHER BRITISH FILMS INCLUDE: *What A Man!* (1938), *The Face at the Window*, *Jamaica Inn* (1939), *Noose* (1948), *Portrait of Clare* (1950), *The Captain's Paradise* (1953).

Adam, Ken (*b* Berlin, 1921). Production designer. German-born designer Adam, in England since 1934, trained as architect at London University, served as RAF pilot during WW2, and entered films as draughtsman on *This Was a Woman* (1948). He made his name as the man responsible for the witty, inventive high-gloss look of the 'BOND' FILMS, for which he concocted ever more lavish and eye-catching sets as the success and budgets for the series rocketed. Also had a very productive association with Stanley KUBRICK on *Dr Strangelove . . .* (1963), with its gleaming and sinister war room, and on the contrastingly mellow TECHNICOLOR beauties of *Barry Lyndon* (1975), for which he won an Oscar. As well, he is responsible for the design of such impressive and varied films as the sumptuous biopic, *The Trials of Oscar Wilde* (1960), the Cold War thriller, *The Ipcress File* (1965), the fantasy, *Chitty Chitty Bang Bang* (1968), and the musical, *Goodbye, Mr Chips* (1969). His most recent work has been mostly on American films, including *In and Out* (1997).

OTHER BRITISH FILMS INCLUDE: (art d) *Night of the Demon* (1957), *Beyond This Place* (1959); (des) *Dr No* (1962), *In the Cool of the Day* (1963), *Goldfinger, Woman of Straw* (1964), *Thunderball* (1965), *Funeral in Berlin* (1966), *You Only Live Twice* (1967), *Sleuth* (1972), *The Spy Who Loved Me* (1977), *Moonraker* (1979, UK/Fr).

Adam, Ronald (*b* Bromyard, 1896 – *d* London, 1979). Actor. Very prolific character player, often in official and professional roles, occasionally sinister, always sober and often stuffy of demeanour. Also wrote several plays which he produced, and was the producer of many more; as well, he wrote a book of memoirs and two war books. Not necessarily known by name to filmgoers, he was a familiar face in scores of British films across five decades, especially in the 40s and 50s when he often made five or more films in a year. There was a lot of television too in his last 20 years. His OBE (1946) seems a just reward for unflagging industry.

BRITISH FILMS INCLUDE: *Song of Freedom* (1936), *The Drum* (1938), *The Foreman Went to France* (1942), *Pink String and Sealing Wax* (1945), *Green for Danger* (1946), *Take My Life* (1947), *Bonnie Prince Charlie* (1948), *Under Capricorn* (1949), *Seven Days to Noon* (1950), *Laughter in Paradise* (1951), *Top Secret* (1952), *The Million Pound Note* (1953), *Reach for the Sky* (1956), *Carlton-Browne of the FO* (1958), *Carry On Regardless* (1961), *Heavens Above!* (1963), *The Ruling Class* (1971).

Adams, Jill (*b* London, 1930). Actress. Leggy blonde, former model, who good-humouredly adorned some engaging light comedies of the 50s, especially to the fore in a couple of BOULTING brothers satires.

BRITISH FILMS INCLUDE: *Forbidden Cargo, The Young Lovers, The Constant Husband* (1955), *Private's Progress, The Green Man, Brothers in Law* (1956), *Doctor in Distress* (1963), *Promise Her Anything* (1965).

Adams, Maud (*b* Lulea, Sweden, 1945). Actress. RN: Wikstrum. Swedish-born Adams, former model, came to fame as the glamorous leading lady of two 'BOND' FILMS: *The Man with the Golden Gun* (1974) and, in the title role, *Octopussy* (1983). Most of the rest were little-seen American and Continental films, of which the best known may be *Rollerball* (1975), and in telemovies.

OTHER BRITISH FILMS: *Killer Force* (1975), *Jane and the Lost City* (1987, UK/US).

Adams, Richard (*b* Berkshire, 1920). Author. Adams' bestsellers, *Watership Down* and *The Plague Dogs* (US), were filmed as cartoons in, respectively, 1978 and 1982, by director-writer Martin Rosen, with starry vocal interpreters (Ralph RICHARDSON, John HURT, etc.) and over-cute animal images. Devotees of the books were severe in their judgements.

Adams, Robert (*b* Georgetown, British Guiana, *c* 1906 – *d* Guyana, *c* 1965). Actor. A former schoolteacher (wrestler according to some sources), this West Indian actor had a good role in Thorold DICKINSON's *Men of Two Worlds* (1946), as the African composer who returns to his native village to help the

District Commissioner overthrow the witch-doctor's power. There were not many rewarding roles for black actors in 30s and 40s British cinema, but the physically imposing Adams landed many of them. He was involved in the first (uncompleted) British film about Britain's black population, *A World Is Turning* (1946). Also acted in the theatre. He is believed to have died in Guyana in 1965, having retired there, disillusioned with the possibilities then open to a black actor in Britain.

OTHER BRITISH FILMS INCLUDE: *Song of Freedom* (1936), *King Solomon's Mines* (1937), *Old Bones of the River* (1938), *It Happened One Sunday* (1944), *Caesar and Cleopatra* (1945), *Old Mother Riley's Jungle Treasure* (1951), *Sapphire* (1959).

Adams, Tom (*b* London, 1938). Actor. Darkly handsome leading man of several 60s films, including the James BOND spoofs, *Licensed to Kill* (1965) and *Somebody's Stolen Our Russian Spy* (1967). From the mid 70s, mainly on television.

OTHER BRITISH FILMS INCLUDE: *A Prize of Arms* (1961), *The Fighting Prince of Donegal* (1966), *Fathom* (1967), *The House That Dripped Blood* (1970), *Mark of the Devil* (1984).

adaptations From the silent period to the present day, British cinema has drawn prolifically on literary and theatrical sources for film material. The received wisdom used to be that British film-makers were less brutal, more 'faithful' in their adaptation of precursor texts than Hollywood vulgarians who would ruthlessly gut fiction and drama in the interests of popular entertainment. Nowadays, British cinema is more likely to be characterised as unadventurous in reworking material from other sources, implying undue reliance on the verbal and too little on the visual. In most recent times, the easy put-down term, 'HERITAGE' CINEMA, has often been closely allied with literary adaptation.

From around 1910, when cinema was firmly established as a narrative art form, British cinema started to make tableau-like versions of classic works, including many adaptations of DICKENS and SHAKESPEARE. A film such as Cecil HEPWORTH and Thomas BENTLEY's *David Copperfield* (1913) looks unbearably static today, with snippets of this very long novel introduced by wordy intertitles, but film-makers were quick to capitalise on the value of a well-known title. As to theatrical adaptations, there was from very early on an attempt to lure West End luminaries, such as Sir Herbert Beerbohm TREE and Sir Frank BENSON, to act in films, which they tended to regard as beneath their dignity even as they lined their pockets, appearing in silent versions of Shakespeare's *Henry VIII* and *Richard III* in 1911.

It was not merely the great classics of English literature that were – and would continue to be – ransacked for the screen. Film versions of reputable middle-brow novelists such as Somerset MAUGHAM, A.J. CRONIN, Graham GREENE and A.E.W. MASON, regional novelists such as David STOREY and John BRAINE, popular West End playwrights such as Noël COWARD and Terence RATTIGAN, crime and mystery writers such as Agatha CHRISTIE and Edgar WALLACE, have continued to take their place among adaptations of Shakespeare, Dickens, Thomas HARDY, Henry JAMES and Jane AUSTEN.

There have been several key phases in the history of British film adaptations. In the 30s, one would not have guessed the deep-seated social problems of British life from the comedies adapted from ALDWYCH FARCES or from Empire-boosting films such as *Sanders of the River* (1935) or *The Four Feathers* (1939), based respectively on novels by Wallace and Mason. Even HITCHCOCK, the most 'cinematic' of British directors of the period, always based his films on novels, including John Buchan's *The 39 Steps* (1935) and Joseph CONRAD's *The Secret Agent* which he filmed as *Sabotage* (1936), though he cared more about film than misplaced fidelity to his source material. Wartime film-making, when it might be argued that British cinema came of age, relied less on adaptation but post-war prestige was closely linked to David LEAN's versions of Dickens, OLIVIER's of Shakespeare, Anthony ASQUITH's of Rattigan, and Carol REED's celebrated dealings with Greene in *The Fallen Idol* (1948) and *The Third Man* (1949).

The adaptation phenomenon received a further boost at the end of the 50s with the 'NEW WAVE' films, based on rougher contemporary novels and plays, including *Room at the Top* (1958), *Look Back in Anger* (1959) and *This Sporting Life* (1963). Running concurrently with these prestige adaptations were HAMMER FILMS' then critically excoriated but immensely popular versions of *Dracula* and *Frankenstein*, each of which went through several permutations. In the floundering British cinema of the late 60s, Ken RUSSELL's audacious version of D.H. LAWRENCE's *Women in Love* (1969) and Joseph LOSEY's *Accident* (1967) and *The Go-Between* (1971) were intelligent attempts to come to terms with both adaptation and the British CLASS system. There were several popular, all-star versions of Agatha Christie, ushered in by *Murder on the Orient Express* (1974), and, over the next three decades, the films of MERCHANT IVORY drew heavily on the works of James and E.M. FORSTER, attracting mixed respect and impatience. There was a burst of Jane Austen films in the 90s, of which the least 'faithful', Patricia ROZEMA's *Mansfield Park* (1999, UK/US), was perhaps the most interesting.

There is no sign of the practice of adaptation's declining. There are heartening suggestions, as in the last-named, or in Iain SOFTLEY's *The Wings of the Dove* (1997), of a willingness to make something clearly new in the process.
BIBLIOG: Brian McFarlane, 'A Literary Cinema? British Films and British Novels', in Charles Barr (ed) *All Our Yesterdays*, 1986.

Addams, Dawn (*b* Felixstowe, 1930 – *d* London, 1985). Actress. For a decade or so, this glamorous brunette had a high profile as much – possibly more – for her hectic and well-publicised romantic life, which included marriage to (1954–71), and divorce from, Prince Vittorio Massimo, as her films. RADA-trained, she was capable of wittier things than she was often given a chance to do, as she showed in Hollywood's *The Moon is Blue* (1953). A journalist before entering films in 1951, and busy in American films (e.g. *Young Bess*, 1953) through most of the 50s, she had the female lead in Harold FRENCH's MGM–British thriller, *The Hour of 13* (1952). CHAPLIN chose her for his leading lady in the lacklustre *A King in New York* (1957), and most of the rest of her career, some of it in Continental films, was undistinguished, though she was seen to decorative advantage in Terence Fisher's *The Two Faces of Dr Jekyll* (1960). Often on the stage in the 60s.
OTHER BRITISH FILMS INCLUDE: *The Silent Enemy* (1958), *Where the Bullets Fly* (1966), *The Vampire Lovers* (1970), *Vault of Horror* (1973, UK/US).

Addinsell, Richard (*b* London, 1904 – *d* London, 1977). Composer. After studying law at Oxford, Addinsell wrote the scores or incidental music for numerous stage shows, including Joyce GRENFELL's famous solo performances and several collaborations, on stage and radio, with playwright Clemence DANE. Entered films in 1936, composing the scores for several important productions for KORDA's LONDON FILMS,

including *Dark Journey* (1937) and *South Riding* (1938). His most famous score is that for the romantic melodrama, *Dangerous Moonlight* (1941), for which he wrote the 'Warsaw Concerto' which contributed much to the film's popularity. During WW2, he supplied the music for a number of official DOCUMENTARIES, such as *Men of the Lightship* (1940) for the MINISTRY OF INFORMATION and *The New Lot* (1943) for the ARMY FILM UNIT. Post-war, he was one of the most sought-after composers in British cinema, carving a special niche in the scoring of COSTUME FILMS.
OTHER BRITISH FILMS: *The Amateur Gentleman* (1936), *Fire Over England* (1937), *Goodbye, Mr Chips*, *The Lion Has Wings* (1939), *Contraband*, *Britain at Bay* (doc), *Gaslight* (1940), *This England*, *Camouflage* (doc), *WRNS* (doc), *Love on the Dole* (1941), *The Day Will Dawn*, *The Big Blockade*, *Troopship* (doc) (1942), *Blithe Spirit* (1945), *A Diary For Timothy* (short) (1946), *The Passionate Friends* (1948), *Under Capricorn* (1949), *The Black Rose* (1950, UK/US), *Encore* (1951), *Sea Devils* (1953), *Beau Brummell* (1954), *The Prince and the Showgirl*, *The Admirable Crichton* (1957), *A Tale of Two Cities* (1958), *Macbeth*, *The Roman Spring of Mrs Stone* (1961), *Waltz of the Toreadors* (1962), *Life at the Top* (1965).

Addison, John (*b* West Chobham, 1920 – *d* Bennington, Vermont, 1998). Composer. In his enormously productive career, Addison composed for the theatre and the concert hall as well as for the screen. Trained at the RCM, he entered films after WW2 through the good offices of Roy BOULTING. He subsequently worked on eight further films for the Boulting brothers, worked across GENRES and STUDIOS throughout the 50s, and adapted readily to the demands of the realist 'NEW WAVE' of the early 60s, especially in the films of Tony RICHARDSON with whom he was associated at the Royal Court Theatre during its ground-breaking seasons in the later 50s. Most of his work after *A Bridge Too Far* in 1977 was for American productions, and he lived in America for some years until his death.
OTHER BRITISH FILMS INCLUDE: *Fame is the Spur* (1947), *The Guinea Pig* (1948, school song), *Pool of London*, *Seven Days to Noon* (1950), *High Treason* (1951), *The Hour of 13* (1952), *The Man Between*, *The 'Maggie'* (1953), *The Black Knight*, *One Good Turn* (1954), *That Lady*, *Josephine and Men*, *Cockleshell Heroes* (1955), *Private's Progress*, *Reach for the Sky* (1956), *The Shiralee*, *Lucky Jim* (1957), *I Was Monty's Double*, *Carlton-Browne of the FO* (1958), *Look Back in Anger* (1959), *The Entertainer* (1960), *A Taste of Honey* (1961), *Go to Blazes*, *The Loneliness of the Long Distance Runner* (1962), *Tom Jones*, *Girl with Green Eyes* (1963), *Guns at Batasi* (1964), *I Was Happy Here* (1965), *The Charge of the Light Brigade* (1968), *Hamlet* (1969), *Sleuth* (1972), *Dead Cert* (1974), *Joseph Andrews* (1976).

Addy, Mark (*b* England, 1963). Actor. Addy was the over-weight, impotent member of *The Full Monty*'s (1997, UK/US) line-up, having been a TV regular since the late 80s in such successes as *A Very Peculiar Practice* (1986) and *The Thin Blue Line* (1995). Starred in Julian Farino's grunge comedy *The Last Yellow* (1999, UK/Ger) and played Fred Flintstone in *The Flintstones in Las Vegas* (2000, US).
OTHER BRITISH FILMS INCLUDE: *Married 2 Malcolm* (1998, UK/Ger).

Adefarasin, Remi (*b* London, 1948). Cinematographer. Trained at Harrow Art School, he made his name as cameraman on several of Mike LEIGH's 80s TV films, including *Four Days in July* (1984), and Dennis POTTER's *Christabel* (1988). In the 90s, he lensed such notable telemovies as *The Lost Language of Cranes* (1991) and Jack CLAYTON's glorious swansong, *Memento Mori* (1992), before coming to prominence for his work on such key films as Anthony MINGHELLA's *Truly Madly*

Deeply (1990) and as second unit DOP he was responsible for much of the swirling romanticism of Minghella's *The English Patient* (1996, UK/US). Nominated for AA and won BAA for *Elizabeth* (1998), gave period glow of a gentler kind to the telemovie, *Emma* (1996), and a ravishing sheen to *Onegin* (1999, UK/US).

OTHER BRITISH FILMS INCLUDE: *The Hummingbird Tree* (1992), *Great Moments in Aviation* (1994, UK/US, TV, some cinemas), *Hollow Reed* (1996, UK/Ger), *Sliding Doors* (1998, UK/US), *The House of Mirth* (2000, UK/US).

Adler, Carine (*b* Rio de Janeiro). Director. An NFTS graduate, she spent some time in the 80s developing screenplays which were not filmed, then made the short, *Fever* (1994). On the basis of her first feature, the confronting *Under the Skin* (1997), which explores family rivalries and sexual appetite, Adler is a major talent, unsparing in her dealings with tough truths.

Adler, Larry (*b* Baltimore, 1914 – *d* London, 2001). Composer. American-born harmonica player who should have been nominated for an Oscar for his irresistibly buoyant theme for *Genevieve* (1953) but, because he was BLACKLISTED at the time, the credit went to music director Muir MATHIESON. He began in films doing specialty spots in Hollywood musicals such as *The Big Broadcast of 1937* (1936), appeared in the British romantic drama, *St Martin's Lane* (1938), with Charles LAUGHTON, returning to England in the 50s as composer on several films.

OTHER BRITISH FILMS: *Calling All Stars* (1937), *Jumping for Joy* (1955), *A Cry from the Streets* (1958), *The Hellions* (1961, UK/Saudi), *King and Country* (1964), *A High Wind in Jamaica* (1965).

BIBLIOG: Autobiography, *It Ain't Necessarily So*, 1985.

Adrian, Max (*b* Enneskillen, N.Ireland, 1903 – *d* Wilford, 1973). Actor. RN: Bor. On stage from 1926, with vast experience in plays classical and modern, in revue and with a one-man show as George Bernard SHAW, he entered films in 1934, mostly in character roles suggesting stylish corruption or idiosyncrasy of one kind or another. His best remembered film work is as the effete dauphin in OLIVIER's *Henry V*, and in the latter part of his long career he had several memorable roles for Ken RUSSELL in whom he seems to have met his flamboyant match. He played the composer Delius in Russell's famous TV film, *Song of Summer* (1968), and subsequently appeared in his big-screen excesses, *The Music Lovers* (1971), *The Devils* (1971) and *The Boy Friend* (1971).

OTHER BRITISH FILMS INCLUDE: *The Primrose Path* (1934), *Kipps, Penn of Pennsylvania* (1941), *The Young Mr Pitt* (1942), *Pool of London* (1950), *The Pickwick Papers* (1952), *Dr Terror's House of Horrors* (1964), *The Deadly Affair* (1966).

advertising films The innovative quality of British advertising films is borne out by those which have survived from the earliest days of cinema and into the TV era. The first examples divided into two types: documentary-style promotion/demonstration films, such as Charles Goodwin Norton's *Vinolia Soap* (*c* 1898), which shows women packaging the product; and playful vignettes, such as Dewar's *The Whisky of His Ancestors* (*c* 1898). For a while, the former dominated, anticipating the strong alliance between film-making and industry in British cinema history (*see* SPONSORED FILM-MAKING).

Post-WW1 saw the emergence of new variations: advertisements disguised as short stories, as in *Daddy's Birthday* (1919),

for Swan Pens; and the snappy commercial, such as *Candy Cushions* (1926). Other celebrities followed Walter FORDE's whimsical tour of the Osram lightbulb factory in *The Economist* (1921): comedian Bobbie Comber soothed his nerves with Classic pipe tobacco in *Sound Advice* (*c* 1934), and cartoonist H.M. Bateman lent his skills to two animated advertisements, *The Boy Who Wanted to Make Pictures* (*c* 1928) for Kodak Pocket Cameras, and *Mr —- Goes Motoring* (*c* 1928), for Shell Motor Spirit. Thus began an enduring tradition of film-makers and other artists turning their hands to advertising films, either through John Grierson's GPO FILM UNIT, producing ANIMATION masterpieces such as Len LYE's *Rainbow Dance* (1936) and Norman McLAREN's *Love on the Wing* (1938), or independently. CAVALCANTI made *Happy in the Morning* (1938) for Ascot Water Heaters; George PÁL created a brilliant series of TECHNICOLOR puppet animation films for Horlicks; and Anson DYER produced Technicolor cartoons for Bush Radios. Maverick genius Richard MASSINGHAM, who made numerous comic MOI films during WW2, raised cinema advertising films to a new level of sophistication with (e.g.) *An Englishman's Home* (1946), for Horlicks, and anticipated the seductive style of TV commercials. British commercial TV, launched in 1955 with the famous 'ice-block' ad for Gibbs SR toothpaste, sustained the inventiveness of British advertising films and many succeeding feature film-makers, including John SCHLESINGER, Ken RUSSELL and Ridley SCOTT nurtured their skills on the genre. Clyde Jeavons

Africa in British film Essentially Africa has provided British cinema with exotic locations in which, more often than not, it situated imperial adventures rather than serious exploration of the problems besetting a continent emerging painfully from Western colonialism and, in many cases, exploitation and oppression. The entry on EMPIRE AND COLONIALISM suggests the range of films made/set in Africa, including KORDA's 30s adventures, such as *Sanders of the River* (1935) and *The Four Feathers* (1939), GAUMONT's *Rhodes of Africa* (1936) and GAINSBOROUGH's *King Solomon's Mines* (1937). Such films characteristically extol the virtues of white civilisation and represent the native populations as either childlike or dangerous, but they were very popular at the time.

Post-war, a change in approach can be detected with Africa no longer standing in so unproblematically as the 'dark - continent' or as some kind of alarming 'other'. Thorold DICKINSON's sympathetic *Men of Two Worlds* (1946) may now seem paternalistic in its account of an educated African returning to his village from London to help whites counter the witch-doctor's influence, but it conceived of Africa in a more complex way than the pre-war adventures. Like Geoffrey BARKAS's silent film, *Palaver* (1926), and John GRIERSON's *Man of Africa* (1953) for GROUP 3, it is one of a small number of African-made British films starring Africans. Films such as Zoltán KORDA's *Cry, the Beloved Country* (1952) and *Simba* (1955) are earnest attempts to explore tragic interracial conflicts. Alongside these seriously intended films are more straightforwardly adventurous pieces: for example, *Diamond City* (1949) and *The Adventurers* (1950), both semi-WESTERNS dealing with mining in South Africa, John HUSTON's well-loved *The African Queen* (1951), a vehicle for two durable stars, *Where No Vultures Fly* (1951) and its sequel, *West of Zanzibar* (1954), based on a game warden's experiences, *Golden Ivory* (1954), a melodrama of sibling rivalry and exploitation, the romance of *Nor the Moon by Night* (1958), with another game warden encountering problems, Cy ENDFIELD's famous *Zulu* (1964), which restages the British–Zulu conflict at Rorke's Drift, and Basil DEARDEN's fine biopic of General Gordon, *Khartoum* (1966). More recent films which have tackled racial issues head-on, albeit in the framework of powerful melodramatic narratives, are two anti-apartheid films, *Cry Freedom* and *A World Apart* (UK/Zimb), and *White Mischief* (1987), based on a real-life murder in Kenya, mounts a sharp critique of colonial society. There are plenty of other examples, with varying degrees of political content, overt or otherwise, of Africa as theme or setting in British cinema, but, for the most part, whatever the motives of the film-makers, it has been represented as exotic, colourful and dangerous.

Agate, James (*b* Manchester, 1877 – *d* London, 1947). Critic. Waspish rather than witty drama critic for, among others, the *Manchester Guardian* and the BBC before becoming the *Sunday Times* critic in 1923. He enjoyed considerable influence in this role, but his work as a film reviewer for the *Tatler* in particular, from 1926 to 1946, and as occasional essayist on the cinema for this and other publications has not worn well. His approach to film was essentially patronising, he adopted a disingenuous philistinism towards those who sought to take it seriously, and his criticism is little more than a series of unsubstantiated and carefully idiosyncratic opinions. His two collected volumes of film criticism (the term is loosely used) are *Around Cinemas* (1946) and *Around Cinemas: Second Series* (1948).
BIBLIOG: Autobiography, *Ego*, Vols 1–9, 1935–49; James Harding, *Agate*, 1986.

agents/agencies. For more than fifty years British agents have been challenged by the giant American agencies. In the 40s and 50s it was the William Morris Agency and MCA (Music Corporation of America); in the 60s and 70s, William Morris, CMA (Creative Management Associates) and IFA (International Famous Agency); in the 80s and 90s, William Morris and ICM (International Creative Management). Throughout the years, small and medium-sized British agencies like those of Christopher MANN, Al PARKER, Fraser & Dunlop and Herbert De LEON kept their offices and most of their clients. The upsurge of brilliant young talent at the end of the 50s and early 60s, gave these agencies, together with new ones like John Redway & Associates, Gregson & Wigan, London Artists and London Management, the tools successfully to challenge the Americans. In the latter part of the 60s, the Grade Organisation, a variety agency, sought to create a single, powerful agency. They bought Gregson & Wigan, London Artists and London Management to form London International, a powerful new British agency with offices in Los Angeles, London and New York. But London International lasted only two years. Since the 70s and 80s, strong British agencies have been formed by the amalgamation of small and medium-sized agencies. Peters, Fraser & Dunlop (PFD) and The Agency are the best examples. London Management continues to prosper as do many smaller, classy agencies. Of the American giants, only ICM survives.
Richard Gregson.

Agland, Phil (*b* Weymouth, 1950). Director. Made his name as a documentarist, for 'Fragile Earth' series in the 80s, then won awards for his work on CHANNEL 4's documentary, *Baka: People of the Rainforest* and the multi-story film, *Beyond the Clouds* (1994). His fascination with a secluded culture under threat from a wider civilisation informs his attractive feature debut, *The Woodlanders* (1997), derived from Thomas HARDY's novel.

Agutter, Jenny (*b* Taunton, 1952). Actress. Distinctively beautiful, Agutter, who trained as a dancer, began her film career as a child in the adventure *East of Sudan* (1964), and in 1971 she made startling impressions in two diverse films. In Lionel JEFFRIES' beguiling *The Railway Children*, she played the resourceful eldest child of the wrongly arrested father (she played the mother in a 2000 TV version), and, in Nicolas ROEG's poetic Australian culture-clash drama *Walkabout*, she was again a teenager whose resources are called into play, this time in appalling circumstances. Since then, what looks like a busy career seems, rather, to suggest how difficult it has been for a young and gifted actress to maintain momentum in British cinema. As a result, she has worked frequently in America (e.g. *Logan's Run*, 1976) and on TV, but only intermittently in British films, where, apart from the horse-loving girl in *Equus* (1977), she has scarcely had a decent role in a decent film since the early 70s.
OTHER BRITISH FILMS INCLUDE: *I Start Counting* (1969), *The Eagle Has Landed* (1976), *Dominique* (1978), *Riddle of the Sands* (1979), *Sweet William* (1979), *An American Werewolf in London* (1981, UK/US), *Blue Juice* (1995).

Aherne, Brian (*b* King's Norton, 1902 – *d* Venice, Florida, 1986). Actor. Most of Aherne's film career was spent in Hollywood where he went in 1933 and appeared in many popular films, such as *My Sister Eileen* (1942), and *Titanic* (1953). Began his British career in silent films, of which Anthony ASQUITH's *Shooting Stars* (1928) was the most notable, establishing himself as an urbane, reliable, if not particularly interesting, leading man, and made a couple of talkies. In 1962 he made *Lancelot and Guinevere* in England for Cornel Wilde. Married to Joan Fontaine (1939–45); in later life wrote his autobiography (*A Proper Job*, 1969) and a biography of his friend George SANDERS (*A Dreadful Man*, 1976). Had a long and distinguished stage career, beginning as a child in 1911.
OTHER BRITISH FILMS: *The Eleventh Commandment* (1924), *The Squire of Long Hadley*, *King of the Castle* (1925), *Safety First* (1926), *A Woman Redeemed* (1927), *Underground* (1928), *The W Plan* (1930), *Madame Guillotine* (1931).

Aherne, Pat (*b* Ireland, 1901 – *d* Los Angeles, 1970). Actor. Brian AHERNE's older brother who had a busy career in British silent films as a tall, handsome hero. Though he continued in talkies in Britain and Hollywood, he never acquired his brother's star status. Most of his talkies career was spent in supporting roles, in such US films as *The Paradine Case* (1947) and *Bwana Devil* (1952). Once married to Renée HOUSTON.
OTHER BRITISH FILMS INCLUDE: *The Cost of Beauty* (1924), *Blinkeyes*, *Born of Fortune* (1926), *Love's Option* (1928), *The Inseparables* (1929), *Return of Bulldog Drummond* (1934), *The Stoker* (1935), *Q Planes*, *Ask a Policeman* (1939), *Thursday's Child*, *Warn That Man* (1943).

Aimée, Anouk (*b* Paris, 1932). Actress. RN: Françoise Dreyfus. Most of this elegant beauty's nearly 70 films were made in France, where she came to fame at 17 in *Les amants de Vérone* (1949), or Italy (*La dolce vita*, 1960). However, she made several memorable appearances in British films, notably in *The Golden Salamander* (1949), *The Man Who Watched Trains Go By* (1952), and *Success is the Best Revenge* (1984, UK/Fr). Her fourth of five husbands was Albert FINNEY.
OTHER BRITISH FILMS INCLUDE: *Forever My Heart* (1954), *Contraband – Spain* (1955), *One Hundred and One Nights* (1995, UK/Fr).

Ainley, Henry (*b* Morley, 1879 – *d* London, 1945). Actor. RN: Riddle. A prominent theatrical celebrity – London stage debut 1900, New York 1903 – Ainley was one of the first major stage actors to become a film star, on screen from 1914.

BRITISH FILMS INCLUDE: *She Stoops to Conquer* (1914), *The Prisoner of Zenda* (1915), *The Manxman* (1916), *Quinneys* (1919), *Money* (1921), *Sally Bishop* (1923), *The First Mrs Fraser* (1932, in which he starred on stage in 1929), *As You Like It* (1936). AS.

Ainley, Richard (*b* London, 1910 – *d* London, 1967). Actor. RN: Riddle. Son of famous stage and silent screen star Henry AINLEY, he appeared with his father in Paul CZINNER's *As You Like It* (1936). Made nine British films, usually in supporting roles, before going to Hollywood in 1940 where he appeared in a further dozen, including *White Cargo* (1942). On stage from 1928.

OTHER BRITISH FILMS: *The Frog* (1937), *Our Fighting Navy, The Gang Show* (1937), *Old Iron, Lily of Laguna* (1938), *There Ain't No Justice, A Stolen Life, An Englishman's Home* (1939).

Aird, Holly (*b* Aldershot, 1969). Actress. While BRANAGH and BONHAM CARTER act furiously in *The Theory of Flight* (1998), the reflective, oval-faced Aird quietly makes her presence felt as Branagh's neglected girlfriend. She starred in the telemovie *The Happy Valley* (1986), set in Kenya, but has generally had supporting roles in films, as in the sexual black comedy, *Intimate Relations* (1996, UK/Can), and *Possession* (2002, UK/US).

OTHER BRITISH FILMS INCLUDE: *Carry On Columbus* (1992), *Fever Pitch* (1997), *Dreaming of Joseph Lees* (1999, UK/US), *The Criminal* (2001, UK/US).

Aird, Jane (*b* Motherwell, Scotland, 1926 – *d* Surrey, 1993). Actress. Supporting player in 50s films, including *The Quatermass Experiment* (1955). Also active on stage, she was married to Guy ROLFE, with whom she appeared in *Dance Little Lady* (1954).

OTHER BRITISH FILMS INCLUDE: *Hunted* (1952), *The Lyons in Paris* (1955), *Quatermass 2* (1957), *The Day the Earth Caught Fire* (1961).

Aitken, Maria (*b* Dublin, 1945). Actress. Tall, slender comedy actress, granddaughter of Lord BEAVERBROOK, famous on stage for witty performances in such plays as *Private Lives* (1980) and *The Women* (1986) and on television, Aitken has so far made only a few films, but was memorably funny as John Cleese's permanently (and justifiably) bad-tempered wife in *A Fish Called Wanda* (1988). The (sort of) sequel, *Fierce Creatures* (1997, UK/US), sadly gave her comic talents little scope. Was married to Nigel DAVENPORT; their son is actor Jack DAVENPORT.

OTHER BRITISH FILMS INCLUDE: *Some Girls Do* (1969), *Mary Queen of Scots* (1971), *Half Moon Street* (1986, UK/US), *The Fool* (1990), *The Grotesque* (1996).

Aked, Muriel (*b* Bingley, 1887 – *d* Settle, 1955). Actress. Archetypal kindly mother or fussy spinster in 40 British films, Aked was on stage from 1916, entered silent films in *A Sister to Assist 'Er* (1922) and starred in its modest 1948 remake. She appeared in some major 30s films, including *Rome Express* (1932), *The Good Companions* (1933), and *A Girl Must Live* (1939), and became a fixture in the 40s. Memorable as Roger LIVESEY's aunt in *The Life and Death of Colonel Blimp* (1943), as Flora ROBSON's friend in the women's internment camp drama, *Two Thousand Women* (1944), as a nosy landlady in *So Evil My Love* (1948), and, in her last film, *The Story of Gilbert and Sullivan* (1953), as Queen Victoria, she never gave a poor performance, her warmth and precision saving her from mere caricature.

OTHER BRITISH FILMS INCLUDE: *Bindle's Cocktail* (1926), *The Middle Watch* (1930), *No Funny Business, Friday the Thirteenth* (1933), *The Night of the Party, Autumn Crocus, Evensong* (1934), *Can You Hear Me Mother?* (1935), *The Silent Battle* (1939), *Cottage to Let* (1941), *The Demi-Paradise* (1943), *The Wicked Lady* (1945), *The Years Between* (1946), *It's Hard to Be Good* (1948), *The Blue Lamp* (1949), *The Happiest Days of Your Life* (1950).

Akomfrah, John (*b* Ghana, 1957) Director, screenwriter. African film-maker who made four films for the Black Audio Collective, all on themes relevant to black experience: (d, sc) *Testament* (1988), *Who Needs a Heart* (1991, UK/Ger), *Seven Songs for Malcolm X* (1993), *The Mothership Connection* (1995, short, d only).

Alcott, Arthur (*b* London, 1894 – *d* Swindon, 1986). Production controller. This was the title most usually associated with Alcott on dozens of film credits from the 40s to the 60s. Entered movies in 1912 as camera assistant on *Sixty Years a Queen* and in varying capacities worked for most film-making companies before becoming production manager at GAINSBOROUGH in the early 40s. The title 'controller' seems first to have been used on *Snowbound* (1948) and he became production controller of PINEWOOD Studios in the early 50s. Major research is required to assess the function and importance of such industry figures. He produced two films near the end of his career: *Linda* (1960) and *Echo of Barbara* (1960).

OTHER BRITISH FILMS INCLUDE: *The Man in Grey* (1943), *Fanny by Gaslight* (1944), *Holiday Camp* (1947), *Diamond City* (1949), *The Long Memory* (1952), *Genevieve* (1953), *Doctor in the House* (1954), *A Town Like Alice* (1956), *A Tale of Two Cities* (1958), *Sapphire* (1959), *Night of the Eagle* (1962).

Alcott, John (*b* Isleworth, 1931 – *d* Cannes, 1986). Cinematographer. The son of Arthur ALCOTT, this cameraman, who died sadly young of a heart attack, had a famous collaboration with Stanley KUBRICK. Having been assistant to ace cameraman Geoffrey UNSWORTH during the 60s, he was asked to photograph the 'Dawn of Man' sequence on *2001: A Space Odyssey* (1968). Promoted to director of photography on Kubrick's notorious *A Clockwork Orange* (1971), contributing notably to the chilly detachment of its vision, he won an Oscar for his extraordinary achievement on Kubrick's *Barry Lyndon* (1975), in which he sought to replicate the effects of the lighting of the film's period, notably in interiors lit by candle. Nothing else in his career can have been as challenging as the four for Kubrick: the last was *The Shining* (1980, UK/US) with its striking use of the Steadicam system. He emigrated to America in 1981, and made only one further British film, *Greystoke . . .* (1984, UK/US). American films include *Under Fire* (1983) and *No Way Out* (1986).

OTHER BRITISH FILMS: *Little Malcolm and His Struggle Against the Eunuchs* (1974), *Overlord* (1975), *March or Die, The Disappearance* (UK/Can) (1977).

BIBLIOG: Duncan Petrie, *The British Cinematographer*, 1996.

Alderton, John (*b* Gainsborough, 1940). Actor. Leading man with a light touch and a flair for comedy which has been more widely displayed on TV than in the cinema. He came to attention in such series as *Please, Sir!* (filmed with most of the regular cast in 1971) and *Upstairs, Downstairs*, but his film career has sputtered rather than catching fire. Married to Pauline COLLINS with whom he co-starred in three television series.

OTHER BRITISH FILMS: *The System* (1964), *Assignment K* (1967), *Duffy* (1968), *Hannibal Brooks* (1968), *Zardoz* (1973), *It Shouldn't Happen to a Vet* (1976), *Clockwork Mice* (1995).

Aldridge, Michael (*b* Glastonbury, 1920 – *d* London, 1994). Actor. Tall and imposing, the shaggy-browed Aldridge most often projected an aloof upper-class mien, but in the television series *Love in a Cold Climate* (1980) and as Pistol in Orson Welles's elegy to Merrie England, *Chimes at Midnight* (1966, Sp/Switz), he also exhibited a finely manic edge. A sporadic film career, but also busy on stage (from 1946) and television.
OTHER BRITISH FILMS: *Bank Holiday Luck* (1947), *Murder in the Cathedral* (1952), *Life for Ruth* (1962), *Mouse on the Moon* (1963), *Follow Me!* (1971), *Bullshot* (1983), *Turtle Diary* (1985), *Clockwise* (1985).

Aldwych farces on film Series of hugely successful film COMEDIES based on the farces by Ben TRAVERS staged at London's Aldwych theatre between 1925 and 1933, utilising the same band of players. The latter included Ralph LYNN, Robertson HARE, Yvonne ARNAUD, Mary BROUGH, Winifred SHOTTER and Tom WALLS, the latter also directing the ADAPTATIONS, albeit in a theatrical manner. There were eight adaptations in all, beginning with *Rookery Nook* in 1930, followed by *Plunder* (1931), *A Night Like This* (1932), *Thark* (1932), *Turkey Time* (1933), *A Cuckoo in the Nest* (1933, remade as *Fast and Loose* in 1954), *Dirty Work* (1934) and *A Cup of Kindness* (1934). One of the farces, *A Bit of a Test*, was not adapted for the screen. A number of other Travers comedies were also filmed during this period with many of the same players, although either based on the author's non-Aldwych stage farces or written directly for the screen. John Oliver.

Alexander, Donald (*b* London, 1913 – *d* Inverness, 1993). Director. DOCUMENTARY film-maker of the 30s and 40s whose work is almost entirely in association with Paul ROTHA, who wrote warmly in 1973 of Alexander's 'sensitive feeling for real people' as exhibited in his *Eastern Valley* (1937).
OTHER BRITISH FILMS INCLUDE: (short, doc) *People in the Park* (1936), *Wealth of a Nation* (1938), *All Those in Favour, Defeat Diphtheria, Five and Under, Our School* (1941), *Life Begins Again, Land Girl* (1942).

Alexander, Terence (*b* London, 1923). Actor. Usually in well-bred roles, Alexander has appeared largely as a supporting actor, often as military officer (as in *Danger Within*, 1958) or as straight man to comedians such as Norman WISDOM (*The Square Peg*, 1958, *The Bulldog Breed*, 1960), MORECAMBE AND WISE (*The Intelligence Men*, 1965), and Frankie HOWERD (*The Runaway Bus*, 1954). First appeared on the London stage in 1950, and often on TV, notably as Monty Dartie in *The Forsyte Saga* (1967) and in a continuing role in *Bergerac* (1981–91).
OTHER BRITISH FILMS INCLUDE: *Comin' Thro' the Rye* (1947), *The Elusive Pimpernel* (1950), *The Gentle Gunman* (1952), *The Green Scarf* (1954), *The One That Got Away* (1957), *The League of Gentlemen* (1960), *Carry On Regardless* (1961), *On the Beat, The Fast Lady* (1962), *Bitter Harvest* (1963), *The Long Duel* (1967), *Only When I Larf* (1968), *The Day of the Jackal* (1973, UK/Fr), *The Internecine Project* (1974).

Alison, Dorothy (*b* Broken Hill, Australia, 1925 – *d* London, 1992). Actress. RN: Dickson. Incisive but sympathetic, Alison was one of the most reliable character players in 50s British cinema. After two Australian films, *The Sons of Matthew* (1949) and the EALING-sponsored *Bitter Springs* (1950), she attracted favourable critical notice as the teacher of the deaf in Ealing's *Mandy* (1952), as Nurse Brace in the Douglas Bader biopic, *Reach for the Sky* (1956), and as the young housewife who rescues a deranged Richard ATTENBOROUGH in *The Man Upstairs* (1958), among others. She returned to Australian film and TV in the early 80s, appearing notably as Lindy Chamberlain's mother in *Evil Angels* (1988, UK/Aust).
OTHER BRITISH FILMS INCLUDE: *Turn the Key Softly, The 'Maggie'* (1953), *The Purple Plain* (1954), *The Silken Affair, The Long Arm* (1956), *The Scamp* (1957), *Life in Emergency Ward 10* (1958), *Georgy Girl* (1966), *A Matter of Innocence* (1967), *Blind Terror* (1971), *Dr Jekyll & Sister Hyde* (1971), *Baxter!* (1972), *Return of the Soldier* (1982).

Allan, Elizabeth (*b* Skegness, 1908 – *d* Hove, 1990). Actress. Slender, blonde heroine of early talkies, successful in mid 30s Hollywood, playing subsidiary roles in such prestige MGM productions as *David Copperfield* and *A Tale of Two Cities* (1935) and *Camille* (1936). Her early British films were prolific rather than distinctive, including *The Lodger* (1932), a modernised REMAKE of HITCHCOCK's silent classic, again with Ivor NOVELLO. When she returned to Britain in the late 30s, her career as a leading lady had lost its momentum, and, after playing Mrs Cibber in *The Great Mr Handel* (1942) and the object of George FORMBY's affections in *He Snoops to Conquer* (1944), she slid somewhat prematurely into character roles, often as neglected or waspish wives. On stage from 1927 at the Old Vic, had TV success on *What's My Line?* in the 50s. Married to production executive W.J. [Bill] O'BRYEN.
OTHER BRITISH FILMS INCLUDE: *Alibi, Black Coffee* (1931), *Service for Ladies* (1932), *The Shadow* (1933), *Java Head* (1934), *Dangerous Medicine* (1938), *Saloon Bar* (1940), *Went the Day Well?* (1942), *That Dangerous Age* (1949), *No Highway* (1951), *Folly to be Wise* (1952), *Twice Upon a Time, The Heart of the Matter* (1953), *Front Page Story* (1953), *The Brain Machine* (1954), *The Grip of the Strangler* (1958).

Allan, Marguerite (*b* St Petersburg, 1909). Actress. Leading lady of the 30s, largely in films which still await a revival of interest, though some are made by directors, including George KING and Adrian BRUNEL, who might repay such attention. Best remembered for Paul STEIN's musical *Blossom Time* (1934), starring Richard TAUBER.
OTHER BRITISH FILMS INCLUDE: *Widdicombe Fair* (1928), *The Plaything* (1929), *Matinee Idol* (1933), *Forbidden Territory* (1934), *Prison Breaker* (1936), *Breach of Promise* (1941).

Allégret, Marc (*b* Basle, Switzerland, 1900 – *d* Paris, 1973). Director. After a distinguished pre-WW2 career in French films, Allégret directed three films in England in the late 40s, and returned to France for the rest of his working life. *Blanche Fury* (1947) is a sumptuous melodrama, sensuous and tough-minded, but his other two British films, *The Naked Heart* (1950), set in Canada, and *Blackmailed* (1950), an uneasy mix of British and French mystery traditions, are disasters. Brother of director Yves Allégret.

Allen, Adrianne (*b* Manchester, 1907 – *d* Montreux, Switzerland, 1993). Actress. Blondely handsome stage actress, RADA-trained Allen had a fitful screen career. She began well in early talkies as *Loose Ends* (1930) *The Stronger Sex* and *The Woman Between* (1931), melodramas quite daring for their time, made one film in Hollywood (*Merrily We Go to Hell*, 1932), and appeared in only five further films, all British, after the war. Her best later role was as Jack WARNER's loyal sister in *The Final Test* (1953). Married (1929–39) to Raymond MASSEY and mother of Daniel and Anna MASSEY.
OTHER BRITISH FILMS: *Black Coffee* (1931), *The Morals of Marcus* (1935), *The October Man* (1947), *Bond Street, Vote for Huggett* (1948), *Meet Mr Malcolm* (1953).

Allen, Chesney (*b* Brighton, 1894 – *d* Midhurst, 1982). Actor, comedian. Allen's name is inextricably associated with Bud FLANAGAN's, and with the CRAZY GANG, the sixsome who won their fame in the MUSIC HALLS, then on the variety stage and the screen. In some ways, Allen seemed the most cerebral of the Gang, though that is not saying much about this bunch of supremely physical pranksters. Viewed in the right frame of mind, they could make one laugh to illness, and some of their films are classics of crazy comedy. Allen (with Flanagan) made his first film, *Wild Boy*, in 1934 and, as part of the Crazy Gang, appeared in *O-Kay for Sound* (1937), *Alf's Button Afloat* (1938), *The Frozen Limits* (1939), *Gasbags* (1940) and *Life is a Circus* (1958).

OTHER BRITISH FILMS (with Flanagan): *The Bailiffs* (1932, short), *A Fire Has Been Arranged* (1935), *Underneath the Arches* (the name of their most famous song) (1937), *We'll Smile Again* (1942), *Theatre Royal* (1943), *Dreaming* (1944), *Here Comes the Sun* (1945): (as and by himself) *Dunkirk* (1958).

BIBLIOG: Maureen Owen, *The Crazy Gang*, 1986.

Allen, Irving (*b* Lemberg, Poland, 1905 – *d* Encino, California, 1987). Producer. RN: Irving Applebaum. Entered films as editor in 1929, produced and/or directed several modest films in Hollywood in the 40s, including *Strange Voyage* (1946), and won Best Short Film AA for *Climbing the Matterhorn* (1947). He went to Europe in 1949 to produce *The Man on the Eiffel Tower* (US/Fr), with a heterogeneous cast including Charles LAUGHTON and skating star Belita. In 1950, he formed WARWICK FILMS in Britain with Albert ('Cubby') BROCCOLI as partner and distribution through Columbia. Warwick turned out a series of proficient action pieces, starring Hollywood actors, such as Alan Ladd (three) and Victor MATURE (five), and including *The Red Beret* (1953) with Ladd, *Cockleshell Heroes* (1955) with José FERRER, and *The Bandit of Zhobe* (1959) with Mature. In the 60s, he turned solo producer, filming in the US (e.g. the Matt Helm films) and in Britain, where he produced *Cromwell* (1970) starring Richard HARRIS.

OTHER BRITISH FILMS INCLUDE: *Hell Below Zero* (1953), *The Black Knight* (1954), *A Prize of Gold* (1955), *Zarak* (1956), *High Flight* (1957), *The Man Inside* (1958), *Killers of Kilimanjaro* (1959), *Hammerhead* (1968).

Allen, Jack (*b* Sandbach, 1907 – *d* Northwood, 1995). Actor. On stage from 1931, Allen (aka John) frequently appeared in films as likeable, jovial professional men, like the small-town lawyer in *Impulse* (1955), or benevolent upper-class types, like the Earl of Ambrose in *The Headless Ghost* (1959). Married to Ruth DUNNING. Much television post-50s.

OTHER BRITISH FILMS INCLUDE: *Cavalier of the Streets* (1937), *The Four Feathers* (1939), *Spy for a Day* (1940), *Bedelia* (1946), *Elizabeth of Ladymead* (1948), *Conspirator* (1949), *Wings of Danger*, *The Sound Barrier* (1952), *The Heart of the Matter* (1953), *Man from Tangier* (1957), *Jack the Ripper* (1958), *Life in Danger* (1959), *The Breaking Point*, *The Queen's Guards* (1961).

Allen, Jim (*b* Manchester, 1926 – *d* Manchester, 1999). Screenwriter. Left-wing television and screenwriter of scenes from working-class life, often associated with the realist films of Ken LOACH. A former miner and building worker, he began his career as a writer for *Coronation Street* and other TV work includes Loach's famed *Days of Hope* (1976), described by one chronicler as a 'Leftist mini-epic about Britain between 1916–26'. He brought a passionately uncompromising approach to all his work, as his three cinema films for Loach attest, his sympathies directed to the underdogs, his anger at their

exploiters. The beleaguered father (Ricky TOMLINSON) in *Raining Stones* (1993) is a typically sympathetic but rigorous character creation.

OTHER BRITISH FILMS: *Hidden Agenda* (1990), *Land and Freedom* (1995, UK/Ger/Sp).

Allen, Keith (*b* Swansea, 1952). Actor. Described by the *New Musical Express* as a 'yob-for-rent', Allen has nonetheless proved a charismatic presence in British films, generally playing dislikeable characters, with great relish. After two minor roles, Allen came to attention as the loaded flat mate, Hugo, in *Shallow Grave* (1994) and as a dealer in *Trainspotting* (1996). Although he works primarily in film and TV (a sympathetic lead in 1999's *Jack of Hearts*), his greatest notoriety comes from pop music circles. Also put in significant work writing, directing and acting in *The Comic Strip* series, which has raised millions of pounds for charity.

OTHER BRITISH FILMS INCLUDE: *Crystal Gazing* (1982), *Loose Connections* (1983), *The Supergrass* (1985), *Comrades* (1986), *Carry On Columbus* (1992), *Captives* (1994), *Blue Juice* (1995), *Loch Ness* (1996), *Twin Town* (1997), *Rancid Aluminium* (2000). Tim Roman.

Allen, Kevin (*b* 1959). Director, actor. Brother of Keith, Allen began directing, writing and producing with the bleak evocation of contemporary Wales, *Twin Town* (1997), and followed this with *The Big Tease* (1999, UK/US, + p), appearing in both. Acting in films since the mid 80s, he was a waiter in the black comedy, *Eat the Rich* (1987), and Andreas in the cult hit, *Trainspotting* (1996). Also much comedy TV, including *French and Saunders* (1987).

OTHER BRITISH FILMS: (a) *The Supergrass* (1985), *The Love Child* (1987), *The Strike* (1988), *Angry Earth* (1989), *Different for Girls* (1996), *Spice World* (1997).

Allen, Lewis (*b* Wellington, Shropshire, 1905 – *d* Santa Monica, California, 2000). Director. Began as stage actor and director before going to Hollywood in the early 40s and directing *The Uninvited* (1944), still one of the most unnerving ghost films. His subsequent films were an uneven bunch, but rarely less than entertaining, including *Our Hearts Were Young and Gay* (1944) and the assassination thriller, *Suddenly* (1954). He made only three films in England, but the first, *So Evil My Love* (1948), part of his Paramount contract, is a minor masterpiece of decorative, fin-de-siècle MELODRAMA. There is less to be said for *Another Time, Another Place* (1958), or *Whirlpool* (1959) in which most of the action is confined to a barge on the Rhine. 1940s Britain would have suited Allen better: his control over a sinister mise-en-scène and response to the brazen oppositions of melodrama might have won him a high place at GAINSBOROUGH.

Allen, Patrick (*b* Malawi, Nyasaland, 1927). Actor. This strong-jawed actor made a superbly intransigent Gradgrind in TV's fine *Hard Times* (1977). In films since 1954 (in *Dial M for Murder*, US), he has etched impressive figures on either side of the law (such as the tough lorry-owner in *The Long Haul*, 1957) in widely assorted films. Latterly, most often seen on television. Married to Sarah LAWSON.

OTHER BRITISH FILMS INCLUDE: *Confession*, 1984 (1955), *Wicked As They Come* (1956), *High Tide at Noon* (1957), *Tread Softly Stranger*, *Dunkirk* (1958), *Jet Storm* (1959), *Captain Clegg* (1962), *The Night of the Generals* (1966, UK/Fr), *Puppet on a Chain* (1970), *The Wild Geese* (1978, UK/Switz), *Who Dares Wins* (1982).

Allen, Sheila (*b* Chard, 1932). Actress. RADA-trained actress on stage since the early 50s, with seasons at the Bristol Old Vic

(1957–58) and the RSC (1966). In occasional supporting roles in films since 1955's *Confession*, with the showier role of an unfaithful wife in *The Alphabet Murders* (1965). Married to director David JONES.

OTHER BRITISH FILMS INCLUDE: *The Malpas Mystery* (1960), *The Prince and the Pauper* (1962), *Children of the Damned* (1963), *Venom* (1971), *The Other Side of the Underneath* (1972), *Pascali's Island* (1988, UK/US).

Allenby, Frank (*b* Hobart, Australia, 1898 – *d* England, 1953). Actor. Authoritative character actor, who began in the theatre in Melbourne in 1917, and made a handful of British films before going to Hollywood to make three more, strikingly in *Madame Bovary* (1949).

BRITISH FILMS: *£5 Man, Return of the Scarlet Pimpernel* (1937), *Second Thoughts* (1938), *Contraband* (1940, unc), *The Black Sheep of Whitehall* (1941), *The Next of Kin* (1942).

Allgood, Sara (*b* Dublin, 1894 – *d* Los Angeles, 1950). Actress. Famed Abbey Theatre actress, on stage from 1904, Allgood became an instantly recognisable comfy mum/housekeeper in innumerable Hollywood films, often set in Britain (*Jane Eyre*, 1943, *Kitty*, 1945) from 1940 on. Made her first film, *Just Peggy* (1918), in Australia while touring in *Peg o' My Heart*. Many of her British films have an Irish slant, but her most famous are those she made for Hitchcock, his first talkie, *Blackmail* (1929), *Juno and the Paycock* (1930, repeating stage role of Juno) and *Sabotage* (1936), and she is cast against type as a socially ambitious matron in *The Passing of the Third Floor Back* (1935). Sister of Maire O'NEILL.

OTHER BRITISH FILMS INCLUDE: *The World, the Flesh and the Devil* (1932), *Irish Hearts, Lily of Killarney* (1934), *Peg of Old Drury, Riders to the Sea* (UK/Ire) (1935), *Pot Luck, Southern Roses* (1936), *Kathleen Mavourneen, Storm in a Teacup, The Sky's the Limit* (1937), *Londonderry Air* (1938), *On the Night of the Fire* (1939).

Alliance Company was launched in 1919 as the first major post-WW1 British production entity by Sir Charles Higham MP (father of the show-business biographer), and with a board including Sir Walter de Frece, A.E. MATTHEWS and Gerald DU MAURIER. (STOLL was formed during WW1, but its first production was post-war.) Harley KNOLES was managing director and director-general of production, with René GUISSART as cinematographer, and the company acquired the studio at St Margarets, TWICKENHAM. Alliance's first production was *Carnival* (1921), with Matheson LANG and Ivor NOVELLO, followed by *The Door That Has No Key* (1921), and *The Bohemian Girl* (1922). It ceased production late in 1922, resurfacing briefly in 1924 with *Love and a Whirlwind*. AS.

Alliance Film Studios Ltd This company was formed in 1946 and controlled film-making at RIVERSIDE (Hammersmith), SOUTHALL and TWICKENHAM (both Middlesex) studios. Riverside had been used for 'QUOTA QUICKIES' production during the 30s, until it was bought by Jack BUCHANAN in 1939 and subsequently sold to Alliance. In 1948, the scandalous *No Orchids for Miss Blandish* was made there, and, in the early 50s, produced a mixture of 'A' and 'B' MOVIES, until the BBC Film Unit took it over for production in 1954. Southall also had a 'Quickies' history during the 30s. When it was acquired by Alliance, it made such films as *Dancing with Crime* (1947) and *Things Happen at Night* (1948) and in the 50s it housed some GROUP 3 productions, including *Time Gentlemen Please!* (1952). Twickenham's long history dated back to 1913, including both 'Quickies' and prestige productions during the 30s, and is still in

operation today, though at the time of its acquisition by Alliance it was the smallest of the three studios. Alliance ceased functioning as a production company in 1960.

Allied Film Makers A consortium of film-makers whose aim was to work together co-operatively and to share in distribution profits. Its key figures were Richard ATTENBOROUGH and Bryan FORBES, subsequently joined by Guy GREEN, Jack HAWKINS and his brother, and the long-established producer-director team, Michael RELPH and Basil DEARDEN. The group, formally constituted in September 1959, was associated for distribution purposes with the RANK ORGANISATION, which backed it financially, by providing 'end money' for its productions. It began well with the box-office success of *The League of Gentlemen* (1960), and *Whistle Down the Wind* (1961), starring Hayley MILLS, was also very profitable, and Dearden's *Victim* (1961), the first mainstream film about homosexuality, eventually made a profit. The group's other films were less commercially successful, including the Forbes–Attenborough production of *Seance on a Wet Afternoon* (1964), which suffered from limited release, and Dearden's excellent *Life for Ruth* (1962), a drama about religious fundamentalism and medical ethics. Rank did not lose money on its support for AFM, but the group finally stopped production in 1964, suffering from inadequate funds to tide it over failures.

BIBLIOG: Alexander Walker, *Hollywood, England*, 1974.

Allister, Claude (*b* London, 1891 – *d* Santa Barbara, California, 1970). Actor. RN: Palmer. Allister left the stock exchange in 1910 for the stage, was wounded in WW1, returned to the West End and touring theatre, and become a fixture of 30s British (and Hollywood) cinema as a monocled 'silly ass'. His type more or less passed with the war, but he made a few more films, including many in Hollywood requiring 'British types', such as *This Above All* (1942) and *Ivy* (1947).

OTHER BRITISH FILMS INCLUDE: *The Midshipmaid* (1932), *The Private Life of Henry VIII* (1933), *The Return of Bulldog Drummond, The Private Life of Don Juan* (1934), *Kiss the Bride Goodbye* (1944), *Gaiety George* (1946), *Quartet, The First Gentleman* (1948).

Altman, John (*b* London, 1949). Composer. Busy as a MONTY PYTHON collaborator since 1979's *Life of Brian* (as arranger), has subsequently worked as composer and/or arranger/musical director/conductor on an interesting range of British films and television. He was music director on two more Pythons (*The Secret Policeman's Other Ball*, 1982, *Erik the Viking*, 1989), conductor on Bertolucci's *The Sheltering Sky* (1990, UK/It), composer on two for Peter CHELSOM (*Hear My Song*, 1991, *Funny Bones*, 1995, UK/US) and on three sweet-tempered small-scale films, *Bhaji on the Beach* (1993), *Beautiful Thing* (1996) and *Little Voice* (1998, UK/US). International work includes arranging period music for *Titanic* (1997, US) and TV composing includes *Peak Practice* (1993 series).

OTHER BRITISH FILMS INCLUDE: (cond) *Foreign Body* (1986), *Everybody Wins* (1990, UK/US); (comp) *Almonds and Raisins* (1983, UK/US), *Bad Behaviour* (1993), *The Matchmaker* (1997, UK/Ire/US).

Alwyn, William (*b* Northampton, 1905 – *d* Southwold, 1985). Composer. As well as composing more than a hundred film scores and many concert works, Alwyn was also a gifted conductor and flautist. He began work in 30s DOCUMENTARIES such as *The Future's in the Air* (1937), following this with factual films for Strand Zoological Films, for Paul ROTHA (*World of Plenty*, 1943), for the CROWN FILM UNIT (*Fires Were Started*, 1942), and for the MOI (*The True Glory*, 1945). Entered feature films with *They Flew Alone* (1942), then worked for virtually every significant British director. Many of his most memorable scores show a willingness to collaborate with and reinforce the melodramatic tensions of a film, as in *Great Day* (1945), *Odd Man Out* (1947) and *Life for Ruth* (1962), but he was equally at home with realist works such as *The Way Ahead* (1944) and *A Night to Remember* (1958). Married composer **Doreen Carwithen** (*b* Haddenham, Bucks, 1922), who scored several British films, including *Boys in Brown* (1949). Created CBE in 1978.

OTHER BRITISH FILMS INCLUDE: *Squadron Leader X* (1942), *Escape to Danger* (1943), *The Rake's Progress* (1945), *Green For Danger* (1946), *So Evil My Love*, *The Fallen Idol* (1948), *The Rocking Horse Winner*, *Madeleine* (1949), *Mandy* (1952), *The Ship that Died of Shame* (1955), *Carve Her Name With Pride* (1958), *The Running Man* (1963).

Alyn, Glen (*b* Melbourne, 1913). Actress. RN: Pointing. Made about 20 films in Britain, mostly in the 30s, when under contract to Warner Bros for whom she made over a dozen films in two years.

BRITISH FILMS INCLUDE: *Head of the Family* (1933), *Trouble in Store* (1934), *Mayfair Melody* (1937), *Sweet Devil*, *The Ware Case* (1938), *A Window in London* (1939), *There's Always a Thursday* (1957).

Amalgamated Studios These studios, newly built at ELSTREE, were acquired by J. Arthur RANK under the nose of John MAXWELL in 1939, thus giving Rank control of the three biggest studios in Britain, along with DENHAM and PINEWOOD. He leased the Amalgamated Studios to the Ministry of Works for storage during the war, and in 1947 sold them to the Prudential Insurance Company, which had invested in film production in the 30s and which in turn sold them to MGM–BRITISH. Under this ownership, the Studios saw the production of lavish Hollywood-style films such as *Edward, My Son* (1949) and *Ivanhoe* (1952). The former Amalgamated Studios had been turned into a replica of a Hollywood studio, and MGM–British continued production there until it was sold in 1970 to a cold storage company.

Amann, Betty (*b* Pirmasens, Germany, *c* 1907 – *d* Westport, Connecticut, 1990). Actress. Between 1926 (*The Kick-Off*) and 1943 (Edgar Ulmer's *Isle of Forgotten Sins*), Amann, of American parents, made films in the US, Germany and the UK. She deserves a footnote in British cinema as the fake 'princess' who briefly distracts the hero from his dull wife in HITCHCOCK's *Rich and Strange* (1932).

OTHER BRITISH FILMS: *The Perfect Lady* (1931), *Strictly Business*, *Pyjamas Preferred* (1932), *Strictly in Confidence*, *Daughters of Today* (1933).

Amber Collective Newcastle-based group which has been making films about working-class life in England's North-East since 1969. Structurally, their films are based on actual lives, the lives preceding the stories. Typically, their films abstain from individual credits and they have notably used actors, like Anna Gascoigne, along with non-professionals. The founders met as film students at London's Regent Street Polytechnic and made their first film, *Maybe*, a 10-minute DOCUMENTARY on the North Shields ferry across the Tyne in 1969. CHANNEL 4 helped finance their first feature film, *Seacoal* (1985) and in 2001 they made their most expensive film, *Like Father*, on a budget of £600,000. Like the much better known Ken LOACH, they have remained true to their socialist principles.

OTHER BRITISH FILMS INCLUDE: *Dream On* (1991), *Eden Valley* (1994), *The Scar* (1997).

Ambler, Eric (*b* London, 1909 – *d* London, 1998). Screenwriter. Along with Graham GREENE, Ambler is perhaps the novelist most closely associated with the British cinema, his writing credits outnumbering Greene's. Before becoming a script consultant to Alexander KORDA in 1938, he worked as engineer and stage actor. During the war, he served with a film combat unit in Italy, then became assistant director of the ARMY FILM UNIT, with responsibility for all educational and morale film-making. Among his most notable wartime achievements was the screenplay (with Peter USTINOV) of *The Way Ahead* (1944) which skilfully blended DOCUMENTARY and fiction, a combination which often marked his later work. Leaving the Army as Lieutenant-Colonel, he joined the RANK ORGANISATION as a screenwriter. Several of his espionage novels had already been adapted to film by others, including *Journey into Fear* (1943) and *The Mask of Dimitrios* (1944) in Hollywood, and, in England, *Hotel Reserve* (1944) was a version of his *Epitaph for a Spy*. As screenwriter, he applied his talents to a range of GENRES wider than those he had practised as a novelist. There are thrillers (*The October Man*, 1947, which he also produced and which was directed by his wartime friend, Roy Ward BAKER), romantic dramas (*The Passionate Friends*, 1948), a biopic (*The Magic Box*, 1951), war films (*The Cruel Sea*, 1952), and comedies (*The Card*, 1952). Was married to Joan HARRISON, Hitchcock's producer, from 1958 until her death in 1994; awarded MBE in 1981.

OTHER BRITISH FILMS: *Highly Dangerous*, *The Clouded Yellow* (1950), *Encore* (1951, 'Gigolo and Gigolette'), *Rough Shoot* (1953), *Lease of Life*, *The Purple Plain* (1954), *A Night to Remember* (1958), *The Wreck of the Mary Deare* (1959, UK/US).

BIBLIOG: Autobiographies, *Here Lies*, 1981; *The Story So Far*, 1993.

Ambler, Joss (*b* Melbourne, 1900 – *d* England, 1959). Actor. Supporting player in British films from 1937, he made forty films in the two decades preceding his death. Versatile and reliable, often as officials (like the jury-resisting Lord Mayor of London in *Penn of Pennsylvania*, 1941) and servicemen, he worked across a wide generic range. Once married to actress June Lang.

OTHER BRITISH FILMS INCLUDE: *The Captain's Orders* (1937), *The Citadel* (1938), *Trouble Brewing* (1939), *Contraband* (1940), *The Next of Kin* (1942), *The Halfway House* (1944), *They Were Sisters* (1945), *Mine Own Executioner* (1947), *Something Money Can't Buy* (1952), *The Long Arm* (1956), *Dunkirk* (1958).

Ambrose (*b* London, 1896 – *d* Leeds, 1971). Bandleader. RN: Bert Ambrose. Appeared with his orchestra in several musical films of the 30s.

BRITISH FILMS: *Soft Lights and Sweet Music* (1936), *Calling All Stars* (1937), *Kicking the Moon Around* (1938).

American response to British silent films American audiences in the early years were unsophisticated, and with eight or more one-reel SHORTS on an average theatre bill they were more than willing to tolerate at least one per evening from the UK. Through 1909, Arthur MELBOURNE-COOPER's Alpha Trading Company, CLARENDON, CRICKS and Martin, HAGGAR, HEPWORTH, R.W. PAUL, the SHEFFIELD PHOTO Co., Charles URBAN, and the WARWICK TRADING CO. were all able to sell their films in the US. The best-known British film of the period, *Rescued by Rover* (1905), found an audience, when released by the American Mutoscope & Biograph Company (which also distributed Gaumont's British productions). But by 1909, the American correspondent of THE BIOSCOPE was reporting that audiences found British films unsuitable, complaining of 'the ponderous humour and the indecision of action which is in them'. French and Italian films became the dominant import from Europe, although, for obvious reasons, Cherry KEARTON's *Roosevelt in Africa* (1910) proved successful, as did educational offerings from Urban.

British films were produced at half the cost of American productions, and it showed. Americans wanted films from Britain, but the only ones that were successful by the early 1910s were those produced in Britain by Edison or Vitagraph and starring John Bunny, Marc McDermott or Miriam Nesbitt. King Baggot's *Ivanhoe* (1913) was popular with American audiences because it was filmed in England and because its star was American. British producers cared little for American criticism: when Hepworth lost its US distributor, it did not consider the possibility that it might be because of inferior product but instead, in the spring of 1914, set up its own American operation, Hepworth American Film Corporation.

By April 1913, *The Bioscope* was reporting 'a total absence of English films of any sort in the States', and the condition remained the same during WW1. There was a breakthrough in 1919, when George PEARSON's *The Better 'Ole* became the first British feature to receive a major US release. In the 20s, a number of British producers, led by Herbert WILCOX, tried to make films for the American market, bringing over (second-echelon) American stars, but failing to improve storylines or production values. Less than 50 British films were reviewed by the *New York Times* between 1914 and 1929, mostly unfavourably. British producers retaliated, not with an increase in the quality of production but rather the establishment of their own American releasing organizations, and the silent era closed with J.D. Williams and John MAXWELL forming World Wide Pictures Corporation in August 1928, to release 50 films a year from Europe, including the entire BIP output. AS.

American response to British sound film The American market presented British sound films with an acute challenge. Despite the common language there were obstacles which made their effective exploitation difficult, including the Hollywood majors' stranglehold over distribution and exhibition, the size, geographical and ethnic diversity of America and, on occasion, censorship restrictions. Yet several key films and GENRES were critically acclaimed and popular including Alexander KORDA's *The Private Life of Henry VIII* (1933), Laurence OLIVIER's *Henry V* (1944, US release 1946), POWELL AND PRESSBURGER's *The Red Shoes* (1948), EALING COMEDIES, the James BOND cycle of the 60s, 'HERITAGE' FILMS such as James IVORY's *A Room With a View* (1985) and romantic comedies including Mike NEWELL's *Four Weddings and a Funeral* (1994).

British films were most acceptable in cities such as New York, Chicago and Los Angeles, while many mid-western audiences claimed that British accents were incomprehensible. Films which fared best were not imitations of Hollywood's output but those which engaged with notions of British national identity such as comedies or historical/costume films. On the whole the Production Code Administration (PCA or the Hays Office) made great efforts to encourage and grant certificates to British films but there were cases when they suffered from the PCA's intervention on moral grounds, for example, Herbert WILCOX's *Nell Gwyn* (1934, US release 1935) was forced to have a different ending from the British version in order to punish the heroine for being the King's mistress. In the case of POWELL AND PRESSBURGER's *Black Narcissus* (1947)

the PCA was unable to prevent the Legion of Decency, the Catholic organisation which dominated American censorship, from insisting on substantial cuts before the film could secure an American release. While the majority of British films do not obtain an American release, in recent years comedies such as *Bean* (1997, UK/US) and *The Full Monty* (1997, UK cast, part-US financed) have been major successes.

BIBLIOG: Anthony Slide, *Banned in the USA*, 1999; Sarah Street, *Transatlantic Crossings: British Feature Films in the USA*, 2002. Sarah Street.

Americans in British silent films At least three American stars, Gene Gauntier, King Baggot and John Bunny, came to the British Isles in the early 1910s to appear in some of the first US films produced on location abroad. American Florence TURNER came to England in 1913, forming her own company, and bringing along her leading man, Tom Powers, excellent in the title role of Hepworth's *Barnaby Rudge* (1915). The first British company to import American stars was LONDON FILM COMPANY, whose first leading ladies were **Edna Flugrath** (*b* New York, 1893 – *d* San Diego, California, 1966) and Jane Gail. The latter was featured in *She Stoops to Conquer* (1914), *The Prisoner of Zenda* (1915) and *Rupert of Hentzau* (1915), among others, before returning to the US in 1915. Flugrath, who was never as big a star as her sisters, Viola Dana and Shirley Mason, was seen in a dozen London films from 1914 and 1915, including *The Ring and the Rajah* (1914) and *A Christmas Carol* (1914). Flugrath was back in England in 1920–21, appearing under the direction of her husband, **Harold Shaw** (*b* Tennessee, 1878 – *d* 1926), in *The Pursuit of Pamela* (1920), *London Pride* (1920), *True Tilda* (1920), *The Land of Mystery* (1920), *Kipps* (1921), and *A Dear Fool* (1921).

In an unusual situation, Thomas Meighan made his screen debut in England in *Dandy Donovan* (1914), while appearing in the West End in *Broadway Jones*. As a result of his appearance in the British film, he was signed to a long-term contract by Famous Players–Lasky, and became a major Hollywood leading man of the 20s. The largest influx of American actors and actresses to British cinema came in the 20s. Evelyn Brent (*b* Tampa, Florida, 1899 – *d* 1975), on screen since 1914, came to London in 1920 to appear in the stage comedy *The Ruined Lady*. When the play finished, she stayed to star in 13 British films: *The Law Divine*, *The Shuttle of Life* (1920), *The Door That Has No Key*, *Demos*, *Sybil*, *Sonia*, *Laughter and Tears* (1921), *Circus Jim*, *The Experiment*, *Trapped by the Mormons*, *Married to a Mormon*, *A Spanish Jade*, and *Pages of Life* (1922). When Brent returned to the US, it was as a 'British Beauty' with a UK career behind her.

Carlyle BLACKWELL both starred in and produced British films. Gertrude McCOY enjoyed a British career equal to her work in the US. Diminutive Marie Doro starred in *A Sinless Sinner* (1919), *Twelve-Ten* (1919) and *Sally Bishop* (1923). Donald CRISP directed himself in *Beside the Bonnie Briar Bush* (1921). Constance Binney was featured in *A Bill of Divorcement* (1922). Anna Q. Nilsson starred in *Three Live Ghosts* (1922), with Norman Kerry, and *The Man from Home* (1922), with James Kirkwood. Bryant Washburn was Joan MORGAN's leading man in *The Road to London* (1921). The minor American actress Wanda Hawley was the star of *Fires of Fate* and *Lights o' London*, both from 1923. Prior to his starring role in *Greed*, Gibson Gowland was seen in the 1923 British films, *The Harbour Lights* and *Hutch Stirs 'Em Up*. The latter starred cowboy hero Charles 'Hutch' Hutchison, who was also featured by IDEAL in

Hurricane Hutch in Many Adventures (1924). Ideal also brought over Seena Owen, who had been 'Princess Beloved' in *Intolerance*, to star in *The Great Well* (1924). The Japanese-American husband and-wife team, Sessue Hayakawa and Tsuru Aoki were starred in two STOLL productions from 1924: *The Great Prince Shan* and *Sen Yat's Devotion*. Jane Novak was featured in *The Blackguard* (1925).

Regal leading lady Alice Joyce starred in *The Passionate Adventure* (1924) and *The Rising Generation* (1928). Sydney CHAPLIN played opposite Betty BALFOUR in *A Little Bit of Fluff* from 1928, and also in that year, Anna May WONG and Gilda Gray starred in *Piccadilly*, and Tallulah Bankhead in *His House in Order*. For his directorial debut, *The Pleasure Garden* (1925), Alfred HITCHCOCK had two American stars, albeit minor, Carmelita Geraghty and Virginia Valli.

The British director most cognisant of the need for American star power in British films was Herbert WILCOX. He brought over **Betty Blythe** (*b* Los Angeles, 1893 – *d* 1972) to star in *Chu Chin Chow* (1923) and *Southern Love* (1924), and Blythe also found time to star in the execrable *She* (1925). Lionel Barrymore appeared for Wilcox in *Decameron Nights* (1924), Pauline Frederick in *Mumsie* (1927), Blanche Sweet in *Woman in White* (1929), and Norman Kerry in *The Bondman* (1929). Wilcox's greatest success in utilizing an American actress was with **Dorothy Gish** (*b* Dayton, Ohio, 1898 – *d* Rapallo, Italy, 1966), featured in *Nell Gwynne, London* (1926), *Madame Pompadour* (1928), and *Tiptoes* (1928), which was also the only British film for quintessential American humourist Will Rogers.

Wilcox's partner, Graham CUTTS, directed another actress closely associated with D.W. Griffith, **Mae Marsh** (*b* Madrid, New Mexico, 1895 – *d* 1968), in *Flames of Passion* (1922), *Paddy the Next Best Thing* (1923) and *The Rat* (1925). **Betty Compson** (*b* Beaver City, Utah, 1897 – *d* Los Angeles, 1974), who had made her British screen debut in Maurice ELVEY's *The Royal Oak* (1923), was also directed to great effect by Cutts in *Woman to Woman* and *The White Shadow* (1924). AS.

Americans in British sound films British films have had only sporadic success in the United States, and this has been a severe limitation to the industry's earnings, but it has never stopped the British industry from trying to lure American film-makers to cross the Atlantic. The rationale was that this would help the distribution of British films in the US. Presumably, some success attended these efforts but never as much as was hoped for. For example, J. Arthur RANK's post-war attempt to capture a slice of the American market was a costly failure.

The importance of the American market for British producers has resulted in many Americans working within the British industry. In the 30s, several of the Hollywood majors set up production in British studios, but they were there – unsurprisingly – to shore up their own interests rather than to promote those of the British industry (*see* HOLLYWOOD STUDIOS IN BRITAIN). The resulting films, often 'QUOTA QUICKIES' were made by American companies to satisfy regulations concerning the screening of a certain percentage of 'British' product. For the most part, however, British producers have actively sought American stars to bolster the marquee value of British films in America. Michael BALCON was among the first to attempt this systematically, during his period as the head of GAUMONT–BRITISH in the early 30s, and it led to appearances by Hollywood stars such as Edward Everett HORTON, British-born Cary GRANT, Robert Young, Sylvia

Sydney and Anna May WONG in British films. There were some major Hollywood–British films of the 30s, usually with star names aimed at US box-offices: e.g. *The Citadel* (1938), directed by King Vidor and starring Rosalind Russell with Robert DONAT, and *A Yank at Oxford* (1937), whose very title hints at its international box-office aspirations, starring Robert TAYLOR and star-to-be Vivien LEIGH; both these were made as part of the MGM–BRITISH operation of the late 30s. Other 30s visitors included directors Sam Wood (*Goodbye, Mr Chips* (1939), William Cameron Menzies, Tim WHELAN, Thornton FREELAND, and documentarist Robert FLAHERTY.

During the 'red scare' of the late 40s/early 50s, Britain became a haven for those on the blacklist because of their suspected Communist sympathies and activities, and the influx of American talent included the directors Cy ENDFIELD, Edward DMYTRYK and Joseph LOSEY, and screenwriters Carl FOREMAN, Ring Lardner, Ben BARZMAN and Donald Ogden Stewart, and actor Larry Parks. It also has been suggested that Gene Kelly, an MGM star at the height of his fame in the early 50s, took up temporary residence and work in Britain at that point to avoid the attention of the investigators.

British films attracted far more popular stars when the Hollywood studios set up British production bases and placed their own contract stars in British-made films. In the 40s and 50s, MGM–BRITISH films featured Elizabeth TAYLOR, Robert TAYLOR and Spencer Tracy and Glenn Ford in what were essentially American films made in British studios. RKO starred Martha Scott with John MILLS in Dmytryk's *So Well Remembered* (1947), Paramount brought British-born Ray MILLAND over for the sumptuous melodrama, *So Evil My Love* (1948), Warners had Patricia NEAL and Ronald REAGAN in Vincent Sherman's *The Hasty Heart* (1949), and Fox's star-heavy *Anastasia* (1956) and *Island in the Sun* (1957) are both technically British. As well, the prolific 'B' MOVIE industry brought in dozens of faded and minor stars (Dale Robertson, Mark Stevens, Brian Donlevy, Hillary Brooke, etc.) to give a transatlantic gloss and acceptability to modest programmers. However, the most significant example of Anglo-American co-production was that pursued by brothers James and John WOOLF, who made *The African Queen* (1951), with Katharine HEPBURN and Humphrey Bogart, *Moulin Rouge* (1953) with Jose FERRER, and the cult favourite, John HUSTON's *Beat the Devil* (1953, UK/It/US).

In the 60s, the pursuit of the youth market and the atmosphere of 'SWINGING LONDON' led to more identifiably British stories, even in trans-Atlantic productions, and films such as *Tom Jones* (1963), *Alfie* (1966), *Georgy Girl* (1966) and the James BOND and BEATLES films found significant success in the United States. During the 60s, American producers invested heavily in British films but withdrew when the rewards failed to match expectations, and the British industry suffered accordingly.

More recently, American funding has continued to play a large and significant role in British film-making. In some cases, American films are made in Britain simply to utilise well-equipped studios, excellent technicians and costs that are low by comparison to Hollywood, but the films themselves can scarcely be defined as British in any significant way. Otherwise, American financing is drawn mainly to British films that will appeal to American audiences. 'HERITAGE' FILMS such as the MERCHANT IVORY productions (*Room With A View*, 1985, *Howards End*, 1990) and *Shakespeare In Love* (1999, UK/US) are one facet of this. Another involves COMEDIES that play upon

Anglo-American rivalries and differences, a winning formula which dates back to *A Yank at Oxford* (1937). The aggressive Jamie Lee Curtis and Kevin Kline, for example, manipulated the repressed John CLEESE and Michael PALIN in *A Fish Called Wanda* (1988), and Andie MacDowell and Julia Roberts offered emotional awakenings to Hugh GRANT's archetypal Englishman in *Four Weddings and a Funeral* (1994) and *Notting Hill* (1999, UK/US), respectively. Even a relatively low-budget film such as *Sliding Doors* (1998, UK/US) was able to attract American financing and distribution when the American actress Gwyneth PALTROW was cast in a leading role. The British media regularly trumpets such films as home-grown successes, but the fact is that much of the money earned returns to the US. Cooperation with Hollywood long ago replaced any real sense of competition or independence for British films, and, for better and for worse, this influenced British film-making for much of the 20th century. Mark Glancy.

Ames, Gerald (*b* London, 1880 – *d* London, 1933). Actor. On stage from 1905, Ames appeared in more than 70 silent films (1914–28). An expert swordsman, he represented Britain at the 1912 Olympic Games. He was active in 1920 in an abortive attempt to unionize screen actors, and also directed himself in a couple of films: *Once Aboard the Lugger* (1920) and *Mr Justice Raffles* (1921).
BRITISH FILMS INCLUDE: *She Stoops to Conquer* (1914), *The Middleman*, *The Prisoner of Zenda* (1915), *Arsene Lupin* (1916), *Adam Bede* (1918), *Alf's Button* (1920), *Tansy* (1921), *The Little People* (1926), *The Rising Generation* (1928). AS.

Amicus Films Although the 60s British HORROR film is most closely identified with HAMMER, other companies including Amicus were involved in the genre. The firm was set up by two Americans, producer/writer Milton SUBOTSKY and Max J. ROSENBERG, and was based at SHEPPERTON STUDIOS. Amicus did make films in other GENRES including the musical *It's Trad, Dad!* (1962), the spy film *Danger Route* (1967), and *A Touch of Love* (1969) adapted from a Margaret Drabble novel, but the company specialised in the horror film, beginning in 1960 with *City of the Dead*. Many of Hammer's personnel worked for Amicus including Peter CUSHING, Christopher LEE, and director Freddie FRANCIS, and Robert BLOCH, author of *Psycho*, wrote a number of their films. The studio's distinctive contribution to the genre was the anthology film such as *Dr Terror's House of Horrors* (1964), *The House That Dripped Blood* (1970), and *Tales from the Crypt* (1972). Tom Ryall.

Amies, Caroline (*b* London, 1951). Production designer. Trained at Harrow Art School, Amies began as assistant or co-art director in the early 80s, and has been responsible for the design of an impressively varied range of films since, including her period recreations in such diverse films as *Carrington* (1994, UK/Fr), set among the Bloomsbury group, and *The Land Girls* (1998, UK/Fr), evoking WW2 rural life.
OTHER BRITISH FILMS INCLUDE: (art d) *Fords on Water* (co-art d), *Darkest England* (short), *Nineteen Nineteen* (1984), *Eat the Rich* (1987); (des) *Wish You Were Here* (1987), *The Dressmaker* (1988), *The Big Man* (1990), *Afraid of the Dark* (1991, UK/Fr), *In the Name of the Father* (UK/Ire/US), *Sister My Sister* (1994), *The Secret Agent* (1996, UK/US), *The Last September* (2000, UK/Fr/Ire).

Amiel, Jon (*b* London, 1948). Director. British-born director who made his name on the television mini-series *The Singing Detective* (1986), directed one feature film, *Queen of Hearts*

(1989), then moved to America, where his films have included *Sommersby* (1993).
OTHER BRITISH FILMS: *The Man Who Knew Too Little* (1997, UK/Ger/US), *Entrapment* (1999, UK/Ger/US).

Amini, Hossein (*b* Iran, 1966). Screenwriter. Wrote two of the finest screenplays of the 90s, *Jude* (1996) and *The Wings of the Dove* (1997, UK/US), both models of ADAPTATION of classic novels – inspired, rigorously cinematic, and illuminating their source works as well. Also, distinguished television work, including BAFTA-winner *Dying of the Light* (1994).
OTHER BRITISH FILMS INCLUDE: *Catch* (1989), *The Four Feathers* (2003, UK/US).

Amis, Sir Kingsley (*b* London, 1922 – *d* London, 1995). Author. Distinguished writer of satirical novels of life in the second half of the 20th century. Works filmed include *Lucky Jim* (1957), *Only Two Can Play* (1961, from novel, *That Uncertain Feeling*) and *Take a Girl Like You* (1970), as well as several for television. He is the father of writer Martin Amis (*b* Oxford, 1949), who wrote the screenplay for Stanley Donen's *Saturn 3* (1980) and whose novel, *The Rachel Papers*, was adapted for the screen in 1989 and *Dead Babies* in 2000 (US), the latter attracting dreadful reviews. As a child, appeared in *A High Wind in Jamaica* (1965).

Amyes, Julian (*b* Cambridge, 1917 – *d* London, 1992) Director. After a couple of appearances as an actor (*High Treason*, 1951, and *Mandy*, 1952), Amyes directed a tough war film, *A Hill in Korea* (1956) and a whimsical romance, *A Miracle in Soho* (1957), and became a prolific television director and executive, notably directing *Dial M for Murder* on television. Married scriptwriter Anne Allan.

Anciano, Dominic (*b* London, 1959). Director, producer, screenwriter. With friend and associate Ray BURDIS, Anciano had a prosperous 80s career as co-producer of music videos and promos for musical stars. In 1988 they produced a short film, *The Universe of Dermot Finn*, and their first feature film, *The Krays*, in 1990. They had a television hit with the semi-documentary series, *Operation Good Guys* (1997) and, maintaining their preference for on-the-set improvisation, produced and directed two blackly comic features in the late 90s – *The Final Cut* (1999, +a) with Ray WINSTONE, Jude LAW and Sadie FROST, and the dire *Love, Honour and Obey* (2000, + sc), with Winstone, Law, Frost and Jonny Lee MILLER. Their work clearly attracts 'hot' young talents.
OTHER BRITISH FILMS INCLUDE: *The Reflecting Skin* (1990), *The Passion of Darkly Noon* (1995, UK/Belg/Ger).

Anderson, Daphne (*b* London, 1922). Actress. On stage since 1937, Anderson appeared in secondary roles in films during the 50s and 60s, most notably as Lucy Lockit in *The Beggar's Opera* (1953) with Laurence OLIVIER, and was also active on television from the 50s.
OTHER BRITISH FILMS INCLUDE: *Trottie True* (1948), *Cloudburst* (1951), *Laughing Anne, Hobson's Choice* (1953), *The Prince and the Showgirl* (1957), *No Time for Tears* (1957), *Snowball* (1960), *Captain Clegg* (1962), *Bitter Harvest* (1963), *I Want What I Want* (1971), *Real Life* (1983).

Anderson, Gene (*b* London, 1931 – *d* London, 1965). Actress. Attractive Cockney-born player, with stage and television experience, first seen on screen as Dora BRYAN's chum in *The Intruder* (1953), though she had done some crowd work before that. She went on to play a number of supporting and leading roles in the years before her tragically early death. Married to Edward JUDD, with whom she acted in *The Shakedown* (1959) and *The Day the Earth Caught Fire* (1961).

OTHER BRITISH FILMS: *Background* (1953), *Doublecross* (1955), *Yangtse Incident* (1956), *The Long Haul* (1957), *The Break* (1962).

Anderson, James (*b* London, 1899 – *d* London, 1964). Director, historian. A librarian with various newsreel companies, Anderson wrote and directed a series of compilation films, narrated by comedians such as Kenneth HORNE, Bob MONKHOUSE and Hughie GREEN: *Echo of Applause* (1946), *Those Were the Days* (1946), *Return Fare to Laughter* (1950), *Made for Laughs* (1952), *All in Good Fun* (1955), and *Crazy Days* (1962). Also an amateur historian of silent cinema: his beautifully-designed, voluminous scrapbooks are now housed at the BFI. AS.

Anderson, Jean (*b* Eastbourne, 1908 – *d* Edenhall, 2001). Actress. Eloquent of face and voice, in a wide range of essentially sympathetic roles, Anderson was one of the great British character actresses, playing nurses, care-worn mothers, matriarchs and astringent companions. She trained at RADA, ran the Players' Theatre during the war, and cut her cinematic teeth in DOCUMENTARIES. She also had notable successes on stage (*Variations on a Theme*, 1958) and television (*The Brothers*, 1972–76). On screen, her dignity and warmth were superbly served by the 1953 hit, *The Kidnappers*.

OTHER BRITISH FILMS: *The Mark of Cain* (scenes deleted) (1947), *Elizabeth of Ladymead* (1948), *The Romantic Age* (1949), *The Franchise Affair* (1950), *Out of True, Life in Her Hands, White Corridors* (1951), *The Brave Don't Cry* (1952), *Johnny on the Run, Street Corner* (1953), *The Dark Stairway, Lease of Life* (1954), *The Secret Tent, A Town Like Alice, Laughing in the Sunshine* (UK/Swe), *The Barretts of Wimpole Street* (1956), *Robbery Under Arms, Lucky Jim* (1957), *Heart of a Child* (1958), *SOS Pacific* (1959), *Spare the Rod* (1961), *The Inspector, The Waltz of The Toreadors* (1962), *The Silent Playground, The Three Lives of Thomasina* (1963), *Half a Sixpence* (1967, UK/US), *Country Dance, Run a Crooked Mile* (1969), *The Night Digger* (1971), *The Lady Vanishes* (1979), *Screamtime* (1983), *Madame Sousatzka* (1988), *Leon the Pig Farmer* (1992), *Simon Magus* (2000, UK/Fr/Ger/It).

Anderson, Lindsay (*b* Bangalore, India, 1923 – *d* Périgueux, France, 1994). Director. To designate Anderson as 'director' is not to minimise his other contributions as writer, critic, actor, and trenchant commentator on all aspects of cinema. Born into the kind of Establishment background he spent much of his adult life denouncing as anachronistic and elitist, he first made his presence felt in 1947 as a founding editor of the short-lived but influential journal, SEQUENCE. Passionate about the possibilities of cinema and how these were so routinely skirted in most British feature film-making at the time, he continued to wage his war of words when *Sequence* folded, in journals such as SIGHT AND SOUND and *New Statesman*, as well as in his use of the film medium itself. He wanted to explore ordinary working lives on film, believing these to be largely ignored in commercial cinema, and so made a series of DOCUMENTARIES which argued for a greater social responsiveness in film-making, winning an Oscar for *Thursday's Children* (1954). Along with Karel REISZ, Tony RICHARDSON and Gavin LAMBERT, in the later 50s he became a major player in the FREE CINEMA MOVEMENT, which provided, in a couple of seasons at the NATIONAL FILM THEATRE, London, a showcase for their short films in a manner which brought them to the attention of critics and art-house audiences.

In Anderson's view, British cinema was bedevilled by emotional timidity, its acquiescence in the divisiveness of the CLASS system, and the fact that Britain had lost its pre-eminence in the post-war world but was unable to face this. The 50s was a prolific but often unadventurous decade in British cinema, and, when Anderson and his friends finally found themselves making feature films, they were determined not to perpetuate what they saw as the glossy stereotypes of the preceding decade. Anderson might have made more films if he'd started earlier, but there is at least no rubbish among his oeuvre, and virtually everything he did testified to his concern for emotional truth, for the cruelties of class, and for the crassness of commercialism. His first film, *This Sporting Life* (1963), which won a British AA (Best Film) is a bruising epic of an inarticulate rugby league footballer's inner life, and his most famous film, *If . . .* (1968), using the public school as a metaphor, deals swingeing blows at the underpinnings of the nation. The central character of *If . . .*, Mick Travis (Malcolm MCDOWELL), reappeared in two subsequent, less popular satirical pieces, *O Lucky Man!* (1973) and *Britannia Hospital* (1982). His final cinema film as director was, surprisingly, the elegiac US-made *The Whales of August* (1987), starring Lillian Gish and Bette Davis.

He also acted in several films, and was the producer of a number of ground-breaking plays at the Royal Court Theatre and elsewhere. As well, he was the author of two books, *The Making of a Film: the Story of 'Secret People'* (1952), and *About John Ford* (1981), the latter a discerning hymn of praise to his idol, concerning whom he narrated a television documentary. His television work included the abrasive, darkly comic Canadian mini-series, *Glory! Glory!* (1989), which took lethal swipes at the phenomenon of television evangelism, and he appeared in a documentary film of his own life, *Is That All There Is?* (1994).

OTHER BRITISH FILMS: (d) (documentaries and shorts) *Meet the Pioneers* (1948), *Idlers that Work* (1949), *Three Installations, Wakefield Express* (1952), *O Dreamland* (1953), *Trunk Conveyor* (1954), *Green and Pleasant Land, The Children Upstairs, Hundred Thousand Children, Henry, Foot And Mouth, £20 a Ton, Energy First* (1955), *Every Day Except Christmas* (1957), *The March to Aldermaston* (co-dir) (1957); (features) *The White Bus, In Celebration* (1974); (a) *Inadmissible Evidence* (1968), *Chariots of Fire* (1981), *Blame It on the Bellboy* (1992, voice only).

BIBLIOG: Erik Hedling, *Lindsay Anderson: Maverick Film-Maker*, 1998; Gavin Lambert, *Mainly About Lindsay Anderson*, 2000.

Anderson, Margaret (*b* Plymouth). Actress. Earliest credits include schoolgirls in *The Romantic Age* (1949) and *The Happiest Days of Your Life* (1950), followed by supporting roles in 'B' MOVIES such as *The Large Rope* (1953) and 'A's such as *The Barefoot Contessa* (1954, US/It). Distinctively pretty, she did much stage and television in the 50s as well. Married actor Guy VERNEY.

OTHER BRITISH FILMS INCLUDE: *River Beat* (1953), *The Quatermass Experiment* (1955), *Reach for the Sky* (1956), *Revenge of the Pink Panther* (1978).

Anderson, Michael (*b* London, 1920). Director. Entered films as office boy at ELSTREE STUDIOS in 1935, acted in a few films, and became assistant director on such high-profile films as *Pygmalion* (1938) and *French Without Tears* (1939). After war service, he became one of the most sought-after first assistants in British cinema, on films such as *Fame is the Spur* (1947) and *School for Secrets* (1946), directed by Peter USTINOV with whom he co-directed *Private Angelo* (1949). He became a busy and proficient genre director in Britain, making melodramas such as *Waterfront* (1950), the charmingly idiotic comedy, *Will Any*

Gentleman . . . ? (1953), the hugely popular war film, *The Dam Busters* (1955), and the excellent frightened-lady thriller, *Chase a Dark Shadow* (1957). He directed the Oscar-winning, starry but unscintillating *Around the World in Eighty Days* (1956, US), thus entering the international phase of his career. His subsequent films were a spotty lot, later petering out in telemovies and little-seen co-productions, though *Logan's Run* (1976, US) has a dazzling first half. Too often, a likeable small-scale storytelling talent seemed to be overwhelmed by large budgets and bland, under-used star casts. His father, **Lawrence Anderson** (*b* London, 1893 – *d* 1939), acted on stage and in British films of the 20s and 30s; his son, **Michael Anderson, Jr** (*b* London, 1943) made several British films, including *The Moonraker* (1957), before embarking on a Hollywood career.

OTHER BRITISH FILMS: *Hell Is Sold Out, Night Was Our Friend* (1951), *The House of the Arrow* (1953), *1984* (1955), *Yangtse Incident* (1956), *Shake Hands with the Devil* (1959, UK/US), *The Naked Edge* (1961), *Operation Crossbow* (1965, UK/It), *The Quiller Memorandum* (1966, UK/US), *Pope Joan* (1972), *Conduct Unbecoming* (1975), *Dominique* (1978).

Anderson, Paul (*b* Newcastle-upon-Tyne, 1965). Director. Young director who made a striking debut with the critically acclaimed *Shopping* (1994), which he also wrote. His skill in handling high-octane action sequences, notably of 'ramraiding' expeditions by joy-riding thieves, has him in demand in Hollywood where subsequent films, the violently actionful *Mortal Kombat* (1995) and *Soldier* (1998, UK/US), were made. *Event Horizon* (1997, UK/US) was shot at PINEWOOD. Owns Impact Pictures with Jeremy Bolt.

OTHER BRITISH FILMS INCLUDE: *Resident Evil* (2002, UK/Ger/US).

Anderson, Rona (*b* Edinburgh, 1926). Actress. Scottish-born actress who came from the stage to play intrepid heroines in many a British 'B' film of the 50s and early 60s, as well as appearing in several more upmarket ventures, such as her first (*Sleeping Car to Trieste*, 1948) and her last to date (*The Prime of Miss Jean Brodie*, 1968). Freshly pretty and good-humoured, she was enjoyable company in such competent double-bill fare as *Double Exposure* (1954) and *Hideout* (1956). Long married to actor Gordon JACKSON, she also acted on the stage (*Pygmalion*, 1984, *The Mousetrap*, 1994) and television.

OTHER BRITISH FILMS INCLUDE: *Floodtide, Poet's Pub* (1949), *Twenty Questions Murder Mystery* (1949), *Her Favourite Husband* (1950, UK/It), *Scrooge* (1951), *Circumstantial Evidence* (1952), *The Black Rider* (1954), *A Time to Kill* (1955), *Soho Incident* (1956), *Man with a Gun* (1958), *The Bay of Saint Michel* (1963), *Devils of Darkness* (1964).

André, Yvonne Actress. French-born André appeared in several British films, including two for Michael Powell: *The Life and Death of Colonel Blimp* (1943) and *The Red Shoes* (1948), in which she played Moira SHEARER's sympathetic dresser.

OTHER BRITISH FILMS: *Neutral Port* (1940), *Secret Mission* (1942), *Bedelia* (1946), *Portrait of Clare* (1950), *The Strange Awakening* (1958), *Return from the Ashes* (1965).

Andrejew, André (*b* St Petersburg, Russia, 1899 – *d* Loudun, France, 1966). Art Director. Educated in Moscow, Andrejew studied art and architecture and became art director under Stanislavski at the Moscow Arts Theatre, subsequently working on the stage in Tiflis, Vienna and Berlin. Entered films in Germany in 1922, and was art director on some notable films including G.W. Pabst's *Pandora's Box* (1928), working also in Prague, Paris and Rome, before coming to England to design Victor SAVILLE's *The Dictator* (1935) and Basil DEAN's life of Mozart, *Whom the Gods Love* (1936, UK/Austria). He returned

to France in 1938 and, after the war, he resumed working for LONDON FILMS, his magnificent sets for *Anna Karenina* (1948) perhaps the film's most potent element. Though often designing sets of period opulence, he was equally at home in the quotidian suburbia of *The Winslow Boy* (1948) and the contemporary unease of post-war Berlin in *The Man Between* (1953).

OTHER BRITISH FILMS INCLUDE: *Escape Me Never* (1935), *The Beloved Vagabond* (1936), *Storm in a Teacup* (1937), *That Dangerous Age* (1949), *My Daughter Joy* (1950), *Melba* (1953), *Anastasia* (1956).

Andress, Ursula (*b* Berne, Switzerland, 1936). Actress. When the Swiss-born Andress emerged, Venus-like, from the sea in *Dr No* (1962), as Honey Ryder, it seemed that a new exotic star had been born. Sadly, little that followed has been able to live up to that high promise: only as HAMMER's *She* (1965) has she subsequently had a role that capitalised on her statuesque presence. She appeared in some high-profile entertainments in the 60s, including *Fun in Acapulco* (1963, US), opposite Elvis Presley, and *The Blue Max* (1966), as well as several co-starring or directed by her then-husband, John Derek, including *Once Before I Die* (1966, US). In recent decades, she has worked mainly in international productions and on television.

OTHER BRITISH FILMS: *What's New, Pussycat?* (1965), *Casino Royale* (1967), *Perfect Friday* (1970), *Clash of the Titans* (1981, UK/US).

Andrews, Anthony (*b* London, 1948). Actor. Handsome blond leading man of 70s and 80s, who came to major prominence as Sebastian Flyte in TV's acclaimed mini-series *Brideshead Revisited* (1981). In TV since 1968, making the jump to the big screen in *Take Me High* (1973), but, though he has worked steadily over two decades the screen has yielded only a few memorable roles: as Hugh in *Under the Volcano* (1984, US) and as Meinertzhagen, apparently German but actually a British secret agent, in *The Lighthorsemen* (1987, Aust). Much of his career has been spent in TV and international co-productions; in 2001, scored a success on stage in *Ghosts*.

OTHER BRITISH FILMS INCLUDE: *Percy's Progress* (1974), *The Holcroft Covenant* (1985), *The Second Victory* (1986), *Haunted* (1995, UK/US).

Andrews, Eamonn (*b* Dublin, 1922 – *d* London, 1987). Presenter. Famous as TV host on such popular programmes as *What's My Line?* (1951–62) and *This Is Your Life* from 1955, Andrews's only contribution to cinema was as narrator or commentator in a few DOCUMENTARIES, as presenter of the stories in *Three Cases of Murder* (1955) and as himself on a TV panel in *Left, Right and Centre* (1959).

OTHER BRITISH FILMS: (narr/comm) *Call of the Islands, The Lilt of the Kilt, Song of Norway* (1955), *HMS Brave Swordsman* (1961).

Andrews, Harry (*b* Tonbridge, 1911 – *d* Salehurst, 1989). Actor. Strong-jawed, imposing character player of myriad British films from 1953 until his death, latterly more often in TV, and also in demand for international films. On stage from 1933, and after army service reappeared at the Old Vic, and his stage career, much of it in the classics, continued unabated as his film work gathered momentum. He played a wide range of roles with a fair smattering of military types, including the avuncular Sergeant in *Ice Cold in Alex* (1958), the ruthless RSM in *The Hill* (1965), and the Brigadier in *Play Dirty* (1968). But he was also at home in comedy, playing the likes of Beryl Reid's gay brother in *Entertaining Mr Sloane* (1969) or the dotty 13th Earl of Gurney in *The Ruling Class* (1971), and slyly undermining the robust, utterly reliable persona honed in so many films. Awarded CBE, 1966.

OTHER BRITISH FILMS: *The Red Beret* (1953), *The Black Knight* (1954), *The Man Who Loved Redheads* (1954), *A Hill in Korea*, *Moby Dick* (1956), *Saint Joan* (UK/US), *I Accuse!* (1957), *The Devil's Disciple*, *A Touch of Larceny*, *In the Nick* (1959), *Circle of Deception* (1960), *Reach for Glory* (1961), *The Inspector*, *Nine Hours to Rama* (1962), *633 Squadron*, *The Informers*, *Nothing But the Best*, *The System* (1963, UK/US), *The Truth About Spring* (1964), *Sands of the Kalahari* (1965), *Modesty Blaise*, *The Deadly Affair*, *The Jokers*, *The Night of the Generals* (UK/Fr) (1966), *The Long Duel*, *I'll Never Forget What's 'is Name* (1967), *The Charge of the Light Brigade*, *The Southern Star* (UK/Fr), *A Dandy in Aspic*, *The Sea Gull* (1968), *Battle of Britain*, *A Nice Girl Like Me*, *Country Dance* (1969), *Wuthering Heights* (1970), *Burke & Hare*, *The Nightcomers*, *I Want What I Want*, *Night Hair Child* (UK/Ger/It/Sp) (1971), *Theatre of Blood*, *Man at the Top*, *The Mackintosh Man*, *The Final Programme* (1973), *The Internecine Project* (1974), *Equus* (1977), *The Medusa Touch* (UK/Fr), *The Big Sleep*, *Watership Down* (voice), *Death on the Nile*, *Superman* (UK/US) (1978), *Hawk the Slayer* (1980), *Mesmerised* (1984, UK/Aust/NZ/US).

Andrews, Dame Julie (*b* Walton-on-Thames, 1935). Actress. RN: Wells. Perhaps if she had been born ten years earlier Andrews might have had a career in British films; equally, though, she might not have become a world star. As it is, her film relationship to British cinema is marginal: *The Americanisation of Emily* (1964, US) was made here, she played celebrated British stage star Gertrude LAWRENCE in the US-made, *Star!* (1968), and starred in *The Tamarind Seed* (1974), *Victor/Victoria* (1982), and *Relative Values* (2000, UK/US), in Gladys COOPER's old stage part. Theatre success in *My Fair Lady* took her to America, where she scored major hits with *Mary Poppins* (1964) and *The Sound of Music* (1965). It seems a shame that she, quintessentially English, has wasted herself on many feeble American films when she could have found feeble films at home – and 'home' needed her more. Created DBE 2000.

Andrews, Naveen (*b* London, 1969). Actor. Trained at the Guildhall School of Music and Drama. Came to fame in TV's *The Buddha of Suburbia* (1993), as the South London son of an Indian father and English mother, and as Kip in *The English Patient* (1996, UK/US). Now appearing in international productions, such as *Drowning on Dry Land* (2000).

OTHER BRITISH FILMS: *London Kills Me* (1991), *Wild West* (1992), *Kama Sutra: A Tale of Love* (1996, UK/Ger/Ind/Jap).

Andrews, W(illiam) C(harles) (*b* London, 1901 – *d* Chiltern, 1986). Art director. Andrews ran his own interior decorating business before entering films in 1932 at GAUMONT–BRITISH as a draughtsman. His first credit as art director was on *The Day Will Dawn* (1942), and, in rapid succession, he made several films for Lance COMFORT (*Squadron Leader X*, 1942), and, especially, Herbert WILCOX (*Yellow Canary*, 1943), among others. His designs, influenced by Alfred JUNGE, were marked by a precision of detail which made their execution straightforward.

OTHER BRITISH FILMS INCLUDE: *Escape to Danger* (1943), *Hotel Reserve* (1944), *I Live in Grosvenor Square*, *Great Day* (1945), *Piccadilly Incident*, *Gaiety George* (1946), *The Courtneys of Curzon Street*, *Mine Own Executioner* (1947), *Spring in Park Lane*, *Elizabeth of Ladymead* (1948), *The Black Rose* (UK/US), *Odette* (1950), *The Lady with a Lamp* (1951), *The Beggar's Opera* (1953), *King's Rhapsody* (1955).

Angel, Daniel M. (*b* London, 1911 – *d* London, 1999). Producer. One of the most respected of British producers, Angel is associated with such directors as Val GUEST, Lewis GILBERT and Joseph LOSEY. Invalided out of the Army in 1944 with the rank of major, he began his film career with a series of

DOCUMENTARY SHORTS, and his first feature was *Murder at the Windmill* (1949); his father-in-law was Vivian Van Damm, who owned London's celebrated Windmill Theatre. Astute in setting up projects, he was also concerned with the creative side, winning the respect of actors and directors.

OTHER BRITISH FILMS: (shorts) *Dancing Thru* (1946), *The King's Horses*, *The King's Music* (1947): (features) *Miss Pilgrim's Progress* (1949), *The Body Said No!*, *Mr Drake's Duck* (1950), *Another Man's Poison* (1951), *Women of Twilight* (1952), *Cosh Boy*, *Albert RN* (1953), *The Sea Shall Not Have Them* (1954), *Escapade* (1955), *Reach for the Sky* (1956), *Seven Thunders* (1957), *Carve Her Name with Pride*, *The Sheriff of Fractured Jaw* (1958), *We Joined the Navy* (1962), *West 11* (1963), *King And Country* (1964), *The Romantic Englishwoman* (1975, UK/Fr).

Angel, Heather (*b* Oxford, 1909 – *d* Montecito, California, 1986). Actress. After a stage career beginning at the Old Vic and a few promising film roles in Britain, the delicately pretty Angel went to Hollywood, where she was kept busy without ever becoming a major star. Better remembered for such American films as *The Informer* (1935) and *Pride and Prejudice* (1940) than for her British films, of which the best known is probably the 1931 version of *The Hound of the Baskervilles*. Married actors Ralph FORBES and Henry WILCOXON and director Robert Sinclair, who was the victim of an unsolved murder.

OTHER BRITISH FILMS INCLUDE: *A Night in Montmartre* (1931), *Frail Women*, *Self-Made Lady*, *After Office Hours* (1932), *Early to Bed* (1933, UK/Ger).

Angelus, Muriel (*b* London, 1909). Actress. RN: Findlay. Blonde beauty of some warmth, Angelus was much in demand as a child model, began in British silent films, and made a few talkies in Britain before going to Hollywood in the late 30s. She made four films there, including *The Great McGinty* (1940) before retiring. Her British films are unremarkable, except for *Hindle Wakes* (1931), in which she has a secondary role. First married actor John STUART.

OTHER BRITISH FILMS INCLUDE: *Sailors Don't Care*, *The Ringer* (1928), *Red Aces* (1929), *No Exit*, *Night Birds* (UK/Ger) (1930), *My Wife's Family* (1931), *So, You Won't Talk?* (1935).

Angers, Avril (*b* Liverpool, 1922). Actress. First appeared at the Palace Pier, Brighton, in 1936, entered films in *The Brass Monkey* (1948), and has worked busily in all the acting media. This character comedienne has played vinegary landladies (*Be My Guest*, 1965) and shrewish mums (Hayley MILLS's, in *The Family Way*, 1966) and other more and less benign comic types with welcome relish.

OTHER BRITISH FILMS INCLUDE: *Miss Pilgrim's Progress* (1949), *Don't Blame the Stork* (1953), *The Green Man* (1956), *Devils of Darkness* (1964), *Two a Penny* (1967), *There's a Girl in My Soup* (1970), *Confessions of a Driving Instructor* (1976).

Anglo-Amalgamated A small but resourceful production/distribution company, A-A was set up in 1945 by two energetic and astute businessmen, Nat COHEN and Stuart LEVY. They began by making low-budget THRILLERS for the bottom half of the double bill and, gambling shrewdly on new talents, showed themselves cleverly attuned to changing market demands, until, in 1969, they were swallowed up in ABPC/EMI. Their earliest productions were half-hour features such as *The Drayton Case* (1953), with plotlines which attested to the unceasing vigilance of Scotland Yard, and with portentous introductions by Edgar LUSTGARTEN. By the 60s, these had given way to hour-long thrillers drawn chiefly from the works of Edgar WALLACE and made at the austere studios at MERTON PARK. But A-A was not limiting itself to 'B' FILM CRIME, the market for which would dry up in a few years: it produced three MUSICALS with the pop star Tommy STEELE (1957–59), all the 'CARRY ON' films up till 1966, and a batch of HORROR films, including *Horrors of the Black Museum* (1959), two Edgar Allan Poe films in collaboration with American International Pictures, *The Masque of the Red Death* (1964, UK/US) and *The Tomb of Ligeia* (1964), and, most famously, Michael POWELL's *Peeping Tom* (1960). In the 60s, the company moved upmarket and allied itself with some of the most important film-makers of the decade, particularly with producer Joseph JANNI and directors John SCHLESINGER and Joseph LOSEY. Janni, previously with RANK and BRITISH LION, brought *A Kind of Loving* (1962) and *Billy Liar!* (1963) to A-A in the first instance, thereby launching Schlesinger's features career, but making producer Peter ROGERS feel A-A was getting too quality-orientated for the 'Carry On' team. The company produced Losey's first British film, *The Sleeping Tiger* (1954), though listing its producer Victor HANBURY as the director instead of the BLACKLISTED Losey. By 1960, Losey's name was on the A-A release *The Criminal*, and Cohen backed *The Go-Between* (1971), though, by that time, A-A had ceased independent existence and the film was released through EMI. A-A also produced that archetypal sixties black comedy, *Nothing But the Best* (1964), and backed the first features of John BOORMAN (*Catch Us If You Can*, 1965) and Ken LOACH (*Poor Cow*, 1967). A good deal of the history of British film-making in the 50s and 60s is encapsulated in the A-A enterprise.

'angry young men' Term coined by the casting director of the Royal Court Theatre and taken up by the media to describe writers who came to prominence in the latter 50s in the wake of the Court's production of *Look Back in Anger* (1956), written by John OSBORNE, the archetypal AYM, in public perception at least. The AYM were vociferously opposed to the Establishment as they saw it, sustaining its privileges through the public school system, the Church of England, and all the subtle and not-so-subtle means open to a class-divided society. The views of these young men, mostly in their mid-thirties and including novelists John BRAINE and Alan SILLITOE, found their way to the screen in such films as *Room at the Top* (1958), with its opportunist working-class protagonist, as much a watershed in film as *Look Back's* Jimmy Porter had been on the stage. Porter's iconoclasm was somewhat muted on the screen by the film star associations of Richard BURTON who played him in Tony RICHARDSON's adaptation (1959). Other films which may be said to have articulated the sorts of class awareness given such a scalding expression in Osborne's play include Karel REISZ's *Saturday Night and Sunday Morning* (1960), Richardson's *The Loneliness of the Long Distance Runner* and Lindsay ANDERSON's *This Sporting Life* (1963). The 'angry young man' tag quickly outlived its usefulness, but it still helps to conjure up a particular moment in British culture, and in terms of the cinema it is one of the 'moments' when British films seemed most in touch with the realities of British life and the wider culture of change.

animation Britain may legitimately claim animation as an indigenous art form. Tom Merry, a lightning sketch artist, J. Stuart BLACKTON (English, but working in New York), Arthur MELBOURNE-COOPER and Walter BOOTH are turn-of-the-century animation pioneers, embracing in their work the caricatural tradition in British image-making. The 'British School' of animation is best epitomised, however, by G.E

Studdy at Gaumont, and book illustrator, Lancelot SPEED, at Neptune Films. Speed made the WW1 PROPAGANDA SHORTS featuring *Bully Boy* (1914), which lampooned the Kaiser, and later adapted A.B. Payne's *Daily Mirror* comic strip, 'Pip, Squeak and Wilfred'.

Britain's standing in the field would have been considerably enhanced but for the loss of Dudley Buxton's film about the sinking of the *Lusitania*, made some three years before Winsor McCay's celebrated 1918 masterpiece about the same event, and the limited acknowledgement of Anson DYER's full-length feature, *The Story of the Flag* (1927), re-cut in the belief that audiences could not watch cartoons for long periods. Dyer's *Old Sam* series also failed to compete against Disney's TECHNICOLOR Mickey Mouse cartoons.

Britain, while encouraging its own artists like Norman McLAREN, has also provided a context for overseas talent to flourish. The 30s saw John GRIERSON's GPO FILM UNIT promote the work of New Zealander, Len LYE, and the emergence of Anthony Gross (*Joie de Vivre*, 1934, and *Foxhunt*, 1935, the first British Technicolor cartoon). Later years saw the development of Canadians, George Dunning (*Yellow Submarine* 1968) and Richard WILLIAMS (*Who Framed Roger Rabbit*, 1988). HALAS AND BATCHELOR, whose work was characterised by Eastern European aesthetics and Disneyesque design, opened in 1940, and became highly influential. The Larkins Studio and Signal Films specialised in making commercials and industrial films, while RANK's Gaumont British Animation, led by ex-Disney director, David HAND, made short films about regional and national idiosyncrasies.

The new post-war commercial era and the emergence of children's television have provided key working contexts for animators. Oliver POSTGATE, Ivor Wood and Gordon Murray created an innocent rural Britain in their children's animation, later up-dated by TVC, COSGROVE HALL, Hibbert Ralph and AARDMAN. The late millennial proliferation of animation courses in British universities and colleges, and CHANNEL 4 funding, inspired more auteurist work, most notably, by women animators creating a distinctive politicised aesthetic. The Leeds Animation Collective (*Out to Lunch* 1989), Joanna Quinn (*Girls Night Out* 1986), Candy Guard (*Fatty Issues* 1990), Erica Russell (*Triangle* 1994), Marjut Rimmenen (*The Stain* 1991), Alison Snowden (with David Fine) (*Bob's Birthday* 1994) and Ruth Lingford (*Pleasures of War* 1998) have created a distinctively feminine aesthetic, which has challenged dominant orthodoxies not merely in British animation, but in the form *per se*. This has been achieved, first, in using the craft-orientation and auteurist control in animation to reconfigure the practice of film-making itself; and second, in the re-definition of aspects of representation, particularly in regard to the depiction of the body, and issues about gender politics and social identity.

The Oscar-winning successes of Bob GODFREY, Daniel Greaves (*Manipulation* 1992), Alison Snowden and David Fine (*Bob's Birthday* 1995), and most particularly, three-time winner, Nick PARK, say much about the success of British animation on the international stage, and its intrinsic impact on all visual cultures in the 21st century. Paul Wells.

Ankers, Evelyn (*b* Valparaiso, Chile, 1918 – *d* Haiku, Hawaii, 1985). Actress. Slender, blonde Ankers made a dozen British films before going to Hollywood where she became film buffs' favourite 'screamer' in a series of Universal horror films. When not in danger from some dreadful creature, she was offering the leading lady a soignée threat for the hero's affections. Some of her British films are well remembered, but not for her tiny parts in most of them. She has leading roles in such lesser ones as *The Claydon Treasure Mystery* and *The Villiers Diamond* (both 1938). Married to Richard Denning.

OTHER BRITISH FILMS INCLUDE: *Rembrandt* (1936), *Knight Without Armour, Fire Over England, Wings of the Morning* (1937), *Over the Moon* (1939).

Annakin, Ken (*b* Beverley, 1914). Director. Annakin travelled widely and worked as a journalist and a salesman before WW2. Invalided out of the RAF, he quickly became involved with DOCUMENTARY film-making before embarking on features, and he made nearly twenty SHORT FILMS such as *A Farm in the Fens* (1945) and *British Criminal Justice* (1946). His first feature, made for GAINSBOROUGH under Sydney BOX's regime, was *Holiday Camp* (1947), which introduced the HUGGETT family, to whose concerns he brought an agreeable feeling for ordinary lives. In the 50s, he had a very successful association with Walt DISNEY for whom he made four popular films. He also made outpost-of-empire films (*The Planter's Wife*, 1952, *The Seekers*, 1954, *Nor the Moon by Night*, 1958), WAR FILMS, ADVENTURES, and several light COMEDIES (including the inventive *Hotel Sahara*, 1951), before moving on to the international phase of his prolific career. He handled large-scale enterprises such as *Those Magnificent Men . . .* (1965) with assurance, but some of his best work is in very accomplished smaller projects like 'The Colonel's Lady' episode of *Quartet* (1948), and *Across the Bridge* (1957), a taut adaptation from Graham GREENE. His most recent films have been made in the US where he now lives. Father of respected agent, the late Jane Annakin. Awarded OBE, 2002.

OTHER BRITISH FILMS: (shorts) *The Sixteen Tasks Of Maintaining Vehicles, We Serve, Cooks, London* (1942), *A Ride with Uncle Joe* (1943), *Black Diamonds, The New Crop, Combined Cadets* (1944), *Crop Rotation, Make Fruitful The Land, Pacific Thrust, We of the West Riding, Three Cadets* (1945), *It Began On The Clyde*, (1946), *Turn It Out* (1947); (features) *Broken Journey, Here Come The Huggetts, Miranda, Vote For Huggett* (1948), *Landfall, The Huggetts Abroad* (1949), *Trio* ('The Verger' and 'Mr Know-All'), *Double Confession* (1950), *The Story of Robin Hood . . .* (1952), *The Sword and the Rose* (1953), *You Know What Sailors Are!* (1954), *Value for Money* (1955), *Loser Takes All, Three Men in a Boat* (1956), *Third Man on the Mountain* (1959), *Swiss Family Robinson* (1960, UK/US), *Very Important Person, The Hellions* (1961, UK/Saudi), *Crooks Anonymous, The Fast Lady* (1962), *The Informers* (1963), *The Long Duel* (1967, + p), *Monte Carlo or Bust!* (1969, UK/Fr/It, + co-sc, p), *Call Of The Wild* (1972, UK/Fr /Ger/It/Sp), *Paper Tiger* (1974), *The Fifth Musketeer* (1979, UK/Austria).

BIBLIOG: Autobiography, *So You Wanna Be a Director?*, 2001.

Annis, Francesca (*b* London, 1945). Actress. Lushly beautiful star of stage and TV as well as screen, Annis trained originally for ballet, then entered films as a child in *The Cat Gang* (1958). Famously played Lady Macbeth's sleep-walking scene in the nude in POLANSKI's *Macbeth* (1971) and acquired another sort of réclame as Lillie Langtry in TV's mini-series, *Lillie* (1978). Much of her career has been spent in TV (e.g. *Reckless*, 1997) and international films; also scored major stage successes as Mrs Erlynne in *Lady Windermere's Fan* (1994), as Gertrude to the Hamlet of Ralph FIENNES, her partner in private life, and as Mrs Alving in *Ghosts* (2001).

OTHER BRITISH FILMS INCLUDE: *Murder Most Foul* (1964), *The Pleasure Girls* (1965), *The Walking Stick* (1970), *Krull* (1983), *The Debt Collector, Onegin* (UK/US) (1999).

Anstey, Edgar (*b* Watford, 1907 – *d* London, 1987). Producer, director. A very important name associated with the British DOCUMENTARY movement, Anstey joined John GRIERSON at the EMPIRE FILM MARKETING BOARD (later the GPO FILM UNIT) from 1930 to 1934, when he left to organise the SHELL FILM UNIT. In 1935, he and Arthur ELTON made, for the Gas, Light and Coke Company, the then-revolutionary documentary, *Housing Problems*, which exposed the grim reality of British slums. He spent three years as production director of *The March of Time* in London. In 1940, he joined the board of directors of the Film Centre, continuing as producer-in-charge of Shell's films. During WW2, he produced many documentaries for the MOI and other official sponsors, was film critic for *The Spectator* (1941–46) and the BBC (1946–49), and the author of *The Development of Film Technique in Britain*. He organised British Transport Films in 1949 and stayed as its head for many years; one of the films he encouraged in this role was John SCHLESINGER's award-winning short *Terminus* (1961). His name appears as director on a few documentaries, but his real importance is in the influence he exerted in the many key administrative roles he filled, including also those of chairman of the BRITISH FILM ACADEMY (1956) and the Society of Film and Television Arts (1967), and a governor of the BFI (1964).

OTHER BRITISH FILMS INCLUDE: (d) *Uncharted Waters* (1933), *Enough to Eat* (1936).

Ant, Adam (*b* London, 1954). Singer, actor. RN: Stuart Goddard. Rock star who led a group called 'Adam and the Ants' in the early 80s before going single, and who also turned to acting at the decade's end. Apart from his first film, Derek JARMAN's *Jubilee* (1978), a punk vision of the 20th-century world, most of his screen work has been US-made and little seen.

Anthony, Lysette (*b* London, 1963). Actress. English beauty, who began her career in television versions of the classics and has subsequently filmed mainly in the US, where she posed nude for *Playboy* as a way of suggesting she was not the English-rose type she looked. In 1998, she starred in the stage musical, *Jackie*; in 2001, in Mike FIGGIS's *Hotel*, as a terrorist.

BRITISH FILMS INCLUDE: *Krull* (1983), *Without a Clue* (1988, UK/US), *The Hour of the Pig* (1993, UK/Fr).

Antony, Scott (*b* Newcastle-upon-Tyne, 1950). Actor. RN: Antony Scott. Juvenile lead of several 70s films, most notably Ken RUSSELL's *Savage Messiah* (1972) as the painter Henri Gaudier-Brzeska.

OTHER BRITISH FILMS: *Mutations* (1973), *Dead Cert* (1974).

Apted, Michael (*b* Ilford, Essex, 1941). Director. Cambridge-educated Apted went into TV in 1963 as assistant to the director of the DOCUMENTARY short *Seven Up*, which explored the lives of several 7-year-old children. Subsequently, Apted followed up the subjects of this film, tracing their paths in further documentaries at ages 21, 28, 35 and 42, and revealing a good deal about opportunity and the British CLASS system in the process. It is arguable that none of his feature work has been so absorbing, but his 70s British films, especially *The Triple Echo* (1972), have some originality and flair. Most of his later work has been in the US, beginning with *Coal Miner's Daughter* (1980), an often-eloquent biography of country singer, Loretta Lynn, and including *Gorky Park* (1983) and *Gorillas in the Mist* (1988). He has made a documentary, focusing on native Americans in *Incident at Oglala* (1991), and directed the BOND item, *The World Is Not Enough* (1999, UK/US). Appeared in

Spies Like Us (1985) and the documentary *Typically British* (1996).

OTHER BRITISH FILMS: *Stardust* (1974), *The Squeeze* (1977), *Agatha* (1978, UK/US), *P'tang Yang Kipperbang* (1982, TV, some cinemas), *Enigma* (2001, UK/Ger/US).

Aquila Productions Small and short-lived production company set up by David RAWNSLEY of the RANK Research Department who had for some years been experimenting with the INDEPENDENT FRAME technique as a means of reducing production costs by having actors perform in front of pre-photographed backgrounds. Aquila was incorporated in 1947 with the express purpose of testing this system. It operated under the Rank umbrella, with Rank, John DAVIS and George Archibald as its directors. Its contract directors and producers were Donald WILSON and Frederick WILSON (unrelated). Though none of its productions enjoyed much success, they are not without interest and are slightly at odds with what was being produced at the time. They include: *A Warning to Wantons* (1948), *Floodtide*, *Poet's Pub*, *Stop Press Girl* (1949). Both Wilsons subsequently went into television, and, though the company was listed for some years in the *British Film and Television Year Book*, the Aquila logo – the eagle with spread wings – appeared on no more films.

Arbeid, Ben (*b* London, 1924 – *d* 1992). Producer. Entered films as production designer on *Svengali* (1954), was production manager on the UK/French co-production *The Hands of Orlac* (1960), and produced some interesting films over the next two decades, including the poetic Western, *Eagle's Wing* (1978) as well as the popular Miss Marple films, *Murder Most Foul* and *Murder Ahoy* (1964, assoc p). Also scriptwriter for TV in the 50s.

OTHER BRITISH FILMS: *The Barber of Stamford Hill*, *Private Potter* (1962), *Children of the Damned* (1963), *The Jokers* (1966), *Assignment K* (1967), *The Hireling* (1973).

Archard, Bernard (*b* London, 1916). Actor. Tall, gaunt, incisive character actor often cast as authority figures. Also on stage and TV, becoming famous as Colonel Pinto in the *Spycatcher* series (1959–61). His first film role was in *The Secret Man* in 1958, perhaps a little late for him to have had quite the busy career in British films which he might have had a decade earlier.

OTHER BRITISH FILMS INCLUDE: *Village of the Damned* (1960), *Man Detained* (1961), *The Password Is Courage* (1962), *Face of a Stranger* (1964), *Play Dirty* (1968), *The File of the Golden Goose* (1969), *Macbeth* (1971), *The Day of the Jackal* (1973, UK/Fr), *The Sea Wolves* (1980, UK/Switz/US), *Krull* (1983).

Archer, Barbara (*b* East Ham, 1934). Actress. Blonde supporting player of the 50s and 60s, at her most vivid (as a vindictive circus performer) in an otherwise negligible 'B' FILM, *Strangers' Meeting* (1957), mostly in very small roles like the perky barmaid, Glad, in *Miracle in Soho* (1957). Born in London's East End, she had a two-year scholarship to RADA before appearing in films and TV.

OTHER BRITISH FILMS INCLUDE: *Jumping for Joy* (1955), *Three Men in a Boat* (1956), *The Feminine Touch* (1956), *Dracula* (1958), *633 Squadron* (1963, UK/US), *Up the Junction* (1967).

Archers Films For a brief period in the latter half of the 40s, several production units, including The Archers, operated independently under the comprehensive title of INDEPENDENT PRODUCERS and under the financial umbrella of the RANK ORGANISATION. Set up in 1942, The Archers was the company

of Michael POWELL and Emeric PRESSBURGER, brought together by Alexander KORDA to make *The Spy in Black* (1939), as a vehicle for Conrad VEIDT, and its success was repeated the following year with *Contraband* (1940). Their fifth film together and the first to be made bearing the logo of the Archers (an arrow striking centre target) was *The Silver Fleet* (1943), which they produced and which Vernon SEWELL directed. Thereafter, their credits most often read 'Produced, Directed and Written by' the two of them, which reflected the closeness of their collaboration, though it was widely known that Powell was actually the director. They made films of great daring: thematically both *The Life and Death of Colonel Blimp* (1943) and *A Canterbury Tale* (1944) can be read as celebrations of Englishness, but not in any straightforward way; *A Matter of Life and Death* (1946) is an astonishing flight of imaginative fancy; *Black Narcissus* (1947) tackles women's sexuality and its repression with a boldness that is still dazzling; and *all* their films are visually striking in a way that stands out in even that exciting era of British film. They employed the services of such key personnel as designer Hein HECKROTH, cinematographer Jack CARDIFF, and many distinctive actors. After the unexpected commercial success of *The Red Shoes* (1948), about which Rank had grave misgivings, they returned to Korda and LONDON FILMS for their next four films. Following Korda's death in 1956, they were back with Rank for the war films, *The Battle of the River Plate* (1956) and *Ill Met By Moonlight* (1957), after which the company was dissolved and Powell and Pressburger went their separate ways. It may well be true to say that no other group in the history of British cinema ever made so dramatically and visually extraordinary a batch of films as The Archers.

OTHER BRITISH FILMS: *I Know Where I'm Going!* (1945), *The End of the River* (1947, directed by Derek TWIST), *The Small Back Room* (1948), *Gone to Earth* (1950), *The Elusive Pimpernel*, *The Tales of Hoffmann* (1951).

BIBLIOG: Ian Christie, *Arrows of Desire*, 1985.

archives The practice of film archiving – the preservation of moving images to make them permanently available – began in Britain in 1919 with the founding of the film archive of the Imperial War Museum, conceived two years earlier as a memorial to the sacrifice and effort represented by WW1. This was the world's first authentic film archive, charged with collecting, preserving and documenting 'all War Cinematograph films'. The unwitting pioneer responsible for this mission was a civil servant and Government 'adviser on cinematograph matters', Edward Foxen Cooper, who articulated most of the basic precepts of film preservation and access. It was not until the 30s that there was a more general recognition of the need for film archives with the creation of Svenska Filmsamfundet (later the Svensk Filminstitutt) in Stockholm in 1933, Goebbels's Reichsfilmarchiv in Berlin in 1934, the Film Department of the Museum of Modern Art in New York and the government-funded BRITISH FILM INSTITUTE's National Film Library in London in 1935, and the Cinémathèque Française in Paris in 1936. With the exception of Sweden, these countries went on to found the INTERNATIONAL FEDERATION OF FILM ARCHIVES (FIAF) in 1938 (put on hold until 1946 by WW2).

The UK's National Film Library – set up 'to maintain a national repository of films of permanent value' – was renamed the National Film Archive in 1955 and subsequently the NATIONAL FILM AND TV ARCHIVE (NFTVA) in the 90s, in recognition of its commitment, since the 50s, to the preservation of national TV. Significantly, and for a while uniquely among the FIAF-founding archives, the NFA declared a formal and equal commitment to the preserving of non-fiction films of all kinds as well as commercial cinema or film as art, citing as examples 'copies of scientific and research films . . . including anthropological films and copies of any films such as NEWS-REELS or DOCUMENTARIES judged to be of importance as historical documents, either socially, politically or economically'. This was the vision of the NFA's founding Curator, Ernest LINDGREN, a major influence on establishing proper policies and practices in film archiving worldwide. The NFTVA is now a part of BFI Collections.

Peculiar to the UK – especially given its compact geographical scale – has also been the emergence since the 70s of a coherent network of officially recognised and funded regional preservation film archives, each with a remit to document, through moving images produced by both amateurs and professionals, the history and society of its region (including cinema production) and to make these educationally available. The first of these very British and important institutions, which complement the two original national archives (the IWM and the NFTVA), was the East Anglian Film Archive (1976), Norwich. This was followed by the Scottish Screen Archive, Glasgow, in the same year, the North West Film Archive, Manchester (1977), the Yorkshire Film Archive, Ripon (1984), the Wessex Film and Sound Archive, Winchester (1988), the UK's fourth national film archive, the Wales Film and TV Archive, Aberystwyth (1989), the South East Film and Video Archive, Brighton (1992), and the South West Film and TV Archive, Plymouth (1993). These, together with the Media Archive for Central England (MACE) and the Northern Region Film and TV Archive, Newcastle upon Tyne, virtually cover the map of mainland Britain in film archiving terms, and make up the Film Archive Forum (FAF), which co-ordinates the archives' activities and joint policy and lobbies for national recognition and funding. The Forum is chaired by the BRITISH UNIVERSITIES FILM AND VIDEO COUNCIL (BUFVC), which also provides a secretariat. Three members of the Forum – the archives of Scotland, Wales and the North West – are also members of FIAF.

BIBLIOG: Penelope Houston, *Keepers of the Frame*, 1994. Clyde Jeavons.

Arden, Robert (*b* London, 1921). Actor. RN: Mark Sharpe. Cockney-born, American-raised former vocalist with AMBROSE's orchestra who turned to acting in the 40s. Working in the radio series *The Adventures of Harry Lime* (derived from *The Third Man*), he met Orson WELLES who gave him his one big chance – as leading man in *Confidential Report* (1955). For the rest, supporting roles in British and, later, American films.

OTHER BRITISH FILMS INCLUDE: *Two Thousand Women* (1944), *The Man from Morocco* (1945), *No Orchids for Miss Blandish* (1948), *Joe Macbeth* (1955), *A King in New York* (1957), *Death Drums Along the River* (1963, UK/Ger/S Af).

Argyle, John F. (*b* Tamworth, 1911 – *d* Salisbury, Rhodesia, 1962). Director, producer, screenwriter. Entered films in 1927 as assistant cameraman at GAINSBOROUGH, and later wrote, directed and produced films for his own production company, and, as a free-lance, for other companies such as ASSOCIATED BRITISH (*The Night Has Eyes*, 1942) and BUTCHER's (*Once a Sinner*, 1950). One of the last British film-makers to hold out against sound, he sometimes acted in his own productions, as in his first, *Thoroughbred* (1931), and was managing director of his

own companies including Argyle Talking Pictures. Finished his career as a maker of travelogues.

OTHER BRITISH FILMS INCLUDE: (p/d, unless noted): *That's His Weakness* (short, + sc), *Flames of Fear* (p, sc, a) (1930), *The Last Tide* (+ sc), *Paradise Alley* (+ sc, a) (1931), *The Final Reckoning* (1932, + sc), *Variety* (1935, p), *Kathleen Mavourneen* (1937, p), *Dark Eyes of London* (1939, p, co-sc), *Thursday's Child* (1943, p), *Send for Paul Temple* (1946), *The Case of Charles Peace* (1949, p), *Island of Venus* (1954, short), *The Land is Green* (1958, short).

Argyle, Pearl (*b* Johannesburg, 1910 – *d* New York, 1947). Actress. Former ballet dancer who starred for Charles Cochrane in his *Midnight Cabaret*, and made a few films in the 30s, most notably *Things to Come* (1936) as Raymond MASSEY's daughter.

OTHER BRITISH FILMS: *That Night in London* (1932), *Chu-Chin-Chow*, *Adventure Limited* (1934), *Royal Cavalcade* (as Anna Pavlova) (1935), *Trust Barclay* (1936).

Aris, Ben (*b* London, 1937). Actor. Former child actor whose first film was *Tom Brown's Schooldays* in 1951. From the mid 60s he has worked steadily, generally in supporting roles, but for some notable directors (Tony RICHARDSON, Lindsay ANDERSON, Ken RUSSELL), and has done a good deal of TV.

OTHER BRITISH FILMS INCLUDE: *The Plague of the Zombies* (1966), *The Charge of the Light Brigade, If . . .* (1968), *Hamlet* (1969, as Rosencrantz), *The Music Lovers* (1971), *The Savage Messiah* (1972), *O Lucky Man!* (1973), *Juggernaut* (1974), *Tommy, Royal Flash* (1975), *Up at the Villa* (2000, UK/US).

Arliss, George (*b* London, 1868 – *d* London, 1946). Actor. RN: George Augustus Andrews. The object of adulation on both sides of the Atlantic for his silent and early talkie films, Arliss was perhaps past his prime when he re-settled in England in 1935. The son of a printer-publisher known as 'the Duke of Bloomsbury', he started his own amateur theatre prior to making his West End debut in 1890. In 1901 he went to the US with Mrs Patrick CAMPBELL's company – and stayed there. Some of his early films, *Disraeli* (1921) and *The Green Goddess* (1923), were adaptations of his stage successes, and both were later refilmed as talkies (in 1929 and 1930), with his wife Florence (Montgomery) Arliss also in the former. He specialised in recreating great men of history, including Disraeli, Rothschild and Voltaire. In 1935, he made *The Iron Duke* (as the Duke of Wellington) for GAUMONT–BRITISH, and after one more US film he returned to live in Britain and to take up a contract with Gaumont–British. By this time, there were beginning to be critical cavils about his mannerisms and his somewhat arch great-man-with-a-twinkle persona, but he was still able to compel the attention even in his last film, *Dr Syn* (1937) as the parson-smuggler. Slight, stooped, well past middle-aged, monocled, he seems an unlikely candidate for stardom, but *star* is what he indubitably was.

OTHER BRITISH FILMS: *The Tunnel, The Guv'nor* (1935), *East Meets West, His Lordship* (1936).

BIBLIOG: Autobiography, *On the Stage*, 1926; *Up the Years from Bloomsbury*, 1927; *My Ten Years in the Studios*, 1940.

Arliss, Leslie (*b* London, 1901 – *d* Jersey, Channel Islands, 1987). Screenwriter, director. Starting as a journalist and critic, Arliss entered British films in 1932 as a writer for THRILLERS, COMEDIES and MUSICALS, the main GENRES of the period. In fact, in all his 30s (and some of his 40s) films, he shares the writing credits with one, two or three others. He began to direct in 1941, sharing the director-writer credit with Norman LEE on *The Farmer's Wife*, based on Eden Philpotts' trusty stage success of RURAL LIFE. In 1942, he directed James MASON in the thriller *The Night Has Eyes*, and, in the following year, the first of the GAINSBOROUGH COSTUME MELODRAMAS, *The Man in Grey*, which made household names of Mason, Phyllis CALVERT and Stewart GRANGER (Margaret LOCKWOOD already was one) and initiated a hugely successful cycle. Arliss was not a greatly gifted or personal director, but, in this film, in *Love Story* (1944), and *The Wicked Lady* (1945), and the neglected *A Man About the House* (1947), he orchestrated some attractive talents before and behind the camera, helping to establish one of the most popular and, at least in hindsight, most influential of British screen genres. Sadly for him, this was virtually the end of his significant career: his attempt to repeat his melodramatic successes in *Idol of Paris* (1948), with its whip-cracking heroines, met only outrage and derision. In the 50s, he directed many short TV films, especially for the series, *Douglas Fairbanks Presents*. Thirty-five years later, Michael WINNER 're-wrote' Arliss's script for *The Wicked Lady*, and directed it to less rewarding results. Often confidently but erroneously described as son of George ARLISS.

OTHER BRITISH FILMS INCLUDE: (co-sc) *Holiday Lovers* (short), *The Innocents of Chicago, Josser on the River* (1932), *Orders Is Orders* (1933), *Road House, Jack Ahoy!* (1934), *Heat Wave* (1935), *Windbag the Sailor, Rhodes of Africa, Everybody Dance* (1936), *Said O'Reilly to McNab* (1937), *Too Dangerous to Live, Come On George!* (1939), *Pastor Hall, For Freedom* (1940), *The Foreman Went to France* (1942), *The Saint Meets the Tiger* (1943); (d, sc) *Saints and Sinners* (1949), *The Woman's Angle* (1952), *Miss Tulip Stays the Night* (1955).

Armitage, Graham (*b* Manchester, 1933 – *d* Johannesburg, 1999) Actor. Supporting player who appeared in several films for Ken RUSSELL in the 70s, as well as playing a flustered boardman in the little seen Cliff RICHARD musical *Take Me High* (1973). Also in international films and TV, including mini-series *Shaka Zulu* (1987).

OTHER BRITISH FILMS INCLUDE: *The Private Life of Sherlock Holmes, Games That Lovers Play* (1970), *The Music Lovers, The Devils, The Boy Friend* (1971), *A Game of Vultures* (1979), *Jane and the Lost City* (1987).

Armstrong, Alun (*b* Annfield Plain, 1946). Actor. Stage and TV actor who has appeared sporadically in films, few of which have given him the scope that, say, the black comedy mini-series, *Underworld* (1998), gave him as a retired gangster and auto-didact. Nevertheless, some notable films: *The French Lieutenant's Woman* (1981), and the US films, *White Hunter, Black Heart* (1990) and *Braveheart* (1995). Most of his 90s work has been in international films, though Mike NEWELL's *An Awfully Big Adventure* (1995) gave him a good supporting role.

OTHER BRITISH FILMS INCLUDE: *Get Carter* (1971), *The 14* (1973), *The Likely Lads* (1976), *A Bridge Too Far* (1977), *Krull* (1983), *London Kills Me* (1991), *Blue Ice* (1992, UK/US), *With or Without You, Onegin* (UK/US), *Greenwich Mean Time* (1999), *Proof of Life* (2001, UK/US).

Armstrong, Craig Composer. Trained at the Royal Academy of Music, now famous as co-writer of the pounding rock score for *Romeo+Juliet* (1996, US) and responsible for the daringly anachronistic rock music for the 18th-century romp, *Plunkett & Macleane* (1999). First composed for Peter MULLAN's short, *Fridge* (1996), and Mullan's feature debut, *Orphans* (1997). He moves effortlessly between classical and pop, and has worked on several big international films, including *The Bone-Collector* (1999, US) and *Moulin Rouge* (2001, Aust/US).

Armstrong, John (*b* Hastings, 1893 – *d* London, 1973). Costume designer. Armstrong was responsible for the costume design of some of the most admired and ambitious films of the 30s. He worked almost exclusively for KORDA at DENHAM, though he did design for Eric POMMER's MAYFLOWER film, *St Martin's Lane* (1938) at ELSTREE. All his work of the decade is notable, contributing to the strong visual appeal of such period pieces as the ground-breaking *The Private Life of Henry VIII* (1933) and such fantasy triumphs as *Things to Come* (1936), on which he shared credit with Korda's other resident designer, René HUBERT, and with Cathleen MANN, and *The Thief of Baghdad* (1940), on which he collaborated with Oliver MESSEL. What remains of Joseph von Sternberg's ill-fated *I Claudius* (1937) gives further evidence of his genius in evoking an historical period, in the interests of both authenticity and audience pleasure. Merle OBERON never looked more stunning than as the diaphanously clad Messalina.

OTHER BRITISH FILMS: *Catherine the Great* (1934), *The Scarlet Pimpernel, Moscow Nights, The Ghost Goes West* (with Hubert) (1935), *As You Like It, The Man Who Could Work Miracles, Rembrandt* (1936), *Hobson's Choice* (1953).

Armstrong, Vic (*b* Farnham Common, 1941). Stunt expert. Winner of the Michael BALCON Award at the 2002 BAFTA ceremony for his contribution to cinema and of an AA for his application of the 'Fan Descender' to increasing safety of stunt persons in high falls. He won a reputation for his imaginative approach to complicated stunts and for his precision in executing them. First worked on the thriller *Arabesque* (1966, UK/US), and his subsequent prolific career included several BOND films as well as *Henry V* (1989) and the US 'Indiana Jones' films. Worked as 2nd unit director on several films, including *Entrapment* (1999, UK/Ger/US), and directed the feature, *The Joshua Tree* (1994, US). His brother, Andy Armstrong is also a stunts expert, who has worked mainly on US films since the later 80s.

OTHER BRITISH FILMS INCLUDE: (a) *Dead Cert* (1974), *Exposé* (1975), *'Copter Kids* (1976); (stunts) *You Only Live Twice* (1967), *On Her Majesty's Secret Service* (1969), *Young Winston* (1972), *Live and Let Die* (1973), *A Bridge Too Far* (1977), *Superman* (1978), *The Long Good Friday* (1979), *Superman II* (1980), *An American Werewolf in London, Never Say Never Again* (UK/US) (1983), *Brazil, The Mission* (1985); (2ud, stunts) *Bear Island* (1979, UK/Can), *Black Beauty* (1994, + a, horse master), *Tomorrow Never Dies* (1997, UK/US), *The World Is Not Enough* (1999, UK/US), *Captain Corelli's Mandolin* (2001, UK/Fr/US), *Die Another Day* (2002, UK/US).

Army Film Unit Like the Navy and the Air Force, the Army recognised the power of film to inform and persuade during WW2 and established its own film production unit, the Army Film Unit, which was not to be confused with the **Directorate of Army Kinematography**, which was responsible for military training films. The AFU was set up in 1940, partly in reaction to the inadequate coverage of the Dunkirk evacuation, and with the encouragement of the War Office. It was intended to liaise with both the newsreel producers and with the MOI's Films Division. By late 1941, its name was changed to the Army Film and Photographic Unit in recognition of the need to integrate the work of still photographers and cinematographers, though the earlier name remained in some quarters, such as PINE-WOOD. The AFPU engaged in some collaborative ventures with the CROWN FILM UNIT (*Wavell's 30,000*, 1941) and with Crown and the RAF FILM UNIT (*Malta*, 1942), but its greatest triumph was *Desert Victory* (1943), the work of David MACDONALD and Roy BOULTING, and its follow-up, *Tunisian Victory* (1944). *Desert Victory*, depicting Montgomery's routing of the Nazis in North Africa, was an enormous success on both sides of the Atlantic, though in the production of both films there was tension due to Anglo-American rivalries. On *Tunisian Victory* the famous American director Frank Capra clashed with Roy Boulting and Hugh STEWART over the undue emphasis on American participation and on the faking of certain events. Brian Desmond HURST's 1946 documentary, *Theirs is the Glory*, a re-enactment of the famous disaster at Arnhem, made use of material shot by the AFPU, and AFPU editors at Pinewood were responsible for cutting the Carol REED–Garson Kanin Oscar-winner, *The True Glory* (1945). The last of its great combat films, *Burma Victory* (1945), was described by Clive Coultass as 'a fitting conclusion to the various productions made by the British service film units during the war'. Other film-makers who had experience with the Army Film Unit included Roy Ward BAKER, Philip LEACOCK, Robert S. BAKER and music director Muir MATHIESON.

BIBLIOG: Clive Coultass, *Images for Battle*, 1989.

Arnall, Julia (*b* Vienna, 1930). Actress. Elegant Austrian-born photographic model, Arnall acted in over a dozen films in Britain following her 1954 debut in *Value for Money*, but failed to make a very vivid impression. Her best chance came as the distraught mother of the kidnapped child in Guy GREEN's tense thriller, *Lost* (1955). Under contract to RANK.

OTHER BRITISH FILMS INCLUDE: *Simon and Laura* (1955), *House of Secrets* (1956), *Mark of the Phoenix* (1957), *The Quiller Memorandum* (1966, UK/US).

Arnatt, John (*b* Petrograd, Russia, 1917 – *d* Surrey, 1999). Actor. Weighty character player, usually in roles suggesting official authority, such as the police superintendent in *Whistle Down the Wind* (1961). Also much TV, including Deputy Sheriff in *The Adventures of Robin Hood* in the 50s and the mini-series of corrupt parliamentary life, *House of Cards*, in 1990. On stage since 1936 after RADA training, and entered films the year after. Was married (1) to actress Betty HUNTLEY-WRIGHT and (2) to broadcaster Sheila Tracy.

OTHER BRITISH FILMS INCLUDE: *Mademoiselle Docteur* (1937), *Dick Barton at Bay* (1950), *Cry, the Beloved Country* (1952), *Forbidden Cargo* (1954), *No Love for Johnnie, Only Two Can Play* (1961), *Our Mother's House* (1967).

Arnaud, Yvonne (*b* Paris, 1892 – *d* London, 1958). Actress. An immediate success on London stage in 1911, and in British films from 1920. Her main screen popularity was in the 30s, especially in Tom WALLS's ADAPTATIONS of famous stage farces by Frederick LONSDALE and Ben TRAVERS. Not at all beautiful, she had an infectious gaiety and comedy gift which are still enjoyable. In the 40s, she played some more sombre character roles (*Tomorrow We Live*, 1942), with a return to an ooh-la-la comic type in *The Ghosts of Berkeley Square* (1947). Her last film was Jacques Tati's *Mon Oncle* (1958).

OTHER BRITISH FILMS: *Desire, The Temptress* (1920), *On Approval, Canaries Sometimes Sing* (1930), *Tons of Money* (1931), *A Cuckoo in the Nest* (1933), *Prince Charming, Lady in Danger* (1934), *Widows Might, Stormy Weather* (1935), *The Improper Duchess, The Gay Adventure* (1936), *Neutral Port* (1940), *I Want to Be an Actress* (short) (1943), *Woman to Woman* (1946).

Arne, Peter (*b* Kuala Lumpur, 1920 – *d* London, 1983). Actor. Victim of an unsolved murder, Malayan-born Arne was busy in the 50s and 60s, most often playing enjoyably furtive and dangerous types, with just an occasional foray into comedy, as in *Chitty Chitty Bang Bang* (1968), but the sinister likes of Benucci in *Breakout* (1959) were more common.

OTHER BRITISH FILMS INCLUDE:*For Those in Peril* (1944), *Saraband for Dead Lovers* (1948), *You Know What Sailors Are!*, *The Purple Plain*

(1954), *Ice Cold in Alex* (1958), *Khartoum* (as Kitchener) (1966), *Straw Dogs* (1971), *Victor/Victoria* (1982).

Arnold, Grace (*b* London, 1899 – *d* London, 1979). Actress. After a long stage career, Arnold entered films in 1939 and played many character roles, particularly at EALING (the vinegary landlady in *It Always Rains on Sunday*, 1947, the devoted but austere housekeeper in *The Loves of Joanna Godden*, 1947). She was one of those cameo players to be counted on for moments of truth and pleasure, whatever the quality of the film. Also TV from 1948.

OTHER BRITISH FILMS INCLUDE: *Men Without Honour* (1939), *Went the Day Well?* (1942), *The Gentle Sex* (1943), *The Way Ahead* (1944), *Hue and Cry* (1946), *My Brother Jonathan* (1948), *Passport to Pimlico* (1949), *Hunted* (1952), *Eight O'Clock Walk* (1954), *The Heroes of Telemark* (1965).

Arnold, Sir Malcolm (*b* Northampton, 1921). Composer. After studying composition with Arthur Jacob at the RCM, Arnold became First Trumpet with the London Philharmonic Orchestra, which he left in 1948 to devote himself to full-time composing and conducting. He has composed the scores for nearly 100 films, almost all of them British, though some had substantial American involvement, including *The Bridge on the River Kwai* (1957) for which he won an Oscar. He worked several times for David LEAN and Carol REED, and many other British film-makers. After beginning with DOCUMENTARIES, he composed for a wide GENRE range including comedies such as *The Belles of St Trinian's* (1954), WAR FILMS (*a Hill in Korea*, 1956), THRILLERS (*Tiger in the Smoke*, 1956), and realist drama (*No Love for Johnnie*, 1961). Awarded CBE in 1970 and knighted in 1993.

OTHER BRITISH FILMS INCLUDE: *Avalanche Patrol* (1947, short), *Charting the Seas* (1948, short), *Britannia Mews* (1949), *No Highway in the Sky* (1951), *The Ringer, The Sound Barrier* (1952), *Albert RN, The Captain's Paradise* (1953), *Hobson's Choice* (1953), *The Night My Number Came Up* (1955), *Dunkirk* (1958), *Blind Date* (1959), *Tunes of Glory, The Angry Silence* (1960), *The Chalk Garden* (1964), *Battle of Britain* (1969, cond).

Arnold, Norman (*b* Culcheth, 1892 – *d* London, 1964). Production designer. With a background including studies in architecture, interior decoration and design, and a series of pictures depicting aerial combat in WW1 for the Imperial War Museum, Arnold came to films in 1920 with Famous Players Lasky, Islington. His elegant, atmospheric designs quickly won him a reputation in the 20s and he worked prolifically into the late 40s, for such producers and/or companies as Herbert WILCOX (*Chu Chin Chow*, 1923, and *Decameron Nights*, 1924, UK/Ger), BRITISH LION, WARNER BROS and GAINS-BOROUGH. Like his designer brother Wilfred ARNOLD, he was associated with HITCHCOCK – as designer on *Juno and the Paycock* (1930) and as co-designer with Wilfred on *Blackmail* (1929). He was adept in designing for THRILLERS (*I See a Dark Stranger*, 1946), COMEDIES (*Hue and Cry*, 1946), and dramas (*The White Unicorn*, 1947, which has a magnificent courtroom design), for Gainsborough high gloss and for EALING's low-key REALISM.

OTHER BRITISH FILMS INCLUDE: *Sally in Our Alley* (1931), *There Goes the Bride* (1932), *Murder Will Out* (1939), *George and Margaret* (1940), *Atlantic Ferry* (1941, with his brother), *They Met in the Dark* (1943), *Mr Emmanuel* (1944), *The Rake's Progress* (1945), *The Blind Goddess* (1948), *Dance Hall* (1950), *The Big Chance* (1957), *Son of Robin Hood* (1959).

Arnold, Wilfred Production designer. Arnold entered films as a draughtsman in 1920, at Famous Players–Lasky, Islington, and had his first credit as art director on Graham CUTTS' *The Rat*, starring Ivor NOVELLO. Made his name as art director on several films for HITCHCOCK, including *The Lodger* (1926), *The Farmer's Wife* (1928), *Blackmail* (1929), *Rich and Strange* and *Number Seventeen* (1932), winning praise for evocative and uncluttered designs, which contributed much to the atmosphere of the films. In the remainder of his career, he worked on a few 'A' films like *The Woman with No Name* (1950), and second features like *Double Exposure* (1954) and *Shadow of Fear* (1963). Brother Norman ARNOLD was also an art director; they worked together on *Atlantic Ferry* (1941).

OTHER BRITISH FILMS INCLUDE: (art d) *The First Born* (1928), *When Knights Were Bold, Talk of the Devil* (1936), *The Saint in London* (1939), *The Ghosts of Berkeley Square* (1947), *Marry Me* (1949), *Reluctant Heroes* (1951), *Horrors of the Black Museum* (1959); (des) *A Stolen Face* (1952), *Wheel of Fate* (1953), *Escapement* (1957), *The Body Stealers* (1969).

Arrighi, Luciana (*b* Australia). Production designer. Arrighi (a cousin of novelist Patrick White) won an Oscar for *Howards End* (1992) and was nominated for *The Remains of the Day* (1993), but had come to attention over 20 years earlier with her superbly evocative design for Ken RUSSELL's *Women in Love* (1969). Her art direction was crucial to audience sense of the developing consciousness of the rebellious heroine in Gillian Armstrong's *My Brilliant Career* (1979, Aust), and she designed *Anna and the King* (1999). Her great strength is in deployment of design as discriminator among persons, temperaments and places. Her sister is actress Niké ARRIGHI.

OTHER BRITISH FILMS INCLUDE: *Sunday Bloody Sunday* (1971), *Return of the Soldier, Privates on Parade* (1982), *The Ploughman's Lunch* (1983), *Madame Sousatzka* (1988), *The Rainbow* (1989), *Close My Eyes* (1991), *Sense and Sensibility* (1995, UK/US), *A Midsummer Night's Dream* (1999, UK/It), *Possession, The Importance of Being Earnest* (2002, UK/US).

Arrighi, Niké (*b* Italy, 1947). Actress. Attractive, fragile-looking Australian-Italian Arrighi was first seen in the gripping HAMMER film, *The Devil Rides Out* (1967), as victim of a satanic cult.

OTHER BRITISH FILMS: *Don't Raise the Bridge, Lower the River* (1967), *Women in Love* (1969), *Countess Dracula* (1970), *Sunday Bloody Sunday* (1971).

art cinema There have been four main phases of activity in Britain, the first occurring in the 20s and 30s when interest in art cinema revolved around film journals, *CLOSE UP* and *Film Art*, the FILM SOCIETY (1925–39) and the DOCUMENTARY FILM MOVEMENT. The Film Society provided an EXHIBITION outlet for foreign-language films and for films which might otherwise have been censored, and nurtured a cultural appreciation for art cinema, particularly amongst the intelligentsia. Within the constraints of official and commercial sponsorship directors such as Len LYE, Alberto CAVALCANTI and Norman McLAREN produced experimental SHORT FILMS including *Colour Box* (1935), *Coal Face* (1935) and *Love On the Wing* (1939) from within the documentary movement. Kenneth MACPHERSON's *Borderline* (1930) represents the most sustained attempt to merge the contributions of avant-garde cinema with a literary aesthetic provided in this case by writer Winifred Bryher and symbolist poet HD.

After the experimental activity of the 30s Britain did not, however, go on to produce an avant-garde cinema, though Humphrey JENNINGS, the 'poet' of the documentary movement, showed a strain of SURREALISM in some of his work. In the second phase of activity, directors working within sound GENRE cinema such as POWELL AND PRESSBURGER introduced

innovatory techniques including the 'composed film' (*The Red Shoes*, 1948 and *The Tales of Hoffmann*, 1951). In the 60s other directors working within the confines of commercial cinema produced distinctive and innovatory works, for example, Lindsay ANDERSON's *If . . .* (1968) and Nicolas ROEG and Donald CAMMELL's *Performance* (1970).

The third major phase of aesthetic interest was 1966–80 when many artists and co-operative film groups attempted to challenge industry traditions and inform film with structuralist critique. Artists attracted to film included Peter Gidal, Malcolm Le Grice and Chris Welsby who presented filmic experiments based on their theoretical writings which were concerned with questions of formalism and time duration. The LONDON FILMMAKERS CO-OP was formed in 1966 with the aim of producing 'oppositional' films in terms of organisation and aesthetics. A number of directors made FEMINIST FILMS which challenged dominant representations of GENDER, particularly Laura Mulvey and Peter WOLLEN's *Riddles of the Sphinx* (1977) and *Amy!* (1980).

During the 80s and 90s, the fourth phase, film-makers such as Sally POTTER, Peter GREENAWAY, Derek JARMAN, Terence DAVIES and Bill DOUGLAS produced films which have been internationally recognised as contributing to a British art film aesthetic which is varied and challenging in terms of political critique, formal experiment and for winning a wider audience for art cinema. The films produced by the SANKOFA Film and Video Collective and the Black Audio Film Collective successfully established a black experimental film-making practice in Britain with films such as *Territories* (1984). ANIMATION has also produced some significant experimental work as well as new developments in video art.

BIBLIOG: Sarah Street, *British National Cinema*, 1997; Michael O'Pray (ed), *The British Avant-Garde Film, 1926-95*, 1996. Sarah Street.

art direction in British silent films. As in the US, the painted backdrop dominated early British films, but unlike its American counterpart, the British silent film industry failed to develop either a standard of cinematic art direction or a name art director of the quality of Wilfred Buckland (who entered films in 1914).

The theatrical tradition of over-dressing a set was prevalent during much of the silent era in most British films. Pictorial artists who entered films, such as Hubert von HERKOMER and Harry FURNISS, seemed more interested in the technical aspects of film-making than in the basic 'look' of their films. Up through the late 1910s, sets were generally flimsy affairs that photographed as such. Only in outdoor locations, where the emphasis was on a natural rather than a conceived 'look' did British films compare favourably with the American output. The films did not necessarily have to be set in the countryside, as with *The Wonderful Story* (1922); the high spot of *Squibs Wins the Calcutta Sweep* (1922), for example, is not in the interior scenes but in the naturalness of the footage shot in Piccadilly Circus.

Art directors of any worth were few, with Walter MURTON deserving of mention, and much later at the end of the silent era, Edward CARRICK, whose work on *The Little People* (1926) is exemplary. AS.

art direction in British sound film *see* **production design**

art-house cinemas *see* **independent and alternative cinemas**

Arthur, George K. (*b* Aberdeen, 1899 – *d* New York, 1985). Actor. RN: Brest. Diminutive and perky personification of the

H.G. WELLS's anti-hero Kipps, in the 1921 film version in which Arthur made his screen debut after a minor stage career. He starred in five further British films, *Wheels of Chance, Lamp in the Desert, A Dear Fool, Flames of Passion* (1922), and *Paddy the Next Best Thing* (1923), before starting a US screen career with *Madness of Youth* (1923), including a series of comedies at MGM, with Karl Dane, beginning with *Rookies* (1927). Began producing UK SHORTS in 1953 with *The Stranger Left No Card*, and later in the decade became US film exporter and distributor. AS.

Arts Council and Lottery The Arts Council's first foray into film-making was to commission films about artists, but in 1972 an additional production fund was established to commission works from film and video artists; both were important sources of funds for the independent sector. The Arts Council was also the major funder of the Regional Arts Associations (later Regional Arts Boards), which helped support regional film and video activity. From 1995 the Arts Councils of England, Wales, Scotland and Northern Ireland became the conduits through which money raised by the National Lottery entered the film industry. In 1996 the four Arts Councils awarded £32m to feature and SHORT FILM projects, of which £19m was distributed by ACEs to 23 features. Although monies have declined somewhat in succeeding years, Lottery funds have clearly been a key factor in the growth of British feature production, recipients including *Stella Does Tricks* (1996), *Wilde* (UK/Ger/Jap/US), *Love and Death on Long Island* (1997, UK/Can), *Love is the Devil* (1998, UK/Fr/Jap), and . Even more significant was the granting of £92m of Lottery monies in 1997 to three new consortia – DNA, THE FILM CONSORTIUM and PATHÉ PICTURES – to enable them to operate like mini-studios for six years, unifying production, DISTRIBUTION and sales. These film franchises are committed to producing over 70 films in this period, although whether they will crack the distribution problem, so long a bugbear for British films, remains to be seen, since only Pathé has a distribution company, although The Film Consortium has secured a distribution deal with UIP. It also has to be pointed out that nothing has yet been done to improve the dire EXHIBITION chances of British films, and that it was revealed in 2000 that all but one (*An Ideal Husband*, 1999, UK/US) of the 14 films funded by Lottery money had flopped. In 2000 the FILM COUNCIL absorbed the responsibilities of ACE's Lottery Film Department. Julian Petley.

Arundell, Denis (*b* London, 1898 – *d* London, 1987). Actor. On stage from 1926, Cambridge-educated Arundell was distinguished in classic and modern drama, as actor, producer (of plays and opera), composer and lyricist. Entered films in 1935 in *The Show Goes On*, with Gracie FIELDS, and achieved great popularity as radio's 'Dr Morelle' (1942–43), was an impressive and sympathetic Charles II in *Penn of Pennsylvania* (1941), and wrote the new lyrics for *Oh, Rosalinda!!* (1955).
OTHER BRITISH FILMS INCLUDE: *The Return of Carol Deane* (1938), *Contraband* (1940), *Pimpernel Smith* (1941), *The Life and Death of Colonel Blimp* (1943), *The Man from Morocco* (1945), *The History of Mr Polly* (1948), *The Tales of Hoffmann* (libretto) (1951).

Ashbourne, Lorraine (*b* 1962). Actress. Remembered best for the suppressed passion of her playing as Pete POSTLE-THWAITE's rebellious daughter in *Distant Voices Still Lives* (1988, UK/Ger), also eloquent as the mother of the soccer-mad hero of *Fever Pitch* (1997), and as TV's Sgt Yvonne Mackay in *City Central* (1998–2000).

OTHER BRITISH FILMS INCLUDE: *The Dressmaker* (1988), *Resurrected* (1989), *Jack & Sarah* (1995, UK/Fr).

Ashcroft, Dame Peggy (*b* London, 1907 – *d* Croydon, 1991). Actress. Dominant star of the British stage for over 50 years, Dame Peggy made no more than 15 films, but some are very memorable. On stage from 1926, she first filmed in 1933 in *The Wandering Jew*, was obliquely sexy and touching as the crofter's wife in *The 39 Steps* (1935), and delectably funny as the affected Fleur in *Quiet Wedding* (1941), then did not film again for nearly 20 years, except for two wartime SHORTS. Never conventionally photogenic, as she aged she played some incisive character roles in both film (*Sunday Bloody Sunday*, 1971, as Glenda JACKSON's astringent mother) and TV (notably as Queen Mary in *Edward and Mrs Simpson*, 1978, and as Barbie, the dim missionary in *Jewel in the Crown*, 1984). Her career in the visual media was crowned by her Oscar for *A Passage to India* (1984). Everything she did was characterised by the sharpest intelligence and truthful feeling. She was created DBE in 1956, but never settled into being a mere *grande dame*.
OTHER BRITISH FILMS: *Rhodes of Africa* (1936), *Channel Incident* (1940, short), *The New Lot* (1943, short), *Tell Me Lies, Secret Ceremony, Three into Two Won't Go* (1968), *Joseph Andrews* (1976), *Hullabaloo Over Georgie and Bonnie's Pictures* (1979, UK/Ind), *Where the Wind Blows* (voice) (1985), *Madame Sousatzka* (1988), *She's Been Away* (1989, TV, some cinemas).
BIBLIOG: Michael Billington, *Peggy Ashcroft*, 1988; Garry O'Connor, *The Secret Woman: A Life of Peggy Ashcroft*, 1997.

Asher, Irving (*b* San Francisco, 1903 – *d* Indio, California, 1985). Producer. Entered films at 16, as assistant director on US silent films. When WARNER BROS bought the TEDDINGTON STUDIOS in 1931, Asher was made production chief, and over the next decade he produced about seventy films. Most were undistinguished 'QUOTA QUICKIES', cheaply made at the rate of about two per month, but they are of interest from the point of view of some of the talent they employed – for instance, Michael POWELL directed *Crown v Stevens* (1936), Lilli PALMER made a much-praised debut in *Crime Unlimited* (1935), and Maurice ELVEY directed Sir Seymour HICKS in *Change for a Sovereign* (1937). Asher's American wife Laura LAPLANTE, starred in several, including one of the best received, *Man of the Moment* (1935), with Douglas FAIRBANKS, Jr Asher left Warners at the end of 1937 to work as associate producer for Alexander KORDA and was engaged as an executive producer for Harefield Productions at DENHAM, under a Korda contract. His name thus appears on such upmarket films as *Q Planes* (1939) and *The Spy in Black* (1939). Back in Hollywood by 1941, and stayed there for the rest of his career.
OTHER BRITISH FILMS INCLUDE: *The Aviator* (1929), *Her Night Out* (1932), *The Thirteenth Candle* (1933), *Something Always Happens* (1934), *Some Day* (1935), *Who Killed John Savage?, It's Not Cricket, Gypsy* (1937), *Ten Days in Paris* (1939), *The Four Feathers* (assoc p) (1939).

Asher, Jack (*b* London, 1916 – *d* 1991). Cinematographer. Entered films in 1930 as assistant cameraman at GAINS-BOROUGH's ISLINGTON STUDIOS on such films as *Friday the Thirteenth* (1933), before becoming camera operator for MGM–BRITISH on the likes of *A Yank at Oxford* (1937). In 1940, he returned to Gainsborough (at SHEPHERD'S BUSH now) as resident camera operator, moving up to director of photography on *Easy Money* in 1948. In the earlier 50s, he shot a number of films for Lewis GILBERT, including *Reach for the Sky* (1956) and the more interesting *Cast a Dark Shadow* (1955), with the camerawork mirroring the hero's ambiguities. At Gainsborough, he was associated with director Terence FISHER on *Portrait from Life* (1948) and from 1957, at HAMMER, he was a major contributor to the resplendent TECHNICOLOR look of the resuscitated HORROR GENRE, ushered in by *The Curse of Frankenstein* (1957). Towards the end of his career, he shot several light comedies directed by his brother, Robert ASHER.

OTHER BRITISH FILMS INCLUDE: *The Astonished Heart* (1950), *Hell Is Sold Out* (1951), *Cosh Boy*, *Albert RN* (1953), *The Young Lovers* (1954), *Dracula*, *The Revenge of Frankenstein* (1958), *The Hound of the Baskervilles*, *The Mummy*, *Follow a Star* (1959), *The Brides of Dracula* (1960), *The Secret of Blood Island* (1964), *The Early Bird* (1965).

Asher, Jane (*b* London, 1946). Actress. First seen as a deaf child in *Mandy* (1952) and other films of the 50s, Asher gained another kind of fame in the 60s as Paul MCCARTNEY's girl-friend. On stage and TV as a child, she has pursued her screen career only sporadically. She was one of Michael CAINE's conquests in *Alfie* (1966), Jane Seymour in *Henry VIII and His Six Wives* (1972), and, nearly forty, Alice's uneasy mother in *Dreamchild* (1985). Married to cartoonist Gerald Scarfe.

OTHER BRITISH FILMS INCLUDE: *Dance Little Lady*, *Adventure in the Hopfields* (1954), *The Quatermass Experiment*, *Charley Moon* (1956), *The Greengage Summer* (1961), *Girl in the Headlines* (1963), *The Buttercup Chain* (1970), *Deep End* (1971, UK/Ger/US), *Runners* (1983), *Success is the Best Revenge* (1984, UK/Fr), *Closing Numbers* (1993).

Asher, Robert (*b* London, 1915 – *d* 1979). Director. After a long apprenticeship as assistant director to such film-makers as Anthony PELISSIER (*The Rocking Horse Winner*, 1949), Robert HAMER (*The Long Memory*, 1952) and Roy Ward BAKER (*A Night to Remember*, 1958), Asher directed his first film, *Follow a Star* in 1959. This starred Norman WISDOM, and Asher proved adept enough at keeping the wheels of farcical humour and easy pathos in motion to do five more with the comedian. He took over from John Paddy CARSTAIRS as the helmsman of the Wisdom films, some of which his brother, Jack ASHER, photographed.

OTHER BRITISH FILMS INCLUDE: (ass d) *The History of Mr Polly* (1948), *Morning Departure* (1950), *The Million Pound Note* (1953), *Man of the Moment* (1955), *Floods of Fear* (1958); (d) *Make Mine Mink*, *The Bulldog Breed* (1960), *On the Beat*, *She'll Have to Go* (1961), *A Stitch in Time* (1963), *The Intelligence Men*, *The Early Bird* (1965), *Press for Time* (1966).

Asherson, Renée (*b* London, 1920). Actress. Shyly attractive leading lady of stage and 40s screen, Asherson began well on film, coming to the screen after Laurence OLIVIER saw her stage success in *The Mask of Virtue* (1943) and chose her to play Princess Katherine in *Henry V* (1944). Subsequently, she worked for Carol REED, Anthony ASQUITH and Michael POWELL, but the roles dried up in the male-dominated 50s genres which offered little for her fragile persona. She continued to work in the theatre, and TV gave her some excellent chances, especially in Jack Clayton's superlative *Memento Mori*, to show how witty she could be. Married to Robert DONAT, with whom she co-starred in *The Cure For Love* (1949). Appeared in Richard ATTENBOROUGH's *Grey Owl* (2000, UK/Can) and *The Others* (2001, Sp/US).

OTHER BRITISH FILMS: *The Way Ahead* (1944), *The Way to the Stars*, *Caesar and Cleopatra* (1945), *Once a Jolly Swagman*, *The Small Back Room* (1948), *Pool of London* (1950), *The Magic Box* (1951), *Malta Story* (1953), *Time Is My Enemy* (1954), *The Day the Earth Caught Fire* (1961), *Rasputin the Mad Monk* (1965), *The Smashing Bird I Used to Know* (1969), *Theatre of Blood* (1973).

Ashfield, Kate (*b* Meriden, 1972). Fetching young star of several urban youth-orientated films of the new century, including *The Low-Down* (2000), for which she won Best Actress in the British Independent Film Awards, and *Late Night Shopping* (2001), in both of which, in different circumstances, she articulates touchingly a longing for commitment. First appeared in *The Princess Caraboo* (1994, US), weathered the disaster of *Guest House Paradiso* (1999), co-starred impressively in the TV mini-series, *Do or Die* (2001, UK/Aust), and has built up a range of theatre credits including *Three Sisters* and *Closer*.

OTHER BRITISH FILMS: *The War Zone* (1999, UK/It), *Christie Malry's Own Double-Entry* (2000, UK/Lux/Neth), *The Last Minute* (2001, UK/US), *Flyfishing* (2002).

Ashton, Roy (*b* Perth, Australia, 1909 – *d* Farnham, Surrey, 1995). Make-up artist. Ashton's filmography tells his story: his film career has been spent almost entirely in the HORROR GENRE, first practising his craft in 1936 on Boris Karloff in *The Man Who Changed His Mind* (literally, that is, not just a matter of vacillation). When HAMMER's famous horror cycle flourished in the late 50s, Ashton came into his own, working on such films as *The Man Who Could Cheat Death* (1959) and *The Brides of Dracula* (1960), and he stayed with the genre for the rest of his career.

OTHER BRITISH FILMS INCLUDE: *Fire Maidens from Outer Space* (1956), *The Mummy* (1959), *The Two Faces of Dr Jekyll* (1960), *The Damned* (1961), *The Kiss of the Vampire* (1962), *Nightmare*, *The Gorgon* (1964), *Fanatic* (1965), *The Reptile* (1966), *Tales from the Crypt* (1972), *The Ghoul* (1975).

Asia in British film Much the most prominently represented Asian country in British cinema is INDIA and this has been dealt with separately. From 30s films such as *The Drum* (1938), through a 50s adventure like *North West Frontier* (1959) to *A Passage to India* (1984), the sub-continent has exerted a fascination over British film-makers, and TV series such as *The Jewel in the Crown* (1984) have perpetuated this. However, there is still a substantial number of British films set in other Asian countries and these range across several GENRES.

WAR FILMS have been well represented. The Burma hospital-set *The Hasty Heart* (1949), was one of the earliest, an ADAPTATION of a popular stage play, as was *The Long and the Short and the Tall* (1960), set in a hut in the Malayan jungle. Both these studio-filmed pieces give a sense of a small sanctuary in dangerous territory. The most famous of the Asian-set war films is David LEAN's *The Bridge on the River Kwai* (1957), about the building of the Burma railway but actually filmed in Ceylon. Other war films include Val GUEST's *The Camp on Blood Island* (1957), criticised for its savagery at the time, Ralph THOMAS's doomed-love story, *The Wind Cannot Read* (1958), set in India and Burma, Guest's *Yesterday's Enemy* (1959), back in the Burmese jungle, as was Robert PARRISH's *The Purple Plain* (1954), and a silly HAMMER war thriller, *The Secret of Blood Island* (1964). Two decades later came Nagisa Oshima's *Merry Christmas Mr Lawrence* (1982, UK/Jap), set in a Japanese p.o.w. camp in Java.

From the late 50s, there was a steady stream of adventure/romances set in various Asian locations, including the BOND piece, *You Only Live Twice* (1967), set in Japan, like the love story, *Seven Nights in Japan* (1976, UK/Fr), the ponderous adaptation of CONRAD's *Lord Jim* (1964) which had the benefit of Freddie YOUNG's gleaming photography, Ronald NEAME's US-backed thriller, *Escape from Zahrain* (1961), and Guy GREEN's romantic comedy, *Pretty Polly* (1967). There was also a handful of more or less POLITICAL DRAMAS located at Asian pressure points, including three set in Malaya: *The Planter's Wife* (1952), *Windom's Way* (1957), and *The Seventh Dawn* (1964), the inspiring 1930-set true story, *The Inn of the Sixth Happiness* (1958), China-set, like *The Devil Never Sleeps* (1962), as well as an unlikely-sounding enterprise, *Welcome to the Club* (1970), allegedly a comedy set in Hiroshima in 1945! Hong Kong was mainly the site of adventure thrillers such as the expensively lumbering RANK failure, *Ferry to Hong Kong* (1959), or the war film, *The Last Grenade* (1969), but there was the exception of the last of the 'Road' films, *The Road to Hong Kong* (1961). Other genres with 'Asian' settings included the musicals *The Mikado* (1939, 1966) and *The Cool Mikado* (1962), and the Hammer horror film, *The Terror of the Tongs* (1960), again set in Hong Kong.

The amount of actual location work varied a good deal, and some films made much more use of Asia as an exotic backdrop than others, but there was a clear trend towards location shooting, even if only for the second unit, in the decades following the war. Apart from the case of India, though, it is perhaps arguable that the strain of Asian-set British film-making never made the impact that its African counterpart did in the history of British cinema. There has been less sense of dealing with the problems of colonialism and imperial adventurism. Two exceptions are *Saigon – Year of the Cat* (1983), set in the last days of the Vietnam war, and *The Killing Fields* (1984), with an American reporter caught up in the horrors of Cambodia after the fall of Phnom Penh.

Asians in British film-making *see* **British-Asian film-making**

Askew, Desmond (*b* London, 1972). Actor. Having appeared as a child actor in *Digital Dreams*, the 1983 documentary about Rolling Stone Bill Wyman, and *Give My Regards to Broad Street* (1984), tow-headed Askew came to adult fame in the US feature, *Go* (1999), as a loose-cannon Brit in the cultural diversity of L.A.

Askey, Arthur (*b* Liverpool, 1900 – *d* London, 1982). Actor. Diminutive (5'2") comedian, who began work as a clerk, joined a concert party in 1924, and had stage and radio experience before entering films in 1937. Known as 'Big-Hearted' Arthur, his catch-phrase was 'Hello, playmates' and his persona was that of the perennially cheerful little bloke for whom winning the girl was rarely a possibility. His films all reflect his MUSIC HALL training; he does his particular turn rather than acts a range of characters. The failure of *Bees in Paradise* (1944) kept him off the screen for ten years. Continued in pantomime until the 70s. Daughter **Anthea Askey** (*b* 1933) appeared with him on TV and radio.

OTHER BRITISH FILMS: *Calling All Stars* (1937), *Band Waggon* (based on his stage show), *Charlie's (Big-Hearted) Aunt* (1940), *The Ghost Train, I Thank You* (1941), *Back Room Boy, King Arthur Was a Gentleman, The Nose Has It* (short) (1942), *Miss London Ltd* (1943), *The Love Match* (1955), *Ramsbottom Rides Again* (1956), *Make Mine a Million* (1959), *Friends and Neighbours* (1959), *The Alf Garnett Saga* (1972), *End of Term* (short) (1977), *Rosie Dixon – Night Nurse* (1978).

BIBLIOG: Autobiography, *Before Your Very Eyes*, 1975.

Askwith, Robin (*b* Southport, 1950). Actor. Youthful leading man of low-budget comedies of the 70s, who began in *If . . .* (1968), but later settled for the 'Confessions of . . .' series. More recently, he has toured the UK and abroad in theatre.

OTHER BRITISH FILMS INCLUDE: *Otley* (1968), *Bless This House* (1972), *Carry On Girls* (1973), *Confessions of a Window Cleaner* (1974), . . . *a Pop Performer* (1975), . . . *a Driving Instructor* (1976), *Let's Get Laid!* (1977), *Britannia Hospital* (1982).

BIBLIOG: Autobiography, *The Confessions of Robin Askwith*, 1999.

Aslan, Grégoire (aka Coco Aslan) (*b* Constantinople, 1908 – *d* Rinsey, 1982). Actor. RN: Krikor Aslanian. Originally a drummer and vocalist with a dance band in Paris, in 50s British cinema, he became a familiar figure in comic or dramatic, heavily sinister or explosive roles.

BRITISH FILMS INCLUDE: *Sleeping Car to Trieste* (1948), *Cage of Gold* (1950), *Innocents in Paris* (1953), *Joe Macbeth* (1955), *Windom's Way* (1957), *Our Man in Havana* (1959), *Village of Daughters* (1962), *The High Bright Sun* (1965).

Asquith, Anthony (*b* London, 1902 – *d* London, 1968). Director. Son of the British Prime Minister, later Lord Oxford and Asquith, 'Puffin' Asquith, as he was widely known, studied film-making in Hollywood after leaving Oxford. He returned to England in 1926 and a year later co-directed his first film, *Shooting Stars* (1928), which he also co-wrote and which was critically well-received. Asquith adapted readily to the coming of SOUND and *A Cottage on Dartmoor* (1929) and *Tell England* (1931), which critics at the time regarded as 'arty', are now seen to be innovative works of an important talent. Sadly, until the end of the 30s, most of his films failed to capitalise on this promise, though even such a light-weight work as *The Lucky Number* (1933) shows his willingness to let the camera tell the story, rather than to rely on the extreme talkiness of much of the period's film-making. He hit his stride in 1938 with a fluent, beautifully acted version of Shaw's *Pygmalion* (1938), the first of his three SHAW films, and *French Without Tears* (1939), the first in his highly successful screen collaborations with playwright Terence RATTIGAN who co-authored the script based on his hit play.

After the charming *Quiet Wedding* (1941), Asquith directed a handful of incisive WAR FILMS, including the pro-Russian comedy of national manners, *The Demi-Paradise* (1943), and in 1945, with a fine screenplay from Rattigan, he made *The Way to the Stars* (1945), a still-moving elegy to lives lived under the emotional constraints engendered by war. His camera trailing through a deserted aerodrome and Jean SIMMONS' singing 'Let him go, let him tarry' in a vast hangar provide two of the vividest images of the period. Such films, and *The Winslow Boy* (1948) and *The Browning Version* (1951), both Rattigan-derived, are civilised, humane and affecting dramas, but his last two films, custom-written by Rattigan, *The VIPs* (1963) and *The Yellow Rolls-Royce* (1964), are lumbering where the earlier work is graceful. Asquith's technique was rarely showy, instead, he uses the resources of the cinema discreetly to reinforce, not to compete with the human drama which was always the focus of his attention, and which his actors repaid by a consistently high level of performance. For 31 years he was president of the Association of Cinema Technicians (ACT) and his allegiance to its goals was greatly admired.

OTHER BRITISH FILMS: *Underground* (1928), *The Runaway Princess* (1929, UK/Ger), *Dance Pretty Lady, Marry Me* (+ sc) (1932), *Letting in the Sunshine* (1933, + sc), *The Unfinished Symphony* (1934, UK/Austria/Ger), *Moscow Nights* (1935), *Guide Dogs for the Blind* (short) (1939), *Channel Incident* (short), *Rush Hour* (short), *Freedom Radio* (1940), *Cottage to Let* (1941), *Uncensored* (1942), *We Dive at Dawn, A Welcome to Britain* (short) (1943), *Two Fathers* (short), *Fanny by Gaslight* (1944), *While the Sun Shines* (1947), *The Woman in Question* (1950), *The Importance of Being Earnest* (1952), *The Net, The Final Test* (1953), *The Young Lovers, Carrington VC* (1954), *On Such a Night* (1955, short), *Orders to Kill, The Doctor's Dilemma* (1958), *Libel* (1959), *The*

Millionairess (1960), *Two Living, One Dead* (1961, UK/Swe), *Guns of Darkness* (1962), *An Evening with the Royal Ballet* (1963).
BIBLIOG: R.J. Minney, *'Puffin' Asquith*, 1973.

Associated British Group Associated British Picture Corporation (ABPC) was established in 1933 by John MAXWELL, a Glaswegian solicitor and film exhibitor, distributor and producer. In 1927, he set up a production company, BRITISH INTERNATIONAL PICTURES (BIP) and in 1928 folded his 29 cinemas into a subsidiary company, Associated British Cinemas (ABC). By the start of WW2, ABPC was generating a healthy profit, mostly from its cinemas. Maxwell and South African I.W. Schlesinger, set up BIP, to take over the ailing BRITISH NATIONAL PICTURES and its ELSTREE studio. Determined to break into foreign – specifically European – markets, Maxwell committed BIP to making high quality films. During the silent era, this often meant co-producing films with European production outfits, which guaranteed access to foreign markets and enabled pooling of production costs. He engaged director Alfred HITCHCOCK, who made ten films for him, including his first sound film *Blackmail* (1929). Other major directors who worked at BIP included E.A. DUPONT and Victor SAVILLE.

When SOUND arrived, Maxwell had to abandon his international ambitions. Production became more expensive and cumbersome: scripts frequently had to be rewritten, and the company often had to engage different stars to cope with the difficulties of acting in a foreign language. He increasingly turned to low-budget productions that could recoup their costs in the UK. The most successful was *My Wife's Family* (1931) a comedy the company remade in 1941 and 1957.

In 1933, Maxwell appointed his scenario editor Walter MYCROFT as head of production, and, under him, the studio produced a run of tightly budgeted COMEDIES, THRILLERS and MUSICALS, including the highly successful *Blossom Time* (1934). Some films, such as *Royal Cavalcade* (1935), were allowed higher budgets, but when Maxwell's attempt to merge his ABC circuit with GAUMONT–BRITISH was blocked by American interests, he decided to make fewer films and concentrate on building up his cinemas. When Maxwell died, his close associate Eric Lightfoot became Managing Director, but when WARNER BROS. bought a 25% share of the company in 1941, it insisted on appointing the aggressive Max Milder as joint Managing Director, a post which he held until April 1945 when he took complete charge by forcing Lightfoot to resign. Warner Bros then wanted to buy a further 12.5% of ABPC, but the Board of Trade would only allow it to do so on two conditions: that it would not sell its shares to a third party without the Board's consent, and that it would sign an agreement designed to ensure that the American company could not outvote the British shareholders. Warners' principal concern was to ensure its American films were booked by the growing ABC cinema chain. Production during WW2 was sparse: all its films were made on low budgets at its smaller, less well-equipped studio in WELWYN. Only *Thursday's Child* (1943) attracted favourable critical comment.

Although ABPC continued financially successful, most of its production activities were limited to co-financing established film-makers, such as Herbert WILCOX (e.g. *I Live in Grosvenor Square*, 1945) and the BOULTING brothers (e.g. *Brighton Rock*, 1947). When the government returned ELSTREE STUDIOS, the company decided to modernise them for hire to independent producers as well as for its own productions. They also had to

increase the production budgets for their own films, as audiences were becoming increasingly critical of indifferent British films. In 1949, Robert CLARK, in charge of production after Milder's death, announced a £2 million investment in ten feature films, at least four of which would be released in the US.

For Clark, a film's story mattered most. He appointed the German émigré Frederick GOTFURT as his scenario editor and recalled his old boss Mycroft as adviser. Among the productions announced (and made) were *The Hasty Heart*, *Private Angelo*, *Landfall*, *No Place For Jennifer* (1949) and *The Dancing Years* (1950). Clark managed a modest profit every year between 1951 and 1957, although often at the expense of the NATIONAL FILM FINANCE CORPORATION which frequently co-financed the company's films by putting up the 'end money'. Clark and his accountants imposed ruthless cost controls whenever a picture went into production, and the company became known as 'Associated Scottish' and Elstree as 'the porridge factory'.

ABPC's biggest success was *The Dam Busters* (1955) which grossed over £400,000 in the UK alone, and *Laughter In Paradise*, *Happy Go Lovely* (1951) and *Angels One Five* (1952) all grossed over £250,000. Despite his commercial success, Clark was unpopular with his fellow directors. He also crossed Jack Warner, resisting the latter's attempt to merge Warners' UK distribution arm with ABPC's and insisting that, if Warners wanted to use ABPC contract star Audrey HEPBURN, then it would have to pay a fee for her services. In a 1958 boardroom coup, Clark was removed as Head of Production, although allowed to remain as a director of the company.

The company steadily diluted its British identity, the distribution arms of ABPC and Warners merging into a single entity, Warner–Pathé Distributors, and American C.J. Latta took over the management of Elstree Studios. A few months later, ABPC bought the assets of ASSOCIATED TALKING PICTURES (ATP), the holding company for EALING Films, but reneged on the undertaking given Michael BALCON that he could continue to produce films for them. ABPC cut production to the minimum, concentrating on cheap COMEDIES featuring TV stars, such as *Sands of the Desert* (1960) with Charlie DRAKE. Few did well at the box-office, but two clean-cut youth MUSICALS starring Cliff RICHARD – *The Young Ones* (1961) and *Summer Holiday* (1962) – were more successful. Apart from these, the company mainly filled its cinemas with films that it part-financed with independent producers, notably HAMMER FILMS which used the company's money to make Gothic HORROR films and contemporary THRILLERS.

ABPC's own films became increasingly out of touch with the times, although the company continued to invest in new technology. In 1964 it equipped its cinemas with magnetic monaural sound and three years later it picked up 30 per cent. of Technicolor Ltd. In 1955, the Independent TV Authority (ITA) had awarded it a commercial TV franchise for the North of England and in 1966 it set up a separate subsidiary, ABC-TV, to produce colour TV films.

By the end of the 60s, the company was ripe for takeover. EMI, the giant entertainment group, initially acquired Warners' shares and in 1969 bought a controlling interest in the company, having finally satisfied the ITA that it would continue to fulfil the terms of the company's TV franchise. Vincent Porter.

Associated Communications Corporation For a few years in the late 70s and early 80s, ACC, run by Lord Lew GRADE, was an important investor in British film. It unashamedly sought to compete with Hollywood and had some successes, including *The Eagle Has Landed* (1976), but it was scuppered as a production company by the disaster of *Raise the Titanic* (1980, US). It also ventured into EXHIBITION and DISTRIBUTION, but along with EMI and GOLDCREST it now resonates with the 80s floundering of the British film industry.

Associated Talking Pictures This was the name given to EALING STUDIOS' production company from 1933 to 1938. This is the period of Basil DEAN's incumbency during which some notable films were made by ATP at Ealing, including Carol REED's *Midshipman Easy* (1935), and Michael POWELL and David LEAN also worked there. Dean left and returned to the theatre in 1938, when Michael BALCON came in to run the studio.

Association of Cinema and Television Technicians *see* **ACT/ACTT/BECTU**

Astell, Betty (aka Elizabeth) (*b* London, 1912). Actress. Astell, with some stage experience, appeared fleetingly in several silent films, such as *The Broken Melody* (1929), but became a regular leading lady in about 25 talkies, many of them long-forgotten 'QUOTA QUICKIES'. She played, variously, ingenues (*This Is the Life*, 1933, with a young Ray MILLAND), gold-diggers (*The Man I Want*, 1934), and ladies with pasts (*Behind Your Back*, 1937). Often played with 30s comics like Frank PETTINGELL and Ernie LOTINGA, moving upmarket to join Jack HULBERT in *Jack of All Trades* (1936) and Will FYFFE in the thriller *The Mind of Mr Reeder* (1939). Married to Cyril FLETCHER, with whom she appeared in *A Piece of Cake* (1948), a strange little fantasy. Also popular as a concert party singer.
OTHER BRITISH FILMS INCLUDE: *Kitty* (1929), *Double Dealing* (1932), *Strike It Rich* (1933), *Josser on the Farm* (1934), *The Vandergilt Diamond Mystery* (1935).

Astley, Edwin (*b* Warrington, Cheshire, 1922 – *d* Goring Heath, 1998). Composer. Astley churned out about 70 scores from the early 50s, many of them for Britain's then-prolific 'B'-FILM industry, including some of the better ones such as *The Heart Within* (1957) and *The Man Who Liked Funerals* (1958). There was also a steady trickle of As, including *To Paris with Love* (1954), *The Mouse That Roared* (1959) and *The World Ten Times Over* (1963). Father of rock star/composer Pete Townshend.
OTHER BRITISH FILMS INCLUDE: *The Crowded Day* (1954), *Dublin Nightmare, A Woman Possessed* (1958), *The Day They Robbed the Bank of England* (1959), *The Phantom of the Opera* (1962).

Atkins, Dame Eileen (*b* London, 1934). Actress. Outstanding stage actress who has only dabbled with films, though sometimes to splendid effect – as Madge, the stage manager, in *The Dresser* (1983) and as Judith Starkadder in *Cold Comfort Farm* (1995, TV, some cinemas). Trained at the Guildhall School, and first on stage in 1952, she has appeared in many critically acclaimed productions of classic and modern plays. Has also done some notable TV work, including a fine Mrs Morel in *Sons and Lovers* (1983), and her interest in the work of Virginia Woolf has now borne fruit on stage, TV (*A Room of One's Own*, based on her one-woman stage show) and screen (her screenplay for *Mrs Dalloway*, 1997, UK/Neth/US, starring Vanessa REDGRAVE, and her role in *The Hours*, 2002, US, some UK shooting). Once married to actor Julian GLOVER. Created DBE, 2001.

OTHER BRITISH FILMS: *Inadmissible Evidence* (1968), *I Don't Want to Be Born* (1975), *Equus* (1977), *'Let Him Have It'* (1991), *Wolf* (1994), *Jack & Sarah* (1995, UK/Fr), *The Avengers* (1998, UK/US), *Women Talking Dirty* (1999), *Wit* (2001, UK/US), *Gosford Park* (2001, UK/Ger/US).

Atkins, Sir Robert (*b* London, 1886 – *d* London, 1972). Actor. Famous theatre actor, RADA-trained, Atkins first appeared on stage in 1906, was in Sir Herbert Tree's company at His Majesty's Theatre, at the Old Vic and at Stratford, playing (and producing) almost every Shakespearean play. Film debut was a version of *Hamlet* in 1913, but he did not film again until 1935, in Herbert WILCOX's *Peg of Old Drury*, as Doctor Johnson.
OTHER BRITISH FILMS INCLUDE: *The Cardinal, Everything is Thunder* (1936), *The Great Mr Handel* (1942), *A Matter of Life and Death* (1946), *The House in the Square* (1951).

Atkinson, Frank (*b* Oldham, 1890 – *d* Pinner, 1963). Actor. After making his film debut in 1920 in *When London Sleeps*, then making nearly 20 films in Hollywood (1928–33), the best-known being *Cavalcade* (1933), Atkinson returned to Britain to make a further 40, usually in small roles, often in co-features in the 50s. Once a circus performer (1902), he collaborated on several 30s screenplays (e.g. *Play Up the Band*, 1935), had considerable stage experience, and played Sam Leech in the TV serial, *Coronation Street*.
OTHER BRITISH FILMS INCLUDE: *Road House* (1934), *A Woman Alone, Sabotage* (1936), *Young and Innocent* (1937), *Pygmalion* (1938), *The Stars Look Down* (1939), *Waterloo Road* (1944), *Great Expectations* (1946), *The Titfield Thunderbolt* (1953), *Three Men in a Boat* (1956), *The Two Faces of Dr Jekyll* (1960), *The Kitchen* (1961).

Atkinson, Rosalind (*b* Wellington, NZ, 1900 – *d* Northwood, Middlesex, 1978). Actress. Respected stage actress for nearly half a century, including several seasons at the Old Vic and the Shakespeare Memorial Theatre, Stratford, Atkinson made very few films, but in two was very noticeable: as Mrs Miller in *Tom Jones* (1963) and as Anne Bancroft's widowed mother in *The Pumpkin Eater* (1964).
OTHER BRITISH FILMS: *Tomorrow We Live* (1936), *Good-Time Girl* (1947).

Atkinson, Rowan (*b* Gosforth, 1955). Actor. Hugely popular for his TV comedy incarnations, first as Edmund Blackadder, from 1983, and then as Mr Bean, from 1989, Atkinson has yet to make a comparable screen impact, though the film SPIN-OFF, *Bean* (1997), undoubtedly intensified awareness of the hapless eponym, especially in the US. Trained as an engineering student, and began his comedy career on the Fringe of the Edinburgh Festival. His first films drew on his sly, shy, zany comedian's persona, among many other entertainers doing their idiosyncratic turns in *The Secret Policeman's Ball* (1981) and *The Secret Policeman's Other Ball* (1982), film records of fund-raisers for Amnesty International. Of his other films, he was probably best served by screenwriter Richard CURTIS in both *The Tall Guy* (1989), as an obnoxious TV comic, and *Four Weddings and a Funeral* (1994), as a hopelessly incompetent officiating clergyman, but was also very funny as the increasingly distraught hotel manager in *The Witches* (1989, US), and provided one of the voices for *The Lion King* (1994, US).
OTHER BRITISH FILMS: *Dead on Time* (short) (1982), *Never Say Never Again* (1983, UK/US), *Maybe Baby* (2000, UK/Fr), *Touch of Weevil* (2002).
BIBLIOG: Bruce Dessau, *Rowan Atkinson*, 1999.

Attenborough, Richard (Lord Attenborough) (*b* Cambridge, 1923). Actor, director, producer. It is no exaggeration to say that Attenborough's is one of the careers most closely associated with the history and maintenance of a British film industry in the last half-century. Of liberal, academically inclined parents, in 1940 he won a scholarship to RADA where he met Sheila SIM, whom he married in 1945 and with whom he co-starred several times on stage (*The Mousetrap*, 1952) and screen (first in *Dancing with Crime*, 1947). Made his film debut in Noël COWARD's *In Which We Serve* (1942) and was instantly noticed as the terrified young stoker. This success, allied to his youthful looks, led to his being cast as delinquents: in *Brighton Rock* (1947), chilling as the murderous Pinkie; in *London Belongs to Me* (1948), as flashy Percy Boon on a manslaughter charge; and in *Boys in Brown* (1949), as a Borstal boy. Condemned to playing roles much younger than his age, he gradually became dissatisfied during the 50s with those offered to him, though he was never less than convincing in them, as in the spiv type in *The Ship that Died of Shame* (1955) and the neurotic lodger in *The Man Upstairs* (1958). A breakthrough came with *The Angry Silence* (1960), for which he and Bryan FORBES set up their own production company, BEAVER FILMS (1959–64), and which dealt in provocative manner with the ostracism of a factory worker during a wildcat strike. In playing the worker, he cut himself off from the conventional GENRE films which were so much a part of 50s British cinema.

He continued to act in substantial character roles often in US films (e.g. *The Flight of the Phoenix*, 1966, *Jurassic Park*, 1993, and its sequel, *The Lost World*, 1997) after making a striking debut as a director with *Oh! What a Lovely War* in 1969, for which he gathered together perhaps the most remarkable all-star cast in British film history. The film showed inventiveness in transferring Joan LITTLEWOOD's memorable pier-end stage representation of the horrors of WW1 to the screen, and since then he has directed and (co-)produced a number of large-scale films. Sometimes the effect has been a little stately, but *Gandhi* (1982, UK/Ind), a project he strove for twenty years to film, has moments of real grandeur and passion, and *Shadowlands* (1993, UK/US), based on the real-life love affair of author C.S. Lewis and an American poet, showed him adept with more intimate material. His liberal views are reflected in such a film as *Cry Freedom* (1987, d, p), which expressed strong anti-apartheid sentiments, and he starred in *10 Rillington Place* (1970) because it chimed with his opposition to capital punishment. He has also directed and/or produced several films in the US including *Magic* (1978) and *A Chorus Line* (1985) but they are not among his most successful work.

He has been an indefatigable champion of the cause of British cinema, as well as playing a diversity of other cultural roles: e.g. he has been governor of the NATIONAL FILM SCHOOL, deputy chairman of CHANNEL 4 TV, vice-president of BAFTA, chairman of RADA, Capitol Radio, GOLDCREST Film and TV, and the BFI, a trustee of the Tate Gallery and a director of Chelsea Football Club. He has in fact achieved a huge amount as actor, director, and producer and as a focus for the *idea* of film as a key element in the national life. Knighted in 1976, and made a Lord in 1994. His younger brother is the celebrated naturalist, Sir David Attenborough, and his daughter is actress **Charlotte Attenborough** who has appeared in several TV films and *Jane Eyre*, 1996.

OTHER BRITISH FILMS: (a) *Schweik's New Adventures*, *The Hundred Pound Window* (1943), *Journey Together* (1945), *A Matter of Life and Death*, *School For Secrets* (1946), *The Man Within* (1947), *The Guinea Pig* (1948), *The Lost People* (1949), *Morning Departure* (1950), *Hell Is Sold Out*, *The Magic Box* (1951), *The Gift Horse, Father's Doing Fine* (1952),

Eight O'Clock Walk (1954), *Private's Progress*, *The Baby and the Battleship*, *Brothers in Law* (1956), *The Scamp* (1957), *Dunkirk*, *The Sea Of Sand*, *Danger Within* (1958), *I'm All Right Jack*, *Jet Storm*, *SOS Pacific* (1959), *League Of Gentlemen* (1960), *Only Two Can Play*, *All Night Long* (1961), *The Dock Brief* (1962), *Séance On A Wet Afternoon* (+ p), *The Third Secret*, *Guns At Batasi* (1964), *The Bliss Of Mrs Blossom*, *Only When I Larf* (1968), *David Copperfield*, *The Magic Christian*, *The Last Grenade* (1969), *Loot, A Severed Head* (1970), *And Then There Were None* (1974), *Conduct Unbecoming, Brannigan* (1975), *The Human Factor* (1979, UK/US), *E=MC²* (1995), *Hamlet* (UK/US) (1996), *Elizabeth* (1998); (p and/or d) *Whistle Down The Wind* (1961), *The L-Shaped Room* (1962), *Young Winston* (1972), *A Bridge Too Far* (1977), *Chaplin* (1992, UK/Fr/It/Jap/US), *Grey Owl* (2000, UK/Can).

BIBLIOG: David Castell, *Richard Attenborough*, 1984; Andy Dougan, *The Actors' Director*, 1994; David Robinson, *Richard Attenborough*, 1992.

Attwood, David (*b* Sheffield, 1952) Director. One of the black directors who contrived to get a couple of features made in the 90s, the better known being *Wild West* (1992), about an Asian country-and-western band in Southall. Also made the 1988 telemovie, *Airbase*.

OTHER BRITISH FILMS: *Saigon Baby* (1995).

Aubrey, Anne (*b* Middlesex, 1937). Actress. Modestly attractive leading lady of a batch of almost ostentatiously forgettable movies made for WARWICK FILMS in the late 50s. Warwick sought to build her as a star, most often opposite Anthony NEWLEY, and there are ADVENTURES, COMEDIES and MUSICALS of little distinction. Aubrey's career was over by 1961, her conventional appeal unlikely to find a place in the new realist cinema of the 60s. Once married to actor Derren NESBITT.

OTHER BRITISH FILMS INCLUDE: *High Flight* (1957), *The Man Inside*, *The Secret Man, Idle on Parade* (1958), *The Bandit of Zhobe, In the Nick*, *Killers of Kilimanjaro, Jazzboat* (1959), *Let's Get Married* (1960), *The Hellions* (1961, UK/Saudi).

Aubrey, Juliet (*b* Fleet, Hampshire, 1968). Actress. Elegantly attractive actress whose few film appearances have illustrated maturity and intelligence. Her most notable film work has been for Michael WINTERBOTTOM in the telefilm *Go Now* (1996), where she played a woman struggling to come to terms with her partner's multiple sclerosis. Awarded BAA for her portrayal of Dorothea Brooke in the BBC mini-series *Middlemarch* (1994).

OTHER BRITISH FILMS: *Food of Love* (1996, UK/Fr), *Welcome to Sarajevo* (1997, UK/US), *Still Crazy* (1998), *Lost Lover* (1999, UK/Fr/It), *Iris* (2002, UK/US). Melinda Hildebrandt.

Auden, W(ystan) H(ugh) (*b* York, 1907 – *d* Vienna, 1973). Writer. Poet and playwright who showed a keen interest in Britain's DOCUMENTARY movement of the 30s, and was warmly welcomed into the GPO FILM UNIT by John GRIERSON. He wrote verse commentary for several of the Unit's most famous films, including *Coal Face* (1935), *Night Mail* (1936), *The Way to the Sea* (1937) and *The Londoners* (1939), and, like composer Benjamin BRITTEN, he brought to them a whiff of high culture which sits oddly with their quotidian concerns. His left-wing sympathies meant, though, that he was genuinely attuned to their point of view. After WW2, he emigrated to America. Came to popular attention again when John HANNAH recited his 'Funeral Blues', in *Four Weddings and a Funeral* (1994).

audience trends The majority preference of British audiences has been for Hollywood's films, so that indigenous productions have never occupied more than 15% of screentime. Within that margin, however, there have been decades when British films have been popular. In the 30s British films were patronised, particularly COMEDIES starring Gracie FIELDS and George FORMBY, in the north of England. In the 30s and 40s there were several studies of the film audience which confirmed that the most frequent cinema-goers were working class, aged 10–24, with female spectators slightly in the majority. MASS-OBSERVATION undertook several studies of audiences during the 30s and WW2, confirming that cinema was the mass entertainment of the majority of the British population. The peak year of cinema-going was 1946 when 1,635 million people went to the cinema. For a brief period in most people's lives, cinema-going was the most important leisure activity, a period which was curtailed by factors such as marriage.

American films and their stars held a fascination for many British audiences, as well as indigenous product, giving rise to fan magazines and the existence of distinct film and fan cultures in Britain. J. Arthur RANKS 'CHARM SCHOOL' of stars in the 40s and 50s attempted to win the loyalty of British fans on a level equivalent to the adulation accorded Hollywood's stars. British GENRES which enjoyed most popularity were comedies and COSTUME MELODRAMAS. In the 50s, however, audiences declined as a whole because of competition from TV and changing leisure patterns. In 1960 annual admissions were 500.80 million, a figure which was further reduced to 72.00 million by 1972. Since then, however, there has been an upturn in cinema attendance owing to the arrival of multiplex cinemas and the increased interest in cinema culture encouraged by the popularity of video, so that by 1997 annual admissions rose to 139.3 million. The number of British films screened in multiplexes is nevertheless by no means high and the upturn in cinema patronage is largely because of increased accessibility of cinema entertainment as well as the location of many multiplex cinemas in other centres of entertainment and leisure, including bowling facilities, shops and restaurants.

Audiences for British films abroad have varied, the American market being largely confined to cities, particularly New York, Chicago and Los Angeles, where film ADAPTATIONS of novels and stage plays, comedies and HAMMER horror films have been popular. The core cinemagoing audience in Britain is aged between 15 and 34 which is reflected in the majority of films shown on British screens. Comedies have done particularly well in recent years including *Four Weddings and a Funeral* (1994), *Bean* and *The Full Monty* (1997, UK/US).

BIBLIOG: J.P. Mayer, *The Sociology of Film*, 1946; Dorothy Sheridan and Jeffrey Richards (eds), *Mass-Observation at the Movies*, 1987. Sarah Street.

Audley, Maxine (*b* London, 1923 – *d* London, 1992). Actress. Striking, dark-haired stage star trained for the stage in both New York and London, making her debut in 1940. She had seasons at Stratford (1949–50, 1955, 1957) as well as appearing in modern plays and the musical *42nd Street* (1986). First film was the short, *The Pleasure Garden* (1952), and she had some memorable supporting roles, including Ada Leverson in *The Trials of Oscar Wilde* (1960), Julia in Val GUEST's excellent thriller *Hell is a City* (1959), and, most famously, Anna MASSEY's blind whisky-drinking mother in Michael POWELL's notorious *Peeping Tom* (1960). She never again had such a rewarding batch and made several very minor 'B' MOVIES, but she was stimulating company. Still appearing on TV just before she died.

OTHER BRITISH FILMS INCLUDE: *The Sleeping Tiger* (1954), *The Barretts of Wimpole Street* (1956), *The Prince and the Showgirl* (1957), *Dunkirk, The Vikings* (1958), *Vengeance* (1962, UK/Ger), *Ricochet, A Jolly Bad Fellow* (1963), *Payment in Kind* (1967), *Frankenstein Must Be Destroyed* (1969), *The Looking Glass War* (1969), *Running Scared* (1972).

Audsley, Mick Editor. Much associated with the films of director Stephen FREARS, Audsley has emerged as a major collaborator in British cinema of the 80s and 90s, with excursions into international films as well, including *Interview with the Vampire* (1994, US). His first credit was on Bill DOUGLAS's austere autobiographical *My Way Home* (1978), and since then he has worked on some of the most interesting British films, including Mike NEWELL's *Dance with a Stranger* (1984) and *Soursweet* (1988), and, for Frears, *My Beautiful Laundrette* (1985), *Sammy and Rosie Get Laid, Prick Up Your Ears* (1987), *The Snapper* (1993), *The Van* (1996, UK/Ire) and *High Fidelity* (2000, UK/US). Also edited Douglas's neglected masterpiece, *Comrades* (1986), and *Captain Corelli's Mandolin* (2001, UK/US).

Aukin, David (*b* London, 1942). Executive. As general manager of the Hampstead Theatre, an important associate of Mike LEIGH when the latter was having difficulties in making feature films and was hired by the BBC to film *Abigail's Party* (1977). In 1990, became head of drama at CHANNEL 4, where he remained influential in setting up the Leigh films, *High Hopes* (1988), *Life is Sweet* (1990) and *Naked* (1993). In 1998, he, Trea Hoving and Colin Leventhal set up the production company, HAL, which has made *Mansfield Park* (1999, UK/US), *Elephant Juice* (2000), *About Adam* (2001, UK/Ire), with several others in preparation. Married to Nancy MECKLER.

Ault, Marie (*b* Wigan, 1870 – *d* London, 1951). Actress. RN: Mary Cragg. Quintessential British character actress, Ault made her stage debut in 1891, and could just as easily portray a stereotypical French character, as witness her role as Mère Colline, the bar owner, in *The Rat* (1925), *The Triumph of the Rat* (1926) and *The Return of the Rat* (1929). Memorable as the landlady in HITCHCOCK's *The Lodger* (1926), she had a major role in the original 1935 stage production of *Love on the Dole*, but a much smaller one in the 1941 screen version.

OTHER BRITISH FILMS INCLUDE: *Class and No Class* (1921), *The Monkey's Paw, Woman to Woman* (1923), *Hindle Wakes* (1927), *Kitty* (1929), *The Speckled Band* (1931), *Major Barbara* (1941), *Cheer the Brave* (1951). AS.

Auric, Georges (*b* Lodève, France, 1899 – *d* Paris, 1983). Composer. Auric began and ended his career in France, but in the middle he contributed musical scores to some memorable British films, starting with *Dead of Night* in 1945 at EALING. He trained at the Paris Conservatoire, and under the composer D'Indy at the Schola Cantorum. He composed his first film score, *Le sang d'un poète*, in 1931, after working prolifically in other musical fields, including ballet. His early scores include those for such famous French films as *A nous la liberté* (1931). In England, he composed the score for eight further Ealing films, as varied as *It Always Rains on Sunday* (1947), *Cage of Gold* (1950) and *The Titfield Thunderbolt* (1953), as well as notable scores for the films of other companies, including *The Queen of Spades* (1948), *The Silent Dust* (1949), a typically stirring melodramatic score, and *The Innocents* (1961). He continued to compose for French films in the post-war decades, scoring such classics as *Du rififi chez les hommes* (1955), and *Lola Montès* (1955). Appointed director of the Paris Opera in 1962.

OTHER BRITISH FILMS: *Caesar and Cleopatra* (1945), *Hue and Cry* (1946), *Another Shore, Corridor of Mirrors* (1948), *The Spider and the Fly, Passport to Pimlico* (1949), *The Galloping Major, The Lavender Hill Mob*

(1951), *The Open Window* (1952, short), *Moulin Rouge* (1953), *The Divided Heart, Father Brown, The Good Die Young* (1954), *The Bespoke Overcoat* (1955, short), *Heaven Knows, Mr Allison* (UK/US), *The Story of Esther Costello, Dangerous Exile, Bonjour Tristesse* (1957), *Next to No Time!* (1958), *The Journey, SOS Pacific* (1959), *The Mind Benders* (1963).

BIBLIOG: Autobiography, *Quand j'étais là*, 1976.

Austen, Jane (*b* Steventon, 1775 – *d* Winchester, 1817). Author. Austen's brilliantly incisive and witty studies of relationships, set in English villages at the turn of the 19th century, were strangely neglected by British film-makers until the 90s when there was a rash of largely successful film adaptations. These were: *Persuasion* (1995, TV, many cinemas), *Sense and Sensibility* (1995, UK/US), *Emma* (1996, one version for the cinema, UK/US, one for TV), and *Mansfield Park* (1999, UK/US). Until then, the 1940 Hollywood version of *Pride and Prejudice* had stood alone, though there had been a telemovie of *Northanger Abbey* (1986) and mini-series made from the other five novels, from the early 60s on, most notably perhaps, the 1996 six-part version of *Pride and Prejudice*, which made a star of Colin FIRTH (as Darcy).

BIBLIOG: Linda Trooste and Sayre Greenfield (eds), *Jane Austen in Hollywood*, 1998.

Australia and British cinema The idea of Australia as a place connoting remoteness or escape is, in days of jet air travel, no longer as potent as it was. In the 1948 film, *My Brother's Keeper*, old lag Jack WARNER wants to go 'to somewhere like South Africa or Australia where it's new and young' and in the 1955 EALING comedy, *Touch and Go*, it comes to stand for a missed opportunity for a fresh start. There is a generalised sense of easy-going classlessness (considerably at odds with the reality) that has tended to characterise the images of Australia purveyed overseas. British cinema's main brush with Australia was Ealing's batch of five films made there: Harry WATT's three – *The Overlanders* (1946), *Eureka Stockade* (1949) and, the studio's last film, *The Siege of Pinchgut* (1959) – Leslie NORMAN's *The Shiralee* (1957), and *Bitter Springs* (1950), directed by Ralph SMART, who also made *Bush Christmas* (1947) there for RANK. Anthony KIMMINS directed *Smiley* (1956) for LONDON FILMS, and its sequel *Smiley Gets a Gun* (1958), and Jack LEE made a lacklustre version of *Robbery Under Arms* (1957). Following the disaster of *Peeping Tom* (1960), Michael POWELL made two modest films in Australia: *They're a Weird Mob* (1966) and *The Age of Consent* (1969), and Tony RICHARDSON made an idiosyncratic version of *Ned Kelly* (1970). At this time, when the local industry was in the doldrums, the British ventures at least seemed to be trying to come to terms with the Australian ethos whereas US films, such as *Kangaroo* (1952) tended to see it as no more than an exotic backdrop. Perhaps the most intelligent British attempt to come to terms with Australia has been Nicolas ROEG's haunting, poetic *Walkabout* (1970). Because there was so little doing in indigenous Australian feature films in the post-war decades, many Australian actors sought careers in British film and theatre: John McCALLUM, Peter FINCH and Keith MICHELL are examples, and even in recent decades, when there has been a major revival, actors such as Judy DAVIS and Geoffrey RUSH have had some of their best chances in Britain (and in the US too). As well, the great Oscar-winning cameraman, Robert KRASKER, could not possibly have sustained a career in Australia in the 40s and 50s, nor could actor-dancer Robert HELPMANN or actresses Margaret JOHNSTON or Coral BROWNE, who left in

the 30s – for good.

auteurism The term 'auteur' was first used in the late 50s by French critics writing for *Cahiers du cinéma* to designate directors who imprinted their films with a personal style, in matters of both thematic preoccupation and style. It was often used to bring to attention American directors who, despite the apparent restrictions of studios and genres, managed to register a distinct personality in their work, and thus deserved to be called the 'authors' of their films. Andrew Sarris offered a systematic reading of the studio years of American cinema from this point of view in *The American Cinema: Directors and Directions 1929–1968* (1968), in which he divided directors into eleven categories, on the basis of how far he was prepared to grant them 'auteur' status. To date, no one has performed this sort of archaeological work on British cinema, but it may be argued that British cinema has suffered from the reckless auteurism which has elevated, say, LEAN, REED and POWELL at various times to such status, thereby neglecting a huge range of interesting work. The case of Gainsborough studios' output in the 40s is an instructive case: it has recently been the subject of much stimulating scholarship, but for a long time its famous MELODRAMAS would never have found their way into serious critical discussion, partly because it would have been difficult to erect auteurist cases for most of the directors involved. Some directors seem to cry out for auteurist exegeses because of the control they appear to have exerted over their work; one thinks of Lindsay ANDERSON, Ken RUSSELL, Derek JARMAN, Mike LEIGH and Peter GREENAWAY. Even so, one would need to adduce other factors, including conditions of production, in coming to terms with their oeuvres. And back in the studio years, directors with a substantial body of work, who may not necessarily qualify for the – in any case outmoded – term 'auteurist', are ripe for, not so much reassessment, as an initial assessment that seeks to place them in the contexts, cultural and industrial, which may help to reveal their worth. Auteurism has served its purpose in bringing to light many American directors who might otherwise now be forgotten; if it could do as much for their British counterparts, this would be a useful start, but not an end.

Autoscope Company was a production entity, founded in 1901 by W.G. BARKER, with offices at 50 Gray's Inn Road, London, and an open-air studio at Stamford Hill. In 1904, it opened the first studio at Ealing (on Ealing Green), and continued in operation until January 1906, when Autoscope merged with the WARWICK TRADING COMPANY. AS.

Auty, Chris Producer. Having acted in Peter GREENAWAY's *The Falls* (1980), Auty became associate producer (*Victory*, 1995, UK/Fr/Ger, released 1998; *Stealing Beauty*, 1996, UK/Fr /It; *Unhold*, 1996, UK/Fr/Ger) or executive producer (*Blood and Wine*, 1996, UK/US; *All the Little Animals*, 1999, UK) in the 90s. In 1999, he became Head of FILM CONSORTIUM.

awards Despite what anyone may say about the vulgarity of the Oscar presentations, the annual awards of the Academy of Motion Picture Arts and Sciences, these are still the most coveted, and many British films have benefited commercially from Oscar victories and even nominations. Sometimes, in fact, as in 1964, Hollywood has seemed perversely determined to overlook the locals and shower the British with honours. The home-grown BAFTA awards are often thought to be more dignified (they have a royal patron), but they still do not carry the prestige or the box-office weight of the Oscars. In 2001, for the first time, they were presented *before* the Oscars, with a view to arousing more interest in them. Other awards worth noting here are the Golden Globe awards, and those deriving from major film festivals. Such awards have had an important place in British film culture and the prestige of the industry, nationally and internationally, providing calling cards for film-makers to work in the wider arena (i.e. usually the US).

See APPENDIX for some of the major awards which British cinema has attracted.

Ayckbourn, Sir Alan (*b* London, 1939). Dramatist. Immense-ly popular and funny chronicler of middle-class anxieties who has been neglected by the screen. Michael WINNER filmed *A Chorus of Disapproval* (1989) to that sort of (undeserved) reaction, the French filmed *Smoking/No Smoking* (1994) and *The Revengers' Comedies* (1998) was a UK/Fr co-production. Why has anyone made this sharp and funny on stage not been filmed by, say, Mike NEWELL? Awarded CBE in 1987, knighted in 1997.

Aylmer, Sir Felix (*b* Corsham, 1889 – *d* Surrey, 1979). Actor. RN: Aylmer-Jones. Oxford-educated Aylmer trained for the stage under Rosina Filippi and made his debut with Sir Seymour HICKS in 1911, beginning an acting career which would span nearly 60 years. From 1930, he appeared in well over a hundred films, most of them British, but some (like his stage appearances) American, typically in shrewd, dignified roles. He was usually cast as professional men, such as doctors and judges, but *Young Man's Fancy* (1939) casts him enjoyably as a parvenu manufacturer and *The Wicked Lady* (1945) as the canting servant who meets a nasty end. Essentially a character actor in films, he nevertheless had three notable starring roles: the courageous elderly Jew (he was himself Jewish) in Nazi Germany in *Mr Emmanuel* (1944), one of *The Ghosts of Berkeley Square* (1947), and the suspected child molester in *Never Take Sweets from a Stranger* (1960). He did so much distinguished work that it is hard to pick the choicest, but the Archbishop of Canterbury in *Henry V* (1944), the vicar in *The Way to the Stars* (1945), and the disappointed schoolmaster in *Separate Tables* (1958, US) stay vividly in the mind for their sharp individuation of small roles. Awarded OBE in 1950 and knighted in 1965, he was President of the BRITISH ACTORS' EQUITY ASSOCIATION from 1949 until 1969. His son David Aylmer (*d* 1964) was also an actor.

OTHER BRITISH FILMS INCLUDE: *Escape* (1930), *The World, the Flesh and the Devil*, *The Lodger* (1932), *The Ghost Camera* (1933), *Night Club Queen*, *The Path of Glory*, *Doctor's Orders* (1934), *The Iron Duke*, *The Ace of Spades* (1935), *Jack of All Trades* (1936), *Tudor Rose*, *Seven Sinners*, *Sensation*, *Dangerous Exile*, *The Mill on the Floss*, *Action for Slander*, *Victoria the Great* (1937), *Bank Holiday*, *Sixty Glorious Years* (1938), *Charley's (Big-Hearted) Aunt*, *Night Train to Munich*, *The Girl in the News* (1940), *Spellbound*, *Quiet Wedding*, *Major Barbara*, *Black Sheep of Whitehall*, *Kipps* (1941), *The Young Mr Pitt*, *Uncensored* (1942), *The Life and Death of Colonel Blimp*, *The Demi-Paradise* (1943), *English Without Tears* (1944), *Caesar and Cleopatra* (1945), *The Years Between* (1946), *Man About the House*, *The October Man* (1947), *Hamlet* (as Polonius) (1948), *Edward, My Son* (1949), *So Long at the Fair*, *Trio* (1950), *The Lady with a Lamp* (1951), *Ivanhoe* (as Isaac of York) (1952), *The Master of*

Ballantrae, *The Angel Who Pawned Her Harp* (1953), *Anastasia* (1956), *Saint Joan* (UK/US), *I Accuse!* (1957), *The Doctor's Dilemma* (1958), *The Mummy* (1959), *Macbeth* (1961), *The Chalk Garden*, *Becket* (1964), *Decline and Fall . . .* (1968).

Aylott, Dave (*b* London, 1885 – *d* Hatfield, 1969). Director. A MUSIC HALL performer, Aylott entered the film industry in the early years of the century, working with WALTURDAW and later spent eight months in charge of James WILLIAMSON's Brighton studio. He joined CRICKS & MARTIN, writing and directing the 'Muggins, VC' series, from 1909, was next with BRITISH AND COLONIAL, where he claimed to have created the 'Lt Daring' series, and then back to Cricks & Martin, directing and often starring in more than 50 SHORTS. Aylott produced the first WW1 film, *War's Grim Reality* (1914) only two days after the outbreak of hostilities. In 1921, he formed Brilliant Photoplays, making one film, *The River of Light* (1921). He ended his directorial career, making SHORTS in 1928–29, and, with the coming of sound, became a prominent make-up man.

BRITISH FEATURE FILMS: (d) *For East Is East* (1913), *The Jade Heart* (1915), *A Soldier and a Man*, *Two Lancashire Lassies in London* (1916, + sc), *Gamblers All* (1919, + sc). AS.

Ayres, Robert (*b* Michigan, 1914 – *d* Hemel Hempstead, 1968). Actor. Michigan-born of British parents, Ayres began work as a stage manager in the Midlands, made his film debut in 1949 and played leading roles in such 'B' MOVIES as *Delayed Action* (1954) and supporting roles in 'A' films such as *A Prize of Gold* (1955), *A Night to Remember* (1958) and *Isadora* (1968). Busy for two decades, he was competent rather than memorable. Also appeared on stage and starred in the TV series, *The Cheaters* (1960–61). Married singer Beryl Edwards.

OTHER BRITISH FILMS INCLUDE: *They Were Not Divided*, *State Secret* (1950), *13 East Street*, *24 Hours of a Woman's Life* (1952), *The Baby and the Battleship* (1956), *Time Lock* (1957), *The Heroes of Telemark* (1965).

Ayres, Rosalind (*b* Birmingham, 1946). Actress. Though pri-marily on TV and stage, Ayres appeared in two 70s films produced by David PUTTNAM and Sandy Lieberson, both starring pop star David ESSEX, and both with a pop music background: *That'll Be the Day* (1973) and *Stardust* (1974). Her subsequent film work has been desultory, including brief vivid bits as Lady Duff Gordon in *Titanic* (1997, US) and Elsa Lanchester in *Gods and Monsters* (1998, UK/US). Married to actor Martin JARVIS.

OTHER BRITISH FILMS INCLUDE: *From Beyond the Grave* (1973), *The Slipper and the Rose* (1976), *Cry Wolf* (1980), *Beautiful People* (1999).

Ayrton, Randle (*b* Chester, 1869 – *d* Stratford-upon-Avon, 1940). Director, actor. Character actor, on stage from 1890, Ayrton directed three silent feature films: *Gates of Duty* (1919), *The Sands of Time* (1919) and the Tallulah Bankhead vehicle *His House in Order* (1928). In 1937, he founded the College of Drama in Stratford, where he first appeared with the New Shakespeare Company in 1924.

BRITISH FILMS INCLUDE: *Profit and Loss* (1917), *The Hanging Judge* (1918), *Chu Chin Chow* (1923, as Kasim Baba), *Southern Love* (1924), *Decameron Nights* (1924, UK/Ger), *Nell Gwynne* (as Charles II), *The Little People* (1926), *The Manxman* (1929), *Two Worlds* (1930), *Dreyfus* (1931), *Me and Marlborough* (1935), *Talk of the Devil* (1936). AS.

Bb

'B' movies A 'B' movie was essentially a low-budget film, quickly made and destined for the bottom half of the double-bill programme which was the commonest mode of exhibition from, roughly, 1930 to 1965. The film shown before interval was characteristically shorter (roughly 55–75 minutes), usually belonging to recognisable THRILLER or COMEDY GENRES, and in modern dress for budgetary reasons. There were also some very short features (about 35 minutes), including the Edgar LUSTGARTEN series, made with an eye on American TV as well as on the double bill. Many American 'B' movies acquired 'sleeper' or cult status, but the British 'B' was virtually unnoticed by critics. This may be the result of the notorious 'QUOTA QUICKIES' of the 30s – films made with shameless speed and meagre budgets to satisfy regulations relating to the EXHIBITION of a certain quota of British films. The obloquy they attracted, for their perfunctory scripting and production values, gave British 'B' movies of ensuing decades a reputation hard to shrug off, even when undeserved.

Wartime restrictions on all film-making in Britain meant that 'B' film-making came almost to a halt, but in the later 40s the RANK ORGANISATION made a conscious effort, more praiseworthy for its intentions than its achievements, to use its HIGHBURY STUDIOS to produce 'B' movies as a showcase for new talents. This experiment produced only eight films, the most notable being the cautionary tale about the perils of drunk driving, Terence FISHER's *To the Public Danger* (1948), but it was a genuine attempt to do something different in this unregarded corner of the British film industry.

In the 50s and early 60s, about 60 second features were made annually in Britain. Some directors, such as Francis SEARLE, Maclean ROGERS, Charles SAUNDERS, and Godfrey GRAYSON made unambitious careers in turning out such films for a steady market. Others, such as Fisher, Ken HUGHES, Lewis GILBERT, Don CHAFFEY and John GILLING used them as a stepping stone to 'A' film-making; and still others, including Lance COMFORT, Arthur CRABTREE, Lawrence HUNTINGTON and Vernon SEWELL, who had made major feature films in the 40s, prolonged their careers in 'B' films. The output dwindled from the mid 60s when the changing exhibition pattern settled for a single main feature, and it was left to TV to take up the once-prolific B-movie genres.

Though the majority of 'B' films were utterly formulaic and undistinguished, there was also a steady trickle of exceptions to the rule which tended to dismiss them all. TEMPEAN FILMS, run by Robert S. BAKER and Monty BERMAN, made a series of pacy, neatly scripted thrillers, often using American stars to encourage US distribution. Among their best are such titles as *The Quiet Woman* (1951), *The Frightened Man* (1952) and *Impulse* (1955), pseudonymously directed by Cy ENDFIELD and

starring Arthur Kennedy. ACT FILMS, set up by the technicians' union to foster employment, made 21 'B' films, including *Private Information* (1952) and *The Last Man to Hang?* (1956, starring Tom CONWAY); and GROUP 3, set up in 1951 by the NATIONAL FILM FINANCE CORPORATION to give new directors a chance, made a series of quirky comedies such as *The Oracle* (1953) with a sub-EALING flavour, and mildly interesting dramas such as *End of the Road* (1954), about the problems of retirement, among films of more obviously A-feature aspirations. Untroubled by such aspirations, pre-horror HAMMER, using such directors as Fisher and Searle, and DANZIGERS and MERTON PARK, setting records for speedy discount filming, churned out dozens of second features, mostly thrillers, in the 50s and early 60s. Even at this level, one could still be surprised by flickers of style and energy, and the field is ripe for further investigation.

BIBLIOG: Brian McFarlane, 'Pulp Fictions: the British B Film', *Film Criticism*, Fall 1996.

Bacon, Mai (*b* Ilkley, 1897 – *d* London, 1981). Actress. On stage from 1915, as actress and sometimes as dancer, Bacon made a dozen or so films, in character roles, between her debut in a tiny role in *The Good Companions* (1933) and her last appearance as the mother in Pete Walker's sex romp, *I Like Birds* (1967). Married to actor Morris HARVEY.

OTHER BRITISH FILMS INCLUDE: *Chick* (1936), *Remember When* (1937), *Riding High, On the Night of the Fire* (1939), *This Man is Mine* (1946), *Up for the Cup, Pool of London* (1950), *Knave of Hearts* (1954, UK/Fr).

Bacon, Max (*b* London, 1906 – *d* London, 1969). Actor. Jewish comedian, also former singer and drummer with AMBROSE's orchestra with whom he made his first three film appearances – *Soft Lights and Sweet Music* (1936), *Calling All Stars* (1937) and *Kicking the Moon Around* (1938). Played several comedy roles for Val GUEST in the early 40s, including a coy head waiter in *Miss London Ltd* (1943) and continued in character roles for a further 20 years.

OTHER BRITISH FILMS INCLUDE: *King Arthur Was a Gentleman* (1942), *Give Us the Moon, Bees in Paradise* (1944), *Pool of London* (1950), *Expresso Bongo* (1959), *The Entertainer* (1960), *Play It Cool* (1962), *The Whisperers* (1966), *Privilege* (1967), *Chitty Chitty Bang Bang* (1968).

Baddeley, Angela (*b* London, 1904 – *d* London, 1976). Actress. RN: Clinton-Baddeley. Stage actress and latterly famous as Mrs Bridges, outspoken cook in TV's *Upstairs, Downstairs* (1971–75), Baddeley made only occasional films. Older sister of Hermione BADDELEY, and on stage from 1915, she first filmed in a modernised version of Conan DOYLE's *The Speckled Band* in 1931. Apart from one small role, she was off the screen for nearly twenty years after *The Citadel* in 1938. She was a sympathetic aunt in *Zoo Baby* and a vividly slatternly Mum in

No Time for Tears (both 1957). Married to theatre actor and producer Glen Byam Shaw.

OTHER BRITISH FILMS: *The Ghost Train* (1931), *Capture, The Safe, Arms and the Man* (1932), *Those Were the Days* (1934), *Quartet* (1948, 'Facts of Life' story), *Tom Jones* (1963).

Baddeley, Hermione (*b* Broseley, 1906 – *d* Los Angeles, 1986). Actress. RN: Clinton-Baddeley. In a more than 60-year career, the youngest of the four Baddeley sisters enjoyed success in all the acting media. On stage from 1918, pre-WW2 she became popular in London stage comedies and revues, drawing on her dancer's training as well as her innate comic flair, several times appearing memorably with the other Hermione – GINGOLD. Too idiosyncratic in appearance and style for conventional pre-war heroines, post-war, she came into her own in films when she repeated her stage success as the blowzy, good-hearted Ida in the BOULTING brothers' film of *Brighton Rock* (1947). She played memorable character roles, including assorted mums and slatterns, until she died. Even in 'B' MOVIES such as *Rag Doll* (1960, as a motherly fortune-teller), she was effortlessly authoritative. Received AAn for her eloquent study of Simone SIGNORET's perceptive and acid-tongued friend in *Room at the Top* (1958), and scored successes on Broadway in the early 60s, when she was signed by Walt Disney for the cook in *Mary Poppins* (1964). The rest of her career was almost entirely spent in US films and TV, where she became a household favourite for her role as fractious cockney cook in the long-running 70s series *Maude*. Her two marriages failed, and she had a long relationship with actor Laurence HARVEY, with whom she first appeared in *There is Another Sun* (1951).

OTHER BRITISH FILMS INCLUDE: *A Daughter in Revolt* (1926), *The Guns of Loos* (1928), *Caste* (1930), *Kipps* (1941), *It Always Rains on Sunday* (1947), *No Room at the Inn, Quartet* (1948), *Passport to Pimlico, Dear Mr Prohack* (1949), *The Woman in Question* (1950), *Tom Brown's Schooldays, Scrooge* (1951), *The Pickwick Papers* (1952), *Cosh Boy, Counterspy* (1953), *The Belles of St Trinian's* (1954), *Jet Storm, Expresso Bongo* (1959), *Up the Front* (1972).

BIBLIOG: Autobiography, *The Unsinkable Hermione Baddeley*, 1984.

Badel, Alan (*b* Manchester, 1923 – *d* Chichester, 1982). Actor. RADA graduate Badel, on stage from 1940, served in the Parachute Regiment (1942–47), after which he played classic and modern roles, with seasons at Stratford and the Old Vic. Some sources give his first film as *The Young Mr Pitt* (1942); if so (one cast list mentions an 'Allan Burdell'), it was in a tiny role. His film career really begins in 1953 with Wendy TOYE's prize-winning short, *The Stranger Left No Card*, and as John the Baptist in Hollywood's *Salome*. With unusual looks and intensity, he was in off-beat character roles from early middle age. His most striking performances included the sexually ambivalent team manager in Lindsay ANDERSON's *This Sporting Life* (1963), a wildly camp Baron de Gunzberg ('half-Admiral of the Fleet, half-maiden aunt') in *Nijinsky* (1980, UK/US) and a memorable Fosco in TV's *The Woman in White* (1978). Married to Yvonne OWEN; father of Sarah BADEL.

OTHER BRITISH FILMS INCLUDE: *Will Any Gentleman . . . ?* (1953), *Three Cases of Murder* (1955), *Children of the Damned* (1963), *Arabesque* (1966, UK/US), *Where's Jack?* (1969), *The Day of the Jackal* (1973, UK/Fr), *The Medusa Touch* (UK/Fr), *Agatha* (UK/US) (1978).

Badel, Sarah (*b* London, 1943). Actress. The daughter of Alan BADEL and Yvonne OWEN has made few films, but was endearingly serene in *Mrs Dalloway* (1997, UK/Neth/US) as the heroine's friend in sonsy middle age. Her main work has been

on stage, several times at Chichester and the National, and TV, where she was an aptly bossy Flora Post in *Cold Comfort Farm* (1968) and a formidable hostess in *Dance to the Music of Time* (1997). Also in the US-made *Not Without My Daughter* (1991).

OTHER BRITISH FILMS INCLUDE: *Every Home Should Have One* (1969), *The Shooting Party* (1984), *Cotton Mary* (1999, UK/Fr/US).

Badland, Annette (*b* Birmingham, 1950). Actress. Very plump actress came to prominence in a series of eye-catching character roles in the 90s. She was the homely mum of one of the boxing youths in *24 7 TwentyFourSeven* (1997), the complacent Lady Alabaster in *Angels and Insects* (1995, UK/US), a barrister in *Hollow Reed* (1996, UK/Ger), and, bravely fat and un-attractive, as Brenda BLETHYN's fishery workmate in *Little Voice* (1998, UK/US), which she had played in the National Theatre version. Has done highly regarded stage work, directed by the likes of Sam Mendes and Stephen DALDRY, and appeared in masses of television.

OTHER BRITISH FILMS INCLUDE: *Jabberwocky* (1977), *Beyond Bedlam* (1993), *Captives* (1994), *The Grotesque* (1996), *Beautiful People* (1999), *Honest* (UK/Fr), *Secret Society* (UK/Ger) (2000), *Mrs Caldicot's Cabbage War, Redemption Road* (2001).

BAFTA The British Academy of Film and TV Arts was founded in 1946 when leading members of the feature film industry formed the BRITISH FILM ACADEMY. In 1958, The Academy amalgamated with The Guild of TV Producers and Directors to form The Society of Film And TV Arts which, in 1976, changed to its present name. In the same year, BAFTA acquired club premises at 195 Piccadilly with two theatres, one seating 213, The Princess Anne, named after its former President and another seating 50, The Run-Run Shaw, named after a major benefactor. Every year there are four Awards Ceremonies for Film, TV, Children's TV and Interactive. Winners are presented with the BAFTA Mask designed by Mitzi Cunliffe. BAFTA has five additional chapters: BAFTA-North, BAFTA-Scotland, BAFTA-Wales, BAFTA-East Coast (NY) and BAFTA-LA. Its total membership is over 3000. Members have a monthly programme of feature films supported by education and training events. Robert Angell.

See also APPENDIX for awards.

Bailey, Claude (*b* London, 1895 – *d* London, 1950). Actor. Dependable character player, chiefly in 40s films, notably as the bluff, suspicious Captain McKelvey in *Bedelia* (1946).

OTHER BRITISH FILMS INCLUDE: *Little Waitress* (1932), *The Unholy Quest* (1934), *Hatter's Castle* (1941), *Unpublished Story* (1942), *The Gentle Sex* (1943), *Don't Take It to Heart!* (1944), *Elizabeth of Ladymead* (1948).

Bailey, John (*b* London, 1915 – *d* London, 1989). Actor. Sturdy character player in British films since the late 40s. His filmography consists almost entirely of THRILLERS, in which he appeared sometimes on the side of the law (e.g. as Detective Inspector Grant in *The Franchise Affair*, 1950), sometimes not, as in the first film in which he made much impression, *Man on the Run* (1949). Last role was as one of Julie WALTERS's clients in *Personal Services*. (1987).

OTHER BRITISH FILMS INCLUDE: *It Happened in Soho* (1948), *Meet Simon Cherry* (1949), *Cairo Road* (1950), *Circle of Danger, High Treason* (1951), *Venetian Bird* (1952), *The Hostage* (1956), *Never Let Go* (1960), *The Wild Little Bunch* (1972).

Bailey, Robin (*b* Hucknall, 1919 – *d* London, 1999). Actor. Though often projecting a patrician image on stage and screen, Bailey not only won his greatest fame as politically incorrect North-of-England working man, Uncle Mort, in TV's *I Didn't*

Know You Cared (1975), but grew up in a Nottinghamshire mining village where his father kept a store. Served in the Army during WW2, first appeared on the London stage in 1947, and made his first film, Peter USTINOV's *Private Angelo*, two years later. Over the next forty years, he worked solidly on the stage (including two Australian stints as Henry Higgins in *My Fair Lady*), played a range of character roles on film (notably the prissy solicitor in *Portrait of Clare*, 1950), and made many TV appearances, finally in *Dance to the Music of Time* (1997). Married actress Patricia Weekes.

OTHER BRITISH FILMS INCLUDE: *His Excellency* (1951), *Folly to be Wise* (1952), *Single-Handed* (1953), *Just My Luck, Hell Drivers* (1957), *The Mouse on the Moon* (1963), *The Whisperers, The Spy with a Cold Nose* (1966), *Danger Route* (1967), *Blind Terror* (1971), *Screamtime* (1983).

Bainbridge, Dame Beryl (*b* Liverpool, 1934). Author. Idiosyncratic novelist/playwright, several of whose books have been filmed for – predictably – minority audiences, who were rewarded, in *An Awfully Big Adventure* (1995) with some dark insights and an acrid whiff of provincial theatre. Also filmed: *Sweet William* (1979) and *The Dressmaker* (1988). She played a small role in *Adult Fun* (1972), a title which aptly sums up her oeuvre. Created DBE in 2000.

Baines, John (*b* 1909). Screenwriter. Playwright as well as screenwriter, Baines was under MGM contract in Hollywood before the war. Returning to Britain, he was with the Films Division of the Ministry of Education (1941–43) and contracted to EALING (1943–45) where he worked on 'The Haunted Mirror' and 'The Ventriloquist's Dummy' sequences of *Dead of Night* (1945). Briefly under contract to INDEPENDENT PRODUCERS, for whom he co-wrote *The Blue Lagoon* (1949), he thereafter freelanced.

OTHER BRITISH FILMS INCLUDE: *Colonel Bogey* (1948), *Hindle Wakes, Derby Day* (1952), *Simba* (1955), *The Big Money* (1958), *Seven Thunders* (1957), *The Hands of Orlac* (1960, UK/Fr).

Baird, Antony (*b* London, 1920). Actor. Tall, lean actor who appeared in a dozen or so films. Best chance came first, as the racing-car driver who has an unnerving hospital experience in *Dead of Night* (1945). Otherwise, bigger roles in minor films such as *Night Comes Too Soon* (1947) or minor roles in bigger films such as *The Ipcress File* (1965), plus some stage and TV.

OTHER BRITISH FILMS INCLUDE: *The Hangman Waits* (1947), *The Winslow Boy* (1948), *Reluctant Heroes* (1951), *Offbeat* (1960), *Carry on Spying* (1964), *The Christmas Tree* (1966).

Baird, Edward ('Teddy') (*b* London, 1901 – *d* London). Producer. RN: Goodman. Entered films in 1928 with BRITISH INSTRUCTIONAL, working in the cutting room, the scenario department, as assistant director and as unit manager. Worked on such notable films as *As You Like It* (1936) and *Elephant Boy* (1937), but mainly associated with Anthony ASQUITH's films, starting with *Tell England* in 1931, as assistant director, then on *Pygmalion* (1938) and *French Without Tears* (1939). In the RAF during WW2, and posted to its Film Unit (1941–46), for which he produced and directed *School for Danger* (finally released in 1946), about the French resistance. Post-war, was assistant producer on Asquith's *While the Sun Shines* (1947) and producer on five further Asquith films: *The Winslow Boy* (1948), *The Woman in Question* (1950), *The Importance of Being Earnest* (1952), *Carrington VC* (1954) and *Two Living, One Dead* (1961, UK/Swe).

OTHER BRITISH FILMS INCLUDE: (ass d) *Dance Pretty Lady* (1932), *A Cuckoo in the Nest* (1933), *Vessel of Wrath* (1938), *Stolen Life* (1939); (p) *Fast and Loose* (1954), *Simon and Laura* (1955), *Don't Panic Chaps* (1959).

Baird, Harry (*b* Georgetown, British Guyana, 1931). Actor. Black actor who appeared in early 'racial problem' films, *Sapphire* (1959), as the murdered girl's terrified dance partner, and *Flame in the Streets* (1961). In the pop-art farrago, *The Touchables* (1968), he played the underworld wrestler who fancies the hero, and he appeared in several big-budget 60s films, including *The Italian Job* (1969), before finishing his career in Italian Westerns such as *Four Gunmen of the Apocalypse* (1975).

OTHER BRITISH FILMS: *A Kid for Two Farthings* (1954), *Killers of Kilimanjaro* (1959), *Offbeat* (1960), *The Mark, The Road to Hong Kong* (1961), *Station Six Sahara* (1963, UK/Ger), *The Whisperers* (1966), *The Oblong Box* (1969), *Cool It Carol!* (1970), *1000 Convicts and a Woman* (1971).

Baird, Roy (*b* Elstree, 1933). Producer, assistant director. Entered films as production manager or assistant director on several films for Lance COMFORT (*The Break*, 1962, *Devils of Darkness*, 1964) and Val GUEST (*The Beauty Jungle*, 1964), then worked with Ken RUSSELL, as associate producer on *Women in Love* (1969), *The Music Lovers* and *The Devils* (1971), and producer on *Mahler* (1974) and *Lisztomania* (1975), as well as on two further films with pop idol Roger DALTREY, *Quadrophenia* (1979) and *McVicar* (1980). Nephew, Stuart BAIRD, is an editor.

OTHER BRITISH FILMS INCLUDE: (p man) *Live It Up* (1963), *Island of Terror* (1966); (ass d) *The Wrong Arm of the Law* (1962), *The Collector* (1965, UK/US), *Casino Royale* (1967); (ex p) *Spring and Port Wine* (1969); (p) *Our Mother's House* (1967), *That'll Be the Day, The Final Programme* (1973), *Buddy's Song* (1990).

Baird, Stuart (*b* Hillingdon, 1948). Editor. Much sought-after editor who turned director on *Executive Decision* (1996, US), after establishing himself with uncredited rescue work on several big-budget US films, including *Tango and Cash* (1989). In Britain, began as assistant to the director on Lindsay ANDERSON's *If . . .* (1968) and Ken RUSSELL's *The Devils* (1971), then edited several films for Russell, starting with *Lisztomania* (1975). Received AAn for editing *Superman* (1978) and *Gorillas in the Mist* (1988, US).

OTHER BRITISH FILMS: *Savage Messiah* (1972, sound e), *Tommy* (1975), *Valentino* (1977), *Superman* (1978), *Outland* (1981), *Five Days One Summer* (1982, UK/US), *The Honorary Consul* (1983), *Revolution* (1985, UK/Nor).

Baker, F(rancis) W(illiam) (*b* Hollesley, 1877 – *d* London, 1950). Producer. Entered films in 1897, served in RAF in WW1, produced several films in the late 1910s, including Maurice ELVEY's fantasy, *Flames* (1918), and subsequently became managing director of BUTCHER's FILM SERVICE. The films he produced for Butcher's in the 30s and 40s were largely knockabout COMEDIES such as *Old Mother Riley MP* (1939) and *Gert and Daisy Clean Up* (1942) or sentimental MUSICALS such as *The Rose of Tralee* (1942) and *My Ain Folk* (1944).

OTHER BRITISH FILMS INCLUDE: *Grit of a Jew* (1917), *Goodbye* (1918), *As He Was Born* (1919), *Jailbirds* (1939), *Pack Up Your Troubles* (1940), *Variety Jubilee, I'll Walk Beside You* (1943), *Demobbed* (1944), *For You Alone* (1945), *I'll Turn to You* (1946).

Baker, George (*b* Varna, Bulgaria, 1929). Actor. Baker, archetypally tall, dark and handsome, was seen on London stage in *Aren't We All?* (1953) by director Guy HAMILTON who cast him in *The Intruder* (1953), a drama of post-war disaffection. Signed by ABPC, he made his name in leading roles for other companies, notably for EALING and WESSEX in two superior war films, *The Ship that Died of Shame* (1955), and *A Hill in Korea* (1956), though he swashbuckled to good effect in ABPC's *The Moonraker* (1957). Later an authoritative character actor, playing in two 'BOND' FILMS, he acquired a new following in the title role of TV's 'Inspector Wexford' mysteries, in which his second wife, Louie Ramsey, played Mrs Wexford. Has also had a successful career as a stage actor and producer, and as a writer.

OTHER BRITISH FILMS INCLUDE: *The Woman for Joe* (1955), *The Feminine Touch*, *The Extra Day* (1956), *These Dangerous Years*, *No Time for Tears* (1957), *Tread Softly Stranger* (1958), *The Finest Hours* (narr) (1964), *Curse of the Fly* (1965), *On Her Majesty's Secret Service*, *Goodbye, Mr Chips* (1969), *The Spy Who Loved Me* (1977), *The Thirty Nine Steps* (1978), *North Sea Hijack* (1979), *For Queen and Country* (1988, UK/US).

Baker, Hylda (*b* Farnworth, 1905 – *d* Epsom, 1986). Actress. On stage since 1918 and a popular comedienne of Midlands and Northern MUSIC HALLS long before entering films, Baker was thoroughly noticed in her first film role – the hero's stroppy Aunt Ada in *Saturday Night and Sunday Morning* in 1960. Appeared in several TV series, including *Best of Friends* (1963), but in only three further films: the sex comedy *She Knows Y'Know* (1962), the realist drama *Up the Junction* (1967), the musical, *Oliver!* (1968), as the harridan wife of undertaker Sowerberry, and TV SPIN-OFF, *Nearest and Dearest* (1972).

Baker, Robert S. (*b* London, 1916). Producer. Co-founder with Monty BERMAN of TEMPEAN FILMS, which produced perhaps the most successful string of British 'B' MOVIES, Baker had a realistic approach to his craft. The aim was to make fast-moving THRILLERS in the American manner, many of them with American stars, including *The Lost Hours* (1952) with Mark Stevens, *Impulse* (1955, + co-sc) with Arthur Kennedy, and *Tiger by the Tail* (1955), with Larry Parks. There were other enjoyable programme-fillers such as *No Trace* (1950), *The Quiet Woman* (1951), and *The Embezzler* (1954) with British stars, supported by sturdy British character actors. As well as co-producing, Baker directed several of these, most of them made for under £20,000 and destined for the bottom half of the double-bill EXHIBITION pattern. When this market showed signs of drying up, Baker and Berman turned to making 'A' films, such as *Sea of Sand* (1958), and the unusual tale of anarchists in Edwardian London, *The Siege of Sidney Street* (1960, co-d/co-p/co-c). An assistant director from 1937, Baker met Berman in the ARMY FILM UNIT during the war. They decided to work as partners post-war, and made their first feature film, *A Date with a Dream*, in 1948. In the 60s, they turned their attention to TV, making such popular series as *The Saint* and *The Persuaders* both with Roger MOORE. Throughout his career, Baker moved easily to meet market demands, in the process producing some lively entertainments.

OTHER BRITISH FILMS: (p, unless noted) *The Way from Germany* (1946, doc), *Melody Club* (1949), *Blackout* (1950, + d), *13 East Street* (+ d), *The Frightened Man*, *The Voice of Merrill*, *Black Orchid* (1952), *The Steel Key* (+ d), *Recoil*, *Love in Pawn*, *Three Steps to the Gallows*, *Escape by Night*, *Deadly Nightshade* (1953), *Double Exposure*, *Delayed Action* (1954), *The Gilded Cage*, *The Reluctant Bride*, *Windfall*, *No Smoking*, *Barbados Quest* (1955), *Passport to Treason* (+ d), *Breakaway*, *Bond of Fear*, *The High Terrace* (1956), *Hour of Decision*, *Stranger in Town*, *Professor Tim** (+ sc) (1957), *Stormy Crossing*, *The Trollenberg Terror*, *Sally's Irish Rogue**, *Blind Spot* (+ co-st), *Blood of the Vampire*, *Jack the Ripper* (+ d, co-c) (1958), *Home is the Hero**, *The Flesh and the Fiends* (1959), *Boyd's Shop**, *The Hellfire Club* (+ d), *The Treasure of Monte Cristo* (+ d) (1960), *What a Carve Up!* (1961), *Crossplot* (1969). *=Made in Dublin.

BIBLIOG: Brian McFarlane, 'Value for Money: Baker and Berman and Tempean Films' in Neil Sinyard and Ian McKillop (eds), *British Cinema in the 50s*, 2003.

Baker, Roy Ward (*b* London, 1916). Director, producer. First known as Roy Baker, he served his apprenticeship at GAINSBOROUGH (1934–39), starting in the sound department. During WW2, first in the Infantry, then in the Army Kinematograph Service, where he met Eric AMBLER. Post-war, he made an auspicious feature film debut directing Ambler's script for *The October Man* (1947) for TWO CITIES, came to the notice of Daryl F. Zanuck with his tense and sombre submarine drama *Morning Departure* (1950), and, as a result, made four films for Fox, including the *noir* thriller *Don't Bother to Knock* (1952), with Marilyn Monroe as a dangerous babysitter, and the excellent 3-D film, *Inferno* (1953). Back in England, he made a series of superior entertainments, characterised by well-wrought screenplays, strong casts performing to edgy effect, and a flair for the evocation of a chilling atmosphere, as in *Tiger in the Smoke* (1956), which has as unsettling a first hour as will be found in British cinema of its decade. His version of the 'Titanic' disaster, *A Night to Remember* (1958), with a script by Ambler and a documentary flavour adding to its authenticity, remains the screen's finest account of the tragedy, James Cameron notwithstanding. He loathed making *The Singer Not the Song* (1960), which has since become a camp classic, showed his versatility in directing the 'Quatermass' sequel, *Quatermass and the Pit*, and Bette Davis as a monster-mum in *The Anniversary* (both 1967). Subsequently, he made several forays in the horror genre which gave him little pleasure, though some, such as *Dr Jekyll & Sister Hyde* (1971), are inventive and darkly witty. As well, he directed a good deal of TV, including the Kenya-set mini-series *The Flame Trees of Thika* (1981).

OTHER BRITISH FILMS: *The Weaker Sex* (1948), *Paper Orchid* (1949), *Highly Dangerous* (1950), *The House in the Square* (1951), *Passage Home* (1955), *Jacqueline* (1956), *The One That Got Away* (1957), *Flame in the Streets*, *The Valiant* (UK/It) (1961), *Two Left Feet* (1963), *Moon Zero Two* (1969), *The Vampire Lovers* (1970), *Asylum* (1972), *And Now the Screaming Starts!*, *The Vault of Horror* (UK/US) (1973), *The Legend of the 7 Gold Vampires* (1974, UK/HK), *The Monster Club* (1980).

BIBLIOG: Autobiography, *The Director's Cut*, 2000.

Baker, Sir Stanley (*b* Ferndale, Wales, 1927 – *d* Malaga, Spain, 1976). Actor. Burly character star discovered for films as a teenager by Sergei NOLBANDOV who cast him in EALING's Yugoslav-set drama *Undercover* (1943). Before his next film, *All Over the Town* in 1949, he worked with Birmingham Rep and did Army service (1946–48). After small film roles, he made his mark as the bullying Bennett in *The Cruel Sea* (1952), when the dangerous edge to his working-class he-man persona emerged powerfully. Busy throughout the rest of the 50s and 60s, he never played conventional leading men: there was always too much sense of threat about him for that: but he created some memorable villains and a few tough heroes in films such as *Knights of the Round Table* (1953, as Modred), *The Good Die Young* (1954, as a broken-down boxer tempted into crime), Cy ENDFIELD's *Hell Drivers* (1957, as an ex-con lured into lorry-driving competitiveness), and Joseph LOSEY's *Blind Date* (1959, as a policeman with a bad cold). In 1967, he gave perhaps his subtlest performance: as the sexually infatuated academic in *Accident* (1967), again for Losey, for whom he also made *The Criminal* (1960) and *Eva* (1962, Fr/It). His later choice of roles may seem wayward, but his charismatic presence meant that he was never dull. Freelancing after ending his contract with

RANK in 1959, he formed his own production company, Oakhurst, which made *The Italian Job* (1969), among others; he appeared in international films such as *Sodom and Gomorrah* (1962, It/US) and *Pepita Jimenez* (1975, Sp); and he personally produced several films, most notably *Zulu* (1964), in which he also starred. Knighted in 1976. Married actress Ellen Martin.

OTHER BRITISH FILMS: *Your Witness, Captain Horatio Hornblower RN* (UK/US) (1950), *The Rossiter Case, Cloudburst, Home to Danger* (1951), *Whispering Smith Hits London* (1952), *The Red Beret, Hell Below Zero, The Tell-Tale Heart* (short) (1953), *Beautiful Stranger* (1954), *Richard III* (1955), *Child in the House, A Hill in Korea, Checkpoint* (1956), *Campbell's Kingdom* (1957), *Violent Playground, Sea Fury* (1958), *The Angry Hills, Yesterday's Enemy, Jet Storm, Hell is a City* (1959), *The Guns of Navarone, A Prize of Arms* (1961), *The Man Who Finally Died* (1962), *Sands of the Kalahari* (1965), *One of Them is Brett* (short, voice only), *Robbery* (+ p) (1967), *Where's Jack?* (+ p), *The Games, The Last Grenade* (1969), *Perfect Friday* (1970), *Innocent Bystanders* (1972).

Baker, Tom (*b* Liverpool, 1934). Actor. A household name as the fourth Dr Who in the BBC's sci-fi series of that name, Baker's big-screen career has been sporadic, including character roles in such international films as *Nicholas and Alexandra* (UK/US, as Rasputin) and Pasolini's *The Canterbury Tales* (Fr/It) both 1971) and several British HORROR films. Nothing in his film work (some in Hollywood) has displaced the image of the tousle-haired Doctor with the long scarf. Second wife was actress Lalla Ward.

OTHER BRITISH FILMS INCLUDE: *The Vault of Horror* (UK/US), *The Golden Voyage of Sinbad, The Mutations* (1973).

Balchin, Nigel (*b* Potterne, 1908 – *d* London, 1970). Author, screenwriter. Cambridge graduate who studied natural science, beginning career as fiction-writer in 1933. During WW2 he was a scientific adviser to the British Army Council, with rank of Brigadier, made his name with *The Small Back Room* (1943), which drew on his wartime experiences, and collaborated with POWELL AND PRESSBURGER on the screenplay for their film version (1949); in 1947, he had adapted *Mine Own Executioner* (1945), his famous psychiatrist-shrink-thyself novel, to film; and in 1960 the BOULTING brothers filmed *A Sort of Traitors* (1949), as *Suspect*, based on Balchin's screenplay. He sometimes adapted other people's books: e.g. *Fame is the Spur* (1947), from Howard Spring's novel of political life; and *The Man Who Never Was* (1955), for which he won a BAA, from Ewen Montagu's tale of wartime ingenuity. He was also author or co-author of original screenplays such as *Josephine and Men* (1955), and *Barabbas* (1961, It, with Christopher Fry). His tautest work dramatises vulnerable men under extreme pressure.

OTHER BRITISH FILMS: *Mandy* (1952, co-sc), *Malta Story* (1953, co-sc), *A Circle of Deception, The Singer Not the Song* (1960).

Balcon, Jill (*b* London, 1925). Actress. Daughter of producer Sir Michael BALCON, wife of the poet Cecil Day-Lewis, and mother of actor Daniel DAY-LEWIS, RADA-trained Balcon worked in repertory and as a BBC announcer before entering films as Madeleine Bray in *Nicholas Nickleby* (1947). She scrapped memorably with Jean KENT in *Good-Time Girl* (1947), but after three more small roles was away from films until two 90s appearances for Derek JARMAN – in *Edward II* (1991) and *Wittgenstein* (1993) – and as Lady Bracknell in the play-within-the-film in *An Ideal Husband* (1999, UK/US).

OTHER BRITISH FILMS: *Saraband for Dead Lovers* (1948), *The Lost People* (1949), *Highly Dangerous* (1950).

Balcon, Sir Michael (*b* Birmingham, 1896 – *d* Hartfield, 1977). Executive, producer. Whatever limitations may now be ascribed to the EALING STUDIOS output of the 40s and 50s, it is undeniably at the centre of any account of the British film industry's most prestigious period – and is above all the achievement of Michael Balcon. In an industry short of Hollywood-style moguls, Balcon emerges, along with Alexander KORDA and J. Arthur RANK, as a key figure, and an obdurately British one too, in his benevolent, somewhat headmasterly approach to the running of a creative organisation. Entered the industry as a regional distributor in 1919, and in 1921 co-founded Victory Motion Pictures with Victor SAVILLE. In 1924, he and Graham CUTTS founded GAINSBOROUGH PICTURES, which he presided over for twelve years, as director of production for GAUMONT–BRITISH from 1931. During his incumbency, he oversaw production of some of HITCHCOCK's most charming entertainments, as well as Jessie MATTHEWS' highly successful MUSICALS.

After two frustrating years in charge of production for MGM–BRITISH, from 1937 until 1959 he was director and production chief at Ealing. When the studio was sold in 1955, he erected a plaque there proclaiming: 'Here during a quarter of a century many films were made projecting Britain and the British character.' This was the most fruitful period of his long career, marked by his capacity to assemble a creative team of writers, directors, actors and others, perhaps unparalleled in British film history. Though it is the famous Ealing comedies, from *Hue and Cry* in 1946 through to *The Ladykillers* in 1955, which are most fondly remembered, the range also included such notable films in realist mode as *San Demetrio–London* (1943), *The Blue Lamp* (1949) and *The Cruel Sea* (1952), a MUSICAL *Champagne Charlie* (1944), the costume romance *Saraband for Dead Lovers* (1948), and the adventure epic *Scott of the Antarctic* (1948). The Ealing vein was played out by the later 50s, but it is a major achievement.

In 1959 he formed BRYANSTON FILMS, and in 1964, amid much controversy, took control of BRITISH LION. Knighted in 1948. Jill BALCON, the actress, is his daughter, and S. Chandos BALCON was his brother.

OTHER BRITISH FILMS INCLUDE (NB During most of his incumbency at Ealing, Balcon assumed the Producer's credit, whereas in fact the Associate Producer carried out the producer's function. The titles following are a selection of his non-Ealing productions): (for Victory) *Woman to Woman* (1923), (for Gainsborough) *The Pleasure Garden* (1925, UK/Ger), *The Lodger* (1926), *Easy Virtue* (1927), *Journey's End* (1930), *Hindle Wakes* (1931), *I Was a Spy, The Good Companions* (1933), *Man of Aran, Evergreen* (1934), *Forever England, The Tunnel, The 39 Steps* (1935), *Tudor Rose* (1936), (for MGM) *A Yank at Oxford* (1937).

BIBLIOG: Autobiography, *A Lifetime in Films*, 1969; Charles Barr, *Ealing Studios*, 1993 (rev ed).

Balcon, S(amuel) Chandos (*b* Waltham St Lawrence, 1891 – *d* Maidenhead, 1947). Associate producer. Was associate producer on several films at GAINSBOROUGH before joining older brother Michael BALCON in this capacity at EALING, where he spent the rest of his career.

BRITISH FILMS INCLUDE: *Everything is Thunder* (1936), *Head Over Heels* (1937), *The Ware Case* (1938), *Cheer Boys Cheer* (1939), *Ships with Wings* (1941), *Went the Day Well?* (1942), *Pink String and Sealing Wax* (1945).

Bale, Christian (*b* Pembroke, 1974). Actor. Partly raised in England, now established in California, Bale came to prominence as the lost child in Steven Spielberg's WW2 adventure *Empire of the Sun* (1987, US). He has since worked in such US films as *Little Women* (1994, as Laurie) and *American Psycho* (1999, US/Can) and notably in such British films as *Henry V* (1989), as the boy carried dead from Agincourt by the King, *The Portrait of a Lady* (1996, UK/US), as the rejected boyish suitor, and *Velvet Goldmine* (1998, UK/US), touching as the provincial lad corrupted by the glamrock scene. On stage at 10, in TV at 12, he appears to have negotiated the transition to adult roles.

OTHER BRITISH FILMS INCLUDE: *The Secret Agent* (1996, UK/US), *Metroland* (1997, UK/Fr/Sp), *All the Little Animals* (1998), *A Midsummer Night's Dream* (1999, UK/It), *Captain Corelli's Mandolin* (2001, UK/Fr/US).

Balfour, Betty (*b* London, 1903 – *d* Weybridge, 1978). Actress. Balfour was the only international star of the British silent cinema, the most popular actress in Britain in the 20s and in 1927 named by the *Daily Mirror* as the country's favourite world star. Gamine-like, she was a consummate screen actress, whose sympathetic portrayals were often tinged with pathos. Her talent was most evident in the 'Squibs' comedy series produced by George PEARSON, while in his *Love, Life and Laughter* (1923) and *Reveille* (1924), she demonstrated a serious side to her character. The partnership ended after *Blinkeyes* (1926), when Pearson's offer to divorce his wife and marry Balfour was rejected by the actress. Made her stage debut in 1913, and was appearing in *Medora* at the Alhambra Theatre when T.A. WELSH and Pearson saw and signed her for *Nothing Else Matters* (1920). After replacing Gertrude LAWRENCE on stage in *The Midnight Follies*, Balfour was back with Pearson with her first starring role in *Mary-Find-the-Gold* (1921). She was equally popular on the Continent, starring in the German films, *Die sieben Töchter der Frau Gyurkovics* (1927) and *Die Regimentstochter* (1929); she starred for Marcel l'Herbier in *Le Diable au Coeur* (1927), for Louis Mercanton in *Monkeynuts* (1928) and for Geza von BOLVARY in *Bright Eyes* (1929). Balfour's sound debut, *The Brat* (1930), based on the 'Squibs' character, was only moderately successful, and her popularity waned in the talkies. 'Britain's Queen of Happiness' was anything but happy in her private life: her 1931 marriage to composer Jimmy Campbell ended in divorce in 1941; and, after a failed stage comeback in 1952, she attempted suicide, and was a recluse for the last 20 years of her life.

OTHER BRITISH FILMS: *Squibs* (1921), *Mord Em'ly, The Wee McGregor's Sweetheart, Squibs Wins the Calcutta Sweep* (1922), *Squibs, MP, Squibs' Honeymoon* (1923), *Satan's Sister, Somebody's Darling* (1925), *The Sea Urchin* (1926), *A Little Bit of Fluff, Paradise* (1928), *The Vagabond Queen* (1929), *Raise the Roof* (1930), *Evergreen, My Old Dutch* (1934), *Forever England, Squibs* (1935), *Eliza Comes to Stay* (1936), *29, Acacia Avenue* (1945). AS.

Balfour, Michael (*b* Kent, 1918 – *d* Surrey, 1997). Actor. Reputedly born in Detroit, rumple-featured, chirpy Balfour was, for two decades the very stuff of which British 'B' MOVIES were made, and accounted, in his numerous barmen, boxers, spivs and drunks, for many of the pleasures incidental to their often-perfunctory plots. After debut with New York's Group Theatre, he was on stage in England in 1936, served with the RAF during WW2, and was in the West End production of *Born Yesterday* (for which he acquired his US background) in 1947. His first film was *Just William's Luck* (1947), and 90 more followed. He was one of the house-invading criminals in *The Small Voice* (1948), a cheerful smuggler in *The Quiet Woman* (1951, for TEMPEAN, in whose films he was a fixture), and assorted low-lifers, with names like Fingers, Chubby and

Barney, in those second features livelier for his presence. There was also a steady trickle of 'A' movies, and when the market for 'B's petered out he found steady work in more ambitious productions such as *The Oblong Box* (1969) and POLANSKI's *Macbeth* (1971), as one of the murderers, and played a scientist in the PINEWOOD-filmed *Batman* in 1989. He also set up his own circus in the late 70s. Married **Kathleen Stuart**, who appeared in his first film.

OTHER BRITISH FILMS INCLUDE: *No Orchids for Miss Blandish* (1948), *Obsession* (1949), *Cage of Gold, Blackout* (1950), *13 East Street* (1952), *Genevieve, River Beat* (1953), *The Gilded Cage, One Good Turn* (1954), *Impulse* (1955), *Reach for the Sky* (1956), *Man from Tangier, Look Back in Anger* (1959), *Carry On Constable, The Hellfire Club* (1960), *The Sicilians* (1964), *Fahrenheit 451* (1966), *The Fixer* (1968), *The Private Life of Sherlock Holmes* (1970), *Joseph Andrews* (1976), *The Krays* (1990).

Ball, Angeline Actress. Up-and-coming 90s player, seen in several British co-productions, including *The Commitments* (1991, UK/US) and *The Gambler* (1997, UK/Hung/Neth). Her best role was as the hero's girlfriend/sister-in-law in *The General* (1998, UK/US). To the US for late 90s films.

OTHER BRITISH FILMS: *Two Nudes Bathing, Brothers in Trouble* (UK/Ger) (1995), *Trojan Eddie* (1996, UK/Ire).

Ball, Vincent (*b* Sydney, 1924). Actor. Strapping Ball worked his way to England on a cargo boat and had his first film work as underwater double for Donald HOUSTON in *The Blue Lagoon* (1948). After RADA training, he embarked on a busy film career, straddling 'A' and 'B' features. Had rewarding roles in *A Town Like Alice* (1956) and *Sea of Sand* (1958), both drawing on his bronzed outdoor image, and typical 'B' FILMS included *Dangerous Voyage* (1954) and *Face in the Night* (1956). His easy good humour made him a popular figure on children's TV in Britain in the 50s, telling tales of Australian life. Later became an authoritative character player in Australia's burgeoning cinema, as in '*Breaker' Morant* (1980).

OTHER BRITISH FILMS INCLUDE: *Talk of a Million* (1951), *The Drayton Case* (1953), *The Black Rider* (1954), *The Blue Peter* (1955), *The Baby and the Battleship* (1956), *Robbery Under Arms* (1957), *Blood of the Vampire, Danger Within* (1958), *Dead Lucky* (1960), *A Matter of WHO* (1961), *Carry on Cruising* (1962), *Mouse on the Moon* (1963), *Oh! What a Lovely War* (1969), *Clinic Xclusive* (1971).

BIBLIOG: Autobiography, *Buck Jones, Where Are You?*, 1997.

Ballantyne, Nell (*b* ? – *d* Glasgow, 1959) Actress. Sturdy Scots player memorable as Morland GRAHAM's loyal wife in *The Shipbuilders* (1943), her first film.

OTHER BRITISH FILMS: *Mr Emmanuel* (1944), *Fortune Lane* (1947), *Bonnie Prince Charlie* (1948), *Laxdale Hall* (1953), *The Bridal Path* (1959).

ballet One of the prestige successes of post-war British cinema was POWELL AND PRESSBURGER's romantic melodrama *The Red Shoes* (1948), set in a highly-coloured version of the ballet world and highlighted by the performance of the eponymous ballet specially composed for the film. The same PRODUCER-DIRECTOR TEAM enjoyed less acclaim with *The Tales of Hoffmann* (1951), which combined opera and ballet and again featured ballet stars, Moira SHEARER and Robert HELPMANN. Shearer danced twice more in British films: in one episode of *The Man Who Loved Redheads* (1945) and, parodying her former roles, in Powell's *Peeping Tom* (1960). Gene Kelly's British-made *Invitation to the Dance* (1954, UK/US), three tales in dance and mime, failed at the box-office; in 1963 four ballets were filmed as *An Evening with the Royal Ballet*, with Margot Fonteyn and Rudolf NUREYEV; and in the 1971 *Tales of Beatrix Potter* Royal Ballet members, in masks, danced the children's stories. Two ambitious dance films were Karel REISZ's *Isadora* (1968), starring Vanessa REDGRAVE as the controversial dancer, and the melodramatic *Nijinsky* (1980, UK/US).

OTHER BRITISH FILMS with ballet sequences included *Dance Pretty Lady* (1932, remade as *Carnival* in 1946), *St Martin's Lane* (1938), *The Little Ballerina* (1947), *Secret People* (1951), *Twice Upon a Time*, *Star of My Night* (1953), *Dance Little Lady* (1954), *Nutcracker* (1982), and, to comic effect, *Make Mine a Million* (1959) and *The Intelligence Men* (1965).

Balmain, Pierre (*b* St Jean-de-Maurienne, France, 1914 – *d* Paris, 1982). Costume designer. Abandoned architecture to study dress designing, working for Edward Molyneux in London before opening his own fashion house in Paris in 1945, also designing for theatre and films. The elegant simplicity which was his trademark was seen in such international films as *Tender is the Night* (1961, US), but most of his screen work (often in collaboration) was in British films such as *The Deep Blue Sea* (1955, with Anna DUSE) and *The Roman Spring of Mrs Stone* (1961, with Beatrice DAWSON). Made Officier de la Légion d'Honneur, 1978.

OTHER BRITISH FILMS INCLUDE: *Night Without Stars* (1951, with Julie Harris), *Mr Topaze* (1961), *In the Cool of the Day* (1963, with Orry-Kelly), *The Devil's Widow* (1971, with Dawson).

Bamber, David (*b* 1954) Actor. Best known for his playing of the outrageous sycophant, Mr Collins, in the 1995 TV version of *Pride and Prejudice*, Bamber also made his mark as the obnoxious yuppy in Mike LEIGH's *High Hopes* (1988). So far, his main work has been for TV, including *The Buddha of Suburbia* (1994), *My Night with Reg* (1996).

OTHER BRITISH FILMS: *Privates on Parade* (1982), *The Doctor and the Devils* (1985), *Dakota Road* (1990).

Bamforth and Co. of Holmfirth, Yorkshire, founded in 1870 by James Bamforth, was a leading manufacturer of postcards and magic lantern slides. In collaboration with William Riley, it began film production circa 1899, but in 1903 abandoned motion pictures in favour of its primary occupation. Bamforth re-entered film production in 1914–15, releasing a number of comedy SHORTS, directed by Cecil BIRCH, featuring Reginald Switz (as Winky), Alf Foy, Lily Ward, and child actress Baby Langley. AS.

Banbury, Frith (*b* Plymouth, 1912). Actor. RN: Frederick Banbury. Prolific stage actor (from 1933) and producer who made a handful of films of which the most significant was *The Life and Death of Colonel Blimp* (1943), as Roger LIVESEY's effeminate school-friend, 'Babyface' Fitzroy.

OTHER BRITISH FILMS INCLUDE: *Snowbound*, *Bond Street*, *The History of Mr Polly* (1948), *The Huggetts Abroad* (1949).

Banerjee, Victor (*b* Calcutta, 1946). Actor. Perceptive Indian player first in Satyajit Ray's *The Chess Players* (1977) and since in several British films, notably David LEAN's *A Passage to India* (1984), in the pivotal role of Dr Aziz, and the MERCHANT IVORY's *Hullabaloo over Georgie and Bonnie's Pictures* (1978, UK/Ind). Starred as an Indian immigrant posing as a doctor in London in *Foreign Body* (1986) and in POLANSKI's *Bitter Moon* (1992, UK/Fr).

Banes, Lionel (*b* Manchester, 1904). Cinematographer. Entered films in 1929 as camera operator at GAINSBOROUGH. At EALING from 1939, he entered the main phase of his career, in 1942, as director of photography and special effects there. In the latter capacity he worked on *Dead of Night* (1945), *Nicholas Nickleby* and *The Loves of Joanna Godden* (1947). He shot five

Ealing films, including *Against the Wind* (1947) and *Passport to Pimlico* (1949). In the latter 50s, his career drifted into 'B' MOVIES and into TV, including 26 short films starring Boris KARLOFF as Colonel March.

OTHER BRITISH FILMS INCLUDE (c, unless noted): *The Captive Heart* (2uc) (1946), *Train of Events*, *The Blue Lamp* (2uc) (1949), *The Magnet* (1950), *The Good Beginning* (1953), *The Night My Number Came Up* (1955), *No Road Back* (1956), *The Surgeon's Knife* (1957), *Grip of the Strangler* (1958), *Submarine X-1* (1968).

Bangura, Roberto (*b* London, 1962). Director. One full-length feature, *The Girl with Brains in Her Feet* (1997), about a teenage girl's athletic and sexual aspirations, and two SHORT FILMS, *Monday* (1995 also produced) and *Sidney's Chair* (1995, + sc, e), suggest Bangura's is a talent to watch. Directed some TV, including *Down to Earth* (2000).

Banks, Leslie (*b* Liverpool, 1890 – *d* London, 1952). Actor. Oxford-educated, on stage from 1911, Banks entered films in Hollywood in the famous horror piece, *The Most Dangerous Game* (1932, aka *The Hounds of Zaroff*), returned to Britain for *Strange Evidence* (1933, UK/US) and became an important character star. A facially-paralysing injury in WW1 left him without the leading man's conventional good looks, but did not preclude interesting roles. He starred for HITCHCOCK in *The Man Who Knew Too Much* (1934) and *Jamaica Inn* (1939), Michael POWELL in *The Fire Raisers* (1933), *Red Ensign* and *The Night of the Party* (1934), Zoltán KORDA in *Sanders of the River* (1935), bearing the white man's burden in Africa, and Thorold DICKINSON in *The Arsenal Stadium Mystery* (1939). His civilised, rugged persona was cleverly exploited in *Went the Day Well?* (1942) as the treacherous squire; he was a memorably inviting Chorus in OLIVIER's *Henry V* (1944); and in his last film, *Madeleine* (1949), he was Ann TODD's oppressive Victorian father. Awarded CBE in 1950.

OTHER BRITISH FILMS: *The Tunnel* (1935), *Debt of Honour*, *The Three Maxims* (1936, UK/Fr), *Wings of the Morning*, *Fire Over England*, *Farewell Again*, *21 Days* (1937), *Dead Man's Shoes*, *Sons of the Sea*, *Guide Dogs for the Blind* (short) (1939), *The Door with Seven Locks*, *Busman's Honeymoon*, *Neutral Port* (1940), *Cottage to Let*, *Ships with Wings*, *Give Us More Ships* (short) (1941), *The Big Blockade* (1942), *Mrs Fitzherbert* (1947), *The Small Back Room* (1949), *Your Witness* (1950).

Banks, Monty (*b* Cesana, Italy, 1897 – *d* Arona, Italy, 1950). Actor, director. RN: Mario Bianchi. Comic dancer who went first to the US in 1914, where he acted in many films, also writing and producing some; in 1928, he came to Britain, where he became a director, occasionally playing bit parts in his own films. Now best remembered as Gracie FIELDS' second husband, he worked prolifically in Britain until 1940 when, under threat of internment, he and Fields returned to the US, where he directed Laurel and Hardy in *Great Guns* (1941) and acted in *Blood and Sand* (1941) and *A Bell for Adano* (1945). Directed Fields in four films, including her British swansong, *Shipyard Sally* (1939), and George FORMBY in the enjoyable *No Limit* (1935).

OTHER BRITISH FILMS INCLUDE: (d, unless noted) *Cocktails* (1928), *His First Car*, *Kiss Me Sergeant* (+ a), *Why Sailors Leave Home* (1930), *Old Soldiers Never Die* (+ a, p), *Poor Old Bill* (1931), *For the Love of Mike* (1932), *You Made Me Love You* (1933, + a), *Falling in Love* (+a), *Father and Son* (1934), *So, You Won't Talk* (1935, + a), *Queen of Hearts* (1936), *We're Going to Be Rich*, *Keep Smiling* (1938); (a) *Weekend Wives* (1928), *Atlantic* (1929), *Hold 'em Jail* (1932).

Bannen, Ian (*b* Airdrie, Scotland, 1928 – *d* Loch Ness, 1999). Actor. Bannen made an easy transformation from handsome young leading man to character player of screen and TV (e.g. curmudgeonly Dr Cameron in *Dr Finlay*, 1993–95). Made stage debut at the Gate Theatre, Dublin, in 1947, and was much praised for his London performance as Jamie in *Long Day's Journey into Night* (1958). Entered films in 1956, starring for the BOULTINGS as the young prince in *Carlton-Browne of the FO* (1958), the romantic lead in *A French Mistress* (1960), and an embittered Korean war veteran in *Suspect* (1960). Notable character roles included the irascible grandfather in *Hope and Glory* (1987) and the conniving Jackie in *Waking Ned* (1999, UK/Fr/US). In recent decades, much in TV and international films; AAn (Supporting Actor) in *The Flight of the Phoenix* (1965, US). Died in car crash.

OTHER BRITISH FILMS INCLUDE: *Private's Progress* (1956), *The Birthday Present* (1957), *Behind the Mask* (1958), *Macbeth* (1961), *Station Six Sahara* (1962, UK/Ger), *Psyche 59* (1963), *Mister Moses* (UK/US), *The Hill* (1965), *Lock Up Your Daughters!* (1969), *Jane Eyre* (1970), *Fright* (1971), *Doomwatch, The Offence* (1972), *The Mackintosh Man* (1973), *Eye of the Needle* (1981), *Gandhi* (1982, UK/Ind), *Defence of the Realm* (1985), *Lamb* (1985), *The Big Man* (1990), *Damage* (1992, UK/Fr), *To Walk with Lions* (UK/Can/Kenya), *Best* (UK/Ire) (2000).

Bannerman, Celia (*b* Abingdon, 1944). Actress. Daughter of dramatist/actress **Kay Bannerman** (*b* Hove, 1919), who wrote several screenplays. First appeared in *The Tamarind Seed* (1974), later in three films for Christine EDZARD: *Biddy* (1983), *Little Dorrit* (1987), *As You Like It* (1992), and *The Land Girls* (1998, UK/Fr). Much stage and TV work.

Bannerman, Margaret (*b* Toronto, Canada, 1896 – *d* Englewood, New Jersey, 1976). Actress. RN: Legrand. On stage 1915, entered films in Maurice ELVEY's *Justice* (1917), made a few British talkies, and finished her career in patrician character roles in such Hollywood films as *Cluny Brown* (1946). Her stage career eclipsed her sporadic screen appearances, but she was a sharply likeable blonde presence in them.

OTHER BRITISH FILMS INCLUDE: *The Gay Lord Quex* (1917), *Hindle Wakes, Goodbye* (1918), *Lady Audley's Secret* (1920, as Lady Audley), *Lily Christine, Two White Arms* (1932), *Over the Garden Wall* (1934), *I Give My Heart* (1935).

Bannister, Trevor (*b* Durrington, 1936). Actor. Best known as insatiably lecherous Mr Lucas, of 'menswear,' in TV's *Are You Being Served?* (1973–83), repeating this role in the film version (1977). Appeared in a few other films including *Au Pair Girls* (1972), *Hostage* (1992), and *Captain Jack* (1998).

Baptiste, Thomas (*b* Georgetown, Guyana, 1936). Actor. Black singer and actor in films since the late 50s, coming to notice as the resident African in the 'liberal' household in *Sunday Bloody Sunday* (1971). Since then roles have not been plentiful, but he has appeared in such US blaxploitation films as *Shaft in Africa* (1973), the UK-Kenya co-production, *Rise and Fall of Idi Amin* (1980) and the telemovie, *Nairobi Affair* (1988).

OTHER BRITISH FILMS INCLUDE: *Beyond This Place* (1959), *Dr Terror's House of Horrors* (1964), *Help!, The Ipcress File* (1965), *Two Gentlemen Sharing* (1969), *The Dogs of War* (1980), *Ama* (1991), *The Secret Laughter of Women* (1999, UK/Can).

Barber, Frances (*b* Wolverhampton, 1958). Actress. Intelligent, distinctively beautiful leading lady on stage and TV (e.g. *The Ice House*, 1997; the Bolter in *Love in a Cold Climate*, 2000) as well as screen. After major success as warm-hearted Rosie in *Sammy and Rosie Get Laid* (1987), she might have been expected to become a full-blown film star, but seems drawn to the kinds of offbeat roles and films which attract critical

attention rather than big audiences. Thus, she was Joe Orton's (Gary OLDMAN) sister in *Prick Up Your Ears* (1987), brassy wife to Oldman in *We Think the World of You* (1988) and obsessed mother of a child who 'sees' fairies in *Photographing Fairies* (1997).

OTHER BRITISH FILMS INCLUDE: *The Missionary* (1981), *Acceptable Levels* (1983), *A Zed & Two Noughts* (1985, UK/Neth), *Castaway* (1986), *Young Soul Rebels* (1991), *Soft Top, Hard Shoulder* (1992), *Still Crazy* (1998), *Esther Kahn* (UK/Fr), *Shiner* (2001).

Barber, Glynis (*b* Johannesburg, 1955). Actress. Attractive South African leading lady whose career has been divided between TV and screen. Played the Patricia ROC role in the 1983 remake of *The Wicked Lady*, inevitably overshadowed by Faye Dunaway's eponym. Has filmed only sporadically since, enjoying most popularity as Makepeace, the well-born policewoman in TV's *Dempsey and Makepeace* (1985–86).

OTHER BRITISH FILMS INCLUDE: *Terror* (1978), *Edge of Sanity* (1988, UK/Hung), *Déjà Vu* (1998, UK/US).

Barber, Paul (*b* Liverpool, 1952). Actor. Black actor who has made the most of limited chances, particularly as Mr Horse in *The Full Monty* (1997, UK/US), and in the TV drama, *The Shoreline* (1985). Reunited with Robert CARLYLE in *The 51st State* (2001, UK/Can/US).

OTHER BRITISH FILMS: *Porridge, The Long Good Friday* (1979), *Madonna and Child* (1980), *Priest* (1994).

Barbour, Joyce (*b* Birmingham, 1901 – *d* London, 1977). Actress. On stage from childhood (1915) and stayed there for 50 years, often in revues and musicals. On screen intermittently from 1920, played supporting roles in ten talkies, sometimes bossy as in *Don't Take It to Heart!* (1944), as the screen wife of her real-life husband Richard BIRD, sometimes dizzy, as in *It Started in Paradise* (1952), as Kay KENDALL's aunt with outmoded fashion ideas. Everley GREGG replaced her in *Brief Encounter* (1945) after shooting began.

OTHER BRITISH FILMS: *Enchantment* (1920), *Diamond Cut Diamond* (1932), *Sabotage* (1936), *The Housemaster* (1938), *Saloon Bar* (1940), *Stop Press Girl* (1949), *The Captain's Paradise* (1953), *The Main Chance* (1964).

Bardot, Brigitte (*b* Paris, 1934). Actress. 'Sex kitten', latterly conservationist, and for over two decades a major icon of French cinema who starred in two British films: *Doctor at Sea* (1955), as Dirk BOGARDE's love interest; and the peculiar Spanish-shot British Western *Shalako* (1968). Otherwise, her career history belongs elsewhere.

Baring, Aubrey (*b* London, 1912 – *d* London, 1987). Producer. Eton- and Cambridge-educated, Baring entered the film industry in 1935, served in the RAF (1939–45), and returned to films as producer on some less happy GAINSBOROUGH efforts, including the notoriously inept *Bad Lord Byron* (1949). In collaboration with Maxwell SETTON he produced some acceptable entertainments for their MAYFLOWER PICTURES CORPORATION, among them the elegant Paris-set thriller *The Spider and the Fly* (1949), the poignant WW2 romance *So Little Time* (1952) and the African adventure *South of Algiers* (1952).

OTHER BRITISH FILMS INCLUDE: *Snowbound* (1948), *Fools Rush In* (1949), *Cairo Road* (1950), *Appointment in London, They Who Dare* (1953), *The Key* (1958), *Cone Of Silence* (1960), *The Wrong Arm of the Law* (1962).

Baring, Norah (*b* Newton Abbot, 1907). Actress. RN: Baker. Gently appealing Baring appeared in three silent films for Anthony ASQUITH – *Underground, The Runaway Princess*

(UK/Ger), *A Cottage on Dartmoor* (1929) – and starred for HITCHCOCK in *Murder!* (1930) and E.A. DUPONT in *Two Worlds* (1930). The rest were mainly second features.

OTHER BRITISH FILMS: *The Celestial City* (1929), *At the Villa Rosa, Should a Doctor Tell?* (1930), *The Lyons Mail* (1931), *The House of Trent* (1933), *Little Stranger* (1934).

Barkas, Geoffrey (*b* Richmond, Surrey, 1896 – *d* Esher, 1979). Director. One of Britain's better directors of his day, Barkas was expert at location filming. A former cinematographer under Sydney BLYTHE, he made one-reelers in Canada in 1923, which became the British *Tall Timber Tales* series (1923). He was associated with BRITISH INSTRUCTIONAL FILMS in the 20s, handled a lot of location direction and shooting on major features of the 30s, and after WW2, Barkas was a producer with Children's Entertainment Films, SHELL FILM UNIT and BP. Won an Oscar for his DOCUMENTARY, *Wings over Everest* (1934, co-d); received both the Military Cross and an OBE.

BRITISH FILMS INCLUDE: (d, unless noted) *Secrets of Nature* series (1923), *Palaver* (1926,+ sc), *The Somme* (1927,+ sc), *Q-Ships* (1928, co-d), *The Third Gun* (1929), *Tell England* (1931, co-d), *Rhodes of Africa* (1936, co-d), *OHMS* (p), *King Solomon's Mines* (2ud) (1937), *The Little Ballerina* (1947, p), *Dusty Bates* (1947, p).

BIBLIOG: Natalie Barkas, *Behind the Camera*, 1934. AS.

Barker, Eric (*b* Thornton Heath, 1912 – *d* Faversham, 1990). Actor. Beginning as a child performer in silent films, then making his mark as a radio actor pre- and post-war, often in partnership with his wife, Pearl HACKNEY, in such popular programmes as *Merry-Go-Round*, short, bespectacled Barker became a sought-after character actor in British films from the later 50s. As the fussing vicar in *Happy is the Bride* (1957) and in such other BOULTING brothers' satires as *Private's Progress* (1956), *Brothers in Law* (1956), for which he won a BAA, and *Heavens Above!* (1963), as well as in several 'CARRY ON' romps, he established a persona of pompous, prissy or put-upon minor officialdom which was a guarantee of at least several minutes of pure pleasure in invariably comic circumstances.

OTHER BRITISH FILMS INCLUDE: *Nelson* (1918), *His Dearest Possession* (1919), *Carry on London, Concert Party* (1937), *On Velvet* (1938), *Blue Murder at St Trinian's* (1957), *Carry on Sergeant, Bachelor of Hearts* (1958), *Left, Right and Centre* (1959), *Carry on Constable, Watch Your Stern* (1960), *On the Fiddle* (1961), *Carry on Cruising, The Fast Lady, On the Beat* (1962), *The Mouse On the Moon, Father Came Too!* (1963), *Carry On Spying* (1964), *Those Magnificent Men . . .* (1965), *Doctor in Clover* (1966), *There's a Girl in My Soup* (1970), *That's Your Funeral* (1972), *Carry On Emmannuelle* (1978).

BIBLIOG: Autobiography, *Steady Barker!*, 1956.

Barker, Ronnie (*b* Bedford, 1929). Actor. Popular, portly British TV comedian, rarely starred in films, but was very funny as an unreliable builder in *Father Came Too!* (1963) and a memorable Friar Tuck in *Robin and Marian* (1976, UK/US). A household name for the series, *The Two Ronnies* (1971–86), in which he and diminutive Ronnie CORBETT got away with an amazing amount of smut without causing the slightest offence, and in 1979 he successfully transferred his cynical old lag from the TV series *Porridge* to the big screen.

OTHER BRITISH FILMS: *The Silent Witness* (1954, short), *Wonderful Things* (1958), *Kill or Cure* (1962), *The Cracksman, Doctor in Distress* (1963), *A Home of Your Own* (short), *The Bargee* (1964), *Runaway Railway* (1965), *The Man Outside, Ghost of a Chance* (1967), *Futtocks End* (1969).

Barker, Sir W(illiam) G(eorge) (*b* London, 1867 – *d* London, 1951). Producer. A pioneering producer, Barker entered films in 1901 with the formation of the AUTOSCOPE COMPANY, becoming head of the WARWICK TRADING COMPANY in 1906, and forming BARKER MOTION PICTURE PHOTOGRAPHY in 1908. His first studio was an open-air stage at Stamford Hill, but in 1902, he purchased property on Ealing Green, and in 1907 built the first covered studio at EALING. Barker gained a reputation for the production of spectacular films wherein art played a secondary role to size and splendour: *Henry VIII* (1911) with Sir Herbert Beerbohm TREE, *East Lynne* (1913), *Sixty Years a Queen* (1913), *Brigadier Gerard* (1915) with Lewis Waller, *Jane Shore* (1915), *and She* (1916) with Alice Delysia. He retired in 1919 and the studios were acquired by GENERAL FILM RENTERS in 1920. Barker's last films are *Her Lonely Soldier* (1919), *The Flag Lieutenant* (1919) *and Odds Against Her* (1919). AS.

Barker Motion Picture Photography Ltd was one of the most prominent of early producers, founded by W.G. BARKER in December 1909 with a studio in EALING (opened 1910). The company's initial film was *Henry VIII* (1911), starring Sir Herbert Beerbohm TREE, and it was the first in a line of prominent dramas, including *East Lynne* (1913), *Sixty Years a Queen* (1913), *Jane Shore* (1915), and *She* (1916). MELODRAMAS and CRIME THRILLERS, featuring a stock company of players headed by Blanche FORSYTHE and Fred PAUL, were the company's staple until WW1, when production slowed and Barker began to produce military dramas such as *Brigadier Gerrard* (1915). Barker's last films (all 1919) were *The Beetle, The Flag Lieutenant, Her Lonely Soldier,* and *Odds against Her*, and in 1920 the company was taken over by GENERAL FILM RENTERS. AS.

Barkworth, Peter (*b* Margate, 1929). Actor. Furrow-browed, RADA-trained TV star of such well-regarded series as *Telford's Change* (1979), on stage from 1948, with a more modest career in the cinema. Glimpsed in small, telling roles for Ralph THOMAS in *No Love for Johnnie* (1961), as a new, eager MP, and as Michael REDGRAVE's discreet valet in *No, My Darling Daughter* (1961), and much later as the anxious aircraft captain in *International Velvet* (1978). He had a small role in the US-made *Patton* (1970).

OTHER BRITISH FILMS INCLUDE: *A Touch of Larceny* (1959), *Tiara Tahiti* (1962), *Downfall* (1964), *Where Eagles Dare* (1968), *Escape from the Dark* (1976, UK/US), *Champions* (1983), *Wilde* (1997, UK/Ger/Jap/US).

Barnabe, Bruno (*b* London, 1905). Actor. RADA-trained Barnabe, on stage from 1923, in films from 1934 (often for John STAFFORD's company), saw war service from 1940–46, and returned to the stage before filming again. Often appeared as a saturnine heavy, like the nightclub doorman in *Pit of Darkness* (1961) or the Pharaoh in *The Mummy's Shroud* (1966). Married Avice LANDONE.

OTHER BRITISH FILMS INCLUDE: *Escape Me Never* (1935), *Wake Up Famous* (1936), *Dreaming Lips* (1937), *Portrait of Alison* (1955), *The Lady is a Square* (1958), *Drop Dead Darling* (1966), *Sinbad and the Eye of the Tiger* (1977).

Barnard, Ivor (*b* London, 1887 – *d* London, 1953). Actor. Hatchet-faced Barnard was an ideal Wemmick in *Great Expectations* (1946), and, during his 20-odd years on screen, lent his spiky features to a memorable gallery of sinister, furtive and mean types. An austere workhouse-board Chairman in *Oliver Twist* (1948), he was still giving the poor a bad time as a duplicitous almoner in *Time Gentlemen Please!* (1952), was a mean-spirited pub habitué in *Great Day* (1945), but briefly and wildly funny as a demented bus-driver in *Don't Take It to Heart!* (1944). On stage from 1908 and screen from 1920 (*The Skin Game*); a major British character actor.

OTHER BRITISH FILMS INCLUDE: *Sally in Our Alley* (1931), *The Blind Spot, Illegal* (1932), *The Good Companions* (1933), *Princess Charming* (1934), *The 39 Steps, Foreign Affaires* (1935), *The Mill on the Floss* (1937), *Pygmalion* (1938), *Cheer Boys Cheer, The Stars Look Down* (1939), *Quiet Wedding* (1941), *The Silver Fleet, Escape to Danger* (1943), *Hotel Reserve, English Without Tears* (1944), *The Wicked Lady, Caesar and Cleopatra* (1945), *So Well Remembered* (1947), *So Evil My Love, The Queen of Spades* (1948), *Madeleine* (1949), *Beat the Devil* (1953, UK/It/US).

Barnes, Barry K. (*b* London, 1906 – *d* London, 1965). Actor. Stylish, sophisticated, RADA-trained leading man on stage from 1927; in films a decade later. In appearance and style, he recalled the US actor Franchot Tone; nearer home, he shared Rex HARRISON's debonair persona. Popular pre-war in *This Man is News* (1938) and *This Man in Paris* (1939), both with Valerie HOBSON, and in *The Girl in the News* (1940) he co-starred with Margaret LOCKWOOD. On stage during WW2; post-war, there were only two further films: with Lockwood again, as a wily insurance investigator, in *Bedelia* (1946) and as a crooked nightclub proprietor in *Dancing with Crime* (1947). Was married (2) to Diana CHURCHILL.

OTHER BRITISH FILMS: *Dodging the Dole* (1936), *You're the Doctor, Who Goes Next?, The Return of the Scarlet Pimpernel, The Ware Case, Prison Without Bars* (1938), *Spies of the Air* (1939), *Two for Danger, Law and Disorder* (1940).

Barnes, Binnie (*b* London, 1905 – *d* Los Angeles, 1998). Actress. Blonde former chorus girl, entered films in 1929, went to Hollywood in 1934, and became a fixture as the heroine's wise-cracking friend or bitchy 'other woman', in the likes of *Holiday* (1938). Her British career, following stage successes, included nearly 20 films in the early 30s, famously as ill-fated Catherine Howard in KORDA's *The Private Life of Henry VIII* (1933). Returned to Britain in 1938 for *The Divorce of Lady X*, as the giddy much-married Lady Mere, having played the lead in the 1933 version, *Counsel's Opinion*, and in the 50s she played in three modest spectacles, technically British but mainly shot in Europe: *Shadow of the Eagle* (1950), *Decameron Nights* (1952), *Malaga* (1954), and produced *Thunderstorm* (1956, UK/Sp). Married Columbia production chief Mike FRANKOVICH.

OTHER BRITISH FILMS INCLUDE: *Love Lies, Dr Josser KC, Out of the Blue* (1931), *Partners Please, The Innocents of Chicago* (1932), *A Taxi to Paradise, Their Night Out, Heads We Go!* (1933), *The Lady is Willing, The Private Life of Don Juan* (1934).

Barnes, John Historian. While so many histories of cinema pay only lip service to the earliest years, John Barnes' five volume series *The Beginnings of the Cinema in England: 1894–1901* demonstrates the considerable riches to be unearthed from the Victorian cinema period alone. An idiosyncractic, un-ashamedly pedantic mix of technical history, biography, rare illustrations and catalogue, volume one was published in 1976, and revised when the full series was eventually re-published under a uniform title in 1996–98. Each volume meticulously documents a year in invention, production and EXHIBITION, making the first, highly creative years of British film uniquely well documented. Luke McKernan.

Barnes, Peter (*b* London, 1931). Dramatist, screenwriter. Former film critic and story editor, Barnes, educated at Stroud Grammar, has worked as a screenwriter in cinema since 1959 (on Sidney HAYERS' *The White Trap*). Co-authored *Ring of Spies* (1963) with Frank LAUNDER, and adapted his own play,

The Ruling Class (1971), to the screen with a success that ought to have been, but was not, followed by other major work. Then, he was Oscar-nominated for his screenplay for the popular romance, *Enchanted April* (1992). Has written (sometimes directed) a good deal of TV, including *Alice in Wonderland* (2000).

OTHER BRITISH FILM: *Offbeat* (1960).

Baron, Elizabeth (*b* 1910). Screenwriter. Entered films as set designer, but worked mainly as screenwriter in the 40s, particularly on Leslie HOWARD's *The Lamp Still Burns* (1943, co-sc) and on Maurice ELVEY's *Beware of Pity* (1946).

OTHER BRITISH FILMS: *Salute John Citizen* (1942), *The Gentle Sex* (1943, unc), *Medal for the General* (1944), *Strawberry Roan* (1945), *Dick Barton Strikes Back* (1949).

Barr, Douglas (*b* 1931). Actor. Entered films as youthful gang member in EALING's ground-breaking comedy, *Hue and Cry* (1946), appeared in two youth-oriented films for John BAXTER, *Fortune Lane* (1947) and *The Last Load* (1948), and starred in *It's Fine to be Young* (1948), the BBC's first teenage comedy series.

OTHER BRITISH FILMS INCLUDE: *Dance Hall, Madeleine* (1949), *One Good Turn* (1951, short).

Barr, Jean-Marc (*b* Bitburg, Germany, 1960). Actor. Hand-some Barr's nearly twenty films have been ubiquitously made (France, US, Denmark, etc.), including the award-winning Scandinavian *Breaking the Waves* (1996, Den/Fr/Neth/Nor/ Swe) and *Dancer in the Dark* (2000, UK/Den/Fin/Fr/Ger/Ice/ Neth/Nor/Swe/US). His wholly British films have been *The Frog Prince* (1984), *Hope and Glory* (1987) as Sammi DAVIS's wartime lover, and *The Scarlet Tunic* (1997), from Thomas HARDY's novella. Trained at Guildhall School; in 1999 directed his first film, *Lovers*, for his own company, Bar-Nothing Productions, set up in 1998. Also stage and TV, in UK and France.

Barr, Patrick (*b* Akola, India, 1908 – *d* London, 1985). Actor. Tall, Oxford-educated former engineer who performed on stage, screen and (most popularly) TV from the 30s until the 80s. Specialised in professional men, always solid, sometimes stolid, playing 20 supporting roles before the war. Post-war, returned to the stage for four years, then was busy in films for two decades. He brought quiet authority to 'B' MOVIES such as *Black Orchid* (1952) and as assorted inspectors, captains and lords in such 'A' movies as *The Lavender Hill Mob* (1951), *The Dam Busters* (1955), *The Satanic Rites of Dracula* (1974) and especially as King Richard in *The Story of Robin Hood . . .* (1952).

OTHER BRITISH FILMS INCLUDE: *Meet My Sister* (1933), *Things to Come* (1936), *Return of the Scarlet Pimpernel* (1937), *The Gaunt Stranger* (1938), *Man on the Run* (1949), *You're Only Young Twice!* (1952), *The Intruder* (1953), *The Brain Machine* (1954), *It's Never Too Late* (1956), *Next to No Time!* (1958), *Billy Liar* (1963), *The Black Windmill* (1974), *The First Great Train Robbery* (1978), *Octopussy* (1983).

Barrett, Jane (*b* London, 1923 – *d* London, 1969). Actress. Pretty brunette on stage from 1938 and radio (over 2000 BBC productions). Sporadic film appearances, starting with *The Citadel* in 1938, then post-war as Derek Bond's wife in *The Captive Heart* (1946). For EALING, she went to Australia for *Eureka Stockade* (1949). Much TV.

OTHER BRITISH FILMS: *Colonel Bogey* (1948), *Time Gentlemen Please!, The Sword and the Rose* (1953), *Bond of Fear* (1956), *Change Partners* (1965).

Barrett, Ray (*b* Brisbane, 1926) Actor. Craggy-featured actor who worked in Australian radio and TV before going to

England in 1958, where he became a fixture in British TV shows like *The Troubleshooters* (1966–71) and appeared in a dozen films including the clever thriller, *Touch of Death* (1962). Returned to Australia in 1975, and became a major figure in its renascent film industry.

OTHER BRITISH FILMS INCLUDE: *Mix Me a Person*, *Jigsaw* (1962), *To Have and to Hold*, *80,000 Suspects* (1963), *The Amorous Milkman* (1974).

Barrett, Sean (*b* London, 1941) Actor. After promising roles as a child actor, especially as the gangling slow-witted Willy in *Bang! You're Dead* (1953), came a disappointing adult career, though he had better opportunities in TV (*Softly, Softly, Z Cars*), radio (member, BBC Drama Company, 1969–71) and theatre (in *Suite and Three Keys*, Noël COWARD's last West End appearance, 1966). Was the resentful son of an Irish widower in *The Genie* (1953), a young Rostov in King Vidor's *War and Peace* (1956, US/It), and the younger brother in *Sons and Lovers* (1960). There were nondescript roles in the ensuing decades, including voice-only roles in animated features *The Dark Crystal* (1982), *Labyrinth* (1986), and a continuing role in TV's *Brush Strokes* in 1986.

OTHER BRITISH FILMS INCLUDE: *Escapade* (1955), *Dunkirk*, *A Cry from the Streets* (1958), *Sink the Bismarck!* (1960), *Great Catherine* (1967), *Robin Hood Junior* (1975).

Barrie, Amanda (*b* Ashton-under-Lyne, 1939). Actress. RN: Broadbent. Pertly pretty Barrie was better known for her TV work (e.g. Alma Sedgwick in *Coronation Street*) than for her limited screen career which reached its apotheosis when she played the eponymous Egyptian in *Carry On Cleo* (1964) to Sid JAMES's Antony. On West End stage from 1961.

OTHER BRITISH FILMS: *Operation Bullshine* (1959), *A Pair of Briefs* (1961), *Doctor in Distress*, *Carry On Cabby* (1963), *I've Gotta Horse* (1965), *One of Our Dinosaurs is Missing* (1975, UK/US).

Barrie, Sir James (*b* Kirriemuir, Scotland, 1860 – *d* London, 1937). Dramatist. Barrie's whimsies have attracted US more than British film-makers in the sound era, but there were a half-dozen British silent versions of his plays including *The Little Minister* (1915) and *What Every Woman Knows* (1917). He also made his own films, including the SHAKESPEARE spoof, *The Real Thing at Last* (1916) and the spoof WESTERN, *How Men Love* (1914), starring Bernard SHAW and G.K. Chesterton! There have been several versions of *Peter Pan*, including a modern reworking as *Second to the Right and Straight on Until Morning* (1980, UK/US) and most recently Steven Spielberg's bloated *Hook* (1991, US); US adaptations of *The Little Minister*, *What Every Woman Knows* (1934) and *Quality Street* (1937); and at least four of *The Admirable Crichton*, the 1957 British version directed by Lewis GILBERT retaining some of the original's feeling for CLASS nuances. Barrie co-authored the screenplay for *As You Like It* (1936), starring Elisabeth BERGNER, with whose waif-like charm he was fascinated.

Barrie, John (*b* New Brighton, 1917 – *d* York, 1980). Actor. Sturdy character player in all acting media, including starring role on TV as Ted Willis's *Sergeant Cork* (1963–64). Effortlessly convincing as the humane police inspector in *Victim* (1961) and the angry, grieving grandfather in *Life for Ruth* (1962), and appeared in *Song of Norway* and *Patton* (1970, US).

OTHER BRITISH FILMS INCLUDE: *The Wild and the Willing* (1962), *Lancelot and Guinevere* (1962), *The Oblong Box* (1969), *The Laughing Girl Murder* (1973).

Barrie, Nigel (*b* Calcutta, 1889 – *d* Los Angeles, 1971). Actor. Well-groomed Hollywood leading man of late 1910s and 20s,

who starred in 38 US features (1917–27), making his debut in the 1916 serial *Beatrice Fairfax*. Career took a nose-dive when he came to England in the 20s and he was reduced to character work. Also active on stage in UK and US; WW1 service with Royal Flying Corps in Canada.

BRITISH FILMS: *The Ringer*, *The Forger* (1928), *The Plaything*, *Under the Greenwood Tree* (1929), *Old Soldiers Never Die*, *Dreyfus* (1931), *Passenger to London* (1937), *Anything to Declare?* (1938). AS.

Barrie, Wendy (*b* Hong Kong, 1912 – *d* Englewood, NJ, 1978). Actress. RN: Jenkins. Came of a distinguished family, and took her acting name from godfather J.M. BARRIE. As much socialite as actress, red-blonde Barrie began her career in the chorus line, was noticed in 1932 by Alexander KORDA, and appeared in several modest films for him (e.g. *Cash*, 1933) and others, before he cast her as Jane Seymour in the hugely popular *The Private Life of Henry VIII* (1933). This proved a major boost, and in 1934 she arrived in Hollywood where she stayed for the rest of her career. She had real charm, was an agreeable actress, but never achieved more than minor leading lady status on screen. Became a popular talk-show host on US TV and appeared as herself in *It Should Happen to You* (1953).

OTHER BRITISH FILMS INCLUDE: *Collision*, *Wedding Rehearsal*, *The Barton Mystery* (1932), *It's a Boy!*, *The House of Trent* (1933), *Murder at the Inn*, *There Goes Susie* (1934).

Barringer, Michael Screenwriter. Very prolific from the late 20s and through most of the 30s, much associated with 'QUOTA QUICKIES' and particularly with director Leslie HISCOTT, on comedies like *Crazy People* (1934) and thrillers like *Death on the Set* (1935), and co-directed *Murder at Covent Garden* (1932) with Hiscott. Also directed *Down Channel* (1929, + sc), and, with Geoffrey BARKAS, co-directed *The Infamous Lady* (1928) and *The Right to Live* (1933, + sc).

OTHER BRITISH FILMS INCLUDE: *That's My Wife* (1933), *Annie, Leave the Room!*, *A Fire Has Been Arranged* (co-sc) (1935), *The Great Barrier* (1937, co-sc), *Sabotage at Sea* (1942), *Dusty Bates* (1947).

Barron, Keith (*b* Mexborough, 1934). Actor. Stern-visaged, sandy-haired star and supporting player of about ten films of the 70s. Made a few minor comedies and several in the horror/fantasy genre, and suddenly appeared again in the 1996 musical, *La Passione*. Did some notable TV work, including *Telford's Change* (1979), as Hannah GORDON's lover.

OTHER BRITISH FILMS INCLUDE: *Baby Love* (1967), *SWALK*, *The Firechasers* (1970), *Nothing But the Night* (1972), *The Land That Time Forgot* (1974), *At the Earth's Core*, *Voyage of the Damned* (1976), *The Elephant Man* (1980, UK/US), *Police 2020* (1997).

Barron, Zelda. Director, continuity. After a long career in continuity on such films as *My Mother's House* (1967) as well as other experience as production supervisor and manager respectively on Lindsay ANDERSON's *If . . .* (1968) and *O Lucky Man!* (1973), Barron directed three little-noticed films in the 80s, and worked as consultant on three films for Warren Beatty – *Reds* (1981), *Love Affair* (1994) and *Bulworth* (1998). Her son is director **Steve Barron** (*b* Dublin, 1956), who has worked primarily in the US, in film, TV and music videos, but recently embarked on two UK films, *Rat* (2000, UK/US) and *Mike Bassett: England Manager* (2001).

OTHER BRITISH FILMS INCLUDE: (cont) *Sebastian* (1967), *Entertaining Mr Sloane* (1969), *Stardust* (1974), *Agatha* (1978, UK/US), *Yanks* (1979); (d) *Secret Places* (1984), *Bulldance* (1989).

Barry, Iris (*b* Birmingham, 1895 – *d* Marseilles, 1969). Critic. To designate Barry in this way is not to diminish her several other claims to grateful attention. One of the earliest female film critics, writing for the *Spectator* (1923–30) and, as film editor, for the *Daily Mail* (1926–30), in 1926 she published *Let's Go to the Pictures*, and was a founding member of the London FILM SOCIETY (1925). Today, she is probably best remembered for her work at New York's Museum of Modern Art: as librarian from 1932, as curator of its archive of books and rare films from 1935, and, from 1947, as its director.

Barry, Joan (*b* London, 1901 – *d* Marbella, Spain, 1989). Actress. RN: Marshman Bell. Probably best remembered for a film in which she did not appear: she dubbed Anny ONDRA's unsuitably accented voice in the sound version of HITCHCOCK's *Blackmail* (1929). A blonde beauty on stage from 1920, she appeared in a couple of silent films. Her main film role was as the dim suburban housewife who blossoms in *Rich and Strange* (1932). She retired on marriage, becoming a prominent society hostess.

OTHER BRITISH FILMS INCLUDE: *Hutch Stirs 'em Up* (1923), *The Happy Ending* (1925), *Atlantic* (1929), *The Outsider* (1931), *Ebb Tide, The First Mrs Fraser, Rome Express* (1932), *Mrs Dane's Defence* (1933).

Barry, John (*b* York, 1933). Composer. RN: Prendergast. One of the most prolific and distinguished names in British (and international) cinema for his film music, Barry had early experience with a military band. A rock'n'roll trumpeter, he formed the 'John Barry Seven' group in the late 50s. First film score was for *Beat Girl* (1959), and he found fame for his work on a dozen BOND adventures, beginning with *Dr No* (1962), and for his Oscar-winning song and score for *Born Free* (1965). Won further Oscars for *The Lion in Winter* (1968), *Out of Africa* (1985, UK/US) and *Dances with Wolves* (1993, US), as well as garnering BAFTA and Golden Globe awards. His credits summarise most of the main shifts in British cinema over the last several decades of the century, though since the early 80s most of his work has been located elsewhere. Formerly married to actress Jane BIRKIN. Awarded OBE in 1999.

OTHER BRITISH FILMS: *Never Let Go* (1960), *The L-Shaped Room, The Amorous Prawn, Mix Me a Person* (1962), *A Jolly Bad Fellow, From Russia with Love, Man in the Middle, The Party's Over* (1963), *Goldfinger, Seance on a Wet Afternoon, Zulu* (1964), *The Knack . . ., The Ipcress File, Thunderball, Four in the Morning, Mister Moses* (UK/US) (1965), *The Wrong Box, The Quiller Memorandum* (UK/US), *Dutchman, The Whisperers* (1966), *You Only Live Twice* (1967), *Deadfall, Boom, Petulia* (1968), *On Her Majesty's Secret Service* (1969), *The Last Valley* (1970), *Diamonds Are Forever, Murphy's War, Mary Queen of Scots, Follow Me!* (1971), *Alice's Adventures in Wonderland* (1972), *The Man with the Golden Gun, The Tamarind Seed* (1974), *The Rocky Horror Picture Show* (1975), *Robin and Marian* (1976, UK/US), *The Deep* (1977, UK/US), *Hanover Street, Moonraker* (UK/Fr) (1979), *Saturn 3* (1980), *Octopussy* (1983), *A View to a Kill* (1985), *The Living Daylights* (1987), *Chaplin* (UK/Fr/It/Jap/US), *Amy Foster* (1997, UK/Fr/US).

Barry, John (*b* London, 1935 – *d* London, 1979). Art director, screenwriter. During his sadly short life, Barry was responsible for the look of some major films, including Stanley KUBRICK's notorious *A Clockwork Orange* (1971), with its confronting design, and the UK-made, US-financed spectaculars, *Star Wars* (1977, AA art d), *Superman* (1978) and *Superman II* (1980). Wrote the story for *Saturn 3* (1980), but Stanley DONEN took over when Barry died of meningitis.

OTHER BRITISH FILMS: *Sitting Target* (1972), *Phase IV* (1973).

Bart, Lionel (*b* London, 1930 – *d* London, 1999). Lyricist, composer. RN: Begleiter. Though unable to read music, East-

Ender Bart had a very successful career in West End musicals, above all with *Oliver!*, a famously tuneful if morally and dramatically diluted version of *Oliver Twist*. Very much a phenomenon of the 60s, he never reached again the heights of *Oliver!* which was adapted to Oscar-winning effect by Carol REED in 1968, and by the early 70s he was bankrupt. His first film score was for Tommy STEELE's *The Duke Wore Jeans* (1958); he wrote the title song for *From Russia with Love* (1963); and his own musical, the period romp *Lock Up Your Daughters!*, was filmed in 1969.

OTHER BRITISH FILMS (comp – score/songs): *In the Nick* (1959), *Never Let Go* (1960), *Sparrows Can't Sing* (1962), *Man in the Middle* (1963), *Danger Route* (1967), *Black Beauty* (1971, UK/Ger/Sp), *The Optimists of Nine Elms* (1973).

Barter, John Producer. Barter and director John BAXTER, colleagues in their theatre days, formed their own company, Baxter and Barter Productions (later reorganised as UK Films), which made its first film in 1935, *A Real Bloke*, in which Barter's wife, Diana BEAUMONT, appeared. With few exceptions, Barter worked as Baxter's producer throughout the 30s.

OTHER BRITISH FILMS INCLUDE: *Birds of a Feather, The Small Man* (1935), *Men of Yesterday* (1936), *The Academy Decides, Overcoat Sam, Song of the Road, Talking Feet* (1937).

Bartholomew, Freddie (*b* Dublin, 1924 – *d* Sarasota, Florida, 1992). Actor. RN: Llewellyn. After two films in Britain as a small child, *Fascination* (1931) and *Toyland* (1932), angel-faced Bartholomew went on to major Hollywood fame as a child star of such films as *David Copperfield* (1935). His appeal dwindled as he matured and, in 1951, he retired, and went into advertising after some TV experience.

Bartlam, Dorothy (*b* Yorkshire, 1908). Actress. Yorkshire-born brunette who came to the screen in 1925 as an extra, via chorus and cabaret, and made about a dozen features, mostly 'QUOTA QUICKIES', in the early 30s. Walter FORDE's *The Ringer* (1931) was her most upmarket opportunity. Published her first novel, *Contrary-Wise* in 1931.

OTHER BRITISH FILMS INCLUDE: *Not Quite a Lady* (1928), *Stranglehold* (1931), *Immediate Possession, Fascination* (1931), *Watch Beverly, Tin Gods* (1932), *Call Me Mame* (1933).

Bartok, Eva (*b* Kecskemet, Hungary, 1929 – *d* London, 1998). Actress. RN: Szöke. Bartok spread an undistinguished career, begun in Hungary in 1947, over several countries, including the US. She was, in truth, more famous for her beauty and her romantic life: her four husbands included Hungarian producer Alexander Paal, responsible for her British debut in *A Tale of Five Cities* (1951), and German star Curt JURGENS, with whom she appeared in several German films. Highlights of her British film career were as Burt Lancaster's love interest in the swashbuckler *The Crimson Pirate* (1952, UK/US) and as a woman charged with euthanasia in *Front Page Story* (1953). Retired to Indonesia in the mid 60s.

OTHER BRITISH FILMS: *Venetian Bird* (1952), *Spaceways, Park Plaza 605* (1953), *Break in the Circle, The Gamma People* (1955), *Operation Amsterdam* (1958), *SOS Pacific* (1959), *Beyond the Curtain* (1960).

BIBLIOG: Autobiography, *Worth Living For*, 1958.

Barton, Margaret (*b* London, 1926). Actress. Looking younger than her years, Barton made an immediate impact in her first two film roles: as the railway buffet assistant in *Brief Encounter* (1945) and, especially, as Robert NEWTON's astute daughter in *Temptation Harbour* (1947), in which virtually every critic singled out her unaffected freshness and poignancy. Not conventionally pretty, and none of her other films gave her such good opportunities, though she was always likeable. RADA-trained, she had a busy stage career for nearly twenty years, scoring a major success in *Pink String and Sealing Wax* in 1943. Many TV plays.

OTHER BRITISH FILMS: *Good-Time Girl* (1947), *Fly Away Peter* (1948), *The Romantic Age, Landfall* (1949), *The Happy Family* (1952), *The Gay Dog* (1954).

Barzman, Ben (*b* Toronto, 1911 – *d* Santa Monica, California, 1989). Screenwriter. Like many Hollywood BLACKLIST victims of the late 40s, Barzman found work in the politically more liberal climate of Britain. Here, he worked with other blacklisted film-makers such as Edward DMYTRYK (*Give Us This Day*, 1949, UK/US) and Joseph LOSEY, for whom he wrote *Time Without Pity* (1957) and co-wrote the ingenious thriller *Blind Date* (1959), but Losey replaced him with Evan Jones on *The Damned* (1961). In the 60s, he began using his own name again and returned to Hollywood. Also worked in France and in 1985 was awarded the Order of Arts and Letters by the French government.

OTHER BRITISH FILMS: *The Heroes of Telemark* (1965), *The Blue Max* (1966).

Basehart, Richard (*b* Zanesville, Ohio, 1914 – *d* Los Angeles, California, 1984). Actor. Never a major star, Basehart was one of the more interesting post-war American actors, often suggesting a quiet, reflective toughness in his persona, as in *Fourteen Hours* (1951) and *Titanic* (1953). Made a handful of British films during the 50s, notably as the disaffected ex-serviceman in *The Good Die Young* (1954) and as Ishmael in *Moby Dick* (1956). Married/divorced actress Valentina CORTESE.

OTHER BRITISH FILMS: *The Stranger's Hand* (1953), *The Extra Day, The Intimate Stranger* (1956), *Passport to China* (1961).

Bass, Alfie (*b* London, 1920 – *d* London, 1987). Actor. Quintessential Cockney player of over 60 British films, as well as a stage career which began at the Unity Theatre in 1939 and considerable TV popularity in the 60s and 70s, from which he is remembered for *The Army Game* and *Bootsie and Snudge*. On screen, short, furrow-browed Bass appeared in several DOCUMENTARIES before his feature debut in *The Bells Go Down* (1943); hovered notably on the wrong side of the law in such EALING films as *It Always Rains on Sunday* (1947, as Dicey Perkins – the name says it all), and as the timid gang-member of the *The Lavender Hill Mob* (1951); and was a memorable Jerry Cruncher in *A Tale of Two Cities* (1958). Repeating his stage role, he co-starred with David KOSSOFF in the award-winning short, *The Bespoke Overcoat* (1955), and stayed close to his Cockney and Jewish roots for most of his career. He epitomises the foundation of character-playing on which the palmy days of British cinema were built.

OTHER BRITISH FILMS INCLUDE: *Holiday Camp* (1947), *The Hasty Heart, Boys in Brown, Man on the Run* (1949), *Pool of London* (1950), *The Galloping Major, High Treason* (1951), *Made in Heaven* (1952), *Top of the Form, The Square Ring* (1953), *A Kid for Two Farthings, Make Me an Offer!, Svengali* (1954), *King's Rhapsody* (1955), *Tiger in the Smoke* (1956), *Hell Drivers* (1957), *I Was Monty's Double* (1958), *The Millionairess* (1960), *Help!* (1965), *Doctor in Clover, Alfie* (1966), *Up the Junction* (1967), *The Fixer* (1968), *Revenge of the Pink Panther* (1978), *Moonraker* (1979, UK/Fr).

Bassett, Linda Actress. Notable 90s character player, in the tradition of Thora HIRD, memorable as the loving English wife of a patriarchally-inclined Pakistani in *East Is East* (2000), as Tom WILKINSON's wife in *Oscar and Lucinda* (1997, Aust/

US), and as a nurse who comically reconciles international tensions in *Beautiful People* (1999).

OTHER BRITISH FILMS INCLUDE: *Paris by Night* (1988), *Newshounds* (1990), *'Let Him Have It'* (1991), *Skallagrigg* (1994), *Haunted* (1995, UK/US), *Alive and Kicking* (1996), *Spoonface Steinberg* (1998).

Bassey, Dame Shirley (*b* Tiger Bay, 1937). Singer. Cardiff-born cabaret singer who appeared as herself in the musical comedy *La Passione* (1997), but has otherwise been heard only on the soundtrack. Sang the theme songs of three BOND films, *Goldfinger* (1964), *Diamonds Are Forever* (1971), and *Moonraker* (1979, UK/Fr), as well as the theme for *The Liquidator* (1965) and John BARRY's 'My love has two faces' for *Deadfall* (1968). Created DBE 2000.

Bastedo, Alexandra (*b* Hove, 1946). Actress. RN: Sharon MacReady. For about twenty years, British-Italian Bastedo popped up decoratively but unmemorably in films made all over the place. Apart from her half-dozen British titles, including the flop *Casino Royale* (1967), she filmed in the US, Ireland, Spain, Switzerland and Canada. Had a success in the 1967 TV series, *The Champions*.

OTHER BRITISH FILMS INCLUDE: *That Riviera Touch* (1966), *The Ghoul* (1975), *Find the Lady* (1976, UK/Can).

Batchelor, Joy (*b* Watford, Hertfordshire, 1914 – *d* London, 1991) and **Halas, John** (*b* Erzsebetfalva, Hungary, 1912 – *d* London, 1995; RN: János Halász). Animators. This husband-and-wife team are the pre-eminent animators of British film history. Halas began work in Budapest, taking over from his Hollywood-bound mentor, George PAL, and was invited to Britain in 1936 to set up a cartoon unit. Batchelor responded to his ad for an assistant, and four years later they married and co-founded Halas–Batchelor Cartoon Films. During the war they made over 60 animated information and PROPAGANDA films and posters for the MOI. Post-war, they worked prolifically, including their most famous film and the first British feature-length cartoon, *Animal Farm* (1954), from Orwell's allegorical novel. Other cartoons which had relatively wide release were *The Owl and the Pussy Cat* (1953, the first 3-D cartoon), *The Monster of Highgate Ponds* (1960) and *The Hoffnung Symphony Orchestra* (1965), and in 1956 they produced *The History of Cinema*, to celebrate 60 years of cinema. In 1960 Halas became the first chairman of the British Animation Group, set up to promote the art of the animated film. Their work was seen at many film festivals and won many awards.

OTHER BRITISH FILMS INCLUDE: *Music Man* (1936), *Pocket Cartoon* (1941), *Dustbin Parade, Filling the Gap* (1942), *Train Trouble* (1943), *The Big Top* (1944), *Handling Ships* (1945), *Charley's New Town* (1947), *Water for Firefighting* (1948), *As Old as the Hills* (1950), *Spring and Winter* (1951), *Coastal Navigation* (1953), *Cars of the Future* (1969), *What is a Computer?* (1970).

Bate, Anthony (*b* Stourbridge, 1928). Actor. Central School-trained actor of superior mien, in theatre since 1953, films since 1957's *High Tide at Noon*, usually in small roles though he starred in *Act of Murder* (1964). Notable TV has included *Smiley's People* (1982).

OTHER BRITISH FILMS: *The Big Day* (1960), *A Prize of Arms* (1961), *Stopover Forever* (1964), *Ghost Story* (1974), *Nelly's Version* (1983), *Give My Regards to Broad Street* (1984).

Bateman, Colin (*b c* 1962). Screenwriter. Bateman's screenplay for *Divorcing Jack* (1998, UK/Fr), was based on his own novel. Himself from Bangor, Bateman wrote *Crossmaheart*

(1999), a story of violence in an Irish town, and set up his own production company, Toddler Films.

OTHER BRITISH FILMS: *Wild About Harry* (UK/Ger/Ire), *The Devil You Know* (2001).

Bates, Sir Alan (*b* Allestree, 1934). Actor. Dominant British star since the early 60s, when he made the transition from the stage (debut in 1955 after national service) to screen in Tony RICHARDSON's *The Entertainer* (1960). RADA-trained, he had five years' stage experience, including *Look Back in Anger* (1956, the Royal Court) and a memorable Edmund in *Long Day's Journey into Night* (1958), before entering films and has always maintained a stage presence. His 60s work included: criminal mistaken for Christ in *Whistle Down the Wind* (1961), decent young man caught in an unpromising marriage in *A Kind of Loving* (1962), suburban social climber who doesn't stop at murder to secure *Nothing But the Best* (1964), Gabriel Oak made believably attractive to the heroine of *Far from the Madding Crowd* (1967), and iconoclast brought to heel by marriage in *Women in Love* (1969). Arguably no other British actor produced a better oeuvre in the decade.

His persona was readily adaptable to troubled integrity or demolishing wit, to sexy leading man or rumpled anti-hero. Later, when such contemporaries as Albert FINNEY and Tom COURTENAY lost their grip on the cinema-going public, Bates went from strength to strength, even in films given the brush-off by the public: for example, the transferred stage successes, *Butley* (1973, UK/Can/US) and *In Celebration* (1974, UK/Can), or Alan BRIDGES' undervalued *The Return of the Soldier* (1982). International films have included *Zorba the Greek* (1964, US/Gr), *The Fixer* (1967, US) for which he won a BAA and, holding his own with Bette Midler, *The Rose* (1978); in the 2000s, he has filmed often but abroad. He has moved easily from leading man (for, say, Julie CHRISTIE and Glenda JACKSON) to character roles. On TV, he has done superb work, as in *An Englishman Abroad* (1983), witty and painful as Guy Burgess. Awarded CBE in 1995. knighted 2003.

OTHER BRITISH FILMS: *Three on a Gas Ring* (1960, short), *The Running Man, The Caretaker* (1963), *Insh'Allah* (1965, short), *Georgy Girl* (1966), *A Day in the Death of Joe Egg, The Three Sisters* (1970), *The Go-Between* (1971), *Second Best* (1972, short), *Royal Flash* (1975), *The Shout* (1978), *Nijinsky* (1980, UK/US), *Quartet* (1981, UK/Fr), *Britannia Hospital* (1982), *The Wicked Lady* (1983), *A Prayer for the Dying* (1987), *We Think the World of You* (1988), *Mister Frost* (UK/Fr), *Hamlet* (UK/US, as Claudius) (1990), *Secret Friends* (1991), *The Grotesque* (1996).

Bates, H(erbert) E(rnest) (*b* Rushden, Northamptonshire, 1905 – *d* Canterbury, 1974). Author. Bates was displeased with the transfer of setting from Kent to Maryland in the screen version of his novel *The Darling Buds of May* (re-named *The Mating Season*, 1959). Otherwise, he was more tolerant than many authors about ADAPTATIONS of his works, British examples including *The Purple Plain* (1954), *Dulcima* (1971), *Triple Echo* (1973), *A Month by the Lake* and *Feast of July* (1995, UK/US). Also co-scripted *The Loves of Joanna Godden* (1947, with Angus MACPHAIL) and *Summer Madness* (1955, UK/US, with David LEAN). Some of his novels have been adapted for TV.

Bates, Michael (*b* Jhansi, India, 1920 – *d* Cambridge, 1978). Actor. Cambridge-educated Bates was an incisive character player for 20 years up till his early death. On stage (from 1947), he had seasons at Stratford (Ontario as well as Warwickshire), the Royal Court, and the West End. On screen, he most often played military officers, as in his first film, *Carrington VC*

(1954), or policemen, notably and comically including Malcolm McDOWELL's tormentor in *The Clockwork Orange* (1971). Comedy with a whiff of danger or madness was his forté. Often seen on TV, in such series as *Clough* (1964) and *It Ain't Half Hot Mum* (1974–77), and appeared in the US film *Patton* (1970).

OTHER BRITISH FILMS INCLUDE: *Dunkirk* (1958), *Bedazzled* (1967), *Hammerhead* (1968), *Oh! What a Lovely War* (1969), *Frenzy* (1972), *No Sex Please – We're British* (1973), *The Bawdy Adventures of Tom Jones* (1975).

Bates, Ralph (*b* Bristol, 1940 – *d* London, 1991). Actor. Most of Bates's career, curtailed by early death, was in the horror genre, as the eponymous researchers in HAMMER's *The Horror of Frankenstein* (1970) and Roy Ward BAKER's inventive *Dr Jekyll & Sister Hyde* (1971), and as Lana TURNER's dangerous son in *Persecution* (1974). TV broadened his range with two seasons of *Poldark* (1977, 1978). Was married to Virginia WETHERELL.

OTHER BRITISH FILMS: *Taste the Blood of Dracula* (1969), *Lust for a Vampire* (1970), *Fear in the Night* (1972), *The Devil Within Her* (1975), *King of the Wind* (1989).

Bateson, Timothy (*b* London, 1926). Actor. Oxford-educated character player who made his film debut as Lord Verisopht in Cavalcanti's *Nicholas Nickleby* (1947). Busiest in the 60s when he appeared in 16 films, including conventional COMEDIES such as *Father Came Too!* (1963), as one of Ronnie BARKER's skiving workmates, and 'SWINGING LONDON' pieces such as *The Knack . . .* (1965), as well as the dentist in *The Italian Job* (1969). TV work includes *Therese Raquin* (1980). Married (1953) to Sheila Shand GIBBS.

OTHER BRITISH FILMS INCLUDE: *Vice Versa* (1948), *White Corridors* (1951), *Richard III* (1955), *Devil's Bait, Yesterday's Enemy* (1959), *Jigsaw, The Golden Rabbit* (starring), *It's Trad, Dad!* (1961), *Crooks Anonymous, Nightmare* (1963), *The Evil of Frankenstein* (1964), *After the Fox, The Wrong Box* (1966), *The Anniversary, Torture Garden* (1967), *Twisted Nerve* (1968), *Loophole* (1980), *A Handful of Dust* (1987), *Les Misérables* (UK/Fr), *The Clandestine Marriage* (1999).

Bath, Hubert (*b* Barnstaple, 1883 – *d* Harefield, 1945). Composer. Trained at the RCM, Bath composed comic operas, cantatas, songs and orchestral works. Also wrote many film scores, of which he was a British pioneer, scoring the first talkie, HITCHCOCK's *Blackmail* (1929), and working for Hitchcock again on *Waltzes from Vienna* (1934) and *The 39 Steps* (1935). In 1933, he joined the GAUMONT–BRITISH music department under Louis LEVY and worked there on such notable films as *Tudor Rose* (1936) and did the rousing score for the Canadian-set adventure, *The Great Barrier* (1937). For MGM, he scored *A Yank at Oxford* (1937) and *The Adventures of Tartu* (1943), and in 1942 returned to LIME GROVE for such popular romances as *Love Story* (1944, source of 'The Cornish Rhapsody') and *They Were Sisters* (1945), as well as composing for such RAF FILM UNIT DOCUMENTARIES as *The Air Plan* and *Operational Height* (1944). His aim was for the score to intensify the emotional effect without drawing attention to itself. Father of John BATH.

OTHER BRITISH FILMS INCLUDE: *Kitty* (1929), *Wings Over Everest* (doc), *Chu-Chin-Chow, Evensong* (1934), *Rhodes of Africa* (source of 'Empire Builders' march') (1936), *Dr Syn* (1937), *Dear Octopus, Millions Like Us* (1943), *A Place of One's Own* (1944).

Bath, John (*b* London, 1916). Composer, music director. Son of composer Hubert BATH, he served with the Army Office film section, editing, composing and conducting music for Army training films during WW2. Post-war, he worked for MERTON

PARK studios as editor, composer and musical director. As well as composing for about 100 DOCUMENTARIES and SHORTS, for RANK, SHELL and other companies, Bath scored several feature films including *The Voice Within* (1945), *Circus Boy* (1947), *Man's Affair* (1949), *See How They Run* (1955), without achieving his father's distinction in this field. Also worked for TV and on Canadian and US films, including Arch Oboler's curiosity, *1+1: Exploring the Kinsey Report* (1961).

Batley, Dorothy (*b* London, 1902 – *d* London, 1983). Actress. A child star in SHORTS directed by her parents, Ernest and Ethyle, Batley made her screen debut in 1910. Two years earlier, she was carried on stage in *East Lynne*, and in 1920, she made her London stage debut in *Charley's Aunt*. Married to Guy NEWALL.
BRITISH FEATURE FILMS INCLUDE: *Bess the Detective's Daughter* (1913), *A Little Child Shall Lead Them* (1914), *The Boys of the Old Brigade* (1916), *The Angel with the Trumpet* (1949), *The Rossiter Case* (1950). AS.

Batley, Ernest C. (*b* 1873 – *d* Bournemouth, 1955) and **Batley, Ethyle** (*b* 1879 – *d* London, 1917). Actors, writers, directors. A husband-and-wife team, responsible for more than 100 films between 1910 and 1917, many starring their daughter Dorothy BATLEY. Ethyle was one of Britain's earliest female directors.
BRITISH FILMS INCLUDE: (d) *A Little Child Shall Lead Them* (d Ethyle), *When London Sleeps* (d Ernest) (1914), *War Is Hell*, *Remember Belgium* (1915, d Ethyle), *The Sins of Youth* (1919, d Ernest). AS.

Bato, Joseph (aka Josef Bato) (*b* Budapest, 1888 – *d*?). Art director. Bato studied architecture and painting (under Matisse) in Paris, entering films in 1930, with a German documentary on mural painting. Came to Britain to work as costume and assistant set designer, working first on *The Thief of Baghdad* (1940). Worked on two ARCHERS' films – *The Life and Death of Colonel Blimp* (1943) and *A Canterbury Tale* (1944) – but returned to the KORDA fold post-war to assist with costumes on *An Ideal Husband* (1947) and *Bonnie Prince Charlie* (1948) and to share the design credit on *The Third Man* (1949), before assuming full credit on several noteworthy films.
OTHER BRITISH FILMS INCLUDE: (art d, unless noted) *The Happiest Days of Your Life* (1950), *Lady Godiva Rides Again* (1951), *The Sound Barrier* (assoc art d), *The Ringer* (des) (1952), *The Intruder*, *The Heart of the Matter* (1953), *An Inspector Calls*, *The Belles of St Trinian's* (1954), *The Deep Blue Sea* (1955, ass a d).

Batty, Sir Archibald (*b* Hatfield, Hertfordshire, 1887 – *d* Budleigh Salterton, 1961). Actor. Distinguished ex-Army officer and Aldwych alumnus, who resembled Tom WALLS, and appeared as assorted military types in the 30s (e.g. Major Bond in *The Drum*, 1938). Also worked as screenwriter with MGM in Hollywood in 1932.
OTHER BRITISH FILMS INCLUDE: *Wives Beware* (1933), *The High Command* (1937), *I See Ice!* (1938), *The Four Feathers*, *The Lion Has Wings* (1939), *The Winslow Boy* (1948).

Bauer, David (aka David Wolfe) (*b* Chicago, *c* 1917 – *d* London, 1973). Actor. RN: Wolfe. Supporting player of about 20 films of the 60s and 70s, including *Live It Up* (1963), as a publicity-mad film producer, and several US films, including *Patton* (1969).
OTHER BRITISH FILMS: *Flat Two* (1962), *Man in the Middle* (1963), *The Mercenaries* (1967), *Inspector Clouseau* (1968), *The Royal Hunt of the Sun*, *Crooks and Coronets* (1969), *Diamonds Are Forever* (1971), *Embassy*, *Endless Night* (1972).

Bax, Sir Arnold (*b* London, 1883 – *d* Cork, 1953). Composer. Trained at Royal Academy of Music, Bax was interested in music as expression of emotional states, as evidenced in his passionate score for David LEAN's *Oliver Twist* (1948), his only feature-film work. During WW2, he composed the score for the RAF, ARMY and CROWN FILM UNITS production, *Malta G.C.* (1942), a tribute to the ordeal of the embattled island. Also composed the score for the award-winning documentary, *Journey Into History* (1952); in 1978, his symphonic poem, 'The Garden of Fand', was used in Ken RUSSELL's TV docu-drama *The Secret Life of Sir Arnold Bax*. Knighted in 1937 and Master of the King's Musick from 1942.

Baxendale, Helen (*b* Litchfield, 1969). After some well-noticed TV, including *Cold Feet* (1997 and since) as Rachel, desperately wanting to be pregnant, and an almost unseen film of *Macbeth* (1997), delicately pretty Baxendale was suddenly in the news for starring roles in 2000: *Ordinary Decent Criminals* (UK/Ger/Ire/US) and *Dead by Monday* (UK/Can).

Baxter, Beryl (*b* Birmingham, 1926). Actress. RN: Ivory. One of the saddest careers in British films. Baxter, on stage at Stratford in 1943, was launched as the star of Leslie ARLISS's wild – and wildly derided – costume-film melodrama, *Idol of Paris* (1948). The somewhat angular Baxter never recovered from the critical walloping and made only two further minor film appearances: in *The Man with the Twisted Lip* (1951) and, fleetingly as the villain's accomplice, in Vernon SEWELL's *Counterspy* (1953). Her stage career lasted a further decade.

Baxter, Clive (*b* 1922 – *d* 1978). Actor. Child actor who appeared in such 30s films as HITCHCOCK's *Young and Innocent* (1937, unc), KORDA's *The Four Feathers* (the hero as a boy) and Carol REED's *The Stars Look Down* (1939). After war service, he returned to the screen in *The Guinea Pig* (1948), but made only three further films.
OTHER BRITISH FILMS: *The Ghost of St Michael's* (1941), *Lady Godiva Rides Again* (1951), *The Blue Peter* (1955), *The Pure Hell of St Trinian's* (1960).

Baxter, Jane (*b* Bremen, Germany, 1909 – *d* London, 1996). Actress. RN: Feodora Forde. Quintessentially English as gentle, gracious Baxter seemed, her mother was half-German and came to England when her Bremen-based English engineer husband was killed. On stage from 1925 to 1978, she was also a popular film heroine of such 30s films as *The Clairvoyant* (1935) and *The Ware Case* (1938), as well as in the Michael POWELL 'quickie', *The Night of the Party* (1934). Much of EALING's class-bound *Ships with Wings* (1941) now seems excruciating but Baxter's charm remains potent. Made two attractive films in Hollywood (*We Live Again*, 1934, and *Enchanted April*, 1935) but disliked the experience. Post-WW2 she made only two further minor films, devoting herself to the stage. First married racing driver Clive Dunfee, killed in 1932 at Brooklands as she watched.
OTHER BRITISH FILMS INCLUDE: *Bed and Breakfast* (1930), *Flat No. 9* (1932), *The Constant Nymph* (1933), *Blossom Time* (1934), *Royal Cavalcade*, *Drake of England* (1935), *Dusty Ermine* (1936), *Confidential Lady* (1939), *The Flemish Farm* (1943), *Death of an Angel*, *All Hallowe'en* (1952).

Baxter, John (*b* Sidcup, 1896 – *d* London, 1975). Director, producer. A theatre manager before entering films as assistant director in 1932, Baxter holds an honourable minor position in British cinema as concerned chronicler of ordinary lives, especially in the 30s when such an agenda was rare. In 1935 he formed his own production company with former theatre colleague John BARTER. His films seem naive today, but are often surprisingly stylish and their heart is always in the right place. His finest film is *Love on the Dole* (1941), the Depression-set ADAPTATION of the stage success, but even pieces as didactic as *Hearts of Humanity* (1936), as moralistic as *Song of the Road* (1937), or as idiotic as *Old Mother Riley in Society* (1940 – *Stella Dallas* in DRAG, really) have beguiling decency of purpose. He made two more ambitious features in the 40s – *The Common Touch* (1941) and *The Shipbuilders* (1943), both with serious themes, a little solemnly treated – as well as popular low-brow comedies with FLANAGAN and ALLEN (*We'll Smile Again*, 1942; *Theatre Royal*, 1943; *Dreaming*, 1944; *Here Comes the Sun*, 1945) and Frank RANDLE (*When You Come Home*, 1947), and several children's films. He also produced most of his own films, and several directed by his 30s assistant Lance COMFORT, and in the early 50s he became managing director for GROUP 3, whose first film, *Judgment Deferred* (1951), he produced and directed. Baxter's work may be simplistic, but it takes real surliness to dislike it.

OTHER BRITISH FILMS (d, unless noted): *Reunion* (1932, assoc d), *Taking Ways, Doss House, Song of the Plough* (1933), *Say It with Flowers, Lest We Forget, Kentucky Minstrels, Flood Tide, Music Hall* (+ st) (1934), *A Real Bloke, The Small Man, Jimmy Boy, Birds of a Feather* (1935), *Sunshine Ahead* (p), *Here and There* (co-d short), *Men of Yesterday* (1936), *Song of the Road, Screen-Struck* (co-p, short), *Overcoat Sam* (co-p, short), *The Academy Decides* (+ co-p), *Talking Feet* (1937), *Stepping Toes* (1938), *Secret Journey, What Would You Do Chums?* (1939), *Laugh It Off, Crook's Tour, Old Mother Riley in Business* (1940), *Old Mother Riley's Ghosts* (1941), *Let the People Sing* (1942), *Old Mother Riley, Detective, When We Are Married* (1943, p), *The Grand Escapade* (1946, + p), *Bank Holiday Luck* (ex p), *Fortune Lane* (+ p) (1947), *Nothing Venture, The Last Load* (1948, + p), *Three Bags Full* (1949, + p), *The Dragon of Pendragon Castle, The Second Mate* (1950), *Ramsbottom Rides Again* (1956, + p), *The Heart Within* (1957, st), *Make Mine a Million* (1959, p).

BIBLIOG: Geoff Brown, with Tony Aldgate, *The Common Touch – The Films of John Baxter*, 1989.

Baxter, Keith (*b* Newport, Wales, 1933). Actor. RN: Baxter-Wright. RADA Bronze Medallist, 1956, and on stage in 1957, Baxter has only dabbled with films, but his eloquently morose Hal in *Chimes at Midnight* (1966, Sp/Switz) was a major contribution to Orson WELLES's masterpiece, and he appeared in several international films.

BRITISH FILMS: *The Barretts of Wimpole Street* (1956), *Family Doctor* (1958), *Peeping Tom* (1960), *Killing Time* (1998).

Baxter, R(odney) K. Neilson (*b* Twickenham, 1909). Producer. Oxford-educated producer of informational films, who began with GAUMONT–BRITISH in the early 30s. Joined SHELL in 1940 to make training films for the Admiralty and the MOI. Post-war, he became a DOCUMENTARY film-maker for Basic Films and film educator, as well as joint editor of the *Penguin Film Review* (1946–49). In the 50s, he worked with Unesco as Visual Aids Adviser. Married Kay MANDER.

Baxter, Stanley (*b* Glasgow, 1926). Actor. Best known for TV's one-man specials which foreground his skill as an impressionist, Baxter has made only limited impact in film. Following his debut as the postman in *Geordie* (1955), he made several likeable – and forgettable – comedies, of which *Crooks Anonymous* (1962) is probably the funniest.

OTHER BRITISH FILMS INCLUDE: *Very Important Person* (1961), *The Fast Lady* (1962), *Father Came Too!* (1963), *Joey Boy* (1965), *Akenfield* (1974).

BIBLIOG: Autobiography, *Stanley Baxter on Screen*, 1981.

Bayldon, Geoffrey (*b* Leeds, 1924). Actor. Rangy, prolific character player of all the acting media, who played many professional men (cynical schoolteacher in *To Sir, with Love*, 1967; boffin in *Assignment K*, 1967) before becoming a household name as a scruffy magician on TV in *Catweazle* (1970–71). Since then, in a wide range of film GENRES and popular TV.

OTHER BRITISH FILMS INCLUDE: *A Night to Remember, Idle on Parade* (1958), *Suspect* (1960), *Greyfriars Bobby* (1961), *Jigsaw* (1962), *A Jolly Bad Fellow* (1963), *Becket* (1964), *Life at the Top* (1965), *Casino Royale* (1967), *Inspector Clouseau* (1968), *Scrooge, The Raging Moon* (1970), *Asylum* (1972), *The Slipper and the Rose* (1976), *The Monster Club* (1980), *Bullshot* (1983), *Madame Sousatzka* (1988), *Tom & Viv* (1994, UK/US).

Bayley, Hilda (*b* London, 1895 – *d* London, 1971). Actress. On stage since 1913, invariably cast in upper-class roles (like Lady Driscoll in George FORMBY's *Much Too Shy*, 1942) in films. Entered films in *Sisters in Arms* (1918), starred in a dozen silents and returned in character roles in the 30s. In *Madonna of the Seven Moons* (1944), her dizzy socialite gushed, 'My dear, with a figure like yours [Phyllis CALVERT's], I should run naked through the hemlock.'

OTHER BRITISH FILMS INCLUDE: *A Soul's Crucifixion* (1919), *Carnival* (1921), *Flames of Passion* (1922), *The Scandal* (1923), *Head Office* (1936), *Jeannie* (1941), *I'll Walk Beside You* (1943), *Give Me the Stars* (1944), *My Brother Jonathan, Elizabeth of Ladymead* (1948), *Madame Louise* (1951).

Bayliss, Peter (*b* London, 1916 [sometimes given as 1922] – *d* London, 2002). Distinctive, beaky-faced character player, briefly in *Caesar and Cleopatra* (1945), then on stage before return to films in *Jet Storm* (1959). His versatility encompassed the drunken illiterate father in *Please, Sir!* (1971) and the campy Lord Grant in *Darling* (1965). Much TV, including Sleary in *Hard Times* (1994).

OTHER BRITISH FILMS INCLUDE: *From Russia with Love* (1963), *The Spy with a Cold Nose* (1966), *Pretty Polly* (1967), *Lock Up Your Daughters!, The Magic Christian* (1969), *Bullshot* (1983), *Hard Road* (1989).

BBC Films BBC theatrical features emerge from the same department responsible for single television dramas. This has long been a source of irritation for those who want the BBC to establish a theatrical arm to rival that of CHANNEL 4. However, funded by the licence fee as it is, the BBC faces certain problems in undertaking purely commercial activities, and possesses neither an in-house distribution arm nor an international sales operation. BBC Films has made around ten theatrical features a year, usually in conjunction with other producers, and its output has included *Face* (1997), *Wilde* (1997, UK/Ger/Jap/US), *Mrs Brown* (1997, UK/Ire/US), *Love Is the Devil* (1998, UK/Fr/Jap), *East is East, Ratcatcher* (1999) and *Billy Elliot* (2000). Its annual budget was recently increased from £10m to £15m by an investment deal with BBC Worldwide, the Corporation's commercial arm, but it has decided to invest more money in fewer, bigger and more commercial films. Julian Petley.

Beach, Ann (*b* Wolverhampton, 1938). Actress. RADA-trained Beach was on TV in 1954, on stage from 1957, appearing often at the Royal Court and the Theatre Royal, Stratford, and in films from *City of the Dead* (1960). Played Polly Garter in the film version of *Under Milk Wood* (1971), but the other media have used her comic talents better. Glimpsed as Hugh GRANT's mother in *Notting Hill* (1999, UK/US). Actress Charlotte COLEMAN was her daughter.

OTHER BRITISH FILMS INCLUDE: *On the Fiddle* (1961), *The Fast Lady* (1962), *Hotel Paradiso* (1966, UK/Fr), *Sebastian* (1967), *The Vanishing Army* (1978).

Beacham, Stephanie (*b* Casablanca, 1949). Actress. RADA-trained Beacham was something of a sensual misfit in British cinema, finding apter opportunities on American TV (as in *The Colbys*). She played opposite Marlon Brando in *The Nightcomers* (1971), a prequel to *The Turn of the Screw*, and most of her other British films were in the HORROR GENRE. Formerly married to John McENERY.

OTHER BRITISH FILMS INCLUDE: *The Games* (1969), *The Devil's Widow* (1971), *And Now the Screaming Starts!* (1973), *House of Mortal Sin* (1975), *Schizo* (1976), *Inseminoid* (1980), *Relative Values* (2000, UK/US).

Beaconsfield Studios Built in 1921 and used intermittently over 70 years. *See* **British Lion Film Corporation Ltd, Independent Artists, National Film and Television School**.

Beadle, Gary (*b* London, 1965). Actor. Apart from his semi-continuing role as the lover of Jennifer SAUNDERS' ex-husband in TV's *Absolutely Fabulous* (1992), Beadle has found limited chances on British screens, where roles for black actors are still scarce. His best part was in *Playing Away* (1986), the inter-racial cricket match comedy.

OTHER BRITISH FILMS INCLUDE: *Absolute Beginners* (1986), *White Mischief* (1987), *Drunk and Disorderly* (1995), *Driven* (1998), *The Imitators* (1999).

Beale, Simon Russell (*b* Penang, Malaysia, 1960). Actor. Surely destined to be a major character actor, chubby Beale, educated at St Paul's Choir School, was a memorable Earl of Moray in *Orlando* (1992, UK/Fr/It/Neth/Russ), kind, exasperated Charles in *Persuasion* (1995, TV, some cinemas), second gravedigger in BRANAGH's *Hamlet* (1996, UK/US), the press lord in *An Ideal Husband* (UK/US), and, especially, hapless Widmerpool in TV's *A Dance to the Music of Time* (1997). An acclaimed Iago in the National Theatre's 1997 *Othello*, Voltaire in *Candide*, an unforgettably moving Hamlet in 2000 and a definitive Uncle Vanya in 2002.

Bean, Sean (*b* Sheffield, 1958). Actor. Strapping, versatile RADA-trained Bean can play handsome heroes and sinister villains with equal facility – *and* without losing his regional accent. After theatre work, including a stint with the RSC, he made his film debut in *Winter Flight* (1984), followed by the violent gambler who poses for *Caravaggio* (1986), made a strong impression in the thriller *Stormy Monday* (1987), and showed off his body (what else?) as the virile Mellors in the telemovie *Lady Chatterley* (1992). Went international as the heavy in *Patriot Games* (1992) and a stiffly uninteresting Vronsky in a dire *Anna Karenina* (1997). Meanwhile, he became a major TV star in the *Sharpe* series (1993–97) as an up-from-the-ranks major in the Napoleonic Wars. He would make a great Flashman. His first wife was actress **Melanie Hill** (*b* Newcastle, *c* 1962), who appeared in *Brassed Off* (1996, UK/US).

OTHER BRITISH FILMS INCLUDE: *War Requiem* (1989), *The Field* (1990, UK/Ire), *Shopping* (1994), *Black Beauty* (1994, UK/US), *GoldenEye* (1995, UK/US), *When Saturday Comes* (1996), *Ronin* (UK/US), *The Canterbury Tales* (UK/Russ, short) (1998), *Essex Boys* (2000).

Beard, John Production designer. Entered films as assistant art director on *Life of Brian* (1979) and worked again for the MONTY PYTHON team on *Brazil* (1985) and *Erik the Viking* (1989). Responsible for the design of such distinctive films as *Map of the Human Heart* (1992, UK/Aust/Fr/Can), the remake of *The Browning Version* (1994) and the masterly *The Wings of the Dove* (1997, UK/US), in which the production design is crucial to understanding the characters' dilemmas, and *The Last Temptation of Christ* (1988, UK/Can).

OTHER BRITISH FILMS (ass art d): *The Wildcats of St Trinian's, Black Angel, Bad Timing* (1980); (art d) *Eureka* (UK/US), *An Unsuitable Job for a Woman* (1981), *Absolute Beginners* (1986), *Splitting Heirs* (1993), *The Lost Son* (1999, UK/Fr).

Beatles, The Pop Group. This phenomenally successful, mop-headed Liverpudlian pop group of the 60s consisted of, John Lennon (*b* Woolton, 1940 – *d* New York, 1980), George Harrison (*b* Liverpool, 1943 – *d* Los Angeles, 2001), Paul McCartney (*b* Allerton, 1942), and Ringo Starr (*b* Dingle, 1940, RN: Richard Starkey). Together, they appeared in the black-and-white hit film, *A Hard Day's Night* (1964), which capitalised on their cheeky insouciance as well as the legendary Mersey sound, the more ambitious but less engaging *Help!* (1965), the 50-minute *Magical Mystery Tour* (1967), and vocally, and in cartoon form only, *Yellow Submarine* (1968), and the DOCUMENTARY *Let It Be* (1970). The 1994 BIOPIC *Backbeat* chronicles their early days together.

In the face of conservative apoplexy, they were awarded MBEs in 1964. Going their separate ways, Harrison, who died of cancer, became executive producer for HANDMADE on such films as *Life of Brian* (1979), *A Private Function* (1984), *Mona Lisa* (1986) and *The Lonely Passion of Judith Hearne* (1987). Seven weeks after his death his single, 'My Sweet Lord', re-released after 31 years, topped the UK charts; Lennon, shot in the streets of New York by a fan, made a number of short films with his second wife, Yoko Ono, and starred in *How I Won the War* (1967); McCartney, who wrote many of the group's songs with Lennon, contributed music to such films as *The Family Way* (1966), *Live and Let Die* (1973), *The Honorary Consul* (1983), and played himself in *Give My Regards to Broad Street* (1984, + sc) and *Eat the Rich* (1987), and was knighted in 1996; and Starr appeared in several features including *Candy* (1968, UK/It/Fr), *The Magic Christian* (1969), *That'll Be the Day* (1973) and *Give My Regards to Broad Street* (1984). Their impact on cinema is arguable, but their films grew out of and fed their fanatical following at the time. Today, they may seem almost wholesome, but they remain indelible icons for a whole generation.

BIBLIOG: Allan Kozinn, *The Beatles*, 1995.

Beaton, Sir Cecil (*b* London, 1904 – *d* Broad Chalke, 1980). Costume designer, production designer. Harrow- and Cambridge-educated Beaton made his name as photographer of theatrical, royal and society luminaries. Began designing for the stage in 1935 and for films in 1941, winning AAs for the flowing elegance of his costume design for *Gigi* (1958, US) and *My Fair Lady* (1964, US) and his art direction on the latter. His films were almost invariably set in high society – or in the demi-monde at least. Made CBE in 1957 and knighted in 1972. Famous for his portraits and idolatry of Garbo, he was the author of seven volumes of autobiography and the subject of several biographies.

BRITISH FILMS: *Major Barbara, Dangerous Moonlight* (1941), *The Young Mr Pitt* (1942), *An Ideal Husband* (1947), *The Truth about Women* (1957), *The Doctor's Dilemma* (1958).

BIBLIOG: Hugo Vickers, *Cecil Beaton*, 1985.

Beaton, Norman (*b* British Guiana, 1934 – *d* Guyana, 1994). Actor. Beaton emigrated to Britain during 60s, distinguishing himself first on stage before starring in several TV series, notably *Empire Road* (1978–79), as a Birmingham landlord, and as the eponymous barber in the sitcom *Desmond's* (1989–94). On screen, he made the most of the meagre chances available to him, such as the charismatic hustler in *Black Joy* (1977) and as the captain of the black cricket team in *Playing Away* (1986).

OTHER BRITISH FILMS: *Up the Chastity Belt* (1971), *Pressure* (1975), *Black Joy* (1977), *Eureka* (1982, UK/US), *Real Life* (1983).

Beatty, Robert (*b* Hamilton, Canada, 1909 – *d* London, 1992). Actor. Amiably rugged leading man in smaller films and second leads in big ones, Beatty had a BA from Toronto and later trained at RADA. Made British stage and film debut in 1938, coming to major notice as 'Yank' in Ealing's wartime drama, *San Demetrio–London* (1943). His lengthy *cv* includes numerous (often American) servicemen (*Against the Wind*, 1947; *Albert RN*, 1953), gangsters (a comic one in *Her Favourite Husband*, 1950), detectives and other easy-going professionals. Some of his more memorable roles in a long career were as the dying gunman's brother in *Odd Man Out* (1947), the boxer struggling to make a comeback in *The Square Ring* (1953), and the troubled airport officer in *Out of the Clouds* (1955). Made his share of 'B' MOVIES, but also appeared in such high-profile enterprises as *Captain Horatio Hornblower RN* (1950, UK/US), *2001: A Space Odyssey* (1968) and *Superman III* (1983). Busy on stage and TV too, he was never a top star but always enjoyable company.

OTHER BRITISH FILMS INCLUDE: *Murder in Soho* (1939), *Dangerous Moonlight* (1941), *The First of the Few* (1942), *It Happened One Sunday* (1944), *Appointment with Crime* (1946), *Green Fingers* (1947), *Portrait from Life, Another Shore, Counterblast* (1948), *Twenty Questions Murder Mystery* (1949), *Calling Bulldog Drummond* (1951), *The Gentle Gunman, The Magic Box* (as Lord Beaverbrook) (1951), *The Net, The Oracle* (1953), *Portrait of Alison* (1955), *Tarzan and the Lost Safari* (1956), *Time Lock* (1957), *The Shakedown* (1959), *The Amorous Prawn* (1962), *Where Eagles Dare* (1968), *Prince for Wales* (1969, doc, assoc p), *Pope Joan* (1972), *The Pink Panther Strikes Again* (1976), *Labyrinth* (1986).

Beaudine, William (*b* New York, 1892 – *d* Canoga Park, California, 1970). Director. Entered films in 1909 as handyman and property boy for D.W. Griffith, and spent most of his 60-year career directing such distinctly non-British double-bill fodder as *Gas House Kids Go West* (1947) and *Pride of the Blue Grass* (1954). However, he directed a dozen films in England from 1934 to 1937, including several very funny farces with the great, intransigently English Will HAY. In such films as *Boys Will Be Boys* (1935) and *Windbag the Sailor* (1936), he at least recognises comic genius when he sees it and keeps out of its way – or kept the way clear for it.

OTHER BRITISH FILMS: *Get Off My Foot, Two Hearts in Harmony, Mr Cohen Takes a Walk, Dandy Dick* (1935), *It's in the Bag, Where There's a Will, Educated Evans* (1936), *Transatlantic Trouble, Said O'Reilly to McNab, Feather Your Nest* (1937).

Beaufoy, Simon (*b* Worth Valley, 1967) Screenwriter. Came to prominence as the writer of the hugely successful comedy of working-class life, *The Full Monty* (1997, UK/US), showing an acute ear for nuances of pain, scabrous humour and poignancy. Worked a similar vein to less effect in the unlikely romance, *Among Giants* (1998), written before *Monty*, but is a talent to be watched when his feeling for people and place is fully engaged. Co-founder of Footprint Films, 1994, which has produced much TV.

OTHER BRITISH FILM: *The Darkest Light* (1999, UK/Fr, + co-d).

Beaumont, Diana (*b* Thames Ditton, 1909 – *d* London, 1964). Actress. On stage from childhood, Beaumont entered films in 1928 (*Adam's Apple*) and was sometimes leading lady in modest films of the period, several of them produced by her first husband John BARTER. By 1940, she was fourth female lead to

Formby in *Let George Do It!*, and her remaining roles were miniscule.

OTHER BRITISH FILMS INCLUDE: *Alibi* (1931), *Side Streets* (1933), *Autumn Crocus* (1934), *A Real Bloke* (1935), *The Secret Voice* (1936), *Black Limelight* (1938), *Hi Gang!* (1941), *Home at Seven* (1952), *Aunt Clara* (1954), *I Was Monty's Double* (1958).

Beaumont, Ena (*b* Dundee – *d* ?). Actress. An athletic leading lady, proud of her shapely body, Beaumont co-founded Garrick in 1919 with Geoffrey MALINS, and starred in *Everybody's Doing It* (1919), *The Rainbow Chasers* (1919), *The Greater Love* (1919), *Patricia Brent, Spinster* (1919), *The Golden Web* (1920), and the *Our Girls and Their Physiques* SERIES (1920).

OTHER BRITISH FILMS INCLUDE: *The Man Who Bought London* (1916), *Adam Bede* (1918), *Watch Your Step* (1920), *All the Winners* (1920), *Settled in Full* (1920), *Watching Eyes* series (1921), *Wheels of Fate* (1922). AS.

Beaumont, Susan (*b* London, 1936). Actress. RN: Black. Daughter of musical comedy actress **Roma Beaumont** (*b* 1913 – *d* London, 2001), who appeared in two negligble 30s films, and theatrical producer Alfred Black (*b* 1913- *d*.2002). Blondely pretty, Beaumont had a brief career in the 50s, starring with Frankie HOWERD in *Jumping for Joy* (1955) and Leslie PHILLIPS in the charming *The Man Who Liked Funerals* (1958). Also on stage, as with Dora BRYAN in *Living for Pleasure* (1958).

OTHER BRITISH FILMS INCLUDE: *The Lyons in Paris* (1954), *Eyewitness* (1956), *High Tide at Noon* (1957), *Carry On Nurse* (1958).

Beaumont, Victor (*b* Berlin, 1912 – *d* 1977). Actor. Education in Berlin and Paris equipped Beaumont for playing a range of foreigners, chiefly Germans, in many British films. So, he was Von Crantz in *The First of the Few* (1942), Jogenkraut in *The Square Peg* (1958), and Colonel Weissner in *Where Eagles Dare* (1968). Minor roles in such US films as *The Kremlin Letter* (1969).

OTHER BRITISH FILMS INCLUDE: *Tomorrow We Live* (1942), *Mark of the Phoenix* (1957), *I Was Monty's Double* (1958), *The Criminal* (1960), *Shoot to Kill* (1960), *Freud* (1962, UK/US), *A Shot in the Dark* (1964), *The Heroes of Telemark* (1965).

Beavan, Jenny (*b* London, 1950) and **Bright, John** Costume designers. Although both costume designers have achieved success individually, it is their collaborations that have been critically acclaimed. Their skilful rendering of historical costume has led to AA and BAA nominations for costume design: for *Maurice* (1987) (AA only), *Howards End* (1992), *The Remains of the Day* (1993) and *Sense and Sensibility* (1995), and Bright for *Room with a View* (1986, joint-AA). Bright founded the costume firm Cosprop.

OTHER BRITISH FILMS: (both) *The Deceivers* (1988), *Jefferson in Paris* (1995); (Beavan) *Hullabaloo Over Georgie and Bonnie's Pictures* (1978, UK/Ind), *Jane Austen in Manhattan* (1980, UK/US), *A Summer Story* (1987), *Impromptu* (1991), *The Bridge* (1991), *Black Beauty* (1994, UK/US), *Jane Eyre* (1996, UK/Fr/It/US), *Metroland* (1997, UK/Fr/Sp), *Tea with Mussolini* (1999, UK/It); (Bright) *Twelfth Night* (1996, UK/US), *Onegin* (1999, UK/US), *The Last September* (UK/Fr/Ire), *The Golden Bowl* (UK/Fr/US) (2000). Fiona Clark.

Beaver Films Production company launched by Bryan FORBES and Richard ATTENBOROUGH in 1960 with *The Angry Silence*, a gesture of protest against anodyne elements of British cinema. Payment for the artists was deferred until the film, made for only £97,000, was in profit. Beaver's other films were the very successful *Whistle Down the Wind* (1961) and the unusual *Seance on a Wet Afternoon* (1964). Operating under the umbrella of ALLIED FILM MAKERS, Beaver showed what artists who cared could achieve. Beaver folded amicably when Forbes went to the US to make *King Rat* (1965).

Beaver, Jack (*b* London, 1900 – *d* 1963). Composer, music director. First associated with music for the silent cinema, Beaver began work on talkies in 1932, scoring *Baroud* (UK/Fr). He worked under Louis LEVY at SHEPHERD'S BUSH on such films as *Channel Crossing* (1933), *The 39 Steps* (1935) and *Doctor Syn* (1937), in collaboration with Hubert BATH; and in 1940 he joined WARNER BROS as composer and musical director, working on such films as *The Prime Minister* (1941). Post-war he worked on a handful of features, including *The Hasty Heart* (1949). The piano concerto he composed for *The Case of the Frightened Lady* (1940) was the prototype of such later works in the mode as 'The Warsaw Concerto' in *Dangerous Moonlight* (1941). Father of composer **Ray Beaver**, who wrote the score for Kevin BROWNLOW's *It Happened Here* (1963).

OTHER BRITISH FILMS INCLUDE: *Wings over Africa* (1936), *The Face at the Window* (1939), *This Was Paris* (1942), *The Peterville Diamond* (1942), *Candlelight in Algeria* (1943), *Gaiety George* (1946), *The Stolen Plans* (1952), *The Clue of the Missing Ape* (1953).

Beaverbrook, Lord (William Maxwell Aitken) (*b* Maple, Ontario, 1879 – *d* Cherkley, 1964). Publisher. In 1916 the then Sir Max Aitken MP established the Canadian War Records Office, which included the services of a cinematographer. The CWRO was absorbed within the War Office Cinematograph Committee, which Aitken headed, thereby controlling the British filmed PROPAGANDA campaign. As Lord Beaverbrook (1917) and Minister of Information (1918) he continued this work, producing DOCUMENTARY features, fiction films (D.W. Griffith's *Hearts of the World*) and a newsreel (*War Office Official Topical Budget*), and demonstrating the power and profitability of film as a propaganda weapon. In the 20s he ran Provincial Cinematograph Theatres and owned a half share in British Pathé and its *Pathé Gazette* newsreel. Active in film industry concerns, it was at a 1921 Cinema Exhibitors Association meeting chaired by Beaverbrook that William FRIESE-GREENE collapsed and died. Beaverbrook had a private cinema at his home in Cherkley, and made dramatised home movies starring his society and literary friends. He had little to do with film after the 20s, instead running the *Daily Express* and becoming Britain's most notable press baron. Luke McKernan.

Bebb, Richard (*b* London, 1927). Actor. Bebb's first film role, as the cocky neophyte batsman and Jack Warner's rival in love in *The Final Test* (1953), was his most notable. Also TV, including Charles II in *The Gay Cavalier* series (1953), and further sporadic films including US-made *King Ralph* (1991). Married Gwen WATFORD.

OTHER BRITISH FILMS INCLUDE: *The Yellow Teddybears*, *A Matter of Choice* (1963), *Pope Joan* (1972), *Born of Fire* (1987), *Cold Comfort Farm* (1995, TV, some cinemas).

Beck, Reginald (*b* St Petersburg, Russia, 1902 – *d* England, 1992). Editor. Doyen of British editors for over 40 years, Beck entered films in 1927, working with Ivor MONTAGU and Adrian BRUNEL, excelling himself on *Henry V* (1944 – he is credited with 'close association' with OLIVIER on this) and, 20 years later, on a string of films for Joseph LOSEY from *Eva* (1962, Fr/It) to *Steaming* (1984). His skilful editing could give distinction to such otherwise pedestrian films as *Serious Charge* (1959), when suddenly the cutting gives urgency to the central sequence.

OTHER BRITISH FILMS INCLUDE: *The Return of Raffles* (1932), *This Man is News* (1938), *The Stars Look Down* (1939), *Freedom Radio* (1940), *Quiet Wedding* (1941), *Unpublished Story* (1942), *The Long Dark Hall* (1951, + co-d), *Twice Upon a Time*, *The Beggar's Opera* (1953), *The Gypsy and the Gentleman* (1957), *Harry Black* (1958), *The Leather Boys* (1963), *Modesty Blaise* (1966), *Accident*, *Robbery* (1967), *Boom*, *Secret Ceremony* (1968), *Figures in a Landscape* (1970), *The Go-Between* (1971), *A Doll's House* (1973, UK/Fr), *The Romantic Englishwoman* (1975, UK/Fr).

Beckinsale, Kate (*b* London, 1973). Actress. Daughter of comedian Richard BECKINSALE and casting director Judy Loe, she was still at Oxford when she entered films. Her dark, vivacious beauty has carried her vividly through some showy roles: a touching Hero in Kenneth BRANAGH's *Much Ado About Nothing* (1993, UK/US); two sublimely self-assured fixits, Flora Post in *Cold Comfort Farm* (1995, TV, some cinemas) and the TV *Emma* (1996); and, in the US, Whit Stillman's lovely elegiac *The Last Days of Disco* (1998), in which assurance takes a tumble. With her looks and wit, she seems made for romantic comedy and is wasted in such overblown stuff as *Pearl Harbor* (2001, US).

OTHER BRITISH FILMS: *Uncovered* (1994, UK/Sp), *Haunted* (1995, UK/US), *Shooting Fish* (1997), *The Golden Bowl* (2000, UK/Fr/US).

Beckinsale, Richard (*b* Nottingham, 1947 – *d* London, 1979). Actor. Popular character comedian whose life was cut tragically short by heart attack. His main success, usually as gullible bumbler, was in such TV series as *The Lovers* (1970–71, filmed in 1973) and the prison-set comedy *Porridge* (1974–77). In the film of the latter he reprised his role as Lenny, as he did in the follow-up TV series, *Going Straight* (1978). Married to casting director Judy Loe, and father of actress Kate BECKINSALE.

OTHER BRITISH FILMS: *Rentadick* (1972), *Three For All* (1974).

Beckley, Tony (*b* Southampton, 1928 – *d* Los Angeles, 1980). Actor. Most often cast as supporting thugs, upmarket in *The Italian Job* (1969) and down- in *Get Carter* (1971), Also a watchful, opportunistic Poins in Orson WELLES's *Chimes at Midnight* (1966, Sp/Switz). TV includes *Callan* (1967).

OTHER BRITISH FILMS: *The Penthouse* (1967), *The Long Day's Dying*, *Lost Continent* (1968), *Assault* (1970), *The Fiend* (1971), *Sitting Target* (1972), *Gold* (1974), *Revenge of the Pink Panther* (1978).

Beckwith, Reginald (*b* York, 1908 – *d* Bourne End, Buckinghamshire, 1965). Actor, author. Jittery, garrulous, pompous or camp, for 25 years and in nearly 80 films, Beckwith was an irresistible character actor in all manner of popular British films (including many for director Val GUEST) – COMEDIES, MUSICALS, WAR FILMS, THRILLERS and costume epics. His henpecked motorist in *Genevieve* (1953) is a high spot in a film full of them; in another vein, he was heroic Lt Bowers in *Scott of the Antarctic* (1948). Film and theatre critic for *Time and Tide* and *The Spectator*, he also wrote successful plays, including *A Soldier for Christmas* and *Boys in Brown*, filmed from his screenplays in 1946 and 1949 respectively. During WW2 he was a war correspondent for the BBC.

OTHER BRITISH FILMS INCLUDE: *Freedom Radio* (1940), *My Brother's Keeper* (1948), *Mr Drake's Duck* (1950), *Another Man's Poison* (1951), *The Titfield Thunderbolt*, *The Million Pound Note* (1953), *Lease of Life*, (1954), *Night of the Demon* (1957), *The Horse's Mouth* (1958), *Expresso Bongo* (1959), *Doctor in Love* (1960), *Lancelot and Guinevere* (1962), *Thunderball* (1965).

BECTU history project Originally the ACTT History Project and the inspiration of Roy Fowler, then chairperson of ACTT's Producers/Directors Section, this ongoing oral history programme was initiated by a small group of long time members of

ACT in 1986. By 2000 they had recorded the recollections of about 500 individuals, representing most professional disciplines, detailing their careers in British film and TV and providing a unique and comprehensive history of them. Original recordings are permanently preserved by the NFTVA while copies are available for research in the BFI library. Roy Fowler.

Beddington, Jack (*b* 1893 – *d* 1959). Administrator. Influential Head of the Films Division of the MOI from 1940 until 1946. A former Director of Publicity for Shell Mex and BP Ltd, he brought necessary drive and expertise to the creation of effective PROPAGANDA, created the SHELL FILM UNIT with Stuart LEGG and Arthur ELTON, enlisted valuable advisers such as Sidney BERNSTEIN, and appointed Ian DALRYMPLE to head the GPO FILM UNIT (later called the CROWN FILM UNIT). He set up an 'Ideas Committee' to consult with producers, and helped promote such key films as *In Which We Serve* (1942) and *The Way Ahead* (1944), and, post-war, supported Humphrey JENNINGS' poetic film collage, *A Diary For Timothy* (1946), and encouraged Michael POWELL to make *A Matter of Life and Death* (1946) in the interests of Anglo-American relations. Beddington had the vision to see that *any* good film might be good propaganda and that the latter was best served by less obvious means. He was the driving force behind Shell's patronage of the arts.

BIBLIOG: Charles Drazin, *The Finest Years: British Cinema of the 1940s*, 1998.

Bedford, Brian (*b* Morley, Yorkshire, 1935). Actor. Since 1966, Bedford's film (and TV) career has been largely US-based, including *Nixon* (1995). Came to prominence on stage (*Five Finger Exercise*, 1958, as the disturbed son) in the later 50s and entered films in 1957, but remains committed to the stage. Was one of Oliver REED's yobbo mates in *The Angry Silence* (1960).

OTHER BRITISH FILMS: *Miracle in Soho* (1957), *Number Six, The Punch and Judy Man* (1962).

Bee Gees, The Pop Group British brothers, **Barry Gibb** (*b* Manchester, 1947), **Maurice Gibb** (*b* Isle of Man, 1949 – *d* Miami, 2003), and **Robin Gibb** (*b* Isle of Man, 1949), with Colin PETERSEN as their drummer, achieved great success with their original score for *Saturday Night Fever* (1977). They provided the music for *SWALK* (1970) and appeared in *Sgt Pepper's Lonely Hearts Club Band* (1978, US/Ger). The three Gibb brothers were awarded CBE, 2002.

Beeby, Bruce (*b* Australia, 1923) Actor. Appeared in over twenty films in the 50s and 60s without making a very strong impression. A handsome enough and convincing presence as a dubious doctor in *The Man in the Road* (1956) and in two Australian-based films, *The Shiralee* (1957) and *Smiley Gets a Gun* (1958).

OTHER BRITISH FILMS INCLUDE: *The Intruder, Front Page Story* (1953), *Impulse* (1955), *Child in the House* (1956), *Payroll, Pit of Darkness* (1961), *Serena* (1962), *Wuthering Heights* (1970).

Beeny, Christopher (*b* Bristol, 1941). Actor. Likably gangling Beeny, in films from childhood, playing the son in TV's *The Grove Family* (1954–57) and its film SPIN-OFF (*It's a Great Day*, 1955), made his mark as the footman Edward in the famed series *Upstairs, Downstairs* (1971–75). Played Albert the porter in the theatre version of *Brief Encounter* (2000).

OTHER BRITISH FILMS: *The Long Memory* (1952), *Trouble in Store, The Little Kidnappers* (1953), *Child's Play* (1954), *Doctor in Distress* (1963), *Pop Pirates* (1984).

Beesley, Max (*b* Burnage, 1971). Actor. Son of jazz drummer Maxton Beesley and singer Chris Marlowe, Beesley, himself also a jazz and rock musician, beguiled viewers with his jack-the-lad title role in TV's *Tom Jones* (1997) and made his film debut two years later as the lovelorn, callipered hero in Mick Davis's *The Match* (1999, UK/Ire/US). In the US, co-starred with Mariah Carey in *Glitter* (2001).

OTHER BRITISH FILMS: *Five Seconds to Spare, It Was an Accident* (UK/Fr) (2000), *Hotel* (UK/It), *The Last Minute* (UK/US) (2001), *Anita and Me* (2002).

Beeson, Paul (*b* London, 1921 – *d* Buckinghamshire, 2001). Cinematographer. Began career as camera assistant at EALING at 17, worked on several films during WW2 as well as serving in the Fleet Air Arm, and was camera operator from 1947 on such films as *Against the Wind* and *Scott of the Antarctic* (1948), working on the latter with Jack CARDIFF. His first film as DOP was *West of Zanzibar* (1954), for Ealing where he stayed until the studio closed in 1958. In the 60s, he was involved with the DISNEY British operation on such films as *Kidnapped* (1960), *The Prince and the Pauper* (1962) and *The Moon Spinners* (1964, UK/US). In later years, he did additional photography on such big international productions as *Raiders of the Lost Ark* (1981) and *Who Framed Roger Rabbit* (1988).

OTHER BRITISH FILMS INCLUDE: (c) *The Feminine Touch* (1956), *The Shiralee* (1957), *The Scapegoat, Dunkirk* (1958), *To Sir, with Love* (1967), *Candleshoe* (1977, UK/US), *The Wolves of Willoughby Chase* (1989).

Begg, Gordon (*b* Aberdeen, 1868 – *d* Los Angeles, 1954). Actor. On stage years before entering films, bald-headed Begg finished his career playing such ancients as Michael WILDING's butler-grandfather in *English Without Tears* (1944), the night porter in *Great Expectations* (1946) and a doddering general in *The Queen of Spades* (1948). Appeared in several British silent films, made four in Hollywood in the 20s, and returned to the UK in *Piccadilly* (1929), and made 20 more.

OTHER BRITISH FILMS INCLUDE: *Wife of a Thief* (1914), *Ask Beccles* (1933), *Penn of Pennsylvania* (1941), *The Million Pound Note* (1953).

Belfrage, Bruce (*b* London, 1901 – *d* Sydney, 1974). Actor. Oxford-educated, on stage in 1923, Belfrage worked for the BBC as casting director (1936–39) and founded the BBC Repertory Company, and returned to the stage after war service. First film, Michael POWELL's quickie thriller, *COD* (1932); subsequently, minor roles such as the prosing Archimandrite in *Warning to Wantons* (1948). Father of agent Julian Belfrage.

OTHER BRITISH FILMS INCLUDE: *Full Circle* (1935), *Hue and Cry* (1946), *Corridor of Mirrors* (1948), *Miss Pilgrim's Progress* (1949), *The Galloping Major* (1951).

Bell, Ann (*b* Wallasey, Cheshire, 1939). Actress. Stage and TV player who appeared in supporting roles in such films as *To Sir, with Love* (1967), as Judy GEESON's anxious mother, and *The Land Girls* (1998, UK/Fr), as Paul BETTANY's dizzy mother. Notable TV includes *The Lost Boys* (1978).

OTHER BRITISH FILMS INCLUDE: *Flat Two* (1962), *The Witches* (1966), *The Reckoning* (1969), *Champions* (1983), *When Saturday Comes* (1996).

Bell, Arnold (*b* England, 1901 – *d* Worthing, 1988). Actor. Prolific in all the acting media, in film since 1919 (*Convict 99*), austere-looking Bell played numerous detectives and military officers, especially in the 50s.

OTHER BRITISH FILMS INCLUDE: *Josser in the Army* (1932), *Doss House* (1933), *Sabotage* (1936), *The Blue Lamp* (1949), *Women of Twilight* (1952), *Appointment in London* (1953), *One Jump Ahead* (1955), *The*

Birthday Present (1957), *Virgin Island* (1958), *An Honourable Murder* (1960), *Seance on a Wet Afternoon* (1964).

Bell, Jamie (*b* Billingham, 1987) Actor. Time will tell whether Bell will have a film career into adulthood, but his playing of the titular *Billy Elliot* (2000) should be noted here. He was utterly inside the anguish of the child on the brink of puberty – and of a father-frightening career as a ballet dancer – and his performance won a BAA. He has since been in several TV shows, including the mini-series *Close and True* (2000).
OTHER BRITISH FILMS: *Who Goes There?*, *Nicholas Nickleby* (UK/US), *Deathwatch* (UK/Ger) (2002).

Bell, Tom (*b* Liverpool, 1932). Actor. Craggy, morose-looking, with a dangerous edge, Bell seems born to play mutinous seamen, or, better still, Morel in the TV mini-series *Sons and Lovers* (1983), opposite Eileen ATKINS. He played Leslie CARON's lover in *The L-Shaped Room* (1962), but mostly his looks pointed to a career as actor rather than film star, in pieces as diverse as *Wish You Were Here* (1987, as Emily LLOYD's scruffy middle-aged seducer), *The Krays* (1990, as Jack 'The Hat' McVitie), and *Prospero's Books* (1991, UK/Fr/It/ Neth).
OTHER BRITISH FILMS INCLUDE: *The Criminal* (1960), *Payroll, The Kitchen, HMS Defiant, A Prize of Arms* (1961), *Ballad in Blue* (1964), *He Who Rides a Tiger* (1965), *The Long Day's Dying* (1968), *Lock Up Your Daughters!* (1969), *Quest for Love* (1971), *Royal Flash* (1975), *The Sailor's Return* (1978), *The Innocent* (1984), *The Rainbow, Resurrected* (1989), *'Let Him Have It'* (1991), *Feast of July* (1995, UK/US), *Amy Foster* (UK/Fr/US), *Preaching to the Perverted* (1997).

Bellamy, George (*b* Bristol, 1866 – *d* London, 1944). Actor. Character player in more than 90 films over 30 years, from 1905; stage debut in 1887. Usually cast as the villain.
BRITISH FILMS INCLUDE: *Wanted a Husband* (1911), *David Garrick* (1912), *A Christmas Carol* (1914), *The Christian, The Prisoner of Zenda* (1915), *Rupert of Hentzau* (1915), *Auld Lang Syne* (1917), *Lorna Doone, Little Dorrit* (1920), *Kipps* (1921), *White Heat* (1926), *Midnight* (1931), *Mixed Doubles* (1933). AS.

Bellan, Ferdinand (aka Fernand) (*b* Vienna, 1897 – *d* Slough, 1976). Art director, costume designer. After entering the film industry in 1919 with UFA, came to London in 1936 and worked for KORDA on such films as *Dark Journey, Knight Without Armour* (1937), *The Drum* (1938) and *The Thief of Baghdad* (1940). He is uncredited on these but over 50 years later his colleague Maurice CARTER claimed that 'he dominated in the background of films', and his sketches are fluid and evocative. During WW2, he worked as assistant art director on such films as *Major Barbara* (1941), *The First of the Few* (1942) and Korda's *Perfect Strangers* (1945). Post-war, he worked on such Korda productions as *An Ideal Husband* (1947), *Bonnie Prince Charlie* (1948) and *The Third Man* (1949). Also acted in several French films.
OTHER BRITISH FILMS: (ass art d) *Summer Madness* (1955, UK/US), *Great Catherine* (1967); (des) *Dangerous Exile* (1957).

Bellew, Dorothy (*b* London, 1891 – *d* ?). Actress. Leading lady in more than 50 films between 1910 and 1918, primarily with CLARENDON.
BRITISH FILMS INCLUDE: *Father and Son* (1910), *Lorna Doone* (1912, title role), *King Charles* (1913), *The Kinema Girl, The Heroine of Mons* (1914), *Disraeli* (1916), *The Lost Chord* (1917), *Lead, Kindly Light* (1918). AS.

Bellingham, Lynda (*b* Montreal, 1948). Actress. Attractive, incisive character player in films from the 70s, seen perhaps at her best in the acrid suburban satire of TV's *At Home with the Braithwaites* (2000–02). Famous as mother in OXO ads family.
BRITISH FILMS INCLUDE: *Sweeney!* (1976), *Stand Up Virgin Soldiers* (1977), *Riding High* (1980), *The Scarlet Tunic* (1997). *Us Begins with You* (1988, UK/US), *Bodywork* (2000).

Belmont, Lara Actress. Breathtaking and heartbreaking as Ray WINSTONE's abused daughter in *The War Zone* (1999, UK/ It), her first film, she has since appeared in *Bread and Roses* (2001, UK/Fr/Ger/It/Sp/Switz/US) and *Long Time Dead* (2002, UK/US).

Belmore, Bertha (*b* Manchester, 1882 – *d* Barcelona, 1953). Actress. Belmore's character names tell it all – Mrs Brummelberg (*Happy*, 1934), Mrs Bloodgood (*Are You a Mason?*, 1934), Mrs Puddlefoot (*Keep It Quiet*, 1934), Lady Milchester (*Hold My Hand*, 1938), Dr Grimstone (*She Couldn't Say No*, 1939) and Mrs Carter-Blake (*The Midas Touch*, 1939). A stately comic presence throughout the 30s. Sister of US-based actor Lionel Belmore.
OTHER BRITISH FILMS INCLUDE: *Blossom Time* (1934), *Royal Cavalcade*, (1935), *Broken Blossoms* (1936), *Weddings Are Wonderful* (1938).

Benda, Georges (*b* Paris). Costume designer. Most of Benda's work is French but he designed sumptuous costumes for three British films: *Knight Without Armour* (1937), starring Marlene DIETRICH, *A Man About the House* (1947) and, most notably, *Saraband for Dead Lovers* (1948).
OTHER BRITISH FILMS: *Bonnie Prince Charlie, Britannia Mews* (1948).

Benfield, John Actor. Watching craggy-visaged Benfield go warily to work in an episode of *Dalziel and Pascoe* (2000), as an opportunistic old lag, or as Kernan in four 'Prime Suspects', one realises that the great tradition of British character acting survives, on TV as well as the big screen, where he has had good parts in *Buster* (1988) and *Beautiful Thing* (1996).
OTHER BRITISH FILMS INCLUDE: *Whoops Apocalypse* (1986), *Hidden Agenda* (1990), *In the Name of the Father* (1993, UK/Ire/US), *Cousin Bette* (1998, UK/US), *24 Hours in London* (2000).

Benham, Joan (*b* London, 1918 – *d* London, 1981). Actress. Best known now as Lady Prudence in TV's *Upstairs, Downstairs* (1971–75), Benham characteristically projected an upper-class image, as with Countess Astrid in *King's Rhapsody* (1955) or Lady Faraday in *The Limbo Line* (1968). She is funniest, though, in *The Man Who Loved Redheads* (1954) as Moira SHEARER's model friend Chloe, shuddering at the thought of 'old' men – 'They talk so high-flown'.
OTHER BRITISH FILMS INCLUDE: *Saturday Island* (1952), *Loser Takes All, Dry Rot* (1956), *Nowhere to Go* (1958), *Tamahine, I Thank a Fool* (1962), *The VIPs* (1963), *Murder Ahoy* (1964), *Tales of Beatrix Potter* (1971), *Rosie Dixon – Night Nurse* (1978).

Benjamin, Arthur (*b* Sydney, 1893 – *d* London, 1960). Composer. After studying at the RCM, Benjamin returned to Sydney Conservatory as Professor, then to England to join the RCM staff, and later spent time in Canada and the US. Entered films in 1934 as composer on HITCHCOCK's *The Man Who Knew Too Much*, for the 1955 remake of which he contributed the 'Storm Cloud Cantata', scored such important British films as *The Scarlet Pimpernel* (1935), *Wings of the Morning* (1937) and *An Ideal Husband* (1947), and DOCUMENTARIES such as *The Cumberland Story* (1947), *The Conquest of Everest* (1953).
OTHER BRITISH FILMS INCLUDE: *The Clairvoyant, Wharves & Strays* (doc), *Turn of the Tide, The Guv'nor* (1935), *Under the Red Robe* (1937),

The Master of Bankdam (1947), *Above Us the Waves* (1955), *Fire Down Below* (1957).

Benjamin, Floella (*b* Trinidad, 1957). Actress. In 1979, Benjamin rightly complained of the scarcity of 'straight parts' for black actresses, having been offered little, apart from children's shows, but roles as prostitutes on TV, and less in cinema films. Had a small role in the horror film, *I Don't Want to Be Born* (1975) and co-starred in *Black Joy* (1977). The chairman of BAFTA, she was appointed an OBE in 2001.

Bennett, Alan (*b* Leeds, 1934). Dramatist, screenwriter, actor. Unrivalled chronicler of middle-class aspirations and quirks, who first made his name as one of the performers in the satirical revue, *Beyond the Fringe* (televised in 1964) with Peter COOK, et al. As playwright, his successes have included *Forty Years On* and *The Madness of George III* (memorably filmed from his screenplay in 1994), and his work for TV, including *An Englishman Abroad* (1983), the story of Coral BROWNE's Moscow meeting with Guy Burgess, and the series of monologues, *Talking Heads* (1978–79, 1998), has been masterly. Other film work has included the witty screenplays for *A Private Function* (1984) and *Prick Up Your Ears* (1987), as well as appearing in *Long Shot* (1978), *The Secret Policeman's Other Ball* (1982), and *Little Dorrit* (1987), and supplying the voice of the Mock Turtle in *Dreamchild* (1985).
BIBLIOG: Alan Bennett, *Writing Home*, 1994.

Bennett, Arnold (*b* Hanley, 1867 – *d* London, 1931). Author. Bennett's work awaits serious ADAPTATION, but *Dear Mr Prohack* (1949) and, especially, *The Card* (1952) drew agreeably on his novels. There were silent versions of *The Old Wives' Tale* (1921) and of his plays *The Great Adventure* (1915) and *Milestones* (1916), and a 1976 mini-series derived from *Clayhanger*. Hollywood twice filmed his novel *Holy Matrimony* – in 1943, and in 1933 as *His Double Life*.

Bennett, Billy (*b* Liverpool, 1887 – *d* Blackpool, 1942). Actor. Scottish character player and former music-hall star who appeared in a handful of 30s films, including the revue-style musical *Calling All Stars* (1937).
OTHER BRITISH FILMS: *Radio Parade of 1935* (1934), *Soft Lights and Sweet Music* (1936), *Almost a Gentleman* (1938, starring role), *Young Man's Fancy* (1939).

Bennett, Charles (*b* Shoreham, 1899 – *d* Los Angeles, 1995). Screenwriter. Perhaps HITCHCOCK's most influential collaborator during the 30s, Bennett has only recently been given some credit for the wit, structure and tone of those beguiling entertainments that preceded the departure of both director and writer for Hollywood. He complained in later life that the director was ungenerous in acknowledging indebtedness. Bennett first appeared on screen in *John Halifax, Gentleman* (1915), and, after WW1 service, became well-known as a playwright, his play providing the basis for Hitchcock's – and Britain's – first talkie, *Blackmail* (1929). Subsequent collaborations included *The Man Who Knew Too Much* (1934; he gets co-author credit on the 1955 version), *The 39 Steps* (1935), *Secret Agent*, *Sabotage* (1936) and *Young and Innocent* (1937). Worked in Hollywood from 1938, on such films as *Foreign Correspondent* (1940), the neat 'Victorian' thriller *Kind Lady* (1951) and the famous stinker, *The Story of Mankind* (1957). In 1949, he returned to England to direct *Madness of the Heart* (1949), a hothouse melodrama with Margaret LOCKWOOD, but the rest of his career was spent in US films, except for co-

screenwriting credits on *Night of the Demon* (1957) and *The City Under the Sea* (1965, UK/US), both for Jacques TOURNEUR.
OTHER BRITISH FILMS INCLUDE: (sc, unless noted) *The Last Hour* (1930, play), *Midnight* (co-sc, play), *Deadlock* (play), *Number Please*, *Two Way Street* (co-sc) (1931), *Partners Please* (1932), *Warn London*, *Gay Love* (1934), *The Clairvoyant*, *Blue Smoke*, *Night Mail* (1935), *King of the Damned* (1936), *King Solomon's Mines* (1937).

Bennett, Compton (*b* Tonbridge Wells, 1900 – *d* London, 1974). Editor/Director. R.N. Robert Compton-Bennett. A former bandleader and commercial artist, Bennett had some amateur film-making experience before working pre-war as editor for LONDON FILMS. He edited PROPAGANDA and instructional films for the British army, at DENHAM and EALING studios (1939–44). His big chance came when Sydney BOX asked him to direct *The Seventh Veil* (1945), a huge box-office success, though it is arguable that the gloomy sex melodrama, *Daybreak* (1946, released 1948) is a more personal production. Lured to Hollywood, he directed respectable adaptations of *The Forsyte Saga* (1949) and *King Solomon's Mines* (1950), though Andrew Marton did the latter's impressive location work. The rest of his career, spent in Britain, was a tailing-off. The wartime romance, *So Little Time* (1952) had some pathos, but the fashion-world melodrama, *It Started in Paradise* (1952), needed more flamboyance than this apparently self-effacing director could summon; and *The Gift Horse* (1952) and *Desperate Moment* (1953) are so-so WAR FILMS. The rest, with the marginal exception of *After the Ball* (1957), a BIOPIC of MUSIC-HALL star, Vesta Tilley, are minor programmers, though *The Flying Scot* (1957) has a tantalising first quarter-hour.
OTHER BRITISH FILMS: (e) *Sanders of the River* (ass e) (1935), *Big Blockade* (1942), *The Flemish Farm* (1943); (d) *Freedom Must Have Wings* (1941, doc), *Find, Fix and Strike* (1942, doc), *Men of Rochdale* (1944, doc), *Julius Caesar* (1945, short), *The Years Between* (1946), *That Woman Opposite* (+ sc), *Man Eater* (1957), *Beyond the Curtain* (1960, + sc), *First Left Past Aden* (1961, doc), *How to Undress in Public Without Undue Embarrassment* (1965, sc).

Bennett, Edward (*b* Cambridge, 1950). Director, screenwriter. Intransigently ART-HOUSE film-maker whose feature film, *Ascendancy* (1982), had an unendearing polemical quality but showed engagement with subject and setting, Belfast 1920. He has directed DOCUMENTARIES (e.g. *Hogarth*, 1977, for the ARTS COUNCIL), telemovies (e.g. *Bye Bye Baby*, 1992, for CHANNEL 4), and a compelling episode of *Dalziel and Pascoe* (1997).
OTHER BRITISH FILMS: *Justine* (1976, p ass, a), *The Life Story of Baal* (1978, d, sc).

Bennett, Eileen (*b* London, 1920). Actress. RADA-trained stage actress who made a number of films in the late 30s/early 40s, returned to the stage in *Arsenic and Old Lace* (1943–45), and went to US in 1946.
BRITISH FILMS INCLUDE: *Trunk Crime*, *The Gang's All Here*, *The Outsider* (1939), *Breach of Promise* (1941), *Much Too Shy* (1942), *Thursday's Child* (1943).

Bennett, Hywel (*b* Garnant, Wales, 1944). Actor. After a notable beginning in *The Family Way* (1966), as Hayley MILLS's husband who has trouble consummating his marriage, Bennett's career seems to have lost impetus. He has kept busy, but more often on TV, including, notably, the *Shelley* series (1979) and *Tinker, Tailor, Soldier, Spy* (1979), and he was strikingly well cast on stage in *Otherwise Engaged* (1977–78). In fact, that title points to a characteristic sad-eyed detachment in his work which may help to explain why major stardom has eluded him. There were good roles in the thriller *Twisted Nerve* (1968) and the black comedy *Loot* (1970), but the excruciating penis-transplant comedy, *Percy* (1971), began the downhill slide.

OTHER BRITISH FILMS INCLUDE: *Virgin Soldiers* (1969), *The Buttercup Chain* (1970), *Endless Night, It's a 2'6" Above the Ground World* (1972), *Deadly Advice* (1994, as Dr Crippen), *Nasty Neighbours* (2000).

Bennett, Jill (*b* Penang, 1930 – *d* London, 1990). Actress. On leaving school in Godalming, Bennett joined Amersham Repertory Company, trained at RADA and began her career at Stratford (1949), when she started a four-year affair with 60-year-old actor Sir Godfrey TEARLE. This relationship inspired John OSBORNE's play, *Time Present* (1968), in which Bennett won awards for her performance. With her striking but idiosyncratic looks – wide eyes, large mouth, skin tight over the cheekbones – she was unlikely to be a conventional film leading lady. However, there is some memorable work: the whale-boat captain in *Hell Below Zero* (1953), the dubious Mrs Duberly in *The Charge of the Light Brigade* (1968), and the mad doctor's devoted assistant in *Britannia Hospital* (1982). She also appeared vividly in such TV as *Paradise Postponed* (1986). Married (1) Ted WILLIS (1962–65) and (2) Osborne (1968–77). She committed suicide, and the scattering of her ashes on the Thames is recorded in the TV documentary of a day in her friend Lindsay ANDERSON's life, *Is That All There Is?* (1994).

OTHER BRITISH FILMS INCLUDE: *The Pleasure Garden,* (1952), *Moulin Rouge* (1953), *Aunt Clara* (1954), *The Extra Day* (1956), *The Criminal* (1960), *The Skull, The Nanny* (1965), *Inadmissible Evidence* (1968), *Julius Caesar* (1970), *Full Circle* (1976, UK/Can), *For Your Eyes Only* (1981), *Lady Jane* (1985), *The Sheltering Sky* (1990, UK/It).

BIBLIOG: Jill Bennett, *Godfrey: A Special Time Remembered*, 1983.

Bennett, John (*b* Beckenham, 1928). Actor. Thin, balding character player in British films and TV for 40 years: in HORROR pieces (*The Curse of the Werewolf,* 1961; *The House that Dripped Blood,* 1970), comedy THRILLERS (*Crooks Anonymous,* 1962; *Kaleidoscope,* 1966), COSTUME DRAMAS (*Henry VIII and His Six Wives,* 1972), modern drama, *Priest* (1994), as a grim Father, and *Antonia and Jane* (1990), a sympathetic Jewish Uncle.

OTHER BRITISH FILMS INCLUDE: *The Syndicate* (1967), *The House in Nightmare Park* (1973), *Eye of the Needle* (1981).

Bennett, Peter (*b* London, 1917 – *d* London, 1989). Actor. Better known on TV (e.g. *The Adventures of Robin Hood*), Bennett played small roles in a number of films, starting as a passer-by thief in *Carry On Constable* (1960) and getting his largest role as the Master of the Otter Hounds in *Tarka the Otter* (1978). Not to be confused with the following actor.

OTHER BRITISH FILMS INCLUDE: *Fate Takes a Hand* (1961), *The Young Detectives* (1963), *Game for Three Losers* (1965).

Bennett, Peter Actor. Supporting actor of 70s and 80s British and international films, including several 'BONDS' – *Moonraker* (1979, UK/Fr), *For Your Eyes Only* (1981), *Octopussy,* 1983, *A View to a Kill,* 1985) and *Indiana Jones and the Temple of Doom* (1984, US).

OTHER BRITISH FILMS INCLUDE: *Full Circle* (1976, UK/Can), *The Dogs of War* (1980), *Highlander* (1986), *For Queen and Country* (1988, UK/US).

Bennett, Richard Rodney (*b* Broadstairs, 1936). Composer. For 40 years a major figure in British film music, now chair of composition at the RCM, Bennett won the 1974 BAA for his

Murder on the Orient Express score. Entered films in 1956 (*Face in the Night*); since involved in such high-profile entertainments as *Billy Liar* (1963), *Far from the Madding Crowd* (1967) and *Yanks* (1979), all for John SCHLESINGER, *Equus* (1977), and Mike NEWELL's two successful romantic comedies, *Enchanted April* (1992) and *Four Weddings and a Funeral* (1994, UK/US). Awarded CBE in 1998, he has worked in the US (*The Brink's Job,* 1978) and for TV (*The Ebony Tower,* 1984).

OTHER BRITISH FILMS: *Interpol, The Safecracker, Song of the Clouds* (doc) (1957), *The Man Inside, Indiscreet* (1958), *Blind Date, The Angry Hills, The Devil's Disciple, The Man Who Could Cheat Death* (1959), *The Mark, Only Two Can Play* (1961), *The Wrong Arm of the Law, The Devil Never Sleeps,* (1962), *Heavens Above!* (1963), *One Way Pendulum* (1964), *The Nanny* (1965), *The Witches* (1966), *Billion Dollar Brain* (1967), *Secret Ceremony* (1968), *Figures in a Landscape, The Buttercup Chain* (1970), *Nicholas and Alexandra* (1971, UK/US), *Lady Caroline Lamb* (1972, UK/It/US), *Voices* (1973), *The Return of the Soldier* (1982), *Swann* (1996, UK/Can).

Benson, Annette (*b* London, 1895 – *d* Santa Clara, California, 1965). Actress. Attractive leading lady who played the film star in *Shooting Stars* (1928) and starred in Warner Bros. first quota picture, *Sir or Madam* (1928). She was one of the few actresses to publish her telephone number in the *Kinematograph Year Book* in the early 30s – but nobody called.

OTHER BRITISH FILMS INCLUDE: *Squibs* (1921), *Squibs Wins the Calcutta Sweep* (1922), *Harbour Lights* (1923), *Afterglow, The Money Habit* (1924), *Downhill* (1927), *The Ringer* (1928), *The Inseparables* (1929), *Deadlock* (1931). AS.

Benson, Sir Frank (*b* Tunbridge Wells, 1858 – *d* London, 1939). Actor. Distinguished if somewhat outmoded actor-manager (1882–1932), primarily associated with Shakespearean roles, Sir Frank Benson is claimed as a mentor by Robert DONAT and Sir Cedric HARDWICKE. With his wife, Lady Constance, he appeared in four heavy-handed screen adaptations from 1911 – *Richard III, Julius Caesar, Macbeth,* and *The Taming of the Shrew* – as well as *Becket* (1923). Knighted in 1916. AS.

Benson, George (*b* Cardiff, 1911 – *d* London, 1983). Actor. Prolific small-part delight, characteristically self-effacing like the man ineffectually ordering a sandwich from Gladys HENSON's no-nonsense stall-keeper in *Highly Dangerous* (1950). The persona was given a sly twist in *The Strange Affair* (1968), as Susan GEORGE's eccentric uncle with a penchant for pornographic snapshots. RADA-trained, on stage from 1929, films from 1932 (*Holiday Lovers*), and much TV.

OTHER BRITISH FILMS INCLUDE: *Keep Fit* (1937), *Young Man's Fancy* (1939), *Convoy* (1940), *The October Man* (1947), *The Captain's Paradise* (1953), *Dracula* (1958), *The Pure Hell of St Trinian's* (1960), *The Private Life of Sherlock Holmes* (1970), *The Creeping Flesh* (1972).

Benson, Harry (*b* Swansea, 1903). Sound recordist. Benson supervised sound mainly on THRILLERS such as *The Night Has Eyes* (1942) and *Cairo Road* (1950), as well as on a couple of farces, *Gert and Daisy's Weekend* and *Banana Ridge* (1941).

OTHER BRITISH FILMS INCLUDE: *Dark Eyes of London* (1939), *East of Piccadilly* (1941), *Thursday's Child* (1943), *Murder Without Crime* (1950), *The Last Moment, Destination Milan* (1954).

Benson, Martin (*b* London, 1918). Actor. Best known for his forbidding Kralahome (what *is* a Kralahome?) in Hollywood's *The King and I* (1956), Benson, for nearly 40 years, could be counted on to give British movie heroes a bad time, as often as not compounding his sinister aura with – worse – a *foreign* threat. His role-call includes Count Mikla (*The Blind Goddess,*

1948), a passport-forging racketeer in *Man from Tangier* (1957), a Maharajah shunning the National Health in *Doctor at Large* (1957), and a Red Chinese General in *Battle Beneath the Earth* (1967). Had his comic moments, as in *Make Mine a Million* (1959), as a TV company chairman, but saturnine, oleaginous villainy was his forté in nearly 80 films, recently in *Angela's Ashes* (1999, UK/US).

OTHER BRITISH FILMS INCLUDE: *I'll Get You for This* (1950), *Wheel of Fate* (1953), *The Flesh is Weak* (1957), *The Pure Hell of St Trinian's, Oscar Wilde* (1960), *Captain Clegg* (1962), *Goldfinger* (1964), *The Magnificent Two* (1967), *The Sea Wolves* (1980, UK/Switz/US).

Bentine, Michael (*b* Watford, 1922 – *d* London 1996). Actor. Anglo-Peruvian member of the Goons radio team in the 40s, transferred less successfully to the screen in *Down Among the Z Men* (1952). Maybe too bizarre for the screen's intransigent realism, Bentine's humour surfaced only fitfully in such films as *Forces' Sweetheart* (1953) and *The Sandwich Man* (1966), both of which he co-wrote. Also popular on stage and TV.

OTHER BRITISH FILMS INCLUDE: *Raising a Riot* (1955), *I Only Arsked!* (1958), *We Joined the Navy* (1962), *Bachelor of Arts* (1969), *Rentadick* (1972).

Bentley, Dick (*b* Melbourne, 1907 – *d* London, 1995). Actor. Australian actor and comedian who became a household voice in British radio as the original 'Ron' in *The Glums*. Made a few COMEDY films around the late 50s/early 60s, including the famous Goonish short, *The Running Jumping & Standing Still Film* (1960).

OTHER BRITISH FILMS: *Desert Mice* (1959), *In the Doghouse, Double Bunk* (1961), *The Girl on the Boat, Tamahine* (1962), *Barry McKenzie Holds His Own* (1974).

Bentley, John (*b* Birmingham, 1916). Actor. Trench-coated tracker-down of indigenous thugs and foreign riff-raff in many 'B' MOVIES in which he pursued a sturdy career. There were occasional 'A' movies – the handsome romantic lead in *The Happiest Days of Your Life* (1950) – but the 'B's needed him more. Always likeable and authoritative, at his best as the sympathetic police inspector in Ken HUGHES' *Confession* (1955). Played Paul Temple three times and 'The Toff' twice; had his own TV series, *African Patrol* (1958) and appeared in the long-running serial *Crossroads* from the mid 60s. Had an unproductive fling with Hollywood in 1957, as second-lead to booze-raddled Errol FLYNN in *Istanbul*.

OTHER BRITISH FILMS INCLUDE: *The Hills of Donegal* (1947), *Calling Paul Temple* (1948), *Torment* (1949), *Paul Temple's Triumph* (1950), *Tread Softly, Salute the Toff, Black Orchid, Hammer the Toff, The Lost Hours, Paul Temple Returns* (1952), *River Beat* (1953), *Golden Ivory* (1954), *The Way Out, The Flaw* (1955), *The Singer Not the Song* (1960), *The Fur Collar* (1962).

Bentley, Thomas (*b* London, 1880 – *d* London, 1953). Director. Best known for his screen ADAPTATIONS of DICKENS. Prior to entering the film industry, he had toured the UK and Australia in Dickensian character studies, and in 1913, he wrote, directed and starred in the two-reel short, *Leaves from the Books of Charles Dickens*, shot at locations cited in the novels. This led to a contract with Cecil HEPWORTH for whom Bentley directed and wrote five Dickens adaptations: *Oliver Twist* (1912), *David Copperfield* (1913), *The Old Curiosity Shop* (1914), *The Chimes* (1914), and *Barnaby Rudge* (1915). When Universal created a British production arm, Trans-Atlantic, in 1915, it hired Bentley, and his first film there was again from Dickens, *Hard Times* (1915). He made two further silent films from Dickens – *The Old Curiosity Shop* and *The Adventures of Mr Pickwick* (1921) –

and one talkie, *The Old Curiosity Shop* (1934). Bentley's films were considered old-fashioned by the 20s, and a decline into 'QUOTA QUICKIES' in the 30s was the obvious career move.

OTHER BRITISH FEATURE FILMS INCLUDE: (d, unless noted) *The Woman Who Dared* (1915), *Milestones* (1916), *The Labour Leader* (1917), *The Divine Gift* (1918), *General Post* (1920), *A Master of Craft* (1922), *Through Fire and Water* (1923), *Money Isn't Everything* (1925), *White Heat* (1926), *Not Quite a Lady* (1928), *Young Woodley* (1930), *Hobson's Choice* (1931), *After Office Hours* (1932, + co-sc), *Hawleys of High Street* (1933), *Those Were the Days* (1934), *Music Hath Charms, Royal Cavalcade* (1935, co-d), *She Knew What She Wanted* (1936, + p), *The Last Chance* (1937), *Marigold* (1938), *Three Silent Men* (1940), *Old Mother Riley's Circus* (1941). AS.

Berens, Harold (*b* Glasgow, 1903 – *d* London, 1995). Actor. Diminutive, beaky, balding, Berens came to movies via variety and radio. He could be 'foreign', sinister or chirpy as his (usually) cameo roles demanded: a friendly barber in *Man from Tangier* (1957), a wary bookseller questioned by police in *The Painted Smile* (1961), and, for laughs, Cecil the Torturer in *Carry on Columbus* (1992).

OTHER BRITISH FILMS INCLUDE: *The Man from Morocco* (1945), *Third Time Lucky* (1949), *A Kid for Two Farthings* (1954), *The Big Money* (1958), *The Pure Hell of St Trinian's* (1960), *The Pink Panther Strikes Again* (1976), *Hear My Song* (1991).

Beresford, Bruce (*b* Sydney, 1940). Director. Beresford, one of the key names in the Australian film revival of the 70s, belongs in this book because he spent an early part of his career in Britain in the mid 60s. He got the job of chairing the BFI's Experimental Film Fund, soon renamed the BRITISH FILM INSTITUTE PRODUCTION BOARD, with a distinguished committee including Karel REISZ and Bryan FORBES. During the years of his incumbency (1966–71), he made several SHORT FILMS, mostly about artists, including *Picasso the Sculptor* (1968). Of his features, only *Barry McKenzie Holds His Own* (1974) and the little-seen *Side by Side* (1975), both starring Barry HUMPHRIES, and the OPERA film, *Aria* (1987, segment) are British-made, and his great successes, including the Oscar-winning *Driving Miss Daisy* (1989), are American.

OTHER BRITISH FILMS INCLUDE: (shorts) *Extravaganza* (1968), *Barbara Hepworth at the Tate* (1969), *Cinema of Raymond Park* (1970).

Bergin, Joan Costume designer. Has worked on several interesting 90s films, starting with *My Left Foot* (1989) and including the Irish-based co-productions *Some Mother's Son* (1996, Ire/US) and *The Boxer* (1998, UK/Ire/US), the off-beat tale of provincial theatre life, *An Awfully Big Adventure* (1995), and *The Winter Guest* (1998, UK/US). To Hollywood for *The Devil's Own* (1997).

Bergman, Ingrid (*b* Stockholm, 1915 – *d* London, 1982). Actress. Celebrated international star whose main career was conducted in 40s Hollywood, then, notoriously, under the direction of her second husband, Roberto Rossellini, in Italy. She made half a dozen notable films in Britain's less moralistic climate: *Under Capricorn* (1949), very touching as the dipsomanic Henrietta; *Anastasia* (1956), in the Oscar-winning role which led Hollywood to forgive her the Rossellini scandal; a charming comedy, *Indiscreet* (1958); *The Inn of the Sixth Happiness* (1958), as a missionary in China; *The Yellow Rolls-Royce* (1964), a cumbersome vehicle; and *Murder on the Orient Express* (1974), for which she won a best supporting actress Oscar.

Bergner,   Elisabeth (*b* Drogobytsch, Ukraine, 1897 – *d* London, 1986). Actress. The fey, gamine charms of this fragile continental leading lady, steered by her director-husband Paul CZINNER, kept her a star in British films during the 30s. Waifs were out of style among the padded shoulders of the 'strong' 40s leading ladies, but Bergner's following had responded to her soulful renderings of the eponymous *Catherine the Great* (1934), the sad mother of an illegitimate tot in *Escape Me Never* (1935), which she had played successfully on London and New York stages, Rosalind in *As You Like It* (1936), the screenplay partly prepared by an admiring J.M. BARRIE; the Thames-bound Gaby of *Dreaming Lips* (1937), and twins, one sweet, one flighty, in *Stolen Life* (1939). On stage in Zurich from 1919, and in German-speaking films from 1923, she was internationally famous in both media by the time she married Czinner in 1931, together leaving Vienna with the rise of Nazism. Her first British film was *The Loves of Ariane* (1931), a remake of her French film, *Ariane*, in turn remade as *Love in the Afternoon* (1957, US). A British subject from 1938, in 1940, she defected from Michael POWELL's *49th Parallel*, refusing to return to Britain after the Canadian location shooting and being replaced by Glynis JOHNS. She went to the US where she made one forgotten film, *Paris Calling* (1941), before returning to the stage for the next 20-odd years, when she resurfaced cinematically in several German films, then the British horror film, *Cry of the Banshee* (1970). As a film star, she flickered fleetingly but authentically.

Beristain,   Gabriel (*b* Mexico, 1949). Cinematographer. Worked on several British films in the 80s, including Derek JARMAN's *Caravaggio* (1986). Since 1990, he has worked chiefly in the US, his work including *Fatal Instinct* (1993), and *The Spanish Prisoner* (1997).
OTHER BRITISH FILMS: *Aria, The Courier* (1987), *Joyriders* (1988, UK/Ire), *Killing Dad, Venus Peter* (1989).

Berkeley,   Ballard (*b* Margate, 1904 – *d* London, 1988). Actor. In films for over 50 years, Berkeley became a household face, if not name, as TV's perpetually well-mannered, non-comprehending Major in *Fawlty Towers* (1975, 1979). Entered films in 1930's *London Melody* and played assorted professionals in several dozen films. Played the law in 'A' films (*They Made Me a Fugitive*, 1947) and 'B's (*Operation Diplomat*, 1953; *Delayed Action*, 1954), a golf-obsessed husband in *Quiet Weekend* (1946), a magistrate in *My Teenage Daughter* (1956), and court clerk in *Hostile Witness* (1968). His chiselled military features became associated with a few minutes of utterly reliable entertainment at whatever level the enterprise. Also a long stage career.
OTHER BRITISH FILMS INCLUDE: *The Chinese Bungalow* (1930), *East Meets West* (1936), *The Outsider* (1939), *In Which We Serve* (1942), *Third Time Lucky* (1949), *The Long Dark Hall* (1951), *After the Ball* (1957), *A Matter of Choice* (1963), *Confessions of a Driving Instructor* (1976), *The Wildcats of St Trinian's* (1980), *Bullshot* (1983).

Berkoff,   Steven (*b* London, 1937). Dramatist, actor. Most of Berkoff's work, political in nature, has been in the theatre, but his unusual intensity in style and appearance has made him a vivid film villain, including the memorably fanatical General Orlov in *Octopussy* (1983). Has filmed internationally (*Rambo: First Blood II*, 1985; *Beverly Hills Cop*, 1984) and done a good deal of TV. Started as an EXTRA in the late 50s, after an East End education.
OTHER BRITISH FILMS INCLUDE: (extra) *I Was Monty's Double, The Captain's Table* (1958), *The Devil's Disciple* (1959); (a) *Slave Girls* (1966),

A Clockwork Orange, Nicholas and Alexandra (1971, UK/US), *Barry Lyndon* (1975), *Joseph Andrews* (1976), *McVicar* (1980), *Outland* (1981), *Revolution* (1985, UK/Nor), *Absolute Beginners* (1986), *The Krays* (1990), *Rancid Aluminium* (2000).

Berman,   Monty (*b* London, 1912 – *d* Monte Carlo, 2002). Costumier. RN: Morris Berman. Son of Russian immigrants, EastEnder Berman began costuming films in the early 30s, was a squadron leader with the RAF in WW2, and post-war ran his family firm of Berman's (established 1884), merging it with Nathan's in 1972. He was responsible for costuming many famous stage productions, including *My Fair Lady*, and for such high-profile films as *The African Queen* (1951), *Lawrence of Arabia* (1962) and the BOND adventures. Awarded MBE for wartime services. Not to be confused with producer of same name.

Berman,   Monty (*b* London, 1913). Producer, cinematographer. RN: Nestor Berman. Berman's film career is closely linked with that of Robert S. BAKER and their production company, TEMPEAN. Berman entered films in 1930, as a camera assistant at TWICKENHAM STUDIOS, and worked as camera operator at TEDDINGTON (1934–38) and EALING (1938–40) STUDIOS. Post-war, after experience with the ARMY FILM UNIT, where he met Baker, the pair financed Tempean's first production, *A Date with a Dream* (1948), with a cast of future stars. In most of their films, Baker was the 'hands-on' producer while Berman lensed them and managed the financial side. Throughout the 50s, they made a steady stream of enjoyable, unpretentious 'B' MOVIES, moving into more ambitious territory when the supporting features market dried up, and later still into some very popular TV series. As cinematographer, Berman achieved some finely atmospheric effects, in 'B's as well as main features such as *The Siege of Sidney Street* (1960). Not to be confused with costumier of the same name.
OTHER BRITISH FILMS (co-p/c, unless noted): *Some Day* (1935, co-c), *The Edge of the World* (1937, co-c only), *Hue and Cry* (1946, cam op), *The End of the River* (cam op), *Daughter of Darkness* (1947, cam op), *The Third Man* (1949, B unit cam op). *See* Robert S. BAKER entry for fuller account of their work together and joint (largely TEMPEAN-based) filmography.
BIBLIOG: Brian McFarlane, 'Value for Money: Baker and Berman and Tempean Films' in Neil Sinyard and Ian McKillop (eds), *British Cinema in the 50s*, 2003.

Bernard,   Chris (*b* Liverpool, 1955) Director. After making the very engaging Liverpool-set Anglo-Russian romantic comedy, *A Letter to Brezhnev* (1985), Bernard's career has been disappointingly sparse: only one further, little-seen film, *A Little Bit of Lippy* (1992), a cross-dressing comedy with surreal touches, and work in a couple of TV series.

Bernard,   James (*b* Nathai Gali, India, 1925 – *d* London, 2001). Composer. Bernard's career was signposted from the start when his first music credits were on the HORROR films, *The Quatermass Experiment* and *X the Unknown* (1956). He did the score for several outpost-of-empire films (*Pacific Destiny*, 1956, *Windom's Way*, 1957, and *Nor the Moon by Night*, 1958); otherwise his career was entirely at the service of HAMMER (and other) horror, starting with *The Curse of Frankenstein* (1957). In 1997, he appeared as himself in a documentary on Hammer: his scores made substantial, sometimes subtle contributions to Hammer's success. Also co-authored the screenplay for *Seven Days to Noon* (1950) and provided music for the restored version of the 1922 classic, *Nosferatu*. Educated at Wellington College, served with the RAF (1943–45), studied at the RCM, then worked at the BBC, composing incidental music for drama, and was invited to Hammer on the recommendation of conductor, John HOLLINGSWORTH.

OTHER BRITISH FILMS INCLUDE: *Dracula, Greece the Immortal Land* (doc) (1958), *The Hound of the Baskervilles* (1959), *The Damned* (1961), *The Gorgon* (1964), *She* (1965), *The Devil Rides Out* (1967), *Frankenstein Must Be Destroyed* (1969), *The Legend of the 7 Golden Vampires* (1974, UK/HK).

Berners, Lord (*b* Arley Park, Shropshire, 1883 – *d* Berkshire, 1950). Composer. Family name Gerald Hugh Tyrwhitt-Wilson. Eton-educated diplomat and largely self-taught musician (though he had some lessons from Stravinsky), as well as painter, Berners composed the score for EALING's *The Halfway House* (1944) and *Nicholas Nickleby* (1947). Also wrote two songs for *Champagne Charlie* (1944).

Bernstein, Sidney Lewis (Lord Bernstein) (*b* Ilford, 1899 – *d* 1993). Executive, producer. Independent exhibitor who became an influential figure in the history of British film and TV. Was founder (1955) and chairman of the Granada group of companies, which included TV, theatres (60 in the mid 50s, often the work of distinguished designers) and publishing, and founder member, and member of the first Council, of the FILM SOCIETY (1924). He became an important link between Government and the film industry during WW2, as films adviser to the MOI (negotiating the US release of *The Next of Kin*, 1942 – he was liaison to the British Embassy in Washington), and as chief of the Film Section of SHAEF (Supreme Headquarters, Allied Expeditionary Forces). He instituted Saturday morning screenings for children for the study of their reactions, and produced *Rope* (1948) and *Under Capricorn* (1949) for HITCHCOCK. His stated aim was to 'entertain intelligently' and he maintained an open, experimental attitude to all aspects of the industry – and a firmly-held faith in British films. He held numerous administrative positions in and out of the industry and was created a life baron in 1969 and awarded a BFI Fellowship in 1984.

Berry, Eric (*b* Streatham, 1913 – *d* Laguna Beach, California, 1993). Actor. General-purpose supporting actor in films since *The Edge of the World* (1937), RADA-trained Berry had a notable stage success in *The Boy Friend* (1954–5) on Broadway. Appeared in several ARCHERS productions, including *The Red Shoes* (1948), was a stolid policeman in *The Intruder* (1953) and a chilly prosecuting counsel in *The Constant Husband* (1954).

OTHER BRITISH FILMS INCLUDE: *Contraband* (1940), *49th Parallel* (1941, unc), *Dear Mr Prohack* (1949), *The Story of Gilbert and Sullivan* (1953), *Double Exposure* (1954).

Berwick Street Film-makers Collective *see* **Lusia Films**

Best, Edna (*b* Hove, 1900 – *d* Geneva, 1974). Actress. Once married to Herbert MARSHALL, Best was an attractive, somewhat staid, blonde leading lady in British films of the 30s and, from 1939, a character player in Hollywood films including *The Ghost and Mrs Muir*, *The Late George Apley* (1947). On stage from 1917 and in films from 1921's *Tilly of Bloomsbury*, she emerged as a talkies star in such films as Victor SAVILLE's *The Faithful Heart* (1933), with Marshall, and *South Riding* (1938), and HITCHCOCK's *The Man Who Knew Too Much* (1934), as the sharp-shooting heroine. Continued to act in the theatre after her last film, *The Iron Curtain* (1948).

OTHER BRITISH FILMS INCLUDE: *Loose Ends, Escape* (1930), *The Calendar, Michael and Mary* (1931), *The Key* (1934), *Prison Without Bars* (1938).

Best, Richard (*b* Hull, 1916). Editor. Entered the cutting rooms at BRITISH AND DOMINION STUDIOS in 1935, and thereafter at most British studios, first as assistant editor and, from *The Lambeth Walk* (1939), with full editor credit on a range of high-profile films. These included such diverse titles as *Fame is the Spur* (1947), *The Dam Busters* (1955), *Yield to the Night* (1956) and *Look Back in Anger* (1959). Married to editor **Noreen Ackland**, who worked several times for Michael POWELL, including *Peeping Tom* (1960).

OTHER BRITISH FILMS INCLUDE: *Desert Victory* (1943), *The Guinea Pig* (1948), *The Dancing Years* (1950), *The Magic Box* (1951), *The Yellow Balloon, The Weak and the Wicked* (1953), *The Moonraker, Woman in a Dressing Gown* (1957), *Ice Cold in Alex* (1958), *School for Scoundrels* (1959), *Go to Blazes* (1962), *The Bargee* (1964), *Otley* (1968), *Dominique* (1978).

Beswick, Martine (*b* Port Antonio, Jamaica, 1941). Actress. Beswick's sex appeal won her small roles in two 'BONDS' (*From Russia with Love*, 1963, and *Thunderball*, 1965), but she is best remembered for her three HAMMER films: *Slave Girls* (1966), as the lead, Kari; *One Million Years BC* (1966); and for playing with relish half the title role in *Dr Jekyll & Sister Hyde* (1971). Most of the rest of her career was spent unremarkably in the US, and in 1992 she was in the Australian-made *Wide Sargasso Sea*.

OTHER BRITISH FILM: *The Penthouse* (1967).

Bett, John Actor. Of his sporadic film appearances over 20 years, Bett is vividly recalled for his gravely dignified DRAG turn as Lady Felicity Ramsden, lady-in-waiting to the royal visitor to *Britannia Hospital* (1982). For the rest, mainly small roles in films with a pronounced Scottish interest: *The Caledonian Account* (1976, short), *Gregory's Girl* (1980), *Scotch Myths* (1982), and the cult success, *Shallow Grave* (1994); also played Peter FIRTH's censorious older brother in POLANSKI's *Tess* (1979, UK/Fr).

OTHER BRITISH FILMS: *The First Great Train Robbery* (1978), *The Pirates of Penzance* (1982), *Tank Malling* (1988), *Truth or Dare* (1996).

Bettany, Paul (*b* London, 1971). Actor. Tall blond actor who played the officer fiancé of one of the *The Land Girls* (1998, UK/Fr) but came to real prominence as wholly vile *Gangster No. 1* (1999), a critical rather than commercial success. Played Steerforth in TV's *David Copperfield* (1999) and to US to film *The Knight's Tale* and *A Beautiful Mind* (2001).

OTHER BRITISH FILMS INCLUDE: *Bent* (1997), *Kiss Kiss Bang Bang, Morality Play* (2002).

Betts, Ernest (*b* London, 1897 – *d* 1975). Screenwriter, critic. Began writing about film in the late 20s, in the avant-garde journal, CLOSE UP, was film critic for the *Evening Standard* (1931–33), wrote for many other journals and London's leading Sunday newspapers, and was the author of two books about cinema: *Inside Pictures* (1970) and *The Film Business* (1973). He also had experience within the industry: he co-authored the screenplays for several 30s films including *Love in Exile* and *Pagliacci* (1936), worked with Filippo DEL GIUDICE in setting up the short-lived Pilgrim Films (1947), and was public relations officer for the British operations of 20TH CENTURY–FOX and MGM in the late 40s and the 50s.

Bevan, Tim (*b* Queenstown, NZ, 1958). Producer. Very influential figure in British cinema from the mid 80s, when he co-founded WORKING TITLE Productions with Sarah RADCLYFFE and produced such to-the-point contemporary dramas as *My Beautiful Laundrette* (1985) and *Sammy and Rosie Get Laid*

(1987). His work has been genuinely international in scope: the Oscar-winning *Fargo* (1996), on which he was executive producer, is technically a British film but culturally American; *Four Weddings and a Funeral* (1994) and *Notting Hill* (1999) involve American finance but are in matters of national identity clearly British; some, like *Loch Ness* (1996), are wholly British, others, like *Bob Roberts* (1992), wholly American. As either producer or executive producer, his name has been on some of the key films of the 20th century's last decade, and he shared a BAA and London Critics' Circle Award for *Elizabeth* (1998) with co-chairman, Eric FELLNER, and they were named producers of the year at the Cinema Expo International, 2001. Married Joely RICHARDSON in 1992, separated in 1997.

OTHER BRITISH FILMS INCLUDE: *Personal Services* (1987), *A World Apart* (1988, UK/Zimb), *Paperhouse, For Queen and Country* (UK/US), *Chicago Joe and the Showgirl, The Tall Guy* (1989), *London Kills Me* (1991), *Map of the Human Heart* (1992, UK/Aust), *Bean, The Borrowers* (1997), *Elizabeth* (1998, + a), *Plunkett & Macleane* (1999), *The Man Who Cried* (UK/Fr/US, ex p), *High Fidelity* (UK/US) (2000), *Bridget Jones's Diary* (UK/Fr/US), *Captain Corelli's Mandolin* (2001, UK/US).

Bewes, Rodney (*b* Bingley, 1937). Actor. Light comedy actor of the 60s TV series, *The Likely Lads*, as the chubby plodder half of the title. He and co-star James BOLAM repeated their roles in the 1976 film version and the 1973 follow-up series, *Whatever Happened to the Likely Lads?*. Bewes' big-screen career has been sporadic, dating back to the early 60s when he played the delusional hero's pal in *Billy Liar!* (1963). Essentially, a *likeable* lad.

OTHER BRITISH FILMS INCLUDE: *A Prize of Arms* (1961), *Heavens Above!* (1963), *San Ferry Ann* (1965), *Spring and Port Wine* (1969), *Jabberwocky* (1977), *Wildcats of St Trinian's* (1980).

Bezencenet, Peter (*b* England, 1914). Editor, director. Entered films in the later 30s, and with the RAF during WW2. Postwar, worked mainly as editor and, especially in the 50s, several times for EALING, beginning with *The Square Ring* (1953), and twice for TEMPEAN in its 'A' film phase: *Jack the Ripper*, 1958, *The Siege of Sidney Street*, 1960. Directed some minor thrillers in the early 60s including *Band of Thieves*, (1962), *A Bomb in the High Street* (1963, co-d), *24 Hours to Kill* (1965).

OTHER BRITISH FILMS INCLUDE: (e) *Conquest of the Air* (1940), *Floodtide* (1949), *The Divided Heart* (1954), *The Feminine Touch* (1956), *Dangerous Exile* (1957), *Floods of Fear* (1958), *Tommy the Toreador* (1959).

Bicat, Nick (*b* 1949). Composer. Began film work on the score for *Dinosaur* (1975, short), composed for a number of tele-movies and mini-series (*Oliver Twist*, 1982; *Lace*, 1984), as well as two films for David HARE, *Wetherby* (1985) and *Strapless* (1988), and Coky GIEDROYC's confronting first feature, *Stella Does Tricks* (1996).

OTHER BRITISH FILMS INCLUDE: *Facelift* (1984), *Stealing Heaven* (1988, UK/Yug), *The Reflecting Skin* (1990), *The Passion of Darkly Noon* (UK/Belg/Ger) (1995).

Biddle, Adrian (*b* London, 1952). Cinematographer. Began as camera operator on Ridley SCOTT's *The Duellists* (1977) and *Alien* (1979, UK/US), and since has lensed such popular features as *Aliens* (1986, US) and *The Mummy* (1999, US). His work has been increasingly international, often, though, on films with a British bias in cast and locations.

OTHER BRITISH FILMS INCLUDE: *The Tall Guy* (1989), *1492: The Conquest of Paradise* (1992, UK/FR/Sp), *Fierce Creatures, Event Horizon* (1997, UK/US), *The World Is Not Enough* (1999, UK/US).

Bidgood, Harry (*b* London, 1898 – *d*?). Composer, music director. The cheery band music that opens George FORMBY's *Let George Do It!* (1940) is typical of Bidgood's contribution to popular fare of the early 40s. A former dance-bandleader, he also conducted the London Symphony Orchestra in the musical *I'll Turn to You* (1946) and was music director on two Vera LYNN films, *We'll Meet Again* (1942) and *One Exciting Night* (1944).

OTHER BRITISH FILMS: (all with Formby) *South American George* (1941), *Get Cracking* (1943), *He Snoops to Conquer* (1944), *I Didn't Do It* (1945), *George in Civvy Street* (1946).

Bikel, Theodore (*b* Vienna, 1924). Actor. Multi-talented Bikel has had careers on stage (the original Captain Von Trapp in *The Sound of Music*), TV (mostly US), and as a folk-singer/guitarist, as well as being a familiar screen actor. His bulky, somewhat morose looks have often condemned him to playing continental villains, but he had one unconventional romantic lead – in the charming fable, *The Kidnappers* (1953), as a Nova Scotian farmer. After a dozen British films, beginning with *The African Queen* (1951, the German naval officer of course), spent most of the rest of his career in America, memorably playing Karpathy, 'that frightful Hungarian', in *My Fair Lady* (1964) and received AAn (supp a) for *The Defiant Ones* (1958). In his teens, he migrated to Palestine, where he acted with Tel Aviv's Habimah Theatre, and had further training at RADA. Has worked in America for the Democratic Party and causes including Jewish relief and Actors' Equity (president 1973–82).

OTHER BRITISH FILMS INCLUDE: *Moulin Rouge, Melba, Desperate Moment* (1953), *The Young Lovers, The Divided Heart, The Colditz Story* (1954), *Above Us the Waves* (1955), *Sands of the Kalahari* (1965), *200 Motels* (1971).

Bilk, Acker (*b* Pensford, 1929) Musician. Bilk appeared with his Paramount Jazz Band in Richard LESTER's first feature film, *It's Trad, Dad!* (1962), starred as himself with his 'trad' music group in the caper comedy, *Band of Thieves* (1962) and co-wrote (with Stanley BLACK) and performed the title theme for *West 11* (1963). Awarded MBE in 2001 for services to music.

Billings, R.H. ('Josh') Critic. Respected reviewer who began writing in 1921 for a minor circuit, joined GAUMONT–BRITISH in 1924, and, from 1928, was for several decades senior film critic of the trade journal, *KINEMATOGRAPH WEEKLY*.

Billington, Kevin (*b* Warrington, Lancs, 1934). Director. Cambridge-educated, BAA-award-winning documentarist (for *Madison Avenue USA*) and director of the BBC's *Henry VIII*, Billington made a handful of cinema films, beginning with *Interlude* (1968), a touching remake of *Intermezzo* set in 'SWINGING LONDON'.

OTHER BRITISH FILMS: *The Rise and Rise of Michael Rimmer* (1970, + p, s), *Voices* (1973), *Reflections* (1984).

Binder, Maurice (*b* New York, 1925 – *d* London, 1991). Title artist. Chiefly known for designing the title graphics of the BOND films, beginning with *Dr No* (1962) and ending with *Licence to Kill* (1989), and arousing state-of-the-art stylistic expectations. The 60-plus films whose titles he designed also included high comedy (*The Grass is Greener*, 1960), period pieces (*Of Human Bondage*, 1964; *The Private Life of Sherlock Holmes*, 1970) and wartime adventures (*Battle of Britain*, 1969; *The Sea Wolves*, 1980, UK/Switz/US). A leader in his field.

OTHER BRITISH FILMS INCLUDE: *The Running Man, I Could Go On Singing, Stolen Hours* (1963), *Repulsion, Thunderball* (1965),

Kaleidoscope, Two for the Road (1966), *Billion Dollar Brain, You Only Live Twice, Fathom* (1967), *On Her Majesty's Secret Service, Country Dance* (1969), *Diamonds Are Forever* (1971), *Live and Let Die* (1973), *The Man with the Golden Gun* (1974), *The Spy Who Loved Me* (1977), *The Wild Geese* (UK/Switz), *Moonraker* (UK/Fr) (1979), *The Awakening* (1980, UK/US), *For Your Eyes Only* (1981), *Octopussy* (1983), *A View to a Kill* (1985), *The Living Daylights* (1987).

Binder, Sybilla (*b* Vienna, 1895 – *d* Dusseldorf, Germany, 1962). Actress. Gaunt but severely handsome Binder often projected a sinister image, as in *Counterblast* (1948), but her Italian servant in *Blanche Fury* (1947) showed generosity of feeling was well within her range. Appeared to effect in some striking 40s MELODRAMAS. On stage from 1925.

OTHER BRITISH FILMS INCLUDE: *Thunder Rock* (1942), *The Night Invader* (1943), *The Man from Morocco, The Latin Quarter* (1945), *Portrait from Life, Idol of Paris* (1948), *The Golden Salamander* (1949).

Binoche, Juliette (*b* Paris, 1964). Actress. Beautiful French star who has broken through into international films in the 90s, beginning with the 1992 UK/US version of *Wuthering Heights*. Her Heathcliff was Ralph FIENNES, her co-star in the inflated but award-winning *The English Patient* (1996, UK/US). In the UK/French co-production, *Damage* (1992), she was memorably poignant as the doom-dispensing lover of son and father, but her most honoured work to date has been in the *Three Colours* series (*Blue*, 1993; *White, Red*, 1994, Fr/Pol/Switz).

OTHER BRITISH FILM: *Chocolat* (2000, US/UK).

biopics Like all national cinemas Britain has contributed its share of biopics both in the silent and sound eras. As well as being subject to CENSORSHIP requirements until the 60s, the general approach usually treats the life of historical and artistic figures both with some degree of artistic licence as well as ignoring any elements offensive to national sensibilities. In the 30s, the unexpected international success of Alexander KORDA's *The Private Life of Henry VIII* (1933) revitalised this GENRE. It led to other films with international casts designed for overseas appeal, such as *Catherine the Great* (1934) starring Elizabeth BERGNER and Douglas FAIRBANKS Jr, *The Iron Duke* (1935) with George ARLISS, and *Rhodes of Africa* (1936) with Walter Huston. Anna NEAGLE also starred in *Victoria the Great* (1937) and its sequel *Sixty Glorious Years* (1938), and as several other notable women of history, including *Nell Gwyn* (1934), *Odette* (1950) and *The Lady with a Lamp* (1951).

Wartime also led to serious biographies such as *Pastor Hall* (1940) and *The First of the Few* (1942). However, later directors such as Ken RUSSELL, in such films as *Lisztomania* (1975) and *Valentino* (1977), ignored the reverential tone seen in artistic biopics such as *The Great Mr Handel* (1942). Despite this, serious biopics still appeared such as Richard ATTEN-BOROUGH's *Young Winston* (1972) and *Gandhi* (1982, UK/Ind).

OTHER BRITISH BIOPICS INCLUDE: *Peg of Old Drury* (1935), *The Young Mr Pitt* (1942), *The Magic Bow* (1946, Paganini), *The Magic Box* (1951), *The Story of Gilbert and Sullivan* (1953), *The Tommy Steele Story* (1957), *Cromwell* (1969), *Elizabeth* (1998), *Topsy-Turvy* (2000). Tony Williams.

Bioscope, The The most respected of British silent film trade periodicals and also the most 'genteel.' Published on a weekly basis from September 18, 1908 until May 4, 1932, when it merged with KINEMATOGRAPH WEEKLY, *The Bioscope* was noted for the honesty of its reporting on the film industry, thanks primarily to John Cabourn, who was its editor from 1908 until his death in 1929. It was forced out of business by an advertising boycott. A complete run survives at the BFI and the journal is available on microfilm from World Microfilms. AS.

Birch, Cecil Director, writer. With BAMFORTH, Birch made more than 40 'Winky' comedy SHORTS and more than 75 other short subjects between 1914 and 1916, together with one feature, *Paula* (1915). AS.

Bird, Antonia (*b* London, 1959). Director. Bird came to prominence with her second feature, *Priest* (1994), the controversial study of a homosexual Catholic priest shunned by his parish. The priest's lover was played by Robert CARLYLE, star of her first film, *Safe* (1993), a grim tale of London's homeless young, and of her fast-moving heist thriller, *Face* (1997), and her bizarre US/UK period adventure, *Ravenous* (1999), whose title hints at its cannibalistic theme. In 1999, Bird, Carlyle and Mark Cousins, in a deal with BBC FILMS, set up 4Ways Pictures, to make a series of films, starting with boxing drama *Benny Lynch*, and a drama-documentary, *Rebekka*. Bird does not flinch from the starker facts of life, and registers them with an assured feel for MELODRAMA.

Bird, John (*b* Nottingham, 1936). Actor. With a background of Cambridge and the Royal Court Theatre (as associate artistic director), Bird entered films in the late 60s. Appeared in *Red and Blue* (1967), the Court-inspired art film for Tony RICHARDSON, and several MONTY PYTHON films, as well as TV comedy including *A Bit of Fry and Laurie* (1991).

OTHER BRITISH FILMS INCLUDE: *The Best House in London* (1968), *A Promise of Bed* (1969), *The Breaking of Bumbo, Take a Girl Like You* (1970), *The Alf Garnett Saga* (1972), *Jabberwocky* (1977), *The Secret Policeman's Other Ball* (1982), *A Fish Called Wanda* (1988).

Bird, Norman (*b* Coalville, 1920). Actor. Character player who works enjoyable variations on a lugubrious persona: hence, one of Jack HAWKINS's vulnerable ring-ins in *The League of Gentlemen* (1960), the terminally meek bank clerk in *Cash on Demand* (1961), Sarah Miles's working-class Dad in *Term of Trial* (1962), and Uncle Fred, devious at the Vicarage dinner table, in *The Virgin and the Gypsy* (1970). In short, a wonderful gallery of under-achievers, especially busy in the mid 60s. Also much TV.

OTHER BRITISH FILMS INCLUDE: *An Inspector Calls* (1954), *Victim* (1961), *Secret Partner* (1961), *Night of the Eagle* (1962), *Maniac* (1963), *The Beauty Jungle,* (1964), *The Hill* (1965), *The Wrong Box* (1966), *A Dandy in Aspic* (1968), *The Raging Moon* (1970), *Hands of the Ripper* (1971), *Young Winston* (1972), *The Medusa Touch* (1978, UK/Fr), *Shadowlands* (1993, UK/US).

Bird, Richard (*b* Liverpool, 1896 – *d* Regina, Canada, 1986). Actor. On stage from 1918, following WW1 service, Bird had a busy career over five decades, often in popular comedies such as *The Happiest Days of Your Life* (1950). Entered films in *Tilly of Bloomsbury* (1931), appearing in 20 light COMEDIES, THRILLERS and MUSICALS during the 30s. Two of his last films suggest his range: the Squadron-Leader with a troubled marriage in *The Halfway House,* and the dual role of put-upon husband (of his real-life wife, actress Joyce BARBOUR) and a ghostly ancestor in the comedy, *Don't Take It to Heart* (both 1944).

OTHER BRITISH FILMS INCLUDE: *The Water Gypsies* (1932), *The Right to Live* (1933), *Night Mail, Royal Cavalcade* (1935), *Sensation* (1936), *Bulldog Drummond at Bay* (1937), *The Girl in the News* (1940), *I'll Walk Beside You* (1943), *Forbidden* (1948), *The City of the Dead* (1960), *Return to Sender* (1963).

Birdsall, Jesse (*b* London, 1963). Actor. In films since late teens, in *Bloody Kids* (1979), and, in view of one conviction for causing bodily harm and another near miss in 1999, it may be that he carries his tough on screen persona into the real world. Brought a nice edge to the village lothario in the last episode of *Inspector Morse* (2000), amply suggesting why there might be so many suspects for his death. Mainly TV in the 90s.

OTHER BRITISH FILMS: *Remembrance* (1982), *Shadey* (1985), *Revolution* (1985, UK/Nor), *Wish You Were Here* (1987), *Beyond Bedlam* (1993).

Birkett, Michael (Lord Birkett) (*b* London, 1929). Producer. Vice-president of the British Board of Film Censors, Birkett came to films in the 50s as 3rd assistant director on *The Ladykillers* (1955). Acted as assistant director on several more films (*Nowhere to Go, Dunkirk* 1958; *The Innocents*, 1961; *Billy Budd*, 1962; *An Evening with the Royal Ballet*, 1963), wrote and directed the short film, *A Soldier's Tale* (1963), and was associate producer on *Some People* (1962) before producing several theatre-related films: *The Caretaker* (1963), *The Marat/Sade . . .* (1966), *A Midsummer Night's Dream* (1968), *King Lear* (1970, UK/Den).

Birkin, Andrew (*b* London, 1945). Director, screenwriter. Son of Judy CAMPBELL, brother of Jane BIRKIN, worked on some idiosyncratic productions, including *The Name of the Rose* (1986, US/Ger, s, a,) and *The Cement Garden* (1993, UK/Fr/Ger, d, s). Was assistant to Stanley KUBRICK on *2001: A Space Odyssey* (1969) and co-wrote Luc Besson's English-speaking *Messenger: The Story of Joan of Arc* (1999).

OTHER BRITISH FILMS INCLUDE: *Popdown* (1968, p m), *The Pied Piper* (1971, s), *The Thief of Baghdad* (1978, UK/Fr, co-s), *After Murder Park* (1997, d, s).

Birkin, Jane (*b* London, 1947). Actress. Though she has acted in almost 60 films and directed two, ex-model Birkin has worked mostly in France, where she so memorably played Dirk BOGARDE's daughter in *Daddy, Nostalgie* (1990). She was the swinging blonde teenager in *Blow-Up* (1966, UK/It), appeared in two Agatha CHRISTIE thrillers, *Death on the Nile* (1978) and *Evil Under the Sun* (1981), and was in a few co-productions. Daughter of actress Judy CAMPBELL, and formerly married to composer John BARRY (1966–68) and composer-singer Serge Gainsbourg (1968–80), she is the mother of actress Charlotte Gainsbourg (*b* 1971), who appeared in *The Cement Garden* (1993, UK/Fr/Ger) and *Jane Eyre* (1996, UK/Fr/It/US). Now married to director Jacques Doillon. Brother Andrew BIRKIN is a screenwriter. Awarded OBE, 2001.

OTHER BRITISH FILMS INCLUDE: *Kaleidoscope* (1966), *Dark Places* (1974), *The Last September* (2000, UK/Ire).

Biro, Lajos (*b* Nagyvarad, Hungary, 1880 – *d* London, 1948). Dramatist, screenwriter. Now best known as screenwriter and executive director of Alexander KORDA's LONDON FILMS, Biro was a journalist and political secretary in Budapest before fleeing to Vienna following the 1918 October Revolution. In Vienna, he began his 23-film collaboration with Korda by writing the screenplay for a version of *The Prince and the Pauper* (1920); and became a popular author and playwright there before going to Hollywood in 1924 to sell his play, *The Czarina*, to Ernst Lubitsch. In 1932, he moved to England, where he worked on three screenplays for GAINSBOROUGH, then either wrote the stories or collaborated on the screenplays of most of Korda's films and became his closest friend. A major influence in the international success of London Films that began with *The Private Life of Henry VIII* (1933) for which he wrote the story.

OTHER BRITISH FILMS: (sc, unless noted) *Michael and Mary, The Ghost Train* (1931), *Service for Ladies, Wedding Rehearsal* (story) (1932), *The*

Faithful Heart, Strange Evidence (unc) (1933), *Catherine the Great* (+ play), *The Private Life of Don Juan* (1934), *The Scarlet Pimpernel, Sanders of the River* (1935), *Rembrandt, The Man Who Could Work Miracles* (unc) (1936), *Under the Red Robe, Dark Journey* ('film play'), *Knight Without Armour, Return of the Scarlet Pimpernel* (1937), *The Drum* (adpt), *The Divorce of Lady X* (adpt) (1939), *Over the Moon* (story), *The Thief of Baghdad* (1940), *An Ideal Husband* (1947), *Storm over the Nile* (1955, add dial).

Birt, Daniel (*b* Mersham, 1907 – *d* London, 1955). Editor, director. It seems unlikely that anyone will try to elevate Oxford-educated Birt to AUTEUR status, but one of his films is striking enough to deserve attention. Birt was a respected editor in pre-war British films, then a maker of DOCUMENTARIES, mostly for Sydney BOX's VERITY FILMS, prior to embarking on features from 1948 until his early death of heart attack in 1955. There are two entertaining pieces starring Valerie HOBSON – a thriller, *Interrupted Journey* (1949), and the divorce drama, *Background* (1953) – but his most striking feature remains his first, *The Three Weird Sisters* (1948). This semi-gothic MELODRAMA has a Welsh setting (like Birt's documentary, *Dai Jones*, 1941), a screenplay by his wife Louise Birt (*b* London, 1910, also a film-maker) and Dylan THOMAS, and Nancy PRICE, Mary CLARE and Mary MERRALL as its formidable 'sisters'; an unsettling film, usually ignored in histories of British cinema. His brush with 'A' features was short-lived and he finished his career with 'B' THRILLERS, SHORTS and TV playlets.

OTHER BRITISH FILMS INCLUDE: (e) *The Lucky Number* (1933), *Variety* (1935), *Woman to Woman* (1946), *Angels One Five* (1952); (d) *Butterfly Bomb* (1944, short), *No Room at the Inn* (1948), *She Shall Have Murder* (1950), *Circumstantial Evidence* (1952), *Meet Mr Malcolm*, (1953), *Laughing in the Sunshine* (1956, UK/Swe).

Bishop, Ed (*b* Brooklyn, NY, 1942). Actor. American player who has worked almost wholly in British film and TV (including *UFO* series, 1970) and is sometimes billed as Edward Bishop.

BRITISH FILMS INCLUDE: *The War Lover* (1962), *The Bedford Incident* (1965), *2001: A Space Odyssey* (1968), *Silver Dream Racer, Saturn 3* (1980), *Nutcracker* (1982), *Testimony* (1987), *Broken Glass* (1996).

Bishop, Terry (*b* London, 1912 – *d* England, 1981). Director. Educated at London University, Bishop had DOCUMENTARY experience before directing features and won an AA for *Daybreak in Udi* (1949), made for the CROWN FILM UNIT. Began as sound assistant in 1930 at TWICKENHAM, but his most fruitful period was in documentary-making during WW2, when he worked as director for the Royal Naval Film Unit and afterwards with Crown. In features, he directed *You're Only Young Twice!* (1952, + sc) for GROUP 3, the Venice festival-winning *Tim Driscoll's Pony* (1955, + sc) for the CHILDREN'S FILM FOUNDATION, and several neat 'B' thrillers, including *Model for Murder* (+ sc) and *Life in Danger* (1959).

OTHER BRITISH FILMS INCLUDE: (d, unless noted) (doc) *Kill That Rat* (1941), *The Western Isles* (1942), *The Royal Mile Edinburgh* (1943), *Five Towns* (1947), *Journey to the Sea* (1952); (features) *West of Zanzibar* (1954, 2ud), *Cover Girl Killer* (1959), *Danger Tomorrow* (1960), *Hair of the Dog* (1961), *Bomb in the High Street* (1963, co-d).

Bisset, Jacqueline (*b* Weybridge, 1944). Actress. RN: Fraser-Bisset. With almost 70 credits, including much TV, Bisset's career remains curiously disappointing, notwithstanding some success in France with directors including François Truffaut. Despite classic beauty, stylish persona and acting talent, she has failed to attract the meaty roles that would have made her a major star as well as a major adornment. A former photographic model, she entered films in Britain, uncredited, in *The Knack . . .* (1965) and, after several more, including *Cul-de-Sac* (1966), went to Hollywood where she starred with Sinatra (*The Detective*, 1968) and Steve McQueen (*Bullitt*, 1968), and produced and starred in *Rich and Famous* (1981), perhaps her best role, as the 'serious' author opposite Candice Bergen's popular novelist.

OTHER BRITISH FILMS INCLUDE: *Drop Dead Darling, Two for the Road* (1966), *Casino Royale* (as Miss Goodthighs) (1967), *Secrets* (1971), *The Deep* (1977, UK/US), *High Season* (1987).

Biziou, Peter (*b* Wales, 1943). Cinematographer. Began in advertising, shooting commercials for Alan PARKER. Won an AA for his work on *Mississippi Burning* (1988, US).

OTHER BRITISH FILMS INCLUDE: *Footsteps* (1974), *Bugsy Malone* (1976), *Time Bandits* (1981), *Pink Floyd The Wall* (1982), *Another Country* (1984), *A World Apart* (1988, UK/Zimb), *City of Joy, Damage* (1992, both UK/FR), *In the Name of the Father* (1993, UK/Ire/US), *Richard III* (1995).

Black, Cilla (*b* Liverpool, 1943). Actress, singer. RN: Priscilla White. Cheerful and tuneful presence in a few films, including *Ferry Cross the Mersey* (1964), *Alfie* (1966), *Work Is a Four Letter Word* (1967) and *Please, Sir!* (1971). Better known as TV presenter and performer. Awarded an OBE in the 1997 New Year's Honours.

Black, Edward (*b* Birmingham, 1900 – *d* London, 1948). Producer. For ten years, Black was a key figure in the production of popular British cinema, particularly for GAINSBOROUGH where he worked as studio manager from 1928. He was appointed Associate Producer of the studio in 1935, and, when Michael BALCON left in 1936, Black and Maurice OSTRER shared the running of the company until 1943. They disagreed about the emphasis of the studio's production programme following the success of *The Man in Grey* (1943), with Black less enthusiastic about the COSTUME MELODRAMAS which became a Gainsborough staple and keener than Ostrer on the realist vein represented by *Millions Like Us* (1943). In 1944 he left to join Alexander KORDA, for whom he produced *A Man About the House* (1947) and the abysmal *Bonnie Prince Charlie* (1948). He also produced several Carol REED films for Twentieth-Century and SHORTS for the MOI in 1941. His is a contribution which awaits further exploration: it goes beyond the films on which his name actually appears.

OTHER BRITISH FILMS INCLUDE: *Tudor Rose* (1936), *Owd Bob, Young and Innocent, Good Morning, Boys!, Dr Syn, Oh, Mr Porter!* (1937), *Strange Boarders, Old Bones of the River, The Lady Vanishes, Crackerjack, Bank Holiday, Alf's Button Afloat* (1938), *Inspector Hornleigh on Holiday, A Girl Must Live, The Frozen Limits, Shipyard Sally, Ask a Policeman* (1939), *Band Waggon, Night Train to Munich, Neutral Port, Gasbags, Charley's Big-Hearted Aunt, Girl in the News* (1940), *Once a Crook, A Letter From Home* (short), *Mr Proudfoot Shows a Light* (short), *Rush Hour* (short), *Kipps, I Thank You, Hi Gang!, The Ghost Train, Cottage to Let* (1941), *The Young Mr Pitt, Uncensored, It's That Man Again, Back Room Boy* (1942), *Miss London Ltd, Give Us the Moon, Dear Octopus, We Dive at Dawn* (1943), *Waterloo Road, Time Flies, Fanny by Gaslight, Two Thousand Women* (1944).

BIBLIOG: Sue Aspinall and Robert Murphy (eds), *Gainsborough Melodrama*, 1983.

Black, Ian Stuart (*b* London, 1915 – *d* 1997). Screenwriter. Ex-RAF (1941–46), he entered films post-war as writer with RANK's INDEPENDENT PRODUCERS, working on such productions as *Take My Life* (1947), *Once a Jolly Swagman* (1948), and *Dear Mr Prohack* (1949). Educated at Manchester University, he wrote

plays and novels as well as film scripts. Film credits were mainly 'B' THRILLERS such as *Shadow of the Past* (1950) and *In the Wake of a Stranger* (1959, based on his novel). TV success with scripts for the likes of *The Saint* (1962). Father of actress Isobel BLACK.

OTHER BRITISH FILMS INCLUDE: *Soho Incident* (1956), *The Long Knife* (1958), *The High Bright Sun* (1965, +story).

Black, Isobel (*b* Edinburgh, 1943). Actress. Brunette daughter of Ian Stuart BLACK, she adorned a few films of the 60s and 70s. Worked mainly in the HORROR genre, as in *Twins of Evil* (1971), though also played the female general's aide in *The Magnificent Two* (1967) and David's gentle mother in *David Copperfield* (1969, TV, some cinemas).

OTHER BRITISH FILMS INCLUDE: *Kiss of the Vampire* (1962), *10 Rillington Place* (1970).

black representation in British films Often overlooked or simply ignored, black actors and film-makers have been working in British films right through the first century of cinema. Bermuda's Ernest Trimmingham was featured in several silents but it was Paul ROBESON, the charismatic African-American actor and singer, who was the first to attain stardom. Though he disowned Alexander KORDA's *Sanders of the River* (1935) for its imperialism, Robeson found British studios more welcoming than US ones. Successful films like *Song of Freedom* (1936), *Jericho* (1937) and *The Proud Valley* (1940) helped establish him as one of Britain's most popular stars, and provided work for other black performers, including the African-American singer Elisabeth WELCH and Robert ADAMS, a former wrestler from Guyana. After Robeson returned to the US, Adams became Britain's leading black actor and had a starring role as an 'educated' African coming into conflict with his own cultural traditions in Thorold DICKINSON's *Men of Two Worlds* (1946).

After the war, with settlers coming to Britain from Africa and the Caribbean, liberal-thinking film directors like Basil DEARDEN and Roy Ward BAKER explored racial conflict in Britain's inner cities. Their films included *Pool of London* (1950), *Sapphire* (1959), which received the BAA for Best British Film, and *Flame in the Streets* (1961). They also provided decent roles for talented black actors like Bermuda's Earl CAMERON and West Africa's Johnny SEKKA. Director Zoltán KORDA, partly responsible for *Sanders of the River*, was at last able to express his true feelings about Africa in *Cry, the Beloved Country* (1952), based on Alan Paton's anti-apartheid novel. On the other hand, Africa remained a colourful, exotic backdrop for white settlers in films like *Where No Vultures Fly*, chosen as the 1951 Royal Film Performance. *A Taste of Honey* (1961) and *The L-Shaped Room* (1962) presented ordinary black characters involved in everyday life, while two critically acclaimed SHORTS, *Ten Bob in Winter* (1963) directed by Jamaica's Lloyd Reckord and *Jemima and Johnny* (1966) directed by South Africa's Lionel NGAKANE, were the first dramas made by black film-makers in Britain. In 1967 Hollywood superstar Sidney POITIER (BAA-winner for *The Defiant Ones*, 1958) came to Britain for *To Sir, with Love*, an unfaithful adaptation of E.R. Braithwaite's novel, based on his experiences as a teacher in London's East End.

Pressure (1975), directed by Trinidadian Horace OVE, is acknowledged as the first feature by a black British director. *Black Joy* (1977), an upbeat comedy, elevated its Guyanese lead actor Norman BEATON to stardom and a Best Film Actor award from the Variety Club of Great Britain, the first to a black British actor. Franco ROSSO's *Babylon* (1980) and Menelik Shabazz's *Burning an Illusion* (1981) explored the lives of second-generation African-Caribbeans in Britain's inner cities. For *Mona Lisa* (1986) Cathy TYSON became the first black British actress nominated for a BAA. Though experienced black British actors were available, the tradition of importing African-Americans for leading roles in British films continued with *Cry Freedom* (1987), *For Queen and Country* (1988, UK/US) and *The Crying Game* (1992).

On the other hand, the independent sector gave a boost to young black film-makers. These included SANKOFA (*The Passion of Remembrance*, 1986), Maureen BLACKWOOD (*Dreaming Rivers*, 1988), Isaac JULIEN (*Young Soul Rebels*, 1991), John AKOMFRAH (*Who Needs a Heart*, 1991) and Ngozi ONWURAH (*Welcome II the Terrordome*, 1995). For Mike LEIGH's *Secrets & Lies* (1996) Marianne JEAN-BAPTISTE earned AA and BAA nominations. Subsequently, she charged BRITISH SCREEN with racism for snubbing her at the Cannes Film Festival and complained that, in spite of her nominations, the British film industry wasn't employing her. At the same time the list of African-American stars drawing audiences to the box-office continued, but the best the British film industry could offer were 'Mr Horse' in *The Full Monty* (1997, UK/US) and 'Scary Spice' in *Spiceworld: The Movie* (1997). Behind the camera, Paul Bucknor co-produced *The Full Monty* (his original idea sparked this international box-office hit) and cinematographer Remi ADEFARASIN won a British AA for *Elizabeth* (1998). The semi-surreal musical extravaganza *Babymother* (1998) found favour with young black audiences, but failed to win critical approval. However, some of the most exciting and innovative British films of the 90s have been SHORTS. Over 60 were made by African-Caribbean and other minority directors including Alrick Riley (*The Concrete Garden*, 1994), Roberto BANGURA (*Sidney's Chair*, 1995), Cyril Nri (*Constance*, 1998) and Treva Etienne (*Driving Miss Crazy*, 1999). BIBLIOG: Peter Noble, *The Negro in Films*, 1948; Stephen Bourne, *Black in the British Frame 1896–1996*, 1998; Onyekachi Wambu and Kevin Arnold, *A Fuller Picture*, 1999. Stephen Bourne.

Black, Stanley (*b* London, 1913 – *d* London, 2002). Composer. Former conductor of the BBC Dance Orchestra and musical director of ASSOCIATED BRITISH Studios, Black was for over 30 years one of the most prolific composers/musical directors in British film. His work covered most GENRES: COMEDIES (*Laughter in Paradise*, 1951; *Too Many Crooks*, 1959), WAR FILMS (*The Long and the Short and the Tall*, 1960), MUSICALS (*Summer Holiday*, 1962), HORROR (*Maniac*, 1963), BIOPICS (*Valentino*, 1977), and 'B' THRILLERS such as *Impulse* (1955) and *The Man in the Back Seat* (1961). There are over 100 titles, as well as many TV commercials. Entered films in 1936, working on the score of *Rhythm Racketeer*, and made feature debut as composer with the 1946 thriller, *Dual Alibi*. OTHER BRITISH FILMS INCLUDE: *It Always Rains on Sunday* (1947), *The Small Voice* (1948), *Shadow of the Past* (1950), *Top Secret* (1952), *Escape By Night* (1953), *Happy Ever After* (1954), *The High Terrace*, *My Teenage Daughter* (1956), *Time Lock*, *The Naked Truth* (1957), *Jack the Ripper* (1958), *Battle of the Sexes* (1959), *The Siege of Sidney Street*, *Hand in Hand* (1960), *House of Mystery*, *The Day the Earth Caught Fire*, *The Young Ones* (1961), *The Pot Carriers* (1962), *The Wicked Lady* (1983).

blacklist Britain did not, of course, practise anything so bizarre and appalling as the McCarthy trials and the resultant anti-Communist blacklist of the late 40s and early 50s, but a number of Hollywood victims of the US madness found refuge in Britain's politically more tolerant climate and re-established careers there, even if initially forced to work under pseudonyms. The most famous is Joseph LOSEY, who went on to make such remarkable British films as *The Servant* (1963) and *The Go-Between* (1971). Others include Cy ENDFIELD, who made some very vigorous action films in Britain, including *Hell Drivers* (1957) and, most famously, *Zulu* (1963), Carl FOREMAN, who produced and wrote *The Guns of Navarone* (1961) and won an AA for writing *The Bridge on the River Kwai* (1957), and the actor Larry Parks. Others included Edward DMYTRYK, who made several British films including *Give Us This Day* (1949, UK/US), starring blacklisted Sam WANAMAKER, director Bernard VORHAUS, who filmed in Britain in the 30s, went to America and was blacklisted, and Larry ADLER who won an AA he couldn't collect for *Genevieve* (1953). There are other less well-known names and this is a complex matter, but it should be noted that such unwilling émigrés often made a major contribution to British cinema in the 50s and 60s.

Blackman, Honor (*b* London, 1925). Actress. Born to working-class parents with intelligent aspirations for her, Blackman made her debut in the BOULTINGS' *Fame is the Spur* (1947) as a youthful revolutionary. Her blonde beauty consigned her to English rose type heroines who got the hero rather than the good lines: witness 1949's *Diamond City* and *A Boy, a Girl and a Bike*, in both of which Diana DORS had the choicer cuts. Her run of 'B' MOVIES in the 50s, of which *Suspended Alibi* (1956) is quite diverting, came to an end when she was cast as a brave mother in *A Night to Remember* (1958) and Norman WISDOM's leading lady in *The Square Peg* (1958). The 60s is her big decade, when she was given some enjoyably bitchy roles. Not only was she, as Pussy Galore in *Goldfinger* (1964), James BOND's sexiest and sharpest leading lady, but she reached major TV stardom in *The Avengers* (1961–64), as leather-clad karate expert Cathy Gale. After that, her career drifted as did the British film industry: there were a few more good roles (*Life at the Top*, 1965; *The Virgin and the Gypsy*, 1970), but she turned more and more to TV and the stage to maintain her career. Was married (2) to Maurice KAUFMANN (1962–75). OTHER BRITISH FILMS INCLUDE: *Daughter of Darkness* (1947), *Conspirator* (1949), *So Long at the Fair* (1950), *Green Grow the Rushes* (1951), *The Rainbow Jacket* (1954), *The Glass Cage* (1955), *Account Rendered* (1957), *A Matter of WHO* (1961), *Serena* (1962), *Shalako*, *Twinky* (1969), *The Cat and the Canary* (1979), *To Walk with Lions* (2000, UK/Can/Kenya, as Joy Adamson), *Bridget Jones's Diary* (2001, UK/Fr/US).

Blackmore, Peter (*b* Clevedon, 1909 – *d* London, 1984). Dramatist, screenwriter. For many years playwrights such as Blackmore, formerly an actor, were a staple of London's West End stage, especially in the light-comedy mode of his famous mermaid farce, *Miranda*, filmed from his screenplay in 1948. He wrote its sequel, *Mad About Men* (1954), and scripts for Norman WISDOM (*Up in the World*, 1956; *Just My Luck*, 1957) and MORECAMBE AND WISE (*The Intelligence Men*, 1965; *That Riviera Touch*, 1966; *The Magnificent Two*, 1967). Quite radically depth-free, his screenplays rattle along with enough one-liners and narrative inventiveness to keep the customers happy. OTHER BRITISH FILMS INCLUDE: *Time Gentlemen Please!* (1952), *All For Mary* (1955), *Make Mine a Million* (1959, co-s), *Make Mine Mink* (1960, add dial), *All at Sea* (1964).

Blackton, J(ames) Stuart (*b* Sheffield, 1875 – *d* Los Angeles, 1941). Producer, director. With his Faversham-born partner,

Albert E. Smith, Blackton was the only Englishman to be the head of a major American studio, having founded in the late 1890s the Vitagraph Company of America, which merged with Warner Bros. in 1925. In 1920, Blackton announced plans to create a British studio. The project failed to materialize, but Blackton did produce and direct three major UK productions: *A Gypsy Cavalier* and, starring Diana MANNERS, *The Glorious Adventure* (1922, in Prizmacolor) and *The Virgin Queen* (1923). All were spectacular costume dramas, but lacked drama and imagination, and the only worthwhile thing to come from them was one of the actors from *The Glorious Adventure*, Victor McLAGLEN, being brought to Hollywood. AS.

Blackwell, Carlyle (*b* Troy, Pennsylvania, 1885 – *d* Miami, Florida, 1955). Actor. Major American leading man of the 1910s, often teamed with Alice Joyce, who began his career in 1909, and worked for Vitagraph, Kalem and World, Blackwell came to the UK to star in J. Stuart BLACKTON's *The Virgin Queen* (1923). Then too old to play juveniles, when he took his shirt off in *She* (1925), it was embarrassing. Returned to US with coming of SOUND, but left acting to his son, Carlyle Blackwell, Jr.
OTHER BRITISH FILMS INCLUDE: *Bulldog Drummond*, *The Beloved Vagabond* (1923), The *Shadow of Egypt* (1924), *Beating the Book* (1926), *The Rolling Road* (1927, + p), *The Wrecker* (1928), *The Crooked Billet* (1929), *Bedrock* (1930, + p, d). AS.

Blackwood, Maureen Director. Black film-maker whose work has so far been chiefly associated with the SANKOFA Film and Video Collective. In 1986, she co-directed and -wrote (with Isaac JULIEN) *The Passion of Remembrance*, and was assistant director on Julien's DOCUMENTARY about poet Langston Hughes, *Looking for Langston* (1989). She directed and wrote *Perfect Image* (1988) and directed *A Family Called Abrew* (1992), a documentary on black Britons involved in boxing and MUSIC HALLS, and the short *Home Away from Home* (1994).

Blair, Barbara Actress. Vivacious blonde (also radio and stage) who made a few enjoyable comedies and dramas in the late 30s, was a memorably bitchy county wife in *Bedelia* (1946), but had dropped way down the cast for her last film, *Tall Headlines* (1952).
OTHER BRITISH FILMS: *Hold My Hand*, *Star of the Circus* (1938), *I Killed the Count*, *Lucky to Me*, *The Outsider* (1939).

Blair, Isla (*b* Bangalore, 1944). Actress. Strikingly attractive, intelligent-looking Blair has done memorable TV work (e.g. *The Final Cut*, 1995) but so far only a few films, getting her best chance as the object of Tom Sizemore's affections in *The Match* (1999, UK/Ire/US). Also in two US/Fr co-productions, *A Flea in Her Ear* (1968) and *Valmont* (1989), and played wife to her real-life husband, Julian GLOVER in *Indiana Jones and the Last Crusade* (1989). Their son is Jamie Glover (*b* London, 1969), square-jawed young actor in several films, including *Closing Numbers* (1993) and, like his mother, he has guested in *Dalziel and Pascoe* (1998).
OTHER BRITISH FILMS INCLUDE: *Doctor Terror's House of Horrors* (1965), *Battle of Britain*, *Taste the Blood of Dracula* (1969).

Blair, Les (*b* Salford, Lancashire, 1941). Director, producer, screenwriter. Has worked typically on films of social concern, unsurprisingly on a couple of occasions for PARALLAX FILMS, the company that has produced Ken LOACH's output of the 90s. Won BAFTA award for *Newshounds* (1990), made for BBC and WORKING TITLE, and was praised for *Bad Behaviour* (1993), a comedy-drama of North London family life, made for

Parallax, FILM FOUR and BRITISH SCREEN.
OTHER BRITISH FILMS INCLUDE: (d) *Going Home*, *Pudding and Pie* (1968, shorts), *Bleak Moments* (1971, p), *Number One* (1984, starring Bob Geldof), *Leave to Remain* (1988), *Jump the Gun* (1997, UK/S Af, +sc).

Blair, Lionel (*b* Montreal, 1931). Actor, choreographer. RN: Ogus. Slight supporting actor, often as dancer in musicals such as *The Cool Mikado* (1962, as Nanky) and the GOLDCREST disaster, *Absolute Beginners* (1986). He did choreography for two WARWICK musicals, *In the Nick* and *Jazzboat* (both 1959), and for *Promise Her Anything* (1965) and *The Magic Christian* (1969). Also on stage, from childhood, and TV (*Name That Tune*, 1983–84).
OTHER BRITISH FILMS INCLUDE: *The Limping Man* (1953), *King's Rhapsody* (1955), *Play It Cool* (1962), *A Hard Day's Night* (1964), *Maroc 7* (1966), *Salt & Pepper* (1968).

Blake, Grey (*b* London, 1917). Actor. On stage from 1935, palely distinguished-looking Blake, under contract to RANK, appeared in a dozen films of the 40s, notably as the iron-lung patient in the air-crash drama, *Broken Journey* (1948). Married (2) to actress Lisa DANIELY.
OTHER BRITISH FILMS INCLUDE: *Java Head* (1934), *Tawny Pipit* (1944), *Jassy* (1947), *Easy Money* (1948), *The Lost People* (1949), *The Dancing Years* (1950) *Paul Temple Returns* (1952).

Blake, Katherine (sometimes **Kathryn**) (*b* Johannesburg, 1928 – *d* London, 1991). Actress. Attractive brunette, touching as a Soho hit man's wife in *Assassin for Hire* (1951), made a handful of films and some TV (as prison governor in the series, *Within These Walls*, 1976). Married to directors (1) David GREENE and (2) Charles JARROTT, for whom she appeared in *Anne of the Thousand Days* (1969).
OTHER BRITISH FILMS: *The Dark Light* (1951), *Hammer the Toff*, *Hunted* (1952), *To Have and to Hold* (1963).

Blake, Yvonne (*b* 1938). Costume Designer. Active in British films since 1966 (*The Idol*, *The Spy with a Cold Nose*), Blake has been involved in some notable international productions, winning shared AAn for *Nicholas and Alexandra* (1971, UK/US) and *The Three Musketeers* (1973, Panama). Also designed costumes for such British-made spectaculars as *Superman* (1978) and *Superman II* (1980), as well as the more intimate *Robin and Marian* (1976, UK/US), but her most recent work has been in the US.
OTHER BRITISH FILMS INCLUDE: *Judith* (1965, UK/Is/US), *Assignment K*, *Charlie Bubbles* (1968), *Country Dance* (1969), *Puppet on a Chain* (1970), *The Eagle Has Landed* (1976), *Green Ice* (1981), *The Return of the Musketeers* (1989, UK/Fr/Sp).

Blakeley, John E(dward) (*b* Manchester, 1889 – *d* Stockport, 1958). Producer, director. Entered the industry in 1908 as a film renter. Much associated with regional comics such as George FORMBY (*Boots! Boots!*, 1934, *Off the Dole*, 1935, both made for MANCUNIAN Films), Duggie WAKEFIELD (*The Penny Pool*, 1937, *Calling All Crooks*, 1938), and Frank RANDLE, in a series of films very popular in the North, with titles such as *Somewhere in England* (1940), . . . *on Leave*, . . . *in Camp* (1942), . . . *in Politics* (1948). These, and the semi-musicals he also made (*Demobbed*, 1944, with warbling Webster BOOTH and wife Anne ZIEGLER), reflected an unsubtle but demotic approach to film-making. In 1947, he founded the Manchester Film Studios where he made such knockabout Randle vehicles as *Cup-Tie Honeymoon* (1947) and *Holidays with Pay* (1948). As the managing director of Mancunian Film Corporation, in a London-centred industry, he deserves a footnote for answering a provincial need for something nearer home. His son Tom BLAKELEY was also a producer.

OTHER BRITISH FILMS INCLUDE: (p/d) *Two Little Drummer Boys* (1928), *Dodging the Dole* (1936), *Under New Management* (1946), *School for Randle* (1949, + s), *Let's Have a Murder* (1950), *It's a Grand Life* (1953), *Trouble with Eve* (1959).

BIBLIOG: Philip Martin Williams & David Williams, *Hooray for Jollywood: The Life of John E. Blakeley and the Mancunian Film Corporation*, 2001.

Blakeley, Tom (*b* London, 1916 – *d* Wilmslow, 1984). Producer. Over fifteen years, Blakeley produced a dozen films, including several crisp 'B's for Lance COMFORT (*Tomorrow at Ten*, 1962, a taut kidnap drama), and three for Francis SEARLE (*Love's a Luxury*, 1952), as well as two HAMMER horrors for Terence FISHER: *Island of Terror* (1966) and *Night of the Big Heat* (1967). Son of John E. BLAKELEY.

OTHER BRITISH FILMS INCLUDE: *Rag Doll* (1960), *The Painted Smile* (1961), *The Break* (1962), *Devils of Darkness* (1964), *Dutchman* (1966, p man).

Blakely, Colin (*b* Bangor, Northern Ireland, 1930 – *d* London, 1987). Actor. Blakely's early death from leukaemia robbed British screen of a major character star. His chunky form and rumpled, good-natured features tended to direct him towards hero's-friend roles, like that in *This Sporting Life* (193), or as Dr Watson in *The Private Life of Sherlock Holmes* (1970), but there was also an impressive toughness and intensity about his work. Early experience with Bangor Operatic Society may have informed his stage performance in Alan AYCKBOURN's *A Chorus of Disapproval* (1986), one among many theatrical successes, and he was a notably moving Kent to OLIVIER's Lear in TV's 1984 *King Lear*. Was married to actress Margaret WHITING.

OTHER BRITISH FILMS INCLUDE: *Saturday Night and Sunday Morning* (1960), *The Informers* (1963), *A Man for All Seasons* (1966), *Charlie Bubbles* (1967), *Decline and Fall . . .* (1968), *Alfred the Great* (1969), *Young Winston* (1972), *The National Health* (1973), *Murder on the Orient Express* (1974), *It Shouldn't Happen to a Vet* (1976), *Equus* (1977), *The Dogs of War* (1980), *Evil Under the Sun* (1981).

Blakiston, Caroline (*b* London, 1933). Actress. Vivid character actress remembered as the woman bent on baring her breasts in *Sunday Bloody Sunday* (1971) and as a brisk county type in *Yanks* (1979), but perhaps even more for her court scene in TV's *The Forsyte Saga* (1967). She was Volumnia to Charles DANCE's *Coriolanus* for the RSC in 1990.

OTHER BRITISH FILMS: *The Trygon Factor*, *The Idol* (1966), *The Magic Christian* (1969), *The Fourth Protocol* (1987).

Blanche, Margaret (*b* Copenhagen) Actress. Leading lady, primarily with Cecil HEPWORTH, in the 1910s, who also appeared in Danish films under her real name, Margaret Jessen.

BRITISH FILMS INCLUDE: *Trelawney of the Wells*, *Comin' Thro' the Rye* (1916), *The Cobweb* (1917), *My Sweetheart* (1918), *Sweet and Twenty* (1919), *The Black Sheep* (1920). AS.

Blanchett, Cate (*b* Melbourne, 1969). Actress. Willowy blonde beauty Blanchett won BAFTA, Golden Globes and other awards and an AAn for her performance as *Elizabeth* (1998). She brought youthful sensuality and intensity to the role, contrasting with her role as priggish Lady Chiltern in *An Ideal Husband* (1999, UK/UN) and the vulnerable opportunist, Lola, in *The Man Who Cried* (2000, UK/Fr/US). Graduated from Sydney's National Institute of Dramatic Art in 1992, did some well-regarded theatre and TV work, and made a major impact in several Australian films, culminating in half the title role in

Oscar and Lucinda (1997, Aust/US), opposite Ralph FIENNES. She went to the US for *Pushing Tin* and *The Talented Mr Ripley* (1999), and seems set for an international career, with roles in each of the *Lord of the Rings* films (2001, 2002, 2003, NZ/US).

OTHER BRITISH FILMS: *Charlotte Gray* (2001, UK/Aust/Ger), *Heaven* (UK//Fr/Ger/It/US) (2002).

Bland, Joyce (*b* London, 1906 – *d* Bournemouth, 1963). Actress. Stage player who starred in some minor films of the 30s, including two for Maclean ROGERS, *The Crime at Blossoms* (1933) and *A Touch of the Moon* (1936), and played supporting roles in bigger films, including Florence NIGHTINGALE in *Sixty Glorious Years* (1938).

OTHER BRITISH FILMS INCLUDE: *Goodnight Vienna*, *The Barton Mystery* (1932), *Spy of Napoleon* (1936), *Dreaming Lips* (1937), *The Citadel* (1938).

Blane, Sue (*b* Wolverhampton, 1949). Costume designer. Blane's sporadic career in films has produced some diverse and flamboyant designs, ranging from *The Rocky Horror Picture Show* (1975), through Peter GREENAWAY's iconoclastic feature debut *The Draughtsman's Contract* (1982) to the sombre historical drama *Lady Jane* (1985) and the stylisation of the failed MUSICAL *Absolute Beginners* (1986). Much praised for her National Theatre designs for *The Relapse* (2001).

OTHER BRITISH FILMS: *Shock Treatment* (1981), *Dream Demon* (1988).

Blessed, Brian (*b* Mexborough, 1936). Actor. It is not surprising to find that so bear-like a presence as Blessed has climbed Mont Blanc and other major peaks. Whatever his role, there is a larger-than-life quality that compels the eye on stage, screen or TV. He is a memorably avuncular Exeter to Kenneth BRANAGH's *Henry V* (1989) and a formidable Ghost in his *Hamlet* (1996, UK/US) and a showy Prince Vultan in *Flash Gordon* (1980). He first came to viewers' attention in TV's *Z Cars* (1962) and was later Richard IV in *Blackadder* and a blustering Squire Western in *Tom Jones* (1997), was in the original theatrical cast of *Cats* in the early 80s, and in many international films such as *Star Wars . . . The Phantom Menace* (1999). Bluff and hearty, or dangerous and dignified, he is inevitably a force to be reckoned with. Married to actress Hildegarde NEIL.

OTHER BRITISH FILMS INCLUDE: *The Christmas Tree* (1966), *Country Dance* (1969), *The Last Valley* (1970), *Henry VIII and His Six Wives* (1972), *The Hound of the Baskervilles* (1983), *Much Ado About Nothing* (1993, UK/US), *The Bruce* (1996), *Macbeth* (1997), *Mumbo Jumbo* (2001).

Blethyn, Brenda (*b* Ramsgate, 1946). Actress. Already a distinguished stage actress, often with London's National Theatre where her gift for comedy was on riotous display in 1977's *Bedroom Farce*, Blethyn suddenly, even improbably, became a film star, albeit an unusual one, in the 90s on the basis of acting range rather than conventional star looks. She had appeared in the US films, *The Witches* (1989) and *A River Runs Through It* (1992), but it was her Oscar-nominated performance in Mike LEIGH's *Secrets & Lies* (1996), as the feckless Cynthia confronted with convulsive truths from her past, which brought her to filmgoers' notice. Subsequently, she has appeared as the raucously exploitative mother bursting out of her cheap clothes in *Little Voice* (1998), contrastingly poignant as the woman dying of cancer in *Girls' Night* (1998), and made several high-profile films in Australia and the US. She thrives under the strong direction that focuses without constricting her eloquence and vibrancy. Awarded OBE, 2003.

OTHER BRITISH FILMS INCLUDE: *Remember Me?* (1996), *Night Train* (1998), *Saving Grace* (2000), *Delaney's Flutter* (2001).

Blezard, John (b Kendal, 1927). Production designer. After training at the Old Vic Theatre School and work in TV, he entered films in the early 60s as art director on such varied fare as *The Hands of Orlac* (1960), *Three on a Spree*, *On the Fiddle* and *Reach for Glory* (1961), and *The Barber of Stamford Hill* (1962). Films as production designer include *First Men in the Moon* (1964), and several for Michael WINNER (*The Wicked Lady*, 1985, *Appointment with Death*, 1988, and *Bullseye!*, 1991), as well as much TV.

OTHER BRITISH FILMS INCLUDE: (art d/des) *Foxhole in Cairo*, *City of the Dead* (1960), *Mix Me a Person*, *The Comedy Man* (1963), *Act of Murder*, *Who Was Maddox?* (1964), *The Liquidator* (1965), *The System*, *That Riviera Touch* (1966), *The Magnificent Two*, *Assignment K* (1967), *Before Winter Comes*, *Only When I Larf* (1968), *Hoffman*, *When Dinosaurs Ruled the Earth* (1969), *Firepower* (1979).

Blick, Newton (b Bristol, 1899 – d Dublin, 1965) Actor. After a successful stage career, culminating in the role of the Tramp with the magic piano in the long-running musical, *Salad Days* (opened 1954), tall, imposing Bristol-born Blick turned to film character work in the 50s and 60s. He brought easy conviction to such roles as the deeply traditional college porter in *Bachelor of Hearts* (1958) and the avuncular, temporising factory boss in *Flame in the Streets* (1961). Continued to work on stage and died in his dressing-room.

OTHER BRITISH FILMS INCLUDE: *Carrington VC* (1954), *The Long Arm* (1956), *The Gypsy and the Gentleman* (1957), *Man in the Moon* (1960), *Term of Trial* (1962), *Lord Jim* (1964).

Bliss, Sir Arthur (b London, 1891 – d London, 1975). Composer. Educated at Rugby, Cambridge and the RCM, Bliss composed only a handful of film scores but some of them are very notable, especially his first – for *Things to Come* (1936). This was an immediate success and performed as a concert suite at the Promenade Concerts. Bliss firmly believed that film music should be able to stand alone in this way, and at least two of his other scores were publicly performed: those for *Conquest of the Air* (1940), which included a twelve-minute suite, and *Men of Two Worlds* (1946), matching the film's lofty aspirations. Wounded during WW1, he spent time in the US in the 20s, was knighted in 1950, appointed Master of the Queen's Musick in 1953, and awarded CH in 1971. Also composed ballets, opera and much chamber music.

OTHER BRITISH FILMS: *Christopher Columbus* (1949), *The Beggar's Opera* (1953), *Welcome the Queen* (1954), *Seven Waves Away* (1956).

Bloch, Robert (b Chicago, 1917 – d Los Angeles, 1994). Screenwriter. Most famous as the author of the original for HITCHCOCK's *Psycho* (1960), Bloch has provided screenplay and/or story for a half-dozen enjoyable British HORROR films for AMICUS in the late 60s and early 70s, four directed by Freddie FRANCIS. Also worked in the US and for TV, always in the horror genre.

BRITISH FILMS: *The Skull*, *The Deadly Bees*, *The Psychopath* (1966), *Torture Garden* (1967), *The House That Dripped Blood* (1970), *Asylum* (1972).

Blomfield, Derek (b London, 1920 – d Brittany, 1964). Actor. Serviceable supporting player in nearly 20 films, who died young of a heart attack on holidays. He is involved, as a child, in the opening street fight of Norman WALKER's homiletic *Turn of the Tide* (1935), joined the BBC Repertory Company 1944–46 and worked solidly on the stage until his death,

starring as the policeman in *The Mousetrap* (1958). Played small roles in 'A' films such as *Hobson's Choice* (1953, as Raymond HUNTLEY's son) and bigger ones in 'B' MOVIES such as *The Flying Dutchman* (1953, as a drunken musician).

OTHER BRITISH FILMS INCLUDE: *Love on Wheels* (1932), *Emil and the Detectives* (1935), *Alibi* (1942), *Night and the City* (1950), *The Golden Arrow* (1952), *Small Hotel* (1957), *East of Sudan* (1964).

Bloom, Claire (b London, 1931). Actress. RN: Blume. Bloom's fragile brunette beauty and intensity caught the attention of reviewers in her first film, the courtroom drama, *The Blind Goddess* (1948), and she became a star in her second, *Limelight* (1951, US), as Charlie CHAPLIN's leading lady. Trained at the Guildhall and Central Schools, appearing first on stage in 1946. Her screen career has divided between British and international films, the latter including *The Brothers Karamazov* (1958) and two for Woody Allen, *Crimes and Misdemeanours* (1989) and *Mighty Aphrodite* (1995). Major British films include *Richard III* (1955, as Lady Anne), *Look Back in Anger* (1959), *The Spy Who Came in from the Cold* (1965), *A Doll's House* (1973, an intelligent if too mature Nora), and *Sammy and Rosie Get Laid* (1987). Has done much notable stage and TV work; on screen, there has been perhaps something too ladylike for major stardom. Married and divorced from Rod STEIGER (1959–69), stage producer Hilliard Elkins (1969–72), and author Philip Roth (1990–95). Her brother John BLOOM is an editor.

OTHER BRITISH FILMS INCLUDE: *Innocents in Paris*, *The Man Between* (1953), *80,000 Suspects*, *The Haunting* (1963), *Three into Two Won't Go* (1968), *A Severed Head* (1970), *Clash of the Titans* (1981), *Déjà Vu* (1984), *A Village Affair*, *Mad Dogs and Englishmen* (1994).

BIBLIOG: Autobiography, *Limelight and After*, 1982.

Bloom, John (b London, 1935). Editor. A former script reader for RANK and Claire BLOOM's younger brother, Bloom has edited nearly fifty British and international films, starting with *The Impersonator* (1961) and including such major productions as *Gandhi* (1982, UK/Ind).

OTHER BRITISH FILMS INCLUDE: *Girl On Approval* (1961), *Man in the Middle*, *The Party's Over* (1963), *Georgy Girl* (1966), *The Lion in Winter* (1968), *The Ritz* (1976), *The French Lieutenant's Woman* (1981), *Damage* (1992, UK/Fr), *A Foreign Field* (1993).

Bloomfield, John Costume designer. Active in British and international films since designing the elaborate period wardrobe for *Henry VIII and His Six Wives* (1972). US films include *Waterworld* (1995).

OTHER BRITISH FILMS INCLUDE: *The Thief of Baghdad* (1978, UK/Fr), *Eye of the Needle* (1981), *The Wicked Lady* (1983), *The Bounty* (1984).

Blunt, Gabrielle (b Herne Bay, 1925). Actress. In the RSC's 1990 *Coriolanus*, Blunt compelled the eye by the sheer attentiveness of her wordless performance. On-screen, she played Catriona, her sights set on mother-ridden Gordon JACKSON, in *Whisky Galore!* (1949) and one of the teachers of the deaf in *Mandy* (1952). Played the Queen Mother in TV's *Diana: Her True Story* (1993).

OTHER BRITISH FILMS INCLUDE: *Tony Draws a Horse*, *The Clouded Yellow* (1950), *Thirty-Six Hours* (1954), *Breath of Life* (1963), *Wilt* (1989).

Bluthal, John (b Poland, 1929). Actor. In Australia since a child, Bluthal alternated between there and the UK, appearing mainly in comedy roles, notably in such popular 60s films as the BEATLES' *A Hard Day's Night* (1964) and *Help!* (1965), and *The Knack . . .* (1965), and as dim Frank in TV's *The Vicar of Dibley* (1994–2000).

OTHER BRITISH FILMS INCLUDE: *Father Came Too!* (1963), *Casino Royale, Follow That Camel* (1967), *Doctor in Trouble* (1970), *Carry On Henry* (1971), *Return of the Pink Panther* (1974), *Superman III* (1983), *Labyrinth* (1986).

Blythe, Betty *see* **Americans in British silent films**

Blythe, John (*b* London, 1921 – *d* Teddington, Middlesex, 1993). Actor. Archetypal spiv and small-time crim in 30 British films, his minor villainy often mitigated by an engaging cheekiness. After 'bits' in *Goodbye, Mr Chips* (1939) and *The Way Ahead* (1944), he was likeable and touching as the son who is killed in *This Happy Breed* (1944), and became a fixture of GAINSBOROUGH films during Sydney BOX's regime in the later 40s. He made five films in which Diana DORS also appeared, and they now seem an enjoyably impudent reminder of more innocent times; they were together again in his last film, *Keep It Up Downstairs* (1976). TV included *Poldark* (1977).

OTHER BRITISH FILMS INCLUDE: *Dear Murderer, Good-Time Girl* (1947), *Portrait from Life, Holiday Camp, Here Come the Huggetts* (1948), *Diamond City, Boys in Brown, A Boy, a Girl and a Bike* (1949), *The Frightened Man* (1952), *Three Steps to the Gallows* (1953), *Doublecross* (1955), *Gaolbreak* (1962), *The VIPs* (1963), *Ups and Downs of a Handyman* (1975).

Blythe, Sydney (*b* England, 1885 – *d*?) Cinematographer. Prolific if unimaginative cameraman, who entered the industry in 1910 as a laboratory assistant, worked exclusively for G.B. SAMUELSON from 1915 to 1926, also serving as his general manager, with New Era from 1927 to 1929 and with Julius HAGEN from 1930 to 1937. Went to Hollywood with Samuelson in 1919–20, but it is not known which of the six films the latter made there were photographed by him.

BRITISH FILMS INCLUDE: *Infelice* (1915), *Gamblers All, Damaged Goods* (1919), *The Game of Life* (co-c), *The Faithful Heart, The Hotel Mouse* (1922), *A Royal Divorce, This England* (1923), *The Unwanted* (1925), *The Somme* (co-c) (1927), *Q-Ships, The Infamous Lady* (1928), *At the Villa Rose* (1930), *Alibi, Black Coffee* (1931), *The Wandering Jew* (1933), *She Shall Have Music* (1935), *A Romance in Flanders* (1937). AS.

Boddey, Martin (*b* Stirling, 1907 – *d* London, 1975). Actor. The founder of Lord's Taverners (1950), this former singer, thick-set and moustached, was a substantial character presence in 50s movies, usually as police inspectors (sympathetically in *Personal Affair*, 1953), coroners, magistrates and other officials.

OTHER BRITISH FILMS INCLUDE: *A Song for Tomorrow* (1948), *The Third Man* (1949), *Seven Days to Noon* (1950), *Laughter in Paradise* (1951), *Cry the Beloved Country* (1952), *Doctor in the House* (1954), *The Iron Petticoat* (1956), *The Square Peg, Carry On Sergeant* (1958), *I'm All Right Jack* (1959), *A Man for All Seasons* (1966).

Boehm, Karlheinz (*b* Darmstadt, Germany, 1929 [or 1927]). Actor. Son of noted conductor Karl Boehm, and known by a variety of mutations (Carl, Karl, Bohm, etc.), he deserves a place here for his haunting portrayal of the sex-obsessed murderer in Michael POWELL's notorious masterpiece, *Peeping Tom* (1960). Also worked in Hollywood (e.g. *The Four Horsemen of the Apocalypse*, 1961), but mostly in Germany.

OTHER BRITISH FILMS: *Too Hot to Handle* (1960), *Come Fly with Me* (1962, UK/US).

Bogarde, Sir Dirk (*b* London, 1921 – *d* London, 1999). Actor, author. RN: Derek Jules Gaspard Ulric Niven van den Bogaerde. Son of the Dutch-born art editor for the London *Times* and a frustrated-actress mother, Bogarde studied as scenic designer and worked as commercial artist, as well as being an unpromising drama student before the war. He first appeared on the stage in 1939 and as a film extra in *Come on*

George [Formby] in the same year. During WW2, served with the Air Photographic Intelligence Unit, had a brief stint as a totally unqualified schoolmaster, was a stage success in *The Power and the Glory* (1947), then went on to become perhaps the most popular and interesting actor in the history of British films.

Bogarde's career of nearly 70 films can be mapped through several key titles. After several films for GAINSBOROUGH, none of them making much impact, he played the charismatic young thug in EALING's *The Blue Lamp* (1949), bringing a violent sexuality to the role that came near to unbalancing the film's sober intentions. He would often, in fact, suggest unsettling currents at work in otherwise modest and/or humdrum films such as *Boys in Brown* (1949), *Cast a Dark Shadow* (1955), *The Spanish Gardener* (1956) and *Libel* (1959), all of which are more compelling for his finding ways of undermining their generic aspirations with his equivocal, watchful intensity.

No doubt it was the astoundingly popular *Doctor in the House* (1954) which initiated the 'Idol of the Odeons' phase, with his Simon Sparrow providing a sanely likeable centre for this skilful ragbag of jokes about the medical profession, and he reprised the role in three of the sequels. As a romantic hero, in comedy (*For Better, for Worse*, 1954) or drama (*The Wind Cannot Read*, 1958), in and out of costume (*Simba*, 1955; *A Tale of Two Cities*, 1958) or uniform (*The Sea Shall Not Have Them*, 1954), in films good and bad, he could do little wrong with audiences during the 50s. For his own part, he grew heartily tired of his image and deliberately sought to change it.

In 1961, he starred as the gay barrister in *Victim*, the first mainstream film to tackle the issue of homosexuality, and, whatever concessions it made to box-office (and the film's courage at the time is worth stressing), its breakthrough status remains. Bogarde, whose own sexuality was always held to be ambivalent, took a calculated risk, probably lost his teenage fans but gained entrée to the more serious roles he craved. As his once-strikingly handsome looks began to change, he acquired a certain sly, furrowed gravitas, which filmgoers registered with rapt attention. His association with US blacklist-fugitive director, Joseph LOSEY, had begun with an enjoyable melodrama, *The Sleeping Tiger* (1954), but it was *The Servant* (1963) which marked the emergence of the new Bogarde – that is, as a great character actor. He played the film's eponym with a riveting aura of opportunism, adducing weapons of sex and class hatred in a blackly comic tussle for power. He made three further films for Losey, including the masterly *Accident* (1967), and thereafter became, in his own words, 'a European actor', memorably associated with Luchino Visconti (*Death in Venice*, 1971, It/Fr, is the key work here), Alain Resnais (*Providence*, 1977, Fr/Switz), Fassbinder (*Despair*, 1978, Ger/Fr), and Bertrand Tavernier for whom he made his eloquent swansong, *Daddy, Nostalgie* (1990, Fr).

He ceased stage work in the mid 50s and did very little television: he was the British *film* actor and star *par excellence*, sometimes making bricks out of straw but also making impressive houses out of bricks. His experiences with Hollywood film-making were uniformly disastrous – his views on, say, *Song Without End* (1960, as Liszt), were almost litigiously frank. In his last two decades, he became a popular author of novels and, covering both his career and his life in France with his friend and manager Anthony FORWOOD, six highly regarded volumes of autobiography. The latter, like his TV interviews, tell the reader just as much as this complex, private man was prepared to reveal.

OTHER BRITISH FILMS: *Dancing with Crime* (1947), *Once a Jolly Swagman*, *Esther Waters* (1948), *Quartet*, *Dear Mr Prohack* (1949), *The Woman in Question*, *So Long at the Fair*, *Blackmailed* (1950), *Penny Princess*, *The Gentle Gunman*, *Hunted* (1952), *They Who Dare*, *Desperate Moment*, *Appointment in London* (1953), *Doctor at Sea* (1955), *Ill Met By Moonlight* (1956), *Campbell's Kingdom*, *Doctor at Large* (1957), *The Doctor's Dilemma* (1958), *Insight: Anthony Asquith* (doc short), *The Singer Not the Song* (1960), *We Joined the Navy* (cameo), *The Password Is Courage*, *HMS Defiant* (1962), *The Mind Benders*, *Doctor in Distress*, *I Could Go On Singing* (1963), *King and Country*, *Hot Enough for June* (1964), *The Epic That Never Was* (doc, TV, some cinemas), *Darling*, *The High Bright Sun* (1965), *Modesty Blaise* (1966), *Our Mother's House*, *Sebastian* (1967), *Oh! What a Lovely War* (1969), *To See Such Fun* (compilation), *A Bridge Too Far* (1977).

BIBLIOG: Margaret Hinxman & Susan d'Arcy, *The Films of Dirk Bogarde*, 1974.

Bolam, James (*b* Sunderland, 1938). Actor. Brought a whiff of regional authenticity to early 60s films such as *A Kind of Loving* and *The Loneliness of the Long Distance Runner* (both 1962), but the Central School-trained actor scored his major successes as laddish Northern boys-about-town in TV's *The Likely Lads* (1964–66) and, more maturely, *When the Boat Comes In* (1975–77). Stage debut at the Royal Court Theatre, 1959, followed by many more performances there (and elsewhere), including *In Celebration* (1969), his role in which he repeated in the 1974 film version (UK/US). Back to big-screen prominence as Kelly MacDONALD's sinisterly avuncular pimp in *Stella Does Tricks* (1996) and the remake of *End of the Affair* (1999, UK/Ger/US).

OTHER BRITISH FILMS INCLUDE: *The Kitchen* (1961), *Murder Most Foul* (1964), *Otley* (1968), *O Lucky Man!* (1973), *The Likely Lads* (1976), *Clockwork Mice* (1995), *It Was an Accident* (2000, UK/Fr).

Boland, Bridget (*b* London, 1913 – *d* Guildford, 1988). Dramatist, screenwriter. Oxford-educated Boland's fame rests chiefly on her chilling 1954 drama, *The Prisoner*, filmed in 1955, with Alec GUINNESS repeating his stage role, as the brain-washed cleric. Co-author of the screenplay for Thorold DICKINSON's *Gaslight* (1940) and author, among a half-dozen others, of King Vidor's *War and Peace* (1956, US/It).

OTHER BRITISH FILMS INCLUDE: *He Found a Star* (1941, co-sc), *The Lost People* (1949, + play), *Anne of the Thousand Days* (1969, co-sc).

Bolt, Jeremy (*b* Uganda) Producer. With director Paul ANDERSON, Bolt formed Impact Pictures in 1992, their first feature being the cult film, *Shopping* (1994). Much of the team's subsequent work has been L.A.-based, but there have been several British films: *Vigo* (1998), with James FRAIN, *There's Only One Jimmy Grimble* (2000, UK/Fr) with Robert CARLYLE, and *The Hole* (2001, UK/Fr), with Thora Birch.

OTHER BRITISH FILMS INCLUDE: (ass p/p/co-p) *Lair of the White Worm* (1988), *The Rainbow* (1989), *Clancy's Kitchen* (co-ex p), *Stiff Upper Lips* (1996), *Event Horizon* (1997, US/UK).

Bolt, Robert (*b* Manchester, 1924 – *d* Petersfield, 1995). Dramatist, screenwriter, director. Bolt, educated at Manchester Grammar School and Manchester University, scored a triumph with his first West End play, *Flowering Cherry* (1958), and another with *A Man for All Seasons* (1960). The film version of the latter (1966) won five Oscars, including those for Best Film and for Bolt's screenplay. It was remade for US TV in 1988. Wrote the screenplays for three of David LEAN's 'big' films: *Lawrence of Arabia* (1962) and the tortuously inflated *Doctor Zhivago* (1965, UK/US, AA/sc) and *Ryan's Daughter* (1970), whose star, Sarah MILES, he twice married. He also wrote and directed Miles in the entertaining but overlong *Lady Caroline Lamb* (1972, UK/It/US). On the evidence, the stroke-afflicted

dramatist was better served by stage than screen. Awarded CBE in 1972. His son **Ben Bolt** (*b* 1952) is a TV drama director.

OTHER BRITISH FILMS: *The Bounty* (1984), *The Mission* (1985).

BIBLIOG: Adrian Turner, *Robert Bolt*, 1988.

Bolton, Guy (*b* Broxbourne, 1885 – *d* London, 1979). Dramatist, screenwriter. Prolific author of plays staged in both Britain and the US of which he became a citizen in 1956, having spent much of his career there. Wrote a number of light-hearted 30s British comedies, and his translation of *Anastasia* from a French play was the basis for the 1956 film.

OTHER BRITISH FILMS INCLUDE: (sc) *Aunt Sally* (1933), *Waltzes from Vienna* (1934, co-sc), *The Guv'nor*, *Man of the Moment* (1935, co-sc), *This'll Make You Whistle* (1936, co-sc, co-story).

Bolton, Peter (*b* Bradford, 1914). Assistant director. Entered films in 1933 and became 1st assistant director in 1936, thereafter spent his entire career in this role, working variously on DOCUMENTARIES such as *Western Approaches* (1944), TWO CITIES productions such as *Trottie True* (1948), several 'CARRY ON' comedies and *A Man for All Seasons* (1966).

Bolvary, Geza Von (*b* Budapest, 1897 – *d* Munich, 1961). Director. An under-rated director of lightweight German comedies and musicals, Bolvary directed four silent Anglo-German productions in Germany, the last two with music and sound effects – *The Ghost Train* (1927), *The Gallant Hussar* (1928), *The Wrecker* (1928), and *Bright Eyes* (1929) – as well as *The Vagabond Queen* (1929). AS.

Bond, Derek (*b* Glasgow, 1919). Actor. On stage from 1937, tall, good-looking Bond was awarded the Military Cross for WW2 service with the Grenadier Guards, entering films in EALING's 1946 POW drama, *The Captive Heart*. Under his Ealing contract, he played the title role in *Nicholas Nickleby* (1947), Googie WITHERS' drowned lover in *The Loves of Joanna Godden* (1947), and gallant Oates in *Scott of the Antarctic* (1948). After some lacklustre RANK contract films in the later 40s (e.g. *Christopher Columbus*, 1949), in the 50s he appeared largely in 'B' MOVIES, some of them, like TEMPEAN's *The Quiet Woman* (1951) and *High Terrace* (1957), rather good. His upper-class style had gone out of fashion, and in middle age he played only a few supporting roles, amusingly mocking his image as a vain actor in *Wonderful Life* (1964). On TV from 1938, and on stage starred in *No Sex Please, We're British*.

OTHER BRITISH FILMS INCLUDE: *Uncle Silas* (1947), *The Weaker Sex*, *Broken Journey* (1948), *Poet's Pub* (1949), *Tony Draws a Horse* (1950), *The Hour of 13* (1952), *Trouble in Store* (1953), *Svengali* (1954), *Press for Time* (1966), *When Eight Bells Toll* (1971).

Bond, Edward (*b* London, 1934). Dramatist, screenwriter. Controversial playwright of *Saved* (1965), in which a baby in a pram is stoned to death, and of *Lear* (1971), a re-working of Shakespeare. Has written two notable screenplays: for Tony RICHARDSON's *Laughter in the Dark* (1969, UK/Fr), adapting NABOKOV, and for Nicolas ROEG's Australian-made *Walkabout* (1970), in which he invested a children's story with unsettling perceptions about cultural differences. Collaborated on the English dialogue for *Blow-Up* (1966, UK/It) and co-authored *Days of Fury* (1973, It/UK).

'Bond' films In 1961 Harry SALTZMAN bought an option on the thriller novels by Ian Fleming and entered into partnership with Albert R. BROCCOLI to produce a series of glamorous action adventures which became the most successful franchise in British cinema history. The Bonds are GENRE films which represent both the last flowering of the old-fashioned imperialist spy THRILLER and the first of the modern high-tech action movies. Although *Dr No* was attacked as 'vicious hokum skilfully designed to appeal to the filmgoer's basest feelings', critical reaction to the Bonds has more often dismissed them as formula entertainments. However, their very longevity makes them a significant production achievement in their own right. Five actors (Sean CONNERY, George Lazenby, Roger MOORE, Timothy DALTON, Pierce BROSNAN) have played the role of Agent 007. All the Bonds have been produced by Eon Productions except the spoof *Casino Royale* (1967) and *Never Say Never Again* (1983, US/UK).

OTHER FILMS: *Dr No* (1962), *From Russia With Love* (1963), *Goldfinger* (1964), *Thunderball* (1965), *You Only Live Twice* (1967), *On Her Majesty's Secret Service* (1969), *Diamonds Are Forever* (1971), *Live and Let Die* (1973), *The Man With the Golden Gun* (1974), *The Spy Who Loved Me* (1977), *Moonraker* (1979, UK/Fr), *For Your Eyes Only* (1981), *Octopussy* (1983), *A View To A Kill* (1985), *The Living Daylights* (1987), *Licence To Kill* (1989), *GoldenEye* (1995, UK/US), *Tomorrow Never Dies* (1997, UK/US), *The World is Not Enough* (1999, UK/US), *Die Another Day* (2002, UK/US).

BIBLIOG: Tony Bennett and Janet Woollacott, *Bond and Beyond*, 1987; James Chapman, *Licence To Thrill: A Cultural History of the James Bond Films*, 1999. James Chapman.

Bond, Gary (*b* Liss, 1940 – *d* London, 1995). Actor. Bond's one major film role was as the bush teacher in the UK/Australian co-production, *Outback* (1971), also known as *Wake in Fright*. In an outback town, he experiences a descent into a personal hell which he helped to make moving and engrossing. His career was curtailed by cancer and, finally, AIDS. He also appeared on stage (e.g. *Design for Living*, 1982) and TV, from as early as an *Avengers* episode in 1961.

OTHER BRITISH FILMS INCLUDE: *Zulu* (1964), *Anne of the Thousand Days* (1969).

Bond, Julian (*b* 1930). Screenwriter. Much associated with TV, including the screenplays for *The Far Pavilions* (1984), Bond also wrote *The Shooting Party* (1984), the elegiac film adapted from Isabel Colegate's novel. Entered the industry in 1952, first working on short instructional films, then on DOCUMENTARIES.

OTHER BRITISH FILMS: *The Witness* (1959), *The Man Outside* (1967, add dial), *Trial by Combat* (1976), *The Whistle Blower* (1986).

Bond, Ralph (*b* London, 1904 – *d* Torbay, 1989). Director, producer. Described by Paul ROTHA as 'the incorruptible left-winger', Bond was an important figure in British DOCUMENTARY film-making, joining John GRIERSON at the EMPIRE MARKETING BOARD FILM UNIT in 1931, for £4 per week. Later became producer and/or director for STRAND FILMS (*Today We Live*, 1937, co-d; *When We Build Again*, 1943, d), REALIST FILMS (*Advance Democracy*, 1938, co-d), World Wide Films (*The Burning Question*, 1945, p), and ACT FILMS (*The Kitchen*, 1961, p super). His work tackled serious problems seriously, and he later became vice-president of the ACTT, and in 1953 became Production Controller for ACT FILMS.

OTHER BRITISH FILMS INCLUDE: (doc) *Neighbours Under Fire*, *Oxford* (1940, both d), *Post 23* (1942, d), *Unity Is Strength* (1944), *Today and Tomorrow*, *A Power in the Land* (1946, d, p); (features) *Don't Panic Chaps* (1959, ex p), *Dead Lucky* (1960, ex p).

Bond, Samantha (*b* London, 1962). Actress. Attractive daughter of actor Philip Bond and producer Pat Sandys (*b* 1926 – *d* 2000), she has played Miss Moneypenny in three 90s 'BOND' FILMS: *GoldenEye* (1995, UK/US), *Tomorrow Never Dies* (1997, UK/US), *The World Is Not Enough* (1999, UK/US). Appeared as a child in *Up Pompeii* and *Not Tonight Darling!* (1971), and in *Erik the Viking* (1989) and *Thacker* (1992). Otherwise, mainly TV, including a sympathetic Mrs Weston in *Emma* (1996).

OTHER BRITISH FILM: *What Rats Won't Do* (1998).

Bonham Carter, Helena (*b* London, 1966). Actress. Because she appeared mostly in period films, critics began to complain of Bonham Carter's limited range. It was as if playing, say, the tragic young queen in *Lady Jane* (1985, her debut), passionate Helena Schlegel in *Howards End* (1992) and driven, resourceful Kate Croy in *The Wings of the Dove* (1997) called on the same emotional and technical resources. Given her impeccable credentials – she is the great-granddaughter of Prime Minister Herbert Asquith (later Lord Oxford and Asquith) and grand-niece of director Anthony ASQUITH, there may have been inverted snobbery in the increasingly predictable commentaries that greeted such roles, especially for her work in four MERCHANT IVORY productions, based on E.M. FORSTER's novels. It was her ardent Lucy Honeychurch in their *Room with a View* (1985) that brought her to real notice, and led her to leave Cambridge.

The image is, however, not all. Her personal life may suggest privilege but has been marked by such misfortunes as her father's paralysis; and her film roles have been more diverse than simplistic appraisal might suggest. She brought real erotic need to her Oscar-nominated performance in *The Wings of the Dove*; was a touching Ophelia in ZEFFIRELLI's *Hamlet* (1990, UK/US); imbued Olivia's parody of love in *Twelfth Night* (1996, UK/US) with delicate comedy; played Woody Allen's wife in *Mighty Aphrodite* (1995, US); and, grungified, finally put paid to the corseted, delicate pre-Raphaelite beauty tag in *Fight Club* (1999, US), as, in her words, an 'obsessive support-group junkie'.

She lived with Kenneth BRANAGH from 1994–99, but the films she made with him – *Mary Shelley's Frankenstein* (1994) and *The Theory of Flight* (1998) – failed commercially. On the brink of international fame, she has been a major British star since the mid 80s. Cousin is TV actor **Crispin Bonham Carter**, who has had small roles in *Howards End* (1992) and *Bridget Jones's Diary* (2001, UK/Fr/US) and played Bingley in TV's *Pride and Prejudice* (1995).

OTHER BRITISH FILMS INCLUDE: *Maurice* (1987), *Where Angels Fear to Tread* (1991), *Margaret's Museum* (1995, UK/Can), *Portraits Chinois* (1996, UK/Fr), *Keep the Aspidistra Flying* (1997), *Carnivale* (1999, Ire/Fr), *Women Talking Dirty* (2001, UK/US).

Bonifas, Paul (*b* Paris, 1902 – *d* Vernouillet, France, 1975). Actor. Lugubrious-looking 'foreigner' in British films during WW2 and after. First in *The Foreman Went to France* (1942), more vividly as an effusive, puzzled insurance investigator in *Bedelia* (1946). In international films until 1975.

OTHER BRITISH FILMS INCLUDE: *Candlelight in Algeria* (1943), *Two Fathers* (short), *Champagne Charlie* (1944), *The Man from Morocco* (1945), *Lisbon Story* (1946), *Take Me to Paris* (1950).

Bonneville, Hugh Actor. With a background in theatre and TV (including an amusing cad in *Take a Girl Like You*, 2000), Bonneville made his film debut in *Mary Shelley's Frankenstein* (1994, UK/US) for Kenneth BRANAGH, followed this with the BOND thriller, *Tomorrow Never Dies* (1997, UK/US), and came to major notice with his role as the hapless stockbroker, in *Notting Hill* (1999, UK/US). Played fatuous Mr Rushworth in *Mansfield Park* (2000, UK/US), and the shy young John Bayley in *Iris* (2002, UK/US), confirming his talent as a subtle character player.

OTHER BRITISH FILMS INCLUDE: *Blow Dry* (UK/Ger/US), *High Heels and Low Lifes* (2001), *My Napoleon* (2002).

Boorman, John (*b* Shepperton, 1933). Director. 'Too rich for their blood,' was Boorman's description of the common reception to his films in Britain. One of the most talented of the 60s generation of English directors, Boorman's contribution to British film is relatively modest. He has never had much time for the concept of NATIONAL CINEMA, and has always veered away from the English cinematic tendency to social REALISM and its tone of irony and restraint in preference for a cinema of myth, dream, passion and imagination. Accordingly most of his best films, such as *Point Blank* (1967) and *Deliverance* (1972), have been made outside England, indeed dealing with the situation of the outsider in a foreign land who, through a journey both physical and psychological, undergoes a baptism of fire.

In Britain, after working in the field of TV documentary with the BBC, Boorman made his film debut with the Dave Clark Five road movie, *Catch Us If You Can* (1965), a SPIN-OFF from the success of *A Hard Day's Night* but with its own individual take on the themes of England and psychological quest. *Leo the Last* (1969), a richly symbolic fable about a foreign aristocrat in London, showed the literary influence of T.S. Eliot and the cinematic influence of HITCHCOCK. *Excalibur* (1981, UK/US) was a stylish examination of the Arthurian legend that had always fascinated Boorman; *Hope and Glory* (1987) a semi-autobiographical memoir of WW2 and an international hit; *The General* (1998, UK/US) a portrait of the Irish gangster Martin Cahill and a prizewinner at Cannes. Also the producer of Neil JORDAN's debut film, *Angel* (1982), Boorman has written about the tribulations of the contemporary film-maker in his book, *Money into Light* (1985), confirming him as one of the most eloquent romantics of the contemporary film scene.

OTHER BRITISH FILMS: *Zardoz* (1973), *Long Shot* (1978), *Emerald Forest* (1985).

BIBLIOG: Michel Ciment, *John Boorman*, 1986. Neil Sinyard.

Booth, Anthony (*b* Liverpool, 1937). Actor. Booth's main claims to fame are two roles: the long-haired 'Scouse git' son-in-law in *Till Death Us Do Part* (1969), based on the TV series (1966–68, 1972, 1974–75), and real-life father-in-law of Prime Minister Tony Blair. Also, Nanette NEWMAN's dodgy boy-friend in *Pit of Darkness* (1961); and in five of the *Confessions of* . . . series.

OTHER BRITISH FILMS INCLUDE: *Suspect* (1960), *The L-Shaped Room* (1962), *The Hi-Jackers* (1963), *Confessions of a Window Cleaner* (1974), . . . *of a Driving Instructor* (1976).

Booth, Connie (*b* Indianapolis, Indiana, 1941). Actress. Booth's adroit comic sense and chirpy blonde prettiness have been inadequately exploited by the cinema. Her fame rests chiefly on her playing of Polly, the hotel maid, in the TV comedy cult favourite, *Fawlty Towers* (1975, 1979), which she co-wrote with John CLEESE, to whom she was married (1968–76). Most other screen appearances have been either in MONTY PYTHON-inspired films (*Monty Python and the Holy Grail*, 1974) or supporting roles in little-seen films, such as the independent *Leon the Pig Farmer* (1992).

OTHER BRITISH FILMS INCLUDE: *Little Lord Fauntleroy* (1980), *The Hound of the Baskervilles* (1983), *The Secret Policeman's Private Parts* (1984), *84 Charing Cross Road* (1986, UK/US), *Hawks* (1988), *American Friends* (1991), *Faith* (1994).

Booth, Harry (*b* London). Director. Responsible for such broad comedies as *On the Buses* (1971), *Mutiny on the Buses* (1972), both drawn from the popular TV series, and the rough-and-ready film studio-set *Go for a Take* (1972, + story), all starring a grimacing Reg VARNEY. In films from 1941, as editor and sound editor before co-producing and -writing the Goons film, *The Case of the Mukkinese Battlehorn* (1956). An oddity in his career was the directing and editing of *A King's Story* (1965, doc), a re-telling of Edward VIII's love affair and abdication. Also TV from early 60s.

OTHER BRITISH FILMS INCLUDE: (d) *River Rivals*, *The Magnificent 6½* (1967, + w both), *The Flying Sorcerer* (+w), *Monet in London* (doc) (1974).

Booth, James (*b* Croydon, 1930). Actor. RN: David Geeves-Booth. Though maybe best known as Ernie Miles in the US TV cult hit, *Twin Peaks* (1990), and most recent work has been in the US, Booth had racked up a substantial body of work in Britain. Trained at RADA and London's Theatre Workshop, appearing in the film version of the latter's *Sparrows Can't Sing* (1962). Played gangster Spider Kelly in two forgettable WARWICK comedies, *In the Nick* and *Jazzboat* (1959), but went on to solid performances in *The Trials of Oscar Wilde* (1960) and as the unlikely hero in *Zulu* (1964). Essentially a character star, his comic talents were exploited in Ken RUSSELL's debut, *French Dressing* (1963), as the naive policeman protagonist of *The Secret of My Success* (1965) and Shirley MacLAINE's secret lover in *The Bliss of Mrs Blossom* (1968).

OTHER BRITISH FILMS INCLUDE: *In the Doghouse*, *The Hellions* (UK/SAf) (1961), *Robbery* (1967), *Revenge* (1971), *Rentadick* (1972), *That'll Be the Day* (1973), *Brannigan* (1975), *Sunburn* (1979, UK/US).

Booth, Walter (*b* England, 1869 – *d* Birmingham, 1938). Director. First and foremost a magician, Booth began making trick films for R.W. PAUL in 1899, introducing drawing into his films, then some basic ANIMATION. In 1906, he joined the CHARLES URBAN TRADING CO, where he directed more than 125 short subjects (including genuine animation and more elaborate trick films, often with SCIENCE-FICTION themes) between 1899 and 1918; one of the first, *The Miser's Doom*, in 1899, ran for 45 feet; and the last was *Tommy's Initiation*, in 1918. AS.

Booth, Webster (*b* Birmingham, 1902 – *d* Llandudno, Wales, 1984). Actor, singer. With his wife Anne ZIEGLER, came sporadically to films via opera, musical comedy and radio. Given their popularity, one must assume their arch style was more suited to the other media than to the camera's scrutiny. Mostly, they appeared as singers in their few films, as in *Waltz Time*, 1945, when they are billed as 'gypsy troubadours'. In the film built around them as 'characters', *The Laughing Lady* (1946), they are simply excruciating whenever they stop singing – and not always when they don't. They were put under contract to BRITISH NATIONAL in 1945, but made only these two films. Together, they also appeared in *Demobbed* (1944) and the South African *Uncle Lord Pete* (1962). Booth's other films as singer were *The Invader*, *The Robber Symphony*, *Sunshine Ahead* (1936) and *The Story of Gilbert and Sullivan* (1953).

Borehamwood Studios Studio situated north of London, this site was chosen by John M. East (1860–1924), a stage and silent screen actor. It opened in 1914 as Neptune Films, which folded in 1921. The premises were later taken over by IDEAL, ROCK, BRITISH NATIONAL, and Associated TV.

Borradaile, Osmond H. (*b* Winnipeg, 1898 – *d* Vancouver, 1999). Cinematographer. Canadian who entered films in 1914 with the Jesse Lasky Company in Hollywood and who went to London in 1930, where he became a cinematographer for the KORDA organisation. He was camera operator on *The Private Life of Henry VIII* (1933), *The Private Life of Don Juan* (1934), and *The Scarlet Pimpernel* (1935); 2nd unit photographer on *Sanders of the River* (1935), *Elephant Boy* (1937), *The Drum* (1938), *The Four Feathers*, *The Lion Has Wings* (1939), *The Trap* (1966, + cam op), specialising in exotic location-shooting; he shot the opening sequence for *The 49th Parallel* (1941), the exteriors for *The Winslow Boy* (1948), was co-cinematographer on *Scott of the Antarctic* (1948) and *Storm over the Nile* (1955), and solo on *The Overlanders* (1946, shot in Australia) and *Saints and Sinners* (1949).

Bosanquet, Simon (*b* London, 1948) Producer. Production manager on such 80s films as *Another Country* (1984) and *Insignificance* (1985), was subsequently associate producer on *White Mischief* (1987) and *Madame Sousatzka* (1988) and co-producer on *Nuns on the Run* (1990), before solo-producing *Afraid of the Dark* (1991, UK/Fr).
OTHER BRITISH FILMS INCLUDE: (p) *Splitting Heirs* (1993, UK/US), *Victory* (1995, UK/Fr/Ger, release 1998), *Onegin* (1999, UK/US).

Boswell, Simon (*b* London, 1954) Composer. Cambridge-educated Boswell began his film career writing scores for Italian horror films, such as Dario Argento's *Creepers* (1984), and for Alejandro Jodorowsky's grotesque *Santa Sangre* (1989, It). His reputation took off as a result of his scores for such British films as the cult success *Shallow Grave* (1994) and *Photographing Fairies* (1997) and TV's *The Lakes* (1997). Scored Michael Hoffman's version of *A Midsummer Night's Dream* (1999, UK/It), and was chosen by Elton JOHN (*Women Talking Dirty*, 2001, UK/US), and Ewan McGREGOR (*Tube Tales*, 1999) and Tim ROTH (*The War Zone*, 1999, UK/It) to score their debuts as, respectively, producer and directors.
OTHER BRITISH FILMS INCLUDE: *Hardware* (1990), *Jack and Sarah* (1995, UK/Fr), *Cousin Bette* (1998, UK/US), *This Year's Love* (1999), *There's Only One Jimmy Grimble* (2000, UK/Fr), *Born Romantic* (2001).

Bouchier, Chili (aka Dorothy) (*b* London 1909 – *d* London, 1999). Actress. Took the name under which she generally appeared from the song 'I Love My Chili Bom-Bom', had the good fortune to live long enough to become a legend of British cinema, with the publicity and the claims in her 1996 autobiography *Shooting Star* far out-stretching her minor importance in films and on stage. However, she did exude a vibrant personality that kept her career alive. Husband (1 of 3) was actor **Harry Milton** (*b* London, 1900 – *d* 1965), who appeared in a few 30s films, including *The King's Cup* (1933), with Bouchier, and (2) was actor **Peter de Greef**, who played Jean KENT's boyfriend in *Champagne Charlie* (1944).
BRITISH FILMS INCLUDE: *A Woman in Pawn* (1927), *Shooting Stars*, *Palais de Danse* (1928), *Carnival* (1931), *Ebb Tide* (1932), *The Ghost Goes West* (1935), *Southern Roses* (1936), *The Dark Stairway* (1938), *Murder in Reverse* (1945), *Mrs Fitzherbert* (1947), *The Counterfeit Plan* (1957), *Dead Lucky* (1960). AS.

Bould, Beckett (*b* 1880 – *d*?). Actor. Former schoolmaster who had a long stage career and on screen as supporting actor, with a gift for regional dialects, from the 30s. Last seen as the sympathetic old-timer in *The Angry Silence* (1960).
OTHER BRITISH FILMS INCLUDE: *Holiday's End* (1937), *The Day Will Dawn* (1942), *The Shipbuilders* (1943), *Anna Karenina* (1948), *Portrait of*

Clare, *Pool of London* (1950), *Lease of Life* (1954), *Let's Be Happy* (1956), *Nowhere to Go* (1958).

Boulter, Rosalyn (*b* Burton-on-Trent, 1917 – *d* Santa Barbara, California, 1997). Actress. On stage from 1935, Central School-trained Boulter played leads in two minor films, *Love at Sea* (1936) and *Return of the Stranger* (1937), then subsided into supporting roles. She played two peripheral dizzy types for Leslie HOWARD in *The First of the Few* (1942) and *The Gentle Sex* (1943), and her last film was the US-made *The Day They Gave Babies Away* (1957). Married director-producer Stanley HAYNES.
OTHER BRITISH FILMS INCLUDE: *A Royal Divorce* (1938), *This Man is Mine*, *George in Civvy Street* (1946), *For Them That Trespass* (1948).

Boulting, John (*b* Bray, 1913 – *d* Sunningdale, 1985) and **Boulting, Roy** (*b* Bray, 1913 – *d* Oxford, 2001). Producers, directors. Twin-brother team who founded Charter Films in 1937 and interchanged the roles of director and producer throughout their long careers. John fought in the Spanish Civil War, and that kind of commitment to social and political issues was a crucial element in much of their film-making. When he returned, they began making supporting features such as *Consider Your Verdict* (1938), which got them and Charter noticed. They made the moving anti-Nazi drama *Pastor Hall* pre-war but its release was delayed for political reasons until 1940. During WW2, John served with the ROYAL AIR FORCE FILM UNIT, and Roy with the ARMY FILM UNIT, for which he made the Oscar-winning DOCUMENTARY *Desert Victory* (1943). In 1942, Roy made the passionately anti-isolationist fantasy, *Thunder Rock*, and two further famous documentaries, *Tunisian Victory* (1944, co-directed with Frank Capra, whose more rhetorical tendencies Boulting tried to restrain) and *Burma Victory* (1945).

Post-war, they determined to make films more relevant to contemporary social realities. Roy's eloquent *Fame is the Spur* (1947) was unpopularly about the frailty of political conviction in the face of ambitious temptations; his *The Guinea Pig* (1948) attacked some of the cruelties of the class and education systems; and John's *Brighton Rock* (1947), though set pre-war, could not have been made then and resonated with post-war malaise. Even their light-hearted satires of the later 50s derive resonance from their persistent willingness to mock the self-importance of such British institutions as the Army (John's *Private Progress*, 1956), the law (John's *Brothers in Law*, 1956), the Foreign Office (Roy's *Carlton-Browne of the FO*, 1958), the trade unions (John's *I'm All Right Jack*, 1959) and the church (*Heavens Above!*, 1963, co-d/co-p).

To finance the making of films of their choice, in the uncertain climate of 50s British cinema, the Boultings periodically made Hollywood films such as Roy's stylish thriller, *Run for the Sun* (1956), for RKO, and *Single-Handed* (1953), for Fox in Britain, and for MGM–BRITISH they made *Seagulls over Sorrento* (1954). They mostly worked together, forming one of those PRODUCER-DIRECTOR TEAMS so influential in British cinema, and they gathered around them a mini-repertory company of actors and other collaborators. Two of their finest joint efforts were the doomsday suspense piece, *Seven Days to Noon* (1950), which made clever use of London locations, and the heartfelt comedy drama, *The Family Way* (1966), starring Hayley MILLS, whom Roy married in 1971. John's main solo films were the documentary *Journey Together* (1945, d, p, sc), for the RAF Film Unit, and the Festival of Britain film *The Magic Box* (1951). Roy's other solo films were: *Heritage of the*

Soil (1937, doc, ass d), *The Landlady* (1938), *Inquest* (1939), *They Serve Abroad* (1942, doc for Army Film Unit), the tense sabotage thriller *High Treason* (1951), *Happy is the Bride* (1957), a sunny-tempered remake of *Quiet Wedding* (1941), and the US-made *The Last Word* (1979). In the event, Roy's directorial career was longer and more varied than John's, but during their crucially productive period, say 1940–60, their contributions were indistinguishable. At their best, they brought urbane wit to bear on seriousness of purpose.

They have not had the serious discussion warranted by their importance in British cinema, not just as film-makers but also for their resolute pursuit of independence from the duopoly of RANK and ABPC which dominated industrial practice in Britain for several decades. In this connection, they were directors of BRITISH LION FILM CORPORATION from 1958 to 1972.

OTHER BRITISH FILMS: *Ripe Earth* (1938, Jp, Rd/e) *The Dawn Guard* (1941, MOI short, Jd, Rp), *Josephine and Men* (1955, Jp, Rd co-s), *Lucky Jim* (1957, Jd, Rp), *Suspect* (1960, co-p, co-d), *A French Mistress* (1960, Jp, Rd co-s), *Rotten to the Core* (1965, Jd, Rp co-s), *Twisted Nerve* (1968, Rd, Jex-p) *There's a Girl in My Soup* (1970, Jp, Rd), *Mr Forbush and the Penguins* (1971, Rd, unc London sequences), *Soft Beds, Hard Battles* (1973, Jp, Rd co-s).

BIBLIOG: Alan Burton *et al* (eds), *The Family Way: The Boulting Brothers and British Film Culture*, 2000.

Boulton, David (aka Davis) (*b* 1911 – *d* 1989). Cinematographer. Beginning as stills photographer on such films as *Gasbags* (1940), *Fame Is the Spur* (1947) and *The Secret Partner* (1961), Boulton later photographed ten films, including the cult horror movie, *The Haunting* (1963) and the US-made *Song of Norway* (1970) and *The Great Waltz* (1972), both directed by Andrew Stone who gave him his first DOP job on the British-made *The Password Is Courage* (1962).

OTHER BRITISH FILMS INCLUDE: (c) *Children of the Damned* (1963), *The Secret of My Success* (1965), *The Frozen Dead, Modesty Blaise* (Amsterdam locations only) (1966), *Danny Jones* (1971).

Boulton, Matthew (*b* Lincoln, 1893 – *d* London, 1962). Actor. From 1937 in Hollywood playing mainly upper-class Brits and assorted officials; before then, in seven British films, of which HITCHCOCK's *Sabotage* (1936) is the most memorable. On stage from 1904 and author of play, *King of Hearts*, filmed in 1936.

OTHER BRITISH FILMS: *His Rest Day* (1927), *To What Red Hell* (1929), *Bed and Breakfast* (1930), *Third Time Lucky, Potiphar's Wife, The Limping Man* (1931).

Boutall, Kathleen Actress. Also on stage, a sturdy supporting player who played the kindly mum worried about children fleeing the nest in *Fly Away Peter* (1948) and sequel *Come Back Peter* (1952) and Margaret BARTON's bossy employer in *Temptation Harbour* (1947), along with a dozen other roles.

OTHER BRITISH FILMS INCLUDE: *A Girl Must Live* (1939), *Uncensored* (1942), *Two Thousand Women* (1944), *The October Man* (1947), *My Brother Jonathan* (1948), *The Woman with No Name* (1950).

Bouwmeester, Theo (*b* Rotterdam, 1871 – *d* Amsterdam, 1956). Director. Born Theodorus Maurits Frenkel, the director adopted the surname of his uncle and mother, Louis and Theodora Bouwmeester, at the time Holland's most celebrated actors. Worked in the UK for HEPWORTH in 1908 and for the Natural Colour Kinematograph Co., filming in KINEMACOLOR, from 1910 to 1912, producing more than 75 SHORTS. Occasionally, he also directed himself as an actor: e.g. in *Checkmated* (1910), *A True Briton* (1911) and *A Whiff of Onion*

(1913). From Britain, he went as a director to Germany (1913–14) and then, in 1915 to the Netherlands, reverting to his real name. AS.

Bovell, Brian (*b* London, 1959). Actor. Most noticeable in *Secrets & Lies* (1996) as Marianne JEAN-BAPTISTE's brother, Bovell has had a good share of the roles available to young black actors in British films and TV, the latter including the mini-series, *Thin Air* (1988).

OTHER BRITISH FILMS: *Babylon* (1980), *Burning an Illusion* (1981), *Real Life* (1983), *Playing Away* (1986), *A Demon in My View* (1991, UK/Ger), *Welcome II the Terrordome* (1995).

Bower, Dallas (*b* London, 1907 – *d* London, 1999). Producer. Now most famous as initiator and associate producer of the wartime success, *Henry V* (1944), Bower had a long career as sound recordist, from 1927, and as pioneer TV producer-director with the BBC TV Service 1936–39. In the latter capacity, he produced operas, ballets, revues, and plays, including some major Shakespearean productions. On-screen, he had acted as associate producer to Paul CZINNER on *Escape Me Never* (1935) and *As You Like It* (1936). Was commissioned in the Royal Corps of Signals in 1939, was Executive Producer of the MOI's Films Division (1940–42), and ensured the interest first of Filippo DEL GIUDICE and then of the RANK ORGANISATION in backing *Henry V*. Bower had hoped to direct but OLIVIER chose to do so as well as to star, and in the intervening years Bower's contribution (for instance, it was he who brought composer William WALTON into the venture) has been undervalued. In 1934, he directed his first film, *Path of Glory* and, post-war, he directed versions of *Alice in Wonderland* (1949, UK/Fr/US, combining puppets and live action) and *The Second Mrs Tanqueray* (1952), two minor US films, and wrote the screenplay for an eight-part children's serial, *Mystery in the Mine*. In 1936, he wrote the book, *Plan for Cinema*.

OTHER BRITISH FILMS: (sd) *Under the Greenwood Tree* (1929), *Such Is the Law, Suspense* (1930), *Other People's Sins* (1931), *Here's George, The City of Paris* (1932); (other) *Supersonic Saucer* (sc), *Into the Light* (short, d) (1956).

BIBLIOG: Brian McFarlane, 'Dallas Bower: The Man Behind Olivier's *Henry V*', *Shakespeare Bulletin*, Winter 1994.

Bowers, Lally (*b* Oldham, 1917 – *d* London, 1984). Actress. On stage from 1936 and due to play Mrs Pearce in *Pygmalion* (1984) just before she died, she filmed infrequently but memorably: as the cowed governess, replaced early, in *The Chalk Garden* (1964), the hearty headmistress in *Our Miss Fred* (1972) and the Queen in *The Slipper and the Rose* (1976). As a kindly, conventional aunt in the 1958 play, *No Concern of Mine*, with an invisible technique and barely fifteen minutes on stage, she quietly made the evening her own.

OTHER BRITISH FILMS INCLUDE: *Tamahine* (1962), *All the Way Up* (1970), *Up Pompeii, Up the Chastity Belt* (1971), *Dracula AD 1972* (1972).

Bowie, David (*b* London, 1947). Singer, actor. RN: Hayward-Jones. One of rock music's most influential figures, Bowie has consistently fought to be recognised as a credible actor. After bit parts in several minor films in the late 60s, Bowie's rise to the heights of rock fame allowed him to appear in the dreamy fantasy, *The Man Who Fell To Earth* (1976). He gave a fine performance in *Merry Christmas Mr Lawrence* (1982) before upstaging a group of puppets in Jim HENSON's *Labyrinth* (1986). Has appeared mainly in American films, often as pop culture icons with profiles as prominent as his own: e.g. as Andy Warhol in *Basquiat* (1996). He has proved to be one of the great visual innovators with many of his video clips (particularly during the 90s) but his filmography remains slight and abstract. Married to model/actress Iman.

OTHER BRITISH FILMS: (a) *Ziggy Stardust and the Spiders from Mars* (1983), *Absolute Beginners* (1986), *Everybody Loves Sunshine* (1999); (comp) *When The Wind Blows, Absolute Beginners* (1986). Tim Roman.

Bowie, Les (*b* Vancouver, 1914 – *d* 1979). Special effects technician. Bowie's career in SPECIAL EFFECTS began at PINEWOOD in the late 40s when he developed expertise in the use of matte shots to preclude the need for undue location work. His high reputation derived essentially from his work in the HORROR GENRE, much of it for HAMMER. Here, he had turned a man into a monster in *The Quatermass Experiment* (1955), created the aura of science with gurgling retorts, green gases and blue electrical charges in *The Evil of Frankenstein* (1964), ensured the imaginative emergence of the alien creatures from their disintegrating spacecraft in *Quatermass and the Pit* (1967), and, in *To the Devil a Daughter* (1976), burnt actor Anthony VALENTINE to a crisp.

OTHER BRITISH FILMS INCLUDE: *Great Expectations* (1946), *The Red Shoes* (1948), *So Long at the Fair* (1950), *The Grip of the Strangler* (1958), *The Curse of the Werewolf* (1961), *Captain Clegg* (1962), *The Quiller Memorandum* (UK/US), *The Reptile, Fahrenheit 451* (1966), *The Mummy's Shroud, Casino Royale** (1967), *Vampire Circus* (1971), *Nothing But the Night, Dracula AD* (1972), *The Satanic Rites of Dracula* (1974), *Superman: The Movie** (1978). *= matte supervisor.

Bowker, Judi (*b* Shawford, 1954). Actress. Delicate of feature and complexion, and a trained ballerina, Bowker, on stage since childhood, has done some fine TV, memorably as Midge Carne in *South Riding* (1974) and Kitty in *Anna Karenina* (1985), but comparatively little cinema. Remembered as Andromeda in *Clash of the Titans* (1981) and free-thinking Lady Olivia in the elegiac *The Shooting Party* (1984).

OTHER BRITISH FILMS: *Brother Sun, Sister Moon* (1972, UK/It), *East of Elephant Rock* (1976).

Bowles, Peter (*b* London, 1936). Actor. Though he has made a dozen or so films, including *Blow-up* (1965, UK/It) and *A Day in the Death of Joe Egg* (1970), as the protagonist's friend in each case, and *The Charge of the Light Brigade* (1968), as Jill BENNETT's cuckolded husband, RADA-trained Bowles only became a household name for his TV work. Tall, moustachioed, urbane, often opportunist, he worked variations on this persona in such popular fare as *Rumpole of the Bailey* (1978–79, 1983, 1987–88, 1991), *To the Manor Born* (1979–81), and *Lytton's Diary* (1985–86), which he co-authored. Also on stage in plays including Osborne's *The Entertainer* (1986) and as Beau Brummell in *The Beau* (2001).

OTHER BRITISH FILMS INCLUDE: *Three Hats for Lisa* (1965), *Eyewitness* (1970), *Endless Night, The Offence* (1972), *The Legend of Hell House* (1973), *The Steal* (1995), *One of the Hollywood Ten* (2000, UK/Sp).

Box, Betty E. (*b* Beckenham, Kent, 1915 – *d* London, 1999). Producer. During a career spanning more than 30 years, Box more than held her own in a male-dominated industry, becoming one of the most consistently successful producers of her generation, with a flair for making genuinely popular British films.

Entered film in 1942, joining brother, Sydney BOX, at VERITY FILMS where she helped produce over 200 wartime SHORTS. Post-war, she made the transition to feature films, co-producing *The Upturned Glass* (1947) at RIVERSIDE STUDIOS. When Sydney took over GAINSBOROUGH STUDIOS in 1946, he appointed her Head of Production at the ISLINGTON studio,

where she produced ten films in two years. While tight budgets and shooting schedules compromised the quality of some of them, Box's time at Islington consolidated her unusual position as a woman producer, and with films such as *When the Bough Breaks* (1947) she was responsible for some of most politically interesting films of the period.

When Gainsborough Studios closed in 1949, Box moved to RANK's PINEWOOD STUDIOS, where her first years were among the toughest of her career. Indeed Box mortgaged her house to provide bridging finance for *The Clouded Yellow* (1950), the first of her 30-odd feature collaborations with director Ralph THOMAS. It is for their popular 'DOCTOR' cycle – from *Doctor in the House* (1954) until *Doctor in Trouble* (1970) – that Box is perhaps best remembered. Although often dismissed as formulaic, they tackled issues of GENDER and CLASS with an irreverence which clearly struck a chord with contemporary audiences.

Box was characteristically modest about her achievements, claiming that she had never regarded herself as a serious filmmaker, but she survived, indeed thrived, during difficult transitional years of British cinema. Her second husband was producer Peter ROGERS.

OTHER BRITISH FILMS: *Dear Murderer* (1947), *The Blind Goddess, Here Come the Huggetts, Vote for Huggett* (1948), *Marry Me, It's Not Cricket, The Huggetts Abroad* (1949), *So Long at the Fair* (1950), *Appointment with Venus* (1951), *The Venetian Bird* (1952), *A Day to Remember* (1953), *Mad About Men* (1954), *Doctor at Sea* (1955) *Checkpoint, The Iron Petticoat* (1956), *Doctor at Large, Campbell's Kingdom* (1957), *A Tale of Two Cities, The Wind Cannot Read, The Thirty Nine Steps* (1958), *Upstairs and Downstairs* (1959), *Conspiracy of Hearts, Doctor in Love* (1960) *No Love for Johnnie, No, My Darling Daughter* (1961), *The Wild and the Willing, A Pair of Briefs* (1962), *Hot Enough for June, Doctor in Distress* (1963), *The High Bright Sun* (1965), *Deadlier than the Male, Doctor in Clover* (1966), *Nobody Runs Forever* (1968), *Some Girls Do* (1969), *Percy* (1971) *It's a 2'6" World Above the Ground* (1972), *Percy's Progress* (1974).

BIBLIOG: Autobiography, *Lifting the Lid*, 2000. Justine Ashby.

Box, John (*b* London, 1920). Production designer. Even a mediocre film such as *First Knight* (1995, US) *looks* wonderful thanks to Box's glittering designs. Educated at the London School of Architecture, he entered films in the late 40s as a draughtsman on such films as *The Woman in Question* (1950) and *The Importance of Being Earnest* (1952). As 'art director', he worked on more than a dozen 50s GENRE films, including six adventures for WARWICK, including *Cockleshell Heroes* (1955) and *Zarak* (1956). He designed for Anthony ASQUITH (*The Young Lovers*, 1954), Carol REED (*Our Man in Havana*, 1959, *Oliver!*, 1968, AA) and, most notably, for David LEAN (*Lawrence of Arabia*, 1962, *Doctor Zhivago*, 1965, UK/US; both AA): i.e, for the best-regarded British directors of their day. The design arguably overwhelms such large-scale films as *Zhivago, Nicholas and Alexandra* (1971, UK/US, AA) and *The Great Gatsby* (1974, US, BAA) but, if so, the responsibility lies elsewhere. He also won BAAs for *A Man for All Seasons* (1966) and *Rollerball* (1975, US), and AAn and BAAn for Lean's *A Passage to India* (1984), and was awarded OBE in 1998. Arguably Britain's most distinguished artist in his field since the 60s.

OTHER BRITISH FILMS: *The Million Pound Note* (1953), *The Black Knight* (1954, assoc art d), *A Prize of Gold* (1955), *The Gamma People, High Flight* (1956), *How to Murder a Rich Uncle, Fire Down Below* (1957), *The Inn of the Sixth Happiness, No Time to Die* (1958), *Our Man in Havana, Left, Right and Centre* (1959), *Two Way Stretch, The World of Suzie Wong* (1960), *The Wild Affair* (1963), *Of Human Bondage* (1964),

The Looking Glass War (1969, p only), *Just Like a Woman* (1992), *Black Beauty* (1994, UK/US).

Box, Muriel (*b* New Malden, 1905 – *d* London, 1991). Director, screenwriter, producer. RN: Baker. Although the 14 films she directed between 1952 and 1964 have received little critical attention, Box was (with Wendy TOYE) one of only two women directors to sustain a career in mainstream British cinema during the 50s and 60s.

Entered films in 1928, as typist at BRITISH INSTRUCTIONAL FILMS, her responsibilities later extended to vetting prospective scripts and working as continuity girl. In 1932, she began a correspondence with Sydney BOX (then an aspiring playwright), offering him advice on scripts. They married in 1935, and their professional collaboration was characteristically pragmatic, with a knack for recognising gaps in the market (e.g. the plays they wrote for women's groups) and attuned to popular tastes.

Although Box's debut as a director is usually given as her first feature, *The Happy Family* (1952), she actually directed as early as 1941 at VERITY FILMS, Sydney's company set up to make wartime DOCUMENTARY SHORTS. In 1943 the couple began producing independent feature films at RIVERSIDE STUDIOS, and this successful period of Box's career culminated in winning an Oscar for the screenplay of *The Seventh Veil* (1945). They were then appointed to take over GAINSBOROUGH STUDIOS with Muriel as Head of the Scenario Department.

The feature films Box directed are generically and thematically varied: *Street Corner* (1953) and *Too Young to Love* (1959) offered commentary on gender issues; *To Dorothy a Son* and *Simon and Laura* (1955) took light-hearted satirical swipes at marital power struggles. After the failure of *Rattle of a Simple Man* 1964) and her separation from Sydney (the couple divorced in 1968; she married Lord Gardiner), Box retired from the film industry. However, she went on to establish a publishing company, Femina Books, and remained an outspoken critic of the sexism of the British film industry until her death in 1991.

OTHER BRITISH FILMS: (d) *The Beachcomber* (1954), *Eyewitness, The Passionate Stranger* (1956), *The Truth About Women* (1957), *Subway in the Sky, This Other Eden* (1959), *The Piper's Tune* (1961).

BIBLIOG: Muriel Box, *Odd Woman Out*, 1974. Justine Ashby.

Box, Sydney (*b* Beckenham, Kent, 1907 – *d* Perth, Australia, 1983). Writer-Producer. During the 30s, Box was a playwright and screenwriter collaborating with his second wife Muriel BOX. In the war he made numerous documentaries as head of VERITY FILMS and produced three films for TWO CITIES, including the witty comedies *On Approval* (1944) and *English Without Tears* (1944). As an independent at RIVERSIDE STUDIOS (1945–46) he established the 'COMPANY OF YOUTH' for potential stars and produced the mildly risqué *29 Acacia Avenue* (1945) and the hugely successful *The Seventh Veil* (1945, AA, Best Screenplay), which combined traditional MELODRAMA with an interest in character psychology, leading to his appointment as production head at GAINSBOROUGH STUDIOS (1947–49). Box's output of over 30 medium-budget films, including those made by his sister Betty BOX at Islington, was impressive, but of uneven quality. His HISTORICAL FILMS, *Bad Lord Byron* (1949) and *Christopher Columbus* (1949), were stilted and the THRILLERS, including *Broken Journey* (1948), wordy and static. More popular were the COMEDIES, notably *Holiday Camp* (1947) that initiated the 'HUGGETTS' series. Most innovative were challenging SOCIAL PROBLEM films,

Good-Time Girl (1947) and *Boys in Brown* (1949), or those exploring male neuroses: *The Years Between* (1946), *Daybreak* (1946, rel 1948), *The Brothers* (1947), *The Upturned Glass, The Man Within* (1948).

In 1951 Box formed London Independent Producers where he produced a similar mixture of films. The finest was *The Prisoner* (1955), a moving Cold War melodrama. By the late fifties Box was more businessman – with interests in theatre, TV and publishing – than film-maker. Illness forced his retirement in 1967. He created a substantial body of films, the best examining controversial social and psychological issues.

OTHER BRITISH FILMS: (shorts/co-p) *Telefootlers, The Roots of Victory* (adpt only) (1941), *Men of Tomorrow, Free House* (1942); (ex p/p): *The Flemish Farm* (1943), *Don't Take It to Heart!, Out of Chaos* (doc) (1944), *Dear Murderer* (+ co-sc), *Jassy* (1947), *My Brother's Keeper, Snowbound, Miranda, The Calendar, Quartet, Easy Money* (+ co-sc) (1948), *The Astonished Heart, Trio, So Long at the Fair* (1950), *Eyewitness* (1956), *Subway in the Sky, Floods of Fear* (1958), *The Long Duel* (1967); (co-p) *OHMS* (1937), *The Sword of the Spirit* (1942), *Men of Rochdale* (1944), *Lost* (1955), *Deadlier Than the Male* (1966); (co-sc, p) *A Girl in a Million* (1946), *Street Corner* (1953), *The Truth About Women* (1958), *Too Young to Love* (1959); (co-sc) *Alibi Inn* (1935), *The Blind Goddess* (1948), *The Happy Family* (1952, + co-p), *The Passionate Stranger* (1956); (sc) *For Dealers Only* (*c* 1937), *Portrait from Life, Here Come the Huggetts* (1948), *Forbidden Cargo* (+ p), *The Beachcomber* (1954), *A King's Story* (1965, doc). Andrew Spicer.

Boxer, John (*b* London, 1909 – *d* 1982). Actor. After stockbroker training, turned to stage in 1928 and entered films in *Royal Cavalcade* (1935), thereafter appearing prolifically as professionals and officials of many kinds, mainly in the 40s and 50s. His characteristic persona was authoritative but he could be comic (like the inept receptionist in *The Black Sheep of Whitehall*, 1941) or sympathetic (like the humane vet in *Heart of a Child*, 1958). Equally prolific on stage (popular in *Seagulls over Sorrento*, 1951, 1952), he appeared in *Gandhi* (1982, UK/Ind) in the year he died.

OTHER BRITISH FILMS INCLUDE: *Fishers of Men* (1939, short), *Convoy* (1940), *In Which We Serve* (1942), *Millions Like Us* (1943), *Waterloo Road, The Halfway House* (1944), *The October Man* (1947), *The Clouded Yellow* (1950), *Encore* (1951), *Diplomatic Passport* (1954), *Bridge on the River Kwai* (1957), *Victim* (1961), *Frenzy, For the Love of Ada* (1972).

Boyd, Don (*b* Nairn, Scotland, 1948). Producer, director. After a childhood spent partly in China, Hong Kong and Uganda, and education in Edinburgh, Boyd studied drama before enrolling in the London Film School in 1968. Graduating in 1970, as bad as a time could be for entering British films, by the end of the decade he had established himself as an independent film-maker to watch. He borrowed money from friends to make his first feature, *Intimate Reflections* (1975, d, p, s), which failed to achieve distribution; *East of Elephant Rock* (1976, d, p, s) drew on childhood memories of the Far East; and he helped to finance *Nighthawks* (1979), a rare account of a homosexual's life in London. He went on to a series of risky propositions including *Sweet William* (1979, ex p), from Beryl BAINBRIDGE's novel of sexual infidelities; *Scum* (1979, ex p), a grim look at Borstal life; Mai ZETTERLING's *Scrubbers* (1982), with women behind bars this time; Derek JARMAN's *The Last of England* (1987, p) and, drawing on Wilfred Owen's poem and Benjamin BRITTEN's music, *War Requiem* (1989, p); and, for his own company, Lexington, *Lucia* (1998, d), which, Donizetti-based, combines his passions for film and opera and stars his daughter Amanda Boyd.

OTHER BRITISH FILMS INCLUDE: *Billiard Balls* (1970, d, short), *International Velvet* (1978, p co-ord), *The Tempest, Hussy, The Great Rock'n'Roll Swindle* (1979, ex p), *Blue Suede Shoes* (1980, doc, ex p), *Aria* (1987, p), *Twenty-One* (1991, d, sc), *The Girl with Brains in Her Feet* (1997, p), *Crossmaheart* (1999, p).

Boyd, Dorothy (*b* Croydon, 1907). Actress. Blonde supporting player or second lead in silent films and 'QUOTA QUICKIES'; on screen 1926 – 1939.
BRITISH FILMS INCLUDE: *The Ball of Fortune* (1926), *Easy Virtue* (1927), *The Constant Nymph* (1928), *Birds of Prey* (1930), *Lily of Killarney* (1934), *Shadowed Eyes* (1939). AS.

Boyd, Stephen (*b* Belfast, 1928 – *d* Los Angeles, 1977). Actor. RN: William Millar. Husky Hollywood-style leading man of just on 50 films in his 20-year career. 50s British cinema should have made better use of this antidote to the tweedy pipe-smokers who dominated and dulled the decade. Apart from one good chance in the teasing war thriller, *The Man Who Never Was* (1955), Hollywood did better by him, especially as the treacherous Messala in *Ben-Hur* (1959), though, in fairness, it also starred him in one of the most risibly awful films ever, *The Oscar* (1966). He almost played Antony opposite Susan Hayward in *Cleopatra* before delays worked in favour of the Burtons. Spent his early childhood in Canada and acted there and in the US before returning to the UK where he debuted in *An Alligator Named Daisy* (1955). Before his premature death from a heart attack, he made a series of lustreless international co-productions.
OTHER BRITISH FILMS: *A Hill in Korea, Seven Waves Away* (1956), *Seven Thunders, Island in the Sun* (1957), *The Inspector* (1962), *The Third Secret* (1964), *Assignment K* (1967), *Shalako* (1968), *The Man Called Noon* (1973), *The Squeeze* (1977).

Boyd, William (*b* Accra, Ghana, 1952). Author, screenwriter, director. Just as it seemed that novelist Boyd's film career would consist mainly of adapting his own and other people's novels into US films, he made his debut as director-screenwriter of *The Trench* (1999, UK/Fr), a Western Front drama with a cast of important new British talent. There was controversy over his co-authorship of *Chaplin* (1992, UK/Fr/It/Jap/US); he shares credit with Bryan FORBES but in fact took over from him. Boyd grew up in Africa, the setting for his US films, *Mr Johnson* (1990) and *A Good Man in Africa* (1994). His screenplay debut was with the excellent telemovie, *Good and Bad at Games* (1983).

Boyle, Catherine (aka Katie) (*b* Florence, 1929). Actress. RN: Catharina di Francavilla. Popular TV personality of the 50s and 60s: she hosted the *Eurovision Song Contest* for many years, and was a panellist on *Juke Box Jury*. Made four films in the 50s – *The House in the Square* (1951), *Not Wanted on Voyage, The Truth about Women* (1957), *Intent to Kill* (1958) – without establishing herself as a screen personality.

Boyle, Danny (*b* Manchester, 1956). Director, producer. Boyle's is one of the success stories of the 90s. How long Britain can hold him is a question, but in his preference for Scottish, Welsh and Northern Ireland settings he resists the usual equation of 'British' with 'English'. His penchant for black comedy came to notice with *Shallow Grave* (1994) and was confirmed by *Trainspotting* (1996), which combined drugs, Iggy Pop, underage sex, Edinburgh grot and several 'hot' young talents, to box-office and critical acclaim. Its refusal of realism, wild black comedy and a curious but tenacious morality made it perhaps the most heartening British film of its year. His third

comedy with Ewan McGREGOR, the US-set *A Life Less Ordinary* (1997), flopped, but he recovered to make *Alien Love Triangle*, a sci-fi love story with Kenneth BRANAGH, and to direct Leonardo DiCaprio in the Thai-set drama, *The Beach* (2000, US). Also produced Alan CLARKE's Northern Ireland TV drama, *Elephant* (1989) and the Swansea-set black comedy *Twin Town* (1997), declining the offer of the fourth in the *Alien* series. Boyle's is a daring, even anarchic talent: it would be a pity for it to be constrained by conventional fare. And in 2001, he was back in Britain's North directing two TV plays for the BBC: *Vacuuming Completely in the Nude* and *Strumpet*, and in the following year he filmed *28 Days Later*.

Brabourne, John (Lord Brabourne) (*b* London, 1924). Producer. Born John Ulick Knatchbull, son of one viceroy of India and son-in-law of another (Lord Mountbatten), this distinguished producer, Eton- and Cambridge-educated, was awarded a CBE in 1993. Entered films in the late 40s as production assistant and in this and related capacities (assistant production manager, unit manager) worked on about a dozen 50s films, including *The Wooden Horse* (1950) and six for the failing Herbert WILCOX (e.g. *Laughing Anne*, 1953; *Trouble in the Glen*, 1954). First film as producer was the Indian adventure, *Harry Black* (1958), on which he took Richard GOODWIN as location manager. Subsequently they became one of the most successful production teams in Britain, their credits including ZEFFIRELLI's ground-breaking *Romeo and Juliet* (1968, UK/It), on which Goodwin was associate producer to Brabourne and Anthony HAVELOCK-ALLAN, *The Tales of Beatrix Potter* (1971), the enjoyable Agatha CHRISTIE all-star romps, beginning with *Murder on the Orient Express* (1974), David LEAN's *A Passage to India* (1984) and the marathon two-part version of *Little Dorrit* (1987), directed by Goodwin's wife, Christine EDZARD. Brabourne's other productions include two popular war films, *Sink the Bismarck!* (1960) and *HMS Defiant* (1962), the film version of OLIVIER's famous *Othello* (1965) and the 'new realist' *Up the Junction* (1967), again with Havelock-Allan. Like the latter in his time, he strengthened the civilised, literary strain of British cinema, and was a creative rather than merely 'financial' producer.
OTHER BRITISH FILMS: (p/ex p) *The Mikado* (1966), *The Dance of Death* (1968), *Smoky Joe's Revenge* (1974), *The 'Copter Kids* (1976), *Seal Island* (1977), *Death on the Nile* (1978), *Stories from a Flying Trunk* (1979), *The Mirror Crack'd* (1980), *Evil Under the Sun* (1981).

Bracken, Brendan (Viscount Bracken) (*b* Kilmallock, Ireland, 1901 – *d* 1958). Administrator. Irish journalist, in Parliament from 1929, and Minister of Information, 1941–45. During this period, the MOI produced many SHORT FILMS, at first based on the experience of the Blitz, later depicting essential war work. The aim was morale-building PROPAGANDA but without giving the public the feeling of being lectured. As well as overseeing shorts and *Warwork News*, the NEWSREEL series produced by the Films Division of the MOI, Bracken was also involved in discussions over several major features. Worries about *In Which We Serve* (1942) being bad for morale having proved groundless, he suggested a similar story to boost the Army. The production which ensued, *The Way Ahead* (1944), was a major success. A close friend of Winston CHURCHILL's, Bracken nevertheless resisted his attempt to stop filming of *The Life and Death of Colonel Blimp* (1943). In 1944, he encouraged the joint UK/US production of the documentary *Tunisian Victory*, but, though he gave muted approval to documentarist Harry WATT's feature *Nine Men* (1942), he was not really in sympathy with the egalitarian sympathies of the DOCU-MENTARY film movement. At the end of the war, he was appointed first lord of the Admiralty in Churchill's caretaker government, having no wish to see the MOI outlast the war.

Braddell, Maurice (*b* Singapore, 1901 – *d* 1990). Actor. Educated at Charterhouse, Oxford and RADA, Braddell appeared in films of the 20s and 30s, starring in KORDA's *Men of Tomorrow* (1932) as a rebellious university student. Also co-wrote *Love, Life and Laughter* (1934), the source play of *It's You I Want* (1936), and the story for *Where's That Fire?* (1939). Went to America, became an artist and appeared as one in Andy Warhol's *Flesh* (1968).

OTHER BRITISH FILMS INCLUDE: *Dawn* (1928), *Master and Man* (1929), *Wolves, Her Reputation* (1931), *Things to Come* (1936).

Braden, Bernard (*b* Vancouver, 1916 – *d* London, 1993). Actor. In Britain since 1938, after Canadian radio experience, had his own very popular radio and TV shows in Britain, and appeared on the London stage as well as in nine films, starting with *Love in Pawn* (1953). Married actress Barbara KELLY in 1942, and they often appeared together, as in *Jet Storm* (1959), as a humorously divorcing couple. Son **Christopher Braden** is a director and appeared as child with Braden in *The Kid from Canada* (1957) and daughter **Kim Braden** is an actress, who appeared in several British films, including *That'll Be the Day* (1973).

OTHER BRITISH FILMS INCLUDE: *The Day the Earth Caught Fire, All Night Long* (1961), *The War Lover* (1962).

BIBLIOG: Autobiography *The Kindness of Strangers*, 1990.

Bradley, David (aka Dai) (*b* Barnsley, Yorks, 1955). Actor. Aged 14, Bradley made an instant impression as the undersized, pinch-faced hero, obsessed with a kestrel, in Ken LOACH's *Kes* (1969). Nothing else in his career could match it. Some TV, including *The Flame Trees of Thika* (1981).

OTHER BRITISH FILMS: *Malachi's Cove* (1973), *Absolution* (1978), *Zulu Dawn* (1979).

Bradley, David (*b* York, 1942) Actor. Character player who worked in an instruments factory for eight years before going to RADA, and made his stage debut in 1968 at Sheffield Playhouse. He has worked with the National Theatre, and has been a great deal on TV, in roles like that of Robson Greene's raddled dad in *Reckless* (1997) and the even more raddled Pitt Crawley in *Vanity Fair* (1998). Suddenly in a rush of films at the turn of the century, including *Blow Dry* (UK/Ger/US), *Gabriel and Me, Harry Potter and the Philosopher's Stone* (UK/US) (2001), as Argus Filch, and the Dogme group's *The King is Alive* (2001).

OTHER BRITISH FILMS INCLUDE: *Another Sunday and Sweet F.A.* (1972), *Prick Up Your Ears* (1987), *Pas de Trois* (2000).

Bradley, Leslie (*b* Aldershot, 1913 – *d* Desert Hot Springs, California). Actor. Characteristically played tough guys like the hoodlum in *No Orchids for Miss Blandish* and 'Basher' in *Noose* (both 1948), but there are detectives, army officers and several Americans among his British films. In the US from 1950, often played British types, as in *King Richard and the Crusaders* (1954).

OTHER BRITISH FILMS INCLUDE: *The Way of Youth* (1934), *Black Limelight* (1938), *Atlantic Ferry* (1941), *The Young Mr Pitt* (1942), *Waterloo Road* (1944), *Anna Karenina* (1948), *A Case for PC 49* (1951).

Bradley, Paul (*b* West Midlands, *c* 1957). Executive producer. Much associated with the films of MERCHANT IVORY, with whom he began as producer's assistant on *Heat and Dust*

(1982), was associate producer on *The Bostonians* (1984, US/UK), *A Room with a View* (1985) and *Maurice* (1987) and executive producer on the team's films from *Howards End* (1992) to *The Golden Bowl* (2000, UK/Fr/US). Co-produced *A Soldier's Daughter Never Cries* (1998, US).

OTHER BRITISH FILMS INCLUDE: *The Remains of the Day* (1993), *Jefferson in Paris, Feast of July* (UK/US) (1995), *Surviving Picasso* (1996, UK/US).

Bradley, Robert 'Buddy' (*b* Harrisburg, Pennsylvania, 1908 – *d* New York, 1972). Choreographer. African-American Bradley's main contribution to British film was his collaboration with Jessie MATTHEWS on dance numbers for *Evergreen* (1934) (he'd arranged the dances for the stage show), and on her *It's Love Again* (1936), *Head Over Heels, Gangway* (1937), and *Sailing Along* (1938). Also helped with her dances in *First A Girl* (1935) and appeared briefly in *Evergreen*, as well as working on several other films, including *Radio Parade of 1935* (1934), and, with Jack BUCHANAN, *Brewster's Millions* (1935) and *This'll Make You Whistle* (1936). His spectacular dance numbers have been compared to Busby Berkeley's.

OTHER BRITISH FILMS: *On the Air* (1934), *Oh, Daddy!, A Fire Has Been Arranged* (1935), *King Arthur Was a Gentleman* (1942), *Walking on Air* (1946).

Brady, Moya (*b* Blackpool). Actress. Supporting player from the late 80s, in such notable and varied films as *Little Dorrit* (1987) and *Nil by Mouth* (1997).

OTHER BRITISH FILMS INCLUDE: *Life is Sweet* (1990), *Mary Reilly* (1996, UK/US), *My Son the Fanatic* (1997).

Bragg, Melvyn (Lord Bragg) (*b* Wigton, 1939). Screenwriter, novelist, presenter. Major figure in British culture of the last third of the 20th century, best known as presenter and editor of TV arts programmes, especially LWT's *South Bank Show* from its inception in 1978, and as Controller of Arts at LWT. In collaboration with Ken RUSSELL, he wrote for the BBC (*The Debussy Film*, 1965) and for Granada (*Clouds of Glory*, 1978). Big screen work includes *Play Dirty* (co-sc), *Isadora* (co-sc, adpt) (1968), Russell's *The Music Lovers* (1971, sc), and *Jesus Christ Superstar* (1973, US, co-sc); *Hullabaloo over Georgie and Bonnie's Pictures* (1978, UK/Ind, ex p); and guest appearances in *Sweet William* (1979) and *The Tall Guy* (1989). Created peer in 1998.

Braham, Henry (*b* 1965). Cinematographer. Braham has worked steadily in the 90s on such diverse films as the caper comedy, *Shooting Fish* (1997), the WW2 rural romance, *The Land Girls* (1998, UK/Fr), in which the look of the film helped to 'write' the period, and the popular Irish-set black comedy, *Waking Ned* (1999, UK/Fr/US). Has also worked on TV, including *Shackleton* (2001).

OTHER BRITISH FILMS: *Soft Top, Hard Shoulders* (1992), *Home Away from Home* (1994, short), *Solitaire for 2* (1995), *Roseanna's Grave* (1997, UK/US), *Crush* (2001).

Brahm, John (*b* Hamburg, 1893 – *d* Malibu, California, 1982). Director. Went to London during the 30s and worked as editor, screenwriter, and production supervisor, and directed his first film there, the re-make of *Broken Blossoms* (1936). Was production supervisor on *Scrooge* and *The Last Journey* (1935). In Hollywood from 1937.

Braine, John (*b* London, 1922 – *d* London, 1986) Author. His breakthrough best-seller, *Room at the Top*, was successfully filmed in 1958, and its sequel, *Life at the Top*, in 1965. TV series,

Man at the Top (1970–72), chronicled further adventures of Joe Lampton, some of them written by Braine.

Braithwaite, Dame Lillian (*b* Ramsgate, 1873 – *d* London, 1948). Actress. Celebrated star of stage and a dozen silent films, who also made several talkies, including *Carnival* (1931) and, just before her death, *A Man About the House* (1947). Married to silent star Gerald LAWRENCE and mother of actress Joyce CAREY.

OTHER BRITISH FILMS INCLUDE: *The Climax* (1915), *Justice, Dombey and Son* (1917), *Castles in Spain* (1920), *Downhill* (1927), *Man of Mayfair* (1931), *The Chinese Puzzle* (1932).

Brambell, Wilfrid (*b* Dublin, 1912 – *d* London, 1985). Actor. After training at the Abbey Theatre, Brambell entered films in *The 39 Steps* (1935). He appeared in nearly 30 others but became a household name with the surprise BBC TV success, *Steptoe and Son* (1962–65, 1970, 1972, 1974). He played the scruffy, conniving old dad of the father-and-son junk-dealer team, and audiences warmed to the odd-couple comedy and occasional pathos. Two mediocre films derived from the series – *Steptoe and Son* (1972) and *Steptoe and Son Ride Again* (1973) – and he can be spotted in early films such as *Dry Rot* (1956), as an obstructive road-worker, and as various other venerable types, notably as Grandad in the BEATLES film, *A Hard Day's Night* (1964). His Steptoe, though, was a true original.

OTHER BRITISH FILMS INCLUDE: *Another Shore* (1948), *The Boys* (1962), *Witchfinder General,* (1968), *Carry On Again Doctor* (1969), '*Death and Transfiguration*' in *The Terence Davies Trilogy* (1983).

Bramble, A.V. (*b* Portsmouth, 1880 – *d* London, 1963). Director, actor. After ten years on the stage, Bramble entered the industry as an actor with BRITISH AND COLONIAL in 1910. Turned to directing in 1916 and made more than 30 films, his only notable achievement being *Shooting Stars* (1928), which he co-directed with Anthony ASQUITH. Ended his career as actor in *Outcast of the Islands* (1951).

BRITISH FILMS INCLUDE: *Jimmy* (1916), *The Laughing Cavalier* (1917), *Bonnie May* (1918), *Wuthering Heights* (1920), *The Card* (1922), *Chick* (1928), *Mrs Dane's Defence* (1933). AS.

Bramhall, Dorothy (*b* Blundellsands) Actress. Apart from starring in the B movie, *The Clouded Crystal* (1948), brunette ex-model Bramhall rarely had enough screen time to make much impression. It says something for her that one remembers bits such as the sharp-spoken nurse in *Take My Life* (1947) and an unyielding secretary in *Encore* (1951). Also on stage.

OTHER BRITISH FILMS INCLUDE: *Love Story* (1944), *I See a Dark Stranger* (1946), *The Weaker Sex* (1948), *Blackmailed* (1950), *A Stolen Face* (1952), *The Lonely House* (1956).

Branagh, Kenneth (*b* Belfast, 1960). Actor, screenwriter, director. White hope of 90s British cinema, Branagh above all reinstated SHAKESPEARE as a bankable name after his triumphant success with *Henry V* (1989), making it accessible, as he said, for 'the *Batman* generation'. His service to the Bard continued with a playful version of *Much Ado About Nothing* (1993, UK/US, + p), again co-starring then-wife (1989–95), Emma THOMPSON, and again assembling a starry cast of stage and screen luminaries. This practice was highlighted in his monumental and daring four-hour *Hamlet* (1996, UK/US), which drew on such varied talents as John GIELGUD, Gérard DEPARDIEU, Julie CHRISTIE and Billy CRYSTAL, kept every word of the original, and illustrated imaginatively several episodes merely referred to in the play. In 1999, he filmed *Love's Labour's Lost* (2000, UK/Fr/US) in a 30s setting, with a score

derived from Gershwin, Porter, etc. He also starred in each of these, most notably as Henry V, and wrote their screenplays; played a fine, rough Iago in Oliver PARKER's respectful *Othello* (1995, UK/US); and directed *In the Bleak Midwinter* (1995, + s), a charming black-and-white comedy about a provincial company staging *Hamlet*.

So far, on screen, his non-Shakespearean ventures have been disappointing. He directed and co-starred in the ensemble comedy *Peter's Friends* (1992, + p), made with some wit and some self-indulgence, and the US-made *Dead Again* (1991), an absurd if mildly enjoyable *noir* melodrama, and *Mary Shelley's Frankenstein* (1994, UK/US, + p), a wearyingly overwrought retelling of the famous overreacher's career. Appeared in Robert Altman's thriller, *The Gingerbread Man* (1997, US) and Woody Allen's *Celebrity* (1998, US), competent but unextended in both. In Britain he starred with his then-partner, Helena BONHAM CARTER, in the barely seen odd-couple romance, *The Theory of Flight* (1998). As an interpreter of Shakespeare, however, his screen contribution has been ground-breaking, justifying some of the less rewarding fund-raisers between Bardic bouts.

Born to a working-class Belfast family, which moved to Reading, where he spent his childhood and developed a taste for theatre, he trained at RADA, winning the Bancroft Award. First appeared in the West End in *Another Country* (1982), and won much acclaim for his Stratford Henry V in 1984. In 1987 he formed the Renaissance Theatre Company, surrounding himself with such actors as Judi DENCH, Derek JACOBI and Richard BRIERS who would appear in his films; also some very notable TV, including *Fortunes of War* (1987). In 1989, aged 28, he impudently published his autobiography, *Beginning*, perhaps not so impudent in the light of the nominations and awards which had already – and would continue to – come his way.

OTHER BRITISH FILMS INCLUDE: (a) *A Month in the Country, High Season* (1987), *Alien Love Triangle* (2001).

Branche, Derrick (*b* Bombay, 1947). Actor. Of Anglo-Indian background, he went to London as a teenager, gaining extensive stage experience. His adaptably exotic good looks made him sought after for southern European as well as Indian parts in several British TV series and international films, most notably the BBC's *The Jewel in the Crown* (1984) and the US film, *The Sicilian* (1987). His most striking role in British film was as the stylishly sleazy Pakistani drug-pusher in *My Beautiful Laundrette* (1985). Recently retired to Goa.

OTHER BRITISH FILMS INCLUDE: *The Golden Lady* (1979, UK/HK), *The Dress* (1984). Ian Britain.

Brandon, Phil (*b* London, 1898 – *d* ?). Associate producer, director. After production experience in the US, entered British films in the 30s, first as actor in *Ouanga* (1934), then as dialogue director or assistant director for KORDA (*The Divorce of Lady X*, 1938, and *Perfect Strangers*, 1945) and others. Directed several minor films in the early 40s, including *We'll Meet Again* (1942), starring Vera LYNN, and *Happidrome* (1943), based on a popular radio show, and produced three 'B' MOVIES in the 50s – *Hindle Wakes, Circumstantial Evidence* (1952), and *House of Blackmail* (1953).

OTHER BRITISH FILMS INCLUDE: (d) *The Missing Million* (1942), *Up with the Lark* (1943); (assoc p) *An Ideal Husband* (1947), *The Fallen Idol* (1948).

Brandt, Ivan (*b* London, 1903 – *d* Scunthorpe, 1972). Actor. RN: Roy Cook. Former architect, on stage from 1927, involved in much BBC drama, and a minor leading man and supporting player in 30s films. His last film work was as the policeman improbably smitten with the excruciating Kitty in *Old Mother Riley, Detective* (1943) and narrator of the DOCUMENTARY *Burma Victory* (1945).

OTHER BRITISH FILMS INCLUDE: *The First Mrs Fraser* (1932), *The Man Who Could Work Miracles* (1936), *On the Night of the Fire* (1939), *The Missing Million* (1942).

Bray Studios Former country house, Down Place, in Berkshire, now famous as the home of HAMMER's output of HORROR films. It was sold in 1949 after which it became Bray Studios, specialising at first in low-budget THRILLERS and film versions of RADIO successes, including *The Man in Black* (1949). It was the success of *The Curse of Frankenstein* (1957) which set it on its new and highly profitable course, under the leadership of James CARRERAS and, later, his son Michael CARRERAS. Since the late 60s, it has had several other landlords but has gone on producing films, TV programmes and commercials, having over 50 years of film-making to its credit.
BIBLIOG: Patricia Warren, *British Film Studios*, 2001 (rev ed).

Brantford, Mickey (*b* London, 1911). Actor. Brantford, who came from a theatrical family and whose sister, Aggie, also played small roles on screen, was a prominent child actor of the 20s, playing Tinker opposite Langhorne BURTON in the 1928 *Sexton Blake* series. A breezy hero in *The Last Journey* (1935).
BRITISH FILMS INCLUDE: *The Man the Army Made* (1917), *The Glorious Adventure* (1922), *This Freedom* (1923), *The Triumph of the Rat* (1926), *Jew Süss* (1934). AS.

Brazzi, Rossano (*b* Bologna, Italy, 1916 – *d* Rome, 1994). Actor. Italian leading man, usually of the 'great lover' type, who made several British films, including *Summer Madness* (1955, UK/US), *The Story of Esther Costello* (1957), and *The Battle of the Villa Fiorita* (1965), in which he beguiled Katharine HEPBURN, Joan Crawford and Maureen O'HARA respectively. Presumably many women shared their weakness because he was a popular international star for forty years, his best role, arguably, as the impotent count in *The Barefoot Contessa* (1954, US).
OTHER BRITISH FILMS: *A Day with Dino* (1965), *The Bobo* (1967), *The Italian Job* (1969).

Breakston, George (*b* Paris, 1922 – *d* Paris, 1973). Director, actor. Appeared as child actor in US, including *Great Expectations* (1934), as young Pip, and made about a dozen international features, including five modest British-backed adventures: *The Boy Who Cried Murder* (1966, UK/Yug), and four starring John BENTLEY – *The Scarlet Spear* (1953, + sc), *Golden Ivory* (1954, + p), *Escape in the Sun* (1955) and *Shadow of Treason* (1963, + sc, p), all Africa-set.

Bredin, Patricia Actress. More noted as singer than actress, Bredin sang the first British entry ('All') in the BBC's Eurovision Song Contest. Appeared in a handful of films, including guest role in *Make Mine a Million* and – her one co-starring part – *Left, Right and Centre* (both 1959).
OTHER BRITISH FILMS: *Desert Mice*, *The Bridal Path* (1959), *The Treasure of Monte Cristo* (1960), *To Have and to Hold* (1963).

Bremner, Ewen (*b* Edinburgh). Actor. One of the 'hotter' British actors of the 90s was the idiosyncratic, pinch-faced Bremner, son of two art teachers. Not only was he on the famous poster for Danny BOYLE's *Trainspotting* (1996), the

decade's cult hit, but worked for such other 90s names as Gillies MACKINNON (*Dreaming*, 1989), Michael WINTERBOTTOM (*Forget About Me*, 1990, UK/Hung), Mike LEIGH (*Naked*, 1993) and Guy RITCHIE (*Snatch*, 2000), and is very much associated with resurgent Scottish cinema (also *The Life of Stuff*, 1997). In US films such as *Pearl Harbor* (2001) and *Black Hawk Down* (2002).
OTHER BRITISH FILMS INCLUDE: *Heavenly Pursuits* (1986), *As You Like It* (1992), *Mojo* (1997), *The Acid House* (1998), *Paranoid* (2000), *Morality Play* (2002).

Brennan, Michael (*b* London, 1912 – *d* Chichester, 1982). Actor. Prison warder, Sergeant-Major, criminal, policeman, security guard, barman: for several decades, burly Brennan was an enjoyable heavy in British films large (*Tom Jones*, 1963, as Newgate jailer) and small (TEMPEAN's *No Trace*, 1950, as low-life tough). Was once John GIELGUD's stage manager, and made stage debut in 1930; was in the Armed Forces (1939–46), and first film was *They Made Me a Fugitive* (1947).
OTHER BRITISH FILMS INCLUDE: *Blanche Fury* (1947), *Morning Departure*, *The Clouded Yellow* (1950), *Ivanhoe*, *13 East Street* (1952), *Up in the World* (1956), *Watch Your Stern* (1960), *Thunderball* (1965), *The Deadly Affair* (1966), *Fright* (1971), *Up the Front*, *Doomwatch* (1972).

Brenon, Herbert (*b* Dublin, 1880 – *d* Los Angeles, 1958). Director. At his peak at Paramount in the 20s with films such as *A Kiss for Cinderella* (1926) and *The Great Gatsby* (1926), Brenon began directing with Carl Laemmle's IMP Company in 1912. Laemmle sent Brenon to Europe in 1913, and he made two films there, both starring King Baggot and Leah Baird: *Ivanhoe* (1913), a tremendous success in the US, and *The Secret of the Air* (1914). Following his success with *War Brides* (1915), Brenon was invited to return to the UK to direct *Victory and Peace* (1918) for the National War Aims Committee, though only a fragment remains to show Ellen TERRY's acting. He then returned to the US, becoming an American citizen. Brenon's career was heading downhill in the mid 30s, when he again came back to Britain. Here he made nine films of which the best is *Housemaster* (1938), with Otto KRUGER in the title role, a graceful ADAPTATION of the Ian HAY play, praised by the playwright. Brenon was also in the UK in 1927, shooting location scenes for the American *Sorrell and Son*, his favourite film.
OTHER BRITISH FILMS INCLUDE: *Living Dangerously* (1936), *Spring Handicap* (1937), *Yellow Sands* (1938), *Black Eyes* (1939), *The Flying Squad* (1940). AS.

Brent, Evelyn *see* **American stars in British silent films**

Brent, Romney (*b* Saltillo, Mexico, 1902 – *d* Mexico City, 1976). Actor. RN Romulo Larralde. Short, dapper actor of character roles in 30s British films, including hero's best friend in *Head Over Heels* (1937), American detective in *Dinner at the Ritz* (1937, + sc), and bland Nazi agent in *Let George Do It!* (1940). Starred on London and Broadway stages, and post-war made several Hollywood films, appearing as King of Spain in *The Adventures of Don Juan* (1948). The author of several plays and screenplays (*The Rat*, 1937), he married Gina MALO.
OTHER BRITISH FILMS INCLUDE: *East Meets West* (1936), *Under the Red Robe*, *School for Husbands* (1937), *On the Night of the Fire* (1939).

Breon, Edmond (*b* Hamilton, Scotland, 1882 – *d* Scotland, 1951). Actor. RN: McLaverty. Made four early films in Hollywood, including *The Dawn Patrol* (1930) and spent the last decade of his life playing upper-class Brits there in such films as *The White Cliffs of Dover* (1944). Became a fixture in 30s British cinema as officers, toffs and silly asses: thus, Colonel

Winterbottom in *Return of the Scarlet Pimpernel* (1937), Lord Fleet in *Wedding Rehearsal* (1932) and Gertrude LAWRENCE's bumbling husband in *No Funny Business* (1933). Stage from 1906.

OTHER BRITISH FILMS INCLUDE: *On Approval* (1930), *Leap Year* (1932), *Mister Cinders* (1934), *A Yank at Oxford* (1937), *Crackerjack* (1938), *Goodbye, Mr Chips* (1939), *Gentleman of Venture* (1940).

Bresslaw, Bernard (*b* London, 1934 – *d* London, 1993). Actor. Tall, pop-eyed, RADA-trained comic actor who became a household name for his role as gormless Pte Arnold Popplewell in TV's *The Army Game* (1957–61), with his plaintive 'I only arsked', the title of his 1957 film. His 40-odd films were almost entirely in comic mode, including 14 'CARRY ON' FILMS, overshadowed by Sidney JAMES and Kenneth WILLIAMS, with occasional upmarket outings like *Morgan: A Suitable Case for Treatment* (1966).

OTHER BRITISH FILMS INCLUDE: *Up in the World* (1956), *Blood of the Vampire* (1958), *Too Many Crooks* (1959), *Carry On Cowboy* (1965), ... *Screaming* (1966), *Follow That Camel* (1967), *Carry On Doctor* (1968), *Up Pompeii* (1971), *Carry On Matron* (1972), ... *Girls* (1973), *Jabberwocky* (1977), *Krull* (1983), *Leon the Pig Farmer* (1992).

Brett, Jeremy (*b* Berkswell, 1933 – *d* London, 1995). Actor. RN: Huggins. Eton-educated and Central School-trained, this handsome, rather saturnine leading man had a busy stage career in classic and modern plays and found fame as, arguably, the subtlest interpreter to date of SHERLOCK HOLMES in the TV series (1984–94). Big-screen stardom eluded him: first seen in *War and Peace* (1956, US/It), his suave persona was at odds with either the new REALISM or the 'SWINGING LONDON' zaniness of 60s British cinema. Best film role was Freddie in *My Fair Lady* (US). Married (1 of 2) Anna MASSEY (1958–62). Terry Manners' cloying biography, *The Man Who Became Sherlock Holmes* (1997), chronicles a tormented life.

BRITISH FILMS: *Macbeth* (1961, as Malcolm), *The Wild and the Willing*, *The Very Edge* (1962), *Girl in the Headlines* (1963), *The Medusa Touch* (1978, UK/Fr), *Mad Dogs and Englishmen* (1994).

Briant, Shane (*b* London, 1946). Actor. Busy in British films and TV in the 70s, notably in *The Mackintosh Man* (1973), the title role of TV's *The Picture of Dorian Gray* (1973) and as Sir Clifford in *Lady Chatterley's Lover* (1981, UK/Fr). In 1983, migrated to Australia where he appeared in TV's *Darlings of the Gods* (1988, as Cecil BEATON) and the Australian-set half of Bill DOUGLAS's masterpiece, *Comrades* (1986, UK).

OTHER BRITISH FILMS INCLUDE: *Demons of the Mind* (1971), *Frankenstein and the Monster from Hell* (1973), *Hawk the Slayer* (1980).

Brickman, Miriam (*b* Reading, 1916 – *d* London, 1977). Casting director. Long before the casting director's name was given a credit to itself, Brickman was acknowledged as a major influence on the life-like patina of films such as Lindsay ANDERSON's *This Sporting Life* (1962) and *If...* (1968) and John SCHLESINGER's *A Kind of Loving* (1962) and *Darling* (1965). London-born, she had worked at the Royal Court Theatre before she began casting films and knew a wide range of new and promising talent. Also worked in the US.

OTHER BRITISH FILMS INCLUDE: *Young Cassidy* (1965), *Straw Dogs*, *Gumshoe* (1971), *Zardoz*, *Don't Look Now* (UK/It) (1973), *The Wilby Conspiracy* (1974), *A Bridge Too Far* (1977).

Bricusse, Leslie (*b* London, 1931). Screenwriter, lyricist, composer. Multi-talented, Cambridge-educated Bricusse wrote the title-song lyrics for *Goldfinger* (1964) and *You Only Live Twice* (1967), won an AA for the song 'Talk to the Animals' in *Doctor Dolittle* (1967, US), wrote the screenplay, music and lyrics for *Scrooge* (1970), and shared AA for original song for *Victor/Victoria* (1982, + co-score). Sadly, his credits attest to British cinema's incapacity in the musical genre: he has worked more for the stage and in the US (e.g. *Hook*, 1991). Awarded OBE, 2001.

OTHER BRITISH FILMS INCLUDE: (comp) *We Joined the Navy* (1962, song), *Stop the World I Want to Get Off* (1966, + sc), *Goodbye, Mr Chips* (1969); (sc) *Charley Moon* (1956), *Bachelor of Hearts* (1958, + songs); (lyricist) *Santa Claus* (1985).

Bridge, Joan (*b* Derbyshire, 1912). Colour consultant, costume designer. Educated at Birmingham University and Birmingham College of Art, became colour director for Dufaycolor in 1937 and joined TECHNICOLOR in 1941. Worked on most British colour films for the next 20 years, and on some continental ones (e.g. *The Golden Coach*, 1952, Fr), credited variously as 'consultant', 'colour control' or 'colour direction', often in association with Natalie KALMUS. She collaborated in COSTUME DESIGN (1964–80) with her partner Elizabeth HAFFENDEN, winning a joint AA for *A Man for All Seasons* (1966).

OTHER BRITISH FILMS INCLUDE: (colour/assoc colour consultant:) *The Life and Death of Colonel Blimp* (1943), *This Happy Breed* (1944), *A Matter of Life and Death* (1946), *Blanche Fury*, *Black Narcissus*, (1947), *Scott of the Antarctic*, *The Red Shoes*, *Trottie True* (1948), *Gone to Earth*, *Pandora and the Flying Dutchman* (1950), *Genevieve*, (1953), *Richard III*, *The Ladykillers*, *Footsteps in the Fog* (1955); (cos des): *The Prime of Miss Jean Brodie* (1968), *The Day of the Jackal* (UK/Fr) (1973), *Hanover Street* (1979).

Bridges, Alan (*b* Liverpool, 1927). Director. Better known for classy TV drama, like *Miss Julie* (1965) and *Rain on the Roof* (1980), he has also done some plangent, undervalued cinema. Came to notice with a superior 'B' film, *Act of Murder* (1964), won the grand prize at Cannes in 1973 for *The Hireling* and the Palme d'Or at Cannes for *The Shooting Party* (1984). These two, and the comparably melancholy *The Return of the Soldier* (1982), three sensitive literary ADAPTATIONS, are his best work, whereas the REMAKE of *Brief Encounter* (1974), starring – with wild disregard for suitability – Sophia Loren and Richard BURTON, was a total disaster. An acute, gentle talent, never quite in vogue, except perhaps with actors who often look their best in his films.

OTHER BRITISH FILMS: *Invasion* (1966), *Out of Season* (1975), *Age of Innocence* (1977, UK/Can), *Very Like a Whale* (1981), *Fire Princess* (1990).

Bridgewater, Leslie Composer, music director. Contributed music to a number of DOCUMENTARY pictures, including *Progress*, *Looking Through* and *Down to Earth*, made post-war at MERTON PARK STUDIOS. Also, musical director on *Beloved Vagabond* (1936) and composer for *Against the Wind* (1947), *Train of Events* (1949), *Stranger at My Door* (1950), *Walk a Crooked Path* (1969, + cond). In the 40s, a well-known conductor and leader of his own orchestra.

Bridie, James (*b* Glasgow, 1888 – *d* Edinburgh, 1951). Dramatist. Contact with screen included three films adapted from his plays – *Flesh and Blood* (1951), *Folly to Be Wise* (1952), and *You're Only Young Twice!* (1952) – and, from a story, *There Was a Crooked Man* (1960). Also wrote the screenplay for *Storm in a Teacup* (1937) and had three brushes with HITCHCOCK: *The Paradine Case* (1947, adpt), *Under Capricorn* (1949, sc) and *Stage Fright* (1950, add dial). Made CBE in 1946.

Briers, Richard (*b* Merton, 1934). Actor. Briers pottered about in British films since 1958 (*Girls at Sea*), and made his West End debut as a frenetic young engineer in *Gilt and Gingerbread* in 1959, but only became a household name with TV's *The Good Life* (1975–78). In films, the engaging, somewhat rumpled-featured character comic has been most fruitfully associated with Kenneth BRANAGH, whose Renaissance Theatre Company RADA-trained Briers joined in 1987. On-screen, has since played a droll, touching Bardolph in *Henry V* (1989), Don Leonato in *Much Ado About Nothing* (1993, UK/US), grandfather in *Frankenstein* (1994, US), an actor playing several roles from Hamlet in *In the Bleak Midwinter* (1995), a wily, intelligent Polonius in *Hamlet* (1996, UK/US) and Nathaniel in *Love's Labour's Lost* (2000, UK/Fr/US), all under Branagh's direction. Awarded OBE, 1989. Married to actress Ann Davies and father of actress Lucy Briers.
OTHER BRITISH FILMS INCLUDE: *Murder She Said*, *A Matter of WHO* (1961), *Doctor in Distress* (1963), *Fathom* (1967), *Rentadick* (1972), *Watership Down* (1978, voice), *A Chorus of Disapproval* (1989), *Peter's Friends* (1992), *Spice World* (1997).

Briggs, Johnny (*b* London, 1935). Actor. Cockney player in films (*Hue and Cry*, 1946) since childhood, better known for TV appearances, especially as Mike Baldwin in *Coronation Street*. Supporting roles in about 25 films, mostly COMEDIES, including several 'CARRY ON's and feeble 70s sex farces, such as *Au Pair Girls* (1972).
OTHER BRITISH FILMS INCLUDE: *Cosh Boy* (1953), *Diplomatic Corpse* (1958), *Sink the Bismarck!* (1960), *HMS Defiant* (1962), *A Stitch in Time* (1963), *The Intelligence Men* (1965), *Carry On Up the Khyber* (1968), *A Man About the House* (1974), *Carry On Behind* (1975).

Brighouse, Harold (*b* Eccles, Lancashire, 1882 – *d* 1958). Dramatist. His famous 1916 play of Lancashire life, *Hobson's Choice* (1916), has been filmed three times: in 1920, 1931 and, most famously, 1954, when David LEAN directed Charles LAUGHTON to splendid effect. Other plays filmed: *The Winning Goal* (1920) and *Children of Jazz* (1923, US).

Bright, John *see* **Beavan, Jenny**

'Brighton School of film-making' There is some veracity to Low Warren's claim in *The Film Game* (1937) that the moving picture was born on the outskirts of Brighton in that Brighton and Hove was the home and workplace of three major film pioneers, A. Esmé COLLINGS, G.A. SMITH and James WILLIAMSON. Associated with the first two was Brighton engineer Alfred Darling, who established his still-extant company in 1894 and become involved in motion picture work in 1896; he built some of the first cinematographic cameras for J. Wrench & Son in 1897. The term 'Brighton School' is credited to the French film historian, Georges Sadoul, who used it in his *Histoire générale du cinéma* (1948). There was no 'school' as such, but a great deal of film activity in the Brighton–Hove area, with William FRIESE-GREENE and Charles URBAN as regular visitors, as well as others working on various aspects of film, photography and colour in particular. AS.

Briley, John (*b* Kalamazoo, Michigan, 1925). Screenwriter. American-born screenwriter in Britain best known for two big ATTENBOROUGH films, *Gandhi* (1982, UK/Ind), for which he won an AA, and *Cry Freedom* (1987, + co-p). International work includes *Molokai: The Story of Father Damien* (2000).
OTHER BRITISH FILMS INCLUDE: *Children of the Damned* (1963), *Hammerhead* (1968), *That Lucky Touch* (1975), *Eagle's Wing*, *The Medusa Touch* (1978, UK/Fr), *Enigma* (1982).

Brilliant, Fredda (aka Alfredda) (*b* Lodz, Poland, 1904 – *d* Carbondale, Illinois, 1999). Screenwriter. Appeared on stage in Australia and US before settling in England where she and her husband, Herbert MARSHALL, the Eisenstein commentator, were involved with productions at the Unity and other theatres. Together they wrote the story for *The Proud Valley* (1940). Post-war, they collaborated on screenplays for children's films, including *Tinker* (1949) and documentaries for Citizen Films, of which she was a director.

Brindley, Madge (*b* ? – *d* 1968) Actress. Large, stern-visaged character player who began as dancer with Pavlova at five, acted on stage and screen, with a six-year gap as a nurse in WW1. In films from 1934 (*General John Regan*), glimpsed in the Casanova Club in *The Third Man* (1949).
OTHER BRITISH FILMS INCLUDE: *Kentucky Minstrels* (1934), *Piccadilly Incident* (1946), *Hobson's Choice* (1953), *The Ladykillers* (1955), *Sailor Beware* (1956), *A Nice Girl Like Me* (1969).

Brinton, Ralph (*b* London, 1895 – *d* ?). Art director. After WW1 service with the Royal Navy, and architectural training (1922–27), entered films in the 30s. Early credits include the first British TECHNICOLOR film, *Wings of the Morning* (1937); in the 40s, he designed four popular TWO CITIES films, *Odd Man Out* (1947), *Sleeping Car to Trieste*, *Trottie True* (1948) and *The Chiltern Hundreds* (1949), and later designed five key 'NEW WAVE' successes – *Room at the Top* (1958, in which his design skilfully differentiates levels of aspiration), *The Entertainer* (1960), *A Taste of Honey* (1961), *The Loneliness of the Long Distance Runner* (1962) and *Tom Jones* (1963).
OTHER BRITISH FILMS INCLUDE: *Rhythm in the Air* (1936), *The Arsenal Stadium Mystery* (1939), *Your Witness* (1950), *Hotel Sahara* (1951), *The Knave of Hearts* (1954, UK/Fr, + cos), *Moby Dick* (1956), *The Gypsy and the Gentleman* (1957), *Isadora* (1968).

Brisson, Carl (*b* Copenhagen, 1893 – *d* Copenhagen, 1958). Actor. RN: Pedersen. Aged fifteen, he was amateur lightweight boxing champion of Denmark, and so it is appropriate he made his UK screen debut as a boxer in HITCHCOCK's *The Ring* (1927). On stage from 1916, and in 1917 appeared in the Danish film, *De mystiske fodspor*. Came to the UK in 1921 as a dancer. After *The Ring*, he appeared in two other silent films, *Hjartas triumf* (1928, Sweden) and *The Manxman* (1929). Brisson was under contract to Paramount in the US (1933–36), starring in such films as *Murder at the Vanities* (1934), later becoming a popular nightclub entertainer. Father of Frederick Brisson and father-in-law of Rosalind Russell.
OTHER BRITISH FILMS: *The American Prisoner* (1929), *Knowing Men* (sound debut), *Song of Soho* (1930), *Prince of Arcadia* (1933), *Two Hearts in Waltz Time* (1934). AS.

British Academy of Film and TV Arts *see* **BAFTA**

British Actors' Equity Association This trade union represents all the acting media – radio, TV, theatre, and film – as well as others involved in the entertainment industry. Though its delegates attend the annual TUC conference to bring members' issues to wider audiences, it is not affiliated to any political party, enabling it to lobby governments of whatever persuasion. Its main function is, of course, the negotiation of acceptable minimum terms and conditions for its members. In 2001, for instance, many well-known actors, including Paul SCOFIELD and Julie WALTERS, backed Equity's campaign to ensure its members had the same pay deals as American colleagues in relation to subsequent uses of their films. It operates not just nationally but also through the Federation of

International Artists and the International Committee for Artistic Freedom. Among well-known actors who have held high positions in the Association at various times are Felix AYLMER, Marius GORING and Michael DENISON.

British Actors' Film Company British Actors' Film Company was founded in 1915 by a group of prominent British stage players, including A.E. MATTHEWS (its managing director), Donald CALTHROP, Leslie HENSON, Owen NARES, Nelson KEYS, and Godfrey TEARLE, determined to rely upon stage actors as its stars. It took over the Herkomer studios at Bushey, but did not release its first film, *The Lifeguardsman*, until 1917. Other films include *The Labour Leader* (1917), *Once Upon a Time* (1918), *The Divine Gift* (1919), and *The Shuttle of Life* (1920). It ceased operations in 1920, when it merged with the ALLIANCE FILM COMPANY; at the end of its days, C. Aubrey SMITH, Leslie HOWARD, Gertrude McCOY, and Adrian BRUNEL were associated with the company. AS.

British and Colonial Kinematograph Company Founded in 1909 by A.H. Bloomfield and J.B. McDOWELL, B and C (as it was known) was a major production company of the 1910s. Its first studio was located at Newstead House, East Finchley, but in 1913, it moved to a new facility on Hoe Street in WALTHAMSTOW. B and C was noted for its early use of LOCATION SHOOTING in England and Wales, and in 1913, it sent a company to the West Indies. It produced the *Lt Daring* series, starring Percy MORAN, beginning in 1911, the *Dick Turpin* series in 1912, and, in 1913, the first British screen spectacle, *The Battle of Waterloo*. Later, it signed stage stars such as Jose Collins and Yvonne ARNAUD, and, in 1919, it attempted to break into the American market with films directed by Herbert BRENON and starring Marie Doro and Gertrude McCOY. The early 20s saw a rapid decline in its production schedule, and in 1924, it declared bankruptcy. AS.

British and Dominion(s) Film Corporation An important film production company during the interwar period formed in 1927/28 by producer/director Herbert WILCOX and actor-comedian Nelson KEYS. It was based at Imperial Studios, part of the ELSTREE complex which Wilcox had helped to establish in the mid 20s. It combined quota production for the American majors with ambitious productions aimed at the American market. A long-term deal with Paramount was signed in 1930 leading to a regular programme of undistinguished quota production, but an alliance with UNITED ARTISTS in 1932 was based on the company supplying quality productions for British and American release. Early successes for the studio included a series of comedy films derived from the ALDWYCH FARCES and featuring Tom WALLS and Ralph LYNN, but the studio is probably best remembered for its films featuring Jack BUCHANAN and Anna NEAGLE, who were among the most popular British stars of the time. Despite the United Artists link, the studio found it difficult to secure success in the American market. The studio was burned down in 1936 and, although the firm survived, it was eventually absorbed into the developing combine that became the RANK ORGANISATION. Tom Ryall.

British-Asian film-making As a result of migration from the former colonies in the post-war period, the ethnic minority population of the UK has grown substantially. The largest of these groups is originally from South Asia (India, Pakistan and Bangladesh) and, at the time of 1991 census, totalled around 1.5 million in number. Such is the size of this community that it has created a small but significant market for Bollywood films in Britain, as indicated by the success of *Kuch Kuch Hota Hai* in 1998 (the most popular foreign-language film of that year). Although certain individuals, such as the Indian-born director Waris HUSSEIN, used Britain as a base from the 60s onwards, it was only during the 70s that a specifically British-Asian cinema, involving either British-Asian film-makers or dealing with British-Asian concerns, began to emerge. One of the first of these films was *A Private Enterprise* (1974), set in Birmingham, and dealing with a young Indian's attempts to set up his own business. This was followed, in the 80s, by INDEPENDENT FILMS from the workshop sector, such as Birmingham Film and Video Workshop's *Mirror Mirror* (1980) and the British-Asian collective Retake's *Majdhar* (1984), in which an abandoned Pakistani wife comes to terms with British society.

The most visible, and commercially successful, film of this period, however, was director Stephen FREARS and writer Hanif KUREISHI's heady mix of COMEDY, romance and social commentary, *My Beautiful Laundrette* (1985). Kureishi (born in London to a Pakistani father and English mother) continued his collaboration with Frears for the anti-Thatcherite polemic *Sammy and Rosie Get Laid* (1987) but directed his own script for *London Kills Me* (1991), an under-appreciated study of social outsiders. Roger MICHELL directed an excellent TV version of Kureishi's novel *The Buddha of Suburbia* (1993) while Udayan PRASAD, the director of *Brothers in Trouble* (1994) – a film about illegal immigrants – made an intelligent version of Kureishi's challenging ADAPTATION of his own short story, *My Son the Fanatic* (1997). What was particularly significant about Kureishi's work was his break with the 'race relations' narratives of earlier British-Asian films and his concern to register the complexity, hybridity and diversity of the experiences of Asians in Britain.

This emphasis on the complexity of British-Asian identities was also found in David ATTWOOD's *Wild West* (1992), an amusing story of young Asians who form a country music band, and in the short films and videos of the writer and political activist Pratibha Parmar who, as in *Khush* (1991), examines the situation of south Asian lesbians and gays. Gurinder CHADHA also charted the changing contours of Asian experience in Britain in her early short *I'm British But . . .* (1989) and in her first feature, *Bhaji on the Beach* (1993), a comic tale of a heterogeneous group of Asians who take a day-trip to the traditional English resort of Blackpool. *Bhaji* was scripted by the successful British-Asian actress, comedian and writer, Meera SYAL, who also wrote and starred in the TV film *My Sister Wife* (1992), dealing with the two wives of a Pakistani businessman. Another British-Asian actor Ayub KHAN-DIN, who played Sammy in *Sammy and Rosie Get Laid* (1987), also adapted his own play about growing up in the north of England in the 70s, for the film version of *East Is East* (2000). Directed by Irishman Damien O'DONNELL, this proved to be one of the surprise hits of the late 90s. As with most of the British-Asian features, this film was funded by CHANNEL 4, which has also supported the work of Indian directors such as Mira NAIR (*Salaam Bombay!* 1988, UK/Fr/Ind; *Mississippi Masala* 1991, UK/US) and Shekhar KAPUR, whose *Elizabeth* (1998), a flamboyant dramatisation of British history, indicates the growing permeability of ethnic and national boundaries in contemporary 'British' film-making. The film version of Kureishi's *Intimacy* (2001, UK/Fr) by the French director Patrice Chereau and Gurinder Chadha's celebration of American ethnic diversity in *What's Cooking?* (2001), set in LA, also confirm this trend.

BIBLIOG: John Hill, *British Cinema in the 1980s: Issues and Themes*, 1999; Sarita Malik, 'Beyond "The Cinema of Duty"? The Pleasures of Hybridity: Black British Films of the 1980s and 1990s' in Andrew Higson (ed), *Dissolving Views: Key Writings on British Cinema*, 1996; Kobena Mercer (ed), *Black Film, British Cinema*, 1988. John Hill.

British Board of Film Censors/British Board of Film Classification *see* **Censorship**

British Council, The Does not engage in film production but with the finished product, in an area in which art and commerce overlap. Its general function is to showcase British cultural developments and, to this end, its film department arranges screenings overseas, assists film-makers in attending significant overseas events and organises seminars on topics such as film marketing. In matters of distribution, it has acted as a clearing-house for SHORT FILMS seeking international festival screenings, and obtains feature film prints, speakers and publicity materials for overseas events, where it often acts as a co-ordinator of British participation. The department is guided by a committee of industry professionals, led since 1999 by producer Duncan KENWORTHY. Whenever possible, it engages in collaborative ventures with such organisations as the BRITISH FILM INSTITUTE and THE FILM COUNCIL. Paul Howson.

British Empire/British Commonwealth of Nations *see* **Empire and colonialism**

British Federation of Film Societies As its name implies, the BFFS co-ordinates the activities of the film societies throughout England, Scotland, and Wales, with regional officers attached to 11 separate, roughly designated geographical areas. It exists to promote the activities of approximately 300 individual Societies. For some time, it distributed free a monthly magazine, *Film*, to all BFFS members.

British Film Academy (BFA) Founded in 1946, a time of high achievement in British cinema, for the advancement of film as an art form, to stimulate informed discussion and research, and to encourage creative film-making. Since 1958 it has been part of the Society of Film and TV Arts. It became known for its awards, now known as the BAFTA awards, which draw attention to excellence in British film-making. The Academy's first Chairman was David LEAN and its director was Roger MANVELL, author and critic.

British Film Academy Awards *see* **BAFTA** and APPENDIX

British Film Commission (BFC) Set up in 1991 and funded by the British government, the BFC mission is to ensure that any film that can be made in Britain *is* made there and has the infrastructure to support it. To achieve this goal, it seeks to promote Britain as an international production centre for film and television and to encourage the use of British locations, services, facilities and personnel. In 2000, it became a division of the FILM COUNCIL, the strategic body for commercial and cultural film activity in the UK. The first British Film Commissioner (1991–97) was Sir Sydney SAMUELSON, son of the industry pioneer, G.B. SAMUELSON, and himself a notable industry figure. In 1997, he was succeeded as Commissioner by Steve Norris who entered the film industry with the RANK ORGANISATION in 1977 and, like his predecessor, is involved in key organisations connected with film and television. Steve Norris.

British Film Institute (BFI) Founded in 1933, the BFI was one of the first nationally-funded cultural film institutions of its kind anywhere in the world, carrying a strong educational remit. 'To distribute films to schools and other approved institutions using non-theatrical films for educational purposes', reads its original mission statement. Its other important brief was to preserve films for posterity and study access, and to this end it set up, in 1935, the National Film Library (later renamed the National Film Archive, and later still the NATIONAL FILM AND TELEVISION ARCHIVE) under Ernest LINDGREN. The BFI's remit was extended in the 50s to include television. In October 1952, the BFI opened its NATIONAL FILM THEATRE, taking over and renaming the 1951 Festival of Britain's Telekinema, which had shown experimental 3-D films, and in October 1957 the present NFT was established close by under Waterloo Bridge. The NFT also became the home of the BFI's annual LONDON FILM FESTIVAL and, in later, more liberal times, the annual Gay and Lesbian Film Festival. The Museum of the Moving Image (MoMI), brainchild of Leslie Hardcastle, Head of the NFT, and David Francis, Curator of the National Film Archive, was created on the premises in 1988, and the BFI's London Imax Cinema opened nearby in 1999. In a number of ventures such as these, the BFI enjoyed generous funding help from the American philanthropist, John Paul Getty Jr.

In an earlier venture, the 1950s, the BFI set up the Experimental Film Fund, an important breeding ground for new film-makers (Karel REISZ, Tony RICHARDSON, Ken RUSSELL and Ridley SCOTT among them). This grew eventually into the BFI PRODUCTION BOARD, making ambitious ART-HOUSE features such as *The Draughtsman's Contract* (1982) and nurturing directors of the calibre of Bill DOUGLAS, Terence DAVIES and Peter GREENAWAY. Alternative funding structures for nationally-subsidised British film (the Lottery, the FILM COUNCIL, and so forth) caused the Board's demise at the end of the 90s.

Today, the BFI is established by Royal Charter and is a registered charity, receiving its Government funding through the FILM COUNCIL. Its current objective, not much different from the original one, is 'to develop greater understanding and appreciation of film, television and the moving image'. This is carried forward by departments devoted to Exhibition, Education, Archive, Marketing, Access and Festivals, the most important elements of which remain the NFT, the NFTVA and its Conservation Centre in Berkhamsted, Hertfordshire, a comprehensive reference library, a massive collection of movie stills, posters and designs, and the BFI's long-running monthly magazine, *SIGHT AND SOUND*. A further aim is to bring all the Institute's activities together in a new BFI Film Centre to be built on London's South Bank, as part of a major arts complex.
BIBLIOG: Ivan Butler, *To Encourage the Art of the Film*, 1971. Clyde Jeavons.

British Film Institute (BFI) Production Board Founded as the Experimental Film Fund in 1952, in the context of the Festival of Britain, the BFI Production Board, as it became known in the 60s when the BFI agreed to administer the small fund, provided the principal support mechanism for formal innovation and radical departures in the content of British film until 1999, when the fund was suspended and its resources diverted into the newly established FILM COUNCIL. The fund's first grants were awarded in 1953 by a board presided over by Michael BALCON and including Thorold DICKINSON and Basil

WRIGHT. The Board's Heads of Production have included Australian director Bruce BERESFORD, Peter Sainsbury, Colin MacCabe, Ben GIBSON, Mamoun Hassan, Barrie Gavin and Roger Shannon. In addition to films about the Arts (an area later taken over by the ARTS COUNCIL Films Department) and support for animators, the first period of the fund coincided with and assisted the FREE CINEMA movement, supporting films by Lindsay ANDERSON, Tony RICHARDSON and others. Other graduates of the fund, for their first short films, included Bill DOUGLAS, Terence DAVIES, Ridley and Tony SCOTT, Sally POTTER, Ken RUSSELL, Stephen FREARS and Derek JARMAN. After 1982 and the completion of Peter GREENAWAY's *The Draughtsman's Contract* and its international success moved the Board into feature production (in alliances with CHANNEL 4 and the BBC), world sales of its titles and the provision of production offices and post-production facilities. At its most productive point in 1998 it was producing four feature films (by Carine ADLER, Jasmin DIZDAR, Andrew KOTTING, John MAYBURY) and ten short films under its NEW DIRECTORS banner. Ben Gibson.

British Instructional Films Ltd Founded in 1919 by H. Bruce WOOLFE, British Instructional specialised in the production of scientific, educational and industrial films, and also made its reputation with features that paid tribute to British heroism: *The Battle of Jutland* (1921), *Ypres* (1925), *Nelson* (1926, with Cedric HARDWICKE in title role) and *The Battles of the Coronel and Falklands* (1927). In 1927, A.F. BUNDY acquired share capital in the company and became chairman, with Woolfe as managing director. On November 8, 1928, the company opened a new studio at Welwyn Garden City, where it produced *The Lost Patrol* (1929), the *Secrets of Nature* series (1929–33) and *England Awake* (1932, co-directed by John Buchan), among others. In 1933, the company was taken over by BRITISH INTERNATIONAL PICTURES and production ceased. AS.

British International Pictures (BIP) see **Associated British Group**

British Lion Film Company was incorporated in 1918 and rented the Neptune studios at Boreham Wood, where Fred Goodwins produced three films directed by A.V. BRAMBLE: *The Non-Conformist Parson*, *A Single Man* and *The Smart Set*. But by mid-1919 the company was bankrupt, losing its principal backer £12,000.

British Lion Film Corporation Ltd was registered in 1927. Its Chairman was Edgar WALLACE, who received £10,000 in the company's shares in return for the film rights to all his novels and plays. By 1929 the company was £50,000 in debt and, to remain competitive in the sound era, it concentrated almost entirely on making 'QUOTA QUICKIES'. When Wallace died in 1932, the company began importing American and European films and limited production to filming cabaret, MUSIC HALL, RADIO and variety entertainers to meet its renter's quota. By mid-1934, it showed a small profit and in 1935 signed a distribution deal with Republic Pictures and returned to producing full-scale features, including a co-production with HAMMER Productions starring Paul ROBESON, *Song Of Freedom* (1936).

With the advent of war, British Lion released several MELODRAMAS shot at BEACONSFIELD, but when the Government requisitioned the studio the company increasingly relied on improved product from Republic Pictures, achieving a record profit of £101,000 in 1944, which enabled it to acquire 50 per cent of the WORTON HALL studio in ISLEWORTH. But in

1945, British Lion was taken over by Alexander KORDA, who quickly bought a controlling interest in SHEPPERTON studios and the remainder of the Worton Hall studio. Korda brought back many of his old team, including Lajos BIRO and George PÉRINAL, and returned to his profligate ways. He directed *An Ideal Husband* (1947), drubbed by the critics, followed by four quality productions, all commercial failures, although *The Fallen Idol* and *The Winslow Boy* (1948) were critical successes; *Anna Karenina* and *Bonnie Prince Charlie* (1948), failed to impress the critics either.

By 1948, the company was again near banktruptcy, but the newly established NATIONAL FILM FINANCE CORPORATION baled Korda out with a £2 million loan, with a further £1 million six months later. A month before the new loan was announced, Korda stepped down to become 'production adviser' and subsequent production budgets were nearly halved. In 1951 the NFFC extended its loan, hoping to recoup revenues from the newly established British Film Production Fund (EADY LEVY). Worton Hall was sold and about two-fifths of the proceeds invested in enlarging Shepperton. But the NFFC's interest charges were crippling, and in June 1954 the Conservative government put the company into receivership. Two new companies were established: British Lion Films Limited and a subsidiary, British Lion Studio Company Limited, to run British Lion's DISTRIBUTION activities and Shepperton studios respectively. A further loan of £569,00 to British Lion Films from the NFFC turned it into a publicly-owned corporation, restricting its activities to managing Shepperton and distributing films. Production activities were limited to loaning advances to independent producers. However, the company was still running at a loss, and, unsurprisingly, in 1957, when the government announced that British Lion was for sale, nobody was interested.

The NFFC restructured the Board of Directors, appointing the BOULTING brothers and LAUNDER AND GILLIAT to it, on condition that they made their future films exclusively for British Lion. The company's main difficulty was that, unlike RANK and ABPC, it did not own any cinemas, so there was no guarantee that its films would receive a circuit release. It therefore expanded its output in an attempt to improve its bargaining power with exhibitors. In 1959 it provided distribution guarantees for a further 13 films, four of which, *Carlton-Browne of the FO* (1958), *I'm All Right Jack*, *The Bridal Path* and *Left, Right and Centre* (1959), were made by the producer members. The remainder came from seven different independent producers. The company steadily moved into profit, much of it from backing films such as *Saturday Night and Sunday Morning* and *Two Way Stretch* (1960).

By 1963, after the success of *Only Two Can Play* (1961), *The Wrong Arm of the Law* and *The L-Shaped Room* (1962), Sir Nutcombe Hume, the new NFFC chairman, wanted British Lion to repay its £591,000 loan to the Corporation. The directors of British Lion refused, partly because they wanted to continue producing films and partly because several of their films could not get a cinema release. In March 1964, when their contracts were due to expire, the NFFC peremptorily bought them out. On 1 April it sold the company for £1.6 million to a consortium (headed by Sir Michael BALCON) of five groups, consisting of the Boulting brothers and Launder and Gilliat; John OSBORNE, Tony RICHARDSON, Oscar Lewenstein and Karel REISZ; Joseph JANNI, John SCHLESINGER and David KINGSLEY; and the American art-house exhibitor Walter Reade Jr. The groups quarrelled with each other; profits fell by

£80,000 and rising costs and the near-monopoly in film bookings in both British and American markets led new chairman Arnold Goodman to ask the government – in vain – for more funds. Although the consortium sold the TV rights to their old films for £250,000, predatory outsiders realised that the company's studio and its back lot were assets ready for stripping.

In 1967, millionaire property owner Max Rayne, took over as Deputy Chairman. The other directors bought out Janni, and David KINGSLEY became Managing Director. He sold more TV rights and floated the company on the stock exchange in order to raise more capital. Even Shepperton studios could not pay its way; and in April 1972, Barclay Securities took the company over, although its plan to sell off the land around Shepperton studios for a housing development foundered because the NFFC had retained the right to veto any voluntary liquidation. Unsurprisingly, the company announced a loss of £1.22 million in November 1972.

Two months later, J.H. Vavasseur took over Barclay Securities, hiving off the company's film-making activities to Great Western Investments, managed by Barry SPIKINGS and Michael DEELEY. After producing *The Man Who Fell to Earth* (1976), Spikings and Deeley went to Hollywood where they made *Nickelodeon* (1976) in association with Columbia and EMI. The latter finally took over Lion International and allowed Spikings and Deeley to join the EMI board. Vincent Porter.

British Mutoscope & Biograph Company The British division of the American Mutoscope & Biograph Company (founded 1895) was created in 1897 and headed by Elias B. Koopman. It built a studio behind London's Tivoli Theatre and produced films not only for EXHIBITION in MUSIC HALLS and fairgrounds but also in peep show-type mutoscope machines. The first public performance of the Biograph in the UK took place at London's Palace Theatre on March 18, 1897. It was a well-capitalised and prestigious film company, its product perhaps the most impressive of the period. The company ceased production in 1907. In *A Victorian Film Enterprise* (1999), Richard Brown and Barry Anthony list more than 600 British Mutoscope & Biograph subjects, including footage of the royal family. AS.

British National Film and Video Catalogue The British National Film Catalogue was established in 1963, when the *Monthly Film Bulletin* was no longer reviewing non-theatrically released material. The annual volumes of the BNFVC have attempted to record all films produced for non-theatrical release in Britain, and serve as a major contributor to the British national filmography. BNFVC is housed by the BRITISH FILM INSTITUTE but published by the British Library, the volumes now being called the *British National Film and Video Guide*. Luke McKernan.

British National Films This company, operating out of British National Studios, built at ELSTREE, was founded by American J.D. Williams who invited Herbert WILCOX to join – which he did for a short while. In the mid 20s, John MAXWELL gained financial control of the company and the studio, changing the name of the latter to British International Studios in 1927. British National is now most associated with the entry of J. Arthur RANK into films: it made his first feature film, *The Turn of the Tide* (1935), difficulties in distributing which led to the setting up of GENERAL FILM DISTRIBUTORS. Rank joined forces with producer John CORFIELD and millionairess Lady YULE to form British National Films as a private company in 1934, and when Rank bought a half-share in PINEWOOD STUDIOS, in 1935, it was planned that British National would use one of its stages, its product to be distributed by GFD. British National, however, never became a major production company, and it produced mainly routine films during the 30s, at WELWYN or WALTON studios, rather than Pinewood. During the war, Lady Yule acquired the ROCK STUDIOS, and a string of undemanding popular films was turned out until the company was wound up in 1948. Among its better known productions were Michael POWELL's *Contraband* (1940), John BAXTER's *Love on the Dole* (1941), Lance COMFORT's *When We Are Married* (1943), Vernon SEWELL's *Latin Quarter* (1945) and Daniel BIRT's *The Three Weird Sisters* (1948). From 1944 to 1948, Louis JACKSON was its executive producer, and was responsible for nearly 30 films. In 1952, the British National Studios were leased for TV production by Douglas FAIRBANKS.

British Screen Finance The British Screen Finance Corporation (as it was originally known) replaced the NATIONAL FILM FINANCE CORPORATION in 1986. It was a private company whose major shareholders were CHANNEL 4, Granada Television, United Artists Screen Entertainment and RANK, but received an annual government grant of £1.5m. Its first Chief Executive was Simon RELPH, followed by Simon PERRY. BSFC's brief was to develop treatments and script drafts to 'encourage the making of British films on a commercially successful basis', and to encourage British talent and original high quality British film work, especially from younger less established producers and directors, across the whole spectrum of British film-making. In 1991 it took on the administration of the European Co-Production Fund which brought in a further £2m. In its first four years it invested over £18m in 44 UK films and by 1997 it was backing 18 films. As a major source of production finance it was involved in a significant percentage of all British low-budget production including *The Last of England* (1987), *Edward II* (1991), *High Hopes* (1988), *Scandal* (1988), *Orlando* (1992, UK/Fr/It/Neth/Russ), *The Crying Game* (1992) and *Butterfly Kiss* (1995). It was absorbed into the FILM COUNCIL in 2000, becoming the conduit for the £22m production finance handled annually by the Council. Julian Petley.

British Society of Cinematographers The BSC, the brainchild of Bert Easey, was formed in September 1949 to promote and encourage the pursuit of the highest standards in the craft of Motion Picture Photography. Freddie YOUNG was the first President. The Society's Club Room is at SHEPPERTON STUDIOS which contains a gallery of Past Presidents and Honours boards. Annually, the BSC holds social events including an Operators' Night, and provides the venue for the Society's Awards, as well as other occasions including New Equipment Shows, varied technical events and 'Question and Answer' screenings at PINEWOOD for members, students and camera technicians. The Society has produced videos of the 'Question and Answer Screenings', as well as a series of 'Portraits' of its members. It also circulates a quarterly newsletter.

The BSC holds strong ties with its US counterpart, the American Society of Cinematographers, and other overseas cinematographer societies. It is also a member of IMAGO, the European Federation of Cinematographers, the Cine Guilds of Great Britain and supports the British Cinematography Scholarship Trust, a post-graduate scholarship for cinematography students, inaugurated in 1996 by **Michael Samuelson**

BSC (*see* G.B. SAMUELSON). Full membership is open to all accredited cinematographers. Along with Associate, Patrons and Friends, membership has grown from its original 55 to 264. Frances Russell.

British Transport Films Founded, for reasons of publicity and information, in 1949 by Edgar ANSTEY who was Films Officer for the British Transport Commission (1949–55). Anstey sought out the best talent (e.g. Arnold BAX, Michael REDGRAVE), and BTF produced a series of notable SHORT FILMS which focused on such matters as the workings of British institutions, the beauties of the British countryside, and, perhaps most famously, Waterloo Station in John SCHLESINGER's award-winning *Terminus* (1961). Anstey was the regular producer and directors included John TAYLOR and Alexander SHAW in the company's heyday until the mid 60s. Its entire library is now administered by the BFI.

OTHER FILMS INCLUDE: *Berth 24* (1950), *Journey into History, Farmer Moving South* (1952), *Snowdrift at Bleath Gill* (1955), *The Land of Robert Burns, Men on the Mend* (1956), *Broad Waterways* (1959).
BIBLIOG: John Reed, *Moving Images*, 1990.

British Universities Film & Video Council The BUFVC exists to support and promote the use of moving images in British higher and further education, across all academic disciplines. Founded in 1948 as the British Universities Film Council, it maintains databases of films in distribution, television and radio broadcasts, and runs courses and conferences. Its database of NEWSREELS came out of the Slade Film History Register, a resource for the study of history through film established in 1969 by Thorold DICKINSON. It is particularly involved in encouraging the development of moving image resources online. Luke McKernan.

Britons in Hollywood The British presence in Hollywood was never stronger than in the 30s and 40s. At the height of the studio system, American producers recruited British writers, directors, producers and stars. One reason for this was the advent of SOUND. 'Talking pictures' placed a premium on actors with well-spoken accents and writers accustomed to dialogue, who could be found in the British theatre. Another reason was the slowly increasing success of British films during this period. As the British industry began to find its feet in the 30s, Hollywood countered the new competition by recruiting the industry's leading talents. The international success of *The Private Life of Henry VIII* (1933) provides a key example. By 1940, the film's writer (Arthur WIMPERIS) and its leading actors (Charles LAUGHTON, Elsa LANCHESTER, Merle OBERON and Binnie BARNES) were in Hollywood, where they escaped from the restrictions placed on British film-making during the war and enjoyed the better facilities, salaries and climate of America's film capital. Indeed, the roster of British talent in Hollywood during the war includes many of the best-known names from the 30s, including directors such as Alfred HITCHCOCK, Robert STEVENSON, Victor SAVILLE and Herbert WILCOX, as well as stars such as Vivien LEIGH, Anna NEAGLE and Laurence OLIVIER. They found ample work, and they often found themselves involved in films that were almost entirely British-orientated, such as *Cavalcade* (1933), *Rebecca* (1940) and *Forever and a Day* (1943), many of whose casts were boosted with such British character actors as Sir C. Aubrey SMITH and Gladys COOPER. These Hollywood 'British' films found favour with both American and British audiences, and their success fuelled the rise of Hollywood's so-called 'British

colony'. Most of these directors and stars did not settle permanently in Hollywood, although Stevenson's career at Disney, which included directing films such as *Mary Poppins* (1964) and *Bedknobs and Broomsticks* (1971), resulted in his attaining the label of 'the most commercially successful director in film history' in the 70s.

After WW2 the decline of the British influence in Hollywood was marked. Hollywood's own 'British' films had largely fallen out of favour with American audiences, and the British industry was no longer seen as a threat. Anna LEE complained that 'Greer GARSON was the last British star they made' in Hollywood, and by the time Dirk BOGARDE arrived in the 50s, he was asked to play romantic Latin-Americans rather than the sophisticated British roles his predecessors had enjoyed. More recently, a trend has developed in which a British accent is used to convey evil. This characterisation is not entirely new, and in fact Basil RATHBONE, Henry DANIELL and George SANDERS can be seen to have established it back in the 30s. Today it dominates and is particularly strong in the action genre; for example, Steven BERKOFF, Peter CUSHING, Jeremy IRONS, Ben KINGSLEY, Alan RICKMAN and Terence STAMP have enjoyed villainous roles in the *Beverly Hills Cop*, *Die Hard*, *Star Wars* and *Superman* films. And directors such as Mike NEWELL, Alan PARKER, Ridley SCOTT and Stephen FREARS work as much in the US as in Britain. Thus, the allure of Hollywood continues to draw some of Britain's best and brightest talents, even if that talent is now put to limited use.
BIBLIOG: Mark Glancy, *When Hollywood Loved Britain*, 1999. Mark Glancy.

Brittain, Ronald (*b* ? – *d* 1981). Actor. Real-life RSM who played, as to the manner born, military types in about ten films, starting with *They Were Not Divided* (1950). He played himself in *You Lucky People* (1955) and Sergeant Britten in *55 Days at Peking* (1962).

OTHER BRITISH FILMS INCLUDE: *Carrington VC* (1954), *The Criminal* (1960), *The Amorous Prawn* (1962), *The Spy with a Cold Nose* (1966).

Britten, Benjamin (Baron of Aldeburgh) (*b* Lowestoft, 1913 – *d* Aldeburgh, 1976). Composer. Leading English composer of his generation, who came to international prominence following success of his opera *Peter Grimes* (1945). Subsequent compositions include *Billy Budd*, *The Turn of the Screw*, *War Requiem*, song-cycles (majority written for his tenor partner Peter Pears), and chamber and orchestral works. Founded English Opera Group (1947) and Aldeburgh Festival (1948). Active as a film music composer, 1935–38, a key figure in the creative team of John Grierson's GPO FILM UNIT. Composed music for *The King's Stamp* and the experimental *Coal Face* (1935), the latter exploring *musique-concrète* techniques (previously developed by Walter LEIGH) and marking his first association with poet W.H. AUDEN. Joined GPO FILM UNIT staff, September 1935, following which he and Auden jointly planned the ambitious *Negroes* (original format aborted, revived as *God's Chillun*, 1938) and *Night Mail* (1936), the most famous British DOCUMENTARY of the period. The combination of Auden's verse commentary, Britten's atmospheric score (for only 12 instruments) and Harry WATT's romantic visuals powerfully evoke the overnight journey of the mail train. The creation of realistic sound effects through musical means was central to the experimental ethos of *Coal Face*, and was further developed in *Night Mail*. Independent documentaries include Paul ROTHA's controversial pacifist film, *Peace of Britain* and the folksong-inspired *Around the Village*

Green (1936). Britten's only feature film score was *Love from a Stranger* (1937), based on an Agatha CHRISTIE short story. *The Instruments of the Orchestra* (1945), an educational film designed to introduce the sounds of the symphony orchestra, has achieved lasting success in the concert hall as *The Young Person's Guide to the Orchestra*. Peerage in 1976. Philip Reed.

Britton, Tony (*b* Birmingham, 1924). Actor. After army service, did notable work on stage, with Stratford (Bassanio to Peggy ASHCROFT's Portia) and Old Vic seasons. Entered films inauspiciously in *Salute the Toff* (1952), became a capable leading man in THRILLERS of various kinds – the hunted man in *The Break* (1962); the hapless 'smuggler' in *The Birthday Present* (1957). As a redundant executive in *Sunday Bloody Sunday* (1971) he was very moving in a character role. On TV, he has mined a polished, upper-middle-class persona in such series as *Don't Wait Up* (1983–90).
OTHER BRITISH FILMS INCLUDE: *Loser Takes All* (1956), *Operation Amsterdam* (1958), *Suspect* (1960), *The Day of the Jackal* (1973), *The People That Time Forgot* (1977), *Agatha* (1978, UK/US).

Broadbent, Jim (*b* Lincoln, 1949). Actor. Bluff, burly, likeable character actor who has won acclaim (and Best Actor at Venice Film Festival) for his interpretation of W.S. Gilbert in Mike LEIGH's *Topsy-Turvy* (2000). Even in the small role of fatuous TV compere in *Time Bandits* (1981), his sleazy bonhomie catches the eye; he is riveting when the phoney nice-guy image slips to reveal the bared teeth in *Little Voice* (1998). Among such others as the cook with aspirations in Leigh's *Life is Sweet* (1990), Miranda RICHARDSON's duplicitous husband in *Enchanted April* (1992), Buckingham in *Richard III* (1995) and the saintly John Bayley in *Iris* (2002, UK/US), for which he won a Best Supporting Oscar, he has racked up as impressive a role-call as any actor currently in British films. Has also filmed internationally, as in Woody Allen's *Bullets Over Broadway* (1994, US) and *Moulin Rouge* (2001, Aust/US). Trained at LAMDA, has worked for the RSC and the National Theatre, and was one half of the two-man stage show, *The National Theatre of Brent*.
OTHER BRITISH FILMS INCLUDE: *The Shout* (1978), *Phoelix* (1979), *Breaking Glass* (1980), *Brazil* (1985), *The Good Father* (1986), *Vroom* (1988), *Erik the Viking* (1989), *The Crying Game* (1992), *Widow's Peak* (1994, UK/US), *The Secret Agent* (1996, UK/US), *The Borrowers* (1997), *Bridget Jones's Diary* (2001, UK/Fr/US).

Broccoli, Albert ('Cubby') R. (*b* New York, 1909 – *d* Los Angeles, 1996). Producer. Now best known as co-producer (with Harry SALTZMAN, until 1976) of the hugely successful BOND films, Broccoli began his career as assistant director at 20th Century–Fox in 1938, and had brief experience as an actors' agent. He moved to England in 1951, where, with Irving ALLEN, he founded WARWICK PICTURES, which produced a series of GENRE films, including the WAR FILMS, *The Red Beret* (1953) and *Cockleshell Heroes* (1955), exotic adventures, *Zarak*, *Safari* (1956) and *Killers of Kilimanjaro* (1959), and pop MUSICALS, *Idle on Parade* (1958) and *Jazzboat* (1959). The mixture of sex, spoof, glamour, thuggery and snobbery made the BONDS a hit from the first, *Dr No* (1962), in which Ursula Andress emerged, bikini-clad, from the surf into the hairy-chested embrace – well, a little later – of Sean CONNERY. Not even changing heroes could dint the box-office appeal of the Bonds, made for Broccoli and Saltzman's Eon Productions.

Brodszky, Nicholas (*b* Odessa, Ukraine, 1905 – *d* Los Angeles, 1958). Composer. Came to Britain during the 30s, and went on

to score many films, including seven for Anthony ASQUITH, starting with *French Without Tears* (1939). His score for *The Way to the Stars* (1945) was available on record. In Hollywood during the 60s, largely at MGM, scoring such films as *Love Me or Leave Me* (1955).
OTHER BRITISH FILMS INCLUDE: *Guilty Melody* (1936), *Freedom Radio*, *Spy for a Day* (1940), *Quiet Wedding* (1941), *The Demi-Paradise* (1943), *Carnival, Beware of Pity* (1946), *A Man About the House* (1947).

Brody, Estelle (*b* New York, 1900 – *d* Malta, 1995). Actress. Briefly in cabaret and on stage, Brody entered films in 1926, as *Mademoiselle from Armentières*. Hailed for her realistic portrayal of a Lancashire girl in *Hindle Wakes* (1927), she starred in the early British talkie, *Kitty* (1929) and made one Hollywood film, *Ann Vickers* (1933). Because of anti-US bias, Brody was publicised as being Canadian-born. Retired to Malta with her second husband in 1969.
OTHER BRITISH FILMS INCLUDE: *White Heat* (1926), *The Glad Eye* (1927), *Sailors Don't Care* (1928), *They Were Not Divided* (1950), *Lilli Marlene* (1951), *Safari* (1956). AS.

Bromhead, A(lfred) C(laude) (*b* Southsea, 1876 – *d* Petersham, 1963). Executive. A major figure in silent cinema, Bromhead founded the British arm of the GAUMONT COMPANY in 1898; in 1922, with brothers Reginald and Herbert, he bought out the interest of Léon Gaumont, and, later, amalgamated the company with distributors W&F and with IDEAL FILMS. Established a film laboratory at SHEPHERD'S BUSH, at which most British films were developed, and next to it, in 1914, he built one of the country's most famous studios. During WW1, Bromhead was a Lieutenant-Colonel, commanding special missions to the Russian and Italian armies, and was awarded the CBE in 1918. Retired in 1929, but during WW2 served as honorary adviser to the Films Division of the MOI. AS.

Bromiley, Dorothy (*b* Manchester, 1930) Actress. Starlet of the 50s who began in Hollywood's *The Girls of Pleasure Island* (1953), then made several films in Britain, including *A Touch of the Sun* (1956), as Frankie HOWERD's leading lady, and two for Joseph LOSEY – *The Criminal* (1960) and *The Servant* (1963).
OTHER BRITISH FILMS: *It's Great to Be Young!* (1956), *Zoo Baby* (1964).

Bron, Eleanor (*b* Edgware, 1938). Actress. Stylish and distinctive revue star who has always seemed a touch *outré* for films, but made a striking Hermione in Ken RUSSELL's *Women in Love* (1969). Successful on stage (e.g. in *The Prime of Miss Jean Brodie*, 1983), radio and TV (who else was bizarre enough to play Patsy's mother in *Absolutely Fabulous*, 1992?), her screen appearances often seem like highly enjoyable 'turns'. Appropriately, her first film was the BEATLES' *Help!* (1965).
OTHER BRITISH FILMS INCLUDE: *Alfie*, *Two for the Road* (1966), *Bedazzled* (1967), *The National Health* (1973), *The Hound of the Baskervilles* (1983), *Turtle Diary* (1985), *Little Dorrit* (1987), *Saint-Ex* (1996), *The House of Mirth* (2000, UK/US).

Brook, Clive (*b* London, 1887 – *d* London, 1974). Actor. Quintessential English gentleman, with prominent stiff upper-lip, who at least in silent films could play other nationalities. His regret was that too often his roles were serious, and an innate, often cynical, comedic streak remained largely hidden. His British career lasted from 1920–24, and embraced 34 films. Three from 1923 with Betty COMPSON – *Woman to Woman*, *The Royal Oak* and *The White Shadow* – led to a Hollywood career, and 56 further films, including Paramount's first talkie, *Interference* (1929) and *Shanghai Express* (1932). Returned to the

UK in 1936, and starred in another 11 features. With the superbly witty high comedy, *On Approval* (1944), he proved himself as good a director as leading man. Also TV from 1956, and authorship of the play *That's What Victor Hugo Said*. Father of Faith BROOK and Lyndon BROOK.

OTHER BRITISH FILMS INCLUDE: *Trent's Last Case* (1920), *This Freedom* (1923), *The Passionate Adventure* (1924), *The Ware Case* (1938), *Convoy* (1940), *The Flemish Farm* (1943), *The Shipbuilders* (1943), *List of Adrian Messenger* (1963, UK/US). AS.

Brook, Faith (*b* York, 1922). Actress. Graceful actress almost invariably in well-bred roles, such as the heroine's mother in *The Eye of the Needle* (1981) and Lady Bexborough in *Mrs Dalloway* (1997, UK/Neth/US), but pleasingly ambiguous in *Chase a Crooked Shadow* (1957). First appeared in *Suspicion* (1941, US), served with the ATS (1942–45), joined the Bristol Old Vic after WW2 and filmed only sporadically. Some notable TV, including *All Passion Spent* (1986). Daughter of Clive BROOK, sister of Lyndon BROOK.

OTHER BRITISH FILMS INCLUDE: *Uneasy Terms* (1948), *Wicked as They Come* (1956), *Across the Bridge* (1957), *The Thirty Nine Steps* (1958, as Nanny), *To Sir, with Love* (1967), *North Sea Hijack* (1979, as Prime Minister).

Brook, Lesley (*b* Folkestone, 1916). Actress. RN: Learoyd. Appealing, gentle-mannered actress of two dozen largely unmemorable films, appearing in eight in 1938, and some lachrymose musicals including *The Rose of Tralee* (1942). Best chances came in Lance COMFORT's *When We Are Married* (1943) and the off-beat 'B' film, *The Fool and the Princess* (1948). On stage before first filming in 1937 (*The Vulture*).

OTHER BRITISH FILMS INCLUDE: *The Return of Carol Deane* (1938), *I'll Walk Beside You*, *The Bells Go Down* (1943), *For You Alone*, *The Trojan Brothers* (1945), *House of Darkness* (1948).

Brook, Lyndon (*b* Los Angeles, 1926). Actor. Short and slight, Clive BROOK's Cambridge-educated son made his West End debut in 1947, entered films in tiny roles in *Trottie True* (1948) and *Train of Events* (1949). Remained a supporting actor in films, getting his best chances as Douglas Bader's pal in *Reach For the Sky* (1956) and the injured navigator in the Burma-jungle adventure, *The Purple Plain* (1954). Some international films, including *Song Without End* (1960, as Wagner), and TV (e.g. *Point Counterpoint*, 1972).

OTHER BRITISH FILMS INCLUDE: *The Passing Stranger* (1954), *One Way Out* (1955), *The Gypsy and the Gentleman* (1957), *The Hireling* (1973), *Who?* (1974), *Defence of the Realm* (1985).

Brook, Sir Peter (*b* London, 1925). Director. Maverick figure whose films have little to do with mainstream British, or any other, cinema. His real career is in the experimental theatre where his productions have often broken new ground, as in his famous 'gymnasium' version of *A Midsummer Night's Dream* (1971). In 1943, still at Oxford, he and Gavin LAMBERT made an amateur film, *A Sentimental Journey* (1943); in 1953, he made a leaden version of *The Beggar's Opera*, with Laurence OLIVIER; in 1966, he filmed his revolutionary stage production, *The Marat/Sade . . .* and in 1970 he made a bleak *King Lear* (UK/Den), starring Paul SCOFIELD. His best-known film is probably *Lord of the Flies* (1963), filmed on location in Puerto Rico as it explored William Golding's dark vision of mankind. His 1979 dealings with Eastern mysticism, *Meetings with Remarkable Men*, a US production with a British cast including his actress wife, Natasha PARRY, had a cult following. He demands a great deal of his audiences, in theatre and film, claiming when he made *Moderato Cantabile* (1960) that he

wasn't 'going to make any concessions' – nor has he, and this may explain why he's made few films.

Brook-Jones, Elwyn (*b* Kuching, Sarawak, 1911 – *d* Reading, 1962). Actor. A concert pianist aged 11, then cabaret artist from 1935, and on screen from 1940's *Dangerous Moonlight*. Heavy-featured purveyor of the sinister, like Jean KENT's slimy employer in *Good-Time Girl* (1947) or the nightclub owner in *The Gilded Cage* (1955), but most memorable as the philo-sophical Tober in *Odd Man Out* (1947). TV from 1947 (*Rope*).

OTHER BRITISH FILMS INCLUDE: *Tomorrow We Live* (1942), *The Small Back Room*, *The Three Weird Sisters*, *The Queen of Spades* (1948), *Judgement Deferred* (1951), *Passport to Shame* (1958), *The Ugly Duckling* (1959).

Brooke, Paul (*b* London, 1944) Actor. Rotund character player, equally at home in roles avuncular, like the Kafka-reading landlord in *Saving Grace* (2000), or vindictive, like the splendidly dreadful McClintock in TV's *Dance to the Music of Time* (1997).

OTHER BRITISH FILMS INCLUDE: *Agatha* (1978, UK/US), *For Your Eyes Only* (1981), *Greystoke . . .* (1984, UK/US), *Revolution* (1985, UK/Nor), *Scandal* (1988), *Splitting Heirs* (1993, UK/US), *Lighthouse* (2000).

Brooke-Taylor, Tim (*b* Buxton, Derbyshire, 1940). Actor. TV comedian, best known for *The Goodies* (1970–77, 1980), as actor and series creator, on screen in two MONTY PYTHON-related films – *Monty Python Meets Beyond the Fringe* (1977) and *The Secret Policeman's Other Ball* (1982) – and several US films. Studied law at Cambridge where he became President of the Footlights Club.

Brookes, Olwyn (aka Olwen) (*b* London, 1902 – *d* 1976). Actress. Welsh supporting player of 20-odd 40s and 50s films; a nicely ambiguous landlady in *Devils of Darkness* (1964).

OTHER BRITISH FILMS INCLUDE: *Caesar and Cleopatra* (1945, unc), *The First Gentleman* (1948), *Valley of Song* (1953), *The Good Companions* (1956), *A Night to Remember*, *Jack the Ripper* (1958), *On the Run* (1969).

Brooks, Beverly (*b* London, 1929 – *d* St Jean Cap Ferrat, 1992). Actress. More famous for being famous (as Viscountess 'Bubbles' Rothermere) than for acting, ex-model Brooks studied at the Webber-Douglas School, was on stage in 1951, films from 1955. Mainly in small roles but had the lead in a mildly diverting 'B' thriller, *Find the Lady* (1956) and was Bader's early girlfriend in *Reach for the Sky* (1956).

OTHER BRITISH FILMS: *Man of the Moment*, *Simon and Laura*, *Lost* (1955).

Brooks, Ray (*b* Brighton, 1939). Actor. As the possessor of *The Knack . . .* (1965), an ultra-trendy 60s comedy, Brooks had his one memorable film role. Otherwise, supporting roles and leads in minor, justly forgotten GENRE movies of the time and was Five of Spades in *Alice's Adventures in Wonderland* (1972).

OTHER BRITISH FILMS INCLUDE: *Some People*, *HMS Defiant* (1962), *Daleks – Invasion Earth 2150 AD* (1966), *Carry On Abroad* (1972), *Tiffany Jones*, *Assassin* (1973).

Broomfield, Nick (*b* London, 1948). Director, screenwriter. Prolific documentarist who has characteristically explored controversial matters, such as police intimidation (*Juvenile Liaison*, 1975; *Juvenile Liaison 2*, 1990), the sex trade (*Chicken Ranch*, 1983; *Heidi Fleiss: Hollywood Madam*, 1995), housing estate conditions (*Behind the Rent Strike*, 1974), and criminal behaviour (*Aileen Wuornos: The Selling of a Serial Killer*, 1994), Mrs Thatcher (*Tracking Down Maggie*, 1994), and the sex-drugs-and-rock scene (*Kurt & Courtney*, 1998). His feature film, *Diamond Skulls* (1989), is a black comedy. Also worked in the US in the early 80s; sometimes produces, photographs and edits his films.

OTHER BRITISH FILMS INCLUDE: *Who Cares?* (1971), *Proud to Be British* (1973), *Whittingham* (1975), *Fort Augustus* (1976), *Lily Tomlin* (1986), *Driving Me Crazy* (1988), *The Leader, His Driver and the Driver's Wife* (1991), *Monster in a Box* (1992), *Fetishes* (1996).

Brosnan, Pierce (*b* Drogheda, Ireland, 1951). Actor. Handsome 90s incarnation of James BOND as tough, elegant and intelligent, in *GoldenEye* (1995), *Tomorrow Never Dies* (1997) and *The World Is Not Enough* (1999) (all UK/US). He nearly missed the role by being unavailable in the 80s when Timothy DALTON took over without distinction. Elsewhere, has starred in international films (e.g. *Mars Attacks!*, 1996; *The Thomas Crown Affair*, 1999, US), and co-produced as well as 'guested' in *The Match* (1999, UK/Ire).Trained at the London Drama Centre, made his London stage debut in 1976 and entered films in *The Long Good Friday* (1979). In 1977 he married actress, **Cassandra Harris**, who appeared in the Bond *For Your Eyes Only* (1981) and died in 1991.

OTHER BRITISH FILMS INCLUDE: *The Mirror Crack'd* (1980, unc), *The Fourth Protocol*, *Taffin* (1987), *The Deceivers* (1988), *The Lawnmower Man* (1992), *Alistair MacLean's Death Train* (1993, UK/US/Yug), *Alistair MacLean's Night Watch* (1995, UK/Croatia/US), *The Disappearance of Kevin Johnson* (1995), *The Nephew* (1998), *The Tailor of Panama* (Ire/US), *Blood and Champagne* (2001), *Die Another Day* (2002, UK/US).

BIBLIOG: York Membery, *Pierce Brosnan*, 1997.

Brough, Mary (*b* London, 1863 – *d* London, 1934). Actress. Made stage debut in 1881 as the maid in Lillie Langtry's stage debut, *She Stoops to Conquer*, but best remembered for her domineering Cockney characterizations. Appeared on stage (1925–29) in a number of ALDWYCH FARCES, and later in the screen versions: *Rookery Nook* (1930), *Plunder* (1931), *Thark* (1932), *A Night Like This* (1932), *A Cuckoo in the Nest* (1933), and *Turkey Time* (1933).

OTHER BRITISH FILMS INCLUDE: *The Brass Bottle* (1914), *The Amazing Quest of Mr Ernest Bliss* (1920), *Squibs* (1921), *The Only Way* (1925), *Wait and See* (1928). AS.

Brown, George H. (*b* London, 1913 – *d* New York, 2001). Producer. Partly educated in Spain where he entered the industry in 1933. Came to England as unit production manager for Pendennis Pictures, set up by Alexander KORDA and Eric POMMER; later worked for Pommer and Charles LAUGHTON's MAYFLOWER PICTURES on *Jamaica Inn* (1939), during which he met Maureen O'HARA, to whom he was briefly (1939–41) married. Was Associate Producer on *49th Parallel* (1941), with the RAF FILM UNIT during WW2, and was associate producer for its *Journey Together* (1945). Post-war he produced many popular films, co-authoring several: the witty *Hotel Sahara* (1951), *Made in Heaven* (1952) and *Desperate Moment* (1953). He worked with such GENRE directors as John Paddy CARSTAIRS (*Sleeping Car to Trieste*, 1948, *The Chiltern Hundreds*, 1949), Ken ANNAKIN (*The Seekers*, 1954) and George POLLOCK (*Rooney*, 1958, *Murder She Said*, 1961). Best-known film is probably John GUILLERMIN's *The Guns at Batasi* (1964), after which his career tapered off.

OTHER BRITISH FILMS INCLUDE: (p, unless noted) *School for Secrets* (1946, co-p), *Vice Versa* (co-p) (1947), *Jacqueline* (1956), *Tommy the Toreador* (1959), *Village of Daughters* (1962), *The Trap* (1966), *Assault* (1970), *Innocent Bystanders* (1972).

Brown, Georgia (*b* London, 1933 – *d* London, 1992). Singer. RN: Lilian Klot. British cabaret performer in occasional films, but best remembered as Nancy in the stage hit *Oliver!* (1960), in London and US. Strong supporting roles in several films: a saloon singer in *A Study in Terror* (1965), a vivid Marfa in *The Fixer* (1969, US), and warm-hearted friend to the paraplegic protagonists in *The Raging Moon* (1970).

OTHER BRITISH FILMS INCLUDE: *Lock Up Your Daughters!* (1969), *Nothing But the Night* (1972), *The Bawdy Adventures of Tom Jones* (1975).

Brown, Janet (*b* Rutherglen, Scotland, 1926). Actress. In *Folly to Be Wise* (1952), pertly pretty singer-impressionist Brown, as a WAAF officer, causes dissension when she asks an ENSA Brains Trust 'What is the basis of a happy marriage?' She never had another comparable moment in films, but was an early TV variety performer. Married actor Peter BUTTERWORTH.

OTHER BRITISH FILMS INCLUDE: *Floodtide* (1949), *The Adding Machine* (1969), *Bless This House* (1972), *For Your Eyes Only* (1981, as Prime Minister).

Brown, Joe (*b* Swaby, 1941). Singer. British pop singer of the 60s rarely seen in films. Two unambitious MUSICALS were built around him – *What a Crazy World* (1963) and *Three Hats for Lisa* (1965). Bigger successes attended his group, Joe Brown and the Bruvvers and his 70s band, Home Brew, and his theatre hit, *Charlie Girl* (1965), co-starring Anna NEAGLE.

OTHER BRITISH FILMS: *Just for Fun!* (1963), *The Beauty Jungle* (1964), *Lionheart* (1968), *Mona Lisa* (1986).

Brown, June (*b* Needham Market, 1927). Actress. Famously 'Dot Cotton', lugubrious gossip in TV's *EastEnders* (1985–93, 1997–), Brown, a fine actress, underused in films, was affecting as Peter FINCH's anxious patient in *Sunday Bloody Sunday* (1971). Married to actors John Garley (deceased) and Robert Arnold.

OTHER BRITISH FILMS INCLUDE: *Inadmissible Evidence* (1968), *Straw Dogs* (1971), *Psychomania* (1972), *Murder by Decree* (1978), *Bean* (1997).

Brown, Pamela (*b* London, 1917 – *d* London, 1975). Actress. Made debut as Juliet at Stratford-on-Avon in 1936, after gaining a gold medal from RADA. Her numerous appearances for the Old Vic, and Broadway triumphs (e.g. opposite GIELGUD in WILDE's *The Importance of Being Earnest*, 1947), were the more remarkable by reason of the debilitating arthritis which she suffered from the age of sixteen. While her work remained predominantly in the theatre, she also made notable screen appearances, commencing with the part of the Dutch school mistress in Michael POWELL's *One of Our Aircraft is Missing* (1942). Her hauntingly enigmatic face, with the great golden eyes which Powell likened to those of a cat, ensured that she was noticed even in secondary roles such as Nicklaus in *The Tales of Hoffmann* (1951) and Jane Shore in OLIVIER's *Richard III* (1955). She and Powell became lovers, and were living together at the time of her death from cancer in 1975. Was married to Peter COPLEY.

OTHER BRITISH FILMS INCLUDE: *I Know Where I'm Going!* (1945), *Alice in Wonderland* (1949), *The Second Mrs Tanqueray* (1952), *Personal Affair* (1953), *The Scapegoat* (1958), *Becket* (1964), *Half a Sixpence* (1967, UK/US), *Secret Ceremony* (1968), *Wuthering Heights* (1970), *Lady Caroline Lamb* (1972, UK/It/Us), *Dracula* (1973, UK/US). Race Mathews.

Brown, Phil (*b* Cambridge, Massachusetts, 1916). Actor. With a background of New York's Group Theater, minor roles in 15 Hollywood films, and McCarthyist scrutiny, Brown moved to England in the late 40s. His first British role, as Sally GRAY's wise-cracking boyfriend in danger of acid-bath demise in *Obsession* (1949), directed by blacklisted Edward DMYTRYK, was probably his best, but he kept working, usually as

Americans abroad, until the 90s, with a small part in *Chaplin* (1992, UK/It/Fr/Jap/US). He was Uncle Owen in *Star Wars* (1977, US).

OTHER BRITISH FILMS INCLUDE: *A King in New York* (1957), *The Bedford Incident* (1965), *Ooh . . . You Are Awful* (1972), *The Romantic Englishwoman* (1975, UK/Fr), *Superman* (1978).

Brown, Robert (*b* Swanage, 1918). Actor. Despite nearly 50 film credits, starting with *Out of True* (1951), burly character player Brown is likely to be best remembered for succeeding Bernard LEE as 'M' in the 'BOND' films, starting with *Octopussy* (1983), having previously played an admiral in the 1977 Bond, *The Spy Who Loved Me*.

OTHER BRITISH FILMS INCLUDE: *Time Gentlemen Please!* (1952), *A Hill in Korea* (1956), *Macbeth* (1961), *Billy Budd* (1962), *One Million Years BC* (1966), *Private Road* (1971), *A View to a Kill* (1985), *The Living Daylights* (1987), *Licence to Kill* (1989).

Browne, Coral (*b* Melbourne, 1913 – *d* Los Angeles, California, 1991). Actress. After three years' stage experience in Australia, Browne came to Britain at 21 and quickly established herself on the West End stage, usually in sophisticated roles. Though she made nearly 30 films, she never became a film star. As a young actress on screen (in, say, *Black Limelight*, 1938, or *Let George* [Formby] *Do It*, 1940), she looked as if she might eat the leading man alive, coming over too strongly for the screen's intimacy. She made a mark in bitchy roles, such as Michael WILDING's spiteful girlfriend (she could have eaten him too) in *The Courtneys of Curzon Street* (1947); scored some major character successes in UK and US films such as *Auntie Mame* (1958, as a gin-sodden actress), as the sluttish Belle in *Dr Crippen* (1962), the dominant Mercy Croft in *The Killing of Sister George* (1968), and the lascivious Lady Claire in *The Ruling Class* (1971). In 1983, in TV's *An Englishman Abroad*, she daringly played herself of 25 years earlier when, touring in Russia with the RSC, she had a chance meeting with defector Guy Burgess. Two years later, she gave a performance of coruscating brilliance and poignancy as Alice Hargreaves, the 'original' Alice in Wonderland, in *Dreamchild*. A notably witty woman (her *bons mots* were legend), she married (2) actor Vincent Price, having been 'murdered' by him in *Theatre of Blood* (1973) – and that, too, seemed a witty thing to do.

OTHER BRITISH FILMS INCLUDE: *Yellow Sands* (1938), *Piccadilly Incident* (1946), *The Roman Spring of Mrs Stone* (1961), *Go to Blazes*, *Tamahine* (1962), *The Night of the Generals* (1966, UK/Fr).

Browne, Irene (*b* London, 1891 – *d* London, 1965). Actress. *Grande dame*-style stage star spread 20-odd films over 45 years, including several in Hollywood in the 30s (e.g. *Cavalcade*, 1933, reprising her stage role). In Britain, she was memorable as Moira SHEARER's guardian in *The Red Shoes* (1948) and in two big roles near the end of her life: Arabella Barrington in *Barnacle Bill* (1957) and the vicar's worldly mother in *Serious Charge* (1959). On stage from 1910.

OTHER BRITISH FILMS INCLUDE: *Drink* (1917), *The Glorious Adventure* (1922), *The Amateur Gentleman* (1936), *Pygmalion* (1938), *Kipps* (1941), *Bad Lord Byron* (1949), *The House in the Square* (1951), *The Wrong Arm of the Law* (1962).

Brownlow, Kevin (*b* Crowborough, 1938). Director, film historian, editor. Britain's leading film historian, whose work includes landmark studies of silent film – e.g. *The Parade's Gone By* (1968), and *Behind the Mask of Innocence* (1990) – and a superb biography of David LEAN (1996) which draws almost

exclusively on a vast range of oral testimony. The affectionate and rigorous research which produced his books has also informed the highly regarded TV series he has made with David Gill: *Hollywood* (1980); *Unknown Chaplin* (1983) and *Cinema Europe: the Other Hollywood* (1995).

Always passionate about cinema, he worked as office boy at World Wide Pictures in 1955; determined to make films, over three years (1952–55), made a short, *The Capture*. He joined forces with the even younger Andrew MOLLO, who worked as editorial assistant, and they scraped together enough money to make *It Happened Here*. Seven years in the making, finally screened in 1964, it is an alarming 'What if?' account of a Nazi invasion of Britain, and, considering it cost £7,000, is staggeringly ambitious, including a Nazi rally in Trafalgar Square. This was not followed by offers of other films to direct, so Brownlow (like Mollo) took editing jobs – he cut Lindsay ANDERSON's *The White Bus* (1967) and Richardson's *Red and Blue* (1967) and *The Charge of the Light Brigade* (1968) – and continued the research for his books.

The other independent film he and Mollo made was *Winstanley* (1975), a defiantly non-commercial historical/political drama, based on the failure of the Leveller and Digger movements during the Civil War. Pessimistic in tone, it is a masterpiece of luminous images of arduous, rain-drenched rural life and of tough, uncompromising intellect. It is a comment on the timid limits of mainstream film-making, that, since then, Brownlow has made no feature film, though he and Mollo were hired to direct *The Breaking of Bumbo* but were got rid of before shooting started. However, he has continued major work of reconstruction on some of the great silent films; the crowning glory is the five-hour frame-by-frame restoration of Abel Gance's *Napoléon* (1927/1979). The result of decades of dedicated care was recognised when the French created him *Chevalier de la Légion d'Honneur*.

As well as the above, he has also made several documentaries, including *Abel Gance: The Charm of Dynamite* (1968), and from 1958 to 1965 edited a great many others.

OTHER BRITISH FILMS (documentaries): *Ascot – A Race Against Time* (1960, + ph, ed), *Nine Dalmuir West* (1962, + ed).

Bruce, Brenda (*b* Prestwich,1919 – *d* London, 1996). Actress. Prolific supporting player, on film, stage and TV over five decades, making a name on stage in plays classic and modern. First on film in 1943's *Millions Like Us*, she brought a wry good humour to a range of roles, from upper-class Mabel Crum in *While the Sun Shines* (1947), to the warm-hearted barmaid in *The Final Test* (1953), to the laconic tart in the opening sequence of *Peeping Tom* (1960). She was briefly in the chase drama, *My Brother's Keeper* (1948), co-directed by Roy RICH whom she married. After his death she married actor Clement McCALLIN.

OTHER BRITISH FILMS INCLUDE: *They Came to a City* (1944, as girl on hillside), *Piccadilly Incident* (1946), *When the Bough Breaks* (1947), *Law and Disorder* (1958), *Nightmare* (1963), *That'll Be the Day* (1973), *Swallows and Amazons* (1974), *Steaming* (1984), *Little Dorrit* (1987), *Antonia and Jane* (1990), *Splitting Heirs* (1993, UK/US).

Bruce, Nigel (*b* Ensenada, Mexico, 1895 – *d* Santa Monica, California, 1953). Actor. Mainly in Hollywood from 1934, but appeared in eleven 30s British films, mostly as bumbling aristocrats, as in *Lord Camber's Ladies* (1932) and *The Scarlet Pimpernel* (1935, as Prince of Wales). Famous in Hollywood as Dr Watson to Basil Rathbone's SHERLOCK HOLMES, and in innumerable British-set films, like HITCHCOCK's *Suspicion* (1941).

OTHER BRITISH FILMS INCLUDE: *Red Aces* (1929), *Escape* (1930), *The Midshipmaid* (1932), *Channel Crossing, I Was a Spy* (1933), *Thunder in the City* (1937).

Brune, Gabrielle (*b* Bournemouth, 1912). Actress. On stage (from 1930) and in cabaret (1937) as well as the odd 30s film, including *Red Pearls* (1930) and, later, sporadic supporting roles, such as Edward CHAPMAN's accommodating secretary in *Mandy* (1952).

OTHER BRITISH FILMS INCLUDE: *The Penny Pool* (1937), *Garrison Follies* (1940), *A Run for Your Money* (1949, as singer) (1952), *The Titfield Thunderbolt* (1953), *Stars in Your Eyes* (1956), *Follow Me!* (1971).

Brunel, Adrian (*b* Brighton, 1892 – *d* Gerrards Cross, 1958). Director, screenwriter. Began as film salesman in 1915, and directed his first film, *The Cost of a Kiss* in 1917, founding MINERVA FILMS with Leslie HOWARD in 1920. Largely forgotten today, he is a pioneer of British production, straddling the silent-sound divide, working prolifically as writer and director, and occasionally as actor. His silent film, *The Man Without Desire* (1923), showed real talent, and if some of his 30s films are 'QUOTA QUICKIES', there are plenty that rose above that perfunctory level. These include the silents *The Vortex* (1927) and *The Constant Nymph* (1928, + s), and the talkies *Elstree Calling* (1930), *Badger's Green* (1934), *While Parents Sleep* (1935) and *The City of Beautiful Nonsense* (1935). He also wrote the Indian film *Shikari* (1932), was co-scriptwriter and associate producer on *Return of the Scarlet Pimpernel* (1937), and acted as production consultant on Howard's *The First of the Few* (1942) and *The Gentle Sex* (1943). In 1949, he published a witty memoir, *Nice Work*, a 'story of low life in British film production'. His work might repay serious excavation. His mother, Adey, wrote plays under the name Dale Laurence, and his son, Christopher, was editor and writer.

OTHER BRITISH FILMS INCLUDE: (d) *Twice Two, Bookworms* (1920), *Too Many Crooks* (1921, + sc), *Lovers in Araby* (+ w, a) (1924), *Blighty* (1927), *The Crooked Billet* (1929), *Follow the Lady* (1933), *Important People* (1934), *Cross Currents* (1935, + sc), *The Rebel Son* (UK/Fr), *The Lion Has Wings* (co-d, co-sc) (1939), *Salvage with a Smile* (1940, short); (sc) *The Face at the Window*, (1920), *Land of Hope and Glory* (1927), *Yellow Caesar* (1940, short, dial, add scenes).

Brunius, Jacques (*b* Paris, 1906 – *d* Exeter, 1967). Actor. RN: Cottance. In Britain from 1950, Brunius made about 20 films, mostly in conventional 'foreign' roles, like the customs official in *The Lavender Hill Mob* (1951) and the angry 'Frenchie' in *Laughing Anne* (1953). Pre-war, in some notable French films including *La bête humaine* (1938), and assistant director on Bunuel's *L'âge d'or* (1930) and Renoir's *Une partie de campagne* (1936).

OTHER BRITISH FILMS INCLUDE: *The Spider and the Fly* (1949, French consultant), *The Wooden Horse* (1950), *Sea Devils* (1953), *Cockleshell Heroes* (1955), *Dangerous Exile* (1957), *Orders to Kill* (1958), *The Yellow Rolls-Royce* (1964).

Bryan, Dora (*b* Southport, 1924). Actress. RN: Broadbent. A regular pleasure of 40s and 50s British films was this chirpy blonde with adaptable nasal voice (Cockney, Lancashire, 'refeened') and scene-stealing comic timing. She played tarts of every hue, starting with warm-hearted Rosie in *The Fallen Idol*, 1948, irresistibly spiteful hussies in *The Cure for Love* (1949) and *Time Gentlemen Please!* (1952), a nosy neighbour in *No Trace* (1950), was very comfy as Gladys, the sultan's wife in *You Know What Sailors Are* (1954), and an extremely dubious head-

mistress in *The Great St Trinian's Train Robbery* (1966). Oddly, after winning a BAA for sluttish, selfish Helen ('Every wrinkle tells a dirty story') in *A Taste of Honey* (1961), she made only a handful more films, but she was so persistently busy on the stage and TV that she can scarcely have noticed. Whether Winnie or Glad or Maisie or Pearl, she assured filmgoers of at least a few minutes of unalloyed joy. On stage from 1935, often in revues but also in *The Merry Wives of Windsor* (1984).

OTHER BRITISH FILMS INCLUDE: *Odd Man Out* (1947), *Traveller's Joy, Now Barabbas Was a Robber, The Interrupted Journey, Don't Ever Leave Me, The Blue Lamp* (1949), *Circle of Danger* (1950), *The Quiet Woman, Lady Godiva Rides Again, No Highway, High Treason, Young Wives' Tale* (1951), *Whispering Smith Hits London, Made in Heaven, The Gift Horse, 13 East Street, The Ringer* (1952), *The Fake, Street Corner, The Intruder* (1953), *Mad About Men* (1954), *You Lucky People, Cockleshell Heroes* (1955), *The Green Man, Child in the House* (1956), *Hello London, Carry On Sergeant* (1958), *Operation Bullshine, Desert Mice* (1959), *Follow That Horse!, The Night We Got the Bird* (1960), *Two a Penny* (1967), *Hands of the Ripper* (1971), *Up the Front* (1972), *Apartment Zero* (1988).

BIBLIOG: Dora Bryan, *According to Dora*, 1987.

Bryan, John (*b* London, 1911 – *d* London, 1969). Producer, production designer. Until his untimely death, Bryan was perhaps Britain's most gifted production designer. Apprenticed to scenic artists at 16, he worked first in stage design. Joined LONDON FILM PRODUCTIONS in 1932, first as draughtsman, assisting Laurence IRVING on *Diamond Cut Diamond* (1932), later as associate art director to Vincent KORDA on *Things to Come* (1936). During the war, he was involved with camouflage. That some of the 40s GAINSBOROUGH MELODRAMAS look so sumptuous may be substantially attributed to his romantic and stylish designs: e.g. *Fanny by Gaslight* (1944) has little connection with realism but evokes superbly the essence of Victorian contrasts of low and high life. After working on Gabriel PASCAL's two previous SHAW films, *Pygmalion* (1938) and *Major Barbara* (1941), he was sought for the ambitious calamity, *Caesar and Cleopatra* (1945), in which his towering evocations of palace and desert dominate proceedings. Post-war, he joined the distinguished CINEGUILD production team: he designed all but one of its output, winning an AA for *Great Expectations* (1946); and there are few better-looking British films than it or the rapturous melodrama, *Blanche Fury* (1947), or *Oliver Twist* (1948) or *The Passionate Friends* (1948), all with cinematographer Guy GREEN. Though he also won an AA for *Becket* (1964), arguably his greatest work is in monochrome. In the 50s and 60s, he produced a dozen films, including *After the Fox* (1966, US/It) and four for ex-Cineguild colleague, Ronald NEAME, including *The Card* (1952), *The Million Pound Note* (1953), *Windom's Way* (1957) and *The Horse's Mouth* (1958), but his greatness lies in his PRODUCTION DESIGN.

OTHER BRITISH FILMS: (art d) *Hearts of Humanity* (1936), *Song of the Road* (1937), *Kicking the Moon Around* (1938), *Stolen Life, The Lambeth Walk, On the Night of the Fire* (1939), *Dangerous Moonlight* (1941), *King Arthur Was a Gentleman* (1942), *It's That Man Again, The Adventures of Tartu, Millions Like Us, Dear Octopus* (1943), *Time Flies, Love Story, Two Thousand Women* (1944), *The Wicked Lady* (1945), *Caravan* (1946); (des) *Take My Life* (1947), *The Golden Salamander* (1949), *Pandora and the Flying Dutchman* (1950), *The Magic Box* (1951), *Great Catherine* (1967); (p:) *The Purple Plain* (1954), *The Spanish Gardener* (1956), *The Secret Place* (1957), *There Was a Crooked Man* (1960), *The Girl on the Boat, Tamahine* (1962), *The Touchables* (1968).

Bryanston Films A consortium of film-makers proposed by Maxwell SETTON and led by Michael BALCON, set up in 1959, including such members as Tony RICHARDSON, Ronald

NEAME, John BRYAN and the team of Leslie PARKYN and Julian WINTLE. Its aim was to drum up financial backing and distribution guarantees for the films it would back. For example, British Lion offered its films an advance guarantee against a 25% fee and 17% of the distributors' gross; the owners of TWICKENHAM studios were also backers. Its successes included the WOODFALL films, *The Entertainer* (1960) and, especially, *Saturday Night and Sunday Morning* (1960). In 1961, it joined forces with the UK arm of Seven Arts, but, though it continued to back independent production, it was, in hindsight, too cautious in its judgements and too modest in its budgets for major success. To its later chagrin, it turned down the chance to back *Tom Jones* (1963). In 1965 it was bought by the TV company, Associated Rediffusion.

Bryant, Gerard (*b* Guildford, 1909). Director, screenwriter. After much experience in writing and directing SHORTS and DOCUMENTARIES for Gaumont–British Magazine, then the GPO FILM UNIT and, from 1941, the CROWN FILM UNIT, he entered feature films post-war. Was production manager on *Western Approaches* (1944) and assistant director on *Seven Days to Noon* (1950), co-wrote the very funny *It's Not Cricket* (1949) and directed *The Tommy Steele Story* (1957).
OTHER BRITISH FILMS INCLUDE: (co-sc) *Hullo Fame* (1940), *The Huggetts Abroad* (1949), *The Secret of the Forest* (1955).

Bryant, Michael (*b* London, 1928 – *d* London, 2002). Actor. Intense blond stage actor (from 1951), who has made sporadic appearances in British films since 1955 (*Passage Home*), including an eye-catching 'churlish priest' in BRANAGH's *Hamlet* (1996), and done some memorable TV, notably as the son in *Talking to a Stranger* (1966). Trained at the Webber-Douglas School, came to prominence as the catalytic German tutor in *Five Finger Exercise* (1958).
OTHER BRITISH FILMS INCLUDE: *A Night to Remember* (1958), *Life for Ruth* (1962), *The Deadly Affair* (1966), *Goodbye, Mr Chips* (1969), *The Ruling Class* (1971), *Gandhi* (1982, UK/Ind).

Bryce, Alex (*b* Larbert, Scotland, 1905 – *d* 2000). Cinematographer, director. Began as clapper-boy at BIP/Elstree and thereafter photographed over 40 routine films (plus co-ph *Sally in Our Alley*, 1931) in the 30s, for Fox–British, BRITISH LION, etc. With the ARMY FILM UNIT during the war, making SHORTS for the MOI. Afterwards worked as location director on *Christopher Columbus* (1949) and *Treasure Island* (1950), and on *Diamond City* (1949, assoc d), *The Adventurers* (1950, assoc d), *Cockleshell Heroes* (assoc d), *The Dark Avenger* (2ud) (1955), etc., as well as continuing to make DOCUMENTARIES.
OTHER BRITISH FILMS INCLUDE: (d, features:) *The End of the Road* (1936), *Against the Tide* (1937), (d doc/shorts:) *Anybody's Bugbear* (1940), *The Siege of Tobruk* (1942); (c:) *The Ringer* (1931), *Josser on the Farm* (1934), *All at Sea, Night Mail, Sexton Blake and the Mademoiselle* (+ d), *Late Extra* (1935).

Bryden, Bill (*b* Greenock, Scotland, 1942). Director. Head of Drama with BBC-Scotland, and awarded CBE in 1993, Bryden's main work has been for TV, for which he wrote *Benny Lynch* (1976). On film, he directed and wrote a segment of *Aria* (1987); was co-author of *The Long Riders* (1980, US), and executive producer of *Down Among the Big Boys* (1993).

Brynner, Yul (*b* Sakhalin Island, Russia, 1915 – *d* New York, 1985). Actor. RN: Taidje Khan. Charismatic shaven-headed international star who made a half-dozen British films, none of them, except *Anastasia* (1956), among his best.

OTHER BRITISH FILMS: *Triple Cross* (1966), *The Double Man, The Long Duel* (1967), *The File of the Golden Goose* (1969), *The Madwoman of Chaillot* (1969), *The Magic Christian* (cameo) (1970).

Buchanan, Jack (*b* Helensburgh, 1890 – *d* London, 1957). Actor. The word 'debonair' seems to have been coined for this elegant song-and-dance man of the 20s and 30s. Younger than Tom WALLS, better-looking than Jack HULBERT, if not as gifted as Fred Astaire, he was Britain's nearest equivalent. Stagestruck from childhood, on stage from 1912, he starred on Broadway with Beatrice LILLIE and Gertrude LAWRENCE in *André Charlot's Revue of 1924*. Always more important on stage than screen, he made a few forgotten silent movies, such as *Auld Lang Syne* (1917), went to Hollywood for *Paris* (1929) and two others. The 30s was his busy time in British film, and if one watches a 'straight' comedy thriller such as *Smash and Grab* (1937, + s, p) one sees a very graceful, insouciant presence, wittily partnered by his favourite co-star, Elsie RANDOLPH. Apart from *'Bulldog' Sees It Through* (1940) and co-producing *Happidrome* (1943), he did not film in the 40s, returned triumphantly in *The Band Wagon* (1953, US), starred in Preston Sturges' ill-fated *Les carnets de Major Thompson* (1955, Fr), and made two more British films: *Josephine and Men* (1955), for the BOULTINGS, and the witless *As Long as They're Happy* (1955), repeating his stage role.
OTHER BRITISH FILMS: *Her Heritage* (1919), *The Audacious Mr Squire* (1923), *The Happy Ending, The Third Round* (1925), *Confetti* (1927), *Toni* (1928), *Man of Mayfair* (1931), *Goodnight Vienna* (1932, + s, d) *Yes Mr Brown, That's a Good Girl* (1933), *Come Out of the Pantry, Brewster's Millions* (1935), *This'll Make You Whistle, When Knights Were Bold* (1936), *The Sky's the Limit* (1937, + s, d, p), *Break the News* (1938), *The Middle Watch, The Gang's All Here, Alias the Bulldog* (1939), *Elstree Story, Giselle* (narr) (1952).
BIBLIOG: Michael Marshall, *Top Hat and Tails*, 1978.

Buchanan, Nigel (*b* Lowestoft, 1921). Actor. Briefly groomed by RANK as a leading man in the late 40s, he failed to survive such dreadful films as *Stop Press Girl* and *Fools Rush In* (1949).
OTHER BRITISH FILMS: *Woman in the Hall* (1947), *Fly Away Peter, Quartet* (1948), *It's Not Cricket* (1949).

Buck, David (*b* London, 1936 – *d* Esher, 1989). Actor. Promising young player of the 60s whose career – and life – were cut short by serious illness. Had the romantic lead in *The Sandwich Man* (1966) and provided the voice of Gimli in *The Lord of the Rings* (1978, US). Was married to actress Madeleine SMITH.
OTHER BRITISH FILMS INCLUDE: *Dr Syn Alias the Scarecrow* (1963), *Mosquito Squadron* (1968), *The Dark Crystal* (1982, voice).

Buck, Jules (*b* St. Louis, Missouri, 1917 – *d* Paris, 2001). Producer. American who, after experience as cinematographer (on John HUSTON's wartime DOCUMENTARIES), associate producer and producer (e.g. on *Fixed Bayonets*, 1951) in the US, came to Britain in the 50s. In 1959, founded Keep Films with actor Peter O'TOOLE, and apart from the comedy, *Operation Snatch* (1962), all his British productions starred O'Toole. They are: *The Day They Robbed the Bank of England* (1959), *Great Catherine* (1967), *Under Milk Wood* (ex p), *The Ruling Class* (1971), *Man Friday* (1975, ex p). Also produced TV series, *OSS* (1957–58).

Buckland, Warwick Director, actor. Director, and occasional actor, at HEPWORTH, responsible for more than 80 SHORTS between 1912 and 1914, starring Flora MORRIS, Gladys SYLVANI, Alma TAYLOR and Chrissie WHITE. Then briefly to production company M.L.B. and, later, independent productions.

BRITISH FILMS INCLUDE: (d) *The Miser and the Maid* (+ a), *A Double Life* (1912), *Two Little Pals* (1913), *The Curtain* (1914), *The Little Mother* (1915). AS.

Buckton, Clifford (*b* Leeds). Actor. Supporting player for several decades, mainly in routine films, with occasional 'A's such as *The Man Who Knew Too Much* (1955, US) and *The Doctor's Dilemma* (1958). Also on stage (London, 1930) and TV.
OTHER BRITISH FILMS INCLUDE: *Lloyd of the CID* (1931), *Father O'Flynn* (1935), *King Arthur Was a Gentleman* (1942), *The Gentle Sex* (1943), *Fame Is the Spur* (1947), *The Fake* (1953), *Pacific Destiny* (1956).

Budd, Roy (*b* London, 1949 – *d* London, 1993). Musician, composer. Jazz pianist who composed the rousing scores for some popular action movies, including *Get Carter* (1971) and *The Wild Geese* (1978, UK/Switz), and several international ones (e.g. *The Stone Killer*, 1973). Died of brain haemorrhage.
OTHER BRITISH FILMS INCLUDE: *Kidnapped* (+ cond), *Something to Hide* (1971), *Steptoe and Son* (1972), *Man at the Top* (1973), *The Sea Wolves* (1980, UK/Switz/US), *Who Dares Wins* (1982).

Bujold, Geneviève (*b* Montreal, 1942). Actress. Waif-like French-Canadian beauty who belongs in this book for two performances: as Anne Boleyn in *Anne of the Thousand Days* (1969) and, very touching, as Annie Crook in *Murder by Decree* (UK/Can). Star of international films since the late 60s.
OTHER BRITISH FILMS: *Adventures of Pinocchio* (1996, UK/Czech/Den/Fr /US), *Eye of the Beholder* (1999, UK/Can).

Bull, Peter (*b* London, 1912 – *d* London, 1984). Actor, author. Eccentric, pudgy, faintly pop-eyed like one of his famous Teddy bear collection, Bull was on stage from 1933, famously creating Pozzo in *Waiting for Godot* (1955), films from 1935, and TV from 1947. He could be droll (*Young Man's Fancy*, 1939; Thwackum in *Tom Jones*, 1963), sinister (as the treacherous landlord in *Oliver Twist*, 1948) or wholly repulsive (twisting Joan GREENWOOD's arm in *Saraband for Dead Lovers*, 1948). US films included *Dr Dolittle* (1967). Awarded DSC for WW2 Royal Navy service, 1941–46.
OTHER BRITISH FILMS INCLUDE: *Sabotage, As You Like It* (1936), *Contraband* (1940), *Quiet Wedding* (1941), *Woman Hater* (1948), *The African Queen* (1951), *The Captain's Paradise* (1953), *The Rebel* (1960), *Dr Strangelove . . .* (1963), *Lock Up Your Daughters!* (1969), *Alice's Adventures in Wonderland* (1972), *The Tempest* (1979).

Bulldog Drummond Breezy, between-wars hero, officer and gentleman, created by 'Sapper' (H[erman] C[yril] McNeile), popular in stories for schoolboys of all ages, incarnated on screen in Britain by Carlyle BLACKWELL (1923), Jack BUCHANAN (1939), Ralph RICHARDSON (1934), Atholl FLEMING (1935), John Lodge (1937), Walter Pidgeon (1951) and Richard JOHNSON (updated and sexed up, in *Deadlier Than the Male*, 1966, and *Some Girls Do*, 1969), and in Hollywood by Ray MILLAND, John Howard, Ron RANDELL and Tom CONWAY.

Bulloch, Jeremy (*b* Market Harborough, 1945). Actor. Trained at Corona Stage Academy, he was on screen and TV from childhood, in the likes of *Spare the Rod* (1961) and later in small supporting roles in such films as the BOND caper, *The Spy Who Loved Me* (1977) and *The Empire Strikes Back* (1980, US). Busier on TV, in sitcoms like *Agony* (1979–81) and drama, such as *Richard II* (1978), as Hotspur.
OTHER BRITISH FILMS INCLUDE: *The Cat Gang* (1958), *Summer Holiday* (1962), *Hoffman* (1969), *Mary Queen of Scots*, 1971).

Bundy, A. Frank (*b* Hanwell, Middlesex, 1908). Producer. Entered films with Herbert WILCOX Productions in 1925,

worked for several companies before joining the BRITISH COUNCIL in 1939 to produce PROPAGANDA films. Joined Sydney BOX in 1946 as associate producer on *Daybreak* (1948), became his personal assistant at GAINSBOROUGH, and worked on *The Man Within, The Brothers, Holiday Camp* (1947), and produced *Easy Money* (1948), *Diamond City, Christopher Columbus* (1949). Later, produced a few minor films such as *Caught in the Net* (1960).

Bunnage, Avis (*b* Manchester, 1923 – *d* Thorpe Bay, 1990). Actor. Busy stage actress, notably with the Royal, Stratford East, where she created blowsy Helen in *A Taste of Honey* (1957), on TV from 1959 and in films since the early 60s. Characteristically cast as slatterns and/or sluts, combining the job descriptions in *The Loneliness of the Long Distance Runner* (1962) as a nasty mum, she finished her career as grandma to *The Krays* (1990). Turbans, fags and sour rejoinders were her tools of trade, though the stage gave her wider scope.
OTHER BRITISH FILMS INCLUDE: *Expresso Bongo* (1959), *Saturday Night and Sunday Morning* (1960), *The L-Shaped Room* (1962), *Tom Jones* (1963), *The Whisperers* (1966), *Panic* (1978), *Gandhi* (1982, UK/Ind).

Burden, Hugh (*b* Colombo, 1913 – *d* London, 1985). Actor. RADA-trained and on the London stage in 1933, maintaining a busy career in the theatre as actor and author of a half-dozen plays. In films from 1937: best remembered for several beautifully exact portraits of modest decency, notably in *The Way Ahead* (1944), as the sycophantic shop assistant who grows in stature during his war experience, and in *Fame is the Spur* (1947), as the socialist who sticks to his principles. Decency could slide into meekness (in *Sleeping Car to Trieste*, 1948, as Finlay CURRIE's put-upon secretary) or weakness (as Leslie BANKS's son in *Ships with Wings*, 1941), but his reticence always compelled attention. Also, several TV series, and his final work was the TV version of *Dr Fischer of Geneva* (1985).
OTHER BRITISH FILMS INCLUDE: *One of Our Aircraft is Missing* (1942), *Ghost Ship* (1952), *No Love for Johnnie* (1961), *The Best House in London* (1968, as Lord Tennyson), *One of Our Dinosaurs is Missing* (1975, UK/US).

Burdis, Ray (*b* London, 1958). Director, producer, screenwriter. In the late 90s, in collaboration with friend Dominic ANCIANO (*see* for details), has produced and directed films with high-profile casts, including Jude LAW and Ray WINSTONE in both *Final Cut* (1998, + a) and *Love, Honour and Obey* (2000, + co-s).
OTHER BRITISH FILMS INCLUDE: (p, d, with Anciano) *The Universe of Dermot Finn* (1988, short), *The Krays, The Reflecting Skin* (1990); *The Death Machine* (1995, a, co-p); (a) *Pressure* (1975), *The Music Machine, Scum* (1979), *Gandhi* (1982, UK/Ind).

Burdon, Albert (*b* South Shields, 1900 – *d* South Shields, 1981). Actor. Popular north-country 'low' comedian of the 30s with MUSIC-HALL experience, usually in gormless roles. Watching him now in, say, *Heat Wave* (1935), in which his innocent abroad is mistaken for a revolutionary, one sees that time has not dealt kindly with his style.
OTHER BRITISH FILMS INCLUDE: *Letting in the Sunshine, It's a Boy!* (1933), *She Knew What She Wanted* (1936), *Jailbirds* (1939).

Burge, Stuart (*b* Brentwood, 1918 – *d* Lymington, 2002). Actor, director. Stage director and former actor, most of whose film work has been theatre-derived, as in transferring OLIVIER's famous National Theatre *Othello* (1965) to screen – not much of a film, but a valuable record. Also, a good deal of prestige TV including two episodes of *Talking Heads 2* (1998). On stage as actor from 1936, as director from 1948.

OTHER BRITISH FILMS: (d) *There Was a Crooked Man* (1960), *Uncle Vanya* (1963), *The Mikado* (1966), *Julius Caesar* (1970).

Burger, Germain (*b* London, 1900). Director, producer. Entered industry with G.B. SAMUELSON in silent days, worked at STOLL STUDIOS as cinematographer (e.g. on Maurice ELVEY's *Innocent*, 1921), before beginning to direct in 1936, *Hard Labour* (short). Other films as director were wholesome animal tales, such as *Sheepdog of the Hills* (1941, + c) or tearful semi-musicals like *Rose of Tralee* (1942). Post-war, he produced DOCUMENTARIES and SHORTS.

OTHER BRITISH FILMS INCLUDE: (d) *Devil's Rock* (1938, +, c, p), *Faithful Forever* (1941, short), *My Ain Folk* (1944).

Burgon, Geoffrey (*b* Hambledon, Hampshire, 1941). Composer. Has worked mainly in TV, on *Brideshead Revisited* (1982) for instance, but has composed several film scores, starting with *Life of Brian* (1979).

OTHER BRITISH FILMS: *The Dogs of War* (1980), *Turtle Diary* (1985), *The Happy Valley* (1986).

Burke, Alfred (*b* Peckham, 1918). Actor. Remembered as the sinister political agitator in *The Angry Silence* (1960), Burke was a busy character actor in 50s and 60s British films, and well-known on TV for *Public Eye* (1965–68), as a seedy investigator. Was Prince of Verona in Stratford's *Romeo and Juliet* (2000).

OTHER BRITISH FILMS INCLUDE: *The Constant Husband* (1954), *Yangtse Incident* (1956), *High Flight* (1957), *The Trials of Oscar Wilde* (1960), *Mix Me a Person* (1962), *The Nanny* (1965), *A Midsummer Night's Dream* (1996).

Burke, Kathy (*b* London, 1964). Actress. Dominant 90s character player, came to notice when awarded best actress at Cannes in 1997 as the battered wife in *Nil by Mouth*. Unconventional-looking and awesomely versatile, she was a bitter Mary Tudor in *Elizabeth* (1998) and a lonely airport cleaner in the romantic comedy, *This Year's Love* (1999), and on TV the range has been evinced in the near-moronic Magda in *Absolutely Fabulous* (1992) and the harridan trollop of *Gimme, Gimme, Gimme* (1999). Born of working-class Irish émigré parents, she was encouraged in acting at school and at 17 she was cast in *Scrubbers* (1982), then played in *Sid and Nancy* (1986) with Gary OLDMAN who remembered her when casting *Nil by Mouth*.

OTHER BRITISH FILMS INCLUDE: *Goodie Two-Shoes* (1983, short), *Straight to Hell* (1986), *Eat the Rich* (1987), *Work Experience* (1989, short), *Hello, Hello, Hello* (short), *After Miss Julie* (1995), *Dancing at Lughnasa* (1998), *Love, Honour and Obey* (2000), *Kevin and Perry Go Large* (2000, as a boy), *Tosspot* (2001).

Burke, Marie (*b* London, 1894 – *d* London, 1988). Actress. RN: Alt. Star of the musical stage who studied in Italy; a dignified presence in nearly 20 British films, often in 'foreign' roles, such as the Argentine socialite in *The Lavender Hill Mob* (1951) or Mama Sopranelli in *The Constant Husband* (1954) or a gypsy in *Devils of Darkness* (1964). Her last, and perhaps best, role was as Peter FINCH's aunt in the bar-mitzvah scene in *Sunday Bloody Sunday* (1971). In US silent films from 1918. Mother of Patricia BURKE.

OTHER BRITISH FILMS INCLUDE: *His House in Order* (1920), *After the Ball* (1932), *Madness of the Heart* (1949), *Odette* (1950), *Miracle in Soho* (1957), *Seance on a Wet Afternoon* (1964).

Burke, Patricia (*b* Milan, 1917). Actress. Attractive, gifted actress and singer, Burke is testimony to British cinema's

incapacity to make good film MUSICALS. On stage from 1933, she scored a hit in *The Lisbon Story* (1943–44), but its leaden filming (1946) failed to transfer her star quality to the screen. Had good melodramatic roles in *The Trojan Brothers* (1945), *While I Live* (1947) and as a wife-in-the-way in *Forbidden* (1948). By mid 50s, reduced to small supporting roles, like twittering Miss Prew in *The Desperate Man* (1959), but further stage success, as in *Charlie Girl* (1968). Daughter of Marie BURKE.

OTHER BRITISH FILMS INCLUDE: *The Impersonator* (1960), *Strangler's Web* (1966), *The Day the Fish Came Out* (1967, UK/Gr), *Soft Beds, Hard Battles* (1973).

Burleigh, Bertram (*b* London, 1893 – *d* ?). Actor. Athletic leading man of silent films, later a cinema manager.

BRITISH FILMS INCLUDE: *Wake Up! or, a Dream of Tomorrow* (1914), *John Halifax, Gentleman* (1915), *A Mother's Influence* (1916), *The Sands of Time* (1919), *Garryowen* (1920), *Becket* (1923), *White Heat* (1926). AS.

Burnaby, Davy (*b* Buckland, Hertfordshire, 1881 – *d* Angmering, 1949). Actor. On stage from 1902, and in films from 1929 (*The Devil's Maze*), almost invariably as monocled spluttering lords, aldermen and colonels, but benignly landowning in *Song of the Road* (1937). Father of **Anne Burnaby**, author of a half-dozen screenplays of the 50s, including *No Time for Tears* (1957).

OTHER BRITISH FILMS INCLUDE: *The Co-Optimists* (1929), *A Shot in the Dark* (1933), *Are You a Mason?* (1934), *Stormy Weather* (1935), *Talking Feet* (1937), *Come on George* (1939).

Burnell, Janet (*b* London – *d* 1999). Actress. Stage supporting player who filmed rarely, memorably as Queen of France in *Henry V* (1944).

OTHER BRITISH FILMS: *Farewell Again* (1937), *Men of Rochdale* (1944), *The Upturned Glass* (1947), *Dear Mr Prohack* (1949), *Invitation to the Wedding* (1983).

Burns, David (*b* New York, 1901 – *d* Philadelphia, 1971). Actor. Stocky American who spent much of the 30s in England, working on the stage and in some films, including such light pieces as *Smash and Grab* (1937) and as a pickpocket outfumbled by *The Saint in London* (1939). Finished career in America.

OTHER BRITISH FILMS INCLUDE: *The Path of Glory* (1934), *The Sky's the Limit* (1937), *St Martin's Lane, Hey! Hey! USA* (1938), *A Girl Must Live*, *The Gang's All Here* (1939).

Burns, Mark (*b* Worcester, 1936). Actor. Handsome second lead, perhaps best remembered for *The Virgin and the Gypsy* (1970), as Honor BLACKMAN's lover, for *Death in Venice* (1971), as Dirk BOGARDE's friend, and as one of Joan COLLINS's men in *The Stud* (1978) and *The Bitch* (1979). Also on stage and TV (e.g. *Sharpe's Honour*, 1994). Entered films in 1960 (*Tunes of Glory*); made three for Michael WINNER in the 60s (*The System, The Jokers*, 1966; *I'll Never Forget What's 'is Name*, 1967), and three later ones: *The Wicked Lady* (1983, as Charles II), *Bullseye!*, (1991) and *Dirty Weekend* (1993).

OTHER BRITISH FILMS INCLUDE: *Juggernaut* (1974), *Champions* (1983), *The Clandestine Marriage* (1999).

Burns, Wilfred (*b* Herefordshire, 1917). Composer. Worked mainly in second features, often with directors Maclean ROGERS and Henry CASS, and for producer Norman COHEN. Some slightly upmarket ventures later in career, including SPIN-OFFS from TV successes, *Till Death Us Do Part* (1969) and *Dad's Army* (1971).

OTHER BRITISH FILMS INCLUDE: *Fools Rush In* (1949, + cond), *Emergency Call* (1952), *There Was a Young Lady* (1953), *West of Suez*

(1957), *The Man Who Couldn't Talk* (1960), *Breath of Life* (1963), *The London Nobody Knows* (1967, doc), *Adolf Hitler – My Part in His Downfall* (1972).

Burrell, Sheila (*b* London, 1922). Actress. Theatre-trained at Webber-Douglas, on London stage from 1944, appearing in new (*The Severed Head*, 1963) and classic plays, including the 1970 Stratford season. Came to screen in three Francis SEARLE programmers – *The Man in Black* (1949, as villainess), *The Rossiter Case* (1950), *Cloudburst* (1951) – and thereafter filmed intermittently for over 40 years, with eye-catching cameos in *Cold Comfort Farm* (1995, TV, some cinemas, as Ada Doom) and *The Woodlanders* (1997) and TV's *Perfect Strangers* (2001). First married to actor Laurence PAYNE.

OTHER BRITISH FILMS INCLUDE: *Black Orchid* (1952), *Double Jeopardy* (1955), *Paranoic* (1962), *Hell Is Empty* (1967), *Laughter in the Dark* (1969, UK/Fr), *Joseph Andrews* (1976), *Jane Eyre* (1996, UK/It/Fr).

Burrows, Saffron (*b* London, 1972). Actress. Tall, graceful beauty whose career quickly took her to Hollywood. Appeared memorably as twins in Mike Figgis's *The Loss of Sexual Innocence* (2000), as well as in his *One Night Stand* (1997), *Miss Julie* (1999), *Time Code* (2000), all US-made, and *Hotel* (2001, UK/US). In 2001, she was a striking presence in *Enigma* (2001, UK/Ger), in which the action partly revolves around her disappearance. Also on stage and on TV, notably with Albert FINNEY in *Karaoke* (1996).

OTHER BRITISH FILMS: *In the Name of the Father* (1993, UK/Ire/US), *Welcome to the Terrordome* (1995), *I Bring You Frankincense* (1996), *Gangster No. 1* (2000, UK/Ger/US).

Burton, Langhorne (*b* Somersby, 1872 – *d* Weymouth, 1949). Actor. Silent era leading man, Burton was the screen's first *Tom Jones* (1917) and starred in the 1928 *Sexton Blake* series. Stage debut in 1900, and in 1914 starred in *The Impossible Woman*, which he filmed in 1918. Fleetingly in one US film, *Marriage License?* (1926).

OTHER BRITISH FILMS INCLUDE: *Turtle Doves* (1914), *God and the Man* (1918), *The Amateur Gentleman* (1920), *Little Dorrit* (1920), *Beside the Bonnie Briar Bush* (1921), *Who Is the Man?* (1924), *Cross Roads* (1930). AS.

Burton, Richard (*b* Pontrhydyfen, Wales, 1925 – *d* Nyon, Switz, 1984). Actor. RN: Jenkins. Archetypal seller-of-birthright-for-mess-of-pottage. Might have been one of the great actors of his day, but settled not merely for stardom but for even merer celebrity. There is still some remarkable work among the cinetrash, including *Who's Afraid of Virginia Woolf?* (1966, US), the tormented preacher in *Night of the Iguana* (1964, US) and, eponymously, *The Spy Who Came in from the Cold* (1965). Famously rescued from Welsh village obscurity by the school-master whose surname he took, he started on stage in 1943, went to Oxford in 1944, served with the RAF (1944–47), and entered films in 1948 with the Welsh-based *The Last Days of Dolwyn*. In this and several other low-key British films, such as *Now Barabbas Was a Robber* (1949) and *Waterfront* (1950), he displayed a watchful brooding intensity, which attracted the interest of Hollywood where he went to star in the romance, *My Cousin Rachel* (1952), *The Robe* (1953, the first CinemaScope film) and others. Meanwhile, he won kudos for his stage Hamlet (1953), with the Old Vic, and repeated the role on Broadway to great acclaim in 1964.

The theatre, with its rigorous ongoing demands, grew less easy to accommodate to a roistering life-style which dominated world headlines when he and Elizabeth TAYLOR, both married

to others, conducted a very public affair during the shooting of *Cleopatra* (1963, UK), a *film maudit* in more ways than one. The filmography hints at a man torn between the desire for prestige and the need for wealth and fame: so, on the one hand, he plays Jimmy Porter (eloquently) in the filmed *Look Back in Anger* (1959) and the title role in *Dr Faustus* (1967, + d); on the other, co-starring with Taylor (whom he twice married and divorced) in *The VIPs* (1963) and *The Sandpiper* (1965, UK) – and having a try for both goals at once in *The Taming of the Shrew* (1966). Returned successfully to the theatre in *Camelot* (1961), winning a New York Drama Critics Award, less successfully with Taylor in *Private Lives* (1983). The mellifluous voice – rather too consciously so in later years – is preserved on the original 1954 recording of Dylan THOMAS's *Under Milk Wood* (filmed in 1971, with Burton as First Voice).

As for the rest of his British film career, there are moments to be salvaged from *Becket* (1964, as Henry II), *Anne of the Thousand Days* (1969, as Henry VIII), especially from *Equus* (1977), as the self-doubting psychiatrist, for which he received his seventh AAn (he never won), and his last film, *Nineteen Eighty-Four* (1984, as O'Brien). In a wayward career, almost as famous for his drinking and his marriages, Burton would intermittently remind audiences of what he could do.

OTHER BRITISH FILMS: *The Woman with No Name* (1950), *Green Grow the Rushes* (1951), *Sea Wife* (1956), *Bitter Victory* (1957, UK/Fr), *Inheritance* (1963, short, voice) *Zulu* (1964, voice), *Boom* (1968), *Where Eagles Dare* (1968), *Villain* (1971), *Brief Encounter* (1974, TV, some cinemas), *The Wild Geese* (UK/Switz), *Absolution, The Medusa Touch* (UK/Fr) (1978), *Tristan and Isolde* (1979, Ire).

BIBLIOG: Melvyn Bragg, *Rich: The Life of Richard Burton*, 1988; Tyrone Steverson, *Richard Burton: A Bio-Bibliography*, 1992.

Burtwell, Frederick (*b* London – *d* England, 1948). Actor. On stage from 1914, a stalwart character player in 30s and 40s British cinema. Can be glimpsed in five Carol REED films, including *Midshipman Easy* (1935), *Laburnum Grove* (1936) and *The Stars Look Down* (1939), as a flustered music-shop owner in *I'll Be Your Sweetheart* (1945) and a solemn butler in *Uncle Silas* (1947), his last film.

OTHER BRITISH FILMS INCLUDE: *A Gentleman of Paris* (1931), *Rembrandt* (1936), *Doctor Syn* (1937), *Much Too Shy* (1942), *The Silver Fleet* (1943), *The Rake's Progress* (1945), *Gaiety George* (1946).

Bush, Dick (*b* Devonport, 1931 – *d* 1997). Cinematographer. Came to attention with TV's *Culloden* (1964), a staged DOCU-MENTARY. Since then often associated with directors Ken RUSSELL, on small screen (e.g. *Isadora*, 1966; *Clouds of Glory*, 1978) and large (*Savage Messiah*, 1972; *Mahler*, 1974; *Tommy*, 1975; *Crimes of Passion*, 1984, US; *Lair of the White Worm*, 1988, UK/US) and Blake Edwards, starting with *Victor/Victoria* (1982). Last years mainly spent on US films, such as *Little Monsters* (1989).

OTHER BRITISH FILMS INCLUDE: *Laughter in the Dark* (1969, UK/Fr), *Twins of Evil* (1971), *Our Miss Fred, Dracula AD 1972* (1972), *In Celebration* (1974, UK/Can), *The Legacy* (1978), *Yanks* (1979).

Bushell, Anthony (*b* Westerham, 1904 – *d* Oxford, 1997). Actor. Tall, dignified, Oxford-educated and RADA-trained player, first on stage in 1924, in films from 1929, starting his screen career in America in *Disraeli* (1929). Appeared in over 50 films as actor, including playing Ffoulkes in both *The Scarlet Pimpernel* (1935) and *The Return of the Scarlet Pimpernel* (1937), a footballer in *The Arsenal Stadium Mystery* (1939), and, as he aged, numerous majors, colonels, brigadiers and a king (*The Black Knight*, 1954). Also directed several films: *The Angel with* the Trumpet (1949, + a), *The Long Dark Hall* (1951, co-d), *The Terror of the Tongs* (1960), *A Woman's Privilege* (1963, short), was associate director on OLIVIER's *Hamlet* (1948, + a, assoc p) and *Richard III* (1955), directed the Antarctic expedition sequence in *Hell Below Zero* (1953), and was second-unit director on *Bhowani Junction* (1955).

OTHER BRITISH FILMS INCLUDE: (a) *Journey's End*, (1930), *The Ghoul*, *Channel Crossing* (1933), *Dark Journey* (1937), *The Small Back Room* (1948), *High Treason* (1951), *A Night to Remember* (1958), *The Queen's Guards* (1960).

Buss, Harry (*b* London, 1874 – *d* Stoke Newington, 1922). Actor, director. Buss played 'Mr Poorluck' in a series of HEPWORTH SHORTS (1910–14) and had small parts in some Hepworth features: *The Vicar of Wakefield* (1913), *The Cloister and the Hearth* (1913) and *The Heart of Midlothian* (1914). In 1913, he also began to direct obscure SHORTS including *Cinderella* (1913), *The Model, Bored, AWS* (1916, + a). AS.

Butcher, Ernest (*b* Burnley, 1885 – *d* London, 1965). Actor. Expert in meek, downtrodden roles, like that of Ethel COLERIDGE's worm-husband who turns in *When We Are Married* (1943), and numerous clerks, porters, etc., several times for John BAXTER. On stage since 1935, films since 1934 (*The Small Man*). Married actress Muriel GEORGE.

OTHER BRITISH FILMS INCLUDE: *Talking Feet, Song of the Road* (1937), *Stepping Toes* (1938), *Pimpernel Smith* (1941), *Tawny Pipit* (1944), *The Years Between* (1946), *Easy Money* (1948), *Background* (1953), *The Desperate Man* (1959).

Butcher's Film Service A renting and equipment company dating back to 1897, which also produced and financed films from time to time. It was named for William Butcher, who committed suicide in 1903. Film makers such as the 'BRIGHTON SCHOOL' pioneer, James WILLIAMSON, were associated with the company during the silent period. In the 30s, the company settled into a pattern of providing low-budget quota pictures to provincial exhibitors in conjunction with other small firms such as NETTLEFOLD PRODUCTIONS. These included a number of films drawn from Britain's MUSIC-HALL traditions including the early Old Mother Riley films featuring Arthur LUCAN and Kitty MACSHANE, and the Gert and Daisy films with Elsie and Doris WATERS. In the post-war period the company operated as a 'B' FILM producer and distributor of mainly crime pictures and was still active in the 60s with films such as *Pit of Darkness* (1961) and *The Night Caller* (1965). Tom Ryall.

Butler, Alexander (*b* Ontario, Canada) Director. Began career with W.G. BARKER in 1913 and again with him in 1918–19; also associated with G.B. SAMUELSON, 1916–17 and 1919–25. Occasional actor as André Beaulieu, as in *My Lady's Dress* (+ d), *The Way of an Eagle* (1918), etc.

OTHER BRITISH FILMS INCLUDE: *A Little Child Shall Lead Them* (1913), *London by Night* (1913), *Just a Girl* (1916), *On Leave* (1918), *Damaged Goods* (1919), *The Ugly Duckling* (1921), *A Royal Divorce* (1923), *Proverbs* series (1925), *Milestone Melodies* series (1925). AS.

Butt, Johnny (*b* England – *d* England, 1930). Actor. Character comedian, primarily in short subjects, Butt appeared in more than 70 films between 1906 and 1930. Starred in two COMEDY SERIES for HEPWORTH: 'Simpkins' (1914) and 'Tubby' (1916).

OTHER BRITISH FILMS INCLUDE: *Hoaxing the Professor* (1906), *Far from the Madding Crowd* (1915), *Nell Gwynne* (1926), *Blackmail* (1929), *A Sister to Assist 'Er* (1930). AS.

Butterworth, Jez (*b* London, 1969). Director, writer. First film was *Mojo* (1997), based on his own play about sex rivalry over a rock'n'roll star, followed by *Birthday Girl* (2001), starring Nicole Kidman and Ben Chaplin and written by his brother **Tom Butterworth** (*b c* 1967).

Butterworth, Peter (*b* London, 1919 – *d* Coventry, 1979). Actor. Chubby comic character player of 50 films, usually as well-meaning ineffectuals. Appeared in many films for director Val GUEST (from *William Comes to Town*, 1948), Richard LESTER (including *Robin and Marian*, 1976, UK/US) and sixteen 'CARRY ONS'. Married actress Janet BROWN.

OTHER BRITISH FILMS INCLUDE: *The Adventures of Jane, Miss Pilgrim's Progress* (1949), *Mr Drake's Duck* (1950), *Penny Princess* (1952), *tom thumb* (1958), *Live Now, Pay Later* (1962), *Prudence and the Pill* (1968), *The Great Train Robbery* (1978).

Bux, Ishaq (*b* Kunpur, India, 1917 – *d* London, 2000). Actor. Played about 15 small Asian character roles in British films: he is a Pakistani in *The Raging Moon* (1970), the Sikh doorman in *Privates on Parade* (1982), and the Maharajah in *The Missionary* (1981). Played Omar in *The Raiders of the Lost Ark* (1981, US).

OTHER BRITISH FILMS INCLUDE: *Inadmissible Evidence* (1968), *Leo the Last* (1969), *The Horseman* (1970), *Rentadick* (1972), *The Vault of Horror* (1973, UK/US), *The Quatermass Conclusion* (1978), *A Passage to India* (1984).

Buxton, Dudley. Animator. Lightning cartoonist responsible for the Tressograph Cartoons, a series of war subjects, introduced in 1914 with the slogan, 'They're British, quite British, you know!' Associated with Anson DYER (1915–16) and the Kine Komedy Kartoons in the later 1910s; for the latter, Buxton made the reconstruction, *The Raid on Zeebrugge* (1918). Made last cartoon series, *Pongo the Pup* in 1924. There was no market for his films in the US and they were no competition to American imports of the period. AS.

Bygraves, Max (*b* London, 1922). Actor. Cockney-born revue entertainer who has dabbled in films, purveying a likeable persona, perhaps best displayed in straight dramatic form in *Spare the Rod* (1961), as a new teacher who wins the confidence of tough kids. Starred in the musical *Charley Moon* (1956) which sank with a boatload of talent. The stage, where he topped the bill at the Palladium, is his métier; also famous for radio's *Educating Archie*.

OTHER BRITISH FILMS INCLUDE: *Bless 'em All* (1948), *Tom Brown's Schooldays* (1951), *A Cry from the Streets* (1958), *Bobbikins* (1959), *The Alf Garnett Saga* (1972, guest).

BIBLIOG: Autobiography, *Max Bygraves*, 1997.

Byrd, Bretton (*b* Ramsgate, 1904) Composer, music director. Byrd joined GAUMONT–BRITISH in 1930, composed and sometimes conducted the score for about 20 light films from the 30s to the 50s, beginning with Jessie MATTHEWS' *It's Love Again* (1936).

OTHER BRITISH FILMS INCLUDE (comp, unless noted): *Seven Sinners* (1936), *Keep Smiling* (1938, m d), *The Saint's Vacation* (1941, m d), *The Goose Steps Out* (1942), *The White Unicorn* (1947), *Tony Draws a Horse* (1950), *Port of Escape* (1956).

Byrne, Alexandra Costume designer. Although Byrne has worked on only a few films, *Persuasion* (1995, TV, some cinemas), *Hamlet* (1996, UK/US) and *Elizabeth* (1998, UK), she has been critically recognised (*Elizabeth* and *Hamlet* both received AAn and BAAn for Costume Design, the former winning a Golden Satellite Award). Her devotion to historical accuracy, passion for detail and attention to the narrative have imbued her costumes with a sense of authenticity and style that has been much noted.

OTHER BRITISH FILMS: *Captain Corelli's Mandolin* (2001, UK/US). Fiona Clark.

Byrne, Eddie (*b* Dublin, 1911 – *d* Dublin, 1981). Actor. Prolific character player of supporting roles in big films such as *Dunkirk* (1958) and starring roles in some minor films such as *Time Gentlemen Please!* (1952), as the layabout blot on the landscape of an idyllic village, and *One Way Out* (1955), as a policeman whose near-retirement is complicated by his family. Byrne's homely features, his relaxed way of inhabiting a role and easy authority with dialogue made him a stalwart of British cinema for over 30 years; even in a horror concoction like *Devils of Darkness* (1964) he confers a few moments of striking reality as a scientist in danger. Appeared in the US films *Mutiny on the Bounty* (1962) and *Star Wars* (1977). Educated in Ireland where he had much stage experience; London stage debut in 1946.

OTHER BRITISH FILMS INCLUDE: *Hungry Hill, Odd Man Out* (1947), *Saints and Sinners* (1949), *The Gentle Gunman* (1952), *Albert RN* (1953), *Children Galore, Aunt Clara* (1954), *Reach for the Sky* (1956), *Floods of Fear* (1958), *The Mummy* (1959), *The Mark* (1961), *The Break* (1962), *The Running Man* (1963), *Sinful Davey* (1968), *Where's Jack?* (1969).

Byrne, Gabriel (*b* Dublin, 1950). Actor. International star of about 50 films whose British career looks distinctly quirky. As against the Hollywood sheen of, say, *Little Women* (1994) or *The Man in the Iron Mask* (1998), one finds *Defence of the Realm* (1985) or *Gothic* (1986), as Lord Byron on a wild night in Switzerland with the Shelleys. Aspired to the priesthood, then teaching, before becoming an actor. A strong unpredictable presence in films from all over the place; also occasional producer, director and writer, sometimes of little-seen Irish (co-)productions. Married (1989–94) to US actress Ellen Barkin.

OTHER BRITISH FILMS INCLUDE (a, unless noted): *Into the West* (1992, + assoc p), *In the Name of the Father* (1993, UK/Ire/US, ex p), *All Things Bright and Beautiful* (1994), *This Is the Sea* (UK/Ire/US), *The Brylcreem Boys* (+ co-p) (1996), *When Brendan Met Trudy* (2000, UK/Ire).

Byrne, John (*b* Paisley, Scotland, 1939). Director, screenwriter. Working-class boy who made it as playwright, after training at the Glasgow School of Art, and adapted two of his own plays for his debut screenplay, *The Slab Boys* (1997), set largely in a Paisley carpet factory of the 50s. Though much praised, the film has been little seen. He has done some highly regarded TV, *Boswell & Johnson's Tour of the Western Isles* (1993), but his only other film is *An Old-Fashioned Picture-Book* (1971, short). Partner of actress Tilda SWINTON.

Byrne, Michael Actor. Blond, sensitive and versatile Central School-trained player of wide-ranging roles in films, as well as having a busy stage and TV career. Held his ground impressively against Alan BATES's atrabilious *Butley* (1973, UK/Can/US) and was a memorably oily solicitor in *The Good Father* (1986). Has filmed internationally (e.g. *Braveheart*, 1995), done much TV, including the *Sharpe* series (1994), and continued to work on stage.

OTHER BRITISH FILMS INCLUDE: *The Scarlet Blade* (1963), *Henry VIII and his Six Wives* (1972), *Conduct Unbecoming* (1975), *A Bridge Too Far* (1977), *Champions* (1983), *Buster* (1988), *Tomorrow Never Dies* (1997, UK/US).

Byron, Kathleen (*b* London, 1922). Actress. Described by Michael POWELL as looking 'secret' and 'witty', Byron brought a mysterious sensuality to British films as rare as it was underused. As Sister Ruth, the nun who goes mad with lust in the Himalayas in *Black Narcissus* (1947), she created some uniquely erotic moments in an often genteel cinema. Powell gave her the chance to be an intelligent leading lady in *The Small Back Room* (1948), and she brought real melodramatic flair to manipulative types in *Madness of the Heart* (1949) and *Prelude to Fame* (1950). After a Hollywood stint for *Young Bess* (1953), she was mostly, and maddeningly, relegated to 'B' MOVIES, but was never less than compelling. Trained at the Old Vic Drama School, she cared more for films than the stage, first filming a 'bit' in *The Young Mr Pitt* (1942). Also did some fine TV, including two adaptations of Henry JAMES (*Portrait of a Lady*, 1968, and *The Golden Bowl*, 1972), and reappeared briefly in three films in the late 90s: *Emma* (1996, UK/US), *Les Misérables* (1998) and *Saving Private Ryan* (1998, US). Her work in the four Powell films has made her something of a cult figure, and she appeared in a TV documentary on her career, *Remembering Sister Ruth* (1997).

OTHER BRITISH FILMS INCLUDE: *The Silver Fleet* (1943), *A Matter of Life and Death* (1946), *The Reluctant Widow* (1950), *Four Days, The House in the Square* (1951), *Star of My Night, Secret Venture* (1954), *Hand in Hand* (1960), *Night of the Eagle* (1962), *Private Road, Twins of Evil* (1971), *Craze* (1973), *The Abdication* (1974), *The Elephant Man* (1980, UK/US).

Cc

Cabot, Sebastian (*b* London, 1918 – *d* Victoria, Canada, 1977). Actor. Portly, usually bearded, character actor, on screen since 1935 (*Foreign Affaires*), after some stage experience. To Hollywood in mid 50s, playing somewhat orotund Brits, sometimes villainous, usually benign, most famously as Mr French in TV's *Family Affair* (1966–70).

OTHER BRITISH FILMS INCLUDE: *Secret Agent* (1936), *They Made Me a Fugitive* (1947), *The Spider and the Fly* (1949), *Midnight Episode* (1950), *Ivanhoe* (1952), *The Captain's Paradise* (1953), *Romeo and Juliet* (1954, UK/It).

Cadell, Jean (*b* Edinburgh, 1884 – *d* London, 1967). Actress. Great Scottish character actor who unforgettably refused to rule out the possibility of cannibalism in *Whisky Galore!* (1949). Even in comedy, she was apt to be forbidding, as in *Quiet Wedding* (1941); she *could* do benevolent, as in *Pygmalion* (1938, as Mrs Pearce); but was more often cast as grim, like the housekeeper in *The Late Edwina Black* (1951). On professional stage from 1908, screen from 1912 (*David Garrick*). In Hollywood for *David Copperfield* (1935).

OTHER BRITISH FILMS INCLUDE: *The Man Who Stayed Home* (1915), *Anna the Adventuress* (1920), *Alf's Button* (1920), *The Naked Man* (1923), *The Loves of Robert Burns, Escape* (1930), *Fires of Fate* (1932), *Timbuctoo* (1933), *Little Friend* (1934), *Whom the Gods Love* (1936, UK/Austria), *Love from a Stranger* (1937), *South Riding* (1938), *Confidential Lady* (1939), *The Young Mr Pitt* (1942), *Dear Octopus* (1943), *I Know Where I'm Going!* (1945), *Jassy, A Man About the House* (1947), *No Place for Jennifer, Madeleine, Marry Me* (1949), *The Reluctant Widow* (1950), *I'm a Stranger* (1952), *Meet Mr Lucifer* (1953), *Let's Be Happy* (1956), *The Little Hut* (1957), *Rockets Galore* (1958), *Upstairs and Downstairs, Serious Charge* (1959), *Very Important Person* (1961).

Caffin, Yvonne (*b* South Africa, 1904 – *d* Wales, 1985). Costume designer. After RADA training, she joined its research staff, and entered the British film industry in 1934, working for GAUMONT–BRITISH and MAYFLOWER pre-war. In war work 1939–41, and with GAINSBOROUGH's ISLINGTON STUDIO from 1942. On her earlier films, such as *Jamaica Inn* (1939) and *They Were Sisters* (1945), she is designated dress, wardrobe, or costume 'supervisor'; her first credit as 'costume designer' was *The Rake's Progress* (1945), her costumes reinforcing temperamental distinctions among Lilli PALMER, Margaret JOHNSTON and Jean KENT. Most of the rest of her prolific career was with RANK, frequently for director Ralph THOMAS and on several 'CARRY ON' films.

OTHER BRITISH FILMS INCLUDE: (supervisor) *Vessel of Wrath* (1938), *Miranda* (1948), *The Woman in Question* (1950), *The Young Lovers* (1954), *Doctor at Large* (1957); (cos des) *When the Bough Breaks, Dear Murderer* (1947), *Doctor in the House* (1954), *An Alligator Named Daisy* (1955), *A Night to Remember* (1958), *North West Frontier* (1959, co-des), *The Singer Not the Song* (1960), *No Love for Johnnie* (1961), *Hot Enough for June* (1964), *Carry On Doctor* (1968), *The Executioner* (1970).

Caffrey, Sean (*b* Belfast, 1940). Actor. Irish supporting player who had the lead opposite Francesca ANNIS in the little-seen *Run with the Wind* (1966) but has since been relegated to often small supporting roles, including two for HAMMER: *The Viking Queen* (1966) and *When Dinosaurs Ruled the Earth* (1969). In TV's *No Hiding Place* (1959–66).

OTHER BRITISH FILMS INCLUDE: *I Was Happy Here* (1965), *The Human Factor* (1979), *Ascendancy* (1982), *Divorcing Jack* (1998, UK/Fr).

Cain, Syd Production designer. Began as draughtsman on *You Know What Sailors Are* (1954), later associated mainly with action films including HITCHCOCK's *Frenzy* (1972), *The Wild Geese* (1978, UK/Switz), and several 'BOND' films: *Dr No* (1962), *From Russia with Love* (1963), *On Her Majesty's Secret Service* (1969), *Live and Let Die* (1973, supervising art d) and, as storyboard artist, *GoldenEye* (1995, UK/US). Early experience with WARWICK FILMS (1955–58); also Hollywood.

OTHER BRITISH FILMS INCLUDE: (ass art d) *Cockleshell Heroes* (1955), *Fire Down Below* (1957), *Lolita* (1961); (art d) *Summer Holiday* (1962), *The High Bright Sun* (1965), *Fahrenheit 451* (1966), *Billion Dollar Brain* (1967), *Gold* (1974); (prod des) *Fear Is the Key* (1972), *Wild Geese II* (1985).

Caine, Hall (*b* Runcorn, 1853 – *d* Isle of Man, 1931). Author. Immensely popular writer of his day and ardent champion of popular leftist causes, Caine made a fortune from his novels, from his stage adaptations and from screen rights. He selected the Isle of Man as the subject for his fiction at the suggestion of Dante Gabriel Rossetti. Caine's novels were filmed in the silent era in both the UK and the US. George Loane TUCKER filmed *The Christian* (1897) in 1915 and *The Traitor Spy* (1939), *The Farmer's Wife* (1941), *I'll Turn to You* (1946), and *The Manxman* was filmed in 1916 and by HITCHCOCK in 1929. AS.

Caine, Sir Michael (*b* Bermondsey, London, 1933). Actor. RN: Maurice Micklewhite. Son of fishporter and charwoman, Caine began in poverty and went on to become one of the most prolific and durable of film stars. After Korean War service, he joined a rep company as assistant stage manager, took easily to acting, and changed his name to Caine after seeing *The Caine Mutiny*. Had walk-on roles in TV and films, including *Sailor Beware* and *A Hill in Korea* (both 1956), but plodded on largely unnoticed, often uncredited, for nearly a decade. Then came the first of those roles in which he has staked out his claim to be a major film actor: this was as the aristocratic officer in *Zulu* (1964). The following year he incarnated Len DEIGHTON's anti-Bond intelligence agent, Harry Palmer, the bespectacled gourmet, in *The Ipcress File* (1965), and completed the hat-trick with *Alfie* (1966), his first Oscar nomination, as a tireless womaniser running out of steam. Off-screen, his freewheeling sex life – he and Terence STAMP shared a King's Road flat and were committed to 'pulling the birds' – merely reinforced his laconic film persona, apparently irresistible to women of all ages. Their very names now conjure up that remotest-seeming of decades, the 60s.

What was also emerging was that he was one of those screen actors who contrives to look as if he is doing nothing while effortlessly inhabiting a range of quite disparate characters, in delineating whom he draws on and extends aspects of a basic personality image. He played Palmer twice more in the 60s, had a big success in the caper movie, *The Italian Job* (1969), in which he held his own with Noël COWARD, found the necessary toughness for *Get Carter* (1971, remade in US, 2000, with Caine in cameo), matched wits with OLIVIER in *Sleuth* (1972), was Julie WALTER's sympathetic lecturer in *Educating Rita* (1983), and a pier-end entrepreneur in *Little Voice* (1998), in which the surface shoddiness peels back to reveal the shoddiness beneath. There are others too, and, when he got sick of paying British taxes and went to live in Hollywood in the late 70s, he kept as impressively busy on the international screen. Won an AA (Supporting Actor) for *Hannah and Her Sisters* (1986, US) and *The Cider House Rules* (2000), as well as becoming an impeccable character star in such movies as: *California Suite* (1978, US), as Maggie SMITH's homosexual husband; a transvestite murderer in *Dressed to Kill* (1980, US); back in Britain as a Soho sleaze in *Mona Lisa* (1986) and a deeply incompetent 'SHERLOCK HOLMES' in *Without a Clue* (1988). He has been very critical of the British film industry, but it has arguably given him most of his best chances.

There is, in a filmography of over 80 titles (plus TV work), inevitably a lot of junk, but his own performances seem teflon-protected from his surrounds on such occasions. And when the material is right, as in *The Man Who Would Be King* (1975, US), few can touch him for conviction and subtlety. In the latter film, his second wife, **Shakira Baksh** (*b* 1947), played her last screen role; his first wife was actress **Patricia Haines** (*b c* 1931 – *d* 1976). Caine now runs his own production company, M & M Productions, with business partner Martin Bregman. Made CBE 1992, knighted and awarded BAFTA fellowship in 2000.

OTHER BRITISH FILMS: *The Steel Bayonet, How to Murder a Rich Uncle, A Woman of Mystery* (1957), *The Two-Headed Spy, Passport to Shame, Blind Spot, Carve Her Name With Pride, The Key, Danger Within* (1958), *The Bulldog Breed, Foxhole in Cairo* (1960), *The Day the Earth Caught Fire* (1961), *The Wrong Arm of the Law, Solo for Sparrow* (1962), *The Wrong Box, Funeral in Berlin* (1966), *Billion Dollar Brain, Woman Times Seven* (1967), *Play Dirty, The Magus, Deadfall* (1968), *Battle of Britain* (1969), *Simon Simon* (short), *The Last Valley* (1970), *Kidnapped, Zee & Co.* (1971), *Pulp* (1972), *The Wilby Conspiracy* (1974), *The Romantic Englishwoman, The Eagle Has Landed* (1976), *Silver Bears, A Bridge Too Far* (1977), *The Honorary Consul* (1983), *The Jigsaw Man* (1984), *Water, The Holcroft Covenant* (1985), *The Whistle Blower* (1986), *The Fourth Protocol* (1987), *Midnight in St Petersburg, Len Deighton's Bullet to Beijing* (UK/Can) (1995), *Blood and Wine* (1996), *Shiner* (2001), *Last Orders* (2002, UK/Ger).

BIBLIOG: Michael Caine, *Acting in Films*, 1990; William Hall, *Arise Sir Michael Caine*, 2000.

Calder, David (*b* Portsmouth, 1946). Actor. Supporting actor of recent decades, in some big films, including *Superman* (1978) and the BOND caper, *The World Is Not Enough* (1999, UK/US), and in several interesting small ones, such as *Moonlighting* (1982), *American Friends* (1991) and, as Martin Donovan's lawyer in a custody battle in *Hollow Reed* (1996, UK/Ger). Had TV success as father in *Bramwell* series (1995–98).

OTHER BRITISH FILMS INCLUDE: *The Disappearance of Harry* (1982), *Defence of the Realm* (1985).

Calder-Marshall, Anna (*b* London, 1947). Actress. Notable stage actress who has merely dabbled with the screen. Had *Wuthering Heights* (1970) been more successful, she might have filmed more. Popped up in the dreadful 1997 *Anna Karenina* (US) as Princess Shcherbatsky.

OTHER BRITISH FILMS: *Two Faces of Evil* (1982), *Saint-Ex* (1996).

Caldicott, Richard (*b* Garnant, Wales, 1908 – *d* London, 1995). Actor. Small-part player, in TV since late 40s, in uncredited 'bits' from 1953 (*The Million Pound Note*), and later in such popular TV shows as *Fawlty Towers* (1975) and the US series *The Beverly Hillbillies* (1967–68).

OTHER BRITISH FILMS INCLUDE: *One Good Turn* (1954), *The Horse's Mouth* (1958), *Dentist on the Job* (1961), *The VIPs* (1963), *The Spy Who Came in from the Cold* (1965), *Adventures of a Private Eye* (1977), *The Fool* (1990).

Cale, John (*b* Swansea, 1940). Composer, singer, musician. Studied in New York with Aaron Copland and, with Lou Reed, founded the rock group Velvet Underground. Always pitched between mainstream rock'n'roll and the avant garde, Cale's full *cv* belongs elsewhere, but he was still recording in the 90s as both soloist and soundtrack composer. His British film scores are *Rhinoceros Hunting in Budapest* (UK/Fr, + a), *I Shot Andy Warhol* (UK/US) (1996), and *House of America* (1997, UK/Neth), and his others include *Something Wild* (1986, US, co-m) and *Basquiat* (1996, US).

Callard, Kay (*b* Canada, 1933). Actress. RN: Katherine Drewry. Pretty lead and second lead in minor British films of the 50s, first seen as nightclub singer in the 'A' war film, *They Who Dare* (1953). Thereafter, sometimes the caring helpmeet, as in *Escapement* (1957), sometimes the opportunist blonde, as in *Find the Lady* (1956), generally good company. Popular in TV's *Knight Errant Limited* (1959, 1960–61). Married to actor Jack McNAUGHTON.

OTHER BRITISH FILMS INCLUDE: *The Stranger Came Home* (1954), *Joe Macbeth* (1955), *The Flying Scot* (1957), *A Woman Possessed* (1958), *Our Cissy* (1974).

Callow, Simon (*b* London, 1949). Actor, author. From box-office assistant at the Old Vic to major character star of 80s and 90s cinema describes portly, jocular Callow's career trajectory. Came to critical attention as Mozart in the National Theatre's *Amadeus* (1980), but had only a small role in the film. MERCHANT IVORY gave him the eye-catching role of the Rev Beebe in *A Room with a View* (1985) and the openly gay Callow crowned a succession of richly enjoyable studies with that of Gareth in *Four Weddings and a Funeral* (1994): his relationship with another man (John HANNAH) and his poignant funeral are among the hit film's highlights. He is wildly funny as the convener of a men's therapy group in *Bedrooms and Hallways* (1999) and as the dour Master of the Revels in *Shakespeare in Love* (1999, UK/US). Has also appeared in American films (e.g. *Mr & Mrs Bridge*, 1990), directed a film, *Ballad of the Sad Café* (1991, US), written biographies of Charles LAUGHTON, Orson WELLES and agent Peggy Ramsay, and a lively semi-autobiography, *Being an Actor*, 1984, and continued to work on stage (e.g. the solo play, *The Mystery of Charles Dickens*, 2000), as actor and director. Made CBE in 1999.

OTHER BRITISH FILMS: *The Good Father* (1986), *Maurice* (1987), *Soft Top, Hard Shoulder, Howards End* (unc) (1992), *Victory* (UK/Fr/Ger, released 1998), *England, My England, Jefferson in Paris* (1995), *The Scarlet Tunic* (1997), *Notting Hill* (1999, UK/US, unc), *Christmas Carol: The Movie* (2001, anim).

Calthrop, Donald (*b* London, 1888 – *d* London, 1940). Actor. In a native industry noted for its character actors, Calthrop stands out as one of the best in the late 20s and 30s. He was a visual performer, who, with his body language, could easily define a role, whether the bullying blackmailer in *Blackmail* (1929), the double-crossing Poole in *Rome Express* (1932), Bob Crachit in *Scrooge* (1935), or the genteel and redundant worker in *Major Barbara* (1941), a role completed the day before he died. A grandson of Dion Boucicault, Calthrop made his stage debut in 1906 and his screen debut ten years later; in real life he became a tragic hero, losing his two eldest sons at Dunkirk.

OTHER BRITISH FILMS INCLUDE: *Wanted a Widow* (1916), *Nelson* (1918), *Atlantic* (1929), *Juno and the Paycock, Murder!* (1930), *Broken Blossoms* (1936), *Fire over England* (1937), *Let George Do It!* (1940). AS.

Calvert, Charles Actor, director. An actor (1909–12), who became a director with CRICKS and Martin in 1913, Calvert directed from 1920 under the name of Captain C.C. Calvert, and ended his career, 1925–28, directing SHORTS.

BRITISH FILMS INCLUDE: (d) *Good for Evil* (1913), *A London Mystery* (1914), *The Avenging Hand* (1915), *Disraeli* (1916, co-d), *The Way of a Man* (1921), *Bonnie Prince Charlie* (1923). AS.

Calvert, Eddie (*b* Preston, 1922 – *d* Johannesburg, 1978). Trumpeter. 'The Man with the Golden Trumpet' performed in *Beyond Mombasa* (1956) and contributed to several soundtracks, including *John and Julie* (1955).

Calvert, Phyllis (*b* London, 1915 – *d* London, 2002). Actress. RN: Bickle. Major star of a major era of British cinema, Calvert's intelligence made supportable, even interesting, a succession of goody-goodies in costume films such as *The Man in Grey* (1943), *Fanny by Gaslight* (1944), *They Were Sisters* (1945), *The Magic Bow* (1946), all for GAINSBOROUGH, for whom she had something meatier as the schizophrenic *Madonna of the Seven Moons* (1944). A dancer until injury turned her to drama, prior to Gainsborough's making her a household name she had slogged away in a dozen films, doing time as George FORMBY's girlfriend in *Let George Do It!* (1940) and as *The Young Mr Pitt*'s (1942) wholly fictitious love interest.

Fighting for more interesting material, she got the cynical journalist instead of the pretty nun in *Two Thousand Women* (1944), was a doctor in Africa in *Men of Two Worlds* (1946), had an appalling time in Hollywood (1947–48), co-produced a couple of duds (*The Golden Madonna*, 1949; *Woman with No Name*, 1950), then had the best part of her career as the mother-with-a-mission in *Mandy* (1952). Gently beautiful as she was, there was always the suspicion of a character actress determined to get out, and under Alexander MACKENDRICK's direction she was very impressive in her fierce determination to put her deaf child's needs first. Her post-*Mandy* career was in character roles, including good ones as Ingrid BERGMAN's sister in *Indiscreet* (1958) and, nearly 40 years later, as Aunt Helena in *Mrs Dalloway* (1997, UK/Neth/US), showing she had lost none of her incisiveness.

Her screen career faded in the late 50s as British cinema changed directions, but she continued to be popular on TV (as agony-column writer in *Kate*, 1970–72; *All Passion Spent*, 1986) and stage (*The Complaisant Lover*, 1959; *The Heiress*, 1989). She was the widow of actor-turned-antiquarian bookseller Peter MURRAY-HILL.

OTHER BRITISH FILMS: *Discord, Anne One Hundred* (1933), *Two Days to Live* (1939), *Neutral Port, Charley's (Big-Hearted) Aunt, They Came by Night* (1940), *Kipps, Inspector Hornleigh Goes to It* (1941), *Uncensored* (1942), *The Root of All Evil* (1947), *Broken Journey* (1948), *Mr Denning* *Drives North* (1951), *The Net* (1953), *It's Never Too Late, Child in the House* (1956), *The Young and the Guilty, A Lady Mislaid* (1958), *Oscar Wilde* (1960, as Constance), *The Battle of the Villa Fiorita* (1965), *Twisted Nerve* (1968), *Oh! What a Lovely War* (1969, as Lady Haig), *The Walking Stick* (1970).

Camarda, Michele (*b* New York, *c*1964). Producer. After study at Boston University, Camarda settled in London in 1985, enrolled in the NATIONAL FILM AND TELEVISION SCHOOL, and won the student award for her graduation film, *This Boy's Story* (1992). In the late 90s, she produced three out-of-the-ordinary films: *Photographing Fairies* (1997), *This Year's Love* and the remarkable, busy-plotted *Wonderland* (1999).

OTHER BRITISH FILMS INCLUDE: *The Soulful Shack* (1988, short), *Say Goodbye* (1989, short), *Born Romantic* (2001).

Cameron, Earl (*b* Pembroke, Bermuda, 1917). Actor. Versatile West Indian who had better opportunities than most black actors in mid-century Britain. Started acting in Bermuda, was in the Merchant Navy during the war, and later did a song-and-dance stint with ENSA, going into rep post-war. First film was EALING's *Pool of London* (1950), in a feelingly presented romance with a white girl, and later had excellent roles in such films as *Sapphire* (1959), as the dead girl's doctor-brother, the foreman facing racial prejudice in *Flame in the Streets* (1961), and the captain ordered to 'assume command' in dangerous circumstances in *Guns at Batasi* (1964). Some TV, including *The Great Kandinsky* (1995).

OTHER BRITISH FILMS: *There Is Another Sun* (1951), *Emergency Call* (1952), *The Heart of the Matter* (1953), *The Woman for Joe, Simba* (1955), *Safari, Odongo* (1956), *Accused, The Heart Within* (starring) (1957), *Killers of Kilimanjaro* (1959), *No Kidding, Tarzan the Magnificent* (1960), *Term of Trial* (1962), *Thunderball* (1965), *The Sandwich Man* (1966), *Two a Penny, Battle Beneath the Earth* (1967), *Two Gentlemen Sharing* (1969), *The Revolutionary* (1970), *A Warm December* (1972, UK/US), *Déjà Vu* (1998, UK/US).

Cameron, John (*b* 1944). Composer. Also conductor or music director on several films, Cameron has been active as composer across several genres, including realist drama (*Kes*, 1969), horror (*Psychomania*, 1972), romantic comedy (*A Touch of Class*, 1972; *Lost and Found*, 1979), adventure (*The Thief of Baghdad*, 1978, UK/Fr) and mystery (*The Mirror Crack'd*, 1980). Considerable TV work, including *Jekyll and Hyde* (1990), and some US films, including *Great Scout and Cathouse Thursday* (1976).

OTHER BRITISH FILMS INCLUDE (comp, unless noted): *Poor Cow* (1967, m d), *The Ruling Class* (1971), *Night Watch* (1973), *Out of Season* (1975), *Nasty Habits* (1976), *Hawks* (1988, + cond), *Driftwood* (1997, UK/Ire).

Cameron, Ken (*b* Wendover, 1915 – *d* Creech St Michael, nr Taunton, 2000). Sound engineer. Educated at Glasgow Academy and Glasgow University, Cameron entered films in 1938, and was sound engineer of the CROWN FILM UNIT during WW2. He was responsible for the evocative, now powerfully nostalgic soundtracks of such major DOCUMENTARY FILMS as *London Can Take It!* (1940), influential in changing US attitudes to the war, *Target for Tonight* (1941), the chronicle of a bombing raid over Germany, and Humphrey JENNINGS' *A Diary For Timothy* (1946). Post-war, he continued with Crown, was awarded an OBE in 1950, and in 1952, after Crown was wound up, founded Anvil Films. He worked on a wide range of films, including intelligent 'B' MOVIES, *Devil's Bait* (1959) and *The Big Day* (1960), 'A's such as *The Beauty Jungle* (1964), and HORROR films, including *Circus of Fear* (1966) and comedies like *Press for Time* (1966).

OTHER BRITISH FILMS INCLUDE: *Fires Were Started* (1943), *Family Portrait* (1950, short), *Greece the Immortal Land* (1958), *Blind Date, The Battle of the Sexes* (1959), *Very Important Person* (1961).

Cammell, Donald (*b* Edinburgh, 1934 – *d* Los Angeles, 1996). Screenwriter, director. For co-writing and co-directing (with Nicolas ROEG) *Performance* (1970), Cammell has a place in this book. It remains one of the key films of its psychedelic time, both an evocation and a critique of a society and an unsettling exploration of dark inner worlds and suppressed identities. Otherwise, in British cinema, he wrote the screenplays for *Duffy* (1968) – for shame! – and for *The Touchables* (1968): no wonder he turned to *Performance* after this almost unwatchable pair: and directed and wrote the little-seen *White of the Eye* (1986). In the US he directed the undervalued scifi thriller, *Demon Seed* (1977). He committed suicide after career disappointments in Hollywood, including the mangling of his last film, the thriller *Wildside* (1995). Despite a meagre output, he remains an oddly compelling figure.

Campbell, Beatrice (*b* Co. Down, N. Ireland, 1922 – *d* London, 1979). Actress. After some stage experience and several tiny roles, this charming actress had a dozen leading roles in the 40s and 50s. She was sweetly flighty in *My Brother Jonathan* (1948), leading to a contract with ABPC, dignified and sympathetic as the blind magnate's wife in *The Silent Dust* (1949), and a characterful love interest in *The Mudlark* (1950) and, opposite real-life husband Nigel PATRICK, in *Grand National Night* (1953). Came in just too late to be a big star; there were scant places for women in films of the tweedy, masculine 50s.

OTHER BRITISH FILMS INCLUDE: *Wanted for Murder* (1946), *No Place for Jennifer* (1949), *The Last Holiday* (1950), *The House in the Square* (1951), *The Master of Ballantrae* (1953).

Campbell, Cheryl (*b* London, 1949). Actress. Unconventionally attractive, LAMDA-trained Campbell may be best remembered as the Scottish missionary's sister in *Chariots of Fire* (1981) and as the acute adulteress in *The Shooting Party* (1984). She always looks as if she knows something crucial and several TV mystery series, such as 'Wexford' and 'Morse', have exploited this aspect of her persona; she was superb as Eileen in *Pennies from Heaven* (1978, mini-series), and a glowingly intelligent Vera Brittain in *Testament of Youth* (1979, mini-series). While films have somewhat neglected her, she scored heavily on stage in *Passion Play* (2000).

OTHER BRITISH FILMS INCLUDE: *McVicar* (1980), *Greystoke . . .* (1984, UK/US), *Monsignor Renard* (1999).

Campbell, Colin (*b* Twickenham, 1937). Actor. Appeared in several films (*The Leather Boys*, 1963, as the troubled young husband; *The High Bright Sun*, 1965, etc.) before making his mark as the unreliable son in TV's *A Family at War* (1970). Since then, his film career has been sporadic, and interspersed with TV.

OTHER BRITISH FILMS INCLUDE: *Bloody Kids* (1979), *Another Time, Another Place* (1983), *My Beautiful Laundrette* (1985), *Nuns on the Run* (1990).

Campbell, Ivar (*b* Otakike, NZ, 1904). Director. Charterhouse-educated former stockbroker who directed, produced and sometimes wrote 'QUOTA QUICKIES' at SOUND CITY during the 30s, fulfilling all three functions on his last, *Too Many Husbands* (1938).

OTHER BRITISH FILMS INCLUDE: (d) *Reunion* (1932), *The Golden Cage, Eyes of Fate* (starring teenage Valerie HOBSON), *Side Streets* (1933),

Designing Women (1934), *The Belles of St Clements* (+ story) (1936), *The Captain's Orders* (1937); (p) *Watch Beverly* (1932), *Doss House* (1933), *White Ensign* (1934); (sc) *How's Chances?* (1934), *Feather Your Nest* (1937, story).

Campbell, Judy (*b* Grantham, 1916). Actress. Of theatrical parents, she is the mother of Jane BIRKIN and Andrew BIRKIN and grandmother of Charlotte GAINSBOURG. On stage from 1935; in 1940's *New Faces*, introduced the song, 'A Nightingale Sang in Berkeley Square'. Tall and graceful, she starred several times for Noël COWARD and was on stage in *Bless the Bride* (1999). Films have been squeezed into gaps left by a busy theatre career: she first filmed in 1940 (*Now You're Talking*, short), did two for EALING (*Saloon Bar, Convoy*, 1940), had her best part as a nurse suspected of murder in *Green for Danger* (1946), was in the lamentable *Bonnie Prince Charlie* (1948), then scarcely filmed again. Appeared in a short film by her son, *Shredni Vashtar* (1981, UK/US), and Agnès Varda's *Le petit amour* (1988) with Gainsbourg. Also wrote plays, including *The Bright One* (1958).

OTHER BRITISH FILMS INCLUDE: *Breach of Promise* (1941), *The World Owes Me a Living* (1945), *Mr Forbush and the Penguins* (1971).

Campbell, Martin (*b* New Zealand). Director. After being involved as production supervisor (*Red, Intimate Games*, 1976) and producer (*Black Joy*, 1977; *Scum*, 1979, assoc p) on some little-seen films, Campbell did some sharp TV (*Edge of Darkness*, 1985) and directed the enjoyable BOND, *GoldenEye* (1995, UK/US, + a).

OTHER BRITISH FILMS: (d) *The Sex Thief* (1973), *Three for All, Eskimo Nell* (1974), *Her Family Jewels* (1976).

Campbell, Patrick (Lord Glenavy) (*b* Dublin, 1913 – *d* London, 1980). Screenwriter, actor. Oxford-educated journalist who wrote screenplays for some British films of the 50s and 60s, including *Lucky Jim* (1957) and the notoriously inept *The Big Money* (1958). Became well-known as TV humorist (and stutterer), especially for appearances on *Call My Bluff*, replacing Robert MORLEY, in the 70s, as captain of one of the 'teams'.

OTHER BRITISH FILMS INCLUDE: (sc) *Helter Skelter* (1949), *Miss Robin Hood* (1952), *The Oracle* (1953), *Law and Disorder* (1958), *Go to Blazes* (1962).

Campion, Gerald (*b* London, 1921 – *d* Agen, France, 2002). Actor. Enjoyably typecast as The Fat Boy ('I wants to make your flesh creep') in *The Pickwick Papers* (1952) and as TV's *Billy Bunter* (1952). Pre-war, RADA-trained Campion was on stage, as in *French Without Tears* (1936) and made uncredited film appearances, as in *The Drum* (1938); in the RAF (1941–46), post-war on stage; and on TV from 1946 and films from 1947 (*Take My Life*), mostly in comedies which exploited his physical bulk. He was TV's Billy Bunter (1952–61). Father of playwright Cyril Campion.

OTHER BRITISH FILMS INCLUDE: *Miranda* (1948), *Top of the Form* (1953), *Up to His Neck* (1954, as Skinny), *Fun at St Fanny's* (1955), *Carry On Sergeant* (1958), *Double Bunk* (1961), *The Sandwich Man* (1966), *Chitty Chitty Bang Bang* (1968), *Little Dorrit* (1987).

Cannan, Denis (*b* Oxford, 1919). Screenwriter. Playwright and ex-actor, Eton-educated Cannan is credited on some interesting films of the 50s and 60s, including two for director Peter BROOK, *The Beggar's Opera* (1953, + a) and the semi-DOCUMENTARY about perceptions of Vietnam, *Tell Me Lies* (1967), for which he wrote the original text.

OTHER BRITISH FILMS INCLUDE: *Don't Bother to Knock* (1961), *Tamahine* (1962), *Sammy Going South* (1963), *A High Wind in Jamaica* (1965).

Canning, Victor (*b* Plymouth, 1911 – *d* Cirencester, 1986). Author. Detective novelist whose works have often been filmed, in Britain once notably (*The Golden Salamander*, 1949), otherwise indifferently, though *Masquerade* (1965), based on *Castle Minerva*, has at least a thrilling climax. HITCHCOCK's last film, *Family Plot* (1976, US) is based on *The Rainbird Pattern*.

OTHER BRITISH ADAPTATIONS: *Venetian Bird* (1952), *A Man on the Beach* (1955, orig st), *The House of the Seven Hawks* (1959), *The Limbo Line* (1968).

Cannon and Ball Comedians. British comedians **Tommy Derbyshire** (*b* Oldham, 1938), and **Robert Harper** (*b* Oldham,1944) from the working-men's club circuit, who rose to dizzy heights on stage as a comic duo, and were famously – and separately – converted to Christianity. They made one film together, *The Boys in Blue* (1983), as comic village policemen, and Ball made two others in America.

Cannon, Danny (*b* London, 1968). Director, screenwriter, producer. After making *Strangers* (1991), for the NATIONAL FILM AND TELEVISION SCHOOL, attracted Hollywood attention with his first feature, *The Young Americans* (1993), a drugs-investigation thriller starring Harvey Keitel. He made *Judge Dredd* (1995) wholly in Britain, with US money, and now seems lost to violent Americana, such as *I Still Know What You Did Last Summer* (1998).

Cannon, Esma (*b* Sydney, 1896 – *d* London, 1972). Actress. For over 25 years in more than 60 films, not to mention TV's *The Rag Trade* (1961–63), this diminutive, bird-like character player was one of the funniest women in films. However, when she wasn't playing nosy spinsters, moronic maids or put-upon drudges (as in *Sailor Beware*, on stage and screen, 1956) for laughs, she could be unexpectedly affecting, as in *Holiday Camp* (1947) as the dim and dizzy Elsie who pays for her romantic illusions with her life and as the mute servant in *Jassy* (1947). In later years, a stand-by in the 'CARRY ON' series.

OTHER BRITISH FILMS INCLUDE: *The Man Behind the Mask* (1936), *I See Ice!* (1938), *Poison Pen*, *The Spy in Black* (1939) *Quiet Wedding* (1941), *The Way Ahead* (1944), *Marry Me* (1949), *Last Holiday* (1950), *The Steel Key* (1953), *Out of the Clouds* (1955), *Jack the Ripper* (1958), *Carry On Constable*, *Doctor in Love* (1960), *What a Carve Up!* (1961), *On the Beat*, *The Fast Lady*, *Carry On Cruising* (1962), *Hide and Seek* (1963).

Cannon Group Founded in 1967, and specialising at first in EXPLOITATION FILMS, this US-based production and distribution company was a significant player in British cinema of the 80s in particular. In 1979 it was bought by the Israeli producers Yoram Globus and Menahen Golan and it was at its most prolifically productive in the mid 80s Cannon, which already owned the Cannon Classic chain, bought Thorn EMI Screen Entertainment, thus acquiring the ABC cinema circuit, which accounted for about a third of UK cinemas. Along with RANK and CHANNEL 4, it was a major investor in BRITISH SCREEN FINANCE CONSORTIUM, the privatised replacement for the NATIONAL FILM FINANCE CORPORATION, but despite its commitment to British production Cannon did not renew its commitment to the BSFC after its first triennium. It is not so much as a production company but as a distributor and exhibitor, spending lavishly to promote its wares at high-profile festivals such as Cannes'

and spearheading the growth of multiplex cinemas, that Cannon figures prominently in British film for over a decade. It bought the MGM studios at ELSTREE in 1988, renaming its multiplexes (and some of its older properties) MGM Cinemas. In 1989, the Italian financier, Giancarli Parretti, acquired Cannon which became part of his Pathé Communications, but just as Cannon suffered serious financial difficulties, so, too, in turn did Parretti's company, and in 1999 Parretti was extradited to the US to face fraud charges. However, for a brief period it was impossible not to be aware of the British-based importance of Cannon: just look at the full-page ad for its six subsidiary companies in the BFI's 1985 *Film and Television Yearbook*, for the range of its activities, which went beyond film production, distribution and exhibition to include also the manufacture of signs and music publication.

Canonero, Milena (*b* Turin). Costume designer. Twice-Oscared, for *Barry Lyndon* (1975, + BAAn) and *Chariots of Fire* (1981, + BAA), with a BAA for *The Cotton Club* (1984, US), at home with contemporary or period costume, Canonero is one of the most honoured designers on either side of the Atlantic. She worked three times with Stanley KUBRICK, providing a key element in the protagonist's confronting 'otherness' in *A Clockwork Orange* (1971). Spent the latter 90s working on US films, including – spectacularly – *Titus* (2000).

OTHER BRITISH FILMS INCLUDE: *The Disappearance* (UK/Can), *Midnight Express* (1978), *The Shining* (1980), *Give My Regards to Broad Street* (1984), *Damage* (1992, UK/Fr), *Death and the Maiden* (UK/Fr/US) (1995), *Camilla* (UK/Can) (1994).

Capaldi, Peter (*b* Glasgow, 1958). Actor, screenwriter. Lead and second lead in 80s and 90s British films, this skinny Scot had his best role in *The Love Child* (1987) as Sheila HANCOCK's grandson. Entered films in *Local Hero* (1983), starred in (with wife Elaine Collins) and co-wrote *Soft Top, Hard Shoulder* (1992), has done masses of TV, including *Tom Jones* (1997), and appeared in such international films as *Dangerous Liaisons* (1988, US) and *Smilla's Feeling for Snow* (1997, Den/Ger/Swe). In 1994, he wrote and directed the AA- and BAA-winning short, *Franz Kafka's It's a Wonderful Life*.

OTHER BRITISH FILMS: (a, unless noted) *Bless My Soul* (1984, short), *Lair of the White Worm* (1988), *December Bride* (1990), *The Lake* (1992), *Captives* (1994), *Bean*, *Shooting Fish* (1997), *What Rats Won't Do* (1998), *Strictly Sinatra* (d, sc), *Mrs Caldicot's Cabbage War* (2001).

Captain Kettle Film Company, The Established in a former roller-skating rink, Towers Hall, Bradford, in 1913 by Henry Hibbert and novelist C.J. Cutliffe-Hyne (author of the 'Captain Kettle' stories); the following year, it produced approximately 30 SHORTS, most starring Connie Somers. AS.

Carby, Fanny (*b* Sutton, Surrey, 1925 – *d* London, 2002). Actress. Theatre actress associated with Joan LITTLEWOOD's Theatre Workshop, Stratford East, in the 60s. Also appeared in many TV series and in about 20 films, starting with *Lost* (1955) and last in *Mrs Dalloway* (1997, UK/Neth/US), usually in small roles, as cleaning ladies and other working-class types.

OTHER BRITISH FILMS INCLUDE: *Women Without Men* (1956), *Some People*, *Sparrows Can't Sing* (1962), *Oh! What a Lovely War* (1969), *The Elephant Man* (1980, UK/US).

Cardiff, Jack (*b* Yarmouth, 1914). Cinematographer, director. RN: John Gran. One of the world's greatest TECHNICOLOR cameramen, Cardiff began as a child actor at 4 and was assistant camera operator at 13, at BIP, acquiring much expertise from working with visiting American cinematographers such as

Harry STRADLING, on films at DENHAM. He was operator on Britain's first Technicolor film, *Wings of the Morning* (1937), and, along with working for STRAND, MOI, World Window and the CROWN FILM UNIT during WW2, he gained further colour film experience on *The Great Mr Handel* (1942), as second unit director on *The Life and Death of Colonel Blimp* (1943), and as cinematographer on the celebrated documentary, *Western Approaches* (1944), set largely in a lifeboat at sea. He worked several times for POWELL AND PRESSBURGER, at his most inventive on *A Matter of Life and Death* (1946), with its strange monochrome Heaven, and *Black Narcissus* (1947, AA), when he drenched the screen in red to signify passion, an effect 'quoted' by Martin Scorsese in *The Age of Innocence* (1993). His lighting and venturesome approach contributed largely to the lush romanticism of such films as *Under Capricorn* (1949), the bizarre *Pandora and the Flying Dutchman* (1950), and *The Barefoot Contessa* (1954, US); and *War and Peace* (1956, US/It) has some visual splendours. However silly such films as *It Started in Paradise* (1952) or *The Vikings* (1958, US) were, they looked better for his mediation.

In 1958, he turned to directing with less notable results. Probably his best film as director is *Sons and Lovers* (1960), though Freddie FRANCIS's loving black-and-white photography is its most haunting feature. Most of the rest, some – such as *My Geisha* (1962, US) – are indifferent, though he did take over *Young Cassidy* (1965) when John FORD became ill. He returned to cinematography in the mid 70s, shooting such films as *The Wicked Lady* (1983) and *Rambo: First Blood II* (1985, UK). Awarded OBE in 2000.

OTHER BRITISH FILMS: (c) (shorts) *Temples of India, Rome Symphony, A Road in India, Petra, Jerusalem, Fox-Hunting in the Roman Campagna, The Eternal Fire* (1938), *River Thames – Yesterday, Main Street of Paris, Peasant Island* (1939), *Queen Cotton, Plastic Surgery in Wartime, The Green Girdle* (1941), *This Is Colour, Out of the Box, Colour in Clay, Western Isles, Border Weave* (1942), *Scottish Mazurka* (1943), *Steel* (1945), *I Know That My Redeemer Liveth* (1952), *Christmas Chorale* (1953), *Vivaldi's Four Seasons* (1991), *The Dance of Shiva* (1998); (features) *Caesar and Cleopatra* (1945, co-c), *The Red Shoes, Scott of the Antarctic* (co-c) (1948), *The Black Rose* (1950, UK/US), *The Magic Box, The African Queen* (1951), *The Master of Ballantrae* (1953), *The Prince and the Showgirl* (1957), *Death on the Nile* (1978), *The Fifth Musketeer* (1979, UK/Austria), *The Dogs of War, The Awakening* (1980, UK/US), *Scandalous* (1983); (d) *Intent to Kill* (1958), *Beyond This Place* (1959), *The Lion* (1962), *The Long Ships* (1963, UK/Yug), *The Liquidator* (1965), *The Mercenaries* (1967), *The Girl on a Motorcycle* (1968, UK/Fr, + ph, adpt), *Penny Gold, Mutations* (1973).

BIBLIOG: Autobiography, *Magic Hour: A Life in the Movies*, 1996.

Carew, James (*b* Goshen, Indiana, 1876 – *d* London, 1938). Actor. A prolific character actor, on stage from 1897 and on screen from 1913, Carew first came to the UK in 1905. In the 30s, he originated the character of Alexander, of 'Alexander and Mose', a black-face cross-talk act on radio with Billy BENNETT. He was the third husband of Ellen TERRY (married 1907).

BRITISH FILMS INCLUDE: *The Fool* (1913), *The Polo Champion* (1915), *Sheba* (1919), *Tansy* (1921), *Owd Bob* (1924), *High Treason* (1929), *The Tunnel* (1935), *Wings over Africa* (1936), *Jericho* (1937), *Glamour Girl* (1938). AS.

Carey, Joyce (*b* London, 1898 – *d* London, 1993). Actress. Daughter of actress Lilian BRAITHWAITE, Carey was on stage from 1918 and stayed there for nearly 70 years, at 86 playing Peter O'TOOLE's mother in *Pygmalion* (1984). She made three silent films, but her screen career really began when she played Bernard MILES's wife in *In Which We Serve* (1942), by Noël COWARD, in whose plays she often starred. Her imposing

screen persona comprehended the pseudo-refined barmaid in *Brief Encounter* (1945), acidulous spinsters (*The Way to the Stars*, 1945; *The Chiltern Hundreds*, 1949; *Libel*, 1959), loving wives (*Cry, the Beloved Country*, 1952), and warm-hearted upper-class aunts (*A Nice Girl Like Me*, 1969). Wrote two plays as Jay Mallory, and received OBE in 1982.

OTHER BRITISH FILMS INCLUDE: *God and the Man, Because* (1918), *Blithe Spirit* (1945), *The October Man, London Belongs to Me* (1948), *Street Corner* (1953), *Loser Takes All* (1956), *Alive and Kicking* (1958), *The VIPs* (1963), *The Black Windmill* (1974).

Carey, Macdonald (*b* Sioux City, Iowa, 1913 – *d* Beverly Hills, California, 1994). Actor. Second-string American star who made a handful of films in Britain, including one of his best, LOSEY's *The Damned* (1961). The others are two mild exotic adventures, *Malaga* (1954) and *Odongo* (1956), and two 1962 thrillers, *Stranglehold* and *The Devil's Agent*. Famous for TV's *Days of Our Lives* (1965–84).

Carey, Richenda (*b* Bitten, 1948). Actress. Though first merely unwelcoming in Mike LEIGH's TV play, *Nuts in May* (1976), Carey's image has become increasingly imperious, very often in upper-class roles, such as mean-mouthed Lady Bradshaw in *Mrs Dalloway* (1997, US/Neth/US). Blood sister to such earlier *grandes dames* as Irene BROWNE and Norma VARDEN. Educated at Rose Bruford College and trained in Rep, often at the Bristol Old Vic, she has done much TV (including *The Choir*) and theatre (including *The Madness of King George*).

OTHER BRITISH FILMS INCLUDE: *P'tang Yang Kipperbang* (1982), *Dealers* (1989), *Loser Takes All* (1990), *Nostradamus* (1994), *Photographing Fairies* (1997), *Whatever Happened to Harold Smith?* (2000).

Cargill, Patrick (*b* London, 1918 – *d* London, 1996). Actor, dramatist. Ex-Indian Army officer, on stage from 1939, in West End and films from 1953, but now most famous for the TV series, *Father Dear Father* (1968–73, 1978–79). In this he played a divorced novelist whose life is constantly disrupted by two teenage daughters, ex-wife, mother, housekeeper and mistress. A film SPIN-OFF was released in 1972. A stylish farceur, he provided some of the few cherishable moments in CHAPLIN's calamitous *A Countess from Hong Kong* (1966) as a disapproving valet. Co-authored the play *Ring for Catty* on which *Carry On Nurse* (1958) and *Twice Round the Daffodils* (1962) were based.

OTHER BRITISH FILMS INCLUDE: *The Sword and the Rose* (1953), *The Night We Dropped a Clanger* (1959), *A Stitch in Time, The Hi-Jackers* (wholly serious as police officer) (1963), *Carry On Jack* (1964), *Help!* (1965), *Hammerhead, Inspector Clouseau* (1968), *Up Pompeii* (1971, as Nero).

Carin, Kate Costume designer. Came to attention in the latter half of the 90s, especially in relation to several Scottish-based or -backed films, such as the black comedy *Shallow Grave* (1994), *Small Faces* (1995), *The Life of Stuff* (1997) and *Gregory's Two Girls* (1999). Also responsible for the 'period' look of *Hideous Kinky* (1998) and for *Spice World* (1997), though how far the famous five controlled their own dress image is at least arguable.

OTHER BRITISH FILMS INCLUDE: *Margaret's Museum* (1995, UK/Can), *Regeneration* (1997, UK/Can), *The 51st State* (2001, UK/Can/US).

Carlson, Veronica (*b* York, 1944). Actress. 'From Yorkshire to Transylvania' summarises this leading lady's career trajectory. Almost all her films have been in the HORROR mode, including some of HAMMER's most notable successes, such as *Frankenstein Must Be Destroyed* (1969). After several small roles, she found her métier in *Dracula Has Risen from the Grave* (1968).

OTHER BRITISH FILMS INCLUDE: *Smashing Time* (1967), *Hammerhead* (1968), *Vampira* (1974), *The Ghoul* (1975), *Flesh and Blood* (1997, UK/US, doc).

Carlyle, Robert (*b* Glasgow, 1961). Actor. Physically slight but commanding star of 90s films and TV, Carlyle had a difficult childhood: deserted while a baby by his mother, brought up by his father whose trade as painter and decorator he followed, before, at 21, deciding to try for an acting career. Very private about his early life, he trained unhappily for three years at the Royal Scottish Academy of Music and Drama, afterwards setting up Rain Dog, his own theatre company and performing for underprivileged young people. He had a role in David HAYMAN's *Silent Scream* (1990) and everything changed in 1991 when Ken LOACH cast him in *Riff-Raff*, as an ex-con building labourer. An immediate success, he later played a Glasgow bus-driver caught up in Nicaraguan politics and romance in Loach's *Carla's Song* (1996).

In the meantime, he collaborated with director Antonia BIRD on the gritty urban drama, *Safe* (1993) and, as the gay priest's lover, in *Priest* (1994), and would go on to star for her in the thieves-fall-out drama, *Face* (1997) and as the cannibal protagonist in *Ravenous* (1999, UK/Czech/Mex/Slovakia/US). As well, he became a household name as the hash-smoking detective in TV's *Hamish Macbeth* (1995–97), whippet-lean and dangerous, and even more threatening as the vicious Begbie in the cult hit, *Trainspotting* (1996). But it was his award-winning role as Gaz, the unemployed Sheffield steelworker-cum-stripper in *The Full Monty* (1997, BAA), that cemented his star reputation, though his acting ability had been thoroughly established in several foregoing films, including Michael WINTERBOTTOM's *Go Now* (1996, TV, some cinemas) as a footballer suffering multiple sclerosis.

It seemed he could do no wrong, and being cast as the villain in the BOND concoction, *The World Is Not Enough* (1999, UK/US), appeared to confirm this, though the period adventure, *Plunkett & Macleane* (1999), was – undeservedly – a flop, despite its violent action and wittily anachronistic pop score. More recent UK/US co-productions, *Angela's Ashes* (1999) and *The Beach* (2000), have broadened his exposure rather than his range, but he remains perhaps the major British star of the 90s. Awarded OBE in 1999. Married to make-up artist, Anastasia Shirley in 1997, and in 1999 he, along with Bird and Mark Cousins, set up 4Way Pictures, to produce a lively-sounding line-up of films.

OTHER BRITISH FILMS: *There's Only One Jimmy Grimble* (UK/Fr) (2000), *Pandaemonium, The 51st State* (2001, UK/Can/US).

Carmichael, Ian (*b* Hull, 1920). Actor. In the latter half of the 50s, Carmichael was one of the most popular of British stars, adept in ringing changes on the image of well-meaning, somewhat bumbling young innocent abroad in a corrupt world. Muriel BOX gave him his first big film chance by insisting on having him reprise his stage success in *Simon and Laura* (1955), as the frazzled young TV producer dealing with temperamental stars. However, it was the BOULTINGS who made him an indisputable star in a series of amiably satirical comedies: *Brothers in Law, Private's Progress* (1956), *Lucky Jim* (1957), *I'm All Right Jack* (1959) and *Heavens Above!* (1963), which took swipes at a range of British institutions, with crises spiralling around the hapless Carmichael. He was also, unlike many British comedians, a satisfactory romantic lead, as he

showed in *Happy is the Bride* (1957), the sunny remake of *Quiet Wedding*, and *Hide and Seek* (1963), an enjoyable comedy thriller.

RADA-trained, he first appeared on stage in 1939 and, after war service in the Army, made a name for himself especially in revue (e.g. *The Lyric Revue*, 1951) and in popular comedies such as *Tunnel of Love* (1957). He had considerable TV success, particularly in *The World of Wooster* (1965–67) and *Lord Peter Wimsey* (1972–75), as upper-class ass and sleuth respectively, and in 1999 appeared in *Wives and Daughters*. As much as anyone, he epitomises the good-natured, un-demanding pleasures of 50s British cinema, and his engaging autobiography, *Will the Real Ian Carmichael?* (1979) rein-forces the screen persona.

OTHER BRITISH FILMS: *Bond Street, Trottie True* (1948), *Dear Mr Prohack* (1949), *Time Gentlemen Please!, Ghost Ship* (1952), *Meet Mr Lucifer* (1953), *Betrayed, The Colditz Story* (1954), *Storm over the Nile* (1955), *The Big Money* (1958), *Left, Right and Centre, School for Scoundrels* (1959), *Light Up the Sky* (1960), *Double Bunk* (1961), *The Amorous Prawn* (1962), *The Case of the 44's* (1964, UK/Den), *Smashing Time* (1967), *The Magnificent Seven Deadly Sins, Lust* (1971), *From Beyond the Grave* (1973), *The Lady Vanishes* (1979), *Diamond Skulls* (1989).

Carminati, Tullio (*b* Zara, Italy, 1894 – *d* Rome, 1971). Actor. RN: Count Tullio Carminati de Brambills. Italian romantic lead who appeared in several British productions for Herbert WILCOX during the mid 30s, including two co-starring Anna NEAGLE, *The Three Maxims* (1936, UK/Fr) and *London Melody* (1937), and acted in international films such as *War and Peace* (1956, US/It) and *The Cardinal* (1963, US) until his death. Active in Hollywood in the 30s, notably in *One Night of Love* (1934).

OTHER BRITISH FILMS: *Sunset in Vienna* (1937), *The Golden Madonna* (1949).

Carney, George (*b* Bristol, 1887 – *d* London, 1947). Actor. Sturdy interpreter of working-class characters, popular on MUSIC HALLS in his youth, and, after one silent film (*Some Waiter*, 1916, + d, sc), became an enjoyable fixture in British films from 1933 (*The Television Follies, Commissionaire*) and had five films released in the year of his death. These latter included two of his best roles: as Jean KENT's brutal father in *Good-Time Girl* and as Hermione BADDELEY's nervous 'boyfriend' in *Brighton Rock*. Other notable ones included two fathers to Wendy HILLER, bluff in *Lancashire Luck* (1937) and business-like in *I Know Where I'm Going!* (1945), John MILLS's father in *In Which We Serve* (1942), and, very poignant, the defeated father in John BAXTER's *Love on the Dole* (1941). He was just the sort one might expect to find associated with Baxter's populist films, in several of which he starred in the mid 30s. He could be comic or touching, venal or upright: in short, a great, natural character actor.

OTHER BRITISH FILMS INCLUDE: *A Real Bloke* (1935), *Dreaming Lips* (1937), *Consider Your Verdict* (1938), *Young Man's Fancy, The Stars Look Down, Come on George* (1939), *Convoy* (1940), *Kipps, The Common Touch* (for Baxter again) (1941), *Hard Steel, Unpublished Story, Thunder Rock* (1942), *Waterloo Road, Tawny Pipit* (1944), *Wanted for Murder* (1946), *The Root of All Evil* (1947).

Carol, Joan (*d* near Narbonne, France, in road accident). Actress. Striking brunette long married to director Vernon SEWELL, for whom she made six of her eight British films. Appeared to best advantage as the adulterous wife in *Ghost Ship* (1952).

OTHER BRITISH FILMS: *Champagne Charlie* (1944), *The Feminine Touch* (1956); for Sewell: *Jack of Diamonds* (1949), *The Dark Light*, *The Black Widow* (1951), *Rogue's Yarn* (1957), *Burke & Hare* (1971).

Carol, John (*b* London, 1910 – *d* London, 1968). Actor. Stage actor, under contract to Warners in the 30s. Had small parts in several films directed by Arthur WOODS, including *The Windmill* (1937) and *The Return of Carol Deane* (1938). Post-war, at Ealing, he was memorable as Googie WITHERS' fancy man, with a slicked-down quiff, in *Pink String and Sealing Wax* (1945), for Robert HAMER. Also in Hamer's *It Always Rains on Sunday* (1947) and *The Spider and the Fly* (1949), and TV's *Boys in Brown* (1949).

OTHER BRITISH FILMS INCLUDE: *Thank Evans* (1938), *Convoy* (1940), *The Silver Fleet* (1943).

Caron, Leslie (*b* Boulogne-Billancourt, France, 1931). Actress, dancer. International star for 50 years, most famously in such Hollywood musicals as *An American in Paris* (1951) and *Gigi* (1958). Also in some notable British films, including *The L-Shaped Room* (1962) as the pregnant single girl, for which she won a BAA, and *Valentino* (1977), as a flamboyant Nazimova. Was married (2 of 3) to British stage and film director, Peter HALL (1956–66); their daughter is actress Jennifer Hall.

OTHER BRITISH FILMS: *The Doctor's Dilemma* (1958), *Guns of Darkness* (1962), *Promise Her Anything* (1965), *James Dean, the First American Teenager* (1975, doc), *Damage* (1992, UK/Fr), *Funny Bones* (1995, UK/US).

Carpenter, Freddie (*b* Melbourne, 1908 – *d* London, 1989). Dancer, choreographer. On stage as dancer in Melbourne from 1925, London from 1929; served in the RAF (1941–44). He arranged dance sequences for several films, including *The Winslow Boy* (1948) – and the disastrous musical, *London Town* (1946); also choreographed several TV specials, but his main allegiance was to the theatre.

OTHER BRITISH FILMS INCLUDE: (dance arranger) *Carnival*, *Gaiety George* (1946), *Here Come the Huggetts* (1948), *Easy Money* (1948), *Diamond City* (1949), *The Love Lottery* (1953).

Carpenter, Paul (*b* Montreal, 1921 – *d* London, 1964). Actor. Canadian leading man in Britain, mostly in second features, though there is a trickle of As, such as *The Weak and the Wicked* (1953). A former singer and ice-hockey player, he played amiable detectives and newspaper men out-thinking the police and rescuing intrepid young women from dangers they could have avoided, but was actually more interesting as weak men, in such films as *Jet Storm* (1959) and as Hillary Brooke's latest lover in *The House Across the Lake* (1954).

OTHER BRITISH FILMS INCLUDE: *School for Secrets* (1946), *Landfall* (1949), *Albert RN* (1953), *The Young Lovers*, *Diplomatic Passport* (1954), *The Hornet's Nest* (1955), *Fire Maidens from Outer Space* (1956), *Intent to Kill* (1958), *Dr Crippen* (1962), *Call Me Bwana* (1963), *The Beauty Jungle* (1964), *Panic* (1965).

Carr, Cameron (*b* Kingston-upon-Thames, 1876 – *d*?). Actor. Carr was a busy character actor in British films from 1909 to 1934, usually associated with villainous roles, but equally adept at police officers.

BRITISH FILMS INCLUDE: *A Turf Conspiracy* (1918), *A Daughter of Eve* (1919), *Trent's Last Case* (1920), *Fox Farm* (1922), *The Qualified Adventurer* (1925), *Poppies of Flanders* (1927), *The Ware Case* (1929), *The W Plan* (1930), *On Thin Ice* (1933), *The Scoop* (1934). AS.

Carr, Jane (*b* Whitley Bay, 1909 – *d* England, 1957). Actress. A popular leading lady of the 30s, from *Let Me Explain, Dear* (1932), Carr made only a few post-war appearances as a stylish

character player, as in a very funny theatre sequence in *It's Not Cricket* (1949) and in *The Saint's Return* (1953). Not to be confused with **Jane Carr** (*b* Loughton, Essex, 1950), who entered films as a teenager in *The Prime of Miss Jean Brodie* (1969) and has since filmed largely abroad or on TV.

OTHER BRITISH FILMS INCLUDE: *Dick Turpin* (1933), *Lord Edgware Dies* (1934), *The Ace of Spades* (1935), *The Lilac Domino* (1937), *Sabotage at Sea*, *Alibi* (1942), *Thirty-Six Hours* (1954).

Carr, Michael (*b* Leeds, 1900 – *d* London, 1968). Composer. Essentially a songwriter for light entertainments such as *Flight from Folly* (1945) and the bizarre *Hello London* (1958). Also wrote songs for the Paul ROBESON vehicle *Jericho* (1937), and composed the hit song 'South of the Border'.

OTHER BRITISH FILMS INCLUDE: *Girls Will Be Boys* (1934), *O-Kay for Sound* (1937), *Front Page Story* (1953), *The Painted Smile* (1961), *Face of a Stranger* (1964, title music).

Carreras, Sir James (*b* London, 1909 – *d* Henley-on-Thames, 1990). Production executive. Leaving Manchester Grammar School at 16, he managed the Oxford cinema, Manchester, and entered the distribution side of the industry in 1934, joining EXCLUSIVE FILMS, formed by his father, Enrique, and Will HAMMER. Rose to Lt-Colonel in WW2, and in 1946 returned as Managing Director of Exclusive, where he actually co-produced one film, *Who Killed Van Loon?* (1947), and oversaw the production of a steady stream of supporting films, mostly thrillers. HAMMER FILMS, established in a country house at BRAY, grew out of Exclusive and began a series of highly profitable HORROR films from the mid 50s, starting with *The Quatermass Experiment* (1955). A very astute man, with an instinct for popular entertainment, Carreras was described as 'managing director of the most successful privately-owned British film company'. He was the Chairman of Hammer Film Productions from 1949 to 1980, was made MBE in 1944 and knighted in 1970. His son was producer Michael CARRERAS.

Carreras, Michael (*b* London, 1927 – *d* London, 1994). Producer, director. Still in his 20s, this son of James CARRERAS was director of EXCLUSIVE FILMS, HAMMER FILMS and BRAY STUDIOS. Worked exclusively for Hammer Films, as producer or executive producer, with occasional directing credits, not on the studio's major productions, but on such pieces as *Parade of the Bands* (1955, short), the travelogue, *Copenhagen* (1956), *The Steel Bayonet* (1957), *What a Crazy World* (1963, + sc), *Slave Girls* (1966, + sc), *The Lost Continent* (1968), and *Shatter* (1974, UK/HK). Presumably his function was primarily to smooth the way for such directors as Terence FISHER or John GILLING, and for 30 years he was one of British cinema's busiest executives.

OTHER BRITISH FILMS (p/exec p): *The Dark Light* (1951), *Never Look Back* (1952), *Blood Orange*, *Mantrap* (1953), *The Stranger Came Home* (+ sc), *Men of Sherwood Forest*, *Mask of Dust*, *Face the Music* (1954, + sc), *Murder by Proxy*, *The Right Person*, *Break in the Circle*; (shorts) *Eric Winstone's Band Show*, *Just For You* (1955), *X the Unknown*, *Dick Turpin – Highwayman*, *Eric Winstone's Stagecoach* (short) (1956), *The Curse of Frankenstein*, *The Camp on Blood Island*, *Quatermass 2*, (1957), *Dracula*, *The Revenge of Frankenstein*, *Ten Seconds to Hell* (1958), *The Hound of the Baskervilles*, *Yesterday's Enemy*, *The Mummy*, *The Man Who Could Cheat Death*, *Hell Is a City* (1959), *Never Take Sweets from a Stranger*, *The Brides of Dracula*, *The Two Faces of Dr Jekyll* (1960), *Taste of Fear*, *The Curse of the Werewolf*, *Cash on Demand*, *The Damned* (1961), *Curse of the Mummy's Tomb* (1964, + co-d, sc), *She* (1965), *One Million Years BC* (1966), *A Challenge for Robin Hood* (1967), *Moon Zero Two* (+ sc), *Crescendo* (1969), *Vampire Circus*, *Blood from the Mummy's Tomb* (1971), *That's Your Funeral*, *Dracula AD 1972*, *Nearest and Dearest*, *Fear in the Night* (1972), *The Lady Vanishes* (1979).

Carrick, Edward (*b* London, 1905 – *d* Thame, 1998). Art director. RN: Craig. Grandson of Ellen TERRY, who adopted professional name of Edward Carrick in order not to appear in the shadow of his great designer father, Edward Gordon Craig. Carrick was a leading figure in British art direction, noted for his intelligence and virtuosity; in the words of his mentor, George PEARSON, 'the supreme master of his art.' Entered the industry in 1928 with Pearson, and became a designer in 1929 with *The Broken Melody* for the director's new company, Welsh–Pearson–Elder. He founded the first UK film school, AAT, in 1937, wrote the first textbook on art direction, *Designing for Films* (1941), and also authored *Art and Design in the British Film* (1948). During WW2, with CROWN FILM UNIT, whose work he recorded in *Meet '. . . the common people . . .'* (undated). Supervising art director at PINEWOOD in 40s. Also active in theatre.

OTHER BRITISH FILMS INCLUDE: *Loyalties* (1933), *Midshipman Easy* (1935), *Target for Tonight* (1941), *Fires Were Started* (1943), *Western Approaches* (1944), *Captain Boycott* (1947), *The Blue Lagoon* (1949), *It Started in Paradise* (1952), *Bachelor of Hearts* (1958), *Tiger Bay, Blind Date* (1959), *Maniac* (1963), *The Nanny* (1965). AS.

Carroll, Madeleine (*b* West Bromwich, 1906 – *d* Marbella, Spain, 1987). Actress. Formerly a school teacher and model, a blonde beauty of ladylike demeanour, Carroll was on stage from 1927 and in films the following year. She made 20 films in Britain, including Victor SAVILLE's WW1 drama, *I Was a Spy* (1933), in which she was very touching, and *The 39 Steps* (1935, as the hand-cuffed heroine) and *The Secret Agent* (1936), establishing the prototype for such later HITCHCOCK heroines as Ingrid BERGMAN and Grace Kelly. From the mid 30s, hers is essentially a Hollywood career, in European-set romances like *The Prisoner of Zenda* (1937) and comedies like *My Favorite Blonde* (1942), and she became an American citizen in 1943, when she married (3 of 4) Sterling Hayden. Following her sister's death during the Blitz, she gave up filming for war relief work and was honoured by France and the US for her wartime and post-war efforts. She made only three further films, including the British alpine-set romance, *White Cradle Inn* (1947). Hers was perhaps a limited talent, but it was exercised with some grace. She was first in a line of English leading ladies Hollywood took to heart, paving the way for Greer GARSON, Deborah KERR and Julie ANDREWS.

OTHER BRITISH FILMS: *What Money Can Buy, The Guns of Loos, The First Born* (1928), *Young Woodley, Escape, Kissing Cup's Race* (1930), *Fascination* (1931), *The Dictator, The Story of Papworth: the Village of Hope* (short) (1935), *It Might Be You!* (1938).

Carruthers, Lito (*b* Athens). Editor. Her imaginative cutting on such popular 40s films as *Madonna of the Seven Moons* (1944) and three major films for Lance COMFORT, his masterpiece, *Temptation Harbour* (1947), *Daughter of Darkness* (1948) and *Silent Dust* (1949), gave way to more routine treatment of more routine assignments in the 50s. Came to England as a child, entered films as production office assistant at LONDON FILMS, and learnt editing skills at EALING, where she cut her first film *Greek Testament* (1942, doc).

OTHER BRITISH FILMS INCLUDE: *The Echo Murders, The Latin Quarter* (1945), *Meet the Navy* (1946), *Obsession* (1949), *Your Witness* (1950), *Valley of Eagles* (1951), *My Death Is a Mockery* (1952), *Conflict of Wings* (1954), *Life in Emergency Ward 10* (1958).

'Carry On' series The most commercially successful and long-running SERIES of COMEDIES in British film history, the 'Carry Ons' began in 1958 with an amiably mediocre farce about army recruits called *Carry On Sergeant*. Its unexpectedly large success suggested to its producer Peter ROGERS that broad comedies about other familiar British social institutions might pay dividends, prompting the making of *Carry On Nurse* (1958), *. . . Teacher* (1959) and *. . . Constable* (1960). The pictures, produced at the rate of one or two per year, quickly became a British institution in their own right, simultaneously drawing huge audiences and dismaying the critics. Rogers produced and Gerald THOMAS directed them all, and the screenwriting baton was passed from Norman HUDIS (who wrote the early 'institutional' scripts) to Talbot ROTHWELL, who had a particular penchant for parodying other film genres – hence the likes of *Carry On Cleo* (1964), *. . . Cowboy* (1965) and *. . . Up the Khyber* (1968), the last of these often acclaimed as the series' triumph. The humour of the series was unabashedly lowbrow, delighting in innuendo, scatology, deliberately terrible puns and unrepentant stereotypes. The repeated use of a core cast of talented comic actors helped to build audience loyalty; the performers most associated with the series include Kenneth WILLIAMS, Joan SIMS, Sid JAMES, Charles HAWTREY, Hattie JACQUES, Kenneth CONNOR and Barbara WINDSOR. The series declined in the 70s, ending with 1978's ill-judged pornography spoof *Carry On Emmannuelle*, for two principal reasons. First, as the original stars aged or moved on, those brought in as intended replacements proved unsatisfying. Second, cultural changes made the seaside postcard attitudes of the 'Carry Ons' look antiquated and coy – though this, paradoxically, has helped them to build a cult following with younger audiences since the 80s. The series briefly re-emerged in 1992 with a thirtieth title, *Carry On Columbus* (1992), but it was strikingly unsuccessful. Andy Medhurst.

Carson, Charles (*b* London, 1885 – *d* London, 1977). Actor. Educated in the UK, US and Germany, and a civil engineer before making stage debut in 1919 and performing over the next 50 years in dozens of modern and classical plays, directing plays for ENSA during WW2. Entered films in 1931 and appeared in over 70 before his last, *Lady Caroline Lamb* (1972, UK/It/US), usually projecting an austere image of integrity (e.g. *Cry, the Beloved Country*, 1952) and/or authority (e.g. *Reach for the Sky*, 1956, as Air Chief Marshal Sir Hugh Dowding). His 'type' was always in demand.

OTHER BRITISH FILMS INCLUDE: *The Loves of Ariane* (UK/Ger), *Many Waters, Dreyfus* (1931), *There Goes the Bride* (1932), *The Broken Melody* (1934), *Sanders of the River* (1935), *Things to Come, Secret Agent,* (1936), *Victoria the Great, Old Mother Riley* (1937), *The Lion Has Wings* (1939), *Pink String and Sealing Wax* (1945), *The Lady with a Lamp* (1951), *The Master of Ballantrae* (1953), *Bobbikins* (1959), *The Trials of Oscar Wilde* (1960), *Macbeth* (1961).

Carson, Jeannie (*b* Pudson, 1928). Actress. RN: Jean Shufflebottom. One of the most deeply dispiriting sights in British cinema is that of Carson dancing and singing a dreadful song as she leaps about on petrol drums outside a decrepit garage in *An Alligator Named Daisy* (1955). The daughter of music hall comedian, Fred Shuff, she was promoted by *Picturegoer* (1954) as 'just the girl to get British studios musical-minded'. She was popular on stage in London (*Love from Judy*, 1954) and New York, and on UK and US television, but film success totally eluded her. Touted as another Jessie MATTHEWS, but no film was ever built round her and on screen she was gratingly 'cute' rather than endearing. Married/divorced actors **Bill Lowe**, who made two minor musicals, *A Date with a Dream* (1948, with Carson) and *Melody Club* (1949), and Biff McGuire.

OTHER BRITISH FILMS: *Love in Pawn* (1953), *As Long as They're Happy* (1955), *Rockets Galore* (1958), *Seven Keys* (1962).

Carson, John (*b* Colombo, Sri Lanka, 1927). Actor. Tall, incisive-looking actor mainly in supporting roles, often in HORROR films, including *Taste the Blood of Dracula* (1969), had leads in a few minor films, such as *Smokescreen* (1964), in which he is nicely ambiguous, and *Act of Murder* (1964). Made several films in South Africa, including *Schweitzer* (1989), and was in such TV series based there as *Shaka Zulu* (1987).
OTHER BRITISH FILMS INCLUDE: *Teheran* (1947), *The Lady Is a Square* (1958), *Master Spy* (1963), *The Plague of the Zombies* (1966), *The Man Who Haunted Himself* (1970), *Kronos* (1972), *Survivor* (1988), *Au Pair* (1994).

Carstairs, John Paddy (*b* London, 1910 – *d* London, 1970). Director, screenwriter. RN: Keys. Son of comedian Nelson KEYS and brother of producer Anthony Nelson KEYS, he produced some snappy entertainments in the later 40s, including *Sleeping Car to Trieste* (1948) and *The Chiltern Hundreds* (1949). In the 50s, he guided comedian Norman WISDOM, from *Trouble in Store* (1953, + co-sc), to massive box-office stardom, through half a dozen cheerfully undemanding films, and thereafter directed little but broad COMEDIES, for the likes of Ronald SHINER and Frankie HOWERD. Entered films in 1928 as assistant cameraman at STOLL studios, and carried out a variety of functions, including screenwriting, for Herbert WILCOX, for MGM–BRITISH and others. Settled to direction from 1936, after two minor efforts in 1930 (*Holiday*, short) and *Paris Plane* (1933, + sc), and served in the Fleet Air Arm during WW2. As well as screenplays, he also wrote three diverting books of memoirs and several novels, and was an exhibited painter, too.
OTHER BRITISH FILMS INCLUDE: (d, sc/co-sc) *Incident in Shanghai* (1938), *Top of the Form* (1953), *One Good Turn* (1954), *Man of the Moment* (1955), *Sands of the Desert* (1960); (d only) *Lassie from Lancashire* (1938), *The Saint in London* (1939), *Spare a Copper* (1940), *Dancing with Crime* (1947), *Fools Rush In* (1949), *Tony Draws a Horse* (1950), *Made in Heaven* (1952), *Jumping for Joy* (1955), *Up in the World* (1956), *Just My Luck* (1957), *The Big Money* (1958), *Tommy the Toreador* (1959), *All at Sea* (1964); (sc/co-sc only) *The Water Gipsies*, *Nine Till Six* (1932), *The Dreamers* (1933), *The Captain's Table* (1936), *The Lambeth Walk* (1939), *Little Big Shot* (1952), *The Crowded Day* (1954, story), *And the Same to You* (1959).

Carter, James (*b* 1902). Production designer. Entered films in 1923 at WORTON HALL STUDIOS, and joined Julius HAGEN at TWICKENHAM in 1929, where he was associated with the production of over 200 films. Was a busy art director, as the designation was, in the 30s, on such well-regarded films of the period as Maurice ELVEY's *The Lodger* (1932) and *I Lived with You* (1933), both with Ivor NOVELLO, *The Wandering Jew* (1933), and most impressively on *The Stars Look Down* (1939) and *Hatter's Castle* (1941), on which his staging of the Tay Bridge disaster won much praise. Worked as associate producer at GRAND NATIONAL (1939–42), for Sydney BOX at RIVERSIDE STUDIOS (1942–46), and for ALLIANCE (1946–48).
OTHER BRITISH FILMS INCLUDE: (art d) *Master and Man* (1929), *The Ghost Camera* (1933), *The Last Journey*, *Scrooge* (1935), *Silver Blaze* (1937), *Under Your Hat*, *Pastor Hall* (1940), *29, Acacia Avenue* (1945), *Daybreak* (1948); (des) *Squibs* (1935); (p) *Daughter of Darkness* (ex p), *Just William's Luck*, *Dancing With Crime*, *They Made Me a Fugitive* (ex p) (1947).

Carter, Jim (*b* Harrogate, 1948). Actor. Respected theatre actor (RSC, National, West End) and with over 60 TV credits, including *The Singing Detective* (1986), Carter became a very

recognisable face in 90s films. He had good, varied roles in such award-winning films as *The Madness of King George* (1994, as Fox), *Richard III* (1995, as Lord Hastings), *Brassed Off* (1996, as colliery bandsman Harry) and best of all as the boatman in *Shakespeare in Love* (1999). Married to Imelda STAUNTON.
OTHER BRITISH FILMS INCLUDE: *Flash Gordon* (1980), *A Private Function* (1984), *A Month in the Country* (1987), *The Rainbow*, *Erik the Viking* (1989), *Crimestrike*, *The Fool* (1990), *Blame It on the Bellboy* (1992), *Black Beauty* (1994), *The Grotesque* (1996), *Keep the Aspidistra Flying* (1997), *The Little Vampire* (2000).

Carter, Maurice (*b* London, 1913 – *d* Buckinghamshire, 2000). Production designer. Credited for design on over 50 films, he worked on an unknown number of others at GAINSBOROUGH, including *Tudor Rose* (1936) and *Bank Holiday* (1938), before securing his first credit on *Bees in Paradise* (1944), having been appointed art director in 1942. In the 30s, he had the experience of working with other masters in his field, such as Alex VETCHINSKY and Alfred JUNGE. *Jassy* (1947) gave him his first brush with TECHNICOLOR, and his design gave the realist drama, *Good-Time Girl* (1947), a convincing surface; in the 50s, he worked steadily for the RANK ORGANISATION on a range of popular GENRES; and became involved in more ambitious, bigger-budgeted productions in the 60s and 70s, including *The Quiller Memorandum* (1966, UK/US) and *The First Great Train Robbery* (1978), and, his two Oscar-nominations, *Becket* (1964) and *Anne of the Thousand Days* (1969).
OTHER BRITISH FILMS INCLUDE: (draughtsman) *We Dive at Dawn* (1943); (ass art d): *The Lady Vanishes* (1938, unc), *Cottage to Let* (1941), *The Young Mr Pitt* (1942); (art d): *Christopher Columbus*, *Bad Lord Byron* (1949), *Trio* (1950), *White Corridors*, *Encore* (1951), *I Believe in You* (1952), *The Seekers* (1954), *The Spanish Gardener* (1956), *Campbell's Kingdom* (1957), *No Love for Johnnie*, *Double Bunk* (1961), *It's Trad, Dad!*, *Lancelot and Guinevere* (1962), *Guns at Batasi*, *The Beauty Jungle* (1964), *Kaleidoscope* (1966), *Battle of Britain* (1969, sup), *10 Rillington Place* (1970), *From Beyond the Grave* (1973), *The People That Time Forgot* (1977, + adpt), *North Sea Hijack* (1979).

Cartier, Rudolph (*b* Vienna, 1904 [also given as 1908] – *d* London, 1994). Screenwriter, director. RN: Katsher. Cartier filmed for Germany's UFA studios before WW2, came to London in 1935, and from 1952 had a long and influential association with the BBC as producer, famously for TV dramas, *The Quatermass Experiment* and *1984* (1954). His connection with cinema is limited: *The Man from Morocco* (1945, original story), *Corridor of Mirrors* (1948, p, sc), *The Man with the Twisted Lip* (1951, short, p), and *Passionate Summer* (1958, d).

Cartlidge, Katrin (*b* London, 1961 – *d* London, 2002). Actress. Apart from British director Mike LEIGH, she worked mainly with foreign film-makers, such as Lars von Trier in *Breaking the Waves* (1996, Den/Fr/Net/Nor/Swe), where her role as a nurse gained international critical acclaim. After a lengthy apprenticeship in the Royal Court Youth Theatre and TV's *Brookside*, Cartlidge was in her early 30s when offered her first major film role in Leigh's *Naked* (1993); as the listless junkie Sophie she won European Actress of the Year. Her idiosyncratic style perfectly suited Leigh's, and she went on to share the lead in his *Career Girls* (1997), for which, as Hannah Mills, she won an *Evening Standard* Film Award. She took on challenging, controversial work, not least her eponymous role in *Claire Dolan* (1998, Fr/US), as the furthest thing from Julia Roberts's version of the screen whore: reserved, elusive and always interesting. Her tragically early death resulted from complications following pneumonia and septicaemia.

OTHER BRITISH FILMS INCLUDE: *Eat the Rich* (1987), *Saint-Ex* (1996), *The Lost Son* (US/Fr/UK), *Topsy-Turvy* (UK/US), *Hotel Splendide* (UK/Fr) (2000). Melinda Hildebrandt.

Cary, Tristram (*b* Oxford, 1925). Composer. Novelist Joyce Cary's son, whose scores often drew on electronic music; he established a studio for its study at the RCM in the 60s. His films range from EALING COMEDY (*The Ladykillers*, 1955) to HAMMER HORROR (*Quatermass and the Pit*, 1967), as well as DOCUMENTARIES and ANIMATED FILMS. Took up an academic appointment in Adelaide, South Australia, in the 80s.

OTHER BRITISH FILMS INCLUDE: *Town on Trial* (1956), *The Little Island* (1958, anim, + sd fx), *The Prince and the Pauper* (1962), *Sammy Going South* (1963), *Twist of Sand* (1968), *Blood from the Mummy's Tomb* (1971), *When the Wind Blows* (1986, anim, m fx).

Case, Gerald (*b* England, 1904 – *d* 1985). Actor. Stage-trained supporting player in films from 1937; with BBC repertory company during WW2; and had a memorable moment, in a career full of military officers and police inspectors, in *Henry V* (1944) when his Westmoreland provides the cue for OLIVIER's St Crispin's Day speech. Mostly in 'B' MOVIES from the 50s.

OTHER BRITISH FILMS INCLUDE: *Museum Mystery* (1937), *The Lion Has Wings* (1939), *In Which We Serve* (1942), *I See a Dark Stranger* (1946), *Landfall* (1949), *Stage Fright* (1950), *Home at Seven*, *Hunted* (1952), *The Flying Scot*, *Barnacle Bill* (1957), *The Lady Is a Square* (1958), *Invasion Quartet* (1961), *Vampyres* (1974).

Cass, Henry (*b* London, 1902 – *d* Hastings, 1989). Director. In commerce 1916–23, then in the theatre as actor (London debut, 1931), then as director of several repertory companies and the Old Vic (1934–35). He remained a regular stage producer long after directing his – and Wendy HILLER's – first film, *Lancashire Lass* (1937). His subsequent film career can be divided into: DOCUMENTARIES for VERITY FILMS during WW2; his post-war features, most popularly the romantic drama, *The Glass Mountain* (1948, + sc), and the child-of-divorce piece, *No Place for Jennifer* (1949); a decline into unremarkable 'B' FILMS; and the Moral Rearmament fables with which he finished his career (on screen and stage). There are some mildly engaging comedies in the post-war period, mostly based on plays (*29 Acacia Avenue*, 1945; *Young Wives' Tale*, 1951) though the best of them, *Last Holiday* (1950), starring Alec GUINNESS, is an original by J.B. PRIESTLEY. Married (2) to actress Joan HOPKINS.

OTHER BRITISH FILMS INCLUDE: (short docs) *HMS Minelayer* (1941), *Common Cause* (1942), *Catholics in Britain* (1944); (features) *Father's Doing Fine*, *Castle in the Air* (1952), *High Terrace*, *The Crooked Sky* (+ p) (1956), *Blood of the Vampire* (1958), *The Hand*, *Boyd's Shop* (1960), *Happy Deathday* (1970, + sc).

Casson, Ann (*b* London, 1915 – *d* London, 1990). Actress. Blonde daughter of Sir Lewis CASSON and Dame Sybil THORNDIKE, who made several early 30s films, including the starring role of the doomed ballerina in *Dance Pretty Lady* (1932). Married to actor Douglas Campbell, with whom she appeared suddenly in the little-seen *I Bought a Vampire Motorcycle* in 1990! On stage from 1921.

OTHER BRITISH FILMS INCLUDE: *Escape* (1930), *The Shadow Between* (1931), *Number Seventeen* (1932), *George and Margaret* (1940).

Casson, Sir Lewis (*b* Birkenhead, 1875 – *d* London, 1969). Actor. Celebrated actor-husband (1908–69) of Dame Sybil THORNDIKE, who filmed occasionally over 35 years, in dignified roles such as the judge in *Little Friend* (1934). Still acting in his 80s. Knighted in 1945; president of Actors' Equity 1940–45.

OTHER BRITISH FILMS INCLUDE: *The Merchant of Venice* (1927, trial scene), *Escape* (1930), *Midshipman Easy* (1935), *Victoria the Great* (1937), *South Riding*, *Sixty Glorious Years* (1938), *The Winslow Boy* (1948), *Shake Hands with the Devil* (1959).

Castle, John (*b* Croydon, 1940). Actor. Interesting actor much seen on TV, notably starring in *Lost Empires* (1986) and as Joan HICKSON's foil in the Miss Marple telemovies, mainly in supporting roles on screen, though he did co-star with Susannah YORK in the Australian adventure, *Eliza Fraser* (1976). Remembered as the painter in *Blow-Up* (1966, UK/It) and one of the squabbling princes in *The Lion in Winter* (1968); also in some international films, such as *RoboCop 3* (1993). Married to screenwriter Maggie Wadey.

OTHER BRITISH FILMS INCLUDE: *Antony and Cleopatra* (1972, UK/Sp/Switz, as Octavius), *Made* (1972), *The Incredible Sarah* (1976, UK/US), *Eagle's Wing* (1978).

Castle, Roy (*b* Scholes, Yorkshire, 1932 – *d* Gerrards Cross, 1994). Actor. Stand-up comedian and tap-dancer who appeared in occasional films, starting with the lamentable musical *Hello London* (1958), as himself. Famous as TV presenter of *Record Breakers* (1972–92). Awarded OBE in 1993.

OTHER BRITISH FILMS INCLUDE: *Dr Terror's House of Horrors* (1964), *Dr Who and the Daleks* (1965), *The Plank* (1967), *Carry On Up the Khyber* (1968), *Legend of the Werewolf* (1974).

Cates, Georgina (*b* London, 1975). Actress. RN: Clare Woodgate. Though she was affecting in the role of the teenager seduced by the provincial theatre in *An Awfully Big Adventure* (1995), the film was not popular and her next British film was the little-seen spoof of MERCHANT IVORY period pieces, *Stiff Upper Lips* (1996). Married to actor Skeet Ulrich, she lives in the US where her later films, including *Big City Blues* (1999), were made.

OTHER BRITISH FILMS: *Au Pair* (1994, UK/Ger/Austria), *Loving* (1995).

Caton-Jones, Michael (*b* Broxburn, Scotland, 1958). Director. Most of his films have been US-made but there are at least two proficient and popular British titles: *Scandal* (1988) and *Memphis Belle* (1990); and the US-made *Rob Roy* (1995) is set in Scotland. A graduate of the National Film School where his SHORTS won attention.

Cattaneo, Peter (*b* London, 1965). Director. After an AA-nominated short film, *Dear Rosie* (1990), and some TV work, Cattaneo directed *The Full Monty* (1997, UK/US), a witty, poignant study of out-of-work Sheffield steel-workers, which became the most commercially successful British film until then. Followed this with *Lucky Break* (2001, UK/Ger/US), a prison-set comedy, at the old EALING STUDIOS. Awarded MBE in 1998.

OTHER BRITISH FILMS: *Budding Prospects* (1999).

Catto, Max (*b* Manchester, 1907 – *d* London, 1992). Author. Popular novelist and playwright, a dozen of whose works have been adapted to the screen, including the play, *They Walk Alone*, as the remarkable Gothic piece, *Daughter of Darkness* (1947), and the novel *Murphy's War*, filmed in 1971. Also (co-)wrote screenplays for *Take Me to Paris* (1950) and *West of Zanzibar* (1954).

OTHER BRITISH FILMS: (adapted works) *The Happy Family* (1936), *The Flanagan Boy* (1953), *A Prize of Gold* (1955), *A Hill in Korea* (1956), *Fire Down Below* (1957), *Ferry to Hong Kong* (1959), *Mister Moses* (1965).

Cavalcanti, Alberto (*b* Rio de Janeiro, 1897 – *d* Paris, 1982). Director, producer. Before he came to Britain, Cavalcanti had already enjoyed a distinguished career as an avant-garde film-maker in France. His *Rien que les heures*, shot in the streets of Paris in 1924, made a huge impact on the British documentarists when it was shown at the FILM SOCIETY in London. In 1934, tired of making routine comedies at Paramount's Billancourt studios, he accepted John GRIERSON's invitation to experiment with SOUND and to pass on his expertise to the young film-makers of the GPO FILM UNIT. More than any other individual, Cavalcanti gave practical meaning to Grierson's definition of DOCUMENTARY as the 'creative interpretation of reality'. While Grierson had always placed an emphasis on the social and educational utility of documentary, Cavalcanti encouraged realist film-making to develop in a more aesthetic direction.

Often uncredited or under-credited for his contributions, Cavalcanti remains one of the unsung individuals in the British cinema. Although he enjoyed only the modest credit of 'sound director', he was the presiding influence over *Night Mail* (1936). Exploiting the full possibilities of montage and sound, the film forged a poetic style and paved the way for the work of two of Cavalcanti's leading disciples at the unit, Len LYE and Humphrey JENNINGS.

In 1940 he joined EALING STUDIOS. Never happy with the word 'documentary' or the often arbitrary distinctions made between factual and fictional film-making, Cavalcanti was able at Ealing to move freely between the two. He supervised both the documentary and feature output of the studio, but also directed a number of features of his own, notably the surreal wartime thriller *Went the Day Well?* (1942), the musical *Champagne Charlie* (1944), which introduced a new sophistication to Ealing comedy, and the chilling 'Ventriloquist's Dummy' episode in the PORTMANTEAU FILM, *Dead of Night* (1945). He made three more features away from Ealing, most notably the crime drama *They Made Me a Fugitive* (1947). He left England in 1950 to help establish a revitalised film industry in his native Brazil.

OTHER BRITISH FILMS INCLUDE: (d) (short, doc) *Pett and Pott* (1934), *Coal Face* (1935), *We Live in Two Worlds* (1937), *Four Barriers* (1938), *Yellow Caesar* (1940), *Greek Testament, Film and Reality* (1942); (features) *Nicholas Nickleby* (1947), *The First Gentleman* (1948), *For Them That Trespass* (1948), *The Monster of Highgate Pond* (1960); (p, doc) *N or NW* (1937), *North Sea* (1938), *Spare Time, The First Days* (1939), *Men of the Lightship* (1940). Charles Drazin.

Cazenove, Christopher (*b* Winchester, 1945). Actor, Fair-haired, affable leading man with aristocratic manner. Ideally suited to MERCHANT IVORY productions *Heat and Dust* (1982) and *The Proprietor* (1996, UK/Fr/Turk/US), but best known for TV work in *The Duchess of Duke Street* (1976–77) and, in the US, as Joan COLLINS's love interest in *Dynasty* (1986–87). Primarily US-based, where he made his stage debut in *Goodbye Fidel* (1980), his films include *Three Men and a Little Lady* (1990). He was impressive as Alec in the London stage version of *Brief Encounter* (2000). Married (1974–94) to Angharad REES.

OTHER BRITISH FILMS INCLUDE: *There's a Girl in My Soup* (1970), *Royal Flash* (1975), *East of Elephant Rock* (1976), *Zulu Dawn* (1979), *Eye of the Needle* (1981), *Souvenir* (1987). AS.

Celi, Adolfo (*b* Messina, Sicily, 1922 – *d* Siena, Italy, 1986). Actor. White-haired Italian character actor, also director and screenwriter, who featured in many international – and ten British – films, and is best remembered as the villain Largo in *Thunderball* (1965).

OTHER BRITISH FILMS INCLUDE: *The Bobo* (1967), *In Search of Gregory* (1969, UK/It), *Fragment of Fear* (1970), *Hitler: The Last Ten Days, The Tempter* (1973, UK/It), *And Then There Were None* (1974).

Cellier, Antoinette (*b* Broadstairs, 1913 – *d* London, 1981). Actress. Attractive daughter of Frank CELLIER, a stage actress who made 15 films in the 30s and 40s, remembered as spirited heroine in the Canada-set adventure, *The Great Barrier* (1937), spinster sister in *Dear Octopus* (1943), and cross queen of island women in *Bees in Paradise* (1944). In TV plays from 1936. Married Sir Bruce SETON.

OTHER BRITISH FILMS INCLUDE: *Late Extra, Royal Cavalcade* (1935), *The Tenth Man* (1936), *At the Villa Rose* (1939), *Headline* (1943), *The End of the River* (1947), *Reach for the Sky* (1956, unc).

Cellier, Frank (*b* Surbiton, 1884 – *d* London, 1948). Actor. Imposing character actor, with no-nonsense features, who played unscrupulous, benign or imperious with equal facility throughout the 30s and 40s. He is in some of GAINSBOROUGH's deftest 30s entertainments, including HITCHCOCK's *The 39 Steps* (1935, as the sheriff), *Tudor Rose* (1936, as Henry VIII) and *The Man Who Changed His Mind* (1936, as a ruthless tycoon), and he was memorable as Deborah KERR's seducer in *Love on the Dole* (1941). He was, in fact, *always* memorable, in the great tradition of British character acting. Father of Antoinette and Peter CELLIER; married (2) **Phyllis Shannaw**, who appeared in several silent films.

OTHER BRITISH FILMS INCLUDE: *Her Reputation* (1931), *Soldiers of the King* (1933), *Jew Süss, Lorna Doone* (1934), *The Passing of the Third Floor Back, The Guv'nor* (1935), *Action for Slander, Non-Stop New York* (1937), *Sixty Glorious Years, The Ware Case* (1938), *Jeannie, Cottage to Let* (1941), *Quiet Weekend* (1946), *The Blind Goddess* (1948).

Cellier, Peter (*b* Barnet, 1928). Actor. Harrow-educated, trained with Leatherhead Rep, Cellier has been a distinctive character player since the 60s, usually in well-bred, urbane roles, such as the three he had in MERCHANT IVORY films, *A Room with a View* (1985), *Howards End* (1992), *Remains of the Day* (1993), as Lord Lexham in *Mrs Dalloway* (1997, UK/Neth/US) and almost the only Caucasian character in *Bhaji on the Beach* (1993). Also much theatre, with RSC and National Theatre seasons, and TV, including most popular series of the last few decades. Son of Frank CELLIER and Phyllis Shannaw, half-brother of Antoinette CELLIER.

OTHER BRITISH FILMS INCLUDE: *Morgan: A Suitable Case for Treatment* (1966), *Young Winston* (1972), *Barry Lyndon, Man Friday* (1975), *Jabberwocky* (1977), *Chariots of Fire* (1981), *Clockwise* (1985), *Personal Services* (1987).

censorship Since 1912, British film censorship has been vested principally in the British Board of Film Censors (from 1985 'Classification' replaced 'Censors'). Although set up voluntarily by the film industry itself and with no mandatory obligations to submit films for approval, it soon became an unwritten law among renters that only certificated films would go on release into cinemas. On the Home Secretary's recommendations, moreover, most local authorities fell into line and accepted the BBFC's rapidly evolving film classifications policy. Working initially under the simple maxim that there should be 'no nudity' or manifestations of 'the figure of Christ', the list of banned subjects was increased to 43 in number by T.P. O'Connor, the Board's second president, dealing essentially with matters of moral concern (prostitution, seduction, pre-marital and extramarital sex, perversion, swearing, etc.) though also with 'controversial' political issues.

With the advent of sound film in the late 20s, the introduction of pre-production scrutiny of scripts or scenarios, together with the existing facility for postproduction review before award of a certificate, ensured conformity of theme and treatment. The GAUMONT–BRITISH PICTURE CORPORATION's proposal to film Walter GREENWOOD's renowned 30s depression novel, *Love on the Dole*, was considered 'very undesirable' on the grounds, for instance, that it threatened to depict 'too much of the tragic and sordid side of poverty'. By contrast, John BAXTER's *A Real Bloke* (1935) was allowed because its unemployed worker 'doesn't whine and whimper but tries to keep his chin up bravely'. In the changed circumstances of WW2 Britain, however, *Love on the Dole* was finally permitted as a film (1941). Its theme was no longer controversial and the need to engage the people directly in the war effort through meaningful PROPAGANDA was paramount. Ironically, albeit under severe control from the MINISTRY OF INFORMATION, British film censorship enjoyed a new measure of relaxation. Though Winston CHURCHILL personally railed against *The Life and Death of Colonel Blimp* (1943), and did much to stall its progress and release, the censorship authorities sensibly realised for their part that nothing could (or perhaps should) ultimately be done to prevent its EXHIBITION in a democracy.

The story of post-war censorship is inextricably linked with the BBFC's desire to lend added 'quality' to British cinema. Thus, the 'X' certificate was introduced in 1951 precisely to invest the category with 'good adult entertainment and films which appeal to an intelligent public'. But it was really only under John TREVELYAN's enlightened stewardship as secretary (1958–71) that notable advances were made on this front. By judiciously (yet still sometimes acrimoniously) courting the 'NEW WAVE' film-makers, in particular, a significant though small body of films was produced (e.g. *Saturday Night and Sunday Morning*, 1960; *A Taste of Honey*, 1961) that signalled a revival in British cinema's fortunes and accorded neatly with the increasing 'permissiveness' of 60s society at large. Owing most to social REALISM for its themes or style and literary pedigree for provenance – the key criteria, as ever, of 'quality' British cinema – they served also to marginalise more demanding films such as Michael POWELL's *Peeping Tom* (1960) which were traditionally deemed to be 'sensational', 'exploitative' and 'offensive' to the mainstream critical consensus. Little appears to have changed in that regard.

'Sex and violence' may have become the ubiquitous watchwords of censorship concern since the 70s but the means whereby they are adjudged remain the same and the dilemmas posed for the BBFC are manifestly similar. How best to balance the prevailing criteria of artistic excellence with the need to take account of public opinion generally as well as the diametrically-opposed yet pervasive forces exerted, in particular, by those demanding greater liberalisation and freedom of expression, on the one hand, and those advocating more restrictions or enhanced limits, on the other? When James FERMAN resigned in 1998, after fully 23 years at the BBFC as, first, the secretary and, latterly, its director, he felt there was evidence of greater tolerance in society and sufficient, at least, to allow of increased latitude over the depiction of sex though not of violence which should continue to be strictly curtailed. Whether his successors agree, or not, remains to be seen.

BIBLIOG: Anthony Aldgate, *Censorship and the Permissive Society, British Cinema and Theatre 1955–1965*, 1995; James C. Robertson, *The Hidden Cinema: British Film Censorship in Action 1913–1972*, 1989; John Trevelyan, *What the Censor Saw*, 1973. Tony Aldgate.

Chadbon, Tom (*b* Luton, 1946). Actor. RADA-trained, on stage from 1967 (often with the Royal Court), TV from 1968 (including a village lothario in *Midsomer Murders*, 2000) and film from 1972 (*The Alf Garnett Saga*), appearing as Angel's censorious brother in *Tess* (1979, UK/Fr).
OTHER BRITISH FILMS INCLUDE: *Juggernaut* (1974), *Dance with a Stranger* (1984), *Shooting Fish* (1997), *A Life for a Life* (1998).

Chadha, Gurinder (*b* Kenya, 1960) Director. Wrote and directed the attractive feature, *Bhaji on the Beach* in 1993, illuminating racial and gender tensions, and has subsequently made several short films, the telemovie *A Nice Arrangement* (1994, + sc), and has filmed in the US and Canada. Married to Paul Mayeda Berges, co-scenarist on her *What's Cooking?* (2001, UK/US). Had a popular success with the football comedy, *Bend It like Beckham* (2002).

Chaffey, Don (*b* Hastings, 1917 – *d* Kawau Island, NZ, 1990). Director. Starting his career in the art department at GAINSBOROUGH in 1944, Chaffey went on to become a workmanlike director for over 30 years, the last mainly in American TV. Among early films he worked on at LIME GROVE STUDIOS are *Madonna of the Seven Moons* (1944) and *The Wicked Lady* (1945); he was assistant art director on *The Rake's Progress* (1945) and art director on *Theirs is the Glory* (1946, doc) and several minor films, before beginning his long career as director. After several thrillers, including *The Man Upstairs* (1958), EXPLOITATION pieces like *The Flesh Is Weak* (1957) and *A Question of Adultery* (1958), on the theme of artificial insemination, and comedies like *Dentist in the Chair* (1960), he made such a success of *Greyfriars Bobby* (1961) that DISNEY retained him for several further features, such as *The Three Lives of Thomasina* (1963) and *Ride the Wild Pony* (US/Australia). As well, he efficiently steered such fantasies as *Jason and the Argonauts* (1963) and *One Million Years BC* (1966), with Ray HARRYHAUSEN's SPECIAL EFFECTS, but his most likeable work is in his child-orientated films, and he directed films for the CHILDREN'S FILM FOUNDATION in the late 40s.
OTHER BRITISH FILMS INCLUDE: (d) *Cape Cargoes* (1948, short), *The Mysterious Poacher* (1949, re-edited 1972), *Time Is My Enemy* (1954), *The Secret Tent* (1956), *Danger Within* (1958), *A Matter of WHO* (1961), *The Crooked Road* (1964), *The Viking Queen* (1966), *Creatures the World Forgot* (1970), *Persecution* (1974).

Chagrin, Francis (*b* Bucharest, 1905 – *d* London, 1972). Composer. After entering French films in 1934, Chagrin settled permanently in England in 1938, working at first on DOCUMENTARY films and MOI PROPAGANDA SHORTS, with titles like *Behind the Guns* (1940) and *Canteen on Wheels* (1941). He also made films for the Dutch Government (1944). His first British feature film scores were for *The Silent Battle* (1939) and *Law and Disorder* (1940), and post-war he worked on a range of mainstream films, such as *Last Holiday* (1950) and several war films, including *The Colditz Story* (1954) and *Danger Within* (1958). His son, **Julian Chagrin** (*b* London, 1940), is an actor and mime, appearing as the latter in *Blow-Up* (1966, UK/It).
OTHER BRITISH FILMS INCLUDE: *Easy Money* (1948), *The Happy Family* (1952), *The Intruder* (1953), *An Inspector Calls*, *The Beachcomber* (1954), *Simba* (1955), *Charley Moon* (1956), *No Time for Tears* (1957), *Greyfriars Bobby* (1961), *In the Cool of the Day* (1963).

Challis, Christopher (*b* London, 1919). Cinematographer. Started his career in the British film industry as a camera assistant on GAUMONT–BRITISH NEWSREELS. During WW2, he served as a cameraman with the RAF, and post-war he worked as camera operator to Jack CARDIFF on his films for the ARCHERS, for whom he shot his first film as cinematographer, *The End of the River* (1947). His most notable work at this time was for Archers, including the black-and-white drama, *The Small Back Room* (1948), with its famous expressionist touches ('some Caligari lighting' as Michael POWELL described it), and the ambitious TECHNICOLOR productions, *Gone to Earth* and *The Elusive Pimpernel* (1950), *The Tales of Hoffmann* (1951), *Oh, Rosalinda!!* (1955), and the war film *The Battle of the River Plate* (1956), as well the black-and-white *Ill Met By Moonlight* (1956). Apart from this often highly imaginative work for Powell, he was extremely busy on other sorts of 50s and 60s film: he is responsible for the wonderfully sunny look of *Genevieve* (1953), shot in trying location circumstances, for the muted Victoriana of *Footsteps in the Fog* (1955), for such large-scale adventure films as *The Adventures of Quentin Durward* (1955), *The Long Ships* (1963) and *Those Magnificent Men . . .* (1965), as well as most of Stanley DONEN's British-made films, including *The Grass Is Greener* (1960) and Billy Wilder's gorgeously decorative *The Private Life of Sherlock Holmes* (1970). He made one or two US films (*The Flame and the Flesh*, 1954; *The Little Prince*, 1974; *Top Secret!*, 1984), but his is essentially a triumphant British career.

OTHER BRITISH FILMS INCLUDE: *Angels One Five* (1952), *Saadia* (1953), *The Spanish Gardener* (1956), *Blind Date* (1959), *Flame in the Streets* (1961), *HMS Defiant* (1962), *The Victors* (1963), *Two for the Road* (1966), *A Dandy in Aspic*, *Chitty Chitty Bang Bang* (1968), *Mary Queen of Scots*, *Follow Me!* (1971), *Mister Quilp* (1974), *The Mirror Crack'd* (1980), *Steaming* (1984).

BIBLIOG: Autobiography, *Are They Really So Awful? A Cameraman's Chronicle*, 1995.

Chamberlain, Cyril (*b* London, 1909 – *d* London, 1974). Actor. Bluff, solidly enjoyable character actor with receding hair, on stage from 1931; started a film career in 1939 but was interrupted by war service (1941–46), after which he appeared in a further 80 films. Usually in small roles, often as policemen, military rankers, officials of various kinds; sometimes shifty, like the deserter-cyclist in *A Boy, a Girl and a Bike* (1949), sometimes comic, as in seven 'CARRY ON' films. Memorable even in tiny roles such as the father of the TV-viewing family in *Simon and Laura* (1955).

OTHER BRITISH FILMS INCLUDE: *Ask a Policeman* (1939), *The Common Touch* (1941), *Dancing with Crime* (1947), *Boys in Brown* (1949), *The Lavender Hill Mob*, *Lady Godiva Rides Again* (1951), *Trouble in Store* (1953), *Above Us the Waves* (1955), *Just My Luck* (1957), *A Night to Remember* (1958), *Carry On Constable* (1960), *Flame in the Streets* (1961), *Carry On Cabby* (1963), *The Great St Trinian's Train Robbery* (1966).

Chamberlain, Richard (*b* Los Angeles, 1935). Actor. American-born actor who has worked in Britain on the stage, screen and TV. Durable, if somewhat bland, star of TV's *Dr Kildare* (1961–66), Chamberlain has had some of his most interesting chances in Britain: as the playboy husband in *Petulia* (1968), Octavius in *Julius Caesar* (1970), Tchaikovsky in Ken RUSSELL's often repellent *The Music Lovers* (1971), Lord Byron in *Lady Caroline Lamb* (1972, UK/It/US), and as Ralph Touchett in TV's *The Portrait of a Lady* (1968). Mostly TV and costume romps in the last two decades, and some return to the stage.

OTHER BRITISH FILMS: *The Madwoman of Chaillot* (1969), *The Count of Monte Cristo* (1974), *The Slipper and the Rose* (1976, as the Prince).

Chance, Naomi (*b* Bath, 1930). Actress. Most at home playing 'mistresses', whether to 'B' FILM leading man, Patrick HOLT, in *Suspended Alibi* (1956), or, as Lily Langtry, to Edward VII in *The Trials of Oscar Wilde* (1960), this striking blonde could also be wholesomely sisterly in *Dangerous Voyage* (1954) or adjust convincingly to the cramped working-class domesticity of *The End of the Road* (1954). On stage from 1947 and TV from 1951, and a welcome presence in 50s 'B' movies.

OTHER BRITISH FILMS INCLUDE: *Wings of Danger* (1952), *Blood Orange* (1953), *The Man Inside* (1958), *He Who Rides the Tiger* (1965).

Chancellor, Anna (*b* London, 1964). Actress. Tall, elegant player who made her mark as Henrietta, jilted at the altar by Hugh GRANT in *Four Weddings and a Funeral* (1994) and as the ineffably snooty Caroline Bingley in TV's *Pride and Prejudice* (1995).

OTHER BRITISH FILMS INCLUDE: *Killing Dad* (1989), *Century* (1993), *Staggered*, *Tom & Viv* (1994, UK/US), *Heart* (1999), *Crush* (2001, UK/Ger).

Chandos, John (*b* Glasgow, 1917 – *d* 1987). Actor. Entered films in 1940 in *49th Parallel* as the penultimate survivor of the Germans fleeing across Canada, initiating a series of corrupt types, such as the child molester whose presence on board helps bring about *The Ship That Died of Shame* and the blackmailer in *One Way Out* (both 1955). There are occasional comedy roles, as in *Doctor at Large* (1957), but he is most vivid as slimy villains.

OTHER BRITISH FILMS INCLUDE: *The Next of Kin* (1942), *Nicholas Nickleby* (1947), *Secret People* (1951), *The Love Lottery* (1953), *Simba* (1955), *The Green Man* (1956), *I Accuse!* (1957), *Jungle Street* (1961).

Channel 4 and British Cinema Launched in 1982, the UK's fourth terrestrial television channel is widely credited with keeping the flame of British film-making alive in the 1980s at a time when successive Conservative Governments refused any kind of state support for the industry. The public Channel 4 Television Corporation established a separate films arm – Film on Four. Its remit was to cross-subsidise British film production with television money to create not only a stream of high quality film drama for the Channel to screen but also throw out a much-needed life-line to the struggling British film industry. Under the leadership of David Rose, Film on Four funded films first for cinema release, prior to subsequent television transmission and some of its early successes were spectacular, including Peter GREENAWAY's *The Draughtsman's Contract* (1982), Neil JORDAN's *Angel* (1982) and Stephen FREARS'/Hanif KUREISHI's *My Beautiful Laundrette* (1985). The 90s saw a more commercially orientated policy but one which often paid box-office dividends in terms of international hits like *Four Weddings and a Funeral* (1994) and *Trainspotting* (1996). In the late 90s, FilmFour, as it was now called, gained its own dedicated subscription TV channel, screening both its own fare and a range of independent, 'challenging' cinema from around the world. However, by July 2002, retrenchment had set in as Channel 4 regained control of its independent film subsidiary, slashing its annual budget for film production largely as the result of a general downturn in TV advertising. Channel 4's contribution to contemporary British cinema had been immense but the demise of FilmFour raised uncomfortable questions about the involvement of television money in film production: for example, to what extent the priorities of commercial television would always in the end take precedence over film and to what extent the scale and ambition of British film-making would always inevitably be reduced to that of low-budget 'television movies' to the detriment of the overall health of both British cinema *and* arguably, indigenous British television drama.

OTHER TITLES INCLUDE: *Walter* (1982), *The Ploughman's Lunch* (1983), *Company of Wolves* (1984), *Wetherby, A Zed & Two Noughts* (1985), *Wish You Were Here* (1987), *The Cook, the Thief, His Wife & Her Lover* (1989), *Riff-Raff, Hear My Song* (1991), *Naked* (1993), *Shallow Grave* (1994), *The Madness of King George, Land and Freedom* (1995), *Brassed Off, Secrets & Lies* (1996), *Velvet Goldmine* (1998), *East Is East* (2000).

BIBLIOG: Peter Ansorge, *From Liverpool to Los Angeles: On Writing for Theatre, Film and Television*, 1997; John Pym, *Film on Four: Ten Years of Film on Four*, 1992. John Cook.

Chaplin, Sir Charles (*b* Walworth, 1889 – *d* Courrier-sur-Vevey, Switzerland, 1977). Actor, director, producer, screenwriter, composer. It is an ironic fact that the screen career of one of the most eminent British film-makers should be largely irrelevant to British cinema. The well-known story embraces the not-very-successful MUSIC HALL parents, the poverty-stricken London childhood, the arrival in New York in 1910 with Fred KARNO's music-hall troupe, and, in 1913, the signing with Mack Sennett of a contract which took him to Hollywood. Once there, he became the most famous film star in the world, working prolifically, but he only filmed in Britain 40 years later when he left the political paranoia of 50s America and settled in Europe. Sadly, the two films he made in Britain at the end of his career, *A King in New York* (1957) and *A Countess from Hong Kong* (1966), failed with critics and public alike, anachronisms with little more than nostalgic interest. The rest of his story – the days of his glory – belongs to another country and in another book.

Chaplin, Geraldine (*b* Santa Monica, California, 1944). Actress. Born in America, the eldest daughter of Charlie CHAPLIN from his marriage to Oona O'Neill (and granddaughter of Eugene), this fragile, graceful beauty has had an interesting international career without ever achieving – perhaps not seeking – certifiable stardom. She first filmed as a child in her father's last American film, *Limelight* (1951), was a touching Tonya in the bloated *Doctor Zhivago* (1965, UK/US), a gracious Queen in *The Three Musketeers* (1973, Panama), and very funny and vulnerable as 'Opal from the BBC' in *Nashville* (1975, US). She did some of her most compelling work for Spanish film-maker, Carlos Saura (with whom she had a long relationship), including the enigmatic *Cria Cuevos* (1976). In 1992, she played her own grandmother in *Chaplin* (UK/US/Fr/It/Jap) and evinced the right social constraint as Winona Ryder's mother in the sublime *The Age of Innocence* (1993). It is not a 'British' career: she is a true product of her heritage: but there are some real grace notes in her British films.

OTHER BRITISH FILMS INCLUDE: *Stranger in the House, Innocent Bystanders* (1972), *The Mirror Crack'd* (1980), *White Mischief* (1987), *The Return of the Musketeers* (1989, UK/Fr/Sp), *To Walk with Lions* (2000).

Chaplin, Sydney (*b* Los Angeles, 1926). Actor. Named for his father's elder half-brother, this son of Charlie CHAPLIN and actor Lita Grey has had only a minor career in international films, including five British productions. Most interesting was Ken HUGHES's *Confession* (1955), as a criminal who is ambivalent at being back in the family nest and falls to his death from a church's organ loft. Had more success on the Broadway musical stage.

OTHER BRITISH FILMS: *Abdullah the Great* (1954), *Follow That Man* (1961), *A Countess from Hong Kong* (1966), *The Adding Machine* (1969).

Chapman, Constance (*b* Weston-super-Mare, 1912). Actress. In films since 1970 after successes in other acting media, including stints with the Bristol Old Vic. She repeated her stage role (and London debut) as the mother in Lindsay ANDERSON's *In Celebration* (1974, UK/Can).

OTHER BRITISH FILMS INCLUDE: *The Raging Moon* (1970), *O Lucky Man!* (1973), *Hedda* (1975), *Clockwise* (1985).

Chapman, Edward (*b* Harrogate, 1901 – *d* Brighton, 1977). Actor. Six years a bank clerk before joining Nottingham Rep in 1924 and entering films in HITCHCOCK's *Juno and the Paycock* (1930) as Captain Boyle. He never looked back and, apart from war service in the RAF (1941–45) was for four decades a solid, stocky tower – or turret – of strength in British films. His characteristic persona conveyed middle-class respectability, mostly benign, but susceptible to dangerous impulse (*The October Man*, 1947), to deviousness (*Mandy*, 1952), to cruelty (*The Intruder*, 1953) and to deflatable pomposity (in Norman WISDOM vehicles, as Mr Grimsdale). The gallery of 80 roles makes choice difficult, but he is perhaps at his most subtly touching as Googie WITHERS' kind, unimaginative husband in *It Always Rains on Sunday* (1947).

OTHER BRITISH FILMS: *Murder!, Caste* (1930), *The Skin Game* (1931), *The Flying Squad, Happy Ever After* (1932), *The Divine Spark, Royal Cavalcade* (narrator), (1935), *Things to Come, Rembrandt* (1936), *The Citadel* (1938), *There Ain't No Justice* (1939), *Ships with Wings, Jeannie* (1941), *Mr Perrin and Mr Traill* (1948), *Madeleine* (1949), *Night and the City, Gone to Earth* (1950), *The Card, The Ringer* (1952), *End of the Road* (1954), *Bhowani Junction* (1995), *X the Unknown* (1956), *The Square Peg* (1958), *Oscar Wilde, The Bulldog Breed* (1960), *The Early Bird* (1965), *The Man Who Haunted Himself* (1970).

Chapman, Graham (*b* Leicester, 1941 – *d* Maidstone, 1989). Actor, screenwriter. An influential member of the MONTY PYTHON group, Chapman met John CLEESE at Cambridge and together they contributed scripts for such TV shows as *Doctor in the House* and for such films as *The Magic Christian* (1969, + a) and *The Rise and Rise of Michael Rimmer* (1970, + a). Their chief claim to fame was the anarchic TV comedy series *Monty Python's Flying Circus* (1969–70, 1972–74) and Chapman's main film credits (a, sc) were on Python-related films such as *And Now for Something Completely Different* (1971), *Monty Python and the Holy Grail* (1974), *The Life of Brian* (1979, as Brian and others), *The Secret Policeman's Other Ball* (1982), *Yellowbeard* (1983).

OTHER BRITISH FILMS INCLUDE: *Doctor in Trouble* (1970, a), *Rentadick* (1972, sc), *The Odd Job* (1978, a, sc, p), *Monty Python's The Meaning of Life* (1983, a, sc, comp), *Love Potion* (1987, p).

Chapman, John (*b* London, 1927 – *d* Périgueux, France, 2001). Writer. Former actor, RADA-trained, who became an immensely successful playwright, the author of such famous farces as *Dry Rot* (1954) and *Simple Spymen* (1958). The former was filmed in 1956; he also wrote screenplays for *Nothing Barred* (1961) and *Not Now, Darling* (1972), from the play by fellow farceur Ray COONEY, and the two co-wrote *There Goes the Bride* (1973), filmed in 1979. Was married to **Betty Impey**, who appeared in a few British films, including *Quatermass 2* (1957).

character actors This term usually implies players other than those in starring roles. If one thinks about it, it tends to suggest that stars aren't acting 'characters', but the generally understood concept is of supporting actors/actresses, often playing 'types' who are recognisable from film to film. They can occasionally play starring roles, but not the conventional male and female leads. Some actors, such as Edward G. Robinson, made careers as character stars; in British film, Alec GUINNESS is perhaps the key instance, though others such as Leslie BANKS, Alastair SIM, Stanley HOLLOWAY, Jack WARNER, Margaret RUTHERFORD or even Robert CARLYLE might qualify for such designation. Occasionally, too, stars in later life become successful character players, as did Phyllis CALVERT, James MASON and Vanessa REDGRAVE.

In British cinema, character actors have been one of the great continuing strengths. Genuine stars with sustained careers in British films are harder to come across, partly because the star-making apparatus, with a few exceptions, was never as efficient as its US counterpart, and partly because, once British actors showed a glimpse of that indefinable 'star quality' – from Leslie HOWARD through Merle OBERON to Ewan McGREGOR – Hollywood was likely to make them unrefusable offers. The character actors, often with backgrounds in the English theatre, tended to stay at home more reliably, though even they were solicited by Hollywood, to add authenticity to British-set American films. They were often to be found acting, sometimes starring, in the THEATRE by night, while filming at DENHAM or ELSTREE by day, and later they provided one of the best reasons for watching British TELEVISION. Survivors such as the great Dora BRYAN recall starring on the West End eight times a week and arriving at studios at crack of dawn to be given their dialogue to learn in the make-up chair.

Though one can still be delighted today by, say, a Robert HARDY or Elizabeth SPRIGGS turning up in *Sense and Sensibility* (1995), the heyday of the character players was probably from the 30s to the late 50s. In the class-stratified way of British cinema of the period, with its roots in the theatre, there were assorted professional men, military types, nightclub-owners and other low-lifers or maids, housewives, tarts and dowagers providing moments of pure pleasure in films substantial and piffling. All films were more entertaining for having on board the likes of Raymond HUNTLEY, endlessly disapproving, Edward CHAPMAN, probably but not certainly respectable, Richard WATTIS wryly anticipating the worst, Michael BALFOUR sailing cheerfully close to the legal wind, or Maurice DENHAM presiding benignly over troubled circumstances – when he wasn't playing a yokel policeman, that is. Among the women, there are the insecurely refined Irene HANDL, the comically predatory Joan SIMS, gossipy Everley GREGG, *grandes dames* such as Ambrosine PHILLPOTTS, drudges like Beatrice VARLEY and comfy housekeepers like Amy VENNESS. The list is endless and includes pairs like Basil RADFORD and Naunton WAYNE, ever-anxious about the cricket, and the entire cast of the 'CARRY ON' series.

The preceding names belong essentially to the studio decades; different character players came to prominence with the 'NEW WAVE' of the early 60s, including Colin BLAKELY, Peter JEFFREY, Michael HORDERN, Billie WHITELAW, Ann LYNN and Gwen NELSON. There were also regional character players, such as Kenneth GRIFFITH, Mervyn JOHNS (Wales), Sara ALLGOOD and Maire O'NEILL from an earlier period, Joseph TOMELTY (Ireland), Gordon JACKSON and Wylie WATSON (Scotland). And as one today admires Richenda CAREY, Kathy BURKE, Ken STOTT, Peter CELLIER or Oliver FORD DAVIES, there seems reason to believe the tradition is not wholly extinct. There is no room here to do more than hint at the riches these actors embody; the breed has not died out but is still required to fill out the texture, the reality of the situations in which their more famous and/or glamorous colleagues occupy the foreground.

Charles, Moie Screenwriter. Entered films with *The Gentle Sex* (1943) as co-author of the screeenplay based on her own story of women at war, provided additional dialogue for the Margaret LOCKWOOD wicked-woman thriller, *Bedelia* (1946) and co-wrote the screenplay for the Lockwood romance, *The White Unicorn* (1947).

OTHER BRITISH FILMS: *When the Bough Breaks* (story), *Master of Bankdam* (co-sc) (1947), *Dark Secret* (1949, sc), *The Scarlet Thread* (co-sc, co-play), *Hell Is Sold Out* (co-sc) (1951), *The Crowded Day* (1954, co-story).

Charles Urban Trading Co. *see* **Urban, Charles**

Charleson, Ian (*b* Edinburgh, 1949 – *d* London, 1990). Actor. First British show business celebrity whose death from AIDS was reported in media, despite his being a closeted gay man who never acknowledged his first screen role as the gay Angel, complete with frontal nudity, in Derek Jarman's *Jubilee* (1978). Gained international stardom as Eric Liddell in *Chariots of Fire* (1981), followed by *Gandhi* (1982, UK/Ind), but also remembered for his theatre work (London debut 1972), including at the National Theatre, *Guys and Dolls* (1982), *Cat on a Hot Tin Roof* (1988) and *Hamlet* (1989), only weeks before his death.

OTHER BRITISH FILMS: *Ascendancy* (1982), *Greystoke* . . . (1984, UK/US), *Car Trouble* (1985). AS.

Charlesworth, John (*b* Hull, 1935 – *d* Birmingham, 1960). Actor. Teenage performer who committed suicide. Was in such films as *Tom Brown's Schooldays* (1951), as East, several CHILDREN'S FILM FOUNDATION productions and 'B' MOVIES, with the occasional 'A' such as *The Angry Silence* (1960). On radio as a child.

OTHER BRITISH FILMS INCLUDE: *Scrooge*, *The Magic Box* (1951), *The Blue Peter* (1955), *Yangtse Incident* (1956), *The Man Upstairs*, *A Question of Adultery* (1958).

'Charm School' *see* **Company of Youth**

Chase, James Hadley (*b* London, 1906 – *d* Corseaux, Switzerland, 1985). Author, screenwriter. Very popular, scarcely subtle crime writer, many of whose novels were set in a violent America of the mind, like his first book, *No Orchids for Miss Blandish*. This was filmed in Britain in 1948 and provoked outrage for its (relatively) frank sexuality and US-style violence. His name appears on the credits of over 30 films, including a half-dozen British and many more French.

OTHER BRITISH FILMS: *I'll Get You for This* (1950, novel), *The Last Page* (1952, play), *The Night Apart* (1959, story), *The Night of the Generals* (1966, UK/Fr, story), *Rough Magic* (1995, UK/Fr, story).

Chater, Geoffrey (*b* Barnet, 1921). Actor. RN: Robinson. After army service (1940–46), Marlborough-educated Chater was on London stage from 1951, with an Old Vic season (1954–55), and in films from 1957. Now remembered as the unctuous Chaplain in *If . . .* (1968), at one point emerging from a drawer in the Headmaster's study. After the mid 70s most of his work was in TV, including classy pieces like *Hotel du Lac* (1986).

OTHER BRITISH FILMS INCLUDE: *Battle of the V-1* (1958), *The Day the Earth Caught Fire* (1961), *10 Rillington Place* (1970), *O Lucky Man!* (1973), *Barry Lyndon* (1975), *Gandhi* (1982, UK/Ind).

Chelsom, Peter (*b* Blackpool, 1956). Actor, director, screenwriter. After some experience as an actor, in films (*Indian Summer*, 1987) and TV (*Cream in My Coffee*, 1980), Chelsom made two quirky films in Britain: *Hear My Song* (1991), set in the Irish area of Liverpool and based in part on the singing and tax-evading activities of tenor Josef Locke (1912–99), and *Funny Bones* (1995, UK/US), set in his native Blackpool and focused on a would-be comedian's search for his British roots. Since these, he has filmed only in America (e.g. *Town and Country*, 2000).

Cherry, Helen (*b* Manchester, 1915 – *d* London, 2001). Actress. 'Gracious' and 'serene': these kinds of epithets are often used to describe Cherry, on stage from 1938 and in films since *The Courtneys of Curzon Street* (1947), now (unfairly) best known as the widow of Trevor HOWARD to whom she was married from 1944 to 1988, bearing up stoically in the face of his roistering ways. She showed wry comedy sense in *Adam and Evelyne* (1949) and *Young Wives' Tale* (1951) and pleasing warmth in thinly written roles in *They Were Not Divided* (1950) and *Tomorrow at Ten* (1962). Some attractive TV, including *Time After Time* (1985), with its cast of irresistible veterans, but her most rewarding work was undoubtedly on the stage, where she had a well-regarded Shakespearean career and continued into the 80s.

OTHER BRITISH FILMS INCLUDE: *Last Holiday, Morning Departure* (1950), *His Excellency* (1951), *Castle in the Air* (1952), *High Flight* (1957), *The Charge of the Light Brigade* (1968), *Conduct Unbecoming* (1975).

Chester, Hal E. (*b* Brooklyn, NY, 1921). Producer. Acted as Hally Chester in 14 Hollywood programmers (1937–41) before turning to production, including ten 'Joe Palooka' films (1946–51), and coming to Britain in 1955 to make *The Weapon*. He produced seven further films there, including the unnerving sci-fi thriller, *The Night of the Demon* (1957, co-p) and nursed the drink-ruined Robert HAMER through his penultimate, *School for Scoundrels* (1959).

OTHER BRITISH FILMS: (p/ex p) *The Two-Headed Spy* (1958), *His and Hers* (1960), *Hide and Seek* (1963), *The Double Man* (1967), *Take a Girl Like You* (1970).

Chetham-Strode, Warren (*b* Pinner, 1897 – *d* Battle, 1974). Author, screenwriter. RN: Reginald Warren Strode. Popular playwright whose most famous work, *The Guinea Pig* (1945), from a script by Chetham-Strode, Bernard MILES and Roy BOULTING, was filmed by the BOULTING brothers (1947), as a post-war approach to social engineering. It was TV's 'Play of the Week' in 1957. His divorce drama, *Background* (1950) was filmed in 1953, and he wrote two Anna NEAGLE vehicles: *Odette* (1950) and *Lady with the Lamp* (1951).

OTHER BRITISH FILMS: *Abdul the Damned* (1935), *A Woman Alone* (1936), *24 Hours of a Woman's Life* (1952).

Chevalier, Albert (*b* London, 1861 – *d* London, 1923). A great Cockney music hall comedian (debut 1876) who performed the mawkish 'My Old Dutch', the comic 'What Cher! or Knocked 'em in the Old Kent Road' and the melodramatic 'A Fallen Star' around the world. He made his screen debut in *The Middleman* (1915), but had his greatest success with *My Old Dutch* (1915), which he also co-wrote, and which was remade in the US in 1926 (without Chevalier's presence) and in the UK in 1934 (in which there is said to be a clip from the 1915 film).

OTHER BRITISH FILMS: *The Bottle* (1915), *The Outrage* (1915, sc), *A Fallen Star* (1916, sc, p). AS.

Cheyney, Peter (*b* Co. Clare, Ireland, 1896 – *d* London, 1951). Author, screenwriter. Mystery writer who created Lemmy Caution (see Jean-Luc Godard's *Alphaville*, 1965) and Slim Callaghan, some of whose adventures have been filmed. In Britain, three films have been derived from his work: *The Wife of General Ling* (1937), and, with Michael RENNIE and Derrick DEMARNEY respectively as Callaghan, *Uneasy Terms* (1948) and *Meet Mr Callaghan* (1954).

child actors Child actors have been popular since cinema's earliest days (think of baby Barbara Hepworth in her father's *Rescued by Rover*, 1905) and some US child stars, such as Jackie Cooper and above all Shirley Temple, achieved huge fame. The received wisdom (perhaps promulgated by British reviewers) used to be that the children in British films were less self-consciously cute, more 'natural' than their American counterparts. There was often a well-bred wistfulness about them that contrasted with trans-Atlantic high spirits (a sort of middle-class decorum that may say something about British behavioural preferences), though avoiding the prissiness of Freddie BARTHOLOMEW when Hollywood nabbed him. There were exceptions to this image of British childhood, notably the cheeky cockney strain exhibited by Harry FOWLER (and others of the 1946 *Hue and Cry* gang) or George COLE. As in most other aspects of British cinema, class is an influential factor here: some children, such as the young William (now James) FOX were characteristically cast in middle- and upper-middle-class roles; Fowler was limited to the class stratum *his* accent suggested.

Another near-axiom is that child stars rarely make the transition to adult careers. There are obvious exceptions in the US, and there are some perhaps less obvious ones in British cinema. Nova PILBEAM, who starred twice for HITCHCOCK in the 30s, acted until 1948, admittedly in less interesting roles; Fowler and Cole went on to have very long careers, Cole becoming a major character star; Fox has had two adult careers divided by a decade's absence in the 70s; Petula CLARK, a somewhat excruciating child star, became far more interesting and attractive in adulthood; Janette SCOTT, child of divorce in *No Place for Jennifer* (1949), continued in films for 15 years; and Jean SIMMONS, enchanting in *The Way to the Stars* (1945) and *Great Expectations* (1946), had a long starring career in Britain and Hollywood.

In the 30s, Pilbeam and her *Tudor Rose* (1936) co-star, Desmond TESTER, and her *Little Friend* (1934) co-star, Jimmy HANLEY, were major teenage actors; so too were the very popular Hughie GREEN, the first of director Carol REED's gifted child players, in *Midshipman Easy* (1935), and KORDA's Indian star, SABU, who had great successes in *The Elephant Boy* (1937) *The Drum* (1938) and *The Thief of Baghdad* (1940) before leaving for Hollywood. Sabu and Hanley certainly maintained adult careers. Hazel ASCOT, star of two musicals, *Talking Feet* (1937) and *Stepping Toes* (1938), and Binkie STUART, touted as the 'British Shirley Temple' (not), were two engaging tots of the period.

In retrospect, the 40s seem dominated by well-spoken Dickensian children – Anthony WAGER as Pip in *Great Expectations* (1946) and John Howard DAVIES, who became a TV producer, as *Oliver Twist* (1948) – and by Reed's seemingly magic powers in directing very small children in *Odd Man Out* (1947), *The Third Man* (1949) and especially Bobby HENREY in *The Fallen Idol* (1948), as well as in the 50s films, *An Outcast of the Islands* (1951) and *A Kid for Two Farthings* (1954), and Mark LESTER as *Oliver!* (1968). The rougher ranks were joined by Anthony NEWLEY, a memorable Dodger in *Oliver Twist*.

In this period, others who won acclaim were: Margaret BARTON, much praised for *Temptation Harbour* (1947); Andrew RAY, who acted for several decades, as *The Mudlark*

(1950); Jeremy SPENSER, who played a musical prodigy in *Prelude to Fame* (1950); Brian SMITH, first donor of *The Browning Version* (1948); Neil NORTH, *The Winslow Boy* (1948) and Lord of the Admiralty in the 1999 version; Mandy MILLER, so eloquent as the deaf mute child in *Mandy* (1952); Jon WHITELEY and Vincent WINTER as *The Kidnappers* (1953); Colin PETERSEN as *The Scamp* (1957); and Pamela FRANKLIN and Martin STEPHENS, terrified/possessed, as *The Innocents* (1961). The phenomenon of the late 50s and the 60s was Hayley MILLS, who brought irresistible cheekiness and spirit to such varied films as *Tiger Bay* (1959) and *Whistle Down the Wind* (1961), in which Alan Barnes, who never acted again, almost stole the show. And in 1969 David BRADLEY gave a remarkable account of deprivation and aspiration in *Kes*.

More recently, Jenny AGUTTER (of *The Railway Children*, 1971) and Christian BALE (the boy in *Henry V*, 1989) have graduated to adult roles; Ben SILVERSTONE, 1994 donor of *The Browning Version*, has since starred in *Get Real* (1999); Sam Bould made a strong impression in *The End of the Affair* (2000, UK/Ger/US); Jamie BELL scored a huge success as *Billy Elliot* (2000) and, slightly older, Lara BELMONT and Freddie CUNLIFFE were very poignant in *The War Zone* (1999, UK/It). Recent cinema has been more persistently youth-centred than it used to be, but the emphasis has not been on very young children so much as twentysomethings.

Child, Jeremy (*b* Woking, 1944). Actor. Expert in upper-class snootiness, as in TV's *First Among Equals* (1986) and *Harnessing Peacocks* (1992). Studied at the Bristol Old Vic Theatre School before entering films in *Privilege* (1967); a valuable character actor since, he could become the Raymond Huntley *de nos jours*.

OTHER BRITISH FILMS INCLUDE: *Play Dirty, Decline and Fall . . .* (1968), *Quest for Love* (1971), *Young Winston* (1972), *The Stud* (1978), *Quadrophenia* (1979), *A Fish Called Wanda* (1988), *The Madness of King George* (1994, UK/US), *Regeneration* (1997), *Whatever Happened to Harold Smith?* (2000).

Children's Film Foundation This organisation came into being in 1950, under the executive leadership of Mary FIELD, who had begun making films for the RANK ORGANISATION in 1944, and with RANK as Chairman of Directors. The CFF was financed from the Levy Fund (*see* EADY LEVY), 1950–84, a plan for charging a small tax on every cinema ticket sold. Its films were essentially wholesome adventures and comedies, focused on the activities and attitudes of children, and there are instructional films about various regions of Britain. The films often featured well-known adult character players and directors such as Don CHAFFEY cut their teeth on them. Some well-known titles include Lewis GILBERT's *The Little Ballerina*, Ralph SMART's Australian-shot *Bush Christmas* and *Dusty Bates* (1947), Chaffey's *The Mysterious Poacher*, and *The Lone Climber*, shot in Austria (both 1950, reissued shortened, 1972).

BIBLIOG: Mary Field, *Good Company*, 1952; Terry Staples, *All Pals Together*, 1997.

Children's Film Unit CFU productions are the result of workshops in all aspects of film, from scripting to post-production, held every Saturday and throughout holiday periods. Its output demands total involvement by all its members (aged from 10–18) under the guidance of Artistic Director Colin FINBOW and industry experts, who have given freely of their time. CHANNEL 4's support over the years has enabled many young people to realise their ambition of working in the film industry and most of the unit's past

students are now working in film and television. Famous actors, such as Glenda JACKSON and Susannah YORK, have appeared in the CFU's productions since its inception in 1981.

Childs, Martin (*b* Bedford, 1954). Production designer. Trained at Leicestershire School of Architecture 1974–78, Childs was art director on films for Kenneth BRANAGH (*Henry V*, 1989; *Peter's Friends*, 1992; *Much Ado About Nothing*, 1993, UK/US) and supervising art director on *The Madness of King George* (1994, UK/US) and *The Portrait of a Lady* (1996, UK/US). Well prepared to assume the mantle of production designer, he received AAn, BAAn for *Mrs Brown* (1997, UK/Ire/US), worked on other period pieces, including the ill-fated *The Clandestine Marriage* (1999), the UK-set, US-financed *Quills* (2000, he received AAn, BAAn) with its asylum setting, and most famously, *Shakespeare in Love* (1999, UK/US). For the last-named, he was Oscared for his exhilarating recreation of Shakespearean London and its theatre world, and, in the Czech–US production, *From Hell* (2001), he recreates another London, that of JACK THE RIPPER. Awarded MBE in 2002.

OTHER BRITISH FILMS: *The Misadventures of Margaret* (1998, UK/Fr/US).

Chitty, Eric (aka **Erik**) (*b* Dover, 1907 – *d* London, 1977). Actor. Well-known as Smith, the tetchy ancient of the school staff, in TV's *Please, Sir!* (1968–72), a role he reprised in the film version, 1971, Chitty was on stage and in TV before WW2. First film credit was in *Contraband* (1940), and thereafter came small character roles in about 25 films, including *The Statue* (1971, UK/US).

OTHER BRITISH FILMS INCLUDE: *Forbidden* (1949), *Footsteps in the Fog* (1955), *The Devil's Disciple* (1959), *Raising the Wind* (1961), *Doctor Zhivago* (1965, UK/US), *The Railway Children* (1971), *The Amazing Mr Blunden* (1972), *Great Expectations* (1975), *Jabberwocky* (1977).

Choudhury, Sarita (*b* London, 1966). Actress. Choudhury's late 90s films have been American, but she has had roles in several British (co-)productions, notably a feminist reworking of *Kama Sutra: A Tale of Love* (1996, UK/Ind/Jap/Ger). Also on stage in America.

OTHER BRITISH FILMS: *Mississippi Masala* (1991, UK/US), *Wild West* (1992), *Fresh Kill* (1994).

Chowdhry, Navin (*b* Bristol, 1971). Actor. Notable as the latest musical prodigy of *Madame Sousatzka* (1988), he also appeared in the US-financed, Europe-set *King of the Wind* (1989), and had a continuing role in the crime series, *Dalziel and Pascoe* (1997), as a police cadet.

Christian, Roger (*b* London, 1944). Director, production designer. Since the mid 90s, has been directing in Hollywood (*The Final Cut*, 1995; *Battlefield Earth*, 2000), having previously worked in the UK. Shared the art direction AA for *Star Wars* (1977), on which he is credited as set decorator. First credit was on Peter HALL's *Akenfield* (1974), and his first as director was *Black Angel* (1980, + p, sc).

OTHER BRITISH FILMS (art d/des unless noted): *Mahler* (1974, assoc art d), *Landscape* (1976, short), *Monty Python's Life of Brian, Alien* (UK/US) (1979), *The Dollar Bottom* (1981, d, short), *The Sender* (1982, UK/US), *Nostradamus* (1994, UK/Ger).

Christie, Dame Agatha (*b* Torquay, 1890 – *d* Wallingford, 1976). Author. RN: Miller. The most successful of all DETECTIVE STORY writers, Christie saw about 20 of her ingenious puzzles adapted to film during her lifetime, 15 of them in Britain, but none perhaps as cleverly as two Hollywood adaptations: *And Then There Were None* (1945) and *Witness for the Prosecution* (1957). Her most famous detectives were the finicky Belgian, Hercule Poirot, and sharp-eyed village spinster, Miss Marple. Margaret RUTHERFORD made four popular appearances as Marple in *Murder She Said* (1961), *Murder at the Gallop* (1963), *Murder Most Foul*, *Murder Ahoy* (1964), but Joan HICKSON's 80s TV incarnation was truer to Christie's concept. Albert FINNEY played Poirot in *Murder on the Orient Express* (1974), a star-studded success which initiated a wave of British Christie-based films: *Death on the Nile* (1978), with Peter USTINOV as Poirot, and, to diminishing returns, *The Mirror Crack'd* (1980), *Evil Under the Sun* (1981, Ustinov again), *Ordeal by Innocence* (1984), and *Appointment with Death* (1988), Ustinov again). Other screen Poirots in Britain have been Austin TREVOR in *Black Coffee*, *Alibi* (1931) and *Lord Edgware Dies* (1934), American Tony Randall in *The Alphabet Murders* (1965), and David SUCHET in the TV series, *Poirot* (1989–93, 1995). A mystery in Christie's own life – an unexplained disappearance in 1926 – was the subject of a film, *Agatha* (1978, UK/US). As well as mysteries she also wrote romances under the pseudonym of Mary Westmacott; these were televised in the late 70s. Twice married, to Colonel Archibald Christie (1914–26), whose name she took, and, from 1930, to archaeologist Max Mallowan. Created DBE in 1971.

OTHER BRITISH FILMS (from her works): *The Passing of Mr Quin* (1928), *Love from a Stranger* (1937), *The Spider's Web* (1960), *Ten Little Indians* (1965), *Endless Night* (1972), *And Then There Were None* (1974), *Ten Little Indians* (1989).

BIBLIOG: Scott Palmer, *The Films of Agatha Christie*, 1993.

Christie, Campbell (*b* Murree, Punjab, 1893 – *d* 1963) and **Dorothy** (*b* Lahore, 1896 – *d* ?). Dramatists. Husband-and-wife team, authors of popular plays, four of which were filmed, including the 1953 court-martial drama, *Carrington VC* (1954), and one of which, *Someone at the Door* (1935) was filmed twice (1936, 1950). Others filmed were *His Excellency* (1950, in 1951) and *Grand National Night* (1946, in 1953). Also co-authored the screenplay for *Jassy* (1947) and wrote dialogue for *The Long Arm* (1956).

Christie, Julie (*b* Chukua, India, 1940). Actress. Arguably the most genuinely glamorous, and one of the most intelligent, of all British stars, Christie brought a gust of new, sensual life into British cinema when she swung insouciantly down a drab northern street in John SCHLESINGER's *Billy Liar*. Trained for the stage at Central School, after an Indian childhood and English education, she first became known as the artificially created girl in TV's *A for Andromeda* (1961), before making her cinema debut in two amusing, lightweight comedies, *Crooks Anonymous* and *The Fast Lady* (1962).

Schlesinger cast her as the silly, superficial, morally thread-bare Diana of *Darling* (1965), for which she won AA, BAA and New York Critics' award, and which is now powerfully resonant of its period, and again as Thomas HARDY's wilful Bathsheba, in *Far from the Madding Crowd* (1967), with other 60s icons, Terence STAMP and Alan BATES. Her Lara intermittently illuminates David LEAN's lumbering *Dr Zhivago* (1965, UK/US) and the colour cameras adored her. Notwithstanding her beauty, she continued to make the running as a serious actress in demanding films such as Joseph LOSEY's *The Go-Between* (1971), as the bored upper-class woman who ruins a boy's life by involving him in her sexual duplicities; Nicolas ROEG's *Don't Look Now* (1973, UK/It), with its famously erotic love scenes between Christie and Donald SUTHERLAND; and in

three US films with Warren Beatty (with whom she was romantically linked): Robert ALTMAN's *McCabe and Mrs Miller* (1971), as a tough Cockney madame out west, *Shampoo* (1975) and *Heaven Can Wait* (1978).

She was greatly in demand, but became much more choosy about her roles as her own political awareness increased ('All you can do is make people more aware of the realities', she said in 1994). This means that some of her later films – *Memoirs of a Survivor* and the DOCUMENTARY, *The Animals Film* (1981), *The Gold Diggers* (1983), Sally POTTER's feminist take on several Hollywood genres – were seen by comparatively few people. However, the talent and the beauty remained undimmed in such British films as *The Return of the Soldier* (1982), Kenneth BRANAGH's *Hamlet* (1996, UK/US), as Gertrude, and, in the US, *Afterglow* (1997), for which she was Oscar-nominated. In 1995, she returned to the stage in a revival of Harold PINTER's *Old Times*, to laudatory reviews.

OTHER BRITISH FILMS: *Young Cassidy* (1965), *Fahrenheit 451* (1966), *Tonite Let's All Make Love in London* (1967, doc), *Petulia* (1968), *In Search of Gregory* (1969), *Heat and Dust* (1982).

BIBLIOG: Michael Feeney Callan, *Julie Christie*, 1984.

Chrystall, Belle (*b* Preston, Lancashire, 1911). Actress. Dark-haired beauty, RADA-trained Chrystall was a notably fresh and natural-seeming lead in 30s British cinema, in such notable films as Victor SAVILLE's *Hindle Wakes* (1931), as the strong-minded mill-girl who has an affair but refuses marriage with the boss's son, and Michael POWELL's first major film, *The Edge of the World* (1937). On stage from 1928.

OTHER BRITISH FILMS INCLUDE: *A Warm Corner* (1930), *Hobson's Choice* (1931), *The Frightened Lady*, *Friday the Thirteenth* (1933), *Key to Harmony* (1935), *Breakers Ahead* (1937), *Yellow Sands*, *Follow Your Star* (1938), *Poison Pen* (1939), *The House of the Arrow* (1940).

Churchill, Diana (*b* London, 1913 – *d* Northwood, Middlesex, 1994). Actress. Mainly on stage (from 1931), the gently pretty Churchill appeared in 16 films, mostly in the 30s. She was a blonde barmaid in *Sensation* (1936), leading lady in several filmed Aldwych farces, and, post-war, a gracious wife to John MILLS's *Scott of the Antarctic* (1948), and 18 years later reappeared in *A Winter's Tale* reprising her stage role of Paulina. Married to actors Barry K. BARNES (*d* 1965), and Mervyn JOHNS. Died after a long struggle with multiple sclerosis.

OTHER BRITISH FILMS: *Sally Bishop* (1932), *Foreign Affaires* (1935), *Pot Luck*, *Dishonour Bright* (1936), *The Housemaster* (1938), *The House of the Arrow* (1940), *The History of Mr Polly* (1948).

Churchill, Donald (*b* Southall, 1930 – *d* Fuengirola, Spain, 1991). Actor. Slight, homely-featured supporting actor who made his first film impression as the friend of the hunted boy in *Victim* (1961) and his last as Watson to Ian RICHARDSON's Holmes in *The Hound of the Baskervilles* (1983). Also, much TV, including *Stanley and the Women* (1991), sometimes as writer. Married to actress Pauline YATES.

OTHER BRITISH FILMS INCLUDE: *Barnacle Bill* (1957), *The Captain's Table* (1958), *The Wild Affair* (1963), *Zeppelin* (1971, sc).

Churchill, Sarah (*b* London, 1914 – *d* London, 1982). Actress. Tall, redheaded daughter of Sir Winston, trained for ballet and made her professional debut in 1936. Entered films in 1937 in *Who's Your Lady Friend?* with first husband Vic OLIVER, and was in the WAAFs (1940–45). Post-war, she made a handful of films, including the Italian *Daniele Cortis* (1946) and the Hollywood musical, *Wedding Bells* (1951), in which she danced and romanced Fred Astaire. She was charmingly astringent in *All Over Town* (1949) and rose to the melodramatic challenge of *Serious Charge* (1959), as a repressed spinster.

OTHER BRITISH FILMS: *Spring Meeting, He Found a Star* (1941, with Oliver), *Fabian of the Yard* (1954).

Churchill, Sir Winston (*b* Blenheim Palace, 1874 – *d* London, 1965). Churchill's association with British cinema has ranged from film subject, to film commentator, and occasional censor. POWELL AND PRESSBURGER's critique of an outmoded military caste in *The Life and Death of Colonel Blimp* (1943) so infuriated Churchill that he tried to stop its production and then its export. In another war film, *The Man Who Never Was* (1955), Peter SELLERS features as the voice of Winston Churchill during a radio broadcast. The most significant celluloid account of Churchill's early years was in Richard ATTENBOROUGH's *Young Winston* (1972), with Simon WARD in the title role. He was also played by Patrick WYMARK in the British film, *Operation Crossbow* (1965, UK/It), and Jack LeVIEN made a documentary of his life, *The Finest Hours* (1964). His own favourite film was alleged to be the unequivocally patriotic *Lady Hamilton* (1941), made in Hollywood by his friend Alexander KORDA. It was learnt in 2000 (a) that he was tempted in 1941 to sell film rights to his book, *Early Life*, to Warner Bros, but was dissuaded by his friend, Brendan BRACKEN, the minister of information; and (b) that actor Norman SHELLEY had stood in vocally for Churchill in some of his famous wartime broadcasts.

Cilento, Diane (*b* Brisbane, 1933). Actress. Described as 'a lick of flame' by one writer, this blonde beauty spent most of her screen career in Britain. The daughter of parents distinguished in the medical world, educated in Australia and the US, she had theatrical training in the US and Britain, where she established herself on stage. In the 50s, a discouraging decade for women in war-dominated British cinema she was lucky enough to get a range of varied leading roles in such films as *Passage Home, The Woman for Joe* (1955), *The Truth about Women* and *The Admirable Crichton*, as Tweeny (1957). In the 60s, she filmed steadily, was Oscar-nominated for *Tom Jones* (1963), was in one of Carol REED's worst films, *The Agony and the Ecstasy* (1965), and married a little-known Scots actor, Sean CONNERY (1962–73), with whom she had a son, actor Jason CONNERY. With the breakup of this marriage in the 70s, she returned to Australia, where she appeared in two films and ran her own theatre company in Queensland. Was married to playwright Anthony SHAFFER from 1985 until his death (2001).

OTHER BRITISH FILMS INCLUDE: *Wings of Danger* (1952), *Jet Storm* (1959), *The Full Treatment* (1960), *The Naked Edge* (1961), *I Thank a Fool* (1962), *Rattle of a Simple Man, The Third Secret* (1964), *Negatives* (1968), *The Wicker Man* (1973).

Cineguild Productions The association on *In Which We Serve* (1942) of director David LEAN, cinematographer Ronald NEAME and (associate) producer Anthony HAVELOCK-ALLAN) was formalised as Cineguild in 1944, formed by Havelock-Allan who invited the others to join, and the resulting production company contributed substantially to the prestige of 40s British cinema. It began with three films derived from Noël COWARD's plays: *This Happy Breed* (1944), *Blithe Spirit* (1945) and, most famously, *Brief Encounter* (1945). The company switched from Coward to DICKENS for its next two successes, *Great Expectations* (1946) and *Oliver Twist* (1948), both much praised. Just before *Brief Encounter*, Cineguild

accepted an invitation to join RANK's INDEPENDENT PRODUCERS (a group including THE ARCHERS and LAUNDER AND GILLIAT's INDIVIDUAL PICTURES), which meant their productions were underwritten by Rank but that they were also given remarkable creative freedom. Cineguild came to an end partly as a result of the partners wanting to do different things. Neame directed the proficient thriller, *Take My Life* (1947), Havelock-Allan bowed out of *Oliver Twist* to produce *Blanche Fury* (1947), and Lean went on to make two films with his then wife Ann TODD: *The Passionate Friends* (1948), taking over the direction of this from Neame, and the sumptuous period piece, *Madeleine* (1949). For seven years Cineguild had a 'quality' reputation out of proportion to the number of films it made.

BIBLIOG: Ronald Neame, *From the Horse's Mouth*, 2002.

Cinema and Television Veterans *see* **pioneers**

cinema architecture Early British film shows were in amusement arcades, 'Travelling Picture Shows' at touring fairs, and in theatres, such as the Empire Music Hall, Leicester Square (1896), then in converted shops, railway arches, etc. Known as 'penny gaffs', the earliest cinemas were of modest size, showing one-reelers. Following the passing of the Cinematograph Act (1909), which imposed fire safety regulations concerning nitrate film projection, there was a cinema-building boom, and early surviving purpose-built cinemas include the Duke of York's, Brighton, and the Electric, Portobello Road, London (both 1910). By 1914 there were over 400 cinemas in Greater London alone. As films became longer and more spectacular, larger cinemas were built in the 20s, seating around 4,000, such as Green's Playhouse Glasgow (1927) and the Davis Theatre Croydon (1928). With the arrival of talkies, a further building boom led to the era of the 30s 'super cinema'. The cinema-going experience became transformed as the viewing environment created a world of fantasy and luxury, a temporary refuge from the mundane, raising audience expectations before the film even started. Smaller cinemas struggled to compete, as from 1929 British-themed 'atmospherics' were built with elaborate decorative interiors, modelled on US 'movie palaces' of the 20s. Especially noteworthy were the London Astorias at Finsbury Park (a mixture of Moorish and Baroque, and the best preserved interior), Streatham (Egyptian) and Brixton (Italian Gardens). There were also spectacular Granadas at Tooting, Woolwich and Clapham Junction, with interiors designed by Theodore Komisarjevsky, and the 4,000-seat Gaumont State Kilburn (Renaissance). By 1934, there were 4,300 cinemas, and 28% had over 1,000 seats. Expanding into middle-class suburbia and exceptionally well-staffed, many larger cinemas had commissionaires (looking like Ruritanian Army Generals), dance halls, smart (but modestly priced) restaurants (until the late 50s), and during intervals the mighty Wurlitzer or Compton organ (complete with coloured lighting sequences) rose from the pit, and variety acts were also featured. Other cinemas were designed in a modern Germanic style, one of the first and best super cinemas in this style being the New Victoria, London (1930). In the same year, the first ODEON was built at Perry Barr, Birmingham. By 1936 Oscar DEUTSCH had built up a chain of 150 cinemas, with the flagship Odeon, Leicester Square (with its black-tiled exterior and its landmark tower) opening in 1937. Unlike the atmospherics, their house style was modern, with sleek curved lines, plain art deco interior, and a powerful exterior, their vast brick or tiled walls and red neon signs dominating the High Street (leading Odeon architects included Harry Weedon, Andrew Mather).

Following the expansion of commercial television (1956–60), over 33% of all cinemas closed – the comedy *The Smallest Show on Earth* (1957) features the mid 50s struggle between 'super' and small cinemas) to make way for retail development. The first cinema was converted to bingo in 1961, and in city centre redevelopments rare new cinemas were usually incorporated in the basement of office blocks. By 1970, the 1945 total of 4,700 cinemas was reduced to 1,529 (mainly single screens). Splitting cinemas was soon to become widespread: screens became much smaller, often with poor sound insulation, and the character of the interior was largely destroyed. Audience expectations were greatly lowered, as, outside of the West End, cinemas became uncomfortable, depressing places to visit, run by a skeleton staff. The generally seedy atmosphere was enchanced by a staple diet of British QUOTA films, mainly low grade HORROR and SEXPLOITATION titles – the environment matched many of the films. With single-screen cinemas now a rarity, the first purpose-built US-style multiplex 'The Point', Milton Keynes (ten screens, operated by US company AMC, later UCI) was constructed in 1985, and by 2000 over 100 multiplexes were built, mainly in out-of-town sites, to a functional 'retail-park rustic' design, with no delusions of grandeur, and largely indistinguishable from the surrounding retail warehouses and bingo halls.

Cinema architecture is concerned with expectation, and, sadly, our expectations have been scaled down, never to be raised again, unless a sense of wonder can be restored by a visit to the BFI's impressive purpose built IMAX Cinema at Waterloo, London, designed by architect Bryan Avery as a multi-storey, glass-enclosed cylinder, illuminated by coloured lighting effects after dark (opened 1999, 477 seats).

See also **cinemas and exhibition**.

BIBLIOG: Richard Gray, *Cinemas in Britain*, 1996; Margaret O'Brien and Allen Eyles (Eds), *Enter the Dream House: memories of cinemas in South London from the twenties to the sixties*, 1993. Roger Philip Mellor.

cinemagazines Weekly magazine films, known also as 'screen magazines' or 'cinemagazines' were a feature of British cinema programmes for fifty years. Charles URBAN pioneered the form with the *Kinemacolor Fashion Gazette* in 1913. *Pathé Pictorial* began in 1918, and over the next two decades there followed *Eve's Film Review, Around the Town, Gaumont Mirror, British Screen Tatler, Ideal Cinemagazine, Gaumont–British Magazine* and *Pathétone Weekly*. *Pathé Pictorial* outlasted them all to close in 1969. Covering such topics as fashion, hobbies, travel, animals and interesting people, the cinemagazines were trivial, escapist and sometimes slyly subversive.

BIBLIOG: Jenny Hammerton, *For Ladies Only? Eve's Film Review: Pathé Cinemagazine 1921–1933*, 2001. Luke McKernan.

cinemas and exhibition The first public show of films in Britain took place in the Great Hall of the Polytechnic Institution, Upper Regent Street, London, commencing 21 February 1896. Film presentations rapidly spread to MUSIC HALLS in London's Leicester Square and then throughout the country, also being presented in hired halls, converted shops, and at fairgrounds by travelling showmen.

As moving pictures passed the novelty stage, purpose-built cinemas were erected in virtually every town and suburb by 1914 and the first national chain, Provincial Cinematograph Theatres (PCT), opened up Picture Houses in the major cities outside London. WW1 and its aftermath stifled expansion until the early 20s when the first truly palatial cinema, PCT's Regent Brighton, opened.

Cinema building resumed in a big way in the late 20s. The new GAUMONT–BRITISH and ASSOCIATED BRITISH combines rapidly added large new cinemas to their older properties and Gaumont took over PCT. These two national circuits established their own weekly release, giving priority to their own productions. Their only rival nationally was Odeon Theatres, an exhibitor only, which from a late start in 1933 became by the end of the decade the third major chain under the astute leadership of Oscar DEUTSCH.

There also existed powerful regional circuits, such as Granada, built up by Cecil and Sidney BERNSTEIN, and the Green brothers' chain in Scotland, but other contenders – County, Union, even British Paramount – were taken over by one or other of the big three. Following Deutsch's early death in 1941, J. Arthur RANK stepped in to run both Odeon and Gaumont but he was forced to keep their cinema circuits separate until 1959.

Rank and ABC carved up the market with ties to particular Hollywood distributors. Although their Odeons, Gaumonts and ABC's (the latter variously named – Regal, Ritz and Savoy being favourites) totalled under 1,000 of Britain's 4,700 cinemas in 1946, when British attendances reached their all-time peak of 1,635 million, the trio dominated the lucrative first run of films. No British picture could expect to make a profit without being released through one of the three chains. American companies restricted themselves to operating London West End flagships like MGM's Empire Leicester Square.

This duopoly continued unchallenged until 1984 when cinema attendances had plummeted to just 54 million and most surviving cinemas had been crudely subdivided. With the immediate success of the first, American-operated, 10-screen multiplex at Milton Keynes in 1985, other American concerns established chains in this country and Hollywood films dominated the box-office. ABC was sold and eventually broken up, while Odeon built multiplexes and further subdivided some of its older traditional sites. Admissions rose to 139.5 million in 1999 and Odeon operated 23% of British screens, almost twice as many as its nearest rival. Overbuilding in areas such as Birmingham (where Europe's largest cinema in terms of screens opened with 30 auditoria) has occurred as increases in seating capacity outstripped the present rise in attendances but multiplexes continue to be planned and built. Allen Eyles.

See also **audience trends**.

cinematography The considerable achievement of British cinematography has consistently been recognised by the sheer number of international awards won by British cameramen, including more than twenty Oscars from 1940 onwards. The artistic potential of cinematography began to be seriously explored in British cinema during the late silent period, primarily due to the increasing number of top-class continental technicians working in British studios as a consequence of pan-European production policies. This trend continued into the sound era with a number of distinguished émigrés such as Georges PÉRINAL, Gunther KRAMPF, Otto KANTUREK and Mutz GREENBAUM (aka Max GREENE) dominating the scene.

Despite the excellence of their work, this foreign presence was resented in certain quarters for impeding the opportunities for British cameramen, with only Freddie YOUNG and Bernard KNOWLES regularly photographing major productions. But the situation soon changed with the coming of WW2, when restrictions on foreign labour allowed a new generation of indigenous talent to emerge at a moment which is generally regarded as an unprecedented 'golden age' of creative achievement in British cinema. Despite an association with sober DOCUMENTARY realism, the 40s is equally marked by a continentally expressionist legacy that clearly inspired young cameramen like Erwin HILLIER, Douglas SLOCOMBE, Guy GREEN and Robert KRASKER. Consequently their work embraces a dominant low-key, high-contrast black-and-white style, epitomised by films like *A Canterbury Tale* (1944), *Dead of Night* (1945), *Great Expectations* (1946), *Odd Man Out* (1947), *Oliver Twist* (1948) and *The Third Man* (1949). Similarly atmospheric work was also being done at this time by established technicians like Young, Greenbaum, Jack COX, Desmond DICKINSON and Otto HELLER.

TECHNICOLOR also began to make its mark, having arrived in Britain in 1936. The initial pre-war colour productions such as *Wings of the Morning* (1937), *The Drum* (1938), *The Four Feathers* (1939) and *The Thief of Baghdad* (1940) tended towards a celebration of exotic landscapes, imperial exploits and fantasy. But British Technicolor scaled new heights after the war primarily through the innovation and artistry of Jack CARDIFF, whose photography on films like *A Matter of Life and Death* (1946), *Black Narcissus* (1947) and *The Red Shoes* (1948) is more distinguished by the subtle use of coloured lighting and filters and sensitive chiaroscuro than their often garish predecessors. Other cinematographers like Young, Krasker, Green and Slocombe also began working in colour, applying the lighting techiques utilised in black and white to create greater depth and atmosphere in the image, while Technicolor trainees like Christopher CHALLIS and Geoffrey UNSWORTH also began lighting features. In the 50s various experiments in muting the vibrant hues of Technicolor were carried out, often against the expressed wishes of the company. Among the most interesting of these is Oswald MORRIS's cinematography on *Moulin Rouge* (1953) and *Moby Dick* (1956).

The 50s witnessed a gradual emergence of a new approach to REALISM involving a greater use of locations, hand-held cameras and natural light and pioneered by technicians like Morris, Gilbert TAYLOR and Freddie FRANCIS on films such as *Knave of Hearts* (1954), *Woman in a Dressing Gown* (1957) and *Saturday Night and Sunday Morning* (1960). But the real breakthrough came with Walter LASSALLY, a cameraman whose sensibility was forged by working regularly on both features and documentaries. His intimate and fluid *cinéma vérité* style on *A Taste of Honey* (1961), *The Loneliness of the Long Distance Runner* (1962) and even the colour period production of *Tom Jones* (1963) constituted a British response to the French *nouvelle vague*. Other DOCUMENTARY trained cinematographers began working in features in the 60s, including Billy WILLIAMS and David WATKIN, and their preference for soft light continued the move away from the harsh contrasts of previous decades.

The 60s proved another innovative period with many British cinematographers increasingly operating in an international arena. Veteran Freddie Young won three Oscars for his work on the epic productions *Lawrence of Arabia* (1962), *Dr Zhivago* (1965, UK/US) and *Ryan's Daughter* (1970). Others like Morris, Krasker, Slocombe, Unsworth, Challis, Heller, Jack HILDYARD, Ted MOORE, Gerry FISHER, Nicolas ROEG, John ALCOTT

produced an array of excellent work in both black-and-white and colour, across a variety of genres, throughout the decade and into the 70s. The demise of the old studios had created a need for new forms of training and feature cinematographers began to emerge out of a variety of fields including documentary, advertising, television and the new film schools, led by the likes of Chris MENGES, Peter SUSCHITZKY, Peter BIZIOU, Roger DEAKINS, Ian WILSON and Roger PRATT who established themselves in the 80s. As faster filmstocks and lighter equipment increased shooting possibilities under a variety of lighting conditions, so cinematographers were required to be increasingly flexible and adaptable, particularly on location. But the art of painting with light presented by the blank canvas of a dark studio set, an environment that has to be literally brought to life with light, has not disappeared altogether: a number of talented cameramen from Alex THOMSON to Brian TUFANO continue to demonstrate the kind of sensibility and skill that has made the reputation of British cinematography internationally renowned.

BIBLIOG: John Huntley, *British Technicolor Films*, 1949; Duncan Petrie, *The British Cinematographer*, 1996. Duncan Petrie.

city life Ever since Augustin Le Prince pointed his prototype movie camera at Leeds Bridge in 1888, film has proved to be a uniquely effective medium in documenting and mythologising the life of Britain's cities. The DOCUMENTARY movement and socialist cine-clubs of the 30s further demonstrated that, in recording the lives and conditions of urban workers, the medium could be a useful political tool. British studio filmmakers were slower to exploit the possibilities of urban locations. Burdened by heavy equipment and the complex negotiations needed to secure permission for filming, they confined their activities largely to the countryside with occasional visits to LONDON. In the early post-war years, however, Carol REED was influential in demonstrating the importance of location shooting in generating an authentic sense of place. *Odd Man Out* (1947), *The Third Man* (1949) and *The Man Between* (1953) atmospherically evoked Belfast, Vienna and Berlin respectively. A few years later and somewhat more prosaically, the NEW WAVE film-makers portrayed some of Britain's Northern cities as stifling zones of confinement for their male working-class protagonists. The tradition persists in films such as *Trainspotting* (1996) and *The Full Monty* (1997, UK/US).

The significance of the city to the CRIME genre has given rise to some of the most memorable depictions of urban environments: Newcastle in *Payroll* (1961), *Get Carter* (1971) and *Stormy Monday* (1987), Manchester in *Hell is a City* (1959), Liverpool in *Violent Playground* (1957) and Glasgow in *Small Faces* (1995). Outside of London's Soho, however, it is Britain's newest city, Brighton, which has been most clearly and repetitiously represented as a centre of sin. From *Brighton Rock* (1947), through *Jigsaw* (1962), *Quadrophenia* (1979) and *Mona Lisa* (1986), to *Dirty Weekend* (1993) and *Circus* (2000, UK/US), Brighton has been the photogenic setting for sex and VIOLENCE, though there are more benign usages in *Genevieve* (1953) and *Be My Guest* (1965). At least it has established a major cinematic presence, unlike Birmingham or Bristol, Leeds or Leicester. Among provincial cities, only Liverpool can rival Brighton's attraction as a film location, but here a gritty REALISM is usually the order of the day: *Waterfront* (1950), *Violent Playground* (1957), the Terence DAVIES Trilogy (1976–83), *Letter to Brezhnev* (1985), and *Priest* (1994), for example. If the cinema comes to play a larger part in tourism in British cities, the maps of standard attractions will need redrafting to include a lot of back streets and tenement blocks. Steve Chibnall.

Clama, Renee (*b* London, 1908). Actress. Dark-haired star of Italian parents, in largely forgotten early talkies, including Victor SAVILLE's *The Sport of Kings* (1931).

OTHER BRITISH FILMS INCLUDE: *Adventurous Youth* (1929), *The Great Game* (1930), *The Stronger Sex* (1931).

Clare, Diane Actress. Most memorable in her early films: as the gormless deb, Clarissa, in *The Reluctant Debutante* (1958, US), the hysterical nurse in *Ice Cold in Alex* (1958) and the Sunday School teacher in *Whistle Down the Wind* (1961); though there were a dozen or more roles in the 60s, including a HAMMER heroine in *The Plague of the Zombies* (1966). TV included *Court Martial* (1965–67).

OTHER BRITISH FILMS INCLUDE: *The Green Helmet* (1961), *Go to Blazes* (1962), *The Haunting* (1963), *The Wrong Box* (1966), *The Trygon Factor* (1966).

Clare, Mary (*b* London, 1894 – *d* London, 1970). Actress. Dominant character star of stage from 1912 and screen from 1920. Of imposing stature and mien, she could be sinister (the 'Baroness' in *The Lady Vanishes*, 1938), ambivalent (*The Next of Kin*, 1942), haughty (the mother-in-law in *Portrait of Clare*, 1950), bossy (*My Brother Jonathan*, 1948), cruelly opportunistic (Mrs Corney in *Oliver Twist*, 1948) or vicious (*The Night Has Eyes*, 1942), and she moved socially up (Duchess of Devonshire in *Mrs Fitzherbert*, 1947) and down (Ma Mutch in *There Ain't No Justice*, 1939), all with effortless ease. In her gallery of 60 films, she was never dull and usually formidable, and it is instructive to watch her bring awful films like *Penny Princess* (1952) to intermittent life, but it is arguable that films never gave her a chance as rewarding as the leading role on stage in COWARD's patriotic *Cavalcade* (1931).

OTHER BRITISH FILMS INCLUDE: *The Skin Game* (1920), *A Prince of Lovers, A Gipsy Cavalier* (1922), *The Outsider* (1931), *The Constant Nymph* (1933), *Say It with Flowers* (star), *Jew Süss, Lorna Doone* (1934), *The Passing of the Third Floor Back* (1935), *Young and Innocent, The Mill on the Floss* (1937), *The Citadel, The Challenge* (1938), *Mrs Pym of Scotland Yard* (star), *A Girl Must Live* (1939), *This Man Is Dangerous* (1941), *Fiddlers Three* (1944), *The Three Weird Sisters* (1948), *Moulin Rouge, The Beggar's Opera* (1953).

Clarence, O(liver) B. (*b* London, 1870 – *d* Hove, 1955). Actor. From romantic stage leading man to toothless old codger (the 'Aged P' in *Great Expectations*, 1946) describes the career of this character player. In over 70 films, he mostly projected a benign and/or eccentric aura, as with the Vicars in *Pygmalion* (1938) and *Uncle Silas* (1947). First filmed in 1914, *Liberty Hall*; last billed as – what else? – 'Old gentleman' in *The Calendar* (1948).

OTHER BRITISH FILMS INCLUDE: *London Pride* (1920), *The Man from Chicago* (1930), *The Bells* (1931), *Goodnight Vienna* (1932), *Friday the Thirteenth* (1933), *The Scarlet Pimpernel, Squibs* (1935), *Seven Sinners* (1936), *Victoria the Great, The Mill on the Floss,* (1937), *Jamaica Inn* (1939), *Return to Yesterday* (1940), *Quiet Wedding, Major Barbara* (1941), *A Place of One's Own, On Approval* (1944), *While the Sun Shines* (1947).

BIBLIOG: Autobiography, *No Complaints*, 1943.

Clarendon Film Company Early producer and distributor, which specialised in comedies – social satire with a nice touch of absurdity – but soon embraced dramas, Clarendon was founded in 1904 by H.V. Lawley (who left the company in 1908)

and Percy STOW, with studios at 16 Limes Road, Croydon. It produced Britain's first three-reel drama, *Saved by Fire!* (1912), made the *Lt Rose* series (1909–15), introduced sound-on-disc films in 1913, and had a prominent, if relatively untalented screenwriter in the 1910s in the regal form of the Marchioness of Townshend. Clarendon was absorbed by HARMA early in 1918. AS.

Clark, Curtis (*b* Oak Ridge, Tennessee). Cinematographer. American long in Britain, where he directed DOCUMENTARIES about popular music (e.g. *British Hustle*, 1978, + c; *Blue Suede Shoes*, 1980), as well as *Cruisin'* (1977), a short about London youth. Most famously, as cinematographer, he shot *The Draughtsman's Contract* (1982), in which the visuals had to keep up with the non-stop dialogue.

OTHER BRITISH FILMS INCLUDE: (c) *Wild Roses* (1966, short), *A Test of Violence* (1970, doc), *Giro City* (1982, TV, some cinemas), *Nelly's Version, Four American Composers* (1983), *Leila and the Wolves* (1984, UK/Leb).

Clark, Ernest (*b* London, 1912 – *d* Hinton St George, Somerset, 1994). Actor. Serious-looking character player and former journalist, on stage from 1937, in the Tank Corps (1939–45) and winner of M.C. during WW2, busy in films from 1948. Played officers in all the services (e.g. *The Dam Busters*, 1955; *The Baby and the Battleship*, 1956), barristers, stockbrokers, prison governors, doctors and other professionals. Had a continuing role as Professor Sir George Loftus in TV's 'Doctor' series in the 70s and early 80s and a long West End stage career. Married (3) Julia LOCKWOOD, daughter of Margaret.

OTHER BRITISH FILMS INCLUDE: *Obsession* (1949), *Seven Days to Noon, The Mudlark* (1950), *Doctor in the House* (1954), *Reach for the Sky* (1956), *The Birthday Present, I Accuse!,* (1957), *A Tale of Two Cities* (1958), *Sink the Bismarck!* (1960), *Tomorrow at Ten* (1962), *Billy Liar* (1963), *The Executioner* (1970), *Gandhi* (1982, UK/Ind), *The Pope Must Die* (1991, UK/US).

Clark, Jameson (*b* Kilbirnie, Scotland, 1907 – *d* Kilbirnie, 1984). Actor. Character player of 'Scottish types' in 20 British films, from *Whisky Galore!* (1949, as Constable Macrae), via *The Kidnappers* and *The 'Maggie'* (1953), to *Greyfriars Bobby* (1961) and *Ring of Bright Water* (1969).

OTHER BRITISH FILMS INCLUDE: *The Brave Don't Cry* (1952), *Laxdale Hall* (1953), *X the Unknown* (1956), *The Long Haul* (1957), *The Bridal Path, The Battle of the Sexes* (1959), *Tunes of Glory* (1960).

Clark, Jim (*b* Boston, Lincolnshire, 1931). Editor. Oscar- and BAFTA-winner for editing *The Killing Fields* (1984), Clark's credits include such key 60s films as *The Innocents* (1961) and *Darling* (1965, first of six for John SCHLESINGER): he is at home on big, sprawling projects and on intimate ones. In an Atlantic-hopping career, he has also worked a good deal in the US on such films as *Midnight Cowboy* (1969), *Marathon Man* (1976) and *The Jackal* (1997). Directed several unremarkable British films including the scattergun satire, *Every Home Should Have One* (1969).

OTHER BRITISH FILMS INCLUDE: (e, unless noted) *The Grass Is Greener* (1960), *Term of Trial* (1962), *The Pumpkin Eater* (1964), *Rentadick* (1972, d), *Yanks* (1979), *Agatha* (1978), *Privates on Parade* (1982), *The Mission* (1985), *Memphis Belle* (1990), *The World Is Not Enough, Onegin* (UK/US), *The Trench* (UK/Fr) (1999).

Clark, Michael (*b* Aberdeen, 1962). Dancer. Brilliant and controversial dancer, trained with the Royal Ballet School, joining the Ballet Rambert in 1981. Appeared in a couple of SHORT FILMS, played a sailor in *Comrades* (1986) and a waiter in Peter GREENAWAY's *The Cook, the Thief, His Wife & Her Lover* (1989, UK/Fr) and co-starred as Caliban in *Prospero's Books* (1991, UK/Fr/It/Neth), Greenaway's wildly inventive reworking of *The Tempest*. Against the resonant classicism of John GIELGUD's Prospero, this shockingly painted creature with bright red genitals helped ensure this was no decorous SHAKESPEAREAN ADAPTATION, but a masterpiece rethought. On stage in Sadler's Wells's *Before and After: The Fall* (2001), Clark, as choreographer, has clearly retained his power to shock.

OTHER BRITISH FILMS: (shorts) *Big Love – An Invitation to Disaster, The Miracle of the Rose* (1984) *Degrees of Blindness* (1988).

Clark, Petula (*b* West Ewell, 1932). Actress, singer. One of the rare child stars who made it into an adult career, and, to some, more attractive as adult performer than as rather prissy teenager. At 11 she had a regular radio programme, *Pet's Parlour*, entertained servicemen during WW2, had a comic strip named for her in *Radio Fun*, and entered films in 1944, in *Medal for the General*. During the latter 40s, she was under contract to RANK and, after the disaster of the MUSICAL *London Town* (1946), was put into the HUGGETTS SERIES, as the precocious youngest daughter. She was unlucky to be a young adult, especially one who could sing, in 50s British cinema, because there was nothing for such talents to do, and her career slid as she appeared in such anodyne enterprises as *Made in Heaven* (1952) and *The Gay Dog* (1954). She had marginally better chances in the hospital drama *White Corridors* (1951) and the comedy *The Card* (1952), but her best screen roles were in two 60s musicals – *Finian's Rainbow* (1968, US) and *Goodbye, Mr Chips* (1969) – made when the genre was declining in popularity.

In 1961, she married a Frenchman and settled anew in France, appearing from time to time in the UK and US as a top singer. Has filmed only once in recent decades, in the children's fantasy, *Never Never Land* (1980), but had major stage success in *Sunset Boulevard* (1996). Created CBE in 1997, recognition of a remarkable career in which films played only a modest role.

OTHER BRITISH FILMS INCLUDE: *I Know Where I'm Going!* (1945), *Vice Versa* (1947), *Here Come the Huggetts* (1948), *The Romantic Age* (1949), *Dance Hall* (1950), *The Runaway Bus* (1953), *That Woman Opposite* (1957), *6.5 Special* (1958).

BIBLIOG: Andrea Kon, *This Is My Song: A Biography of Petula Clark*, 1983.

Clark, Robert (*b* Paisley, Scotland, 1905 – *d* Cambridgeshire, 1984). Executive. Former lawyer who entered films at ELSTREE in 1929, was in charge of WELWYN STUDIOS from 1935. He was a director of ASSOCIATED BRITISH PICTURE CORPORATION from 1945 until his resignation in 1969. He was an astute but prudent head of production, who took credit on such films as *The Dam Busters* (1955) and *No Time for Tears* (1957), although his real contribution was to put ABPC in profit during the 50s, acquiring a reputation for tough dealing. He was removed as Head of Production in 1958, but stayed on as a director of the company.

BIBLIOG: Patricia Warren, *Elstree: the British Hollywood*, 1983.

Clark, Trilby (*b* Australia, 1903). Actress. A plain-looking ingenue who made films on three continents but no impact anywhere. On stage in Australia and on screen there in 1920 (*The Breaking of the Drought*). Second female lead in 11 minor Hollywood features from 1923–27, including *Just off Broadway* (1924).

BRITISH FILMS INCLUDE: *Carry On!* (1927), *Maria Marten* (1928), *Chick, God's Clay, The Devil's Maze* (1929), *Harmony Heaven, Night Porter* (1930). AS.

Clarke, Alan (*b* Liverpool, 1935 – *d* London, 1990). Director. Much of Clarke's work was for TV, but he was responsible for two confronting films of rough working-class life, notably the graphic Borstal drama, *Scum* (1979, from TV play), for BERWICK STREET FILM-MAKERS COLLECTIVE, and starring a very young Ray WINSTONE, and the exploration of teenage sex on a housing estate, *Rita, Sue and Bob Too* (1986). His final TV film, *The Firm* (1988), was an abrasive vision of football violence and, by extension, a critique of Thatcherism. He favoured an apparently detached, 'documentary' film-making style, but this in no way lessened his impact. Died of cancer.

OTHER BRITISH FILMS: *Achilles Heel* (1973), *Billy the Kid and the Green Baize Vampire* (1985).

BIBLIOG: Richard Kelly (ed), *Alan Clarke*, 1998.

Clarke, Angela (*b* Liverpool, 1969). Actress. Vivid, loud and engaging performer of Liverpudlian types, first on screen as Teresa's sister in *A Letter to Brezhnev* (1985); later as one of the girls-on-the-town in Mike OCKRENT's *Dancin' Thru the Dark* (1990) and in TV's *Soldier, Soldier* (1991). Sister of Margi and screenwriter Frank CLARKE. Not to be confused with the American character actress of the same name.

OTHER BRITISH FILMS: *Blonde Fist, Bernard and the Genie* (1991), *Land and Freedom* (1995, UK/Ger/Sp).

Clarke, Frank Screenwriter. Brother of Margi and Angela CLARKE, who wrote the marvellously vernacular screenplay for *A Letter to Brezhnev* (1985) and directed his sisters in *Blonde Fist* (1991). Also wrote *The Fruit Machine* (1988), a thriller with a sympathetically presented gay love story, and runs Orion Production and Casting Agency, Liverpool.

Clarke, Margi (*b* Kirkby, Lancashire, 1955). Actress. Former TV presenter who made an indelible impression as the bold, blonde chicken-processer, Teresa, in *A Letter to Brezhnev* (1985), but who has had little chance in films to shine so vivaciously since. Well-known for TV's *The Good Sex Guide* (1994).

OTHER BRITISH FILMS: *The Dressmaker* (1988), *Strike It Rich* (1990, UK/US), *Blonde Fist* (1991).

Clarke, T(homas) E(rnest) B(ennett) (*b* Watford, 1907 – *d* Surrey, 1989). Screenwriter. Celebrated EALING alumnus, widely known as Tibby, who won an Oscar for his screenplay for *The Lavender Hill Mob* (1951). Worked in journalism, advertising and the police force before coming to Ealing (1943–57), and this varied experience feeds the naturalistic observation underpinning such eccentric comedies as *Hue and Cry* (1946), *Passport to Pimlico* (1949, AAn), *The Lavender Hill Mob*, and *The Titfield Thunderbolt* (1953). Though his name is associated with these affectionately remembered comedies, two points should be noted: he also wrote serious films such as Basil DEARDEN's *The Blue Lamp* (1949), a tribute to the London police; and he did *not* write the more astringent Ealing comedies, such as *Kind Hearts and Coronets* (1949) or *The Man in the White Suit* (1951). His sensibility seems to have chimed most harmoniously with director Charles CRICHTON, for whom he wrote seven screenplays, including the post-Ealing *Law and Disorder* (1958), and with Dearden, for whom he worked on six. His post-Ealing films included versions of *A Tale of Two Cities* (1958) and *Sons and Lovers* (1960), though he preferred original screenplays, and the US-backed, creatively

British caper, *A Man Could Get Killed* (1966). Awarded the OBE in 1952, and published his autobiography, *This Is Where I Came In*, in 1974, as well as writing 15 novels and a stage play.

OTHER BRITISH FILMS: *Champagne Charlie* (new music and lyrics), *The Halfway House* (co-sc), *For Those in Peril* (1944), *Johnny Frenchman*, *Dead of Night* (co-sc) (1945), *Against the Wind* (1947), *Train of Events* (1949, co-sc), *The Magnet* (1950), *Encore* (1951, co-sc), *The Rainbow Jacket* (1954), *Who Done It?* (1956), *Barnacle Bill* (1957), *Gideon's Day* (1958), *The Horse Without a Head* (1963), *A Hitch in Time* (1978).

BIBLIOG: Charles Barr, *Ealing Studios*, 1993.

Clarke, Warren (*b* Oldham, Lancashire, 1947). Actor. Thick-set character player, best remembered as the droog Dim in *A Clockwork Orange* (1971), his first film, and as TV's crotch-scratching, uncouth but morally unassailable Dalziel in five seasons of the idiosyncratic police series *Dalziel and Pascoe* (since 1996) – and much other excellent TV. Directed the US film, *Inside Edge*, in 1992.

OTHER BRITISH FILMS INCLUDE: *Antony and Cleopatra* (1972, UK/Sp/Switz), *O Lucky Man!* (1973), *Enigma* (1982), *Angels* (1992), *Greenfingers* (2001).

Clarke-Smith, D(ouglas) A. (*b* Montrose, Scotland, 1888 – *d* Withyham, 1959). Actor. Somewhat raffish-looking, mousta-chioed character player (and pig-breeder), wildly prolific on stage from 1913 to 1953 (three-and-a-half columns in *Who's Who in the Theatre*) and almost 60 films after *Atlantic* (1929). Worked for HITCHCOCK and Victor SAVILLE in the 30s, rejoined the Army in WW2 (1939–44) and post-war was seen in seven films, including *Quo Vadis* (1951, US) and, as the hectoring attorney Dodson, *The Pickwick Papers* (1952), and much TV drama.

OTHER BRITISH FILMS INCLUDE: *The Frightened Lady* (1932), *I Was a Spy*, *The Good Companions*, *Friday the Thirteenth* (1933), *The Man Who Knew Too Much*, *Lorna Doone* (1934), *Sabotage* (1936), *Dangerous Fingers* (1938), *Frieda* (1947), *Something Money Can't Buy* (1952), *The Baby and the Battleship* (1956).

class Economic and social divisions and consciousness of social distinctions (in terms of dress, speech, and manners) have been a continuing feature of British society. It is hardly surprising therefore that social class should also have impacted upon British cinema. It has done so in three main ways: in relation to film production, the audiences for film, and the representations of class apparent in British films. Film production is an expensive business requiring specific cultural and technical competences. For this reason British film-making, as elsewhere, has been primarily a middle-class activity and critics have often argued that this has led to a cinema that is also middle-class in outlook. Thus, Jeffrey Richards (in *The Age of the Dream Palace*) suggests that British cinema in the 30s manifests a middle-class consensus while Raymond Durgnat (in *A Mirror for England*) describes the period 1945–58 as 'a climax period for middle-class cinema'. There have been intermittent attempts to broaden access to film production, as in the 30s when groups such as the WORKERS' FILM AND PHOTO LEAGUE were active and in the 80s when there was a growth in grassroots FILM AND VIDEO WORKSHOPS (such as AMBER in the north of England), but these have remained activities on the margins of (or in active opposition to) the commercial mainstream.

However, while British film production may have been predominantly middle-class in character, the largest group of cinemagoers in Britain – at least until recently – has been the urban working class. Thus, while different sections of the population have always attended the cinema, it was the young working-class male who was the most habitual cinemagoer in Britain during the 30s and 40s. It was not necessarily British films, however, that were most attractive to this spectator and it has often been claimed that Hollywood films, which dominated the British box-office from the 20s onwards, succeeded in providing pleasures and satisfactions that a more 'respectable', middle-class British cinema failed to deliver. Thus, while there has been a tradition of popular British COMEDY – stretching from the films of George FORMBY and Gracie FIELDS in the 30s through to the 'CARRY ON' series in the 60s and 70s – which has often defied notions of 'good taste', British cinema has more commonly been identified with a pursuit of 'quality' via literary ADAPTATION and historical recreation on the one hand or social responsibility and 'REALISM' on the other.

Whereas the first of these strands (as in the COSTUME DRAMA or 'HERITAGE' FILMS) has often been associated with representation of the upper classes and upper-middle class, the 'realist' tradition has more commonly displayed a concern to show the working class. This tradition has its roots in the DOCUMENTARY movement of the 30s, and its emphasis upon the dignity of labour. It carried into wartime dramas (such as *In Which We Serve*, 1942, and *Millions Like Us*, 1943) in which the idea of the nation pulling together to win the war entailed stories involving a microcosm of British society. The 'NEW WAVE' or 'kitchen sink' films of the late 50s and early 60s (such as *Saturday Night And Sunday Morning*, 1960, and *A Kind Of Loving*, 1962) renewed interest in working-class characters but at a time when the working class was perceived as being in a state of decline as a result of 'affluence' and consumerism. This sense of decline reached a certain terminus in films of the 90s, such as *Brassed Off* (1996, UK/US) and *The Full Monty* (1997, UK/US) in which working-class characters faced the new realities of de-industrialisation and mass UNEMPLOY-MENT.

The essentially benign character of a film such as *The Full Monty* (with its utopian moment of triumph in the face of adversity) reveals the continuing preference of British cinema for narratives of 'consensus' rather than conflict. Although British films have revealed a recurring fascination with the workings of British society, they have consistently shied away from representations of open class conflict (the television work of Ken LOACH in the 60s and 70s – such as *The Big Flame*, 1969, and *The Rank and File*, 1971 – perhaps comes closest). This is partly for institutional reasons (such as CENSORSHIP) but also for aesthetic reasons, insofar as the conventions of narrativity and realism characteristic of mainstream cinema typically work against a satisfactory representation of collective (rather than individual) action and social and economic (rather than interpersonal) relations.

BIBLIOG: Raymond Durgnat, *A Mirror for England*, 1970; John Hill, *Sex, Class and Realism: British Cinema 1956–63*, 1986; Jeffrey Richards, *The Age of the Dream Palace: Cinema and Society 1930–1939*, 1984. John Hill.

Clavell, James (*b* Sydney, 1922 – *d* Vevey, Switz, 1994). Screenwriter, author, director. A captain with the British Royal Artillery, who spent much of WW2 in a Japanese prisoner-of-war camp, an experience he used in writing *King Rat* (filmed 1965). Many of his novels have been either filmed or made into TV mini-series (e.g. *Noble House*, 1988); he became a screen-writer in 1958 (*The Fly*, US); wrote several British films, beginning with *633 Squadron* (1964, UK/US), and also directed the sentimental hit, *To Sir, with Love* (1967, + sc, p), *Where's Jack?* (1969), *The Last Valley* (1970, + sc, p).

Clay, Jim (*b* Middlesbrough, 1958). Production designer. One of the most intelligently sumptuous productions of the last few years, *Onegin* (1999, UK/US), owes a great deal to Clay's design, with its telling contrasts of, say, panelled warmth and the chill whiteness of the setting for the dénouement. He created the WW1 claustrophobia of *The Trench* (1999, UK/Fr), and achieved a *noir* gloss in TV's *The Singing Detective* (1986). The failings of *Captain Corelli's Mandolin* (2001, UK/US/Fr) cannot be laid at his door. Trained at the Teesside College of Art, he has worked as an architect, with the BBC Design Department, and, since 1986, as freelance film designer.

OTHER BRITISH FILMS INCLUDE: *Circle of Friends* (1995, Ire/US), *Queen of Hearts* (1989), *The Crying Game* (1992), *Felicia's Journey* (1999, UK/Can), *Maybe Baby* (2000, UK/Fr), *About a Boy* (2002).

Clay, Nicholas (*b* London, 1946 – *d* London, 2000). Actor. Husky leading man of the Old Vic in the early 70s and of a few 80s British films, including *Excalibur* (US money, UK personnel), as Lancelot, a suspect in *Evil Under the Sun* and gamekeeper Mellors in *Lady Chatterley's Lover* (all 1981). He was also Tristan in the Irish *Tristan and Isolde* (1979). Later work mostly for TV, including *The Odyssey* (1997) as Menelaus.

OTHER BRITISH FILMS: *The Damned* (1961), *The Night Digger*, *The Darwin Adventure* (1971), *The Hound of the Baskervilles* (1983).

Clayton, Jack (*b* Brighton, 1921 – *d* Slough, 1995). Director, producer. Joining Alexander KORDA's LONDON FILMS at the age of 14, having appeared as a child in *Dark Red Roses* (1929), Clayton had a 20-year apprenticeship in the film industry, working his way up from third assistant director to producer before making his mark as a director with a SHORT FILM, *The Bespoke Overcoat* (1955), which won international awards including an Oscar. (During WW2 he served with the RAF FILM UNIT, directing DOCUMENTARIES.) His feature film debut, *Room at the Top* (1958), had a sensational impact, ushering in the British 'NEW WAVE' and often credited with bringing a new frankness to the British screen in its depiction of CLASS and sexual relationships. Clayton, however, was impervious to film fashion and his subsequent works, although all based on literary sources, were personal and private dramas, affirmations of human dignity and dominated by gallant loners and romantic dreamers.A brilliant horror film, *The Innocents* (1961), adapted from Henry JAMES, enhanced his reputation, as did the marital drama, *The Pumpkin Eater* (1964), scripted by Harold PINTER. But *Our Mother's House* (1967) was too defiantly quirky to find much of an audience (Spielberg has since expressed great admiration for it). It prefaced a difficult period in his career, during which a number of projects were cancelled, often at the last minute. His film in Hollywood of *The Great Gatsby* (1974) was savaged by the press (though Tennessee Williams loved it); and in 1978 he suffered a disabling stroke that for a while deprived him of speech. Nevertheless, he made a strong comeback in the 80s, with a long-cherished project, *The Lonely Passion of Judith Hearne* (1987).

His final work was the beautifully crafted, blackly comic TV, *Memento Mori* (1992). Fastidious and uncompromising, Clayton was a hero to his peers for his absolute artistic integrity. His *oeuvre* is small but choice. He married and divorced actresses Christine NORDEN and Katherine KATH

and was married to Haya HARAREET for many years until his death.

BIBLIOG: G.M.A. Gaston, *Jack Clayton: A Guide to References and Resources*, 1981; Neil Sinyard, *Jack Clayton*, 2000. Neil Sinyard.

Clayton, Sue (*b* Newcastle-upon-Tyne). Director. Clayton has been involved in several socially-committed films, including *Women and the Welfare State* (1977), an exploration of attitudes of the state to single mothers, *The Song of the Shirt* (1979, + sc), and, as production manager, *Veronica 4 Rose* (1982), young lesbians in a heterosexist society, made for LUSIA FILMS.

OTHER BRITISH FILMS INCLUDE: *Heartsongs* (1992, short), *The Disappearance of Finbar* (1996, UK/Fr/Ire/Swe, + sc).

Cleese, John (*b* Weston-super-Mare, 1939). Actor, screenwriter, producer. Dominant in British comedy since the 60s, tall (6'4"), eccentric Cambridge law graduate, Cleese is associated with such landmark TV series as *The Frost Report* (1966) and the iconoclastic *Monty Python's Flying Circus* (1969–70, 1972–74) on which his cohorts included Graham CHAPMAN, Eric IDLE, Michael PALIN, Terry JONES and director Terry GILLIAM. With these, he would go on to bring MONTY PYTHON to the cinema in *And Now for Something Completely Different* (1971), *Monty Python and the Holy Grail* (1974), . . . *Life of Brian* (1979), *The Secret Policeman's Ball* (1979) and . . . *Other Ball* (1982), and *Monty Python's The Meaning of Life* (1983), on which he wrote as well as acted. The wild inventiveness revealed in 'Python' was harnessed to different anarchic effect in the TV series, *Fawlty Towers* (1975, 1979), co-written and performed with his then-wife (1968–76) Connie BOOTH, and perhaps the funniest ever British sitcom. He had a great success (AAn/BAAn, sc; BAA a) in 1988 with *A Fish Called Wanda* (+ co-d, p), which he failed to duplicate in the follow-up *Fierce Creatures* (1997, UK/US), played 'R' in the 1999 BOND, *The World Is Not Enough* (UK/US), and was in several US films, including *Silverado* (1985) and the film version of the cult children's book, *Harry Potter and the Philosopher's Stone* (2001, UK/US). He also founded Video Arts Ltd, which produced some witty business training films. His varied contributions stamp him a polymath of British comedy in the last third of the 20th century.

OTHER BRITISH FILMS (a, unless noted): *The Bliss of Mrs Blossom*, *Interlude*, *The Best House in London* (1968), *The Magic Christian* (1969), *The Rise and Rise of Michael Rimmer* (1970), *Rentadick* (1972, sc), *It's a 2'6" Above the Ground World* (1972), *Romance with a Double Bass* (1974, short, + sc), *The Strange Case of the End of Civilisation As We Know It* (1977, + sc), *Time Bandits* (1981), *The Great Muppet Caper* (1981), *Privates on Parade*, *Strictly Private* (short) (1982), *Clockwise* (1985), *The Wind in the Willows* (1996), *Parting Shots* (1998).

Clemens, Brian (aka Tony O'Grady) (*b* Croydon, 1931). Screenwriter. Clemens sweated on the 'B' MOVIE treadmill of the 50s, occasionally coming up with something enjoyable such as 1958's *A Woman Possessed* (she was Margaretta SCOTT), before breaking into more ambitious – if not always more enjoyable – features post-1960. *Dr Jekyll & Sister Hyde* (1971, + p, comp) is written with some wit, and there are sadistically calculated frissons in *Blind Terror* (1971). Mostly TV after the early 70s.

OTHER BRITISH FILMS INCLUDE: (sc) *Operation Murder* (1956), *Three Sundays to Live*, *The Betrayal*, *At the Stroke of Nine* (1957), *Moment of Indiscretion* (1958), *Web of Suspicion* (1959), *An Honourable Murder* (1960), *Station Six – Sahara* (1962), *And Soon the Darkness* (1970), *Captain Kronos: Vampire Hunter* (1972, + d, p).

Clement, Dick (*b* Westcliff-on-Sea, 1937). Screenwriter, director. Clement's career is almost wholly bound up with that of his co-writer **Ian LaFrenais** (*b* Newcastle-upon-Tyne, 1936): they made their names with the very witty TV series *The Likely Lads* (1964–66), which spawned a follow-up, *Whatever Happened to the Likely Lads?* (1973–74), and a film (1976). There was other brilliant TV, including *Porridge* (1974–77), with sequel, *Going Straight* (1978), and film SPIN-OFF (1979, + d). Their cinema work began with *The Jokers* (1966) and *Hannibal Brooks* (1968), both for Michael WINNER, who hasn't had such writing since, and *Otley* (1968), which Clement also directed. LaFrenais almost always shared the writing credit with Clement, but sometimes – *Catch Me a Spy* (1971, assoc p), *Porridge* (+ 2ud), *Bullshot* (1983) and *Water* (1985, directed by Clement) – also produced. They won a BAA for their screenplay for *The Commitments* (1991). They have worked in the US (*The Prisoner of Zenda*, 1979, co-sc; *Vice-Versa*, 1988, co-p, co-sc), and won numerous awards for *Tracey Takes On* (1993–99), but their wit seems essentially British and they genuinely raised the standard of TV writing.

OTHER BRITISH FILMS (co-sc unless note): *A Severed Head* (1970, d Clement), *Villain* (1971), *To Russia with Elton* (1979, doc, + co-d, p LaF), *Never Say Never Again* (1983, UK/US, co-add dial), *Roseanna's Grave* (1997, UK/US), *Still Crazy* (1998). LaFrenais alone: *The Touchables* (1968, sc), *The Virgin Soldiers* (1969, add dial), *Look at Yourself* (short), *Percy's Progress* (1974).

Clements, Sir John (*b* London, 1910 – *d* London, 1988). Actor. Tall, distinguished stage actor, knighted 1968, who filmed sporadically over 50 years, from young leading man in *Once in a New Moon* (1935) to cameos in *Gandhi* (1982, UK/Ind) and *The Jigsaw Man* (1984). Had his best roles in the 30s, including the young socialist in *South Riding* (1938) and, while under contract to KORDA, the hero accused of cowardice in *The Four Feathers* (1939), but there are a few interesting later roles, such as the idealist hero of *They Came to a City* (1944) and the philandering composer in *Train of Events* (1949). On stage from 1930; it remained his prime allegiance. Married (2) to actress Kay HAMMOND.

OTHER BRITISH FILMS INCLUDE: *Things to Come, Rembrandt* (1936), *The Housemaster* (1938), *Convoy* (1940), *This England, Ships with Wings* (1941), *Tomorrow We Live* (1942), *The Silent Enemy* (1958), *The Mind Benders* (1963).

Cliff, Laddie (*b* Bristol, 1891 – *d* Valais, Switzerland, 1937). Actor. RN: Clifford Perry. On stage as a child, first London pantomime in 1900, he was later a member of *The Co-Optimists* (film version, 1929) concert party revue and made his film debut in *The Card* (1922), later appearing with Stanley LUPINO in several 30s comedies. Married (2) Phyllis MONKMAN.

OTHER BRITISH FILMS INCLUDE: *On with the Dance* (1927), *The Sleeping Car* (1933), *Happy* (1934), *Sporting Love* (1936), *Over She Goes* (1937).

Cliffe, Fred E. (*b* 1885 – *d* Berkshire, 1957). Composer, lyricist. Cliffe wrote songs (music and lyrics) and sometimes other music for nine films starring George FORMBY: *No Limit* (1935), *Keep Your Seats, Please* (1936), *Keep Fit, Feather Your Nest* (1937), *I See Ice!, It's in the Air* (1938), *Come On George, Trouble Brewing* (1939), *Let George Do It!* (1940).

Clifford, Hubert (*b* Bairnsdale, Victoria, 1904). Composer. Trained first in Melbourne, then in London under Ralph Vaughan WILLIAMS at the RCM, Clifford entered films during WW2, composing scores for PROPAGANDA films, such as *Road to Moscow* and *Battle of Britain* (1944, for MOI). He also worked for the BBC during WW2, then became Professor of Composition at the Royal Academy of Music in 1944, prior to being appointed KORDA's Music Director at LONDON FILMS in 1947. Here he worked on (as music director or conductor) such notable films as *The Winslow Boy* and *The Fallen Idol* (1948). In the 50s, he composed the score for varied genre films, including the chase drama, *Hunted* (1952), the thriller, *Hell Drivers*, and war film, *The One That Got Away* (1957) and the comedy, *Bachelor of Hearts* (1958). He also wrote about film music.

OTHER BRITISH FILMS INCLUDE: (m d) *An Ideal Husband* (1947), *Pandora and the Flying Dutchman* (1950), *Cry, the Beloved Country* (1952); (cond) *Mine Own Executioner* (1947), *The Happiest Days of Your Life, Seven Days to Noon* (1950; (comp) (doc) *The Second Freedom* (1943), *General Election*, (1945), *The Road to Canterbury* (1952); (features) *The Dark Man* (1950), *River Beat* (1953), *House of Secrets* (1956).

Clifford, Jill (*b* Radlett, 1931). Actress. RN: Clifford-Turner. Brunette starlet of the early 50s, first in *No Highway* (1951). Discovered by Ben LYON.

OTHER BRITISH FILMS INCLUDE: *The House in the Square* (1951), *Venetian Bird* (1952), *Just My Luck* (1957).

Clifford, Peggy Ann (*b* Bournemouth, 1921). Actress. After playing the hearty Maud, whom the Duke of Chalfont has settled on as 'good breedin' stock' in *Kind Hearts and Coronets* (1949), the substantial Clifford settled early into character roles in many a 50s RANK film, as expostulating maids, cooks and landladies.

OTHER BRITISH FILMS INCLUDE: *Chance of a Lifetime* (1950), *Man of the Moment, Lost* (1955), *Doctor at Large* (1957), *Sparrows Can't Sing, On the Beat* (1962), *Carry On Cleo* (1964), *Under Milk Wood* (1971, as Bessie Bighead), *Murder by Decree* (1978).

Clift, Denison (*b* Omaha, 1892 – *d* Los Angeles, 1961). Screenwriter, director. A man of many trades, Clift was a scriptwriter for William Fox in 1918, appointed head of its writing team the following year, and in 1920, promoted to director. He was hired by IDEAL as writer/director: *The Diamond Necklace, Demos, A Woman of No Importance, Sonia, The Old Wives' Tale* (1921), *Bentley's Conscience, Diana of the Crossways, A Bill of Divorcement* (1922), *This Freedom, Out to Win,* and *The Loves of Mary, Queen of Scots* (1923). He returned to the US in 1924, again to direct for Fox, and later worked on the script for Cecil B. DeMille's *King of Kings* (1927). Between 1926 and 1936, Clift had four plays produced on Broadway; in the 20s and 30s, he returned occasionally to the UK; in the 30s and 40s, a number of his plays, novels and short stories were adapted for the screen.

OTHER BRITISH FILMS INCLUDE: *Paradise* (1928), *Power over Men* (sc), *Taxi for Two* (co-d), *High Seas* (1929), *All That Glitters* (1936, + sc), *The Last Adventurers* (1937). AS.

Clive, Colin (*b* St-Malo, France, 1898 – *d* Los Angeles, 1937). Actor. Son of a British Colonel, and descended from the legendary Clive of India, he turned to the stage when a serious knee injury concluded his military career. On stage from 1919, he memorably created the role of Stanhope in *Journey's End*, which he repeated in the film version (1930, UK/US) directed by his friend, James WHALE. Most of the rest of his career was spent in Hollywood where he played in Whale's *Bride of Frankenstein* (1935). Married (1929) to Jeanne De CASALIS until his death from TB, exacerbated by alcoholism.

OTHER BRITISH FILMS: *A Matter of Good Taste* (1930), *The Stronger Sex* (1931), *Lily Christine* (1932).

Clore, Leon (*b* Brighton, 1918 – *d* London, 1992). Producer. DOCUMENTARY film-maker who made a few features, including two for FREE CINEMA colleague Karel REISZ, *Morgan: A Suitable Case for Treatment* (1966) and *The French Lieutenant's Woman* (1981). Much associated with INDEPENDENT FILM-MAKERS, Anthony SIMMONS (e.g. *Sunday By the Sea*, 1953, + ed; *Bow Bells*, 1954, doc, short), and John KRISH (e.g. *I Want to Go to School*, 1959, *Return to Life*, 1960, *Mr Marsh Comes to School*, 1961). Other Free Cinema titles include Lindsay ANDERSON's *Every Day Except Christmas* (1957) and Reisz's *We Are the Lambeth Boys* (1959).
OTHER BRITISH FILMS INCLUDE: *The Conquest of Everest* (1953, doc, AAn), *The Passing Stranger* (ex p) (1954), *Time Without Pity* (co-p), *Virgin Island* (1958), *All Neat in Black Stockings* (1969).

Close, Ivy (*b* Stockon-on-Tees, 1893 – *d* Goring-on-Thames, 1968). Actress. After winning the 1911 *Daily Mirror* Beauty Contest, Ivy Close starred in a series of films directed by her husband Elwin NEAME. She had a brief US career with the Kalem Company in 1916 and starred for Abel Gance in *La Roue* (1922). Mother of **Derek Neame** (*see* Elwin NEAME) and Ronald NEAME.
BRITISH FILMS INCLUDE: *The Lady of Shallot* (1912), *Darkest London* (1915), *The Ware Case* (1917), *The Flag Lieutenant* (1919), *Expiation* (1922). AS.

Close Up Although this journal was short-lived (July 1927-December 1933), it provided a forum for 'serious' criticism of international cinema. Edited by Kenneth MACPHERSON, who was assisted by Bryher [Winifred Ellerman], much of the vigorous debate about CENSORSHIP and the state of the British film industry in the 1920s and 30s centred around this publication. Contributors included Ivor MONTAGU, Ernest BETTS and Ralph BOND as well as Gertrude Stein and Dorothy M. Richardson. The journal was given much impetus by its championship of the Soviet cinema, in particular the work of Eisenstein and Pudovkin, and the cinemas of Germany and France.
BIBLIOG: James Donald *et al* (eds), *Close Up, 1927–33: Cinema and Modernism*, 1998; Rachael Low, *The History of the British Film: 1918–1929*, 1971. Deane Williams.

Cloutier, Suzanne (*b* Ottawa, 1927). Actress. Formerly married (1954–71) to Peter USTINOV, this actress appeared as a maid who gets to romance a film star in *Derby Day* (1952) and someone's girlfriend in *Doctor in the House* (1954), but is best remembered as Orson WELLES's Desdemona in *Othello* (1952, Morocco).

Clowes, St John L. (*b* 1907). Screenwriter, director. Best known now as the director and writer of the notorious *No Orchids for Miss Blandish* (1948), which Oswald MITCHELL took over when Clowes became ill. Trained for the Navy at Dartmouth, he left the service to join BIP in 1927, and in the 30s made several 'QUOTA QUICKIES', such as *Dora* (1933, d, sc, e) and *Grand Prix* (1934, d, sc, p). There were two wartime SHORTS for STRAND, *A Welcome to Britain* (assoc p) and *Battle for Music* (sc) (1943) and his 'perfect murder' play, *Dear Murderer* was stylishly filmed in 1947.
OTHER BRITISH FILMS INCLUDE: *Who's Your Father?* (1935, p sup), *Things Happen at Night* (1948, p, sc).

Clunes, Alec (*b* Brixton, 1912 – *d* London, 1970). Actor. RN: Alexander dem Sherriff Clunes. Of theatrical parents, suave-seeming Clunes began in advertising and journalism before his professional stage debut in 1933 initiated a distinguished career as actor, producer and manager, including seasons at Stratford and the Old Vic, as well as modern plays. Entered films in 1940, making several appearances at EALING, including *Let George Do It!*, *Saloon Bar* and *Convoy*. Post-war, he filmed very rarely but was memorable as Hastings in *Richard III* (1955) and the distraught father in the kidnap thriller, *Tomorrow at Ten* (1962). His son is actor Martin CLUNES.
OTHER BRITISH FILMS INCLUDE: *Convoy* (1940), *One of Our Aircraft is Missing* (1942), *Now Barabbas Was a Robber* (1949), *Melba* (1953), *Tiger in the Smoke* (1956).

Clunes, Martin (*b* London, 1961). Actor. Lanky and hefty, this gifted comic actor was very busy in 90s TV and found fame in *Men Behaving Badly* (1992, 1993–98, 2002) as the terminally laddish Gary. In films, he directed and starred in the little-seen but droll *Staggered* (1994), was the bickering bourgeois husband in *The Acid House* and a swaggering Burbage in *Shakespeare in Love* (1999). Son of Alec CLUNES; married (1) actress Lucy Aston and (2) producer of *Staggered*, Philippa Braithwaite.
OTHER BRITISH FILMS: *The Ballad of Kid Divine, Carry On Columbus* (1992), *It's Good to Talk* (1997, short), *The Revengers' Comedies* (1998, UK/Fr), *Saving Grace* (2000).

Clyde, June (*b* St Joseph, Missouri, 1909 – *d* Fort Lauderdale, Florida, 1987). Actress. RN: Tetrazini. Began career as child in vaudeville, made 25 indifferent films in Hollywood before moving there in 1935 with her husband, director Thornton FREELAND. A blonde musical comedy actress, she starred in 15 British musicals and comedies during the latter 30s, including *Charing Cross Road* (1935), opposite John MILLS, and *Land Without Music* (1936), co-starring Richard TAUBER. Post-war, she was back in Britain in character roles, often as brash Americans, as in *Treasure Hunt* (1952), and often on stage.
OTHER BRITISH FILMS INCLUDE: *She Shall Have Music* (1935), *Aren't Men Beasts?* (1937), *Night Without Stars* (1951), *The Love Lottery* (1953), *The Story of Esther Costello, After the Ball* (1957).

coal mining The British cinema's sporadic forays into the mining industry were tempered by the censor's dictum against material featuring industrial disputes or union activity (mining was notorious for its militancy). Consequently, those mining films that surfaced tended to stress communality as against conflict, with the inevitable pit disaster uniting management and worker. Even DOCUMENTARIES like *Coal Face* (1935) were more poetic than realistic. Notable exceptions that attempted a more truthful depiction of mining were *The Citadel* (1938), *The Stars Look Down* (1939), *The Proud Valley* (1940) and *The Brave Don't Cry* (1952), wherein the harsh working and social conditions were brought to greater prominence. Post-war nationalisation saw the new National Coal Board institute its own film unit to promote the industry, including *Mining Review*, a regular magazine film, but features set in the industry were few. Jill CRAIGIE's *Blue Scar* (1949) was a noteworthy exception. The ravages wrought by THATCHERISM have been depicted in two films: *The Big Man* (1990) and *Brassed Off* (1996, UK/US). John Oliver.

Coates, Anne V. (*b* Reigate, 1925). Editor. The niece of J. Arthur RANK, Coates wrote in 1963, 'I got into the industry through influence'. Maybe, but she stayed to become one of its most respected editors, on nearly 50 films, starting as assistant editor on such films as *The History of Mr Polly* (1948) and *The Chiltern Hundreds* (1949). Her first credit as editor was on *The Pickwick Papers* (1952); she won an Oscar for *Lawrence of Arabia* (1962), worked on such popular films as *Murder on the the the*

Orient Express (1974) and *The Eagle Has Landed* (1976), and in recent years on such Hollywood films as *Erin Brockovich* (2000). Married to director Douglas HICKOX; mother of US-based director Anthony Hickox.

OTHER BRITISH FILMS INCLUDE: *Grand National Night* (1953), *Lost* (1955), *The Horse's Mouth* (1958), *Tunes of Glory* (1960), *Becket* (1964), *Young Cassidy* (1965), *The Bofors Gun* (1968), *Follow Me!* (1971), *Bequest to the Nation* (1973), *Greystoke . . .* (1984, UK/US), *Lady Jane* (1985), *Chaplin* (1992, UK/Fr/It/Jap/US).

Coates, Eric (*b* Hucknall, 1886 – *d* London, 1957). Composer. Wrote only four film scores but two of them were very memorable: 'The Eighth Army March' for the film *Nine Men* (1942) and, above all, the stirring march for *The Dam Busters* (1955), now so redolent of both WW2 and its 50s film representations.

OTHER BRITISH FILMS: *The Old Curiosity Shop* (1934), *High Flight* (1957).

Cockrell, Gary Actor. Supporting player and second lead of the 60s, in some notable films, including *Lolita* (1961) and *Twilight's Last Gleaming* (1977, US/Ger), without making much impact.

OTHER BRITISH FILMS INCLUDE: *Tarzan the Magnificent* (1960), *On the Fiddle* (1961), *Tiara Tahiti*, *The War Lover* (1962), *Blaze of Glory* (star) (1963), *The Bedford Incident* (1965).

Codrington, Ann (*b* Kasauli, India, 1895 – *d* ?). Actress. Stage actress who filmed occasionally after 1935 debut in *The Price of Wisdom*. On stage from 1915 and with the BBC Repertory Players (1942–45). Mother of actress Patricia HILLIARD.

OTHER BRITISH FILMS INCLUDE: *Lucky Days* (1935), *I'll Turn to You* (1946), *No Place for Jennifer* (1949), *Portrait of Clare*, *Stage Fright* (1950), *The Lady with a Lamp* (1951).

Coe, Peter (*b* London, 1929 – *d* Byfleet, 1987). Director. First resident director of the Mermaid Theatre from 1959, when he scored a big success with the pastiche 18th century romp, *Lock Up Your Daughters*, which he filmed in 1969 to less acclaim, despite a high-powered cast. Died in a car accident.

Coen, Guido Producer. Purveyor of proficient 'B' MOVIE THRILLERS, most often in collaboration with director Charles SAUNDERS, with whom he turned out 15 such items, starting with *Meet Mr Callaghan* (1954), for companies such as Kenilworth, Fortress and Theatrecraft. Also produced Vernon SEWELL's fine suspense thriller, *Strongroom* (1962).

OTHER BRITISH FILMS INCLUDE: *She Shall Have Murder* (1950), *The Hornet's Nest* (1955), *Behind the Headlines* (1956), *There's Always a Thursday* (1957), *Jungle Street*, *Dangerous Afternoon* (1961), *Baby Love* (+ sc), *The Penthouse* (1967), *Burke & Hare* (1971).

Coffey, Denise (*b* Aldershot, 1936). Actress. Trained at Glasgow College of Drama, on stage from 1954, and her first film was *The Wild and the Willing* (1962). Played the heroine's mousy little friend Peg in *Georgy Girl* (1966), and has had supporting roles in a further half-dozen films.

OTHER BRITISH FILMS INCLUDE: *Waltz of the Toreadors* (1962), *Percy* (1971), *Another Time, Another Place* (1983), *Saving Grace* (2000).

Coffin, Adeline Hayden Actress. This ageing character actress in silent films, who often appeared in aristocratic roles, was married to the prominent stage actor Hayden Coffin (1862–1935) and was often billed as Mrs Hayden Coffin.

BRITISH FILMS INCLUDE: *The Manxman* (1916), *The Sands of Time* (1919), *The Prodigal Son* (1923), *The Triumph of the Rat* (1926), *Other People's Sins* (1931). AS.

Cohen, Nat (*b* London, 1905 – *d* London, 1988). Executive. Entered industry in 1930 as cinema-owner and in 1942 formed ANGLO-AMALGAMATED production and distribution partnership with Stuart LEVY. They were responsible for the EDGAR WALLACE series of the 50s, the first dozen 'CARRY ON' films, and more prestigious productions in the 60s. When A-A was absorbed by EMI, Cohen joined its board, Levy having died in 1966, and eventually became head of Anglo-EMI. Last worked as executive producer on *Clockwise* (1985). He is one of those influential figures whose names do not necessarily appear in film credits, and his negotiations are behind such successes as John SCHLESINGER's *A Kind of Loving* (1962) and *Darling* (1965), and *Murder on the Orient Express* (1974). Alexander Walker described him as 'a more urbane version of the one-man bands who used to be studio bosses in Hollywood's heyday'.

Cohen, Norman (*b* Dublin, 1936 – *d* Van Nuys, California, 1983). Director. Irish-born maker of DOCUMENTARY and fiction films, who began as editor on 'B' MOVIES such as *A Guy Called Caesar* (1962) and later directed a run of 70s comedies, including several in the 'Confessions of . . .' SERIES. Directed several short films in Ireland (e.g. *Brendan Behan's Dublin* (1966) and *Burning Rubber* (1981, doc) in US.

OTHER BRITISH FILMS INCLUDE: (d, unless noted) *Breath of Life* (1963, p), *The Runaway* (1964, e), *The London Nobody Knows* (1967, doc), *Till Death Us Do Part* (1969), *Dad's Army* (1971), *Confessions of a Window Cleaner* (1974, ex p), *. . . of a Pop Performer* (1975), *. . . of a Driving Instructor* (1976), *Stand Up Virgin Soldiers* (1977).

Coke, Peter (*b* Southsea, 1913). Actor. RADA bronze medallist, on stage from 1934, and playwright whose *Breath of Spring* (1958) was filmed as *Make Mine Mink* (1960). In films from 1937 (*Missing, Believed Married*) in supporting roles, with the Royal Artillery 1940–46, followed by return to the stage, and for 15 years he was radio's Paul Temple.

OTHER BRITISH FILMS INCLUDE: *Keep Smiling* (1938), *Cheer Boys Cheer* (1939), *The Broken Horseshoe* (1953), *John and Julie* (1955), *The Extra Day, Carry On Admiral* (1957), *Up the Creek* (1958).

Cole, George (*b* London, 1925). Actor. Cole's 60-year career gives the lie to the notion that child actors fail to go on to adult success. He became a major character star, hurdling the decades with ease as he refurbished his persona from that of cockney kid ('I was paid to be cheeky and people clapped me for it', he said in 1990), to awkward, often shy young man, to 'Flash Harry' of four ST TRINIAN's capers, to TV's wonderfully shifty 'Arfer Daley' in *Minder* (1979–84, 1988–94). Yet even these significant transmutations leave out much of a remarkable career.

On stage from 14, in the chorus of *White Horse Inn* (1939), in Blackpool; then, in Birmingham and London, *Cottage to Let* (1940), in which the star was Alastair SIM, who took Cole under his wing and would play so influential a role in his career. They were both cast by Anthony ASQUITH in the film version of *Cottage* (1941), Cole as the resourceful evacuee who helps unmask an unlikely spy. Looking younger than his years, he played another evacuee in *Those Kids from Town* (1942) and, very touchingly, the boy in *Henry V* (1944), and was in the RAF (1943–47). The obsessive kite-flyer in an episode of *Quartet* (1948) is probably the best of his gauche young men, though he plays his part in the tense build-up of the submarine drama, *Morning Departure* (1950). He played the younger – to Sim's older – *Scrooge* (1951) and they acted together in eight more films, including the ST TRINIAN'S SERIES in which their comic styles complemented each other: Sim is all restrained outrage, Cole grotesque spivvery. Along the way, there were serious roles, such as the cockney promoted to officer in *The Intruder* (1953) and the Sergeant in *A Prize of Gold* (1955), and in 1971 he played the straight role of an anxious husband in *Fright* (1971). Also appeared in two international botches: *Cleopatra* (1963 – as Caesar's deaf-mute barber) and *The Bluebird* (1976 – as The Dog).

Not only are there 40-odd films, but as well Cole was very fortunate with his TV work: not just *Minder*, but *A Life of Bliss* (1960–61), reprising the shy bachelor character he had played on radio, *A Man of Our Times* (1968), which marked his transition to middle-aged roles, and the broadly droll *Blott on the Landscape* (1985). He also appeared in over 30 plays, including several by James BRIDIE. Married to actresses (1) Eileen MOORE (1954–62) and (2) Penny MORELL (1964–).

OTHER BRITISH FILMS INCLUDE: *Nero* (1940, short), *The Demi-Paradise* (1943), *Journey Together* (1945), *My Brother's Keeper* (1948), *The Spider and the Fly* (1949), *Gone to Earth* (1950), *Laughter in Paradise* (1951), *Top Secret* (1952), *Happy Ever After*, *The Belles of St Trinian's*, (1954), *The Green Man* (1956), *Too Many Crooks* (1959), *Dr Syn Alias the Scarecrow* (1963), *One Way Pendulum* (1964), *The Great St Trinian's Train Robbery* (1966), *Mary Reilly* (1996, UK/US), *Station Jim* (2001).

Cole, Sidney (*b* London, 1908 – *d* London [Ealing], 1998). Editor, producer. An important member of the EALING family during its heyday, 1942–52. Educated at the LSE, to which he attributed his Leftist sympathies, he first worked for STOLL PRODUCTIONS, then with BIP, Ealing and others before going to Spain in 1938 with Thorold DICKINSON to make DOCUMENTARIES. He edited such notable films as *Gaslight* (1940) and *Pimpernel Smith* (1941), before rejoining Ealing, where he was variously editor (*Went the Day Well?*, 1942), supervising editor (*San Demetrio–London*, 1943), associate producer (*Dead of Night*, (1945), producer (*Secret People*, 1951), co-screenwriter (*They Came to a City*, 1944, + assoc p), and director (segment of *Train of Events*, 1949). Given that 'associate producer' at Ealing meant, in effect, 'producer', the title Michael BALCON took for himself on virtually every film, the fact that Cole was assigned to *Scott of the Antarctic* (1948) in this role points to his prestige at the studio. In the late 50s and the 60s, he turned to TV.

From 1935, he was active in the ACT (later ACTT, BECTU) and was on the board of its production company ACT FILMS, for which he produced *The Kitchen* (1961). He had also been an early supporter of the FILM SOCIETY.

OTHER BRITISH FILMS: (e) *Mr Cinders* (1934), *Midshipman Easy* (1935), *The High Command* (1937), *Behind Spanish Lines*, *Spanish ABC* (1938, shorts, co-ed, co-d), *Roads Across Britain* (1939, short, d), *Breach of Promise* (1941), *Our Film* (short), *Nine Men* (1942); (sup e) *The Bells Go Down* (1943), *The Halfway House* (1944); (assoc p) *The Loves of Joanna Godden*, *Against the Wind* (1949), *The Magnet* (1950), *Escapade* (1955).

Coleby, A.E. (*b* London, 1876 – *d* London, 1930). Actor, director. Coleby was a former race-course bookie, a tough, burly gent with a sense of humour – after listing his work in the *Kinematograph Year Book*, he concluded the entry, 'also a good comedian' – who directed mediocre action pictures, in which he often appeared. In all, he directed, sometimes wrote and often appeared in more than 700 films, primarily SHORTS, between 1907 and 1930. Among the dross are *The Call of the Road* (1920), which marked the debut of Victor McLAGLEN, and the immensely long and tedious *The Prodigal Son* (1923), shot on location in Iceland. Companies with which Coleby was

associated are Cricks & Martin, PATHÉ, I.E. Davidson, and STOLL; he left the last in 1924 and formed the FHC Company at Esher with R.H. CRICKS.

BRITISH FEATURE FILMS INCLUDE: (d) *The Treasure of Heaven* (1916, + a), *Thelma* (1918, co-d), *The Silver Lining* (1919), *The Way of the World* (1920, + a, sc), *The Fifth Form at St Dominic's*, *Froggy's Little Brother* (1921, + sc), *Unto Each Other* (1929, co-d), *Over the Sticks* (1930, co-d). AS.

Coleman, Bryan (*b* London, 1911). Actor. On stage before entering films in the 30s when his first credit seems to have been *Sword of Honour* (1939), though some sources list *Broken Blossoms* and *The Mill on the Floss* (1936). After WW2 service (1940–45), he filmed very sparingly over the next 45 years, best remembered as the architect seduced to Linden TRAVERS' purposes in *Jassy* (1947).

OTHER BRITISH FILMS INCLUDE: *Train of Events* (1949), *The Planter's Wife* (1952), *Suspended Alibi*, *Reach for the Sky* (1956), *Crooks Anonymous* (1962), *Zeppelin* (1971), *Mona Lisa* (1986).

Coleman, Charlotte (*b* London, 1968 – *d* London, 2001). Actress. Wonderfully funny as the bizarre, punkish Scarlett in *Four Weddings and a Funeral* (1994), Coleman had already shown her mettle in TV's *Oranges Are Not the Only Fruit* (1990) as the teenage lesbian daughter of Geraldine McEWAN. Short and distinctive, and a self-confessed tearaway as a teenager, she was one of the smartest young faces in 90s British film, and always in good company, but was still awaiting a hit film built around her at the time of her tragically early death from asthma. Daughter of actress Ann BEACH and TV producer Francis Coleman.

OTHER BRITISH FILMS INCLUDE: *Map of the Human Heart* (1992, UK/Aust/Can/Fr), *The Young Poisoner's Handbook* (1995, UK/Ger), *The Revengers' Comedies* (1998, UK/Fr), *Beautiful People* (1999), *Bodywork* (2000).

Coleridge, Ethel (*b* South Milton, Devon,1883 – *d* London, 1976). Actress. RN: Coleridge-Tucker. Unforgettably hatchet-faced, bullying Clara Soppit in *When We Are Married* (1943), Coleridge worked variations on this persona in nearly 20 films: witness the lugubrious lighthousekeeper's wife in *The Loves of Joanna Godden* (1947) and the moronic cleaning ladies of *A Piece of Cake* and *Penny and the Pownall Case* (1948). On stage from 1905 and in adaptations of plays in the 30s; in the 40s, in several HIGHBURY STUDIOS second features.

OTHER BRITISH FILMS: *Rookery Nook* (1930), *Plunder* (1931), *Laburnum Grove* (1936), *Women Aren't Angels* (1942), *Murder in Reverse* (1945), *Song for Tomorrow*, *The Fallen Idol* (1948).

Coleridge, Sylvia (*b* Darjeerling, India, 1912 – *d* London, 1986). Actress. Mainly associated with the stage, from 1931, at the Old Vic (1962–64), she appeared in occasional films, including *Tess* (1979, UK/Fr) as Mrs D'Urbeville. Some TV, including *Bleak House* (1985), as Miss Flyte.

OTHER BRITISH FILMS INCLUDE: *Cross My Heart* (1937), *Jailbirds*, *I Met a Murderer* (1939), *The Raging Moon* (1970), *Secret Places* (1984).

Coles, Michael Actor. Supporting player of the 60s and 70s, seen mostly on TV, and in such SPIN-OFFS as *Dr Who and the Daleks* (1965). Started film career in 'B' MOVIES at MERTON PARK: *Man Detained* (1961) and *Solo for Sparrow* (1962).

OTHER BRITISH FILMS INCLUDE: *Private Potter*, *HMS Defiant*, (1963), *A Touch of Love* (1969), *The Wicker Man* (1973), *The Satanic Rites of Dracula* (1974), *Sweeney!* (1976), *Dirty Weekend* (1993).

Colicos, John (*b* Toronto, 1928 – *d* Toronto, 2000) Actor. Famous for uncanny impersonation of CHURCHILL in the play, *Soldiers* (1968), Colicos made a handful of British films of

which only *Anne of the Thousand Days* (1969), as devious Thomas Cromwell, gave him anything worth doing. Many striking, oleaginous Hollywood character roles, like the cuckolded husband in *The Postman Always Rings Twice* (1981).
OTHER BRITISH FILMS: *Appointment in London* (1953), *Passport to Treason, Barbados Quest* (1955), *Bond of Fear* (1956).

Colin, Ian (*b* Livingstone, South Africa, 1910). Actor. RN: Wetherell. Tall, lean supporting actor, in bigger roles pre-war (e.g. lead in *Wings over Africa*, 1936), later in small parts like Adrienne CORRI's neglectful husband in *The Big Chance* (1957). Was Inspector Lomax in TV's *The Quatermass Experiment* (1953).
OTHER BRITISH FILMS INCLUDE: *A Moorland Tragedy* (1933), *Late Extra*, (1935), *Men of Yesterday* (1936), *The Outsider* (1939), *The Winslow Boy, The Queen of Spades* (1948), *The White Trap* (1959), *Strongroom* (1962).

Colin, Jean (*b* Brighton, 1905 – *d* London, 1989). Actress. Pretty blonde leading lady of 30s MUSICALS and COMEDIES, including *Charing Cross Road* (1935) and, notably, *The Mikado* (1939), as Yum-Yum. Returned in character roles in *Last Holiday* (1950), as Sidney JAMES's vulgar wife, and *Laxdale Hall* (1953). On stage from 1925 to mid 50s.
OTHER BRITISH FILMS INCLUDE: *A Dear Liar* (1925), *Compromising Daphne* (1930), *Lord Babs* (1932), *Mad About Money* (1938), *Bob's Your Uncle* (1941).

Colin, Sid (*b* London, 1915 – *d* London, 1989). Screenwriter. Comedy writer for radio, TV and films, including the endlessly suggestive *Up Pompeii* (1971). Also sang and played guitar for AMBROSE's band and wrote the hit song, 'If I only had wings' for the RAF.
OTHER BRITISH FILMS INCLUDE: *Starlight Serenade* (1943, short), *The Brass Monkey* (1948, comp), *The Golden Arrow* (1952, co-sc), *The Ugly Duckling* (1959), *Carry On Spying* (1964), *Up the Chastity Belt* (1971), *Percy's Progress* (1974).

Colleano, Bonar (*b* New York, 1924 – *d* Birkenhead, 1958). Actor. RN: Sullivan. Charismatic American-born actor who went to Britain when he was 12. After experience from childhood with Ringling Brothers' Circus and in his family's famous circus and music hall act, he entered films in 1944, and enlivened nearly 30 with his wise-cracking, dame-stalking persona. He is irresistibly good-humoured as gum-chewing Friselli in *The Way to the Stars* (1945), one of the heroine's international suitors in *While the Sun Shines* (1947) and a womanising Sergeant in *Sleeping Car to Trieste* (1948), more sinister as a deserter in *Good-Time Girl* (1947). He was the archetypal brash GI ('overpaid, over sexed and over here') in 40s films, but kept working, though in less rewarding material, until his untimely death in a car accident. Married (2) actress Susan SHAW, who declined into alcoholism after his death. Stage work included Stanley in *A Streetcar Named Desire* (1949) with Vivien Leigh.
OTHER BRITISH FILMS: *Starlight Serenade* (1943, short), *Wanted for Murder, A Matter of Life and Death* (1946), *Once a Jolly Swagman, Merry-Go-Round, One Night with You* (1949), *Give Us This Day* (1949), *Dance Hall, Pool of London* (1950), *A Tale of Five Cities* (1951), *Is Your Honeymoon Really Necessary?, Escape by Night* (1953), *Time Is My Enemy, The Sea Shall Not Have Them, The Flame and the Flesh* (UK/US) (1954), *Joe Macbeth, No Love for Judy* (narr) (1955), *Zarak, Stars in Your Eyes* (1956), *Interpol, Fire Down Below, Death over My Shoulder* (1957), *Them Nice Americans, The Man Inside, No Time to Die* (1958).

Colley, Kenneth (*b* Manchester, 1937). Actor. Incisive supporting player, in films since the mid 60s, including five for Ken RUSSELL, starting with *The Music Lovers* (1971), and showing

up particularly well as the TV current affairs editor in *Giro City* (1982). Also in *The Empire Strikes Back* (1980, US) and *Return of the Jedi* (1983, US).
OTHER BRITISH FILMS INCLUDE: *Seventy Deadly Pills* (1963), *The Jokers* (1966), *Performance* (1970), *The Devils* (1971), *Mahler, Juggernaut* (1974), *Lisztomania* (1975), *Jabberwocky* (1977), *Monty Python's Life of Brian* (1979), *The Rainbow* (1989), *Brassed Off* (1996, UK/US), *Hold Back the Night* (UK/It), *Holding On* (1999).

Collie, Stephanie (*b* Warrington, 1963) Costume designer. Trained at Cheltenham Art College and London College of Fashion, she assisted on two Kenneth BRANAGH productions, *Peter's Friends* (1992) and *Much Ado About Nothing* (1993, UK/US). Has since specialised in films which seem to limit the designer's art to the mundane and/or scruffy end of the spectrum, including *Among Giants* (1998) and *Lock, Stock and Two Smoking Barrels* (1999), in which however the costumes still contrive to distinguish between members of the respective ensembles.
OTHER BRITISH FILMS INCLUDE: *Swan Song* (1992, short), *The Innocent Sleep* (1995), *Stiff Upper Lips* (1996, UK/Ind), *Greenwich Mean Time* (1999), *Shiner* (2001).

Collier, Constance (*b* Windsor, 1878 – *d* New York, 1955). Actress, dramatist. RN: Hardie. Celebrated British actress but not, mostly, in British films, though some of her Hollywood-based *grandes dames* are in British-set films, such as *Kitty* (1945). She appeared in five British films of the 20s and 30s, including *Bleak House* (1920), as Lady Deadlock, and *Thunder in the City* (1937), and post-war returned to play Lady Markby in *An Ideal Husband* (1947). With Ivor NOVELLO, she co-authored two plays later filmed as vehicles for him: *Downhill* (1927) and *The Rat* (1925, remade 1937).
OTHER BRITISH FILMS: *The Impossible Woman* (1919), *The Bohemian Girl* (1922), *Clothes and the Woman* (1937).

Collier, Lionel (*b* 1892 – *d* ?). Critic. During the 40s and 50s, Collier's 'Shop for Your Films' in *Picturegoer* was an unaffected fans' guide to new films. Oxford-educated, he had served in WW1, after which he wrote film criticism for, among others, *Evening News, Sunday Express* and *Reynolds News*, and in the 40s and early 50s his clear synoptic accounts of releases, with unpretentious evaluative comment, offered the sort of service no longer available to the average filmgoer. He applauded British films whenever he could, but was not at all xenophobic about it. **Margaret Hinxman** (*b* London, 1924) replaced him as chief reviewer for *Picturegoer* in the 50s. He also reviewed for the trade publication, KINEMATOGRAPH WEEKLY.

Collier, Patience (*b* London, 1911 – *d* London, 1987). Actress. RN: Rene Ritcher. Distinctively sharp-featured character star of all the acting media: on stage since leaving RADA in 1932, in classic and modern roles and at least once very funny in revue (*Living for Pleasure*, 1958); she made over 2,000 radio broadcasts and was on TV from 1950; entered films in 1962 in Norman WISDOM's *The Girl in the Boat*. She made a meal of some rich character roles, including Flossie Fagan in *Decline and Fall . . .* (1968), a snooty agency manageress in *Every Home Should Have One* (1969), Grandma in *Fiddler on the Roof* (1971, US), and especially the vinegary Mrs Poulteney in *The French Lieutenant's Woman* (1981).
OTHER BRITISH FILMS INCLUDE: *Baby Love* (1967), *Countess Dracula* (1970), *National Health* (1973).

Collin, John (*b* Burnley, 1931 – *d* 1987). Actor. Sturdy character player of films and TV, including five years of *Z Cars* (1973–78).

He was the hapless Durbeyfield in *Tess* (1979, UK/Fr) but his best screen role was in the US-made *Star!* (1968) as Gertrude LAWRENCE's first husband.

OTHER BRITISH FILMS INCLUDE: *Against the Tide* (1965), *The Witches* (1966), *Before Winter Comes* (1968), *Man at the Top* (1973), *The Errand* (1980).

Collings, A(rthur) Esmé (*b* Weston-super-Mare, 1859 – *d* Eastbourne, Sussex, 1936) Pioneer. A portrait photographer in Brighton, who had a partnership with William FRIESE-GREENE beginning in 1885, Collings began filming later in 1896, with *The Lord Mayor's Show* and a drama, *The Broken Melody*, among others. Though he was associated with the 'BRIGHTON SCHOOL' of film-makers, his interest in cinematography does not appear to have extended beyond 1898, at which time he was active as a painter of miniatures and water colours. Despite the best efforts of historian John BARNES, little is known of Collings. AS.

Collins, Alf (*b* London, 1865 – *d* London, 1951). Director, actor. Former MUSIC HALL comedian who directed and sometimes acted in more than 50 fast-moving SHORTS, including the earliest British 'chase' films, for GAUMONT between 1902 and 1910. In 1908, he directed Harry LAUDER in *Harry Lauder in a Hurry*, and at the end of his career, in 1912, directed at least one dramatic short, *A Maid of the Alps*. AS.

Collins, Anthony (*b* Hastings, 1893 – *d* Los Angeles, 1964). Composer, conductor. Former orchestral player with the LSO, entered films in 1937 as composer-conductor on *Victoria the Great*, the first of 13 collaborations with Herbert WILCOX, both in the US on such films as *Nurse Edith Cavell* (1939) and *Irene* (1940) and Britain. Post-war, he scored for Wilcox through thick – *Piccadilly Incident* (1946) – and thin – *Laughing Anne* (1953). An oddity on his credits is Luis Buñuel's *The Adventures of Robinson Crusoe* (1954).

OTHER BRITISH FILMS: *The Rat* (1937), *I Live in Grosvenor Square* (1945), *The Courtneys of Curzon Street* (1947), *Odette* (1950), *The Lady with a Lamp* (1951), *Trent's Last Case*, *Derby Day* (1952).

Collins, Edwin J. (*b* 1875 – *d* ?). Actor, director. An actor with Cricks & Martin from 1910–11, and a director of more than 50 SHORTS (between 1912 and 1923) for the same company and later for H.B. PARKINSON.

BRITISH FEATURE FILMS INCLUDE: (d) *Eugene Aram* (1914), *God and the Man* (1918), *The Starting Point* (1919), *Calvary*, *Foul Play* (1920), *Stella*, *Miss Charity* (1921), *A Gamble with Hearts* (1923), *What Money Can Buy* (1928). AS.

Collins, Jackie (*b* London, 1937). Actress, author. Before settling in the US and to international notoriety as the author of such 'sizzling' works as *The Stud* (1978), filmed from her screenplay and starring sister Joan, Collins appeared decoratively and fleetingly in some justly forgotten British films, such as *Rock You Sinners* (1957). Married Oscar Lerman, producer of *The World Is Full of Married Men* (1979), based on her novel and screenplay.

OTHER BRITISH FILMS INCLUDE: *They Never Learn* (1956), *Barnacle Bill*, *The Safecracker* (1957), *Passport to Shame* (1958).

Collins, Joan (*b* London, 1933). Actress. Someone (Oscar Levant??) once said: 'I knew Joan Collins when she was older than she is today', highlighting the remarkable way in which she seems to have hurdled the decades, with – still intact – that glamour that British film-makers hardly knew what to do with. After three small roles, she was thoroughly noticed as sultry sexpots in *I Believe in You* (1952), *Cosh Boy* and *Turn the Key Softly* (1953). There was perhaps never a suitable decade for Collins in British films, but it certainly wasn't the tweedy 50s. Small wonder she went to Hollywood which made her a star in such films as *Land of the Pharaohs* (1955) and *The Virgin Queen* (1955).

A star, but not a superstar: that was finally achieved, in her 50s, by TV's *Dynasty* (1982–89), as arch-bitch Alexis Carrington, weaving a tangled web of seduction and treachery among Denver's oil-rich. Her own life had some of the elements of such lush soaps. The daughter of a theatrical booking agent, she married serially: to Maxwell REED who beat her; Anthony NEWLEY who gave her two children and put her in a dreadful film; producer **Ron Kass** (*b* Philadelphia, 1935; he presented her as 'Fontaine Khaled' in *The Stud*, 1978, and *The Bitch*, 1979, both from sister Jackie's novels); and Swedish businessman Peter Holm. All ended in divorce and were interspersed with high-profile romances with the likes of Warren BEATTY, and in 2002 married Peruvian theatre manager Percy Gibson, 32 years her junior. Noel LANGLEY who directed her in *Our Girl Friday* (1953) called her 'a baby temptress'; Hollywood turned her into an adult one, but, to be fair, she has kept on working while most of her contemporaries are forgotten. In the 70s, she made a string of HORROR films in Britain, then a batch of sex romps, and in the 80s she was mainly seen on American TV. After all this time, she can still surprise one by being fun as well as glamorous as she does in *In the Bleak Midwinter* (1995), as . . . what? A star of course.

OTHER BRITISH FILMS INCLUDE: *Lady Godiva Rides Again*, *Judgment Deferred* (1951), *Decameron Nights* (1952), *The Square Ring* (1953), *The Good Die Young* (1954), *Sea Wife* (1956), *Island in the Sun* (1957), *Can Hieronymus Merkin Ever Forget . . .* (1969, for Newley), *Quest for Love*, *Revenge* (1971), *Tales That Witness Madness* (1973), *The Big Sleep* (1978), *Sunburn* (1979), *Nutcracker* (1982), *The Clandestine Marriage* (1999, + assoc p).

Collins, Lewis (*b* Birkenhead, 1946). Actor. Came to prominence as the tough agent Bodie in TV's fast-moving thriller series, *The Professionals* (1977–83), but found only two nondescript roles in British films, *Confessions of a Driving Instructor* (1976) and *Who Dares Wins* (1982), as well as several little-seen co-productions.

Collins, Pauline (*b* Exmouth, 1940). Actress. Though much-awarded for her stage and film starring role as *Shirley Valentine* (1989, UK/US, BAA, AAn), a put-upon London housewife who finds romance and fulfilment in Greece, Collins' main career has been in TV. There, she made her name as the ambitious parlourmaid Sarah in *Upstairs, Downstairs* (1971–75), playing opposite husband John ALDERTON, with whom she co-starred in the spin-off series, *Thomas and Sarah* (1979). First film was *Secrets of a Windmill Girl* (1965); her few others include *City of Joy* (1992, UK/Fr), *Mutters Courage* (1995, UK/Austria/Ire/Ger) and *Paradise Road* (1997, US/Aust), in which she gave a moving study in goodness as a nun in a Japanese prisoner-of-war camp. Awarded OBE, 2001.

Collins, Phil (*b* London, 1951). Singer, lyricist, actor. A performer from childhood (the Artful Dodger in *Oliver!* on stage; a screaming fan in the BEATLES' film, *Help!* (1964); a children's film, *Calamity the Cow* (1967)), Collins found fame as a rock and pop singer in the US and the UK, especially in the 80s. Short and homely, he had one hit after another with rock band Genesis. On film his sympathetic performance as train robber *Buster* (1988) suggested there may yet be a career as a character player when the music stops.

OTHER BRITISH FILMS: *Genesis – A Band in Concert* (1976, doc), *The Secret Policeman's Other Ball* (1982), *Calliope* (1993, short), *Balto* (1995, anim, voice).

Collinson, Peter (*b* Cleethorpes, 1938 – *d* Santa Monica, California, 1980). Director. In his short but prolific career, Collinson often seemed to bring to film a flashiness derived from his experience on TV commercials. His early films – *Up the Junction*, *The Penthouse* (+ sc) (1967) – found little critical favour but the caper thriller, *The Italian Job* (1969), with its famous car chase (actually the work of the 2ud), was a major commercial success, and *Fright* (1971) has some genuinely scary moments among its absurdities. Sadly, his last film, *The Earthling* (1980, Aust/US), is almost a total, risible disaster.

OTHER BRITISH FILMS: *The Long Day's Dying* (1968), *You Can't Win 'Em All* (1970), *Straight on Till Morning* (+ p), *Innocent Bystanders* (1972), *The Man Called Noon* (1973, UK/It/Sp), *And Then There Were None* (1974), *The Spiral Staircase*, *The Sell-out* (1975), *Tomorrow Never Comes* (1977, UK/Can).

Colonial Film Unit This was a DOCUMENTARY production company founded in 1939 to make films of special interest to audiences in what was then the British Empire. The use of film in the colonies was funded by the Colonial Development and Welfare Act (1940), and CFU set up four production units in West Africa in the early 40s, funded partly by the British Government, partly by the territories involved. The function of the Unit's films was essentially that of education and PROPAGANDA, some of it intended to counteract the effects of the 'Americanisation' of Empire culture. Its films were distributed by the Central Office of Information and are now held by Overseas Film and TV. Silent film director George PEARSON went to the CFU as Head of Production and stayed there until his retirement in 1956. The Unit ceased production in 1955.

colonialism *see* **Empire and colonialism**

colour Natural colour motion pictures are additive or subtractive in principle. Additive processes variously work to the principle of adding together the three primary colours – red, green and blue – to create the desired synthesis. Subtractive processes start with white light, and essentially remove the colours not needed. The latter is the principle on which all colour cinematography now is based, but colour television operates on the additive principle. In the silent era distinction needed to be made between the pioneering natural colour systems, and the artificial means of adding colour: hand-painting (first introduced in Britain by R.W. PAUL in 1896); stencil colour (imported from France and often used in fashion items in NEWSREELS, and seen as late as 1930 in *Elstree Calling*); and the tinting and toning method of applying general colours to entire scenes which remained standard practice until the arrival of sound films.

Early colour systems were additive, using various methods to record and reproduce colour information with black-and-white originals. Edward R. Turner patented a three-colour system with rotating colour filters in 1899 which never worked in practice, but Charles URBAN purchased the rights and his associate G.A. SMITH in 1906 invented an ingenious compromise using just red and green filters to give an adequate colour record. KINEMACOLOR became the colour sensation of the pre-WWI period, before falling foul of a court case raised by the rival Biocolour system of William FRIESE-GREENE. The colour fringing caused by the two colour components not being in complete synchronisation, caused by the subject moving between alternate colour exposures, limited Kinemacolor's success; and a problem inherent in all additive systems was that the colour filters absorbed much of the light, rendering them unsuitable for studio work. J. Stuart BLACKTON brought the American system Prizmacolor to Britain to film *The Glorious Adventure* (1922), and Claude FRIESE-GREENE improved greatly on his father's work in his beautiful two-colour travel series *The Open Road* (1924–25), but two-colour subtractive TECHNICOLOR (using colour dyes) was now being seen in British cinemas in such American titles as *Ben-Hur* (1925) and *The Black Pirate* (1926).

Three-colour Technicolor film production began in Britain with *Wings of the Morning* (1937). Expensive, and jealously guarded by its dictatorial 'consultant' Natalie KALMUS, Technicolor in the 1930s was only seen in some ANIMATION films and the prestigious feature films of Alexander KORDA. A number of rival systems emerged, mostly used for advertising and animation: Gasparcolor, Chemicolor, Dunning Colour, and Dufaycolor, which worked on the additive principle, and was used creatively by Humphrey JENNINGS in some of his early work, and by Maurice ELVEY in one feature film, *Sons of the Sea* (1939). Dufay was also available to the narrow gauge home movie market, as were Kodachrome and Agfacolor.

Three-strip Technicolor continued to be the only colour system used in British feature films until the emergence of single-strip Eastmancolor in 1950. In that time great cinematographers such as Jack CARDIFF, Geoffrey UNSWORTH, Christopher CHALLIS and Freddie YOUNG produced the rich and glorious Technicolor productions of British cinema's heyday. With the introduction of Eastmancolor, colour became progressively more common, particularly necessary as an attraction not yet available on the rival medium, television. The last British A-feature made in black-and-white was *Bunny Lake is Missing* (1965), though occasional independent titles have appeared in recent years e.g. Shane Meadows' *24 7 TwentyFourSeven* (1997). Colour is now so wholly naturalistic that it is effectively unnoticed, except in the hands of a few colour-conscious directors. Derek JARMAN has probably been the most creative user of colour in recent years, most remarkably in his single-colour reverie *Blue* (1993). In considering Britain's colour film heritage, however, it is important to note that for fifty years production was predominantly in monochrome, now largely associated with the irrevocable past in the general consciousness. The need for colour has affected the commercial availability of Britain's monochrome film heritage, as black-and-white videos become harder to sell. The success of the television series *The Second World War in Colour* (1999) has only increased a sense that monochrome is losing its meaning for people. THE NATIONAL FILM AND TELEVISION ARCHIVE's restorations of Britain's Technicolor heritage have done much to increase appreciation of this grand period in British film history, but there needs to be equal education concerning the value and the beauties of monochrome, if a great part of Britain's film past is not gradually to slip out of view forever.

BIBLIOG: Brian Coe, *The History of Movie Photography*, 1981; Adrian Klein, *Colour Cinematography*, 1936; Derek Jarman, *Chroma*, 1995. Luke McKernan.

Coltrane, Robbie (*b* Glasgow, 1950). Actor. RN: Anthony McMillan. Heavy-set Scots comic actor with proven capacity for more dramatic work. Served apprenticeship at Edinburgh's renowned Traverse Theatre, worked extensively as a nightclub comedian, and gained mass popularity as a member of TV's *Comic Strip* team. Coltrane appeared in numerous minor film roles throughout the 80s, of which the most notable are Bob HOSKINS' endearing friend Thomas in *Mona Lisa* (1986), and Falstaff in BRANAGH's *Henry V* (1989). Coltrane teamed with Eric IDLE in the irreverent farce *Nuns on the Run* (1990), and followed this with the eponymous role in the satire *The Pope Must Die* (1991, UK/US), broadening his international appeal as a potential leading actor. Coltrane returned to TV for his most serious, best-known role to date, as the volatile criminal psychologist Fitz in *Cracker* (1993–96), for which he won three BAAs as best TV actor. In 2000 he won the role of gamekeeper Hagrid in *Harry Potter and the Philosopher's Stone* (2001, UK/US).

OTHER BRITISH FILMS INCLUDE: *Britannia Hospital* (1982), *Krull*, *Loose Connections* (1983), *Revolution* (UK/Nor), *Defence of the Realm* (1985), *Absolute Beginners*, *Caravaggio* (1986), *Eat the Rich* (1987), *The Fruit Machine* (1988), *Slipstream* (1989), *GoldenEye* (1995, UK/US), *The World Is Not Enough* (1999, UK/US), *Delaney's Flutter* (2001). Melinda Hildebrandt.

Columbia–British Hollywood company which had a fifty-year history of distributing British films in the US, starting with *The Song You Gave Me* (1933), including some major titles such as *The Beloved Vagabond* (1936), *State Secret* (1950) and many from HAMMER during the 50s and 60s, along with a good many second features. It entered pre-war British production only tentatively: its first British production was *The Lady Is Willing* (1934), a minor drama starring Leslie HOWARD, but mainly it backed the production of independent companies such as Irving ASHER's at DENHAM. In the 50s it engaged in a DISTRIBUTION deal with WARWICK FILMS, many of these action dramas with US stars (e.g. *Hell Below Zero*, 1953, starring Alan Ladd), and in the 60s some of its most successful productions were British-made, including *Lawrence of Arabia* (1962), *A Man for All Seasons* (1966) and *Oliver!* (1968).

comedy A major British film GENRE, comedy has over the course of the 20th century adopted various forms, including chase and gag films, musicals, 'comedian comedy', allegory and satire, variety, parody and burlesque, and television sitcom. In early British films (e.g. *Our New Errand Boy*, 1905), the chase and the gag prevail over narrative form, and the filming of MUSIC HALL sketches was a common form of silent film comedy. However, with the rise of the studio system and the virtual disappearance of artisan film-making, comedy was linked to narrative. For example, from 1912 to 1922, 'Pimple', played by Fred EVANS (in over 180 short films), satirised cultural and political stereotypes, and a film such as *Squibs Wins the Calcutta Sweep* (1922) is a fusion of gag, slapstick, and physical humour linked to a familial and romance plot.

In the early SOUND era, a popular form of comedy is identified with two female stars – Gracie FIELDS and Jessie MATTHEWS. Fields was one of many British film performers who brought their music hall inheritance to the screen. Her musical comedies were identified with a working-class milieu: she is the catalyst who unifies the community through her skill at impersonation, singing talent, and common sense. Rarely is romance a central feature of her films. (Her successor in popular sentimental comedy of the 50s was Norman WISDOM, who creates, then prevails over, chaos, as in *Trouble in Store*, 1953). By contrast, the 'dancing divinity', Matthews, escapes from an everyday existence of work through her ingenuity at disguise and her superb talent at mimicry, song, and dance, her

comedies more aligned to Hollywood forms of entertainment. Relying, like Gracie, on regional dialect and working-class humour, George FORMBY, another regional actor promoted by Basil DEAN, was identified with the ukelele and with music-hall entertainment.

The zest of the music hall tradition also informed the 30s and 40s films of the CRAZY GANG, Arthur LUCAN (Old Mother Riley), Leslie FULLER, Frank RANDLE, Tommy TRINDER and others. In another vein, the eccentric figure of Will HAY combined slapstick and satire. In films directed by Marcel VARNEL such as *Oh! Mr Porter* (1937) *Old Bones of the River* (1938), and in *Boys Will Be Boys* (directed by William BEAUDINE, 1935), his long, gangly persona is the epitome of irreverence. He violates moral and social codes as schoolmaster, railway stationmaster, or imperial civil servant, and his films, strung together by verbal and physical gags, expose corrupt institutions.

Perhaps the most popular comedies internationally, around the mid-century, were those produced at EALING under Michael BALCON, including such films as *Passport to Pimlico* (1949), *Kind Hearts and Coronets* (1949), *The Lavender Hill Mob* (1951) and *The Man in the White Suit* (1951). Ealing's 'team spirit' produced films that poked fun at the government, bureaucracy, repressive rituals and customs, and class snobbery through the concerted efforts of a group of writers (T.E.B. CLARKE), directors (e.g. Robert HAMER, Charles CRICHTON), and actors (Alec GUINNESS, Basil RADFORD, Joan GREENWOOD among others).

The 'DOCTOR' series, a cycle of films starring Dirk BOGARDE, focused on the medical profession, a favourite target of British comedy, the humour partly derived from the series' 50s focus on tenuous masculinity. The great tradition of British character comedy was upheld in the 50s by such notable exemplars as Alastair SIM, Margaret RUTHERFORD, George COLE and Joyce GRENFELL, while broader comedy was popularly dispensed by Cockney-style Ronald SHINER and Brian RIX and Wisdom's little-man-with-aspirations.

The 'CARRY ON' films, produced from the late 50s to the 70s, offered a different, more ribald, earthy form of humour, identified with a repertory group of actors (e. g. Charles HAWTRY, Sidney JAMES, Joan SIMS, Kenneth WILLIAMS, Kenneth CONNOR, Hattie JACQUES) who tackled, in broadly satiric, slapstick fashion, such British institutions and preoccupations as the Army, the medical profession, patriotism, leisure life, and sport. The youth-orientated 60s, with its concept of 'SWINGING LONDON', produced such exuberant comic fare as *The Knack . . .* (1965), *Georgy Girl* (1966) and *Here We Go Round the Mulberry Bush* (1967), as well as the darker effects of *Nothing But the Best* (1964).

Satiric comedy, in more 'intellectual' form than in the 'CARRY ON' series, is also characteristic of MONTY PYTHON, whose 70s and 80s work bridges film and TELEVISION. The Pythons thrived on contemporary allusions to politics, the royal family, the British reverence for tradition and history, sexual politics, television, and cinema. Like the comedy SERIES that preceded them, the Pythons depended on a familiar group of actors and a sketchy, episodic structure. The international aspirations of British comedy were exemplified by the series of 'Pink Panther' films in the 70s, directed by Blake Edwards and starring Peter SELLERS as bungling Inspector Clouseau.

During the Thatcher years, satire flourished, and one of the harshest social satires was *Britannia Hospital* (1982), which uses the hospital as a microcosm of British society and draws on parody, caricature, and invective in its indictment of contemporary institutions and mores. Similarly, *A Private Function* (1984), starring Python Michael PALIN, Maggie SMITH, and a hapless pig to be slaughtered, is set in the 40s during the celebration of Philip and Elizabeth's marriage. The 'private function' is allegorised as the body politic to reveal the inhumane face of British post-war society.

Comedy has found renewed life on television. *The Black Adder* (later, *Blackadder*), *Are You Being Served?* and *Absolutely Fabulous* (*AbFab*) are among the more recent British comedy series on television that have attracted international audiences. These programmes follow many of the successful strategies characteristic of British comedy: eccentricity of character, risqué physical humour pertaining to the body, topical political allusions in their treatment of family, gender and class relations, and a discernible self-reflexivity about media. Comedy continued to be profitable in 90s British cinema as witnessed by the international success of such films as *Four Weddings and a Funeral* (1994), *The Full Monty* (1997, UK/US), *Shakespeare in Love* (1999, UK/US) and *Notting Hill* (1999, UK/US). Marcia Landy.

Comfort, John (*b* London, 1935). Production manager. Son of director Lance COMFORT, he entered the industry through uncredited work on his father's films in the 50s and has been involved in 40 projects, most often as production manager/supervisor, sometimes (*Britannia Hospital*, 1982; *A Fish Called Wanda*, 1988) associate producer. Also involved in US films, most recently *101 Dalmatians* (1996).

OTHER BRITISH FILMS INCLUDE: (ass d): *Dr Blood's Coffin* (1960); (pr super): *Mahler* (1974), *Shock Treatment* (1981); (pr man): *Touch of Death, Tomorrow at Ten, Jigsaw, The Break* (1962), *Blind Corner* (1963), *Oh! What a Lovely War* (1969); (assoc. prod.): *Under Milk Wood* (1971), *Breaking Glass* (1980).

Comfort, Lance (*b* London, 1908 – *d* Worthing, 1966). Director. One of the most underrated of British directors, Comfort had a long apprenticeship from 1926 until he directed his first feature, *Penn of Pennsylvania*, in 1941. He had worked as an animator, camera operator at EALING, ISLINGTON, SOUTHALL and other studios, then, from 1932, as sound recordist at STOLL STUDIOS, Cricklewood. He directed many documentaries, including medical SHORTS, before becoming 'technical supervisor' or 'assistant director' on films for John BAXTER, being appointed technical supervisor at BRITISH NATIONAL in 1939, and acting in these capacities on Baxter's *Love on the Dole* (1941). He also made a series of short films for children in 1938–39, one of them, *Toddlers and a Pup*, featuring his son John COMFORT.

Comfort scored a major melodramatic triumph with his second film, *Hatter's Castle* (1941), made several proficient thrillers and a charming regional comedy, *When We Are Married* (1943) during WW2, then a string of compelling films with strong melodramatic strains: *Great Day* (1945); the *noirish* wicked woman thriller, *Bedelia* (1946); his moody masterwork, *Temptation Harbour* (1947); the sensual gothic of *Daughter of Darkness* (1947); and the soured pastoral of *Silent Dust* (1949). His luck ran out with the romance *Portrait of Clare* (1950), and he spent the rest of his career until his untimely death in co-features and 'B' MOVIES. However, some of his work in these straitened circumstances is excellent, making a virtue out of financial constraint: *Bang! You're Dead* (1953) is a haunting work of post-war malaise in a very ambiguous rural setting; *Make Mine a Million* (1959) is a broadly funny satire on TV; and

there are two tense minor thrillers, *Touch of Death* and *Tomorrow at Ten* (1962), worth anyone's attention. As well, during the 50s, he produced masses of TV for *Douglas Fairbanks Jr Presents*, *Crown Theatre* and others. A very enjoyable minor talent who deserves to be rediscovered. Married dancer Peggy Lamb.

OTHER BRITISH FILMS (d, unless noted): *Those Kids from Town, Squadron Leader X* (1942), *Escape to Danger, Old Mother Riley, Detective* (1943), *Hotel Reserve* (1944), *Home to Danger* (1951, p), *The Girl on the Pier, The Genie, The Triangle* (1953), *Eight O'Clock Walk, The Last Moment* (1954), *Port of Escape* (p), *The Man in the Road, Atom at Spithead* (probably unreleased), *Face in the Night* (1956), *At the Stroke of Nine, The Man from Tangier* (1957), *The Ugly Duckling* (1959), *Rag Doll* (1960), *The Breaking Point, Pit of Darkness* (1961), *The Break, The Painted Smile, Band of Thieves* (p) (1962), *The Switch* (co-p), *Live It Up, Blind Corner* (1963), *Devils of Darkness, Be My Guest* (1965).

BIBLIOG: Brian McFarlane, *Lance Comfort*, 1999.

Company of Youth This was a project developed by producer Sydney BOX at RIVERSIDE STUDIOS to groom young people for stardom, casting them in small roles in big pictures or in bigger roles in minor films, bolstered by more experienced players. When Box joined the RANK ORGANISATION in 1947, he took the Company with him and it metamorphosed into the derided Rank Charm School. Those enrolled were paid a small salary and trained in matters of speech and deportment, presided over by former RADA instructor Molly TERRAINE. Alumni who went on to better things included Christopher LEE, Diana DORS, Jane HYLTON and Anthony STEEL.

Compson, Betty *see* **American stars in British silent films**

Compton, Fay (*b* London, 1894 – *d* London, 1978). Actress. Theatrical luminary, born to an actor-manager father, Edward Compton (1854–1918) and on stage from 1911, staying there for over 50 years. She famously starred in such modern plays as Somerset MAUGHAM's *The Circle* (1921) and Dodie SMITH's *Autumn Crocus* (1931), which she filmed (1934), as well as classic roles, including both Ophelia and Gertrude. Never quite a film *star*, though she made over 40 films, and starred in about half these in the 20s and 30s, by 1931 she was playing the hero's mother in *Tell England* and the heroine's in *The Mill on the Floss* (1937), having become rather severe-looking in early middle-age. As a character actress, she had moving moments as Queen Victoria in *The Prime Minister* (1941), was a humane Rosie in *Odd Man Out* (1947), a tired prostitute in *Aunt Clara* (1954), and the disgusting old Grandma in *The Virgin and the Gypsy* (1970). She was also a fine Emilia in Orson WELLES's *Othello* (1952, Morocco), and filmed twice in Hollywood: *Fashions in Love* (1929) and *Lady Possessed* (1952). On TV she was Aunt Ann in *The Forsyte Saga* (1967) and had a high old time as Aunt Ada Doom in *Cold Comfort Farm* (1968). Her four husbands included actors Leon QUARTERMAINE (3) and Ralph MICHAEL (4), her son was the director Anthony PELISSIER, of her first marriage, and her brother was the novelist Compton MacKenzie. Created CBE 1975.

OTHER BRITISH FILMS INCLUDE: *She Stoops to Conquer* (1914), *A Woman of No Importance* (1921), *The Loves of Mary, Queen of Scots* (1923), *Robinson Crusoe* (1927), *Uneasy Virtue* (1931), *Waltzes from Vienna* (1934), *So This Is London* (1939), *Nicholas Nickleby* (1947), *London Belongs to Me* (1948), *Laughter in Paradise* (1951), *Town on Trial* (1956), *The Haunting* (1963).

Compton, Juliette (*b* Columbus, Georgia, 1899 – *d* Pasadena, California, 1989). Actress. A dark Southern beauty, briefly a *Ziegfeld Follies* showgirl, Compton starred in a number of late silent British films before returning to her native America. There, between 1930 and 1941, she appeared in more than 25 features, including *Berkeley Square* (1933) and *That Hamilton Woman* (1941). A 1942 divorce from wealthy Britisher James Bartram was very messy, with her accusing him of delighting in wearing female attire and him introducing nude photographs of her in evidence.

BRITISH FILMS INCLUDE: *Human Desires* (1924), *Afraid of Love* (1925), *Nell Gwynne*, *The Chinese Bungalow* (1926), *The Fake* (1927), *The Intruder* (1928), *Woman to Woman* (1929). AS.

Connaughton, Shane (*b* Redhills, Co. Cavan, *c* 1947). Screenwriter, actor. Nominated with Jim SHERIDAN for AA and BAA for best adapted screenplay for *My Left Foot* (1989), based on the life of author Christy Brown. His other screenplays have included *The Dollar Bottom* (1981), *Every Picture Tells a Story* (1984), and *Run of the Country* (1995, Ire/US). He also acted in *The Miracle* (1991), *The Playboys* (1992, UK/Ire/US), *The Lord of the Dance* (2001, UK).

Connell, Maureen (*b* Nairobi, 1931). Actress. Interesting rather than conventionally pretty, Connell showed up well in the African adventure, *Golden Ivory* (1954), contrasting with Susan STEPHEN's anodyne leading lady, and displayed some comedy flair in *Lucky Jim* (1957). Featured by John FORD in *The Rising of the Moon* (1957, Ire/US); generally, minor roles in 'A' films (including *Skyjacked*, 1972, US), some 'B' MOVIE leads, and some TV.

OTHER BRITISH FILMS INCLUDE: *Barbados Quest* (1955), *Town on Trial* (1956), *The Man Upstairs*, *Next to No Time!* (1958), *Danger by My Side* (1962).

Connell, Thelma (aka Myers) (*b* London – *d* Monaco, 1976). Editor. Respected editor of over 30 films, much associated with LAUNDER AND GILLIAT in the 40s and 50s, operating as Myers in the 40s films, which included *The Rake's Progress* (1945) and *Green for Danger* (1946). Entered films in 1935, as secretary to Basil DEAN at EALING, spent three years as CONTINUITY 'girl' at DENHAM, and cut her first film, *In Which We Serve*, in 1942 under David LEAN's supervision. Her first film as Connell is Launder's *Lady Godiva Rides Again* (1951).

OTHER BRITISH FILMS INCLUDE: (as Myers) *The Life and Death of Colonel Blimp* (1943), *I See a Dark Stranger* (1946), *The Mudlark*, *State Secret* (1950); (as Connell) *Folly to Be Wise* (1952), *The Belles of St Trinian's* (1954), *Geordie* (1955), *Only Two Can Play* (1961), *Ring of Spies*, *Hide and Seek* (1963), *The Hill* (1965), *Alfie* (1966, BAAn), *Blind Terror* (1971), *Endless Night* (1972), *Ransom* (1974).

Connery, Jason (*b* London, 1963). Actor. Son of actors Sean CONNERY and Diane CILENTO, Connery has pursued a modest career, unfortunately appearing often in films which have had the most limited – or no – release, like the Harry Palmer sequel, *Bullet to Beijing* (UK/Can) or *Macbeth* (1997), co-starring Helen BAXENDALE. In Australia, he appeared with Cilento in *The Boy Who Had Everything* (1984), but the film had no local release. He had more luck starring in TV's *Robin of Sherwood* series (1986) when he replaced the lead actor Michael Praed. Married (1996) actress **Mia Sara** (*b* New York, 1967), who was in *Bullet to Beijing*.

OTHER BRITISH FILMS: *Dream One* (1984, UK/Fr), *Tank Malling* (1988), *The Beauty and the Beast* (1992, voice), *Jamila* (1993), *Urban Ghost Story* (1998).

Connery, Sir Sean (*b* Edinburgh, 1930). Actor. Left school at 15 and escaped a poor Edinburgh background, first by joining the British Navy and, later on, the stage (in the London chorus of *South Pacific*, 1951) and 50s movies in which he characteristically played low-lifers. *Dr No* (1962) changed all that: 'Sean Connery is James Bond', the publicity announced, and the world's box-offices couldn't have been more pleased. Nearly 40 years later, he remains the most popular incarnation of Ian Fleming's snobbish macho hero, though Fleming did not originally approve the casting. Dressed in a tuxedo while mixing martinis, pummelling villains with pretensions to international domination, and romancing a string of nubile young women, of whom only Honor BLACKMAN was a match for him, he became Britain's most successful film star – and export. The working-class villains he played in early movies like *The Frightened City* (1961) no doubt feed into the ferocity one often feels to be lurking beneath the suave Bondian surface. He played Bond half a dozen times before surrendering the role, returning in 1983 in the aptly named *Never Say Never Again* (UK/US). 'I don't want to be Bond all the time', he said, and his feuding with Bond producer, Cubby BROCCOLI, no doubt strengthened his resolve to put Bond behind him.

The 'BOND' FILMS shouldn't be allowed to obscure the range of his abilities. Not only did he become one of the world's most bankable stars, but also one of its best actors. Not, it must be added, mainly in his British films, though some of these have real merits: the romantic melodrama, *Woman of Straw* (1964); two for Sidney Lumet – the gripping war film, *The Hill* (1965) and *The Offence* (1972), in which he plays an obsessive cop; and the heist thriller, *The First Great Train Robbery* (1978). In the US, HITCHCOCK's *Marnie* (1964) and three mid 70s titles warrant special mention: John HUSTON's *The Man Who Would Be King* and the romantic adventure, *The Wind and the Lion* (1975), and the elegiac *Robin and Marian* (1976, UK/US), perhaps his most moving work on film. His 90s films, on several of which he is also executive producer, and full producer on *Entrapment* (1999, UK/US), are all of US origin, as was *The Untouchables* (1987) for which he won a best supporting actor Oscar. He won a BAA for *The Name of the Rose* (1986, Fr/Ger/It). If the Bond films won him an international following, it was these others which won him critical respect.

He has been a vocal supporter of Scottish nationalism, which, it was alleged, cost him a knighthood in 1998. This omission was made good in the 2000 New Year honours. His first marriage (1962–73) was to actress Diane CILENTO, and their actor son, Jason CONNERY played Ian Fleming, James Bond's creator, in the telemovie *Spymaker: The Secret Life of Ian Fleming* (1990). He has lived in Spain for many years with his second wife, artist Micheline Roquebrune.

OTHER BRITISH FILMS: *Lilacs in the Spring* (1954), *No Road Back* (1956), *Time Lock*, *Action of the Tiger*, *Hell Drivers* (1957), *Another Time, Another Place* (1958), *Tarzan's Greatest Adventure* (1959), *On the Fiddle* (1961), *From Russia with Love* (1963), *Goldfinger* (1964), *Thunderball* (1965), *You Only Live Twice* (1967), *Shalako* (1968), *Diamonds Are Forever* (1971), *Zardoz* (1973), *Murder on the Orient Express*, *Ransom* (1974), *A Bridge Too Far* (1977), *Time Bandits*, *Outland* (1981), *G'Olé* (1982, doc, narr), *Sean Connery's Edinburgh* (short, narr), *Sword of the Valiant* (1983), *Film No. 1* (short, voice), *Highlander* (1986).

BIBLIOG: Michael Feeney Callan, *Sean Connery*, 1993.

Connolly, Billy (*b* Anderston, Glasgow, 1942). Actor. Unlike his preceding fellow-countryman, wildly popular Connolly is not an ardent nationalist, but they share a poverty-stricken childhood. He worked as baker, bookshop assistant, welder and member of the Parachute Battalion of the Territorial Army before buying a banjo and forming The Humblebums. He grew more interested in a comedy career and the group disbanded in

1971. He became a stand-up comedian with long greasy hair and a talent for non-stop rude one-liners. His films have been a motley collection: there are concert films like *The Secret Policeman's Ball* (1979) and . . . *Other Ball* (1982), supporting roles, usually comic, in such films as *Water* (1985), and *The Big Man* (1990), and substantial starring roles in *Mrs Brown* (1997, UK/Ire/US), as outspoken John Brown, Queen Victoria's influential Highland gillie, and *The Debt Collector* (1999), as an ex-crim-turned-sculptor. He lived in the US for some time and has appeared in TV and films there, including *Beautiful Joe* (2000) with Sharon Stone. The years have tamed the anarchic streak somewhat, but the capacity to surprise – shock – shouldn't be underestimated. Married (2) actress Pamela STEPHENSON in 1989.

OTHER BRITISH FILMS INCLUDE: *Absolution* (1978), *Bullshot* (1983), *Dreaming* (1989), *Middleton's Changeling* (1997), *Gabriel and Me* (2001).
BIBLIOG: Pamela Stephenson, *Billy*, 2001.

Connor, Edric (*b* Mayaro, Trinidad, 1913 – *d* London, 1969). Actor, producer. The first black actor in Shakespeare at Stratford when, in 1958, he played – or, with operatic power, *sang* – Gower in Tony RICHARDSON's *Pericles*. Trained in engineering in Trinidad and London, he first appeared on the BBC in 1944, and in 1946 his programme, *Serenade in Sepia*, was transferred to TV. His first film role was as Canada Lee's selfish brother in *Cry, the Beloved Country* (1952), and though he made a further dozen, including several (e.g. *King of Kings*, 1961) for US companies, none except *Virgin Island* (1958) gave him the opportunities his charismatic talents and imposing presence deserved. He died still young, having been an inspiration to many other black performers in post-war Britain.

OTHER BRITISH FILMS INCLUDE: *West of Zanzibar* (1954), *Moby Dick* (1956), *Fire Down Below* (1957), *Nobody Runs Forever* (1968).

Connor, Kenneth (*b* London, 1918 – *d* Harrow, 1993). Actor. Short, lugubrious-looking player whose easily stirred anxiety contributed regularly to the comedy of the 'CARRY ON' SERIES. After his small role in *Poison Pen* (1939), war service intervened; after this, he made a name for funny voices on radio, re-entered films with *Don't Say Die* (1950), and appeared in such 50s TV as *A Show Called Fred* (1956). 'Carry On' took up most of the rest of his film career, but he was also briefly funny as a distraught expectant father in *Make Mine a Million* (1959). His *'Carry Ons'* were: . . . *Sergeant*, . . . *Nurse* (1958), . . . *Teacher* (1959), . . . *Constable* (1960), . . . *Regardless* (1961), . . . *Cruising* (1962), . . . *Cabby* (1963), . . . *Cleo* (1964), . . . *Up the Jungle* (1970), . . . *Henry* (1971), . . . *Matron*, . . . *Abroad* (1972), . . . *Girls* (1973), . . . *Dick* (1974), . . . *Behind* (1975), . . . *England* (1976), . . . *Emmannuelle* (1978). On stage during the later 60s and TV in the 80s. His son, Jeremy Connor, is an actor.

OTHER BRITISH FILMS INCLUDE: *Miss Robin Hood* (1952), *The Ladykillers* (1955), *Davy* (1957), *Dentist on the Job, What a Carve Up!*, (1961), *Gonks Go Beat, Cuckoo Patrol* (1965).

Connor, Kevin (*b* London, 1937). Director, editor. Began his career in British films during the 60s as a second assistant editor, sound recordist, then as editor on such ambitious pieces as Richard ATTENBOROUGH's *Oh! What a Lovely War* (1969) and *Young Winston* (1972). In the 70s, he had his chance as director on a series of imaginative fantasies, including *From Beyond the Grave* (1973) and *Arabian Adventure* (1979), after which he made *Motel Hell* (1980) in the US and has worked mainly in TV there ever since.

OTHER BRITISH FILMS: (e) *Bloomfield* (UK/Isr), *Hitler: The Last Ten Days* (1973, UK/It); (sd) *Lancelot and Guinevere* (1962), *The Sailor from Gibraltar* (1967); (d) *The Land That Time Forgot* (1974), *At the Earth's Core* (1976), *Warlords of Atlantis* (1978).

Conrad, Jess (*b* London, 1936). Singer, actor. Pop singer who has filmed intermittently over 30 years, especially in the 60s. He had a central role in his fourth film, *Rag Doll* (1960), as a singer with a penchant for burglary, but his films have been secondary to his singing career. Some TV, including the improbably bronzed tennis pro in *The Body in the Library* (1984), and a TV documentary on his life was made in 2001.

OTHER BRITISH FILMS INCLUDE: *Too Young to Love* (1959), *The Boys, The Queen's Guards* (1961), *The Assassination Bureau* (1968), *The Great Rock'n'Roll Swindle* (1979), *Absolute Beginners* (1986), *The Punk* (1993).

Conrad, Joseph (*b* Berdichev, Poland, 1857 – *d* Canterbury, 1924). Author. HITCHCOCK's adaptation of *The Secret Agent* as *Sabotage* (1936) was British cinema's first brush with the sombre novelist; there were two sightings in the 50s – Carol REED's intelligent *Outcast of the Islands* (1951) and Herbert WILCOX's *Laughing Anne* (1953), a disastrous version of *Between the Tides* made as a Margaret LOCKWOOD vehicle; Peter O'TOOLE starred as *Lord Jim* in 1964; and Ridley Scott's first feature *The Duellists* (1977), from the story *The Duel*, may well be the finest Conrad film to date, though Francis Ford Coppola's US reworking of *The Heart of Darkness* as *Apocalypse Now* (1979) was powerful indeed. More recent ventures include *Victory* (1995, UK/Fr/Ger, released 1998), TV's *Nostromo* (1996), *The Secret Agent* (1996, UK/US) and *Amy Foster* (1997, UK/Fr/US).

BIBLIOG: Gene M. Moore, *Conrad on Film*, 1997.

Conroy, Ruaidhri (*b* Dublin, 1978). Actor. Young Irish actor who made some strong impressions in the 90s, in Mike NEWELL's fanciful Dublin-set *Into the West* (1992) and in *Clockwork Mice* (1995), as the intense, troubled student who finds a passion for running.

OTHER BRITISH FILMS INCLUDE: *Hear My Song* (1991), *The Serpent's Kiss* (1997, UK/Fr/Ger), *When the Sky Falls* (2000, UK/Ire/US).

Considine, Paddy (*b* Burton-on-Trent, 1974). Actor. Considine made a powerfully unsettling impression as the deceptive, dangerous misfit Morell in Shane MEADOWS' *A Room for Romeo Brass* (1999), and followed this with the sweet-tempered Alfie in *The Last Resort* (2001). Not conventionally handsome, he is a charismatic performer, who has been rushed from film to film, for directors including David KANE (*Born Romantic*, 2001), Michael WINTERBOTTOM (24 *Hour Party People*, 2002) and Jim SHERIDAN (*East of Harlem*, 2002).

OTHER BRITISH FILMS: *Happy Now, The Martins* (2001), *Doctor Sleep* (2002).

Constanduros, Denis (*b* Sutton, Surrey, 1910 – *d* Salisbury, 1978). Screenwriter. Nephew to Mabel CONSTANDUROS with whom he co-wrote screenplays for *Holiday Camp* (1947) and the three succeeding HUGGETT films. Great-grandfather, Thomas Tilling, founded London buses.

Constanduros, Mabel (*b* London, 1880 – *d* Chichester, 1957). RN: Tilling. Actress, screenwriter, dramatist. Central School-trained as an actress, in radio from 1925, on stage from 1929, and films at least from 1933 (some sources say she was in silent films). Better known as author of radio programmes, including *The Buggins Family*, and stage plays, of which the mildly daring (too much so for J. Arthur RANK) 29, *Acacia Avenue* (co-written with nephew Denis) was filmed in 1945. With Denis and several others she co-authored *Holiday Camp* (1947) and three HUGGETT sequels: *Here Come the Huggetts, Vote for Huggett*

RIGHT *Comin' Thro' the Rye* (1923, d.Cecil Hepworth), popular silent film romance.

Cecil Hepworth, pioneer director.

Betty Balfour, star of silent films.

RIGHT *The Rat* (1925, d.Graham Cutts), romantic thriller, starring Ivor Novello.

ABOVE **Sir Alexander Korda**, producer, director, studio head.

ABOVE RIGHT *The Private Life of Henry VIII* (1933, d.Alexander Korda), internationally successful costume drama, with Charles Laughton, Elsa Lanchester.

RIGHT *The Last Journey* (1935, d.Bernard Vorhaus), thriller, with Eliot Makeham, Eve Grey.

BELOW **Sir Alfred Hitchcock**, director, long in Hollywood.

Sir John Mills, star actor.

Phyllis Calvert, star actress.

ABOVE **Lance Comfort**, director (second from left).

BELOW **Stewart Granger**, star actor, later in Hollywood.

Muir Mathieson, music director, composer, conductor.

ABOVE **Jack Cardiff**, cinematographer, later director.

LEFT **Jean Kent**, star actress.

BELOW **Carmen Dillon,** production designer.

(1948) and *The Huggetts Abroad* (1949). Acted in about a dozen films, of which the last was *Easy Money* (1948) as Petula CLARK's Grandma.

OTHER BRITISH FILMS INCLUDE (a, unless noted): *Radio Parade* (1933), *Where's George?* (1935), *Stars on Parade* (1936), *Salute John Citizen*, *Rose of Tralee* (1942), *Variety Jubilee* (dial), *I'll Walk Beside You* (story) (1943), *Medal for the General* (1944), *Caravan* (co-sc) (1946), *The White Unicorn* (1947).

Conti, Tom (*b* Paisley, Scotland, 1941). Actor. Short, charismatic, witty actor who came to notice in Frederic RAPHAEL's brilliant TV plays, *The Glittering Prizes* (1976), and followed this with Alan AYCKBOURN's droll trilogy, *The Norman Conquests* (1977). Film has offered few comparable rewards: he worked for Joseph LOSEY (*Galileo*, 1974, UK/Can), Ridley SCOTT (*The Duellists*, 1977) and Nagisa Oshima (*Merry Christmas Mr Lawrence*, 1982, UK/Jap) without repeating his television impact. Much of the 80s and 90s was spent in US films and TV, receiving an AAn for *Reuben, Reuben* (1983) but gradually settling into supporting roles. He was Pauline COLLINS's Greek fling in *Shirley Valentine* (1989, UK/US), but she got the plaudits. Stage-trained at the Glasgow College of Drama, he won a 1979 Tony for his performance as the paraplegic in *Whose Life Is It Anyway?*. Also a trained classical pianist, he starred in the stage musical, *They're Playing Our Song* (1980). Married actress Kara Wilson in 1967.

OTHER BRITISH FILMS INCLUDE: *Flame* (1974), *Full Circle* (UK/Can), *Eclipse* (1976), *Heavenly Pursuits* (1986), *Us Begins with You* (UK/US), *Something to Believe In* (UK/Ger) (1998).

continuity personnel Right from the earliest filming, because of the need for accuracy and for each shot to match with the one that would follow it in the finished film, the job of the 'Continuity Girl' (old title) or 'Script Supervisor' (new) was born. (In the US the term was never used: 'script clerk', later 'script girl' was the title.) In Britain, the position was almost invariably filled by a woman, hence the gendered title. As silent films gave way to 'talkies' the need for additional information to aid the director in his task became obvious and a continuity girl became a vital part of the crew. Observation, adaptability, diplomacy and absolute dedication to the job were required. She had to note everything on the set concerned with every shot, timing, length of shot (when a shot begins and ends in the script), what the artists are wearing, including hair-styles, how many takes are made, which are to be printed or why they were cut. When all these notes are complete, she ensures all the scenes in the script have been accounted for and how long the film is likely to run. She makes a report on every shot, giving the above information, including details of lens and filters used, for benefit of the camera department, plus – if on exteriors – the time of day and prevailing weather. This report is sent to the director and editor so that he has a full documentation of what to expect in the 'rushes'. In the event of retakes, she has all the information to hand for all departments.

In the early days it was a case of feeling one's way, for no training schools existed, but as time went by the continuity girl had an assistant, who learnt the task by example. Today, many directors come from TV, bringing with them their PA/CONs, who have the benefit of referring to video recording or takes. Some notable 'continuity girls' of the past were: Alma REVILLE (HITCHCOCK's wife), Tilly DAY, Angela MARTELLI, Phyllis Crocker (at EALING in the 40s and 50s), and Maggie Unsworth (who worked a lot with David LEAN). Elaine Schreyeck.

Conway, Gordon (*b* Cleburne, Texas, 1894 – *d* Fredericksburg, Virginia, 1956). Costume designer. She worked in Britain in the early 30s and designed two dozen popular films, including several for director Victor SAVILLE (e;g., *The Good Companions*, 1933) and actresses such as Jessie MATTHEWS and Madeleine CARROLL.

OTHER BRITISH FILMS: *Sunshine Susie* (1931), *Rome Express* (1932), *The Faithful Heart, Soldiers of the King, I Was a Spy, Friday the Thirteenth, Britannia of Billingsgate, The Constant Nymph* (1933), *Red Ensign* (1934).

Conway, Tom (*b* St Petersburg, 1904 – *d* Los Angeles, 1967). Actor. RN: Sanders. Brother of actor George SANDERS, the suave, moustached Conway appeared in dozens of Hollywood B movies from 1940, often as 'The Falcon', and in seven minor British thrillers of the 50s, starting with *Park Plaza 605* (1953). Married (2) and divorced actress Queenie LEONARD.

OTHER BRITISH FILMS: *Blood Orange* (1953), *Barbados Quest* (1955), *Copenhagen* (short, narr), *Breakaway, The Last Man to Hang?, Operation Murder* (1956).

Conyers, D'Arcy (*b* Tanganyika, 1919 – *d* 1972). Actor, director. Conyers acted in a half-dozen films before beginning to direct in 1955, after which he made light entertainments, such as *The Night We Dropped a Clanger* (1959) and *In the Doghouse* (1961), and several for children. He sometimes also produced and wrote his own films.

OTHER BRITISH FILMS INCLUDE: (a) *Ha'penny Breeze* (1950, + p), *Golden Arrow, Wings of Danger* (1952), *The Blue Peter* (1955); (d) *The Secret of the Forest* (1955, + sc), *The Devil's Pass* (1957, + sc, p), *The Night We Got the Bird* (1960, + sc, p), *Nothing Barred* (1961).

Conyngham, Fred (*b* Sydney, 1901 – *d* ?). Actor, dancer. Son of actor-manager, Conyngham first appeared as a speciality dancer, then in musical theatre, and played supports and some leads in British 'B' MOVIES, starting with *The Indiscretions of Eve* (1932).

OTHER BRITISH FILMS INCLUDE: *Radio Parade of 1935* (1934), *School for Stars, Key to Harmony, The Crouching Beast* (1935), *Ball at Savoy* (1936), *The Minstrel Boy, Rose of Tralee* (1937).

Coogan, Steve (*b* Manchester, 1965). Actor. Hugely popular TV comedian (*Coogan's Run*, 1995; *'I'm Alan Partridge'*, 1997) whose screen career took off with his starring role in the CRIME caper film, *The Parole Officer* (2001), as an honest but inept probation officer framed for murder, followed by the lead in Michael WINTERBOTTOM's Manchester-set pop musical comedy, *24 Hour Party People* (2002).

OTHER BRITISH FILMS: *The Wind in the Willows* (1996), *The Revengers' Comedies* (1998).

Cook, Peter (*b* Torquay, 1937 – *d* London, 1995). Actor, humorist. Educated at Cambridge, where he became president of the Footlights Club. Subsequently joined forces with Dudley MOORE, David FROST, Alan BENNETT and Jonathan MILLER to produce the award-winning comedy group 'Beyond the Fringe'. Cook and Moore in partnership later formed a memorable comic duo, the one lanky and lugubrious, the other short and perky, and they appeared together in the British comedies, *The Wrong Box* (1966), *Bedazzled* (1967, + co-sc), *The Bed-Sitting Room, Monte Carlo or Bust!* (UK/Fr/It) (1969), and a spoof version of *The Hound of the Baskervilles* (1977, + co-sc). When they went their separate ways, neither ever seemed so funny again: while Moore continued his career in the US, Cook's was mainly British-based until his untimely death, though he appeared in such US films as *Yellowbeard* (1983, + co-sc) and *The Princess Bride* (1987). He was the founder of the irreverent satirical journal, *Private Eye*. Married (2 of 3) to actress Judy HUXTABLE.

OTHER BRITISH FILMS INCLUDE: *A Dandy in Aspic* (1968), *The Secret Policeman's Ball* (1979), *The Secret Policeman's Other Ball* (1982), *Supergirl* (1984), *Without a Clue* (1988), *Black Beauty* (1994, UK/US).

Cook, Ron (*b* South Shields, 1948). Actor. After small roles in a few films, including Mike LEIGH's *Secrets & Lies* (1996), and a stage background that includes RSC and Royal Court seasons, Cook made a strong impression in Leigh's *Topsy-Turvy* (2000, UK/US) with a beautifully judged performance as the watchful D'Oyly Carte, manager of the Savoy Theatre and referee between the warring Gilbert and Sullivan.

OTHER BRITISH FILMS INCLUDE: *Secrets of a Superstud* (1975), *The Magic Shop*, *Scandalous* (1983), *Number One* (1984), *The Cook, the Thief, His Wife & Her Lover* (1989, UK/Fr), *Turbulence* (1990), *Lucky Break* (2001, UK/Ger/US).

Cookson, Georgina (*b* Mevagissey, 1918). Actress. Benenden-educated and RADA-trained, Cookson entered films in *Millions Like Us* (1943) and has appeared sparingly since. She was Stewart GRANGER's jilted bride in the opening scene of *Woman Hater* (1948) and very funny as Terry-THOMAS's acidulous and unillusioned wife in *The Naked Truth* (1957). On stage from 1939, and some TV, including the *Kipling* series (1964).

OTHER BRITISH FILMS INCLUDE: *I Didn't Do It* (1945), *Your Money or Your Wife* (1960), *Five Golden Hours* (1961), *Woman of Straw* (1964), *Darling* (1965).

Coombe, Carol (*b* Perth, Australia, 1911 – *d* London, 1966). Actress. Blonde daughter of Australian theatre magnate who went to Britain in 1930, entered films in 1931 (*The Ghost Train*) and made West End debut in 1932. One source lists a further dozen films, including *Sally in Our Alley* (1931), in which her participation may be uncredited.

OTHER BRITISH FILMS: *The Rasp* (1931), *The Strangler*, *Help Yourself* (1932), *My Lucky Star* (1933), *The Man Without a Face* (1935).

Coombs, Pat (*b* London, 1926 – *d* London, 2002). Actress. Popular TV comic, with beanpole figure and simpering manner, very well used in *The Dick Emery Show*, on which she was a regular, and she appeared in the SPIN-OFF film, *Ooh . . . You Are Awful* (1972). Several of her ten films were spin-offs, including *On the Buses* (1971), but she also played Spike MILLIGAN's mother in *Adolf Hitler – My Part in His Downfall* (1972).

OTHER BRITISH FILMS: *Follow a Star* (1959), *A Stitch in Time* (1963), *Cry Wolf*, *Carry On Doctor* (1968), *. . . Again Doctor*, *Till Death Us Do Part* (1969), *On the Buses*, *Dad's Army* (1971).

Cooney, Ray (*b* London, 1932). Playwright, screenwriter. Boy actor on stage from 1946, and in 1948 film, *My Brother Jonathan*, and hugely successful comedy playwright, stage director and manager, who presented *Your Money or Your Wife*, which ran for over nine years. In 2000, Fox was negotiating with Cooney to film this hit farce. He has acted in some of his own plays and in the film versions of *Not Now, Darling* (1972, + co-d) and *Not Now, Comrade* (1976, + co-d, co-sc). He produced the ADAPTATION of his play *There Goes the Bride* (1979, + sc) and was executive producer of the US version of Brian Clark's serious comedy, *Whose Life Is It Anyway?* (1981).

OTHER BRITISH FILMS: (a) *The Night We Dropped a Clanger* (1959), *The Hand* (1960, + co-sc); (co-sc/sc) *The Night We Got the Bird* (1960), *What a Carve Up!* (1961), *One for the Pot* (1968), *Why Not Stay for Breakfast?* (1979, + p).

Coop, Denys (*b* Reading, 1920 – *d* London, 1981). Cinematographer. During WW2, served with the photographic section of the Fleet Air Arm and later with the ARMY FILM UNIT. His cinema career began as assistant before the war; post-war, he was camera operator on such notable films as *The Fallen Idol* (1948) and *The Third Man* (1949). Fulfilled this function for over a decade before becoming director of photography, first on *The Girl on the Boat* (1962), then on several key products of the British 'NEW WAVE', including *A Kind of Loving* (1962), *Billy Liar* and, most notably, *This Sporting Life* (1963), in which his camera renders both the physicalities and the emotional texture of the film. Shot several films for Otto Preminger, including his last, *Rosebud* (1975, US), and shared AA for the special visual effects of *Superman* (1978).

OTHER BRITISH FILMS INCLUDE: (cam op) *The Man Between* (1953), *Richard III* (1955), *Saint Joan* (1957, UK/US), *Bonjour Tristesse* (1957), *Libel* (1959), *Lolita* (1961), *Ryan's Daughter* (1970, 2u –storm sequence); (c)*The Mind Benders* (1963), *King and Country* (1964), *Bunny Lake is Missing* (1965), *Drop Dead Darling* (1966), *The Birthday Party* (1968), *10 Rillington Place* (1970), *Asylum* (1972), *The Vault of Horror* (1973), *Inserts* (1974).

Cooper, D(ouglas) P(ercival). (*b* Stourbridge, ? – *d* 1973). Cinematographer. A busy, reliable if uninspired cameraman, Cooper claimed to have photographed more than 200 films by 1929. He began his career as a cinema manager and in 1908 started filming travel and interest SHORTS. In 1918, he was hired by D.W. Griffith to film the sequences for *Hearts of the World* shot in England. Cooper was associated with director A.E. COLEBY in the late 1910s and early 20s, with STOLL for the remainder of the decade, and with Charter Films in the late 30s. Father of Wilkie COOPER.

BRITISH FILMS INCLUDE: *The Exploits of Parker* (1917), *The Peacemaker* (1922), *The Prehistoric Man* (1924), *The Wonderful Wooing* (1925), *Guns of Loos* (1928, co-c), *London Melody* (1930), *Betrayed* (1932), *Consider Your Verdict* (1938), *Inquest* (1939), *The Greed of William Hart* (1948). AS.

Cooper, Frederick (*b* London, 1890 – *d* London, 1945). Actor. Primarily a stage actor, Cooper was a ghostly figure in *Thunder Rock* (1942) and a gaunt-faced Nym in *Henry V* (1944); in ten other unremarkable films.

OTHER BRITISH FILMS INCLUDE: *The Skin Game* (1920), *Every Mother's Son* (1926), *Remembrance* (1928), *Jericho* (1937), *Escape to Danger* (1943), *They Knew Mr Knight* (1945).

Cooper, Garry (*b* Hull, 1955). Actor. Craggy-featured stage actor of wide experience, who has had supporting roles in some distinctive films, notably as Davide in Derek JARMAN's *Caravaggio* (1986). Much TV, including such popular series as *Dalziel and Pascoe* and as the prole neighbour in *At Home with the Braithwaites* (2000–02).

OTHER BRITISH FILMS: *Quadrophenia* (1979), *P'tang Yang Kipperbang* (1982), *Nineteen Eighty-Four* (1984), *My Beautiful Laundrette* (1985), *London Kills Me* (1991), *Beautiful Thing* (1996).

Cooper, George (*b* Leeds, 1916). Actor. Tough-looking character player, remembered as moorland pub landlord in *Hell Is a City* (1959) and rightly outraged cuckold in *Tom Jones* (1963). Compelling rather than likeable.

OTHER BRITISH FILMS INCLUDE: *The Passing Stranger* (1954), *Violent Playground* (1957), *Nightmare* (1963), *Life at the Top* (1965), *The Strange Affair* (1968), *On Her Majesty's Secret Service* (1969), *Bless This House* (1972), *The Black Windmill* (1974).

Cooper, George A. (*b* 1886 – *d* Surrey, 1947). Director. A director of primarily silent SHORTS (from 1922), who made features for GAUMONT in 1924, and graduated to 'QUOTA QUICKIES' in the 30s, Cooper generally edited his own films and from 1926–28 was responsible for a series of Phonofilm (early sound) SHORTS. Also an actor, reporter, film editor, and playwright.

BRITISH FEATURE FILMS INCLUDE: *Claude Duval, The Eleventh Commandment* (1924), *Somebody's Darling* (1925), *Master and Man* (1929, + sc), *The World, the Flesh and the Devil* (1932), *The Roof, Mannequin* (1933), *The Case for the Crown* (1935), *Royal Eagle* (1936, co-d), *Old Mother Riley at Home* (1945, sc), *Loyal Heart* (1946, sc). AS.

Cooper, Dame Gladys (*b* London, 1888 – *d* Remenham, 1971). Actress. Legendary beauty of the British theatre made her debut in 1905 and died during the revival of *The Chalk Garden* in London in 1971. She was WW1's most popular pin-up girl, but, as the nearly five columns her career requires in *Who's Who in the Theatre* (1972) makes clear, also became a formidable, much-sought actress. While she featured in nine British silents from 1913, co-starring with George ARLISS in *The Iron Duke* in 1935, her screen career really began in Hollywood in 1940. Played over 30 aristocratic, warm-hearted or vindictive elderly women, and was thrice Oscar-nominated: for *Now Voyager* (1942), *The Song of Bernadette* (1943) and *My Fair Lady* (1964). She filmed in England just three more times: as blind Clara in *Beware of Pity* (1946), to steal *The Man Who Loved Redheads* (1954) in its last ten minutes, and in *A Nice Girl Like Me* (1969). Was memorable TV matriarch of suave swindlers in series, *The Rogues* (1964). Married (3 of 3) actor Philip Merivale, and her two daughters of previous marriages married actors Robert MORLEY and Robert HARDY.

OTHER BRITISH FILMS INCLUDE: *The Eleventh Commandment* (1913), *The Real Thing at Last* (1916), *Masks and Faces* (1917), *Unmarried* (1920), *The Bohemian Girl* (1922), *Bonnie Prince Charlie* (1923, as Flora MacDonald).

BIBLIOG: Autobiography *Gladys Cooper*, 1931; Sheridan Morley, *Gladys Cooper*, 1979.

Cooper, Melville (*b* Birmingham, 1896 – *d* Los Angeles, 1973). Actor. On stage from 1914 at Stratford-on-Avon, he made eight films in Britain in the early 30s, including *The Scarlet Pimpernel* (1935), after which he took his sniffy, strutting persona to Hollywood. He made well over 50 films there, famously as the sycophantic Mr Collins in *Pride and Prejudice* (1940).

OTHER BRITISH FILMS INCLUDE: *The Calendar* (1931), *Two White Arms* (1932), *The Private Life of Don Juan* (1934).

Cooper, Richard (*b* Harrow-on-the-Hill, 1893 – *d* 1947). Actor. Appeared in 25 films in the 30s, many of them 'QUOTA QUICKIES' for Julius HAGEN's Real Art Productions, though there are some 'A' films for Walter FORDE early on, including *Lord Richard in the Pantry* (1930), in which he starred as the eponymous nobleman.

OTHER BRITISH FILMS INCLUDE: *At the Villa Rose* (1930), *Black Coffee* (1931), *Lord Edgware Dies* (1934), *The Ace Of Spades* (1935), *Stepping Toes* (1938), *Shipyard Sally* (1939), *Inspector Hornleigh Goes to It* (1941).

Cooper, Rowena Actress. Intelligent-looking player who has been more often on TV (*Late Starter*) and stage (excellent in 1994 revival of David Storey's *Home*) than on screen. She had a vivid short role in *Shooting Fish* (1997).

OTHER BRITISH FILMS: *Dentist in the Chair* (1960), *Memoirs of a Survivor* (1981), *Secret Friends* (1991), *Our Boy* (1997).

Cooper, Wilkie (*b* London, 1911 – *d* Worthing, 2001). Cinematographer. Son of cameraman D.P. COOPER, he began acting as a teenager, before switching interest to the camera department.

After several films as camera operator, he had his first cinematographer's credit on *Conquest of the Air* (1940). He was at EALING during the war and, post-war, often with LAUNDER AND GILLIAT, his unobtrusive style suiting their restrained, literate screenplays. He secured some striking effects in *Silent Dust* (1949) in rendering a blind man's perception of the world, and in the 60s, perhaps a little surprisingly, he was associated with such FANTASY films as *The Siege of the Saxons* (1963) and *First Men in the Moon* (1964), working several times with special effects genius Ray HARRYHAUSEN and director Nathan JURAN. Married actress **Peggy Bryan** (*b* 1916 – *d* Worthing, 1996) who appeared in a few British films, including *Dead of Night* (1945).

OTHER BRITISH FILMS INCLUDE: (c): *Ships with Wings* (1941), *The Foreman Went to France, Went the Day Well?* (1942), *The Halfway House, Champagne Charlie* (1944), *The Rake's Progress* (1945), *I See a Dark Stranger, Green for Danger* (1946), *Captain Boycott, Mine Own Executioner* (1947), *The Hasty Heart* (1949), *Stage Fright* (1950), *The Pickwick Papers* (1952), *Svengali* (1954), *The Admirable Crichton* (1957), *Sea of Sand* (1958), *Jason and the Argonauts* (1963), *One Million Years BC* (1966), *Cromwell* (1970, 2uc).

Co-operative Movement and film The British Consumer Co-operative Movement was a pioneer of the industrial film and possibly the first Labour Movement organisation in the world to use the cinema in its propaganda. The Co-operative Movement, an association of working-class consumers, had developed rapidly since the mid-1800s, so that by the turn of the century 1,229 local distributive societies with a membership of 1,500,000 controlled a combined annual trade of over £50m. Local co-op societies sponsored film shows as early as 1897, and the first films of the Movement's factories were available from 1899/1900. In the decade before WW1, all of the Movement's factories and workshops were filmed and the central federal body, the Co-operative Wholesale Society, was operating a film lecture service for the benefit of local societies. From around 1914/15, some co-operative societies established cinemas for the entertainment of their members, while other societies became involved in film-making and commissioning to record their commercial and cultural activities. By the 30s, an impressive array of film work had been undertaken by co-operators, to the extent that one contemporary authority claimed that the Movement was 'probably the principal film maker and buyer outside the trade itself'. Co-operation had come to film appreciably before the trade unions and the Labour Party, and in the mid 30s was instrumental in bringing those two Labour organisations to cinema PROPAGANDA; first of all with the Workers' Film Association (1938), and later the National Film Association (1946–53). Following the demise of those bodies the oppositional character of Co-operative cinema declined and film was used primarily to serve trade, which it continued to do until the late 60s. The Co-operative Movement enjoyed a creditable seven decades of experience with film, whereby the screen was used for propaganda, education, publicity and entertainment, all in the service of working-class families and a moralistic conception of consumption.

BIBLIOG: Alan Burton, *The British Co-operative Movement Film Catalogue*, 1997. Alan Burton.

Coote, Robert (*b* London, 1909 – *d* New York, 1982). Actor. Son of actor Bert Coote, he spent most of his film career in the US, playing amiable if dim upper-class types in such British-set films as *Forever Amber* and *The Ghost and Mrs Muir* (1947). Tiny roles in *Sally in Our Alley* (1931) and *Loyalties* (1933) preceded his Hollywood career, and, after serving as squadron leader with the Canadian Air Force during WW2, he filmed sporadically in Britain, most memorably as the bumbling Bunny in the last scenes of *The League of Gentlemen* (1960), and was Roderigo in Orson WELLES's *Othello* (1952, US/Fr). Played Colonel Pickering in the original production of *My Fair Lady* (1956).

OTHER BRITISH FILMS INCLUDE: *A Matter of Life and Death* (1946), *The Constant Husband* (1954), *The Horse's Mouth* (1958), *The VIPs* (1963), *Theatre of Blood* (1973).

Cope, Kenneth (*b* Liverpool, 1931). Actor. In British films from the mid 50s, a forceful supporting actor and sometimes lead, typically convincing as a junior policeman in *Tomorrow at Ten* (1962) and as young thug who falls for the girl taken hostage in *Naked Fury* (1959) – and, later, in comic roles in two 'CARRY ON' films. Popular on TV, especially for *Coronation Street* (1961) and *That Was the Week That Was* (1962–63).

OTHER BRITISH FILMS INCLUDE: *X the Unknown*, (1956), *Dunkirk* (1958), *The Criminal* (1960), *The Damned* (1961), *A Twist of Sand* (1968), *Carry On at Your Convenience* (1971), *Carry On Matron* (1972), *Juggernaut* (1974).

Copeland, James (*b* Helensburgh, Scotland, 1923 – *d c* 2002). Actor. Craggy-visaged Scots character player, educated at Glasgow's College of Drama and active with the Citizens' Theatre before entering films in the early 50s. Typically cast as one of the more cautious *Innocents in Paris* (1953), and still playing in Scots-set pieces such as *The Big Man* as late as 1991. Much TV, including four episodes of *Dr Who* (1968–69) as Selris.

OTHER BRITISH FILMS INCLUDE: *Laxdale Hall*, *The 'Maggie'* (1953), *You Lucky People* (1955), *The Private Life of Sherlock Holmes* (1970).

Copeland, Stewart (*b* Alexandria, Virginia, 1952). Composer. Formerly drummer and vocalist with The Police, he went solo with some success in the early 80s. Has written a great deal of music for TV and US films; in Britain, has worked with Ken LOACH on three films: *Hidden Agenda* (1990), *Riff-Raff* (1991), *Raining Stones* (1993).

OTHER BRITISH FILMS: *Urgh! A Music War* (1981, doc, a), *Decadence* (1993), *The Leopard Son* (1996, doc).

Copley, Peter (*b* Bushey Heath, 1915). Actor. Ascetic-looking Copley (he would look at home under the cowl of a very austere order) trained at the Old Vic School and first appeared on stage at the Vic in 1932. Entered films in *Farewell Again* (1937); was with the Royal Navy during WW2, and the Old Vic company 1945–50. Also a legal expert, called to the bar in 1963. His postwar films reveal degrees of grimness, but there is range in, say, the prison chaplain in *Time Without Pity* (1957), the blackmailed homosexual in *Victim* (1961) and the quibbling colonel in *King and Country* (1964). In 2001, he was much praised on stage as Justice Shallow in *Henry IV, Part I*. He married (1 of 3) Pamela BROWN.

OTHER BRITISH FILMS INCLUDE: *The Golden Salamander* (1949), *The Card* (1952), *Just My Luck* (1957), *The Knack . . .*, *Help!* (1965), *Quatermass and the Pit* (1967), *Frankenstein Must Be Destroyed* (1969), *Hennessy* (1975), *Little Lord Fauntleroy* (1980).

Coppel, Alec (*b* Australia, 1907 – *d* London, 1972). Screenwriter. Novelist and playwright whose best work for the cinema may be his sharply nasty screenplay for *Obsession* (1949), the enjoyably twisty *Mr Denning Drives North* (1951) and the comic invention of *The Captain's Paradise* (1953, AAn), all from his

originals. At Elstree before WW2; also worked in Hollywood, notably on *Vertigo* (1958, co-sc).

OTHER BRITISH FILMS INCLUDE: *Over the Moon* (1939), *Woman Hater* (1948), *No Highway* (1951), *Hell Below Zero* (1953), *The Bliss of Mrs Blossom* (1968, + play).

Coquillon, John (aka Johnny, Jean) (*b* Canada, 1933 – *d* 1987). Cinematographer. Beginning as a clapper-boy (e.g. on *Fame Is the Spur* (1947), Coquillon spent time filming documentaries in Africa and second unit work for African-set features such as *Call Me Bwana* (1963) and *The Last Safari* (1967). His most notable work was on the now-cult film, *Witchfinder General* (1968), and three for Sam Peckinpah, the Cornwall-set *Straw Dogs* (1971), *Pat Garrett and Billy the Kid* (1973, US) and *Cross of Iron* (1977, UK/Ger), complementing visually their violent challenges.

OTHER BRITISH FILMS INCLUDE: *The Last Rhino* (+ co-p), *Girl on Approval* (1961), *Cup Fever* (1965), *The Oblong Box* (1969), *Cry of the Banshee* (1970), *The Triple Echo*, *The National Health* (1973), *The Four Feathers*, *The Thirty Nine Steps* (1978), *Clockwise* (1985).

Corbett, Harry H. (*b* Rangoon, 1925 – *d* Hastings, 1982). Actor. Best-known as Harold, the oft-exasperated son of a wily old rag-and-bone man, in TV's popular *Steptoe and Son* (1962–65, 1970, 1974). The son of a British army officer, Corbett had already learned his craft in a dozen plays at the Theatre Workshop, Stratford East, continued to act on stage and made about 30 films, but never really escaped the *Steptoe* connection. Two disappointing film SPIN-OFFS were made – *Steptoe and Son* (1972) and *Steptoe and Son Ride Again* (1973) – and the series was remade in America as *Sanford and Son* (1972–76). Entered films in *Nowhere to Go* (1958), was a tough prison warden in *Floods of Fear* (1958), and had his best role as a northerner who falls for a London prostitute in *Rattle of a Simple Man* (1964). He added the H to his name to avoid confusion with a popular ventriloquist of the same name. Married (1 of 2) Susan STEAFEL, father of TV actress Susannah Corbett. Created OBE in 1976.

OTHER BRITISH FILMS INCLUDE: *Shake Hands with the Devil* (1959, UK/US), *The Big Day* (1960), *Sparrows Can't Sing* (1962), *Sammy Going South* (1963), *Carry On Screaming* (1966), *Percy's Progress* (1974, as Prime Minister), *Silver Dream Racer* (1980).

Corbett, Leonora (*b* London, 1907 – *d* Vleuton, Netherlands, 1960). Actress. Tall, glamorous, Oxford-educated stage star, and lead in a dozen 30s films, from Victor SAVILLE's *Love on Wheels* (1932), and including *The Constant Nymph* (1933), as the 'other woman', and a crook's sympathetic 'secretary' in *Wild Boy* (1934).

OTHER BRITISH FILMS INCLUDE: *Friday the Thirteenth* (1933), *Royal Cavalcade* (1935), *Living Dangerously* (1936), *Night Alone* (1938), *Under Your Hat*, (1940).

Corbett, Ronnie (*b* Edinburgh, 1930). Actor. Diminutive comic most famous for his TV partnership with bulky Ronnie BARKER in the long-running, often outrageously funny series *The Two Ronnies* (1971–86). After RAF service, entered films in *You're Only Young Twice!* (1952). Droll enough as the harassed bank employee and suspected porn-customer in *No Sex Please – We're British* (1973), but he misses Barker to act against. Much TV and stage work. Created OBE, 1978.

OTHER BRITISH FILMS INCLUDE: *Rockets Galore* (1958), *Casino Royale* (1967), *Some Will – Some Won't* (1969), *Fierce Creatures* (1997, UK/US).

Cordell, Cathleen (*b* New York, 1916 – *d* Los Angeles, 1997). Actress. RADA-trained stage actress (from 1933) who warrants a brief mention as the vividly duplicitous maid Nancy in *Gaslight* (1940). Was Mog Habbijam in *Major Barbara* (1941), but the rest of her career is in US films (*The Return of the Living Dead*, 1985, was last) and TV.

Cordell, Frank (*b* 1918 – *d* Sussex, 1980). Composer, conductor. Oscar-nominated for *Cromwell* (1970), Cordell spent most of his career scoring routine fare, such as *The Captain's Table* (1958), but his music was important to the epic sweep of *Khartoum* (1966).

OTHER BRITISH FILMS INCLUDE: *The Voice of Merrill* (1952), *The Rebel* (1960), *The Bargee* (1964), *Ring of Bright Water* (1969, + cond), *Trial by Combat* (1976).

Corduner, Allan (*b c* 1951). Actor. Long-respected on stage, where he was in the Tony-winning musical, *Titanic* (1997) and Caryl Churchill's *Serious Money*, London and New York, and in TV and, indeed, films since the early 80s, Corduner came finally to filmgoers' notice in Mike LEIGH's *Topsy-Turvy* (2000, UK/US). He played the sybaritic, culturally ambitious Sullivan to Jim BROADBENT's bourgeois Gilbert, in that loving warts-and-all view of theatrical life. His TV work includes two brushes with Joseph CONRAD – Nicolas ROEG's *Heart of Darkness* (1994) and the mini-series, *Nostromo* (1996) – and there are several US films, including *Talk Radio* (1988) and *The Impostors* (1999).

OTHER BRITISH FILMS INCLUDE: (features) *Yentl* (1983, UK/US), *Antonia and Jane* (1990), *Carry On Columbus* (1992), *Alive and Kicking* (1996), *The Search for John Gissing* (2001, UK/US).

Corfield, John (*b* Liverpool, 1893 – *d* ?). Producer. Educated for the law at Liverpool University, fought in WW1 and entered films in 1935. Produced *The Turn of the Tide* for BRITISH NATIONAL FILMS and joined the company's board with Lady YULE and J. Arthur RANK, bringing this pair into commercial film production. He stayed with British National, where his highpoint was Thorold DICKINSON's eloquent *Gaslight* (1940), until 1943 when he formed his own company and made *Headline* (1943) and two Margaret LOCKWOOD vehicles, *Bedelia* (1946) and *The White Unicorn* (1947). Then, he and Harold HUTH formed Burham Productions and filmed *My Sister and I* (1948) and *Look Before You Love* (1948).

OTHER BRITISH FILMS INCLUDE: *Debt of Honour* (1936), *Dead Men Tell No Tales* (1938), *Contraband* (1940), *One of Our Aircraft Is Missing* (1942, co-p), *Penny and the Pownall Case* (1948).

Cornelius, Henry (*b* Cape Town, 1913 – *d* London, 1958). Director, screenwriter. South African who grew up and studied drama in Berlin, leaving for France with the rise of Nazism, Cornelius directed only a handful of films but one of them was *Genevieve* (1953, + p), so that his place in the story is secure. In few films do simple-seeming ingredients blend so felicitously, even if none of its four stars was first choice. Cornelius came to Britain in the 30s and found work at DENHAM, first as English-speaking editor of René Clair's *The Ghost Goes West* (1935), later editing *The Drum* (1938) and *The Four Feathers* (1939). After working briefly with CAVALCANTI at the GPO FILM UNIT, he returned to South Africa where he made (p, d, e, a) 15 propaganda films, and in 1943 he joined EALING at Cavalcanti's invitation, as associate producer on *Painted Boats* (1945) and, later, *Hue and Cry* (1946), in which DOCUMENTARY and fantasy rubbed shoulders as they did in his directorial debut *Passport to Pimlico* (1949). He was thus a formative element in launching the concept of 'Ealing comedy', and *Genevieve*, centred on a vintage-car race from London to Brighton, has been described

as the most Ealing film never made at Ealing. He died after just two more films, including a somewhat dowdy version of *I Am a Camera* (1955).

OTHER BRITISH FILMS: (d, sc) *The Galloping Major* (1951), *Next to No Time* (1958).

Cornwell, Judy (*b* London, 1940) Actress. There is a plump cosy sensuality about Cornwell that made her ideal for Somerset MAUGHAM's sonsy Rosie in TV's *Cakes and Ale* (1975) or the slatternly Daisy in *Keeping Up Appearances* (1990–95). She started in films in her early 20s (*Dr Terror's House of Horrors*, 1964; *Two for the Road*, 1966), but, after starring with Marty FELDMAN in *Every Home Should Have One* (1969), settled into character roles such as housekeeper Nellie in *Wuthering Heights* (1970) and the fatly sighing Mrs Musgrove in *Persuasion* (1995, TV, some cinemas). Stage and TV have given her more varied chances.

OTHER BRITISH FILMS INCLUDE: *Cry Wolf* (1968), *Country Dance* (1969), *Cry Freedom* (1987), *Mad Cows* (1999).

Corri, Adrienne (*b* Edinburgh, 1931). Actress. Rightly described in *Picturegoer* (1953) as having 'no nice-little-girl-next-door nonsense about her', the red-haired, sinuous, RADA-trained Corri was on stage from 1948, had a screen bit in *The Romantic Age* (1949) and starred in her next, Jean Renoir's *The River* (1951, US). A cinema not notably stocked with sexy leading ladies might have made better use of her, but she made the most of what came her way: the frustrated daughter in *The Kidnappers* (1953), the pianist daughter in *Lease of Life* (1954), a seductress in the neat B movie, *The Big Chance* (1957, and the raped Mrs Alexander in *A Clockwork Orange* (1971), among thirty-odd others, including international epics such as *Quo Vadis* (1951, US) and *Dr Zhivago* (1965, UK/US). Married to Daniel MASSEY (1961–67).

OTHER BRITISH FILMS INCLUDE: *Make Me An Offer!* (1954), *Three Men in a Boat*, *The Feminine Touch* (1956), *The Rough and the Smooth* (1959), *Bunny Lake Is Missing* (1965), *Cry Wolf* (1968), *Vampire Circus* (1971), *The Human Factor* (1979).

Cortese, Valentina (*b* Milan, 1925). Actress. Beautiful Italian star of international films, with a strong emotional acting style, Cortese had time in Hollywood in the late 40s/early 50s, and married Richard BASEHART. She appeared in five UK films, first as Michael DENISON's wartime love interest in *The Glass Mountain* (1948) and also notably as part of the European community caught up with anarchists in *Secret People* (1951). Won BAA for her role in *Day for Night* (1973, Fr/It).

OTHER BRITISH FILMS: *Shadow of the Eagle* (1950), *Brother Sun, Sister Moon* (1972, UK/It), *The Adventures of Baron Munchausen* (1988, UK/Ger/It).

Cosgrove Hall Films Cosgrove Hall (formerly 'Stopframe'), founded by Brian Cosgrove and Mark Hall, in 1976 as a subsidiary company within Thames Television, became internationally successful with children's animated series like *Dangermouse*, *Count Duckula* and *Wind in the Willows*. Relaunched as Cosgrove Hall Films in 1993, following the loss of Thames' ITV franchise, the company has consolidated its international status with *Animal Shelf*, *Noddy* and *Little Grey Rabbit*; its combination of traditional cel and model ANIMATION, and quality literary adaptations representing an intrinsic Englishness in the global marketplace. Cosgrove Hall's features include *The Wind in the Willows* (1983) and *Truckers* (1991). Paul Wells.

Cossins, James (*b* Beckenham, 1933 – *d* London, 1997). Actor. Character turn in over 30 films, most often official or officious (e.g. *Gandhi*, 1982, UK/Ind), but best remembered as Bette DAVIS's transvestite son in *The Anniversary* (1967). The great days of the British film character player were almost over before he started, but he made his mark even in brief roles and poor films.

OTHER BRITISH FILMS INCLUDE: *Darling* (1965), *Privilege, How I Won the War* (1967), *SWALK* (1970), *Young Winston* (1972), *The First Great Train Robbery* (1978), *The Masks of Death* (1984).

Costigan, George (*b* Portsmouth, 1947). Actor. He was the eponymous Bob in *Rita, Sue and Bob Too* (1986), cheerily lubricious seducer/seducee of teenage girls, and was very touching as the husband coming to terms with his wife's death in *Girls' Night* (1998, UK/US). Much of his work has been on TV, including the Bastard in *King John* (1984) and the P.D. James thriller, *A Mind to Murder* (1995), and in theatre he devised *Trust Byron*, in homage to his poet hero.

OTHER BRITISH FILMS INCLUDE: *The Sailor's Return* (1978), *Bloody Kids* (1979), *Shirley Valentine* (1989, UK/US), *Safe, The Hawk* (1993), *Paranoid* (2000).

costume design In Britain, as elsewhere, it was common practice in the early years for players to supply their own contemporary wardrobes. Period costumes and accessesories tended to be rented from theatrical costume houses, such as BJ Simmons, Berman's, and Angels. Studio wardrobe departments were a later phenomenon. Designers came from various backgrounds, primarily fashion, illustration, or theatre. The pioneering Gordon CONWAY, an American, heralded from all three. She first came on the British film scene in the mid-1920s, contributing to GAINSBOROUGH productions; by the early 30s Conway headed the first studio costume department in Britain, at GAUMONT–BRITISH at SHEPHERD'S BUSH, though this proved short-lived. Even the big KORDA productions in the 30s, credited to names like Oliver MESSEL and John ARMSTRONG, had their clothes mainly executed or supplied by BJ Simmons. British cinema could boast no glamour fashion names like Hollywood's Adrian or Travis Banton, although occasionally some names from the world of *haute couture* were called in, such as Molyneux, STRASSNER, or Norman HARTNELL. Instead, British designers excelled as craftsmen, or period costume experts.

In the 40s studio costume departments in Britain finally came into their own. Yvonne CAFFIN reigned at Gainsborough's ISLINGTON STUDIO, while at Shepherd's Bush Elizabeth HAFFENDEN created the garb for the Gainsborough MELODRAMAS, and trained the next wave of designers, including Julie HARRIS and Joan ELLACOTT. Haffenden, who later designed for MGM–BRITISH's costume spectacles in the 50s, was a leading specialist in period costume. Others were Oliver MESSEL (*Caesar and Cleopatra*, 1945), Cecil BEATON (*An Ideal Husband*, 1947; *Anna Karenina*, 1948), Roger FURSE (*Henry V*, 1944), and Sophie Harris of the firm of Motley, working with Margaret FURSE (LEAN's *Great Expectations*, 1946; *Oliver Twist*, 1948).

Wartime rationing in the 40s naturally had an effect on wardrobe, its limitations providing a challenge to designers like Anthony MENDLESON, hired as EALING's first official costume designer in 1947. A master at creating clothes for character, Mendleson designed for the major Ealing comedies, though the clothes were still made up by costume houses. Most contemporary fashions were bought at department stores, shops, or from specific couturiers.

In the 40s Anna NEAGLE was the leading clothes-horse for British fashion designers; *Maytime in Mayfair* (1949) featured a TECHNICOLOR fashion show showcasing the industry's 'New Look', including creations by Victor Stiebel and Norman HARTNELL. In the 50s, the RANK ORGANISATION's chief designer, Julie Harris, designed for a wide variety of films; her duties also included designing clothes for Rank stars and starlets for personal appearances, premieres, and festivals.

By the 60s, studio designers also had to stay on top of – or in some cases anticipate – the latest trends of 'SWINGING LONDON', from mini-skirts to Carnaby Street tailoring. Prime examples are Jocelyn RICKARDS's mod clothes for the models in Antonioni's *Blow-Up* (1966, UK/It), and Julie Harris's clothes for the young BEATLES fans in *A Hard Day's Night* (1964) and the BOND girls in *Casino Royale* (1967). Nor should one forget the avant-garde cavegirl fashions created by Carl TOMS for Raquel Welch for HAMMER's prehistoric epic *One Million Years BC* (1966), particularly the bikini constructed of doeskin.

During the 60s, British designers finally began gaining all-important American recognition for their work. In 1966 Harris became the first British costume designer to win an Oscar, for costume design in black-and-white, for *Darling*; Phyllis DALTON, another industry veteran, won that same year for colour design (*Doctor Zhivago*, UK/US). The 60s also saw the rise of Shirley RUSSELL, whose eclectic blend of vintage clothes and original designs continued to enliven the films of Ken RUSSELL until the late 70s (*Women in Love*, 1969; *The Boy Friend*, 1971; *Tommy*, 1975).

The 80s and 90s were dominated by James ACHESON, who won Oscars for three period dramas, *The Last Emperor* (1987, China/It), *Dangerous Liaisons* (1988, US), and *Restoration* (1995, UK/US). John BLOOMFIELD first came to the fore with the television success of *The Six Wives of Henry VIII* (1970), a noteworthy example of invention triumphing over budget; he now specialises in big, quirky Hollywood productions like *Robin Hood: Prince of Thieves* (1991) and *Waterworld* (1995).

The current art of British costume design is strongly identified with HERITAGE cinema and literary ADAPTATIONS. Designers need to be *au fait* with a range of period styles, from Tudor finery to the very different Englands of Jane AUSTEN and DICKENS, from Victorian plush through to WW2 austerity and 70s punk glam. The insatiable demand for 'quality' product helps offset the growing trend in British 'realist' films for no costumes at all, beyond perhaps torn jeans and football scarfs, down to 'the full monty'. Catherine A. Surowiec.

costume melodrama This is a form which has been spasmodically successful at the British box-office but has received little favour with critics. During the silent cinema period, costume film played a small role in overall output. The films of Herbert WILCOX, including *The Only Way* and *Nell Gwynne* (1926) were important, along with some prestigious ADAPTATIONS of SHAKESPEARE, including *Richard III* (1913), and DICKENS, such as Maurice ELVEY's *Bleak House* (1920). In the 30s, a range of producer/directors made significant innovations, either by presenting real historical figures in a new way, or by making imaginary characters re-draw the boundaries between sacred and profane behaviour. Alexander KORDA, in such films as *The Scarlet Pimpernel* (1935), used the aristocracy as a symbol of a broader mode of imaginative life which was available to all. Michael BALCON, in films such as *Jew Süss* (1934) used the costume mode as a liberal critique of injustice, whereas Herbert WILCOX used history in *Victoria the Great* (1937) to assuage audience's anxieties about social change. With the coming of war, the MINISTRY OF INFOR-MATION initially encouraged films which presented history as valuable PROPAGANDA lessons, but it eventually came to favour films with a modern setting. Costume film during WW2 was dominated by the radical innovations at GAINSBOROUGH, which used popular novels by female novelists. In such films as *The Man in Grey* (1943) and *The Wicked Lady* (1945), Gainsborough presented vibrant, bad women who were symbolically linked with marginal figures such as GYPSIES and aristocrats. The films themselves were cheaply made, but they used the full resources of decor and costume in order to usher the audience into a land beyond the constraints of common sense.

In post-war British cinema, the costume mode became increasingly varied and fragmented. Some production companies used historical settings, but gave minimal attention to history as such: *Great Expectations* (1946) is an example of such a 'quality' costume film. Other companies tried to emulate the 'bad woman' MELODRAMAS of Gainsborough with extravaganzas such as *Idol of Paris* (1948). Michael Balcon at Ealing made an ill-advised attempt to combine the costume mode with the discourse of realism in such films as *Nicholas Nickleby* (1947). By the end of the 40s, the costume melodrama was in serious decline because of the changes in audience demography and because many of the proponents of the genre had gone into artistic decline.

In the 50s, British costume film lost its sureness of touch. A range of films was made in which middle-class heroes were socially and culturally unstable – *The Card* (1952), for example – but with the exception of *A Tale of Two Cities* (195 8), they did very little box-office business. Profitable costume melodramas in Britain in the 50s were financed by American production companies, who were able to take full advantage of the EADY LEVY. Costume films made in Britain by MGM and DISNEY were qualitatively different from the home-grown product. The Americans chose to make films with Scottish settings; and in such films as *Rob Roy* . . . (1953), they deployed the genre as a means of celebrating an energetic masculinity which endorsed individualism and challenged legitimacy.

Costume film in 60s cinema was a minority practice, and was progressively squeezed by social REALISM. Only Tony RICHARDSON, with *Tom Jones* (1963) and *The Charge of the Light Brigade* (1968) engaged with the genre, and these films displayed an anarchic inventiveness towards the traditions of costume film. Their sense of sophisticated play with melodramatic convention was replicated in a few 70s films – *Royal Flash* (1975), for example. It is tempting to categorise Ken RUSSELL's *The Devils* (1971) as a costume melodrama, since it is characterised by emotional excess and unusual garments. By the same token, Derek JARMAN's *Sebastiane* (1971) might also be included in the canon.

By the early 80s, costume melodrama had become riven by irony and self-referentiality. The films of MERCHANT IVORY changed everything. In such films as *Room With a View* (1985) the more polemical aspects of the genre were reined in, and history became pretty once more. The patina of emotional restraint was laid over the past. MERCHANT IVORY's dominance of the costume film was broken in the 90s by 'outsiders' to the business: by a woman director (Sally POTTER) with the 1993 *Orlando* (UK/Fr/It/Neth/Russ), and by an Indian director (Shekhar KAPUR) with *Elizabeth* (1998). Both films were profoundly innovatory, and both managed to make substantial profits by a radical reinterpretation of the past.

BIBLIOG:Sue Harper, *Picturing the Past: the Rise and Fall of the British Costume Film* 1994; Pam Cook, *Fashioning the Nation: Costume and Identity in British Cinema*, 1996. Sue Harper.

Cotes, Peter   (*b* Maidenhead, 1912 – *d* Chipping Norton, 1998). RN: Sydney Boulting. Actor, producer. Elder brother of the BOULTING twins, Cotes had a many-faceted career, especially as controversial stage director, importing the outspoken US drama, *Pick-Up Girl* (1946), to the London stage and attracting the unlikely approval of Queen Mary, and championing such club theatres as the Lindsey and Bolton's. On stage since childhood, and trained at the Italia Conti school, he became famous (and rich?) as the first producer of *The Mousetrap* (1952), wisely insisting on a royalty rather than a flat fee. Became senior drama producer at Associated Rediffusion in the 50s, but his main commitment was to the theatre where he directed nearly 70 productions. With all this activity, he really only grazed the surface of British cinema: as actor (from *Pal o' Mine*, 1936 to *The Upturned Glass*, 1947); as dialogue director at GAINSBOROUGH from 1947 (e.g. on *Miranda*, 1948); and as director (*The Right Person*, 1955, short; *The Young and the Guilty*, 1958). Married (2) Joan MILLER with whom he often worked.

OTHER BRITISH FILMS INCLUDE: (a) *Pastor Hall* (1940), *The Gentle Sex* (1943), *The Way to the Stars* (1945), *Beware of Pity* (1946).

Cotten, Joseph   (*b* Petersburg, Virginia, 1906 – *d* Westwood, California, 1994). Actor. Elegant, urbane American lead of over 80 films, who made a couple of memorable appearances in British films: as an innocent abroad in *The Third Man* and as convict-turned-gentleman in *Under Capricorn* (1949). Married (2) Patricia MEDINA.

OTHER BRITISH FILMS: *Some May Live* (1967), *Petulia* (1968), *The Abominable Dr Phibes* (1971).

BIBLIOG: Autobiography, *Vanity Will Get You Somewhere*, 1987.

Cotton, Oliver   (*b* London, 1944). Actor. Has worked mainly in the US, as in *Eleni* (1985). First appeared in *Here We Go Round the Mulberry Bush* (1967), played Monks in *Oliver Twist* (1982, TV, some cinemas), both for Clive DONNER. Also in *The Innocent Sleep* (1995), and strikingly in TV's *The Borgias* (1981) and *The Camomile Lawn* (1992).

Cottrell-Boyce, Frank   Screenwriter. Among other work, has written four very diverse films for Michael WINTERBOTTOM, starting with the compelling road movie, *Butterfly Kiss* (1995), and including the clever transposition of Thomas HARDY's *The Mayor of Casterbridge* (2001, UK/Can/Fr) to the snowbound goldfields of California's Sierras. He had also written Winterbottom's TV film, *Forget About Me* (1990, UK/Hung).

OTHER BRITISH FILMS: *Saint-Ex* (1996), *Welcome to Sarajevo* (1997, UK/US), *24 Hour Party People, A Revenger's Tragedy* (2002).

Cotts, Campbell   (*b* London, 1902 – *d* London, 1964). Actor. RN: Sir Campbell Mitchell-Cotts. Baronet, rotund of frame and orotund of phrase, who took to films in the late 40s, providing moments of enjoyable expostulation in such productions as *Dear Mr Prohack* (1949) and *Last Holiday* (1950). Formerly a barrister and holder of high offices.

OTHER BRITISH FILMS INCLUDE: *Trottie True* (1948), *Encore* (1951), *The Hour of 13* (1952), *Three Men in a Boat, The Good Companions* (1956), *Doctor at Large* (1957).

Coulouris, George   (*b* Manchester, 1903 – *d* London, 1989). Actor. Son of Greek immigrant father and English mother, educated at Manchester Grammar School and trained at

Central School, Coulouris was on stage at the Old Vic in 1926 and Broadway in 1929. In 1937, he played Mark Antony in Orson WELLES's modern-dress *Julius Caesar*, and having made three minor 30s appearances in US films, followed Welles to Hollywood for *Citizen Kane* (1941), thereafter becoming one of the world's most respected character actors. Mostly sinister, as in *Watch on the Rhine* (1943), sometimes floridly 'foreign' as in *A Song to Remember* (1945), in 1950, after being BLACKLISTED in the McCarthy era, he returned to Britain, working steadily on the stage and compelling attention in a further 50-odd good, bad and indifferent films. These included several of the 'DOCTOR' series, and more serious pieces such as *Outcast of the Islands* (1951) and *Conspiracy of Hearts* (1960).

OTHER BRITISH FILMS INCLUDE: *Appointment with Venus* (1951), *Venetian Bird* (1952), *The Runaway Bus* (1953), *Doctor in the House* (1954), *Doctor at Sea* (1955), *Seven Thunders* (1957), *Law and Disorder, No Time to Die* (1958), *Surprise Package, Bluebeard's Ten Honeymoons* (1960), *Arabesque* (1966, UK/US), *The Assassination Bureau* (1968), *Mahler, Murder on the Orient Express* (1974), *The Ritz* (1976).

Coulter, Michael (*b* Glasgow, 1952). Cinematographer. Most often associated with the films of fellow Scot, Bill FORSYTH, from *That Sinking Feeling* (1979) on, Coulter has worked with some of the key directorial talents of the 80s and 90s, including Terence DAVIES, on *The Long Day Closes* (1992), in which his mellow images contribute much to the film's elegiac tone, and Mike NEWELL, on *Four Weddings and a Funeral* (1994), giving a dewy freshness to its youthful gaiety.

OTHER BRITISH FILMS INCLUDE: *Gregory's Girl* (1980), *Local Hero* (1983), *Comfort and Joy* (1984), *No Surrender* (UK/Can), *Restless Natives* (1985), *The Good Father, Heavenly Pursuits* (1986), *Housekeeping, The Dead* (landscape photography) (1987), *The Dressmaker* (1988), *Diamond Skulls* (1989), *Where Angels Fear to Tread* (1991), *The Neon Bible, Sense and Sensibility* (1995, UK/US), *Notting Hill* (1999, UK/US), *Mansfield Park* (2000, UK/US).

Coulthard, Raymond Actor. Promising young actor of the late 90s, on stage (the 1998 revival of *Black Comedy*), TV (as Frank Churchill in *Emma*, 1996) and screen (*The English Patient*, 1996, UK/US; *The Furnace*, 2000).

Couper, Barbara (*b* London, 1903 – *d* Watford, 1992). Actress. On stage from 1925, star of classic roles, as in the 1936 Stratford season, and modern plays such as *Women of Twilight* (1952). Occasional films from 1944 (*Heaven Is Round the Corner*), mostly in dignified roles, such as the prison doctor in *The Weak and the Wicked* (1953). Was married to BBC producer Howard Rose.

OTHER BRITISH FILMS INCLUDE: *Dark Secret, The Last Days of Dolwyn* (1949), *The Lady with a Lamp* (1951), *Face in the Night* (1956), *The Great St Trinian's Train Robbery* (1966), *Goodbye, Mr Chips* (1969).

Coupland, Diana (*b* Leeds, 1929). Actress. Entered film by providing Lana TURNER's singing voice in *The Flame and the Flesh* (1954); thereafter, mixed film and TV, reprising her role of Sid JAMES's wife in *Bless This House* (1971–76) in the 1972 film spin-off. Her best role was probably as James MASON's long-suffering wife in *Spring and Port Wine* (1969).

OTHER BRITISH FILMS INCLUDE: *The Millionairess* (1960), *The Family Way* (1966), *Charlie Bubbles* (1967), *The Best Pair of Legs in the Business* (1972).

Courant, Curt (*b* Berlin, 1899 – *d* Los Angeles, 1968). Cinematographer. In German films from 1916. During the 30s, he worked in Britain, mostly for GAUMONT–BRITISH, and in France, e.g. *La Bête Humaine* (1938) and *Le Jour Se Lève* (1939). Famous for his atmospheric low-key lighting, and occasionally

an exquisitely luminous, soft-focus style, e.g. the British REMAKE of *Broken Blossoms* (1936). Courant also worked with HITCHCOCK on *The Man Who Knew Too Much* (1934), before moving to Hollywood in 1941.

OTHER BRITISH FILMS INCLUDE: *Perfect Understanding* (1933), *The Iron Duke, Me And Marlborough* (1935), *Man In The Mirror, Dusty Ermine, Spy of Napoleon* (1936). Tim Bergfelder.

Court, Hazel (*b* Sutton Coldfield, 1926). Actress. Redhead whose beauty was only fully revealed in the stylish TECHNICOLOR HORROR films she made for HAMMER, starting with *The Curse of Frankenstein* (1957). The last third of her career was in this GENRE, either for Hammer or for Roger Corman (e.g. *The Raven*, 1963, US), co-starring with such horrorcrats as Christopher LEE and Vincent PRICE. However, she had been much touted in the 40s as a leading lady at GAINSBOROUGH, and, after playing sisters to Sally GRAY (*Carnival*, 1946) and Phyllis CALVERT (*The Root of All Evil*, 1947), she was starred in *Meet Me at Dawn* (1947) and, most noticeably, in *Holiday Camp* (1947), as the eldest HUGGETT daughter. In the early 50s, the RANK star system having lost steam, she declined into 'B' MOVIES, starring several times with husband (1949–63) Dermot WALSH, as in *Ghost Ship* (1952) and *Counterspy* (1953). She divorced Walsh, married American actor-director Don Taylor (1964), and settled in the US, where she guested in many TV series and also established herself as a sculptress.

OTHER BRITISH FILMS INCLUDE: *Dreaming* (1944), *Gaiety George* (1946), *Dear Murderer* (1947), *Bond Street, My Sister and I* (1948), *Forbidden* (1949), *Devil Girl from Mars* (1954), *The Narrowing Circle* (1956), *The Man Who Could Cheat Death* (1959), *Dr Blood's Coffin* (1960), *The Masque of the Red Death* (1964, UK/US).

Courtenay, Margaret (*b* Cardiff, 1923 – *d* Northwood, Middlesex, 1996). Actress. Of stately demeanour, Courtenay characteristically played formidable women on stage, TV, and only rarely on screen, between the first, *Touch and Go* (1955), and the last, *The Mirror Crack'd* (1980).

OTHER BRITISH FILMS INCLUDE: *Isadora, Hot Millions* (1968), *Under Milk Wood* (1971), *Ooh . . . You Are Awful* (1972), *Royal Flash* (1975).

Courtenay, Syd Actor, screenwriter. Much associated with broadly comic Leslie FULLER for whom he wrote revue material and, in the 30s, film scripts, starting with *Why Sailors Leave Home* (1930), often acting in Fuller's vehicles. One interesting exception was the screenplay for Michael POWELL's *The Man Behind the Mask* (1936).

OTHER BRITISH FILMS INCLUDE: (a/sc, unless noted) *Not So Quiet on the Western Front* (a), *Kiss Me Sergeant* (play, a) (1930), *Old Spanish Customers* (1932), *The Outcast* (sc) (1934), *The Stoker* (1935), *Everything Is Rhythm* (sc) (1936), *Sing As You Swing* (d, sc) (1937).

Courtenay, Sir Tom (*b* Hull, 1937). Actor. With his gaunt face and slight frame, this RADA-trained actor represented for a generation of filmgoers resistance to the status quo. Unlike his burlier ANGRY YOUNG MEN contemporaries, Albert FINNEY and Alan BATES, Courtenay conveyed his strength through posture, quiet intonation and the expressiveness of his eyes. This eloquence, coupled with a regional accent (confronting at the time), proved a powerful combination in his signature role in *The Loneliness of the Long Distance Runner* (1962), and made him a star of the British NEW WAVE of films tackling social problems during the 60s. However, despite compelling performances in *Billy Liar* (1963), LOSEY's *King and Country* (1964), and the epic *Doctor Zhivago* (1965, UK/US, AAAn/supp a), when the decade closed and the wave had ebbed, Courtenay's star status diminished. During the next decade he concentrated mainly on the stage, until making a notable return to films in 1983 with *The Dresser* (AAAn/a, BAAn/a), playing a prissy, dedicated assistant to a vainglorious stage actor. Courtenay brings wonderful panache to the role he had already performed to great acclaim on the London and Broadway stages, and is at once versatile and moving, and he has devastating moments as the distraught father in '*Let Him Have It*' (1991). Divorced from stage actress **Cheryl Kennedy** (*b* Enfield, 1947), who appeared in a few films in the 70s. Knighted in 2001.

OTHER BRITISH FILMS: *Private Potter* (1962), *Operation Crossbow* (1965, UK/It), *The Night of the Generals* (1966, UK/Fr), *The Day the Fish Came Out* (1967, UK/Gr), *A Dandy in Aspic*, *Otley* (1968), *One Day in the Life of Ivan Denisovich* (1970, UK/Nor/US), *Catch Me a Spy* (UK/Fr/US), *The Last Butterfly* (1991, UK/Czech/Fr), *The Boy From Mercury* (1996, UK/Fr), *Whatever Happened to Harold Smith?* (2000), *Last Orders* (2001, UK/Ger).

BIBLIOG: Autobiography, *Dear Tom: Letters from Home*, 2002. Melinda Hildebrandt.

Courtneidge, Dame Cicely (*b* Sydney, 1892 – *d* London, 1980). Actress. Much-loved character star of stage (debut 1901), in comedies, variety and revue, and an indefatigable touring player until she was nearly 80. She transferred her good-natured, rib-nudging comic style to the screen in 1929, and appeared in a dozen popular comedies, often with husband Jack HULBERT, including *Jack's the Boy* (1932) and *Falling for You* (1933), and *Me and Marlborough* (1935), in which, disguised as a man, she joins Marlborough's army to prove her husband's innocence of spying. Though never subtle, she was immensely popular in the 30s. She was out of films from 1940 until 1955, but in 1960 gave her best film performance, as an ageing lesbian music-hall star, in *The L-Shaped Room*, and several cameos followed. With age, the somewhat wearing zaniness of her persona had mellowed. Created CBE in 1951, DBE in 1972.

OTHER BRITISH FILMS INCLUDE: *Elstree Calling* (1930), *The Ghost Train* (1931), *Happy Ever After* (1932, UK/Ger), *Soldiers of the King* (1933), *Things Are Looking Up* (1935), *Everybody Dance* (1936), *Take My Tip* (1937), *Under Your Hat* (1940), *Miss Tulip Stays the Night* (1955), *Those Magnificent Men . . .* (1965), *The Wrong Box* (1966), *Not Now, Darling* (1972).

BIBLIOG: Autobiography, *Cicely*, 1953.

Cowan, Maurice (*b* London, 1891 – *d* 1974). Producer. Former journalist (from 1919) and theatrical producer (1925–31), then editor of *Illustrated* and *Picturegoer* for many years. Worked on several screenplays in the 40s, including *I Live in Grosvenor Square* (1945), *Wanted for Murder*, *Spring Song* (story) (1946) and *Meet Me at Dawn* (1947); resigned editorship of *Picturegoer* in 1948; and became a producer and sometimes writer, as on two Norman WISDOM vehicles, *Trouble in Store* (1953) and *One Good Turn* (1954). TV's *The Six Wives of Henry VIII* (1970) was based on an idea of his.

OTHER BRITISH FILMS (p): *Derby Day*, *Home at Seven* (1952), *Turn the Key Softly* (1953, + sc), *The Gypsy and the Gentleman* (1957), *Operation Amsterdam* (1958), *Watch It, Sailor!* (1960).

Cowan, Theo (*b* Letchworth, 1917 – *d* London, 1991). Publicist. Having worked in the GAUMONT–BRITISH publicity department before war service (1939–46), post-war he joined GAINSBOROUGH and in 1947 was appointed manager of RANK's Personal Appearances division, an important publicity arm of the time, and in 1955 became Rank's Controller of Publicity. Dirk BOGARDE was one of his stellar responsibilities, maintained in the 60s on the Bogarde–Joseph LOSEY films,

King and Country (1964) and *Accident* (1967).

Coward, Sir Noël (*b* Teddington, Middlesex, 1899 – *d* Blue Harbor, Jamaica, 1973). Director, screenwriter, dramatist, producer, actor. Showbusiness polymath whose dealings with film, while not exactly peripheral to his career, have always seemed to occupy a secondary place in it. There were: the stirring wartime naval tribute, *In Which We Serve* (1942), which he wrote, produced, starred in and co-directed with David LEAN, and which brought him a Special AA; film adaptations of his plays, notably the three directed by Lean – *This Happy Breed* (1944, + m), *Blithe Spirit* (1945) and, most memorably, the poignant drama of near-adultery, *Brief Encounter* (1945, based on the play *Still Life*), all screen-written and produced by Coward; and in later years a series of stylish film cameo roles in such films as *Our Man in Havana* (1959) and *The Italian Job* (1969). In 1999, his centenary, a flurry of filming projects was announced: *Blithe Spirit* (with Rupert EVERETT), *Hay Fever* (with Joanna LUMLEY) and *Relative Values* (2000, UK/US, with Julie ANDREWS).

On stage from childhood (1913), and in the D.W. Griffith film *Hearts of the World* in 1918, he then turned serious attention to the stage, as playwright and composer. Reinventing himself as the epitome of upper-class sophistication, he wrote plays which represent a benchmark of wit in 20th-century drama: *Hay Fever* (1925), *Private Lives* (1930), and *Design for Living* (1933), both filmed by Hollywood (1931, 1933), and *Blithe Spirit*. These are plays in which people in evening dress speak to each other in some of the best one-liners of the age and in plays built on the firmest structural procedures. As well there were musicals, like *Bitter Sweet* (1929, filmed in 1933 with Anna NEAGLE, and in Hollywood, 1940) and the patriotic extravaganza, *Cavalcade* (1931), filmed in Hollywood (1933), a ballet, short stories, novels, autobiographies and innumerable songs and cabaret appearances. The new realists eclipsed him briefly in the 50s and 60s, but it seems likely that his appeal will outlast theirs. Daniel MASSEY played him on screen in *Star!* (1968).

OTHER BRITISH FILMS: *The Queen Was in the Parlour* (UK/Ger, play), *The Vortex* (play) (1927), *The Little Damozel* (1933, m), *The Astonished Heart* (1950, play, sc, m, a), *Meet Me Tonight* (1952, from *Tonight at 8.30*), *Surprise Package* (a), *The Grass is Greener* (songs) (1960), *Bunny Lake Is Missing* (1965, a), *Pretty Polly* (1967, story), *Boom* (1968, a), *Brief Encounter* (1974, play).

BIBLIOG: Autobiographies, *Present Indicative*, 1937; *Future Indefinite*, 1954; *Past Conditional*, 1982.

Cox, Alex (*b* Wirral, 1954). Director, screenwriter. Independent film-maker, most of whose work has been outside Britain, including the cult feature, *Repo Man* (1984, US), based on a job he once held repossessing cars. Read for law at Oxford, switched to film studies at Bristol University and UCLA. Highlight of his work in British film is *Sid and Nancy* (1986), the violently downbeat account of the life and death of Sid Vicious of the Sex Pistols and his groupie girlfriend, Nancy Spungen.

OTHER BRITISH FILMS: *Nearly Wide Awake* (1979, a), *Straight to Hell* (1986, d, sc), *Red Hot and Blue* (1990, doc, co-d), *Kurosawa: The Last Emperor* (1999, doc, d).

Cox, Brian (*b* Dundee, 1946). Actor, director. Stage-trained actor whose film work has been mainly either for TV, including *The Lost Language of Cranes* (1991) and *Sharpe* (1993), or in America, where he has appeared in such films as *Manhunter* (1986, as the first Hannibal Lecktor), *The Long Kiss Goodnight* (1996) and *Rushmore* (1997). In his first British film, *In Celebration* (1974, UK/Can), he repeated his stage role from

David STOREY's play, and he had important roles in Ken LOACH's *Hidden Agenda* (1990) and Jim SHERIDAN's *The Boxer* (1998, UK/Ire/US). His son is actor **Alan Cox** (*b* 1970), seen in *Mrs Dalloway* (1997, UK/Neth/US). Awarded CBE, 2003.

OTHER BRITISH FILMS: *Grushko* (1993), *The Prince of Jutland* (1994, UK/Den/Fr/Ger), *Mad About Mambo, Saltwater* (Ire) (2000), *Morality Play, Strictly Sinatra* (2001).

Cox, Jack (*b* London, 1896 – *d* Surrey, 1960). Cinematographer. His 45-year career started as director's assistant in 1913 and spanned nearly 90 films, and, in the silent period, he collaborated 11 times with Maurice ELVEY. There was no doubt plenty of dross among his films, but there are two clear high spots of activity: credited variously as John, Jack and J.J., he shot ten of HITCHCOCK's films at BIP, from *The Ring* (1927) to *Number 17* (1932), and including Britain's first talkie, *Blackmail* (1929), with its moody atmospherics; and, in the early 40s, he shot some of GAINSBOROUGH's romantic melodramas, imbuing a film such as *Madonna of the Seven Moons* (1944) with a delirious chiaroscuro essential to its meaning.

OTHER BRITISH FILMS INCLUDE: *The Passionate Friends* (1922), *The Wandering Jew* (1923), *White Slippers* (1924), *The Chinese Bungalow* (1926), *Hindle Wakes* (1927), *The Farmer's Wife, Champagne* (1928), *The Manxman* (1929), *Murder!* (1930), *The Skin Game* (1931), *Rich and Strange* (1932), *Red Wagon* (1934), *The Man Who Changed His Mind, Windbag the Sailor* (1936), *Dr Syn* (1937), *The Lady Vanishes* (1938), *A Girl Must Live* (1939), *They Came by Night* (1940), *Cottage to Let* (1941), *Millions Like Us* (co-c) (1943), *Two Thousand Women* (1944), *The Wicked Lady, They Were Sisters* (1945), *Holiday Camp* (1947), *The Cure for Love, Mr Drake's Duck* (1950), *One Good Turn* (1954), *Up in the World* (1956), *The Square Peg* (1958).

Cox, John (*b* Leicester, 1908), Sound recordist. Oscar-winner for the sounds of desert storms in *Lawrence of Arabia* (1962) and nominated for *Becket* (1964) and *The Guns of Navarone* (1961), and BAA-nominated for *Oliver!* (1968, co-sd), Cox had one of the longest careers in British film. Began with *Gaumont Sound News* and recorded his first feature, *The Bells*, at WEMBLEY STUDIOS in 1931, and remained there as chief sound engineer until war service (1939–42), then working with the ARMY FILM UNIT until 1945. Post-war, he was in charge of sound for BRITISH LION, working at various studios and for the most famous names in British film history.

OTHER BRITISH FILMS INCLUDE: (sd) *Pett and Pott* (short), *Death at Broadcasting House* (1934), *Melody Express* (1937), *The Wooden Horse, Gone to Earth* (1950), *Tales of Hoffman* (1951), *The Bridge on the River Kwai* (1957), *The Horse's Mouth* (1958), *The Grass is Greener* (1960), *The Innocents* (1961), *Dr Strangelove . . .* (1963), *King and Country* (1964), *Othello* (1965), *Modesty Blaise* (1966); (sound sup) *The New Lot* (1943, doc, short), *An Ideal Husband* (1947), *The Winslow Boy, The Fallen Idol* (1948), *The Third Man* (1949), *The Man Between, Hobson's Choice* (1953), *The Man Who Loved Redheads* (1954), *Storm over the Nile* (1955), *A Hill in Korea, The Green Man* (1956), *Room at the Top* (1958), *Tunes of Glory* (1960), *The Servant* (1963), *Oliver!* (1968).

Cox, Vivian A. (*b* Bangalore, India, 1915). Producer. Cambridge-educated Cox entered films in 1946 as personal assistant to Sydney Box, with whom he co-authored *Bad Lord Byron* (1949), the book of the film. He produced about a dozen routine comedies and thrillers; two interesting exceptions were *Father Brown* (1954) and *The Prisoner* (1955).

OTHER BRITISH FILMS INCLUDE: (p, unless noted) *Tread Softly* (1952), *Lost* (1955), *Bachelor of Hearts* (1958), *Deadly Record* (1959, + co-sc), *We Joined the Navy* (1962, assoc p), *The Long Duel* (1967, co-p).

Crabtree, Arthur (*b* Shipley, Lancashire, 1900 – *d* Worthing, 1975). Director, cinematographer. In films from 1929 as

assistant cameraman at BIP, becoming camera operator at GAUMONT–BRITISH in 1932 and DOP in 1935 on several Michael POWELL films. Until 1944, he provided luminous images in such varied films as *Kipps* (1941), the realist *Waterloo Road* (1944) and the lush GAINSBOROUGH MELODRAMAS, *The Man in Grey* (1943) and the very handsome *Fanny by Gaslight* (1944), in which his lighting so eloquently complemented John BRYAN's Victorian production design. He directed the next Gainsborough melodrama himself, the potently resonant *Madonna of the Seven Moons* (1944). Sadly, he did not live long enough to see his work of this period revalued. He slumped in the 50s, as did several A directors of the 40s (e.g. Lance COMFORT, Bernard KNOWLES), spending most of the decade in second features or in making half-hour films for TV, for *Douglas Fairbanks Presents* and others, though the horror films at the end of his career, *Fiend Without a Face* (1957) and *The Horrors of the Black Museum* (1959), which has some particularly nasty moments, have their admirers.

OTHER BRITISH FILMS INCLUDE: (c) *The Love Test* (1935), *Oh, Mr Porter!, The Great Barrier* (1937), *Bank Holiday, Convict 99* (1938), *For Freedom, Charley's (Big-Hearted) Aunt* (1940), *South American George, Rush Hour* (short) (1941), *Uncensored* (1942), *Dear Octopus* (1943); (d) *They Were Sisters* (1945), *Caravan* (1946), *Dear Murderer* (1947), *The Calendar, Quartet* ('The Kite') (1948), *Hindle Wakes* (1952), *West of Suez* (1957).

Craig, Daniel (*b* Chester, 1968) Actor. Craig left a modest Liverpool background as a teenager to try for an acting career in London, was accepted into the National Youth Theatre in 1989, had a year in the National Theatre (appearing in *Angels in America*), then came to notice as Geordie, the failed musician, in TV's *Our Friends in the North* (1996). On the big screen, he had two major roles: artist Francis Bacon's proletarian lover in *Love Is the Devil* (1998, UK/Fr/Jap) and the platoon Sergeant in the Battle of the Somme drama, *The Trench* (1999, UK/Fr). To both he brought an imposingly rugged presence which has led to his being in demand since.

OTHER BRITISH FILMS INCLUDE: *Ghengis Cohn* (1993), *Saint-Ex* (1996), *Elizabeth* (1998), *Hotel Splendide, Some Voices* (2000).

Craig, Sir Gordon (*b* Peterborough, 1891 – *d* Totnes). Executive, producer. Came to film via theatrical production and after WW1 service in the Royal Artillery. Joined the Regent Film Company in 1921 and became chairman of New Era which produced the notable WAR FILMS *The Somme* (1927) and *Q-Ships* (1928) and several films directed by G.B. SAMUELSON, including *Inquest* (1931). Knighted in 1929, he was much associated with Movietone News from the mid 30s.

OTHER BRITISH FILMS: *Down Channel, The Co-Optimists* (1929), *The Other Woman, Jealousy* (1931), *Threads, Collision, The Callbox Mystery* (1932), *The Crucifix.* (1934).

Craig, Michael (*b* Poona, India, 1929). Actor. Former merchant seaman, born of military father in India, Craig left the Navy in 1949. Spotted for films while working at Oxford Playhouse, was given work as extra in 1950, then small parts in such films as *The Malta Story* and *The Love Lottery* (1953). Briefly under contract to TEMPEAN FILMS. Tall and handsome, he was obvious casting for romantic leads in thrillers such as *House of Secrets* (1956), comedies such as *Upstairs and Downstairs* (1959) and adventures like *Nor the Moon by Night* (1958). One of the last RANK contract artists, he was given, generally, parts turned down by Dirk BOGARDE and grew dissatisfied with the limitations in which these GENRE films confined him, though he played with easy authority. He had more rewarding assignments in *Sapphire* (1959), as a racist policeman, and in *The Angry Silence* (1960), the film about a wildcat strike, which he helped to write and in which he played against type as a weak-willed lothario. In the 60s, he gave fine performances as the tormented fundamentalist father of a critically ill daughter in *Life for Ruth* (1962), as the lover of his friend's wife in *Life at the Top* (1965), and as Gertrude LAWRENCE's lover in *Star!* (1968, US). For most of his career, he was more intelligent than the material he worked on, but he made the most of his chances, including the title role in the Australian film, *The Irishman* (1978). Has lived in Australia since the early 70s and acted there on stage, screen and TV, becoming a household name in the series *GP* in the 90s. Married (2) to actress Sue Walker.

OTHER BRITISH FILMS INCLUDE: *The Embezzler* (1954), *Yield to the Night*, *Eyewitness*, *The Black Tent* (1956), *Campbell's Kingdom* (1957), *Sea of Sand*, *The Silent Enemy* (1958), *Doctor in Love* (1960), *Payroll, A Pair of Briefs* (1961), *Modesty Blaise* (1966), *The Royal Hunt of the Sun*, *Country Dance* (1969), *The Vault of Horror* (1973, UK/US).

Craig, Stuart (*b* Norwich). Production designer. Associated with some of the most high-profile British films of the 80s and 90s, Craig won Oscars for *Gandhi* (1982, UK/Ind), *Dangerous Liaisons* (1988, US) and *The English Patient* (1996, UK/US), and a BAA for *The Elephant Man* (1980, UK/US). His best work has fed films of a sweeping romanticism and powerful feeling for place, as in his several for Richard ATTENBOROUGH. Awarded OBE, 2003.

OTHER BRITISH FILMS INCLUDE: (art d/des) *A Bridge Too Far* (1977), *Superman* (1978), *Greystoke...* (UK/US), *Cal* (1984), *The Mission* (1985), *Cry Freedom* (1987), *Memphis Belle* (1990), *Chaplin* (1992, UK/Fr/It/Jap/US), *Shadowlands* (1993, UK/US), *Mary Reilly* (1996, UK/US), *Notting Hill* (1999, UK/US), *Harry Potter and the Philosopher's Stone* (2001, UK/US).

Craig, Wendy (*b* Sacriston, 1934). Actress. Awarded a 1963 BAA (Most Promising Newcomer) for her work as the displaced fiancée in *The Servant*, Central School-trained Craig became famous for several TV series, including *Not in Front of the Children* (1967–70) and *Butterflies* (1978–83). In 1970, the Variety Club named her TV Personality of the Year. Films never found much use for her off-centre prettiness and likeable, self-deprecating humour. In 2000, she returned to the stage to play Mrs Malaprop in *The Rivals* at Stratford.

OTHER BRITISH FILMS INCLUDE: *Room at the Top* (1958), *The Mind Benders* (1963), *The Nanny* (1965), *I'll Never Forget What's 'is Name* (1967).

Craigie, Jill (*b* London, 1914 – *d* London, 1999). Director, screenwriter. One of the first women directors in British cinema, Craigie was essentially a documentarist in her approach. A socialist from her unhappy schooldays, she worked first as a journalist. At 19, she married alcoholic sculptor Claude Begbie-Clench, followed by another brief marriage to screenwriter and director, Jeffrey DELL, with whom she collaborated on the screenplay of *The Flemish Farm* (1943). This was made for TWO CITIES studios for which she directed and wrote two DOCUMENTARIES, *Out of Chaos* (1944), about British artists in wartime, and *The Way We Live* (1946), a then-innovative study of a family emerging from the ruins of war-ravaged Plymouth. Despite some criticism of its simplistic politics, her feature film, *Blue Scar* (1949), set in a Welsh mining village, won enthusiastic support from the documentary filmmakers. In the 50s, she wrote the screenplays for feature films, *The Million Pound Note* (1953) and *Windom's Way* (1957), but

at intervals during the rest of her life made documentaries on subjects close to her heart: e.g. *The Woman's Rebellion* (1952), a BBC radio programme on female suffrage, and in 1995, *Two Hours from London*, on the situation in Yugoslavia. While filming in Plymouth, she met the Labour politician (later party leader, 1980–83) Michael Foot; they lived together for some years, finally marrying in 1949 and remained married until her death 50 years later.

OTHER BRITISH FILMS: *Make-Up* (1937, a), *Children of the Ruins* (1948, doc, d), *To Be a Woman* (1951, doc, d, p, sc).

Cranham, Kenneth (*b* Dunfermline, 1944). Actor. Distinctively craggy-looking supporting player, much seen on TV, including the title role of the disillusioned returned serviceman in *Shine On Harvey Moon* (1982–85) and as Silas Wegg in *Our Mutual Friend* (1998). On screen since *Oliver!* (1968, as Noah Claypole) and in about 20 British films since, including *Prospero's Books* (1991, as Sebastian) and *The Boxer* (1998, UK/Ire/US). Married (1) actress Diana QUICK and (2) actress Fiona Victory.

OTHER BRITISH FILMS: *Fragment of Fear* (1970), *Vampira* (1974), *Joseph Andrews* (1976), *Hellbound: Hellraiser II* (1988), *Under Suspicion* (1991), *Vigo* (1998, UK/Fr), *The Last Yellow* (1999, UK/Ger), *Kevin & Perry Go Large* (UK/US), *Gangster No. 1* (UK/Ger/Ire) (2000), *Born Romantic*, *Shiner* (2001).

Cranmer Court Studios Situated at Clapham, these studios were used in the early part of the 20th century by, among others, producers Bertram PHILLIPS and Harry B. PARKINSON. The studios were used, often for SHORT FILMS, until the end of the 20s.

Craven, Gemma (*b* Dublin, 1950). Actress. Leading lady of a few films, most notably as Cinderella in *The Slipper and the Rose* (1976). On stage opposite Tom CONTI in the musical, *They're Playing Our Song* (1980) and Minna to Richard Burton's Wagner in the TV marathon, *Wagner* (1983, some cinemas).

OTHER BRITISH FILMS INCLUDE: *Why Not Stay for Breakfast?* (1979), *The Mystery of Edwin Drood* (1993), *The Last Bus Home* (1997, Ire), *The Hole* (2001, UK/Fr).

Craven Park Studios Studios founded in Harlesden, London, by Thomas WELSH and George PEARSON of The Welsh Pearson Company Limited in 1918 and closed in 1926, in the wake of the General Strike. During the early 20s, popular films starring Betty BALFOUR, Annette BENSON and Mabel POULTON were made here.

Crawford, Andrew (*b* Glasgow, 1917). Actor. Former publicist who entered films in the late 40s, getting his best chance in *Trottie True* (1948), as Sid, Jean KENT's cheerful balloonist admirer. RANK put him into a dozen films in short order, but, amiable and competent as he was, he never quite made it as a star. On TV from 1951.

OTHER BRITISH FILMS INCLUDE: *Dear Murderer, The Man Within, The Brothers* (1947), *London Belongs to Me, Broken Journey* (1948), *Boys in Brown* (1949), *Morning Departure, Trio* (1950), *One Wild Oat* (1951), *The Queen's Guards* (1961), *Julius Caesar* (1970).

Crawford, Anne (*b* Haifa, Israel, 1920 – *d* London, 1956). Actress. Came to England as a child and made 23 films before her sadly early death from leukaemia. After a 'bit' in *They Flew Alone* (1942), cool blonde Crawford was under contract with WARNERS for whom she made four films before being taken on by GAINSBOROUGH, where her well-bred tones made her a dull heroine in *Caravan* (1946) but a vividly selfish hedonist in *They*

Were Sisters (1945). Once or twice, as in *Tony Draws a Horse* and *Trio* (1950), she showed an under-used sense of comedy, and she is a nicely treacherous Morgan LeFay in *The Knights of the Round Table* (1953). Too often, though, the invincibly upper-class vowels keep audience sympathy at bay, even if the character might warrant it, as in *Daughter of Darkness* (1947), when one roots for the murderess instead. To Hollywood for *Thunder on the Hill* (1951).

OTHER BRITISH FILMS: *The Peterville Diamond* (1942), *The Dark Tower*, *The Night Invader*, *The Hundred Pound Window*, *Headline*, *Millions Like Us* (1943), *Two Thousand Women* (1944), *Bedelia* (1946), *The Master of Bankdam* (1947), *It's Hard to Be Good*, *The Blind Goddess*, *Night Beat* (1948), *Street Corner* (1953), *Mad About Men* (1954).

Crawford, John (*b* 1926). Actor. Tough-looking American lead and second lead who filmed in Britain in the late 50s and early 60s, most impressively as the dangerous Murphy in *Floods of Fear* (1958) and the criminal on the run in *Hell Is a City* (1959).

OTHER BRITISH FILMS INCLUDE: *Intent to Kill*, *Orders to Kill*, *The Key* (1958), *Piccadilly Third Stop* (1960), *The Impersonator*, *The Long Shadow* (1961), *Jason and the Argonauts* (1963).

Crawford, Michael (*b* Salisbury, 1942). Actor, singer. RN: Dumble-Smith. In films since his teens, Crawford is now known world-wide for his TV series, *Some Mothers Do 'Ave 'Em* (1973–75, 1978), as the gormless Frank Spencer, and for creating the title role in Andrew Lloyd-Webber's musical *Phantom of the Opera* (1986), for which he won numerous awards in the UK and US. On-screen, he had some major opportunities after his debut in *Soapbox Derby* (1957), in films such as *The Knack . . .* (1965) and *The Jokers* (1966), but these are not films that have worn well, despite their popularity at the time. There were several American films, including *Hello Dolly* (1969), but since the 70s, almost all his work has been on stage or TV or in recordings. Awarded OBE 1987.

OTHER BRITISH FILMS INCLUDE: *A French Mistress* (1960), *Two Living, One Dead* (1961), *The War Lover* (1962), *Two Left Feet* (1963), *How I Won the War* (1967), *The Games* (1969), *Alice's Adventures in Wonderland* (1972).

BIBLIOG: Autobiography, *Parcel Arrived Safely: Tied with String*, 1999.

Crazy Gang, The Six fiercely robust and subversive clowns, the Crazy Gang comprised three comedy double acts (NERVO and KNOX, FLANAGAN and ALLEN, NAUGHTON and GOLD) originally brought together for stage shows at the London Palladium in the early 30s. One such show, *O-Kay For Sound*, became their first film in 1937, and, although its cinematic technique was rudimentary, it remains a brilliant record of their comic skills, which drew on circus acrobatics, slapstick, quickfire cross-talk and a healthy disregard for social and cultural hierarchies. Further films included *Alf's Button Afloat* (1938), *The Frozen Limits* (1939) and *Gasbags* (1940), wherein they uncover a secret German training camp for Hitler impersonators. After WW2, they concentrated on stage work, though *Life Is A Circus* (1958) was an affectionate valedictory for the by-then elderly Gang. Andy Medhurst.

Creasey, John (*b* London, 1908 – *d* Bodenham, Wiltshire, 1973). Author. Creator of the 'Toff', the society sleuth, about whose investigations two films were made in the 50s – *Salute the Toff* and *Hammer the Toff* (1952) – with John BENTLEY starring. The TV series *Gideon's Way* (1964–65) and *The Baron* (1966–67) were based on Creasey's pseudonymously written novels.

Creed-Miles, Charlie (*b* London, 1972). Actor. Rapidly rising young actor of the 90s who came to notice as an asylum inmate in *The Young Poisoner's Handbook* (1995), Ian HOLM's sidekick in *The Fifth Element* (1997, Fr), and a heroin addict in Gary OLDMAN's punishing *Nil by Mouth* (1997). Has child by actress Samantha MORTON.

OTHER BRITISH FILMS: *London Kills Me*, *'Let Him Have It'* (1991), *The Punk and the Princess* (re-cut version of *The Punk*, 1993), *Super Grass* (short) (1994), *Bad English 1: Tales of a Son of a Brit*, *Glastonbury the Movie* (doc) (1995), *Woundings* (1998), *The Last Yellow* (1999, UK/Ger), *Essex Boys* (2000), *Station Jim* (2001).

Cribbins, Bernard (*b* Oldham, 1928). Actor. Popular comedian with somewhat lugubrious expression and suggestion of incompetence, which he made excellent use of as Nervous O'Toole in *The Wrong Arm of the Law* (1962), in a couple of 'CARRY ON' films (he played Albert Poop-Decker in *Carry On Jack*, 1964) and as the warm-hearted railway porter in *The Railway Children* (1971). Also popular on TV as narrator of *The Wombles* (1973) and as a recording artist of comedy songs.

OTHER BRITISH FILMS INCLUDE: *Davy* (1957), *Tommy the Toreador*, *Make Mine a Million* (1959), *Two Way Stretch* (1960), *The Girl on the Boat* (1962), *Crooks in Cloisters*, *Carry On Spying* (1964), *She* (1966), *Casino Royale*, *Ghost of a Chance* (1967), *Frenzy* (1972), *The Water Babies* (1975), *Night Ferry* (1976), *Carry On Columbus* (1992).

Crichton, Charles (*b* Wallasey, Cheshire, 1910 – *d* London, 1999). Director. Oxford-educated Crichton's career can be divided into four main parts. He entered British films in the 30s as an editor with LONDON FILMS and was involved with such prestige productions as *Sanders of the River* (1935) and *Things to Come* (1936) before moving on to EALING, where he edited several more films including *The Big Blockade*, *Nine Men* (1942, + assoc p) and PROPAGANDA DOCUMENTARIES.

The second stage is the most important: he became the quintessential Ealing director, the man who made the films most affectionately associated in the public mind with the studio, combining a whimsical imagination with a flair for surface REALISM. He began directing in semi-documentary vein with *For Those in Peril* (1944), about the work of Air-Sea Rescue boats, and *Painted Boats* (1945), a lyrical account of aspects of the English canal system, but it was as a director of COMEDIES, in conjunction with screenwriter T.E.B. CLARKE, that he won greatest popularity. In 1946 his *Hue and Cry*, a tale of kids in post-war London outwitting a gang of crooks which has been using a comic strip to convey information, launched the brand product that became known as 'Ealing comedy', a term that, 50 years later, still stirs fond recollection. Crichton's other great success in the genre was *The Lavender Hill Mob* (1951), in which a mild-mannered bank clerk masterminds a bullion theft from the Bank of England. These were truly inventive comedies making imaginative use of locations; they deserve their reputations, though it could be argued that they have less bite to them than others from the Ealing stable, such as *Kind Hearts and Coronets* (1949) or *The Man in the White Suit* (1951). Certainly, Crichton's other Ealing comedies, *Another Shore* (1948), *The Titfield Thunderbolt* (1953) and *The Love Lottery* (1954) are comparatively feeble. He also made non-comedies at Ealing, including the unusual war film, *Against the Wind* (1947) and *The Divided Heart* (1954), in which a child becomes a battleground in post-war Europe.

Post-Ealing, Crichton, like some of his colleagues, rather lost his way. There are incidental felicities in *Law and Disorder* (1958) and *The Battle of the Sexes* (1959), but this third stage of his career really belongs to television, where he directed episodes of such popular 60s series as *Danger Man* and *The Avengers*. There were three more little-regarded feature films in the 60s and a frustrating 1963 visit to Hollywood to direct *Birdman of Alcatraz*, from which he withdrew halfway after disagreements with star Burt Lancaster.

The fourth stage is no more than a coda: John CLEESE, with whom he had worked on business training films, brought him back at 78 to direct the hit comedy, *A Fish Called Wanda* (1988), for which he received AAn (d, co-sc) and BAAn/d. Cleese's name appears as co-director, but that seems to have been for insurance purposes and Crichton enjoyed an Indian summer of esteem. His was a gentle talent but at its best his work also exhibited an underlying structural shrewdness and a sharp observer's eye.

OTHER BRITISH FILMS: (ass ed/ed/co-ed) *Men of Tomorrow* (1932), *Cash, The Private Life of Henry VIII, The Girl from Maxim's* (1933), *Twenty-One Days, The Elephant Boy* (1937), *Prison Without Bars* (1938), *The Thief of Baghdad, Old Bill and Son, Yellow Caesar** (1940), *The Young Veterans*, Guest Of Honour*, Find, Fix And Strike** (1942), *Greek Testament** (1942); (d:) *Dead of Night* (1945), *Train Of Events* (1949), *Dance Hall* (1950), *Hunted* (1952), *The Man in the Sky* (1956), *Floods Of Fear* (1958), *The Boy Who Stole A Million* (1960), *The Third Secret* (1964), *He Who Rides A Tiger* (1965). *= doc.

cricket *see* sport

Cricklewood Studios, London In 1920, theatre owner Sir Oswald STOLL bought a disused aeroplane factory and converted it into a film studio. STOLL PICTURE PRODUCTIONS followed the current trend, making ADAPTATIONS of popular stage plays and novels. Additional revenue came from renting out the studios to other production companies such as Welsh–Pearson, BUTCHERS and the BRITISH AND DOMINIONS COMPANY. In 1922 American director J.Stuart BLACKTON made *The Glorious Adventure* with Lady Diana MANNERS and Victor McLAGLEN, generally considered to be Britain's first feature in colour using the two-colour Prizma system. In the 20s Sir Frank BENSON, George ROBEY, Lillian HALL-DAVIS, Betty BALFOUR, and Brian AHERNE appeared in Cricklewood productions. The studio made a number of 'QUOTA QUICKIES' in the 30s and, in spite of some modernisation in 1937 and a few successful films including the LUCAN-McSHANE, *Old Mother Riley* SERIES, British film production was dwindling and the studios were sold in 1938.
BIBLIOG: Patricia Warren. *British Film Studios – An Illustrated History*, 2001. Patricia Warren.

Cricks, G(eorge) H(oward) (*b* Woodford, Essex, 1861 – *d* Surrey, 1936). Producer. Cricks was an amateur photographer, who began making films for George Harrison and Co. Ltd, *c* 1900. In 1901, he founded Cricks and Sharp with H.M. Sharp, with a studio at Mitcham, Surrey, and began production, primarily of comedy SHORTS. In February 1908, the company was renamed Cricks and Martin Ltd as Cricks took on a new partner, J.H. Martin, and a new studio at Croydon. The company was still making comedies and trick films when the partnership was dissolved in January 1913, at which point the output was very old-fashioned. Cricks continued in production through 1918; the early films he directed himself, the later ones were the work of A.E. COLEBY, Charles CALVERT and Will KELLINO. In the 1920s, Cricks operated the Croydon Film Co. Ltd and Pictos, Limited; in 1926, he formed FHC (Faith, Hope and Charity) Company with Coleby and produced a few SHORTS at a studio in Esher, Surrey. A son,

Reginald Howard Cricks (*d* 1967), was a noted technical authority on the cinema, and was instrumental in the founding of the British Kinematograph Society. AS.

crime films As one might expect in a country where theatrical melodrama made folk devils of Sweeney Todd, the Demon Barber of Fleet Street and Squire Corder, the murderer of Maria Marten in the Red Barn, crime was a favoured subject for early British film-makers. In 1905 two versions were made of the life and death of homicidal Sheffield burglar Charles Peace and the exploits of *Chicago May: the Modern Adventuress* were brought to the screen in 1909. After 1912, however, the flow of crime films was filtered through the British Board of Film Censors, which prohibited the depiction of real criminals, of scenes in prison, and of criminal activity that might be imitated. Thus the characteristic crimes of the inter-war years – smash and grab raids, safe-breaking and racecourse protection rackets – were almost wholly absent from British films of the period. When film-makers did venture beyond country house mysteries and the activities of gentlemanly sleuths, it was for the re-staging of traditional melodramas such as *Maria Marten* (1935) or to the more contemporary fantasies of Edgar Wallace like *Dark Eyes of London* (1939).

Two fine adaptations were made of the low-life novels of James Curtis, *They Drive by Night* (1938) and *There Ain't No Justice* (1939), but it was the Second World War, with its legacy of black marketeers, deserters and maladjusted ex-servicemen, which launched the first wave of films to deal convincingly with the underworld. Between 1947 and 1950 films like *Appointment with Crime* (1946), *Dancing with Crime, Brighton Rock, It Always Rains on Sunday, Black Memory, They Made Me a Fugitive, Good-Time Girl* (1947), *Night Beat, Noose* (1948) and *Night and the City* (1950, UK/US) presented a world populated by racketeers, deserters, ineffectual policemen, and vulnerable, exploited women.

By the end of the 40s the public's flirtation with the black market had turned sour and a return to law and order was welcomed. *The Blue Lamp* (1949) caught the mood precisely, crystallising concern with juvenile delinquents and showing the ordinary uniformed policeman – a hitherto neglected and despised figure – in a wholly positive light. It beckoned in a decade of what Raymond Durgnat called 'copperolatory', and films like *The Long Arm* (1956) and *Gideon's Day* (1958) are reverentially respectful of the English policeman. However, in the 'B' MOVIE jungle, spivs still flourished. Slightly relaxed CENSORSHIP rules allowed the filming of 30s crime novels such as Laurence Meynell's *The Creaking Chair* (as *Street of Shadows* in 1953), Bruce Graeme's *Suspense* (as *Face in the Night* in 1956) and Robert Westerby's *Wide Boys Never Work* (as *Soho Incident* in 1956) and they rubbed shoulders with crime melodramas such as *Hell Drivers* and *The Long Haul* (1957) and salacious exposés like *The Flesh is Weak* (1957) and *Passport to Shame* (1958).

In 1960 *The Criminal, Hell is a City* and *Never Let Go* began a cycle of films which were gloomily pessimistic about the pervasiveness of crime and the ethical problems involved in combating it effectively. However, like *Offbeat* (1960), *Payroll* (1961), *The Small World of Sammy Lee* (1962) and *The Informers* (1963), they are invigorated by NEW WAVE concerns for REALISM and authenticity. The switch from black-and-white to colour which occurred around the middle of the decade and the demise of the 'B' film caused a dramatic reduction in the number of crime films made; but those films which were made fed more directly off the reality of criminal life. *Robbery* (1967) was solidly based on the Great Train Robbery of 1963; *The Strange Affair* (1968) combined the corrupt policemen exposed in the Challenor affair with the sadistic gangsters exposed by the trial of the Richardson gang. *Villain* (1971) featured an East End gangster who, like Ronald Kray, was a sadistic homosexual devoted to his mother. *Performance* (1970) and *Get Carter* (1971) have less obvious real life parallels but they are both informed by the seedy ethos of the late 60s where permissiveness had turned to pornography and idealism to corruption.

Get Carter, a macabre, witty, revenge tragedy had no real successor. *The Squeeze* (1977), which has an alcoholic ex-policeman (Stacey Keach) hunting down the vicious gangsters who have kidnapped his ex-wife, comes closest, but it is a much less charismatic affair. *The Long Good Friday* (1979), with its gangster overlord looking forward to the huge profits to be made from the redevelopment of London's docklands, seems uncannily prescient of what was to happen to Britain in the 80s under Margaret Thatcher. Other anti-Thatcherite films also linked business and crime – most notably *Stormy Monday* (1987) and *The Cook, the Thief, His Wife & Her Lover* (1989, UK/Fr) – but in the 90s, films like the futuristic *Shopping* (1994) and the black yuppie comedy *Shallow Grave* (1994) were more concerned with post-modern stylisation than with the reality of the British underworld.

Writers, like policemen, need to cultivate contacts in the underworld if they want to find out what is going on, and such contacts are difficult to maintain. The traditional working-class families who supplied the hardmen of the 60s and 70s have died out, leaving serious crime the preserve of criminal businessmen who operate among a network of gun clubs, golf clubs and masonic lodges, and maintain contacts with bankers and policemen and international racketeers. It is an unattractive world, difficult to penetrate, and the British film industry, perhaps wisely, has steered clear of it. The most commercially successful British crime film of recent years, *Lock, Stock and Two Smoking Barrels* (1998) is a lively, violent updating of the criminal capers of *The Lavender Hill Mob* (1951) and *The Italian Job*, and the successors it has spawned, such as *Circus* (UK/US), *Honest* (UK/Fr), *Essex Boys*, *Gangster No. 1* (UK/Ger/Ire), *Rancid Aluminium*, *Love Honour and Obey* (2000), *Sexy Beast* (2001, UK/Sp/US), look back with nostalgia on an underworld that no longer exists.

BIBLIOG: Raymond Durgnat, *A Mirror for England*, 1970; Robert Murphy, 'Riff Raff' in Charles Barr (ed), *All Our Yesterdays*, 1986; Steve Chibnall and Robert Murphy (eds), *British Crime Cinema*, 1999. Robert Murphy.

Crisham, Walter (*b* Worcester, Massachusetts, 1913). Actor. New York and London stage actor and choreographer, distinctively long-jawed, who entered films in 1935 (*Opening Night*) and appeared occasionally in the 40s and 50s, most vividly as gangster Eddie in *No Orchids for Miss Blandish* (1948) and the flamboyant Dessosse in *Moulin Rouge* (1953).

OTHER BRITISH FILMS INCLUDE: *They Met in the Dark* (1943), *Her Favourite Husband* (1950, UK/It), *The Captain's Paradise* (1953), *The Beachcomber* (1954), *Joe Macbeth* (1955).

Crisp, Donald (*b* Aberfeldy, Scotland, 1880 – *d* Los Angeles, 1974). Actor, director. Legendary figure from early silent days in Hollywood, where he often played Brits, as in *National Velvet* (1944). He directed four British silent films in 1920–21 and his penultimate role was in the British *Greyfriars Bobby* (1961).

OTHER BRITISH FILMS (d): *Beside the Bonnie Briar Bush* (+ a), *Appearances*, *The Princess of New York* (1921, UK/US), *Tell Your Children* (1922).

Crisp, Quentin (*b* London, 1908 – *d* Manchester, 1999). Author, actor. RN: Denis Pratt. Wildly and courageously flamboyant personality who insisted the world take note of him and his homosexuality – and it did. He emphasised his effeminacy in dress and makeup, and, after a series of jobs including nude modelling, he was catapulted into fame by the TV-filming of his autobiography, *The Naked Civil Servant* (1975), in which John HURT played Crisp. This led to a career as an actor and he appeared in three British films – an experimental *Hamlet* (1976), in which he played Polonius, *The Bride* (1985) and *Orlando* (1992, UK/Fr/It/Neth/Russ) as Queen Elizabeth 1 – and in several US films. He lived in New York from 1980.

critics/criticism A Leavisite hostility to mass culture, an educational aversion to new disciplines, a cultural preference for the literary over the visual: all these factors have hindered the cinema's claim for serious critical attention in this country. From 1927 to 1933, the influential journal *CLOSE UP* engaged in critical discussion of such matters as CENSORSHIP and the merits of Soviet Cinema. In the 30s, John GRIERSON had become a powerful polemicist for film but chiefly seeing its value in its capacity to dramatise 'real life' or 'the living scene'. More flexible was Graham GREENE, whose evocative film reviews embraced the cinema's capacity for poetry and popularity. The standard of his journalism inspired perceptive successors like Dilys POWELL, C.A. LEJEUNE and Richard WINNINGTON. However, Lindsay ANDERSON introduced a valuable belligerence to the debate, berating critics for their facile values, attacking British cinema for its timidity and calling for films of passion and commitment. His attacks sometimes graced the pages of the BFI's *SIGHT AND SOUND*, whose pre-eminence as Britain's top film journal was challenged in the 60s by *MOVIE*, whose critics (e.g. V.F. Perkins, Robin Wood) lauded Hollywood auteurism; and then in the 70s by *SCREEN*, whose dense pages included influential articles from theorists like Peter WOLLEN, Stephen Heath and Laura MULVEY. In this battle of ideas and ideologies amongst British critics, the achievements of British cinema tended to be sidelined until historians such as Charles Barr and Jeffrey Richards rectified the omission. Whether the critical establishment has sufficiently encouraged its NATIONAL CINEMA remains debatable.One still recalls Ken RUSSELL's attack on Alexander Walker with a rolled-up *Evening Standard* after the latter had lambasted Russell's *The Devils* (1971). Asked years later whether he regretted doing that, Russell replied: 'Yes – it should have been an iron bar.' Neil Sinyard.

Croft, Peter (*b* 1917). Actor. Supporting player of a dozen films of the 30s and 40s, with breaks for Merchant Navy service (1946–47) and the London stage (1947–49). Last film was *Poet's Pub* (1949), as the hero-poet's ex-Cambridge chum. Became a TV director on such series as *Black Arrow* (1972–75).

OTHER BRITISH FILMS INCLUDE: *King of the Damned*, *East Meets West* (1936), *OHMS*, *A Yank at Oxford* (1937), *The Goose Steps Out*, *Flying Fortress* (1942), *Escape* (1948).

Croise, Hugh (*b* Cornwall – *d*?). Director. Hugh Croise studied opera, singing in Italy, Germany and the US, and painting and design at the Slade School, before entering the film industry in 1911 as a 'bit' player. Also active in German cinema in the 20s, Croise was primarily a director/writer of obscure SHORTS and equally obscure feature films before his career ended with the coming of sound.

BRITISH FEATURE FILMS INCLUDE: *Judged by Appearances* (1916), *Four Men in a Van* (1921, + sc), *The Ball of Fortune* (1926, + sc). AS.

Crompton, Richmal (*b* Bury, Lancashire, 1890 – *d* Chislehurst, 1969). Author. Creator of scapegrace schoolboy 'William Brown' whose adventures spawned three films – *Just William* (1939, starring Dickie Lupino), and *Just William's Luck* (1947) and *William Comes to Town* (1948), both starring William Graham – and several TV series between 1956 and 1995.

Cronin, A(rchibald) J(oseph) (*b* Cardross, Scotland, 1896 – *d* Montreux, Switzerland, 1981). Author. This novelist's glum tracts of hardship, whether down the mines or in bleak Scottish villages, were best-sellers from the 30s to the 50s. They provided the basis for five British films: *The Citadel* (1938), *The Stars Look Down* (1939), *Hatter's Castle* (1941), *The Spanish Gardener* (1956), *Beyond This Place* (1959), all arguably more compelling entertainments than their lugubrious sources. Hollywood adaptations included *The Keys of the Kingdom* (1944) and *The Green Years* (1956).

Cropper, Anna (*b* Brierfield, 1938). Actress. Versatile Central School-trained character player mostly on TV, including *Jewel in the Crown* (1984) and *Castles* (1995), with few screen appearances since debut in *All Neat in Black Stockings* (1969). Married TV actor William Roache; mother of Linus ROACHE. OTHER BRITISH FILMS: *Cromwell* (1970), *Footsteps* (1974, short), *Praying Mantis* (1982), *Nanou* (1986), *The Affair* (1995).

Crosbie, Annette (*b* Edinburgh, 1934). Actress. Star of such TV series as *Doctor Finlay* (1993–95) and *One Foot in the Grave* (1990), who has made less impact on screen. Of her dozen or so films, she is best remembered as the twinkly-eyed (she *does* twinkle) fairy godmother in *The Slipper and the Rose* (1976). It is good to see her rather too-sweet persona take on a touch of vinegar occasionally, as in *Shooting Fish* (1997). Awarded OBE 1998.

OTHER BRITISH FILMS INCLUDE: *The Bridal Path* (1959), *Sky West and Crooked* (1965), *Follow Me!* (1971), *The Pope Must Die* (1991, UK/US), *Leon the Pig Farmer* (1992), *The Debt Collector* (1999).

Cross, Ben (*b* London, 1947). Actor. RADA-trained and with stage experience with the RSC and Prospect Theatre Company, dark, intense-looking Cross's film career has been curiously disappointing following his flying start in *Chariots of Fire* (1981). Of the two young stars of that Oscar-winner, Ian CHARLESON is now dead and Cross has confined himself largely to TV, most famously in *The Far Pavilions* (1984), and to little-seen international films, of which the best-known may be *First Knight* (1995, US), in which he played an imposing villain. OTHER BRITISH FILMS INCLUDE: *Great Expectations* (1975), *A Bridge Too Far* (1977), *Paperhouse* (1988), *Robert Rylands' Last Journey* (1996).

Cross, Beverley (*b* London, 1931 – *d* London, 1998). Writer. Distinguished playwright and librettist of operas, Cross also wrote six screenplays, including *Genghis Khan* (1965, US), *Half a Sixpence* (1967), based on his own libretto, and *Clash of the Titans* (1981, UK/US), in which his wife (3), Maggie SMITH starred.

OTHER BRITISH FILMS: *The Long Ships* (UK/Yug), *Jason and the Argonauts* (1963), *Sinbad and the Eye of the Tiger* (1977, + story).

Cross, Eric (*b* 1902). Cinematographer. For three decades Cross was one of the stalwarts of British cinematography,

perhaps competent rather than innovative, but he brings a real pastoral freshness to such films as *Tawny Pipit*, *Don't Take It to Heart* (1944) and *The Kidnappers* (1953), and his edgy images contribute to the tension of such on-the-run dramas as *The One That Got Away* (1957) and *Tiger Bay* (1959), and even to such 50s 'B' MOVIES as *Black Orchid* (1952). Entered films as stills photographer in 1927 and was chief cameraman at WEMBLEY STUDIOS before becoming director of photography in 1933, and was chief cinematographer for RANK's *This Modern Age* (1946–50).

OTHER BRITISH FILMS INCLUDE: *The Bells* (1931, ass c), *On Thin Ice*, *The Lure* (1933), *The Secret of the Loch* (underwater ph), *Mastership* (1934), *Turn of the Tide*, *The Mystery of the Marie Celeste* (1935), *Song of Freedom* (1936), *Sons of the Sea* (1939), *Ships with Wings*, *The Black Sheep of Whitehall* (1941), *The Flemish Farm* (1943), *Quiet Weekend* (1946), *The Chance of a Lifetime*, *The Dark Man* (1950), *Private Information*, *Hunted* (1952), *Glad Tidings* (1953), *Simba*, *Tiger by the Tail*, *Escapade* (1955), *Three Men in a Boat*, *Private's Progress*, *The High Terrace* (1956), *High Tide at Noon* (1957), *Crosstrap* (1961).

Cross, Hugh (*b* London, 1925 – *d* London, 1989). Actor. Pleasant young RADA-trained lead and supporting player of the 40s, who played the older brother in the two 'William' films – *Just William's Luck* (1947) and *William Comes to Town* (1948) and William's sorely-tried father in the TV series, *Just William* (1976). Best role was in the BOULTINGS' thriller, *Seven Days to Noon* (1950).

OTHER BRITISH FILMS INCLUDE: *Millions Like Us* (1943), *Warning to Wantons* (1948), *Svengali* (1954), *The Court Martial of Major Keller* (1964).

Cross, Pippa Producer. Was made head of Granada Film (1995), established in 1989 as a subsidiary of the Granada Media Group. She has been credited usually as executive producer on Granada's films, though on earlier ones such as *Jack & Sarah* (1995, UK/Fr) and *August* (1996) she is co-producer. The enterprising group had a success with *Girls' Night* (1998, UK/US) and a flop with *Rogue Trader* (1999). Also, *The Weekend* (1999, UK/US, ex p), *The House of Mirth* (2000, UK/US, co-ex p), *Essex Boys* (2000, ex p), *The Hole* (2001, UK/Fr, co-p with Jeremy BOLT).

Crossley, Syd (*b* London, 1885 – *d* Redruth, 1960). Actor. Former vaudevillian in the US where he began his film career in 1925, tall, somewhat pop-eyed Crossley returned to Britain in 1929 and appeared in nearly 90 supporting roles, mostly as comic cockneys over the next ten years. Mainly in long-forgotten comedies, with a few upmarket excursions such as *The Ghost Goes West* (1935) and *Victoria the Great* (1937). At his busiest he averaged about 10 films a year.

OTHER BRITISH FILMS INCLUDE: *Atlantic* (1929), *Never Trouble Trouble*, *The Mayor's Nest*, *For the Love of Mike* (1932), *You Made Me Love You*, *Perfect Understanding*, *Letting in the Sunshine*, *Leave It to Me*, *The King's Cup*, *The Bermondsey Kid* (1933), *Music Hath Charms*, *Me and Marlborough* (1935), *Queen of Hearts*, *The Man Behind the Mask* (1936), *Boys Will Be Girls*, *Young and Innocent* (1937), *We're Going to Be Rich* (1938), *Come On George!* (1939), *Old Mother Riley's Circus* (1941).

Crowden, Graham (*b* Edinburgh, 1922). Actor. Dominant character player of mad-eyed eccentrics, shambling scholars, since the 60s in film, on stage since 40s walk-ons at Stratford, with National, RSC and Chichester seasons, and eight years at the Royal Court (1957–65). Here he met Lindsay ANDERSON in whose films, *If . . .* (1968), *O Lucky Man!* (1973) and *Britannia Hospital* (1982, as a Frankenstein-type surgeon), he appeared. He could be imposingly tall and dignified, but there was always the enjoyable promise of hidden nuttiness: he could be aristocratic, or just crackers. He has also done masses of excellent TV work, including *A Very Peculiar Practice* (1986, 1988), as the boozing head of an odd medical centre, and as the maverick inmate of a retirement home in *Waiting for God* (1990–94). Married actress Phyllida Hewat.

OTHER BRITISH FILMS: *The Bridal Path* (1959, unc), *Don't Bother to Knock* (1961, unc), *We Joined the Navy* (1962, unc), *Dead Man's Chest* (1965), *Morgan: A Suitable Case for Treatment* (1966), *The Virgin Soldiers, Leo the Last* (1969), *Percy, Up the Chastity Belt, The Ruling Class* (1971), *The Amazing Mr Blunden* (1972), *Jabberwocky* (1977), *For Your Eyes Only, The Missionary* (1981), *The Company of Wolves* (1984), *The Innocent Sleep* (1995), *I Want You, The Sea Change* (UK/Sp) (1998), *Possession* (2002, UK/US).

Crowden, Sarah (*b* Edinburgh, 1955). Actress. Began career as Assistant Stage Manager in 1974 and has since worked with the RSC and the Almeida Theatre, and at Chichester. Much TV including *Lovejoy* (1986), and a scattering of films, including *Orlando* (1992, UK/Fr/It/Neth/Russ) as Queen Mary. Daughter of Graham CROWDEN and actress Phyllida Hewat, whose daughter she played in TV's *The Rainbow* (1989).

OTHER BRITISH FILMS: *Billy the Kid and the Green Baize Vampire* (1985), *Erik the Viking* (1989), *The Wind in the Willows* (1996), *The Man Who Knew Too Little* (1997, UK/Ger/US).

Crowe, Eileen (*b* Dublin, 1898 – *d* Dublin, 1978). Actress. RN: Eilleen Judge. Abbey Theatre actress whose dozen films include four American, *The Quiet Man* (1952, as the Vicar's wife) the most notable. Her British films, from *Hungry Hill* (1947), all had an Irish production or location component. Married to actor F.J. McCORMICK.

OTHER BRITISH FILMS INCLUDE: *Home Is the Hero, Shake Hands with the Devil* (UK/US) (1959), *Boyd's Shop* (Ire), *A Terrible Beauty* (1960), *Girl with Green Eyes* (1964).

Crowe, Sara (*b c* 1966). Actress. Best remembered as the first bride (and cause of Hugh GRANT's solecism) in *Four Weddings and a Funeral* (1994), this blonde young comedienne has appeared in occasional films and TV commercials and series, such as *Haggard* (1990–92, as Fanny Foulacre).

OTHER BRITISH FILMS INCLUDE: *Carry On Columbus* (1992), *The Steal* (1995), *Caught in the Act* (1996).

Crown Film Unit This renaming of the GPO Film Unit came about when the MINISTRY OF INFORMATION was charged with controlling wartime PROPAGANDA production. With the backing of a single government department and the wartime social purpose, this unit produced some of Britain's most influential DOCUMENTARIES including *Target for Tonight* (1941) and *Western Approaches* (1944). Crown also saw the emergence of what many consider to be the documentary film movement's poet, Humphrey JENNINGS. Jennings believed strongly in the healing process of art and that all experience, regardless of contradiction, could be reconciled through a reliance on an almost mythological idea of England. In films such as *London Can Take It!* (1940), *Listen to Britain* (1942), *Fires Were Started* (1943) and *A Diary For Timothy* (1946), he eschewed traditional documentary cohesion in favour of a mosaic of everyday life providing a model for the later FREE CINEMA film-makers, in particular Lindsay ANDERSON. Deane Williams.

Croydon, John (*b* London, 1907). Executive producer. In films for 35 years in varying capacities: in the 30s, accountant, assistant studio manager (GAUMONT–BRITISH), studio manager (GAINSBOROUGH, then GAUMONT); in the 40s, production manager for Irving ASHER Productions, then to EALING as production supervisor and associate producer (on *Champagne Charlie*, 1944, *Dead of Night*, 1945, *Nicholas Nickleby*, 1947). When RANK developed a scheme to make 'B' MOVIES at HIGHBURY STUDIOS, 1947–49, Croydon was appointed producer-in-charge of the short-lived enterprise, of which only *To the Public Danger* (1948) can stand scrutiny. During the 50s, he produced such 'A' features as *White Corridors* (1951) but was as often working on second features such as *The Delavine Affair* (1954) and short children's films such as *Five O'Clock Finish* (1954) and *Playground Express* (1955, + co-sc), both directed by his Highbury colleague John IRWIN. At the end of the decade, he produced several HORROR films, including *Fiend Without a Face* (1957), and near the end of his interesting career he was associate producer on *The Entertainer* (1960) and produced *High Wind in Jamaica* (1965).

OTHER BRITISH FILMS INCLUDE: (pr man/super) *Spare a Copper, Yellow Caesar* (short), *Conquest of the Air* (1940), *The Big Blockade, The Foreman Went to France, Went the Day Well?* (1942); (p) *Food for Thought* (1940, short), *A Piece of Cake, Trouble in the Air, Love in Waiting, Colonel Bogey, Badger's Green, Song for Tomorrow* (1948, all Highbury), *One Wild Oat* (1951), *Golden Ivory* (1954), *1984* (1955), *Tarzan and the Lost Safari* (1956), *Corridors of Blood* (1958), *The Projected Man* (1966).

Cruickshank, Andrew (*b* Aberdeen, 1907 – *d* London, 1988). Actor. Weightily imposing actor of serious mien, born to play judges and colonels, lords and doctors, winning household fame as crusty Dr Cameron in TV's *Dr Finlay's Casebook* (1962–71). On the London stage 1930 and in films 1938, as Robert Burns in *Auld Lang Syne*, and after five years in the army (1940–45) he returned to films in 1947, surviving a role in the notoriously idiotic *Idol of Paris* (1948), to appear in a further two dozen films as men of substance and authority.

OTHER BRITISH FILMS INCLUDE: *The Mark of Cain* (1948), *Forbidden, Paper Orchid* (1949), *Your Witness* (1950), *Where No Vultures Fly* (1951), *The Cruel Sea* (1952), *Richard III* (1955), *The Battle of the River Plate* (1956), *Innocent Sinners* (1958), *Kidnapped* (1960), *Greyfriars Bobby* (1961), *Murder Most Foul* (1964).

Crutchley, Rosalie (*b* London, 1921 – *d* London, 1997). Actress. Dark-eyed and intense (she often played 'foreign'), Crutchley made a striking debut as the violinist who gets murdered in her first film *Take My Life* (1947). Thereafter, she was more often dangerous than endangered, most notably as the shroud-knitting Madame DeFarge in *A Tale of Two Cities* (1958). She seemed always destined for character roles rather than leads, suggesting too much complexity for most of the latter, and she does superbly by Peter FINCH's neglected wife in *No Love for Johnnie* (1961). On stage from 1938, mainly in films and TV after 1960, and a conspicuous wedding guest in *Four Weddings and a Funeral* (1994). On TV, she was playing Goneril as early as 1949, and, as Katherine Parr, dourly outlasted Henry VIII in both *The Six Wives of Henry VIII* (1970) and *Elizabeth R* (1971). Married (2) and divorced actor **Peter Ashmore**.

OTHER BRITISH FILMS INCLUDE: *Give Us This Day* (1949), *Prelude to Fame* (1950), *The Sword and the Rose* (1953), *Make Me An Offer!* (1954), *The Spanish Gardener* (1956), *Sons and Lovers* (1960), *The Haunting* (1963), *Creatures the World Forgot* (1970), *And Now the Screaming Starts!* (1973), *Mahler* (1974), *A World Apart* (UK/Zimb), *Little Dorrit* (1987), *The Fool* (1990), *Saint-Ex* (1996).

Cuka, Frances (*b* London, 1936). Actress. After Guildhall training and a few small parts with the Theatre Workshop, she came to critical attention on stage in *A Taste of Honey* (1957), as the pregnant Jo. Expressive rather than pretty, she has appeared in few films, most prominently as Catherine of Aragon in *Henry VIII and His Six Wives* (1972). She was also in the US films, *The Watcher in the Woods* (1982) and *The Mountains of the Moon* (1990).

OTHER BRITISH FILMS: *Over the Odds* (1961), *Scrooge* (1970, as Mrs Cratchit), *Hide and Seek* (1972), *Afraid of the Dark* (1991, UK/Fr), *Snow White: A Tale of Terror* (1996, US/UK).

Culley, Frederick (*b* Plymouth, 1879 – *d* Newbury, Berkshire, 1942). Actor. On stage for many years, often in Cyril MAUDE's companies; made at least one silent film, *The Suicide Club* (1914) and was in some notable KORDA productions in the 30s, including *The Drum* (1938), as raj representative, Dr Murphy.

OTHER BRITISH FILMS INCLUDE: *Madame Guillotine* (1931), *Once a Thief* (1935), *The Rat, Knight Without Armour* (1937), *Special Edition* (1938), *Four Feathers* (1939), *Conquest of the Air* (1940), *The Young Mr Pitt* (1942), *The Bells Go Down* (1943).

Culver, Michael (*b* London, 1938) Actor. Tall, austere-looking actor who has made a vivid impression on TV (e.g. as Maclean in *Philby, Burgess and Maclean*, 1977, and in *Secret Army*, 1977) and occasional films, including *A Passage to India* (1984), as police officer McBryde, and *The Empire Strikes Back* (1980, US). Son of Roland CULVER.

OTHER BRITISH FILMS: *Crossplot* (1969), *Goodbye, Mr Chips* (1969), *The Fast Kill* (1972), *Conduct Unbecoming* (1975).

Culver, Roland (*b* London, 1900 – *d* Henley-on-Thames, 1984). Actor. His autobiography, which scarcely mentions his films, was called *Not Quite a Gentleman* (1979), but it would have taken a very practised cinemagoing eye to notice the difference as he made his way through about 90 films. He could be corrupt as in *The Ship That Died of Shame* (1955) or blinkered and blustery as in *Rockets Galore* (1958), but rarely ungentlemanly. After WW1 experience as a RAF pilot, he trained at RADA. Starred on the stage (debut 1924), and was moving as the *non*-gentleman father in *Five Finger Exercise* (1958), but not on screen, which gave him good character roles within a quite narrow range, though the deftness of his timing and his way with a dry line shouldn't be underestimated. There are numerous lords and colonels among his films, but a rare exception in a minor film – a tenacious police inspector in *The Late Edwina Black* (1951) – stays in the mind among such clubbable types as John JUSTIN's old friend in *The Man Who Loved Redheads* (1954). In Hollywood, 1946–49, initially to play a benign aristocrat in *To Each His Own* (1946), and on TV he was a memorable Duke of Omnium in *The Pallisers* (1974). His son is actor Michael CULVER.

OTHER BRITISH FILMS INCLUDE: *Fascination 77, Park Lane* (1931), *Her First Affaire* (1932), *French Without Tears* (1939), *Night Train to Munich, Fingers* (1940), *Quiet Wedding, This England* (1941), *Talk About Jacqueline, Secret Mission, The First of the Few, The Day Will Dawn* (1942), *Dear Octopus* (1943), *Give Us the Moon, On Approval, English Without Tears* (1944), *Dead of Night, Perfect Strangers* (1945), *Wanted for Murder* (1946), *Trio* (1950), *Hotel Sahara, The Magic Box* (1951), *Rough Shoot* (1953), *Touch and Go, An Alligator Named Daisy* (1955), *Bonjour Tristesse, The Vicious Circle* (1957), *Term of Trial, The Fast Lady* (1962), *The Yellow Rolls-Royce* (1964), *Thunderball* (1965), *Bequest to the Nation, The Mackintosh Man* (1973), *The Missionary* (1981), *Britannia Hospital* (1982).

Cumming, Alan (*b* Perthshire, Scotland, 1965). Actor. Daring, Pan-like actor who often plays eccentric, sexually ambiguous characters, hovering between mischief and villainy. His scoundrel's progress began as Minnie DRIVER's oily, over-

eager suitor in *Circle of Friends* (1995, Ire/US). Appearances in high-profile films such as *GoldenEye* (1995, UK/US), *Emma* (1996, UK/US), and the suitably camp *Spice World* (1997), enhanced his healthy reputation as an actor (Olivier Award for *Accidental Death of an Anarchist*, 1991; Tony Award for his lascivious MC in the 1998 Broadway revival of *Cabaret*). Has continued to choose provocative roles: a hideously made-up Lord in *Plunkett & Macleane* (1999), the corrupt Saturninus (again, as though in drag) in the audacious *Titus* (2000, UK/US) and the suggestive hotel clerk in Kubrick's *Eyes Wide Shut* (1999, UK/US), where, in just a few minutes, he upstaged Tom Cruise. Made his directorial feature film debut with *The Anniversary Party* (2001, US, + co-p, s), starring Kevin Kline. Divorced from actress Hilary Lyon.

OTHER BRITISH FILMS INCLUDE: *Passing Glory* (1986, short), *Prague* (1992, UK/Fr), *Second Best* (1994, UK/US). Melinda Hildebrandt.

Cummings, Constance (*b* Seattle, 1910). Actress. RN: Halverstadt. Settled in England during the mid 30s, after experience as Broadway dancer and 20 US films, including *The Criminal Code* (1931). First British film was *Channel Crossing* (1933), and post-1936 she filmed only in Britain, with leading roles in such films as *Busman's Honeymoon* (1940) as Dorothy Sayers' heroine, Harriet Vane, EALING's wartime adventure, *The Foreman Went to France* (1942), and the sorely-tried second wife in *Blithe Spirit* (1945). After that, she played character roles of which the best was probably the efficiency expert in *The Battle of the Sexes* (1959), enshrining her sharply sophisticated comedy sense. Built a substantial reputation on the London stage (with sorties to Broadway), and was a heart-breaking Mary Tyrone, opposite OLIVIER, in *Long Day's Journey into Night* (1971), filmed (1973) for TV. Married British dramatist and producer Benn W. LEVY (1933 to 1973, his death).

OTHER BRITISH FILMS INCLUDE: *Heads We Go!* (1933), *Seven Sinners* (1936), *This England* (1941), *Into the Blue* (1950), *Three's Company* (1953), *John and Julie* (1955), *The Intimate Stranger* (1956), *Sammy Going South* (1963), *Jane Eyre* (1970).

Cummins, Peggy (*b* Prestatyn, Wales, 1925). Actress. In films as a teenager, Cummins is now most famous for two American roles: one she was imported to play but in the event didn't (the title role in *Forever Amber*, 1948); and the other as a wildly sensual young tearaway in *Gun Crazy* (1949), a classic *film noir*. Nothing else in her career can touch this, and she could have used some of its tough sexiness in *Hell Drivers* (1957), an otherwise admirable British *noir*. She is, though, always acceptable company in mild comedies like *English Without Tears* (1944), as the heroine's kid sister, the glamour arm of a con-team in *Always a Bride* (1953), a mild Anglo-version of *The Lady Eve*, and *The Captain's Table* (1958, when she still looked 18).

OTHER BRITISH FILMS: *Dr O'Dowd* (1940), *Salute John Citizen* (1942), *Old Mother Riley, Detective* (1943), *Welcome Mr Washington* (1944), *Escape* (1948), *That Dangerous Age* (1949), *My Daughter Joy* (1950), *Who Goes There!* (1951), *Meet Mr Lucifer, Street Corner, The Love Lottery* (1953), *The March Hare* (1956), *Night of the Demon, Carry On Admiral* (1957), *Your Money or Your Wife, Dentist in the Chair* (1960), *In the Doghouse* (1961).

Cunliffe, Freddie Actor. Made a very impressive debut as the watchful son who sees his family destroyed by abuse in *The War Zone* (1999, UK/It), his pinched and pimply features wearing the pain.

Cunningham, Neil (*b* Kent, 1942 – *d* London, 1987). Actor. Supporting player who appeared in some notable films of the

70s and 80s, remembered as the duplicitous estate manager in *The Draughtsman's Contract* (1982) and the kindly Foreign Office functionary in *A Letter to Brezhnev* (1985).

OTHER BRITISH FILMS: *Hardcore* (1977), *Bloody Kids*, *The Tempest* (1979), *Victor/Victoria* (1982), *The Supergrass*, *My Beautiful Laundrette* (1985), *Eat the Rich* (1987).

Cunynghame, Sir David (*b* Sarawak, 1905 – *d* London, 1978). Production manager. RN: David St Leger Brooke Selwyn. Very important executive figure in the history of LONDON FILMS and one of Alexander KORDA's most significant associates, both in the 30s and post-war, when he also became a director of BRITISH LION, controlling both SHEPPERTON and ISLEWORTH STUDIOS. Became 11th baronet in 1941.

Curram, Roland (*b* Brighton, 1932). Actor. RADA-trained, with extensive stage and TV credits (including Freddie in *Eldorado*, 1993–94), slightly-built Curran had one starring role, as a mental outpatient in *The Secret Playground* (1963), and vivid supporting roles in *Darling* (1965), as the heroine's gay friend, and as the 'hunted' Eldrich in the old boys' dinner sequence of *I'll Never Forget What's 'is Name* (1967). Was married to actress Sheila GISH.

OTHER BRITISH FILMS INCLUDE: *The Good Beginning* (1953), *Up to His Neck* (1954), *Dunkirk*, *The Captain's Table* (1958), *Peeping Tom* (1960), *Panic* (1965), *Decline and Fall . . .* (1968), *Ooh . . . You Are Awful* (1972), *Hardcore* (1977), *Madame Sousatzka* (1988).

Currie, Finlay (*b* Edinburgh, 1878 – *d* Gerrards Cross, 1968). Actor. Monumental character player who terrified a generation of schoolchildren, and not a few adults, when, as Magwitch in David LEAN's *Great Expectations* (1946), he leapt out at the young Pip in a gloomy cemetery. Formerly an organist and choirmaster, and on stage from 1898 and in films from 1931's *The Old Man*, the craggy, white-haired Currie continued to act into his 80s, often dour and forbidding, sometimes merely irascible as in *The Mudlark* (as gillie John Brown) and *Trio* (1950), sometimes zealous as in *Quo Vadis* (1951, US), as St Peter, and occasionally benign, the reluctant retiree (a role he never sought in life) in the tender 'B' MOVIE, *The End of the Road* (1954). He worked in Hollywood in the early 50s and the 60s, and made *Kangaroo* (1952) in Australia, where he had toured earlier in the century. Married to American musical comedy star, Maude Courtney, with whom he formed a stage team in the 1890s.

OTHER BRITISH FILMS INCLUDE: *Rome Express*, *The Frightened Lady* (1932), *The Good Companions* (1933), *Heat Wave* (1935), *Edge of the World*, (1937), *49th Parallel* (1941), *Thunder Rock* (1942), *The Shipbuilders*, *The Bells Go Down*, (1943), *I Know Where I'm Going!* (1945), *School for Secrets* (1946), *The Brothers* (1947), *So Evil My Love*, *Sleeping Car to Trieste*, *Mr Perrin and Mr Traill*, *My Brother Jonathan*, *The History of Mr Polly* (1948), *Treasure Island* (1950), *Ivanhoe* (1952), *Rob Roy . . .* (1953), *King's Rhapsody* (1955), *Dangerous Exile*, *Campbell's Kingdom* (1957), *Kidnapped*, *Hand in Hand* (1960), *Billy Liar*, *Murder at the Gallop* (1963), *Bunny Lake Is Missing*, *The Battle of the Villa Fiorita* (1965).

Curry, Julian (*b* Dartington Hall, Devon, 1937). Actor. Supporting actor probably best known as the fastidious Erskine-Browne in TV's *Rumpole of the Bailey* (from 1978), seen in a few films, including *Smashing Time* (1967), *The Missionary* (1981), *Terry on the Fence* (1985) and *Loch Ness* (1996).

Curry, Tim (*b* Cheshire, 1946). Actor, singer. The career of Dr Frank N. Furter, the mad scientist of the cult stage show and film version, *The Rocky Horror Picture Show* (1975), belongs only tangentially here. Curry appeared in three other British

films, *The Shout* (1978), *The Ploughman's Lunch* (1983) and *Sorted* (2000, UK/US). The rest of his prolific career has been spent on stage (he played Mozart in *Amadeus* on Broadway), as a recording artist, on TV and international films, such as *Oscar* (1991) and *Home Alone 2* (1992).

Cursitor Street Studios These three small stages in Camden were used by independent companies between 1947 and the early 50s. Among others, Paul ROTHA produced his *History of Writing*, *History of Printing* and *The World is Rich* at Camden during the 40s. By the mid 50s, the premises were no longer used as a film studio.

Curtis, Richard (*b* New Zealand, 1956). Screenwriter. Born of Australian parents, brought up in several continents, and educated at Harrow and Oxford, Curtis began his writing career on TV's *Not the Nine O'Clock News* (1979–80, 1982), and went on to become the premier comedy screenwriter in 90s Britain. His sharp eye for middle-class mores, for the simply idiotic in human behaviour, and for the gratifications of romantic comedy have helped to account for some of the most popular British films ever, including *Four Weddings and a Funeral* (1994, p, sc – AAn, BAAn) and *Notting Hill* (1999, UK/US, p, sc), both starring Hugh GRANT, and *Bean* (1997, p, sc), starring Rowan ATKINSON, with whom he had worked on the 80s TV series, *Blackadder*. Made CBE in 2000. His partner is script editor/broadcaster Emma Freud.

OTHER BRITISH FILMS INCLUDE: *The Tall Guy* (1989, sc, a), *Bridget Jones's Diary* (2001, UK/Fr/US).

Curtis, Sarah Producer. Came to prominence as the producer of some attractive entertainments in the latter 90s, most notably *Mrs Brown* (1997, UK/Ire/US). Married director Iain SOFTLEY.

OTHER BRITISH FILMS INCLUDE: *Bad Behaviour* (1993), *Backbeat* (1994, co-p), *The Englishman Who Went Up . . .* (1995), *The Governess* (1998, UK/Fr), *Mansfield Park* (1999, UK/US), *Charlotte Gray* (2001, UK/Aust/US).

Curwen, Patrick (*b* London, 1884 – *d* England, 1949). Actor. Oxford-educated character player in supporting roles from 1931 (*The Ringer*), usually as professional men, like the five doctors he played. On stage from 1907, and a well-known broadcaster.

OTHER BRITISH FILMS INCLUDE: *Loyalties* (1933), *Hearts of Humanity* (1936), *Sea Fort* (short, narr), *Return to Yesterday* (1940), *The Man in Grey*, *The Lamp Still Burns* (1943), *Mr Emmanuel*, *Don't Take It to Heart* (1944), *The Rake's Progress* (1945), *Green Fingers* (1947), *Nothing Venture* (1948).

Curzon, George (*b* Amersham, 1896 – *d* London, 1976). Actor. Former naval officer (back in the Navy in WW2), whose most famous moment in films occurred in *Young and Innocent* (1937) when the camera tracks across a hotel ballroom, from a high angle to an extreme close-up of his guilty twitching eyes. The son of actress Ellis Jeffries, he appeared in a further 30-odd films, including three as Sexton Blake, and was on stage from 1924.

OTHER BRITISH FILMS INCLUDE: *Escape* (1930), *Chin Chin Chinaman* (1931), *Her First Affaire* (1932), *The Man Who Knew Too Much*, *Java Head* (1934), *Strange Boarders*, *Sexton Blake and the Hooded Terror* (1938), *Q Planes*, *Jamaica Inn* (1939), *Jassy*, *Uncle Silas* (1947), *That Dangerous Age* (1949), *The Cruel Sea* (1952), *Woman of Straw* (1964).

Cusack, Cyril (*b* Durban, 1910 – *d* London, 1993). Actor. Notable Irish character player, on stage aged seven and film the following year (*Knocknagow*, 1918), joined the Abbey Theatre in

1932, and first appeared on the London stage in 1936. Despite maintaining a busy stage career, he became a very recognisable film presence, especially in the post-war period, memorably in POWELL AND PRESSBURGER's *The Small Back Room* (1948), as a stammering corporal, *Gone to Earth* (1950) as Jennifer JONES's clergyman husband, and, enjoying himself, as the duplicitous Chauvelin in *The Elusive Pimpernel* (1950). But even in much less distinctive films, *he* was distinctive: as a dipsomanic inmate of a dubious hospital in *Man in the Road* (1956), his dissecting eye and verbal asperity command the attention. Too stocky for a leading man, he went on acting until his death, last appearing in Christine EDZARD's *As You Like It* and *Far and Away* (Ire/US) (1992). Occasionally filmed in the US, first in *Soldiers Three* (1951), and did much notable television, including his last, *Memento Mori* (1992). Four of his children – Sinead, Sorcha, Niamh and Catherine – are actresses.

OTHER BRITISH FILMS: *Late Extra, The Man Without a Face* (1935), *Servants All* (1936), *Once a Crook, Inspector Hornleigh Goes to It* (1941), *Odd Man Out* (1947), *Once a Jolly Swagman, Esther Waters, Escape* (1948), *All Over the Town, The Blue Lagoon* (1949), *The Last Moment, Destination Milan* (1954), *Passage Home, The Man Who Never Was* (1955), *The Spanish Gardener, Ill Met By Moonlight, Jacqueline* (1956), *Miracle in Soho, Rising of the Moon* (Ire/US) (1957), *Cradle of Genius* (doc), *Gideon's Day, Floods of Fear* (1958), *Shake Hands with the Devil* (1959, UK/US), *A Terrible Beauty, Johnny Nobody* (1960), *I Thank a Fool, Waltz of the Toreadors* (1962), *80,000 Suspects, The Spy Who Came in from the Cold, I Was Happy Here* (1965), *Fahrenheit 451* (1966), *Oedipus the King* (1967), *Country Dance, David Copperfield* (1969), *King Lear* (UK/Den) (1970), *The Devil's Widow* (1971), *The Homecoming, The Day of the Jackal* (UK/Fr) (1973), *Juggernaut, The Abdication* (1974), *Children of Rage* (1975, UK/Is/It), *Andrina* (1981), *The Outcasts* (1982), *Nineteen Eighty-Four* (1984), *Little Dorrit* (1987), *My Left Foot* (1989), *The Fool* (1990).

Cusack, Sinead (*b* Dalkey, Ireland, 1948). Actress. When not playing Shakespeare with the RSC (she was a fine Beatrice in 1984) or appearing on quality TV (*Twelfth Night*, 1980), she has made doggedly uncommercial forays into cinema, since 1969 (*Alfred the Great*), with a minor success in the Australian film *My Mother Frank* (2000). Cyril CUSACK's daughter; married actor Jeremy IRONS (1978).

OTHER BRITISH FILMS INCLUDE: *David Copperfield* (as Emily), *Hoffman* (1969), *The Devil's Widow* (1971), *Venus Peter* (1989), *Waterland* (1992), *Bad Behaviour* (1993), *The Cement Garden* (1993, UK/Fr/Ger), *Uncovered* (1994), *Stealing Beauty* (1996, UK/Fr/It), *Dream* (2002).

Cushing, Peter (*b* Kenley, Surrey, 1913 – *d* Canterbury, 1994). Actor. Trained at London's Guildhall School of Music and Drama, Cushing began his career in pre-war Hollywood in *The Man in the Iron Mask* (1939) and made several films there before starting in Britain with *Hamlet* (1948), as a vividly exquisite Osric. In the early 50s, he worked mainly in the theatre (he was in OLIVIER's 1951 St James Theatre season), had a TV triumph in *1984* (1954), and was very moving as Deborah KERR's cuckolded husband in *The End of the Affair* (1954). His film career took off when he played the eponymous over-reacher in HAMMER's *The Curse of Frankenstein* (1957), establishing him at once as a cult hero of the HORROR film aficionados, with Christopher LEE as the monster. These two, along with director Terence FISHER, now metonymically evoke the oeuvre of this most successful British studio. As well as playing the Baron half a dozen times, he also memorably incarnated Dr Van Helsing in several reprises of the Dracula myth, including the wonderfully stylish *The Brides of Dracula* (1960). His chiselled features, refined, even ascetic speech and

bearing, his intense *belief* in the scientific mumbo-jumbo he was given to say, are now so firmly embedded in the public mind that it is an effort of will to remember that he played many other roles, including SHERLOCK HOLMES. It is arguable, though, that his most incisive performance is as the thin-lipped bank manager under fearful strain in the excellent 'B' thriller, *Cash on Demand* (1961). Created OBE in 1989.

OTHER BRITISH FILMS: *Moulin Rouge* (1953), *The Black Knight* (1954), *Time Without Pity, The Abominable Snowman, Violent Playground* (1957), *Dracula, The Revenge of Frankenstein* (1958), *John Paul Jones, The Hound of the Baskervilles, The Mummy* (1959), *The Flesh and the Fiends, Cone of Silence, Sword of Sherwood Forest, Suspect* (1960), *Fury at Smuggler's Bay, The Hellfire Club, The Naked Edge* (1961), *Captain Clegg, The Man Who Finally Died, The Devil's Agent* (UK/Ger) (1962), *The Evil of Frankenstein, The Gorgon, Dr Terror's House of Horrors* (1964), *She, Dr Who and the Daleks, The Skull* (1965), *Island of Terror, Daleks – Invasion Earth 2150 AD* (1966), *Corruption, Frankenstein Created Woman, Some May Live, Night Of The Big Heat, Torture Garden, Caves of Steel, The Mummy's Shroud* (narr) (1967), *Blood Beast Terror* (1968), *Frankenstein Must Be Destroyed, Doctors Wear Scarlet, Scream and Scream Again, One More Time* (1969), *The House That Dripped Blood, The Vampire Lovers, I, Monster, Incense For The Damned* (1970), *Twins of Evil* (1971), *Tales From The Crypt, Dracula AD 1972, Nothing But the Night, Fear in the Night, Dr Phibes Rises Again, Asylum, The Creeping Flesh, Horror Express* (UK/Sp) (1972), *Frankenstein and the Monster from Hell, The Satanic Rites of Dracula, And Now the Screaming Starts!, From Beyond The Grave* (1973), *The Beast Must Die, The Legend of the 7 Golden Vampires* (UK/HK), *Madhouse, Legend of the Werewolf, Shatter* (UK/HK) (1974), *The Ghoul* (1975), *The Devil's Men* (UK/US), *At the Earth's Core, Trial By Combat* (1976), *The Uncanny* (UK/Can) (1977), *Arabian Adventure* (1979), *Touch Of The Sun* (UK/Zam), *House Of The Long Shadows* (1982), *Sword of the Valiant* (1983), *Biggles* (1986).

BIBLIOG: *An Autobiography*, 1986; *Past Forgetting*, 1988.

Cuthbertson, Allan (*b* Perth, Australia, 1920 – *d* London, 1988). Actor. Australian actor in Britain since 1947, superb conveyer of icy disdain, whether as marital bully in *Room at the Top* (1958), or would-be killer in *Portrait of Alison* (1955), or imperious military types, as in *Tunes of Glory* (1960) – or in a 1975 episode of *Fawlty Towers* as a twitching Colonel whose wife cowers behind him. Also played haughty Brits in such international enterprises as *Cast a Giant Shadow* (1965, US). When most benign, condescending; when not, malevolent; when*ever*, riveting.

OTHER BRITISH FILMS INCLUDE: *Carrington VC* (1954), *Anastasia, The Passionate Stranger* (1956), *Barnacle Bill* (1957), *Ice Cold in Alex, I Was Monty's Double* (1958), *The Stranglers of Bombay* (1959), *The Malpas Mystery* (1960), *The Guns of Navarone* (1961), *Term of Trial* (1962), *Life at the Top* (1965), *Press for Time* (1966), *Sinful Davey* (1968), *Performance* (1970), *The Mirror Crack'd, The Sea Wolves* (UK/Switz/US) (1980).

Cuthbertson, Iain (*b* Glasgow, 1930). Actor. Commanding performer whose first professional work was on radio, followed by the stage in Glasgow in 1955. Made film debut as the wrongly arrested father in *The Railway Children* (1971), and has filmed sporadically since, usually in upper-class roles, such as Lord Hailsham in *Scandal* (1988) and Saskia REEVES's urbanely autocratic publisher-boss in *Antonia and Jane* (1990). Once married to Scottish actress **Anne Kristen** (*b* Glasgow, 1937 – *d* Leith, 1996), who appeared in a few films. Much TV, including Dr Arnold in *Tom Brown's Schooldays* (1971).

OTHER BRITISH FILMS INCLUDE: *Up the Chastity Belt* (1971), *The Assam Garden* (1985), *'Let Him Have It'* (1991), *The Tichborne Claimant* (1998).

Cutler, Kate (*b* London, 1870 – *d* London, 1955). Actress. Character player on stage from 1888 and in 14 films from 1929's *Dark Red Roses* until *Pygmalion* (1938), in which she is billed simply as 'Grand Old Lady'. Typically cast as upper-class aunts and assorted dowagers, as in *Action for Slander* (1937).

OTHER BRITISH FILMS INCLUDE: *Such Is the Law* (1930), *Wedding Rehearsal* (1932), *Lord of the Manor* (1933), *Moscow Nights* (1935), *When Knights Were Bold* (1936), *The Perfect Crime* (1937).

Cutts, Graham (*b* Brighton, 1885 – *d* London, 1958). Director. Iris BARRY's description of the films of Graham Cutts as 'certainly above the general British level' is an understatement. He was, without question, the finest of the country's directors in the 20s. A former exhibitor, Cutts began his directorial career in 1922 with *While London Sleeps* for H.B. PARKINSON. That same year, he went into partnership with Herbert WILCOX, directing *The Wonderful Story* (1922), *The Flames of Passion* (1922), and *Paddy the Next Best Thing* (1923). *Woman to Woman* (1923), starring Betty COMPSON, enhanced Cutts's career, but it was with *The Rat* (1925, + sc), *The Sea Urchin* and *The Triumph of the Rat* (1926, + sc) that he proved his originality, editing within the camera, fluidly moving it from one character to another as the story develops. It was Cutts who enhanced Wilcox's reputation as a producer, was Michael BALCON's first director, and was on hand when Balcon co-founded PICCADILLY PICTURES. Unfortunately, his private life was a mess and he began to resent the rise to popularity of Alfred HITCHCOCK, who was involved in a number of his films as screenwriter or art director. It would have been nice to report that Hitchcock was influenced by Cutts, but their styles are so patently different. Cutts did some good work in talkies, notably with a production number that literally moves the sets in Gracie FIELDS's *Looking on the Bright Side* (1932), with the fast-paced Stanley LUPINO musical, *Over She Goes* (1937) and in capturing the spirit of Richmal CROMPTON's schoolboy hero in *Just William* (1939). If it is true, as Hitchcock claims, that Cutts was assigned as an assistant to him on *The Thirty Nine Steps*, it is a pathetic end to a notable career.

OTHER BRITISH FEATURE FILMS: *The Sign of Four* (1923, co-d), *The White Shadow, The Prude's Fall, The Passionate Adventure* (1924), *The Blackguard* (1925), *The Queen Was in the Parlour* (+ sc), *The Rolling Road, Confetti* (1927), *God's Clay, Glorious Youth* (1928), *The Return of the Rat* (1929), *The Temperance Fete, Love on the Spot* (1932), *As Good as New, Three Men in a Boat* (1933), *Oh, Daddy!, Car of Dreams* (1935, co-d), *Aren't Men Beasts?, Let's Make a Night of It* (1937), *She Couldn't Say No* (1939). AS.

Cutts, Patricia (aka Wayne) (*b* London, 1926 – *d* London, 1974). Actress. Daughter of Graham CUTTS, RADA-trained, she first filmed as a child in *Self-Made Lady* (1932) and as an adult in the RAF film, *Flying with Prudence* (1946). Attractive but perhaps not distinctive enough for stardom, she had leads opposite Robert Montgomery in *Your Witness* (1950) and Danny Kaye, in Hollywood (1955–57), in *Merry Andrew* (1958), but is most fun as the flapper Bubbles in *The Man Who Loved Redheads* (1954). Committed suicide.

OTHER BRITISH FILMS INCLUDE: *Just William's Luck* (1947), *Madness of the Heart* (1949), *Those People Next Door* (1952), *The Happiness of 3 Women* (1954), *Private Road* (1971).

Czinner, Paul (*b* Budapest, 1890 – *d* London, 1972). Director. First filmed in Austria in 1919. In the 20s there were frequent collaborations with his later wife, actress Elisabeth BERGNER. His first British film was the Pola Negri vehicle *The Woman He Scorned* (1929). In the 30s he directed most of Bergner's British films, richly stylised melodramas based on continental literary or dramatic sources. Working for the RANK ORGANISATION in the 50s and 60s, Czinner directed a number of skilful DOCUMENTARIES of European ballet and opera productions.

OTHER BRITISH FILMS INCLUDE: *Catherine the Great* (co-d, 1934), *Escape Me Never* (1935), *As You Like It* (1936), *Dreaming Lips* (1937), *Stolen Life* (1939), *Don Giovanni* (1954), *The Bolshoi Ballet* (1957), *The Royal Ballet* (1959), *Der Rosenkavalier* (1961), *Romeo and Juliet* (1966). Tim Bergfelder.

D'Abbes, Ingram *see* **Sherie, Fenn**

D'Abo, Maryam (*b* London, 1960) Actress. Daughter of Dutch father and Russian mother, D'Abo was girlfriend to Timothy DALTON's James Bond in *The Living Daylights* (1987). Nothing significant since; only small roles in *Leon the Pig Farmer* (1992) and *The Browning Version* (1994) and several little-seen international films.
OTHER BRITISH FILMS INCLUDE: *Xtro* (1982), *Solitaire for 2* (1995), *The Sea Change* (1998), *The Point Men* (2001).

Dade, Stephen (*b* Beckenham, 1909). Cinematographer. Camera assistant at GAUMONT–BRITISH from 1927, working on such films as *Gangway* (1937) and HITCHCOCK's *Sabotage* (1936) and *Young and Innocent* (1937), until he became a lighting cameraman in the early 40s. Made nearly 50 films (including some undistinguished 'B' MOVIES), and became noted for the distinct quality of his colour photography on such films as *Zulu* (1964), but his black-and-white work on such GAINSBOROUGH films as *Caravan* (1946) and *Good-Time Girl* (1947) is often sharply effective.
OTHER BRITISH FILMS INCLUDE: (c) *Sailors Don't Care* (1940), *Somewhere in Camp* (1942), *Get Cracking* (1943), *Demobbed* (1944), *A Place of One's Own* (1945), *Dear Murderer*, *The Brothers* (1947), *Snowbound* (1948), *Christopher Columbus*, *Bad Lord Byron* (1949), *The Late Edwina Black* (1951), *The Sea Shall Not Have Them* (1954), *The Flesh Is Weak* (1957), *The Angry Hills* (1959), *Doctor Blood's Coffin* (1960), *Don't Talk to Strange Men*, *Serena* (1962), *The Crooked Road* (UK/Yug) (1964), *The City Under the Sea* (1965), *The Vulture*, *The Viking Queen* (UK/Can/US) (1966), *On the Run* (1969).

Dahl, Roald (*b* Llandaff, Wales, 1916 – *d* Oxford, 1990). Author. Popular author of eccentric children's tales and ghost stories, some of the latter televised as *Tales of the Unexpected* (1979). Wrote the screenplay for *You Only Live Twice* (1967), co-wrote *Chitty Chitty Bang Bang* (1968), and wrote *The Night Digger* (1971) which starred his then-wife (2 of 3, 1953–83) Patricia NEAL. Several of his stories, which usually took the child's point of view, were adapted by others, including *Willy Wonka and the Chocolate Factory* (1971, US) and *Danny, the Champion of the World* (1989).

Dainton, Patricia (aka Joanne Dainton) (*b* Hamilton, England, 1930). Actress. Pretty blonde who had a big chance as leading lady in *The Dancing Years* (1950), but most of her others were 'B' MOVIES, some of them rather good, like *The Third Alibi* (1961), in which she played a terminally ill murderess. Daughter of agent Vivienne Black.
OTHER BRITISH FILMS INCLUDE: *The Bells Go Down* (1943), *Uncle Silas* (1947), *Tread Softly*, *Castle in the Air*, *Paul Temple Returns* (1952), *Operation Diplomat* (1953), *No Road Back* (1956), *At the Stroke of Nine* (1957), *Ticket to Paradise* (1960).

Dalby, Amy (*b* 1888 – *d* 1969). Actress. Tiny stage actress who came to films in her 50s, after a long stage career, and played spinsters (a teacher in *The Night Has Eyes*, 1942) and kindly aunts (one of those Margaret LOCKWOOD rebels against in *The Wicked Lady*, 1945) over 25 years.
OTHER BRITISH FILMS INCLUDE: *Penn of Pennsylvania* (1941), *Millions Like Us*, *The Gentle Sex*, *Dear Octopus* (1943), *Waterloo Road* (1944), *The White Unicorn* (1947), *Home to Danger* (1951), *The Straw Man* (1953), *The Man Upstairs* (1958), *The Haunting* (1963), *The Secret of My Success* (1965), *Smashing Time* (1967).

Dalby, Stephen (*b* 1910). Sound recordist. Entered film industry in 1930 and was sound recordist/supervisor at EALING during the BALCON years, from *The Gaunt Stranger* (1938) until *The Siege of Pinchgut* (1959). Post-Ealing, he remained very busy, working on 40 further productions, totally eclectic as to genre, status and nationality.
OTHER BRITISH FILMS INCLUDE: *The High Command* (1937), *The Ware Case* (1938), *Come On George!*, *Cheer Boys Cheer* (1939), *The Proud Valley* (1940), *Hue and Cry* (1946), *Frieda*, *It Always Rains on Sunday* (1947), *Daybreak* (made 1946), *Scott of the Antarctic*, *Saraband for Dead Lovers* (1948), *Whisky Galore!*, *Passport to Pimlico*, *Kind Hearts and Coronets*, *The Blue Lamp* (1949), *Cage of Gold* (1950), *Secret People*, *The Man in the White Suit*, *The Lavender Hill Mob* (1951), *I Believe in You*, *Mandy*, *The Cruel Sea* (1952), *The 'Maggie'*, *The Square Ring* (1953), *The Divided Heart*, *Lease of Life* (1954), *Touch and Go*, *The Ladykillers*, *The Night My Number Came Up*, *The Ship That Died of Shame* (1955), *The Feminine Touch*, *Who Done It?* (1956), *Davy*, *Barnacle Bill*, *The Shiralee* (1957), *Nowhere to Go*, *Dunkirk* (1958), *Touch of Death*, *Strongroom*, *The Quare Fellow*, *The Loneliness of the Long Distance Runner*, *Emergency* (1962), *A Hard Day's Night* (1964), *Repulsion*, *Help!*, *A High Wind in Jamaica* (1965), *Cul-de-Sac* (1966).

Daldry, Stephen (*b* England, 1961). Director. Former director of the Royal Court Theatre and director of the long-running, critically lauded *An Inspector Calls* (1992), scored a hit with his first feature, *Billy Elliot* (2000), in which he showed himself a fluent master of his new medium. His follow-up film was *The Hours* (2002, US), starring Nicole Kidman as Virginia WOOLF.
OTHER BRITISH FILMS: *Eight* (1998, short).

Dale, Jim (*b* Rothwell, Northamptonshire, 1935). Actor, singer, lyricist. Trained for ballet before debut as stage comedian in 1951, and also enjoyed some success as a pop singer. Wonderfully droll on stage in such diverse plays as *The National Health* and *The Merchant of Venice* (both Old Vic, 1970), tall, cheerful Dale has never quite had roles that give him enough scope on screen. He appeared in eleven 'CARRY ON' capers, but, funny as he is there, he is almost too subtle to make his presence felt among all those bold farceurs, though he is the only pleasure on hand in the series' finale, *Carry On Columbus* (1992), in the title role. His best screen chances in Britain were probably in the little-seen ADAPTATION of *The National Health* (1973) and as Spike MILLIGAN in *Adolf Hitler – My Part in His Downfall* (1972). Became popular in such Disney films as *Pete's Dragon* (1977), won a Tony for the title role in *Barnum* on Broadway, and wrote the Oscar-nominated lyrics for the title song for *Georgy Girl* (1966).

OTHER BRITISH FILMS INCLUDE: *6.5 Special* (1958), *The Iron Maiden*, *Carry On Cabby* (1963), . . . *Spying*, . . . *Jack*, . . . *Cleo* (1964), . . . *Cowboy*, *The Big Job* (1965), *Carry On Screaming*, *Don't Lose Your Head*, *The Winter's Tale* (1966), *The Plank*, *Follow That Camel* (1967), *Carry On Doctor*, *Shalako* (song lyrics) (1968), *Carry On Again Doctor* (1969), *Joseph Andrews* (1976), *Scandalous* (1983).

Dall, Evelyn (*b* New York, 1920). Actress. Likeable blonde American nightclub singer who featured in British MUSICAL FILMS (1936–44), perhaps seen at her best in the naive but funny time-travel comedy, *Time Flies* (1944).

OTHER BRITISH FILMS INCLUDE: *Soft Lights and Sweet Music* (1936), *Kicking the Moon Around* (1938), *King Arthur Was a Gentleman* (1942), *Miss London Ltd* (1943).

Dallas, Julian (*b* High Wycombe, 1920 – *d* Swindon, Wiltshire, 1997). Actor. RN: Scott Forbes. Tall, good-looking actor who showed mild promise in several British films, such as *This Was a Woman* (1948), was lured to Hollywood (as Scott Forbes) in 1950 and got lost in the shuffle, playing second leads in such films as *Rocky Mountain* (1950, US). Made only two further British films: *Subterfuge* (1968) and *The Mind of Mr Soames* (1969), and acted in British television (e.g. *Emergency – Ward 10*) during the 60s.

OTHER BRITISH FILMS: *The Hundred Pound Window* (1943), *Night Boat to Dublin* (1946), *Mrs Fitzherbert* (1947), *But Not in Vain* (1948), *The Reluctant Widow* (1950).

Dalrymple, Ian (*b* Johannesburg, 1903 – *d* London, 1989). Editor, director, screenwriter, producer. Educated at Rugby and Cambridge, he began as a film editor (1927–35) for GAUMONT–BRITISH/GAINSBOROUGH on films such as *The Ghost Train* (1931) and *Evergreen* (1934), before turning to screenwriting in 1933, sharing the credit on *The Good Companions* (1933 + ass p) and an Oscar for the *Pygmalion* (1938) screenplay. An erudite man, his influence was felt in British films for more than 30 years. In 1940, he was appointed producer with the CROWN FILM UNIT, and produced some of the most famous wartime documentaries, including *Words for Battle* (1941). He then worked briefly for KORDA–MGM (*Perfect Strangers*, 1945); and in 1946 his WESSEX PRODUCTIONS was set up as part of RANK's INDEPENDENT PRODUCERS. For Wessex, his most successful film was the wartime escape drama, *The Wooden Horse* (1950), but the company continued to produce until 1962 (*Mix Me a Person*, sc). Not really a director by instinct or inclination, he did in fact (co-)direct six films.

OTHER BRITISH FILMS INCLUDE: (e) *Sunshine Susie* (1931), *Rome Express*, *Jack's the Boy* (1932), *The Faithful Heart*, *The Ghoul* (1933), *Little Friend* (1934), *Her Last Affaire* (+sc), *The Iron Duke*, *Turn of the Tide* (1935); (ass p/prod ass) *It'a Boy!*, *I Was a Spy*, *Friday the Thirteenth* (1933); (p) *Channel Crossing* (1933), *The Lion Has Wings* (1939, assoc p), *The Heart of Britain* (1941, short, +sc), *Malta G.C.*, *Coastal Command*, *Listen to Britain* (1942, shorts), *We Sail at Midnight* (1943), *Western Approaches* (1944), *Woman in the Hall* (1947, + sc), *Once a Jolly Swagman* (1948), *Dear Mr Prohack* (+ sc), *All Over the Town* (1949), *Family Portrait* (1950, short), *Royal Heritage*, *Clearing the Lines* (1952, shorts), *The Heart of the Matter* (1953, + sc), *Raising a Riot* (1955, + sc), *The Admirable Crichton* (1957), *A Cry from the Streets* (1958); (sc only) *The Brown Wallet* (1936), *Action for Slander* (1937, add dial), *South Riding*, *The Citadel*, *The Divorce of Lady X* (1938, co-sc), *French Without Tears*, *Q Planes*, *A Window in London* (co-sc) (1939), *Pimpernel Smith* (1941, co-sc), *A Hill in Korea* (1956, co-sc); (d/co-d) : *Modern Orphans of the Storm* (1937, short, co-d), *Old Bill and Son*, *Sea Fort* (short) (1940, +sc), *Storm in a Teacup* (1937, co-d, + sc), *Esther Waters* (1948, co-d, p), *Bank of England* (1960).

BIBLIOG: Charles Drazin, *The Finest Years: British Cinema of the 1940s*, 1998.

Dalton, Phyllis (*b* London, 1925). Costume designer. Entered films as a seamstress on OLIVIER's *Henry V* (1944) and 45 years later won an AA for designing the costumes for Kenneth BRANAGH's version (1989). After training at Ealing Art School, she became assistant to Yvonne CAFFIN at GAINSBOROUGH in 1946, working on such films as *Dear Murderer* (1947), *Miranda* and *Quartet* (1948). Her most notable work as designer has been in period films, including two for David LEAN, *Lawrence of Arabia* (1962) and *Doctor Zhivago* (1965, UK/US, AA/cos), Branagh's *Much Ado about Nothing* (1993, UK/US), and *The Hireling* (1973, BAA/cos). Received a BAFTA Special Award in 1994.

OTHER BRITISH FILMS INCLUDE: *Your Witness* (1950), *Rob Roy . . .* (1953), *One Good Turn* (1954), *Passage Home* (1955), *Zarak* (1956), *Island in the Sun* (1957), *Carve Her Name With Pride* (1958), *Our Man in Havana* (1959), *The World of Suzie Wong* (1960), *Becket*, *Lord Jim* (1964), *Oliver!* (1968, AAn/cos, BAAn/cos), *Fragment of Fear* (1970), *The Water Babies* (1975, UK/Pol), *Voyage of the Damned* (1976), *Eagle's Wing* (1978), *The Mirror Crack'd*, *The Awakening* (UK/US) (1980), *A Private Function* (1984), *Stealing Heaven* (1988, UK/Yug).

Dalton, Timothy (*b* Colwyn Bay, Wales, 1946). Actor. Tall (6'2"), dark and improbably handsome, like the old-time film idol he never quite became, Dalton has had a varied career on stage, screen and TV. He played with the National Youth Theatre in 1964, did a stint at RADA and quit to join Birmingham Rep. Has had some success as a classical actor, notably with the RSC and the Prospect Theatre Co. in the mid 70s, and roles in many TV series, including a fine Rochester in *Jane Eyre* (1983) and Rhett Butler in *Scarlett* (1994), but, apart from his two appearances as James BOND, his screen career has been disappointing. He was an unusually saturnine Bond in *The Living Daylights* (1987) and *Licence to Kill* (1989), admired more by critics than the public. Other notable film roles included costume pieces such as *The Lion in Winter* (1968), *Cromwell* (1970), *Mary Queen of Scots* (1971, as Darnley), giving scope for well-bred derring-do. Had a long relationship with Vanessa REDGRAVE, whose husband he played in *Mary and Agatha* (1978).

OTHER BRITISH FILMS INCLUDE: *Wuthering Heights* (1970, as Heathcliff), *Flash Gordon* (1980), *The Doctor and the Devils* (1985), *Hawks* (1988), *Possessed* (2002, UK/US).

Daltrey, Roger (*b* London, 1944). Singer, actor, composer, producer. Former lead singer with rock band The Who, then a solo performer from 1973, Daltrey came to filmgoers' attention in leading roles in two Ken RUSSELL features: *Lisztomania* (1975), offering a very free interpretation of Liszt's life, and in the title role of the rock-opera, *Tommy* (1975). He broadened his acting range as the eponymous criminal in *McVicar* (1980), and his wonderfully sleazy Soho pop impresario in *Like It Is* (1998) suggested he could have a new career as a character actor.

OTHER BRITISH FILMS INCLUDE: (a, unless noted) *The Legacy* (1978), *Quadrophenia* (1979, ex p, m d), *Pop Pirates* (1984), *Buddy's Song* (1990, + m d), *Best* (2000, UK/Ire), *The Chemical Wedding* (2001).

Daly, John (*b* London, 1936) Producer. Son of a cockney dockworker, the enterprising Daly, with actor David HEMMINGS, founded Hemdale in 1967, originally as a talent agency, then as a company producing low-budget films. Daly bought Hemmings out in 1971 and Hemdale hit the bigtime in the US with *The Terminator* (1984) and *Platoon* (1986), Daly acquiring a reputation as a guileful operator – though both PALACE and GOLDCREST which had dealings with him would have qualified their praise quite strongly. Most of his work has been in the US, but he was executive producer on *Buster* (1988) and *Hidden Agenda* (1990), the Ken LOACH film made in collaboration with Hemdale.

OTHER BRITISH FILMS: *The Passage* (1978, ex p), *Sunburn* (1979, UK/US, co-sc), *High Risk* (1981, US/UK).

Daly, Mark (*b* Edinburgh, 1887 – *d* 1957). Actor. On stage from 1906, often in pantomime and variety, and in films from 1930, this cheery Scots character actor was busy in the 30s in small but sometimes vivid roles like that of 'Arty' Jones, an enterprising prisoner ('I'll bash yer face to a jelly', he warns Will HAY) in *Good Morning Boys* (1937).

OTHER BRITISH FILMS INCLUDE: *East Lynne on the Western Front* (1931), *A Cuckoo in the Nest* (1933), *The Ghost Goes West* (1935), *The Man Who Could Work Miracles* (1936), *Wings of the Morning, Knight Without Armour* (1937), *Q Planes* (1939), *The Farmer's Wife* (1941), *The Next of Kin, The Big Blockade* (1942), *Bonnie Prince Charlie* (1948), *The Card* (1952), *Lease of Life* (1954), *Footsteps in the Fog* (1955), *The Gelignite Gang, The Feminine Touch* (1956), *The Tommy Steele Story, The Shiralee* (1957).

Dampier, Claude (*b* London, 1879 – *d* London, 1955). Actor. RN: Cowan. Stage comedian popular in 30s films, characteristically cast as bumblers and bumpkins, like the village lawyer, Septimus Earwicker in *Riding High* (1937).

OTHER BRITISH FILMS INCLUDE: *No Monkey Business, Boys Will Be Boys* (1935), *Such Is Life* (1936), *Sing As You Swing* (1937), *Don't Take It to Heart* (1944), *Meet Mr Malcolm* (1953), *Climb Up the Wall* (1960).

dance British cinema has generally been flat-footed. While BALLET has often featured notably, it is generally as a special event, and in ordinary dance routines British feet have seldom moved with the instinctive grace of an Astaire or Rogers. Jack BUCHANAN had such grace, but British films seldom gave him the opportunities that he found on the stage. Jessie MATTHEWS, 'the Dancing Divinity', created memorable routines with American choreographer Buddy BRADLEY, notably the sinuous 'Dancing on the Ceiling' in *Evergreen* (1934). Home-grown choreographer Wendy TOYE devised imaginative routines for Lilian HARVEY and Anna NEAGLE, and even somehow for Margaret LOCKWOOD in *I'll Be Your Sweetheart* (1945), but her finest work was in the SHORT FILMS she directed, especially the hypnotic *The Stranger Left No Card* (1952), with its metronomic beat. Outside of conventional MUSICALS (and few would care to recall Freddie CARPENTER's disastrous choreography for *London Town*), there have been a few memorable dance routines, including Jack HULBERT's anarchic saunter through Selfridges in *Love on Wheels* (1932), even John MILLS' quick shoe-shuffle in *The Green Cockatoo* (1937), but American dance is best done by Americans, the Nicholas Brothers in *Calling All Stars* (1937) or Johnny Nit in *Everything is Rhythm* (1936). Luke McKernan.

Dance, Charles (*b* Redditch, 1946). Actor. In earlier decades tall, blond Dance would have become a big romantic star, instead of an intermittently interesting character actor. Despite his patrician persona, he had a disturbed lower-middle-class childhood in Plymouth (sometimes given as his birthplace). Trained at art school at Plymouth and later Leicester, he was privately coached in acting and joined the RSC in 1975, entering films in *For Your Eyes Only* (1981). His role as a British soldier in turbulent India in the TV mini-series, *The Jewel in the Crown* (1984), made him famous, establishing him as a thinking woman's sex symbol. However, his film roles have not generally promoted this image, though there were elements of it in *White Mischief* (1987), in which he played a corrupt British colonial. His international films include *The Last Action Hero* (1993, US) and *Michael Collins* (1996, US), but these have been in supporting roles. In Britain, his best work was as Meryl Streep's sorely tried diplomat husband in *Plenty* (1985, US-financed), and a subdued cameo as Derek Du Pré in *Hilary and Jackie* (1998). He seems to choose his roles carefully and remains a star manqué as far as the cinema goes.

OTHER BRITISH FILMS INCLUDE: *The McGuffin* (1985), *Hidden City* (1987), *Pascali's Island* (1988, UK/US), *Century* (1993), *Us Begins with You* (UK/US), *What Rats Won't Do* (1998), *Dark Blue World* (2001, UK/Czech).

Dane, Clemence (*b* London, 1888 – *d* London, 1965). Playwright, screenwriter. RN: Winifred Ashton. Took pseudonym from name of London church, St Clement Danes. Also acted on stage, from 1913, as Diana Cortis. Her first play, *A Bill of Divorcement* (1921), was an immediate hit and was filmed three times: in Britain in 1922, with Fay COMPTON, and twice in the US (1932, 1940), and her novel, *Enter Sir John* provided the basis for HITCHCOCK's *Murder!* (1930). She won an AA for Best Original Story for *Perfect Strangers* (1945) and (co-)wrote several other screenplays. Appointed CBE in 1953.

OTHER BRITISH FILMS INCLUDE: (sc) *The Amateur Gentleman* (1936, co-sc), *Farewell Again, Fire Over England* (1937, co-sc), *St Martin's Lane* (1938), *Salute John Citizen* (1942, co-sc), *Bonnie Prince Charlie* (1948).

Daneman, Paul (*b* London, 1925 – *d* London, 2001). Actor. After RAF service in WW2, trained at RADA, was on stage from 1947 (as front legs of a horse), and entered films in *Peril for the Guy* (1956). He had a pleasing lightness of touch which was shown to better effect on TV as an excellent Mr Knightley in *Emma* (1960); he was also a riveting Richard III in *An Age of Kings* (1960); and he had several seasons with the Old Vic, but cinema success largely escaped him.

OTHER BRITISH FILMS INCLUDE: *Time Without Pity* (1957), *The Clue of the New Pin* (1960), *Zulu* (1964), *How I Won the War* (1967), *Oh! What a Lovely War* (1969).

Daniel, Jennifer (*b* Pontypool, 1938). Actress. Pleasing Welsh actress much seen on TV and in a handful of films, including two minor HAMMER horrors: *The Kiss of the Vampire* (1962) and *The Reptile* (1966). Once married to actor Dinsdale LANDON.

OTHER BRITISH FILMS: *Marriage of Convenience* (1960), *The Clue of the Silver Key* (1961), *Return to Sender* (1963).

Daniels, Bebe (*b* Dallas, 1901 – *d* London, 1971). Actress. Daniels became one of the best-loved British RADIO and TELEVISION performers largely because she was an American who, with husband Ben LYON, sat out the Blitz in London, spending most of her later years in London as the star, and often writer, of the radio series *Hi Gang!* (1940–41, 1949) and, of course, *Life with the Lyons* (on radio 1950–61 and on television 1957 and 1961). Prior to coming to the UK, Daniels had been a major US star, on screen since 1910, Harold Lloyd's leading lady in the 1910s, a DeMille star in the late 1910s and early 20s, and a

Paramount star of the 20s, but none of her British films does her justice. An adopted son **Richard Lyon** (*b* 1934) made several American films as a child including *The Unseen* (1945), and the British film *The Headless Ghost* (1959), as well as two 'Lyons' films.

BRITISH FILMS: *A Southern Maid* (1933), *The Song You Gave Me* (1933), *Not Wanted on Voyage* (1937), *The Return of Carol Deane* (1938), *Hi Gang!* (1941), *Life with the Lyons*, *The Lyons in Paris* (1954). AS.

Daniels, Ben Actor. (*b* 1964) Supporting actor, LAMDA-trained and mostly on stage, but appeared in a few films of the 90s, following his debut in *Wish You Were Here* (1987), and the telemovie *The Lost Language of Cranes* (1991). Played amusingly the mother's dopey hippy boyfriend in *Beautiful Thing* (1996).

OTHER BRITISH FILMS: *Truth or Dare* (1996), *I Want You* (1998), *Fanny and Elvis* (1999).

Daniels, Phil (*b* London, 1958). Actor. First in films as child (*Anoop and the Elephant*, 1972), Daniels came from a working-class background to fame, starring in *Quadrophenia* (1979), the musical based on Mods-and-Rockers conflict. Many of his films have been concerned with rock music and scruffy urban life, and he has favoured a 'bad boy' image. He enjoyed brief pop star fame when he recorded 'Parklife' with the band Blur.

OTHER BRITISH FILMS INCLUDE: *Scum* (1979), *The Class of Miss MacMichael* (1978), *Breaking Glass* (1980), *Number One* (1984), *Billy the Kid and the Green Baize Vampire*, *The Bride* (1985), *Bad Behaviour* (1993), *After Miss Julie* (1995), *Still Crazy* (1998), *Chicken Run* (2000, anim, voice).

Daniely, Lisa (*b* Reading, 1930). Actress. RN: Elizabeth Bodington. Shapely brunette who began promisingly as *Lilli Marlene* (1950) and starred in the remake of *Hindle Wakes* (1952), but spent a good deal of her career in DANZIGERS' second features, including *An Honourable Murder* (1960), a modern business-world version of *Julius Caesar*. In recent decades, she has done TV under her real name. Educated in France and RADA; married to Grey BLAKE.

OTHER BRITISH FILMS INCLUDE: *The Wedding of Lilli Marlene* (1953), *Tiger by the Tail* (1955), *The Vicious Circle* (1957), *The Man in the Road* (1956), *The Tommy Steele Story* (1957), *High Jump* (1958), *Curse of Simba* (1964), *Souvenir* (1987).

Danischewsky, Monja (*b* Archangel, Russian 1911 – *d* Farnham, Surrey, 1994). Screenwriter, producer, publicity director. When his family migrated to England, he was educated at the Royal College of Art, and was a painter and journalist before entering the film industry as a publicist. Worked at several studios, including MGM–BRITISH before joining EALING as publicity director in 1938 and spent most of his career there, both as screenwriter and (associate-)producer. He filled the latter role on *Whisky Galore!* (1949), over which he had some conflict ('a miserable if successful collaboration' he later wrote) with director Alexander MACKENDRICK, and produced *The Galloping Major* (1951, + sc) for British Lion. He produced and wrote several films post-Ealing, including *Battle of the Sexes* (1959, p, sc) and *Topkapi* (1964, US), but is now best remembered for his publicist's contribution to the Ealing public image.

OTHER BRITISH FILMS: (p, sc) *Meet Mr Lucifer* (1953), *The Love Lottery* (1954), *Two and Two Make Six* (1962), *Mister Moses* (1965); (sc/co-sc only) *Undercover* (1943), *Bitter Springs* (1950), *Rockets Galore* (1958), *That Lucky Touch* (1975, adapt). As John Danischewsky: *Run Wild, Run Free* (1969, p).

BIBLIOG: Autobiography, *White Russian, Red Face*, 1966.

Dankworth, John (aka Johnny) (*b* Woodford, Essex, 1927). Composer. Key participant in such 60s films as *Saturday Night and Sunday Morning* (1960), *Darling* (1965) and, especially, Joseph LOSEY's *The Servant* (1963, + unc appearance) to which his moody score contributes so atmospherically. His wife from 1958, Cleo LAINE, sang his evocative theme song, 'All Gone', in the latter, and he worked on three other Losey films. Dankworth studied at the Royal Academy of Music (1944 –1946), formed the Johnny Dankworth Seven in 1950, and from 1953 to 1964 had a jazz band featuring Laine, with whom he has established a major performance centre at Milton Keynes. He appeared in *Contrast in Rhythm*, *Parade of the Bands* (1955, short), and *6.5 Special* (1958), and was a guest artiste in *All Night Long* (1961).

OTHER BRITISH FILMS: (comp) *We Are the Lambeth Boys* (1959, doc), *The Criminal* (1960), *A Game Called Scruggs*, *Sands of the Kalahari*, *Return from the Ashes* (1965), *The Idol* (+ cond), *Modesty Blaise*, *Morgan: A Suitable Case for Treatment* (1966), *The Last Safari*, *Accident*, *Fathom* (1967), *The Magus*, *I Love You, I Hate You*, *Salt & Pepper* (short) (1968), *The Last Grenade* (1969), *Perfect Friday*, *10 Rillington Place* (cond) (1970), *Strike It Rich* (1990, UK/US, unc).

BIBLIOG: *Cleo and John: A Biography of the Dankworths*, 1976.

Danquah, Paul (*b* London). Actor. Son of a Ghanian politician father and English mother, Danquah played the black sailor who has a brief affair with and impregnates the schoolgirl heroine (Rita TUSHINGHAM) in *A Taste of Honey* (1961) and was much praised for the sensitivity of his work. Law-trained and admitted to the bar in 1958, he acted in several British films of the 60s and appeared in such TV series as *The Avengers* (1961). Now lives in Morocco.

OTHER BRITISH FILMS: *That Riviera Touch*, *Maroc 7* (1966), *Smashing Time* (1967).

Danziger, Edward (*b* ?) and **Harry** (*b c* 1920). Producers. *See* **Danzigers, The**

Danzigers, The Notorious British film production company, founded by the Danziger brothers, Edward J. and Harry Lee, American citizens who came to Britain in 1950. Edward had studied law, and assisted at the Nuremberg War Crimes Tribunal; Harry took courses in music at the New York Academy. By the late 40s, the brothers were working in New York City, dubbing foreign films into English. Arriving in the UK, they used SHEPPERTON, RIVERSIDE and MGM–BRITISH studios to produce their first films, including the cult classic *Devil Girl From Mars* (1954). After trying to purchase BEACONSFIELD STUDIOS, and then TWICKENHAM STUDIOS, for a proposed slate of low-budget productions with no success, the brothers decided to build an entirely new facility, which they dubbed New Elstree Studios. The studio, located on Elstree Road, Elstree, Hertfordshire, was opened in 1956, and had six sound stages, a seven acre back-lot, and a staff of more than 200 workers. The Danzigers made it clear that their aim was to make TV shows and feature films as economically as possible. As proof of this, their average budget for a feature was between £15,000 and £17,500, although from time to time they would splurge on a relatively big-budget film like the CinemaScope science-fiction epic *Satellite in the Sky* (1956). More typical of their output were such 'B' MOVIES as *Feet of Clay* (1960), *Man Accused* (1959), *High Jump* (1958), *Sentenced For Life* (1959) and many others, shot on schedules of 5 to 10 days. They had an international TV hit with their series *Mark Saber, Detective*; typically, two episodes of the series were completed every five days. By 1961, however, increased production costs made the profit margin impossibly slim, and the studio closed in December. Though undeniably cheap and shoddy, the Danzigers's films nevertheless portrayed a world of hopeless nihilism and brutal economy, offering a more accurate picture of contemporary lower-middle-class British life than most would care to admit.

OTHER BRITISH FILMS INCLUDE: *Alias John Preston* (1955), *A Date at Midnight* (1959), *The Spider's Web*, *An Honourable Murder* (1960), *Return of a Stranger* (1962), dozens more. Wheeler Winston Dixon.

D'Aragon, Lionel Actor. On stage from 1903 and on screen from 1913, D'Aragon was a busy villain, but always in supporting roles, in more than 40 silent films.

BRITISH FILMS INCLUDE: *A Sporting Chance* (1913), *Eugene Aram* (1914), *The Price He Paid* (1916), *The First Men in the Moon* (1919), *Rodney Stone* (1920), *The Virgin Queen* (1923), *Eugene Aram* (1924), *Quinneys* (1927), *Q-Ships* (1928). AS.

Dare, Daphne (*b* Yeovil, 1929 – *d* London, 2000). Costume designer. Dare's early credits include designing for TV's *Doctor Who* (1963); on film, she was mostly associated with Ken LOACH, starting with *Kes* (1969) and, in general, with modern-dress films.

OTHER BRITISH FILMS: *Every Home Should Have One* (1969), *Family Life*, *Gumshoe* (1971), *Hidden City* (1987), *Hidden Agenda* (1990), *Century* (1993), *Land and Freedom* (1995, UK/Ger/Sp), *Carla's Song* (1996, UK/Ger/Sp).

Dare, Phyllis (*b* London, 1890 – *d* Brighton, 1975) Actress. Sister of Zena DARE, with whom she made her stage debut in 1899 and stayed there for the next half-century; made several long-forgotten films, including *Marigold* (1938) as Sophie STEWART's disgraced actress mother.

OTHER BRITISH FILMS: *The Argentine Tango and Other Dances* (1913), *Dr Wake's Patient* (1916), *The Common Law* (1923), *Crime on the Hill* (1933), *Debt of Honour* (1936).

Dare, Zena (*b* London, 1885 – *d* London, 1975). Actress. Married into aristocracy (second son of Lord Esher), but managed a long stage career (starting 1899 and including Mrs Higgins in *My Fair Lady*, in the later 50s) and a handful of films: *No. 5 John Street* (1921), *A Night in London* (1928. UK/Ger), *The Return of Carol Deane* (1938) and, as a sort of well-bred procuress, *Over the Moon* (1939).

Darling, W. Scott (*b* Toronto, 1898 – *d* Santa Monica, California, 1951). Screenwriter. Prolific screenwriter, the first of whose nearly 100 films was released in 1920 and the last in 1952, the year after he drowned. In the 30s, he wrote the screenplays for 16 British programmers, all for Warner Bros/First National, many of them directed by George KING and John DAUMERY. In Hollywood, he wrote dozens of unpretentious genre films for Fox and Universal.

BRITISH FILMS INCLUDE: *High Society*, *Her Night Out* (1932), *Long Live the King*, *Naughty Cinderella* (story), *I Adore You* (story), *The Bermondsey Kid* (1933), *Guest of Honour*, *Church Mouse* (1934).

Darnborough, Anthony (*b* Weybridge, 1913 – *d* Weybridge, 2000). Producer. Worked as a journalist from 1932, and after distinguished WW2 service (1939–45) joined Sydney BOX at RIVERSIDE STUDIOS, as uncredited assistant on such films as *The Seventh Veil* (1945) and *Daybreak* (1946, rel 1948). Joining the RANK ORGANISATION in 1946, he became a respected producer on nearly 20 films, including the three Somerset MAUGHAM compendia: *Quartet* (1948), *Trio* (1950) and *Encore* (1951). He also co-directed two films with Terence FISHER: *The Astonished Heart* and *So Long at the Fair* (1950). It has been alleged that his career was shortened because he fell foul of Rank's managing director, John DAVIS. Briefly engaged, amid much publicity, to Glynis JOHNS in 1951.

OTHER BRITISH FILMS: *Dear Murderer* (1947), *Portrait from Life*, *The Calendar*, *My Brother's Keeper* (1948), *Traveller's Joy*, *Helter Skelter*, *Boys in Brown* (1949), *Highly Dangerous* (1950), *The Net*, *Personal Affair* (1953), *To Paris with Love* (1954), *The Baby and the Battleship* (1956).

Daumery, John (*b* Brussels, 1898 – *d* Lausanne, Switzerland, 1934). Director. Churned out 15 'QUOTA QUICKIES' in the 30s, mostly at Warner's TEDDINGTON STUDIOS, and responsible for all French versions of WARNER BROS films. Served with Belgian Army in WW1. Also directed several French-language films as Jean Daumery.

BRITISH FILMS INCLUDE: *Rough Waters* (1930), *A Letter of Warning*, *Postal Orders* (1932), *Meet My Sister*, *Naughty Cinderella* (1933), *Without You*, *Over the Garden Wall* (1934).

Dauphin, Claude (*b* Corbeil, France, 1903 – *d* Paris, 1978). Actor. The sort of French actor who will always be described as 'suave', outside France at least. After starting as a set designer, he acted in nearly 100 films, mostly French, but some US (e.g. *Rosebud*, 1975) and a half-dozen British, including *English Without Tears* (1944), as a Frenchman wise in the ways of love (of course). His sophisticated Gallic delivery was a reliable source of pleasure in films such as *Madame Rosa* (1977, Fr), the year before his death. Married (2 of 3) actress **Maria Mauban** (*b* Marseilles, 1924), who appeared in two 1950 British films, *Cairo Road* and *Cage of Gold*.

OTHER BRITISH FILMS: *Présence au combat* (1945, UK/Fr), *Innocents in Paris* (1953), *The Full Treatment* (1960), *Tiara Tahiti* (1962), *Two for the Road* (1966), *The Madwoman of Chaillot* (1969).

Davenport, A. Bromley (*b* Bagington, 1867 – *d* London, 1946). Actor. He is one of the ancient Chelsea Pensioners whose comments provide a choral commentary on the war in *The Way Ahead* (1944), his last film. On stage from 1892, he made about 50 films, most of them in the 30s.

OTHER BRITISH FILMS INCLUDE: *The Great Gay Road* (1920), *Fox Farm*, *A Maid of the Silver Sea* (1922), *Sally Bishop* (1923), *Somebody's Darling* (1925), *A Sister to Assist 'er* (1927), *The American Prisoner* (1929), *Mischief* (1931), *Lord Camber's Ladies* (1932), *The Scarlet Pimpernel* (1934), *Owd Bob* (1938), *Jamaica Inn* (1939), *Love on the Dole* (1941), *The Young Mr Pitt*, *Those Kids from Town* (1942).

Davenport, Jack (*b* Suffolk, 1973). Actor. Son of actors Maria AITKEN and Nigel DAVENPORT, this good-looking young actor made his mark as the agreeably swinish barrister, Miles, in the cult TV series, *This Life* (1996). So far, he has had only minor roles in films, starting with *Fierce Creatures* (1997, UK/US), on which he'd asked John CLEESE to let him be a runner, and more noticeably in *The Talented Mr Ripley* (1999, US) as the sympathetic gay who is murdered.

OTHER BRITISH FILMS INCLUDE: *The Wisdom of Crocodiles* (1998), *The Cookie Thief* (1999, short), *Not Afraid, Not Afraid* (2001).

Davenport, Nigel (*b* Shelford, Cambridge, 1928). Actor. Cheltenham- and Oxford-educated Davenport, on stage from 1952, was a striking character actor from the start, at least from his role as the Police Sergeant in *Peeping Tom* (1960). Everything he played was imbued with an imposing burly authority, which stood him in good stead in such costume pieces as *A Man for All Seasons* (1966, as the Duke of Norfolk) and *Mary Queen of Scots* (1971, as Lord Bothwell), but equally as lion-loving George Adamson in *Living Free* (1972). Has also appeared in US films, including *Nighthawks* (1981). He has had a busy television career, too, embracing impoverished gentleman-farmer, Carne, in *South Riding* (1974) and bluff Dan Peggotty in *David Copperfield* (1999). His first film was *Look Back in Anger* (1959), apt in view of his having been a member of the English Stage Company's first season at the Royal Court Theatre in 1956. Married (2, 1972–80) and divorced Maria AITKEN; actor Jack DAVENPORT is their son.

OTHER BRITISH FILMS INCLUDE: *Desert Mice* (1959), *Lunch Hour* (1962), *Ladies Who Do, In the Cool of the Day* (1963), *The Verdict, The Third Secret* (1964), *Sands of the Kalahari, Life at the Top, A High Wind in Jamaica* (1965), *Sebastian* (1967), *The Strange Affair, Play Dirty, Sinful Davey* (1968), *The Virgin Soldiers, The Royal Hunt of the Sun* (1969), *The Last Valley, No Blade of Grass* (1970), *Villain* (1971), *Charley One-Eye* (1973), *Stand Up Virgin Soldiers* (1977), *The London Connection* (1979), *Chariots of Fire* (1981), *Greystoke . . .* (UK/US), *A Christmas Carol* (TV, some cinemas) (1984), *Caravaggio* (1986), *Without a Clue* (1988), *Mumbo Jumbo* (2001).

Davey, Shaun (*b* Belfast). Composer. Best known as a classical composer, whose concert pieces include suites and concertos, and work written for the theatre, including Dublin's Abbey Theatre and the RSC, Davey has also composed the score for TV (e.g. *David Copperfield*, 1999) and for the films, *Loving* (1995), *Twelfth Night* (1996, UK/US), *A Further Gesture* (1997, UK/Sp), and *Waking Ned* (1999, UK/Fr/US).

David, Eleanor (*b* Lincolnshire, 1956). Actress. Stage actress, with the RSC (e.g. in *Les Liaisons Dangereuses*) and other companies, as well as a good deal of TV, including *Paradise Postponed* (1986), David has appeared in about a dozen films, since her debut as the selfish mother in *The Rocking Horse Winner* (1982, short). She co-starred in Bill FORSYTH's *Comfort and Joy* (1984) and played Sullivan's mistress, Fanny Ronalds, in *Topsy-Turvy* (2000).

OTHER BRITISH FILMS INCLUDE: *Pink Floyd The Wall* (1982), *Facelift* (1984), *84 Charing Cross Road* (1986), *London Kills Me* (1991), *The Guilty* (1993).

David, Joanna (*b* Lancaster, 1947). Actress. Appealingly vulnerable in TV's *Rebecca* (1979), as Mrs de Winter, and *Fame Is the Spur* (1982), as the suffragette heroine, she conveys strength beneath a frail exterior. Much outstanding TV and stage work, comparatively few films, but notable as a Dorset wife in *Comrades* (1986) and mutely noticeable as Mrs Baring in *Rogue Trader* (1999). Partner of Edward FOX and mother of Emilia FOX.

OTHER BRITISH FILMS INCLUDE: *Sympathy for the Devil* (1968), *The Smashing Bird I Used to Know* (1969), *Sleepwalker* (1984), *Secret Friends* (1991), *Cotton Mary* (1999).

Davidson, Jaye (*b* Riverside, California, 1965). Actor. In Britain from age 2, the androgynous Davidson, involved in the fashion world, was discovered by casting director Susie FIGGIS while looking for someone to play Dil, the black girlfriend who proves to be a man in *The Crying Game* (1992). He was Oscar- and BAFTA-nominated for the role, and allegedly received US$1m for his follow-up role in *Stargate* (1994).

Davidtz, Embeth (*b* Trenton, New Jersey, 1966) Actress. RN: Gretta Milano. US-born but raised from early childhood in South Africa, now appearing in international films, most famously *Schindler's List* (1993), as the Jewish maid. Her British films have included: *A Private Life* (1988, UK/SA), *Feast of July* (1995, UK/US), *Simon Magus* (2000, UK/Ger/It, as a Silesian baker), and, most vividly, as the manipulative Mary Crawford in *Mansfield Park* (1999, UK/US).

OTHER BRITISH FILMS INCLUDE: *The Hole, Bridget Jones's Diary* (2001, UK/Fr/US).

Davies, Betty Ann (*b* London, 1910 – *d* Manchester, 1955). Actress. Though she died sadly young, following an appendectomy, she remains a vivid figure in British films, especially post-war, as embittered or downtrodden women. She was the prostitute killed accidentally in *Escape* (1948), the shrewish Miriam in *The History of Mr Polly* (1948), the careworn mother in *The Blue Lamp* (1949), Raymond HUNTLEY's cruelly-used wife in *Trio* (1950), the shrill Doris in *Meet Me Tonight* (1952), and the teacher who yearns for 'the courage to kill myself' in *The Belles of St Trinian's* (1954). It was a surprise to see how attractive she still was as the mother of the *Cosh Boy* (1953). One of the original Cochran Young Ladies, she played some chirpy leads and second leads in the 30s and was back on stage, 1940–47. Aunt of John Howard DAVIES.

OTHER BRITISH FILMS INCLUDE: *My Old Duchess* (1933), *She Knew What She Wanted* (1936), *Silver Top* (1938), *Kipps* (1941), *It Always Rains on Sunday* (1947), *To the Public Danger, The Passionate Friends* (1948), *The Man in Black, Now Barabbas Was a Robber* (1949), *Outcast of the Islands* (1951), *Grand National Night* (1953), *Alias John Preston* (1955).

Davies, Irving *see* **Stone, Paddy**

Davies, Jack (*b* London, 1913 – *d* California, 1994). Screenwriter. Noted concoctor of screen comedies from the days of Will HAY, though he is often uncredited here, and later for Mario ZAMPI (*Laughter in Paradise*, 1951, and others), the 'DOCTOR' films, six for Norman WISDOM (who always gave Davies major credit), and *Those Magnificent Men . . .* (1965) and its sequel, *Monte Carlo or Bust!* (1969, UK/Fr/It). Entered the industry in 1932, did stints as film critic for the *Daily Sketch* (1938) and the *Sunday Graphic* (1948), and during WW2 wrote RAF instructional films. At his most prolific in the 50s and 60s, with a firm grip on public taste. Father of John Howard DAVIES.

OTHER BRITISH FILMS (sc/co-sc): *Mister Cinders, Radio Parade of 1935, Love at Second Sight* (1934), *Mimi, Heart's Desire, Music Hath Charms, Dance Band* (1935), *The Tenth Man, A Star Fell from Heaven, One in a Million, Someone at the Door* (1936), *Convict 99* (1938), *Trouble in the Air* (1948), *Top Secret, Curtain Up* (1952), *Happy Ever After* (1954), *Jumping for Joy, Doctor at Sea, An Alligator Named Daisy* (1955), *Up in the World, True as a Turtle* (1956), *High Flight* (1957), *The Square Peg, I Only Arsked!* (1958), *Follow a Star, Don't Panic Chaps, The Ugly Duckling* (1959), *The Bulldog Breed, It Started in Naples* (1960), *Nearly a Nasty Accident, Very Important Person* (1961), *On the Beat, The Fast Lady, Crooks Anonymous, Seven Keys* (1962), *A Stitch in Time, Father Came Too!* (1963), *The Early Bird* (1965), *Doctor in Clover* (1966), *Some Will – Some Won't* (1969, + story), *Doctor in Trouble* (1970), *Paper Tiger* (1974), *The Comeback* (1977, sd), *The Sailor's Return* (1978, sd), *North Sea Hijack* (1979).

Davies, John Howard (*b* London, 1939). Actor. Son of scriptwriter Jack DAVIES, he began as the angel-faced child hero of David LEAN's *Oliver Twist* (1948) and followed this with the torment of *The Rocking Horse Winner* (1949). After completing his education, he had a new career as an important TV director and/or producer of comedy series, and his name is on such cutting-edge enterprises as *Steptoe and Son* (1962), *Monty Python's Flying Circus* (1969–70, 1972–74), *Fawlty Towers* (1975), *Mr Bean* (1989).

OTHER BRITISH FILMS: *Tom Brown's Schooldays, The Magic Box* (1951).

Davies, Petra (*b* Wales) Actress. Dark-haired, attractive star of a few minor movies, with small roles in major ones like *Stage Fright* (1950). Married Jack MAY with whom she appeared in the children's film, *Swarm in May* (1983).

OTHER BRITISH FILMS: *Girdle of Gold* (1952), *The Man Who Loved Redheads* (1954), *The Silent Invasion, Two-Letter Alibi* (1961).

Davies, Rupert (*b* Liverpool, 1916 – *d* London, 1976). Actor. RN: Lisburn Gwynne. Famous TV interpreter of Simenon's pipe-smoking, Pernod-quaffing 'Maigret' (1960–63) with a long career as a character actor on screen, in such diverse films as *The Spy Who Came in from the Cold* (1965), as Smiley, and, as the Monsignor, in *Dracula Has Risen from the Grave* (1968). He had a rare starring role in Desmond DAVIS's *The Uncle* (1964); avuncular was, in fact, how he appeared, though he did not have the title role. A memorable Count Rostov in TV's *War and Peace* (1972), and a couple of international films, including *The Night Visitor* (1971, US).

OTHER BRITISH FILMS INCLUDE: *Health in Our Time* (1948, short), *Private Angelo* (1949), *Seven Days to Noon* (1950), *The Traitor* (1957), *Sea Fury, The Key* (1958), *Sapphire, Bobbikins* (1959), *The Criminal* (1960), *The Brides of Fu Manchu* (1966), *Submarine X-1, Witchfinder General, The Curse of the Crimson Altar* (1968), *The Oblong Box* (1969), *Zeppelin* (1971), *Frightmare* (1974).

Davies, Terence (*b* Liverpool, 1945). Director. Uncompromising director of some of the most innovative, harrowing, and hauntingly lyrical films of recent times, exploring processes of memory and creativity in associative, elliptical compositions closer to music than to traditional narrative.

Davies's Catholic working-class background is explored in the autobiographical films made between 1976 and 1992. In his trilogy – *Children* (1976), *Madonna and Child* (1980), and *Death and Transfiguration* (1983) – painful childhood memories are augmented by an imagined old age and death, in stark, powerful imagery recalling Bresson and Bergman. The same bleakness fills *Distant Voices Still Lives* (1988, UK/Ger), his recreation of life rendered intolerable by a brutal father. Proceeding by memory association from one family gathering to the next, the film is remarkable for the expressive fluency of its camera, and its innovative use of music, particularly popular song. Music performs a similarly dynamic function in *The Long Day Closes* (1992), a subjective exploration of childhood after the father's death, dominated by the security of home, and by his overwhelming passion for cinema, particularly for American musicals. The slow, reflective camera delights in the detailed vision of childhood, creating lyrical compositions of light and texture which lie outside time. Far from sentimental, the film reminds us of the black terrors constantly lurking beneath this magical world.

Davies next turned to literary sources. *The Neon Bible* (1995, UK/US) is adapted from the novel written by sixteen-year-old John Kennedy Toole, and, set in Georgia in the 40s, the film paints a vivid portrait of small-town America. *The House of Mirth* (2000, UK/US), adapted from Edith Wharton's novel of New York high society mores, reveals, through masterly close-ups, tracking and dissolves, the independence and fierce inner 'morality'of the penniless and beautiful heroine *and* her brittle vulnerability. Wendy Everett.

Davies, Windsor (*b* London, 1930). Actor. Bulky, bluff and often blustery character player, familiar from TV's *It Ain't Half Hot Mum* (1974–77) and *Never the Twain* (1981–83, 1986–89). In films since 1964, mostly in comedy, including several 'CARRY ON' capers, to which he would have seemed ideally suited. Born to play explosive Sergeants.

OTHER BRITISH FILMS INCLUDE: *Murder Most Foul* (1964), *The Alphabet Murders* (1965), *Drop Dead Darling* (1966), *Frankenstein Must Be Destroyed* (1969), *Endless Night* (1972), *Mister Quilp* (1974), *Carry On*

Behind (1975), *Not Now, Comrade, Confessions of a Driving Instructor* (1976), *Playbirds* (1978).

Davis, Allan (*b* London, 1913 – *d* London, 2001). Director. Now best remembered as producer of *No Sex Please, We're British* (1971–87), the world's longest-running stage comedy. Began as a chorus boy, served with the Army (1939–46), became director of Bristol Old Vic in 1939, made one long-forgotten film in Hollywood, *Rogue's March* (1952), and returned to England to direct several pocket THRILLERS in the Edgar WALLACE and the Edgar LUSTGARTEN SERIES at MERTON PARK STUDIOS.

OTHER BRITISH FILMS INCLUDE: *The Man Who Had Everything* (1954), *The Clue of the New Pin* (1960), *Wings of Death* (1961).

Davis, Bette (*b* Lowell, Massachusetts, 1908 – *d* Neuilly-sur-Seine, France, 1989). Actress. Legendary American actress-star, whose bulging eyes and way with a cigarette made her an impersonator's gift but couldn't disguise her greatness on the screen for over 50 years. In her declining years, made six British films, none of them among her finest, but *Death on the Nile* (1978) is certainly one of the most enjoyable ADAPTATIONS from Agatha CHRISTIE.

OTHER BRITISH FILMS: *Another Man's Poison* (1951 – her producer thought she was a 'cow'), *The Nanny* (1965), *The Anniversary* (1967), *Connecting Rooms* (1969), *Madame Sin* (1972).

Davis, Carl (*b* New York, 1936). Composer. One of the great names in British film music, not just for such BAA-winning scores as that for *The French Lieutenant's Woman* (1981) or as music director for Mike LEIGH's *Topsy-Turvy* (2000), but also for his scores for Kevin BROWNLOW's lovingly restored silent classics, including *Greed* (1925) and *Napoléon* (1927). He has also scored such notable TV series as *The World at War* (1973–74) and *Dance to the Music of Time* (1997), has composed for many stage productions and is a conductor with the London Philharmonic Orchestra. Married actress **Jean Boht** (*b* Bebington, 1936), who appeared in several British films including *Distant Voices Still Lives* (1988, UK/Ger).

OTHER BRITISH FILMS INCLUDE: *The Bofors Gun, Praise Marx and Pass the Ammunition* (1968), *Up the Chastity Belt, Up Pompeii, I, Monster* (1971), *Rentadick, The Lovers!* (1972), *The National Health* (1973), *Man Friday* (1975), *The Sailor's Return* (1978), *The Secret Policeman's Other Ball* (1982), *Champions* (1983, + cond), *Scandal* (1988), *The Rainbow* (+ cond) (1989), *D.W. Griffith: Father of Film* (1993, UK/US, doc), *Widow's Peak* (1994, UK/US).

Davis, Desmond (*b* London, 1928). Director. Following training with the ARMY FILM UNIT, Davis entered films in 1948, worked as focus-puller (*The Embezzler*, 1954), camera operator (*A Taste of Honey*, 1961; *Freud*, 1962; *Tom Jones*, 1963), before eventually directing a few films. His first films, two wistful Irish-set romances, *Girl with Green Eyes* (1963) and *I Was Happy Here* (1965), and the chamber work, *The Uncle* (1964), suggested a sensitive talent, but, among later films, *A Nice Girl Like Me* (1969) and *Ordeal by Innocence* (1984), from Agatha CHRISTIE, simply put talented casts through excruciating paces. Since the last-named, he has been restricted to TV production. Was once married to actress Lueen McGRATH. Not to be confused with Desmond Davis (1907–59) a British writer-director, mainly on TV but worked on several films from the late 40s..

OTHER BRITISH FILMS INCLUDE: (cam op) *Strangers' Meeting, The Heart Within* (1957), *The Trollenberg Terror* (1958), *Taste of Fear* (1961); (c) *Behemoth the Sea Monster* (1958); (d) *Stop the Merry-Go-Round*

(1952, short), *Smashing Time* (1967), *Clash of the Titans* (1981, UK/US), *The Country Girls* (1983).

Davis, Gilbert (*b* Johannesburg, 1899 – *d* Montreux, Switzerland, 1983). Actor. Stage actor, in films from 1932, including a batch for Ealing in the late 40s (e.g. the genial 'governor'of Edward CHAPMAN's local in *It Always Rains on Sunday* (1947). Married to Winifred SHOTTER.
OTHER BRITISH FILMS INCLUDE: *Service for Ladies* (1932), *The Good Companions* (1933), *The Amateur Gentleman* (1936), *The Silver Blaze* (1937), *The Loves of Joanna Godden*, *Frieda*, *Against the Wind* (1947), *Snowbound* (1948), *Passport to Pimlico* (1949), *Mr Drake's Duck* (1950), *The Galloping Major* (1951), *Quatermass 2* (1957), *Desert Mice* (1959), *The Entertainer* (1960).

Davis, Sir John (*b* London, 1906 – *d* 1993). Executive. One of the most influential and unpopular figures in the British film industry, who rescued the RANK ORGANISATION from financial chaos in the late 40s but, in doing so, led such film-makers as David LEAN to look elsewhere. Educated at the City of London School and a member of the Chartered Institute of Secretaries, he was secretary to several companies before joining ODEON Theatres in 1938 as accountant and later as managing director. He met RANK in 1938 and retained a lifelong admiration for him, becoming managing director of the Rank companies, which embraced production, DISTRIBUTION and EXHIBITION, in the late 40s. He was largely responsible for moving Rank's production activities wholly to PINEWOOD, and for the collapse of INDEPENDENT PRODUCERS, the creative umbrella Rank had erected over some major talents in the 40s. He appointed the American Earl ST JOHN as Executive Producer at Pinewood and some would argue created an ensuing homogenisation of the product. Davis was the director of numerous companies associated with Rank, but always disclaimed – disingenuously perhaps – any wish to interfere in the creative aspects of film-making. He famously advocated clean 'family films' without, apparently, noticing in the 50s that television, which he disdained, was catering for this market. Was married to and divorced from actress Dinah SHERIDAN.
BIBLIOG: Geoffrey MacNab, *J. Arthur Rank and the British Film Industry*, 1993; Charles Drazin, *The Finest Years: British Cinema of the 1940s*, 1998.

Davis, Judy (*b* Perth, Australia, 1956). Actress. One of the major stars of the Australian film revival of the 70s and 80s, winning acclaim and awards, including BAA, for her playing of the feminist heroine of *My Brilliant Career* (1979). Her international career began unpropitiously with a dim British political thriller, *Who Dares Wins* (1982), but she received a deserved AAn for her next: David LEAN's *A Passage to India* (1984), in which, despite well-reported clashes with the director, she brilliantly captured the honourable, maddening Adela. Her British films have included the bizarre *The Naked Lunch* (1992, UK/Can) and two costume pieces: the comparatively conventional *Where Angels Fear to Tread* (1991), from E.M. Forster's novel, and the high camp *Impromptu* (1991), as George Sand. Most of her 90s work has been in the US, including several for Woody Allen. Married to actor Colin Friels.
OTHER BRITISH FILM: *Blood and Wine* (1996, UK/US).

Davis, Mick (*b* Glasgow). Director, screenwriter. Davis wrote the screenplay for *Love in Paris* (1997, UK/Fr/US), one of the least necessary sequels ever – to *9½ Weeks*. If this is not to be

held against him, he may need to do something tougher than his directorial debut, *The Match* (1999, UK/Ire/US, + sc), a soft-centred sports-and-disability movie set in the Scottish Highlands.

Davis, Phil (aka Philip) (*b* South Ockendon, Essex, 1953). Actor. Very endearing as the kind-hearted Marxist who has set up house with Ruth SHEEN in Mike LEIGH's *High Hopes* (1988), National Youth Theatre alumnus Davis, who grew up in the East End, has been playing somewhat off-centre roles for over 20 years. In TV's *North Square* (2000), his charismatic chief clerk commands the screen while surrounded by actors who tower over him. A major character star who has also directed theatre and TV as well as two modestly well-regarded features, *I.D.* (1995, +a UK/Ger), about police and football hooligans, and *Hold Back the Night* (1999), an uncosily engaging piece about unlikely people finding support from each other.
OTHER BRITISH FILMS INCLUDE: *Mister Quilp* (1974), *Quadrophenia* (1979), *Pink Floyd The Wall* (1982), *The Bounty* (1984), *Underworld* (1985), *Comrades* (1986), *In the Name of the Father* (1993, UK/Ire/US), *Crimetime*, *Secrets & Lies*, *Different for Girls* (1996), *Face*, *Photographing Fairies* (1997), *Still Crazy* (1998).

Davis, Redd (*b* 1897 – *d* ?). Director. Canadian who began his career as an actor with the Edison Company, directed a few 20s films in Hollywood, and went to England with Monty BANKS in 1928 and directed over 20 'QUOTA QUICKIES' in the 30s. These were mostly light films featuring popular comics of the day, including FLANAGAN and ALLEN (in *Underneath the Arches*, 1937) and Claude ALLISTER, and musical revues.
OTHER BRITISH FILMS INCLUDE: *The Bells of St Mary's* (1928), *Ask Beccles*, *The Umbrella* (1933), *Easy Money* (1934), *Say It with Diamonds* (1935), *Calling All Stars*, *Variety Hour* (1937), *Anything to Declare?* (1938), *That's the Ticket* (1940), *The Balloon Goes Up* (1942).

Davis, Rex (*b* 1890 – *d* ?). Actor. Virile leading man of silent films, who earned the Military Cross during WW1.
BRITISH FILMS INCLUDE: *A Sporting Chance* (1913), *For Her People*, *Polly's Progress* (1914), *Rodney Stone* (1920), *All Sorts and Conditions of Men* (1921), *The Making of the Gordons*, *A Race for a Bride* (1922), *Married Love*, *A Couple of Down and Outs* (1923), *Every Mother's Son* (1926), *Motherland* (1927). AS.

Davis, Sammi (*b* Kidderminster, 1964). Actress. Noticed at once in her debut role as a prostitute in *Mona Lisa* (1986), blonde, vivacious Davis might have been expected to make a bigger splash subsequently. In the event, she has appeared in some interesting roles (Dawn, straining at the sexual leash, in John BOORMAN's WW2 family drama, *Hope and Glory*, 1987; Ursula Brangwen in Ken RUSSELL's *The Rainbow*, 1989) without becoming a major figure. Has worked on TV and in the US, where she appeared in *Horseplayer* (1990), directed by Kurt Voss whom she married.
OTHER BRITISH FILMS INCLUDE: *A Prayer for the Dying* (1987), *Consuming Passions* (UK/US), *The Lair of the White Worm* (1988).

Davis, Stringer (*b* Birkenhead, 1896 – *d* Chalfont St Peter, 1973). Actor. Married to Margaret RUTHERFORD in 1945 when still in the Army, Davis's main career was that of devoted husband. As a function of this role, he appeared in about 20 of her films, notably as 'Mr Stringer' in her Miss Marple series, beginning with *Murder She Said* (1961). Appears to have been as self-effacing as the roles he played.
OTHER BRITISH FILMS INCLUDE: *Miranda* (1948) *The Happiest Days of Your Life* (1950), *Curtain Up* (1952), *Innocents in Paris* (1953), *Aunt Clara* (1954), *The March Hare* (1956), *Just My Luck* (1957), *I'm All Right Jack* (1959), *The VIPs*, *Murder Most Foul* (1964).

Davis, Tyrrell (aka Tyrell) (*b* Surbiton). Actor. Tall, Cambridge-educated actor on London and New York stage, in US films from 1928 and British from 1934 to 1938, including leading role in *Under Proof* (1936) as a comic coward who wins through.

OTHER BRITISH FILMS: *Freedom of the Seas, Designing Women* (1934), *All at Sea, Smith's Wives* (1935), *Dinner at the Ritz* (1937), *Strange Boarders, Second Best Bed* (1938).

Davison, Peter (*b* London, 1951). Actor. Likeable TV performer in such popular series as *Dr Who* (1981–84) and *All Creatures Great and Small* (1978–90), but only rarely in films, such as *Black Beauty* (1994, UK/US) and *Parting Shots* (1998), as the hero's chum. Muddied his nice-guy persona satisfyingly as the incompetent suburban adulterer in TV's *At Home with the Braithwaites* (2000–02).

Dawe, Cedric (*b* London, 1906 – *d* Chartridge, 1996). Production designer. Versatile over a range of genres, Dawe could equally recreate the grim realities of the Korean War in *A Hill in Korea* (1956), the sci-fi fantasy of *The Day of the Triffids* (1962), the period squalor of *Where's Jack?* (1969) and, best of all, the moody *film noir* waterfront atmospherics of *Temptation Harbour* (1947). In his long career (1934–69), he was one of the most serviceable art directors in British cinema's prolific decades. He joined BIP after designing for the US stage 1927–33; served in the Army 1940–46; and became art director at ASSOCIATED BRITISH in 1946.

OTHER BRITISH FILMS INCLUDE: (des/a d/sets) *Girls Will Be Boys* (1934) *Mimi* (1935), *Glamorous Night,* (1937), *The Housemaster* (1938), *The Gang's All Here, Poison Pen, The Outsider* (1939), *Quartet* (1948), *So Long at the Fair* (1950), *Another Man's Poison* (1951), *Street Corner* (1953), *Man of the Moment, Lost* (1955), *Across the Bridge* (1957), *Floods of Fear* (1958), *Carry On Doctor* (1968).

Dawson, Anthony (*b* Edinburgh, 1916 – *d* Sussex, 1992). Actor. Now best remembered as Grace KELLY's would-be murderer in *Dial M for Murder* (1954, US), tall, gaunt, RADA-trained Dawson, exuded a faintly disreputable, minor-public-school suavity in over 20 British films and some international ones. Made his debut in *The Way Ahead* (1944) following WW2 service (1939–42).

OTHER BRITISH FILMS INCLUDE: *The Way to the Stars* (1945), *The Queen of Spades* (1948), *The Wooden Horse* (1950), *The Long Dark Hall* (1951), *That Lady* (1955), *Tiger Bay, Libel* (1959), *Offbeat* (1960), *Dr No* (1962), *From Russia with Love* (1963), *The Jigsaw Man* (1984).

Dawson, Beatrice (*b* Lincoln, 1908 – *d* Yorkshire, 1976). Costume designer. Whatever else such films as *Trottie True* (1948), *Pandora and the Flying Dutchman* (1950), *The Importance of Being Earnest* (1952), *The Servant* (1963) and *Modesty Blaise* (1966) have going for them, they all have the advantage of Dawson's fluent, meticulous designs, and their generic range points to her versatility. Trained at Slade School of Art and Chelsea Polytechnic, she designed for the fashion world and the stage as well as the screen. Won AAn for *The Pickwick Papers* (1952) and BAAn for *Of Human Bondage, Woman of Straw* (1964) and *A Doll's House* (1973).

OTHER BRITISH FILMS: *Night Beat, London Belongs to Me* (1948), *Dear Mr Prohack* (1949), *The Reluctant Widow, State Secret* (1950), *Tom Brown's Schooldays* (1951), *Penny Princess* (1952), *Grand National Night* (1953), *The Black Knight, Svengali, Dance Little Lady* (1954), *Footsteps in the Fog* (1955, co-cos des), *The Black Tent* (1956), *The Prince and the Showgirl, Manuela, The Abominable Snowman* (1957), *The Wind Cannot Read, Life Is a Circus, A Tale of Two Cities, The Key* (1958), *Expresso Bongo* (1959, co-cos des), *Faces in the Dark, The Full Treatment* (1960),

The Day the Earth Caught Fire, Macbeth (1961), *Waltz of the Toreadors, The L-Shaped Room, Term of Trial* (1962), *I Could Go On Singing, Stolen Hours* (co-des) (1963), *The Beauty Jungle* (1964, co-cos des), *The Intelligence Men, Where the Spies Are, Life at the Top, Promise Her Anything, Masquerade* (1965), *Accident* (1967, co-cos des), *The Assassination Bureau, Guns in the Heather, Only When I Larf, Mrs Brown, You've Got a Lovely Daughter* (1968), *The Last Grenade* (1969), *The Man Who Haunted Himself, Three Sisters* (1970), *Zee & Co., Tam-Lin* (co-cos des) (1971), *The Bawdy Adventures of Tom Jones* (1975).

Day, Ernest (*b* 1927). Cinematographer, director. Camera operator from the mid 50s, on several WARWICK films, on three LEAN epics – *Lawrence of Arabia* (1962), *Dr Zhivago* (1965) and *Ryan's Daughter* (1970) – and several BOND films, before his first film as cinematographer, *Running Scared* (1972). Received AAn and BAAn for his work on *A Passage to India* (1984). Also directed *Green Ice* (1981), replacing Anthony SIMMONS, and *Waltz Across Texas* (1982, US), and has worked mostly in the US and on TV in recent times.

OTHER BRITISH FILMS INCLUDE: (cam op) *Cockleshell Heroes, The Gamma People* (1955), *You Only Live Twice* (1967), *A Clockwork Orange* (1971), *Juggernaut* (1974); (c) *Made* (1972), *Revenge of the Pink Panther* (1978), *The Burning Secret* (1988); (2ud) *The Spy Who Loved Me* (1977), *Moonraker* (1979, UK/Fr).

Day, Frances (*b* New York, 1907 – *d* Brighton, 1984). Actress. Popular on the London stage from 1925, as actress and singer, exuberant blonde Day, of Russian–German lineage, entered films in *The Price of Divorce* (1928), made about a dozen light entertainments in the 30s, but scarcely filmed again post-war. It was a surprise when she turned up in, say, *There's Always a Thursday* (1957), as Charles VICTOR's supposed girlfriend. She continued to appear on stage and on TV with her own vocal group, 'The Four Knights'.

OTHER BRITISH FILMS INCLUDE: *Big Business* (1930), *The First Mrs Fraser* (1932), *The Girl from Maxim's* (1933), *Dreams Come True* (1936), *Who's Your Lady Friend?* (1937), *Kicking the Moon Around* (1938), *Room for Two* (1940), *Fiddlers Three* (1944), *Tread Softly* (1952), *Climb Up the Wall* (1960).

Day, Jill (*b* Brighton, 1930 – *d* Kingston-upon-Thames, 1990). Singer, actress. RN: Yvonne Page. Popular as singer with well-known bands, on stage and TV, Day sang in *Always a Bride* (1953) and had one starring role in films, in the mildly amusing *All for Mary* (1955). That, as far as films went, was it.

Day, Robert (*b* London, 1922). Director. Day did time as a camera operator from 1948 to 1956, before getting his chance to direct *The Green Man* (1956), a very funny black comedy from a LAUNDER AND GILLIAT screenplay and with a cast of notable comics, led by Alastair SIM. He directed a further 11 British films, including one of Peter SELLERS' best comedies, *Two Way Stretch* (1960), several HORROR films, including two with Boris KARLOFF, and a rejuvenescent *Tarzan the Magnificent* (1960). He moved to America in the mid 60s and since then his once-bright talent has been buried in the graveyard of US telemovies. Married actress Dorothy Provine in 1969.

OTHER BRITISH FILMS INCLUDE (cam op) *Silent Dust, Obsession, Give Us This Day* (1949), *The Wooden Horse* (1950), *The Man Between* (1953), *An Inspector Calls* (1954), *1984* (1955); (d) *Strangers' Meeting* (1957), *Corridors of Blood, Grip of the Strangler, Life in Emergency Ward 10* (1958), *Bobbikins* (1959), *The Rebel* (1960), *Operation Snatch* (1962), *She* (1965).

Day, Tilly (*b* London, 1903 – *d* London, 1994) Continuity. Doyenne of the 'continuity girls', as they were called, Day's name appeared on dozens of films from the 40s to the 60s, and directors praised her legendary meticulousness. Her first credits include *The Mystery of the Marie Celeste* (1935) for continuity, for 'script supervision' on *Variety* (1935), and as editor on *Blarney* (1938, UK/Ire).

OTHER BRITISH FILMS INCLUDE: (cont) *Vice Versa* (1947), *The Rocking Horse Winner* (1949), *Venetian Bird* (1952), *The Kidnappers, Personal Affair* (1953), *Mad About Men* (1954), *Lost* (1955), *Jacqueline* (1956), *Too Many Crooks, Sapphire* (1959), *The Brides of Dracula* (1960), *Private Potter, Captain Clegg* (1962), *Jane Eyre* (1970), *Up Pompeii* (1971); (sc super) *Gaiety George* (1946), *Malta Story* (1953), *The Beachcomber* (1954), *The Woman for Joe* (1956), *The Stranglers of Bombay* (1959). *Hell Drivers* (1957).

Day, Vera (*b* London, 1933). Actress. If the somewhat raddled blonde sitting at a card table in *Lock, Stock and Two Smoking Barrels* (1998) looks familiar to filmgoers of a certain age, it is because she was the once-sassy starlet of 20-odd features of the 50s and 60s. Former model, typist, waitress and receptionist, she got a chance in the chorus of Jack Hylton's revue *Wish You Were Here* (1952), which led to an uncredited bit in Val GUEST's *Dance Little Lady* (1954). She had the lead in the comedy, *Fun at St Fanny's* (1955), and small roles in bigger films like *The Prince and the Showgirl* (1957), in which the presence of Marilyn Monroe again drew attention to British cinema's incapacity (notwithstanding Diana DORS) to create indigenous blonde bombshells. Day had some success on stage and radio, and hung on gamely in films for a decade.

OTHER BRITISH FILMS INCLUDE: *The Crowded Day, A Kid for Two Farthings* (1955), *The Flesh Is Weak, Quatermass 2, Hell Drivers* (1957), *Up the Creek, I Was Monty's Double* (1958), *Grip of the Strangler, Too Many Crooks* (1959), *Watch It Sailor!* (1961), *A Stitch in Time* (1963), *Saturday Night Out* (1964).

Day, W. Percy (*b* Luton, 1878 – *d* Los Angeles, 1965). Special effects director. Affectionately known as 'Poppa', Day was a major contributor to the technical development of British films. Trained as photographer with W.J. Roberts and as artist at the Royal Academy of Art, London, 1901–06, he became a noted portraitist, before entering films in 1919 at Elstree's IDEAL FILMS to create special effects. During the 20s he worked in the French cinema, where he introduced the glass shot and the technique of matte painting, before returning to England in 1932. He worked mainly for KORDA in the 30s, not always credited, on such films as *The Private Life of Henry VIII* (1933) and *Things to Come* (1936), and ten years later, after work on a range of distinguished films, including several for POWELL AND PRESSBURGER, he was appointed Director of Special Effects for Korda's LONDON FILMS. Powell wrote 40 years later of Day's work in creating the whirlpool sequence in *I Know Where I'm Going!* (1945) and eulogised him with: ' . . . he commanded respect and admiration from all who worked with him, because he *knew*' – his craft, that is. Also appeared in a small role in *Napoléon* (1927), and was created OBE in 1948.

OTHER BRITISH FILMS INCLUDE: *The Scarlet Pimpernel, Sanders of the River* (1935), *Victoria the Great* (1937), *The Drum* (1938), *The Four Feathers* (1939), *The Thief of Baghdad* (1940, 'scenic backgrounds'), *Secret Mission, The First of the Few* (1942), *The Life and Death of Colonel Blimp, The Demi-Paradise* (1943), *This Happy Breed* (1944), *A Canterbury Tale, Henry V* (1944), *Caesar and Cleopatra, Perfect Strangers* (1945), *Men of Two Worlds, A Matter of Life and Death* (1946), *Black Narcissus, An Ideal Husband, A Man About the House, Mine Own Executioner* (1947), *The Winslow Boy, Bonnie Prince Charlie, The Fallen Idol, Anna Karenina* (1948), *The Last Days of Dolwyn* (1949), *Gone to Earth, The Mudlark, The Elusive Pimpernel, Pandora and the Flying Dutchman* (1950).

Day, Will (*b* Luton, 1873 – *d* London, 1936). Pioneer, historian. A professional cyclist, pioneer motorist and aeronaut, and a figure closely associated with John Logie Baird and the invention of television, Will Day was the first historian of the British film industry. Taught the craft of magic lantern projection by his father, Day began exhibiting films in 1898; he was general manager of Walter Tyler Ltd, Tyler Apparatus Co. Ltd and Jury's Kine Supplies Ltd before founding his own motion picture equipment company, Will Day Ltd in 1913. He produced *Royal Remembrances* for GAUMONT in 1928. Day acquired one of the largest collections of early film equipment and documents and also authored the unpublished volume on the origins of the motion picture, *25,000 Years to Trap a Shadow*. His collection (the published catalogue of which appeared in 1930) was housed for many years at the Science Museum, South Kensington, before being acquired at auction in the 60s by the Cinémathèque Française. AS.

Day-Lewis, Daniel (*b* London, 1957). Actor. Major star of the 80s and 90s, who in 1999, temporarily, renounced acting to take up shoemaking. The son of poet laureate Cecil Day-Lewis (*b* 1904 – *d* 1978) and second wife, actress Jill BALCON, and grandson of EALING STUDIOS head, Sir Michael BALCON, he dropped out of school (Sevenoaks, followed by Bedales) and got a bit part in *Sunday Bloody Sunday* (1971). Deciding to take acting seriously, he trained at the Bristol Old Vic and joined the RSC in the later 70s. After several small film roles, including one as a young thug in *Gandhi* (1982, UK/Ind), he made an indelible impression in 1985 with two roles so widely contrasted that it was hard to believe the same actor played them: the stuffy Cecil Vyse in MERCHANT IVORY's *A Room with a View* and the gay punk in *My Beautiful Laundrette*.

This kind of versatility continued to mark his career, so that he remained primarily an actor rather than a film star, and the seal was set on it with his AA- and BAA-award winning performance of cerebral palsy victim Christy Brown in *My Left Foot* (1989), the first of three films for Irish director, Jim SHERIDAN. The other two were as one of the wrongly-gaoled 'Guildford four' in *In the Name of the Father* (1993, UK/Ire/US; AAn, BAAn), and the title role in *The Boxer* (1998, UK/Ire/US). In the meantime, he had established himself in US films: *The Unbearable Lightness of Being* (1988), erotic drama set against the 1968 Soviet invasion of Czechoslovakia; the adventure *The Last of the Mohicans* (1992, BAAn), for which he rebuilt his body to good box-office effect; Martin Scorsese's masterpiece, *The Age of Innocence* (1993), as the honourable, frustrated apex of a romantic triangle; and as the honourable, frustrated John Proctor in *The Crucible* (1996).

Following the latter, he married Arthur Miller's daughter, Rebecca, having previously had a long relationship with French star, Isabelle Adjani. His stage career took a serious tumble when he withdrew from the National Theatre's *Hamlet* in 1989, claiming exhaustion; he was replaced by understudy Jeremy NORTHAM. The tall, intense, darkly good-looking Day-Lewis was famous for his total immersion in a role, but this perhaps means that acting is for him more stressful than shoemaking. Returned to acting in *Gangs of New York* (2001).

OTHER BRITISH FILMS: *The Bounty* (1984), *The Insurance Man* (1985), *Nanou* (1986, UK/Fr), *Eversmile, New Jersey* (1989, UK/Arg).

Deacon, Brian (*b* Oxford, 1949). Actor. Slightly built Deacon made a strong impression as the young soldier who deserts and poses as Glenda JACKSON's sister in *The Triple Echo* (1972), his first film. Since, his only film of interest has been Peter GREENAWAY's *A Zed & Two Noughts* (1985, UK/Neth), in

which he and his brother **Eric Deacon** (*b* Oxford, 1950) played twins. Did some notable TV, including Oswald in *Ghosts* (1977), played the title role in the US-made *Jesus* (1979), and was affecting as the understanding husband in the stage version of *Brief Encounter* (2000). Was married to actress Rula LENSKA.
OTHER BRITISH FILMS: *Vampyres* (1974), *Nelly's Version* (1983).

Deakins, Roger (*b* Torquay, 1949). Cinematographer. Since 1990, Deakins, graduate of the National Film School, has worked mainly in the US, winning three Oscar nominations, for the prison drama, *The Shawshank Redemption* (1994), Scorsese's lyrically beautiful *Kundun* (1997), and *Fargo* (1996). He began his British career working on DOCUMENTARIES and SHORTS, such as *Welcome to Britain* (1976), a look at Britain's immigration laws, *Blue Suede Shoes* (1980), a chronicling of the early days of rock'n'roll, and *The Animals Film* (1981), a high-profile documentary on aspects of animal abuse. His fiction-film career took off with two muted-colour pieces for director Michael RADFORD, *Another Time, Another Place* (1983), and *Nineteen Eighty-Four* (1984), followed by some of the most distinctive British films of the 80s, including *Defence of the Realm* (1985), *Sid and Nancy* (1986), *White Mischief* (1987) and the tough, glossy thriller, *Stormy Monday* (1987), all of more than routine visual interest.
OTHER BRITISH FILMS INCLUDE: *Horseboy, Farmer's Hunt* (1974, shorts), *Cruel Passion* (1977), *Box On* (1979, short), *Memoirs of a Survivor* (1981), *The Innocent* (1984), *Personal Services, The Kitchen Toto* (1987), *Pascali's Island* (1988, UK/US).

Dean, Basil (*b* Croydon, 1888 – *d* London, 1978). Director, producer, writer. On stage from 1906, he acted in many plays until 1916, and post-WW1 became an important West End and New York producer of plays such as *The Constant Nymph* (1925, + co-auth) and *Autumn Crocus* (1931), both of which he later transferred (p, d) to the screen, the former twice (in 1928 and, with his third wife, Victoria HOPPER, in 1933) and the latter in 1934 (+ p, co-sc). A major figure in pre-WW2 theatre and film, in 1939 he became founding director of ENSA (Entertainments National Service Association, aka Every Night Something Awful) which operated throughout WW2.

In 1929, having directed an old friend, Clive BROOK, in *The Return of Sherlock Holmes* in the US, he founded ASSOCIATED TALKING PICTURES (ATP), but his first feature, *Escape* (1930), based on John GALSWORTHY's play, was a commercial failure. He then initiated the building of EALING STUDIOS, 'the first in England designed specifically for talkie production' (Rachael Low). There, through most of the 30s, Dean, as producer and/or director, scored big commercial successes with Gracie FIELDS and George FORMBY, Northern MUSIC-HALL stars who found near-universal favour.

When it became clear that the DISTRIBUTION agreement Dean had made with the US company, RKO, was never going to be favourable to him, ATP registered British Associated Film Distributors to ensure the appropriate presentation of its films. During Dean's incumbency at Ealing, such soon-to-be-famous film-makers as Carol REED, David LEAN, Thorold DICKINSON and Michael POWELL got their first credits, and it is often remarked that Dean was more notable as a producer than as a director. The films he directed, including *Autumn Crocus, Lorna Doone* (1934, + p), *Whom the Gods Love* (1936, + p), suggested by Mozart's life, and *21 Days* (1937, + p, co-sc) suffered from staginess, and after 1937 he directed no more films but maintained his theatre career. As well as writing a number of plays, he also authored *The Theatre at War* (1955)

and two volumes of autobiography. Created MBE (1918) and CBE (1947).
OTHER BRITISH FILMS INCLUDE: (p, unless noted) *Birds of Prey* (1930, + p, sc), *Sally in Our Alley* (1931), *The Water Gipsies* (+ sc), *Nine Till Six* (+ d), *Looking on the Bright Side* (+ d, sc, orig st) (1932), *Loyalties* (+ d) (1933), *Sing As We Go!* (+ d), *Java Head* (1934), *No Limit, Midshipman Easy, Look Up and Laugh* (+d) (1935), *Queen of Hearts, Laburnum Grove, Sensation* (orig play) (1936), *The Show Goes On* (+ d, sc), *Keep Fit, Feather Your Nest* (1937), *Penny Paradise* (+ sc), *It's in the Air* (1938).
BIBLIOG: *Seven Ages: An Autobiography 1888–1927*, 1970; *Mind's Eye: An Autobiography 1927–1972*, 1973.

Dean, Isabel (*b* Aldridge, 1918 – *d* England, 1997). Actress. RN: Hodgkinson. Theatre critic Harold Hobson described Dean as 'the most undervalued actress' of the English stage, on which she first appeared in 1939. Of a serene, patrician beauty, she was nearly 30 when she entered films, where leading roles eluded her, but she gave some attractive supporting performances: e.g. as Trevor HOWARD's about-to-be-betrayed wife in *The Passionate Friends* (1948), Gilbert's long-suffering wife in *The Story of Gilbert and Sullivan* (1953) and John CASSAVETES' understandably critical mother-in-law in *Virgin Island* (1958). A good deal of TV, including *I, Claudius* (1976), and several US films, including *Five Days One Summer* (1982). Married and divorced writer William FAIRCHILD.
OTHER BRITISH FILMS INCLUDE: *The Last Page* (1952), *Twice Upon a Time* (1953), *Davy* (1957), *A High Wind in Jamaica* (1965), *Inadmissible Evidence* (1968), *Oh! What a Lovely War* (1969), *The Bawdy Adventures of Tom Jones* (1975), *The Bad Sister* (1983).

Dean, Ivor (*b* 1917 – *d* 1974). Actor. Bald-headed character player best known as Simon Templar's frustrated Scotland Yard contact in TV's *The Saint* (1962–69). Also appeared in about a dozen films, beginning with 'B' MOVIE, *Cloak and Dagger* (1955) and ending, as a Bishop, in the comedy *Never Mind the Quality, Feel the Width* (1972).
OTHER BRITISH FILMS INCLUDE: *The Sicilians* (1964), *Stranger in the House* (1967), *Theatre of Death* (1966), *Salt & Pepper, Where Eagles Dare* (1968), *The Oblong Box, Crooks and Coronets* (1969), *Dr Jekyll and Mr Hyde* (1971).

Deans, Marjorie (*b* London). Screenwriter. Interesting peripheral figure, now remembered for her collaboration on the screenplays of two of Gabriel PASCAL's adaptations of SHAW's plays, *Major Barbara* (1941) and *Caesar and Cleopatra* (1945), about the latter of which she wrote a book-length production account called *Meetings at the Sphinx* (1947). She co-wrote a further 17 films between 1934 and 1950, and in 1950 wrote *and* directed *The Girl is Mine*, inconsequential stuff, but the rarity of a woman director then should be noted. Began as script girl for GAUMONT–BRITISH and worked for several other companies, including BIP.
OTHER BRITISH FILMS: (co-sc) *The Great Defender, Catherine the Great* (1934), *Drake of England, Royal Cavalcade* (1935), *Living Dangerously, Sensation, Wings over Africa* (1936), *Kathleen Mavourneen, Aren't Men Beasts?* (1937), *Talk About Jacqueline* (1942), *Rhythm Serenade* (1943), *Woman to Woman* (1946), *The Girl Who Couldn't Quite* (1949).

Dearden, Basil (*b* Westcliff-on-Sea, 1911 – *d* London, 1971). Director, producer, screenwriter. RN: Dear. For a long time, the films of DEARDEN and his regular producer, Michael RELPH, were cavalierly dismissed as representing the journeyman strain of EALING film-making, and their later, 'SOCIAL PROBLEM' FILMS were seen as predictably packaging 'issues' in safely conventional narrative modes. In 1993, critic Charles Barr offered a tentative reassessment of Dearden's importance in the Ealing canon and in 1997 a book of essays devoted to his films appeared. It is now less easy to elide the achievement under patronising adjectives like 'liberal' and 'safe'; Dearden's films offer, among other rewards, a fascinating barometer of public taste at its most nearly consensual over three decades.

He began his career as theatre actor, was stage manager to Basil DEAN whose assistant at Ealing he later became (he changed his surname to avoid confusion). Apart from uncredited work with Dean, he worked on eight Ealing films, including five George FORMBY comedies, before starting to direct, at first in collaboration with Will HAY, on *Black Sheep of Whitehall* (1941), *The Goose Steps Out* (1942), and *My Learned Friend* (1943). He went solo with *The Bells Go Down* (1943), a wartime tribute to the Auxiliary Fire Service. As one considers his next dozen or so Ealing films, it is hard to justify the workhorse tag he acquired. *The Halfway House* (1944) is a philosophical fantasy; *They Came to a City* (1944), from J.B. Priestley's play, is a striking if static social engineering tract; he directs 'The Hearse Driver' sequence in the PORTMANTEAU HORROR film, *Dead of Night* (1945); *The Captive Heart* (1946) remains an affecting POW drama; *Frieda* (1947) mines the what-shall-we-do-with-the-Germans-now? theme for potent melodramatic effect; *Saraband for Dead Lovers* (1948) is a costume melodrama, gorgeous-looking thanks to Relph's production design and Douglas SLOCOMBE's colour photography; *The Blue Lamp* (1949) may be superficially a tribute to the police force, but its power is in the representation of its seductive criminal element. And so on. There are dull films in the 50s, but not many and *The Ship That Died of Shame* (1955) holds up well in its metaphoric account of post-war decline.

When Ealing finished in 1958, the Dearden–Relph team continued productively until Dearden's tragic death in a car accident on the M1 in 1971. They made the social problem films for which they are now, perhaps, best known: including *Sapphire* (1959), a murder thriller with race-relations complication; *Victim* (1961), the first mainstream film to broach the issue of homosexuality; and *Life for Ruth* (1962), a powerful account of fundamentalist religious belief in the context of family grief. The melodramatic strand so skilfully worked here was apparent in some of Dearden's Ealing work, and is there in later pieces such as *Woman of Straw* (1964) and his last, the science-fiction thriller, *The Man Who Haunted Himself* (1970). Perhaps it was essentially this streak which led to his being so undervalued at the time. As well there are the stirring imperial epic, *Khartoum* (1966), and the action-packed period spoof, *The Assassination Bureau* (1968). What might have been praised as versatility was too often denigrated as mere impersonal efficiency.

Married Melissa STRIBLING, who appeared in four of his films, including the witty heist thriller, *The League of Gentlemen* (1960), and was the father of director James DEARDEN.

OTHER BRITISH FILMS: (ass d) *It's in the Bag, Penny Paradise* (1938), *Come On, George!* (1939), *Young Veteran* (1941); (co-sc) *This Man Is News* (1938), *Let George Do It!* (1940); (assoc p) *Spare a Copper* (1940), *Turned Out Nice Again* (1941); (d) *Train of Events* (1949, 2 episodes), *Cage of Gold, Pool of London* (1950), *I Believe in You* (co-d), *The Gentle Gunman* (1952), *The Square Ring* (1953), *The Rainbow Jacket* (1954), *Out of the Clouds* (1955), *Who Done It?* (1956), *The Smallest Show on Earth, Violent Playground* (1957), *Man in the Moon* (1960), *The Secret Partner, All Night Long* (1961), *The Mind Benders, A Place to Go* (1963), *Masquerade* (1965), *Only When I Larf* (1968); (p – all d, Relph) *Davy* (1957), *Rockets Galore* (1958), *Desert Mice* (1959).

BIBLIOG: Alan Burton *et al* (eds), *Liberal Directions: Basil Dearden and Post-war British Film Culture*, 1997.

Dearden, James (*b* London, 1949). Director, screenwriter. Oxford-educated son of Basil DEARDEN, he came to prominence as screenwriter for *Fatal Attraction* (1987), a huge commercial (and scandalous) success, directed in Hollywood by fellow-Brit Adrian Lyne, for whom he also co-scripted *Lolita* (1997, US/Fr). In Britain, he directed several short films, including *Diversion* (1980), a preliminary sketch for *Fatal Attraction*, then *The Cold Room* (1984) for US cable, cinemas elsewhere, followed by the mildly attractive period piece, *Pascali's Island* (1988, UK/US, + sc), and the disastrous *Rogue Trader* (1999, + p, sc), in which he botched a potentially gripping story.

OTHER BRITISH FILMS INCLUDE: (d) *Contraption* (1977, +sc), *Panic* (1978, + p), *Diversion* (1980, short).

Dearing, R(oger) E(dward) (*b* Suffolk, 1893 – *d* Ruislip, 1968). Editor, associate producer. In the film business from 1912, he became the leading (and, by several accounts, dictatorial) editor for GAUMONT–BRITISH and GAINSBOROUGH during the 30s, so that his name is on many Will HAY films, making a contribution to their pacy fun. He was associate producer on *Madonna of the Seven Moons* (1944) and thereafter fulfilled such functions as 'production supervisor'.

OTHER BRITISH FILMS INCLUDE: (e, unless noted) *No Lady, Hindle Wakes* (1931), *Friday the Thirteenth* (1933), *Windbag the Sailor* (1936), *Oh, Mr Porter!, Good Morning, Boys!, Doctor Syn* (1937), *Old Bones of the River, The Lady Vanishes, Convict 99* (1938), *Ask a Policeman* (1939), *Gasbags, Night Train to Munich, They Came by Night* (1940), *Kipps, Cottage to Let* (1941), *The Young Mr Pitt, Uncensored, King Arthur Was a Gentleman* (1942), *Millions Like Us, The Man in Grey, It's That Man Again* (super e), *We Dive at Dawn* (1943), *Fanny by Gaslight, Two Thousand Women* (1944); (ass to p) *Escape* (1948), *The Black Rose* (1950); (p super) *Single-Handed* (1953), *The Mouse on the Moon* (1963).

De Banzie, Brenda (*b* Manchester, 1915 – *d* Haywards Heath, 1981). Actress. Forceful blonde character actress who had one great starring role, the dominant Maggie in *Hobson's Choice* (1953), to which she brought steel and warmth. She thereafter played a range of overbearing spinsters (like the one after James Robertson JUSTICE in *Doctor at Sea*, 1955) or more malevolent types like the kidnapper in *The Man Who Knew Too Much* (1955, US) or the procuress in *Passport to Shame* (1958). However, she could be benign, like the Scots missionary in *The Purple Plain* (1954), and she is very touching as worn-out Phoebe in *The Entertainer* (1960), reprising her stage role. On stage from the mid 30s, in London from 1942, she was in films as an EXTRA before and during WW2.

OTHER BRITISH FILMS INCLUDE: *The Long Dark Hall* (1951), *The Happiness of 3 Women* (1954), *A Kid for Two Farthings, As Long as They're Happy* (1955), *House of Secrets* (1956), *The Thirty Nine Steps* (1958), *Too Many Crooks* (1959), *The Mark, Flame in the Streets, A Pair of Briefs* (1961), *I Thank a Fool* (1962), *Pretty Polly* (1967).

De Carlo, Yvonne (*b* Vancouver, 1922). Actress. RN: Peggy Middleton. Famously pretty star of many an idiotic Eastern or Western in Hollywood, she showed an unexpected gift for comedy in some of her British films: as the versatile mistress of the proprietor of *Hotel Sahara* (1951), as Alec GUINNESS's exotic wife yearning for domesticity in *The Captain's Paradise* (1953), and in the very funny Irish-set *Happy Ever After* (1954).

OTHER BRITISH FILMS: *Sea Devils* (1953), *American Gothic* (1987).

De Casalis, Jeanne (*b* Basutoland, 1899 – *d* London, 1966). Made her stage debut in 1919 at Cannes, after studying under French and Russian teachers. She worked on stage, especially in comedy, RADIO, where she created the popular character of gossipy 'Mrs Feather', and in films from 1925 (*Settled Out of Court*). After two more silent films, she made nearly 20 sound films, typically as rather scatter-brained, upper-class eccentrics, as in *Cottage to Let* (1941) and as the warm-hearted novelist in *Those Kids from Town* (1942), Married (1) to actor Colin CLIVE until his death in 1937. She also wrote several books and plays.

OTHER BRITISH FILMS INCLUDE: *The Glad Wife* (1927), *Knowing Men* (1930), *Radio Parade* (1933), *Nell Gwyn* (1934), *Jamaica Inn* (1939), *Sailors Three, Charley's (Big-Hearted) Aunt* (1940), *They Met in the Dark* (1943), *Medal for the General* (1944), *Woman Hater* (1948), *Twenty Questions Murder Mystery* (1949).

Decker, Diana (*b* New York, 1926). Actress. Pretty, vivacious American actress in Britain, from her debut as helpful shopgirl in *San Demetrio–London* (1943) until her last role as duplicitous satanist in *Devils of Darkness* (1964). She starred in *Is Your Honeymoon Really Necessary?* (1953) and *The Betrayal* (1957), but generally provided good-humoured support. Much TV in the 50s.

OTHER BRITISH FILMS INCLUDE: *Fiddlers Three* (1944), *Meet Me at Dawn* (1947), *Murder at the Windmill* (1949), *Knave of Hearts* (1954), *A Yank in Ermine* (1955), *Lolita* (1961).

Deckers, Eugene (*b* France, 1917 – *d* 1977). Actor. One of postwar British cinema's resident 'foreigners' who played clerks and colonels, waiters and Nazis, and, in comedy (*The Lavender Hill Mob*, 1951, as a customs official) and drama (*The Longest Day*, 1962, as Nazi officer), he stayed busy for twenty years. Perhaps best recalled as one of Yvonne DE CARLO's lovers-of-all-nations in *Hotel Sahara* (1951). Also a stage actor, he came to Britain when France was liberated; on TV from 1947.

OTHER BRITISH FILMS INCLUDE: *Woman to Woman* (1946), *Against the Wind* (1947), *Madeleine* (1949), *Highly Dangerous, So Long at the Fair* (1950), *The Colditz Story* (1954), *The Iron Petticoat* (1956), *North West Frontier* (1959), *Hell Is Empty* (1967), *The Assassination Bureau* (1968).

De Cordova, Leander (*b* Jamaica, 1878 – *d* Los Angeles, 1969). Director, actor. A former stage actor, his first US credit is as assistant director on *Romeo and Juliet* (1916). He continued as assistant director or director in the US and was also studio manager for Goldwyn and others. In 1921, he provided the screenplay for the British feature, *Roses In the Dust*, and then was in South Africa directing Joan MORGAN in *Swallow* (1922). Appeared in at least three British films, *Fires of Fate* (1923), *I Will Repay* (1923) and *The Secret Kingdom* (1925), and directed Betty BLYTHE in the British production of *She* (1925), shot in Berlin. From the late 20s through the 40s, he was involved in various American 'B' pictures, by 1946 reduced to playing a servant in *Gilda*. AS.

De Courville, Albert (*b* Croydon, 1887 – *d* London, 1960). Director. After making a reputation as director of theatrical revue, he made 20 light films, THRILLERS, MUSICALS and COMEDIES, during the 30s, including two made on the Continent. Among the more notable were *The Midshipmaid* (1932), starring Jessie MATTHEWS, who called him 'raving bloody mad', and *The Lambeth Walk* (1939), adapted from the popular stage musical, with Lupino LANE, and he directed Charles LAUGHTON's first film, *Wolves* (1930).

OTHER BRITISH FILMS: *There Goes the Bride* (1932), *This is the Life* (1933), *Wild Boy* (1934, + story), *Charing Cross Road, The Case of Gabriel Perry* (1935), *Strangers on Honeymoon, Seven Sinners* (1936), *Oh, Boy!, Crackerjack* (1938), *An Englishman's Home* (1939).

BIBLIOG: Memoirs, *I Tell You*, 1929.

Deeley, Michael (*b* 1932). Producer. Producer of several idiosyncratic films, including the Goons short, *The Case of the*

Mukkinese Battlehorn (1955, co-p), Lindsay ANDERSON's *The White Bus* (assoc p) and *The Man Who Fell to Earth* (1976), as well as popular successes such as *The Italian Job* (1969) and *Murphy's War* (1971). Still in his twenties, he edited episodes of TV's *Robin Hood* (1955–59); and he was general manager for WOODFALL FILMS in the early 60s. In the later 60s, he set up Oakhurst company with Stanley BAKER, making *Robbery* (1967, co-p) and *Where's Jack?* (1969, ex p), and became managing director of BRITISH LION in 1973. When EMI bought British Lion in 1976, Deeley joined its board, along with Barry SPIKINGS with whom he co-produced several films including *The Deer Hunter* (1978, US), for which he won AA. Also in the US, produced his most famous film, *Blade Runner* (1982).

OTHER BRITISH FILMS INCLUDE: *At the Stroke of Nine* (1957, co-p, co-sc), *One Way Pendulum* (1964), *The Knack . . .* (1965, co-assoc p), *The Long Day's Dying* (1968), *Conduct Unbecoming* (1975).

DeForest, Lee (*b* Council Bluffs, Iowa, 1873 – *d* Los Angeles, 1961). Inventor, producer. DeForest's 1906 invention of the audion tube gave birth to the electronics industry and made possible the modern sound-on-film motion picture. In order to promote his invention to the film industry, DeForest began producing sound shorts as early as 1919 (many of which are preserved at the Library of Congress), and from 1925 to 1929 his 'phonofilms' were also produced at a UK studio in Clapham, featuring stars of the stage and MUSIC HALL. Some were collected together in 1932 as 'Musical Medley' and 'Camera Cocktails.' AS.

Deghy, Guy (*b* Budapest, 1912 – *d* London, 1992). Actor. In continental films from 1934, in British films since 1944 (*Mr Emmanuel*) as all-purpose foreigner: he is Nicole MAUREY's Italian 'artistic adviser' in *The Constant Husband* (1954), a Russian scientist in *The Mouse on the Moon* (1963) and a German major in *Where Eagles Dare* (1968). To British filmmakers, one foreigner was much like another, and Deghy made a good thing of this delusion. Also, some TV (*The Avengers*, 1961; *Bergerac*, 1981) and some international films, such as *The Greek Tycoon* (1978).

OTHER BRITISH FILMS INCLUDE: *Against the Wind* (1947), *The Divided Heart, The Colditz Story* (1954), *Lost* (1955), *The House of the Seven Hawks* (1959), *Surprise Package* (1960), *Sammy Going South, The Comedy Man* (1963), *Operation Crossbow* (1965, UK/It), *The Looking Glass War* (1969), *Cry of the Banshee* (1970), *Success is the Best Revenge* (1984).

De Grunwald, Anatole (*b* St Petersburg, 1910 – *d* London, 1967). Producer, screenwriter. The son of a Czarist diplomat, he fled to England during the Revolution, and was educated at Cambridge and the Sorbonne. Entered films in 1939, was much associated with directors Anthony ASQUITH and Harold FRENCH, and writer Terence RATTIGAN, and became an important figure in 40s British cinema, as writer and producer, in some very *English* enterprises. His first important screenplay was *French Without Tears* (1939), co-written with Rattigan for Asquith, a collaboration repeated on *Quiet Wedding* (1941), *The Way to the Stars* (1945), *While the Sun Shines* (1947) and *The Winslow Boy* (1948); he appeared in *Insight* (1960), a documentary on Asquith's work. He was involved as writer with FRENCH on *Jeannie* (1941), *Secret Mission, Unpublished Story, The Day Will Dawn* (1942), and *English Without Tears* (1944, + p). Was producer and writer for TWO CITIES before becoming an independent producer on such films as *Libel* (1959) and *The VIPs* (1963) for Asquith, and *The Queen of Spades* and *Now Barabbas Was a Robber* (+ sc) (1949). His brother, **Dimitri De**

Grunwald (*b* St Petersburg, 1914 – *d* Hove, 1990, also produced a number of films, including *The Millionairess* (1960), *Mr Topaze* (1961), *The Dock Brief* (1962) and *That Lucky Touch* (1975).

OTHER BRITISH FILMS: (sc/co-sc) *Spy for a Day, Freedom Radio, Discoveries* (1940), *Pimpernel Smith, Penn of Pennsylvania, Cottage to Let, Major Barbara* (1941), *Tomorrow We Live, The First of the Few* (1942), *They Met in the Dark* (1943), *The Last Days of Dolwyn* (1949), *Home at Seven, Women of Twilight* (1952); (p, sc) *The Demi-Paradise* (1943), *Bond Street* (1948), *Flesh and Blood* (1951), *Treasure Hunt, Golden Arrow, The Holly and the Ivy* (1952), *Innocents in Paris* (1953), *The Doctor's Dilemma* (1958), *I Thank a Fool, Come Fly with Me* (1962).

Dehn, Paul (*b* Manchester, 1912 – *d* London, 1976). Screenwriter, critic. Oxford-educated Dehn was film critic for the *Sunday Referee* (1936–68) and with the *Sunday Chronicle* (1946–53), following war service (1939–45). He shared an Oscar for the taut, topical screenplay of *Seven Days to Noon* (1950) and won a BAA for his *Orders to Kill* (1958) screenplay. He also wrote the BOND lark, *Goldfinger* (1964), and, in the US, three of the *Planet of the Apes* series (1970, 1971, 1972). Versatile in several media and modes.

OTHER BRITISH FILMS INCLUDE (sc, unless noted): *Moulin Rouge* (1953, lyrics), *On Such a Night* (short), *I Am a Camera* (lyrics) (1955), *The Innocents* (1961, lyrics), *The Spy Who Came in from the Cold* (1965), *The Deadly Affair* (BAAn) (1966), *Fragment of Fear* (1970, + p), *Murder on the Orient Express* (1974, AAn).

Deighton, Len (*b* London, 1929). Author, screenwriter. Creator of the anti-romantic secret agent/gourmet, Harry Palmer, played by Michael CAINE, in several ADAPTATIONS: *The Ipcress File* (1965), *Funeral in Berlin* (1966), *Billion Dollar Brain* (1967), and resurrected in *Bullet to Beijing* (1995, UK/Can/Russ). His novels provided the basis for *Only When I Larf* (1968, + p), and *Spy Story* (1976), and he worked uncredited on the screenplay for *Oh! What a Lovely War* (1969). Famous gastronome as well.

De Keyser, David (*b* London, 1927). Actor. Enjoyable character player mainly seen on TV(e.g. giving some bite to the idiocies of *The House of Eliott*, 1991, as a sorely tried legal adviser). His films are an idiosyncratic mix of little-seen shorts, including *The Plain Man's Guide to Advertising* (1961, anim, voice) and *Balham: Gateway to the South* (1977); offbeat features like *Leon the Pig Farmer* (1992) and David HARE's *The Designated Mourner* (1977); and mainstream entertainments like *Diamonds Are Forever* (1971) and *A Touch of Class* (1972), and the odd US film, like *King David* (1985).

OTHER BRITISH FILMS INCLUDE: *Catch Us If You Can* (1965), *On Her Majesty's Secret Service* (1969), *Voyage of the Damned* (1976), *Valentino* (1977, as Joseph Schenck), *Yentl* (UK/US), *The Ploughman's Lunch* (1983), *Sunshine* (2000, UK/Austria/Can/Ger/Hung).

De La Haye, Ina (*b* St Petersburg, 1906 – *d* Ticehurst, 1972). Actress. RADA-trained and also a singer, she entered films in 1928 (*Paradise*), played the Grand Duchess Olga in *You Can't Take It with You* in London (1937), was an indefatigable concert singer during WW2, and post-war appeared in about a dozen films, invariably in 'foreign' roles, such as Tamara TOUMANOVA's maid in *The Private Life of Sherlock Holmes* (1970), her last film.

OTHER BRITISH FILMS INCLUDE: *Give Us This Day* (1949), *Top Secret* (1952), *Dance Little Lady* (1954), *I Am a Camera* (1955), *The Spanish Gardener, Anastasia* (1956), *Isadora* (1968).

De La Roche, Catherine (*b* Ukraine, 1907 – *d* Wellington, NZ, 1997). Critic. A reader at EALING and DENHAM before WW2 and Films Officer with the MOI, 1943–45, she became a

respected writer on film for many journals (*Picturegoer, Films and Filming, Sequence*) and books (*Penguin Film Review*) in the 40s and 50s.

De La Tour, Frances (*b* Bovingdon, 1944). Actress. When she played the dopey Maude in *Every Home Should Have One* (1969) and the hearty sports mistress in *Our Miss Fred* (1972), it looked as if she might become the Joyce GRENFELL *de nos jours*. In fact, her screen career has been sporadic, and she had better roles in the theatre and more fun in TV's *Rising Damp* (1974–78), reprising her role as gauche Miss Jones in the SPIN-OFF film (1980). Scored a major theatre success in the 2000 revival of *Fallen Angels*. Married and separated from Tom KEMPINSKI.

OTHER BRITISH FILMS INCLUDE: *Country Dance* (1969), *To the Devil a Daughter* (1976), *Wombling Free* (1977), *Loser Takes All* (1990, UK/US).

Delamar, Michael (aka Mickey) (*b* Lebanon, 1908). Producer, production manager. In films as stunt man from 1928, then in varied capacities (producer of shorts, production manager, assistant director, etc) in the 30s, was production manager with the RANK ORGANISATION in the mid 40s, associate producer with GRAND NATIONAL PICTURES (1945–47), and production manager with EXCLUSIVE/HAMMER from 1953. Also produced several films in the 50s, including *Mask of Dust* (1954), *Break in the Circle* (1955) and *Serious Charge* (1959, + sc).

OTHER BRITISH FILMS INCLUDE: *Make-Up* (1937, ass d), *Under Your Hat* (1940, p man), *Fahrenheit 451* (1966, assoc p).

De Lane Lea, William (*b* 1900 – *d* 1964). Executive. Pioneer of sound dubbing processes and of production of English-language versions of Continental films, including Vittorio De Sica's *L'Oro di Napoli* (1954). Directed two films in the 50s, *Model Girl* (1954, short) and *No Love for Judy* (1955), both written and produced by his son, **Jacques De Lane Lea** (*b* Paris, 1931) production manager, sometimes producer, on a number of minor films of the 50s and 60s. Became managing director of De Lane Lea Ltd on his father's death.

Delaney, Maureen (aka Delany) (*b* Kilkenny, Ireland, 1888 – *d* London, 1961). Actress. Memorable character player with long Abbey Theatre experience, in British films from 1947. She was vividly treacherous in *Odd Man Out* (1947) and the terminally grumpy Aunt Bridget in *The Holly and the Ivy* (1952); usually in roles which drew on her Irish background.

OTHER BRITISH FILMS INCLUDE: *Captain Boycott* (1947), *The Mark of Cain, So Evil My Love* (1948), *Saints and Sinners, Under Capricorn* (1949), *Night and the City* (1950, UK/US), *Jacqueline* (1956), *The Story of Esther Costello, The Scamp* (1957), *The Doctor's Dilemma* (1958).

Delaney, Pauline (*b* Dublin). Actress. Best remembered for her ripe charms as Alan BATES's widow-on-the-make landlady in *Nothing But the Best* (1964), ready to try blackmail if seduction fails. Most of her screen roles (also active on stage) drew on her Irish origins, including Sister Flannagan in *Percy* (1971).

OTHER BRITISH FILMS INCLUDE: *Rooney, Innocent Sinners* (1958), *A Question of Suspense* (1961), *The Quare Fellow* (1962), *Young Cassidy* (1965), *Brannigan* (1975), *Trenchcoat* (1983).

Delaney, Shelagh (*b* Salford, 1939). Dramatist. Barely 20 when her play *A Taste of Honey* (1957) was staged to acclaim in London, and later New York. It was filmed in 1961 (mostly in Salford) by Tony RICHARDSON, with whom she co-wrote the screenplay and shared a BAA. A lyrical realist, the author of other plays and a novelist, she wrote screenplays for Lindsay

ANDERSON's *The White Bus* (+ story), for *Charlie Bubbles* (1967), *Dance with a Stranger* (1984), locating the tragic end of Ruth Ellis in a cruel class context, and the telemovie, *The Railway Station Man* (1992).

De Lautour, Charles (aka De la Tour) (*b* Vancouver, 1909). Director. In 1916 came to England where he later worked as actor and director in the theatre prior to entering documentary film-making with STRAND (1940–44). Credited with three 'B' MOVIES in the 50s, but the nifty Hollywood-influenced *noir* thriller, *Impulse* (1955), which bears his name, was really directed by US blacklistee, Cy ENDFIELD, as was *The Limping Man* (1953). They formally co-directed *Child in the House* (1956).

OTHER BRITISH FILMS INCLUDE: (d, shorts, unless noted) *Oxford* (1940, ass d), *Coalminer* (1944) *Subject Discussed* (1944), *British Industries Fair* (1948), *Farmer Moving South* (1952, co-d), *Song of the Canaries* (1957).

Delderfield, R(onald) F(rederick) (*b* London, 1912 – *d* Sidmouth, 1972). Author, dramatist, screenwriter. Former journalist, later successful playwright and novelist, several of whose works have been filmed, including *All Over the Town* (1948, story), *Glad Tidings* (1953, play), famously *Carry On Sergeant* (1958, story) and *On the Fiddle* (1961, novel). Wrote screenplays from his plays for *Worm's Eye View* (1951), *Now and Forever* (1955), *Where There's a Will* (1955). His work has a strong regional flavour and has also been adapted to TV series, notably *To Serve Them All My Days* (1980).

OTHER BRITISH FILMS (sc): *Value for Money, Keep It Clean* (1955), *Home and Away* (1956, add dial).

De Leon, Herbert (*b* Panama, 1907 – *d* London, 1979) Agent. Representative of many famous artistes of stage, screen and television (including Jean KENT, Dora BRYAN), and brother of playwright Jack De Leon (*b* Panama, 1897 – *d*?), several of whose plays were filmed, including *Jury's Evidence* (1936), with Margaret LOCKWOOD, and who started the Q Theatre, Kew, in 1924.

Delerue, Georges (*b* Roubaix, France, 1925 – *d* Los Angeles, 1992). Composer. Prolific composer of French and international films, responsible for the scores of such notable 60s British films as *The Pumpkin Eater* (1964), *A Man for All Seasons* (1966) and *Women in Love* (1969, BAAn). Nominated for several Oscars and won for *A Little Romance* (1979, US), and favoured by such directors as Fred ZINNEMANN and Jack CLAYTON.

OTHER BRITISH FILMS INCLUDE: *French Dressing* (1963), *Our Mother's House* (1967, + cond), *The Day of the Jackal* (1973, UK/Fr).

Delfont, Bernard (Lord Delfont) (*b* Tokmak, Russia, 1909 – *d* Angmering, 1994). Entrepreneur. RN: Barnet Winogradsky. Theatre impresario in UK from 1941; presented shows on ITV from the mid 50s; and, in 1967, joined the EMI (Electrical and Musical Industries) board as EMI was planning to take over ABPC and rival RANK, becoming a major force in production, DISTRIBUTION and EXHIBITION. As head of EMI's film division, he appointed Bryan FORBES head of production in 1969 for a stormy few years. Knighted in 1974, for 'services to charity', and made a life peer in 1976. Brother of Lord [Lew] GRADE with whom he clashed over the production of rival *Titanic* films in 1979; both had their sights set on international – i.e. US – success, and to some extent achieved this, with films like *Murder on the Orient Express* (1974). Delfont refused to finance *Life of Brian* (1979) on grounds of blasphemy. He became chief executive officer of EMI in 1979 and resigned in 1980, a late-arriving but colourful figure on the British film scene.

BIBLIOG: Autobiography (with Barry Turner), *East End, West End*, 1990.

Delgado, Roger (*b* London, 1918 – *d* Turkey, 1973). Actor. Typically cast in sinister 'foreign' roles, this Cockney-born son of a Spanish father and French mother made 30 films over two decades, playing 'nasty spy' (*Storm over the Nile*, 1955), colonels, policemen and doctors of many nations, and a tong enforcer in *The Terror of the Tongs* (1960). It was the same on TV – he was a villainous Mendoza in *Sir Francis Drake* (1961–62). Killed in car crash.

OTHER BRITISH FILMS INCLUDE: *The Captain's Paradise* (1953), *The Belles of St Trinian's* (1954), *The Battle of the River Plate* (1956), *Sea Fury* (1958), *The Singer not the Song* (1960), *Village of Daughters* (1962), *The Running Man* (1963), *Masquerade* (1965), *Antony and Cleopatra* (1972, UK/Sp/Switz, as Soothsayer).

Del Giudice, Filippo (*b* Trani, Italy, 1892 – *d* Florence, Italy, 1961). Producer. Brought up in Rome, he trained as a lawyer and worked for the Vatican. In 1933 he fled fascist Italy for England and entered films four years later when, with Mario ZAMPI, he founded TWO CITIES. Early successes included the 1939 film version of Terence RATTIGAN's play *French without Tears* and one of the first anti-Nazi films of the war, *Freedom Radio* (1940). But both Del Giudice and Zampi were nonetheless interned as enemy aliens in 1940. Del Giudice managed to negotiate his early release and relaunched Two Cities with the production of Noël COWARD's *In Which We Serve* (1942). Its spectacular success paved the way for some of the most ambitious British films to be made during the war. Del Giudice considered himself to be an 'administrator of talents' rather than a producer. His prestige productions tended to be built around well-known directors, writers or actors, who would be granted an exceptional degree of creative autonomy. For a while this policy made Two Cities the most exciting film company in Britain, but soon cost it its independence. In 1944, to raise the finance for Laurence OLIVIER's risky and very expensive production of *Henry V* (1944), Del Giudice surrendered a controlling interest to the RANK ORGANISATION. Some great successes followed, including *The Way to the Stars* (1945), *Odd Man Out* (1947) and *Hamlet* (1948), but there were also some expensive failures, notably Thorold DICKINSON's *Men of Two Worlds* (1946). As costs mounted, Rank sought to impose increasing control over Two Cities. Unhappy with these restrictions, Del Giudice resigned in 1947 to form a new company, Pilgrim Pictures. Three films were made – the BOULTING brothers' *The Guinea Pig* (1948), Bernard MILES's *Chance of a Lifetime* (1950) and Peter USTINOV's *Private Angelo* (1949) – but they were not box-office successes and Del Giudice struggled to raise finance. He returned to Italy in 1950, and, although he made some comeback attempts, never produced another film. He died on New Year's Eve, 1961.

OTHER BRITISH FILMS INCLUDE: *The Demi-Paradise, The Gentle Sex* (1943), *This Happy Breed, Mr Emmanuel, Tawny Pipit* (1944), *Blithe Spirit* (1945), *Beware of Pity, School for Secrets* (1946), *Vice Versa, The October Man, Fame is the Spur* (1947). Charles Drazin.

Dell, Jeffrey (*b* Shoreham-by-Sea, 1899 – *d* Sussex, 1985). Actor, screenwriter, author. A writer from the 30s, both in Hollywood and the UK, and author of *Nobody Ordered Wolves*, a well-regarded satirical novel of the film industry, Dell tried his hand four times at directing, achieving one minor success with the charming comedy, *Don't Take It to Heart* (1944, + sc). Most of the rest of his career was spent (co-)writing films for the BOULTING brothers, including such institutional satires as *Lucky Jim* (1957). Several films were adapted from his plays, including *Payment Deferred* (1932, US). Was briefly married in the 40s to Jill CRAIGIE, with whom he co-wrote *The Flemish Farm* (1943, + d).

OTHER BRITISH FILMS INCLUDE: (co-sc, unless noted) *Sanders of the River* (1935), *Night Alone* (1938, play), *Spies of the Air* (1939, play), *Freedom Radio* (1940), *The Saint's Vacation* (1941), *Thunder Rock* (1942), *It's Hard to Be Good* (1948, d, sc), *The Dark Man* (1950, d, sc), *Brothers in Law* (1956), *Happy is the Bride* (1957), *Carlton-Browne of the FO* (1958), *A French Mistress*, *Suspect* (1960), *The Family Way* (1966, adapt).

Delta Pictures Housed in the small, one-stage studio in Bushey, Herts, this company made 'QUOTA QUICKIES' in the 30s, often directed by Widgey NEWMAN.

De Marney, Derrick (*b* London, 1906 – *d* London, 1978). Actor. Handsome, vigorous leading man of Irish and French ancestry, on the London stage from 1926 and in films from 1928 (*The Valley of Ghosts, Two Little Drummer Boys*). With brother Terence DE MARNEY, he formed Concanen Productions (named for their mother) and produced wartime shorts, such as *Diary of a Polish Airman* (1942), and several features, including Leslie HOWARD's *The Gentle Sex* (1943, co-p) and *She Shall Have Murder* (1950). As actor, his best-known roles include HITCHCOCK's man-on-the-run in *Young and Innocent* (1937), the sculptor hero in the long-unseen grand Guignol, *Latin Quarter* (1945, + co-p), the dangerous *Uncle Silas* (1947) and Peter CHEYNEY's detective in *Meet Mr Callaghan* (1954), a role he had created on stage (1952).

OTHER BRITISH FILMS INCLUDE: (a, unless noted) *Adventurous Youth* (1929), *The Laughter of Fools* (1933), *The Scarlet Pimpernel* (1935), *Things to Come* (1936), *Victoria the Great* (as Disraeli) (1937), *Dangerous Moonlight* (1941), *The First of the Few* (1942), *Sleeping Car to Trieste* (1948), *No Way Back* (1949, p, co-sc), *Private's Progress* (1956), *The Projected Man* (1966).

De Marney, Terence (*b* London, 1909 – *d* London, 1971). Actor. Brother of Derrick DE MARNEY, whom he resembled and with whom he formed Concanen producing company, for which he starred in *No Way Back* (1949). There was overlap in their careers, including playing Peter CHEYNEY's Slim Callaghan on stage; they fell out when Terence mounted a rival production of a Callaghan saga. His British screen career is less distinctive than Derrick's and he spent over a decade in US films, including *The Silver Chalice* (1952), returning to England for a few films and some TV before his death by railway accident. Also wrote several plays in collaboration, including *Wanted for Murder* (filmed 1946), and was a regular radio performer. Married (2) actress Beryl MEASOR.

OTHER BRITISH FILMS INCLUDE: *The Eternal Feminine* (1931), *Little Napoleon, Eyes of Fate* (1933), *Thunder in the City* (1937), *I Killed the Count* (1939), *They Met in the Dark* (1943), *Dual Alibi* (1947), *Separation* (1967), *The Strange Affair* (1968), *All Neat in Black Stockings* (1969).

Demongeot, Mylène (*b* Nice, France, 1936). Actress. Among her 70 films, Demongeot appeared in several British productions of the 50s and 60s, typically as blonde diversions from the hero's domestic affiliations, as in *Upstairs and Downstairs* (1959), as *au pair*, Ingrid (Sweden, France, it's all the same to 50s' British films), or more ambitiously as Locha, coming between priest and bandit in *The Singer Not the Song* (1960). Her real career lies elsewhere.

OTHER BRITISH FILMS: *It's a Wonderful World* (1956), *Bonjour Tristesse* (1957), *Doctor in Distress* (1963).

Dempster, Austin (*b* 1921 – *d* Surrey, 1975). Cinematographer. Camera operator from the mid 40s, on several films for Herbert WILCOX, which meant working with ace cinematographer Max GREENE, starting with *Piccadilly Incident* (1946); cinematographer from 1968, on *Bedazzled*.

OTHER BRITISH FILMS INCLUDE: (cam op) *They Came to a City* (1944), *Maytime in Mayfair* (1949), *Odette* (1950), *The Beggar's Opera* (1953), *The Bridal Path* (1959), *Tunes of Glory* (1960), *The Queen's Guards* (1961), *Two for the Road* (1966, 2uc); (c) *Otley* (1968), *The Looking Glass War* (1969), *Loot, A Severed Head* (1970), *Tales of Beatrix Potter* (1971), *A Touch of Class* (1972).

Dempster, Hugh (*b* London, 1900 – *d* Chicago, 1987). Actor. On stage from 1920 and films from 1924 (*The Great Well*), usually in supporting roles, often of a blusterous nature: viz, the caught-out philanderer, Oblonsky, in *Anna Karenina* (1948), the besotted Lord Augustus in *The Fan* (1949, US) and the bibulous clubman in *The House Across the Lake* (1954). Toured the US 1957–63 as Pickering in *My Fair Lady*.

OTHER BRITISH FILMS INCLUDE: *The Vanished Hand* (1928), *Blossom Time* (1934), *The Scarlet Pimpernel* (1935), *Bell-Bottom George, He Snoops to Conquer, Heaven Is Round the Corner* (1944), *The Way to the Stars, The Trojan Brothers* (1945), *School for Secrets* (1946), *While the Sun Shines* (1947), *Paul Temple's Triumph* (1950), *Father Brown* (1954), *The Extra Day* (1956), *The Curse of Frankenstein* (1957).

Dempsey, Richard (*b c* 1973) Actor. Guildhall-trained actor/singer who has been very busy on stage since his early teens (with the RSC, 2000) and TV (*Wives and Daughters*, 2000) and has appeared in a few films, including *Prince of Jutland* (1994, UK/Fr/Den/Ger) and *24 Hours in London* (2000).

Denbigh-Russell, Grace Actress. One of those character players who vivify moments in British films: in *Great Expectations* (1946), wispy Denbigh-Russell as Mrs Wopsle asked plaintively 'Why is it the young are never grateful?' at the early Christmas dinner scene – and never appeared again. Much stage and some TV.

OTHER BRITISH FILMS INCLUDE: *My Brother Jonathan, The Small Voice* (1948), *The Dark Man, The Mudlark* (1950), *Lost* (1955), *The Camp on Blood Island* (1957), *The Night We Got the Bird* (1960), *The Young Detectives* (1963, serial x8).

Dench, Dame Judi (*b* York, 1934). Actress. One of the most respected and *liked* actresses of the last third of the 20th century, Dench has been heaped with honours for her stage work, in plays classic and modern, and her TV series – *A Fine Romance* (1981–84), opposite her late husband Michael WILLIAMS, and *As Time Goes By* (1992–2002) – brought her vast new audiences. But, in 1994, she was still saying '. . . filming doesn't come naturally to me, . . . and I don't enjoy it very much'. As the decade wore on, she became in fact a film *star*, 30-odd years after her film debut in Charles CRICHTON's long-forgotten *The Third Secret* (1964). She had huge successes as Cleopatra, Viola, Madame Ranyevskaya and the ordinary housewife in *Pack of Lies* (1983) on stage, on which she first appeared as Ophelia in 1957, but film work remained incidental.

Her early films are hard to see (e.g. *Four in the Morning*, 1965, BAA as promising newcomer) and at least one, Tony RICHARDSON's disastrous *Dead Cert* (1974), is hard to watch, with Dench striding around stables in a red pants-suit. Despite her disclaimers, though, in the 80s she did superb character work: as a flamboyant novelist in *A Room with a View* (1985,

BAA, supp a), a touchingly restrained Nora Doel in *84 Charing Cross Road* (1986, US-financed, BAAn), and a wonderful Mistress Quickly, dirty and tear-stained, in *Henry V* (1989). Then in the 90s, she came to filmgoers' consciousness as never before: as a feminist M in the BOND films, *GoldenEye* (1995), *Tomorrow Never Dies* (1997), *The World Is Not Enough* (1999), and *Die Another Day* (2002) (all UK/US) putting Pierce Bond BROSNAN crisply in his place; as Queen Victoria, her first major starring role in films, in *Mrs Brown* (1997, UK/Ire/US, BAA/a and AAn); her glorious 8-minute stint as Queen Elizabeth in *Shakespeare in Love* (1999, UK/US), for which she won both the AA denied her the year before and a BAA; and *Iris* (2002, UK/US), for which she won a BAA for her playing of Iris Murdoch and should have won another Oscar too. She received the Women in Film and Television Lifetime Achievement Award in 1997.

It is easy when writing about her merely to list the awards, to chart the popularity and the versatility; it is less easy to encapsulate the moments of sheer pleasure – of greatness as a performer in all the media – which are her legacy. The career of this short, pretty, not conventionally beautiful woman, with a faintly husky voice, deserves serious analysis, certainly something better than John Miller's hagiography, *Judi Dench* (1998). She is the mother of actress **Finty Williams**, who has appeared in several films, and the sister of stage actor Jeffery Dench.

OTHER BRITISH FILMS INCLUDE: *A Study in Terror, He Who Rides the Tiger* (1965), *A Midsummer Night's Dream* (1968), *Luther* (1973, UK/Can/US), *Wetherby* (1985, BAAn), *The Angelic Conversation* (1985, voice), *A Handful of Dust* (1987), *Jack and Sarah* (1995, UK/Fr), *Hamlet* (1996, US/UK, as Hecuba!), *Tea with Mussolini* (1999), *Into the Arms of Strangers* (2000, UK/US, doc, narr) *Therese Raquin* (2001).

Denham Studios By 1935 Alexander KORDA, the Hungarian émigré, was a film impresario of international stature who had apparently rejuvenated England's film industry with his productions of *The Private Life of Henry VIII* (1933) and *The Scarlet Pimpernel* (1935). Korda capitalised on his box-office success by securing funding from the Prudential Assurance Company to underwrite future productions and finance the construction of his own studio. Building the massive Denham Studios started in late summer 1935 on a 165-acre site near Denham village in Buckinghamshire. The complex was designed by Jack Okey, who had been responsible for the First National and Paramount Studios in Hollywood.

The largest production facility in the country opened in May 1936, boasting seven sound stages, workshops for every craft, restaurants and dressing-rooms fit for Hollywood stars and a new TECHNICOLOR laboratory. This was to be a dream factory whose movies would have 'prestige, pomp, magic and madness', according to KORDA. Unfortunately, many believed the 'madness' was in actually building the studios so large in the first place and taking on the financial burden of 2,000 employees. The design of the studios was also criticised, with its ribbon layout requiring lengthy walks between departments that were next-door neighbours in other facilities.

Korda was hard pressed to utilise the studios fully even with tenant producers supplementing his own productions. It was a non-Korda film which was first on the floor at Denham – Max SCHACH's *Southern Roses* (1936) – although Korda's *The Ghost Goes West* (1935), *Things to Come* and *The Man Who Could Work Miracles* (1936) had all used the back-lot for exteriors while the studios were being finished. *Knight Without Armour* (1937) was the kind of extravagant 'Hollywood' style picture

Korda wanted to make at Denham and Marlene DIETRICH's temporary residence at the studios kept Denham in the spotlight. In reality, however, there were too few films being made there, and with competition from PINEWOOD, opened in September 1936, and the fallout from the infamous film companies' 'crash' of 1937, Prudential were considering winding up the operation as early as April of that year. Within months, Prudential effectively operated Denham as Korda relinquished control and saw his beloved studios merged with RANK's Pinewood Studios in 1939.

Pictures continued to be made at Denham, including some of Britain's most notable films, but they were not Korda pictures and under corporate control there was little effort expended to ensure the survival of Denham Studios. For a man seemingly able to reinvent himself and relaunch his career at will the loss of Denham Studios was a crushing blow nonetheless. DISNEY's *Robin Hood* (1952) brought the curtain down on Denham Studios' role as a major full-time film studio and the site served various commercial uses before being demolished for an industrial park.

Other films of note made at Denham Studios include *Rembrandt* (1936), *A Yank at Oxford* (1937), *South Riding* (1938), *Thief of Baghdad* (partial) (1940), *In Which We Serve* (1942), *The Life and Death of Colonel Blimp* (1943), and *Brief Encounter* (partial) (1945). Martin Stockham.

Denham, Maurice (*b* Beckenham, 1909 – *d* London, 2002). Actor. One of the great British character players, with over 100 films to his credit, as many TV roles (most famously as Judi DENCH's father in *Talking to a Stranger*, 1966) and a great deal of theatre, where he began in 1934, giving up a career as an engineer. He became famous on RADIO for *ITMA*, before WW2 army service, and post-war for *Much-Binding-in-the-Marsh*. His bald head and invincibly intelligent look became a fixture in British films for 50 years, often as officials, chilly (the force-feeding doctor in *Fame Is the Spur* (1947) or benign (Major Fraser in *Blanche Fury*, 1947), and military men of every rank, but he could also be shifty as in *Street Corner* (1953), seriously sinister as the child molester in *Eight O'Clock Walk* (1954), despairing as Blore in *The Purple Plain* (1954, BAAn) and defeated as Peggy ASHCROFT's husband in *Sunday Bloody Sunday* (1971), and marvellously funny, as, say, the craven vicar in *Once Upon a Dream*, the yokel policeman in *Poet's Pub*, or, above all, as the mad Nazi spy at large in rural England in *It's Not Cricket* (all 1949). His is a gallery with few equals. Awarded OBE, 1992.

OTHER BRITISH FILMS: *The Upturned Glass, Dear Murderer* (scenes cut), *They Made Me a Fugitive, Take My Life, Jassy, Captain Boycott, The Man Within, The End of the River, Holiday Camp* (1947), *Daybreak, Look Before You Love, London Belongs to Me, Here Come the Huggetts, Escape, Easy Money, Quartet, The Blind Goddess, My Brother's Keeper, Oliver Twist, Miranda* (1948), *Traveller's Joy, The Spider and the Fly, Landfall, Don't Ever Leave Me, A Boy, a Girl and a Bike, The Blue Lagoon, Madness of the Heart* (1949), *No Highway* (1951), *The Million Pound Note, Malta Story, Time Bomb, The Net* (1953), *The Power to Fly* (short), *Carrington VC, Animal Farm* (voice) (1954), *Simon and Laura, Doctor at Sea* (1955), *Checkpoint, Toto and the Poachers* (1956), *Man With a Dog* (short), *Night of the Demon, Barnacle Bill* (1957), *The Captain's Table* (1958), *Our Man in Havana* (1959), *Two Way Stretch, Sink the Bismarck!* (1960), *The Mark, Invasion Quartet, The Last Rhino, The Greengage Summer* (1961), *HMS Defiant, Paranoiac* (1962), *The King's Breakfast* (short), *The Set-Up* (1963), *Downfall, The 7th Dawn* (US/UK), *The Uncle, Hysteria* (1964), *Operation Crossbow* (UK/It), *The Night Caller, The Legend of Young Dick Turpin, The Heroes of Telemark, Those Magnificent Men . . . , The Nanny, The Alphabet Murders* (1965), *Torture Garden, The Long*

Duel, Danger Route, Attack on the Iron Coast (UK/US) (1967), *Negatives, The Best House in London* (1968), *A Touch of Love, Some Girls Do* (1969), *The Virgin and the Gypsy, Countess Dracula* (1970), *Luther* (UK/Can/US), *The Day of the Jackal* (UK/Fr) (1973), *Shout at the Devil* (1976), *The Enchanted Sail* (1977, short), *Recluse* (1979, short), *The Chain* (1984), *Mr Love* (1985), *The Last Journey of Robert Rylands* (1996, UK/Sp).

Denham, Reginald (*b* London, 1894 – *d* Englewood, New Jersey, 1983). Director, dramatist. Essentially a man of the theatre, initially as actor from 1913, then as writer and director, most famously co-authoring *Ladies in Retirement* (1939), filmed in Hollywood, 1941, and, as *The Mad Room*, 1969. In the 30s, he directed, sometimes produced and wrote about 25 films, including many 'QUOTA QUICKIES'. Theatre claimed him in the 40s and 50s, but he returned to co-direct *Anna of Brooklyn* (1958, US/It). Married (1 of 3) actress Moyna McGill (1919–24) and (2) Mary NEWLAND who starred in two of his films – the thrillers, *Death at Broadcasting House* (1934) and *The Silent Passenger* (1935).

OTHER BRITISH FILMS INCLUDE: (d, unless noted) *Nothing Else Matters* (1920, a), *Man of Mayfair* (add dial), *These Charming People* (dial consultant) (1931), *Ebb Tide* (1932, co-sc), *The Primrose Path* (+ p), *Lucky Loser, Brides to Be* (+ p) (1934), *Lucky Days* (1935), *Kate Plus Ten* (1938), *Trunk Crime* (play), *Blind Folly* (1939).
BIBLIOG: Autobiography, *Stars in My Hair*, 1958.

Denis, Armand (*b* Brussels, 1897 – *d* Langta, Kenya, 1971) and **Denis, Michaela** (*b* London, 1914 – *d* Kenya, 2003). Explorers and producers who made two films for EALING from their travels: *Under the Southern Cross* (1954), *Beneath the Barrier Reef* (1955). Later became well-known TV personalities.

Denison, Michael (*b* Doncaster, 1915 – *d* Amersham, 1998). Actor. Invariably gentlemanly leading man, Harrow- and Oxford-educated Denison had a popular run of films for a decade, 1947–57. Theatre-trained at Webber-Douglas School, he was on stage from 1938, had two brief film roles pre-war, was in army intelligence 1940–46, after which he re-embarked on a 50-year career in the theatre, often co-starring with his wife, Dulcie GRAY. A chance recollection by director Harold FRENCH brought him the starring role opposite Gray in *My Brother Jonathan*, which proved the British box-office hit of 1948, and they were promoted as a team in the popular romance, *The Glass Mountain* (1948), and in *The Franchise Affair* (1950), *There Was a Young Lady* (1953) and *Angels One Five* (1952), though not romantically linked in the latter. He also held his own in a dream cast for Anthony ASQUITH's *The Importance of Being Earnest* (1952) as Algernon. He had a successful TV series in/as *Boyd Q.C.* (1956–65), but his heart was really in the theatre and he and Gray were appearing in Peter Hall's production of *An Ideal Husband*, in London and New York, for several years from 1992. In 1992, he suddenly reappeared in films, as an elderly don in *Shadowlands* (UK/US), revealing a new screen authority. His versatility was displayed more amply on stage; on screen, in the more limited range available to him, he was an intelligent, wholly likeable performer. He was active in Equity, serving as vice-president, 1952–53 and 1961–63, and was the author of two very engaging volumes of memoirs, *Overture and Beginners* (1973) and *Double Act* (1985). He and Gray, married for nearly 60 years, were each awarded the CBE in 1983.

OTHER BRITISH FILMS: *Inspector Hornleigh on Holiday* (1939, unc), *Tilly of Bloomsbury* (1940), *Hungry Hill* (1947), *The Blind Goddess* (1948), *Landfall* (1949), *The Magic Box* (1951), *Tall Headlines* (1952),

Contraband – Spain (1955), *The Truth about Women* (1957), *Faces in the Dark* (1960), *Dark River* (1990).

Dennis, John Sound recordist. In films from 1930 in the sound departments at ELSTREE and BRITISH AND DOMINIONS STUDIOS, then at PINEWOOD from its earliest days, as well as several other studios. He worked subsequently for such directors as Leslie HOWARD (*The First of the Few*, 1942), Anthony ASQUITH (*The Browning Version*, 1951) and Basil DEARDEN (*Khartoum*, 1968). Appointed chief production mixer at Pinewood in 1946; it is now difficult to determine his input for individual films.

OTHER BRITISH FILMS INCLUDE (sd mixer/recordist, prod mixer): *Come Out of the Pantry* (1935), *When Knights Were Bold* (1936), *The Arsenal Stadium Mystery* (1939), *Pimpernel Smith* (1941), *The Silver Fleet* (1943), *Henry V* (1944), *Black Narcissus* (1947), *The Woman in Question* (1950), *The Importance of Being Earnest* (1952), *Mad About Men* (1954), *Value for Money* (1955), *Swiss Family Robinson* (1960), *Dr No* (1962), *The Assassination Bureau* (1968).

Densham, Dennis and **Ray** (*b* London, 1921) Cinematographers. Twins who entered the industry in the 30s, Dennis as clapper boy who made his way up by 1940 to camera operator for CROWN FILM UNIT on such films as *Fires Were Started* (1943) and as cinematographer on GROUP 3 features like *Make Me An Offer!* (1954). Ray became assistant cameraman at EALING, and later worked mainly on DOCUMENTARIES and SHORT FILMS, often with director Denis KAVANAGH. Ray died in 2000.

OTHER BRITISH FILMS INCLUDE: (Dennis) Shorts: *By Sea and Land* (1944), *Faster than Sound* (1949), *Eagles of the Fleet* (1950), *Trouble with Junia* (1967); Features: *Man of Africa* (1953), *Child's Play* (1954), *Devil on Horseback* (1954). (Ray) *Spotlight on Glamour* (short), *Eyes That Kill* (1947), *Soho Conspiracy* (1950), *Commando – The Story of the Green Beret* (1952, doc).

Dent, Alan (*b* Ayr, 1905). Writer. Worked as film (and literary and drama) critic for various upmarket publications, including *Tatler* and *Illustrated London News*, before and after war service (1943–45), and was text editor and adviser on OLIVIER's SHAKESPEARE films, *Henry V* (1944), *Hamlet* (1948), and *Richard III* (1955), models of careful pruning and cinematic rethinking. He was also James AGATE's secretary and protégé.

Denton, Geoffrey (*b* Eltham). Actor. General purpose character player, several times as policemen and a convincingly corrupt businessman in *Touch of Death* (1962).

OTHER BRITISH FILMS INCLUDE: *Adam and Evelyne* (1949), *The Net* (1953), *The Horrors of the Black Museum* (1959), *The Breaking Point* (1961), *The Mind Benders* (1963), *A Dandy in Aspic* (1968), *Nothing But the Night* (1972).

De Rouen, Reed (*b* Green Bay, Wisconsin, 1921). Actor. Tough-acting character player, usually in low-budget CRIME MOVIES, often with director Charles SAUNDERS, for whom he played a brutal gang boss in *The Naked Fury* (1959). Also wrote stories for *The Six Men* (+ a) and *Miss Robin Hood* (1952).

OTHER BRITISH FILMS INCLUDE: *The Strangers Came* (1949), *Top Secret* (1952), *Sea Devils* (1953), *The Sheriff of Fractured Jaw* (1958), *There Was a Crooked Man* (1960), *The Traitors* (1962), *Billion Dollar Brain* (1967), *Baxter!* (1972).

De Sarigny, Peter (*b* South Africa, 1911). Producer. Entered industry in 1936, gaining experience in production before RAF service (1940–46), after which he joined the BOULTING brothers as associate producer on *Fame Is the Spur* (1947). In the 50s, he produced several films for RANK.

OTHER BRITISH FILMS: *Pastor Hall* (1940, ass d); (assoc p) *Brighton Rock* (1947), *Seven Days to Noon* (1950); (p) *Malta Story* (1953, + co-sc), *Simba* (1955), *True as a Turtle* (1956), *Never Let Go* (1960, + story), *Waltz of the Toreadors* (1962).

Desmond, Florence (*b* London, 1905 – *d* Guildford, 1993). Actress. Though popular as a leading lady in the 30s, Desmond's real claim to fame was as a brilliant impersonator of stage and screen stars. Trained as a dancer, on stage from 1915, in revue and cabaret from 1925, she made one Hollywood film, *Mr Skitch* (1933), and nearly 20 in Britain, often playing characters called Flo or Florrie, perhaps an acknowledgment of her standing. She appeared with Gracie FIELDS in *Sally in Our Alley* (1931), as spoilt Florrie, and as George FORMBY's leading lady in *No Limit* (1935), exhibiting a cheery blonde chirpiness in her film persona. Post-war, she made only three more films: *Three Came Home* (1950, US), *Charley Moon* (1956) and *Some Girls Do* (1969), none of which hinted at the star she had been – and still was in cabaret and on stage, as in *Auntie Mame* (1958) with Beatrice LILLIE.

OTHER BRITISH FILMS INCLUDE: *Road to Fortune* (1930), *Murder on the Second Floor*, *High Society* (1932), *Radio Parade*, *My Lucky Star* (1933), *Gay Love* (1934), *Accused* (1936), *Kicking the Moon Around* (1938), *Hoots Mon!* (1939).

BIBLIOG: Autobiography, *Florence Desmond*, 1953.

Desmonde, Jerry (*b* Middlesbrough, 1908 – *d* London, 1967). Actor. After long experience on the MUSIC-HALL stage, he came to the screen with his theatre partner Sid FIELD in the 1946 disaster, *London Town*, and was Field's foil again in *Cardboard Cavalier* (1949). His long-nosed sniffiness made him an equally good straight man for Norman WISDOM in seven films, and he became a household name for such TV shows as *The $64,000 Question* (1956–58), having appeared in TV demonstration programmes in 1931.

OTHER BRITISH FILMS INCLUDE: *The Perfect Woman* (1949), *Trouble in Store* (1953), *Man of the Moment* (1955), *Up in the World* (1956), *Just My Luck, A King in New York* (1957), *Follow a Star* (1959), *Carry On Regardless* (1961), *A Kind of Loving* (1962), *A Stitch in Time* (1963), *The Beauty Jungle* (1964), *The Early Bird* (1965).

Desni, Tamara (*b* Kharkov, Russia, 1913). Actress. Darkly beautiful Russian-born leading lady in Britain from 1932, then in a run of genre films, starting with *Falling for You* (1933). There is a touch of the sexy temptress about her, well displayed in such films as *Fire Over England* and *The Squeaker* (1937). Married actors (1) Bruce SETON and (2) Raymond LOVELL.

OTHER BRITISH FILMS INCLUDE: *Jack Ahoy!* (1934), *Love in Exile* (1936), *Diplomatic Lover* (1939), *Flight from Folly* (1945), *Send for Paul Temple* (1946), *The Hills of Donegal* (1947), *Dick Barton at Bay* (1950).

Desny, Ivan (*b* Peking, 1922). Actor. China-born to Russian parents but raised in Paris and interned by the Germans during WW2, tall, distinguished Desny came to Britain to play Ann TODD's unlucky lover in *Madeleine* (1949), and in a very long international (mainly German) career, including Ophuls's sublime *Lola Montès* (1955), appeared in a half-dozen further British films.

OTHER BRITISH FILMS INCLUDE: *Anastasia* (1956), *Number Six* (1962), *Mayerling* (1968), *The Adventures of Gerard* (1970, UK/It/Switz), *Who?* (1974, UK/Ger), *Paper Tiger* (1974).

De Souza, Edward (*b* Hull, 1932). Actor. Dark-haired, RADA-trained stage actor who appeared in a dozen films from the early 60s, starting with *The Roman Spring of Mrs Stone* (1961) and starring in *The Phantom of the Opera* (1962) as romantic lead. Played Joseph Bonaparte in TV's *Napoleon in Love* (1974).

OTHER BRITISH FILMS INCLUDE: *The Kiss of the Vampire* (1962), *The Main Chance* (1964), *The Spy Who Loved Me* (1977), *Home Before Midnight*, *The Thirty Nine Steps* (1978), *The Return of the Soldier* (1982), *Jane Eyre* (1996, UK/Fr/It/US).

detective films Think of 'detective' in a Hollywood context and one thinks of the hardboiled private eye defying crooks and cops in his quest for truth down mean urban streets, an image that British cinema at best has only parodied, as in Stephen FREARS's *Gumshoe* (1971).The British version tends to take the form of amateur sleuth, whether it be Margaret RUTHERFORD's Miss Marple or Alec GUINNESS's Father Brown or even Hermione BADDELEY's Ida in *Brighton Rock* (1947), tenaciously clinging to notions of right and wrong in a world about to be consumed by evil. Alastair SIM gave the characterisation his inimitable twist of eccentricity in films such as *Green for Danger* (1946) and *An Inspector Calls* (1954). Stanley BAKER offered sharp characterisations of police detectives with a class chip on their shoulder in Joseph LOSEY's *Blind Date* and Val GUEST's *Hell is a City* (1959), roles which undermined the implicit complacency of the detective hero – our 'interpreter of coincidence and violence', as Gavin LAMBERT has termed him – and showed men brutalised by the world they had to deal with. However, the aristocratic gentleman detective, who uses his superior skills of reasoning to unmask a villain, remains a popular British prototype, embodied to perfection in the character of SHERLOCK HOLMES. He has been incarnated many times on screen and never better than by ROBERT STEPHENS in Billy Wilder's *The Private Life of Sherlock Holmes* (1970), an affectionate exploration of the gap between legend and reality in which the master detective's powers of rational deduction are revealed as precarious, even tragic, compensation for his wounded romanticism. Neil Sinyard.

De Toth, André (*b* Mako, Hungary, 1913 – *d* Los Angeles, 2002). Director, A maverick Hollywood director from 1943, who directed his first films in Hungary in 1939. At his best with *film noir* and adult Westerns, de Toth was responsible for *The Two-Headed Spy* (1958), a sometimes sadistic study of the Nazi terror, and the very dark and violent *Play Dirty* (1968). Had worked earlier for director Zoltán KORDA on *Elephant Boy* (1937), *The Drum* (1938) and *The Four Feathers* (1939) and as second unit director on *Jungle Book* (1942); also worked with Michael POWELL on *The Thief of Baghdad* (1940), as associate director (unc) on *Lawrence of Arabia* (1962), as director of the flying sequences on *Superman* (1978), and as producer of *Billion Dollar Brain* (1967). AS.

Deutsch, David (*b* Birmingham, 1926 – *d* London, 1992). Producer. Son of Oscar DEUTSCH, in films from 1949 as assistant editor, on such films as *Traveller's Joy* (1949) and *The Intruder* (1953), then as assistant to Sydney BOX on such films as *The Prisoner* (1955), before becoming a producer on *Blind Date* (1959).

OTHER BRITISH FILMS INCLUDE (p, unless noted): *High Tide at Noon*, *The One That Got Away* (1957, assoc p), *Floods of Fear* (1958, assoc p), *Play It Cool* (1962), *Nothing But the Best* (1964), *Catch Us If You Can* (1965), *Interlude* (1968), *A Day in the Death of Joe Egg* (1970), *The Day of the Jackal* (1973, co-p).

Deutsch, Oscar (*b* Birmingham, 1893 – *d* 1941). Exhibitor. The founder of the Odeon cinema circuit was the son of a Hungarian emigrant who had prospered in scrap metal. Entered film industry in the 20s with school friends Michael

BALCON and Victor SAVILLE, who went into production, while Deutsch became a prominent exhibitor, at first shrewdly capitalising on the value of cinemas to provincial businessmen. By 1933, he had 26 cinemas, called Odeons, alleged to be an acronym for 'Oscar Deutsch Entertains Our Nation', and by 1937 there were 250, with the Leicester Square Odeon opened as the flagship. The Odeons were famously stylish and comfortable, catering to the increased middle-class respectability of the cinema, and bringing the idea of the 'picture palace' to Britain. Unlike the other two big circuits, ABC and GAUMONT–BRITISH, Odeon was not affiliated with production. When Deutsch died of cancer, his accountant, John DAVIS, became joint, then sole, managing director. Deutsch's widow sold out to J. Arthur RANK, thus helping cement his pre-eminent position in the British film industry.

Devereaux, Ed (*b* Australia, 1925). Actor. Supporting actor who has made numerous films in Britain but has remained intransigently Australian in his rugged looks and bearing. On stage from childhood, then much in musical theatre, he played small roles in Australian films, usually made by British companies, and including *Eureka Stockade* (1949) and *The Shiralee* (1957 – his part was shot in London). In British films from 1958, he appeared in five 'CARRY ONS', and many other popular comedies such as *The Captain's Table* (1958), *The Wrong Arm of the Law* (1962), and, quite touchingly, as David HEMMING's sorely tried father in the teen musical, *Live It Up* (1963). On TV, he was an authoritative Beaverbrook, another tough colonial, in *Edward and Mrs Simpson* (1978).

OTHER BRITISH FILMS INCLUDE: *Carry On Sergeant, . . . Nurse* (1958), *Watch Your Stern* (1960), *Carry On Regardless, Very Important Person* (1961), *Mix Me a Person, Carry on Cruising* (1962), *Carry On Jack* (1964), *Bless This House* (1972), *I Bought a Vampire Motorcycle* (1990).

Deverell, John (*b* 1880 – *d* Haywards Heath, 1965). Actor. Stage actor from 1900 who appeared as upper-class asses (*Above Rubies*, 1932) and professionals (the Judge in *Marry the Girl*, 1935) in a dozen 30s supporting roles.

OTHER BRITISH FILMS INCLUDE: *John Forrest Finds Himself* (1920), *Children of Chance* (1930), *Alibi* (1931), *The Path of Glory, The King of Paris* (1934), *The Divine Spark* (1935), *The Street Singer* (1937), *Incident in Shanghai* (1938).

Devine, George (*b* London, 1910 – *d* London, 1966). Actor. Hugely important figure in 20th century stage history in Britain, Oxford-educated Devine merely dabbled with the screen, where he made most impression in his last film, *Tom Jones* (1963), as Squire Allworthy. Married Sophia Harris of MOTLEY, the firm of stage designers for whom Devine was secretary and manager (1932–35). He was appointed Artistic Director of the English Stage Company at the Royal Court Theatre in 1955, ushering in a period of crucial change with *Look Back in Anger* (1956), in the film version of which he played the small role of the doctor.

OTHER BRITISH FILMS: *The Silent Battle* (1939), *The Card* (1952), *The Million Pound Note, The Beggar's Opera* (1953), *Time Without Pity* (1957).

Devlin, J.G. (*b* Belfast, 1907 – *d* Belfast, 1991) Actor. Irish character player of stage and TV who came to the screen when he was 50 in the Belfast-set *Jacqueline* (1956) and was last in *Far and Away* (1992, US/Ire).

OTHER BRITISH FILMS INCLUDE: *The Rising of the Moon* (1957), *Darby O'Gill and the Little People* (1959), *Johnny Nobody* (1960), *The Frightened City* (1961), *I Thank a Fool* (1962), *The Comedy Man* (1963), *The Reckoning* (1969), *The Alf Garnett Saga* (1972), *Sir Henry at Rawlinson*

End (1980), *No Surrender* (1985), *The Raggedy Rawney* (1988), *The Miracle* (1991).

Devlin, William (*b* Aberdeen, 1911 – *d* Somerset, 1987). Actor. Oxford-educated stage actor who had Old Vic, Stratford and Abbey Theatre seasons and made a few films either side of WW2 service, 1939–45, usually in dignified roles.

BRITISH FILMS INCLUDE: *The Mill on the Floss, Concerning Mr Martin* (1937), *Jamaica Inn* (1939), *Treasure Island* (1950), *Blood of the Vampire* (1958), *Oscar Wilde* (1960), *The Shuttered Room* (1966).

Dew, Desmond (*b* 1912). Sound recordist. Dew's name is on the credits for some of the most significant films of the mid 40s, when he worked for POWELL (*A Canterbury Tale*, 1944), ASQUITH (*The Demi-Paradise*, 1943), LEAN (*Brief Encounter*, 1945) and REED (*Odd Man Out*, 1947). Educated at Manchester University and entered films in 1935, working on *Things to Come* (1936).

OTHER BRITISH FILMS INCLUDE: *In Which We Serve* (1942), *The Silver Fleet, The Life and Death of Colonel Blimp* (1943), *The Way Ahead, This Happy Breed, Tawny Pipit, Henry V* (1944), *Blithe Spirit, Great Day, Caesar and Cleopatra, The Way to the Stars* (1945), *Great Expectations, Gaiety George* (1946), *The October Man, Blanche Fury, Uncle Silas* (1947), *Hamlet, Idol of Paris, So Evil My Love, Trottie True, The Red Shoes* (1948), *The Chiltern Hundreds* (1949).

Dewhurst, George W. Actor, director, screenwriter. A stage actor with the Liverpool Rep and in the West End, Dewhurst was an actor on screen from 1918 to 1947, and a screenwriter from 1920 to 1947. In 1924, he conceived the notion to produce films in Blackpool, and, four years later, formed Lancashire Screen Productions. As a director, he made *A Sister to Assist 'Er*, based on the play by John le Breton and the MUSIC HALL sketch by Fred EMNEY, five times, in 1922, 1927, 1930, 1938, and 1948, each time contributing the screenplay.

OTHER BRITISH FILMS INCLUDE: (d) *The Homemaker* (+ p) (1918), *A Great Coup* (1919), *The Shadow Between* (1920, + sc), *Lonesome Farm, The Doubles* (1922), *The Uninvited Guest* (1923, + p, sc), *What the Butler Saw* (1924, + p, sc), *Bright Young Things* (1927, sc). AS.

De Wolfe Music Library In Wardour Street, established in 1909, it is reputed to have the world's largest collection of 'ready canned' film music.

De Wolff, Francis (*b* Southminster, Essex, 1913 – *d* 1984). Actor. Bulky, black-bearded character actor of often awesome mien, unusually benign as Squire Brown in *Tom Brown's Schooldays* (1951), comically villainous as the blustering, would-be takeover-merchant in *The Smallest Show on Earth* (1957). Lent his burly, RADA-trained presence to adventure films, comedies, musicals, thrillers, and horror items like *The Man Who Could Cheat Death* (1959), often playing sinister foreigners.

OTHER BRITISH FILMS INCLUDE: *Flame in the Heather* (1935), *Fire Over England* (1937), *Trottie True* (1948), *Under Capricorn* (1949), *Treasure Island* (1950), *Scrooge* (1951), *Ivanhoe* (1952), *Moulin Rouge, The Kidnappers* (1953), *King's Rhapsody, Geordie* (1955), *The Hound of the Baskervilles* (1959), *The Two Faces of Dr Jekyll* (1960), *The Siege of the Saxons, The Three Lives of Thomasina, From Russia With Love* (1963), *Carry On Cleo, The Black Torment* (1964), *Licensed to Kill* (1965), *Sinful Davey* (1968).

Dewsbury, Ralph (*b* 1881 – *d* 1921). Director. Co-founder in 1913 of LONDON FILM COMPANY and its joint managing director until 1916 when he joined the Royal Flying Corps. Directed five films for London – *The King's Outcast, Whoso Diggeth a Pit* (1915), *His Daughter's Dilemma, Partners at Last, and The Man in Motley* (1916) – and returned from active duty in 1917 to direct one more, *Everybody's Business*. His last film as director and producer was *The Golden Dawn* (1921). AS.

Dickens and British silent cinema Thomas BENTLEY is the British director most closely associated with the many silent screen ADAPTATIONS of the works of Charles Dickens (*b* Landford, Portsmouth, 1812 – *d* Gad's Hill, nr Rochester, 1870), and his *Oliver Twist* (1912) was the first British feature film. In all, there are at least 99 silent film adaptations from Dickens worldwide, beginning with *Death of Nancy Sykes*, filmed by the American Mutoscope Company in 1897, and ending with Herbert WILCOX's superior production of *The Only Way* (1925), starring Sir John MARTIN-HARVEY in his renowned theatrical version of *A Tale of Two Cities*. Other key British Dickens films include: R.W. PAUL's *Scrooge, or Marley's Ghost* (1901), Bentley's *David Copperfield* (1913) and *Barnaby Rudge* (1915), the Vitagraph series of scenes from *Pickwick Papers* (1913), and Maurice ELVEY's *Bleak House* (1920). AS.

Dickens and British sound cinema Dickens's novels have always attracted British film-makers. Nevertheless, after a century of Dickens ADAPTATIONS, two films dominate: *Great Expectations* (1946) and *Oliver Twist* (1948), both directed by David LEAN, who captured something essential about the novelist's mastery of narrative, complexity of character and criticism of society. Both contained unforgettable scenes of Dickensian nightmare – the opening graveyard scene of *Great Expectations*, where Pip encounters the escaped convict; the murder of Nancy in *Oliver Twist*, whose horror is implied by the frantic efforts of Sykes's dog to get out of the room. No other Dickens film can match them: indeed British film has rarely been Dickensian. His social rage and range, the believable extravagance of characterisation, the surreal vision and storytelling ingenuity – in other words, the Dickens who influenced Griffith, entranced Eisenstein and moved Chaplin – are qualities that have mostly eluded directors, who have rendered him as a tepid classic who tells a good yarn. Nevertheless, there have been some worthwhile attempts, including *The Old Curiosity Shop* (1934), EALING's *Nicholas Nickleby* (1947), *Scrooge* (1951), starring Alastair SIM, *A Tale of Two Cities* (1958), with Dirk BOGARDE as hero, Carol REED's Oscar-winning *Oliver!* (1968), and, most remarkably, Christine EDZARD's six-hour *Little Dorrit* (1987). Neil Sinyard.

Dickinson, Desmond (*b* London, 1902 – *d* Surrey, 1986). Cinematographer. One of the most prolific and distinguished cameramen in British film, Dickinson entered films in 1919, graduated to being chief cameraman for STOLL PICTURES in 1928, making several dozen low-budget films, mainly at CRICKLEWOOD STUDIOS. During WW2 he made DOCUMENTARIES for the MOI, and became involved again with Thorold DICKINSON, for whom he had photographed *The Arsenal Stadium Mystery* (1939) and documentary short, *Westward Ho!* (1940), on the ambitious feature, *Men of Two Worlds* (1946). Much of this was shot in Tanganyika, under very difficult lighting conditions, and much had to be recreated in the studios. This film and OLIVIER's *Hamlet* (1948) put Dickinson into the top end of his field: the TECHNICOLOR challenges of *Men of Two Worlds* were scarcely more demanding than the fluidly tracking, depth-of-field effect Olivier wanted. He won the Venice Film Festival award and the BAA for *Hamlet*.

During the next ten years, he moved easily between colour and black-and-white, as films like *The Rocking Horse Winner*

(1949), with its hard contrasts, and *The Importance of Being Earnest* (1952), a triumph of brightly sunny artifice, testify. He continued to work until the mid 70s, but the assignments generally grew less stimulating, including some visually uninspired Miss Marple thrillers (*Murder Most Foul, Murder Ahoy*, 1964) and a batch of unmemorable horror films. To a violent urban thriller, *The Frightened City* (1961), he brought an edgy grey realism.

OTHER BRITISH FILMS: (c, unless noted): *A Woman Redeemed* (1927, ass c), *The Price of Divorce* (1928), *COD – A Mellow Drama* (1929, co-d), *Such Is the Law* (1930), *Other People's Sins, The Great Gay Road* (1931), *Here's George, Threads* (1932), *Love's Old Sweet Song, Dick Turpin, Daughters of Today, Commissionaire* (1933), *Song at Eventide, Danny Boy, Romance in Rhythm, Grand Prix* (1934), *Variety, A Real Bloke, City of Beautiful Nonsense, Strictly Illegal, Barnacle Bill, Cock o' the North, The Small Man* (1935), *King of Hearts, Lieutenant Daring, RN, Stars on Parade, Sunshine Ahead* (1936), *Song of the Forge, Holiday's End* (1937), *Take Off That Hat, Scruffy, Chips* (1938), *The Door With Seven Locks, Yesterday Is Over Your Shoulder* (doc) (1940), *Her Father's Daughter* (1941, short, d), *They Flew Alone, Secret Mission* (1942, fx), *Thursday's Child* (1943), *Hungry Hill* (1947), *The History of Mr Polly* (1948), *Madness of the Heart* (1949), *The Woman in Question, Morning Departure* (1950), *The Browning Version, Encore* (1951), *Meet Me Tonight* (1952), *Meet Mr Lucifer, The Net, The Man Between* (1953), *Carrington VC* (1954), *The Last Man to Hang?, The Black Tent* (1956), *Action of the Tiger, Fire Down Below* (1957), *Orders to Kill, Intent to Kill* (1958), *The Horrors of the Black Museum* (1959), *Foxhole in Cairo, The City of the Dead, Moment of Danger, Konga, The Hands of Orlac* (UK/Fr) (1960), *Mary Had a Little . . . , The Devil's Daffodil* (UK/Ger) (1961), *Two and Two Make Six, Sparrows Can't Sing* (1962), *Cairo* (1963), *A Study in Terror, The Alphabet Murders, Dr Zhivago* (UK/US, 2uc) (1965), *Berserk!, Baby Love* (1967), *Decline and Fall . . .* (1968), *Crooks and Coronets* (1969), *Trog, The Beast in the Cellar, Doctors Wear Scarlet* (1970), *Whoever Slew Auntie Roo?, Nobody Ordered Love, The Fiend, Burke & Hare* (1971), *Tower of Evil* (1972, UK/US), *The Man from Nowhere* (1976).

Dickinson, Thorold (*b* Bristol, 1903 – *d* Oxford, 1984). Director. Dickinson, with ASQUITH, GRIERSON, and CAVALCANTI, belonged to a generation whose careers were beset by industry crises, prejudices, and a World War. His contribution to cinema was more substantial than his rare, albeit prestigious, screen credits suggest. Entering the industry in 1925, as French interpreter to George PEARSON, he became Chief Editor at ATP (forerunner of EALING STUDIOS), where, appalled by industry working conditions, he instigated the trade union coup which installed a dynamic leadership, and remained vice-President of the ACT until 1953.

His directorial career began with *The High Command* (1937), a murder mystery ranging from the IRA to the colonial establishment in West Africa. After actuality films for the Spanish Republican cause, he resumed his career with *The Arsenal Stadium Mystery*, an enjoyable 'B' FILM (1939), and then enjoyed critical and commercial success with *Gaslight* (1940), the co-originator of the COSTUME MELODRAMA cycle pursued by GAINSBOROUGH. *The Prime Minister* (1941), with John GIELGUD as Disraeli, made a historical parallel with Britain's lone stand, through 1940–41, against Fascist expansionism. For the MOI, the War Office, and the Army, his films ranged from *Yesterday Is Over Your Shoulder*, which 'starred' the first rude word on British screens ('Bugger the neighbours!'), to *The Next of Kin* (1942), a military training film whose impact on service personnel induced Churchill to recommend its wider release; it gratified both public taste for Hitchcockian suspense (but with an *un*happy end), and the intellectuals' taste for the 'semi-documentary' aesthetic (effectively, neo-realism). After reorganising Army film production, and initiating *The Way Ahead* (1944), Dickinson spent three years producing *Men of Two Worlds* (1946), a mega-budget spectacular for the Colonial Office and RANK. Responding, like *A Matter of Life and Death* and *Caesar and Cleopatra*, to US disapproval of the British Empire, it's less akin to the KORDA Empire spectaculars starring SABU than to the BALCON films starring Paul ROBESON.

The Queen of Spades (1948), from Pushkin's tale of obsessional gambling, was a virtuoso demonstration of passionate aestheticism, and a worthy contrast with Eisenstein's late style. *Secret People*, his widely admired return to the political thriller, was Ealing's great bid for the European market, but the English Communist Party's campaign against it deterred the studio from launching it boldly. (The Stalinist objections, based on a misreading, were later reprised, egregiously, by *Screen*).

Hill 24 Does Not Answer (1952) was a Rossellini-like account of the founding of the State of Israel, which was still a white hope of the liberal left, and led to his 1956 appointment as Head of Film Production at the United Nations. The Suez War footage in *Blue Vanguard* (1956) provoked French, British, and Israeli threats to withdraw from the UN were the film released.

Having been a guiding spirit of the London FILM SOCIETY, he wrote copiously on film aesthetics. At University College, London, 1960–71, he pioneered Film Studies in Britain, nurturing a diversity of creative and critical talents, from Bellochio to Barry Salt. His powerful cinematic style was unique in British film, and can only be described as a mixture of Eisenstein (for strong editing) and Cukor (for mercurially sensitive acting). The left-liberal ideas which subtend his films await the – inevitable – demise of political correctness.

BIBLIOG: Jeffrey Richards, *Thorold Dickinson*, 1986; Lindsay Anderson, *Making A Film: Secret People*, 1951. Raymond Durgnat.

Dickson, Andrew Composer. Much of Dickson's composing for films has been for director Mike LEIGH, their association having begun on *Meantime* (1983, TV, some cinemas). He won the European Film Award for best composer for *High Hopes* (1988).

OTHER BRITISH FILMS: *Naked* (1993), *Someone Else's America* (1995, UK/Fr/Ger), *Secrets & Lies* (1996).

Dickson, Paul (*b* Cardiff, 1920). Director. Began his film career in 1940 as a photographer with the ARMY FILM UNIT, worked as an assistant to Paul ROTHA, and went on to win a reputation as a DOCUMENTARY film-maker. He won plaudits particularly for *The Undefeated* (1950), the study of a disabled pilot who remakes his life, and *David* (1951), a story of Welsh coalfields life through the eyes of a school caretaker. His feature films, including *Star of My Night* (1954), a romantic melodrama involving a ballerina and an artist who is going blind, were disappointing by comparison, and he later went into TV.

OTHER BRITISH FILMS: (doc/short) *Country Homes* (1947), *Personal Hygiene* (1948), *Chick's Day* (1950, co-d), *The Javanese Dagger*, *The Sable Scarf* (1953), *The Man Who Stayed Alive* (1955), *The Film That Never Was*, *A Dill-Pickle* (1957), *Nine Dalmuir West* (1962, narr); (features) *Gilbert Harding Speaking of Murder* (1953), *Satellite in the Sky* (1956), *The Depraved* (1957), *A Matter of Who* (1961, story).

Dickson, William Kennedy Laurie (*b* St Bue, France, 1860 – *d* Twickenham, 1935). Pioneer. French-born Britisher generally considered to have been crucial to Edison's 'invention' of the motion picture. An electrical engineer Dickson came to the US in 1879, joined Thomas Edison's laboratory staff in 1883, and was lead engineer in the inventor's work on the concept of

motion pictures later filming a number of subjects in the famed Black Maria studio. In 1895, left Edison to co-found the American Mutoscope Company. In 1897, with wife and sister Antonia (1858–1903), to UK, where he shot many subjects for BRITISH MUTOSCOPE & BIOGRAPH COMPANY; also filmed Pope Leo XIII in the Vatican Gardens (1898) and the Boer War. Author of *The Life and Inventions of Thomas A. Edison*, with Antonia Dickson (1894), *History of the Kinetograph, Kinetoscope and Kineto-Phonograph*, with Antonia Dickson (1895), and *The Biograph in Battle* (1901). First rescued from Edison's shadow by historians for his technical genius, Dickson's considerable artistry is now gaining praise with the happy discovery of more British Biograph films in recent years. AS.

Dietrich, Marlene (*b* Schöneberg, Germany, 1901 – *d* Paris, 1992). Actress. RN: Maria Dietrich von Losch. Legendarily beautiful star, discovered in Berlin, made into an international star in Hollywood by director Joseph von Sternberg and assorted, brilliant cameramen, Dietrich made only three British films but she is memorable in all of them. She is the gorgeously attired Countess on the run in the romantic adventure, *Knight Without Armour* (1937), and glamorous stars (what else *would* she play?) in both HITCHCOCK's *Stage Fright* (1950) and the aircraft-set drama, *No Highway* (1951). The rest of her remarkable career belongs elsewhere.

Diffring, Anton (*b* Koblenz, 1918 – *d* Chateauneuf-de-Grasse, France, 1989). Actor. Left Nazi Germany for Canada, where he worked on stage, had tiny roles in two British films in 1940 (*Neutral Port*, *Convoy*), then settled to a film career in Britain in 1950. Like many expatriate German actors, he played Nazi officers in war films such as *The Sea Shall Not Have Them* (1954) and foreigners of mostly sinister cast in dozens of other films, like *The Traitor* (1957) which ends with him madly playing the piano as soldiers close in to arrest him; and he also starred in several horror films, including *The Man Who Could Cheat Death* (1959) and *Circus of Horrors* (1960). His blond, chiselled features might in other times have led to romantic leads; as it was, he mostly played despicable. In many international films in later years.

OTHER BRITISH FILMS INCLUDE: *State Secret* (1950), *Hotel Sahara* (1951), *The Red Beret*, *Albert RN*, *Never Let Me Go* (1953), *The Colditz Story* (1954), *House of Secrets* (1956), *A Question of Adultery* (1958), *The Heroes of Telemark* (1965), *Fahrenheit 451* (1966), *Where Eagles Dare* (1968), *Zeppelin* (1971), *Valentino* (1977).

Dighton, John (*b* London, 1909 – *d* 1989). Screenwriter, playwright. Charterhouse- and Cambridge-educated Dighton was a key figure in British film-writing for over two decades, as well as being the author of one of the funniest stage farces, *The Happiest Days of Your Life* (1947), brilliantly filmed in 1950 from his screenplay. Another play, *Who Goes There!* (1951) was filmed in 1952. Came to films in the mid 30s and enjoyed his most prolific and distinguished period at EALING during the 40s, when, in collaboration with Angus MACPHAIL and others, he worked on such varied projects as *Saloon Bar* (1940), *Went the Day Well?* (1942), *Champagne Charlie* (1944) and *Kind Hearts and Coronets* (1949). His comic touch is perhaps both broader and more verbal than some of his collaborators'. He shared Oscar nominations for *The Man in the White Suit* (1951) and *Roman Holiday* (1953, US), finest flower of his post-Ealing period.

OTHER BRITISH FILMS INCLUDE: (co-sc, unless noted) *Hail and Farewell* (1936), *The Vulture* (1937), *It's in the Blood*, (1938), *Sailors Three* (co-story), *Let George Do It!*, *The Briggs Family* (sc) (1940), *The Ghost of*

St Michael's (+ co-story), *The Black Sheep of Whitehall* (+ co-story) (1941), *The Next of Kin*, *The Foreman Went to France* (1942), *Undercover*, *My Learned Friend* (1943), *Nicholas Nickleby* (1947, sc), *Saraband for Dead Lovers* (1948), *Folly to Be Wise* (1952), *The Barretts of Wimpole Street* (1956, sc), *Summer of the Seventeenth Doll* (UK/Aus, sc), *The Devil's Disciple* (1959).

Dignam, Basil (*b* Sheffield, 1905 – *d* England, 1979). Actor. Former lumberjack who came to the screen in his mid 40s after stage experience and played innumerable professional men. A few samples: doctors in *The Intimate Stranger* (1956) and *Sapphire* (1959), police inspectors in *Them Nice Americans* (1958) and *A Cry from the Streets* (1958), military officers in *The Safecracker* (1957) and *Where the Spies Are* (1965), and so on and on. Mostly small roles, but his square, reliable features helped to fix them in the mind. Brother of Mark DIGNAM, married to Mona WASHBOURNE.

OTHER BRITISH FILMS INCLUDE: *The Lady with a Lamp*, (1951), *Hammer the Toff* (1952), *There Was a Young Lady* (1953), *Touch and Go*, (1955), *Private's Progress*, *Yangtse Incident* (1956), *The Spaniard's Curse*, (1957), *Room at the Top*, *Corridors of Blood* (1958), *I'm All Right Jack* (1959), *The Spider's Web*, *Suspect* (1960), *Life for Ruth* (1962), *Heavens Above!*, *80,000 Suspects* (1963), *The Amorous Adventures of Moll Flanders* (1965), *The Jokers* (1966), *I'll Never Forget What's 'is Name* (1967), *Twisted Nerve* (1968), *The Games* (1969), *10 Rillington Place* (1970).

Dignam, Mark (*b* London, 1909 – *d* London, 1989). Actor. On stage first with Sheffield Repertory Company in 1930, then in London from 1932, with Old Vic and Stratford seasons. An imposingly authoritative figure, he made a splendid Malvolio in 1958, and, though he made fewer films than brother Basil DIGNAM, whom he much resembled, he had generally larger roles, such as the Captain of the Ark Royal in *Sink the Bismarck!* (1960) and Merlin in *Lancelot and Guinevere* (1962). Married to stage actress Helen Christie (2 of 3). Also, a good deal of TV, from as far back as 1939.

OTHER BRITISH FILMS INCLUDE: *Who Killed Jack Robins?* (1940), *Train of Events* (1949), *Murder in the Cathedral* (1952), *The 'Maggie'* (1953), *Lease of Life* (unc), *Carrington VC* (1954), *The Prisoner*, *Escapade* (1955), *The Pure Hell of St Trinian's* (1960), *Tom Jones* (1963), *The Charge of the Light Brigade* (1968), *Hamlet* (1969), *Memoirs of a Survivor* (1981), *On the Black Hill* (1987).

Dillane, Stephen (*b* London, 1957). Actor. Intelligent, austerely good-looking actor who has established a high reputation on the stage in plays as varied as *Hamlet* and *Angels in America*, all in the 90s, has yet to make a comparable mark in films, perhaps uninterested in being a conventional film star. He briefly tried – and hated – journalism after leaving Exeter University, trained for the stage at the Bristol Old Vic theatre school, and first appeared in films in 1987 (*Business as Usual*). Became well-known to televiewers in *The Rector's Wife* (1993) and was a more-than-usually sympathetic Karenin in *Anna Karenina* (2000). On-screen, his best chances have been as Horatio to Mel Gibson's *Hamlet* (1990, UK/US) and the compassionate journalist in *Welcome to Sarajevo* (1997, UK/US).

OTHER BRITISH FILMS INCLUDE: *Firelight* (1997), *Love and Rage* (1998, Ire/Ger), *The Darkest Light* (1999, UK/Fr), *Ordinary Decent Criminal* (2000, UK/Ger/Ire/US).

Dilley, Leslie (*b* Rhondda, Wales) Production designer. Co-recipient of AAs for his work on *Star Wars* (1977) and *Raiders of the Lost Ark* (1981), Dilley has worked mainly in the US but made a half-dozen British films from 1978 to 1983, including *Superman* (1978, co-des) and the often-remarkable *Alien* (1979, UK/US, co-des), both hugely dependent on their design.

OTHER BRITISH FILMS: *Black Angel* (1980, p), *An American Werewolf in London* (UK/US), *Eureka* (1982, UK/US, super a d), *Never Say Never Again* (1983, UK/US, super a d).

Dillon, Carmen (*b* London, 1908 – *d* Hove, 2000). Production designer. One of the most respected British designers, Dillon trained as an architect before entering films in 1935 as an assistant at FOX–BRITISH PICTURES' WEMBLEY STUDIOS. After five minor films, she worked with Paul SHERIFF on Anthony ASQUITH's *French Without Tears* (1939), establishing two important working relationships. She collaborated with Sheriff in the design of four further Asquith films, including the elegiac *The Way to the Stars* (1945), and later solo-designed several more for Asquith: her versatility is demonstrated by the contrast in the lifeless schoolmaster's residence in *The Browning Version* (1951) and the lush period elegance of *The Importance of Being Earnest* (1952). She had three famous brushes with SHAKESPEARE and OLIVIER: on the delicate blend of realism and stylisation in *Henry V* (1944, shared AAn with Sheriff), on the sombre, massive pillars and winding corridors of *Hamlet* (1948, shared AA with Roger FURSE) and on *Richard III* (1956, with Furse); she also designed Olivier's *The Prince and the Showgirl* (1957).

Through the 50s and 60s, she remained constantly in work, whether it was for the DISNEY organisation, on 'CARRY ON' and 'DOCTOR' movies, which she enjoyed, elsewhere giving distinction to routine fare like *Miracle in Soho* (1957), while relishing the challenges of two for Joseph LOSEY, recreating academe in *Accident* (1967) and refurbishing a neglected country mansion for *The Go-Between* (1971), both BAA-nominated, as was her work on *Lady Caroline Lamb* (1972, UK/It/US) and *Julia* (1977, US). Hers was a meticulous art, but she insisted it was interpretive rather than creative. An older sister, Una, founded Dillon's Bookshop.

OTHER BRITISH FILMS: (art d/des, unless noted): *The £5 Man* (1937), *The Claydon Treasure Mystery*, *Father o' Nine*, *The Last Barricade*, *Murder in the Family* (1938), *The Mikado* (1939), *Freedom Radio* (1940, ass art d), *Quiet Wedding* (1941, ass art d), *Unpublished Story*, *Secret Mission* (1942), *The Gentle Sex*, *The Demi-Paradise* (1943), *White Cradle Inn*, *Vice Versa* (1947), *Woman Hater* (1948), *Cardboard Cavalier*, *The Rocking Horse Winner* (1949), *The Woman in Question*, *The Reluctant Widow* (1950), *The Story of Robin Hood . . .*, *Meet Me Tonight* (1952), *The Sword and the Rose*, *Rob Roy . . .* (1953), *One Good Turn*, *Doctor in the House* (1954) *Simon and Laura*, *Doctor at Sea* (1955), *Checkpoint*, *The Iron Petticoat* (1956), *A Tale of Two Cities* (1958), *Sapphire* (1959), *Carry On Constable*, *Watch Your Stern*, *Make Mine Mink*, *Kidnapped*, *Please Turn Over*, *No Kidding* (1960), *Raising the Wind*, *The Naked Edge* (1961), *Twice Round the Daffodils*, *Carry On Cruising* (1962), *The Iron Maiden* (1963), *The Chalk Garden* (1964), *The Battle of the Villa Fiorita* (US/UK), *The Intelligence Men*, *Sky West and Crooked* (1965), *A Dandy in Aspic*, *Sinful Davey*, *Otley* (1968), *The Rise and Rise of Michael Rimmer* (1970), *Catch Me a Spy* (UK/Fr/US), *Bequest to the Nation*, *Butley* (UK/Can/UK) (1973), *The Sailor's Return* (1978).

Dimbleby, Richard (*b* Brentford, 1913 – *d* London, 1965). Broadcaster. Famous first as a war correspondent, then as a broadcaster on state occasions like the coronation (1953), and later as the compère of such respected TV programmes as *Panorama*, from 1953 until his death. He appeared as his recognisable avuncular self in four films: *Twenty Questions Murder Mystery* (1949), *John and Julie* (1955), *Rockets Galore* (1958), *Libel* (1959). Awarded OBE (1945) and CBE (1959).

Dines, Gordon (*b* London, 1911 – *d* Ealing, London, 1982). Cinematographer. Entered films as teenage camera assistant at BIP's ELSTREE STUDIOS, and worked uncredited on such films as *The White Sheik* (1928) and *Blackmail* (1929), moving on to EALING (in its ATP period in the mid 30s). Here, he was, first, camera operator, later cinematographer, working on many George FORMBY comedies, then was with the Royal Navy (1940–46). Reached his period of greatest distinction at postwar Ealing, where his contrasty black-and-white images powerfully reinforced the drama of such films as *Nicholas Nickleby* and *Frieda* (1947) while he contributed influentially to the semi-DOCUMENTARY texture of such films as *The Blue Lamp* (1949) and *Secret People* (1951). His post-Ealing career was less distinguished.

OTHER BRITISH FILMS INCLUDE: (c, unless noted) *Rome Express* (1932, cam ass), *Dreams Come True* (1936, co-c), *Keep Fit* (1937, co-c), *Penny Paradise* (co-c), *The Ware Case* (cam op), *The Gaunt Stranger* (co-c) (1938), *The Four Just Men* (cam op), *Young Man's Fancy* (cam op), *Come On George!* (cam op) (1939), *Saloon Bar* (cam op), *Spare a Copper* (cam op) (1940), *Train of Events* (1949), *Pool of London* (1950), *The Gentle Gunman, I Believe in You, The Cruel Sea* (1952), *The Square Ring* (co-c), *The 'Maggie'* (1953), *The Crowded Day, The Colditz Story* (1954), *You Lucky People, The Ship That Died of Shame* (1955), *Yangtse Incident, The Long Arm* (1956), *These Dangerous Years, Wonderful Things* (1957), *The Lady is a Square* (1958), *The Siege of Pinchgut, The Navy Lark* (1959), *Circle of Deception* (1960), *Bomb in the High Street* (1963), *Bread* (1971).

Dinsdale, Reece (*b* Normanton, Yorkshire, 1959). Actor. Played Guildenstern in Kenneth BRANAGH's *Hamlet* (1996, UK/US), but unfortunately the films in which he has starred have been little seen: *i.d.* (1995), as an ambitious police officer; and *Romance and Rejection* (1996), as a struggling composer. Much on TV, notably in *Threads* (1984), the nuclear drama.

OTHER BRITISH FILM: *A Private Function* (1984).

Dionisotti, Paola (*b* Turin, 1946). Actress. Eloquent actress seen mostly on TV, suddenly making an Agatha CHRISTIE thriller seem profound in a few moments of vengeful grief in *A Murder Is Announced* (1985). Very scattered films since 1978 debut in *The Sailor's Return*. Scored a major stage success as the tenacious heroine of *Further Than the Furthest Thing* (2000, 2001).

OTHER BRITISH FILMS: *Fords on Water* (1984), *The Tichborne Claimant, Les Misérables, Vigo* (1998, UK/Fr), *Intimacy* (2001, UK/Fr).

Disney Organisation In the early 50s, Walt Disney set up offices in Pall Mall, London, and produced a series of popular, Technicolored entertainments, such as *The Story of Robin Hood and His Merrie Men* (1952), *The Sword and the Rose, Rob Roy . . .* (1953), *Third Man on the Mountain* (1959), *Kidnapped* (1960), *Greyfriars Bobby, In Search of the Castaways* (1961), *The Prince and the Pauper* (1962), *The Horse Without a Head, Dr Syn Alias the Scarecrow, The Three Lives of Thomasina* (1963), *The Moon Spinners* (1964) and *The Fighting Prince of Donegal* (1966). Many of these were filmed on location: e.g. *Swiss Family Robinson* (1960) was filmed wholly in Tobago; most were executed on the 'storyboard' principle, which appealed to some British film-makers, like Ken ANNAKIN, but not to others, such as Carmen DILLON. Disney–British used directors Annakin and Don CHAFFEY several times, as well as Dillon and cameraman Guy GREEN, actors like Richard TODD and Susan HAMPSHIRE, and made an international star of Hayley MILLS. The Disney British films are tarred with the wholesome brush of their transatlantic siblings, but they were undoubtedly proficient and gave work to many British actors and technicians.

distribution Britain's film distributors first established themselves in London's Cecil Court, off Charing Cross Road, which was nicknamed Flicker Alley, then migrated to Soho, so many setting up shop in Wardour Street that its name became synonymous with the film trade. Initially selling films outright, distributors soon switched to renting them and have been known within the trade until recent times as 'renters'. Companies established branch offices in major cities or, in the case of smaller concerns, hired local agents.

The two major combines that emerged in the late 20s, GAUMONT–BRITISH and ASSOCIATED BRITISH (initially BRITISH INTERNATIONAL PICTURES), had distribution companies to supply their films to their own chain of cinemas and other outlets. The American majors sometimes formed local partnerships (Jury–Metro–Goldwyn) to release their productions in Britain but subsequently established their own distribution companies, sponsoring 'QUOTA QUICKIES' and sometimes (as in the case of UNITED ARTISTS) important British productions to meet their legal obligations to distribute a percentage of domestic output. Only UNIVERSAL relied on a local company, GENERAL FILM DISTRIBUTORS (later part of the RANK ORGANISATION), as a result of GFD's investment in the company in 1936.

Almost all distributors had ties to either the Odeon or Gaumont chains (under combined J. Arthur RANK management from 1948) or ABC for first run release; BRITISH LION was the major exception, trading with either group. After GFD (later Rank Film Distributors) and Associated British Pathé (later EMI), British Lion was the third major source of British-made pictures in the boom years of the 40s and 50s, although all the Hollywood majors backed films in Britain and distributed them internationally, to use frozen funds, to take advantage of good exchange rates and British technical expertise, or to obtain suitable, realistic settings for a particular subject.

The decline in attendances forced local mergers, often between Hollywood and Britain (Warner–Pathé, Fox–Rank); then American films were released through international partnerships like CIC (Universal and Paramount), later UIP (with the addition of MGM for many years). A proliferation of small distributors has come and gone, but the rise of multiplexes has encouraged many newcomers handling smaller, often British pictures. The box-office dominance of Hollywood films has meant that British productions no longer enjoy regular widespread popularity as in the boom years of cinemagoing, but depend on the occasional hit (*Four Weddings and a Funeral*, 1994; *The Full Monty*, 1997, UK/US) to reach the masses, while foreign-language pictures have been confined to a tiny ART-HOUSE sector. Allen Eyles.

Dixon, Adele (*b* London, 1908 – *d* Manchester, 1992). Actress. On stage from childhood, RADA-trained Dixon made few films, memorably as the unsympathetic wife in *Woman to Woman* (1946). Frequently broadcast with BBC radio.

OTHER BRITISH FILMS: *Uneasy Virtue* (1931), *The Happy Husband* (1932), *Calling the Tune* (1936), *Banana Ridge* (1941).

Dixon, G. Campbell (*b* Ouse, Tasmania, 1895 – *d* 1960). Critic, dramatist. Respected commentator on the film scene of the 40s and 50s, when he was film reviewer for the *Daily Telegraph*. He was also the editor of the first *International Film Annual* (1957), a still highly readable collection, as well as of several books and plays, including *Ashenden* (derived from Somerset MAUGHAM's novel) on which HITCHCOCK's *Secret Agent* (1936) is based. President of the Critics' Circle (1950–51).

Dizdar, Jasmin (*b* Zenica, Bosnia, 1961). Director. Émigré Yugoslav and graduate of FAMU, Prague's film school, Dizdar won acclaim, at Cannes and other European festivals with his first feature, *Beautiful People* (1999). His aims were to show 'London from a foreigner's point of view' and 'how the media use war to make drama', using five loosely interrelated stories. The screenplay was commissioned by the BFI. His student film, *After Silence* (1987), won awards in Europe.

Djalili, Omid (*b* London, 1965) Actor. Internationally popular stand-up comedian, of Iranian refugee parents, who has appeared in several British films, including *Notting Hill* (UK/US – he sells Hugh GRANT the catalytic orange juice), *Mad Cows* and *The World Is Not Enough* (UK/US) (1999), the US film, *The Mummy* (1999), and *Gladiator* (2000, UK/US), and regularly on TV comedy shows, including Alexei Sayle's *Merry-go-round*.

Dmytryk, Edward (*b* Grand Forks, Canada, 1908 – *d* Encino, California, 1999). Director. Most of his career was located in the US, but, in the later 40s, following the House UnAmerican Activities Committee's witch-hunt, he was one of the 'Hollywood Ten' (former communists) sentenced to a year's gaol, after which he made three films in Britain's more politically tolerant climate. These were: the turgid romantic drama, *So Well Remembered* (1947), the socially alert *Give Us This Day* and the acid-bath murder thriller, *Obsession* (1949), before returning to Hollywood to remake his career, avoiding the BLACKLIST by testifying against former colleagues. He chronicles these experiences in his second volume of autobiography, *Odd Man Out: A Memoir of the Hollywood Ten* (1996).
OTHER BRITISH FILMS: *The End of the Affair* (1954), *Shalako* (1968), *The 'Human' Factor* (1975, UK/US).

DNA Films One of the three LOTTERY-funded franchises (others were the French-based PATHÉ Pictures and The FILM CONSORTIUM), DNA was formed by Duncan KENWORTHY and Andrew MACDONALD, and set up in 1997 as part of a move by the ARTS COUNCIL to rationalise production, DISTRIBUTION and sales, with guaranteed finance for six years. The aim was to help stabilise British film output, and DNA Films planned to make three films per year. Its first release was the poorly received black comedy, *Beautiful Creatures* (2001).

Dobie, Alan (*b* Wombwell, 1932). Actor. Somewhat morose-seeming actor who has had his best chances on TV (e.g. as Prince Andrei in *War and Peace*, 1972; the hapless Stephen in *Hard Times*, 1977). In films since 1962 (*Seven Keys*), probably best remembered as the German prisoner in *The Long Day's Dying* (1968). Married (1) Rachel ROBERTS (1955–61).
OTHER BRITISH FILMS INCLUDE: *The Comedy Man* (1963), *The Charge of the Light Brigade* (1968), *Alfred the Great* (1969), *Madame Sin* (1972), *White Mischief* (1987).

Dobtcheff, Vernon (*b* Nimes, France, 1934). Actor. In films from the mid 60s, Dobtcheff has maintained a busy career in British and international films and TV. His chiselled features and somewhat remote demeanour have secured him mainly unsympathetic roles, like that of the severe professor in *Hilary and Jackie* (1998) and the spy Reynaldo in ZEFFIRELLI's *Hamlet* (1990, UK/US).
OTHER BRITISH FILMS INCLUDE: *The Hidden Face* (1965), *Baby Love* (1967), *A Dandy in Aspic* (1968), *Anne of the Thousand Days* (1969), *The Beast in the Cellar* (1970), *Mary Queen of Scots* (1971), *The Day of the Jackal* (UK/Fr) (1973), *Murder on the Orient Express* (1974), *Joseph Andrews* (1976), *The Spy Who Loved Me* (1977), *Nutcracker, Enigma* (UK/Fr) (1982), *Mata Hari* (1984), *Caravaggio* (1986), *Testimony* (1987), *Pascali's Island* (UK/US), *Madame Sousatzka* (1988), *The Krays* (1990),*'Let Him Have It'* (1991), *Jude, St Ives, Vigo* (Fr/UK) (1998), *Dreaming of Joseph Lees* (1999, UK/US).

'Doctor' series Richard Gordon's best-seller, *A Doctor in the House* (1952), little more than a collection of amusing anecdotes deriving their humour from the vicissitudes of doctors in training and, later, practice, gave rise to the popular 1954 film, starring Dirk BOGARDE as Dr Simon Sparrow. The simple ingredients were stirred with skill and gaiety, and inevitable successors, based on Gordon's follow-ups, *Doctor at Sea* (1955) and *Doctor at Large* (1957), maintained a good standard of invention, which tailed off in the remaining four, in which the *Doctor* was . . . *in Love* (1960), . . . *in Distress* (1963), . . . *in Clover* (1967) and . . . *in Trouble* (1970). All seven were directed by Ralph THOMAS and produced by Betty BOX for the RANK ORGANISATION. Bogarde starred in the first three and in *Distress*; Michael CRAIG and Leslie PHILLIPS had leads in the later ones. There were TV spin-offs at intervals between 1969 and 1991.

documentary animation A peculiarly (though not exclusively) British genre that has flourished since the advent, in 1981, of CHANNEL 4 television, which encouraged and commissioned a wide range of new animation projects, often focussing on strong social issues and true experiences, such as Marjut Rimminen's *Some Protection* (1988), about legal injustices to women; Tim Webb's *A is for Autism* (1992), about autistic children; Paul Vester's arguably ironic *Abductees* (1995), using sound interviews with people claiming to have been abducted by aliens; Gillian Lacey's *Gotta Get Out* (1995), about claustrophobia; Vivienne Jones's *Touch Wood* (1996), about compulsive obsessive disorder; and Sylvie Bringas and Orly Yadin's *Silence* (1998), about a child survivor of the Holocaust. Whilst the introduction and creative application of more flexible animation techniques has given life to this genre of film-making, it has a deep historical background, which can be traced back through the information films of HALAS AND BATCHELOR in the 40s, 50s and 60s, Norman McLaren's early polemics (such as *Hell Unlimited*, 1936), the DOCUMENTARY MOVEMENT's GPO-sponsored experimental animation films of the 30s (especially those of LEN LYE), political propaganda cartoons of the 20s, George Studdy's and others' anti-German lampoons of the Great War – all the way to Tom Merry's 'lightning sketches' of such figures as Kaiser Wilhelm and Count Bismarck in 1895, some of British cinema's first moving images. One of the attractions of documentary production of this kind is its ability to present difficult, sometimes abstract and often intimate subject-matter honestly, concisely and imaginatively without being voyeuristic or resorting to the falsity of dramatisation. This has led to a variety of practitioners entering the genre, often with popular success, such as Bob GODFREY (*Marx for Beginners*, 1987) and the Aardman team (*Conversation Pieces*, 1983, and *Creature Comforts*, 1989). Orly Yadin.

documentary film in Britain Between 1896 and 1910 most documentaries made in Britain were either SHORT FILMS which employed trick effects within a context of staged or re-staged events, such as Cecil HEPWORTH's *How It Feels to be Run Over* (1900) and Alfred COLLINS' *A Derby Day Incident* (1903); ACTUALITY recordings of events such as royal and state occasions, wars or sporting events; heavily 'reconstructed' films of actual events, such as James WILLIAMSON's *Attack on a Chinese Mission Station* (1900) and films which drew on pre-existing traditions of literary and theatrical convention and popular culture, as in William HAGGAR's *The Life of Charles Peace* (1905). Other films, commonly known as 'industrials', had more explicit instructional objectives, as with the corporate public relations films which appeared from 1904 onwards, including *The Story of a Piece of Slate* (1904), *Bootmaking* (1906), *Life on the Oxo Cattle Ranch* (1911) and *The Manchester Ship Canal* (1912). One of the most important producers of the period was Charles URBAN, whose companies made films with an educational aspect designed to put 'Nature on the Stage', including shorts such as *Through the Microscope* (1907) and *Rodents and Their Habits* (1908).

During WW1 Britain embarked upon a major programme of PROPAGANDA film production. Short films such as *The Wonderful Organization of the Royal Army Medical Corps* (1916) were followed by longer films such as *The Battle of the Somme* (1916), *The Battle of the Ancre* (1917), *The German Retreat and the Battle of Arras* (1917), *The Great German Retreat and the Battle of Perrone* (1917) and *The Capture of Messines* (1917). During the inter-war period a considerable number of actuality films were also made dealing with social and political issues. Some of these were made by local councils, promoting public awareness of various social and health hazards. Others were made by political organizations such as the Communist Party of Great Britain (CPGB), and by politically committed film-making organizations such as Kino, the WORKERS FILM AND PHOTO LEAGUE and the PROGRESSIVE FILM INSTITUTE (PFI).

A very important group of committed films was made during the Spanish Civil War by the PFI, which, in 1936, sent to Spain a unit which included Ivor MONTAGU, Sidney COLE, Thorold DICKINSON and Norman McLAREN. Its first film, *Defence of Madrid* (1936), was followed by *News From Spain*, *Crimes Against Madrid* (1937), *Spanish ABC*, *Behind The Spanish Lines*, and *Testament of Non-Intervention* (1938). Other important 30s films, associated with the Spanish Civil War and the struggle against appeasement, included Montagu's *Peace and Plenty* (1939), and McLaren's *Hell Unlimited* (1936).

Alongside these radical film-making organizations, another film movement emerged during the 30s which was to have a significant influence on the development of British film culture. In 1929 John GRIERSON made *Drifters*, a film made in the style of Soviet montage film-making. Following its success, Grierson went on to establish the documentary film movement, appointing directors such as Basil WRIGHT, Paul ROTHA, Arthur ELTON, Edgar ANSTEY, Robert FLAHERTY, Stuart LEGG, John TAYLOR, Donald TAYLOR and Marion GRIERSON. In 1934 the documentary film movement was transferred to the Post Office, and the GPO FILM UNIT was established; it produced documentary films until 1940, when it became part of the MINISTRY OF INFORMATION (MOI), and changed its name to the CROWN FILM UNIT. During this period, directors such as Harry WATT, Humphrey JENNINGS, Alberto CAVALCANTI, Len LYE, Norman McLaren, Alexander SHAW, Jack HOLMES and Pat JACKSON were appointed.

Grierson's first theory of documentary film, as embodied in *Drifters*, contained many modernist aspects. However, his views gradually changed, until, by 1941, he had abandoned the formalist *avant-gardism* of *Drifters*, and had adopted a more strident, didactic approach to film-making. In the mid 30s he and some of his associates left the GPO Film Unit to found a number of independent documentary production units. There,

they made films such as *Children at School* (Wright, 1937) in Grierson's preferred didactic style. Divisions also began to appear between Grierson and his associates and the film-makers remaining at the GPO, now led by Cavalcanti. Under Cavalcanti, the GPO Film Unit developed a different approach to film-making between 1937 and 1940, evidenced in impressionistic documentaries such as *Spare Time* (Jennings, 1939), and dramatised documentaries such as *North Sea* (Watt, 1938). During WW2, the documentary film movement at Crown also produced a series of feature-length dramatised documentaries, including *Target For Tonight* (Watt, 1941), *Coastal Command* (Holmes, 1942) and *Western Approaches* (Jackson, 1944).

As the documentary film movement declined after 1955, the tradition was carried forward in the films of FREE CINEMA. However, there was little continuity between the documentary film movement and Free Cinema, whose film-makers rejected the models of journalistic documentary film-making advocated by Grierson. Free Cinema did, however, distinguish between Grierson and his associates on the one hand, and Humphrey Jennings on the other, and regarded Jennings's *Spare Time* and *Listen to Britain* as the model upon which a new documentary practice could be created.

Free Cinema film-makers such as Lindsay ANDERSON emphasised the poetic qualities of the documentary film. The first programme of Free Cinema screenings took place in August 1956 and consisted of *O Dreamland* (Anderson, 1953) *Momma Don't Allow* (Tony RICHARDSON and Karel REISZ, 1955) and *Together* (Lorenza Mazzetti, 1953). The first programme of screenings was then followed by five others, between 1956 and 1959, and included *Every Day Except Christmas* (Anderson, 1957), and *We Are The Lambeth Boys* (Reisz, 1959).

No one, over-arching movement in documentary film-making has emerged between 1960 and the present. Instead, a wide variety of film-making has appeared, ranging from *ciné vérité* (*Decisions*, Roger Graef, 1975–76), political modernist documentary (*Song of the Shirt*, Sue CLAYTON and Jonathan Curling, 1981), reflexive documentary (*Heidi Fleiss: Hollywood Madam*, Nick BROOMFIELD, 1995), postmodernist documentary (*Handsworth Songs*, John AKOMFRAH, 1986) and social realist documentary (*Hidden Voices*, Mike Grigsby, 1995). The drama documentary has also emerged as a major television genre, in films such as *The War Game* (Peter WATKINS, 1966) and *Death of a Princess* (Anthony Thomas, 1980). Dramatised reconstruction also combines with *avant-gardist* reflexivity in films such as Peter GREENAWAY's *Act of God* (1980). However, despite this range, the *tradition* represented by the documentary film movement remains a touchstone for contemporary film-makers who work either within or against the grain of that tradition.

BIBLIOG: Paul Rotha, *Documentary Diary*, 1973; Ian Aitken (ed), *The Documentary Film Movement: An Anthology*, 1998. Ian Aitken.

Dodd, Ken (*b* Knotty Ash, 1927) Comedian. Famed TV comic who has scarcely touched films, but was glimpsed (in an unShakespearean insert) as Yorick in BRANAGH's eclectically cast *Hamlet* (1996, UK/US). Was the second ninja in *The Ninja Mission* (1984) and Mr Mouse in the 2000 telemovie, *Alice in Wonderland*. Awards include OBE (1982).

Dodds, Olive (*b* London, 1912 – *d* Northwood, Middlesex, 1999). Casting director. An influential figure in post-war British cinema, Dodds, born with a withered arm, trained as a secretary and in 1930 took a position with the Ministry of

Agriculture and worked for the government Public Relations Department during WW2, before joining the RANK ORGANISATION. From 1949, she was in charge of Rank's contract artistes, coaching the likes of Diana DORS and Dirk BOGARDE for stardom and heading the (in)famous Rank 'CHARM SCHOOL'. As casting director, she was in constant cahoots with the likes of producer Betty BOX, whom she assisted in the casting of the 'DOCTOR' films. In the 60s, she turned to TV, first with ATV, then with Yorkshire, and continued to work into her seventies.

Doleman, Guy (b Hamilton, NZ, 1923 – d Los Angeles, 1996). Actor. Began his career in such indigenous and overseas-initiated films as were available in Australia in the late 40s and the 50s. He had roles in the British-backed *His Majesty O'Keefe* (1953) and *Smiley* (1956), and in the American *On the Beach* (1959), before heading for Britain where he found a niche as Colonel Ross in the Harry Palmer spy thrillers, *The Ipcress File* (1965), *The Funeral in Berlin* (1966) and *Billion Dollar Brain* (1967). Spent the last years of his career in Australia.

OTHER BRITISH FILMS: *The Partner* (1963), *Boy with a Flute* (1964, short), *The System* (1964), *Thunderball* (1965), *The Idol, The Deadly Bees* (1966), *A Twist of Sand* (1968).

Donald, James (b Aberdeen, 1917 – d Wiltshire, 1993). Actor. Donald is best known as the Army doctor who looks down on the wreckage of *The Bridge on the River Kwai* (1957) and speaks the final lines, 'Madness, madness'. This is exactly the kind of role – sardonic, introspective, abrasive – in which he had specialised since playing another doctor for the same director, David LEAN, in the naval epic *In Which We Serve* (1942), followed by the most intelligent and least amenable of the Army recruits in *The Way Ahead* (1944). A career dedicated primarily to stage work, and to supporting film roles, was broken by a short period of post-war stardom, which he owed to his lean good looks and to his ability to project the idealism of the scientific visionary. His medical pioneer in *White Corridors* (1951) and his aircraft designer in *The Net* (1953) have a convincing intensity. As the unvisionary 50s wore on, British cinema ceased to offer such roles, and Donald was overtaken by safer and tweedier male stars. He did, however, have another moment of glory in Hammer's *Quatermass and the Pit* (1967), where his Professor Roney, another sardonic idealist, saves the world from destruction.

OTHER BRITISH FILMS: *One of Our Aircraft is Missing* (unc), *Went the Day Well?, The Missing Million* (1942), *San Demetrio–London* (1943), *Broken Journey, The Small Voice, Trottie True* (1948), *Edward, My Son* (1949), *Cage of Gold* (1950), *The Pickwick Papers, The Gift Horse, Brandy for the Parson* (1952), *Beau Brummell* (1954), *Third Man on the Mountain* (1959), *The Jokers* (1966), *Hannibal Brooks* (1968), *David Copperfield, The Royal Hunt of the Sun* (1969), *Conduct Unbecoming* (1975), *The Big Sleep* (1978). Charles Barr.

Donat, Robert (b Manchester, 1905 – d London, 1958). Actor. In the 30s, Donat was perhaps the nearest British equivalent to a Hollywood star, his image forged under the guidance of Alexander KORDA. Tall, handsome in the romantic manner, and possessed of a mellifluous speaking voice, he made his stage debut in 1921, often playing with major provincial repertory theatres, as well as in West End and Old Vic successes. Dogged by bad health, he ironically came to the fore in films requiring a dashing display: as Thomas Culpepper in *The Private Life of Henry VIII* (1933), the dual role of laird and ghost in *The Ghost Goes West* (1935), the secret agent caught up in the Russian Revolution in *Knight Without Armour* (1937) and

another, very athletic secret agent in HITCHCOCK's *The 39 Steps* (1935).

But it is his last 30s role for which he is best known: the shy schoolmaster who blooms under love and becomes an institution for generations of schoolboys in *Goodbye, Mr Chips* (1939). Class-ridden and sentimental perhaps, it remains extraordinarily touching in his Oscar-winning performance, and it ushers in the Donat of the post-war years. He could do comedy – the suburban worm who thrives during war in *Perfect Strangers* (1945) or the broad Lancashire farce of *The Cure for Love* (1949, + d) – and the charismatic 'turn' – Parnell in *Captain Boycott* (1947), and the supercilious defence counsel in *The Winslow Boy* (1948), who warms to the spectacle of unassailable right. However, it is for the tenderness of *Chips*, of the defeated inventor in *The Magic Box* (1951) and the ailing clergyman in *Lease of Life* (1954, BAAn) and the dying Mandarin in *The Inn of the Sixth Happiness* (1958), that one most cherishes him. Other stars had his dash; it is hard to think of another major star who could so move an audience with the sheer delicacy of his emotional shading in these roles. His last words on the screen (to Ingrid BERGMAN) were: 'We shall not see each other again, I think. Farewell.' If that sounds sentimental, try watching and listening without weeping.

He made *The Count of Monte Cristo* (1934) in Hollywood, but did not care to repeat the experience. Married (2) Renée ASHERSON.

OTHER BRITISH FILMS: *That Night in London, Men of Tomorrow* (1932), *Cash* (1933), *The Citadel* (1938, AAn), *The Young Mr Pitt* (1942), *The Adventures of Tartu, The New Lot* (doc) (1943), *The Stained Glass at Fairford* (1956, narr).

BIBLIOG: Kenneth Barrow, *Mr Chips: The Life of Robert Donat*, 1985.

Donen, Stanley (b Columbia, S. Carolina, 1924). Director. Famous director of MGM musicals from the late 40s on, who made a half-dozen attractive romantic comedies in Britain, including the Cary GRANT–Ingrid BERGMAN soufflé, *Indiscreet* (1958), and, with Grant again, *The Grass Is Greener* (1960).

OTHER BRITISH FILMS: *Surprise Package* (1960), *Two for the Road, Arabesque* (UK/US) (1966), *Bedazzled* (1967), *Saturn 3* (1980).

Donisthorpe, Wordsworth (b Leeds, 1847 – d Hindhead, 1914). Pioneer. A barrister, and the inventor, in 1889, of the Kinesigraph camera, with which, a year later, he shot footage of Trafalgar Square. Also actively involved in chess, poll tax and languages; his story is told in Stephen Herbert's *Industry, Liberty, and a Vision* (1998). AS.

Donlan, Yolande (b Jersey City, 1920). Actress. Blonde star with air of frivolity and French accent, daughter of character actor James Donlan, who played small roles in US films (1936–44). Went to UK in 1947 to star in stage production of *Born Yesterday*, and subsequent British screen career. Married (2) Val GUEST, who directed her in *Miss Pilgrim's Progress* (1949), *The Body Said No!, Mr Drake's Duck* (1950), *They Can't Hang Me* (1955), *Expresso Bongo* (1959), *80,000 Suspects* (1963). Wrote autobiography, *Shake the Stars Down/Third Time Lucky* (1976) and travel book *Sand in My Mink* (1955).

OTHER BRITISH FILMS: *Traveller's Joy* (1949), *Tarzan and the Lost Safari* (1956), *Seven Nights in Japan* (1976, UK/Fr). AS.

Donnelly, Donal (b Bradford, Yorkshire, 1931). Actor. Yorkshire-born but trained and made debut at the Gate Theatre, Dublin in 1952. Has continued to work on stage and TV, mainly in Irish roles, as well as appearing in a dozen scattered films, from *The Rising of the Moon* (1957, Ire/US). First noticed as Dandy

NICHOLS's lodger in *The Knack . . .* (1965), evicted for being a secret painter. Recent films have been Irish co-productions, including *Love and Rage* (1998, Ire/Can).

OTHER BRITISH FILMS INCLUDE: *Gideon's Day* (1958), *I'm All Right Jack*, *Shake Hands with the Devil* (UK/US) (1959), *Young Cassidy*, *Up Jumped a Swagman* (1965), *The Dead* (1987, UK/Ger/US).

Donner, Clive (*b* London, 1926). Director. Began as an assistant film editor at DENHAM STUDIOS in 1940 and had his first editor's credit on *Scrooge* (1951). His directorial debut was the taut little thriller, *The Secret Place* (1957), and in the 60s he made such interesting films as the daring Pinter adaptation, *The Caretaker* (1963), and the smart black social comedy, *Nothing But the Best* (1964). He showed some real visual flair, but since 1970, he has made undistinguished films and telemovies on both sides of the Atlantic, the early promise hard to discern in the likes of *The Nude Bomb* (1980).

OTHER BRITISH FILMS: (e) *The Card, Meet Me Tonight* (1952), *The Million Pound Note, Genevieve* (1953), *The Purple Plain* (1954), *I Am a Camera* (1955); (d) *Heart of a Child* (1958), *Marriage of Convenience* (1960), *Some People* (1962), *Here We Go Round the Mulberry Bush* (1967), *Alfred the Great* (1969), *Vampira* (1974), *The Thief of Baghdad* (1978, UK/Fr), *A Christmas Carol* (1984, TV, some cinemas), *Stealing Heaven* (1988, UK/Yug).

Donohoe, Amanda (*b* London, 1962). Actress. Too sexually alluring to find enough demanding work in British films, Donohoe has also worked extensively in the US cinema and TV, including an award-winning stint as lesbian Cara Jean Lamb in *LA Law* (1990–92). In British films, she was a sexy distraction from the absurdity of *Castaway* (1986), a snake goddess in Ken RUSSELL's *The Lair of the White Worm* (1988) and a lesbian seductress in his *The Rainbow* (1989).

OTHER BRITISH FILMS INCLUDE: *Foreign Body* (1986), *Tank Malling* (1988), *Diamond Skulls* (1989), *Paper Mask* (1990), *The Madness of King George* (1994, UK/US), *Circus* (2000, UK/US), *Wild About Harry* (2001, UK/Ger/Ire).

Doonan, Patric (*b* Derby, 1925 – *d* London, 1958). Actor. Very gifted, intense young actor, specialising in tough working-class roles. RADA-trained, he was on stage in 1942, in the armed forces 1944–48, and on screen in 1948's *Once a Jolly Swagman*, but came to prominence as Dirk BOGARDE's criminal associate in *The Blue Lamp* (1949). Inexplicably his roles declined in the 50s and he committed suicide. He was the son of comedian George Doonan and brother of actor Anthony Doonan, and married actress Aud Johanson.

OTHER BRITISH FILMS: *Train of Events, All Over the Town, A Run for Your Money* (1949), *Highly Dangerous, Blackout* (1950), *The Man in the White Suit, The Lavender Hill Mob, High Treason, Calling Bulldog Drummond, Appointment with Venus* (1951), *I'm a Stranger, The Gift Horse, The Gentle Gunman* (1952), *Wheel of Fate, The Red Beret, The Net, The Case of Gracie Budd* (short) (1953), *What Every Woman Wants, Seagulls over Sorrento* (1954), *John and Julie, Cockleshell Heroes* (1955).

Doré, Edna (*b* 1922). Actress. RN: Gorring. Usually seen as stubborn old women, Doré became widely known as Mo Butcher in TV's *EastEnders* (1988–92). Film roles have been few but noticeable: as tearaway David McCALLUM's indulgent Mum in *Jungle Street* (1961); the disoriented grandma in *High Hopes* (1988) for which she won a European Film Award; and the tough old gran who unforgettably sang 'Can't help lovin' that man of mine' in *Nil by Mouth* (1997). Married actor/screenwriter **Alexander Doré**.

OTHER BRITISH FILMS: *More Deadly than the Male* (1959), *My Little Eye* (1992), *Les Misérables* (1998).

Dorne, Sandra (*b* Keighley, 1925 – *d* London, 1992). Actress. RN: Joanna Smith. Archetypal blonde floozie of innumerable 'B' MOVIES, occasionally the heroine, as in *The Gelignite Gang* (1956), more often good-time girls at best, like Judy ('Where's that hunk of man?' she demands) in *13 East Street* (1952), or, simply, 'Whore in traffic' in *Joseph Andrews* (1976). Good company, though, and it was fun to see her again in 1987's black comedy, *Eat the Rich*. Married actor Patrick HOLT (1954–92).

OTHER BRITISH FILMS: *Eyes That Kill* (1947), *Once a Jolly Swagman* (1948), *Traveller's Joy, All Over the Town* (1949), *Never Say Die, The Clouded Yellow* (1950), *Happy Go Lovely* (1951), *Golden Arrow, Hindle Wakes* (1952), *The Yellow Balloon, The Weak and the Wicked, The Beggar's Opera* (1953), *Police Dog, Alias John Preston* (1955), *The Iron Petticoat* (1956), *Three Sundays to Live* (1957), *Orders to Kill* (1958), *The Malpas Mystery* (1960), *The Amorous Prawn* (1962), *All Coppers Are . . .* (1971), *Playbirds* (1978).

Dornhelm, Robert (*b* Timisoara, Romania, 1947). Director. Went to Vienna in 1960, has made two films in Britain: *Digital Dreams* (1983), about Bill Wyman of the Rolling Stones, and *A Further Gesture* (1997, UK/Ire/Ger/Jap), about an IRA terrorist starting life again in New York. Also filmed in the US.

Dors, Diana (*b* Swindon, Wiltshire, 1931 – *d* Windsor, 1984). Actress. RN: Fluck. Dors became stereotyped as blonde glamour girl, having few opportunities for dramatic roles, the main exceptions being *Yield to the Night* (1956), as the woman condemned to hang, and *Deep End* (1970). Her early parts were as post-war 'good-time girls' in films such as *The Shop at Corner* (1946), *Dancing with Crime*, (1947), *Good-Time Girl* (1947) and the first three HUGGETT films. Although she played the slatternly Nancy in David LEAN's *Oliver Twist* (1948), she quickly became type-cast in sexpot roles, as in *An Alligator Named Daisy* (1955). But even in such harmless enterprises as this, or *Value for Money* or *As Long As They're Happy* (1955), she brings a welcome easy sensuality to British cinema. Certainly in the 50s she had few if any rivals in this matter, and she had a sort of genius for attracting publicity, whether through her love life or her mink bikini. However, she later moved impressively to character roles in films such as *The Amazing Mr Blunden* (1972) and *Steaming* (1984). She also filmed, not very successfully in Hollywood, and is the author of several volumes of undemanding autobiography.

OTHER BRITISH FILMS: *Holiday Camp* (1947), *My Sister and I, Penny and the Pownall Case* (1948), *The Calendar, It's Not Cricket, A Boy, A Girl, and A Bike, Diamond City* (1949), *Dance Hall* (1950), *Worm's Eye View, Lady Godiva Rides Again* (1951), *The Last Page, My Wife's Lodger, The Weak and the Wicked, Is Your Honeymoon Really Necessary?* (1952), *It's A Grand Life, The Great Game* (1953), *The Saint's Return, A Kid for Two Farthings* (1954), *Miss Tulip Stays the Night* (1955), *The Long Haul* (1957), *Passport to Shame, Tread Softly Stranger* (1958), *Berserk!* (1967), *Mrs Gibbons' Boys* (1962), *Baby Love* (1967), *There's A Girl in My Soup* (1970), *Hannie Caulder* (1971), *Nothing But the Night* (1972), *Theatre of Blood, Steptoe and Son Ride Again, From Beyond the Grave* (1973), *Craze, Bedtime with Rosie, The Amorous Milkman* (1974), *Confessions of a Driving Instructor* (1976), *The Groove Room, Adventures of A Private Eye* (1977), *Confessions from the Galaxy Affair, The Plank* (1979), *Dr Jekyll and Mr Hyde* (1980), *The Unicorn* (1983).

BIBLIOG: Autobiography, *Dors by Diana*, 1981. Tony Williams.

Dotrice, Karen (*b* Guernsey, 1955). Actress. Daughter of Roy DOTRICE and sister of Michele, she had her most famous role in *Mary Poppins* (1964) in Hollywood, but she began with DISNEY in Britain in *The Three Lives of Thomasina* (1963). As an adult, she has appeared on TV, including *Napoleon in Love* (1974) and in only two further films: *Joseph Andrews* (1976), *The Thirty Nine Steps* (1978).

Dotrice, Michele (*b* Cleethorpes, 1947). Actress. Daughter of Roy DOTRICE, she began her career later than her younger sister, Karen. Has made only a handful of films, including *Jane Eyre* (1970), but has become an enjoyable TV character actress in middle age, as in *Midsomer Murders* (1997). Married to Edward WOODWARD.

OTHER BRITISH FILMS: *The Witches* (1966), *And Soon the Darkness*, *Blood on Satan's Claw* (1970), *Not Now, Comrade* (1976).

Dotrice, Roy (*b* Guernsey, 1923). Actor. Gained interest in acting while POW during WW2, was in varied rep (1945–55) before forming the Guernsey Repertory Company (1955–57), and with the RSC (1961–65), building up to leads. Best known for his one-man show, *Brief Lives* (1967, 1969), as aged John Aubrey, he entered films in *The Criminal* (1960), and has been busy on screen and TV ever since, in the US and Britain, where his best film part was as the heroine's decrepit father in *Lock Up Your Daughters!* (1969).

OTHER BRITISH FILMS INCLUDE: *The Heroes of Telemark* (1965), *A Twist of Sand* (1968), *Toomorrow, The Buttercup Chain* (1970), *Hide and Seek* (1972), *Not Now, Comrade* (1976), *The Colour of Funny* (1999).

Douglas Home, William *see* **Home, William Douglas**

Douglas, Angela (*b* Gerrards Cross, Bucks, 1940). Actress. Pretty fair-haired, blue-eyed actress, with theatre experience, who married Kenneth MORE after acting with him in *Some People* (1962) and *The Comedy Man* (1963). Her comedy sense landed her in several 'CARRY ONS': . . . *Cowboy* (1965), . . . *Screaming* (1966), . . . *Up the Khyber* (1968). Her sister, Sarah Douglas (*b* Stratford-upon-Avon, 1952), also appeared in a few British films (e.g. *Dracula*, 1973; *The People that Time Forgot*, 1977) before embarking on a career in US films and TV.

OTHER BRITISH FILMS INCLUDE: *The Shakedown* (1959), *The Gentle Terror* (1962), *Maroc 7* (1966), *Follow That Camel* (1967), *Digby, the Biggest Dog in the World* (1973), *Hamlet* (1996, UK/US).

Douglas, Bill (*b* Newcraighall, Scotland, 1934 – *d* Barnstaple, 1991). Director. Despite a comparatively small body of work, Bill Douglas remains one of the most original film-poets in British cinema history. His masterpiece remains the celebrated autobiographical trilogy – *My Childhood* (1972), *My Ain Folk* (1973) and *My Way Home* (1978) – produced under the auspices of the BFI production board. Shot in an austere, monochrome style it recounts the material and emotional privations of the film-maker's childhood in a Scottish mining village in the aftermath of WW2. The haunting images of harsh poverty and suffering, forcing the audience to look at, contemplate and understand the world and emotions of his filmic alter-ego, Jamie, drew critical comparisons with such masters as Dovzhenko, Dreyer, Satyajit Ray and Bresson. In addition to the unadorned stillness of the shots, the trilogy is also distinguished by a carefully crafted elliptical narrative structure, a demonstration of the emotional and intellectual power of editing rarely seen since the days of Soviet montage cinema.

It took Douglas eight years to realise his next film, *Comrades* (1986), the story of the Tolpuddle Martyrs, six farm labourers who were arrested, tried and transported to Australia in 1834 for forming a trade union. This three-hour film continued his interest in the struggle and redemption of ordinary people and the virtues of community and comradeship. The story is told through the eyes of a travelling magic lanternist and the film contains numerous references to pre-cinematic optical devices and entertainments including the camera obscura, the peep show and the panorama. This fascination also informed Douglas's other life as a collector of artefacts, ephemera and books relating to the history and pre-history of cinema. After his death this collection was donated to the University of Exeter where it is displayed in the Bill Douglas Centre, a museum honouring his legacy.

BIBLIOG: Eddie Dick *et al* (eds). *Bill Douglas: A Lanternist's Account*, 1993. Duncan Petrie.

Douglas, Howard (*b* Scotland, 1896 – *d* ?). Actor. Prolific character player of stage (from 1912, with Sir Herbert TREE) and films, often, in middle age, as professional men, like the silver-haired doctor in *Dear Murderer* (1947). In RAF in WW1 and WW2.

OTHER BRITISH FILMS INCLUDE: *Death at Broadcasting House* (1934), *No Limit* (1935), *Brief Ecstasy, Fire Over England* (1937), *The Challenge* (1938), *The Rake's Progress* (1945), *Spring Song, Hue and Cry* (1946), *They Made Me a Fugitive* (1947), *Miranda* (1948), *Man on the Run* (1949), *Stage Fright, State Secret, The Mudlark* (1950), *Stolen Face* (1952), *Meet Mr Callaghan* (1954), *Whistle Down the Wind* (1961), *The Heroes of Telemark* (1965).

Douglas, Jack (*b* Newcastle-upon-Tyne, 1927). Actor. Comedian who collaborated with Joe Baker and Des O'Connor on TV programmes and appeared almost exclusively in 'CARRY ON' films: . . . *Matron*, . . . *Abroad* (1972), . . . *Girls* (1973), . . . *Dick* (1974, as Sgt Jock Strapp), . . . *Behind* (1975), . . . *England* (1976), . . . *Emmannuelle* (1978), . . . *Columbus* (1992). Also in the TV series, *Carry On Laughing* (1975).

OTHER BRITISH FILMS: *Nearly a Nasty Accident* (1961), *Bloody Kids* (1979), *The Shillingbury Blowers* (1980).

Douglas, Lilian Actress. Busy second lead and occasional leading lady in 20s films.

BRITISH FILMS: *Little Mother, A Sporting Double, A Master of Craft, When Greek Meets Greek, The Sporting Interest* (1922), *Paddy-the-Next-Best-Thing, The Hypocrites, In the Blood* (1923), *The Jungle Woman* (1926), *Pearl of the South Seas* (1927). AS.

Douglas, Robert (*b* Bletchley, Bucks, 1909 – *d* California, 1999). Actor, director. RN: Finlayson. While he never became a top star, Douglas was a compelling screen presence, especially in urbanely villainous roles, preferably with sword in hand. A world-class swordsman, he may now be best remembered for his duel with Errol FLYNN in *The Adventures of Don Juan* (1948, US) and swashbuckling in the MGM–British *Ivanhoe* (1952). RADA-trained, on stage from 1927 (London 1928) and on Broadway 1929, he entered films in 1931 and made nine before serving in the Fleet Air Arm (1939–45), including *Over the Moon* (1939), with Merle OBERON, and the mountaineering drama, *The Challenge* (1938), both for KORDA. Post-war, he had a prolifically villainous career in Hollywood and later became a TV director on many popular US series. Married (1 of 2) actress Dorothy HYSON (1935–43).

OTHER BRITISH FILMS INCLUDE: *PC Josser* (1931), *Death Drives Through* (1935), *Our Fighting Navy* (1937), *The Lion Has Wings* (1939), *The Chinese Bungalow* (1940), *The End of the River* (1947), *Night Train to Paris* (1964, d).

Dowie, Freda (*b* Carlisle, 1928). Actress. Trained as a drama teacher at Central School and has combined acting with teaching. Came to attention with her stunning performance as the careworn, battered wife in Terence Davies' *Distant Voices Still Lives* (1988, UK/Ger). Other films have been few, including two for Michael WINTERBOTTOM: *Butterfly Kiss* (1995) and *Jude* (1996); some notable TV, including *Oranges Are Not the Only Fruit* (1990) and *Our Friends in the North* (1996).

OTHER BRITISH FILMS: *Subterfuge* (1968), *Cover Her Face* (1985), *The Monk* (1990, UK/Sp), *Maisie's Catch*, *Trick of the Light* (2000, shorts).

Dowling, Joan (*b* Laindon, 1929 – *d* London, 1954). Actress. As spunky tomboy in *Hue and Cry* (1946) or Cockney waif, touchingly vulnerable in *No Room at the Inn* (1948), Dowling was a young actress of impressive range, with a gift for pathos. On stage from 1943 and under contract to ABPC in later 40s, her career faltered as she matured, and she committed suicide. Was married to Harry FOWLER.
OTHER BRITISH FILMS: *For Them That Trespass*, *Bond Street* (1948), *Train of Events*, *A Man's Affair*, *Landfall* (1949), *Murder Without Crime*, *Pool of London* (1950), *The Magic Box* (1951), *24 Hours of a Woman's Life*, *Women of Twilight* (1952), *The Case of Gracie Budd* (1953, short).

Down, Lesley-Anne (*b* London, 1955). Actress. Delicately lovely brunette, in films from her teens, but really came to attention for her role as Lady Georgina Worsley in the TV series *Upstairs, Downstairs* (1971–75). She had the female lead in *The First Great Train Robbery* (1978), but generally her British films were disappointing – like her subsequent US ones. Many telemovies and mini-series, including *North and South* (1985, US) and its sequels. Married (1 of 3) director William Friedkin (1982–85).
OTHER BRITISH FILMS: *The Smashing Bird I Used to Know* (1969), *Assault*, *Countess Dracula* (1970), *Pope Joan* (1972), *Brannigan* (1975), *The Pink Panther Strikes Again* (1976), *Hanover Street* (1979).

Doxatt-Pratt, B(ernard) E(dwin) (*b* Upper Norwood, 1886 – *d* ?). Director. Directed feature films between 1920 and 1922 for Anglo-Hollandia, a production company formed by Maurits Binger and distributor Granger's Exclusives, utilizing the studios of the former in Haarlem, Holland. Despite interesting casts and storylines, the films were antiquated in direction and low in production values. Early in the 30s, Doxatt-Pratt abandoned wife and children (one of whom, Norman, sometimes appeared in his films) and simply disappeared.
BRITISH FILMS: (co-d) *Fate's Plaything*, *Hidden Life*, *John Heriot's Wife*, *The Little Hour of Peter Wells*, *Nurse Brown*, *Joy*, *As God Made Her* (+ sc) (1920), *Circus Jim* (1922, co- director); (d) *The Skin Game*, *Laughter and Tears*, *The Other Person* (1921), *My Lord the Chauffeur* (1927). AS.

Doyle, Sir Arthur Conan (*b* Edinburgh, 1859 – *d* Crowborough, 1930). Author. Though some other of Doyle's fictions have been filmed, including three versions of *The Lost World* (1960, 1992, and on TV, 1999, all US, and 2001, UK) and *The Adventures of Gerard* (1970, UK/It/Switz), the screen – like the world – has been overwhelmingly preoccupied with his master detective, SHERLOCK HOLMES, and Holmes's prosaic sidekick, Dr Watson. He was much filmed in Britain in the 30s and in a popular low-budget series in the US in the mid 40s. His creations have also given rise to pastiche entertainments, in fiction and film, some of rare quality, like Billy Wilder's *The Private Life of Sherlock Holmes* (1970). Knighted in 1902.

Doyle, Patrick (*b* Uddingston, Scotland, 1953). Composer, actor. Doyle, who studied at the Royal Scottish Academy of Music and Drama, has achieved much of his success as Kenneth BRANAGH's first choice for film scoring. However he has also worked with other British directors such as Mike NEWELL (*Into The West*, 1992) as well as Americans such as Brian De Palma (*Carlito's Way*, 1993). Doyle joined Branagh at the Renaissance Theatre Company in 1987. His first musical project was the ambitious and masterful *Henry V* (1989, + a). Though the music for this film was heroic and dramatic, the generally sunny tone of much of Doyle's work has lent itself

beautifully to such comedies as *Much Ado About Nothing* (1993, UK/US) and *Sense and Sensibility* (1995, UK/US) for which he won a BAA. Doyle has also appeared in minor roles in many of Branagh's films but his first acting role dates back to 1981, when he appeared in *Chariots of Fire*.
OTHER BRITISH FILMS INCLUDE: (comp) *Dead Again* (1991, UK/US, + a), *Hamlet* (1996, UK/US), *Love's Labour's Lost* (2000, UK/Fr/US, + a); (a) *In The Bleak Midwinter* (1995). Tim Roman.

Doyle, Roddy (*b* Dublin, 1958). Author, screenwriter. Doyle's novels of Irish life have been popularly adapted to the screen in Alan PARKER's *The Commitments* (1991) and Stephen FREARS's *The Snapper* (1993) and *The Van* (1996). Doyle worked on all three screenplays and their affection for their subjects survives intact; in 2000 he wrote the original screenplay for *When Brendan Met Trudy* (UK/Ire). Won the Booker Prize (1993) for his novel, *Paddy Clark Ha Ha Ha*.

Doyle, Tony (*b* Frenchpark, Ireland, 1942 – *d* London, 2000). Actor. Trained as actor after leaving Trinity College, Dublin, Doyle was best known for several key, finely differentiated TV roles: priest in *The Riordans* (1965), police chief in *Between the Lines* (1992), shifty businessman in *Ballykissangel* (1996) and violent, moody widower in *Amongst Women* (1998). Beside these, his films, including *Damage* (1993, UK/Fr), have seemed incidental.
OTHER BRITISH FILMS INCLUDE: *Ulysses* (1967, UK/US), *Loophole* (1980), *Who Dares Wins* (1982), *Secret Friends* (1991), *Circle of Friends* (1995, Ire/US), *The Boxer* (UK/Ire/US), *I Went Down* (1998, UK/Ire/Sp).

drag performances British audiences have a seemingly unquenchable thirst for men in frocks, and most film comedians and many comic actors have at some time been obliged to don drag. Among the more memorable are Alastair SIM as the headmistress in the ST TRINIAN'S SERIES, Kenneth CONNOR as a putative glamour girl in *Carry On Cabby* (1963), Sid FIELD as a 17th-century matron in *Cardboard Cavalier* (1949) and Dennis QUILLEY as a showbiz queen in *Privates On Parade* (1982). Lurking behind such performances are both the shadow of the pantomime dame and also, though in more complex ways, the use of drag and camp in gay and queer subcultures. Drag isn't entirely confined to comedy, however, being used more as a shock tactic or a plot tease in thrillers and mysteries that range from HITCHCOCK's early sound picture *Murder!* (1930) to Neil JORDAN's *The Crying Game* (1992). Women dressing as men is far rarer, in any genre, though Jessie MATTHEWS in *First A Girl* (1935) deserves a mention, as does the Laurel and Hardy act performed by British actresses Beryl REID and Susannah YORK in the US-made *The Killing of Sister George* (1968). Andy Medhurst.

Drake, Charlie (*b* London, 1925). Actor. RN: Springall. In TV from the early 50s, with his own comedy series in 1958 and 1960. Short of stature, outrageous of demeanour and bizarre of accent, he is clearly an acquired taste; cinema audiences never acquired it in great numbers, as they watched mind-numbing pieces like *Petticoat Pirates* (1961) and *The Cracksman* (1963).
OTHER BRITISH FILMS: *The Golden Link* (1954), *Sands of the Desert* (1960), *Mister Ten Per Cent* (1967), *Professor Popper's Problems* (1974), *To See Such Fun* (1977).

Drake, Fabia (*b* Herne Bay, 1904 – *d* London, 1990). Actress. RN: Ethel McGlinchy. Screen debut as a child in *Masks and Faces* (1917) preceded stage career, in Shakespearean and other classic roles, and pre-war TV; in film, settled into enjoyable battleaxedom with such post-WW2 roles as Lady Cotton in

Poet's Pub, opera-mad Miss Gelding (a name for allegory) in *All Over the Town* (1949) and a scandalised nanny in *Young Wives' Tale* (1951). Often titled, invariably formidable, she was still exercising her craft in the/her 80s: in TV's *The Jewel in the Crown* (1984), in *A Room with a View* and the US-made *Year of the Dragon* (1985), in which she did not play the title role. Awarded OBE in 1987.

OTHER BRITISH FILMS INCLUDE: *Meet Mr Penny* (1938), *London Belongs to Me* (1948), *White Corridors* (1951), *The Hour of 13* (1952), *Fast and Loose* (1954), *All for Mary* (1955), *The Good Companions* (1956), *Girls at Sea* (1958), *Operation Bullshine* (1959), *A Nice Girl Like Me* (1969), *The Devil's Widow* (1971), *Sweet Virgin* (1974), *Valmont* (1989).

BIBLIOG: Autobiography, *Blind Fortune*, 1978.

Draper, Peter (*b* 1925). Dramatist, screenwriter. Wrote two archetypal 60s films for Michael WINNER – *The System* (1964) and *I'll Never Forget What's 'is Name* (1967) – catching some of the decade's glitz, but has done little since. Also wrote *The Buttercup Chain* (1970) and some of TV's *Poldark* (1975).

Drayton, Alfred (*b* Brighton, 1881 – *d* London, 1949). Actor. RN: Varick. Marvellously entertaining bullet-head, forever on the brink of explosion, much associated, in the latter part of his career, with Robertson HARE, with whom he appeared in stage farces often transferred to the screen, as with *Aren't Men Beasts?* (1937) and *Women Aren't Angels* (1942). He also expostulated with/against other comedians of the day, such as Leslie HENSON and Albert BURDON, and when he wasn't expostulating he could be convincingly corrupt, as in *The Halfway House* (1944), or vicious as Mr Squeers in *Nicholas Nickleby* (1947), and he and Joan HICKSON are a very funny nouveau riche couple in *Don't Take It to Heart* (1944). Apparently choleric in real life too, he collapsed during a performance of *One Wild Oat* and died next morning.

OTHER BRITISH FILMS: *Iron Justice* (1915), *A Little Bit of Fluff* (1919), *A Temporary Gentleman*, *The Honeypot* (1920), *A Scandal in Bohemia*, *Love Maggie* (1921), *The W Plan*, *The Squeaker* (1931), *Happy Ending*, *Brown Sugar*, *The Calendar* (1931), *Lord Babs* (1932), *The Little Damozel*, *It's a Boy!*, *Friday the Thirteenth*, *Falling for You* (1933), *Radio Parade of 1935*, *Jack Ahoy!*, *Lady in Danger*, *Red Ensign* (1934), *Oh, Daddy!*, *Me and Marlborough*, *Look Up and Laugh*, *First A Girl* (1935), *Tropical Trouble*, *The Crimson Circle* (1936), *A Spot of Bother* (1938), *So This is London* (1939), *Banana Ridge* (1941), *The Big Blockade* (1942), *They Knew Mr Knight* (1945), *Things Happen at Night* (1948).

Dresdel, Sonia (*b* Hornsea, 1909 – *d* Canterbury, 1976). Actress. RN: Lois Obee. It is surprising to find she made only about a dozen films: she is such a vivid melodramatic presence in them that they seem more numerous in the memory. RADA-trained, she had a long stage career, from 1931, was a famous Hedda Gabler (1942, 1943, 1955), and excelled as women of strong, sometimes murderous emotion. Entered films in *The World Owes Me a Living* (1945), did cherishably wicked things in *While I Live* (1947) and *This Was a Woman* (1948), and was mutely vengeful in *The Break* (1962), but her most indelible impression was as Ralph RICHARDSON's harridan wife in *The Fallen Idol* (1948). Sadly, we shall probably not see such actresses again.

OTHER BRITISH FILMS: *The Clouded Yellow* (1950), *The Third Visitor* (1951), *The Secret Tent* (1956), *Death Over My Shoulder* (1957), *The Trials of Oscar Wilde* (1960), *The Last of the Long-Haired Boys* (1968), *Lady Caroline Lamb* (1972, UK/It/US).

Dreyfus, James (*b* London, 1968). Actor. Made his name as Constable Goody in TV's *The Thin Blue Line* (1995) and has since made an endearing impression in cinema as Hugh GRANT's fey bookshop assistant in *Notting Hill* (1999). Was also in two gay-orientated comedies, *Thin Ice* (1994) and *Boyfriends* (1996), as well as *Richard III* (1995) and *Being Considered* (2000).

Driver, Betty (*b* Leicester, 1920). Actress. Formerly a singer, leading lady of a few very light 30s entertainments, including *Penny Paradise* (1938) and *Let's Be Famous* (1939); became a household name for continuing role of Betty Turpin in TV's *Coronation Street* from 1969.

Driver, Edgar (*b* London, 1887 – *d* 1964). Actor. Stocky, balding character player, much seen in the 30s films of John BAXTER, often as a chirpy character called Tich – a transport driver who, unlike the hero, switches from horses to vans in *Song of the Road* (1937).

OTHER BRITISH FILMS INCLUDE: *Song of the Plough*, *Doss House* (1933), *White Ensign*, *Designing Women* (1934), *A Real Bloke*, *Jimmy Boy* (1935), *Men of Yesterday*, *Hearts of Humanity* (1936), *Victoria the Great*, *Talking Feet* (1937), *Stepping Toes* (1938), *The Common Touch* (1941), *We'll Smile Again* (1942), *Demobbed* (1944, unc), *Judgement Deferred* (1951), *The Big Chance* (1957), *The King's Breakfast* (1963, short).

Driver, Minnie (*b* London, 1971). Actress. Raised in Barbados, now settled in the US, it seems the unconventionally beautiful, intelligent, Bedales-educated Driver will now film only sporadically in Britain. This is bad news for British films as her work in several diverse films suggests: as the plump frump of *Circle of Friends* (Ire/US); as the suddenly impoverished Jewess, who remakes her identity to earn a living in *The Governess* (1998, UK/Fr); and as waspish Mabel Chiltern in *An Ideal Husband* (1999, UK/US). In the US, she was Oscar-nominated for her supporting role in *Good Will Hunting* (1997) and made a dozen films there in five years, including the charming romance, *Return to Me* (2000). Trained at Webber-Douglas, she at once found TV work. Set up a production company with sister Kate – The Two Drivers – and made *At Satchem Farm* (1998).

OTHER BRITISH FILMS INCLUDE: *Cruel Train* (1995), *GoldenEye* (1995, UK/US), *High Heels and Low Lifes* (2001, UK/US).

Drury, Weston (*b* London, 1892 – *d* 1983) and **Drury, Weston Jr** (*b* Leeds, 1916). Casting directors. Weston Sr, former stage actor and producer, entered films in 1929 and worked as casting director for several companies, including Warners before joining the RANK ORGANISATION in that capacity (1945–48), and, later, Associated Rediffusion. His son, after working at GAINSBOROUGH, followed his father at Rank in 1949 and stayed until 1971. He was later responsible for casting such BOND adventures as *Live and Let Die* (1973) and *Moonraker* (1979, UK/Fr) and for such high-profile TV series as *The Return of the Saint* (1978–79). Active in casting until 1983.

Dryhurst, Edward (*b* Desborough, 1904 – *d* London, 1989). Screenwriter, producer, director. Entered industry at 15, as office boy at IDEAL FILM COMPANY and in 1922 wrote and directed (as Edward Roberts) a two-reeler called *Hims – Ancient and Modern*. Went to Hollywood in 1924 where he worked for various companies, including Universal, in the publicity department. Back in Britain he collaborated on several screenplays, his first credits being on *Kidnapped* and *The Woman from China* (1930). Busy throughout the 30s, mainly as writer, on modest genre pieces, he went somewhat upmarket in the 40s, writing screenplays for such as *The Man from Morocco* (1945) and *Master of Bankdam* (1947, co-sc, co-p), and producing films for his own company, including two directed by Edmond GRÉVILLE, *Noose* (1948, + co-sc) and *The Romantic Age* (1949, + co-sc). In 1987, he published an autobiography, *Gilt off the Gingerbread*, with frank accounts of getting on in the industry and somewhat leering details of his sexual adventurings.

OTHER BRITISH FILMS INCLUDE (sc, unless noted): *Dangerous Seas* (1931, + d), *Commissionaire* (1933, d), *Dial 999* (p), *The Claydon Treasure Mystery* (1938), *The Case of the Frightened Lady* (1940), *This Man is Dangerous*, *Atlantic Ferry* (co-sc) (1941), *This Was Paris* (1942), *Get Cracking* (1943, co-sc), *The Agitator* (1945), *While I Live* (1947, p), *Castle in the Air* (1952, co-sc, p), *It's Never Too Late* (1956), *Stranger in Town* (1957, co-sc).

Dudley, Anne (*b* Chatham, Kent, 1956). Composer. Anne Dudley's film scores have been rare but are associated with some of Britain's most successful films. Classically trained at England's RCM, Dudley got her start as protégée of pop producer Trevor Horn and, in 1983, formed the influential electronic group 'The Art Of Noise'. The group's success throughout the 80s gave Dudley a base from which to move into film scoring and her music for the Phil COLLINS' vehicle *Buster* (1988) won her a British Music Award. She also scored Neil JORDAN's international breakthrough film, *The Crying Game* (1992). After working with Michael Flately to conduct the music for his 'Lord Of The Dance' spectaculars, Dudley won an Oscar for her score for *The Full Monty* (1997, UK/US).

OTHER BRITISH FILMS INCLUDE: *The Misadventures of Mr Wilt* (1989), *The Pope Must Die* (UK/US), *The Miracle* (1991, UK/Ire), *The Grotesque*, *When Saturday Comes*, *Hollow Reed* (1996, UK/Fr). Tim Roman.

Dudley-Ward, Penelope (*b* London, 1919 – *d* London, 1982). Actress. Marriage to director Carol REED seems to have put paid to the film career of this radiantly lovely actress who came from a society background, her mother Freda having been the mistress of Edward, Prince of Wales, for 16 years, and her father a Liberal MP. Her fresh-minted beauty and gaiety make her very welcome company in such male-dominated films as *Convoy* (1940), *In Which We Serve* (1942) and especially as David NIVEN's wife in *The Way Ahead* (1944). Funny as a silly socialite in *The Citadel* (1938) and entrancing as the girl who converts Russian engineer Laurence OLIVIER to things British in *The Demi-Paradise* (1943), she had a fine light comedy touch. Her stage career outlasted her film work by several years.

OTHER BRITISH FILMS: *Escape Me Never*, *Moscow Nights* (1935), *Hell's Cargo* (1939), *The Case of the Frightened Lady*, *Dangerous Comment* (1940), *Major Barbara* (1941), *English Without Tears* (1944).

Duering, Carl (*b* Berlin, 1923). Actor. RN: Gerald Fox. Entered films and TV in early 50s, usually playing foreigners, most of whom, like Peter ILLING's thuggish off-sider in *Escapement* (1957), were up to no good. Playing Dr Brodsky in *A Clockwork Orange* (1971) was probably the highpoint of his film career; recent decades spent mostly on TV.

OTHER BRITISH FILMS INCLUDE: *Appointment in London*, *The Red Beret* (1953), *The Divided Heart*, *The Colditz Story* (1954), *The Battle of the V-1* (1958), *The Guns of Navarone* (1961), *Strip Tease Murder* (1963), *Arabesque* (1966, UK/US), *Gold* (1974), *Voyage of the Damned* (1976), *The Waiting Time* (1999), *Saltwater* (2000, UK/Ire/Sp).

Duffell, Bee (*b* Belfast, 1914 – *d* 1974). Actress. After 10 years' acting experience in Belfast and Dublin, she came to the West End in 1951 and filmed the following year, in the lamentable *Treasure Hunt* (1952), and occasionally over the next 20 years.

OTHER BRITISH FILMS INCLUDE: *Duel in the Jungle* (1954), *A Night to Remember* (1958), *Tamahine* (1962), *The Victors* (1963), *Fahrenheit 451* (1966), *The Double Man*, *Quatermass and the Pit* (1967), *Wonderwall* (1968), *Monty Python and the Holy Grail* (1974).

Duffell, Peter (*b* 1924). Director. In 1972, having spent the 60s on MERTON PARK thrillerettes, Duffell directed and co-scripted one of the most intelligent adaptations of Graham GREENE, *England Made Me* (UK/Yug), capturing the seediness and danger of the original, and enshrining a great Greenean interpretation in Michael HORDERN's Minty. There was nothing in his *cv* before this to suggest Duffell could do it, and nothing after to remind one that he had. He was 2ud on *Superman* (1978) and since then has been mainly involved with TV, including the brilliantly acted anecdote, *Caught on a Train* (1980) and the lush oriental soap, *The Far Pavilions* (1984).

OTHER BRITISH FILMS INCLUDE: *The Silent Weapon* (short), *Partners in Crime* (1961), *Men of Inchinnan* (1962, short), *Company of Fools* (1966, short, + co-sc), *Payment in Kind* (1967, short, + co-sc), *The House That Dripped Blood* (1970), *Inside Out* (1975), *Letters to an Unknown Lover* (1985, UK/Fr).

Duggan, Tommy (*b* Ireland, 1909 – *d* 1998) Actor. Irish character player on London stage, then, after RAF service, in small roles for 50 years, starting with *Dangerous Moonlight* (1941). Made several minor US films at the end of the 50s and, on TV, he was Judge Roy Bean in *Lillie* (1978).

OTHER BRITISH FILMS INCLUDE: *Thunder Rock*, *Flying Fortress* (1942), *A Matter of Life and Death* (1946), *Good-Time Girl* (1947), *Bonnie Prince Charlie* (1948), *The Elusive Pimpernel* (1950), *Lady Godiva Rides Again* (1951), *Happy Ever After*, *The Belles of St Trinian's* (1954), *Don't Bother to Knock* (1961), *The Fur Collar* (1962), *The Adding Machine* (1969), *The Revolutionary* (1970), *Superman II* (1980).

Duke, Ivy (*b* London, 1896 – *d* ?). Actress. A leading lady, who often appeared on screen with her husband, Guy NEWALL, Duke made her stage debut in 1915, left the theatre to star in films in 1918, and returned to the stage in 1924.

BRITISH FILMS: *I Will*, *The March Hare*, *Fancy Dress*, *The Garden of Resurrection* (1919), *Duke's Son*, *Testimony* (1920), *The Bigamist* (1921), *Beauty and the Beast*, *The Persistent Lovers*, *Boy Woodburn* (1922), *The Starlit Garden* (1923), *The Great Prince Shan*, *Decameron Nights* (1924), *A Knight in London* (1929). AS.

Du Maurier, Dame Daphne (*b* London, 1907 – *d* Par, 1989). Author. One of the most popular best-selling novelists of the inter-war period, especially for the Gothic romance, *Rebecca*, filmed in Hollywood by HITCHCOCK and in two British TV versions (1979, 1997). Hollywood also filmed *Frenchman's Creek* (1944) and *My Cousin Rachel* (1952), skilful distillations of women's emotional needs and conflicts. Hitchcock did poorly by *Jamaica Inn* (1939) in Britain and made the brilliantly apocalyptic *The Birds* (1963), from her novella, in the US. Other British films derived from her work are: *The Years Between* (1946, from play), the turgid *Hungry Hill* (1947), *The Scapegoat* (1958) and Nicolas ROEG's erotically charged nightmare, *Don't Look Now* (1973, UK/It). Her father was actor Gerald DU MAURIER and her grandfather George Du Maurier, author of *Trilby*, filmed in Britain as *Svengali* in 1954. Made DBE in 1969. In 2000, Kate WINSLET was announced as starring in a film derived from a controversial biography of Daphne Du Maurier which depicts her as bisexual and the lover of Gertrude LAWRENCE.

Du Maurier, Sir Gerald (*b* London, 1873 – *d* London, 1934). Actor. The most celebrated actor-manager of his day, generally regarded as having brought a new naturalism to bear on popular drama. He made three silent films but disliked filming, though, towards the end of his life, for financial reasons, he made six talkies, including *Escape* (1930), as John GALSWORTHY's beleaguered hero-on-the-run, and *Jew Süss*, released in the year he died. In 1929, Basil DEAN had persuaded him to join the board of ASSOCIATED TALKING PICTURES. Father of Daphne DU MAURIER, he was knighted in 1922.

OTHER BRITISH FILMS: *Masks and Faces, Justice* (1917), *Unmarried* (1920), *Lord Camber's Ladies* (1932), *I Was a Spy* (1933), *The Scotland Yard Mystery, Catherine the Great* (1934).

Dunbar, Adrian (*b* Enniskillen, Ireland, 1958). Actor. Trained at Guildhall School of Music and Drama, sharp-featured, intelligent Dunbar has run up an impressive list of credits in the acting media. He has appeared in classic and modern plays, at the National Theatre and the Manchester Exchange among others, in TV mini-series, such as *Melissa* (1997) and the tele-drama *Tough Love* (2000), and nearly 20 films. Gained serious screen attention as the likeable wheeler-dealer, Micky O'Neill, in *Hear My Song* (1991, + co-sc), and followed this with telling roles in *The Crying Game* (1992), *Richard III* (1995, as Tyrell) and *The General* (1998). His role in *Star Wars . . . The Phantom Menace* (1999) was cut. Has the wit for comedy and the intensity for drama.

OTHER BRITISH FILMS INCLUDE: *Sky Bandits* (1986), *A World Apart* (1987, UK/Zim), *The Dawning* (1988), *My Left Foot, Dealers* (1989), *The Playboys* (1992, Ire/US), *Widows' Peak* (1994, UK/US), *Halcyon Days, Innocent Lies* (UK/Fr) *The Near Room* (1995), *The Wedding Tackle* (2000), *Wild About Harry* (2001, UK/Ger/Ire).

Duncan, Archie (*b* Glasgow, 1914 – *d* London, 1979). Actor. Tall, solid character actor (and former electric welder), Duncan brought his imposing presence to over 30 roles, often with Scottish affiliations, including the shipyard manager in *Floodtide* (1949) and Dugal MacGregor in *Rob Roy . . .* (1953), but also a sturdy Beaudricourt in *St Joan* (1957, UK/US).

OTHER BRITISH FILMS INCLUDE: *Counterblast* (1948), *Bad Lord Byron, The Gorbals Story* (1949), *The Elusive Pimpernel, Circle of Danger* (1950), *Green Grow the Rushes* (1951), *The Story of Robin Hood . . .*, *Castle in the Air, The Brave Don't Cry, You're Only Young Twice!* (1952), *Laxdale Hall, Street Corner* (1953), *Trouble in the Glen* (1954), *X the Unknown* (1956), *The Devil's Pass* (1957), *Harry Black* (1958), *Lancelot and Guinevere* (1962), *The Mouse on the Moon* (1963), *The Man Outside* (1967), *Ring of Bright Water* (1969), *The Wilby Conspiracy* (1974).

Duncan, Lindsay (*b* Edinburgh, 1950). Actress. Though she played the female lead of the feminist who advertises for a co-driver to Munich in *Loose Connections* (1983), Duncan was never quite a film *star*. Central School-trained, she has, how-ever, become one of the most interesting character actresses in contemporary British cinema, as indicated by her perfor-mances as an unusually youthful Lady Markby in *An Ideal Husband* (1999, UK/US) and, vividly, in the dual role of Lady Bertram, drugged out of her mind, *and* her careworn sister in *Mansfield Park* (2000, UK/US). In such diverse TV series as *GBH* (1991, BAAn) and *Oliver Twist* (1999, as Oliver's vindictive stepmother) and on stage in the PINTER double, *Celebration/ The Room* (2000), she rounded off a remarkable mid-life flowering in her career in all the acting media. Provided the voice for TC-14 in *Star Wars . . . The Phantom Menace* (1999). Married actor Hilton MCRAE.

OTHER BRITISH FILMS INCLUDE: *Grown Ups* (1980), *Samson and Delilah* (1984, short), *Prick Up Your Ears* (1987), *The Reflecting Skin* (1990), *A Midsummer Night's Dream* (1996, Titania/Hippolyta).

Dundas, David (*b* Oxford, 1945). Composer. Associated with director Bruce ROBINSON on the cult comedy hit, *Withnail & I* (1986), and *How to Get Ahead in Advertising* (1989, co-comp), having earlier scored Barney PLATTS-MILLS's independent feature, *Private Road* (1971), in which Robinson had starred.

OTHER BRITISH FILMS: *Dark City* (1990), *Freddie as F.R.O.7* (1992, co-comp).

Dunham, Maudie (*b* Essex, 1902 – *d* London, 1982). Actress. Dunham enjoyed a short-lived career usually as a second female lead; appeared in nine films for producer G.B. SAMUELSON, including three he made in the US in the 1920s: *Love in the Wilderness, The Night Riders, The Ugly Duckling*.

BRITISH FILMS: *The Lads of the Village, The Beetle* (1919), *The Winning Goal, All the Winners* (1920), *Love Maggie, Mr Pim Passes By, The Magistrate, Laughter and Tears, Sheer Bluff* (1921), *Sinister Street* (1922), *The Parting of the Ways – Psalm 57* (1927), *What Money Can Buy* (1928). AS.

Dunn, Clive (*b* London, 1921). Actor. Having been a POW in Austria for two years during WW2 must have given Dunn some wry moments when he became a household favourite as Lance-Corporal Jack Jones in TV's cosy *Dad's Army* (1968–77) and the SPIN-OFF film (1971). His other credits are in a ragbag of modestly funny and/or merely trendy comedies.

OTHER BRITISH FILMS INCLUDE: *Treasure of San Teresa* (1959), *What a Whopper!* (1961), *The Fast Lady* (1962), *The Mouse on the Moon* (1963), *Just Like a Woman* (1966), *The Bliss of Mrs Blossom* (1968), *The Magic Christian, Crooks and Coronets* (1969).

Dunn, Geoffrey (*b* London, 1903). Actor. Prolific stage actor, director and translator of operas, who appeared in a few films, as, e.g. the tall, beaky would-be house-buyer in *Father Came Too!* (1963).

OTHER BRITISH FILMS: *While the Sun Shines* (1947), *Queen of Spades* (1949), *Ghost Ship* (1952), *I Am a Camera* (1955), *Crooks Anonymous, Lancelot and Guinevere, Doomsday at Eleven* (1962), *The Leather Boys* (1963).

Dunn, Nell (*b* London, 1936). Playwright, screenwriter. Chronicler of working-class life whose novels, *Up the Junction* and *Poor Cow*, were both filmed in 1967, by Peter COLLINSON and Ken LOACH respectively. Her play, *Steaming*, a serious spin on 'ladies' night in a Turkish bath', was the basis for Joseph LOSEY's last film (1984).

Dunn, Valentine (*b* Glasgow, 1904 – *d* Virginia Water, 1980). Actress. Serviceable supporting player of stage and screen, mainly of the 40s, when she played a young wife called to do war work in *Millions Like Us* (1943), a sharp-talking barmaid in *Great Day* (1945) and the hero's chintzy mother in *Song for Tomorrow* (1948).

OTHER BRITISH FILMS INCLUDE: *His Lordship Regrets* (1938), *Beyond Our Horizon* (1939), *Banana Ridge, Quiet Wedding* (1941), *Salute John Citizen* (1942), *Loyal Heart* (1946), *Gone to Earth* (1950), *Valley of Song* (1953).

Dunning, Ruth (*b* Prestatyn, 1911 – *d* London, 1983). Actress. On stage in 1935, first film – *Save a Little Sunshine* – in 1938, found fame in *The Grove Family* (1954–57), Britains' first TV soap, as nice lower-middle-class Mrs Grove, repeating the role in the cinema SPIN-OFF, *It's a Great Day* (1955). In film, she had leads in some 'B' MOVIES, including quite good ones like *Dangerous Afternoon* (1961), and in the little seen curiosity *Intimate Relations* (1953), but was essentially a reliable sup-porting actress. Married actor Jack ALLEN.

OTHER BRITISH FILMS INCLUDE: *Man of the Moment* (1955), *Urge to Kill, And Women Shall Weep* (1960), *The Three Lives of Thomasina* (1963), *Hoffman* (1969), *The House in Nightmare Park* (1973), *The Black Panther* (1977).

Dupont, E(wald) A(ndré) (*b* Zeitz, Saxony, 1891 – *d* Los Angeles, 1956). Director. Responsible for one genuine screen masterpiece in his native Germany, *Variete/Variety* (1925), his two UK silent films as director, *Moulin Rouge* (1928) and *Piccadilly* (1929), are brilliant examples of German expressionism; his three British talkies, *Atlantic* (1930), *Two Worlds* (1930) and *Cape Forlorn* (1931), represent early sound films at their worst. Also produced and co-wrote *Madame Pompadour* (1928). A later US career failed to produce any works of lasting value. AS.

Duprez, Fred (*b* 1884 – *d* at sea, 1938). Actor. Balding, beaky American vaudevillian who became a popular character actor in British films of the 30s, very funny as the fast-talking studio boss in *O-Kay for Sound* (1937). His first screen credit was as co-writer of *My Wife's Family* (1931), based on his stage comedy, filmed again in 1941 and 1956, and most of his films are light comedies and musicals typical of the period. Father of June DUPREZ.

OTHER BRITISH FILMS INCLUDE: *My Old Duchess* (1933), *Without You, Love, Life and Laughter, Danny Boy* (1934), *No Monkey Business, Lend Me Your Wife* (1935), *Reasonable Doubt, Queen of Hearts, The Big Noise* (1936), *Kathleen Mavourneen, Café Colette, Shooting Stars* (1937), *Take Off That Hat, Hey! Hey! USA* (1938).

Du Prez, John (*b* Sheffield, 1946). Composer. Recent work has been mainly in US movies, but he became known for his 80s British film scores, including some of the decade's most successful comedies: *Monty Python's The Meaning of Life* (1983), *A Private Function* (1984, + cond), *Personal Services* (1987) and *A Fish Called Wanda* (1988). In the 90s, Ninja Turtles seemed to hi-jack his career.

OTHER BRITISH FILMS: *Bullshot* (1983, + a), *She'll Be Wearing Pink Pyjamas* (1984, + cond), *A Chorus of Disapproval* (1989), *Carry On Columbus* (1992), *The Wind in the Willows* (1996).

Duprez, June (*b* London, 1918 – *d* London, 1984). Actress. This delicately lovely actress had her biggest success – as the Princess in the fantasy, *The Thief of Baghdad* (1940) – on the eve of WW2, then went to Hollywood where her career never again found momentum. She had two good roles there, in *None But the Lonely Heart* (1944) and *And Then There Were None* (1945), but nothing to work on the myth-making potential of the *Thief*'s success. She disliked Hollywood and blamed her agent, Myron Selznick, for not furthering her interests and retired in 1947, returning for the Canadian oddity, *One Plus One* in 1961. Her earlier British films included *The Four Feathers* (1939) as the hero's fiancée who believes him a coward.

OTHER BRITISH FILMS: *The Crimson Circle, The Cardinal* (1936), *The Spy in Black, The Lion Has Wings* (1939).

Dupuis, Paul (*b* Montreal, 1916 – *d* Saint Saureun, Canada, 1976). Actor. French-Canadian leading man briefly popular in British films during the later 40s. A radio announcer in Canada before war service, he was first seen in Ealing's *Johnny Frenchman* (1945), though one source claims an uncredited bit in *Yellow Canary* (1943). Mostly cast as romantic Frenchman, he had his best chances as the police inspector in *Sleeping Car to Trieste* (1948) and as the Duke of Burgundy in *Passport to Pimlico* (1949), and also co-starred with Margaret LOCKWOOD in the florid novelette, *Madness of the Heart* (1949).

OTHER BRITISH FILMS: *The Laughing Lady* (1946), *The White Unicorn, Against the Wind* (1947), *The Romantic Age* (1949), *The Reluctant Widow* (1950), *Life in Her Hands* (1951, unc).

Durrant, Frederick W. Director. Minor silent director, responsible for the first version of *The Picture of Dorian Gray* (1916) with Henry Victor in the title role. Under contract to W.G. BARKER, 1914–16, and to G.B. SAMUELSON in 1920.

OTHER BRITISH FILMS: *If England Were Invaded* (1914), *Cassell's Profession, The Girl Who Didn't Care* (1915), *What Every Woman Knows* (1917), *Women Who Win* (1919), *The Husband Hunter, A Temporary Gentleman* (1920), *No. 7 Brick Row* (1922). AS.

Durbridge, Francis (*b* Hull, 1912 – *d* London, 1998). Screenwriter, author. Creator of the RADIO hero, novelist-detective Paul Temple, whose exploits were filmed three times: *Send for Paul Temple* (1946, + co-sc), *Calling Paul Temple* (1948, + co-sc) and *Paul Temple Returns* (1952). Other films based on his TV serials were: *The Broken Horseshoe* (1953), *The Teckman Mystery* (1954, + co-sc), *Portrait of Alison* (1955), *The Vicious Circle* (1957, + sc), and *Operation Diplomat* (1953) based on his story. Later TV series included *The World of Tim Frazer* (1960–61) and *Melissa* (1964, 1997).

Dury, Ian (*b* Upminster, 1942 – *d* London, 2000). Actor, singer, composer. Former lead singer with rock bands 'Kilburn & the High Roads' (1971–75) and 'Ian Dury and the Blockheads' (1977–81), working-class Dury trained at the Royal College of Art before going in for rock and developed an interest in acting after the two – only moderately successful – bands folded. However, he had acquired a cult following, and it would need a cultist's devotion to track down most of his films. Apart from *The Cook, the Thief, His Wife & Her Lover* (1989, UK/Fr), none of them is exactly well-known. His last, *Middleton's Changeling* (1997), gave him a starring role but is not likely to have endeared itself to his fans.

OTHER BRITISH FILMS: *Fundamental Frolics* (1981), *Ian Dury* (1983, doc), *Number One* (1984), *Rocinante* (1986), *The Raggedy Rawney* (1988), *Bearskin – an Urban Fairytale* (UK/Port) (1989), *Split Second* (1992), *Skallagrigg* (1994), *Crow: City of Angels, Different for Girls* (1996), *Underworld* (1997).

Duse, Anna (*b* Wilmslow, 1908 – *d* Lauzerte, France, 1992). Costume designer. Active in films for 25 years post-war, she worked often with LAUNDER AND GILLIAT, contributing to the outrageous demeanour of the St Trinian's monstresses, and on two of the MORECAMBE & WISE films: *That Riviera Touch* (1966) and *The Magnificent Two* (1967). Reliable and workmanlike rather than inspired. Married film composer Temple ABADY (*d* 1970).

OTHER BRITISH FILMS INCLUDE: *It Happened One Sunday* (1944), *The Man From Morocco* (1945), *Quiet Weekend,* (1946), *Noose* (1948), *Lady Godiva Rides Again* (1951), *Folly to Be Wise* (1952), *Isn't Life Wonderful!* (1953), *The Constant Husband, The Belles of St Trinian's, A Kid for Two Farthings* (1954), *The Deep Blue Sea, Geordie* (1955), *The Extra Day, The Green Man* (1956), *Alive and Kicking* (1958), *Decline and Fall . . .* (1968, co-cos des), *The Most Dangerous Man in the World, Carry On Again Doctor* (1969).

Duvitski, Janine Actress. Eccentric character player who came to attention as love-lorn assistant to the vile retirement home manager in TV's *Waiting for God* (1990–94), then as demented supplicant to the King in *The Madness of King George* (1994) and anxious sycophant in TV's *Vanity Fair* (1998).

OTHER BRITISH FILMS INCLUDE: *Jabberwocky* (1977), *The First Great Train Robbery* (1978), *Breaking Glass* (1980), *The Missionary* (1981), *The Bride* (1985), *East of Ipswich* (1987), *Drowning by Numbers* (1988, UK/Neth), *Amy Foster* (1997, UK/Fr/US), *About a Boy* (2002, UK/Fr/Ger/US).

Dvorak, Ann (*b* New York, 1912 – *d* Honolulu, 1979). Actress. Stylish American actress who made four films in Britain during WW2 while then-husband, Leslie Fenton (*b* Liverpool, 1902 – *d* Montecito, California, 1978), was in the Royal Navy. Praised particularly as the former fiancée of a Nazi spy in *Squadron*

Leader X (1942), with director Lance COMFORT and co-star Eric PORTMAN, all three reunited for *Escape to Danger* (1943). Fenton directed two British features: *FP1* (1933, UK/Ger) and *The Saint's Vacation* (1941).

OTHER BRITISH FILMS: *This Was Paris* (1942), *There's a Future in It* (1943, short, co-d Fenton).

Dwoskin, Stephen (*b* New York, 1939). Director, cinematographer. Based in UK since 1964, Dwoskin's early work was associated with the LONDON FILM-MAKERS' CO-OPERATIVE, which he co-founded in 1966 to encourage experimental filmmaking, and later The Other Cinema. He had made short films in the US as part of Andy Warhol's circle prior to this. His films explore interior states (e.g. *Soliloquy*, 1967, UK/US; *Moment*, 1970), often subtly reflecting his viewpoint as a severely disabled man. He has filmed for CHANNEL 4, the BFI PRODUCTION BOARD, ZDF, ARTE and La Sept. His best-known feature films are probably *Dyn Amo* (1972), set in a strip-club, and *Trying To Kiss the Moon* (1995), his first openly autobiographical work. A retrospective of his work was shown at the 1995 Vue Sur Les Docs, Marseilles.

OTHER BRITISH FILMS INCLUDE: (short, d) *Naissant* (1964, UK/US), *Chinese Checkers* (1965, UK/US), *Me, Myself and I* (1969, UK/US), *Trixi*, (1970); (feature, d) *Times For* (1970), *Death and the Devil* (1973, UK/Ger), *Central Bazaar* (1973); (d/c/sc/e) *Behindert* (1974, + a, p, UK/Ger), *The Silent Cry* (1977, co-sc, co-e, + p, co-m, UK/Ger/Fr) *Shadows from Light* (1983, co-c, + p, doc), *Ballet Black* (1986, + p, doc). David Curtis.

Dwyer, Hilary (*b* Liverpool, 1945). Actress, producer. RN: Heath. Vivaciously attractive actress seen mainly in horror pictures, most notably in Michael REEVES' *Witchfinder General* (1968); also Isabella Linton in *Wuthering Heights* (1970). Later, as Hilary Heath (her real name), she became a producer, associated with TV mini-series derived from novels by Daphne DU MAURIER (*Jamaica Inn*, 1985; *Rebecca*, 1997; *Frenchman's Creek*, 1998), and has co-produced two notable cinema films: *An Awfully Big Adventure* (1995) and Gary OLDMAN's excoriating *Nil by Mouth* (1997).

OTHER BRITISH FILMS: (a) *Two Gentlemen Sharing, Thin Air, The Oblong Box, The File of the Golden Goose* (1969), *Cry of the Banshee* (1970).

Dwyer, Leslie (*b* London, 1906 – *d* Truro, 1986). Actor. Good-natured, jaunty Cockney standby in dozens of films, always recognisable, always enjoyable, sometimes, as in *The Way Ahead* (1944), as ex-travel agent Beck, or sharing a middle-aged romance with Megs JENKINS in *A Boy, a Girl and a Bike* (1949), given – and relishing – a real character to create. On stage from 1916 and in silent films from 1921 (*The Fifth Form at St Dominic's*), his main film career begins during WW2.

OTHER BRITISH FILMS INCLUDE: *The Flag Lieutenant* (1932) *In Which We Serve* (1942), *The Lamp Still Burns* (1943), *Perfect Strangers, Great Day* (1945), *Night Boat to Dublin, Piccadilly Incident* (1946), *Temptation Harbour, When the Bough Breaks, The Little Ballerina* (1947), *Bond Street, The Calendar* (1948), *Bad Lord Byron, Poet's Pub, Now Barabbas Was a Robber, It's Not Cricket* (1949), *Lilli Marlene, Double Confession* (1950), *There is Another Sun, Smart Alec, Judgement Deferred* (1951), *My Wife's Lodger, The Hour of 13, Hindle Wakes* (1952), *Marilyn* (1953), *The Good Die Young, The Black Rider* (1954), *Where There's a Will* (1955), *Face in the Night* (1956), *Stormy Crossing, The Thirty Nine Steps* (1958), *Left, Right and Centre* (1959), *I've Gotta Horse, Monster of Terror* (1965), *Crooks and Coronets* (1969), *Dominique* (1978).

Dyall, Franklin (*b* Liverpool, 1874 – *d* Worthing, 1950). Actor. On stage from 1894, he made a handful of silent films, including *Easy Virtue* (1927) for HITCHCOCK. Talkie debut was in the

'Titanic'-inspired *Atlantic* (1929), followed by 20 others, including major films like *The Private Life of Henry VIII* (1933) as Thomas Cromwell. Married to Mary MERRALL. Father of Valentine DYALL.

OTHER BRITISH FILMS INCLUDE: *Esther* (1916), *The Garden of Resurrection* (1919), *Duke's Son* (1920, d), *Alibi, The Ringer* (1931), *Men of Steel* (1932), *The Iron Duke* (1935), *Fire Over England* (1937), *All at Sea* (1939), *Conquest of the Air* (1940), *Yellow Canary* (1943), *Bonnie Prince Charlie* (1948).

Dyall, Valentine (*b* London, 1908 – *d* London, 1985). Actor. Most famous for the velvety voice in which he weekly introduced a long-running radio series with 'This is your storyteller . . . the Man in Black', a film derived from which he narrated in 1949. Harrow- and Oxford-educated son of stage and screen actor Franklin DYALL, he was on stage from 1930, entering films 12 years later. A ubiquitous and usually lugubrious presence in films, his two best remembered roles are those of the Duke of Burgundy in *Henry V* (1944), summing up the aftermath of battle, and the coldly censorious Stephen in *Brief Encounter* (1945), bitterly ironic at Trevor HOWARD's expense. In his last years, he was in several BBC TV Shakespearean productions.

OTHER BRITISH FILMS INCLUDE: *Much Too Shy* (1942, unc), *The Silver Fleet, Yellow Canary* (1943), *Hotel Reserve*, (1944), *I Know Where I'm Going!, Latin Quarter* (1945), *Night Boat to Dublin* (1946), *The White Unicorn* (1947), *Corridor of Mirrors* (1948), *Man On the Run, The Queen of Spades, Christopher Columbus* (narr) (1949), *The Body Said No!* (1950), *Ivanhoe, Paul Temple Returns, Salute the Toff* (1952), *The Final Test* (1953), *Suspended Alibi* (1956), *City of the Dead* (1960), *The Haunting* (1963), *The Wrong Box* (1966), *Casino Royale* (1967), *The Slipper and the Rose* (1976), *Britannia Hospital* (1982).

Dyer, Anson (*b* Patcham, 1876 – *d* Cheltenham, 1962). Animator. The most prominent of early British cartoonists, who had a background in stained glass and was at one time hailed as the country's answer to Walt Disney, Dyer is now little known and his work had small impact on the art or craft of ANIMATION. After study at the Brighton School of Art, Dyer entered the industry in 1915, producing three *Dicky Dee* cartoons for British and Colonial. He continued animation work with the Cartoon Film Company and Kine Komedy Kartoons (*Agitated Adverts* and *Peter's Picture Poem*, both from 1918, are preserved in the National Film and Television Archive), and in 1919 joined Cecil HEPWORTH's company, producing a series of *Cartoon Burlesques* and the *Kiddiegraph* series. In 1927, he created what would have been Britain's first animated feature, *The Story of the Flag*, but producer Archibald Nettlefold decided to release it as a series of shorts. Nettlefold did, however, finance Dyer's cartoon studio, Anglia Films, which began production in 1935 with *Sam and His Musket*. In 1939, Dyer formed Analysis Films to produce shorts for the MOI and other government agencies; as he had done earlier, Dyer also produced SPONSORED FILMS at Analysis, such as *Adventures of Soupy* (1947) for Symington's Soups. His last Analysis film was *Who Robbed the Robins* (1947) and his last production was *Fowl Play* (1950). AS.

Dyer, Danny (*b c* 1978). Actor. East Ender who shot to recognition as the drug-fuelled Moff in Justin KERRIGAN's *Human Traffic* (1999, UK/Ire). An agent saw him perform in a high school drama class and got him his first professional role in TV's *Prime Suspect 3* (1993). Since his success in *Human Traffic*, he has been rushed from film to film, and he has been touted to play the lead in a new film about Sid Vicious. He revoiced one of the leads for Luc Besson's *Taxi* (1999) for British consumption.

OTHER BRITISH FILMS: *Loving* (1995), *The Trench* (1999, UK/Fr), *Greenfingers* (UK/US), *High Heels and Low Lifes, Mean Machine* (UK/US) (2001).

Dyneley, Peter (*b* Hastings, 1921 – *d* 1977). Actor. Essentially a small-part supporting actor in 'A' films, like *The Young Lovers* (1954), Dyneley played leads in some minor films, including several with his wife Jane HYLTON. They are especially effective as adulterous wife and vengeful husband in *House of Mystery* (1961). In 1976, bearded and silver-haired, he played Celia JOHNSON's husband in the TV drama, *The Dame of Sark*.

OTHER BRITISH FILMS INCLUDE: *Hell Below Zero* (1953), *Beau Brummell* (1954), *Laughing in the Sunshine* (UK/Swe), *The Battle of the River Plate* (unc) (1956), *The Whole Truth, The Golden Disc* (1958), *Deadly Record* (1959), *The Roman Spring of Mrs Stone* (1961), *Call Me Bwana* (1963), *Green for Ireland* (1967, Ire, short, narr), *Thunderbird 6* (1968, voice), *The Executioner* (1970).

Dyson, Noel (*b* Newton Heath, 1916 – *d* 1995). Actress. Character player on stage since 1948 and in films since 1953, when she played the thermos-bearing gallery regular ('I never miss a murder') at the Old Bailey in *Eight O'Clock Walk*. Now best known on TV as Nanny in *Father Dear Father* (1968–73, 1978–79), a role she reprised in the feeble film SPIN-OFF in 1972.

OTHER BRITISH FILMS INCLUDE: *Carry On Constable* (1960), *The Silent Invasion* (1961), *Carry On Cabby* (1963), *Press for Time* (1966), *Champions* (1983), *Super Grass* (1994).

Ee

Eady, David (*b* London, 1924). Director. Son of Sir Wilfred Eady, Eady made several DOCUMENTARIES before being put under contract to LONDON FILMS where he was an assistant cutter on *The Third Man* (1949) and edited *Cry the Beloved Country* (1952), before directing an episode of *Three Cases of Murder* (1955). Directed several unusual 'B' MOVIES in the 50s: *The Heart Within* (1957), a racial-problem thriller; the engaging, wittily written *The Man Who Liked Funerals* (1958); and the oddly attractive *Zoo Baby* (1960, made 1957) about a small boy who steals a coatimundi from the zoo. Later career included further DOCUMENTARIES and children's films.

OTHER BRITISH FILMS INCLUDE: (d, unless noted) *Bridge of Time* (1950, short, + sc), *Edinburgh, The Road to Canterbury* (1952, shorts, + sc), *Malaga* (1954, 2ud), *In the Wake of a Stranger, The Crowning Touch* (1959), *Faces in the Dark* (1960), *The Verdict* (1964), *Operation Third Form* (1966, + co-sc), *Anoop and the Elephant, Hide and Seek* (1972), *The Laughing Girl Murder* (1973), *Where's Johnny* (1974, + co-p), *The Hostages* (1975), *Night Ferry, Echo of the Badlands* (co-d) (1976), *Deep Waters, Play Safe* (BAAn) (1978), *Danger on Dartmoor* (1980), *The Perils of Easy* (1986, short).

Eady levy Named for Sir Wilfred Eady, the Treasury official who devised the scheme. Introduced in 1950 as a temporary, voluntary measure to aid film production, then enshrined as a regular form of support for the film industry in the Cinematograph Films Act of 1957. It provided for a redistribution of revenue, achieved by an additional tax on box-office receipts. Part of its fruits was paid back to producers in proportion to the earnings of their films and part to the NATIONAL FILM FINANCE CORPORATION, the BFI and the CHILDREN'S FILM FOUNDATION. It clearly respected box-office success but its abolition in 1985 was a further setback to producers in already constrained times.

Ealing Studios The London suburb of Ealing has been a centre for film-making since the early 1900s. Will BARKER's original studio was replaced in 1931 by the existing one, built by ASSOCIATED TALKING PICTURES, but it was only when Michael BALCON took over as Head of Production from Basil DEAN in 1938 that the place, and the name, began to be associated with a distinctive body of films. In 1955 Balcon sold the studio, which has since been used by the BBC, and then by a variety of independents; his attempt to continue the Ealing operation on alien soil was short-lived. The term 'Ealing' essentially refers to the set of nearly 100 films made by the company under Balcon's management, and released between 1938 and 1959.

Ealing has become identified above all with COMEDY, and with a particular style and ethos: gentle, cosy, whimsical. While this stereotyping is understandable, it is far from being the whole truth. The company's output evolved over the years, and it was never homogeneous; indeed, it is precisely the variety, and the internal tensions, that give the work its energy and its continuing interest.

Already an experienced producer, Balcon set himself at Ealing to select and build, at a time when war was imminent, a team dedicated to making films that were 'absolutely rooted in the soil of this country'. Many of his long-term producers and directors, such as Sidney COLE, Charles FREND, Charles CRICHTON and Robert HAMER, were recruited as editors and then promoted; Harry WATT and Alberto CAVALCANTI were directors already, brought in from the government's CROWN FILM UNIT so that their expertise in DOCUMENTARY could enhance the REALISM of the studio's war films. This policy paid off in films like Cavalcanti's *Went the Day Well?* (1942), Watt's *Nine Men*, and Frend and Hamer's *San Demetrio–London* (1943).

Ealing had, by then, made a number of comedies with George FORMBY, Tommy TRINDER, and Will HAY, but it now concentrated increasingly on dramas, ranging from the Australian cattle-drive epic *The Overlanders* (1946) to *Scott of the Antarctic* (1948). Only with the release in 1949 of *Whisky Galore!*, *Passport to Pimlico* and *Kind Hearts and Coronets* did the concept of 'Ealing Comedy' become established, though there had been isolated predecessors such as *Hue and Cry* (1946). Comedies continued to constitute only a small proportion of the ouput; some of them flopped, but the best, such as *The Ladykillers* (1955), have proved more memorable than the dramas, with occasional exceptions like the police drama *The Blue Lamp* (1949) and the return to WW2 in *The Cruel Sea* (1952).

Comedy was a fertile post-war GENRE for Ealing because it enabled topical issues, with which Balcon's team had been conditioned to deal, to be dramatised not solemnly but in the liberating form of FANTASY. In late 40s Britain, the austerity of wartime dragged on; the protagonists of the comedies are therapeutically released into the fulfilment of their desires. But the films are more complex than this simple wish-fulfilment model suggests. First, the nature of the release is limited; *Passport to Pimlico* ends up seeming positively nostalgic for the wartime world of controls and rationing. Second, there is a clear gulf between the two main sub-sets of Ealing comedy. Those scripted by Ealing's most influential writer, T.E.B. CLARKE, such as *Passport to Pimlico, The Lavender Hill Mob* (1951) and *The Titfield Thunderbolt* (1953), are indulgent to their characters, courting such descriptions as cosy and whimsical; those directed by Ealing's main post-war recruit, Alexander MACKENDRICK, none of them written by Clarke, demonstrate a more ruthless analytical intelligence, and suggest that good intentions and goodwill are in themselves of limited value. The key texts here are *Whisky Galore!* and *The Man in the White Suit* (1951), along with Robert Hamer's *Kind Hearts and Coronets*, arguably his and Ealing's masterpiece.

The fascination of Ealing is that its films embody a 20-year continuity, responding to the exigencies of war and its aftermath in a manner that is both coherent and complex. Most of the individuals named above worked there for more than a decade; the studio's most prolific director, Basil DEARDEN, made 18 films between 1942 and 1956, covering a remarkable range both in GENRE and in style, and his body of work needs to be seen alongside the more spectacular achievements of Hamer and Mackendrick if the full significance of the studio's output is to be understood.

In 2000, the Ealing studios were bought for £10,000,000 by a consortium comprising FRAGILE FILMS (responsible for such successes as *Spice World*, 1997, and *An Ideal Husband*, 1999, UK/US), the property developers Manhattan Loft Company and The Idea Factory, a digital development company based in San Francisco. In the three years prior to this, it had been used by the NATIONAL FILM AND TELEVISION SCHOOL as a training facility for producers. The latest owners announced a film-making programme of 20 films in five years.

BIBLIOGRAPHY: Charles Barr, *Ealing Studios*, 1977, 3rd edition 1999; Patricia Warren, *British Film Studios*, 1995, rev. ed. 2001. Charles Barr.

Earle, Josephine (*b* New York, 1892 – *d* New York, 1929). Actress. After US appearances in 10 feature films in 1916 and 1917, Earle came to the UK as a leading lady, returning briefly to New York in 1920 for a stage appearance.

BRITISH FILMS INCLUDE: *Branded* (1920), *The Way of a Man* (1921), *Woman to Woman* (1923), *Unto Each Other* (1929), *Raise the Roof* (1930). AS.

Easdale, Brian (*b* Manchester, 1909 – *d* London, 1995). Composer. Came to fame for his work on nine POWELL and/or PRESSBURGER's films, beginning with *Black Narcissus* (1947) and winning an Oscar for *The Red Shoes* (1948), for which he composed the title BALLET. Powell found him 'the ideal musical collaborator', creating a sort of 'opera' in which 'music, emotion, image and voices all blended together into a new and splendid whole'. Trained at the RCM, his pre-Powell experiences included writing concert music, music for the theatre, and, during WW2 when he was in the Royal Artillery, he was often assigned to writing music for DOCUMENTARIES, as he had begun to do in 1936, for the GPO and CROWN FILM UNIT.

OTHER BRITISH FILMS INCLUDE: (short/doc) *Kew Gardens, Big Money* (1937), *Men in Danger* (1939), *Ferry Pilot* (1942); (features) *The Small Back Room* (1948), *Gone to Earth, The Elusive Pimpernel* (1950, + cond), *Outcast of the Islands* (1951), *The Green Scarf* (1954), *The Battle of the River Plate* (1956), *Miracle in Soho* (1957), *Peeping Tom* (1960), *The Queen's Guards* (1961), *Return to the Edge of the World* (1978).

Eastman, Brian (*b c* 1949) Producer. Winner of the Alexander KORDA Award for *Shadowlands* (1993, UK/US, co-p), Eastman was a busy producer of the 90s, especially on TV where he has been involved with ADAPTATIONS of Agatha CHRISTIE and Tom Sharpe, whose *Wilt* he filmed for cinema in 1989.

OTHER BRITISH FILMS INCLUDE: *Whoops Apocalypse* (1986), *Under Suspicion* (1991), *Firelight* (1997, UK/US), *Up on the Roof* (1997, co-p).

Easton, Jock Stunts expert. A Captain in WW2, Easton set up post-war a stunt agency in Soho, in partnership with **Joe Powell**, drawing on highly disciplined ex-servicemen to perform the dangerous stunts that often made stars look so brave.

Films for which they provided the stunts include *The Crimson Pirate* (1952), *Knights of the Round Table* (1953), *Moby Dick* (1956) and *The Curse of Frankenstein* (1957).

Eaton, Andrew (*b* Derry, *c* 1960). Producer. Cambridge-educated former BBC researcher who has teamed up to great effect with brilliant director Michael WINTERBOTTOM. They first worked together on TV's *Family* (1993), then formed Revolution Films, which made *Go Now* (1996), the moving study of a laddish character afflicted with multiple sclerosis, followed by, among others, the rigorously tragic *Jude* (1996), the dazzling multi-storied *Wonderland* (1999), and *The Claim* (2001, UK/Can/Fr), an audacious reworking of Thomas HARDY again. The Winterbottom–Eaton–Revolution group is producing some of the most remarkable work in British film.

OTHER BRITISH FILMS INCLUDE: *The James Gang, Resurrection Man* (1997), *I Want You* (1998), *With or Without You* (1999).

Eaton, Mick (*b* Nottingham, 1954). Director. Independent film-maker whose 80s and 90s work in offbeat film and TV production, including *Darkest England* (1984, + sc), was rewarded in 1999 with an MBE. He has had the support of CHANNEL 4, BBC FILMS and the BFI. TV work has included the screenplay for the docu-drama, *Why Lockerbie?* (1990).

OTHER BRITISH FILMS INCLUDE: *A Description of the World* (1981, short, + p, co-sc), *Fellow Traveller* (1989, sc), *Border Crossing* (1993, UK/Ger, co-sc).

Eaton, Shirley (*b* London, 1937). Actress. Memorable as the girl fatally gilded in *Goldfinger* (1964), Eaton had already made 20 mostly *un*memorable films before it and did virtually nothing memorable after it. A shapely blonde, she trained at the Aida FOSTER School, made her West End debut in 1954 and was used as decoration in many 50s comedies, starting with *You Know What Sailors Are* (1954), and making her way through 'DOCTOR' and 'CARRY ON' films. She had most fun in *Sailor Beware* (1956) and *The Naked Truth* (1957), where she was lively as well as nubile. The RANK ORGANISATION bought up her contract with LONDON FILMS – and did with her what it always did with pretty girls.

OTHER BRITISH FILMS INCLUDE: *Doctor in the House* (1954), *The Love Match* (1955), *Three Men in a Boat, Charley Moon* (1956), *Doctor at Large, A Date with Disaster* (1957), *Further Up the Creek, Carry On Sergeant, . . . Nurse* (1958), *. . . Constable* (1960), *Ten Little Indians* (1965), *The Blood of Fu Manchu* (1968).

Eaton, Wallas (*b* Leicester, 1917 – *d* Australia, 1995). Actor. Cambridge-educated character player on stage from 1936 and in occasional films from the late 40s, playing an embarrassed waiter in *This Sporting Life* (1963), and in Australia from the mid 70s. Much TV, including series, *Up Pompeii* (1971).

OTHER BRITISH FILMS INCLUDE: *Dual Alibi* (1947), *A Man's Affair* (1949), *Chelsea Story* (1951), *Operation Cupid* (1959), *Two Way Stretch* (1960), *Inspector Clouseau, Isadora* (1968), *O Lucky Man!* (1973).

Eatwell, Brian (*b* London, 1939). Production designer. BAA-nominated for his design for *The Three Musketeers* (1973), Eatwell has worked largely in the US since the early 70s. Cut his teeth on some trendy 60s British fare, including *Here We Go Round the Mulberry Bush, 30 Is a Dangerous Age, Cynthia* (1967) and the stylishly acrid *The Strange Affair* (1968), was assistant to Jocelyn HERBERT on *If . . .* (1968), and art director on two highly idiosyncratic films for Nicolas ROEG – *Walkabout* (1970, Aust), in which design underscores the film's cultural binarism, and *The Man Who Fell to Earth* (1976).

OTHER BRITISH FILMS INCLUDE: *The Shuttered Room* (1966), *I Start Counting* (1969), *The Abominable Dr Phibes* (1971), *Madame Sin* (1972), *Silent Cries* (1993).

Eberts, Jake (*b* Montreal, 1941). Executive. Founder and chief executive officer of GOLDCREST FILMS, the company that brought most prestige to British films in the 80s, with such Oscar triumphs as *Chariots of Fire* (1981) and *Gandhi* (1982, UK/Ind). A graduate of Harvard Business School with no particular interest in film until he became involved in raising money for the animated film version of *Watership Down* (1978), he became engrossed in the development of projects by major film-makers. This latter was important to him: he cannot be said to have promoted the careers of unknowns, but under his leadership such film-makers as Richard ATTENBOROUGH, David PUTTNAM and John BOORMAN received the kind of support from Goldcrest that is not common in post-studio decades. Resigned from Goldcrest in 1984 but returned in late 1985 at the invitation of its board to try (vainly) to rescue it financially, and resigned again in 1987. Has since worked for Allied Film-makers, functioning as producer or executive producer on some of its films. In 1990, he co-authored (with Terry Ilott), *My Indecision Is Final* an absorbing account of his Goldcrest years, emerging as a man of probity, with a taste for quality film production.

Eccles, Donald (*b* Nafferton, 1908 – *d* Brighton, 1986). Actor. Worked first in insurance; on stage in 1930 and stayed there for 50 years, including several seasons at Stratford. Much TV, including *I, Claudius* (1976), but few films, including *The Dresser* (1984), as a mincing thespian abused thus: 'You're meant to be the Duke of Venice, not the Queen of the May'.
OTHER BRITISH FILMS: *A Taste of Money* (1960), *Backfire!* (1962), *A Midsummer Night's Dream* (1968, as Starveling), *The Quatermass Conclusion* (1978), *A Private Function* (1984).

Eccleston, Christopher (*b* Salford, 1964). Actor. Attractive, bony-faced actor who brings a strong physical presence to film and television roles. Though not strictly a descendant of the ANGRY YOUNG MEN tradition, Central School-trained Eccleston has played roles that reveal commitment to his working-class background. His dedication to truthfulness is reflected in his film debut as the simple-minded Derek in '*Let Him Have It*' (1991), and maintained in his characterisation of the unhinged David in *Shallow Grave* (1994) and his poignant portrayal of Hardy's tragic *Jude* (1996). These led to international exposure in films such as *Elizabeth* (1998) and David Cronenberg's *eXistenZ* (1999, UK/Can). On TV he has favoured socially-conscious film-makers like Alan Bleasdale (*b* Liverpool, 1946; screenwriter for *No Surrender*, 1985), Alan CLARKE and Ken LOACH; most memorable in the Jimmy McGOVERN-scripted *Cracker* (1993–94) and the series, *Clocking Off* (2000). In 2000, he played the valet Jean in the West End production of Strindberg's *Miss Julie*, and in 2001 he starred on TV in Danny BOYLE's *Strumpet*, and as a notable Iago.
OTHER BRITISH FILMS INCLUDE: *Anchoress* (1993, UK/Belg), *Heart*, *With or Without You* (1999). Melinda Hildebrandt.

Eckman, Sam Jr (*b* New York, 1891 – *d* New York, 1976). Executive. Entered film industry in 1910 as exhibitor with his father, took charge of the New York office of Goldwyn Pictures in 1917, and, post-amalgamation with Metro (1924), was made manager of Eastern Division and, in 1927, managing director of MGM's British operation. Became a powerful figure in the British FILM SOCIETY, attracting some criticism when MGM allowed rubbishy films to be shown under its aegis to meet the quota requirements of the Cinematograph Act of 1927, but in late 1936 securing the services of Michael BALCON to oversee the production of high quality films, starting with *A Yank at Oxford* (1937). MGM's production programme was interrupted by WW2, but was resumed post-war. Eckman was awarded an Honorary OBE in 1947 and garnered an impressive number of other honours during his time in Britain.

Eclair Film Company, Limited Officially became operational in London on 28 January 1913, as the British arm of Société Française des Films et Cinématographe Eclair, founded in France in 1907, active in the US since 1911. Pre-1913, Eclair films were released in the UK by the Tyler Film Co. In 1912, it had produced a series of *Sherlock Holmes* shorts in England, continuing a tradition of producing detective dramas, begun in 1908 with the Nick Carter series. Eclair produced a British newsreel, *Eclair Journal*, until 1916, but its activities here basically ended with the outbreak of WW1. AS.

Eddington, Paul (*b* London, 1927 – *d* London, 1995). Actor. One of the best-known figures on British TV, Eddington starred in such popular sitcoms as *The Good Life* (1975–78), as Penelope KEITH's long-suffering husband, and *Yes Minister* (1980–82) and its sequel, when Eddington's character has secured top job, *Yes Prime Minister* (1986–88). Also a notable stage actor, from 1944 to 1994 when he co-starred magisterially with *Good Life* neighbour, Richard BRIERS in *Home*. Films were no more than a drop in his career bucket, starting unmemorably with *Jet Storm* (1959) and continuing thus. His autobiography, *So Far, So Good* (1995) all but omits them. Made CBE in 1987.
OTHER BRITISH FILMS: *The Man Who Was Nobody* (1960), *Ring of Spies* (1963), *The Devil Rides Out* (1967), *The Amazing Mr Blunden, Baxter!* (1972).

Ede, Nic Costume designer. Worked as wardrobe supervisor on such early 80s films as *Eureka* (UK/US), *Gandhi* (UK/Ind) (1982) and *Greystoke . . .* (1984, UK/US) before assuming full designer responsibility on such varied mainstream fare as *A World Apart* (1987, UK/Zimb) and *Relative Values* (2000, UK/US).
OTHER BRITISH FILMS INCLUDE: *The Tempest* (1979), *Paperhouse, Joyriders* (1988), *A Foreign Field* (1993), *Loch Ness* (1996), *Wilde* (UK/Ger/Jap/US), *Resurrection Man* (1997).

Eden, Mark (*b* London, 1928). Actor. RN: Douglas Malin. Handsome leading-man type who never quite became one except in 'B' MOVIES like *Game for Three Losers* (1965) but made a mark as Leslie CARON's ex-lover in *The L-Shaped Room* (1962), as Barbara SHELLEY's lover in *Blind Corner* (1963) and as the father of the kidnapped child in *Seance on a Wet Afternoon* (1964). Had a continuing role in TV's 'Peter Wimsey' series (1972–75). Married TV actress Sue Nicholls.
OTHER BRITISH FILMS INCLUDE: *The Password Is Courage* (1962), *The Partner, Heavens Above!* (1963), *Doctor Zhivago* (UK/US), *The Pleasure Girls* (1965), *Arthur? Arthur!* (1969, unreleased), *Richard's Things* (1980).

Edgar, G. Marriott (*b* Colvend, Scotland, 1880 – *d* London, 1951). Screenwriter. After much experience in writing for the stage, turned to films in the mid 30s and collaborated, usually with J.O.C. ORTON and/or Val GUEST on many comedies for Will HAY, Arthur ASKEY and the CRAZY GANG. These are full of wild invention and tailored to the personalities of their stars.

BRITISH FILMS INCLUDE: (co-sc, unless noted) *Here's George* (sc, a) (1932), *Windbag the Sailor* (1936), *O-Kay for Sound, Oh, Mr Porter!, Good Morning, Boys!* (1937), *Old Bones of the River, Hey! Hey! USA!, Alf's Button Afloat, Convict 99* (1938), *The Frozen Limits* (1939), *Band Waggon, Gasbags, Charley's (Big-Hearted) Aunt* (1940), *I Thank You, Hi Gang!, The Ghost Train* (1941), *King Arthur Was a Gentleman, Back Room Boy* (1942), *Miss London Ltd* (+ co-story), *Bees in Paradise* (1944), *Top of the Form* (1953, co-story).

Edgar-Bruce, Toni (*b* London, 1892 – *d* Chertsey, 1966). Actress. Daughter of Edgar Bruce, stage actor/manager, she at one time owned the Prince of Wales Theatre. Her main career was in the theatre, but she had some memorable screen moments, usually in upper-class roles of imperious demeanour, like Lady Houston, dismissive of airpower in *The First of the Few* (1942), and the snobbish Mrs Harbottle-Smith who fortuitously breaks her leg in *Derby Day* (1952).
OTHER BRITISH FILMS INCLUDE: *Duke's Son* (1920), *A Warm Corner* (1930), *Tell England* (1931), *Mannequin* (1933), *Boys Will Be Girls* (1937), *Too Dangerous to Live* (1939), *Heaven Is Round the Corner* (1944), *Waltz Time* (1945).

Edge, Francis (*b* London, 1923). Producer. Entered film industry in 1941 with GAINSBOROUGH where he was assistant editor on *Millions Like Us* (1943). As producer, he joined John TEMPLE-SMITH in founding Major Productions. The films they made, four directed by Peter Graham SCOTT, were distinctly minor, but nevertheless enjoyable, especially *The Big Chance* (1957).
OTHER BRITISH FILMS: (p) *Profile* (1954), *On Such a Night* (1955, assoc p) *Hideout, Find the Lady* (1956), *Account Rendered* (1957); (co-sc, with Temple-Smith) *Home to Danger* (1951), *Black Orchid* (1952).

editing Noël COWARD said that there are only three creative jobs in film-making, writer, director and editor, because they are the storytellers. After each day's shoot the processed film (the rushes or dailies) is sent to the cutting-rooms where it is synchronised with the SOUND. As each scene is completed, the editor cuts it together to make the first (or rough) cut. Each scene is shot from different angles – long shots, medium shots, close-ups, etc. It is the editor's job to piece these together and, through variations in the selection and length of each shot, the right tempo is arrived at. As filming progresses, so the cut grows until the whole film is assembled. The advantage of film over, say, theatre is that director and editor can focus the audience's attention on what they (the storytellers) want them to see. At the next stage, the editor and director, through numerous corrections, shortening and sometimes eliminating entire scenes, achieve the final cut. Then music and sound effects are laid to synchronise with the picture, after which these tracks are mixed together to give the film its final form.

Montage sequences were much in use in British film until the 50s, to illustrate, say, the passage of time or a collage of images. A typical montage might be of a theatrical troupe on tour, dissolving from a performance in a city to a train going past, to a performance in another town, with the name of the town superimposed, then a close-up of the train wheels, and so on. Or a montage might show the leaves of a calendar falling to indicate the passage of days, weeks or months, or the passage of seasons by shots of a tree changing from spring into summer, then autumn and winter. In British films of the period, there are striking montage sequences in such varied films as *The Way Ahead* (1944), where the montage depicts a series of training exercises, and *Uncle Silas* (1947) to represent a nightmarish journey.

In British cinema there has been a strong tradition of editors associated with particular directors and companies. For instance, Alfred ROOME worked in the 30s on Tom WALLS's versions of ALDWYCH FARCES and in the 50s and 60s for RANK and Ralph THOMAS and on the 'CARRY ON' films; Sidney COLE was supervising editor on many 40s EALING films, as well as associate producer; Jack HARRIS worked for CINEGUILD in the 40s; Russell LLOYD edited ten films (US as well as UK) for John HUSTON, Reginald BECK a dozen for Joseph LOSEY, and Jonathan MORRIS all of Ken LOACH's 90s films. There is also a British tendency for editors to gravitate towards direction, most notably David LEAN, others including Leslie NORMAN, Charles CRICHTON, Anthony HARVEY, Peter HUNT, Fergus McDONELL, Kevin CONNOR, Thorold DICKINSON, and Peter Graham SCOTT. Teddy Darvas.

Edmondson, Adrian (*b* Bradford, Yorkshire, 1957). Actor. Chiefly known as a TV comedian, Edmondson has appeared in several British films (*The Supergrass*, 1985; *Eat the Rich*, 1987; *The Pope Must Die*, 1991, UK/US; *Guest House Paradiso*, 1999, + d, sc) without enhancing his reputation. Many guest spots on TV, including several with wife Jennifer SAUNDERS (e.g. *Absolutely Fabulous*).

Edmunds, Robert Screenwriter. Co-author of about 15 films between 1933 and 1940, mostly comedies, including a couple for Will HAY, with whom he shared credit on *Boys Will Be Boys* (1935), and *The Clairvoyant* (1935), co-written with Charles BENNETT.
OTHER BRITISH FILMS INCLUDE: *Medicine Man* (1933), *My Song for You* (1934), *Where There's a Will* (1936), *The Lambeth Walk* (1939, + cont), *Band Waggon* (1940).

Edney, Beatie (*b* London, 1963). Actress. Daughter of actress Sylvia SYMS, Edney first appeared as a small child in a long-lost film, *A Day at the Beach* (1969). Since the 80s, she has been seen in some classy TV, including *The Tenant of Wildfell Hall* (1996), in international films including Bruce BERESFORD's *Mr Johnson* (1990, US), and a handful of British ones, notably as one of the accused in *In the Name of the Father* (1993, UK/Ire/US).
OTHER BRITISH FILMS INCLUDE: *Highlander* (1986), *A Handful of Dust* (1987), *Wildflowers* (1989).

Edwardes, Olga (*b* Johannesburg, 1917). Actress. First appeared at Open Air Theatre in 1935 and subsequently in the West End and at Stratford. Only a handful of films, including *Caesar and Cleopatra* (1945) as Charmian, and the intrepid heroine of *Black Orchid* (1952).
OTHER BRITISH FILMS: *The Dominant Sex* (1937), *Contraband* (1940), *The Angel with the Trumpet* (1949), *Scrooge, The Six Men* (1951).

Edwards, Blake (*b* Tulsa, Oklahoma, 1922). Director. Belongs in this book primarily as the director of the 'Pink Panther' films, whose inspired lunacy made an international star of Peter SELLERS. Following the success of the first, *The Pink Panther* (1963), all but one of the rest are (technically) British. His other British films include the romantic drama, *The Tamarind Seed* (1974, + sc) and the charming cross-dresssing comedy *Victor/Victoria* (1982, + p, sc), both starring wife Julie ANDREWS. Admired for his sophisticated staging of slapstick action – and for bringing out the best in some manic actors.
OTHER BRITISH FILMS: (d, p, co-sc, unless noted) *A Shot in the Dark* (1964), *Casino Royale* (1967, sc contrib), *Inspector Clouseau* (1968, orig character only), *Return of the Pink Panther, Gift of Laughter* (doc, participant) (1974), *The Pink Panther Strikes Again* (1976), *Revenge of the*

Pink Panther (1978, + story), *Trail of the Pink Panther* (1982), *Curse of the Pink Panther* (1983).

Edwards, Glynn (*b* Malaya, 1931). Actor. Sugar plantation manager before becoming a character player of wide theatre and film experience. Now best known as Dave, the drinking-club owner with the lived-in face, in TV's *Minder* (1978–85, 1988–94). His easy, likeable conviction was clear as early as in *Smokescreen* (1964), as a police inspector investigating an insurance racket. Married (1 of 3) Yootha JOYCE.

OTHER BRITISH FILMS INCLUDE: *The Heart Within* (1957), *Sparrows Can't Sing* (1962), *The Hi-Jackers* (1963), *Zulu* (1964), *The Ipcress File* (1965), *Robbery* (1967), *Get Carter, Burke & Hare, Under Milk Wood* (1971), *11 Harrowhouse* (1974), *Rising Damp* (1980), *Champions* (1983).

Edwards, Henry (*b* Weston-super-Mare, 1883 – *d* Chobham, 1952). Actor, director, writer, producer. Closely associated with Cecil HEPWORTH, who described him as 'my greatest colleague', Edwards generally played sensitive and caring heroes, often directing and writing for himself. Female fans were thrilled when he showed off his body in *The Naked Man* (1923, + d, sc), but were equally delighted when he married his leading lady, Chrissie WHITE, in 1922. Edwards was a stage actor, who made his film debut in *Clancarty* (1914) for the LONDON FILM COMPANY; in 1914, he joined Florence TURNER's company, becoming her first British leading man, writer and later director, on such films as *East Is East* (1916). From Turner, he moved to Hepworth, where his films, including *Towards the Light* (1918, + sc, a), were basically independent productions. In 1927, Edwards founded producer/distributor WP Film Company with W.B. Williams and Julius HAGEN, making two films starring Edwards, *The Fake* and *Further Adventures of the Flag Lieutenant* (both 1927). He was again associated with Hagen in 1929 with the formation of TWICKENHAM FILM STUDIOS, starring in its first production, *Ringing the Changes* (1929). Edwards's last entrepreneurial effort was the formation of TEDDINGTON FILM STUDIOS in 1931, which he sold to WARNER BROS. after making only one film. As a director, he could be innovative, making, for example, Britain's first silent feature without subtitles, *Lily of the Alley* (1923, + sc, a). He was a major figure in British film history.

OTHER BRITISH FILMS: (d, unless noted) *A Welsh Singer, Doorsteps* (1916, + sc, a), *Merely Mr Stubbs* (+ sc, a), *Dick Carson Winds Through* (+ sc, a), *Broken Threads* (+ a) (1917), *The Hanging Judge* (+ sc, a), *The Message* (+ a), *Against the Grain* (+ a), *Old Mother Hubbard, Anna* (+ a), *Her Savings Saved* (+ a), *The Poet's Windfall* (+ a), *The Inevitable, What's the Use of Grumbling, The Secret* (+ a) (1918), *Her Dearest Possession, The Kinsman, Possession, The City of Beautiful Nonsense* (1919, + a), *A Temporary Vagabond* (+ sc), *Aylwin, The Amazing Quest of Mr Ernest Bliss, John Forest Finds Himself* (1920, + a), *The Lunatic at Large, The Bargain* (+ sc) (1921, + a), *Tit for Tat* (1922, + co-sc, a), *Boden's Boy* (1923, + a), *The World of Wonderful Reality* (1924, + sc, a), *Owd Bob, King of the Castle, A Girl of London* (1925), *One Colombo Night, The Island of Despair* (1926), *The Girl in the Night* (+ p, sc, a), *Stranglehold* (+ p, sc) (1931), *The Flag Lieutenant* (+ a), *The Barton Mystery, Brother Alfred* (1932), *General John Regan* (+ a), *Discord, One Precious Year, Lord of the Manor, Anne One Hundred, Purse Strings* (1933), *The Man Who Changed His Name, The Lash, Lord Edgware Dies, Are you a Mason?* (1934), *D'Ye Ken John Peel?, The Rocks of Valpré, The Lad, Vintage Wine, Squibs, Scrooge, The Private Secretary* (1935), *In the Soup, Eliza Comes to Stay, Juggernaut* (1936), *Beauty and the Barge, The Vicar of Bray, Song of the Forge* (1937). AS.

Edwards, Hilton (*b* London, 1903 – *d* Dublin, 1982). Actor, director. In 1928, he founded the Gate Theatre with fellow actor and partner Micheál MACLIAMMÓIR and gave Orson WELLES

his first acting job there in 1931. On screen, vivid as Brabantio in Welles's *Othello* (1952, US/Fr) and the blind, melancholy homosexual H.P. in *Victim* (1961). Directed some Irish films, including *From Time to Time* (1953).

OTHER BRITISH FILMS INCLUDE: *Call of the Blood* (1948), *She Didn't Say No* (1957), *Cat and Mouse* (1958), *The Quare Fellow* (1962), *The Wrong Box* (1966), *Half a Sixpence* (1967, UK/US).

Edwards, Jeillo (*b* Freetown, Sierra Leone, 1942). Actor. Educated in Freetown and Norwood Technical College. Noticed as the housing-estate mother of the Mama Cass-fan in *Beautiful Thing* (1996) and the TV drama-documentary *A Skirt Through History (The Two Marys)* (1994), as a woman born to slavery.

OTHER BRITISH FILMS INCLUDE: *Black Joy* (1977), *Britannia Hospital* (1982), *The Line, the Cross and the Curve* (1993), *Great Moments in Aviation* (1994, TV, some cinemas), *Paris, Brixton* (1997, short).

Edwards, Jimmy (*b* London, 1920 – *d* London, 1988). Actor. Former variety comedian famous for his huge handle-bar moustache, his outrageously blustering manner, and his radio (*Take It From Here*) and TV work (*Whack-O!*, 1953–60, 1971–72). Sporadic screen appearances never quite made him a film favourite: some early dire comedies, like *Trouble in the Air* (1948), *Helter Skelter* (1949) and *Treasure Hunt* (1952), would have sunk a career less securely anchored elsewhere. Won a DFC in the RAF and post-war started at the Windmill Theatre, subsequently playing himself in *Murder at the Windmill* (1949).

OTHER BRITISH FILMS INCLUDE: *Innocents in Paris* (1953), *An Alligator Named Daisy* (1955), *Three Men in a Boat* (1956), *Bottoms Up* (1959), *Nearly a Nasty Accident* (1961), *The Plank* (1967), *The Bed-Sitting Room*, (1969), *I Am a Groupie* (1971), *To See Such Fun* (1977).

Edwards, Maudie (*b* Neath, Wales, 1906 – *d* London, 1991). Actress. On stage from age 4, she appeared in occasional films over thirty years and dubbed the singing voices of such stars as Margaret LOCKWOOD, with whom she appeared in *I'll Be Your Sweetheart* (1945) as a helpful landlady.

OTHER BRITISH FILMS INCLUDE: *The Flying Doctor* (1937, UK/Aust), *The Shipbuilders* (1943), *Murder in Reverse* (1945), *School for Randle* (1949), *The Ugly Duckling* (1959), *Only Two Can Play* (1961), *Burke & Hare, Under Milk Wood* (1971).

Edwards, Meredith (*b* Rhosllanerchrugog, Wales, 1917 – *d* Abergele, Wales, 1999). Actor. Aptly, he played Owen Glendower, the fanatical Welshman, in the Old Vic's *Henry IV, Pt I*, after WW2 in which he was a conscientious objector. For a man fiercely proud of his Welshness, his film roles, especially at EALING, were mostly stereotyped Taffs, like the rugby supporter up in London in *A Run for Your Money* or the police choirmaster in *The Blue Lamp* (1949). Played numerous other policemen and soldiers, dying memorably in *Dunkirk* (1958) with Welsh on his lips, and bringing a whiff of authenticity to often clichéd roles. Involved in Welsh-language performances at Theatr Clwyd, near Mold, in recent years.

OTHER BRITISH FILMS INCLUDE: *Midnight Episode, The Magnet* (1950), *Where No Vultures Fly, The Lavender Hill Mob* (1951), *The Cruel Sea, The Gift Horse* (1952), *A Day to Remember* (1953), *Devil on Horseback* (1954), *Lost* (1955), *The Long Arm, Town on Trial* (1956), *Escapement* (1957), *Tiger Bay* (1959), *The Trials of Oscar Wilde* (1960), *Flame in the Streets, Only Two Can Play* (1961), *The Great St Trinian's Train Robbery* (1966).

Edzard, Christine (*b* Paris, 1945). Director. Of German-Polish parentage and with a background in theatre design, she met her husband, producer Richard GOODWIN, working on ZEFFIRELLI's *Romeo and Juliet* (1968). No one could accuse her of courting commercial favour, but she had substantial ART-

HOUSE success with her 6-hour *Little Dorrit* (1987, d, sc), which received AAn and BAAn for its adapted screenplay. Her version of *As You Like It* (1992, d, p, e) was sharply intelligent but too bleak for popularity, and in 2001 she filmed *A Midsummer Night's Dream* with a cast of schoolchildren. She and Goodwin formed Sands Films which has produced most of their films, and have a reputation for 19th-century costume design.

OTHER BRITISH FILMS INCLUDE: (d, unless noted) *Tales of Beatrix Potter* (1971, des, sc), *Stories from a Flying Trunk* (1979, + sc), *The Nightingale* (1981, short, anim, co-d), *Biddy* (1983, + sc), *The Fool* (1990), *IMAX Nutcracker* (1997, + sc, cos).

Egan, Beresford (*b* London, 1905 – *d* London, 1984). Actor. Journalist and novelist before entering films in 1942, after discharge from the services, he made four films with director Vernon SEWELL, most vividly as a murderous sculptor in *Latin Quarter* (1945), on which he collaborated on the costume design.

OTHER BRITISH FILMS INCLUDE: *The Silver Fleet* (1943), *A Canterbury Tale* (1944), *Latin Quarter* (1945), *The Ghosts of Berkeley Square* (1947, cos), *Dangerous Voyage* (1954), *Joe MacBeth* (1955).

Egan, Peter (*b* London, 1946). Actor. Won a BAA as Best Newcomer for *The Hireling* (1973) as Sarah MILES's smoothly upper-class MP admirer, but made only a handful of further cinema films, including *Chariots of Fire* (1981) as the Duke of Sutherland. He has done much more TV, enjoyably unpleasant in *Paradise Postponed* (1986), and extensive theatre. Married to actress Myra Frances.

OTHER BRITISH FILMS INCLUDE: *One Brief Summer* (1969), *Callan* (1974, reprising TV role), *Hennessy* (1975), *Bean* (1997).

Egbert, Albert (*b c* London, 1879 – *d* London, 1942) and **Egbert, Seth** (*b* London, *c* 1878 – *d* London, 1944). Actors. Popular music hall comedians, the Egbert brothers made a film career out of their act from 1912 to 1936. They were Inkey (Albert) and Co (Seth) in *Inkey and Co, Inkey and Co in Business* and *Inkey and Co – Glad Eye* (all 1913), and the 'Happy Dustmen' (Bill and Walter) in *The Happy Dustmen, The Dustman's Holiday* (1913), *The Happy Dustmen Play Golf, The Happy Dustmen's Christmas* (1914), *The Dustmen's Nightmare* (1915), *The Dustman's Wedding*, and *The Dustmen's Outing* (1916).

OTHER BRITISH FILMS INCLUDE: *The Coster's Honeymoon, Yiddle on My Fiddle* (1912), *Further Adventures of the Flag Lieutenant* (1927), *Old Timers* (1936). AS.

Ege, Julie (*b* Sandnes, Norway, 1943). Actress. Norwegian photographic model and former Miss Norway who appeared in British features during the 70s, usually in the role of blonde bombshell, for which nature had equipped her, and often as a disruption to British domesticity, as in *Every Home Should Have One* (1969). In 1978 returned to Norway where she now works as a trained nurse.

OTHER BRITISH FILMS INCLUDE: *On Her Majesty's Secret Service* (1969), *Creatures the World Forgot* (1970), *Up Pompeii* (1971), *Rentadick* (1972), *Percy's Progress* (1974).

Eggar, Samantha (*b* London, 1939). Actress. RN: Eggars. Gifted auburn-haired beauty who mysteriously failed to become a major star after her success (AAn, BAA, other awards) as the kidnapped heroine of William Wyler's *The Collector* (1965, UK/US), co-starring man-of-the-moment Terence STAMP. Discovered by Betty BOX who cast her in *The Wild and the Willing* (1962) and *Doctor in Distress* (1963), she was affecting as Crippen's mistress in *Crippen* (1962). For the rest of her prolific career, she co-starred in few big US films, notably *The Molly Maguires* (1970) and *The Seven-Per-Cent Solution* (1976), and did time in nondescript US telemovies and horror movies. In 1972 she starred with Yul BRYNNER in the TV series, *Anna and the King*, cancelled after one season. Married actor-director Tom Stern.

OTHER BRITISH FILMS: *Psyche 59* (1963), *Return from the Ashes* (1965), *The Walking Stick* (1970), *Welcome to Blood City, The Uncanny* (1977, UK/Can).

Eggerth, Marta (*b* Budapest, 1912). Actress, singer. A popular leading lady in German musical films, Eggerth had only sporadic success in Britain, including *My Heart Is Calling* (1934), co-starring husband, tenor Jan KIEPURA, and less still in supporting roles in Hollywood, in *For Me and My Gal* (1942) and *Presenting Lily Mars* (1943).

OTHER BRITISH FILMS: *Where Is This Lady?* (1932), *Unfinished Symphony* (1934, UK/Austria/Ger), *The Divine Spark* (1935, UK/It).

Ehle, Jennifer (*b* North Carolina, 1969). Actress. Central School-trained Ehle won the 1996 BAA for playing a sexy, intelligent Elizabeth Bennett in the BBC TV ADAPTATION of *Pride and Prejudice*. Since that success, has played a POW in *Paradise Road* (US/Aus), Mrs Oscar Wilde in *Wilde* (1997, UK/Ger/Jap/US), Kevin McKIDD's (sort of) girlfriend in *Bedrooms and Hallways* (1999), Ralph FIENNES' Jewish wife in *Sunshine* (2000, UK/Austria/Can/Ger/Hung) and starred in *Possession* (2002, UK/US), without quite matching her TV and theatre kudos. Won a Tony for her Broadway performance in *The Real Thing* (2000) and starred in the TV series, *Melissa* (1997). Daughter of actress Rosemary HARRIS and US writer John Ehle.

OTHER BRITISH FILMS INCLUDE: *Backbeat* (1994), *This Year's Love* (1999).

Ekberg, Anita (*b* Malmö, Sweden, 1931). Actress. Beauty queen – 'Miss Sweden', 1951 – who has become an international celebrity, if not a famous actress. Began in a string of forgettable US films, touching prestige with *War and Peace* (1956, US/It), had three undistinguished WARWICK FILMS in Britain (*Zarak*, 1956; *Interpol*, 1957; *The Man Inside*, 1958), and achieved a sort of iconic status in Fellini's *La dolce vita* (1960, It). In recent decades, she has filmed all over the place as, in whatever role, an overpowering blonde. Married (1 of 2) Anthony STEEL (1956–59).

OTHER BRITISH FILMS: *Call Me Bwana* (1963), *The Alphabet Murders* (1965).

Ekland, Britt (*b* Stockholm, 1942). Actress. RN: Eklund. Not to be confused with several other Nordic sex symbols – it is hard *not* to confuse her with, say, Elke SOMMER – she, somewhat surprisingly, hung on for a quarter-century after her showy starring role in *The Night They Raided Minsky's* (1968). Of her 40-odd films, about 15 were British, most famously the gangster classic, *Get Carter* (1971), the (oc)cult horror, *The Wicker Man* (1973) and the Profumo-based *Scandal* (1988). An acceptable actress, she became more famous for her off-screen life, including marriage to Peter SELLERS (1964–68), with whom she appeared in *After the Fox* (1966, US/It) and *The Bobo* (1967), and a tempestuous, headlining liaison with Rod Stewart.

OTHER BRITISH FILMS INCLUDE: *The Double Man* (1967), *Percy* (1971), *Endless Night, Asylum, Baxter!* (1972), *The Man with the Golden Gun* (1974), *Royal Flash* (1975), *The Monster Club* (1980).

BIBLIOG: Autobiography, *True Britt*, 1980.

Elder, Clarence (*b* Glasgow). Production designer. Educated at Glasgow University, he became supervising art director at ASSOCIATED BRITISH in the 30s, was camouflage supervisor during WW2, and post-war co-directed and wrote *Silver Darlings* (1946). Designed some ambitious films of their time, including the musical, *Blossom Time* (1934) and the historical piece, *Drake of England* (1935).

OTHER BRITISH FILMS INCLUDE (a d, or co-a d, unless noted): *The Yellow Mask, Bill and Coo* (1931), *The Maid of the Mountains* (1932), *Radio Parade of 1935* (1934), *Royal Cavalcade, Abdul the Damned* (1935), *Music Hath Charms, Invitation to the Waltz, Heart's Desire* (1937), *The Little Singer* (1956, short, d).

Elder, T(homas) C(oates) (*b* Manchester, 1870 – *d* ?). Executive. Elder began his career as a writer, who, in 1899, 'ghosted' the best-seller *Dan Leno: Hys Booke*. In 1920, he was appointed a director of STOLL PICTURE PRODUCTIONS, remaining with the company until 1927. Became joint managing director of Welsh–Pearson–Elder when the company was incorporated on 16 February 1928, and co-wrote the screenplay for its production of *The Broken Melody* (1929). Ceased to be involved in films in the early 30s. AS.

Eldridge, John (*b* Folkestone, 1917 – *d* 1961). Screenwriter, director. Haileybury-educated, entered industry as assistant editor in 1936, joined STRAND FILMS in 1940 and embarked on the DOCUMENTARIES which occupied much of his career, continuing to do so at Greenpark Productions in the late 40s. Eight of his wartime films were scripted by Dylan THOMAS. The rest of his career until his early death was divided among EALING (as co-screenwriter on *Pool of London*, 1950, and others), GROUP 3, where he directed three modest films, of which *Conflict of Wings* (1954) has pastoral charm and a serious theme, and several children's films. With William ROSE he was BAA-nominated for two screenplays: *The Man in the Sky* (1956) and *The Smallest Show on Earth* (1957).

OTHER BRITISH FILMS INCLUDE: (d, unless noted) (doc, short) *Village School, Story of Michael Flaherty* (1940), *War Front, Tank Patrol, Architects of England* (1941), *Young Farmers, Black Mountain, New Towns for Old* (1942), *Our Country, Conquest of a Germ* (1944), *A City Reborn, A Soldier Comes Home* (1945), *Waverley Steps, Three Dawns to Sydney* (+ sc) (1948); (features) *Brandy for the Parson* (1952), *Laxdale Hall* (1953, + co-sc), *Out of the Clouds* (1955, co-sc), *Operation Amsterdam* (1958, co-sc), *The Boy Who Stole a Million* (1960, co-sc), *Some People* (1962, sc).

Eles, Sandor (*b* Budapest, 1936 – *d* 2000). Actor. Hungarian leading man and, later, supporting actor in British films, playing the Doctor's assistant in *The Evil of Frankenstein* (1964) and the handsome young Hussar who falls victim to *Countess Dracula* (1970), as well as other assorted foreigners. TV work includes Ken RUSSELL's *Isadora Duncan* (1966).

OTHER BRITISH FILMS INCLUDE: *The Rebel* (1960), *Guns of Darkness* (1962), *French Dressing* (1963), *San Ferry Ann* (1965), *The Magnificent Two* (1967), *And Soon the Darkness* (1970), *Surviving Picasso* (1996).

Elgar, Avril (*b* Halifax, 1932). Actress. Educated in India and England, trained at Old Vic Theatre School and on stage from 1952, Elgar came to attention in John OSBORNE's *Epitaph for George Dillon* (1958). Has also done much TV, including the gaunt mother in *The Stars Look Down* (1975), but only rare films, starting with *Room at the Top* (1958), as one of the office staff. Married James MAXWELL.

OTHER BRITISH FILMS INCLUDE: *She Always Gets Their Man* (1962), *Ladies Who Do* (1963), *Spring and Port Wine* (1969), *Betrayal* (1982), *Wilde* (1997, UK/Ger/Jap/US, as Lady Bracknell).

Ellacott, Joan (*b* London, 1920). Costume designer. Studied dress design at Birmingham, Northampton and Bromley Schools of Arts and Crafts; in WAAF during WW2, entering films as Elizabeth HAFFENDEN's assistant on *Jassy* (1947) at GAINSBOROUGH. Forty-odd films later she finished her career on *The Lady and the Highwayman* (1988) for the restored 'Gainsborough Pictures'. In between, most of her work was on modern films for RANK across a characteristic GENRE range, including Norman WISDOM, WAR FILMS and 'CARRY ON'.

OTHER BRITISH FILMS INCLUDE: *Snowbound* (1948), *The Happiest Days of Your Life* (1950), *The Long Memory, Curtain Up* (1952), *The Kidnappers* (1953), *Mad About Men* (1954), *All for Mary* (1955), *Tiger in the Smoke* (1956), *The Violent Playground* (1957), *Carry On Sergeant, Floods of Fear, The Captain's Table* (1958), *Suddenly, Last Summer* (1959), *The League of Gentlemen* (1960), *A Stitch in Time* (1963), *Carry On Jack* (1964).

Ellenshaw, Peter (*b* London, 1914). Special effects artist, designer. Worked mainly as a matte artist on some very distinguished British films, including *Black Narcissus* (1947), on which such work was very important in sustaining the Himalayan illusion. In the 50s, he took up with DISNEY in Britain and the rest of his career, much of it in Disney's US films, was spent with that Organisation, sharing an AA for *Mary Poppins* (1964) and thrice AA-nominated for US films – *Bedknobs and Broomsticks* (1971) and *Island at the Top of the World* (1974) for art direction and *The Black Hole* (1979) for special effects. Mostly uncredited on his 30s films. Married daughter of special effects director Percy 'Poppa' DAY.

OTHER BRITISH FILMS INCLUDE (ass/matte artist, unless noted): *The Ghost Goes West* (1935), *Things to Come, Rembrandt, The Man Who Could Work Miracles* (1936), *Elephant Boy, Victoria the Great* (1937), *The Drum* (1938), *The Four Feathers* (1939), *The Thief of Baghdad* (1940), *A Matter of Life and Death* (1946), *The Red Shoes* (1948), *Treasure Island,* (1950), *The Story of Robin Hood . . .* (1952), *Rob Roy . . .* (1953), *Kidnapped* (1960, sfx, UK/US), *In Search of the Castaways* (1961, sfx), *The Fighting Prince of Donegal* (1966, sfx).

Elliott, Denholm (*b* London, 1922 – *d* Ibiza, Spain, 1992). Actor. One of the great CHARACTER ACTORS, with an enormously productive stage, TV and screen career. Trained at RADA; served with the RAF (1940–45), including three years as POW; post-war, on stage from 1945, usually in notable new plays, like T.S. Eliot's *The Confidential Clerk* (1953) though there was also a Stratford season in 1960. On-screen from 1949 (*Dear Mr Prohack*), he was an only moderately interesting young leading man in the likes of *The Sound Barrier* (1952) and *Pacific Destiny* (1956). There was perhaps something too shy, too cautious, about him for conventional stardom, and he looked sensitive rather than handsome.

His real ascendancy began with *Nothing But the Best* (1964) as the seedy, minor-public-school man who is Alan BATES's social mentor, and almost everything he did after this had a touch of this persona – wry, a bit battered, cynical. Whether the films were dross or gold, he never failed to rivet the attention, whether as the abortionist in *Alfie* (1966), a decadently trendy parent in the execrable *Here We Go Round the Mulberry Bush* (1967), an embittered Krogstad in *The Doll's House* (1973), snobbish Dr Swaby in *A Private Function* (1984, BAA/supp a), warm-hearted Mr Emerson in *A Room with a View* (1985, AAn, BAAn/supp a) or the decent drunken journalist in *Defence of the Realm* (1985, BAA/supp a).

There were international films as well, including *Raiders of the Lost Ark* (1981), *Trading Places* (1983, BAA/supp a) and *The Razor's Edge* (1984), in Clifton Webb's original role, and masses of memorable TV: the seedy butler in *Blade on the Feather* (1980), cynical Philip in *Hotel du Lac* (1986) and George Smiley in *A Murder of Quality* (1991). There are over 120 major film and TV credits, and it is hard to encapsulate their versatile understanding and immaculate technique briefly. Married (1) Virginia McKenna. Second wife, Susan Elliott, collaborated on a biography, *Denholm Elliott – Quest for Love* (1994). Died of AIDS complications.

OTHER BRITISH FILMS: *The Holly and the Ivy*, *The Ringer*, *The Cruel Sea* (1952), *They Who Dare*, *The Heart of the Matter* (1953), *Lease of Life*, *The Man Who Loved Redheads* (1954), *The Night My Number Came Up* (1955), *Station Six Sahara* (1962), *The High Bright Sun*, *You Must Be Joking!* (1965), *The Spy with a Cold Nose*, *Maroc 7* (1966), *The Rise and Rise of Michael Rimmer*, *The House That Dripped Blood* (1970), *Percy*, *Quest for Love* (1971), *Madame Sin* (1972), *The Vault of Horror* (1973, UK/US), *Percy's Progress* (1974), *Russian Roulette* (1975), *To the Devil a Daughter*, *Voyage of the Damned* (1976), *A Bridge Too Far* (1977), *Watership Down* (1978), *The Hound of the Baskervilles* (1977), *Sweeney 2* (1978), *Game for Vultures* (1979), *Bad Timing*, *Rising Damp* (1980), *The Missionary* (1981), *Brimstone & Treacle* (1982), *The Wicked Lady*, *The Hound of the Baskervilles* (1983), *Underworld* (1985), *The Whoopee Boys* (1986), *Maurice* (1987), *Stealing Heaven* (UK/Yug), *Return from the River Kwai* (1988), *Killing Dad* (1989).

Elliott, W. Gerald Screenwriter. Working almost invariably in collaboration, Elliott was involved in nearly 30 films in the latter 30s, mostly crime THRILLERS, some derived from Edgar WALLACE, but also several of John BAXTER's homilies, including *Hearts of Humanity* (1936) and *Song of the Road* (1937). Co-writers included Ian HAY and Adrian BRUNEL.

OTHER BRITISH FILMS INCLUDE: *Birds of a Feather*, *Cross Currents* (1935), *Café Mascot* (1936), *The Frog*, *Museum Mystery*, *Double Exposures* (1937), *The Return of the Frog* (1938), *Inspector Hornleigh*, *All at Sea* (1939), *The Great Mr Handel* (1942).

Ellis, Mary (*b* New York, 1897 – *d* London, 2003). Actress. RN: Elsas. Achieved considerable success in stage musicals, as well as in straight dramas, such as *The Browning Version* (1948), as viperish Millie Crocker-Harris. Trained first for art, then for singing, she was on stage in New York in 1918, London 1930. Made several films in Hollywood in the 30s, and a handful in Britain: *Bella Donna* (1934), as a dangerous beauty; *Glamorous Night* (1937), rallying gypsies to save a Ruritanian king; *The Three Worlds of Gulliver* (1960), as Queen of Brobdignag; guest role in *The Magic Box* (1951). Married (2 of 3) Basil SYDNEY. Lived to be over one hundred.

Ellis, Vivian (*b* London, 1904 – *d* London, 1996). Composer, lyricist. Educated at Cheltenham College, trained as concert pianist, Ellis emerged as a prolific composer of light-hearted stage musicals and film scores, including *Mr Cinders* (1934), which he wrote for the stage in 1929 (restaged in 1982), and several romantic comedies starring Jack HULBERT. Also wrote many popular romantic songs, Greta GYNT's 'Lady Spiv' number in *Easy Money* (1948), several novels and two volumes of autobiography. Made CBE, 1984.

OTHER BRITISH FILMS INCLUDE: (comp/co-comp) *Elstree Calling* (1930), *Out of the Blue* (1931), *Lord Babs*, *Jack's the Boy*, *The Water Gipsies* (1932), *Falling for You* (1933), *Over the Garden Wall* (1934), *Public Nuisance No. 1* (1936), *Who's Your Lady Friend?* (1937), *Brimstone & Treacle* (1982, song).

Elmes, Guy (*b* London, 1920). Screenwriter. Former journalist who entered industry in 1945 and (co-)authored some interesting screenplays in the 50s, beginning with the Malayan-set drama, *The Planter's Wife* (1952) and including the fascinating oddity, *Bang! You're Dead* (1953), with its child's-

eye-view of a shabby world. Also had a part in the musical farrago, *Hello London* (1958). International work includes *The Night Visitor* (1971, US).

OTHER BRITISH FILMS INCLUDE: *The Stranger's Hand*, *The Flanagan Boy* (1953), *Across the Bridge* (1957), *Nor the Moon by Night* (1958), *Serious Charge* (1959), *Stranglehold* (1962, + story), *The Biggest Bank Robbery* (1980, + story).

Elphick, John (*b* Hartley, 1903). Production designer. Trained architect, who began film career as set decorator at EALING in 1934, also working at other studios before being promoted to art director in 1944 at GAINSBOROUGH, where his first credit was on the decorative Victorian ghost story, *A Place of One's Own* (1944). Elsewhere he was location art director in Egypt on *Caesar and Cleopatra* (1945) and chief assistant art director (to John BRYAN) on *Great Expectations* (1946). Of later films, including a number of 'B' MOVIES, his most impressive work was on the HORROR FILMS with which he finished his career, especially his recreation of 1820s Edinburgh in *The Flesh and the Fiends* (1959).

OTHER BRITISH FILMS INCLUDE: *When the Bough Breaks*, *Dear Murderer* (1947), *The Calendar* (1948), *The Lost People*, *Helter Skelter* (1949), *Seven Days to Noon* (1950), *Private Information* (1952), *Women Without Men*, *Town on Trial* (1956), *Fiend Without a Face* (1957), *Grip of the Strangler* (1958).

Elphick, Michael (*b* Chichester, 1946 – *d* London, 2002). Actor. Prominent, burly character actor of screen and TV, usually cast as rough diamonds, with stress often on rough rather than diamond. He was probably best known for such TV roles as the hero's scruffy father at odds with the heroine's genteel mother in *Three Up, Two Down* (1985–89), ex-fireman *Boon* (1986) and a gruffly devoted Barkis in *David Copperfield* (1999). Films began with *Where's Jack?* and *Hamlet* (1969) and there was a steady trickle subsequently, including a Supporting Actor BAAn for *Gorky Park* (1983, US), and a droll turn as a yokel in *Withnail and I* (1986), as well as assorted policemen and thugs.

OTHER BRITISH FILMS INCLUDE: *The Buttercup Chain*, *The Cry of the Banshee* (1970), *Blind Terror* (1971), *O Lucky Man!* (1973), *Quadrophenia* (1979), *Privates on Parade* (1982), *Ordeal by Innocence* (1984), *The Supergrass* (1985), *Little Dorrit* (1987), *The Krays*, *Buddy's Song* (1990), *'Let Him Have It'* (1991), *Richard III* (1995).

Elphinstone, Derek (*b* 1913). Actor. Non-descript supporting player of the officer-and-gentleman variety in occasional films, of which his role as the ship's First Officer in *In Which We Serve* (1942) is the most prominent. Also on stage as actor and producer.

OTHER BRITISH FILMS INCLUDE: *East Meets West* (1936), *The Four Feathers* (1939), *Convoy* (1940), *The Day Will Dawn* (1942), *Night Boat to Dublin* (1946), *The Red Shoes* (1948), *Distant Trumpet* (1952), *Secret People* (1951).

Elsom, Isobel (*b* Chesterton, 1893 – *d* Los Angeles, 1981). Actress. An attractive blonde leading lady in silent films, later a character actress in talkies, often playing elegant society ladies. Made stage debut in the chorus of *The Quaker Girl* (1911) and film debut in *A Prehistoric Love Story* (1915). Among her more than 20 British silent films are *Milestones* (1916), *The Elder Miss Blossom* (1918), *In Bondage* (1919), *Nance* (1920), *The Sign of Four* (1923), *The Last Witness* (1925), *Human Law* (1926). Came to the US in 1926, appearing on stage in *The Ghost Train*, and to Hollywood in 1941 for the screen version of *Ladies in Retirement*, in which she had starred on Broadway in 1939. Among her American films are *Monsieur Verdoux* (1947) and

My Fair Lady (1964). Married to (1) Maurice ELVEY and (2) Carl HARBORD (1947 to 1958, his death).

BRITISH SOUND FILMS: *The Other Woman, Stranglehold* (1931), *The Crooked Lady, Illegal* (1932), *The Thirteenth Candle* (1933), *The Primrose Path* (1934). AS.

Elstree Studios Film studio complex attached to Elstree, the small town in once-rural Hertfordshire. Sometimes called the 'British Hollywood', the name refers to a total of six separate studios of varying size and fame that were set up in the area at different times. These combined to produce the largest and most vibrant film community in the history of British film, albeit one frequently subject to financial and other misfortunes. The first of the Elstree studios to open was Neptune Studios in 1914, in its day the finest in England, and in its brief life was responsible for numerous patriotic silent films before closing in 1921, after which time new studios were set up in the area and Elstree had its golden time. In 1927 the newly formed BRITISH INTERNATIONAL PICTURES, which later became ASSOCIATED BRITISH, commenced operations. Among its early notable productions was HITCHCOCK's *Blackmail* (1929), the first British all-talkie, and one of ABPC's most famous Elstree films was *The Dam Busters* (1955).

Later decades saw increasing American involvement, culminating in the 'Star Wars' and 'Indiana Jones' trilogies. Eventually ownership of the site passed to the Brent Walker Entertainment Group, which in 1988 attempted to revive the Elstree legend through its GOLDCREST STUDIOS venture. After the failure of Goldcrest, partial redevelopment of the site and protracted legal disputation the remaining film facilities were sold to the Hertsmere Borough Council. Another major facility which flourished under American patronage started life in 1935 as AMALGAMATED STUDIOS and in 1948 became the MGM–BRITISH Studios, initially specialising in opulent costume dramas and later playing host to such immense projects as Stanley KUBRICK's *2001: A Space Odyssey* (1968) before 1970 when it too closed and later was sold off. Two tribute films from the earlier times, *Elstree Calling* (1930) and *The Elstree Story* (1952), are a legacy of Elstree's golden years, the former a collection of sketches, including several directed by HITCHCOCK, the latter a compilation spanning 25 years of film-making.

BIBLIOG. Patricia Warren, *Elstree: The British Hollywood*, 1982. Simon Caterson.

Elton, Sir Arthur, Bt (*b* London, 1906 – *d* London, 1973). Producer. Marlborough- and Cambridge-educated, in films from 1927, at GAINSBOROUGH. He was then successively with the EMPIRE MARKETING FILM BOARD (1930), the Ministry of Labour (1934–35), the GPO FILM UNIT (1934–37), co-founded the FILM CENTRE with John GRIERSON and Basil WRIGHT in 1937 and returned to work with it from 1945 to 1949, after being production supervisor with the MINISTRY OF INFORMATION during WW2. He also had a period post-war with SHELL FILM UNIT and his name is ineradicably associated with British DOCUMENTARY film production. Liberal left-leaning in his orientation, and with a special interest in scientific and technical subjects, his influence goes beyond individual credits, but some of the films with which he was associated, usually as producer, are: *Shadow on the Mountain* (1930), *Upstream* (1931), *Aero-Engine, Voice of the World* (1932), *Workers and Jobs, Housing Problems* (1935), *Village School* (1940), *A Welcome to Britain* (1943), *Two Fathers* (1944), *How to Spray* (1946), among many others. His brother **Ralph Elton** (*b* Bradford-on-Avon,

1914 – *d* Clevedon, 1968) was also involved in documentary film-making before and during WW2, on such films as: *Roadways* (co-d) (1937), *Factory Front* (co-d), *Communique* (1940) and *Coastal Command* (1942, 2ud).

Elton, Ben (*b* London, 1959). Actor, author, dramatist, screenwriter. Brilliant satirical writer of novels, including *Inconceivable* (1999), a semi-autobiographical reworking of the problems of conception, staged successfully (2001) but filmed badly as *Maybe Baby* (2000), of several West End hit plays, and of such TV series as *Blackadder* in its five incarnations, first in 1983, and *The Thin Blue Line* (1995). Also a stand-up comic of ferocious wit, which British film comedy could use. In films, so far he has appeared in *The Secret Policeman's Third Ball* (1987) and as Verges in *Much Ado about Nothing* (1993), as well as directing and writing *Maybe Baby*.

Elton, Ray (*b* Cardiff, 1914). Cinematographer. Entered films in 1933 as camera assistant at TWICKENHAM STUDIOS, was promoted to lighting cameraman at STOLL in 1937, where he worked on DOCUMENTARIES. Continued to make documentary shorts during WW2, turning to features for GAINSBOROUGH in the latter 40s. His location shooting for *A Boy, a Girl and a Bike* (1949) brings a refreshingly outdoor touch to the often studio-bound filming of the time. From the mid 50s, under contract to Film Producers' Guild.

OTHER BRITISH FILMS INCLUDE: (doc, short) *Our Island Nation, The League at Work* (1937), *Soldier, Sailor* (1944); (features) *Miranda, The Blind Goddess, Quartet* (1948), *Last Holiday* (1950), *Four Days, Two on the Tiles* (1951), *Song of Paris* (1952).

Elvey, Maurice (*b* Darlington, 1887 – *d* Brighton, 1967). Director. RN: William Seward Folkard. The longest-serving and most prolific film director in British cinema history, Elvey made over 300 features and numerous shorts between 1913 and 1957, when the loss of an eye caused him to retire. Despite (or more likely because of) his high productivity and eclecticism, he has been undeservedly neglected and undervalued. In fact, he was much more than just a competent journeyman, proving particularly adept at adapting classic novels and plays, and his astonishing output contained many films of originality and quality, including a number of box-office successes. Poor and uneducated as a child, Elvey began his career as a teenage actor at the Theatre Royal, Nottingham, before directing (and acting in) his first film, *The Fallen Idol* (1913). His films of the silent period were probably his best work, most notably *Nelson* (1918), *At the Villa Rose* (1920), *The Hound of the Baskervilles, The Adventures of Sherlock Holmes* (series, 1921), *The Wandering Jew* (1923), *Mademoiselle from Armentières, The Flag Lieutenant* (1926), *Roses of Picardy, Hindle Wakes* (+ co-p) (1927), *High Treason* (sound, 1929), and the extraordinary *The Life Story of David Lloyd George* (1918), a uniquely stylised, contemporary hagiography of the British Prime Minister, a precursor of docu-drama, politically suppressed and not seen publicly until its 1996 restoration and revival by the Wales Film and Television Archive. Elvey's sound films are best remembered for his collaborations with Gracie FIELDS (*Sally in Our Alley*, 1931; *Love, Life and Laughter*, 1934) and Cicely COURTNEIDGE (*Soldiers of the King*, 1933; *Under Your Hat*, 1940), a science-fiction drama, *The Tunnel* (1935), *The Clairvoyant* (1935), several decent contributions to the war effort (*For Freedom*, 1940; *Salute John Citizen*, 1942; *The Lamp Still Burns*, 1943); the tragic romance, *Beware of Pity* (1946), the taut and handsome murder drama, *The Late Edwina Black*

(1951), and some later comedies, such as *Dry Rot* (1956). Also worked briefly in Hollywood and on the Continent. Was once married to Isobel ELSOM.

OTHER BRITISH FILMS: *Maria Marten or The Mystery of the Red Barn, The Great Gold Robbery, Bridegrooms Beware!!* (1913), *The Suicide Club, The Sound of Her Voice, Beautiful Jim, The Loss of Birkenhead, Inquisitive Ike, Black-Eyed Susan, Her Luck in London, The Cup Final Mystery, It's a Long, Long Way to Tipperary, The Bells of Rheims* (1914), *The Idol of Paris, A Will of Her Own, There's Good in Everyone, Midshipman Easy, Love in a Wood, London's Yellow Peril, Honeymoon for Three, Home, Her Nameless Child, Grip, Gilbert Gets Tiger-itis, Gilbert Dying to Die, From Shopgirl to Duchess, The Greatest Wish in the World, Fine Feathers, Florence Nightingale, Charity Ann, Meg, the Lady* (1915), *When Knights Were Bold* (+ p), *Vice Versa, The Princess of Happy Chance, Mother Love, Esther* (+ sc), *Driven* (+ sc) (1916), *The King's Daughter, The Woman Who Was Nothing, Smith, Justice, Mary-Girl, The Grit of a Jew, The Gay Lord Quex, Flames, Dombey and Son* (+ p) (1917), *Nelson; The Story of England's Immortal Naval Hero* (+ p), *Hindle Wakes, Goodbye, Adam Bede* (1918), *The Rocks of Valpré, The Swindler, The Victory Leaders, Mr Wu, God's Good Man, Comradeship, Keeper of the Door, The Elusive Pimpernel* (1919), *The Tavern Knight, A Question of Trust, The Hundredth Chance, Bleak House, The Amateur Gentleman, The Tragedy of a Comic Song* (1920), *Yellow Face, The Tiger of San Pedro, The Solitary Cyclist, A Scandal in Bohemia, The Resident Patient, The Red-Haired League, The Priory School, The Noble Bachelor, The Man with the Twisted Lip, Innocent, A Gentleman of France, The Fruitful Vine, The Empty House, The Dying Detective, The Devil's Foot, The Copper Beeches, A Case of Identity, The Beryl Coronet, A Romance of Wastdale* (1921), *Running Water, Man and His Kingdom, Dick Turpin's Ride to York, A Debt of Honour, The Passionate Friends* (1922), *The Battle of Worcester* (doc short), *Charles Augustus Milverton, Guy Fawkes, The Sign of Four* (+ sc), *The Royal Oak, Don Quixote, Sally Bishop* (1923), *The Love Story of Aliette Brunton, Slaves of Destiny, Henry, King of Navarre* (1924), *The Phantom Gambler* (1925), *Human Law* (UK/Ger), *The Woman Tempted* (+ co-p), *Windsor Castle, The Tower of London, Kenilworth Castle and Amy Robsart, Glamis Castle, Baddesley Manor – The Phantom Gambler* (1926), *The Arcadians* (co-p committee), *The Glad Eye* (co-p), *Quinneys* (1927), *Smashing Through* (co-p), *The Flight Commander, You Know What Sailors Are, What Money Can Buy, Sailors Don't Care* (co-p), *The Physician* (p exec), *Palaise de danse* (+ p), *Mademoiselle Parley-Voo, Balaclava* (1928), *Guy Fawkes, The School for Scandal* (+ p) (1930), *Potiphar's Wife, A Honeymoon Adventure* (1931), *The Water Gipsies, The Marriage Bond, The Lodger, In a Monastery Garden, Frail Women, Diamond Cut Diamond* (1932), *The Wandering Jew, This Week of Grace, I Lived with You, The Lost Chord* (1933), *Road House, Princess Charming, My Song for You* (UK/Ger), *Lily of Killarney* (1934), *The Clairvoyant, The Tunnel, Heat Wave* (1935), *Spy of Napoleon, The Man in the Mirror* (1936), *Who Killed John Savage?, A Romance in Flanders, Melody and Romance* (+ sc), *Clothes and the Woman* (d of p), *Change for a Sovereign* (1937), *Who Goes Next?, Return of the Frog, Lightning Conductor* (1938), *Sword of Honour* (+ p), *Sons of the Sea* (+ co-sc), *The Spider* (1939), *Goofer Trouble* (short), *Room for Two,* (1940), *The Gentle Sex* (1943, co-d, unc), *Medal for the General* (1944), *Strawberry Roan* (1945), *The Third Visitor* (1951), *My Wife's Lodger* (1952), *Is Your Honeymoon Really Necessary?, House of Blackmail, The Great Game* (1953), *What Every Woman Wants, The Harassed Hero, The Happiness of 3 Women, The Gay Dog* (1954), *You Lucky People, Room in the House, Fun at St Fanny's* (1955), *Stars in Your Eyes, The Last Man to Hang?* (1956), *Second Fiddle* (1957). Clyde Jeavons.

Elvin, George (*b* Buckhurst Hill, 1907 – *d* Southend, Essex, 1984). Executive. Chartered accountant who in 1934 became famously the General Secretary of the ACT, and stayed so until 1969. Held other important posts representing workers' rights, including secretary of the Film Industry Employees Council.

Elvin, June (*b* London, 1925). Actress. 40s starlet who made a few films, including *Nicholas Nickleby* (1947, as Mrs Snevecelli) before fading from view. On stage with ENSA during WW2, then briefly under contract to EALING.

OTHER BRITISH FILMS INCLUDE: *Hue and Cry* (1946, unc), *The Small Back Room* (1948), *Judgment Deferred* (1951), *Salute the Toff* (1952), *Too Hot to Handle* (1960).

Elvin, Violetta (*b* Moscow, 1925). Dancer. RN: Violetta Prokhorova. Soloist with the Bolshoi Ballet, later Covent Garden and Sadler's Wells, Elvin made three film appearances: as a gypsy dancer in *Queen of Spades* (1949), as a scheming 'other woman' in *Twice Upon a Time* (1953), and in *Melba* (1953) as – what else? – a prima ballerina.

Elwes, Cary (*b* London, 1962). Actor. Son of painter Dominic Elwes and interior designer Tessa Kennedy, handsome Harrow-educated Elwes was, appropriately enough, first noticed in public-schoolboy roles in *Another Country* and *Oxford Blues* (1984, UK/US). Had his first starring role as Lord Dudley in *Lady Jane* (1985), opposite Helena BONHAM CARTER; has since worked predominantly in America, in popular films such as *Glory* (1989), and, eponymously, *Robin Hood: Men in Tights* (1993).

OTHER BRITISH FILMS INCLUDE: *The Bride* (1985), *Maschenka* (1987, UK/Ger/Fr/Fin), *The Informant* (1996), *Shadow of the Vampire* (2001, UK/Lux/US).

Emary, Barbara K. (*b* London, 1908). Screenwriter. In films from 1933, at SOUND CITY, and associated for over 20 years with the films of John BAXTER, first as uncredited assistant, then as co-author and continuity on *Stepping Toes* (1938). Thereafter, she was usually credited as co-screenwriter, sometimes as production manager (e.g. on *The Shipbuilders*, 1943) or associate producer (on *Make Mine a Million*, 1959, produced by Baxter).

OTHER BRITISH FILMS INCLUDE (sc/co-sc, unless noted): *Secret Journey* (cont), (1939), *Old Mother Riley in Society* (+ cont), *Crook's Tour* (adapt) (1940), *Love on the Dole, The Common Touch* (1941), *Let the People Sing, We'll Smile Again* (1942), *When We Are Married, Old Mother Riley, Detective* (1943), *Fortune Lane* (1947, assoc p), *The Second Mate* (1950, assoc p, co-sc), *Judgment Deferred* (1951, assoc p), *Ramsbottom Rides Again* (1956, assoc p).

Embassy Pictures *see* **George King**

Emerton, Roy (*b* Burford, Oxfordshire, 1892 – *d* England, 1944). Actor. Hefty character player of stage and screen, whose pre-acting jobs, as stevedore, miner and others, are easy to credit. Very busy in the 30s, as, for example, Jane Grey's executioner in *Tudor Rose* (1936) or the heroine's burly foreman father in *The Great Barrier* (1937), and just before his death a fine Bardolph in *Henry V* (1944). Married Catherine LACEY.

OTHER BRITISH FILMS INCLUDE: *Shadows* (1931), *That Night in London, The Sign of Four* (1932), *Lorna Doone* (as Carver Doone) *Java Head* (1934), *Everything Is Thunder* (1936), *Doctor Syn, Big Fella* (1937), *The Drum, Convict 99* (1938), *The Thief of Baghdad, Busman's Honeymoon* (1940), *The Young Mr Pitt* (1942), *Time Flies, Love Story* (1944).

Emery, Dick (*b* London, 1918 – *d* London, 1983). Actor. Most famous for his TV show (1972) with catchcry of 'Ooh . . . You are awful!', which became the title of the movie (1972) built around his various bizarre personae, several of them in DRAG. Funny as he was, he never took off in cinema.

OTHER BRITISH FILMS INCLUDE: *The Case of the Mukkinese Battlehorn* (1955), *Follow a Star* (1959), *Crooks Anonymous, The Fast Lady, The Wrong Arm of the Law* (1962), *Just for Fun!* (1963), *Baby Love* (1967), *Yellow Submarine* (1968, anim, voice), *Find the Lady* (1976).

EMI Electrical and Musical Industries (EMI) was a British show business conglomerate which, in the later 60s, aimed to become a force in film production-exhibition-distribution. In several stages it took over ASSOCIATED BRITISH PICTURE CORPORATION, with its ELSTREE STUDIOS, first buying out the Warner–Seven Arts share in ABPC. By 1969, the latter had been replaced by EMI–Elstree, MGM agreed to co-finance some Elstree films, rather than pursue its own production pro-gramme at Borehamwood, and actor-director Bryan FORBES was made head of production and managing director of EMI–MGM. For a couple of years Forbes tried valiantly to produce films which would keep the company financially viable, and there were solid successes with *The Railway Children* and *Tales of Beatrix Potter* (1971) and a major *succès d'estime* with *The Go-Between* (1971). However, the studio was probably overcommitted to productions not likely to be major box-office successes; there were difficult labour relations; and late in 1971, committed to a no-redundancy policy, Forbes resigned. By 1973, MGM had withdrawn its participation, and the studio's permanent staff had been halved. There were odd hits in the 70s, such as *Murder on the Orient Express* (1974), but the company continued to have financial difficulties and was bought in 1979 by Thorn, the electrical conglomerate. Thorn–EMI worked to attract American majors to use the Elstree studio facilities and to embrace television as well as film production. In 1986, the amalgamated company was bought by the CANNON GROUP, so ending EMI's dream of becoming a major player in British film.
BIBLIOG: Alexander Walker, *Hollywood, England*, 1974.

Emlyn, Endaf (*b* Pwllheli, Wales, 1945). Director, screen-writer. Emlyn's inadequately distributed films chronicle the Wales of several decades ago with affection and detachment, often from a child's point of view, as with *The Making of Maps* (1995), and sometimes, as in *Gaucho* (1983), uniting this vision to a familiar genre, like that of political thriller.
OTHER BRITISH FILMS (d, sc/co-sc): *Storms of August* (1988), *One Full Moon* (1991), *Leaving Lenin* (1993).

Emmett, E(dward) V.H. (*b* London, 1902 – *d* London, 1971). Commentator, screenwriter, producer. Emmett's familiar, jocular commentary sets the ensuing tone for *On Approval* (1944), one of the wittiest films made in Britain, and it as commentator that he is best remembered, sometimes appearing *in* the film, sometimes not. He also contributed to the screenplays of such films as *Sabotage* (1936) and *Young Man's Fancy* (1939), and played commentators of several kinds in *Wings of the Morning* (1937), *The Arsenal Stadium Mystery* (1939) and *For Freedom* (1940). A former journalist, he joined *Gaumont Sound News* in 1930 as a cutter, becoming also a commentator when it became *Gaumont British News* (1934), and stayed until 1944, when he was appointed producer-director-writer for GB INSTRUCTIONAL. Also, associate pro-ducer at EALING in the latter 40s, on films such as *Passport to Pimlico* (1949), and last heard as narrator on *Carry On Cleo* (1964).
OTHER BRITISH FILMS INCLUDE (narr/comm, unless noted): *The Camels are Coming* (1934), *The Lion Has Wings* (1939, + co-sc), *Sailors Three* (1940), *Get Cracking* (1943), *Easy Money* (1948), *Gentlemen – the Queen* (1953, + w), *Churchill, Man of the Century* (1955), *Private's Progress, South of Sahara* (short) (1956); (co-sc/sc): *Non-Stop New York* (1937, add dial), *The Ware Case* (1938), *Bothered By a Beard* (1945, + d, p, short), *Dance Hall* (1950, + assoc p).

Emmott, Basil (*b* London, 1894 – *d* Chichester, 1976). Cine-matographer. With over 140 films to his credit, Emmott had one of the most prolific careers in British cinema. He made his name with the famous DOCUMENTARY *Drifters* (1929), contributing to the poetic REALISM of the struggle between men and nature and to the bustle of ordinary shore lives. It may be true to say that nothing else in his career offered a comparable challenge, though it could be claimed that his pre-*noir* images for Warner Bros in the 30s, as in *They Drive by Night* (1939), stand out from his many journeyman chores of the period. And, in the 'B' MOVIE THRILLERS at the end of his career, his moody atmospherics collude with director Lance COMFORT's dark vision, in such films as *The Painted Smile* (1961), *The Break* (1962) and, making good use of a deceptive PASTORAL setting, *Touch of Death* (1962).
OTHER BRITISH FILMS INCLUDE: (c, unless noted) *Rob Roy* (1922, co-c), *The Glad Eye, The Arcadians* (1927, co-c), *Sailors Don't Care* (1928, co-c), *To What Red Hell* (c), *The Feather* (1929), *The Great Game* (1930, co-c), *Chin Chin Chinaman, The Rosary*, (1931), *The Silver Greyhound, The Missing Rembrandt* (1932), *Out of the Past, I Adore You* (1933), *Something Always Happens* (1934), *Mr Cohen Takes a Walk* (1935), *Crown v Stevens, Irish for Luck, Educated Evans* (1936), *It's Not Cricket, The Compulsory Wife, The Singing Cop* (1937), *The Return of Carol Deane, Many Tanks Mr Atkins* (1938), *Too Dangerous to Live, Hoots Mon!, His Brother's Keeper, The Good Old Days, The Midas Touch* (1939), *Sailors Three, Two for Danger, George and Margaret* (1940), *The Prime Minister, Atlantic Ferry* (1941), *This Was Paris, Flying Fortress* (1942), *It's That Man Again* (1943), *It Happened One Sunday, Time Flies* (1944), *The Man from Morocco* (1945), *Master of Bankdam* (1947), *The Brass Monkey* (1948), *Paper Orchid* (1949), *The Case of . . . Gracie Budd, . . . the Black Falcon, . . . Soho Red* (1953, shorts), *The Green Buddha* (1954), *Johnny, You're Wanted, Joe MacBeth, Cross Channel* (1955), *Wicked as They Come* (1956), *The Long Haul* (1957), *Battle of the V-1, I Was Monty's Double* (1958), *Rag Doll* (1960), *Pit of Darkness, The Breaking Point* (1961), *Strongroom, Tomorrow at Ten* (1962), *Live it Up, Blind Corner* (1963), *Curse of the Fly, Be My Guest* (1965).

Emney, Fred (*b* London, 1900 – *d* Bognor Regis, 1980). Actor. Son of a celebrated MUSIC HALL actor of the same name, on stage from 1915, mostly in musicals, comedy and variety, including ten years in American vaudeville (1920–31), Emney had a dawdling career in films. Appeared in about 30 in 40 years, invariably in comedy, and often in characters given to bluster, like the star role in the 1955 farce, *Fun at St Fanny's*. His films were at their most upmarket in the 60s, when he appeared in *Those Magnificent Men . . .* , *Bunny Lake Is Missing* (1965) and *Oliver!* (1968, as the workhouse chairman).

Empire and colonialism The films of Empire and colonialism were Britain's contribution to GENRE cinema. Largely pro-duced by Alexander KORDA's LONDON FILMS in the 30s with substantial support from brother Zoltán, these films were blatantly nationalist and colonialist in much the same way as the American Western embodies certain imperialist myths about the US. In *Sanders of the River* (1935), *The Drum* (1938), and *The Four Feathers* (1939), the protagonists are clean-cut British civil servants, physicians, or professional military men. The antagonists are rebellious Africans, Indians, Asians, and Irish who foment sedition, pitting British against foreigners. They are suggestible and vulnerable to manipulation, owing to their 'childlike', if not savage, and primitive state. It falls to the British presence to establish order with only a handful of men and at great personal sacrifice. The landscape of the films is crucial to these motifs, underscoring a binary distinction between British civilisation versus 'orientalist' barbarism.

'Home' is associated with upper-class splendour exemplified by the big house in *The Four Feathers*. This setting contrasts with the 'outposts' of the empire identified with nature, often with the jungle where 'natives', camouflaged by their clothing and painted bodies can attack without warning. British colonial offices are identified with globes, maps, and portraits of British monarchs. INDIA is distinguished from AFRICA, though the nature of political threat is transposable: in *The Drum*, the Indian enemy is identified with rugged mountain passes, also exoticism, architectural splendour, and excessiveness in clothes, jewels, furniture and architecture. Both *The Drum* and *Sanders of the River* convey that (a) running an empire can be managed by thrifty and trustworthy public servants; (b) aggression is always initiated by the natives; and (c) colonial rule is necessary given the state of chaos and disorganisation of non-Christian and non-British cultures. Political 'wisdom' resides in designating important intermediaries who can be trusted to keep their own people in line.

Another aspect of the films which seems more directly related to economic, not governing, issues is the quest for treasure exemplified by *King Solomon's Mines* (1937). The indigenous people are divided between helpers and traitors: one who assists, a princely figure with authority to lead the British to treasure and to ritual secrets, and one who defies, an unruly figure who works actively against the British presence. Films of empire and colonialism continued in the post-war era but with modification. These films cover a range of themes: conflicts between tradition and modernity in Africa (*Men of Two Worlds*, 1946), commercial exploitation of African tribesmen (*Where No Vultures Fly*, 1951; *West of Zanzibar*,1954); violence against the British in the movement toward independence (*Simba*, 1955; *Zulu*, 1964); films that dramatise conflict in outposts of empire such as New Zealand and the Far East (*The Seekers*, 1954; *The Beachcomber*, 1954; and *Windom's Way*, 1957). Some films were REMAKES (*Storm over the Nile*, 1955) of earlier popular empire films.

In recent decades, ATTENBOROUGH's *Gandhi* (1982, UK/Ind), a BIOPIC, was an epic treatment of Indian struggles for independence and *In the Name of the Father* (1993, UK/Ire/US) addressed the Anglo-Irish conflict. British cinema also produced parodies of the Empire film, e.g. *Old Bones of the River* (1938) and the hilarious *Carry On Up the Khyber* 1968), and there have been notable ADAPTATIONS of novels which take a seriously jaundiced view of British colonial activities, including *Outcast of the Islands* (1951), *The Heart of the Matter* (1953), *Lord Jim* (1964), and *A Passage to India* (1984). Marcia Landy.

Empire Marketing Board Film Unit If one wanted to trace the origins of what is now called the British DOCUMENTARY MOVEMENT back to a particular moment, it would be John GRIERSON's appointment to the Empire Marketing Board. This occurred in 1928 after he had returned from the US and met EMB secretary Stephen TALLENTS, who had a clear sense of the sorts of subjects he considered suitable for films, essentially extolling in lively fashion the virtues of British institutions and attitudes. Grierson's first EMB film *Drifters* (1929) is the film accepted as beginning the movement and it enabled Grierson to set up a Film Unit within the Board employing Basil WRIGHT, John TAYLOR, Arthur ELTON, Paul ROTHA and Edgar ANSTEY. The Unit produced about 100 films between January 1931 and July 1933, when it became part of the Public Relations Department of the General Post Office. The Film Unit was only a part – a radical one – of the EMB, which was a government body promoting trade throughout the British Empire through posters, exhibitions, newspapers, pamphlets and the like, before Grierson turned up and persuaded Tallents to include film as well. Although often maligned, the impressionistic *Industrial Britain* (1931), shot largely by Robert FLAHERTY, with some input from Grierson and others, remains the greatest of the Unit's productions. Deane Williams.

Endfield, Cy (*b* Scranton, Pennsylvania, 1914 – *d* Shipston-on-Stour, 1995). Director. Yale-educated Endfield came to Britain in the early 50s when the McCarthy hearings led to a blacklisting that put paid to his modest US career, just as it was reaching new distinction with the lynch-mob drama, *The Sound of Fury* (1950). His British work is superior to the 'Joe Palooka' series typical of his earlier US films: the highlights are *Hell Drivers* (1957, + co-sc), a powerful melodrama of truck-driving rivalries in a charmless midlands setting; and the military epic, *Zulu* (1964, + co-p, co-sc); but it is all workmanlike, vigorous stuff like the 'B' FILM, *Impulse* (1955), which he directed but for which Charles De LAUTOUR is credited. He adopted several names (C. Raker, Hugh Raker, etc) during the period just after the BLACKLIST. Served with the Army Signal Corps during WW2.

OTHER BRITISH FILMS: *Colonel March Investigates*, *The Limping Man* (unc) (1953), *The Master Plan* (1954, as Hugh Raker), *The Secret* (+ sc) (1955), *Child in the House* (1956, co-d, + sc), *Sea Fury* (+story), *Jet Storm* (1959, + co-sc), *Mysterious Island* (1961), *Hide and Seek* (1963), *Sands of the Kalahari* (1965), *Universal Soldier* (1971, + sc).

Engel, Susan (*b* Vienna, 1935). Actress. Educated at the Sorbonne and Bristol Universities, this stage actress has made few films, but has appeared with distinction, especially as Regan in *King Lear* (1970, UK/Den) and Alan BATES's estranged wife in *Butley* (1973). Her work has commanding stillness and intelligence.

OTHER BRITISH FILMS INCLUDE: *Inspector Clouseau* (1968), *Charlie Bubbles* (1967), *Ascendancy* (1982), *Shadey* (1985), *Damage* (1992, UK/Fr).

Engelen, Paul (*b* Walton-on-Thames, 1949). Make-up artist. BAA-winning (for *Greystoke* . . . , 1984, UK/US) make-up specialist has worked on – from his corner – some of the most demanding films of the last 20 years, and been Oscar-nominated for *Greystoke* . . . and *Frankenstein* (1994, UK/US) and BAA-nominated for *Batman* (1989, UK/US) and *The Emerald Forest* (1985).

OTHER BRITISH FILMS INCLUDE: *Pulp* (1972), *The Man with the Golden Gun* (1974), *That Lucky Touch* (1975), *The Hound of the Baskervilles*, *The Spy Who Loved Me* (1977), *The Wild Geese* (1978, UK/Switz), *Moonraker* (UK/Fr), *North Sea Hijack* (1979), *Trail of the Pink Panther*, *Pink Floyd The Wall*, *Victor/Victoria* (1982), *Superman III* (1983), *The Bounty* (1984), *Santa Claus, Revolution* (sup) (UK/Nor) (1985), *A Fish Called Wanda* (sup), *Stealing Heaven* (UK/Yug) (1988), *The Sheltering Sky* (1990, UK/It), *Much Ado About Nothing* (UK/US), *Splitting Heirs* (1993), *Restoration* (1995, US/UK), *Gladiator* (2000, UK/US).

English, Arthur (*b* Aldershot, 1919 – *d* Camberley, 1995). Actor. Best known as the shambling irreverent janitor, Mr Harman, in TV's politically incorrect series *Are You Being Served?* (1973–83) and the SPIN-OFF movie (1977). First film role was as a lorry-driver in *The Hi-Jackers* (1963).

OTHER BRITISH FILMS INCLUDE: *Echo of Diana* (1963), *Percy* (1971), *For the Love of Ada* (1972), *The Boys in Blue* (1983).

Enigma Productions *see* **Puttnam, David**

Eno, Brian (*b* Woodbridge, Suffolk, 1948). Composer. Formerly a founder-member of Roxy Music (1971), he later worked solo and became a well-regarded producer of such rock musicians as David BOWIE. His work in film has been chiefly for ART-HOUSE directors like Peter GREENAWAY (*Vertical Features Remake*, 1978, title music; *The Falls*, 1980) and Derek JARMAN (*Sebastiane*, 1976; *Jubilee*, 1978). Main career belongs elsewhere.

OTHER BRITISH FILMS INCLUDE: *Berlin Horse* (1970, short), *The Devil's Men, Resistance* (doc) (1976), *Glitterbug* (1994, doc), *The Million Dollar Hotel* (2000, UK/Ger/US, songs).

episodic (or portmanteau) films British cinema seems particularly drawn to the episodic or portmanteau film, where a number of personal narratives are presented, generally with some linking thread. *Friday the Thirteenth* (1933), *Train of Events* (1949) and *Laughter in Paradise* (1951) are among the most typical examples. G.B. SAMUELSON started the trend, with historical dramas such as *Milestones* (1916) showing the experiences of different family members over successive generations. A variation on the theme is the compendium film featuring a number of short stories, of which the most typical example is *Quartet* (1948), a sophisticated entertainment based on four Somerset MAUGHAM stories, and popular enough to result in the similarly-constructed Maugham sequels *Trio* (1950) and *Encore* (1951). EALING's *Dead of Night* (1945) represents the short story compendium at its peak. The tradition of the portmanteau or short story film continues in modern British cinema, with the multiple, interlocking life stories on show in *This Year's Love* (1999) and the three Irving Welsh stories that comprise *The Acid House* (1998). Luke McKernan.

Eros A comparatively small distribution company which was responsible for getting screened much of the 'B' MOVIE output in the late 40s and the 50s, as well as reissuing top Hollywood films from most major studios. Production companies such as TEMPEAN used Eros regularly, and directors like Francis SEARLE and Vernon SEWELL recalled its usefulness when major distributors (RANK and ABC) showed little interest in working with smaller production outfits. Phil Hyams, chairman in its key period, and his brother Sid Hyams, managing director, entered the industry in 1912 as cinema owners, forming Eros post-WW2. In the mid 50s, Eros became involved in the production of such independently produced 'A' films as *The Man Who Watched Trains Go By* (1952) and *The Sea Shall Not Have Them* (1954). It went into liquidation in 1961.

Erskine, Eileen (*b* Nottingham, 1914 – *d* Chiddingfold, 1995). Actress. Demure stage actress who made few films, memorably flaring up against character, in *This Happy Breed*, touching as Hugh BURDEN's anxious wife in *The Way Ahead* (1944), and a composed, knowing Biddy in *Great Expectations* (1946). Went to Hollywood in the late 40s with husband Philip FRIEND and played two minor roles there. In TV's *The Pallisers* (1974), and the author of a very attractive memoir, *Scenes from a Life* (2000), published posthumously. Her son is TV director, Martyn Friend.

OTHER BRITISH FILMS: *The Midas Touch* (1939), *Sheepdog of the Hills* (1941, unc).

Esher Studio A one-stage studio opened in 1913. It had only minor success and its activities seem to have ended with the production of short films, by Henry AINLEY, in the early 20s. Two directors who worked there were Geoffrey MALINS and A.V. BRAMBLE.

Esmond, Annie (*b* Surrey, 1873 – *d* London, 1945). Actress. First in the West End theatre in 1894, Esmond became a prolific supporting player in films, from 1917, busiest in the 30s, when she played maids and nannies, with the occasional 'great lady' thrown in. She was nanny to the *Dear Octopus* (1943) family, and Lady Plumtree to a pack of unruly evacuees in *Gert and Daisy's Weekend* (1941). John GIELGUD gives a touching account of her illegitimacy and dogged, solitary life in *Backward Glances* (1972).

OTHER BRITISH FILMS INCLUDE: *Dawn* (1917), *Damaged Goods, Possession, The Right Element* (1919), *Innocent* (1921), *The Sins Ye Do* (1924), *Tiptoes* (1927), *Alf's Button* (1930), *The Outsider* (1931), *Men of Tomorrow* (1932), *The Good Companions* (1933), *Abdul the Damned, The Scarlet Pimpernel* (1935), *Stolen Life* (1939), *Saloon Bar* (1940), *Let the People Sing* (1942), dozens more.

Esmond, Carl (*b* Vienna, 1905). Actor. RN: Willy Eichberger. Esmond, handsome leading man of the Berlin theatre, fled the Nazi regime to find haven in London in 1933. He appeared in British films until 1938, when he went to Hollywood and settled there, playing Nazi swine in wartime melodramas like *First Comes Courage* (1943). In 30s Britain, he played romantic foreigners on stage and in three films: *Evensong, Blossom Time* (1934), and *Invitation to the Waltz* (1935).

Esmond, Jill (*b* London, 1908 – *d* London, 1990). Actress. Born to theatrical parents, playwright/actor-manager H.V. Esmond and actress Eva MOORE, Bedales-educated and RADA-trained Esmond was on stage at 14, and when she married Laurence OLIVIER in 1930 was considerably more famous than he. In Hollywood in the early 30s, she gave up the chance of the lead in *A Bill of Divorcement* (1932) to return with him to London; but the marriage ended in divorce in 1940. Esmond's second film was HITCHCOCK's *The Skin Game* (1931) and, in this and *No Funny Business* (1933), opposite a somewhat wooden Olivier, she showed naturalness and intelligence as a screen actress. During WW2, she took her small son, Tarquin, to Hollywood where she played incisive Englishwomen in a dozen films, helping authenticate dubious English-set production design. Post-war, she was excellent in three more British films, and retired in 1955 after two further US films, becoming active in the administration of theatrical charities.

OTHER BRITISH FILMS: *The Chinese Bungalow* (1930), *The Eternal Feminine* (1931), *FP1* (1933, UK/Ger), *Bedelia* (1946), *Escape* (1948), *Private Information* (1952).

Essex, David (*b* Plaistow, 1947). Actor. Hugely popular British pop star of the 70s, adored by teenage girls for his blue-eyed, tousled looks. Apart from recording hits like 'Rock On' (1974), Cockney Essex starred on stage in *Godspell* and in a handful of movies built around his gifts and appeal: *That'll Be the Day* (1973), *Stardust* (1974) and *Silver Dream Racer* (1980). Awarded OBE, 1999.

OTHER BRITISH FILMS: *Carry On Henry, Assault* (1970), *All Coppers Are . . .* (1971).

Estridge, Robin (*b* England, 1920). Screenwriter. Estridge had written ten novels before beginning his screenwriting career, which was at its busiest in the 50s, when he wrote popular films such as the Cold War romance, *The Young Lovers* (1954, co-sc, BAA) and the period adventures *Dangerous Exile* (1957) and

North West Frontier (1959, BAAn). Wrote novel and screenplay for his last film, *Permission to Kill* (1975).

OTHER BRITISH FILMS INCLUDE: *A Day to Remember* (1953), *Simba* (co-sc) (1955), *Checkpoint* (1956), *No Kidding* (1960), *Eye of the Devil* (1956).

Eurimages Name given to the film fund of the Council of Europe as part of a pan-European cinema scheme, founded in 1989, to offer completion money (up to £600,000 or 20% of the budget) to projects involving at least three member countries, and to ensure distribution and exhibition of European films. Britain did not join until 1993 and withdrew in 1996, after receiving support for such projects as Peter GREENAWAY's *The Pillow Book* (1996, UK/Fr/Lux/Neth). The new Labour Government, elected in 1997, pledged re-entry. Eurimages fostered the production of some interesting films, while raising again the issue of what constituted a 'British film'.

BIBLIOG: Robert Murphy (ed), *British Cinema of the 90s*, 2000.

Europeans in British film Throughout its history, British cinema has had productive exchanges with other European film cultures. In the mid 20s, directors Alfred HITCHCOCK and Graham CUTTS worked in Germany, where they were influenced by continental approaches to set design and lighting. In the late 20s and early 30s, BIP and GAUMONT–BRITISH co-operated with German and French companies on multilingual co-productions, part of a pan-European strategy to counter Hollywood dominance. As a result of these strategies and the subsequent rise of fascism in Europe, a large number of continental film-makers, actors, and technicians worked in Britain in the 30s and 40s, arguably the most 'European' and culturally hybrid period in British film history. The legacy in British cinema of émigré producers (Alexander KORDA, Max SCHACH, Josef SOMLO, Friedrich ZELNIK, Marcel HELLMAN), cinematographers (Günter KRAMPF, Max GREENE, Otto HELLER, Erwin HILLIER), production designers (Alfred JUNGE, Oscar WERNDORFF, Vincent KORDA, Ernö METZNER, Ferdinand BELLAN), composers (Allan GRAY, Hans MAY, Walter GOEHR, Mischa SPOLIANSKY), and screenwriters (Lajos BIRO, Emeric PRESSBURGER, Wolfgang WILHELM) has been immense. The impact of European stars (Conrad VEIDT, Elisabeth BERGNER, Richard TAUBER) and directors (Berthold VIERTEL, Karl GRUNE, Paul CZINNER, E.A. DUPONT), on the other hand, was frequently more short-lived. After the war, British cinema often used imported European actors as glamorous exotics (Mai ZETTERLING, Greta GYNT, Brigitte BARDOT, Simone SIGNORET, Leslie CARON, Hildegarde NEFF, Britt EKLAND, Juliette BINOCHE, and men such as Rossano BRAZZI and Ivan DESNY), while it continued to attract new generations of émigré directors (Roman POLANSKI, Jerzy SKOLIMOVSKY) and other visitors from the Continent (François Truffaut, Michelangelo Antonioni, Andi Engel).

BIBLIOG: Richard Maltby, Andrew Higson (eds), *Film Europe and Film America. Cinema, Commerce, and Cultural Exchange 1920–1939*, 1999. Tim Bergfelder.

Eustrel, Anthony (*b* London, 1903 – *d* Los Angeles, 1979). Actor. On stage from 1927, with experience in touring companies, at Stratford and the Open Air Theatre, Regent's Park, Eustrel entered films in 1936, under contract to John STAFFORD, in *Second Bureau*. Appeared in several British films, including *Caesar and Cleopatra* (1945), before going to Hollywood in the 50s, playing professional Brits in a range of genres, including a butler in *Goodbye Charlie* (1964).

OTHER BRITISH FILMS INCLUDE: *Under the Red Robe* (1937), *Gasbags* (1940), *The Silver Fleet*, *The Adventures of Tartu* (1943), *I Know Where I'm Going!* (1945), *The Story of Robin Hood* . . . (1952).

Evans, Barry (*b* Guildford, 1945 – *d* Claybrooke Magna, 1997). Actor. Evans began by starring in the 'swinging 60s' feature, *Here We Go Round the Mulberry Bush* (1967), became popular in TV's *Doctor in the House* (1969–70) series and sequel *Doctor at Large* (1971), as the young protagonist, Mike Upton, replacing the original Simon Sparrow. His career dwindled sadly and he was working as a taxi driver at the time of his death, caused by a blow during a robbery at his house.

OTHER BRITISH FILMS: *Alfred the Great* (1969), *Die Screaming, Marianne* (1970), *Adventures of a Taxi Driver* (1975), *Under the Doctor* (1976), *The Mystery of Edwin Drood* (1993).

Evans, Betsan Morris Director. From television, Evans made a not wholly successful but visually daring, cinema debut with *Dad Savage* (1998), a thriller set in flat East Anglian countryside. On TV, by contrast, she directed Pinero's social melodrama of an earlier age, *Lady Audley's Secret* (2000).

OTHER BRITISH FILMS: *Spoonface Steinberg* (1998).

Evans, Clifford (*b* Senghenydd, Wales, 1912 – *d* Senghenydd, Wales, 1985). Actor. Sincere, sympathetic, earnest: these are epithets that come to mind in relation to the lean-faced Evans's performances. It is an image honed in such roles as *Penn of Pennsylvania* (1941), the decent heroes of *Love on the Dole* (1941) and *The Foreman Went to France* (1942). On London and New York stages before entering films, Evans never recovered career momentum after WW2 service (1942–46) and the failure of *The Silver Darlings* (1946), the semi-documentary he also co-directed. Subsequently, he appeared almost entirely in small roles and 'B' MOVIES, playing Stryker of Scotland Yard in about a dozen short films, called *The Case of* . . . *Gracie Budd* (1953), . . . *Diamond Annie* (1954), etc. Married actress **Hermione Hannen** (*b* London, 1913), who appeared in *The Life of the Party* (1934).

OTHER BRITISH FILMS INCLUDE: *The River House Mystery* (1935), *At the Villa Rose* (1939), *The Proud Valley*, *Freedom Radio* (1940), *The Flemish Farm* (1943), *While I Live* (1947), *A Run for Your Money* (story) (1949), *Face in the Night* (1956), *The Violent Playground* (1957), *The Heart Within*, *At the Stroke of Nine* (1959), *The Curse of the Werewolf* (1961), *The Long Ships* (1963), *A Twist of Sand* (1968).

Evans, David Director. Made his directorial debut with an acceptable, if not exactly exhilarating, version of Nick Hornby's *Fever Pitch* in 1997, and followed it with the little-seen *Our Boy* (1997) and a TV drama, *Passion Killers* (1999).

Evans, David A. (*b* Wales, 1893 – *d* Los Angeles, 1966). Screenwriter. Cambridge-educated novelist who entered films in 1936, writing ten 'QUOTA QUICKIES' for FOX–BRITISH at WEMBLEY. After RAF service (1940–45), he collaborated on a half-dozen more films before leaving for Hollywood in 1951. *Boomerang* (1934) was based on his play and *You Must Get Married* (1937) on his novel.

OTHER BRITISH FILMS INCLUDE: (sc/co-sc) *Irish and Proud of It* (1936), *The Villiers Diamond* (1938), *I'll Turn to You* (1946), *Snowbound* (1948), *The Late Edwina Black*, *The Third Visitor* (1951).

Evans, Dame Edith (*b* London, 1888 – *d* Cranbrook, 1976). Actress. Justly celebrated stage star (from 1912), of classic and modern roles (at Stratford, the Old Vic, the West End, Broadway), made DBE in 1946 and loaded with honorary doctorates (London, Oxford, Cambridge), she went on to accrue almost comparable honours as a screen character actress. For those who never saw her on stage, her definitive performance as Lady Bracknell was carefully preserved, like a fly in amber, in Anthony ASQUITH's *The Importance of Being Earnest* (1952): the magisterial bearing, the vowel-heavy delivery ('a ha-a-a-andbag?'), the total command of the mise-en-scène, are wonders to behold, but the transition to screen has been truly made. She made three long-forgotten silent films (though *East Is East*, 1916, has its admirers), then over 30 years later returned to mesmerise filmgoers with her role as the ancient countess who has sold her soul for success at cards in *The Queen of Spades* (1948). It is one of the great performances in a British film; so, too, is her tiny role as Ma Tanner in *Look Back in Anger* (1959), or an outraged Miss Western in *Tom Jones* (1963, AAn), or the imperiously dotty Mrs St Maugham in *The Chalk Garden* (1964, AAn) or the frightened old lady in *The Whisperers* (1966, BAA, AAn). She acted until she died, in films not always worthy of her, a curiously solitary figure crowned with laurels of every kind.

OTHER BRITISH FILMS: *A Welsh Singer, Honeymoon for Three* (1915), *The Last Days of Dolwyn* (1949), *Young Cassidy* (1965), *Prudence and the Pill* (1968), *The Madwoman of Chaillot, Crooks and Coronets, David Copperfield* (1969), *Scrooge* (1970), *A Doll's House, Craze* (1973), *The Slipper and the Rose, Nasty Habits* (1976).

BIBLIOG: Bryan Forbes, *Ned's Girl: the Life of Edith Evans*, 1977.

Evans, Edward (*b* London, 1914 – *d* Longsdon, 2001). Actor. From a Welsh theatrical family which discouraged his acting aspirations, Evans became a very popular TV soap opera star, first as the lower-middle-class father of *The Grove Family* (1954–57), starring in the SPIN-OFF film version, *It's a Great Day* (1955). This was followed by many other TV roles, including that of corner-shop owner Lionel Petty in *Coronation Street* (1965–66). After WW2 army service, he made his stage debut in 1947 and was in TV from 1948. Pre-war, he did stunt work and unbilled bit roles in films, and he returned to films in 1948, mostly in small roles, including many policemen, as in *London Belongs to Me* (1948).

OTHER BRITISH FILMS INCLUDE: *The Small Voice* (1948), *Secret People* (1951), *I Believe in You* (1952), *Deadly Nightshade, Valley of Song, Appointment in London, Cosh Boy, Grand National Night* (1953), *The Man Upstairs* (1958), *The Trials of Oscar Wilde* (1960), *Blind Corner* (1963), *Till Death Do Us Part* (1969), *10 Rillington Place* (1970), *Sunday Bloody Sunday* (1971), *Out of Season* (1975), *Lifeforce* (1985).

Evans, Fred (*b* London, 1889 – *d* London, 1951). Actor. A former MUSIC HALL and circus performer, Evans was a knockabout comedian, who was starred by Cricks & Martin in 1910–11 in the 'Charley Smiler' SERIES. In 1912, he came into his own on screen as the grotesque slapstick character 'Pimple,' who was starred in almost one film a week through 1918, all written and directed by Evans in association with his brother Joe. Compared with American slapstick, theirs was unsophisticated fare, but Evans did prove himself adept at starring in parodies of well-known films of the era, such as *Pimple's Ivanhoe* (1913), *The House of Distemperley* (1914), *Pimple's Million Dollar Mystery, Pimple's Three Weeks* (1915), *Pimple's The Whip* (1917), and *Pimple's Better 'Ole* (1918). AS.

Evans, Jessie (*b* Mountain Ash, S. Wales, 1918 – *d* Canterbury, 1983). Actress. Former nurse, a stage actress from 1943, in companies with Emlyn WILLIAMS and John GIELGUD, she appeared on TV from 1950 and in occasional films from 1952.

BRITISH FILMS INCLUDE: *Aunt Clara* (1954), *Raising a Riot* (1955), *The Extra Day* (1956), *Doctor in Distress* (1963), *Countess Dracula* (1970), *Mistress Pamela* (1973).

Evans, Joe (*b* England, 1891 – *d* Brighton, 1967). Director, actor. On-screen from 1912–18, Evans (not to be confused with the American actor of the same name) directed himself in a series of comedy shorts, often playing the character of Joey. He also co-directed and sometimes appeared in the 'Pimple' films, starring his brother Fred EVANS. Joe and Fred's uncle is the legendary British music hall comedian, Will Evans, who co-founded the Sunny South and Sealight Film Company at Shoreham-on-Sea in 1914. AS.

Evans, Lee (*b* Avonmouth, 1962). Actor. Retired from boxing at 21, then followed his father's lead as a physical, stand-up comedian, and appeared first in films in the acrid *Funny Bones* (1995, UK/US) – as a comic. Since then, he has been sought – and found – by Hollywood, appearing in *There's Something About Mary* (1998, US), the UK–French sci-fi hit, *The Fifth Element* (1997), and *Tosspot* (2001, UK), and has his own TV show.

Evans, Lyn (*b* Llanelly, Wales, 1898 – *d* ?). Actor. On stage with his father from 1912 and in two dozen films of the 40s and 50s, though one source claims he was in *The Rat* (1925). Balding Evans was usually in small bits, like the bemused pub landlord in *Miranda* (1948) or the sceptical policeman in *A Boy, a Girl and a Bike* (1949). Married actress **Nuna Davey**, the bitchy Mrs Rowlandson in *Brief Encounter* (1945).

OTHER BRITISH FILMS INCLUDE: *Jeannie* (1941), *The Years Between* (1946), *They Made Me a Fugitive* (1947), *Daybreak, The Small Voice, Quartet* (1948), *Marry Me, Kind Hearts and Coronets, Christopher Columbus* (1949), *Lady Godiva Rides Again, White Corridors* (1951), *The Card* (1952).

Evans, Marc (*b* Carmarthen, Wales, 1960). Director. Welsh director of little-seen films, though *House of America* (1997, UK/Neth), in which the children of a deserting father long to follow him to America, attracted some attention. Also directed an unsettling TV version of Ruth RENDELL's *Master of the Moor* (1994).

OTHER BRITISH FILMS INCLUDE: *Johnny Be Good* (1984, short), *Arthur's Departure* (1995, + co-sc), *Resurrection Man* (1997).

Evans, Maurice (*b* Dorchester, 1901 – *d* Rottingdean, 1989). Actor. Distinguished theatre star, on the professional stage from 1926, playing major roles in Britain and the US, notably as Hamlet on Broadway, 1938. Made a few insignificant films in Britain in the 30s, starring in Dallas BOWER's *The Path of Glory* (1934), not filming again until *Kind Lady* (1951, US) and only three more times in Britain, notably as Sullivan in *The Story of Gilbert and Sullivan* (1953). He filmed a lacklustre *Macbeth* (1961), but the rest of his film career is mainly in US movies, famously *Rosemary's Baby* (1968) and as Dr Zaius in the 'Planet of the Apes' films (1968, 1970), and TV, including several seasons of *Bewitched* from 1964. A US citizen from 1941, during WW2 he headed the Army Entertainment Section, Central Pacific Theatre.

OTHER BRITISH FILMS INCLUDE: *White Cargo* (1929), *Raise the Roof* (1930), *Cupboard Love* (1931), *Wedding Rehearsal* (1932), *The Only Girl* (1933), *By-Pass to Happiness* (1934), *Scrooge, Checkmate* (1935), *Thin Air* (1969).

Evans, Peggy (*b* Sheffield, 1925). Actress. Slender blonde supporting actress (alumnus of the 'Charm School') of a few 40s and 50s films, most vividly as Dirk BOGARDE's increasingly terrified girlfriend in *The Blue Lamp* (1949), and star of two footling HIGHBURY STUDIOS pieces, *Penny and the Pownall Case* (1948) and *Love in Waiting* (1948). Married to actor **Michael Howard** (*b* Holywell Green, 1916 – *d* London, 1988), who had small roles in a few films, including *A Canterbury Tale* (1944).

OTHER BRITISH FILMS INCLUDE: *Charley's (Big-Hearted) Aunt* (1940), *School for Secrets* (1946), *Look Before You Love* (1948), *Calling Bulldog Drummond* (1951).

Evans, Stephen (*b c* 1946). Producer. Much associated with the literary-adaptation strand of 90s British cinema, he received a BAAn for *The Madness of King George* (1994); was (exec-)producer of several Kenneth BRANAGH films: *Henry V* (1989), *Peter's Friends* (1992) and *Much Ado About Nothing* (1993, UK/US); and co-producer of the under-valued *Twelfth Night* (1996, UK/US) and the brilliant *The Wings of the Dove* (1997, UK/US). A stockbroker by profession, he began as financial adviser to Branagh's Renaissance Theatre and Film Companies.

OTHER BRITISH FILMS: *The Grotesque* (1996, ex p), *The Luzhin Defence* (2000, UK/Fr/It, co-p).

Eve, Trevor (*b* Birmingham, 1951). Actor. Eve's main successes have been on the stage (e.g. his award-winning performance as Astrov in *Uncle Vanya*, 1996) and TV (e.g. the amiable West Country private eye in *Shoestring*, 1979–80; prestige literary adaptations). His best film chance was as Jonathan Harker in *Dracula* (1979), US-financed with British cast, like his later *Possession* (2002).

BRITISH FILMS INCLUDE: *Children* (1976), *Scandal* (1988), *Don't Get Me Started* (1994), *Appetite* (1998).

Everest, Barbara (*b* London, 1890 – *d* London, 1968). Actress. On stage from 1912 – in Shakespeare, Shaw, many modern plays – and films from 1916, Everest remained busy until her death, usually projecting a warm, motherly image. After a dozen British silents and 30 more in the 30s, including character roles as servants (*The Passing of the Third Floor Back*, 1935) and society ladies (*The Prime Minister*, 1941), she went to Hollywood to perform the same mix (see *Gaslight* and *Jane Eyre*, 1943), returning to Britain post-war. On stage she played the hero's confused, well-meaning mother in *Frieda* (1946), repeating her role in the 1947 film, and gave memorable performances as mother to Eric PORTMAN in *Wanted for Murder* (1946) and to another murderer, Ann TODD, in *Madeleine* (1949).

OTHER BRITISH FILMS INCLUDE: *The Man Without a Soul* (1916), *Not Guilty, The Auction* (1919), *Fox Farm* (1922), *There Goes the Bride, The Lodger* (1932), *Scrooge* (1935), *Men of Yesterday* (1936), *This Man is Dangerous* (1941), *Children of Chance* (1949), *Tony Draws a Horse* (1950), *An Inspector Calls* (1954), *The Damned* (1961), *Rotten to the Core* (1965).

Everett, Dany Costume designer. Main achievement was the designs for the fine TV adaptation, *Dance to the Music of Time* (1997), its shifts in time, place and temperament often signalled in the costumes. Other work includes the comedy of paternal love, *Jack & Sarah* (1995, UK/Fr), and *August* (1996), a relocating of *Uncle Vanya* to 1890 Wales.

Everett, Rupert (*b* Norfolk, 1959). Actor. In 1997 Everett became a certified film *star* by playing a supporting role as Julia Roberts' gay chum in the overrated US comedy, *My Best Friend's Wedding*, which brought him several awards, including a BAA. Interviews confirmed his gay identity and his refusal to hide it in a Hollywood usually nervous on this matter. Born to wealthy parents, educated at Ampleforth College and, after a self-confessed stint as a prostitute, trained for the stage at Central School, he had West End success in *Another Country* (1982), as a young Guy Burgess type, repeating the role on film

(1984). Between that and his late 90s *réclame*, he made some curious choices, the most interesting of which were the moody, Venice-set sexual drama, *The Comfort of Strangers* (1990, UK/It) and as the indolent, waspish Prince of Wales in *The Madness of King George* (1994, UK/US). None of his international films was a popular success (including Robert Altman's *Prêt-à-Porter*, 1994): some, indeed, were scarcely seen: then, with *Shakespeare in Love* (1999, UK/US, as Marlowe), *An Ideal Husband* (UK/US, as a languid Lord Goring) and *A Midsummer Night's Dream* (UK/It) (1999), it was hard to avoid him, and not many wanted to. He has been nominated for – and often won – awards across a wide spectrum of prestige, and seems to have become a cult favourite.

OTHER BRITISH FILMS: *A Shocking Accident* (1982), *Real Life, The Bloody Chamber* (short) (1983), *Remembrance of Things Fast* (1993), *B. Monkey* (1998, UK/It/US).

Everyman Cinema Famous ART-HOUSE cinema in Hampstead, London, converted from a theatre to a small (285 seats) repertory cinema in 1933, showing foreign-language films, the great classics of world cinema, as well as a sprinkling of more obviously popular fare. It retained its original ambience until 1999, when it was refurbished as the Pullman Everyman, but it has since passed to other hands, is called the Everyman again and programmes new releases.

Exclusive Films Ltd Incorporated in 1935, founded by Enrique Carreras and Will (Hinds) HAMMER, as a distribution company. In the immediate post-war years, Exclusive began to produce 'B' MOVIES, such as *Dick Barton – Special Agent* (1948) and its sequel *Dick Barton Strikes Back* (1949), sometimes using the two-stage studio at Marylebone. It still operated as a distributor – of minor American films, especially from the Lippert organisation with which it went on to co-produce many features. In 1947, HAMMER FILMS was set up to rationalise the productions in which Exclusive was involved. Within a few years it was established at BRAY, Exclusive distributing its productions, which often starred second-string American actors and were usually in thriller – and sometimes light comedy – vein. Between 1947 and 1963, Hammer/Exclusive released 68 second features and had their first 'A' hit with the horror film, *The Quatermass Experiment* (1955).

See **Carreras, Sir James**

exhibition *see* **cinemas and exhibition**

exploitation films The exploitation era, at its height in the 70s, is remembered for a large number of poor quality soft-core SEX COMEDIES and a handful of intense HORROR films. Independent producers were encouraged in the 50s by government subsidy (the EADY LEVY) and relaxation of CENSORSHIP. Early films, often quasi-DOCUMENTARIES about naturism, most famously Harrison MARKS's *Naked As Nature Intended* (1961), were made by men connected with glamour photography and MUSIC HALL. Their milieu, beauty contests and nude revues, is accurately satirised in *Lady Godiva Rides Again* (1951). Marks's discovery Pamela GREEN, a prominent sex symbol of the period, appears in POWELL's *Peeping Tom* (1960), which draws on clandestine, shabby aspects of the business. In 1960 showmen Michael KLINGER and Tony TENSER began exploiting a legal loophole, not plugged until 1985, which allowed uncertificated films to play to club members. Klinger and Tenser also produced and distributed exploitation films, giving opportunities to many young directors, notably Roman POLANSKI, whose *Repulsion* (1965) was an early mainstream crossover. Another protégé, Robert HARTFORD-DAVIS, went on to direct the manic *Corruption* (1967).

Britain's most prolific and successful exploitation directors, Stanley A. LONG, Derek FORD and Pete WALKER, all began work in the 60s. Long and Ford, enthusiastic hacks, initially specialised in exposés of suburban 'depravity', but later moved into sex COMEDY. Walker went in the opposite direction, graduating from *School For Sex* (1968) to atmospheric psychological THRILLERS, including *House of Whipcord* (1974) and *Frightmare* (1974), in which young women are persecuted by older authority figures. The most interesting exploitation films of the 70s are those in which extreme sex and horror are combined. The unique *Secrets of Sex* (1969) is the product of its director Antony Balch's avant-garde background. *Symptoms* and *Vampyres* (1974) comprise the best work of Jose Larraz, who seemed to lose his touch when he returned to his native Spain and forsook the influence of Polanski. Among the puerile sex comedies of the 70s, *Confessions of a Window Cleaner* (1974) and three sequels were so popular that they hastened first the coarsening, then the end, of the 'CARRY ON' SERIES. Porn baron David Sullivan triumphed with one of the worst films ever made, *Come Play With Me* (1977), directed by Marks and featuring Sullivan's favourite model, Mary MILLINGTON. The film's four-year London run made Millington the last star of exploitation, which ended in 1981 with another Sullivan production, *Emmanuelle in Soho*. The industry collapsed primarily with the introduction of video and termination of the Eady fund, although, by the late 70s, audiences had begun to tire of the general inferiority of the product.

OTHER BRITISH EXPLOITATION FILMS INCLUDE: *The Flesh Is Weak* (1957), *Horrors of the Black Museum* (1959), *Circus of Horrors* (1960), *The Yellow Teddybears* (1963), *The Wife Swappers* (1969), *Cool It Carol!* (1970), *Eskimo Nell, Can You Keep It Up For a Week?* (1974), *Exposé* (1975), *The Stud* (1978), *Inseminoid* (1980).

BIBLIOG: David McGillivray, *Doing Rude Things*, 1992; Jonathan Rigby, *English Gothic*, 2000; Simon Sheridan, *Keeping the British End Up*, 2001. David McGillivray.

Exton, Clive (*b* 1930). Dramatist, screenwriter. Of the 'ANGRY YOUNG MAN' generation, Exton alone made his name on TV, with a series of minutely observed realist dramas, beginning with *No Fixed Abode*. Educated at Christ's Hospital and trained as an actor, a bad one he claimed, he went on to collaborate with Francis DURBRIDGE on *The World of Tim Frazer* (1960–61) and to adapt P.G. WODEHOUSE, Agatha CHRISTIE and Ruth RENDELL. He moved some distance from the plays that made his name, but without loss of proficiency. Sporadic cinema work includes two for Karel REISZ, *Night Must Fall* (1964) and *Isadora* (1968), neither of which wholly worked, an adaptation of Joe ORTON's *Entertaining Mr Sloane* (1969), and, his best screenplay, *10 Rillington Place* (1970), based on the 40s

'Christie murders'. He seems now to have settled to TV as his prime medium.

OTHER BRITISH FILMS: *A Place to Go* (1963, add dial), *Running Scared* (co-sc), *Doomwatch* (1972), *The House in Nightmare Park* (1973, co-sc), *The Awakening* (1980, co-sc).

extras Very small-part cast members, usually without lines, often to form part of a crowd; in Britain, represented by FILM ARTISTES ASSOCIATION.

Eyre, Peter (*b* New York, 1942). Actor. Reliable character player of stage and TV, offering enjoyably snooty upper-middle-class types, lay and clerical, in various detective series, including *Dalziel and Pascoe* (1996). Films have been intermittent, but with some incisive moments: as Tesman to Glenda JACKSON's *Hedda* (1975), the Pope in *Orlando* (1992, UK/Fr/It/Neth/Russ), and Lord Halifax in *The Remains of the Day* (1993), for MERCHANT IVORY, for whom he has worked several times, playing the Henry JAMES-lookalike seller of *The Golden Bowl* (2000, UK/Fr/US).

OTHER BRITISH FILMS INCLUDE: *Julius Caesar* (1970, as Cinna the poet), *Mahler* (1974), *Maurice* (1987), '*Let Him Have It*' (1991), *Surviving Picasso* (1996, UK/US), *The Tango Lesson* (1997, UK/Arg/Fr/Ger/Jap).

Eyre, Sir Richard (*b* Barnstaple, 1943). Director. One of the top echelon theatrical producers of recent decades; director of the Royal National Theatre, 1988–97; former BBC director and producer; made CBE in 1992 and knighted in 1997: in a career crowded with achievement and honours, film has played a disappointingly small role. His first feature, *Ploughman's Lunch* (1983), a wry state-of-the-nation piece, captured some critical attention, but was too acrid for popular consumption; *Loose Connections* (1983) was a picaresque romantic comedy somewhat short on charm; and, since then, the post-Falklands TV drama, *Tumbledown* (1989), has been his most challenging film work. In 2000, recalling his own mother's experience of Alzheimer's, he began work on a film about novelist Iris Murdoch (*Iris*, 2002, UK/US), co-written with his *Tumbledown* collaborator, Charles Wood. Wrote and directed the TV series *Changing Stages* (2000), a survey of world theatre. Married to TV producer Sue Birtwistle.

OTHER BRITISH FILMS: *Laughterhouse* (1984), *The Insurance Man* (1985), *Richard III* (1995, co-sc, ex p).

Eziashi, Maynard (*b* London, 1965) Actor. Of Nigerian origin, Eziashi trained at Rose Bruford School of Speech and Drama (1986–89) and has since worked on radio (BBC plays), TV (e.g. *Bad Boy Blue*) and stage (e.g. *The Island*). In film, he played the title role in *Mister Johnson* (1990) and was in *A Good Man in Africa* (1994), both US-backed productions directed by Bruce Beresford. British films have included *Twenty-One* (1991, UK/US) and *Bad Boys* (1994), co-starring Clive OWEN.

Ff

factual series Early short factual and 'CINEMAGAZINE' series included *Astra Gazette*, *Gaumont Graphic*, *Eclair Journal* and *Eve's Film Review* (for women's interests). There were several later noteworthy series. *This Modern Age* (1946–50) was produced by RANK as a British answer to *The March of Time*, each monthly film covering a current affairs topic, and aiming for a 'balanced' explanatory style. 41 x 20-minute films were made between *Homes for All* (1946) and *Turkey: Key to the Middle East* (1950), and released to Rank cinemas, *The True Fact of Japan* (1950) winning a BAFTA Special Award. Sergei NOLBANDOV was supervising producer; commentaries were read by Robert HARRIS, music supervised by Muir MATHIESON. According to cynics, they were Rank's attempt to keep in the good books of the Labour government.

Mining Review (1947–83), produced by National Coal Board/ Data Films, was a monthly 20- (later 10-) minute cinemagazine series (over 350 episodes), with cinema distribution limited to mining areas, featuring 'the miner at work and leisure', with commentary often by John SLATER. Malcolm ARNOLD wrote the early music, and, in a 1949 edition, Paul ROBESON visits Wales and sings to the miners. *Pathé Pictorial* (1918–69), produced by ASSOCIATED BRITISH PATHÉ, was a light-toned 10-minute weekly cinemagazine, regularly in colour from 1955, variously known as *Pathé Pictorial* (1918–30), *Pathé Sound Pictorial* (1931–35), *Pathé New Sound Pictorial* (1936–44), *New Pathé Pictorial* (1944–55) and *Colour Pathé Pictorial* (1955–69).

Rank also produced *Look at Life* (1959–69), which replaced Gaumont–British News in 1959 on the two Rank circuits. Over 500 x 10-minute colour weekly SHORTS on general interest subjects were produced. Rarely, a complex subject was covered (e.g. *The Common Market/EEC*), warranting a two-reel film. Edward A. Candy was Head of Production, commentaries read by Tim TURNER. Although *Pathé Pictorial* and *Look at Life* had a longer shelf-life in cinemas than the weekly NEWSREEL, they were rarely little more than time-fillers. With the spread of colour television, colour film was no longer a novelty by 1969, and there was no cultural or economic reason to continue production. Roger Philip Mellor

Fairbanks, Douglas Jr (*b* New York, 1909 – *d* New York, 2000). Actor. Son of the legendary swashbuckler, Fairbanks emerged from his father's shadow to carve out his own career. In films from 1923 and on stage from 1927, pre-WW2 he had appeared in over 60 films, as a debonair leading man. Many were routine, but some, like *Little Caesar* (1930) and (as the villainous Rupert of Hentzau) *The Prisoner of Zenda* (1937), allowed some versatility. In 1934, Alexander KORDA imaginatively cast him as the half-mad Grand Duke Peter in *Catherine the Great*. A committed Anglophile, he made six further British films in the 1930s, as actor or producer, and after distinguished WW2 work, and four unexceptional post-war Hollywood films, he returned to England. Starred in the excellent thriller, *State Secret*, and the comedy, *Mr Drake's Duck* (1950), then turned to TV production. He produced and sometimes starred in several dozen half-hour telefilms, made at BRITISH NATIONAL studios at ELSTREE, primarily for US television. On several occasions, batches of three of these short films, often with excellent casts and directed by the likes of Lance COMFORT and Lawrence HUNTINGTON, were spliced together with a commentary by Fairbanks and released as cinema films in Britain. Examples of this practice are: *The Triangle* (1953) and *Forever My Heart* (1954).

Lived in London for many years after his retirement from the screen in the mid 50s, engaging in business and philanthropic enterprises and famously becoming a friend to royalty. Awarded honorary knighthood in 1949. Married (1 of 3) Joan Crawford (1929–33).

OTHER BRITISH FILMS: (a, unless noted) *Mimi, Man of the Moment* (1935), *The Amateur Gentleman* (+ ex p), *Crime over London* (co-p), *Accused* (+ co-p) (1936), *Jump for Glory* (1937, +co-p), *Another Man's Poison* (1951, co-p), *Destination Milan* (1954, + p c), *The Enchanted Doll* (1955, short), *The Silken Affair* (1956, p), *Chase a Crooked Shadow* (1957, p), *Red and Blue* (1967).

Fairbrother, Sydney (*b* London, 1872 – *d* London, 1941). Actress. One of those wonderfully eccentric ageing character actresses endemic in British film and theatre. On both stage and screen, she would carry her cat along with her, hidden within her bosom. On stage from 1889; from 1912 to 1914, she starred in MUSIC HALL with Fred EMNEY in the sketch, 'A Sister to Assist 'er'. Was memorable as Mahbubah on stage in *Chu-Chin-Chow*, recreating the role in the 1934 film, and is very funny as a temperance fanatic in *The Last Journey* (1935).

BRITISH FILMS INCLUDE: *Iron Justice* (1915), *Auld Lang Syne* (1917), *The Temporary Gentleman* (1920), *Sally Bishop* (1923), *Reveille* (1924), *Nell Gwynne* (1926), *Excess Baggage* (1933), *Gay Love* (1934), *Brewster's Millions* (1935), *King Solomon's Mines* (1937), *Little Dolly Daydream* (1938). AS.

Fairchild, William (*b* Boscastle, 1918 – *d* 2000). Screenwriter, director. Educated at Dartmouth Naval College, and invalided out of the Navy (as Lt-Commander) in 1946, he entered films in 1947, working on scripts for RANK'S HIGHBURY STUDIOS, starting with *Colonel Bogey* (1948, co-sc). During the 50s, he worked on screenplays for such popular films as *Morning Departure* (1950) and *Front Page Story* (1953, adapt), two films proficiently drawing roles for large casts, and directed and wrote *John and Julie* (1955), *The Extra Day* (1956), *The Silent Enemy* (1958), all modestly attractive films. Also wrote several

plays produced in the West End and the TV series, *199 Park Lane* (1965) and, winning a Writers Guild Award, the US film, *Star!* (1968). Married and divorced from Isabel DEAN.
OTHER BRITISH FILMS INCLUDE: (sc) *Song for Tomorrow, Penny and the Pownall Case* (1948), *Outcast of the Islands* (1951), *The Net* (1953), *The Seekers* (1954), *Passage Home*, (1955), *Embassy* (1972); (co-sc): *The Gift Horse* (1952), *The Malta Story* (1953), *Value for Money* (1955), *The Horsemasters* (1961, + d).

Fairhurst, Lyn (*b* Warrington, 1921 – *d* London, 2002). Screenwriter. Author of five screenplays for Lance COMFORT, including the excellent thriller *Touch of Death* (1962), the good-natured teen musicals, *Live It Up* (1963), which has some acutely written scenes from family life, and *Be My Guest* (1965), the Gothic thriller *Devils of Darkness* (1964), and the Comfort-produced heist film, *Band of Thieves* (1962). Also a TV and radio presenter.

Fairlie, Gerard (*b* 1899 – *d* 1983). Screenwriter. A former Guards officer and boxing champion, and a novelist, twice adapted – *A Shot in the Dark* (1933) and *'Bulldog' Sees It Through* (1940). Busiest in the 30s, working several times for Julius HAGEN at TWICKENHAM. 'Sapper's' model for Bulldog Drummond, he wrote several Drummond novels after his author friend died.
OTHER BRITISH FILMS INCLUDE: (sc) *Open All Night* (1934), *The Big Noise* (1936); (co-sc), *Jack Ahoy!* (1934), *Bulldog Jack* (1935), *The Lonely Road*, *Chick* (1936), *Conspirator* (1949, with Sally Benson), *Calling Bulldog Drummond* (1951, + story).
BIBLIOG: Autobiography, *With Prejudice*, 1952.

Faith, Adam (*b* London, 1940 – *d* Stoke, 2003). Actor, singer. RN: Terence Nelhams. 'Drink's for squares, man': in such words, hinting at darker depravities, does Faith announce his rebel's credentials in his debut film, *Beat Girl* (1959). It is not his fault that yesterday's iconoclasts look so tame forty years on. A good-looking, popular teen singing star of the late 50s and early 60s, he first hit success with John BARRY's 'Drumbeat' series. A competent actor, he gave two impressive thug studies in *Never Let Go* (1960) and *Mix Me a Person* (1962), ably supported (BAAn) David ESSEX in *Stardust* (1974) and Roger DALTREY in *McVicar* (1980), and had some success on TV, notably in the Soho street-life series *Budgie* (1971–72), as an aspiring loser, and in *Love Hurts* (1992–94). He went into music management in the 1970s.
OTHER BRITISH FILMS: *What a Whopper!*, *What a Carve Up!* (1961), *Yesterday's Hero* (1979), *Cliff Richards and the Shadows* (1979).
BIBLIOG: Autobiography, *Acts of Faith*, 1996.

Faithfull, Geoffrey (*b* Walton-on-Thames, 1894 – *d* 1979). Cinematographer, director. Closely associated with Cecil HEPWORTH as his primary cinematographer, he was, according to director Adrian BRUNEL, 'Always excellent, helpful and cheerful' – if never innovative. Faithfull joined Hepworth straight from school in 1907, within a year of his brother Stanley's joining the company. He worked in various production capacities at the studio, and there is no definitive record of which Hepworth films he actually shot. Remained at WALTON-ON-THAMES after Hepworth sold the studio, and even lived there through the early 50s. His later films were mostly minor, but he was always busy, finding time to shoot two TV series, *Mark Saber* (1955–58) and *Espionage* (1962) and also advertisements for Pearl and Dean in the mid 50s. In 1945, he directed two insignificant productions: *For You Alone* (1945) and *I'll Turn to You* (1946).

OTHER BRITISH FILMS INCLUDE: (c) *The Funeral of King Edward VII* (1910, co-c), *The Cobweb* (1917), *Tansy* (1921), *Comin' Thro' the Rye* (1923), *Wait and See* (1928), *Deadlock, Rynox* (1931), *Her First Affaire* (1932), *Boomerang, Falling in Love* (1934), *Busman's Holiday* (1936), *Sheepdog of the Hills* (1941), *Kiss the Bride Goodbye* (1944), *Send for Paul Temple* (1946), *The Glass Mountain* (1948), *The Lavender Hill Mob* (1951, 2u co-c), *Marilyn, River Beat* (1953), *The Blue Peter* (co-c), *Stock Car* (1955), *Man from Tangier* (1957), *Corridors of Blood* (1958), *Bobbikins* (1959), *Village of the Damned* (1960), *Murder She Said* (1961), *On the Beat* (1962), *The Sicilians* (1964), *Cry Wolf* (1968, co-c). AS.

Faithfull, Marianne (*b* London, 1947). Actress. It is hard not to warm to a reinvented 60s icon who refers to her life as 'a triumph of style over substance abuse'. Perhaps still most famous as former girlfriend of Mick JAGGER, with whom (and others) she was involved in a drug scandal, she made a comeback in 1979, displaying a newly husky delivery, with 'Broken English'. The daughter of Baroness Erisso and a WW2 British spy, she remains one of the most compelling survivors of her generation's heady days. On film, she is at her most 60s-ish in *I'll Never Forget What's 'is Name* (1967), as a mistress discarded early by Oliver REED, and as *The Girl on a Motorcycle* (1968, UK/Fr), and she is a touchingly vulnerable Ophelia in Tony RICHARDSON's *Hamlet* (1969). Still filming, with new authority, in the 90s in such films as *Shopping*, 1994. Mark Hodkinson's biography, *As Tears Go By*, named for the first Jagger–Keith Richard song, which she recorded, appeared in 1993.
OTHER BRITISH FILMS INCLUDE: *Sympathy for the Devil* (1968), *Ghost Story* (1974), *Dreaming* (1989), *Moondance* (1994, UK/Ire/US), *The Rolling Stones Rock and Roll Circus* (1996, doc), *Crimetime* (1996), *Intimacy* (2001, UK/Fr).
BIBLIOG: Autobiography, *Faithfull*, 1992.

Falklands War and British film The few British cinematic responses to the nation's 1982 dispute with Argentina were conditioned by the sanitised, celebratory treatment of the fighting orchestrated by the Ministry of Defence and enthusiastically promoted by the media. The Thatcher government's representation of the war as an emblematic vindication of its economic and industrial policies and a dramatic endorsement of its revisionist social agenda was first critiqued in Richard EYRE's *The Ploughman's Lunch* (1983), from a script by Ian McEWAN, which highlights the perils of surrendering a firm perspective on the past to the personal and political ambitions of the present day. Five years later, Eyre returned to the South Atlantic with *Tumbledown* (1989) from a screenplay by Charles WOOD. The film challenges the mythic narrative of the war as a journey to national and individual wholeness by laying bare the brutality of the fighting and the indifference of Government and public to its wounded survivors. Paul GREENGRASS's *Resurrected* (1989) tells the (true) story of a simple soldier, missing, presumed killed in action, and subsequently memorialised by the military and his community, who unexpectedly resurfaces. His uninspiring ordinariness challenges the lexicon of celebration which embalmed the war. A black paratrooper in the Falklands, Reuben James, the hero of Martin STELLMAN's *For Queen and Country* (1988, UK/US) returns to the North London housing estate of his childhood to find that recent changes to the Nationality Act mean that he faces deportation to the West Indies of his parents. *For Queen and Country* demonstrates that the ideal of national/familial unity so zealously promoted by politicians during the war failed to heal divisions of race, colour and class.

BIBLIO: James Aulich (ed), *Framing the Falklands*, 1992; Kevin Foster, *Fighting Fictions*, 1999. Kevin Foster.

Fancey, E(dwin) J. (*b* Richmond, Surrey, 1901 – *d* Surrey, 1980). Executive, producer. In distribution before WW2, in post-war years he (co-)produced nearly 20 minor films, distributed by New Realm or DUK Films, of both of which he was managing director. He regularly used such personnel as director Maclean ROGERS and cameraman Geoffrey FAITHFULL, as in the thriller, *Flannelfoot* (1953).

OTHER BRITISH FILMS INCLUDE: *The Balloon Goes Up* (1942, UK/Fr), *Up with the Lark* (1943), *Soho Conspiracy* (1950), *Potter of the Yard* (short) (1952), *Behind the Headlines* (1953), *Johnny on the Spot* (1954), *They Never Learn* (+ co-sc), *Fighting Mad* (co-p) (1956), *The Traitor* (1957), *Crocodile Safari* (1967, co-sc).

fantasy Despite being prevalent in British cinema, fantasy films and films exhibiting fantasy properties have often been neglected by the dominant cultural and historical accounts. British film writing has traditionally embraced a realist aesthetic – the effect of what Julian Petley terms the 'hegemony of the DOCUMENTARY spirit' – and viewed adversely those films regarded as stylistically abstract, expressionistic, illusionary and surreal.

Silent cinema, influenced by French pioneer Georges Méliès, was fascinated with the fantasy effects that film could produce and such elements were prominent in the imaginative trick films of the 'BRIGHTON SCHOOL'. Trick films emphasised cinema's magic and illusion, and the early experimental short, Walter BOOTH's *The '?' Motorist* (1906) depicted a flying car through the use of superimposition and miniatures. Transformation narratives were also a feature and human-animal metamorphosis occurs in *The Fakir's Spell* (1914), and *Heba the Snake Woman* (1915). Many fantasies made during and immediately after WW2 – the GAINSBOROUGH melodramas, British *FILM NOIR* and the films of Michael POWELL and Emeric PRESSBURGER – were largely studio-based, and focused on the creation of visual depth and excess. The fantasy in these films was arguably a reflection and articulation of the tension, trauma and unfulfilled desires of British audiences of the time. The films also offered an escape from British reality, and, as with the colonial fantasies and those of lost civilisations, projected distant lands associated with the exotic and esoteric.

Fantasy is also present in the horrors of HAMMER and AMICUS, the 60s 'SWINGING LONDON' films, and British sexploitation; the films of Richard LESTER, Ken RUSSELL, Jim HENSON, and Bob GODFREY, to name a few. Elements appear in film moments depicting hallucination, the effects of excessive alcohol (*The Small Back Room*, 1949), and the taking of drugs (*Trainspotting*, 1996); dreams (*Let George Do It!*, 1940) and daydreams (*Billy Liar*, 1963); wish-fulfilment (*Madonna of the Seven Moons*, 1944) and anxiety (*How to Get Ahead in Advertising*, 1989); and sexual obsession (*Black Narcissus*, 1946, and *Deep End*, 1970).

A fantasy GENRE can be discerned as falling between HORROR and SCIENCE-FICTION. This includes fairytales such as *The Dark Crystal* (1982), and *Labyrinth* (1986); sword-and-sorcery costumers and magical quests such as *Excalibur* (1981, UK/US), and *Krull* (1983); spiritual tussles such as *A Matter of Life and Death* (1946) and *Meet Mr Lucifer* (1953); mythical creations as in *Jason and the Argonauts* (1963) and the mermaid film *Miranda* (1948); colossal creature features *Konga* (1960) and *Gorgo* (1960); the prehistoric action films, *One Million Years BC* (1966) and *When Dinosaurs Ruled the Earth* (1969);

lost civilisation 'epics', *She* (1965) and *Warlords of Atlantis* (1978); colonial fantasies, *King Solomon's Mines* (1937) and *The Thief of Baghdad* (1940, 1978); and the Edgar Rice Burroughs adventures *At the Earth's Core* (1976) and *The People that Time Forgot* (1977).

The colossal creature films of the late 50s and early 60s are fantasies of mass destruction, revisiting images of British wartime terror and the Blitz *and* constructing allegories of atomic age fears. Similar exploitation and the creation of film cycles are apparent in the prehistoric action films of the late 60s and early 70s, and the *Star Wars*-inspired legends of films such as *Krull* (1983). But unable to compete with Hollywood, contemporary British fantasy is perhaps now most prominent in American films. British technicians and PINEWOOD and SHEPPERTON studios are recognised as world-class in the creation of visual effects and models, which have been employed spectacularly in foreign productions.

Other British films, across a wide GENRE range, with major fantasy elements include: *The Red Shoes*, *A Piece of Cake* (1948), *The Tales of Hoffmann* (1951), *Behemoth the Sea Monster* (1958), *It Happened Here* (1963), *The Lost Continent*, *Yellow Submarine* (1968), *The Man Who Haunted Himself*, *Trog* (1970), *The Love Pill* (1971), *White Cargo* (1973), *The Shout* (1978), *The Company of Wolves* (1984).

BIBLIOG: Julian Petley, 'The Lost Continent', in Charles Barr (ed), *All Our Yesterdays: 90 Years of British Cinema*, 1986. Ian Conrich.

Farebrother, Violet (*b* Grimsby, 1888 – *d* Eastbourne, 1969). Actress. Latterly a formidable character player in such roles as the circus-owner in *The Woman for Joe* (1955), Farebrother began on stage in 1907 and toured in Shakespeare with Frank Benson's company, playing on film Queen Elizabeth in his *Richard III* (1911). Played a jury member in HITCHCOCK's *Murder!* (1930).

OTHER BRITISH FILMS INCLUDE: *Easy Virtue*, *Downhill* (1927), *At the Villa Rose* (1930), *Nine Forty-Five* (1934), *It's Not Cricket* (1937), *Cup-Tie Honeymoon* (1947), *Look Before You Love* (1948), *An Alligator Named Daisy* (1955), *Fortune Is a Woman* (1957).

Farmer, Suzan (*b* Tonbridge, 1942). Actress. Supporting player seen in films of the 60s, several of them for HAMMER FILMS, like *Dracula – Prince of Darkness* (1965). Was married to Ian McSHANE (1965–68).

OTHER BRITISH FILMS INCLUDE: *633 Squadron* (UK/US), *The Devil-Ship Pirates*, *The Scarlet Blade* (1963), *Monster of Terror*, *Rasputin the Mad Monk* (1965), *Persecution* (1974).

Farnon, Robert (*b* Toronto, 1917). Composer, arranger, conductor. *Spring in Park Lane* was a box office-hit of 1948, and Farnon's appealing musical score was a significant element: in late 40s British cinema, his arrangements of lush orchestral string sounds had no equal. Farnon's scoring for film and radio transported austerity-wearied audiences into a world of glamour and romance. He broadcast with orchestras on arriving from Canada in 1944 as conductor of the Canadian Band of the Allied Expeditionary Forces. Much associated with Herbert WILCOX's films, he worked on other musicals such as *Where's Charley?* (1952) and *Expresso Bongo* (1959), also providing a stirring, romantic score for *Captain Horatio Hornblower RN* (1950, UK/US).

OTHER BRITISH FILMS INCLUDE: *Piccadilly Incident* (1946), *The Courtneys of Curzon Street* (1947), *Elizabeth of Ladymead* (1948), *Maytime in Mayfair* (1949), *The Dancing Years*, *Circle of Danger* (1950), *Lilacs in the Spring* (1954), *King's Rhapsody* (1955), *It's a Wonderful*

World (1956), *The Truth About Spring* (1964), *Friend or Foe* (1982). Roger Phillip Mellor.

Farr, Derek (*b* London, 1912 – *d* London, 1986). Actor. Former schoolmaster who began his stage career in 1937 (London 1939), and after three bit roles was cast by Anthony Asquith in *Freedom Radio* (1940) and as the bridegroom in *Quiet Wedding* (1941). After WW2 service (1942–45), he returned to leading man roles, usually as the nice young man, even when he was a *Man on the Run* (1949), leaving serious villainy to others (say, Eric Portman in *Wanted for Murder*, 1946). Played a criminal, however, in *Bond Street* (1948), had four leading roles for Lance Comfort, most notably in *Silent Dust* (1949) and *Bang! You're Dead* (1953), comedy roles in *Value for Money* (1955) and *Doctor at Large* (1957), and did creditable TV work in *Nightingale's Boys* (1975) and *Winter Sunlight* (1984). Married (1) stage actress Carol Lynne and (2) Muriel Pavlow, his romantic lead in *The Shop at Sly Corner* (1946).

OTHER BRITISH FILMS INCLUDE: *Q Planes, The Outsider* (1939, unc), *Spellbound* (1941), *Quiet Weekend* (1946), *Teheran* (1947), *Noose* (1948), *Murder Without Crime, Double Confession* (1950), *The Young Wives' Tale, Reluctant Heroes* (1951), *Front Page Story* (1953), *Eight O'Clock Walk* (1954), *The Dam Busters* (1955), *Town on Trial, The Man in the Road* (1956), *The Vicious Circle* (1957), *Attempt to Kill* (1961), *Pope Joan* (1972).

Farrar, David (*b* London, 1908 – *d* Natal, South Africa, 1995). Actor. Farrar, riding high in critical and popular esteem, went to Hollywood and, though he enjoyed the glamour, it ruined his career, via films such as *The Golden Horde* (1951) and *The Black Shield of Falworth* (1954), usually in two-dimensional villain roles. A strongly virile figure, he had served a ten-year apprenticeship in British films before making his mark in Michael Powell's *Black Narcissus* (1947), as the district agent who stirs up sexual tensions in a Himalayan convent. There were two other striking roles for Powell – as the lame bomb-disposal expert in *The Small Back Room* (1948) and the swaggering squire in *Gone to Earth* (1950) – and substantial leads for Ealing in *Frieda* (1947) and *Cage of Gold* (1950). This burst of star filming climaxed a career begun in 1937, after a stint at journalism and stage experience from 1932: he played Sexton Blake twice, had small parts in big films, like *Went the Day Well?* (1942), starred in Ealing's semi-documentary about the Air-Sea Rescue Service, *For Those in Peril* (1944), and made several poor films at British National, including *Lisbon Story* (1946), before hitting his stride in the late 40s. Retired when he was just over 50, unwilling to play 'the heroine's father' as he did in *Beat Girl* (1959), depriving British cinema of an interesting mix of sneering authority and sensitivity, and eventually moving to South Africa.

OTHER BRITISH FILMS INCLUDE: *Head Over Heels, Return of a Stranger* (unc), *Silver Top, Sexton Blake and the Hooded Terror* (1938), *Goofer Trouble* (1940, short), *Sheepdog of the Hills, Danny Boy* (1941), *Suspected Person* (1942), *They Met in the Dark, The Night Invader, Headline, The Hundred Pound Window* (1943), *Meet Sexton Blake* (1944), *The Echo Murders, The Trojan Brothers, The World Owes Me a Living* (1945), *Mr Perrin and Mr Traill* (1948), *Diamond City* (1949), *Night Without Stars, The Late Edwina Black* (1951), *Duel in the Jungle, Lilacs in the Spring* (1954), *Lost* (1955), *The Battle of the River Plate* (1956), *I Accuse!* (1957), *Son of Robin Hood* (1958), *The Webster Boy* (1962).

BIBLIOG: Autobiography, *No Royal Road*, 1948.

Farrell, Charles (*b* Dublin, 1900 – *d* London, 1988). Actor. Educated in Canada, on London stage from 1921, in about 50 British films from 1931, and enjoyable supporting company even in such dire trivia as *Hornet's Nest* (1955), as, typically, an inept low-lifer called Posh Peterson. Said to have appeared in many Vitagraph comedies in the US from the teens and in Britain he often played vaguely American characters. Not to be confused with the Hollywood star Charles Farrell.

OTHER BRITISH FILMS INCLUDE: *The House Opposite* (1931), *Jack's the Boy* (1932), *Boys Will Be Boys* (1935), *Dangerous Moonlight* (1941), *The Way to the Stars* (1945, as American orderly), *They Made Me a Fugitive* (1947), *Night and the City* (1950, UK/US), *The Crimson Pirate* (1952), *The Sheriff of Fractured Jaw* (1958), *Sebastian* (1967), *Countess Dracula* (1970), *The Abominable Dr Phibes* (1971).

Farrell, Colin (*b* Dublin, *c* 1976). Actor. Promising young actor of the late 90s, who dropped out of Dublin's Gaiety Drama School and quickly became popular locally in TV's *Ballykissangel*. After a couple of roles in such British films as *The War Zone* (1999, UK/It), he has been nabbed by Hollywood for starring roles in the likes of *Jesse James* (2001).

Farrell, Nicholas (*b* Essex, 1955). Actor. Perhaps Farrell *could* play a villain, but he projects such an image of decency and dogged, indeed *doggy*, devotion that it is a shock to find him even merely unpleasant as a parliamentary secretary in *Plunkett & Macleane* (1999). He has a strong record of stage work with the RSC, playing Laertes to Kenneth Branagh's Hamlet (he was a wonderful Horatio in Branagh's film, *Hamlet*, 1996, UK/US), with the Bristol Old Vic, and in the West End, co-starring with Maggie Smith in Alan Bennett's *The Lady in the Van* (2000). On TV he first came to attention making something interesting of Edmund Bertram in *Mansfield Park* (1983) and as well-meaning Teddy in *Jewel in the Crown* (1984). His film roles have been rare but choice: the athlete Aubrey in *Chariots of Fire* (1981), Derek in *Playing Away* (1986), Montano in *Othello*, an actor playing Laertes in Branagh's *In the Bleak Midwinter* (1995), Antonio in *Twelfth Night* (1996, UK/US) and the frazzled, humane doctor in *Beautiful People* (1999).

OTHER BRITISH FILMS INCLUDE: *The Rocking Horse Winner* (1982, short), *Greystoke . . .* (1984, UK/US), *Bloody Sunday* (2002).

Faulds, Andrew (*b* Esoko, Tanganyika, 1923 – *d* Stratford-on-Avon, 2000). Actor. Born to Scottish missionary parents in Africa and educated at Glasgow University, tall, imposing Faulds had three years with the RSC, several television series and about 20 films behind him when he entered Parliament in 1966. Persuaded by Paul Robeson to join the Labour Party, he was elected member for Smethwick (1966–74) and Warley East (1974–97) and was famously outspoken. Acted only inter-mittently after 1966, though he did appear in four films for Ken Russell, in whom he may have met his flamboyant match, playing Richard Strauss in *Lisztomania* (1975). Always authoritative, even in smallish roles like the treacherous climber in *The Trollenberg Terror* (1958), or as Westmoreland in *Chimes at Midnight* (1966, Sp/Switz) – on which he did his best to ensure Orson Welles paid the actors' salaries.

OTHER BRITISH FILMS INCLUDE: *The Card* (1952), *The Million Pound Note* (1953), *The One That Got Away* (1957), *Danger Within, Sea of Sand* (1958), *Payroll* (1961), *The Charge of the Light Brigade* (1968), *The Music Lovers, The Devils* (1971), *Young Winston* (1972), *Mahler* (1974).

Faulkner, James (*b* London, 1948). Actor. Dark, intense character actor, notably effective in unpleasant roles, such as Bentley Drummle, providing an acid note in the sugary 1975 version of *Great Expectations*, and as a caddish officer in *Conduct Unbecoming* (1975). Much TV, persuasively suggesting danger-ous possibilities in, for example, *Devices and Desires* (1991).

OTHER BRITISH FILMS INCLUDE: *The Abdication* (1974), *Priest of Love* (1980), *Eureka* (1982), *Carry On Columbus* (1992), *All the Little Animals*, *Vigo* (UK/Fr) (1998), *Bridget Jones's Diary* (2001, UK/Fr/US).

Faulkner, Keith (*b* 1936). Actor. Fair, slightly built, character actor who vividly played two nervous young criminals in films for Vernon SEWELL – *The Man in the Back Seat* (1961) and *Strongroom* (1962) – and small roles in 10 other films, as well as being a children's TV favourite. Not to be confused with **Keith Falkner** who made a few films in the late 30s.

OTHER BRITISH FILMS INCLUDE: *Adam and Evelyne* (1949), *Johnny on the Run* (1953), *The Blue Peter* (1955), *Tunes of Glory* (1960), *Payroll* (1961), *It's All Happening* (1963).

Faulkner, Trader (*b* Sydney, 1930). Actor. Australian stage actor who came to England post-war and made a handful of films, as well as appearing on stage and TV, notably as Prince John in *Richard the Lionheart* (1962). Author of *Peter Finch: A Biography*, 1979.

BRITISH FILMS: *Mr Denning Drives North* (1951), *A Killer Walks* (1952), *Macbeth* (1961, as Seyton), *The Spanish Sword* (1962), *The Bay of Saint Michel* (1963), *A High Wind in Jamaica* (1965), *The Murder Game* (1965).

Faulkner, W(illiam) G(eorge) (*b* 1864 – *d* ?). Film critic. Former schoolteacher who became a journalist; maybe the first regular film reviewer in Britain. He was film editor for the London *Evening News* from 1910–21 after which he started his own *Film Review*. In 1922, he was one of the founders of the British Association of Film Directors.

Fawcett, L'Estrange (*b* Southport) Producer. Cheltenham- and Cambridge-educated, former *Morning Post* journalist and film critic who produced about a dozen early talkies, including Maurice ELVEY's *High Treason* (1929, + sc).

OTHER BRITISH FILMS INCLUDE: *Thread o' Scarlet*, *The Night Porter* (+ co-sc), *Greek Street*, *Alf's Button* (+ sc) (1930), *No Lady*, *Down River*, *Bracelets* (1931).

Fay, W(illiam) G(eorge) (*b* Dublin, 1872 – *d* London, 1947). Actor. Usually benign old character actor of the 30s and 40s, mainly in roles drawing on his Irish background, like that of Father Tom in *Odd Man Out* (1947). He was a director of Dublin's Abbey Theatre as well as one of its leading players, and he and his brother, Frank, founded a touring company in the late 1890s.

OTHER BRITISH FILMS INCLUDE: *The Blarney Stone* (1933), *Storm in a Teacup* (1937), *This Man Is Dangerous*, *Spellbound* (1941), *London Town* (1946), *Temptation Harbour* (1947), *Oliver Twist* (1948).

Faye, Janina (*b* London, 1948). Actress. Best remembered for two childhood appearances in films with hortatory titles, *Never Take Sweets from a Stranger* (1960) and *Don't Talk to Strange Men* (1962), menaced by dangerous men in both, and by big weeds in *The Day of the Triffids* (1962). Slim pickings since.

OTHER BRITISH FILMS INCLUDE: *Dracula* (1958), *The Two Faces of Dr Jekyll*, *The Hands of Orlac* (1960), *The Beauty Jungle* (1964), *The Smashing Bird I Used to Know* (1969).

Faye, Randall (*b* US). Director, screenwriter, producer. American who started (1926) and finished (1947) his career in the US but produced and/or directed 'B' MOVIES in Britain, including the amiable farce, *Such is Life* (1936), starring Gene GERRARD.

OTHER BRITISH FILMS INCLUDE: (sc) *Call Me Mame*, *As Good As New* (1933), *Father and Son* (1934); (co-sc) *Harmony Heaven*, *Song of Soho* (1930), *The Face at the Window* (1939, co-scenario/dialogue); (d/p) *This Green Hell* (+ sc), *If I Were Rich*, *Luck of the Turf* (1936); (d) *Hyde Park* (1934, + sc), *Mr Stringfellow Says No* (1937, + co-sc).

Fazan, Eleanor (*b* Kenya, 1930). Choreographer. Trained as dancer at Sadler's Wells Ballet School, first appeared on stage as dancer and actress, then from the mid 50s was (co-)director or choreographer of many West End and Chichester productions. Her film and TV work has been mainly as choreographer, though she acted in several films, including *Value for Money* (1955), *Savage Messiah* (1972) and *O Lucky Man!* (1973). Responsible for the dances in several BBC SHAKESPEARE productions, she choreographed such diverse and notable films as *Oh! What a Lovely War* (1969) and *Yanks* (1979), and was responsible for the delirious 'Blue Danube' sequence in *Heaven's Gate* (1981, US). Married and divorced composer Stanley MYERS.

OTHER BRITISH FILMS INCLUDE: (a) *A Game Called Scruggs* (1965), *Inadmissible Evidence* (1968); (choreography) *Follow a Star* (1959), *The Ruling Class* (1971), *Lady Caroline Lamb* (1972, UK/US/It), *Joseph Andrews* (1976), *A Christmas Carol* (1984), *Cold Comfort Farm* (1995), *St Ives* (1998).

Feast, Michael (*b* Brighton, 1946). Actor. Having played the statue in Peter GREENAWAY's *The Draughtsman's Contract* (1982) and the god Hermes, in silver overalls, in Tony HARRISON's bravely inventive *Prometheus* (1999), Feast hardly seems bent on a mainstream career. More conventionally on TV, he was in Miss Marple's *Caribbean Mystery* (1989) and the police telemovie, *Touching Evil* (1999).

OTHER BRITISH FILMS INCLUDE: *I Start Counting* (1969), *Private Road* (1971, + co-comp), *Brother Sun, Sister Moon* (1972, UK/It), *Sweet Virgin* (1974), *The Music Machine* (1979), *McVicar* (1980), *Velvet Goldmine* (1998, UK/US).

Federation of Film Societies *see* **British Federation of Film Societies**

Feldman, Marty (*b* London, 1934 – *d* Mexico City, 1982). Actor. Pop-eyed Feldman was a successful radio writer, with credits for *Round the Horne* (1965–69), and TV comic before entering films in *The Bed-Sitting Room* (1969). With his farouche looks, he was never likely to be a leading man, and his attempt at being one in *Every Home Should Have One* (1969, + co-sc) founders. His most successful film work was in the US, notably in *Young Frankenstein* (1974), as the Doctor's assistant with the movable hunchback, and he specialised in spoofing popular classic fictions. Died on location while filming *Yellowbeard* (1983) in Mexico.

OTHER BRITISH FILMS: *The Magnificent Seven Deadly Sins* (1971, + co-sc), *To See Such Fun* (1977), *Group Madness* (1983, doc).

Feller, Catherine (*b* Paris). Actress. Supporting player of the late 50s and the 60s, having first appeared as a schoolgirl in *The Belles of St Trinian's* (1954). Starred in two minor thrillers: *The Malpas Mystery* (1960) and *Murder in Eden* (1961). On stage from 1954, TV from 1955.

OTHER BRITISH FILMS INCLUDE: *The Gypsy and the Gentleman* (1957), *The Curse of the Werewolf* (1961), *Waltz of the Toreadors* (1962), *San Ferry Ann* (1965).

Fellner, Eric (*b* 1960). Producer. Educated at Cranleigh School, former video producer, now co-chairman with Tim BEVAN of WORKING TITLE, one of the most successful production companies in 80s and 90s Britain. Shared BAA and AAn for *Elizabeth* (1998). Worked as (co-)producer on such films as *Sid and Nancy* (1986), *Pascali's Island* (1988, UK/US) and *Hidden Agenda* (1990, co-p) before joining Working Title, with whom he has been involved in US films such as *Dead Man*

Walking (1995, ex p).

OTHER BRITISH FILMS (co-p, unless noted): *Straight to Hell* (1986), *The Rachel Papers* (1989, co-ex p), *Wild West* (1992, p), *The Hawk* (ex p), *No Worries* (1993), *Four Weddings and a Funeral* (1994, co-ex p), *French Kiss* (1995, UK/Fr), *Loch Ness* (1996, co-ex p), *Bean, The Borrowers* (1997), *What Rats Won't Do* (1998), *Plunkett & Macleane, Notting Hill* (UK/US, co-ex p) (1999), *The Man Who Cried* (2000, UK/Fr/US, ex p), *Bridget Jones's Diary, Captain Corelli's Mandolin* (2001, UK/US).

Fellowes, Julian (*b* Cairo, 1949). Actor. Enjoyable, round-faced character player, Ampleforth- and Cambridge-educated and Webber-Douglas-trained. Mostly on TV – e.g. in *Monarch of the Glen* (1999, 2000), as the devious Kilwillie – but he has also been noticeable in several films, including *Shadowlands* (1993, UK/US), as a don, in the WW1 drama, *Regeneration* (1997), and *Baby – Secret of the Lost Legend* (1985) for Disney-US. Has also written scripts for the BBC and for Robert Altman's *Gosford Park* (2001, UK/Ger/US); for this witty, insightful take on the country-house mystery, he won an Oscar.

OTHER BRITISH FILMS INCLUDE: *Full Circle* (1976, UK/Can), *Priest of Love* (1980), *Damage* (1992, UK/Fr), *Jane Eyre* (1996, UK/Fr/It/US), *Tomorrow Never Dies* (1997, UK/US).

Felton, Felix (*b* US, 1911 – *d* London, 1972). Actor. Tubby supporting player, in small roles in the 50s mainly, such as Dr Slammer in *The Pickwick Papers* (1952) and the police commissaire in *Escapement* (1957).

OTHER BRITISH FILMS INCLUDE: *Lady Godiva Rides Again, Night Was Our Friend* (1951), *The Beggar's Opera* (1953), *Doctor in the House* (1954), *Confession* (1955), *Pacific Destiny* (1956), *Just My Luck* (1957), *It's Trad, Dad!* (1962), *Chitty Chitty Bang Bang* (1968), *Up in the Air* (1969).

female stars British cinema has consistently lacked the industrial basis for a strong STAR SYSTEM and, even though the full-blown Hollywood system has fragmented into a more celebrity-based set-up, British performers still have to go to America for a stable industrial base. More importantly, despite the consistent press hunt for British stars, British audiences have stubbornly shown a preference for the demotic appeal of Hollywood stars as the focus for cultural identification. For British female stars, in particular, the automatic association of Hollywood with glamour has placed them in the difficult position of directly competing with their American rivals or finding different grounds on which to claim stardom: nationality, performance and class have all been used as distinctive markers.

Not that British stars couldn't be glamorous. Freda Bruce Lockhart, in the dire days of the 50s when actresses had to compete with old cars for the attention of their male co-stars, asserted that it was a legend that 'British film girls are frigid, too lady-like and passionless' (*Picturegoer*, 14 April 1956). But since British 'girls' have to be different from the Hollywood stars whose sexuality was their hallmark, there is always a tendency either to emphasise a fair and innocent English type of beauty or a vivacious naturalness which can be more tomboylike than vamp. Even stars who are strongly associated with glamour, like Jessie MATTHEWS, are described as natural and unaffected, while the English-rose tag has clung to a variety of British stars. The period when female stars were consistently acknowledged as glamorous occurred when national ambition, studio system and cultural questions about the role of women came together briefly at GAINSBOROUGH towards the end of WW2. Ebullient, escapist historical dramas like *Fanny by Gaslight* (1944) and *The Wicked Lady* (1945) specifically used the trappings of stardom to express the frustrations and desires of their female audiences

and made stars like Margaret LOCKWOOD, Phyllis CALVERT, Patricia ROC and Jean KENT temporarily glamorous. By contrast, Kay KENDALL, whose star image was strongly associated with style and elegance, was notoriously underused by RANK a decade later and left to pursue her career in America.

Gainsborough's successes owed much to an international outlook which welcomed European influences but probably the most successful female stars of the studio period were those who worked with the national preoccupations of British cinema and stood for particular aspects of British culture. Thus, Gracie FIELDS combined down-to-earth ordinariness with MUSIC HALL vigour and used her extraordinary voice to generate a feeling of unity and hopefulness in MUSICALS with a realist setting; Anna NEAGLE brought dignity to strong female roles which linked British identity with past glories. In both cases, the star personae could be placed within the context of the values which British cinema professed – REALISM, restraint and ordinariness; they asserted a national identity which was reliable and resilient, characteristics which made up for lack of sexual glamour by constructing an image of national pride.

Performance was also important in marking out British stars. From the silent period, London's studios were populated by performers who would catch the train in the evenings to appear in the theatres or music halls where they had made their name and British stars, such as Maggie SMITH and Judi DENCH, continue to work extensively outside film, with television taking the place of music hall as a source of stars. In addition, British cinema is associated with repertory casting which emphasises group playing and character acting. This has encouraged stars themselves to value the cultural prestige of theatre and to seek a career which oscillated between film and stage, sometimes with a detrimental effect on their film star career. This emphasis on acting also developed into a particularly British performance style which draws attention to acting as work so that the performer is praised for the skill of a professional rather than the innate talent of the star. This has led to acclaim for some rather unlikely female stars, the Dames of the British theatre who grace British 'HERITAGE' FILMS, in particular, with what are often highly mannered and condescending performances. The emphasis on group performances, while generally offering a much wider range of parts to actors, has also allowed some character actresses such as Margaret RUTHERFORD to emerge as popular stars.

Finally, class remains critical to the development and reception of British female stars. Stars like Betty BALFOUR and Gracie Fields were defined by their regional star images and often restricted to comedy but other female stars were relentlessly tutored into the 'tairrably refained' accents (*Picturegoer*, 9 July 1955) which ironically made them incomprehensible to American audiences. RANK's 'CHARM SCHOOL', an unsuccessful effort to replicate the Hollywood studio system, even tried to make Diana DORS conform to such class-bound standards. While the 'British New Wave' let in some working-class male stars, it did less for actresses, and the biggest female star of the sixties, the middle-class Julie CHRISTIE, quickly moved from British youth icon to international star in co-productions set in the past. Female stars of the 80s and 90s, such as Helena BONHAM CARTER, took a similar route and found, in popular 'HERITAGE' films, roles which made star persona out of middle-class manners, 'good' acting and historical costumes. As the British education system made going to drama school even more difficult for working-class aspirants at the end of the century, the upper-middle-class image of actresses like Emma

THOMPSON and Kate WINSLET led to a welcome for them from Hollywood as classy examples of British cinema's female stars.

BIBLIOG: Geoffrey Macnab, *Searching for Stars*, 2000; Sarah Street, *British National Cinema*, 1997. Christine Geraghty.

feminism and British cinema Women were involved in the development of cinema in Britain from the first. Largely unacknowledged and unresearched, they worked as script-writers and studio personnel, or in the shadow of husbands, fathers and brothers – for example, Alma REVILLE, Joan MORGAN, Ruby GRIERSON, and Betty and Muriel BOX, who in the 50s emerged into relative autonomy as, respectively producer and director, representing, along with Wendy TOYE, the only mainstream WOMEN FILM-MAKERS prior to the emergence of 'second wave' feminism's impact in the 70s. This differed from the earlier suffrage movement in recognising the role of representation in forming GENDER and sexual identities at both institutional and personal levels. Thus, mass-mediated images in advertising, television and films were a prime target for critical analysis and for an emerging, independent oppositional practice.

However, not only is feminism strongly international in outlook, eschewing national identities as themselves based on an oppressive positioning of 'woman', but British cinema has been overshadowed by Hollywood in entertainment and Europe in ART CINEMA. Thus while establishing in the 70s an internationally influential critical discourse, British feminism oscillated between opposing Hollywood and exploring European avant-garde practices. Its initial impact on British cinema, then, appears in initiatives by groups such as the London Women's Film Group (1972–77), which developed women's training, production and distribution, followed closely by the Sheffield Film Co-op (1973–91) and the Leeds Women's Animation Workshop (1976–); distribution outlets, Cinema of Women and Circles, and the black film-making collective, SANKOFA (1983–) which addressed feminism in relation to black issues. The LWFG had considerable influence within the Independent Film-makers Association, which in turn impacted on the ACTT, leading to the first union survey of gendered employment practices and an agreement to recognise grant-aided workshops, thus easing the way for women to participate in professional film-making.

While initially turning to DOCUMENTARY, British feminists led the way in developing out of the neo-Marxist and post-structural debates of the 1960s and 70s an anti-realist feminist THEORY and film practice. Laura MULVEY in her inter-nationally influential 'Visual Pleasure and Narrative Cinema' (1975), drew from semiotic and psychoanalytic theorisation of 'classic Hollywood narrative' to argue that the position from which the spectator engaged with fiction film was already con-structed as masculine, turning on the fetishistic overvaluation or voyeuristic investigation and punishment of the specu-larised figure of woman. While this model produced its own formal and intellectual frisson in films deconstructing femininity, maternity, sexual difference and identity such as Mulvey and Peter WOLLEN's *Penthesilea* (1974) and *Riddles of the Sphinx* (1977), Sally POTTER's *Thriller* (1979) or Sankofa's *Passion of Remembrance* (1986), it provoked questions about the relation between historically located female audiences and female screen images and about how to connect with popular consciousness and pleasures – questions explored through a feminist focus on GENRES central to women and through the

return in the 80s to national film histories.

New interest in the till then, 'unknown' British cinema (Alan Lovell, 1997), opened up two major strands in a feminist engagement with British film history. Firstly, the 'homefront film' of WW2, mixing fiction and documentary, highlighted the narrative and ideological tensions focused around the figure of woman as the self-sacrificial and maternal symbolic centre of its cross-class national address, at the same time acknowledging the increasing demand on women to leave the home to fill industrial roles vacated by men. Conversely, feminist involvement in the historical rediscovery of GAINSBOROUGH studios explored its infamous COSTUME MELODRAMA genre of the 40s, involving aristocrats, orphans, highwaymen, GYPSIES which so delighted female audiences and shocked the establishment with their reckless disregard for wartime and post-war austerities and their indulgence in dressing-up, disguise and unstable identities. This apparent opposition between 'official', realist, middle-class, masculin-ised as opposed to a transgressive, excessive, lower-class, feminised cinema may well dissolve into a new dialogic conception as the heterogeneous nature of British film-making is mapped through a wider range of genres (including revaluation of the 'HERITAGE FILM'), historical research recovers insights from the neglected area of women's film criticism. For example, Dorothy Richardson (1873–1957) and Iris BARRY (1895–1969), both refused the distinction between 'art' and 'entertainment', hailed the connection between the new aesthetics of cinema and the new audience of women it created. Also, films by directors like Potter, Christine EDZARD, Lezli-An BARRETT and Gurinder CHADHA are developing strategies that both appeal to cultural recognitions and offer, via a transformative play with class, gender and ethnic forms – including costume, popular fictions, social rituals and docu-ments, media stereotypes and images – excursions into new articulations of pleasure and identities.

BIBLIOG: Antonia Lant, *Blackout: Reinventing Women for Wartime British Cinema*, 1991; Cook, *Fashioning the Nation:Costume and Identity in British Cinema*, 1996; Sue Harper, *Women in British Cinema: Mad, Bad and Dangerous to Know*, 2000. Christine Gledhill.

Fenemore, Hilda (*b* London, 1919). Actress. Pleasant-looking character actress in films from 1948 (*Esther Waters*), often in motherly roles as in *The Young and the Guilty* (1958) and *The Tommy Steele Story* (1957), or as charladies, etc, as in *Strongroom* (1962). Much TV, including *Dixon of Dock Green*.

OTHER BRITISH FILMS INCLUDE: *Saturday Island* (1952), *The End of the Road* (1954), *The Safecracker* (1957), *Innocent Sinners*, *Carry On Nurse* (1958), *Witchcraft* (1964), *I Want What I Want* (1971), *Full Circle* (1976, UK/Can), *Absolution* (1978).

Fennell, Albert (*b* London, 1920 – *d* Malden, 1988). Producer. Best known as co-producer of TV's *The Avengers* in the later 60s and executive producer on *The Professionals* (1977–83), but also involved in some significant films at the start of the 60s: *Peeping Tom* (assoc p), *Tunes of Glory* (ex p) (1960), *The Innocents* (1961, ex p) and *This Sporting Life* (1963, ex p). Entered industry in 1941 as assistant studio manager for GAINSBOROUGH, at ISLINGTON, then at LIME GROVE, working as production supervisor on such films as *The Wicked Lady* (1945), *Caravan*, *The Magic Bow* (1946).

OTHER BRITISH FILMS INCLUDE (p/co-p, unless noted): *The Cure for Love* (1949, co-sc), *Park Plaza 605* (1953, + co-sc), *The Green Scarf* (1954), *The Horse's Mouth* (ex p), *Next to No Time!* (1958), *Bitter Harvest* (1963), *Dr Jekyll & Sister Hyde* (1971), *The Legend of Hell House* (1973).

Fenton, George (*b* Bromley, Kent, 1949). Composer. Successful composer on major British and American films for more than 20 years. Classically trained, he found fame with his collaborative score for *Gandhi* (1982, UK/Ind, AAn), and proved adaptable across many musical and film GENRES. His astutely contextual music for Ken LOACH films (*Land and Freedom*, 1994, UK/Ger/Sp; *My Name Is Joe*, 1998, UK/Fr/Ger/It/Sp) has been attuned to the film-maker's vision. Produced powerful scores for *Dangerous Liaisons* (1988, US, AAn), *Shadowlands* (1993, UK/US), and *The Madness Of King George* (1994, UK/US). Founded the Association of Professional Composers.

OTHER BRITISH FILMS INCLUDE: *Hussy* (1979), *The Company Of Wolves* (1984, UK/US), *Cry Freedom* (AAn), *A Handful of Dust, White Mischief* (1987), *The Dressmaker* (1988), *Ladybird Ladybird* (1994), *Carla's Song* (1996, UK/Ger/Sp), *The Woodlanders* (1997), *Bread And Roses* (2000, UK/Fr/Ger/It/Sp). Tim Roman.

Fenton, Leslie *see* **Dvorak, Ann**

Ferguson, Craig (*b* Glasgow, 1964). Actor, screenwriter. Well-known as snooty Nigel Wick in TV's *The Drew Carey Show* (1996–2000), former musician (drums and guitar) and stand-up comedian, Ferguson seems poised for serious stardom after *The Big Tease* (1999, + co-ex p, co-sc), about a gay Scottish hairdresser who wrongly thinks he's about to have a big adventure in LA, and *Saving Grace* (2000, + co-p, co-sc), in which he instructs Brenda BLETHYN in the business of marijuana-growing.

OTHER BRITISH FILMS: *Born Romantic* (2001).

Ferman, James (*b* New York, 1930 – *d* London, 2002). Executive, director. Former TV director who in 1975 became Director of the British Board of Film Censors (now Classification), until 1999. Won a reputation for steering a diplomatic course between moral conservatism and anything-goes, and his period of office was complicated by the advent of video. Experience as a film-maker made him an unusual – and perhaps unusually sympathetic – figure as a censor.

Ferrer, José (*b* Santurce, Puerto Rico, 1912 – *d* Coral Gables, Florida, 1992). Actor. Won AA for *Cyrano de Bergerac* (1950, US) and AAn for playing Toulouse-Lautrec in *Moulin Rouge* (1953), the most famous of his eight British films, which included two he also directed: the war film, *Cockleshell Heroes* (1955), and *I Accuse!* (1957), an account of the Dreyfus (Ferrer) affair. Main career is in US films and, latterly, TV. Was married to actresses Rosemary Clooney and Uta Hagen, among others.

OTHER BRITISH FILMS: *Beautiful Stranger* (1954, song comp), *Lawrence of Arabia* (1962, as Bey of Derea), *Nine Hours to Rama* (1962), *Voyage of the Damned* (1976), *The Fifth Musketeer* (1979, UK/Austria).

Ferrer, Mel (*b* Elberon, New Jersey, 1917). Actor. American star who has made several British films and was a fine King Arthur in *Knights of the Round Table* (1953). Married to Audrey HEPBURN (1954–68).

OTHER BRITISH FILMS: *Oh, Rosalinda!!* (1955), *The Hands of Orlac* (1960, UK/Fr), *A Time for Loving* (1971), *Embassy* (1972), *Brannigan* (1975).

Ferris, Barbara (*b* London, 1940). Actress. Ferris received her best notices for the disruptive young woman in *Interlude* (1968) and her star career might have been longer if her next film, *A Nice Girl Like Me* (1969) had been less of a syrupy, trendy mess. A former fashion model, she appeared in some quite eye-catching films, including *Term of Trial* (1962) and the pop musical, *Catch Us If You Can* (1965). More recently, in character roles and on TV (*Where the Heart Is*, 1997).

OTHER BRITISH FILMS INCLUDE: *Five Guineas a Week* (1956), *tom thumb* (1958), *Sparrows Can't Sing* (1962), *Bitter Harvest* (1963), *The System* (1964), *A Chorus of Disapproval* (1989), *The Krays* (1990).

festivals The United Kingdom is currently home to more than thirty film and television festivals, competitive and non-competitive, ranging from those with the broadest of remits to those dedicated to more closely-defined areas such as DOCUMENTARIES or CRIME FILMS, and to other events for special interest groups of many kinds.

The longest-established festivals are the LONDON FILM FESTIVAL, organised by the BRITISH FILM INSTITUTE since 1957, and the Edinburgh International Film Festival which claims to be the world's oldest continually running film festival, having been held annually since 1947. Other UK events include Bradford's Bite the Mango, the largest Black and Asian festival in Europe, the Sheffield International Documentary Festival, and Wildscreen, a biennial wildlife event held in Bristol since 1982. The BFI also organises the London Jewish Film Festival and the London Lesbian and Gay Film Festival, selections from which (as with the London Film Festival) tour the UK after their London screenings. Elaine Burrows.

Ffrangçon-Davies, Dame Gwen (*b* London, 1891 – *d* Halstead, 1992). Actress. Superb stage actress who made only a handful of films in 40 years, but she was an eloquent Mary Tudor ('Though I may feel pity, I can show no mercy' she tells Jane Grey) in *Tudor Rose* (1936) and a compelling satanist in *The Devil Rides Out* (1967). On stage from 1911, she was a heart-breaking Mary Tyrone in *Long Day's Journey into Night* (1958), and was in many TV plays, including a pre-war *Gaslight* (1939). Created DBE in 1991 at age 100.

OTHER BRITISH FILMS: *The Witches* (1966), *The Burning* (1967, short), *Leo the Last* (1969).

Fiander, Lewis (*b* Melbourne, 1938). Actor. Stylish, sharp-featured Australian actor in Britain since the early 60s, first in films in 1962 (*The Password Is Courage*) and later in several HORROR films, including *I Start Counting* (1969) and *The Doctor and the Devils* (1985). Much TV – e.g. Darcy in *Pride and Prejudice* (1967) – and stage hits in the RSC's *Wild Oats* (1977) and in *My Fair Lady* in Australia (1987).

OTHER BRITISH FILMS INCLUDE: *Dr Jekyll & Sister Hyde* (1971), *Dr Phibes Rides Again* (1972), *The Abdication* (1974), *Sweeney 2* (1978).

Field, Alexander (*b* London, 1892 – *d* London, 1971). Actor. On stage from 1913 in Manchester, as singer and actor, and in supporting roles in about 40 films, sometimes uncredited. Busiest in the 30s; post-war (on stage 1945–49) reduced to very small film roles like that of the farmer in *Blanche Fury* (1947) and the anxious old gang member in *The Naked Fury* (1959).

OTHER BRITISH FILMS INCLUDE: *The Woman Juror* (1926), *Third Time Lucky* (1931), *Dick Turpin* (1933), *Invitation to the Waltz* (1935), *Limelight* (1936), *Dark Eyes of London* (1939), *The Next of Kin* (1942), *Poet's Pub* (1949), *There's Always a Thursday* (1957).

Field, Jonathan (*b* Redhill, Surrey, 1912). Actor. Educated at Reigate Grammar School and in theatre from 1931, first as composer, sometimes as producer and playwright. Films from 1937, always in small roles like those of the French messenger in *Henry V* (1944) or the anxious organist in the inane *Fools Rush In* (1949). In many early TV plays.

OTHER BRITISH FILMS INCLUDE: *Bedtime Story* (1938), *He Found a Star* (1941), *Salute John Citizen* (1942), *Millions Like Us* (1943), *I'll Be Your*

Sweetheart (1945), *Worm's Eye View* (1951), *Father's Doing Fine* (1952), *The High Terrace* (1956).

Field, Mary (*b* London, 1896 – *d* Worthing, 1968). Executive, director. Graduate of the University of London and a former history and English teacher who entered film industry in 1926 as education manager for BRITISH INSTRUCTIONAL FILMS. Though now best remembered as executive officer for RANK's CHILDREN'S FILM FOUNDATION, begun in 1950, she had a long career in DOCUMENTARY and educational film-making: with BIF from 1927 to 1933, when the company was taken over by BRITISH INTERNATIONAL PICTURES and production ceased; as board member of GB INSTRUCTIONAL FILMS, for which she was involved in making the *Secrets of Life* and *Secrets of Nature* series, in collaboration with Percy SMITH. From 1944 she began making children's films for the RANK ORGANISATION, acting as executive producer on the films shown in the J. Arthur Rank Children's Cinema Clubs. Had real interest in what would capture youthful attention, in the importance of films tailored to this end, and in their reactions to what they saw. When the Children's Entertainment Films unit which she led was shut down, as a result of Rank's cutbacks, the government funded the CFF with Rank as chairman and Field as executive officer. Given the membership of the clubs (several millions by 1955) she was in an influential position, and the films she oversaw were essentially wholesome adventures. She was a member of the BRITISH BOARD OF FILM CENSORS (1951–55); made president of the International Centre of Films for Children of Unesco in 1958; and in 1959 she left films to become consultant to ABC-TV and ATV's children's programmes. Awarded OBE, 1951.
BIBLIOG: Mary Field, *Good Company*, 1952; Geoffrey Macnab, *J. Arthur Rank and the British Film Industry*, 1993.

Field, Shirley Anne (*b* London, 1936). Actress. The remarkable thing about Field is that she has survived and become more interesting with the years. A Cockney child, she became a 'beauty queen' and landed tiny parts in several films, including *Simon and Laura* and *Lost* (1955), without making much impression beyond that of exceptionally pretty ingenue. She made a merit of vapidity in *Peeping Tom* (1960) and was rewarded with the roles of Doreen who finally snares Albert FINNEY for domesticity in *Saturday Night and Sunday Morning* (1960) and Tina who seduces Laurence OLIVIER in *The Entertainer* (1960). She did what she could with what the 60s offered: sister to thuggish Oliver REED in *The Damned* (1961) and one of *Alfie*'s (1966) girls. Out of films for a decade, then back with new confidence as Saeed JAFFREY's warm-hearted mistress in *My Beautiful Laundrette* (1985) and there were glowing character studies in *Hear My Song* (1991) and TV's *Lady Chatterley* (1992), and, on stage, as shady lady Lottie Grady, in *When We Are Married* (1996).
OTHER BRITISH FILMS INCLUDE: *The Horrors of the Black Museum*, *Beat Girl* (1959), *Man in the Moon* (1960), *The War Lover* (1962), *Doctor in Clover* (1966), *The Rachel Papers* (1989), *UFO* (1993), *Christie Malry's Own Double-Entry* (2000, UK/Neth/Lux).
BIBLIOG: Autobiography, *A Time for Love*, 1991.

Field, Sid (*b* Birmingham, 1904 – *d* London, 1950). Actor. After many years in MUSIC HALLS, achieved West End stardom in the revues, *Strike a New Note*, and its follow-up, *Strike It Again* (1943). Revered by such peers as Norman WISDOM, he never found film success. After a feeble comedy, *That's the Ticket* (1941), he made only two more films: the disastrous and expensive musical misfire, *London Town* (1946), which at least

preserves several of his variety turns, and, for RANK, as a barrow boy in *Cardboard Cavalier* (1949), a Cromwellian romp, funnier than received wisdom has it. So, glimpses of a great comedian in what might just have been the wrong medium.
BIBLIOG: John Fisher, *What a Performance!*, 1975.

Fielding, Fenella (*b* London, 1934). Actress. Anglo-Rumanian leading lady with delectably fruity voice and seductive manner, inadequately used by film. A former secretary, first on stage in 1954, irresistible in *Valmouth* (1958–59), she is essentially a revue star, despite creditable appearances in Ibsen and Chekhov and touring in *Lady Windermere's Fan* in 2000. She tends to happen *to* films rather than become part of their texture. Just look at her 'turns' in *The Old Dark House* (1962) or, as Lady Eager, the name epitomising the role, in *Lock Up Your Daughters!* (1969).
OTHER BRITISH FILMS INCLUDE: *Follow a Star* (1959), *Doctor in Love*, *Foxhole in Cairo* (1960), *No Love for Johnnie*, *Carry On Regardless* (1961), *Doctor in Distress* (1963), *Drop Dead Darling*, *Carry On Screaming* (1966), *Guest House Paradiso* (1999).

Fielding, Henry (*b* Sharpham Park, Somerset, 1707 – *d* Lisbon, 1754). Author. Fielding's masterpiece of rollicking, picaresque romantic adventure, *Tom Jones*, was exuberantly filmed by Tony RICHARDSON in 1963; in 1975 a much more single-mindedly sexed-up version appeared as *The Bawdy Adventures of Tom Jones*; and there was a TV mini-series in 1997. Richardson returned to Fielding with a lacklustre version of *Joseph Andrews* (1976), and, in 1969, there was a somewhat rib-nudging version of the stage musical *Lock Up Your Daughters!*, based on Fielding's play, *Rape Upon Rape*.

Fielding, Marjorie (*b* Gloucester, 1892 – *d* London, 1956). Actress. Educated at Cheltenham Ladies' College and on stage from 1913, small, decisive Fielding entered films in 1938 (*Second Thoughts*) and became an indispensable character player, usually briskly sympathetic, memorable in everything she did. She was endearing as Mildred Royd, the bride's harassed mother in *Quiet Wedding* (1941) and again in *Quiet Weekend* (1946), reprising stage roles; very moving as Lizzie Lightowler, the early Labourite who has kept the faith, in *Fame Is the Spur* (1947), and, making bricks from straw, as Aunt Cathie in *Portrait of Clare* (1950); very funny as the Western fiction addict in *The Lavender Hill Mob* (1951); and intelligently registering blinkered goodwill as the grandmother in *Mandy* (1952). Last on stage as a domineering guest at the *Small Hotel* (1955).
OTHER BRITISH FILMS: *Jeannie* (1941), *Yellow Canary*, *The Demi-Paradise* (1943), *Spring in Park Lane*, *Easy Money* (1948), *Conspirator*, *The Chiltern Hundreds* (1949), *The Mudlark*, *Trio*, *Sanatorium*, *The Franchise Affair*, *Circle of Danger* (1950), *The Magic Box*, *The Woman's Angle* (1952), *The Net*, *Rob Roy* ... (1953), *Laughing in the Sunshine* (1956, UK/Swe).

Fields, Dame Gracie (*b* Rochdale, 1898 – *d* Capri, 1979). Actress, singer. Though she never greatly cared for the film-making processes, pleasantly plain and invincibly cheerful Fields became one of the most popular stars of British cinema, appealing across classes and regions. Born above a fish-and-chip shop, she sang her way from MUSIC HALL to cinema screen to the London Palladium – and to semi-retirement in Capri. She held on to her working-class ordinariness and therein lay her appeal; and her films, carefully balancing her star quality against an all-hands-to-the-pump consensus, were just the thing for Depression-hit Britain. Their optimistic titles tell almost all: *Looking on the Bright Side* (1932), *Sing As We Go!* (1934), *Look Up and Laugh* (1935), *Keep Smiling* (1938). The image of her leading the workers in song at the end of *Sing As We Go!* (the title song is an anthem for the times) absolutely encapsulates her appeal as indomitable, one of us but more enterprising, vindicating her faith in people treating each other decently. In British films until 1939, when she travelled to America to continue her acting career in Hollywood, where she made four features, most notably *Holy Matrimony* (1943), and sang 'Wish Me Luck' in a 1942 two-reeler, *Young and Beautiful*. Married (2 of 3) director Monty BANKS who taught her to overcome her 'dread' of films and who, as an Italian about to be interned in WW2 Britain, was a major reason for her leaving Britain. It was some time before she was forgiven for her apparent desertion, but her wartime efforts had their effect and her hit, 'Wish Me Luck', became a wartime rallying song. Created DBE in 1979.

OTHER BRITISH FILMS: *Sally in Our Alley* (1931), *This Week of Grace* (1933), *Love, Life and Laughter* (1934), *Queen of Hearts* (1936), *The Show Goes On* (1937), *We're Going to Be Rich* (1938), *Shipyard Sally* (1939).

BIBLIOG: Autobiography, *Sing As We Go*, 1960; Peter Hudson, *Gracie Fields: Her Life in Pictures*, 1989; David Bret, *Gracie Fields*, 1985.

Fiennes, Joseph (*b* Salisbury, 1970). Actor. Handsome, smouldering younger brother of Ralph FIENNES and director Martha FIENNES, Joseph has had a remarkably rapid ascent. Youngest of a nomadic, artistic family, he worked with the Young Vic Theatre Company, trained at the Guildhall School, and quickly found high-profile work in the West End, notably as the tutor in *A Month in the Country* (1994). Also appeared on TV, including *The Vacillations of Poppy Carew* (1995), before his cinema debut in Bertolucci's *Stealing Beauty* (1996, UK/Fr/It). His *annus mirabilis* was 1998, with starring roles in *Elizabeth*, as the Queen's lover, and as *Shakespeare in Love* with Gwyneth PALTROW. Funny, sexy and smart in the latter, he might have been expected to make one hit after another, but chose to return to the theatre, making a triumphant RSC debut in Dennis POTTER's *Son of Man* (1999), and then filmed the much-vilified black comedy, *Rancid Aluminium* (2000). Other films have been interspersed with his RSC work. His romantic life is well-reported if not especially stable.

OTHER BRITISH FILMS: *Martha, Meet Frank, Daniel and Laurence* (1998), *Enemy at the Gates* (2001, UK/Ger/Ire/US), *Killing Me Softly, Dust* (2002, UK/US).

Fiennes, Martha (*b* 1964). Director. Sister of Ralph and Joseph FIENNES, who directed Ralph in her first film, *Onegin* (1999, UK/US), a handsome and moving ADAPTATION of Pushkin's poetic novel. Studied film at Harrow College, and produced music videos and commercials.

Fiennes, Ralph (*b* Suffolk, 1962). Actor. Considering how utterly English Fiennes seems in his gentlemanly, held-down sensuality, it is surprising to note that only four films of his prolific 1990s output are British. *The English Patient* (1996), which established him as a thinking woman's heart-throb and won him AAn and BAAn, may seem creatively British in terms of chief personnel, but is US-financed; his next, *Oscar and Lucinda* (1997), in which he undermined his romantic image by playing a gawky, ginger-haired eccentric, is a US-Australian production. Arguably, though, his finest work to date has been in British films as two men tormented by unexpected love: the aristocratic dilettante in *Onegin* (1999, UK/US), directed by sister Martha FIENNES; and Graham GREENE's embittered author in *The End of the Affair* (2000, UK/Ger/US, BAAn/a).

His other US films include *Schindler's List* (1993, BAA, AAn/ supp a) as the Nazi Commandant, a role for which he famously put on 30 pounds, and the cheating contestant in *Quiz Show* (1994). The record for versatility and serious application would be hard to match in the late 20th century cinema.

The eldest of a gifted family (brother is Joseph FIENNES), he had art school training before RADA, and joined the RSC in 1988. He has stacked up an awesome list of theatre performances, including a Tony-winning Hamlet on Broadway (1995), with Francesca ANNIS (for whom he left wife Alex KINGSTON) as Gertrude, and a double at the Almeida, London, with *Richard II* and *Coriolanus* (2000).

OTHER BRITISH FILMS: *Wuthering Heights* (1992), *The Baby of Mâcon* (1993), *Sunshine* (2000, UK/Austria/Can/Ger/Hung).

BIBLIOG: York Membery, *Ralph Fiennes: The Biography*, 1997.

Figgis, Mike (*b* Carlisle, 1948). Director, writer, composer, cinematographer, producer. In the Introduction to *Projections 10* (1999), John BOORMAN describes the multi-talented Figgis, the book's guest editor, as 'a guerilla fighter, lean and fast', a profile which neatly registers Figgis's adventuresome approach to film-making since leaving Britain for the US in the late 80s. His feature debut, *Stormy Monday* (1987), a stylish thriller set in Newcastle, provided his entry visa to Hollywood, but his work there has become increasingly experimental, moving from the relatively conventional cop drama of *Internal Affairs* (1990) through the defiant obscurities of *The Loss of Sexual Innocence* (2000, UK/US), which was partially shot in Kenya where the British-born Figgis lived until he was eight, to the risky, multi-screened audaciousness of *Time Code* (2000). His only other British film to date has been *The Browning Version* 1994), a solid ADAPTATION of Terence RATTIGAN's play. His career highlight, so far, has been the much-lauded *Leaving Las Vegas* (1995). Cousin of Susie FIGGIS. Tom Ryan.

Figgis, Susie (*b* Kenya). Casting director. Figgis made news in 2000 when she quit *Harry Potter* because she insisted on an all-British cast. She has been involved in casting most of the major British films of the last two decades, including several for GOLDCREST (e.g. *The Mission*, 1985) and PALACE (including *The Crying Game*, 1993) and the huge box-office success of *The Full Monty* (1997, UK/US). Cousin of Mike FIGGIS.

OTHER BRITISH FILMS INCLUDE: *Heat and Dust* (1982), *The Company of Wolves, The Killing Fields, Comfort and Joy* (1984), *Turtle Diary* (1985), *Comrades, Absolute Beginners, Mona Lisa* (1986), *Wish You Were Here, Cry Freedom, A World Apart* (UK/Zimb) (1987), *Scandal* (1988), *War Requiem* (1989), *The Big Man* (1990), *Chaplin* (UK/Fr/It/Jap/US) (1992), *The Browning Version* (1994), *Land and Freedom* (UK/Ger/Sp), *An Awfully Big Adventure* (1995), *Hollow Reed* (1996, UK/Ger), *The Butcher Boy* (Ire/US), *The Woodlanders* (1997), *Velvet Goldmine* (US), *Hideous Kinky* (UK/Fr) (1998), *Gregory's Two Girls, The End of the Affair* (UK/Ger/US) (1999), *Purely Belter* (2000, + sound), *Killing Me Softly* (2001).

Fildes, Audrey (*b* Liverpool, 1922). Actress. Old Vic-trained stage actress who warrants a fleeting mention here for being touchingly real as Dennis PRICE's *déclassée* mother, and the cause of his career of elegant homicide, in *Kind Hearts and Coronets* (1949). Also in *While I Live* (1947) as Olwen, who gives her name to the film's famous theme song.

film and video workshops The workshop ideal of film as an oppositional, collective and essentially *social* practice is rooted in the INDEPENDENT CINEMA of the 1930s and the radical cultural politics of 1968. The workshops' heyday came in 1981 with the Workshop Declaration – an agreement between the

ACTT and CHANNEL 4, the BRITISH FILM INSTITUTE and the regional Arts Associations – by which the union permitted lower rates of pay and crewing levels and the Channel provided revenue funding for certain workshops (as opposed simply to commissioning one-off programmes from them). This kind of financial security greatly enabled the growth of the workshop sector. However, by 1990 the broadcasting climate had changed, along with the wider political one, and both the Channel and the BFI ceased revenue funding, leaving the workshops in the same position as any other small independent producer.

BIBLIOG: British Council, *Landmarks* 1989; Margaret Dickinson, *Rogue Reels*, 1999. Julian Petley.

Film Artistes Association The Film Artistes Guild, forerunner of the FAA, was formed in 1928 and affiliated with the Trades Union Council in 1930. As the FAA, from 1932, it was inundated with requests for membership during the Depression years, and was committed to regularising rates of pay for EXTRAS (small-part and background players). During WW2, the depleted FAA workforce took part in many of the PROPAGANDA films produced to boost morale, though it was later found that during the war casting agencies had used non-union labour, sometimes exploiting the situation. An alliance was later formed (October 1947) between British film producers and the FAA, resulting in the formation of a film casting association, later known as Central Casting, in an agreement signed by J. Arthur RANK among others. Detailed terms and conditions were negotiated for providing suitable background artistes. Following stringent trades union reforms under the Thatcher government, Central Casting, the sole representative of background artistes, was dissolved. Seeking amalgamation with another union, the former FAA merged with BECTU (the Broadcasting, Entertainment, Cinematograph & Theatre Union) in July 1995. Roy Lansford.

Film Centre The origins of Film Centre, founded in 1938, lie in John GRIERSON's belief that, by 1936, the DOCUMENTARY film movement needed to expand out from the State sponsored GPO FILM UNIT. Grierson was finding working within the Post Office too constraining, and, consequently, he attempted to develop documentary film units within a number of corporate institutions, such as Shell International. In order to maintain a degree of cohesion within the movement, and establish a degree of contact with new film units such as SHELL, STRAND and REALIST, and, in addition, to help the field of documentary film-making generally, an umbrella organisation was set up, whose role was to act as an enabling and supportive body. Initially, Paul ROTHA, Arthur ELTON, Edgar ANSTEY and Donald TAYLOR participated in the establishment of Associated Realist Film Producers, which was founded in 1935 in order to manage film production sponsored by companies such as Shell and the Gas and Coke Corporation (who sponsored *Housing Problems*, amongst other films). In 1937, Film Centre was established by Basil WRIGHT, Elton, Stuart LEGG and J.P.R. Golightly, and ARFP developed into a more general organisation dedicted to the advancement of the documentary film. Film Centre acted as a promotional organ for the documentary movement outside of the State, and managed films commissioned by organisations such as Shell, Imperial Airways and the Films of Scotland Committee. Film Centre's first films were Wright's *Children at School* (1937), and John TAYLOR's *The Smoke Menace* (1937). Ian Aitken.

Film Consortium The biggest of the three Lottery-funded franchises (others were DNA, formed by Duncan KENWORTHY and Andrew MACDONALD, and the French-based PATHÉ PICTURES) set up in 1997 as part of a move by the ARTS COUNCIL to rationalise production, distribution and sales, with guaranteed finance for six years. Film Consortium brought together SCALA (Steve WOOLLEY, Nik POWELL), PARALLAX (Ken LOACH, Sally HIBBIN) and Skreba-Greenpoint (Simon RELPH, Ann SCOTT). In August 2000, Alan PARKER, Chairman of the FILM COUNCIL, warned the Consortium that, following a series of commercial and critical failures, including *Hideous Kinky* (1998, UK/Fr) and *Janice Beard: 45 wpm* (2000), it was in danger of losing its franchise. It was revealed that it had been bought by a former meat-processing company, Civilian Content.

Film Council This was set up in April 2000 as the strategic agency for both developing a sustainable and entrepreneurial film industry and enhancing the wider film culture by improving access to, and education about, the moving image. Its establishment follows recommendations made in the 1998 report of the Film Policy Review Group, *A Bigger Picture*. It now channels all public funding for film production previously allocated to other bodies by the Department for Culture, Media and Sport (with the exception of the grant to the NATIONAL FILM AND TELEVISION SCHOOL), having absorbed the responsibilities of the ARTS COUNCIL of England's Lottery Film Department, the BRITISH FILM COMMISSION, The BRITISH FILM INSTITUTE PRODUCTION BOARD and BRITISH SCREEN FINANCE. The BFI is now funded primarily by the FILM COUNCIL, and it was restructured during 1998/9 to take account of the Council's cultural and educational objectives for film. Julian Petley.

Film Europe Term now given to efforts to produce a pan-European cinema in the 20s and early 30s, loosely co-ordinated through a series of trade congresses. (It is an anglicisation of 'Film-Europa', the term then used by the German press.) Designed to enable European film-makers to compete more equitably with Hollywood, strategies included co-productions, reciprocal distribution deals and exchange of personnel between the strongest players in the European market (especially Germany, Britain, France, Italy). The conversion to sound saw the production of different language versions of the same film. Nationalist politics in the 30s put an end to Film Europe, although many émigrés from the German cinema found work in Paris and London.

BIBLIOG: Andrew Higson and Richard Maltby (eds), *'Film Europe' and 'Film America': Cinema, Commerce and Cultural Exchange, 1920–1939*, 1999. Andrew Higson.

Film Industry Defence Organisation Organised by British renters and exhibitors in 1958 in an attempt to prevent old feature films being sold to TV. The body disintegrated in 1964 after a five-year period in which renters feared reprisals if they attempted to sell their product. Finally, the matter was laid to rest on the understanding that no film of major box-office potential would be shown on TV for at least five years.

film noir The term *film noir*, traditionally associated with 40s and 50s Hollywood cinema, has in recent years been applied to the formal, thematic and historical attributes of other film cultures, including Britain's. In 1947, without reference to the then-unknown term '*film noir*', Arthur Vesselo, reviewing *They Made Me a Fugitive* in SIGHT AND SOUND, objected to its 'morbid burrowings', which he saw as part of a disturbing post-war trend in the British cinema. Vesselo, in his attack, pointed to specific recurring thematic characteristics of this trend which included an 'unpleasant undertone' coupled with a pervasive sense 'of frustrated violence'. More pertinent was his objection to 'the inversion and disordering of moral values' and a 'groping into the grimier recesses of the mind'. These aspects had entered the CRIME GENRE in the 40s as part of a general weakening of the world's polarisation into moral absolutes, presenting a more graduated moral structure which emanated from their pessimistic depiction of an alienated society, devoid of communal strength. This is evident in *On the Night of the Fire* (1939), described by American film historian William K. Everson as 'Britain's first bona fide *film noir*', and, when Kobling (Ralph RICHARDSON) steals £100, he sets off a chain of events which culminate in death for him and his wife.

This 1939 film is an early, stylised example of the alienation and entrapment in a hostile community that troubled Vesselo, and others, after WW2. The wartime desire for communal solidarity, along with the need to project a sense of optimism and faith, militated against these fatalistic motifs' continuing after 1939. However, in the early 40s, low-budget Gothic thrillers like *The Night Has Eyes* (1942) paved the way for the more full-blown perversities of *film noir*, including a popular cycle of films depicting female murderers immediately post-war. This cycle included: *Pink String and Sealing Wax* (1945), where Pearl (Googie WITHERS) poisons her brutal husband; Margaret LOCKWOOD as *Bedelia* (1946), from the novel by Vera Caspary, author of *Laura*, who poisons her first three husbands for their insurance money, then attempts to repeat the action with her latest husband; Vivien (Greta GYNT) in *Dear Murderer* (1947) who poisons her husband because he murdered her former lover and threatens her current beau; and Olivia Harwood (Ann TODD) in *So Evil My Love* (1948), who kills both her employer's husband and her own lover. Perhaps the most extreme example of this pattern was Lance COMFORT's *Daughter of Darkness* (1947) in which childlike Emmy Beaudine's (Siobhan McKENNA) latent nymphomania is released through her murderous reaction towards the men she attracts.

The inability to adjust to civilian life was a recurring post-war motif in *film noir* and, when disillusioned ex-RAF officer Clem (Trevor HOWARD) enters the world of black marketeers in *They Made Me a Fugitive* (1947), he find himself framed for robbery and murder. War-related psychological problems also trouble Sammy Rice (David FARRAR) in *The Small Back Room* (1948), and trigger Adam Lucien's (Kieron MOORE) seemingly unmotivated attacks on his wife in *Mine Own Executioner* (1947). This motif of maladjusted ex-servicemen in films such as *Silent Dust* (1949) continued briefly into the 50s with *The Good Die Young* (1954).

Other factors which provoked mental instability included a bus accident in *The October Man* (1947), a thriller which locates a disturbing microcosm of post-war neuroses in a West London boarding house. Jealousy brought on by the actions of a selfish wife leads Robert NEWTON to devise a convoluted plan to kill his wife's lover in *Obsession* (1949), while another ambitious wife provokes her husband (Paul Douglas) to kill his gangster boss in Ken HUGHES's *Joe Macbeth* (1955). HUGHES's earlier film, *House Across the Lake* (1954), reworks aspects of *Double Indemnity* as a greedy wife seduces a stranger into participating in the death of her husband. Repressed homosexual desire unbalances lawyer Dirk BOGARDE in *Victim*

(1961); circumstances lead to the imprisonment of conductor Hugh WILLIAMS in *Take My Life* (1947) and husband Rex HARRISON in *The Long Dark Hall* (1951); and the theft of the family motor car drives salesman Richard TODD to the edge in the underrated *Never Let Go* (1960).

In the 80s and 90s this pattern of tormented and morally ambivalent protagonists, set against visual and other references to *film noir*, continued in films as seemingly different as *Dance With a Stranger* (1984), *Stormy Monday* (1987), *Under Suspicion* (1991), *Shallow Grave* (1994) and *Wings of the Dove* (1997, UK/US). Geoff Mayer.

Film on Four *see* **Channel 4 and British cinema**

Film Society, The The Film Society was founded in 1925 to screen significant foreign productions that could not otherwise be seen in Britain, often through the restrictive attitude of the British Board of Film Censors. Its organisers included the film exhibitor Sidney BERNSTEIN, film critics Iris BARRY and Ivor MONTAGU, and film-maker Adrian BRUNEL, while its founder members included George Bernard SHAW and H.G. WELLS.

Its Sunday afternoon screenings at London West End cinemas became a hugely popular cultural event, attracting over 1,500 people, and they had a strong influence in introducing the latest ideas in technique and subject matter from abroad through the showing of such films as *Die Freudlose Gasse* (1925) and *Berlin: Die Sinfonie Der Grosstadt* (1927). Many historically significant films were also revived, including examples of German expressionism like *Das Cabinet des Dr Caligari*. Important new Russian productions, banned by the Censor, were imported and film-makers like Pudovkin and Eisenstein came over to speak to members, leading to press accusations that the Society was politically motivated. British DOCUMENTARIES were regularly featured in the 30s. The Film Society continued until 1939, even though ART-HOUSE CINEMAS, such as the ACADEMY in Oxford Street, had been successfully established to take over much of its function.

BIBLIOG: Jamie Sexton, 'The Film Society and the Creation of an Alternative Film Culture in Britain in the 1920s', in Andrew Higson (ed), *Young and Innocent? The Cinema in Britain, 1896–1930*, 2002. Allen Eyles.

finance and British cinema The major sources of finance for British films have been commercial and private capital, facilitated by a degree of protective state LEGISLATION and, since 1995, by monies from the NATIONAL LOTTERY.

The major difficulties of financing British films have related to: Hollywood's domination of the home market; the unstable nature of film production and its reputation as a risky business; the decline in cinema admissions since the 1950s; and the contentious question of how to define a British film. In the silent period thousands of short films were financed and produced by individuals and small companies, including Cecil HEPWORTH and the SHEFFIELD PHOTO COMPANY. As demand for film entertainment increased, so did the supply of films from Europe and America, resulting in an EXHIBITION boom. Consequently, the largest British film company before WW1 was Provincial Cinematograph Theatres which established a production subsidiary and studios. The company was backed by members of the 'Establishment', including Lord Ashfield and Lord Beaverbrook, and in 1929 was absorbed by one of the largest film companies of the 30s, the GAUMONT–BRITISH PICTURE CORPORATION, a vertically-integrated company financed by Isidore and Maurice OSTRER. The trend of financing films from box-office profits was firmly established by Gaumont–British and its major rival, the ASSOCIATED BRITISH PICTURE CORPORATION, a company financed by Scottish solicitor John MAXWELL. In the 30s film production attracted sponsorship from respected institutions such as the National Westminster Bank and the Prudential Assurance Company which financed Alexander KORDA's LONDON FILM PRODUCTIONS.

Despite the advances made by British films, the City of London became wary after many new film companies went bankrupt in the 'crash' of 1937. Competition from American films and the new companies' financial instability resulted in a loss of confidence in British cinema as an investment opportunity, despite protective LEGISLATION. During and after WW2 the film industry recovered and expanded, mainly due to the output of the RANK ORGANISATION, a major company which had absorbed Gaumont–British in 1941 and was rivalled only by Associated British in the 40s and 50s. Both organisations, the 'duopoly', were controversial with their respective links with American majors, UNIVERSAL and WARNER BROS, and because of their domination over production, DISTRIBUTION and EXHIBITION, leading to frequent criticism as companies occupying monopoly status. In the late 50s and early 60s, however, INDEPENDENT PRODUCTION units, with no direct links with the 'duopoly' and associated with the British NEW WAVE, attracted positive critical attention and commercial success. Ironically, this paved the way for an influx of American finance for British films in the 60s, an aim of the Board of Trade's film policy since 1938. In the 70s much of this external support was withdrawn, leaving the industry weak and unstable, without a strong indigenous financial infrastructure to compensate and with cinema admissions in sharp decline. When the Conservative government dismantled all existing protective legislation in the 80s and phased-out tax allowances, the industry found it difficult to sustain the brief period of increased confidence following the Oscars and box-office success of *Chariots of Fire* (1981). Increased commercial and technical interdependence of the film and television industries resulted in television companies investing in film production, most notably CHANNEL 4, and to a lesser extent the BBC, ITV and cable companies such as BSkyB. Co-productions with European countries provided some additional finance, but resulted in debates about the definition of a 'British' film. In 1995 the film industry received a major injection of capital from the NATIONAL LOTTERY, at first distributed via the ARTS COUNCIL but since 2000 by the state-sponsored FILM COUNCIL which was formed 'to pursue an integrated strategy for film culture and the film industry' with an annual budget of £54 million at its disposal. At first the Lottery monies were controversial in that many films were funded but few were able to obtain a theatrical release, drawing attention to the importance of linking production finance with DISTRIBUTION. Three Lottery-funded franchises were awarded in 1997 to PATHÉ PICTURES, The FILM CONSORTIUM and DNA FILMS in order to unify production, distribution and exhibition. The proliferation of outlets for filmed entertainment – cinema, television, video, DVD and the Internet – has expanded the potential number of screens for British films, but Hollywood remains the dominant force in a global market. Tax incentives were reinstated to encourage film-making in Britain, adding up to a package designed by the Labour government to overcome many of the financial problems experienced by the British cinema in the 20th century.

BIBLIOG. Margaret Dickinson and Sarah Street, *Cinema and State*, 1985; British Institute, *Film and Television Handbook*, 2000. Sarah Street.

Finbow, Colin (*b* Ipswich, 1940). Director. Trained at Ipswich College of Art and Goldsmith's College, this prolific director of children's films during the 80s and 90s also produced and wrote most of his films. Usually made for the CHILDREN'S FILM UNIT, plus some for TV, they all featured youthful protagonists, but sometimes well-known adult actors, such as Susannah YORK (*Daemon*, 1986) and Glenda JACKSON (*Doombeach*, 1989) appear.

OTHER BRITISH FILMS INCLUDE: *The Custard Boys* (1979), *A Swarm in May* (1983), *Mr Skeeter* (1985), *School for Vandals* (1986), *Take Cover* (1987), *Infantile Disorders* (1988), *Hard Road* (1989), *Survivors* (1990), *How's Business* (1992), *Awayday* (1997).

Finch, Jon (*b* Caterham, 1942). Actor. Somewhat morose leading man, with theatre background, who had his best run of films in the early 70s: as POLANSKI's *Macbeth* (1971), making the Scot young, brooding and dangerous; as the man wrongly sought for murder in HITCHCOCK's *Frenzy* (1972), in which his interestingly ambivalent persona suggests he *might* be guilty; and as *Lady Caroline Lamb*'s (1972, UK/It/US) unenviable husband. Nothing very interesting since, except perhaps *Giro City* (1982, TV, some cinemas), and some TV, including Bolingbroke in *Richard II* (1978).

OTHER BRITISH FILMS INCLUDE: *The Vampire Lovers* (1970), *Sunday Bloody Sunday* (1971), *The Final Programme* (1973), *Death on the Nile* (1978), *Breaking Glass* (1980), *The Threat* (1982), *Witching Time* (1985), *Darklands* (1996).

Finch, Nigel (*b* Tenterden, 1949 – *d* London, 1995). Director, producer. Best known as director of *Stonewall* (1995), which records the outbreaks of violence between gay activists and the police around Stonewall Bar in New York, 1969. His other work was mainly for BBC television, for which he began work as a researcher in the 70s, editing the *Arena* series (1975–78) and later making the telemovie, *The Lost Language of Cranes* (1991), in which the father of a gay son comes to terms with his own sexuality. Died of an AIDS-related illness.

Finch, Peter (*b* London, 1916 – *d* Beverley Hills, California, 1977). Actor. Charismatic leading man, who filmed internationally, winning a posthumous AA and BAA for the overwrought *Network* (1976, US), but remained essentially a British star. Born in England and raised in Australia from age 10 (his own accounts of his unconventional youth are notoriously variable), he came back to England in the late 40s, having been spotted in Australia by OLIVIER, who cast him in the Old Vic's *Daphne Laureola*. He appeared in a half-dozen Australian films, before and during WW2; his first British film role was as the murderer in EALING's *Train of Events* (1949). Thereafter, films dominated his career. He seemed to work non-stop during the 50s, appearing as the Sheriff of Nottingham in *The Story of Robin Hood . . .* (1952), D'Oyly Carte in *The Story of Gilbert and Sullivan* (1953), the cultivated thief Flambeau in *Father Brown* (1954), the vain TV star in *Simon and Laura* (1955), gallant Aussie Joe Harmon in the POW drama, *A Town Like Alice* (1956, BAA), the dignified German captain of the *Graf Spee*, in *The Battle of the River Plate* (1956), and – his own favourite – the swagman in Ealing's Australian-set *The Shiralee* (1957). It is a showy line-up of leading roles, and he filled them with consummate, stylish ease.

However, the best was still to be. Not the odd skirmish with Hollywood, such as *Elephant Walk* (1954) or the negligible *The*

Sins of Rachel Cade (1961) or even Robert Aldrich's enjoyably florid *The Legend of Lylah Clare* (1968), but his greatest roles in British cinema. He was an infinitely moving, wearily witty Wilde in *The Trials of Oscar Wilde* (1960, BAA/a), dead-behind-the-eyes as the shallow, opportunist politician in *No Love for Johnnie* (1961, BAA/a), believably unfaithful husband to too-fecund wife in *The Pumpkin Eater* (1964), an alarmingly obsessive Boldwood in *Far from the Madding Crowd* (1967), wonderfully humane, sympathetic and resigned as the homosexual doctor in *Sunday Bloody Sunday* (1971, BAA/a, AAn/a), and a persuasively battered Nelson in *Bequest to the Nation* (1973). It is arguable that no other actor ever chalked up such a rewarding *cv* in British films, and he accumulated the awards to bolster this view.

There were tired and bad films among all these, but he emerged unscathed. Dead of a heart attack at 61, he did not emerge unscathed from a life of well-publicised hell-raising, and several biographies chronicle the affairs and the booze, but a serious appraisal of a great actor remains to be written.

OTHER BRITISH FILMS: *Eureka Stockade* (1949), *The Wooden Horse*, *The Miniver Story* (1950), *The Heart of the Matter* (1953), *Make Me An Offer!* (1954), *Passage Home, Josephine and Men, The Dark Avenger* (1955), *Robbery Under Arms, Windom's Way* (BAAn) (1957), *Operation Amsterdam* (1958), *Kidnapped* (1960), *I Thank a Fool* (1962), *In the Cool of the Day, Girl with Green Eyes* (1963), *First Men in the Moon* (1964), *Judith* (1966, US/UK/Isr), *Something to Hide* (1971), *England Made Me* (1972, UK/Yug), *The Abdication* (1974).

BIBLIOG: Trader Faulkner, *Peter Finch*, 1979; Elaine Dundy, *Finch, Bloody Finch*, 1980.

Findlay, Deborah Actress. Ubiquitously and vividly on view on TV – a village gossip in *Wives and Daughters* (1999) and the pietistic Countess Lydia in *Anna Karenina* (2000) – Findlay could become a major British character actress. Film so far has limited her to small roles in *Truly Madly Deeply* (1990), *Jack & Sarah* (1995) and, as the priest's sister, *The End of the Affair* (2000, UK/Ger/US).

Finlay, Frank (*b* Farnworth, 1926). Actor. Without the star's conventional good looks, Finlay has become a much-respected character actor. RADA-trained and on stage from 1957, he triumphed as Iago to OLIVIER's Othello at the National in 1964, and in the 1965 film version for which he received a BAAn. He played striking supporting roles in many films, from 1962 (as a tetchy railway clerk in *The Loneliness of the Long Distance Runner*), including the chaplain, prosing on about the value of games – as he pats a boy's knee – in *I'll Never Forget What's 'is Name* (1967), Inspector Lestrade in *A Study in Terror* (1965) and *Murder by Decree* (1978), and, very touchingly, Glenda JACKSON's bemused, decent husband in *The Return of the Soldier* (1982, BAAn/supp a). Has filmed internationally (e.g. *The Molly Maguires*, 1970, US; *The Three/Four Musketeers*, 1973/74, Panama/Spain) and also done a great deal of highly regarded TV, including the very popular Surrey-set, sex-dominated saga, *A Bouquet of Barbed Wire* (1976), and Charles STURRIDGE's mammoth *Longitude* (2000). Created CBE, 1984.

OTHER BRITISH FILMS INCLUDE: *Private Potter, Life for Ruth* (1962), *The Wild Affair, The Informers* (1963), *Hot Enough for June* (1964), *The Jokers, The Deadly Bees* (1966), *Robbery* (1967), *Twisted Nerve* (1968), *Cromwell, Assault* (1970), *Sitting Target* (1972), *The Wild Geese* (UK/Switz), *Enigma* (UK/Fr) (1982), *The Ploughman's Lunch* (1983), *Dreaming of Joseph Lees* (1999, US/UK).

Finn, Arthur (*b* Buffalo, NY) Actor, director. American actor who made some films there in 1912, then entered the UK film industry as actor with BRITISH AND COLONIAL in 1913. The

following year, he co-founded the Weston–Finn Company (later known as the Regent Company), with STUDIOS in Bayswater, and became known for the character of Finn in *Detective Finn; or, in the Heart of London, Detective Finn and the Foreign Spies* and *The Great Python Robbery* (all 1914). He concentrated on a stage career (1919–34), appearing in comedies, dramas and revues, but returned to the screen in 1935 playing American character parts.

OTHER BRITISH FILMS INCLUDE: (a, unless noted) *The Master Crook, A Son of Japan, The Ragged Prince* (1913), *The Bishop's Silence, The Girl Next Door* (+ d), *Your Name Brown?* (d), *What a Kiss Will Do* (+d), *Self-Accused* (1914), *Wild Oats* (1915), *Forty Winks* (1920, d), *Annie, Leave the Room!, Say It with Diamonds* (1935), *The Three Maxims* (1936), *What Would You Do Chums?* (1939). AS.

Finney, Albert (*b* Salford, 1936). Actor. A successful stage actor before his film career began with a small role in *The Entertainer* (1960) for Tony RICHARDSON, a director he had worked with in the theatre, and he and Richardson became key figures of the British NEW WAVE of social REALISM. Distinctive because of his powerful voice, resonant of his Northern origins, Finney first made his name in Karel REISZ's *Saturday Night and Sunday Morning* (1960), playing Arthur Seaton, a lathe worker who refuses to 'let the bastards grind you down'. He conquered US audiences and critics with his spirited portrayal of *Tom Jones* (1963, AAn/a), but shied away from further romantic parts, preferring a variety of character roles, including a psychopath in *Night Must Fall* (1964, + p), the title role in the musical, *Scrooge* (1970), an idiosyncratically conceived Hercule Poirot in *Murder on the Orient Express* (1974, AAn/a), and a bombastic theatre actor in *The Dresser* (1983, AAn/a). While such choices demonstrate his resistance to stardom, Finney has gained widespread respect playing men who are forces to be reckoned with, and as a result, continues to gain quality work across the media: on TV in Dennis POTTER's *Karaoke* (1996), and *Cold Lazarus* (1996); on stage in the 1996 West End production of *Art*; in film, *Erin Brockovich* (2000, US, AAn/supp a) opposite box-office magnet Julia Roberts. Finney is divorced from actresses Jane WENHAM (1957–61) and Anouk AIMÉE (1970–78).

OTHER BRITISH FILMS: *The Inheritance, The Victors* (1963), *Two for the Road* (1966), *Charlie Bubbles* (1967, + d), *Gumshoe* (1971), *Alpha Beta* (1972), *The Duellists* (1977), *Loophole* (1980), *The Biko Inquest* (1984, + d), *The Playboys* (1992, Ire/US), *The Browning Version, A Man of No Importance* (UK/Ire) (1994), *The Run of the Country* (1995, Ire/US), *Simpatico* (1999, UK/Fr/US).

BIBLIOG: Quentin Falk, *Albert Finney in Character*, 1992. Melinda Hildebrandt.

Firbank, Ann (*b* Secunderabad, India, 1933). Actress. Graceful player of upper-(middle-)class types, like the society woman in the café in *The Servant* (1963), Stanley BAKER's neglected wife in *Accident* (1967), the doctor's wife in the lamentable 1974 *Brief Encounter* (TV, some cinemas), Raj-upholding Mrs Callender in *A Passage to India* (1984), and Lady Bradley in *Anna and the King* (1999, US).

OTHER BRITISH FILMS INCLUDE: *Carry On Nurse, Behind the Mask* (1958), *A Severed Head* (1970), *Sunday Bloody Sunday* (1971), *Foreign Body* (1986), *Strapless* (1988).

Firth, Anne (*b* Westcliff-on-Sea, 1918 – *d* 1967). Actress. George FORMBY's leading ladies usually went on to more illustrious things, but Firth did very little after *Bell-Bottom George* (1944), though she was a briefly gracious Oriana Wilson in *Scott of the Antarctic* (1948).

OTHER BRITISH FILMS: *The Goose Steps Out*, *The First of the Few*, *Suspected Person* (1942), *Demobbed* (1944), *Vengeance Is Mine* (1948).

Firth, Colin (*b* Grayshott, 1960). Actor. For a moment in the 1990s, there can scarcely have been a woman or girlchild unaware of the minutiae of the life of TV's Mr Darcy (BAAn). *Pride and Prejudice* (1995) over with, the surlily handsome Firth has striven to reinvent himself as an actor in varied films: *The English Patient* (1996, UK/US) as the cuckolded husband; *Fever Pitch* (1997) as a fanatical Arsenal supporter; *Shakespeare in Love* (1999, UK/US) as an unromantic Lord Wessex; and as Julie ANDREWS' quizzical nephew in *Relative Values* (2000, UK/US). Maybe he is *meant* to be a sex symbol; the result of going in for character lurches means that major film stardom eludes him, unless *Bridget Jones's Diary* (2001, UK/Fr/US), as another Darcy, does the trick.

Born to academic parents, trained at Chalk Farm Drama Centre, made West End debut in *Another Country* (1982) as a Communist sixth-former, reprising the role in the film (1984). Early films also included *A Month in the Country* (1987), as a WW1-scarred veteran, the very quirky, Buenos Aires-set *Apartment Zero* (1988) and *Valmont* (1989, UK/Fr), opposite Meg Tilly by whom he has a son. There has been some US work (*A Thousand Acres*, 1997), a return to the stage in 1999, and some notable TV, including the post-Falklands drama *Tumbledown* (1989, BAAn) and *The Deep Blue Sea* (1994) as that pickled adolescent, Freddie Page.

OTHER BRITISH FILMS INCLUDE: *Nineteen Nineteen* (1984), *Out of the Blue* (1991), *The Hour of the Pig* (1993, UK/Fr), *Playmaker* (1994, UK/US), *Circle of Friends* (1995, Ire/US), *The Secret Laughter of Women* (1999, UK/Can), *The Importance of Being Earnest* (2002, UK/US), *Love Actually* (2003).

Firth, Peter (*b* Bradford, Yorkshire, 1953). Actor. Still associated with his award-winning role of the horse-obsessed adolescent in *Equus* (stage 1973, film 1977), fair, slight Firth has given intelligent performances in a range of films without reaching star status. On stage from childhood and in films from 1972's *Brother Sun, Sister Moon* (UK/It) and *Diamonds on Wheels* (DISNEY children's thriller), he had juvenile leads in *Aces High* (1976, UK/Fr), *Joseph Andrews* (1976, in the title role but upstaged by Ann-Margret's bosom), *Tess* (1979, UK/Fr, as Angel Clare), the allegorical *The Aerodrome* (1983, TV, some cinemas), and the charming fable of love's tenacity, *A Letter to Brezhnev* (1985). Latterly, he has moved into character roles, memorable as Dr Craig in *Shadowlands* (1993, UK/US) and as the harassed stage manager in *An Awfully Big Adventure* (1995), since when he has worked in TV and the US (e.g. *Amistad*, 1997).

OTHER BRITISH FILMS: *White Elephant* (1984), *Lifeforce* (1985), *Born of Fire* (1987), *Tree of Hands* (1988).

Fisher, Gerry (*b* London, 1926). Cinematographer. Had long experience as focus-puller, then as camera operator on major films such as *The Bridge on the River Kwai* (1957), before coming to prominence as LOSEY's preferred cinematographer. He gave a slumbrous feel to the gardens and colleges of *Accident* (1967), caught the oppressive summer heat of *The Go-Between* (1971, BAAn) and the claustrophobic chill of *A Doll's House* (1973, UK/Fr), and also worked on Losey's European films. Sad to report that so distinguished a collaborator has, in recent years, worked almost entirely abroad.

OTHER BRITISH FILMS INCLUDE: (cam op) *Suddenly, Last Summer* (1959), *The Millionairess* (1960), *Guns of Darkness* (1962), *Night Must Fall*, *Guns at Batasi* (1964), *Bunny Lake is Missing* (1965); (c) *Sebastian*

(1967), *Interlude*, *Secret Ceremony*, *The Sea Gull* (1968), *Hamlet* (1969), *Ned Kelly* (1970), *Blind Terror* (1971), *The Offence* (1972), *Bequest to the Nation*, *Butley* (US/Can/UK) (1973), *Juggernaut* (1974), *The Romantic Englishwoman* (UK/Fr), *Brannigan* (1975), *Aces High* (1976, UK/Fr, BAAn/c), *The Holcroft Covenant* (1985), *Highlander* (1986, European scenes), *Black Rainbow* (1989).

Fisher, Terence (*b* London, 1904 – *d* Twickenham, 1980). Director. Arguably the most important director of the Gothic cinema in the second half of the 20th century, Fisher early apprenticed himself as an editor on various projects at WARNER BROS' UK studio during the 30s and early 40s, before getting his first chance at direction with *Colonel Bogey* (1948), a modest programme picture for HIGHBURY STUDIOS. This was followed by the more successful *To the Public Danger* (1948), based on Patrick Hamilton's famous radio play on the perils of drunken driving, but apart from a couple of 'nervous A' pictures (*Portrait from Life*, 1948, with Mai ZETTERLING; and *The Astonished Heart*, 1950), co-directed with Antony DARNBOROUGH, Fisher remained stuck in dreary poverty-row crime thrillers, comedies, and other marginal films, working for such companies as Highbury, EROS, and HAMMER FILMS. Hammer Studios, however, was about to change both Fisher's life, and the entire face of British Gothic HORROR film-making. In 1956, Hammer decided to take, for what was such a small company, a major risk. Following the success of their 'Quatermass' series of science-fiction thrillers, Hammer decided to put nearly all their financing into *The Curse of Frankenstein* (1957), the studio's first feature in colour, with Fisher directing. The film was an international box-office hit, and Fisher quickly followed it with *Dracula* (1958). These two films, starring Peter CUSHING and Christopher LEE, effectively set Fisher on the track he was to pursue for the rest of his career. A conscientious craftsman who always came in on time and under budget, Fisher used his skills as an editor to keep coverage to an absolute minimum. He brought depth, flair, and a unique Gothic sensibility to all his work. Although his films included copious quantities of then-unprecedented graphic violence, Fisher once commented that his works were not really 'horror films. They're fairy tales for adults.'

OTHER BRITISH FILMS INCLUDE: *Home to Danger* (1951), *Children Galore* (1954), *The Mummy* (1959), *The Brides of Dracula* (1960), *The Curse of the Werewolf* (1961), *The Gorgon* (1964), *The Earth Dies Screaming* (1964), *Dracula-Prince of Darkness* (1965), *The Devil Rides Out* (1967), *Frankenstein Must Be Destroyed* (1969), *Frankenstein and the Monster from Hell* (1973).

BIBLIOG: Wheeler Winston Dixon, *The Charm of Evil: The Life and Times of Terence Fisher*, 1991; Peter Hutchings, *Terence Fisher*, 2001. Wheeler Winston Dixon.

Fisz, S. Benjamin (*b* Warsaw, 1922 – *d* London, 1989). Producer. Came to England pre-WW2, served in the RAF and the Polish Air Force, and in the 50s began to produce in Britain. Associated with action adventures, including the excellent *Hell Drivers* (1957), directed by frequent associate Cy ENDFIELD, and co-produced *Battle of Britain* (1969).

OTHER BRITISH FILMS INCLUDE: *Child in the House* (1956), *Sea Fury* (1958), *On the Fiddle* (1961), *The Heroes of Telemark* (1965), *A Town Called Bastard* (1971, UK/Sp), *Aces High* (1976, UK/Fr), *The Jigsaw Man* (1984).

Fitzgerald, Barry (*b* Dublin, 1888 – *d* Dublin, 1961). Actor. RN: William Shields. His long career of playing irascible leprechauns and the like was bookended by a few British films, of which *Happy Ever After* (1954) is the most enjoyable, smelling least of peat and cloverleaf. Hollywood, where he conducted most of his career, encouraged his professional Irishry and gave him a Best Supporting Oscar (*and* a Best Actor nomination) for doing it in *Going My Way* (1944). Brother of actor Arthur Shields.

OTHER BRITISH FILMS: *Juno and the Paycock* (1930), *When Knights Were Bold* (1936), *Rooney, Cradle of Genius* (doc) (1958), *Broth of a Boy* (1959).

Fitzgerald, Geraldine (*b* Dublin, 1914). Actress. One of the most beautiful women in British films of the 30s, Fitzgerald had Dublin stage experience from 1932 before making such films as *Turn of the Tide* (1935), J. Arthur RANK's entry to professional film-making. An archetypal Irish redhead with green eyes, perfect features and a slightly husky voice, along with an incisive acting talent: what was British cinema to do with all this? The answer, sadly, is very little. Only *The Mill on the Floss* (1937), as a fine, vivid Maggie Tulliver, challenged her; after that she was whisked off to Hollywood to play Isabella in *Wuthering Heights* (1939) in which she (AAn) alone looked as if she'd read the book. She had interesting roles in the US, like the second Mrs *Wilson* (1944), but always looked too intelligent for major stardom. Filmed in England only twice more: brilliant as the tippling adultress in *So Evil My Love* (1948) and as the suspected companion of *The Late Edwina Black* (1951). Became a potent stage actress in the US, especially in *Long Day's Journey into Night* (1971), and went on doing occasional films and TV until the early 1990s. The son of her first marriage is director Michael LINDSAY-HOGG and Tara FITZGERALD is her great-niece.

OTHER BRITISH FILMS: *Radio Parade of 1935* (1934), *Open All Night, Blind Justice* (1934), *Three Witnesses, The Lad, Ace of Spades, Department Store* (1935), *Debt of Honour, Café Mascot* (1936).

Fitzgerald, Tara (*b* London, 1967). Actress. RN: Callaby. Fast-rising young star of the 90s, a black-haired, somewhat gamine beauty who had enviable roles on stage (Ophelia to Ralph FIENNES' Hamlet in 1995; Sophocles' *Antigone*, 1999), TV (especially *The Camomile Lawn*, 1992; *The Tenant of Wildfell Hall*, 1996, in the lead), and film, starting with *Hear My Song* (1991) as Adrian DUNBAR's girlfriend. She made two with Hugh GRANT – the soft-centred *Sirens* (1994, UK/Aust) and *The Englishman Who Went Up . . .* (1995), but it was the flugelhorn-playing love interest for Ewan McGREGOR in the generally tough-minded *Brassed Off* (1996, UK/US) that fixed her in the public mind. Great-niece to Geraldine FITZGERALD.

OTHER BRITISH FILMS INCLUDE: *A Man of No Importance* (1994, UK/Ire), *Conquest* (1998), *Rancid Aluminium* (2000), *Dark Blue World* (2001).

Fitzgerald, Walter (*b* Keyham, 1896 – *d* London, 1976). Actor. Stalwart character player of the 40s and 50s; former stockbroker who then trained at RADA; on London stage in 1924, and made one film in 1932, *Murder at Covent Garden*, returning to the screen in *In Which We Serve* (1942). Usually in professional or service roles, he moved easily between sympathetic and severe: he was the middle-aged farmer in love with Sheila SIM in *Great Day* (1945), the hectoring patriarch in *Blanche Fury* (1947), an understanding doctor in *The Fallen Idol* (1948), a memorable Squire Trelawney in *Treasure Island* (1950), the Dean of the Cathedral in *Lease of Life* (1954) and Admirals, austere in *HMS Defiant* and comic in *We Joined the Navy* (1962). His sort of actor was the backbone of British cinema for two decades, a guarantee of authenticity even when the plot was challenging this. Married (1 of 2) Rosalie CRUTCHLEY.

OTHER BRITISH FILMS INCLUDE: *Squadron Leader X* (1942), *San Demetrio–London* (1943), *Mine Own Executioner* (1947), *The Winslow Boy, This Was a Woman, The Small Back Room* (1948), *Edward, My Son* (1949), *The Pickwick Papers, The Ringer, The Cruel Sea* (1952), *Twice Upon a Time, The Net, Appointment in London, Personal Affair, Our Girl Friday, Front Page Story* (1953), *Cockleshell Heroes* (1955), *The Birthday Present* (1957), *Third Man on the Mountain* (1959).

Fitzhamon, Lewin (*b* Aldingham, 1869 – *d* London, 1961). Director. A former MUSIC HALL entertainer, who became Cecil HEPWORTH's first director in 1904, making more than 600 shorts, including one classic of the cinema, *Rescued by Rover* (1905). Hepworth considered his 'original and sprightly ideas had a considerable effect upon our work.' In 1912, he formed Fitz Films in WALTHAMSTOW, which *The Bioscope* described as 'essentially English, in the best sense of the word', often featuring animals as their heroes. Ended his career in 1913–14, directing shorts for various old-fashioned producers. Made no feature-length productions. AS.

Fitzpatrick, James A. (*b* Shelton, Connecticut, 1895 – *d* Palm Springs, 1980). Director. American pioneer of 'Traveltalks', of often stupefying banality, who directed five modest features in 1930s Britain, including *Auld Lang Syne* (1937), a 'biography' of Robert Burns, starring Andrew CRUICKSHANK.

OTHER BRITISH FILMS:*David Livingstone, The Captain's Table* (1936), *The Last Rose of Summer, The Bells of St Mary's* (1937).

Flaherty, Robert (*b* Iron Mountain, Michigan, 1884 – *d* Dummerston, Vermont, 1951). Director. Cited as a major influence on John GRIERSON, Flaherty indirectly became part of the mythology of the British DOCUMENTARY movement when Grierson proclaimed 'of course, *Moana* (1926) being a visual account of events in the daily life of a Polynesian youth and his family, has documentary value.' He had made his name with *Nanook of the North* (1922, d, p, sc, ed, ph), a study of Eskimo survival in a harsh landscape, but was constantly frustrated by his dealings with Hollywood over his films, and after problems with *White Shadows in the South Seas* (1928) and *Tabu* (1930) he went to Britain to join forces with Grierson. Flaherty began the project that became the unfairly maligned *Industrial Britain* (1931) for the EMPIRE MARKETING BOARD. Although this film evinces the nostalgia that permeated all his works, this has often been complicated by the understanding that it was completed by Grierson, Basil WRIGHT and Arthur ELTON. Flaherty returned to Britain to rework his perennial theme of humanity against the elements in *Man of Aran* (1934) for GAINSBOROUGH. Flaherty's location shooting was also successfully combined with Zoltán KORDA's studio footage for *Elephant Boy* (1937). The rest of his career produced only two more US films. Deane Williams.

Flanagan, Bud (*b* London, 1896 – *d* Kingston, Surrey, 1968). Actor. RN: Reuben Weintrop. Broad comedy half of the Flanagan and (Chesney) ALLEN double-act component of the CRAZY GANG. He went to America before WW1 and worked with many comics before joining Allen and the Gang in 1931, entering films in 1932, filming at TWICKENHAM and GAINSBOROUGH. He made only two films without Allen: *Judgment Deferred* (1951) and *The Wild Affair* (1963). Also a composer and singer of sentimental songs, he had a television series, *Bud*, in 1963.

See **Allen, Chesney** and **Crazy Gang** for films made together.

Flanagan, Fionnula (*b* Dublin, 1941). Actress. Most of Abbey Theatre-trained Flanagan's work has been for American TV, including her Emmy-winning role in *Rich Man, Poor Man* (1976), but she has also won a reputation as theatrical interpreter of James JOYCE. First film was *Ulysses* (1967, UK/US) in which she was a vivid Gertie MacDowell, and all her subsequent British features have had an Irish setting or theme. In *Some Mother's Son* (1996, Ire/US), she is very moving (and funny) as the mother of an IRA prisoner.

OTHER BRITISH FILMS: *Sinful Davey* (1968), *Reflections* (1984), *Waking Ned* (1999, UK/Fr/US), *With or Without You* (1999).

Fleet, James (*b* Staffordshire, 1955). Actor. Best known as the floppy-haired, diffident, near-moronic Hugo in TV's *The Vicar of Dibley* (1994–2000), Fleet first appeared briefly as a parliamentary secretary in *Defence of the Realm* (1985) before emerging in the 90s as a major comic find in films such as *Four Weddings and a Funeral* (1994), as the craven John Dashwood in *Sense and Sensibility* (1995, UK/US), and as an endearing bungler out of his depth with gangsters in TV's *Underworld* (1997).

OTHER BRITISH FILMS INCLUDE: *Electric Moon* (1992), *The Grotesque, Remember Me?* (1996), *Three Steps to Heaven* (1995), *Kevin & Perry Go Large* (2000, UK/US).

Fleetwood, Susan (*b* St Andrews, 1944 – *d* Salisbury, 1995). Actress. Dead sadly young from cancer, statuesque, RADA-trained Fleetwood was a gifted stage actress who had several seasons with the RSC, co-founded the Liverpool Everyman theatre, and was a gauchely affecting Ophelia to Ian MCKELLEN's Hamlet (1971), which was filmed for TV (1972). Films are few but memorable, including haughty colonial types in *Heat and Dust* (1982) and *White Mischief* (1987) and, especially, as the gravely well-meaning, blinkered Lady Russell in *Persuasion* (1995, TV, cinemas). Her brother Mick was the drummer with Fleetwood Mac.

OTHER BRITISH FILMS: *Clash of the Titans* (1981, as Athena), *Dream Demon* (1988), *The Krays* (1990).

Fleming, Atholl (*b* London, 1894 – *d*?). Actor. Tall ex-accountant, educated at City of London School, on stage from 1924 and in supporting roles in 30s films, playing a *hors-de-combat* Bulldog Drummond in *Bulldog Jack* (1935).

OTHER BRITISH FILMS INCLUDE: *Tin Gods* (1932), *Mixed Doubles* (1933), *Little Friend* (1934), *Non-Stop New York, OHMS* (1937).

Fleming, Ian (*b* Melbourne, 1888 – *d* London, 1969). Actor. RN: Macfarlane. Australian actor of much stage experience, from 1904, in both London and the provinces. Entered films in 1926 (*Second to None*) and made nearly 100, good and bad, memorable and forgotten, and often uncredited. He was Watson to Arthur WONTNER's Holmes in the 30s and was assorted officers and professional gents for the next three decades.

OTHER BRITISH FILMS INCLUDE: *The School for Scandal* (1930), *The Triumph of Sherlock Holmes* (1935), *Silver Blaze* (1937), *Jeannie, Hatter's Castle* (1941), *We Dive at Dawn, The New Lot* (doc) (1943), *I Didn't Do It* (1945), *Captain Boycott* (1947), *Quartet, For Them That Trespass* (1948), *The Voice of Merrill* (1952), *The Seekers, Delayed Action* (1954), *The Trials of Oscar Wilde* (1960), *No, My Darling Daughter* (1961), *The Return of Mr Moto* (1965).

Fleming, Ian (*b* London, 1908 – *d* Canterbury, 1964). Author. Eton- and Sandhurst-educated creator of James BOND, whose adventures became the subject of some of the most popular British films, following the success of the first, *Dr No* (1962). Secret agent, bedroom athlete, martini-mixer, Bond first appeared in the 1935 novel, *Casino Royale*, filmed unhappily in

1967. Fleming had been a foreign correspondent with Reuters, famously reporting a spy trial in Russia, a banker (in the family bank) and stockbroker, and a senior naval intelligence officer during WW2. This was a useful background to draw on for Bond, whom he wrote about at his Jamaica showplace, 'Goldeneye', the name of a film (1995, UK/US) based on his characters. He was the younger brother of explorer Peter Fleming, who married Celia JOHNSON. In 1990, a biographical telemovie, *The Secret Life of Ian Fleming*, starring Jason CONNERY, appeared.

OTHER BRITISH FILMS: (adapted from his novels) *From Russia with Love* (1963, + a), *Goldfinger* (1964), *You Only Live Twice* (1967), *On Her Majesty's Secret Service* (1969), *Diamonds Are Forever* (1971), *Live and Let Die* (1973), *The Man with the Golden Gun* (1974), *The Spy Who Loved Me* (1977), *Moonraker* (1979, UK/Fr); (Fleming characters) *Licence to Kill* (1989, + novel, story), *GoldenEye* (1995, UK/US), *Tomorrow Never Dies* (1997, UK/US), *The World Is Not Enough* (1999, US/UK); (co-story): *Thunderball* (1965), *Never Say Never Again* (1983, UK/US); (stories): *Chitty Chitty Bang Bang* (1968), *For Your Eyes Only* (1981), *Octopussy* (1983); (story): *A View to a Kill* (1985), *The Living Daylights* (1987).

Fleming, Rachael (*b* Lancashire, *c* 1965). Costume designer. Designing for *Trainspotting* (1996), in which she also made an uncredited appearance as Renton's nurse, brought Fleming to prominence. She provided subtly evocative ordinary-to-low-life designs for Michael WINTERBOTTOM's early films, *Butterfly Kiss* (1995) and *Go Now* (1996), as well as for the sophisticated theatrical types of *The Leading Man* (1996), and has gone on to such eye-catching projects as *The Beach* (2000, UK/US) and *Bridget Jones' Diary* (2001, UK/Fr/US).

OTHER BRITISH FILMS INCLUDE: *Under the Sun* (1992), *Saint-Ex* (1996), *Twin Town, A Life Less Ordinary* (1997), *I Want You, Dad Savage* (1998), *Rogue Trader* (1999).

Flemyng, Gordon (*b* Glasgow, 1934 – *d* London, 1995). Director. Flemyng's film career began at MERTON PARK, on EDGAR WALLACE mysteries, and in the 60s he looked briefly promising as director of *Dr Who and the Daleks* (1965) and *Daleks – Invasion Earth 2150 AD* (1966), and of the Shavian adaptation *Great Catherine* (1967). He came from TV and that, from 1970, in unremembered telemovies, was where he finally returned.

OTHER BRITISH FILMS: *Solo for Sparrow* (1962), *Just for Fun!, Five to One* (1963), *The Last Grenade* (1969).

Flemyng, Jason (*b* London, 1967). Actor. Up-and-coming, red-headed young leading actor of the 90s, in TV (as the new doctor in *Doctor Finlay*, 1993) and such smart films as *Lock, Stock and Two Smoking Barrels* (1998). He is actually more interesting as Joely RICHARDSON's perhaps brutal live-in boyfriend in *Hollow Reed* (1996, UK/Ger), a taut film that passed almost unnoticed. Also in international films, including *Rob Roy* (1995, US) and re-voiced a lead role in Luc Besson's *Taxi* (1999) for English-speaking release.

OTHER BRITISH FILMS INCLUDE: *Stealing Beauty* (UK/Fr/It), *Alive and Kicking* (1996), *The James Gang, The Life of Stuff, Spice World* (1997), *Snatch* (2000), *Mean Machine* (2001, UK/US).

Flemyng, Robert (*b* Liverpool, 1912 – *d* London, 1995). Actor. Former medical student, Haileybury-educated Flemyng was first on London stage in 1931 and was busy there and on Broadway throughout the 30s. Filmed only once – as Jessie MATTHEWS' leading man in *Head Over Heels* (1937) – before WW2 service, for which he was awarded the Military Cross and the OBE (Military). Returned to the stage in *While the Sun Shines* (1945) and to films in *Bond Street* and *The Guinea Pig*

(1948), playing the sympathetic housemaster in the latter. Usually played sympathetic professionals, albeit crisply so, as in *The Blue Lamp* (1949), or sardonically, as in *Cast a Dark Shadow* (1955), properly suspicious of Dirk BOGARDE in both cases. Too reserved for stardom perhaps, but always a drily intelligent presence. Much TV, appearing in *The Choir* (1995) just before he died.

OTHER BRITISH FILMS INCLUDE: *Conspirator* (1949), *The Man Who Never Was* (1955), *Let's Be Happy* (1956), *Windom's Way* (1957), *A Touch of Larceny, Blind Date* (1959), *The Quiller Memorandum* (UK/US), *The Deadly Affair* (1966), *Battle of Britain* (1969), *The Firechasers* (1970), *Young Winston* (1972), *The Four Feathers, The Thirty Nine Steps* (1978), *Paris By Night* (1988), *Shadowlands* (1993, UK/US).

Fletcher, Cyril (*b* Watford, 1913). Actor. Star of stage and revue who made a few films, the only notable one being *Nicholas Nickleby* (1947), in which he played a flamboyant Mantalini. Other appearances in *Yellow Canary* (1943), as himself, and *A Piece of Cake* (1948), one of the silliest films ever made. Married to Betty ASTELL.

BIBLIOG: Autobiography, *Nice One, Cyril*, 1978.

Fletcher, Dexter (*b* London, 1966). Actor. In films from childhood, as Baby Face in *Bugsy Malone* (1976), the boy who frees *The Elephant Man* (1980, UK/US) from the freak show, and Al Pacino's son in the GOLDCREST-wrecking *Revolution* (1985, UK/Nor). Very popular with young people as Spike in TV's *Press Gang* (1989–93), he has made his mark as an adult actor in *Lock, Stock and Two Smoking Barrels* (1998) and *Topsy-Turvy* (2000, UK/US). His brothers, **Steve Fletcher** and **Graham Fletcher Cook**, made several films each, including *The Raggedy Rawney* (1988) with Dexter.

OTHER BRITISH FILMS INCLUDE: *The Long Good Friday* (1979), *The Bounty* (1984), *Caravaggio* (1986), *When the Whales Came, The Rachel Papers* (1989), *Jude* (1996), *Pandaemonium* (2001).

Flugrath, Edna *see* **Americans in British silent films**

Flynn, Errol (Hobart, 1909 – *d* Vancouver, 1959). Actor. Celebrated roisterer, film star and actor, in descending order, Flynn scarcely belongs in this book. However, he did appear in five British films: *Murder in Monte Carlo* (1935), before Hollywood fame overtook him, and four in the mid 50s when the booze had half-ruined him and Hollywood was losing interest. There were two mild period cloak-and-dagger jobs – *The Master of Ballantrae* (1953) and *The Dark Avenger* (1955) – and two dire retro musicals with Anna NEAGLE, whose own prime was passing, *Lilacs in the Spring* (1954) and *King's Rhapsody* (1955), but it was too late to arrest the slide and he was dead four years later. In Hollywood, he often played Brits, as in *The Adventures of Robin Hood* (1938).

Fogwell, Reginald G. (*b* Dartmouth, ? – *d* England, ?). Producer, director, screenwriter. Made about a dozen films in the early 30s, in the usual THRILLER GENRE of the period, with MUSICAL and COMEDY exceptions. Former publicity manager for Fox–British, he spent time in Hollywood, and wrote *Flames of Desire* (1924).

BRITISH FILMS INCLUDE (co/p, co/sc, unless noted): *The Warning, The Imposter* (1929, d, sc), *Cross Roads* (1930, + d), *Madame Guillotine* (1931, + d), *Betrayal* (1932, + d), *Prince of Arcadia* (1933), *Two Hearts in Waltz Time* (1934), *Murder at the Cabaret* (1936, + d).

Fogwell, Roy (*b* London, 1901 – *d*?). Cinematographer. Educated at St Joseph's College, in films as camera assistant in 1930, and later worked at VERITY FILMS in WW2 and at GAINSBOROUGH as chief exterior cameraman, on such films as *King Arthur Was a Gentleman* (1942), *Miss London Ltd, We Dive at Dawn* (1943), *Bees in Paradise, Love Story* (1944). Under contract to RANK (1947–49), he photographed several minor films, such as *Trouble in the Air* (1948).

OTHER BRITISH FILMS INCLUDE: (c, unless noted) *Dora* (1933, co-c), *The Ghost Train* (2uc) (1941), *The Young Mr Pitt* (2uc), *Millions Like Us* (co-c), *Bell-Bottom George* (1944), *To the Public Danger* (co-c), *Fly Away Peter* (1948), *Those People Next Door* (1952).

Foley, George Actor. Villain of the silent screen, who ended his career playing heavy opposite Walter FORDE in 1926 two-reel comedies.

BRITISH FILMS INCLUDE: *Adventures of Dick Turpin* (1912), *The Battle of Waterloo* (1913), *The Life of Shakespeare* (1914), *The Ware Case* (1917), *Because* (1918), *Little Dorrit, Trent's Last Case* (1920), *The Road to London* (1921), *A Romance of Mayfair* (1925). AS.

Foot, Geoffrey (*b* London, 1915). Editor. Latymer-educated, in films from 1934 at EALING until 1937, then assistant editor at LONDON FILMS (1938–39) and MAYFLOWER (1939–40) before becoming editor with CROWN FILM UNIT. Following WW2 service with the ARMY KINEMATOGRAPH SERVICE, he edited for CINEGUILD, cutting *The Passionate Friends* (1948) and *Madeleine* (1949) for David LEAN, as well as Lean's later *The Sound Barrier* (1952). His later career descended to *Confessions of a Pop Performer* (1975) and its puerile successors.

OTHER BRITISH FILMS INCLUDE: *They Flew Alone* (1942), *Take My Life* (1947), *Rob Roy . . .* (1953), *Value for Money* (1955), *The Bridal Path, Jazzboat* (1959), *The Trials of Oscar Wilde* (1960), *The Long Ships* (1963, UK/Yug), *The Great St Trinian's Train Robbery* (1966), *Run Wild, Run Free* (1969), *The Legend of Hell House* (1973), *Rosie Dixon – Night Nurse* (1978), *Sunburn* (1979, UK/US).

Forbes, Bryan (*b* London, 1926). Actor, screenwriter, director, producer. RN: John Clarke. To this list of descriptors might be added studio head and author. He has had one of the most varied careers in British cinema, influential at several levels, and his Cockney background did not make it easy for him – he was once rejected for a role because he wasn't 'officer material'! RADA-trained and on the London stage from 1945, he did military service (1945–48) before embarking on his film career, though he had appeared in the short, *The Tired Men* (1943). He played a steady stream of supporting roles in the late 40s and the 50s, most notably as the seducer-son of the bourgeois family upheaval when *An Inspector Calls* (1954), as well as numerous servicemen. During this time, he also wrote for *Picturegoer* under various pseudonyms.

He began screenwriting with uncredited stints on Alan Ladd films for WARWICK, *The Red Beret* and *Hell Below Zero* (both 1953), coming into his own with two films at the end of the decade – the controversial wildcat strike drama *The Angry Silence* (1960) and the witty heist caper, *The League of Gentlemen* (1960), in both of which he also acted. In their diverse ways, on matters of class and contemporary issues, these were important films. The former received an AAn, the latter a BAAn, as did *Only Two Can Play* (1961). To produce *The Angry Silence*, he and Richard ATTENBOROUGH formed BEAVER FILMS, which became part of the ALLIED FILM MAKERS consortium.

His directing debut, *Whistle Down the Wind* (1961, BAAn for best film), happened when Guy GREEN pulled out. Thereafter he directed a dozen films in which realism (*The L-Shaped Room*, 1962, + sc), romance (*The Raging Moon*, 1970, + sc), period comedy (*The Wrong Box*, 1966, + p) and fantasy (*The

Slipper and the Rose, 1976, + co-sc) found their place, films noted for their discreet observation of place and character, accuracy of dialogue, and sympathetic handling of actors. Especially, he has shown himself adept at getting the best out of larger-than-life players like Cicely COURTNEIDGE, giving the performance of her career in *The L-Shaped Room*, Kim Stanley in *Seance on a Wet Afternoon* (1964, + co-p, sc) and Dame Edith EVANS in *The Whisperers* (1966, + sc). Also directed several US films, including *King Rat* (1965), and took over *The Madwoman of Chaillot* (1969) when John HUSTON pulled out.

In 1969, he became head of production and managing director of EMI–MGM, trying to produce films which would keep the company financially viable, without creating any redundancies. Though there were some successes (e.g. *The Railway Children* and *The Go-Between*, 1971), there were insoluble labour problems and policy clashes and Forbes resigned in late 1971. In recent decades, he has written two unusually lively volumes of autobiography, a heartfelt memoir of Edith Evans, *Ned's Girl*, 1977, and a string of entertaining novels.

Married (1) Constance SMITH (1951–54) and (2) Nanette NEWMAN (1954 on), who has starred in several of his films.

OTHER BRITISH FILMS (a): *Smith, Our Friend* (1946, short), *The Small Back Room* (1948), *Dear Mr Prohack, All Over the Town* (1949), *Saturday Night* (short), *The Wooden Horse* (1950), *Green Grow the Rushes* (1951), *Appointment in London, Wheel of Fate, Sea Devils, The Million Pound Note* (1953), *Up to His Neck, The Colditz Story* (1954), *Passage Home, Now and Forever* (1955), *Satellite in the Sky, It's Great to Be Young!, The Baby and the Battleship* (+ add scenes, dial), *The Extra Day* (1956), *Quatermass 2* (1957), *I Was Monty's Double* (+ sc), *The Key* (1958), *Yesterday's Enemy* (1959), *Guns of Navarone* (1961), *A Shot in the Dark, Of Human Bondage* (+ co-d, sc) (1964), *Un danseur: Rudolph Nureyev* (1972, narr, Fr/UK), *Restless Natives* (1985); (d/sc): *Deadfall* (1968), *Better Late Than Never* (1983), *International Velvet* (1978, + p, a); (sc/co-sc): *The Black Knight* (1954), *Cockleshell Heroes* (1955), *The Black Tent, House of Secrets* (1956), *The Captain's Table, Danger Within* (1958), *SOS Pacific* (1959, dial) *Man in the Moon* (1960), *Station Six Sahara* (1962), *The High Bright Sun* (1965), *Chaplin* (1992, UK/Fr/It/Jap/US).

Forbes, Meriel (*b* London, 1913 – *d* London, 2000). Actress.
RN: Forbes-Robertson. That she is now chiefly remembered as the widow of Sir Ralph RICHARDSON does injustice to a charming actress with a comedy flair of which films made too little use. Actor-manager Frank Forbes-Robertson's daughter, she was an established West End actress by the time she met Richardson, whom she married in 1944, two years after the death of his first wife. She made only 16 films in 25 years but is memorable as Griffith JONES's *nouveau riche* fiancée in *Young Man's Fancy* (1939) and the spirited barmaid whose evidence clears Richardson of a murder charge in *Home at Seven* (1952). Played Lady Constance in TV's *Blandings Castle* (1967) with her husband.

OTHER BRITISH FILMS INCLUDE: *Borrow a Million* (1934), *Over the Moon, Come On George!* (1939), *The Day Will Dawn* (1942), *The Gentle Sex, The Bells Go Down* (1943), *The Captive Heart* (1946), *The Long Dark Hall* (1951), *Oh! What a Lovely War* (1969).

Forbes, Ralph (*b* London, 1905 – *d* New York, 1951). Actor. A
good-looking, lightweight performer, Forbes began his career in the UK, but came to the US in 1924 and began a lengthy stage and screen career there, marrying two well-known actresses, Ruth Chatterton and Heather ANGEL. His American films include *Beau Geste* (1926) and *Romeo and Juliet* (1936). His mother, **Mary Forbes** (*b* London, 1883 – *d* Beaumont, Ca, 1974), made a few silent films in Britain before moving to the US

where she often played upper-class Brits in such films as *The Picture of Dorian Gray* (1945), and his sister Brenda Forbes (*b* London, 1909) also made several US films including *Mrs Miniver* (1942).

BRITISH FILMS: *The Fifth Form at St Dominic's, A Lowland Cinderella* (1921), *Comin' Thro' the Rye* (1923), *Owd Bob, Reveille* (1924). AS.

Forbes, Scott *see* Dallas, Julian

Forbes-Robertson, Sir Johnston (*b* London, 1853 – *d* St
Margaret's Bay, 1937). Actor. Made his stage debut in 1874, played Romeo to Mrs Patrick Campbell's Juliet in 1895, and was the finest Hamlet of his day. A 1913 film version of *Hamlet* is a record of his famous farewell performance at Drury Lane, and he is impressive in the title role of *The Passing of the Third Floor Back* (1917), which also serves as a record of a characterisation created on stage in 1908. Forbes-Robertson made one other film: *Masks and Faces* (1917). AS.

Ford, Cecil (*b* Dublin, 1910 – *d* Reading, 1980). Associate
producer. Worked as production manager on 'big' films like *The Bridge on the River Kwai* (1957), *The Inn of the Sixth Happiness* (1958) and *Young Winston* (1972), as assistant director, location manager, especially on Irish-set films, and, once, as actor (*West of Kerry*, 1938, UK/Ire), in films spread over 40 years.

OTHER BRITISH FILMS INCLUDE: (ass d) *It's Hard to Be Good* (1948), *Mogambo* (UK/US), *Appointment in London* (1953); (assoc p, unless noted) *Summer of the Seventeenth Doll* (1959, UK/Aust), *The Guns of Navarone* (1961, p), *The Devil Never Sleeps* (1962), *633 Squadron* (1963, UK/US, p), *A Shot in the Dark* (1964), *All Creatures Great and Small* (1974), *It Shouldn't Happen to a Vet* (1976).

Ford, Derek (*b* Essex, 1926 – *d* Bromley, Kent, 1995). Director,
screenwriter. More prolific than distinguished, Ford's output is largely in EXPLOITATION genres, such titles as *Scream and Die* (sc, super e) and *Keep It Up, Jack!* (d, co-sc) (1973) suggesting the range. Sometimes co-wrote with brother **Donald Ford**, including one of his more 'respectable' ventures, the SHERLOCK HOLMES thriller, *A Study in Terror* (1965).

OTHER BRITISH FILMS INCLUDE: (co-sc) *The Yellow Teddybears* (1963), *Corruption* (1967), *Hell Boats* (1969), *Venom* (1971); (d/sc) *A Promise of Bed* (1969), *The Sexplorer* (1975), *What's Up Nurse?* (1977), *What's Up Superdoc?* (1978); (d/co-sc) *The Wife Swappers, Groupie Girl* (1970).

Ford, John (*b* Cape Elisabeth, Maine, 1894 – *d* Palm Desert,
California, 1973). Director. Great Irish-American film-maker, famous for his Westerns above all, who made a very few British films: *Mogambo* (1953, UK/US), *The Rising of the Moon* (1957, Ire) and *Gideon's Day* (1958), and *Young Cassidy* (1965), which Jack CARDIFF took over when Ford became ill. There are felicities in all these films, but the source of Ford's huge reputation lies elsewhere.

Ford, Mick (*b* Croydon, 1952) Actor. More familiar to TV
audiences, from such programmes as *Silent Witness* (1997) and *Fish* (2000), and theatre (*Art*, 1998), than to filmgoers. The wiry, curly-haired Ford has, however, had some substantial roles, since entering films in *The Sailor's Return* (1978) and co-starred with Trevor HOWARD in *Light Years Away* (1980, Fr/Switz).

OTHER BRITISH FILMS INCLUDE: *Scum* (1979), *The Fourth Protocol* (1987), *How to Get Ahead in Advertising* (1989).

Ford, Wallace (*b* Bolton, Lancashire, 1898 – *d* Los Angeles,
1966) Actor. Went to Hollywood in the 30s and became a popular lead and later character actor, last in *A Patch of Blue*

(1965), as a kindly drunken grandpa. Returned to Britain for three films: *Jericho* (1937), as a US racketeer in the British army in *OHMS* (1937), and *Mad About Money* (1938).

Ford Davies, Oliver (*b* London, 1939). Actor. Probably best-known as the incorruptible head of chambers in TV's *Kavanagh QC* (1994–95), an unusually persuasive study in civilised decency. Urbane and middle-aged, educated at King's School Canterbury and Oxford, he was briefly glimpsed as the Minister in his first film, *Defence of the Realm* (1985), as the Dean of Windsor in *Mrs Brown* (1997, UK/Ire/US) and in such US films as Sio Bibble in *Star Wars . . . The Phanton Menace* (1999). Best chances so far on TV and stage, the latter including long stints with the RSC and National Theatre, and a season with Ralph FIENNES in *Richard II* and *Coriolanus* (2000).
OTHER BRITISH FILMS: *Luther* (1973, UK/Can/US), *Scandal* (1988), *Paper Mask* (1990), *Sense and Sensibility* (1995, UK/US), *Mrs Dalloway* (1997, UK/Neth/US), *An Ideal Husband* (1999, UK/US), *Whatever Happened to Harold Smith?* (2000), *Blow Dry* (2001, UK/Ger/US).

Forde, Brinsley (*b* Guyana, 1952). Actor. Lead singer with the British reggae group, ASWAD, Forde had several small roles in films and the lead in *Babylon* (1980), a drama concerned with emerging black culture in Britain.
OTHER BRITISH FILMS: *The Magnificent 6½* (1967), *Leo the Last* (1969), *Diamonds Are Forever* (1971), *Please, Sir!* (1971).

Forde, Florrie (*b* Melbourne, 1876 – *d* Aberdeen, 1940). Actress. Forde made her stage debut as a legitimate actress in Sydney, 1893; came to Britain in 1897 and quickly became a popular MUSIC-HALL performer and principal boy. Forde specialised in songs with sing-a-long choruses, such as 'Down at the Old Bull and Bush', 'Has Anybody Here Seen Kelly?', and 'Hold Your Hand Out, Naughty Boy', all of which she sang to great effect in the delightfully sentimental *Say It with Flowers* (1934).
OTHER BRITISH FILMS: *My Old Dutch* (1934), *Royal Cavalcade* (1935). AS.

Forde, Walter (*b* Bradford, 1898 – *d* Los Angeles, 1984). Actor, director. RN: Thomas Seymour Woolford. The best British screen comedian of the 20s who became one of the top British directors of the 30s and 40s, and whose meek, bespectacled manner belied a determined and forceful personality. A knockabout comedian on stage in the 1910s, Forde made his film debut in 1919 with a one-reel short, *The Wanderer*, followed by a SERIES of two-reel SHORTS, which he also wrote. To Hollywood briefly in 1923, where, after a career as a Universal comedian failed, he took up house-painting. In the late 20s, he turned to editing, but, in 1928, began a new career as feature film director with *Wait and See*, in which he also starred. He graduated to dramas, including *The Ghost Train* (1931), *Condemned to Death* (1932) and his masterwork, *Rome Express* (1932), with its international cast and atmospheric set. Forde hit his stride with MUSICALS such as *Chu-Chin-Chow* (1934) and *Land without Music* (1936), with THRILLERS such as *The Four Just Men* (1939), and directing a group of fellow comedians, including Jack HULBERT in *Jack Ahoy!* (1934), Arthur ASKEY in *Charley's (Big-Hearted) Aunt* (1940), Tommy TRINDER in *Sailors Three* (1940), Tommy HANDLEY in *It's That Man Again* (1943), Sid FIELD in *Cardboard Cavalier* (1949), and the 'Inspector Hornleigh' series with Gordon HARKER. Retired to the US in 1954 with his wife, Culley, the former editor Adeline Culley, who served as his scriptgirl, constant companion and collaborator.

OTHER BRITISH FILMS INCLUDE: (d, unless noted) *The Handy Man, Never Say Die, Fishing for Trouble* (1920, + a, sc), *The Economist* (a), *Walter's Winning Ways* (a, sc), *Walter Finds a Father* (a, sc) (1921), *Walter Wins a Wager, Walter's Trying Frolics, Walter Makes a Movie, Walter Wants Work* (1922, co-d with father, Tom Seymour, + a, + sc). *Walter the Sleuth* (1926, + c, sc), *What Next?* (1928, a, co-sc), *Lord Richard in the Pantry* (1930), *The Ringer* (1931), *Lord Babs* (1932), *Jack's the Boy, Orders Is Orders* (1933), *Bulldog Jack, Forever England* (1935), *King of the Damned* (1936), *Cheer, Boys, Cheer, Inspector Hornleigh on Holiday* (1939), *Saloon Bar* (1940), *Flying Fortress* (1942), *Time Flies, One Exciting Night* (1944), *The Master of Bankdam* (1947).
BIBLIOG: Geoff Brown, *Walter Forde*, 1982. AS.

Foreman, Carl (*b* Chicago, 1914 – *d* Beverley Hills, California, 1984). Screenwriter, producer. American BLACKLIST victim of the McCarthy hearings, Foreman had had a distinguished career as writer and/or producer of such socially aware films as *The Men* (1950, AAn) and *High Noon* (1952, AAn), before leaving for the comparative political tolerance of Britain. Even there, he had first to work under another name (Derek Frye) on such films as *The Sleeping Tiger* (1954), directed pseudo-nymously by fellow-blacklistee Joseph LOSEY, and *Born for Trouble* (1955), and the Academy would not allow him to collect the Oscar for the screenplay of *Bridge on the River Kwai* (1957). In mellower times, and with his own company, Open Road, established since 1958's *The Key* (p, sc), he was nominated for the screenplays of *The Guns of Navarone* (1961) and *Young Winston* (1972), and went on to produce, write and direct *The Victors* (1963), a rather heavy-handed anti-war epic, and somewhat surprisingly to produce both *Born Free* (1965) and *Living Free* (1972). Though it gathered momentum in Britain, his career was virtually over by the time he returned to Hollywood in 1975. Created CBE in 1970.
OTHER BRITISH FILMS: *The Mouse That Roared* (1959, co-p), *Otley* (1968, ex p), *The Virgin Soldiers* (1969, ex p), *Force 10 from Navarone* (1978, ex p, story).

Forester, C(ecil) S(cott) (*b* Cairo, 1899 – *d* Fullerton, California, 1966). Author. Educated at Dulwich College, Forester was one of the great popular storytellers of the century, his adventures characterised by a confidence-creating concern for authenticity of detail. His most famous creation is the eponymous *Captain Horatio Hornblower RN* (filmed 1950, UK/US), also the subject of TV series (1998–99). Other films from his works include several US-made (e.g. the wartime propaganda piece, *Eagle Squadron*, 1942; *The Pride and the Passion*, 1957, from *The Gun*) and the British-made *Brown on Resolution* (1935), its remake *Single-Handed* (1953), *The African Queen* (1951) and *Sink the Bismarck!* (1960).

Forlong, Michael (*b* Wanganui, NZ, *c* 1914 – *d* Javea, Spain, 2000). Director. Entered films in 1937 in NZ, after working in theatre and radio there; also filmed in India and Norway (*Suicide Mission*, 1954, d, p, sc), becoming known for 2nd unit work on such films as *Alexander the Great* and *Odongo* (1956) and EALING's Australian-made *Bitter Springs* (1950). He directed/produced/wrote several modest films in the 60s and 70s.
OTHER BRITISH FILMS: *Dunkirk* (1958, assoc p); (d) *The Green Helmet, Over the Odds* (1961), *Stork Talk* (1962); (d, p, sc/co-sc) *Lionheart* (1968), *Raising the Roof* (1971), *Rangi's Catch* (1972, serial).

Forman, Sir Denis (*b* Moffat, Scotland, 1917). Executive. Cambridge-educated Forman became interested in the training possibilities of film in the Army in WW2. Post-war, he joined the Film Division of the Central Office of Information, becoming its chief production officer in 1948. As director of the BFI (1949–55), having been encouraged to apply for the post by John GRIERSON, with whom he had worked at the CROWN FILM UNIT, he set about revivifying the Institute and its chief publication, SIGHT AND SOUND; was also Chairman of its Board of Governors, 1971–73. In 1955 he joined Granada Television as Joint Managing Director, becoming chairman (1975) when Lord [Sidney] BERNSTEIN retired, overseeing such prestigious productions as *The Jewel in the Crown* (1984). Much respected and crowned with awards (e.g. BFI Fellowship, 1993), he has been an influential commentator on as well as administrator of British film and TV, and his views are preserved in such publications as *The Cinema 1951* (1951) and *The Film and the Public* (1955). Hugh HUDSON's *My Life So Far* (2000) derives from Forman's early life.

Formby, George (b Wigan, 1904 – d Preston, Lancashire, 1961). Actor. 'I wasn't very good but people seemed to like me', remarked Formby and for several years he was Britain's most popular film star, and one of the highest-paid. Beginning in northern MUSIC HALLS, where his father, George Sr, billed as 'The Wigan Nightingale', had been a popular singing comedian, he became known in the south only with movie success in the mid 30s. He played essentially gormless incompetents, aspiring to various kinds of professional success (as, say, cyclist or jockey) and even more improbably to a middle-class girlfriend, usually in the clutches of some caddish type with a moustache. Invariably he scored on both counts, in such films as *No Limit* (1935), *Keep Fit* (1937), and *Trouble Brewing* (1939). These artless narratives, interspersed with songs of Formby's own composition and accompanied by him on the ukelele, are unpretentiously skilful in their balance between broad comedy and action, laced with his shy ordinariness. The sly sexual content of some of the songs is sung with such a toothy grin and air of innocence that offence was kept at bay. Love scenes, with the likes of Phyllis CALVERT (who marvelled at the brilliance of his timing), Dinah SHERIDAN, Linden TRAVERS, Kay WALSH and Googie WITHERS were, allegedly, controlled with a stopwatch by Formby's ever-watchful wife **Beryl Formby** who appeared with him in *Boots! Boots!* (1934, + co-sc) and *Off the Dole* (1935, + co-sc). When he got engaged shortly after her death (1960), he explained that her drinking had long undermined the happiness of their marriage. He is comic ancestor to Norman WISDOM.

OTHER BRITISH FILMS (a, unless noted): *By the Shortest of Heads* (1915), *Keep Your Seats, Please* (1936), *Feather Your Nest* (1937), *It's in the Air, I See Ice!* (1938, + co-m, lyrics), *Come on George!* (1939, + co-m, lyrics), *Let George Do It!* (+ co-m, lyrics), *Spare a Copper* (1940), *Turned Out Nice Again*, *South American George* (1941), *We'll Meet Again* (assoc p), *Much Too Shy* (1942), *Get Cracking* (1943), *Bell-Bottom George, He Snoops to Conquer* (1944), *I Didn't Do It* (1945), *George in Civvy Street* (1946).

Forrest, John (b Connecticut, 1931). Actor. On stage from 1945 and entered films as young Herbert Pocket in *Great Expectations* (1946). Played schoolboys in *The Guinea Pig* (1948) and (Flashman, no less) in *Tom Brown's Schooldays* (1951).

OTHER BRITISH FILMS INCLUDE: *Bonnie Prince Charlie* (1948), *Adam and Evelyne* (1949), *The Franchise Affair* (1950), *The Gift Horse* (1952), *Very Important Person* (1961), *The Bawdy Adventures of Tom Jones* (1975).

Forrestal, Terry (b Chesterfield, 1948 – d Norway, 2000). Stunt coordinator. After travelling the world and starting a medical course, Forrestal joined the Territorial Army in 1975, graduated to the SAS at Hereford, serving in Ireland, and left in

the mid 80s to concentrate on films. He became one of filmdom's leading stunt coordinators, very daring and imaginative but thorough in his planning. He worked on such international films as *Batman* (1989) and *Titanic* (1997, + a), but mostly on such British successes as *The Killing Fields* (1984), combat sequences being a specialty of his, *Mona Lisa* (1986), *Trainspotting* (1996) and *Elizabeth* (1998). He died in a 'base-jumping' accident in Norway when something went wrong with a parachute jump from a 900-metre cliff.

OTHER BRITISH FILMS INCLUDE: *The Long Good Friday* (1979), *Flash Gordon* (1980, a), *An American Werewolf in London* (1981, UK/US), *Krull* (1983), *Greystoke . . .* (1984, UK/US), *Brazil* (+ a), *Insignificance* (1985), *Bellman & True* (1987), *Without a Clue* (1988, US/UK), *The Young Americans* (1993), *Shopping* (1994), *Loch Ness* (1996), *The Full Monty* (US/UK), *Amy Foster* (UK/Fr/US), *The Borrowers* (1997), *Martha, Meet Frank, Daniel and Laurence* (1998).

Forster, E(dward) M(organ) (b London, 1879 – d Coventry, 1970). Author. Film-makers gave Forster's novels a wide berth until the 80s, when suddenly five were filmed in rapid succession. David LEAN's last film was *A Passage to India* (1984), then there were three by MERCHANT IVORY: *A Room with a View* (1985), the team's first mainstream success; *Maurice* (1987), from the novel suppressed in Forster's life-time because of its overtly homosexual themes; and *Howards End* (1992), a finely crafted chronicle of class and sex conflict; and *Where Angels Fear to Tread* (1991), directed by Charles STURRIDGE. There was a TV version of *A Passage* in 1965, and Forster wrote a commentary for Humphrey JENNINGS' DOCUMENTARY, *Diary for Timothy* (1946).

Forster-Jones, Glenna (b Sierra Leone, 1945). Actress. There have been few major roles for black actresses in British films and Forster-Jones had some good parts in the 60s, especially as the girl saved from prostitution by *Leo the Last* (1969), but nothing much since.

OTHER BRITISH FILMS: *Sympathy for the Devil, Joanna* (1968), *The Spy's Wife* (1971, short), *The Human Factor* (1979, UK/US), *Flash Gordon* (1980), *The Punk* (1993).

Forsyth, Bill (b Glasgow, 1947). Director, screenwriter. After working on DOCUMENTARIES and other SHORTS, he came to prominence with the charming *Gregory's Girl* (1980, + sc), the romance of a shy soccer hero and the girl who insists on joining his team. This was written, directed and played with an acute and sensitive feeling for teenage life and found a wide, appreciative audience. It was followed by the equally attractive *Local Hero* (1983, + sc), a latter-day EALING-style piece about an American tycoon outmanoeuvred by Scottish islanders, with a sharp aftertaste that suggested MACKENDRICK rather than the softer Ealing alumni, and *Comfort and Joy* (1984), which adroitly combined burgeoning romance and an ice cream war in Glasgow. After two unremarkable US films, *Housekeeping* (1987, + sc), which has a certain cult following, and *Breaking In* (1989), he returned to Britain for a major flop, *Being Human* (1994), with Robin Williams and, as if to recoup credit, *Gregory's Two Girls* (1999). Forsyth's is a gentle talent, nourished by the observation of human singularity and free of easy sentimentality.

OTHER BRITISH FILMS: (shorts) *Mackintosh 1868–1928* (1968, e), *Mirror* (1970, a), *Islands of the West* (1972, d), *Shapes in the Water* (1974, d), *Robert Adam – Architect* (1975, d), *Tree Country* (1976, d), *Long Shot* (1978, a); (feature, d/sc): *That Sinking Feeling* (1979, + p).

Forsyth, Bruce (b London, 1928). Actor. Best known as a remorselessly jocular TV games show host (e.g. *The Generation*

Game, 1971–77, reprised 1990–94), Forsyth trained as a dancer, made stage debut in 1942, and went on to work mainly in variety. Quit TV in 2000, with widely targeted acrimonious swipes. So far, films have scarcely detained him, and his best role was as Gertrude LAWRENCE's father in *Star!* (1968).

BRITISH FILMS: *Can Hieronymous Merkin Ever Forget . . .* (1969), *The Magnificent Seven Deadly Sins* (1971), *Pavlova: A Woman for All Time* (1983), *House!* (2000).

Forsyth, Frederick (*b* Ashford, Kent, 1938). Author. Best-selling novelist, several times adapted to the British screen. The most popular film was probably *The Day of the Jackal* (1973, UK/Fr), about an assassination attempt on General De Gaulle; others include *The Odessa File* (1974, UK/Ger), *The Dogs of War* (1980), *The Fourth Protocol* (1987, + co-ex p, sc), and TV adaptations of his work, in the series *Frederick Forsyth Presents* (1989–90).

Forsythe, Blanche Actress. A leading lady with BARKER MOTION PICTURE PHOTOGRAPHY and star of its two best known films, *East Lynne* (1913) and *Jane Shore* (1915). Described tersely by Rachael Low as a 'plump demure English girl.'

OTHER BRITISH FILMS INCLUDE: *How Vandyke Won His Wife* (1912), *A Little Girl Shall Lead Them, Sixty Years a Queen* (1913), *Jim the Fireman* (1914), *Brigadier Gerard* (1915), *A Just Deception* (1917). AS.

Fortescue, Kenneth (*b* Kew). Actor. After leaving Dulwich College and RADA, Fortescue had considerable radio and theatre experience before entering films in the late 50s as juvenile lead in such films as *Desert Mice* (1959). Showed promise in comedy but good roles failed to materialise.

OTHER BRITISH FILMS INCLUDE: *The Barretts of Wimpole Street* (1956), *High Flight* (1957), *Don't Bother to Knock* (1961), *Lawrence of Arabia* (1962), *The Brides of Fu Manchu* (1966), *Up the Front* (1972), *The Mirror Crack'd* (1980).

Forwood, Anthony (*b* Weymouth, 1920 – *d* London, 1988). Actor. Former stage actor and agent, and in a dozen minor films (*Black Widow*, 1951) or minor roles (John MCCALLUM's ex-RAF pal in *Travellers' Joy*, 1949), before becoming personal manager of Dirk BOGARDE. They shared a house in Provence for many years and Bogarde has written movingly of their friendship and of Forwood's death. Formerly married to Glynis JOHNS; Gareth Forwood (*see* Glynis JOHNS) is their son.

OTHER BRITISH FILMS INCLUDE: *The Man in Black* (1949), *Captain Horatio Hornblower RN* (1950, UK/US), *The Story of Robin Hood . . .* (1952), *Appointment in London* (1953), *Five Days* (1954).

Foss, Kenelm (*b* Croydon, 1885 – *d* London, 1963). Director, writer. A busy rather than important director and writer, who entered films in 1915 with the LONDON FILM COMPANY, collaborating with George Loane TUCKER, as writer on *The Shulamite* (1915), *The Manxman* (1916), etc, after an earlier career in the theatre as an actor, manager and producer. Tried his hand unsuccessfully at independent production in 1919 and 1920; ended life as owner of a snack bar.

OTHER BRITISH FILMS INCLUDE: (sc) *The Man without a Soul* (1916), *The Grit of a Jew* (1917), *Peace, Perfect Peace, The Wages of Sin* (1918); (d) *A Little Bit of Fluff* (1919, + sc), *A Bachelor Husband* (1920), *The Headmaster, The Double Event, The Wonderful Year* (1921, + sc), *Dicky Montieth, The House of Peril* (1922, + sc). AS.

Foster, Aida (*b* London). Agent. Before becoming a theatrical agent in 1944, she had run a dance (and later more general) school since 1929. Her best known discovery was Jean SIMMONS, but there were many others in the 40s. Closed the School in 1970 but continued to run the Aida Foster Theatrical Agency.

Foster, Barry (*b* Beeston, Nottinghamshire,1930 – *d* Guildford, 2002). Actor. Sandy-haired supporting actor, an enjoyable smart alec in *The Family Way* (1966) and sleazily charming murderer in HITCHCOCK's *Frenzy* (1972), as well as regular ranker in 50s WAR FILMS. Trained at Central School, on London stage from 1955, very arresting in *Passion Play* (1984), and much excellent TV, including the starring role in crime series *Van der Valk* (1972–73, 1977, 1991–92).

OTHER BRITISH FILMS INCLUDE: *Yangtse Incident* (1956), *Sea of Sand, Dunkirk* (1958), *Yesterday's Enemy* (1959), *Surprise Package* (1960), *Playback* (1962), *King and Country* (1964), *Robbery* (1967), *Twisted Nerve* (1968), *Ryan's Daughter* (1970), *Sweeney!* (1976), *The Wild Geese* (1978, UK/Switz), *Heat and Dust* (1982), *The Whistle Blower* (1986), *Maurice* (1987), *Rancid Aluminium* (2000).

Foster, Dianne (*b* Edmonton, Canada, 1928). Actress. RN: Laruska. Attractive brunette Canadian who came to Britain as a child, began work as a model, and was briefly under contract to TEMPEAN FILMS, appearing in two superior 'B' MOVIES, *The Quiet Woman* (1951) and *The Lost Hours* (1952). She had the romantic lead in *Isn't Life Wonderful!* (1953), was signed by Columbia, relocated to the US and returned to Britain only for John FORD's *Gideon's Day* (1958). Retired in 1963.

Foster, Dorothy Actress. A leading lady from 1910 to 1913 with the BRITISH AND COLONIAL KINEMATOGRAPH COMPANY, seen in the films shot by the company in Wales and Cornwall and often featured in the *Lt Daring* series.

BRITISH FILMS INCLUDE: *The Baby, the Boy and the Teddy Bear* (1910), *A Soldier's Sweetheart* (1911), *Hamlet, A Cornish Romance, A Factory Girl's Honour* (1912), *The Planter's Daughter* (1913). AS.

Foster, Dudley (*b* Harrogate, 1925 – *d* London, 1973). Actor. Supporting player of TV and films, from 1962 as a detective in *Term of Trial*. Second-last film role was as a thin-lipped undertaker killed in a 'chicken' race to the cemetery with his rival, in *That's Your Funeral* (1972). Committed suicide.

OTHER BRITISH FILMS INCLUDE: *Ricochet* (1963), *A Study in Terror* (1965), *Where's Jack?* (1969), *Wuthering Heights* (1970), *Dulcima* (1971), *Follow Me!* (1972), *Mistress Pamela* (1973).

Foster, Julia (*b* Lewes, 1941). Actress. Entered films as one of the girls who go off for the weekend with Tom COURTENAY and friend in *The Loneliness of the Long Distance Runner* (1962), showed touching vulnerability and warmth as one of *Alfie's* (1966) cast-offs, and charm and gaiety as Tommy STEELE's leading lady in *Half a Sixpence* (1967, UK/US). Films cut out in the early 70s, but she continued on stage, including title role in *Lulu* (1970) and TV, including Margaret of Anjou in *Henry VI* (1983).

OTHER BRITISH FILMS INCLUDE: *The Small World of Sammy Lee* (1962), *One Way Pendulum, The System* (1964), *Percy, All Coppers Are . . .* (1971), *The Great McGonagall* (1974).

Fowlds, Derek (*b* London, 1937). Actor. Diffident-seeming supporting actor, RADA-trained, who became a household name and face as whipping-boy Bernard in TV's *Yes Minister* (1980–82) and *Yes Prime Minister* (1986–88), and, surprisingly aged, as tetchy Sgt Blaketon in *Heartbeat* (1992–2001). His dozen films have given him nothing so choice.

BRITISH FILMS INCLUDE: *We Joined the Navy, Tamahine* (1962), *Doctor in Distress* (1963), *East of Sudan* (1964), *Frankenstein Created Woman* (1966), *Tower of Evil* (1972), *Mistress Pamela* (1973), *They Never Slept* (1990).

Fowle, H(enry) E(dward) ('Chick') (*b* London – *d* England, 1995). Cinematographer. With a background in DOCUMEN-

TARY film-making, Fowle shot many wartime and post-war SHORT FILMS, including several famous ones for Humphrey JENNINGS, such as *Spare Time* (1939), *Listen to Britain* (1942) and *The Cumberland Story* (1947), helping to realise Jennings' poetic vision. Post-war, he entered features, under contract to WESSEX FILMS, lensing two for CROWN colleague, Jack LEE, *The Woman in the Hall* (1947) and *Once a Jolly Swagman* (1948), whose hour-long documentary, *Children on Trial* (1946) he also photographed. From the 50s on worked in Brazil, influenced no doubt by his association with CROWN alumnus CAVALCANTI.

OTHER BRITISH FILMS INCLUDE: (doc, short, co-c) *The King's Stamp* (1935), *Night Mail* (1936), *North Sea* (1938), *Britain Can Take It* (1940); (doc, c): *News for the Navy* (1938), *Men in Danger* (1939), *Health in War* (1940), *We Sail at Midnight* (1943, cam op, UK/US), (feature, co-c): *Esther Waters* (1948); (feature, c): *Dear Mr Prohack* (1949), *Morning Departure* (1950, add c).

Fowler, Harry (*b* Lambeth, London, 1926). Actor. Former newspaper boy interviewed by Roy RICH on radio's *In Town Tonight* and cast as evacuee in *Those Kids from Town* (1942). Skinny, beaky-nosed, an authentic Cockney and a natural actor, he was virtually never out of work again, irresistibly resourceful and cheeky in several EALING films ('Ealing was like a university to me', he said in 1992), most notably as the leader of the kids' gang in *Hue and Cry* (1946). He played whatever came along: 'B' MOVIES, such as *The Last Page* and *13 East Street* (1952) and smaller roles in main features including *High Treason* (1951), *The Pickwick Papers* (1952, as Sam Weller) and *Lawrence of Arabia* (1962). He early developed an effortlessly authoritative presence, so that even in brief appearances, like the sullen young tearaway in the opening scenes of *Tomorrow at Ten* (1962) or the milkman in a moment with Bette DAVIS in *The Nanny* (1965), or in films of surpassing idiocy like *Fire Maidens from Outer Space* (1956), he stays in the mind. In later years (with the moustache that made him look his age rather than the teenager he suggested well into his 30s), he popped up in TV's *World's End* (1981) or an episode of *The Bill*, as reliably entertaining as ever. His first wife was actress Joan DOWLING (1951 until her death, 1954). Awarded MBE, 1970.

OTHER BRITISH FILMS INCLUDE: *Went the Day Well?* (1942), *The Demi-Paradise* (1943), *Don't Take It to Heart!*, *Champagne Charlie* (1944), *Painted Boats* (1945), *Trouble in the Air* (1948), *Once a Sinner*, *Dance Hall* (1950), *There Is Another Sun* (1951), *I Believe in You*, *Angels One Five* (1952), *Top of the Form*, *A Day to Remember* (1953), *Up to His Neck*, *Conflict of Wings* (1954), *The Blue Peter*, *Stock Car* (1955), *Behind the Headlines* (1956), *The Birthday Present*, *West of Suez*, *Lucky Jim* (1957), *I Was Monty's Double*, *The Diplomatic Corpse*, *Idle on Parade* (1958), *The Heart of a Man* (1959), *Crooks Anonymous* (1962), *Ladies Who Do*, *Father Came Too!*, *Clash by Night* (1963), *Life at the Top* (1965), *Doctor in Clover* (1966), *George and Mildred* (1980), *Just a Walk in the Dark* (1983, short), *Chicago Joe and the Showgirl* (1989).

Fox, Bernard (*b* England, 1930). Actor. Made a handful of British films, including two for Vernon SEWELL, *Soho Incident* and *Home and Away* (1956), often as blusterous types, before heading for the US and a long career on TV (notably in *Bewitched*, 1967–72) and the occasional film, including *Titanic* (1997). In later years, best known as M.C. at Mayfair Music Hall, Santa Monica.

OTHER BRITISH FILMS: *The Counterfeit Plan*, *Blue Murder at St Trinian's*, *The Safecracker* (1957), *A Night to Remember* (1958).

Fox, Edward (*b* London, 1937). Actor. Eldest son of agent Robin Fox, brother of JAMES FOX, has quietly racked up a very impressive list of theatre, television and film credits, including nearly 40 of the latter since first seen in bit roles – as a barman in *This Sporting Life* (1963), for instance. Even in bits he was noticeable, and he went on to hone his very English persona so as to suggest with equal conviction generosity, as in his beautiful performance as Trimingham in *The Go-Between* (1971, BAA), sympathetic cynicism, as in his world-battered Krogstad in *A Doll's House* (1973, UK/Fr), or bitterness, as the second-rate actor in *The Dresser* (1983). He has perhaps the most *courteous* smile in films, but it doesn't always mean the same. Harrow-educated Fox had a major starring role as the cold-blooded assassin in *The Day of the Jackal* (1973), was Harold MacMillan to the life on stage in *Letter of Resignation* (1998), and has done remarkable TV, including the indolent Harthouse in *Hard Times* (1977) and disreputable Uncle Giles in *Dance to the Music of Time* (1997). Once married to Tracy REED; his partner of over 30 years is Joanna DAVID and their daughter is Emilia Fox, both seen in TV's *Pride and Prejudice* (1995). Awarded OBE, 2003.

OTHER BRITISH FILMS INCLUDE: *The Mind Benders* (1963), *Morgan: A Suitable Case for Treatment*, *Life At the Top*, *The Frozen Dead*, *The Jokers* (1966), *The Long Duel*, *The Naked Runner* (1967), *Battle of Britain*, *Oh! What a Lovely War* (1969), *The Breaking of Bumbo* (1970), *Galileo* (1974, UK/Can), *A Bridge Too Far*, *The Duellists* (1977), *The Big Sleep*, *Force 10 From Navarone* (1978), *The Cat and The Canary* (1979), *The Mirror Crack'd* (1980), *Gandhi* (1982, UK/Ind), *Never Say Never Again* (UK/US), *The Shooting Party*, *The Bounty* (1984), *Wild Geese II* (1985), *Return from the River Kwai* (1988), *A Feast at Midnight* (1994), *A Month by the Lake* (1995, US/UK), *Prince Valiant* (UK/Ire/US), *After Murder Park* (1997), *Lost in Space* (1998, UK/US), *The Importance of Being Earnest* (2002, UK/US).

Fox, James (*b* London, 1939). Actor. Younger brother of Edward FOX, he began as child actor (William Fox), playing the son in *The Miniver Story* (1950) and starring as the mendacious owner of *The Magnet* (1950). As adult, he changed his name from William (to avoid confusion with character actor William FOX) to James, made a vivid impression as the public-school competitor for Tom COURTENAY in *The Loneliness of the Long Distance Runner* (1962) and was a brilliant foil to Dirk BOGARDE in *The Servant* (1963, BAA/best newcomer) in which his blond good looks were subsumed into an overriding vacuity, a supine need to be waited on. Thirty years later he gave a resonant reworking of this character in *The Remains of the Day* (1993), a well-meaning fascist now nannied by a devoted butler. In between, he gave a string of excellent performances in such diverse fare as *Those Magnificent Men . . .* (1965), as an engaging young flyer, and *Performance* (1970), as a vicious thug with an increasing problem of identity; took over a decade off to work with a religious group; and returned in the 80s to become, like his brother, a major character star. He seems natural casting for patrician types, as in Bill DOUGLAS's wonderful *Comrades* (1986), but his Fielding in *A Passage to India* (1984) is a deeply felt liberal, his chilling Karenin is the *only* thing worth attention in *Anna Karenina* (1997, US), and, in TV's *The Choir* (1995), he is persuasively mean-minded. Other US films include *Thoroughly Modern Millie* (1967) and *Patriot Games* (1992).

OTHER BRITISH FILMS: *Tamahine* (1962), *Duffy*, *Isadora* (1968), *Runners*, *Pavlova: A Woman for All Time* (UK/Russia) (1983) *Greystoke . . .* (UK/US), *Film No. 1* (short) (1984), *Absolute Beginners*, *The Whistle Blower* (1986), *High Season* (1987), *She's Been Away* (1989, TV, some cinemas), *The Russia House* (1990), *Afraid of the Dark* (1991, UK/Fr), *Hostage*, *As You Like It* (1992), *The Shadow Run*, *Mickey Blue*

Eyes (1999, UK/US), *The Golden Bowl* (US/Fr/UK), *All Forgotten* (UK/US) (2000), *Sexy Beast* (UK/Sp/US) (2001).

BIBLIOG: Autobiography, *Comeback*, 1983.

Fox, Kerry (*b* Wellington, NZ, 1966). Actress. Brilliant international star (though more actress than star) of the 90s, first noticed as tormented NZ novelist Janet Frame in Jane Campion's biopic, *An Angel at My Table* (1992), with a frizz of red hair and striking intensity of feeling. Since then, she has filmed in Australia (very affecting in the little-seen *The Sound of One Hand Clapping*, 1998), Canada (*The Hanging Garden*, 1997, UK/Can), Kenya (*To Walk with Lions*, 2000, UK/Can/Kenya) and the UK. Her most eye-catching British films are the black comedy cult success, *Shallow Grave* (1994), as one of the Edinburgh flatmates trying to dispose of a body, and *Welcome to Sarajevo* (1997, UK/US) as the TV producer after more 'graphic' footage; and in 2001 she was involved in some controversially frank sex scenes in *Intimacy* (UK/Fr).

OTHER BRITISH FILMS: *Friends* (1993, UK/Fr), *Saigon Baby* (1995), *The Wisdom of Crocodiles* (1998), *The Darkest Light, Fanny and Elvis* (1999), *The Point Men* (2001).

Fox, William (*b* Manila, Philippines, 1911 – *d* 1987). Actor. Central School-trained character actor, on stage from 1930, appearing in London and New York, with the BBC Repertory Company (1952–53, 1963–65), and in a handful of films, including *She Always Gets Their Man* (1962) as a fake millionaire in yachting attire. Married (2) Patricia HILLIARD.

OTHER BRITISH FILMS: *The Secret Partner* (1961), *What Every Woman Wants* (1962), *Ransom* (1974), *Mata Hari* (1984).

Fox–British Pictures Throughout the 30s, Fox made 'QUOTA QUICKIES' at its WEMBLEY STUDIOS, to comply with the law relating to the quota of British films exhibitors were required to screen. This law led Fox–British to produce its own shoddy second features cheaply rather than acquiring them from other companies. Some higher-level productions there included Maurice ELVEY's *Who Goes Next?* (1938), shortly after which Fox decided to close Wembley.

See **Hollywood studios in Britain**.

Foxwell, Ivan (*b* London, 1914 – *d* Lincoln, 2002). Producer. The son of the author of the children's comic book, *Tiger Tim*, Wellington-educated Foxwell entered the industry in 1932, as technical assistant at BRITISH AND DOMINIONS PRODUCTIONS, as a result of a chance meeting with Tom WALLS. He also worked with several other companies before going to Paris in 1937, working as producer with Curtis Bernhardt on *Carrefour* (1938, Fr) among other films. After WW2 service (1939–46), he returned to British films as producer and co-screenwriter on about ten films, including a lively, varied batch of four with director Guy HAMILTON: *The Intruder* (1953, p), an undervalued study of post-war malaise; the POW escape film, *The Colditz Story* (1954); an erotic melodrama, *Manuela* (1957); and a romantic comedy, *A Touch of Larceny* (1959, BAAn for sc). His second wife, from 1992, was actress Zena MARSHALL.

OTHER BRITISH FILMS (p, co-sc, unless noted): *No Room at the Inn* (1948), *Guilt Is My Shadow* (1950), *24 Hours of a Woman's Life* (1952), *Tiara Tahiti* (1962, BAAn for sc), *The Quiller Memorandum* (1966, UK/US, p), *Decline and Fall* ... (1968).

Fragile Films This company, set up in 1996, has been largely responsible for such successful films as *Spice World* (1997) and *An Ideal Husband* (1999, UK/US), and bought EALING STUDIOS in 2000, with a view to turning it into 'a next generation digital studio, the first of its kind in Europe', said

Uri Fruchtmann, its co-founder (with Barnaby Thompson).

Frain, James (*b* Leeds, 1968). Actor. Central School-trained actor of the 90s, dark, slight and intense, who has come to notice on stage (with the Peter Hall Company, 1993, and with the RSC, 1995), on TV (as sensitive, lame Philip Wakem in *The Mill on the Floss*, 1997) and in a string of high-profile films. In *Loch Ness* (1996), he was an earnest young Scot; he was the Spanish Ambassador in *Elizabeth* (1998, UK); the French filmmaker *Vigo* (1998, UK/Fr); conductor Daniel Barenboim in *Hilary and Jackie* (1998); and the short-lived Bassanius in *Titus* (2000, UK/US), one of a number of international productions, also including *Sunshine* (2000, UK/Austria/Can/Ger/Hung), as Ralph FIENNES' quick-tempered brother.

OTHER BRITISH FILMS INCLUDE: *Shadowlands* (1993, UK/US), *An Awfully Big Adventure, Nothing Personal* (1995), *What Rats Won't Do* (1998), *The Count of Monte Cristo* (2002, UK/US).

Frampton, Harry (*b* Kingston-on-Thames, *c* 1915 – *d* Weybridge, *c* 1992). Make-up artist. For over 30 years, a distinguished practitioner of his craft, with credits on many EALING films, especially those of Basil DEARDEN for whom he often worked after Dearden left Ealing. His triumph, though, must surely have been turning Alec GUINNESS into eight different people in *Kind Hearts and Coronets* (1949). Son, Peter FRAMPTON, is also a make-up artist.

OTHER BRITISH FILMS INCLUDE: *Frieda* (1947), *Scott of the Antarctic, Saraband for Dead Lovers* (1948), *Passport to Pimlico, The Blue Lamp* (1949), *Cage of Gold, Pool of London* (1950), *Mandy, The Gentle Gunman* (1952), *Lease of Life, The Rainbow Jacket* (1954), *The Ship That Died of Shame* (1955), *The Smallest Show on Earth* (1957), *Nowhere to Go* (1958), *The League of Gentlemen* (1960), *Victim, Spare the Rod* (1961), *Life for Ruth, The L-Shaped Room* (1962), *The Mind Benders* (1963), *Masquerade, The Fighting Prince of Donegal* (1966), *The Assassination Bureau* (1968), *Frenzy* (1972), *Victor/Victoria* (1982).

Frampton, Peter (*b* Weybridge, 1950) Make-up artist. Oscared for *Braveheart* (1995, UK/US, + BAAn) and shared-BAA for *Greystoke* . . . (1984, UK/US), Frampton has been involved in some key British films of recent decades, including *The Emerald Forest* (1985, co-BAAn), *Withnail & I* (1986) and *Henry V* (1989). Son of Harry FRAMPTON, with whom he worked on several of his earliest films, including *Straw Dogs, I, Monster* (1971) and *Frenzy* (1972).

OTHER BRITISH FILMS INCLUDE: *Death Line* (1972), *Trail of the Pink Panther, Pink Floyd The Wall, Victor/Victoria* (1982), *Lady Jane* (1985), *Absolute Beginners, Sid and Nancy* (BAAn) (1986), *Without a Clue, Pascali's Island* (1988, UK/US), *Under Suspicion* (1991), *Peter's Friends* (1992), *Little Buddha* (1993, UK/Fr).

France and British cinema The first commercial film programme in Britain was French, courtesy of the Lumières. French companies were prominent in the pre-WW1 years, GAUMONT and PATHÉ each establishing local production bases and NEWSREELS which kept their names before the British public for decades. French stars in British films are almost invariably debonair, sophisticated or uninhibited lovers: Maurice Chevalier teamed with Jack BUCHANAN in René Clair's *Break the News* (1938); Michèle MORGAN in *The Fallen Idol* (1948); Françoise ROSAY and Paul DUPUIS, EALING's resident (Canadian-)Frenchman, in *Johnny Frenchman* (1945); Simone SIGNORET in *Room at the Top* (1958); Brigitte BARDOT in *Doctor at Sea* (1955). French directors in Britain include René Clair (*The Ghost Goes West*), Jacques Feyder (*Knight Without Armour*); Edmond GREVILLE (*Brief Ecstasy*), and the *nouvelle vague* brought François Truffaut

(*Fahrenheit 451*) and even Jean-Luc Godard (*One Plus One*). France as a theme in British films has usually meant 'gay Paree', as visited by the *Innocents in Paris* (1953), thrilled at their first flight to this exotic other land, or the similarly simpleminded *The Lyons in Paris* (1954), though it has more sinister connotations in *So Long at the Fair* (1950). Among the more memorable French-themed titles are *Moulin Rouge* (1928), showing the heartache behind the glamour; *Henry V* (1944), where the French at Agincourt, for reasons of PROPAGANDA, represent Nazi Germany; Alec GUINNESS and Stanley HOLLOWAY's descent of the Eiffel Tower in *The Lavender Hill Mob* (1951); Edward FOX as the chilling would-be assassin of De Gaulle in *The Day of the Jackal* (1973, UK/Fr); and the immaculate recreation of the 1924 Paris Olympic Games in *Chariots of Fire* (1981). Two of the most notable French-themed films, however, take place in London: Rene Clément's witty, sexy *Knave of Hearts* (1954), with Gérard Philipe as the knowing Frenchman working his romantic way through the city; and *Passport to Pimlico* (1949), where an escape from post-war austerity is in learning that Pimlico is really part of Burgundy. Peter SELLERS' Inspector Clouseau in the *Pink Panther* films is a grotesque comic turn that is now thankfully rather out of date. Luke McKernan.

France, C(harles) V(ernon) (*b* Bradford, 1868 – *d* Gerrards Cross, 1949). Actor. The sort of stage actor (from 1891) who will always be described as 'distinguished', and possibly was: it means he usually played Squires and Admirals and spent a lot of time in dinner jackets. France made a couple of silents, including *The Blue Bird* (1910, as Time), then returned in 1930 to play 20-odd upper-class types, including Jill ESMOND's intransigent father in *The Skin Game* (1931), the Archbishop of Canterbury in *Victoria the Great* (1937) and, stiff as he tended to be on screen, still touching as the Vicar in *Went the Day Well?* (1942).

OTHER BRITISH FILMS INCLUDE: *The Loves of Robert Burns* (1930), *Black Coffee* (1931), *Royal Cavalcade, Scrooge* (1935), *Broken Blossoms* (1936), *A Yank at Oxford* (1937), *Night Train to Munich* (1940), *The Halfway House* (1944).

Francis, Derek (*b* Brighton, 1923 – *d* London, 1984). Actor. Specialist in pompous, professional men, like the heroine's unsympathetic father in *Bitter Harvest* (1963) or Lord Kingsclere in *The Wicked Lady* (1983), and at his best in TV's *Winter Sunlight* (1984) as an oppressively selfish husband. Five 'CARRY ONS' dealt his pomposity some blows.

OTHER BRITISH FILMS INCLUDE: *The Criminal* (1960), *No Love for Johnnie* (1961), *Backfire!, Captain Clegg* (1962), *The Comedy Man* (1963), *The Tomb of Ligeia* (1964), *Press for Time* (1966), *Carry On Doctor* (1968), . . . *Camping* (1969), *Scrooge* (1970), *Carry on Abroad* (1972), *Jabberwocky* (1977), *A Christmas Carol* (1984).

Francis, Freddie (*b* London, 1917). Cinematographer, director. One of the greatest of all cinematographers, he has won two AAs: for *Sons and Lovers* (1960) and *Glory* (1989, US). In 1999, he completed filming of David Lynch's *The Straight Story* (1999) in 28 days of arduous location shooting in Iowa. Starting as clapper-loader, Francis advanced through the ranks to assistant cameraman, and during WW2 was camera operator in the ARMY KINEMATOGRAPHIC UNIT. After the war, he worked on such films as *Mine Own Executioner* (1947), *Outcast of the Islands* (1951), *Beat the Devil* (1953, UK/It/US), and *Moby Dick* (1956, + 2ud, unc), until he was given *A Hill in Korea* (1956) as full-fledged cinematographer. Francis continued in this role on such films as *Time Without Pity* (1957), *Room at the*

Top (1958), *Saturday Night and Sunday Morning* (1960), and *The Innocents* (1961), before breaking into feature direction with *Two and Two Make Six* (1962) and *The Brain* (1962). However, it was HAMMER which gave Francis his biggest break, assigning him the direction of the suspense film *Paranoiac* (1962), which immediately put him on the map as a HORROR director, though he maintains he has little affection for the genre. Nevertheless, with such films as *Dr Terror's House of Horrors* (1964), *The Skull* (1965) and *Torture Garden* (1967), he became irrevocably typecast as a horror film-maker. In disgust, Francis withdrew from directing and was chosen to shoot David Lynch's first major feature film, *The Elephant Man* (1980, UK/US). His work as cinematographer since, including *The French Lieutenant's Woman* (1981) and *The Executioner's Song* (1982), has confirmed his reputation as one of Britain's finest craftsmen.

OTHER BRITISH FILMS INCLUDE: (cam op) *The Small Back Room* (1948), *Golden Salamander* (1949), *The Elusive Pimpernel, Gone to Earth* (1950), *Angels One Five* (1952), *Moulin Rouge* (1953); (c) *The Scamp* (1957), *Virgin Island, Next to No Time!* (1958), *Battle of the Sexes* (1959), *Never Take Sweets from a Stranger* (1960), *Night Must Fall* (1964), *The Jigsaw Man* (1984), *Memed My Hawk* (1984), *Rainbow* (1996, UK/Can), *Ghosthunter* (2000, short, consultant); (d) *Nightmare* (1963), *The Evil of Frankenstein, Hysteria* (1964), *The Psychopath, The Deadly Bees* (1966), *Dracula Has Risen From the Grave* (1968), *Mumsy, Nanny, Sonny and Girly* (1969), *Trog* (1970), *Tales from the Crypt, The Creeping Flesh* (1972), *Craze* (1973), *Son of Dracula, Legend of the Werewolf* (1974), *The Ghoul* (1975), *The Doctor and the Devils* (1985).

BIBLIOG: Wheeler Winston Dixon, *The Films of Freddie Francis*, 1991. Wheeler Winston Dixon.

Francis, Karl (*b* Bedwas, Gwent, 1943). Director. Strongly political Welsh director of dramas often centred on coalmining and other aspects of national experience. Outside Wales, best known for *Giro City* (1982, + sc), a highly critical examination of media practice in reporting Northern Ireland strife.

OTHER BRITISH FILMS INCLUDE: (d) *Children of the Coalface* (1977), *Rebecca's Daughters* (1992, UK/Ger); (d/sc) *Angry Earth* (1989), *Morphine and Dolly Mixtures* (1990), *Streetlife* (1995); (d/[co-]sc/[co-]p) *Above Us the Earth* (1977), *Milwyr Bychan* (1986), *One of the Hollywood Ten* (2000, UK/Sp).

Frank, Amy (*b* Susice, Czechoslovakia, 1896 – *d* Berlin, 1980). Actress. Educated in Vienna and on European stages and screens before London debut in 1939, Frank had one good role in British films – as George III's Queen in *The First Gentleman* (1948) – and minor ones in *While the Sun Shines* (1947) and *Broken Journey* (1948).

Frank, Charles (*b* Belgium, 1910). Director. Former expert in dubbing Continental films into English, he directed one delirious Gothic piece, *Uncle Silas* (1947), in which he skilfully orchestrated acting, production and costume design, music and editing to maximum melodramatic effect – and consequently was hardly ever given a chance again in Britain.

OTHER BRITISH FILMS: *Malachi's Cove* (1950), *The Late Edwina Black* (1951, co-sc), *Intimate Relations* (1953, + co-sc).

Frankau, Ronald (*b* London, 1894 – *d* Eastbourne, 1951). Actor. Eton-educated comedian of stage, radio and screen, most popular in the 30s, beginning with *Potiphar's Wife* and as the auctioneer in *The Skin Game* (1931).

OTHER BRITISH FILMS INCLUDE: *Radio Parade of 1935* (1934), *The Show's the Thing* (1936), *His Brother's Keeper* (1939), *Much Too Shy* (1942, sc), *What Do We Do Now?* (1945), *Dual Alibi* (1947), *The Ghosts of Berkeley Square* (1947).

Frankel, Benjamin (*b* London, 1906 – *d* London, 1973). Composer, music director. Studied at Guildhall School of Music and Trinity College of Music, did further study in pre-war Germany, and entered films as songwriter and/or music director on such light entertainments as *Radio Parade of 1935* (1934) and *Public Nuisance No. 1* (1936). During WW2 he worked on numerous short films for MOI, CROWN and the BRITISH COUNCIL. Post-war he was greatly in demand as composer and/or conductor on many well-regarded films, including *The Seventh Veil* (1945), *The Importance of Being Earnest* (1952), and across the popular GENRES, with a special flair for comedy scoring, evinced in the sunny *Happy is the Bride* (1957); while his 1961 score for the horror film, *Curse of the Werewolf*, was notably influenced by Schoenberg's twelve-tone serialism. Also had a high reputation for his West End play scores, concert pieces, and an opera, *Marching Song*, based on John Whiting's play.

OTHER BRITISH FILMS INCLUDE: (comp/cond) *Give Us This Day* (1949, UK/US), *So Long at the Fair* (1950), *Hotel Sahara* (1951), *The Final Test* (1953), *The Man Who Loved Redheads* (1954), *Footsteps in the Fog, The Prisoner* (1955), *Orders to Kill* (1958), *Libel* (1959), *The Old Dark House* (1962); (comp) *Love in Exile* (1936), *Flight from Folly* (1945), *The Years Between, Girl in a Million* (1946), *Mine Own Executioner, Dear Murderer* (1947), *Daybreak, Trottie True, Bond Street* (1948), *Night and the City* (1950, UK/US), *The Man in the White Suit* (1951), *Malaga, Aunt Clara* (1954), *Surprise Package* (1960); (cond) *The Singing Cop* (1937), *The Young Lovers* (1954); (comp/m d) *The Clouded Yellow* (1950), *Lost* (1955); (m d) *Music Hath Charms* (1935), *He Found a Star* (1941), *On Such a Night* (1955, short).

Frankel, Cyril (*b* London, 1921 – *d* London, 1973). Director. Former documentary film-maker with the CROWN FILM UNIT and GROUP 3, entered films 1947, after WW2 service. Made his first feature, *Man of Africa* (1953), entirely in Africa, with John GRIERSON as producer. Most of his films are modestly attractive without being very exciting, like *It's Great to Be Young!* (1956), a fresh enough youth musical for a kind of youth who was going out of style. However, the horror film, *The Witches* (1966), has some genuinely scary moments and *Never Take Sweets from a Stranger* (1960), rather daringly tackles the theme of child molestation, both showing the benefits of HAMMER's more full-blooded approach. Directed much TV, including episodes of *The Avengers* (1961), and also the US-financed *Permission to Kill* (1975).

OTHER BRITISH FILMS INCLUDE: *Explorers of the Depths* (+ co-sc), *Eagles of the Fleet* (1950), *Devil on Horseback, Make Me An Offer!* (1954), *No Time for Tears* (1957), *Alive and Kicking* (1958), *On the Fiddle, Don't Bother to Knock* (1961), *The Very Edge* (1962), *The Trygon Factor* (1966).

Frankel, Mark (*b* London, 1962 – *d* London, 1996). Actor. A motor cycle accident cut tragically short the promising career of the charismatic Frankel. Trained for stage at Webber-Douglas, he came to critical and popular attention as the young man in search of a parent in *Leon the Pig Farmer* (1992) and such TV as *Season of Giants* (1991, UK/US/It) in which he played young Michelangelo.

OTHER BRITISH FILMS: *Solitaire for 2* (1995) and *Roseanna's Grave* (1997).

Franklin, Gretchen (*b* London, 1911). Actress. Famous on stage in the *Sweet and Low* revues at the Ambassadors' Theatre, London, in the 40s, and decades later a household name and face as increasingly senile Ethel Skinner in the long-running *EastEnders* (1985–93), then special appearances, prior to her mercy killing by Dot Cotton in 2000). Entered films in 1955 thriller, *Before I Wake*, and played character roles on film

(including US-made *Ragtime*, 1981) and TV over the next three decades.

OTHER BRITISH FILMS INCLUDE: *Cloak without Dagger* (1955), *The High Terrace* (1956), *Flame in the Streets* (1961), *Help!* (1965), *How I Won the War* (1967), *Twisted Nerve* (1968), *The Quatermass Conclusion* (1978).

Franklin, Pamela (*b* Yokohama, 1950). Actress. Small and dark, Franklin unfortunately had her best role – one of the 'possessed' children in Jack CLAYTON's *The Innocents* (1961) – when she was 11 years old and rarely had another to come near it. She made the most of what did, including the oldest daughter of the bereft family in Clayton's *Our Mother's House* (1967) and the duplicitous Sandy (BAAn) in *The Prime of Miss Jean Brodie* (1968). Finished her career in US television and in LA repertory theatre.

OTHER BRITISH FILMS INCLUDE: *The Lion* (1962), *The Third Secret* (1964), *The Nanny* (1965), *Sinful Davey* (1968), *And Soon the Darkness* (1970), *The Legend of Hell House* (1973).

Franklyn, Leo (*b* London, 1897 – *d* London, 1975). Actor. Stage actor (from 1916), much associated with Brian RIX at the Whitehall Theatre, and the titles of some of his few films suggest allegiance to this connection, *viz*: *The Night We Dropped a Clanger, And the Same to You* (1959) and *The Night We Got the Bird* (1960), all with Rix. Father of William FRANKLYN.

OTHER BRITISH FILMS: *Two Minutes' Silence* (1934), *Keep Fit* (1937), *I've Got a Horse* (1938), *Nothing Barred* (1961).

Franklyn, William (*b* London, 1925). Actor. Polished, suave leading man and latterly character actor in film and TV, whose practised charm could convincingly suggest various kinds of repression: wartime treachery in *Danger Within* (1958), opportunism in *The Big Day* (1960) or the anxieties of the amnesiac hero in *Pit of Darkness* (1961). Guested on *French and Saunders* (2000). Son of Leo FRANKLYN.

OTHER BRITISH FILMS INCLUDE: *The Secret People* (1951), *Time Is My Enemy* (1954), *Above Us the Waves* (1955), *Quatermass 2* (1957), *The Snorkel* (1958), *Fury at Smugglers Bay* (1960), *Cul-de-Sac* (1966), *The Satanic Rites of Dracula* (1974), *Nutcracker* (1982), *Splitting Heirs* (1993), *Robert Rylands' Last Journey* (1996, UK/Sp).

Frankovich, M(ike) J. (*b* Bisbee, Arizona, 1910 – *d* Los Angeles, 1992). Producer, executive. Adopted son of comedian Joe E. Brown, former UCLA sports champion Frankovich made some late 30s/early 40s film appearances as sports announcers, and after WW2 service spent some time with Republic Pictures before coming to Europe in 1949. In charge of Columbia Pictures' British division, he produced some variable GENRE films for Columbia's distribution, including the entertaining 'Victorian' MELODRAMA, *Footsteps in the Fog* (1955, co-p, ex p) and the Shakespeare pastiche, *Joe MacBeth* (1955). In 1962 he was made supervisor of Columbia's international productions and in 1963 vice-president of the company's production arm. Married Binnie BARNES.

OTHER BRITISH FILMS: *Decameron Nights* (1952), *Beyond Mombasa, Wicked as They Come* (1956, co-p), *The Looking Glass War* (1969, ex p), *There's a Girl in My Soup* (1970, co-p).

Fraser, Bill (*b* Perth, Scotland, 1908 – *d* Bushey, 1987). Actor. Big, burly Scots actor, on stage from 1931, London in 1940, in films from 1936's *Murder in the Family*, billed as W. Simpson Fraser. In 1941's *The Common Touch* (as Bill Fraser), in the RAF (1941–46), and thereafter an increasingly popular character player in all the media, including long-running TV successes in

The Army Game (1958–60) as CSM Snudge, reprising this blusterer in *Bootsie and Snudge* (1960–63). On stage he had seasons at Chichester, Stratford and the Old Vic, starring at the latter as *The Good-natured Man* (1971), and formed and ran the Worthing Repertory Company for many years. Always memorable in films, whether the pompous stage manager in *Meet Me Tonight* (1952) or the publisher who won't 'publish drivel unless it's by someone important' in *The Man Who Liked Funerals* (1958); even as racing dignitary Sir Cresswell in Tony RICHARDSON's disastrous *Dead Cert* (1974) his bluff presence ensures some relief.

OTHER BRITISH FILMS INCLUDE: *Helter Skelter* (1949), *Lady in the Fog* (1952), *The Captain's Paradise, Time Bomb* (1953), *Charley Moon* (1956), *Second Fiddle, Just My Luck* (1957), *The Fast Lady* (1962), *Masquerade* (1965), *All the Way Up* (1970), *Up the Chastity Belt, Up Pompeii* (1971), *Up the Front, That's Your Funeral, Not Now, Darling* (1972), *Eye of the Needle* (1981), *Cover Her Face* (1985), *Little Dorrit* (1987).

Fraser, Helen (*b* Oldham, 1942). Actress. Supporting player of film (as a girlfriend of *Billy Liar*, 1963), TV (Mrs Moreland in *Northanger Abbey*, 1987; a cynical policewoman in *Bad Girls*, 2000) and stage (a brusque WAAF in *Absolute Hell*, 1995, at the National), with comic sense. Also in the US films, *Start the Revolution Without Me* (1969) and *Gorillas in the Mist* (1988). Married sound recordist Peter HANDFORD.

OTHER BRITISH FILMS: *The Uncle* (1964), *Repulsion* (1965), *The Birthday Party* (1968), *Something to Hide* (1971), *Joseph Andrews* (1976).

Fraser, John (*b* Glasgow, 1931). Actor. Youthful-looking leading man of the 50s and 60s, playing romantic heroes like Inigo in *The Good Companions* (1956) and Susannah YORK's Corporal boyfriend in *Tunes of Glory* (1960), but making his strongest impression, atypically, as Bosie (BAAn) in *The Trials of Oscar Wilde* (1960). Educated at Glasgow High School, began BBC appearances as a schoolboy, did a stint in the Army and joined the Glasgow Citizens' Theatre in 1950; in the 50s, under contract to ABPC for whom he made *The Dam Busters* (1955). Mainly on stage in recent years.

OTHER BRITISH FILMS INCLUDE: *The Good Beginning, Valley of Song* (1953), *Touch and Go* (1955), *The Wind Cannot Read* (1958), *The Horsemasters* (1961), *Waltz of the Toreadors, Tamahine* (1962), *Repulsion, A Study in Terror* (1965), *Isadora* (1968), *Truth or Dare* (1996).

Fraser, Laura (*b* Glasgow, 1975). Actress. Beautiful raven-haired newcomer of the 90s, first noticed as Joanne, who urges bashful art student Alan to ask her out, in *Little Faces* (1996). She had good roles – and deserves them – in *Divorcing Jack* (1998, UK/Fr) and, very affecting, as Lavinia, sans tongue, sans hands, in the Grand Guignol *Titus* (2000, UK/US).

OTHER BRITISH FILMS INCLUDE: *Good Day for the Bad Guys* (1995, short), *Paris, Brixton* (1997, short), *Cousin Bette* (1998), *Virtual Sexuality, The Match* (UK/Ire/US) (1999), *Whatever Happened to Harold Smith?, Kevin & Perry Go Large* (UK/US) (2000), *Station Jim* (2001).

Fraser, Liz (*b* London, 1933). Actress. RN: Winch. May seem like a busty 'CARRY ON' blonde in popular recollection (she is in four of the series), but is in fact a fine actress with about 40 films to her credit. She is very funny as Peter SELLERS's daughter with an eye on boarder Ian CARMICHAEL in *I'm All Right Jack* (1959), toughly convincing as a hard-bitten dance 'hostess' in *The Painted Smile* (1961) and as Barry FOSTER's disillusioned wife in *The Family Way* (1966).

OTHER BRITISH FILMS INCLUDE: *Touch and Go* (1955, unc), *The Night We Dropped a Clanger, Desert Mice* (1959), *Doctor in Love, Two Way Stretch, The Bulldog Breed, The Rebel* (1960), *Watch it, Sailor!, Double*

Bunk, Carry on Regardless (1961), *Carry On Cruising, Live Now, Pay Later, The Amorous Prawn* (1962), *Up the Junction* (1967), *Dad's Army* (1971), *Hide and Seek* (1972), *Three for All* (1974), *Carry On Behind* (1975), *Rosie Dixon – Night Nurse* (1978), *The Great Rock'n'Roll Swindle* (1979), *Chicago Joe and the Showgirl* (1989).

Fraser, Moyra (*b* Sydney, 1923). Actress. With Sadler's Wells Ballet from 1937 till 1945, then in straight theatre roles, including revue, to which her eccentric comedy style is well-suited. Film roles have been few but choice, like Ethel the flapper in *The Man Who Loved Redheads* (1954) and Madame Dubonnet in *The Boy Friend* (1971). TV appearances include *As Time Goes By* (1993). Sister of Shelagh FRASER; married (1940–51) to author Duncan Sutherland.

OTHER BRITISH FILMS: *Madeleine* (1949), *Left, Right and Centre* (1959), *The VIPs* (1963), *Here We Go Round the Mulberrry Bush* (1967), *Prudence and the Pill* (1968), *A Handful of Dust* (1987).

Fraser, Ronald (*b* Ashton-under-Lyne, 1930 – *d* London, 1997). Actor. Sometimes pugnacious, sometimes dopily pompous, RADA-trained, pudgy-faced Fraser was a consummate character player, coming to notice as the plodding Lance-Corporal of the isolated patrol in *The Long and the Short and the Tall* (1960). He had substantial roles throughout the next 20 years, most often in comedy in which he excelled, though the starring roles of ex-Malayan rubber planter, Basil Allenby-Johnson, in TV's *The Misfit* (1970–71) and Falstaff in the Open Air Theatre's *The Merry Wives of Windsor* (1984) probably represent the apogee of his comic achievement. The spectacle of Fraser huffing, puffing and bluffing his way through several dozen film roles, across classes and genres, is one of the pleasures of later 20th-century British cinema. Also in such US films as *The Flight of the Phoenix* (1965) and *The Killing of Sister George* (1968).

OTHER BRITISH FILMS INCLUDE: *Bobbikins* (1959), *There Was a Crooked Man* (1960), *Don't Bother to Knock* (1961), *Private Potter, The Pot Carriers, The Punch and Judy Man* (1962), *The Girl in the Headlines* (1963), *Crooks in Cloisters, The Beauty Jungle* (1964), *The Whisperers* (1966), *Fathom, Sebastian* (1967), *Sinful Davey* (1968), *Rentadick, Ooh . . . You Are Awful* (1972), *Swallows and Amazons, Percy's Progress, Paper Tiger* (1974), *The Wild Geese* (1978, UK/Switz), *Absolute Beginners* (1986), *Scandal* (1988), *'Let Him Have It'* (1991), *The Mystery of Edwin Drood* (1993).

Fraser, Shelagh (*b* Purley, Surrey, 1923 – *d* London, 2000). Actress. Demure-looking character player adept at suggesting inner strength, as in her best known role – as Jean Ashton, Liverpool mother of *A Family at War* (1970–72). From 1938 on stage, with a wider range of roles than the generally retiring females she played in such films as *The Master of Bankdam* (1947) or *Raising a Riot* (1955), though she did get to play vulgar Lady Orreyd in *The Second Mrs Tanqueray* (1952). A younger generation will remember her as Aunt Beru in *Star Wars* (1977, US). Also a frequent radio actress, a playwright and author of children's books. Sister of Moyra FRASER. Once married to director Anthony SQUIRE.

OTHER BRITISH FILMS INCLUDE: *Welcome Mr Washington* (1944), *The History of Mr Polly* (1948), *Salute the Toff* (1952), *The Last Man to Hang?* (1956), *The Witches* (1966), *A Touch of Love, Thin Air* (1969), *Doomwatch* (1972), *Persecution* (1974), *Hope and Glory* (1987).

Frears, Stephen (*b* Leicester, 1941). Director. Although Stephen Frears got a taste for film-making as an assistant to Lindsay ANDERSON on *If . . .* (1968), much of his early career was spent working in TV, most notably on *Six Plays by Alan Bennett*. During the 1970s, the amiable private-eye comedy-thriller *Gumshoe* (1971) and the forthright social realism of *Bloody Kids* (1979) made it clear that he was to become a force in British cinema, although it wasn't until the mid 80s – with *My Beautiful Laundrette* (1985) and *Sammy and Rosie Get Laid* (1987) – that he emerged as a major figure. Since then he has continued to divide his time between film and TV, Britain and the US, working on projects as various as *Dangerous Liaisons* (1988, US), *The Van* (1996, UK/Ire), *High Fidelity* (UK/US), the live-to-air TV version of *Fail-Safe* (both 2000), and *Liam* (2001, UK/Ger/It). One of Frears' most distinctive characteristics is his ability to switch modes with ease – from conventional genre fare (even including a latterday Western, *The Hi-Lo Country*, 1998, US) to social dramas and comedies (like *Prick Up Your Ears*, 1987, and *High Fidelity*). He has also long viewed himself as part of a team rather than an auteur, his work regularly distinguished by the impressive array of collaborators he's been able to gather around him.

OTHER BRITISH FILMS: *Morgan: A Suitable Case for Treatment* (1966, ass to d), *The Burning* (1967, short), *Incident* (1971, short), *Long Shot* (1978), *Saigon – Year of the Cat* (1983, TV, some cinemas), *The Hit* (1984), *The Snapper* (1993), *Satan at His Best* (1995, doc, ex p), *Mary Reilly* (1996, UK/US). Tom Ryan.

Frederick, Lynne (*b* Hillingdon, 1954 – *d* Los Angeles, 1994). Actress. Now best remembered as Peter SELLERS' widow (married 1977 until his 1980 death) and was once married to David FROST, Frederick had a modest film career. Began as a teenager in Cornel WILDE's eco-thriller *No Blade of Grass* (1970), had a small role in *Nicholas and Alexandra* (1971, UK/US), was a charming Isabel Boncassen in TV's *The Pallisers* (1974), co-starred as Princess Flavia with Sellers in *The Prisoner of Zenda* (1979) – and died sadly young.

OTHER BRITISH FILMS: *Vampire Circus* (1971), *The Amazing Mr Blunden, Henry VIII and His Six Wives* (1972), *Phase IV* (1973), *Voyage of the Damned* (1976).

Free Cinema The freedom of Free Cinema was an attitude of mind which linked the 'poetry of everyday life' which Lindsay ANDERSON had written about in the journal SEQUENCE to the 'ordinary lives' of the British NEW WAVE. As an event, Free Cinema consisted of six programmes of films shown at the NATIONAL FILM THEATRE in London between 1956 and 1959. What made the films 'Free' was a free expression of personality which escaped the routines of commercial cinema or the standard British DOCUMENTARY. The model was the poetry of Humphrey JENNINGS's documentaries rather than the social responsibiltiy of GRIERSON. 'These films are free', declared a programme hand-out, 'in the sense that their statements are entirely personal.' The notion of a Free Cinema had something of the aspirational quality which attached to the notion of oppositional 'independence' in the Independent Film-makers Association in Britain in the late 70s. The programmes were assembled by a group which included Anderson, Karel REISZ, John Fletcher, and Walter LASSALLY, and included films – mainly documentaries, with a few ANIMATIONS – by Anderson (*O Dreamland*, 1953; *The Wakefield Express*, 1952; *Every Day Except Christmas*, 1957), Reisz (*Momma Don't Allow*, 1956; *We Are the Lambeth Boys*, 1959), Tony RICHARDSON (*Momma Don't Allow*, 1956), Norman McLAREN (*Neighbours*, 1953), Franju (*Le Sang des bêtes*, 1956), Lenica and Borowczyck (*Once Upon a Time*, 1957; *Dom*, 1957), Lorenza Mazzetti (*Together*, 1956), POLANSKI (*Two Men and a Wardrobe*, 1957), Goretta and Tanner (*Nice Time*, 1957), Truffaut (*Les Mistons*, 1957) and Chabrol (*Le Beau Serge*, 1958). Appearing in 1956, Free Cinema

was the first expression in the cinema of the shift in British culture which was happening in the Royal Court Theatre around *Look Back in Anger* (1956), a theatrical revolution whose flame had been lit, at least in part, by Anderson and Richardson. John Caughie.

Freeland, Thornton (*b* Hope, N. Dakota, 1898 – *d* Fort Lauderdale, Florida, 1987). Director. Teenage actor who joined Vitagraph studios in 1916 and worked in many capacities before directing his first film in 1929. After directing *Flying Down to Rio* (1933) and a dozen other GENRE films, he moved to England to direct *Brewster's Millions* (1935). He directed a further nine there, mostly comedies, including *Over the Moon* (1939) with Merle OBERON, before returning to the US when war broke out, serving with the American forces. Post-war he was back in England to make three more films, of which his last, *Dear Mr Prohack* (1949), from Arnold BENNETT's play, is the most notable, showing a mildly agreeable light touch. Married to American actress June CLYDE; they lived in Britain for many years.

OTHER BRITISH FILMS INCLUDE: *The Amateur Gentleman, Skylarks* (1936), *Jericho* (1937), *Hold My Hand* (1938), *The Gang's All Here, So This is London* (1939), *Meet Me at Dawn* (1947), *The Brass Monkey* (1948, + co-sc).

Freeman, Paul (*b* Barnet, 1943). Actor. Protean player who moves easily between the RSC (e.g, *Hamlet*, 1997) and entertaining film villainy, including arch-rival to Indiana Jones in *Raiders of the Lost Ark* (1981, US) or Moriarty in the Sherlock Holmes spoof, *Without a Clue* (1988). Has filmed internationally and done some excellent TV, including a formidable tycoon in *The Dark Room* (1999). Married to actress Maggie Scott whom he met while filming *The Dogs of War* (1980) in Africa.

OTHER BRITISH FILMS INCLUDE: *Feelings* (1975), *The Long Good Friday* (1979), *An Unsuitable Job for a Woman* (1981), *Shanghai Surprise* (1986), *A World Apart* (1987, UK/Zimb), *Grushko* (1993).

Freeman, Robert (*b* Cambridge, 1935). Director. Former fashion director and title artist on the BEATLES films, *A Hard Day's Night* (1964) and *Help!* (1965), who directed one unspeakable British film, *The Touchables* (1968), for which the 'original idea' is also his responsibility.

French, Dawn (*b* Holyhead, Wales, 1957). Actress, comedienne. Vast, and vastly amusing, comedienne famous for her TV collaborations with Jennifer SAUNDERS (they created *French and Saunders*, 1987–88) and such solo series as *Murder Most Horrid* (1991) and as *The Vicar of Dibley* (premiered in 1994). The screen, in disasters like *Maybe Baby* (2000, UK/Fr), has not used her comic gifts, but she was very funny on stage as a bossy wife in *When We Are Married* (1996). Married comedian Lenny HENRY in 1984.

OTHER BRITISH FILMS INCLUDE: *The Supergrass* (1985), *Eat the Rich* (1987), *The Strike* (1988), *The Adventures of Pinocchio* (1996, UK/Fr/Ger/Czech/US).

French, Harold (*b* London, 1900 – *d* London, 1997). Actor, director. On stage from childhood, enrolled with the Italia Conti acting school, French became a popular London stage star, before taking to direction in 1934 and having a major success with *French Without Tears* (1936). From a modest background, he became known as producer of stage plays of upper-class life. In films, also, he began as a very young actor (*The Land of Mystery*, 1920), appearing in about 20 largely forgotten early 30s films, mostly light comedies and thrillers. He co-wrote several screenplays in the late 30s before settling to direction for the rest of his career.

After three minor films he was appointed director of *Major Barbara* (1941) but found producer Gabriel PASCAL, almost impossible to work with and in 1991 claimed that most of the film was directed by David LEAN. French became a proficient director of middle-of-the-range entertainments, characterised by smooth storytelling and fine performances. He had some notable successes: *Jeannie* (1941), a Scots-Cinderella story; *Dear Octopus* (1943), a warmly human version of Dodie Smith's hit play; *My Brother Jonathan* (1948), the most commercially successful British film of its year; and episodes in each of the MAUGHAM compendia ('Sanatorium' in *Trio*, especially fine). Above all an actor's director, he gets memorable performances from Celia JOHNSON as the unhappy daughter in *Dear Octopus*, Felix AYLMER as *Mr Emmanuel* (1944), a Jew in Nazi Germany, Claire BLOOM, making her debut in *The Blind Goddess* (1948), Claude RAINS as *The Man Who Watched Trains Go By* (1952, +sc) and Gladys COOPER as the understanding wife of *The Man Who Loved Redheads* (1954). Wrote two very witty volumes of autobiography: *I Swore I Never Would* (1970) and *I Thought I Never Could* (1973). Uncle of Hugh French (*see* Eve LISTER).

OTHER BRITISH FILMS INCLUDE: (a) *The Hypocrites* (1923), *Jealousy*, (1931) *When London Sleeps* (1932) *Mannequin* (1933), *The Girl in the Crowd* (1934), *The Diplomatic Lover* (1939); (co-sc) *Accused, Crime Over London* (1936), *Jump for Glory* (1937); (d – complete) *The Cavalier of the Streets* (1937), *Dead Men Are Dangerous* (1939), *The House of the Arrow* (1940), *Our Film* (short), *Unpublished Story, Talk About Jacqueline, Secret Mission, The Day Will Dawn* (1942), *English Without Tears* (1944), *Quiet Weekend* (1946), *White Cradle Inn* (1947, + co-sc), *Quartet* (1948, 'The Alien Corn'), *Adam and Evelyne* (1949, + p), *The Dancing Years* (1950), *Encore* (1951, 'Gigolo and Gigolette'), *The Hour of 13* (1952), *Rob Roy . . . , Isn't Life Wonderful!* (1953), *Forbidden Cargo* (1954).

French, Leslie (*b* Bromley, 1904 – *d* Ewell, 1999). Actor. A dozen films spread over 50 years suggests that the diminutive French had other things in mind – and so he did. He was, from his teens, a tireless stage performer, particularly in Shakespeare, and especially as Ariel in *The Tempest*. His near-nude appearance in this role inspired both protest and the statue on the façade of London's Broadcasting House. Much associated with the Open Air Theatre, London, and with theatre in Capetown, which presented him with the Key to the City. In such international films as *The Leopard* (1963, It/Fr) and *Death in Venice* (1971, It/Fr), but memorable in only one of his British films: as the wrong victim of *Orders to Kill* (1958).

OTHER BRITISH FILMS INCLUDE: *Peg of Old Drury* (1935), *The Scapegoat* (1958©, *The Singer Not the Song* (1960), *Invitation to the Wedding* (1983), *The Living Daylights* (1987).

Frend, Charles (*b* Pulborough, 1909 – *d* London, 1977). Editor, director. One of Michael BALCON's young Oxbridge men at EALING where he was most famous as director of big, male-dominated action dramas like *Scott of the Antarctic* (1948) and *The Cruel Sea* (1952). He also directed there (taking over from Robert HAMER) the stirring war film, *San Demetrio–London* (1943, + co-sc), the vivid PASTORAL of *The Loves of Joanna Godden* (1947) and the elegiac *Lease of Life* (1954), but he is curiously less known and perhaps less individual than the other Ealing directors. He began as editor, working on such HITCHCOCK films as *Secret Agent, Sabotage* (1936) and *Young and Innocent* (1937), before joining MGM–BRITISH for *A Yank at Oxford* (1937) and following Balcon to Ealing. His career tapered off when Ealing ceased operation in 1958, and he ended

as 2ud on the pretentious dud, *Ryan's Daughter* (1970).

OTHER BRITISH FILMS INCLUDE: (e) *Arms and the Man* (1932, co-e), *Waltzes from Vienna* (1934), *The Tunnel* (1935), *The Great Barrier* (1937), *The Citadel* (1938), *Goodbye, Mr Chips, The Lion Has Wings* (doc) (1939), *Conquest of the Air* (1940, doc, sup e, narr), *Major Barbara* (1941); (d) *The Foreman Went to France, The Big Blockade* (doc, + co-sc) (1942), *Return of the Vikings* (1944, doc), *Johnny Frenchman* (1945), *A Run for Your Money* (1949, + co-sc), *The Magnet* (1950), *The Long Arm* (1956), *Barnacle Bill* (1957), *Cone of Silence* (1960), *Girl on Approval* (1961), *The Sky Bike* (1967, + sc, story), *Guns in the Heather* (1968, 2ud).

Freshman, William A. (*b* Sydney, 1902 – *d* London, 1980). Actor, director. A healthy, fresh-faced young leading man, Freshman came to the UK aged seven. He entered the industry with GAUMONT in 1918, working as an apprentice in various departments, before touring in repertory. At the end of his acting career, including films on the continent, he was associate producer for ASSOCIATED BRITISH in 1937. In 1939, he returned to Australia to produce, write and direct *Ants in His Pants* for Cinesound. During WW2, he served as deputy assistant of Army Kinematography. Freshman's last credit is as co-director and co-screenwriter of *Teheran* (1947).

BRITISH FILMS INCLUDE: *The First Men in the Moon* (1919), *The Fifth Form at St Dominic's* (1921), *Faust, The Sporting Twelve* series (1922), *The Guns of Loos* (1928), *Greek Street, Thread o' Scarlet* (1930), *FPI, Lucky Blaze* (1933), *The Scarlet Pimpernel* (1935), *Limelight* (1936), *The Man at the Gate* (1941). AS.

Frewin, Leslie R. (*b* London). Publicist. After some time in theatrical production and administration, Frewin entered films as publicity assistant at GAINSBOROUGH's ISLINGTON STUDIOS, working on some very notable films such as *The Lady Vanishes* and *Bank Holiday* (1938), before WW2 service (1940–46). Post-war he returned to Gainsborough as assistant publicity director at LIME GROVE STUDIOS, then joined ABPC as publicity director (1948–56), responsible for such key films as *The Dam Busters* (1955), leaving to set up his own public relations company, handling many famous stars. Author of several books, including *Blonde Venus: A Life of Marlene Dietrich* (1955) and later had his own publishing company.

Fricker, Brenda (*b* Dublin, 1945). Actress. Formidably gifted actress who had been in small roles in films for over 20 years before sudden fame as Christy Brown's mother in *My Left Foot* (1989) for which she won Supporting Actress AA. Since then, she has been in constant demand for film and TV, in Britain (*The Field*, 1990, UK/Ire) and in the US (*Home Alone 2*, 1992; *Moll Flanders*, 1996). Forceful rather than pretty, she is a character asset to any film.

OTHER BRITISH FILMS INCLUDE: *Of Human Bondage* (1964), *Sinful Davey* (1968), *The Quatermass Conclusion* (1978), *Bloody Kids* (1979), *The Woman Who Married Clark Gable* (1985), *Utz* (1992, UK/Ger), *A Man of No Importance* (1994, UK/Ire), *Swann* (1996, UK/Can), *Resurrection Man* (1997), *The War Bride* (2000).

Friel, Anna (*b* Rochdale, 1976). Actress. Thin, gamine, sexy Friel is so far famous for exposure other than on screen: for the first lesbian kiss in a British TV soap, as Beth in *Brookside* (1993); on stage, as a stripper in Patrick Marber's confronting play, *Closer* (1998–99, London and Broadway); in any number of tabloids, drawing the ire of fellow actress Samantha MORTON for stripping for a Breast Cancer Care photo; and for her raunchy outspokenness in interviews. On screen, she was the most coarse-speaking, sexually willing of *The Land Girls* (1998, UK/Fr); an enjoyably scatty Hermia in *A Midsummer Night's Dream* (UK/It), the sexy wife of Ewan McGREGOR's

Rogue Trader (1999) and single Mum Maddy in *Mad Cows* (1999). She holds her own in all of these but none has been a commercial or critical success; she, though, remains intelligently newsworthy. Following relationships with Darren Day and Robbie Williams, her partner is now David FREWLIS.

OTHER BRITISH FILMS: *The Stringer* (1997, UK/Russ), *St Ives* (1998), *The War Bride* (2000, UK/Can), *Me Without You* (2001).

Friend, Philip (*b* Horsham, 1914 – *d* Chiddingfold, 1987). Actor. Traditionally tall, dark and handsome leading man in British films from 1939, after some stage experience; in Hollywood (1947–52) with modest success in swashbucklers like *Buccaneer's Girl* (1950) and Brit-set romances like *My Own True Love* and *Enchantment* (1948). Back in Britain, he made a dozen or so films (including obvious 'B's like *Cloak Without Dagger*, 1955) without quite regaining the momentum of his early 40s career in such films as *In Which We Serve* (1942) and *Great Day* (1945), in which he is pleasantly breezy with well-played serious moments. Was married to Eileen ERSKINE; TV director Martyn Friend is their son.

OTHER BRITISH FILMS INCLUDE: *Inquest, The Midas Touch* (1939), *Dangerous Moonlight, Sheepdog of the Hills, Pimpernel Smith* (1941), *The Next of Kin* (1942), *We Dive at Dawn, The Bells Go Down, The Flemish Farm* (1943), *Desperate Moment, Background* (1953), *The Diamond* (1954), *Son of Robin Hood* (1958), *The Vulture* (1966, UK/Can/US).

Friese-Greene, Claude (*b* 1898 – *d* 1943). Cinematographer. Son of pioneer William FRIESE-GREENE, he was involved in photographic work from an early age and after WW1 specialised in aerial cinematography, experimented in the 20s with colour photography and was (co-)cinematographer on dozens of films of the usual 30s GENRES. His moody black-and-white adds a frisson to a thriller like *Black Limelight* (1938), though his work is essentially functional, and, as to that for *On Approval* (1944), one can at least say that he doesn't get in the way of a peerless cast.

OTHER BRITISH FILMS INCLUDE: (co-c) *The Middle Watch* (1930), *The Maid of the Mountains* (1932), *Girls Will Be Boys* (1934), *Music Hath Charms, Drake of England* (1935), *The Great Mr Handel* (1942, + co-c); (c) *Widecombe Fair* (1928), *Elstree Calling, Young Woodley* (1930), *Mr Bill the Conqueror* (1932), *No Monkey Business* (1935), *Crime Over London* (1936), *The Saint in London, The Middle Watch, The Gang's All Here* (1939), *The Farmer's Wife* (1941), *Hard Steel* (1942).

Friese-Greene, William (*b* Bristol, 1855 – *d* London, 1921). Pioneer. William Friese-Greene is a legend in British cinema, the man whose work was usurped by others in the US and France, and who died a pauper after making an impassioned speech on behalf of the British film industry, with only the price of a cinema ticket in his pocket. His life is devotedly if sometimes misleadingly recorded by Ray Allister in *Friese-Greene: Close-up of an Inventor* (1948), complete with a list of his various patents from 1889 to 1921. Sadly, as historian Brian Coe has written, his work must be considered 'an interesting but unfruitful attempt to solve the basic mechanical and photographic problems involved in kinematography'. Allister's biography was filmed in 1951 as the star-studded and leaden *The Magic Box*, which did about as much for the art of British cinema as did Friese-Greene for its craft. However, recent researches have found more to value in his work, including his experiments with the Biocolour film system, which he conducted in the 1900s and teens. His son, Claude, was a prolific, journeyman cinematographer. AS.

Frinton, Freddie (*b* Grimsby, 1909 – *d* Poole, 1968). Actor. Better known for his TV sitcom, *Meet the Wife* (1964–65), with Thora HIRD, than for his half-dozen anaemic film comedies, such as *Trouble in the Air* (1948), in which he plays a butler-cum-bellringer, drunk on cooking sherry. Many people, especially in Germany for some reason, are fond of his TV sketch, *Dinner for One* (1963); others find it quite radically laugh-free.

OTHER BRITISH FILMS: *Penny Points to Paradise* (1951), *Forces' Sweetheart* (1953), *Stars in Your Eyes* (1956), *Make Mine Mink* (1960), *What a Whopper!* (1961).

Fröbe, Gert (*b* Planitz, Germany, 1912 – *d* Munich, 1988). Actor. Best known in the title role of *Goldfinger* (1964), which launched him as a thickset, crew-cut villain in international films, Fröbe had already made over 60 films in his native Germany, beginning in 1948. A former Nazi-party member, he had actually helped Jews to escape detection, but even so had problems getting a post-war career started. His brand of villainy often benefits from a comic touch, as in *Those Magnificent Men . . .* (1965).

OTHER BRITISH FILMS: *A High Wind in Jamaica* (1965), *Triple Cross* (1966, UK/Fr/Ger), *Rocket to the Moon* (1967), *Chitty Chitty Bang Bang* (1968), *Monte Carlo or Bust!* (1969, UK/Fr/It), *And Then There Were None* (1974).

Frost, Sir David (*b* Tenterden, 1939). Entertainer, producer. Cambridge-educated Frost was one of the 60s figures who made British TV so stimulating, via such ground-breaking satirical commentative programmes as *That Was the Week That Was* (1962–63) and *The Frost Report* (1966–67), demonstrating a hard-hitting interview technique. His impact on cinema has been muted: he appeared as a reporter in *The VIPs* (1963) and was executive producer on *The Rise and Rise of Michael Rimmer* (1970), *Charley One-Eye* (1973), *The Slipper and the Rose* (1976), (co-)productions for Paradine, his own company. Married (1 of 2) Lynne FREDERICK (1981–82). Knighted in 1993.

Frost, Sadie (*b* London, 1967). Actress. Youthful tearaway – from Italia Conti School at 11, to teenage punkdom in Liverpool – who has become one of the smart names of British cinema without ever actually being in a good/popular film. After some stage experience in Manchester, she married (1988–97) Gary KEMP, actor and Spandau Ballet frontman, and starred with him in *The Krays* (1990). In 1994, she co-starred with Jude LAW in the urban grunge thriller, *Shopping*, and they married in 1997. Along with Sean PERTWEE, Ewan McGREGOR and Jonny LEE MILLER, they founded the production company NATURAL NYLON. Frost and some of these people have been in some dreadful films, like *Love, Honour and Obey* (2000). She is very pretty and engaging even in trash like that; perhaps NN will beome more discriminating.

OTHER BRITISH FILMS INCLUDE: *A Horse Called Jester* (1979), *Diamond Skulls* (1989), *Splitting Heirs* (1993), *Bent* (1997, UK/Jap/US), *Final Cut, An Ideal Husband* (UK/US), *Captain Jack* (1998), *Rancid Aluminium* (2000).

Fry, Stephen (*b* London, 1957). Actor. And comedian, columnist, novelist, autobiographer and commentator on late 20th-century society as well. Educated at Uppingham and Stout's Hill schools, then, after a three-month spell in prison for credit-card fraud, had a successful career at Cambridge where he began doing comedy with the Footlights Club and made friends with Emma THOMPSON and Hugh LAURIE. The latter became his comedy partner, both on stage and on TV's *A Bit of Fry and Laurie* (1989–92) and *Jeeves and Wooster*

(1990–93) and both appeared in various seasons of *Blackadder* (from 1983). As well as masses of other TV, and re-scripting the stage hit, *Me and My Girl*, he has appeared in a steady stream of films, starring in *Peter's Friends* (1992), a semi-reunion of his Footlights chums and others, and, in the role he was born to play, *Wilde* (1997, UK/Ger/Jap/US) – not just because, as both gay and Jewish, he had insider knowledge of being an outsider, but because of his strong physical resemblance to Wilde and because of the multiplicity of his achievements.

OTHER BRITISH FILMS INCLUDE: *The Good Father* (1986), *A Handful of Dust*, *The Secret Policeman's Third Ball* (1987), *A Fish Called Wanda* (1988), *The Steal, Cold Comfort Farm* (TV, some cinemas) (1995), *The Wind in the Willows* (1996), *Spice World* (1997), *The Tichborne Claimant* (1998), *Whatever Happened to Harold Smith?*, *Best* (UK/Ire), *Relative Values* (UK/US), *Sabotage* (UK/Fr/Sp) (2000).

BIBLIOG: Autobiography *Moab Is My Washpot*, 1997.

Fuest, Robert (*b* London, 1927). Director. For a couple of years in the early 70s, especially following the success of the horror film, *The Abominable Dr Phibes* (1971), Fuest might have become a cult director, but from lack of either opportunity or inclination he failed to build on this and worked only sporadically and mostly in TV thereafter. Formerly a painter and designer; also (co-)wrote some of his screenplays.

OTHER BRITISH FILMS: (d, unless noted) *Just Like a Woman* (1966, + sc), *Wuthering Heights, And Soon the Darkness* (1970), *Dr Phibes Rises Again* (1972, + co-sc), *The Final Programme* (1973, + sc, des), *Marie Curie, The Road to Mandalay* (1977, short).

Fulford, Christopher Actor. Among a lot of TV, including *Tom Jones* (1997, as Mr Square), and a stage appearance in a controversial reworking of the assassination of Becket, *Four Nights in Knaresborough* (1999), Fulford has made a trickle of films and was endearingly droll as the gay hero's straight friend into therapy in *Bedrooms and Hallways* (1999).

OTHER BRITISH FILMS INCLUDE: *The Ploughman's Lunch* (1983), *Wetherby* (1985), *A Prayer for the Dying* (1987), *Resurrected* (1989), *Immortal Beloved* (1994, UK/US), *One of the Hollywood Ten* (2000, UK/Sp).

Fuller, Leslie (*b* London, 1889 – *d* Margate, 1948). Actor. BRITISH INTERNATIONAL PICTURES made a popular 30s star of this bluff, broad comedian with his concert party background and his sad-sack demeanour. Many of his films, from *Not So Quiet on the Western Front* (1930), were written by Syd COURTENAY, his former concert-party colleague. Married **Nan Bates** who appeared with him in *The Pride of the Force* (1933).

OTHER BRITISH FILMS INCLUDE: *Kiss Me Sergeant* (1930), *Poor Old Bill* (1931), *Hawleys of High Street* (1933), *Captain Bill* (1935), *Boys Will Be Girls* (1937), *The Middle Watch* (1939), *My Wife's Family* (1941), *Front Line Kids* (1942), *What Do We Do Now?* (1945).

Fuller, Rosalinde (*b* Portsmouth, 1892 – *d* London, 1982). Actress. Trained singer and prolific stage actress (from 1920) who appeared in a handful of 30s films, most prominently *The Song of the Plough* (1933). Awarded MBE, 1966.

OTHER BRITISH FILMS: *The Unwritten Law* (1929), *The Message* (1930, short), *Perfect Understanding* (1933), *The Immortal Gentleman, Escape Me Never* (1935).

Fullerton, Fiona (*b* Kaduna, Nigeria, 1956). Actress. Made film debut as a child in *Run Wild, Run Free* (1969), starred in a musical version of *Alice's Adventures in Wonderland* (1972), drifted into TV (enjoyably in *Hazard of Hearts*, 1987, an unashamed bodice-ripper) and made only a few further films. Was married to Simon MacCORKINDALE.

OTHER BRITISH FILMS: *The Human Factor* (1979, UK/US), *A View to a Kill* (1985).

Furber, Douglas (*b* London, 1885 – *d* London, 1961). Screenwriter. Author of popular musical comedies and revues who worked sometimes solo, sometimes in collaboration, sometimes provided story, sometimes the lyrics or dialogue, for about 20 cheerful entertainments of 30s cinema, most notably songs for *The Good Companions* (1933) and for *The Lambeth Walk* (1939, + co-book).

OTHER BRITISH FILMS INCLUDE: *The Gay Deceiver* (1926, titles); (co-sc) *Happy Ever After* (UK/Ger), *The Maid of the Mountains* (1932), *Falling for You* (1933, + lyrics), *Come Out of the Pantry, Brewster's Millions* (dial) (1935), *When Knights Were Bold, Queen of Hearts* (dial) (1936), *The Sky's the Limit* (1937), *So This is London* (1939); (story) *Money Means Nothing* (1932), *Soldiers of the King* (1933), *Oh, Boy!* (1938); (lyrics) *Elstree Calling* (1930), *Love on Wheels, Jack's the Boy* (+ co-play) (1932), *That's a Good Girl* (1933, + a, co-sc, play).

Furie, Sidney J. (*b* Toronto, 1933). Director. Began work in Canadian TV in the late 50s before moving to England where he secured several modest successes in the early 60s, including two popular MUSICALS with Cliff RICHARD, *The Young Ones* (1961) and *Wonderful Life* (1964) and two critically praised dramas of restless youth, *The Boys* (1962, + p) and *The Leather Boys* (1963). He seemed a fresh, innovative talent, not quite in line with other strands of contemporary British film-making, flashy perhaps, but also zestful. He scored a box-office hit with *The Ipcress File* (1965, BAA Best Picture), a Len DEIGHTON spy thriller, and was thereafter lost to – and in – Hollywood (first there: *The Appaloosa*, 1966) where he continues to work in film and TV.

OTHER BRITISH FILMS: *Dr Blood's Coffin* (1960), *The Snake Woman, During One Night* (+ p), *Three on a Spree* (1961), *The Naked Runner* (1967).

Furneaux, Yvonne (*b* Roubaix, France, 1928). Actress. RN: Elisabeth Scarcherd. French-born, Oxford-educated and RADA-trained actress who made nearly 30 films without registering much more than a darkly attractive presence. In films from 1952, she had small roles in *Meet Me Tonight* and several others before appearing twice with the ageing, raddled Errol FLYNN, in *The Master of Ballantrae* (1953) and *The Dark Avenger* (1955), and with Marcello Mastroianni in *La dolce vita* (1960, It); she had good roles for POLANSKI in *Repulsion* (1965) and Claude Chabrol in *Champagne Murders* (1966, Fr), but none of these ever quite made her a star.

OTHER BRITISH FILMS: *24 Hours of a Woman's Life* (1952), *The Genie, The House of the Arrow, The Beggar's Opera* (1953), *Cross Channel* (1955), *The Mummy* (1959).

Furniss, John (*b* London, 1935). Costume designer. What films such as *The Go-Between* (1971, BAAn cos), *England Made Me* (1972, UK/Yug) and *Daisy Miller* (1974, AAn cos) have in common is their immaculate period costume design and they represent some of Furniss's best work, costume signifying character at every turn. In films since 1966, with *The Blue Max* (1966), for which he won a BAAn.

OTHER BRITISH FILMS INCLUDE: *The Viking Queen* (1966), *The Long Duel* (1967), *Mr Forbush and the Penguins* (1971), *Endless Night* (1972), *Sleuth, A Doll's House* (UK/Fr), *Soft Battles, Hard Beds* (1973), *Wombling Free* (1977), *International Velvet* (1978).

Furniss, Harry (*b* Wexford, 1864 – *d* Hastings, 1925). Animator. A highly regarded cartoonist for *Punch*, Harry Furniss was brought to the US by Thomas A. Edison, Inc. in 1911, acquiring stories, writing scenarios and appearing on screen in a number of short subjects. Returned to the UK in 1913 and settled in Hastings, where he produced a couple of SERIES, *Peace and War Pencillings* and *Winchelsea and Its Environs* (both 1914), featuring his creation of 'lightning sketches', and he also became a commentator on the motion picture, authoring an early text, *Our Lady Cinema* (1914), He can be seen in George PEARSON's *The Little People* (1926). AS.

Furse, Jill (*b* Camberley, 1915 – *d* 1944). Actress. Sweet-faced young actress, sister of Judith and Roger FURSE, who died tragically young, after appearing memorably in only two films: as the home-loving heroine of *There Ain't No Justice* (1939) and as John MILLS' wife in *Goodbye, Mr Chips* (1939).

Furse, Judith (*b* Deepcut, 1912 – *d* England, 1974). Actress. Large, hearty and often formidable character player, Old Vic-trained sister to Jill and Roger FURSE, who made about 40 films, usually lending her bulk to comic effect. The names of some of her characters invoke her persona: she was Dame Maud Hackshaw in *Blue Murder at St Trinian's* (1957), 'Battle-axe woman' in *Carry On Cabby* (1963), and 'Traction engine driver' in *The Iron Maiden* (1963). She was an obvious 'CARRY ON' choice for mannish viragos, but once or twice extended her range: as Greer GARSON's holiday companion in *Goodbye, Mr Chips* (1939), the probation officer in *Serious Charge* (1959) and, especially, as Sister Briony, sent for her 'strength' to St Faith's in *Black Narcissus* (1947).

OTHER BRITISH FILMS INCLUDE: *A Canterbury Tale* (1944), *Johnny Frenchman* (1945), *Quiet Weekend* (1946), *Dear Mr Prohack* (1949), *The Browning Version, The Man in the White Suit* (1951), *I Believe in You* (1952), *Mad About Men* (1954), *Doctor at Large* (1957), *Further Up the Creek* (1958), *Carry On Regardless* (1961), *Live Now, Pay Later, I Thank a Fool* (1962), *Carry On Spying* (1964), *Sky West and Crooked* (1965), *Sinful Davey* (1968), *Twinky* (1969).

Furse, Margaret (*b* London, 1911 – *d* London, 1974). Costume designer. RN: Watts. Was married (2) to Roger FURSE (1936–51), with whom she worked as an assistant on *Henry V* (1944), her first film. Most famous for her designs for costume films: she won AA and BAAn for *Anne of the Thousand Days* (1969), won BAA and AAn for *Becket* (1964), and other AAn for *The Mudlark* (1950), *The Lion in Winter* (1968), *Scrooge* (1970) and *Mary Queen of Scots* (1971), and BAAn for *Young Cassidy* (1965) and the modern-set *A Shot in the Dark* (1964). She was with CINEGUILD in the late 40s, costuming Ann TODD in *The Passionate Friends* (1948) and *Madeleine* (1949), and with both RANK and DISNEY in the 50s and 60s. Married (1) to author and critic Stephen WATTS.

OTHER BRITISH FILMS INCLUDE: *Great Expectations* (ass), *Carnival* (1946), *Blanche Fury* (1947, ass), *Oliver Twist* (1948), *The House in the Square* (1951), *The Million Pound Note* (1953), *Windom's Way* (1957), *The Inn of the Sixth Happiness* (1958), *Sons and Lovers, Kidnapped* (1960), *The Horsemasters, Greyfriars Bobby* (1961), *In Search of the Castaways, The Prince and the Pauper* (1962), *The Three Lives of Thomasina* (1963), *The Trap* (1966), *Great Catherine* (1967), *Sinful Davey* (1968), *A Bequest to the Nation, A Delicate Balance* (UK/US/Can) (1973).

Furse, Roger (*b* Ightham, 1903 – *d* Corfu, 1972). Production designer. Educated at Eton and at the Slade School for Fine Arts, with further study in Paris and work in the US, Furse began stage design in 1934 and had several notable years with the Old Vic. In the Navy 1940–45, and released to design costumes and armour for *Henry V* (1944). He won Oscars for the black-and-white glories of both costume design and art direction (shared with Carmen DILLON) on OLIVIER's *Hamlet* (1948), and also designed his *Richard III* (1955) and *The Prince and the Showgirl* (1957). He was Royal Designer for Industry, 1949. Was married (1 of 2) to Margaret FURSE, and was brother to Jill and Judith FURSE.

OTHER BRITISH FILMS (art d/des, unless noted): *The True Glory* (UK/US), *Burma Victory* (1945), *Odd Man Out* (1947), *Under Capricorn, The Angel with the Trumpet* (1949, cos des), *Ivanhoe* (1952, cos des, co-art d), *Knights of the Round Table* (1953, cos des), *Saint Joan* (UK/US), *Bonjour Tristesse* (1957), *The Roman Spring of Mrs Stone, The Road to Hong Kong* (1961).

Furst, Anton (*b* Wendens Ambo, 1944 – *d* Los Angeles, 1991). Production designer. Oscar-winner for designing *Batman* (1989), a US film largely made at PINEWOOD. Trained as architect and with experience in lighting rock concerts, he was uncredited assistant on *Alien* (UK/US) and *Moonraker* (UK/Fr) (1979), and did superb work in recreating Vietnam in the Home Counties for *Full Metal Jacket* (1987). To Hollywood in the late 80s; committed suicide.

OTHER BRITISH FILMS: *Lady Chatterley's Lover, An Unsuitable Job for a Woman* (1981), *The Company of Wolves, The Frog Prince* (1984).

Fury, Billy (*b* Liverpool, 1941 – *d* London, 1983). Actor. RN: Ronald Wycherley. Durable rock star who could also act, and did so in three films: *Play It Cool* (1962), *I've Gotta Horse* (1965), *That'll Be the Day* (1973). Began his recording career in 1959, and became a popular TV performer, with something of Elvis Presley's sexual charisma. Died sadly young of heart disease.

Fyffe, Will (*b* Dundee, 1885 – *d* St Andrews, 1947). Actor. A popular Scottish MUSIC HALL entertainer – debut 1916 – best remembered for the song 'I Belong to Glasgow'. Unlike his fellow music-hall performers, Fyffe always played character roles on screen rather than appearing in his stage persona, revealing impressive range. He was seen on stage in the late 20s and early 30s and made one American film, *Rulers of the Sea* (1939). His British films included: *King of Hearts* (1936) as the heroine's docker father; the attractive regional drama, *Owd Bob* (1938), as a drunken, irascible Scots shepherd; *Heaven Is Round the Corner* (1943) acting as a sort of Cupid to the young lovers; and, in a fine sympathetic swansong, *The Brothers* (1947). His death resulted from a fall from a hotel bedroom window.

OTHER BRITISH FILMS: *Elstree Calling* (1930), *Happy* (1934), *Rolling Home* (1935), *Debt of Honour, Love in Exile* (1936), *Annie Laurie* (1936), *Men of Yesterday* (1936), *Well Done, Henry* (1937), *Cotton Queen* (1937), *Said O'Reilly to McNab* (1937), *The Mind of Mr Reeder* (1939), *The Missing People* (1939), *They Came by Night, For Freedom, Neutral Port* (1940), *The Prime Minister* (1941), *Give Me the Stars* (1944). AS.

Gg

Gabel, Scilla (*b* Rimini, Italy, 1937). Actress. Pneumatic star of international, mainly Italian films, including such 60s toga tales as *Revenge of the Gladiators* (1965). Appeared to purely decorative effect in three British films: *Tarzan's Greatest Adventure* (1959), *Village of Daughters* (1962) and *Modesty Blaise* (1966).

Gable, Christopher (*b* London, 1940 – *d* Halifax, 1998). Actor. Though he died so young, of cancer, Gable had been a star of the Royal Ballet since 1960, co-starring with fellow alumnus of its Ballet School, Lynn Seymour, in *The Invitation*. With handsome looks and physique, he became a popular ballet star during the 60s, venturing into straight theatre at the end of the decade, with the RSC. His film career is almost entirely associated with director Ken RUSSELL, for whom he first, and memorably, played self-effacing Eric Fenby to Max ADRIAN's Delius in TV's *Song of Summer* (1968). This was followed by five RUSSELL films: *Women in Love* (1969), as doomed Tibby Lupton; *The Music Lovers* (1971); *The Boy Friend* (1971), in which he shared the choreography credit as well as starring with TWIGGY; *The Lair of the White Worm* (1988) and *The Rainbow* (1989); and Bryan FORBES' *The Slipper and the Rose* (1976). Awarded CBE in 1996.

Gabriel, John (*b* London, 1914 – *d* Surrey, 1998) Actor. Tall, lean, general purpose supporting actor, mainly in 'B' FILMS of the 50s and 60s, quite memorably dislikeable in *The Lost Hours* (1952), also in such TV series as *Bergerac* (1981). Appeared in several US films, including *King David* (1985), and his credits are often confused with younger US actor of same name.
OTHER BRITISH FILMS INCLUDE: *Highly Dangerous* (1950), *Secret People* (1951), *The Master Plan* (1954), *The Cat Gang, Corridors of Blood* (1958), *The Curse of the Werewolf* (1961), *The Siege of the Saxons* (1963), *Oh! What a Lovely War* (1969).

Gachet, Alice Actress, teacher. Teacher of French drama at RADA who instructed Renée ASHERSON as Princess Katherine in *Henry V* (1944), and played several small roles in British films: as a hotel manageress in *Bedelia* (1946), and two for Herbert WILCOX: *The Courtneys of Curzon Street* (1947, as a French maid) and *The Man Who Wouldn't Talk* (1957).

Gadd, Renee (*b* Bahia Blanca, Argentina, 1908). Actress. Now best remembered for her small, sharply-observed character roles in the 40s, including Raymond HUNTLEY's bad-tempered wife in *They Came to a City* (1944) or the uppity motorist in *The Blue Lamp* (1949). However, as a pretty blonde under contract to BIP, she had made over 20 modest British films in the 30s, plus three in the US, without reaching stardom, and the roles got smaller as the decade moved on. Came to England on holiday, stayed, trained for ballet, and had a stage career in both Shakespeare and musical comedy.
OTHER BRITISH FILMS INCLUDE: *Aren't We All?, Josser Joins the Navy* (1932), *Letting in the Sunshine* (1933), *Happy* (1934), *Where's Sally?, The Crimson Circle* (1936), *Brief Ecstasy* (1937), *Meet Mr Penny* (1938), *Unpublished Story* (1942), *Dead of Night* (1945), *Frieda, Good-Time Girl* (1947).

Gaffney, Liam (*b* Lucan, Ireland, 1911). Actor. After experience with Dublin's Abbey Theatre, Gaffney played supporting roles in a dozen or so films from 1936 (*Irish and Proud of It*), including Norwood Beverley, a florid repertory actor, in *Curtain Up* (1952). Often in films with Irish elements, such as *Captain Boycott* (1947).
OTHER FILMS INCLUDE: *Macushla* (1937), *The Londonderry Air* (1938), *Dr O'Dowd* (1940), *The Case of Charles Peace* (1949), *Bad Lord Byron* (1949, as Tom Moore), *Women of Twilight* (1952), *Rooney* (1958), *The Trials of Oscar Wilde* (1960), *Island of Terror* (1966).

Gail, Zoe (*b* Cape Town, 1920). Actress. RN: Stapleton. 'Introduced' and, as far as films go, 'farewelled' in *No Orchids for Miss Blandish* (1948). A willowy blonde, she gets a mention for singing a good song well, as Slim Grissom's ex-floozie. Some success in cabaret, on stage (first in Johannesburg), and on TV's *I've Got a Secret* (1956). Married (1) Hubert GREGG.

Gainsborough and Gaumont–British Picture Corporation

Gainsborough was founded in 1924 by Michael BALCON, and in 1927 became associated with the Gaumont–British Picture Corporation, which was set up by the OSTRER brothers. Balcon became director of production for both companies. Gaumont–British, the mother company based at SHEPHERD'S BUSH, produced 'quality' pictures, while Gainsborough's studios at ISLINGTON were dedicated to lower-status fare.

Gaumont–British was a subsidiary of the French production company GAUMONT, which had bought the land for a studio at Shepherd's Bush in 1912 and begun producing by 1914. It was a solely British company from 1922, with a film-making history which preceded the joining up with Gainsborough, and was an EXHIBITION giant in Britain by the late 20s, with 280 cinemas in 1929. With its DISTRIBUTION interests as well, it was a prime example of the vertical integration at work in the film industry.

Under Balcon, Gaumont–British was responsible for some prestigious films, such as *I Was a Spy* (1933), *Jew Süss* (1934) and *The Passing of the Third Floor Black* (1935). Such films attempted to broaden contemporary definitions of national identity, and they experimented with new methods of set construction. In the less ambitious comedies, such as *Cuckoo in the Nest* (1933), or musicals such as *Soldiers of the King* (1933), Balcon left the team unhampered to produce cheap and profitable fare.

Under Balcon's aegis, both Gaumont–British and Gainsborough provided a link to Continental, and specifically German, film practices. Balcon had links with UFA, and in 1925 he encouraged Alfred HITCHCOCK to study German methods *in situ*. Gainsborough also specialised in the production of multilingual films in the late 20s/early 30s. As the German industry became uncomfortable for some artistes in the 30s, both Balcon's companies offered employment to displaced personnel, including Conrad VEIDT, Elizabeth BERGNER, Berthold VIERTEL, Mutz GREENBAUM and Alfred JUNGE. In 1936 Balcon left for MGM–BRITISH, and the internationalist days of Gaumont–British were over. The Gaumont–British studio at Shepherd's Bush was closed, and J. Arthur RANK acquired substantial interests in Gainsborough. Henceforth, Maurice Ostrer became more involved in production, and producer Ted BLACK was more influential in the running of the studio. Black had an unerring sense of British popular taste, and production was skewed to the home market with such films as *Oh, Mr Porter!* (1937) and *Owd Bob* (1938).

With the outbreak of war, Gainsborough was poised to dominate the popular market. Rank had a hands-off policy on the company, and the Ostrers gave Black his head in the orchestration of film topics. From 1942, a crucial figure in the Gainsborough production team was R.J. MINNEY, a successful novelist and former Hollywood scriptwriter. Minney and Black inaugurated a series of COSTUME MELODRAMAS at Gainsborough which dominated the domestic market from 1942 to 1946. These were based on recent popular books by female novelists, foregrounding GYPSIES, wanton women and lustful aristocrats. They were made into films which mined a rich seam in British popular culture and were visually extravagant and morally ambivalent: films such as *The Man in Grey* (1943), *Madonna of the Seven Moons* (1944), *The Wicked Lady* (1945) and *Caravan* (1946). Black and Minney encouraged the careers of a new breed of British stars – Margaret LOCKWOOD, James MASON, Stewart GRANGER, Patricia ROC – who were democratic in their manner, and the *female* side of the British audience took them to their hearts. Critics and male viewers excoriated the Gainsborough costume melodramas, but for female fans the historical pleasures and sexual mayhem performed an important function.

From 1942 to 1946, Black and Minney also specialised in two other film genres: comedy and modern-dress melodramas. With the latter, the same themes as the costume melos were rehearsed. *Love Story* (1944), and *They Were Sisters* (1945) dealt with desire, anger and sartorial envy. The comedies were more heterogeneous and lacked the box-office instincts of the melodramas. Tommy HANDLEY's *Time Flies* (1944) was intellectually inventive but a box-office failure, and the Arthur ASKEY films such as *Bees in Paradise* (1944) performed unevenly and were often misogynist.

After 1946, Rank's henchmen began to intervene more directly in production, and one by one the disillusioned Gainsborough specialists left. The Ostrers resigned, Black went to MGM, Minney left film production and Rank wished to appoint a successor who would continue their popular melodrama trajectory. He chose Sydney BOX, mistakenly thinking that his *The Seventh Veil* (1945) provided the right pedigree. But Box was essentially interested in verisimilitude of method and appearance. Films such as *Here Come the Huggetts* (1948) and *A Boy, a Girl and a Bike* (1949) were predicated on social REALISM. Box's output was uneven, and he was hampered by inexperience, bad planning and expensive LOCATION work.

Gainsborough's dominance at the box-office declined drastically, and Rank cut his losses by closing the studio in 1950.

However, Box ushered in some important innovations in film practice. He appointed his sister Betty BOX as producer at the ISLINGTON arm of Gainsborough, and gave her sufficient autonomy to develop a substantial career. Indeed, she was, from late 1946 and right throughout the 50s, the only major female producer in the British industry. She produced a range of COMEDIES at Gainsborough, such as *Miranda* (1948), which were professional and popular, and some CRIME THRILLERS, such as *The Blind Goddess* (1948), which were more mediocre. Sydney Box also furthered the career of his wife Muriel BOX while at Gainsborough, promoting her to head of the Scenario Department. Muriel wrote a number of ground-breaking scripts, in which her FEMINISM was much in evidence. Such films as *The Brothers* (1947) and *Good-Time Girl* (1947) have scripts which nuance female desire and its punishment in an unusually explicit way.

As well as feature production, Gaumont–British engaged in three other areas of film-making. Under the name of GB INSTRUCTIONAL, it was involved in DOCUMENTARY, specializing in films for the educational market. Mary FIELD was one of the most important of its directors, making her name in school films about biology and history. Second, Gaumont entered the competitive NEWSREEL market with Gaumont–British News; its competent newsreeels had wide showings in circuit cinemas. Third, in the mid 40s, RANK set up GB Animation, under American David HAND, but this venture was less successful, never rivalling the popularity of its US competition.

BIBLIOG: Pam Cook (ed), *Gainsborough Pictures*, 1997; Sue Harper, *Picturing the Past: the Rise and Fall of the British Costume Film*, 1994, and *Women in British Cinema*, 2000. Sue Harper.

Gainsbourg, Charlotte (*b* London, 1971). Actress. Daughter of French director Serge Gainsbourg and actress Jane BIRKIN, and granddaughter of actress Judy CAMPBELL, she has filmed primarily in France, but has appeared in two British co-productions: *The Cement Garden* (1993, UK/Fr/Ger), directed by uncle Andrew BIRKIN, and, eponymously, in *Jane Eyre* (1996, UK/Fr/It/US).

OTHER BRITISH FILMS: *The Intruder* (1999, UK/Can).

Galer, Andrea Costume designer. Famously designed Richard E. GRANT's long, actorish coat in *Withnail & I* (1986), but she had already made a name for her designs for Julie CHRISTIE in *Don't Look Now* (1973, UK/It). As well as designing for films, to which she returned after ten years of child-raising, and for pop stars, she also designs for the public, showing her wares on the internet. As with her designs for *Mansfield Park* (1999, UK/US), she subtly accommodates period accuracy to contemporary acceptability.

OTHER BRITISH FILMS INCLUDE: *Brothers in Trouble* (1995), *Letters from the East* (1996), *Love and Death on Long Island*, *Firelight* (1997).

Galleon, George (*b* Argentina). Actor. Lead and second lead of a few light 30s films, usually in upper-class roles, most notably as Wendy HILLER's love interest in *Lancashire Luck* (1937). She remembered him in 1991 as a 'beautiful creature' who had a disappointing career.

OTHER BRITISH FILMS: *Ship's Concert*, *The Windmill*, *Mayfair Melody*, *The Man Who Made Diamonds* (1937), *The Singing Cop*, *It's in the Blood* (1938).

Gallone, Carmine (*b* Taggia, Italy, 1886 – *d* Frascati, Italy, 1972). Director. Italian director who divided his creative talents between Italy, Germany, Japan, and Britain. Many of his films were of operatic inspiration; his British films are almost all MUSICALS of one kind or other and are, if not unwatchable, largely unseeable today, though they star major 30s players such as Jan KIEPURA, whose *My Heart is Calling* (1934) *can* sometimes be seen on TV. He began making films in Italy in 1914, directed the first German talkie (*Land Without Women*) in 1929, and was much involved in European co-productions.
OTHER BRITISH FILMS INCLUDE: *City of Pleasure* (1928), *King of the Ritz* (1933), *Two Hearts in Waltz Time* (1934), *The Divine Spark* (1935).

Galsworthy, John (*b* Kingston Hill, Surrey, 1867 – *d* London, 1933). Author. Galsworthy's most famous connection with film was via the hugely popular and prestigious BBC TV serialisation of *The Forsyte Saga* (1967), which quite eclipsed the Hollywood film of 1949. He had acted in a couple of silent films (*School Days*, 1921, and *Island Wives*, 1922, US); his play, *Justice*, was filmed in 1917; and, in the early 30s, as a result of his friendship with Basil DEAN, he allowed his play, *Escape* (1930), to be filmed, starring Gerald DU MAURIER. It was filmed again by Fox in Britain in 1948, with Rex HARRISON. In 1931, HITCHCOCK made a fluently cinematic treatment of *The Skin Game* and in 1933 Dean filmed *Loyalties*, starring Basil RATHBONE, for the newly formed ASSOCIATED TALKING PICTURES. His short story, 'The First and the Last' was filmed as *21 Days* (1937), with a screenplay by Graham GREENE who later derided it, and excerpts were used to satirical effect in *The End of the Affair* (2000, UK/Ger/US); and another story, 'The Apple Tree', was filmed as *A Summer Story* (1987).

Galton, Ray (*b* London, 1930). Writer. With co-writer Alan SIMPSON, a legendary figure in British television, generally considered responsible for the success of Tony HANCOCK, for whom Galton began writing material on radio in 1952. Also co-scripted Hancock's feature film, *The Rebel* (1960). Other television work includes *Steptoe and Son*, *Citizen James and Clochemerle*. Made unsuccessful attempts at a US career with Simpson at Screen Gems in 1965 and with Johnny Speight at ABC in 1979. Awarded OBE 2000.
OTHER BRITISH FILMS: (co-sc) *The Wrong Arm of the Law* (1962), *The Bargee* (1964), *The Spy with a Cold Nose* (1966), *Loot* (1970), *Up the Chastity Belt* (1971), *Steptoe and Son* (1972), *Steptoe and Son Ride Again* (1973). AS.

Galvani, Dino (*b* Milan, 1890 – *d* London, 1960). Actor. Intended for the priesthood, Galvani made his stage debut in Milan in 1902, in London 1921, entered films in the late 20s and stayed on to play dozens of 'continental types', like the Italian professor in *Father Brown* (1954).
OTHER BRITISH FILMS INCLUDE: *Blighty* (1927), *Adam's Apple* (1928), *Adventurous Atlantic* (1929), *Kidnapped* (1930), *The Missing Rembrandt* (1932), *Princess Charming* (1934), *Strange Boarders* (1938), *It's That Man Again* (1943), *Sleeping Car to Trieste* (1948), *Always a Bride* (1953), *Checkpoint* (1956), *Danger Within* (1958), *Bluebeard's Ten Honeymoons* (1960).

Gambon, Sir Michael (*b* Dublin, 1940). Actor. Tall, hefty and in every possible way dominant actor of the late 20th century, equally distinguished on stage (his 1982 King Lear at Stratford was an unforgettable old lion at bay, and he won unending plaudits for playing PINTER's tramp in *The Caretaker*, 2000), TV (winning BAAs for *The Singing Detective*, 1986, and *Wives and Daughters*, 1999), and film. He can fill a stage with the sheer *size* of his interpretation; unlike some great stage performers, though, he knows exactly how to reduce the scale to the minute scrutiny of the camera. He started on the National Theatre stage in its inaugural season of 1963 and entered films in 1965, in *Othello*, the screened record of OLIVIER's triumph. There were a few small film roles and a bigger one as the aquarium keeper in *Turtle Diary* (1985), but he really came to filmgoers' attention as the vile thief, Albert Spica, in Peter GREENAWAY's extraordinary *The Cook, the Thief, His Wife & Her Lover* (1989, UK/Fr). This finely honed study in disgusting cruelty offered remarkable contrasts with the unctuous headmaster in *The Browning Version* (1994) or the seedy Lionel Croy in *The Wings of the Dove* (1997, UK/US). International films have included *Sleepy Hollow* (UK/Ger) and *The Insider* (US) (1999). Made CBE in 1992, knighted in 1998, he is well on the way to national treasurehood, without succumbing to luvviedom.
OTHER BRITISH FILMS: *Nothing but the Night* (1972), *The Beast Must Die* (1974), *Paris by Night* (1988), *The Rachel Papers* (1989), *A Man of No Importance* (1994), *Two Deaths, Nothing Personal, Midnight in St Petersburg, Len Deighton's Bullet to Beijing* (UK/Can/CIS), *The Innocent Sleep* (1995), *Mary Reilly* (1996, UK/US), *The Gambler* (1997, UK/Neth/Hung), *Dancing at Lughnasa* (1998, UK/US/Ire), *Plunkett & Macleane, Dead on Time* (short) (1999), *The Last September* (2000, UK/Fr/Ire), *High Heels and Low Lifes* (UK/US), *Christmas Carol: The Movie* (voice, anim), *Gosford Park* (UK/Ger/US), *Charlotte Gray* (UK/Aust/US) (2001), *Chequered Past* (2002).

Gamley, Douglas (*b* Melbourne, 1924 – *d* London, 1998). Composer. After competent 'prentice work in generally undistinguished GENRE fare in the 50s, Gamley found his niche in HORROR films, starting with *The Horror of It All* (1964). Apart from a stint with MONTY PYTHON in 1971, he remained with this genre for the rest of his career.
OTHER BRITISH FILMS INCLUDE: (co-comp) *Land of Laughter* (1957), *Carry On Cruising* (1962), *Enigma* (1982); (cond): *The Roman Spring of Mrs Stone* (1961), *Rotten to the Core* (1965); (m d): *The Girl on a Motorcycle* (1968, UK/Fr), *Sunday Bloody Sunday* (1971); (comp): *The Admirable Crichton* (1957), *tom thumb, Gideon's Day* (1958), *Beyond This Place* (1959), *The Grass Is Greener* (m arr) (1960), *Spring and Port Wine* (1969), *And Now for Something Completely Different* (1971), *Tales from the Crypt, Asylum* (1972), *The Vault of Horror* (1973, UK/US), *The Land That Time Forgot* (1974), *The Monster Club* (1980).

Ganatra, Nitin Chandra (*b* Kisum, Kenya, 1968). Actor. Studied in Britain (Bristol University) and trained in Italy under director Jerzy Grotowski, Ganatra has been busy on stage, to acclaim in *To the Green Fields Beyond* (2000), as the Blake-reading Sikh soldier. Also worked in TV (*This Life, The Sins*, etc) and radio; his film work, including *Truly Madly Deeply* (1991), as a ghost, and *Secrets & Lies* (1996), has been less prolific but still noticeable.
OTHER BRITISH FILMS INCLUDE: *Guru in Seven* (1998), *Second Generation* (2000), *Shooters* (2001).

Gardner, Ava (*b* Smithfield, N. Carolina, 1922 – *d* London, 1990). Actress. Comprehensively gorgeous international star whom the years only served to make more so, with a streak of tough-minded humour as well. She was manufactured by MGM, who admittedly had prime material to work on, and made only a half-dozen British films, but she was memorable as Pandora in the bizarre *Pandora and the Flying Dutchman* (1950), as Queen Guinevere in *Knights of the Round Table* (1953), and as Mabel Dodge in *Priest of Love* (1980). Disillusioned with Hollywood, she lived her last years in London.
OTHER BRITISH FILMS: *Mogambo* (1953, UK/US), *Mayerling* (1968, UK/Fr), *The Devil's Widow* (1971), *The Cassandra Crossing* (1976).

Gardner, Joan (*b* Chesham, 1914 – *d* Beverly Hills, 1999). Actress. Alexander KORDA starlet of 30s who met and married his brother, Zoltán KORDA, and moved with him in 1940 to Hollywood, where she became a prominent socialite. Rumour had it that Zoltán married her because she could drive and he could not. Voice heard in two US animated features: *Gay Purree* (1962) and *Mister Magoo's Holiday Festival* (1970).
BRITISH FILMS INCLUDE: *Catherine the Great* (1934), *The Scarlet Pimpernel* (1935), *The Man Who Could Work Miracles*, *Wings over Africa* (1936), *Dark Journey* (1937), *The Challenge* (1938). AS.

Garnett, Tony (*b* Birmingham, 1935). Producer. For more than 35 years Tony Garnett has not only charted but taken an active role in promoting social and even legislative change through the forceful advocacy of his work, most notably with TV's *Cathy Come Home* (1966). Starting as actor, he moved into TV, taking a leading role as story editor for the *The Wednesday Play*, where Dennis POTTER, Ken LOACH and others came to notice. Garnett's later collaborations with LOACH at Kestrel Films included the influential *Kes* (1969). His 1982 film, *Handgun* (p, d, sc), made in the US by Kestrel for EMI, was powerful and thought-provoking in his best British manner. After a brief residence in Los Angeles, where he otherwise worked without much pleasure or distinction (e.g. on *Earth Girls Are Easy*, 1989) and a stint as a director, he returned to England in 1992. His more recent TV work, *This Life* (1996) and *The Cops* (1998) revealed undimmed his sensitive eye for the nuances of cultural change and his fearless exposure of the nation's social ills.
OTHER BRITISH FILMS INCLUDE: (a) *The Boys* (1962), *The Rivals*, *Incident at Midnight* (1963); (p, unless noted) *Kes* (1969, + co-sc), *Family Life* (1971), *Black Jack* (1979), *Prostitute* (1980), *Beautiful Thing* (1996). Kevin Foster.

Garrick, John (*b* Brighton, 1902 – *d* San Francisco, 1966). Actor. RN: Reginald Dandy. Filmed in Hollywood until the early 30s, then returned to England to make 20 MUSICALS, including *Chu-Chin-Chow* (1934) and other GENRE pieces, with major roles in RANK's first commercial venture, *Turn of the Tide* (1935), as one of the feuding Lunns, and the comedy, *Riding High* (1937) as the blacksmith hero.
OTHER BRITISH FILMS INCLUDE: *Anything Might Happen* (1934), *The Rocks of Valpré*, *His Majesty and Co.* (1935), *A Woman Alone*, (1936), *Sunset in Vienna*, *Knight for a Day* (1937), *Special Edition* (1938).

Garson, Greer (*b* London, 1904 – *d* Dallas, 1996). Actress. Legendarily ladylike Hollywood star, two of whose legends – her birth place and date (*not* Belfast, *not* 1908) – were exploded only after her death. She made only two UK films: the durably affecting *Goodbye, Mr Chips* (1939), as the woman who humanises Chips, and the unjustly despised *The Miniver Story* (1950), sequel to her AA-winning *Mrs Miniver* (1942, US), but she was a pioneer of British TV, appearing in such dramas as *Twelfth Night* and *School for Scandal* (1937), and had already made a name on the London stage. Her star outshone virtually all others in wartime Hollywood; she went into immediate and irreversible decline afterwards, last appearing as herself in the documentary, *Directed by William Wyler* (1986).
BIBLIOG: Michael Troyan, *A Rose for Mrs Miniver. The Life of Greer Garson*. 1999.

Garwood, Norman (*b* Birmingham, 1947). Production designer. Garwood's career has been roughly divided between Britain till 1985 and Hollywood since. In Britain he was associated with the surrealities of Terry GILLIAM's *Time*

Bandits (1981) and *Brazil* (1985), for which he won a BAA and AAn, and with two Richard LONCRAINE oddities, *The Missionary* (1981) and *Brimstone & Treacle* (1982). Also received AAn for US films, *Glory* (1989) and (the vulgar excesses of) *Hook* (1991).
OTHER BRITISH FILMS: *Bullshot* (1983), *Water* (1985), *Shadey*, *Link* (1985), *Being Human* (1994), *Lost in Space* (1998, UK/US).

Gastoni, Lisa (*b* Alassio, Italy, 1935). Actress. Came to England in 1948, trained as architect and became photographic model before entering films. Between 1953 and 1961, the attractive brunette made 20 films in Britain, before returning to her native Italy where she made a further 30-odd, including LOSEY's *Eva* (1962, It/Fr) and the quite potent sexual melodrama, *Scandalo* (1976). In her UK films, she had leads in 'B' MOVIES like *Man from Tangier* (1957) and *The Breaking Point* (1961), essentially as glamorous distractions, and supporting roles in bigger films, though she is virtually the only woman in the popular comedy, *The Baby and the Battleship* (1956). More fun than some of the more solemn Continental imports of the 50s.
OTHER BRITISH FILMS INCLUDE: *The Runaway Bus* (1953), *Dance Little Lady* (1954), *Man of the Moment* (1955), *Three Men in a Boat* (1956), *The Truth about Women* (1957), *Family Doctor*, *Hello London* (as herself) (1958), *Visa to Canton* (1960).

Gates, Tudor (*b* London, 1930). Screenwriter. Mostly associated with EXPLOITATION genres, though at upmarket levels. In the industry from 1954, he wrote screenplays for many popular TV series, including *Colditz* (1972–74) and *Sweeney* (1975–76), as well as novels and stage plays. His films included HORROR tales such as *Twins of Evil* (1971) and sex romps such as *Intimate Games* (1976), as well as *Barbarella* (1967, It/Fr) and *The Optimists of Nine Elms* (1973).
OTHER BRITISH FILMS INCLUDE: *Dateline Diamonds* (1965), *Lust for a Vampire*, *Fright* (1971), *The Love Box* (1972), *Three for All* (1974), *Confessions of the Naughty Nymphos* (1980).

Gauge, Alexander (*b* Wenchow, China, 1914 – *d* Woking, 1960). Actor. Tubby actor who was of course Friar Tuck in TV's *Robin Hood* (1955), Gauge was a sort of mini-Sydney Greenstreet in British films (often 'B' MOVIES) of the 50s. Thus, he was Mr Tupman in *The Pickwick Papers* (1952), a shifty advertising boss in *Double Exposure* (1954), the posh-talking head of a bunch of crooks in *The Hornet's Nest* (1955), and, in a touch of the ART-HOUSE, Henry II in George HOELLERING's *Murder in the Cathedral* (1952).
OTHER BRITISH FILMS INCLUDE: *The Interrupted Journey* (1949), *Will Any Gentleman . . . ?*, *The Square Ring*, *Counterspy* (1953), *Fast and Loose*, *Dance Little Lady* (1954), *Before I Wake*, *The Reluctant Bride*, (1955), *The Iron Petticoat*, *Port of Escape*, *The Green Man* (1956), *Nothing Barred* (1961).

Gaumont is the oldest extant film company in the world, having been founded in 1895 as La Société Léon Gaumont et Cie in France by Léon Gaumont (*b* 1863 – *d* 1946). In 1896, Gaumont appointed his secretary Alice Guy as his and the world's first female director. In September 1898, A.C. BROMHEAD and T.A. WELSH opened a British branch in London, and it developed into a major producer and distributor of many UK films, aside from those of Gaumont. In 1913, Gaumont erected the first purpose-built glass studio at London's LIME GROVE, and, in 1922, the British organisation was acquired by financier Isidore OSTRER. AS.

Gaumont–British Instructional Films *see* **GB Instructional Films**

Gaumont–British Picture Corporation *see* **Gainsborough and Gaumont–British**

Gausden, Sidney Production designer. Worked on a half-dozen inspirational films directed by Norman WALKER, including *Hard Steel* (1942), *The Great Mr Handel* (1942 – his most lavish work), and the drab homiletic, *They Knew Mr Knight* (1945). Directed one religious film, *The Permanent Way* (1944).

OTHER BRITISH FILMS: *Beyond Our Horizon, The First Easter* (1939, shorts), *The Man at the Gate* (1941).

Gawthorne, Peter (*b* Laoighis, Ireland, 1884 – *d* London, 1962). Actor. Extremely busy character actor, usually cast in authoritarian roles, such as police, the military or the aristocracy, including the Duke of Richmond in *The Iron Duke* (1935). On stage from 1906, often in musical comedy, and began film career in Hollywood (1929–31).

OTHER BRITISH FILMS INCLUDE: *The Lodger, The Flag Lieutenant* (1932), *Dirty Work* (1934), *No Limit* (1935), *Windbag the Sailor* (1936), *Gangway, Good Morning, Boys!, Brief Ecstasy* (1937), *Riding High, Convict 99* (1938), *Ask a Policeman* (1939), *They Came by Night* (1940), *Gasbags, Pimpernel Smith, Love on the Dole* (1941), *Bell-Bottom George* (1944), *Murder in Reverse* (1945), *This Man Is Mine* (1946), *Paul Temple Returns* (1952), *Five Days* (1954). AS.

gay and lesbian representation Censorship ensured that portrayals of gays and lesbians in British cinema were suppressed before the 60s, though many lesbians, gays and bisexuals existed in front of – and behind – the camera. They included actors Charles LAUGHTON, Ivor NOVELLO, Ernest THESIGER, John GIELGUD, Mary MORRIS, Anton WALBROOK, Eric PORTMAN, Dennis PRICE and Michael WARD; directors Anthony 'Puffin' ASQUITH and Brian Desmond HURST; composers Benjamin BRITTEN and Richard 'Warsaw Concerto' ADDINSELL; and screenwriters Terence RATTIGAN and Paul DEHN (AA winner for *Seven Days to Noon*). In the hands of director James WHALE, the anti-war drama *Journey's End* (1930) – a British production made in Hollywood – became a haunting vision of homo-emotional male-bonding. Alfred HITCHCOCK stereotyped gays as perverse killers, such as the transvestite in *Murder!* (1930) and later in *Rope* (1948, US). On a lighter note, it is almost impossible to find a British musical-comedy star who didn't enjoy periodic cross-dressing, such as Cicely COURTNEIDGE (*Soldiers of the King*, 1933), Jessie MATTHEWS (*First A Girl*, 1935) and Tommy TRINDER (*Fiddlers Three*, 1944). The gay subtext in *Brief Encounter* (1945) comes from its source, writer/producer Noël COWARD, with a perhaps covertly gay character in Stephen Lynn, played by Valentine DYALL. In 1990 Richard KWIETNIOWSKI reworked *Brief Encounter* as *Flames of Passion*, a short gay romantic drama. Occasional gay roles surfaced in the films of POWELL AND PRESSBURGER including the effete French aristocrat in *A Matter of Life and Death* (1946) and the ballet impresario based on Diaghilev in *The Red Shoes* (1948). For years, Charles HAWTREY and Kenneth WILLIAMS camped it up in the popular 'CARRY ON' series. In 1960 two films about Oscar WILDE were passed by the British Board of Film Censors, though neither permitted any physical contact between men, or mentioned the word homosexuality. Gay characters in *A Taste of Honey* (1961), *The L-Shaped Room* (1962) and *The Leather Boys* (1963) were sympathetically drawn, and they were obliquely signified in *The League of Gentlemen* (1960) and *This Sporting Life* (1963), but it was DEARDEN and RELPH's *Victim* (1961), a thriller about the blackmailing of gays, that had the biggest impact. Its star, Dirk BOGARDE, was often associated with gay/camp roles (*The Spanish Gardener, The Servant, Modesty Blaise, Death in Venice*). After the 1967 Sexual Offences Act partially decriminalised 'homosexual practices', John SCHLESINGER made *Sunday Bloody Sunday* (1971), an intelligent exploration of a bisexual triangle, though Derek JARMAN's *Sebastiane* (1976) was truly the first British gay film. An outspoken activist, openly gay Jarman went on to become the British film industry's *enfant terrible*. Other openly gay directors who emerged at this time included Terence DAVIES (his 'trilogy', 1976–83, was a critically acclaimed, if depressing vision of a Catholic gay man's life) and Ron PECK (*Nighthawks*). In the 80s public schools provided the setting for *Another Country* (1984) and MERCHANT IVORY's *Maurice* (1987), based on E.M. FORSTER's long-unpublished novel. *My Beautiful Laundrette* (1985), crossing gay with mixed-race theme, was originally made for TV, but found an international cinema audience. Underrated Liverpudlian writer Frank CLARKE deserved more attention – and opportunities to work in film – after *The Fruit Machine* (1988). *Framed Youth*, made by the Lesbian and Gay Video Project in 1983, won the John GRIERSON Award for Best Documentary. Some members of the project (Constantine Giannaris, Isaac JULIEN) went on to become part of the 'New Queer Cinema' movement with Jarman whose adaptation of Christopher Marlowe's *Edward II* (1991) was acclaimed. Towards the end of the 80s AIDS began to influence some film-makers, including Jarman who succumbed to the illness in 1994. In 1988 the London Lesbian and Gay Film Festival was launched. Mainstream films with gay characters and themes that have been pushing the boundaries further include *Prick Up Your Ears* (1987), *The Krays* (1990), *Young Soul Rebels* (1991), *Priest* (1994), *Beautiful Thing* (1996), *Wilde* (1997, UK/Ger/Jap/US), *Get Real* and *Like It Is* (both 1999).

Lesbians have been ill-served in British cinema and mostly restricted to stereotypes. In *Two Thousand Women* (1944) trouser-wearing Phyllis CALVERT reveals to her room-mate she once had a crush on a girl at school. Freda JACKSON played a mannish farm owner in *A Canterbury Tale* (1944) and Pamela BROWN was the wild, sexually ambiguous Catriona in *I Know Where I'm Going!* (1945). Important breakthroughs came when popular, well-known actresses began to accept sympathetic – if underwritten – lesbian roles. These included Cicely Courtneidge (*The L-Shaped Room*, 1962), Sylvia SYMS (*The World Ten Times Over*, 1963) and Claire BLOOM (*The Haunting*, 1963). In spite of Beryl REID's *tour de force* as a lesbian soap star, *The Killing of Sister George* (1968) exploited the sensational aspects of its lesbian theme. Predatory lesbian vampires surfaced in HAMMER horrors and Vanessa REDGRAVE played a repressed lesbian in Merchant Ivory's *The Bostonians* (1984, UK/US). Ken RUSSELL's adaptation of D.H. LAWRENCE's *The Rainbow* (1989) featured Sammi DAVIS as the North Country girl who falls in love with her teacher. Fiona Cunningham Reid's *Thin Ice* (1994), a believable lesbian love story, won the Audience Award at the Turin Lesbian and Gay Film Festival.

BIBLIOG: Stephen Bourne, *Brief Encounters – Lesbians and Gays in British Cinema 1930–71*, 1996; Keith Howes, *Broadcasting It – An Encyclopaedia of Homosexuality on Film, Radio, and TV in the UK 1923–1993*, 1993. Stephen Bourne.

Gay, Noel (*b* Wakefield, 1898 – *d* London, 1954). Composer. RN: Reginald Armitage. Cambridge- and RCM-educated composer and songwriter who contributed songs and music to about 20 light entertainments of the 30s and early 40s. Co-author of the stage musical, *For Me and My Girl*, filmed in 1939 as *The Lambeth Walk*, named for its hit song, heard again nearly 50 years later in *The Land Girls* (1998, UK/Fr), he composed music and/or songs for the likes of Jessie MATTHEWS, Cicely COURTNEIDGE and Arthur ASKEY, and new words and music for *Champagne Charlie* (1944).

OTHER BRITISH FILMS: (co-m) *You Made Me Love You, Facing the Music, No Funny Business* (1933), *Things Are Looking Up* (1935), *Lassie From Lancashire* (1938), *Time Flies* (1944); (m) *There Goes the Bride, The Midshipmaid* (1932), *Soldiers of the King* (1933), *Me and Marlborough* (1935), *Our Fighting Navy* (1937), *I Thank You* (1941).

Gayson, Eunice (*b* London, 1931). Actress. RN: Sargaison. In October 1955, *Picturegoer* felt Gayson was 'the girl with possibly the biggest drawing power among Britain's up-and-coming actresses'. In the event, Gayson, who had opera training and a stage background, never became more than a RANK starling, with second female leads in films like *Dance Little Lady* (1954), *Out of the Clouds* (1955), and *Zarak* (1956). She acted in numerous TV playlets for *Douglas Fairbanks Presents* during the 50s, was Sylvia Trench in the first two BOND movies, *Dr No* (1962) and *From Russia with Love* (1963), was the Countess in the London production of *The Sound of Music* (1972), and has scarcely been heard of since.

OTHER BRITISH FILMS INCLUDE: *My Brother Jonathan* (1948), *Dance Hall* (1950), *Miss Robin Hood* (1952), *Street Corner* (1953), *The Last Man to Hang?* (1956), *Light Fingers* (starring role), *The Revenge of Frankenstein, Hello London* (1958).

GB Instructional Films Founded in 1933 by H. Bruce WOOLFE as a subsidiary of the GAUMONT–BRITISH PICTURE CORPORATION to make educational films for schools. Key early films include the *Secrets of Life* series by Mary FIELD and Percy Smith, Paul ROTHA's *Shipyard* (1935) and Field's *This was England* (1935). The range of educational films covered language, literature, history, geography, sports and science, characterised by their use of animated maps, diagrams and pictograms. As with most other DOCUMENTARY units, GB Instructional produced a plethora of wartime films for the government and Services. The Children's Film Department, later Children's Entertainment Films, was also established during the war. This was ultimately run by Field and expanded after the war with the addition of directors including Lewis GILBERT, Ralph SMART and Philip LEACOCK. At this time Donald Carter took over from Woolfe but the company was hit badly by the film industry slump of the early 50s. Children's Entertainment Films was closed down and GB Instructional assimilated into its parent company with a change of name to the Specialised Film Unit. Sarah Easen.

Geeson, Judy (*b* Arundel, 1948). Actress. Educated at the Corona Stage School, Geeson began her professional career on TV, before entering films in 1963 and coming to notice in *To Sir, with Love* (1967), as the pretty blonde student who falls in love with 'Sir'. There were good roles in *Three into Two Won't Go* (1968) and, as the wife of the tragic victim, in *10 Rillington Place* (1970), but, though she kept filming, often in insignificant comedies and horror films, her best chances were arguably in TV, with continuing roles in *The Newcomers* (1965–69), *Poldark* (1975) and *Danger UXB* (1979). Theatre seasons in the 70s with the RSC and the Young Vic. Sister of Sally GEESON; once married to actor Kristoffer Tabori.

OTHER BRITISH FILMS INCLUDE: *Wings of Mystery* (1963), *Berserk!* (1967), *Prudence and the Pill* (1968), *The Executioner* (1970), *Doomwatch* (1972), *Percy's Progress* (1974), *Brannigan* (1975), *The Eagle Has Landed, Carry On England* (1976), *Dominique* (1978), *The Duke* (1999, UK/Can).

Geeson, Sally (*b* Cuckfield, 1950). Actress. Judy GEESON's younger sister, best known as Sid JAMES's teenage daughter in TV's *Bless This House* (1971–76), a role she played in the 1972 movie SPIN-OFF. Entered films as Norman WISDOM's leading lady in *What's Good for the Goose* (1969), but thereafter had only small roles in a handful of films.

OTHER BRITISH FILMS: *The Oblong Box* (1969), *The Cry of the Banshee* (1970), *Mr Forbush and the Penguins* (1971), *Carry On Abroad* (1972), . . . *Girls* (1973).

Geldof, Bob (*b* Dun Laoghaire, Ireland, 1954). Singer. The career of this remarkable pop star belongs properly in another book, but the former lead singer with 'The Boomtown Rats' has made a few guest appearances in films, in *Spice World* (1997) and notably in the Amnesty-inspired revue films, *The Secret Policeman's Other Ball* (1982) and *The Secret Policeman's Third Ball* (1987), as well as starring in *Pink Floyd The Wall* (1982). Awarded honorary knighthood 1986, and BAFTA television award 1985.

gender representation The repressed, emotionally stunted upper-class male, characterised by his 'stiff upper lip', has provided the model for the quintessential Englishman for decades. Rooted in the image of the public school boy, this figure, personified by the likes of Clive BROOK and Herbert MARSHALL in the 30s, is distinguished by masochism and martyrdom. He is often a-sexual, or uneasy with his sexuality, from Peter O'TOOLE in *Lawrence of Arabia* (1962) and Alec GUINNESS in *The Bridge on the River Kwai* (1957) to Anthony HOPKINS in *Remains of the Day* (1993) and Ralph FIENNES in *The End of the Affair* (2000, UK/Ger/US). Even the expressive Ivor NOVELLO, 'Britain's answer to Valentino' in the 20s, betrayed more than a hint of hysteria in HITCHCOCK's *The Lodger* (1926) and GAINSBOROUGH's *Rat* trilogy. In the late 40s, when gender boundaries shifted dramatically, the twisted, brooding sexuality of James MASON was contrasted with the upright athleticism of Stewart GRANGER, a strapping example of the upwardly mobile post-war New Man. Granger may be the nearest thing Britain has to offer in response to American heroes such as John Wayne, Henry Fonda and Rock Hudson, 'natural' men who retained their virility in the face of emasculation. English masculinity seems to have more affinity with European tortured romantic figures such as Anton WALBROOK and Conrad VEIDT, both popular with British audiences.

The late 50s and 60s gave birth to new masculine identities with strong class and regional dimensions. Working-class rebels Albert FINNEY in *Saturday Night and Sunday Morning* (1960) and Richard HARRIS in *This Sporting Life* (1963) exhibited a sullen physicality akin to Marlon Brando's. With *Dr No* in 1962 British cinema's most enduring masculine persona was born. James BOND – from Sean CONNERY to Pierce BROSNAN – is the epitome of understated, ironic English masculinity, sardonically commenting on his sexual insecurities even as he embraces New Lad culture. Bond's working-class equivalent, Michael CAINE as *Alfie* (1966), never achieved the same international status. However, raffish East End reprobates, who first found popularity with Caine and Terence STAMP in the 60s, enjoyed a revival in *Lock, Stock and Two Smoking Barrels* (1998) and *Snatch* (2000).

Female identities in British cinema are generally more robust and transgressive. Between the wars, modern femininity was characterised as androgynous and essentially mobile. Tomboy Jessie MATTHEWS in Victor SAVILLE's *Sunshine Susie* (1931) and *First A Girl* (1935) was the archetypal social climber living off her wits, while a swashbuckling Anna NEAGLE cross-dressed in *Peg of Old Drury* (1935) as well as displaying matriarchal authority as Queen Victoria in *Sixty Glorious Years* (1938). Flora ROBSON's magnificently mannish Empress Elizabeth in *Catherine the Great* (1934) outshone both Elisabeth BERGNER as Catherine and Douglas FAIRBANKS JR as the foppish Grand Duke Peter. English women from Madeleine CARROLL in *The 39 Steps* (1935) to Margaret LOCKWOOD in *The Lady Vanishes* (1938) were independent adventurers equal to their male counterparts, a trend which continued into the 40s with wicked ladies such as Jean KENT in *Caravan* (1946) and Phyllis CALVERT in *Madonna of the Seven Moons* (1944). Even a pillar of propriety such as Celia JOHNSON found herself morally compromised in *Brief Encounter* (1945).

In the 50s, the fabric of society continued to fray as women gained power in the home and the workplace. Blonde bombshell Diana DORS literally embodied the pleasures and perils of consumerist excess in *A Kid for Two Farthings* (1954), while the supremely elegant Kay KENDALL engaged in battles of the sexes with Kenneth MORE in *Genevieve* (1953) and Peter FINCH in Muriel BOX's *Simon and Laura* (1955). In the 60s, youthful rebels such as Julie CHRISTIE in John SCHLESINGER's *Darling* (1965) and Rita TUSHINGHAM in Tony RICHARDSON's *A Taste of Honey* (1961) and, later, Glenda JACKSON in Ken RUSSELL's *Women in Love* (1969) resisted the resigned suffering of mature sirens Simone SIGNORET in *Room at the Top* (1958) and Rachel ROBERTS in *This Sporting Life*. An army of Bond girls from Honor BLACKMAN in *Goldfinger* (1964) to Judi DENCH as 'M' in *GoldenEye* (1995) has given 007 a run for his money, even if their FEMINISM appears somewhat cartoon-like. Recently, film-makers have turned to the past to explore gender, as with Sally POTTER's anthem to androgyny *Orlando* (1992, UK/Fr/It/Neth/Russia) and MERCHANT IVORY's period costume films such as *Maurice* (1987) and *Howards End* (1992). BIBLIOG: Sue Harper, *Women in British Cinema*, 2000; Andrew Spicer, *Typical Men: The Representation of Masculinity in Popular British Cinema*, 2001. Pam Cook.

General Film Distributors Established in 1935 by C.M. WOOLF with the compensation he received after leaving GAUMONT–BRITISH, GFD introduced the symbol of the man with the gong. In the following year it was fully taken over by the General Cinema Finance Corporation, which gave GFD the security of a tie-up with Universal, whose product it now distributed in the UK, as well as that of Gaumont, and it became a DISTRIBUTION giant as well as investing in production. By the early 40s, GFD was part of J. Arthur RANK's empire, which, with its control of both the Odeon and Gaumont circuits, now embraced production, distribution and EXHIBITION. GFD took over the distribution of EALING STUDIOS' films, after Rank invested in the company, from 1947 to 1956. In 1955, it was renamed J. Arthur Rank Film Distributors, later shortened to Rank Film Distributors. Following the loss of the lucrative UNIVERSAL output in the early 70s, the company continued to handle British and, increasingly, foreign productions until it was sold to Carlton, along with Rank's highly profitable cinema screen advertising company, in 1997. Carlton immediately closed down the film distribution side. Allen Eyles.

General Film Renting Co. Ltd was founded to distribute British films, many from G.B. SAMUELSON, in February 1920 by accountant Harold Denton Hardwick (*b* Epsom, 1882 – *d*?), who had entered the film industry in 1913 and operated a couple of small cinema circuits. It also took over the BARKER MOTION PICTURE PHOTOGRAPHY studio as a rental facility. General ceased operations in 1924. AS.

Genn, Leo (*b* London, 1905 – *d* London, 1978). Actor. A practising barrister before becoming an actor, Genn was educated at the City of London School and Cambridge University. Made his professional stage debut in 1930, was with the Old Vic from 1934 to 1936, and had much theatrical experience (in London and the US) pre- and post-WW2, in which he served with the Royal Artillery. He was assistant prosecutor for the Belsen war crimes trial. First commanded filmgoers' attention with a superbly sardonic Constable of France in *Henry V* (1944), though he'd made a dozen films before. In a sturdy post-war film career, his mellifluous voice and pipe-smoking urbanity seem to have comforted myriad middle-class female fans, though he was a bit too muted for serious stardom. He made three Hollywood films in the 40s, notably, as a sympathetic (of course) psychiatrist in *The Snake Pit* (1948) and received AAn (supp a) for *Quo Vadis* (1951). His best British roles included the divorcing father in *No Place for Jennifer* (1949), one of the instigators of *The Wooden Horse* (1950) escape, and Starbuck in *Moby Dick* (1956). Married dancer Marguerite van Praag.

OTHER BRITISH FILMS INCLUDE: (doc, narr) *Ripe Earth* (1938), *Land of Laughter* (1957), *Greece the Immortal Land* (1958), *Greek Sculpture* (1959); (a, features) *The Immortal Gentleman* (1935), *The Rat* (1937), *The Girl in the News*, *Contraband* (1940), *The Way Ahead* (1944), *Green for Danger* (1946), *The Miniver Story* (1950), *24 Hours of a Woman's Life* (1952), *Personal Affair* (1953), *The Green Scarf* (1954), *I Accuse!* (1957), *Ten Little Indians* (1965), *Endless Night* (1972), *The Mackintosh Man* (1973), *Frightmare* (1974).

genre As in literary criticism, genre is a term used in film CRITICISM to designate categories into which narrative films are grouped. The term, genre system, characterizes a mode of production, not merely types of films. Before WWI, British films were sometimes the product of individual artisans and less governed by type and more by subject matter, e.g. trick films, gags, chase films, ACTUALITIES, and spectacle, made by such PIONEERS as Walter R. BOOTH, G.W. SMITH, and Cecil HEPWORTH. (Recent studies, however, have modified the 'cottage industry' image of early British cinema, finding evidence that it was often a proficiently and profitably organised business.)

Financial and cultural factors dictated the change from shorter to longer narrative in the middle teens. Film-making moved from the home and makeshift workshop to the studio. A concentrated and coordinated system of production, DISTRIBUTION and EXHIBITION (vertical integration) developed in the inter-war years in Britain resembling that of Hollywood. STUDIOS became identified with genre films bearing common technical and stylistic characteristics and associated with particular directors and stars.

Popular genres in British cinema were COMEDY, MELO-DRAMA, MUSICALS, WAR FILMS, HISTORICAL FILMS, COSTUME DRAMAS, ADVENTURE FILMS, EMPIRE FILMS, THRILLERS, DETECTIVE FILMS, HORROR, and SCIENCE-FICTION. KORDA'S LONDON FILMS were associated with historical, biographical films, adventure, and films of EMPIRE expensively mounted, e.g. *Sanders of the River* (1935), *The Drum* (1938) and *The Four Feathers* (1939), featuring images of high-minded British colonial administrators or military men, who epitomised the civilizing benevolence of the British Empire in a style often reminiscent of the Hollywood WESTERN.

EALING was associated with a range of genres: comedies, musicals, detective films, war films, melodramas, and in the 50s with a series of SOCIAL PROBLEM FILMS identified with Basil DEARDEN, but, in terms of international recognition, the studio is best known for its comedies, identified by the studio name and by the leadership of Michael BALCON whose guidance provided a common ethos. *Hue and Cry* (1946), *Whisky Galore!*, *Passport to Pimlico*, *Kind Hearts and Coronets* (1949) *The Man in the White Suit*, *The Lavender Hill Mob* (1951), and *The Ladykillers* (1955) were representative of these Ealing films. RANK, meanwhile, had enormous success with the 'DOCTOR' SERIES, begun in 1954 with *Doctor in the House*, and the BOULTING brothers initiated a popular series of 'institutional' satires, starting with the Army in *Private's Progress* (1956) and subsequently taking on trade unions, the church and the law. Another brand of film comedy, the 'CARRY ON' series (directed by Gerald THOMAS at PINEWOOD), was also popular from the 50s through the 70s, boasting a repertory cast of actors (e.g. Charles HAWTREY, Sid JAMES, etc,). These ribald and irreverent films parodied British institutions: the medical profession, the army and navy, leisure life and sports. imperial themes and cinema itself.

GAINSBOROUGH STUDIOS, like Ealing, produced a range of genres, including the famous 30s comedies starring Will HAY, but became particularly identified with popular costume melodramas and a repertoire of actors (e.g. Margaret LOCKWOOD, Patricia ROC, James MASON, Phyllis CALVERT, and Stewart GRANGER) in such films as *The Man in Grey* (1943), *Fanny by Gaslight* (1944), *The Wicked Lady* (1945), *They Were Sisters* (1945) and *Jassy* (1947), films associated largely with studio and stars, rather than with directors and with an escapist response to wartime DOCUMENTARIES and feature films. However, the war film was an important British genre, as if the war itself had given British films a subject and styles it could do best, exemplified during WW2 by *The Life and Death of Colonel Blimp* (1943) and *Millions Like Us* (1943) and ten years later with such box-office successes as *The Dam Busters* (1955).

Another major British genre is the HORROR film. Although slow in developing, owing in part to strict CENSORSHIP, the genre became internationally popular in the 50s, becoming largely associated with HAMMER FILMS under the leadership of James and Michael CARRERAS, Jimmy SANGSTER and director Terence FISHER. Beginning with *The Quatermass Experiment* (1955) the studio went on to produce cycles of *Frankenstein* and *Dracula* films that became overtly sexual in the late 60s and 70s. The two major actors for these films, largely directed by Terence Fisher, were Christopher LEE and Peter CUSHING, who lent to these productions – e.g. *The Curse of Frankenstein* (1957), *The Horror of Dracula* (1958), and *Stranglers of Bombay* (1959) – a certain grace, dandyism, and sophistication. The science-fiction film, with some famous exemplars in the 30s, such as *The Tunnel* (1935), *The Man Who Changed His Mind* (1936), and *Things to Come* (1936), became very popular in the post-WW2 era, the best-known including *Seven Days to Noon* (1950), *The Quatermass Experiment* (1955) and *The Day the Earth Caught Fire* (1961).

The 50s and 60s saw a number of films, influenced by Italian neorealism, the French New Wave, and by Labourite philosophy, that undertook to dramatize prevailing 'social problems' (e.g. juvenile delinquency, capital punishment, sexual promiscuity, homosexuality), in such films as *The Blue Lamp* (1949), *Yield to the Night* (1956), *The Weak and the Wicked* (1953), and *Victim* (1961), featuring such actors as Dirk BOGARDE, Diana DORS and Joan COLLINS.

From the 60s to the present, the genre system, tied as it is to a form of studio production, has undergone a series of transmutations. No longer supported by a predictable studio system, reliable and steady forms of financing, it is more subject to the vicissitudes of the national and international financial market. From WOODFALL's 'kitchen sink' realist dramas to 'SWINGING LONDON' films (identified with such stars as Tom COURTENAY, Michael CAINE, Julie CHRISTIE, Rita TUSHINGHAM, Lynn and Vanessa REDGRAVE), to more recent less classifiable films such as *The Crying Game* (1992) and *Carrington* (1994, UK/Fr), the old genre forms have either gone into decline or been hybridised. Strictly genre films have been largely replaced, apart from a late-20th century gangster cycle, by *auteur* texts (e.g. those of Terence DAVIES, Derek JARMAN, Sally POTTER, Neil JORDAN), CHANNEL 4 and INDEPENDENT and regional productions that address cultural, ethnic, racial, sexual, and feminist issues in style and subject matter (e.g. *My Beautiful Laundrette*, 1985; *Sammy and Rosie Get Laid*, 1987; *Bhaji on the Beach*, 1993), television and docu-drama (e.g. *Dance with a Stranger* (1984), and foreign-financed 'epic' films, 'HERITAGE' FILMS, and classic novels on film.

BIBLIOG: Marcia Landy, *British Genres: Cinema and Society, 1930–1960*, 1991. Marcia Landy.

George, Isabel (*b* London, 1929) Actress. With some stage experience in rep and the West End, this attractive, rather sad-eyed RADA-trained brunette had only a modest film career in the early 50s, her best role being as one of the policewomen in *Street Corner* (1953).

OTHER BRITISH FILMS INCLUDE: *Death is a Number* (1951), *Girdle of Gold*, (1952), *The Beggar's Opera*, *Twice Upon a Time*, *River Beat* (1953), *The Love Match* (1954).

George, Muriel (*b* London, 1883 – *d* Brighton, 1965). Actress. Short plump character player, equally adept at benign (the postmistress in *Went the Day Well?*, 1942) or bossy (Esma CANNON's bullying employer in *Last Holiday*, 1950). Married (2) Ernest BUTCHER, with whom she formed a concert party, 'The Bunch of Keys', which toured MUSIC HALLS for 12 years, post-WW1. On the West End stage throughout the 30s and 40s, and in films over the same period. Last seen as the televiewing grandma in *Simon and Laura* (1955).

OTHER BRITISH FILMS INCLUDE: *His Lordship* (1932), *Nell Gwyn* (1934), *Limelight* (1936), *Song of the Road* (1937), *Crackerjack* (1938), *Freedom Radio* (1940), *Quiet Wedding*, *Mr Proudfoot Shows a Light* (short), *Cottage to Let* (1941), *They Flew Alone*, *Alibi* (1942), *Dear Octopus* (1943), *A Place of One's Own*, *Perfect Strangers*, *I'll Be Your Sweetheart* (1945), *The Years Between* (1946), *The Dancing Years* (1950).

George, Susan (*b* Surbiton, 1950). Actress. On stage aged 12 in *The Sound of Music*, in TV's *Swallows and Amazons* in 1963, and on screen in *Cup Fever*, 1965. Film producers quickly exploited her jail-bait sexiness in such films as *The Strange Affair* (1968 – very strange it was, too) and, most famously, in Sam Peckinpah's *Straw Dogs* (1971), as the victim of yokel lust. Her pouting sensuality shone through even such anodyne enterprises as *Spring and Port Wine* (1969), as James MASON's recalcitrant daughter, and as the baby-sitter in *Fright* (1971 – what were the parents thinking of?). What were British films to do with this commodity? Send it to America of course, where George slunk unforgettably through *Mandingo* (1975) and others. She kept working on either side of the Atlantic, often in TV, and in 1988 co-produced *Stealing Heaven* (UK/Yug) with husband Simon MacCorkindale whom she married in 1984.

OTHER BRITISH FILMS INCLUDE: *Up the Junction, The Sorcerers, The Billion Dollar Brain* (1967), *All Neat in Black Stockings, Twinky, The Looking Glass War* (1969), *Out of Season* (1975), *Venom* (1981), *The Jigsaw Man* (1984).

George, Terry (*b* Belfast, 1952). Director, screenwriter. His British films have all been co-productions with Ireland and/or the US, and all three are either set there or have Irish subject matter. They are: *In the Name of the Father* (1993, UK/Ire/US, co-sc, co-p – shared AAn/sc and BAAn/sc), the story of the trial of the Guildford 'bombers'; *Some Mother's Son* (1996, Ire/US, d, co-sc), a polemic directed against British treatment of political prisoners; and *The Boxer* (1998, UK/Ire/US), in which a former IRA prisoner seeks to remake his life. Once himself interned for suspected IRA sympathies, he has worked in the US most recently.

Geraldo (*b* London, 1904 – *d* Vevey, 1974). Orchestra leader. RN: Gerald Bright. Geraldo and his dance-band orchestra enlivened some light entertainments of the 30s and 40s, including *Limelight* (1936), with Anna NEAGLE, and *We'll Meet Again* (1942), with Vera LYNN. Usually appeared as himself or as an unnamed orchestra leader. He was also music director on a couple of films – *Brewster's Millions* (1935, co-m d), *The Three Maxims* (1936) and *Our Fighting Navy* (1937) – and music director for Scottish Television from the late 50s.

Geray, Steven (*b* Ungvár, Austria-Hungary, now Uzhgorod, Ukraine, 1904 – *d* Mesa, Arizona, 1973). Actor. After establishing himself as a stage actor in Hungary, where he also made two films, Geray made eight films in Britain, starting with *Dance Band* (1935). Inevitably cast as continental 'types', he from time to time delivered something more distinctive in the 100 US films he made from 1941 on, especially in the early *film noir*-ish 40s, culminating in a star role in *So Dark the Night* in 1946. His British films, apart from *The High Command* (1937), were no more than a stepping-stone.

OTHER BRITISH FILMS INCLUDE: *The Student's Romance* (1935), *A Star Fell from Heaven* (1936), *Premiere* (1938), *Inspector Hornleigh* (1939).

Germaine, Mary (*b* Biarritz, France, 1933). Actress. Creamy blonde heroine of several 'B' FILMS and second lead of a few 'A's of the 50s, more distinctive than most, but, though she acquitted herself well in the likes of *Where's Charley?* (1952), the musical version of *Charley's Aunt*, and *The Floating Dutchman* (1953), the decade was no kinder to her than to women in general, and especially to young pretty ones. They rarely had the chance to be anything more.

OTHER BRITISH FILMS INCLUDE: *Laughter in Paradise* (1951), *The Night Won't Talk, Father's Doing Fine, Women of Twilight* (1952), *Flannelfoot, House of Blackmail* (1953), *The Green Buddha* (1954).

Gerrard, Gene (*b* London, 1889 – *d* Sidmouth, 1971). Actor. A star of stage musical comedy and operetta, who made his debut as stooge to comedian George MOZART in 1910, Gerrard was more a comedic support than leading man in the Jack BUCHANAN mould. Often partnered on screen with Molly LAMONT.

BRITISH FILMS INCLUDE: *Out of the Blue* (+ co-d) (1931), *Brother Alfred, Lucky Girl* (+ co-d) (1932), *Leave It to Me* (+ co-sc), *The Love Nest* (+ co-sc) (1933), *The Guv'nor, No Monkey Business* (1935), *Such Is Life* (1936), *Glamour Girl* (1938, d), *Dumb Dora Discovers Tobacco* (1945). AS.

Gibbs, Anthony (*b* 1925). Editor. Associated with some key 60s films, including several for Tony RICHARDSON – editing is obviously crucial to the structure of *The Loneliness of the Long Distance Runner* (1962), which constantly cuts from past to present in piecing together its protagonist's disaffection with the status quo. Also worked several times for Richard LESTER, on some very modish pieces, and on Nicolas ROEG and Donald CAMMELL's *echt*-60s diagnosis, *Performance* (1970).

OTHER BRITISH FILMS INCLUDE: (e) *Offbeat, Oscar Wilde* (1960), *The Snake Woman, A Taste of Honey* (1961), *Tiara Tahiti* (1962), *Tom Jones* (1963), *The Knack . . .* (1965), *Mademoiselle* (1966, UK/Fr), *The Birthday Party, Petulia* (1968), *Juggernaut, The Black Windmill* (1974), *A Bridge Too Far* (1977), *The Dogs of War, The Wildcats of St Trinian's* (1980).

Gibbs, Gerald (*b* 1907 – *d* 1990). Cinematographer. In films from 1928, as camera assistant at STOLL STUDIOS at CRICKLEWOOD, and stayed there until the studio closed in 1938, with a brief spell at BIP. While under contract to EALING (1941–43), he was camera operator on *Went the Day Well?* (1942) and *The Bells Go Down* (1943), and later in the decade, after time with BRITISH NATIONAL (1943–45), was cinematographer on Ealing's *Whisky Galore!* (1949). His versatility may be suggested by comparing the luminous images of the latter with the hard urban edge he brought to *No Orchids for Miss Blandish* (1948), his preceding credit. Spent much of the 50s photographing 'B' FILMS, but won a BAAn for *Station Six Sahara* in 1963.

OTHER BRITISH FILMS INCLUDE: (co-d) *COD – A Mellow Drama* (1929); (co-c) *Meet My Sister* (1933), *Loyal Heart* (1946), *The Accused* (1953), *Cloak Without Dagger* (1955), *A Prize of Arms* (1961); (c) *Shadowed Eyes* (1939), *Don Chicago* (1945), *Your Witness* (1950), *Night Was Our Friend* (1951), *There Was a Young Lady* (1953), *Delayed Action* (1954), *Room in the House* (1955), *X the Unknown, The Green Man* (1956), *Fortune Is a Woman, Quatermass 2, Blue Murder at St Trinian's* (1957), *The Man Upstairs* (1958), *Follow That Man* (1961), *The Boys, The Webster Boy* (1962), *The Leather Boys, Devil Doll* (1963), *Hostile Witness* (1968).

Gibbs, Sheila Shand (*b* Dundee, 1930). Actress. Attractive blonde, blue-eyed Scottish player who was in TV from 1949 but made only a handful of films, including the US-made *The Seven-Per-Cent Solution* (1976). Married actor Timothy BATESON.

BRITISH FILMS: *Mr Denning Drives North* (1951), *A Killer Walks* (1952), *The Great Game, The 'Maggie'* (1953).

Gibbs, Suzanne (*b* Reading, 1937). Actress. Child player whose first role, the sprightly but doomed Lavinia, crucial to the division of sympathies, in *Blanche Fury* (1947), was her best. Thereafter, parts diminished in size and significance, ending with an uncredited bit role in *Lolita* (1961).

OTHER BRITISH FILMS: *Britannia Mews* (1948), *Stage Fright, The Dragon of Pendragon Castle* (1950), *Miss Robin Hood* (1952).

Gibson, Alan (*b* London, Canada, 1938 – *d* London, 1987). Director. Worked prolifically in TV from 1964, before entering films in 1968, as co-director of *Journey into Midnight* (1968), and thereafter often in the HORROR mode, including *Dracula AD 1972* (1972). Made frequent returns to TV, directing such high-profile work as *A Woman Called Golda* and *Witness for the Prosecution* (1982).

OTHER BRITISH FILMS: *Crescendo* (1969), *Goodbye Gemini* (1970), *The Satanic Rites of Dracula* (1974), *Martin's Day* (1985).

Gibson, Ben (*b* London, 1958). Executive. As head of BFI PRODUCTION BOARD 1989–97, he was the executive producer on such interesting, off-centre films as *Young Soul Rebels* (1991), *Stella Does Tricks* (1996), *Under the Skin* (1997) and *Love Is the Devil* (1998, UK/Fr/Jap, + a), focusing as they do on issues of race and sexuality. In 1997 he became co-director of Seven Arts Productions (1997), and in 2000 director of the London International Film School.

OTHER BRITISH FILMS INCLUDE: (ex p/co-ex p) *Silent Scream* (1990), *The Long Day Closes* (1992), *Loaded* (1994), *Madagascar Skin* (1995), *Gallivant* (1996), *Beautiful People* (1999).

Gibson, Brian (*b* London, 1942). Director. Award-winning TV director (for *Blue Remembered Hills*, 1979), who began on BBC medical and scientific DOCUMENTARIES (e.g. for *Horizon*) and has directed films in both UK and US. His British films include *Breaking Glass* (1980, + sc), a tale of rock-world manipulation, and *Still Crazy* (1998), chock-a-block with trendy, bankable talents, and very funny. Married to US actress Lynn Whitfield.

Gibson, Sue Cinematographer. First came to attention in 1991, with the FILM FOUR fantasy, *Secret Friends*, starring Alan BATES, and the attractive drama-with-music, *Hear My Song* (1991), following this with the glowing images of Marleen Gorris's version of *Mrs Dalloway* (1997, UK/Neth/US), in which the eponym's day shimmers before us as it does in her mind. Since then, mainly on TV projects.

OTHER BRITISH FILMS INCLUDE: *The Search for John Gissing* (2001, UK/US).

Giedroyc, Coky Director. After TV experience, she confronted filmgoers with *Stella Does Tricks* (1996), a bleak and sometimes blackly comic account of a Scottish prostitute's vicissitudes in London. Her other British films include the short, *The Future Lasts a Long Time* (1996), with Samantha MORTON, and *Women Talking Dirty* (2001, UK/US), starrily cast with Helena BONHAM CARTER, Gina McKEE, James PUREFOY and Eileen ATKINS. Her sister **Mel Giedroyc** (*b* Epsom, 1968) is a TV actress.

Gielgud, Sir John (*b* London, 1904 – *d* Aylesbury, Buckinghamshire, 2000). Actor. Not many actors rack up film credits over eight decades, and perhaps especially not when it takes them half their lives to believe fully in film as an actor's medium. By the end of his life (and he was still acting in his last year, crossly changing his agent at 96 because of a failure to cast him in a TV version of *David Copperfield*), he was a consummate screen actor. He had won an AA for the butler role in *Arthur* (1981, US), but this engaging bit of froth obscures the real greatness of his film work, above all in his Shakespearean roles. These latter included: the austere, conspiratorial Cassius in *Julius Caesar* (1953), stealing the notices from an all-star cast; an affecting Clarence in his rival OLIVIER's *Richard III* (1955); an unforgettably poignant Henry IV, chilled with pain, age and disappointment, in WELLES's elegiac *Chimes at Midnight* (1966, Sp/Switz); and reaching an apotheosis in Peter GREENAWAY's audacious reworking of *The Tempest* as *Prospero's Books* (1991), in which his Prospero, bravely naked for some of the time, set the seal on a lifetime's achievement in bringing Shakespeare, and this role in particular, to life.

Born to a famous acting family – his great-aunt was the celebrated Ellen TERRY, great-uncle Fred Terry came to fame as *The Scarlet Pimpernel*, grandmother Kate Terry Gielgud memorably played Cordelia at 14, his brother **Val Gielgud** (*b* 1900 – *d* 1981) was a playwright and (mainly radio) producer

who appeared in a few films – he was stagestruck from the first. Educated at Westminster School and, after training at RADA, made his stage debut in 1921. The stage was the great allegiance of his life and he played a huge range of classical and modern roles, his theatrical career occupying eight columns in the last volume of *Who's Who in the Theatre* (1972). He was not an impressive young romantic lead (his 1924 Romeo was all poetry and too little passion) and the physicalities of Othello (1961, Stratford) were beyond him. Not much else was, though, and in 1970, a decade after Olivier had embraced the ANGRY YOUNG MEN, Lindsay ANDERSON co-starred him with Ralph RICHARDSON in David STOREY's play, *Home*. In one magisterial leap, he had moved conclusively into the modern idiom.

In his final decades, film (and TV – see *Brideshead Revisited*, 1981, for example) claimed more of his attention. Apart from an engaging Inigo Jollifant in Victor SAVILLE's *The Good Companions* (1933) and starring in HITCHCOCK's *The Secret Agent* (1936), his early film work is largely insignificant. By the end, he had become a great film character actor – not just in SHAKESPEARE, but in such treasurable roles as the dying writer in Alain Resnais' *Providence* (1977, Fr/Switz), the hell-fire priest in *A Portrait of the Artist as a Young Man* (1977), the suave diplomat who utters a four-letter word with aplomb in *Plenty* (1985, UK/US), the zealous environmentalist in *The Shooting Party* (1984), and Mr Touchett, ancient, wise and generous, in *The Portrait of a Lady* (1996, UK/US).

He was heaped with honours for his work in all the acting media and a 1953 charge for homosexual soliciting caused no dent in the public acclaim in which he was held, though it caused him great unhappiness. He was knighted earlier in 1953, received honorary doctorates from prestigious universities, and was made *Chevalier de la Légion d'Honneur*; he was the author of volumes of autobiography (*Early Stages*, 1939; *An Actor in His Time*, 1979) and of reflections on the craft of acting (*Stage Directions*, 1963; *Acting Shakespeare*, 1991); he recorded a great deal of poetry (including his famous one-man show, *The Ages of Man*) and drama (including *Hamlet* and *The Importance of Being Earnest*); he produced both straight plays and opera; and he masterminded some of the greatest theatrical seasons of the century. In terms of the performing arts, it is no exaggeration to say that he towered over the century; cinema was lucky to secure its share of his last few decades.

OTHER BRITISH FILMS: *Who Is the Man?* (1924), *The Clue of the New Pin* (1929), *Insult* (1932), *The Prime Minister, An Airman's Letter to His Mother* (1941), *Unfinished Journey* (1944, comm, doc), *Hamlet* (1948, voice, ucr), *The Barretts of Wimpole Street* (1956), *Saint Joan* (1957, UK/US), *Greece the Immortal Land* (1958, voice, doc), *Becket* (1964), *Sebastian* (1967), *The Charge of the Light Brigade* (1968), *Oh! What a Lovely War* (1969), *Julius Caesar* (1970), *Gold, 11 Harrowhouse, Murder on the Orient Express, Galileo* (UK/Can) (1974), *Aces High* (UK/Fr), *Joseph Andrews* (1976), *Murder by Decree* (1978, UK/Can), *The Human Factor* (1979, UK/US), *Priest of Love* (1980), *Chariots of Fire* (1981), *Gandhi* (1982, UK/Ind), *The Wicked Lady, Scandalous, Invitation to the Wedding* (1983), *The Whistle Blower* (1986), *Loser Takes All* (1990, UK/US), *Haunted* (1995, UK/US), *Shine* (UK/Aust), *Hamlet* (UK/US) (1996), *Elizabeth, The Tichborne Claimant* (1998), *Catastrophe* (2000, short).

BIBLIOG: Jonathan Croall, *Gielgud: A Theatrical Life*, 2001.

Gifford, Alan (*b* Taunton, Massachusetts, 1911 – *d* Blairgowrie, Scotland, 1989). Actor. RN: John Lennox. Somewhat gaunt actor who, having made his debut in the Australian 'western', *The Kangaroo Kid* (1950), spent almost all his career in British films. Oscillating between minor roles in 'A's like *Isadora* (1968) and bringing a touch of authority to 'B's like

Time Lock (1957), as the anxious bank manager, or *Flying Scot* (1957), as criminal boss, he also found time for some striking TV, notably as the devious Osmond in *The Portrait of a Lady* (1968).

OTHER BRITISH FILMS INCLUDE: *Lilacs in the Spring* (1954), *Satellite in the Sky*, *The Iron Petticoat* (1956), *Across the Bridge*, *Escapement* (1957), *Too Young to Love* (1959), *Devil Doll* (1963), *Carry On Cowboy* (1965), *2001: A Space Odyssey* (1968), *Who Dares Wins* (1982).

Gifford, Denis (*b* London, 1927 – *d* London, 2000). Film historian. The author of over 60 well-researched studies such as *The Movie Makers: Chaplin* (1974) and a definitive directory of *Entertainers in British Films* (1998), an authority on comic magazines, and a writer for radio and TV, Gifford laid the basis for much further study of British cinema with his indispensable *British Film Catalogue 1895–1970* (1973). This landmark work was being re-edited and updated at the time of his death, and in 2001 was published with fiction and non-fiction volumes.

Gifford, Harry (*b c*1887 – *d* London, 1960). Composer. RN: Gifford Folkard. Contributed songs, usually music and lyrics, to seven George FORMBY films of the later 30s, starting with *No Limit* (1935).

OTHER BRITISH FILMS: *Keep Your Seats, Please* (1936), *Keep Fit, Feather Your Nest* (1937), *It's in the Air* (1938), *Trouble Brewing, Come On George* (1939), *Let George Do It!* (1940).

Gilbert, Brian (*b c*1960) Director. With some background in TV, Gilbert has directed several films in Britain, including two which focus sympathetically on literary protagonists, *Tom & Viv* (1994, BAAn/best film), an episode in the life of T.S. Eliot, and *Wilde* (1997, UK/Ger/Jap/US), starring Stephen FRY. Has also worked on US films, including *Not Without My Daughter* (1991).

OTHER BRITISH FILMS INCLUDE: *The Devotee* (1982, short), *The Frog Prince* (1984, + adapt), *This Is the Sea* (1996, UK/US/Ire), *The Gathering* (2002).

Gilbert, Lewis (*b* London, 1920). Director. The son of MUSIC-HALL parents, Gilbert entered films as a child actor, appearing in over 70 films, the last of which was *The Divorce of Lady X* (1938). Worked with the RAF FILM UNIT during WW2, and, post-war, directed DOCUMENTARIES at GB INSTRUCTIONAL, before directing the children's film, *The Little Ballerina* (1947) and ten 'B' FILMS, including the engaging village comedy, *Time Gentlemen Please!* (1952). Throughout the 50s and 60s, he worked very busily, across a range of GENRES, but making his name with a string of popular WAR FILMS, including *Reach for the Sky* (1956, + co-sc), based on the life of flying ace, Douglas Bader, *Carve Her Name With Pride* (1958, + co-sc) and *Sink the Bismarck!* (1960). In fact, two less well-known thrillers, *The Good Die Young* (1954, + co-sc), fuelled by post-war malaise, and *Cast a Dark Shadow* (1955), with Dirk BOGARDE teasing his romantic image, are more interesting – both very well-acted and enjoyably unwholesome. He went on to direct three BONDS (one with CONNERY, two with Roger MOORE), the quintessential 60s hit, *Alfie* (1966, + p, AAn, BAAn/best film), with its suburban lothario running out of birds and steam, and two 80s films, derived from plays by Willy RUSSELL, with feminist themes and showcasing strong actresses – *Educating Rita* (1983, + p, BAA/best film), with Julie WALTERS, and *Shirley Valentine* (1989, + p, BAAn/best film), with Pauline COLLINS. His is a survivor's career: a skilled, unpretentious craftsman, hurdling the decades and their changing tastes, and grabbing opportunities as they occur. As a freelancer, he has only himself to take the credit.

OTHER BRITISH FILMS: (co-p) *Harmony Lane* (1954, short); (sc) *Marry Me* (1949, co-sc), *Emergency* (1962, co-story); (d, unless noted) (doc, short) *Sailors Do Care* (1944), *The Ten-Year Plan* (1945), *Under One Roof, Arctic Harvest* (1946), *Fishing Grounds of the World* (1947); (features) *Once a Sinner* (1950), *There Is Another Sun, Scarlet Thread* (1951), *Emergency Call, Cosh Boy* (+ co-sc), *Albert RN, Johnny On the Run* (+ p) (1953), *The Sea Shall Not Have Them* (1954, + co-sc), *The Admirable Crichton* (1957), *A Cry from the Streets* (1958), *Ferry to Hong Kong* (1959, + co-sc), *Light Up the Sky* (1960, + p), *The Greengage Summer* (1961), *HMS Defiant* (1962), *The 7th Dawn* (1964, UK/US), *You Only Live Twice* (1967), *Friends* (1971, + p, story), *Paul and Michelle* (1974, + story), *Seven Nights in Japan* (1976, UK/Fr, + p), *The Spy Who Loved Me* (1977), *Moonraker* (1979, UK/Fr, + a), *Not Quite Jerusalem* (1984), *Haunted* (1995, UK/US, + co-p), *Before You Go* (2002).

Gilbert, Terry (*b* Bond's Main, 1932 – *d* Worthing, Sussex, 2001). Dancer, choreographer. Like cinema's *Billy Elliot*, Gilbert was a miner's son, born in a tough (Derbyshire) mining village; unlike Elliot, he did not encounter opposition when he started ballet classes in Chesterfield. After establishing himself as a principal dancer, he began choreographing, and his main work on film was in this role and on four films for Ken RUSSELL – *Women in Love* (1969), *The Music Lovers* (1971), *The Devils*, *The Boy Friend* (1971). He also appeared in several films as a dancer, including two Cliff RICHARD MUSICALS – *The Young Ones* (1961) and *Summer Holiday* (1962). Married dancer Selena Wylie in 1954.

OTHER BRITISH FILMS INCLUDE: (dancer) *Invitation to the Dance* (1954, UK/US), *Chitty Chitty Bang Bang* (1968); (choreographer) *Don't Lose Your Head* (1966), *Billion Dollar Brain* (1967), *Henry VIII and His Six Wives* (1972), *The Elephant Man* (1980), *Aria* (1987, 'The Masked Ball' segment), *Four Weddings and a Funeral* (1994).

Gilbert, W.S. (*b* London, 1836 – *d* Harrow Weald, 1911), and, **Sullivan, Sir Arthur** (*b* London, 1842 – *d* London, 1900). Composers. There are two British, more or less biographical films based on the careers of the celebrated pair: LAUNDER AND GILLIAT's somewhat ponderous affair, *The Story of Gilbert and Sullivan* (1953), starring Robert MORLEY and Maurice EVANS; and Mike LEIGH's glowing testimonial to the theatrical spirit, *Topsy-Turvy* (2000), starring Jim BROADBENT and Allan CORDUNER. There was an early British TECHNICOLOR version of *The Mikado* in 1938, a modern-dress parody by Michael WINNER, *The Cool Mikado* (1962), a HALAS AND BATCHELOR animated version of *Ruddigore* (1967), and another animated story, *Dick Deadeye – or Duty Done* (1975), featuring characters from the best-known operas and many of the songs; and in 1982 there was a film version of Joseph Papp's production of *The Pirates of Penzance*, starring Kevin Kline. Films such as *Rentadick* (1972) have featured excerpts from the operettas; there were several animated shorts which drew inspiration from them, including *The Monarch of the Sea* (1974), based on a song from *HMS Pinafore*; and there have been many TV adaptations of G&S.

Gill, Basil (*b* Birkenhead, 1877 – *d* Hove, 1955). Actor. A prominent stage actor (1897–1944), Gill did occasional screen work (1911–38). On stage, he played Messala in *Ben-Hur* in London (1902) and on a US tour (1902–03), but is best remembered for his Shakespearean roles.

BRITISH FILMS INCLUDE: *Henry VIII* (1911), *The Ragged Messenger* (1917), *The Rocks of Valpré* (1919), *High Treason* (1929), *The Wandering Jew* (1933), *Rembrandt* (1936), *The Citadel* (1938). AS.

Gill, Maud Actress. Character player with stage experience who played supporting roles in about a dozen 30s films, typically cast as duchess in *Excess Baggage* (1933) and lady's maid in *Such Is the Law* (1930).

OTHER BRITISH FILMS INCLUDE: *The Farmer's Wife* (1928), *A Sister to Assist 'er* (1930), *Mischief* (1931), *Lilies of the Field* (1934), *Look Up and Laugh* (1935), *Keep Your Seats, Please* (1936).

Gill, Tom (*b* Newcastle-upon-Tyne, 1916 – *d* London, 1971). Actor. Minor supporting player who began both stage and screen careers in 1935; regular on TV series, *The Invisible Man* and *The Third Man*. Film roles were often camp cameos, as in *The Wedding of Lilli Marlene* (1953). During WW2 he went to prison as scapegoat in a homosexual scandal, but his careeer continued unabated afterwards.

BRITISH FILMS INCLUDE: *Midshipman Easy* (1935), *The High Command* (1937), *This Man Is News* (1938), *The First Gentleman* (1948), *Hotel Sahara*, *Lady Godiva Rides Again* (1951), *Simon and Laura* (1955), *Wicked as They Come*, *The Good Companions* (1956), *Up the Creek*, *Further Up the Creek* (1958), *The Yellow Rolls-Royce* (1964), *A Nice Girl Like Me* (1969). AS.

Gillen, Aiden (*b* Dublin, 1968). Actor. Slight, dark, intense-looking Gillen has made his name in TV, as the gay PR man in CHANNEL 4's *Queer as Folk* (1999–2000), on stage, particularly as Ariel in *The Tempest* (2000) and as *Platanov* (2001) for the Almeida, and on screen, in two Irish-set films, *Circle of Friends* (1995, Ire/US), and *Some Mother's Son* (1996, Ire/US), as Helen MIRREN's son imprisoned for IRA involvement, and as the likeable protagonist in the casually engaging *The Low-Down* (2001).

OTHER BRITISH FILMS: *The Lonely Passion of Judith Hearne* (1987), *The Courier* (1987, Ire), *Safe* (1993), *Mojo* (1997), *The Final Curtain* (UK/US), *My Kingdom* (2001).

Gillett, Aden (*b* Aden, 1958). Actor. Tall, RADA-trained Gillett was in a major theatrical success, Stephen DALDRY's *An Inspector Calls* (1992), came to widespread attention as amiable Jack Maddox in *The House of Eliott*, starting in 1991, in fact did much theatre and TV, but little film. He was in the Australian romantic comedy, *Under the Lighthouse Dancing* (1995), played the householder in the endearing fantasy, *The Borrowers* (1997), and made the stick-like figure of the daughter's fiancé in *The Winslow Boy* (1999, UK/US) humanly believable.

OTHER BRITISH FILMS INCLUDE: *Shadow of the Vampire* (2001, UK/Lux/US).

Gilliam, Terry (*b* Minneapolis, 1940). Director, screenwriter. Sole American member of the revered MONTY PYTHON comedy ensemble, now a successful film-maker in his own right. Original Python member John CLEESE recruited him to design the now-famous and entirely bizarre cutout ANIMATION for the TV series, *Monty Python's Flying Circus*. Gilliam joined Monty Python on their inevitable foray into films, as animator, collaborative screenwriter, actor and occasional director. Of the films made by the group with Gilliam's substantial involvement, *Monty Python and the Holy Grail* (1974, a/anim/co-d/co-sc), *Life of Brian* (1979, a/co-sc/anim), and *The Meaning of Life* (1983, a/co-d/anim d/co-sc), are certified international cult-classics. Gilliam's more individual efforts as director like, *Time Bandits* (1981, + co-sc/p), *Brazil* (1985, + a, co-sc) and *Twelve Monkeys* (1995, US) maintained a Pythonesque satire while revealing a deep pessimism that makes them unsettling rather than conventional.

OTHER BRITISH FILMS: (shorts, d) *Story Time* (1970), *The Miracle of Flight* (1974), *The Crimson Permanent Assurance* (1983); (features, a/co-sc/d) *And Now for Something Completely Different* (1971, + anim), *Jabberwocky* (1977), *The Secret Policeman's Private Parts* (1984, a), *The*

Adventures of Baron Munchausen (1988, UK/Ger/It). Melinda Hildebrandt.

Gilliat, Leslie (*b* New Malden, 1917). Producer, production manager. Often collaborated with his brother Sidney GILLIAT, acting as location manager (*Captain Boycott*, 1947), production manager (*State Secret*, 1950), associate producer on eight LAUNDER and Gilliat films of the later 50s, and producer on three still later ones (*Only Two Can Play*, 1961; *The Great St Trinian's Train Robbery*, 1966; *Endless Night* (1972).

OTHER BRITISH FILMS INCLUDE: (assoc p) *Geordie* (1955), *The Green Man* (1956), *Fortune Is a Woman*, *The Smallest Show on Earth* (1957), *The Bridal Path*, *Left, Right and Centre* (1959), *The Pure Hell of St Trinian's* (1960), *A Dandy in Aspic* (1968); (p) *The Amorous Prawn* (1962), *Joey Boy* (1965), *The Virgin Soldiers* (1969, co-), *The Buttercup Chain* (1970, ex p).

Gilliat, Sidney *see* **Launder and Gilliat**

Gilliatt, Penelope (*b* London, 1932 – *d* London, 1993). Critic, screenwriter. The third wife of John OSBORNE, Gilliatt was film reviewer for the *Observer* during the 60s and for *The New Yorker*, alternating with Pauline Kael, in the 70s, until she left under a cloud. A perceptive, if sometimes irritatingly mannered and even patronising critic, she also contributed – and received AAn and BAAn for – the finely sophisticated screenplay for *Sunday Bloody Sunday* (1971).

BIBLIOG: Penelope Gilliatt, *Unholy Fools*, 1993 (film and theatre criticism).

Gillie, Jean (*b* London, 1915 – *d* London, 1949). Actress. Pretty blonde Gillie died sadly young, having made her name as a dancer on stage and (mostly) wisecracking second lead in 20 films, including two in Hollywood – *Decoy* (1946) and *The Macomber Affair* (1947). She is a chirpy land girl in *Tawny Pipit* (1944) and the girl who claims 'I want a change . . . and I'm going to get it' in *The Gentle Sex* (1943).

OTHER BRITISH FILMS INCLUDE: *While Parents Sleep* (1935), *Sweet Devil* (1938), *Tilly of Bloomsbury* (1940), *The Saint Meets the Tiger* (1943), *Flight from Folly* (1945).

Gilling, John (*b* London, 1912 – *d* Madrid, 1984). Screenwriter, director. Had experience in the US and entered British films before doing WW2 service in the Royal Navy, and (co-)wrote a few minor films in the late 40s, including Laurence HARVEY's first, *House of Darkness* (1948). However, Gilling's career is chiefly, if unequally, divided among three companies: TEMPEAN, WARWICK and HAMMER. Now best known for his contributions (often as writer) to the HORROR genre for Hammer, it is worth recording how efficiently he directed and wrote a string of 'B' FILMS for Tempean. These adroit variants on CRIME themes include such enjoyable second features as *No Trace* (1950), *The Quiet Woman* (1951) and *The Voice of Merrill* (1952), and the strange little character piece, *The Embezzler* (1954). Producer Robert S BAKER found him wholly reliable, though some of his actors (including Diana DORS) thought him abrasive. For Warwick, he made eight, mainly ACTION FILMS, such as *High Flight* (1957, + co-sc) and *The Bandit of Zhobe* (1959, + sc), as part of its bid for internationalism. His introduction to horror was on Tempean producer Baker's 'A' venture, *The Flesh and the Fiends* (1959, + story); he then made nearly 20 films in this and related genres, nine of them for Hammer, including *Shadow of the Cat* (1961), *The Gorgon* (1964, sc only) and *The Plague of the Zombies* (1966). These and other films have their frissons, but Gilling lacked the transforming poetic touch of horror*meister* Terence FISHER.

Directed one film in Spain, *The Devil's Cross* (1975), and retired there, becoming a painter. Married actress **Lorraine Clewes**, who appeared in a few films including two for her husband – *The Challenge* (1959, + sc) and *The Pirates of Blood River* (1961, + co-sc).

OTHER BRITISH FILMS INCLUDE: (co-sc) *Guilt is My Shadow* (1950), *The Steel Key* (1953), *Impulse* (1955), *Trog* (1970, story); (sc) *Black Memory* (1947), *The Man in Black* (1949), *Blackout* (1950), *The Lost Hours*, *13 East Street* (1952), *Bond of Fear* (1956), *Killers of Kilimanjaro* (1959), *The Secret of Blood Island* (1964); (d) *Wings Over Africa* (1937, ass), *Deadly Nightshade* (1953), *The Gilded Cage* (1955), *Interpol* (1957), *Idle on Parade* (1958), *The Night Caller* (1965); (d/sc/co-sc – complete) *Escape from Broadmoor* (1948), *A Matter of Murder* (1949), *The Frightened Man* (1952), *Recoil*, *Escape by Night* (1953), *3 Steps to the Gallows*, *Double Exposure* (1954), *Tiger by the Tail*, *The Gamma People* (1955), *Odongo* (1956), *The Man Inside* (1958), *Fury at Smugglers Bay* (1960, + p, story), *The Scarlet Blade* (1963), *The Brigand of Kandahar*, *Panic* (+ co-story) (1965), *The Mummy's Shroud* (1966).

Gilmore, Peter (*b* Leipzig, 1931). Actor. Sandy-haired, RADA-trained Gilmore may still be best known for playing the shipping line founder in TV's *The Onedin Line* (1971–80), but he has also appeared in 25 films, including ten in the 'CARRY ON' series. Was married to actress **Jan Waters** (*b* Bournemouth, 1937), who made a few films, including *Touch of Death* (1962) and *Corruption* (1967), and was on stage from 1960.

OTHER BRITISH FILMS INCLUDE: *Master Spy* (1963), *Carry On Jack*, . . . *Cleo* (1964), *The Jokers*, *The Great St Trinian's Train Robbery* (1966), *Carry On Doctor*, . . . *Up the Khyber* (1968), *Carry On Again Doctor* (1969), . . . *Henry*, *The Abominable Dr Phibes* (1971), *The Lonely Passion of Judith Hearne* (1987), *Carry On Columbus* (1992).

Gingold, Hermione (*b* London, 1897 – *d* New York, 1987). Actress. Celebrated revue star and straight actress on UK and US stages (debut 1908), Gingold is now indelibly associated with her touching role as Leslie CARON's grandmother in *Gigi* (1958), and especially for singing 'I Remember It Well' with Maurice Chevalier. Noted for her sardonic wit, she famously partnered Hermione BADDELEY in several revues and in the 1949 revival of Noël COWARD's *Fallen Angels*, and they played in two films together, *The Pickwick Papers* (1952) and *Cosh Boy* (1953). She filmed sporadically in Britain from 1932, but generally had better roles in the US, as in *Bell, Book and Candle* (1958) and *The Music Man* (1962), as the outraged – and outrageous – mayoress. On the whole, though she enlivened every film in which she appeared, her strange looks and bizarre talents were better suited to the theatrical stage; in her way, she is as much a one-off as Groucho Marx. Married and divorced (1) publisher Michael Joseph and (2) screenwriter, playwright and lyricist Eric MASCHWITZ.

OTHER BRITISH FILMS INCLUDE: *Merry Comes to Town* (1937), *Meet Mr Penny* (1938), *The Butler's Dilemma* (1943), *Our Girl Friday* (1953), *Promise Her Anything* (1965), *Jules Verne's Rocket to the Moon* (1967).

BIBLIOG: Autobiographies: *The World Is Square*, 1958; *Sirens Should Be Seen and Not Heard*, 1963; *Growing Old Disgracefully*, 1989.

Gish, Dorothy see **Americans in British silent films**

Gladwell, David (*b* Gloucester, 1935). Director. Entered films in the late 50s, and has turned his hand to various aspects of the industry, including the editing of two features for Lindsay ANDERSON – *If . . .* (1968), *O Lucky Man!* (1973) – and the directing of a bleak piece of future shock, *Memoirs of a Survivor* (1981, + co-sc). The failure of this ambitious enterprise seems to have stunted his career. Has also been a TV editor.

OTHER BRITISH FILMS INCLUDE: (doc/short, e) *Terminus* (1961, ass), *Time to Heal* (1963), *Reaching Out* (1968), *Film* (1979); (doc/short, d) *The Great Steam Fair* (1964, co-d, + e, comm), *28B Camden Street* (1965), *Requiem for a Village* (1975, + sc, e); (features, e) *Recluse* (1979), *Nineteen Nineteen* (1984).

Glazer, Jonathan (*b* London, 1965). Director. After an award-winning TV ad for Guinness, and a background in music videos, Glazer, trained in art school, made a successful feature debut with the narratively taut and visually striking gangster movie, *Sexy Beast* (2001, UK/Sp/US), which won the Best British Independent Film Award, and Glazer was named Best Director.

Gleeson, Brendan (*b* Dublin, *c* 1954). Actor. The winner of the London Critics' Award for his robust, humanly complex playing of criminal Martin Cahill in *The General* (1998, UK/US), former schoolteacher Gleeson made a mark in the 90s in a range of largely Irish-set/based films, like *The Field* (1990). With the likeable looks of a somewhat broken-down boxer, he made a strong impression in tough roles, as a priest in Neil JORDAN's *The Butcher Boy* (1997, UK/Ire) and IRA founder Michael Collins in TV's *The Treaty* (1991). Having embarked on an international career in the late 90s, he must hope not again to be in anything as stupid as *Mission: Impossible 2*(2000, US/Aust); he went on to work for Steven Spielberg in *AI: Artificial Intelligence* (2001) and Martin Scorsese in *Gangs of New York* (2002).

OTHER BRITISH FILMS INCLUDE: *Into the West* (1992), *The Snapper* (1993), *Love Lies Bleeding* (1994), *Trojan Eddie* (1996), *I Went Down* (1998, UK/Ire/Sp), *Wild About Harry*, *The Tailor of Panama* (Ire/US) (2001), *28 Days Later* (2002).

Glen, Iain (*b* Edinburgh, 1961). Actor. Educated at the University of Aberdeen and trained at RADA (Bancroft medal-winner), tall, austere-looking Glen has had major successes on TV, in such diverse pieces as: the costume romance *Wives and Daughters* (1999), as a cad; the Gothic Victoriana of *The Wyvern Mystery* (2000); and the contemporary drama of a conflict-ridden family, *Anchor Me* (2000). On stage, he was Henry V for the RSC in 1994 and famously co-starred with Nicole Kidman in *The Blue Room* (1998). Without yet being a major *film* name, he has had a string of interesting roles in the 90s, including his award-winning murderer in *Silent Scream* (1990) and Hamlet in *Rosencrantz and Guilderstern Are Dead* (1990, US); and his leading role in the US-made *Lara Croft: Tomb Raider* (2001) may change his film star status. Married to Susannah HARKER, with whom he starred in TV's *Adam Bede* (1991).

OTHER BRITISH FILMS INCLUDE: *Paris by Night* (1988), *Fools of Fortune* (1989), *The Young Americans* (1993), *Paranoid* (2000), *Beautiful Creatures*, *Gabriel & Me* (2001).

Glen, John (*b* Sunbury-on-Thames, 1932). Editor, director. After experience as editor and/or as second unit director on such action films as *Gold* (1974) and *The Spy Who Loved Me* (1977), Glen got his chance to direct on *For Your Eyes Only* (1981), after which he became the regular BOND director of the 80s. In the 90s, he has been involved with TV (including an appearance in *The James Bond Story*, 1999) and international films, including *Christopher Columbus: The Discovery* (1992).

OTHER BRITISH FILMS INCLUDE: (e, unless noted) *The Extra Day*, *The Scamp* (1957, sd e), *On Her Majesty's Secret Service* (1969, + 2ud), *Pulp* (1972), *A Doll's House* (1973), *Dead Cert* (1974), *Conduct Unbecoming* (1975), *The Wild Geese* (UK/Switz, + 2ud), *Superman* (1978), *Moonraker* (1979, UK/Fr, 2ud), *The Sea Wolves* (1980, UK/Switz/US); (d) *Octopussy* (1983), *A View to a Kill* (1985), *The Living Daylights* (1987), *Licence to Kill* (1989).

Glendenning, Raymond (*b* Newport, Wales, 1907 – *d* Buckinghamshire, 1974). Sports commentator. Made guest or cameo appearances, often as announcers, in a dozen films, typically as a racing commentator, as in *The Rainbow Jacket* (1954), sometimes as unseen narrator, as in *Derby Day* (1952).

OTHER BRITISH FILMS INCLUDE: (commentator/narrator, unless noted) *Asking for Trouble* (1942), *Cameramen at War* (doc), *Dreaming* (a) (1944), *XIVth Olympiad: The Glory of Sport* (1948, doc), *The Galloping Major* (1951), *Dry Rot* (1956), *Make Mine a Million* (1959, a), *The Iron Maiden* (1963).

Glenister, Philip (*b* Harrow, 1963). Actor. Rugged TV actor, an authoritative presence in such series as *Vanity Fair* (1998) as faithful Dobbin and, especially, as the factory foreman in *Clocking Off* (1999), who has to date made only a few films, including *London Kills Me* (1991), *i.d.* (1995) and *The Perfect Blue* (1997). Possibly one to watch. Brother is actor **Robert Glenister** (*see* Amanda REDMAN).

Glenne, Daphne (*b* 1900 – *d* ?). Actress. Ingenue billed by producer W.G. BARKER as 'England's Own Picture Girl'; career ended with that of her producer-mentor in 1920.

BRITISH FILMS INCLUDE: *On Leave* (1918), *The Ticket-of-Leave Man* (1918), *Her Lonely Soldier* (1919), *The Lamp of Destiny* (1919), *The Ever-Open Door* (1920). AS.

Glenville, Peter (*b* London, 1913 – *d* New York, 1996). Actor, director. Educated at Oxford where he began his acting career, and son of stage actors Shaun Glenville, and Dorothy Ward, he put his matinee idol looks to work in a few films, notably as a gigolo in *Madonna of the Seven Moons* (1944) and a spiv in *Good-Time Girl* (1947), before turning to direction with the sombre drama, *The Prisoner* (1955). He made an intelligent, talky stab at Anouilh's *Becket* (1964, AAn/d) and the modern drama of a teacher accused of assault by his pupil, *Term of Trial* (1962, + sc), which won a Venice Film Festival award. His most attractive film as director may have been the US-made Tennessee Williams ADAPTATION, *Summer and Smoke* (1961), which he had produced successfully on the London stage, and in 1962 *Films and Filming* dubbed him 'the first really international British film maker since HITCHCOCK'. However, he never wholly shook off the theatricality and/or literariness of the sources of most of his films.

OTHER BRITISH FILMS: (a) *His Brother's Keeper* (1939), *Two for Danger, Return to Yesterday* (1940), *Uncensored* (1942), *Heaven Is Round the Corner* (1944); (d) *Hotel Paradiso* (1966, UK/Fr + d, co-sc).

Gliddon, John (*b* St Alban's, 1897 – *d* Worthing, 1990). Agent. One of the most famous agents of the 40s and 50s, when his clients included Deborah KERR, Kathleen BYRON, Vivien LEIGH and Sally GRAY (enough, really, to build a reputation for prestige on), as well as James DONALD and Michael RENNIE, Gliddon began as an actor with Sir Philip Ben Greet's Shakespearean Company. He also appeared in a half-dozen silent films, 1919–20, and directed and wrote two more: *Senorita, Pins and Needles* (1921). After experience as film executive and journalist, he set up as an agent in 1934, with offices in Regent Street, London.

OTHER BRITISH FILMS: (a) *The Sands of Time, The Power of Right, The Laundry Girl* (1919), *The Temptress, The Rank Outsider* (1920), *The Dawn of Truth* (1920).

Glover, Brian (*b* Sheffield, 1934 – *d* London, 1997). Actor. Busy, burly character actor, formerly a wrestler known as 'Leon Arris, the Man from Paris', who entered films as the bullying games master in *Kes* (1969) and worked steadily thereafter.

Appeared in popular TV shows such as *The Sweeney* (1975) and *The Bill* (1983). Died of a brain tumour.

OTHER BRITISH FILMS INCLUDE: *O Lucky Man!* (1973), *Mister Quilp* (1974), *Joseph Andrews, Sweeney!* (1976), *Britannia Hospital* (1982), *The Company of Wolves* (1984), *Leon the Pig Farmer* (1992), *Stiff Upper Lips* (1996), *Up 'n' Under* (1997).

Glover, Julian (*b* London, 1935). Actor. Versatile RADA-trained character actor on stage from 1953 and in films from 1963 (a lieutenant in *Tom Jones*). He has played official types, like the aggressive Colonel investigating the other-worldly arrival in *Quatermass and the Pit* (1967), the hectoring police officer in the little seen *Dead Cert* (1974), and Kristatos in *For Your Eyes Only* (1981), all with apt military bearing. Also international films such as *The Empire Strikes Back* (1980) and *Indiana Jones and the Last Crusade* (1989); much plushy TV, including *QB VII* (1974) and *Nancy Astor* (1984); and a controversial King Lear (2001) at the Globe. Married (1) Eileen ATKINS and (2) Isla BLAIR, and his son by Blair is actor **Jamie Glover** (*b* London, 1969).

OTHER BRITISH FILMS INCLUDE: *Girl with Green Eyes* (1963), *I Was Happy Here* (1965), *Theatre of Death* (1966), *Alfred the Great* (1969), *Wuthering Heights* (1970), *Nicholas and Alexandra* (1971, UK/US), *Antony and Cleopatra* (1972, UK/Sp/Switz, as Proculeius), *Juggernaut* (1974), *Heat and Dust* (1982), *Cry Freedom, The Fourth Protocol* (1987), *Vatel* (2000, UK/Fr).

Glyn, Elinor (*b* Jersey, Channel Islands, 1864 – *d* London, 1943). Writer, director. Her name is synonymous with sex, thanks to her 1907 novel *Three Weeks*, her popularization of the word 'It' to symbolize sex appeal, and her identification of Clara Bow as the personification of 'It.' *Three Weeks* was first filmed in the US in 1915, and that same year, Fred EVANS as Pimple made the parody, *Pimple's Three Weeks (without the Option)*. In the UK, she formed Elinor Glyn Productions Ltd in 1929 and directed two features, *Knowing Men* and *The Price of Things* (1930), both mediocre in production and storyline. AS.

Glyn-Jones, John (*b* London, 1909). Actor. Engaging Welsh character player, equally at home as a sympathetic priest in *Heart of a Child* (1958), a sardonic boffin in *Man in the Moon* (1960) or the fussy insurance assessor in *Smokescreen* (1964). Entered films in 1939 and was director of BBC TV, 1947–51, writing and producing some early series and plays.

OTHER BRITISH FILMS INCLUDE: *Convoy* (1940), *Vice Versa* (1947), *The Long Memory* (1952), *Carrington VC* (1954), *Value for Money* (1955), *I'm All Right Jack* (1959), *Two Way Stretch* (1960), *Waltz of the Toreadors, Go to Blazes* (1962), *Heavens Above!* (1963), *The 'Copter Kids* (1976).

Glynne, Angela (*b* Staines, 1933). Actress. An appealing child player in such lachrymose enterprises as *Rose of Tralee* (1942) and in comedy as the hoydenish Barbara in *The Happiest Days of Your Life* (1950), she left films after a couple of small roles as a young woman – in *The House Across the Lake* and *36 Hours* (1954).

OTHER BRITISH FILMS INCLUDE: *Bank Holiday* (1938), *Hard Steel, Those Kids from Town* (1942), *Give Me the Stars* (1944), *Fortune Lane* (1947), *The Last Load* (1948).

Glynne, Mary (*b* Penarth, Wales, 1898 – *d* London, 1954). Actress. Always very regal in silent films, but on stage (debut 1908), she had played Wendy in *Peter Pan* (1912 and 1913) and Oliver in *Oliver Twist* (1912). Her most prominent film was *Beside the Bonnie Briar Bush* (1921, UK/US), in which she played opposite and was directed by Donald CRISP, but the *New York Times* found her 'not particularly effective'. A cousin of John

GIELGUD's, she was a sympathetic Miss Trant in *The Good Companions* (1933). Married actor Dennis NEILSEN-TERRY.

OTHER BRITISH FILMS INCLUDE: *His Last Defence* (1919), *The Call of Youth* (1920), *Mystery Road* (1921), *Inquest* (1931), *The Lost Chord* (1933), *Outcast* (1934), *Scrooge, Royal Cavalcade* (1935), *Cavalcade of the Stars* (1938). AS.

Glynne, Maureen (*b* London, 1928). Actress. On stage aged three, she entered films in the late 30s with uncredited roles in, among others, *Sixty Glorious Years, A Royal Divorce* (1938) and *The Outsider* (1939), and was briefly under contract to GRAND NATIONAL PICTURES. Married Peter HAMMOND.

OTHER BRITISH FILMS: *Medal for the General* (1944), *The Turners of Prospect Road* (1947), *The Guinea Pig* (1948), *The Franchise Affair* (1950).

Godber, John (*b* Hemsworth, 1956). Director. Innovative theatre director, founder of the Hull Truck Theatre Company, author and producer of plays for it, and writer of TV series (including 11 episodes of *Brookside*, 1982), Godber directed his first feature, *Up 'n' Under* (1997), based on one of his plays. It concerned the harnessing of a bunch of no-hopers into a football side. Alleged to have turned down Mark ADDY's role in *The Full Monty* (1997).

Goddard, Alf (*b* London, 1897 – *d* Harlow, 1981). Actor. A very busy screen tough guy, active in films from 1923 (starting as stunt man) to 1953, Goddard was a former boxer and stuntman, with the looks to match. It seems appropriate he should have played a PT instructor in *The Way Ahead* (1944), training British actors in how to be tough.

OTHER BRITISH FILMS INCLUDE: *The Sign of Four* (1923), *Mademoiselle from Armentières* (1926), *Downhill* (1927), *High Treason* (1929), *Too Many Wives* (1933), *No Limit* (1935), *Song of Freedom* (1936), *Non-Stop New York, King Solomon's Mines* (1937), *The Drum, Convict 99* (1938), *Return to Yesterday* (1940), *South American George* (1941), *The Young Mr Pitt* (1942), *The Way to the Stars, Perfect Strangers* (1945), *Innocents in Paris* (1953). AS.

Goddard, Willoughby (*b* Bicester, 1926). Actor. Chubby character player in films since the mid 50s (there is an early uncredited appearance in *The Million Pound Note*, 1953), as Sergeants, squires and sirs, usually sympathetic, and much on TV. On stage from 1943, London 1948; best remembered as Landburgher Gessler in TV's *William Tell* (1958–59).

OTHER BRITISH FILMS INCLUDE: *The Green Man* (1956), *Heart of a Child* (1958), *The Millionairess* (1960), *Double Bunk* (1961), *Carry On Cruising* (1962), *The Wrong Box* (1966), *The Charge of the Light Brigade* (1968), *Joseph Andrews* (1976), *Jabberwocky* (1977).

Godden, Rumer (*b* Eastbourne, 1907 – *d* Thornhill, Dumfriesshire, 1998). Author. Raised in India which provided the setting for two of her most famous novels, *The River* (filmed by Jean Renoir, 1951, US/Ind) and *Black Narcissus*, Godden was fascinated with the sub-continent, returning to England just before Indian independence was achieved. *Black Narcissus*, magnificently filmed by POWELL AND PRESSBURGER in 1947, though Godden disliked it, may be read on many levels, one of which is a presage of the passing of British rule in India. Other films from her novels include: *Innocent Sinners* (1958, from *An Episode of Sparrows*), *The Greengage Summer* (1961), a sensitive study of burgeoning female sexuality, and *The Battle of the Villa Fiorita* (1965).

Godfrey, Bob (*b* West Maitland, Australia 1922) Animator. The wholly anglicised Godfrey learned his trade at the Larkins Studio before becoming a founder member of Biographic films, and a committed comic auteurist, specialising in irony

and innuendo. Godfrey's absurdism may be traced in the FREE CINEMA politics of *Polygamous Polonius* (1959); his mock-erotic EXPLOITATION films of the 70s, *Henry 9 'til 5* (1970) and *Kama Sutra Rides Again* (1971); and his children's ANIMATION, *Roobarb and Custard* and *Henry's Cat*. His Oscar-winning musical DOCUMENTARY *Great* (1975) critiqued Victorian restraint in a burlesque biography of engineer Isambard Kingdom Brunel. His best work, with scriptwriter, Stan Hayward, works as a surreal satire on the social identity of the 'small' man, and the inhibitions of British masculinity.

OTHER BRITISH FILMS INCLUDE: *Watch the Birdie* (1954), *Do-It-Yourself Cartoon Kit* (1961), *Alf, Bill and Fred, The Rise and Fall of Emily Sprod* (1964), *Two Off the Cuff* (1967), *Dream Doll* (1979). Paul Wells.

Godfrey, Derek (*b* London, 1924 – *d* London, 1983). Actor. Prominent stage actor – debut 1949 – who appeared with Old Vic and RSC, and played secondary roles on screen and television. Married actress Diana Fairfax.

BRITISH FILMS INCLUDE: *Guns of Darkness* (1962), *The Vengeance of She, A Midsummer Night's Dream* (1968), *Julius Caesar* (1970), *Hands of the Ripper* (1971). AS.

Godfrey, Peter (*b* London, 1899 – *d* Los Angeles, 1970). Actor, director. After directing two thrillers, *Thread o' Scarlet* (1930), *Down River* (1931) and acting in three films – *Leave It to Me, Heads We Go!* (1933) and *Good Morning, Boys!* (1937) – Godfrey went to America where he directed, among others, the enjoyable melodramas, *The Two Mrs Carrolls* (1947) and *The Woman in White* (1948). Also acted in several US films in his first years there. From the mid 50s he became a TV director. Married actress Renee (Hall) Godfrey.

Godsell, Vanda (*b* England, 1918 – *d* London, 1990). Actress. Vivid blonde character player, at her best as Mrs Weaver in *This Sporting Life* (1963), spiteful when her advances are spurned by Richard HARRIS. Busiest in the 60s, roles ranged from the Prioress in *The Sword of Sherwood Forest* (1960) to 'Tart' in *Night Without Pity* (1962), the latter typical of her more characteristic mode.

OTHER BRITISH FILMS INCLUDE: *The Large Rope* (1953), *The Frightened City* (1961), *The Wrong Arm of the Law, The Waltz of the Toreadors, Term of Trial* (1962), *The Victors, 80,000 Suspects* (1963), *A Shot in the Dark, The Earth Dies Screaming* (1964), *The Wrong Box* (1966), *The Pink Panther Strikes Again* (1976).

Godwin, Frank (*b* London, 1917). Director, screenwriter, producer. Former accountant, then stage and cabaret producer-writer, who entered films with the RANK ORGANISATION in 1943, being appointed assistant to executive producer Earl ST JOHN in 1950. Worked as associate producer on *Penny Princess* (1952) and produced his first film, *Portrait of Alison* (1955), independently for ANGLO-AMALGAMATED. In 1956, he formed a partnership with writer Ted WILLIS and J. LEE-THOMPSON, and they made the realist dramas *Woman in a Dressing Gown* (1957) and *No Trees in the Street* (1958). His later career included a number of children's films, several of which he also directed.

OTHER BRITISH FILMS INCLUDE: (p or co-p, unless noted) *Operation Bullshine* (1959), *The Small World of Sammy Lee* (1962), *Lust for a Vampire* (1970, lyricist), *Demons of the Mind* (1972, + co-story), *Sky Pirates* (1976, short), *The Boy Who Never Was, Electric Eskimo* (1979, short, + d), *Terry on the Fence* (1985, + d, sc).

Goehr, Walter (*b* Berlin, 1903 – *d* London, 1960). Composer, conductor. A former pupil of Arnold Schönberg, Goehr went to Britain in 1933, working initially as a conductor for Columbia and HMV, later also in films, where he often collaborated with Allan GRAY. Goehr composed several film scores, most notably for David LEAN's *Great Expectations* (1946).

OTHER BRITISH FILMS INCLUDE: *Brief Ecstasy* (1937, m d); (comp) *What A Man!* (1938), *I'll Get You for This* (1950); (cond) *The Volunteer* (1943), *A Canterbury Tale* (1944), *I Know Where I'm Going!* (1945), *A Matter of Life and Death* (1946). Tim Bergfelder.

Gold, Jack (*b* London, 1930). Director. Entered films in 1955, first directing a BFI short, *The Visit*, in 1959, and having experience as an editor with BBC TV in the 60s. There is a maverick heterogeneity about his *cv*: consider the toughly unlikeable *The Reckoning* (1969); the witty screen transfer of Peter NICHOLS's stage satire, *The National Health* (1973); *Aces High* (1976) – an airborne remake of *Journey's End*; a surprisingly acceptable *Little Lord Fauntleroy* (1980), made for US television, in cinemas elsewhere; and the house-selling comedy, *The Chain* (1984). None of these has been widely seen, yet all have their rewards, especially those of a director who knows how to deploy strong casts. Some of his TV work has also been notable, especially *Catholics* (1973, some cinemas) and *The Naked Civil Servant* (1975), a mordant, compassionate version of the life of Quentin CRISP; and since the mid 80s he has worked wholly in TV, including a strongly cast version of *The Return of the Native* (1994).

OTHER BRITISH FILMS: *Living Jazz* (1960, doc), *The Bofors Gun* (1968), *Who?* (1974), *Man Friday* (1975), *The Medusa Touch* (UK/Fr, + co-op), *The Sailor's Return* (1978), *Praying Mantis* (1982).

Gold, Jimmy (*b* Glasgow, 1886 – *d* Harrow, 1967). Actor. RN: James McGonigal. Slapstick comedian who, along with his comic partner of 35 years, former house-painter **Charlie Naughton** (*b* Glasgow, 1887 – *d* London, 1976), was part of the famous CRAZY GANG in the later 30s. They appeared first in films as a pair: in *My Lucky Star* (1933), *Cock o' the North* (1935), as incompetent detectives in *Highland Fling* (1936), and *Wise Guys* (1937), directed by Harry Langdon, US comedian. They then starred with the whole Gang in *O-Kay for Sound* (1937), *Alf's Button Afloat* (1938), *The Frozen Limits* (1939), *Gasbags* (1940) and *Life Is a Circus* (1958).

Goldbacher, Sandra (*b c* 1960). Director, screenwriter. Television documentary film-maker Goldbacher came to the attention of producer Sarah CURTIS who gave her the chance to direct her first feature, the underrated *The Governess* (1998, UK/Fr). This grew out of a 'diary' Goldbacher wrote from the point of view of the film's heroine who must come to terms with her Jewish identity and her personal ambitions. This very promising start was followed by the US-made *The Devil's Chimney* (1999) and *Me Without You* (2001, + sc), a study of friends growing up in outer London in the 70s and 80s. TV work includes the award-winning short *Seventeen* (1994).

Goldblatt, Stephen (*b* South Africa). Cinematographer. Now established in high-budget US enterprises, Goldblatt's early British work could hardly have seemed to point him towards *Lethal Weapon* (1987, sequel 1989). He started on a HALAS AND BACHELOR animated piece, *This Love Thing* (1970), and followed with DOCUMENTARY work such as *Foto: Sven Nykvist* (1973) and *The Alternative Miss World* (1980) and a batch of oddly assorted features, including *The Mangrove Nine* (1973 – conflict in Notting Hill), *Breaking Glass* (1980 – a female rock singer's vicissitudes), the space Western, *Outland*

(1981), and the undervalued *The Return of the Soldier* (1982).

Goldcrest Films Canadian Jake Eberts founded Goldcrest in 1977, as a development finance company for feature film projects. Its first investment was a modest £11,250 in Ken LOACH's *Black Jack* (1979), a box-office failure. Some years later, and in stark contrast, its final venture as an independent company involved a massive investment of around £35 million in three films – *Revolution* (1985, UK/Nor), *The Mission* (1985) and *Absolute Beginners* (1986). The films did share one feature with Loach's film – box-office failure – but the losses on the high-budget pictures brought Goldcrest to the brink of bankruptcy and it was sold to the Brent Walker group in 1987. During the intervening years, with financial backing from the Pearson Longman media conglomerate, Goldcrest became a leading name in British cinema and a major source of production finance for British films. David PUTTNAM and Richard ATTENBOROUGH joined the company's board as non-executive directors, and Sandy Lieberson was head of production for a brief period. After the success of *Chariots of Fire* (1981), in which Goldcrest had a modest investment, the company became closely identified with the renaissance of the British film with a number of its titles winning prestigious Oscars. It was involved in various ways, from modest development support to major production financing, in many important films of the period including *Gandhi* (1982, UK/Ind), *Local Hero* (1983), *The Killing Fields, Cal, The Dresser, Dance with a Stranger* (1984), *A Room with a View* (1985), and *Hope and Glory* (1987).

BIBLIOG: Jake Eberts and Terry Ilott, *My Indecision Is Final*, 1990. Tom Ryall.

Golden, Michael (*b* Bray, Ireland, 1913). Actor. Formerly in the Civil Service and on stage from 1932 with the Abbey Theatre, in London from 1943, in the Stratford 1947 season, and on screen first in *A Canterbury Tale* (1944), Golden played supporting roles in about 30 films. Sometimes on the side of the law, as in *Pool of London* (1950), as a customs officer; on the other side, as the traditional small-time crim in *The Blue Lamp* (1949), both for Basil DEARDEN for whom he appeared in two further films. Also in a dozen 'B' FILMS of the 50s.

OTHER BRITISH FILMS INCLUDE: *Hungry Hill* (1947), *Noose* (1948), *Cry, the Beloved Country, The Gentle Gunman* (1952), *Operation Diplomat, The Square Ring* (1953), *Thirty-Six Hours, The Green Scarf* (1954), *Murder by Proxy* (1955), *Women Without Men* (1956), *The Man Without a Body* (1957), *Tread Softly Stranger* (1958), *Murder She Said* (1961).

Goldie, F. Wyndham (*b* Rochester, 1896 – *d* London, 1957). Actor. Supporting player good at colonial roles, from Cecil Rhodes in *Victoria the Great* (1937) to Commissioner Sanders in *Old Bones of the River* (1938). Major stage career – debut 1922 – with the Liverpool Rep from 1927 to 1934; war service (1914–18) and in WW2 with RAF, 1940–46; and on stage for three years following. Also on TV from 1946. His wife, Grace Wyndham Goldie, was a key figure in BBC current affairs TV programmes.

OTHER BRITISH FILMS INCLUDE: *Lorna Doone* (1934), *Under the Red Robe* (1937), *Sixty Glorious Years* (1938), *The Arsenal Stadium Mystery* (1939), *Night Train to Munich, The Girl in the News* (1940), *Seven Days to Noon* (1950), *Brothers in Law* (1956). AS.

Golding, Louis (*b* Manchester, 1896 – *d* Manchester, 1958). Author, screenwriter. Oxford-educated novelist, popular between wars, whose best-known novel was *Magnolia Street* (1931), dealing with Jewish/Gentile conflict in Manchester. He worked on a number of screenplays in Hollywood (with David O. Selznick) and in Britain, where he wrote the dialogue for Bernard VORHAUS's *Cotton Queen* (1937), authored the screenplays for *The Proud Valley* (1940, co-sc) and *Theirs is the Glory* (1946), and was the co-author of the story for *Freedom Radio* (1940). Most notably, *Magnolia Street* was sensitively adapted to the screen as *Mr Emmanuel* (1944), after which he tried vainly to do more films with Greta GYNT as his heroine Elsie Silver.

Goldner, Charles (*b* Vienna, 1900 – *d* London, 1955). Actor. Very likeable character player who came to films after a stage career in Vienna and London, and was allegedly fluent in nine languages. In nearly 30 British films (he'd begun in Vienna), he could be effortlessly – and charmingly – corrupt, like Colleoni, the suave criminal who never dirties his hands, in *Brighton Rock* (1947), or touching, as in his scene with Mary MERRALL, as a couple of old troupers in *Encore* (1951), or cynically aware of human weakness, as in *The End of the Affair* (1954), his last British film.

OTHER BRITISH FILMS INCLUDE: *Room for Two* (1940), *Mr Emmanuel* (1944), *Flight from Folly* (1945), *Bond Street, Bonnie Prince Charlie, No Orchids for Miss Blandish* (1948), *Give Us This Day* (UK/US), *Dear Mr Prohack* (1949), *Shadow of the Eagle, I'll Get You for This* (1950), *Secret People* (1951), *Top Secret* (1952), *The Captain's Paradise* (1953), *Duel in the Jungle* (1954).

Goldsmith, Isadore (*b* Vienna, 1893 – *d* Putney, Vermont, 1964). RN: Goldschmidt. Producer. European manager of BIP and its German subsidiary Südfilm from 1925, he was independent producer in Britain from 1933. From 1936 frequently collaborated with Max SCHACH, co-founder of the company Grafton. Among his 30s films, the best-known today is Carol REED's *The Stars Look Down* (1939). In the 40s, Goldsmith collaborated with director Lance COMFORT on *Hatter's Castle* (1941) and the Margaret LOCKWOOD melodrama *Bedelia* (1946, + co-sc), after which he left for Hollywood.

OTHER BRITISH FILMS: *Southern Roses* (1936), *A Woman Alone* (1936), *Whom The Gods Love* (1936), *Mademoiselle Docteur* (1937), *The Lilac Domino* (1937), *I Killed The Count* (1939), *The Voice Within* (1945). Tim Bergfelder.

Goodall, Louise (*b* Glasgow, 1962). Actress. Eloquent player who came to prominence as the social worker who falls for the reformed alcoholic in Ken LOACH's masterly *My Name Is Joe* (1998), winning several award nominations for her performance. Educated in Glasgow schools, she worked in semi-professional theatre companies until 1983, co-founding the Unit One Theatre Company. Since then, as well as theatre, a good deal of TV, including *Jolly: A Life* (1995), film debut in the small role of a prostitute in *Silent Scream* (1990), and was Robert CARLYLE's earlier girlfriend in Loach's *Carla's Song* (1996, UK/Ger/Sp).

OTHER BRITISH FILMS INCLUDE: *Aberdeen* (2000, UK/Nor/Swe).

Goodhew, Philip (*b* Aldershot, 1960). Director, screenwriter. Studied playwriting at Manchester University, had acting experience in the 80s in the theatre and on TV, including the sharp telemovie, *Good and Bad at Games* (1983), and a stint in *Crossroads* (1985–88). Made his debut as film director with the black comedy, *Intimate Relations* (1996, UK/Can), with Julie WALTERS who, like her daughter, takes sailor lodger, Rupert GRAVES, as lover.

OTHER BRITISH FILM: *Another Life* (2001).

Goodliffe, Michael (*b* Bebington, Cheshire, 1914 – *d* 1976). Actor. Indispensable character player of the 50s and 60s, Oxford-educated son-of-the-vicarage Goodliffe was on stage from 1936, at Stratford (1936 –39), in the Army and a prisoner-of-war during WW2, and entered films in *The Small Back Room* (1948). Played numerous officers and gentlemen, in such films as *The One That Got Away* (1957) and *Sink the Bismarck!* (1960), with easy conviction, but was even more satisfying as the troubled professionals for whom his lean, incisive features seemed to equip him: the disfigured preacher in *The End of the Affair* (1954) or the designer of the 'Titanic' in *A Night to Remember* (1958). Also in a few international films (e.g. *The Fixer*, 1968) and some TV, including an early performance as Tybalt in *Romeo and Juliet* (1947). Committed suicide while hospitalised.

OTHER BRITISH FILMS INCLUDE: *The Wooden Horse, Family Portrait* (doc, narr) (1950), *Cry, the Beloved Country* (1952), *Sea Devils, Rob Roy . . .* (1953), *Wicked as They Come* (1956), *Fortune Is a Woman, The Camp on Blood Island* (1957), *Carve Her Name With Pride* (1958), *The Battle of the Sexes* (1959), *Peeping Tom, The Trials of Oscar Wilde* (1960), *The Day the Earth Caught Fire, No Love for Johnnie* (1961), *80,000 Suspects* (1963), *The Jokers* (1966), *Cromwell* (1970), *Henry VIII and His Six Wives* (1972), *The Man with the Golden Gun* (1974), *To the Devil a Daughter* (1976, UK/Ger).

Goodner, Carol (*b* New York, 1904 – *d* Katonah, NY, 2001). Actress. Busy second lead and occasional star of largely insignificant films of the 30s, who was strangely never tapped by Hollywood. Major US stage star – debut 1908; London debut 1927 – who was memorable as Lorraine Sheldon in *The Man Who Came to Dinner* (1939).

BRITISH FILMS INCLUDE: *Those Who Love* (1929), *The Ringer* (1931), *There Goes the Bride* (1932), *Red Ensign* (1934), *Music Hath Charms* (1935), *The Frog* (1937), *A Royal Divorce* (1938). AS.

Goodwin, Harold (*b* Wombwell, 1917). Actor. Vividly doleful, raw-boned purveyor of about 50 enjoyable small roles in British films of the 50s and 60s. First noticed as the gormless under-porter in *The Happiest Days of Your Life* (1950), then in a wide range of 'A' and 'B' FILMS: thus, he is the call boy in *The Prince and the Showgirl* (1957) and, Scouse, the nervous lorry-driver in *The Hi-Jackers* (1963). Also, TV in the 70s and 80s. Not to be confused with the documentary producer Harold Goodwin (*b* London, 1908) who worked for GB INSTRUCTIONAL FILMS in the late 40s.

OTHER BRITISH FILMS INCLUDE: *The Magnet, Dance Hall* (1950), *The Man in the White Suit, Appointment with Venus* (1951), *Angels One Five, The Cruel Sea* (1952), *The Million Pound Note* (1953), *The Dam Busters, The Ladykillers* (1955), *Zarak* (1956), *The Bridge on the River Kwai, Barnacle Bill* (1957), *Sea of Sand* (1958), *Wrong Number, The Mummy* (1959), *The Bulldog Breed* (1960), *Phantom of the Opera* (1962), *The Curse of the Mummy's Tomb* (1964), *Frankenstein Must Be Destroyed* (1969), *Jabberwocky* (1977).

Goodwin, Ron (*b* Plymouth, 1929 – *d* Brimpton Common, Berkshire, 2003). Composer, conductor. Prolific composer of film music since the early 50s, when he began writing scores for DOCUMENTARIES, while also writing arrangements for the leading bands and orchestras of the day, including GERALDO. Trained at the Guildhall School of Music, he was musical director of Parlophone Records from 1950, and began broadcasting with his own orchestra. His feature film scores were first heard in *The Man with a Gun* (1958) and *Whirlpool* (1959) and, on the nearly 60 that followed, he was often conductor or music director as well as composer. Much of his work was for ACTION FILMS (like *Those Magnificent Men . . . ,*

1965), but he is equally adept with COMEDIES (e.g. two for MORECAMBE AND WISE) or MELODRAMA (e.g. *I Thank a Fool*, 1962, + m d; *Of Human Bondage*, 1964, + cond). Often guest conductor with famous orchestras, has won several Ivor NOVELLO Awards, including one in 1994 for Lifetime Achievement.

OTHER BRITISH FILMS INCLUDE: (m d only) *The Witness* (1959), *The Clue of the New Pin* (1960); (comp/m d) *Lancelot and Guinevere* (1962), *Children of the Damned* (1963), *Murder Most Foul* (1964); comp/cond) *633 Squadron* (1963, UK/US), *Murder Ahoy* (1964), *The Alphabet Murders* (1965), *The Trap* (1966), *Where Eagles Dare* (1968), *Battle of Britain* (1969), *The Executioner* (1970), *Frenzy* (1972), *Candleshoe* (1977), *Force 10 from Navarone* (1978); (comp) *In the Nick* (1959), *Village of the Damned*, *The Trials of Oscar Wilde* (1960), *Village of Daughters*, *The Day of the Triffids* (1962), *Murder at the Gallop* (1963), *Operation Crossbow* (1965, UK/It), *That Riviera Touch* (1966), *The Magnificent Two* (1967), *Monte Carlo or Bust!* (1969, UK/Fr/It).

Goodwins, Fred (*b* London, 1891 – *d* London, 1923). Director. A British journalist in the US, who had earlier appeared on stage, Goodwins has small roles in a number of Charlie CHAPLIN shorts from 1915, including *A Night Out*, *The Tramp*, *Shanghaied*, and *Police* (1916). Other US films include *For Husbands Only* (1918) and *Common Clay* (1919), followed by about ten in Britain.

BRITISH FILMS: (d) *The Artistic Temperament*, *The Chinese Puzzle* (1919), *The Ever-Open Door*, *The Department Store*, *The Impossible Man*, *The Noble Art*, *Colonel Newcombe*, *The Scarlet Kiss*, *Build Thy House* (1920), *Blood Money*, (1921, + a). AS.

Goolden, Richard (*b* London, 1895 – *d* London, 1981). Actor. Charterhouse- and Oxford-educated stage actor (from 1923) in many Shakespearean and other roles, who appeared in nearly 20 films spread over 40 years. Became famous in the 30s for his radio series, 'Mr Penny', which he also took on stage tours and transferred to film as *Meet Mr Penny* in 1938.

OTHER BRITISH FILMS INCLUDE: *Once in a New Moon* (1935), *School for Husbands* (1937), *Mistaken Identity* (1942), *Headline* (1943), *Vengeance Is Mine* (1948), *The Weapon* (1956), *In the Doghouse* (1961), *It's All Happening* (1963), *Joseph Andrews* (1976).

Gopal, Ram (*b* Bangalore, India, 1917) Actor. Famous Indian dancer and actor, on stage in London from 1939, who appeared in several British films, including *The Planter's Wife* (1952), set in Malaya, *The Purple Plain* (1954), set in Burma, and *The Blue Peter* (1955), as a Malaysian who wonders if his country might benefit from the Outward Bound programme at the film's centre.

Gordon, Colin (*b* Ceylon, 1911 – *d* Haslemere, 1972). Actor. Cherishable British character player, Marlborough- and Oxford-educated Gordon, on stage from 1934, came to films after spending WW2 in the Army (1940–46). He was essentially a comic performer, somewhat in the manner of Richard WATTIS; that is, he could be prissy, officious or healthily sardonic. In fact, he won an award for playing on stage Wattis's film role in *The Happiest Days of Your Life* (1950). However, perhaps his very finest film performance, among 60-odd, was in a different mode: he plays the bank manager humanised into self-awareness by the barely evaded threat of death in *Strongroom* (1962). Also on stage in New York and in a lot of TV, including *A Life of Bliss* (1960–61) and *The Baron* (1966).

OTHER BRITISH FILMS INCLUDE: *Traveller's Joy* (1949), *Circle of Danger* (1950), *Laughter in Paradise* (1951), *Mandy, Folly to Be Wise* (1952), *Grand National Night* (1953), *Escapade* (1955), *The Green Man* (1956), *The One That Got Away* (1957), *Virgin Island, The Doctor's Dilemma* (1958), *The Mouse That Roared* (1959), *Please Turn Over, The Big Day*

(1960), *Very Important Person* (1961), *The Boys, Night of the Eagle* (1962), *The Running Man, Heavens Above!, The Pink Panther* (1963), *The Great St Trinian's Train Robbery, The Family Way* (1966).

Gordon, Dorothy (*b* London, 1924). Actress. Former child actress who, at nearly 30, was very funny – and convincing – as Stanley HOLLOWAY's snivelling, adenoidal schoolgirl daughter in the 'Fumed Oak' segment of *Meet Me Tonight* (1952) and as the former aspirant to Willie Mossop pushed aside by Brenda DEBANZIE in *Hobson's Choice* (1953). Usually appeared looking doggedly plain. Daughter of actors **Nora Gordon** (*b* West Hartlepool, 1893 – *d* London, 1970) and **Leonard Sharp** (*b* Watford, Herts, 1890 – *d* Watford, Herts, 1958), who both played small roles in British films from the 30s to the 50s.

OTHER BRITISH FILMS INCLUDE: *The Silver Fleet* (1943), *Women of Twilight* (1952), *Love in Pawn* (1953), *Lost, All for Mary* (1955), *Grip of the Strangler, Life in Emergency Ward 10* (1958), *Sons and Lovers, Never Let Go* (1960), *The Secret Partner* (1961).

Gordon, Hal (*b* London, 1894 – *d* 1946). Actor. Tubby former law clerk and much later pub landlord, who was popular in the 30s as comic dimwit foil for stars, or in support of more famous comedians such as Lupino LANE and George FORMBY, often for BIP. Starred in a few SHORT FILMS such as *East of Ludgate Hill* (1937) and *Father o' Nine* (1938) for Fox–British. Made 70 films; on MUSIC HALL stage from 1912.

OTHER BRITISH FILMS INCLUDE: *Windjammer* (1930), *Bill and Coo* (1931), *Indiscretions of Eve* (1932), *Invitation to the Waltz* (1935), *Sabotage, Queen of Hearts* (1936), *Victoria the Great, Keep Fit* (1937), *It's in the Air* (1938), *Come on George!* (1939), *Let George Do It!* (1940), *Old Mother Riley, Detective* (1943), *I'll Turn to You* (1946, ucr).

Gordon, Hannah (*b* Edinburgh, 1941). Actress. Beautiful and charming actress, more often on stage (memorably in *Winter Journey*, 1983) and TV (notably as Virginia Bellamy in *Upstairs, Downstairs*, 1971, and as Peter BARKWORTH's wandering wife in *Telford's Change*, 1979) than on screen, where she played Anthony HOPKINS' wife in *The Elephant Man* (1980, UK-made, US-financed) and co-starred with Terence STAMP in *Tire à Part* (1997, Fr).

OTHER BRITISH FILMS INCLUDE: *Spring and Port Wine* (1969), *Alfie Darling* (1975), *The Big Sleep* (1978).

Gordon, Michael S. (*b* England, 1909). Screenwriter, director, editor. Often confused with the blacklisted American director of the same name, born in the same year, this Michael Gordon, Cambridge-educated, served his apprenticeship as editor with GAUMONT–BRITISH, worked as editor with the CROWN FILM UNIT during WW2, and edited the famous DOCUMENTARY, *Theirs is the Glory* (1946). He shared writing credits on two WESSEX films, *Esther Waters* (1948) and *All Over the Town* (1949) and directed *Wherever She Goes* (1953, Aust), a pedestrian biopic about pianist Eileen JOYCE. Edited a further five films in the 50s.

OTHER BRITISH FILMS INCLUDE: (e, unless noted) *Seven Sinners* (1936), *King Solomon's Mines* (1937), *Coastal Command* (1942, doc), *Malta Story* (1953, 2ud), *Simba* (1955), *Safari* (1956), *Night of the Demon* (1957).

Gordon-Sinclair, John (*b* Glasgow, 1962). Actor. As a gangling teenager, this actor (who keeps ringing changes on the parts of his name) came to prominence as the hero of Bill FORSYTH's *Gregory's Girl* (1980), the charming comedy of football and adolescence for which he won a BAAn and which spawned a less successful sequel 20 years on, *Gregory's Two Girls* (1999, UK/Ger). Between these two, his career has lost some of the expected momentum, but he has worked in TV and in a half-dozen or so films, including the US-backed *Half Moon Street* and *Walter and June* (1986).

OTHER BRITISH FILMS INCLUDE: *That Sinking Feeling* (1979), *Local Hero* (1983), *The Girl in the Picture* (1985, starring), *The Brylcreem Boys* (1996).

Goring, Marius (*b* Newport, Isle of Wight, 1912 – *d* Rushlake Green, 1998). Actor. Educated at Perse School Cambridge and at several European universities, Goring, in nearly 50 films, maintained an urbane image – when, that is, he wasn't being notably sinister. Wholly British as he was, he was remarkably adept at suggesting foreigners, sometimes merely decadent (like the playboy in *The Barefoot Contessa*, 1954), sometimes actual Nazi swine (as in *Pastor Hall*, 1940; *I Was Monty's Double*, 1958). The stage (in London from 1927) was his first love: he had several Old Vic seasons in the 30s, playing a range of Shakespearean roles, including a much-praised Feste in *Twelfth Night* (1937), and seasons at Stratford. Also toured a great deal, in plays classic and modern, and during WW2, having joined the Army in 1940, was appointed supervisor of BBC radio productions broadcasting to Germany.

In 1990, he said that he'd enjoyed some of his television work, citing *The Old Men at the Zoo* (1983) as example, 'much more than most of my films'. However, his film work stands up very well. He valued the films he made for Michael POWELL above the rest: *The Spy in Black* (1939), as a U-boat captain; *A Matter of Life and Death* (1946), as the effete heavenly 'conductor' who complains of the absence of Technicolor 'up there'; *The Red Shoes* (1948), as the young composer in love with the doomed ballerina; and *Ill Met by Moonlight* (1956), as another Nazi. However, there were other felicities among his film work, including the increasingly deranged schoolmaster in *Mr Perrin and Mr Traill* (1948), the musician obsessed with Ava GARDNER in *Pandora and the Flying Dutchman* (1950), an equivocal ballet teacher in *Circle of Danger* (1950) and another, sympathetic German officer in *So Little Time* (1952). On TV he was a finely flamboyant *Scarlet Pimpernel* (1954) and a gruff ('Bugger Bognor') George V in *Edward and Mrs Simpson* (1978).

As well as his very rich acting career in all the media, he was a vigorous supporter of ACTORS' EQUITY, fighting as far as the courts, to maintain its political neutrality so as to strengthen its position with governments of whatever persuasion. He co-founded the union in 1929 and was twice its vice-president (1963–65, 1975–82). He was appointed a Fellow of the Royal Society of Literature in 1979 and CBE in 1991. His second wife was actress Lucie MANNHEIM (1941, until her death in 1976), and in 1977 he married television producer Prudence Fitzgerald.

OTHER BRITISH FILMS INCLUDE: *Consider Your Verdict* (1938), *Flying Fifty-Five* (1939), *Big Blockade* (1942, doc), *The Night Invader* (1943), *The True Story of Lili Marlene* (1944, doc), *Take My Life* (1947), *Highly Dangerous*, *Odette* (1950), *The Man Who Watched Trains Go By* (1952), *The Adventures of Quentin Durward* (1955), *The Moonraker* (1957), *Whirlpool* (1959), *Beyond the Curtain* (1960), *The Inspector* (1962), *Zeppelin* (1971), *Strike It Rich* (1990).

Gorton, Assheton Production designer. In a somewhat sparse career – only 20 films in nearly 40 years, Gorton has clear highspots: the evocation of 'SWINGING LONDON' (BAAn) in *Blow-Up* (1966, UK/It), the northern rigours of *Get Carter* (1971), and the double vision of Victorian England and contemporary London (AAn and BAAn) in *The French*

Lieutenant's Woman (1981). Since the last, has worked mainly in US films.

OTHER BRITISH FILMS INCLUDE: *The Knack . . .* (1965), *The Bliss of Mrs Blossom*, *Wonderwall* (1968), *The Magic Christian*, *The Bed Sitting Room* (1969), *Revolution* (1985, UK/Nor), *Shadow of the Vampire* (2001, UK/Lux/US).

Goss, Helen (*b* London, 1903). Actress. Supporting player of nearly 30 British films, Goss was a drama teacher as well, at one time in charge of the RANK CHARM SCHOOL intake. In films, she slid up and down the social scale: as pub landlord Wilfrid LAWSON's missus in *Fanny by Gaslight* (1944) and barmaid in *Pink String and Sealing Wax* (1945), on the one hand; on the other, colonial lady in *The Planter's Wife* (1952) and dowager in *Half a Sixpence* (1967, UK/US).

OTHER BRITISH FILMS INCLUDE: *Important People* (1934), *Dear Octopus* (1943), *The Wicked Lady*, *They Were Sisters* (1945), *The Mark of Cain* (1948), *Stage Fright* (1950), *The Pickwick Papers* (1952), *Gideon's Day*, *Carry On Sergeant* (1958), *The Two Faces of Dr Jekyll* (1960), *Jane Eyre* (1970).

Gossage, John W. (*b* Liverpool, 1905 – *d* 1997). Producer. One of those figures who hovers round the industry (he entered it in 1935 as producer for Reunion Films) in several capacities, never quite making his mark in any of them. Was associate producer in the later 30s; served in the RAF in WW2 (1939–46); was production manager post-war on *Uncle Silas* (1947) and *Hamlet* (1948); involved in a handful of mildly interesting 50s films, including *Angels One Five* (1952, p).

OTHER BRITISH FILMS: (p, unless noted) *Skylarks* (1936), *The Housemaster* (1938, assoc p), *Yellow Sands*, *Marigold*, *The Outsider*, *The Gang's All Here* (1939), *Green Grow the Rushes* (1951), *The Gamma People* (1955, + co-sc), *Family Doctor* (1958, co-adpt).

Gotell, Walter (*b* Bonn, Germany, 1924 – *d* London, 1997). Actor. Frequently cast as suspicious foreigners in British and international productions, including *The African Queen* (1951), *Guns Of Navarone* (1961), and *The Spy Who Came In From The Cold* (1965). His best known role was KGB General Gogol in the James BOND series (first appearance in *The Spy Who Loved Me*, 1977), a character Gotell imbued with mischievous irony. Had continuing role of Chief Constable in *Softly Softly: Task Force* (1970–76).

OTHER BRITISH FILMS INCLUDE: *The Goose Steps Out*, *Squadron Leader X* (1942), *Two Thousand Women* (1944), *The Wooden Horse* (1950), *Albert RN* (1953), *Ice-Cold In Alex*, *I Was Monty's Double* (1958), *Sink the Bismarck!* (1960), *From Russia With Love* (1963), *Endless Night* (1972), *The Stud* (1978), *Moonraker* (1979, UK/Fr), *For Your Eyes Only* (1981), *Octopussy* (1983), *A View To A Kill* (1985), *The Living Daylights* (1987). Tim Bergfelder.

Gotfurt, Frederick (*b* Berlin, 1901 – *d* London, 1973). RN: Fritz Gotfurcht. Writer, producer, scenario editor. Formerly a theatre critic in Germany, Gotfurt turned scriptwriter in British exile. From 1949 he became scenario editor at ABPC, responsible for acquisition of literary sources and the development of screenplays. Made mostly uncredited script contributions to films such as *The Dam Busters* (1955), *Yield To The Night* (1956), and *Ice Cold in Alex* (1958).

OTHER BRITISH FILMS INCLUDE (credited work only): *The Girl In The Taxi* (UK/Fr, 1937), *It Happened One Sunday* (1944, + co-p), *Temptation Harbour* (1947), *Talk Of A Million* (1951), *A Lady Mislaid* (1958). Tim Bergfelder.

Gott, Barbara (*b* Stirling, Scotland, 1872 – *d* London, 1944). Actress. Plump character actress, who made her first film, *Betta the Gypsy* in 1918, and whose stage career (London debut 1913,

New York debut 1936) was more important than her work on screen.

OTHER BRITISH FILMS INCLUDE: *The Romance of Lady Hamilton* (1919), *Downhill* (1927), *Not Quite a Lady* (1928), *Sally in Our Alley* (1931), *The Good Companions* (1933), *The Beloved Vagabond* (1936), *Pastor Hall* (1940). AS.

Gough, Michael (*b* Malaya, 1917). Actor. Tall, gaunt, intense actor who, after stage experience from 1936, entered films in 1947 as Valerie HOBSON's ineffectual husband in *Blanche Fury*. A survivor, he was still in demand 50 years later for international films, including *The Age of Innocence* (1993) and *Sleepy Hollow* (1999, Ger/US), and had become established in four big-budget comic-book films (1989, 1992, 1995, 1997) as Batman's manservant. Among his dozens of British films, one recalls him as the outlaw Irish tinker in Paul ROTHA's *No Resting Place* (1951), as Joan GREENWOOD's unpromising fiancé in *The Man in the White Suit* (1951), as the murderer, Dighton, in *Richard III* (1955), as the unnoticing father in *The Go-Between* (1971) and the ancient retainer Firs in *The Cherry Orchard* (2000) – and many more, maintaining a steady stage career the while. He was on TV from 1946, in episodes of popular series and in plays and mini-series. Married actresses (1) Diana Graves and (2) Anne (Annie) LEON.

OTHER BRITISH FILMS INCLUDE: *Saraband for Dead Lovers, The Small Back Room* (1948), *Night Was Our Friend* (1951), *Rob Roy . . .* (1953), *Ill Met by Moonlight* (1956), *The Horse's Mouth* (1958), *Dr Terror's House of Horrors* (1964), *Berserk!* (1967), *Women in Love* (1969), *Savage Messiah* (1972), *The Legend of Hell House* (1973), *Venom* (1981), *The Dresser* (1983), *Caravaggio* (1986), *Strapless* (1988), *'Let Him Have It'* (1991), *Wittgenstein* (1993), *What Rats Won't Do, St Ives* (1998).

Goulding, Alfred (*b* Katoomba, Australia, 1896 – *d* Los Angeles, 1972). Director. Vaudeville comedian who entered films in 1917 in Hollywood and joined Harold Lloyd's company as a director in 1919. Turned to feature film direction at MGM in 1925, with many Hollywood films. Work in Britain is relatively negligible, but when Goulding returned to Hollywood he directed Laurel and Hardy in their last major success, *A Chump at Oxford* (1940). Active through 60s.

BRITISH FILMS INCLUDES: *One Good Turn, Everything Is Rhythm* (1936), *Splinters in the Air* (1937), *Dick Barton — Special Agent* (also co-sc), *The Dark Road* (1948), *The Devil's Jest* (1954). AS.

government intervention *see* **legislation**

Gowers, Patrick (*b* 1936). Composer. While most of Gowers' scores have been for TV, notably for the definitive 80s SHERLOCK HOLMES series with Jeremy BRETT, there is still some notable film music, including the organ prelude for *Marat-Sade* (1966) and the scores for *The Virgin and the Gypsy* (1970, + cond), the semi-documentary on David Hockney's work, *A Bigger Splash* (1974) and the eloquent if little-seen *Stevie* [Smith, that is] (1978).

OTHER BRITISH FILMS INCLUDE: *Hamlet* (1969), *The Boy Who Turned Yellow* (1972, electronic music), *Whoops Apocalypse* (1986).

Gowland, Gibson (*b* Durham, 1872 – *d* London, 1951). Actor. Big, lumbering man whose appearance harmed his potential for major roles, but who is legendary as a result of two films for Erich von Stroheim: *Blind Husbands* (1918) and *Greed* (1925). Started career on stage in UK, and appeared on screen here in 20s and 30s in supporting roles, but made final film appearances in US in the 40s.

BRITISH FILMS INCLUDE: *The Harbour Lights* (1923), *The Private Life of Don Juan* (1934), *King of the Damned* (1936), *Cotton Queen* (1937). AS.

GPO Film Unit After the demise of the EMPIRE MARKETING BOARD, John GRIERSON and Stephen TALLENTS transferred that organisation's Film Unit to the General Post Office in 1934. Although the organisations were distinct, there was some overlap with the SPONSORED PRODUCTIONS *Song of Ceylon* (1934) and *BBC – The Voice of Britain* (1935) having their origins in the earlier organisation. Along with the talented personnel already on hand, Brazilian Alberto CAVALCANTI, who had a background in the French experimental cinema, joined the Unit bringing with him a peculiar understanding of film technique, including editing and sound manipulation. Len LYE, Humphrey JENNINGS and Norman McLAREN also brought a variety of film-making approaches. Despite the constraints that the world economic depression brought to bear on all government organisations, as well as the pressures exerted on the government to abandon the Unit in favour of private commercial interests in SHORT FILM production, the GPO Film Unit produced some of the best films of the DOCUMENTARY movement. These include *North Sea* (1938), *Song of Ceylon*, *Pett and Pott* (1934), *Coal Face* (1935), *Night Mail* (1936) and *Spare Time* (1939). With Grierson promulgating the development of a collaborative approach to film production, the Unit produced a number of films with exceptional personnel involved. This aspect is evidenced in the likes of Cavalcanti, Stuart LEGG, Harry WATT and Evelyn Spice participating in *BBC – The Voice of Britain* and in the contributions of Watt, Basil WRIGHT, Cavalcanti, W.H. AUDEN, and Benjamin BRITTEN to the production of *Night Mail*, which set a benchmark for international documentary film. As war broke out, the Unit was transferred to the MINISTRY OF INFORMATION which saw the emergence of Jennings as a major creative force with the likes of *London Can Take It!* (1940) and *Heart of Britain* (1941). In 1939 the GPO Film Unit was renamed the CROWN FILM UNIT to serve the war effort. Deane Williams.

Graber, Sheila (*b* South Shields, 1940) Director. An often unsung, but profoundly influential animator, specialising in promoting art and ANIMATION in schools, colleges, and local communities, and in her pioneering work as an independent woman animator.

BRITISH FILMS INCLUDE: *Boy and the Microscope* (1972), *Michelangelo* (1975), *Four Views of Landscape* (1976), *Howayy the Lasses* (1977), *Mondrian, William Blake* (1978), *The Face in Art* (1982), *My River Tyne* (1986), *Heidi's Horse* (1989). Paul Wells.

Grace, Nickolas (*b* Liverpool, 1947). Actor. There is such an enjoyably exotic whiff to Grace's performances that it comes as a surprise to note his Merseyside background. Apart from masses of eye-catching TV, like his role as Anthony Blanche in *Brideshead Revisited* (1982), Central School-trained Grace has compelled the attention in several prominent supporting roles in films: as Harry Hamilton-Paul in *Heat and Dust* (1982), as Bertrand Russell in *Tom & Viv* (1994) and as the Vicomte de Nanjac in *An Ideal Husband* (1999, UK/US). Much experience as stage actor and director, often in Shakespeare.

OTHER BRITISH FILMS INCLUDE: *City of the Dead* (1960), *Salome's Last Dance, Dream Demon* (1988), *Shooting Fish* (1997), *The Golden Bowl* (2000, UK/Fr/US).

Grade, Leslie (*b* London, 1916 – *d* South of France, 1979). Agent. RN: Winogradsky. Well-established theatrical agent, in partnership with his brother Lew GRADE. Much involved in TV production, especially in regard to popular commercial TV programmes. In films, he managed Sarah MILES and thus came to influence the production circumstances of *The Servant* (1963). He headed, with brothers Lew and Bernard DELFONT, the powerful Grade Organisation which, in the 70s, sought to extend its activities by joining with EMI. By all accounts the most retiring, business-orientated of the three brothers, he did not aspire to creative participation in show business.

BIBLIOG: Hunter Davies, *The Grades – The First Family of British Entertainment*, 1981.

Grade, Lew (Lord Grade) (*b* Tomak, Kazakhstan, 1906 – *d* London, 1998). Producer. RN: Lewis Winogradsky. Grade's Russian origins, Jewishness, and flamboyant personality suggest a Hollywood tycoon and, indeed, in the latter stages of his show business career his company – ITC, part of the Associated Communications Company – made an ambitious attempt to become a major player in the international film industry. Grade, with his brother Leslie GRADE, was a key force in the rise of commercial TV in Britain selling programmes such as *The Saint* and *The Avengers* to US television. This enabled him to attract investment for an expensive film programme aimed at the American market and he was involved in the production of around one hundred films including *The Return of the Pink Panther* (1974), *The Cassandra Crossing* (1976), *The Medusa Touch* (1978, UK/Fr), and *Escape to Athena* (1979), using international stars such as Peter SELLERS, Ava Gardner, Roger MOORE, David NIVEN, Sophia LOREN, Omar SHARIF, Richard BURTON, and Alec GUINNESS. Critical opinion on the films has been hard with one writer describing them as 'rootless productions of no relevance to any nation, lacking purpose or passion'. The spectacular failure of *Raise the Titanic* (1980), backed by his company ITC, provided an irresistible source of metaphor for the demise of Grade's company. Knighted in 1969, created a life peer, Baron Grade of Elstree. His other brother was Bernard, later Lord, DELFONT.

BIBLIOG: Autobiography, *Still Dancing*, 1987; Hunter Davies, *The Grades – The First Family of British Entertainment*, 1981. Tom Ryall.

Grade, Michael (*b* London, 1943) Executive. Son of Leslie GRADE, he was formerly an agent with London Management, head of production for LWT, head of CHANNEL 4 and First Leisure, from which he resigned to become Chairman of PINEWOOD STUDIOS in 2000. He headed a management buyout of Pinewood for £62m, committed to turning it into 'a multi-media production centre', with the aim of continuing to attract Hollywood blockbusters *and* to make more British films. In February 2001, he finalised the amalgamation of Pinewood and SHEPPERTON STUDIOS (owned by Ridley and Tony SCOTT), and in 2002 he announced plans for extending production to studios in Toronto.

Graetz, Paul (*b* Glogau, Germany, 1890 – *d* Los Angeles, 1937). Actor. A regular collaborator of Max Reinhardt and Ernst Lubitsch in German films of the 20s, Graetz was a diminutive character actor, often in tragi-comic parts. In Britain since 1933, one of his rare starring roles was in *Mr Cohen Takes A Walk* (1935), as a Jewish tramp.

OTHER BRITISH FILMS INCLUDE: *The Red Wagon, Blossom Time, Jew Süss* (1934), *Bulldog Jack, Mimi, Car Of Dreams* (1935). Tim Bergfelder.

Graham, Genine (*b* London, 1926). Actress. Had big opportunities on stage in London as the eponymous mermaid in *Miranda* (1947) and in New York in *The Millionairess* (1952), and had her own TV series, *Mail Call* (1955–56). She made about a dozen films, but usually had small parts in small films,

like the usherette in *Murder at the Windmill* (1949).

OTHER BRITISH FILMS INCLUDE: *Idol of Paris* (1948), *Hell Below Zero* (1953), *Dangerous Cargo* (1954), *Time to Remember* (1962), *The Vault of Horror* (1973, UK/US).

Graham, Morland (*b* Glasgow, 1890 – *d* London, 1949). Actor. Memorable character actor on stage from 1908 (London 1922), and in films of the 30s and 40s. Best screen roles included Shields, wartime batman and later shipyard employee of Clive BROOK in *The Shipbuilders* (1943), 'good old Sir Thomas Erpingham', whose cloak the King borrows, in *Henry V* (1944), and McFarish, one of the feuding patriarchs, in *The Brothers* (1947).

OTHER BRITISH FILMS INCLUDE: *The Private Life of Don Juan* (1934), *The Scarlet Pimpernel, Moscow Nights* (1935), *Jamaica Inn* (1939), *Old Bill and Son, Freedom Radio* (1940), *This England, Ships with Wings* (1941), *The Young Mr Pitt* (1942), *Medal for the General* (1944), *Gaiety George* (1946), *Bonnie Prince Charlie* (1948), *Whisky Galore!* (1949).

Graham, Richard (*b* Farnborough, 1960). Actor. Supporting actor in films since the mid 80s, most notably as Genghis in *My Beautiful Laundrette* (1985) and co-starring with Reese DINSDALE in *i.d.* (1995), as the senior police officer investigating football hooliganism; also had a small role in *Titanic* (1997, US). Educated in Hailsham, Sussex, and trained at East 15 Acting School, he has worked for Bristol Old Vic and Glasgow Citizens' Theatre as well as much TV (e.g. *Inspector Morse*, 1987; *A Touch of Frost*, 1992).

OTHER BRITISH FILMS INCLUDE: *The Bounty* (1984), *Return from the River Kwai* (1988), *24 Hours in London* (2000), *Arthur's Dyke* (2001)..

Grahame, Margot (*b* Canterbury, 1911 – *d* London, 1982). Actress. Popular blonde leading lady of 30s British films and flamboyant brunette character player of a half-dozen or so late 40s/50s films. The highpoint of her career was playing the prostitute Katie (AAn) in John FORD's 1935 drama, *The Informer*, after which she made over a dozen unremarkable Hollywood films before returning to Britain to play the vain film star in *Broken Journey* (1948), the suspicious wife of a besotted schoolmaster in *The Romantic Age* (1949) and several other over-the-top ladies. Apparently overweight, she was cruelly replaced by Binnie BARNES in *Shadow of the Eagle* (1950). TV debut in 1951. Raised in Durban, she had a stage career before entering films. Married (1 of 2) to actor Francis LISTER.

OTHER BRITISH FILMS INCLUDE: *Rookery Nook* (1930), *Uneasy Virtue* (1931), *The Innocents of Chicago* (1932), *Sorrell and Son* (1933), *Broken Melody* (1934), *Crime Over London* (1936), *I'll Get You for This* (1950), *Venetian Bird* (1952), *The Beggar's Opera* (1953), *Saint Joan* (1957, UK/US).

Grainer, Ron (*b* Atherton, Australia, 1922 – *d* Cuckfield, 1981). Composer. Well known for such stage successes as *Robert and Elizabeth* (1964) and theme music for such TV series as *Maigret* and *Dr Who*, and, just before his death, the mini-series, *Edward and Mrs Simpson* (1978). Grainer came into his own as a film composer with his work on popular 60s films like *A Kind of Loving* (1962, + cond), *Nothing But the Best* (1964) and *To Sir, with Love* (1967).

OTHER BRITISH FILMS INCLUDE: (comp, unless noted) *Terminus* (1961, doc, + cond), *The Dock Brief, Station Six Sahara* (UK/Ger) (1962), *The Man on the Moon* (1963), *Night Must Fall* (+ cond), *The Finest Hours* (doc) (1964), *Only When I Larf, The Assassination Bureau* (1968), *Lock Up Your Daughters!* (+ cond), *Hoffman* (1969), *Steptoe and Son* (theme m), *Mutiny on the Buses* (1972), *Steptoe and Son Ride Again* (1973, theme m), *Cat and Mouse* (1974, UK/US).

Grainger, Gawn (*b* Glasgow, 1940). Actor. Versatile stage actor who began his career in rep, later at the Bristol Old Vic in many leading roles, joined the National Theatre in 1972, and worked in the West End and on Broadway. He has also written several plays for the theatre and TV plays and series episodes (e.g. *Minder*). In the 90s, he scored acting successes in all three media: as Helen MIRREN's kind, simple husband in *A Month in the Country* on stage (1994), on TV in many series such as *Dalziel and Pascoe* (1998), and on screen as the cynical Dr Lloyd in *August* (1996), Anthony HOPKINS' transposition of *Uncle Vanya* to Wales. Married to Zoë WANAMAKER.

OTHER BRITISH FILMS INCLUDE: *Joseph Andrews, The Incredible Sarah* (UK/US) (1976), *The Raggedy Rawney* (1988), *Love and Death on Long Island* (1997).

Granada Cinemas *see* cinemas and exhibition

Grand National Pictures Company founded in 1938 by Maurice J WILSON who built the HIGHBURY STUDIOS which he leased pre-WW2 to independent companies and post-war was used by RANK for second features. Grand National's moment of highest prestige was as distributor of *The Stars Look Down* (1939). It made and/or distributed a few modest features in the 40s and early 50s, including *Under Your Hat* (1940), *The Voice Within* (1945, d. Wilson) *The Flamingo Affair, The Turners of Prospect Road* (d. Wilson) (1947) and *A Tale of Five Cities* (1951). Grand National (i.e. Wilson) turned attention to distribution after the mid 50s.

Granger, Stewart (*b* London, 1913 – *d* Santa Monica, California, 1993). Actor. RN: James Stewart. Although active in British cinema since 1933, Granger shot to stardom after appearing in a supporting role in the GAINSBOROUGH COSTUME MELODRAMA *The Man in Grey* (1943). He had changed his real name for obvious professional reasons and successfully appeared in popular GAINSBOROUGH productions such as *Fanny By Gaslight, Love Story, Madonna of the Seven Moons* (1944) and *The Magic Bow* (1946), with contemporary stars such as Margaret LOCKWOOD, Phyllis CALVERT, James MASON, and Patricia ROC. Demobilised from wartime service for health reasons, Granger's handsome looks, athletic physique, and masculine profile made him one of 40s British cinema's key romantic leading men and brought him to the attention of Hollywood and an MGM contract which lasted until 1960, and which in turn brought him international stardom in such capers as *Scaramouche* (1952). Married first to actress Elspeth MARCH and second to Jean SIMMONS, with whom he co-starred in the romantic comedy, *Adam and Evelyne* (1949), the historical romance, *Young Bess* (1953, US), and the underrated 'Victorian' thriller, *Footsteps in the Fog* (1955).

Despite frequent typecasting, Granger could often produce interesting performances such as his 'spiv' role in *Waterloo Road*, (1945) and the doomed romantic leads in *Blanche Fury* (1947) and *Saraband for Dead Lovers* (1948), who were victims of a ruthless CLASS structure. After freelancing in Europe during the 60s and 70s he began to appear frequently on TV, one of his last roles being as Prince Philip in *The Royal Romance of Charles and Diana* (1982).

OTHER BRITISH FILMS: *A Southern Maid* (1933), *Over the Garden Wall, Give Her A Ring* (1934), *Mademoiselle Docteur, So This is London* (1939), *Convoy* (1940), *Thursday's Child* (1943), *The Lamp Still Burns* (1943), *Caesar and Cleopatra* (1945), *Caravan* (1946), *Captain Boycott* (1947), *Woman Hater* (1948), *Beau Brummell* (1954), *Bhowani Junction* (1955),

Harry Black (1958), *The Secret Partner* (1961), *The Crooked Road* (1964), *The Trygon Factor* (1966), *The Wild Geese* (1978).

BIBLIOG: Stewart Granger, *Sparks Fly Upwards*, 1981. Tony Williams.

Grant, Arthur (*b* 1915 – *d* 1972). Cinematographer. Best remembered for his highly efficient and effective work on many HORROR films produced during the 60s at HAMMER, where his speed made him welcome in days of tight budgets. Though he is undoubtedly partly responsible for the gothic beauties of some of those films, it is worth noting that he had served a very long apprenticeship, beginning as camera operator in the early 30s. His first films as cinematographer were minor rural MELODRAMAS like *Loyal Heart* (1946) and *The Hills of Donegal* (1947), and some of his Hammer horrors still reflect a yearning for the PASTORAL, given more obvious scope in his early 50s films for GROUP 3, such as *Laxdale Hall* (1953). However, he worked competently across a GENRE range as wide as that traversed by his frequent collaborator, director Val GUEST.

OTHER BRITISH FILMS INCLUDE: (cam op) *Rynox* (1931), *Weddings Are Wonderful* (1938), *Salute John Citizen* (1942), *When We Are Married* (1943), *Master of Bankdam* (1947); (c) *I'll Turn to You* (1946), *The Brave Don't Cry* (1952), *Background* (1953), *Conflict of Wings* (1954), *The Blue Peter* (1955), *Dry Rot, The Extra Day* (1956), *Count Five and Die* (1957), *Up the Creek, Danger Within* (1958), *Yesterday's Enemy, Hell Is a City* (1959), *The Curse of the Werewolf, Cash on Demand, The Damned* (1961), *Jigsaw, Paranoiac, The Old Dark House* (1962), *80,000 Suspects* (1963), *The Reptile, They're a Weird Mob* (UK/Aust), *The Witches* (1966), *Quatermass and the Pit, The Devil Rides Out* (1967), *Frankenstein Must Be Destroyed* (1969), *Blood From the Mummy's Tomb* (1971), *Fear in the Night* (1972).

BIBLIOG: Duncan Petrie, *The British Cinematographer*, 1996.

Grant, Cary (*b* Bristol, 1904 – *d* Davenport, Iowa, 1986). Actor. RN: Archibald Leach. One of the greatest of all film actors, whose adroitness and teasing complexity have been charted at length, belongs in this book only because (a) he was English by birth and it remained part of his universally attractive persona and (b) he appeared in a handful of British-made films. These included: the minor comedy, *The Amazing Quest of Ernest Bliss* (1936); and two deft romantic comedies (of which he was master) for Stanley DONEN, *Indiscreet* (1958) and *The Grass Is Greener* (1960).

Grant, Cy (*b* British Guiana, 1917) Actor. Grant made a striking impression as one of the survivors in *Sea Wife* (1956), but there was not much doing for black actors in 50s British cinema. He had roles in *Safari* (1956) and *At the Earth's Core* (1976); appeared in a DOCUMENTARY about the Antilles, *Calypso* (1958, It/Fr); and the US-made *Shaft in Africa* (1973).

Grant, Hugh (*b* London, 1960). Actor. Two tedious things everyone knows about Grant: he is 'floppy-haired' and he was arrested in Los Angeles in 1995 for engaging in 'a lewd act'. These scraps of information to one side, he is arguably the most persuasive romantic comedy lead in several decades. He had been trundling along unexceptionally for some years, having made his first film *Privileged* (1982) while he was still at Oxford. He had done well enough in MERCHANT IVORY's *Maurice* (1987), had fun as Chopin in the camp BIOPIC, *Impromptu* (1991) and been affable as Lord Darlington's reporter nephew in *Remains of the Day* (1993). Then everything changed when he starred as the diffident hero of *Four Weddings and a Funeral* (1994), bumbling priapically to the inevitable final embrace, and revealing a technique and timing which led to comparisons with that other Grant, Cary. In 1995 releases, he honed this persona in *The Englishman Who Went Up . . .* as the eponym educated by Celtic canniness, brought agreeable life to Jane AUSTEN's wettest hero in the deft version of *Sense and Sensibility* (1995, UK/US), and even in the execrable US comedy, *Nine Months*, though perhaps his best performance was as the affected theatre company boss in *An Awfully Big Adventure* (1995). It took four years to reinstate himself in the censorious eyes of the ticket-buying public after his arrest, but he finally did so with *Notting Hill* (1999, UK/US), a charming feel-good romance in which Julia Roberts this time persuades him to take the emotional plunge. His timing, his way of testing and savouring dialogue, particularly Richard CURTIS's (in his two major hits), and his obvious good looks, have made him in demand internationally, as in the New York comedies, *Mickey Blue Eyes* (1999) and *Small Time Crooks* (2000), and he nabbed a key romantic comedy lead as sleazy Daniel in *Bridget Jones's Diary* (2001, UK/Fr/US). He lived with actress-model Elizabeth HURLEY for 13 years, until 2000, forming their own company, Simian Films, which produced the thriller, *Extreme Measures* (1996, UK/US).

OTHER BRITISH FILMS: *White Mischief* (1987), *The Lure of the White Worm*, *The Dawning* (1988), *The Big Man* (1990), *Bitter Moon* (1992, UK/Fr), *Sirens* (1994, UK/Aust), *Restoration* (1995, UK/US), *Intolerable Cruelty*, *About a Boy* (2002, UK/Fr/Ger/US).

BIBLIOG: Jody Tresidder, *Hugh Grant*, 1996.

Grant, Richard E(ster) (*b* Mbabane, Swaziland, 1957). Actor. RN: Huysen. British cinema needs lanky, witty Grant more than he needs it and should use him more and better. He can be a brilliant comic performer as he showed in the cult favourite, *Withnail and I* (1987) or as Aguecheek in *Twelfth Night* (1996, UK/US); he can do the straight romantic lead as in *Jack & Sarah* (1995, UK/Fr); he gave a restrained account of aristocratic Warburton in *The Portrait of a Lady* (1996, UK/US); savoured the extravagance of Gorgeous Gus in *The Match* (1999); and, in the US, enjoyed the malice of Larry Lefferts in *The Age of Innocence* (1993) and the outrageous campery of *Prêt-à-Porter* (1994). Educated at University of Capetown, he came to England in 1982, worked on stage and TV (he was a surprisingly muted Scarlet Pimpernel in the 1998, 1999 series), and is now in demand for films everywhere.

OTHER BRITISH FILMS INCLUDE: *Hidden City* (1987), *How to Get Ahead in Advertising* (1989), *Franz Kafka's It's a Wonderful Life* (1993, short), *The Food of Love* (1996), *Keep the Aspidistra Flying*, *Spice World* (1997), *St Ives*, *Cash in Hand* (1998), *Cocozza's Way*, *The Little Vampire* (UK/Ger/Neth), *Gosford Park* (UK/Ger/US) (2001).

BIBLIOG: *With Nails – The Film Diaries of Richard E. Grant*, 1996.

Granville, Fred Leroy (*b* Warrnambool, Australia, 1886 – *d* London, 1932). Director. Granville enjoyed an exotic career, working for 18 years with his father's South Seas trading company, before entering the film industry in 1908 as a cinematographer. He photographed 16 feature films in the US, beginning with *Rescue of the Stefansson Arctic Expedition* (1914). When British producer G.B. SAMUELSON came to Hollywood, Granville joined his company, and directed his then-wife Peggy HYLAND in several films including *The Honeypot* (1920), *Love Maggie* (1921), and *Forbidden Cargoes* (1925).

OTHER BRITISH FILMS: *The Beloved Vagabond* (1923), *The Sins Ye Do* (1924), *A Dear Liar* (1925). AS.

Graves, George (*b* London, 1876 – *d* London, 1949). Actor. Blustered his way as hearty colonels and the like in about a dozen films during the 30s. On stage from his early teens.

BRITISH FILMS INCLUDE: *Jerry Builders* (1930), *The Crooked Lady* (1932), *Royal Cavalcade*, *Heart's Desire* (1935), *The Tenth Man* (1936).

Graves, Peter (Lord Graves) (*b* London, 1911 – *d* France, 1994). Actor. Real-life aristocrat who frequently played ditto on stage and screen, Harrow-educated Graves was a popular leading man of the stage (often in musical comedy, as well as straight drama) from the mid 30s, eventually playing, as so many English actors past middle age do, Lord Caversham in *An Ideal Husband* (1969). Entered films in *Kipps* (1941), followed by a series of dimmish GAINSBOROUGH musical comedies, of which *I'll Be Your Sweetheart* (1945) was the most attractive, and suaved his way through several Herbert WILCOX vehicles, including *Spring in Park Lane* (1948) and *Maytime in Mayfair* (1949), disdained by Anna NEAGLE in both. He was the Prince of Wales in *The Laughing Lady* (1946) and again in *Mrs Fitzherbert* (1947) and Prince Albert to Neagle's *Lady with a Lamp* (1951). Soldiered on (there *are* several military characters) in supporting roles on film and TV until the 90s. Married actress **Vanessa Lee** (*b* London, 1920), who played his wife in the US farrago, *The Adventurers* (1970), her only film. Not to be confused with US actor of the same name.

OTHER BRITISH FILMS INCLUDE: *King Arthur Was a Gentleman* (1942), *Give Us the Moon* (1944), *Waltz Time* (1945), *Gaiety George* (1946), *Encore* (1951), *Derby Day* (1952), *Lilacs in the Spring* (1954), *The Admirable Crichton* (1957), *The Wrong Box* (1966), *How I Won the War* (1967), *The Magic Christian* (1969), *The Slipper and the Rose* (1976).

Graves, Rupert (*b* Weston-Super-Mare, 1963). Actor. Though he made his name in a series of upper-class roles in costume pieces (Freddie in *A Room with a View*, 1985; the disruptive John Beaver in *A Handful of Dust*, 1987), he actually ran away from his provincial home to join a circus at 15. When he wasn't in costume, he was apt to be nude, as in his first major role as the hero's working-class lover in *Maurice* (1987); by the time he made *Where Angels Fear to Tread* (1991), he had cornered the market in E.M. FORSTER ADAPTATIONS. Revealed unsuspected depths in two tormented roles: as the doomed son of Jeremy IRONS in *Damage* (1992, UK/Fr) and the suicidal Septimus in *Mrs Dalloway* (1997, UK/Neth/US); was convincingly vile as the drunken husband in the mini-series *The Tenant of Wildfell Hall* (1996) and the seducer Patrick in *Take a Girl Like You* (2000); and scored on Broadway in *Closer* (1998–99) and as slick, nasty Mick in *The Caretaker* (2000), the London production honouring playwright Harold PINTER's 70th birthday.

OTHER BRITISH FILMS INCLUDE: *Good and Bad at Games* (1983, TV, some cinemas), *The Madness of King George* (1994, US/UK), *Different for Girls* (1996), *Bent* (1997, UK/US/Jap), *The Revengers' Comedies* (1998, UK/Fr), *Dreaming of Joseph Lees* (1999, UK/US), *Room to Rent* (2000, UK/Fr), *The eXtremists* (2002).

Gray, Allan (*b* Tarnow, Poland, 1902 – *d* Amersham, 1973). RN: Josef Zmigrod. Composer. Trained in Berlin under Arnold Schönberg, Gray was an established composer for stage, cabaret, and screen before his emigration in 1933. His film scores in Britain were playfully eclectic in style, alternating between haunting romanticism, catchy melodies, and occasional stark modernist touches. Gray's arguably most experimental work can be found in his collaborations with POWELL AND PRESSBURGER, particularly in *I Know Where I'm Going!* (1945), where he inventively used Scottish folklore, and in *A Matter of Life and Death* (1946), where ticking clocks and repetitive piano scales evoke the monotony of celestial afterlife.

OTHER BRITISH FILMS INCLUDE: *Emil And The Detectives* (1935), *The Challenge* (1938), *The Silver Fleet, The Life And Death Of Colonel Blimp* (1943), *A Canterbury Tale* (1944), *Latin Quarter* (1945), *MrPerrin and MrTraill* (1948), *Madness Of The Heart* (1949), *The Late Edwina Black, The African Queen* (UK/US) (1951), *The Planter's Wife* (1952), *Women of Twilight* (1955), *The Big Hunt* (1958). Tim Bergfelder.

Gray, Carole (*b* South Africa, 1940). Actress. Gray co-starred with Cliff RICHARD in her first film, *The Young Ones* (1961), was quite striking as a jealous lady vampire in *Devils of Darkness* (1964), but she never made much impression on filmgoers and ended the decade and her film career with an uncredited bit in *Oh! What a Lovely War* (1969).

OTHER BRITISH FILMS: *Rattle of a Simple Man* (1964), *Curse of the Fly* (1965, co-starring), *The Brides of Fu Manchu, Island of Terror* (1966).

Gray, Charles (*b* Bournemouth, 1928 – *d* London, 2000). Actor. Of aristocratic voice and bearing, former estate agent Gray made a memorable villain in such films as the BOND caper, *Diamonds Are Forever* (1971), playing the malevolent Blofeld with a white cat to underline his decadence. On stage from 1952 (as 'Charles the Wrestler' in *As You Like It*, Regent's Park), the 6-foot, silver-haired Gray had Old Vic and Broadway seasons, but his main career was on screens large and small. Famous in the 80s as TV's Mycroft in the 'SHERLOCK HOLMES' series; a memorable 'Claudius', on- and off-stage in the wonderful *An Englishman Abroad* (1983); brilliantly type-cast as Pandarus in the BBC's *Troilus and Cressida* (1981); and guest in innumerable popular series.

On-screen from the late 50s (a caddish ladies' man in the 'B' movie, *The Desperate Man*, 1959), he made a major impact as icily evil Mocata in the masterly HAMMER occult piece, *The Devil Rides Out* (1967). He was an authoritative Essex in *Cromwell* (1970), threw himself into the cult camp nonsense of *The Rocky Horror Picture Show* (1975), and appeared in several nondescript US films, including *The Secret War of Harry Frigg* (1967). His mellifluous tones were in demand for narrations (e.g. *On the Game*, 1973, a documentary about prostitution's history), and from the early 80s TV claimed him increasingly. Provided Jack HAWKINS's 'voice' when Hawkins lost his own through throat cancer.

OTHER BRITISH FILMS INCLUDE: *I Accuse!* (1957), *Follow a Star* (1959), *The Entertainer* (1960), *The Night of the Generals* (1966, UK/Fr), *You Only Live Twice* (1967), *The Mosquito Squadron* (1968), *The Executioner* (1970), *The Beast Must Die* (1974), *Seven Nights in Japan* (1976, UK/Fr), *The Mirror Crack'd* (1980), *The Tichborne Claimant* (1998).

Gray, Donald (*b* Fort Beaufort, South Africa, 1914 – *d* Fort Beaufort, South Africa, 1978). Actor. RN: Eldred Tidbury. Best known as the one-armed actor (result of wartime service in France in 1944), who starred as detective Mark Saber in the 1955–60 TV series, and in a few minor 50s films, including *Saturday Island* (1952), a desert island romance, and *The Secret Tent* (1956). Last seen on TV on *Emmerdale Farm* in 1972.

OTHER BRITISH FILMS INCLUDE: *The Belles of St Clements* (1936), *Murder in the Family, 13 Men and a Gun* (1938), *The Four Feathers* (1939), *We'll Meet Again* (1942), *The Quatermass Experiment* (1955), *Satellite in the Sky* (1956). AS.

Gray, Dulcie (*b* Kuala Lumpur, Malay States, 1919). Actress. Gifted and undervalued film actress who was so busy on stage for over 50 years, often co-starring with her husband Michael DENISON, and later on TV (notably as Kate in *Howard's Way*, 1985–90), that she may not have noticed the end of her film career. Studied at the Webber-Douglas School, on stage first in *Hay Fever* (1939), and in the mid 90s she and Denison played in

An Ideal Husband for several years in London and New York. They were both awarded the CBE in 1983. She is memorable in several of her 40s films: as a servant played without stereotypical comic patronage in *A Place of One's Own* (1944), true and touching as the gentle Charlotte driven to alcoholism and suicide in *They Were Sisters* (1945), and as the spirited, firm-minded Ellen who saves her threatened sister in *A Man About the House* (1947). There was real vivacity and intelligence in all her performances, and she and Denison were teamed attractively on several occasions, to best effect in the romantic MELODRAMA, *The Glass Mountain* (1948). In her last cinema film, *A Man Could Be Killed* (1966, UK/US), she shows how funny she could be, given half a chance, and she was a memorable Miss Marple on stage in *A Murder Has Been Announced* (1977). Also wrote plays and detective novels, some of which were adapted to radio.

OTHER BRITISH FILMS: *Banana Ridge* (1941, unc), *Victory Wedding* (short), *Madonna of the Seven Moons, Two Thousand Women* (1944), *The Years Between, Wanted for Murder* (1946), *Mine Own Executioner* (1947), *The Franchise Affair* (1950), *Angels One Five* (1952), *There Was a Young Lady* (1953).

Gray, Elspet (*b* Inverness, 1929). Actress. From an inconsequential ingenue under contract to GAINSBOROUGH in 1948, Elspet Gray has developed into a deft portrayer of no-nonsense, sensible and organised characters primarily on television but also occasionally on screen (as in 1994's *Four Weddings and a Funeral* as Laura's mother). Had only one starring role in films, in the minor *Johnny on the Spot* (1954), but, on TV, left her mark in *Solo* (1981) and *Tenko* (1984). With husband Brian RIX, she has appeared on stage in *Reluctant Heroes* (1950) and its film version (1952), in the 1988 revival of *Dry Rot*, and on the radio sitcom *One Man's Meat* (1964).

OTHER BRITISH FILMS INCLUDE: *The Blind Goddess* (1948), *Love in Waiting* (1948), *Brandy for the Parson* (1952), *The Girl in a Swing* (1988). AS.

Gray, Eve (*b* Brighton, 1904). Actress. Blue-eyed blonde beauty who made an easy transition from silents to sounds, alternating leads and supporting roles, often cast as characters with names such as Toots (*The Bermondsey Kid*, 1933), Mavis (*The Crimson Candle*, 1934), Daisy (*The Last Journey*, 1935), or Cutie (*They Didn't Know*, 1936). Leading lady to Errol FLYNN in his first UK film, *Murder at Monte Carlo* (1935). Some international reputation thanks to second female lead in E.A. DUPONT's *Moulin Rouge* (1928), but generally criticised for artificial acting. Grew up in Australia, where she made stage debut, UK stage in 1924; some German films in late 20s. Was also a vocalist.

OTHER BRITISH FILMS INCLUDE: *The Silver Lining* (1927), *Smashing Through* (1928), *Night Birds* (1930), *The Flaw* (1933), *What's in a Name?* (1934), *Scrooge* (1935), *Silver Blaze* (1937), *One Good Turn* (1951). AS.

Gray, Nadia (*b* Roumania, 1923 – *d* New York, 1994). Actress. RN: Kujnir-Herescu. Auburn-haired beauty who brought an exotic touch to a few post-war British films, of which the best were the elegant thriller, *The Spider and the Fly* (1949), and the spy comedy, *Top Secret* (1952). Before this, she had appeared on the European stage, and most of her film career was spent in French and Italian productions, most notably Fellini's *La dolce vita* (1960, It/Fr). Very decorative, she had a rarely exploited comedy touch, which Stanley DONEN tapped in *Two for the Road* (1966), and, on marrying for the second time, she relocated to New York where she became a night-club entertainer.

OTHER BRITISH FILMS: *Night Without Stars, Valley of the Eagles* (1951), *The Captain's Table* (1958), *Mr Topaze* (1961), *Maniac* (1963), *The Crooked Road* (1964, UK/Yug), *The Naked Runner* (1967).

Gray, Sally (*b* London, 1918). Actress. Possessed of one of the most attractive voices in British films – husky, devoid of cut-glass vowels – as well as gravely beautiful face, Gray began in films in her teens (*School for Scandal*, 1930), returned in 1935, made nearly 20 films culminating in the wartime romantic hit, *Dangerous Moonlight* (1941), was off the screen for several years (a nervous breakdown was alleged), then returned to make her strongest bid for stardom. This latter involved a series of attractive MELODRAMAS, all of which stand up well today: they include: the hospital thriller, *Green for Danger* (1946); the decorative Victoriana of *Carnival* (1946) and *The Mark of Cain* (1948); two films which, in their different ways, capture some of the essence of post-war Britain, *They Made Me a Fugitive* (1947) and *Silent Dust* (1949); and the *film noir* piece, *Obsession* (1949), in which she plays Robert NEWTON's faithless wife.

Her range was wider than this list suggests: trained at Fay COMPTON's School of Dramatic Art, she was also well established in the theatre, in revue and musical comedy, before embarking on a series of light COMEDIES, MUSICALS and THRILLERS in the 30s (including two in the 'Saint' series), films at some remove from her post-war work. In 1943, she scored a major stage success in the title role of *My Sister Eileen* in London. She retired in 1952 to marry Lord Oranmore and lived in Ireland for some time.

OTHER BRITISH FILMS: *Lucky Days, Cross Currents, Checkmate* (1935), *Cheer Up!, Calling the Tune* (1936), *Saturday Night Revue, Café Colette, Over She Goes* (1937), *Mr Reeder in Room 13, Lightning Conductor, Hold My Hand* (1938), *Sword of Honour, The Saint in London, A Window in London, The Lambeth Walk* (1939), *Honeymoon Merry-Go-Round* (1940), *The Saint's Vacation* (1941), *Escape Route* (1952).

Gray, Simon (*b* Hayling Island, 1936). Dramatist, author, screenwriter. Best known for such mordantly witty plays as *Butley* (1971) and *Otherwise Engaged* (1977), Westminster- and Cambridge-educated and former academic, Gray has written two sharply incisive screenplays: he adapted *Butley* (1973, UK/Can/US), retaining Alan BATES in the title role; and *A Month in the Country* (1987), an allegorical account of restoring church frescoes and broken lives. His TV includes a version of his sardonic *Quartermaine's Terms* (1987). Also a novelist.

Gray, Vernon (*b* Saskatoon, Canada, 1930). Actor. After theatrical experience in Canada, drama school and two TV shows in New York, Gray played juvenile leads in several 50s British films. He was Alec GUINNESS's son in the limp romantic comedy *To Paris with Love* (1954) and he and Janette SCOTT were eloping lovers in the even sillier romance *Now and Forever* (1955).

OTHER BRITISH FILMS: *A Day to Remember* (1953), *The Gold Express* (1955), *The Barretts of Wimpole Street* (1956).

Gray, Willoughby (*b* London, 1916 – *d* 1993). Actor. On stage since childhood, Gray also played many roles in TV's *The Adventures of Robin Hood* throughout 1955 and his last work was as the Earl of Drune in *Robin Hood: The Movie* (1991, US). Among other theatre and TV work, he fitted in about a dozen British films, always in small roles, often as professionals, like the Coroner in the racing drama, *Dead Cert* (1974).

OTHER BRITISH FILMS INCLUDE: *The Mark of Cain* (1948), *Seven Days to Noon* (1950), *Top Secret* (1952), *Richard III* (1955), *The Man Outside* (1967), *Young Winston* (1972), *Absolution* (1978), *The Hit* (1984), *A View to a Kill* (1985).

Graysmark, John (*b* London). Production designer. After uncredited work as draughtsman on *Lawrence of Arabia* (1962) and others, Graysmark began as art director in the early 70s before achieving the title of 'production designer' on 1981's *Ragtime* (US). Since then he has worked mainly on US films, including *White Hunter, Black Heart* (1990).

OTHER BRITISH FILMS INCLUDE: (art d, unless noted) *The Walking Stick* (1970), *Young Winston* (1972), *The Man with the Golden Gun* (1974, co-art d), *The Big Sleep* (1978); (super art d) *Escape to Athena* (1979), *Flash Gordon* (1980); (des) *The Bounty* (1984), *Lifeforce* (1985).

Grayson, Godfrey (*b* Birkenhead, 1913 – *d* Surrey, 1998). Director. With the marginal exception of a (leaden-paced) version of Agatha CHRISTIE, *The Spider's Web* (1960), Grayson never made anything other than 'B' MOVIES. Entered films as cutter at Warners' TEDDINGTON STUDIOS in 1934, had experience with Warners and MGM in Hollywood as assistant editor, but it must be said that not much of it rubbed off. During WW2 he worked with the ARMY FILM UNIT on some of its famous DOCUMENTARIES, was location director on GAINS-BOROUGH's *Snowbound* (1948), before beginning to direct features. *The Adventures of PC 49* (1949), about a gentleman copper looking for post-war excitement, and *Dick Barton Strikes Back* (1949) and *Dick Barton at Bay* (1950), written by his twin brother **Ambrose Grayson** and based on the exploits of the radio serial hero, are hearty blood-and-thunder pieces for the undemanding. On the other hand, films like *So Evil, So Young* (1961), a girls' reformatory drama, and *She Always Gets Their Man* (1962), about provincial girls hunting for chaps in London, are about as inept as 'B' movies can be, with idiotic stories and dreadful dialogue, tricked out with irrelevantly flashy editing. Also directed the 1955 afternoon TV slot area: *Flickwiz*. His earlier films were made for HAMMER/EXCLUSIVE, the later ones for the notorious discount film-makers, the DANZIGERS.

OTHER BRITISH FILMS INCLUDE: *Meet Simon Cherry* (1949, + sc, story), *Room to Let* (+ sc), *What the Butler Saw* (1950), *The Fake* (1953, sc. Ambrose), *Black Ice* (1957), *A Woman's Temptation* (1959), *An Honorable Murder* (1960), *The Pursuers* (1961), *The Battleaxe* (1962).

Green, Danny (*b* London, 1903 – *d* 1973). Actor. Hulking, balding, six-foot Cockney who specialised in none-too-bright thugs, like One-Round whom he famously played in *The Ladykillers* (1955). Educated in London and US, he began filming in Britain in 1929 (*The Crooked Billet, The Silent House, Atlantic*), there were a few 30s roles, and then his career as a character presence took off. He is a member of Stewart GRANGER's gang in *Madonna of the Seven Moons* (1944), and *No Orchids for Miss Blandish* (1948) was old home week for him. Had small roles in the US features, *The 7th Voyage of Sinbad* (1958) and *The Fixer* (1968).

OTHER BRITISH FILMS INCLUDE: *Naughty Husbands* (1930), *Things Are Looking Up* (1935), *Non-Stop New York* (1937), *Fiddlers Three* (1944), *The Man Within, Good-Time Girl* (1947), *State Secret, Mr Drake's Duck* (1951), *Little Big Shot* (1952), *Laughing Anne* (1953), *A Kid for Two Farthings* (1954), *Interpol* (1957), *Beyond This Place* (1959), *The Fast Lady* (1962), *Smashing Time* (1967).

Green, David (*b* London, 1948). Director. TV director who made a modest success with *Buster* (1988), a zippy if senti-mentalised version of the great train robber as family man. Since then, he has filmed mainly in the US, including *Firebirds* (1990), two more recent UK films scarcely seen: *Solomon and Gaenor* (1999, ex p) and *Breathtaking* (2000, d). Not to be confused with director David GREENE.

OTHER BRITISH FILM: *Car Trouble* (1985).

Green, Guy (*b* Frome, 1913). Cinematographer, director. David LEAN recommended Green to Carol REED as cameraman for *The Way Ahead* (1944), thus launching a major career as cinematographer, and in 1947 he won an AA for lensing Lean's *Great Expectations*, though it is arguable that his brooding chiaroscuro on Lean's *Oliver Twist* (1948) and *Madeleine* (1949) is even more sophisticated. What needs no arguing is that Green, in films since 1929, was for a decade one of the world's most distinguished black-and-white cinematographers, and in the sumptuous-looking period MELODRAMA, *Blanche Fury* (1947), showed equal proficiency in colour. He worked as camera assistant at ELSTREE from the mid 30s, and his name is on some important films as (assistant) camera operator from *Song of the Plough* (1933) until *This Happy Breed* (1944). He took to direction in 1953, cutting his teeth on smartly paced 'B' FILMS such as *River Beat* (1953) and *Portrait of Alison* (1955), claiming in 1992 that he found being a cameraman 'an excellent preparation [for directing] because you then have no fear of the mechanics of it'. He directed two controversial films in Britain: the drama of a wildcat strike, *The Angry Silence* (1960), and the child molestation piece, *The Mark* (1961), winning kudos for both, and leading to working on bigger-budget but not necessarily more interesting US films, such as *Diamond Head* (1962), the weepie *A Patch of Blue* (1965, + sc), which won several AA nominations, and the lush inanities of *Once Is Not Enough* (1974). To keep his hand in, he also directed a number of telemovies but never found this a satisfying format.

OTHER BRITISH FILMS: (cam op) *Spellbound* (1941), *One of Our Aircraft is Missing*, *In Which We Serve* (1942), *The Way to the Stars* (1945, 2uc); (c) *Escape to Danger* (1943), *Carnival* (1946), *Take My Life* (1947), *The Passionate Friends* (1948), *Adam and Evelyne* (1949), *Captain Horatio Hornblower RN* (1950, UK/US), *Night Without Stars* (1951), *The Story of Robin Hood* . . . , *The Hour of 13*, *Decameron Nights* (1952), *Rob Roy* . . . , *The Beggar's Opera* (1953), *For Better, for Worse*, *Souls in Conflict* (1954), *I Am a Camera*, *The Dark Avenger* (1955); (d) *Lost* (1955), *House of Secrets* (1956), *The Snorkel*, *Sea of Sand* (1958), *SOS Pacific* (1959), *Pretty Polly* (1967), *Magus* (1968), *Luther* (1973, UK/Can/US).

Green, Harry (*b* New York, 1892 – *d* London, 1958). Actor. RN: Henry Blitzer. Short, jovial character player who made 20-odd light films in America, the musical *Marry Me* (1932), with George ROBEY in Britain, and spent the last decade of his life there, playing supporting roles in such films as *Joe Macbeth* (1955), with SHAKESPEARE relocated to the underworld.

OTHER BRITISH FILMS: *A Date with a Dream* (1948), *Glad Tidings* (1953), *An Alligator Named Daisy* (1955), *A King in New York* (1957), *Next to No Time!* (1958).

Green, Hughie (*b* London, 1920 – *d* London, 1997). Actor. Child performer noted for impersonations on radio and on screen in *Music Hall Parade* (1939), in which he imitates Lionel Barrymore, Charles LAUGHTON, Nellie WALLACE, and others. Played opposite Margaret LOCKWOOD in *Midshipman Easy* (1935) and tried to emulate its success with *Melody and Romance* (1937), again with Lockwood. In later years noted as the host on radio and TV of *Opportunity Knocks* and, on TV, of *Double Your Money*. Long legal feud with BBC in which he claimed he was blacklisted. Revealed as father of Paula Yates just before he died.

OTHER BRITISH FILMS: *Little Friend* (1934), *Radio Pirates* (1935), *Down Our Alley* (1939), *Paper Orchid* (1949), *What's Up Superdoc?* (1978).
BIBLIOG: Autobiography, *Opportunity Knocked*, 1965. AS.

Green, Janet (*b* Hitchin, 1908 – *d* Beaconsfield, 1993). Screenwriter, dramatist. Former actress, in ALDWYCH FARCES (1930–34), and a playwright whose thriller, *Murder Mistaken* (1952), produced in London by her husband, John McCORMICK, was subsequently turned into a novel (co-authored by Leonard Gribble) and an excellent film, *Cast a Dark Shadow* (1955). She wrote three screenplays (the latter two co-authored by McCormick) for SOCIAL PROBLEM FILMS directed by Basil DEARDEN: *Sapphire* (1959), dealing with racial problems; *Victim* (1961), the first mainstream film to focus on homosexuality; and *Life for Ruth* (1962), about the tragic effects of fundamentalist beliefs. In each case, a melodramatic story line was skilfully meshed with social responsibility. She and McCormick also wrote the screenplay for John FORD's last film, *Seven Women* (1965, US).

OTHER BRITISH FILMS: (co-sc) *The Clouded Yellow* (1950), *The Good Beginning* (1953), *The Long Arm* (1956); (sc) *Lost* (1955), *Eyewitness* (1956), *The Gypsy and the Gentleman* (1957).

Green, Martyn (*b* London, 1899 – *d* Los Angeles, 1975). Singer. Though he acted in straight plays in the second half of his career, mainly in the US, RCM-trained Green was essentially an exponent of GILBERT AND SULLIVAN, succeeding Henry Lytton in the famous comedy roles. In his very sparse film career, he played Ko-Ko in a popular TECHNICOLOR version of *The Mikado* (1939), and in the 1953 biopic, *The Story of Gilbert and Sullivan*, he played celebrated G&S actor George Grossmith and sang a half-dozen roles from the operettas. He appeared in the US films, *A Lovely Way to Die* (1968) and *The Iceman Cometh* (1973), and his voice was heard in an animated version of *Cyrano* (1974). Lost a leg in a grisly car park accident in New York.

Green, Nigel (*b* Pretoria, South Africa, 1924 – *d* Brighton, 1972). Actor. Imposing character player, RADA-trained after brief period as engineering student, Green hit his stride in the mid 60s with a run of choice roles: the strong reliable colour Sergeant in *Zulu* (1964), the duplicitous Dalby in *The Ipcress File* (1965), and General Wolseley in *Khartoum* (1966). He thereafter mixed US films, including *The Kremlin Letter* (1969), with such British fare as *The Ruling Class* (1971), until his untimely death from an accidental overdose of sleeping pills. Noticeable in films as minor as *Pit of Darkness* (1961, as the hero's doctor), he was a serious loss to character acting ranks.

OTHER BRITISH FILMS INCLUDE: *Meet Mr Malcolm* (1953), *The Sea Shall Not Have Them* (1954), *Find the Lady* (1956), *The Gypsy and the Gentleman* (1957), *Beat Girl* (1959), *The League of Gentlemen* (1960), *Jason and the Argonauts* (1963), *The Masque of the Red Death* (1964, UK/US), *The Skull* (1965), *Let's Kill Uncle*, *Deadlier Than the Male* (1966), *Africa – Texas Style* (1967), *Play Dirty* (1968), *Countess Dracula* (1970).

Green, Pamela (*b* Kingston-upon-Thames, *c* 1929). Actress, model. Best known to (more or less) mainstream filmgoers as the scarred model who becomes a victim of *Peeping Tom* (1960), Green was better known to those with more recherché tastes as the star of nudie romps with names like *Naked As Nature Intended* (1961), directed by her then-partner George HARRISON MARKS. Also famous as a model for magazines, and in later years was a member of the Yarmouth Women's Institute, on the Isle of Wight, where she and her present partner run a photographic studio.

OTHER BRITISH FILMS: *The Window Dresser*, *Xcitement*, *Gypsy Fire*, *Witches' Brew* (late 50s, dates uncertain), *The Day the Earth Caught Fire* (1961, unc), *The Chimney Sweeps* (1963), *The Naked World* of *Harrison Marks* (1965), *Legend of the Werewolf* (1974), *Under the Bed* (1976).

Green, Philip (*b* London, 1911 – *d* Ireland, 1982). Composer. One of the most prolific film composers in British cinema, utterly protean in his moving from, say, the chirpy accompaniments to half a dozen Norman WISDOM comedies, starting with *The Man of the Moment* (1955), to Basil DEARDEN's moody social problem pieces and his strange, jazz-drenched retelling of *Othello* in *All Night Long* (1961). If his scores are not especially memorable, it may be because they were so entirely at the service of the films for which they were written. Also conducted some of the scores he composed.

OTHER BRITISH FILMS INCLUDE: (m d) *While the Sun Shines* (1947), *The Golden Disc* (1958); (comp/cond) *Conflict of Wings* (1954), *Up in the World* (1956), *The League Of Gentleman* (1960), *Masquerade* (1965); (comp) *For Them That Trespass* (1948), *Landfall* (1949), *Young Wives' Tale* (1951), *24 Hours of a Woman's Life* (1952), *John and Julie* (1955), *The Extra Day* (1956), *The Violent Playground*, *Just My Luck* (1957), *The Square Peg*, *Innocent Sinners*, *Hello London*, *Operation Amsterdam*, *Life in Emergency Ward 10* (1958), *Sapphire*, *Upstairs and Downstairs*, *A Touch of Larceny* (1959), *The Bulldog Breed*, *The Singer Not the Song* (1960), *Victim*, *Flame in the Streets* (1961), *On the Beat* (1962), *A Stitch in Time* (1963), *The Intelligence Men* (1965).

Green, S(id) C. (*b* 1928). Screenwriter. Revered comedians, MORECAMBE AND WISE, never remotely equalled their TV popularity on screen, but this was not the fault of some quite neat and funny screenplays by Green and co-writer R.M. HILLS. Who wrote what is now academic; all have some good jokes. Like Morecambe in *The Magnificent Two* (1967) grandly identifying with the leader he impersonates in South America: 'These are my people', says Morecambe. '*Your* people are in Manchester,' punctures Ernie.

OTHER BRITISH FILMS: *The Intelligence Men* (1965), *That Riviera Touch* (1966).

Greenaway, Peter (*b* Newport, Wales, 1942). Director, screenwriter. Some regard the audacious Greenaway as a daring, stimulating innovator; others dismiss him as obscure and pretentious; very few who have seen his intransigently ART-HOUSE oeuvre are indifferent. His background as a painter, his intellectual's fascination with ideas, his wide-ranging preoccupations (social, political, literary, aesthetic) have made him unique among British film-makers, and he has claimed that his passion for films derives from seeing European art-house cinema in the late 50s/early 60s. He trained as a painter and entered films as an editor with the Central Office of Information, before embarking on a series of short films in which he teases audiences and himself with bizarre motifs and images, lists and numbers. Such films include *Windows* (1974) and *H is for House* (1976), and the very long *The Falls* (1980), biographies of 92 people whose names begin with 'Fall'.

His first commercial feature, *The Draughtsman's Contract* (1982), was an art-house hit and it played with GENRES such as the country house romance and the DETECTIVE THRILLER to unaccustomed ends. With its incessant dialogue, it made the film's imagery work hard not to be overwhelmed by the verbal. For the next ten years, Greenaway, greatly aided by such regular collaborators as his Dutch producer, Kees KESANDER, and his wildly gifted cameraman, Sacha VIERNY, continued to make obdurately esoteric films, which somehow found large enough audiences to keep the enterprise afloat. It cannot be said that films such as *A Zed & Two Noughts* (1985, UK/Neth), in which he explored his fascination with the idea of twinship, or

Drowning by Numbers (1988, UK/Neth), in which the steady parade of numbers 1 to 100 is counterpointed by the arbitrariness of human behaviour, set out to woo audiences. He expects his viewers to *work* and for a decade enough were prepared to. The black anti-Thatcherite fable, *The Cook, the Thief, His Wife & Her Lover* (1989, UK/Fr), was a confronting mix of sex, eating, excrement and cruelty, culminating in an outrageous cannibalistic image, and the whole shot through with visual and aural effects of disconcerting beauty. *Prospero's Books* (1991, UK/Fr/It/Neth) is a mesmeric version of *The Tempest*, enshrining John GIELGUD's interpretation of the master magician among a welter of technical wizardry which seems apt for the text.

Since then he has lost some of the partisanship which applauded his daring in enterprises like *The Baby of Mâcon* (1993, UK/Fr/Ger/Neth), in which audiences watch audiences watching grotesque and sometimes horrifying spectacles, and *The Pillow Book* (1996, UK/Fr/Lux/Neth), which combines his passionate interests in calligraphy, sexuality, other cultures and nudity. As to the latter, his little-seen *8 ½ Women* (1999, UK/Ger/Lux/Neth) seems to have pushed even his loyal defenders too far, with its insistence on nudity, its incessant preoccupation with sexuality, including a brush with incest.

OTHER BRITISH FILMS INCLUDE: (shorts) *Intervals* (1973), *Water Wrackets*, *A Walk Through H* (+ sc, e, des), *Vertical Features Remake* (+ p, sc, c, e) (1978), *The Bridge* (1997); (features) *The Belly of an Architect* (1987, UK/It).

BIBLIOG: Alan Woods, *Being Naked Playing Dead: The Art of Peter Greenaway*, 1996.

Greenbaum, Mutz *see* **Greene, Max**

Greene, David (*b* London, 1921 – *d* Ojai, California, 2003). Actor, director. After doing a range of jobs pre-war, then being invalided out of the Royal Navy, Greene trained at RADA and made a few unremarkable appearances as an actor in such films as *Daughter of Darkness* (1947, as victim to the homicidal heroine) and *The Golden Madonna* (1949). Spent over a decade as a TV director in Canada and the US before returning to Britain to direct his first feature film, *The Shuttered Room* (1966), which won some praise for its Gothic frissons. His next, *The Strange Affair* (1968), an acrid drama of a young policeman's corruption, stands up much better than most of the evanescent entertainments of its time, of which his spy spoof, *Sebastian* (1967), starring Dirk BOGARDE, is more typical. British cinema failed to capitalise on his obvious talent, and most of the rest of his career was spent in US telemovies, including remakes of such famous films as *Whatever Happened to Baby Jane?* and *Night of the Hunter* (1991) and episodes of *Hill Street Blues*. Now best remembered for *Godspell* (1973, US). Was married to actress Kathryn BLAKE. Not to be confused with director David GREEN.

OTHER BRITISH FILMS: (a) *The Small Voice* (1948), *The Wooden Horse* (1950), *The Dark Light* (1951); (d) *I Start Counting* (1969), *Madame Sin* (1972, for TV, some cinemas).

Greene, Graham (*b* Berkhamsted, 1904 – *d* Vevey, Switzerland, 1991). Novelist, screenwriter, critic. His contribution to British cinema is probably the greatest of any novelist of his – or indeed any other – generation. Collaborations with Carol REED – *The Fallen Idol* (1948), *The Third Man* (1949), *Our Man in Havana* (1959) – and the BOULTINGS' *Brighton Rock* (1947) are especially notable. Virtually all his novels and novellas have been filmed, with Greene adapting *Our Man in Havana* and *The Comedians* (1967, US) and writing and co-producing *The*

Stranger's Hand (1953, UK/It). He also adapted *Saint Joan* (1957, UK/US) from SHAW's play. His career as a critic began in the 30s with stints at *The Spectator* and *Night and Day*. The latter publication was forced to close as a result of damages awarded in a libel action brought against the publishers by Twentieth Century-Fox when Greene, in a review of the studio's *Wee Willie Winkie* (1937), queried the sexual exploitation of the film's child star Shirley Temple. Greene was an outspoken and influential critic, and wrote an unfavourable review of Alexander KORDA's *Twenty-One Days* (1937), for which Greene himself had adapted John GALSWORTHY's novel *The First and the Last*. He was similarly unimpressed with Joseph MANKIEWICZ's version of his novel *The Quiet American* (1957, US) and campaigned against the film's release in Britain. Greene makes a brief appearance in François Truffaut's *Day for Night* (1973, Fr) as 'Henry Graham', an insurance man watching the rushes of a doomed film.

BIBLIOG: Quentin Falk, *Travels in Greeneland: The Cinema of Graham Greene*, 1990 (rev ed); David Parkinson (ed), *Mornings in the Dark: The Graham Greene Film Reader*, 1993. Simon Caterson.

Greene, Leon Actor. Greene's career trajectory takes in seven years as principal bass with the D'Oyly Carte Opera Company as well as supporting roles in several of the 'CARRY ON' series and *The Adventures of . . . a Private Eye* (1977) and *. . . a Plumber's Mate* (1978), with an early striking bit as Christopher LEE's anti-Satanist offsider in *The Devil Rides Out* (1967), and much TV, including *A Man Called Intrepid* (1979).

OTHER BRITISH FILMS INCLUDE: *Don't Lose Your Head* (1966), *Carry On . . . Henry*, *. . . at Your Convenience* (1971), *11 Harrowhouse* (1974), *Royal Flash* (1975), *The Ritz* (1976), *The Squeeze* (1977), *The Human Factor* (1979, UK/US), *The Return of the Musketeers* (1989, UK/Fr/Sp).

Greene, Max (*b* Berlin, 1896 – *d* Findon, Sussex, 1968). Cinematographer, director. RN: Mutz Greenbaum. In German films from 1915, Greene worked in British cinema from the early 30s, initially for GAUMONT–BRITISH, later a frequent collaborator of Herbert WILCOX and the BOULTING brothers, for whose *Thunder Rock* (1942) he was responsible for making the FANTASY sequences both real and other-worldly. Hallmarks of his images were unusual angles, a legacy of his training in German cinema, and depth of field. A nominal co-director on *Escape to Danger* (1943) and *Hotel Reserve* (1944), Greene's only solo directorial effort was *The Man from Morocco* (1944), an atmospheric drama about remnants of the International Brigade in early WW2. Worked under his real name until 1940.

OTHER BRITISH FILMS INCLUDE: *Hindle Wakes, Sunshine Susie* (1931), *The Constant Nymph* (1933), *Bulldog Jack* (1935), *Tudor Rose, Strangers On Honeymoon* (1936), *The Return of the Scarlet Pimpernel, Climbing High* (1938), *The Stars Look Down* (1939), *Pastor Hall* (1940), *Pimpernel Smith* (1941), *Hatter's Castle* (1941), *Thunder Rock* (1942), *The Yellow Canary* (1943), *Wanted For Murder* (1946), *The Courtneys Of Curzon Street* (1947), *Spring In Park Lane, So Evil My Love* (1948), *Maytime In Mayfair* (1949), *Night And The City* (1950, UK/US), *Lucky Jim* (1957), *Carlton-Browne Of The FO* (1958), *I'm All Right Jack* (1959), *Suspect* (1960), *Heavens Above!* (1963). Tim Bergfelder.

Greene, Richard (*b* Plymouth, 1918 – *d* North Walsham, 1985). Actor. Handsome, swashbuckling leading man who made his name in Hollywood and later played the title role in TV's *Robin Hood* (1955–58). After screen debut in *Sing As We Go!* (1934), from which his one scene was cut, Greene signed a seven-year contract with 20th Century–Fox in 1938 and came to Hollywood, where his films include *The Hound of the Baskervilles* and *Stanley and Livingstone* (1939). After war service, returned to UK and a career on stage and screen (including the lead in the musical BIOPIC *Gaiety George*, 1946), punctuated by a second spell in Hollywood, including *Forever Amber* (1947). Later films were unimportant and income from *Robin Hood* helped Greene retire in style. Married to Patricia MEDINA (1941–51).

OTHER BRITISH FILMS INCLUDE: *Unpublished Story, Flying Fortress* (1942), *Yellow Canary* (1943), *Don't Take It to Heart!* (1944), *That Dangerous Age, Now Barabbas was a Robber* (1949), *My Daughter Joy, Shadow of the Eagle* (1950), *Sword of Sherwood Forest* (1960), *The Blood of Fu Manchu* (1968), *Tales from the Crypt* (1972). AS.

Greenpoint Films A loose association of ten film-makers, formed by Simon RELPH and Ann SCOTT, along with – among others – Richard EYRE and Mike NEWELL, who have turned out about 30 films in the last two decades. Titles include: *Loose Connections, The Ploughman's Lunch* (1983), *The Good Father* (1986), *Enchanted April* (1992), and *Hideous Kinky* (1998). It is one of the companies under the FILM CONSORTIUM Lottery Film Franchise.

Greenwood, Edwin (*b* London, 1895 – *d* 1939). Art director, director, screenwriter. A stage director and actor from 1912 onwards, Greenwood was art director for IDEAL from 1919 to 1921, and a minor director in the 20s. After seeing Greenwood's *To What Red Hell* (1929), CLOSE UP remarked there was 'no reason why he should ever make another picture' – he didn't. His career as screenwriter proved more distinguished and he worked on several films for HITCHCOCK in the 30s.

OTHER BRITISH FILMS INCLUDE: (d) *Wonder Women of the World* series (1922), *Gems of Literature* series, *Heartstrings* (1923), *The Art of Love* series (1925), *What Money Can Buy* (1928, + sc), *The Co-Optimists* (1929); (sc, unless noted) *The Love Race* (1931), *Lord Camber's Ladies* (1932), *The Man Who Knew Too Much* (co-sc), *While Parents Sleep* (1935), *East Meets West* (1936, + play), *Young and Innocent* (1937, co-sc), *Jamaica Inn* (1939, a). AS.

Greenwood, Jack (*b* 1919). Producer. Studio manager of MERTON PARK STUDIOS and wildly prolific producer of modest 'B' FILMS for a decade from 1958, until the market for such fare dried up. Most of his titles were in three SERIES – the *Edgar Wallace Mysteries, Scotland Yard* and *Scales of Justice* – and most were totally formulaic but he did give director Alan BRIDGES his start on two superior pieces: *Act of Murder* (1964) and *Invasion* (1966) and in 1960 he produced Joseph LOSEY's *The Criminal*. He occasionally ventured away from Merton Park Productions, as on the stylish if sadistic *Horrors of the Black Museum* (1959).

OTHER BRITISH FILMS INCLUDE: *Man with a Gun* (1958), *The Desperate Man* (1959), *The Clue of the Twisted Candle* (1960), *The Man at the Carlton Tower* (1961), *Playback* (1962), *A Woman's Privilege* (1963), *Downfall* (1964), *Change Partners* (1965), *Strangler's Web* (1966), *Payment in Kind* (1967), dozens more.

Greenwood, Joan (*b* London, 1921 – *d* London, 1987). Actress. Irresistible leading lady of some of the most enduring British films, seductive of voice, face and figure, searching the language – and indeed the world – for booby traps, Greenwood's performance record must be nearly unrivalled among British leading ladies. RADA-trained and on stage from 1938 (delectably malicious as Hattie in *The Grass Is Greener*, 1958; sharply ambiguous in *The Chalk Garden*, 1971), she was in films from 1940. She was one of *The Gentle Sex* (1943) celebrated in Leslie HOWARD's film, was a sympathetic helper for *The October Man* (1947), and a doomed Sophie Dorothea in

Saraband for Dead Lovers (1948), but it was as the female lead in a series of benchmark COMEDIES that she made herself indispensable to British films. In *Whisky Galore!* and *Kind Hearts and Coronets* (1949), she is the drily beguiling Peggy and the wonderfully minxish Sibella respectively; she deflects Alec GUINNESS from his experiments in *The Man in the White Suit* (1951, 'What could I do?' she asks, as if it wasn't obvious) and she is, in her way, as imperishably Gwendolyn as Edith EVANS is Lady Bracknell in *The Importance of Being Earnest* (1952). She did better in America than some of her contemporaries (cf. *Moonfleet*, 1955, and *Stage Struck*, 1958). She played character roles back in Britain but remained a *star* till the end, which came after *Little Dorrit* (1987), as Mrs Clennam, and it was good to see her brilliant at the finish. There was some TV and stage work but she is above all a British *film* star, the genuine article. Never, it seems, very ambitious, she had a late but happy marriage to actor André MORELL and worked only fitfully after that.

OTHER BRITISH FILMS: *John Smith Wakes Up* (1940, short), *My Wife's Family*, *He Found a Star* (1941), *They Knew Mr Knight, Latin Quarter* (1945), *A Girl in a Million* (1946), *The Man Within, The White Unicorn* (1947), *Bad Lord Byron* (1949), *Flesh and Blood, Young Wives' Tale* (1951), *Knave of Hearts, Father Brown* (1954), *Mysterious Island* (1961), *The Amorous Prawn* (1962), *Tom Jones* (1963), *The Moon Spinners* (1964, UK/US), *Girl Stroke Boy* (1971), *The Water Babies* (1975, UK/Pol), *The Uncanny, The Hound of the Baskervilles* (1977).

Greenwood, John (*b* London, 1889 – *d* Lewes, 1975). Composer. RCM-trained Greenwood composed symphonies, a ballet and other works, which he often conducted with major orchestras, as well as the scores for about 30 films. He worked on important 30s films such as *Man of Aran* (1934), *Elephant Boy* (1937) and *The Drum* (1938, co-comp), proved equally at home with such wartime subjects as *The Gentle Sex* and *San Demetrio–London* (1943) and with two of the Somerset MAUGHAM compendia, *Quartet* (1948) and *Trio* (1950), and scored Humphrey JENNINGS' last documentary, *Family Portrait* (1950). Won Venice Film Festival award for his score for *The Last Days of Dolwyn* (1949).

OTHER BRITISH FILMS INCLUDE: *To What Red Hell* (1929), *The Constant Nymph* (1933, co-comp), *East Meets West* (1936), *Contraband* (1940), *Pimpernel Smith* (1941), *Nine Men, The Lamp Still Burns* (1943), *Hungry Hill, Frieda* (1947), *Eureka Stockade* (1949), *Another Man's Poison* (1951), *The Gentle Gunman* (1952), *Grand National Night* (1953).

Greenwood, Rosamund (*b* Leeds – *d* 1997). Actress. Trained at Central School and on stage from early 30s, the somewhat twittery Greenwood was born to play WILDE's Miss Prism, which she did on TV in 1981. Elsewhere, she played assorted spinsters, like Miss Ogle, distressingly impregnated by aliens in *Village of the Damned* (1960). Very funny on stage as gauche Agnes Gooch to Beatrice LILLIE's *Auntie Mame* (1958).

OTHER BRITISH FILMS: *Men Are Not Gods* (1936), *The Peterville Diamond* (1942), *Give Us the Moon* (1944), *Night of the Demon* (1957), *Idle on Parade* (1958), *Term of Trial* (1962), *A Severed Head* (1970), *Stand Up Virgin Soldiers* (1977), *The Missionary* (1981), *Winnie* (short, starring role) (1984).

Greenwood, Walter (*b* Salford, Lancs, 1903 – *d* Isle of Man, 1974). Screenwriter. Playwright and novelist, born and educated in Salford, Greenwood had a fervent sympathy for the underprivileged. Made his name with his first novel, *Love on the Dole* (1933), which subsequently became a play (1934, co-author Ronald Gow) and was filmed by John BAXTER in 1941 (co-scripted by Greenwood). It took four years for the censors to

allow this harshly compassionate drama to be filmed. His very funny play, *Rod of Iron* (1945), was filmed under its later title, *The Cure for Love* (1949, + add dial).

OTHER BRITISH FILMS: *Where's George?*, *No Limit* (1935, story), *Eureka Stockade* (1949, co-sc), *Chance of a Lifetime* (1950).

Gregg, Colin (*b* Cheltenham, 1947). Director. Gregg's career has been fitful, initiated by independently made SHORT FILMS, including the BFI-funded romance, *The Flying Man* (1972), and *Before the Bough Breaks* (1975), dealing with the problems of handicapped children. His cinema features to date are two sensitive, slightly off-centre pieces: *Lamb* (1985), charting the relationship between a disillusioned priest and a young boy, and *We Think the World of You* (1988), in which a middle-aged homosexual displaces his affections on to his jailed lover's dog. Some TV, including a handsome version of *To the Lighthouse* (1983).

OTHER BRITISH FILMS: (shorts) *Sunset and Beyond* (1969), *Begging the Ring* (1978), *The Trespasser* (1988).

Gregg, Everley (*b* Bishop Stoke, 1900 – *d* Beaconsfield, 1959). Actress. RADA-trained stage actress, often in Noël COWARD's plays, and the apogee of her screen career was playing garrulous Dolly Messiter in *Brief Encounter* (1945), replacing Joyce BARBOUR after production had begun. Always memorable, in roles large and small, hearty or vinegary, she slid up and down the social scale, favouring the upper end. She was Catherine Parr passively outliving the king in *The Private Life of Henry VIII* (1933) and a somewhat butch viscountess in *Lost* (1955), Kay Walsh's nurse in *In Which We Serve* (1942), snivelling Sarah Pocket in *Great Expectations* (1946), and, penultimately, the Mayoress muttering her preference for 'the Lancers' at the ball in *Room at the Top* (1958).

OTHER BRITISH FILMS INCLUDE: *The Ghost Goes West, The Scoundrel* (1935), *Pygmalion* (1938), *Freedom Radio* (1940), *Uncensored* (1942), *The Demi-Paradise* (1943), *I See a Dark Stranger* (1946), *The Astonished Heart, Stage Fright* (1950), *Moulin Rouge* (1953), *Father Brown* (1954), *The Man Who Never Was* (1955), *Deadly Record* (1959).

Gregg, Hubert (*b* London, 1914). Actor, lyricist, screenwriter. Multi-talented, Webber-Douglas-trained actor, on stage from 1933, with several Shakespearean seasons at the Regent's Park Open Air Theatre as well as touring experience as actor and director, and writer of lyrics and music for plays and revues. On film, the short, dapper Gregg was Phyllis CALVERT's rich but spineless fiancé in *The Root of All Evil* (1947), wicked Prince John in *The Story of Robin Hood . . .* (1952), and the spluttering, legalistic Pusey in *The 'Maggie'* (1953), among over a dozen sharp character studies. Also wrote lyrics for *Doctor at Sea* (1955, + a). Married (1) Zoë GAIL (2) Pat KIRKWOOD.

OTHER BRITISH FILMS INCLUDE: (a) *In Which We Serve* (1942), *29, Acacia Avenue* (1945), *Once Upon a Dream, Landfall* (1949), *Svengali* (1954), *Simon and Laura* (1955); (co-/sc) *Stars in Your Eyes, Three Men in a Boat* (1956), *After the Ball* (1957, + orig. TV play).

Gregory, Thea (*b* 1929). Actress. Attractive lead and second lead of a half-dozen mid 50s mostly 'B' FILMS. Began in a tiny role in EALING's *The Magnet* (1950). Married John GREGSON, male lead of *The Weak and the Wicked* (1953), in which she had a small part.

OTHER BRITISH FILMS INCLUDE: *The Scarlet Spear* (1953), *Profile, The Golden Link, Five Days* (1954), *Satellite in the Sky* (1956).

Gregson, John (*b* Liverpool, 1919 – *d* Porlock, 1975). Actor. Agreeable 50s leading man, variously described as having 'an Irish background' and as being 'born in Scotland' where he began acting, Liverpudlian Gregson actually began work as a telephone engineer, engaged in amateur theatricals and, after WW2 service in the Royal Navy, joined the Liverpool Old Vic, appearing on the London stage in 1948. He became, though, essentially a film actor – the word 'star' seems almost too glitzy for so unassuming a presence. After a few small roles, including the policeman hero-worshipped by a little girl in *The Lavender Hill Mob* (1951), he was given the male lead as the engineer in love with Celia JOHNSON in the undervalued *The Holly and the Ivy*, and played the former miner, now heading the rescue team, in *The Brave Don't Cry* and the volunteer reserve pilot, 'Septic' Baird, in *Angels One Five* (all 1952).

The film that clinched his popularity, and the highlight of his RANK contract, was *Genevieve* (1953), in which (non-driver that he was) he played vintage-car owner Alan McKimm. He brought absolutely the right adolescent fanaticism to the part and at the end behaves with a touching courtesy that reminds his wife of why she married him. By playing it 'straight', Gregson achieves one of the best comic performances of the decade. He made 25 more films, but it is arguable that he never had another role as good. However, he is always solidly convincing – watch him in such contrasting roles as the harassed Captain in the comedy, *The Captain's Table* (1958) and the determined police inspector in *Tomorrow at Ten* (1962). TV included starring in the police series, *Gideon's Way* (1964–65) and he played the British padre in the US film, *The Longest Day* (1962). Was married to actress Thea GREGORY.

OTHER BRITISH FILMS: *Saraband for Dead Lovers, Scott of the Antarctic, London Belongs to Me* (1948), *Whisky Galore!, Train of Events* (1949), *Treasure Island, Cairo Road* (1950), *Venetian Bird* (1952), *The Weak and the Wicked, The Titfield Thunderbolt* (1953), *To Dorothy a Son, The Crowded Day, Conflict of Wings* (1954), *Three Cases of Murder, Value for Money, Above Us the Waves* (1955), *The Battle of the River Plate, True as a Turtle, Jacqueline* (1956), *Miracle in Soho* (1957), *Sea of Sand, Rooney* (1958), *SOS Pacific* (1959), *Hand in Hand, Faces in the Dark, The Treasure of Monte Cristo* (1960), *The Frightened City* (1961), *Live Now – Pay Later* (1962), *The Night of the Generals* (1966, UK/Fr), *Fright* (1971).

Grenfell, Joyce (*b* London, 1910 – *d* London, 1979). Actress. RN: Phipps. Immortalised as toothy, gauche games mistress, Gossage ('Call me Sausage'), in *The Happiest Days of Your Life* (1950), former journalist Grenfell invaded over 20 often-unexceptional British films, creating moments of treasurable idiocy. She is wonderfully exasperated with Alastair SIM's further postponement of their wedding ('I've been home three weeks and I've had a bath') in *Laughter in Paradise* (1951), is all fringe and jangling beads as the hotel proprietress in *Genevieve* (1953), was several times hilariously love-lorn Policewoman (later Sergeant) Ruby Gates in the ST TRINIAN'S SERIES. As a celebrated monologuist, gently caricaturing the middle classes, she showed wider emotional range than films ever explored. Appeared in many revues, as well as her own inimitable one-woman shows, which she wrote and with which she toured extensively. She was living proof that you could be a sharp satirist without – miraculously – descending to malice; she is as English as glee-singing and much more fun. Awarded OBE in 1946.

OTHER BRITISH FILMS: *A Letter from Home* (1941, short), *The Lamp Still Burns, The Demi-Paradise* (1943), *While the Sun Shines* (1947), *A Run for Your Money, Poet's Pub, Alice in Wonderland* (voice) (1949), *Stage Fright* (1950), *The Magic Box, The Galloping Major* (1951), *The Pickwick Papers* (1952), *The Million Pound Note* (1953), *The Belles of St Trinian's, Forbidden Cargo* (1954), *The Good Companions* (1956), *Happy is the Bride, Blue Murder at St Trinian's* (1957), *The Pure Hell of St*

Trinian's (1960), *The Old Dark House* (1962, UK/US), *The Yellow Rolls-Royce* (1964).

BIBLIOG: *Joyce Grenfell Requests the Pleasure*, 1976.

Gréville, Edmond T. (*b* Nice, 1906 – *d* Nice, 1966). Director. No less a critic than Graham GREENE thought Gréville had 'an impeccable cinematic eye' and praised him for his treatment of sexual passion in *Brief Ecstasy* (1937), even if *Mademoiselle Docteur* (1937, UK/Fr – English version only) had a 'really shocking script'. Of English–French parentage, after making some experimental SHORTS, he began film-making in Paris (as an actor in René Clair's *Sous les toits de Paris*, 1930), directing seven films there before coming to England, where his first film was *Gypsy Melody* (1936), a Ruritanian musical starring Lupe Velez. During WW2, he filmed in occupied France, and returned to England to make the lively 'spiv' THRILLER, *Noose* (1948), which marshals a lot of urban action convincingly. Of his other British films, *Beat Girl* (1959) is perhaps the most interesting, evoking vividly a vanished world where to be wild and young was to haunt coffee bars. Committed suicide, bringing to end a sombre, idiosyncratic career.

OTHER BRITISH FILMS: *Secret Lives* (1937), *What a Man!* (1938), *But Not in Vain* (1948, UK and Dutch versions, + p, sc), *The Romantic Age* (1949), *Guilty?* (1956, UK/Fr), *The Hands of Orlac* (1960, UK/Fr).

Grewal, Shani (*b* Punjab, 1958). Director. Grewal made three films in the 90s, none of which was widely seen: *After Midnight* (1990, UK/Ire); *Double X: The Name of the Game* (1992), which was described severely as a throwback to British 'B' FILMS of the 50s, though it at least brought Norman WISDOM back to the screen; and *Guru in Seven* (1998), a sort of Asian–British *Alfie*, starring Nitin Chandra GANATRA, and made on a budget of £33,000.

Grey, Anne (*b* Lincoln, 1907). Actress. RN: Aileen Ewing. Bit player of late silents who became the dignified leading lady of over 40 talkies, often teamed with Tom WALLS and, in her last two films, with Harry Agar LYONS. Film career led to stage debut in 1931, but nothing important. Briefly in Hollywood with actor-husband Lester MATTHEWS, 1935–36, where she made *Bonnie Scotland* (1935) with Laurel and Hardy.

BRITISH FILMS INCLUDE: *The Constant Nymph* (1928), *Master and Man, Taxi for Two* (1929), *The Brat* (1930), *The Calendar* (1931), *Number Seventeen* (1932), *The Faithful Heart, The Wandering Jew* (1933), *Road House* (1934), *Dr Sin Fang* (1937), *Chinatown Nights* (1938). AS.

Griem, Helmut (*b* Hamburg, Germany, 1932). Actor. German stage and screen actor who has worked for R.W. Fassbinder, Volker Schlöndorff, and Luchino Visconti (*The Damned*, 1969, *Ludwig*, 1972). In international productions he is frequently cast as a Nazi officer (*The Mackenzie Break*, 1970, US) or as an aristocratic dandy (*Cabaret*, US, 1972).

BRITISH FILMS INCLUDE: *Children of Rage* (UK/Israel/It, 1975), *Voyage Of The Damned* (1976), *Sergeant Steiner* (UK/Ger, 1978), *The Second Victory* (UK/Ger, 1986). Tim Bergfelder.

Grierson, John (*b* Deanston, Scotland, 1898 – *d* Bath, 1972) Director, producer, administrator. Founder of the British DOCUMENTARY FILM MOVEMENT, Grierson was strongly influenced by the Presbyterian idealism of his father, Robert, and the politically conscious radicalism of his mother, Jane. After education at Stirling High School he read philosophy and literature at Glasgow University, and graduated in moral philosophy, logic and metaphysics in 1923. In 1924 he was awarded a Rockefeller scholarship to study at the University of Chicago. He rejected the critiques of democratic practice then being mounted by figures such as Harold Lasswell and Walter Lippmann, and argued, instead, that film could be used as a means to sustain democracy. He first began to write on the cinema in 1925 in the *Chicago Evening Post*, and helped edit the English titles for Sergei Eisenstein's *Battleship Potemkin* in 1926. In 1927 he returned to Britain and was appointed Assistant Films Officer at the EMPIRE MARKETING BOARD. There, he argued that a new type of film was required to represent the relationship between the citizen and the state. This was the basis of his well known description of documentary film as the 'creative treatment of actuality', and of his first film as a director, *Drifters* (1929).

Grierson used the success of *Drifters* to establish the EMB FILM UNIT, employing film-makers such as Basil WRIGHT, Paul ROTHA, Robert FLAHERTY, Stuart LEGG, Arthur ELTON, John TAYLOR, Donald TAYLOR, Edgar ANSTEY, and Grierson's sister – Marion GRIERSON. When the EMB was dissolved in 1933 Grierson and his film-makers joined the Post Office, and established the GPO FILM UNIT, employing Alberto CAVALCANTI, Humphrey JENNINGS, Len LYE, Alexander SHAW, Jack HOLMES, Pat JACKSON and Harry WATT. In 1937 Grierson left the GPO Film Unit to establish FILM CENTRE, and also encouraged other film-makers to establish independent documentary film-making organisations. This led to the formation of the SHELL, REALIST, and STRAND Film Units.

In 1939, Grierson was appointed as first Film Commissioner of the National Film Board of Canada. He left in 1945 and, in 1948, returned to Britain in order to take up an appointment as Controller, Film, at the Central Office of Information, resigning his post in 1950. In 1951, he was placed in charge of GROUP 3, a production arm of the NATIONAL FILM FINANCE CORPORATION. However, the films made were rarely successful, and Group 3 ceased production in July 1955. From October 1957 to 1967 he presented the television programme *This Wonderful World* for Scottish Television, making 350 programmes over this period.

Grierson was one of the most important – and controversial – figures in British film culture. Not only was he the founder of the British documentary film movement, but he also played a role in influencing the REALIST CINEMA which emerged in Britain during the WW2, and the development of television current affairs and documentary television in series such as *World In Action*. He was also an important theorist of the cinema. However, Grierson has also been criticised on the grounds that he initiated a practice of and approach to documentary film-making which was insufficiently radical or oppositional, and which obstructed the development of a more avant-garde or politically progressive British documentary tradition. In addition, during the 1970s, and under the auspices of anti-realist 'SCREEN theory', he was (mistakenly) accused of developing a 'naive-realist' theory of documentary representation. More recently, the issue of elitism within Grierson's ideology has arisen, and he has been accused of harbouring proto-fascist ideals. This, again, is mistaken, and Grierson's ideology is more clearly associated with strands of progressive social democratic corporatist thinking which emerged in Britain during the inter-war period. Ian Aitken.

Grierson, Marion (*b* Stirling, Scotland, 1907 – *d* Edinburgh, 1999). Director, producer. Marion Grierson joined brother John GRIERSON at the EMB FILM UNIT, where she worked between 1930 and 1934, initially starting as an editor, before progressing to director after 1932. Between 1935 and 1946 she worked as a director for the STRAND film company and the CROWN FILM UNIT, and also worked as an editor on one of the house journals of the DOCUMENTARY FILM MOVEMENT, *World Film News*. Left film-making in 1946 to take a degree in psychology at London University, thereafter pursuing a career as a social worker in Glasgow and worked on youth-related problems until her retirement.

BRITISH FILMS INCLUDE: *Britain's Countryside* (1932), *So This is London* (1933), *The Key to Scotland*, *Village Harvest* (1935), *London on Parade* (1937), *Civil Engineering* (1946). Ian Aitken.

Grierson, Ruby (*b* Stirling, Scotland, 1904 – *d* at sea, 1940) Director. Sister of John and Marion GRIERSON; trained as a teacher, and only entered the film industry in 1935, when she began work with the STRAND FILM COMPANY. Between 1938 and 1940 she worked with the REALIST FILM UNIT. She died in 1940, when the ship on which she was sailing, full of children being evacuated from London to Canada, was torpedoed and sunk.

BRITISH FILMS INCLUDE: *London Wakes Up* (1936), *Animals Looking At You* (1937), *The Zoo and You* (1938), *What's For Dinner?*, *Green Food For Health*, *They Also Serve* (1940). Ian Aitken.

Griffies, Ethel (*b* Sheffield, 1878 – *d* London, 1975). Actress. On stage age two, and in London from 1901, she lived to be the oldest – let alone the longest-working – actress in English. Apart from her stage career on both sides of the Atlantic, the severe-looking Griffies made over 80 films, most of them in Hollywood (famously, when she was 85, in *The Birds*, 1963), often in Brit-set pieces like *The White Cliffs of Dover* (1944), as the cross lady on the train, or as Aunt Branwell in *Devotion* (1946). In the UK, she appeared in two silent films, three 30s films, and had a great swansong as grandma to *Billy Liar* (1963). The second husband she outlived was actor **Edward Cooper** (*b* ? – *d* 1945), who made a few films in the UK (e.g. *The Life and Death of Colonel Blimp*, 1943) and the US (e.g. *Kitty*, 1945).

OTHER BRITISH FILMS: *The Cost of a Kiss* (1917), *Hard Cash* (1921), *Twice Branded*, *Not So Dusty*, *Guilty Melody* (1936).

Griffin, Josephine (*b* London, 1928). Actress. One of the many pretty blondes who decorated British films in the 50s. She was rushed through ten quite decent films in three years without being given a chance to register more than a sympathetic presence, as, for instance, the 'nice, sensible girl' who 'protects' (and contrasts with) Gloria Grahame in *The Man Who Never Was* (1955).

OTHER BRITISH FILMS INCLUDE: *The House of the Arrow* (1953), *The Crowded Day* (1954), *Room in the House*, *Portrait of Alison* (1955), *The Spanish Gardener*, *The Extra Day* (1956).

Griffith, Hugh (*b* Anglesey, 1912 – *d* London, 1980). Actor. With a touch of the farouche, wild-eyed Griffith was a formidable character player, the highlight of whose 40-year film career was winning a supporting actor Oscar as the Sheikh in *Ben-Hur* (1959, US), though his wildly blusterous Squire Western in *Tom Jones* (1963, AAn) is just as film-stealing. Formerly a bank clerk, RADA-trained (Bancroft Gold Medallist) Griffith was on stage from 1939, had seasons at Stratford, the Old Vic, on Broadway, and did a lot of touring, with King Lear his favourite role. Entered films also in 1939 and quickly showed he didn't need much screentime to make his presence felt: witness the Lord High Steward in the penultimate episode of *Kind Hearts and Coronets* (1949), the fire-breathing Professor Welch in *Lucky Jim* (1957), the vengeful magistrate in

Oliver! (1968), to choose three almost at random. In his last 20 years, much in demand for international films.

OTHER BRITISH FILMS INCLUDE: *Neutral Port* (1940), *The Silver Darlings* (1946), *The Three Weird Sisters, So Evil My Love, London Belongs to Me* (1948), *The Last Days of Dolwyn* (1949), *Gone to Earth* (1950), *The Titfield Thunderbolt* (1953), *Passage Home* (1955), *The Good Companions* (1956), *Term of Trial* (1962), *The Bargee* (1964), *The Sailor from Gibraltar* (1967), *Cry of the Banshee* (1970), *The Abominable Dr Phibes* (1971), *Dr Phibes Rises Again* (1972), *Legend of the Werewolf* (1974), *Joseph Andrews* (1976), *The Hound of the Baskervilles* (1977).

Griffith, Kenneth (*b* Tenby, 1921). Actor. As a young man, Griffith played slight, dark weasels, weaklings and spivs of every hue, making his mark ineradicably as blackmailing Archie Fellowes in *The Shop at Sly Corner* (1946), a role he also played on stage and TV. After which it was hard to trust him, even as clergyman (*Heavens Above!*, 1963) or medical orderly (*The Wild Geese*, 1978, UK/Switz), and certainly not as the nightclub owner in *The Painted Smile* (1961), though the BOULTING brothers gave him some good comedy chances. Sixty films and 50 years after Archie, he played two delightful character bits: the irascible old guest in *Four Weddings and a Funeral* (1994) and the Rev. Jones in *The Englishman Who Went Up . . .* (1995). Notable TV included memorable Napoleons in *War and Peace* (1963) and *The Man on the Rock* (1975), and *Curious Journeys*, about the Irish 1916 Easter Rebellion; his polemical *Hang Up Your Brightest Colours*, on Michael Collins, was banned. Outspoken on controversial matters, he turned down a role in *Patriot Games* (1992, US) because of its simplistic view of IRA violence. Has returned intermittently to the stage, as in Terence RATTIGAN's *Cause Célèbre* (1977). Also has a reputation as a military historian.

OTHER BRITISH FILMS INCLUDE: *Channel Incident* (1940, short), *Love on the Dole, Hard Steel* (1941), *Fame Is the Spur* (1947), *Bond Street* (1948), *Waterfront* (1950), *High Treason* (1951), *The Prisoner, 1984* (1955), *Private's Progress, Tiger in the Smoke* (1956), *The Naked Truth, Lucky Jim, Chain of Events* (1957), *A Night to Remember* (1958), *Tiger Bay, Libel, I'm All Right Jack* (1959), *Suspect, Circus of Horrors* (1960), *Only Two Can Play* (1961), *The Whisperers* (1966), *The Lion in Winter, The Assassination Bureau* (1968), *Revenge* (1971), *Callan* (1974), *Sea Wolves* (1980, UK/US/Switz), *Who Dares Wins* (1982), *Very Annie Mary* (2001, UK/Fr).

BIBLIOG: Autobiography, *The Fool's Paradise*, 1994.

Griffiths, Fred (*b* Ludlow, 1912 – *d* London, 1994). Actor. Former fireman (he played one in *Fires Were Started*, 1943), who became a small-part fixture, often uncredited, in British films, especially in the 50s. Characteristically seen as taxi drivers (*John and Julie*, 1955; *There Was a Crooked Man*, 1960; *Carry On Regardless*, 1961; *Billion Dollar Brain*, 1967; *Perfect Friday, Carry On Loving*, 1970; *Love Thy Neighbour*, 1973 – was he just a good driver?) and, earlier, spivs (*Passport to Pimlico*, 1949; *Double Confession*, 1950).

OTHER BRITISH FILMS INCLUDE: *Nine Men* (1942), *It Always Rains on Sunday* (1947), *Stop Press Girl* (1949), *The Lavender Hill Mob* (1951), *The Cruel Sea* (1952), *Bang! You're Dead* (1953), *The Sleeping Tiger* (1954), *Lost, The Ladykillers* (1955), *Sailor Beware* (1956), *The Horse's Mouth, Carry On Nurse, Dunkirk* (1958), *I'm All Right Jack* (1959), *Dad's Army* (1971), *The Chiffy Kids* (1976).

Griffiths, Jane (*b* Peacehaven, 1929 – *d* England, 1975). Actress. Conventionally pretty brunette who trained at Sadlers Wells Ballet School and entered films as a child in *The Derelict* (1937) and *Pandamonium* (1939). After stage experience, returned to films in 1949, and had the female lead (when Dinah SHERIDAN was unavailable) opposite Gregory PECK in *The Million Pound Note* (1953). But her career never took off and she was reduced to leads in such mildly enjoyable 'B' FILMS as *The Traitor* (1957) and *The Third Alibi* (1961). On stage throughout the 50s and 60s.

OTHER BRITISH FILMS INCLUDE: *Now Barabbas Was a Robber* (1949, unc), *Double Confession* (1950), *The Green Scarf* (1954), *Tread Softly Stranger* (1958), *Dead Man's Evidence* (1962).

Griffiths, Lucy (*b* Birley, Hertfordshire, 1919 – *d* London, 1982). Actress. In films from 1952, Griffiths seemed to settle into playing nosy spinsters from her mid 30s, in the likes of *Children Galore* (1954), in which she runs the village shop as a gossip site, or *The Third Alibi* (1961), as a smugly insinuating telephonist (re the heroine: 'She certainly doesn't have many lonely nights'). TV also from 1952; appeared in episodes of *The Prisoner* (1967). May have made a half-dozen uncredited early appearances, in, e.g. *Genevieve* and *Personal Affair* (1953); later in career, a 'CARRY ON' standby.

OTHER BRITISH FILMS INCLUDE: *The Ladykillers* (1955), *Jack the Ripper* (1958), *Please Turn Over* (1959), *Murder She Said, Carry On Regardless* (1961), *Murder Ahoy* (1964), *Stranger in the House* (1967), *Carry On Doctor* (1968), *Under Milk Wood, Follow Me!* (1971), *No Sex Please – We're British* (1973), *The Hound of the Baskervilles* (1977).

Griffiths, Rachel (*b* Melbourne, 1967). Actress. Versatile Australian player of tough, intense, strong-minded roles who established herself as Toni Collette's free-wheeling friend in *Muriel's Wedding* (1994) and several other Australian films before inevitably being enticed overseas. She made a believably sensuous figure of Hardy's hoydenish Arabella in *Jude* (1996); won an AAn for her compelling account of the put-upon sister in *Hilary and Jackie* (1998); and she and Pete POSTLETHWAITE dropped their clothes but not their reputations with *Among Giants* (1998). In real life she went topless in protest against casino development in Melbourne: the kind of daring she showed here is paralleled in her career moves. She has worked in Hollywood as well as the UK, but returns to Australia to act in films (*Me Myself I*, 1999) and stage (*The Doll's House*, 1998).

OTHER BRITISH FILMS: *My Son the Fanatic* (1997), *Divorcing Jack* (1998, UK/Fr), *Blow Dry* (UK/Ger/US), *Very Annie Mary* (UK/Fr) (2001)

Griffiths, Richard (*b* Stockton-on-Tees, 1947). Actor. Rotund and much in demand since his household-name-making role as the policeman-turned-gourmet chef in TV's *Pie in the Sky* (1994–95). He had been with the RSC for ten years and trundling along in film character roles since the mid 70s. One recalls his snubbing Michael PALIN in *A Private Function* (1984) and his cumbersome lechery in *Withnail and I* (1986). Now sought for international films such as *Sleepy Hollow* (1999, US/Ger) and *Harry Potter and the Philosopher's Stone* (2001, UK/US), he still delights viewers in such lethally witty studies as the time-serving gourmand politician in TV's *In the Red* (1998).

OTHER BRITISH FILMS INCLUDE: *It Shouldn't Happen to a Vet* (1976), *Chariots of Fire* (1981), *Britannia Hospital, Gandhi* (UK/Ind) (1982), *Greystoke . . .* (1984, UK/US), *Shanghai Surprise* (1986), *Funny Bones* (1995), *Vatel* (2000, UK/Fr).

Grose, Lionel (*b* London, 1908). Casting director, actor. With a stage career in the US and Britain before war service (1942–46), Grose appeared in a dozen films, including *In Which We Serve* (1942), usually in small roles, before setting up as a casting director in the 50s. He worked for such independents as Douglas FAIRBANKS and DANZIGER Productions and for a time was studio controller at the Danzigers' New Elstree Studios, which turned out second features and TV programmes until closure in 1965.

OTHER BRITISH FILMS: (a) *49th Parallel* (1941), *We Dive at Dawn* (1943), *Blanche Fury* (1947), *Madness of the Heart* (1949), *Hindle Wakes* (1952); (assoc p) *Miss MacTaggart Won't Lie Down* (1966).

Grossmith, George Jr (*b* London, 1874 – *d* London, 1935). Actor. This famous son of a famous father made his stage debut in 1892 and quickly became a musical-comedy star, often likened to George M. Cohan because, like the American, he also wrote his own songs and shows. A minor British film career, starting with *A Gaiety Duet* (1909), and three Hollywood feature films in the 30s.

OTHER BRITISH FILMS: *Winning a Widow* (1910), *The Argentine Tango* (1913), *Service for Ladies, Wedding Rehearsal* (1932), *The Girl from Maxim's* (1933), *Princess Charming* (1934).

BIBLIOG: Autobiography, *G.G. – Reminiscences*, 1933. AS.

Grossmith, Lawrence (*b* London, 1877 – *d* Los Angeles, 1944). Actor. Supporting player, generally characterizing the rich and powerful, including Sir Henry Baskerville in *Silver Blaze* (1937). Stage debut 1896 and major career in music hall and the legitimate theatre. First came to US in 1898 with Lily Langtry, and ended his career there 1939–44 with roles in *Journey for Margaret* (1942), *Gaslight* (1944), etc. Brother of George GROSSMITH and brother-in-law of Vernon and Irene Castle.

OTHER BRITISH FILMS INCLUDE: *The Brass Bottle* (1914), *Tiger Bay* (1933), *Rolling in Money, Sing As We Go!* (1934), *It Happened in Paris* (1935), *Men Are Not Gods* (1936), *Smash and Grab* (1937). AS.

Group 3 State-subsidised film company that survived from March 1951 until February 1956. Funded by the NATIONAL FILM FINANCE CORPORATION (NFFC), the Labour administration intended the group to be a stepping stone for young film-makers. It was the third of the NFFC's group production schemes – the other two were co-financed by RANK and ABPC respectively – which all sought to combine producer independence, a continuous programme of production that would benefit from economies of scale and help achieve financial stability by cross-collateralising the films' revenues.

NFFC Managing Director John Lawrie and the group's chairman Michael BALCON, appointed John GRIERSON as managing director. The intention was to make 'story documentaries' which blended DOCUMENTARY and fiction on budgets averaging £50,000. Unfortunately Grierson had no experience of the discipline of turning ideas into lively and coherent feature scripts. He was so slow starting that the unit's first film, *Judgement Deferred* (1951), Joan COLLINS's screen debut, was made by established director John BAXTER, who was the group's production controller at their SOUTHALL studios. Many of the group's 22 films had sub-EALING plots, achieved little critical success and unsurprisingly were released as second features. Even *The Brave Don't Cry*, which Grierson scripted and co-produced with director Philip LEACOCK using a cast of non-professional actors, and which won universal acclaim at the 1952 Edinburgh Festival, was held up and poorly released by Associated British Film Distributors. In 1954 Grierson resigned through illness and Lawrie and Balcon soon followed.

By mid 1955, the NFFC realised that Group 3's type of middle-budget production was not suited to current exhibition patterns and that only one of its films, *Conquest of Everest* (1953), would be likely to recover its costs. The following year, having lost nearly half a million pounds, the NFFC sold the group off to become Beaconsfield Films Ltd.

Despite the group's commercial failure, many of its young film-makers, including Lewis GILBERT (*Time Gentlemen Please!*), John GUILLERMIN (*Miss Robin Hood*) and Cyril FRANKEL (*Devil On Horseback, Man of Africa* and *Make Me An Offer!*), went on to make substantial contributions to the British film industry. Vincent Porter.

Groves, Fred (*b* London, 1880 – *d* London, 1955). Actor. Stolid leading man in silent films who graduated to character roles with coming of sound; on screen 1913–50; on stage 1896–1945.

OTHER BRITISH FILMS INCLUDE: *Maria Marten* (1913), *Midshipman Easy* (1915), *Garryowen* (1920), *Squibs, MP* (1923), *Escape* (1930), *An Ideal Husband* (1947), *Up for the Cup* (1950). AS.

Gruffudd, Ioan (*b* Cardiff, 1974). Actor. Born to a strongly religious background, with teacher parents, Gruffudd (pronounced: Yo-an Griffith) was a popular teenage figure in the Welsh-language soap, *People of the Valley* (1987–94) and trained at RADA. In films, he had a line in *Titanic* (1997, US), played John Gray in *Wilde* (1997, UK/Ger/Jap/US), and starred in the Welsh–Jewish love story, *Solomon and Gaenor* (1999), in which he played the Jew. His reputation has been firmly established on TV, as Horatio Hornblower in two series (1998–99) and as Pip in an interesting, idiosyncratic *Great Expectations* (1999). His handsome appearance and a compelling intensity in his playing have led him to be rushed from one feature film to another at the turn of the century, including a stab at Hollywood stardom in *102 Dalmatians* (2000).

OTHER BRITISH FILMS: *Very Annie Mary* (UK/Fr), *Another Life, Happy Now* (2001), *The Gathering* (2002).

Grune, Karl (*b* Vienna, 1890 – *d* Bournemouth, 1962). Director. Working in German cinema of the 20s, and best-known for his social-realist drama *The Street* (1923), Grune came to Britain in 1933, a business associate of producer Max SCHACH. Grune's British films were visually opulent and operatic historical costume dramas, receiving scornful reviews from critic Graham GREENE. After Schach's companies collapsed, Grune retired, but he re-emerged a decade later to co-produce *The Silver Darlings* (1946).

OTHER BRITISH FILMS: *Abdul The Damned* (1935), *The Marriage of Corbal, Pagliacci* (1936). Tim Bergfelder.

Guard, Christopher (*b* London, 1953). Actor. His work has been mainly on TV. Co-starring with Julie CHRISTIE in the pleasure-free *Memoirs of a Survivor* (1981) did nothing for his fledgling career in films, but he had a continuing role in TV's *Casualty* (1993–94) and was in the film version of *A Little Night Music* (1977, US/Ger/Austria). Son of actors **Philip Guard**, who appeared in a couple of films, including *Caravan* (1946), and Charlotte MITCHELL, and brother of Dominic GUARD.

OTHER BRITISH FILM: *Loophole* (1980).

Guard, Dominic (*b* London, 1956). Actor. Came to immediate notice as *The Go-Between* (1971), then seen as Lord Nelson's son in *Bequest to the Nation* (1973) and as the young aristocrat in the influential Australian film *Picnic at Hanging Rock* (1975). Subsequent appearances sporadic. Son of actors Philip Guard and Charlotte MITCHELL, and brother of Christopher GUARD.

OTHER BRITISH FILMS INCLUDE: *SWALK* (1970), *The Count of Monte Cristo* (1974, TV, some cinemas), *Absolution* (1978), *An Unsuitable Job for a Woman* (1981), *Gandhi* (1982, UK/Ind).

Gudrun, Ann (*b* Campsie, Scotland, 1930). Actress. RN: Gudrun Ure. Rather pertly pretty, auburn-haired supporting player of a few mid 50s films, most visible as Bonar

COLLEANO's fiancée in *The Sea Shall Not Have Them* (1954). Also, radio and TV, and early experience with Glasgow Citizens' Theatre, as well as co-starring with Orson WELLES in *Othello* in London (1951). Reverted to original name later in acting career, as, for instance, as TV's *Supergran* (1985–87).

OTHER BRITISH FILMS INCLUDE: *The Million Pound Note* (1953), *Trouble in the Glen, Doctor in the House, The Diamond* (1954).

Guest, Val (*b* London, 1911). Director, screenwriter, producer. Guest is the British GENRE film-maker *par excellence*. After spending the 30s as (co-)screenwriter on scripts for some of the leading comics of the day, including Will HAY and the CRAZY GANG, he began directing in the early 40s, in most cases still working on the screenplays. He made COMEDIES (*Up the Creek*, 1958, + co-sc unc), SCIENCE-FICTION (*The Quatermass Experiment*, (1955, + co-sc), MUSICALS (*Expresso Bongo*, 1959, + p), WAR FILMS (*Camp on Blood Island*, 1957, + co-sc), COSTUME ADVENTURES (*Men of Sherwood Forest*, 1954), THRILLERS (*Jigsaw*, 1962, + p, sc), SPY STORIES (*Where the Spies Are*, 1965, + p, co-sc), and the list gives only one example of each, whereas in most cases there were a half-dozen or more. He was the least pretentious of directors, but his films were never less than skilfully crafted.

A frustrated actor, he became a film journalist as the London-based columnist for *Hollywood Reporter*, before starting work on that string of famous comedies at GAUMONT–BRITISH (*Oh, Mr Porter*, 1937, and *The Frozen Limits*, 1939, are classics of their zany kind). The first films he directed were in this line, starting with *Miss London Ltd* (1943, + co-sc, lyrics), starring Arthur ASKEY. There were several more sophisticated comedies in the late 40s starring his second wife Yolande DONLAN, including *Mr Drake's Duck* (1950, + sc), but it was in the mid 50s that he hit his stride, particularly with the inventive science-fiction films – *The Day the Earth Caught Fire*, 1961, + p, co-sc) and *Quatermass* are now regarded as classics of the genre – and tough urban thrillers, including *Hell Is a City* (1959, + sc). His career trailed off, like the British industry at large, in the 70s and he eventually retired to California, but he has left a body of films which acts as a reliable barometer of public taste over several decades.

OTHER BRITISH FILMS: (sc/co-sc, unless noted – includes) *The Maid of the Mountains* (1932), *No Monkey Business* (1935), *Public Nuisance No. 1* (1936), *Good Morning, Boys! O-Kay for Sound* (1937), *Old Bones of the River, Convict 99* (1938), *Ask a Policeman, Where's That Fire?* (1939), *Band Waggon, Gasbags* (1940), *The Ghost Train, I Thank You* (1941), *Back Room Boy* (1942), *London Town* (1946), *Another Man's Poison* (1951), *Dentist in the Chair* (1960); (d, co-/sc, unless noted – complete) *The Nose Has It* (1942, short, d), *Give Us the Moon, Bees in Paradise* (1944), *I'll Be Your Sweetheart* (1945), *Just William's Luck* (1947), *William Comes to Town* (1948), *Murder at the Windmill, Miss Pilgrim's Progress* (1949), *The Body Said No!* (1950), *Penny Princess* (1952), *The Runaway Bus* (1953, + p), *Life with the Lyons, Dance Little Lady, The Lyons in Paris* (1954), *They Can't Hang Me, Break in the Circle* (1955), *The Weapon* (d), *It's a Wonderful World* (1956), *Carry On Admiral, Quatermass 2, The Abominable Snowman* (d) (1957), *Life Is a Circus, Further Up the Creek* (1958), *Yesterday's Enemy* (d) (1959), *The Full Treatment* (1960, + p), *80,000 Suspects* (1963, + p), *The Beauty Jungle* (1964, + p), *Casino Royale* (co-d), *Assignment K* (1967), *When Dinosaurs Ruled the Earth* (1969), *Toomorrow* (1970), *Au Pair Girls* (1972), *Confessions of a Window Cleaner* (1974, d), *The Diamond Mercenaries* (1975, d), *The Shillingbury Blowers* (d), *Dangerous Davies – The Last Detective* (1980), *The Boys in Blue* (1983). BIBLIOG: Autobiography, *So You Want to Be in Pictures*, 2001.

Guillermin, John (*b* London, 1925). Screenwriter, director. Guillermin, who made arguably the best Tarzan film ever (*Tarzan's Greatest Adventure*, 1958), was most comfortable working within familiar GENRE conventions. He left for Hollywood in the 60s and directed a number of big-budget films, including the all-star extravaganza *Towering Inferno* (1974), the dull remake of *King Kong* (1976) and the even more abysmal *King Kong Lives* (1986). Far more successful were the British films he directed from the mid 50s (*Town on Trial*, 1957) to the mid 60s (*Guns at Batasi*, 1964).

Educated at the City of London School, followed by WW2 service with the RAF, and a brief period working on DOCUMENTARIES in France, Guillermin entered British films in the late 40s with his script for *Melody in the Dark* (1948). A series of low-budget THRILLERS followed, including *Four Days* (1951) and *Double Jeopardy* (1955), before he graduated to more substantial films, including *Town on Trial*, a police film with a strong cast, including John MILLS, Charles COBURN and Derek FARR. Such generic fare, including the WAR FILM, *I Was Monty's Double* (1958), suited Guillermin and in 1960 he directed two CRIME MELODRAMAS, *The Day They Robbed the Bank of England* (1959) and *Never Let Go* (+ co-story), which, with more than a touch of *film noir*, gave Richard TODD arguably his best screen role as an unsuccessful salesman tracking the thieves who stole his car. After the French-based drama *Rapture* (1965), Guillermin worked mainly for Hollywood companies, beginning with the commercially successful *The Blue Max* (1966), with George Peppard as a WW1 German ace, followed by two US films starring Peppard, *PJ* (1968), and *House of Cards* (1968). In 1970 Guillermin, emulating the Italian Western, with its combination of sex and violence and generic conventions, filmed *El Condor* (1970, US) in Spain, and thereafter worked mainly on large-budget Hollywood films with *Sheena* (1984), starring Tanya Roberts as queen of the jungle, the lowest point in his career.

OTHER BRITISH FILMS INCLUDE: (sc) *High Jinks in Society* (1949, co-); (d) *Torment* (1949, + sc, p), *Song of Paris* (1952), *The Crowded Day* (1954), *The Whole Truth* (1958), *Waltz of the Toreadors* (1962), *Death on the Nile* (1978); (d/co-sc) *Operation Diplomat* (1953), *Tarzan Goes to India* (1962). Geoff Mayer.

Guillory, Sienna (*b* London, 1975). Actress. Fragile-looking blonde who caught to perfection Kingsley AMIS's Jenny Bunn in the mini-series, *Take a Girl Like You* (2000), and confirmed this promise with one of the leads in *Late Night Shopping* (2001, UK/Ger) as Susie who 'seduces' someone over the hospital bed of her comatose boyfriend. Her partner is Nick MORAN with whom she appeared in the SHORT FILMS, *The Future Lasts a Long Time* (1996) and *The Rules of Engagement* (1999).

OTHER BRITISH FILMS INCLUDE: *Sorted* (UK/US), *Kiss Kiss (Bang Bang), Going Down* (short) (2000), *Superstition* (2001, UK/Lux/Neth).

Guinness, Sir Alec (*b* London, 1914 – *d* Midhurst, 2000). Actor. Of the great acting knights of the 20th century, none so whole-heartedly embraced the cinema as the chameleon Guinness. True, he began on the stage in 1934, having trained with the Fay Compton School (and privately with Martita HUNT), and would return to it regularly, with laudable results. Pre-war he joined the Old Vic, playing a wide range of supporting roles and a famous modern-dress Hamlet in 1938. After WW2 service in the Royal Navy, he starred in such diverse plays as T.S. Eliot's *The Cocktail Party* (1950), Terence RATTIGAN's *Ross* (1960), winning the Evening Standard Award for the title role, and as the blind protagonist of John MORTIMER's *A Voyage Round My Father* (1971).

Household fame, though, came with films. An extra in *Evensong* (1934), he didn't film again until his beautifully exact

Herbert Pocket in David LEAN's *Great Expectations* (1946), followed by his controversially repulsive Fagin in *Oliver Twist* (1948) and the series of EALING comedies with which, to this day, his name is most tenaciously associated. (Except of course by the very young who know him only as Obi-Wan in *Star Wars*, 1977, US, for which he famously took a percentage and needed never to work again.) There are seven of these comedies, most memorable of which are the immaculate *Kind Hearts and Coronets* (1949), in which he played eight members of a ducal family, *The Lavender Hill Mob* (1951), as the mild bank clerk dreaming larcenously of gold bars, *The Man in the White Suit* (1951), as an inventor in the grip of an *idée fixe*, and *The Ladykillers* (1955), as the unctuous, snaggle-toothed leader of a gang of incompetent crooks. In 1989, he claimed never to feel comfortable playing characters too like himself, and most of these films allow physical disguise to complement the inner obsessions. His own physical appearance as a young man was pleasantly ordinary rather than glamorously film starrish.

Ealing made him one of the great character stars of British films, but there are other treasurable performances as well: on-the-make Denry in *The Card* (1952); the Cardinal under interrogation in *The Prisoner* (1955); the madly zealous Captain Nicholson in *The Bridge on the River Kwai* (1957), for which he won the Oscar; the hard-drinking extroverted Jock in *Tunes of Glory* (1960); and a touching Charles I in the underrated *Cromwell* (1970). There were miscalculations too; he would have agreed that the heroes of such romantic comedies as *The Captain's Paradise* (1953) and *To Paris with Love* (1954) might have been better served by Rex HARRISON, and his six-film association with Lean came to an inglorious end with his black-face turn as Godbole in *A Passage to India* (1984).

Though there is a steady trickle of international films, dating back to *The Swan* (1956), he remains an essentially British phenomenon. He continued to act almost until his death, submerging himself in an amazing array of characters. Despite being heaped with honours – CBE in 1955, knighthood in 1959, Companion of Honour in 1994, as well as numerous acting awards – he remained the most private of celebrities, keeping his real self for his real life. He married actress Merula Salaman in 1938 and their son **Matthew Guinness** (*b* 1940) had small roles in a number of films, first playing his father as a boy in *The Card*.

OTHER BRITISH FILMS: *A Run for Your Money* (1949), *The Mudlark*, *Last Holiday* (1950), *Malta Story* (1953), *Father Brown* (1954), *Barnacle Bill* (1957), *The Scapegoat*, *The Horse's Mouth* (1958), *Our Man in Havana* (1959), *HMS Defiant*, *Lawrence of Arabia* (1962), *Doctor Zhivago* (UK/US), *Hotel Paradiso* (UK/Fr) (1966), *Scrooge* (1970), *Brother Sun, Sister Moon* (1972, UK/It), *Hitler: The Last Ten Days* (1973, UK/It), *Little Lord Fauntleroy* (1980), *Little Dorrit* (1987), *A Foreign Field* (1993), *Mute Witness* (1995, UK/Russ, unc). BIBLIOG: Autobiographies, *Blessings in Disguise*, 1985; *My Name Escapes Me*, 1997; Kenneth von Gunden, *Alec Guinness: The Films*, 1987.

Guissart, René (*b* Nice, 1888 – *d* 1960). Cinematographer. Made his name in the US (1916–20), after working as a cameraman with the Eclair Company in Paris. Hired in the UK by Harley KNOLES, who brought him to ALLIANCE in 1920 as possibly the country's highest paid cameraman. After filming Alliance's *The Bohemian Girl* (1922), he worked with Graham CUTTS on *Flames of Passion* (1922) and *Paddy-the-Next-Best-Thing* (1923) and Herbert WILCOX on *Chu Chin Chow* (1923) and *Southern Love* (1924). He was always associated with major British silent films, often with American stars, but returned to the US in 1921, 1922, 1923, and 1924, and co-photographed *Ben-Hur* (1925). Between 1931 and 1932, Guissart photographed or

directed eight French- or Spanish-language features at Joinville, France, and in 1938 directed one British film, *Sweet Devil*, with Bobby HOWES.

OTHER BRITISH FILMS INCLUDE: *Land of Hope and Glory* (1927), *Tommy Atkins* (1928, co-c), *High Seas*, *The American Prisoner* (1929), *The Brat* (1930). AS.

Gunn, Gilbert (*b* Glasgow, *c* 1912). Director. Educated at Glasgow High School and University, Gunn worked in the 30s as playwright and stage producer, then as screenwriter at ASSOCIATED BRITISH. During WW2 and after, he directed over 50 short DOCUMENTARIES for, among others, the MOI and the Central Office of Information. Post-war he rejoined ABPC, as director and writer, his best-known film probably the good-natured services comedy *Operation Bullshine* (1959, + co-sc).

OTHER BRITISH FILMS INCLUDE: *Save a Little Sunshine* (1938, sc), *The Farmer's Wife* (1941, a); (d, unless noted) (doc, short) *Women Away from Home* (1942), *Canteen Command* (1943), *Tyneside Story* (1944), *Routine Job* (1946), *Beethoven or Boogie* (1949); (features, d, unless noted) *Landfall* (1949, co-sc), *Elstree Story* (1952, + p, sc), *The Valley of Song* (1953), *My Wife's Family* (1956, +sc), *The Strange World of Planet X*, *Girls at Sea* (1958), *What a Whopper!* (1961), *Wings of Mystery* (+ sc) (1963).

Gunning, Christopher (*b* Cheltenham, 1944). Composer. Most of Gunning's work has been for TV: he has been associated with adaptations of Agatha CHRISTIE and the lushly absurd *Reckless* (1997), and he shared a BAA for the scoring of the mini-series, *Middlemarch* (1994). His film scores have been an eclectic bunch, including the SPIN-OFFS from TV, *Ooh . . . You Are Awful* (1972) and *Man About the House* (1974), Lindsay ANDERSON's fine screen version of his stage success, *In Celebration* (1974, UK/Can), and an undervalued *film noir*, *Under Suspicion* (1991).

OTHER BRITISH FILMS INCLUDE: *Goodbye Gemini* (1970), *Nicholas and Alexandra* (UK/US, cond, addit m), *Hands of the Ripper* (1971), *When the Whales Came* (1989), *Firelight* (1997).

Gurney, Rachel (*b* Eton, 1927 – *d* Holt, Norfolk, 2001). Actress. Graceful star of stage and especially TV, where she famously played Lady Marjory Bellamy in *Upstairs, Downstairs* (1971) and was a finely ambiguous Madame Merle in *The Portrait of a Lady* (1968). Trained at Webber-Douglas and on the London stage from 1946, she made few films and usually in unworthy roles, starting with *Tom Brown's Schooldays* (1951).

OTHER BRITISH FILMS INCLUDE: *Room in the House* (1955), *A Touch of Larceny* (1959), *Funeral in Berlin* (1966), *I Want What I Want* (1971).

Guthridge, John Editor. Worked on roughly two major films per year from 1948, with the RANK ORGANISATION (TWO CITIES), to 1965, at the end of his career editing ten films for Basil DEARDEN, achieving some powerful effects of cutting in, for example, the court scenes of *Life for Ruth* (1962). Entered the film industry in Spain with MGM in the 30s and came to England in 1935, working uncredited on such films as *Fire Over England* (1937) and *Prison Without Bars* (1938), before WW2 service with the RAF and its Film Unit.

OTHER BRITISH FILMS INCLUDE: *Vice Versa* (1948), *Give Us This Day* (1949, UK/US), *The Woman in Question* (1950), *The Browning Version* (1951), *The Importance of Being Earnest* (1952), *The Seekers* (1954), *An Alligator Named Daisy* (1955), *Tiger in the Smoke* (1956), *Hell Drivers* (1957), *Innocent Sinners* (1958), *Sapphire* (1959), *The League of Gentlemen*, *Man in the Moon* (1960), *Victim*, *All Night Long* (1961), *The Mind Benders* (1963), *A Woman of Straw* (1964), *Masquerade* (1965).

Guthrie, Sir Tyrone (*b* Tunbridge Wells, 1900 – *d* Dublin, 1971). Actor. Celebrated man of the theatre, most famous as

Artistic Director of the Shakespearean Festival, Stratford, Ontario for many years, filming his production of *Oedipus Rex* (1955) in 1957. He appeared in two British films as actor: *Vessel of Wrath*, *Sidewalks of London* (1938). Knighted in 1961.

Gutowski, Gene (*b* Lodz, Poland, 1925). Producer. Having previously worked for American TV, Gutowski came to Britain in the late 50s. In the early 60s he was the manager of a German-financed production company, CCC-London, before forming Cadre Films, a production partnership with Roman POLANSKI. Also worked with another Polish exile director, Jerzy SKOLIMOWSKY.

BRITISH FILMS INCLUDE: *Station Six Sahara* (1962), *Vengeance* (1962), *Repulsion* (1965), *Cul-de-Sac* (1966), *The Fearless Vampire Killers* (1967), *Romance of a Horsethief* (1969), *The Adventures of Gerard*, *The Private Life of Sherlock Holmes* (1970). Tim Bergfelder.

Guyler, Deryck (*b* Wallasey, Cheshire, 1914 – *d* Brisbane, 1999). Actor. Comic supporting player with a background in radio, including Tommy HANDLEY's *ITMA*, which he joined in 1947. Became a popular TV character, especially as Potter, the grumpy school caretaker in *Please, Sir!* (1968–72), a role he repeated in the film SPIN-OFF (1971).

OTHER BRITISH FILMS INCLUDE: *Mad About Men* (1954), *The Fast Lady* (1962), *Nurse on Wheels* (1963), *A Hard Day's Night*, *Smokescreen* (1964), *Carry On Doctor* (1968), *No Sex, Please – We're British* (1973), *One of Our Dinosaurs is Missing* (1975).

Gwenn, Edmund (*b* Glamorgan, Wales, 1875 – *d* Los Angeles, 1959). Actor. Elfin-like quality coupled with a kind and under-standing voice made Gwenn a popular character actor both in Britain and the UK. He began making Hollywood films in the mid 30s – *Sylvia Scarlett* (1936) and more than 40 more – and reached the apex of his career there in 1947, playing Santa Claus in *Miracle on 34th Street*. Gwenn was thrown out of the family home when he declared his intention to be an actor, with his civil servant father calling him 'a rogue and a vagabond [who would] end in the gutter.' Stage debut 1895 led to Gwenn's becoming a favourite of George Bernard SHAW, who cast him in *Major Barbara* and several more plays, and insisted he be cast in the 1931 film, *How He Lied to Her Husband*. Starred on stage in the 1920 and 1929 productions of *The Skin Game*, and in the 1920 and 1931 film ADAPTATIONS. His British roles of the 30s (e.g. in *South Riding*, 1938) often have an edge blurred later in Hollywood. Died in the Motion Picture Country House, where ill health and financial problems took him in 1958.

OTHER BRITISH FILMS INCLUDE: *The Real Thing at Last* (1916), *Unmarried* (1920), *Hindle Wakes* (1931), *The Good Companions*, *I Was a Spy*, *Channel Crossing*, *Friday the Thirteenth* (1933), *Waltzes from Vienna*, *Java Head*, *Spring in the Air* (1934), *Laburnum Grove* (1936), *A Yank at Oxford* (1937), *An Englishman's Home* (1939). AS.

Gwillim, Jack (*b* Canterbury, 1909 – *d* Los Angeles, 2001). Actor. Tall, imposing and prolific character player, typically in military roles since his screen debut as Captain Parry in *The Battle of the River Plate* (1956), in which his naval bearing commanded respect. His *cv* is littered with admirals, air commodores, kings and brigadiers, both on screen and TV. Has also filmed in the US (e.g. *Blind Date*, 1987), and had a long stage career including Stratford and Old Vic seasons.

OTHER BRITISH FILMS INCLUDE: *The One That Got Away* (1957), *North West Frontier* (1959), *Sink the Bismarck!*, *Circus of Horrors* (1960), *The Inspector*, *Lawrence of Arabia* (1962), *Sammy Going South* (1963), *Thunderball* (1965), *A Man for All Seasons* (1966), *Battle of Britain* (1969), *Cromwell* (1970), *Clash of the Titans* (1981, UK/US).

Gwynn, Michael (*b* Bath, 1916 – *d* London, 1976). Actor. Character actor who made stage debut in 1938 and came to prominence in a Shaw season at the Arts Theatre, leading to role as Christopher ISHERWOOD in *I Am a Camera* (1954). On-screen has been featured in a number of major costume epics: Cimber in *Cleopatra* (1963, US), Hermes in *Jason and the Argonauts* (1963), and Cornelius in *The Fall of the Roman Empire* (1964, US). Also much TV work.

OTHER BRITISH FILMS INCLUDE: *The Secret Place* (1957), *The Revenge of Frankenstein*, *Dunkirk*, *The Doctor's Dilemma* (1958), *Village of the Damned* (1960), *What a Carve Up!* (1961), *Some People* (1962), *Catch Us If You Can* (1965), *The Virgin Soldiers* (1969), *Spy Story* (1976). AS.

Gynt, Greta (*b* Oslo, 1916 – *d* London, 2000). Actress. RN: Margarethe Woxholt. Slinky blonde Gynt (actually brunette) was just the ticket for austerity-ridden post-war Britain. She exuded a reckless sexuality and a glamorous, hedonistic bravura which were at the other end of the spectrum from, say, Celia JOHNSON's image of devotion to duty. She began dancing and acting in her native Norway, pushed by an ambitious mother, came to England when she was 19, and played in about a dozen films in the 30s, of which only *Dark Eyes of London*, with Bela LUGOSI, and *The Arsenal Stadium Mystery* (1939) are worth remembering.

She came into her own briefly in the 40s, with a surprisingly touching performance as Jewish Elsie Silver in *Mr Emmanuel* (1944), forceful as a loyal wife proving her husband's innocence in the excellent thriller, *Take My Life* (1947), a lushly promis-cuous murderess in *Dear Murderer* (1947), and a night club singer (she sings 'Shady Lady Spiv') in *Easy Money* (1948). She could do nothing with *London Town* (1946), nor could anyone else, was miscast as a boys' school matron in *Mr Perrin and Mr Traill* (1948), was absurdly misused by Hollywood in *Soldiers Three* (1951), and when she returned to Britain her career foundered on 'B' FILMS and television playlets, masquerading as films.

Her private life was always a boon to gossip writers: she married four times, first to agent Christopher MANN, and was said to be the mistress of producer Filippo DEL GIUDICE.

OTHER BRITISH FILMS INCLUDE: *It Happened in Paris* (1935, as Grete Woxholt), *Boys Will Be Girls* (1937), *The Second Best Bed* (1938), *Too Dangerous to Live*, *The Middle Watch* (1939), *Crooks' Tour*, *Bulldog Sees It Through* (1940), *The Common Touch* (1941), *Tomorrow We Live* (1942), *It's That Man Again* (1943), *The Calendar* (1948), *The Shadow of the Eagle*, *I'll Get You for This* (1950), *The Ringer* (1952), *The Last Moment*, *Forbidden Cargo* (1954), *The Blue Peter*, *See How They Run* (1955), *Fortune Is a Woman* (1957), *Bluebeard's Ten Honeymoons* (1960), *The Runaway* (1964).

gypsies In early cinema, gypsies were demonised as drunks, thieves and child-abusers, a threat to the stability of the bourgeois Edwardian family (*Rescued by Rover*, 1905). Later, in films such as *The Romany* (1923) and *Romany Love* (1931), they became romantic and exotic figures, a trend culminating in the gender-bending antics of the weird and wonderful *Wings of the Morning* (1937), the first British feature in TECHNICOLOR. Gypsies were more than just local colour in GAINSBOROUGH costume films such as *Caravan* (1946) and *Jassy* (1947), where they received sympathetic treatment, but by 1957, in Joseph LOSEY's *The Gypsy and the Gentleman*, Melina Mercouri was cast as a promiscuous, amoral social parasite. In 1971's *The Virgin and the Gypsy*, Franco NERO was a figure of romantic passion, but in Guy RITCHIE's caper film, *Snatch* (2000), Brad Pitt's rakish gypsy thief did little to redeem the image created in Losey's film. Pam Cook.

Hh

Haas, Dolly .(*b* 1910, Hamburg – *d* New York, 1994). Actress. Gamine star of German film comedies of the early 30s, Haas proved a remarkable tragedienne in the REMAKE of *Broken Blossoms* (1936), directed by her first husband, John BRAHM. From Britain she emigrated to America, where she worked almost exclusively in theatre, except for a notable supporting role in Alfred HITCHCOCK's *I Confess* (1953). She was one of the subjects of Rosa von Praunheim's documentary, *Dolly, Lotte and Maria* (1987, Ger).
OTHER BRITISH FILMS: *Girls Will Be Boys* (1934), *Spy Of Napoleon* (1936). Tim Bergfelder.

Habberfield, Mary Sound editor. Worked at Ealing from 1941 as dubbing editor on most of the company's films, though she was also assistant editor to Sidney COLE on *The Bells Go Down* (1943). Became sound editor for SHELL FILM UNIT, 1954.
OTHER BRITISH FILMS INCLUDE: *The Foreman Went to France* (1942), *San Demetrio–London* (1943), *For Those in Peril* (1944), *Johnny Frenchman, Dead of Night* (1945), *Hue and Cry* (1946), *The Loves of Joanna Godden, Against the Wind* (1947), *Mandy, I Believe in You* (1952), *The 'Maggie'* (1953), *The Colditz Story* (1954).

Hackney, Alan (*b* Manchester, 1924). Screenwriter. Comedy writer best known for his all-encompassing approach to satirical targets – corrupt bosses, skiving employees, sentimental communists, etc. – in the BOULTING brothers' *I'm All Right Jack* (1959). He also provided the story for the Boultings' *Private's Progress* (1956). Almost all his films are in comic mode, but *Jack* is probably the most fondly remembered; it is a long way downhill to *Double Take* (1972).
OTHER BRITISH FILMS INCLUDE: *Watch Your Stern, Two Way Stretch* (add dial) (1960), *You Must Be Joking!* (1965), *Decline and Fall . . .* (1968).

Hackney, Pearl (*b* Burton-upon-Trent, 1916) Actress. Supporting player of films, TV and radio, long married to actor Eric BARKER with whom she had played in radio serials such as *Merry-Go-Round*, before WW2. Small roles in films, including four for director Pete WALKER, starting with *Cool It Carol* (1970).
OTHER BRITISH FILMS INCLUDE: *Tiffany Jones* (1973), *Schizo* (1976), *Stand Up Virgin Soldiers* (1977), *Yanks* (1979), *The Ploughman's Lunch* (1983), *Laughterhouse* (1984).

Haddon, Peter (*b* Rawtenstall, 1898 – *d* London, 1962). Actor. RN: Peter Tidsley. Comedic supporting player and occasional leading man in films from 1934, often in aristocratic roles, (notably Lord Peter Wimsey in *The Silent Passenger* (1935). Very busy on stage (from 1920) as actor, producer and director, and in 50s long associated with weekly rep at the Wimbledon Theatre. Studied medicine at Cambridge.

OTHER BRITISH FILMS INCLUDE: *Lizzie's Last Leap* (1924), *Alf's Button, Greek Street* (1930), *Death at Broadcasting House* (1934), *No Monkey Business* (1935), *Over the Moon* (1939), *Helter Skelter* (1949), *The Second Mrs Tanqueray* (1952). AS.

Hafenrichter, Oswald (*b* Oplomitz, Yugoslavia 1899 – *d* London, 1973). Editor. A communist refugee from Nazi Germany, Hafenrichter edited DOCUMENTARY SHORTS for the MINISTRY OF INFORMATION during WW2. Later joined Alexander KORDA's LONDON FILMS, his most prestigious assignment being Carol REED's *The Third Man* (1949). In the 50s he followed a call from Alberto CAVALCANTI to Brazil, and contributed as an editor and scriptwriter to several productions, including the internationally acclaimed *O Cangaceiro* (1953). After his return to Britain, Hafenrichter worked on an eclectic range of films, including blockbusters such as *The Guns Of Navarone* (1961), and HAMMER HORRORS.
OTHER BRITISH FILMS INCLUDE: *An Ideal Husband* (1947), *The Fallen Idol* (1948), *The Happiest Days Of Your Life* (1950), *The Smallest Show On Earth* (1957), *Jet Storm* (1959), *Foxhole In Cairo* (1960), *Sparrows Can't Sing* (1962), *The Skull* (1965), *The Trygon Factor, The Deadly Bees* (1966), *Cry Of The Banshee* (1970), *The Vault Of Horror* (1973, UK/US). Tim Bergfelder.

Haffenden, Elizabeth (*b* Croydon, 1906 – *d* London, 1976). Costume designer. Although Haffenden, educated at Croydon School of Art, is best known for her flamboyant, stylish designs for 40s GAINSBOROUGH period romances such as *The Wicked Lady* (1945), she had an illustrious career in theatre and cinema spanning 40 years. After the demise of Gainsborough in 1949, as resident costume designer for MGM–BRITISH she worked on historical extravaganzas such as *Beau Brummell* (1954) and *The Adventures of Quentin Durward* (1955). From 1959 she worked freelance in association with her close friend Joan BRIDGE, and they won Oscars for *Ben-Hur* (1959, US) and *A Man for All Seasons* (1966). During the 60s and 70s Haffenden and Bridge worked on many box-office successes, including *The Prime of Miss Jean Brodie* (1968). She started pre-production work on *Julia* (1977), but died before production began.
OTHER BRITISH FILMS: *Wedding Group* (1936), *The Young Mr Pitt* (1942), *The Man in Grey* (1943), *Give Us the Moon, Madonna of the Seven Moons, Love Story, Fanny by Gaslight, Two Thousand Women* (1944), *A Place of One's Own, I'll Be Your Sweetheart* (1945), *Caravan, The Magic Bow, Bedelia* (Margaret Lockwood's dresses) (1946), *The Man Within, Uncle Silas, Jassy* (1947), *Call of the Blood* (1948, UK/It, Kay Hammond's costumes), *Bad Lord Byron, The Spider and the Fly* (Nadia Gray's costumes), *Christopher Columbus* (1949), *Portrait of Clare, So Long at the Fair* (dresses) (1950), *The Late Edwina Black* (1951), *The Story of Gilbert and Sullivan* (1953, co-cos), *Footsteps in the Fog, The Dark Avenger* (1955), *Moby Dick, The Barretts of Wimpole Street* (1956), *Heaven Knows, Mr Allison* (UK/US), *I Accuse!* (1957), *Kill or Cure*

(wardrobe), *Village of Daughters, I Thank a Fool* (1962); (with Joan Bridge) *The Amorous Adventures of Moll Flanders, The Liquidator* (1965), *Drop Dead Darling* (1966), *Half a Sixpence* (1967, UK/US), *Chitty Chitty Bang Bang* (1968), *Pope Joan* (1972), *The Day of the Jackal* (UK/Fr), *Luther* (UK/Can/US), *The Homecoming* (1973, UK/US), *Great Expectations, Conduct Unbecoming* (1975).

BIBLIOG: Pam Cook, *Fashioning the Nation: Costume and Identity in British Cinema*, 1996. Pam Cook.

Hagen, Julius (*b* Hamburg, 1884 – *d* London, 1940). Producer, studio head. Flamboyant and energetic figure in British cinema of the 20s and 30s, the innovative producer of bilingual pictures in the early 30s, and closely associated with TWICKENHAM STUDIOS, which he ran from 1927 to 1938. Hagen began his career in his father's cigar business, and was involved in theatrical production, before entering film industry with Ruffells', the rental firm, and later as UK manager for UNIVERSAL. In 1919, he co-founded the distributors W&F Film Service; in 1923, he became manager of the BRITISH AND COLONIAL Studios; in 1928 he founded STRAND FILM CO; and a year earlier, he formed W&P Film Company, setting up production at Twickenham. Here, Hagen specialised in 'QUOTA QUICKIES', but in 1935, he created JH Productions, to produce more lavish films, such as *Broken Blossoms* (bringing D.W. Griffith to the UK as would-be director), *Spy of Napoleon* (starring American Richard Barthelmess) and *Juggernaut* (with Boris KARLOFF) (all 1936). In late 1935, he bought Consolidated Studios at ELSTREE to augment his Twickenham resources. Sadly, in 1938, Hagen declared bankruptcy and died two years later, a broken man, with half-a-million pounds in debts.

OTHER BRITISH FILMS INCLUDE: *All the World's a Stage* (1917), *Paint and Passion, Love and Lobster* (1918), *The Fake* (1927), *To What Red Hell* (1929), *At the Villa Rose* (1930), *Alibi* (1931), *When London Sleeps, Hundred to One* (1932), *The Wandering Jew, The Ghost Camera* (1933), *Lord Edgware Dies, Lily of Killarney, The Lash* (1934), *Scrooge, Annie, Leave the Room!, The Last Journey* (1935), *Dusty Ermine* (1936), *Silver Blaze* (1937), *Make It Three* (1938), *The Face at the Window* (1939).

BIBLIOG: Linda Wood, 'Julius Hagen and Twickenham Film Studios', in *The Unknown 30s*, 1998.

Haggar, William (*b* London, 1851 – *d* Aberdare, Wales, 1924). Pioneer. Producing between 30 and 60 short subjects between 1902 and 1908, Haggar is the major Welsh film pioneer. A travelling fairground showman, he first screened films at Aberavon in 1898. Haggar's most important work is *The Life of Charles Peace*, shot in Pembroke in 1905, with son, Walter, as Peace; the film makes unusual use of cross-cutting, displays remarkable vitality, and features what was at the time considered a gruesome hanging. Haggar's other films, both comedies and dramas, include *Phantom Ride through Swansea* (1902), *A Desperate Poaching Affray* (1903), *The Salmon Poachers* (1905), *A Message from the Sea* (1905), and *The Maid of Cefn Ydfa* (1908). The last was remade by Haggar in 1914 featuring Will FYFFE in a supporting role. AS.

Haggard, Sir H(enry) Rider (*b* West Bradenham, 1856 – *d* London, 1925). Author. Adventure novelist whose novels *She* and *King Solomon's Mines* have been filmed numerous times. *She* was first filmed in silent days, with two British versions (1916, 1925), then famously in the US in 1935, with Helen Gahagan, and in Britain, with Ursula ANDRESS in the HAMMER version (1965), and its sequel, *The Vengeance of She* (1967). *King Solomon's Mines* filmed in Britain in 1937, starring Paul ROBESON and Cedric HARDWICKE, was given the lavish Technicolor and star treatment in the Hollywood MGM version of 1950, and became a US/South African co-production

in 1985. There have been other reworkings too of these imperial adventures. A diary 'discovered' in 2001 suggests that Haggard's views were less imperialist and more on the side of native land rights than would have been supposed.

BIBLIOG: Philip Leibfried, *Rudyard Kipling and Sir Henry Rider Haggard on Screen, Stage, Radio and Television*, 2000.

Haggard, Piers (*b* London, 1939). Director. Minor director of films whose work has been mainly for TV, including *Pennies from Heaven* (1978) and four episodes of *Quatermass* (1979), which, however, were edited to form a feature film, *The Quatermass Conclusion* (1978). Started in the theatre, working at the Royal Court and the National Theatres; TV from 1965. Son of Stephen HAGGARD.

OTHER BRITISH FILMS: (d, unless noted) *Blow-Up* (1966, a), *I Can't . . . I Can't* (1969, Ire), *Blood on Satan's Claw* (1971, + addit material), *Venom* (1981), *A Summer Story* (1987), *Conquest* (1998, UK/Can).

Haggard, Stephen (*b* Guatemala City, 1912 – *d* Middle East, 1943). Actor. Died in WW2 so sadly young that his career was barely under way, at least in films, but he was a vivid Nelson in *The Young Mr Pitt* (1942). Now most remembered for *The Craft of Comedy* (1944), co-authored with Athene SEYLER, with whose husband, Nicholas HANNEN he appeared in the Richard MASSINGHAM short *Fear and Peter Brown* (1940). Father of Piers HAGGARD.

OTHER BRITISH FILMS: *Whom the Gods Love* (1936), *Jamaica Inn* (1939).

Haig, David (*b* Aldershot, 1955) Actor. RN: David Haig Collum Ward. Short, dark, balding, and distinctive character player, who famously played Harold Nicolson in TV's *Portrait of a Marriage* (1990), Detective Inspector Grim in the spoof police series, *The Thin Blue Line* (1995), and a paedophile park-keeper in *Talking Heads 2* (1998). On-screen, he had a memorable role as the rapacious second groom in *Four Weddings and a Funeral* (1994). The Rugby-educated actor has also written two plays, and he starred brilliantly in Alan AYCKBOURN's *House* and *Garden* plays (2000).

OTHER BRITISH FILMS INCLUDES: *Dark Enemy* (1984), *Morons from Outer Space* (1985), *The Alamut Ambush* (1986).

Haigh, Kenneth (*b* Mexborough, 1930). Actor. Trained at Central School, Haigh originated the role of truculent Jimmy Porter in the London and Broadway productions of John OSBORNE's *Look Back in Anger* (1956, 1957). On Irish stage from 1952, London from 1954; played Mark Antony in *Julius Caesar* at Stratford (1963). The ANGRY YOUNG MAN persona he helped create was honed further in *My Teenage Daughter* (1956) and *High Flight* (1957), in the TV series, *Man at the Top* (1970–72), derived from John BRAINE's characters, and in the SPIN-OFF movie (1973). He also played two historical achievers: Napoleon in *Eagle in a Cage* (1970) and Richard Burton, the explorer, not the roisterer, in TV's *The Search for the Nile* (1971). Appeared in several US films, including *A Lovely Way to Die* (1968) and was made Hon. Professor, Yale Drama School.

OTHER BRITISH FILMS INCLUDE: *Saint Joan* (1957, UK/US), *A Hard Day's Night* (1964, unc), *The Deadly Affair* (1966), *Robin and Marian* (1976, UK/US), *The Bitch* (1979), *Wild Geese II* (1985), *Shuttlecock* (1991).

Haigh, Peter (*b* London, 1925 – *d* London, 2001). Presenter, actor. TV personality who appeared in a few films, including guest spots in *Band of Thieves* (1962) and *Live It Up* (1963), and played a magistrate in *Witchfinder General* (1968). Also narrated the animated feature, *The Commonwealth* (1962), but his real fame was as founder-presenter of TV's *Picture Parade* (1956–62), an early magazine programme, and as compère of several other popular shows of the 50s and 60s. Was married to Jill ADAMS (1957–64).

Halas and Batchelor and **Halas, John** *see* **Batchelor, Joy**

Haldane, Bert Director. A former associate of Fred KARNO, Haldane directed more than 300 films, primarily shorts, between 1910 and 1922. He was closely associated with producers Cecil HEPWORTH and W.G. BARKER, and co-directed *Jane Shore* (1915), a prominent epic of its day.

OTHER BRITISH FILMS INCLUDE: *The Road to Ruin* (1913, co-dir), *The Lure of London, The Lights o' London* (1914), *Tommy Atkins, Five Nights, Do unto Others, Brigadier Gerard, Jack Tar* (1915), *The Ticket-of-Leave Man* (1918), *The Romance of Lady Hamilton* (1919), *The Grip of Iron, Mary Latimer, Nun* (1920). AS.

Hale, Binnie (*b* Liverpool, 1899 – *d* Hastings, 1984). Actress. RN: Beatrice Mary Hale-Monro. Actress. Star of musical comedy and revue – stage debut 1916 – remembered with affection for starring roles in *No, No, Nanette* (1925) and *Sunny* (1926), and often featured opposite Bobby HOWES. With the exception of *Hyde Park Corner* (1935), films gave her little opportunity to sing effectively. Sister of Sonnie HALE; married Jack RAINE, mother of Patricia RAINE.

OTHER BRITISH FILMS INCLUDE: *On with the Dance* (1927), *This Is the Life* (1933), *The Phantom Light* (1935), *Take a Chance, Love from a Stranger* (1937). AS.

Hale, Georgina (*b* Ilford, 1943). Actress. Is she essentially an over-the-top performer or has she just coincidentally attracted a run of flamboyant roles, several of them, unsurprisingly, for Ken RUSSELL? Not for nothing was she cast to play the Bette DAVIS character as a young woman in *The Watcher in the Woods* (1982). In 1966 entered TV where she played the wife of small-time loser *Budgie* (1971–72), and, in 1969, films.

OTHER BRITISH FILMS INCLUDE: *Eagle in a Cage* (1970), *The Boy Friend, The Devils* (1971), *Butley* (1973, UK//Can/US), *Mahler* (1974, as Alma Mahler), *Lisztomania* (1975), *Voyage of the Damned* (1976), *Valentino* (1977), *McVicar* (1980), *Castaway* (1986), *Preaching to the Perverted* (1997).

Hale, Sonnie (*b* London, 1902 – *d* London, 1959). Actor, director, screenwriter. RN: Robert Hale-Monro. There must have been something more to Hale than meets the eye to have had two of the most famous stars of the day fighting over him. He married first Evelyn LAYE, then, an acrimonious divorce case later, Jessie MATTHEWS. On the face of it, he was a mildly talented actor and singer whose film career went sharply down hill after the 30s. At his peak, he co-starred with Matthews in *Evergreen* (1934), *It's Love Again* and *First A Girl* (1935), and directed her in *Gangway, Head Over Heels* (1937) and *Sailing Along* (1938, + sc); even at his peak there was something dislikeable about his persona. Post-war, he appeared only in the disastrous *London Town* (1946), though he continued on stage (debut 1921) until the mid 50s.

OTHER BRITISH FILMS INCLUDE: *Tell Me Tonight* (1932), *Friday the Thirteenth* (1933), *Wild Boy, My Song for You* (1934), *Marry the Girl* (1935), *Let's Be Famous* (1939), *Fiddlers Three* (1944).

Hall, Adelaide (*b* New York, 1901 – *d* London, 1993). Singer. American-born jazz singer sadly under-used in films. In Britain from 1938 she became a popular all-round entertainer. Sang 'Be Still, My Heart' in *The Thief of Baghdad* (1940) but, apart from a couple of Pathé newsreels and the documentary *Sophisticated Lady* (1989), her only other screen appearance – in *Night and the City* (1950) – was cut.

BIBLIOG: Stephen Bourne, *Sophisticated Lady – A Celebration of Adelaide Hall*, 2001. Stephen Bourne.

Hall, Cameron (*b* Hull, 1897 – *d* Sidmouth, 1983). Actor. Sturdy small-part actor with a long stage background in the US (his first film, *Adventure's End*, 1933, was made there) and Britain, and much TV since the 40s (*Morning Departure*, 1946). In over 30 films, he could be briefly memorable as, for example, the drunk singing 'Bless 'em All' while being booked by Anthony STEEL in *The Blue Lamp* (1949) or the café owner demanding his 'cut' from a robbery in *Impulse* (1955). Starred in film series *At Home with the Hardwickes* (1952).

OTHER BRITISH FILMS INCLUDE: *Yes Madam?* (1938), *Neutral Port* (1940), *Spellbound, South American George* (1941), *Mr Emmanuel* (1944), *Beware of Pity* (1946), *My Brother Jonathan* (1948), *Madeleine* (1949), *Once a Sinner* (1950), *Cosh Boy* (1953), *Footsteps in the Fog* (1955), *Blood of the Vampire* (1958), *Saturday Night and Sunday Morning* (1960), *Rotten to the Core* (1965).

Hall, Harvey Actor. RN: Hallsmith. Strong-jawed, sandy-haired purveyor of both villainy and authority in about 15 films, including the lecherous butler in *The Vampire Lovers* (1970) and a military policeman in *Up the Front* (1972). Also TV work in such series as *The Persuaders!* (1971). Left acting in 1974 to become a schoolmaster.

OTHER BRITISH FILMS INCLUDE: *The Mouse on the Moon* (1963), *Zulu* (1964), *Lust for a Vampire* (1970), *Twins of Evil* (1971), *The Sex Thief* (1973).

Hall, Lee (*b* Newcastle-upon-Tyne, 1966). Screenwriter. Came to attention with his moving 1997 radio play, *Spoonface Steinberg*, filmed the following year by director Betsan Morris EVANS, and in 2000 shared in the plaudits for *Billy Elliot* with a screenplay whose toughness kept the feelgood factor under control. His second screenplay, *Gabriel & Me* (2001) combines some of the motifs of both – a determined child and an imminent family death.

Hall, Sir Peter (*b* Bury St Edmunds, 1930). Director. Dominant figure in British theatre in second half of the 20th century, educated at Perse School and Cambridge University, Hall has had a fitful screen career, directing a half-dozen films of more or less coterie appeal in over 30 years. His major interests fairly clearly lie in the theatre: he began professional directing in 1953; had many seasons at Stratford, creating the RSC as a permanent ensemble; directed numerous plays classical and new, as well as opera; succeeded Laurence OLIVIER as Director of the National Theatre; formed his own theatre company in the 90s; and in 1996 became artistic director at London's Old Vic theatre. Films include: a version of his stage production of *A Midsummer Night's Dream* (1968); a drama of sexual tensions, *Three into Two Won't Go* (1968); the chronicle of village life, *Akenfield* (1974); and, made for TV but also shown in cinemas, *She's Been Away* (1989), starring Peggy ASHCROFT. Acted in *The Pedestrian* (1974, Ger/Switz). His other TV work includes *The Wars of the Roses* (1964) and *The Camomile Lawn* (1992), with a cast of stars-in-the-making. Heaped with honours, he was made CBE in 1963 and knighted in 1977. First wife was Leslie CARON (1956–65).

OTHER BRITISH FILMS: *Work Is a Four Letter Word* (1967), *Perfect Friday* (1970), *The Homecoming* (1973, UK/US).

BIBLIOG: *Peter Hall's Diaries*, 1983; Autobiography, *Making an Exhibition of Myself*, 1993; Stephen Fay, *Power Play*, 1995.

Hall, Willis (*b* Leeds, 1929). Screenwriter. Willis had an out-standing ear for the cadences and patter of working-class and regional speech as revealed in the play which established his name, *The Long and the Short and the Tall* (1959, filmed 1960) and was an influential figure in 60s theatre and film. Enjoyed a prolific screenwriting association with Keith WATERHOUSE through the 60s, including *Billy Liar* (1963, BAAn/sc, from their 1959 play; later a TV series, 1973–74) before migrating to TV work (e.g. *Queenie's Castle*, 1970–72; *Budgie*, 1971–72) and children's fiction. Married (1) Jill BENNETT.

OTHER BRITISH FILMS: (all co-sc, with Waterhouse) *Whistle Down the Wind* (1961, BAAn/sc), *The Valiant* (1961), *A Kind of Loving* (1962, BAAn/sc), *West 11* (1963), *Man in the Middle*, 1963, *Pretty Polly*, 1967, *Lock Up Your Daughters!* (1969). Kevin Foster.

Hallard, C(harles) M(aitland) (*b* Edinburgh, 1865 – *d* Farnham, 1942). Actor. Leading man of silent films, whose first 11 features were for G.B. SAMUELSON, and who played character roles in talkies, usually members of the landed classes, and even Winston CHURCHILL in *Royal Cavalcade* (1935). Stage debut with Frank Benson in 1889, and star of two J.M. BARRIE plays, *The Little Minister* (1897) and *What Every Woman Knows* (1909).

OTHER BRITISH FILMS INCLUDE: *The Elder Miss Blossom* (1918), *Convict 99*, *The Bridal Chair* (1919), *The Husband Hunter* (1920), *The Pauper Millionaire* (1922), *Carry On!* (1927), *Tell England* (1931), *On Secret Service* (1933), *Night Mail*, *Moscow Nights* (1935), *King of the Damned* (1936), *The Sky's the Limit* (1937). AS.

Hallatt, May (aka Hallett) (*b* Scarborough, 1876 – *d* London, 1969). Actress. Eccentric-looking player of eccentric characters, best remembered as the aged retainer of the palace-turned-nunnery in *Black Narcissus* (1947), as the spinster racing fan in *Separate Tables* (1958, US), recreating her stage role, and as a batty author of penny-dreadfuls in *The Gold Express* (1955). On stage from 1896, she made about 20 films. Mother of actor Neil HALLATT.

OTHER BRITISH FILMS INCLUDE: *Eyes of Fate* (1933), *The Dark Eyes of London*, *The Lambeth Walk* (1939), *Painted Boats* (1945), *The Spider and the Fly* (1949), *The Pickwick Papers* (1952), *Grand National Night* (1953), *Room at the Top* (1958), *Make Mine Mink* (1960), *Bitter Harvest* (1963).

Hallatt, Neil (aka Hallett) Actor. Son of May HALLATT, a supporting actor playing policemen and officers from the mid 50s, in a mixture of 'A' and 'B' FILMS and some lamentably limp sex romps of the 70s, including the suavely-titled *Can You Keep It Up for a Week?* (1974). Well, actors have to eat. Also appeared in some popular TV, such as *Ghost Squad* (1961–64) and *The Informer* (1966–67).

OTHER BRITISH FILMS INCLUDE: *Three Steps in the Dark* (1953), *X The Unknown* (1956), *Model for Murder* (1959), *Transatlantic* (1960), *Rotten to the Core* (1965), *SWALK* (1970), *Keep It Up Downstairs* (1976), *The Four Feathers* (1978), *4D Special Agents* (1981).

Hall-Davis, Lilian (*b* London, 1901 – *d* London, 1933). Actress. 'An actress of hard efficiency and no charm,' wrote CLOSE UP, 'she cannot help failing to appeal to you, to me, and it is to her credit that she is efficient.' It seems a harsh indictment of a blonde beauty who never failed to give her best often in films unworthy of anyone's talent. Depressed at lack of work, Hall-Davis committed suicide in 1933; actress Joan MORGAN used her life and death as the subject for her first novel, *Camera* (1940).

BRITISH FILMS INCLUDE: *The Admirable Crichton* (1918), *The Honeypot* (1920), *Love Maggie* (1921), *The Faithful Heart* (1922), *A Royal Divorce* (1923), *I Pagliacci* (1923), *Roses of Picardy*, *The Ring* (1927), *The Farmer's Wife* (1928), *Many Waters* (1931). AS.

Halstan, Margaret (*b* London, 1879 – *d* Hornchurch, 1967). Actress. In later years a majestic character player (literally so as the Queen of Transylvania in the original Drury Lane *My Fair Lady*, 1958) in such films as *The Holly and the Ivy* (1952), very grand and strange as Aunt Lydia. Often imbued her upper-class roles with a nice sense of their absurdities. Her stage career, begun in 1895, embracing SHAKESPEARE, SHAW, BARRIE etc, occupies four columns in *Who's Who in the Theatre* (1957). Hers is the first signature (as Examiner) on Laurence OLIVIER's 'Dramatic Certificate' from Central School. Made *Protect Your Daughters* in Hollywood in 1933.

OTHER BRITISH FILMS INCLUDE: *Profit and the Loss* (1917), *Tell Your Children* (1922), *The Middle Watch* (1930), *Drake of England* (1935), *Old Mother Riley in Society* (as Duchess) (1940), *Quiet Wedding* (1941), *Touch and Go* (1955), *The Feminine Touch* (1956).

Hambling, Arthur (*b* Reading, 1888 – *d* Surrey, 1952). Actor. On stage from 1912 and in 40-odd films from the early 30s to the early 50s, often playing authority figures, including policemen, like the Detective-Sergeant in *The Gaunt Stranger* (1938) and Colonel Tremaine in *Derby Day* (1952). However, he also played a railway porter (*Don't Take It to Heart!* (1944) and a barman (*It's Not Cricket*, 1949). Some sources suggest he began in silent films.

OTHER BRITISH FILMS INCLUDE: *Thread o' Scarlet* (1930), *A Night in Montmartre* (1931), *Lorna Doone* (1934), *The Scarlet Pimpernel*, *Midshipman Easy* (1935), *A Romance in Flanders* (1937), *At the Villa Rose* (1939), *The Common Touch*, *Pimpernel Smith* (1941), *They Flew Alone* (1942), *Henry V*, *Demobbed* (1944), *Johnny Frenchman* (1945), *Odd Man Out*, *It Always Rains on Sunday*, *Daughter of Darkness* (1947), *Train of Events* (1949), *The Lavender Hill Mob* (1951), *Time Bomb* (1953).

Hambling, Gerry (*b* Surrey, 1926). Editor. Former sound editor who, after apprenticeship in conventional 50s British cinema, has worked many times with Alan PARKER, and received AAn for his work on Parker's *Midnight Express* (1978), *Fame* (1980, US), *Mississippi Burning* (1988, US), *The Commitments* (1991, UK/US) and *Evita* (1996, UK/US), and Jim SHERIDAN's *In the Name of the Father* (1993, UK/Ire/US). He, at least, recovered from the GOLDCREST disaster, *Absolute Beginners* (1986).

OTHER BRITISH FILMS INCLUDE: (dubbing/sd e) *The Beggar's Opera* (1953), *The Servant* (1963), *Wuthering Heights* (1970, co-); (e, shorts) *Our School* (1962, co-e), *The Chairman's Wife* (1971), *Footsteps* (1974); (e, features) *Trent's Last Case* (1952, ass), *Dry Rot* (1956), *The Whole Truth* (1958), *Left, Right and Centre* (1959, co-e), *The Bulldog Breed* (1960), *The Kitchen* (1961), *The Early Bird* (1965), *That Riviera Touch*, *The Magnificent Two* (1967), *Bugsy Malone* (1976), *Pink Floyd The Wall* (1982), *Another Country* (1984), *City of Joy* (1992, UK/Fr), *The Boxer* (1998, co-e, UK/Ire/US), *Angela's Ashes* (1999, UK/US).

Hamer, Robert (*b* Kidderminster, 1911 – *d* London, 1963). Director. Hamer destroyed himself with drink, as everyone knows, driven by demons which may have included closeted homosexuality; sad for him, but, for us, the Cambridge-educated EALING alumnus was responsible for some of the most vivid achievements of 40s British cinema. He began in the cutting room at DENHAM in 1938, as editor on such films as *Vessel of Wrath* (1938), before fetching up in 1940 at Ealing, where he edited several films before beginning his illustrious career as director. In the interim, he worked on DOCU-MENTARIES for the GPO FILM UNIT.

After uncredited co-directorial work on *Fiddlers Three* and *San Demetrio–London* (+ assoc p) (1943), he directed the 'Haunted Mirror' sequence in the famous PORTMANTEAU thriller, *Dead of Night* (1945), and followed this with the stylish

MELODRAMA, *Pink String and Sealing Wax* (1945) and the REALISM of *It Always Rains on Sunday* (1947), both starring the great Googie WITHERS, who valued him above her other directors. His masterpiece was *Kind Hearts and Coronets* (1949), to this day perhaps the wittiest and most impassioned black COMEDY in British cinema. Away from Ealing he faltered, though *The Spider and the Fly* (1949) is an elegant and feeling THRILLER. Many other directors could have done as well or better with the froth of *To Paris with Love* (1954); *The Scapegoat* (1958) is a turgid adaptation of Daphne DU MAURIER; and, despite his having the credit, *School for Scoundrels* (1959) seems to have been only partly his work.

The son of actor **Gerald Hamer** (*b* 1886 – *d* 1972), mostly in British-set Hollywood films, he lived with Herbert WILCOX's daughter, Pamela, who, without naming him except as 'Robert', has given a moving account of his descent into early death in *Between Hell and Charing Cross* (1977).

OTHER BRITISH FILMS: (e) *St Martin's Lane* (1938, co-e), *Jamaica Inn* (1939), *La Cause Commune, French Communiqué* (1940, doc, + sc), *Mastery at Sea* (+ sc), *Turned Out Nice Again* (e, unc), *Ships With Wings* (1941), *The Foreman Went to France* (1942), *My Learned Friend* (1943); (d) *The Loves of Joanna Godden* (1947, co-d, unc), *His Excellency* (1951), *The Long Memory* (1952), *Father Brown* (1954), *Bernard Shaw* (1957, d, short). BIBLIOG: 'Robert Hamer' in Charles Drazin, *The Finest Years: British Cinema of the 1940s*, 1998.

Hamilton, Guy (*b* Paris, 1922). Director. Educated at Haileybury, Hamilton began his career in 1939 as an apprentice at Victorine Studios, Nice. Came to Britain in 1940, worked with British–Paramount News, and served with the Navy during WW2. In the post-war years, he became the most sought-after assistant director in British films, his reputation based on his work with such directors as Carol REED (on *The Fallen Idol*, 1948; *The Third Man*, 1949) and John HUSTON (on *The African Queen*, 1951). When he began to direct his own films, he proved a very proficient craftsman, with at times an urbane approach to GENRE material.

Reed advised him to begin with a thriller and the result was *The Ringer* (1952), a briskly entertaining version of Edgar WALLACE, and the films that followed showed a flair for economical storytelling and are all strongly cast. *The Intruder* (1953) is an undervalued drama of post-war malaise; *An Inspector Calls* (1954) is PRIESTLEY's morality play given cinematic force with a finely ambiguous leading role from Alastair SIM; *The Colditz Story* (1954) is one of the most popular and intelligent of the 50s POW films; *Manuela* (1957) is a love story with an erotic tension then rare in British films; and *A Touch of Larceny* (1959) is a witty romantic comedy with Cold War touches. The international phase of his career includes piloting four BOND japes (starting with *Goldfinger*, 1964) to box-office success and a couple of all-star Agatha CHRISTIE THRILLERS, but the essentially *British* achievements of the 50s are perhaps his most distinctive achievement. Married actress KERIMA, star of *Outcast of the Islands* (1951) on which Hamilton was assistant director.

OTHER BRITISH FILMS: (ass d, include) *They Made Me a Fugitive* (1947), *Anna Karenina* (1948), *State Secret* (1950); (d, complete) *Charley Moon* (1956), *The Devil's Disciple* (1959), *The Party's Over, Man in the Middle* (1963), *Funeral in Berlin* (1966), *Battle of Britain* (1969), *Diamonds Are Forever* (1971), *Live and Let Die* (1973), *The Man with the Golden Gun* (1974), *The Spy Who Loved Me* (1977, unc pre-production), *Force 10 from Navarone* (1978), *The Mirror Crack'd* (1980), *Evil Under the Sun* (1981).

Hamilton, Patrick (*b* Hassocks, 1904 – *d* 1962). Author, dramatist. Former actor, on stage from 1921, he is the author of

Gas Light (1938), filmed as *Gaslight* in Britain in 1940, to superbly sinister effect, and much more elaborately in Hollywood in 1944. His novel *Hangover Square* was filmed in Hollywood in 1945 and his play *Rope* (1929) by HITCHCOCK (1948, US). He wrote the screenplay for the cautionary drink-driving tale, *To the Public Danger* (1948, + radio play).

Hamilton, Suzanna (*b* London, 1960). Actress. In films from childhood (*Swallows and Amazons*, 1974), Hamilton had good parts in two 1980s films: as the crippled daughter who is raped in *Brimstone & Treacle* (1982), from Dennis POTTER's play, and as Julia in *Nineteen Eighty-Four* (1984). However, neither film was popular, and she spent most of the rest of her career in TV. Central School-trained, she also had stage experience.

OTHER BRITISH FILMS INCLUDE: *Tess* (1979, UK/Fr), *The Wildcats of St Trinian's* (1980), *Wetherby* (1985), *Tales of a Vampire* (1992).

Hamlett, Dilys (*b* Tidworth, 1928 – *d* Cupar, Scotland, 2002). Actress. Former secretary who trained at the Old Vic School, first appearing on the London stage in 1952; played Ophelia at Stratford in 1956 and won praise as wife to *Brand* in 1959. Filmed sporadically (first, *Mix Me a Person*, 1962) and was in some popular TV series, such as 'Miss Marple' (*The Moving Finger*, 1985). Married/divorced director Caspar WREDE in whose *The Barber of Stamford Hill* (1962) she acted.

OTHER BRITISH FILMS INCLUDE: *Assault* (1970), *What Changed Charley Farthing?* (1974), *Hollow Reed* (1996, UK/Ger).

Hamley-Clifford, Molly (*b* Exeter,1887 – *d* London, 1956). Actress. Supporting player of stage and screen, in a few silent films and then in 20 talkies, in which she slid up and down the social scale (from landlady in *What a Night!*, 1931, to Baroness Hekla in *Contraband*, 1940). William (later James) FOX has a run-in with her in her formidable mode in *The Magnet* (1950).

OTHER BRITISH FILMS INCLUDE: *Milestones* (1916), *Spinner o' Dreams* (1918), *Temptation* (1935), *Mademoiselle Docteur* (1937), *Easy Riches* (1938), *Dark Secret* (1949), *Street of Shadows, Meet Mr Lucifer* (1953).

Hamm, Nick Director. Won a BAA for Best Short Film with *The Harmfulness of Tobacco* (1991) and has presented Rik MAYALL shows, but big-screen success has been elusive: his romantic comedy, *Martha, Meet Frank, Daniel and Laurence* (1998), presumably aimed at *Four Weddings and a Funeral* (1994) audiences, was a charmless flop. In 2001, he directed *American Beauty* star, Thora Birch, in the much more impressive suspense thriller, *The Hole* (UK/Fr).

OTHER BRITISH FILM: *Out of the Blue* (1991), *Deed Poll* (2002, short, co-d).

Hammer Films Ltd Without doubt the most important Gothic HORROR film studio of the 50s and 60s on an international scale, and the most financially successful independent film studio in British cinema history, Hammer Films was founded in 1934 by William Hinds, a jeweller who sometimes performed as a comedian in MUSIC HALL under the stage name **Will Hammer** (*b* London, 1887 – *d* Guildford, 1957, in a freak cycling accident). The company's first film was *The Public Life of Henry the Ninth* (1935), a parody of Alexander Korda's *The Private Life of Henry VIII* (1933), a modest programme picture, in which both Hammer and his partner George MOZARD appeared. Other early Hammer releases included *The Mystery of the Marie Celeste* (1935), with Bela Lugosi, and *Song of Freedom* (1936) with Paul ROBESON. In 1937, Hammer formed a partnership with distributor Enrique Carreras, whose company, EXCLUSIVE FILMS, began to release Hammer's output, concentrating on reissues of earlier product until 1948. In that year, Hammer/Exclusive produced *River Patrol* (1948), *Dick Barton, Special Agent* (1948), and other modest programme films. All were commercially successful, and Hammer Films Ltd was officially incorporated in 1949, with William Hinds, his son Anthony HINDS, Enrique Carreras, and his son James CARRERAS as sole partners. The first studios were located in a manor house named Dial Close at Cookham Dene, Berkshire. Hammer immediately began churning out a large number of films, most of them police THRILLERS and MYSTERIES. About this time, director Terence FISHER became associated with the company, and future screenwriter Jimmy SANGSTER signed on as an assistant director. In 1950, Hammer moved studios to a manor house in BRAY, but production continued much as before, with modest programme THRILLERS dominating the company's output.

In 1956, Hammer secured the rights to a BBC SCIENCE-FICTION radio serial, which led to the production of *X the Unknown* (1956), a rather graphic (for the period) science-fiction thriller. Box-office response to this was so pronounced that Hammer commissioned a survey to find out precisely what had enticed so many viewers to the cinema: was it the science-fiction angle, or the horror and violence? 'Horror and violence' was the overwhelming verdict, and Hammer launched into their first colour production, *The Curse of Frankenstein*, in 1956, which established the studio as a worldwide phenomenon for years ahead. The film truly launched the career of director Fisher, who, working with cameraman Freddie FRANCIS, became Hammer's most prolific director; the film's stars, Peter CUSHING and Christopher LEE, became the most famous horror film stars since Boris KARLOFF and Bela Lugosi. Shot in lurid colour by the brilliant cameraman Jack ASHER, with a screenplay from first-time scenarist Sangster, superb period sets by the gifted Bernard ROBINSON, and a haunting music score by James BERNARD, *The Curse of Frankenstein* shattered box-office records internationally.

Hammer immediately began turning out a torrent of stylish horror films, including *Dracula* (1958), *The Mummy* (1959), *The Brides of Dracula* (1960), *The Curse of the Werewolf* (1961), *The Gorgon* (1964), *Dracula – Prince of Darkness* (1965), and *The Devil Rides Out* (1967), all directed by Fisher; and *Paranoiac* (1962), *Nightmare* (1963), *The Evil of Frankenstein* (1964), *Hysteria* (1964), and *Dracula Has Risen From the Grave* (1968), all directed by Francis. Other directors who also worked for Hammer as Gothic specialists included Roy Ward BAKER, John GILLING, and even Joseph LOSEY, whose brilliant *The Damned* (1961) was initially shelved by Hammer as being 'too experimental' before being released. However, by the early 70s, when Fisher directed his last Hammer film, *Frankenstein and the Monster From Hell* (1973), Hammer had moved from Bray, and much of the flavour and atmosphere that made its early films so memorable was irrevocably lost. Changing standards and styles, too, took their toll: George Romero's *Night of the Living Dead* (1968) introduced a new level of graphic violence to the screen, to which Hammer responded with increased doses of nudity and violence (in such films as Sangster's regrettable *Lust for a Vampire*, 1971), but it was too little, too late. Hammer's last film was Peter SYKES's *To the Devil a Daughter* (1976, UK/Ger), a disappointing conclusion to the career of a studio that redefined the modern horror film. However, Hammer's overall reputation remains untarnished, and the studio's films influenced an entire new generation of film-makers, and viewers.

BIBLIOG: David Pirie, *A Heritage of Horror: The English Gothic Cinema*, 1973; Denis Meikle, *A History of Horrors: The Rise and Fall of the House of Hammer*, 1986; Peter Hutchings, *Hammer and Beyond: The British Horror Film*, 1993. Wheeler Winston Dixon.

Hammer, Will *see* **Hammer Films Ltd**

Hammond, Kay (*b* London, 1909 – *d* Brighton, 1980). Actress. RN: Dorothy Standing. Very popular, blondely glamorous stage star with distinctive, seductive voice, Hammond studied at RADA and made her London debut in 1927, scoring major successes in the original productions of *French Without Tears* (1936–38) and *Blithe Spirit* (1941–44). She repeated her role of the malicious ghost Elvira in the film of *Blithe Spirit* (1946), but though she appeared in about 25 films, including several early US talkies (D.W. Griffith's *Abraham Lincoln*, 1930, for one), she never became a major film star. She was the daughter of stage actor **Sir Guy Standing** (*b* London, 1873 – *d* Hollywood Hills, California, 1937) who filmed in Hollywood, notably in *The Lives of a Bengal Lancer* (1935), and was the mother of actor John STANDING, son of her first marriage to Sir Ronald Leon, Bt. Her second husband was actor Sir John CLEMENTS, with whom she often appeared on stage, as in the 'Grecian' romp, *The Rape of the Belt* (1958).
OTHER BRITISH FILMS INCLUDE: *Children of Chance* (1930), *Carnival* (1931), *Britannia of Billingsgate, Bitter Sweet* (1933), *Jeannie* (1941), *Call of the Blood* (1948), *Five Golden Hours* (1961, UK/It).

Hammond, Peter (*b* London, 1923). Actor, director. RN: Hill. Just when it seemed that perennial cheery teenager Hammond would have to grow up on screen, he reinvented himself as a successful director of TV series and plays, including *The White Rabbit* (1967) and *The Return of Sherlock Holmes* (1986, 1988). Educated at Harrow Art School, he had some stage experience before entering films in *They Knew Mr Knight* (1945), and had a continuing role as Petula CLARK's daft boyfriend in the HUGGETT films, having played a Huggett *son* in *Holiday Camp* (1947), and was an even dafter boyfriend called Pieface in *Fly Away Peter* (1948) and *Come Back Peter* (1952). Also directed the Lancashire-set comedy, *Spring and Port Wine* (1969). Married to former actress, Maureen GLYNNE. (Not to be confused with Peter Hammond, publicist for Rank, etc.)
OTHER BRITISH FILMS INCLUDE: (a) *Here Come the Huggetts, Vote for Huggett* (1948), *The Huggetts Abroad* (1949), *Morning Departure, The Adventurers* (1950), *Father's Doing Fine* (1952), *Confession* (1955), *X the Unknown, It's Never Too Late* (1956), *Model for Murder* (1959).

Hammond, Roger (*b* 1936). Actor. Supporting actor of films and TV since the mid 60s, graduating from, say, one of Sandy Dennis's raffish friends in *A Touch of Love* (1969) to jovial Mr Musgrove in *Persuasion* (1995, TV, some cinemas) and Sir Roysten in TV's *Drop the Dead Donkey* (1990–98).
OTHER BRITISH FILMS INCLUDE: *Lock Up Your Daughters!* (1969), *Private Road* (1971), *Royal Flash* (1975), *Little Dorrit* (1987), *Madame Sousatzka* (1988), *Orlando* (1992, UK/Fr/It/Neth/Russ), *The Madness of King George* (1994, UK/US), *Richard III* (1995), *The Clandestine Marriage* (1999), *Redemption Road* (2001).

Hampshire, Susan (*b* London, 1942). Actress. Spotted on a train by someone casting the role of Jean SIMMONS as a child in *The Woman in the Hall* (1947), she was tested and cast. Smitten with the acting bug, she finished her education and went into the theatre, making her debut in *Expresso Bongo* (1958), repeating her role as a twittering deb in the 1959 film version. She had the female leads in the Cliff RICHARD musical, *Wonderful Life*, and

Karel REISZ's updating of *Night Must Fall* (1964), and was taken up by the DISNEY Organisation for *The Three Lives of Thomasina* (1963), which cast her as a witch, and *The Fighting Prince of Donegal* (1966). Though exceptionally pretty and charming, she was, in her own 1994 words, 'not easily accepted because of her middle-class background' at a time when a rougher, more northern persona would have served her better.

Though she found her film career 'disappointing', there is no doubt that she triumphed on TV, from *The Andromeda Breakthrough* (1962) on, and is now identified with a string of classic serials. Won Emmy Awards for the determined Fleur Forsyte in *The Forsyte Saga* (1967), which set a kind of benchmark for the genre, for manipulative Sarah in *The First Churchills* (1969), and for ambitious Becky Sharp in *Vanity Fair* (1971), perhaps surpassing them all as Glencora, growing from heedless youth to tender age in *The Pallisers* (1974). Certainly, these gave her chances beyond any in film, and the beauty and charm were revealed intact, along with touches of mature wit, in the Scottish-set mini-series, *Monarch of the Glen* (1999, 2000).

She wrote a memoir *Susan's Story* (1981), chronicling her struggles with dyslexia and received an OBE in 1995 for her work in this cause. Married (1) director Pierre Granier-Deferre (their son is assistant director **Christopher Granier-Deferre**, *b* 1970, whose films include *The Golden Bowl*, 2000, UK/Fr/US), and (2) Sir Eddie Kulukundis, who contributed to National Film Archive restorations.

OTHER BRITISH FILMS INCLUDE: *David Copperfield, The Trygon Factor* (1966), *Monte Carlo or Bust!* (1969, UK/Fr/It), *A Time for Loving* (1971), *Living Free, Baffled!* (1972).

Hampton, Christopher (*b* Fayal, Azores, 1946). Dramatist, screenwriter, director. In the news in the late 90s as translator of Yasmina Reza's plays, *Art* (1996) and *Conversations after a Burial* (2000), Hampton had his own considerable theatrical reputation for plays such as *The Philanthropist* (1970), *Tales from Hollywood* (1983–84, at London's National Theatre) and his version of *Dangerous Liaisons*, filmed in 1988 (US), won Adapted Screenplay AA and BAA. His first screenplay was for the Claire BLOOM version of *The Doll's House* (1973) and he has since adapted Graham GREENE's *Honorary Consul* (1983) and CONRAD's *The Secret Agent* (1996, UK/US) as well as writing screenplays for *The Good Father* (1986), *Carrington* (1994, UK/Fr, BAAn), *Total Eclipse* (UK/Belg/Fr) (1995), and *Mary Reilly* (1996, UK/US). For TV he provided witty adaptations of *The History Man* (1981) and *Hotel du Lac* (1986).

Hampton, Louise (*b* Stockport, 1881 – *d* London, 1954). Actress. Stage actress (from childhood) who filmed intermittently for several decades, in character parts like that of Ian Hunter's doting cook in *Bedelia* (1946).

OTHER BRITISH FILMS INCLUDE: *The Eleventh Commandment* (1924), *His Lordship Goes to Press* (1938), *Goodbye, Mr Chips* (1939), *Busman's Honeymoon* (1940), *Scrooge* (1951), *Background* (1953).

Hanbury, Victor (*b* London, 1897 – *d* London, 1954). Director, producer. Interesting peripheral figure in British films, now perhaps best remembered as the producer whose name appears as director on blacklistee Joseph LOSEY's first British film, *The Sleeping Tiger* (1954). He had directed some 'very bad' pictures (his own description) in the 30s when he worked chiefly for producer John STAFFORD's company: they had first collaborated on *The Beggar Student* (1931, d. Hanbury; Stafford, co-sc, prod ass) and Hanbury then made about a dozen films for Stafford's company, sometimes in affiliation

with RKO. In the 40s, after WW2 service in the Navy, he produced five films for director Lance COMFORT, including several of Comfort's best – *Squadron Leader X* (1942), *Great Day* (1945), and *Daughter of Darkness* (1947) – and he shares the directing credit on *Escape to Danger* (1943) and *Hotel Reserve* (1944), though contemporary sources make clear he was really producer. Finished his career producing 'B' FILMS, including three for director Wolf RILLA (Insignia Films) and Guy GREEN's directorial debut, *River Beat* (1953).

OTHER BRITISH FILMS INCLUDE: (d/co-d, unless noted) *Where Is This Lady?* (1932), *Dick Turpin* (1933), *There Goes Susie* (+co-sc, co-p), *Spring in the Air* (1934), *Ball at Savoy, Second Bureau* (1936), *Gentleman of Venture* (1940); (p, unless noted) *They Flew Alone* (1942, assoc p), *Noose for a Lady* (1952), *Glad Tidings, The Large Rope* (1953).

Hancock, Sheila (*b* Blackgang, Isle of Wight, 1933). Actress. Viewers with long memories will remember sharp-featured, expressive Hancock as one of Miriam KARLIN's obstreperous co-workers in *The Rag Trade* (1961–63) – she was the slim sardonic one. Several decades later she was playing a *grande dame* in TV's *The Buccaneers* (1995), having enjoyed a busy career on stage (UK, US) and TV and filming fitfully but memorably in the intervening years. Also a regular on the radio programme, *Just a Minute*. Of working-class background, educated at Dartford County Grammar and RADA-trained, she was on the London stage from 1958, replacing Joan SIMS in *Breath of Spring*. In film from 1960 (*Doctor in Love*), she was the maid Dora in *Night Must Fall* and Senna Pod in *Carry On Cleo* (1964), and, repeating her stage role, locked horns with Bette DAVIS in *The Anniversary* (1967); was the disapproving mother-in-law of *Buster* (1988) – well, you would be; and gave the only bite to *Love and Death on Long Island* (1997) as John HURT's housekeeper. Her second husband was John THAW.

OTHER BRITISH FILMS INCLUDE: *The Bulldog Breed* (1960), *Girl on the Boat* (1962), *The Moon Spinners* (1964), *How I Won the War* (1967), *The Wildcats of St Trinian's* (1980), *The Love Child* (1987), *Hawks* (1988), *A Business Affair* (1994), *Hold Back the Night* (1999).

Hancock, Tony (*b* Birmingham, 1924 – *d* Sydney, 1968). Actor. Cult comedian whose image of human frailty originated in the creation of writers Ray GALTON and Alan SIMPSON, and together they made him the most popular comic in late 50s Britain. Even with their help, his 1960 film, *The Rebel*, was hardly a success; without them, his career and his life became a disaster, and, disillusioned and deluded, Hancock committed suicide while on Australian tour. Began his career while in the RAF during WW2, later appearing in pantomime, at London's Windmill Theatre, and on radio, before becoming a star on radio and TV with *Hancock's Half Hour*. At the height of his fame, he was certainly one of the most original and popular figures on British TV, and many of his half-hour studies in neurotic self-absorption and paranoia remain classics of TV comedy. Cinema scarcely tapped his genius.

OTHER BRITISH FILMS: *Orders Are Orders* (1954), *The Punch and Judy Man* (1962), *Those Magnificent Men . . .* (1965), *The Wrong Box* (1966).

BIBLOG: Philip Oakes, *Tony Hancock*, 1975; Cliff Goodwin, *When the Wind Changed: The Life and Death of Tony Hancock*, 1999. AS.

Hand, David (*b* Plainfield, New Jersey, 1900 – *d* San Luis Obispo, California, 1986). Animator. Educated at the Academy of Fine Arts in Chicago, Hand worked on Andy Gump cartoons in 1919, joining the staff at the John Bray studios, before moving on to be a director at the Fleischer studios, and to prominence at the Disney studio as the Supervising Director of *Snow White and the Seven Dwarfs* (1937) and *Bambi* (1941). His expertise in cartoon shorts at Disney – most notably in seminal and influential works like *The Country Cousin* (1936) – won him an invitation to head J.Arthur RANK's GB Animation initiative at Cookham in 1947, and the influence of the Disney aesthetic is clear in the *Animaland* cartoons, featuring Ginger Nutt, and the *Musical Paintbox* series looking at national and regional landmarks and eccentricities. With the closure of the studio in 1949, Hand returned to the United States.

OTHER BRITISH FILMS INCLUDE: *Bee Bother, Forest Dragon, The Cuckoo, Christmas Circus* (1947), *Yorkshire Ditty, Wales* (1948) *Cornwall, Devon Whey, Sketches of Scotland* (1949). Paul Wells.

Hand, Mat Actor. This promising young actor played the dreadlocked boy who has a drug overdose in *24 7 TwentyFourSeven* (1997), and was in two short films, *Where's the Money, Ronnie?* and *Small Time* (1996), all three for director Shane MEADOWS.

Hand, Slim (*b* London, 1902). Director. RN: Harry Hand. In the industry from 1920 at Famous Players–Lasky Studios, Hand had various functions in British cinema: sound recordist at GAUMONT–BRITISH in the 30s on such films as *Man of Aran* (1934) and *The Clairvoyant* (1935); assistant director at G-B on such notable films as *King Solomon's Mines* (1937) and *South Riding* (1938); then production manager at EALING, with a break for WW2 service (1939–45). In 1948, he directed *Penny and the Pownall Case*, for the RANK ORGANISATION's HIGHBURY STUDIOS, a thriller in comic-strip mode, before returning to Ealing as production manager on such films as *The Lavender Hill Mob* (1951).

OTHER BRITISH FILMS INCLUDE: (sd) *The Ghost Train* (1931), *Jack's the Boy* (1932), *Friday the Thirteenth* (1933), *The Camels are Coming* (1934), *Stormy Weather* (1935); (ass s) *The Green Cockatoo* (1937); (p man) *The Four Just Men, Cheer Boys Cheer* (1939), *Return to Yesterday* (1940), *Hue and Cry* (1946), *It Always Rains on Sunday* (1947), *Train of Events* (1949), *Dance Hall* (1950).

Handford, Peter (*b* Four Elms, Nr Edenbridge, 1919). Sound recordist. From a vicarage background, Handford, determined on a career in films, entered the industry in 1936 as sound loader at LONDON FILMS, and learnt his craft on the job. After spending WW2 in the Army (1939–45), with time in the ARMY FILM UNIT, he had his first credit on the Italian-made US film, *Black Magic* (1949), followed by HITCHCOCK's *Under Capricorn* (1949). He then worked for Herbert WILCOX six times, and in the 60s for such prominent directors as Tony RICHARDSON, John SCHLESINGER, Karel REISZ and Joseph LOSEY, particularly enjoying the challenges of location shooting. In the 80s, he worked on large-scale international productions, winning the AA and BAA for sound on *Out of Africa* (1985) and AAn for *Gorillas in the Mist* (1988). An acknowledged authority on train sounds. Married to actress Helen FRASER.

OTHER BRITISH FILMS INCLUDE: (co-/sd rec) *Odette* (1950), *Trent's Last Case* (1952), *The Beggar's Opera* (1953), *Lilacs in the Spring, Seagulls Over Sorrento,* (1954), *Summer Madness* (1955), *Private's Progress* (1956), *Happy is the Bride* (1957), *Room at the Top* (1958), *Saturday Night and Sunday Morning, Sons and Lovers, The Entertainer* (1960), *Billy Liar, Tom Jones* (1963), *The Pumpkin Eater* (1964), *Darling* (1965), *Morgan: A Suitable Case for Treatment* (1966), *Charlie Bubbles* (1967), *The Railway Children, The Go-Between* (1971), *Frenzy* (1972, mixer), *Murder on the Orient Express* (1974), *The Romantic Englishwoman* (1975, UK/Fr), *Steaming* (1984), *Hope and Glory* (1987).

Handl, Irene (*b* London, 1901 – *d* London, 1987). Actress, author. In reviewing *The Key* (1958), Basil WRIGHT referred to 'one of those brief moments of sheer joy which Irene Handl . . . brings to British films'. Plump-faced, wheedling or reprimanding, she made her stage and film debut in 1937 and in over 100 films those moments of 'sheer joy' were for 50 years one of the rewards of British film-watching. And yet her appearances are often not just 'turns': in a short time she could establish the sense of a whole life, as she does in *Temptation Harbour* (1947), as the carnival MC's bored wife casually picking her teeth; or as Peter SELLERS' no-nonsense wife in *I'm All Right Jack* (1959). Of course she is fun, too, as the beaming cinema organist in *Brief Encounter* (1945) or an extravagantly earringed schoolmistress in *The Belles of St Trinian's* (1954). Major success on stage with *Goodnight Mrs Puffin* (1961–63, London, Australia), and on TV with *For the Love of Ada* (1970–71, filmed 1972). Also a novelist of some reputation.

OTHER BRITISH FILMS INCLUDE: *Missing, Believed Married* (1937), *Strange Boarders* (1938), *Mr Proudfoot Shows a Light* (1941, short), *Dear Octopus* (1943), *Great Day* (1945), *The Shop at Sly Corner* (1946), *The History of Mr Polly* (1948), *Silent Dust, Cardboard Cavalier* (1949), *Young Wives' Tale* (1951), *Top Secret* (1952), *A Kid for Two Farthings* (1954), *Brothers in Law* (1956), *Carry On Nurse* (1958), *Two Way Stretch, A French Mistress, Carry On Constable* (1960), *Heavens Above!* (1963), *Morgan: A Suitable Case for Treatment* (1966), *The Italian Job* (1969), *The Private Life of Sherlock Holmes* (1970), *The Hound of the Baskervilles* (1977), *Absolute Beginners* (1986), dozens more.

Handley, Tommy (*b* Liverpool, 1893 – *d* London, 1949). Actor. Legendary radio comedian – debut 1925 – who starred in *It's That Man Again* (ITMA, filmed 1943) from 1939 until his sudden death, which resulted in national mourning. Often appeared in *Pathé Pictorial* and similar shorts, including some with Ronald FRANKAU as 'Murgatroyd and Winterbotton'.

OTHER BRITISH FILMS: *Elstree Calling* (1930), *BBC Musical's 2* (1936, reissued 1947 as *Making the Grade*), *Two Men in a Box* (1938), *Time Flies, Bob in the Pound, Poppy Poopah's Pennies* (1944).

BIBLIOG: Autobiography, *Handley's Pages,* 1938; Bill Grundy, *That Man,* 1977. AS.

HandMade Films Production company established by former BEATLE, George HARRISON, and Denis O'Brien to fund the second MONTY PYTHON film, *Life of Brian* (1979), and over the next 15 years produced some of the most popular and critically acclaimed British films – and some of the direst. The former include: *The Long Good Friday* (1979), *Time Bandits* (1981), *A Private Function* (1984), *Mona Lisa* (1986) and the cult comedy *Withnail & I* (1986), as well as the superbly made though uncommercial *The Lonely Passion of Judith Hearne* (1988). A major flop was *Shanghai Surprise* (1986). In 1994, the company was bought by Canada's Paragon Entertainment Corporation for a reported $8.5 million and Harrison successfully sued O'Brien over losses incurred by the latter in his capacity as manager of HandMade.

Hanley, Jenny (*b* Gerrards Cross, 1947). Actress. Daughter of actors Dinah SHERIDAN and Jimmy HANLEY, better known as a TV personality on such shows as *Magpie* (1968), and in other TV series, than in films where she has usually appeared in small roles. She had the female lead in two horror films: *Scars of Dracula* (1970) and *The Flesh and Blood Show* (1972).

OTHER BRITISH FILMS INCLUDE: *On Her Majesty's Secret Service* (1969), *The Devil's Widow* (1971), *Percy's Progress* (1974, as Miss Teenage Lust), *Alfie Darling* (1975).

Hanley, Jimmy (*b* Norwich, 1918 – *d* London, 1970). Actor. On stage from 1930 and in films as a teenager – e.g. co-starring with

Nova PILBEAM in *Little Friend* (1934) and as one of Will HAY's pupils in *Boys Will Be Boys* (1935) – Hanley matured quickly into an excellent character player of the 40s and 50s. Trained at the Italia Conti Stage School and did WW2 service 1939–44. He could adapt easily from the likeable 'boy-next-door' types he played in *Holiday Camp* (1947) and the 'HUGGETT' sequels, in the third of which (*The Huggetts Abroad*, 1949), he is married to real-life wife, Dinah SHERIDAN, to the brash ex-car salesman, Stainer, in *The Way Ahead* (1944), to the sceptical English soldier in *Henry V* (1944), to the petty crim, Whitey, in *It Always Rains on Sunday* (1947), and, in his best remembered role, to the upright young cop in *The Blue Lamp* (1949). His career faltered in the 50s when his first marriage broke up, but he continued to work in the theatre. There was an easy likeable authority about his work, in roles chiefly sympathetic. His second wife was actress **Margaret Avery**, who played Anthony NEWLEY's girlfriend in *A Boy, a Girl and a Bike* (1949). He and SHERIDAN are parents of Jenny HANLEY and Jeremy Hanley, chairman of the Conservative party in 1994–95. Died sadly young of cancer.

OTHER BRITISH FILMS INCLUDE: *Red Wagon* (1934), *The Tunnel, Brown on Resolution* (1935), *Housemaster* (1938), *There Ain't No Justice* (1939), *Gaslight* (1940), *Salute John Citizen* (1942), *The Gentle Sex* (1943), *Kiss the Bride Goodbye* (1944), *Murder in Reverse, 29, Acacia Avenue* (1945), *The Captive Heart* (1946), *Master of Bankdam* (1947), *Here Come the Huggetts* (1948), *Boys in Brown* (1949), *Room to Let* (1950), *The Galloping Major* (1951), *The Black Rider* (1954), *The Deep Blue Sea* (1955), *The Lost Continent* (1968).

Hannaford, David (*b* London, 1942) Actor. Refreshingly natural child actor of late 40s/early 50s, remembered for two 1954 releases: *Eight O'Clock Walk*, as the child whose testimony sets the action in train; and *The End of the Road*, as Finlay CURRIE's affectionate grandson, called – one is sorry to say – Barney Wee.

OTHER BRITISH FILMS INCLUDE: *The Last Load* (1948), *Now Barabbas Was a Robber* (1949), *The Second Mate* (1950), *The Pickwick Papers* (1952), *Jumping for Joy* (1955), *Carry On Admiral* (1957).

Hannah, John (*b* East Kilbride, Scotland, 1962). Actor. Handsome, rather saturnine young actor who has become an international star despite well-founded critical indifference to his US films, *The Mummy* (1999) and *The Mummy Returns* (2001), in which he played Rachel WEISZ's foppish brother. A former electrician who later trained at a Glasgow drama school, he won prominence when he read W.H. AUDEN's poem as Simon CALLOW's bereaved lover in *Four Weddings and a Funeral* (1994). Those who could penetrate the accents found the TV police series *McCallum* (1995) and *Rebus* (2000) rewarding, and he revealed a comic gift opposite Gwyneth PALTROW in the popular romantic comedy, *Sliding Doors* (1998). Co-founder of Clerkenwell Films (1998), he is married to actress **Joanna Roth**, who played Ophelia in *Rosencrantz and Guildenstern Are Dead* (1990, US).

OTHER BRITISH FILMS INCLUDE: *Harbour Beat* (1990, UK/Aust), *The Innocent Sleep* (1995), *The James Gang, Resurrection Man* (1997), *The Intruder* (1999), *Circus* (2000, UK/US), *Pandaemonium* (2001, UK/US), *Before You Go* (2002).

Hannan, Peter (*b* Australia, 1941). Cinematographer. In Britain since the 70s, he was responsible for the distinctive look of such varied films as *Dance with a Stranger* (1984), with its hard bright evocation of the 50s, *Withnail & I* (1986), where the look of the comfortless countryside contributed to the fun, and *The Lonely Passion of Judith Hearne* (1987), set in a drably-

caught Dublin. Was 2nd unit cinematographer on *Sleepy Hollow* (1999, US/Ger).

OTHER BRITISH FILMS INCLUDE: *Radio Wonderful* (1973, doc), *Full Circle* (1976, UK/Can), *The Stud* (1978), *The Missionary* (1981), *Brimstone & Treacle* (1982), *Turtle Diary, Insignificance* (1985), *A Handful of Dust* (1987), *Milk* (1999).

Hannen, Nicholas (*b* London, 1881 – *d* London, 1972). Actor. Venerable stage actor, from 1910, of gauntly impressive mien (he was called 'Beau'), starred in dozens of classical and modern plays, toured South Africa with his own company (1929) and Egypt and Australia (1932–33) with a repertory of 13 plays. Somehow, he contrived to fit about 25 films into an almost non-stop theatre career, and struck vivid cameos as the Duke of Exeter in *Henry V* (1944) and the disapproving Colonel Watherstone in *The Winslow Boy* (1948). Had a famously long-running romance with actress Athene SEYLER whom he married in 1960 after the death of his first wife (m. 1907) and with whom he starred in the first Somerset MAUGHAM piece on TV, *The Breadwinner* (1938). Received the OBE (military) for his WW1 Army service (1915–18). Daughter was RADA-trained actress **Hermione Hannen** (*b* London, 1913 – *d* Shrewsbury, 1988), who appeared in *The Life of the Party* (1934), and was married in turn to actors Anthony QUAYLE and Clifford EVANS.

OTHER BRITISH FILMS INCLUDE: *FP1* (1933, UK/Ger), *The Dictator* (1935), *Marigold* (1938), *Spy for a Day* (1940), *The Prime Minister* (1941), *Hell Is Sold Out* (1951), *Richard III* (1955), *Sea Wife* (1956), *Dunkirk* (1958), *Term of Trial* (1962).

Hanray, Lawrence (*b* London, 1874 – *d* London, 1947). Actor. Dignified character player, educated at the City of London School, on stage from 1892, and in over 60 films from 1923's *The Pipes of Pan*. Very often in period roles, including several for KORDA, such as Thomas Cranmer in *The Private Life of Henry VIII* (1933), Burke in *The Scarlet Pimpernel* (1935) and the French Ambassador in *Fire Over England* (1937), but dignity did not deter him from appearing in *Old Mother Riley's Circus* (1941) or *My Learned Friend* (1943).

OTHER BRITISH FILMS INCLUDE: *Her Reputation* (1931), (1932), *The Faithful Heart, The Good Companions* (1933), *Catherine the Great, Chu-Chin-Chow, Lorna Doone* (1934), *Brewster's Millions* (1935), *Rembrandt, The Man Who Could Work Miracles* (1936), *Smash and Grab, Action for Slander, 21 Days* (1937), *Quiet Wedding, Hatter's Castle* (1941), *On Approval, Hotel Reserve* (1944), *Mine Own Executioner, Nicholas Nickleby* (1947).

Hanslip, Ann (*b* London, 1934). Actress. RADA-trained actress who had a run of supporting roles in the early 50s, including Yum-Yum in 'The Mikado' sequence in *The Story of Gilbert and Sullivan* (1953) and the ingenue with a head cold in *Where There's a Will* (1955), in which she tells George COLE to 'Shut up, you cheap little spiv'.

OTHER BRITISH FILMS INCLUDE: *Lady Godiva Rides Again* (1951), *Knights of the Round Table* (1953), *The Pursuers* (1961).

Hanson, Barry (*b* Bradford, 1943). Producer. TV and film producer whose most notable achievement was to get the classic gangster film, *The Long Good Friday* (1979), made for the GRADE organisation in the period of its ruinously expensive *Raise the Titanic* (1980). He worked at Thames Television in the 70s, and went on to produce several more movies and Ken RUSSELL's TV film of *Lady Chatterley* (1992).

OTHER BRITISH FILMS INCLUDE: *Bloody Kids* (1979), *Runners* (1983), *Morons from Outer Space* (1985), *Out of the Blue* (1991), *Dead Romantic* (1992, ex p).

Harareet, Haya (*b* Haifa, Israel, 1931). Actress, screenwriter. Having performed on stage and screen in Israel, including the lead in Thorold DICKINSON's *Hill 24 Doesn't Answer* (1955), she came to international prominence as Esther in *Ben-Hur* (1959), and subsequently filmed in Britain (*The Secret Partner*, 1961), the US (*The Interns*, 1962) and elsewhere. Married Jack CLAYTON, whose *Our Mother's House* (1967) she co-authored.

Harbord, Carl (*b* Salcombe, 1902 – *d* Los Angeles, 1958). Actor. Popular on stage from early 20s, then in nearly 20 British films in the next decade, most famously as the upper-class young hero killed at Gallipoli in *Tell England* (1931). Married Isobel ELSOM with whom he starred in *The Christmas Present*, a very early BBC TV drama. Went to Hollywood in late 30s and played supporting roles in such Brit-set enterprises as *Eagle Squadron* (1942) and *Dressed to Kill* (1946).

OTHER BRITISH FILMS INCLUDE: *The Marquis of Bolibar* (1928), *Such Is the Law* (1930), *Fascination* (1931), *Dance Pretty Lady* (1932), *The Scarlet Pimpernel* (1935), *The Cavalier of the Streets* (1937), *Beyond Our Horizon* (1939).

Harcourt, James (*b* Headingley, 1873 – *d* London, 1951). Actor. On stage from 1902, entered films in 1931, and appeared in 30 over the ensuing two decades. (One source suggests a 1916 film.) Short and balding, he is a prosing (and bewigged) Fox in *Penn of Pennsylvania* (1941) and Robert NEWTON's ancient butler in *Obsession* (1949). With the Old Vic in the mid 40s.

OTHER BRITISH FILMS INCLUDE: *Hobson's Choice* (1931), *Song of the Plough* (1933), *The Old Curiosity Shop* (1934), *Seven Sinners, Laburnum Grove* (1936), *The Stars Look Down* (1939), *Night Train to Munich* (1940), *Love on the Dole* (1941), *The Young Mr Pitt* (1942), *He Snoops to Conquer* (1944), *The Captive Heart* (1946), *Meet Me at Dawn* (1947).

Hardie, Kate (*b* London, 1968). Actress. Daughter of **Bill Oddie** (*b* Oldham, Lancs, 1941), star of TV's *The Goodies* (1970–77, 1980) and jazz singer Jean Hart, Hardie (the name amalgamates her parents') is small, dark and vivacious. On-screen since her teens, she has made a dozen films and been vivid enough in them to be better known than she is; especially notable as the heroin-addicted teenage prostitute in *Mona Lisa* (1986), the former prostitute-turned-croupier in *Croupier* (1998, UK/Fr/Ger/Ire), and Christopher ECCLESTON's increasingly uneasy wife in the little-seen *Heart* (1999).

OTHER BRITISH FILMS INCLUDE: *Runners* (1983), *Revolution* (1985, UK/Nor), *Cry Freedom* (1987), *Tree of Hands* (1988), *The Krays* (1990), *Safe* (1993), *Jack & Sarah* (1995, UK/Fr), *The Announcement* (2000, UK/US).

Harding, Gilbert (*b* Hereford, 1907 – *d* London, 1960). Actor. Rotund, acidulous Harding was in about a dozen films, but not actually *of* them, usually playing himself or a pundit of some kind, as in *Gilbert Harding Speaking of Murder* (1953). Cambridge-educated and a former schoolmaster, he was with the BBC from 1940, then became a sort of institution on TV, on the panel game, *What's My Line?* (1951–60) and with his own show *Harding Finds Out*. On John Freeman's *Face to Face* (1960), he famously broke down under intense personal probing about his response to his mother's death. Films scarcely exploited his household name status and persona.

OTHER BRITISH FILMS INCLUDE: *The Gentle Gunman* (1952), *The Oracle* (the voice of the Oracle), *Meet Mr Lucifer* (1953), *An Alligator Named Daisy* (1955), *Expresso Bongo, Left, Right and Centre* (1959).

Harding, Lyn (*b* St Brides Wentlooge, Wales, 1867 – *d* London, 1952). Actor. RN: David Llewellyn Harding. Vast, over-the-top actor who was on stage from 1890 and in films from 1920 (*The Barton Mystery, A Bachelor Husband*); was Henry VIII in *When Knighthood Was in Flower* (1922, US), and a famous Professor Moriarty on stage and screen (*The Triumph of Sherlock Holmes*, 1935; *Silver Blaze*, 1937); and Robert DONAT's headmaster in *Goodbye, Mr Chips* (1939). A former draper's apprentice, he acted until his mid 70s, frequently in villainous roles.

OTHER BRITISH FILMS INCLUDE: *Les Misérables* (1922), *Land of Hope and Glory* (1927), *The Speckled Band* (1931), *The Constant Nymph* (1933), *Wild Boy* (1934), *Escape Me Never* (1935), *Fire Over England, Knight Without Armour* (1937), *The Prime Minister* (1941).

Hardwick, Paul (*b* Bridlington, 1918 – *d* London, 1983). Actor. Above all, a Shakespearean actor, first on stage in *Antony and Cleopatra* (1946), later a contract player with the RSC from 1961. Educated at University of Birmingham, he merely dabbled with films, including the roles of Capulet in *Romeo and Juliet* (1968, UK/It) and Messala in *Julius Caesar* (1970). On TV, was John of Gaunt in *Richard II* (1970) and was in the RSC's televised *The Wars of the Roses* (1964).

OTHER BRITISH FILMS: *A Night to Remember* (1958), *A Man for All Seasons, The Deadly Affair* (1966), *The Long Duel* (1967), *Octopussy* (1983).

Hardwicke, Sir Cedric (*b* Lye, 1893 – *d* New York, 1964). Actor. The main film career of this illustrious film character actor belongs to Hollywood, where he first went in 1934, and returned in the late 30s, staying to play dozens of dignified persons, sometimes villainous (Mr Jones in *Victory*, 1940), occasionally benign (the old actor in *I Remember Mama*, 1948), at times imperious (Senator Cabot Lodge in *Wilson*, 1944). From 1912, after RADA training, he had a very long and distinguished stage career in London and New York, excelling as an interpreter of SHAW, whose fifth favourite actor he was (the first four were the Marx Brothers). Knighted in 1934.

His British films are comparatively few, but there are still more than 20 and some of his roles are choice. After a couple of silents – *Riches and Rogues* (1913) and *Nelson* (1926) – he began filming in earnest in 1931 (*Dreyfus*), and had excellent chances as the bullying Scots author, McBane, in *Rome Express* (1932), a ringleted Charles II in *Nell Gwyn* (1934), the emotional artist Theotocopulos in *Things to Come* and the scheming Earl of Warwick in *Tudor Rose* (1936), and Allan Quartermain in *King Solomon's Mines* (1937). After WW2 (he had served in the Army in WWI), he made several more films in Britain: he was a malevolent Uncle Ralph in *Nicholas Nickleby* (1947), a moving, obdurate figure as father of *The Winslow Boy* (1948), and, finally, in *The Pumpkin Eater* (1964), as Anne Bancroft's intimidating father. 'Intimidating' was perhaps what he did best, but the range is wide and the pickings rich: he was apparently always short of cash which was bad luck for him but not for filmgoers as it meant he played over 80 roles with consummate authority. His first wife was actress Helena PICKARD, and Edward HARDWICKE is their son.

OTHER BRITISH FILMS: *Orders Is Orders, The Ghoul* (1933), *The Lady Is Willing, The King of Paris, Jew Süss, Bella Donna* (1934), *Peg of Old Drury* (1935), *Laburnum Grove, Calling the Tune* (1936), *French Town* (1945, short), *Beware of Pity* (1946), *Now Barabbas Was a Robber* (1949), *Richard III* (1955).

BIBLIOG: Autobiography, *A Victorian in Orbit*, 1960.

Hardwicke, Edward (*b* London, 1932). Actor. The son of Helena PICKARD and Sir Cedric HARDWICKE, who wrote of him, 'Edward was doomed to be an actor. Barry Jackson was his godfather. My son made his debut at the age of seven at the

Malvern Festival'. After RADA and RAF service (1951–52), was on London stage from 1954, and in films from 1953 (*Hell Below Zero*). Has something of his father's gravitas in his film persona, but his most memorable role, as C.S. Lewis's brother in *Shadowlands* (1993, UK/US) has a very touchingly understated emotional base. Much TV, famously as Dr Watson to Jeremy BRETT's Holmes in the 80s. Married stage actress Anne Iddon; daughter Emma is also an actress.

OTHER BRITISH FILMS INCLUDE: *Othello* (1965), *The Reckoning* (1969), *The Day of the Jackal* (1973, UK/Fr), *Full Circle* (1976, UK/Can), *'Let Him Have It'* (1991), *Richard III* (1995), *Hollow Reed* (1996), *Elizabeth*, *Parting Shots* (1998), *She* (2001, UK/Bulg/Can/It).

Hardy, Forsyth (*b* Bathgate, Scotland, 1910 – *d* Scotland, 1994). Critic, writer. Film journalist with *The Scotsman* from 1930, editor of *Cinema Quarterly* (1932–35), and producer of over 150 short films for the Films of Scotland Committee (1955–75), Hardy is now best known as the author of two books on the work of fellow Scot, pioneer documentarist, John GRIERSON: *Grierson on Documentary* (1946) and *John Grierson: A Documentary Biography* (1979).

Hardy, Robert (*b* Cheltenham, 1925). Actor. After touring with the Stratford Memorial Theatre Company, Hardy first appeared on the London stage in 1952 and has maintained a stage presence ever since, but his greatest fame probably derives from his TV work. In two famous SHAKESPEARE-based mini-series he was Prince Hal to Sean CONNERY's Hotspur in *An Age of Kings* (1960), dazzled as Coriolanus in *The Spread of the Eagle* (1963), and in two George Eliot adaptations he was a wonderfully languid, disdainful Grandcourt in *Daniel Deronda* (1970) and foolish flustered Mr Brooke in *Middlemarch* (1994). Most famously he starred as vet Siegfried Farnon in *All Creatures Great and Small* (1978–90). On the big screen he has made the most of more limited opportunities, notably as decent Lord Lilburn in *The Shooting Party* (1984), as Sir John Middleton, full of innuendo in *Sense and Sensibility* (1995, UK/US), and, inevitably, as blustering Lord Caversham in *An Ideal Husband* (1998, UK/US). Married to Gladys COOPER's daughter, Sally Pearson.

OTHER BRITISH FILMS INCLUDE: *The Spy Who Came in from the Cold* (1965), *Berserk!* (1967), *10 Rillington Place* (1970), *Young Winston*, *Psychomania* (1972), *Mrs Dalloway* (1997, UK/Neth/US), *The Tichborne Claimant* (1998).

Hardy, Robin (*b* Surrey, 1929). Director. After making one innovatory, intelligent, genuinely unsettling piece of gothic horror, *The Wicker Man* (1973), he has directed one unseen Irish thriller, *The Fantasist* (1986) and written the screenplay for *Bulldance* (1989), also little seen.

Hardy, Thomas (*b* Bockhampton, 1840 – *d* Dorchester, 1928). Author. The great 'Wessex' novels (except *Return of the Native*, a 1994 mini-series) have all been filmed for the big screen: *Tess of the D'Urbevilles* (1913, US; 1924, US; and, as *Tess*, 1979, UK/Fr, d. Roman POLANSKI, and as *Prem Granth*, 1996, Ind); *Far from the Madding Crowd* (1915; 1967, d. John SCHLESINGER, with Julie CHRISTIE as Bathsheba); *Jude* (1996, a bleak masterpiece by Michael WINTERBOTTOM); *The Woodlanders* (1997, d. documentarist Phil AGLAND); and *The Mayor of Casterbridge*, re-set in snowbound California, as *The Claim* (2001, UK/Can/Fr, WINTERBOTTOM again). There have also been several mini-series, and film versions of *Under the Greenwood Tree* (1929) and *The Melancholy Hussar* (as *The Scarlet Tunic*, 1997). Hardy's love of the 'Wessex' countryside is a lure for film-makers; the trick is not to let the scenery outshine the characters or the work they do.

Hare, Sir David (*b* Hastings, 1947). Dramatist, screenwriter, director. RN: David Rippon. One of the most important figures in contemporary British theatre, where his plays, including *Fanshen* (1975), *Plenty* (1978) and *Pravda* (1985) have explored decline in national morality and authority, Cambridge-educated Hare has made a provocative rather than prolific contribution to British cinema. He had made his name with the TV films, *Licking Hitler* (1977) and *Dreams of Leaving* (1980), before turning to the cinema. His first feature, *Wetherby* (1985, + sc), is an unsettling account of suicide and difficult relationships; his screenplay for Fred Schepisi's *Plenty* (1985, UK/US) explores post-war disillusionment; he directed *Strapless* (1988, + sc), in which the personal and the political are again seen as illuminating each other with results far from serene; and he wrote the deeply disturbing family tragedy, *Damage* (1992, UK/Fr, + co-p). Knighted in 1998.

OTHER BRITISH FILMS: *Paris by Night* (1988, d, sc), *The Secret Rapture* (1993, sc, co-p), *The Designated Mourner* (1997, d, co-p).

Hare, Doris (*b* Bargoed, Wales, 1905 – *d* 2000). Actress. How long some actors live – and how long they work! Hare first appeared on stage aged three; 86 years later she appeared in her last film, *Second Best* (1994, UK/US). Made her name in revue in the 30s, toured internationally, acted on Broadway and at the Old Vic, and already seemed ancient as Grannie Tooke on stage in *Valmouth* in 1958–59, a decade before household fame as Reg VARNEY's slatternly Mum (replacing Cicely COURTNEIDGE) in the vulgar but undeniably popular sitcom, *On the Buses* (1969–73), and its three film SPIN-OFFS, *On the Buses* (1971), *Mutiny on the Buses* (1972) and *Holiday on the Buses* (1973). Made MBE in 1941 for wartime broadcasting services – she was compere of *Shipmates Ashore* – to the Royal Navy.

OTHER BRITISH FILMS INCLUDE: *Night Mail* (1935), *Luck of the Navy* (1938), *Here Come the Huggetts*, *The History of Mr Polly* (1948), *Dance Hall* (1950), *Tiger by the Tail* (1955), *The League of Gentlemen* (1960), *A Place to Go* (1963), *Confessions . . . of a Pop Performer* (1975), *. . . of a Driving Instructor* (1976), *. . . from a Holiday Camp* (1977), *Nuns on the Run* (1990).

Hare, Robertson (*b* London, 1891 – *d* Northwood, Middlesex, 1979). Actor. During the 30s, the diminutive, plummy-voiced Hare, on stage from 1911, was an indispensable part of the team that produced the ALDWYCH FARCES, a series of comedies based on the plays of Ben TRAVERS. Hare was usually cast as a pompous, hen-pecked husband ripe for comic humiliation, although his best part was as the motor-biking vicar in *Cuckoo in the Nest* (1933). Hare's work away from the Aldwych team was less memorable although he did achieve some success late in his career with the TV situation comedy *All Gas and Gaiters* (1967, 1969–71).

OTHER BRITISH FILMS INCLUDE: *Rookery Nook* (1930), *Plunder* (1931), *Thark* (1932), *Friday the Thirteenth* (1933), *Dirty Work*, *A Cup of Kindness* (1934), *Car of Dreams*, *Stormy Weather* (1935), *Jack of all Trades*, *Pot Luck* (1936), *So This Is London* (1939), *Banana Ridge* (1941), *He Snoops to Conquer* (1944), *Things Happen at Night* (1948), *One Wild Oat* (1951), *Three Men in a Boat*, *My Wife's Family* (1956), *The Young Ones* (1961), *Crooks Anonymous* (1962), *Hotel Paradiso* (1966, UK/Fr), *Raising the Roof* (1971).

BIBLIOG: Autobiography, *Yours Indubitably*, 1956. Peter Hutchings.

Harker, Gordon (*b* London, 1885 – *d* London, 1967). Actor. Lugubrious, shifty, aggressive, occasionally chirpy, Cockney Harker, of the protruding lower lip, was a cherished fixture in

British films for 30 years, starting with several appearances in fellow-EastEnder Alfred HITCHCOCK's films, including *The Ring* (1927), *The Farmer's Wife* and *Champagne* (1928). He was extremely busy throughout the 30s, in such popular thrillers as *The Ringer* (1931) and *Rome Express* (1932), as well as ex-convict Faker Brown in the wild comedy of *Boys Will Be Boys* (1935). He starred as *Inspector Hornleigh* (1939) and in the sequels, *Inspector Hornleigh on Holiday* (1939) and *Inspector Hornleigh Goes to It* (1941); did a lovely cameo as a casually corruptible pub-keeper in *Bang! You're Dead* (1953); and starred in his penultimate film, *Small Hotel* (1957), as the devious waiter, matching wits with Marie LOHR, in the role he had created on stage, 50-odd years after entering the profession as prompter to Fred Terry. A stocky tower of strength in over 60 films, it is good to know he had the chance to play Alfred Dolittle in an early TV performance of *Pygmalion* (1948).

OTHER BRITISH FILMS INCLUDE: *The Return of the Rat* (1929), *Elstree Calling* (1930), *The Sport of Kings* (1931), *The Lucky Number, Britannia of Billingsgate* (1933), *Dirty Work* (1934), *The Phantom Light* (1935), *The Frog* (1937), *Saloon Bar* (1940), *29, Acacia Avenue* (1945), *Her Favourite Husband* (UK/It), *The Second Mate* (1950), *Derby Day* (1952), *Left, Right and Centre* (1959).

Harker, Susannah (*b* London, 1965). Actress. Best known to date for her TV work as doomed Mattie Storin in the TV trilogy, *House of Cards* (1990), *To Play the King* (1994) and *The Final Cut* (1995), and as firmly gentle Jane in *Pride and Prejudice* (1995). On screen, supporting parts in *White Mischief* (1987) and *Surviving Picasso* (1996, UK/US), *A Dry White Season* (1989, US), and *Intimacy* (2001, UK/Fr). Married actor Iain GLEN, her *Adam Bede* (1991, TV) co-star, and sister of **Caroline Harker** (*b* 1966), Mrs Fitzherbert in *The Madness of King George* (1994, UK/US) and in much TV. They are the daughters of stage actors Polly Adams and Richard Owens.

Harkin, Dennis (*b* London, 1918). Actor. On stage from 1939, he played supporting roles in the later 40s, including Margaret BARTON's follower in *Brief Encounter* (1945) and one of the card-sharpers taught a lesson by Jack WARNER in *Holiday Camp* (1947).

OTHER BRITISH FILMS INCLUDE: *Waterloo Road* (1944), *Jassy, Dusty Bates* (serial) (1947), *Easy Money* (1948), *Home to Danger* (1951).

Harlow, John (*b* Ross-on-Wye, 1896 – *d* England, ?) Screenwriter, director. Post-WW1 service, he had varied theatrical experience, including concert-party actor and manager of the Kingsway Theatre, before entering films in 1927 as assistant director at ELSTREE. His chief prominence came with some pacy thrillers in the 40s, including two Sexton Blake adventures starring David FARRAR, *Meet Sexton Blake* (1944, + sc) and *The Echo Murders* (1945, + sc), two gripping melodramas with William HARTNELL, *The Agitator* (1945) and *Appointment with Crime* (1946, + sc), the enjoyably foolish *While I Live* (1947, + co-sc), distinguished by its theme tune, 'The Dream of Olwen', and a barnstorming performance from Sonia DRESDEL. After directing and co-writing two 'Old Mother Riley' comedies (*OMR's New Venture*, 1949; *OMR, Headmistress*, 1950), his career tapered off in unmemorable 'B' MOVIES, including one for TEMPEAN (*Delayed Action*, 1954) but the producers found his approach old-fashioned by then.

OTHER BRITISH FILMS INCLUDE: (d, unless noted) *The Informer* (1929, ass d), *Two Worlds* (1930, a), *Master and Man, Bagged* (1934), *Spellbound* (1941), *This Was Paris* (1942), *The Dark Tower, Headline* (1943), *Candles at Nine* (1944), *Green Fingers* (1947), *Those People Next Door* (1952), *The Blue Parrot, Alf's Baby* (1953), *Dangerous Cargo* (1954).

Harma & Co. Ltd was a production entity, owned by Harry Maze Jenks, and headed by Martin THORNTON, assisted by actor Harry LORRAINE and A.C. Hunter. Harma specialised in dramas, starring Marjorie VILLIS and James KNIGHT. A successor to the CLARENDON FILM COMPANY, Harma was, in turn, reorganised in January 1921 as Associated Exhibitors Film Company (AEFC). AS.

Harman, A(rthur), Jympson (*b* Hastings, 1891 – *d* Petersfield, 1988). Critic. RN: Arthur Jympson. At *Evening News* from 1907 and post-WW1 service returned there to become its film critic in 1921, holding this position for nearly 40 years and becoming President of the Critics' Circle. Published *Good Films: How to Appreciate Them* (1946). His son is editor John JYMPSON.

Harper, Frank (*b* London, 1962). Actor. The chubby robber in *Kevin & Perry Go Large* (2000, UK/US) was educated at the (Thomas) Malory Secondary Modern School, Catford, then spent ten years working at Smithfield meat market, before making his stage debut in 1985. His first film was *For Queen and Country* (1988, UK/US) and his most notable film work so far has been in the two Shane MEADOWS features: *24 7 TwentyFourSeven* (1997) and *A Room for Romeo Brass* (1999, UK/Can), and as Michael CAINE's loyal henchman in *Shiner* (2001). He has continued to work on stage (*The Novice*, at the Almeida, 2000) and done a lot of TV, including *Other People's Children* (2000), as a harassed, likeable divorcé trying to do the right thing by his kids.

OTHER BRITISH FILMS INCLUDE: *In the Name of the Father* (1993, UK/Ire/US), *Lock, Stock and Two Smoking Barrels* (1998), *Lucky Break* (UK/Ger/US), *The Last Minute* (UK/US), *The Search for John Gissing* (UK/US) (2001), *Club Le Monde, Bend It like Beckham* (UK/Ger) (2002).

Harper, Gerald (*b* London, 1929). Actor. RADA-trained, former medical student, on London stage in 1951, Harper usually projected an upper-class persona, as in *The Admirable Crichton* (1957), as the nitwit Hon. Ernest Woolley, or as the hopeful adulterer, Mr Todhunter, in the dire 1979 remake of *The Lady Vanishes*. Probably now best known for the TV series, *Adam Adamant Lives* (1966–67), and *Hadleigh* (1969–76), in both of which he played the title roles, as gentleman-adventurer and country squire respectively. Married to stage actress **Jane Downs**, who, like Harper, appeared in *A Night to Remember* (1958), as Kenneth MORE's wife.

OTHER BRITISH FILMS INCLUDE: *Tiger in the Smoke, The Extra Day* (1956), *The League of Gentlemen, Tunes of Glory* (1960), *The Young Ones* (1961), *Wonderful Life* (1964).

Harper, Kenneth Producer. Former agent with MCA who became an independent producer in the mid 50s, and is particularly associated with three MUSICALS starring Cliff RICHARD: *The Young Ones* (1961), *Summer Holiday* (1962) and *Wonderful Life* (1964).

OTHER BRITISH FILMS INCLUDE: *For Better, for Worse* (1954), *Yield to the Night* (1956), *Passionate Summer* (1958, co-p), *Go to Blazes* (1962), *French Dressing* (1963), *Prudence and the Pill* (1968, co-p), *The Virgin and the Gypsy* (1970), *Take Me High* (1973).

Harris, Caroline Costume designer. Notable designer of the late 90s, especially known for her work in period dramas such as *Othello* (1995, UK/US) and *An Ideal Husband* (1999, UK/US).

OTHER BRITISH FILMS INCLUDE: *In the Bleak Midwinter* (1995), *Amy Foster* (1997, UK/Fr/US), *Still Crazy* (UK/US), *Croupier* (UK/Fr/Ger/Ire), *The Governess* (1998, UK/Fr), *Very Annie Mary* (2001, UK/Fr).

Harris, Damian (*b* London, 1958). Director, screenwriter. Son of Richard **Harris**, brother of Jared **Harris**. Having appeared as a child in *Otley* (1968), he directed *The Rachel Papers* (1989), an intermittently witty version of Martin **Amis**'s novel, and several US films, including *Deceived* (1991) and *Mercy* (2000). Married to actress **Annabel Brooks** (*b c* 1962) who has appeared in several films, including *Love Is the Devil* (1998, UK/Fr/Jap).

Harris, Henry (*b* London, 1899 – *d* 1971). Cinematographer. Entered the industry in 1913 as projectionist and assistant cameraman. After service with the Royal Flying Corps during WW1, he became a cinematographer with Pathé Frères in Paris, and gained a reputation on the continent. His 1923 British film, *Man without Desire*, directed by Adrian **Brunel**, shot in Germany and on location in Venice, displays the influence of German cinema. Harris also filmed the Brunel parody shorts, including *A Typical Budget* and *Cut It Out* (both 1925). With the coming of sound, Harris alternated 'quota quickies', often for Paramount–British, with 'A' pictures. In the 40s, he became chief of the special effects department at **Denham** and **Pinewood Studios**, creating the special effects for *I Know Where I'm Going!* (1945), *Caesar and Cleopatra* (1945), *A Matter of Life and Death* (1946), *Odd Man Out* (1947), and *Hamlet* (1948), etc. His photographic career ended where it began – in Paris in 1950 with *Garou-Garou le Passé-Muraille*.
OTHER BRITISH FILMS INCLUDE: *The Boy Woodburn* (1922), *The Runaway Princess* (1929, co-c), *The Wonderful Story* (1932), *Purse Strings* (1933), *Badger's Green* (1934), *Brewster's Millions* (1935), *Limelight* (1936), *The Street Singer* (1937), *Brief Ecstasy* (1937), *This Man in Paris*, *The Stars Look Down* (1939, co-c). AS.

Harris, Jack (*b* South Farnborough, 1905 – *d* Yeovil, 1971). Editor. One of the great British editors, Harris entered films in 1921 with the **Gaumont** Company, acquired very diverse experience before going to **Twickenham Studios** in 1929, first as assistant director, then as editor. His period of chief eminence was as editor for **Cineguild** in the 40s when he was responsible for the creative cutting of such films as *Brief Encounter* (1945), *Great Expectations* (1946), *Blanche Fury* (1947), *Oliver Twist* (1948). He worked at **Pinewood**, **Ealing** and **Warner Bros** in the 50s on a range of GENRE films.
OTHER BRITISH FILMS: (sup e, include) *Broken Blossoms* (1936), *The Angelus* (1937), *Pastor Hall* (1940), *The Common Touch* (1941), *When We Are Married*, *Old Mother Riley, Detective*, *The Demi-Paradise* (1943), *Take My Life* (1947), *Meet Mr Lucifer* (1953); (co-/e, complete) *Lord Richard in the Pantry* (1930), *Black Coffee*, *The Sleeping Cardinal* (+ 2ud), *Splinters in the Navy* (1931), *When London Sleeps*, *The Lodger*, *Frail Women*, *The Missing Rembrandt* (1932), *I Lived with You*, *Called Back* (co-d only), *The Shadow*, *The Wandering Jew* (1933), *The Broken Melody*, *Lily of Killarney* (1934), *The Last Journey*, *Scrooge*, *D'Ye Ken John Peel?*, *The Triumph of Sherlock Holmes*, *Squibs*, *The Morals of Marcus* (1935), *Spy of Napoleon*, *Eliza Comes to Stay*, *Juggernaut*, *Dusty Ermine*, *In the Soup* (1936), *Beauty and the Barge* (1937), *The Face at the Window* (1939), *Sailors Don't Care*, *Crimes at the Dark House* (1940), *Old Mother Riley's Ghosts* (1941), *Salute John Citizen* (1942), *This Happy Breed* (1944), *Blithe Spirit* (1945), *Once a Jolly Swagman*, *The Passionate Friends* (1948), *The Golden Salamander* (1949), *Captain Horatio Hornblower RN* (1950, UK/US), *Where No Vultures Fly* (1951), *The Master of Ballantrae* (1953), *The Rainbow Jacket* (1954), *Out of the Clouds*, *The Ladykillers* (1955), *Barnacle Bill*, *The Prince and the Showgirl* (1957), *Indiscreet*, *The Scapegoat* (1958), *Billy Budd* (1962), *Sammy Going South* (1963), *The Chalk Garden* (1964), *He Who Rides a Tiger* (1965), *Work is a Four Letter Word*, *Mister Ten Per Cent* (1967), *A Midsummer Night's Dream* (1968), *Three Sisters*, *Take a Girl Like You* (1970).

Harris, Jared (*b* London, 1961). Actor. Son of Richard **Harris**. Best known for his uncanny portrayal of Andy Warhol in the 1996 feature *I Shot Andy Warhol* (UK/US), a role he reprised in *54* (1998, US). He has worked as much in the US as in Britain where his first role was in brother Damian **Harris**'s *The Rachel Papers* (1989).
OTHER BRITISH FILMS INCLUDE: *Far and Away* (1992, Ire/US), *Lost in Space* (UK/US), *B. Monkey* (UK/It/US) (1998), *The Weekend* (1999, UK/US), *Morality Play* (2002).

Harris, Julie (*b* London, 1921). Costume designer. Oscar-winning designer for *Darling* (1965), Harris trained at Chelsea Art School and entered films after serving with the ATS during WW2. Taken on as assistant to Elizabeth **Haffenden** at **Gainsborough**, she had her first credit on *Holiday Camp* (1947) and later designed for the Somerset **Maugham** films, *Quartet* (1948), *Trio* (1950) and *Encore* (1951). When **Lime Grove Studio** closed, she went to **Pinewood** where she designed for the usual **Rank** GENRE mix of the 50s – THRILLERS, romances and COMEDIES – mostly in modern dress and often for director Ken **Annakin**, but there were later a few opportunities for period clothes in such films as *The Gypsy and the Gentleman* (1957) and *The Slipper and the Rose* (1976). While keeping abreast of contemporary fashions, she was also very alert to costume as signifier of class, temperament and nationality. She famously designed the mink bikini Diana **Dors** wore at the 1955 Venice Film Festival.
OTHER BRITISH FILMS INCLUDE: *Good-Time Girl* (1947), *Traveller's Joy* (1949), *The Clouded Yellow* (1950), *Hotel Sahara*, *Another Man's Poison* (1951), *The Net*, *Desperate Moment* (1953), *You Know What Sailors Are!*, *The Seekers* (1954), *Value for Money*, *Simon and Laura*, *Cast a Dark Shadow* (1955), *Miracle in Soho* (1957), *Sapphire*, *North West Frontier* (Lauren Bacall's dresses) (1959), *The Greengage Summer*, *All Night Long* (1961), *The Chalk Garden*, *A Hard Day's Night* (1964), *Help!* (1965), *Casino Royale* (1967, co-cos), *Goodbye, Mr Chips* (1969), *The Private Life of Sherlock Holmes* (1970), *Frenzy* (1972), *Live and Let Die* (1973), *Lost and Found* (1979), *The Hound of the Baskervilles* (1983).

Harris, Julie (*b* Grosse Pointe, Michigan, 1925). Actress. Idiosyncratic and much respected American stage and screen star, Harris has made a half-dozen distinctive appearances in British films, most notably in *I Am a Camera* (1955), in which she played wild child Sally Bowles when Dorothy **Tutin** declined to reprise her stage role. Most famous film role was as disturbed adolescent in *The Member of the Wedding* (1953, US), played when she was 28.
OTHER BRITISH FILMS: *The Truth About Women* (1957), *Sally's Irish Rogue* (1958, Ire), *The Haunting* (1963), *Voyage of the Damned* (1976), *Gentle into the Night* (1996, UK/It/Fr).

Harris, Richard (*b* Limerick, Ireland, 1930 – *d* London, 2002). Actor. A fiercely individualistic performer, as unconventional in his public as in his private life, becoming a star as the masochistic North Country rugby player in *This Sporting Life* (1963), and appearing on both screen (1966, US) and stage as King Arthur in *Camelot*. Rabelaisian in his drinking, and yet wrote fiction and poetry, reading it at New York's Lincoln Center in 1972 and publishing his first book of verse the following year. After RADA he joined Joan **Littlewood**'s Theatre Workshop, Stratford East, where he appeared in *The Quare Fellow*. Made his screen debut in *Alive and Kicking* (1958) under contract to **Associated British**, and his 6'2" frame led to a string of action heroes, including *The Heroes of Telemark* (1965), and he was an impressive *Cromwell* (1970). Has starred for Antonioni in *Red Desert* (1964, It) and in many Hollywood films, including *A Man Called Horse* (1970) and its sequels, and *Gladiator* (2000, UK/US). Oscar-nominated for *This Sporting*

Life and *The Field* (1990, UK/Ire). Second wife (1974–82) actress Ann Turkel. Sons by his first wife are director Damian HARRIS and actor Jared HARRIS.

OTHER BRITISH FILMS INCLUDE: *Shake Hands with the Devil* (1959, UK/US), *The Long and the Short and the Tall, The Guns of Navarone* (1961), *Bloomfield* (1969, UK/Israel, d), *To Walk with Lions* (2000, UK/Can/Kenya), *Harry Potter and the Philosopher's Stone* (UK/US) *My Kingdom* (2001), *Harry Potter and the Chamber of Secrets, The Count of Monte Cristo* (2002, UK/Ire/US).

BIBLIOG: Michael Feeney Callan, *Richard Harris: A Sporting Life*, 1990; Gus Smith, *Richard Harris: Actor by Accident*. AS.

Harris, Robert (*b* Weston-super-Mare, 1900 – *d* Northwood, Middlesex, 1995). Actor. Sherbourne- and Oxford-educated, this RADA-trained stage actor, often at Stratford and the Old Vic, on Broadway and the West End, played many Shakespearean and other classical roles from 1923. Entered films in 1930 (*The 'W' Plan*), lending his austere looks to such dignified roles as the Cardinal in *That Lady* (1955). Also filmed in the US, but not to be confused with the American actor, Robert B Harris, active in the 50s and 60s.

OTHER BRITISH FILMS INCLUDE: *How He Lied to Her Husband* (1931), *The Life and Death of Colonel Blimp* (1943), *The True Glory* (1945, UK/US, narr), *Bad Lord Byron* (1949), *Seven Waves Away* (1956), *Oscar Wilde* (1960), *Decline and Fall . . .* (1968), *Young Winston* (1972), *Lady Caroline Lamb* (1972, UK/It/US), *Ransom* (1974).

Harris, Rosemary (*b* Ashby, Suffolk, 1930). Actress. Much respected stage actress who has merely flirted, though to seductive effect, with the screen since playing Mrs Fitzherbert in *Beau Brummell* (1954). Began her stage career in Bognor Regis (1948), followed by time in rep and at RADA, before making her New York debut in 1952 and London the next year. Came to fame as *The Seven Year Itch* girl in London (1953), and then played her way through SHAKESPEARE, SHAW and others with the most reputable companies, winning awards (e.g. a Tony for *The Lion in Winter*, 1966) on the way. Somewhat eccentrically, she was cast as Peter FINCH's outback Australian girlfriend in *The Shiralee* (1957), has filmed in the US (*The Boys from Brazil*, 1978), done some major TV, including an all-star *Uncle Vanya* (1963, some cinemas), and was Oscar-nominated for her supporting role in *Tom & Viv* (1994, UK/US). She is the mother of Jennifer EHLE; both appeared in *Sunshine* (2000, UK/Austria/Can/Ger/Hung), playing the same character at different ages.

OTHER BRITISH FILMS: *The Ploughman's Lunch* (1983), *The Bridge* (1991), *Hamlet* (1996, UK/US), *Blow Dry* (2001, UK/Ger/US).

Harris, Vernon (*b* Folkstone, 1905 – *d* Yeovil, 1990). Screenwriter. Harris's career is almost wholly entwined with that of director Lewis GILBERT for whom he wrote or co-wrote 17 films. Gilbert claimed (1990) that Harris's 'real strength was as a script editor', that they 'would lay out the scenario together' and get a dialogue expert to complete the task. Together they achieved immense box-office success with such films as *Reach for the Sky* (1956), *Carve Her Name With Pride* (1958) and the two BOND adventures, *The Spy Who Loved Me* (1977, sc e) and *Moonraker* (1979, UK/Fr, sc e). Received BAAn for *Three Men in a Boat* (1957) and AAn for *Oliver!* (1968). A former actor, he scripted BBC radio series *Band Waggon* (1938, filmed 1939).

OTHER BRITISH FILMS INCLUDE: (a) *Joy-Ride* (1935, + sc), *Tropical Trouble* (+ sc), *Show Flat* (1936), *The Last Barricade, The Gables Mystery* (1938); (co-orig story) *There Was a Young Lady* (1953), *Emergency* (1962); (co-sc/sc) *The Improper Duchess* (1936), *The Adventures of PC 49* (1949), *Emergency Call* (1952), *Cosh Boy, Albert RN* (1953), *The Good Die Young, The Sea Shall Not Have Them* (1954), *The Admirable Crichton*

(1957), *A Cry from the Streets* (1958), *Ferry to Hong Kong* (1959), *Light Up the Sky* (1960), *Friends* (1971), *Paul and Michelle* (1974); (sc e) *Educating Rita* (1983), *Shirley Valentine* (1989, UK/US).

Harrison, Cathryn (*b* London, 1959). Actress. Delicate-featured blonde had her best film chances in the 70s: in Robert Altman's *Images* (1972, Ire), Louis Malle's *Black Moon* (1975, Fr/Ger) and the Australian girl-and-horse saga, *Blue Fire Lady* (1978). Had small roles in several 80s films, including *The Dresser* (1983), but found more interesting work on TV in the 90s, including leading roles in mini-series, *Portrait of a Marriage* (1990) as silly, stormy Violet Trefusis and *The Choir* (1995). Her grandfather was Rex HARRISON, and father, Noel Harrison (*b* London, 1933), appeared in a handful of films in the 60s, and, like his daughter, was in *Déjà Vu* (1998, UK/US).

OTHER BRITISH FILMS INCLUDE: *The Pied Piper* (1971), *The Happy Valley* (1986), *Eat the Rich, A Handful of Dust* (1987), *Thin Ice* (1994).

Harrison, George *see* **Beatles, The**

Harrison, Joan (*b* Guildford, 1907 – *d* London, 1994). Writer, producer. The personification of the 'cool blonde' of the HITCHCOCK films, Sorbonne-educated Harrison went to work for him as his secretary in 1935, became his screenwriter on *Jamaica Inn* (1939), went with him to the US, co-wrote *Rebecca* (1940), *Foreign Correspondent* (1940), *Suspicion* (1941), and *Saboteur* (1942), and later produced the TV series *Alfred Hitchcock Presents* (1955–62). Like writer Charles BENNETT, Harrison is a major, and yet shadowy, figure in the director's career. She became a producer in 1944 with *Phantom Lady*, and among her credits are two UK features, *Your Witness* and *Circle of Danger* (both 1950). Married Eric AMBLER in 1958, and returned to UK in 1982 in ill health. AS.

Harrison, Kathleen (*b* Blackburn, 1892 – *d* London, 1995). Actress. Not just an actress, but really an institution in British films in which she created moments of comic naturalism and poignancy over nearly 50 years and in about 80 films. Considering she was also frequently on stage from 1926, after RADA training, as well as radio and numerous TV appearances, it is as well she lived to be 103 to accommodate it all. She came clean about her birthdate just before her 100th birthday, having knocked six years off previously. Though she became identified as the Cockney maid or mum *par excellence*, she was born to middle-class parents and learnt to speak the Cockney dialect while rehearsing *Pygmalion* at RADA. On stage her range is exemplified in three famous roles: Violet the maid who announces the triumphant news in *The Winslow Boy* (1946), unforgettably repeating the role on film (1948); kind, vulgar Mrs Ashworth in *Waters of the Moon* (1951), and Nanny, with a cliché for all occasions, in *All for Mary* (1954), repeating her starring role on film (1955). As *Mrs Thursday* (1966), she had an instant TV hit.

It is probably with the HUGGETTS series she is most firmly identified. She and Jack WARNER were introduced as Mr and Mrs Huggett, a no-nonsense working-class couple, in *Holiday Camp* (1947). They proved so popular that three films and a radio programme followed based on the Huggett family life. A great DICKENS enthusiast, she also played memorable roles in *Oliver Twist* (1948, as the virago Mrs Sowerberry), in *Scrooge* (1951) and *The Pickwick Papers* (1952). But the gallery is so crowded it is hard to choose: even in a decades-forgotten melodrama, *Waterfront* (1950), as Robert NEWTON's long-suffering wife, she could register the sharp pain of real experience.

OTHER BRITISH FILMS: *Our Boys* (1915), *Hobson's Choice* (1931), *The Man from Toronto, The Ghoul* (1933), *What Happened Then?, The Great Defender* (1934), *Dandy Dick, Line Engaged* (1935), *Everybody Dance, Broken Blossoms* (1936), *Wanted, Aren't Men Beasts?* (1937), *I've Got a Horse, Bank Holiday, Almost a Gentleman, Convict 99* (1938), *I Killed the Count, Home from Home, A Girl Must Live, Discoveries, The Outsider* (1939), *They Came By Night, Tilly of Bloomsbury, The Flying Squad, Girl in the News* (1940), *Major Barbara, Once a Crook, Kipps, I Thank You, The Ghost Train, Letter from Home* (short) (1941), *In Which We Serve, Much Too Shy* (1942), *The New Lot* (doc), *Dear Octopus* (1943), *It Happened One Sunday, Meet Sexton Blake* (1944), *Great Day* (1945), *I See a Dark Stranger* (ucr), *Wanted for Murder, The Shop at Sly Corner* (1946), *Temptation Harbour* (1947), *Bond Street, Here Come the Huggetts, Vote for Huggett* (1948), *Now Barabbas Was a Robber, Landfall, The Huggetts Abroad* (1949), *Trio, Double Confession* (1950), *The Magic Box* (1951), *Golden Arrow, The Happy Family* (1952), *Turn the Key Softly, The Dog and the Diamonds* (1953), *Lilacs in the Spring* (1954), *Where There's a Will, Cast a Dark Shadow* (1955), *It's a Wonderful World, Home and Away* (1956), *Seven Thunders* (1957), *The Big Money, A Cry from the Streets, Alive and Kicking* (1958), *On the Fiddle* (1961), *Mrs Gibbons' Boys, The Fast Lady* (1962), *West 11* (1963), *Lock Up Your Daughters!* (1969), *The London Connection* (1979).

Harrison, Sir Rex (*b* Huyton, 1908 – *d* New York, 1990). Actor. No one could do better that particular thing Harrison did: the quizzical, elegant, sexually predatory man-about-town. The film that enshrines the persona most vividly is *The Rake's Progress* (1945), in which he plays the caddish philanderer who redeems himself in WW2 (Harrison himself had served in the RAF). The facts of his own life are not entirely remote from the type he made his own on stage (from 1924) and screen (from 1930): he married five times, including three rounds with famous actresses – Lilli PALMER (2), Kay KENDALL (3), and RACHEL ROBERTS (4) – and seems to have left much to be desired as husband and home-maker; and he was famously involved with American star Carole Landis who, allegedly, killed herself for love of him. The press of course dubbed him 'Sexy Rexy', and this personal history made him safe casting as the ageing homosexual in the British-set, French-made, US-financed *Staircase* (1969). The other great role of his life was his Tony-winning Henry Higgins in *My Fair Lady* (1956–58), for repeating which on screen he won an Oscar (1964, US). Curmudgeonly, misogynistic, talking his way through his songs, hectoring and charming the audience as he did Eliza, he recreated SHAW's original perhaps definitively.

He wore a lot of dinner jackets in 30s British theatre and had a moderate innings in pre-war cinema (e.g. a society doctor in *The Citadel*, 1938; a breezily intrepid hero in *Night Train to Munich*, 1940). Post-war, he hit his stride with *Blithe Spirit* (1945), had major US success with *Anna and the King of Siam* (1946), and from then on was more likely to be filming in Hollywood (or anywhere, really) than Britain. Among his later films, *Cleopatra* (1963, US) gave him a fine chance as witty, cynical Caesar; there was much, of course, to be cynical about. He was starring on Broadway in *The Circle* when he died. Knighted in 1989).

OTHER BRITISH FILMS: *School for Scandal, The Great Game* (1930), *Leave It to Blanche, Get Your Man* (1934), *All at Sea* (1935), *Men Are Not Gods* (1936), *Storm in a Teacup, School for Husbands* (1937), *St Martin's Lane* (1938), *Ten Days in Paris, The Silent Battle, Over the Moon* (1939), *Major Barbara* (1941), *I Live in Grosvenor Square* (1945), *Escape* (1948), *The Long Dark Hall* (1951, + assoc p), *The Constant Husband* (1954), *The Yellow Rolls-Royce* (1964), *The Fifth Musketeer* (1979, UK/Austria).

BIBLIOG: Autobiographies, *Rex*, 1974, *A Damned Serious Business: A Life in Comedy*, 1991; Alexander Walker, *Rex Harrison*, 1998.

Harrison, Tony (*b* Leeds, 1937). Director, writer. Anyone who makes a two-hour film in verse, based on Aeschylus's *Prometheus Bound* and transferred to the unemployed coalminers of Northern England, clearly has a streak of the heroic in his make-up. This difficult, intensely demanding film, *Prometheus* (1999), was first screened at the Locarno Film Festival; unsurprisingly, it has had only limited showings since. Also a poet and translator for the stage, and maker of TV verse films, including *V* (1987), controversial for its liberal use of swear words. Married to opera star Teresa Stratas.

Harrison Marks, George (*b* London, 1926 – *d* London, 1997). Director, producer. Originally a stand-up comic, he became the best known purveyor of soft-core porn among British film-makers. There are only five feature films among his EXPLOITATION output, but as well masses of short subjects, as it were. Before his death from cancer, he was preoccupied with the erotic aspects of corporal punishment. Lived for eight years with model/actress Pamela GREEN, star of his most famous film, *Naked As Nature Intended* (1961) – Marks persistently did his bit for nature.

OTHER BRITISH FILMS INCLUDE: *The Chimney Sweeps* (1963), *Pattern of Evil* (1961), *The Nine Ages of Nakedness* (1969), *Come Play with Me* (1977).

Harryhausen, Ray (*b* Los Angeles, 1920). Special effects. One of the finest and most distinctive exponents of stop-motion model ANIMATION, Harryhausen learned his craft in emulation of Willis H. O'Brien, the pioneering animator of *King Kong* (1933). He worked as assistant to O'Brien on *Mighty Joe Young* (1949), claiming that he did most of the animation himself. Subsequent credits include *The Beast from 20,000 Fathoms* (1953) and *It Came from Beneath the Sea* (1955), both of which required him to animate atomically-mutated gargantua and integrate them with live action; 'Dynamation' was the name he later gave to his interpretation of this process. In 1958 he turned to fantastic and mythical subjects with *The 7th Voyage of Sinbad*, followed later by the British-produced *Jason and the Argonauts* (1963), *The Golden Voyage of Sinbad* (1973), *Sinbad and the Eye of the Tiger* (1977) and *Clash of the Titans* (1981, UK/US), after which he retired. He moved to London in 1969 to be nearer to the European locations required for these projects, and to utilise RANK film studios' advanced travelling matte processes. Next to today's computer-generated movie monsters, his creations may seem quaint, but his meticulous hands-on approach lends them a characteristic style of motion which reveals the hand of an artist. Dan North.

Hart, Diane (*b* Bedford, 1926 – *d* London, 2002). Actress. Touted as an auburn-haired British Eve Arden type, Hart, in 1941 the youngest-ever RADA enrollee, needed better breaks than she ever had in British films to realise such potential. On stage (from 1943), she had more rewarding roles: e.g. Bessie in *The Chiltern Hundreds* (London, 1947; Broadway, 1949) and Susan in *The Little Hut* (1952). In films from late 40s, she was cheerful company in such programme fodder as *Happy Go Lovely* (1951) as Vera-Ellen's adenoidal Scots girl friend (1952), but the 'B' FILM, *One Jump Ahead* (1955), gave her her best chance to sparkle. Famously litigious, she was also famous as a corset-designer.

OTHER BRITISH FILMS INCLUDE: *The House in the Square* (1951), *You're Only Young Twice!, Something Money Can't Buy, Father's Doing Fine* (1952), *My Wife's Family* (1956), *Enter Inspector Duval* (1961), *Games That Lovers Play* (1970).

Hart, Ian (*b* Liverpool, 1964). Actor. Intense performer who often plays idealistic young men in crisis, Hart was perfectly cast as fellow-Liverpudlian and legendary BEATLE John LENNON in Iain SOFTLEY's fine drama *Backbeat* (1994), reprising a role he had played in *The Hours and Times* (1992, US). In Ken LOACH's Spanish Civil War film, *Land and Freedom* (1995, UK/Ger/Sp), he gave a remarkable performance as Dave Carne, a naive Liverpudlian bound up in tragic circumstances. Roles as Martin Donovan's gay lover in *Hollow Reed* (1996, UK/Ger), shiftless Dan in Michael WINTER-BOTTOM's *Wonderland* (1999), shabby private detective Parkis in *The End of the Affair* (2000, UK/Ger/US), and the desperate father in *Liam* (2001, UK/Ger/It), demonstrate his adaptable, risk-taking talent.

OTHER BRITISH FILMS INCLUDE: *No Surrender* (1985, UK/Can), *The Englishman Who Went Up . . .* , *Clockwork Mice*, *Nothing Personal* (UK/Ire) (1995), *B. Monkey* (1998, UK/It/US), *This Year's Love* (1999), *Best* (UK/Ire), *Born Romantic*, *Harry Potter and the Philosopher's Stone* (2001, UK/US), *Killing Me Softly* (2002). Melinda Hildebrandt.

Hartford-Davis, Robert (*b* England, 1923 – *d* Los Angeles, 1977). Producer, director. Entered films in 1939 at TEDDING-TON STUDIOS, and worked as camera and cutting assistant before going to the US to study, becoming a TV producer in 1955. His first feature as director was the 'B' THRILLER, *Crosstrap* (1961), but most of his work is of the EXPLOITATION variety, ranging (according to David McGillivray) 'from dreadful to dazzling', including the musical, *Gonks Go Beat* (1965, d, p, co-story), and the lamentable episodic comedy, *The Sandwich Man* (1966, d, co-sc), as well as more predictable fare. Ended his career in minor US films and TV.

OTHER BRITISH FILMS INCLUDE: (shorts) *The Man on the Cliff* (d), *Dollars for Sale* (p, sc) (1955), *Stranger in the City* (1961, d, p, sc); (features, d/p unless noted) *The Yellow Teddybears* (1963), *Saturday Night Out* (+ co-story), *Black Torment* (1964), *Press for Time* (1966, p), *The Smashing Bird I Used to Know* (1969, d), *Doctors Wear Scarlet* (1970), *The Fiend* (1971).

Hartley, Richard (*b* Holmfirth, 1944). Composer, music director. Responsible for the score of such disparately interesting films as Nicolas ROEG's *Bad Timing* (1980, + cond), several for Mike NEWELL, including *Dance with a Stranger* (1984) in which his score helps to evoke the distant 50s and the emotional pain of the film's theme, and *An Awfully Big Adventure* (1995), where the music plays on acrid nostalgia.

OTHER BRITISH FILMS INCLUDE: (m d) *The Rocky Horror Picture Show*, *The Romantic Englishwoman* (1975, UK/Fr, + comp); (comp) *Aces High* (1976, UK/Fr, + cond), *Shock Treatment* (+ cond, m arr, musician), *Bad Blood* (UK/NZ) (1981), *Foreign Skies* (add m), *The Good Father* (1986), *Soursweet*, *Tree of Hands* (1988), *Rough Magic*, *Victory* (UK/Fr/Ger) (1995, released 1998), *Stealing Beauty* (UK/Fr/It), *The Brylcreem Boys* (1996), *All the Little Animals* (1998), *Rogue Trader* (1999), *When Brendan Met Trudy* (UK/Ire), *The Martins* (2001).

Hartnell, Sir Norman (*b* London, 1901 – *d* Windsor, 1979). Costume designer. Cambridge-educated Hartnell started his own dressmaking business in 1923, and received a royal warrant in 1940. His dresses for Queen Elizabeth, Princess Margaret and the Queen Mother were suitable, dowdy and dull, making him an ideal costume designer for British films, and his house, Norman Hartnell Ltd, supplied the wardrobe for many from 1930–63. Appeared as himself in Humphrey JENNINGS's *Design for Spring* (1938). Knighted 1977.

BRITISH FILMS INCLUDE: *Such Is the Law* (1930), *Princess Charming* (1934), *Two's Company* (1936), *Non-Stop New York* (1937), *Sailing Along*, *Climbing High* (1938), *Ships with Wings* (1941), *The Demi-Paradise*

(1943), *Nowhere to Go* (1958), *Suddenly, Last Summer* (1959), *Never Put It in Writing* (1963).

BIBLIOG: Autobiography: *Silver and Gold*, 1955. AS.

Hartnell, William (aka Billy) (*b* Seaton, 1908 – *d* London, 1975). Actor. Before playing the first *Dr Who*, Hartnell, on stage from 1924, was a familiar face in British cinema portraying tough Sergeants and underworld types. However, despite stereotyped roles, the actor often delivered varied inflexions to his part. Former apprentice jockey, he first appeared on stage in 1924 and appeared in films from the early 30s onwards. He could play both light leads and character roles. He came to notice playing the firm Sergeant in *The Way Ahead* (1944) which led to a brief period as leading man in the crime dramas *Murder in Reverse* (1945), *Appointment with Crime* (1946) as well as playing the title role in the political morality film *The Agitator* (1945).

During the 50s, Hartnell soon became stereotypically cast as a Sergeant in serious films and comedies such as *Private's Progress* (1956) and *Carry on Sergeant* (1958), but with some interesting character variants from time to time, like soft-spoken Dallow in *Brighton Rock* (1947) and the ambivalent hanger-on to the rugby star in *This Sporting Life* (1963).

OTHER BRITISH FILMS: *The Lure* (1933), *Seeing is Believing* (1934), *Farewell Again* (1937), *Murder Will Out* (1939), *They Came By Night* (1940), *Suspected Person* (1942), *Odd Man Out*, *Temptation Harbour* (1947), *Escape* (1948), *Now Barabbas Was a P·bber*, *The Lost People* (1949), *Double Confession* (1950), *The Magic Box* (1951), *The Holly and the Ivy*, *The Ringer*, *The Pickwick Papers* (1952), *Will Any Gentleman?* (1953), *Yangtse Incident* (1956), *Hell Drivers* (1957), *And the Same to You* (1959), *Heavens Above!* (1963).

BIBLIOG: Jessica Carney, *Who's There? The Life and Career of William Hartnell*, 1996. Tony Williams.

Hartog, Simon (*b* London, 1940 – *d* London, 1992). Activist. After playing the American GI who precipitates a nuclear attack in Peter WATKINS' *The War Game* (1966), Hartog helped found THE LONDON FILMMAKERS COOPERATIVE, then played a crucial role in the IFA and the campaign for CHANNEL 4. In the 70s he researched the ACTT's nationalisation proposals, then put theory into practice as adviser to the post-colonial government in Mozambique. The three series of *Visions: Cinema* (Channel 4) made by Large Door, the company he started with John Ellis, reflected his passion for World Cinema and opposition to CENSORSHIP. David Curtis.

Harvey, Anthony (*b* London, 1931). Editor, director. Best known for directing *The Lion in Winter* (1968), for which he had an AAn and won a Directors' Guild award, Harvey entered films as a child actor in *Caesar and Cleopatra* (1945). Became an editor, working often on the BOULTING brothers' films of the 50s, and later on KUBRICK's *Dr Strangelove . . .* (1963). The films he has directed are an eclectic lot: consider *Dutchman* (1966), an allegorical sex-and-race piece set on a Manhattan subway; the engaging SHERLOCK HOLMES fantasy, *They Might Be Giants* (1971, US); *Eagle's Wing* (1978), a Western of haunting images; and *The Patricia Neal Story* (1991, co-d, TV, some cinemas).

OTHER BRITISH FILMS INCLUDE: (e) *Seagulls Over Sorrento* (1954, ass e), *Private's Progress*, *Brothers in Law* (1956), *Happy is the Bride* (1957), *Tread Softly Stranger* (1958), *I'm All Right Jack* (1959), *The Angry Silence* (1960), *Lolita* (1961), *The Spy Who Came in from the Cold* (1965), *The Whisperers* (1966); (d) *Giacometti* (1967, short, + e), *The Abdication* (1974), *Richard's Things* (1980).

Harvey, Forrester (b London, 1880 – d Laguna Beach, California, 1945). Actor. Character player who made some silent films in 20s Britain before moving to Hollywood where he often appeared in Brit-set films like *Rebecca* (1940).

BRITISH FILMS INCLUDE: *The Lilac Sunbonnet* (1922), *Somebody's Darling* (1925), *Nell Gwynne*, *The Flag Lieutenant* (1926), *The Ring* (1927), *Moulin Rouge* (1928), *Ringing the Changes* (1929).

Harvey, Frank Jr (b Manchester, 1912 – d Ottery St Mary, 1981). Dramatist, screenwriter. The author of some popular plays, including *Saloon Bar* (1939, filmed 1940) and *Elizabeth of Ladymead* (1948, filmed later that year from his screenplay), his screen career was much involved with the BOULTING brothers, who filmed *Brighton Rock* (1947) which Harvey had adapted to the stage. For them he (co-)wrote such successes as *Seven Days to Noon* (1950), *Private's Progress* (1956, BAAn/sc) and *I'm All Right Jack* (1959, shared BAA/sc). Not to be confused with father, stage actor Frank Harvey.

OTHER BRITISH FILMS INCLUDE: (co-sc, unless noted) *Burma Victory* (1945), *My Brother's Keeper* (sc), *Portrait from Life* (1948), *High Treason* (1951), *The Long Memory* (1952), *Seagulls Over Sorrento* (1954), *Josephine and Men* (1955), *Brothers in Law* (1956), *The Thirty Nine Steps* (1958, sc), *Danger Within* (1958), *No, My Darling Daughter* (1961, sc), *Heavens Above!* (1963).

Harvey, Laurence (b Yomishkis, Lithuania, 1927 – d London, 1973). Actor. Real name: Hirsch Skikne – also cited as Larushka Mischa Skikne. Harvey was in the right place at the right time just once: his performance (AAn, BAAn) as Joe Lampton in *Room at the Top* (1958) remains a significant indicator of the winds of change in British cinema. He is the screen's answer to the theatre's Jimmy Porter, much more so than the screen's own Jimmy Porter as filtered through Richard BURTON's mellifluous tones. Harvey's last moments as he gets into the bridal car to be driven to 'the top' remain a moving statement of ambition achieved at the cost of self-betrayal. His performance as the working-class man on the make opened the doors for Tom COURTENAY, Albert FINNEY and others who breasted the NEW WAVE of British cinema. Unlike them, though, he tended to draw critical opprobrium for most of his work.

He wasn't a newcomer when he played Joe. Educated in South Africa, he came to England to study at RADA and quite soon became a by-word for living picturesquely beyond his means. Means, that is, generated by a series of modest programmers like *Man on the Run* (1949), the lead in 'B' FILMS such as *The Scarlet Thread* (1951), playing charming wastrels across the social spectrum in, e.g., *I Believe in You* (1952) and *The Good Die Young* (1954), made for ROMULUS to whom he was under contract; doing a somewhat wooden Romeo for Castellani in *Romeo and Juliet* (1954, UK/It) – and so on. Then Joe made him a major star for a while, sought on both sides of the Atlantic. In the US he played opposite Elizabeth TAYLOR (you couldn't aspire higher in 1960) in *Butterfield 8* and his characteristic affectlessness was brilliantly used in John FRANKENHEIMER's *The Manchurian Candidate* (1962). Back in Britain, he reprised Joe in *Life at the Top* (1965), more respectable than most sequels and owing much to the continuities he brought it, and was well-served by the intelligently observed superficialities of *Darling* (1965). He died sadly young (of cancer) after another dozen or so indifferent films shot all over the place, with an ineptitude that knew no geographic barriers. Also directed *The Ceremony* (1963, US/Sp). Married (1) Margaret LEIGHTON (1957–61) and (2) Joan Cohn (1968–72), widow of fabled ogre Harry.

OTHER BRITISH FILMS: *House of Darkness* (1948), *The Man from Yesterday*, *Landfall* (1949), *The Dancing Years* (bit part), *The Black Rose* (UK/US), *Cairo Road* (1950), *There Is Another Sun* (1951), *A Killer Walks*, *Women of Twilight* (1952), *Innocents in Paris* (1953), *Storm over the Nile*, *I Am a Camera* (1955), *Three Men in a Boat* (1956), *After the Ball*, *The Truth About Women* (1957), *The Silent Enemy* (1958), *Expresso Bongo* (1959), *The Long and the Short and the Tall* (1960), *The Running Man* (1963), *Of Human Bondage* (1964), *The Spy with a Cold Nose*, *The Winter's Tale* (1966), *A Dandy in Aspic* (1968, + add d), *The Magic Christian* (1969), *Night Watch* (1973).

BIBLIOG: Emmett and Des Hickey, *The Prince: Laurence Harvey*, 1975.

Harvey, Lilian (b London, 1906 – d Juan-les-Pins, France, 1968). Actress. A romantic ingenue and accomplished comedienne in German films of the 20s, Harvey became a truly 'European' star in the early 30s in French, German, and British multi-lingual co-productions. Her biggest success was the costume operetta *Congress Dances* (1931, UK/Ger). She also starred in three Hollywood films before her career petered out in the late 30s, perhaps because she stayed too long in Nazi Germany.

OTHER BRITISH FILMS: *A Knight in London* (1929), *Love Waltz*, *The Temporary Widow* (1930), *Happy Ever After* (1932), *The Only Girl* (1933), *Invitation To The Waltz* (1935), *Did I Betray?/Black Roses* (1937).

BIBLIOG: Hans Borgen, *The Lilian Harvey Story*, 1974. Tim Bergfelder.

Harvey, Morris (b London, 1877 – d 1944). Actor. Former stockbroker, who went on to success on London and New York stage, and appeared in about 20 films mainly in the 30s, in small roles like that of the poulterer in *Scrooge* (1935) and the pawnbroker in *21 Days* (1937). Married Mai BACON.

OTHER BRITISH FILMS INCLUDE: *Cash* (1933), *Sing As We Go!* (1934), *Crown v Stevens* (1936), *Crook's Tour* (1940), *The Great Mr Handel* (1942).

Harvey, Richard (b Enfield, 1944). Composer. Most of his work has been for TV, and he shared a BAA for the music for mini-series, *GBH* (1991). He scored three contrasting 80s films – *Steaming* (1984), *Defence of the Realm* (1985), *The Assam Garden* (1985) – but has since worked on little-seen films.

OTHER BRITISH FILMS INCLUDE: *Lady Chatterley's Lover* (1981, co-comp), *The Honorary Consul* (1983, add m), *Paper Mask* (1990), *Deadly Advice* (1994), *Captain Jack* (1998).

Harvey, Tim Production designer. After doing notable work on major TV series like *I, Claudius* (1976) and *Fortunes of War* (1987), starring Kenneth BRANAGH, Harvey has designed all Branagh's films. The success of *Henry V* (1989), shot entirely at SHEPPERTON, with stunning use of studio sets to introduce the drama, was followed by very different effects in *Much Ado About Nothing* (1993, UK/US), for which he designed additions to an actual 14th-century Tuscan villa. For *Mary Shelley's Frankenstein* (1994), US-financed but made almost entirely at Shepperton, Harvey recreated an 18th-century Swiss town as well as an Arctic ice-scape, and for the four-hour *Hamlet* (1996, UK/US), which had Blenheim Palace for exteriors, Harvey used five Shepperton soundstages to recreate elaborate interiors. Nominated for AA for *Hamlet* and BAA for *Henry V*, *Frankenstein*, and *Hamlet*.

OTHER BRITISH FILMS INCLUDE: *Peter's Friends* (1992), *In the Bleak Midwinter* (1995), *Othello* (1995, UK/US), *Love's Labour's Lost* (2000, UK/Fr/US), *Last Orders* (2002, UK/Ger).

Harvey, Walter J. (b Norfolk, 1903) Cinematographer. Immensely prolific craftsman who worked mainly in second features, but sometimes gave these an unexpected sheen, as he does for Francis SEARLE's grim *Cloudburst* (1951) and Ken

HUGHES's moody *The House Across the Lake* (1954), and made occasional forays into main feature territory – he photographed Marie TEMPEST in *Yellow Sands* (1938) and the monstrous Other in *The Quatermass Experiment* (1955).

OTHER BRITISH FILMS INCLUDE: (co-c) *Man From Chicago* (1930), *Love Lies, Hobson's Choice* (1931), *Facing the Music* (1933), *The Flying Squad* (1940); (c) *His Wife's Mother* (1932), *The Love Nest* (1933), *Sensation* (1936), *Bulldog Drummond at Bay* (1937), *Just William* (1939), *Spellbound* (1941), *They Keep the Wheels Turning* (1942, short), *Song of Tomorrow* (1948), *The Rossiter Case* (1950), *A Case for PC 49* (1951), *Stolen Face, The Last Page* (1952), *Life with the Lyons* (1954), *One Way Out, The Glass Cage* (1955), *Women Without Men* (1956), *The Big Chance, The End of the Line* (1957), *Jungle Street* (1961), *Shadow of Fear, The Hi-jackers* (1963), *The Runaway* (1964).

Harwood, Ronald (*b* Cape Town, 1934). Dramatist, screenwriter. In England since 1951, trained as actor at RADA and joined Donald WOLFIT's company in 1953. His experiences here provided the basis for his best-known play, *The Dresser* (1980), filmed in 1983, and he received AAn and BAAn for his screenplay. It is an affectionate, witty evocation of a now vanished acting tradition, and it starred Tom COURTENAY and Albert FINNEY, two actors with whom Harwood's career has been linked. Two of his earlier screenplays, *Private Potter* (1962, co-sc) and *One Day in the Life of Ivan Denisovich* (1971, UK/Nor/US), both directed by Caspar WREDE, starred Courtenay, and he received another BAAn for *The Browning Version* (1994), starring Finney as the embittered schoolmaster. His career on stage and TV is also impressive. AA in 2003 for screenplay (adaptation) for *The Pianist* (UK/Ger/Pol).

OTHER BRITISH FILMS INCLUDE: *The Barber of Stamford Hill* (1962, + orig TV play), *A High Wind in Jamaica* (1965, co-sc), *Eyewitness* (1970), *The Doctor and the Devils* (1985), *The Pianist* (2001, UK/Fr/Ger/Pol, co-sc).

Harwood, Shuna (*b* Thaxted, 1940). Costume designer. From Richard LONCRAINE's *Richard III* (1995), for which she won a BAA and AAn, to contemporary romantic comedy, *Notting Hill* (1999, UK/US), suggests the range of Harwood's work, which also includes three offbeat projects for Nicolas ROEG – *Bad Timing* (1980, add cos), *Insignificance* (1985) and *Track 29* (1988). A graduate of the Royal College of Art, she was a magazine fashion editor before entering films in 1976.

OTHER BRITISH FILMS INCLUDE: *Full Circle* (1976, UK/Can), *The Odd Job* (1978), *The Missionary* (1981), *Brimstone & Treacle* (1982), *Personal Services, Wish You Were Here, Aria* (segment) (1987), *The Land Girls* (1998, UK/Fr), *Bride of the Wind* (2001, UK/Ger).

Hassall, Imogen (*b* Woking, 1942 – *d* London, 1980). Actress. Ingenue of a few 60s and 70s films, including some of the EXPLOITATION variety, such as *Licensed to Love and Kill* (1979). Played the gypsy's wife in *The Virgin and the Gypsy* (1970), but with very limited screen time, and appeared in several TV series, including *The Saint* (1962). Died of a drug overdose.

OTHER BRITISH FILMS INCLUDE: *The Mind Benders* (1963), *The Early Bird* (1965), *Mumsy, Nanny, Sonny and Girly* (1969), *Toomorrow, Carry On Loving, Doctors Wear Scarlet* (1970), *White Cargo* (1973).

Hassé, Charles (*b* Algeria 1904 – *d* Grosseto, Italy, 2002). Director, editor. Joined **GPO FILM UNIT** 1934, and directed *War & Order* (1940), *Venture Adventure* (1941), *Christmas Under Fire* (1941) for the CROWN FILM UNIT. Then moved to EALING where he edited a half-dozen films including *My Learned Friend* (1943), *Dead of Night* (1945) and *Hue and Cry* (1946), after which he freelanced and edited many films including *My Brother Jonathan* (1948), *Private Angelo* (1949)

and *Albert RN* (1953). In 1958 he went to Kuwait under contract to **FILM CENTRE** and edited several films, including *Sweat Without Tears* (1959).

OTHER BRITISH FILMS INCLUDE: (e) *The Halfway House, Champagne Charlie* (1944, *The Captive Heart* (1946), *Midnight Episode* (1950), *Night Was Our Friend* (1951), *Emergency Call* (1952), *Cosh Boy* (1953), *It's Never Too Late* (1956), *She Didn't Say No* (1957), *Close-up on Kuwait* (1961). Rodney Giesler.

Hastings, Hugh (*b* Sydney, 1917). Actor, dramatist. After a diversity of jobs in Australia, came to UK in 1936. After WW2 Royal Navy service, he acted in a number of plays before finding success as the author of *Seagulls Over Sorrento* (1949), subsequently adapted to the screen (1954). He collaborated on the screenplays for *It Started in Paradise* and *The Gift Horse* (1952), and several decades later appeared in small character roles in *Dad's Army* (1971) and three children's films.

OTHER BRITISH FILMS: (a) *Captain Stirrick* (1982), *A Swarm in May* (1983), *School for Vandals* (1986).

Hauser, Philo (*b* Graz, Austria, 1915). Actor. Austrian stage actor who emigrated to Britain in 1939 via Belgium. On London stage from 1942, in British cinema mainly confined to small supporting parts, often typecast in stereotypical Teutonic roles. Occasionally also in international productions (*Exodus*, 1960).

BRITISH FILMS INCLUDE: *Against The Wind* (1947), *Portrait From Life* (1948), *The Lost People, Give Us This Day* (UK/US) (1949), *Lilli Marlene* (1950), *Hell Below Zero* (1953, UK/US), *The Divided Heart* (1954), *Desert Mice* (1959), *The Password Is Courage* (1962), *The Heroes of Telemark* (1965). Tim Bergfelder.

Havelock-Allan, Sir Anthony (*b* Darlington, 1904 – *d* London, 2003). Producer. One of the most distinguished producers in British film history, Havelock-Allan entered the industry in 1933 as casting director and producer's assistant, after working at several other jobs. He became personal assistant to Captain NORTON (later Lord Grantley) at Pinewood, and produced a great many 'QUOTA QUICKIES' during the 30s, for PARAMOUNT, BRITISH AND DOMINIONS, and PINEBROOK, for which he produced his first real success, *This Man is News* (1938), starring Valerie HOBSON, who became his first wife. During the 40s, he was associated with the prestige arm of British film production through work for TWO CITIES (*In Which We Serve*, 1942, assoc p) and his founding of CINEGUILD, with David LEAN and Ronald NEAME, an independent production unit under the RANK umbrella. Some of its films included *Brief Encounter* (1945, co-sc, co-ex p), *Great Expectations* (1946, co-sc, ex p) and *Oliver Twist* (1948, ex p), films which raised the reputation of British cinema internationally. He made four more films with Hobson at this time, the most notable of which are the sumptuous MELODRAMA, *Blanche Fury* (1947) and the threatened-household thriller, *The Small Voice* (1948), and produced two for Anthony ASQUITH, *The Young Lovers* (1954) and *Orders to Kill* (1958). His 60s credits, including ZEFFIRELLI's ground-breaking *Romeo and Juliet* (1968, UK/It), point to his interest in the other arts, and his final film, *Ryan's Daughter* (1970), reunited him with David LEAN. He also held many important executive positions in the film industry. Despite what other reference books say, he never married US actress Marguerite Chapman.

OTHER BRITISH FILMS: (p, unless noted) *Badger's Green* (1934), *The Village Squire, School for Stars, The Price of Wisdom, Once a Thief, The Mad Hatters, Lucky Days, Key to Harmony, Jubilee Window, Gentlemen's Agreement, Expert's Opinion, Cross Currents, Checkmate* (1935), *Ticket of Leave, Wednesday's Luck, Two on a Doorstep, Show Flat, The Secret Voice, The Scarab Murder Case, Paybox Adventure, Murder by Rope, Love at Sea,*

House Broken, Grand Finale, The Belles of St Clements (1936), *Night Ride, Museum Mystery, Mr Smith Carries On, Missing, Believed Married, The Last Curtain, Lancashire Luck, Holiday's End, The Fatal Hour, Cross My Heart, Cavalier of the Streets* (1937), *Incident in Shanghai, A Spot of Bother, Lightning Conductor* (1938), *This Man in Paris, The Silent Battle, Stolen Life* (assoc p), *The Lambeth Walk* (1939), *From the Four Corners* (1941, short, d), *Unpublished Story* (+ co-story) (1942), *This Happy Breed* (1944, co-p, co-sc), *Blithe Spirit* (+ co-sc) (1945), *Take My Life* (1947), *The Interrupted Journey* (1949), *Shadow of the Eagle* (1950), *Never Take No for an Answer* (1951), *Meet Me Tonight* (1952), *The Quare Fellow* (1962), *An Evening with the Royal Ballet* (co-p, co-d) (1963), *Othello* (1965, co-p), *The Mikado* (1966, co-p), *Up the Junction* (1967, co-p).

Havers, Nigel (*b* London, 1949). Actor. Son of Baron Havers, former Attorney General and Lord Chancellor, tall, chisel-featured Havers has generally had his best chances on TV, in mini-series such as *The Glittering Prizes* (1976) and *A Horseman Riding By* (1978) and the sitcom, *Don't Wait Up* (1983), though by the time he starred in *Dangerfield* (1995) he was looking his age without any compensating character interest. He had two good film roles: the benign aristocrat in *Chariots of Fire* (1981) and the wet Ronnie Heslop in *A Passage to India* (1984). Was a stylish Algy in the National Theatre's *The Importance of Being Earnest* (1982–83).

OTHER BRITISH FILMS: *Pope Joan* (1972), *Full Circle* (1976, UK/Can), *The Whistle Blower* (1986), *Element of Doubt* (1996).

Hawk, Jeremy (*b* Johannesburg, 1918 – *d* Reading, 2002). Actor. RN: Cedric Lange. Harrow-educated, RADA-trained, elegant supporting actor of stage (London from 1940, followed by revues and plays) and screen from early 40s, as in *In Which We Serve* (1942). Often seen as straight man to comedians such as Benny HILL (in *Who Done It?*, 1956, plus TV appearances) and suave TV compere. Married/divorced Joan HEAL; their daughter is TV actress, Belinda Lang (*b* London, 1953).

OTHER BRITISH FILMS INCLUDE: *The Peterville Diamond* (1942), *Lucky Jim* (1957), *Dentist on the Job* (1961), *The Trygon Factor* (1966), *The Return of the Pink Panther* (1974), *Stealing Heaven* (1988), *Elizabeth* (1998).

Hawkesworth, John (*b* London, 1920). Producer, art director. Entered films in the late 40s working in various art department capacities on such films as *The Fallen Idol* (1948) and *The Third Man* (1949, as an assistant to Vincent KORDA). Later became producer of such TV series as *Upstairs, Downstairs* (1971, + sc) and the SHERLOCK HOLMES series of the 80s.

OTHER BRITISH FILMS INCLUDE: (art d) *State Secret* (1950, ass), *The Sound Barrier* (1952, co-art d), *Father Brown* (1954), *The Prisoner, The Man Who Never Was* (1955); (p) *Windom's Way* (1957, assoc p), *Tiger Bay* (1959, + co-sc).

Hawkins, Jack (*b* London, 1910 – *d* London, 1973). Actor. Square-jawed actor who exploited his rich vocal tones to endow the countless figures of authority he played with a formidable screen presence. A child performer, Hawkins scored his first film role in 1921 in *The Four Just Men* and made his theatrical debut in London at age 12, playing the elf king in *Where the Rainbow Ends*. Years of minor screen work followed, as did his marriage (1932–42) to Jessica TANDY, and a stint in India during WW2 as Colonel in ENSA (the entertainment arm of Britain's armed forces). Serious fame came in the 50s with his roles as Captain Ericson in *The Cruel Sea* and the gruffly humane teacher of deaf children in *Mandy* (1952), the paternalistic Merton in *The Intruder* (1953), Major Warden, the fervent demolition expert of *The Bridge on the River Kwai* (1957), and his most commanding turn of all, Quintus Arrius

('Your eyes are full of hate, 41') in *Ben-Hur* (1959, US). In 1960, it was interesting to see him submit his officer-and-gentleman persona to some scrutiny in *The League of Gentlemen*, and he remained in regular demand in British and international films. In 1966, cancer of the larynx destroyed his voice though not his desire to act. Hawkins appeared in films right up until his death, miming the dialogue that was dubbed in post-production by either Charles GRAY or Robert RIETTY.

OTHER BRITISH FILMS: *Birds of Prey* (1930), *The Lodger* (1932), *A Shot in the Dark, The Jewel, I Lived with You, The Good Companions, The Lost Chord* (1933), *Death at Broadcasting House, Autumn Crocus* (1934), *Peg of Old Drury* (1935), *The Frog, Beauty and the Barge* (1937), *Who Goes Next?, A Royal Divorce* (1938), *Murder Will Out* (1939), *The Flying Squad* (1940), *The Next of Kin* (1942), *The Fallen Idol, Bonnie Prince Charlie, The Small Back Room* (1948), *The Elusive Pimpernel, State Secret, The Black Rose* (UK/US), *The Adventurers* (1950), *No Highway* (1951), *Home at Seven, The Planter's Wife, Angels One Five* (1952), *Twice Upon a Time, Malta Story, Front Page Story* (1953), *The Seekers* (1954), *Touch and Go, The Prisoner* (1955), *The Long Arm, The Man in the Sky* (1956), *Fortune Is a Woman* (1957), *The Two-Headed Spy, Gideon's Day* (1958), *The League of Gentlemen* (1960), *Lawrence of Arabia* (1962), *Zulu, The Third Secret, Guns at Batasi, Lord Jim* (1964), *Masquerade, Judith* (UK/Israel/US) (1965), *Great Catherine* (1967), *Shalako* (1968), *Monte Carlo or Bust!* (UK/Fr/It), *Oh! What a Lovely War, Twinky* (1969), *The Adventures of Gerard* (UK/It/Switz), *Jane Eyre* (1970), *When Eight Bells Toll, The Ruling Class* (co-p), *Kidnapped* (1971), *Young Winston* (1972), *Theatre of Blood, Tales That Witness Madness* (1973).

BIBLIOG: Autobiography, *Anything for a Quiet Life*, 1973. Melinda Hildebrandt.

Hawksworth, Johnny Composer. Worked on about a dozen idiosyncratically diverse films in the 60s and 70s, including three with animator Bob GODFREY – *Bang, Whatever Happened to Uncle Fred?* (1967), *Henry 9 'til 5* (1970).

OTHER BRITISH FILMS INCLUDE: (comp, unless noted) *The Naked World of Harrison Marks* (1965, + m d), *Goal! World Cup 1966* (1966, UK/Liecht, doc), *The Penthouse* (1967), *Kama Sutra Rides Again* (1971, anim, + cond), *Justine* (1976).

Hawthorne, David (*b* Kettering, 1888 – *d* Folkestone, 1942). Actor. Starring roles in film from 1920 led to a stage career in 1924 for this actor who played the screen's second *Rob Roy* (1922) and was featured opposite Tallulah Bankhead in *His House in Order* (1928). Supporting roles on screen from 1931.

OTHER BRITISH FILMS INCLUDE: *Testimony* (1920), *The Mating of Marcus* (1924), *The Other Woman* (1931), *Laburnum Grove* (1936). AS.

Hawthorne, Sir Nigel (*b* Coventry, 1929 – *d* Radwell, Hertfordshire, 2001). Actor. Perhaps the greatest character star in British films since Alec GUINNESS, Hawthorne, raised in South Africa, in Britain from 1951, had a long slow climb to a very assured summit. First on stage in Capetown, where he attended university, then on West End stage in 1962. On TV from mid 50s, he came first to popular attention as the endlessly manipulative Sir Humphrey, whose reiterated *Yes Minister* (1980–82) and later *Yes Prime Minister* (1986–88) was a sure sign of devious disagreement with his superior. First film was *Young Winston* (1972) and there were a few minor roles over the next decade, including the US film, *Firefox* (1982), and he was becoming well known on TV. It was his playing on screen of his award-winning National Theatre role in *The Madness of King George* (1994, UK/US) which led to his being sought for international films. As the loving, demented King, he created an unforgettable portrait and followed this by a moving account of the Duke of Clarence in *Richard III* (1995) and a superbly haughty, self-deluding Malvolio in Trevor NUNN's

LEFT **Robert Krasker**, cinematographer.

ABOVE **Sir David Lean**, director, former editor.

BELOW LEFT **Fame Is the Spur** (1947), drama, with Michael Redgrave, Jean Shepheard.

BELOW *Temptation Harbour* (1947, d.Lance Comfort), film noir thriller, with Robert Newton, William Hartnell.

RIGHT *Blanche Fury* (1947, d.Marc Allegret),
with Stewart Granger, Valerie Hobson.

BELOW **Kathleen Byron**, leading actress, here
in *Black Narcissus*.

ABOVE *The Fallen Idol* (1948, d.Carol Reed),
drama, with Bobby Henrey.

RIGHT *Trottie True* (1948, d.Brian Desmond
Hurst), musical romance, with Jean Kent
(left).

perhaps undervalued *Twelfth Night* (1996, UK/US). In 1999, he gave a definitive account of *The Winslow Boy*'s father, intransigent in seeing right done, but his other 1999 release, *The Clandestine Marriage* (+ assoc p), got appalling reviews, and allegedly cost him a lot of his own invested money. It took more than this, though, to obstruct a career so firmly established in all the acting media – and in the public regard. He was awarded CBE in 1987 and knighted in 1999, to add to the swag of honours bestowed for his acting, including BAAs for *King George* and the TV series, *The Fragile Heart* (1996), and a Tony for his Broadway role in *Shadowlands* (1991).

OTHER BRITISH FILMS: *Watership Down* (voice), *Sweeney 2*, *The Sailor's Return* (1978), *Memoirs of a Father*, *The Knowledge* (1981), *Gandhi* (1982, UK/Ind), *Dead on Time* (1982), *The Chain* (1984), *Turtle Diary* (1985), *Fleabites* (1991), *Freddie as F.R.O.7* (1992).

Hawtrey, Charles (*b* Hounslow, 1914 – *d* Walmer, 1988). Actor. RN: Hartree. On stage from 1925 and in London from 1927, in children's plays, the paper-thin, twittery Hawtrey became famous for his participation in the 'CARRY ON' series, where his camp behaviour and pursuit of the opposite sex lent sexual ambiguity to his persona. His morning-dressed, mother-ridden traveller will clearly find Spain a liberating experience in *Carry On Abroad* (1972), though he is funnier in . . . *Constable* (1960), as Constable Constable. In films since the early 30s, he cut his teeth on several Will HAY comedies, including *Good Morning, Boys!* (1937) and had made about 30 films, supporting other comedians, such as Benny HILL in *Who Done It?* (1956), before finding his 'Carry On' niche, which he finally deserted as a result of a row over billing. In 2000, his blue-plaqued house in Deal was in the news when it came up for sale. Not to be confused with stage actor **Charles Hawtrey** who appeared in several silent films, including *A Message from Mars* (1913).

OTHER BRITISH FILMS INCLUDE: *Marry Me* (1932), *Sabotage* (1936), *The Ghost of St Michael's* (1941), *A Canterbury Tale* (1944), *The End of the River* (1947), *The Galloping Major* (1951), *Man of the Moment* (1955), *The March Hare*, *Who Done It?* (1956), *I Only Arsked!*, *Carry On Sergeant*, . . . *Nurse* (1958), . . . *Teacher* (1959), *Please Turn Over* (1960), *Dentist on the Job*, *Carry On Regardless* (1961), . . . *Cabby* (1963), . . . *Spying*, . . . *Jack*, . . . *Cleo* (1964), . . . *Cowboy* (1965), . . . *Screaming*, . . . *Don't Lose Your Head* (1966), *Follow That Camel* (1967), *Carry On Up the Khyber*, . . . *Doctor* (1968), *Zeta One*, *Carry On Camping*, . . . *Again Doctor* (1969), . . . *Up the Jungle*, . . . *Loving* (1970), . . . *Henry*, . . . *at Your Convenience* (1971), . . . *Matron* (1972).

BIBLIOG: Roger Lewis, *Charles Hawtrey 1914–1988: The Man Who Was Private Widdle*, 2001.

Hay, Ian (*b* Chorlton, 1876 – *d* Petersfield, 1952). Dramatist, screenwriter. RN: John Hay Beith. Popular playwright many of whose light entertainments were filmed, especially in the 30s. Among the films derived from his plays were *Tilly of Bloomsbury* (1921, 1931, 1940), *The Middle Watch* (1930, 1939, co-authored with his frequent collaborator, Stephen King-Hall) and, most notably, *The Housemaster* (1938). He also (co-)wrote several screenplays, including *I Was a Spy* (1933), and had dialogue credit for three HITCHCOCK thrillers: *The 39 Steps* (1935), *The Secret Agent*, *Sabotage* (1936). As Major-General Beith, in WW1, he received the MC, and in 1918 he was made CBE.

OTHER BRITISH FILMS: (plays filmed) *The Happy Ending* (1925, 1931), *Tommy Atkins* (1928), *The Sport of Kings* (1931), *The Midshipmaid* (1932, co-play), *Orders Is Orders* (1933, 1954, co-play), *Leave It to Me* (1933, co-play), *All at Sea* (play, co-sc), *Admirals All* (co-play, co-sc) (1935), *The Frog* (1937, play, co-sc), *Carry On Admiral* (1957, co-play), *Girls at Sea* (1958, co-play); (sc/co-sc) *Me and Marlborough* (1935), *The Man Behind*

the Mask (1936), *Keep Your Seats, Please* (1936), *Farewell Again* (1937), *Return of the Frog* (1938), *An Englishman's Home* (1939).

Hay, Will (*b* Stockton-on-Tees, 1888 – *d* London, 1949). Actor. Comic genius who created a genuinely original persona which worked variations on the tattered, shifty 'professional', whether teacher (*Boys Will Be Boys*, 1935, + co-sc; *Good Morning Boys*, 1937; *Ghost of St Michael's*, 1941, + co-d), barrister (*My Learned Friend*, 1943, + co-d) prison governor (*Convict 99*, 1939) or stationmaster (*Oh, Mr Porter!*, 1937, perhaps his masterpiece). In whatever circumstances, he was always required to deceive both superiors and inferiors, the latter proving sharper at detecting the radical incompetence beneath his seedy dignity. Accompanied by fat boy Graham MOFFATT and toothless old codger Moore MARRIOTT in half a dozen films for GAINSBOROUGH, directed usually by Frenchman Marcel VARNEL or American William BEAUDINE, he created a comic oeuvre as endearing and enduring as any in British cinema. When he went to EALING in 1941, he co-directed (with Basil DEARDEN) as well as starring, and in another Ealing film, *The Big Blockade* (1942) he broke with his baffled inefficiency to play a straight role. In private life, apparently a very serious man with a profound interest in astronomy, he published *Through My Telescope* (1935).

OTHER BRITISH FILMS: *Those Were the Days*, *Radio Parade of 1935* (1934), *Dandy Dick* (1935, + co-sc), *Where There's a Will*, *Windbag the Sailor* (1936, + co-sc), *Old Bones of the River*, *Hey! Hey! USA* (1938), *Where's That Fire?*, *Ask a Policeman* (1939), *Go to Blazes* (short), *The Goose Steps Out* (+ co-d), *The Black Sheep of Whitehall* (1941), *To See Such Fun* (1977, compilation).

BIBLIOG: John Fisher, *Funny Way to Be a Hero*, 1973; Ray Seaton, *Good Morning Boys*, 1978.

Hayden, Linda (*b* London, 1953). Actress. Still in her teens, Hayden made a striking debut in the unsettling *Baby Love* (1967), and spent most of the rest of her career in EXPLOITATION FILMS of various kinds, sexual and HORROR, though she was involved in more innocuous fare on TV (e.g. *Village Hall*, *Robin's Nest*). Was in the US film, *The Boys from Brazil* (1978), and on TV thereafter.

OTHER BRITISH FILMS INCLUDE: *Taste the Blood of Dracula* (1969), *Something to Hide* (1971), *Night Watch* (1973), *Confessions of a Window Cleaner* (1974), *Let's Get Laid!*, *Confessions from a Holiday Camp* (1977).

Hayden-Coffin, Adelin *see* **Coffin, Adelaide Hayden**

Haye, Helen (*b* Assam, India, 1874 – *d* London, 1957). Actress. Not to be confused with US star Helen Hayes (both played the Dowager Empress in *Anastasia*: Haye on the London stage and TV in 1953, when she was nearly 80; Hayes in the 1956 film), Haye was a white-haired, impressively dignified, usually titled presence in 50 British films. Made stage debut in 1898, and, after a handful of silent films, including *The Skin Game* (1920), her role in which she repeated for HITCHCOCK's talkie version in 1931, she filmed frequently and recognisably: e.g. as the enigmatic wife of the master criminal in *The 39 Steps* (1935); James MASON's inexplicably doting mother in *The Man in Grey* (1943); unusually benign, as the wife celebrating her golden wedding, in *Dear Octopus* (1943); and Stewart Granger's snobbish mother in *Fanny by Gaslight* (1944).

OTHER BRITISH FILMS INCLUDE: *Masks and Faces* (1917), *Bleak House* (1920), *Tilly of Bloomsbury* (1921), *Altantic* (1929), *The Congress Dances* (1931, UK/Ger), *This Week of Grace* (1933), *Drake of England* (1935), *St Martin's Lane* (1938), *The Spy in Black*, *A Girl Must Live* (1939), *Kipps* (1941), *Madonna of the Seven Moons* (1944), *A Place of One's Own* (1945),

Anna Karenina (1948), *Hobson's Choice* (1953), *Richard III* (1955), *The Gypsy and the Gentleman* (1957).

Hayers, Sidney (*b* Edinburgh, 1921 – *d* Altea, Spain, 2000). Editor, director. In films since 1941, first in sound department, then as cutter – as sound editor, then editor, on such films as *Warning to Wantons* (1948), *A Town Like Alice* (1956) and *A Night to Remember* (1958). His films as director are a motley lot, mostly THRILLERS like *Payroll* (1961), which have at least the virtue of energy, and several quite inventive HORROR films, including the unsettling black-and-white occult piece, *Night of the Eagle* (1962). Perhaps his most interesting film is *The Trap* (1966, UK/Can), the outdoors melodrama set in British Columbia, with the then-potent starpower of Rita TUSHING-HAM and Oliver REED. He directed episodes of such TV series as *The Professionals* (1978–79), but, from about 1980, his work was almost exclusively for US television, including series like *Remington Steele* (1982) before retiring to Spain with former actress wife **Erika Remberg** (*b* Medan, Indonesia, 1932), who made about 30 films, three of them in Britain, including Hayers' *Circus of Horrors* (1960).

OTHER BRITISH FILMS INCLUDE: (e) *While the Sun Shines* (1947, sound e), *Prelude to Fame* (1950), *White Corridors* (1952), *Recoil* (1953), *Romeo and Juliet* (1954, UK/It), *House of Secrets* (1956), *The One That Got Away* (1957), *Violent Moment* (+ d) (1958), *Tiger Bay* (1959); (d) *Operation Amsterdam* (1958, ass), *The White Trap* (1959), *This Is My Street* (1963), *Finders Keepers* (1966), *Assault* (1970), *All Coppers Are . . .* (1971), *Deadly Strangers, What Changed Charley Farthing?* (1974, + co-p, UK/Sp), *A Bridge Too Far* (1977, ass).

Hayes, Elton (*b* Bletchley, 1915 – *d* Bury St Edmunds, 2001). Actor, singer. Popular radio singer, with his own show, who made his film debut in *Date with a Dream* (1948), the musical which launched TEMPEAN FILMS, and had two further roles in British films: as Allan-a-Dale (who else?) in *The Story of Robin Hood . . .* (1952) and as the Troubadour (what else?) in *The Black Knight* (1954). Two further Canadian films.

Hayes, George (*b* London, 1888 – *d* London, 1967). Actor. On stage from 1912 and subsequently in many classic plays, with Old Vic and Stratford seasons; in films from 1934 (*No Quarter*, short). Busy in later 30s films, but best known to filmgoers as the scarred convict Compeyson in *Great Expectations* (1946), where he made the most of some striking close-ups. Unlikely to be confused with Hollywood's George 'Gabby' Hayes.

OTHER BRITISH FILMS INCLUDE: *The Guv'nor* (1935), *Strange Boarders*, (1938), *Come on George!* (1939), *Spy for a Day, Freedom Radio* (1940), *Esther Waters, For Them That Trespass* (1948).

Hayes, Melvyn (*b* London, 1935). Actor. Short, sharp-featured and sharp-eyed comic player, popular especially on TV, where he played the Artful Dodger in a 1962 version of *Oliver Twist* and as Bombardier 'Gloria' Beaumont in *It Ain't Half Hot, Mum* (1974–81). On-screen, first noticed as Moira SHEARER's Cockney brother, Sydney, sent by Ma to fetch her home, in *The Man Who Loved Redheads* (1954) and, looking youthful, played teenagers for several more years. Had good supporting roles in Cliff RICHARD's musicals, starting with *The Young Ones* (1961). Married to actress Wendy Padbury.

OTHER BRITISH FILMS INCLUDE: *Face the Music* (1954), *The Good Companions* (1956), *The Curse of Frankenstein* (1957), *No Trees in the Street* (1958), *Bottoms Up* (1959), *Summer Holiday* (1962), *Crooks in Cloisters* (1964), *Man About the House* (1974), *Carry On England* (1976), *Santa Claus* (1985).

Hayes, Patricia (*b* London, 1909 – *d* London, 1998). Actress. Though in films since 1938 (*Follow Your Star*), tiny, comic

Hayes, usually playing Cockney maids and the like, as in *When We Are Married* (1943), only came to real prominence on TV, as foil in comedy series such as *Hancock's Half Hour* in the 50s and *The Benny Hill Show* in the 60s, but especially for her BAA-winning performance as *Edna, the Inebriate Woman* (1971), a fiercely independent vagrant. She never had a comparable film role, though she has some very funny moments in *A Fish Called Wanda* (1988) – and masses more TV. Mother of actor Richard O'CALLAGHAN.

OTHER BRITISH FILMS INCLUDE: *Went the Day Well?* (1942), *Great Day* (1945), *Nicholas Nickleby* (1947), *The Love Match* (1955), *The Battle of the Sexes* (1959), *The Bargee* (1964), *The Terrornauts* (1967), *Carry On Doctor* (1968), *Fragment of Fear* (1970), *Danger on Dartmoor* (1980), *Little Dorrit* (1987), *War Requiem* (1989), *The Fool* (1990), *The Steal* (1995).

Haygarth, Tony (aka Anthony) (*b* Liverpool, 1945). Actor. Distinctive, later bearded, somewhat pudgy-faced supporting player, who made an impression in his first credited role, as the cynical schoolmaster who warns David HEMMINGS against 'the knight errantry fantasy' in *Unman, Wittering and Zigo* (1971), and ten years later starring in the science-fiction sitcom, *Kinvig* (1981), and later still in *Our Friends in the North*. Strong performances as the heroine's father in *The Woodlanders* (1997), and in National Theatre productions of *Glengarry Glen Ross* and, as Caliban, *The Tempest*.

OTHER BRITISH FILMS INCLUDE: *Let's Get Laid* (1977), *The Human Factor* (1979), *McVicar* (1980), *Britannia Hospital* (1982), *A Private Function* (1984), *Dreamchild* (voice of Mad Hatter), *Clockwise* (1985), *A Month in the Country* (1987), *The Dressmaker* (1988), *The Trial* (1992), *Amy Foster* (1997, UK/Fr/US), *Chicken Run* (2000, UK/US, voice).

Hayman, David (*b* Glasgow, 1950). Actor, director. Lean, balding actor who has excelled at playing Scots (or Irish) hard men, in such films as *My Name Is Joe* (1998, UK/Fr/Ger/It/Sp), as vicious drug dealer and gangleader, and *Ordinary Decent Criminal* (2000, UK/Ger/Ire/US), as Kevin Spacey's gangster colleague. More benign as Sarah MILES's soldier husband in *Hope and Glory* (1987), he was very busy in the 90s, including the recurring role of tough cop Walker in four seasons of *Trial & Retribution* (1997–2000), and stints as director, on such films as *Silent Scream* (1990) and *The Hawk* (1993), and several TV series.

OTHER BRITISH FILMS INCLUDE: (a) *The Adman, Never Say Die!* (1980, shorts), *Eye of the Needle* (1981), *Sid and Nancy* (1986), *Twin Town, Regeneration* (UK/US), *The Boxer* (UK/Ire/US) (1997), *The Match* (1999, UK/Ire/US), *Best* (2000, UK/Ire), *The Tailor of Panama* (2001, Ire/US).

Haynes, Arthur (*b* London, 1914 – *d* London, 1966). Actor. Obstreperous and often cruel TV comedian whose tramp character was created for him by Johnny SPEIGHT. Only three film appearances: in 1945 MINISTRY OF INFORMATION short *Food Flash*, as Rock Hudson's taxi driver in *Strange Bedfellows* (1965, UK) and as Tarquin Wendover in *Doctor in Clover* (1966). AS.

Haynes, H. Manning (*b* Lyminster, 1888 – *d* Surrey, 1967). Actor, Director. An actor on stage from 1906 and on screen, 1914–20, who, in 1921, became a director of minor silent films and 'QUOTA QUICKIES.'

BRITISH FILMS INCLUDE (d): *Monty Works the Wires* (1921, co-d), *London Love* (1926), *The Ware Case* (1929), *Should a Doctor Tell?* (1930), *Tomorrow We Live* (1936, + sc), *Coming of Age* (1938), *The Man at the Gate* (1941, sc). AS.

Haystead, Mercy (*b* London, 1932). Actress. RADA-trained Haystead had a minor career in film of the 50s, starting with the female lead (a stowaway tropical princess) in *What the Butler Saw* (1950), but never quite getting a role good enough to click. On West End stage from 1956 and in the TV series, *The Count of Monte Cristo* (1956).

OTHER BRITISH FILMS INCLUDE: *Chelsea Story* (1951), *Private Information, Sing Along with Me* (1952), *The Beggar's Opera* (1953), *The Admirable Crichton* (1957), *Dentist on the Job* (1961), *Death Trap* (1962).

Hayter, James (*b* Lonuvias, India, 1907 – *d* Spain, 1983). Actor. Hayter's exotic birth and death places seem all wrong for one who so completely enshrined indigenous types over 40 years of films. On stage from 1925, in many West End plays, including *My Fair Lady* (1959), taking over the role of Doolittle from Stanley HOLLOWAY and touring with it in 1964–65, short, stocky Hayter entered films in *Sensation* (1936). Apart from WW2 service (1940–45), he was thereafter on screen almost continuously, with major roles as the Verger in the first episode of *Trio* and one of the doomed submariners in *Morning Departure* (1950), in 1952 as Friar Tuck (of course) in *The Story of Robin Hood* . . . and triumphantly as Pickwick in *The Pickwick Papers*, and as Mr Memory in the otherwise largely unmemorable *The Thirty Nine Steps* (1958). But there are 80 films to choose from and the pickings are choice. Also much TV from the late 40s when he starred in *Pinwright's Progress* (1946–47).

OTHER BRITISH FILMS INCLUDE: *Marigold* (1938), *Come on George* (1939), *Sailors Three* (1940), *The October Man, Nicholas Nickleby* (1947), *Quartet, Once a Jolly Swagman, No Room at the Inn, My Brother Jonathan* (1948), *Silent Dust, The Blue Lagoon, The Spider and the Fly, Passport to Pimlico* (1949), *Waterfront, Your Witness, Night and the City* (UK/US) (1950), *Tom Brown's Schooldays* (1951), *A Day to Remember, Always a Bride* (1953), *For Better, for Worse, Beau Brummell* (1954), *Touch and Go, See How They Run* (1955), *Seven Waves Away* (1956), *The Heart Within* (1957), *The Key, I Was Monty's Double* (1958), *Go to Blazes* (1962), *Stranger in the House* (1967), *Oliver!* (1968), *David Copperfield* (1969), *The Horror of Frankenstein* (1970), *Burke & Hare, Not Tonight Darling!* (1971), *The Bawdy Adventures of Tom Jones* (1975).

Haythorne, Joan (*b* London, 1915 – *d* London, 1987). Actress. RN: Haythornthwaite. Stylish stage leading lady in such popular matinee fare as *Miranda* (1947), Swiss-educated and RADA-trained Haythorne entered films in 1946 as wife of boffin Raymond HUNTLEY in *School for Secrets*. She had some broad fun as Michael SHEPLEY's wife in the filmed *Dry Rot* (1956), but more often films gave her severely dignified roles, such as a prison governor in *The Weak and the Wicked* (1953) and a reform school matron in *So Evil, So Young* (1961), tediously intoning about 'honour'.

OTHER BRITISH FILMS INCLUDE: *Jassy* (1947), *The Browning Version* (1951), *Svengali* (1954), *The Feminine Touch* (1956), *Very Important Person, The Frightened City* (1961), *Decline and Fall* . . . (1968), *Countess Dracula* (1970).

Hayward, Henry (*b* Cheltenham, 1889 – *d* ?). Make-up artist. Educated at Cheltenham Training College, Hayward entered film industry in 1931, his first film *The Return of Raffles*. Worked at several studios before becoming make-up supervisor for BRITISH NATIONAL FILMS, including the 'Old Mother Riley' SERIES in which his craft must have received some challenges.

OTHER BRITISH FILMS INCLUDE: *When We Are Married* (1943), *Medal for the General* (1944), *Murder in Reverse, Latin Quarter* (1945), *Lisbon Story, Laughing Lady, Woman to Woman* (1946), *The Ghosts of Berkeley Square, Mrs Fitzherbert* (1947), *My Brother Jonathan* (for ABPC), *No Room at the Inn* (1948).

Hayward, Louis (*b* Johannesburg, 1909 – *d* Palm Springs, California, 1985). Actor. RN: Seafield Grant. Swashbuckling

hero, who portrayed 'The Saint' on screen in US, and appeared in a handful of British films as well as the TV series, *The Pursuers* (1961), which he also co-produced. To UK at age two, and educated here and in France. Began stage career here, playing Renfield in *Dracula* (1931). Made Broadway debut in 1934, and Hollywood debut the following year, active through 1973. Hayward became a US citizen in 1941, serving, with distinction, in the Marine Corps. Married Ida LUPINO (1939–45).

BRITISH FILMS: *Self-Made Lady* (1932), *The Thirteenth Candle, The Man Outside, I'll Stick to You, Chelsea Life, Sorrell and Son* (1933), *The Love Test* (1935), *The Saint's Return* (1953). AS.

Hayward, Richard (*b* England, 1892 – *d* 1964). Actor. Moving to Ireland as a child, during the 20s he wrote and acted for local theatre and radio before co-founding Belfast Repertory Players in 1929. An enthusiast for Ulster dialect and folk culture, he flourished as a singer of local songs and ballads. Acted and sang in Ireland's first 'sound' film *The Voice of Ireland* (1932) before teaming up with Donovan PEDELTY's Crusade Films to make a series of 'QUOTA QUICKIES', involving Belfast Repertory Players and partly filmed in Ireland. Also responsible for the first film to be completely shot in Northern Ireland, *Devil's Rock* (1938). Subsequently, mainly involved in making DOCUMENTARY SHORTS and Irish travelogues, often tied in with his travel books.

OTHER BRITISH FILMS INCLUDE: *Flame in the Heather* (1935), *The Luck of the Irish* (1935), *Shipmates o' Mine* (1936), *The Early Bird* (1936), *Irish and Proud of It* (1936), *Devil's Rock* (1938), *In the Footsteps of St Patrick* (1939), *Simple Silage* (1942), *Back Home in Ireland* (1946) *A Night to Remember* (1958). John Hill.

Hazell, Hy (*b* London, 1920 – *d* London, 1970). Actress. RN: Hyacinth Hazel Higgins. On stage from childhood, long-legged, blonde, witty, elegant Hazell toured with ENSA during WW2, had much experience of pantomime and cabaret, and was a splendid 'mature' beauty queen in *Expresso Bongo* (1959). Films, in a word, wasted her talent: in bits from 1943 – as Derna Hazell in *The Dummy Talks* and *My Learned Friend* – she made over 20, most of which gave her nothing worth doing. A marginal exception was the wisecracking newspaper comedy, *Paper Orchid* (1949), where she at least starred; just before her tragic death (by choking) she was reduced to a few caustic moments at the end of *Every Home Should Have One* (1969).

OTHER BRITISH FILMS INCLUDE: *Just William's Luck* (1947), *Celia* (1949), *The Lady Craved Excitement, The Franchise Affair* (1950), *The Yellow Balloon* (1953), *Up in the World, Anastasia* (1956), *The Whole Truth* (1958), *Five Golden Hours* (1961).

Head, Murray (*b* London, 1946). Actor. Handsome young actor who had two good chances early in his film career: as Hayley MILLS's leering brother-in-law in *The Family Way* (1966) and as the self-absorbed object of Glenda JACKSON's and Peter FINCH's affections in *Sunday Bloody Sunday* (1971). Since then, he has been usually more interested in his musical career, either as composer or singer (he sang Judas in the original *Jesus Christ Superstar* album and starred on stage in *Chess* (1984), and has appeared in several French films which failed to cross the Channel, and in TV's *North Square* (2000). Brother of actor **Anthony Head** (*b* London, 1954), who appeared in a few films including *A Prayer for the Dying* (1987), and became popular as Giles in TV's *Buffy, the Vampire Slayer*, from 1997.

OTHER BRITISH FILMS: *Two Weeks in September* (1967, UK/Fr), *Gawain and the Green Knight* (1973), *White Mischief* (1987).

Headey, Lena (aka Heady) (*b* Huddersfield, 1974). Actress. Brunette beauty who has resisted categorisation as costume drama décor (as she threatened to become in earlier films) by appearing as a gangster's girlfriend in *Face* (1997), as the lesbian prostitute in TV's *Band of Gold* (1995), and as a nasty teen in the US-made *Gossip* (2001). Nevertheless, her most striking screen work to date has been in two period ADAPTATIONS: she is the best friend when young of *Mrs Dalloway* (1997, UK/Neth/US) and very touching as Liv TYLER's sister in *Onegin* (1999, UK/US). In demand internationally from 2000.

OTHER BRITISH FILMS INCLUDE: *Waterland* (1992, UK/US), *The Remains of the Day*, *Century* (1993), *The Grotesque* (1996), *Aberdeen* (UK/Nor/Swe), *The Parole Officer* (2001), *Possession* (UK/US), *Anazapta* (2002), *The Actors* (2003).

Heal, Joan (*b* Vobster, 1922 – *d* London, 1998). Actress. Like Diane HART whose style Heal's somewhat resembled, and with whom she twice appeared (*Happy Go Lovely*, 1950; *The Pickwick Papers*, 1952, as sisters), she was ill-used by 50s British cinema. On stage she had a major success in *Grab Me a Gondola* (1956–58), as the blonde sexpot at the Venice Film Festival aspiring to play Portia, though less than fully literate. On-screen, a brief scene of outraged suspicion as Sydney TAFLER's wife in *Make Mine Mink* (1960) was about as good as it got. Served with WRNS during WW2 and was married (1 of 2) to Jeremy HAWK; their daughter is TV actress, Belinda Lang (*b* London, 1953).

OTHER BRITISH FILMS INCLUDE: *Flesh and Blood* (1951), *The Good Die Young* (1954), *Tiger by the Tail* (1955), *Live Now, Pay Later* (1962), *Heavens Above!* (1963), *'Let Him Have It'* (1991).

Hearne, Richard (*b* Norwich, 1909 – *d* Bearstead, 1979). Actor. On stage from six months and a veteran of circus, revue, pantomime, etc, before making his film debut as a drunk in *Give Her a Ring* (1934). In the persona of 'Mr Pastry', the walrus-moustached village storekeeper, who first appeared in *For the Children* (1946), he became established as a great favourite with young viewers in his own and other series, and recreated the character several times on film, starting with *Helter Skelter* (1949). His range was wider than this but nothing else was so popular.

OTHER BRITISH FILMS INCLUDE: *Millions* (1936), *Miss London Ltd* (1943), *One Night with You* (1948), *Something in the City*, *Captain Horatio Hornblower RN* (1950), *Madame Louise* (1951), *Miss Robin Hood* (1952), *Tons of Trouble* (1956).

Heath, Gordon (*b* New York, 1918 – *d* Paris, 1991). Actor. Black American in Britain during the 50s who came to attention in Kenneth Tynan's version of *Othello* (1950) and played the role again in Tony RICHARDSON's BBC TV production (1955). He found Britain (and even more so Paris where he lived with his partner) more racially tolerant than the US, but, even so, roles for black actors were scarce. He was in a few international films, including Orson WELLES's *Mr Arkadin* (1955, Sp/Switz), but is best remembered as the arrogant barrister in *Sapphire* (1959).

OTHER BRITISH FILMS: *Man of Africa* (1953, narr), *Animal Farm* (1954, anim, narr), *Passionate Summer* (1958), *The Madwoman of Chaillot* (1969).

Heath, Hilary *see* **Dwyer, Hilary**

Heathcote, Thomas (*b* Simla, India, 1917 – *d* London, 1986). Actor. Somewhat dour-looking, furrow-browed character player who entered films and TV in the late 40s, and appeared in about 30 films over the next three decades. A protégé of

Laurence OLIVIER who gave him a tiny role in *Hamlet* (1948) and in 1949 he starred in *Antigone* on TV where he generally had better chances.

OTHER BRITISH FILMS INCLUDE: *Cloudburst* (1951), *The Sword and the Rose* (1953), *The Seekers* (1954), *Tiger in the Smoke* (1956), *A Night to Remember* (1958), *Village of the Damned* (1960), *Billy Budd* (1962), *A Man for All Seasons* (1966), *Quatermass and the Pit* (1967), *Julius Caesar* (1970), *Burke & Hare* (1971), *Trial by Combat* (1976), *The Jigsaw Man*, *The Shooting Party* (1984).

Heatherly, Clifford (*b* Preston, Lancs, 1888 – *d* London, 1937). Actor. RN: Lamb. Busy supporting actor of the 20s and 30s, who made screen debut in 1911 adaptation of theatre production of *Henry VIII*. A major stage actor – debut 1909 – with his own company (1916); also many musical comedy roles on stage, including *Bitter Sweet* (1929, screen 1933).

OTHER BRITISH FILMS INCLUDE: *Bleak House* (1920), *Yellow Face* (1921), *Roses of Picardy* (1927), *Champagne* (1928), *High Treason* (1929), *My Old China*, *The Love Habit* (1931), *Goodnight Vienna*, *Happy Ever After* (1932), *Smithy* (1933), *Catherine the Great* (1934), *No Monkey Business* (1935), *Café Mascot* (1936), *It's Not Cricket* (1937). AS.

Heckroth, Hein (*b* Giessen, Germany, 1901 – *d* Amsterdam, 1970) Production and costume designer. A surrealist painter, and a production designer for German theatre and ballet, Heckroth emigrated to Britain in 1935. Entered British films as costume designer for *Caesar And Cleopatra* (1945), and then worked in the same capacity for POWELL AND PRESSBURGER, before becoming their principal production designer in 1948. His best work, on *The Red Shoes* (1948, AA) and *The Tales Of Hoffmann* (1951), reveals Heckroth's formative influences in SURREALISM, as well as his affinities to the BALLET, to striking effect. On *Black Narcissus* (1947), he memorably created the Himalayan palace/convent at PINEWOOD. His later work, including HITCHCOCK's *Torn Curtain* (1966), continued meticulous, but tended more towards the conventional.

OTHER BRITISH FILMS: *A Matter of Life and Death* (1946), *The Small Back Room* (1948), *Gone To Earth* (1950), *The Elusive Pimpernel* (1950), *The Story of Gilbert and Sullivan* (1953), *Oh, Rosalinda!!* (1955), *The Battle of The River Plate* (1956).

BIBLIOG: Catherine A. Surowiec, *Accent on Design: Four European Art Directors*, 1992. Tim Bergfelder.

Hedley, Jack (*b* London, 1930). Actor. RN: Hawkins. Likeable, slightly rumpled-looking leading man in films and TV from the late 50s. First major success was in the title role of TV's *The World of Tim Frazer* (1960–61); also in the POW series, *Colditz* (1972–74), and much else, including an episode of *Dalziel and Pascoe* as an unwelcome revenant. On-screen, he had a pleasing classlessness and ease: he is Billie WHITELAW's policeman boyfriend in *Make Mine Mink* (1960), cheery medical student Griffiths in *Of Human Bondage* (1964), Bette DAVIS's intimidated son in *The Anniversary* (1967), and, one is sorry to add, Sophia LOREN's nice husband in the lamentable televersion of *Brief Encounter* (1974).

OTHER BRITISH FILMS INCLUDE: *Behind the Mask* (1958), *Cone of Silence* (1960), *Lawrence of Arabia*, *Nine Hours to Rama* (1962), *The Secret of Blood Island* (1964), *How I Won the War* (1967), *Goodbye, Mr Chips* (1969), *For Your Eyes Only* (1981).

Heinz, Gerard (*b* Hamburg, 1904 – *d* London,1972). RN: Gerhard Hinze. Actor. Heinz, a communist émigré from Nazi-Germany, was a prolific supporting actor in British films from the 40s. His screen characters often had an austere and intense demeanour that either suggested ruthless fanaticism or moral authority. He had a rare sympathetic part as the child's ambassador father in *The Fallen Idol* (1948) and a rare leading one in the SPY THRILLER *Highway To Battle* (1960).

OTHER BRITISH FILMS INCLUDE: *Thunder Rock* (1942), *Caravan* (1946), *Frieda* (1947), *Broken Journey* (1948), *State Secret, The Clouded Yellow* (1950), *His Excellency* (1951), *The Cruel Sea* (1952), *The Prisoner* (1955), *The Man Inside* (1958), *Mystery Submarine* (1962), *Devils Of Darkness* (1964), *The Heroes Of Telemark* (UK/US 1965), *Venom* (1971). Tim Bergfelder.

Heller, John G. (*b* Teplica Sanov, Czechoslovakia). Actor. European character player in 'A' films like *The Colditz Story* (1954) as a German guard and 'B' FILMS like *Cloak Without Dagger* (1955) as a shifty-looking dress designer. Almost invariably played sinister foreigners, mostly German.

OTHER BRITISH FILMS INCLUDE: *Battle of the V-1, I Was Monty's Double* (1958), *The Breaking Point* (1961), *Operation Crossbow* (1965, UK/It), *The Double Man* (1967), *Where Eagles Dare* (1968), *Revenge of the Pink Panther* (1978).

Heller, Lukas (*b* Kiel, Germany, 1930 – *d* London, 1988). Screenwriter. Much associated with US director Robert Aldrich, for whom he wrote such popular films as *Whatever Happened to Baby Jane?* (1962, US) and the UK/US co-production, *The Dirty Dozen* (1967).

OTHER BRITISH FILMS: *Sapphire* (1959, add dial), *Never Back Losers* (1961), *Candidate for Murder* (1962), *Hot Enough for June* (1964).

Heller, Otto (*b* Prague, 1896 – *d* London, 1970). Cinematographer. Began his career while serving with the Austrian Army, when, in 1916, he shot the funeral of Emperor Franz Josef. In Czech films from 1918, Heller worked in numerous countries in the 20s and 30s. From 1940, a highly prolific and diverse career in British cinema. Famous for his high contrast black-and-white photography, as in *The Queen Of Spades* (1948), he also demonstrated an expressive use of colour in *The Ladykillers* (1955) and *Peeping Tom* (1960).

OTHER BRITISH FILMS INCLUDE: *The Amazing Quest Of Ernest Bliss* (1936), *Mademoiselle Docteur* (1937), *Alibi, Tomorrow We Live* (1942), *The Night Invader, They Met In The Dark* (1943), *Mr Emmanuel* (1944), *I Live In Grosvenor Square* (1945), *Night Boat to Dublin* (1946), *They Made Me a Fugitive* (1947), *Noose* (1948), *The Square Ring* (1953), *The Rainbow Jacket, The Divided Heart* (1954), *Richard III* (1955), *The Passionate Stranger* (1956), *Manuela* (1957), *Victim* (1961), *Life For Ruth* (1962), *The Curse Of The Mummy's Tomb* (1964), *The Ipcress File* (1965), *Alfie, Funeral In Berlin* (1966), *Bloomfield* (1969).

BIBLIOG: Duncan Petrie, *The British Cinematographer*, 1996. Tim Bergfelder.

Hellman, Marcel (*b* Bucharest, 1898 – *d* 1985). Producer. Hellman came to Britain in the mid 30s via Berlin and Paris. Sometimes derided as the 'KORDA of the shoe-string budget', Hellman was a distinctly idiosyncratic presence in British cinema, mostly on 'B' MOVIES, until the late 60s. He is reported to be the model for the producer in Cameron MacCabe's 1937 novel about the British film industry, *The Face On The Cutting Room Floor*.

BRITISH FILMS INCLUDE: *Crime over London* (1937), *Secret Mission* (1942), *They Met in the Dark* (1943), *Wanted for Murder* (1946), *North West Frontier* (1959), *The Amorous Adventures of Moll Flanders* (1965), *Mayerling* (1968). Tim Bergfelder.

Helm, Brigitte (*b* Berlin, 1906 – *d* Ascona, Switzerland 1996). Actress. RN: Schittenhelm. After her iconic debut in Fritz Lang's *Metropolis* (1927), the classically beautiful Helm became, albeit briefly, an international star. Mostly portraying glacial, blonde sirens, she was ideally cast as a statuesque, enigmatic desert queen in *The Mistress of Atlantis* (UK/Fr/Ger, 1932). In 1935 she retired from film-making, and lived the rest of her life out of the public eye.

OTHER BRITISH FILMS: *The Blue Danube* (1932). Tim Bergfelder.

Helmore, Tom (*b* London, 1904 – *d* Longboat Key, Florida, 1995). Actor. Smooth second lead in British films of the 30s, who began as an extra in 1924, had small roles in HITCHCOCK's *The Ring* (1927), *The Secret Agent* (1936), went to Hollywood in the 40s and stayed there, often playing Brits, but most noticed as duplicitous Gavin Elster in *Vertigo* (1958).

OTHER BRITISH FILMS INCLUDE: *White Cargo* (1929), *The Barton Mystery* (1932), *The King's Cup* (1933), *The Riverside Murder* (1935), *Not Wanted on Voyage* (1937), *Shadowed Eyes* (1939).

Helpmann, Sir Robert (*b* Mount Gambier, Australia, 1909 – *d* Sydney, 1986). Actor, dancer, choreographer. Known primarily for his stage (and administrative) work in drama and BALLET in Australia and Britain (from 1933), Helpmann contributed to eleven British feature films between 1942 and 1972. In every one he danced or acted melodramatic character roles: e.g. most famously as the autocratic dance impresario in *The Red Shoes* (1948), for which he was the choreographer; outrageously camp as the Dutchman in *One of Our Aircraft is Missing* (1942), the villain's friend in *Caravan* (1946) and Prince Tuan in *55 Days at Peking* (1962); and the crooked clergyman in *The Big Money* (1958). Who but Helpmann could be cast as the Mad Hatter in *Alice's Adventures in Wonderland* (1972)? In later years, he returned several times to film in Australia. Made CBE, 1964; knighted, 1968.

OTHER BRITISH FILMS: *Henry V* (1944), *Caravan* (1946), *The Tales of Hoffmann* (1951), *The Iron Petticoat* (1956), *The Soldier's Tale* (1964), *The Quiller Memorandum* (1966, UK/US), *Chitty Chitty Bang Bang* (1968). Anne Bittner.

Hemming, Lindy Costume designer. Prolific designer of the 80s and 90s, Hemming has shown herself adept across an impressive range of GENRES. Her keen observational eye takes in contemporary Britain, evident in social realist works (*My Beautiful Laundrette*, 1985; *Life is Sweet*, 1990; *Hear My Song*, 1991; *Naked*, 1993), as well as the BOND FANTASIES (*GoldenEye*, 1995, *Tomorrow Never Dies*, 1997, *The World is Not Enough*, 1999, all UK/US), romantic COMEDY (*Four Weddings and a Funeral*, 1994, BAAn/cos), and COSTUME DRAMA, winning the 2000 AA for *Topsy-Turvy* (UK/US).

OTHER BRITISH FILMS INCLUDE: *Laughterhouse* (1984), *Comfort and Joy* (1984), *Wetherby* (1985), *High Hopes* (1988), *Queen of Hearts* (1989), *The Krays* (1990), *Waterland* (1992), *Sister My Sister* (1994), *Funny Bones* (1995), *Little Voice* (1998), *The Trench* (1999), *The Man Who Cried* (2000, UK/Fr/US), *Lara Croft: Tomb Raider* (2001, UK/Ger/Jap/US). Fiona Clark.

Hemmings, David (*b* Guildford, 1941). Actor, producer, director. Initially studied painting at the Epsom School of Art and then, having been a boy soprano, went back to singing briefly in his early 20s. Looking not unlike a depraved cherub he began his film career as a child actor in *The Rainbow Jacket* (1954, UK), then played several roles as rebellious youth (engagingly so in *Live It Up*, 1963) before rising to stardom playing a fashion photographer in the existential thriller *Blow-Up* (1966, UK/Italy). He played a number of leading roles (a convincingly troubled schoolmaster in *Unman, Wittering and Zigo*, 1971, + co-p), before his career took a new turn and he directed his first film *Running Scared* (1972). Founded the HEMDALE CORPORATION with business partner John DALY, to give the actor greater control both before and behind the camera. He has spent the greater part of the last two decades working in TV; more recent roles include that of Cassius in *Gladiator* (2000, UK/US). Married (2) Gayle HUNNICUTT (1968–74), with whom he co-starred in *Fragment of Fear* (1970). OTHER BRITISH FILMS INCLUDE: (a) *The Heart Within, Saint Joan* (1957), *The Painted Smile* (1961), *Some People* (1962), *The System* (1964), *Be My Guest* (1965), *The Charge of the Light Brigade, Only When I Larf, The Long Day's Dying, The Best House in London* (1968), *Alfred the Great* (1969), *The Walking Stick* (1970), *Juggernaut, Mister Quilp* (1974), *Murder By Decree* (1978, UK/Can) (1978); (d) *Running Scared* (1972), *The 14* (1973), *Spy Game* (UK/US), *Mean Machine* (UK/US) (2001), *Last Orders* (2002, UK/Ger). Anne-Marie Thomas.

Hempel, Anouska (*b* Wellington, NZ, 1947). Actress. Retired from the screen since marrying Lord Weinberg, a London hotelier, Hempel now works as a fashion designer and takes part in her husband's business. First appeared as an Australian girl in *On Her Majesty's Secret Service* (1969) and starred in *Tiffany Jones* (1973), based on the *Daily Mail* comic strip adventures of a London model. Often on TV, she is perhaps the only actress to give her name to a hotel.
OTHER BRITISH FILMS: *The Scars of Dracula* (1970), *The Magnificent Seven Deadly Sins* (1971), *Go for a Take* (1972, as a film star), *Double Exposure* (1976).

Henderson, Dickie (*b* London, 1922 – *d* London, 1985). Actor, singer. Short, sharp-featured entertainer who had his own TV show (1960–65, 1968, 1971), began his career as a child in the US film, *Cavalcade*, and appeared in a couple of British films, *Time Without Pity* (1957) and, as himself, in *Make Mine a Million* (1959). Much on stage from 1938, usually as a single variety act. Son of MUSIC HALL comedian **Dick Henderson**, who appeared in a couple of British films, including *Things Are Looking Up* (1935), in which Dickie played his son.

Henderson, Don (*b* Epping, 1931 – *d* Warwick, 1996). Actor. Imposing character player, usually seen in roles requiring authority and dignity, like the exiled Duke and his usurper in the bleak *As You Like It* or, to comic effect, the Bosun in *Carry On Columbus* (both 1992). A respected stage actor, he was with the RSC from 1966 to 1972, and had wide TV and radio experience as well. Married to actress **Shirley Stelfox** (*b* 1941) with whom he appeared in the telemovie, *Pat and Margaret* (1994) and who appeared in a few films, including *Personal Services* (1987).
OTHER BRITISH FILMS INCLUDE: *A Midsummer Night's Dream* (1968), *Callan* (1974), *The Ghoul* (title role), *Brannigan* (1975), *Voyage of the Damned* (1976), *The Big Sleep* (1978), *Brazil* (1985), *The Fool* (1990), *The Trial* (1992), *The Baby of Mâcon* (1993, UK/Fr/Ger/Neth), *The Wind in the Willows* (1996).

Henderson, Jane (*b* England, 1925 – *d* London, 1965). Actress. Supporting player who died sadly young after appearing in a few films: *The Angel with the Trumpet* (1949), *The Heart of the Matter* (1953), *The Belles of St Trinian's, The Green Scarf* (1954).

Henderson, John Director. After acting in a few films, including *Another Time, Another Place* (1983), he turned to directing, mainly on TV (e.g. *Return of the Borrowers*, 1996), but also made the mildly engaging *Loch Ness* (1996) and the scattergun spoof of the pop music scene, *Bring Me the Head of Mavis Davis* (1998).

Henderson, Shirley (*b* Dunfermline, Scotland, 1966). Actress. Trained at the Guildhall School, lovely, intense-looking Henderson has racked up some classy credits since the mid 90s when she first appeared with Robert CARLYLE in the Scottish-based TV series, *Hamish Macbeth* (1995). She was Ewen

BREMNER's unfortunate girlfriend in *Trainspotting* (1996), leading Savoy actress, Leonora Braham, in Mike LEIGH's *Topsy-Turvy* (2000, UK/US), Bridget's chum in *Bridget Jones's Diary* (2001, UK/Fr/US), and, above all, single mum Debbie in *Wonderland* (1999) and Annie in *The Claim* (2001, UK/Can/Fr), both for director Michael WINTERBOTTOM. She also played Morag in the US-financed *Rob Roy* (1995).
OTHER BRITISH FILMS: *Dreaming* (1989), *Villa des roses* (UK/Fr/Can), *24 Hour Party People, Doctor Sleep* (2002).

Hendry, Ian (*b* Ipswich, 1931 – *d* London, 1984). Actor. Twice nominated for BAAs, for *Live Now, Pay Later* (1962), as best newcomer to leading roles, and *Get Carter* (1971) as hoodlum Eric Paice, toughly urban Hendry was one of the most promising actors around in the 60s and 70s. Central School-trained, he had stage and TV experience, including a season with *The Avengers* (1961) and the starring role in the series *The Lotus Eaters* (1973), as well as an impressive list of film credits before his untimely death from undisclosed cause. He entered films in a tiny role in *Room at the Top* (1958), and quickly established himself as a characterful leading man, in such films as *Girl in the Headlines* (1963) and *The Beauty Jungle* (1964), and Roman POLANSKI starred him in *Repulsion* (1965), but he was declared bankrupt in 1980. Married (1963–71) to actress Janet MUNRO.
OTHER BRITISH FILMS INCLUDE: *Sink the Bismarck!* (1960), *Children of the Damned* (1963), *The Hill* (1965), *Cry Wolf* (1969), *The McKenzie Break* (1970), *Tales from the Crypt* (1972), *Theatre of Blood, Assassin* (1973), *The Bitch* (1979), *McVicar* (1980).

Heneker, David (*b* Southsea, 1906 – *d* Llwyndyrys, Wales, 2001). Songwriter. Former Regular Army officer (1925–48), who became a music and lyrics writer, often in collaboration, for such popular stage shows as *Expresso Bongo* (1958), *Charlie Girl* (1965) and *Half a Sixpence* (1963). The latter was also filmed (1967, UK/US), and Heneker's other credits included: *The Two Faces of Dr Jekyll* (1960, co-comp), *The Truth about Spring* (1964, title song), *I've Gotta Horse* (1965, songs).

Henfrey, Janet (*b* Aldershot) Actress. Excellent character player with strong theatre background over several decades, including RSC seasons. She has excelled at playing spinster types on film, kind, stern or fussy, in such films as *Mrs Dalloway* (1997, UK/Neth/US), and in *An Ideal Husband* (1999, UK/US)she plays – of course – Miss Prism in the play-within-the-film. On TV in the 90s, she had an amusing continuing role in *As Time Goes By*, as Frank MIDDLEMASS's severe house-keeper.
OTHER BRITISH FILMS INCLUDE: *It's All Happening* (1963), *The Tamarind Seed* (1974), *Lady Jane* (1985), *Foreign Body* (1986), *The Cook, the Thief, His Wife & Her Lover* (1989, UK/Fr), *Amy Foster* (UK/Fr/US), *Les Misérables* (1998, UK/Ger/US), *Blow Dry* (2001, UK/Ger/US).

Henreid, Paul (*b* Trieste, 1908 – *d* Santa Monica, California, 1992). Actor. RN: von Hernreid. In Britain in the late 30s after fleeing his native Austria, the suave Henreid had already filmed in Europe before making a handful of films in Britain en route to Warner Bros in Hollywood where he famously lit two cigarettes at once in *Now Voyager* and kept his ideals *and* Ingrid BERGMAN in *Casablanca* (1942). Never quite a top star, he stayed busy for several decades as actor and director. In Britain, he was Robert DONAT's climbing pal in *Goodbye, Mr Chips* (1939), a Nazi in *Night Train to Munich* (1940), and in the 50s appeared in two minor Terence FISHER thrillers – *Stolen Face* (1952) and *Mantrap* (1953).

OTHER BRITISH FILMS: *Victoria the Great* (1937), *An Englishman's Home* (1939), *Under Your Hat* (1940), *Ballad in Blue* (1964, d, co-story), *Operation Crossbow* (1965, UK/It), *The Madwoman of Chaillot* (1969).

Henrey, Bobby (*b* Villers-sur-Mer, Calvados, France, 1939). Actor. Son of French refugees who lived in Piccadilly during the war, Henrey in *The Fallen Idol* (1948), under the sensitive direction of Carol REED, gave a miraculous performance at age eight, as the ambassador's son whose idolising of his father's butler leads to lies and crises. He made only one more film – *The Wonder Kid* (1951, + German version) – but his small place in British film history is secure.
BIBLIOG: (Mrs) Robert Henrey, *A Film Star in Belgrave Square*, 1948.

Henry, Joan (*b* London, 1914 – *d* London, 2000). Author, screenwriter. Wife (2 of 3) of J LEE-THOMPSON, who made films from two of her novels, both dealing with women in prison: *The Weak and the Wicked* (1953, from *Who Lie in Gaol*, + co-sc) and *Yield to the Night* (1956, + co-sc/BAAn). Also wrote the screenplay for *Passionate Summer* (1958).

Henry, Lenny (*b* Dudley, 1958). Actor. Brilliant black comedian with a unique style, Henry has enjoyed tremendous success on British TV and as stand-up comic, but failed to make an impact on screen. Disney failed to make him a US star with *True Identity* (1991), as an African-American posing as a white man. In 1992, Henry launched his own production company, Crucial. Married (1984) to Dawn FRENCH.
BRITISH FILMS: *The Secret Policeman's Third Ball* (1987), *Lenny Live and Unleashed*, *Work Experience* (1989), *Robo Vampire* (1993).
BIBLIOG: Autobiography, *The Quest for the Big Woof*, 1991. AS.

Henshall, Douglas (*b* Glasgow, 1967). Actor. One of the Scots who swaggered south in the 90s helping to invigorate British films, reddish-haired Henshall has done striking work in film and TV without a major hit to establish him firmly with audiences. On TV, he was brilliant as the sadistic Corporal Berry in *Lipstick on Your Collar* (1993), the irresponsible father of the *Kid in the Corner* (1999) and the troubled, ultimately serene Levin in *Anna Karenina* (2000). On screen, he was equally riveting as the insolent, jeering Edgar, incestuously in love with his sister in *Angels and Insects* (1995, UK/US), the injured brother in Peter MULLAN's inadequately seen *Orphans* (1997), a story of Glaswegian family torments, and the laddish, unfaithful tattooist in *This Year's Love* (1999).
OTHER BRITISH FILMS INCLUDE: *The Big Man* (1990), *Down Among the Big Boys* (1993), *Fast Food* (1998), *The Lawless Heart, Silent Cry* (2002).

Henson, Basil (*b* London, 1918 – *d* Sevenoaks, 1990). Actor. Supporting actor in films and TV since the late 50s, with a continuing role in TV's sitcom, *Kate* (1970). Usually in small roles, like those of the police inspector in *The Walking Stick* (1970) and the furious monk in *Galileo* (1974, UK/Can). Served with the Indian Army in WW2 and made stage debut in 1946, playing Malvolio to Vivien LEIGH's Viola in *Twelfth Night* (1955). Married to Patricia RAINE.
OTHER BRITISH FILMS INCLUDE: *Inside Information* (1957), *The Guilty Party, Dr Crippen* (1962), *Darling* (1965), *The Frozen Dead* (1966), *Cromwell* (1970), *The Final Programme* (1973), *Shadey* (1985).

Henson, Gladys (*b* Dublin, 1897 – *d* London, 1983). Actress. RN: Gunn. Durable, fondly remembered character player of dozens of working-class mums, nannies, nurses, landladies and barmaids, sometimes lovable, sometimes viragos. Highspot of her career was as Mrs Dixon, crumpling in grief at the news of her husband's death in *The Blue Lamp* (1949), but she was also comically memorable as the harpy Mrs Larkins in *The History of Mr Polly* (1948), Dora BRYAN's termagant mother in *The Cure for Love* (1949), the school matron in *The Happiest Days of Your Life* (1950) and Gordon HARKER's grumpy wife, Glad, in *Derby Day* (1952). Convent-educated and trained at Stedman's Academy, she was on stage from 1910 (as an Oyster in *Alice in Wonderland*) and steadily thereafter, mainly in modern plays; in films from 1943, and much TV from 1948, including a long stint as Grannie in *The Newcomers* (1965–69). Married and divorced Leslie HENSON.
OTHER BRITISH FILMS INCLUDE: *The Demi-Paradise* (1943), *The Captive Heart* (1946), *Temptation Harbour, Frieda, It Always Rains on Sunday* (1947), *London Belongs to Me* (1948), *Train of Events* (1949), *The Magnet, Cage of Gold* (1950), *I Believe in You* (1952), *Meet Mr Lucifer* (1953), *Doctor at Large, The Prince and the Showgirl, Davy* (1957), *The Trials of Oscar Wilde* (1960), *No Love for Johnnie* (1961), *The Leather Boys* (1963), *The Legend of Young Dick Turpin, The Bawdy Adventures of Tom Jones* (1975).

Henson, Jim (*b* Greenville, Mississippi, 1936 – *d* New York, 1990). Director, producer, screenwriter. Most famous for his creation of the 'Muppets', among whom he also provided the voice of Kermit the Frog and several others. Having been featured in the US television series, *Sesame Street* from 1969, they went on to have their 'own' show and to be the subjects of two British films: *The Muppet Movie* (1979, + p, voices) and *The Great Muppet Caper* (1981, + d, voices), as well as *The Muppets Take Manhattan* (1984, US). The multi-talented Henson was involved in two other British films: *The Dark Crystal* (1982, co-d, co-p, voices) and *Labyrinth* (1986), and Jim Henson's Creature Shop was responsible for the brilliant, idiosyncratic depiction of characters from *Alice in Wonderland* in the undervalued story of the 'real' Alice, *Dreamchild* (1985). Jim Henson Productions continues to produce children's entertainment, usually involving FANTASY and puppetry.
BIBLIOG: Christopher Finch, *Jim Henson: The Works*, 1994.

Henson, Leslie (*b* London, 1891 – *d* London, 1957). Actor. Ebullient comedian who had the audacity to portray CHAPLIN in *The Real Thing at Last* (1916) and was so popular a star, on stage especially, that he later played himself in *The Demi-Paradise* (1943). On stage from 1910, made London debut in 1912, Broadway in 1914. His films were almost invariably based on stage comedies, and he repeated his roles in the film versions of *A Warm Corner* (1930) and *It's a Boy!* (1933). In the RFC in WW1, he and Basil DEAN co-founded ENSA in WW2. Married (2 of 3) Gladys HENSON; father of Nicky HENSON.
OTHER BRITISH FILMS: *Wanted a Widow, The Lifeguardsman* (1916), *Broken Bottles* (+ d, sc), *Alf's Button* (1920), *Tons of Money* (1924, co-p), *On with the Dance* (1927), *The Sport of Kings* (1931), *The Girl from Maxim's* (1933) *Oh, Daddy!* (1935), *Home and Away* (1956).
BIBLIOG: Autobiographies, *My Laugh Story*, 1926; *Yours Faithfully*, 1948. AS.

Henson, Nicky (*b* London, 1945). Actor. Swaggering, good-looking leading man, at his best on stage or television, the son of Leslie HENSON. Married to Una STUBBS (1969–75). Typical of his film work is the title role in *The Bawdy Adventures of Tom Jones* (1975); never quite a film *star*.
OTHER BRITISH FILMS INCLUDE: *Father Came Too!* (1963), *The Jokers* (1966), *Witchfinder General* (1968), *Crooks and Coronets* (1969), *The Love Ban* (1973), *Vampira* (1974), *Class Act* (1994). AS.

Hepburn, Audrey (*b* Brussels, 1929 – *d* Tolo Chenaz, Switzerland, 1993). Actress. RN: Edda van Heemstra Hepburn-Ruston. One of the indisputable glories of cinema in the second half of the 20th century – and a standing rebuke to British starmakers that they let her get away, so that she only just belongs in this book at all. The daughter of a Dutch baroness and a British banker, she endured serious wartime privation in Nazi-occupied Holland. Post-war, she trained as a dancer, and screen-tested in Amsterdam where she made her first film. Worked on stage in Britain where any number of people claim to have 'discovered' her; had a few small roles for ABPC, and can be glimpsed in *One Wild Oat* and *Laughter in Paradise* (1951), as well as two better parts in the Ealing films, *The Lavender Hill Mob* and, as a dancer, *Secret People* (1951). Even in these far from wonderful opportunities, her willowy beauty, gamine charm and sense of comedy are visible enough to make one wonder why she wasn't instantly built into a star. Paramount signed her to co-star with Gregory PECK in William Wyler's *Roman Holiday* (1953), for which she won an Oscar, and the rest, as they say, is history – history studded with nominations and awards. Married (1 of 2) Mel FERRER.

OTHER BRITISH FILMS: *Young Wives' Tale* (1951), *Monte Carlo Baby* (1952, UK/Fr), *Two for the Road* (1966).

BIBLIOG: Alexander Walker, *Audrey: Her Real Story*, 1994.

Hepburn, Katharine (*b* Hartford, Connecticut, 1907). Actress. Perhaps the most honoured female star in film history, with four Oscars and two BAAs, plus many other nominations and awards, she made about a half-dozen British films, including two of her most memorable: *The African Queen* (1951), as the doughty spinster who civilises Humphrey Bogart, and *The Lion in Winter* (1968, AA, BAA), as wry and regal Eleanor of Aquitaine. She and Venice vie for attention in David LEAN's *Summer Madness* (1955, UK/US); she is mismatched with Bob Hope in *The Iron Petticoat* (1956); is as bizarre as need be in *Suddenly, Last Summer* (1959), can't do too much with the whimsy of *The Madwoman of Chaillot* (1969), and is gravely witty in the Albee adaptation, *A Delicate Balance* (1973, UK/Can/US), in which she and Paul SCOFIELD play together like two elegant glasses of fine, dry sherry. The last 20 years were given over mainly to TV, including two telemovies for her old mentor, George Cukor, the UK/US co-productions, *Love Among the Ruins* (1975) and *The Corn Is Green* (1979). The rest of her coruscating career belongs elsewhere.

BIBLIOG: Barbara Leaming, *Katharine Hepburn*, 1995.

Hepton, Bernard (*b* Bradford, Yorks, 1925). Actor. An infrequent screen actor, often playing haughty, usually upper-class types, Hepton has found fruitful chances in TV, notably as Toby Esterhase in the John LE CARRÉ mini-series, *Tinker, Tailor, Soldier, Spy* (1979), as a pinched, Oxbridge-schooled veteran of the spy trade, and *Smiley's People* (1982), as a fur-hat-wearing, 'antique'-dealing charlatan. As well as other excellent small-screen work in, say, *Elizabeth R* (1971), Hepton's brief appearances in films like *Get Carter* (1971), *Voyage of the Damned* (1976) and *Shadey* (1985) provide further evidence of his deliciously eccentric style.

OTHER BRITISH FILMS INCLUDE: *Henry VIII and His Six Wives* (1972), *Barry Lyndon* (1975), *Gandhi* (1982, UK/Ind), *The Holcroft Covenant* (1985), *Stealing Heaven* (1988, UK/Yug). Melinda Hildebrandt.

Hepworth, Cecil (*b* London, 1874 – *d* London, 1953) Producer, director. Along with Birt ACRES, Robert PAUL, G.A SMITH and James WILLIAMSON, Hepworth, son of magic lanternist T.C. Hepworth (author of *The Book of the Lantern*), is recognised as one of the great pioneers of British cinema. He also had the longest active career of them, finally succumbing to bankruptcy in 1924. During a 25-year career, Hepworth, primarily an inventor by nature, was without a doubt one of the most respected of the early British film-makers, though clearly towards the end his style was outdated. He began as a commentator on the new medium in journals, and published the first British book on CINEMATOGRAPHY, *The ABC of the Cinematograph*, in 1897. Initially, he worked in the industry for Charles URBAN, before setting up his own company in 1899. At first he concentrated on ACTUALITY subjects, finally achieving success with his coverage of the funeral of Queen Victoria in January 1901. He brought wit and invention to his early subjects, notably *How It Feels to Be Run Over*, and *Explosion of a Motor Car* (1900), and early on experimented with longer films, producing an 800-ft *Alice in Wonderland* in 1903.

In 1905 Hepworth produced one of the most important, and certainly the most celebrated, surviving British film of the period, *Rescued by Rover*, under the direction of his collaborator, Lewin FITZHAMON. He expanded his purpose-built studio at WALTON-ON-THAMES, and went on to gather around himself a unique stock company of players, including Henry EDWARDS, Violet HOPSON, Stewart ROME and Chrissie WHITE. Around 1908, he created a synchronised sound-on disc system, the Vivaphone, which enjoyed a brief popularity, and Hepworth produced several hundred Vivaphone shorts. The system finally failed for the usual reasons: the lack of amplification and the challenge of synchronising both record and picture.

In 1911 he made the transition to feature production, including several DICKENS adaptations and a feature version of *Hamlet* starring Sir Johnston FORBES-ROBERTSON. An excellent photographer and painter, his films were renowned for their pictorial beauty, but suffered owing to Hepworth's traditional approach to film language and construction. He emphasised the landscape in his pictures, both natural beauty and the beauty of the English stately home, which in turn was emphasised in his choice of subject matter, generally ADAPTATIONS of Victorian novels. He was distrustful of EDITING and close-ups, preferring to shoot scenes in depth and in single shots, and preferring to fade out and in between sequences. As a result, by the early 20s his style was out of step with the American style now dominant in British cinemas, and, though respected by the trade, to audiences his films seemed distant, old-fashioned and slow. After a stock issue to fund ambitious expansion plans was badly under-subscribed, his company, Hepworth Picture Plays, failed in 1924. He continued working in the industry, making trailers for the National Screen Service in the 30s, and 'Food Flashes' for the MINISTRY OF INFORMATION during WW2. In his later years, he was chairman of the History Research Committee of the BRITISH FILM INSTITUTE, out of which, importantly, emerged Rachael LOW's *History of the British Film*.

OTHER BRITISH FEATURE FILMS INCLUDE (d): *The Basilisk* (1914), *The Baby on the Barge* (1915), *Trelawney of the Wells*, *Annie Laurie* (1916), *Nearer My God to Thee* (1917), *Sheba* (1919), *Anna the Adventuress* (1920), *Wild Heather*, *Tansy* (1921), *Mist in the Valley*, *Comin' Thro' the Rye* (1923), *The House of Marney* (1926).

BIBLIOG: Autobiography, *Came the Dawn*, 1951. Simon Brown and Anthony Slide.

Herbert, Sir A(lan) P(atrick) (*b* Elstead, 1890 – *d* London, 1971). Author, lyricist. Politician and barrister (though he never practised), he had much theatrical success as a writer of revues, comic operas and musicals, and also contributed songs, lyrics and/or additional dialogue to a half-dozen films: *Windjammer* (1930, dial), *Sally in Our Alley* (1931, songs), *Tell England* (1931, add dial), *The Water Gipsies* (1932, from his novel, songs), *Waltz Time* (1933, sc, lyrics), *King's Rhapsody* (1955, add dial). The TV programme, *Misleading Cases* (1967–68, 1971), was derived from his writings about legal absurdities. Father of Jocelyn HERBERT.

Herbert, Jocelyn (*b* London, 1917 – *d* 2003). Production designer. The daughter of A.P. HERBERT, she shared an AA for the design of her first film (as colour consultant), the exhilarating version of *Tom Jones* (1963), directed by Tony RICHARDSON for whom she worked again three times (*Hamlet*, 1969; *Ned Kelly*, 1970; *The Hotel New Hampshire*, 1984, US). Her career is caught up with the remarkable efflorescence of talent at the Royal Court Theatre in the latter 50s and her films reveal the connection: apart from Richardson, she also worked in films three times with Lindsay ANDERSON (*If . . .*, 1968; *O Lucky Man!*, 1973; *The Whales of August*, 1987, US) and with Karel REISZ (*Isadora*, 1968). Designed for the National Theatre, and recreated on film her design for the OLIVIER *Othello*, 1965, and designed Tony HARRISON's venturesome *Prometheus* (1999).

Herbert, Percy (*b* London, 1925 – *d* London, 1992). Actor. Tough, sandy-haired Cockney character player, who made a corner in truculent rankers in such British war films as *A Hill in Korea* (1956), *The Bridge on the River Kwai* (1957), *Yesterday's Enemy* (1959), and especially as the RSM in *Tunes of Glory* (1960). He could also do policemen and crooks and 'CARRY ON' comedy (. . . *Jack*, 1964; . . . *Cowboy*, 1965) with equal facility, was even a burly Baron in *Becket* (1964). Attributed his acting start to the intervention of Sybil THORNDIKE and went on to play in over 60 films, including several US productions (*Too Late the Hero*, 1970, as – naturally – a Sergeant), and to star as a Scot in the US television series, *Cimarron Strip* (1967).

OTHER BRITISH FILMS INCLUDE: *The Cockleshell Heroes, The Night My Number Came Up* (1955), *Quatermass 2, Night of the Demon* (1957), *No Time to Die, Sea of Sand* (1958), *A Touch of Larceny* (1959), *The Guns of Navarone* (1961), *Guns at Batasi* (1964), *Bunny Lake is Missing* (1965), *The Viking Queen* (1966), *The Royal Hunt of the Sun* (1969), *The Mackintosh Man* (1973), *Valentino* (1977), *The Wild Geese* (1978, UK/Switz), *The Sea Wolves* (1980, UK/Switz/US).

'heritage' cinema Term coined to describe the seeming conjunction of period costume films and the heritage industry in the 80s and 90s, although it is possible to trace a much longer connection between British film-making and heritage discourses and practices. In the 80s and 90s, this connection was played out in the films' museum aesthetic, a concern for period fidelity leading to the spectacular display of heritage attractions (landscapes, architecture, interiors, costumes) and a particular view of the national past. Such properties sometimes went on display in museums, while tourists were encouraged to visit the locations featured in the films. Following the success of *Chariots of Fire* in 1981 (and *Brideshead Revisited*, 1981, on TV), there have been several cycles of COSTUME DRAMAS with a period British (usually English) setting. Most prominent are MERCHANT IVORY's ADAPTATIONS of E.M. FORSTER, *A Room With a View* (1985), *Maurice* (1987), and *Howards End* (1992), celebrated for their tasteful, soft-edged pictorial recreations of the Edwardian past. See also their Kazuo Ishiguro adaptation, *The Remains of the Day* (1993) and two Forster novels adapted by others: *A Passage to India* (1985) and *Where Angels Fear to Tread* (1991). The former was also part of the 'Raj revival' of the mid 80s.

After the Forster cycle came 'Austenmania', with *Sense and Sensibility* (1995), *Emma* (1996) and *Mansfield Park* (2000) (all UK/US), as well as several TV adaptations. Other heritage-rich adaptations include versions of Evelyn WAUGH's *A Handful of Dust* (1987), Henry JAMES's *The Wings of the Dove* (1997, UK/US), Thomas Hardy's *Jude* (1996) and *The Woodlanders* (1997) and Virginia Woolf's *Orlando* (1992, UK/Fr/It/Neth/Russ) and *Mrs Dalloway* (1997, UK/Neth/US), as well as the work of SHAKESPEARE and DICKENS. The literary connection also figures in a series of BIOPICS: *Shadowlands* (1993, UK/US, about C.S. Lewis), *Tom & Viv* (1994, UK/US, about T.S. Eliot's relationship with his wife), *Carrington* (1994, UK/Fr, which also features Lytton Strachey), *Wilde* (1997, UK/Ger/Jap/US), and *Shakespeare in Love* (1999, UK/US, a comic version of an imagined moment in Shakespeare's life). Another cycle includes fictionalised accounts of ROYALTY: *The Madness of King George* (1994, UK/US), *Mrs Brown* (1997, UK/Ire/US) and *Elizabeth* (1998). These quality period COSTUME DRAMAS have played a crucial role in the process of imagining nationhood, telling symbolic stories of CLASS, GENDER, ethnicity, and identity set in PASTORAL English landscapes and picturesque houses.

Critics have argued over whether heritage films are inherently conservative or liberal; studies of reception demonstrate that they can be read in both ways. Audiences for these films have tended to be older, more middle-class and more female than mainstream audiences. While the natural home for many of the films would seem to be the ART-HOUSE, most have also had a limited run in mainstream cinemas, but some have scored substantial success. Despite the ostensible Englishness of such films, they have depended on the interest of American distributors, whether small independent companies or the 'classics' divisions opened by the majors, to exploit such fare. BIBLIOG: Andrew Higson, *English Heritage, English Cinema*, 2001. Andrew Higson.

Herkomer, Sir Hubert von (*b* Waal, Bavaria, 1849 – *d* Bushey, 1914). Producer. A noted painter and Royal Academician, he founded the Herkomer School of Art at Bushey in 1883. Early in 1913, he transformed an amateur theatre in the garden of his Bushey home, Lululand, into a studio, and with his son, Siegfried, entered film production. The films were artistic in nature with a minimum of subtitles but lacking in commercial potential. 'As a film producer he was anxious to do too much; in the result, he did nothing', wrote Low Warren in *The Film Game* (1937). The studios were taken over by the BRITISH ACTORS' FILM COMPANY, and were used in recent years as a home base by Stanley KUBRICK. BRITISH FILMS INCLUDE: *The White Witch, His Choice* (+ a), *Love in a Teashop* (1913), *The Grit of a Dandy, A Highwayman's Honour* (+ a) (1914). BIBLIOG: Michael Pritchard, *Sir Hubert von Herkomer and Film-making in Bushey*, 1987. AS.

Herlie, Eileen (*b* Glasgow, 1920). Actress. RN: O'Herlihy. On stage from 1938, and in London, 1942, as Mrs De Winter in *Rebecca*. A striking brunette who played strong theatrical leads in plays such as *The Eagle Has Two Heads* (1946–47) and *The Second Mrs Tanqueray* (1944–45, 1950), Herlie has never seemed very interested in a film career. After a small role in *Hungry Hill* (1947), she came to attention as Gertrude in *Hamlet* (1948), her interpretation powerfully suggesting folly's being made to acknowledge itself (she repeated the role with Richard BURTON in a TV version, 1964, US). Her other films offer her only moderate rewards. Had success in the long-running US television soap, *All My Children* (from 1976).

OTHER BRITISH FILMS: *The Angel with the Trumpet* (1949), *The Story of Gilbert and Sullivan, Isn't Life Wonderful!* (1953), *For Better, for Worse* (1954), *She Didn't Say No* (1957), *The Sea Gull* (1968).

Herman, Mark (*b* Bridlington, 1954). Director. Not many people saw Herman's first feature, the Venice-set black comedy, *Blame It on the Bellboy* (1992, + sc), though it is quite engaging, but huge numbers responded to his next, *Brassed Off* (1996, UK/US, + sc), a tough-minded comedy-drama, about brass bands, unemployed colliery workers, and masculine uncertainties. The former art school student and animator went on to two further provincially-set successes: *Little Voice* (1998, + sc), with its rich evocation of seaside culture, and *Purely Belter* (2000), the comedy-drama based around Newcastle United football team, recalling his first film, the short *See You at Wembley, Frankie Walsh* (1986). The feelgood potential of a Herman film is usually kept in its place by sourly truthful and uncomfortable insights.

Heron, Joyce (*b* Port Said, 1916 – *d* London, 1980). Actress. Fine-boned, elegant West End stage star (from 1937, after training at Embassy Theatre School), Heron filmed only intermittently from 1942 (*Women Aren't Angels*). Played character roles, like the prison matron in *The Weak and the Wicked* (1953); was in TV from 1946, and played Lady Berkhamsted in *Upstairs, Downstairs* (1974). Married and divorced Ralph MICHAEL.

OTHER BRITISH FILMS INCLUDE: *Twilight Hour* (1944), *Don Chicago* (1945), *The Body Said No!* (1950), *Three Cornered Fate* (1955), *Au Pair Girls* (1972).

Hervey, Grizelda (*b* Plomesgate, Suffolk, 1901 – *d* London, 1980). Actress. Stage actress who began with the Benson Company in the provinces in 1919 and also had much radio experience. Played supporting roles in a few films, including several for Herbert WILCOX, starting with *London Melody* (1937); last seen as Derek BOND's suspicious wife in *Gideon's Day* (1958). Also in US films, including *The Informer* (1935).

OTHER BRITISH FILMS INCLUDE: *Up to the Neck* (1933), *Yellow Canary* (1943), *Oh, Rosalinda!!* (1955), *My Teenage Daughter* (1956).

Heslop, Charles (*b* Thames Ditton, 1883 – *d* London, 1966). Actor. Light comedy actor with many years of stage experience, from 1903; ran his own concert party, 'The Brownies' (1908–21, with break for WW1 service), and was in London, in comedy and panto, from 1915; and was in experimental TV in 1930, and a TV regular from the late 30s. His supporting roles in films were mostly in comic vein, like the timid vicar rebuked for hypocrisy by Mary MERRALL in *The Late Edwina Black* (1951).

OTHER BRITISH FILMS INCLUDE: *Hobson's Choice* (1920, 1931), *This Is the Life* (1933), *Waltzes from Vienna* (1934), *Crackerjack* (1938), *The Lambeth Walk* (1939), *Flying Fortress* (1942), *The Second Mate* (1950), *Follow a Star* (1959), *A Pair of Briefs* (1961), *The Prince and the Pauper* (1962).

Hess, Dame Myra (*b* London, 1890 – *d* London, 1966). Concert pianist. During WW2, she organised lunchtime concerts in London's National Gallery, and in Humphrey JENNINGS's masterly wartime collage, *Listen to Britain* (1942), she is memorably seen performing before an audience including the Queen. Made DBE in 1941.

Hessler, Gordon (*b* Berlin, 1925). Director, producer. German-born of English–Danish parentage, Hessler had experience in DOCUMENTARY and in TV, including episodes of *The Alfred Hitchcock Hour*, before his features debut with

Catacombs (1964). He acquired some reputation as a HORROR film-maker with a flair for claustrophobic tensions in *Scream and Scream Again*, *The Oblong Box* (+ p) (1969) and *Cry of the Banshee* (1970, + p), as well as for the FANTASY *The Golden Voyage of Sinbad* (1973). Since then, he has filmed largely in the US, and often for TV.

OTHER BRITISH FILMS: *The Last Shot You Hear* (1968), *Embassy* (1972), *Girl in a Swing* (1988, + sc).

Hewitt, Henry (*b* London, 1885 – *d* Newbury, 1968). Actor. Bald and beaky supporting player in films from middle age, after stage career dating back to 1905. Usually seen as professional men, like the news editor in *The Day Will Dawn* (1942) or the Minister of Health in *Top Secret* (1952). On stage (e.g. *The Doctor's Dilemma*, 1956) and screen (*The Naked Truth*, 1957) well into his 70s.

OTHER BRITISH FILMS INCLUDE: *The School for Scandal* (1930), *The First Mrs Fraser* (1932), *Jew Süss* (1934), *Rembrandt* (1936), *The High Command* (1937), *Sailors Three* (1940), *The Young Mr Pitt* (1942), *London Belongs to Me* (1948), *Train of Events* (1949), *Where's Charley?*, *Emergency Call* (1952), *Rob Roy . . .* , *Isn't Life Wonderful!* (1953), *Brothers in Law* (1956).

Hewitt, Peter (*b* Brighton, Sussex, 1962). Director. After making the cult success, *Bill & Ted's Excellent Adventure* (1991, US) and other US-based film and TV work, Hewitt won praise for the charming and inventive British fantasy, *The Borrowers* (1997), and what has been called the 'magical-realist fable' of punk aspiration, *Whatever Happened to Harold Smith?* (2000). A lightly likeable talent.

OTHER BRITISH FILMS: *Thunderpants* (2002).

Heyman, John (*b* Leipzig, 1933). Agent, producer. Oxford-educated Heyman entered film industry in 1955, worked on the public relations side at first, then as editor and producer of SHORT FILMS, before making his feature debut as producer of *Privilege* (1967), archetypal disposable 60s fable of hysterical youth and the media, for his own company World Film Services. With Norman PRIGGEN, he co-produced three Joseph LOSEY films: *Boom*, *Secret Ceremony* (1968), and *The Go-Between* (1971) and was executive producer on Losey's *A Doll's House* (1973, UK/Fr) and David LEAN's *A Passage to India* (1984). Also produced some notable TV, including *Between the Lines*.

OTHER BRITISH FILMS: *Twinky* (1969, p), *Bloomfield* (1969, UK/Israel, co-p), *Hitler: The Last Ten Days* (1973, UK/It, ex p), *DARYL* (1985, p).

Heyman, Norma (*b* Cheshire, 1940). Producer. RN: Pownall. Since receiving a shared AAn as co-producer of *Dangerous Liaisons* (1988, US), Heyman has been involved in some interesting if not wholly successful ventures, including *Sister My Sister* (1994), Christopher HAMPTON's *The Secret Agent* (1996, UK/US), and the critically acclaimed but not widely popular *Gangster No 1* (2000, UK/Ger). Has her own company, NFH Productions.

OTHER BRITISH FILMS INCLUDE: *Empire State* (1987), *Buster* (1988), *The Innocent* (1993, UK/Ger), *Mary Reilly* (1996, UK/US), *Kiss Kiss (Bang Bang)* (2000, ex p).

Heywood, Anne (*b* Birmingham, 1930). Actress. RN: Violet Pretty. Perhaps Britain's only talented sex kitten, who posed nude in the October 1967 issue of *Playboy*, and of whom Marlon Brando proclaimed she had 'very sexy nostrils.' Producer Raymond STROSS, whom she married in 1960 (until his death, 1988), launched Heywood as an international star; their first UK film together, *The Fox* (1968), with its nudity and lesbian theme, paved the way for other adult films and was socially ahead of its time. Heywood worked as an usherette at a Birmingham cinema before becoming 'Miss Great Britain' and hosting *The Violet Pretty Show* on TV, changing her name when she became a RANK starlet. Had some good roles, as in *Violent Playground* (1957) and *The Most Dangerous Man in the World* (1969), but never became a major star.

OTHER BRITISH FILMS INCLUDE: *Lady Godiva Rides Again* (1951), *Dangerous Exile, Doctor at Large* (1957), *Floods of Fear* (1958), *Heart of a Man, Upstairs and Downstairs* (1959), *A Terrible Beauty* (1960), *Vengeance* (1962), *I Want What I Want* (1971). AS.

Heywood, Pat (*b* England, 1927). Actress. BAA-nominated for her first film role, the Nurse in *Romeo and Juliet* (1968, UK/It), Heywood has a single moment of emotional genius in *Young Winston* (1972), as a soldier's mother to whom Churchill calls out a greeting at a public gathering. Much TV, and two Italian-made films for ZEFFIRELLI, with largely British participation: *Young Toscanini* (1988, UK/Fr/It) and *Sparrow* (1993, UK/It).

OTHER BRITISH FILMS INCLUDE: *10 Rillington Place* (1970), *Whoever Slew Auntie Roo?* (1971), *Bequest to the Nation* (1973), *Wish You Were Here* (1987).

Hibbert, Geoffrey (*b* Hull, 1924 – *d* Epsom, 1969). Actor. Webber-Douglas-trained purveyor of callow young men hurtled prematurely into adult experience, as in two 1941 films for John BAXTER: Harry who gets his girlfriend pregnant in *Love on the Dole* and Peter, forced by his father's sudden death to run a large firm, in *The Common Touch*. After WW2 service (1942–46) he was on stage for several years, and his most substantial film role was as the murderous Steenie in *Secret People* (1951). In 1968, he appeared in the TV series, *Oh Brother!*, and died shortly after of a heart attack.

OTHER BRITISH FILMS: *In Which We Serve, The Next of Kin* (1942), *The Shipbuilders* (1943), *Emergency Call* (1952), *Albert RN* (1953), *For Better, for Worse* (1954), *Orders to Kill, I Was Monty's Double* (1958), *Live Now, Pay Later* (1962), *Heavens Above!* (1963).

Hibbin, Sally (*b* London, 1953). Producer. Noted for her collaboration with Ken LOACH through his most critically acclaimed and commercially successful period in the early-to-mid 1990s. She is attached to the production company, PARALLAX, for which all her films have been made. In the 80s, she worked in TV, producing demanding shows like *A Very British Coup* (1988). Daughter of **Nina Hibbin** film critic for the *Daily Worker* and *Morning Star* from 1959 to 1972. Sally Hibbin also reviewed and wrote about film, including *The Official James Bond Movie Book*, 1989, and the Hibbins, *mère et fille*, wrote *What a Carry On – The Official Story of the Carry On Film Series*, 1988.

BRITISH FILMS INCLUDE: (p) *Riff-Raff* (1991), *Raining Stones* (1993, BAAn), *Ladybird Ladybird* (1994), *i.d.* (1995), *Carla's Song* (1996, UK/Ger/Sp, BAAn); (ex p) *Bad Behaviour* (1993), *The Englishman Who Went Up . . .* (1995), *Land and Freedom* (1995, UK/Ger/US), *Liam* (2001, UK/Ger/It). Kevin Foster.

Hickox, Douglas (*b* London, 1929 – *d* London, 1988). Director. Pre-director experience included production assistant at PINEWOOD, second-unit director, and maker of commercials for the award-winning Illustra Films which he co-founded in the 60s. As assistant director, he worked on over a dozen films, starting with *Prelude to Fame* (1950), several HORROR films and a Miss Marple mystery, *Murder She Said* (1961). As director, he is best remembered for the film version of Joe Orton's black comedy, *Entertaining Mr Sloane* (1969) and

the spoof horror film, *Theatre of Blood* (1973). Both these showed a darker wit than was to be found elsewhere in his work. Was married to editor Anne V. COATES and father of US-based director, Anthony Hickox.

OTHER BRITISH FILMS INCLUDE: (ass d/2ud) *Appointment in London* (1953), *Grip of the Strangler* (1958), *The Snake Woman* (1961); (d) *It's All Over Town* (1963), *Just for You* (1964, + co-orig idea), *Sitting Target* (1972), *Brannigan* (1975), *The Hound of the Baskervilles* (1983).

Hicks, Barbara (*b* Wolverhampton, 1924). Actress. In the admirable tradition of British character actresses, Hicks has been injecting films with moments of beaky asperity, comic or serious, for over 40 years, as well as masses of TV, including several Miss Marple mysteries with her great compeer, Joan HICKSON, and as Tempest Sidebottome – a name to conjure with – in *Memento Mori* (1992). She began to be noticed in one of the few female roles in *I Was Monty's Double* (1958) and as a barking Sergeant in *Operation Bullshine* (1959), and was still being noticed in *Up at the Villa* in 2000 (UK/US).

OTHER BRITISH FILMS INCLUDE: *Background* (1953), *Sailor Beware* (1956), *A Touch of Larceny* (1959), *Hand in Hand* (1960), *Smokescreen* (1964), *The Charge of the Light Brigade* (1968), *Evil Under the Sun* (1981), *Britannia Hospital* (1982), *Brazil* (1985), *We Think the World of You* (1988), *Howards End, Orlando* UK/Fr/It/Neth/Russ) (1992), *Remember Me?* (1996, as 'elderly sister' – well, of course).

Hicks, Sir Seymour (*b* St Helier, Jersey, 1871 – *d* Fleet, Hampshire, 1949). Director, actor, screenwriter. Celebrated star of the London stage, a great farceur and a comic singer who had much success in revue and became an actor-manager, founding the Aldwych Theatre, home of the famous farces, in 1906. In films from 1913, starring as/in *Scrooge*, a role he repeated in the 1935 version (+ co-sc), he appeared several times with his famous wife Ellaline TERRISS, as in *Always Tell Your Wife* (1923, + co-d) and *Glamour* (1931, + co-d, sc), and in old age in a series of rich character roles, culminating in his decent, tricycling grandee in *Silent Dust* (1949). Also gave HITCHCOCK his first work as director when he called on him to replace Hugh CROISE on the comedy SHORT, *Always Tell Your Wife* (1923). Knighted in 1935.

OTHER BRITISH FILMS INCLUDE: *A Prehistoric Love Story* (1915, + co-sc), *Blighty* (1927), *Sleeping Partners* (1930, + d, sc), *The Secret of the Loch* (1934), *Royal Cavalcade, Vintage Wine* (co-sc) (1935), *Change for a Sovereign* (1937, + sc), *Young Man's Fancy* (1939), *Pastor Hall, Busman's Honeymoon* (1940), *Fame Is the Spur* (1947).

BIBLIOG: Autobiographies, *Between Ourselves*,1930; *Me and My Missus*, 1939.

Hickson, Joan (*b* Kingsthorpe, 1906 – *d* London, 1998). Actress. It is not given to many CHARACTER PLAYERS to achieve stardom in their late 70s, but that is what happened to Hickson when she appeared on TV as Miss Marple, after well over 80 films spanning a half-century. Small, birdlike in her concentration, invincibly intelligent and deceptively cosy, she eclipsed previous Marples, her success tending to elide the long preceding career of solid achievement. RADA-trained and on stage from 1927 (with a Tony-winning role in *Bedroom Farce*, 1977), on screen she often provided two minutes of sheer joy as turbaned landladies, cooks standing on their dignity or barmaids dispensing acid rejoinders with warm beer, or the nouveau riche Mrs Pike in *Don't Take It to Heart!* (1944), or the old lady on an outing and wittering on about missing sherry glasses in *Clockwise* (1985). However, when the occasion demanded, she could do full-length character studies, like the working-class mother in *The Guinea Pig* (1948) or Alan BATES's relentlessly smoking, interfering, chattering mother in *A Day in the Death of Joe Egg* (1970), both repeating stage roles. Her status as national treasure was recognised with an OBE in 1987.

OTHER BRITISH FILMS INCLUDE: *Trouble in Store* (1934), *The Man Who Could Work Miracles* (1936), *Love from a Stranger* (1937), *The Rake's Progress, The Trojan Brothers* (1945), *I See a Dark Stranger* (1946), *This Was a Woman, It's Hard to Be Good* (1948), *Seven Days to Noon* (1950), *High Treason* (1951), *The Card* (1952), *The Million Pound Note, Deadly Nightshade* (1953), *The House Across the Lake, Mad About Men, Doctor in the House* (1954), *Simon and Laura, Lost* (1955), *Child in the House, Sea Wife* (1956), *Happy is the Bride* (1957), *The Horse's Mouth, Law and Disorder* (1958), *Please Turn Over, Carry On Constable* (1960), *Murder She Said, Carry On Regardless* (1961), *Crooks Anonymous* (1962), *Heavens Above!* (1963), *Carry On Loving* (1970), *Theatre of Blood* (1973), *Yanks* (1979), *The Wicked Lady* (1983), *Century* (1993).

Higgins, Anthony (aka Anthony Corlan) (*b* Northampton, 1947). Actor. First made an impression playing louche young men like the imprisoned 'art dealer' in *Quartet* (1981) and the equivocal eponym in *The Draughtsman's Contract* (1982). He never approximated the conventional leading man type, and it was an imaginative stretch to accept him as OLIVIER in the mini-series *Darlings of the Gods* (1988, UK/Aust), but he has had a rewarding career as a character actor. Has worked internationally, as in *For Love or Money* (1993, US).

OTHER BRITISH FILMS INCLUDE: *Taste the Blood of Dracula* (1969), *Voyage of the Damned* (1976), *She'll Be Wearing Pink Pyjamas* (1984), *Nostradamus* (1994, UK/Ger), *The Last Minute* (2001, UK/US).

Higgins, Ken (*b* London, 1919). Cinematographer. Came to prominence in the 60s, especially for his black-and-white photography on Ken RUSSELL's TV biopic, *Elgar* (1962) and on *Darling* (1965) and *Georgy Girl* (1966), catching the febrile, of-the-moment feel of that evanescent period. Entered films as camera trainee with the GPO FILM UNIT in 1934, was with the ARMY FILM UNIT (1940–45), and worked on *XIVth Olympiad: The Glory of Sport* (1948, doc).

OTHER BRITISH FILMS INCLUDE: *Terminus* (1961, short), *French Dressing* (1963), *Wonderful Life* (1964), *Up Jumped a Swagman* (1965), *Stranger in the House* (1967), *Salt & Pepper, Hot Millions* (1968), *The Virgin Soldiers* (1969), *Julius Caesar, Games That Lovers Play* (1970).

Highbury Studios A small London-based studio, Highbury was built in 1937 and quickly became associated with the production of 'QUOTA QUICKIES'. After WW2, it was bought by the RANK ORGANISATION which produced a series of short features there designed to give experience to untested actors, often members of the Rank 'CHARM SCHOOL', and other creative personnel. Highbury's best films were all directed by Terence FISHER, who would later become British HORROR's main director. His *Colonel Bogey* (1948) was a charming ghost story while *To the Public Danger* (1948) was a convincing portrayal of post-war ennui. The remainder of the Highbury product was less impressive, with this no doubt hastening Rank's abandonment of the Highbury experiment. Other Highbury films included *Penny and the Pownall Case, Trouble in the Air, A Song for Tomorrow, Fly Away Peter, Love in Waiting, A Piece of Cake* (1948) and *Badger's Green* (1949). Peter Hutchings.

Hilary, Jennifer (*b* Frimley, 1942). Actress. Delicately attractive, RADA-trained (Bancroft Gold Medallist) on stage from 1961, in London and New York, and in occasional films since her debut in *Becket* (1964). Also some TV, including the mini-series, *The Sun Also Rises* (1984).

OTHER BRITISH FILMS INCLUDE: *The Heroes of Telemark* (1965), *The Idol* (1966), *One Brief Summer* (1969), *North Sea Hijack* (1979).

Hildyard, David Sound recordist. Shared Oscar-winner for *Fiddler on the Roof* (1971), brother of cinematographer Jack HILDYARD, he entered films as boom operator after WW2 on such films as *A Matter of Life and Death* (1946), and worked as sound recordist on a wide range of popular films from the mid 50s to the late 80s.

OTHER BRITISH FILMS INCLUDE: (sd/sd recordist), *Bermuda Affair* (1956), *Bonjour Tristesse* (1957), *The Hellions* (1961, UK/Saudi), *The Lion* (1962), *Judith* (1965, UK/Isr/US), *Puppet on a Chain* (1970), *North Sea Hijack* (1979), *The Sea Wolves* (1980, UK/Switz/US), *The Pirates of Penzance* (1982), *Yentl* (UK/US), *Champions* (1983), *Turtle Diary* (1985), *Without a Clue* (1988, UK/US).

Hildyard, Jack (*b* London, 1908 – *d* London, 1990). Cinematographer. A major cameraman yet one with no discernible style. Most closely associated with David LEAN on *Hobson's Choice* (1953), *The Sound Barrier* (1952), *Summer Madness* (1955) and *The Bridge on the River Kwai* (1957), for which he won an Oscar. A favourite with US directors working in the UK, and some US films, including *Topaz* (1959) *55 Days at Peking* (1962) and his last, *Lion of the Desert* (1980), which proved that without Lean, Hildyard's desert photography could be unimpressive. Began as clapper boy at ELSTREE in 1932, became camera operator in 1937, and cinematographer in 1945. Brother of David HILDYARD.

OTHER BRITISH FILMS INCLUDE: *Caesar and Cleopatra* (1945, co-c), *While the Sun Shines, Vice Versa* (1947), *Sleeping Car to Trieste* (1948), *The Chiltern Hundreds* (1949), *Hotel Sahara* (1951), *The Heart of the Matter* (1953), *The Deep Blue Sea* (1955), *Anastasia* (1956), *Suddenly, Last Summer* (1959), *The Sundowners* (1960), *Live Now, Pay Later* (1962), *The VIPs* (1963), *Modesty Blaise* (1966), *Casino Royale* (1967), *Puppet on a Chain* (1970), *The Beast Must Die* (1974), *The Wild Geese* (1978, UK/Switz). AS.

Hill, Arthur (*b* Melfort, Canada, 1922). Actor. Tall, slight actor on stage in London from 1948, who most famously played George in the original Broadway and London productions of *Who's Afraid of Virginia Woolf?* (1962–64). His main film and TV careers have been conducted in the US and Canada, but he appeared in about a dozen British films from 1949 (*Miss Pilgrim's Progress*) to 1955 (Kenneth MORE's chum in *The Deep Blue Sea*), without making much impression. Returned at long intervals to make several more British films, including *A Bridge Too Far* (1977), typically playing a US Medical Colonel.

OTHER BRITISH FILMS INCLUDE: *Mr Drake's Duck* (1950), *The Scarlet Thread* (1951), *A Day to Remember* (1953), *The Crowded Day* (1954), *Petulia* (1968), *The Most Dangerous Man in the World* (1969).

Hill, Benny (*b* Southampton, 1925 – *d* Teddington, 1992). Actor. One of the most internationally successful of British comedians, whose fame was comparable to that of even CHAPLIN or Stan Laurel. Borrowing heavily from British MUSIC HALL, Hill emphasised sexual innuendo with cherubim innocence; it was all politically incorrect and, ultimately, Hill's lonely private life was as sad as the frustrated men that his comedy featured. Hill's career began in the late 30s, but he came to fame on BBC Television in 1952, moving to Thames Television in 1969. Apart from *The Best of Benny Hill*, a 1974 compilation of his television skits, Hill's film appearances fail to capture his comedic persona.

OTHER BRITISH FILMS: *Who Done It?* (1956), *Light Up the Sky* (1960), *Those Magnificent Men . . .* (1965), *Chitty Chitty Bang Bang* (1968), *The Waiters, The Italian Job* (1969).

BIBLIOG: Robert Ross, *Merry Master of Mirth*, 2000. AS.

Hill, Bernard (*b* Manchester, 1944). Actor. Forceful character player, occasionally in leading roles, as in *Drowning by*

Numbers (1988, UK/Neth) as the coroner in love with three identically named women, or the computer engineer in *Bellman & True* (1987), but more often in substantial character parts, like the insensitive husband of *Shirley Valentine* (1989, UK/US) or Egeus in *A Midsummer Night's Dream* (1999, UK/It) or Captain Smith in *Titanic* (1997, US). On TV, made his name and won a Best Actor BAA for *Boys from the Blackstuff* (1982), played York in the BBC's *Henry VI* (1983), and an alarming Magwitch in *Great Expectations* (1999); has been in demand for international films, including *Lord of the Rings* (2001, US/NZ).

OTHER BRITISH FILMS INCLUDE: *It Could Happen to You* (1975), *Trial by Combat* (1976), *Gandhi* (1982, UK/Ind), *Runners* (1983), *The Bounty*, *The Chain* (1984), *Restless Natives* (1985), *Skallagrigg* (1994), *The Wind in the Willows* (1996), *The Criminal* (2001, UK/US).

Hill, James (*b* Eldwick, 1919 – *d* London, 1994). Director. Former documentarist and SHORT FILM director, who won an AA for his short *Giuseppina* (1959), directed the popular *Born Free* (1965), and should not be confused with the US producer who co-founded Hecht–Hill–Lancaster and married Rita Hayworth. The British Hill made a quirky collection of films, including the ACT FILMS production, *The Kitchen* (1961), from Arnold Wesker's play, and often showed special interest in animals: see also *An Elephant Called Slowly* (1969, + co-sc, co-p), *Black Beauty* (1971, UK/Ger/Sp, + add dial), and *The Belstone Fox* (1973, + sc). Also a great deal of TV, including *Worzel Gummidge* (1979, + p), which, like much of his work, was tailored to juvenile audiences.

OTHER BRITISH FILMS INCLUDE: (short/doc, d) *Paper Chain* (1946), *Behind the Flame* (1948), *District Nurse, Britain's Comet* (1952), *Home-Made Car* (1963, + p, BAAn), *The Specialist* (1966), *The Lions Are Free* (1967), *The Lion at World's End* (1971, co-d, + co-p, co-sc); (feature, d) *Reach for the Sky* (1956, ass), *The Mystery in the Mine* (1959 + co-sc), *Lunch Hour, The Dock Brief* (1962), *A Study in Terror* (1965), *Captain Nemo and the Underwater City* (1969), *The Young Visiters* (1984, + p, adptn).

Hill, Sinclair (*b* Surbiton, 1896 – *d* Chapel-en-le-Frith, 1945). Director, writer. Hill was a busy young man, joining Tyler Films as an office boy at the age of 16, becoming adviser to Italia Films a year later, and manager of New Agency Film Company in London at the age of 18. In October 1919, he became an actor for Maurice ELVEY and switched to screenwriting when his adaptation of *The Tavern Knight* (1920) was accepted for filming. Hill became a director with STOLL in 1920, becoming the company's managing director seven years later. Awarded OBE for his WW1 career, ending with rank of major. Hill's films are a mix of the interesting (e.g. the pseudo-WESTERN *The Man from Toronto*, 1933) and the mediocre.

OTHER BRITISH FEATURE FILMS INCLUDE: (d, sc, unless noted) *The Tidal Wave* (1920), *Half a Truth* (d), *The Experiment* (d), *Expiation, The Nonentity* (1922), *The Conspirators, White Slippers* (1924), *The Qualified Adventurer* (1925), *The Chinese Bungalow, The King's Highway* (1927, d); (d, unless noted) *The Guns of Loos* (+ story), *The Price of Divorce* (1928), *Greek Street* (1930), *The Great Gay Road* (1931), *The First Mrs Fraser* (1932), *Britannia of Billingsgate* (1933), *Hyde Park Corner* (1935), *The Cardinal* (1936), *Follow Your Star* (1938, + co-sc). AS.

Hiller, Dame Wendy (*b* Bramhall, 1912 – *d* 2003). Actress. There was simply no one like her in British films: her sculpted, unconventionally beautiful face, distinctive voice and the intelligent intensity of her playing marked her as exceptional. Essentially a stage actress, she made only 15 cinema films in 50 years but how choice so many of them were: in Anthony ASQUITH's *Pygmalion* (1938), she was the definitive Eliza for a generation, receiving an AAn; in *I Know Where I'm Going!*

(1945), she is irresistibly engaging and finally touching as the headstrong heroine losing her grip on her life when she falls in love – and though she hated working with director Michael POWELL; in *Separate Tables* (1958, US), she won an AA for her supporting role as the lonely, generous hotel manager; she is D.H. LAWRENCE's bitter, passionate Mrs Morel to the life in *Sons and Lovers* (1960); very moving as the great-hearted, simple Alice More in *A Man for All Seasons* (1966, another AAn/supp a); making bricks from Agatha CHRISTIE's straw as the Princess in *Murder on the Orient Express* (1974); and austerely dominant as Auntie in *The Lonely Passion of Judith Hearne* (1987), her screen swansong.

Alongside this gallery is a great stage career, begun in Manchester in 1930, and brought to early notice with the role of Sally in her husband (1937–93), Ronald Gow's play, *Love on the Dole* in 1934, repeating the role on Broadway to which she would often return. It was her playing of *St Joan* and *Pygmalion* at the Malvern Festival which led SHAW to recommend her for the lead in the films of *Pygmalion* and *Major Barbara* (1941). She had enormous successes in classical plays (as in her Old Vic season, 1955–56) and such new plays as *The Heiress* (1950) and *Flowering Cherry* (1958). On TV, she chose with similar care and to similar effect, her range encompassing the outraged spinster of *Clochemerle* (1972) and the wise, humane Lady Slane, who, *All Passion Spent* (1986), is determined to remake her life in widowhood. Most actors have to put up with a certain amount of dross; Wendy Hiller seems to have avoided it. Awarded OBE in 1971 and DBE in 1975.

OTHER BRITISH FILMS: *Lancashire Luck* (1937), *To Be a Woman* (1951, doc, comm), *Single-Handed* (1953), *How to Murder a Rich Uncle, Bernard Shaw* (doc) (1957), *David Copperfield* (1969), *Voyage of the Damned* (1976), *The Cat and the Canary* (1979), *Attracta* (1983).

Hilliard, Patricia (*b* Quetta, India, 1916 – *d* Ditchling, 2001). Actress. RADA-trained actress who appeared in films (*The Girl in the Crowd, The Private Life of Don Juan*, 1934) before her 1935 stage debut. After several starring roles in the 30s, she stopped filming in 1942 (*The Missing Million*), and gave up theatre for radio in the early 50s. She was the daughter of Ann CODRINGTON and stepdaughter of **Stafford Hilliard**, who also appeared in a number of 30s films, including *The Wandering Jew* (1933) and *The Rebel Son* (1939), usually in small character roles. Was married to actor William FOX.

OTHER BRITISH FILMS INCLUDE: *The Ghost Goes West* (1935), *Things to Come* (1936), *Farewell Again* (1937), *A Gentleman's Gentleman* (1939).

Hillier, Erwin (*b* Berlin, 1911). Cinematographer. Trained at Germany's UFA studios, Hillier's breakthrough in Britain was his work for POWELL AND PRESSBURGER on *A Canterbury Tale* (1944) and *I Know Where I'm Going!* (1945), which showed his affinity for high-contrast, chiaroscuro lighting, angled compositions, and a keen eye for romantic landscapes. After the war, he became a regular collaborator of director Michael ANDERSON, where Hillier's work retained a strong *noirish* feel well into the 60s (*Chase A Crooked Shadow*, 1957, *The Naked Edge*, 1961, *The Quiller Memorandum*, 1966, UK/US), although their best-known work together is the WAR FILM *The Dam Busters* (1955), with its spectacular aerial shots.

OTHER BRITISH FILMS INCLUDE: (c, unless noted) *Jack Ahoy!* (cam op), *Little Friend* (cam ass) 1934), *Brown on Resolution* (1935, cam op), *Protection of Fruit* (1940, doc), *Defeat Diphtheria* (1941, doc), *The Silver Fleet* (1943), *Great Day* (1945), *London Town* (1946), *The October Man* (1947), *The Mark of Cain, Mr Perrin and Mr Traill* (1948), *The Interrupted Journey* (1949), *Shadow of the Eagle* (1950), *Where's Charley?* (1952), *Will Any Gentleman . . .?* (1953), *Duel in the Jungle* (1954), *Shake*

Hands with the Devil (1959, UK/US), *The Long and the Short and the Tall* (1960), *The Pot Carriers, Go To Blazes* (1962), *Sammy Going South* (1963), *Operation Crossbow* (1965, UK/It), *The Shoes of the Fisherman* (1968).

BIBLIOG: Duncan Petrie, *The British Cinematographer*, 1996. Tim Bergfelder.

Hills, R(ichard) M. (*b* 1926 – *d* Sussex, 1996). Screenwriter. In the industry since 1933, and in Hollywood writing for four years, Hills ('Dick') was the co-author (with Sid Green) of the *Morecambe And Wise Show* and of the three films starring the adored duo: *The Intelligence Men* (1965), *That Riviera Touch* (1966), *The Magnificent Two* (1967). None of these really succeeded as films, but each has moments of felicitous writing. Hills otherwise worked entirely in TV.

Hilton, James (*b* Leigh, Lancashire, 1900 – *d* Long Beach, California, 1954). Author, screenwriter. Best-selling middle-brow novelist most of whose articulations of middle-class fantasies transferred successfully to the screen. Cambridge-educated Hilton settled in Hollywood in 1935, and shared an AA/sc for *Mrs Miniver* (1942, US). His Shangri-La romance, *Lost Horizon* (1937) was twice filmed by Hollywood: lustrously in 1937, ludicrously in 1972. Now most famous for his novella, *Goodbye, Mr Chips*, that hymn to the English public school, filmed twice in Britain: in 1939, with Robert DONAT winning an AA in the title role, and as a musical in 1969. Other British films made from his novels are *Knight Without Armour* (1937) and *So Well Remembered* (1947), for which he provided the narration, as he did in the opening scene of MGM's masterly ADAPT-ATION of his romance, *Random Harvest* (1942, US).

Hinds, Anthony (*b* Ruislip, 1922). Producer. Son of the founder of HAMMER FILMS (William Hinds), educated at St Paul's School and in films since 1946 with EXCLUSIVE FILMS, producing a great many modest thrillers, before hitting the spot with *The Quatermass Experiment* in 1955. He also pro-duced the TV series *Journey to the Unknown* (1968). Under the pseudonym 'John Elder', he was a prolific screenwriter and from the mid 60s he concentrated on this activity, returning to production for *The Lost Continent* (1968). A very influential figure in the Hammer success story.

OTHER BRITISH FILMS INCLUDE: (sc) *Captain Clegg* (1962), *Rasputin The Mad Monk* (1965), *Frankenstein Created Woman* (1966), *Taste the Blood of Dracula* (1969), *The Scars of Dracula* (1970), *Legend of the Werewolf* (1974), *The Ghoul* (1975); (p) *The Adventures of PC 49, The Man in Black* (1949), *Room to Let* (1950), *Cloudburst* (1951), *The Last Page* (1952), *The House Across the Lake* (1954), *X the Unknown, Women Without Men* (1956), *The Curse of Frankenstein, The Camp on Blood Island* (1957), *Dracula, The Revenge of Frankenstein* (1958), *The Hound of the Baskervilles, The Stranglers of Bombay* (1959), *The Brides of Dracula* (1960), *The Curse of the Werewolf* (1961, + sc), *The Evil of Frankenstein* (1964, + sc), *The Nanny* (ex), *Fanatic* (1965), *Lost Continent* (1968, ex).

Hinds, Ciaran (*b* Belfast, 1954). Actor. Rugged, charismatic actor who came to prominence in the 90s. He had appeared in supporting roles in *Excalibur* (1981, UK/US) and *The Cook, the Thief, His Wife & Her Lover* (1989, UK/Fr), when he suddenly made his presence felt with a brusque, unconventional reading of Captain Wentworth in *Persuasion* (1995, TV, some cinemas), perhaps the most intelligent of the AUSTEN ADAPTATIONS. Since then, he has done imposing work in unsympathetic roles in the Irish-set drama, *Some Mother's Son* (1996, Ire/US) and *The Lost Son* (1999, UK/Fr/US) as well as building a solid TV list, including *Jane Eyre* (1997), as a perfectly cast Rochester. Educated at Queen's University, Belfast, and RADA-trained, he

has mastered all the acting media, winning plaudits on London and Broadway stages for his role in *Closer* (1998–99), having experience with such major companies as the Glasgow Citizens' Theatre (1979–85) and the RSC (1991, 1993).

OTHER BRITISH FILMS INCLUDE: *December Bride* (1990, Ire), *Circle of Friends* (1995, Ire/US), *Mary Reilly* (1996, UK/US), *The Life of Stuff* (1997), *Titanic Town* (1998, UK/Fr/Ger).

Hines, Ronald (*b* London, 1929). Actor. Best known for his TV work, including *The Marriage Lines* (1963–66), as Richard BRIERS's neighbour, and *Not in Front of the Children* (1968–70), replacing Paul DANEMAN as Wendy CRAIG's husband. Has appeared in character roles in about a dozen films since the late 50s, including 'B' FILMS like *The Hi-Jackers* (1963), as a treacherous lorry-driver, and 'A's like *Young Winston* (1972) as an adjutant.

OTHER BRITISH FILMS INCLUDE: *Dunkirk* (1958), *The Angry Silence* (1960), *Whistle Down the Wind, House of Mystery* (1961), *Seance on a Wet Afternoon* (1964), *Take Me High* (1973).

Hinton, Mary (*b* London, 1896 – *d* Exbury, 1979). Actress. RN: Emily Forster. In *Trottie True* (1948), Hinton played a Duchess melting towards her music-hall daughter-in-law; in life, the daughter of Baron Forster and a GBE mother, took to the stage in 1925, in Australia, toured with Seymour HICKS (1927), and thereafter became a popular West End star, usually in upper-class roles, but also as kind, harassed Mrs Ellis in *Great Day* (1945). On-screen sporadically but often vividly from 1935: e.g. as Lady Castlemaine in *Penn of Pennsylvania* (1941) and an anxious mother in *Broken Journey* (1948). Also in early TV at Alexandra Palace.

OTHER BRITISH FILMS INCLUDE: *Once in a New Moon* (1935), *Poison Pen* (1939), *Gaslight* (1940), *Hatter's Castle* (1941), *Quartet* (1948), *White Corridors* (1951), *The Crowded Day* (1954).

Hird, Dame Thora (*b* Morecambe, 1911 – *d* London, 2003). Actress. Hird's status as national treasure was confirmed by the awards of OBE in 1983 and DBE in 1993, but long before those she was secure in the country's affections as a result of playing dozens of instantly recognisable characters in film and TV, the latter including several years as presenter on the religious pro-gramme, *Songs of Praise*, from the mid 70s to the early 90s. Her salty good humour, her glorying in her humble Lancashire origins, her sharp tongue and her oft-proclaimed faith made her a homely icon. On stage in Morecambe from childhood, she came to films in 1941's *Spellbound*, and for the next 60 years she was incessantly on screen, TV or stage. Her film cameos included an ATS girl in *Went the Day Well?* (1942), an internee scrubbing floors in baggy shorts in *Two Thousand Women* (1944), the lugubrious Mrs Gaye in *The Weaker Sex* (1948), a sour almshouse manager in *Time Gentlemen Please!* (1952), the housekeeper with TV aspirations in *Simon and Laura* (1955), a slatternly and malicious landlady with turban and fag in *Lost* (1955), and so – endlessly – on. But, lest it be thought that such one-note delights defined her range, look at the vicious mother-in-law in *A Kind of Loving* (1962): this is a fully rounded portrayal of narrow, mean-spirited lower-middle-class snobbery; and thereafter her roles were more consistently substantial. She starred in the TV series, *The First Lady* (1968–69) as an independently-minded councillor, was in the all-star dark comedy, *Memento Mori* (1992) as the housekeeper in a nursing home, and was unforgettable in two seasons of Alan BENNETT's *Talking Heads* (1988, 1998). She was a comic turn in many a British film, but she was also a great actress. Her daughter is former actress Janette SCOTT.

OTHER BRITISH FILMS: *The Black Sheep of Whitehall* (1941), *The Next of Kin*, *The Foreman Went to France*, *Big Blockade* (1942), *The Courtneys of Curzon Street* (1947), *Corridor of Mirrors*, *Portrait of Life*, *Once a Jolly Swagman*, *My Brother Jonathan* (1948), *Madness of the Heart*, *Maytime in Mayfair*, *Fools Rush In*, *Conspirator*, *Boys in Brown*, *A Boy, a Girl and a Bike*, *The Cure for Love* (1949), *Once a Sinner*, *The Magnet* (1950), *The Magic Box*, *The Galloping Major* (1951), *The Lost Hours*, *The Long Memory*, *The Frightened Man*, *Emergency Call* (1952), *Street Corner*, *Turn the Key Softly*, *Personal Affair*, *The Great Game*, *A Day to Remember*, *Background*, *Don't Blame the Stork* (1953), *One Good Turn*, *For Better, for Worse*, *The Crowded Day* (1954), *The Quatermass Experiment*, *Tiger by the Tail*, *The Love Match*, *Lost* (1955), *Women Without Men*, *Sailor Beware*, *Home and Away*, *The Good Companions* (1956), *These Dangerous Years* (1957), *Further Up the Creek*, *A Clean Sweep* (1958), *The Entertainer* (1960), *Over the Odds* (1961), *Term of Trial* (1962), *Bitter Harvest* (1963), *Rattle of a Simple Man* (1964), *Some Will – Some Won't* (1969), *The Nightcomers* (1971), *Consuming Passions* (1988, UK/US), *Julie and the Cadillacs* (1999).
BIBLIOG: Autobiography, *Scene and Hird*, 1976.

Hiscott, Leslie (*b* London, 1894 – *d* London, 1968). Director. Generally considered the man who put the 'quickie' into 'QUOTA QUICKIES', but some, such as *A Fire Has Been Arranged* (1935), with FLANAGAN and ALLEN, and *Annie, Leave the Room!* (1935), are surprisingly good. Entered film industry in 1919 as an assistant director in Italy and the UK, associated with Graham CUTTS, George PEARSON and Famous Players–British. His work with UK directors in England in the 20s obviously helped hone his skills at speedy and efficient film-making. At his best when teamed with screenwriter Michael BARRINGER.
OTHER BRITISH FILMS INCLUDE: (d, unless noted) *Mrs May Comedies* series (1925), *This Marriage Business* (1927, + sc), *At the Villa Rose*, *The House of the Arrow* (1930), *A Night in Montmartre* (1931), *When London Sleeps* (1932), *Strike It Rich*, *Marooned* (1933), *She Shall Have Music* (1935), *The Interrupted Honeymoon* (1936), *Ship's Concert* (1937), *Tilly of Bloomsbury* (1940), *Sabotage at Sea* (1942), *The Time of His Life* (1955, + co-sc), *Tons of Trouble* (1956, + co-sc). AS.

historical films The British historical film followed the lead set by popular literature and the education system in the celebration of military victories, the transformation of disasters into acts of heroic sacrifice, and the deification of national heroes. The films also mythologised the monarchy, and, by association, the establishment, thus serving to legitimise the status quo. This was also achieved, as Jeffrey Richards has argued, by the personalisation of the monarchy, through such films as *The Virgin Queen* (1923), *Nell Gwyn* (1926 and 1934), and, most famously, Alexander KORDA's *The Private Life of Henry VIII* (1933) and Herbert WILCOX's two reverential paeans to Queen Victoria, *Victoria The Great* (1937) and *Sixty Glorious Years* (1938). The latter films also served another purpose touched on by historical films – the celebration of EMPIRE. *Rhodes of Africa* (1936) and *David Livingstone* (1936), for example, demonstrated the value and benefits that British imperialism had bestowed on subject peoples.

Historical treatments also provided the means of circum-navigating the rigours of British CENSORSHIP which forbade the treatment of controversial subjects. This is visibly demonstrated in *Fire Over England* (1937), with its analogy between 16th-century Spain and Nazi Germany. Historical analogies continued into the early war years in *This England* (1941), *The Prime Minister* (1941) and *The Young Mr Pitt* (1942), where the achievements of the past were compared to the present wartime situation. Historical films went into decline in the latter years of the war, being superseded by GAINS-BOROUGH's COSTUME MELODRAMAS, wherein fictitious characters were used within vague historical contexts. The post-war box-office disasters of *Bonnie Prince Charlie* (1948), *Christopher Columbus* and *Bad Lord Byron* (1949) probably did not help their cause, and the 50s tended to celebrate recent rather than past history through a plethora of WAR FILMS.

More recent historical films have also reflected contemporary ideology, but now they began to question the past and not merely to glorify it. The military madness behind *The Charge of the Light Brigade* (1968), the agrarian poverty of *Winstanley* (1975), the establishment anti-Semitism on display in *Chariots of Fire* (1981) and the anti-unionism in *Comrades* (1986) all serve to exemplify this change.
BIBLIOG: Jeffrey Richards, *The Age of the Dream Palace*, 1984; Sue Harper, *Picturing The Past*, 1994. John Oliver.
See also **heritage cinema**.

Hitchcock, Sir Alfred (*b* London, 1899 – *d* Los Angeles, 1980). Director. Nowadays Hitchcock is remembered for his great Hollywood films, particularly *Rear Window* (1954), *Vertigo* (1958), *Psycho* (1960) and *The Birds* (1963) with an affectionate backglance at *The 39 Steps* (1935) and *The Lady Vanishes* (1938) and an acknowledgement of *Blackmail* (1929) as the first fully-fledged British talkie. It is easy to forget that he had already made eight sound films when he embarked on *The 39 Steps* and that his nine silent films had established him as Britain's most promising director before SOUND was invented.

He had begun work in the film industry designing and writing title cards for the American company, Famous Players–Lasky. By 1924, when the Americans moved out and their ISLINGTON STUDIOS were taken over by Michael BALCON's GAINSBOROUGH PICTURES, Hitchcock had been promoted to assistant director and in 1926 he made his debut as director with *The Pleasure Garden*. Four more films followed for Gainsborough – *The Mountain Eagle*, *The Lodger* (1926), *Downhill* and *Easy Virtue* (1927) – before Hitchcock was poached by John MAXWELL for BRITISH INTERNATIONAL PICTURES (BIP), an ambitious new company with purpose-built studios at ELSTREE. The silent films he made at Elstree share common themes and stylistic traits, which mark Hitchcock as a mature practitioner of the art of silent cinema. He shows an unexpected feeling for the English landscape in *The Farmer's Wife* (1928) and a facility for oddball romantic comedy in *Champagne* (1928); and extraordinary sequences, such as the boxer's hallucination of his wife's infidelity in *The Ring* (1927), and the dissolve in *The Manxman* (1928) from the wife's plunge into the harbour to the inkwell of the judge (her lover) who will try her for attempted suicide, indicate an exceptional virtuosity.

Hitchcock eagerly seized the opportunities offered by sound. The sequence in *Blackmail* where a chattering neighbour's constant repetition of the word 'knife' grates on the nerves of the guilty heroine; the way in which Sir John, the discontented juror in *Murder!* (1930), voices his thoughts while shaving in the mirror, showed that he could be as inventive with sound as he was with pictures. In *Rich and Strange* (1932), where a young married couple (not unlike Hitchcock and his wife Alma REVILLE) are given the opportunity to escape their dull suburban existence on a world cruise, he showed it was possible to combine the sophisticated visual fluency of a silent film with the greater psychological complexity dialogue allowed. Unfortunately, the film was neither a critical nor a commercial success and by 1933 Hitchcock's career seemed to be drifting into the doldrums. After making *Waltzes from Vienna* (1933) as an independent production, he rejoined Michael Balcon, now head of production at BIP's main rival, GAUMONT–BRITISH, to make *The Man Who Knew Too Much* (1934).

The six thrillers Hitchcock made at Gaumont–British restored the reputation he had established with *The Lodger* and *Blackmail*. Their plots are complex and exciting but they are always subsidiary to the personal dilemmas of the characters; villains are fascinating and intriguing; romances are enlivened with conflict; and settings, even when unostentatious studio sets, create a convincing and resonant world. *The 39 Steps* is the most satisfactory combination of these elements but its successors have their own virtues: the edgy distrust which permeates *The Secret Agent* (1936); the melancholy evocation of pinched lives in *Sabotage* (1936); the exuberant enthusiasm of *Young and Innocent* (1937). *The Lady Vanishes* (1938) was made after Hitchcock had signed a contract with David Selznick which would take him to Hollywood and the next phase of his career, and had been written by Frank LAUNDER and Sidney GILLIAT for another director. But Hitchcock turns what might have been a routine assignment into a masterpiece: he creates within the confines of a few railway carriages a microcosm of Europe on the brink of war, establishing a highly effective comic romantic partnership between Margaret LOCKWOOD's plucky heroine and Michael REDGRAVE's eccentric musicologist.

Hitchcock was to spend the next 40 years in Hollywood, returning briefly to make two short PROPAGANDA films in 1944, and *Under Capricorn* (1949) and *Stage Fright* (1950). His penultimate film, *Frenzy* (1972), is set in a cosily old-fashioned London, but, as in *The Lodger*, it is the site for terrifying sexual violence and nightmarish black comedy. As if to close the circle, the psychopathic villain, like his own father, is a greengrocer.

BIBLIOG: Raymond Durgnat, *The Strange Case of Alfred Hitchcock*, 1974; Tom Ryall, *Alfred Hitchcock and the British Cinema*, 1986; Jane Sloan, *Alfred Hitchcock: A Filmography and Bibliography*, 1995. Charles Barr, *English Hitchcock*, 1999. Robert Murphy.

Hobbes, Peter (*b* Dover, 1917 – *d c*1996). Actor. Son of Hollywood-based character actor, Halliwell Hobbes (*b* 1877 – *d* 1962), he made a few small-part US appearances (theatre callboy in *Top Hat*, 1935), and post-war played supporting roles in some British films, including the sympathetic housemaster in *The Courtneys of Curzon Street* (1947). In US since early 60s.

OTHER BRITISH FILMS INCLUDE: *I Live in Grosvenor Square* (1945), *My Brother Jonathan* (1948), *24 Hours of a Woman's Life* (1952), *The Night of the Demon*, *The Barretts of Wimpole Street* (1956).

Hobbs, Christopher (*b c*1945). Production designer. Also an artist and sculptor, Hobbs was associated with the design of some of the most enterprising British films from the late 70s. He worked several times each with Derek JARMAN, starting with *Sebastiane* (1976, title design, + a) and *Jubilee* (1978), Ken RUSSELL, on *Gothic* (1986) and *Salome's Last Dance* (1988), and Terence DAVIES, on *The Long Day Closes* (1992) and *The Neon Bible* (1995, UK/US). His designs for the TV gothic mini-series, *Gormenghast* (2000), drawing eclectically on Asian architecture, attracted much attention.

OTHER BRITISH FILMS: (des) *Caravaggio* (1986), *The Last of England* (+ a), *Aria* (segment) (1987), *Edward II* (1991, + a), *Deadly Advice* (1994), *Velvet Goldmine* (1998, UK/US), *Mansfield Park* (2000, UK/US).

Hobbs, Jack (*b* London, 1893 – *d* Brighton, 1968). Actor. Bit player on screen who graduated to minor, generally lightweight leading man, and ended film career playing minor roles in two

George FORMBY features. Very busy on stage from 1906, including more than 2,200 performances in the Whitehall farce, *Worm's Eye View* (from 1945).

BRITISH FILMS INCLUDE: *Love's Legacy* (1915), *The Lady Clare* (1919), *The Skin Game* (1920), *The Crimson Circle* (1922), *The Happy Ending* (1925), *Dr Josser KC* (1931), *Josser Joins the Navy* (1932), *Car of Dreams*, *No Limit* (1935), *Millions* (1936), *Leave It to Me, Intimate Relations* (1937), *It's in the Air, Miracles Do Happen* (1938), *Let George Do It!* (1940). AS.

Hobson, Valerie (*b* Larne, Northern Ireland, 1917 – *d* London, 1998). Actress. A great beauty who became an impressive actress, elegant redheaded Hobson landed some very choice roles in the later 40s, and is perhaps at her best in those which permit her to exercise her talent for high comedy. She originally trained as a dancer until she grew too tall, and made her stage debut aged 15 in *Ball at Savoy* at Drury Lane, where, symmetrically enough, she made her final acting appearance as the governess in *The King and I* (1953), for which she won wide acclaim and to play which she had to pass up the female lead in *Father Brown* (1954).

Her film career began in modest British films – in, for example, *Badger's Green* (1934) – before she took off in her teens for Hollywood where she made about a half-dozen films, of which only *The Bride of Frankenstein* (1935) is memorable. On return to England, there were a few more minor films before TECHNICOLOR made her a star in KORDA's *The Drum* (1938). She then had successes in two comedy thrillers, *This Man is News* (1938) and its sequel, *This Man in Paris* (1939), produced by Anthony HAVELOCK-ALLAN whom she married in 1939. For her favourite director, Michael POWELL, she appeared to advantage in two popular wartime SPY THRILLERS, *The Spy in Black* (1939) and *Contraband* (1940), establishing her as an attractive, ladylike but spirited heroine. Her post-war period of great achievement includes: a properly icy Estella in *Great Expectations* (1946); the passionate, ambitious heroine of *Blanche Fury* (1947), her personal favourite; the priggish Edith in *Kind Hearts and Coronets* (1949), an exquisite comic performance as someone who takes life very seriously; and the extravagant, cold-hearted Hester in *The Rocking Horse Winner* (1949). Her last film, *Knave of Hearts* (1954), showed her again as a mistress of subtle comedy.

She retired to marry politician John Profumo to whom she remained married until her death, weathering the security scandal of 1963, after which he resigned, and both spent much of their time in charitable work. The author David Profumo is their son.

OTHER BRITISH FILMS: *Eyes of Fate* (1933), *Two Hearts in Waltz Time, The Path of Glory* (1934), *Oh! What a Night!* (1935), *The Secret of Stamboul, No Escape* (1936), *Jump for Glory* (1937), *Q Planes, The Silent Battle* (1939), *Atlantic Ferry* (1941), *Unpublished Story* (1942), *The Adventures of Tartu* (1943), *The Years Between* (1946), *The Small Voice* (1948), *The Interrupted Journey, Train of Events* (1949), *Who Goes There!* (1951), *Meet Me Tonight, The Voice of Merrill, The Card* (1952).

Hodge, Douglas (*b* Plymouth, 1960). Actor. Dark, intense actor who has had his best chances on TV in such varied roles as Adam, caught up in hideous crime, in *A Fatal Inversion* (1991) and Dr Lydgate in *Middlemarch* (1994), but who so far has had only modest supporting roles on film. He was Bosey in Ken RUSSELL's bizarre *Salome's Last Dance* (1988, US/UK) and had a good courtroom scene in *Hollow Reed* (1996, UK/Ger). Had stage seasons with London's Almeida and National Theatres and scored a success in the revival of *The Caretaker* (2000).

OTHER BRITISH FILMS INCLUDE: *Diamond Skulls*, *Dealers* (1989), *The Trial* (1992), *Saigon Baby* (1995).

Hodge, John (*b* Glasgow, 1963). Screenwriter, actor. Regular writer of director Danny BOYLE and producer Andrew MACDONALD's films, including *Shallow Grave* (1994, + a), *Trainspotting* (1996, + a), for which he won an AA and a BAAn for adapted screenplay, as well as several other awards and nominations, *A Life Less Ordinary* (1997) and *The Beach* (2000, US). Trained as a doctor of medicine.
OTHER BRITISH FILMS INCLUDE: *Alien Love Triangle*, *The Final Curtain* (UK/US) (2001).

Hodge, Patricia (*b* Cleethorpes, 1946). Actress. Exquisitely delicate blonde who is better known for such TV roles as Phyllida in the 'Rumpole' series (from 1978), the impeccably groomed Mary in *The Lives and Loves of a She-Devil* (1990), and the bored Monica in *Hotel du Lac* (1986), than for her films. She had the lead in the enigmatic PINTER-scripted film, *Betrayal* (1982), but otherwise stage and TV have used her patrician – metaphoric as well as literal – persona more profitably than film has.
OTHER BRITISH FILMS INCLUDE: *The Disappearance* (1977, UK/Can), *Rosie Dixon – Night Nurse* (1978), *Riding High* (1980), *The Leading Man* (1996), *Jilting Joe* (1997), *Before You Go* (2002).

Hodges, Adrian Screenwriter. Former film trade reporter (for *Screen International* until 1990) and reader of screenplays, and responsible for a finely diagnostic TV version of *Great Expectations* (1999), Hodges has shown an interesting, rather literary talent in his screenplays for *The Bridge* (1991), based on the story behind Impressionist painter Philip Wilson Steer's painting 'The Bridge', *Tom & Viv* (1994, UK/US, co-sc), based on T.S. Eliot's first marriage, and *Metroland* (1997, UK/Fr/Sp).

Hodges, Ken (*b* London, 1922 – *d* 1993). Cinematographer. Entered films in 1940, had a longish apprenticeship as camera operator, then as cinematographer on SHORTS, before beginning his prolific feature career. Much of the latter is utterly routine (e.g. the 'Confessions' series), but he could rise to the challenge of more interesting material, such as the mining drama, *The Brave Don't Cry* (1952, co-c), and his three diverse films for Peter MEDAK: *Negatives* (1968), *A Day in the Death of Joe Egg* (1970), *The Ruling Class* (1971).
OTHER BRITISH FILMS INCLUDE: (cam op) *Master of Bankdam* (1947, ass), *Laxdale Hall*, *Street Corner* (1953); (c) *Morning Departure* (1950, underwater ph), *Behemoth the Sea Monster* (1958), *Faces in the Dark* (1960), *Emergency* (1962), *The Comedy Man* (1963), *The Jokers*, *The Great St Trinian's Train Robbery*, *The Shuttered Room* (1966), *Inadmissible Evidence* (1968, co-c), *Baffled!* (1972), *No Sex, Please – We're British* (1973), *Confessions of a Driving Instructor* (1976), *Stand Up Virgin Soldiers* (1977), *Nelson's Touch* (1979).

Hodges, Mike (*b* Bristol, 1932). Director. Spent ten years cutting his teeth on TV fare in the 60s before making his screen debut with the now-cult classic, *Get Carter* (1971, + sc), a gangster movie thought very violent in its day. To realise its merits, one has only to consider the dire Hollywood remake (2000). Nothing else in his *cv* comes near this tough, raw piece; not *Pulp* (1972), with its bizarre cast and erratic spoofing; or the sci-fi parody, *Morons from Outer Space* (1985). He has filmed only sparsely, and, though some mild fun may be had from *Flash Gordon* (1980), his success with *Carter* and *Croupier* (1998, UK/Fr/Ger/Ire, but re-released in the UK, 2000, after sleeper success in the US) suggest his talent lies to one side of his jokey preferences. Has also worked in US films (*The*

Terminal Man, 1974, + p, sc) and TV.
OTHER BRITISH FILMS INCLUDE: *Polygamous Polonius Revisited* (1984, anim, p), *A Prayer for the Dying* (1987).

Hoellering, George (*b* Baden, Austria, 1898 – *d* London, 1980). Producer, director, exhibitor. Formerly producer in Germany (*Kuhle Wampe*, 1932) and Hungary (*Hortobagy*, 1935, +d, sc, e). In the early 40s Hoellering made several DOCUMENTARY SHORTS for the MOI, and in 1952 the feature-length *Murder in the Cathedral*. Managing director of Film Traders Ltd, responsible for renting notable foreign films, he was also, from 1939 until his death, the managing director of London's ACADEMY CINEMA, which screened many such films.
OTHER BRITISH FILMS: (short/doc) *Eyes On The Target* (1942), *Water Saving* (1942), *Salvage Saves Shipping* (1943), *Message From Canterbury* (1944), *Paper Possibilities* (1945), *30,000 Years Of Modern Art* (1970). Tim Bergfelder.

Hoey, Dennis (*b* London, 1893 – *d* Palm Beach, Florida, 1960). Actor, singer. RN: Samuel Hyams. Now revered by cultists as the bone-headed Inspector Lestrade in the SHERLOCK HOLMES series made in Hollywood in the early 40s, tall, dominant Hoey, a former stock exchange clerk, had established himself as a character actor (he never looked like a leading man) in about 20 British films of the 30s, including *Tell England* (1931), as the padre, and *Chu-Chin-Chow* (1934). In 1941, went to the US where he spent the rest of his career, often in Brit-set pieces like *Kitty* (1945), as Paulette Goddard's brutal husband. On stage from 1918.
OTHER BRITISH FILMS INCLUDE: *The Man from Chicago* (1930), *The Maid of the Mountains* (1932), *The Good Companions* (1933), *Jew Süss* (1934), *Brewster's Millions* (1935), *Did I Betray?* (1937).

Hoey, Iris (*b* London, 1885 – *d* London, 1979). Actress. First on stage 1903 and thereafter constantly for over 50 years, RADA-trained Hoey by comparison merely flirted with film, and is probably best remembered as the bizarre Ysabel, the society columnist in *Pygmalion* (1938). Busy in largely forgotten films of the 30s, and briefly funny in *Poet's Pub* (1949) as a dowager who proclaims: 'When I was young *all* Americans were millionaires.' Married actors (1) Max Leeds and (2) Cyril RAYMOND.
OTHER BRITISH FILMS INCLUDE: *East Lynne* (1922), *Her Reputation* (1931), *Royal Cavalcade* (1935), *Living Dangerously* (1936), *The Perfect Crime* (1937), *Jane Steps Out* (1938), *The Midas Touch* (1939), *The Girl Who Couldn't Quite* (1949).

Hoffe, Monckton (*b* Connemara, Ireland, 1880 – *d* London, 1951). Dramatist, screenwriter. RN: Hoffe-Miles. A prominent playwright, his work included *The Little Damozel* (1909), filmed in 1916 and 1933; *Panthea* (1913), US-filmed in 1917; and *The Faithful Heart* (1922), filmed 1933. Also acted on stage and occasionally in films, such as *The Lady with a Lamp* (1951). At MGM (1932–39) as a screenwriter. For British films of the 30s, he generally wrote dialogue only.
BRITISH FILMS: *Michael and Mary* (1931), *Bitter Sweet* (1933), *Runaway Queen* (1934), *Haunted Honeymoon*, *Busman's Honeymoon* (1940), *Daybreak* (1946). AS.

Hogan, Brenda (*b* Birkenhead, 1928). Actress. Trained with Liverpool Rep and toured in *Dr Jekyll and Mr Hyde* with Basil DEAN before making screen debut in *The Fatal Night* (1948). Had her best chance as Richard ATTENBOROUGH's adolescent romantic interest in *The Guinea Pig* (1948); made few more films, including *The Admirable Crichton* (1957), as the imperious maid, Fisher. Married Donald HOUSTON.

OTHER BRITISH FILMS INCLUDE: *Noose* (1948), *Adam and Evelyne*, *Private Angelo* (1949), *Encore* (1951), *Saturday Island* (1952), *Lost* (1955), *Trouble with Eve* (1959).

Hogg, Ian (*b* Newcastle-upon-Tyne, 1937). Actor. Trained at Drama Centre, London, on stage first in 1964, then on screen in 1966 repeating his theatre role in the film version of Peter BROOK's *The Marat/Sade . . .* (1966). He has played supporting roles in a dozen or more films, including the little-seen *Dead Cert* (1974), as a luckless steeplechaser, and starred as Detective Sergeant Rockliffe for two TV seasons in *Rockliffe's Babies* (1987) and *Rockliffe's Folly* (1988).

OTHER BRITISH FILMS INCLUDE: *Tell Me Lies* (1967), *King Lear* (1970, UK/Ger, as Edmund), *Macbeth* (), *The Hireling* (1973), *Hennessy* (1975), *The Legacy* (1978), *Lady Jane* (1985), *Little Dorrit* (1987), *The Pleasure Principle* (1991).

Holden, Jan (*b* Southport, 1931). Actress. Not every actress can claim that she played one of *The Fire Maidens from Outer Space* (1956) as Holden can – if she dares. She was a competent and attractive lead and second lead in a mix of main and second features (often for the DANZIGERS) in the 50s. Married to Edwin RICHFIELD.

OTHER BRITISH FILMS INCLUDE: *The Hornet's Nest* (1955), *Assignment Redhead* (1956), *High Flight, Quatermass 2* (1957), *A Woman Possessed* (1959), *Never Let Go* (1960), *Work Is a Four Letter Word* (1967), *The Best House in London* (1968), *Dominique* (1978).

Holden, William (*b* O'Fallon, Illinois, 1918 – *d* Santa Monica, California, 1981). Actor. RN: William Beedle. Major American star, especially of the 50s after he cast off his nice-guy persona to play a heel in *Sunset Boulevard* (1950). Appeared in a few British films of which the most notable are David LEAN's *The Bridge on the River Kwai* (1957) and Carol REED's moody *The Key* (1958), in both of which he gives an important international gloss to the proceedings.

OTHER BRITISH FILMS: *The World of Suzie Wong* (1960), *The Devil Never Sleeps, The Lion* (1962), *The 7th Dawn* (1964, UK/US), *Casino Royale* (1967), *Escape to Athena* (1979, unc).

Holder, Ram John (*b* Guyana, *c* 1934). Actor. Tall, now grizzled, West Indian actor who has had a substantial share of the roles available to black actors in mainstream British cinema, since his first eye-catching turn as a predatory gay in *Two Gentlemen Sharing* (1969). Became best known as lollipop man, Porkpie, in the barber-shop sitcom, *Desmond's* (1989–94) and in the 1995 spin-off series, *Porkpie*, in which he has won a lottery. He has also done notable stage work with London's National Theatre and the Bristol Old Vic (title role in *Julius Caesar*).

OTHER BRITISH FILMS: *Leo the Last* (1969), *Pressure* (1975), *Britannia Hospital* (1982), *My Beautiful Laundrette* (1985), *The Passion of Remembrance, Playing Away* (1986), *Virtual Sexuality* (1999), *Lucky Break* (2001, UK/Ger/US).

Holder, Roy (*b* Birmingham, 1946). Actor. First seen as the school chum of the boy who thinks he's seen Jesus in *Whistle Down the Wind* (1961), Holder nabbed a few juvenile roles in the 60s, like Peter, the Nurse's servant, in *Romeo and Juliet* (1968, UK/It) and another servant in *The Taming of the Shrew* (1967, US/It), and, with TV (e.g. the lead in *Spearhead*, 1978–79) and films, hung on for over 30 years. Best film role was probably as the inept thief in *Loot* (1970).

OTHER BRITISH FILMS INCLUDE: *Term of Trial* (1962), *Murder Ahoy* (1964), *Othello* (1965), *The Virgin Soldiers* (1969), *The Virgin and the Gypsy* (1970), *Psychomania* (1972), *Mack the Knife* (1989).

Holland, Rodney Editor. Worked first as sound editor on some very distinguished early 70s films, like *Don't Look Now* (1973, UK/It) and *Barry Lyndon* (1975), then in the 80s and 90s as editor in TV and on such films as *The Company of Wolves* (1984) and *Alive and Kicking* (1996).

OTHER BRITISH FILMS INCLUDE: (sd e) *Private Road, Gumshoe* (1971), *Images* (1972), *Caravan to Vaccares* (1974), *Cross of Iron* (1977), *Bad Timing* 1980, dial e); (e) *Scrubbers* (1982), *No Surrender, The Assam Garden* (1985), *Diamond Skulls* (1989).

Hollander, Tom (*b* Oxford, 1969). Actor. Short, dark, droll actor, hilarious as the flamboyant gay, in serious danger from 'the fashion police', in *Bedrooms and Hallways* (1999), Cambridge-educated Hollander did his best with the ill-conceived *Martha, Meet Frank, Daniel and Laurence* (1998), as the guy with least chance of winning the heroine, and, in quite other vein, compelling as an unsympathetic British diplomat in *Some Mother's Son* (1996, Ire/US). Successful on London and New York stage as the tiresome Bosie in *The Judas Kiss* (1998) and as the ailing Byronesque Osborne in TV's *Wives and Daughters* (1999).

OTHER BRITISH FILMS INCLUDE: *True Blue* (1996), *The Clandestine Marriage* (1999), *Maybe Baby* (2000, UK/Fr), *The Lawless Heart, Enigma* (UK/Ger/US), *Gosford Park* (2001, UK/Ger/US).

Holles, Antony (*b* London, 1901 – *d* London, 1950). Actor. With over 70 films in 20 years, short, dark Holles was prolific in small roles, adept as foreigners, like the Italian film director 'jumping around' the market in *Britannia of Billingsgate* (1933), working-class types, like Sergeant Bassett in *A Canterbury Tale* (1944) and minor functionaries of many kinds. Had a bigger chance in a drag turn in Michael POWELL's *Hotel Splendide* (1932). Educated at Latymer School, on stage from 1916, in *Charley's Aunt*.

OTHER BRITISH FILMS INCLUDE: *The Will* (1921), *Star Reporter* (1931), *The Lodger* (1932), *Loyalties, Forging Ahead* (1933), *Brewster's Millions* (1935), *Things to Come, Seven Sinners, Sensation* (1936), *Dark Journey, Smash and Grab, Action for Slander* (1937), *They Drive By Night* (1939), *Neutral Port* (1940), *Tomorrow We Live, Talk About Jacqueline* (1942), *English Without Tears* (1944), *Caesar and Cleopatra* (1945), *Carnival, The Magic Bow* (1946), *Bonnie Prince Charlie* (1948), *The Rocking Horse Winner* (1949).

Hollingsworth, John (*b* London, 1916 – *d* London, 1963). Music director. Educated at the Guildhall School of Music, Hollingsworth began his professional career with the London Symphony Orchestra at the age of 23. In the RAF, 1940, became associate conductor of the Royal Air Force Symphony Orchestra, and began association with DOCUMENTARY FILM production conducting the score for *Target for Tonight* (1941). He worked exclusively as a music director on documentaries until 1945 when he collaborated with Muir MATHIESON on the adaptation of Rachmaninov's music for *Brief Encounter* (1945). He is seen on screen as the conductor in *The Mark of Cain* (1948). Left film in the late 40s when he joined Covent Garden as a conductor, but returned (1954–63) to be HAMMER's first music director until his death from tuberculosis.

OTHER BRITISH FILMS INCLUDE: (doc, short) *Cornish Village, Crofters* (1944), *Burma Victory, Three Cadets* (1945), *A Soldier Returns, Jungle Mariner, The Glen Is Ours* (1946), *Boy Builders, North-East Corner* (1947); (features) *The Silver Darlings* (1946), *When the Bough Breaks* (1947), *The Quatermass Experiment* (1955), *X the Unknown* (1956), *The Curse of Frankenstein* (1957), *Dracula* (1958), *The Hound of the Baskervilles, The Mummy* (1959), *The Brides of Dracula* (1960), *Taste of Fear, The Damned* (1961), *Paranoiac* (1962). AS.

Holloway, Julian (*b* Watlington, Oxfordshire, 1944). Actor. Harrow-educated, RADA-trained son of Stanley Holloway, with much stage experience, including *The Norman Conquests* (1975) and, on Broadway, *My Fair Lady* (1992–93) and over 200 TV performances, including *Rebecca* (1979) as a marvellously venal Jack Favell. Entered films in such swinging 60s fare as *Five to One* (1963), *A Hard Day's Night* (1964) and *The Knack . . .* (1965), and did a half-dozen Carry Ons, as well as several officer roles, as in *Young Winston* (1972). First married to Zena Walker. Model **Sophie Dahl** (*b* 1979), who has appeared in a few British films, including *Mad Cows* (1999) and *Best* (2000, UK/Ire) is his daughter by **Tessa Dahl** (*b* 1957) who had small roles in such British films as *Royal Flash* (1975) and *The Slipper and the Rose* (1976).

OTHER BRITISH FILMS INCLUDE: (a, unless noted) *Catch Us If You Can* (ass d) (1965), *The Jokers* (1966), *Follow That Camel* (1967), *Carry On Up the Khyber*, . . . *Doctor* (1968), . . . *Camping, Scream and Scream Again* (1969), *Carry On Loving* (1970), *The Spy's Wife* (+ p, co-sc) (1971), *The Stud* (1974), *Porridge, The Great Rock'n'Roll Swindle* (1979), *Loophole* (1980, co-p).

Holloway, Stanley (*b* East Ham, 1890 – *d* Littlehampton, 1982). Actor, comedian, singer. One of the best-loved British entertainers of the 20th century, Holloway first trained for opera, then, post-WW1 infantry service, became a seaside concert artist and MUSIC HALL performer, making his London stage debut in 1919, enduringly famous for his rendition of the classic monologue, 'Albert and the Lion'. Made one silent film, *The Rotters* (1921), but entered films in earnest in the 30s, revealing a huge demotic appeal that was noticeable in an essentially middle-class cinema. His first talkie was a film version of his concert-party revue, *The Co-Optimists* (1929), and some of his other 30s movies enabled him to film his famous monologues (e.g. *Sam and His Musket* and *Drummed Out*, 1935, anim, voice), but his real fame as a character star came in the 40s.

He brings a bluff lower-middle to middle-class solidity and authenticity to such roles as the former Parliament House stoker in *The Way Ahead* (1944), the next-door neighbour in *This Happy Breed* (1944), the Police Sergeant in *Wanted for Murder* (1946), the bottom-smacking porter in *Brief Encounter* (1945), the shopkeeper-councillor in *Passport to Pimlico* (1949), Alec Guinness's souvenir-making colleague ('Anne 'athaway cottages for string') in *The Lavender Hill Mob* (1951), the embattled householder in *The Happy Family* (1952), the turning-worm husband in *Meet Me Tonight* (1952, 'Fumed Oak' episode), the true Labour man who tells MP Peter Finch 'You learnt the words but not the music' in *No Love for Johnnie* (1961) – and so on. As well, there are cherishable breaks with realism in, say, his Vincent Crummles in *Nicholas Nickleby* (1947) and the Gravedigger in *Hamlet* (1948). And, for many people, the crowning achievement of a great career was his originating of Doolittle in *My Fair Lady* (1964, US, AAn), his famous song from which, 'Wiv a little bit of luck', provided the title for his 1969 autobiography. By then, he'd become an institution on stage, screen and TV. Father of Julian Holloway.

OTHER BRITISH FILMS: *The Girl from Maxim's, Sleeping Car* (1933), *Sing As We Go!, Road House, Love at Second Sight, Lily of Killarney* (1934), *In Town Tonight, D'Ye Ken John Peel?, Squibs, Play Up the Band* (1935), *Beat the Retreat, Alt! 'oo Goes There?* (anim), *Sam's Medal* (anim) (1936), *The Vicar of Bray, Song of the Forge, Sam Small Leaves Town, Cotton Queen, Our Island Nation* (doc) (1937), *Co-Operette* (1939, short), *Albert's Savings* (short), *Highlights of Variety* (1940), *Major Barbara* (1941), *Salute John Citizen* (1942), *Savings Cavalcade* (1943, short), *Champagne Charlie* (1944), *The Way to the Stars, Caesar and Cleopatra* (1945), *Carnival* (1946), *Meet Me at Dawn* (1947), *One Night With You, Snowbound, The Winslow Boy, Noose, Another Shore* (1948), *The Perfect Woman* (1949), *Midnight Episode* (1950), *Lady Godiva Rides Again, One Wild Oat, The Magic Box, Painter and Poet* (short, voice), *Sailor's Consolation* (short, voice) (1951), *The Titfield Thunderbolt, Meet Mr Lucifer, A Day to Remember, The Beggar's Opera* (1953), *Fast and Loose* (1954), *Jumping for Joy, An Alligator Named Daisy* (1955), *No Trees in the Street, Hello London, Alive and Kicking* (1958), *On the Fiddle, Ten Little Indians* (1965), *The Sandwich Man, That Swinging City* (1966), *Mrs Brown, You've Got a Lovely Daughter* (1968), *The Private Life of Sherlock Holmes* (1970), *Flight of the Doves* (1971), *Up the Front* (1972).

Hollywood studios in Britain Famous Players–Lasky (Paramount) set up a studio in Islington in 1920 but it was not until after the 1927 'quota' legislation that other American majors followed suit. Thereafter Hollywood firms wanting to distribute American pictures in Britain had to ensure that a proportion of their annual film offerings were British-made, and while some commissioned or acquired films from British firms to meet their obligations, others set up studios and embarked upon quota production in a systematic way.

WARNER BROS. registered a British company in 1931, and leased TEDDINGTON STUDIOS which they eventually bought and modernised. Among the 100-odd films made at the studio were *The Girl in the Crowd* (1934) one of a number of quota pictures directed by MICHAEL POWELL, an early Errol Flynn picture, *Murder at Monte Carlo* (1935), and *They Drive By Night* (1938), one of the best crime pictures of the period. Warners continued to use the studio but, following its substantial investment in the ASSOCIATED BRITISH PICTURE CORPORATION, production was switched to the ABPC Studios at ELSTREE.

FOX also set up a British production branch in 1931 with the company leasing the WEMBLEY STUDIOS which they eventually bought and as quota production was stepped up during the decade. The schedules included a couple of Powell films, and *Late Extra* (1935) notable for the first screen appearance of JAMES MASON.

MGM–BRITISH was set up in 1936 with a commitment to the production of 'quality films' rather than the low-budget 'QUOTA QUICKIE' production associated with American companies. Revised quota legislation encouraged bigger budgets and the company made three films at DENHAM STUDIOS including *Goodbye, Mr Chips* (1939) which enjoyed considerable success both in Britain and America as A-grade pictures.During WW2, with the freezing of the US majors' British earnings, RKO set up RKO RADIO BRITISH Productions Ltd. Though the exile firm began with a film in the parent company's low budget 'Saint' series, it went on to make films such as *Dangerous Moonlight* (1941) and *They Flew Alone* (1942) starring ANTON WALBROOK and ANNA NEAGLE respectively. Later in the war, MGM acquired their own studio with the purchase of the AMALGAMATED STUDIOS at BOREHAMWOOD (ELSTREE) and its British-based production was resumed in the late 40s with *Edward, My Son* (1949). Also, MGM's first CinemaScope picture – *Knights of the Round Table* – was made at Borehamwood in 1953 as one of a number of big-budget spectaculars made on a 'runaway' basis. The company continued to make films in Britain until the late 60s but closed down their Borehamwood facilities in 1970. Among their final productions was a musical remake of one of the original MGM–British titles from the late thirties – *Goodbye, Mr Chips* (1969). Tom Ryall.

Holm, Sir Ian (*b* Ilford, Essex, 1931). Actor. RN: Ian Holm Cuthbert. Trained at RADA, and for some years on the London stage, before making his screen debut in *The Bofors Gun* (1968), for which he won a BAA as best supporting actor. This award was also given for *Chariots of Fire* (1981) in addition to an AAn for the same performance. Holm has distinguished himself as one of the leading CHARACTER ACTORS of his generation, with roles as varied as the robot in *Alien* (1979, UK/US), the petty but evil bureaucrat in *Brazil* (1985), Fluellen in *Henry V* (1989) and Polonius in *Hamlet* (1990, UK/US). He gave much admired performances in leading roles as Lewis Carroll in *Dreamchild* (1985) and in *The Sweet Hereafter* (1997, Can). Has also done a great deal of superb TV, including *The Lost Boys* (1978), as J.M. BARRIE, and a brave *King Lear* (1998), and he resumed his stage career in 2001, in a revival of Harold PINTER's *The Home-coming*, the play that made his name. Awarded CBE in 1989, knighted in 1998. Married (2) to Penelope WILTON; they divorced in 2001.

OTHER BRITISH FILMS INCLUDE: *Oh! What A Lovely War* (1969), *Mary Queen of Scots* (1971), *Young Winston* (1972), *The Homecoming* (1973, UK/US), *Juggernaut* (1974), *Time Bandits* (1981), *Dance with a Stranger*, *Laughterhouse* (1984), *Wetherby* (1985), *The Madness of King George* (1994, UK/US), *Loch Ness* (1996), *eXistenZ* (1999, UK/Can/Fr), *Simon Magus* (2000, UK/Ger/It), *Esther Kahn* (2001, UK/Fr), *The Emperor's New Clothes* (2002). Simon Caterson.

Holm, Sonia (*b* Sutton, 1920 – *d* Oxford, 1974). Actress. RN: Freeborn. Sweet-faced, slightly melancholy-looking alumnus of RANK's COMPANY OF YOUTH, in RADA and rep pre-war. An ex-WAAF radar operator, she was given such a role in *School for Secrets* (1946), and then modest second leads in the likes of Rank's *Miranda* and *Broken Journey* (1948), and a better chance as John McCALLUM's fiancée in *The Loves of Joanna Godden* (1947) and his love interest in *The Calendar* (1948). Married/divorced actor Patrick HOLT.

OTHER BRITISH FILMS INCLUDE: *Warning to Wantons* (1948), *Bad Lord Byron*, *Stop Press Girl* (1949), *13 East Street* (1952), *The Crowded Day* (1954).

Holmes, Jack B. (*b* Bickley, Kent, 1901 – *d* 1968) Director, producer. Began work as editor, scriptwriter and director with GAUMONT–BRITISH INSTRUCTIONAL FILMS. Between 1935 and 1938 worked as a director and producer of the STRAND FILM COMPANY on films such as *The Way to the Sea* (1937), and, between 1938 and 1945, with the GPO FILM UNIT and CROWN FILM UNIT, with whom he was producer-in-charge (1943–46). Between 1954 and 1961 worked for SHELL to produce films in Egypt, Africa and Asia. Between 1965 and 1968 he produced films for the CHILDREN'S FILM FOUNDATION. His most important film was Crown's war-time feature-length documentary *Coastal Command* (1942), which he directed and co-wrote.

OTHER BRITISH FILMS INCLUDE: *The Islanders* (1939), *Merchant Seamen*, *Ordinary People* (co-d) (1941), *The Centre* (1947), *Berth 24* (1950). Ian Aitken.

Holmes, Phillips (*b* Grand Rapids, Michigan, 1907 – *d* Armstrong, Canada, 1942). Actor. Blond, sensitive Hollywood leading man (1928–36), whose career was ruined through alcohol and drug addiction. An Anglophile, Holmes died while serving with the Royal Canadian Air Force. Son of actor Taylor Holmes.

BRITISH FILMS: *Ten Minute Alibi*, *The Divine Spark* (1935), *The Dominant Sex* (1937), *Housemaster* (1938). AS.

Holmes, Richard (*b* Epping, *c* 1963). Producer. With director Stefan SCHWARTZ, runs production company known as the Gruber Brothers, scoring a success with the scam comedy *Shooting Fish* (1997, co-p, co-sc). Is managing director of WhiteCliff Film and Television and acts under the name Otto Jarman; e.g. as prison guard in *Shooting Fish*, and in TV's *As Time Goes By*. Married to Catherine RUSSELL.

OTHER BRITISH FILMS INCLUDE: *The Joyriders* (1988, UK/Ire, a), *Soft Top, Hard Shoulder* (1992, p), *Waking Ned* (1999, UK/Fr/US, co-p), *The Jolly Boys Last Stand* (ex p), *The Abduction Club* (co-p) (2001).

Holmes-Paul, R. (*b* Norwich, 1892 – *d* ?) Production designer. Much associated with John BAXTER's films, often giving them a not unpleasing studio-bound look, and seen at best in the bleakness of *Love on the Dole* (1941) and the lovingly created Victoriana of Lance COMFORT's *When We Are Married* (1943), produced by Baxter. Under contract to BRITISH NATIONAL, for whom he designed many GENRE pieces in the 40s.

OTHER BRITISH FILMS: (des) *Stamboul* (UK/US), *Man of Mayfair* (1931), *Service for Ladies* (1932), *The High Command* (1937); (art d) *Strange Evidence* (UK/US) (1933), *Death at Broadcasting House* (1934), *Brief Ecstasy* (1937), *The Common Touch* (1941), *Murder in Reverse* (1945), *Woman to Woman*, *Lisbon Story* (1946), *Dual Alibi*, *Mrs Fitzherbert* (1947), *Uneasy Terms* (1948), *Lilli Marlene* (1950), *The Final Test* (1953).

Holt, Patrick (*b* Cheltenham, 1912 – *d* London, 1993). Actor. RN: Parsons. Handsome six-footer who entered films (as Parsons) just before WW2, had a distinguished military career (1940–46), and post-war was put under contract by RANK. Not quite distinctive enough for major stardom, he nevertheless had a prolific career in film and TV over 50 years. Had supporting roles in 'A' features like *Frieda* and *The October Man* (1947), but was essentially a stalwart of the thriving 'B' FILM industry of the 50s, playing leads in neat thrillers like *Suspended Alibi* (1956) and, surprisingly, the villain in *The Gelignite Gang* (1956). When this trade dried up, he found a pretty steady stream of smallish roles which called for a dignified elderly mien, like that of the Colonel in *Playing Away* (1986). Married (1) Sonia HOLM (1947–53) and (2) Sandra DORNE (1954–92, her death), appearing with both in *13 East Street* (1952).

OTHER BRITISH FILMS INCLUDE: *The Return of the Frog* (1938), *Convoy*, (1940), *Hungry Hill*, *When the Bough Breaks* (1947), *The Mark of Cain*, *Portrait from Life* (1948), *Boys in Brown*, *A Boy, a Girl and a Bike* (1949), *Ivanhoe*, *Come Back Peter* (1952), *The Golden Link* (1954), *Fortune Is a Woman*, *There's Always a Thursday* (1957), *I Was Monty's Double* (1958), *Too Hot to Handle* (1960), *The Frightened City* (1961), *Serena* (1962), *Guns at Batasi* (1964), *Thunderball* (1965), *When Dinosaurs Ruled the Earth* (1969), *Cromwell* (1970), *Psychomania*, *Young Winston* (1972), *Legend of the Werewolf* (1974), *Priest of Love* (1980), *The Whistle Blower* (1986), *Loser Takes All* (1990, UK/US).

Holt, Seth (*b* Palestine, 1923 – *d* London, 1971). Director. Former editor and associate producer for EALING (on some of its most famous films), and for a time Robert HAMER's brother-in-law, Holt's early death robbed British cinema of a promising talent. He directed one of Ealing's last films, the moody, noirish *Nowhere to Go* (1958) and edited a couple of films post-Ealing (*The Battle of the Sexes*, 1959; *Saturday Night and Sunday Morning*, 1960). His *Taste of Fear* (1961) for HAMMER is a highly efficient piece of Grand Guignol and Bette DAVIS thought him 'ruthless' when he directed her in *The Nanny* (1965), with the result that she gave one of her most restrained performances in years. He had to withdraw from producing *If . . .* (1968) and died (heart disease and alcoholism) while making his last film, Hammer's *Blood from the Mummy's Tomb* (1971).

OTHER BRITISH FILMS INCLUDE: (e/co-e) *Champagne Charlie* (1944), *Hue and Cry* (1946), *Frieda* (1947), *Scott of the Antarctic*, (1948), *Kind Hearts and Coronets*, *The Spider and the Fly* (1949), *Dance Hall* (1950), *The Lavender Hill Mob* (1951), *Mandy* (1952); (asssoc p) *Touch and Go*, *The Ladykillers* (1955), *The Man in the Sky* (1956); (d) *Wildlife in Danger* (1946, doc, d), *Station Six Sahara* (1962), *Danger Route* (1967).

Home, William Douglas (*b* Edinburgh, 1912). Screenwriter, dramatist. Son of 13th Earl of Home, educated at Eton and Oxford and trained at RADA, Home was admirably equipped to chronicle the upper-class world which is the milieu for his most famous plays and the films derived from them, *The Chiltern Hundreds* (1947, filmed 1949, + co-sc) and *The Reluctant Debutante* (1955, filmed 1958, US, + sc). A more sombre play, *Now Barabbas* (1947), was filmed in 1949. Brother Alec was Prime Minister (1963–64).

OTHER BRITISH FILMS INCLUDE: (co-sc) *Sleeping Car to Trieste* (1948), *Hotel Sahara* (1951), *Made in Heaven* (1952), *The Colditz Story* (1954).

Homolka, Oscar (aka Oskar) (*b* Vienna, 1898 – *d* Kent, 1978). Actor. Trained at Vienna's Royal Dramatic Academy, bulky, heavy-featured Homolka appeared on stage in Austria and Germany, and in many German films before coming to England soon after Hitler came to power. Made three British films, notably HITCHCOCK's *Sabotage* (1936) as the anarchist stabbed to death by Sylvia Sydney, before continuing on to the US in 1936. He played villains and occasionally jovial, accented foreigners there, winning an AAn for *I Remember Mama* (1948), and periodically returned to the UK to play such roles as the fence in *The Shop at Sly Corner* (1946) and, from the mid 60s, when he played Colonel Stok in two Harry Palmer spy thrillers, *Funeral in Berlin* (1966) and *Billion Dollar Brain* (1967), he worked almost entirely in Britain until his death. Married (1) **Grete Mosheim**, who appeared in the 1935 British film, *Car of Dreams*, and (4), from 1949 until her death, **Joan Tetzel** (*b* New York, 1921 – *d* 1977), who made several British films, including *Hell Below Zero* (1953).

OTHER BRITISH FILMS INCLUDE: *Rhodes of Africa* (as Kruger) (1936), *Top Secret* (1952), *The Key* (1958), *The Long Ships* (1963, UK/Yug), *The Madwoman of Chaillot* (1969), *The Tamarind Seed* (1974).

Honri, Baynham (*b* London, 1903 – *d* Lightwater, 1987). Sound recordist. RN: Percy Baynham Henry Thompson. Entered industry in 1921 at STOLL STUDIOS, of which he later became general manager until WW2, having had experience of sound recording at GAINSBOROUGH and TWICKENHAM. In 1944 he worked with John BAXTER, for whom he was associate producer on several films and directed and produced *Bank Holiday Luck* (1947); was also technical supervisor at EALING briefly in the later 40s/early 50s. President of the British Kinematograph Society in the mid 50s.

OTHER BRITISH FILMS INCLUDE: (studio man/tech super) *Another Shore* (1948), *Whisky Galore!* (1949); (sd rec) *The Lodger* (1932), *Squibs* (1935), *Broken Blossoms* (1936); (sd) *Lord Richard in the Pantry* (1930), *Condemned to Death* (1932), *The Broken Melody*, *Bella Donna* (1934), *Scrooge*, *The Rocks of Valpré*, *The Last Journey* (1935), *Dusty Ermine* (1936), *The Vicar of Bray* (1937), *Freedom Radio* (1940).

BIBLIOG: Baynam Honri, 'British Studios – A Technical Survey', in Peter Noble (ed), *British Film Yearbook 1947–48*, 1947.

Hood, Noel (*b* Bristol, 1909 – *d* 1979). Actress. Beginning as she was to continue, Hood was first seen as Basil RADFORD's aseptic sister and Naunton WAYNE's unlikely fiancée in *Crook's Tour* (1940), and thereafter maintained a career as a series of acidulous spinsters and haughty titled ladies. In TV from the mid 50s.

OTHER BRITISH FILMS INCLUDE: *The Million Pound Note* (1953), *The Constant Husband* (1954), *The Curse of Frankenstein*, *How to Murder a Rich Uncle* (1957), *The Inn of the Sixth Happiness* (1958), *Devil's Bait*, *Bobbikins* (1959), *Two Way Stretch* (1960), *Tamahine* (1962), *Time Flies* (1971).

Hook, Henry (aka Harry) (*b* England, 1959). Director. Went to live in Kenya aged four and most of his film work has had African subjects, his best known film being *The Kitchen Toto* (1987, + sc). Prior to that he directed several short films, then edited *Lord of the Flies* (1990, US), did some TV (episodes of *Silent Witness*, 1996), and directed *St Ives* (1998).

Hope, Bob (*b* London, 1903). Actor. Legendary comedian who emigrated to America aged three and became an institution there, especially for his association with Bing Crosby and Dorothy Lamour in the 'Road' series, the last and least of which is the British-made *Road to Hong Kong* (1961). In 1943, he appeared in Anthony ASQUITH's documentary *Welcome to Britain*; his other three British features are not among his best, and *The Iron Petticoat* (1956), with Katharine HEPBURN, was pretty dismal stuff, with two great stars failing to strike sparks from each other.

OTHER BRITISH FILMS: *Call Me Bwana* (1963), *The Muppet Movie* (1979).

Hope, Dawn (*b* Sheffield). Actress. Appeared in the award-winning *Black Joy* (1977), but has otherwise not found parts plentiful, being relegated to small roles like the Jamaican nurse in *Richard's Things* (1980). Some TV in the 90s, including *Waiting for God* (1990).

OTHER BRITISH FILMS: *SWALK* (1970), *Midnight Breaks* (1988).

Hope, Vida (*b* Liverpool, 1918 – *d* Chelmsford, 1963). Actress. Rough-hewn character actress, willing to play unglamorous and unattractive characters like Fanny Squeers in *Nicholas Nickleby*, duplicitous Mrs Fenshaw in *They Made Me a Fugitive* (1947), or the tough-minded union official in *The Man in the White Suit* (1951). A former journalist and amateur actress, she appeared first on the professional stage in 1939, and, apart from acting in an interesting range of plays (from *Peer Gynt* to *Tobacco Road*), she also devised, starred in and produced *The Punch Revue* (1955). Repeated her stage role of the vicious, finally repentant Jess in the film of *Women of Twilight* (1952) and staged the musical numbers in *Charley Moon* (1956, + a). Married director Derek TWIST. Died tragically young in a road accident.

OTHER BRITISH FILMS INCLUDE: *Champagne Charlie* (1944), *The Way to the Stars* (1945), *Beware of Pity*, *Hue and Cry* (1946), *It Always Rains on Sunday* (1947), *The Mark of Cain* (1948), *The Interrupted Journey* (1949), *The Woman in Question* (1950), *Green Grow the Rushes* (1951), *Angels One Five* (1952), *The Broken Horseshoe* (1953), *Lease of Life* (1954), *In the Doghouse* (1961).

Hopkins, Sir Anthony (*b* Port Talbot, S. Wales, 1937). Actor, director. Trained at the Welsh College of Music and Drama, Cardiff, and RADA. In 1965 he auditioned for the National Theatre before Laurence OLIVIER who was to become his mentor. Critically acclaimed for his stage work, including his award-winning role in *Pravda* (1985) and, at the National, *King Lear* (1986) and *Antony and Cleopatra* (1987), as well as playing the psychiatrist in *Equus* on Broadway (1974–75). He made his film debut in *The White Bus* (1967) and has shown his versatility many times since: as Richard the Lionheart in *The Lion in Winter* (1968), Claudius in *Hamlet* (1969), John Avery in *The Looking Glass War* (1969) and an explosive Captain Bligh in *The Bounty* (1984). Possibly best known for his mesmerising portrayal of Hannibal 'the Cannibal' Lecter in *Silence of the Lambs* (1991, US), for which he won an AA and a BAA, but he won less praise for the sequel, *Hannibal* (2001, US). He has great ability to transform himself and to penetrate the emotional depths of his characters: witness his portrayal of C.S. Lewis in *Shadowlands* (1993, UK/US), for which he won a BAA, and his other BAA-performance as Stevens the butler in *Remains of the Day* (1993). In 1990 he starred in and directed *August* (1994), a Welsh-set version of *Uncle Vanya*, and over three decades has done much noteworthy TV work. Made CBE in 1987 and knighted in 1993, he became an American citizen in 2000, and much of his recent film work, including the title roles in *Nixon* (1995) and *Titus* (2000, UK/US), was US-produced.

OTHER BRITISH FILMS: *When Eight Bells Toll* (1971), *Young Winston* (1972), *A Doll's House* (1973), *All Creatures Great and Small*, *Juggernaut* (1974), *A Bridge Too Far* (1977), *International Velvet* (1978), *The Hunchback of Notre Dame* (1982), *A Married Man* (1984), *The Good Father* (1986), *84 Charing Cross Road* (1986, UK/US), *The Dawning* (1988), *A Chorus of Disapproval* (1989), *Howards End* (1992), *Chaplin* (UK/Fr/It/Jap/US), *The Trial* (1992), *The Innocent* (1993, UK/Ger), *Surviving Picasso* (UK/US) (1996).

BIBLIOG: Quentin Falk, *Anthony Hopkins – Too Good to Waste*, 1989; Michael Feeney Callan, *Anthony Hopkins*, 1989. Anne-Marie Thomas.

Hopkins, Antony (*b* London, 1921). Composer. RN: Reynolds. Responsible for 15 film scores from the late 40s, starting with a jocular contribution to Peter USTINOV's Victorian pastiche, *Vice Versa* (1947) and ending with Ustinov's *Billy Budd* (1962, + m d), perhaps his most notable score. RCM-trained, he is also a pianist and has composed sonatas, chamber music and a one-act opera.

OTHER BRITISH FILMS INCLUDE: *Here Come the Huggetts* (1948), *The Pickwick Papers* (1952, + m d), *Child's Play* (1954), *The Blue Peter*, *Cast a Dark Shadow* (1955), *Seven Thunders* (1957).

Hopkins, Joan (*b* London, 1915). Actress. Eloquent of face and voice, this RADA-trained actress, on stage from 1938, had small, uncredited roles in *Alibi* and *Squadron Leader X* (1942). She made her name on stage (1946) as the ill-fated Princess Charlotte in *The First Gentleman*, repeating the role on screen, 1948, but with less acclaim. She is a charmingly natural heroine in two thrillers, *Man on the Run* (1949) and *Double Confession* (1950), her last film. Also, some TV including *Othello* and *The Admirable Crichton* (1950). Married director Henry CASS.

OTHER BRITISH FILMS: *We Dive at Dawn* (1943), *Temptation Harbour* (1947), *The Weaker Sex* (1948).

Hopkins, John (*b* London, 1931 – *d* Los Angeles, 1998). Screen-writer. Best known for his TV work, including a series of *Z Cars* scripts and, most notably, his four interlocking family dramas, *Talking to a Stranger* (1966). He wrote sporadically for the screen, but the unsettling drama of police interrogation, *The Offence* (1972), and the SHERLOCK HOLMES pastiche, *Murder by Decree* (1978, UK/Can), indicate his range and his tough quality. Married (2) Shirley KNIGHT (1969 to his death).

OTHER BRITISH FILMS: *Two Left Feet* (1963, co-sc), *Thunderball* (1965, co-sc), *The Holcroft Covenant* (1985, co-sc).

Hopper, Victoria (*b* Vancouver, 1909). Actress. After training for opera, Hopper made her stage debut as *Martine* (1933). She was spotted by Carol REED and cast by Basil DEAN in *The Constant Nymph* (1933). Marriage to Dean the following year resulted in a handful of starring roles on screen, none of which suggest that here was a major film talent, though she is aptly charming as Lucy in *The Mill on the Floss* (1937).

OTHER BRITISH FILMS: *Lorna Doone* (1934), *Whom the Gods Love*, *Laburnum Grove*, *The Lonely Road* (1936), *Escape from Broadmoor* (1948). AS.

Hopson, Violet (*b* San Francisco, 1891 – *d*?). Actress. A dark-haired, cold-faced beauty, Hopson has a modernistic look, reminiscent of her American contemporary, actress Miriam Cooper. She was closely associated with Cecil HEPWORTH – who promoted her as a 'Dear Delightful Villainess' – from 1912 to 1917, and then worked with director Walter WEST at Broadwest, Walter West Productions and Violet Hopson Productions. Minor roles in a few talkies.

BRITISH FILMS INCLUDE: *The Vicar of Wakefield* (1913), *The Chimes* (1914), *Barnaby Rudge* (1915), *Trelawney of the Wells* (1916), *Comin' Thro' the Rye* (1916), *The Cobweb* (1917), *A Turf Conspiracy* (1918), *In the Gloaming* (1919), *Kissing Cup's Race* (1920,+ p), *The Scarlet Lady* (1922, + p), *Remembrance*, *Widecombe Fair* (1928). AS.

Hordern, Sir Michael (*b* Berkhamsted, 1911 – *d* Oxford, 1995). Actor. Former teacher and sales rep who had one line in *A Girl Must Live* and a fleeting bit in *Band Waggon* (1940), before WW2 service in the Royal Navy (1940–45), returned to the stage in 1947, to TV (*Morning Departure*) and films (*School for Secrets, Girl in a Million*) in 1946 – and thereafter never stopped. Despite claiming in 1990 that he had 'never been ambitious', he had one of the most productive careers of any 20th-century British actor. He had several seasons at Stratford and the Old Vic, playing many of the great classic roles – Lear, Prospero, Brutus, Pastor Manders in *Ghosts*, as well as new plays – and there was masses of rich TV, culminating in *Memento Mori* (1992) and, as Farebrother, in *Middlemarch* (1994 – why didn't someone make this when he was young enough to play a definitive Casaubon?).

Besides all this were nearly 100 films. Even in the 30-odd small roles he did in the decade after WW2, he was distinctive as policemen and officials of various kinds; then, from about 1955 he started to have more significant parts. He was Commander Lindsay with a nightmare story to tell in *The Night My Number Came Up* (1955), the embittered, jealous father of the little boy in *The Spanish Gardener* and the Resident Commissioner in *Pacific Destiny* (1956), the Governor of Gibraltar in *I Was Monty's Double* (1958), a fine Banquo in a dreadful *Macbeth* (1961). He had even more rewarding roles in the 60s, including Ashe in *The Spy Who Came in from the Cold* (1965), a great comedy turn in *A Funny Thing Happened on the Way to the Forum* (1966, UK/US), and Thomas Boleyn in *Anne of a Thousand Days* (1969), to choose three among many; and in 1972, as the seedy journalist Minty in *England Made Me* (UK/Yug), he gives perhaps the quintessential Greenean performance of any adaptation of Greene's work. In or out of uniform, in costume or modern dress, he was an unassuming pillar of British cinema for several decades.

OTHER BRITISH FILMS: *Mine Own Executioner*, *Good-Time Girl* (1947), *Night Beat*, *The Small Voice*, *Portrait from Life* (1948), *Train of Events*, *Passport to Pimlico* (1949), *The Astonished Heart*, *Trio*, *Highly Dangerous* (1950), *Flesh and Blood*, *Tom Brown's Schooldays*, *Scrooge*, *The Magic Box* (1951), *The Story of Robin Hood . . .*, *The Hour of 13*, *The Card* (1952), *Street Corner*, *Personal Affair*, *The Heart of the Matter*, *Grand National Night* (1953), *You Know What Sailors Are!*, *Forbidden Cargo*, *The Beachcomber*, *The Constant Husband* (1954), *Storm over the Nile*, *The Dark Avenger*, *The Man Who Never Was* (1955), *The Baby and the Battleship* (1956), *No Time for Tears*, *Windom's Way*, *The Spaniard's Curse*, *I Accuse!* (1957), *Girls at Sea* (1958), *Sink the Bismarck!*, *Moment of Danger*, *Man in the Moon* (1960), *Dr Syn Alias the Scarecrow*, *The VIPs* (1963), *The Yellow Rolls-Royce* (1964), *Khartoum*, *The Jokers* (1966), *How I Won the War*, *I'll Never Forget What's 'is Name* (1967), *Prudence and* the Pill, Where Eagles Dare (1968), Some Will – Some Won't, The Bed Sitting Room, Futtocks End (1969), Up Pompeii, Girl Stroke Boy, Demons of the Mind, The Pied Piper, A Christmas Carol (UK/US) (1971), Alice's Adventures in Wonderland (1972), The Mackintosh Man, Theatre of Blood (1973), Juggernaut, Mister Quilp (1974), Royal Flash, Barry Lyndon (narr) (1975), The Slipper and the Rose: The Story of Cinderella, Joseph Andrews (1976), Watership Down (anim), The Medusa Touch (UK/Fr) (1978), The Wildcats of St Trinian's (1980), The Missionary (1981), Gandhi (1982, UK/Ind), Group Madness (1983, doc), Lady Jane (1985), Labyrinth, Comrades (1986), Diamond Skulls (1989), The Fool (1990), The Beauty and the Beast, Freddie as F.R.O.7 (1992, anim).

BIBLIOG: Autobiography, A World Elsewhere, 1993.

Horn, Camilla (b Frankfurt am Main, Germany, 1906 – d Gilching, Germany, 1996). Actress. F.W. Murnau's Faust (1926) made Horn an international star, and brought her, briefly, to Hollywood. In the early 30s she provided continental glamour in a number of British films, her image changed from naive ingenue to blonde siren. During WW2 she made several films in Italy.

BRITISH FILMS: The Return Of Raffles (1932), Matinee Idol (1933), The Love Nest (1933), The Luck Of A Sailor (1934). Tim Bergfelder.

Hornbeck, William (b Los Angeles, 1901 – d Ventura, California, 1983). Editor. Went to UK in 1934, after entering the US industry at 15, and during the 30s he was either editor or supervising editor of Alexander KORDA's productions from The Scarlet Pimpernel (1935) to The Thief of Baghdad (1940). Following the outbreak of WW2, he returned to the US, where his first credit was as editor of Korda's That Hamilton Woman (1941) and where he spent the rest of his illustrious career, winning an Oscar for editing A Place in the Sun (1951).

OTHER BRITISH FILMS INCLUDE: (e/super e) Sanders of the River (co-e), The Ghost Goes West (1935), Things to Come, Rembrandt, The Man Who Could Work Miracles (1936), Dark Journey, Elephant Boy, Knight Without Armour, Return of the Scarlet Pimpernel (1937), The Divorce of Lady X, The Drum (1938), Over the Moon, Q Planes, Four Feathers, The Spy in Black, The Lion Has Wings (1939), Suddenly, Last Summer (1959).

Horne, David (b Balcombe, 1898 – d London, 1970). Actor. Imposing character player, ex-Grenadier Guard (the training tells in his film persona) and amateur actor before professional stage debut in 1925, where, typically, he played the Victorian paterfamilias in Pink String and Sealing Wax (1943). Entered films in 1933, and usually played professional and military types – such as the prosecuting counsel in Don't Take It to Heart! (1944), Ann TODD's doctor in The Seventh Veil (1945), the judge in Street Corner (1953) and Admiral Southbound in Dentist on the Job (1961). On TV from 1946 (The Importance of Being Earnest).

OTHER BRITISH FILMS INCLUDE: Lord of the Manor (1933), Badger's Green (1934), Gentlemen's Agreement, Royal Cavalcade (co-p only) (1935), Seven Sinners (1936), The Mill on the Floss (1937), The Stars Look Down (1939), Return to Yesterday, Night Train to Munich (1940), The First of the Few (1942), Yellow Canary (1943), The Wicked Lady, They Were Sisters, The Rake's Progress (1945), Caravan, Men of Two Worlds, Gaiety George (1946), The Man Within (1947), Once Upon a Dream, Madeleine (1949), The Intruder (1953), Beau Brummell (1954), The Prince and the Showgirl (1957), The Devil's Disciple (1959), Nurse on Wheels (1963), Diamonds for Breakfast (1968).

Horne, Geoffrey (b Buenos Aires, 1933). Actor. Under a Columbia contract in the late 50s, this handsome actor had good roles in two British films – The Bridge on the River Kwai and Bonjour Tristesse (both 1957) – and then was lost to international films (like Tempest, 1958, in which he starred) and

serial marriages, including one to actress Collin Wilcox.

Horne, Kenneth (b London, 1900 – d London, 1975). Playwright. Author of popular light plays, several of which were adapted to the screen (including Fools Rush In, 1946, filmed 1949, and A Lady Mislaid, 1948, filmed 1958). Also wrote some screenplays, including Aunt Clara (1954). Not to be confused with comedian/broadcaster of the same name.

OTHER BRITISH FILMS INCLUDE: Almost a Honeymoon (1938), The Spider (1939), Sailors Don't Care (1940).

Hornung, E(rnest) W(illiam) (b Middlesborough, 1866 – d St Jean du Luz, France, 1921). Author. His most famous creation, A.J. Raffles, the gentleman burglar and cricketer, was portrayed in Hollywood by John Barrymore (1918), Ronald Colman (1930), David NIVEN (1940) and in Britain by George Barraud in The Return of Raffles (1932), and in the 1977 TV series by Anthony VALENTINE. His stories, Stingaree (1905), were filmed in Hollywood in 1915 and 1934. Hornung was brother-in-law to Conan DOYLE, who disapproved of a criminal hero, however well-bred.

Horrocks, Jane (b Rossendale Valley, Lancashire, 1964). Actress. Very gifted young star of the 90s, who kept coming to attention in new ways. Working-class, RADA-trained, then with the RSC, first widely noticed as the stroppy, anorexic daughter in Mike LEIGH's Life is Sweet (1990), from whose breasts David THEWLIS licked melted chocolate. She followed this with TV's Absolutely Fabulous (1992–95) as Jennifer SAUNDERS' moronic assistant Bubble, for whom thought constituted hard labour, and she was the funniest thing in the pilot for Mirrorball (2000), the AbFab follow-up. There were major theatre successes, as a Lady Macbeth who urinates on stage (of the Greenwich Theatre) and in The Rise and Fall of Little Voice (1992). She followed this by receiving a BAAn for reprising her role in this, as the introverted girl with a brilliant gift for mimicking famous singers, in the film version, Little Voice (1998), and revealing her own remarkable singing voice. In 2000, she released an album entitled The Further Adventures of Little Voice, classic songs with big-band backing.

OTHER BRITISH FILMS INCLUDE: The Dressmaker (1988), Memphis Belle (1990), Deadly Advice (1994), Second Best (1994, UK/US), Some Kind of a Life (1995),), Bring Me the Head of Mavis Davis (1998), Chicken Run (UK/US, anim, voice), Born Romantic, Christmas Carol: The Movie (2001).

horror Just as the English Gothic novel of the Romantic period flourished in reaction against the sedateness of 18th-century neoclassical culture, so the British horror film has revelled in offering an alternative to the predominant realist, rationalist mode of the national cinema, gleefully exaggerating its melancholy and morbidity and releasing its repression – to the horror of some critical commentators. With varying prolificacy the horror GENRE has been an element in popular British cinema at least since the 30s, with such films as The Ghoul (1933) and Dark Eyes of London (1939), or the 1942 Gothic piece, The Night Has Eyes, and the Hellraiser films of the late 80s and Beyond Bedlam (1994), attesting to its durability.

There have been two main cinematic traditions in Britain for rendering horror – the subtle and the suggestive as against the sensual and sensational. In the former case, rather as Henry JAMES argued in his Preface to the classic ghost story, The Turn of the Screw, directors have felt that horror is more effective when evoked in the mind and imagination of the spectator rather than through visual explicitness. The horror here is in the spirit of place, the terror of the unseen, the deceptiveness of appearance, and the slow revelation of the dark underside of human personality. Distinguished examples in this tradition include the Ealing compendium *Dead of Night* (1945), with its eerie suggestion of *déjà-vu* and never-ending nightmare; Thorold DICKINSON's stylish ADAPTATION of Pushkin, *The Queen of Spades* (1948), with its inventive use of soundtrack to suggest supernatural visitation; Jacques Tourneur's *Night of the Demon* (1957), an M.R. James adaptation which, until the finale, is all suggestion and implied terror; and Jack CLAYTON's masterly adaptation of the afore-mentioned Henry James novella, *The Innocents* (1961), where the horror lies in the ambiguity of the visual presentation and the psychological derangement of the heroine.

Spearheaded by the productions of HAMMER studios in the 50s, the other tradition eschewed restraint and relished the gore. Hammer brought colour and blood into British film, defying good taste in its X-rated excesses and in its overt sexuality, with Christopher LEE's Count Dracula a disturbingly seductive figure, both personification of evil and sexual liberator. For many critics at this time, the horror film was a lowly form, pandering to the sadistic instincts of the mass audience. C.A. LEJEUNE famously described *The Curse of Frankenstein* (1957) as 'among the half-dozen most repulsive films I have ever encountered.' Some laughed off the Hammer films as jokey Grand Guignol, but two deadly serious works in the genre became arguably the most controversial films of the British cinema. Michael POWELL's *Peeping Tom* (1960), an extraordinary study of a serial-killer with a murderous movie camera, which implicated the audience in the hero's tortured voyeurism, provoked critical outrage on a scale that virtually ended Powell's directing career. Similarly, Michael REEVES's *Witchfinder General* (1968), a ferociously pessimistic study of bigotry and brutality in 17th-century England, was widely condemned for its extremes of violence and only later defended for its stylistic daring and its seriousness of purpose.

Gradually the horror film has come to be recognised as one of the major GENRES of British film. Thematically, its exploration of the unconscious, its socio-psychological explanation of human behaviour, its uncovering of the hypocrisy behind Victorian respectability, its critique of scientific arrogance, have tapped into many contemporary fears. Visually it has provided the scope for the kind of stylistic flair not readily associated with a national cinema prized for its DOCUMENTARY-style sobriety and social REALISM. In the place of the three Rs of British cinema – realism, rationalism, restraint – it has contibuted three Es: excess, eccentricity, exuberance. The effect has been vulgar or liberating, according to taste.

OTHER KEY BRITISH HORROR FILMS: *The Masque of the Red Death* (1964), *Quatermass and the Pit* (1967), *The Devil Rides Out* (1967), *Hands of the Ripper* (1971), *The Wicker Man* (1973).

BIBLIOG: David Pirie, *A Heritage of Horror: the English Gothic Cinema*, 1973; Peter Hutchings, *Hammer and Beyond: the British Horror Film*, 1993. Neil Sinyard.

Horsbrugh, Walter (*b* Scarborough, 1904 – *d* London, 1972). Actor. Long-faced, bespectacled character player, educated at St Paul's School, London, and trained as an engineer before taking up acting. Much stage and radio experience before entering films in *All Over the Town* (1948). Usually played dignified professionals, like the Cabinet Minister in *Top Secret* (1952) – or the butler in his last film, *The Abominable Dr Phibes* (1971).

OTHER BRITISH FILMS INCLUDE: *The Romantic Age* (1949), *Laxdale Hall*, *Innocents in Paris* (1953), *The Green Scarf* (1954), *Suspended Alibi* (1956), *Night of the Demon* (1957), *The Lady Is a Square* (1958), *The Share Out* (1962), *One Way Pendulum* (1964), *The Knack . . .* (1965), *The Walking Stick* (1970).

Horsfall, Bernard (*b* Bishop's Stortford, 1930). Actor. Character player always in professional roles, often as military men, including Sergeant Prideaux in *Guns at Batasi* (1964) and General Edgar in *Gandhi* (1982, UK/Ind). Also, lots of TV, such as *The Jewel in the Crown* (1984) and *Dr Bell and Mr Doyle* (1999), and Balliol in *Braveheart* (1995, US).

OTHER BRITISH FILMS INCLUDE: *High Flight*, *The Steel Bayonet* (1957), *The Angry Silence* (1960), *On Her Majesty's Secret Service* (1969), *Quest for Love* (1971), *Gold* (1974), *Shout at the Devil* (1976).

Horsley, John (*b* Westcliff-on-Sea, 1920). Actor. Stalwart character player of stage from 1938, films from 1950, and TV from 1959. In his long and prolific film career, after WW2 service in the Army, he played innumerable policemen, his easy authoritative demeanour usually ensuring his placement in the upper echelons of the force, like the Inspectors in *The Quiet Woman* (1951), *Recoil* and *Deadly Nightshade* (1953), all directed by John GILLING for Robert BAKER and Monty BERMAN's company, TEMPEAN, with whom Horsley had a long and harmonious working relationship. Also played many other professionals and officers; was in several main features for EALING (e.g. *Dunkirk*, 1958) and other companies; had a small role in *Ben-Hur* (1959, US), stage seasons at the Old Vic, and a continuing role in TV's *The Fall and Rise of Reginald Perrin* (1976). A working actor *par excellence*.

OTHER BRITISH FILMS INCLUDE: *Highly Dangerous* (1950), *The Frightened Man*, *The Lost Hours*, *The Long Memory* (1952), *Time Bomb*, *Single-Handed* (1953), *Father Brown*, *Double Exposure* (1954), *Above Us the Waves*, *Barbados Quest* (1955), *Breakaway*, *The Weapon* (1956), *Hell Drivers*, *Barnacle Bill* (1957), *Carry On Nurse* (1958), *Wrong Number* (1959), *Sink the Bismarck!* (1960), *Serena*, *Jigsaw*, *The Comedy Man* (1963), *Panic* (1965), *The Doctor and the Devils* (1985), *The Fourth Protocol* (1987), *Stanley's Dragon* (1994).

Horton, Edward Everett (*b* Brooklyn, 1886 – *d* Los Angeles, 1970). Actor, archetypal screen fusspot, who appeared in prissy character roles in more than 120 films from 1922–70. In the 30s, Horton starred in a handful of unmemorable British features: *Soldiers of the King*, *It's a Boy!* (1933), *The Private Secretary* (1935), *The Man in the Mirror* (1936), and *The Gang's All Here* (1939). AS.

Hoskins, Bob (*b* Bury St Edmunds, 1942). Actor. Short and stocky character star whose physical attributes have not been a barrier to his considerable success in films. First appeared on screen in 1972, and, by the late 70s, a starring role in Dennis POTTER's TV series *Pennies from Heaven* (1978), and his portrayal of Harold Shand in the cult CRIME film, *The Long Good Friday* (1979), had already demonstrated the malleability of his talent. Despite his strong Cockney accent, he spent the 80s playing anything from New York gangster Owney Madden in *The Cotton Club* (1984, US), to George, the hard man with a soft centre in *Mona Lisa* (1986, AAn/a), or the object of Maggie SMITH's tragic affection in *The Lonely Passion of Judith Hearne* (1987). Though also in international box-office hits like *Who Framed Roger Rabbit* (1988, US), and *Hook* (1991, US), Hoskins often works in low-budget local films like *24 7 TwentyFourSeven* (1997), in which he shines as the inspirational Alan Darcy. Whether playing a serial killer (*Felicia's Journey*, 1999, UK/Can), or a famous politician (uncannily like

Krushchev in *Enemy at the Gates*, 2001, UK/Ger/Ire/US), he is a compelling film presence.

OTHER BRITISH FILMS: (a, unless noted) *Up the Front* (1972), *The National Health* (1973), *Inserts, Royal Flash* (1975), *Pink Floyd The Wall* (1982), *The Honorary Consul* (1983), *The Woman Who Married Clark Gable* (short, UK/Ire), *Brazil* (1985), *The Secret Policeman's Third Ball, A Prayer for the Dying* (1987), *The Raggedy Rawney* (1988, + d), *Rue Saint-Sulpice* (1991, UK/Fr), *The Big Freeze* (1994, UK/Fin), *Balto* (1995, anim, UK/US), *Rainbow* (UK/Can, + d), *The Secret Agent* (UK/US, + exec p) (1996), *Spice World* (1997), *Cousin Bette* (UK/US), *Parting Shots, Captain Jack* (1998), *A Room for Romeo Brass* (UK/Can), *Let the Good Times Roll* (short) (1999), *Tortoise vs Hare* (anim) (2002). Melinda Hildebrandt.

Hough, Harold Director. An early director of one- and half-reel shorts, Hough began his career with GAUMONT, producing 1904 dramas such as *Man the Lifeboat* and *The Story of a Colliery Disaster* and reconstructions, such as *The Bombardment of Port Henry* and *Garrotting a Motor Car*. He later turned to comedy, and in 1906 formed his own company, Norwood, where he made *Attack in the Rear* (1906), *Jones' Birthday* (1907), etc. AS.

Hough, John (*b* London, 1941). Director. After TV experience in the 60s (for example, on *The Avengers*), Hough had a success with the stylish HAMMER HORROR film, *Twins of Evil* (1971), intelligently complex about matters of Puritans and sexuality, creating a powerful sense of oppositions at work. Since then, he has become one of those directors who have filmed largely in the US, much of it for TV, without ever fulfilling the early promise, though there are minor pleasures in *The Return from Witch Mountain* (1978, US), with Bette DAVIS, and *Biggles* (1986), for the boy in all of us. Among some ludicrous horror films are three also ludicrous but mildly enjoyable TV bodice-rippers, *A Hazard of Hearts* (1987), *The Lady and the Highwayman* (1988) and *Duel of Hearts* (1992), *après* GAINS-BOROUGH – some distance *après*, quite unresonant, but not devoid of melodramatic fun.

OTHER BRITISH FILMS INCLUDE: *Wolfshead: the Legend of Robin Hood* (1969), *Eyewitness* (1970), *The Legend of Hell House* (1973), *American Gothic* (1987), *Something to Believe in* (1998, + co-p, co-sc).

Houston, Donald (*b* Tonypandy, Wales, 1923 – *d* Coimbra, Portugal, 1991). Actor. Husky leading man of *The Blue Lagoon* (1949), who began as a touring actor in 1940, was in the RAF (1943–46), and on the London stage from 1947. For the rest of his life, he maintained a steady career in theatre, TV (including starring in *Moonbase 3*, 1973), and films. On stage he had his most challenging time with the Old Vic (1959–60). He was featured in films like *A Run for Your Money* (1949), as a Welsh football fan in London, *Dance Hall* (1950), as Natasha PARRY's conventional fiancé, and as one of the starring quartet in *Doctor in the House* (1954), but he never became a major star. However, he moved easily between 'A' films, in character parts by the mid 50s in such films as *Yangtse Incident* (1956) and memorably as Laurence HARVEY's decent friend in *Room at the Top* (1958), and 'B' FILMS, such as the enjoyably silly *Find the Lady* (1956), in which he played leads. Married Brenda HOGAN. Older brother of Glyn HOUSTON.

OTHER BRITISH FILMS INCLUDE: *Crow Hollow* (1952), *Small Town Story, The Red Beret, The Large Rope* (1953), *The Girl in the Picture* (1956), *The Man Upstairs, A Question of Adultery, Danger Within* (1958), *The Mark* (1961), *Twice Round the Daffodils, The Prince and the Pauper* (1962), *Maniac, Doctor in Distress* (1963), *Carry On Jack* (1964), *The Viking Queen* (1966), *Where Eagles Dare* (1968), *Tales That Witness Madness* (1973), *Voyage of the Damned* (1976), *Clash of the Titans* (1981, UK/US).

Houston, Glyn (*b* Tonypandy, Wales, 1926). Actor. The younger brother of Donald HOUSTON. Houston has appeared in supporting roles in just about every GENRE in post-war British cinema, including CRIME, HORROR, the SOCIAL PROBLEM film, COMEDY and SCIENCE FICTION. He is one of those reassuringly familiar talents upon which British cinema relies but who rarely receive much recognition. In the 70s, he was Bunter to Ian CARMICHAEL's Lord Peter Wimsey for a BBC TV series.

BRITISH FILMS INCLUDE: *The Blue Lamp* (1949), *The Cruel Sea* (1952), *River Beat* (1953), *The Sleeping Tiger, The Sea Shall Not Have Them* (1954), *Lost* (1955), *The Long Arm* (1956), *The Battle of the Sexes* (1959), *Circus of Horrors* (1960), *Payroll, Flame in the Streets* (1961), *A Stitch in Time* (1963), *One Way Pendulum, The Secret of Blood Island* (1964), *Are You Being Served?* (1977), *The Sea Wolves* (1980, UK/Switz/US), *The Mystery of Edwin Drood* (1993). Peter Hutchings.

Houston, Penelope Critic. Co-founder with Lindsay ANDERSON and others of the short-lived but influential magazine, SEQUENCE, Oxford-educated Houston joined the journal SIGHT AND SOUND in late 1950, as assistant to editor Gavin LAMBERT. She became its editor in 1956 and remained so until 1990, during which time it remained a civilised, perhaps somewhat staid, forum for discussion of international film. Author of several books on film, including *The Contemporary Cinema* (1963) and *Keepers of the Frame* (1994).

Houston, Renée (*b* Johnstone, Renfrewshire, 1902 – *d* London, 1980). Actress. Exuberant, flamboyant character player of dozens of films, who began her professional career in 1916 as half of the singing-dancing 'Houston Sisters' act, appeared in variety theatres all over England and toured overseas, and thereafter was often seen in revues, pantomimes and musical comedies, as well as straight plays, including Charles LAUGHTON's last, *The Party* (1958), as his good-natured, 'common' friend. In the 30s, she had leads in a few light films, including *Come into My Parlour* (1932), with her second husband, Pat AHERNE, *Fine Feathers* (1937), on which she met Donald CHURCHILL, who became her third, and *Happy Days Are Here Again* (1936, + story), a semi-autobiographical revue with sister Billie. Post-war, she became a vivid supporting player, especially effective in roles suggestive of a certain experienced, overblown sexuality, as with prisoner-of-war Ebbey in *A Town Like Alice* (1956) or Sara Monday, ex-wife and model of Gulley Jimson in *The Horse's Mouth* (1958).

OTHER BRITISH FILMS INCLUDE: *Blighty* (1927), *Mister Cinders* (1934), *No Monkey Business* (1935), *A Girl Must Live* (1939), *Old Bill and Son* (1940), *Two Thousand Women* (1944), *Lady Godiva Rides Again* (1951), *The Belles of St Trinian's* (1954), *Time Without Pity* (1957), *The Flesh and the Fiends* (1959), *The Phantom of the Opera, Tomorrow at Ten* (1962), *Nurse on Wheels, Carry On Cabby* (1963), *Repulsion* (1965), *Cul-de-sac, The Spy with a Cold Nose* (1966), *Legend of the Werewolf* (1974).

BIBLIOG: Autobiography, *Don't Fence Me In*, 1974.

Howard, Alan (*b* London, 1937). Actor. Son of actor Arthur HOWARD, nephew of Leslie HOWARD and of Fay COMPTON, on stage from 1958 and in films from 1960. Whereas he has persistently done significant theatre, including seasons at the Royal Court, Stratford (Oberon/Theseus in Peter BROOK's famous *Midsummer Night's Dream*, 1970–71), Vladimir in the 1997 Old Vic revival of *Waiting for Godot* and the sexual obsesssive, Schoning, in the Almeida's revival of *Lulu* (2001), only in two of his dozen films has he made much impression: as Rob LOWE's tutor (uphill work) in *Oxford Blues* (1984), and Helen MIRREN's brutally murdered lover in *The Cook, the*

Thief, His Wife and Her Lover (1989, UK/US). First film role was as the weak-minded friend of the gay suicide in *Victim* (1961).

OTHER BRITISH FILMS INCLUDE: *The Heroes of Telemark* (1965), *Work Is a Four Letter Word* (1967), *Strapless* (1988), *The Return of the Musketeers* (1989), *The Secret Rapture* (1993).

Howard, Arthur (*b* London, 1910 – *d* London, 1995). Actor. RN: Steiner. Brother of Leslie HOWARD, father of Alan HOWARD, and somewhat overshadowed by both, not even mentioned in Leslie Ruth Howard's *A Quite Remarkable Father* (1959). In films from the mid 30s, he played teachers, clerks and other minor functionaries in several dozen films, and made many uncredited appearances. Perhaps most memorable as the minor school headmaster who accidentally became a wartime icon in *The Intruder* (1953), and on TV as Jimmy EDWARDS's witless sidekick in *Whack-O!* (1956–60).

OTHER BRITISH FILMS INCLUDE: *The Lady is Willing* (1934), *London Belongs to Me* (1948), *Passport to Pimlico* (1949), *The Happiest Days of Your Life*, *Cage of Gold* (1950), *The Man in the White Suit* (1951), *Albert RN* (1953), *The Belles of St Trinian's*, *Knave of Hearts* (UK/Fr), *The Constant Husband* (1954), *One Way Out*, (1955), *Nowhere to Go* (1958), *Libel* (1959), *Watch it, Sailor!* (1961), *Ladies Who Do* (1963), *Jane Eyre* (1970), *Steptoe and Son* (1972), *Full Circle* (1976, UK/Can), *Moonraker* (1979, UK/Fr), *The Trail of the Pink Panther* (1982), *Another Country* (1984), dozens more.

Howard, Irene (*b* London, 1903 – *d* London, 1981). Casting director. Sister of Leslie and Arthur HOWARD, she began as a stage actress before setting up as casting director after helping Leslie cast *Pimpernel Smith* (1941) and *The Gentle Sex* (1943). As casting director for TWO CITIES, she worked on such films as *The Lamp Still Burns* (1943) and *Henry V* (1944). In 1946, was appointed casting director for MGM–BRITISH, for the likes of *Edward, My Son* (1949) and *Knights of the Round Table* (1953), and also worked for EALING in the later 50s, on, for example, *The Shiralee* (1957).

OTHER BRITISH FILMS INCLUDE: *In Which We Serve* (1942), *The Way Ahead* (1944), *Blithe Spirit*, *The Way to the Stars* (1945), *Men of Two Worlds* (1946), *Odd Man Out*, *Uncle Silas* (1947), *Ivanhoe* (1952), *Beau Brummell* (1954), *Bhowani Junction* (1955), *The Barretts of Wimpole Street* (1956), *The Secret Partner* (1961), *Murder at the Gallop*, *The Haunting*, *Children of the Damned* (1963), *Doctor Zhivago* (1965, UK/US), *Blow-Up* (1966, UK/It).

Howard, Joyce (*b* London, 1922). Actress. Sweet-faced, blonde, RADA-trained lead and second lead in a dozen films of the 40s. On stage first, made a touching film impression as Helen, pregnant by her unemployed boyfriend in *Love on the Dole* (1941), vivid as the light-minded member of *The Gentle Sex* (1943), sobered by experience, and affecting as the ill-fated *Mrs Fitzherbert* (1947). If the latter had been a stronger film, she might have had a longer career. Married Basil SYDNEY.

OTHER BRITISH FILMS INCLUDE: *Freedom Radio* (1940), *The Common Touch* (1941), *Talk About Jacqueline*, *The Night Has Eyes* (1942), *They Met in the Dark* (1943), *Appointment with Crime*, *Woman to Woman* (1946), *Shadow of the Past* (1950).

Howard, Leslie (*b* London, 1893 – *d* en route by air from Portugal, 1943). Actor, director, producer. RN: Steiner. Though born to Hungarian parents not long in Britain, Howard characteristically presented a sensitive, at times almost dreamy and slightly effete Englishman who underplayed his roles from *The Scarlet Pimpernel* (1935) to Ashley Wilkes in *Gone with the Wind* (1939, US). Following WW1 shell-shock, he took up acting, establishing himself on the stage and joining with Adrian BRUNEL and others to form British Comedy Films Ltd (name changed later to MINERVA Films), at Bushey. Despite a

Hollywood career in much of the 30s, he remained a highly patriotic and popular Britisher, fighting the Nazis in *Pimpernel Smith* (1941, +d, p), inventing the Spitfire in *The First of the Few* (1942, + d, co-p), which reunited him with Brunel who served as co-producer, and paternally celebrating the ATS in *The Gentle Sex* (1943, d), in which he appears briefly at the start. There was national mourning when he lost his life when the commercial plane in which he was travelling was shot down by a German war plane. His most famous screen role, however, is as Higgins in *Pygmalion* (1938), which he co-directed with Anthony ASQUITH, and which remains the benchmark for filmed SHAW. Both his son, actor Ronald HOWARD, and daughter, Ruth, have written of him in, respectively, *In Search of My Father* (1982) and *A Quite Remarkable Father* (1959). His brother was Arthur HOWARD and nephew is Alan HOWARD.

OTHER BRITISH FILMS: (a, unless noted) *The Heroine of Mons* (1914), *The Happy Warrior* (1917), *The Lackey and the Lady* (1919), *Five Pounds Reward*, *Bookworms*, *The Bump* (p), *Twice Two* (p), *Too Many Cooks* (p), *The Temporary Lady* (p) (1920), *Service for Ladies* (1932), *The Lady Is Willing* (1934), *49th Parallel*, *From the Four Corners* (short), *The White Eagle* (short, doc) (1941), *In Which We Serve* (1942, voice only), *The Lamp Still Burns* (p), *War in the Mediterranean* (short, doc, narr) (1943). AS.

Howard, Lionelle (*b* Cirencester, ? – *d* ?). Actor. Intelligent and well-educated leading man, who appeared in more than 80 silent films, Howard had a somewhat languid and delicate appearance that made him perfect for certain types of villainous roles. He entered the industry in 1911, working in all areas of production before settling down to acting in 1914.

BRITISH FILMS INCLUDE: *Old St Paul's* (1914), *Barnaby Rudge*, *Her Boy* (1915), *Trelawney of the Wells* (1916), *Three Men in a Boat* (1920), *The Wonderful Year* (1921), *One Arabian Knight* (1923, as Aladdin), *Not For Sale* (1924). AS.

Howard, Norah (*b* London, 1901 – *d* New York, 1968). Actress. Supporting actress of the 30s. On stage from 1913, in popular plays like *Bitter Sweet* (1929) and *Love from a Stranger* (1937), famous for introducing the song, 'Other People's Children' in revue, and a regular radio performer, she is engaging on film as the wise-cracking secretary who nabs the boss in *Car of Dreams* (1935).

OTHER BRITISH FILMS INCLUDE: *The W Plan* (1930), *A Cuckoo in the Nest*, *Love, Life and Laughter* (1934), *Fighting Stock* (1935), *The Big Noise* (1936), *I've Got a Horse* (1938), *An Englishman's Home*, *The Lambeth Walk* (1939).

Howard, Ronald (*b* London, 1918 – *d* London, 1996). Actor. Son of Leslie HOWARD, formerly a journalist and in the Navy during WW2, this blond six-footer had a long but somewhat lacklustre film career. He was an amiable leading man in *While the Sun Shines* (1947), was Michael DENISON's charming, irresponsible brother in *My Brother Jonathan* (1948) and the heroine's first husband in *Portrait of Clare* (1950), but after 1950 he settled into 'B' FILMS, like *Black Orchid* (1952) as a doctor accused of murdering his wife, and supporting roles in bigger films. Perhaps too much like his father to establish a clear film persona, but he had a TV following for his SHERLOCK HOLMES in 1954–55.

OTHER BRITISH FILMS INCLUDE: *Pimpernel Smith* (1941, ucr), *Bond Street*, *Night Beat* (1948), *The Queen of Spades*, *Now Barabbas Was a Robber* (1949), *The Browning Version*, *Assassin for Hire* (1951), *Street Corner* (1953), *Hideout* (1956), *No Trees in the Street*, *Gideon's Day* (1958), *Man Accused* (1959), *The Spider's Web* (1960), *The Naked Edge* (UK/US), *Murder She Said* (1961), *Live Now, Pay Later* (1962), *The Siege of the Saxons*, *Nurse on Wheels* (1963), *The Curse of the Mummy's Tomb* (1964), *Africa – Texas Style* (1967), *Persecution* (1974).

Howard, Sydney (*b* Yeadon, 1885 – *d* London, 1946). Actor. On stage from 1912 and in films from 1930, this once popular comedian is almost wholly – and most unjustly – forgotten today. He had earlier toured in revues, served in WW1, and returned to the stage in 1919, reaching London in 1927. He made one US film, *Transatlantic Merry Go Round* (1934) and co-starred with Gracie FIELDS in *Shipyard Sally* (1939). To watch him at work as the florid-spoken, tipsily dignified photographer in *When We Are Married* (1943) is to be aware of a unique comic talent, appreciated in his time by no less a critic than Graham GREENE. His films are not readily available but he is well worth pursuing.

OTHER BRITISH FILMS INCLUDE: *Splinters* (1929), *French Leave* (1930), *Up for the Cup*, *Splinters in the Navy* (1931), *Night of the Garter* (1933), *Where's George?* (1935), *Splinters in the Air* (1937), *What a Man!* (1938), *Tilly of Bloomsbury* (1940), *Once a Crook*, *Mr Proudfoot Shows a Light* (short) (1941), *Flight from Folly* (1945).

Howard, Trevor (*b* Cliftonville, Kent, 1913 – *d* Bushey, 1988). After small roles in *The Way Ahead* (1944) and *The Way to the Stars* (1945), Howard played the object of Celia JOHNSON's tremulously awakened love in David LEAN's *Brief Encounter* (1945). His grave, courteous charm made him a star at once, and he played another married woman's lover for Lean in *The Passionate Friends* (1948). He offered a new kind of male lead in British films: steady, middle-class, reassuring, as he so brilliantly is in *I See a Dark Stranger* (1946) and, especially, as Major Calloway in *The Third Man* (1949), but also capable of suggesting neurosis under the tweedy demeanour. It is a shock to find him unshaven and on the run in *They Made Me a Fugitive* (1947), but the stereotype of English gent continues to founder in very compelling ways: he is hopelessly degenerate in *Outcast of the Islands* (1951), morally tormented in *The Heart of the Matter* (1953), sexually infatuated with *Manuela* (1957), and D.H. LAWRENCE's rambunctious, defeated Morel to the life in *Sons and Lovers* (1960). There was plenty of conventional stuff along the way and, like so many of his peers, he settled into character cameos in later life, but for over ten years he was a major British actor. RADA-trained, he made his West End debut in 1938 and entered films when he was invalided out of the Royal Artillery in 1943. Married to Helen CHERRY.

OTHER BRITISH FILMS: *Green for Danger* (1946), *So Well Remembered*, (1947), *Golden Salamander* (1949), *Odette*, *The Clouded Yellow* (1950), *Lady Godiva Rides Again* (guest role), *Gift Horse* (1951), *April in Portugal* (narrator), *Cockleshell Heroes* (1955), *Interpol* (1957), *The Key* (1958), *The Lion* (1962), *Man in the Middle* (1963), *Operation Crossbow* (1965, UK/It), *Triple Cross* (1966), *Battle of Britain*, *Twinky* (1969), *Catch Me a Spy*, *Mary Queen of Scots*, *Kidnapped* (1971), *Pope Joan*, *The Offence* (1972), *A Doll's House* (UK/Fr), *Craze* (1973), *11 Harrowhouse*, *Persecution*, *The Count of Monte Cristo*, *Who?* (1974), *Hennessy*, *Conduct Unbecoming*, *The Bawdy Adventures of Tom Jones* (1975), *Aces High* (1976, UK/Fr), *Superman*, *Stevie* (1978), *The Sea Wolves* (UK/Switz/US), *Sir Henry at Rawlinson End* (1980), *The Missionary*, *Gandhi* (1982, UK/Ind), *Sword of the Valiant* (1983), *White Mischief* (1987).

BIBLIOG: Vivienne Knight, *Trevor Howard: A Gentleman and a Player*, 1986; Trevor Munn, *Trevor Howard: The Man and His Films*, 1990.

Howard, William K. (*b* St Mary's, Ohio, 1899 – *d* Los Angeles, 1954). Director. Sandwiched between long bouts of routine US movies, this engineering graduate, in movies since 1920, who fell foul of the Hollywood majors, made four films in Britain in the later 30s. *Fire Over England* (1937) has some virtuoso sequences in depicting the Armada, and the film has massive sets by Lazare MEERSON; *The Squeaker* and *The Green Cockatoo* (1937) are lively thrillers; and *Over the Moon* (1939) is a feeble,

Technicolored romantic comedy with Merle OBERON as an heiress. Back in the US in 1939, he took to second features and, with renewed vigour, the bottle.

Howe, James Wong (*b* Kwantung, China, 1899 – *d* Los Angeles, 1976). Cinematographer. Celebrated Hollywood craftsman who won two Oscars (*The Rose Tattoo*, 1955; *Hud*, 1963) and seven further nominations, and was brought over to England during the mid 30s by KORDA to work at DENHAM STUDIOS. He gave a lustrous glow to *Fire Over England* (1937), doing justice to Lazare MEERSON's sets and the beauty of Vivien LEIGH and Tamara DESNI. Unlike his associate, William K. HOWARD, he went back to even greater distinction in Hollywood.

OTHER BRITISH FILMS: *Farewell Again* (interiors), *Under the Red Robe* (co-c) (1937), *It Might Be You!* (1938, short, epilogue c).

Howell, John (*b* London, 1914). Production designer. Entered film industry in the art department of GAINSBOROUGH FILMS (1932–37), was at SOUND CITY until WW2 service with the RAF (1939–42) and afterwards with the RAF FILM UNIT until 1945, getting his first art director credit on its *Journey Together* (1945). He designed a further 35 films, including three for the BOULTING brothers in the later 40s: *Fame Is the Spur*, *Brighton Rock* (1947) and *The Guinea Pig* (1948), in all of them his designs intelligently complementing the films' meanings. He received a BAAn for his design for *Khartoum* (1966).

OTHER BRITISH FILMS INCLUDE: (art d) *The Guinea Pig* (1948), *The Dancing Years* (1950), *The Net* (1953), *Forbidden Cargo* (1954), *Simba* (1955), *The Baby and the Battleship* (1956), *Manuela* (1957), *Orders to Kill* (1958), *Third Man on the Mountain* (1959), *The Young Ones* (1961), *The Mouse on the Moon* (1963), *Khartoum*, *The Deadly Affair* (1966), *Casino Royale* (co-) (1967), *Tales of Beatrix Potter* (1971), *Soft Beds, Hard Battles* (1973); (des) *The Prime of Miss Jean Brodie* (1968), *The Walking Stick* (1970), *Embassy* (1972).

Howell, Peter (*b* London, 1919). Actor. After his late 50s stardom in the medical soap opera *Emergency – Ward 10*, it was surprising that British cinema, unlike theatre and television, was strangely intermittent in its use of Peter Howell's talents. His prison governor in *Scum* (1979) and college president in *Shadowlands* (1993) demonstrate the charisma he brings to patrician roles, in which a smooth exterior may conceal a ruthless core; he was especially shrewdly cast as Ernest, head of the extended family, in Stephen POLIAKOFF's ambitious TV film *Perfect Strangers* (2001).

OTHER BRITISH FILMS INCLUDE: *Hell-fire Club* (1960), *Raising the Wind* (1961), *Devil-Ship Pirates* (1963), *The Errand* (1980), *Bellman & True* (1987). Charles Barr.

Howells, Jack (*b* Abertysswg, Wales, 1913 – *d* Penarth, Wales, 1990). Director, screenwriter. Educated at University of Wales and best known for his imaginative DOCUMENTARY, *Dylan Thomas* (1961), in which on screen participant Richard BURTON reads from the poet's work. In film from 1945, he wrote many SHORT FILMS for Associated British Pathé, including *Scrapbook for 1933* (1949) and several in the 'Wealth of the World' series, as well as the screenplay for the feature films, *Front Page Story* and *Skid Kids* (1953). Also worked much in TV.

OTHER BRITISH FILMS INCLUDE: *The Peaceful Years* (1948), *Elstree Story* (1952).

Howells, Michael (*b* Staffordshire, 1957). Production designer. Trained at Cheltenham and Camberwell Schools of Art, Howells came to the fore in the 90s with his handsome designs for the period films, *Emma* (1996, UK/US) and *An Ideal Husband* (1999, UK/US). His first film credit was as assistant art director on *The Cook, the Thief, His Wife & Her Lover* (1989, UK/Fr) – perhaps this turned him towards the less confronting literary ADAPTATIONS. He has worked in the US (e.g. on Mike FIGGIS's *Miss Julie*, 1999) and TV (e.g. *Shackleton*, 2001).

OTHER BRITISH FILMS INCLUDE: *Orlando* (1992, UK/Fr/It/Neth/Russ, art d), *Second Best* (1994, UK/US), *Fairytale: A True Story* (1997, UK/US), *Disgrace* (2001).

Howells, Ursula (*b* London, 1922). Actress. Distinctively stylish actress with attractively husky voice and upper-class mien, who never had quite the film career she deserved. First on stage with Dundee Rep in 1939, London in 1945, she entered films in 1951's *Flesh and Blood*, but was more thoroughly noticed as the society dipso in *I Believe in You* (1952). She pottered on in 'B' films such as *Account Rendered* (1957) as Griffith JONES's faithless, neurotic wife, with small roles in main features like *The Constant Husband* (1954), and was better served on stage (e.g, Ruth in the 1970 revival of *Blithe Spirit*) and TV (a touching Mrs Gradgrind in *Hard Times*, 1977; elegantly homicidal in *A Murder Is Announced*, 1985).

OTHER BRITISH FILMS INCLUDE: *The Weak and the Wicked* (1953), *The Gilded Cage* (1955), *The Long Arm* (1956), *West of Suez* (1957), *80,000 Suspects* (1963), *The Sicilians* (1964), *Mumsy, Nanny, Sonny and Girly*, *Crossplot* (1969), *The Tichborne Claimant* (1998).

Howerd, Frankie (*b* York, 1922 – *d* London, 1992). Actor. RN: Francis Howard. First realised his talent for comedy while entertaining troops during his WW2 service with the Royal Artillery, and post-war landed a spot with BBC radio's *Variety Bandbox*, staying for over two years. On stage from 1950, playing key comedy roles in *Charley's Aunt* (1955), *A Midsummer Night's Dream* (1957, as Bottom) and *A Funny Thing Happened on the Way to the Forum* (1963, UK/US). In films and on TV's *Up Pompeii* (1970, filmed in 1971), he honed an inimitable innuendo- and pun-ridden style, all outrageously camp and sexist, taking the audience into his confidence with direct address. TV possibly suited him best, but there are some very funny film performances, dating back to the aggrieved barrow boy in *The Ladykillers* (1955), and, when the films' plots couldn't properly contain him, he just pushed them aside and went on his lubricious way.

OTHER BRITISH FILMS: *The Runaway Bus* (1953), *Jumping for Joy, An Alligator Named Daisy* (1955), *A Touch of the Sun* (1956), *Further Up the Creek* (1958), *Watch It, Sailor!* (1961), *The Fast Lady, The Cool Mikado* (1962), *The Mouse on the Moon* (1963), *The Great St Trinian's Train Robbery* (1966), *Carry On Doctor* (1968), *Carry On Up the Jungle* (1970), *Up the Chastity Belt* (1971), *Up the Front* (1972), *The House in Nightmare Park* (1973).

BIBLIOG: Autobiography, *On the Way I Lost It*, 1976; Robert Ross, *The Complete Frankie Howerd*, 2001.

Howes, Bobby (*b* London, 1895 – *d* London, 1972). Actor. Short, engaging song-and-dance man of the 30s theatre, who made a dozen films, beginning with the silent *The Guns of Loos* (1928). Much experience in MUSIC HALLS, cabaret, musical comedy and pantomime, but never really a film star, though he is enjoyable company in such trifles as *Sweet Devil* (1938), and played the back legs of a stage horse in *The Trojan Brothers* (1945). Father of Sally Ann HOWES.

OTHER BRITISH FILMS INCLUDE: *Third Time Lucky* (1931), *Over the Garden Wall* (1934), *Please Teacher* (1937), *Happy Go Lovely* (1951), *The Good Companions* (1956), *Watch It, Sailor!* (1961).

Howes, Sally Ann (*b* London, 1930). Actress. Graceful, talented daughter of Bobby HOWES and, like her father, has had more sustained success on stage than in films, which she began in 1943's *Thursday's Child*, as the teenager who becomes a film star, then throws it away. She had four good roles for EALING in the mid 40s –the child of estranged parents in *The Halfway House* (1944), Mervyn JOHNS's resentful daughter in *Pink String and Sealing Wax* (1945), the teenager at the Christmas party in *Dead of Night* (1945), and Kate Nickleby in *Nicholas Nickleby* (1947). After that, her career tapered off and she was in some of the worst British films, including *Stop Press Girl* (1949). Replaced Julie ANDREWS in *My Fair Lady* (1958) on Broadway, and has done intermittent TV. Was married to composer Richard Adler.

OTHER BRITISH FILMS INCLUDE: *Anna Karenina, The History of Mr Polly* (1948), *Fools Rush In* (1949), *The Admirable Crichton* (1957), *Chitty Chitty Bang Bang* (1968), *Death Ship* (1980, UK/Can).

Howitt, Peter (*b* Manchester, 1957). Director. Had a big commercial success with his first film as director, the 'what if' romantic comedy, *Sliding Doors* (1998, + sc, a), starring Gwyneth PALTROW. Prior to that, he had acted in TV and in the films, *In the Name of the Father* (1993, UK/Ire/US) and *Some Mother's Son* (1996, Ire/US). He and friend Douglas McFerran have set up their own production company, Power Pictures, in 1999. Not to be confused with designer of the same name.

Howlett, Noel (*b* Maidstone, 1901 – *d* London, 1984). Actor. Educated at King's School, Canterbury, this former theological student and schoolmaster took to rep theatre in mid 30s, films from 1936 (*Men Are Not Gods*). First noticed as Vivien LEIGH's elderly husband in *A Yank at Oxford* (1937), and, after WW2 service with ENSA (1941–45), played lawyers, doctors, vicars and other professionals for the next 30 years, including judges two years in a row in *When the Bough Breaks* (1947) and *The Mark of Cain* (1948), Dirk BOGARDE's loyal clerk in *Victim* (1961) and the feeble headmaster in TV's *Please, Sir!* (1968–72) and its film SPIN-OFF (1971).

OTHER BRITISH FILMS INCLUDE: *The Proud Valley* (1940), *The White Unicorn, Good-Time Girl* (1947), *The Winslow Boy, Scott of the Antarctic, The Calendar* (1948), *Scrooge, The Reluctant Widow* (1950), *Cloudburst* (1951), *Father Brown, One Good Turn* (1954), *Nowhere to Go* (1958), *The Battle of the Sexes* (1959), *Tomorrow at Ten* (1962), *Murder at the Gallop* (1963), *Woman of Straw* (1964), *Quatermass and the Pit* (1967).

Hudd, Roy (*b* Croydon, 1936). Actor. Popular TV performer, often as stand-up comic and famous for his impersonations of Max MILLER, chirpy, big-eyed Hudd has made only a few films, including *Up the Chastity Belt* (1971) as Nick the Pick.

OTHER BRITISH FILMS: *The Blood Beast Terror* (1967), *Up Pompeii, The Magnificent Seven Deadly Sins* (1971), *The Alf Garnett Saga* (1972).

Hudd, Walter (*b* London, 1898 – *d* London, 1963). Actor. On stage, 1919, then on tour with Fred Terry's company, Hudd toured with his own company to various camps and worksites during WW2 (1942–45), as well as maintaining a busy acting career on stage and screen. In the 30s, he was with KORDA in *Rembrandt* (1936) and *Elephant Boy* (1937), and played a treacherous solicitor in *Black Limelight* (1938). Post-war, he looked increasingly ascetic, playing George CARNEY's prim secretary in *I Know Where I'm Going!* (1945), Algy's manservant in *The Importance of Being Earnest* (1952), and various dignified professionals until he died. Was one of those announced as playing T.E. LAWRENCE, in 1936, and was Drama Director at Central School in the 50s.

OTHER BRITISH FILMS INCLUDE: *Moscow Nights* (1935), *Housemaster* (1938), *Major Barbara* (1941), *Love Story* (1944), *I Live in Grosvenor Square* (1945), *Escape* (1948), *Cosh Boy* (1953), *The Good Die Young* (1954), *Cast a Dark Shadow* (1955), *Reach for the Sky* (1956), *The Man Upstairs* (1958), *Look Back in Anger* (1959), *Sink the Bismarck!*, *Life for Ruth* (1962).

Hudis, Norman (*b* London, 1923). Screenwriter. Best known as the writer of the first half-dozen 'CARRY ON' SERIES, set in various institutions (army, hospital, school, etc) and credited by producer Peter ROGERS as having more 'heart' than the other writers in the series, which may also mean he was capable of the sentimental elements of films like *Twice Round the Daffodils* (1962) and *Nurse on Wheels* (1963). He had (co-) written over a dozen pre-'Carry On' scripts, including the trim 'B' THRILLER, *The Flying Scot* (1957); he also co-wrote *Mr Ten Per Cent* (1967) for Charlie DRAKE, alas. Went to Hollywood to work in TV.
OTHER BRITISH FILMS INCLUDE: (sc/co-sc) *Face in the Night*, *Breakaway* (1956), *The Tommy Steele Story*, *Mark of the Phoenix* (1957), *The Duke Wore Jeans*, *6.5 Special*, *Carry On Sergeant*, . . . *Nurse* (1958), . . . *Teacher* (1959), . . . *Constable*, *Please Turn Over* (1960), *Carry On Regardless* (1961), . . . *Cruising* (1962), *A Monkey's Tale* (1999, UK/Fr/Ger, anim).

Hudson, Hugh (*b* London, 1936). Director. Winning the AA and BAA for *Chariots of Fire* (1981), former TV commercials- and DOCUMENTARY-maker Hudson looked like the hope of the British side. This tale of two athletes at the 1924 Olympic Games won critical and commercial favour for its skilful melding of popular elments. Allegedly a difficult, perfectionist director, he has done nothing comparably successful since: his other two British films, both co-productions, the overblown *Greystoke* . . . (1984, UK/US, + co-p) and the disastrous and wasteful *Revolution* (1985, UK/Nor) hastened the failure of GOLDCREST FILMS. He has since filmed internationally – and unobtrusively – including the little-seen *My Life So Far* (2000), based on Denis FORMAN's early life.
BIBLIOG: Jake Eberts & Terry Ilott, *My Indecision Is Final: The Rise and Fall of Goldcrest Films*, 1990.

Huggetts, the The Cockney Huggett family first appeared in Ken ANNAKIN's feature film debut, *Holiday Camp* (1947). Headed by Jack WARNER and Kathleen HARRISON as Joe and Ethel, the family later moved from supporting to leading players in *Here Come the Huggetts*, *Vote for Huggett* (1948) and *The Huggetts Abroad* (1949), all directed by ANNAKIN. Jane HYLTON, Susan SHAW, Petula CLARK, Jimmy HANLEY and Dinah SHERIDAN also played family members at various times, with Diana DORS as a disruptive cousin. The Huggetts also appeared in a popular BBC radio series which ran from 1953 to 1961. Tony Williams.

Hughes, Harry (*b* London – *d* ?). Director. Having entered film industry in 1907 as editor and scenario writer with PATHÉ, he finally became a director in the 20s with NETTLEFOLD PRODUCTIONS and, in the 30s, with BIP, where he made such GENRE pieces as the sentimental crime drama, *Song at Eventide* (1934), and the musical, *The Mountains o' Mourne* (1938, + p).
OTHER BRITISH FILMS INCLUDE: (d, unless noted) *A Daughter in Revolt* (1926), *The Hellcat*, *Troublesome Wives* (1928), *The Man at Six* (+ co-sc), *Glamour* (co-d) (1931), *Bachelor's Baby* (1932, + sc), *Facing the Music* (1933), *Womanhood* (1934), *Tropical Trouble* (1936), *The Last Chance* (1937, sc), *Dead Men Are Dangerous* (1939, co-sc).

Hughes, Ken (*b* Liverpool, 1922 – *d* Los Angeles, 2001). Director, screenwriter. The film-maker most consistently identified during the 50s with the CRIME STORIES which were then a staple of British production. Nearly always providing his own scripts, he progressed from modest 'B' MOVIES and several half-hour featurettes in the 'Scotland Yard' SERIES to slick, medium-budget productions with imported Hollywood players and in some cases – *Joe Macbeth* (1955), *Wicked As They Come* (1956) – notional American settings. Probably his most accomplished thrillers were the trucking MELODRAMA, *The Long Haul* (1957), and *The Small World of Sammy Lee* (1962), a doubly personal venture in that it was adapted from his 1958 teleplay, *Sammy*, and was set in Soho, subject of a prizewinning short he made as an amateur in 1943. Away from crime, he made the polished *The Trials of Oscar Wilde* (1960), but the big-budget *Cromwell* (1970) provided an unhappy compromise with history. Personal difficulties later caused his career to falter.
OTHER BRITISH FILMS INCLUDE: *Wide Boy* (1952), *The House Across the Lake*, *The Brain Machine*, *Little Red Monkey* (1954), *Timeslip*, *Confession* (1955), *Jazzboat*, *In the Nick* (1959), *Of Human Bondage* (1964), *Drop Dead Darling* (1966), *Casino Royale* (1967, co-d), *The Internecine Project* (1974), *Alfie Darling* (1975). Tim Pulleine.

Hughes, Roddy (*b* Portmadoc, N. Wales, 1891 – *d* 1970). Actor. Oxford-educated former schoolmaster, who took to the stage in 1916 and films in 1931, thereafter popping up chubbily in over 60 small roles, including cherubic Tim Linkinwater, with Athene SEYLER in the marriage lineup at the end of *Nicholas Nickleby* (1947), and one of the prosing clubmen in the opening scene of *Obsession* (1949). Much TV from 1948.
OTHER BRITISH FILMS INCLUDE: *Reunion* (1932), *The Old Curiosity Shop* (1934), *Men of Yesterday* (1936), *Poison Pen* (1939), *Under Your Hat* (1940), *Hatter's Castle*, *The Black Sheep of Whitehall* (1941), *George in Civvy Street*, *Silver Darlings* (1946), *The Small Back Room* (1948), *Scrooge*, *The Man in the White Suit* (1951), *The Million Pound Note* (1953), *One Jump Ahead*, *See How They Run* (1955), *Corridors of Blood* (1958).

Hulbert, Claude (*b* London, 1900 – *d* Sydney, 1964). Actor. Upper-class 'silly ass', Cambridge-educated comedian on stage from 1920, starring in *Sunny* (1926), *Oh, Kay!* (1927), etc. He was too busy with films to pursue a stage career in 30s, appearing in over 30 light comedies, such as the very funny ADAPTATIONS of ALDWYCH FARCES, *Thark* (1930) and *A Cup of Kindness* (1934), and *The Interrupted Honeymoon* (1936). Returned to stage for *The Hulbert Follies* (1941), etc, and often broadcast with wife Enid Trevor (m. 1924); they also co-starred in the film, *Ship's Concert* (1937). In later years ran a chain of laundrettes. Brother of Jack HULBERT.
OTHER BRITISH FILMS INCLUDE: *Champagne* (1928), *Let Me Explain*, *Dear* (1932), *Heads We Go!* (1933), *Lilies of the Field* (1934), *Bulldog Jack* (1935), *Where's Sally?* (1936), *It's Not Cricket* (1937), *Sailors Three* (1940), *The Ghost of St Michael's* (1941), *London Town* (1946), *The Ghosts of Berkeley Square* (1947), *Cardboard Cavalier* (1949), *Fun at St Fanny's* (1955). AS.

Hulbert, Jack (*b* Ely, 1892 – *d* London, 1978). Actor. With little discernible talent beyond a toothy grin, a long chin and a large nose, Westminster- and Cambridge-educated Hulbert displayed considerable charisma as a light comedian, performing to perfection a nonsense song such as 'The Flies Crawled up the Window' in *Jack's the Boy* (1932) or the cheery 'My Hat's on the Side of My Head' in *Jack Ahoy!* (1934). Made his stage debut in 1913, and three years later married his partner, Cicely COURTNEIDGE, with whom he appeared in several then-popular film comedies, including *Happy Ever After* (1932) and *Falling for You* (1933). His style now belongs very much to the

30s, but there was an engaging breeziness that carried him through a dozen or so light-hearted films as well as maintaining, well into his 70s, a very busy stage career. Brother of Claude HULBERT.

OTHER BRITISH FILMS INCLUDE: *Elstree Calling* (1930), *The Ghost Train* (1931), *The Camels are Coming* (1934), *Bulldog Jack* (1935), *Jack of All Trades* (1936), *Katie Plus Ten* (1938), *Under Your Hat* (1940), *Into the Blue* (1950), *The Spider's Web* (1960), *Not Now, Darling* (1972).

BIBLIOG: Autobiography, *The Little Woman Is Always Right*, 1975. AS.

Hulme, Anthony (*b* Dolgelly, Wales, 1902). Actor. On stage before entering films in 1938, then in the RAF from 1940 to 1946, Hulme was the low-key and not very convincing leading man in Daniel BIRT's choice piece of Grand Guignol, *The Three Weird Sisters* (1948), an insufficiently dashing Temple in *Send for Paul Temple* (1946), and, better cast, Charles II in the farce, *Cardboard Cavalier* (1949).

OTHER BRITISH FILMS INCLUDE: *The Frozen Limits* (1939), *They Came by Night* (1940), *The Body Vanishes* (1942), *Up with the Lark* (1943), *It's a Grand Life* (1953).

Hume, Alan (*b* London, 1924). Cinematographer. Among the 80-odd films he has shot since he first started getting credits in the early 50s, Hume has had his name on 17 of the 'CARRY ON' SERIES, including several of the best such as *Carry On Cleo* (1964), on several BOND films, including *For Your Eyes Only* (1981) and the famous opening sequence of *The Spy Who Loved Me* (1977), as well as HORROR films, COMEDIES like *A Fish Called Wanda* (1988), and SCIENCE-FICTION like *Return of the Jedi* (1983, US). He began at DENHAM in 1942, was assistant to Guy GREEN at CINEGUILD in the later 40s, and was still in demand in the 90s, especially on telemovies.

OTHER BRITISH FILMS INCLUDE: (focus-puller) *They Came to a City* (1944); (cam op) *Prelude to Fame* (1950), *The End of the Affair* (1954), *Carry On Sergeant* (1958), . . . *Constable* (1960); (c) *No Kidding* (1960), *In the Doghouse*, *Carry On Regardless* (1961), . . . *Cruising, Kiss of the Vampire* (1962), *Carry On Cabby* (1963), . . . *Spying*, . . . *Jack, Dr Terror's House of Horrors* (1964), *The Big Job*, *Carry On Cowboy* (1965), . . . *Screaming, Don't Lose Your Head* (1966), *Follow That Camel* (1967), *The Bofors Gun* (1968), *Perfect Friday* (1970), *Zeppelin, Carry On Henry* (1971), . . . *Abroad, Bless This House, Not Now, Darling* (1972), *The Legend of Hell House, From Beyond the Grave* (1973), *The Land That Time Forgot* (1974), *Carry On Emmannuelle* (1978), *Eye of the Needle* (1981), *Octopussy* (1983), *A View to a Kill* (1985), *Without a Clue* (1988, UK/US), *Shirley Valentine* (1989, UK/US), *Carry On Columbus* (1992).

Hume, Benita (*b* London, 1907 – *d* Egerton, 1967). Actress. Dark and sombre-looking leading lady, who was married to Ronald Colman (1938) and whose innate sense of humour may have helped in a 1958 marriage to George SANDERS. Stage debut 1924, and a star in 1929's *Symphony in Two Flats*, in which she both starred on screen and made her New York debut in 1930. A busy actress in such British films as *Easy Virtue* (1927), *Lord Camber's Ladies* (1932) and *The Private Life of Don Juan* (1934), Hume went to Hollywood in the mid 30s, but never became a film star. With Colman, she starred in *The Hall of Ivy* on radio (1950–52) and TV (1954–55).

OTHER BRITISH FILMS INCLUDE: *The Happy Ending* (1925), *Second to None* (1926), *The Constant Nymph* (1928), *High Treason* (1929), *The Happy Ending* (1931), *Sally Bishop* (1932), *Jew Süss* (1934), *18 Minutes* (1935). AS.

Hume, Marjorie (*b* Yarmouth, 1900 – *d* Oxshott, 1976). Actress. When Jesse L. Lasky signed Hume to star in PARAMOUNT's first British production, *The Great Day* (1920), *The Moving Picture World* hailed her as 'a versatile and expressive actress, with artistic imagination and big reserves

of emotional power'. Despite the praise, Hume's career, which was lengthy and encouraged at the beginning by Ellen TERRY, went nowhere – least of all to Hollywood. Returned to play a few character roles in the 50s, as in *Children Galore* (1954).

OTHER BRITISH FILMS INCLUDE: *Her Greatest Performance* (1916), *Keeper of the Door* (1919), *Bluff* (1921), *This Marriage Business* (1927), *Young Woodley* (1929), *Member of the Jury* (1937), *The Curse of Frankenstein* (1957). AS.

Humphreys, Cecil (*b* Cheltenham, 1883 – *d* New York, 1947). Actor. The *New York Times* critic Brooks Atkinson described Humphreys' work on stage in *The Circle* (1938) as 'sufficiently good' – and that phrase just about sums up the career of an actor closely associated with the stage from 1900, the author of four plays, and a character player on screen, often associated with villainous roles, like that of Sir Percival Glyde in *The Woman in White* (1929). Humphreys made several US films, including *The Razor's Edge* (1946).

OTHER BRITISH FILMS INCLUDE: *The Lifeguardsman* (1916), *The Sorrows of Satan* (1917), *The Elusive Pimpernel* (1919), *The Four Just Men* (1921), *The Glorious Adventure* (1922), *Strictly in Confidence* (1933), *Chick* (1936). AS.

Humphreys, Gerry (*b* Llandrindod Wells, 1931). Sound recordist. Fantastically prolific Humpreys has been associated with over 200 films since the mid 60s, and, variously credited as sound mixer, dubbing mixer, sound (re-)recordist, sound editor, etc, he has worked for virtually every notable director in British films since. These include POLANSKI, Tony RICHARDSON, Richard LESTER, Joseph LOSEY and Richard ATTENBOROUGH, sharing BAA/sd for *A Bridge Too Far* (1977) and *Cry Freedom* (1987), plus shared AAn and BAAn for *Gandhi* (1982, UK/Ind).

OTHER BRITISH FILMS INCLUDE: (dubbing mixer/rec) *Cul-de-sac* (1966), *Petulia* (1968), *The Italian Job*, *Country Dance* (1969); (sound rec/re-rec mixer) *Repulsion* (1965), *Accident* (1967), *The Charge of the Light Brigade* (1968), *Oh! What a Lovely War*, *Kes* (1969), *Sunday Bloody Sunday* (1971), *A Doll's House* (UK/Fr), *The Mackintosh Man* (1973), *Mahler* (1974), *Royal Flash*, *The Romantic Englishwoman* (UK/Fr), *Overlord* (1975), *Eagle's Wing* (1978), *Superman II* (1980), *Eureka* (UK/US), *The Bounty* (1984), *The Emerald Forest* (1985), *White Mischief* (1987), *A Fish Called Wanda* (1988), *The Sheltering Sky* (1990, UK/It), *The Playboys* (Ire/US), *Chaplin* (UK/Fr/It/Jap/US) (1992), *Shadowlands* (1993, co-sd), *Circle of Friends* (1995, Ire/US), *Tea with Mussolini* (1999, UK/It), *Grey Owl* (2000, UK/Can, sd).

Humphries, Barry (*b* Melbourne, 1934). Actor. Melbourne University-educated Humphries is one of Australia's most famous expatriates, known especially for his dazzling one-man stage and TV shows, in the guise of suburban diva Dame Edna Everage and slobbering Minister of the Yarts, Les Patterson. Based in London from the 60s, he has really only dabbled in films, albeit in several continents. He played Edna in *The Adventures of Barry McKenzie* (1972, Aust) and several roles in the UK sequel, *Barry McKenzie Holds His Own* (1974). He is somewhat lost in straight character roles (as in *The Leading Man*, 1996) and in other circumstances is apt to eat up the screen. Perhaps the live audience, whether on stage or TV studio, is what he needs for the display of his lethal satiric gifts.

OTHER BRITISH FILMS INCLUDE: *Bedazzled* (1967), *The Bliss of Mrs Blossom* (1968), *Percy's Progress* (1974), *Shock Treatment* (1981), *The Secret Policeman's Other Ball* (1982), *Spice World* (1997).

BIBLIOG: Autobiography, *More Please*, 1992.

Hunnicutt, Gayle (*b* Fort Worth, Texas, 1943). Actress. Brunette beauty who settled in England when she married

David HEMMINGS (1967–74) and improved her career prospects, though somehow she has never quite achieved what one might have expected. Best role was opposite Hemmings in *Fragment of Fear* (1970); also worked in TV (e.g. *A Woman of Substance*, 1983) and on the English stage from 1974. Now married to Simon Jenkins, author and journalist.

OTHER BRITISH FILMS INCLUDE: *The Freelance* (1970), *Running Scared* (1972), *The Spiral Staircase*, *The Sellout* (1975).

Hunt, Gareth (*b* London, 1943). Actor. Floridly handsome actor who enjoyed success as agent Gambit in TV's *The New Avengers* (1976–77) but has had only a sporadic screen career, typically playing the womanising amateur actor in *A Chorus of Disapproval* (1989).

OTHER BRITISH FILMS INCLUDE: *For the Love of Ada* (1972), *The World Is Full of Married Men* (1979), *Funny Money* (1982), *It Couldn't Happen Here* (1989), *Fierce Creatures* (1997, UK/US), *Parting Shots* (1998).

Hunt, Martita (*b* Buenos Aires, 1900 – *d* London, 1969). Actress. Wildly eccentric (in life it seems, as well as on screen), Hunt was one of the great British CHARACTER ACTRESSES, now best remembered as reclusive, embittered Miss Havisham (a role she had played in the Rudolph Steiner Hall in 1939) in David LEAN's *Great Expectations* (1946), in which she was about as Dickensian as a living person can get. In England from age 10, on stage from 1921, playing all kinds of commanding roles (if they weren't commanding before she got to them, they certainly were when she'd done with them), from the Tsarina in *Rasputin* (1929) to the Grand Duchess in *The Sleeping Prince* (1953). Appeared in the silent film, *A Rank Outsider* (1920), but her real film career began with *Service for Ladies* and *Love on Wheels* (1932). She is Lady Jane Grey's ambitious mother in *Tudor Rose* (1936), an awesome Mrs Glegg in *The Mill on the Floss* (1937) and a no-nonsense Duchess making a rich marriage for her son in *A Young Man's Fancy* (1939). But her real ascendancy derives from her work from the mid 40s on: she is one of the oppressive family circle in *The Wicked Lady* (1945), Raymond HUNTLEY's suspicious mother in *So Evil My Love* (1948), the Queen, naturally, in *The Story of Robin Hood . . .* (1952), a faded grande dame of the music hall circuit in *Meet Me Tonight* (1952), the Baroness, stretching her autocratic command, 'Wine', into four syllables in *The Brides of Dracula* (1960). So the list goes on, almost every bizarre incarnation deserving to be noted.

OTHER BRITISH FILMS: *Youth Will Be Served* (short), *I Was a Spy*, *Friday the Thirteenth* (1933), *Too Many Millions* (1934), *Mr What's-His-Name*, *First A Girl*, *The Case of Gabriel Perry* (1935), *King of the Damned*, *When Knights Were Bold*, *Sabotage*, *Pot Luck*, *The Interrupted Honeymoon* (1936), *Farewell Again*, *Paradise for Two*, *Good Morning, Boys!* (1937), *Strange Boarders*, *Second Best Bed*, *Prison Without Bars*, *Everything Happens to Me* (1938), *Goodbye, Mr Chips*, *Trouble Brewing*, *Old Mother Riley Joins Up*, *The Nursemaid Who Disappeared*, *The Middle Watch*, *The Good Old Days*, *A Girl Must Live*, *At the Villa Rose* (1939), *Miss Knowall* (short), *Miss Grant Goes to the Door* (short), *Tilly of Bloomsbury*, *Freedom Radio* (1940), *Quiet Wedding*, *East of Piccadilly*, *The Seventh Survivor* (1941), *They Flew Alone*, *Talk About Jacqueline*, *Sabotage at Sea*, *Lady from Lisbon* (1942), *The Man in Grey* (1943), *Welcome Mr Washington* (1944), *The Ghosts of Berkeley Square*, *The Little Ballerina* (1947), *Anna Karenina*, *My Sister and I* (1948), *Treasure Hunt*, *It Started in Paradise*, *Folly to be Wise* (1952), *Melba* (1953), *King's Rhapsody* (1955), *The March Hare*, *Three Men in a Boat*, *Anastasia* (1956), *The Admirable Crichton*, *Dangerous Exile*, *Bonjour Tristesse* (1957), *Bottoms Up* (1959), *Mr Topaze* (1961), *Becket* (1964), *Bunny Lake is Missing* (1965), *The Best House in London* (1968).

Hunt, Peter (*b* London, 1928 – *d* Santa Monica, California, 2002). Editor, director. In films since the early 40s, doing whatever came along, working as editorial assistant, on DOCUMENTARIES and features for the RANK ORGANISATION. From the mid 50s, he was editor for WESSEX FILMS (e.g. *A Hill in Korea*, 1956; *The Admirable Crichton*, 1957), then for other companies, editing several early BOND films, before being given his chance to direct. This came with the least successful Bond, *On Her Majesty's Secret Service* (1969, + a), and he never directed another, but went on to make lacklustre adventures such as *Gold* (1974) and *Shout at the Devil* (1976). His most recent work saw him back as supervising editor on *The Desperate Hours* (1990, US).

OTHER BRITISH FILMS INCLUDE: (a) *Touch and Go* (1955), *The Hands of Orlac* (1960); (p assoc) *Chitty Chitty Bang Bang* (1968); (d) *The Jigsaw Man* (1984, 2ud), *Wild Geese II* (1985); (e) *Wheel of Fate* (1953, sound), *Stranger from Venus* (1954), *Doublecross* (1955), *The Secret Tent* (1956), *A Cry from the Streets* (1958), *Sink the Bismarck!* (1960), *The Greengage Summer* (1961), *Dr No* (1962), *From Russia with Love* (1963), *Goldfinger* (1964), *The Ipcress File* (1965), *You Only Live Twice* (1967, + 2ud).

Hunter, Ian (*b* Kenilworth, nr Cape Town, 1900 – *d* Northwood, 1975). Actor. Dependable, somewhat stolid leading man who became a ditto character player as he aged. Just made it into WW1, was on stage from 1919 and persistently in the West End, with sorties to Broadway and, from 1924, balanced films with his theatre work. He appeared in over 20 films in Britain, including several for HITCHCOCK, before settling in Hollywood in the mid 30s. He found a very profitable niche as English gents in such Brit-set enterprises as *The Adventures of Robin Hood* (1938) as King Richard, and he depicted upright decency in several dozen films, playing Bette DAVIS's leading man in *The Girl from 10th Avenue* (1935). Returned to England during WW2 to join the Navy, and post-war played a series of dull heroes (one is on Margaret LOCKWOOD's side as she plans his demise in *Bedelia*, 1946), before succumbing to supporting status as Group Captains and the like. He repeated his stage role from *Edward, My Son* (1948) on film the following year. Appointed Artistic Director of the Edinburgh Festival in 1950 and the Bath Festival in 1955.

OTHER BRITISH FILMS INCLUDE: *Not for Sale* (1924), *The Ring*, *Downhill*, *Easy Virtue* (1927), *Escape* (1930), *Sally in Our Alley* (1931), *The Man from Toronto* (1933), *The Night of the Party* (1934), *White Cradle Inn*, *The White Unicorn* (1947), *It Started in Paradise* (1952), *Appointment in London* (1953), *Eight O'Clock Walk* (1954), *The Battle of the River Plate* (1956), *North West Frontier* (1959), *The Queen's Guards* (1961), *Guns of Darkness* (1962).

Hunter, T(homas) Hayes (*b* Philadelphia, 1882 – *d* London, 1944). Director. Mediocre film-maker who directed a number of Edgar WALLACE THRILLERS and the cult HORROR classic, *The Ghoul* (1933). Stage manager with David Belasco, Hayes entered films in UK in 1914 and directed 15 unmemorable features there. In 1937 he opened British–American Film Agency, Inc. in Hollywood, but returned to UK in 1943, becoming an agent and head of Film Rights Ltd and English Theatre Guild Ltd; clients included SABU, Richard GREENE, Flora ROBSON, and Robert MORLEY.

OTHER BRITISH FILMS INCLUDE: *One of the Best* (1927), *A South Sea Bubble* (1928), *The Silver King* (1929), *The Calendar* (1931), *Sally Bishop* (1932), *Josser on the Farm* (1934). AS.

Huntington, Lawrence (*b* London, 1900 – *d* London, 1968). Director, screenwriter. One of the undervalued British directors, Huntington was in the industry from silent days, directed a few undistinguished films in the 30s, peaked in the 40s, and declined into 'B' FILMS and television playlets, often for *Douglas Fairbanks Presents* in the 50s. It is a paradigmatic career, like Lance COMFORT's or Daniel BIRT's, though Huntington lacks the melodramatic intensity of either at their most febrile. His best work includes: the hearty spy thriller, *Night Train to Dublin* (1945), with Robert NEWTON as almost-conventional hero; the psychological dramas, *Wanted for Murder* (1946), starring Eric PORTMAN as a mother-fixated strangler, and *The Upturned Glass* (1947), with James MASON as the brain surgeon/strangler; and, best of all, the school-set drama, *Mr Perrin and Mr Traill* (1948), which gets a brilliant performance from Marius GORING as another neurotic who lives with his mother. There is a clearly recurring interest in obsessive figures, and these films are all marked by tight compositions, enhanced by sharply contrasted lighting from such noted practitioners as Erwin HILLIER and Max GREENE.

He made a couple of pleasant films with Dulcie GRAY (*The Franchise Affair*, 1950, + co-sc; *There Was a Young Lady*, 1953), but generally his second features are less taut than COMFORT's, and, among his last work, his script for *The Oblong Box* (1969) has some style and edge but, *Death Drums Along the River* (1963, UK/Ger/Zanz), is a feeble Technicolor remake of *Sanders of the River*. Father of actress **Sheila Huntington**, who appeared in a few films of the late 40s, including *The Upturned Glass*.

OTHER BRITISH FILMS: (d) *Two on a Doorstep, Café Mascot, Strange Cargo, Full Speed Ahead* (+ p, screen story) (1936), *Screen Struck, Twin Faces, Passenger to London* (+ p) (1937), *Dial 999* (1938), *This Man is Dangerous, Tower of Terror* (1941), *Women Aren't Angels* (1942, + co-sc), *When the Bough Breaks* (1947), *Thought to Kill, The Genie* (1953, co-), *Tony* (short), *The Red Dress* (co-) (1954), *The Clock* (1955), *Stranglehold* (1962); (d, sc) *After Many Years* (1930), *Romance in Rhythm* (1934, + p), *Bad Boy* (1938), *The Bank Messenger Mystery* (1940), *Suspected Person* (1942), *Warn That Man* (1943), *Man on the Run* (1949, + p), *Destination Milan* (1954, co-d), *Contraband – Spain* (1955), *Deadly Record* (1959), co-sc), *The Fur Collar* (1962, + p), *The Vulture* (1966, + p, UK/Can/US); (p) *Lieutenant Daring, RN* (1936), *The Trunk* (1960); (sc) *I Killed the Count* (1939, co-), *One Wild Oat* (1951, co-), *Deadly Nightshade* (1953), *Impulse* (1955, co-), *A Question of Suspense* (1961).

BIBLIOG: Brian McFarlane, 'Lance Comfort, Lawrence Huntington and the British Program Feature Film', in Dixon, W.W. (ed), *Re-Viewing British Cinema 1900–1922*, 1994.

Huntley, John (*b* London, 1921). Film historian. First a tea boy at pre-war DENHAM, Huntley was in the armed services, 1940–45, working often as lecturer and projectionist, and post-war joining the RANK ORGANISATION as music and sound technician under Muir MATHIESON. He published two important pioneering books in the late 40s: *British Film Music* (1947) and *British Technicolor Films* (1949). After two years with the Telekinema (later the NATIONAL FILM THEATRE) he began a 23-year association with the BRITISH FILM INSTITUTE, as programme officer initially, and later as head of the Regional Unit of the BFI. He also set up the Huntley Film Archives, and did frequent radio and TV broadcasts.

Huntley, Raymond (*b* Birmingham, 1904 – *d* London, 1990). Actor. As the brow furrowed, the eyes narrowed and a wintry smile played about thinning lips, it would be clear that Huntley was about to perform some small bureaucratic coup that would leave someone else distinctly uncomfortable. Educated and trained (with Barry Jackson's rep company) in Birmingham, he became one of the indispensable British CHARACTER ACTORS for nearly 40 years, on stage from 1922, and in films from 1934. The stage gave him wider opportunity, in plays as varied as

Dracula (1927, title role), *Private Lives* (1944) and the board-room drama, *Any Other Business?* (1958). On TV he was well-known as the crusty family solicitor in *Upstairs, Downstairs* (1971–75). In films, he guaranteed a few minutes of satisfaction as the innumerable civil servants, disapproving bank managers and sourpusses of every kind with whom he adorned films good, bad and indifferent. When he was given a more extended role, such as the pious windbag husband in *When We Are Married* (1943), the self-important salesman-turned-soldier in *The Way Ahead* (1944), a Nazi spy in *I See a Dark Stranger* (1946), the mother-ridden husband in danger of being poisoned in *So Evil My Love* (1948), or the embittered tuber-cular husband in *Trio* (1950), it was clear that he was more than a turn: he was a major actor.

OTHER BRITISH FILMS: *What Happened Then?* (1934), *Can You Hear Me Mother?* (1935), *Rembrandt* (1936), *Knight Without Armour, Dinner at the Ritz* (1937), *Night Train to Munich, Freedom Radio* (1940), *Pimpernel Smith, Once a Crook, Inspector Hornleigh Goes to It, The Ghost Train, The Ghost of St Michael's* (1941), *The Day Will Dawn* (1942), *The New Lot* (doc) (1943), *They Came to a City* (1944), *School for Secrets* (1946), *Broken Journey, Mr Perrin and Mr Traill, It's Hard to Be Good* (1948), *Passport to Pimlico* (1949), *The Long Dark Hall, The House in the Square, Mr Denning Drives North* (1951), *The Last Page* (1952), *Laxdale Hall, Glad Tidings, Meet Mr Lucifer, Hobson's Choice* (1953), *The Teckman Mystery, Aunt Clara, Orders Are Orders, The Constant Husband* (1954), *The Prisoner, The Dam Busters, Geordie, Doctor at Sea* (1955), *The Last Man to Hang?, The Green Man, Town on Trial, Brothers in Law* (1956), *Innocent Meeting, Room at the Top, Carlton-Browne of the FO, Next to No Time!* (1958), *The Mummy, I'm All Right Jack, Our Man in Havana, Bottoms Up* (1959), *Suspect, Sands of the Desert, Make Mine Mink, A French Mistress, Follow That Horse!, The Pure Hell of St Trinian's* (1960), *Only Two Can Play* (1961), *Waltz of the Toreadors, Crooks Anonymous, On the Beat* (1962), *The Yellow Teddybears, Nurse on Wheels, Father Came Too!* (1963), *The Black Torment* (1964), *Rotten to the Core* (1965), *The Great St Trinian's Train Robbery* (1966), *Hot Millions, Hostile Witness* (1968), *The Adding Machine, Arthur! Arthur!* (1969, unreleased), *Young Winston, That's Your Funeral* (1972), *Symptoms* (1974).

Huntley-Wright, Betty (*b* London, 1911). Actress. Studied singing and dancing, made stage debut in 1927, and was in many operettas, pantomimes and musical comedies, including *The Boyfriend* (1957–58) as Mme Dubonnet. Occasional films, including a tiny role in HITCHCOCK's *Waltzes from Vienna* (1934) and several other 30s musicals as second lead. Daughter of stage actor **Huntley Wright** (1869–1943), who made several films, including *Look Up and Laugh* (1935), with Gracie FIELDS. Married (2) and divorced John ARNATT.

OTHER BRITISH FILMS INCLUDE: *Commissionaire* (1933), *The Last Waltz* (1936, UK/Fr), *Meet Sexton Blake* (1944), *The First Gentleman* (1948), *The Brute* (1976).

Hurley, Elizabeth (*b* Basingstoke, 1965). Actress, model, producer. Best known for wearing a Versace dress held together with giant safety pins, also known as the face of Estée Lauder. Her film debut was in *Aria* (1987) and she has appeared in a number of films since, including *Beyond Bedlam* (1993), and *Bedazzled* (2000). Together with former partner Hugh GRANT she set up SIMIAN FILMS and produced *Extreme Measures* (1996, UK/US) and co-produced *Mickey Blue Eyes* (1999, UK/US). Anne-Marie Thomas.

Hurran, Nick (*b* 1959). Director. On the strength of *Girls' Night* (1998, UK/US), Hurran at very least knows how to let two brilliant actresses (Brenda BLETHYN and Julie WALTERS) do their stuff to major emotional effect and to work towards climaxes that grow persuasively from our knowledge of them. His follow-up, the romantic comedy, *Virtual Sexuality* (1999), has some real wit and charm, and his subsequent TV work – *Happy Birthday Shakespeare, Take a Girl Like You* (2000) – confirms a very likeable talent.

OTHER BRITISH FILMS: *Plots with a View* (2002, UK/US).

Hurst, Brian Desmond (*b* Castlereagh, Ireland, 1895 – *d* London, 1986). Director, screenwriter. In Hollywood as assistant to John FORD, his cousin, before returning to England in 1934 to make ten films pre-war, including a version of Poe's *The Tell-Tale Heart* (1934), a lively thriller, *Sensation* (1936), and the grimly impressive *On the Night of the Fire* (1939), which has been described as Britain's first *film noir*. His first major success was the wartime romantic MELODRAMA, *Dangerous Moonlight* (1941), which introduced Richard ADINSELL's 'Warsaw Concerto'. During WW2, he made several DOCUMENTARY shorts and filmed the feature-length documentary, *Theirs is the Glory* (1946), a reconstruction of the 1944 airborne operation at Arnhem, but his most distinctive work is in his post-war films. These include: the meandering but intermittently forceful saga of feuding families, *Hungry Hill* (1947), with some well-executed set pieces; the charming musical romance, *Trottie True* (1948), with Jean KENT's MUSIC HALL star marrying into the aristocracy and thereby providing an oblique comment on post-war class relations; the bold, airless domestic melodrama of *The Mark of Cain* (1948), with its superbly oppressive art direction; and *Scrooge* (1951), still the definitive version of *The Christmas Carol*. The rest of his 50s films are a mixed bag. *Dangerous Exile* (1957) is a COSTUME ADVENTURE with some real feeling for the genre, but *Malta Story* (1953) is a drab wartime tale, *Simba* (1955) is a simplified account of the Mau Mau terror in East Africa, fatally undermined by its romantic interest, *Behind the Mask* (1958), is a dull hospital film, short of either realism or melodramatic flair, and *His and Hers* (1960) is one of the silliest comedies of the period. At his best, Hurst made the most of an enjoyably florid taste, but the industry as it was kept pointing him in other directions.

OTHER BRITISH FILMS: (d, unless noted) *Irish Hearts* (1934, + sc), *Riders to the Sea* (1935, UK/Ire, + co-p), *The Tenth Man, Ourselves Alone* (co-d) (1936), *Glamorous Night* (1937), *Prison Without Bars* (1938), *The Lion Has Wings* (1939, co-d), *Miss Grant Goes to the Door, The Call for Arms* (1940, doc, shorts), *Alibi* (1942), *The Hundred Pound Window, A Letter from Ulster* (doc, short) (1943), *Tom Brown's Schooldays* (1951, p), *The Black Tent* (1956), *The Playboy of the Western World* (1962, UK/Ire, + sc).

BIBLIOG: Brian McElroy, 'British Filmmaking in the 1930s and 1940s: The Example of Brian Desmond Hurst', in Dixon, W.W. (ed), *Re-Viewing British Cinema 1900–1922*, 1994.

Hurst, David (*b* Berlin, 1926). Actor. In England since childhood, Hurst has appeared in cabaret, variety, radio and TV, and on film has played a string of eccentric, usually 'foreign' roles, starting with Wolfgang Winkel in *The Perfect Woman* (1949), as a waiter dispensing romantic wisdom. For the rest, his role-call includes Beckstein (*Always a Bride*, 1953), Mantalini (*Mad About Men*, 1954) and, last to date, Perelli (*After the Ball*, 1957). Since then TV and US movies, including *Hello Dolly* (1969) – as Rudolph Reisenweber. On London stage in *Romanoff and Juliet* (1956), as a spy.

OTHER BRITISH FILMS INCLUDE: *Tony Draws a Horse* (1950), *Venetian Bird, Top Secret* (1952), *Rough Shoot* (1953), *One Good Turn* (1954), *As Long As They're Happy, All for Mary* (1955), *The Intimate Stranger* (1956).

Hurst, Veronica (*b* Malta, 1931). Actress. RN: Patricia Hurst. Pretty, shapely blonde (to England in 1939), who, after RADA

training, was on stage in 1950 and in films the following year. After a small role in *Laughter in Paradise* (1951), she had the second lead in *Angels One Five* (1952), after which Hollywood put her through *The Maze* (1953), a 3-D thriller of not much more than curiosity value. On return to England, she gradually slipped into 'B' FILMS, some of more than ordinary interest, including *Bang! You're Dead* (1953), as the barmaid in a difficult love triangle, which she invested with some genuine sensuality. Married William SYLVESTER.

OTHER BRITISH FILMS INCLUDE: *Will Any Gentleman . . . ?, The Yellow Balloon* (1953), *The Gilded Cage* (1955), *Peeping Tom* (1960), *Live It Up* (1963), *Licensed to Kill* (1965).

Hurt, John (*b* Chesterfield, Derby, 1940). Actor. Immensely bold RADA-trained actor, recognised internationally for his richly varied characterisations of outsiders, such as the defiant homosexual Quentin CRISP in TV's *The Naked Civil Servant* (1975), or Winston Smith, the government functionary who illegally falls in love in *Nineteen Eighty-Four* (1984). Other roles represent something physically strange, like Kane, impregnated by an otherworldly parasite in *Alien* (1979, UK/US), or the disfigured John Merrick in David Lynch's dark masterpiece, *The Elephant Man* (1980, US-financed/UK-shot and -set, BAA/a). Hurt has also taken on characters who are psychologically unhinged, most vividly his outrageously camp Caligula in TV's *I, Claudius* (1976). His trademark deep, rasping voice has garnered him occasional parts in animated features and work as the narrator of TV specials and documentaries. Divides his acting time between the UK and the US.

OTHER BRITISH FILMS INCLUDE: *The Wild and the Willing* (1962), *A Man for All Seasons* (1966), *Sinful Davey, Before Winter Comes* (1968), *10 Rillington Place* (1970), *Mr Forbush and the Penguins, The Pied Piper* (1971), *The Ghoul* (1975), *East of Elephant Rock* (1976), *Midnight Express, The Shout* (1978), *Champions* (1983), *The Hit* (1984), *White Mischief, Aria* (1987), *Scandal* (1988), *The Field* (1990, UK/Ire), *Great Moments in Aviation* (1994, UK/US), *Love and Death on Long Island* (1997, UK/Can), *All the Little Animals* (1998), *Captain Corelli's Mandolin* (UK/Fr/US), *Harry Potter and the Philosopher's Stone* (UK/US), *Tabloid* (2001), *Miranda* (2002). Melinda Hildebrandt.

Hussein, Waris (*b* Lucknow, India, 1938). Director. Most of Hussein's work has been for TV, much of it in the US, though he did some quality drama in Britain, including the mini-series, *Shoulder to Shoulder* (1974) and *Edward and Mrs Simpson* (1978). His first feature for the big screen was *A Touch of Love* (1969), an undervalued ADAPTATION of Margaret Drabble's *The Millstone*, and he followed this with the attractive children's film, *SWALK* (1970), and the costume drama, *Henry VIII and His Six Wives* (1972), inspired by the TV series, *The Six Wives of Henry VIII* (1970), also starring Keith MICHELL.

OTHER BRITISH FILM: *The Sixth Happiness* (1997).

Hussey, Olivia (*b* Buenos Aires, Argentina, 1951). Actress. Hussey had made two films before and 30-odd films and TV appearances since, but she remains firmly associated with ZEFFIRELLI's 1968 *Romeo and Juliet* (UK/It), famously playing the tragic teenage lover at almost the right age. She and Leonard WHITING brought a poignant youth and beauty to their roles that more than compensated for lack of experience. Hussey had substantial supporting roles in *Death on the Nile* (1978) and *The Cat and the Canary* (1979), but the Juliet legend persisted in the public mind; certainly, a dreadful film such as the *Lost Horizon* (1973, US) remake would not dislodge it. Married (2 of 4) US actor Dean Paul Martin.

OTHER BRITISH FILMS: *The Battle of the Villa Fiorita*, *Cup Fever* (1965), *All the Right Noises* (1969).

Huston, John (*b* Nevada, Missouri, 1906 – *d* Middletown, Rhode Island, 1987). Director. Legendary American film-maker, who made his name as director, after a decade as a screenwriter, with *The Maltese Falcon* (1941). He belongs in this book largely because of a series of Anglo-American productions he made in Britain and various exotic locations in the 50s. His first was *The African Queen* (1951, + co-sc), the much-loved adventure romance between the gin-swilling owner of the eponymous craft and a spinster missionary, respectively played by Humphrey Bogart and Katharine HEPBURN. He made two further films for the WOOLF brothers' firm, Romulus: the popular though scarcely authentic biography of Toulouse-Lautrec, *Moulin Rouge*, and the idiosyncratic cult favourite, *Beat the Devil* (UK/It/US)(1953, + co-sc). He became an Irish citizen in 1964 and made several more British films, without repeating the success of his first, but his last film, *The Dead* (1987, UK/Ger/US), from a James JOYCE novella, is as eloquently lovely an epitaph as film-maker ever had.

OTHER BRITISH FILMS: *It Happened in Paris* (co-sc), *Death Drives Through* (co-story) (1935), *Moby Dick* (1956, + co-sc), *Heaven Knows, Mr Allison* (1957, UK/US, + co-sc), *Casino Royale* (1967, co-d, + co-sc, a), *Sinful Davey* (1968), *The Mackintosh Man* (1973).

BIBLIOG: Autobiography, *An Open Book*, 1981; Lawrence Gobel, *The Hustons*, 1990.

Hutcheson, David (*b* Craigmore, Bute, Scotland, 1905 – *d* London, 1976). Actor. Educated at Tonbridge School and on stage from 1926, this agreeable light second lead and character actor, long-faced and beaky, often monocled, was adept in COMEDY, like the would-be gourmet in *Sleeping Car to Trieste* (1948), or THRILLERS, like *Circle of Danger* (1950), or as the hero's best friend, as in *Something Money Can't Buy* (1952), usually projecting an upper-middle-class image. War service (1942–45) and long gaps for stage work, including Australasian tour as Pickering in *My Fair Lady* (1961–62).

OTHER BRITISH FILMS INCLUDE: *Romance in Rhythm* (1934), *The Love Test* (1935), *The Sky's the Limit* (1937), *The Middle Watch* (1939), *Convoy* (1940), *The Next of Kin* (1942), *The Life and Death of Colonel Blimp* (1943), *The Trojan Brothers* (1945), *Vice Versa* (1947), *Woman Hater* (1948), *The Elusive Pimpernel* (1950), *Encore* (1951), *Law and Disorder* (1958), *The Evil of Frankenstein* (1964), *The Abominable Dr Phibes* (1971), *The National Health* (1973).

Hutchinson, Leslie ('Hutch') (*b* Grenada, West Indies, 1900 – *d* London, 1969). Actor. Fey West Indian singer/pianist, popular with London café society, and with a style similar to that of Bobby Short. On-screen, always as himself, in a number of Pathetone shorts and a handful of features: *Big Business* (1930), *Cock o' the North* (1935), *Beloved Imposter* (1936), *Happidrome* (1943), *Lucky Mascot* (1948), *Treasure of San Teresa* (1959).

BIBLIOG: Charlotte Breese, *Hutch*, 2000. AS.

Huth, Harold (*b* Huddersfield, 1892 – *d* London, 1967). Actor, producer, director. Well known as actor on stage and screen who retired from acting owing to ill-health after a busy career in 30s British films. In the late 30s, he was casting director for MGM–BRITISH, and began to direct in 1939, though none of the films he directed was of much distinction. As producer, he was associated with some popular films, including such GAINSBOROUGH melodramas as *They Were Sisters* (1945) and *Caravan* (1946). He finished his career as a producer with WARWICK FILMS, most notably on *The Trials of Oscar Wilde*

(1960). In the late 40s, he and John CORFIELD formed Burnham Productions which made *My Sister and I* and *Look Before You Love* (1948, + co-p).

OTHER BRITISH FILMS INCLUDE: (a) *Sir or Madam* (1928), *The Silver King*, (1929), *Guilt* (1931), *Rome Express* (1932), *The Ghoul* (1933), *The Camels are Coming* (1934), *Blackmailed* (1950, + p); (d) *Hell's Cargo* (1939), *Bulldog Sees It Through* (1940), *East of Piccadilly* (1941), *Night Beat* (1948, + p), *The Hostage* (1956); (assoc p) *Busman's Honeymoon* (1940), *Pimpernel Smith* (1941), *The Bandit of Zhobe* (1959); (p) *Love Story* (1944), *The White Unicorn*, *Root of All Evil* (1947), *Police Dog* (1955), *Jazzboat*, *In the Nick* (1959), *The Hellions* (1961, + co-sc, UK/SAf).

Hutton, Brian G. (*b* New York, 1935). Director. US film-maker who began as an actor (in, for example, Elvis Presley's *King Creole*, 1958), turned director and made his most successful film in Britain, the boys' own WW2 adventure, *Where Eagles Dare* (1968), as well as two melodramatic vehicles for Elizabeth TAYLOR – *Zee & Co.* (1971) and *Night Watch* (1973). His career has scarcely prospered since.

Hutton, Robert (*b* Kingston, NY, 1920 – *d* Kingston, NY, 1994). Actor, screenwriter. His brief and modest Hollywood stardom, a product of wartime scarcity among leading men, was well behind him before tall, boyish Hutton sought to prolong his career in a series of undistinguished British programmers. There were two in the 50s, *The Man Without a Body* and *Man from Tangier* (1957), then a return to the US for the likes of *The Slime People* (1962), before coming back to Britain to finish his career, mainly in horror films such as *Cry of the Banshee* (1970). Also co-wrote the Lana TURNER British film, *Persecution* (1974).

OTHER BRITISH FILMS INCLUDE: *The Secret Door* (1962, UK/US, + assoc p), *The Sicilians* (1964), *Finders Keepers* (1966), *You Only Live Twice*, *Torture Garden* (1967), *Tales from the Crypt*, *The Cherry Picker* (1972).

Hyde-White, Wilfrid (*b* Bourton-on-the-Water, 1903 – *d* Woodland Hills, California, 1991). Actor. RN: White. Supremely unctuous character player, adept at smoothly honed sycophancy – as, for example, the literary chairman of *The Third Man* (1949), the headmaster in *The Browning Version* (1948), and one of the wealthy brothers in *The Million Pound Note* (1953). With his plummy tones and sleekly coiffed appearance, he usually played upper-class, but there is a smattering of fake smoothies, like crim Soapie Stevens in *Two Way Stretch* (1960), or the merely deferential like the jeweller in *Bond Street* (1948). However, it is hopeless trying to limit the highlights in such a career, which spanned fifty years, every type of British film and not a few international ones, most famously as that arch-gent, Colonel Pickering, in *My Fair Lady* (1964, US). Marlborough-educated and RADA-trained, he was first on stage in 1922, scoring a major hit as the father of *The Reluctant Debutante* (1955) and screen since 1936. His son **Alex Hyde-White** (*b* London, 1959) has acted in several films including *Biggles* (1986) and *Pretty Woman* (1987, US).

OTHER BRITISH FILMS INCLUDE: *Josser on the Farm* (1934), *Night Mail* (1935), *Rembrandt* (1936), *Elephant Boy* (1937), *I've Got a Horse* (1938), *Poison Pen*, *The Lambeth Walk* (1939), *Turned Out Nice Again* (1941), *Lady from Lisbon* (1942), *The Demi-Paradise* (1943), *Appointment with Crime*, *Night Boat to Dublin*, *Wanted for Murder* (1946), *While the Sun Shines*, *The Ghosts of Berkeley Square* (1947), *My Brother's Keeper*, *The Passionate Friends*, *Quartet* (1948), *That Dangerous Age*, *Conspirator*, *The Angel with the Trumpet* (1949), *The Mudlark*, *Trio*, *Mr Drake's Duck* (1950), *No Highway*, *Outcast of the Islands* (1951), *Top Secret* (1952), *The Story of Gilbert and Sullivan* (1953), *The Rainbow Jacket* (1954), *See How They Run* (1955), *My Teenage Daughter* (1956), *The Truth About Women*,

Wonderful Things (1957), *Up the Creek, Carry On Nurse* (1958), *North West Frontier* (1959), *On the Fiddle* (1961), *Crooks Anonymous* (1962), *You Must Be Joking!* (1965), *Our Man in Marrakesh* (1966), *Sumuru* (1967), *Fragment of Fear* (1970), *The Cat and the Canary* (1979), *Fanny Hill* (1983).

Hyland, Peggy (*b* Birmingham, 1895 – *d*?). Actress. RN: Gladys Hutchinson. A classic brunette beauty, married to Fred LeRoy GRANVILLE, Peggy Hyland had a major US career (1915–20), starring in some 28 features and enjoying a two-year contract with Fox. In 1922, she produced, directed and starred in *With Father's Help* for her own company in Britain, followed by a smattering of British silents.

OTHER BRITISH FILMS INCLUDE: *In the Ranks* (1914), *John Halifax, Gentleman, Fetters of Fear* (1915), *Sally Bishop* (1916), *The Honeypot* (1920), *Love Maggie* (1921), *Forbidden Cargoes* (1925). AS.

Hylton, Jack (*b* Bolton, Lancashire, 1892 – *d* London, 1965). Bandleader, producer. Now best remembered as a theatrical impresario of the 40s and 50s, he had his own band from 1924, and was famous on MUSIC HALL and RADIO. He appeared with his band in two 30s MUSICALS, *She Shall Have Music* (1935) and *Band Waggon* (1940), and in the 1943 DOCUMENTARY about the London Philharmonic Orchestra, *Battle for Music*.

Hylton, Jane (*b* London, 1925 – *d* Glasgow, 1979). Actress. RN: Gwen Clark. RADA-trained, with rep experience, in film from 1945 and a member of Sydney BOX's COMPANY OF YOUTH, Hylton ought to have become a big star. A symptomatic figure, she was attractive and distinctive enough, could suggest passion more persuasively than most, and could cross the social divides with unusual facility. RANK had her under contract and largely wasted her: the maid in *Dear Murderer* (1947), the oldest daughter in *Here Come the Huggetts* (1948), and the star of the fashion-world drama, *It Started in Paradise* (1952), which muffed its melodramatic potential and looked merely old-fashioned. Her best chances came elsewhere: at EALING for *Passport to Pimlico* (1949), as Molly carrying a torch for fishmonger John SLATER, and as self-sacrificing Mary ('Mary' rarely has fun in British films) in *Dance Hall* (1950); the firm-minded pub-keeper in TEMPEAN's excellent second feature, *The Quiet Woman*, and the woman having a nervous breakdown in CROWN's *Out of True* (1951); and the prisoner punished by the death of her child for 'liking men too much' in ABPC's *The Weak and the Wicked* (1953). Even in later 'B' FILMS like *Devil's Bait* (1959) and *House of Mystery* (1961, with second husband Peter DYNELEY), her earthiness and ambiguity make her interesting to watch. Also did some notable TV, including Guinevere in *The Adventures of Sir Lancelot* (1956)

and *The Four Seasons of Rosie Carr* (1964), and just before her premature death was very fine on the National stage in *The Madras House* (1978). First husband was producer Euan LLOYD.

OTHER BRITISH FILMS INCLUDE: *A Girl in a Million* (1946), *Jassy, Holiday Camp* (1947), *My Brother's Keeper, My Sister and I* (1948), *The Tall Headlines* (1952), *Secret Venture* (1955), *Laughing in the Sunshine* (1956, UK/Swe), *Night Train for Inverness* (1959), *Circus of Horrors* (1960), *The Wild Geese* (1978, UK/Switz).

Hyson, Dorothy (*b* Chicago, 1914 – *d* London, 1996). Actress. Delightful ingenue with heart-shaped face, blue eyes and blonde hair, who inspired the Rodgers and Hart song, 'The Most Beautiful Girl in the World'. Daughter of **Dorothy Dickson** (*b* Kansas City, 1896 – *d* London, 1995), who appeared in three British films, including *Channel Crossing* (1933), and choreographer Carl Hyson, she came to UK with parents in 1921, made London stage debut in 1927 and became a major West End star. Her films were almost all made in the 30s, and she finally played George FORMBY's leading lady in *Spare a Copper* (1940). Her 1933 contract with Basil DEAN led to a nervous breakdown. Married Robert DOUGLAS (1935–45) and Anthony QUAYLE (1947).

OTHER BRITISH FILMS INCLUDE: *The Ghoul, Turkey Time* (1933), *Sing As We Go!, Happy, A Cup of Kindness* (1934), *You Will Remember* (1940). AS.

Hytner, Nicholas (*b* 1967). Director. Manchester Grammar-educated theatre director who came to films triumphantly with his 1994 adaptation of Alan BENNETT's *The Madness of King George* (UK/US), which he had produced in 1991 at London's National Theatre, where he was an associate director, before being made its Artistic Director in 2001. His subsequent films have been US-made: *The Crucible* (1996), from Arthur Miller's screenplay, and the charming comedy, *The Object of My Affection* (1998). Has also worked for the RSC, directed opera in many cities and brought it to TV; and in 1989 directed the musical play, *Miss Saigon*.

Hytten, Olaf (*b* Glasgow, 1888 – *d* Los Angeles, California, 1955). Actor. Prolific character actor who died one day after filming a scene with Bette Davis in *The Virgin Queen* (1955, US). Despite being born in Glasgow, he was the quintessential English servant on screen. As much a success on the New York as London stage in 1910s and 20s, Hytten appeared in some 20 British silent films, beginning with *Knave of Diamonds* (1921).

OTHER BRITISH FILMS INCLUDE: *Trapped by the Mormons* (1922), *Chu Chin Chow* (1923). AS.

Ii

Ibbetson, Arthur (*b* Bishop Auckland, 1922 – *d* Hillingdon, Middlesex, 1997). Cinematographer. Served a long apprenticeship as camera assistant, camera operator and second unit cinematographer, before getting his first full credit on Ronald NEAME's *The Horse's Mouth* (1958). After this lush opportunity for lingering over Gulley Jimson's canvasses, he did sterling black-and-white work on several interesting contemporary dramas for ALLIED FILM MAKERS, including *Whistle Down the Wind* (1961), and in Neame's 1963 colour drama, *I Could Go On Singing*, he catches memorable images of Judy Garland at the top of her harrowing form. Of his later films, *The Railway Children* (1970) and *Little Lord Fauntleroy* (1980) charmingly capture the look of a bygone era and of children's illustrated books. Received AAn for *Anne of the Thousand Days* (1969) and BAAn for *Nine Hours to Rama* (1962) and *The Chalk Garden* (1964).

OTHER BRITISH FILMS INCLUDE: (focus-puller) *Brief Encounter* (1945); (cam op) *Hotel Reserve* (1944), *Great Day* (1945), *Captain Boycott* (2uc), *Fame is the Spur* (2uc), *Vice Versa* (1947), *Warning to Wantons* (1948), *The Spider and the Fly* (1949), *Circle of Danger* (1950), *The Magic Box* (1951, assoc), *The Beggar's Opera* (1953), *The Man Who Never Was* (1955), *Moby Dick* (1956); (c) *The Blue Lagoon* (1949, co-c), *Saturday Island* (1952, co-c), *Melba* (1953, co-c), *The Bridal Path* (1959), *The League of Gentlemen*, *The Angry Silence*, *Tunes of Glory* (1960), *Murder at the Gallop* (1963), *Fanatic* (1965), *A Countess from Hong Kong* (1966), *Where Eagles Dare* (1968), *When Eight Bells Toll* (1971), *A Doll's House* (1973), *Out of Season* (1975), *The Bounty* (1984).

Ideal Film Company Founded in 1911 as a distributor, Ideal entered production in 1915 with Simon ROWSON in charge and Fred PAUL as production head. The latter directed the company's first film, *Whoso Is without Sin* (1916). Ideal quickly became known for its stage and literary ADAPTATIONS, including *The Second Mrs Tanqueray*, *Lady Windermere's Fan*, *The Fallen Star*, *The Vicar of Wakefield* (1916), *Masks and Faces* (1917), and *The Gay Lord Quex* (1918). After a hiatus in the late 1910s, Ideal again became a busy producer in the 20s, with further adaptations, including *Bleak House*, *Wuthering Heights* (1920), *A Woman of No Importance*, *The Adventures of Mr Pickwick* (1921), *A Bill of Divorcement*, and *The Card* (1922). It ceased production in 1924 and merged with GAUMONT–BRITISH in 1927. The Ideal name was revived the following year with the Tallulah Bankhead vehicle *His House in Order*, *Maria Marten* and *Sweeney Todd*. AS.

Idle, Eric (*b* South Shields, 1943). Actor. Educated at Cambridge with other MONTY PYTHON alumni, John CLEESE and Graham CHAPMAN, and most of his film work has been involved, as actor, co-writer and composer, with the Python gang. He has, for instance, multiple roles in each of *And Now for Something Completely Different* (1971, + co-sc), *Monty Python and the Holy Grail* (1974, + co-sc, as, *inter alia*, 'Sir Lancelot's Trusty Steed'), *Life of Brian* (1979, + co-sc, co-m) and *The Meaning of Life* (1983, + co-sc, co-m). He *looks* less bizarre than some of the Pythons, but the looks are not to be trusted. In the 90s, he appeared chiefly in US films (e.g. *Casper*, 1995) and TV, and was composer on *As Good As It Gets* (1997, US). Married (1 of 2, 1969–75) to actress **Lyn Ashley** who appeared in several films, including *Quest for Love* (1971).

OTHER BRITISH FILMS INCLUDE: *Side by Side* (1975), *The Secret Policeman's Private Parts* (1984), *The Adventures of Baron Munchausen* (1988, UK/Ger/It, + co-m), *Nuns on the Run* (1990), *Splitting Heirs* (1993, + ex p, sc), *The Wind in the Willows* (1996).

Ifans, Rhys (*b* Ruthin, Wales, 1966). Actor. RN: Evans. Lanky, Welsh-speaking star who made his film debut in *August* (1996), the Wales-set adaptation of *Uncle Vanya*, but came to prominence in *Notting Hill* (1999, UK/US) as Hugh GRANT's crotch-scratching flatmate in greying underpants. The Guildhall-trained actor has been in constant demand since, though it must be said that two of the demands he answered – *Love, Honour and Obey* and *Kevin & Perry Go Large* (2000, UK/US) – could have finished many a career for good. In the US, he had a major role in *Shipping News* (2001). His brother, **Llyr Ifans** (*b* Ruthin) is also an actor, and they starred together in *Twin Town* (1997).

OTHER BRITISH FILMS INCLUDE: *You're Dead*, *Dancing at Lughnasa* (UK/Ire/US) (1998), *Heart*, *Janice Beard: 45 wpm* (2000), *Rancid Aluminium* (2000), *The 51st State* (2001, UK/Can/US).

Ifield, Frank (*b* Coventry, 1937). Singer. British-born Ifield grew up in Australia, where he successfully pursued a singing (and yodelling) career and came to England in 1960 to further recording success. His one film, *Up Jumped a Swagman* (1965), shows a movie persona accomplished and charming enough to have warranted more.

Illing, Peter (*b* Vienna, Austria, 1899 – *d* London, 1966). Actor. RN: Peter Ihle. Exiled from his native Austria in 1937, Illing specialised in his British (and occasionally Hollywood) films in shady, sweaty and inscrutable foreigners, often of Mediterranean or Middle Eastern origin. Usually cast in minor supporting parts, he had a more substantial role as a jovial Italian patriarch in Emeric PRESSBURGER's *Miracle In Soho* (1957).

OTHER BRITISH FILMS INCLUDE: *The End Of the River* (1947), *Against the Wind* (1947), *Eureka Stockade* (1949), *State Secret* (1950), *Outcast of the Islands* (1951), *Never Let Me Go* (1953), *The Young Lovers* (1954), *Svengali*, *Bhowani Junction* (US/UK) (1955), *Manuela*, *Escapement* (1957), *Blind Date* (1959), *Nine Hours To Rama* (1963), *Devils Of Darkness* (1964). Tim Bergfelder.

Imi, Tony (*b* London, 1937). Cinematographer. Entered films in 1959, but his first solo feature credit was a decade away on

The Raging Moon (1970) for Bryan FORBES for whom he subsequently shot *The Slipper and the Rose* (1976), in which his delicate colour enhanced the film's fairy-tale quality, and *International Velvet* (1978). Much of his work has been on routine US television, but he contributed to the kinetic energies of Paul Anderson's *Shopping* (1994), about 'ramraiding' young hooligans.

OTHER BRITISH FILMS INCLUDE: (shorts) *Junket 89* (1970), *Edward Burra* (1973), *The Firefighters* (1974), *Bismarck* (1975); (features) *Inadmissible Evidence* (1968, co-c), *Dulcima* (1971), *The Likely Lads* (1976), *North Sea Hijack* (1979), *Not Quite Jerusalem* (1984), *Empire State* (1987), *Buster* (1988), *Downtime* (1997, UK/Fr), *Goodbye Charlie Bright* (2001), *Silent Cry* (2002).

Imrie, Celia (*b* Guildford, 1952). Actress. Droll character player best known for her appearances in Victoria WOOD's TV shows, including *Victoria Wood – As Seen on TV* (1986) and *Dinnerladies* (1998), as the bumbling personnel manager, but equally effective as a crisp politician in an episode of *Dalziel and Pascoe* (2000) and worried but warm as Sadie in *Love in a Cold Climate* (2000). On stage, she has appeared at the National and the Chichester Festival, and on screen she has appeared twice for Kenneth BRANAGH: in *Frankenstein* (1994, UK/US) and the comedy of provincial theatre, *In the Bleak Midwinter* (1965). She gave a sharp account of an insensitive mother in *Hilary and Jackie* (1998), and was glimpsed in *Star Wars . . . The Phantom Menace* (1999, US).

OTHER BRITISH FILMS INCLUDE: *Assassin* (1973), *The Wicked Lady* (1983), *Highlander* (1986), *The Borrowers* (1997, UK/US), *Dead in the Water* (2001), *Thunderpants* (2002, UK/Ger).

Ince, Ralph (*b* Boston, Mass., 1886 – *d* London, 1937). Actor, director. Youngest of the three US film-maker brothers (John and Thomas are the others), he began his career as an actor in 1907, and played in and/or directed nearly 200 films all up, the last 22 in England between 1934 and 1937. Mostly 'QUOTA QUICKIES,' some of these sound lively crime thrillers which might repay excavation, if they exist. They include *Murder at Monte Carlo* (1935), starring Errol FLYNN on his way to Hollywood. Killed in a car crash.

OTHER BRITISH FILMS INCLUDE: *Love at Second Sight*, *A Glimpse of Paradise* (1934), *So You Won't Talk?*, *Rolling Home*, *Black Mask* (1935), *Twelve Good Men*, *Jury's Evidence* (1936), *The Vulture*, *It's Not Cricket* (1937).

Independent Artists Production company set up by Julian WINTLE at PINEWOOD, its first film being the thriller *The Dark Man* (1950). The company's films were produced by Wintle until 1958 when he took on Leslie PARKYN as his partner and shifted Independent Artists to BEACONSFIELD STUDIOS which became available when Sydney BOX decided to leave. The company produced an interesting mixture of films, including notable 'A' films such as *The One That Got Away* (1957) and *This Sporting Life* (1963) and interesting 'B' FILMS such as *The Big Day* (1960) and *The Man in the Back Seat* (1961). Its last production was *The Belstone Fox* (1973).

BIBLIOG: Anne Francis, *Julian Wintle. A Memoir*, 1984.

independent, art-house and alternative cinemas By the mid 30s most cinemas were independent, with the largest circuits (ABC and Gaumont–British) controlling only 10% of total exhibition. These circuits were less dominant in the North, where 'industrial halls' were looking for cut-price product, like that provided by MANCUNIAN FILMS, that would appeal to their audiences. Many independents, grouped into small regional/county chains, under the same ownership, relied heavily on double-bills and reissues. In a desperate attempt to attract the shrinking audiences of the mid 50s and to cut costs, many smaller independents played cut-price US imports of the 'teenage monster' variety, but to no avail: between 1956–60, most cinema closures were small independent second/third-run houses.

London art-houses included the Paris-Pullman, the ACADEMY, and Cameo-Poly, all now closed. The Telekinema, constructed on the South Bank for the Festival of Britain, became the BFI-supported NATIONAL FILM THEATRE, opened in 1952, moving to purpose-built premises in 1957. The first art-house outside London was the Cosmo, Glasgow (1939), and the Classic revivals/art-house chain introduced many European films to other cities in the 50s and 60s. In London there were also several small cinemas, the Berkeley, Gala-Royal, Continentale, showing mainly French films, although in the 50s, mainstream continental films, such as *Rififi* (1955), were widely shown on the RANK circuits. Art-house cinemas could attract large audiences for films with the 'X' CERTIFICATE, which were marketed as risqué or controversial, as with *La Dolce Vita* (1960, It). The first subsidised regional film theatre (Bristol), opened in 1967, and by the 80s, there was a regional consortium, a small 'circuit' of 30 independent cinemas serviced by the BFI.

The Film Society movement, including THE FILM SOCIETY (London, 1925), was traditionally an important outlet for alternative films. In the 30s a socialist film movement developed through the Worker's Theatre Movement, evolving into Kino, a distributor of features and DOCUMENTARIES to a national network of film societies, working men's clubs, and selected independent cinemas. The LONDON FILM-MAKERS' COOPERATIVE was founded in 1966 to facilitate 'open screenings' of such films at universities, bookshops and other venues. British alternative cinema exhibitors include the NFT, the Institute of Contemporary Arts (ICA), and arts centres/galleries. Other past alternative forms of exhibition included mobile cinemas (especially in 30s and 40s) operating from vans, setting up their 16mm/35mm equipment in workers' canteens, town and village halls, usually screening documentaries, often accompanied by a speaker. More recently, Asian community cinemas are screening 'Bollywood' films in Southall, Birmingham and other centres, and a small number of special cinemas, such as the IMAX at Waterloo and the Pictureville Cinerama Cinema, Bradford.

News cinemas (until the 60s) were located in large cities, and at major railway termini. The Daily Bioscope, Bishopsgate (1906) was the first news cinema and the Cameo Piccadilly (1930) was the first sound news theatre. Programmes were repeated hourly, typically consisting of a newsreel, cartoon, comedy short, and a travelogue/documentary perhaps from BRITISH TRANSPORT FILMS. Roger Philip Mellor.

See also **cinemas and exhibition**.

independent film-making in Britain 'Independent film' isn't a precise description. It has been applied to a variety of different phenomena including groups like the WORKERS' FILM AND PHOTO LEAGUE of the 30s, the LONDON FILM-MAKERS' CO-OP of the 60s and the WORKSHOP MOVEMENT of the 80s. It has also been applied to film-makers as disparate as Norman McLAREN, Lindsay ANDERSON, Derek JARMAN, and Ken LOACH. Although it has been mainly used in relation to film making, it has frequently encompassed DISTRIBUTION and EXHIBITION.

However, it is possible to recognise three versions of independence which have been present in some form when claims to independent status have been made. The first version values economic freedom. The central preoccupation is with finding financial support from sources outside the established film industry. The second values political freedom. It looks for the possibility of expressing oppositional (almost exclusively left-wing) political views. The third values aesthetic freedom. It gives priority to developing innovative forms of cinematic expression. All three versions are usually present, though in different proportions, whenever film-makers have claimed to be independent.

The two periods when independent film has had a substantial presence in the British cinema were during the 30s and from the mid 70s to the early 90s. In the 30s independence was conceived of principally in political terms. Faced by what seemed to be the final collapse of capitalism and the rise of Fascism, film enthusiasts with left-wing sympathies sought ways of using the cinema as a form of political intervention. The cinematic inspiration for the films which emerged was the 20s Soviet cinema, NEWSREEL, DOCUMENTARY and agit-prop being the favoured forms. The interest of most of these films is tied to the political events they were a response to, but *Bread* (1934), *Hell Unlimited* (1936), and *Peace and Plenty* (1939), are all films whose energy and invention make them still worth watching.

Like the 30s movement, the independent movement which developed in the late 70s had a political inspiration. In this case it was the critique of capitalism which came out of the 1968 student rebellions, especially as these ideas were translated into film-making by Jean-Luc Godard. Mainly because of Godard's influence, the politics were closely tied to an avant-garde aesthetic. It was argued that to be effective, a political challenge required a formal challenge. Films which most fully embody these ideas include *Riddles of the Sphinx* (1977), *Song of the Shirt* (1979), *Handsworth Songs* (1986) and *Looking for Langston* (1989).

Beginning with the magazine *CLOSE UP* in the 20s, there has also been a consistent tradition of independent film-making maintained by film-makers who relate strongly to developments in the visual arts. In the 60s and 70s this tradition was re-energised by the work of the LONDON FILM-MAKERS CO-OP. While it has never been completely separate from the other independent traditions, its focus has been on formal innovation, aimed especially at detaching the cinema from its literary connections. By its nature, it tends to be a cinema of individual artists. Derek Jarman and Peter GREENAWAY are two film-makers from this tradition who have established international reputations.

Isaac JULIEN's work demonstrates the difficulty of making fine distinctions amongst independent film-makers. In the 80s and early 90s he was a member of a black workshop. With the demise of the WORKSHOP MOVEMENT, his work moved closer to the visual arts, so much so that in 2001, it was nominated for the Turner prize.
BIBLIOG: Bert Hogenkamp, *Deadly Parallels*, 1986; Margaret Dickinson (ed), *Rogue Reels – Oppositional Film in Britain 1945–90*, 1999. Alan Lovell.

Independent Frame This method was used briefly by RANK Studios in the late 40s as a cost-cutting method of film production, involving extensive use of back-projected materials to cut down on location shooting, 'doubling' the actors whenever possible in long shots to avoid the necessity of stars going on location, and a completely detailed storyboard to make sure that location and studio footage were properly matched. The most famous of the films made using this method was Montgomery TULLY's *Boys in Brown* (1949), starring Richard ATTENBOROUGH and Dirk BOGARDE as inmates in a juvenile prison. After an extensive pre-production period supervised by Rank art director David RAWNSLEY, during which various actors 'doubled' for the film's protagonists for silent location shooting, and numerous process background plates were shot for later use, the actors completed their roles in less than two weeks, never once setting foot outside the studio. However, the inherent artificiality and static camera placement necessitated by the continual use of process photography made the Independent Frame system unpopular with directors as well as actors, and the system was abandoned shortly thereafter. Other films which used the system included *Warning to Wantons* (1948) and *Prelude to Fame* (1950).
BIBLIOG: Wheeler Winston Dixon, 'The Doubled Image: Montgomery Tully's *Boys in Brown* (1949) and the Independent Frame Process', in *Re-Viewing British Cinema 1900–1992*, 1994. Wheeler Winston Dixon.

Independent Producers This was the umbrella name which sheltered various individual production companies financed by the RANK ORGANISATION. It was incorporated in February 1942, under the chairmanship of George Archibald, who had held many executive posts in the British film industry. In the later 40s, IP accounted for much of the 'quality' arm of British film-making. Its initial aim was to centralise production facilities and for the film-makers it offered the independence that could only come from the protection of a major company like Rank, and directors such as Michael POWELL and David LEAN testified at various times to the idyllic nature of such working conditions, whatever they later said. The production units which operated under IP included THE ARCHERS (Powell and Pressburger), CINEGUILD (Lean, Anthony HAVELOCK-ALLAN, Ronald NEAME, etc), INDIVIDUAL PICTURES (LAUNDER & GILLIAT), WESSEX FILMS (Ian DALRYMPLE). In 1947, AQUILA (Donald WILSON, Frederick WILSON) joined the consortium. Of earlier members of the IP group, Leslie HOWARD was killed before he could make a film for it and Marcel HELLMAN withdrew after two modest films. The very freedom which Rank allowed his film-makers led to some criticism of the latter on grounds of self-indulgence, though the prestige it had brought to British cinema, before it was wound up in late 1948 and the Rank enterprise transferred to PINEWOOD, had been enormous.

India and British film The era of EMPIRE, and a singular preoccupation with how the British saw themselves and the culture they colonised, underpin British feature film images of India. Mostly adapted from books, the films are rooted in the English literary tradition of Empire novelists, like Rudyard KIPLING and, more equivocally, E.M FORSTER. Within that tradition, impressions have modulated over the decades as the circumstances and meaning of Empire have changed. Classic Kiplingesque evocations of colonial India, such as *The Drum* (1938), were popular in the 30s. In the 50s, films like *North West Frontier* (1959) nostalgically revisited the lost British Raj, but by 1968 it was ripe for parody in *Carry On Up the Khyber* (1968). Heavyweight historical and literary dramatisations marked a renewed interest in British India in the 80s, with such films as *Gandhi* (1982, UK/Ind) and *A Passage to India* (1984). With little interest in India since then, audiences still await a British film dealing with the post-colonial years, though the telemovie,

Staying On (1980), deals explicitly with this period, even if its main characters were ex-Raj. Stephen Guy.

Individual Pictures One of the production units which operated within the RANK company, INDEPENDENT PRO-DUCERS, in the 40s, this was the baby of Frank LAUNDER and Sidney GILLIAT. Its first production was *The Rake's Progress* (1945) and it turned out a string of civilised entertainments, culminating in *The Happiest Days of Your Life* (1950), after which Launder and Gilliat transferred to LONDON FILMS. Less obviously canted towards the 'literary' prestige of its sister company, CINEGUILD, and less visually daring than THE ARCHERS, Individual Pictures productions are marked by perceptive, sophisticated screenplays, wit in dialogue and situation, and a high level of acting performance, across a GENRE range which includes realist drama, SPY THRILLER, DETECTIVE STORY and slapstick COMEDY.

Ingham, Barrie (*b* Halifax, 1934). Actor. Former Royal Artillery officer, on stage since 1956 and with the RSC 1967–68; in occasional films from 1961, starring in *A Challenge for Robin Hood* (1967). Much TV in both US (played John Barrymore in *My Wicked, Wicked Ways*, 1985) and UK.

OTHER BRITISH FILMS INCLUDE: *The Fourth Square* (1961), *Tiara Tahiti*, *Number Six* (1962), *Dr Who and the Daleks* (1965), *Invasion, Day of the Jackal* (1973, UK/Fr).

Inman, John (*b* Bishop Auckland, 1935). Actor. Played the outrageous gay shop assistant Mr Humphries in TV's *Are You Being Served?* (1973–83), ever solicitous about the inside-leg measurements, repeated this caricature in the film SPIN-OFF (1977), and did a guest spot in *The Tall Guy* (1989).

Innes, George (*b* London, 1938). Actor. Supporting actor in films since 1962, much on TV where he played Alfred, the footman in the early episodes of *Upstairs, Downstairs* (1971), and often in working-class roles, but a monk in *Pope Joan* (1972) and a Sergeant in *A Bridge Too Far* (1977).

OTHER BRITISH FILMS INCLUDE: *Billy Liar* (1963), *Charlie Bubbles* (1967), *The Italian Job* (1969), *Gumshoe* (1971), *Sweeney 2* (1978), *Quadrophenia* (1979), *Ordeal by Innocence* (1984), *Morons from Outer Space* (1985).

Innes, Hammond (*b* Horsham, 1913 – *d* Suffolk, 1998). Writer. Prolific author of once-popular, now dated adventure stories, usually set in difficult terrains. Film ADAPTATIONS include *Snowbound* (1948, from *The Lonely Skier*, 1947), *Hell Below Zero* (1953, from *The White South*, 1949), *Campbell's Kingdom* (1957, + co-sc, novel 1952), *The Wreck of the Mary Deare* (1959, US, mainly UK-set and personnel, novel 1956). Awarded CBE in 1978.

Innocent, Harold (*b* Coventry, 1933 – *d* London, 1993). Actor. Plump actor whose villainous and sinister demeanour in films belied his name. Impressive as corrupt Bishop of Hereford in *Robin Hood: Prince of Thieves* (1991, US) and the dignified Duke of Burgundy in *Henry V* (1989). Busy supporting and character actor on stage – debut with Birmingham Rep in mid 50s – who was in TV from 1959 to 1962 and later in such films as *Every Home Should Have One* (1969) and *Loot* (1970), and Fellini's *Casanova* (1974, It).

OTHER BRITISH FILMS INCLUDE: *Yellow Dog* (1973), *Galileo* (1974, UK/Can), *Brazil* (1985), *Little Dorrit* (1987), *Buster, The Tall Guy, Without a Clue* (UK/US) (1989). AS.

International Federation of Film Archives (FIAF) Known by its French acronym, FIAF (Fédération Internationale des Archives du Film), this organisation was co-founded in 1938 by the film ARCHIVES of London, Berlin, New York and Paris, interrupted by WW2, and reconvened in Paris in 1946, by which time new archives had been established in Brussels, Basel, Prague, Amsterdam and Warsaw. Today, FIAF has more than 125 affiliates throughout the world. Its main aim is to '[bring] together institutions dedicated in each country to the collection and preservation of films, both as elements of cultural heritage and as historical documents'. Its chief activities are: the maintaining of common standards of preservation, cataloguing, documentation, access and programming; repatriation of lost films; exchange of prints for exhibition in cinémathèques; and training of film archivists.

BIBLIOG: Penelope Houston, *Keepers of the Frame*, 1994. Clyde Jeavons.

Ireland and British cinema Before the 1970s, when film-making became more established in Ireland, most Irish-themed films were produced by British and American companies. Early in the century, British pioneers Robert PAUL and Arthur MELBOURNE-COOPER arrived in Ireland and shot and exhibited films such as *Whaling Afloat and Ashore* (1908) and *A Cattle Drive in Galway* (1908). The 1910s and 20s saw the production of HISTORICAL DRAMAS including *Michael Dwyer* (1912), the comic *Mike Murphy* cycle, and ADAPTATIONS of Dion Boucicault plays, *The Lily of Killarney* (1922), and *The Colleen Bawn* (1924). The 30s saw the production of musical comedies including *Irish for Luck* (1936) and *The Rose of Tralee* (1937), and a significant War of Independence drama, *Ourselves Alone* (1936), directed by Irish-born Brian Desmond HURST. Robert FLAHERTY's classic DOCUMENTARY, *Man of Aran*, was filmed in the West of Ireland in 1934.

In the post-Independence years, British films suffered official and unofficial CENSORSHIP in Ireland. The jingoism of historical films such as *The Private Life of Henry VIII* (1933), passed the Free State's Censorship of Films Act (1923), but were occasionally interrupted by riots or protests: a print of Alfred HITCHCOCK's Sean O'Casey adaptation, *Juno and the Paycock* (1930), was seized and publicly burned by nationalists. Official censorship, perceiving some British films as 'immoral', banned, for example, *Brief Encounter*, in 1945. During WW2, Ireland's neutrality heightened the separatist attitude to Britain – many NEWSREEL and PROPAGANDA films were banned. *I See a Dark Stranger* (1946) and *Night Boat to Dublin* (1947) dramatised Ireland's neutrality.

Irish actors such as Jimmy O'DEA and Barry FITZGERALD found continuous work in British films featuring the 'Oirish' character. The popular 'Old Mother Riley' cycle featured Irish actors Arthur LUCAN and Kitty McSHANE.

When, in 1958, the Irish government established Ardmore Studios, policy on indigenous film-making was quickly scrapped in favour of British (and American) productions. These included Paul ROTHA's *No Resting Place* (1951), *The Quare Fellow* (1962), an adaptation of Brendan Behan's play. British films dealing with political VIOLENCE have been criticised for misappropriating issues relating to Anglo-Irish history and politics through a simplified humanist perspective. Thus, James MASON's IRA man, Johnny, in *Odd Man Out* (1947), or John MILLS's Terence in *The Gentle Gunman* (1952), find redemption in their realisation of the inhumanity of their actions. However, recent films by Irish film-makers – Pat O'CONNOR's *Cal* (1984), Neil JORDAN's *Angel* (1982, Ire), and Thaddeus O'SULLIVAN's *Nothing Personal* (1995, UK/Ire) – have been criticised for taking the same path. Irish subject matter continues to feature in British mainstream films. Working-class REALISM has been reworked in *The Commitments* (1991, UK/US), *The Snapper* (1993), and *The Van* (1996, UK/Ire), all based on books by Dubliner Roddy DOYLE, and gangster movies in John BOORMAN's film on Dublin underworld criminal, Martin Cahill, *The General* (1998, UK/US). Boorman's 2001 feature, *The Tailor of Panama* (Ire/US), starring Pierce BROSNAN, was also shot in Ireland.

The BBC, CHANNEL 4, and the BFI have continued to provide support for challenging Irish films like Joe Comerford's *Down the Corner* (1977, UK/Ire) and *Traveller* (1981, Ire), Thaddeus O'Sullivan's *December Bride* (1990, Ire) and Paddy Breathnach's *I Went Down* (1998, UK/Ire/Sp). Eugene Finn.

Ireland, Anthony (*b* Peru, 1902 – *d* London, 1957). Actor. Cheltenham-educated six-footer, on stage from 1925 in US and UK, in RAF intelligence in WW2, and seen in character roles in films, mainly in the 30s. He was, for instance, a stereotyped untrustworthy and amorous foreigner in *Sweet Devil* (1938).
OTHER BRITISH FILMS INCLUDE: *Big Business* (1930), *These Charming People* (1931), *The Water Gipsies* (1932), *White Ensign* (1934), *The Three Maxims, Juggernaut* (1936), *Just Like a Woman* (1938), *The Prime Minister* (1941), *The Gambler and the Lady* (1952), *I Accuse* (1957).

Ireland, Jill (*b* Hounslow, 1936 – *d* Malibu, California, 1990). Actress. Trained as a dancer, on stage at 12, in films first as dancer in *Oh, Rosalinda!!* (1955), this fragile-looking blonde had about 15 roles in British films of the 50s and early 60s, including a few female leads, as in *Robbery Under Arms* (1957). Then came 'B' FILMS such as *The Desperate Man* (1959), as a village reporter, and *Jungle Street* (1961), as a stripper who tangles with a thief played by David MCCALLUM, who became her first husband (1957–67), and with whom she co-starred in several episodes of TV's *The Man from Uncle*. Relocated to America, was married to Charles Bronson from 1964 until her death from cancer, and rarely appeared in films without him.
OTHER BRITISH FILMS INCLUDE: *Simon and Laura* (1955), *Three Men in a Boat* (1956), *Hell Drivers* (1957), *Carry On Nurse* (1958), *So Evil, So Young, Raising the Wind* (1961), *The Battleaxe* (1962).
BIBLIOG: Autobiographies, *Life Wish*, 1987; *Life Lines*, 1989.

Irons, Jeremy (*b* St Helens, Isle of Wight, 1948). Actor, director. Tall elegant actor, sometimes thought of as a thinking woman's sex symbol, for his lean good looks, air of faintly brooding melancholy and eloquent articulation. In spite of all this, the Sherborne-educated star is in fact a considerable actor, a fact which became clear in his early 80s, BAA-nominated pair: as the lovelorn Charles Ryder in TV's *Brideshead Revisited* (1981) and *The French Lieutenant's Woman* (1981), in a – sort of – dual role. Trained at the Bristol Old Vic Drama School, he made his London stage debut as John the Baptist in *Godspell* (1973) and has continued to do highly regarded theatre work, such as his Tony-winning role in *The Real Thing* (1984) and a languid, finally moving *Richard II* (1986) at Stratford.

His first film was *Nijinsky* (1980, UK/US), as Fokine, and his subsequent film work suggests an actor who chooses his roles sparingly. He was a convincing Polish labourer stranded in London in *Moonlighting* (1982), an adulterous lover in the film version of Pinter's *Betrayal* (1982), a courageous missionary, admittedly upstaged by the music, in *The Mission* (1985), the hapless star of the amateur light opera company in *A Chorus of Disappproval* (1989), and the wretched husband and father in *Damage* (1992, UK/Fr). In Australia, bizarrely, he played in a version of *The Wild Duck* (1983); in the US, he won an Oscar as

Claus von Bülow in *Reversal of Fortune* (1990), was a pair of insane twin gynaecologists in *Dead Ringers* (1988, Can), the voice of Scar in *The Lion King* (1994), the obligatory well-spoken Brit villain in *Die Hard: With a Vengeance* (1995), and a finely touching Humbert in the remake of *Lolita* (1997). Married (2, in 1978) to Sinead CUSACK, he acted with their son Sam Irons and his father-in-law, Cyril CUSACK, in the charming telemovie, *Danny, the Champion of the World* (1989). He is a major cinema figure of the last two decades.
OTHER BRITISH FILMS: *Waterland* (1992), *Stealing Beauty* (1996, UK/Fr/It), *The Man in the Iron Mask* (1998, UK/US), *Faeries* (1999, anim, voice), *The Fourth Angel* (2001).

Irvin, John (*b* Newcastle, 1940). Director. Came to films via SHORTS in the early 60s, directed some quality TV, including the intelligent drama of mid-life crisis, *The Nearly Man* (1974) and a rigorous version of *Hard Times* (1977), and began feature-filming with *The Dogs at War* (1980). *Turtle Diary* (1985) was an engaging animal-rights comedy-drama, and a vehicle for charismatic stars, *Shiner* (2001) features Michael CAINE and some gruelling VIOLENCE, but *A Month by the Lake* (1995, UK/US) was a totally inert piece of pictorialism, devoid of interest. Also works in the US (e.g. *Hamburger Hill*, 1987); at best, a director worth noting.
OTHER BRITISH FILMS INCLUDE: (d) (shorts) *Inheritance* (+ sc), *Gala Day* + sc) (1963), *Bedtime* (1967), *Bismarck* (1975); (features) *Champions* (1983), *Widow's Peak* (1994, UK/US), *The Fourth Angel* (2001).

Irving, Ellis (*b* Sydney, 1902 – *d*?). Actor. On stage in Tasmania in 1923, he came to London in 1930 after theatrical experience in Australia, to which he several times returned on tour, in 1954 with wife Sophie STEWART in *Dear Charles*. Essentially a stage actor, he made about 20 films, including a half-dozen in Hollywood in 1940. He is the gentleman-crook hero of *Black Mask* (1935), but most of his film roles are small, like the auctioneer who sells Phyllis CALVERT's farm in *The Root of All Evil* (1947).
OTHER BRITISH FILMS INCLUDE: *The Bermondsey Kid* (1933), *Murder at Monte Carlo* (1935), *As You Like It* (1936), *Went the Day Well?* (1942), *Strawberry Roan, Murder in Reverse* (1945), *Green Fingers* (1947), *Rough Shoot* (1953), *Strictly Confidential* (1959).

Irving, Ernest (*b* Godalming, 1878 – *d* London, 1953). Music director, composer. Musical director for many London theatres from Edwardian era onwards, who also composed incidental music for many plays. Entered film industry in 1930 as Music Director with ASSOCIATED TALKING PICTURES, on such films as *Escape* (1930), becoming Music Director at EALING 1934, a position he held into the 1950s. Irving also composed scores or songs for about ten films, starting with *Saloon Bar* (1940).
OTHER BRITISH FILMS INCLUDE: (m d) *Java Head* (1934), *Midshipman Easy* (1935), *Laburnum Grove* (1936), *The Gaunt Stranger* (1938), *Young Man's Fancy* (1939), *The Proud Valley* (1940), *The Next of Kin, Went the Day Well?* (1942), *The Halfway House* (1944), *Pink String and Sealing Wax* (1945), *Frieda, It Always Rains on Sunday* (1947), *Saraband for Dead Lovers, Scott of the Antarctic* (1948), *Passport to Pimlico, The Blue Lamp* (1949), *The Man in the White Suit* (1951), *Mandy* (1952), *The Cruel Sea* (1953); (comp) *The Ghost of St Michael's, The Black Sheep of Whitehall* (1941), *The Great Mr Handel, The Goose Steps Out* (1942), *My Learned Friend* (1943), *Champagne Charlie* (1944), *Whisky Galore!, A Run for Your Money* (1949), *Bitter Springs* (1950). AS.

Irving, Laurence (*b* London, 1897 – *d* London, 1988). Production designer. Grandson of actor Sir Henry Irving, he went to Hollywood in the late 20s to work on *The Iron Mask* (1929), returned to England in the 30s and designed a half-dozen films. The notable ones are *Pygmalion* (1938), vividly evoking a cross-class range of settings, including a lavish ballroom, and *Uncle Silas* (1947, + p), in which his design is a key element in a gothic near-masterpiece. Also an exhibited artist, a book illustrator (especially of sea voyages), his grandfather's biographer, and a distinguished stage designer. Served in RAF in both World Wars, receiving the Croix de Guerre, 1916, and the OBE (military) in 1944.

OTHER BRITISH FILMS: *77 Park Lane* (1931), *Diamond Cut Diamond* (1932), *Colonel Blood* (1933, co-des), *Moonlight Sonata* (1937).

Irwin, John (*b* Dublin). Producer, director. Former actor who had a brief career in British films, directing two features for RANK's HIGHBURY STUDIOS experiment, one of them the modestly pleasing *Badger's Green*, the other, the totally inane fantasy, *A Piece of Cake* (1948). After that, he made five SHORT FILMS, several of them starring Peter BUTTERWORTH, as a mechanic, funfair operator, etc. In TV, he edited and produced *Kaleidescope* (1946–53), a popular BBC magazine programme, and in 1961 he produced *First World War*, a series written by A.J.P. Taylor.

OTHER BRITISH FILMS: (shorts) *Mr Marionette* (1949), *Five O'Clock Finish*, *Black in the Face* (1954), *Playground Express*, *That's an Order* (1955).

Isaacs, Jason (*b* Liverpool, 1963). Actor. Graduated in law from Bristol University but switched to acting and attended London's Central School. Made his film debut in Mel Smith's *The Tall Guy* (1989), then appeared in a variety of TV and stage roles before landing the role of scientist Quincy in *Armageddon* (1998, US). Has ranged from market trader in *Shopping* (1994) to vicious IRA thug in *Divorcing Jack* (1998, UK/Fr) to priest in *The End of the Affair* (1999, UK/Ger/US). With his steely blue eyes and commanding voice he was particularly convincing as the evil Colonel Tavington in *The Patriot* (2000, US), further demonstrating his versatility in *Sweet November* (2001, US) by appearing as a drag queen.

OTHER BRITISH FILMS: *Solitaire for Two* (1995), *The Last Minute* (2001, UK/US). Anne-Marie Thomas.

Isaacs, Sir Jeremy (*b* Glasgow, 1932). Administrator. Heaped with honours for his services to arts which have to date not included cinema. He has received BAFTA and BFI Fellowships (1984, 1986) and his contributions to British TV have included production of current affairs programmes for Granada Television, from 1958, of the BBC documentary *The World at War* (1975), and serving as first executive of CHANNEL 4 (1981–87). Became general director of the Royal Opera House in 1988 and was knighted in 1996.

Isherwood, Christopher (*b* Disley, Cheshire, 1904 – *d* Los Angeles, 1986). Author, screenwriter. Novelist and playwright who became a US citizen in 1946. He co-authored the sensitive and, for its time, quite daring divorce drama, *Little Friend* (1934); the film *I Am a Camera* (1955) traces its origins back to his Berlin stories, as does the musical version, *Cabaret* (1972, US); and he co-authored Tony RICHARDSON's *The Sailor of Gibraltar* (1967). Also wrote several Hollywood screenplays, including that for Richardson's *The Loved One* (1965).

Isleworth Studios Having purchased the Worton Hall estate in 1914, G.B. SAMUELSON commenced production with the first screen appearance of SHERLOCK HOLMES in *A Study In Scarlet*, directed by George PEARSON. The studios were enlarged in 1916 and also leased out, in part, to other companies, achieving a reputation for high-quality films until being taken over by GENERAL FILM RENTING CO. in 1920 who sold to British Screen Productions in 1928. During the 30s Isleworth was leased to various companies making 'QUOTA QUICKIES' for clients such as UNITED ARTISTS. In 1934 Alexander KORDA leased the studios and there followed a complex deal with Douglas Fairbanks Snr and FAIRBANKS Jr, who was to star in *Catherine the Great* and produce films. In 1935 Rene Clair made *The Ghost Goes West* there with Robert DONAT. The studios were closed in 1939 and reopened in 1944 by new owners, BRITISH LION FILM CORPORATION. In 1946/7 KORDA bought controlling shares in the company, which also operated SHEPPERTON STUDIOS. In 1949 Richard BURTON made his debut there in *The Last Days Of Dolwyn* and some scenes from *The Fallen Idol* (1948) and *The African Queen* (1951) were also shot at ISLEWORTH. Financial difficulties curtailed production in 1951 and the studio was sold to the National Coal Board in 1952.

BIBLIOG: Patricia Warren. *British Film Studios – An Illustrated History*, 2001. Patricia Warren.

Islington Studios In 1919 American Famous Players–Lasky Company founded the Famous Players–Lasky British Producers Ltd, at Islington. Early productions in 1920 directed by American Hugh Ford, were *The Great Day* and *The Call Of Youth* starring Ben WEBSTER. In 1924 the studios were sold to Michael Balcon and his associates and in the same year GAINSBOROUGH PICTURES was formed with director Graham CUTTS. In 1926 Alfred HITCHCOCK, who had worked as Cutts's assistant, directed *The Lodger*, followed by *Downhill* and *Easy Virtue*. In 1928 Gainsborough was absorbed into GAUMONT–BRITISH PICTURE CORPORATION, a conglomerate which owned SHEPHERD'S BUSH STUDIO, and Gainsborough productions were then made at both studios. In the 30s, directors Walter FORDE and Victor SAVILLE came to the fore and Islington films starred Jessie MATTHEWS, Cedric HARDWICKE, John MILLS, Boris KARLOFF and comedian Will HAY. Balcon left Gaumont–British in 1936 and producer Edward BLACK reorganised the studio. Financial disaster struck Islington in 1937 and C.M. WOOLF and J. Arthur RANK announced a complicated rescue package, further helped by 20TH CENTURY–FOX who decided to make films there until the outbreak of war in 1939. Islington was reopened shortly after the war by the J. ARTHUR RANK ORGANISATION which acquired full control and in 1946 Sydney BOX became head of production for Islington and Shepherd's Bush. Post-war productions included *Miranda* and *Here Come The Huggetts* (1948). The crisis in the Rank film empire in the late 40s necessitated the sale of the studios in 1949. In June, 1999 the *Times* stated that part of the site was being redeveloped for 'film-making', but in 2000 it was used for the Almeida Theatre productions, *Richard II* and *Coriolanus*, both starring Ralph FIENNES.

BIBLIOG: Patricia Warren. *British Film Studios – An Illustrated History*, 2001. Patricia Warren.

Ives, Douglas (*b* Sheffield, 1909 – *d* London, 1969). Actor. Supporting player of small roles in 50s and early 60s comedies, such as *Doctor in the House* (1954) and *Carry On Regardless* (1961), as a mad patient, and dramas like *Miracle in Soho* (1957) and, as a farmer involved with thieves, in *The Big Chance* (1957). TV from 1952.

OTHER BRITISH FILMS INCLUDE: *Brandy for the Parson* (1952), *Innocents in Paris* (1953), *Out of the Clouds* (1955), *Left, Right and Centre* (1959), *Raising the Wind* (1961), *Live It Up* (1963), *Be My Guest* (1965).

Ivory, James (*b* Berkeley, California, 1928). Director. American film-maker long associated with producer Ismail MERCHANT with whom he began making India-set films in the 60s and 70s, including the masterpiece *Autobiography of a Princess* (1975) and a subtle version of Henry JAMES's *The Europeans* (1979). There were some endearingly idiosyncratic pieces like *Jane Austen in Manhattan* (1980, UK/US), enshrining a great star performance from Anne Baxter; then in 1985 the team had a major box-office success with *A Room with a View*, following this with further ADAPTATIONS of E.M. FORSTER and James, but in the 90s Ivory fell somewhat out of critical favour with failures such as *Jefferson in Paris* (1995) and *Surviving Picasso* (1996, UK/US). However, there were still cherishable performances to be had from Anthony HOPKINS and Vanessa REDGRAVE in *Howards End* (1992) and from Hopkins, Emma THOMPSON and James FOX in *The Remains of the Day* (1993), and in 2000 he returned to James with *The Golden Bowl* (UK/Fr/US), making an intelligent stab at a very difficult, late work. His attention to details of period and place has always been impeccable. Among his US films, *Mr & Mrs Bridge* (1990), is a beautifully played account of a marriage.

OTHER BRITISH FILMS: *Adventures of a Brown Man in Search of Civilisation* (1971), *Hullabaloo Over Georgie and Bonnie's Pictures* (1978, UK/Ind, TV, some cinemas), *Quartet* (1981), *Heat and Dust, The Courtesan of Bombay* (co-devisor) (1982), *The Bostonians* (1984, UK/US), *Maurice* (1987), *A Soldier's Daughter Never Cries* (1998, UK/US, + co-sc).

See also **Merchant Ivory**.

Izzard, Eddie (*b* Aden, Yemen, 1962). Actor. Emmy-winner for his solo TV show, *Eddie Izzard: Dress to Kill* (1998), famous as a stand-up comedian for his scathing social comment and for his transvestism, Izzard only began in the late 90s what promises to be a very productive screen career. He was a member of the anarchists' group in *The Secret Agent* (1996, UK/US), a manipulative manager in *Velvet Goldmine* (1998), and is now in demand on both sides of the Atlantic, playing Charlie CHAPLIN in *The Cat's Meow* (2002, UK/Can/Ger).

OTHER BRITISH FILMS INCLUDE: *Circus* (UK/US), *The Criminal* (UK/US) (2000), *Shadow of the Vampire* (2001, UK/Lux/US), *A Revenger's Tragedy* (2002).

Jj

J.H. Productions In 1935, Julius HAGEN bought WHITEHALL STUDIOS at ELSTREE, and set up J.H. Productions to provide a 'quality' complement to the 'QUOTA QUICKIES' he had produced at TWICKENHAM. However, he was not commercially successful with more ambitious productions, including *Broken Blossoms* (1936), and in 1937 the company was in receivership. It had experienced difficulties in getting satisfactory UK releases and had none in the US.

BIBLIOG: Linda Wood, 'Julius Hagen and Twickenham Film Studios', in *The Unknown 30s*, 1998.

Jack the Ripper The notorious killer of five prostitutes in London's East End in 1888 quickly became the source of penny-dreadful narratives, though the puzzle of his identity was not 'solved' until Robert S. BAKER and Monty BERMAN's *Jack the Ripper* (1958). Previously Ivor NOVELLO was suspected of being a Ripper-like killer in Alfred HITCHCOCK's *The Lodger* (1926) and again in Maurice ELVEY's REMAKE (1932). SHERLOCK HOLMES has twice unmasked the Ripper, in *A Study in Terror* (1965) and *Murder By Decree* (1978, UK/Can), with different resolutions on each occasion.

OTHER BRITISH FILMS: *Hands of the Ripper* (1971), *Jack the Ripper* (1988), *From Hell* (2001, UK/US). James Chapman.

Jackley, Nat (*b* Sunderland, Lancs, 1909 – *d* London, 1988). Actor. Former MUSIC HALL comic, part of a travelling troupe as a child and on stage from 1931. Appeared in occasional films from 1944 (the variety comedy, *Demobbed*), and turned up decades later in character roles in *Yanks* (1979) and *Ploughman's Lunch* (1983). On TV he starred in *Nat's in the Belfry* (1956), two specials, co-written by his wife Marianne Lincoln, and played Snout in the BBC's *Midsummer Night's Dream* (1981).

OTHER BRITISH FILMS: *Under New Management* (1946), *Stars in Your Eyes* (1956), *Magical Mystery Tour* (1967), *Mrs Brown, You've Got a Lovely Daughter* (1968).

Jackson, Barry (*b* Birmingham, 1938). Actor. Strong supporting player who had a continuing role as Dr Bullard in *Midsomer Murders* (1997) and character roles in a dozen or more films, including *Alfred the Great* (1969), but generally better chances on TV and stage, playing in *Peace in Our Time* at the Royal Court.

OTHER BRITISH FILMS INCLUDE: *Girl on the Roof* (1961), *Strangler's Web* (1966), *The Bofors Gun* (1968), *Ryan's Daughter*, *The Raging Moon* (1970), *Barry Lyndon* (1975), *Aces High* (1976, UK/Fr), *The Shooting Party* (1984), *Mr Love* (1985).

Jackson, Freda (*b* Nottingham, 1909 – *d* Northamptonshire, 1990). Actress. The great harridan of British cinema, unforgettably bullying young Pip in *Great Expectations* (1946) as hatchet-faced Mrs Joe. Indeed, she was generally giving someone a bad time, whether as the vicious proprietress of a home for evacuees in *No Room at the Inn* (1948, repeating her stage success), or exploiter of 'fallen' women in *Women of Twilight* (1952) and *The Flesh Is Weak* (1957), or 'The Vengeance', relishing mass executions, in *A Tale of Two Cities* (1958), and – the bizarre leading the macabre – Martita HUNT's servant in *The Brides of Dracula* (1960), but she was merely butch in *A Canterbury Tale* (1944) and somewhat muted as Mistress Quickly in *Henry V* (1944). Educated at Nottingham University College and on stage from 1934, she had a long and distinguished theatrical career, with seasons at Stratford (*The Taming of the Shrew*, 1940–41) and the Old Vic (custom-built for Goneril in *King Lear*, 1952).

OTHER BRITISH FILMS INCLUDE: *Mountains o' Mourne* (1938), *Beware of Pity* (1946), *Flesh and Blood* (1951), *The Good Die Young* (1954), *Bhowani Junction* (1955, UK/US), *The Last Man to Hang?* (1956), *Greyfriars Bobby* (1961), *Tom Jones* (1963), *The Third Secret* (1964), *The Jokers* (1966), *The Clash of the Titans* (1981, UK/US).

Jackson, Glenda (*b* Birkenhead, 1936). Actress. The screen's loss was politics' gain when dominant actress Jackson successfully stood as Labour MP for Hampstead and Highgate in 1992, and has not filmed since, giving herself whole-heartedly to her political responsibilities. A bricklayer's daughter, early determined on an acting career, she trained at RADA and first appeared on stage in 1957, her big chance coming in 1964 when Peter BROOK cast her as assassin Charlotte Corday in his Theatre of Cruelty production *The Marat/Sade . . .*, transferred to the screen in 1966. She would continue to appear on the stage, notably, for the RSC, as Ophelia in Peter HALL's *Hamlet* (1965), as Hedda Gabler (1975, filmed as *Hedda*, 1975) and, to mixed reception, with Alan HOWARD in *Antony and Cleopatra* (1978).

She can be spotted sitting on a piano in a party scene in *This Sporting Life* (1963), but, apart from the RSC transfers, her film career really began with her magisterial Oscar-winning Gudrun in Ken RUSSELL's daring adaptation of *Women in Love* (1969). Her blazing intelligence, sexual challenge and abrasiveness were at the service of a superbly written role in a film with a passion rare in the annals of British cinema. She came to films just as the bottom was falling out of the domestic industry which makes more remarkable the roles she *did* get: she vies, with painful conviction (and for a BAA), for a share of Murray HEAD's affections in *Sunday Bloody Sunday* (1971); is perhaps the screen's greatest Elizabeth I, charismatic and commanding, both in *Mary Queen of Scots* (1971) and TV's *Elizabeth R* (1971); a sensual, whorish Emma Hamilton (making Vivien LEIGH's seem like a debutante) in *Bequest to the Nation* (1973); a sardonic Sister Alexandra in *Nasty Habits* (1976); a tautly moving figure as *Stevie* [Smith] (1978); very affecting as the dowdy housewife whose life is disrupted by *The Return of the Soldier* (1982). Virtually everything is worth noting, including her second Oscar role in *A Touch of Class* (1972), though comedy is not her forté, the title role in *The Patricia Neal Story* (1981, TV, some cinemas) and other TV including *A Murder of Quality* (1991). Perhaps not since the heyday of Googie WITHERS was there so potent a British screen actress. Awarded CBE, 1978. Was married (1958–76) to former stage actor and designer, Roy Hodges. Stood unsuccessfully for Mayor of London in 2000.

OTHER BRITISH FILMS: *Benefit of the Doubt* (1965), *Tell Me Lies* (1967), *Negatives* (1968), *The Music Lovers* (1970), *The Boy Friend* (1971), *The Triple Echo* (1972), *The Maids* (1974, UK/Can), *The Romantic English-woman* (UK/Fr), *The Tempter* (UK/It) (1975), *The Incredible Sarah* (1976, UK/US), *The Class of Miss MacMichael* (1978), *Lost and Found* (1979), *Giro City* (1982, TV, some cinemas), *Turtle Diary* (1985), *Business as Usual* (1987), *The Rainbow* (1989), *Doombeach, King of the Wind* (1989).

BIBLIOG: Ian Woodward, *Glenda Jackson: A Study in Fire and Ice*, 1985.

Jackson, Gordon (*b* Glasgow, 1923 – *d* London, 1990). Actor. Educated in Glasgow and trained as a draughtsman, sandy-haired Scots character player Jackson worked steadily in British films for nearly 50 years, probably without ever giving a poor performance. After stage and radio experience in Scotland, he made his London theatrical debut in 1951, but was essentially a film actor, though, arguably, his greatest fame came with his Emmy-winning role as butler Hudson in TV's *Upstairs, Downstairs* (1971–75). He always regarded his time at EALING in the 40s as the highlight of his film career, and his unaffected naturalness before the cameras resulted in memorable performances in such films as *San Demetrio–London* (1943), *Pink String and Sealing Wax* (1945) as the young man swayed by a seductive Googie WITHERS, and as the mother-ridden George Campbell in *Whisky Galore!* (1949). An unassuming man, regarding himself as merely 'a Scots type', he did whatever was offered and from the early 50s that included 'B' FILMS, such as *Windfall* (1955), as well as a continuing stream of supporting roles in major films, including two beautifully judged studies in friendship: in *Tunes of Glory* (1960) and, as a superb Horatio in specs, to Nicol WILLIAMSON's *Hamlet* (1969), repeating his stage role. Married to Rona ANDERSON from 1951. Received OBE in 1979.

OTHER BRITISH FILMS INCLUDE: *One of Our Aircraft is Missing, The Foreman Went to France, Nine Men* (1942), *Millions Like Us* (1943), *The Captive Heart* (1946), *Against the Wind* (1947), *Floodtide, Eureka Stockade* (1949), *Bitter Springs* (1950), *Castle in the Air* (1952), *Meet Mr Lucifer* (1953), *The Quatermass Experiment, Passage Home* (1955), *Sailor Beware, Pacific Destiny, The Baby and the Battleship* (1956), *Hell Drivers* (1957), *Rockets Galore, Blind Spot* (1958), *Yesterday's Enemy, Devil's Bait, The Bridal Path, Blind Date* (1959), *Snowball, Cone of Silence* (1960), *Greyfriars Bobby* (1961), *Those Magnificent Men . . . , The Ipcress File* (1965), *Triple Cross* (1966, UK/Fr/Ger), *The Prime of Miss Jean Brodie* (1968), *Run Wild, Run Free* (1969), *Scrooge* (1970), *Kidnapped* (1971), *Madame Sin* (1972), *The Shooting Party* (1984), *The Whistle Blower* (1986).

Jackson, Louis H. (*b* London, 1904 – *d* ?). Producer. Chairman and governing director of Anglo-American Film Corporation (1939–46) and executive producer for BRITISH NATIONAL FILMS from 1944 to 1948. During this time, apart from some dire Paul STEIN MUSICALS (e.g. *Lisbon Story*, 1946), he produced several films of more than passing interest, including two THRILLERS with William HARTNELL, *Murder in Reverse*

(1945) and *Appointment with Crime* (1946), Vernon SEWELL's long-lost Grand Guignol, *Latin Quarter* (1945), Montgomery TULLY's costume romance, *Mrs Fitzherbert* (1947), and Daniel BIRT's all-stops-out melodrama, *The Three Weird Sisters* (1948). His is a busy *cv* worth investigating.

OTHER BRITISH FILMS INCLUDE: *A Medal for the General* (1944), *Strawberry Roan, Waltz Time, The Echo Murders, The World Owes Me a Living, The Trojan Brothers* (1945), *Meet the Navy, Laughing Lady* (1946), *Dual Alibi, Green Fingers, The Ghosts of Berkeley Square* (1947), *Uneasy Terms, Counterblast* (1948).

Jackson, Pat (*b* London, 1916). Director. A noted DOCU-MENTARY film-maker, Jackson worked as director and producer for the GPO FILM UNIT and CROWN FILM UNIT from 1934 to 1944. His most influential documentary film was *Western Approaches* (1944), the film which led Alexander KORDA to bring him to MGM and Hollywood. It explored the dangers experienced by the Merchant Navy and was the first major 'story documentary' to use TECHNICOLOR, for which cinematographer Jack CARDIFF was much praised. It was Crown's most prestigious wartime documentary in terms of resources, and was particularly successful in recreating the experiences of sailors adrift on a lifeboat.

Jackson prospered at Crown, alongside talents such as Humphrey JENNINGS, but failed to make a big impression as a feature film director after leaving Crown. He directed several notable films, but four disastrous years in America (1944–48), unable to make any films other than *Shadow on the Wall* (1949) because of contractual obligations, hindered his subsequent career. Back in England Jackson made *White Corridors* (1951, + co-sc), a hospital-set film which combined successfully documentary technique with the fiction film. Its multi-narrative approach provided a model for later films (including his own *The Feminine Touch*, 1956, made for EALING) and TV series set in hospitals. It was followed by ten further features, of which the most important is probably *The Birthday Present* (1957), a downbeat drama about false accusation and the loss of social standing in the face of authority.

OTHER BRITISH FILMS: *Something Money Can't Buy* (1952), *Virgin Island* (1958), *Snowball* (1960), *What a Carve Up!* (1961), *Seven Keys, Don't Talk to Strange Men* (1962), *Seven Deadly Pills* (1964), *Dead End Creek* (1964, 6-part serial).

BIBLIOG: Autobiography, *Retake Please! : Night Mail to Western Approaches*, 1998. Ian Aitken.

Jackson, Philip (*b* Retford, 1948). Actor. Excellent, craggy-faced character player of films and TV who had been around since the mid 70s, but really caught filmgoers' attention with three striking performances in the later 90s: as the sardonic Jim in *Brassed Off* (1996, UK/US), the lubricious telephone repair man in *Little Voice* and the greedy cuckold in *Girls' Night* (1998, UK/US). On TV he has played Inspector Japp in about a dozen ADAPTATIONS of Agatha CHRISTIE's 'Poirot' novels (1988–2001), and has worked for Mike LEIGH on stage and on screen in *High Hopes* (1988), as Edna DORÉ's vilely jocose son-in-law.

OTHER BRITISH FILMS INCLUDE: *Pressure* (1975), *Switch Off* (1977), *Scum* (1979), *Give My Regards to Broad Street* (1984), *The Doctor and the Devils* (1985), *The Fourth Protocol* (1987), *Cousin Bette* (UK/US), *What Rats Won't Do* (1998), *Mike Bassett: England Manager* (2001, UK/US).

Jackson, Ray (*b* 1931 – *d* London, 1989). Actor. In films from 1947 as David FARRAR's brother in *Frieda*, he had his best chance as the poet son of cricketing legend, Jack WARNER, in *The Final Test* (1953), but his film career was finished by the end of the 50s.

OTHER BRITISH FILMS INCLUDE: *Seagulls Over Sorrento* (1954), *Lost* (1955), *Yangtse Incident* (1956), *These Dangerous Years* (1957), *Dunkirk* (1958).

Jacob Street Studios Created in 1984 from an old dog-biscuit factory in Southwark, these studios produced some idiosyncratic pieces such as *Prick Up Your Ears* (1987) and *The Cement Garden* (1993), as well as the mainstream 'Highlander' films (1986, 1990, 1994) and commercials and TV productions, but by 2000 the studios which once had seven sound stages were no longer listed in the BFI's *Film and Television Handbook*.

Jacobi, Sir Derek (*b* Leytonstone, 1938). Actor. Blue-eyed, leonine-featured actor with a precise baritone voice, who quietly channels his emotions into often-tortured roles. Homosexuals feature widely in his repertoire of such characters, including Guy Burgess in *Philby, Burgess and Maclean* (TV, 1977), Alan Turing in stage (first 1986) and television (1996) productions of *Breaking the Code*, and painter Francis Bacon in *Love is the Devil* (1998, UK/Fr/Jap). Also played Hitler in the ABC television production of *Inside the Third Reich* (1982), but audiences seem to prefer him in gentler roles, such as the title character in TV's *I, Claudius* (1976), as Arthur Clennam in *Little Dorrit* (1987) and the priest *Cadfael* (first seen on TV in 1994). Began career at Birmingham Rep in 1960, was seen by Laurence OLIVIER and asked to join National Theatre Company in 1963, and was a prominent member of the Actors' Company in the early 70s. Despite performances in 1982 television version of *The Hunchback of Notre Dame*, and the films *Dead Again* (1991, US/UK) and *Gladiator* (2000, US/UK), Jacobi has not made a strong mark in UK cinema, and remains committed to the stage. Knighted 1994.

OTHER BRITISH FILMS: *Othello* (1965), *Interlude* (1968), *Blue Blood, The Odessa File* (UK/Ger) (1974), *The Medusa Touch* (1978, UK/Fr), *The Human Factor* (1979), *Henry V* (1989), *The Fool* (1990), *Hamlet* (1996, UK/US), *Gosford Park* (UK/Ger/US), *Revelation, A Revenger's Tragedy* (2002). AS.

Jacques, Hattie (*b* Sandgate, 1922 – *d* London, 1980). Actress. Monumental star of the 'CARRY ON' SERIES, usually cast as formidable hospital matrons (at least four) or man-devouring predators whose affections were apt to strike terror in weak-kneed men, and she strikes an engagingly exotic note as Floella in *Carry On Abroad* (1972). On stage since 1944, often in pantomimes and revues, and on radio in *ITMA* (1948–49) and *Educating Archie* (1950–54), she was on screen for over a decade before she began to 'carry on'. She can be spotted singing in the thieves' pub in *Oliver Twist* (1948), does a music hall turn with Bill OWEN and Jean KENT in *Trottie True* (1948), but, as with the rest of the 'Carry On' team, once she established her persona in the series it was hard to think of her as anything else. She also had a notable TV career, especially as twin sister of the eponymous *Sykes* (1960–65, 1971–79). Married and divorced (1949–65) actor John LE MESURIER.

OTHER BRITISH FILMS INCLUDE: *Green for Danger* (1946), *Nicholas Nickleby* (1947), *Chance of a Lifetime* (1950), *Scrooge* (1951), *The Pickwick Papers, The Pleasure Garden* (1952), *Up to His Neck* (1954), *The Square Peg, Carry On Sergeant, . . . Nurse* (1958), *. . . Teacher, The Night We Dropped a Clanger* (1959), *Watch Your Stern, Make Mine Mink, Carry On Constable* (1960), *. . . On Regardless* (1961), *The Punch and Judy Man* (1962), *Carry On Cabby* (1963), *The Bobo* (1967), *Carry On Doctor* (1968), *Monte Carlo or Bust!* (UK/It/Fr), *Carry On Camping, . . . Again Doctor* (1969), *Carry On Loving* (1970), *. . . at Your Convenience* (1971), *. . . Matron* (1972), *. . . Dick* (1974), *That's Carry On* (1977).

Jaeger, Frederick (*b* Berlin, 1928). Actor. Character player of brisk, military mien, whether as the German major in *The Passage* (1978) or as Colonel Melchett in TV's *The Body in the Library* (1984). In England since 1939 and on stage from 1949. Also in international films, including *Scorpio* (1973) and *Nijinsky* (1980, UK/US).

OTHER BRITISH FILMS INCLUDE: *The Black Tent* (1956), *The One That Got Away* (1957), *I Was Monty's Double* (1958), *Mystery Submarine* (1962), *The Looking Glass War* (1969), *Voyage of the Damned* (1976), *Cold Comfort Farm* (1995, TV, some cinemas).

Jaffé, Carl (*b* Hamburg, 1902 – *d* London, 1974). Actor. An authoritative presence, Jaffé, a Jewish refugee from Nazi Germany, portrayed scientists (*First Man Into Space*, 1959), aristocrats (*The Roman Spring Of Mrs Stone*, 1961), and, like many German exiles, a fair share of Nazi officers (*Appointment in London*, 1953) and Eastern European villains. During the war, Jaffé worked as a German newsreader for the BBC.

OTHER BRITISH FILMS INCLUDE: *Over the Moon, The Saint In London* (US/UK), *The Lion Has Wings* (1939), *Gasbags* (1940), *Squadron Leader X* (1942), *The Life And Death Of Colonel Blimp, The Night Invader* (1943), *Two Thousand Women* (1944), *The Man From Morocco* (1945), *The Dancing Years* (1948), *State Secret* (1950), *Lilli Marlene* (1950), *Desperate Moment* (1953), *Cross Channel* (1955), *The Traitor* (1957), *The Battle of the V-1, Operation Amsterdam* (1958), *The Double Man* (1967). Tim Bergfelder.

Jaffrey, Madhur (*b* Delhi, 1933). Actress, screenwriter. RN: Madhur Bahadur. RADA-trained actress, almost as well known for her Indian cookery books and TV series as for her films. She was the Princess in the MERCHANT IVORY masterwork, *Autobiography of a Princess* (1975), the Begum in *Heat and Dust* (1982), having appeared in two of their Indian films, *Shakespeare Wallah* (1965) and *The Guru* (1969), and Deborah KERR's homesick Surrey neighbour in *The Assam Garden* (1985). Also in international films, including *Vanya on 42nd Street* (1994). Married (1) Saeed JAFFREY (divorced 1969); (2) violinist Sanford Allen.

OTHER BRITISH FILMS INCLUDE: *Cotton Mary* (1999, UK/Fr/US).

Jaffrey, Saeed (*b* Maler Kotla, India, 1929). Actor, screenwriter. Prolific player in British and international films, trained at RADA and with experience at London's National Theatre. He has given ebullient performances in such high-profile British films as *A Passage to India* (1984) and *My Beautiful Laundrette* (1985), for which he received a BAAn, and TV as *Staying On* (1979) and *The Jewel in the Crown* (1984), and was in such US films as *The Razor's Edge* (1984) and many Indian films. Awarded OBE, 1995. Divorced (1969) Madhur JAFFREY.

OTHER BRITISH FILMS INCLUDE: *The Wilby Conspiracy* (1974), *Hullabaloo over Georgie and Bonnie's Pictures* (1978, UK/Ind), *Once Again* (1979), *Heat and Dust* (Urdu dialogue), *Gandhi* (UK/Ind) (1982), *The Deceivers* (1988), *Second Generation* (2000), *Mr In-Between* (2001).

Jagger, Sir Mick (*b* Dartford, 1943). Singer, actor. Lead singer with The Rolling Stones who, somewhat surprisingly, was still going strong as he neared 60, which is some sort of comment on lifestyle. As a film actor, he is of little consequence except that his particular louche charisma was brilliantly exploited by Nicolas ROEG and Donald CAMMELL in *Performance* (1970), that hymn and epitaph to 60s excess. His *Ned Kelly* (1970) is of interest largely to cultists, and most of his other films have been of the rockumentary type. He has seven children by a range of mothers and his private life has been of continuing interest to the tabloids, even now that he is a grandfather. His own production company is called Jagged Films, and his first feature production, *Enigma* (2001, UK/Ger/US), about Britain's WW2 code-breaking activities, opened to enthusiastic reviews. In 2000, he said he intended an epic on the life of fellow 60s icon, Che Guevara. Knighted in 2002.

OTHER BRITISH FILMS INCLUDE: (a, unless noted) *Charlie Is My Darling* (1965, doc, + m, songs), *Tonite Let's All Make Love in London* (1967, doc), *Sympathy for the Devil* (1968), *The Rolling Stones Rock and Roll Circus* (1996, doc), *Bent* (1997, UK/Jap/US), *Donald Cammell: the Ultimate Performance* (1998, doc).

Jago, June Actress. Protean Australian player who, after antipodean theatrical experience, came to London with the first production of *Summer of the Seventeenth Doll* in 1959 and stayed to perform with many British companies, including the Royal Court and the RSC. Among her half-dozen British films, she had her best role in *Please Turn Over* (1960) as the spinsterish Gladys who gets a more vibrant love life in the film's fantasy scenes. Filmed in Australia in the 80s.

OTHER BRITISH FILMS: *The Captain's Table* (1958), *No Kidding* (1960), *Carry On Regardless* (1961), . . . *Doctor* (1968), *The Games* (1969), *SWALK* (1970).

Jamal, Ahmed Alauddin (*b* Lucknow, India, 1950). Director, screenwriter. Film-maker who went to UK in 1974 where he has explored on film the experiences of Asian (particularly Pakistani) immigrants in the UK, foregrounding cultural differences and racial harassment.

BRITISH FILMS INCLUDE: (d) *Majdhar* (+ sc), *Living in Danger* (1984, doc) *Hotel London* (1987, short, + sc).

James Bond *see* **Bond films**

James, Geraldine (*b* Maidenhead, 1950). Actress. Tall, blonde, intelligent-looking actress who has had her best opportunities on TV – as, for instance, the increasingly stroppy wife of *The History Man* (1981), the independently-minded Sarah in *The Jewel in the Crown* (1984), the niece who helps Peggy ASHCROFT escape from a mental institution in *She's Been Away* (1989, some cinemas). On the big screen, the outback teacher in *No Worries* (1993, UK/Aust) gave her more to do than most of her films.

OTHER BRITISH FILMS INCLUDE: *Bloody Kids* (1979), *Gandhi* (1982, UK/Ind), *The Tall Guy* (1989), *The Bridge* (1991), *The Luzhin Defence* (UK/Fr), *All Forgotten* (UK/US) (2000).

James, Henry (*b* New York, 1843 – *d* Rye, 1916). Author. Magisterial chronicler of the inner life, through processes of novelistic dramatisation, James has generally been extremely fortunate in ADAPTATION. American but long resident in England, much preoccupied with the 'complex fate' of Americans coming to terms with Europe, he was largely neglected, in screen terms, in his native America, apart from William Wyler's *The Heiress* (1949), derived from a Broadway adaptation of *Washington Square*, and the undervalued *Daisy Miller* (1974). The British versions of his work include Jack CLAYTON's wonderfully ambivalent black-and-white nightmare world of *The Innocents* (1961), from *The Turn of the Screw*, the MERCHANT IVORY adaptations of *The Europeans* (1979), *The Bostonians* (1984, UK/US) and *The Golden Bowl* (2000, UK/Fr/US), Jane Campion's uneven *The Portrait of a Lady* (1996, UK/US), and, best of all, Iain SOFTLEY's passionate, rigorously intelligent *The Wings of the Dove* (1997, UK/US). Michael WINNER's *The Nightcomers* (1971) is a sort of vulgar prequel to *The Turn of the Screw*, of which there have been frequent TV adaptations, and there was a fine TV *Portrait of a Lady* (1968).

James, Horace (*b* Trinidad – *d* Trinidad, 2000). Actor. More important on TV, where he was a regular in *Compact* (1964) and collaborated on the scripts for *Rainbow City* (1967), where his insider view of a black man's problems in British society was important to the authenticity of the series. On cinema screens, he was seen in *Guns at Batasi* (1964) and *The Lost Continent* (1968).

James, Oscar (*b* Trinidad). Actor. In the original cast of the TV serial, *EastEnders* (1985–87), though he felt his character was not fully developed, and in Horace OVÉ's *Pressure* (1975), claimed as Britain's first black feature. He had small roles in such US films as *Last Night at the Alamo* (1983) but has not found roles plentiful post-*EastEnders*.

OTHER BRITISH FILMS INCLUDE: *Naked Evil* (1966), *All the Right Noises* (1969), *Gumshoe* (1971), *Black Joy* (1977), *Water* (1985), *Hardware* (1990).

James, Sidney (*b* Johannesburg, 1913 – *d* Sunderland, Tyne-and-Wear, 1976). Actor. RN: Cohen. In Britain from 1946, former ladies' hairdresser James is now best remembered for the incurably lascivious persona he honed to such comic effect in the 'CARRY ON' SERIES, but in fact he had appeared in almost 80 films before appearing as Sergeant Frank Wilkins in the very funny *Carry On Constable* (1960). He had played barmen, as in the notorious *No Orchids for Miss Blandish* and *The Small Back Room*, as Knucksie (1948), taxi drivers (*Father's Doing Fine*, 1952), cops (*Cosh Boy*, 1953) and a deeply incompetent crook in *The Lavender Hill Mob* (1951), and even a country gent in *The Man in Black* (1949). He also famously played Tony HANCOCK's sidekick in TV's *Hancock's Half-Hour* (1956–60), derived from their radio show, but 'Carry On' gradually eclipsed everything in this wildly prolific career. At best homely of mien, with a filthy laugh, ever with an eye to the main chance, sexual or financial or both, he was perhaps the keystone which held the series together. Mostly playing characters called Sid(ney), memorably as Sir Sidney Ruff-Diamond in *Carry On Up the Khyber* (1968), he had his finest hour as Mark Antony in *Carry On Cleo* (1964) and as Johnny Finger, the Rumpo Kid in *Carry On Cowboy* (1965). For his last ten years, he was as much institution as actor. Only well after his death on stage at the Empire, Sunderland, did the darker side of the legend – the gambling, drinking, the broken marriages and the unhappy affair with co-star Barbara WINDSOR – become widely known. In 2000, the National Theatre staged a play which drew on some of this material: *Cleo, Camping, Emmanuelle and Dick.*

OTHER BRITISH FILMS INCLUDE: *It Always Rains on Sunday* (1947), *Once a Jolly Swagman* (1948), *Paper Orchid* (1949), *Last Holiday* (1950), *I Believe in You* (1952), *The Titfield Thunderbolt* (1953), *The House Across the Lake, A Kid for Two Farthings* (1954), *John and Julie, Joe Macbeth* (1955), *Wicked as They Come, The Iron Petticoat* (1956), *Hell Drivers, The Story of Esther Costello* (1957), *The Silent Enemy, The Thirty Nine Steps* (1958), *Make Mine a Million* (1959), *The Pure Hell of St Trinian's* (1960), *Carry On Regardless, What a Carve Up!* (1961), *Carry On Cruising* (1962), . . . *Cabby* (1963), *The Beauty Jungle* (1964), *Three Hats for Lisa, Carry On Cowboy, The Big Job* (1965), *Don't Lose Your Head* (1966), *Carry On Doctor* (1968), . . . *Again Doctor*, . . . *Camping* (1969), . . . *Up the Jungle*, . . . *Loving* (1970), . . . *Henry*, . . . *at Your Convenience* (1971), . . . *Matron*, . . . *Abroad* (1972), . . . *Girls* (1973), . . . *Dick* (1974), *That's Carry On* (1977).

Jameson, Pauline (*b* Heacham, 1920). Actress. RADA-trained, on stage from 1938 and in London from 1942, she was in the company that reopened the Old Vic in 1950, and played many strong women on stage. Her first film role was as a hospital nurse in *Esther Waters* (1948) and she had good roles in such diverse films as *I Could Go On Singing* (1963) and *Murder Most Foul* (1964), without ever quite becoming a recognisable character figure. Most striking as the embittered Mrs Catherick in TV's *The Woman in White* (1978).

OTHER BRITISH FILMS INCLUDE: *The Queen of Spades* (1949), *The Black Knight* (1954), *The Millionairess* (1960), *Crooks Anonymous* (1962), *Doctor in Distress* (1963), *Night Watch* (1973), *Joseph Andrews* (1976).

Janni, Joseph (*b* Milan, 1916 – *d* London, 1994). Producer. In Britain since 1939, after studying at Milan University and Rome Film School. Among Janni's early productions are the operatic *The Glass Mountain* (1949, which he co-wrote), Pat JACKSON's hospital drama *White Corridors* (1951), and an adaptation of Nevil Shute's *A Town Like Alice* (1956). In the 60s he became associated with the NEW WAVE, through a productive partnership with director John SCHLESINGER which lasted, intermittently, until the late 70s, and led to such high-profile films as *Darling* (1965) and *Sunday Bloody Sunday* (1971). As producer, he enjoyed the respect of directors and actors alike.

OTHER BRITISH FILMS INCLUDE: *Romeo and Juliet* (1954), *Robbery Under Arms* (1957), *The Captain's Table* (1959), *A Kind of Loving* (1962), *Billy Liar* (1963), *Modesty Blaise* (1966), *Far from The Madding Crowd* (1967), *Poor Cow* (1967), *In Search Of Gregory* (1969), *Made* (1972), *Yanks* (1979). Tim Bergfelder.

Jardine, Betty (*b* Manchester, 1903 – *d* Bournemouth, 1945). Actress. Strong young actress who died in childbirth, having appeared in nine films. She was a tough land-girl in *A Canterbury Tale* and the traitor who brawls with Jean KENT in *Two Thousand Women* (1944), her last two films.

OTHER BRITISH FILMS INCLUDE: *Almost a Honeymoon* (1938), *The Girl in the News* (1940), *Kipps*, *The Ghost Train* (1941), *We'll Meet Again* (1942), *Rhythm Serenade* (1943).

Jarman, Derek (*b* Northwood, Middlesex, 1942 – *d* London, 1994). Director. Self-described as a painter who made films, Slade-trained Jarman's films and his life were a fight against the mainstream. The productions (often shot in Super 8mm) lack a definable style and are often angry diatribes against a country and society that failed to accept Jarman's homosexuality or cure his AIDS (he was diagnosed HIV-positive in 1986). The ultimate British queer film-maker, Jarman entered the Slade School in 1963, where his interest in theatre design developed, leading to 1967 employment at the Royal Opera House, Covent Garden, and 1970 work as a designer for Ken RUSSELL. He first came to filmgoers' attention with the homoerotic *Sebastiane* (1976), with its frontal nudity and Latin dialogue. The punk-laden *Jubilee* (1978) established Jarman's angry style of film-making; *Caravaggio* (1986) is more accessible, but his last film, *Blue* (1993), marks a return to a challenging approach to the audience, with Jarman narrating primarily from his journals and the visuals consisting of nothing more than a screen-filled blue colour field. His 1979 version of *The Tempest* (1979), however, is apart from the eruption of Elizabeth WELCH singing 'Stormy Weather' with a chorus of sailors, surprisingly (and intelligently) restrained. Also, author of 12 books, including *Dancing Ledge* (1984), *Modern Nature: The Journals of Derek Jarman* (1991), *Derek Jarman's Garden* (1995), and *Kicking the Pricks* (1997).

OTHER BRITISH FILMS INCLUDE: *The Tempest* (1979), *Imaging October* (1984), *The Angelic Conversion* (1985), *Aria* (segment), *The Last of England* (1987), *War Requiem*, *Pet Shop Boys Concert* (1989), *The Garden* (1990), *Edward II* (1991), *Wittgenstein* (1993).

BIBLIOG: Michael O'Pray, *Derek Jarman: Dreams of England*, 1996. AS.

Jarre, Maurice (*b* Lyons, France, 1924). Composer. Triple Oscar-winner for his score for David LEAN's *Lawrence of Arabia* (1962), his first British work, for *Doctor Zhivago* (1965, UK/US) with its romantic 'Lara's Theme' which became a popular single, and for *A Passage to India* (1984). These lush scores made him one of the most sought-after film composers and he received AAn for several US films, including the thriller, *Witness* (1985), the African adventure, *Gorillas in the Mist* (1988), and the romantic fantasy *Ghost* (1990). Trained at the Paris Conservatoire, and for a time in the 50s the musical director of the Théâtre Nationale Populaire, he wrote his first film score for the 1952 short, *Hotel des Invalides*. He has been in enormous demand internationally, contributing to the emotional power of *Sunshine* (2000, UK/Austria/Can/Ger/Hung). Once married to actress Dany Saval. One son is Kevin Jarre, the US-based screenwriter, and another is the popular composer Jean-Michel Jarre.

OTHER BRITISH FILMS INCLUDE: (comp, unless noted) *The Collector* (1965, UK/US), *The Night of the Generals* (1966, UK/Fr, + cond), *Isadora* (1968), *Ryan's Daughter* (1970, + cond), *Pope Joan* (1972), *The Mackintosh Man* (1973, + cond), *Great Expectations* (1975, + cond), *Shout at the Devil* (1976, + cond), *March or Die* (1977, + cond), *The Bride* (1985, + cond).

Jarrott, Charles (*b* London, 1927). Director. After some UK experience as rep actor and director, he went to Canada in 1953 and worked for the Ottawa Theatre and the Canadian Broadcasting Corporation. He made four British films, including the rather ponderous costume dramas, *Anne of the Thousand Days* (1969) and *Mary Queen of Scots* (1971). Relocating to the US, he made such expensive clinkers as *Lost Horizon* (1973) and *The Other Side of Midnight* (1977), and has been involved in TV series as well as maintaining a string of little-seen features. Became a US resident in 1983. Married to actress Katharine BLAKE.

OTHER BRITISH FILMS INCLUDE: *Time to Remember* (1962), *Escape from the Dark* (1976).

Jarvis, Martin (*b* Cheltenham, 1941). Actor. Caught attention on TV as young Jolyon ('Jon') Forsyte in *The Forsyte Saga* (1967) and as a superbly sycophantic Uriah Heep in *David Copperfield* (1974). Films have been rare: *Secrets of a Windmill Girl* (1965), *Taste the Blood of Dracula* (1969), *Buster* (1988), *Calliope* (1993), and he played Duff Gordon in *Titanic* (1997, US). In 2000, scored a stage success in the revival of Peter NICHOLS' *Passion Play*. Married Rosalind AYRES, 1974.

Jason, David (*b* London, 1940). Actor. RN: White. Television star of such series as *Only Fools and Horses* (1981, hugely popular as South London wide boy, Del), *Porterhouse Blue* (1987, for which he won a BAA), and *A Touch of Frost* (1992). So far, only occasional films, including *Under Milk Wood* (1971), as Nogood Boyo, and *Royal Flash* (1975), as the Mayor. Brother of TV actor Arthur White.

OTHER BRITISH FILMS INCLUDE: *White Cargo* (1973), *Wombling Free* (1977, voice), *The Odd Job* (1978), *The BFG* (1989, voice).

Jay, Ernest (*b* London, 1893 – *d* London, 1957). Actor. Character player on stage from 1917 and in films from 1933, usually as bald, rather fussy professionals, like the boffin in *School for Secrets* (1946) or lawyer Calamy in *Blanche Fury* (1947).

OTHER BRITISH FILMS INCLUDE: *Tiger Bay* (1933), *Broken Blossoms* (1936), *I See Ice!* (1938), *Don't Take It to Heart!* (1944), *Vice Versa* (1947), *So Evil My Love* (1948), *Edward, My Son* (1949), *The Franchise Affair*

(1950), *Top Secret*, *I Believe in You* (1952), *Grand National Night* (1953), *Who Done It?* (1956), *The Curse of Frankenstein* (1957).

Jayne, Jennifer (*b* Yorkshire, 1931). Actress. RN: Jennifer Jones. Changing her name to avoid confusion with the US star, this attractive supporting player and occasional lead pottered around British films for nearly 40 years. She and Janet MUNRO were a mind-reading act in the SCIENCE-FICTION thriller, *The Trollenberg Terror* (1958); she was Norman WISDOM's leading lady in *On the Beat* (1962); and she wrote two HORROR films, *Tales That Witness Madness* (1973) and *Son of Dracula* (1974), under the name Jay Fairbanks. Was in popular TV series like *William Tell* (1958, as Frau Tell) and *Whiplash* (1961).

OTHER BRITISH FILMS INCLUDE: *Once a Jolly Swagman* (1948), *The Blue Lamp* (1949), *The Man Who Wouldn't Talk* (1957), *Raising the Wind* (1961), *Clash by Night* (1963), *They Came from Outer Space* (1967), *The Medusa Touch* (1978, UK/Fr), *The Jigsaw Man* (1984), *The Doctor and the Devils* (1985).

Jayston, Michael (*b* Nottingham, 1935). Actor. RN: James. Somewhat saturnine leading man of all the acting media. A former accountant, he trained at the Guildhall School and first appeared on stage in 1962, with subsequent seasons at Bristol Old Vic and Stratford, proving himself equally adept in SHAKESPEARE or Noël COWARD (*Private Lives*, 1980). On screen since 1968's *A Midsummer Night's Dream*, he was co-starred in the epic, *Nicholas and Alexandra* (1971, US/UK), when Rex HARRISON was unavailable, and impressively repeated his 1967 stage role in the film version of PINTER's *The Homecoming* (1973, US/UK), but never became a film *star*. Some accomplished TV, including *Tinker, Tailor, Soldier, Spy* (1979) and *Cluedo* (1991).

OTHER BRITISH FILMS INCLUDE: *Cromwell* (1970), *Follow Me!* (1971), *Bequest to the Nation*, *Craze* (1973), *The Internecine Project* (1974), *Dominique* (1978), *Element of Doubt* (1996).

Jean, the Vitagraph dog (*b* New York – *d* 1916). Actress. With all due respect to the star of *Rescued by Rover*, Jean was Britain's first dog star, appearing in support of Florence TURNER in various productions from 1913–15, beginning with *Jean's Evidence* (1913). Jean, a collie owned and trained by director Larry Trimble, made her debut with the Vitagraph Company in 1909, and was one of the most popular actresses on the lot. Died at the height of her fame. AS.

Jean, Vadim (*b* Bristol, 1966). Director, screenwriter, producer. Enterprising film-maker of the 90s who began by co-directing and -producing *Leon the Pig Farmer* (1992), the comedy of Jewish life and artificial insemination, then directed the science-fiction thriller *Beyond Bedlam* (1993, + co-sc), the humane classroom drama, *Clockwork Mice* (1995), and the sincere but rather too soulful *One More Kiss* (1999), and was 'additional unit director' on *Event Horizon* (1997, UK/US).

OTHER BRITISH FILMS INCLUDE: *The Real Howard Spitz* (1998, UK/Can).

Jean-Baptiste, Marianne (*b* London, 1967) Actress. RADA-trained actress who made an impressive debut in Mike LEIGH's *Secrets & Lies* (1996), in which she gave a quietly compassionate performance as an adopted black woman who discovers her white birth-mother, receiving Supporting Actress BAAn and AAn, the first black Britisher to achieve the latter. However, aside from a composer credit on Leigh's subsequent feature *Career Girls* (1997) and the telemovie *The Man* (1999), Jean-Baptiste was unable to build on this promise in British film. Citing racial discrimination after her exclusion from a parade

of young British stars at the 50th anniversary of the Cannes Film Festival in 1997, she left for America and has worked there almost exclusively since.

OTHER BRITISH FILMS: *London Kills Me* (1991), *New Year's Day* (2001, UK/Fr), *Spy Game* (2002, UK/US). Melinda Hildebrandt.

Jeans, Isabel (*b* London, 1891 – *d* London, 1985). Actress. Regal and beautiful actress of stage and screen, Jeans is memorable as Zélie de Chaumet, the French aristocrat interested in a bit of 'rough' in the unlikely form of Ivor NOVELLO, in *The Rat*; she appeared in both the 1924 and 1927 stage productions of the play and also three screen ADAPTATIONS: *The Rat* (1925), *The Triumph of the Rat* (1926), and *The Return of the Rat* (1929). American audiences know her best as Aunt Alicia in *Gigi* (1958); other US films include *Tovarich* (1937), and *A Breath of Scandal* (1960). Made her stage debut in 1909 as a daffodil in *Pinkie and the Fairie*, first came to the US in 1915, and made her TV debut in 1955. Was married to Claude RAINS and to playwright Gilbert WAKEFIELD.

OTHER BRITISH FILMS INCLUDE: *The Profligate* (1917), *Tilly of Bloomsbury* (1921), *Downhill, Easy Virtue* (1927), *Sally Bishop* (1932), *Rolling in Money* (1934), *The Crouching Beast* (1935), *Banana Ridge* (1941), *Great Day* (1945), *Elizabeth of Ladymead* (1948), *Heavens Above!* (1963), *The Magic Christian* (1969). AS.

Jeans, Ursula (*b* Simla, India, 1906 – *d* London, 1973). Actress. RN: McMinn. So ineffably gracious is her image in later years, it is hard to recall that Jeans came to prominence as Fanny, the butler's upwardly mobile daughter in the US-made *Cavalcade* (1933). Fair-haired, blue-eyed, RADA-trained and on stage from 1925, she played 'Colonel's lady' types (like Lady Windham in 1959's *North West Frontier*) as to the manner born, but her most fully achieved screen role was as the middle-class widow dealing with the problems of post-war austerity in *The Weaker Sex* (1948). Had a wider range of roles on stage, including several Old Vic seasons, and showed a charming comic talent on many occasions. Married (1) to actor **Robin Irvine** (*b* Ireland, 1899 – *d* ?), who made a half-dozen films in the late 20s/early 30s, including HITCHCOCK's *Downhill* and *Easy Virtue* (1927) and (2) Roger LIVESEY, with whom she often appeared on stage and in the film, *The Life and Death of Colonel Blimp* (1943).

OTHER BRITISH FILMS INCLUDE: *The Gipsy Cavalier* (1922), *The Virgin Queen* (1923), *SOS* (1928), *The Love Habit* (1931), *The Barton Mystery* (1932), *Friday the Thirteenth* (1933), *Dark Journey* (1937), *Over the Moon* (1939), *Mr Emmanuel* (1944), *Gaiety George* (1946), *The Woman in the Hall* (1947), *The Night My Number Came Up* (1955), *The Queen's Guards* (1961), *The Battle of the Villa Fiorita* (1965).

Jeayes, Allan (*b* London, 1885 – *d* London, 1963). Actor. Educated at Merchant Taylor's School and a former farmer, strong-featured Jeayes began on stage in 1906, in London, 1910, and appeared in dozens of plays, classical and modern, over the next 50 years. Entered films in 1918 as William Hamilton in *Nelson*, and by the 30s had settled into playing colonels (*Catherine the Great*, 1934), lords (*The Scarlet Pimpernel*, 1935), inspectors (*The Squeaker*, 1937) and General Faversham in *The Four Feathers* (1939). He was a fixture in KORDA's 30s films, and was also memorable as the unsympathetic mine-owner in *The Stars Look Down* (1939) and land-owner Weatherby in *Blanche Fury* (1947).

OTHER BRITISH FILMS INCLUDE: *A Gentleman of France* (1921), *The Third Round* (1925), *The Ghost Train* (1931), *Sanders of the River* (1935), *Things to Come, Rembrandt* (1936), *Elephant Boy, Knight Without Armour, Action for Slander* (1937), *They Drive by Night*, (1939), *The Thief of Baghdad, The Proud Valley, Convoy* (1940), *Pimpernel Smith* (1941),

The Shipbuilders (1943), *Dead of Night* (1945), *The Man Within* (1947), *Obsession* (1949), *The Reluctant Widow* (1950), *Reach for Glory* (1961).

Jefford, Barbara (*b* Plymstock, 1930). Actress. Greatly respected stage actress who has merely dabbled with film, though her tour de force as Molly Bloom in *Ulysses* (1967, UK/US) won her a BAAn. A RADA Gold Medallist, she has played most of SHAKESPEARE's heroines, with Stratford and Old Vic seasons, and was a celebrated *St Joan* (1959–60). Her films are an eccentric lot and include the starring role in *Lust for a Vampire* (1970), *Hitler: The Last Ten Days* (1973, UK/It) as Magda Goebbels, *Where Angels Fear to Tread* (1991) as Mrs Herriton, and Fellini's *And the Ship Sails On* (1983, It). On TV did her best to give a bit of bite to the marshmallow of *The House of Eliott* (1991) as autocratic Aunt Lydia. Married and divorced actor Terence LONGDON. Awarded OBE in 1965.

OTHER BRITISH FILMS INCLUDE: *A Midsummer Night's Dream*, *The Bofors Gun* (1968), *Nelly's Version* (1983), *When the Whales Came* (1989).

Jeffrey, Peter (*b* Bristol, 1929 – *d* Stratford-upon-Avon, 2000). Actor. From his 20-odd films, Jeffrey is now probably best remembered for the three films he did for Lindsay ANDERSON: *If . . .* (1968), as the super-executive headmaster; *O Lucky Man!* (1973), as both coffee-factory boss and prison governor; and *Britannia Hospital* (1982), as the sceptical senior surgeon. Harrow- and Cambridge-educated, a former teacher, he played with the Bristol Old Vic, the National and the RSC. He belongs to the great tradition of versatile, utterly dependable British CHARACTER ACTORS, as he showed on TV as well, in such diverse fare as *Middlemarch* (1994), as the unmasked hypocrite Bulstrode, and *Our Friends in the North* (1996).

OTHER BRITISH FILMS INCLUDE: *Becket* (1964), *The Early Bird* (1965), *That Riviera Touch* (1966), *Anne of the Thousand Days* (1969), *Countess Dracula* (1970), *Kidnapped* (1971), *The Odessa File* (1974, UK/Ger), *Midnight Express* (1978), *The Adventures of Baron Munchausen* (1988, UK/It/Ger).

Jeffries, Lionel (*b* London, 1926). Actor, director. Expert purveyor of knuckle-headed choler in dozens of films, Jeffries also proved a director of subtlety in at least one film, the charming colour version of *The Railway Children* (1971). He in fact showed himself a very capable director of children's films, but it is as a character player, specialising in doomed obduracy, that he will be remembered. Bald from an early age, he has played inept crooks and policemen as well as more benign figures later in his long career. Among his 70-odd films, highlights include the fanatical Marquis of Queensberry in *The Trials of Oscar Wilde* (1960), the inevitably outwitted Inspector 'Nosey' Parker in the comedy crime caper *The Wrong Arm of the Law* (1962) and Grandpa Potts in *Chitty Chitty Bang Bang* (1968), and he also appeared in international films, including *Camelot* (1967), as King Pellinore. On TV, he and Peggy ASCHCROFT scored a notably moving success in *Cream in My Coffee* (1980) as an elderly couple overcome with the rage of growing old.

OTHER BRITISH FILMS INCLUDE: (a) *Stage Fright* (1950), *Will Any Gentleman?* (1953), *The Colditz Story* (1954), *The Quatermass Experiment, Windfall* (1955), *The Baby and the Battleship, The High Terrace* (1956), *Doctor at Large, Barnacle Bill* (1957), *The Revenge of Frankenstein, Orders to Kill, Up the Creek, Dunkirk* (1958), *Jazzboat* (1959), *Please Turn Over, Two Way Stretch* (1960), *Mrs Gibbons' Boys* (1962), *The Truth About Spring, Murder Ahoy* (1964), *The Secret of My Success* (1965), *The Spy with a Cold Nose* (1966), *Twinky* (1969), *Whoever Slew Auntie Roo?* (1971), *Royal Flash* (1975), *A Chorus of Disapproval*

(1989); (d, sc) *The Amazing Mr Blunden, Baxter!*; (d) (1972), *The Water Babies* (1975, UK/Pol, + add dial), *Wombling Free* (1977).

Jeffs, Waller (*b* London, 1861 – *d* Stratford-upon-Avon, 1941). Pioneer. Jeffs was a pioneer exhibitor in the Midlands, first screening films at Birmingham's Curzon Hall in 1899. He filmed a number of ACTUALITIES in the Birmingham area in the early 1900s, including footage of Joseph Chamberlain, and was also active as an exhibitor in Derby and Nottingham. In the 1920s, he retired to manage a cinema in Stratford-upon-Avon. BIBLIOG: John H. Bird, *Cinema Parade*, 1947. AS.

Jenkins, Amy (*b* London, 1967) Screenwriter. Best known as the creator of the groundbreaking TV series, *This Life* (1996), made a disappointing cinema feature debut with *Elephant Juice* (2000), which she also co-produced with its director Sam MILLER. The territory overlapped *This Life*, but the effect was attenuated. Educated at Pimlico Comprehensive School, read law at University College London, and wrote and directed the short film *Blink* (1998) for Channel 4, and wrote and directed a segment of the PORTMANTEAU feature film *Tube Tales* for Sky Premiere (1999).

Jenkins, Megs (*b* Birkenhead, 1917 – *d* Suffolk, 1998). Actress. RN: Muguette Jenkins. Fondly regarded character player who made a corner in plumply comfortable, reassuring mothers, governesses and housekeepers. Dropping her ambition to be a ballet dancer, she joined Liverpool Playhouse in 1933 and stayed four years, and in London made her name in several Emlyn WILLIAMS plays, starting with *The Light of Heart* (1940), working mostly in modern plays, such as the revival of *The Winslow Boy* (1970). On screen, she was first noticed as Welsh Gwen in *Millions Like Us* (1943), was a nurse under suspicion in *Green for Danger* (1946), cast to type as the Plump Woman in *The History of Mr Polly* (1948), had a middle-aged romance with Leslie DWYER in *A Boy, a Girl and a Bike* (1949), was kindly mother and sister respectively in *No Place for Jennifer* (1949) and *The Cruel Sea* (1953), and so on, saving perhaps her most notable performance for Jack CLAYTON's *The Innocents* (1961), as the housekeeper whose grasp of goodness is the children's only hope. She repeated the role on TV 13 years later. Her achievement over-all was to be good and yet not dull.

OTHER BRITISH FILMS INCLUDE: *Poison Pen* (1939), *The Lamp Still Burns* (1943), *Painted Boats* (1945), *The Brothers* (1947), *White Corridors, Secret People* (1951), *Personal Affair* (1953), *Out of the Clouds, John and Julie* (1955), *The Story of Esther Costello* (1957), *Indiscreet* (1958), *Tiger Bay* (1959), *Conspiracy of Hearts* (1960), *Life for Ruth* (1962), *Murder Most Foul* (1964), *Oliver!* (1968), *David Copperfield* (1969), *Asylum* (1972).

Jennings, Alex (*b* Upminster, 1957). Actor. Educated at Warwick University and trained at the Bristol Old Vic Theatre School, Jennings spent four years with the National Youth Theatre, has had a busy career with the RSC and London's National Theatre, on radio and TV (including *Smiley's People*, 1982, and the title role in the serial, *Ashenden*, 1991), but has so far made few films. However, he was an expertly opportunist Lord Mark in *The Wings of the Dove* (1997, UK/US) and played both Theseus and Oberon (as he had with the RSC in 1995) in *A Midsummer Night's Dream* (1999, UK/It).

OTHER BRITISH FILMS: *War Requiem* (1989), *The Four Feathers* (2003, UK/US).

Jennings, Gladys (*b* Oxford, 1902 – *d* Oxfordshire, 1994). Actress. A stage performer, Jennings entered films in 1919 as a second female lead with BRITISH ACTORS' FILM COMPANY in

The Lady Clare, The Face at the Window (1919) and *The Shuttle of Life* (1920).

OTHER BRITISH FILMS INCLUDE: *In the Night* (1920), *Rob Roy* (1922), *Becket* (1923), *Hindle Wakes* (1927), *Lilies of the Field* (1934), *Alibi Inn* (1935). AS.

Jennings, Humphrey (*b* Walberswick, Suffolk, 1907 – *d* Poros, Greece, 1950) Director. Studied English at Cambridge, and, after graduating, worked as painter and poet, with a particular interest in SURREALISM, and helped to organise the influential Surrealist Exhibition of 1936 in London. Between 1934 and 1936 Jennings worked as designer, editor and actor at the GPO FILM UNIT. Between 1936 and 1938 he worked with Len LYE at the SHELL FILM UNIT, before returning to the GPO Film Unit (later CROWN FILM UNIT) between 1938 and 1949. In 1936 he founded the MASS-OBSERVATION movement, with anthropologist Tom Harrisson and poet Charles Madge. Between 1949 and 1950 he worked as a director for WESSEX FILMS. In 1950 Jennings died during an accident whilst film-making in Greece. He also left the text of a book on the English Industrial Revolution, entitled *Pandemonium*, finally published in 1985.

His most important films (often greatly abetted by his editor Stewart MCALLISTER) include: *Spare Time* (1939), one of the most poetic and aesthetically significant films to emerge from the British DOCUMENTARY FILM MOVEMENT; *Words for Battle* (1941, + sc), which ends with Laurence OLIVIER reciting the Gettysburg address as tanks rumble through Parliament Square; *Listen to Britain* (1942, co-d, co-e), a film which used sound and music to sum up Jennings' conception of an English national identity rooted in both city and country; and *A Diary for Timothy* (1946), a collage of expectations for a baby born as the War ends, written by E.M. FORSTER and narrated by Michael REDGRAVE. *Fires Were Started* (1943, + sc), depicting a wartime day and night in the National Fire Service, is perhaps the most successful of the feature-length 'drama-documentaries' to emerge from the Crown Film Unit during the War, though *The Silent Village* (1943), which reconstructs the tragedy of the Czech village of Lidice in terms of a Welsh mining village had it been taken over by the Germans, is still very powerful. He is the great poet of the documentary movement.

OTHER BRITISH FILMS INCLUDE: (doc/short) (d, unless noted) *Post-Haste, Locomotives, Pett and Pott* (sets) (1934), *BBC – The Voice of Britain* (a), *Birth of a Robot* (co-d), *Story of the Wheel* (1935), *Farewell Topsails* (1937), *Making Fashion, Penny Journey, The Farm, Design for Spring, Speaking from America, English Harvest* (1938), *The First Days* (co-d), *SS Ionian* (1939), *Cargoes* (shortened version of *SS Ionian*), *Spring Offensive, Welfare of the Workers, London Can Take It!, Britain Can Take It* (1940, co-d), *The Heart of Britain* (1941), *The Eighty Days* (+ p), *The True Story of Lili Marlene* (+ sc), *V 1* (1944), *A Defeated People, Town Meeting of the World* (comm) (1946), *The Cumberland Story* (1947, + sc), *Dim Little Island* (1948, + p) and *Family Portrait* (1950, +sc).
BIBLIOG: Mary-Lou Jennings, *Humphrey Jennings: Film-Maker, Painter, Poet*, 1982; Kevin Jackson, *The Humphrey Jennings Film Reader*, 1993. Ian Aitken.

Jerome, Jerome K(lapka) (*b* Walsall, 1859 – *d* Ewelme, Chilterns, 1927). Writer. Former railway worker most famous for *Three Men in a Boat* (comic novel), and *The Passing of the Third Floor Back* (morality play), which have both been filmed several times. In Britain, *Three Men* was twice filmed as a silent (1915, as *Hanging a Picture*, and 1920) and twice as a talkie (1933, 1956), and as a TV adaptation in 1975. *The Passing*, was filmed twice in Britain, in 1918 and, with Conrad VEIDT as the godlike stranger, in 1935.

Jerrold, Mary (*b* London, 1877 – *d* London, 1955). Actress. Lovable character player of stage (from 1896) and screen (from *Midnight Gambols*, 1919), usually as kindly wives, mothers (John JUSTIN's in *The Gentle Sex*, 1943; Renée ASHERSON's in *The Way Ahead*, 1944) and aunts. She was especially subtle as Marius GORING's far-from-possessive mother in *Mr Perrin and Mr Traill* (1948) and contrasted effectively with austere spinster sister Jean CADELL in the marriage broker trade in *Marry Me* (1949). Married **Hubert Harben** (*b* 1878 – *d* 1941) who appeared in a number of silent and 30s British films, including several made from ALDWYCH FARCES. Their children were **Philip Harben** (*b* London, 1906 – *d* London 1970), who made a few films and was a celebrated TV chef, and **Joan Harben** (*b* London, 1909 – *d* London, 1953), who appeared in *The Man in the White Suit* (1951).

OTHER BRITISH FILMS INCLUDE: *Candytuft* (1921), *The W Plan* (1930), *Alibi* (1931), *Friday the Thirteenth* (1933), *Spring in the Air* (1934), *Fighting Stock* (1935), *Jack of All Trades* (1936), *Jamaica Inn* (1939), *Return to Yesterday* (1940), *Talk About Jacqueline* (1942), *The Magic Bow* (1946), *Colonel Bogey, Woman Hater* (1948), *The Queen of Spades* (1949), *Meet Me Tonight* (1952), *Top of the Form* (1953).

Jessel, Patricia (*b* Hong Kong, 1920 – *d* London, 1968). Actress. Trained by Italia Conti, Jessel was first on stage in 1933, and, after several years' rep experience, joined the Stratford season 1943–44, playing major roles, and won a Tony and other awards for her 1954 lead (UK, US) in *Witness for the Prosecution*. Her early death robbed the screen of a vivid supporting actress, so enjoyably seen in her last film, *A Funny Thing Happened on the Way to the Forum* (1966, UK/US) as Michael HORDERN's dragon wife.

OTHER BRITISH FILMS INCLUDE: *The Flesh Is Weak* (1957), *The Man Upstairs* (1958), *Model for Murder* (1959), *A Jolly Bad Fellow* (1963).

Jewell, Jimmy (*b* Sheffield, 1909 – *d* London, 1995). Actor. RN: Marsh. North Country comedian who was long partnered with his cousin Ben WARRISS. Turned to straight acting on stage in 1975 as Willie Clarke in *The Sunshine Boys* and achieved major success.

BRITISH FILMS: *Rhythm Serenade* (1943), *What a Carry On!* (1949), *Let's Have a Murder* (1950), *The Man Who Had Power Over Women* (1970), *Nearest and Dearest* (1972), *Rocinante* (1986), *The Krays* (1990).
BIBLIOG: Autobiography, *Three Times Lucky*, 1982. AS.

Jewesbury, Edward (*b* London, 1917 – *d* Surrey, 2002). Actor. Supporting player of TV (since the mid 70s) and film, most notable on screen for his roles in Kenneth BRANAGH's productions, starting with a memorable stint as 'good old Sir Thomas Erpingham' in *Henry V* (1989).

OTHER BRITISH FILMS INCLUDE: *Little Dorrit* (1987), *We Think the World of You* (1988), *Peter's Friends* (1992), *Much Ado About Nothing* (1993, UK/US), *Richard III, In the Bleak Midwinter* (1995), *Preaching to the Perverted, Mrs Dalloway* (UK/Neth/US) (1997), *Beautiful People* (1999).

Jewish representation The Jews first settled in England after the Norman Conquest. They were expelled by Edward I in 1290, but later readmitted by Oliver Cromwell during his Protectorship (1653–58). Jews have always had a marginal presence in England, numbering 400 in 1690 to 350,000 today. Yet despite this, they have been prominent in English society and represented in films from the beginning of English cinema. The earliest films portrayed Jews as either venal and grasping (*The Robbers and the Jew*, 1908; *A Bad Day for Levinsky*, 1909; *The Antique Vase*, 1913), or as dangerous subversives (*The Invaders*, 1909). However, films more sympathetic to Jews were made during the 20s and 30s, perhaps in response to anti-semitism. These included *Motherland* (1927), produced by Jewish film-maker G.B. SAMUELSON, *Loyalties* (1933), directed by Basil DEAN, and two screen adaptations of E. Temple Thurston's equivocal play *The Wandering Jew* (1923, 1934), both versions directed by Maurice ELVEY. Michael BALCON, the Jewish father of post-war EALING prestige, produced *Jew Süss* for GAUMONT–BRITISH in 1934. Starring Conrad VEIDT in a powerful performance, this was a condemnation of anti-semitism at a time when few films world-wide dared to broach political issues or speak the word 'Jew'. Just as forthright was *Mr Emmanuel* (1944), starring Felix AYLMER as the elderly hero of Louis GOLDING's popular novel, *Magnolia Street*.

Notwithstanding Alec GUINNESS's gross but brilliant portrait of Fagin in *Oliver Twist* (1948), Jews in English films have been shown with increasing realism since WW2. Such films as *Make Me an Offer!* (1954), *A Kid for Two Farthings* (1954), *The Bespoke Overcoat* (1955, AA/short), *Expresso Bongo* (1959), and *The Barber of Stamford Hill* (1963), all show Jews as equal members of a pluralist society. Difficult themes such as racial hatred and religious bigotry are treated with maturity in *Conspiracy of Hearts* (1960), *Hand in Hand* (1960), *Reach for Glory* (1961), *Ulysses* (1967), *Solomon and Gaenor* (1999), *Simon Magus* (2000, UK/Ger/It), and *Liam* (2001, UK/Ger/It). *Chariots of Fire* (1981) was a significant attempt to show how social mistrust and dislike of Jews is bound up with class prejudice, while *Sunday Bloody Sunday* (1971) was an important breakthrough in the normalising of a Jewish character in a major film. The self-parodying *Leon the Pig Farmer* (1992) and the inclusion of Jewish gangsters in *Snatch* (2000) are further evidence of a move towards the comfortable acceptance of Jews in British life.

OTHER RELEVANT BRITISH FILMS INCLUDE: *The Merchant of Venice* (1916), *General Post* (1920), *The Prime Minister* (1941), *Ivanhoe* (1952), *Svengali* (1955), *Sparrows Can't Sing* (1962), *The Deadly Affair* (1966), *Oliver!* (1968), *Antonia and Jane* (1990), *The Tango Lesson* (1997), *The Governess* (1998, UK/Fr), *Esther Kahn* (UK/Fr), *The Man Who Cried* (UK/Fr/US) (2000). Jan Epstein.

Jhabvala, Ruth Prawer (*b* Cologne, 1927). Author, screenwriter. Twice Oscared for her work (*A Room with a View*, 1986; *Howards End*, 1992; both BAAn/sc), she is best known for her collaboration with MERCHANT IVORY, for whom she wrote her first screenplay in 1963, *The Householder*, based on her own novel. Of Polish-Jewish parents who fled to England in 1939, she studied English at London University, married an Indian architect and moved to Delhi in 1951. Her writing career began here and was much concerned with coming to terms with Anglo-Indian culture conflict. Her association with Merchant Ivory included: original screenplays such as *The Guru* (1969, UK/Ind), *Autobiography of a Princess* (1975), *Hullabaloo over Georgie and Bonnie's Pictures* (1978, UK/Ind) and the witty *Jane Austen in Manhattan* (1980, UK/US); and ADAPTATIONS of her own novels, including *Heat and Dust* (1982, BAA/sc) and of other authors, notably Henry JAMES (e.g. *The Europeans*, 1979; *The Golden Bowl*, 2000, UK/Fr/US). With a fine eye for the cinematic, understanding that the verbal must sometimes play second fiddle to the visual, she has shown respect for authors she adapts, more perhaps than one might sometimes wish. Has lived in New York since 1975. Awarded CBE, 1998.

OTHER BRITISH FILMS INCLUDE: *Quartet* (1981, UK/Fr), *The Bostonians* (1984, UK/US), *Madame Sousatzka* (1988, co-sc), *The Remains of the Day* (1993, AAn, BAAn), *Jefferson in Paris* (1995), *A Soldier's Daughter Never Cries* (1998, UK/US).

Joffé, Roland (*b* London, 1945). Director, screenwriter. This grandson of sculptor Jacob Epstein, with substantial theatre and TV experience, made a spectacular film debut (AAn/d) with *The Killing Fields* (1984), based on the experiences of a US reporter in Cambodia after the fall of Phnom Penh. He followed this with the visually and aurally magnificent *The Mission* (1985), which didn't quite replicate the earlier success, and has since filmed internationally, to calamitous effect in *The Scarlet Letter* (1995, + p), one of the worst ADAPTATIONS ever of a great novel. His penchant for exotic settings was reasserted in the Calcutta-set *City of Joy* (1992, UK/Fr), made for Lightmotive, his own production company. Married to Jane LAPOTAIRE (1971–80), his subsequent partner was actress Cherie LUNGHI.

OTHER BRITISH FILMS INCLUDE: *Vatel* (2000, UK/Fr).

John, David (*b* Bedford, 1945 – *d* London, 2002). Sound recordist. Entered the industry in the editing department at DENHAM but soon turned to sound recording, and was quickly associated with such high-profile 80s films as *The Long Good Friday* (1980), *The Dresser* (1983) and *Scandal* (1988), moving into large-scale ACTION movies like the BOND number, *GoldenEye* (1995, UK/US). Noted for his sensitivity to actors' voices and for the contribution of sound to atmosphere; for instance, to the scary quality of a film like *The Haunting* (1999, US).

OTHER BRITISH FILMS INCLUDE: *Scum* (1979), *Absolute Beginners*, *84 Charing Cross Road* (UK/US), *Mona Lisa* (1986), *Memphis Belle* (1990), *The Jackal* (1997, UK/Fr/Ger/Jap/US), *Les Misérables* (1998, UK/Ger/US), *Entrapment* (1999, UK/US).

John, Sir Elton (*b* Pinner, 1947). Singer. RN: Reginald Dwight. Hugely successful British popstar of the 70s who has lasted and been rewarded with honours – CBE in 1996, knighthood in 1998 – and the friendship of Diana, Princess of Wales, at whose funeral he sang his song, 'Candle in the Wind'. His main career belongs in another book but he has appeared in a few British films, most memorably in Ken RUSSELL's *Tommy* (1975) and most often in guest spots, as in *Spice World* (1997).

OTHER BRITISH FILMS INCLUDE: *Friends* (1971, comp), *Born to Boogie* (1972, a), *High Fidelity* (2000, UK/US, song), *Women Talking Dirty* (2001, co-comp, ex p, m super).

John, Errol (*b* Gulf of Paria, Trinidad, 1924 – *d* London, 1988). Actor. Prominent black actor and writer of talent and sophistication, who played Othello at the Old Vic in 1963. To UK after WW2, making stage debut in 1947. Frequent US films included *The Nun's Story* (1959) and *PT109* (1963). Received Guggenheim Fellowship for Creative Writing, with his best known work, *Moon on a Rainbow Shawl*, adapted for radio in 1958, for TV in 1960, performed at Royal Court Theatre in 1958 and on Broadway in 1962. Active in black causes in later years.

BRITISH FILMS INCLUDE: *The Heart of the Matter* (1953), *Simba* (1955), *Man in the Middle* (1963), *Guns at Batasi* (1964). AS.

John, Martyn Production designer. Worked as art director (i.e. now subsidiary to production designer) on some notable films across a generic range, from the sumptuous period recreation of *The Wings of the Dove* (1997, UK/US) to the contemporary romantic comedy, *Sliding Doors* (1998, UK/US). Later designed large-scale works such as *Londinium* and *The Criminal* (UK/US) (2000).

OTHER BRITISH FILMS INCLUDE: *UFO* (1993), *The Browning Version* (1994, ass art d), *Jude* (1996, co-art d), *The Search for John Gissing* (2002, UK/US).

John, Rosamund (*b* London, 1913 – *d* London, 1998). Actress. RN: Jones. Forever being described as 'gentle-mannered', John was in fact tough-minded and sharp-witted, and the screen persona is not nearly as anodyne as many accounts suggest. She entered films in 1943 as a Scots girl in *The Secret of the Loch*, and was on stage the following year. In 1989, she claimed the stage was her 'first love' but she was lucky enough in her 16 films to create an indelible image of integrity, strength and femininity. She attributed her early 40s ascendancy in film to Leslie HOWARD, for whom she made three films in a row: *The First of the Few* (1942), very touching as Spitfire inventor Mitchell's wife; *The Gentle Sex*, as one of seven ATS girls; and *The Lamp Still Burns* (1943), as a trainee architect-turned-nurse. But her best roles were still to come. As the pub landlady Toddy in Anthony ASQUITH's *The Way to the Stars* (1945) and the suffragette wife of a temporising politician in *Fame Is the Spur* (1947), she is very poignant indeed, surface restraint clearly no more than a mask for depth of feeling; and in *Green for Danger* (1946), LAUNDER AND GILLIAT's witty thriller, her sweet-faced reserve is used to brilliant effect. She retired from acting when she married her second husband, politician John Silkin, whom she met when he canvassed her, and, a committed socialist herself, gladly lent him her support. She was for many years a magistrate in Kent. First married to editor Russell LLOYD.

OTHER BRITISH FILMS: *Tawny Pipit, Soldier, Sailor* (1944), *When the Bough Breaks, The Upturned Glass* (1947), *No Place for Jennifer* (1949), *She Shall Have Murder* (1950), *Never Look Back* (1952), *Street Corner* (1953), *Operation Murder* (1956).

Johns, Glynis (*b* Durban, 1923). Actress. Husky-voiced charmer, trained as a ballet dancer and on stage from 1935, she played the malicious child in the London production of *The Children's Hour* (1936) and first appeared in film as the hero's motherless daughter in *South Riding* (1938). Her screen career blossomed in the 40s and 50s, from the time she played her real-life father Mervyn JOHNS' daughter in the wartime FANTASY, *The Halfway House* (1944). A fetching Mabel Chiltern in *An Ideal Husband* (1947), she became a fully-fledged star as the mermaid, *Miranda* (1948), reprising the role in *Mad About Men* (1954), and played 20 leading parts in 50s COMEDIES (*Josephine and Men*, 1955), dramas (*Personal Affair*, 1953, as a schoolgirl obsessed with a married teacher; *The Weak and the Wicked*, 1953, as a middle-class girl in gaol for gambling fraud); COSTUME ROMANCES (DISNEY's *The Sword and the Rose*, 1953, as Mary Tudor; *The Seekers*, 1954); and the wartime comedy-adventure, *Appointment with Venus* (1951). In truth, popular as she was, she sometimes seemed imprisoned by a too-cute persona. Her Hollywood career, effectively begun with her role as the stewardess in *No Highway* (1951) for FOX–BRITISH, gave her limited opportunities, best remembered of which is that of suffragette Mrs Banks in *Mary Poppins* (1964). However, she has stayed the course and now plays grandmas in films like *Superstar* (1999). Nominated for a Supporting Actress Oscar for *The Sundowners* (1960), she won a Tony for her stage lead in *A Little Night Music* (1973). Married (1 of 4) Anthony FORWOOD, by whom she had a son, **Gareth Forwood** (*b* London, 1945), who appeared in several films, including *Gandhi* (1982, UK/Ind), and she had a well-publicised engagement to producer Antony DARNBOROUGH.

OTHER BRITISH FILMS INCLUDE: *Prison Without Bars* (1938), *49th Parallel* (1941), *Adventures of Tartu* (1943), *Perfect Strangers* (1945), *Frieda* (1947), *Dear Mr Prohack* (1949), *State Secret* (1950), *Encore* (1951), *The Card* (1952), *The Seekers, The Beachcomber* (1954), *Loser Takes All*

(1956), *Shake Hands with the Devil* (1959, UK/US), *Lock Up Your Daughters!* (1969), *Under Milk Wood* (1971), *The Vault of Horror* (1973, UK/US).

Johns, Harriette (*b* Perth, Scotland, 1922). Actress. RADA-trained stage actress, on stage from 1938, drove a lorry during WW2 (1940–43) and post-war appeared in a run of largely modern plays, including *Edward, My Son* (1948), as the magnate's mistress. Also played in the film version (1949) but in a much smaller role; in *Meet Mr Callaghan* (1954), though, she recreated her stage leading role. Few films, but plenty of TV and theatre.

OTHER BRITISH FILMS INCLUDE: *An Ideal Husband* (1947), *A Night to Remember* (1958), *The Yellow Teddy Bears* (1963), *Happy Deathday* (1970).

Johns, Mervyn (*b* Pembroke, Wales, 1899 – *d* Northwood, Middlesex, 1992). Actor. Stalwart character player of over 60 films, short and stocky Johns was equally convincing when doing benign, like the ghostly innkeeper in the wartime morality piece, *The Halfway House* (1944), co-starring daughter Glynis JOHNS, or shabby, like the small business man sent to gaol in *Edward, My Son* (1949), or courageous, like Greaser John Boyle in *San Demetrio–London* (1943), or morally equivocal, like the doctor in *The Vicious Circle* (1957). The gentle exterior could be used to teasingly ambiguous effect, as in *The Next of Kin* (1942), in which he played a traitor. On stage for over 40 years from 1923; in films from 1934, playing first and second features, in films good and bad, without striking a false note. His time at EALING in the 40s was probably the highlight of his career, including his tyrannical Victorian paterfamilias in *Pink String and Sealing Wax* and the man with the disturbing dream in *Dead of Night* (1945), but he was also a notable Bob Cratchit in *Scrooge* (1951) and Friar Lawrence in *Romeo and Juliet* (1954, UK/It) and he continued in substantial supporting roles until the 70s. First married to concert pianist, Alys Maude Steele-Payne, and, after long widowhood, to Diana CHURCHILL.

OTHER BRITISH FILMS INCLUDE: *Lady in Danger* (1934), *Storm in a Teacup* (1937), *Jamaica Inn* (1939), *The Girl in the News* (1940), *Went the Day Well?* (1942), *The Bells Go Down* (1943), *They Knew Mr Knight* (1945), *The Captive Heart* (1946), *Easy Money, Counterblast* (1948), *Tony Draws a Horse* (1950), *The Tall Headlines* (1952), *Valley of Song* (1953), *1984* (1955), *Moby Dick, Find the Lady* (1956), *The Surgeon's Knife, The Gypsy and the Gentleman* (1957), *Never Let Go* (1960), *No Love for Johnnie* (1961), *The Day of the Triffids* (1962), *The Victors, 80,000 Suspects* (1963), *The Heroes of Telemark* (1965), *The National Health* (1973).

Johns, Stratford (*b* Pietermaritzburg, South Africa, 1925 – *d* Heveningham, 2002). Actor. Bald and portly, Johns was an unlikely starter for household fame, which is what he won on TV as Det. Inspector Barlow in TV's *Z Cars*, of the 60s and 70s, and the spin-offs, *Softly, Softly* and *Barlow at Large*, with Johns working his way up the constabulary hierarchy. In fact, he played many cops and other functionaries in films before and after his TV debut: he plays constables in *Who Done It?, Tiger in the Smoke* and *The Long Arm* (1956) and 20 years later is Chief Commissioner in *The Strange Case of the End of Civilisation As We Know It* (1977). In 1988, he played Herod in *Salome's Last Dance*. His volatile domestic life brought him unwelcome publicity when his wife had him arrested for assault in 1988.

OTHER BRITISH FILMS INCLUDE: *The Ship That Died of Shame* (1955), *The One That Got Away* (1957), *Hand in Hand* (1960), *Cromwell* (1970), *George and Mildred* (1980), *Dance with a Stranger* (1984), *Wild Geese II*

(1985), *Foreign Body* (1986), *The Lair of the White Worm* (1988), *Splitting Heirs* (1993).

Johnson, Dame Celia (*b* Richmond, Surrey, 1908 – *d* Nettlebed, 1982). Actress. A late recruit to the screen, Johnson quickly acquired iconic status in British cinema and has maintained it, despite how few films she made. It is probably the eyes, as she acknowledged: she stares at the audience and breaks its heart as she sees her would-be lover, Trevor HOWARD, head off to catch his train out of her life in *Brief Encounter* (1945, AAn/actress). This is the definitive Johnson role: she makes utterly real all the constraints (and comforts) of a decent middle-class woman's life: but there are other cherishable performances, too. In another COWARD-LEAN film, *This Happy Breed* (1944), though her accent wobbles a bit at times, she is the stoical lower-middle class housewife and mother to the life, unbearably moving as she comes to terms with the defection – and return – of her rebellious younger daughter. As the self-sacrificing daughter of a benignly selfish parson in *The Holly and the Ivy* (1952) and as a conscientious probation officer in *I Believe in You* (1952), she makes goodness interesting and touching. That she could also do comedy is seen in *The Captain's Paradise* (1953), parodying her usual image. She can do nothing with the awful Coward piece, *The Astonished Heart* (1950 – 'I'll just have a tray in my room') and is miscast in *A Kid for Two Farthings* (1954). No doubt stage (from 1928 to 1982, in SHAKESPEARE, RATTIGAN, Ibsen, COWARD, etc) and perhaps TV (from 1937 to 1982, especially *Staying On*, 1980) gave her more varied opportunities, but for the best of what she did on screen filmgoers should be grateful. Married explorer Peter Fleming and mother of TV actress **Lucy Fleming** (*b* Nettlebed, 1947), seen in *Pride and Prejudice* (1995). Awarded CBE in 1958 and DBE in 1981.

OTHER BRITISH FILMS: *Letter from Home* (1941, short), *In Which We Serve*, *We Serve* (short) (1942), *Dear Octopus* (1943), *The Good Companions* (1956), *The Prime of Miss Jean Brodie* (1958).

BIBLIOG: Lucy Fleming, *Celia Johnson*, 1991.

Johnson, David (*b* Nottingham, 1954). Cinematographer. Educated in Nottingham where he worked briefly in the theatre, before joining SAMUELSON's Film Services in 1974, obtaining there a full technical knowledge of camera equipment. Assisted on such films as *Alien* (1979, UK/US) and *Clash of the Titans* (1981, UK/US). His cinematographer credits include such high-profile 90s films as *Hilary and Jackie* (1998) and, for some time, the only box-office success of the LOTTERY-assisted films, *An Ideal Husband* (1999, UK/US). He also shot *Othello* (1995, UK/US), which, intelligent and sumptuous as it was, lacked the excitement of, say, Orson WELLES's hand-to-mouth production of 1952.

OTHER BRITISH FILMS INCLUDE: *Saint-Ex* (1996), *Martha, Meet Frank, Daniel and Laurence* (1998), *Honest* (2000, UK/Fr), *The Martins* (2001), *Football, Resident Evil* (UK/Ger/US) (2002).

Johnson, Fred (*b* Dublin, 1899 – *d* London, 1971) Actor. With the Abbey Theatre, 1929 – 46, before coming to England in 1947, when he appeared as the prison chaplain in *The Mark of Cain* (1948) and various police and other professionals after that. Solemn-faced and often bespectacled, he was busy on London and Broadway stages.

OTHER BRITISH FILMS INCLUDE: *Another Shore* (1948), *Adam and Evelyne* (1949), *No Resting Place* (1951), *The Long Memory* (1952), *Happy Ever After* (1954), *The Quatermass Experiment* (1955), *The Curse of Frankenstein* (1957), *The Brides of Dracula* (1960), *The Greengage Summer* (1961), *Young Cassidy* (1965), *Where's Jack?* (1969).

Johnson, Katie (*b* Clayton, Yorkshire, 1878 – *d* London, 1957). Actress. Not many achieve stardom in their 70s, but that is what happened to Johnson after her BAA role as the little old lady whose Victorian rectitude outlasts and outwits a gang of thieves in *The Ladykillers* (1955). On the stage from 1894 and in numerous small film roles from 1932's *After Office Hours*, she played many old ladies, including a German spy in *I See a Dark Stranger* (1946). Sadly, she died just two years and two films after her breakthrough.

OTHER BRITISH FILMS INCLUDE: *Strictly in Confidence* (1933), *Laburnum Grove* (1936), *The Rat* (1937), *Marigold* (1938), *Freedom Radio* (1940), *Jeannie* (1941), *He Snoops to Conquer* (1944), *The Shop at Sly Corner*, *The Years Between* (1946), *Meet Me at Dawn* (1947), *I Believe in You* (1952), *The Rainbow Jacket* (1954), *John and Julie* (1955), *How to Murder a Rich Uncle* (1957).

Johnson, Laurie (*b* London, 1927) Composer, conductor, producer. RCM-trained, Johnson entered films as orchestrator for music director Louis LEVY on ABPC's *The Good Companions* (1956). During the early 60s, Johnson developed a fresh modern sound combining big band jazz riffs with Latin rhythms and smooth string textures. Early memorable film scores included *Tiger Bay* (1959), *Bitter Harvest* (1963), *The Beauty Jungle* (1964) and an orchestration of 'When Johnny Comes Marching Home' for *Dr Strangelove . . .* (1963). His themes were everywhere on TV in the 60s, including the Diana RIGG series of *The Avengers* (1966–69). Also wrote music for West End musicals (*Lock Up Your Daughters*), band and classical compositions, and, more recently, was a co-producer of costume drama TV movies, such as *A Hazard of Hearts* (1987, + p).

OTHER BRITISH FILMS INCLUDE: (comp/arr/cond) *The Moonraker* (1957), *No Trees in the Street* (1958), *Operation Bullshine* (1959), *Siege of the Saxons* (1963), *Hot Millions* (1968), *The Belstone Fox* (1973), *Hedda* (1975), *It Shouldn't Happen To A Vet* (1976). Roger Philip Mellor.

Johnson, Pauline (*b* Cardiff, 1900 – *d* Sherborne, 1947). Actress. A pretty and vivacious actress, Pauline Johnson began her film career in 1920 opposite Leslie HOWARD in *Bookworms* and ended it in 1929 opposite Ray MILLAND in *The Flying Scotsman*. She was Walter FORDE's leading lady in *Wait and See* (1928), *What Next?* (1928) and *Would You Believe It?* (1929).

OTHER BRITISH FILMS INCLUDE: *Love at the Wheel* (1921), *A Sailor Tramp* (1922), *The Bohemian Girl* (1927), *The Wrecker* (1928), *Little Miss London* (1929). AS.

Johnson, Richard (*b* Upminster, 1927). Actor. Durable star of the British acting media, who entered RADA at 16, was on stage first a spear-carrier to Gielgud's Hamlet (1944) and 50 years later soldiers on in television dramas. Was Laertes in Peter BROOK's *Hamlet* (1953), the first British production in post-Revolution Moscow, and with the RSC, 1957–58, as Romeo, Pericles and others. An early film was *Calling Bulldog Drummond* (1951) and he later played the lead in two updated Drummond adventures: *Deadlier than the Male* (1966) and *Some Girls Do* (1969). Made a lot of films in the 60s and 70s, and, if he never became a major star, he was often an interesting actor, ranging from HORROR (*The Haunting*, 1963) to epic (*Khartoum*, 1966) to SHAKESPEARE (*Julius Caesar*, 1970, as Cassius) and the costume romp, *Moll Flanders* (1965), opposite Kim Novak whom he briefly married. His first wife was actress **Sheila Sweet** who appeared in a few films of the 50s, including *Conflict of Wings* (1954). In the mid 80s, he joined Glenda JACKSON, Albert FINNEY and others in a short-lived venture, United British Artists, to provide a base for the production of modest-budgeted films, such as *Turtle Diary* (1985, + a), but uncongenial government measures helped its demise.

OTHER BRITISH FILMS INCLUDE: (a, unless noted) *Captain Horatio Hornblower RN* (1950, UK/US), *80,000 Suspects* (1963), *The Pumpkin Eater* (1964), *Operation Crossbow* (1965, UK/It), *Oedipus the King* (1967), *A Twist of Sand* (1968), *Henessey* (1975, + story), *The Four Feathers* (1978), *The Monster Club* (1980), *Lady Jane* (1985), *Castaway* (1986, ex p), *The Lonely Passion of Judith Hearne* (1987, co-p), *Milk* (1999).

Johnson, Van (*b* Rhode Island, 1916). Actor. Freckle-faced bobby-sox hero of 40s US films who, rather surprisingly, held on as a character actor, latterly on TV for the most part. In the 50s, as his star waned, he made four films in Britain: totally miscast in *The End of the Affair* (1954), he acquitted himself adequately in the others – *Action of the Tiger* (1957), *Subway in the Sky* (1958), *Beyond This Place* (1959).

Johnston, Margaret (*b* Sydney, 1918 – *d* Kingston-upon-Thames, 2002) Actress. Despite giving a string of memorable performances, this gravely beautiful actress never became a major star. She studied law at Sydney University, trained at RADA, and was on the London stage from 1939. After a fleeting appearance in *The Prime Minister* (1941), she reappeared to excellent effect in the 1946 classic, *The Rake's Progress*, as the woman who has Rex HARRISON's number but also loves him; she made touching the spinster's repressed passion in *A Man About the House* (1947); but kept vanishing for returns to the stage so that her film career never built momentum. The box-office (and, largely, critical) failure of *Portrait of Clare* (1950), which should have been a star vehicle for her, was a stumbling-block, but there are still other fine performances to savour, including the careworn second wife in *The Magic Box* (1951), the bossy lady exec in a suit in *Knave of Hearts* (1954, UK/Fr), and the bitchy wife in *Life at the Top* (1965). She married agent Al PARKER and when he died she took over the running of his agency, which catered for such top talents as James MASON and Helen MIRREN.

OTHER BRITISH FILMS: *Touch and Go* (1955), *Night of the Eagle* (1962), *Girl in the Headlines* (1963), *The Psychopath* (1966), *Sebastian* (1967).

Johnston, Oliver (*b* Beaconsfield, 1888 – *d* London, 1966). Actor. Minor character actor, who specialised in elderly professional men; also on stage (from 1929) and television. He had a substantial role as Jaumier in CHAPLIN's *A King in New York* (1957) and the comedian also cast him, in a lesser part, in *A Countess from Hong Kong* (1966).

OTHER BRITISH FILMS INCLUDE: *Kate Plus Ten* (1938), *Stolen Life* (1939), *The Good Beginning* (1953), *Room in the House* (1955), *Indiscreet, Nowhere to Go* (1958), *A Touch of Larceny* (1959), *Kidnapped* (1960), *Dr Crippen* (1962), *The Tomb of Ligeia* (1964), *You Must Be Joking!* (1965). AS.

Johnston, Sue (*b* Warrington, 1943). Actress. Her marvellously subtle incarnation of put-upon, working-class housewifedom in TV's *The Royle Family* (1998–2000; BAAn/ comedy performance, 1998) is perhaps her finest hour, but she is a character player to relish even in smaller roles such as Philip JACKSON's wife in *Brassed Off* (1996, UK/US) and Robert CARLYLE's Mum in *Face* (1997). Also had popular continuing roles in TV's *Brookside* (1982-) and *Medics* (1992–95).

OTHER BRITISH FILMS: *Preaching to the Perverted* (1997), *New Year's Day* (2001, UK/Fr).

Jones, Barry (*b* Guernsey, Channel Islands, 1893 – *d* Guernsey, 1981). Actor. Stocky character who had one starring role, which he played with disquieting conviction, as the professor who sets the government a dangerous challenge in *Seven Days to Noon*

(1950). He was on stage, 1921, having served in the army in WW1, and in films from 1931, though his main screen career came post-WW2 service. He usually played professional men, sometimes villainous, like Professor Logan in the remake of *The Thirty Nine Steps* (1958). He appeared in a number of Hollywood films in the 50s, including *Brigadoon* (1954), as the schoolmaster, and as Aristotle no less in *Alexander the Great* (1956). Films and TV all but displaced stage work from the early 50s; he played Julius Caesar in the mini-series, *The Spread of the Eagle* (1963).

OTHER BRITISH FILMS INCLUDE: *Number Seventeen* (1932), *Murder in the Family* (1938), *Squadron Leader X* (1942), *Frieda, Dancing with Crime* (1947), *That Dangerous Age, Madeleine* (1949), *The Clouded Yellow* (1950), *White Corridors* (1951), *Saint Joan* (1957), *A Study in Terror* (1965).

Jones, David (*b* Poole, 1934). Director, screenwriter, producer. Jones's screen career as director includes the elliptical, backward-moving *Betrayal* (1982), from PINTER, the pleasant opening out of *84 Charing Cross Road* (1986, UK/US), and, again from a Pinter screenplay, a listless version of *The Trial* (1992). Initially a stage director, he was company director for the RSC's first London season, 1970–71; recently, he has worked in US television. Married Sheila ALLEN.

OTHER BRITISH FILMS INCLUDE: *Fallen Angel* (1989, doc, ex p).

Jones, Emrys (*b* Manchester, 1915 – *d* Johannesburg, 1972). Actor. Perennially youthful-looking actor on stage from 1937, in Donald WOLFIT's company, subsequently starring in such popular plays as *The Hasty Heart* (1945) and *Dial 'M' for Murder* (1952, 1954). Briefly noticed as a radio operator in *One of Our Aircraft is Missing* (1942), he made 20 further films, likeable in such supporting roles as the unmarried father in *Holiday Camp* (1947) and a sympathetic Robbie Ross in *The Trials of Oscar Wilde* (1960), and an adequate lead in such 'B' FILMS as *Deadly Nightshade* (1953), in a dual role, and *Serena* (1962). Radio and TV experience. Married (1) to Pauline Bentley who appeared with him in *Blue Scar* (1949) and (2) Anne Ridler who appeared in *Camp on Blood Island* (1957) and *633 Squadron* (1963, UK/US).

OTHER BRITISH FILMS INCLUDE: *The Shipbuilders* (1943), *Give Me the Stars* (1944), *The Wicked Lady* (1945), *Beware of Pity* (1946), *Nicholas Nickleby* (1947), *This Was a Woman* (1948), *Dark Secret* (1949), *Three Cases of Murder* (1955), *The Shield of Faith* (1956), *On the Run* (1963).

Jones, Evan (*b* Portland, Jamaica, 1927). Author, screenwriter. Began writing for BBC television in 1956, he made his mark in cinema as writer on four films for Joseph LOSEY: *The Damned* (1961), *Eva* (1962, Fr/It), the rigorous and moving *King and Country* (1964) and the camply comic (Dirk BOGARDE, pegged out in the desert sun, calls: 'Champagne!') *Modesty Blaise* (1966). Since then, his career has been all over the place and short on the distinction one might have expected, though screenplays for two Australian films, *Wake in Fright* (1971) and *Kangaroo* (1986), catch the idiom convincingly.

OTHER BRITISH FILMS INCLUDE: *Funeral in Berlin* (1966), *Two Gentlemen Sharing* (1969), *Ghost in the Noonday Sun* (1974), *Champions* (1983).

Jones, Freddie (*b* Stoke-on-Trent, 1927). Actor. There is an enjoyable touch of old-time barnstormer in some of Jones's work, like for instance his cruel exploiter of *The Elephant Man* (1980, US-financed, UK-made). Entered the profession in mid 50s, training at the Rose Buford College of Speech and Drama, and played small roles in films starting with *Marat/Sade* . . . (1966). Made his mark as an obsessive scientist in *Frankenstein*

Must Be Destroyed (1969), and played in several further HORROR films, as well as, *inter alia*, Pompey in *Antony and Cleopatra* (1972, UK/Sp/Switz), the Vicar in *Comrades* (1986) and Harald the Missionary in *Erik the Viking* (1989), and such international films as *Dune* (1984) and masses of TV, looking as deranged as ever as Adam Lambsbreath in *Cold Comfort Farm* (1995, TV, some cinemas). A great eccentric.

OTHER BRITISH FILMS INCLUDE: *Accident, Far from the Madding Crowd* (1967), *The Man Who Haunted Himself, Assault* (1970), *Kidnapped* (1971), *Juggernaut, Son of Dracula* (1974), *Krull* (1983), *Consuming Passions* (1988, UK/US), *The Mystery of Edwin Drood* (1993), *What Rats Won't Do* (1998), *My Life So Far* (UK/US), *House!* (2000).

Jones, Gemma (*b* London, 1942). Actress. Daughter of Griffith JONES and sister of Nicholas JONES, RADA-trained, this slender, attractive player settled rather early into character roles, perhaps in the wake of her TV success as *The Duchess of Duke Street* (1976–77), based on the real-life Rosa Lewis of the Cavendish Hotel. Her career began to move in 1971, with a fine stage performance as Kenneth MORE's wife in *Getting On* and the honourable Fleda Vletch in the mini-series, *The Spoils of Poynton*, from Henry JAMES. Entered films in *The Devils* (1971) but has mostly played mothers, not always in very rewarding roles: Mrs Dashwood in *Sense and Sensibility* (1995, UK/US) and (very touching) the mother of *The Winslow Boy* (1999, US-made, UK cast) are perhaps the best, but she was unexpectedly funny as Bridget's mother in *Bridget Jones's Diary* (2001, UK/Fr/US).

OTHER BRITISH FILMS INCLUDE: *On the Black Hill* (1987), *Paperhouse* (1988), *Feast of July* (1995, UK/US), *Wilde* (1997, UK/Ger/Jap/US, as Bosie's mother), *Cotton Mary* (1999, UK/Fr/US).

Jones, Griff Rhys *see* **Rhys Jones, Griff**

Jones, Griffith (*b* London, 1910). Actor. Tall, elegant RADA gold-medallist and on stage from 1930, Jones had a long film career without becoming a major film *star*. His good looks won him a succession of light hero roles in 30s films such as *Escape Me Never* and the Jessie MATTHEWS musical, *First A Girl* (1935) and Robert STEVENSON's charming *Young Man's Fancy* (1939), but it was in second lead roles like those in *A Yank at Oxford* (1937), *The Wicked Lady* and *The Rake's Progress* (1945) that he established a somewhat limiting gentlemanly persona. It took a couple of tough 1947 roles (the thugs, Danny, in *Good-Time Girl*, and, especially, the vile Narcy in *They Made Me A Fugitive*) to reveal a wider range – and suggest some seismic changes might be at work in British cinema (and society). As far as Jones was concerned, these were the highlights and he spent the rest of his film career largely in 'B' FILMS, sometimes bringing a touch of distinction to these, as in *Account Rendered* (1957), and he was always busy on stage. Father of Gemma and Nicholas JONES.

OTHER BRITISH FILMS INCLUDE: *Money Talks* (1932), *Catherine the Great* (1934), *The Mill on the Floss* (1937), *The Day Will Dawn, Uncensored* (1942), *Henry V* (1944), *Miranda, Look Before You Love* (1948), *Once Upon a Dream* (1949), *The Sea Shall Not Have Them, The Scarlet Web* (1954), *Face in the Night* (1956), *The Truth About Women* (1957), *Strangler's Web* (1966), *Decline and Fall . . .* (1968).

Jones, James Cellan (*b* Swansea, 1930). Director. Much respected TV director whose work has included an intelligent version of *The Portrait of a Lady* (1968), the BBC's very funny *The Comedy of Errors* (1983), and the mini-series, *Fortunes of War* (1987). Won a BAA/d for the series, *Jenny: Lady Randolph Churchill* (1975). His cinema films are *A Bequest to the Nation* (1973), a perhaps authentic but unengrossing version of the Nelson-Lady Hamilton amour, and *Married 2 Malcolm* (1998, UK/Ger).

Jones, Jennifer (*b* Tulsa, Oklahoma, 1920). Actress. RN: Phyllis Isley. Oscared for *Song of Bernadette* (1944), this American star, a fragile, faintly tormented-looking beauty, made four British films. Two of these – Michael POWELL's lushly romantic *Gone to Earth* (1950) and John HUSTON's delectable shaggy dog story, *Beat the Devil* (1953, UK/It/US) – are among her best films; the other two – a remake of *The Barretts of Wimpole Street* (1956) and *The Idol* (1966) – are not. Married (1 of 3) to actor Robert Walker (1939–44) and (2) to David O Selznick (1949–65, his death).

Jones, Kenneth V. (*b* Bletchley, Buckinghamshire, 1924). Composer. A professor at the RCM, he entered films in 1950 and wrote the scores for about 50 films, including a batch for WARWICK FILMS in the later 50s, and otherwise ranging generically from *The Horse's Mouth* (1958, + dance arr) to *Tarzan the Magnificent* (1960), *Dr Crippen* (1962) and *Battle Beneath the Earth* (1967).

OTHER BRITISH FILMS INCLUDE: (dance music) *The Horrors of the Black Museum, Too Young to Love* (1959); (comp/ m d) *Vengeance* (1962, UK/Ger), *Psyche 59* (1963); (comp/cond) *Passport to Shame* (1958), *Cairo* (1963), *The Tomb of Ligeia* (1964), *Whoever Slew Auntie Roo?* (1971), *The Brute* (1976); (comp) *Sea Wife* (1956), *High Flight, Fire Down Below* (1957), *Indiscreet* (1958), *The Bandit of Zhobe, Ferry to Hong Kong* (1959), *Two Way Stretch* (1960), *The Green Helmet* (1961), *Tarzan Goes to India* (1962), *Tower of Evil* (1972, UK/US).

Jones, Mary (*b* Rhayader, Wales, 1915 – *d* 1990). Actress. Agreeable supporting player who appeared in a dozen films, including an uncredited bit as Anthony BUSHELL's secretary in *The Battle of the River Plate* (1956). Made a minor meal of a bitchy wife who defenestrates in *Account Rendered* (1957).

OTHER BRITISH FILMS INCLUDE: *Trottie True* (1948), *Black Orchid* (1952), *One Jump Ahead, Timeslip* (1955), *The Big Chance* (1957), *The Promise* (1969), *Under Milk Wood* (1971).

Jones, Nicholas (*b* London, 1946). Actor. Educated at Westminster School and trained at RADA (in stage management) and Bristol Old Vic Theatre School (acting), he had RSC and National Theatre seasons and scored a major TV success as dynamic Captain Triggers in the *Wings* (1976–77) series, was enjoyably and ineptly devious in *Kavanagh QC* (1994–95), and relished swinish Bob Duport in *A Dance to the Music of Time* (1997). Best film roles to date: twittish Charles in *Daisy Miller* (1974, US) and Jennifer EHLE's outraged father in *This Year's Love* (1999). Son of Griffith JONES and brother of Gemma JONES.

OTHER BRITISH FILMS INCLUDE: *Wolfshead: the Legend of Robin Hood* (1969), *Cromwell* (1970), *The Blockhouse* (1973), *When the Whales Came* (1989).

Jones, Paul (*b* Portsmouth, 1942). Actor. RN: Paul Pond. Lead singer and harmonica player with the 60s group 'Manfred Mann', and founder of the 'Blues Band' in 1979, he played the lead (a pop idol) in Peter WATKINS's fable of the times, *Privilege* (1967), and starred in *The Committee* (1968), and the HORROR film, *Demons of the Mind* (1971). Much on TV, including even a stint on *Songs of Praise* (1980).

Jones, Peter (*b* Wem, 1920 – *d* England, 2000). Actor. From the moment he appeared on screen as the hapless milord in search of forbidden pleasures in *Fanny by Gaslight* (1944), the die was cast for Jones, who found household fame as inept boss Fenner in TV's *The Rag Trade* (1961–63, 1977–78), constantly outsmarted by wily shop steward, Miriam KARLIN. He is in dozens of films – WAR FILMS (*Angels One Five*, 1952; *Albert RN*,

1953), 'CARRY ON' SERIES (. . . *Doctor*, 1968; . . . *England*, 1976), and COMEDIES of every hue – and almost always his persona suggests he shouldn't be taken too seriously and that events will overwhelm him. Much TV, including an episode of *Midsomer Murders* a couple of years before his death, and famous on RADIO for his long-running participation in the game pro- gramme *Just a Minute* (1967, last in 1999). On stage from 1936, London 1942; in the original cast of T.S. Eliot's *The Confidential Clerk* (1953) and Peter NICHOLS's *Forget-Me-Not- Lane* (1971).

OTHER BRITISH FILMS INCLUDE: *Dead of Night* (1945), *Vice Versa* (1947), *Private Angelo* (1949), *Chance of a Lifetime* (1950), *The Browning Version* (1951), *The Long Memory* (1952), *John and Julie* (1955), *Private's Progress* (1956), *Blue Murder at St Trinian's* (1957), *Danger Within* (1958), *Never Let Go*, *The Bulldog Breed* (1960), *Father Came Too!* (1963), *Press for Time* (1966), *Hot Millions* (1968), *Return of the Pink Panther* (1974), *Chariots of Fire* (1981), *Milk* (1999).

Jones, Terry (*b* Colwyn Bay, Wales, 1942). Actor, director, screenwriter. One of the MONTY PYTHON group, multi- talented, Oxford-educated Jones (the others were at Cambridge) came to TV in the mid 60s, scoring with such comedy series as *Do Not Adjust Your Set* (1968–69, a, sc) and *The Complete and Utter History of Britain* (1969). He joined the cult Python group with *Monty Python's Flying Circus* (1969–70, 1972–74); was in their first cinema film, *And Now for Something Completely Different* (1971, + co-sc); and co-directed and co- wrote *Monty Python and the Holy Grail* (1974) and the savagely satirical *Life of Brian* (1979, + a) and *The Meaning of Life* (1983, + a). These wild swipes at Just About Everything, allied to a wild visual style, have retained their popularity with a new generation of viewers. In different mode, he also directed *Personal Services* (1987), based on the life of brothel-keeper, Cynthia Payne, and directed and wrote *The Wind in the Willows* (1996, + a, songs), featuring several Python alumni. Also the author of several children's books.

OTHER BRITISH FILMS INCLUDE: *The Secret Policeman's Ball* (1979, a, co-sc), *The Secret Policeman's Other Ball* (1982, a), *The Secret Policeman's Private Parts* (1984, a), *Labyrinth* (1986, sc), *Erik the Viking* (1989, d, a), *The Chemical Wedding* (2001, d).

Jones, Trevor (*b* Cape Town, 1949). Composer. Came to England when 17, trained at the Royal Academy of Music, and worked as music reviewer at the BBC for four years; has scored 70 film and TV programmes since the late 70s. He was music arranger on MONTY PYTHON's *Life of Brian* (1979), colla- borated with Jim HENSON on several films, including *The Dark Crystal* (1982, co-synthesiser of electronic sounds), and has gone on to score such popular and diverse films as *Richard III* (1995), *Brassed Off* (1996, UK/US) and *Notting Hill* (1999, UK/US). Also worked on big US films including *The Last of the Mohicans* (1992) and *Thirteen Days* (2001).

OTHER BRITISH FILMS INCLUDE: (comp, unless noted) *Bovver Boots* (1977, short, co-comp), *Black Angel* (short), *Brothers and Sisters* (1980, + cond), *The Dollar Bottom* (short, + cond), *Time Bandits* (co-m) (1981), *The Sender* (1982, UK/US), *Labyrinth* (1986), *In the Name of the Father* (1993, UK/Ire/US), *Loch Ness* (1996), *Titanic Town* (1998, UK/Ire).

Jones, Vinnie (*b* Watford, 1965). Actor. Former Wimbledon footballer and one of soccer's toughest heroes, who embarked on a new career as East End enforcer in Guy RITCHIE's popular gangster movie, *Lock, Stock and Two Smoking Barrels* (1998), and was retained by Ritchie for his follow-up, even more impenetrably plotted shoot-fest, *Snatch* (2000), and for the lead in his biopic of bare-knuckle boxer Lenny McLean.

Chosen by John Travolta to play villain in his $156m thriller *Swordfish* (2000), and may well be largely lost to Hollywood where he took to the lifestyle and where the immobility of his features will be less conspicuous.

OTHER BRITISH FILMS: *Mean Machine* (2001).

Jordan, Neil (*b* Sligo, Ireland, 1950). Director, screenwriter, producer. Imaginative Irish film-maker whose films move easily between representations of the monstrous and the poetic. His directorial career began with *Angel* (1982, + sc, Ire), where Jordan favourite Stephen REA played a saxophonist whose quiet regard for a deaf-mute girl led to murder. The superbly realised *noir* thriller *Mona Lisa* (1986, + co-sc) and the now-legendary (*that* scene) *The Crying Game* (1992, + sc, AAsc) contain moments of tenderness between ill-fated couples in environments fraught with danger. Religion also dominates the narrative landscape of Jordan films, like *The Butcher Boy* (1997, Ire/US, + sc, exec p) and his ADAPTATION of Graham GREENE's *The End of the Affair* (1999, UK/Ger/US, + sc, co-p), where in the context of war a woman is compelled to choose between her lover and God. Jordan's efforts in the US (*High Spirits*, 1988, + sc; *We're No Angels*, 1989; *Interview with the Vampire*, 1994; *In Dreams*, 1998, + sc) have been patchy with the exception of *Michael Collins* (1996, + sc), suggesting that a personal connection to stories results in his best work.

OTHER BRITISH FILMS: *Traveller* (1981, Ire, sc), *The Company of Wolves* (1984, d, co-sc), *The Courier* (1987, Ire, ex p), *The Miracle* (1991, UK/Ire, d, sc), *The Last September* (1999, UK/Fr/Ire, ex p), *The Good Thief* (2002, UK/Can/Fr/Ire). Melinda Hildebrandt.

Jordan, Patrick (*b* Harrow, 1923). Actor. Character player who has played policemen (*Bunny Lake Is Missing*, 1965) and murderers (*Emergency*, 1962), and military men, Sergeants (*The Victors*, 1963) and officers (*Play Dirty*, 1968), in over 30 movies, starting with a run of 'B' FILMS.

OTHER BRITISH FILMS INCLUDE: *A Ray of Sunshine* (1950), *Profile*, *The Embezzler* (1954), *Cloak Without Dagger* (1955), *The Battle of the River Plate* (1956), *The Angry Hills* (1959), *Rag Doll* (1960), *The Break* (1962), *The Heroes of Telemark* (1965), *You Only Live Twice*, *Robbery* (1967), *Perfect Friday*, *Jane Eyre* (1970), *The Slipper and the Rose* (1976).

Josephs, Wilfred (*b* Newcastle-upon-Tyne, 1927 – *d* London, 1997). Composer. Wrote the score for perhaps the best British 'B' FILM, *Cash on Demand* (1961), considerably increasing its painful tension, and thereafter adapted to the generic demands of HORROR films (*The Deadly Bees*, 1966), THRILLERS (*Callan*, 1974) and children's films (*Swallows and Amazons*, 1974). Also scored high-profile TV series, including *I, Claudius* (1976) and the title music for *Norman Conquests* (1978).

OTHER BRITISH FILMS INCLUDE: *Night Without Pity* (+ cond), *The Webster Boy* (1962), *Fanatic* (1965), *Dark Places* (1973), *All Creatures Great and Small* (1974), *The Uncanny* (1977, UK/Can), *Martin's Day* (1985, UK/Can).

Jourdan, Louis (*b* Marseilles, 1919). Actor. RN: Gandre. Charming and handsome leading man, who made screen debut in France in 1939, and achieved international stardom later thanks to such Hollywood films as *The Paradine Case* (1948), *Letter from an Unknown Woman* (1948) and *Gigi* (1958). His British films, all starring roles, did nothing for his career or status as an actor.

BRITISH FILMS: *Dangerous Exile* (1957), *The VIPs* (1963), *The Count of Monte Cristo* (1974), *Octopussy* (1983). AS.

Joyce, Eileen (*b* Zeehan, Tasmania, 1912 – *d* Westerham, 1991). Pianist. Joyce's remarkable career belongs in other volumes, but she deserves noting here for two films, released within months of each other, in which she is heard but not seen. She is all over the soundtrack of *Brief Encounter* (1945), playing the Rachmaninov concerto to great emotional effect, and she dubbed the playing of the traumatised heroine, Ann TODD, in *The Seventh Veil* (1945). Appeared as a musician in *A Girl in a Million* (1946) and *Trent's Last Case* (1952), and dubbed Schubert's 'Impromptu in E flat major' while Françoise ROSAY 'played' in *Quartet* (1948). A drab BIOPIC of her early life, *Wherever She Goes*, appeared in 1951 (Aust). Lived with agent Christopher MANN for 37 years but never married him.

BIBLIOG: Richard Davis, *Eileen Joyce: A Portrait*, 2001.

Joyce, James (*b* Dublin, 1882 – *d* Zurich, 1941). Author, dramatist. Few authors can have seemed less likely cinematic material, but in the event there have been some brave tries: bravest of all is Mary Ellen Bute's *Passages from 'Finnegans Wake'* (1965, US), about as resolutely ART-HOUSE as a film could be; Joseph STRICK's *Ulysses* (1967, UK/US) enshrines gallant performances from Milo O'Shea as Bloom and Barbara JEFFORD as Molly; Strick's *A Portrait of the Artist as a Young Man* (1977) captured in surprising degree the dialectic of the novel's last section; and John HUSTON's *The Dead* (1987, UK/Ger/US) is one of the great films of its decade. In December 1909, backed by three somewhat inept Italian businessmen, Joyce opened Dublin's first cinema, the 'Volta', and he was an enthusiastic filmgoer despite his failing eyesight. Ewan McGREGOR played Joyce in *Nora* (2000, UK/Ger/Ire/It), based on the life of Joyce's wife.

Joyce, Yootha (*b* London, 1927 – *d* London, 1980). Actress. Baleful-eyed blonde character player seen at her predatory best in two films for Jack CLAYTON – *The Pumpkin Eater* (1964), in a beauty-salon cameo of matchless malice, and *Our Mother's House* (1967), as a nosy neighbour. Very popular on TV as Mildred Roper in *Man About the House* (1973–76) and its follow-up *George and Mildred* (1976–78), and appeared in the SPIN-OFF FILMS made from each, 1974 and 1980 respectively.

OTHER BRITISH FILMS INCLUDE: *A Place to Go* (1963), *Catch Us If You Can* (1965), *A Man for All Seasons* (1966), *Charlie Bubbles* (1967), *Fragment of Fear, Burke & Hare* (1971), *Steptoe & Son Ride Again* (1973).

Judd, Edward (*b* Shanghai, 1932). Actor. Strong-featured lead and second lead in several decades of British films, having started as a teenager in 1948 (*The Small Voice, The Guinea Pig, Once a Jolly Swagman*). Played military officers (e.g. in *Mystery Submarine*, 1962), a doctor dealing with alien *Invasion* (1966), Susan Hayward's racing-driver lover in *Stolen Hours* (1963, UK/US), the journalist hero in *The Day the Earth Caught Fire* (1961), and turned up in several HORROR films later in his career. Also on stage and TV, starring in *Intrigue* (1966). Was married to Gene ANDERSON until her death in 1965.

OTHER BRITISH FILMS INCLUDE: *The Good Die Young* (1954), *X the Unknown* (1956), *The Man Upstairs, Carry On Sergeant* (1958), *Sink the Bismarck!, The Criminal* (1960), *First Men in the Moon* (1964), *The Vengeance of She* (1967), *Living Free* (1972), *O Lucky Man!, Assassin* (1973), *The Kitchen Toto* (1987).

Julien, Isaac (*b* London, 1960). Director, screenwriter, producer. Intellectual, with a post in cultural studies at Harvard, artist and theorist, Julien has produced a respected body of work which constitutes a critique of BLACK/GAY REPRESENTATION. Opposed to essentialist stereotyping, he claims to work *from* but not *for* the black/gay position, and his

best known (if not commercially successful) feature, *Young Soul Rebels* (1991), depicts relationships across racial and sexual divides. He has also directed DOCUMENTARIES about black activists and writers: *Looking for Langston* (1989) and *Frantz Fanon: Black Skin, White Mask* (1996). A graduate of St Martin's School of Art, he is also involved in innovative art exhibitions and was nominated for the 2001 Turner Prize for art.

OTHER BRITISH FILMS INCLUDE: (d, unless noted) *Who Killed Colin Roach?* (1983, doc, short, c, e), *The Passion of Remembrance* (1986, co-d, co-sc), *This Is Not an AIDS Ad* (1987, short), *The Attendant, The Darker Side of Black* (1993, shorts, + co-sc).

June (*b* Blackpool, 1901 – *d* New York, 1985). Actress. RN: June Tripp. A popular star of musical comedy and revue in the 1910s, 20s and 30s – debut 1911 – who donned a wig for the role of Daisy Bunting in *The Lodger* (1926) and became HITCHCOCK's first stereotypical blonde heroine. Retired from stage (1929–32) following her first marriage to Lord Inverclyde. Played a VAD girl in her Hollywood film, *Forever and a Day* (1943).

OTHER BRITISH FILMS: *Auld Robin Gray* (1918), *The Yellow Claw* (1921), *Riding for a King* (1926).

BIBLIOG: Autobiography, *The Whole Story*, 1932; *The Glass Ladder*, 1960. AS.

Junge, Alfred (*b* Görlitz, Germany, 1886 – *d* Bad Kissingen, Germany, 1964). Production designer. Junge, in film from 1920, as art director at Berlin's UFA studios, came to Britain in the mid 20s with director E.A. DUPONT, and spent the rest of his career there. He headed GAUMONT–BRITISH's production department between 1932 and 1937 at a time when its head, Michael BALCON, was trying to compete with Hollywood, and where his craftsmanship and technical expertise influenced many British directors and other technicians. At Gaumont–British, SHEPHERD'S BUSH STUDIOS, he gave a distinctive look to such generically diverse films as *The Ghoul* (1933), the wonderfully glamorous Jessie MATTHEWS musical, *Evergreen* (1934), and to several HITCHCOCK THRILLERS, and, at MGM–British, to the nostalgically recreated public school world of *Goodbye, Mr Chips* (1939). His greatest artistic triumphs, though, were his collaborations with POWELL AND PRESSBURGER in the 40s, particularly *A Matter of Life and Death* (1946), with its 'staircase to Heaven' and celestial court, and *Black Narcissus* (AA, 1947), the latter magically recreating the Himalayan convent in PINEWOOD and Horsham, Surrey. Michael Powell later rated him as 'probably the greatest art director that films have ever known'. In the 50s he headed MGM–BRITISH's production department, responsible for transatlantic productions such as *Ivanhoe* (1952).

OTHER BRITISH FILMS INCLUDE: *Moulin Rouge* (1928), *Piccadilly* (1929), *Two Worlds* (1930), *Cape Forlorn* (1931), *Service For Ladies* (1932), *The Good Companions, I Was A Spy, Friday The Thirteenth, The Constant Nymph* (1933), *Red Ensign, Little Friend, Evensong, Jew Süss, The Man Who Knew Too Much*, (1934), *Bulldog Jack* (1935), *It's Love Again* (1936), *King Solomon's Mines, Young And Innocent* (1937), *Climbing High, The Citadel* (1938), *Contraband, Gaslight* (1940), *The Life And Death Of Colonel Blimp* (1942), *The Silver Fleet* (1943), *A Canterbury Tale* (1944), *I Know Where I'm Going!* (1945), *The Hour of 13* (1952), *Seagulls Over Sorrento* (1954), *The Barretts Of Wimpole Street* (1956).

BIBLIOG: Catherine A. Surowiec, *Accent on Design: Four European Art Directors*, 1992. Tim Bergfelder.

Junkin, John (*b* London, 1930). Actor, screenwriter. Tall, gawky and latterly balding comedian, much on TV, including *Marty* (1968–69), as foil to Marty FELDMAN, and many other comedy shows including his own, often writing for others as well as himself. A former schoolteacher, on the big screen he was funny as Shake, part of the BEATLES' entourage in *A Hard Day's Night* (1964) and appeared, usually in comic roles in about 20 other films, mainly in the 60s and 70s.

OTHER BRITISH FILMS INCLUDE: *The Break* (1962), *The Pumpkin Eater* (1964), *The Wrong Box* (1966), *How I Won the War* (1967), *Confessions of a Driving Instructor* (1976) . . . *from a Holiday Camp, Rosie Dixon – Night Nurse* (1978), *A Handful of Dust* (1987), *Chicago Joe and the Showgirl* (1989).

Jupp, Ralph T. (*b* Walsall, 1875 – *d* Buckinghamshire, 1921). Exhibitor. Was co-founder in 1909 and managing director of Provincial Cinematograph Theatres Ltd, the first important UK cinema circuit. In 1912, he co-founded the Cinematograph Exhibitors' Association of Great Britain and was its first president, and, in 1914, founded Associated Provincial Picture Houses. A year earlier, he formed the LONDON FILM COMPANY in a serious effort to make quality British films. Ill health in 1916 forced Jupp to withdraw from the industry, and in May 1918, he sold his interest in Provincial Cinematograph Theatres to Sir William JURY. AS.

Juran, Nathan (*b* Vienna, 1907 – *d* Palos Verdes Estates, California, 2002). Director. Former art director, Juran became a competent director of routine Westerns, thrillers and scifi sagas in Hollywood, before coming to the UK to make three modestly enjoyable features in the mid 60s: the costume action piece, *The Siege of the Saxons* (1963), the space romp, *First Men in the Moon* (with Ray HARRYHAUSEN effects), and – *après* (by some distance) *The African Queen – East of Suez* (1964).

Jürgens, Curt (*b* Munich, 1915 – *d* Vienna, 1982). Actor. Tall, heavy-built star of over 100 European, British, and Hollywood productions, Jürgens portrayed imposing villains and slightly dissolute heroes. As a Chinese warlord in *The Inn Of The Sixth Happiness* (1958) he romanced Ingrid BERGMAN, while his megalomaniac millionaire in *The Spy Who Loved Me* (1977) became a memorable villain of the James BOND series. As a leading man, though, he lacked the on screen presence to save a dull adventure like *Ferry To Hong Kong* (1959). Among Jürgens' five wives was actress Eva BARTOK (1955–56).

OTHER BRITISH FILMS INCLUDE: *Bitter Victory* (1957, UK/Fr), *Hide and Seek, Psyche 59* (1963), *Lord Jim* (1964), *The Assassination Bureau* (1969), *Battle Of Britain* (1969), *Nicholas and Alexandra* (1971, UK/US), *The Vault of Horror* (1973, UK/US). Tim Bergfelder.

Jury, Sir William (*b* London, 1870 – *d* London, 1944). Distributor. A rough-and-ready, major renter or distributor in the early years of British cinema, who was so important that, from 1924 to 1927, MGM films were distributed in the UK as Jury–Metro–Goldwyn Ltd releases. A self-made-man, he began his career as a fairground showman, forming Jury's Imperial Pictures and, in 1918, taking over Provincial Cinematograph Theatres. During WW1, he was a member of both the War Office Cinematograph Committee and of the MOI's cinematograph division. Knighted in 1918 (first from the film industry to be so honoured) for his work in organizing the supply of films from the Western Front, Italy and the Middle East. Retired in 1927, but continued his philanthropic work with the Cinematograph Trade Benevolent Fund, and in November 1935, he presented Glebelands to the Fund as a convalescent home. AS.

Justice, James Robertson (*b* Wigtown, Scotland, 1905 – *d* Kings Somborne, 1975). Actor. Irascible character player who

began acting when nearly 40 at the Players' Theatre in 1944 and entered films in the same year (*Champagne Charlie, Fiddlers Three, For Those in Peril*). Also a journalist and naturalist, as well as a falconry expert, he had made about 30 films before the role of senior surgeon, Sir Lancelot Spratt, in *Doctor in the House* (1954) and its sequels made his booming, bearded figure and sarcastic locutions popular with filmgoers. He was never required to do anything very subtle, but what he did was enough to keep him extremely busy for 25 years, and included the strong simple Evans in *Scott of the Antarctic* (1948), Little John (of course) in *The Story of Robin Hood* . . . (1952) and Henry VIII in *The Sword and the Rose* (1953). Also filmed in Hollywood, in *David and Bathsheba, Anne of the Indies* (1951), and others.

OTHER BRITISH FILMS INCLUDE: *Vice Versa, Against the Wind* (1947), *Whisky Galore!, Poet's Pub* (1949), *The Magnet* (1950), *The Voice of Merrill* (1952), *Rob Roy* . . . (1953), *Doctor at Sea, An Alligator Named Daisy* (1955), *Moby Dick* (1956), *Doctor at Large* (1957), *Orders to Kill* (1958), *Doctor in Love* (1960), *The Guns of Navarone* (1961), *Crooks Anonymous* (1962), *Father Came Too!, Doctor in Distress* (1963), *Those Magnificent Men* . . . (1965), *Doctor in Clover* (1966), *Chitty Chitty Bang Bang* (1968), *Doctor in Trouble* (1970).

Justin, John (*b* London, 1917 – *d* London, 2002). Actor. RN: John Justinian De Ledesma. Tall, handsome leading man who grew up in Argentina. On stage from 1933, then trained at RADA before London debut in 1938. KORDA signed him to star in *The Thief of Baghdad*, released at the end of 1940. WW2 service (1940–45) as a RAF pilot intervened; he was released to play Joyce HOWARD's young man in the ATS hymn, *The Gentle Sex* (1943). Post-war, he returned to the theatre, with a Stratford season in 1948, but in the 50s he was mostly in films. If he never regained the momentum which might have followed *The Thief*, and though he didn't fit the tweedy 50s male stereotype, he had some good opportunities: the pilot who survives in *The Sound Barrier* (1952), the hero with an *idée fixe* in the charming *The Man Who Loved Redheads* (1954), and the Governor's aide in the star-studded *Island in the Sun* (1957, UK/US). Never a major star, but an agreeable, intelligent leading man who later adapted to character work in three Ken RUSSELL films: *Savage Messiah* (1972), *Lisztomania* (1975) and *Valentino* (1977). Married (2 of 3) and divorced Barbara MURRAY.

OTHER BRITISH FILMS INCLUDE: *Journey Together* (1945), *Call of the Blood* (1948, UK/It), *The Angel with the Trumpet* (1949), *Hot Ice* (1952), *Melba, The Village* (UK/Switz) (1953), *Seagulls Over Sorrento, The Teckman Mystery* (1954), *Guilty?* (UK/Fr), *Safari* (1956), *The Spider's Web* (1960), *The Big Sleep* (1978).

Jympson, John (*b* London, 1930). Editor. Part of the effervescent, if not indeed evanescent, charm of the BEATLES' *A Hard Day's Night* (1964) is attributable to Jympson's sprightly cutting. After minor cutting chores on such 50s films as *The Ship That Died of Shame* (1955) and *I Was Monty's Double* (1958), Jympson, trained at EALING, worked solidly throughout the 60s, on big films like *Zulu* (1964), *The Bedford Incident* (1965) and *Where Eagles Dare* (1968), cut HITCHCOCK's penultimate, London-set thriller, *Frenzy* (1972), received a BAAn for editing the hit comedy, *A Fish Called Wanda* (1988), but in the 80s and 90s worked as much in the US as the UK before ill-health forced retirement. Son of A. Jympson HARMAN.

OTHER BRITISH FILMS INCLUDE: *Suspect* (1960), *A Prize of Arms* (1961), *Sands of the Kalahari* (1965), *Kaleidoscope* (1966), *Deadfall* (1968), *The Walking Stick* (1970), *Night Watch* (1973), *Mister Quilp* (1974), *Green Ice* (1981), *Circle of Friends* (Ire/US), *Haunted* (UK/US) (1995), *Mad Cows* (1999).

Kaley, Vi Actress. Small-part character player of 30 films from 1931 to 1953, often cast as charwoman (*Lloyd of the CID*, 1931; *Children of the Fog*, 1937) or landlady, in *The Man Without a Face* (1935) and the title role in Roy BOULTING's short film, *The Landlady* (1938).

OTHER BRITISH FILMS: *A Royal Demand* (1933), *The Gay Old Dog* (1935), *Men of Yesterday* (1936), *Victoria the Great, Talking Feet* (1937), *Father o' Nine* (1938), *The Day Will Dawn* (1942), *Old Mother Riley, Detective* (1943), *The Trojan Brothers* (1945), *Vice Versa* (1947), *Noose, The Weaker Sex* (1948), *The Mudlark* (1950), *My Wife's Lodger* (1952), *Cosh Boy* (1953).

Kalipha, Stefan (aka Stephen) (*b* Trinidad, *c* 1939). Actor. West Indian actor who secured a better-than-average share of the limited roles available to black actors in British film and TV in the 80s and 90s, including *Playing Away* (1986), but the roles have usually been small. Also fleetingly in a few US films, including *Indiana Jones and the Last Crusade* (1989).

OTHER BRITISH FILMS INCLUDE: *Events* (1969, + co-d), *Black Joy* (1977), *The Biggest Bank Robbery, Babylon* (1980), *For Your Eyes Only* (1981), *Superman III* (1983), *Water* (1985), *Born of Fire* (1987), *Scandal* (1988).

Kalmus, Natalie (*b* Boston, 1892 – *d* Boston, 1965). Colour consultant. Infamous figure in the history of colour cinematography, who often fought with cinematographers and art directors and is generally considered to have contributed little to the films on which her name appears. The TECHNICOLOR system was invented in large part by Herbert T. Kalmus, who had married Natalie Dunphy in 1903. When she divorced him in 1922, the divorce settlement gave her the right to place her name as Color Consultant on all Technicolor productions. When Technicolour (*sic*) Ltd was formed in the UK in 1935, she was shipped to England, where her name appeared on the first British Technicolor production, *Wings of the Morning* (1937), and stayed here for a number of years. Following a series of bitter lawsuits, her name was finally removed from Technicolor films in 1949, after which Joan BRIDGE became British Techicolor consultant. AS.

Kamen, Michael (*b* New York, 1948). Composer. Educated at Julliard School of Music and leader of the New York Rock Ensemble before taking to film music, Kamen has written over 80 scores for film and TV, including a good deal for US movies, such as *Die Hard* (1988) and *Robin Hood: Prince of Thieves* (1991). In Britain, he has worked on such diverse films as *Mona Lisa* and *Highlander* (1984), the BOND caper, *Licence to Kill* (1989), *The Krays* (1990) and *Winter Guest* (1998, UK/US) on which his blamelessly resonant piano score stood no chance against turgid script and direction. He has been prolific and inventive.

OTHER BRITISH FILMS INCLUDE: (comp, unless noted) *Venom* (1981), *Pink Floyd The Wall* (1982, arr, cond), *Brazil* (+ orch, arr) (1985), *Rita, Sue and Bob Too* (1986), *For Queen and Country* (1988, UK/US), 'Let Him Have It' (1991), *Circle of Friends* (1995, Ire/US), *Event Horizon* (1997, UK/US, + cond, orch).

Kane, David Director, screenwriter. After TV experience, Kane made his big-screen debut as writer-director of the witty, perceptive PORTMANTEAU film, *This Year's Love* (1999), in which he directed a cast of attractive young talents to excellent effect. His TV film, *Ruffian Hearts* (1994), was similarly concerned with interconnecting relationships, as was his follow-up film, *Born Romantic* (2001), with its salsa-club background.

Kanievska, Marek (*b* London, 1952). Director. Despite an auspicious feature debut with *Another Country* (1984), the screen adaptation of Julian Mitchell's drama of sexual and political rebellion, he directed only two further films, neither of them British. Also directed the TV drama series, *Muck and Brass* (1984).

Kann, Lily (aka Lilly, Khan) (*b* Peitz, Spreewald, Germany, 1898 – *d* Sussex, 1978). Actress. Cosy, all-purpose 'foreign' character player of the 40s and 50s, long in Britain and memorable as Queen Charlotte in *Mrs Fitzherbert* (1947), the refugee in *The Clouded Yellow* (1950), and the comforting housekeeper in the divorce drama, *Background* (1953).

OTHER BRITISH FILMS INCLUDE: *Escape to Danger, The Flemish Farm* (1943), *Latin Quarter* (1945), *Woman to Woman* (1946), *The White Unicorn* (1947), *Now Barabbas Was a Robber, The Third Man* (1949), *Street Corner* (1953), *Eight O'Clock Walk, A Kid for Two Farthings* (1954), *No Trees in the Street* (1958), *Whirlpool* (1959).

Kanner, Alexis (*b* Bagnères, France, 1942). Actor, director. Montreal-educated Kanner was an early regular in TV's *Softly, Softly* (1966–70) who appeared in scattered films of the 60s and 70s. His best part was probably as the modish young creep spongeing off Bette DAVIS in the little-seen *Connecting Rooms* (1969). In several international films.

OTHER BRITISH FILMS INCLUDE: *Reach for Glory* (1961), *We Joined the Navy* (1962), *Crossplot* (1969), *Goodbye Gemini* (1970).

Kanturek, Otto (*b* Vienna, Austria 1897 – *d* 1941). Cinematographer, director. Kanturek photographed numerous German feature films in the 20s, before moving to Britain later in the decade. Frequently working with Max SCHACH and Karl GRUNE, Kanturek also directed the film operetta *The Student's Romance* (1935). He was killed in an air crash while shooting *A Yank in the RAF* (1941).

OTHER BRITISH FILMS INCLUDE: *The Queen Was in the Parlour* (UK/Ger 1927), *Blossom Time, Mr Cinders* (1934), *Music Hath Charms* (co-ph. 1935), *Pagliacci* (1936), *Over She Goes* (1937), *The Housemaster* (1938), *Hold My Hand* (1938), *Premiere* (1938), *Queer Cargo* (1938), *So This Is London* (1939), *Shipyard Sally* (1939), *Night Train to Munich* (1940), *The Girl in the News* (1940). Tim Bergfelder.

Kapoor, Shashi (*b* Calcutta, 1938). Actor. Immensely popular Indian star of over 200 films, who has occasionally appeared in British productions. He played Hayley MILLS's boyfriend in *Pretty Polly* (1967), but is best known in the West for his performances in the MERCHANT IVORY films, *The Householder* (1963, Ind), *Shakespeare Wallah* (1965, Ind) and, co-starring his wife Jennifer Kendal (*b* Southport, Lancs, 1934 – *d* London, 1984), *Bombay Talkie* (1970, Ind). He was the Nawab in *Heat and Dust* (1982), in which Kendal also appeared.
OTHER BRITISH FILMS INCLUDE: *Sammy and Rosie Get Laid* (1987), *The Deceivers* (1988), *In Custody* (1993).

Kapur, Shekhar (*b* Lahore, 1945). Director. Kapur came to Western attention with *Bandit Queen* (1994), a UK/Indian co-production based on a famous Indian woman outlaw. His first wholly British film was *Elizabeth* (1998), a powerful MELODRAMA of the Virgin Queen's violent life, at some remove from the safeties of 'HERITAGE FILMS'. Both dramatised the conflicts faced by strong women in surviving, and he was nominated for a BAA/d for *Elizabeth*. His next English-speaking film was *The Four Feathers* (2003, UK/US).

Karas, Anton (*b* Vienna, 1906 – *d* Vienna, 1985). Composer. Deserves at least a footnote in British cinema history as composer of the famous zither score for *The Third Man* (1949). A former performer in a Viennese wine-cellar, he made a major contribution to the film's atmosphere, and did a guest turn the following year in *Come Dance with Me*.
BIBLIOG: Charles Drazin, *In Search of The Third Man*, 1999.

Karen, Anna (*b* Natal, South Africa, 1936). Actress. The acting highlight of former stripper Karen's acting career was probably playing Reg VARNEY's plain sister Olive in TV's *On the Buses* (1969–73) and the film SPIN-OFFS, *On the Buses* (1971), *Mutiny on the Buses* (1972) and *Holiday on the Buses* (1973). Highlights do not often come lower. Married to US actor Jeff Morrow until his death in 1993.
OTHER BRITISH FILMS INCLUDE: *Poor Cow* (1967), *Carry On Camping*, . . . *Loving* (1970), *Beautiful Thing* (1996).

Karina, Anna (*b* Copenhagen, 1940). Actress. RN: Hanne Karin Bayer. A former model, famously associated with French director Jean-Luc Godard whom she married (1961–67), she is essentially a European star though she appeared in four British films. The first was a numbingly unfunny farce, *She'll Have to Go* (1961); the others were more interesting: *The Magus* and *Before Winter Comes* (1968), and *Laughter in the Dark* (1969, UK/Fr), Tony RICHARDSON's version of NABOKOV's dark novel. Her post-Godard career included *Vivre Ensemble* (1973), which she wrote and directed as well as acted in, and the US film *Justine* (1969), messily derived from Lawrence Durrell's novel.

Karlin, Miriam (*b* London, 1925). Actress. RN: Samuels. RADA-trained Karlin first appeared on wartime ENSA tours, then in London from 1946. Stage career included several revues (e.g. *For Adults Only*, 1958) in which she excelled: she had a droll way with innuendo and could make a simple statement resonate suggestively. Became a popular TV favourite with *The Rag Trade* (1961–63), as Paddy, the whistle-blowing shop steward and bane of boss Fenner's life. Screen gave her only limited chances but she grabbed them with relish, as she does with the coarse chorus girl in *The Entertainer*, the anxious Jewish mother in *Hand in Hand* (both 1960), and, particularly, the Cat Lady in *A Clockwork Orange* (1971).

OTHER BRITISH FILMS INCLUDE: *Down Among the Z Men* (1952), *The Deep Blue Sea* (1955), *Room at the Top* (1958), *The Millionairess* (1960), *Watch It Sailor!*, *On the Fiddle* (1961), *I Thank a Fool* (1962), *Heavens Above!*, *Ladies Who Do* (1963), *Mahler* (1974), *Utz* (1992), *The Man Who Cried* (2000, UK/Fr/US).

Karloff, Boris (*b* London, 1887 – *d* Midhurst, Sussex, 1969). Actor. RN: William Henry Pratt. Karloff's most famous role as the monster in *Frankenstein* (1931, US) made him a legend but it did little – or perhaps too much – for his career; he is far more memorable as Ned in *The Criminal Code* earlier the same year. The actor began his screen career in the US in 1916 with *The Dumb Girl of Portici* and, in all, made 164 feature films, mostly American. The British-made *The Ghoul* (1933) was no doubt influenced by his US success in the HORROR genre, as were some later UK appearances. Also had TV series, *Colonel March of Scotland Yard* (1953–55), three episodes of which were compiled as the feature, *Colonel March Investigates* (1953).
OTHER BRITISH FILMS: *The Man Who Changed His Mind*, *Juggernaut* (1936), *Grip of the Strangler* (1958), *Corridors of Blood* (1962, filmed in 1958), *The Sorcerers* (1967), *The Crimson Cult* (1970). AS.

Karno, Fred (*b* Exeter, 1886 – *d* Lilliput, Dorset, 1941). Comedian. Famous MUSIC HALL comic who appeared in and/or contributed story material to a few films in the 30s. His comic sketches provided the basis for such films as *Oh! What a Duchess* (1933, from his sketch, 'Mumming Birds'), *Don't Rush Me* (1936, made for his own production company) and *Jailbirds* (1939). Though his own film career is minor, the stage sketches performed for his companies had an important effect on silent film comedy, and those who worked for him at various times included such film luminaries as Charlie CHAPLIN, Max MILLER and Will HAY.
OTHER BRITISH FILMS INCLUDE: (co-sc/sc, unless noted) *Early Birds* (1923, a), *The Bailiffs* (+ a), *Bad Companions* (1932, orig story), *Tooth Will Out*, *Sign Please* (1933, short), *Post Haste* (1934, short).

Kasander, Kees (*b* Gorinchem, Holland, 1951). Producer. Kasander's great contribution to British cinema has been his ability to arrange finance for Peter GREENAWAY's idiosyncratic oeuvre. Not everyone cares for the latter, but there is no denying that it is unique in British cinema, and in 1994 Greenaway praised his producer for ' . . . financing difficult projects. Every credit for the continuity must go to him.'
BRITISH FILMS: *A Zed & Two Noughts* (1985, UK/Neth), *Drowning by Numbers* (1988, UK/Neth), *Death in the Seine* (1989, short, UK/Fr/Neth), *The Cook, the Thief, His Wife & Her Lover* (1989, UK/Fr), *Prospero's Books* (1991, UK/Fr/It/Neth), *The Baby of Mâcon* (1993, UK/Fr/Ger/Neth), *The Prince of Jutland* (1994, UK/Fr/Den/Ger, co-p), *The Pillow Book* (1996, UK/Fr/Lux/Neth), *Crush Proof* (1998, UK/Ger/Ire/Neth), *8 ½ Women* (1999, UK/Lux/Neth), *Christie Malry's Own Double-Entry* (2000, UK/Lux/Neth).

Kasket, Harold (*b* London, 1926 – *d* London, 2002). Actor. Former impressionist whose first film was *No Orchids for Miss Blandish* (1948), plump-faced Kasket spent most of his time in films as foreigners, sinister or otherwise, and often of Eastern extraction. Thus he is the owner of the *Moulin Rouge* (1953), the Arab captain in *The Naked Earth* (1957), Jose in *Tommy the Toreador* (1959) and Mohammed Lufti in *Arabesque* (1966, UK/US). Didn't look English enough to play the Englishman he was. Joined ENSA in 1945; was on TV often from 1950, finally in *War and Remembrance* (1989), and also on stage, including a Stratford season in the early 50s, and Uncle Max in the original London production of *The Sound of Music* (1961–64).

OTHER BRITISH FILMS INCLUDE: *Children of Chance* (1949), *Hotel Sahara* (1951), *The House of the Arrow* (1953), *A Kid for Two Farthings* (1954), *Out of the Clouds*, *Doctor at Sea* (1955), *Manuela* (1957), *SOS Pacific*, *Whirlpool* (1959), *The Greengage Summer* (1961), *Nine Hours to Rama* (1962, UK/US), *Follow That Camel* (1967), *Where's Jack* (1969), *Trail of the Pink Panther* (1982).

Kath, Katherine (*b* Paris, 1928). Actress. French actress who made a striking impression in her first British film, *Moulin Rouge* (1953), as the dancer La Goulue. She made about a dozen further British films, with strong roles in *Subway in the Sky* (1958) and as Catherine de Medici in *Mary Queen of Scots* (1971), and also appeared on TV. She was the second wife of Jack CLAYTON.
OTHER BRITISH FILMS INCLUDE: *Anastasia* (1956), *The Seven Thunders* (1957), *The High Bright Sun* (1965), *The Assassination Bureau* (1968), *Cruel Passion* (1977).

Kaufmann, Maurice (*b* Gorleston, 1928 – *d* London, 1997). Actor. Dark, somewhat saturnine-looking supporting player in about three dozen movies, sometimes the lead in such 'B' FILMS as *Zoo Baby* (1957), as a child-rescuing newsreel cameraman, or as young tenant of Vernon SEWELL's superior *House of Mystery* (1961). Married and divorced from Honor BLACKMAN, with whom he appeared in *Fright* (1971), as a police inspector. Also some TV, including the *Douglas Fairbanks Presents* series (1957).
OTHER BRITISH FILMS INCLUDE: *The Angel Who Pawned Her Harp* (1953), *The Quatermass Experiment* (1955), *It's a Wonderful World*, *Find the Lady* (1956), *Fire Down Below*, *Campbell's Kingdom* (1957), *Life in Emergency Ward 10* (1958), *A Shot in the Dark* (1964), *Fanatic* (1965), *Circus of Fear* (1966), *Cry Wolf* (1968), *Bloomfield* (1969, UK/Israel), *The Abominable Dr Phibes* (1971).

Kavanagh, Denis (*b* Carlow, Ireland, 1906 – *d* Moreton-in-Marsh, 1984). Director. Entered film industry in Hollywood in 1926, working at Paramount and Warners as assistant director, coming to Britain in 1931, and continuing as assistant director at various studios. Turned to DOCUMENTARY in 1937, to work with GB INSTRUCTIONAL; served in the RAF (1939–42) and post-war devoted himself largely to documentary film-making, several times for E.J. FANCEY Productions.
OTHER BRITISH FILMS INCLUDE: (ass d) *The Silver Fleet* (1943); (e) *The Wallet* (1952); (p man) *Sweet Beat* (1959); (d, short) *Spotlight on Dogs* (1945), *The Dover Road* (1946), *Information Please* (1948), *Twinkling Fingers* (1950), *Sicilian Memories* (1958); (d, feature) *Starlight Serenade* (1943, + co-sc), *Night Comes Too Soon* (1947), *Fighting Mad* (1956), *Rock You Sinners* (1957).

Kay, Bernard (*b* Bolton, Lancs, 1928). Actor. Trained at the Old Vic School, this busy TV actor (e.g. in *A Very British Coup*, 1988) had supporting roles in about a dozen films of the 60s and 70s, including a small role in *Dr Zhivago* (1965, UK/US) and a larger one in the HORROR film, *Trog* (1970).
OTHER BRITISH FILMS INCLUDE: *Carry on Sergeant* (1958), *Torture Garden* (1967), *Sweeney!* (1976), *Sinbad and the Eye of the Tiger* (1977).

Kay, Charles (*b* Coventry, 1930). Actor. Educated at Birmingham University and a RADA Gold Medallist, Kay first appeared on the London stage in *Roots* (1959) and has had seasons with the Royal Court, Stratford and the National. Entered films in *Bachelor of Hearts* (1958), as a student. His air of faint – or not so faint – superiority suited the calculating Archbishop of Canterbury in *Henry V* (1989), Charlotte COLEMAN's snooty upper-crust father in *Beautiful People* (1999), and his TV appearances in, say, *The Victorians* (1963) and *Fall of Eagles* (1974), as Tsar Nicholas.

OTHER BRITISH FILMS INCLUDE: *Piccadilly Third Stop* (1960), *The Wild and the Willing* (1962), *The Deadly Affair* (1966), *Hennessy* (1975), *School for Vandals* (1986).

Kaye, Davy (*b* London, 1916 – *d* Paradise Island, Bahamas, 1988). Actor. Diminutive (4'11") comedian, popular in the 60s, who appeared in about a dozen films, including a couple of the 'CARRY ON' SERIES (. . . *Cowboy*, 1965; . . . *at Your Convenience*, 1971), and, appropriately, as the Mouse in *Alice's Adventures in Wonderland* (1972). In variety from the mid 30s.
OTHER BRITISH FILMS INCLUDE: *Everything Is Rhythm* (1936), *Fun at St Fanny's* (1955), *The Millionairess* (1960), *The Wrong Arm of the Law*, *The Pot Carriers* (1962), *Crooks in Cloisters* (1964), *Chitty Chitty Bang Bang* (1968), *The Magnificent Seven Deadly Sins* (1971, as 'Sloth').

Keach, Stacy (*b* Savannah, Georgia, 1941). Actor. Son of a US-based British actor and drama teacher, Keach trained at LAMDA. In his prolific career, he made a half-dozen British films, playing the title role in *Luther* (1973, UK/Can/US), narrating *James Dean, the First American Teenager* (1975, doc) and *The Duellists* (1977), and acting in *Hamburger Hamlet* (1975) for the National Film School, *Conduct Unbecoming* (1975) and *The Squeeze* (1977). Won notoriety when gaoled in Britain for smuggling drugs in 1984 and critical plaudits for his London stage performance in *Art* (1998).

Kean, Marie (*b* Rush, Co. Dublin, 1922 – *d* Dublin, 1994). Actress. Irish character player in about 15 British films, mostly with Irish settings, including *Ryan's Daughter* (1970), *Barry Lyndon* (1975) as the eponymous hero's mother, and *The Lonely Passion of Judith Hearne* (1987) as the landlady-mother of the repulsive Bernard. On stage at Dublin's Gaiety from 1947.
OTHER BRITISH FILMS INCLUDE: *Jacqueline* (1956), *Rooney*, *Sally's Irish Rogue* (Ire) (1958), *The Quare Fellow* (1962), *Girl with Green Eyes* (1963), *I Was Happy Here* (1965), *Cul-de-Sac* (1966), *Angel* (1982), *The Dead* (1987, UK/Ger/US).

Keane, John Composer. As well as scoring about ten, somewhat idiosyncratic, films, including *Hideous Kinky* (1998, UK/Fr), Keane has worked on some notable TV, such as *A Very British Coup* (1988), the US-made *Tales of the City* (1993) and the *Hornblower* series, gaining a BAA for his 1998 score for this.
OTHER BRITISH FILMS: *The Kitchen Toto* (1987), *Resurrected* (1989), *The Hummingbird Tree* (1992), *One Man's War* (1993, UK/US), *Small Faces* (1995), *Monsignor Renard* (1999).

Kearton, Cherry (*b* Thwaite, Swaledale, Yorkshire, 1871 – *d* Edgware, 1940). Cinematographer, producer. A once-famous name, Kearton was the author of more than 20 books on naturalism, including *Cherry Kearton's Travels* (1941), the first to illustrate natural history books with photographs. Along with his brother Richard, he was a pioneer cinematographer of big game and wild animal subjects. In 1903, he filmed the first record of a dirigible flight over London, in 1909; he made a film of Theodore Roosevelt's African hunting expedition; contributed NEWSREEL footage in the early days of WW1; and had his own studio in Clapham. He was the last owner of the WARWICK TRADING COMPANY and the Royal Geographical Society still awards an annual medal in his name for wildlife photography.
BRITISH FILMS INCLUDE: *Sea Bird Colonies* (1907, shot with brother Richard) (1911), *Our Boys* (1915), *Wild Life across the World* (1923), *With Cherry Kearton in the Jungle* (1926), *Tembi* (1929). AS.

Keats, Viola (*b* Doune, Scotland, 1911 – *d* Brighton, 1998). Actress. RADA Gold Medallist on stage from 1930, in London, New York, and, as Blanche DuBois, Australia (1950). Appeared in about 20 films, half in the 30s, including *The Guv'nor* (1935), as the romantic lead made wiser by George ARLISS's simplistic philosophies, and half from 1957, in character roles like the unsympathetic mother of a club-footed daughter in *No Time for Tears* (1957).

OTHER BRITISH FILMS: *Too Many Wives, Double Wedding* (1933), *The Night of the Party* (1934), *Her Last Affaire* (1935), *A Woman Alone* (1936), *She Didn't Say No* (1957), *The Roman Spring of Mrs Stone* (1961), *Tamahine* (1962), *Witchcraft* (1964), *The Witches* (1966).

Kedrova, Lila (*b* Petrograd, Russia, 1918 – *d* Sault St Marie, Canada, 2000). Actress. Oscar-winner (+ BAAn) for her touching portrayal of dying Madame Hortense in *Zorba the Greek* (1964, US/Gr), this larger-than-life character player lived and acted mostly in France, but there was a sprinkling of English-speaking films, including HITCHCOCK's *Torn Curtain* (1966, US) and a half-dozen British, starting with Alexander MACKENDRICK's *A High Wind in Jamaica* (1965), as a bar owner. On stage until the early 90s.

OTHER BRITISH FILMS INCLUDE: *Time for Loving* (1971), *Soft Beds, Hard Battles* (1973), *Sword of the Valiant* (1983).

Keel, Howard (*b* Gillespie, Illinois, 1917). Actor. Popular, rugged star of Hollywood musicals, Keel (then called Harold) was starring in *Oklahoma!* on the London stage when Anthony HAVELOCK-ALLAN cast him as the house-invading thug in *The Small Voice* (1948). Critically acclaimed, he was taken up by MGM, returning to Britain for two further films: the US-set *Floods of Fear* (1958), again as a runaway convict, and SCIENCE-FICTION thriller, *The Day of the Triffids* (1962). On London stage again in *Ambassador* (1971).

Keen, Geoffrey (*b* London, 1916). Actor. Indispensable, wildly prolific character player of COMEDY (the motor cycle cop in *Genevieve*, 1953), THRILLERS (the baker in the lively 'B' film, *Devil's Bait*, 1959), realist drama (the chaplain in *Yield to the Night*, 1956; the sympathetic, tetchy works manager in *The Angry Silence*, 1960), and BONDAGE (Minister of Defence in five 007 capers, starting with *The Spy Who Loved Me*, 1977), of cockneys (*It's Hard to Be Good*, 1948) and gents (*Carrington VC*, 1954). Virtually everything he did deserves noting for its immaculate timing, its detailed attention to what gives life to a role, small or large. Son of Malcolm KEEN, he was a RADA Gold Medallist, on stage from 1932, with several Stratford seasons, and during WW2 he toured for four years in 'Stars in Battle Dress', and entered feature films in 1946. Married (1 of 2) Hazel TERRY.

OTHER BRITISH FILMS INCLUDE: *The New Lot* (1943, doc), *Odd Man Out* (1947), *The Small Back Room* (1948), *The Third Man* (1949), *Seven Days to Noon, Chance of a Lifetime* (1950), *High Treason* (1951), *Cry, the Beloved Country, Hunted* (1952), *Turn the Key Softly, The 'Maggie'* (1953), *The Divided Heart* (1954), *Storm over the Nile, The Man Who Never Was* (1955), *A Town Like Alice, The Spanish Gardener, Sailor Beware, Town on Trial* (1956), *Doctor at Large, The Birthday Present* (1957), *Nowhere to Go* (1958), *Beyond This Place* (1959), *Sink the Bismarck!* (1960), *Spare the Rod, No Love for Johnnie* (1961), *The Inspector* (1962), *The Mind Benders* (1963), *Doctor Zhivago* (UK/US), *Born Free* (1965), *Taste the Blood of Dracula* (1969), *Cromwell* (1970), *Moonraker* (1979, UK/Fr), *For Your Eyes Only* (1981), *Octopussy* (1983), *A View to a Kill* (1985), *The Living Daylights* (1987).

Keen, Malcolm (*b* Bristol, 1887 – *d* London, 1970). Actor. A leading man who later became a character player, Keen made his stage debut in 1902 and his screen debut in *Jimmy* in 1916. Had a brief US career in the early 50s, appearing in *Lorna Doone* (1951) and others, and playing Marley's Ghost in a 1951 TV

version of *A Christmas Carol*. His son is Geoffrey KEEN; they both appeared in the sombre drama, *The Birthday Present* (1957).

BRITISH FILMS INCLUDE: *The Lost Chord* (1917), *The Skin Game* (1920), *A Bill of Divorcement* (1922), *The Lodger* (1926), *The Manxman* (1929), *Wolves* (1930), *Whispering Tongues* (1934), *Sixty Glorious Years* (1938), *Rob Roy . . .* (1953), *Macbeth* (1961), *Two and Two Make Six* (1962). AS.

Keen, Pat Actress. Reliable character player of occasional films and much TV. First on screen as Alan BATES's sympathetic sister in *A Kind of Loving* (1962) and comic as the chain-smoking director of an Academy in *The Rachel Papers* (1989).

OTHER BRITISH FILMS INCLUDE: *Memoirs of a Survivor* (1981), *Clockwise* (1985), *Without a Clue* (UK/US), *We Think the World of You* (1988), *Shadowlands* (1993, UK/US), *Cold Comfort Farm* (1995, TV, some cinemas).

Keene, Ralph (*b* Mysore, India, 1902 – *d* England, 1963). Director. Documentarist with MOI, British Transport, etc, who often focused on animal studies, including what Paul ROTHA described as 'six excellent films for the Zoological Sociey in collaboration with Professor Julian Huxley'. Was producer/director at the STRAND FILM COMPANY, he and Donald TAYLOR having taken over Julius HAGEN's feature company in 1935; and, from 1940 to 1947, was co-founder and producer at Greenpark Productions. He was adviser and producer for the Government Film Unit in Ceylon (1951–53) and was producer and scriptwriter for British Transport Films (1955–63).

BRITISH FILMS INCLUDE: *Statue Parade* (1936), *The Green Girdle* (1941), *London* (1942), *We of the West Riding* (1945), *Cyprus Is an Island* (1946), *Five Towns* (1947), *Three Dawns to Sydney* (1948). Ian Aitken.

Keiller, Patrick (*b* Blackpool, 1950). Director. Independent film-maker of obdurately ART-HOUSE fare, some of it produced by the BFI (e.g. *London*, 1994, + CHANNEL 4, d, sc); *Robinson in Space* (1996, + BBC SCREEN, d, sc), both narrated by Paul SCOFIELD. He has also directed several short films including *Stonebridge Park* (1984) and *Norwood* (1996), and the feature *The Dilapidated Dwelling* (2000, + d, sc).

Keir, Andrew (*b* Glasgow, 1926 – *d* London, 1997). Actor. Scottish character player, former member of the Glasgow Citizens' Theatre Company, in films since 1950, often in films with Scottish settings or themes, including the mining disaster drama, *The Brave Don't Cry* (1952), *Laxdale Hall* (1953) and *Tunes of Glory* (1960), as well as costume dramas (*Mary Queen of Scots*, 1971) and horror pieces (*Blood from the Mummy's Tomb*, 1971), but best remembered as Professor Quatermass in *Quatermass and the Pit* (1967). Often played (bearded) stern authority figures. Also in TV series including *Ivanhoe* (1958) and *Adam Smith* (1971–73). His daughter is actress **Julie T Wallace** who has appeared in several films, including *The Living Daylights* (1987) and the TV drama, *The Life and Loves of a She-Devil* (1986). Other children, Sean and Deirdre, are TV producers.

OTHER BRITISH FILMS INCLUDE: *The 'Maggie'* (1953), *High Flight* (1957), *A Night to Remember* (1958), *Lord Jim* (1964), *The Fighting Prince of Donegal, The Viking Queen* (1966), *Royal Hunt of the Sun* (1969), *The Thirty Nine Steps, Absolution* (1978).

Keir, David (*b* Dundee, 1884 – *d* ?). Actor. Filmed in South Africa and India before first British film, *The Ghost Goes West* (1935), after which he appeared in small roles in 40 films, including various Scottish 'types' as in *The Captive Heart* (1946)

as the father of Gordon JACKSON's fiancée, and the Duke of Argyll's servant in *Rob Roy* . . . (1953), his last.
OTHER BRITISH FILMS INCLUDE: *Hearts of Humanity* (1936), *Talking Feet* (1937), *This Man Is News* (1938), *The Arsenal Stadium Mystery* (1939), *Hatter's Castle* (1941), *Tomorrow We Live* (1942), *The Shipbuilders, The Demi-Paradise* (1943), *English Without Tears, Tawny Pipit* (1944), *Pink String and Sealing Wax* (1945), *Bedelia* (1946), *While the Sun Shines, The Brothers* (1947), *Blue Scar* (1949), *The Last Page* (1952).

Keitel, Harvey (*b* Brooklyn, NY, 1939). Actor, producer. Dominant American character star who has appeared in a half-dozen British films, most notably as one of *The Duellists* (1977), Ridley SCOTT's impressive feature debut, in the poetic 'Western', *Eagle's Wing* (1978), and Nicolas ROEG's drama of obsession, *Bad Timing* (1980) as the police inspector.
OTHER BRITISH FILMS INCLUDE: *Saturn 3* (1980), *The Young Americans* (1993), *Head Above Water* (1996, UK/US).

Keith, Penelope (*b* Sutton, Surrey, 1940). Actress. RN: Hatfield. Witty, statuesque comedienne whose main fame has been acquired via the TV series, *The Good Life* (1975–78) and *To the Manor Born* (1979–81), mining a haughty but vulnerable persona for rich comic rewards. Her cinema roles have been sporadic and, with the marginal exceptions of the teutonic nanny in *Every Home Should Have One* (1969) and gauche, innocent Dorothy Brett in *Priest of Love* (1980), scarcely worth noting. On stage, she was a splendid Judith Bliss in *Hay Fever* (1983–84). Awarded OBE in 1989, and appointed High Sheriff of Surrey in 2002.
OTHER BRITISH FILMS INCLUDE: *Carry On Doctor* (1968), *Take a Girl Like You* (1970), *Rentadick* (1972), *The Hound of the Baskervilles* (1977).

Keith, Sheila (*b* Aberdeen, 1920). Actress. Webber-Douglas-trained player much on stage and TV, Keith had supporting roles in a dozen or so British films of the 70s and 80s, most notably appearing in five paranoid horror films directed by Peter WALKER, including the *House of Whipcord* (1974), *Frightmare* (1974) and *House of Mortal Sin* 1975).
OTHER BRITISH FILMS INCLUDE: *Ooh . . . You Are Awful* (1972), *The Confessional* (1975), *The House of Long Shadows* (1983), *Clockwise* (1985).

Kellett, Bob (*b* Lancaster, 1927). Director. In the 70s, Kellett directed several TV comics in film SPIN-OFFS of TV series: Frankie HOWERD in *Up the Chastity Belt, Up Pompeii* (1971), and *Up the Front* (1972), and the entire TV casts for *The Alf Garnett Saga* (1972) and *Are You Being Served?* (1977); as well as directing drag star Danny LA RUE in his one feature film, *Our Miss Fred* (1972). His 1971 comedy, *Girl Stroke Boy* had its admirers, but his career seemed to peter out after the 70s.
OTHER BRITISH FILMS INCLUDE: (d, unless noted) *A Home of Your Own* (1964, p), *San Ferry Ann* (1965, p), *Futtocks End* (1969, + p), *Don't Just Lie There, Say Something!* (1973), *Tightrope to Terror* (1982, + sc), *Haunted* (1995, UK/US, co-sc).

Kellino, Pamela (aka Pamela Mason) (*b* Westgate-on-Sea, Kent, 1916 – *d* Los Angeles, 1966). Actress, screenwriter. Daughter of film executive Isidore OSTRER, married first to director Roy KELLINO, then to James MASON (1941–64), she later became a vitriolic gossip columnist. As a teenager, she had appeared in *Jew Süss* (1934); the credits of her next film, *I Met a Murderer* (1939), reek of family history: director and cinematographer, Roy Kellino; producers, Pamela and Roy Kellino, James Mason; screenplay, Pamela Kellino and Mason, from her story. Father Ostrer declined to distribute it. By the time it was made, Pamela had separated from Kellino and was living with Mason. In her undistinguished film career, she gave her best

performance as Mason's neglected daughter in *They Were Sisters* (1945).
OTHER BRITISH FILMS INCLUDE: *The Upturned Glass* (1947), *Pandora and the Flying Dutchman* (1950).

Kellino, Roy (*b* London, 1912 – *d* Los Angeles, 1956). Cinematographer, director. Son of silent film director W.P. KELLINO, for whom he worked as a child actor, he was involved in several aspects of film-making without quite achieving distinction in any. Apart from acting, he also directed seven films, including *I Met a Murderer* (1939, + co-p, c), starring his wife Pamela KELLINO and her lover, James MASON, and *Charade* (1953, US), starring the Masons, was second unit director on *Great Expectations* (1946) and directed and co-wrote a grimly telling 'B' FILM, *Guilt Is My Shadow* (1950). Also worked as special effects director and cinematographer (at EALING, 1940–45), producer and writer.
OTHER BRITISH FILMS INCLUDE: (a) *Rob Roy* (1922), *The Further Adventures of the Flag Lieutenant* (1927); (c) *Jew Süss* (co-c), *The Phantom Light, Foreign Affaires* (1935), *OHMS, Aren't Men Beasts?* (1937), *The Proud Valley, Convoy* (co-c) (1940), *Nine Men* (1942), *Johnny Frenchman* (1945); (d) *Catch As Catch Can* (1937), *The Silken Affair* (1956); (fx) *Spare a Copper, Sailors Three* (1940, co-fx), *The Big Blockade* (1942), *San Demetrio–London*, (1943), *The Halfway House, They Came to a City* (1944, co-fx).

Kellino, W(illiam) P(hillip) (*b* London, 1873 – *d* 1958). Director. A former MUSIC HALL acrobat and clown, Kellino entered the film industry in 1910 with the Ec-Ko Company. In 1915, he produced one-reel comedies for CRICKS and Martin, and in the 1920s, he was associated with GAUMONT and STOLL. After years directing more than 90 shorts, Kellino directed a number of major silent features and early talkies, and was active through 1936. Father of Roy KELLINO.
BRITISH FILMS INCLUDE: *Rob Roy* (1922), *Young Lochinvar* (1923), *The Colleen Bawn* (1924), *Sailors Don't Care* (1928), *Alf's Carpet* (1929), *Alf's Button* (1930). AS.

Kellner, William (*b* Austria, 1900). Art director. Educated at Vienna University, became a British citizen and entered film industry in 1942. Shared AAn for work on *Saraband for Dead Lovers* (1948) and *Suddenly Last Summer* (1959), after working as draughtsman on several ARCHERS productions, including *Black Narcissus* (1947), and on *Brief Encounter* (1945). Some of his most stylish work was for EALING where he designed *Kind Hearts and Coronets* (1949) and *Secret People* (1951).
OTHER BRITISH FILMS INCLUDE: (draughtsman) *A Canterbury Tale* (1944), *A Matter of Life and Death* (1946); (art d) *The Queen of Spades* (1949), *The Wooden Horse* (1950), *The Lavender Hill Mob* (1951), *I Am a Camera* (1955), *The Admirable Crichton* (1957), *Jack the Ripper* (1958), *The Siege of Sidney Street* (1960), *The Kitchen* (1961), *The VIPs* (1963), *Othello* (1965).

Kelly, Barbara (*b* Vancouver, 1923). Actress. Blonde comedienne who started radio career in Canada, coming to England in 1947 and making her London stage debut in 1948. Married to Canadian actor, Bernard BRADEN, with whom she worked on British radio and TV in the 50s; she was also in *What's My Line?* from 1951. She acted in several light films of the early 50s, most memorably as Mrs Clodfelter Dunn in *Castle in the Air* (1952).
OTHER BRITISH FILMS: *A Tale of Five Cities* (1951), *Glad Tidings, Love in Pawn* (1953), *Jet Storm* (1959).

Kelly, Clare (aka Claire) (*b* Manchester, 1912 – *d* Bath, 2001). Actress. Attractively sympathetic character actress of the 60s and 70s, who played a barmaid in the BEATLES romp, *A Hard*

Day's Night (1964) and had a more substantial role as Bill OWEN's wife in *Georgy Girl* (1966).

OTHER BRITISH FILMS INCLUDE: *Five to One* (1963), *The Whisperers* (1966), *Inadmissible Evidence* (1968), *And Soon the Darkness* (1970), *The Fourth Protocol* (1987).

Kelly, David (*b* Dublin, 1929). Actor. Supporting actor in British and Irish films since the 70s, including co-productions such as *A Man of No Importance* (1994, UK/Ire), as Albert FINNEY's beaky, malapropistic mate, Baldy, and *Waking Ned* (1999, UK/Fr/US), in which he posed as the title character. Wide stage experience in several European countries and on TV since 1958, including *Emmerdale* and his own Irish TV programme, but now most famous as Mr O'Reilly in the 'The Builders' episode of *Fawlty Towers*, his poor workmanship leading Basil to threaten him with a garden gnome.

OTHER BRITISH FILMS INCLUDE: *Dublin Nightmare* (1958), *The Quare Fellow* (1962), *The Italian Job* (1969), *The McKenzie Break* (1970), *A Portrait of the Artist as a Young Man* (1979), *Anne Devlin* (Ire), *The Jigsaw Man* (1984), *Joyriders* (1988, UK/Ire), *Into the West* (1992, UK/Ire/US), *The Van* (1996, UK/Ire), *Ordinary Decent Criminal* (2000, UK/Ger/Ire/US), *Mean Machine* (2001, UK/US).

Kelly, James (*b* Birkenhead, 1931 – *d* London, 1978). Screenwriter. Co-author with **Peter Miller** (*b* London, 1935) of two neat thrillers, *Tomorrow at Ten* (1962) and *Blind Corner* (1963) and was co-adaptor with Miller on *Three on a Spree* and *Dr Blood's Coffin* (1960). Directed *Beast in the Cellar* (1971, + sc) and the English-speaking version of *Night Hair Child* (1971), and co-wrote the Hollywood film, *W* (1974).

Kelly, Judy (*b* Naviabri, Australia, 1913). Actress. Pretty brunette who won a film-test competition in Australia, came to Elstree on three months' test, and stayed in Britain to become a modestly popular lead and second lead, often as smart 'other women', in 30-odd light films of the 30s. Now perhaps best remembered as a traitor in *Tomorrow We Live* (1942), the wife of the crashed racing-car driver in the 'Hearse driver' episode of *Dead of Night* (1945), and a jealous dance hostess in *Dancing with Crime* (1947).

OTHER BRITISH FILMS INCLUDE: *Adam's Apple* (1928), *The Private Life of Henry VIII*, *Mannequin* (1933), *Royal Cavalcade* (1935), *Boys Will Be Girls*, *Over She Goes* (1937), *Jane Steps Out* (1938), *The Midas Touch* (1939), *Saloon Bar* (1940), *It Happened One Sunday* (1944), *Warning to Wantons* (1948).

Kelsall, Moultrie (*b* Bearsden, Scotland, 1901 – *d* Blair Logie, Scotland, 1980). Actor. Character player often featured in films with Scottish backgrounds, such as *The Master of Ballantrae* (1953), *The 'Maggie'*, *Trouble in the Glen* (1954), *The Battle of the Sexes* (1959), and *Greyfriars Bobby* (1961). Trained as a lawyer, with a degree from Glasgow University, Kelsall was a founding member, in 1927, of the Scottish National Players and a broadcaster and producer with the BBC as early as 1931. In films from 1948.

OTHER BRITISH FILMS INCLUDE: *Landfall* (1949), *Last Holiday* (1950), *The Lavender Hill Mob* (1951), *You're Only Young Twice!*, *The Hour of 13* (1952), *Albert RN* (1953), *The Sea Shall Not Have Them* (1954), *The Adventures of Quentin Durward* (1956), *Violent Playground* (1957), *Beyond This Place*, *North West Frontier* (1959), *The Birthday Party* (1970). AS.

Kemp, Gary (*b* London, 1959). Actor, guitarist, lyricist. Former member of 80s rock group Spandau Ballet, which he and his brother, **Martin Kemp** (*b* London, 1961) co-founded in 1979. The band enjoyed success in the US and UK until the mid 80s, but finally broke up in 1990. The brothers co-starred successfully in the film *The Krays* (1990), playing the East End gangsters. Gary appeared in the children's film, *Hide and Seek* (1972), and in several international films, as well as *Paper Marriage* (1991, UK/Pol) and *Dog Eat Dog* (2001). He was married to Sadie FROST (1988–97). Martin has made a half-dozen or so international, mainly US films, and two further British ones: *Monk Dawson* (1997), as a sleazy tabloid editor, and *Sugar Town* (1999).

Kemp, Jeremy (*b* Chesterfield, Derbyshire, 1934). Actor. RN: Edmund Walker. Central School-trained and on stage from 1957, at the Old Vic the following year, this tall, ruddy character player of somewhat forbidding countenance came to fame in TV's *Z Cars* (1962–65), and in recent decades has appeared mainly on TV. In films, he was genuinely imposing in such works as *The Blue Max* (1966), *Darling Lili* (1970, US) and, as a psychotic policeman, *The Strange Affair* (1968). He played a very small role in *Four Weddings and a Funeral* (1994), and, in 1995, he was properly authoritative as the hero's upper-class patron in *Angels and Insects* (UK/US).

OTHER BRITISH FILMS INCLUDE: *Dr Terror's House of Horrors* (1964), *Operation Crossbow* (1965, UK/It), *Assignment K* (1967), *The Games* (1969), *Eyewitness* (1970), *Pope Joan* (1972), *The Belstone Fox* (1973), *East of Elephant Rock* (1976), *A Bridge Too Far* (1977), *The Return of the Soldier* (1982), *When the Whales Came* (1989).

Kemp, Martin *see* **Kemp, Gary**

Kempinksi, Tom (*b* London, 1938). Actor. Character player of films and TV, especially in the late 60s/early 70s, often cast as police officers and other professionals. Married and separated from Frances DE LA TOUR.

BRITISH FILMS INCLUDE: *The Damned* (1961), *Othello* (1965), *The Whisperers* (1966), *The Reckoning* (1969), *Gumshoe* (1971), *Adult Fun* (1972).

Kemplen, Ralph (*b* London, 1912). Editor. Winner of BAA (+ AAn) for editing *The Day of the Jackal* (1973, UK/Fr), Kemplen entered films in 1928, worked first as assistant editor, and subsequently cut many famous films, including *Moulin Rouge* (1953, AAn/e), *Freud* (1962) and *A Man for All Seasons* (1966). Much favoured by US directors working in Britain.

OTHER BRITISH FILMS INCLUDE: *The Frightened Lady* (1932), *Jack Ahoy!* (1934), *Broken Blossoms* (1936), *Young Man's Fancy* (1939, co-e), *Channel Incident* (1940, short), *The Saint's Vacation* (1941), *Carnival* (1946), *Uncle Silas* (1947), *Mr Perrin and Mr Traill*, *Trottie True* (1948), *Pandora and the Flying Dutchman* (1950), *The African Queen* (1951), *Beat the Devil* (1953, UK/It/US), *The Good Die Young* (1954), *The Story of Esther Costello* (1957), *Room at the Top* (1958), *The Roman Spring of Mrs Stone* (1961), *Oliver!* (1968), *Goodbye, Mr Chips* (1969), *The Odessa File* (1974, UK/Ger), *The Dark Crystal* (1982).

Kempson, Rachel (*b* Dartmouth, Devon, 1910 – *d* 2003). Actress. Now perhaps best known as widow of Michael REDGRAVE and mother of Vanessa, Lynn and Corin REDGRAVE, RADA-trained Kempson was on stage from 1933, at Stratford, returning several times, as well as appearing in many modern plays. She had a small role in *Jeannie* (1941), and was given the female lead (with Redgrave) in *The Captive Heart* (1946), but never became a film star. There was something gravely reserved about her, but she played about 20 character roles, including Charles Boyer's querulous invalid wife in *A Woman's Vengeance* (1948, US), and worked regularly on TV (e.g. in *The Jewel in the Crown*, 1984).

OTHER BRITISH FILMS INCLUDE: *Tom Jones* (1963), *Curse of the Fly* (1965), *Georgy Girl* (1966), *The Charge of the Light Brigade* (1968), *A Touch of Love* (1969), *Jane Eyre* (1970), *Little Lord Fauntleroy* (1980),

Stealing Heaven (1988, UK/Yug), *She's Been Away* (1989, TV, some cinemas), *Déjà Vu* (1998, UK/US).

BIBLIOG: Autobiography, *A Family and Its Fortunes*, 1986.

Kemp-Welch, Joan (*b* London, 1906 – *d* London, 1999). Actress. Roedean-educated theatre actress, on stage from 1927, later a distinguished director for Manchester Rep and other companies, and later still a TV director, winning the Desmond Davis Award for her services to television in 1963, along with several other awards. As a screen player, she made a dozen films in the 30s and 40s, most memorably as Robert NEWTON's girlfriend, Aggie, in *Busman's Honeymoon* (1940) and as Amy Johnson's mother in *They Flew Alone* (1942): her real importance is elsewhere. Married TV director Peter Moffat.

OTHER BRITISH FILMS INCLUDE: *Veteran of Waterloo* (1933), *Once a Thief* (1935), *School for Husbands* (1937), *The Citadel* (1938), *Pimpernel Smith*, *Jeannie* (1941), *Hard Steel* (1942), *Rhythm Serenade* (1943).

Kendal, Felicity (*b* Birmingham, 1946). Actress. Famously cute star of TV's *The Good Life* (1975–78), actually made of much sterner stuff as she showed in later TV, such as *The Camomile Lawn* (1992), and on stage in, for instance, *The Real Thing* (1982–83), by real-life partner of eight years, Tom STOPPARD, or the brilliant revival of *Fallen Angels* (2000), directed by second husband, Michael Rudman (m.1983). Has shown little interest in the cinema: born of actor parents who ran a touring company in India, she first appeared in MERCHANT IVORY's affectionate tribute to them, *Shakespeare Wallah* (1965), and has since been in *Valentino* (1977), as June Mathis, and *Parting Shots* (1998). Sister was Jennifer KENDAL; first husband was actor **Drewe Henley**, who had small roles in a few British films, including *Nothing But the Best* (1964).

Kendal, Jennifer see **Kapoor, Shashi**

Kendall, Henry (*b* London, 1897 – *d* France, 1962). Actor. Lightweight leading man whose performances were generally elegantly effete, as in *The Ghost Camera* (1933). Most notable perhaps in HITCHCOCK's *Rich and Strange* (1932), as the suburban husband who blossoms with travel. Also had a major stage career – debut 1914 – as both actor and director. Brother of William KENDALL.

OTHER BRITISH FILMS INCLUDE: *Mr Pim Passes By* (1921), *French Leave* (1930), *The Flaw* (1933), *Death at Broadcasting House* (1934), *Lend Me Your Wife* (1935), *It's Not Cricket* (+ sc), *School for Husbands* (1937), *29, Acacia Avenue* (1945), *The Voice of Merrill* (1952), *An Alligator Named Daisy* (1955), *Nothing Barred* (1961).

BIBLIOG: Autobiography, *I Remember Romano's*, 1960. AS.

Kendall, Kay (*b* Withernsea, 1926 – *d* London, 1959). Actress. RN: Justine Kendall McCarthy. First on stage with sister Kim, and granddaughter of musical comedy star Marie Kendall, long-legged, gorgeous Kendall blew a trumpet on screen in *Genevieve* (1953) and was at once a genuine star. Time ran tragically short for her, but she glittered with sophisticated wit and glamour as few British female stars have. After uncredited bits, she had a big role in the clunking *London Town* (1946), and, after this setback, returned to rep, not filming again until 1950 (*Dance Hall*). In *Lady Godiva Rides Again* (1951) she looks good and wisecracks well as the beauty queen's sister, and is a languidly funny socialite in *It Started in Paradise* (1952), which won her a RANK contract. Not that this gave her much joy: she is a wittily expensive dinner date in *Doctor in the House* (1954), but only *Simon and Laura* (1955), opposite Peter FINCH, allows her to stretch the talents so irresistibly shown in *Genevieve*. The

rest is Hollywood; *Les Girls* (1957), which she stole, hilariously; *The Reluctant Debutante* (1958, Paris-made), as the dizzy socialite married to real-life husband, Rex HARRISON; and *Once More with Feeling* (1959). She established herself as a great comedienne as well as a great beauty, then she was dead.

OTHER BRITISH FILMS INCLUDE: *Fiddlers Three*, *Dreaming*, *Champagne Charlie* (1944), *Waltz Time*, *Caesar and Cleopatra* (1945), *Wings of Danger*, *Curtain Up* (1952), *Mantrap*, *Street of Shadows*, *The Square Ring*, *Meet Mr Lucifer* (1953), *Fast and Loose*, *The Constant Husband*, *Abdullah the Great* (UK/Egypt) (1954), *The Adventures of Quentin Durward* (1955).

Kendall, Suzy (*b* Belper, 1944). Actress. RN: Frieda Harrison. Former model who first appeared in films as a debutante modelled as 'Everybody's Dream Girl' in *Up Jumped a Swagman* (1965). An *echt*-60s bouffante blonde, she is glimpsed as a squabbling girlfriend in *The Sandwich Man* (1966) and a sympathetic music teacher in *To Sir, with Love* (1967), had more substantial roles in two films for Peter COLLINSON: as the slumming socialite in *Up the Junction* (1967) and the terrorised girl in *The Penthouse* (1967). In the 70s she worked abroad, as well as appearing in a couple of British HORROR films, *Tales That Witness Madness* and *Craze* (1973). Was married (1966–68) to Dudley MOORE, her co-star in *30 Is a Dangerous Age, Cynthia* (1967).

OTHER BRITISH FILMS INCLUDE: *The Liquidator*, *Thunderball* (1965), *Circus of Fear* (1966), *Assault* (1970), *Fear Is the Key* (1972).

Kendall, Victor Screenwriter. Author/co-author of two dozen modest GENRE films of the decade 1929–39, including comedies like *Money for Nothing* (1932), and thrillers like *Dead Men Are Dangerous* (1939, co-sc), and most notably the screenplay for E.A. DUPONT's *Atlantic* (1929).

OTHER BRITISH FILMS INCLUDE: (co-sc) *Weekend Wives* (1928, co-story), *The Flying Scotsman* (1929), *Night Birds* (1930, UK/Ger), *The Maid of the Mountains* (1932), *Mr Reeder in Room 13* (1938); (sc) *Young Woodley* (1930), *Fascination* (1931), *Dick Turpin* (1933).

Kendall, William (*b* London, 1903 – *d* 1984). Actor. In business before taking up acting, the Sevenoaks-educated Kendall was on stage from 1923, often in musical comedy, repeating his stage roles in two Jack BUCHANAN films, *That's a Good Girl* (1933) and *This'll Make You Whistle* (1936). Returned to films in (usually upper-class) character roles in the 50s and also appeared in a lot of early TV drama. Brother of Henry KENDALL.

OTHER BRITISH FILMS INCLUDE: *Goodnight Vienna* (1932), *The King's Cup* (1933), *Debt of Honour* (1936), *Sweet Devil* (1938), *Blind Folly* (1939), *Dance Little Lady* (1954), *Jumping for Joy* (1955), *Idle on Parade* (1958), *A Touch of Larceny* (1959), *The Trials of Oscar Wilde* (1960), *The Jokers* (1966), *The Assassination Bureau* (1968).

Kennaway, James (*b* Perthshire, Scotland, 1928 – *d* Eton, 1968). Author, screenwriter. Nominated for AA and BAA for his tensely characterful screenplay for *Tunes of Glory* (1960), he wrote a handful of others before his untimely death in a car accident. *Country Dance* (1969), derived from his novel and play, touches on the then-taboo subject of incest.

OTHER BRITISH FILMS INCLUDE: *Violent Playground* (1957), *The Mind Benders* (1963), *Battle of Britain* (1969, co-sc), *The Dollar Bottom* (1981, novel).

Kennedy, Joyce (*b* London, 1898 – *d* London, 1943). Actress. RADA-Gold Medallist, on stage from 1920, and in a dozen 30s films, mostly in supporting roles, like that of Lady Bracebury in *Debt of Honour* (1936). Daughter of author/theologian Stoddart Kennedy.

OTHER BRITISH FILMS INCLUDE: *The Man from Chicago* (1930), *Say It with Music* (1932), *The Return of Bulldog Drummond* (1934), *Seven Sinners* (1936), *The Nursemaid Who Disappeared* (1939).

Kennedy, Margaret (*b* London, 1896 – *d* Adderbury, 1967). Author, screenwriter. Now more or less unreadable, her 1924 best-seller *The Constant Nymph* (also turned into a play with Basil DEAN) was filmed four times (1928, 1933, for British TV in 1938, and in Hollywood 1943). The intensely romantic play, *Escape Me Never* (1933) was filmed in Britain with Elizabeth BERGNER in 1935 (+ co-sc) and in Hollywood in 1947. Oxford-educated Kennedy also (co-)authored a dozen other screenplays, including the excellent thriller, *Take My Life* (1947).

OTHER BRITISH FILMS INCLUDE: (co-sc, unless noted) *The Old Curiosity Shop*, *Little Friend* (with Christopher ISHERWOOD, etc) (1934), *Whom the Gods Love* (1936, UK/Austria, sc), *Dreaming Lips* (1937), *Stolen Life*, *The Midas Touch* (+ novel) (1938), *The Man in Grey* (1943), *One Exciting Night* (1944, add dial).

BIBLIOG: Autobiography, *Where Stands a Winged Sentry*, 1937.

Kenney, James (*b* London, 1930 – *d* London, 1982). Actor. Promising player of adolescent roles in late 40s/early 50s who, perhaps because he maintained a very youthful appearance, never became a star, though he appeared in over 20 films, mainly in the 50s, and most notably as *Cosh Boy* (1953), repeating his 1951 stage role. Trained at Italia Conti Stage School and was on stage from 1944, having a major success as the pop idol in *Expresso Bongo* (1958–59). Said to be in 1942's *The Young Mr Pitt*, he finished his movie career in forgotten 'B' FILMS.

OTHER BRITISH FILMS INCLUDE: *Circus Boy* (1947), *The Guinea Pig* (1948), *Captain Horatio Hornblower RN* (1950, UK/US), *Outcast of the Islands* (1951), *The Gift Horse* (1952), *The Good Die Young*, *The Sea Shall Not Have Them* (1954), *Above Us the Waves* (1955), *The Gelignite Gang*, *The Yangtse Incident* (1956), *Seven Thunders* (1957), *Ambush in Leopard Street* (1962).

Kenny, Sean (*b* Portroe, Ireland, 1929 – *d* London, 1973). Production designer. Celebrated stage designer of, among others, *Oliver!* (1960) and the National Theatre's *Hamlet* (1963), who designed only two films – *I Thank a Fool* (1962) and *Stop the World, I Want to Get Off* (1966) – and died young.

Kensit, Patsy (*b* London, 1968). Actress. Youthful film veteran, who appeared as a tot in *For the Love of Ada* (1972) and as Mia Farrow's daughter in *The Great Gatsby* (1974), and serial bride of rock stars (Dan Donovan, 1988–91; Jim Kerr, 1992–96; Liam Gallagher, 1997–2000), this fragile-looking blonde, born to East End poverty, has still to establish herself securely in films. She was in the disastrous musical, *Absolute Beginners* (1986), in Michael WINNER's unfairly savaged *A Chorus of Disapproval* (1989), in the witty but not widely seen *Blame It on the Bellboy* (1992), and used her beauty and eroticism to good purpose in *Angels and Insects* (1995, UK/US). She co-starred more or less unnoticeably with Mel Gibson in *Lethal Weapon 2* (1989) and plays the wife of the football hero in *Best* (2000, UK/Ire). Perhaps if she is serious about not marrying any more rockers, she will devote herself more single-mindedly to her career.

OTHER BRITISH FILMS INCLUDE: *Hennessy* (1975), *Hanover Street* (1979), *Twenty-One* (1991), *The Turn of the Screw* (1992), *Janice Beard: 45 wpm* (2000), *Darkness Falling* (2002, UK/Can).

Kent, Jean (*b* London, 1921). Actress. RN: Joan Summerfield. Archetypal 40s star who made her way from MUSIC HALL to film studio, from supporting roles to showy vehicles, who very successfully applied herself to what the RANK ORGANISATION required of her, knew what it was to be a star and how to carry it off. First appeared on stage as a child dancer in 1932, known for a while as Jean Carr, was in several revues and then, in the 40s, devoted herself almost entirely to the screen, winning a popular reputation as a 'bad girl'. After two 1935 films, she gathered steam in the war years, first in support of famous comics, including Tommy HANDLEY in *It's That Man Again* (1943) and Arthur ASKEY in *Bees in Paradise* (1944), then making her first serious mark as the ambitious Lucy in *Fanny by Gaslight* (1944). In her potent sexiness, she contrasted sharply with Phyllis CALVERT as Fanny, and in *Madonna of the Seven Moons* (1944) and *The Magic Bow* (1946), and with a too-refined Anne CRAWFORD in *Caravan* (1946), and made the most of a few touching moments as James MASON's doxy in *The Wicked Lady* (1945). Her big starring chances came with the strong cautionary tale, *Good-Time Girl* (1948), as the prostitute in *Bond Street Story*, with *Trottie True* (1948), a chorus-girl-to-duchess romance that allowed her to sing and dance, with the *Rashomon*-like *The Woman in Question* (1950), and most powerfully as the vindictive Millie in *The Browning Version* (1951). Ironically, playing this realistically unpleasant 40-year-old, perhaps her best role ever, was also her last lead in an 'A' film. She played supporting roles and 'B' FILM leads in the 50s, but essentially had to look to the stage (*The Deep Blue Sea*, 1954) and TV (*Sir Francis Drake*, 1961–62, as Elizabeth I) for rewarding work. She had a tough, versatile talent that post-50s British cinema wasted. Married (1946 till 1989, his death) Jusuf Ramart (later Hurst) (*b* Vienna, 1918 – *d* Newmarket, 1989), who appeared in *Caravan* and *The Queen of Spades* (1948), before giving up acting.

OTHER BRITISH FILMS: *The Rocks of Valpré* (as Joan Summerfield), *Who's Your Father?* (1935), *Hello Fame* (1940), *Miss London Ltd*, *Warn That Man* (1943), *Waterloo Road*, *Soldier, Sailor*, *Champagne Charlie*, *Two Thousand Women* (1944), *The Rake's Progress* (1945), *Carnival* (1946), *The Man Within*, *The Loves of Joanna Godden* (1947), *Sleeping Car to Trieste* (1948), *Her Favourite Husband* (UK/It), *The Reluctant Widow* (1950), *The Lost Hours* (1952), *Before I Wake* (1955), *The Prince and the Showgirl*, *Bonjour Tristesse* (1957), *Grip of the Strangler* (1958), *Beyond This Place* (1959), *Please Turn Over*, *Bluebeard's Ten Honeymoons* (1960), *Shout at the Devil* (1976).

Kent, Keneth (*b* Liverpool, 1892 – *d* London, 1963). Actor, singer. RADA-trained and on stage from 1912, where he had major successes in such plays as *Charley's Aunt* (1917) and *The Shop at Sly Corner* (1944), in the lead role played by Oscar HOMOLKA on screen (1946) but by Kent on TV (also 1946). Seen in occasional films from 1938, including the notoriously idiotic *Idol of Paris* (1948), as Napoleon III.

OTHER BRITISH FILMS INCLUDE: *Luck of the Navy* (1938), *At the Villa Rose* (1939), *Night Train to Munich* (1940), *Dangerous Moonlight* (1941), *A Time to Kill* (1955).

Kenworthy, Duncan (*b* Yorkshire, 1950). Producer. Cambridge-educated Kenworthy, along with Richard CURTIS and Andrew MACDONALD, formed DNA FILMS in 1997. He had TV experience on *Sesame Street* in the US, producing *The Muppet Show* (1976–81) and *The Storyteller* series (1988–91), in association with Jim HENSON. In 1994 he produced the phenomenally successful (BAA, AAn) *Four Weddings and a Funeral*, repeating the pattern with *Notting Hill* (1999, UK/US, BAAn). Awarded OBE 1999.

OTHER BRITISH FILMS: *The Dark Crystal* (1982, assoc p), *Dreamchild* (1985, co-p), *Lawn Dogs* (1997, UK/US), *Beautiful Creatures, Cocozza's Way* (2001), *The Final Curtain* (2002).

Kerima (*b* Algiers, 1925). Actress. Exotic star of international films who made a striking impression in Carol REED's *Outcast of the Islands* (1951), as the native girl who fires Trevor HOWARD's passion. Her other English-speaking films were: *Land of the Pharaohs* (1955, US), *The Quiet American* (1957, US) and *The Love Box* (1972). Married (2) Guy HAMILTON.

Kerr, Bill (*b* Cape Town, 1922). Actor. Began as child actor in Australia in 1933 (as 'Willie Kerr'), in both films and on stage, and went to Britain in 1947, becoming popular on radio and TV (e.g. *Hancock's Half Hour*, 1956–60; *Citizen James*, 1960–62), as well as appearing in a dozen or so films. His good-humoured persona was honed in such films as *Appointment in London* (1953), as a flying officer friend of Dirk BOGARDE, and as a cheery soldier in *The Night My Number Came Up* (1955). On returning to live in Australia in the later 70s, he has become a respected character actor in such films as *Gallipoli* (1981) and *Dusty* (1982).

OTHER BRITISH FILMS INCLUDE: *Penny Points to Paradise* (1951), *You Know What Sailors Are* (1954), *The Dam Busters* (1955), *The Captain's Table* (1958), *The Wrong Arm of the Law* (1962), *Doctor in Clover* (1966), *The House of Mortal Sin* (1975).

Kerr, Deborah (*b* Helensburgh, Scotland, 1921). Actress. RN: Kerr-Trimmer. When Kerr went to Hollywood in 1947, British cinema lost a prime talent. She returned from time to time but without doing work to be compared with what she had achieved in the 40s. Gabriel PASCAL brought her to the screen as Jenny Hill in *Major Barbara* (1941) and her wonderfully fresh natural beauty and incisiveness of playing were on show in John BAXTER's *Love on the Dole* and Lance COMFORT's *Hatter's Castle* (1941), in both as women who stumble sexually, by altruistic design in the former, through heartless seduction in the latter. Michael POWELL (who had cut her brief role in *Contraband*, 1940) made her a major star by giving her the triple role of the heroines in *The Life and Death of Colonel Blimp* (1943) and four years later cast her unforgettably as Sister Clodagh, forced to confront her own repressions in the Himalayan setting of *Black Narcissus*. This and the nympho-maniacal army wife in *From Here to Eternity* (1953, US), utterly subverting any residual gentility in her image, may well be her best work on film. However, there are plenty of other rewards: the dowdy wife who blossoms in wartime in *Perfect Strangers* (1945); the assertive Irish spy in *I See a Dark Stranger* (1946); the wife who falls into dipsomania in *Edward, My Son* (1949); 'I' in *The King and I* (1956, US); Gladys COOPER's put-upon daughter in *Separate Tables* (1958, US); the wonderfully ambiguous governess in *The Innocents* (1961); and the prickly memsahib adjusting to the home counties in her last film, *The Assam Garden* (1985).

Stage-trained in Bristol, she would sometimes return to the theatre, most notably in *Tea and Sympathy* (1953), repeating her role in the film version (1956), and there was occasional TV, including the telemovie remake of *Witness for the Prosecution* (1982), but she was pre-eminently a *film* star. Awarded a BFI Fellowship (1986), a Special BAA Award (1990), and a CBE (1998). Married (1) flying ace Anthony Bartley and (2) Holly-wood screenwriter Peter Viertel.

OTHER BRITISH FILMS: *Penn of Pennsylvania* (1941), *The Day Will Dawn* (1942), *The End of the Affair* (1954), *Heaven Knows, Mr Allison* (UK/US), *Bonjour Tristesse* (1957), *The Grass is Greener* (1960), *The Naked Edge* (UK/US), *The Chalk Garden* (1964), *Casino Royale* (1967), *Prudence and the Pill* (1968).

BIBLIOG: Eric Braun, *Deborah Kerr*, 1977.

Kerr, Fred (aka Frederick) (*b* London, 1858 – *d* London, 1933). Actor. RN: Keen. Charterhouse and Cambridge-educated player, popular on stage and screen, in US (about a dozen early talkies, including *Frankenstein*, 1931, as the old Baron) and UK films, the latter usually in dominant upper-class roles, as in *The Midshipmaid* (1932). Father of Geoffrey KERR.

OTHER BRITISH FILMS INCLUDE: *The Lifeguardsman* (1916), *12.10* (1919), *The Man from Toronto, Lord of the Manor* (1933).

Kerr, Geoffrey (*b* London, 1895 – *d* Aldershot, 1971). Screen-writer. RN: Keen. Charterhouse-educated son of Fred, on stage from 1913, in US from 1920, on both stage and screen. Also a playwright (e.g. of *Cottage to Let*, 1940, filmed 1941) and (co-) screenwriter of about ten British films, including the comedy, *Sweet Devil* (1938), and *Jassy* (1947). Married (1926–43) US actress June Walker; father of actor John Kerr.

OTHER BRITISH FILMS INCLUDE: (co-sc) *The Tenth Man, Living Dangerously* (1936), *Break the News* (1938), *The Calendar* (1948), *Fools Rush In* (1949); *Under Your Hat* (1940, co-author of play).

Kerridge, Mary (*b* London, 1914 – *d* Windsor, 1999). Actress. Briefly secretary and model before her stage debut in 1934, she helped her husband, producer **John Counsell** (*b* Beckenham, 1905 – *d* 1987, in a couple of 30s films), to run the Theatre Royal, Windsor. Her greatest stage success was starring in *Anastasia* (1953), a role she repeated on TV. Made only a few films, but was a vividly unhappy Dolly in *Anna Karenina* (1948) and a poignant Queen in *Richard III* (1955). Daughter **Elizabeth Counsell** played small roles in a few films of the 60s/70s, including *Hot Millions* (1968).

OTHER BRITISH FILMS: *Paradise for Two* (1937, uncr), *Under the Frozen Falls* (1948), *The Blue Peter* (1955), *The Duke Wore Jeans, Law and Disorder* (1958), *Curse of Simba* (1964).

Kerrigan, Justin (*b* 1974). Director, screenwriter. Enjoyed critical success (including several award nominations) with his first film, *Human Traffic* (1999), an amiable, stylistically lively exploration of the lives of six twentysomething clubbers in Cardiff.

Kesson, David Cinematographer. A prominent American cameraman of the 1910s and 20s, Kesson came to the UK in 1924 with director Marshall Neilan and star Blanche Sweet to shoot exterior scenes at Stonehenge for *Tess of the D'Urbevilles* (1924) and in Scotland for *The Sporting Venus* (1925). Also filmed exteriors for an ADAPTATION of Rebecca West's *Return of the Soldier*, which Sweet tried unsuccessfully to produce. Kesson was back in England in 1928 filming *The Bondman* for Herbert WILCOX, and Sweet asked that he stay on to be her cameraman on *The Woman in White* (1929). AS.

Kestelman, Sara (*b* London, 1944). Actress. Central School-trained stage actress, who has made a few films, starting with *Zardoz* (1972) as May, and done a good deal of plushy TV, including *Anna Karenina* (2000), as Vronsky's mother. Starred in the Australian-made romantic drama, *Break of Day* (1977).

OTHER BRITISH FILMS INCLUDE: *Lisztomania* (1975), *Lady Jane* (1985), *Mind Games* (2000).

Keys, Anthony Nelson (*b* London, 1911 – *d* Kingston-upon-Thames, 1985). Producer. Not as well known as his father,

Nelson **Keys**, or his brother John Paddy **Carstairs**, Keys was still a prominent figure in British film production of the 50s and 60s, closely associated with **Hammer**, where he had earlier been an associate producer. After service in the **Army Film & Photographic Unit**, 1940–46, Keys became an assistant director, production manager and associate producer. As a production manager, he worked on *Contraband* (1940), *Snowbound* (1948), *Bad Lord Byron* (1949), and *Women of Twilight* (1952), etc. Retired to care for his ailing wife.

OTHER BRITISH FILMS INCLUDE: (assoc p) *Dancing with Crime* (1947), *Albert RN* (1953), *Reach for the Sky* (1956), *The Curse of Frankenstein* (1957), *Dracula, The Revenge of Frankenstein* (1958), *The Mummy* (1959), *The Brides of Dracula* (1960), *The Damned* (1963); (p) *The Pirates of Blood River* (1962), *The Scarlet Blade* (1963), *The Secret of Blood Island* (1965), *The Witches* (1966), *Quatermass and the Pit* (1967), *The Devil Rides Out* (1968), *Nothing But the Night* (1972). AS.

Keys, Nelson (*b* London, 1886 – *d* London, 1939). Actor. A musical comedy star whose revue appearances include the 1924 *Ziegfeld Follies*. He appeared in about 20 films, starting with the COMEDY SHORTS, *Drowsy Dick Dreams He's a Burglar* and *Drowsy Dick's Dream* (1910). His son John Paddy **Carstairs** wrote his biography: *Bunch* (1941).

OTHER BRITISH FILMS INCLUDE: *Alone I Did It* (1914), *Once Upon a Time* (1918), *Mumsie* (1927), *Splinters* (1930), *Almost a Divorce* (1931), *The Last Journey* (1935), *Dreams Come True* (1936), *Knight for a Day* (1937). AS.

Khan Din, Ayub (*b* Salford, Lancs, 1961). Actor, screenwriter. Now best known as the writer of *East Is East* (2000), BAA/best film-winner, he also appeared in two important 80s films foregrounding Anglo-Asian relations: *My Beautiful Laundrette* (1985) and *Sammy and Rosie Get Laid* (1987, as Sammy). *East Is East*, based on his play, has a wonderful ear for dialogue and understanding of painful comedy.

Kidron, Beeban (*b* London, 1961). Director. Made her name with the celebrated, BAA-winning TV series, *Oranges Are Not the Only Fruit* (1990), with its sensitive exploration of a young girl's awareness of her lesbian sexuality, and went on to make *Antonia and Jane* (1990), a study of a long-lasting friendship between a female odd-couple. She worked in the US with moderate success on *Used People* (1992) and *To Wong Foo, Thanks for Everything, Julie Newmar* (1994), and back in Britain made the little-seen CONRAD adaptation, *Amy Foster* (1997, UK/Fr/US, + co-p). A graduate of the NATIONAL FILM AND TELEVISION SCHOOL, and a quirkily likeable talent.

OTHER BRITISH FILMS INCLUDE: *Vroom* (1988, d), *Alex* (1990, short, d, sc), *Great Moments in Aviation* (1994, UK/US).

Kiel, Richard (*b* Redford, Michigan, 1939). Actor. Famous as the seemingly indestructible seven-foot villain, Jaws, of two BOND movies, *The Spy Who Loved Me* (1977) and *Moonraker* (1979, UK/Fr). He has been a dangerous presence in about 30 other films, including, memorably, Clint Eastwood's *Pale Rider* (1985, US).

OTHER BRITISH FILM: *Force 10 from Navarone* (1978).

Kiepura, Jan (*b* Sosnowiec, Poland, 1902 – *d* New York, 1966). Singer, actor. Romantic tenor and international star of light stage and screen operettas in the 20s and 1930s, often paired with his wife, soprano Marta **Eggerth**. In the early 30s he starred in a number of British–European co-productions. From 1939 he continued his career in the US.

BRITISH FILMS: *City of Song* (1931), *Tell Me Tonight* (1932), *My Song For You* (1934), *My Heart Is Calling* (1934). Tim Bergfelder.

Kier, Udo (*b* Cologne, 1944). Actor. Prolific character player with well over 100 international film and TV credits, a few of them (not necessarily the most interesting) with British credentials. His first film was Mike **Sarne**'s British short, *The Road to Saint Tropez* (1966), but his other British films, with the marginal exception of the multi-national co-production, *Dancer in the Dark* (2000, UK/Den/Fin/Fr/Ger/Ice/It/Neth/Nor/Swe/US), do not compare in interest with those he made for Rainer Fassbinder (*Lili Marleen*, 1980; *Lola*, 1982, Ger) or Gus Van Sant's *My Own Private Idaho* (1991, US).

OTHER BRITISH FILMS INCLUDE: *Exposé* (1975), *Prince Valiant* (1997, UK/Ger/Ire/US), *Shadow of the Vampire* (UK/Lux/US), *The Last Minute* (UK/US) (2001), *Revelation* (2002).

Kilburn, Terry (*b* London, 1926). Actor. RN: Kilbourne. Though one of those CHILD ACTORS who didn't enjoy major adult careers, Kilburn made 20-odd films before he became too old for juvenile roles. Apart from a couple of adult roles – in the British-made *Fiend Without a Face* (1957) and *Lolita* (1961) – he made another career on stage and as a drama teacher in the US. Of vaudeville parents, he began in Hollywood but had his most memorable screen time as four generations of fresh-faced Colley schoolboys in *Goodbye, Mr Chips* (1939). In post-war Hollywood, he had continuing role in four 'BULLDOG DRUMMOND' second features.

Kimmins, Anthony (*b* Harrow, 1901 – *d* Hurstpierpoint, 1964). Director, screenwriter, actor, producer. A former naval officer, this craftsmanlike film-maker was at his best with breezy COMEDIES such as the George **Formby** films he directed and co-wrote pre-war at EALING, including *Trouble Brewing* (1939), and the more sophisticated romantic comedy, *The Captain's Paradise* (1953, + p). Pre-WW2 naval service, he had acted in a couple of films, then (co-)wrote and/or directed 20 popular light entertainments. He wrote for Gracie **Fields** (e.g. *The Show Goes On*, 1937) and several times for Carol **Reed** including *Midshipman Easy* (1935), as well as being Formby's regular supplier of good-natured, slyly ambiguous dialogue and routines. Post-war, he made the edgy, visually stylish, psychological melodrama *Mine Own Executioner* (1947, + co-p), before having the misfortune to be the director (one among several) whose name fetches up on the screen for *Bonnie Prince Charlie* (1948). Of the rest, *Mr Denning Drives North* (1951, + co-p) is a nicely twisty thriller, *Aunt Clara* (1954, + co-p) is a sentimental comedy just about redeemed by Margaret **Rutherford**, and the Australian-made *Smiley* (1956) has a pleasing freshness. Also a playwright: his 1932 play, *While Parents Sleep* was filmed in 1935, and his last film, *The Amorous Prawn* (1962, d, + co-sc), was based on his 1960 success. Awarded OBE in 1946.

OTHER BRITISH FILMS INCLUDE: (a) *The Golden Cage* (1933), *White Ensign* (1934); (sc/co-sc/dial/story) *Queen of Hearts, Laburnum Grove* (1936), *Keep Fit* (+ d), *Good Morning, Boys!* (1937), *I See Ice!* (1938, + d), *Top of the Form* (1953); (play) *The Night Club Queen* (1934): (d, sc) *By-Pass to Happiness* (1934), *All at Sea* (1935), *It's in the Air* (1938); (d) *How's Chances?* (1934), *Flesh and Blood* (1951); (d, p) *Who Goes There!* (1951), *Smiley Gets a Gun* (1958, + sc).

Kinemacolor was the first commercially successful natural COLOUR film process, a two-colour additive system, involving photography through red-orange and blue-green gelatin filters, and projection through the same coloured filters at 32 frames per second. Englishmen Frederick Marshall Lee and Edward Raymond Turner, who were granted a patent in 1899, devised an unworkable three-colour system. In 1903, Charles **Urban**

acquired the patent rights from Turner's widow, and the system was subsequently developed by G.A. SMITH (patent No. S.F. 26,671 in 1906) and named as Kinemacolor in 1909. The *British Journal of Photography* commented, 'The process achieved is so satisfactory that we are warranted in saying that the process should be commercially valuable in a very short time'.

Urban assured that initial success with the formation of the Natural Color Kinematograph Company in March 1909, and production of the first Kinemacolor drama, *The Story of Napoleon*, released in November 1910. The coronation of George V was filmed in Kinemacolor, and on September 14 and 15, 1911, a Kinemacolor programme was presented before the King and Queen Mary at Balmoral Castle. Urban established a studio in the South of France and also converted the studio of James WILLIAMSON in Brighton to Kinemacolor production, and in April 1911, he leased London's Scala Theatre as a permanent home for Kinemacolor presentations. Aside from many short subjects, Urban also produced in Kinemacolor *The Coronation Durbar at Delhi* (1912), part of a larger film show called *With Our King and Queen Through India*, as well as *Round the World in Two Hours* (1912), *The World, the Flesh and the Devil* (1914), which was the first colour feature film, *Little Lord Fauntleroy* and *With the Fighting Forces in Europe* (1914).

Urban also established the Kinemacolor Company of America in 1910. There were other rival colour systems at the time, notably William FRIESE-GREENE's Bicolour process, marketed by Brighton-based Biocolour Limited, the Gaumont Coloured Films and the Ulysses three-colour process, introduced in 1914. In December 1913, Biocolour brought a court case against Kinemacolor; Urban won originally, but lost on appeal the following year; lawsuits by rival concerns ended Urban's colour monopoly, but Kinemacolor was the inspiration for the many colour systems that followed. Production ceased, and the company was liquidated, resurfacing as Color Films Ltd.

BIBLIOG: D.B. Thomas, *The First Colour Motion Pictures*, 1969. AS.

Kinematograph Weekly provides a definitive overview of the history of the British film industry for more than three-quarters of its existence, being the longest surviving trade paper. First published on June 15, 1899 as the *Optical Magic Lantern Journal and Photographic Enlarger*, edited from 1904 by Theodore Brown, who left for a short time but returned when it became the *Kinematograph and Lantern Weekly* on May 16, 1907, and the *Kinematograph Weekly* on December 4, 1919. Four other editors, Low Warren (1912–17), Frank Tilley (1918–24), S.G. Rayment (1926–45) and Bill Altria (1955–71) are most closely associated with the 'Kine' as it was fondly called. It ceased publication on September 25, 1971 when it merged with Britain's only other trade publication, *Today's Cinema*. An almost complete run exists at the BRITISH FILM INSTITUTE, and the journal is available on microfilm from World Microfilms. AS.

Kinematograph Renters' Society Founded by film distributors in 1915 for collective bargaining power, and protection against exhibitors. Now known as Society of Film Distributors.

King, Dave (*b* Twickenham, 1929 – *d* London, 2002). Comedian. In *Go to Blazes* (1962), a droll comedy about imaginative if inept crooks, King revealed an engaging comic persona – shrewd, streetwise, chipper – that was only very rarely exploited in films. Had some TV success in the 50s with his own show (1955–57) which he also presented at the London

Hippodrome, then returned as a character player in such fare as mini-series *Pennies from Heaven* (1978) and the gangster thriller, *The Long Good Friday* (1979).

OTHER BRITISH FILMS INCLUDE: *Up the Chastity Belt* (1971), *The Ritz* (1976), *Golden Lady* (1979), *Revolution* (1985, UK/Nor).

King, George (*b* London, 1899 – *d* London, 1966). Director, producer. It is hard to conceive now of a director making 70 films, except perhaps in TV, where King's formulaic approach might have found its home. He had wide experience of film-making, as agent, writer of title cards in the 20s, assistant director, then producer of – generally – films more prestigious than had fallen his lot as a 30s director of 'QUOTA QUICKIES', including *The First of the Few* (1942, co-p) and *Eight O'Clock Walk* (1954). In the 30s, he churned out the GENRE staples of the period: fluffy COMEDIES, like *Too Many Wives* (1933), THRILLERS like *Man Without a Face* (1935, + co-p), and barn-storming MELODRAMAS like *Sweeney Todd, The Demon Barber of Fleet Street* (1936), starring the redoubtable Tod SLAUGHTER. He ventured successfully upmarket with his wartime films, *Tomorrow We Live* (1942) and *Candlelight in Algeria* (1943), and post-war made an agreeable MUSICAL BIOPIC, *Gaiety George* (1946), a tense film version of the popular stage CRIME melodrama, *The Shop at Sly Corner* (1946), and, finally, the taut but grim romantic MYSTERY, *Forbidden* (1949).

OTHER BRITISH FILMS INCLUDE: (d) *Leave It to Me* (1930), *Midnight* (1931), *Men of Steel* (1932), *High Finance* (1933), *Full Circle* (1935), *The Crimes of Stephen Hawke* (1936), *The Face at the Window* (1939), *George and Margaret* (1940); (p) *Maria Marten, or The Murder in the Red Barn* (1935), *Riding High* (1937); (d, p) *Deadlock* (1931), *Little Stranger* (+ sc), *Get Your Man* (1934), *Merry Comes to Town* (1937), *Sexton Blake and the Hooded Terror* (1938), *The Chinese Bungalow* (1940).

King, Ivan (*b* 1922). Production designer. After architecture studies, then war service (1940–44), King began in films as draughtsman on *The Seventh Veil* (1945), was then assistant art director before getting his full credit on *Silver Darlings* (1946). Much of his work was on routine films, but even on such thick-ear stuff as *Dick Barton Strikes Back* (1949) the look of the film, with its use of Blackpool Tower, is partly due to him. He does serviceable work on such varied fare as the Irish-set *Happy Ever After* (1954), the messy domesticity of *It's Never Too Late* (1956) and his use of farm, fair and church in *Daughter of Darkness* (1947) helps create the kinds of opposition at this strange film's heart.

OTHER BRITISH FILMS INCLUDE: *The Interrupted Journey* (1949), *Shadow of the Past* (1950), *Laughter in Paradise* (1951), *Top Secret* (1952), *Rough Shoot* (1953), *See How They Run* (1955), *Wonderful Things, The Naked Truth* (1957), *Too Many Crooks* (1959), *Hand in Hand, Village of the Damned* (1960), *Operation Snatch* (1962), *Crossplot* (1969).

King, Philip (*b* Beverley, 1904 – *d* Brighton, 1979). Dramatist. Began as actor for seven years in Harrogate, subsequently the author of a run of popular plays, often in collaboration with Falkland Cary (*b* Kildare, Ireland, 1897 – *d* Surrey, 1989), who also shared screenplay credits with him on *Sailor Beware* (1956) and *Watch It Sailor!* (1961), adapted from their 1950 and 1960 plays. Others of King's plays filmed were: *Curtain Up* (1952, derived from *On Monday Next*, 1949), a farce about weekly rep; the frantic, long-running *See How They Run* (1955), set in a country vicarage; and the melodramatic *Serious Charge* (1959), in which a vicar is accused of molesting a teenage boy. Also acted as the prison doctor in *Eight O'Clock Walk* (1954).

King, Sydney (aka Sidney) (b 1910). Actor. Former journalist, educated at Hull Grammar School, King played mainly dapper upper-middle-class types in a dozen films, including the heroine's brother in *Quiet Wedding* (1941) and Greta GYNT's bounderish ex-boyfriend in *The Calendar* (1948).

OTHER BRITISH FILMS INCLUDE: *The Sleeping Cardinal* (1931), *The King's Cup* (1933), *The Gables Mystery* (1938), *Cottage to Let* (1941), *Flying Fortress* (1942), *The Glass Mountain* (1948), *The Silent Enemy* (1958).

Kingsley, Sir Ben (b Snainton, 1943) Actor. RN: Krishna Bhanji. Of Anglo-Indian parentage, he joined the RSC in 1967 and spent the next 15 years appearing mainly on stage. He made his film debut as Royale in *Fear is the Key* (1972) and appeared briefly in *Hard Labour* (1973). After almost a decade he returned to film when he was cast in the title role in *Gandhi* (1982, UK/Ind), winning AA and BAA for his subtle and compelling performance. Demonstrated his versatility in a variety of roles since, including Shostakovich in *Testimony* (1987), clever Dr Watson in *Without a Clue* (1988, UK/US), Itzhak Stern in *Schindler's List* (1993, US), Dr Roberto Miranda meeting his nemesis in *Death and the Maiden* (1995, UK/Fr/US), a very intelligent Feste in *Twelfth Night* (1996, UK/US), and terrifying as the gangster bent on recruiting former colleague Ray WINSTONE in *Sexy Beast* (2001, UK/Sp/US). Has also worked extensively in international films, including, *Bugsy*, 1991, US) and on TV, including *Silas Marner* (1985). Knighted in 2002.

OTHER BRITISH FILMS: *Betrayal* (1982), *Turtle Diary* (1985), *Maurice* (1987), *Pascali's Island* (1988, US/UK), *Slipstream* (1989), *The Children* (1990, UK/Ger), *Freddie as F.R.O.7* (1992, voice), *Photographing Fairies* (1997), *Parting Shots* (1998), *Rules of Engagement* (2000), *The Triumph of Love* (2001). Anne-Marie Thomas.

Kingsley, David (b 1917). Administrator. Old Etonian former accountant, Kingsley held several very important managerial positions in the British film industry, including those of Secretary (1949–50) and later Managing Director (1954) of the NATIONAL FILM FINANCE CORPORATION, a director and later (1958) Managing Director of BRITISH LION FILMS LTD and its associated companies. In 1989, Roy BOULTING, Board member of British Lion, credited Kingsley with turning its fortunes around and for keeping it independent.

Kingston, Alex (b London, 1963). Actress. Voluptuous RADA-trained actress with extensive stage experience, including RSC seasons, who keeps making news. In 1996, she was Moll (BAA/n) in a racy TV version of *The Adventures of Moll Flanders* (1996); she endured a much-publicised divorce from actor Ralph FIENNES (m.1993–97); in the US, she became a TV star with her role as Dr Elizabeth Corday in the long-running *ER* (1994–); then, in 2000, two years after it was made, *Croupier* (1998, UK/Fr/Ger/Ire), in which she has a showy role as the South African gambler, became a surprise hit in the US and elsewhere. Half-German, she has now married a German journalist.

OTHER BRITISH FILMS INCLUDE: *The Cook, the Thief, His Wife & Her Lover* (1989, UK/Fr), *Carrington* (1994, UK/Fr), *Saint-Ex* (1996), *Essex Boys* (2000).

Kinnear, Roy (b Wigan, 1934 – d Madrid, 1988). Actor. Tubby, balding character comic, who tragically died after a horse-riding accident while filming *Return of the Musketeers* (1989, UK/Fr/Sp) in Spain. RADA-trained, he spent a lot of acting time with the Theatre Workshop, Stratford, from the late 50s. His screen career got under way in the 60s, and he was very funny in Ken RUSSELL's little-regarded cinema debut, *French*

Dressing (1963). He was much associated with the films of Richard LESTER, including *Help!* (1965), the surreal *The Bed Sitting Room* (1969), was the ship's social director in *Juggernaut* (1974), and the lackey Planchet in *The Three* (and *Four*) *Musketeers* (1973, Panama; 1974, Panama, Sp).

OTHER BRITISH FILMS INCLUDE: *The Millionairess* (1960), *The Boys, Tiara Tahiti, Sparrows Can't Sing* (1962), *Heavens Above!* (1963), *The Hill* (1965), *The Deadly Affair* (1966), *Lock Up Your Daughters!* (1969), *Scrooge* (1970), *Madame Sin, The Alf Garnett Saga* (1972), *Not Now, Comrade* (1976), *The Hound of the Baskervilles* (1977), *The London Connection* (1979), *Just Ask for Diamond* (1988, UK/US).

Kinnoch, Ronald (b Dundee, 1910). Producer. Educated in Edinburgh and Paris, Kinnoch entered films in 1932, and worked as assistant director and unit manager during the 30s. After WW2 service (1940–45), he worked as production manager for TWO CITIES before beginning to produce for ACT FILMS, for which he produced (and co-wrote) the heartfelt second feature, *Private Information* (1952), and was later associate producer of *The Ipcress File* (1965).

OTHER BRITISH FILMS INCLUDE: (prod man) *Hungry Hill* (1947), *The Winslow Boy* (1948), *Night and the City* (1950); (p/co-p) *Escape Route* (1952), *That Lady* (1954), *Fire Down Below* (1957), *The Secret Man* (1958, + d), *Village of the Damned* (1960, + co-sc), *Invasion Quartet* (1961), *Cairo, Inadmissible Evidence* (1968).

Kinski, Klaus (b Zoppot, East Prussia, 1926 – d Lagunitas, California, 1991). Actor. RN: Nikolaus Nakszynski. An excessive and volatile personality on screen and off, but also a unique talent, Kinski portrayed disturbed and menacing characters in countless international productions. Best known for his collaborations with Sergio Leone (*For A Few Dollars More*, 1965) and Werner Herzog (*Nosferatu*, 1979, *Fitzcarraldo*, 1981), he appeared in a dozen British films. His daughter is actress Nastassia KINSKI.

BRITISH FILMS INCLUDE: *The Devil's Daffodil* (UK/Ger, 1961), *Traitor's Gate* (UK/Ger), *Doctor Zhivago* (UK/US) (1965), *Circus Of Fear* (1966), *Our Man In Marrakesh* (1966), *Hell Is Empty* (UK/It 1966), *Lifespan* (1974), *Venom* (1981). Tim Bergfelder.

Kinski, Nastassia (b West Berlin, 1961). Actress. RN: Nakszynski. Beautiful daughter of Klaus KINSKI, who has starred in some British films, including the HORROR piece, *To The Devil A Daughter* (1976, UK/Ger); *Tess* (1979, UK/Fr), as Thomas HARDY's blighted heroine; and more recently in another film derived from Hardy, *The Claim* (2001, UK/Can/Fr). Now living in the US, she has worked very busily in the new millennium.

OTHER BRITISH FILMS: *Terminal Velocity* (1994), *Playing by Heart* (1998), *The Lost Son* (1999, UK/Fr/US).

Kipling, Rudyard (b Bombay, 1865 – d London, 1936). Author. Celebrated novelist and poet of EMPIRE, raised in INDIA, whose novels and stories have provided the basis for many films, but mostly in a Raj-besotted pre-war Hollywood, when films such as *Wee Willie Winkie* (1937) and *Gunga Din* (1939) were very popular. These and such post-war US films as *Kim* (1950), *Soldiers Three* (1951) and *The Man Who Would Be King* (1975) are stocked with British actors. In Britain, *Elephant Boy* (1937) was based on *Toomai of the Elephants*, and Lindsay ANDERSON's *If . . .* (1968) borrows its title ironically from Kipling's poem. A morsel: his short story, 'Mrs Bathurst' (1904), uses a film show as the turning point of its narrative.

BIBLIOG: Philip Leibfried, *Rudyard Kipling and Sir Henry Rider Haggard on Screen, Stage, Radio and Television*, 2000.

Kirby, Joyce (*b* St Margaret's-on-Thames, 1915) Actress. Diminutive (5'1") blonde dancer in Cochrane shows, on stage from childhood, and in a dozen largely forgotten 30s films, of which *The Midshipmaid* (1932) and *Britannia of Billingsgate* (1933) are the best-known – but not for her tiny roles in them. She had co-starring roles in two long-unseen films for Arthur WOODS, *Mayfair Melody* and *The Compulsory Wife* (1937).
OTHER BRITISH FILMS INCLUDE: *It's a Boy!*, *The Fire Raisers* (1933), *Are You a Mason?* (1934), *Hail and Farewell* (1936), *Ship's Concert* (1937).

Kirkwood, Pat (*b* Pendleton, 1921). Actress. Singing in variety as a teenager, and on radio from 1936, Kirkwood started in films in *Save a Little Sunshine* (1938) and played opposite George FORMBY in *Come on George* (1939). Primarily a stage performer, she became the queen of 40s West End musicals and revue. After an unsuccessful Hollywood musical film, *No Leave, No Love* (MGM, 1946), she returned to England and a more dramatic role in *Once a Sinner* (1950). Had her own BBC television show in the 50s, and triumphantly played MUSIC HALL stars Marie Lloyd and Vesta Tilley in TV's *Our Marie* (1953) and *The Great Little Tilley* (1956), the latter adapted for the colour film *After the Ball* (1957). Sadly, her vitality is not captured well on film. Married (3) Hubert GREGG.
OTHER BRITISH FILMS: *Me and My Pal* (1939), *Band Waggon* (1940), *Flight from Folly* (1945), *Stars in Your Eyes* (1956).
BIBLIOG: Autobiography, *The Time of My Life*, 1999. Roger Philip Mellor.

Kirwan, Dervla (*b* Dublin, 1971). Actress. Spirited, likeable Celtic beauty, best known for her TV work as pub-keeping Assumpta in *Ballykissangel* (1996–99) and the endangered Jinx in *The Dark Room* (1999). She has worked steadily on stage from 1988, but her films have been few, her main chance coming with the lead in Michael WINTERBOTTOM's *With or Without You* (1999).
OTHER BRITISH FILMS: *The Fantasist* (1986, Ire), *December Bride* (1990), *War of the Buttons* (1994).

Kirwan, Kitty Actress. Ancient character player in Celtic fringe roles, including Mrs Campbell whose anniversary is celebrated in *I Know Where I'm Going!* (1945) and Grannie in *Odd Man Out* (1947).
OTHER BRITISH FILMS: *The Vicar of Bray*, *Macushla*, *The Edge of the World* (1937), *Floodtide* (1949).

Kirwan, Patrick (*b* London, 1899 – *d* London, 1984). Screenwriter. Well-known as critic and playwright, Kirwan began writing screenplays in the mid 30s and was the author of the original stories on which the WAR FILMS, *Escape to Danger* (1943) and *The Captive Heart* (1946), were based. Most of his screenwriting, across the usual GENRE range, is proficient rather than inventive, but *The Arsenal Stadium Mystery* (1939) and *Dear Octopus* (1943) offer something more, and in two very different genres.
OTHER BRITISH FILMS INCLUDE: (co-sc) *Riders to the Sea* (1935, UK/Ire), *Wings over Africa* (1936), *The Drum* (1938), *On the Night of the Fire* (1939), *Convoy* (1940), *Ships with Wings* (1941), *The Day Will Dawn* (1942), *The Chiltern Hundreds* (1949), *Hotel Sahara* (+ co-story) (1951), *Desperate Moment* (1953), *Jacqueline* (1956), *This Other Eden* (Ire), *Broth of a Boy* (Ire), *Tommy the Toreador* (1959); (sc) *The Fake* (1954), *Rooney* (1958).

Kitchin, Jack (aka C.D. Milner-Kitchin, Milner Kitchin) (*b* US, 1901 – *d* ?). Producer, editor. Brought up from 1904 and educated in Canada, he entered films in Hollywood in 1929 as editor at RKO, returning to England in 1934 and working at EALING as supervising editor, as well as (associate) producer of

several George FORMBY films, until WW2 service (1939–45). During this time, he was closely associated with director Basil DEAN, for whom he first worked as editor on *Birds of Prey* (1930). Post-war, he co-produced *Mine Own Executioner* (1947).
OTHER BRITISH FILMS INCLUDE: (e, super e) *Lorna Doone* (1934), *No Limit* (1935), *Queen of Hearts* (1936), *Keep Fit, I See Ice!* (1938); (p, assoc p, co-p) *Penny Paradise* (co-p), *It's in the Air* (assoc) (1938), *Trouble Brewing, Come on George!* (1939, p).

Kitchen, Michael (*b* Leicester, 1948). Actor. Charismatic character player of TV (see *Caught on a Train*, 1980; *To Play the King*, 1990, as a Prince Charles figure; *Oliver Twist*, 1999, many others) and screen, where he has played Intelligence Officer Bill Tanner in two BOND films, *GoldenEye* (1995, UK/US) and *The World Is Not Enough* (1999, UK/US). He conveys intelligent likability (as in *Mrs Dalloway*, 1997, UK/Neth/US), but can also suggest dangerous possibilities as in the opening episode of *Pie in the Sky* (1994). Some international films, including *Out of Africa* (1985, UK/US).
OTHER BRITISH FILMS INCLUDE: *Unman, Wittering and Zigo* (1971), *Dracula* (1973), *Breaking Glass* (1980), *Enchanted April*, *The Trial* (1992), *The Guilty* (1993), *Proof of Life* (UK/US), *New Year's Day* (UK/Fr) (2001).

Klinger, Michael (*b* London, 1921 – *d* Watford, 1989). Producer. Son of immigrant Polish tailor, former disc jockey, strip-club manager and film distributor, Klinger entered films as co-producer, with Tony TENSER, of such EXPLOITATION films as *Naked As Nature Intended* (1961). Aspiring higher than this, and having earned enough to do so, he became involved with POLANSKI's *Repulsion* (1965, ex p) and *Cul-de-Sac* (1966), and produced two films for Mike HODGES, *Get Carter* (1971) and *Pulp* (1972). In the 70s, he interspersed his more upmarket ventures with several entries in the 'Confessions of . . .' SERIES, and the failure of his last film, *Riding High* (1980, co-p) apparently ruined him.
OTHER BRITISH FILMS INCLUDE: (p, unless noted) *The Yellow Teddy Bears* (1963, co-p), *London in the Raw* (1964, doc), *A Study in Terror* (co-p), *Primitive London* (1965), *The Projected Man* (1966, co-p), *The Penthouse* (co-ex p), *Baby Love* (ex p, co-sc) (1967), *Something to Hide* (1971), *Gold*, *Confessions of a Window Cleaner* (ex p) (1974), *Shout at the Devil*, *Confessions of a Driving Instructor* (ex p) (1976), *Tomorrow Never Comes* (1977, co-p).

Kneale, Nigel (*b* Isle of Man, 1922). Screenwriter. BBC staff writer who found instant fame as the creator of TV's *The Quatermass Experiment* (1953), which brought a new dimension of intelligence to bear on British SCIENCE-FICTION film. It was adapted to the big screen in 1955 by HAMMER, whose fortunes it greatly enhanced, and there were three sequels: *Quatermass 2* (1957), the very exciting *Quatermass and the Pit* (1967) and *The Quatermass Conclusion* (1978), on all of which he worked as (co-)screenwriter. His other film work includes two BAA-nominated screenplays, for WOODFALL: *Look Back in Anger* (1959) and *The Entertainer* (1960, co-written with John OSBORNE), both skilfully 'opened out'.
OTHER BRITISH FILMS: *The Abominable Snowman* (1957), *HMS Defiant* (1962, co-sc), *First Man in the Moon* (1964, co-sc), *The Witches* (1966), *Gentry* (1987).

Knef, Hildegarde *see* **Neff, Hildegarde**

Knight, Castleton (*b* Battle, 1894 – *d* Battle, 1972). Director. RN: Leonard Castleton-Knight. Directed a few early British (sound added) talkies, including *The Kissing Cup's Race* (1931, + co-sc), and produced GAUMONT–BRITISH NEWSREELS in the 30s, but is now best remembered as maker of DOCU-MENTARIES chronicling public events: *Theirs Is the Glory* (1946, p), recreating the Battle of Arnhem, *XIVth Olympiad: The Glory of Sport* (1948, p, d), *Royal Wedding* (1947, d), and *A Queen Is Crowned* (1953, p, d), which was Oscar-nominated, and which probably accounts for his being awarded an OBE.

OTHER BRITISH FILMS INCLUDE: (d, unless noted) *The Flying Scotsman* (1929), *For Freedom* (1940, co-d), *Sons of the Air, The Second Battle of London* (+ p) (1944, doc), *Gentlemen – The Queen!* (1953, + p), *Churchill, Man of the Century* (1955, doc).

Knight, David (*b* Niagara Falls, US, 1928). Actor. RN: Mintz. California-educated leading man who taught drama before coming to England in 1952 to take up a scholarship to RADA. Tall, pleasant-looking and agreeable, he starred successfully in his first film, *The Young Lovers* (1954), Anthony ASQUITH's cold-war romance, but, though never less than convincing in his subsequent ten British films (e.g. as the distraught young father in *Lost*, 1955), he never became a major star. Also stage from the mid 50s, as a useful American in London in such fare as *The Caine Mutiny Court Martial* (1956) and *The Trial of Mary Dugan* (1958), and on TV from the late 50s.

OTHER BRITISH FILMS INCLUDE: *Out of the Clouds, On Such a Night* (short) (1955), *Eyewitness* (1956), *Across the Bridge* (1957), *Battle of the V-1* (1958), *Nightmare* (1963).

Knight, Esmond (*b* East Sheen 1906 – *d* Egypt 1987). Actor. Near-blindness suffered in naval action early in WW2 scarcely disturbed Knight's progress from handsome romantic lead to solid character actor; indeed it arguably gave extra depth to roles like the Village Idiot in *A Canterbury Tale* (1944) – in which he also played a soldier and narrated the Chaucerian Prologue – and the Holy Man in *Black Narcissus* (1947). These were two of the many films he made for Michael POWELL between his screen debut in *77 Park Lane* (1931) and *The Boy who Turned Yellow* (1972); his talismanic status for Powell is confirmed by his casting as the artfully-named PINEWOOD director Arthur Baden in *Peeping Tom* (1960). Other notable roles include the young Johann Strauss in HITCHCOCK's *Waltzes from Vienna* (1933), Fluellen in *Henry V* (1944), and the father, alongside his own wife Nora SWINBURNE, in Renoir's *The River* (1951, US).

OTHER BRITISH FILMS INCLUDE: *The Ringer* (1931), *The Bermondsey Kid* (1933), *Dandy Dick* (1935), *Pagliacci* (1936), *The Arsenal Stadium Mystery* (1939), *Contraband* (1940), *The Silver Fleet* (1943), *The Halfway House* (1944), *The End of the River, Holiday Camp* (1947), *The Red Shoes, Hamlet* (1948), *Gone to Earth* (1950), *Richard III* (1955), *Sink the Bismarck!* (1960), *The Spy Who Came in from the Cold* (1965), *Where's Jack* (1969).

BIBLIOG: Esmond Knight, *Seeking the Bubble*, 1942. Charles Barr.

Knight, James (*b* Canterbury, 1891 – *d* 1947). Actor. A virile leading man in silent films who later became a minor character player, Knight made more than 60 films, including a number for HARMA between 1918 and 1922, in which he was Marjorie VILLIS's leading man.

BRITISH FILMS INCLUDE: *The Happy Warrior* (1917), *The Man Who Forgot* (1919), *Beautiful Kitty* (1923), *A Safe Affair* (1931), *The Life and Death of Colonel Blimp* (1943), *Johnny Frenchman* (1945), *My Sister and I* (1948). AS.

Knight, Rosalind (*b* London, 1933). Actress. Daughter of Esmond KNIGHT and Nora SWINBURNE, Knight entered films and TV in the later 50s. She has appeared in many popular TV programmes, including *The Adventures of Sherlock Holmes* (1984) and *Heartbeat* (2000), and her film work, largely in comic vein, has included two in the 'ST TRINIAN'S' SERIES

(student in *Blue Murder at . . .*, 1957; teacher in *Wildcats of . . .*, 1980), two 'CARRY ON' romps (*. . . Nurse*, 1958; *. . . Teacher*, 1959), Mrs Fitzpatrick, object of dalliance with *Tom Jones* (1963), and several very funny moments in *About a Boy* (2002, (UK/Fr/Ger/US) as an out-of-it mother-in-law (sort of).

OTHER BRITISH FILMS INCLUDE: *The Horse's Mouth* (1958), *The Kitchen* (1961), *Diamonds for Breakfast* (1968), *Start the Revolution Without Me* (1969), *Mister Quilp* (1974), *The Lady Vanishes* (1979), *Prick Up Your Ears* (1987), *Afraid of the Dark* (1991, UK/Fr).

Knight, Shirley (*b* Goessel, Kans, 1937). Actress. Notable stage-trained American actress who entered films in the early 60s, vividly remembered in *Sweet Bird of Youth* (1962, AAn) and *The Group* (1966), and in her long career appeared in five British (co-) productions: *Dutchman* (1966), *Petulia* (1968), *Secrets* (1971), *Juggernaut* (1974) and *The Sender* (1982, UK/US). She has continued to play character roles in international films. Married screenwriter John HOPKINS (1969 to 1989, his death).

Knight, Vivienne (*b* Ipswich, 1918). Publicist, screenwriter. Former fashion designer and journalist who became publicity director for the ARCHERS (1943–51), cutting her promotional teeth on the tricky *A Canterbury Tale* (1944), later acting as intermediary between the Archers and KORDA on *The Tales of Hoffman* (1951). Moved on to EALING in 1951, as publicity director, becoming associate producer in 1954, and, with husband Patrick CAMPBELL, co-wrote several screenplays, including *Law and Disorder* (1958, with T.E.B. Clarke), *Go to Blazes* (1962) and *Girl in the Headlines* (1963). Wrote *A Gentleman and a Player* (1988), the biography of Trevor HOWARD.

Knode, Charles Costume designer. His early work was on MONTY PYTHON films, in which he took advantage of the considerable scope they offered. Since then he has worked on the BOND film, *Never Say Never Again* (1983, UK/US), won a BAA and an AAn for his designs for *Braveheart* (1995, US) and shared a BAA for costume design for *Blade Runner* (1982, US). Despite these heterogeneous assignments, he has more recently settled into the world of TV classic ADAPTATIONS.

OTHER BRITISH FILMS INCLUDE: (cos, unless noted) *Monty Python and the Holy Grail* (1974, co-cos), *The Hound of the Baskervilles* (1977), *1492: Conquest of Paradise* (co-cos) (1992), *Snow White: A Tale of Terror* (1996, UK/US, co-cos).

Knoles, Harley (*b* Rotherham, 1880 – *d* London, 1936). Producer, director. Knoles was described by *The Moving Picture World* as 'the best director of motion pictures England ever sent to America', responsible for more than 25 US features from 1915 to 1920; he also acted opposite Helen Gardner in *Cleopatra* (1912). When Knoles was named as head of ALLIANCE FILM CORPORATION in the UK in 1919, he claimed that no-one there was aware he was English. For Alliance he directed its most prestigious productions: *Carnival* (1921), with Matheson LANG and Ivor NOVELLO, *The Door That Has No Key* (1921), with Evelyn BRENT, and *The Bohemian Girl* (1922), with Gladys COOPER and Novello. Also directed in Canada and again in the US in 1926.

OTHER BRITISH FILMS: *Land of Hope and Glory* (1927), *The White Sheik* (1927), *The Rising Generation* (1928, co-director). AS.

Knopfler, Mark (*b* Glasgow, 1949). Composer, guitarist, singer. Lead singer from 1977 of Dire Straits which won international success and lasted until 1995. His first film score was for Bill FORSYTH's EALING-style *Local Hero* (1983), and he also scored *Comfort and Joy* (1984), another Scottish-set FORSYTH comedy, as well as the drama of Ulster-set *Cal* (1984). He has also worked in the US, notably on *The Princess Bride* (1987) and *Wag the Dog* (1997).

OTHER BRITISH FILMS INCLUDE: *The Secret Policeman's Other Ball* (1987, performer), *Metroland* (1997, UK/Fr/Sp, m, performer).

Knowles, Bernard (*b* Manchester, 1900 – *d* Taplow, Bucks, 1975). Director, cinematographer. Celebrated cameraman who, like so many of his craft in Britain, aspired to direct and did so with diminishing results after a promising start with the charming ghost story, *A Place of One's Own* (1945). With GAINSBOROUGH in the 40s he directed tosh-fests like *The Magic Bow* (1946), the life-story, to use the term with outrageous looseness, of Paganini, and *The White Unicorn* (1947), a soppy MELODRAMA of unhappy women and unreliable men. He did what he could with the strange but not uninteresting *The Man Within* (1947) and the enjoyable melodramatics of *Jassy* (1947), and he made something worthwhile of the displaced persons drama, *The Lost People* (1949). From the early 50s, his career tapered off into 'B' FILMS, and he didn't have the élan of, say, Lance COMFORT or Lawrence HUNTINGTON to bring life to their threadbare plots. Like those two, he also worked in 50s TV, including episodes of *Ivanhoe* (1958).

A former press photographer on the *Detroit News*, he became the first British cameraman to light a TECHNICOLOR film, *The Mikado* (1939), for which he received special recognition for technical achievement by the American Academy, he was responsible for lighting such films as *The 39 Steps* (1935), plus four further HITCHCOCK films, being responsible for the celebrated tracking shot across the hotel floor in *Young and Innocent* (1937), and *Gaslight* (1940). Very little in his directorial career seems as distinguished as the kinds of frisson his black-and-white images help to create in those films, and he was just as adept in lighter films such as those he did for ASQUITH, including *The Demi-Paradise* (1943) in which he lit the radiant Penelope DUDLEY WARD as she deserved. His brother was Cyril KNOWLES.

OTHER BRITISH FILMS INCLUDE: (cam ass/op) *Squibs' Honeymoon* (1923), *Reveille* (1924), (c) *Dawn* (1928), *King Solomon's Mines* (1937); *The Hound of the Baskervilles* (1931), *Marry Me* (1932), *The Good Companions, Falling for You* (1933), *Jew Süss, Jack Ahoy!* (1934), *Brown on Resolution* (1935), *Secret Agent, Rhodes of Africa, Sabotage, East Meets West* (1936), *Jamaica Inn, French Without Tears* (1939), *Channel Incident* (short), *Freedom Radio* (1940), *Quiet Wedding* (1941), *Secret Mission* (1942), *The Day Will Dawn* (1943), *English Without Tears, Love Story* (1944); (d) *Easy Money* (1948), *The Reluctant Widow* (1950), *The Triangle* (episode 3), *Thought to Kill* (episode 3), *Park Plaza 605* (+ co-sc) (1953), *Barbados Quest* (1955), *Frozen Alive* (1964).

Knowles, Cyril (*b* Manchester, 1905 – *d* Rome, 1961). Cinematographer. Brother of Bernard KNOWLES, he entered the industry in 1927 as camera assistant for Welsh–Pearson Ltd, and spent much time as camera operator, often on films shot by his brother, and developed a reputation for location shooting. The latter involved him with the African exteriors for *King Solomon's Mines* (1937), the Alpine exteriors for *Snowbound* (1948), and location and special effects photography on *Christopher Columbus* (1949). In the 50s, he did 2nd unit work for WARWICK on such films as *Fire Down Below* (1957) and *The Bandit of Zhobe* (1959). During WW2 he worked on War Office training films; post-war, he was contracted to GAINSBOROUGH.

OTHER BRITISH FILMS INCLUDE: (cam op) *Gaslight* (1940), *Cottage to Let* (1941), *The Day Will Dawn* (1942), *The Demi-Paradise* (1943), *Moulin Rouge* (1953); (2uc) *The Sword and the Rose* (1953), *No Time to Die* (1958), *Fury at Smugglers Bay* (1960); (exterior c) *Caravan* (1946),

The Calendar (1948); (c) *Illegal* (1932), *The Open Window* (1952, doc), *Zarak* (1956, co-c), *Land of Laughter* (1957, doc).

Knowles, Patric (*b* Horsforth, 1911 – *d* Los Angeles, 1995). Actor. Patrician leading man who made his mark in Hollywood opposite Errol FLYNN in *The Charge of the Light Brigade* (1936) and *The Adventures of Robin Hood* (1938), and was memorable in *How Green Was My Valley* (1941). Worked on stage at Abbey Theatre, Dublin, and often played up his supposed Irish background in Hollywood. Discovered by Irving ASHER and brought to Hollywood by Warner Bros after a dozen or so British films, from 1932 (*Men of Tomorrow*), usually as second lead. War service with Royal Canadian Flying Corps. Long-time resident of San Fernando Valley, honorary mayor of Tarzana.

OTHER BRITISH FILMS INCLUDE: *Irish Hearts* (1934), *Abdul the Damned, Royal Cavalcade, The Guv'nor* (1935), *Crown v Stevens, Irish for Luck* (1936). AS.

Knox, Alexander (*b* Strathroy, Ontario, 1907 – *d* Berwick-upon-Tweed, 1995). Actor. Distinguished and intelligent performer of stage (from 1930) and screen, best remembered in the title role of *Wilson* (1944). Knox began his film career in the UK in 1938, but his best roles are in American films, such as *Sister Kenny* (1946) and *The Judge Steps Out* (1949, *Indian Summer* in UK), both of which he co-wrote. However, he had some strong roles in such 50s British films as *The Divided Heart* (1954) and *The Night My Number Came Up* (1955), when American BLACKLIST forced his return to UK. In 1944, married **Doris Nolan** (*b* New York, 1916 – *d* Berwick-upon-Tweed, 1998), who appeared in three British films; *The Servant* (1963), *Juggernaut* (1974) and *The Romantic Englishwoman* (1975, UK/Fr). A collection of Knox's writings was published as *On Actors and Acting* (1998).

OTHER BRITISH FILMS INCLUDE: *The Gaunt Stranger* (1938), *Cheer Boys Cheer* (1939), *Reach for the Sky* (1956), *Chase a Crooked Shadow* (1957), *Oscar Wilde* (1960), *The Damned* (1961), *Woman of Straw* (1964), *Modesty Blaise, Khartoum* (1966), *Accident, You Only Live Twice* (1967), *Shalako* (1968). AS.

Knox, Teddy (*b* Gateshead-on-Tyne, 1895 – *d* Salcombe, 1974). Actor. *See* **Crazy Gang, The**

Konstam, Anna (*b* London, 1914). Actress. RADA-trained theatre actress who made a half-dozen films, starting with an uncredited bit in HITCHCOCK's *Young and Innocent* (1937) and finishing with *Waterloo Road* (1944), apart from a small role in the little-seen 1972 film, *All the Advantages*. Her best chance was as Molly, who befriends an ex-prisoner in *They Drive by Night* (1938).

OTHER BRITISH FILMS: *Too Dangerous to Live* (1939), *Saloon Bar, The Midas Touch* (1940).

Konstam, Phyllis (*b* London, 1907 – *d* Stoke St Gregory, 1976). Actress. RN: Kohnstamm. Stage actress, first with the Comédie Francaise in 1923. She made a few early talkies, including four for HITCHCOCK: bits in *Champagne* (1928) and, as a gossiping neighbour, *Blackmail* (1929), and substantial roles in *Murder!* (1930), as Doucie (she 'can play anything from a Gladys Cooper to a Marie Lloyd part'), and *The Skin Game* (1931), as Chloë with a past. Her film career faltered thereafter, though she made several US films, including *The Voice of the Hurricane* (1964). Married tennis player 'Bunny' Austin.

OTHER BRITISH FILMS INCLUDE: *Escape, Compromising Daphne* (1930), *Tilly of Bloomsbury* (1931, as Tilly), *A Gentleman of Paris* (1931), *The Kindled Flame* (1939).

BIBLIOG: Autobiography, *A Mixed Double*, 1969.

Korda, Sir Alexander (*b* Puszta Turpaszto, Turkeve, Hungary, 1893 – *d* London, 1956). Director, producer. RN: Kellner. After an international career as both a producer and director in his native Hungary, Austria, Germany and Hollywood, Alexander Korda (his brothers were Vincent KORDA and Zoltán KORDA) began to work for Paramount in France, in 1930. After directing *Rive Gauche* and, notably, Marcel Pagnol's *Marius* (1931), he made two films for Paramount in Britain, *Service for Ladies* and *Women who Play*, before setting up LONDON FILM PRODUCTIONS in February 1932. In the course of the next year he produced five 'QUOTA QUICKIES' for Paramount and two first features for GAUMONT–BRITISH, *Wedding Rehearsal* and *The Girl From Maxim's*. But it was the worldwide success of *The Private Life of Henry the VIII* (1933), with Charles LAUGHTON in the title role, that established him as Britain's leading producer. Made in the face of considerable financial difficulty, Korda could find no British film company that would support the venture, and the film was finally made with the support of the Italian banker Giuseppe De Toeplitz and the American distribution company UNITED ARTISTS. Delighted with the success of *Henry VIII*, United Artists gave Korda a long-term distribution contract in 1934, and in September 1935 Korda joined Charlie CHAPLIN, Mary Pickford and Samuel Goldwyn as an owner-member of the company.

A string of bold and very expensive Hollywood-style productions followed. The notable successes included *The Scarlet Pimpernel* (1934) *Catherine the Great* (1934) and *The Ghost Goes West* (1936). But there were also costly failures. Korda's production of H.G. WELLS's *Things to Come* (1936) was hailed as a landmark in film history which, according to the *Daily Telegraph*, 'made stories of the future such as *Metropolis* look like "Quota Quickies"', but it would recover scarcely more than half its then colossal production cost of £240,000. *Rembrandt* (1936) was an admirable and handsomely produced biography but scarcely a commercial success.

In 1936, with the financial backing of the Prudential Assurance Company, Korda opened Europe's biggest film studio at DENHAM in Buckinghamshire. The only film he was to direct there himself was *Rembrandt*, as he gave over more and more of his time to administration of the large studio. The highlights included *Elephant Boy* (1937), *Knight without Armour* (1937) and a Technicolor production of *The Four Feathers* (1939), but as a whole Korda's programme of films still failed to to match its enormous production cost. By 1938 the debt of London Film Productions exceeded £2 million, and the Prudential Assurance Company took over control of London Film Productions and Denham Studios.

Setting up a new company, Alexander Korda Film Productions, Korda remained at Denham as a tenant producer, and, in a timely change of fortune, made one of his most spectacular and commercially successful films, *The Thief of Baghdad* (1940). With the onset of the war, he made the PROPAGANDA semi-documentary *The Lion has Wings* (1939) in only two weeks, and then transferred his activities to Hollywood. Here he directed *That Hamilton Woman* (1941) with the covert support of the British MINISTRY OF INFORMATION, and, during 1940–41, when America was still neutral, played a key although necessarily unacknowledged role in persuading Hollywood to support the British war effort. Through his association with United Artists, he was also instrumental in securing the distribution in America of such important British wartime films as *In Which We Serve* (1942) and *One of Our Aircraft is Missing* (1942).

He was knighted in 1942 and returned to England the following year as production head of MGM–BRITISH. But wartime restrictions and the scarcity of studio space meant that only one film would result from the association, *Perfect Strangers*, with Robert DONAT and Deborah KERR. In 1944, Korda bought back London Film Productions from the Prudential for £100,000, and after resigning from MGM in October 1945, proceeded to build up a second film empire that would encompass SHEPPERTON STUDIOS and the BRITISH LION distribution company. *An Ideal Husband* (1947), the last film that Korda would direct himself, and Julien Duvivier's *Anna Karenina* (1948) were typical of the lavish but also somewhat leaden costume epics that followed. Film after film failed at the box-office and British Lion was only able to continue with the aid in 1949 of a £3m loan from the British Government. This sum was finally deemed irrecoverable, despite the major commercial success of *The Third Man* (1949), and a receiver appointed for BRITISH LION in June 1954.

With finance from an American property tycoon Robert Dowling, Korda produced one last successful programme of films, which included David LEAN's *Summer Madness* (UK/US) and OLIVIER's *Richard III* (1955), so that it might be said that this most colourful mogul of British film finished on a high note. His first and second of three wives were actresses Maria Corda and Merle OBERON. He died in 1956.

OTHER BRITISH FILMS INCLUDE: (d) *The Private Life of Don Juan* (1934); (p) *Sanders of the River* (1935), *The Man Who Could Work Miracles* (1937), *The Drum, The Divorce of Lady X* (1938); (ex p) *Bonnie Prince Charlie* (1948), *The Winslow Boy* (1948), *The Third Man* (1949), *The Elusive Pimpernel* (1950), *Cry, the Beloved Country* (1951), *The Sound Barrier* (1952), *The Story of Gilbert and Sullivan* (1953), *Storm over the Nile* (1955).

BIBLIOG: Michael Korda, *Charmed Lives*, 1980; Karol Kulik, *Alexander Korda: The Man Who Could Work Miracles*, 1975. Charles Drazin.

Korda, Vincent (*b* Puszta Turpaszto, Turkeve, Hungary, 1896 – *d* London, 1979). Production designer. RN: Kellner. Trained as a painter at Budapest Academy of Art, and at the Academies of several other cities. Most often associated with his brothers Alexander and Zoltán KORDA, he became famous in his own right as designer of such LONDON FILMS productions as *The Private Life of Henry VIII* (1933), *The Thief of Baghdad* (1940, AA/art d), for the futuristic vision of *Things to Come* and the solidly evoked world of *Rembrandt* (1936). As distinct from these period or fanciful achievements, he scored major successes with two films celebrating European cities: his production design for *The Third Man* (1949) colludes unforgettably with Robert KRASKER's camera to recreate the ruined, melancholy beauty of post-war Vienna; and in *Summer Madness* (1955, UK/US) he has considerable help from Venice in providing a setting for the heroine's romantic awakening. He was with Alexander KORDA at MGM–BRITISH for *Perfect Strangers* (1945) and followed him to the re-formed LONDON FILMS in 1946. His credits all represent a high level of artistic flair and respected accomplishment; the least driven of the three brothers, he in fact had the longest career. His first wife was actress Gertrude MUSGROVE, the mother of Michael Korda, who wrote the excellent *Charmed Lives* (1979), about the Korda family, and a shoddy best-seller, *Queenie* (1985), based transparently but scurrilously on the life of Auntie Merle OBERON.

OTHER BRITISH FILMS INCLUDE: (sets) *The Scarlet Pimpernel, The Ghost Goes West* (1935), *The Squeaker* (1937), *Over the Moon* (1939), *The Fallen Idol* (1948); (p des) *Men of Tomorrow* (1932), *Sanders of the River*

(1935), *Elephant Boy* (1937), *The Drum* (1938), *The Four Feathers* (1939), *Major Barbara* (1941), *Bonnie Prince Charlie* (1948), *Outcast of the Islands* (1951), *The Holly and the Ivy* (co-des), *The Sound Barrier* (1952), *The Deep Blue Sea* (1955); (art d) *Catherine the Great* (1934), *Men Are Not Gods*, *The Man Who Could Work Miracles* (1936), *Prison Without Bars*, *The Challenge* (1938, sup), *Q Planes*, *The Lion Has Wings* (1939), *An Ideal Husband* (1947), *Home at Seven* (1952, co-des), *The Yellow Rolls-Royce* (1964, European sequences).

BIBLIOG: Catherine A. Surowiec, *Accent on Design: Four European Art Directors*, 1992.

Korda, Zoltán (*b* Puszta Turpaszto, Turkeve, Hungary, 1895 – *d* Los Angeles, 1961). Director. RN: Kellner. A former officer in the Hungarian army, Korda was responsible for some major epics of military achievement when he came to work with brothers Alexander and Vincent at LONDON FILMS in the 30s. Though Alex was a committed imperialist, and his view no doubt dominated the way the films finally appeared, the socialistically inclined Zoltán managed to ensure that some sense of oppressed peoples emerges in such adventures as *Sanders of the River* (1935), *The Drum* (1938) and *The Four Feathers* (1939), the latter two of which are still very rousing, filmed with a clear sense of their epic potential. A former editor and cameraman, who had worked in Hungary and Hollywood, he was perhaps a more gifted director than his more famous brother, whom he accompanied to Hollywood in the early 40s and made at least three more than usually interesting films: *Sahara* (1944), a tough WW2 story starring Humphrey Bogart; *The Macomber Affair* (1947), a compromised but still incisive version of Hemingway's short story; and *A Woman's Vengeance* (1948), a powerful adaptation of Aldous Huxley's 'The Giaconda Smile', with a riveting performance from Jessica TANDY. He made only two further British films – the bravely well-meaning, somewhat ponderous anti-apartheid piece, *Cry, the Beloved Country* (1952), and, co-directing with Terence YOUNG, *Storm over the Nile* (1955), an inferior remake of *The Four Feathers*. Married to actress Joan GARDNER from 1930 until his death.

OTHER BRITISH FILMS INCLUDE: *Men of Tomorrow* (1932).

Kortner, Fritz (*b* Vienna, 1892 – *d* Berlin, 1970). Actor, director, producer. RN: Kohn. Illustrious figure of German stage and film (from 1918, with titles including *Pandora's Box*, 1928), Kortner was forced to flee the Nazi regime. He stopped in Britain long enough to appear in six films, playing assorted foreigners – Austrian in *Evensong* and Arab in *Chu-Chin-Chow* (1934), Turkish in *The Crouching Beast* and *Abdul the Damned* (1935) and 'Grovnian' in *Midnight Menace* (1937). Finally finding refuge in Hollywood in 1938, he was similarly typecast, but in the high-gloss finish of *The Razor's Edge* (1946) his philosophical Kosti briefly suggests another order of reality. By 1949 he was back in Germany where, as actor and director, he had won such high renown as an adventurous interpreter of the classics.

OTHER BRITISH FILMS INCLUDE: *Little Friend* (1934).

Kossoff, David (*b* London, 1919). Actor. Former interior designer and aircraft draftsman who studied privately for the stage, making his London debut in 1942 at the Unity where he devised many shows for services personnel. He was with the BBC Repertory Company (1945–51), thereafter on stage where he famously created the role of Morry in *The Bespoke Overcoat* (1953), reprising it in Jack CLAYTON's award-winning film version (1955). Entering films in *The Good Beginning* (1953), he has played nearly three dozen character roles, often as

foreigners, as in *The Young Lovers* (1954), usually sympathetic, as in *A Kid for Two Farthings* (1954). Also became well known on TV for *The Larkins* (1958–60, 1963–64), as the henpecked but resourceful husband, and he played this role in the film SPIN-OFF, *Inn for Trouble* (1959). He is a noted British purveyor of Jewish lore and humour. His son was Paul Kossoff, the late guitarist with the band, 'Free'.

OTHER BRITISH FILMS INCLUDE: *Svengali* (1954), *The Woman for Joe*, *I Am a Camera*, *1984* (1955), *The Iron Petticoat* (1956), *Indiscreet, Innocent Sinners* (1958), *Jet Storm, The Mouse That Roared* (1959), *Conspiracy of Hearts* (1960), *Summer Holiday* (1962), *The London Connection* (1979), *Staggered* (1994).

Kotcheff, Ted (*b* Toronto, 1931). Director. Educated at University of Toronto, drama director at Canadian Broadcasting Corporation in 1955, Kotcheff began his film directing career in Britain where he made three more than averagely interesting films: *Tiara Tahiti* (1962), a COMEDY of character and CLASS; *Life at the Top* (1965), a rare sequel which didn't dishonour its notable precursor; and *Two Gentlemen Sharing* (1969), an agreeable exercise in race relations. *Billy Two Hats* (1973) is technically but in no other significant sense British. The rest is Hollywood and Canada.

Kötting, Andrew Director. Artist as well as film-maker, Kötting had made several well-regarded SHORT FILMS, including *Self Heal* (1987) and *Hoi Polloi* (1990), before coming to wider attention with *Gallivant* (1996), the DOCUMENTARY in which he charted a journey round coastal Britain with his elderly grandmother and severely disabled daughter. His next feature was *This Filthy Earth* (2001), an evocation of rural hardship, with surreal comic touches.

Kove, Kenneth (*b* London, 1893 – *d* 1965). Actor. Had stage experience as 'silly-ass' comic in ALDWYCH FARCES, and was in two dozen 30s light COMEDIES and MYSTERIES, typically cast as a village vicar in *The Man from Toronto* (1933), and in roles with larky names like Codlin, a fisherman in *The Scarlet Pimpernel* (1934) and Cyril Chattaway in *Marry the Girl* (1935). He then made only scattered appearances after 1940, culminating in *Dr Terror's House of Horrors* (1964).

OTHER BRITISH FILMS INCLUDE: *Murder!* (1930), *Out of the Blue* (1931), *Her First Affaire* (1932), *Song of the Plough* (1933), *Radio Pirates, Look Up and Laugh* (1935), *Talking Feet* (1937), *Asking for Trouble* (1942), *They Knew Mr Knight* (1945), *Stage Fright* (1950), *Golden Arrow* (1952), *Raising the Wind* (1961), *The Evil of Frankenstein* (1964).

Krabbé, Jeroen (*b* Amsterdam, 1944). Actor, director. In his wide-ranging international career, this tall, imposing Dutch stage and screen star came to attention in films for Dutch director, Paul Verhoeven, including *The Fourth Man* (1979), and has made vivid impressions in several British films. He was memorable as the defector Koskov in the BOND caper, *The Living Daylights* (1987), a sympathetic Gus Roth, anti-apartheid activist in *A World Apart* (1987, UK/Zimb), and an equivocal Ivanov in *Scandal* (1988). Also Hollywood films, including *The Fugitive* (1993).

OTHER BRITISH FILMS INCLUDE: *Turtle Diary* (1985), *Immortal Beloved* (1994, UK/US), *An Ideal Husband* (1999, UK/US).

Krampf, Günther (*b* Vienna, 1899 – *d* London, 1950) Cinematographer. Krampf was a highly regarded cameraman in Germany in the 20s, shooting such notable films as Robert Wiene's *The Hands of Orlac* (1924) and, above all, G.W. Pabst's *Pandora's Box* (1928), much of whose effectiveness was due to his inspired lighting. Came to Britain in 1931 to work on co-productions at ELSTREE, and was under contract at GAUMONT–BRITISH from 1932, praised for his visual inventiveness and technical expertise, particularly his use of mobile cameras and back-projection, which he showcased in *Rome Express* (1932). Like fellow émigrés Curt COURANT and Max GREENE, Krampf used chiaroscuro lighting and soft-focus lenses to often highly atmospheric effect, pre-empting the visual style of 1940s *film noir*. His post-war films are generally less distinguished, with the major exception of *Fame Is the Spur* (1947), in whose latter sequences Krampf's subjective camera work captures brilliantly the protagonist's decline.

OTHER BRITISH FILMS INCLUDE: *The Outsider* (1931), *The Bells* (1931), *The First Mrs Fraser* (1932), *The Lucky Number*, *The Ghoul* (1933), *Little Friend* (1934), *The Tunnel* (1935), *Everything Is Thunder* (1936), *Marigold* (1938), *On the Night of The Fire* (1939), *Convoy* (1940), *The Black Sheep of Whitehall* (1941), *The Night Has Eyes* (1942), *Bon Voyage* (1944, short), *Aventure Malgache* (1944, short), *Latin Quarter* (1945), *Meet Me at Dawn* (1947), *This Was a Woman* (1947), *Portrait of Clare* (1950), *The Franchise Affair* (1950). Tim Bergfelder.

Krasker, Robert (*b* Perth, Australia, 1913 – *d* London, 1981). Cinematographer. Australian who arrived in Britain in 1932, via photographic studies in Paris and Dresden, and found work at KORDA's LONDON FILMS, where he became senior camera operator, usually for Georges PÉRINAL. After two shared cinematographer credits, he had his first solo stint on *The Gentle Sex* (1943), and spent the rest of the 40s lighting such honoured films as the TECHNICOLOR triumph of *Henry V* (1944), and *Brief Encounter* (1945), *Odd Man Out* (1947) and *The Third Man* (1949), for which his magisterial black-and-white images, often unnervingly tilted, brought him an Oscar. In this notable trio of films, his camera work is as crucial an element as any in establishing their *film noir* affiliations, observational realism constantly in tension with the rendering of anguished inner states. Virtually everything he did was notable, whether evoking Renaissance Verona in *Romeo and Juliet* (1954, UK/It), the harsh black-and-white realities of *The Criminal* (1960), or the epic sweep of *El Cid* (1961, US/It), in 70mm Technirama, one of the several international films he photographed. He shot his last feature, the Canadian-set, *The Trap* in 1966, after which he retired because of ill-health.

OTHER BRITISH FILMS INCLUDE: (cam op) *Things to Come*, *Rembrandt*, *Men Are Not Gods* (1936), *The Squeaker* (1937), *The Thief of Baghdad* (1940), *One of Our Aircraft is Missing* (1942); (c) *Saint Meets the Tiger* (1941, co-c), *The Lamp Still Burns* (1943), *Uncle Silas* (1947), *Bonnie Prince Charlie* (1948), *The Angel With the Trumpet* (1949), *State Secret* (1950), *Another Man's Poison* (1951), *Cry, the Beloved Country* (1952), *Never Let Me Go*, *Malta Story* (1953), *That Lady* (1955), *The Rising of the Moon* (Ire/US), *The Story of Esther Costello* (1957), *Behind the Mask*, *The Doctor's Dilemma* (1958), *Libel* (1959), *Guns of Darkness*, *Billy Budd* (1962), *The Running Man* (1963), *The Collector* (UK/US), *The Heroes of Telemark* (1965).

BIBLIOG: Duncan Petrie, *The British Cinematographer*, 1996.

Krish, John (*b* London, 1923). Director. Cut his teeth on DOCUMENTARY, joining the CROWN FILM UNIT cutting room in 1940, and working as editor for the ARMY FILM UNIT, 1942–45. Post-war, he directed shorts for Public Relationship Films (e.g. *Health in Our Time*, 1948) and BRITISH TRANSPORT FILMS (*Away for the Day*, 1952), then did a run of the half-hour 'Stryker of the Yard' SERIES for Republic, and directed *Companions in Crime* (1954), made by linking two Stryker stories. In the early 60s, he made several short instructional films for producer Leon CLORE (*Our School*, 1962, + sc), as well as working on TV series such as *The Avengers* (1961), before,

rather surprisingly, landing the Evelyn WAUGH-derived *Decline and Fall* . . . (1968). It has been an idiosyncratic career, with children's films and documentaries and TV commercials interspersed with the odd feature, including the SCIENCE-FICTION piece, *Unearthly Stranger* (1963) and the US-made *Jesus* (1979).

OTHER BRITISH FILMS INCLUDE: (shorts) *What's in a Number?* (+ sc), *Jet-Propelled Germs* (1948), *The Case of the Bogus Count*, . . . *the Black Falcon* (1953), . . . *Canary Jones*, . . . *the Second Shot* (1954), *Mr Marsh Goes to School*, *They Took Us to Sea* (1961, + sc), *Searching* (1974); (features) *The Salvage Gang* (1958, + sc), (1981), *Out of the Darkness* (1985).

Krishnamma, Suri (*b* London). Director. After two shorts (*Mohammed's Daughter*, 1986; *Water's Edge*, 1988), made the attractive feature, *A Man of No Importance* (1994, UK/Ire), starring Albert FINNEY as a gay Dublin bus conductor with theatrical aspirations. Since then, he has made the BBC telemovie, *O Mary This London* (1994), a couple of superior episodes of *Dalziel and Pascoe* (1999), and the feature, *New Year's Day* (2001, UK/Fr), an unsettling account of two schoolboys on the rampage.

Kruger, Hardy (*b* Berlin, 1928) Actor. A blond, boyishly handsome, but brooding type, Kruger portrayed strong-willed and moody characters in German and international cinema. His role as a German POW in his first British film, *The One That Got Away* (1956), won him popularity and critical acclaim and he had appropriate charm for the COMEDY, *Bachelor Of Hearts* (1958). In US productions Kruger provided the German element in *Hatari!* (1961) and the all-male environment of *The Flight Of The Phoenix* (1965).

OTHER BRITISH FILMS INCLUDE: *Blind Date* (1959), *Barry Lyndon* (1975), *Paper Tiger* (1974), *A Bridge Too Far* (1977). Tim Bergfelder.

Kruger, Otto (*b* Toledo, Ohio, 1885 – *d* Los Angeles, 1974). Actor. The super-urbane, silver-haired Kruger brought his high polish to bear on a half-dozen British films of the 30s, most notably as *The Housemaster* (1938), in which suavity is tempered by sympathetic understanding. All told he appeared in over 80 films, moving easily from leading man to highly enjoyable character actor in such varied films as *High Noon* (1952) and *Sex and the Single Girl* (1964), his penultimate role.

OTHER BRITISH FILMS: *Living Dangerously* (1936), *Glamorous Night* (1937), *Star of the Circus* (1938), *The Gang's All Here*, *Black Eyes* (1939).

Kubrick, Stanley (*b* New York City, 1928 – *d* Harpenden, 1999). Director, writer, producer. Kubrick will rightly be remembered as one of the major film-makers of the 20th century. Although he made only 13 features from the low-budget *Fear and Desire* (1953) to his final masterpiece *Eyes Wide Shut* (1999), his life and work have been the subject of at least 20 book-length analyses and countless critical articles. Moved to England permanently in the early 60s, not long after shooting *Lolita* (1961) at the ABPC studios. However, while he showed no interest in returning to the US, especially after the fiasco of *One-Eyed Jacks*, from which he was removed in 1958 during pre-production, and the tensions during the making of *Spartacus* (1960), his subsequent work still bore the marks of a sensibility shaped elsewhere. Their influences may be traced far afield – in the cinemas of Ophuls, von Sternberg, Fellini and WELLES – but all of Kubrick's remaining films, from *Dr Strangelove* . . . (1963) to *Eyes Wide Shut*, were shot in the UK, with occasional second unit work featuring US locations, but most of them are distinctively American in style, setting and allusion, and the grand scale on which they are imagined.

2001: A Space Odyssey (1968) ambitiously transported SCIENCE-FICTION on to an entirely different level both in terms of its technical accomplishment and its metaphoric thrust; *The Shining* (1980, UK/US) uses a Stephen King novel as the starting-point for its tale of a psychotic writer trapped in a maze of his own making; *Full Metal Jacket* (1987) ponders the moral consequences of the US presence in Vietnam; and *Eyes Wide Shut* (1999) unfolds in a glittering Manhattan that is as dazzling to the eye as it is precarious for the soul. Only the controversial *A Clockwork Orange* (1971) and the rigorously ironic *Barry Lyndon* (1975), both based on novels by distinguished English writers, feel like British films.

There seem to be as many views of Kubrick as there are collaborators or critics who have spoken or written about him and his work. A recluse? A perfectionist? Precious? An artist more interested in effect than feeling? Nihilistic? Humanist? Trite? Penetrating? But the work of few film-makers has been anticipated with the same enthusiasm, discussed for-and-against with the same passion, or able to boast the same remarkable consistency of achievement.

BIBLIOG: Alexander Walker, *Stanley Kubrick: A Visual Analysis*, 2000; Michel Ciment, *Kubrick: The Definitive Edition*, 2001; Gene D. Phillips, ed., *Stanley Kubrick: Interviews*, 2001. Tom Ryan.

Kun, Magda (*b* Szaszergen, Hungary, 1912 – *d* London, 1945). Actress. Star of Hungarian films and stage in the 30s, since 1935 based in Britain, a lively, tempestuous actress, often cast as a temperamental continental in COMEDIES and MUSICALS. She also had a minor supporting part with Michael REDGRAVE in *Dead Of Night* (1945). Married to actor Steven GERAY.

OTHER BRITISH FILMS INCLUDE: *Dance Band* (1935), *Room For Two* (1940), *Old Mother Riley Overseas* (1943), *Heaven Is Round the Corner*, *Meet Sexton Blake* (1944). Tim Bergfelder.

Kureishi, Hanif (*b* Bromley, Kent, 1954). Screenwriter, director. Influential purveyor of Anglo-Asian relationships in evocatively created London settings, Kureishi, of Pakistani descent, came first to notice as the author of the screenplay for *My Beautiful Laundrette* (1985), with its unusually subtle rendering of sex, race and class issues. It received an AAn/sc and won the New York Critics' Award for best screenplay. Some of these preoccupations recurred in the generational and other conflicts of *Sammy and Rosie Get Laid* (1987) and the richly detailed dramas of interracial life in the TV mini-series, *The Buddha of Suburbia* (1993), which he adapted from his own novel, as he did the screenplays for *My Son the Fanatic* (1997, UK/Fr) and *Intimacy* (2001, UK/Fr). The latter was so sexually explicit that, it is said, he had to seek production in France. He both directed and wrote the critically panned *London Kills Me* (1991), another study of youthful London lives.

Kwan, Nancy (*b* Hong Kong, 1939). Actress. Of Chinese father and English mother, Kwan grew up in England where she trained with the Royal Ballet. Her film career got off to a flying start with the title role in *The World of Susie Wong* (1960), in which she played a beautiful prostitute, and her first Hollywood film, the musical, *Flower Drum Song* (1961). She was the seductively disruptive *Tamahine* (1962), but by the end of a decade which hadn't much use for her exoticism she faded from British view. She has subsequently made about twenty international films, mainly for the S.E. Asian market, and TV

appearances, as in *Noble House* (1988).

OTHER BRITISH FILMS INCLUDE: *The Main Attraction* (1962), *The Wild Affair* (1963), *Drop Dead Darling* (1966).

Kwietniowski, Richard (*b* London, 1957). Director, screenwriter, cinematographer. After a decade of making little-seen curiosities, mostly shorts and mostly on gay themes, including *Flames of Passion* (1990, + sc), a wordless reworking of *Brief Encounter*, he directed and co-wrote the wish-fulfilment fantasy, *Love and Death on Long Island* (1997, UK/Can), starring John HURT as an unworldly author besotted with a porn-film hunk. At this late stage he won a BAA as 'Most Promising Newcomer in British Film'. It was hard to see why (given his age and previous credits), though it may be charitable to say he did what he could with a sentimental story. His SHORT FILMS have won several awards.

OTHER BRITISH FILMS INCLUDE: (d, unless noted; shorts) *Next Week's Rent* (1986, + p), *Alfalfa* (1987, + p), *The Ballad of Reading Gaol* (1990, + sc), *The Cost of Love* (1991).

Kwouk, Burt (*b* Manchester, 1930). Actor. Raised in Shanghai, Kwouk made about 35 films, most of them British, starting with *The Inn of the Sixth Happiness* (1958). He is best remembered as Peter SELLERS's over-zealous right-hand man, Cato Fong, in the 'Clouseau' films, starting with *A Shot in the Dark* (1964), and he played Sellers's servant again in the Paris-made *The Fiendish Plot of Fu Manchu* (1990).

OTHER BRITISH FILMS INCLUDE: *Yesterday's Enemy* (1959), *The Devil Never Sleeps* (1962), *Goldfinger* (1964), *The Brides of Fu Manchu* (1966), *Casino Royale, You Only Live Twice* (1967), *Nobody Runs Forever* (1968), *Return of the Pink Panther* (1974), *The Pink Panther Strikes Again* (1976), *Revenge of the Pink Panther* (1978), *Carry On Columbus, Leon the Pig Farmer* (1992).

Kydd, Sam (*b* Belfast, 1917 – *d* London, 1982). Actor. Utterly indispensable character player who appeared in about 150 films, often in small uncredited roles. His lean, angular features were frequently seen above uniforms, whether of mess waiter in *Angels One Five* (1952), or naval rating in *Single-Handed* (1953), or Police Sergeant in *The Quatermass Experiment* (1955). He played shifty crooks and stroppy shop stewards, moving effortlessly from posh affairs like *Father Brown* (1954) to budget items like *Soho Incident* (1956). It was in fact hard to miss him in 50s British cinema – and no one with an eye for authenticity of character would have wanted to. He entered films after WW2 service playing a POW in *The Captive Heart* (1946) and he stayed there (when he wasn't on TV, as in *Crane*, 1963–65) till he died.

OTHER BRITISH FILMS INCLUDE: *They Made Me A Fugitive* (1947), *To the Public Danger, Scott of the Antarctic, Trottie True* (1948), *Obsession, Passport to Pimlico, The Cure for Love* (1949), *Cage of Gold, Seven Days to Noon, Chance of a Lifetime, The Clouded Yellow* (1950), *Assassin for Hire, Secret People* (1951), *Hunted, The Voice of Merrill, The Brave Don't Cry, The Cruel Sea* (1952), *Time Bomb, The Saint's Return* (1953), *The Embezzler, A Kid for Two Farthings* (1954), *As Long as They're Happy, The Ladykillers* (1955), *The Baby and the Battleship, Tiger in the Smoke* (1956), *Happy is the Bride, Dangerous Exile* (1957), *I Was Monty's Double, The Captain's Table, Further Up the Creek* (1958), *I'm All Right Jack, Libel* (1959), *The Treasure of Monte Cristo* (1960), *The Iron Maiden* (1963), *Smokescreen* (1964), *Smashing Time* (1967), *Moon Zero Two* (1969), *10 Rillington Place* (1970), *Up the Chastity Belt* (1971), *Steptoe & Son Ride Again* (1973), *Confessions of a Window Cleaner* (1974), *Great Expectations* (1975), *Yesterday's Hero* (1979), *Eye of the Needle* (1981).

L

Labarr, Marta Actress. Dark-haired beauty who had some experience in continental films before her British debut in *Ball at Savoy* (1936), making a further half-dozen before her last, *Teheran* (1947), in which she played a Russian ballerina who foils a plot to assassinate President Roosevelt in Persia. Truly. And in *The Singing Cop* (1937), she was an opera diva intrepidly moonlighting as a spy.

OTHER BRITISH FILMS INCLUDE: *Second Bureau* (1936), *Break the News* (1938), *Traitor Spy* (1939), *Gentleman of Venture* (1940).

La Bern, Arthur (*b* London, 1909 – *d* London, 1990). Novelist, screenwriter. Former journalist and war correspondent, La Bern was a popular novelist of the 40s, particularly, when two of his novels were filmed – *It Always Rains on Sunday* and *Night Darkens the Street*, filmed as *Good-Time Girl* (1947). These were novels coming to grips with the rise of crime in post-war London, and the films achieved a comparably tough realism. Other films based on his novels were *Paper Orchid* (1949) and *Frenzy* (1972, from his *Goodbye Piccadilly, Farewell Leicester Square*). He also wrote a half-dozen screenplays for minor crime thrillers, mostly based on stories by Edgar WALLACE.

OTHER BRITISH FILMS INCLUDE: *Freedom to Die*, *Dead Man's Evidence* (+ story) (1962), *Accidental Death* (1963), *The Verdict* (1964).

Lacey, Catherine (*b* London, 1904 – *d* London, 1979). Actress. Distinguished stage star who first appeared in 1925 with Mrs Patrick CAMPBELL, rapidly winning a major reputation and playing four starring roles at Stratford in 1935. A brilliant Queen Elizabeth in Schiller's *Mary Stuart* (1958), she was equally forceful in modern plays. First screen role was as the 'nun' in high heels in *The Lady Vanishes* (1938), and there were 20 further impeccable film character studies, including the drunken Miss Porter in *Pink String and Sealing Wax* (1945), the sympathetic landlady, played without a touch of class condescension, in *The October Man* (1947), the finally hysterical Mrs Waggett in *Whisky Galore!* (1949) and the inane, ossified Lady Mountsett in *The Servant* (1963). Also successful on TV, including a 1947 version of *Gaslight*. Married (2 of 3) actor Roy EMERTON.

OTHER BRITISH FILMS INCLUDE: *Poison Pen* (1939), *I Know Where I'm Going!* (1945), *Carnival* (1946), *The White Unicorn* (1947), *Another Sky* (1955), *Innocent Sinners*, *Rockets Galore* (1958), *The Sorcerers* (1967), *The Private Life of Sherlock Holmes* (1970).

Lacey, Ronald (*b* Harrow, 1935 – *d* London, 1991). Actor. Reliable and versatile character player in films since 1962, Lacey played a memorable village idiot in *The Fearless Vampire Killers* (1967), Toht in *The Raiders of the Lost Ark* (1981, US) and stolid Lestrade in *The Hound of the Baskervilles* (1983). Appeared in many international productions and much TV including episodes of *Porridge* (1974) and *Tropic* (1979). Both his daughters, Rebecca and Ingrid, are actresses.

OTHER BRITISH FILMS INCLUDE: *The Boys* (1962), *Of Human Bondage* (1964), *How I Won the War* (1967), *Crucible of Terror* (1971), *The Likely Lads* (1976), *Sword of the Valiant* (1983), *Valmont* (1989, UK/Fr).

Lachman, Harry (*b* La Salle, Illinois, 1886 – *d* Beverly Hills, California, 1975). Director. Equally important as a painter, Lachman studied art in Paris in 1911, entering films in 1925 as assistant to Rex Ingram in Nice. There he also met the young Michael POWELL, whose early career he abetted, and they collaborated on a SERIES called *Travelaughs* in the late 20s. In the UK, he directed for BIP and PARAMOUNT–BRITISH, turning out quality films, with a distinctive visual style, that led to work in Hollywood from 1933 to 1942. Best-known US production is *Dante's Inferno* (1935); his best-known British film is the thriller *They Came by Night* (1940).

OTHER BRITISH FILMS INCLUDE: *Weekend Wives* (1928), *The Yellow Mask*, *Song of Soho* (1930), *The Love Habit*, *The Outsider* (+ co-sc) (1931), *Aren't We All?* (1932). AS.

Lack, Simon (*b* Cleland, Scotland, 1913 – *d* London, 1980). Actor. RN: Macalpine. First on stage in Edinburgh (1935) and just getting his stage and film career moving when WW2 service (1940–46) intervened. He played William's older brother in *Just William* (1939), and post-war played a dozen supporting roles, including an Air Chief Marshal in *The Longest Day* (1962, US) and Menteith in *Macbeth* (1961), the role he played in a 1954 TV production.

OTHER BRITISH FILMS INCLUDE: *Goodbye, Mr Chips* (1939), *The Proud Valley* (1940), *Bonnie Prince Charlie* (1948), *Port of Escape* (1956), *The Cone of Silence* (1960), *Dr Syn Alias the Scarecrow* (1963), *All at Sea* (1969), *Trog* (1970).

Laffan, Patricia (*b* London, 1919). Actress. Tallish, imperious-looking lead and second lead acquired a sort of camp cult status as Nyah, *Devil Girl from Mars* (1954), who has fetched up at John LAURIE's Scottish inn in her quest for male replenishments for Mars. She was a striking Poppaea in *Quo Vadis* (1951); otherwise, the 50s was just the wrong decade for her to make a serious mark on British films. Trained at the Webber-Douglas, she made her debut with the Oxford Playhouse (1937). Sometimes listed as being in such 30s films as *One Good Turn* (1936) and *Pygmalion* (1938); if so, in very small, uncredited roles. On TV from 1948 and Polly in radio's *Mrs Dale's Diary* in the early 50s. Not to be confused (as if she *could* be confused – with *anyone*) with contemporary character actor **Pat Laffan**, who has appeared in several films including *The Snapper* (1993).

OTHER BRITISH FILMS INCLUDE: (unconfirmed) *Glamour Girl*, *The Citadel* (1938), *Major Barbara* (1941), *Waltz Time* (1945); (confirmed) *The Rake's Progress* (1945), *Caravan*, *I See a Dark Stranger*

(1946), *Escape Route* (1952), *Rough Shoot* (1953), *Crooks in Cloisters* (1964).

La Frenais, Ian (*b* 1936). Screenwriter. *See* **Clement, Dick**

Laine, Dame Cleo (*b* Southall, 1927). Actress. RN: Clementina Campbell. The wonderfully throaty voice of Laine singing 'All gone' is a major element in the pervasive melancholy of *The Servant* (1963). She and her siblings, of Jamaican father and English mother, appeared as street urchins in *The Thief of Baghdad* (1940) and her few film appearances are all as performers, such as the singer in *The Roman Spring of Mrs Stone* (1961). Essentially a concert hall star, she also scored successes in musical plays including *Valmouth* (1958–59), as village masseuse, Mrs Yaj, and *The Mystery of Edwin Drood*, for which she won several awards, and on TV, as, for instance, one of *The Last of the Blonde Bombshells* (2000). Married since 1958 to John **Dankworth** with whose jazz band she first sang at 25. Made DBE in 1997.

OTHER BRITISH FILMS INCLUDE: *6.5 Special* (1958), *The Third Alibi* (1961), *Where Has Poor Mickey Gone?* (1964).

BIBLIOG: Graham Collier, *Cleo and John: A Biography of the Dankworths*. London, 1976.

Laird, Jenny (*b* Manchester, 1912 – *d* London, 2001). Actress. Now best remembered as gentle-hearted Sister Honey in *Black Narcissus* (1947), London University-educated Laird appeared in 20 films, including EALING's semi-DOCUMENTARY, *Painted Boats* (1945), in which she had the lead. For the rest, she had small roles such as the would-be helpful neighbour in *The Long Dark Hall* (1951), played another nun in *Conspiracy of Hearts* (1960), was often on TV from 1947 (e.g. *Shoulder to Shoulder*, 1974), and on stage (from 1936) in London and New York. She was the second wife of John Fernald, stage director (who directed Laird in *Heartbreak House*, 1950) and Principal of RADA (1955–65), and they co-authored the play, *And No Birds Sing* (1945).

OTHER BRITISH FILMS INCLUDE: *The Last Chance* (1937), *Lily of Laguna* (1938), *The Lamp Still Burns* (1943), *Beware of Pity* (1946), *Your Witness* (1950), *Life in Her Hands* (1951), *Face in the Night* (1956), *Village of the Damned* (1960).

Laird, Trevor (*b* London, 1957). Actor. Black actor who has been in some films significant for their exploration of racial issues, including *Babylon* (1980) and *Burning an Illusion* (1981). Probably best known for *Secrets & Lies* (1996), as the brother of Hortense, suddenly confronting the idea of a slatternly white mother. Had a very good TV role in *Undercover Heart* (1998).

OTHER BRITISH FILMS INCLUDE: *Quadrophenia, The Long Good Friday* (1979), *Water* (1985), *Slipstream* (1989), *Love, Honour and Obey* (2000).

Lake, Alan (*b* Stoke-on-Trent, 1941 – *d* Windsor, 1984). Actor. Best known as Diana **Dors**' third husband, from 1968 until her death in 1984, he also spent twelve months (1970–71) in prison for his share in a pub brawl, and finally committed suicide. His film credits are uninspiring; his 70s films, including his star vehicle, *Confessions from the David Galaxy Affair* (1979), are mostly in the EXPLOITATION genre.

OTHER BRITISH FILMS INCLUDE: *Sky West and Crooked* (1965), *Charlie Bubbles* (1967), *Hide and Seek* (1972), *Percy's Progress, The Amorous Milkman* (1974), *Playbirds* (1978), *Yesterday's Hero* (1979), *Don't Open Till Christmas* (1984).

Lamac, Karel (*b* Prague, 1897 – *d* Hamburg, 1952). Director. Had a prolific directing career in Czech cinema of the 20s, frequently in collaboration with Anny **Ondra** (whom he married) and Otto **Heller**. From the late 20s, he made mainly German films, before emigrating to Britain in 1939. Lamac's British films include an update of the quintessentially Czech fable about the soldier Schweijk (*Schweik's New Adventures*, 1943, + co-sc). Post-war, he returned to Germany.

OTHER BRITISH FILMS: *They Met In The Dark* (1943), *It Happened One Sunday* (1944). Tim Bergfelder.

Lamb, Charles (*b* London, 1900 – *d* London, 1989). Actor. Worried-looking character player of about 40 films, busiest in the 50s and 60s. He is the put-upon father in *Come Back Peter* (1952), but usually in smaller roles, like the carpenter in *School for Scoundrels* (1959). A former engineer, on stage from 1924, in films from 1941's *Once a Crook*, and on TV from 1947, including the 1979 *Quatermass* series.

OTHER BRITISH FILMS INCLUDE: *The Lavender Hill Mob* (1951), *The Intruder* (1953), *John and Julie* (1955), *Lucky Jim* (1957), *Jack the Ripper* (1958), *The Shakedown* (1959), *The Criminal* (1960), *Hide and Seek* (1963), *Life at the Top* (1965), *Quatermass and the Pit* (1967), *Hands of the Ripper* (1971), *The Tall Guy* (1989).

Lambert, Gavin (*b* Wincanton, 1924). Critic, author. Like his friend Lindsay **Anderson**, Lambert was educated at Cheltenham and Oxford, and, with Anderson and others, founded the short-lived but influential journal, SEQUENCE, while still at Oxford. He edited SIGHT AND SOUND from 1949 to 1955, then wrote and directed *Another Sky* (1955), made in Morocco. Went to live in Hollywood as a screenwriter and personal assistant to director Nicholas Ray, whose *Bitter Victory* (1957, UK/Fr) he co-wrote. Among his British films, he was nominated for a shared AA/sc for *Sons and Lovers* (1960), a skilful job of compression, and wrote *The Roman Spring of Mrs Stone* (1961), adapting Tennessee Williams' novel. The author of several novels with Hollywood settings (e.g. *Inside Daisy Clover*, 1963) and books about such figures as George Cukor, most recently he has written *Mainly About Lindsay Anderson* (2000), which also reveals a good deal about himself and their contrasting responses to their homosexuality. He contributed to Stephen **Frears**'s film in the centenary History of Cinema series, *Typically British* (1996). An American citizen since 1964.

OTHER BRITISH FILMS: (add material) *I Know What I Want, Whoever Slew Auntie Roo?* (1971).

Lambert, Jack (*b* Ardrossan, Scotland, 1899 – *d* London, 1976). Actor. Stern-faced Scots character player, former sanitary engineer and amateur boxer, in films from 1931. Came to attention when released from WW2 service in the Army to head the cast of EALING's DOCUMENTARY-style war film, *Nine Men* (1942). Lambert, demobbed as Lieutenant-Colonel, played a tough sergeant. Post-war, contracted to Ealing, playing the padre in *The Captive Heart* (1946); post-Ealing, made over two dozen films, including main features like *Storm over the Nile* (1955) as the Colonel, 'B' FILMS like *The Lost Hours* (1952), as a worried air traffic controller, and in-betweens like *Floodtide* (1949), in which, as Rona **Anderson**'s father, he seemed made up to look like Arthur **Rank**. On stage from 1928 and TV from 1939. Not to be confused with American actor of the same name.

OTHER BRITISH FILMS INCLUDE: *A Honeymoon Adventure* (1931), *The Ghost Goes West* (1935), *Hue and Cry* (1946), *Dear Murderer* (1947), *Eureka Stockade* (1949), *Twice Upon a Time* (1953), *Lost* (1955), *Son of Robin Hood* (1958, as Will Scarlet), *The Shakedown* (1959), *Greyfriars Bobby* (1961), *Dracula – Prince of Darkness* (1965).

Lambert, Verity (*b* London, 1935). Producer. Lambert began her career in TV in 1954, going on to produce such popular programmes as *Doctor Who* (1963–66, some episodes),

W Somerset Maugham (1969–70), *Budgie* (1971–72), *The Naked Civil Servant* (1975), and *GBH* (1991, ex p). The cinema films on which she has worked include the lovely, underrated *Dreamchild* (1985, co-ex p) and *Evil Angels* (1988, UK/Aust, p). Awarded OBE, 2002.

OTHER BRITISH FILMS: (ex p) *The Sailor's Return* (1978), *Link, Clockwise, Morons from Outer Space* (1985).

Lamble, Lloyd (*b* Melbourne, 1914). Actor. Sturdy, reliable character player who made one Australian film, *Strong Is the Seed* (1949), and, in the absence of an indigenous industry, came to England – and made a further three dozen. With an air of quiet authority, he was often cast as policemen, like Superintendent Kemp-Bird in several of the ST TRINIAN'S SERIES, or in such 'B' FILMS as *There's Always a Thursday* (1957). From the 60s, more often in TV, with a continuing role in *Crossroads* from 1964; played Quentin Crisp's father in *The Naked Civil Servant* (1975).

OTHER BRITISH FILMS INCLUDE: *Curtain Up* (1952), *Background* (1953), *The Belles of St Trinian's, Profile* (1954), *The Man Who Never Was* (1955), *Barnacle Bill* (1957), *Dunkirk* (1958), *The Trials of Oscar Wilde, The Pure Hell of St Trinian's* (1960), *Term of Trial* (1962), *And Now the Screaming Starts!* (1973).

Lamont, Duncan (*b* Lisbon, 1918 – *d* Tonbridge, 1978). Actor. RN: Driscoll. Raised in Scotland, this rugged six-footer had considerable pre-war stage experience, entering films in the early 50s. Very busy throughout the decade, whether as villain (e.g. Count William de la Marck in *The Adventures of Quentin Durward*, 1955) or the dangerous Defarge in *A Tale of Two Cities* (1958) or duplicitous in the cause of friendship, like the soldier-turned-farmer in *The Intruder* (1953). There is the usual 50s range of policemen and soldiers, mostly in main features, but also in 'B' FILMS, such as *The End of the Road* (1954), as the decent but worried son of Finlay CURRIE. Much TV too, including *The Quatermass Experiment* (1953). Married to actress **Patricia Driscoll** (*b* Clonakilty, Ireland, 1927), who appeared in a few 50s films, including *Charley Moon* (1956), opposite Max BYGRAVES, and had some success on TV, as a children's show host and as Marian in *Robin Hood*.

OTHER BRITISH FILMS INCLUDE: *Waterfront* (1950), *The Man in the White Suit* (1951), *The Lost Hours* (1952), *The Final Test* (1953), *The Teckman Mystery* (1954), *Passage Home* (1955), *The Thirty Nine Steps* (1958), *A Touch of Larceny* (1959), *Murder at the Gallop* (1963), *Arabesque* (1966, UK/US), *Quatermass and the Pit* (1967), *Battle of Britain* (1969), *Burke & Hare* (1971), *The Creeping Flesh* (1972), *Escape from the Dark* (1976, UK/US).

Lamont, Molly (*b* Boksburg, South Africa, 1910 – *d* Los Angeles, California, 2001). Actress. Former beauty contest-winner, whose prize was a trip to England and a film test, she became a popular and prolific leading lady of 30s British films, mostly for BIP, though for WARNERS–BRITISH she made *Murder at Monte Carlo* (1935), the film that sent Errol FLYNN to Hollywood. In Hollywood herself from 1936, she became a notable character actress, often as 'other women' (as in *The Awful Truth*, 1937), but really fine as a bullied wife in *The Suspect* (1944).

OTHER BRITISH FILMS INCLUDE: *My Wife's Family, Shadows* (1931), *Lord Camber's Ladies, The Last Coupon* (1932), *Letting in the Sunshine* (1933), *White Ensign* (1934), *Oh! What a Night!, Alibi Inn* (1935).

Lamont, Peter (*b* London, 1929). Production designer. Now much associated with the BOND films, Lamont began as draughtsman on such films as *The Importance of Being Earnest* (1952), then as set decorator, on (e.g.) *This Sporting Life* (1963) and *Thunderball* (1965), then as art director for the first time on

Sleuth (1972). In this capacity he worked on several more Bond films before getting his first 'production designer' credit on *For Your Eyes Only* (1981). Since then, he has been a regular Bond collaborator, as the films' design has grown ever more extravagantly eye-catching. Also worked in Hollywood, and, however silly one may find aspects of *Titanic* (1997), there is no gainsaying its fabulous design, for which he shared a deserved Oscar and a BAAn. Shared awards on other films such as *Fiddler on the Roof* (1971, US), *The Spy Who Loved Me* (1977) and *Aliens* (1986, US).

OTHER BRITISH FILMS INCLUDE: (set dresser/decorator, ass art d) *The Night of the Eagle* (1962), *Chitty Chitty Bang Bang* (1968), *On Her Majesty's Secret Service* (1969), *Diamonds Are Forever* (1971); (art d) *Live and Let Die* (1973), *The Man with the Golden Gun* (1974), *Moonraker* (1979, UK/Fr); (des) *Octopussy* (1983), *A View to a Kill* (1985), *The Living Daylights* (1987), *Consuming Passions* (1988, UK/US), *Licence to Kill* (1989), *GoldenEye* (1995, UK/US), *The World Is Not Enough* (1999, UK/US), *Die Another Day* (2002, UK/US).

Lanchester, Elsa (*b* Lewisham, 1902 – *d* Woodland Hills, California, 1986). Actress. Eccentric character player, long in Hollywood with husband Charles LAUGHTON, now best remembered, wild-haired and hissing-voiced, as *The Bride of Frankenstein* (1935), or of his 'monster', and as her creator, Mary Shelley. Trained as a dancer (as a child danced with Isadora Duncan's troupe), on stage from 1922, she ran a cabaret in London called 'The Cave of Harmony', frequented by Evelyn WAUGH, with whom she appeared in the amateur film, *The Scarlet Woman* (1924), never screened publicly. She made about a dozen British films before settling in America, most memorable as Anne of Cleves whose wit enables her to keep her head in *The Private Life of Henry VIII* (1933), as the devoted servant of *Rembrandt* (1936), and the missionary in *The Vessel of Wrath* (1938), all opposite Laughton. Her main career is American and she received AAn for *Come to the Stable* (1949) and *Witness for the Prosecution* (1957), again with Laughton, to whom, despite his homosexual leanings, she remained married until his death.

OTHER BRITISH FILMS INCLUDE: *One of the Best* (1927), *The Constant Nymph* (1928), *The Love Habit, Potiphar's Wife* (1931), *The Private Life of Don Juan* (1934), *The Ghost Goes West* (1935).

Landau, Leslie (*b* London, 1904). Producer, screenwriter. Educated at Cheltenham and in Germany, in films from 1924, as NEWSREELS editor and as DOCUMENTARY director, before making several features for FOX–BRITISH. He produced an early 'B' film for Michael POWELL, *The Love Test* (1935), and the last 'A' film for Lance COMFORT, *Portrait of Clare* (1950, + co-sc). In Hollywood in the later 30s, and worked in England on PROPAGANDA films during WW2. Also a playwright, he co-wrote the very successful *My Brother Jonathan* (1948).

OTHER BRITISH FILMS: *The Riverside Murder* (co-sc), *The Dark World* (p, co-story) (1935), *Wedding Group* (1936, p).

Landen, Dinsdale (*b* Margate, 1932). Actor. Educated at King's School, Rochester, trained at Florence Moore Theatre Studios, Hove; on stage from 1948, in London from 1955, providing a sane foil as nephew Patrick to Beatrice LILLIE's *Auntie Mame* (1958–59). In fact he showed a sense of comedy which films have scarcely exploited, except in such marginal enterprises as *Every Home Should Have One* (1969), as a sex-obsessed vicar. Never quite a leading man in films, he settled for character roles, often of military figures, as in *Young Winston* (1972). Much TV, including *The Glittering Prizes* (1976). Once married to actress Jennifer DANIEL.

OTHER BRITISH FILMS INCLUDE: *The League of Gentlemen* (1960), *A Jolly Bad Fellow* (1963), *Mosquito Squadron* (1968), *International Velvet* (1978), *Morons from Outer Space* (1985), *The Steal* (1995).

Landi, Elissa (*b* Venice, 1904 – *d* New York, 1948). Actress. RN: Elizabeth Kuenhelt Alleged to be descended from royal house of Austria, Landi, exquisitely lovely, and lively too, had a disappointing career in Hollywood, except for the lead in *The Count of Monte Cristo* (1934), though she is better remembered as the Christian heroine of *Sign of the Cross* (1932). Educated in England, on London stage from 1924, she made six late British silents, including Herbert WILCOX's *London* (1926) and, as Brian AHERNE's shopgirl sweetheart, Anthony ASQUITH's *Underground* (1928), and two early talkies made by Elinor GLYN, *Knowing Men* and *The Price of Things* (1930). In 1930 she left for Broadway and subsequently Hollywood, returned briefly to Britain for *Köenigsmark* (1935) and *The Amateur Gentleman* (1936), stopped filming in 1937, reappeared surprisingly in *Corregidor* (1943) and five years later died of cancer. Also wrote several novels.

OTHER BRITISH FILMS: *The Marquis of Bolibar, Synd* (UK/Swe) (1928), *The Inseparables* (1929), *Children of Chance* (1930).

Landi, Marla (*b* Turin, 1931). Actress. RN: Scarafia. Dark-haired beauty and model, who played leads in a few minor 50s films, including the dismal *The Hornet's Nest* (1955), as a photographic model, and *Dublin Nightmare* (1958), a cutprice Celtic *Third Man*. Moved upmarket as David KNIGHT's anxious girlfriend in *Across the Bridge* (1957) and as Cecile, yearning for Spain and sinking in English quicksand in *The Hound of the Baskervilles* (1959).

OTHER BRITISH FILMS: *The Golden Link* (1954), *First Man into Space* (1958), *The Pirates of Blood River* (1961), *The Murder Game* (1965).

Landone, Avice (*b* Quetta, India, 1908 – *d* London, 1976). Actress. RN: Spitta. Supporting player of 30 films, mainly in the 50s, and mainly as middle-class wives or mothers, like those she played in 1956's *True as a Turtle* (as yacht-owning Cecil PARKER's wife) and *Reach for the Sky* (as Douglas Bader's mother), with a sprinkling of nurses, as in *The Wind Cannot Read* (1958). Unusually kinky as kinky Dennis PRICE's wife in her last film, *The Adventures of Barry McKenzie* (1972, UK/Aust). On London stage from 1938 and married to actor Bruno BARNABE.

OTHER BRITISH FILMS INCLUDE: *The Franchise Affair* (1950), *White Corridors* (1951), *Operation Diplomat* (1953), *The Embezzler* (1954), *Carve Her Name With Pride* (1958), *The Leather Boys* (1963), *Nothing But the Best* (1964), *Two Gentlemen Sharing* (1969), *Blood on Satan's Claw* (1970).

Lane, Jackie (aka Jocelyn Lane) (*b* Vienna, 1937). Actress. RN: Jackie Bolton. Educated in New York, at 14 came to England where she trained as a dancer; at 17 she was put under contract to WARWICK FILMS, which put her in the travelogue short, *April in Portugal* (1955) and a bit part in *The Gamma People* (1955). Anna NEAGLE then used her in big roles in two films, *These Dangerous Years* (1957) and *Wonderful Things* (1957), but the Neagle–WILCOX era had passed, and her career languished. Hollywood was little better – *vide* AIP's *Hell's Belles* (1969). Sister of Mara LANE.

OTHER BRITISH FILMS INCLUDE: *Men of Sherwood Forest* (1954), *The Truth About Women* (1957), *The Angry Hills, Jet Storm* (1959).

Lane, Lupino (*b* London, 1892 – *d* London, 1959). Actor, director. A member of a celebrated theatrical family who came to England from Italy in 1632, Lane was a brilliant acrobatic comedian on stage (from 1896) and screen. Made his film debut in 1915; silent films include *A Wife in a Hurry* (1916), *The Missing Link* (1917), *Love and Lobster* (1918), and *A Lot about a Lottery* (1920). First came to the US in 1920 and was immediately popular, giving excellent performances as a refugee in D.W. Griffith's *Isn't Life Wonderful* (1924) and as Maurice Chevalier's valet in Ernst Lubitsch's *The Love Parade* (1929). Lane's biggest stage success was in *Me and My Girl* (1937), in which he created 'The Lambeth Walk'; disappointingly filmed in 1939 as *The Lambeth Walk*. Brother to Wallace LUPINO; cousin to Stanley and Ida LUPINO.

OTHER BRITISH FILMS INCLUDE: (a) *The Man in Possession* (1915), *The Dummy* (1916), *Splash Me Nicely* (1917), *The Yellow Mask* (1930), *A Southern Maid* (1933), *Trust the Navy* (1935), *Hot News* (1936); (d, unless noted) *No Lady* (+a), *The Love Race* (co-d) (1931), *Innocents of Chicago* (+ p, co-sc), *Old Spanish Customers* (1932), *Letting in the Sunshine* (1933), *My Old Duchess* (1933).

BIBLIOG: Autobiography, *How to be a Comedian*, 1945; *Born to Star*, 1957. AS.

Lane, Mara (*b* Vienna, 1930). Actress. RN: Dorothy Bolton. Misguidedly touted as Britain's answer to Monroe, the brunette Lane had a few small roles in early 50s British films. She played in *Something Money Can't Buy* (1952) what she actually never became – a film star – and she was a glamorous misfit in the ridiculous *Treasure Hunt* (1952). From 1954, she was in US and European films of little account. Married Prince Alfonso Hohenlohe. Sister of Jackie LANE.

OTHER BRITISH FILMS INCLUDE: *Hell Is Sold Out* (1951), *It Started in Paradise* (1952), *Innocents in Paris* (1953).

Lang, Gordon (*b* Combe Martin, 1912). Cinematographer. In films from 1931, with GAINSBOROUGH's camera department, promoted to camera operator before WW2, partly spent with the ARMY FILM UNIT (1942–46). Post-war, with Gainsborough as operator on films like *Good-Time Girl* and *The Brothers* (1947). His first job as DOP was HIGHBURY's *Colonel Bogey* (1948), he shot the Italian location scenes for *Bad Lord Byron* (1949) and a further ten features of no great distinction, with the marginal exceptions of *My Brother's Keeper* (1948) and the very funny *It's Not Cricket* (1949), but his camerawork is only – and properly – functional, uninfluenced by his association with the moody atmospherics of 1947.

OTHER BRITISH FILMS INCLUDE: *Boys in Brown* (1949, co-c), *Ha'penny Breeze* (1950, co-c), *A Tale of Five Cities* (1951), *Distant Trumpet* (1952), *Innocents in Paris* (1953).

Lang, Harold (*b* London, 1922 – *d* Cairo, 1970). Actor. RADA Gold Medallist who had seasons with London's Arts Theatre and toured with the Stratford company. He devised, performed in and toured world-wide with the inventive *Macbeth in Camera* in the 60s. In about 35 films from 1949, often as shifty characters like the ex-pug in *Cloudburst* (1951) or Susan SHAW's draft-dodging, flat-footed seducer in *The Intruder* (1953), and finally in HORROR FILMS, including *The Psychopath* (1966).

OTHER BRITISH FILMS INCLUDE: *The Spider and the Fly* (1949), *Calling Bulldog Drummond* (1951), *The Long Memory* (1952), *The Saint's Return, Street Corner* (1953), *Dance Little Lady* (1954), *The Quatermass Experiment* (1955), *Paranoiac* (1962), *Dr Terror's House of Horrors* (1964).

Lang, Matheson (*b* Montreal, 1879 – *d* Bridgetown, Barbados, 1948). Actor. A prominent actor-manager of the old school, Lang made his stage debut in 1897 and recreated four of his greatest roles on screen: *Mr Wu* (1919, on stage 1913), Silvio Steno in *Carnival*, which he also co-wrote (1921 and 1931, on stage 1920), Matathias in *The Wandering Jew* (1923, on stage 1920), and Huan Sing in *The Chinese Bungalow* (1926 and 1930, on stage 1925). Still a commanding presence in such 30s roles as the financier about to be exposed in *Channel Crossing* (1933) and the father suing his wife for divorce in *Little Friend* (1934). A clergyman's son who defied family opposition by going on the stage, he was a rare matinee idol of the period who took seriously to films.

OTHER BRITISH FILMS INCLUDE: *The Merchant of Venice* (1916), *Everybody's Business* (1917), *Victory and Peace* (1918), *Dick Turpin's Ride to York* (1922), *White Slippers* (1924), *The Secret Kingdom* (1925), *The King's Highway* (1927), *Triumph of the Scarlet Pimpernel* (1928), *Drake of England* (1935), *The Cardinal* (1936).

BIBLIOG: Autobiography, *Mr Wu Looks Back*, 1940. AS.

Lang, Robert (*b* Bristol, 1934). Actor. Expert purveyor of choleric types, like Colonel Protheroe in TV's *Murder at the Vicarage* (1986) or Lord Hibbott in *Four Weddings and a Funeral* (1994). Former meteorologist, trained at Old Vic Theatre School, first on London stage in 1957, joined the National Theatre in 1963, and in 1965 reprised on film his stage performance as Roderigo in *Othello*. Has done more TV than film but has been an enjoyable character presence in British films for several decades, in films as varied as *The Great Train Robbery* (1978), as a police inspector, and *Wilde* (1997, UK/Ger/Jap/US), as C.O. Humphries.

OTHER BRITISH FILMS INCLUDE: *School for Secrets* (1946), *The Dark Man* (1950), *Catch Us If You Can* (1965), *Interlude*, *The Dance of Death* (1968), *Savage Messiah* (1972), *Shout at the Devil* (1976), *Hawks* (1988), *The Trial* (1992), *Some Mother's Son* (1996, Ire/US).

Langley, Bryan (aka Brian) (*b* London, 1909). Cinematographer, special effects. Educated at Wellington School, Langley entered films as assistant cameraman in 1926, had his first cinematographer's credit on *No Exit* (1930) and was busy throughout the 30s, mostly on routine films, with occasional upmarket jobs, like *Blossom Time* (1934) and *Royal Cavalcade* (1935). After Middle and Far East service with the ARMY FILM UNIT (1940–45), he shot only a few more films, including location work for *Piccadilly Incident* (1946) and exteriors for *Bond Street* (1948). From 1948, he turned his attention to SPECIAL EFFECTS photography, on such films as *1984* (1955) and, from 1951, to travelling matte work on such films as *Green Grow the Rushes* (1951).

OTHER BRITISH FILMS INCLUDE: (c/co-c) *Number Seventeen* (1932), *No Funny Business* (1933), *Music Hath Charms* (1935), *Living Dangerously* (1936), *Dark Eyes of London* (1939), *Spare a Copper* (1940), *The Tower of Terror* (1941), *When the Bough Breaks* (1947), *The Monkey's Paw* (1948); (fx c) *The Weaker Sex* (1948), *Cardboard Cavalier*, *The Perfect Woman* (mattes) (1949), *Angels One Five* (1952), *Reach for the Sky* (1956).

Langley, Noel *b* Durban, 1911 – *d* Desert Hot Springs, California, 1980). Writer. Described as 'a pixie nonconformist at MGM', Langley is primarily remembered as the co-writer of the screenplay for *The Wizard of Oz* (1939), along with other Hollywood films, and the play, *Edward, My Son* (1947), co-authored with Robert MORLEY and filmed, without Langley's participation, in 1949. He first came to Hollywood in 1936, returned to UK in 1946. He wrote screenplays for several light comedies and literary ADAPTATIONS, directed a star-studded version of *The Pickwick Papers* (1952, + co-p, sc) and a REMAKE of *Svengali* (1954, + sc), then ending his career in Hollywood. Married (2) **Pamela Deeming**, who was in a couple of 'B' FILMS, *The Girl Is Mine* and *Dangerous Assignment* (1950).

OTHER BRITISH FILMS INCLUDE: *King of the Damned*, *The Secret of Stamboul* (1936, co-sc), *Cardboard Cavalier*, *Adam and Evelyne* (co-sc) (1949), *Trio* (1950, co-sc), *Tom Brown's Schooldays*, *Scrooge* (1951), *Ivanhoe* (co-sc), *Father's Doing Fine* (from his play, *Little Lambs Eat Ivy*) (1952), *Knights of the Round Table* (co-sc), *Our Girl Friday* (+ d) (1953). AS.

Langton, David (*b* Motherwell, Scotland, 1912 – *d* Stratford-upon-Avon, 1994). Actor. RN: Basil Langton-Dodds. Now best remembered for his patrician Lord Bellamy in TV's *Upstairs, Downstairs* (1971–75), Langton was on stage from the early 30s and, post-WW2 service, in leading roles. Merely dabbled in films, but can be spotted in such bizarrely eclectic affairs as *Saint Joan* (1957, UK/US), *The Pumpkin Eater* and *A Hard Day's Night* (1964). Much TV including Lord Mountbatten (whom he resembled) in *Charles & Diana: A Royal Love Story* (1982) and theatre, including co-starring with Diana RIGG in *Night and Day* (1979). Father of Simon LANGTON.

OTHER BRITISH FILMS INCLUDE: *The Ship That Died of Shame* (1955), *The Liquidator* (1965), *The Hound of the Baskervilles* (1983), *The Whistle Blower* (1986).

Langton, Simon (*b* Amersham, 1941). Director. Respected TV director who had early credits on episodes of *Upstairs, Downstairs* (1975), did *Smiley's People* in 1982, won a BAA/d for the Grand Guignol mini-series *Mother Love* (1989), and had a popular success with *Pride and Prejudice* (1995, BAAn). On-screen so far, there have been *The Whistle Blower* (1986) and *Headhunters* (1992), and in late 1999 he was reported to be filming the life of Mario Lanza. Son of David LANGTON.

Lansbury, Angela (*b* London, 1925). Actress. An Oscar-nominee while in her teens, as the pert maid in *Gaslight* (1944), pushed from film to film by MGM without becoming a leading lady, it seems that her pouty looks and acid delivery always pointed towards character roles rather than romantic leads. Granddaughter of British Labour leader George Lansbury and daughter of actress Moyna MacGill who sent her to the Webber-Douglas school, then out of wartime England to America in 1940. And that is where most of her very long career, on screen, stage (she had a huge Tony-winning success as *Mame*, 1966) and TV (monotonously nominated for Emmys for *Murder, She Wrote* over the past two decades), has taken place, but there has been a minor stream of British films, the most notable of which are probably *Death on the Nile* (1978), as the outrageous novelist, Salome Otterbourne, and *The Company of Wolves* (1984), as Granny. Awarded BAFTA Life Achievement award in 1991, CBE in 1994.

OTHER BRITISH FILMS INCLUDE: *In the Cool of the Day* (1963), *The Lady Vanishes* (1979), *The Mirror Crack'd* (1980), *The Pirates of Penzance* (1982).

La Plante, Laura (*b* St Louis, 1904 – *d* Los Angeles, 1996). Actress. Pert blonde of silent films and early talkies, noted for her bobbed hair and comedic style, on screen primarily in Hollywood from 1921 to 1957. After divorcing her first husband, director William Seiter (m.1926), in 1934, she immediately married Irving ASHER in Paris, soon after he had been named production chief of WARNER BROS. BRITISH. For Asher, she starred in five British features: *Her Imaginary Lover* (1933), *The Girl in Possession*, *The Church Mouse* (1934), *The Widow's Might*, *Man of the Moment* (1935). AS.

Lapotaire, Jane (*b* Ipswich, 1944). Actress. Eight films in over 30 years suggest that Lapotaire's main interests lie elsewhere, on the stage to be precise, with seasons at the Bristol Old Vic, the National and Stratford. She has done more TV, including a version of her famous 1980 stage show, *Piaf* (1984), but her films are spread out between the minor crime thriller, *Crescendo* (1969), and *There's Only One Jimmy Grimble* (2000), as a wizened old hag – which she emphatically is not. But the films do little justice to her potential for passionate intensity. Married director Roland JOFFÉ (1971–80).

OTHER BRITISH FILMS INCLUDE: *Antony and Cleopatra* (as Charmian) (1972), *Eureka* (1982, US/UK), *Lady Jane* (1985), *Surviving Picasso* (1996, UK/US), *Shooting Fish* (1997).

La Rue, Danny (*b* Cork, 1927). Actor. RN: Daniel Carroll. Famous drag star of stage and TV, he has made only one film, the moderately amusing *Our Miss Fred* (1972), in which the plot about helping a school party to escape from Germany seemed to constrain him. Some sources claim an uncredited bit in *Every Day's a Holiday* (1964). Awarded OBE, 2002.

Lassally, Walter (*b* Berlin, 1926). Cinematographer. A key figure in the British NEW WAVE, Lassally came to Britain as a refugee from Nazi Germany. He has worked solidly in British and international films for fifty years, starting as a clapper boy, then filming semi-professionally with friend Derek YORK (*Smith, Our Friend*, 1946, short, + co-p). He also wrote many magazine articles about film-making from the late 40s. After directing a number of DOCUMENTARIES and SHORTS, several for FREE CINEMA directors, including Tony RICHARDSON's *Momma Don't Allow* (1955), Lindsay ANDERSON's *Every Day Except Christmas* (1957) and Karel REISZ's *We Are the Lambeth Boys* (1959), he followed these directors into feature films and contributed to the look of the new British realist cinema of the late 50s/early 60s. He shot three notable features for Richardson: *A Taste of Honey* (1961) with its melancholy black-and-white rendering of England's north; *The Loneliness of the Long Distance Runner* (1962) in which his images – of the liberating effect of the early morning runs intercut with recollections of shabby urban confinement – contribute strikingly to the film's polemic; and *Tom Jones* (1963), an exuberantly, spring-fresh version of an 18th-century novel, shot with up-to-the-moment technology. He then did several films for Greek director, Michael Cacoyannis, and won an AA for his work on *Zorba the Greek* (1964, US/Gr). In 1972 he began his association with director James IVORY by shooting *Savages*, which remains one of his favourite films. His other MERCHANT IVORY films include *Autobiography of a Princess* (1975), and the Indian-set *Heat and Dust* (1982), in which he gave the 20s sequences a soft 'period' glow that contrasted with the more brightly-lit, often hand-held look of the modern scenes. Tirelessly innovative, he went on working well into the 90s (e.g. *The Little Dolphins*, 1993, Gr), after most of his Free Cinema colleagues had died or retired.

OTHER BRITISH FILMS INCLUDE: (shorts) *Three Installations* (1951), *The Pleasure Garden*, *Wakefield Express* (1952), *Sunday By the Sea* (1953), *Bow Bells*, *Thursday's Children* (1954), *Green and Pleasant Land*, *Foot and Mouth*, *The Children Upstairs* (1955), *Together* (add ph), *Simon* (1956), *Bernard Shaw* (co-c) (1957), *The Peaches* (1964, short), *Silent Film* (1997); (features) *The Passing Stranger* (1954), *Another Sky* (1955), *Beat Girl* (1959), *Psyche 59* (1963), *The Day the Fish Came Out* (UK/Gr), *Oedipus the King* (1967), *Joanna*, *Three Into Two Won't Go* (1968), *The Adding Machine*, *Twinky* (1969), *To Kill a Clown* (1971), *The Seaweed Children* (1973), *Hullabaloo Over Georgie and Bonnie's Pictures* (1978, UK/Ind), *Memoirs of a Survivor* (1981), *Tuxedo Warrior* (1982), *The Bostonians* (1984, UK/US), *The Deceivers* (1988), *Diary of a Madman* (1992, Ire).

BIBLIOG: Autobiography, *Itinerant Cameraman*, 1987.

Latham, Philip (*b* Leigh-on-Sea, 1929). Actor. Long-faced, somewhat lugubrious-looking actor who is best remembered for his superbly played Plantagenet Palliser in TV's *The Pallisers* (1974), growing touchingly in warmth and moral authority. He appeared in about a dozen feature films in the 60s and 70s, having his biggest role in the Len DEIGHTON adaptation, *Spy Story* (1976).

OTHER BRITISH FILMS INCLUDE: *The Monster of Highgate Ponds* (1960), *Ring of Spies* (1963), *Dracula – Prince of Darkness* (1965), *Force 10 from Navarone* (1978).

Latimer, Hugh (*b* Haslemere, 1913). Actor. Cambridge-educated supporting player of about 20 films of the 50s and 60s, including two 'B' MOVIES for Vernon SEWELL: *Ghost Ship* (1952), as faithless Joan CAROL's lover; and *Counterspy* (1953) as a police inspector. Central School-trained, he was on stage from 1936, resuming career after WW2 service (1940–46) and doing time in radio's *Mrs Dale's Diary*.

OTHER BRITISH FILMS INCLUDE: *Corridor of Mirrors* (1948), *Someone at the Door* (1950), *The Million Pound Note* (1953), *The Horse's Mouth* (1958), *Sink the Bismarck!* (1960), *Girl in the Headlines* (1963), *Jane Eyre* (1970).

Lauchlan, Agnes (aka Laughlan) (*b* London, 1905 – *d* 1993). Actress. RADA-trained supporting actress of stage (debut 1924; Madame Arcati in *Blithe Spirit*, 1942–43) and screen, who eventually had a continuing TV role as Patrick CARGILL's mother in *The Many Wives of Patrick* (1976–78). Usually in dignified roles; she played Queen Charlotte in *The Young Mr Pitt* (1942), but film work was sporadic.

OTHER BRITISH FILMS INCLUDE: *Oh, Mr Porter!* (1937), *Alf's Button Afloat* (1938), *The Spy in Black* (1939), *The Black Sheep of Whitehall* (1941), *Once Upon a Dream* (1949), *The Whole Truth* (1958).

Lauder, Sir Harry (*b* Edinburgh, 1870 – *d* Strathaven, Scotland, 1950). Actor. Lauder was once Scotland's major contribution to world popular culture, although his songs and humour today seem oddly quaint. He generally sang on screen the songs that made him famous, such as 'I Love a Lassie' and 'Roamin' in the Gloamin'' and 'She Is Ma Daisy' (all filmed 1931); he lip-synched six songs in *Auld Lang Syne* (1929), starred in the Harry Lauder Songs SERIES (1931), made six 'Singing Pictures' with experimental sound for GAUMONT in 1907 and another 14 experimental sound SHORTS for the American Cort-Kitsee Talking Pictures and Selig in 1914. Knighted in 1919.

OTHER BRITISH FILMS: *Harry Lauder in a Hurry* (1908), *Golfing* (1913), *A Trip Down the Clyde* (1922), *Huntingtower* (1927), *The End of the Road* (1936). AS.

Laughton, Charles (*b* Scarborough, 1899 – *d* Los Angeles, 1962). Actor. RADA-trained Laughton is important in British cinema because of *The Private Life of Henry VIII* (1933) which brought international recognition, but his greatest work is in the US, to which he came in 1932 as the unusual hero of *The Old Dark House*. He will be remembered for roles such as a perverted Nero in *The Sign of the Cross* (1932), the overbearing father in *The Barretts of Wimpole Street* (1934), Captain Bligh in *Mutiny on the Bounty* (1935), the title character in *The Hunchback of Notre Dame* (1939), and, above all, for *The Night of the Hunter* (1955), which he directed, and which is one of the greatest of all films. There is an intensity of purpose to Laughton's performances which require an audience's attention, and he is a difficult actor to analyse, thanks in part to the basic simplicity of his playing in, for example, the aborted *I Claudius* (1937). After a 1926 stage debut, Laughton played major roles in seven separate London theatrical productions the following year. Post-war he returned to British films only once more, but how memorable he was – as the patriarch brought to heel in *Hobson's Choice* (1953).

In 1929, he married Elsa LANCHESTER who accepted if not condoned his homosexuality, and there is both a loving and farcical quality to the marriage which the couple often brought to roles together on screen, beginning with Laughton's first two films, directed by Ivor MONTAGU and based on stories by H.G. WELLS, the comedy SHORTS *Bluebottles* and *Day Dreams* (1928), and including memorably *Rembrandt* (1936) and *Vessel of Wrath* (1938).

OTHER BRITISH FILMS: *Piccadilly* (1929), *Wolves* (1930), *Down River* (1931), *St Martin's Lane* (1938), *Jamaica Inn* (1939).
BIBLIOG: Simon Callow, *Charles Laughton*, 1987. AS.

Launder, Frank *see* Launder and Gilliat

Launder and Gilliat. **Frank Launder** (*b* Hitchin, 1906 – *d* Monte Carlo, Monaco, 1997) and **Sidney Gilliat** (*b* Cheshire, 1908 – *d* Pewsey Vale, 1994). Screenwriters, producers, directors. In the 40s and 50s, Launder and Gilliat were, along with POWELL AND PRESSBURGER, the most distinctive and talented British film partnership, writing, producing and directing perceptive, witty, and sympathetic films around British character and eccentricity. Their major films, all black-and-white, are in the GAUMONT–BRITISH tradition. *Millions Like Us* (1943, L/G co-d, co-sc), *Waterloo Road* (1944, G d, sc), *The Rake's Progress* (1945, G d; G/L co-p, co-sc), *I See a Dark Stranger* (1946, L d; L/G co-p, co-sc), and *Green for Danger* (1946, G d, co-sc; L/G co-p) are finely crafted quiet satires, close in tone to that of affectionate cartoonists of the period such as Fougasse and David Langdon. Even *The Rake's Progress* offers less the biting edge of William Hogarth's etchings, from which it takes its name, than the compassionate worlds of Osbert Lancaster and Nicolas Bentley. Later they found inspiration in Ronald SEARLE's illustrations for their series of ST TRINIAN'S films. They were less comfortable with conventional dramas such as *Captain Boycott* (1947, L d/co-s; L/G co-p), *London Belongs to Me* (1947, G d/co-sc; L/G co-p) and *State Secret* (1950, L p; G d/p/sc), where their own subtle script-writing skills were constricted. *Captain Boycott* experienced production difficulties, *London Belongs to Me* was too complex a novel for a successful screen ADAPTATION, and *State Secret*, which had its own mythical language especially created for it, lacked the authenticity that gave conviction to *The Third Man*. They instinctively returned to comedy, although their two films featuring Peter SELLERS, *Two Way Stretch* (1960, L/G co-ex p) and *Only Two Can Play* (1961, S d; S/L co-p), rely over-heavily on the actor. Although they attempted broad COMEDY in their later works, their forté is more sophisticated, replete with character study. *I See a Dark Stranger* and *Green for Danger*, although completed after 1945, involve spying for the enemy and were deeply embedded in feelings about the war. In the former, a young Irish girl continually bungles her attempts to strike a blow for national independence by working for the Germans, and, in the end, finds romance with a British army officer who compromises his position by covering for her. The latter pokes fun at what Gilliat described as the British 'omniscient detective figure' and is, characteristically, full of fine detail.

As 30s screenwriters, they worked on many outstanding features, including *Rome Express* (1932, Gilliat only), *A Yank at Oxford* (1937, Gilliat co-story) and *The Lady Vanishes* (1938, G/L

sc). Their partnership as writer-directors began with the WW2 PROPAGANDA short, *Partners in Crime* (1942) and quickly led to *Millions Like Us* (1943), which GAINSBOROUGH took over from the MINISTRY OF INFORMATION and which was the only feature they co-directed. A simple propaganda idea about women conscripted into munitions manufacture becomes, in their hands, a pivotal film of WW2, where actuality footage can be seen in the background of the fictional story. At a time when other films are full of forced patriotism, the sequence which makes it immediately identifiable as a work of Launder and Gilliat is of the father 'abandoned' by a family engaged on war work and left to look after himself at home. His socks are full of holes, there are dirty dishes piled up in the sink, and the cat snatches the best part of his fish and chips. It remains an important, if imperfect, period piece, celebrating the collectivism of the period. Peace and change are cautiously anticipated but the factory foreman (Eric PORTMAN), who is courting a socialite (Anne CRAWFORD), finds it difficult to imagine a future in which class ceases to be the defining feature of British society and refuses to marry her until he sees the transformation with his own eyes.

Launder and Gilliat's masterpiece, *The Rake's Progress* was for their own company, INDIVIDUAL PICTURES and financed by J. Arthur RANK. A sweeping portrait of upper-class England from the end of WW1 to the middle of WW2, it can be compared to Powell and Pressburger's *The Life and Death of Colonel Blimp* (1943). It delicately lampoons the class-ridden attitudes and public school system which encourage an élite of playboys and scoundrels to survive on a combination of audacity and nepotism. The central character (Rex HARRISON), son of a Conservative MP, begins and ends his life as a profligate sybarite. He is sent down from Oxford, found idle employment among South America's coffee plantations, fritters away his fortune, takes up motor racing, extorts money by marrying a young Jewish refugee in Vienna immediately after the Anschluss in 1938, but falls into decline when he accidentally kills his father in a car. The war revives his cavalier spirit, but he is killed when he recklessly takes his armoured car over an almost certainly mined bridge. An army officer, on hearing his dying words were 'something about it being a good year', sees him as the kind of soldier who has helped turn the tide of war by sacrificing his life. In fact, he was commenting on the quality of the champagne, a bottle of which he was holding in his hand as he died.

Of the two, Gilliat is the stronger director, preferring to emphasise quiet comic eccentricity and dialogue more than technique. Launder's strength is in handling pace and farce and he has a greater sense of comic exaggeration. In the end, the films directed by Gilliat are more enduring, but together they formed a formidable combination, deeply steeped in the British tradition of self-mockery. Launder was married to actress Bernadette O'FARRELL, who appeared in several of his films.

OTHER BRITISH FILMS: **Launder:** (titles) *Cocktails* (1928); (add/dial) *The Compulsory Husband* (+ dubbing), *Harmony Heaven, The W Plan* (1930), (sc e) *Windbag the Sailor* (1936), *Good Morning, Boys!, O-Kay for Sound, Doctor Syn* (1937), *Owd Bob, Convict 99, Alf's Button Afloat, Hey! Hey! USA!, Old Bones of the River, Bank Holiday,* (1938), *The Frozen Limits* (1939); (story) *Oh, Mr Porter!* (1937), *Inspector Hornleigh Goes To It* (1940); (co-sc) *Song of Soho, The Middle Watch, Children of Chance* (1930), *Keepers of Youth* (1931), *Arms and the Man, For the Love of Mike, The Last Coupon* (1932), *Hawleys of High Street, A Southern Maid* (1933), *Those Were the Days* (1934), *Emil and the Detectives, So You Won't Talk?, Mr What's-His-Name, I Give My Heart, Get Off My Foot, The Black*

Mask (1935), *Where's Sally?*, *Educated Evans* (1936), *We Dive at Dawn* (1943); (sc) *How He Lied to Her Husband* (1931), *After Office Hours*, *You Made Me Love You, Happy* (1934), *Rolling Home* (1935), *A Girl Must Live* (1939), *Soldier, Sailor* (1944); (d) *Two Thousand Women* (1944, + sc); (comm) *The Lions Are Free* (1967).

Gilliat: (titles) *Toni, Champagne, Adam's Apple, Weekend Wives* (1928); (research) *The Manxman* (1928); (ass d) *Would You Believe It?* (1929, + add gags, titles, a), *Red Pearls* (1930, + sc contrib), *You'd Be Surprised!* (1930, + a, sd fx, w), *The Last Hour* (1930, + sd fx); (sc contrib) *Lord Richard in the Pantry, Bed and Breakfast* (1930), *Third Time Lucky, The Ringer, The Ghost Train* (1931), *Jack's the Boy, Lord Babs* (1932), *The Ghost Train* (1941); (story) *Falling for You, Friday the Thirteenth* (co-) (1933), *Jack Ahoy!* (1934, co-), *Up to His Neck* (1954, co-orig), *The Boys In Blue* (1983, orig); (co-sc) *The Happy Ending* (ucr), *A Gentleman of Paris* (1931), *Orders Is Orders* (1933), *Chu-Chin-Chow* (1934, + co-dial, add lyrics) *Bulldog Jack* (1935), *Twelve Good Men, Strangers on Honeymoon, King of the Damned, Seven Sinners* (1936), *Take My Tip* (1937), *Jamaica Inn* (+ dial), (1939), *Unpublished Story* (1942, unc); (sc) *A Night in Marseilles, Two Way Street* (1931) *Sign Please* (short), *Post Haste* (short), *Facing the Music* (+ co-story/scen) (1933), *My Heart is Calling* (1934), *The Gaunt Stranger* (1938), *The Girl in the News* (1940), *Mr Proudfoot Shows a Light* (short), *You're Telling Me* (short), *From the Four Corners* (short), *Kipps* (1941); (co-assoc p) *Tudor Rose, Where There's a Will* (+ co-story), *The Man Who Changed His Mind* (+ co-sc), *Everybody Dance* (1936); (p consultant) *The Wildcats of St Trinian's* (1980).

Launder and Gilliat: *Under the Greenwood Tree* (1929, L add dial/co-scen; G cost/lit adv), *Strange Boarders* (L sc, e; G co-sc), *Ask a Policeman* (L sc, e; G story), *Inspector Hornleigh on Holiday* (L/G sc) (1939), *They Came by Night* (L/G sc), *Night Train to Munich* (L/G sc), *Crooks' Tour* (L/G orig radio series) (1940), *The Young Mr Pitt* (L/G sc), *Uncensored* (L/G orig sc) (1942), *The Blue Lagoon* (1949, L d, p, co-sc; G p), *The Happiest Days of Your Life* (1950, L d, p, co-sc; G p) (1950), *Lady Godiva Rides Again* (1951, L d, p, co-sc; G p), *Folly to Be Wise* (1952, L d, p, co-sc; G p), *The Story of Gilbert and Sullivan* (1953, L p; G d, p, co-sc), *The Belles of St Trinian's* (L d, p, co-sc; G p, co-sc), *The Constant Husband* (L p; G d, p, co-sc), *Geordie* (1955, L d, p, sc; G p, sc), *The Green Man* (1956, L/G co-p, co-sc, co-play), *Fortune Is a Woman* (L p, sc; G d, p, sc), *The Smallest Show on Earth* (L/G co-p), *Blue Murder at St Trinian's* (L d, p, co-sc; G p, co-sc) (1957), *The Bridal Path* (L d, p, co-sc; G p), *Left, Right and Centre* (L p; G d, p, sc, co-story) (1959), *The Pure Hell of St Trinian's* (1960, L d, p, co-sc; G p, co-sc), *Ring of Spies* (1963, L co-sc; G p), *Joey Boy* (1965, L d, co-sc), *The Great St Trinian's Train Robbery* (1966, L d, co-sc, co-story; G d, ex p, co-story), *Endless Night* (L ex p; G d, sc), *Ooh . . . You Are Awful* (L/G co-ex p) (1972).

BIBLIOG: Geoff Brown, *Launder and Gilliat*, 1977; Bruce Babington, *Launder and Gilliat*, 2002. Kevin Gough-Yates.

Laurence, Michael (*b* Dublin, 1918). Actor. RN: Michael Clarke. Husky Irish actor, whose desert-island advances the shipwrecked Anna NEAGLE resisted in *Piccadilly Incident* (1946) only to find herself married to him in the once-controversial 'flapper' episode of *Elizabeth of Ladymead* (1948). Frank LAUNDER saw him on the Dublin stage and brought him to England for a film test, but his career was short-lived, even with John GLIDDON as agent. He played Cassio in Orson WELLES's *Othello* (1951, Morocco) and appeared in the 1977 documentary on the film's making.

OTHER BRITISH FILMS: *Carnival* (1946), *For Them That Trespass* (1948), *Return to Glennascaul* (1951, Ire).

Laurenson, James (*b* New Zealand, 1935). Actor. Craggy, LAMDA-trained actor busier on stage and TV than on screen, where he was first seen as the post-WW1 preacher in *Women in Love* (1969). Made his strongest impression on TV as the Aboriginal detective *Boney* (1972, Aust), played in blackface make-up, and as the seducer of *Esther Waters* (1977). In 2000, he had a stage success in the revival of Peter NICHOLS's *Passion Play*.

OTHER BRITISH FILMS INCLUDE: *The Magic Christian, Assault* (1970), *The Monster Club* (1980), *Pink Floyd The Wall* (1982), *The Cat's Meow* (2002, UK/Can/Ger).

Laurie, Hugh (*b* Oxford, 1959). Actor. Tall, drily droll, Eton-educated Laurie, took to acting at Cambridge, becoming President of the Footlights Club (as well as rowing star). Became a household name and face (well, in certain kinds of household) for such TV work as the various *Blackadder* series of the 80s and for *A Bit of Fry and Laurie* (1989). His first film role, apart from a 'turn' in *The Secret Policeman's Third Ball* (1987), was in David HARE's *Strapless* (1988); he was one of *Peter's Friends* (1992), with Cambridge chums Emma THOMPSON and Stephen FRY; did a superb Mr Palmer in *Sense and Sensibility* (1995, UK/US), speechless at the inanity of wife Imelda STAUNTON; was defeated by the radically wit-free *Maybe Baby* (2000, UK/Fr); and had a go at Hollywood stardom with the mildly engaging *Stuart Little* (2000), though in danger of being upstaged by a mouse. His cerebral zaniness may belong more to the revue sketch than the conventional narrative film.

OTHER BRITISH FILMS INCLUDE: *The Borrowers, Spice World* (1997), *The Man in the Iron Mask, Cousin Bette* (1998, UK/US), *Girl from Rio* (2001, UK/Sp).

Laurie, John (Dumfries, 1897 – *d* Chalfont St Peter, 1980). Actor. Hugely prolific Scots character player, Central School-trained, on stage 1921 after WW1 service, and in films since 1930's *Juno and the Paycock*, having first trained as an architect. Gaunt-faced and intense, he came to attention in his third film, HITCHCOCK's *The 39 Steps* (1935), as the jealous crofter, and was memorable again and again, in three 1944 films: *The Way Ahead*, as the farmer recruit; *Fanny by Gaslight*, as propietor of 'The Shades' brothel; and as Captain Jamie in *Henry V*. He was in all three of OLIVIER's SHAKESPEARE films, not surprising for someone who spent so much time playing the Bard at Stratford, the Old Vic and the Open Air, Regent's Park. There was also a great deal of TV, most popularly as Fraser in *Dad's Army* (1968–77; also in the film version, 1971), and he finally appeared looking sprightly but (as you might after such a career) frail in *Return to the Edge of the World* (1978), as one of the surviving participants of Michael POWELL's 1937 romantic melodrama, *The Edge of the World*. Did such actors ever have a holiday?

OTHER BRITISH FILMS INCLUDE: *Red Ensign* (1934), *Her Last Affaire* (1935), *Tudor Rose, As You Like It* (1936), *Jericho* (1937), *The Ware Case* (1938), *Q Planes, The Four Feathers* (1939), *Sailors Three* (1940), *Dangerous Moonlight, Old Mother Riley's Ghosts* (1941), *The Life and Death of Colonel Blimp, The Lamp Still Burns, The Gentle Sex, The Demi-Paradise, The New Lot* (short) (1943), *Medal for the General* (1944), *The Agitator, I Know Where I'm Going!, Great Day* (1945), *School for Secrets* (1946), *The Brothers, Uncle Silas, Jassy* (1947), *Hamlet, Bonnie Prince Charlie* (1948), *Madeleine* (1949), *Trio* (1950), *Laughter in Paradise, Encore* (1951), *Tread Softly* (1952), *Hobson's Choice* (1953), *Richard III* (1955), *Campbell's Kingdom* (1957), *Rockets Galore* (1958), *Kidnapped* (1960), *The Siege of the Saxons* (1963), *Mister Ten Per Cent* (1967), *The Abominable Dr Phibes* (1971).

Laverick, June (*b* Redcar, 1931) Actress, dancer. At her peak (1959–60), she was starring in three films, a West End musical, *When in Rome*, and a popular TV sitcom *The Dickie Henderson Show* (1960–65, 1968, 1971). A trained dancer, she had appeared at Covent Garden (1950) and in the chorus of the musical *Gay's the Word* (1951). Selected by RANK for her perfect English looks, cast as the pretty English girl in *It Happened in Rome* (1956, It), she had two more Rank starring roles: in Joseph LOSEY's *The*

Gypsy and the Gentleman (1957), and *Follow a Star* (1959), with Norman WISDOM. Adept at portraying Princesses (*The Duke Wore Jeans*, 1958) and fair ladies (*Son of Robin Hood*, 1958), she never had opportunity to do more.

OTHER BRITISH FILMS: *The Flesh and the Fiends* (1959). Roger Philip Mellor.

Lavi, Daliah (*b* Haifa, 1940). Actress. RN: Levenbuch. Elegant, olive-complexioned brunette Israeli actress who adorned international films in the 60s. A former dancer, she appeared in eight British films, most notably as the girl in *Lord Jim* (1964).

OTHER BRITISH FILMS INCLUDE: *Ten Little Indians* (1965), *The Spy with a Cold Nose* (1966), *Nobody Runs Forever* (1968), *Some Girls Do* (1969), *Catlow* (1971, UK/US-set).

Law, Jude (*b* London, 1972). Actor. Handsome actor who came to international fame as the murdered golden boy in *The Talented Mr Ripley* (1999, US), winning a BAA and AAn, among other nominations and awards. And deservedly so for a highly intelligent performance. He has not merely traded on his good looks, but has done some daring roles, including the petulant Bosie in *Wilde* (1997, UK/Ger/Jap/US), Kevin SPACEY's dangerous lover in *Midnight in the Garden of Good and Evil* (1997) and the Russian country-boy soldier in *Enemy at the Gates* (2001, UK/Ger/Ire/US). There were ill-advised choices like *Love, Honour and Obey* (2000), but there is a sense of someone determined to make his own career; having made about 15 films since his first – *Shopping* (1994), on which he met his wife, Sadie FROST – it seems he is more than usually adept at this, and is in demand in the US as well as the UK. Spielberg starred him in *AI* and Sam MENDES in *The Road to Perdition* (2002, US). The son of South London teachers, he joined the National Youth Theatre at 13, had a small part in the TV soap, *Families* (1990), and won a Tony nomination for the role he played (London and Broadway) in *Les Parents Terribles*. He and Frost and actor friends founded the production company NATURAL NYLON, with Law as SHAKESPEARE in *Marlowe* (2003).

OTHER BRITISH FILMS INCLUDE: *I Love You, I Love You Not* (1996, UK/Fr/Ger/US), *Bent* (1997, UK/Jap/US), *Final Cut*, *The Wisdom of Crocodiles* (1998), *eXistenZ* (1999, UK/Can/Fr).

Law, Phyllida (*b* Glasgow, 1932). Actress. Sharp-featured, often acerbic character player who had some noticeable roles in the 90s: especially the dryly spoken housekeeper to *Peter's Friends* (1992), who included real-life daughter Emma THOMPSON; Emma's harpie mother in the gloomy Scots-set *The Winter Guest* (1998, UK/US); deaf, benignly uncomprehending Mrs Bates in *Emma* (1996, UK/US), mother to her other daughter Sophie THOMPSON; and village busybody in *Saving Grace* (2000). Also, long stage and TV career. Was married to actor Eric Thompson until his death (1982).

OTHER BRITISH FILMS INCLUDE: *Otley* (1968), *Tree of Hands* (1988), *Much Ado About Nothing* (1993, UK/US), *I Want You* (1998), *Mad Cows* (1999, UK/Fr/It).

Lawford, Peter (*b* London, 1923 – *d* Los Angeles, 1984). Actor. It seems amazing that one so modestly gifted should have hung on so long and made so many films. More famous as a member of Frank Sinatra's tedious 'Rat Pack' and as President Kennedy's brother-in-law (m.Patricia Kennedy 1954–66, 1 of 4; their son, Christopher Lawford is an actor) than as actor, he made two British films as a child, played dozens of debonair types in Hollywood, usually Brits (as in *The White Cliffs of Dover*, 1944), sometimes not, as in the charming musical *Good*

News (1947). Made only four more British films, of which only *The Hour of 13* (1952) is of the slightest interest.

OTHER BRITISH FILMS: *Salt & Pepper* (1968), *One More Time* (1969), *Where Is Parsifal?* (1983).

BIBLIOG: James Spada, *Peter Lawford*, 1991.

Lawrence, D.H. (*b* Eastwood, Nottinghamshire, 1885 – *d* Vence, France, 1930). Author. Despite the daunting problems his novels would seem to offer adapters, notably their pre-occupation with articulating inner states, several excellent films have eventuated, British and otherwise, and some for TV. Ken RUSSELL's *Women in Love* (1969) is some kind of masterpiece, audacious not so much for two nude men wrestling as for its prolonged discussions of ideas; the 1949 version of *The Rocking Horse Winner* is a tough, unsettling film; *Sons and Lovers* (1960) does decently by Lawrence's quasi-autobiography; and *The Virgin and the Gypsy* (1970) assembles the novella's oppositions with sensuous percipience. Other Lawrence-derived films include *The Fox* (1968, US) and *Kangaroo* (1986, Aust), and Ian McKELLEN made a convincing stab at playing Lawrence in *Priest of Love* (1980).

OTHER BRITISH FILMS: (adpt from Lawrence) *The Trespasser* (short), *Lady Chatterley's Lover* (UK/Fr) (1981), *The Rocking Horse Winner* (1982, short), *Samson and Delilah* (1984, short), *The Rainbow* (1989), *Lady Chatterley* (1992, TV, some cinemas).

Lawrence, Delphi (*b* Herefordshire, 1932). Actress. Slinky lead, often untrustworthy, of many a 'B' MOVIE of the 50s (*Blood Orange*, 1953; *The Gold Express*, 1958), with a RANK contract. RADA-trained with rep experience, she had supporting roles in upmarket enterprises like *Bunny Lake Is Missing* (1965) and small bits in several US films, including *Cops and Robbers* (1973).

OTHER BRITISH FILMS INCLUDE: *Meet Mr Callaghan* (1954), *Barbados Quest* (1955), *The Feminine Touch*, *It's Never Too Late* (1956), *Just My Luck* (1957), *Too Many Crooks* (1959), *Cone of Silence* (1960), *On the Run* (1963),.

Lawrence, Gerald (*b* London, 1873 – *d* London, 1957). Actor, director. A Shakespearean stage actor – debut 1893 – who acted in and directed the occasional silent film, playing the title role in *David Garrick* (1912).

OTHER BRITISH FILMS INCLUDE: (a, unless noted) *Henry VIII* (1911), *A Widow's Son* (+ d, sc), *Enoch Arden* (sc), *His Just Deserts* (d, sc) (1914), *The Romany Rye* (1915), *The Grand Babylon Hotel* (1916), *Carrots* (1917), *An Affair of Honour* (1922), *The Iron Duke* (1935). AS.

Lawrence, Gertrude (*b* London, 1898 – *d* New York, 1952). Actress. RN: Alexandra Dagmar Lawrence-Klasan. Luminous and adored stage star (debut 1908) whom the screen simply refused to love. On stage she starred in drama, comedy and musicals (was in *The King and I* at the time of her death); on screen she played in several forgettable 30s comedies, was touching as housekeeper Geertje in *Rembrandt* and flamboyant in *Men Are Not Gods* (1936), and a coruscating Amanda in *The Glass Menagerie* (1950, US), then she was untimely dead. Hollywood filmed her autobiography, *Star!* (1968), with Julie ANDREWS.

OTHER BRITISH FILMS: *Aren't We All?*, *Lord Camber's Ladies* (1932), *No Funny Business* (1933), *Mimi* (1935).

Lawrence, Josie (*b* Old Hill, 1959). Actress. Tall comedienne who has done a lot of TV, including her own show, *Josie* (1991), and the comedy series, *Outside Edge* (1994). On film, she was touching as well as comic in *Enchanted April* (1992), as the sad-faced, put-upon wife of Alfred MOLINA, but film has occupied her little. In 2001, she scored a London stage success in *The King and I.*

OTHER BRITISH FILMS: *Riders of the Storm* (1986, UK/US), *Married 2 Malcolm* (1998).

Lawrence, Patricia (*b* Andover, 1925 – *d* London, 1993). Actress. Demure-looking character player much on TV, as in *Tenko* (1981–82, 1984) and sporadically on screen, in small parts like one of the wedding guests in *Howards End* (1992).

OTHER BRITISH FILMS INCLUDE: *Blue Murder at St Trinian's* (1957), *The Hireling, O Lucky Man!* (1973), *A Room with a View* (1985).

Lawrence, Quentin (*b* Gravesend, 1920 – *d* Halifax, 1979). Director. Apart from making what may be the best British 'B' MOVIE, *Cash on Demand* (1961), Lawrence is better known for his TV work (episodes of *The Avengers*, 1961; *Danger Man*, 1964; and *The Baron*, 1966) than for his obdurately uninspired remaining features. *The Trollenberg Terror* (1958) has its frissons, but *The Man Who Finally Died* (1962) is lumbering and *The Secret of Blood Island* (1964) is idiotic.

OTHER BRITISH FILMS: *Playback* (1962), *We Shall See* (1964).

Lawrence, Stephanie (*b* Hayling Island, 1949 – *d* London, 2000). Actress. Musical comedy star, famous for impersonations of Dietrich and others, as well as the hit musical, *Blood Brothers* (1989–93), for which she won a Tony nomination. Very rare films include *Buster* (1988) as Franny Reynolds.

OTHER BRITISH FILMS: *O Lucky Man!* (1973), *The Likely Lads* (1976).

Lawrence, T(homas) E(dward) (*b* Tremadoc, Wales, 1888 – *d* Clouds Hill, 1935). Writer. There was talk of BIOPICS about the life of the legendary Lawrence from the 30s when Alexander KORDA bought the rights to Lawrence's abridged biography, *Revolt in the Desert* (1927), at various times announcing Leslie HOWARD, Robert DONAT, Walter HUDD, John CLEMENTS and Laurence OLIVIER for the title role. With WW2 imminent, the project was shelved. In the late 50s, Anthony ASQUITH and Terence RATTIGAN worked on an aborted story about the fabled adventurer with Dirk BOGARDE to play the lead. When RANK vetoed this venture, the screenplay went on to become a play, *Ross* (1960), and David LEAN made *Lawrence of Arabia* (1962), starring ascetic-looking hell-raiser Peter O'TOOLE, when Marlon Brando proved unavailable and Albert FINNEY unwilling. The rest is history. Lawrence himself appeared in Lowell Thomas's *With Allenby in Palestine and Lawrence in Arabia* (1919, US), and he has been played in TV movies by Ralph FIENNES in *Dangerous Man: Lawrence of Arabia* (1990) and Douglas HENSHALL in *Adventures of Young Indiana Jones: The Daredevils of the Desert* (1999).

Lawson, Arthur (*b* Sunderland, 1908). Production designer. Worked as engineer before entering the industry in 1932. During the 30s and 40s he worked in the art departments of LIME GROVE, EALING, PINEWOOD and other studios, and was assistant art director to Alfred JUNGE on several POWELL AND PRESSBURGER films. Shared an Oscar with Hein HECKROTH for the vividly imaginative design of *The Red Shoes* (1948) and was nominated again for *The Bedford Incident* (1965), but the Powell films were his creative highspot.

OTHER BRITISH FILMS: (ass/assoc art d) *The Life and Death of Colonel Blimp* (1943), *The Way Ahead* (1944), *A Matter of Life and Death* (1946), *Oh, Rosalinda!!* (1955); (art d) *Black Narcissus* (1947), *The Elusive Pimpernel, Gone to Earth* (1950), *The Tales of Hoffmann* (1951), *Folly to Be Wise* (1952), *Twice Upon a Time* (1953), *Sea Wife* (1956), *Harry Black*

(1958), *Peeping Tom* (1960), *HMS Defiant* (1962), *The Leather Boys* (1963, des), *Lost Continent* (1968).

Lawson, Dennis (aka Denis) (*b* Perthshire, 1947). Actor. Stage star of such successes as *Pal Joey* (1980) and *Mr Cinders* (1982–83), Lawson has filmed only occasionally, most noticeably as Wedge in *Star Wars* (1977), *The Empire Strikes Back* (1980) and *Return of the Jedi* (1983), and as Urquhart, village landlord and rabbit-stewer in *Local Hero* (1983). Uncle of Ewan McGREGOR.

OTHER BRITISH FILMS INCLUDE: *Dinosaur* (1975), *The Chain* (1984).

Lawson, Leigh (*b* Atherstone, 1943). Actor. Heavy-featured actor of stage (ambivalent and unsettling in *Old Times*, 1995), TV (*Love Among the Ruins*, 1975; *Disraeli*, 1978) and screen. He played the penis-transplant hero of *Percy's Progress* (1974) and the sensual seducer of *Tess* (1979) – one expects him to twirl a moustache – but in recent decades most often on the small screen. Had a long relationship with Hayley MILLS; married to actress-model TWIGGY.

OTHER BRITISH FILMS INCLUDE: *Brother Sun, Sister Moon* (1972), *Ghost Story* (1974), *Madame Sousatzka* (1988), *Out of Depth* (1999).

Lawson, Sarah (*b* London, 1928). Actress. Pleasant, intractably wholesome, leading lady of the 50s and 60s, who began in main features like *You Know What Sailors Are* (1954), as Donald SINDEN's romantic interest, but declined into such unexceptional 'B' MOVIES as *Links of Justice* (1958), going upmarket again with *The Devil Rides Out* (1967) and *Battle of Britain* (1969), but in minor roles. Some rep experience, having formed her own company for a season at Felixstowe; also, played the Governor in the final series of *Within These Walls* (1978). Married to Patrick ALLEN.

OTHER BRITISH FILMS INCLUDE: *The Browning Version* (1951), *Street Corner* (1953), *The Blue Peter* (1955), *It's Never Too Late* (1956), *On the Run* (1963), *The Stud* (1978).

Lawson, Tony (*b* London, 1944). Editor. Educated at King Alfred's School, London, and trained on the job, first working on DOCUMENTARIES for four years before moving into features as assistant editor on such films as *The Prime of Miss Jean Brodie* (1969). After assisting on *Don't Look Now* (1973, UK/It) he became Nicolas ROEG's regular editor, contributing notably to their mosaic approach to narrative.

OTHER BRITISH FILMS INCLUDE: *Straw Dogs* (1971), *Barry Lyndon* (1975), *Bad Timing* (1980), *Eureka* (1982, UK/US), *The Bounty, Castaway* (1986), *Aria* (1987), *Track 29* (1988), *Tom & Viv* (1994, UK/US), *Victory* (UK/Fr/Ger) (1995, released 1998), *The Butcher Boy* (1997, Ire/US), *The End of the Affair* (2000, UK/Ger/US), *Blow Dry* (2001, UK/Ger/US).

Lawson, Wilfrid (*b* Bradford, Yorks, 1900 – *d* London, 1966). Actor. RN: Worsnop. Strongly-built, good-looking actor, noted for his natural performance style, who, even as a young man, played older character parts. Excellent as Alfred Doolittle in *Pygmalion* (1938), which he played on stage as early as 1927, and as the haunting *Pastor Hall* (1940), he went on to play authoritative character roles in British films until the late 60s, including good-natured Chunks in *Fanny by Gaslight* (1944). His American career began with *Ladies in Love* (1936) and included *The Long Voyage Home* (1940), but alcohol problems and abrasive manner hurt his career and may have been responsible for his losing major parts. Stage debut 1916, with his best role as the father in 1935 revival of *The Barretts of Wimpole Street*, in which he toured UK in 1947.

OTHER BRITISH FILMS INCLUDE: *East Lynne on the Western Front* (1931), *Turn of the Tide* (1935) *Bank Holiday, The Gaunt Stranger* (1938),

Stolen Life (1939), *Jeannie, The Tower of Terror* (1941), *The Night Has Eyes, The Great Mr Handel* (1942), *The Turners of Prospect Road* (1947), *The Prisoner* (1955), *Hell Drivers, The Naked Truth* (1957), *Room at the Top* (1958), *Expresso Bongo* (1959), *The Naked Edge* (1961, UK/US), *Tom Jones* (1963), *The Wrong Box, The Viking Queen* (1966). AS.

Lawton, Frank (*b* London, 1904 – *d* London, 1969). Actor. Dapper leading man of 30s films, in UK, from *Young Woodley* (1930, repeating his stage success), and the US, notably in *Cavalcade* (1933) and as the adult *David Copperfield* (1935). After war service (1939–45), played character roles in such British films as *The Winslow Boy* (1948), as Kate's spineless suitor, and *A Night to Remember* (1958), as the White Star Line's Managing Director. On stage from 1923, he had his main career there, but also ran up an interesting film role-call, usually of upper-middle-class types. Married to Evelyn LAYE from 1934.
OTHER BRITISH FILMS: *Birds of Prey* (1930), *The Skin Game, The Outsider* (1931), *Friday the Thirteenth* (1933), *The Mill on the Floss* (1937), *The Four Just Men* (1939), *Went the Day Well?* (1942), *Rough Shoot* (1953), *Doublecross* (1955), *Gideon's Day* (1958), *The Queen's Guards* (1961).

Laye, Dilys (*b* London, 1934). Actress. RN: Lay. Trained at the Aida FOSTER School and on stage from 1948, when she also made her film debut playing Jean KENT as a child in *Trottie True*. The rest of her film career was spent chiefly in comedy, including four in the 'CARRY ON' SERIES, while appearing steadily on stage and TV (e.g. *The Bed-Sit Girl*, 1965, and a stint in *Coronation Street*, 2000).
OTHER BRITISH FILMS INCLUDE: *The Belles of St Trinian's* (1954), *Doctor at Large* (1957), *Please Turn Over* (1960), *Carry On Cruising, On the Beat* (1962), *Carry On Spying* (1964), . . . *Doctor* (1968), . . . *Camping* (1969), *Voices* (1995).

Laye, Evelyn (*b* London, 1900 – *d* London, 1996). Actress. Golden-haired soprano with a fragile complexion, who was a major musical comedy star – debut 1915 – at her best on screen in *Evensong* (1934), as an opera singer modelled after Nellie Melba. Her career declined in the 40s but she made a comeback on stage with *Wedding in Paris* (1954) and *The Amorous Prawn* (1959). Never a major film star, she had two Hollywood films, *One Heavenly Night* (1931) and *The Night Is Young* (1934), and two British character roles in the 60s. Married Sonnie HALE (acrimoniously dissolved 1926) and Frank LAWTON (1934).
OTHER BRITISH FILMS INCLUDE: *The Luck of the Navy* (1927), *Waltz Time* (1933), *Princess Charming* (1934), *Make Mine a Million* (1959), *Theatre of Death* (1966), *Say Hello to Yesterday* (1970).
BIBLIOG: Autobiography, *Boo to My Friends*, 1958. AS.

Leach, Rosemary (*b* Much Wenlock, Shropshire, 1935). Actress. Twice BAA-nominated for strong supporting roles, as David ESSEX's shopkeeping mother in *That'll Be the Day* (1973) and as Helena BONHAM CARTER's dim upper-class mum in *A Room with a View* (1985), Leach even managed to be affecting as a deserted wife in the wretched *Brief Encounter* (1974) REMAKE. On stage from 1961, she has also done much quality TV, including the lead in *Cider with Rosie* (1970) and *The Jewel in the Crown* (1984).
OTHER BRITISH FILMS INCLUDE: *Face of a Stranger* (1964), *Turtle Diary* (1985), *The Mystery of Edwin Drood* (1993), *Whatever Happened to Harold Smith?, Breathtaking* (2000).

Leacock, Philip (*b* London, 1917 – *d* London, 1990). Director. Bedales-educated Leacock began working in DOCUMENTARIES in 1935, and went to Spain in 1938 to work with Thorold DICKINSON on the Civil War films, *Spanish ABC* (ass d) and *Behind Spanish Lines* (ass e). During WW2 he was involved with the ARMY FILM UNIT and acted as adviser on army procedures on Carol REED's *The Way Ahead* (1944); post-war, he joined the CROWN FILM UNIT. Apart from some location shooting in Cornwall for *Mr Perrin and Mr Traill* (1948), his work at this time was essentially in documentary. In the early 50s, he made three modest features which bridged the gap between documentary and fiction: *Out of True*, about treatment of mental patients, and *Life in Her Hands*, about nursing (1951), and the moving COALMINING disaster film, *The Brave Don't Cry* (1952). He showed a capacity to combine narrative rhythms with a realistically observed mise-en-scène, which stood him in good stead for the rest of his British career.

In 1953, he directed the charming fable, *The Kidnappers*, convincingly set in Nova Scotia, PINEWOOD, establishing a reputation for sensitive handling of CHILD ACTORS which would be useful in subsequent films: *Escapade* (1955), about schoolboys and a peace petition; *The Spanish Gardener* (1956) reuniting him with *Kidnappers* boy, Jon WHITELEY, *Innocent Sinners* (1958), in which children try to cultivate a bomb-site garden in London; and *Hand in Hand* (1960), about the barrier-breaking friendship between Jewish and Catholic children. He first went to America in 1955, but his US output, largely of episodes in TV series, represents a sad decline in a liberal, imaginative talent. Only his first two features – *Take a Giant Step* and *The Rabbit Trap* (1959) – recall his best British work. He was the brother of documentarist Richard Leacock, who worked wholly on American films.
OTHER BRITISH FILMS INCLUDE: (short/doc) *Kew Gardens* (1937), *The Londoners* (1939, ass d), *The Story of Wool* (1940), *Deadly Lampshade* (1948), *Festival in London* (1951); (features) *Riders of the New Forest* (1946), *Appointment in London* (1953), *High Tide at Noon* (1957), *Reach for Glory* (1961), *The War Lover, Tamahine* (1962), *Baffled!* (1972, + p).

Lean, Sir David (*b* Croydon, 1908 – *d* London, 1991). Director. The son of Quaker parents, David Lean was expected to avoid the cinema. When, one afternoon, he slipped in to *The Hound of the Baskervilles* (1921), it had an incredible impact on the 13-year-old schoolboy. From that moment, he was lost to the ordinary world. His father announced he was sending his academically brilliant younger brother, Edward, to Oxford, 'but frankly, David, you're not worth it.'

He was so miserable working in his father's office that he was allowed to go into the film business in 1927, and, remarkably, he joined the director of *The Hound of the Baskervilles*, Maurice ELVEY, on *Quinneys* (1927). By 1930 he was cutting *Gaumont Sound News*, and felt at home in a studio. He came to recognise the perils of 'QUOTA QUICKIES' and while he was happy to edit them, he refused to direct them, waiting for something worthwhile. Meanwhile, he watched closely what directors did on the floor, editing his pictures by night. He became the best editor in the country – he cut *Pygmalion* (1938) and *49th Parallel* (1941) – and when Noël COWARD was looking for a technician to help him make *In Which We Serve* (1942), he was advised to take Lean.

Coward was so impressed with his protégé that he left him to do more and more of the directing. Lean joined producer Anthony HAVELOCK-ALLAN and cameraman Ronald NEAME in CINEGUILD PRODUCTIONS to undertake further Coward productions. *This Happy Breed* (1944), the story of a suburban family between the wars, was one of the top-box office attractions in wartime Britain. Coward felt that Lean did less than justice to his favourite play, *Blithe Spirit* (1945), and critics decided that Lean had no sense of humour, but a few years later he made a first-class version of *Hobson's Choice*. In 1945, Lean directed (AAn/d) *Brief Encounter*; based on a Coward one-act play and starring Celia JOHNSON and Trevor HOWARD. After a disastrous preview, at which the audience screamed with laughter, the film became a classic.

Lean's two DICKENS ADAPTATIONS are still regarded as among the finest of all British films. *Great Expectations* (1946, AAn/d) has a shock opening in a lonely graveyard, when Pip encounters the convict, and the stylisation suited the outsize characters and incidents. Lean's second wife, Kay WALSH, cracked the impossible opening to *Oliver Twist* (1948) with a wild storm, and a pregnant girl staggering to the workhouse. In these Dickens films Lean never puts a foot wrong; whereas his next two films, *The Passionate Friends* (1948) and *Madeleine* (1949), were regarded as handsome but cold tributes to his third wife, Ann TODD.

Lean's enthusiasm for scientific progress shone through *The Sound Barrier* (1952, BAA/film), about the first pilot to fly faster than sound. He progressed from modest British pictures to international epics via *Summer Madness* (1955, UK/US, AAn/d), a romance with Katharine HEPBURN, given scale by its location shooting in Venice. During production he was sent by Sam SPIEGEL a novel by Pierre Boule, *The Bridge on the River Kwai* (1957, UK). Spiegel had offered the Carl FOREMAN script to a number of bankable directors who turned it down. Lean felt like doing so, too, but he was undergoing a divorce and was nearly broke. He battled over the script with several writers, battled over the production with Spiegel and battled with the actors – and emerged with a film which won several Academy Awards (including Best Director and Film). Spiegel rewarded him with *Lawrence of Arabia* (1962, BAA/film, AA/film/d and others), which fulfilled his passion for the ancient world, British eccentricity, and – particularly – the desert. He was heartbroken when Spiegel pulled him out of the desert and forced him to finish the film in Spain. Nevertheless, he produced a masterpiece, revived to astonishing acclaim in the 80s.

He followed *Lawrence* with another epic, *Dr Zhivago* (1965, UK/US, AAn/d/film), which the critics did not like but the public adored. Lean startled the film world by giving the role of Zhivago to his Egyptian discovery from *Lawrence*, Omar SHARIF. The film made staggering sums of money. In 1970, he made *Ryan's Daughter*, such an old-fashioned picture that the critics devoured it – and Lean. He liked to say he gave up making films for 14 years; in fact, he settled in the South Pacific, trying to make a version of *Mutiny on the Bounty*, but his ideas were too ambitious for his backers. He returned to England, and was given *A Passage to India* (1984, AAn/d/film) by producers Richard GOODWIN and Lord BRABOURNE and this time the critics hailed his return. He was so encouraged that he embarked on a film of Joseph Conrad's *Nostromo*, but he died just before shooting was due to start.

OTHER BRITISH FILMS INCLUDE: (e) *The Night Porter* (1930), *These Charming People* (1931), *Insult* (1932), *Money for Speed*, *Matinee Idol*, *Song of the Plough*, *The Ghost Camera*, *Tiger Bay*, *The Fortunate Fool* (1933), *Dangerous Ground*, *The Secret of the Loch*, *Java Head* (co-e) (1934), *Escape Me Never*, *The Crouching Beast*, *Turn of the Tide* (1935), *Ball at Savoy*, *As You Like It* (1936), *Dreaming Lips*, *The Wife of General Ling*, *The Last Adventurers* (1937), *Spies of the Air*, *French Without Tears* (1939), *Spy for a Day* (1940), *Major Barbara* (1941, super e, ass d), *One of Our Aircraft Is Missing* (1942).

BIBLIOG: Kevin Brownlow, *David Lean*, 1996; Adrian Turner, *Robert Bolt*, 1998. Kevin Brownlow.

Leavesden Studio This complex, located on the site of a Hertfordshire aerodrome formerly owned by Rolls-Royce and set in 280 acres but within easy reach of London, was built in 1994. The first film produced there was *GoldenEye* and thereafter it was used for such lavish productions as *Mortal Kombat 2* (1997) and the *Star Wars* prequel, *The Phantom Menace* (1998), American producers finding attractive reasons for filming in Britain. Other films made at least partly here were *An Ideal Husband* (1999, UK/US) and *Onegin* (1999, UK/US), and the producers of *Harry Potter and the Philosopher's Stone* (2001, UK/US) leased the entire studios for much of 2000–01.

BIBLIOG: Patricia Warren, *British Film Studios*, 2001.

Le Breton, Flora (*b* Croydon, 1898 – *d* ?). Actress. A petite and charming leading lady of the 20s, at her best in J. Stuart BLACKTON's *The Glorious Adventure* (1922, UK/US) and *A Gipsy Cavalier* (1922). Made her US stage debut in *Lass o' Laughter* (1924); but her six Hollywood features between 1924 and 1930, the best of which is *Charley's Aunt* (1930), did nothing for her.

OTHER BRITISH FILMS INCLUDE: *La Poupée* (1920), *The Crimson Circle* (1922), *I Will Repay* (1923), *Tons of Money* (1924), *The Rolling Road* (1927). AS.

Lee, Anna (*b* Ightham, 1913). Actress. RN: Joanna Winnifrith. Daughter of the vicarage, trained at Royal Albert Hall, this sweet-faced, spirited blonde made over 20 British films in the 30s. Some were 'QUOTA QUICKIES' but she made the most of the real chances that came her way: she contrasts nicely with Jessie MATTHEWS in *First A Girl* (1935), handles gamely the intrepid heroines of *King Solomon's Mines* (1937) and *Non-Stop New York* (1937), both directed by first husband (1933–44) Robert STEVENSON, as were her last two films prior to accompanying Stevenson to Hollywood. These show her at her best: as the circus performer who marries an aristocrat in *Young Man's Fancy* (1939) and the aspiring provincial actress in *Return to Yesterday* (1940). She was charming and characterful in these films, as she was, without being a major star, in the 30-odd films she made in Hollywood, including those she made for John FORD, and she became a TV favourite in the long-running soap, *General Hospital* (from 1978). Her children, Venetia Stevenson and Jeffrey Byron, are both actors. Her third husband (1970 till 1985, his death) was playwright Robert Nathan.

OTHER BRITISH FILMS INCLUDE: *Ebb Tide* (1932), *Mayfair Girl* (1933), *The Camels are Coming* (1934), *Heat Wave* (1935), *The Man Who Changed His Mind* (1936), *OHMS* (1937), *The Four Just Men* (1939), *Gideon's Day* (1958).

Lee, Belinda (*b* Budleigh Salterton, 1935 – *d* San Bernardino, California, 1961) Actress. After RADA, Nottingham Playhouse and several small film roles, Lee secured a RANK contract from 1955, assisted by magazine promotions from studio photographer husband (1954–59), Cornell LUCAS. She revealed a gift for comedy in *Who Done It?* (1956) with Benny HILL, and her quiet beauty suited such low-key roles as Julia in *Miracle in Soho* (1957). In 1957, a publicity stunt at Cannes brought offers to appear in Italy as femmes fatales in sword-and-sandal epics, followed by other European films. There was a scandal – an affair with a Prince who was a Vatican dignitary – which led to a dual suicide attempt in 1958, followed by divorce action by Lucas. Died in a car accident in 1961.

OTHER BRITISH FILMS INCLUDE: *The Runaway Bus* (1953), *Footsteps in the Fog*, *Man of the Moment* (1955), *The Feminine Touch*, *Eyewitness* (1956), *The Secret Place*, *Dangerous Exile* (1957), *Nor the Moon by Night* (1958). Roger Philip Mellor.

Lee, Bernard (*b* London, 1908 – *d* London, 1981). Actor. Stalwart character player for nearly 50 years, RADA-trained, on stage in 1914 in a sketch with his actor father, and as adult from 1926, touring as Stanhope in *Journey's End* in 1930. After a few films in the 30s, when he was constantly busy on stage, he was in the Army (1940–46) and post-war hit his stride as a film actor. He played innumerable Inspectors (Cherry in *The Blue Lamp*, 1949), Superintendents (regularly in the Edgar WALLACE mysteries of the early 60s), Brigadiers, Colonels and the like, his fame coming to rest as 'M' in the first eleven BOND movies. For some, though, the lasting image of Lee is as Sergeant Paine in *The Third Man* (1949), dogged and loyal, shot by Harry Lime to no purpose – or perhaps the troubled father in *Whistle Down the Wind* (1961). To pick one at odds with his usually benign persona, there is bullying Bert Connelly, beautifully exact, in *The Angry Silence* (1960). It is just possible he gave a poor performance in his 80-plus films, but it is hard to think of one. He was grandfather of Jonny Lee MILLER.

OTHER BRITISH FILMS INCLUDE: *Double Event* (1934), *Rhodes of Africa* (1936), *The Frozen Limits* (1939), *This Man is Mine* (1946), *The Fallen Idol*, *Quartet* (1948), *Morning Departure*, *Odette* (1950), *White Corridors* (1951), *Beat the Devil* (UK/It/US), *The Yellow Balloon* (1953), *The Rainbow Jacket* (1954), *The Battle of the River Plate* (1956), *Across the Bridge* (1957), *Dunkirk*, *Danger Within* (1958), *Kidnapped* (1960), *Dr No* (1962), *From Russia with Love*, *A Place to Go* (1963), *Goldfinger* (1964), *The Spy Who Came in from the Cold*, *Thunderball* (1965), *You Only Live Twice* (1967), *On Her Majesty's Secret Service* (1969), *10 Rillington Place* (1970), *Diamonds are Forever*, *Dulcima* (1971), *Live and Let Die* (1973), *The Man with the Golden Gun* (1974), *The Spy Who Loved Me* (1977), *Moonraker* (1979, UK/Fr).

Lee, Christopher (*b* London, 1922). Actor. Lee is one of the more unlikely graduates of the Rank CHARM SCHOOL, J. Arthur RANK's training institution for young film actors. He appeared in small roles in numerous British films from the late 40s onwards before landing the apparently thankless role of the mute creature in HAMMER's *The Curse of Frankenstein* (1957). The success of this film led to Lee's being cast in the role that made his name, the vampire in Hammer's *Dracula* (1958). The film offered a more explicitly sexual version of vampirism than had earlier versions, and Lee's brooding performance was a vital contribution to its worldwide success. Wary of typecasting Lee refused to play Dracula again for several years and instead appeared in character roles until his vampiric comeback in *Dracula – Prince of Darkness* (1965). This was the first of several increasingly poor Dracula sequels, and Lee himself later expressed some disappointment over the quality of the material he had to work with. He appeared to much greater effect in *The Devil Rides Out* (1967), one of the best Hammer horrors, and was also a notable presence in the cult film *The Wicker Man* (1973). Since the 60s Lee's career has been mainly an international one, but his star persona still has strong links with British HORROR, as his casting in *Sleepy Hollow* (1999, US/Ger), Tim Burton's homage to Hammer horror, testifies. Awarded CBE, 2001.

OTHER BRITISH FILMS INCLUDE: *Penny and the Pownall Case*, *Scott of the Antarctic* (1948), *Prelude to Fame*, *They Were Not Divided* (1950), *Moulin Rouge* (1953), *Final Column*, *Storm over the Nile*, *Cockleshell Heroes* (1955), *The Battle of the River Plate*, *Private's Progress* (1956), *Fortune Is a Woman*, *The Truth About Women* (1957), *A Tale of Two Cities*, *Corridors of Blood* (1958), *The Man Who Could Cheat Death*, *The Mummy*, *The Hound of the Baskervilles*, *Beat Girl* (1959), *The Two Faces of Dr Jekyll*, *The Terror of the Tongs*, *The Hands of Orlac* (UK/Fr) (1960), *Taste of Fear* (1961), *The Gorgon*, *Dr Terror's House of Horrors* (1964), *The Skull*, *The Face of Fu Manchu*, *She*, *Rasputin the Mad Monk* (1965), *Circus of Fear*, *The Brides of Fu Manchu*, *Theatre of Death* (1966), *The Vengeance of Fu Manchu* (1967), *Curse of the Crimson Altar*, *Dracula Has Risen from the Grave*, *The Face of Eve* (UK/Sp) (1968), *The Oblong Box*,

Scream and Scream Again (1969), *Scars of Dracula*, *The Private Life of Sherlock Holmes*, *Julius Caesar* (1970), *Nothing But the Night*, *Dracula AD 1972*, *The Creeping Flesh* (1972), *Dark Places*, *The Satanic Rites of Dracula* (1974), *The Man with the Golden Gun* (1974), *To the Devil a Daughter* (1976, UK/Ger), *The Passage* (1978), *House Of The Long Shadows* (1982), *The Rainbow Thief* (1990), *Funny Man* (1994).

BIBLIOG: Autobiography, *Tall, Dark and Gruesome*, 1997. Peter Hutchings.

Lee, Doris (*b* Harrow, 1926). Costume designer. Trained at Harrow School of Art, Lee began film work at LIME GROVE STUDIOS, working as assistant on a string of GAINSBOROUGH films, including *Fanny by Gaslight* (1944). Also worked on (mainly) period films (e.g, *Uncle Silas*, 1947; *The First Gentleman*, 1948) for other companies.

OTHER BRITISH FILMS INCLUDE: (ass cos des) *Love Story* (1944), *I'll Be Your Sweetheart*, *The Wicked Lady* (1945), *Caravan* (1946), *Christopher Columbus* (1949), *The Spider and the Fly* (1949), *The Card* (1952); (cos des) *Time Flies* (1944), *The Master of Bankdam* (1947), *Diamond City* (1949), *Scrooge* (1951).

Lee, Jack (*b* Slad, 1913 – *d* Sydney, 2002). Director. Between 1938 and 1946, Lee was with the GPO FILM UNIT and CROWN FILM UNIT, and worked as a freelance feature film director from 1946 onwards. His most influential DOCUMENTARY film was *Close Quarters* (1943), one of a number of 'story-documentaries' which emerged from Crown during the war years. Lee's most important feature films were *The Wooden Horse* (1950, + co-sc), *A Town Like Alice* (1956) and *Circle of Deception* (1960). *The Wooden Horse*, for WESSEX FILMS, was produced by Ian DALRYMPLE, who was in charge of Crown during WW2. Although, conforming to many of the standard stereotypes relating to the POW film, it is also marked by a convincing degree of REALISM which reflects Lee and Dalrymple's background in documentary; and *Alice*, a major commercial success, is similarly characterised by a tone of understated, resilient heroism, this time in relation to a group of women prisoners. Like these two films, *Circle of Deception* also focuses on how the individual suffers at the hands of an inhuman or uncaring system, and an opposition between the ordinary, humane individual, and official or authoritarian forces, runs through all three. Lee retired to Australia in the early 60s. Brother of author Laurie Lee.

OTHER BRITISH FILMS INCLUDE: (d) (documentaries) *The Pilot Is Safe* (1941), *Close Quarters* (1943, + sc), *The Eighth Plague* (1945), *Children on Trial* (1946, + co-sc); (features) *The Woman in the Hall* (1947, + co-sc), *Once a Jolly Swagman* (1948, + co-sc), *South of Algiers* (1952), *Turn the Key Softly* (1953, + co-sc), *Robbery Under Arms* (1957), *The Captain's Table* (1958). Ian Aitken.

Lee, Margaret (*b* London, 1939). Actress. Most of her career has been in little-seen European films, but she appeared in a handful of British films, mostly of the HORROR genre, like *Circus of Fear* (1966). Also in the ludicrous 1970 remake of *Dorian Gray* (It/Ger).

OTHER BRITISH FILMS: *Our Man in Marrakesh* (1966), *Five Golden Dragons* (1967), *Venus in Furs* (UK/Ger/It/US), *Night of the Blood Monster* (UK/Ger/It/Sp) (1969).

Lee, Norman H. (*b* Sutton, Surrey, 1898 – *d* London, 1963). Director, screenwriter. Prolific film-maker of largely forgotten 30s GENRE films, some popular in their time, like *Dr Josser KC* (1931, d, p, sc) and its successors, mostly for BIP and ABPC. Discharged from the Navy (he had also served in WW1), he participated in some curiosities, like *The Girl Who Couldn't Quite* (1949), from Leo MARKS's play, and worked mainly as a writer. His first film work was on Southern Rhodesian animal films.

OTHER BRITISH FILMS INCLUDE: (d, unless noted) *The Lure of the Atlantic* (1929), *The Night Patrol* (1930), *Josser on the River* (+ p, co-sc), *Josser Joins the Navy* (+ p), *Josser in the Army* (1932), *The Outcast* (+ co-sc), *Doctor's Orders* (1934), *Royal Cavalcade* (1935, co-d), *No Escape* (1936), *Bulldog Drummond at Bay* (1937), *The Monkey's Paw* (1948, + co-sc), *The Case of Charles Peace* (1949, + co-sc); (co-sc) *My Wife's Family* (1941), *He Snoops to Conquer* (1944), *Idol of Paris* (1948).

Lee Miller, Jonny *see* **Miller, Jonny Lee**

Lee Thompson, J. *see* **Thompson, J(ohn) Lee**

Leech, Richard (*b* Dublin, 1922). Actor. RN: McClelland. Arts graduate from Trinity College, Dublin, then medical student, he practised as a doctor for a year before turning to acting, and made London debut in 1948, later playing such roles as Henry VIII in *A Man for All Seasons* (1960). His strong build and dignified manner brought him many service officers (e.g. *The Dam Busters*, 1955; *Gandhi*, 1982, UK/Ind), police inspectors (*The Wild and the Willing*, 1962) and – no training is ever wasted – doctors (*The Shooting Party*, 1984). Also plenty of TV, including *The Doctors* (1969–71) and *Smiley's People* (1982).

OTHER BRITISH FILMS INCLUDE: *The Temptress* (1949), *The Prisoner* (1955), *The Good Companions* (1956), *The Birthday Present* (1957), *A Night to Remember*, *The Horse's Mouth* (1958), *Tunes of Glory* (1960), *Life at the Top* (1965), *Young Winston* (1972), *Champions* (1983), *A Handful of Dust* (1987).

Leeman, Dicky (*b* Shanghai, 1912). Director. Essentially a TV producer, Leeman entered films as a child actor, before going over to the technical side in 1933, working as assistant director in the 30s at various studios, including DENHAM and ELSTREE. After RAF service (1939–45), he again worked as assistant director, on such films as *Daughter of Darkness* (1947), and then directed his sole feature, *A Date with a Dream* (1948, + co-sc), an ingenuous musical for the newly constituted TEMPEAN FILMS, of whose initial board he was a director. However, from the early 50s he went into TV and produced many programmes for the BBC and ATV.

OTHER BRITISH FILMS INCLUDE: (ass d) *They Made Me a Fugitive* (1947), *Prelude to Fame* (1950); (d) *Going Shopping with Elizabeth Allan* (1955, short).

Lees, Tamara (*b* Vienna, 1925). Actress. RN: Mapplebeck. RANK starlet, who played minor roles in British films, like the gangster's girlfriend in *Her Favourite Husband* (1950, UK/It), but was a major performer in more than 30 Italian productions of 50s. Her first husband was Bonar COLLEANO.

OTHER BRITISH FILMS INCLUDE: *While the Sun Shines* (1947), *Bond Street*, *Trottie True* (1948). AS.

Legg, Stuart (*b* London, 1910 – *d* Wiltshire, 1988). Director. Entered films in 1931, as director and film editor with GAUMONT–BRITISH INSTRUCTIONAL FILMS. From 1932 to 1937, he was director and producer at the EMB and GPO FILM UNITS; he worked with the STRAND FILM COMPANY (1938–39); and from 1939 to 1948, worked with John GRIERSON at the National Film Board of Canada. From 1948 to 1950 he produced *World in Action* for the CROWN FILM UNIT. From 1950 to 1964, he worked for FILM CENTRE International, mainly producing films for SHELL, and then retired. Most influential films include (as co-director) the GPO's *BBC – The Voice of Britain* (EMB, 1935), in which George Bernard SHAW, H.G. WELLS, David Low and others appeared, for salaries of £5 each. H. Forsyth HARDY praised it as 'always more of an illumination than a summary'. Legg also wrote an eloquent narration for Ruby GRIERSON's *Today We Live* (1937).

OTHER BRITISH FILMS INCLUDE: (d, unless noted; doc) *Varsity* (1930), *Savings Bank*, *Pett and Pott* (assoc, + co-sc), *The New Operator* (1934), *Coal Face* (1935, co-sd), *Night Mail* (1936, comm), *Roadways* (1937, co-d), *Wings Over Empire* (1939), *Churchill's Island* (1941); (p) *Wealth of a Nation* (1938), *Inside Fighting China* (1942, + sc, e), *Inside France* (1944), *Spotlight on the Colonies* (1950), *Song of the Clouds* (1957). Ian Aitken.

Leggatt, Alison (*b* London, 1904 – *d* London, 1990). Actress. Central School Gold Medallist, on stage from 1924, Leggatt had a long theatrical career, much associated with Noël COWARD, though her *cv* also embraces John OSBORNE and N.F. Simpson's *One Way Pendulum* (1959), recreating her role in the latter on screen in 1964. Her screen persona is usually disapproving, as in *Encore* (1951), as Nigel PATRICK's outraged sister-in-law, projecting a gentler image in such later films as *Nothing But the Best* (1964), as Alan BATES's unsuspecting mother, and *Far from the Madding Crowd* (1967), as Julie CHRISTIE's aunt. However, her screen highlight is her first major role, derived from Coward: she is wonderfully funny as hypochondriac Aunt Sylvia, given to Higher Thought and off-key singing, in *This Happy Breed* (1944). In her over-50-year career, she also did some notable TV, including *Sanctuary* (1967–68) and *The Edwardians* (1972).

OTHER BRITISH FILMS INCLUDE: *Nine Till Six* (1932), *Waterloo Road* (1944), *Here Come the Huggetts* (1948), *Marry Me* (1949), *The Card* (1952), *Touch and Go* (1955), *Never Take Sweets from a Stranger* (1960), *Goodbye, Mr Chips* (1969), *The Hireling* (1973).

legislation British legislation for the cinema was intended to protect film production from American competition. The first Cinematograph Act 1909, however, related to the licensing of cinemas and the safety of audiences. The implementation of the Act gave rise to the informal system of film CENSORSHIP which was established in 1912. The government responded to pressure from producers, industrialists and those who were concerned about the popularity of Hollywood's films, by devising the Cinematograph Films Act, 1927. This made it a statutory requirement that renters and exhibitors should handle and screen a certain percentage of British films, 7.5% and 5% respectively in the first instance, increasing in stages until 1935. The Act applied to long films designated 'British' according to a definition which was based primarily on the nationality of a production's labour input. It also attempted, with little success, to outlaw booking malpractices which had given American films an unfair advantage. Although the Act was criticised for encouraging the production of cheap 'QUOTA QUICKIES', films made purely to satisfy the letter of the law while flouting its spirit, it resulted in an increase in production and encouraged the development of an infrastructure which was largely responsible for the survival of the industry in WW2 and its subsequent expansion. In 1938 a second Cinematograph Films Act became law, reaffirming the 'quota' system but modifying it so that short films were also protected and, to prevent 'quickies', all films had to have cost a stipulated minimum sum. A controversial addition was the sanctioning of expensive 'multiple' credit quota films which encouraged American companies producing in Britain.

WW2 disrupted the first years of the new Act, but quota protectionism was reaffirmed by the 1948 Cinematograph Films Act, which abolished the renters' quota and fixed the exhibitors' at 45%. In 1950 the figure was reduced to 30% where it remained until the abolition of quotas in 1983. In all, the system provided some market protection but was criticised for ignoring the crucial question of production FINANCE. The Labour government, 1945–51, instituted the other major elements of protective legislation for the cinema. Immediately after WW2 the combination of a fuel and exchange crisis prompted severe criticism of the amount of dollars which American companies remitted to the US in respect of their films shown in Britain. In August 1947 a 75% customs duty was imposed on the value of imported films, also known as the 'Dalton Duty', which resulted in a boycott of the British market by the Motion Picture Producers of America. An agreement was reached in March 1948 whereby the boycott was lifted and the American companies agreed to maintain a stipulated minimum of 'blocked' dollar earnings in Britain in the hope that a percentage would be used to produce films in Britain.

A more extensive attempt to bolster British production, however, was the establishment of the NATIONAL FILM FINANCE CORPORATION (NFFC) in 1949. £5 million was made available to the Corporation as a contribution to 'end' money which was allocated to producers via BRITISH LION, a DISTRIBUTION company. Many significant British films were funded with NFFC support, including *The Third Man* (1949) and *Saturday Night and Sunday Morning* (1960), but its monies were reduced over the years until it was abolished in 1985 by the Conservative government.

The final element of state support was the British Film Production Fund, established in 1950 and also known as the 'EADY LEVY'. This was the result of a compromise between the government and the film trade which for years had complained bitterly about having to pay Entertainments Tax. Exhibitors had been paying Entertainments Tax out of box-office takings since 1916 in ever-increasing tranches. During WW2, when cinema attendances were high, the tax was raised three times but none of the monies were used to assist film production. In exchange for a reduction of the tax and permission to raise seat prices the film trade agreed to the Eady Levy which required them to pay a percentage of box-office receipts into the Production Fund. The Fund was made statutory in 1957 but it was wound up in 1985 after much criticism that the major beneficiaries had been American companies producing films in Britain. A more positive aspect of the Fund was its allocation of support to the BRITISH FILM INSTITUTE, the Experimental Film Fund, the NATIONAL FILM SCHOOL and the CHILDREN'S FILM FOUNDATION.

Since the cessation of these major elements of state support for British cinema there have been several initiatives intended to encourage indigenous production but none has resulted in long-term official commitment to subsidise the film industry. BRITISH SCREEN was established as a successor to the NFFC as a consortium of dominant film and television interests with some degree of support from the British Treasury and in 1997 the Labour Government appointed a minister with special responsibility for the film industry who established a Film Policy Review Group whose report, *A Bigger Picture* (1998), emphasised the importance of effective distribution. Tax incentives were also instituted to encourage film production. In 2000 three major sources of funding – British Screen, the NATIONAL LOTTERY and BRITISH FILM INSTITUTE PRODUCTION BOARD – were merged as the FILM COUNCIL, a government-funded body which represents a renewed state commitment to supporting the British film industry.

BIBLIOG: Margaret Dickinson and Sarah Street, *Cinema and State* (1985). Sarah Street.

Lehmann, Beatrix (*b* Bourne End, 1903 – *d* London, 1979). Actress. Dominant, RADA-trained stage actress, from 1924, who had notable successes in SHAKESPEARE, Ibsen, O'Neill and Tennessee Williams. Often on TV, she was a brilliant Volumnia in *Spread of the Eagle* (1963), an aptly dessicated Mrs Touchett in *The Portrait of a Lady* (1968). Her screen work was sporadic, but usually compelling, right up to her last gasp in *The Cat and the Canary* (1979). The word 'idiosyncratic' might have been coined for her. Elected President of Equity in 1945. Sister to novelist Rosamund Lehmann and poet-publisher John Lehmann.

OTHER BRITISH FILMS INCLUDE: *The Passing of the Third Floor Back* (1935), *The Rat* (1937), *Candles at Nine* (1944), *The Key* (1958), *Psyche 59* (1963), *The Spy Who Came In from the Cold* (1965).

Lehmann, Carla (*b* Winnipeg, 1917 – *d* Windsor, 1990). Actress. Popular RADA-trained blonde star of stage (including several ALDWYCH FARCES) and screen, especially during WW2. Signed by RANK, she made several war adventures, including two with James MASON – *Secret Mission* (1942) and *Candlelight in Algeria* (1943) – but her best work is in her last film, *Fame Is the Spur* (1947), as the warm-hearted Lady Lettice. Retired after second marriage and cultivated her notable garden in Berkshire.

OTHER BRITISH FILMS INCLUDE: *Luck of the Navy* (1938), *Sailors Three* (1940), *Cottage to Let* (1941), *Talk About Jacqueline*, *Flying Fortress* (1942), *29, Acacia Avenue* (1945).

Lehmann, Olga (*b* Chile, 1912 – *d* Saffron Walden, 2001). Costume designer. Also a portrait and sketch artist, who did the paintings for Vernon SEWELL's fantasy, *The Ghosts of Berkeley Square* (1947), and designed the costumes for a dozen or so films and much TV over the next few decades. Some versatility is seen in the homely outback clothes for *Robbery Under Arms* (1957), the WAR FILM *The Guns of Navarone* (1961) and the Scottish gear for *Kidnapped* (1971). Trained at the Slade School where she was awarded scholarships and prizes, and in the 30s her murals were included in major exhibitions. Post-war, she became closely involved with film-making, working for such companies as RANK, MGM–BRITISH and ASSOCIATED BRITISH.

OTHER BRITISH FILMS INCLUDE: *The Gamma People* (1955), *tom thumb*, *The Scapegoat* (1958), *The Victors* (1963), *The Four Feathers* (1978), *Little Lord Fauntleroy* (1980).

Leigh, J(ack) L.V. Actor, director. Actor on screen from 1912 to 1919, who played second lead, Conway Bass, in the 1916 'Ultus' SERIES: *Ultus, the Man from the Dead*, *Ultus and the Grey Lady*, *Ultus and the Secret of the Night*. Later became a director.

OTHER BRITISH FILMS INCLUDE: (d) *Farmer Spudd and the Missus Take a Trip to Town* (1915), *'Twixt Cup and Lip* (1916), *The Adventures of Eve* series, *The Key of the World* (1918), *The First Men in the Moon* (1919). AS.

Leigh, Mike (*b* Salford, 1943). Director. Leigh may have seemed one of the key figures in 90s British cinema, but his had been a long apprenticeship, with nearly two decades spent, through no wish of his own, on stage and little-seen TV films, some of them very striking, often in blackly comic style. Some, including *Nuts in May* (1976), *Abigail's Party* (1977) and *Meantime* (1983, some cinemas), are now on video. After *Bleak Moments* (1971) – and the title is indicative of much of his work – he did not film for the cinema again until 1988's *High Hopes*, in which he so vividly contrasts the pair who have made a successful career of yuppie greed with the gentle herbivores who care for each other, and for others. It was a triumph of REALISM streaked with an anarchic Swiftian satire: his films are not realism *ordinaire* as, say, Ken LOACH's are; they demand a flexibility of response to their sometimes unsettling modal shifts. This is true of his next films: *Life is Sweet* (1990), the very dark *Naked* (1993), the masterly *Secrets & Lies* (1996, UK/US, AAn/d/sc), which brought him nearer the mainstream and which won BAA/sc and several other nominations, and the chamber work, *Career Girls* (1997). None of these, however, could have prepared his followers for the warmth of his unsentimentally affectionate tribute to the theatrical life in the GILBERT AND SULLIVAN biopic, *Topsy-Turvy* (2000, UK/US, AAn/sc). He is a risk-taking director: witness the long, semi-articulate monologue given to David THEWLIS in *Naked*, or the stunning nine-minute take in *Secrets & Lies* in which Brenda BLETHYN and Marianne JEAN-BAPTISTE come to terms with each other, or the sudden intrusive comic touches. His actors, like those named or Jim BROADBENT, Timothy SPALL and Lesley MANVILLE, reward him with performances of amazing truth, the result apparently of much improvisation and rehearsal *before* the carefully controlled shooting. His stage training at RADA has not been wasted, though it was always films he wanted to get into, and he transferred to the London Film School. Was married to Alison STEADMAN.

OTHER BRITISH FILMS: *All or Nothing* (2002, UK/Fr).

BIBLIOG: Michael Coveney, *The World According to Mike Leigh*, 1996; Howie Movshovitz (ed), *Mike Leigh Interviews*, 2000; Ray Carney and Leonard Quart, *The Films of Mike Leigh*, 2000.

Leigh, Suzanna (*b* Reading, 1945). Actress. RN: Smyth. Trained at Webber-Douglas and entered films as EXTRA in *tom thumb* (1958). Showed some gift for publicity, making the most of her US stint as Elvis Presley's leading lady in *Paradise, Hawaiian Style* (1966). On return to England, mostly in HORROR films, including *Son of Dracula* (1974).

OTHER BRITISH FILMS, INCLUDE: *Oscar Wilde* (1960), *The Pleasure Girls* (1965), *The Deadly Bees* (1966), *Lost Continent* (1968), *Lust for a Vampire* (1970), *The Fiend* (1971).

Leigh, Vivien (*b* Darjeeling, India, 1913 – *d* London, 1967). Actress. RN: Vivian Hartley. Legendary beauty whose film fame rests largely on her two Oscar-winning US roles: in *Gone with the Wind* (1939), for which she was chosen to play the wilful Scarlett O'Hara at the end of the most famous casting search in film history, and in *A Streetcar Named Desire* (1951), this time as a faded Southern belle, in a performance of much fragile pathos. Trained at RADA, she always claimed the stage (debut 1935) as her first allegiance, though the jury remained divided about her work in classical drama. Entered films in 1935, getting her first major chance in *Fire Over England* (1937), as romantic interest of future husband Laurence OLIVIER, and then was vivid enough in several late 30s films of which the best remembered is *A Yank at Oxford* (1937), playing a minx who anticipates Scarlett. There were romantic-tragic successes in two US films – *Waterloo Bridge* (1940) and *That Hamilton Woman* (1941) – but her post-war British films saw her unequal to the demands of *Caesar and Cleopatra* (1945), *Anna Karenina* (1948) and *The Deep Blue Sea* (1955). As her health deteriorated and her wildly overdocumented marriage to Olivier broke up, she was poignant in two roles for women of a certain age: *The Roman Spring of Mrs Stone* (1961) and *Ship of Fools* (1965).

OTHER BRITISH FILMS: *The Village Squire, Things Are Looking Up, Look Up and Laugh, Gentleman's Agreement* (1935), *Dark Journey, Storm in a Teacup* (1937), *St Martin's Lane* (1938).

BIBLIOG: Anne Edwards, *Vivien Leigh*, 1977; Alexander Walker, *Vivien*, 1987.

Leigh, Walter (*b* London, 1905 – *d* nr.Tobruk, Libya, 1942). Composer. Post-Cambridge, he began his career in films with the GPO FILM UNIT, where he composed scores for several films, the most famous being for *Song of Ceylon* (1934, doc). Also composed for CAVALCANTI's witty short film, *Pett and Pott* (1934) and for Michael POWELL's *His Lordship* (1932, + lyrics). Killed in action.

OTHER BRITISH FILMS INCLUDE: *6.30 Collection* (1934, short), *Fairy of the Phone* (1936, short), *The Fourth Estate* (doc), *Squadron 992* (short) (1940).

Leigh-Hunt, Barbara (*b* Bath, 1935). Actor. Stage actress who has been much seen on TV (a vividly grim Lady Catherine de Bourgh in *Pride and Prejudice*, 1995), but little on screen. She was memorably strangled in her first, *Frenzy* (1972), dourly outlasted the king in *Henry VIII and his Six Wives* (1972) and popped up as Vice-Principal of the Royal Ballet School panel in *Billy Elliot* (2000). Married Richard PASCO in 1967.

OTHER BRITISH FILMS: *Bequest to the Nation* (1973), *Keep the Aspidistra Flying* (1997), *The Martins, Iris* (UK/US) (2001).

Leigh-Hunt, Ronald (*b* London, 1916). Actor. Authoritative character man who slid convincingly into military and law officer roles in a dozen 50s 'B' MOVIES, in, for example, *Paul Temple Returns* (1952, as Police Inspector) and *Assignment Redhead* (1956, as Colonel Fentriss), and played supporting professionals of various kinds in another 20 films. Now best remembered as King Arthur in *The Adventures of Sir Lancelot* (1956–57), replacing Bruce SETON after the early episodes.

OTHER BRITISH FILMS INCLUDE: *Blackout* (1950), *Flannelfoot* (1953), *Tiger by the Tail* (1955), *Zoo Baby* (1957), *Oscar Wilde* (1960), *Very Important Person* (1961), *The Third Secret* (1964), *Khartoum* (1966), *Hostile Witness* (1968), *Clegg* (1969), *Baxter!* (1972).

Leighton, Margaret (*b* Barnt Green, 1922 – *d* Chichester, 1976). Actress. Elegant and eloquent beauty of aristocratic mien, on stage from 1938 and films ten years later, after establishing credentials in Birmingham Rep and Old Vic seasons from 1942 to 1947. In films, she brought the right warmth and steel to the role of Kate Winslow, suffragette sister of *The Winslow Boy* (1948), survived such stinkers as *Bonnie Prince Charlie* (1948) and *The Astonished Heart* (1950), was affecting as the unhappy, tippling daughter in *The Holly and the Ivy* (1952) and aptly vindictive as David NIVEN's wife in *Carrington VC* (1954), receiving a BAAn for the latter. Her finest film performance was as Julie CHRISTIE's seething neurotic mother in *The Go-Between* (1971, BAA/supp actress, AAn). She was in some dud films but she could transmute dross momentarily into gold; and she makes the long slog of *Lady Caroline Lamb* (1972, UK/It/US) worthwhile for the way she delivers the last line. Joseph LOSEY called her 'the great and marvellous Margaret Leighton', but her British films scarcely deserved her. Some notable TV, including *A Day by the Sea*, Tony awards for *Separate Tables* (1956) and *Night of the Iguana* (1962), at least one fine US film, *The Best Man* (1964). Married (1) publisher Max Reinhardt, (2) Laurence HARVEY (1957–61), (3) Michael WILDING (1963 until her death from multiple sclerosis).

OTHER BRITISH FILMS: *Under Capricorn* (1949), *The Elusive Pimpernel* (1950), *Calling Bulldog Drummond* (1951), *Home at Seven* (1952), *The Teckman Mystery, The Good Die Young, The Constant Husband* (1954), *The Passionate Stranger* (1956), *Waltz of the Toreadors* (1962), *The Madwoman of Chaillot* (1969), *Zee & Co.* (1972), *Bequest to the Nation*,

From Beyond the Grave (1973), *Galileo* (1974, UK/Can), *Great Expectations* (1975, as Miss Havisham), *Trial by Combat* (1976).

Leister, Frederick (*b* London, 1885 – *d* London, 1966). Actor. Character player on stage from 1906, after working briefly as lawyer's articled clerk, appeared in many new and classic plays, and served in the Army in WW1 (1915–18). Made several dozen films, usually in upper-class and professional roles, mostly upright men like the husband celebrating his golden wedding in *Dear Octopus* (1943) but occasionally less admirable, like Martha Scott's jailed extortionist father in *So Well Remembered* (1947). Married Dora Luther, direct descendant of Martin.

OTHER BRITISH FILMS: *Bracelets* (1931), *The Iron Duke* (1935), *Whom the Gods Love* (1936, UK/Aus), *King Solomon's Mines*, *OHMS* (1937), *Sixty Glorious Years* (1938), *Goodbye, Mr Chips* (1939), *The Prime Minister* (1941), *The Next of Kin* (1942), *The Shipbuilders* (1943), *The Captive Heart* (1946), *Escape*, *Quartet* (1948), *Dear Mr Prohack* (1949), *Top Secret* (1952), *The End of the Affair* (1954), *The Dam Busters* (1955), *The Naked Edge* (1961, UK/US).

Lejeune, C(aroline) A(lice) (*b* Manchester, 1897 – *d* London, 1973). Film critic. The first regular female film reviewer, she began with the *Manchester Guardian* (1922–28), then joined the *Observer*, with whom she stayed for 32 years. She acquired a reputation for wit, but often this was at the service of a middle-class disdain for the popular art she was meant to be reviewing. Her taste was for the British 'quality' film, which meant generally the decorously literary or the understated realist. Hollywood was an easy target for her and she aimed at it relentlessly. Hindsight has been much kinder to the other 'Sunday lady', Dilys POWELL; Lejeune simply never seemed to take the cinema seriously, as if it were not an art form to compare with others.

BIBLIOG: Autobiography, *Thank You for Having Me*, 1964; Anthony Lejeune (ed), *The C.A. Lejeune Film Reader*, 1991.

Leland, David (*b* Cambridge, 1947). Actor, director, screenwriter. Leland had experience as actor at the Royal Court Theatre and in several films, including *Time Bandits* (1981), as well as writing for theatre and TV. It is a dispersed career which has, however, brought him rewards such as a BAA for his big-screen script, *Wish You Were Here* (1987, + d), an acute if somewhat downbeat study in adolescent sexuality, and nominations for the gritty insights of the street-life study, *Mona Lisa* (1986, co-BAAn) and the more raucous pleasures of *Personal Services* (1987, + a), the racy story of madam, Cynthia Payne. There is something muted about the films he has directed, as if real vigour might be cheapening, but there is also a real feel for milieu in *The Big Man* (1990), about unemployment and bare-knuckle boxing in Scotland, and *The Land Girls* (1998, UK/Fr), in which three young women come to terms with the facts of rural life in WW2. Has also directed music videos for such names as Bob Dylan and Ringo STARR.

OTHER BRITISH FILMS INCLUDE: (a) *One Brief Summer* (1969) *Julius Caesar*, *The Scars of Dracula*, *Underground* (1970), *The Pied Piper* (1971), *The Missionary* (1981); (d) *Checking Out* (1988).

Le Mesurier, John (*b* Bedford, 1912 – *d* Ramsgate, 1983). RN: John Elton Halliley. Le Mesurier became so closely associated with the role of ex-public school Sgt. Arthur Wilson in the TV series (1968–77) and film of *Dad's Army* (1971), that one may forget that he appeared in over 100 films, often in one-scene cameos. Worked in a legal office before taking up acting, first in repertory at Birmingham, then with small roles in 'B' FILMS. He became a jobbing character actor of the 50s and 60s, appearing in West End plays, numerous films and TV episodes,

his persona making him ideal for bishops, neurotic high-ranking military officers – or racket-running from Dockland warehouses. Few films stand out, but he was well used by the BOULTING brothers in *Private's Progress* (1956), in which he memorably played an army psychiatrist with a 'tic', and in *I'm All Right Jack* (1959), his comic genius was much in evidence as a sinister 'time and motion' expert. His best sustained screen acting is probably in Dennis Potter's TV play *Traitor* (1971). One of the most widely recognised and loved faces in British films, his trademark expressions included a world-weary sigh, a twitch, grimace and raised eyebrow. Married (2 of 3) Hattie JACQUES (1949–65).

OTHER BRITISH FILMS INCLUDE: *Death in the Hand* (1948), *Old Mother Riley's New Venture* (1949), *The Baby and the Battleship* (1956), *Happy is the Bride* (1957), *Law and Disorder*, *Too Many Crooks* (1959), *Follow a Star*, *School for Scoundrels* (1959), *Never Let Go*, *The Rebel*, *The Bulldog Breed* (1960), *Only Two Can Play* (1961), *Village of Daughters*, *The Wrong Arm of the Law* (1962), *The Pink Panther* (1963), *The Wrong Box* (1966), *The Italian Job* (1969), *Doctor in Trouble* (1970), *Jabberwocky* (1977).

BIBLIOG: John Le Mesurier, *A Jobbing Actor*, 1985; Joan LeMesurier, *Dear John*, 2001. Roger Philip Mellor.

Lemkow, Tutte (*b* Oslo, 1918 – *d* London, 1991). Actor. Small, dark dancer/choreographer with a touch of the farouche, who came to England in 1946 with wife Mai ZETTERLING and child, tried for a ballet career but ended up playing small parts in films, starting with *The Lost People* (1949), in which Zetterling starred. The marriage broke down, but he had a solid enough career playing eccentric foreigners in WAR FILMS, COMEDIES and THRILLERS, and as choreographer for films with dance sequences, like *The Captain's Paradise* (1953, + a), as well as dancer on several TV shows.

OTHER BRITISH FILMS INCLUDE: (a) *Moulin Rouge* (1953), *The Iron Petticoat*, *Anastasia* (1956), *Too Many Crooks* (1959), *The Siege of Sidney Street*, *The Guns of Navarone* (1961), *The Victors* (1963), *A Shot in the Dark* (1964), *The Wrong Box* (1966), *Fathom* (1967), *Theatre of Blood* (1973); (choreographer) *High Flight*, *Fire Down Below* (1957), *Casino Royale* (1967).

Lemont, John V. (*b* Toronto, 1914). Director. Educated in Canada, US and Britain, he entered films in 1934 and was a producer and director with the ARMY FILM UNIT during WW2. Under contract with ABPC post-war but directed no feature until *The Green Buddha* in 1954. All his films were either SHORTS, DOCUMENTARIES, children's films or 'B' MOVIES, with the exception of one rather good gangster thriller, *The Frightened City* (1961, + co-p, co-story). Also worked a good deal in TV as writer and producer of series (e.g. *The Errol Flynn Theatre*, 1957) and advertising magazine programmes.

OTHER BRITISH FILMS INCLUDE: *Witness in the Dark* (+ co-sc), *The Shakedown* (+ co-sc, story) (1959), *Konga* (1960); (p, shorts), *Deep Waters* (1978, + sc, story).

Lennard, Robert (*b* London, 1910). Casting director. Influential figure in 50s and 60s British cinema, Lennard famously discovered Audrey HEPBURN dancing at 'Ciro's' but, though ABPC signed her to a contract, it never managed to do anything useful with her. Lennard began as office-boy in the 30s, with GAUMONT–BRITISH for a while, then worked as Casting Director Weston DRURY's assistant at BIP, before joining the Fire Service in WW2. Post-war, Robert CLARK, chief at ABPC, appointed Lennard casting director and his first coup was the signing of Richard TODD, who became a star on the strength of *The Hasty Heart* (1949). Lennard believed fervently in the importance of stars to the industry and in the theatre as the crucial training ground. Among those he gathered in were Sylvia SYMS, Laurence HARVEY and George BAKER; it is probably not Lennard's fault that ABPC rarely made the best use of the talent it had on hand.

OTHER BRITISH FILMS INCLUDE: *Stage Fright* (1950), *The Weak and the Wicked* (1953), *Happy Ever After* (1954), *The Dam Busters, 1984* (1955), *Yield to the Night* (1956), *Woman in a Dressing Gown, Night of the Demon* (1957), *Indiscreet* (1958), *Look Back in Anger* (1959), *The Roman Spring of Mrs Stone, The Young Ones* (1961), *Billy Budd* (1962), *Sammy Going South* (1963), *A Man for All Seasons* (1966).

Lennox, Annie (*b* Aberdeen, 1954). Singer. Popular singer with the group 'The Eurythmics', whose performances have been the subject of film and TV DOCUMENTARIES, including *Brand New Day* (1987) which chronicles her and Dave Stewart with the group in Japan. She appeared briefly in *Revolution* (1985, UK/Nor) and, as a singer, in *Edward II* (1991). Married to producer **Uri Fruchtmann** (*b* Israel, *c* 1955), responsible for *Spice World* (1997).

Leno, Dan (*b* London, 1860 – *d* London, 1904). Actor. Legendary MUSIC HALL star, who was billed as 'The Funniest Man on Earth,' appeared in a handful of SHORTS, which like his recordings fail to do justice to his talent. They include *The Rats, Dan Leno's Attempt to Master the Cycle, Dan Leno's Cricket Match* (1900), *Dan Leno's Day Out* (the only one which survives), *Dan Leno Musical Director* (1901), *Bluebeard* (1902). AS.

Lenska, Rula (*b* St Neots, 1947). Actress. RN: Countess Roza-Maria Laura Leopoldnya Lubienska. Became an instant TV star in 1976 with *Rock Follies*, but had only minor roles in minor films. A law suit prevented the public from seeing her one starring role in *Queen Kong* (1976, UK/Fr/It). Optimistically billed as an 'international star' in the US, in Alberto VO5 hairspray commercials (1977–80). Married/divorced Brian DEACON and Dennis WATERMAN.

OTHER BRITISH FILMS: *Soft Beds, Hard Battles* (1973), *Alfie Darling, Royal Flash* (1975), *It Could Happen to You* (1975). AS.

Lenya, Lotte (*b* Penzing, Austria, 1898 – *d* New York, 1981). Actress. Celebrated stage star, first married to Kurt Weill (1926–50, his death), entered films in Germany in Brecht's *The Threepenny Opera* (1931), and belongs in this book for two striking performances in British film: as the procuress in *The Roman Spring of Mrs Stone* (1961) and as dangerous Rosa Klebb, one of BOND's most formidable adversaries, in *From Russia with Love* (1963).

Leon, Anne (Annie) (*b* London, 1925). Actress. Made an appealing debut, as the wife of a pilot (Bryan FORBES), who is killed in *Appointment in London* (1953), but this was followed only by insignificant bits – like one of the office girls in *Room at the Top* (1958). Married Michael GOUGH.

OTHER BRITISH FILMS: *Reach for the Sky* (1956), *Carve Her Name With Pride* (1958), *Mr Topaze* (1961).

Leon, Valerie (*b* London, 1945). Actress. Tall leading and supporting actress of the 60s and 70s, whose *cv* includes several 'CARRY ON's and two 'BOND' FILMS, a lingerie-clad answer to an ad in *No Sex, Please – We're British* (1973) and a formidable Madame Defarge in TV's *A Tale of Two Cities* (1989). Was married to TV producer Michael Mills until his 1988 death.

OTHER BRITISH FILMS INCLUDE: *Smashing Time* (1967), *Carry On Up the Khyber* (1968), . . . *Camping,* . . . *Doctor* (1969), *Blood from the Mummy's Tomb* (1971), *Carry On Matron* (1972), . . . *Girls* (1973), *The*

Spy Who Loved Me (1977), *Revenge of the Pink Panther* (1978), *Never Say Never Again* (1983, UK/US).

Leonard, Hugh (*b* Dublin, 1926). Screenwriter. RN: John Keys Byrne. Leonard's credits include a number of TV literary ADAPTATIONS (e.g. the excellent series, *Country Matters*, 1974, from H.E. BATES and A.E. Coppard), and an eclectic half-dozen films. To his shame, he authored *Percy* (1971); to his credit is Kevin BILLINGTON's sensitive *Interlude* (1968).

OTHER BRITISH FILMS: *Broth of a Boy* (1959, Ire, play); (sc) *Great Catherine* (1967), *Our Miss Fred* (1972), *Widows' Peak* (1994, UK/US).

Leonard, Queenie (*b* London, 1905 – *d* Los Angeles, 2002). Actress. RN: Pearl Walker. Lively supporting actress in some 30s British films, including Gracie FIELDS's *The Show Goes On* (1937); went to Hollywood and played dozens of maids and the like from the early 40s until 1964, often in such Brit-set films as *The Lodger* (1944). Married and divorced (1) art director L.P. WILLIAMS (1936–47) and (2) actor Tom CONWAY (1958–63).

OTHER BRITISH FILMS INCLUDE: *Who Killed Doc Robin?* (1931, short), *Romance in Rhythm* (1934), *Limelight* (1936), *Moonlight Sonata* (1937), *Kate Plus Ten* (1938).

Le Prevost, Nicholas (*b* Wiltshire, 1947). Actor. Supporting player of 80s and 90s TV (e.g. *A Fatal Inversion*, 1991) and films (e.g. *Shakespeare in Love*, 1999, UK/US, as Gwyneth PALTROW's socially ambitious father).

OTHER BRITISH FILMS INCLUDE: *Crystal Gazing* (1982), *Clockwise* (1985), *The Land Girls* (1998, UK/Fr), *Being Considered* (2000).

LePrince, Louis Aimé Augustin (*b* Metz, France, 1841 – *d* France, 1890). Pioneer. Thanks to the mythology of the motion picture, Louis Aimé Augustin LePrince is not remembered for having made what is arguably the first motion picture film, in October 1888 – of Leeds Bridge, the city to which he moved in 1866; or for having applied for a US patent on January 10, 1888 for 'apparatus for producing animated photographic pictures' – apparatus now in the Science Museum, London. Rather, he is known for his mysterious disappearance on a train between Dijon and Paris on September 16, 1890. The LePrince story is told in highly personalised fashion by Christopher Rawlence in *The Missing Reel* (1990). AS.

lesbianism *see* **gay and lesbian representation**

Lesley, Carole (*b* Chelmsford, 1935 – *d* New Barnet, 1974). Actress. RN: Maureen Rippingdale. On stage and screen from 13, in the chorus from 16, a contract with ABPC, then a few goodish parts in films before her luck ran out, and she committed suicide. Probably best remembered as Yvonne MITCHELL's worldly-wise friend in *Woman in a Dressing Gown* (1957) and as Herbert LOM's moll in *No Trees in the Street* (1958), both for J. Lee Thompson, reputedly infatuated with her.

OTHER BRITISH FILMS INCLUDE: *The Embezzler* (1954), *These Dangerous Years* (1957), *Operation Bullshine* (1959), *The Pot Carriers* (1962).

Lesslie, Colin (*b* ? – *d* 1974). Producer. Began as actor in the 30s, served with the Irish Guards during WW2, and in 1949 set up his own production company for which he produced Paul ROTHA's critically acclaimed study of the life of an itinerant Irish tinker, *No Resting Place* (1951, + co-sc). Also freelanced, notably on *Tunes of Glory* (1960).

OTHER BRITISH FILMS INCLUDE: (a) *All at Sea, The Ghost Goes West* (1935), *A Yank at Oxford* (1937); (p) *Her Favourite Husband* (1950,

UK/It), *Aunt Clara* (1954), *Charley Moon* (1956), *Danger Within* (1958, p).

Lester, Adrian (*b* Birmingham, 1970). Actor. Came to attention as the high-minded (if not for long) presidential aide in *Primary Colors* (1998, US) and has since appeared in a half-dozen or so UK (co-)productions. Whether the short supply of good roles for black actors will force him to live in the US remains to be seen. Played Hamlet for Peter BROOK in Paris (2000).
BRITISH FILMS: *Up on the Roof* (1997), *Love's Labour's Lost* (UK/Fr/US, as Dumaine), *Best* (UK/Ire), *Maybe Baby* (UK/Fr), *Born Romantic* (2001), *The Final Curtain, Dust* (2002, UK/US).

Lester, Bruce (aka Lister) (*b* Johannesburg, 1912). Actor. RN: Lister. In Britain from infancy, this amiable-looking actor was long in Hollywood where he played Bingley in *Pride and Prejudice* (1940) as to the manner/manor born. His British films include *Death at Broadcasting House* (1934) and the post-war oddity, *The Fool and the Princess* (1948), then back to Hollywood. Under contract to WARNER–BRITISH in the 30s.
OTHER BRITISH FILMS INCLUDE: *Badger's Green* (1934), *Crime Over London* (1936), *Ship's Concert* (1937), *Quiet Please* (1938), *But Not in Vain* (1948), *Celia* (1949).

Lester, Mark (*b* Oxford, 1958). Actor. Lester began acting as an angel-faced child, starring as *Oliver!* (1968) in manner so definitive that it is hard to imagine him now with wife and children and an osteopath's practice. He was to the life the exquisitely mannered tot, uncorrupted by the surrounding crime and brutality, that Dickens so clearly had in mind. He'd made several films before this, including Jack CLAYTON's dark fable, *Our Mother's House* (1967) and a further half-dozen or so, but failed to shake off the image of 'asking for more'.
OTHER BRITISH FILMS INCLUDE: *Fahrenheit 451* (1966), *Run Wild, Run Free* (1969), *Eyewitness, SWALK* (1970), *Whoever Slew Auntie Roo?*, *Black Beauty* (UK/It/Sp) (1971), *Redneck* (1972).

Lester, Richard (*b* Philadelphia, 1932). Director. Primarily remembered for a golden period when he directed the BEATLES' films, *A Hard Day's Night* (1964) and *Help!* (1965) and the joyous youth comedy *The Knack . . .* (1965) which won the Golden Palm at Cannes. Such credentials immediately identified Lester with the stylistic dash and social rebelliousness of 'SWINGING LONDON' and the so-called permissive generation, an association he found hard to live down.
    Lester had settled in England in the mid 50s. Two modest, visually striking features, *It's Trad, Dad!* (1962) and *The Mouse on the Moon* (1963) attracted attention, but his calling card for the Beatles was his short, *The Running Jumping Standing Still Film* (1959) whose zany humour corresponded with their own. Their collaboration clicked; their films together ran, jumped, rarely stood still; in Manny Farber's phrase, the 'day of the Lesteroid' had arrived.
    It could not last, and as the mood of the decade darkened, so did Lester's films. *How I Won the War* (1967) bleakly mocked the ambiguous heroics of war and WAR FILMS, while *The Bed-Sitting Room* (1969) was a surreal comedy about the Bomb, with London now sinking, not swinging. In between, Lester returned to America to make his masterpiece, *Petulia* (1968, UK/US), which poignantly anatomised the death throes of America's 'summer of love'. After the 60s, Lester's work ranged from the bracing adventurism of *The Three Musketeers* (1973, Panama) to the tender tragedy of *Robin and Marian* (1976, UK/US). In *Juggernaut* (1974), a subtle political commentary

simmered beneath the surfaces of a tense thriller. The career momentum was flagging, though, and when a key player Roy KINNEAR was tragically killed while filming *The Return of the Musketeers* (1989, UK/Fr/Sp), Lester decided to retire. His visual quick-wittedness and sceptical intelligence are much missed.
OTHER BRITISH FILMS: *The World Is Your Oyster* (1965, short), *Mondo Teeno* (1967, UK/US, doc, co-d), *Royal Flash* (1975), *The Ritz* (1976), *Superman II* (1980), *Superman III* (1983), *Get Back* (1991, doc).
BIBLIOG: Neil Sinyard, *The Films of Richard Lester*, 1985; Andrew Yule, *The Man Who 'Framed' the Beatles: A Biography of Richard Lester*, 1994. Neil Sinyard.

Lestocq, Humphrey (*b* London, 1919 – *d* London, 1984). Actor. Insignificant screen career with never a major role and scarcely a major film, but television immortality as presenter on BBC children's programme, *Whirligig*, along with puppet, Mr Turnip, beginning in November 1950.
BRITISH FILMS INCLUDE: *Once a Sinner* (1950), *Two on the Tiles* (1951), *Angels One Five* (1952), *Meet Mr Lucifer* (1953), *Conflict of Wings* (1954), *The Third Alibi* (1961), *Waltz of the Toreadors* (1962). AS.

Letts, Barry (*b* Leicester, 1925). Actor. After acting in a half-dozen films, including the HIGHBURY cautionary tale, *To the Public Danger* (1948), as Susan SHAW's disaffected boyfriend, as Cherry-Gerrard in *Scott of the Antarctic* (1948), and one of the cycling team in *A Boy, a Girl and a Bike* (1949), Letts became a TV actor and producer/director. He produced many literary serials (e.g. *The Invisible Man*, 1984) and did time with *EastEnders* (1985). Brother of Pauline LETTS.
OTHER BRITISH FILMS: *San Demetrio–London* (1943), *Frieda* (1947), *The Cruel Sea* (1952).

Letts, Pauline (*b* Loughborough, 1917 – *d* Isleworth, 2001). Actress. RADA-trained actress on stage 1935, with Stratford and Old Vic seasons, scoring a major success as the unhappy wife in *Edward, My Son* (1948), and in occasional films since 1945's *Pink String and Sealing Wax*. Also on TV, including two ADAPTATIONS produced by brother Barry LETTS, *Nicholas Nickleby* (1977), as thespian Mrs Crummles, and *The Old Curiosity Shop* (1979).
OTHER BRITISH FILMS INCLUDE: *Girl on Approval* (1961), *Eye of the Devil* (1966), *Gawain and the Green Knight* (1973), *Turtle Diary* (1985).

Le Vien, Jack (*b* New York, 1918 – *d* London, 1999). Documentary producer. Reporter and editor for Pathé News after WW2 service. Famous for compilation films on the lives of 20th-century myth-makers, he won an Oscar for *The Black Fox* (1962, US), his documentary on the life of Hitler, narrated by Marlene Dietrich, and was Oscar-nominated for his DOCUMENTARIES, *The Finest Hours* (1964), a tribute to CHURCHILL, and *A King's Story* (1965), which pieced together the life of the Duke of Windsor until his 1936 abdication.
OTHER BRITISH FILMS: *The Other World of Winston Churchill* (1964, doc), *England Made Me* (1972, UK/Yug), *A Question of Choice* (1983).

Levy, Benn W. (*b* London, 1900 – *d* Oxford, 1973). Screenwriter, dramatist. Oxford-educated author and adapter of many plays, including the delightful classical spoof, *The Rape of the Belt* (1958), starring his wife (1933, till his death) Constance CUMMINGS. Several of his plays were adapted to film (e.g. his *Ever Green* became *Evergreen*, 1934) and he wrote screenplays for such 30s films as *The Dictator* (1935). Also wrote dialogue for the sound version of HITCHCOCK's *Blackmail* (1929), and worked on some US films, including *The Devil and the Deep* (1932). MP for Eton and Slough, 1945–50. Awarded MBE 1944.

OTHER BRITISH FILMS INCLUDE: *The Temporary Widow* (1930, UK/Ger, co-sc), *Lord Camber's Ladies* (1932, d, co-sc), *The Unfinished Symphony* (1934, UK/Austria/Ger, 1934, sc).

Levy, Louis (*b* London, 1893 – *d* Slough, 1957). Music director. A legendary figure in British music associated with so many films not as a composer but as a musical director, sometimes credited as the first person to develop the theme song in film. Studied violin under Guido Papini and made professional debut at age ten. A leading cinema conductor of the silent era, Levy became musical director at GAINSBOROUGH/GAUMONT–BRITISH in 1929, and was responsible for the music in all films shot at LIME GROVE until 1949, in which year he moved to ASSOCIATED BRITISH. Associate producer on one film, *I'll Be Your Sweetheart* (1945).

OTHER BRITISH FILMS INCLUDE: *Balaclava* (1928), *High Treason* (1929), *Sunshine Susie* (1931), *The Lucky Number* (1933), *Evergreen, The Man Who Knew Too Much* (1934), *My Heart Is Calling, The 39 Steps,* (1935), *Tudor Rose, It's Love Again, Oh! Mr Porter, Sabotage* (1936), *The Great Barrier, Young and Innocent* (1937), *Bank Holiday, Convict 99, The Lady Vanishes, Pygmalion, The Citadel* (1938), *Goodbye, Mr Chips, Shipyard Sally* (1939), *Cottage to Let, Kipps* (1941), *The Man in Grey, Millions Like Us* (1943), *Fanny by Gaslight, Two Thousand Women* (1944), *Waterloo Road, They Were Sisters, The Wicked Lady* (1945), *The Idol of Paris, The Queen of Spades* (1948), *The Dancing Years, Stage Fright* (1950), *The Dam Busters, 1984* (1955), *Moby Dick, Yield to the Night, The Good Companions* (1956).

BIBLIOG: Autobiography, *Music for the Movie*, 1948. AS.

Levy, Stuart (*b* London, 1908 – *d* London, 1966). Producer. In 1942 formed ANGLO-AMALGAMATED production and distribution partnership with Nat COHEN. They were responsible for the Edgar WALLACE series of the 50s, the first dozen 'CARRY ON' films, and more prestigious productions in the 60s, including *A Kind of Loving* (1962) and *Darling* (1965). He and Cohen also operated under Bruton Film Productions and Insignia Films. Sometimes listed as 'executive producer', sometimes he and Cohen simply 'present' (as with *Ghost Ship*, 1952). What is certain is that they were a very active pair in the 50s and 60s.

Lewis, Cecil (*b* Birkenhead, 1898 – *d* London, 1997). Novelist, screenwriter, director. One of the founders of the BBC (1922) and its first deputy director, Lewis shared an Oscar for the screenplay of *Pygmalion* (1938), and directed and co-wrote two other 30s ADAPTATIONS of SHAW, at Shaw's instigation, *How He Lied to Her Husband* (1931, short) and *Arms and the Man* (1932). Also a WW1 flying ace, his novel provided the basis for *Aces High* (1976, UK/Fr), about the exploits of the Royal Flying Corps.

OTHER BRITISH FILMS: *Gipsy Blood* (1931, d, co-sc), *The Indiscretions of Eve* (1932, d, p, sc, m), *Leave It to Me* (1933), *Café Mascot* (1936, sc, story).

Lewis, Fiona (*b* Westcliff-on-Sea, 1946). Actress. *Lisztomania* (1975) opens with the composer kissing the breasts of Lewis (as Marie) until her irate husband interrupts. The brunette beauty appeared in several HORROR films, including the 1973 *Dracula* (UK/US) in which she was vampirised by Jack PALANCE. Also in US films, including *Drum* (1976), sensationalised sequel to *Mandingo* (1975).

OTHER BRITISH FILMS INCLUDE: *Dance of the Vampires* (1967), *Where's Jack?* (1969), *Villain* (1971), *Dr Phibes Rises Again* (1972), *Blue Blood* (1973).

Lewis, Gary (*b* Glasgow, *c* 1957). Actor. Since his debut in the cult *film noir*, *Shallow Grave*, in 1994, masterly Scots character actor (and former street-sweeper) Lewis has been in constant

demand, with two searing performances as inarticulate fathers imploding with frustrated feeling: in the TV series *Life Support* (1999), as the father with a son dying of leukaemia, and as the miner-dad of *Billy Elliot* (2000), coming to terms with his son's passion for dance. As well, he riveted attention as the grieving brother who refuses to leave his mother's coffin in *Orphans* (1997), directed by Peter MULLAN, for whom Lewis had appeared in two earlier, short films: *Good Day for the Bad Guys* (1995) and *Fridge* (1996). Martin Scorsese cast him in *Gangs of New York* (2002).

OTHER BRITISH FILMS INCLUDE: *Ruffian Hearts* (1994), *Carla's Song* (1996, UK/Ger/Sp), *My Name Is Joe* (1998), *The Match* (UK/Ire/US), *Gregory's Two Girls* (1999), *East Is East* (2000), *One Life Stand, Shiner, Rob of the Rovers* (2001).

Lewis, Jay (*b* Warwickshire, 1914 – *d* London, 1969). Director, producer. After theatrical experience, Lewis joined BIP in 1933, and during the 30s acted as assistant director and producer for various companies. He and Sydney BOX formed VERITY FILMS in 1940, making short DOCUMENTARIES and instructional films, until Lewis joined the ARMY FILM UNIT (1942–45). He continued with this kind of film-making post-war before embarking on feature film production with *A Man's Affair* (1949, d, p, co-sc). He then produced the critically and commercially successful *Morning Departure* (1950) and directed several more films including the punchy *Live Now, Pay Later* (1962).

OTHER BRITISH FILMS INCLUDE: (shorts) *Crime Doesn't Pay* (*c* 1935), *Little White Lies* (1940, d), *The Roots of Victory* (d), *Queen's Messengers* (d, p) (1941), *Knights of St John* (1942, d), *Home of Your Own* (1946, d, co-sc); (features) *Front Page Story* (1953, p, co-sc), *The Baby and the Battleship* (1956, d, co-sc), *Invasion Quartet* (1961, d).

Lewis, Michael J. (*b* Aberystwyth, 1939). Composer. Entered films in 1968, winning the Ivor Novello Award for best score with his debut film, *The Madwoman of Chaillot*. He maintained a steady output, often as conductor as well, over the next few decades, in film and TV, and in recent years he has worked mainly in America.

OTHER BRITISH FILMS INCLUDE: (comp/cond) *The Man Who Haunted Himself, Julius Caesar* (1970), *Unman, Wittering and Zigo* (1971), *Running Scared, Baxter!* (1972), *The Passage* (1978), *North Sea Hijack* (1979), *The Hound of the Baskervilles* (1983).

Lewis, Ronald (*b* Port Talbot, Wales, 1928 – *d* London, 1982). Actor. RADA-trained, with rep and West End experience, this rather sombre, darkly handsome actor entered films in 1953's *The Square Ring*. Under contract to LONDON FILMS, but most of his roles were for other companies, including RANK and HAMMER. He is a strong presence in such diverse films as *Bachelor of Hearts* (1958), the Gothic *Taste of Fear* (1961) and *Billy Budd* (1962), but the roles dwindled sharply in the 70s. He committed suicide. Married to actress **Norah Gorsen** (*b* Portland, Dorset, 1933), with whom he worked at the Regent's Park Open Air Theatre and who starred in *Geordie* (1955).

OTHER BRITISH FILMS INCLUDE: *Storm over the Nile, The Prisoner* (1955), *Sailor Beware, A Hill in Korea* (1956), *The Secret Place, Robbery Under Arms* (1957), *The Wind Cannot Read* (1958), *Conspiracy of Hearts* (1960), *Jigsaw* (1962), *The Siege of the Saxons, Nurse on Wheels* (1963), *Friends* (1971), *Paul and Michelle* (1974, UK/Fr).

Lewis, Stephen (*b* London, 1936). Actor. Supporting player best known as the by-the-book bus inspector in TV's *On the Buses* (1969–73, + co-sc some episodes), repeating his role in the three film SPIN-OFFS, and the series *The Last of the Summer Wine* (1988). Played the suavely named Crapper in *Adventures* *of a Plumber's Mate* (1978); character actor in a bad period for his kind. Mainly TV in the 80s and 90s.

OTHER BRITISH FILMS INCLUDE: *A Prize of Arms* (1961), *Sparrows Can't Sing* (1962, + co-sc), *On the Buses* (1971), *Mutiny on the Buses* (1972), *Holiday on the Buses* (1973), *Adventures of a Taxi Driver* (1975), *Personal Services* (1987), *The Krays* (1990).

Lexington Production company. Set up in 1996 by producer Don BOYD, its aim to make non-conventional films, the first being *Lucia* (1998).

Lexy, Edward (*b* London, 1897 – *d* Dublin, 1970). Actor. RN: Gerald Little. Short, severe, even pugnacious-looking supporting player of numerous choleric types, like Colonel Jenkins in *Blanche Fury* (1947). Came to attention as Inspector Hollis in the likeable pre-war comedy THRILLERS, *This Man Is News* (1938) and *This Man in Paris* (1939). Educated for the Army, then the law, then made stage debut at Dublin's Gate Theatre, 1935; after WW2 service (1940–46), he was in immediate demand for character roles, and remained so until his death.

OTHER BRITISH FILMS INCLUDE: *Knight Without Armour, Action for Slander* (1937), *The Divorce of Lady X, Sixty Glorious Years* (1938), *The Spider, The Outsider* (1939), *Spare a Copper, The Proud Valley* (1940), *School for Secrets, Piccadilly Incident* (1946), *Temptation Harbour, Good-Time Girl* (1947), *The Winslow Boy* (1948), *Cloudburst* (1951), *The Happy Family* (1952), *Orders Are Orders* (1954), *Up in the World* (1956), *The Story of Esther Costello, The Man Who Wouldn't Talk* (1957).

Leyton, John (*b* Frinton-on-Sea, 1938). Actor. With some success as a 60s pop singer, the craggy-featured Leyton had a limited film career, with the romantic lead in *Guns at Batasi* (1964) offering perhaps his best role. On TV he sang some mournful ballads on *Thank Your Lucky Stars* (1961–66); unlike many teen idols, he went on to an adult career.

OTHER BRITISH FILMS INCLUDE: *The Great Escape, It's Trad Dad!* (as himself) (1962), *The Idol* (1966), *Schizo* (1976), *Dangerous Davies – the Last Detective* (1980).

Leyton Studio Former horse-tram shed which operated as a studio from 1914 to about 1924. Owned by the J.B. Davidson Film Company, it was also used by actor-director A.E. COLEBY, and the actors Percy MORAN and Victor McLAGLEN starred in films made there.

Lieven, Albert (*b* Hohenstein, East Prussia, 1906 – *d* London, 1971). Actor. In British films since 1939. Blond, blue-eyed, and with a brusque, military demeanour, Lieven was equally adept at playing romantic leads, as in *Beware Of Pity* (1945) or as one of Ann TODD's suitors in *The Seventh Veil* (1945), and snarling Nazi villains, as in *Frieda* (1947). Was married to (3) Valerie WHITE and (4) Susan SHAW.

OTHER BRITISH FILMS INCLUDE: *Spy For A Day* (1939), *Convoy, Let George Do It!* (1940), *The Young Mr Pitt* (1942), *The Yellow Canary* (1943), *English Without Tears* (1944), *Sleeping Car To Trieste* (1948), *Hotel Sahara* (1951), *Conspiracy Of Hearts* (1960), *Death Trap* (1962), *Death Drums Along the River* (UK/Ger/S Af), *The Victors* (US/UK) (1963), *City Of Fear* (1965). Tim Bergfelder.

Lijertwood, Lucita (*b* Trinidad, 1921). Actress. West Indian player who had a few roles in British films of the 70s and 80s, including Horace OVE's drama of black generational conflict, *Pressure* (1975), was last seen in a small role in *Playing Away* (1986). Has had some TV work, as in a 1981 episode of *Only Fools and Horses.*

OTHER BRITISH FILMS INCLUDE: *Leo the Last* (1969), *The Squeeze* (1977), *Pink Floyd The Wall* (1982), *Water* (1985).

Lill, Denis (*b* Hamilton, NZ, 1942). Actor. Much of Lill's work has been for TV, including Rodolphe, lover of *Madame Bovary* (1975), and decent, foolish Giles in *Rebecca* (1997). In films, he was in Mike NEWELL's UK/NZ co-production *Bad Blood* (1981), and had small roles in such late 90s films as *Mrs Dalloway* (1997, UK/Neth/US) as the doctor.

OTHER BRITISH FILMS INCLUDE: *The Eagle Has Landed* (1976), *Richard III* (1995), *Evita* (1996, UK/US), *Fierce Creatures* (1997, UK/US).

Lillie, Beatrice (*b* Toronto, 1898 – *d* Henley-on-Thames, 1989). RN:Constance Sylvia Munston. Just possibly the funniest woman of the 20th century, Lillie could quell with a glance, hinting suspicion of nameless depravities. Stage and radio were her true media and, from her first film (*Exit Smiling*, 1926, US) to her last (*Thoroughly Modern Millie*, 1967, US – as a white slaver, yet), she scarcely averaged one a decade. She belongs in this book for *On Approval* (1944), in which she yawns as she sings 'Drink to me only . . . ' and imbues a line like 'You'll find the dinghy by the jetty' with a wealth of dark meaning. Married Sir Robert Peel (1920–34, his death); fell victim to Alzheimer's Disease many years before her death.

OTHER BRITISH FILM: *A Welcome to Britain* (1943).

BIBILOG: Beatrice Lillie, *Every Other Inch a Lady*, 1973; Bruce Laffey, *Beatrice Lillie: The Funniest Woman in the World*, 1989.

Lime Grove Studios *see* **Shepherd's Bush Studios**

Lincoln, Andrew (*b* Hull, 1973). Actor. RN: Clutterbuck. As 'Egg', the moral centre of TV's cult series *This Life* (1996–98), Lincoln was so definitively decent and smart and self-knowing, that he has had to work hard to escape the image. RADA-trained, he returned to the theatre to tackle *Blue/Orange* (2000), a play about mental illness. On TV he played a gay man dying of AIDS in *Hushabye Mountain* and the manic lead in *Teachers* (2000), and on screen appeared in the clubbers' tale, *Human Traffic* (1999, UK/Ire), and as an unrecognisable thug in *Gangster No. 1* (2000).

OTHER BRITISH FILMS INCLUDE: *Boston Kickout* (1995), *Understanding Jane* (1998), *Offending Angels* (2000).

Lind, Gillian (*b* India, 1904 – *d* Lewes, 1983). Actress. Occasional character performer on screen, but more active on stage (debut 1922; a memorable Mrs Penniman in *The Heiress*, 1949) and TV (from 1949). Married Cyril RAYMOND.

BRITISH FILMS INCLUDE: *Condemned to Death* (1932), *Open All Night* (1934), *The Oracle, The Heart of the Matter* (1953), *Aunt Clara* (1954), *Fear in the Night* (1972), *And Now the Screaming Starts!* (1973). AS.

Linden, Jenny (*b* Worthing, 1939). Actress. With a look of Debbie Reynolds which served her well as she whipped Alan BATES into shape in her most famous role as one of the *Women in Love* (1969), Linden has had a spotty screen career since. Repeated on screen her stage role of Mrs Elvsted to Glenda JACKSON's *Hedda* (1975), but most of her post-70s film work has been for TV, including a season in the spy drama, *Charlie Muffin* (1983).

OTHER BRITISH FILMS INCLUDE: *Nightmare* (1963), *A Severed Head* (1970), *Vampira* (1974), *Valentino* (1977).

Linder, Cec (*b* Timmins, Ontario, 1921 – *d* Toronto, 1992). Actor. Brought up in Canada, Linder spent a lot of time playing Americans on the British stage (e.g. *The Trial of Mary Dugan*, 1958) and screen (e.g. *Lolita*, 1961). Worked steadily up to his death, best remembered as BOND's CIA opposite number in *Goldfinger* (1964), and often on TV or in international films.

OTHER BRITISH FILMS INCLUDE: *Subway in the Sky* (1958), *SOS Pacific*, *Jet Storm* (1959), *The Verdict* (1964), *A Touch of Class* (1972), *Super Bitch* (1973, UK/It), *Tomorrow Never Comes* (1977, UK/Can), *Lost and Found* (1979).

Lindgren, Ernest (*b* London, 1910 – *d* Totteridge, 1973). Film archivist. Lindgren was curator of the NATIONAL FILM ARCHIVE from its inception in 1935 to his death in 1973. He joined the BRITISH FILM INSTITUTE as Information Officer in 1934, but was soon given the newly-established National Film Library to run. He established the principles and practices of film preservation which have been the mainstay of film archiving in Britain and around the world ever since. His professional life saw an unceasing battle with the BFI over funds, with the film industry over acquisition of materials, and with the INTERNATIONAL FEDERATION OF FILM ARCHIVES (FIAF) over the faction that preferred the romantic cinephilia of Henri Langlois to Lindgren's relentless insistence on working for a posterity that never seemed to come. In truth he was far more committed to access than his detractors have allowed, but he understood that it should never be at the expense of preservation. Lindgren was not as much fun as Langlois, but he was right. Luke McKernan.

Lindo, Olga (London, 1898 – *d* London, 1968). Actress. Strong, distinctive character player, short but imposing, on stage from 1913, at Drury Lane, and in films from 1927, in *A Window in Piccadilly* (1928). She played many wives: loyal but misunderstood in *The Last Journey* (1935), mischievous in *Return to Yesterday* (1940), complacent-riding-for-a-fall in *When We Are Married* (1943), frightened in *Sapphire* (1959). Perhaps best of all as the haughty, uncharitable Mrs Birling in *An Inspector Calls* (1954), and funny as Arthur ASKEY's landlady in her third for Lance COMFORT, *Make Mine a Million* (1959). Valuable company in 30 films, she was also on stage constantly.

OTHER BRITISH FILMS INCLUDE: *Royal Cavalcade* (1935), *The Stars Look Down* (1939), *Alibi* (1942), *Time Flies* (1944), *The Rake's Progress* (1945), *I See a Dark Stranger, Bedelia* (1946), *Obsession, Train of Events* (1949), *Yield to the Night, The Extra Day* (1956), *Woman in a Dressing Gown* (1957), *Dr Crippen* (1962).

Lindsay, James (*b* Devonshire, 1869 – *d* Melbourne, 1928). Actor. A busy performer in more than 50 silent films, often as the villain, from 1914 to 1927, having begun his stage career in 1894.

BRITISH FILMS INCLUDE: *The Cry of the Captive* (1914), *The Second Mrs Tanqueray* (also on stage), *The Lyons Mail* (1916), *The Admirable Crichton* (1918), *Damaged Goods* (1919), *The Rat* (1925, also on stage). AS.

Lindsay, John (*b* Glasgow, 1949). Director, exhibitor. Former stills photographer who became Britain's leading maker of blue movies in the 70s, some of them featuring porn star, Mary MILLINGTON. Prosecuted for exhibiting obscene films, he was imprisoned for a year, after which he sold his film clubs, called 'Taboo', exhibition venues (though not the only ones) for his hardcore products, and retired from the business. His feature films include titles such as *The Love Pill* (1971, p, story), *The Porn-Brokers* (1973, + a, p, c) and *The Hot Girls* (1974), but it was his hardcore shorts that made him notorious.

BIBLIOG: David Kerekes, 'Jolly Hockey Sticks!: The Career of John Lindsay, Britain's 'Taboo' Film-maker of the Seventies', in Jack Stevenson (ed), *Fleshpot: Cinema's Sexual Myth Makers & Taboo Breakers*, 2000.

Lindsay, Robert (*b* Ilkeston, 1949). Actor. RN: Stevenson. Versatile character star of stage, TV and screen whose prowess

and reputation reached new heights in the 90s. Son of an ex-naval man, RADA-trained Lindsay first came to notice in TV's *Citizen Smith* (1977–80), as self-appointed leader of the Tooting Popular Front, and has done a dazzling range of TV since, including five BBC SHAKESPEARE productions (he was Benedick in *Much Ado About Nothing*, 1984), Fagin in *Oliver Twist* (1999), Captain Pellew in six *Hornblower* films (1998–2001), and a BAA-winning ruthless council boss in *GBH* (1991). Highlights of his theatre work include *Richard III* (1998) for the RSC, and his Tony-winning success in the revival of *Me and My Girl*. Big-screen work has been relatively modest, but he is a compelling presence as a slick politician in *Divorcing Jack* (1998, UK/Fr), and he played the title role in *Bert Rigby, You're a Fool* (1989, US), with his then-partner, actress Diana Weston (*b* Canada, 1953), as his screen wife.

OTHER BRITISH FILMS INCLUDE: *That'll Be the Day* (1973), *Three for All* (1974), *Genghis Cohn* (1993), *Remember Me?* (1996), *Fierce Creatures* (1997, UK/US).

Lindsay-Hogg, Michael (*b* New York, 1940). Director. Distinguished director of US and UK television, including *Brideshead Revisited* (1981, co-d), Lindsay-Hogg has so far made only a smattering of films. His early DOCUMENTARY on the BEATLES, *Let It Be* (1970), and *Nasty Habits* (1976), his witty ADAPTATION of Muriel Sparks's witty 1974 novel, *The Abbess of Crewe*, may still be his best film work. Son of Geraldine FITZGERALD.

OTHER BRITISH FILMS INCLUDE: *The Object of Beauty* (1991, UK/US, + sc), *The Rolling Stones Rock and Roll Circus* (doc), *Guy* (UK/Ger) (1996), *Waiting for Godot* (2001, Ire).

Lindsell, R(eginald) Stuart (*b* Biggleswade, 1898 – *d* ?). Actor. Silver-haired character player of upper-class types in 40s and 50s films. He was the local grandee who snubs Robert NEWTON in *Hatter's Castle* (1941), hapless Cabinet Minister father of *Fanny by Gaslight* (1944), choosing death before dishonour, and the anxious father of the iron-lung passenger in *Broken Journey* (1948). More dignified than exciting.

OTHER BRITISH FILMS INCLUDE: *The Young Mr Pitt* (1942), *The Man in Grey* (1943), *Night Boat to Dublin* (1946), *My Brother Jonathan, Escape* (1948), *Passport to Pimlico, Christopher Columbus* (1949), *Once a Sinner* (1950), *High Treason* (1951), *West of Zanzibar* (1954).

Lion, Leon M. (*b* London, 1879 – *d* Brighton, 1947). Actor. A character actor who usually received star billing, Lion was a major theatrical (debut 1896) figure, as actor and manager (responsible for some 70 plays between 1918 and 1939). He appeared in the 1919 and 1932 screen adaptations of his play, *The Chinese Puzzle*, and starred as a tramp in HITCHCOCK's *Number Seventeen* (1932). Named Chevalier of the Legion of Honour 1928.

OTHER BRITISH FILMS INCLUDE: *Grip* (1915), *Hard Times* (1915), *Chin Chin Chinaman* (1931), *Lady in Danger* (1934), *Strange Boarders, Crackerjack* (1938).

BIBLIOG: Autobiography: *The Surprise of My Life*, 1948. AS.

Lipman, Maureen (*b* Hull, 1946). Actress. In films since 1967's *Up the Junction*, LAMDA-trained Lipman has remained essentially a stage star, scoring recently such notably varied successes as *Oklahoma!* (1998, also on TV) and *Peggy for You* (2000), as legendary agent Peggy Ramsay. On TV she has played in SHAKESPEARE (*Love's Labour's Lost*) and Alan AYCKBOURN (*Absurd Person Singular*) (1985); on screen, she has had a dozen supporting roles, including Julie WALTERS' friend in *Educating Rita* (1983) and Countess Esmeralda in

Carry On Columbus (1992), but films haven't made of her the Eve Arden-ish use they might. Married to screenwriter Jack ROSENTHAL since 1973; awarded CBE in 1999.

OTHER BRITISH FILMS: *The Smashing Bird I Used to Know* (1969), *Gumshoe* (1971), *The Wildcats of St Trinian's* (1980), *Water* (1985), *Solomon and Gaenor* (1999), *The Pianist* (2002, UK/Fr/Ger/Pol).

Lippert, Robert L. (*b* San Francisco, 1909 – *d* Oakland, California, 1976). Producer. American exhibitor and producer of many second features, mostly Westerns; in 1950 entered into a deal with James CARRERAS to make co-productions with EXCLUSIVE. Such films, with Lippert Films co-credited, usually starred somewhat passé American stars, like Zachary Scott in *Wings of Danger*, Cesar Romero in *Lady in the Fog*, and George Brent in *The Last Page* (all 1952). In the 60s, he produced a series of THRILLERS for his own company, starting with *Witchcraft* (1964), nostalgically starring Lon Chaney Jr. Lippert was interested in film as commodity rather than art, and probably achieved his goals.

OTHER BRITISH FILMS INCLUDE: (p/co-p) *Night Train to Paris, The Earth Dies Screaming* (1964), *Curse of the Fly* (1965), *The Last Shot You Hear* (1968).

Lipscomb, W(illiam) P(ercy) (*b* Merton, Surrey, 1887 – *d* London, 1958). Screenwriter. Prolific and notable screenwriter and occasional producer, who, from 1929, wrote several screenplays, including *The Good Companions* (1933), in the UK before going to Hollywood in 1934. Worked there on such films as *A Tale of Two Cities* (1935) and returned to England to share an Oscar for the screenplay of *Pygmalion* (1938). Worked as writer-producer on *Beware of Pity* (1946) and *The Mark of Cain* (1948) for TWO CITIES and was scenario editor for EALING (1947–51), co-authoring several films there and doing a very successful ADAPTATION of *A Town Like Alice* (1956) for RANK.

OTHER BRITISH FILMS INCLUDE: (sc) *Splinters* (1929), *On Approval* (1930), *The Speckled Band* (1931), *There Goes the Bride* (1932), *Loyalties, Colonel Blood* (+ d) (1933), *Make Me An Offer!* (1954, + p); (co-sc) *Rookery Nook* (1930), *I Was a Spy* (1933), *The King of Paris* (1934), *Caesar and Cleopatra* (1945), *Bitter Springs* (1950), *Where No Vultures Fly* (1951), *Robbery Under Arms* (1957), *Dunkirk* (1958).

Lister, Eve (*b* Brighton, 1913 – *d* London, 1997). Actress. Supporting and occasionally leading brunette player of mid 30s GENRE films, including a George FORMBY comedy, *No Limit* (1935), and an early Michael POWELL film, *The Girl in the Crowd* (1934). Briefly popular, then gone. On stage from childhood; replaced Valerie HOBSON in *The King and I* (1955). Married (1) **Hugh French** (*b* London, 1910 – *d* Los Angeles, 1976), who filmed mainly in Hollywood but also made a couple of British films, including *Shadow of the Eagle* (1950), before turning agent. Married (2) **Bernard Hunter** (*b* Hartlepool, 1920), who appeared in a few early 60s films, including *Invasion Quartet* (1961).

OTHER BRITISH FILMS INCLUDE: *Hyde Park, A Glimpse of Paradise* (1934), *Birds of a Feather* (1935), *Sunshine Ahead, Men of Yesterday* (1936).

Lister, Francis (London, 1899 – *d* London, 1951). Actor. Suave character player of stage (mostly – first in 1914) and screen, where he began in 1921 and had a few colourful roles in the 40s, as, for instance, the Duke of Orleans in *Henry V* (1944) and the florid Lord Kingsclere in *The Wicked Lady* (1945). Also filmed in Hollywood in the mid 30s. Married (1) Nora SWINBURNE, (2) Margot GRAHAME.

OTHER BRITISH FILMS INCLUDE: *Branded* (1921), *Comin' Thro' the Rye* (1923), *Atlantic* (1929), *Jack's the Boy* (1932), *Sensation* (1936), *The Return*

of the Scarlet Pimpernel (1937), *The Hundred Pound Window* (1943), *Christopher Columbus* (1949), *Home to Danger* (1951).

Lister, Moira (*b* Cape Town, 1923). Actress. Willowy, blue-eyed blonde of screen and stage, primarily latter. Child actress on stage with Seymour HICKS, making Johannesburg debut 1929 (London 1937; New York 1948). Came to attention as Ray MILLAND's mistress in *So Evil My Love* (1948), and played leads (*Pool of London*, 1950) and second leads (*White Corridors*, 1951) throughout the 50s. Starred in 1951 French film farce, *Mon Phoque et Elles*, and read the opening commentary in *Hiroshima Mon Amour* (1959).

OTHER BRITISH FILMS INCLUDE: *The Shipbuilders* (1943), *Love Story* (1944), *Uneasy Terms, Once a Jolly Swagman* (1948), *A Run for Your Money* (1949), *Something Money Can't Buy, The Cruel Sea* (1952), *Grand National Night, Trouble in Store* (1953), *The Deep Blue Sea* (1955), *Seven Waves Away* (1956), *Joey Boy* (1965), *Not Now, Darling* (1972).

BIBLIOG: Autobiography, *The Very Merry Moira*, 1969. AS.

literature and film The most obvious kind of relationship that exists between literature and British film is the ADAPTATION of literary texts to the screen, a phenomenon almost as old as cinema. In Britain, with the exception of the WW2 period, when perhaps the national life was throwing up subjects of more urgent concern, the adaptation of classic and popular works has gone on apace – from silent-screen versions of SHAKESPEARE and DICKENS to 90s 'HERITAGE' film-making in which, say, E.M. FORSTER has been much filmed against backgrounds of listed buildings. Given the literary bias of most British reviewers, it was not surprising that, in earlier decades at least, they generally bewailed infidelity to the antecedent texts. The NEW WAVE period, say 1958–63, saw a more marked congruence between the literary culture and what film was doing with literature than at any other time: the ANGRY YOUNG MEN of literature were adapted by their cinematic counterparts (Tony RICHARDSON films John OSBORNE, etc) and for once cinema seemed to enjoy parity with literature. It is revealing, though, that all the films of this period *are* adapted from novels or plays.

But there are other aspects of the relationship between British film and the older form which are worth noting. It has often been claimed that British culture has favoured the verbal over the visual, resulting in a pantheon of authors and very few comparably privileged visual artists. In film, there is some evidence of this. There is often a stronger reliance on dialogue than one would expect in American films, and only a rare film like Peter GREENAWAY's *The Draughtsman's Contract* (1982) seriously *exploits* this tendency; most (inferior) directors just succumb to it. Nevertheless, this point of view has been exaggerated: one has only to think of the oeuvre of Michael POWELL, David LEAN or Ken RUSSELL, or even lesser figures like Lance COMFORT and Lawrence HUNTINGTON to point to the visual power of which British cinema was capable.

British cinema has a record of attracting major literary figures to work on its screenplays, with generally happier results than in Hollywood where the famous came to make fortunes and bite hand-feeders. Christopher Isherwood wrote *Little Friend* in 1934; W.H. AUDEN worked on such famous DOCUMENTARY films as *Night Mail* (1935); and another poet, Dylan THOMAS stayed sober long enough to make some surprising contributions to both SHORTS and feature films. Playwrights from Ben TRAVERS, through Noël COWARD and Terence RATTIGAN, to Ronald HARWOOD and Christopher

HAMPTON, all wrote significant screenplays, sometimes – but not always – adapting their own work. And, most influentially, such novelists as Graham GREENE (also a notably perceptive film reviewer in the 30s), Eric AMBLER and Ian MCEWAN provided important screenplays, both adapted and original, the former two having very productive collaborations with, respectively, directors Carol REED and Roy Ward BAKER.

Finally, there has been a small group of films which has gone beyond conventional adaptation to explore literature in other ways. Gavin MILLAR's *Dreamchild* (1985), drawing on Lewis Carroll's life and work, on the life of the 'real' Alice in Wonderland, as child and old woman, on the relations of FANTASY to reality, is an example of a more innovative approach to the often vexed literature-film connections, as are Greenaway's *Prospero's Books* (1991, UK/Fr/It/Neth) and Patricia ROZEMA's *Mansfield Park* (1999, UK/US).

Little, Natasha (*b* Liverpool, 1970). Actress. Guildhall-trained, she made her mark in TV, notably as insinuating Rachel in the cult series, *This Life* (1997) and as Becky Sharp in *Vanity Fair* (1998), her exquisite features and complexion teasing the bitchy demands of the roles. Has made a half-dozen films since, including the disastrous *The Clandestine Marriage* (1999) and the unspeakable *Kevin & Perry Go Large* (2000, UK/US, as Anne Boleyn), and was hacked to bits in *The Criminal* (2001, UK/US). She deserved better and got it in *Another Life* (2001), a 20s drama of adultery and murder.

OTHER BRITISH FILMS: *Greenfingers* (UK/US), *The Island of the Mapmaker's Wife* (2001).

Littlewood, Joan (*b* London, 1914 – *d* London, 2002). Director. Co-founder of the Theatre Workshop, Stratford, East London, in 1945, and hugely influential theatre producer from the 50s, when such groundbreaking plays as *The Hostage* and *A Taste of Honey* (1957) and *Oh! What a Lovely War* (1963) transferred to the West End. The latter two were successfully filmed (1961 and 1969) and she directed and wrote the screenplay of the film version of *Sparrers* [*Sparrows* for the film] *Can't Sing* (1963), starring Workshop alumni James BOOTH and Barbara WINDSOR.

Litvak, Anatole (*b* Kiev, Ukraine, 1902 – *d* Neuilly-sur-Seine, 1974). Director. RN: Litwak. A Jewish refugee from Nazi Germany, Litvak had a 40-year career, most of it spent in making superior Hollywood films like *Tovarich* (1937) and the AA-nominated *The Snake Pit* (1948). He made two pre-war British films and 20 years later directed Vivien LEIGH in *The Deep Blue Sea* (1955, + p) and Ingrid BERGMAN in *Anastasia* (1956), two popular romantic MELODRAMAS. Most famous for the tragic love story, *Mayerling* (1936, UK/Fr), which opened Hollywood's doors to him. Married (1) Miriam Hopkins (1937–39).

OTHER BRITISH FILMS: *Tell Me Tonight* (1932, UK/Fr/Ger), *Sleeping Car* (1933), *Meet Me at Dawn* (1947, story), *The Night of the Generals* (UK/Fr).

Livesey, Barrie (*b* Barry, Wales, 1904). Actor. Brother of Jack and Roger and son of Sam LIVESEY, Barrie appeared in supporting roles and a few leads in a dozen films, starting with *The Old Curiosity Shop* (1921) and finishing with *They Were Sisters* (1945) as hedonist Anne CRAWFORD's long-suffering husband. Starred with his father in *The Commissionaire* (1933).

OTHER BRITISH FILMS INCLUDE: *The Blue Squadron* (1934), *Variety* (1935), *Rembrandt* (1936).

Livesey, Jack (*b* Barry, Wales, 1901 – *d* Burbank, California, 1961). Actor. Brother of Barrie and Roger and son of Sam LIVESEY, on London stage, from 1917, in a range of popular plays, including *Showboat* (1929) and *The Ringer* (1931), and in about 20 films from 1933 (*The Wandering Jew, Song of the Plough*), dropping the white man's burden in Will HAY's lap in *Old Bones of the River* (1938), and finishing with small roles in US films like *That Touch of Mink* (1962).

OTHER BRITISH FILMS INCLUDE: *Variety* (1935), *Rembrandt* (1936), *Penny Paradise* (1938), *The World Owes Me a Living* (1945), *The First Gentleman* (1948), *Paul Temple's Triumph* (1950).

Livesey, Roger (*b* Barry, Wales, 1906 – *d* Walford, 1976). Actor. Best known of the Livesey acting brothers, a character star more than a character player, Livesey is most fondly remembered for his screen roles in the films of Michael POWELL: *The Life and Death of Colonel Blimp* (1943, as the hero who ages through three wars), *I Know Where I'm Going!* (1945 – his most famous romantic role as the laird who teaches Wendy HILLER about life and love) and *A Matter of Life and Death* (1946, as the benign neurologist-philosopher, Reeves). Other notable roles include the lead in Peter USTINOV's *Vice Versa* (1947), the bogus clergyman in *The League of Gentlemen* (1960), OLIVIER's father in *The Entertainer* (1960) and the Gravedigger in *Hamlet* (1969). Made stage debut in 1917, Broadway 1936; often teamed on stage with wife Ursula JEANS. Last major role in *The Pallisers* (BBC, 1974). His bluff presence and inimitably husky tones made him, perhaps surprisingly, a maturely attractive figure to women.

OTHER BRITISH FILMS: *Where the Rainbow Ends, The Four Feathers* (1921), *Married Love* (1923), *East Lynne on the Western Front* (1931), *A Veteran of Waterloo, A Cuckoo in the Nest* (1933), *Blind Justice, Lorna Doone* (1934), *The Price of Wisdom, Midshipman Easy* (1935), *Rembrandt* (1936), *The Drum, Keep Smiling* (1938), *Spies of the Air, Rebel Son* (1939), *The Girl in the News* (1940), *That Dangerous Age* (1949), *Green Grow the Rushes* (1951), *The Intimate Stranger* (1956), *No, My Darling Daughter* (1961), *Of Human Bondage* (1964), *Oedipus the King* (1967), *Futtocks End* (1969). AS.

Livesey, Sam (*b* Flintshire, 1873 – *d* London, 1936). Actor. First on stage in infancy and much experience thereafter; first in silent films, followed by about 30 talkies in rapid succession until his early death. In some famous 30s films, including RANK's first foray into cinema, *Turn of the Tide* (1935), as one of the feuding patriarchs, as the grumpy headsman in *The Private Life of Henry VIII* (1933), and finally as the obdurate and litigious Mr Tulliver in *The Mill on the Floss* (1937). Father of Jack, Barrie and Roger LIVESEY.

OTHER BRITISH FILMS INCLUDE: *One Summer's Day* (1917), *The Sins of Youth* (1919), *All the Winners* (1920), *Foolish Monte Carlo* (1922), *Maisie's Marriage* (1923), *Blackmail* (1929), *Young Woodley* (1930), *The Hound of the Baskervilles, Dreyfus* (1931), *Jew Süss, The Great Defender* (1934), *Moscow Nights* (1935), *Rembrandt* (1936), *Wings of the Morning* (1937).

Llewellyn, Fewlass (*b* Hull, 1866 – *d* England, 1941). Actor. Welsh character actor, on stage from 1890; appeared in several silent films and about 20 thrillers and comedies of the 30s, usually in dignified roles, like the Dean in *Good Morning, Boys!* (1937). A former engineer, he was also a playwright and producer.

OTHER BRITISH FILMS INCLUDE: *Dombey and Son* (1917), *Goodbye* (1918), *This Freedom* (1923), *The Flag Lieutenant* (1926), *The Outsider* (1931), *Ask Beccles* (1933), *Red Ensign* (1934), *The Phantom Light, Stormy Weather* (1935), *Brief Ecstasy* (1937), *Stolen Life, The Outsider* (1939).

Llewellyn, Suzette Actress. Black player who has been in some striking films since first seen in *Playing Away* (1986), including a major role in *Welcome II the Terrordome* (1995), with its vision of a violent future, and had a continuing role in TV's *Hope and Glory* (2000).

OTHER BRITISH FILMS: *Personal Services* (1987), *Sammy and Rosie Get Laid* (1987), *For Queen and Country* (1988), *Babymother* (1998).

Llewelyn, Desmond (*b* Newport, 1915 – *d* Firle, E. Sussex, 1999). Actor. Llewelyn, after being turned down for the police force, trained at RADA, entered films in 1939, was a POW for five years in WW2, and resumed his acting career post-war. He had played about a dozen film roles before being cast as 'Q', James Bond's irascible gadget-dispensing supervisor in *From Russia with Love* (1963) – and spent the rest of his career in BOND FILMS, dispensing with his Welsh accent for the role. The role brought him fame, but he regretted the loss of other opportunities. He was killed in a car crash.

OTHER BRITISH FILMS INCLUDE: *Ask a Policeman* (1939, ucr), *They Were Not Divided* (1950), *Knights of the Round Table* (1953), *A Night to Remember* (1958), *Only Two Can Play* (1961), *Goldfinger* (1964), *Thunderball* (1965), *You Only Live Twice* (1967), *On Her Majesty's Secret Service* (1969), *Diamonds are Forever* (1971), *The Man with the Golden Gun* (1974), *The Spy Who Loved Me* (1977), *Moonraker* (1979, UK/Fr), *For Your Eyes Only* (1981), *Octopussy* (1983), *A View to a Kill* (1985), *The Living Daylights* (1987), *Licence to Kill* (1989), *GoldenEye* (1995, UK/US), *Tomorrow Never Dies* (1997, UK/US), *The World is Not Enough* (1999, UK/US).

BIBLIOG: Sandy Hernu, *'Q' – the Authorised Biography of Desmond Llewelyn*, 1999.

Lloyd, Emily (*b* London, 1970). Actress. Daughter of Roger LLOYD-PACK, granddaughter of Charles LLOYD-PACK, she erupted on to the screen as the cheeky 50s teenager ('Up yer bum!' was her favoured riposte) in *Wish You Were Here* (1987), receiving a BAAn, but her subsequent career has been disappointing. She had roles in several US films, including *In Country* (1989), opposite Bruce Willis, but problems interfered with her working for some time, though she returned to films in *The Honeytrap* (2001).

OTHER BRITISH FILMS INCLUDE: *Chicago Joe and the Showgirl* (1989), *When Saturday Comes* (1996), *Welcome to Sarajevo* (1997, UK/US), *Woundings* (1998).

Lloyd, Euan (*b* Rugby, 1923). Producer. Entered industry in 1955 on ABPC's EXHIBITION arm, then directed a couple of SHORT FILMS (e.g. *April in Portugal*, 1955) before finding his métier as producer, scoring a major commercial success with *The Wild Geese* (1978), *Who Dares Wins* (1982) and *Wild Geese II* (1985), films skilfully targeting international markets.

OTHER BRITISH FILMS INCLUDE: (d, shorts) *Invitation to Monte Carlo* (UK/US, + co-sc), *The Inheritance* (1963, + p); (p) *Genghis Khan* (1965, Ger/It/Yug), *Shalako* (1968), *Catlow* (1971), *The Sea Wolves* (1980, UK/Switz/US).

Lloyd, Frederick (*b* London, 1880 – *d* Hove, 1949). Actor. On stage from 1905, this character player of the 30s actually made one silent film, *Princess Clementina* (1911). He usually played officers, as in *Tell England* (1931), and gentlemen, like the legal type in *Twenty-One Days* (1937), and his last role was as the aptly grim-visaged Grimwig in *Oliver Twist* (1948).

OTHER BRITISH FILMS INCLUDE: *Balaclava* (1928), *The Hound of the Baskervilles*, *A Gentleman of Paris* (1931), *Blossom Time* (1934), *Royal Cavalcade* (1935), *Weddings Are Wonderful* (1938).

Lloyd, Hugh (*b* Chester, 1923). Actor. Short, anxious character player from the 60s, usually in comedy roles in such films as *Go to Blazes* (1962), as a fireman, and *Father Came Too!* (1963), as Mary Queen of Scots in a village pageant, but touchingly Chekhovian in *August* (1996), as Prosser whose wife has long gone. He and Terry SCOTT teamed in *Hugh and I* (1962–67), with Lloyd doing his fussy turn. By 1999, ready to play the Aged P in TV's *Great Expectations*.

OTHER BRITISH FILMS INCLUDE: *It's Trad, Dad!* (1961), *The Punch and Judy Man* (1962), *The Mouse on the Moon* (1963), *White Cargo* (1973), *Quadrophenia* (1979), *Venom* (1981), *The Clandestine Marriage* (1999).

Lloyd, Jeremy (*b* London, 1932). Actor, screenwriter. Character player usually in upper-class roles, whether for comic effect (e.g. *We Joined the Navy*, 1962) or serious (*Death Drums Along the River*, 1963, UK/Ger/S Af – very pukka). Also directed and co-scripted episodes of TV's politically incorrect series, *Are You Being Served?* (1973–83) and *'Allo, 'Allo* (1984–92) as well as many other radio and TV shows, and wrote for and appeared in *Laugh-In* (1969–70). Was married to Joanna LUMLEY.

OTHER BRITISH FILMS: (a, unless noted) *School for Scoundrels* (1959), *Crooks Anonymous* (1962), *A Hard Day's Night* (1964), *Help!* (1965), *The Wrong Box* (1966), *The Long Duel*, *Smashing Time* (1967), *Goodbye, Mr Chips* (1969), *Murder on the Orient Express* (1974), *Are You Being Served?* (1977, ex p, co-sc).

Lloyd, Russell (*b* Swansea, 1916). Editor. Entered films in the 30s in the cutting room of Alexander KORDA's LONDON FILMS, working under William HORNBECK, and getting his first credit on *The Squeaker* (1937). Transferred to PINEWOOD just before WW2, serving in the Navy and seconded at one stage to work for the CROWN FILM UNIT on *Close Quarters* (1943) at Pinewood. Post-war, starting with *Moby Dick* (1956), he had a long association with director John HUSTON, who allowed him creative freedom. He cut nine further films for this mostly British-based American film-maker, receiving AAn for *The Man Who Would Be King* (1975). Also co-directed *The Last Days of Dolwyn* (1949, + e) and was second-unit director on *Anna Karenina* (1948, + e) and *Treasure Island* (1950). Married (1 of 2) Rosamund JOHN.

OTHER BRITISH FILMS INCLUDE: *The Green Cockatoo* (1937), *School for Secrets* (1946), *I'll Get You for This* (1950), *Rough Shoot* (1953), *The Sea Shall Not Have Them* (1954), *Heaven Knows, Mr Allison* (UK/US), *The Naked Earth*, *Count Five and Die* (1957), *The Lion* (1962), *The Wild Affair*, *Bitter Harvest* (1963), *Of Human Bondage* (1964), *Sinful Davey* (1968), *The Mackintosh Man* (1973), *In Celebration* (1974, UK/Can), *Absolute Beginners* (1986).

Lloyd, Sue (*b* Aldeburgh, 1939). Actress. Comely lead, usually blonde, who came to notice as Harry Palmer's female interest in *The Ipcress File* (1965) and made the most of the slim pickings for her kind of actress in British films over the next couple of decades. Television treated her better with continuing roles in *The Baron* (1966–67) as an intelligence agent (brunette) and *Crossroads* (1975–88) as Barbara Brady.

OTHER BRITISH FILMS INCLUDE: *Hysteria* (1964), *That Riviera Touch* (1966), *Where's Jack?*, *Twinky* (1969), *Percy* (1971), *Revenge of the Pink Panther*, *The Stud* (1978), *Eat the Rich* (1987), *Bullet to Beijing* (1995, UK/Can/CIS).

Lloyd-Pack, Charles (*b* London, 1902 – *d* London, 1983). Actor. Of his five dozen roles, many were of the meek variety, like the small, flustery solicitor in *The Constant Husband* (1954) or the nervous hairdresser in *Victim* (1961). Apart from a pre-war comedy, *The House of the Spaniard* (1936), the first film on which he is certainly credited is the sabotage THRILLER, *High Treason* (1951), but he may have had several previous uncredited roles (e.g. in *The Passionate Friends*, 1948). Father of Roger LLOYD-PACK and grandfather of Emily LLOYD.

OTHER BRITISH FILMS INCLUDE: *The Gift Horse* (1952), *River Beat* (1953), *Aunt Clara* (1954), *Yield to the Night* (1956), *Quatermass 2*, *Interpol* (1957), *Dracula, The Revenge of Frankenstein* (1958), *The Man Who Would Cheat Death* (1959), *Only Two Can Play, The Kitchen* (1961), *Crooks Anonymous* (1962), *The Third Secret* (1964), *Bedazzled* (1967), *If . . .* (1968), *Madame Sin* (1972), *The Mirror Crack'd* (1980).

Lloyd-Pack, Roger (*b* London, 1944). Actor. Son of Charles LLOYD-PACK, father of Emily LLOYD, he is now most widely known as Trigger in the series *Only Fools and Horses*, in the 80s and early 90s, and as the malodorous Owen on the vestry of *The Vicar of Dibley* (1994–2000), a man of very basic instincts. Also seen as the lugubrious undertaker, Sowerberry, in TV's *Oliver Twist* (1999), but yet to make comparable impact in films, in which he has had small roles since the late 60s, when he played the spy Reynaldo in Tony RICHARDSON's *Hamlet* (1969), and more recently Joely RICHARDSON's solicitor in *Hollow Reed* (1996). Some small roles in US films, including *Cuba* (1979).

OTHER BRITISH FILMS INCLUDE: *The Magus* (1968), *The Go-Between* (1971), *Fright* (1971), *Nineteen Eighty-Four* (1984), *Prick Up Your Ears* (1987), *Object of Beauty* (1991, UK/US) (1991), *The Young Poisoner's Handbook* (1995, UK/Fr/Ger),.

Lloyd Webber, Andrew (*b* London, 1948). Composer. Some would credit him with single-handedly arresting the decline of English theatre; others would suggest his work lacks variety; he is, in any case, a wildly successful man of the theatre who has only dabbled with film. His scores have been heard in *Jesus Christ Superstar* (1973, US – AAn/m) and *Evita* (1996, UK/US – AA/best song, BAAn/m), ADAPTATIONS of his stage successes; claimed in 2001 that what he really wanted was to compose a hit pop song. Also scored *Gumshoe* (1971) and *The Odessa File* (1974, UK/Ger). Knighted, 1993; made life peer, 1997. Married (2 of 3) stage star Sarah Brightman.

Loach, Kenneth (*b* Nuneaton, 1936). Director. Loach's uncompromising cinema attacks social injustice, in the face of virulent criticism by the Establishment, particularly during the Thatcher years. His first love was theatre, and after reading law at Oxford (where he was President of the University Dramatic Society, and Secretary of the Experimental Theatre Club), he worked in repertory until 1963, when he became a trainee director at the BBC. His earliest TV assignments included *Z-Cars*, an innovative series about a Merseyside police force, and the experimental 'Wednesday Plays' with their rigorous portrayals of contemporary British working-class life. *Up the Junction* (1965), *Cathy Come Home* (1966), and *In Two Minds* (1967), for example, not only established his talent, but also transformed public awareness of issues such as homelessness by giving voice to traditionally marginalised figures. One consequence of the broadcasting of *Cathy Come Home* was the creation of Shelter, the charity for the homeless, making Loach one of few directors whose films have provoked genuine social change.

His first feature, *Poor Cow* (1967), was not wholly successful but foreshadowed techniques and concerns that would shape his later work, and his second film, *Kes* (1969), established his international reputation. Based on Barry Hines's novel, *Kes* creates a moving portrait of an alienated and lonely child briefly finding hope through his relationship with a kestrel. Its stark images recalling Bresson, its naturalism suggesting links with the British DOCUMENTARY movement, the French New

Wave, and Italian Neo-Realism, *Kes* achieved enduring cult status.

Loach's preoccupation with the socially marginalised continued throughout the 70s in narratives dealing with issues such as schizophrenia, poverty, and working-class despair. His mini-series, *Days of Hope* (1975), written by Jim ALLEN, dealing with social and political conflicts of the period 1916–26, is a key work of this period. Following the 1979 election he used documentary to attack Thatcher's extremist policies, and he found it increasingly difficult to obtain funding. However, his reputation soared again in the 90s: *Hidden Agenda* (1990) won the Special Jury Prize at Cannes, while the humanitarian discourse of films such as *Riff-Raff* (1991), *Raining Stones* (1993), and *Ladybird Ladybird* (1994), powerfully combined bleak accounts of Thatcher's social legacy with humour, compassion, and sensitivity. Similarly, the harsh depiction of poverty, drugs, and crime in *My Name is Joe* (1998) is counterbalanced by Loach's homage to football (his other passion). More recently, *Land and Freedom* (1995), and *Carla's Song* (1996, UK/Ger/Sp) situate social injustice and betrayal within broader historical and geographical contexts, while *Bread and Roses* (2001), his first US film, is set in Los Angeles, and deals with the exploitation of illegal immigrant workers.

OTHER BRITISH FILMS: *Family Life, Talk about Work, After a Lifetime* (1971), *Black Jack* (1979), *Looks and Smiles* (1981), *Fatherland* (1986, UK/Fr/Ger) (1986).

BIBLIOG: George McKnight (ed), *Agent of Challenge and Change: The Films of Ken Loach*, 1997; Graham Fuller (ed), *Loach on Loach*, 1998. Wendy Everett.

locations As early as the 1910s, Will BARKER was using actual LONDON locations for filming a crime series, and Cecil HEPWORTH used Lulworth Cove pre-war and celebrated the English countryside in later films such as *Comin' Thro' the Rye* (1923). In the 30s, location-filming was largely seen as the preserve of the DOCUMENTARY movement, with features predominantly studio-based, and HITCHCOCK recreating Scottish glens (complete with live sheep) at LIME GROVE for *The 39 Steps* (1935). With *The Edge of the World* (1937) Michael POWELL broke new ground by taking cast and crew to the Scottish island of Foula (representing St Kilda) for several arduous weeks, and *The Four Feathers* (1939) was the first of many British epics involving extensive overseas location-shooting.

During WW2, feature-length documentaries such as *Fires Were Started* (1943) and *Western Approaches* (1944, filmed at sea in TECHNICOLOR) used non-professional actors in real locations. This trend was continued into post-war films by EALING, which ventured into London streets for *Hue and Cry* (1946), *It Always Rains on Sunday* (1947), *Passport to Pimlico* (1949), exploring Romney Marsh in *The Loves of Joanna Godden* (1947) and Barra, Outer Hebrides in *Whisky Galore!* (1949). However, studio lighting was deemed essential by director Carol REED for presenting an expressionist view of Belfast docks in *Odd Man Out* (1947), and exteriors were partly re-created at DENHAM.

By 1960, the liberating influence of French *nouvelle vague* and the *cinéma vérité* documentary style was affecting younger British directors. The British NEW WAVE extensively used location-filming, in the films of Tony RICHARDSON (*A Taste of Honey*, 1961; *The Loneliness of the Long Distance Runner*, 1962), Karel REISZ and others. *The Caretaker* (Clive DONNER, 1963) was the first British feature to be shot inside a modest house, in

Hackney. However, vividly conveying the atmosphere of a location is a rare, sensitive skill, and locations quickly become a cliché when used mindlessly, as in many brightly coloured 'SWINGING LONDON' films. Contrast this with US exile Joseph LOSEY's masterly visual depictions of Chelsea (*The Servant*, 1963), Oxford (*Accident*, 1967), and rural Norfolk (*The Go-Between*, 1971), suggesting it may take an outsider to direct a questioning camera at aspects of the British scene natives take for granted.

Far from being more 'real' than the studio, a location can also be seen as another set to be 'dressed' to the film maker's requirements. The process often involves manipulation, constructing settings not naturally there, to present an idealised environment, or a totally fabricated one, perhaps somewhere in another country: North Wales as a walled Chinese city in *Inn of the Sixth Happiness* (1958), or the derelict 300-acre Beckton gasworks as war-torn Vietnam, for *Full Metal Jacket* (1987). A location can be 'enhanced' by adding to what is already there as when an entire village was built in remote County Kerry for *Ryan's Daughter* (1970). More recently, films from the MERCHANT IVORY team and their imitators have constructed an enchanted heritage view of Britain, replete with indicators of wealth, power and nostalgia for a past golden age. The selection of film locations also has a role to play in the representation of national identity for WALES, SCOTLAND, NORTHERN IRELAND and IRELAND, and for images of CITY LIFE, PASTORAL, VILLAGE LIFE and RURAL LIFE.

BIBLIOG: Brian Pendreigh, *On Location : The film fan's guide to Britain and Ireland*, 1995; Mark Adams, *Movie Locations: a guide to Britain and Ireland*, 2000. Roger Philip Mellor.

Locke, Harry (*b* London, 1912 – *d* Worthing, Sussex, 1987). Actor. Another of those wildly prolific small-part character players in whom British cinema abounds. On stage in 1931, in the Intelligence Corps during WW2 (1940–46), post-war he pursued a career as popular stand-up comedian and as purveyor of lower-orders cheerfulness (e.g. as Superintendent John MILLS's offsider in *Town on Trial* (1956) in about six dozen films. Often cast as barmen, cab-drivers and the like, he was in some very famous films, starting with *Piccadilly Incident* (1946) but is probably known by name only to dedicated buffs.
OTHER BRITISH FILMS INCLUDE: *No Room at the Inn* (1948), *Passport to Pimlico* (1949), *Treasure Island* (1950), *Angels One Five* (1952), *Doctor in the House* (1954), *Reach for the Sky* (1956), *Woman in a Dressing Gown* (1957), *Nowhere to Go* (1958), *I'm All Right Jack* (1959), *On the Fiddle* (1961), *Tiara Tahiti*, *Crooks Anonymous* (1962), *Heavens Above!* (1963), *The Early Bird* (1965), *Alfie* (1966), *Carry On Doctor* (1968), *The Creeping Flesh* (1972).

Locke, Philip (*b* London, 1928). Actor. Primarily a stage actor, Locke once created a moment of high camp as a Cardinal excommunicated for baptising a dog before the high altar in the musical *Valmouth* (1958–59). Plenty of TV and about 20 films, usually in small roles, like one of Ronnie BARKER's skiving workmates in *Father Came Too!* (1963), a brief touch of menace in *Thunderball* (1965) and a dignified senator in *Othello* (1995, UK/US).
OTHER BRITISH FILMS INCLUDE: *Cloak Without Dagger* (1955), *Heart of a Child* (1958), *The Girl on the Boat* (1962), *Porridge* (1979), *Ascendancy* (1982), *Stealing Heaven* (1988, UK/Yug), *Tom & Viv* (1994, UK/US), *Wilde* (1997, UK/Ger/Jap/US).

Lockhart, Calvin (*b* Nassau, Bahamas, 1934). Actor. RN: Cooper. Handsome West Indian actor who played the black lover of *Joanna* (1968), one of the more ill-advised films of the often-foolish 60s, and starred in the AMICUS HORROR, *The Beast Must Die* (1974), but who has in the main been lost to US films and TV, including a continuing role in *Dynasty* (1981).
OTHER BRITISH FILMS INCLUDE: *The Mercenaries* (1967), *A Dandy in Aspic*, *Nobody Runs Forever* (1968), *Leo the Last* (1969).

Lockhart, Robert Composer. Active in British films since the mid 80s, he scored the second of Terence DAVIES' reveries on a Liverpool childhood, *The Long Day Closes* (1992), and was music arranger on Davies' US-set *The Neon Bible* (1995, UK/US).
OTHER BRITISH FILMS: *On the Black Hill* (1987), *Cold Comfort Farm* (1995, + m arr), *All Souls' Day* (1997, Ire).

Lockton, Joan (*b* London, 1904). Actress. Leading lady of the 20s, under contract to STOLL from 1924 to 1927.
BRITISH FILMS INCLUDE: *No More Servants for Me* (1918), *The Hour of Trial*, *Pillars of Society* (1920), *Miss Charity* (1921), *Whispering* (1922), *White Slippers* (1924), *Confessions* (1925), *A Woman Redeemed* (1927). AS.

Lockwood, Julia (*b* Bournemouth, 1941). Actress. RN: Leon. Child player of the 50s who barely continued her career into adulthood. Appeared first with her mother, Margaret LOCKWOOD, in *Hungry Hill* (1947), as a tot, and had her best role in *Please Turn Over* (1960) as an imaginative teenager whose flights of fancy are acted out to the embarrassment of her family. Known as 'Toots', as every fan magazine reader knew. Was married to actor Ernest CLARK.
OTHER BRITISH FILMS: *The Flying Eye* (1955), *My Teenage Daughter* (1956), *The Solitary Child* (1958), *No Kidding* (1960).

Lockwood, Margaret (*b* Carica, India, 1916 – *d* London, 1990). Actress. RADA-trained, Lockwood was first on stage at the age of 12 and on screen at 18. Although capable of playing a variety of leading roles as in *Lorna Doone* (1934), *The Lady Vanishes* (1938), with just the right light touch, *The Stars Look Down* (1939), in an early unsympathetic role, *Night Train to Munich* (1940), and *Love Story* (1944), as the afflicted pianist heroine, she shot to fame playing the calculating Hester in *The Man in Grey* (1943) and repeated her success by playing the title role in *The Wicked Lady* (1945). In *Jassy* (1947), Lockwood and Patricia ROC exchanged the roles of villainess and heroine they played in the earlier film. For a time Lockwood was the top female box-office star in British cinema until replaced by Anna NEAGLE in the late 40s. Lockwood's devious 'wicked lady' roles in GAINSBOROUGH MELODRAMAS and other films such as *Bedelia* (1946) echoed the new-found freedom of British women performing male-defined occupations during wartime, temporarily free from patriarchal control.

After escaping from Gainsborough wicked lady roles, Lockwood attempted different parts in the family saga, *Hungry Hill* (1947), and the slapstick *Cardboard Cavalier* (1949) which affected her popularity, which her 50s films with Herbert WILCOX did nothing to restore. After the box-office failure of one of her strongest performances, in *Cast A Dark Shadow* (1955), she returned to stage (scoring a success as Mrs Cheveley in *An Ideal Husband*, 1966) and moved into television. In 1965 she starred as the proprietor in the TV series 'The Flying Swan' and appeared on the right side of the law in the ITV series 'Justice' (1971–74). Her last screen appearance was as a wicked stepmother in *The Slipper and the Rose* (1976).
OTHER BRITISH FILMS: *The Case of Gabrielle Perry*, *Some Day*, *Honours Easy*, *Man of the Moment*, *Midshipman Easy* (1935), *Jury's Evidence. The Amateur Gentleman*, *Beloved Vagabond*, *Irish for Luck* (1936), *The Street*

Singer, Who's Your Lady Friend?, *Dr Syn*, *Melody and Romance* (1937), *Owd Bob*, *Bank Holiday* (1938), *A Girl Must Live*, *Susannah of the Mountains*, *Rulers of the Sea* (1939), *Girl in the News* (1940), *Quiet Wedding* (1941), *Alibi* (1942), *Dear Octopus* (1943), *Give Us the Moon* (1944), *A Place of One's Own*, *I'll Be Your Sweetheart* (1945), *The White Unicorn* (1947), *Look Before You Love* (1948), *Madness of the Heart* (1949), *Highly Dangerous* (1950), *Trent's Last Case* (1952), *Laughing Anne* (1953), *Trouble in the Glen* (1954).

BIBLIOG: Autobiography, *Lucky Star*, 1955; Hilton Tims, *Once a Wicked Lady*, 1989; Bruce Babington, 'Queen of British hearts: Margaret Lockwood revisited', in Babington (ed), *British Stars and Stardom*, 2001. Tony Williams.

Lockwood, Preston (*b* West Ham, 1912 – *d* London, 1996). Actor. Prolific radio actor, a member of the BBC repertory company of the 40s, and much on stage and TV, often as church and legal dignitaries, but only in films from 1970's *Julius Caesar* (as Trebonius).

OTHER BRITISH FILMS INCLUDE: *Lady Caroline Lamb* (1972, UK/It/US), *Ransom* (1974), *Absolution* (1978), *Time Bandits* (1981), *Scandalous* (1983), *The Fool* (1990).

Loder, John (*b* London, 1898 – *d* Selbourne, 1988). Actor. RN: Lowe. Loder was tall and adequately handsome, with conventionally upper-class demeanour, but scarcely interesting enough to account for the tenacious way he held on to his screen career for over 30 prolific years. Eton- and Sandhurst-educated, he served in WW1 with the Hussars at Gallipoli, made his debut in German silent films, appeared in a dozen mainly Hollywood films until 1931, then became a popular leading man in British films of the 30s. He co-starred (though not romantically) with Gracie FIELDS in *Sing As We Go!* (1934), played stalwart leading men to Merle OBERON in *The Battle* (1934, UK/Fr), Margaret LOCKWOOD in *Owd Bob* (1938), and Anna LEE in *The Man Who Changed His Mind* (1936), *King Solomon's Mines* and *Non-Stop New York* (1937). In Hollywood again from 1940, he was love interest twice to Bette DAVIS and in 1947 to Hedy Lamarr (*Dishonored Lady*) whom he married (3 of 5), having become a US citizen. He made a handful of films in Britain from the mid 50s without in any way modifying his screen reputation as decent, dependable and rather dull. Retired with fifth wife to run her ranch in Argentina.

OTHER BRITISH FILMS INCLUDE: *The First Born* (1928), *Wedding Rehearsal* (1932), *The Private Life of Henry VIII* (1933), *Java Head*, *Lorna Doone* (1934), *Sabotage*, *Queen of Hearts* (1936), *Doctor Syn* (1937), *The Silent Battle* (1939), *Small Hotel* (1957), *Gideon's Day* (1958), *The Firechasers* (1970).

BIBLIOG: Autobiography, *Hollywood Hussar*, 1977.

Lodge, David (*b* Rochester, 1921). Actor. After his 1955 film debut in *Cockleshell Heroes*, Lodge seems scarcely to have drawn breath as his burly, moustachioed presence, usually to comic, sometimes more belligerent, effect provided one of the character delights of the ensuing decade or so. His range of thick proles, in and out of uniform, in such films as *I'm All Right Jack* (1959, card-playing malingerer) and *The League of Gentlemen* (1960, military), and in regular comic support to Peter SELLERS, is evidence of the continuity of British CHARACTER ACTING, and he was also noticeable in such TV series as *United!* (1965–66) as an Association Football manager of a team down on its luck. Came from a background of MUSIC HALL and circus.

OTHER BRITISH FILMS INCLUDE: *Private's Progress* (1956), *The Naked Truth* (1957), *I Only Arsked!* (1958), *Yesterday's Enemy* (1959), *Never Let Go*, *Watch Your Stern*, *Two Way Stretch* (1960), *Carry On Regardless* (1961), *Go to Blazes*, *The Dock Brief* (1962), *Guns at Batasi* (1964), *The*

Early Bird (1965), *The Wrong Box* (1966), *Only When I Larf* (1968), *Hoffman* (1969), *The Railway Children*, *On the Buses*, (1971), *Carry On Girls* (1973), . . . *Dick* (1974), . . . *Behind* (1975), . . . *England* (1976), *Edge of Sanity* (1988, UK/Hun).

BIBLIOG: Autobiography, *Up the Ladder to Obscurity*, 1986.

Lodge, Jean (*b* Hull, 1927). Actress. Prettily brunette, pleasant lead and second lead of – mainly – 'B' MOVIES of the 50s and 60s, like the perfunctory *Dangerous Voyage* (1954), with occasional mildly upmarket ventures such as *Brandy for the Parson* (1952) and *The Black Knight* (1954). Spotted for films while at Windsor Rep, she began in TV in 1949. Married Alfred SHAUGHNESSY in 1948.

OTHER BRITISH FILMS INCLUDE: *Dick Barton Strikes Back* (1949), *The Dancing Years* (1950), *White Corridors* (1951), *Johnny on the Spot* (1954), *The Hellfire Club* (1960), *Accidental Death* (1963), *Invasion* (1966).

Lodge, John (*b* Washington, DC, 1903 – *d* New York, 1985). Actor. Handsome leading man of stage and screen who came from a prominent Boston political family. Had a Hollywood career in 30s, notably as dashing Prince Alexei opposite Marlene Dietrich in *The Scarlet Empress* (1934), followed by French, Italian and British films (1935–39). This grandson of Senator Henry Cabot Lodge later became Governor of Connecticut (1951–55), and US Ambassador to Spain (1955–61) and Argentina (1969–73).

BRITISH FILMS INCLUDE: *Ourselves Alone*, *The Tenth Man* (1936), *Sensation*, *Bulldog Drummond at Bay* (1937), *Premiere*, *Queer Cargo*, *Bank Holiday* (1938). AS.

Logan, Jimmy (*b* Glasgow, 1928 – *d* Clydebank, Scotland, 2001). Popular Scottish comedian whose roots were in the MUSIC HALL and he became famous for his sharply observed, essentially good-natured parodies of Scottish working-class life and as an interpreter of Sir Harry LAUDER. Migrated easily from theatre to TV where he had his own show (1957–61). Appeared in only a half-dozen films, beginning with *Floodtide* (1949), a drama of the Glasgow shipyards, as Gordon JACKSON's larky chum. Awarded OBE 1996.

OTHER BRITISH FILMS: *The Wild Affair* (1963), *Carry On Abroad* (1972), *Carry On Girls* (1973), *Lucia* (1998), *The Debt Collector* (1999), *My Life So Far* (2000, UK/US).

Logan, Phyllis (*b* Paisley, Scotland, 1956). Actress. Versatile, attractive auburn-haired actress who entered films in the far-from-propitious mid 80s and has combined cinema and TV. Came to attention in Michael RADFORD's *Another Time, Another Place* (1983) as the frustrated young farmer's wife who has a wartime affair with an Italian internee, and, in complete contrast, played the continuing role of Lady Jane Felsham in the East Anglian-set detective series, *Lovejoy* (1986, 1991–92, 1993). Small but showy roles in late 90s films, *Secrets & Lies* (1996) and *Shooting Fish* (1997).

OTHER BRITISH FILMS INCLUDE: *The Chain*, *Nineteen Eighty-Four* (1984), *The Doctor and the Devils* (1985), *The Kitchen Toto* (1987), *Silent Cries* (1993, UK/US).

Lohr, Marie (*b* Sydney, 1890 – *d* Brighton, 1975). Actress. Upper-class benevolence was Lohr's stock-in-trade, whether as Professor Higgins's long-suffering mother in *Pygmalion* (1938) or the courageous lady of the manor in *Went the Day Well?* (1942) or the severe aunt disapproving of *The Rake's Progress* (1945), but these were all more than stereotyped portrayals. So were her conventional, unhappy mother of *The Winslow Boy* (1948), the haughty, morally rigorous dowager in *Small Hotel* (1957) and her charming comic turn as another dowager, actually part of a light-fingered gang in *Always a Bride* (1953). On stage in Sydney in 1894, London in 1901, and thereafter acted her way through five columns of entries in *Who's Who in the Theatre* (1972). Her films spanned 50 years and she rose majestically above the duds that inevitably came her way, such as *The Magic Bow* (1946).

OTHER BRITISH FILMS INCLUDE: *The Real Thing at Last* (1916), *Aren't We All?* (1932), *My Heart Is Calling* (1934), *Foreign Affaires*, *Fighting Stock* (1935), *South Riding* (1938), *Major Barbara* (1941, Lady Brit), *Twilight Hour* (1944), *Anna Karenina*, *Counterblast* (1948), *Silent Dust* (1949), *Out of the Clouds*, *Escapade* (1955), *A Town Like Alice* (1956), *Carlton-Browne of the FO* (1958), *Great Catherine* (1967).

Lom, Herbert (*b* Prague, 1917). Actor. RN: Herbert Charles Angelo Cuchacevich ze Schluderpacheru. 'In English eyes all foreigners are sinister', said Herbert Lom, resignedly in 1991, accounting for the large number of reprehensible types which have fallen to the lot of the aristocratic, educated and erudite veteran of 100 films. Certainly he had more than his share of crooks, usually executing their villainy with a degree of continental suavity, as in *Night and the City* (1950, UK/US) and *North West Frontier* (1959), parodying this in *The Ladykillers* (1955), and he was a vile seducer in *No Trees in the Street* (1958). However, he also played Napoleon twice (*The Young Mr Pitt*, 1941; *War and Peace*, 1956, US/It), was first seriously noticed as Ann TODD's psychiatrist (a role he repeated on stage, 1951) in *The Seventh Veil* (1945), was an all-but saintly lorry driver in *Hell Drivers* (1957), and found new and different fame as the dithering, frustrated Inspector Dreyfus in the 'Pink Panther' films. On stage he played the King opposite Valerie HOBSON in *The King and I* (1955–56). An escapee from the Germans in the late 30s, having acted in Czech plays and films, he was seconded from the Army in WW2 to work in the Czech and German section of the BBC.

OTHER BRITISH FILMS: *Mein Kampf, My Crimes* (1940), *Tomorrow We Live*, *Secret Mission* (1942), *The Dark Tower* (1943), *Hotel Reserve* (1944), *Night Boat to Dublin*, *Appointment with Crime* (1946), *Dual Alibi*, *Good-Time Girl* (1947), *Snowbound*, *Portrait from Life*, *The Brass Monkey* (1948), *The Golden Salamander* (1949), *State Secret*, *The Black Rose* (UK/US), *Cage of Gold* (1950), *Hell Is Sold Out*, *Mr Denning Drives North*, *Two on the Tiles* (1951), *Whispering Smith Hits London*, *The Man Who Watched Trains Go By* (1952), *The Ringer*, *The Net*, *Rough Shoot*, *Star of India* (UK/It), *The Love Lottery* (1953), *Beautiful Stranger* (1954), *Action of the Tiger*, *Fire Down Below*, *Chase a Crooked Shadow*, *I Accuse!* (1957), *Passport to Shame*, (1958) *Intent to Kill*, *Third Man on the Mountain* (1959), *Mysterious Island*, *Mr Topaze*, *The Frightened City* (1961), *The Phantom of the Opera*, *Tiara Tahiti* (1962), *The Horse Without a Head* (1963), *A Shot in the Dark* (1964), *Return from the Ashes* (1965), *Our Man in Marrakesh* (1966), *The Face of Eve* (UK/Sp), *99 Women* (UK/Ger/It/Sp) (1968), *Mister Jerico*, *Doppelgänger* (1969), *Asylum* (1972), . . . *And Now the Screaming Starts!*, *Dark Places* (1973), *And Then There Were None*, *The Return of the Pink Panther* (1974), *The Pink Panther Strikes Again* (1976), *The Revenge of the Pink Panther* (1978), *The Lady Vanishes* (1979), *Trail of the Pink Panther* (1982), *Curse of the Pink Panther* (1983), *Memed My Hawk* (1984), *Whoops Apocalypse* (1986), *The Pope Must Die* (1991, UK/US).

Lomas, Herbert (*b* Burnley, 1886 – *d* Devon, 1961). Actor. RADA-trained and on stage from 1906, the severe-looking Lomas played titled chaps (Sir Ensor Doone in *Lorna Doone*, 1934) and humble farmers (*The Man Within*, 1947) with equal facility. Is perhaps best remembered as the husband whose golden wedding is celebrated by the ceilidh in *I Know Where I'm Going!* (1945). Crowned a versatile stage career with the role of the endearing but selfish clergyman in *The Holly and the Ivy* (1950), recreating the role on TV.

OTHER BRITISH FILMS INCLUDE: *Hobson's Choice* (1931), *Perfect Understanding* (1933), *Java Head* (1934), *The Ghost Goes West* (1935), *Rembrandt* (1936), *South Riding* (1938), *Jamaica Inn*, *Over the Moon* (1939), *The Ghost Train* (1941), *They Met in the Dark* (1943), *Master of Bankdam* (1947), *The Guinea Pig* (1948), *The Net* (1953).

Loncraine, Richard (*b* Cheltenham, 1946). Director. In 1995, Loncraine directed one of the most innovative and intelligent ADAPTATIONS of SHAKESPEARE in his brilliantly cast *Richard III*, for which he co-wrote the screenplay with star Ian MCKELLEN and which received a BAAn for Best Picture. Since then, he has not made a British film, though there have been several US titles mooted. Coming from an acting family, he originally intended to be an actor (he had a small role in *Sunday Bloody Sunday*, 1971), but changed direction after three years at the Film School of the Royal College of Art. Won a BAA/d for TV's *Blade on the Feather* (1980) and was nominated again for *Wide-Eyed and Legless* (1994). His films have been an idiosyncratic bunch, including the Edwardian comedy of clerical intentions, *The Missionary* (1981) and the unsettling Dennis POTTER piece, *Brimstone & Treacle* (1982), a kind of *Teorama* in reverse. Also produced hundreds of commercials.

OTHER BRITISH FILMS INCLUDE: (2ud) *Rentadick* (1972); (d) *Flame* (1974), *Full Circle* (1976, UK/Can), *Bellman & True* (1987, + co-sc); (story) *Professor Popper's Problems* (1974).

London Film Commission This agency was formed in 1995 to stimulate and facilitate filming in London, which had never been easy in the way that filming reputedly was/is in large US cities. Its aim was to attract off-shore filming to London and its initial grant of £100,000 from the Department of National Heritage was for this purpose. It successfully met the demands of *Mission: Impossible* (1996), but by 1998 it had to look to the government for financial support, having failed to attract private-sector finance.

London Film Company, unrelated to the later Alexander KORDA organisation, was founded in 1913 by the cinema circuit Provincial Cinematograph Theatres, and had studios at St Margarets, Twickenham. Headed by Ralph JUPP and Ralph DEWSBURY, the company boasted two US directors, Harold SHAW and George Loane TUCKER, and two US stars, **Edna Flugrath** (*b* New York, 1893 – *d* San Diego, California, 1966), who made a couple of British films for the company, and Jane Gail. London's first release was *The House of Temperley* (1913), directed by Shaw and starring Ben WEBSTER and Charles MAUDE; its most important film was an adaptation of Hall CAINE's *The Manxman* (1916), directed by Tucker. London ceased production in 1918, but renewed its operation in 1919–20. AS.

London Film Festival The London Film Festival, staged annually since 1957 under the aegis of the BRITISH FILM INSTITUTE, was the earliest of the now proliferating non-competitive 'festival of festivals' events, and is one of the world's oldest film festivals. (At the time of its creation, the only other regular festivals were Cannes, Venice, Berlin, the alternating Moscow–Karlovy Vary event and the DOCU-MENTARY festivals of Edinburgh and Oberhausen.). The invention of two critics, Derek Prouse, then programming London's NATIONAL FILM THEATRE where the event was staged, and Dilys POWELL, the first festival was sponsored by Powell's newspaper, *The Sunday Times*. Derek Prouse's successors as director were generally critics, in turn David Robinson (1959 only), Richard Roud, Ken Wlaschin, Derek

Malcolm and Sheila Whitaker. Roud was instrumental in creating the New York Film Festival, which for several years he directed in tandem with London, as a twin event.

The programme of the first London Festival consisted of only 15 films – among them new works by Visconti, Clair, Fellini, Ray, Kurosawa, Bergman and Wajda, the last four of whom were still new names on the international scene. By the mid 80s, in line with a world-wide inflation of film festivals, London's annual programme had expanded to almost 200 films, with a variety of new venues supplementing the festival's original home at the NATIONAL FILM THEATRE. The proportion of English-language films also increased; by 2000 these represented some 40% of the whole programme. Though the programme continued to feature foreign-language films – often providing their only chance of exposure in Britain – from the late 90s, under a new director, Adrian Wootton – the festival gave the impression of bias towards commercial and especially Hollywood cinema. In 2000, with the acquisition of a major new sponsor, the festival became the Regus London Film Festival. David Robinson.

London Filmmakers Co-operative Inspired by the non-profit co-operative distribution agency set up in New York by Jonas Mekas, the LFMC was founded in 1966 by poet Bob Cobbing, Simon HARTOG, Steve DWOSKIN and others to promote experimental film. The involvement of Malcolm LeGrice (b Plymouth, 1941) led to the establishment of a film-workshop, uniquely including film-printing and processing equipment alongside editing. Housed in a succession of warehouse spaces throughout the 70s and 80s, the LFMC held weekly screenings of new British work and international classics. Associated artists include Peter Gidal (b New York, 1946), author of the polemic *Theory and Definition of Structural/Materialist Film* (1976), Annabel Nicolson (b London, 1946) William Raban (b Fakenham, 1948) and David Larcher (b London, 1940). A sister organisation London Video Arts (LVA) (later London Electronic Arts) was established in 1976 by David Hall (b Leicester, 1937), Tamara Krikorian (b Bridport, 1944), Stuart Marshall (b Manchester, 1949 – d London, 1993) and others, and a break-away group founded the women's distribution agency, Circles, in 1980. In 1999 LEA and LFMC merged to form Lux, housed in purpose-built premises, where many of the same objectives were pursued, but the Lux cinema closed, mid some controversy, in 2002.
BIBLIOG: Stephen Dwoskin, *Film Is*, 1975; Malcolm Legrice, *Abstract Film & Beyond*, 1977; Mike O'Pray, *The British Avant-Garde Film*, 1996. David Curtis.

London Films For a brief shining moment in the history of British cinema, the sight and sound of Big Ben and the words LONDON FILM PRODUCTIONS was as much a guarantee of big-budget escapism as any of the trademarks of the Hollywood studios. The irony was that this British iconography was utilised by a group of Hungarians led by Alexander KORDA, the eldest of three brothers, who had arrived in London in November 1931. The KORDAS along with actor George GROSSMITH Snr, writer Lajos BIRO, and assorted financiers, started London Film Productions in February 1932 from offices at 22 Grosvenor Street in London's Mayfair.

KORDA immediately established a STUDIO SYSTEM of operation whereby stock actors were assembled, including Wendy BARRIE, Joan GARDNER, Merle OBERON, Robert DONAT, Emlyn WILLIAMS and John LODER. Many were to appear in London Films' first independent feature, *Wedding Rehearsal* (1932). The production artists recruited by KORDA included cinematographers Georges PERINAL and Osmond BORRODAILE, film editor William HORNBECK and composer Miklos ROSZA. Production manager Sir David CUNYNGHAME was a major figure, ultimately running the business in the later years.

London Films' second independent feature established the company and KORDA worldwide. *The Private Life of Henry VIII* (1933), a critical and commercial success, identified London Films with historical subject matter, usually British, and given international appeal by its polyglot creators with the help of bankable Hollywood stars, in this case Charles LAUGHTON. *Henry VIII*'s success enabled the construction of the company's purpose-built studios at DENHAM, where Hollywood made a fleeting touchdown in the Buckinghamshire countryside. In a few years London Films produced *The Scarlet Pimpernel* (1935), *Knight Without Armour* (1937), the 'EMPIRE FILMS' *Sanders of the River* (1935), *The Drum* (1938), *The Four Feathers* (1939), and the FANTASY epics *The Thief of Baghdad* (1940) and *The Jungle Book* (1942). The latter pictures were completed from KORDA's wartime base in Hollywood after Denham Studios was lost to the financiers and the company temporarily wrested out of Korda's control. The American pictures were actually produced by Alexander Korda Films Inc. though they have long been regarded as London Films output.

PROPAGANDA heartbreaker *That Hamilton Woman* (1941) was the highpoint of the Hollywood years and once back in London Korda based London Films in sumptuous offices at 144 Piccadilly. The company continued to be a magnet for such cinema and literary talent as Terence RATTIGAN, Graham GREENE, Carol REED and Laurence OLIVIER, despite lurching from one financial crisis to another.

By the early 50s the company was more a financing and co-production vehicle though still involved with some memorable pictures. London Films' last feature slate, produced in association with John WOOLF, included *Storm over the Nile* (1955), *The Deep Blue Sea* (1955) and *Richard III* (1956).

Korda died in 1956 and London Films ceased to be a major independent production company. It was revived in the mid 70s, without any Korda interest, and operates as a television producer and distributor. Martin Stockham.

London on film London has always been central as a location and as a theme in British films. Beyond its status and readily recognisable features, the fact that it housed or had nearby almost all the British film studios has made it an almost inescapable presence in the history of British film-making. Will BARKER, who established film studios at EALING, used London as both a theme and a location in a series of crime dramas in the 1910s, such as *Trapped by the London Sharks* (1916). Three decades later, Michael BALCON's Ealing Studios similarly made a virtue of their London identity and use of recognisable locations, with *Hue and Cry* (1946), *Passport to Pimlico* (1949), *The Blue Lamp* (1949), *The Lavender Hill Mob* (1951), and *The Ladykillers* (1955). Every London location seems to have inspired its own particular feature film: Covent Garden (*Pygmalion*, 1938), Petticoat Lane (*A Kid for Two Farthings*, 1954), Hampstead (*Truly Madly Deeply*, 1990), Soho (*Expresso Bongo*, 1959), and the eponymous *Pool of London* (1950), *Waterloo Road* (1944) and *Notting Hill* (1999, UK/US), and indeed there was a 'SWINGING LONDON' sub-genre in the 60s making much use of famous landmarks. Stanley KUBRICK

played the most with a location's recognisability, when the Vietnam War was recreated for *Full Metal Jacket* (1987) in what still seemed all too obviously Docklands. A past London of the imagination has been memorably recreated in *The Glorious Adventure* (1922, UK/US, featuring the Great Fire of London), *Henry V* (1944), *Tom Jones* (1963), *Hope and Glory* (1987) and both *Oliver Twist* (1948, John BRYAN's designs inspired by Doré's illustrations) and *Oliver!* (1968). Certain actual London locations reappear in film after film, notably the warehouses of Shad Thames (*Oliver!*, 1968; *The Elephant Man*, 1980; *Bridget Jones's Diary*, 2001, UK/Fr/US), and Cheney Road behind King's Cross Station (*The Ladykillers*, 1955; Ian McKELLEN's *Richard III*, 1995). Hollywood film-makers have been memorably cavalier with London's imagery and culture, most grossly so with *Mary Poppins* (1964), though RANK's gaudy musical *London Town* (1946) showed that a British studio could be equally vulgar. René CLÉMENT's Gallic take on London manners in *Knave of Hearts* (1954), however, was refreshingly subtle. Vivid use of unusual or unlovely London locations has been a hallmark of more recent British films, notably *The Long Good Friday* (1979, perhaps the quintessential London film), *Close My Eyes* (1991), *My Beautiful Laundrette* (1985), *Nil by Mouth* (1997), *Wonderland* (1999) and gangland capers set in South London such as *The Krays* (1990) and *Lock, Stock and Two Smoking Barrels* (1998). The LONDON FILM COMMISSION now exists to promote and facilitate the use of London locations in film productions.
BIBLIOG: Colin Sorensen, *London on Film*, 1996. Luke McKernan.

Long, Stanley A. (*b* London, 1933) Director, producer, cinematographer. Though in the film industry for over 30 years, most of them spent in EXPLOITATION genres, Long directed only seven features, including three in the *Adventures of . . .* series: *Adventures of a Taxi Driver* (1976, + co-p), *. . . a Private Eye* (1977, + p), *. . . a Plumber's Mate* (1978). Had cinematographer credits on such titles as *Nudes of the World* (1961, + sc) and *Take Off Your Clothes and Live!* (1962), and made DOCUMENTARIES for the Ministry of Defence (1968–69).
OTHER BRITISH FILMS INCLUDE: (c) *West End Jungle* (1961), *Kill* (1962), *Primitive London* (1965), *The Sorcerers, Terror of the Blood Beast* (1967); (d) *Naughty!* (doc, + p, co-sc), *Bread* (+ p) (1971), *On the Game* (1973, doc, + co-p), *It Could Happen to You* (1975, + p), *Dreamhouse* (1981, co-d, co-p); (p) *A Promise of Bed* (1969), *Groupie Girl* (1970, + c), *Eskimo Nell* (1974).

Longden, John (*b* West Indies, 1900 – *d* Barnstaple, 1971). Actor. Tall, serious-looking former mining engineer who became a popular star of late silent and 30s films, including several for HITCHCOCK. He is the heroine's grave detective boyfriend in *Blackmail* (1929) and the detective inspector in *Young and Innocent* (1937), among others. Made three films in Australia in the 30s, including *The Silence of Dean Maitland* (1935), did WW2 service (1942–45), and post-war slipped into supporting roles. There was an alleged drinking problem, but he nevertheless remained a busy character player, working several times for the ARCHERS (*A Matter of Life and Death*, 1946, narrator) and at EALING (*Pool of London*, 1950), before settling into 'B' MOVIES.
OTHER BRITISH FILMS INCLUDE: *Quinneys* (1927), *The Flight Commander* (1928), *Atlantic* (1929), *Elstree Calling* (1930), *The Skin Game, The Ringer* (1931), *The Gaunt Stranger* (1938), *Q Planes, Jamaica Inn* (1939), *Contraband* (1940), *The Common Touch* (1941), *One of Our Aircraft is Missing, The Rose of Tralee* (1942), *The Silver Fleet* (1943), *Anna Karenina* (1948), *The Elusive Pimpernel* (1950), *Meet Mr Callaghan* (1954), *Quatermass 2* (1957), *Lancelot and Guinevere* (1962).

Longdon, Terence (*b* Newark on Trent, 1922). Actor. Post-WW2 service, tall, fair-haired Longdon trained at RADA and from 1968 played over 1,000 performances in *The Secretary Bird*. On-screen from early 50s, mostly in supporting roles in 'A' films (*The Man Who Never Was*, 1955; as Sean CONNERY's chum in *Another Time, Another Place*, 1958) and several 'CARRY ONS', with the odd 'B' MOVIE lead, as in *Clash by Night* (1963). Married and divorced from Barbara JEFFORD.
OTHER BRITISH FILMS INCLUDE: *Never Look Back* (1952), *Angels One Five* (1952), *The Woman for Joe* (1955), *Dangerous Exile* (1957), *Carry On Sergeant, . . . Nurse* (1958), *. . . Constable* (1960), *. . . Regardless* (1961), *The Sea Wolves* (1980, UK/Switz/US), *Letters from the East* (1996, UK/Fin/Ger/Swe).

Longfellow, Malvina (*b* Virginia, US, 1890 – *d* ?). Actress. This attractive, dark-haired, American-born performer played the quintessential English heroine, Emma Hamilton, in *Nelson* (1918) and *The Romance of Lady Hamilton* (1919). Her career ended with the coming of sound.
OTHER BRITISH FILMS INCLUDE: *Holy Orders* (1917), *Thelma* (1918), *Adam Bede* (1918), *Betta the Gypsy* (1918), *Unmarried* (1920), *Moth and Rust* (1921), *The Last Crusade* (1922), *The Wandering Jew* (1923), *The Celestial City* (1929). AS.

Longhurst, Henry B(irt) (*b* Brighton, 1891 – *d* Tonbridge, 1970). Actor. Usually bespectacled, often disapproving of aspect, in several dozen small roles from the early 30s, typically as professionals, like military men or policemen, or the doctor in *The Belles of St Trinian's* (1954).
OTHER BRITISH FILMS: *Let Me Explain, Dear* (1932), *Bulldog Jack* (1935), *Crackerjack* (1938), *Old Mother Riley, MP* (1939), *A Place of One's Own, Perfect Strangers* (1945), *His Excellency* (1951), *The Captain's Paradise* (1953), *Mad About Men* (1954), *The Quatermass Experiment* (1955), *Private's Progress* (1956), *Gideon's Day* (1958), *Heavens Above!* (1963), *Circus of Fear* (1966).

Lonsdale, Frederick (*b* Jersey, 1881 – *d* London, 1954). Dramatist. Popular playwright, particularly of the 20s, noted for his sophisticated, witty dealings with upper-class life. Among his works filmed are: *Canaries Sometimes Sing* (1930), starring and directed by Tom WALLS; *Aren't We All?* (1932), starring Gertrude LAWRENCE; and *On Approval*, filmed in 1930, again directed by Walls, and most famously in 1944, with Clive BROOK as director-star and Beatrice LILLIE. Lonsdale also collaborated on several screenplays, including the US flag-waver *Forever and a Day* (1943).
OTHER BRITISH FILMS: (play adapted, unless noted) *The Fake* (1927, + co-sc), *Women Who Play* (from *Spring Cleaning*), *The Maid of the Mountains* (1932), *Just Smith* (1933), *The Private Life of Don Juan* (1934, co-sc).

Lonsdale, Michel (*b* Paris, 1931). Actor. Son of a British military officer, Lonsdale won distinction on the French stage before turning whole-heartedly to the cinema, where he has racked up over 100 roles, including a dozen in British films. The plump-faced actor received a BAAn for his supporting role of Detective Lebel in *The Day of the Jackal* (1973, UK/US) and was a noteworthy opponent for BOND in *Moonraker* (1979, UK/Fr), as Hugo Drax, hellbent on world domination.
OTHER BRITISH FILMS INCLUDE: *The Romantic Englishwoman* (1975, UK/Fr), *The Passage* (1978), *Chariots of Fire* (1981), *The Remains of the Day* (1993), *Jefferson in Paris* (1995).

Loraine, Violet (*b* London, 1887 – *d* Newcastle, 1956). Actress. A plain-looking actress of the musical stage, Loraine starred opposite George ROBEY in the most popular shows of WW1, *The Bing Boys Are Here* (1916) and *The Bing Girls Are There*

(1917). In the former, she sang, with Robey, 'If You Were the Only Girl in the World', captured on film in *The King's People* (1937) and a 1939 *Pathé Gazette*, and in the latter, 'Let the Great Big World Keep Turning', recorded on film in *Road House* (1934). Loraine appeared in only one other British feature, *Britannia of Billingsgate* (1933). Sister of actor Ernest SEFTON. AS.

Lord, Justine Actress. Attractive 'B' MOVIE lead and supporting player in 'A' films of the 60s, who gave a very striking performance as the disturbed wife in Alan BRIDGES' well-regarded 'B' thriller, *Act of Murder* (1964) – and never had such a good role again. Some TV, including *The Doctors* (1969–71) and *Crossroads* (1975).
OTHER BRITISH FILMS INCLUDE: *Tamahine* (1962), *Incident at Midnight* (1963), *Doctor in Clover* (1966), *Twenty-Nine* (1969).

Lord, Peter *see* **Aardman Animation**

Loren, Sophia (*b* Rome, 1934). Actress. RN: Sofia Villani Scicolone. Legendarily voluptuous Italian star of international films, including a few British ones. She was Carol REED's enigmatic heroine in *The Key* (1958), lacked the comic dazzle needed for SHAW's Epifania in the leaden *The Millionairess* (1960), was a graceful leading lady in the espionage THRILLER, *Arabesque* (1966, UK/US), but could do nothing to save either CHAPLIN's *A Countess from Hong Kong* (1966) or the totally misconceived REMAKE of *Brief Encounter* (1974). Her real celebrity as actress, as distinct from great beauty, lies elsewhere.
OTHER BRITISH FILMS: *Operation Crossbow* (1965, UK/It), *Judith* (1965, UK/Israel/US), *The Cassandra Crossing* (1976, UK/Ger/It).

Lorenz, Margo (*b* Vienna). Actress. Of Anglo-Austrian parents and educated in England, Lorenz began her very short screen career as stand-in to Ava GARDNER on *The Barefoot Contessa* (1954, US/It). Played the female lead in EALING's PORTMANTEAU drama, *Out of the Clouds*, amid considerable publicity; appeared in a short film, *The Right Person* and a TV version of *Thunder Rock*, all 1955; and that was that.

Lorimer, Glennis (*b* London, 1913). Actress. In 16 films of the 30s, with a few female leads, as in *Ask a Policeman* (1939), and supporting roles in bigger affairs like *Rhodes of Africa* (1936), the petite Lorimer, daughter of Henry OSTRER, found lasting fame of a kind as the GAINSBOROUGH Lady (there may have been others; she is the best known), nodding graciously in an oval frame to introduce the studio's output. Possibly uncredited in other early 30s films.
OTHER BRITISH FILMS INCLUDE: *Britannia of Billingsgate* (1933), *Jew Süss* (1934), *Car of Dreams* (1935), *Alf's Button Afloat* (1938).

Lorraine, Guido (*b* Kracow, Poland, 1912). Actor. Trained for the stage in Poland, so he naturally played Nazis (*The Red Beret*, 1953), Arabs (*Port Afrique*, 1956) and even a Pole (*The Colditz Story*, 1954), in line with the idea of heterogeneous otherness that obtained in 50s British cinema. The sardonic-looking Lorraine may have had his best role in the comedy, *Hotel Sahara* (1951), as the Italian captain who lays siege to Yvonne DE CARLO. Also London stage and TV, and, as a singer, radio and cabaret.
OTHER BRITISH FILMS INCLUDE: *The Passionate Friends* (1948), *State Secret* (1950), *Encore* (1951, as Russian Prince), *Top Secret* (1952), *The Village* (UK/Switz) (1953), *Father Brown* (1954), *Above Us the Waves* (1955), *That Woman Opposite* (1957), *Great Van Robbery* (1959).

Lorraine, Harry (*b* Brighton, *c* 1878 – *d* Astoria, New York, 1934). Actor, director. RN: Henry Herd. Active from 1912 to

1929, former stunt man Lorraine is best remembered for having played 'Lieutenant Daring' in the SERIES of the same name (1913–14), and was noted for performing his own stunts. Lorraine made his debut as Little John in *Robin Hood Outlawed* (1912, short). He also directed a handful of films, including *Big Money* (1918), and *The Further Exploits of Sexton Blake: The Mystery of the SS Olympic* (1919).
OTHER BRITISH FILMS INCLUDE: (a) *Lieutenant Daring and the Mystery of Room 41* (1913), *Lieutenant Daring, Aerial Scout, Detective Daring and the Thames Coiners* (+ d) (1914), *The Happy Warrior* (1917), *The Woman and Officer 26* (a, co-d, sc), *Pillars of Society* (p) (1920), *Sweeney Todd* (1928), *Stranger Than Fiction* (1930). AS.

Lorre, Peter (*b* Rosenberg, Hungary, 1904 – *d* Los Angeles, 1964). Actor. RN: Ladislav Loewenstein. A star in Germany as the child murderer in *M* (1931), short Jewish Lorre fled Nazism in 1933 and went on to have a highly prolific Hollywood career and his melancholy, dangerous persona became the object of innumerable impersonations. He made four British films, including his English-speaking debut as the very sinister Abbott in HITCHCOCK's *The Man Who Knew Too Much* (1934), played the experienced killer, the 'General', in *Secret Agent* (1936). Active until his death by heart attack.
OTHER BRITISH FILMS: *Double Confession* (1950), *Beat the Devil* (1953, UK/It/US).

Losey, Joseph (*b* La Crosse, Wisconsin, 1909 – *d* London, 1984). Director. Perhaps the most famous victim of the notorious McCarthy BLACKLIST, Losey left medical studies to pursue a theatrical career. His pre-film career included work as small-part stage actor, book and theatre reviewer for several newspapers, and director of the political *Living Newspaper* productions in the later 30s. His first films were documentaries and industrial shorts before MGM took him on to produce entries in its series, *Crime Does Not Pay*. Post-WW2 service, he made several notable features, modest in scope but all contriving to imbue genre material – fantasy, thrillers – with an unsettling concern for difficult relationships and social maladies. Declining to appear before the House UnAmerican Activities Committee to answer charges of Communism, he fled to England where he made his first film, the enjoyably florid melodrama, *The Sleeping Tiger* (1954) under the name of Victor HANBURY, and it introduced him to Dirk BOGARDE, with whom he would make four brilliant 60s films. (He also used the name Joseph Walton on *The Intimate Stranger* (1956).

His British career is mainly a 60s phenomenon in which one brilliant film follows another. *The Gypsy and the Gentleman* (1957) is a famously panned film, but in its homing in on the British CLASS system it is instructive as a precursor of such mature masterpieces as *The Servant* (1963), *King and Country* (1964, + co-p), *Accident* (1967, + co-p, BAAn/film) and *The Go-Between* (1971, BAAn/d). With *The Servant*, he seemed to catch an entire society in moral decay and recorded its collapse in a darkly poetic visual style – sublime gliding cameras, inspired angles to catch the most revealing detail – that lifted the film clear of the critically favoured preoccupation with REALISM. The theme of class is crucial to the military trial at the heart of *King and Country*; it is complexly interwoven with issues of SEXUALITY and the academic life in *Accident*; and *The Go-Between* unforgettably records that combination of simmering passions and social repressiveness that cripples lives. All but the last of these star Bogarde, whose status as *actor* was lifted to new heights by his association with Losey, as was Stanley BAKER's in the rigorous thrillers, *Blind Date* (1959) and *The Criminal* (1960), as well as *Accident* and *Eva* (1962, Fr/It).

There were some less successful collaborations, like that with Elizabeth TAYLOR in *Boom* (1968) and *Secret Ceremony* (1968), and Jane FONDA reputedly resisted his direction on *The Doll's House* (1973, UK/Fr), but its fierce polemical life doesn't suffer from their frictions. The 70s were not generally kind to him, but his version of *Don Giovanni* (1979, Fr/Ger/It) rounds off the decade with what may well become the benchmark for filmed OPERA. The story of Losey's re-finding his career in England, and bringing a distinctively non-British sensibility to bear on some very British subjects, as well as a craftsmanship that had few if any peers in Britain, is one of the triumphs of cinema in this country.

OTHER BRITISH FILMS: *A Man on the Beach* (1955, short), *The Intimate Stranger* (1956), *Time Without Pity* (1957), *First on the Road* (1960, short), *The Damned* (1961), *Modesty Blaise* (1966), *Figures in a Landscape* (1970), *Galileo* (1974, UK/Can, + co-sc), *The Romantic Englishwoman* (1975, UK/Fr), *Steaming* (1984).

BIBLIOG: Tom Milne, *Losey on Losey*, 1967; Michel Ciment, *Conversations with Losey*, 1985.

Lotinga, Ernie (*b* Sunderland, 1876 – *d* London, 1951). Actor. Slapstick comic, popular in revues and variety, who made stage debut as Dan Roy in 1898 and US debut in 1909. With the exception of *Smith's Wives* (1935), he always played the character of Jimmy Josser, in various mutations, on screen.

OTHER BRITISH FILMS INCLUDE: *The Raw Recruit, The Orderly Room* (1928), *Josser, KC, Acci-dental Treatment* (1929), *PC Josser* (1931), *Josser Joins the Navy, Josser on the River* (1932), *Josser on the Farm* (1934), *Love Up the Pole* (1936). AS.

Lotis, Denis (*b* Johannesburg, 1928). Actor, singer. Popular singing star of the 50s and 60s who appeared in a few films, several times in guest roles as in *It's a Wonderful World* (1956), *The Golden Disc* (1958) and *Make Mine a Million* (1959). First of his few 'acting' roles was in *The Extra Day* (1956). Also had his own commercial radio show, was a TV regular on *The Tin Pan Alley Show* (1956), and starred on stage in the musical *Harmony Close*.

OTHER BRITISH FILMS INCLUDE: *Sword of Sherwood Forest* (1960), *She'll Have to Go* (1961), *What Every Woman Wants* (1962).

Lott, Barbara (*b* Richmond, Surrey, 1920 – *d* London, 2002). Actress. Character player more often on TV, as, for example, Ronnie CORBETT's domineering mother in *Sorry!* (1981–88), but noticeable as the haughty wife of the classics master in *Unman, Wittering and Zigo* (1971).

OTHER BRITISH FILMS INCLUDE: *Three Silent Men* (1940), *The Party's Over* (1963), *The Pillow Book* (1996, UK/Fr/Lux/Neth).

Loudon, Norman (*b* Campbelltown, Scotland, 1902 – *d* ?). Producer. In the early 1930s, Loudon bought the country house, Lyttleton Park, Shepperton, established SOUND CITY STUDIOS, and turned out a run of 'QUOTA QUICKIES', with himself producing for directors including Ivar CAMPBELL and Adrian BRUNEL. In the mid 30s, he moved out of production, except in relation to John BAXTER's films, and Sound City became, as Rachael LOW says, 'a studio-owning company', and in 1946 its studios were acquired by LONDON FILMS.

BRITISH FILMS INCLUDE: (p) *Reunion* (1932), *Side Streets, The Golden Cage, Eyes of Fate, Colonel Blood* (1933), *Youthful Folly, Menace, White Ensign* (1934), *Rolling Home, Radio Pirates* (1935).

Love, Bessie (*b* Midland, Texas, 1898 – *d* London, 1986). Actress. RN: Juanita Horton. Pert star of American silents from 1916, who made easy transition to talkies with *The Broadway Melody* (1929). Went to UK in 1935, and had a lengthy British career, generally in roles with little importance except that an American accent was required, as in *Journey Together* (1945), but more than memorable as the mother in *Isadora* (1968) and telephone operator in *Sunday Bloody Sunday* (1971). Also on stage, including 1972 musical version of *Gone with the Wind*, and a brief 1958 appearance in her own play, *The Homecoming*. Married producer-writer William B. Hawks (1929–36).

OTHER BRITISH FILMS INCLUDE: *Live Again* (1936), *Atlantic Ferry* (1941), *The Magic Box, No Highway* (1951), *Beau Brummell* (1954), *Nowhere to Go* (1958), *Children of the Damned* (1963), *On Her Majesty's Secret Service* (1969), *The Ritz* (1976), *Lady Chatterley's Lover* (1981, UK/Fr).

BIBLIOG: Autobiography, *From Hollywood with Love*, 1977. AS.

Lovejoy, Ray (*b* London, 1939 – *d* London, 2001). Editor. Oscar-nominated for editing *Aliens* (1986, US), Lovejoy began his career as assistant editor on *Dr Strangelove . . .* (1963) and went on to edit Stanley KUBRICK's *2001: A Space Odyssey* (1968), for which one would have expected at least another nomination. Worked in the US for most of the 80s.

OTHER BRITISH FILMS INCLUDE: *The Ruling Class* (1971), *Fear Is the Key* (1972), *Never Too Young to Rock* (1975), *The Shining* (1980, UK/US), *Krull, The Dresser* (1983), *'Let Him Have It'* (1991), *Rainbow* (1996, UK/Can), *Lost in Space* (1998, UK/US), *The Quickie* (2001, UK/Fr/Ger).

Lovegrove, Arthur (*b* London, 1913 – *d* Richmond, Surrey, 1981). Actor. Bald, quizzical supporting player in small roles (like Sgt Bromley in *The Quatermass Experiment*, 1955) from the post-war period until his death, last glimpsed as the man at the newstand in *Memoirs of a Survivor* (1981). On TV from 1946.

OTHER BRITISH FILMS INCLUDE: *Noose* (1948), *Night and the City* (1950), *Emergency Call* (1952), *A Kid for Two Farthings* (1954), *Passage Home, Lost* (1955), *Carry On Admiral* (1957), *Yesterday's Enemy, Wrong Number* (1959), *Crooks Anonymous* (1962), *Carry On Cowboy* (1965), *Eye of the Needle* (1981).

Lovell, Raymond (*b* Montreal, 1900 – *d* London, 1953). Actor. Icon of post-war corruption, characteristically cravatted for suave villainy – and immensely enjoyable about it. Of tubby but still elegant appearance (one suspected he was dressed by blackmarket contacts), it was a slight surprise to find him as a simple garage owner in *The Way Ahead* (1944). Much more typical were the Prince Regent in *The Man in Grey* (1943), dubious Duclos in *Hotel Reserve* (1944), Ray MILLAND's shifty offsider in *So Evil My Love*, silly Lord Willie in morning dress at the races in *The Calendar* (1948) and a pompous, self-serving town councillor in *Time Gentlemen Please!* (1952). Trained for medicine at Cambridge, he was on the stage in the 20s. As for films he, as much as any actor, evokes the post-war years, when pleasure could only be bought at a price, moral and financial. Married and divorced from Tamara DESNI.

OTHER BRITISH FILMS INCLUDE: *The Third Clue* (1934), *The Case of Gabriel Perry* (1935), *King of the Damned* (1936), *Murder Tomorrow* (1938), *Contraband* (1940), *49th Parallel, The Common Touch* (1941), *The Young Mr Pitt, Uncensored* (1942), *Caesar and Cleopatra* (1945), *Night Boat to Dublin, Appointment with Crime* (1946), *The End of the River* (1947), *My Brother's Keeper, The Three Weird Sisters, Easy Money, The Blind Goddess, Quartet* (1948), *Once Upon a Dream, Bad Lord Byron, Madness of the Heart, The Romantic Age, Fools Rush In* (1949), *The Mudlark* (1950), *The Pickwick Papers* (1952), *The Steel Key* (1953).

Low, Rachael Film historian. Perhaps the major figure in the excavation of early British film history, Low presented her findings, in prose of exemplary precision and even-handedness in seven volumes: *The History of the British Film*: Vol 1 *1896–1906* (1949, with Roger MANVELL); Vol 2 *1906–14* (1949); Vol 3 *1914–18* (1950); Vol 4 *1918–29* (1971); *The History of the British Film* (1929–39): Vol 5 *Documentary and Educational Films of the 30s* (1979); *Films of Comment and Persuasion of the 30s* (1979); *Film Making in 30s Britain* (1985). Initiated by the History Committee of the BRITISH FILM INSTITUTE, they are a great scholarly achievement. Daughter of celebrated political cartoonist David Low.

Lowe, Arthur (*b* Hayfield, Derbyshire 1915 – *d* Birmingham 1982). Actor. Varied small roles in *Kind Hearts and Coronets* (1949), *The Spider and the Fly* (1949) and *The Green Man* (1956) led to notable collaborations with director Lindsay ANDERSON, including the team manager in *This Sporting Life* (1963), the weak schoolmaster in *If . . .* (1968) and the roles of Mr Duff, Charley Johnson and Dr Munda in *O Lucky Man!* (1973). For the latter, he won a British AA (Best Supporting Actor). He was renowned as the pompous Captain Mainwaring in the television comedy series *Dad's Army*, a role he repeated on radio, stage and in the 1971 SPIN-OFF film. He also received acclaim as the drunken butler in *The Ruling Class* (1971) and even in the appalling 1979 REMAKE of *The Lady Vanishes* he is an honourable Charters, upholding the tradition of Basil RADFORD's cricket-obsessive.

OTHER BRITISH FILMS INCLUDE: *London Belongs to Me* (1948), *Final Appointment* (1954), *One Way Out* (1955), *Stranger in Town, Hour of Decision* (1957), *Follow That Horse!* (1960), *Go to Blazes* (1962), *The White Bus* (1967), *The Bed Sitting Room* (1969), *Adolf Hitler – My Part in His Downfall* (1972), *Theatre of Blood, No Sex Please – We're British* (1973), *Man About the House* (1974), *The Bawdy Adventures of Tom Jones* (1975), *Sweet William* (1979), *Britannia Hospital* (1982).

BIBLIOG: Stephen Lowe, *Arthur Lowe: Dad's Memory*, 1997. Matthew Caterson.

Lowe, Barry (*b* Southport, 1931). Actor. Entered films in the mid 50s as a youthful character player. Appeared in several films for Val GUEST, starting with *The Quatermass Experiment* (1955), but had arguably his best role as the chipper member of Peter CUSHING's browbeaten staff in the fine THRILLER, *Cash on Demand* (1961). From mid 60s, his career went into TV series.

OTHER BRITISH FILMS INCLUDE: *They Can't Hang Me* (1955), *Quatermass 2, Manuela* (1957), *Up the Creek* (1958), *Yesterday's Enemy, Expresso Bongo* (1959), *Hands of the Ripper* (1971).

Lowe, Len (*b* London, 1916 – *d* 1999). Actor. With his brother Bill, formed a very popular pre-war variety duo, after experience as straight actor and as vocalist and guitarist with Jack HYLTON's band. Post-war they appeared together in two minor musicals, *Date with a Dream* (1948) and *Melody Club* (1949), the first two productions of TEMPEAN FILMS. Bill married Jeannie CARSON and went to the US where he became a TV director; Len formed another comedy double, 'Lowe and Ladd', with his older brother Don. He appeared in two more films but turned more to TV where he played straight man to such comics as Peter SELLERS and Dick EMERY.

OTHER BRITISH FILMS: *A Countess from Hong Kong* (1966), *Carry On Loving* (1970).

Lowe, Olga (*b* Durban, 1919). Actress. Trained as a dancer in Johannesburg and later toured the Americas, dancing at one stage with Carmen Miranda's troupe, Lowe came to England in 1946 and appeared in a great deal of theatre, often in musicals, including *Guys and Dolls*. Made her film debut in the MUSICAL, *Trottie True* (1948), as Ruby Rubarto and let herself go as the brothel madame in *Carry On Abroad* (1972). Married to (1)

stage producer John Toré until his death in 1959 and (2) actor **Keith Morris**, who has appeared in several British films, including *The Spy Who Loved Me* (1977).

OTHER BRITISH FILMS INCLUDE: *State Secret* (1950), *Hotel Sahara* (1951), *So Little Time* (1952), *Oh, Rosalinda!!* (1955), *Where Eagles Dare* (1968), *Riddle of the Sands* (1979).

Lucan, Arthur (*b* Sibsey, 1887 – *d* Barnsley, 1954). Actor. RN: Towle. From 1937 to 1952, fifteen rough-and-ready comedies featuring Lucan in DRAG as Old Mother Riley, with his real-life wife, Kitty MCSHANE, as his daughter Kitty, were persisently popular with (perhaps undiscriminating) audiences. Lucan/ OMR engaged in wild slapstick, wore his washerwoman's weeds without the slightest attempt at gender conviction, did violence to the language and invariably thwarted the pompous and the nefarious. The links with MUSIC HALL are obvious and account for the bizarre charm of the films. Lucan (in show business from 1900) and McShane first appeared as themselves in *Bridget's Night Out* (1935), *Stars on Parade* (1936) and *Kathleen Mavourneen* (1937). *Old Mother Riley* (1937) began the series; they separated in 1951 and McShane is not in the last, *Mother Riley Meets the Vampire* (1952). Their popularity spawned and was fanned by a comic strip version of their antics in *Radio Fun* in the 40s.

OTHER BRITISH FILMS: *Old Mother Riley in Paris* (1938), . . . *MP*, . . . *Joins Up* (1939), . . . *in Society*, . . . *in Business* (1940), . . . *'s Ghosts*, . . . *'s Circus* (1941), . . . *Overseas*, . . . *Detective* (1943), . . . *at Home* (1945), . . . *'s New Venture* (1949), . . . *Headmistress* (1950), . . . *'s Jungle Treasure* (1951).

Lucas, Cornel (*b* London, 1920). Stills photographer. To turn the pages of *Heads & Tails: The Film Portraits of Cornel Lucas* (1988) is to understand Lucas's reputation as Britain's most famous stills photographer. He started photography aged 13, then got a job as a lab technician with RANK, was with the RAF photographic group during WW2, and post-war settled at PINEWOOD. He contributed significantly to the star-building process, giving the likes of Joan COLLINS, Kay KENDALL, Dirk BOGARDE and Belinda LEE (his first wife) the patina of Hollywood glamour. He is now married to the daughter of Linden TRAVERS and one of his most striking portraits is of these two beautiful women.

BIBLIOG: *Heads & Tales: The Film Portraits of Cornel Lucas*, 1988.

Lucas, Leighton (*b* London, 1903 – *d* London, 1982). Composer. A solo ballet dancer while still a boy, Lucas was distinguished as conductor (e.g. with the BBC Orchestra) as well as for composing. In the 30s he worked with Louis LEVY on many GAUMONT–BRITISH films, including *The Ghoul* and *Waltz Time* (1933), received his first composer credit with *Hyde Park Corner* (1935), made at WELWYN, was with the RAF during WW2, scoring several DOCUMENTARIES such as *Target for Tonight* (1941, for CROWN), *A Date with a Tank* (1945, for the ARMY FILM UNIT) and *Ship Busters* (1945, for the RAF FILM UNIT). Among his post-war features, *Portrait of Clare* (1950) draws skilfully on Schumann and others to romantic effect, and he shares *The Dam Busters* (1955) credit for incidental music with Eric COATES.

OTHER BRITISH FILMS INCLUDE: (comp, unless noted) (doc) *The Key to Scotland* (1935), *Pacific Thrust, We of the West Riding* (1945); (features) *Now Barabbas Was a Robber* (1949), *The Weak and the Wicked* (1953), *Yangtse Incident* (1956), *Ice Cold in Alex* (1958), *The Millionairess* (1960, cond), *Mr Topaze* (1961, m arr).

Lucas, William (*b* Manchester, 1925). Actor. Experienced on stage before entering films in the mid 50s, Lucas made a very persuasive thug in two superior 'B' MOVIES for Lance COMFORT: *Touch of Death* and *The Break* (1962) and was properly tormented as the older Morel son in *Sons and Lovers* (1960). His forceful persona should have guaranteed a stronger film career, but in fact his main work was on stage and TV, the latter including the lead in the series, *The Adventures of Black Beauty* (1972–74).

OTHER BRITISH FILMS INCLUDE: *Lost* (1955), *High Flight* (1957), *Breakout* (1959), *Payroll* (1961), *Bitter Harvest* (1963), *Tower of Evil* (1972, UK/US), *Man at the Top* (1973).

Luckham, Cyril (*b* Salisbury, 1907 – *d* London, 1989). Actor. Trained for the Navy and took to the stage when invalided out in 1931, was in rep until his London debut in 1944 and, though he made about 20 films, he remained predominantly a theatre actor, with notable Stratford seasons. Typically cast in films as silver-haired dignitaries, like the magistrate he played in *The Birthday Present* (1957), or Archbishop Cranmer in *A Man for All Seasons* (1966), or, on TV, Bishop Grantly in *The Barchester Chronicles* (1982).

OTHER BRITISH FILMS INCLUDE: *Murder in Reverse* (1945), *Out of the Clouds* (1955), *How to Murder a Rich Uncle* (1957), *Billy Budd* (1962), *The Pumpkin Eater* (1964), *Anne of the Thousand Days* (1969), *Mr Forbush and the Penguins* (1971), *Seal Island* (1977).

Lucoque, Horace Lisle (*b* 1887 – *d* London, 1925). Director, producer. After co-directing **Alice Delysia** (*b* Paris, 1889 – *d* ?, also in *Evensong*, 1934) in *She* (1916), Lucoque formed his own company, with studios in London's Ebury Street, producing *The Four Feathers* (1915) and *The Rugged Path* (1918), and producing and directing *Beau Brocade*, *Tatterly*, *Fairyland* (1916), and *Dawn* (1917). Moving to a studio at Kew Bridge, he produced *Three Men in a Boat* (1920), and produced and directed *Lorna Doone* and *Castles in Spain* (1920). His last film as a director was *Where the Rainbow Ends* (1921), and in 1925, a despondent Lucoque declared bankruptcy and committed suicide. His wife, Nellie E., was often his scenarist. AS.

Luczyc-Wyhowski, Hugo (*b* 1957). Production designer. He has been responsible for the design of some of the most provocative films of the last two decades, notably *My Beautiful Laundrette* (1985), *Prick Up Your Ears* (1987), the corrosive *Nil by Mouth* (1997) and the caper film, *Snatch* (2000, UK/US), all of which evoke worlds and social groups outside the tourist images of LONDON.

OTHER BRITISH FILMS INCLUDE: *Car Trouble* (1985), *Sammy and Rosie Get Laid*, *Personal Services* (1987), *Waterland* (1992, UK/US), *Mojo* (1997), *Cousin Bette* (1998, UK/US), *Dirty Pretty Things* (2002, UK).

Ludlow, Patrick (*b* London, 1903 – *d* London, 1996). Actor. On stage from 1915 in *Peter Pan*, Ludlow remained a stage actor, with his own touring company from 1943. He made 20-odd films in the 30s, mostly light comedies, repeated his stage role of Lord Henry in *Bitter Sweet* (1933), and was in the original *Old Mother Riley* (1937); abandoned films in 1942, and reappeared only three more times – in *Children Galore* (1954) and *The Great St Trinian's Train Robbery* and *Modesty Blaise* (1966).

OTHER BRITISH FILMS INCLUDE: *The Third Gun* (1929), *His Lordship* (1932), *Chelsea Life* (1933), *Evergreen* (1934), *Seven Sinners* (1936), *The Rose of Tralee* (1937), *Goodbye, Mr Chips*, *Old Mother Riley, MP* (1939), *We'll Meet Again* (1942).

Lukas, Paul (*b* Budapest, 1894 – *d* Tangier, 1971). Actor. Tall, handsome, debonair European leading man who could play hero and heavy, as he did so well as the charming but villainous Dr Hartz in *The Lady Vanishes* (1938). Began career on stage in native Hungary, to Germany in 1915, when he made film debut, and went to Hollywood in mid 20s, winning an Oscar for *Watch on the Rhine* (1943), in which he also starred on stage. Moved to Tangier in 1961.

OTHER BRITISH FILMS: *Brief Ecstasy*, *Dinner at the Ritz*, *The Mutiny of the Elsinore* (1937), *A Window in London* (1939). AS.

Lulu (*b* Glasgow, Scotland, 1948). Actress. RN: Marie Lawrie. Found fame as a singer when she made the Top Ten with her recording of 'Shout' (1964) and a series of subsequent raucous hits in the mid 60s. Came to filmgoers' attention when she played in *To Sir, with Love* (1967), for which she also sang the title song, but attractive and likeable as she was she has not pursued a film career, and it was a surprise when she came back as Tom COURTENAY's tarty wife in *Whatever Happened to Harold Smith?* (2000). Has done much more TV and had her own series in the 60s.

OTHER BRITISH FILMS: *Gonks Go Beat* (1965, as herself, with 'The Luvvers'), *Hot Millions* (1968, sang title song), *The Man with the Golden Gun* (1974, sang title song).

Lumet, Sidney (*b* Philadelphia, 1924). Director. Respected US film-maker whose 40-year career, full of passionately wrought melodramas, included six British films (or UK co-productions): the rigorous war drama, *The Hill* (1965), the convoluted LeCarré-based thriller, *The Deadly Affair* (1966, + p); a strongly but perhaps too heterogeneously cast ADAPTATION of *The Sea Gull* (1968, UK/US, + p); the psychological drama, *The Offence* (1972); *Murder on the Orient Express* (1974, UK/US), which launched the all-star Agatha CHRISTIE series and which is one of Lumet's most *enjoyable* films; and the frenzies of *Equus* (1977).

Lumière presentations in Britain The first screening of the Lumière brothers, Louis and Auguste, took place in Paris on March 22, 1895, and the film shown was *Sortie d'usine/Workers Leaving the Factory*. The first programme shown in Britain, including *L'arrivée d'un train/The Arrival of a Train*, was at the Marlborough Hall of the Regent Street Polytechnic, London, on February 20, 1896, with the public paying an admission fee of one shilling. The films were brought to the UK by Felicien Trewey, a conjuror, juggler and circus performer, who was the Lumières' British business manager, and also appeared in several of the films, including *La partie d'écarte/The Card Game* and *Assiettes tournantes/Spinning Plates*. Trewey initiated the screenings but they were subsequently mostly presented by Alexandre Promio. The Lumière programme moved from Regent Street on March 9, 1896 to the Empire Theatre of Varieties in Leicester Square, where it ran for 18 months. Subsequently, Trewey introduced motion pictures to Cardiff (April 1896), Birmingham (May 1896), Manchester (May 1896), and Belfast and Dublin (October 1896). Trewey also began making films in England, and, by 1897, the Lumière catalogue featured 13 SHORTS shot in London, including *Outside of the Empire*. The Lumière films were distributed in the UK later by the WARWICK TRADING COMPANY. As the output of new films from Lumière dried up, Trewey disbanded his UK operation and retired to Asnières near Paris. AS.

Lumley, Joanna (*b* Srinagar, Kashmir, 1946). Actress. Now synonymous with Bolly-swigging Patsy in the ground-breaking TV comedy series, *Absolutely Fabulous* (1992) co-starring Jennifer SAUNDERS, tall elegant Lumley had been in the business for a quarter-century before that. A former model, she entered films in 1969's *Some Girls Do*, had small parts in several other films, including the almost unseen *The Breaking of Bumbo* (1970), and appeared in a series of clinkers in the late 90s (*Parting Shots*, 1998; *Mad Cows*, 1999; *Maybe Baby*, 2000, UK/Fr). She had major TV success with *The New Avengers* (1976–77), and in 2000 she and Saunders were commissioned to do a new sitcom, *Mirrorball*. Film stardom may have eluded her, but she could be a huge character asset. Married (1) Jeremy LLOYD, (2) conductor Stephen Barlow.

OTHER BRITISH FILMS INCLUDE: *On Her Majesty's Secret Service* (1969), *Games That Lovers Play* (1970), *The Devil's Woman* (1971), *Trail of the Pink Panther* (1982), *Shirley Valentine* (1989, UK/US), *Cold Comfort Farm* (1995, TV, some cinemas), *Prince Valiant* (1997, UK/Ger/Ire/US), *The Cat's Meow* (2002, UK/Can/Ger).

BIBLIOG: Joanna Lumley, *Stare Back and Smile*, 1989.

Lunghi, Cherie (*b* Nottingham, 1952). Actress. Vibrant, dark-haired Anglo-Italian beauty whose screen career was off to a spectacular start when she played Guenevere in the medieval romance *Excalibur* (1981), but has proceeded fitfully since. Arguably, she has had better chances on TV, as in *The Monocled Mutineer* (1986) or in the title role of *The Manageress* (1989–90), as the woman who runs a football team, and on stage she was one of the brilliant quartet in the 2000 revival of Peter NICHOLS's confronting *Passion Play*. Has a daughter by director Roland JOFFE.

OTHER BRITISH FILMS: *Praying Mantis*, *Oliver Twist* (1982, as Nancy), *The Sign of Four* (1983), *Parker* (1984), *The Mission* (1985), *Silent Cries* (1993, UK/US), *Jack & Sarah* (1995, UK/Fr).

Lupino, Ida (*b* London, 1918 – *d* Burbank, California, 1995). Actress, director. Daughter of Stanley LUPINO and niece of Lupino LANE, Lupino is now famous as the woman who had the most sustained career as a Hollywood film and TV director, and this after – and sometimes concurrently with – a fine career as a toughly dramatic actress, notably in *The Hard Way* (1944). She made six films in Britain while still in her teens, and is a perky heroine in, for example, Bernard VORHAUS's *The Ghost Camera* (1933). Married (1) Louis HAYWARD (1938–45), (2) Collier Young (1948–52), (3) Howard Duff (1952–84).

OTHER BRITISH FILMS: *Her First Affaire* (1932), *Prince of Arcadia*, *Money for Speed*, *I Lived with You*, *High Finance* (1933).

Lupino, Stanley (*b* London, 1893 – *d* Los Angeles, 1942). Actor. RN: Hook. A star of musical comedy, who made his stage debut in 1900 as a monkey in pantomime, Lupino was an all-round energetic performer, as much acrobat, singer and dancer as actor, and became a major star in pantomime, musical theatre and revue. His performance of 'I Don't Want to Go to Bed' in *Sleepless Nights* (1932) is evidence of his unique talent and the tragedy that he never made as many films as he should. He produced as well as starred in two cheerful comedies, *Honeymoon for Three* (1935), and *Cheer Up!* (1936). A member of a famous acting and performing family, he is father of Ida LUPINO, cousin of Wallace LUPINO and Lupino LANE.

OTHER BRITISH FILMS: *Love Lies*, *The Love Race* (1931), *King of the Ritz*, *Facing the Music*, *You Made Me Love You* (1933), *Happy* (1934), *Sporting Love* (1936), *Over She Goes* (1937), *Hold My Hand* (1938), *Lucky to Me* (1939).

BIBLIOG: Autobiography, *From the Stocks to the Stars*, 1934. AS.

Lupino, Wallace (*b* Edinburgh, 1898 – *d* Ashford, 1961). Actor. RN: Lane. Lesser member of a famous family, who appeared in his brother Lupino LANE's stage hit, *Me and My Girl* (1937) as Parchester. Stage debut in 1906 in pantomime, in which, and in variety, he spent most of his career; in Educational Comedies in UK from 1923; in 30s, played Wally in

a series of comedies directed by John HARLOW; and was effective as PC Winch in *The Man Who Could Work Miracles* (1936). Cousin of Stanley LUPINO and Ida LUPINO.

OTHER BRITISH FILMS INCLUDE: *The Blunders of Mr Butterbun* series (1918), *Children of Chance* (1930), *The Maid of the Mountains* (1932), *The Student's Romance* (1935), *Shipmates o' Mine* (1936), *21 Days* (1937), *The Lambeth Walk* (1939), *Waterloo Road* (1944). AS.

Lusia Films Production company which became a base for radical and experimental film. Initially a successful producer of public relations films, Lusia changed course in 1968 when one of the directors, Richard Mordaunt, made its resources available to Cinema Action (1968–93) which was to become one of the most important Leftist film groups of the 70s. Productions include *The UCS Struggle* (1971) *The Miners' Film* (1974/5), *So that You Can Live* (1981) *Rocinante* (1986). Key members included Gustav (Schlacke) Lamche, Ann Lamche, Eduardo Guedes, Humphrey Trevelyan and Marc Karlin. In 1971, the latter two left to form **Berwick Street Collective** and Richard Mordaunt joined them bringing Lusia with him. The Collective dispersed after completing the critically acclaimed *Night Cleaners* (1975) but Mark Karlin (1943 -1999) continued to work from Lusia to make politically challenging films. The film magazine *Vertigo* was launched from its premises in 1993. Margaret Dickinson.

Lustgarten, Edgar (*b* Manchester, 1907 – *d* London, 1978). Journalist, broadcaster. Between 1953 and 1967, the impassive Lustgarten 'hosted' over 50 pocket-sized thrillers in the 'Scotland Yard' (to 1961) and 'Scales of Justice' (1962–67) series. These were made at MERTON PARK by directors such as Ken HUGHES and Montgomery TULLY, and starring Russell NAPIER in the first series, and were screened regularly on ABC cinema programmes. Lustgarten was also a novelist, screen-writer and writer about famous trials. The Narrator (Charles GRAY) in *The Rocky Horror Picture Show* (1975) parodies him.

BRITISH FILMS INCLUDE: (sc) *The Man Who Wouldn't Talk* (1957), *Rockets Galore* (1958, unc); (novel) *The Long Dark Hall* (1951), *Game for Three Losers* (1965); (presenter) *The Drayton Case* (1953), *Fatal Journey* (1954), *Wall of Death* (1956), *Inside Information* (1957), *Crime of Honour* (1958), *The Ghost Train Murder* (1959), *Wings of Death* (1961), *The Guilty Party* (1962), *The Hidden Face* (1965), *Payment in Kind* (1967).

Lutyens, Elizabeth (*b* London, 1906 – *d* London, 1983). Composer. Began composing for films in the mid 40s, scoring such CROWN DOCUMENTARIES as *Jungle Mariner* (1944) and *The Way from Germany* (1946). Also composed for RADIO and TV (*The White Falcon*, 1956), as well as for about 20 features, including several 60s HORROR films, and SHORTS. The originality of her 'serious' compositions (e.g. the cantata *De Amore*, 1957) meant that acceptance came to her later in life, and film composing was a financial godsend. Daughter of Sir Edwin Lutyens (1869–44), the famous architect, she studied at the RCM.

OTHER BRITISH FILMS INCLUDE: *Penny and the Pownall Case* (1948), *To Be a Woman*, *Out of True* (1951, shorts), *Bermuda Affair* (1956), *Never Take Sweets from a Stranger* (1960), *Don't Bother to Knock* (1961), *Paranoiac* (1962), *The Earth Dies Screaming* (1964), *The Skull* (1965), *Theatre of Death*, *The Psychopath* (1966), *The Terrornauts* (1967).

Lye, Len (*b* Christchurch, New Zealand, 1901 – *d* Warwick, Rhode Island, 1980). Animator. An innovator in experimental cinema who also worked within the mainstream of film-making, Lye is the creator of 'direct' film-making, camera-less films made by painting or scratching the film emulsion. Lye's work as an animator embraces puppet films, such as *The Birth* *of a Robot* (1935); experiments with colour, such as *Rainbow Dance* (1936); a fantasy sequence in *Mad about Money* (1938); combining ANIMATION with live action, as in *When the Pie Was Opened* (1941); and jump-cutting, as in *Rhythm* (1953). A striking figure with a bald head and pointed goatee, Lye learned film-making in Australia and embarked on anthropological studies in Samoa before moving to the UK in 1926. Associated with the GPO FILM UNIT in the 30s and the British MINISTRY OF INFORMATION during WW2, Lye went to the US in 1944 to work on *March of Time*. He was also a painter, kinetic sculptor and genetic theorist, who exhibited in the 1936 International Surrealist Exhibition in London. Lye is the author of two books, *No Trouble* (1930) and *Figures of Motion* (1982) and many articles, 1935–81, and the subject of the documentary, *Doodlin': Impressions of Len Lye* by Keith Griffiths (1987).

OTHER BRITISH FILMS INCLUDE: *Tusalava* (1929), *A Colour Box*, *Kaleidoscope* (1935), *Trade Tattoo* (1937), *Swinging the Lambeth Walk*, *Profile of Britain* (1940), *Newspaper Train* (1942), *Work Party* (1943), *Cameramen at War* (1944). AS.

Lye, Reg (*b* Sydney, 1912 – *d* 1988). Actor. Lye's career is bookended by Australia, where he was a respected character actor for such films as *Sunday Too Far Away* (1965), as a drunken shearer with bleak prospects. Appeared in two Australian-set British films, *Smiley* (1956) and *The Shiralee* (1957), then made about a dozen British films in the 60s and 70s.

OTHER BRITISH FILMS INCLUDE: *The Wrong Arm of the Law* (1962), *The Wrong Box* (1966), *The Lost Continent* (1968), *The Games* (1969), *10 Rillington Place* (1970), *Dracula* (1973, UK/US), *Tarka the Otter* (1978).

Lyel, Viola (*b* Hull, 1900 – *d* London, 1972). Actress. RN: Violet Watson. Trained at the Guildhall School of Music and the Old Vic School, on stage from 1918 and for over 50 years, Lyel also made two dozen films, starting in 1930. Usually in comic roles, she starred as Maggie in the 1931 version of *Hobson's Choice*, and as character player post-war had most scope as the parish spinster who takes to the cooking sherry in *See How They Run* (1955); on stage she played everything from the Queen in *Hamlet* (1944, Stratford) to Miss Preen in *The Man Who Came to Dinner* (1941–44).

OTHER BRITISH FILMS INCLUDE: *Thread o' Scarlet* (1930), *Marry Me* (1932), *Channel Crossing* (1933), *Night Mail* (1935), *Quiet Wedding*, *The Farmer's Wife* (1941), *Wanted for Murder* (1946), *Mr Perrin and Mr Traill* (1948), *It's Not Cricket* (1949), *Isn't Life Wonderful!* (1953), *Suspended Alibi* (1956).

Lynch, Alfred (*b* London, 1932). Actor. Character player, often in cockney roles as in *On the Fiddle* (1961), a services comedy in which, as a London wide boy, he co-starred effectively with Sean CONNERY, and at his best in *The Hill* (1965), as the POW who breaks under the strain of sadistic treatment. Had stage experience with the Theatre Workshop, Stratford, East London, where he created the title role in Brendan Behan's *The Hostage* (1958), and extensive TV, including *Manhunt* (1970).

OTHER BRITISH FILMS INCLUDE: *Look Back in Anger* (1959), *The Password Is Courage* (1962), *The Sea Gull* (1968), *Joseph Andrews* (1976), *Loophole* (1980), *The Krays* (1990), *Second Best* (1994, UK/US).

Lynch, Joe (*b* Mallow, Co. Cork – *d* Alicante, Spain, 2001). Actor. Best known for his TV roles as the Catholic trouser-maker in *Never Mind the Quality, Feel the Width* (1967–71; cinema SPIN-OFF, 1972) and as one of Elsie Tanner's boyfriends in *Coronation Street* (1978–79), Lynch also had a strong background of Irish theatre (much work with Dublin's Abbey,

Gate and Gaiety) and radio. Made a clutch of films in the early 60s, including such Irish-set pieces as *A Terrible Beauty* (1960) and had his biggest film chance as Blazes Boylan in Joseph STRICK's *Ulysses* (1967, UK/US). In later years, a big favourite on Irish TV.

OTHER BRITISH FILMS INCLUDE: *The Siege of Sidney Street* (1960), *Girl with Green Eyes* (1963), *Young Cassidy* (1965), *Loot* (1970), *The Mackintosh Man* (1973).

Lynch, Kenny (*b* London, 1939). Actor. Eastender who has played small roles in a few films, suffering from the shortage of worthwhile roles for black actors. Better known on TV, he played himself in *The Alf Garnett Saga* (1972), as suspected father to Alf's expected grandchild, and a bus conductor interrupting a snogging couple in *Carry On Loving* (1970).

OTHER BRITISH FILMS INCLUDE: *Just for Fun!* (1963), *Dr Terror's House of Horrors* (1964, + songs), *The Plank* (1967), *Confessions from the David Galaxy Affair* (1979).

Lynch, John (*b* Coventry, 1962). Actor. Central School-trained actor who has specialised in intense roles, such as the eponymous *Cal* (1981, BAAn/newcomer) and *Best* (2000, UK/Ire), one of the accused in *In the Name of the Father* (1993, UK/Ire/US), the psychiatric patient in *Angel Baby* (1995, Aust/US) and Bobby Sands in *Some Mother's Son* (1996, Ire/US). Unsurprisingly perhaps, he seemed to lack the necessary light touch for *Sliding Doors* (1998, UK/US). He is married to director **Mary McGuckian** (*b* N Ireland, 1963), in whose film, *This Is the Sea* (1996, UK/Ire/US), he co-starred, and his sister is Susan LYNCH.

OTHER BRITISH FILMS INCLUDE: *Hardware* (UK/US), *1871* (1990), *Edward II*, *Out of the Blue* (1991), *Nothing Personal* (1995).

Lynch, Susan (*b* Newry, N. Ireland, *c* 1971). Actress. Like brother John LYNCH, she trained at Central School, and they were both in *The Secret of Roan Inish* (1994), in which she won acclaim as the Selkie, half-human, half-seal. Made a very striking TV debut in *Cracker* (1993), as a murderous young woman; shared a Screen Actors' Guild Award for the cast of *Waking Ned* (1999, UK/Fr/US); and co-starred memorably with Ewan McGREGOR as *Nora* [Barnacle] (2000, UK/Ger/It/Ire). Also international films, including *From Hell* (2001, Czech/US), as a JACK THE RIPPER victim.

OTHER BRITISH FILMS INCLUDE: *Downtime* (1997, UK/Fr), *Beautiful Creatures*, *Happy Now*, *The Mapmaker* (Ire) (2001).

Lynn, Ann (*b* London, 1934). Actress. Granddaughter of farceur Ralph LYNN, the rather grave-faced Ann was anything but – her roles tended to the intense, and she was excellent in the lead as the woman trapped in a bank's *Strongroom* (1962), in Anthony SIMMONS's melancholy *Four in the Morning* (1965), and as a bitchy wife in *I'll Never Forget What's 'is Name* (1967).

OTHER BRITISH FILMS INCLUDE: *Johnny, You're Wanted* (1955), *Naked Fury* (1959), *Flame in the Streets* (1961), *HMS Defiant* (1962), *The Party's Over* (1963), *A Shot in the Dark*, *The Uncle* (1964), *Baby Love* (1967), *Hitler: The Last Ten Days* (1973, UK/It).

Lynn, Leni (*b* Waterbury, Connecticut, 1925). Actress, singer. After five Hollywood films including *Babes in Arms* (1939), this pretty songstress made four musicals in Britain in the mid 40s, beginning with the sentimental romance *Heaven Is Round the Corner* (1944) and followed this with a ditto, *Give Me the Stars* (1944), with same director Maclean ROGERS and co-star, Will FYFFE. Success eluded her and she had secondary roles only in her other two films: *Gaiety George* and *Spring Song* (1946), but she fared better on stage.

Lynn, Ralph (*b* Manchester, 1882 – *d* London, 1962). Actor. Character comedian famous for his monocle and toothy grin, and generally considered the quintessential 'silly ass' Englishman. Made stage debut in Wigan, 1900 (Broadway 1913, after years of touring; London 1914); also a theatrical producer, most notably of *Is Your Honeymoon Really Necessary?*, in which he starred from 1944–47. Closely associated with Tom WALLS in the ALDWYCH FARCES of Ben TRAVERS beginning in 1922, and in which he was featured on screen; *Rookery Nook* (1930), *Plunder* (1931), *Mischief* (1931), *The Chance of a Night-Time* (1931, + co-d), *A Night Like This* (1932), *Thark* (1932), *Turkey Time* (1933), *Dirty Work* (1934), and *Stormy Weather* (1935). His brand of comedy may now seem dated, but it was immensely popular in its time and even today his timing and intonation can still delight on film. Father of Robert LYNN; grandfather of Ann LYNN.

OTHER BRITISH FILMS INCLUDE: *Peace and Quiet* (1929), *Tons of Money* (1931), *Just My Luck, Summer Lightning* (1933), *Fighting Stock, Foreign Affaires* (1935), *In the Soup, Pot Luck* (1936), *The Adventures of Rex* (1959 serial). AS.

Lynn, Robert (*b* London, 1918 – *d* London, 1982). Director. Began and ended his career as assistant director. Starting at Twickenham Studio in 1936, the Charterhouse-educated son of Ralph LYNN served in the Royal Artillery 1939–46, worked for RANK's HIGHBURY STUDIOS post-war, then on a wide range of films before getting his chance to direct about ten modest productions, of which the most notable was *Dr Crippen* (1962). Continued as assistant director, production manager or 2nd unit director (e.g. on *Superman*, 1978; *Superman*, 1980) for the rest of his career.

OTHER BRITISH FILMS INCLUDE: (ass d, unless noted), *Black Narcissus* (1947), *A Song for Tomorrow, A Piece of Cake* (1948), *A Boy, a Girl and a Bike* (1949), *Murder Without Crime* (1950), *An Inspector Calls* (1954), *Dracula* (1958), *Performance* (p man), *The Railway Children* (p) (1970), *Dracula AD 1972* (1972); (d) *Postman's Knock, Information Received* (1961), *Take Me Over, Blaze of Glory* (1963), *Mozambique* (1964, UK/Zanz), *Change Partners* (1965).

Lynn, Dame Vera (*b* London, 1917). Singer. RN: Vera Welsh. Much loved singer of wartime Britain, when she was known as 'the Forces' Sweetheart', her hit song, 'We'll Meet Again' becoming almost a national anthem, the pleasant-faced but not very photogenic Lynn never made it as a film star. She appeared in three minor 40s musicals, starting with *We'll Meet Again* (1942), but post-war, while her popularity has always been high, she was a recording, concert hall and TV star. Her other films were *Rhythm Serenade* (1943) and *One Exciting Night* (1944). On film, her most famous moment is probably her soundtrack singing of 'We'll Meet Again' in *Dr Strangelove . . .* (1963), to the accompaniment of rising atomic clouds.

Lynne, Gillian (*b* Bromley, 1927). Choreographer. With an extensive background of theatre work in Britain (RSC, revival of *My Fair Lady*) and the US, as well as many high-profile TV specials, Lynne has had only limited time for the screen. Her occasional films scarcely represent her best work, but there are modest dance pleasures in *Wonderful Life* (1964) and *Half a Sixpence* (1967, UK/US).

OTHER BRITISH FILMS INCLUDE: *Every Day's a Holiday* (1964), *Three Hats for Lisa* (1965), *Mister Quilp* (1974), *Yentl* (1983, UK/US), *Mr Love* (1985).

Lyon, Ben (*b* Atlanta, 1901 – *d* at sea, 1979). Actor. With his wife Bebe DANIELS, much beloved American stars thanks to their wartime stay in the UK and their radio series, *Hi Gang!* (1940–41, 1949) and *Life with the Lyons* (1950–61), with film version in 1954. Had a long career in Hollywood from 1917, including a classic, over-the-top performance as the cowardly Monte Rutledge in *Hell's Angels* (1930). Often credited with discovering Marilyn Monroe while casting director at 20th Century–Fox in 1940s. Awarded OBE, 1977. Following Bebe's death, married actress Marian Nixon (1972) and was on cruise with her aboard *QEII* when he died.

OTHER BRITISH FILMS: *I Spy* (1933), *Mad about Money* (1938), *I Killed the Count, Confidential Lady* (1939), *Hi, Gang!* (1941), *This Was Paris* (1942), *The Dark Tower* (1943), *The Lyons in Paris* (1954). AS.

Lyon, Richard *see* **Daniels, Bebe**

Lyons, Harry Agar (*b* Ireland, 1878 – *d* ?). Actor. A villain on stage and screen, Lyons was active in film from 1908 to 1937. He was the screen's first Fu Manchu in two series from STOLL: *The Mystery of Fu Manchu* (1923) and *The Further Mysteries of Dr Fu Manchu* (1924). Unable to play Fu Manchu later, he created Dr Sin Fang and played him in a 1928 series of that name and also in two feature films, *Dr Sin Fang* (1937) and *Chinatown Nights* (1938).

OTHER BRITISH FILMS INCLUDE: *East Lynne* (1913), *Little Lord Fauntleroy* (1914), *The Warrior Strain* (1918), *The Man Who Forgot* (1919), *Henry, King of Navarre* (1924), *Luck of the Navy* (1927). AS.

Mm

McAleese, Peter Producer. After experience as 2nd unit director/assistant director on such films as *In the Name of the Father* (1993, UK/Ire/US) and as line producer on two more, McAleese went on to produce one of the most popular films of 2001, *Bridget Jones's Diary* (UK/Fr/US).

OTHER BRITISH FILMS INCLUDE: (2ud/ass d unless noted) *Bad Behaviour* (1993), *Highlander III* (1994, UK/Can/Fr, line p) *When Saturday Comes, The Leading Man* (1996), *Intimacy* (2001, UK/Fr, p) *Twin Town, Spice World* (co-p) (1997), *Complicity* (2000).

McAllister, Stewart (*b* Scotland, 1914 – *d* Lanark, Scotland, 1963) Despite having spent much of his working life in the shadow of Humphrey JENNINGS, McAllister's name has since grown to mythical status amongst scholars of British DOCUMENTARY film. In suffering the fate of many technicians, McAllister's hand in the editing of any particular film is often clouded by the collaborative approach to film making often adopted by the British documentary movement. Nevertheless, it can be said that McAllister was responsible for the sophisticated editing of Jennings' CROWN FILM UNIT documentaries *Heart of Britain* (1941), *Words for Battle* (1941), *Listen To Britain* (1942), *Fires Were Started* (1943), *The Silent Village* (1943) and *Family Portrait* (1950). He also edited Harry WATT's *Target for Tonight* (1941). His genius lay in his ability to contribute creatively to any film on which he worked, elevating him from mere technician to a status more often reserved for directors.

BIBLIOG: Dai Vaughan, *Portrait of an Invisible Man: The Working Life of Stewart McAllister, Film Editor*, 1983. Deane Williams.

McAnally, Ray (*b* Buncrana, Ireland, 1926 – *d* Arklow, Ireland, 1989). Actor. Authoritative Irish character actor who received BAAs for playing Christy Brown's father in *My Left Foot* and for his TV performance in *A Very British Coup* (1988), and an earlier BAAn for *The Mission* (1985). On stage in Donegal from 1942 and London from 1962, playing George in *Who's Afraid of Virginia Woolf?* (1964). He entered films in the 1957 Irish-set *Professor Tim*, but his film career really only took off in the 80s, when it was almost too late, but there is enough evidence to define a major talent.

OTHER BRITISH FILMS INCLUDE: *She Didn't Say No* (1957), *Shake Hands with the Devil* (1959, UK/US), *Billy Budd* (1962), *The Looking Glass War* (1969), *Fear Is the Key* (1972), *Angel* (1982, Ire), *Cal* (1984), *No Surrender* (1985, UK/Can), *White Mischief* (1987), *The Fourth Protocol, Empire State* (1987), *Venus Peter* (1989).

McAninch, Cal (*b* Scotland). Actor. Interesting young actor of the 90s who played the AIDS sufferer in *Nervous Energy* (1995), was vividly disruptive as the young doctor who invades the lives of *The Woodlanders* (1997), and has generally made the most of the supporting roles that have come his way, and of the

TV lead as the unsuspecting young husband in *Best of Both Worlds* (2000).

OTHER BRITISH FILMS INCLUDE: *Splitting Heirs* (1993), *The Lost Son* (1999, UK/Fr), *Best* (2000, UK/Ire), *Breathtaking, The Point Men* (UK/Fr/Lux) (2001).

MacArthur, James (*b* Los Angeles, 1937). Actor. Cleancut young American actor of the 50s and early 60s, mainly remembered for TV's *Hawaii Five-O* (1968–79) and for work with the DISNEY ORGANISATION, for whom he made three British films: *Third Man on the Mountain* (1959), *Swiss Family Robinson* (UK/US) and *Kidnapped* (1960), and played Hayley MILLS's love interest in *The Truth About Spring* (1964). Adopted son of playwright Charles MacArthur and actress Helen Hayes (*b* Washington D.C., 1900 – *d* Nyack, New York, 1993), who memorably starred in the British film, *Anastasia* (1956).

OTHER BRITISH FILM: *The Bedford Incident* (1965).

McAuliffe, Nicola (*b* Surrey, 1955). Actress. Gifted and inventive actress of TV (*Surgical Spirit*, 1989–95) and stage (e.g. Queen Victoria in the RSC's panto-musical *Poppy*, 1983–84), but with only three – admittedly vivid – screen appearances: in *The Doctor and the Devils* (1985), *Bedrooms and Hallways* (1999) and as Lady Crombie in *Plunkett & Macleane* (1999, UK/Czech).

MacBean, L(udovic) C(harles) (*b* Glasgow, *c* 1874 – *d* Tunbridge Wells, 1929). Director, screenwriter. Initially a screenwriter of 'Big Ben' SHORTS for Union in 1914, MacBean began co-directing with Fred PAUL for G.B. SAMUELSON in 1915. In 1922, he authored *Kinematograph Studio Technique*.

BRITISH FILMS INCLUDE: (d, unless noted) *The Angels of Mons* (co-d), *Infelice* (co-d), *The Ways of the World* (+ sc), *Harry the Swell* (sc) (1915, + sc), *Love* (1916), *Forgive Us Our Trespasses* (1919), *The Dawn of Truth* (1920, + p, sc), *Bladys of the Stewpony* (1921). AS.

McCallin, Clement (*b* London, 1913 – *d* London, 1977). Actor. Stowe-educated, RADA-trained stage actor, performing from 1931, with seasons at the Old Vic (1935–56) and several at Stratford, WW2 service with the Army (1940–45), and a spell in Australia in the latter 50s/early 60s. In a dawdling film career, he made only a dozen films in 30 years. He starred in the lively 'B' film, *The Rossiter Case* (1950); the rest are small roles. Married (2) to Brenda BRUCE when he died.

OTHER BRITISH FILMS INCLUDE: *Stolen Life* (1939), *The Queen of Spades, Edward, My Son* (1949), *The Story of Robin Hood . . .* (1952), *Rough Shoot* (1953), *Happy Deathday* (1970).

McCallum, David (*b* Glasgow, 1932). Actor. This boyish-looking, slight and short, performer with sensitive features, once described as 'a sexy Scot,' is more a character actor than a leading man. RADA-trained, he began his career with a RANK contract, appearing in substantial roles in such films as *The Violent Playground* (1957), *A Night to Remember* (1958), and *The Long and the Short and the Tall* (1960). Active as much on TV as in film, became an international star as the mysterious Russian, Illya Kuryakin, in the American TV series *The Man from UNCLE* (1964–67) and played Judas Iscariot in *The Greatest Story Ever Told* (1965). First wife was Jill IRELAND (1957–67). Not to be confused with US sound editor of same name, or with his own violinist father **David McCallum**, who appeared in *Prelude to Fame* and *Last Holiday* (1950).

OTHER BRITISH FILMS INCLUDE: *The Secret Place, Robbery Under Arms* (1957), *Billy Budd* (1962), *The Great Escape* (1962, UK/US), *Mosquito Squadron* (1968), *Hear My Song* (1991), *Dirty Weekend* (1993). AS.

McCallum, Gordon (*b* Chicago, 1919 – *d* Sherborne, 1989). Sound recordist. Entered the industry in 1935, in the sound department at ELSTREE STUDIOS, and subsequently at PINEWOOD (1936–38), DENHAM (1939–45) and then, from 1946, back at Pinewood, where he was dubbing mixer on all films made there. His post-war credits alone run to hundreds. Won shared-AA for *Fiddler on the Roof* (1971, US); had shared-AAn for *Ryan's Daughter* (1970), *Diamonds Are Forever* (1971) and *Superman* (1978); and won a shared-BAA for *Jesus Christ Superstar* (1973, US) and six other shared BAA nominations.

OTHER BRITISH FILMS INCLUDE: (sd) *I Know Where I'm Going!* (1945), *The Red Shoes* (1948), *As Long as They're Happy* (1955), *Eyewitness, Checkpoint* (1956), *Across the Bridge* (1957), *North West Frontier* (1959), *Swiss Family Robinson* (UK/US), *Peeping Tom* (+ mixer, rec) (1960), *The Tamarind Seed* (1974); (sd rec/re-rec/mixer) *Great Expectations, Green for Danger* (1946), *Blanche Fury, Black Narcissus* (dubbing) (1947), *Oliver Twist, The Passionate Friends, So Evil My Love, London Belongs to Me* (1948), *Obsession, Madeleine* (1949), *The Woman in Question, The Clouded Yellow* (1950), *The Browning Version, White Corridors, High Treason* (1951), *The Importance of Being Earnest* (1952), *Genevieve, The Final Test* (1953), *Doctor in the House* (1954), *Simon and Laura* (1955), *A Town Like Alice* (1956), *The One That Got Away* (1957), *A Night to Remember, Carry On Sergeant* (1958), *No Love for Johnnie* (1961), *Tiara Tahiti, Life for Ruth* (1962), *This Sporting Life,* (1963), *Goldfinger, Carry On Cleo* (1964), *Khartoum* (1966), *You Only Live Twice* (1967), *The Prime of Miss Jean Brodie* (1968), *Battle of Britain* (1969), *The Private Life of Sherlock Holmes* (1970), *The Devils* (1971), *Frenzy* (1972), *The Odessa File* (1974, UK/Ger), *McVicar* (1980), *Victor/Victoria* (1982), *Octopussy* (1983), *Greystoke . . .* (1984, UK/US), dozens more.

McCallum, John (*b* Brisbane, 1918). Actor. Handsome, vigorous leading man of nearly 20 features from the late 40s to the mid 50s, when he, with his wife Googie WITHERS, returned to Australia to live, and whence they have commuted regularly to act on British stages. He had trained for the stage at RADA and had begun his film career in Australia after WW2 service, returning to the UK in 1947. He brought an unaffected virile presence to such films as *The Root of All Evil* (1947) and, particularly, in the EALING dramas, *The Loves of Joanna Godden* and, as a criminal on the run, *It Always Rains on Sunday* (1947), both co-starring Withers, with whom he made four more films. He is also very fine as the compromised police detective in *The Long Memory* (1952).

Back in Australia, apart from running J.C. Williamson's theatres, he acted in many plays, often with Withers, as in *The Deep Blue Sea* (1955), and played an important, often behind-scenes role in the resurgence of the long-dormant Australian cinema. His production of Michael POWELL's *They're a Weird Mob* (1966, UK/Aust) was a key precursor of the revival of the 70s. He was also prominent in the development of local TV, including the hugely popular, *Skippy* (1967–68). Daughter

Joanna McCallum is a stage and TV actress. Made CBE, 1971.

OTHER BRITISH FILMS: *The Calendar, Miranda* (1948), *A Boy, a Girl and a Bike* (1949), *The Woman in Question* (1950), *Valley of Eagles, The Magic Box, Lady Godiva Rides Again* (1951), *Derby Day, Trent's Last Case, The Long Memory* (1952), *Melba* (1953), *Devil on Horseback, Trouble in the Glen* (1954), *Port of Escape, Smiley* (1956).

McCallum, Neil (*b* Henley, Canada, 1929 – *d* Reading, 1976). Actor. Burly character actor specializing in tough guy roles, like one of the escaped convicts in *The Siege of Pinchgut* (1959); also occasional leads in minor productions. Starred in TV's *Vendetta* (1966–68), as a gang-busting investigator on the Mafia trail.

OTHER BRITISH FILMS INCLUDE: *On the Run* (1958), *Foxhole in Cairo* (1960), *The Inspector, The War Lover* (1962), *Witchcraft, Catacombs* (+ co-p) (1964), *The Lost Continent* (1968), *Quest for Love* (1971). AS.

McCann, Donal (*b* Dublin, 1944 – *d* Harold's Cross, Ireland, 1999). Actor. Respected Irish actor, much associated with performing the works of Sean O'CASEY. Son of one-time Mayor of Dublin, McCann trained at the Abbey School, and entered films in the Irish-set DISNEY caper, *The Fighting Prince of Donegal* (1966). Appeared in several films for John HUSTON, including the superb *The Dead* (1987, UK/Ger/US), in which he starred with impressive quiet passion, and on TV he was a suitably romantic figure as Phineas Finn, the Irish MP, in *The Pallisers* (1974). He starred in *Poitin* (1977), the first Irish-language feature film, and successfully juggled stage, film and TV until his untimely death from cancer.

OTHER BRITISH FILMS INCLUDE: *Sinful Davey* (1968), *The Mackintosh Man* (1973), *Angel* (1982, Ire), *Cal* (1984), *Mr Love* (1985), *December Bride* (1990, Ire), *The Miracle* (1991, UK/Ire), *Innocent Lies* (1995, UK/Fr), *Stealing Beauty* (1996, UK/Fr/It), *The Nephew* (1998, Ire).

McCarthy, Michael (*b* Birmingham, 1917 – *d* St Leonard's, 1959). Director. After a long apprenticeship – he entered films at Julius HAGEN's TWICKENHAM STUDIOS in 1934, moving on as assistant director with DENHAM, EALING and CROWN – he directed dozens of DOCUMENTARIES for VERITY FILMS and the Film Producers' Guild, as well as children's films, in the post-war years. Also directed several 'B' MOVIES, including the unusually tense and humane *Assassin for Hire* (1951) and a couple of upmarket features, including *It's Never Too Late* (1956) and *Operation Amsterdam* (1958, + co-sc). Also directed TV playlets for Douglas FAIRBANKS in the mid 50s, as well as acting in occasional films.

OTHER BRITISH FILMS INCLUDE: (ass d) *San Demetrio–London* (1943), *The Halfway House, Fiddlers Three* (1944); (a) *No Highway* (1951), *Wheel of Fate, Forces' Sweetheart* (1953); (d) *Mystery Junction* (1951), *Crow's Hollow* (1952), *Shadow of a Man* (1954, + co-sc), *The Traitor* (1957, + sc); (other) *Painted Boats* (co-story), *Johnny Frenchman* (2ud) (1945).

McCarthy, Neil (*b* Lincoln, 1932 – *d* Hampshire, 1985). Actor. Former teacher and supporting player of film and TV (since 1958), usually in tough roles, such as Sgt Burton in *The Hill* (1965) and TV's *The View from Daniel Pike* (1971) in which he arm-wrestles the even tougher protagonist.

OTHER BRITISH FILMS INCLUDE: *The Criminal, Offbeat* (1960), *We Joined the Navy* (1962), *Zulu* (1964), *Where Eagles Dare* (1968), *Follow Me!* (1971), *Trial by Combat* (1976), *The Monster Club* (1980), *Time Bandits* (1981).

McCartney, Sir Paul *see* **Beatles, The**

McClory, Kevin (*b* Dublin, 1926). Director, producer. After working as location manager on *Cockleshell Heroes* (1955) and 2nd unit director on *Moby Dick* and *Around the World in Eighty Days* (1956), enjoyed a minor *succès d'estime* with the art-house fable, *The Boy and the Bridge* (1959, + co-sc). Nothing came of this, in film terms, except that he produced *Thunderball* (1965, + co-story, a) and its remake, *Never Say Never Again* (1983, UK/US).

MacCorkindale, Simon (*b* Ely, 1952). Actor. Handsome leading man, who was once considered for James BOND. Named 'Most Promising Newcomer on Screen' by *London Evening News* in 1979, but work in UK is minimal compared to success in US on TV in *Falcon Crest* (1984–86) and others. Formed UK production company, Amy International, with second wife Susan GEORGE (married 1984), with *Stealing Heaven* (1988, UK/Yug) their first film. Also occasional producer, director and screenwriter. Married/divorced Fiona FULLERTON
OTHER BRITISH FILMS: *Juggernaut* (1974), *Death on the Nile* (1978), *The Riddle of the Sands* (1979). AS.

McCormack, Catherine (*b* Alton, Hants, 1972). Actress. Charming, intelligent actress who has been immensely busy since her first film, *Loaded* (UK/Ger/NZ) in 1994. She followed this with the tragic Murron in *Braveheart* (1995, US) – and a dozen or more features since, both UK and US. She was Christina, unmarried-with-child in 1936 Ireland, in *Dancing at Lughnasa* (1998, UK/Ire/US); the nicely-spoken Stella in *The Land Girls* (1998, UK/Fr); and in *This Year's Love* (1999) the bride who discovers on her wedding day that her bridegroom has been persistently unfaithful throughout their engagement. Landed major starring roles in such films as *The Tailor of Panama* (Ire/US) and *The Spy Game* (UK/US) (2001), opposite Pierce BROSNAN and Brad Pitt, respectively, and co-starred with Julie WALTERS and Ben Daniels in the National Theatre's superb revival of *All My Sons* (2000). Few new actresses have had such chances – or used them better.
OTHER BRITISH FILMS INCLUDE: *Tashunga* (1995, UK/Fr/It/Nor), *Born Romantic* (2001), *Shadow of the Vampire* (2001, UK/Lux/US).

McCormack, John (*b* Athlone, Ireland, 1884 – *d* Moore Abbey, Ireland, 1945). Actor, singer. Milan-trained opera singer who took American citizenship in 1919, and became a much-loved singer of doleful love songs, like 'The Rose of Tralee'. Appeared in the US romance, *Song o' My Heart* (1930), and the first British TECHNICOLOR feature, *Wings of the Morning* (1937), as himself.

McCormick, F.J. (*b* Skerries, Ireland, 1891 – *d* Dublin, 1947). Actor. RN: Peter Judge. Celebrated Irish character actor of over 400 stage performances and one unforgettable film role – as Shell, who tries to sell the wounded hero of *Odd Man Out* (1947) to the authorities. Played Captain Brennan in John FORD's US version of *The Plough and the Stars* (1936) and the small role of Old Tim in *Hungry Hill* (1947). Was married to Eileen CROWE.

McCourt, Emer Actress. Came to attention as Robert CARLYLE's girlfriend in *Riff-Raff* (1991), having starred in the Derry Film & Video Collective's production of *Hush-A-Bye Baby* (1989). She has persistently played characters of scruffy, streetwise intensity and produced the engaging club-scene comedy-drama *Human Traffic* (1999, UK/Ire).
OTHER BRITISH FILMS INCLUDE: *London Kills Me* (1991), *Boston Kickout* (1995), *Sunset Heights* (1997, Ire).

McCowen, Alec (*b* Tunbridge Wells, 1925). Actor. RADA-trained classical actor who made stage debut 1942. More at home in theatre than film, making London stage debut in 1950 and Broadway, 1951. Noted for one-man shows of *Kipling*

(1984) and *St Mark's Gospel* (1977), for which he won a Tony award. Memorable film roles include Fay COMPTON's murderer son in *Town on Trial* (1956), Michael REDGRAVE's endangered son in *Time Without Pity* (1957), the police inspector with gourmet-cook wife in *Frenzy* (1972), Acting High Commissioner in *Cry Freedom* (1987) and Sillerton Jackson in *The Age of Innocence* (1993, US). Awarded CBE 1986.
OTHER BRITISH FILMS INCLUDE: *The Cruel Sea* (1952), *The Deep Blue Sea* (1955), *The Long Arm, The Good Companions* (1956), *The One That Got Away* (1957), *A Night to Remember* (1958), *The Doctor's Dilemma* (1958), *The Loneliness of the Long Distance Runner* (1962), *The Witches* (1966), *Stevie* (1978), *Hanover Street* (1979), *Never Say Never Again* (1983, UK/US), *The Assam Garden* (1985), *Henry V* (1989), *The American* (1998, voice).
BIBLIOG: Autobiography, *Double Bill*, 1980. AS.

McCoy, Gertrude (*b* Rome, Georgia, 1896 – *d* Atlanta, Georgia, 1967). Actress. American leading lady who began her career with Edison in 1911; McCoy was married to Duncan McRae (died 1931), a stage producer in the UK and US, with whom she worked at the start of her British career at British Actors'.
BRITISH FILMS INCLUDE: *Castle of Dreams* (1919), *Tangled Hearts* (1920), *Christie Johnstone* (1921), *Tell Your Children* (1922), *A Royal Divorce* (1923), *Nets of Destiny* (1924), *Nelson* (1926). AS.

McCracken, Esther (*b* Newcastle-upon-Tyne, 1907 – *d* 1971). Playwright. RN: Armstrong. Former actress with Newcastle Rep, she was the author of three plays successfully filmed: *Quiet Wedding* (1938, filmed 1941 and, as *Happy is the Bride*, 1957), *Quiet Weekend* (1941, filmed 1946) and *The Weaker Sex* (play, *No Medals*, 1944; filmed 1948), all dealing gently and amusingly with middle-class life.

McCrory, Helen (*b* London, 1968). Actress. Distinctively beautiful, McCrory came to attention in some very striking roles in the later 90s, including TV's *The Fragile Heart* (1996), *Anna Karenina* (2000), as Anna, and the legal series, *North Square* (2000). Educated in Europe and Africa and trained at the Drama Centre, London, she has done high-profile stage work with the National, the RSC, the Donmar Warehouse, and was acclaimed for the Almeida's *Platanov* (2001). In films, her star has risen via roles in Jim McBride's *Uncovered* (1994) and the critically praised thriller, *Dad Savage* (1998), opposite *Anna Karenina* co-star, Kevin McKIDD.
OTHER BRITISH FILMS INCLUDE: *Streetlife* (1995), *The James Gang* (1997, UK/Can), *Hotel Splendide* (2000), *Charlotte Gray* (UK/Aust/US) (2001), *The Count of Monte Cristo* (2002, UK/US).

MacDermot, Robert (*b* Poona, India, 1908 – *d* London, 1964). Screenwriter. RN: Barbour. Educated at Stowe and Oxford, MacDermot was a former actor, and playwright, often collaborating with his wife, Diana MORGAN. During WW2, he was responsible for the BBC's Forces Programme, and he wrote two short films for STRAND: *Neighbours Under Fire* (1940) and *The Green Girdle* (1941). Post-war he became story editor for RANK, working (uncredited) on screenplays for *Colonel Bogey*, *Mr Perrin and Mr Traill* and *Sleeping Car to Trieste* (1948). In 1948 he left Rank to join the BBC as director of Television Drama.

McDermott, Hugh (*b* Edinburgh, 1908 – *d* London, 1972). Actor. Though Scots by birth and Irish by parentage, he played a remarkable number of American wise guys in post-war British films, as in *Good-Time Girl* (1947) and *No Orchids for Miss Blandish* (1948) and in several plays, such as *The Glass*

Menagerie (1948). When not roughing people up, as he was in these two, he offered a somewhat coarser version of Nigel PATRICK's insouciant persona at its less trustworthy, as for instance in *The Seventh Veil* (1945), as 'the apostle of a new religion called swing'. A former golf pro and sportswriter; in films from 1936 and on stage from 1938.

OTHER BRITISH FILMS INCLUDE: *The Captain's Table* (1936), *The Divorce of Lady X* (1938), *The Saint in London* (1939), *Pimpernel Smith* (1941), *The Young Mr Pitt* (1942), *This Man Is Mine* (1946), *Lilli Marlene* (1950), *Trent's Last Case* (1952), *The Man Who Wouldn't Talk* (1957), *Guns in the Heather* (1968), *The Adding Machine* (1969), *Chato's Land* (1971).

Macdonald, Andrew (*b* Glasgow, 1966). Producer. One of the most powerful British producers since the 1994 black comedy hit, BAA-winner *Shallow Grave* (1994) and the even more cultishly successful *Trainspotting* (1996, BAAn), on both of which (and on the less successful *A Life Less Ordinary*, 1997) he was associated with Figment Films, with director Danny BOYLE and writer John HODGE. He and Boyle were executive producers on *Twin Town* (1997) and he negotiated a deal with 20th Century–Fox to invest substantially in Figment/Boyle's *The Beach* (2000, UK/US). In 1997, he and Duncan KENWORTHY founded the mini-studio, DNA Films, which got off to a poorly received start with *Beautiful Creatures* (2001). He is the grandson of Emeric PRESSBURGER and brother of Kevin MACDONALD.

OTHER BRITISH FILMS: *Parole Officer, Alien Love Triangle* (2001), *The Final Curtain, 28 Days Later* (2002).

MacDonald, David (*b* Helensburgh, Scotland, 1904 – *d* England, 1983). Director. Different explanations, including various personal difficulties, are advanced for the relative collapse of MacDonald's once-promising career. Certainly, after 1950 he made only one further 'A' feature, the breezy SWASHBUCKLER, *The Moonraker* (1957). Former manager of a rubber plantation in Malaya, he went to Hollywood in 1929 and worked with Cecil B. DeMille, whose facility with the overblown MacDonald might profitably have invoked on the tedious *Christopher Columbus* and the absurd *Bad Lord Byron* (1949). Before these disasters set in he had been doing very nicely.

Pre-war, he had made his name with two zesty comedy thrillers, *This Man Is News* (1938) and its follow-up, *This Man in Paris* (1939), both starring Barry K BARNES and Valerie HOBSON, as a reporter and his girlfriend, doing duty as British Thin Man and wife. During WW2, he directed the DOCUMENTARY *Men of the Lightship* (1940) for CROWN, and produced two famous records of war with director Roy BOULTING, *Desert Victory* (1943) and *Burma Victory* (1945), both for the ARMY FILM UNIT. Post-war, there are three enjoyable MELODRAMAS: *The Brothers* (1947, + co-adpt), a stirring tale of passions of love and hate on Skye and with two genuinely ferocious episodes; the vigorous, if somewhat over-plotted cautionary tale, *Good-Time Girl* (1947); and *Snowbound* (1948), an Alpine-set thriller of post-war greed. These are the last gasp of his control over his material. After the BOX-era disasters, he made two dull African adventures, *Diamond City* (1949) and *The Adventurers* (1950), then descended into 'B' MOVIES, of which *Devil Girl from Mars* (1954) has a camp-cult following and *Small Hotel* (1957) has a certain quiet charm. He didn't film for the last 20 years of his life. TV experience in the 50s, including episodes of *Ivanhoe*, and produced and directed the Australian-set *The Flying Doctor* (1960–61).

OTHER BRITISH FILMS INCLUDE: (d) *Double Alibi* (1937), *Dead Men Tell No Tales* (1938), *The Midas Touch* (1939), *This England* (1941), *Left of the Line* (1944, doc), *Cairo Road* (1950), *Tread Softly, The Lost Hours* (1952), *Three Cornered Fate, Alias John Preston* (1955), *A Lady Mislaid* (1958), *The Petticoat Pirates* (1961).

McDonald, Gary (*b* London, 1961). Actor. Impressive black actor whose main work to date has been on stage – he has worked at the Theatre Workshop, with the National, the Royal Court and the Black Theatre Co-op among others – and TV, including roles in *EastEnders*, *The Bill* (1983) and *Between the Lines* (1992). He starred in the CHANNEL 4 feature, *Shooting Stars* (1990), was in the US-made *The Spanish Prisoner* (1997) and has been associated with director Isaac JULIEN in *Passion of Remembrance* (1986) and *Young Soul Rebels* (1991).

OTHER BRITISH FILMS INCLUDE: *Burning an Illusion* (1981), *Elphida* (1987), *Secrets & Lies* (1996).

Macdonald, Kelly (*b* Glasgow, 1976). Actress. Like most associated with *Trainspotting* (1996), Macdonald's career took off from here. Since playing Ewan McGREGOR's surprising one-night stand, she has done a dozen films, most poignantly as the teenage prostitute in *Stella Does Tricks* (1996) and as the feisty girl who charms a schizophrenic Daniel CRAIG in *Some Voices* (2000); and more than holds her own in the all-star cast of Robert Altman's British country-house thriller, *Gosford Park* (2001, UK/Ger/US).

OTHER BRITISH FILMS INCLUDE: *Cousin Bette* (UK/US), *Elizabeth* (1998), *My Life So Far* (UK/US), *The Loss of Sexual Innocence* (UK/US), *House!* (2000), *Cocozza's Way* (2001).

Macdonald, Kevin (*b* Glasgow, 1967). Oxford-educated brother of Andrew MACDONALD and grandson of Emeric PRESSBURGER, whose sympathetic biography, *Emeric Pressburger: The Life and Death of a Screenwriter* (1994), he wrote, Macdonald is a DOCUMENTARY film-maker. His films include the Oscar-winning *One Day in September* (1999, UK/Switz/Ger), about the terrorist attack at the 1972 Munich Olympics, and CHANNEL 4's *Humphrey Jennings* (2000). Married to production designer **Tatiana Lund**, who designed *Monday* (1995).

OTHER BRITISH FILMS: (doc) *Howard Hawks: American Artist* (1996), *Donald Cammell: The Ultimate Performance* (1998, co-d).

McDonald, Peter (*b* Dublin, 1972). Actor. Graduate of University College Dublin where he began acting, MacDonald made his feature debut in the gangster thriller *I Went Down* (1998, UK/Ire/Sp). Since then, he has made several features in rapid succession, including *Nora* (2000, UK/Ger/Ire/It), as Stanislaus Joyce, *Saltwater* (2000, Ire), for which he won an Irish Film and Television Award, and the lead in the romantic comedy *When Brendan Met Trudy* (2001, UK/Ire).

OTHER BRITISH FILMS INCLUDE: *Captain Jack* (1998), *Felicia's Journey* (1999, UK/Can), *Blow Dry* (2001, UK/Ger/US).

MacDonald, Philip (*b* Scotland, 1899 – *d* Woodland Hills, California, 1981). Author, screenwriter. Prolific author of mystery novels, often with a strong comedy element, several of which were adapted to the screen, culminating with two British-set US films, *23 Paces to Baker Street* (1956) and *The List of Adrian Messenger* (1963), a good example of the jokey approach to murder which he favoured. Also wrote many screenplays for both US (in the 30s and 40s) and British (mainly 30s) films. Grandson of Scottish poet and novelist, George MacDonald.

OTHER BRITISH FILMS INCLUDE: (novels/stories) *The Rasp, Rynox, The Star Reporter* (+ co-sc) (1931), *COD* (1932), *Who Killed John Savage?*

(1937, from novel *Rynox*), *Circle of Danger* (1950, from *White Heather*, + sc), *The Hour of 13* (1952, from *X v Rex*).

MacDonald, Richard (*b* Bristol, 1919 – *d* Los Angeles, 1993). Production designer. Nominated for several BAAs (e.g. *King and Country*, 1964), MacDonald's prestige now rests largely on his work with Joseph LOSEY. He was teaching in art school and painting when Losey met him and they developed a system that came to be called 'predesigning', completing the work of the scriptwriter before shooting began. Losey later praised the richly imaginative, sometimes excessive ideas MacDonald brought to their often-combustible collaboration: the results, on such diverse films as *The Servant* (1963) and *Modesty Blaise* (1966), speak eloquently for his talents. Spent his last 20 years almost entirely in the US.

OTHER BRITISH FILMS INCLUDE: *The Criminal* (1960), *Far from the Madding Crowd* (1967), *Secret Ceremony* (1968), *Boom, Bloomfield* (UK/Israel) (1969), *A Severed Head* (1970), *The Go-Between* (1971, title des), *A Doll's House* (1973, title des), *Galileo* (1974, UK/Can), *The Romantic Englishwoman* (1975, UK/Fr), *Supergirl* (1984).

McDonell, Fergus (*b* Tunbridge Wells, 1910 – *d* Norwich, 1984). Editor, director. In films from 1934 as assistant editor, and later a notable editor on such prestigious films as *The Way Ahead* (1944), *The Way to the Stars* (1945) and *Odd Man Out* (1947), McDonell became, by several accounts, a somewhat nervous director. However, the three features he directed are all interesting: the besieged-household drama, *The Small Voice* (1948); the child-prodigy melodrama, *Prelude to Fame* (1950); and the ACT feature about council housing corruption, *Private Information* (1952). At very least, he was able to sustain tension in three genres, and obtained impressive performances from his three leading ladies, Valerie HOBSON, Kathleen BYRON and Jill ESMOND respectively. He then spent the rest of the 50s working as editor and sometimes director on SHORTS, mainly DOCUMENTARIES, for the National Film Board of Canada, returning to England in the early 60s to edit a dozen features, including such diverse pieces as *Nothing But the Best* (1964) and *Khartoum* (1966).

OTHER BRITISH FILMS INCLUDE: (e) *Catch As Catch Can* (1937), *I Met a Murderer* (1939), *On Approval* (1944), *Some People* (1962), *The Caretaker* (1963), *Four in the Morning* (1965), *Charlie Bubbles* (1967), *Alfred the Great* (1969), *Unman, Wittering and Zigo* (1971), *Yellow Dog* (1973).

McDougall, Charles Director. Notable TV director, of BAA-winning (Best Single Drama) for *Hillsborough* (1996), and of episodes of multi-award-winning *Queer as Folk* (1999) and the US hit series, *Sex and the City* (2000–01), he has so far directed only one film, the challenging emotional piece, *Heart* (1999).

MacDougall, Roger (*b* Bearsden, Scotland, 1910 – *d* Northwood, 1993). Screenwriter. Wrote for BBC radio in late 30s, transferring to films with *This Man Is News*, and later writing and directing educational DOCUMENTARIES for Merlin Film Company (1942–49). Was cousin to Alexander MACKENDRICK with whom he collaborated on three 90-second 'instructional' films for the MOI and, famously, on the AA-nominated screenplay for *The Man in the White Suit* (1951), derived from MacDougall's play. He also co-authored many other British comedy screenplays, including those for *A Touch of Larceny* (1959) and *The Mouse That Roared* (1959). His plays included *To Dorothy a Son* (1950, filmed 1954), *The Gentle Gunman* (1950, filmed 1952) and *Escapade* (1952, filmed 1955). Taught at UCLA (1963–70), and miraculously cured himself of life-threatening illness during that time.

OTHER BRITISH FILMS INCLUDE: (co-sc) *This Man in Paris*, *Cheer Boys Cheer* (1939), *Spare a Copper* (1940), *The Bells Go Down*, *The Foreman Went to France* (1942). AS.

McDowall, Betty (*b* Sydney, 1933). Actress. Quietly appealing actress, first on screen in the Australian *Always Another Dawn* (1947); especially good at 'ordinary' housewives, like the increasingly distraught one in *Time Lock* (1957) and as John GREGSON's patient wife in *Tomorrow at Ten* (1962), and a spirited almoner in *Jack the Ripper* (1958). Also appeared on TV and in a few US films, including *The Omen* (1976).

OTHER BRITISH FILMS INCLUDE: *Interpol* (1957), *She Didn't Say No* (1958), *Spare the Rod* (1961), *First Men in the Moon* (1964).

MacDowell, Andie (*b* Gaffeny, S. Carolina, 1958). Actress. Lovely US player who has appeared in several high-profile British (co-)productions, most notably as the woman with whom Hugh GRANT falls seriously in love in *Four Weddings and a Funeral* (1994) and even survived, touchingly, the awfulness of *Crush* (2001). Came to major attention in *sex, lies and videotape* (1989, US).

OTHER BRITISH FILMS: *Greystoke . . .* (1984, UK/US), *The Object of Beauty* (1991, UK/US).

McDowell, J(ohn) B(enjamin) (*b* London, 1877 – *d* Pitsea, Essex, 1954). Producer, cinematographer. McDowell co-founded the BRITISH AND COLONIAL KINEMATOGRAPH COMPANY in 1909, after earlier involvement with WALTURDAW, but his primary importance in film history is as one of the Official War Cinematographers with the War Office Cinematograph Committee. Along with Geoffrey MALINS, he is responsible for *The King Visits His Armies in the Great Advance*, *The Battle of the Somme* (1916) and *The German Retreat and the Battle of Arras* (1917). AS.

McDowell, Malcolm (*b* Leeds, 1943). Actor. There seems almost to be a stage missing in McDowell's career, somewhere between the rebellious and/or violent youths of his two most famous roles – Mick Travis in Lindsay ANDERSON's *If . . .* (1968) and Alex in Stanley KUBRICK's *A Clockwork Orange* (1971) – and the somewhat flashy character roles of his later years. His two most important directors conferred on him a sort of iconic status that failed to shade into more predictable leading man roles; perhaps there was something too surly for romantic leads, though he does well enough by Flashman in *Royal Flash* (1975), but nothing ever suited him as well as the schoolboy rebel and the dangerous droog. Anderson used him and his Travis persona twice more, in *O Lucky Man!* (1973) and *Britannia Hospital* (1982), neither of which caught the youthful public's fancy as *If . . .* had. His career since the early 80s has been largely US-based – and largely unmemorable, even, that is, when seen. *Time After Time* (1979), in which he played H.G. WELLS, is a semi-exception. In 2000, he gave a critically acclaimed character performance as a barking old gangster in *Gangster No. 1*. Married (2 of 3) to Mary Steenbergen (1980–90).

OTHER BRITISH FILMS INCLUDE: *Poor Cow* (1967, scenes cut), *Figures in a Landscape*, *The Raging Moon* (1970), *Aces High*, *Voyage of the Damned* (1976), *The Passage* (1978), *My Life So Far* (2000, UK/US), *The Chemical Wedding* (2001).

McElhinney, Ian (*b* Belfast, 1948). Actor. Has degrees from Edinburgh and Brandeis (Boston) Universities, and worked at the Abbey and Gate Theatres, Dublin, and with the RSC and Royal Court, London. The tall, burly, fair-haired character player has had some vivid moments in film as, for instance, the right-hand man of the corrupt Prime Minister in *Divorcing Jack*

(1998, UK/Fr) and 'Uncle' Andrew in *Small Faces* (1995), and starring roles in the Irish feature *Reefer and the Model* (1987) and the New Zealand-set *The Grasscutter* (1990). On TV, he had continuing roles in two very different series: *Hornblower* (1998, 2000) and *Queer as Folk* (1999, 2000).

OTHER BRITISH FILMS INCLUDE: *Acceptable Levels* (1983), *Lamb* (1985), *A Prayer for the Dying* (1987), *Hidden Agenda* (1990), *Hamlet* (UK/US), *The Boy from Mercury* (UK/Fr) (1996), *The Boxer* (1998, UK/Ire/US), *The Mapmaker* (2001, Ire).

McElhone, Natascha (*b* London, 1971). Actress. Tall, beautiful young actress in films from the mid 90s, dividing her time between the UK and the US. The daughter of Fleet Street journalists, she trained at LAMDA and was glimpsed as a snooty art gallery assistant in an episode of *Absolutely Fabulous* (1992) She made her first mark as the artist's free-spirited mistress in *Surviving Picasso* (1996, UK/US); had a new-minted freshness as *Mrs Dalloway* (1997, UK/Neth/US) when a girl; and was a touchingly direct Lauren/Sylvia, Jim Carrey's lost love, in *The Truman Show* (1998, US). Now lives mainly in the US.

OTHER BRITISH FILMS: *What Rats Won't Do* (1998), *Love's Labour's Lost* (2000, UK/Fr/US), *Killing Me Softly* (2002).

McEnery, John (*b* Birmingham, 1943). Actor. After a bit role in *Othello* (1965), came to popular and critical attention (with BAAn) as a sardonic and moving Mercutio in ZEFFIRELLI's *Romeo and Juliet* (1968); and was Osric to Mel GIBSON's *Hamlet* (1990, UK/US). On TV was ideally cast as John Rokesmith in *Our Mutual Friend* (1976) and as the cynically chivalrous chum of *The Scarlet Pimpernel* (1999). On stage from 1963, joined the National in 1966, also had RSC seasons, and in 2001 he was a notable Fool in the Globe's *Lear* (2001). It has been a busy career, with film merely one of his media, the stress on character rather than stardom.

OTHER BRITISH FILMS INCLUDE: *Bartleby* (1970, title role), *Nicholas and Alexandra* (1971, UK/US), *The Land That Time Forgot* (1974), *Schizo* (1976), *The Duellists* (1977), *Little Dorrit* (1987), *The Krays* (1990), *Black Beauty* (1994, UK/US).

McEnery, Peter (*b* Walsall, 1940). Actor. On stage from 1958, often with the RSC from 1961, and in films from 1959. Had the looks for a romantic leading man, but fulfilled this function only rarely, as in the DISNEY adventures, *The Moon Spinners* (1964, UK/US) and (as) *The Fighting Prince of Donegal* (1966). More adventurous roles include the young gay hounded to suicide in *Victim* (1961), the son seduced by father's second wife in *La Curée* (1966, Fr/It), and the object of the kinky affections of a middle-aged brother and sister in *Entertaining Mr Sloane* (1969). Married/divorced TV actress Julie Peasgood.

OTHER BRITISH FILMS INCLUDE: *Beat Girl* (1959), *Tunes of Glory* (1960), *Negatives* (1968), *The Adventures of Gerard* (1970, UK/It/Switz, title role), *Tales That Witness Madness* (1973), *The Cat and the Canary* (1979).

McEwan, Geraldine (*b* Old Windsor, 1932). Actress. Stage star (debut 1946, Windsor; 1951 London) who mixed modern drama such as *Member of the Wedding* (1957) with a Shakespeare season at Stratford the next year, playing a wonderfully funny Olivia in *Twelfth Night*. By the time she turned her attention to films, it was largely a matter of character roles, notably as Alice in BRANAGH's *Henry V* (1989) and Mortianna in *Robin Hood: Prince of Thieves* (1991, US). On TV she was a magisterial Mrs Proudie in *The Barchester Chronicles* (1982), acquired a cult following in *Mapp & Lucia* (1985–86, as Lucia), and was brilliant as the narrow evangelist mother in *Oranges Are Not the Only Fruit* (1990). Married

Hugh Cruttwell (*b* Singapore, 1918 – *d* London, 2002), RADA Principal (1966–84) and consultant to Branagh on several films from *Henry V* onwards.

OTHER BRITISH FILMS INCLUDE: *There Was a Young Lady* (1953), *Dance of Death* (1968), *Escape from the Dark* (1976), *Foreign Body* (1986), *Love's Labour's Lost* (UK/Fr/US), *The Contaminated Man* (UK/Ger/US) (2000).

McEwan, Ian (*b* Aldershot, 1948). Author, screenwriter. Novelist often concerned with the bizarre or with ambivalent sexuality, as in two famous works that have been filmed: *The Comfort of Strangers* (1990, UK/It) and *The Cement Garden* (1993, UK/Ger). Wrote the screenplays for the acrid state-of-the-nation piece, *The Ploughman's Lunch* (1983), and for *Soursweet* (1988), in which a young Hong Kong couple seek their fortune in London, as well as adapting his own novel for *The Innocent* (1993, UK/Ger) and his story for *The Good Son* (1993, US). Awarded CBE, 1999.

McFadyen, Angus (*b* Scotland, 1963) Actor. Raised in France, educated at Edinburgh University where he began his acting career, McFadyen came to prominence as (a) Robert the Bruce in *Braveheart* (1995) and (b) as partner to Catherine ZETA-JONES until 1996. Mostly in US films, including *Cradle Will Rock* (1999, as young Orson WELLES) and *Titus* (2000, UK/US, as Lucius); some eye-catching TV, including *The Lost Language of Cranes* (1991), as the gay son who precipitates a family crisis.

OTHER BRITISH FILMS: *The Brylcreem Boys* (1996), *Second Skin* (2000, UK/Can/Zanz), *Styx* (2001, UK/US).

McGann, Mark (*b* Liverpool, 1961). Actor. Younger brother of Paul McGANN, whom he resembles and with whom (plus other brothers, Joe and Stephen) he starred in TV's historical drama, *The Hanging Gale* (1995). Supporting roles in a few films, including the brother of the doomed boy in *'Let Him Have It'* (1991). **Joe McGann** (*b* Liverpool, 1958) was also in *No Surrender* (1985, UK/Can), and **Stephen McGann** (*b* Liverpool, 1963) was in *Business as Usual* (1987), two of Paul's other films.

OTHER BRITISH FILMS: *No Surrender* (1985, UK/Can), *Endgame* (2001).

McGann, Paul (*b* Liverpool, 1960). Actor. In a career spanning two decades, McGann is best remembered for his debut performance in the cult classic *Withnail & I* (1986), Bruce ROBINSON's feature about two out-of-work actors who share a seedy Camden Town flat. He played 'I', the comparative straight-man to Richard E. GRANT's insanely melodramatic Withnail. Despite this encouraging introduction to cinema, McGann has made only sporadic film appearances, starring in Ken RUSSELL's *The Rainbow* (1989), and little-seen features, *Dealers* (1989), *Paper Mask* (1990), and *Downtime* (1997, UK/Fr). However, his diverse TV work has ranged from a dashing army officer in *The Monocled Mutineer* (1986), to the eighth *Doctor Who* in a 1996 telemovie, reintroducing him to cult status material. Brothers Mark, Stephen and Joe are also actors.

OTHER BRITISH FILMS: *Tree of Hands* (1988), *The Monk* (1990, UK/Sp), *Afraid of the Dark* (1991, UK/Fr), *My Kingdom* (2001). Melinda Hildebrandt.

McGann, William (*b* Pittsburgh, 1893 – *d* Woodland Hills, California, 1977). Director. Minor director for WARNER BROS. who made nine 'QUOTA QUICKIES' for them at their TEDDINGTON STUDIOS in 1932–33. Returned to America, directing 30 undistinguished films before becoming a special effects expert at Warners for the last ten years of his career. His first British film, *Illegal* (1932), has been described as 'aggressively glum'.

OTHER BRITISH FILMS INCLUDE: *The Silver Greyhound, Murder on the Second Floor, Her Night Out* (1932), *Long Live the King* (1933).

McGarvey, Seamus (*b* Armagh, NI, 1967). Cinematographer. Trained at Polytechnic of Central London in the 80s/early 90s, and began as a stills photograher before becoming clapper loader and focus-puller with various DOPS. His cold bright light is one of the strengths of *Winter Guest* (1998, UK/US) as it is in a much finer film, Tim ROTH's *The War Zone* (1999, UK/It), and he was chosen to shoot Stephen DALDRY's first US film, *The Hours* (2002).

OTHER BRITISH FILMS INCLUDE: *Butterfly Kiss* (1995), *Jump the Gun* (UK/S Af), *The Slab Boys* (1997), *Wit* (UK/US), *Enigma* (UK/Ger/US) (2001).

MacGinley, Sean (*b* Donegal). Actor. With gaunt, angular face, McGinley has been a compelling, sometimes unsettling presence in films and TV from 1990 particularly. He played Brendan GLEESON's hapless offsider in *The General* (1998, UK/US) and even in the usually anodyne *Midsomer Murders* series he showed what a real character actor could do in the episode, *Who Killed Cock Robin?* (1997). Most of his films have been set in Ireland (*The Field*, 1990) or on Irish themes (*The Informant*, 1997, Ire/US), but he had a major role in Michael WINTERBOTTOM's *The Claim* (2001, UK/Can/Fr). With actress wife, **Marie Mullen**, with whom he appeared in *The Disappearance of Finbar* (1996, UK/Ire/Swe) and *The Butcher Boy* (1997, Ire/US), he co-founded the Druid Theatre in Galway.

OTHER BRITISH FILMS INCLUDE: *Fools of Fortune* (1989), *Circle of Friends* (1995, Ire/US), *Resurrection Man* (1997), *Simon Magus* (2000, UK/Ger/It).

MacGinnis, Niall (*b* Dublin, 1913). Actor. Very busy character actor, usually in robust Irish – or other regional – roles. Trained as a doctor at Trinity College (served as surgeon lieutenant with Royal Navy in WW2) and began acting at Peacock Theatre, Dublin, in 1931. In 1934, made London stage debut and film debut, being noticed in 1935 as John Lunn in J. Arthur RANK's first film, *Turn of the Tide*. Had rare starring roles in Michael POWELL's Scottish-set *The Edge of the World* (1937) and the charming wartime PASTORAL, *Tawny Pipit* (1944), and was a vigorous Levin in *Anna Karenina* (1948), a jocular Green Knight in *Knights of the Round Table* (1953) and an alarming occultist in *Night of the Demon* (1957). Some Hollywood films among his six dozen features.

OTHER BRITISH FILMS INCLUDE: *The Luck of the Irish* (1935), *The Last Adventurers* (1937), *Mountains o' Mourne* (1938), *49th Parallel* (1941), *We Dive at Dawn* (1943), *Henry V* (1944), *Captain Boycott* (1947), *Hamlet* (1948), *Chance of a Lifetime* (1950), *Talk of a Million* (1951), *Hell Below Zero* (1953), *Shake Hands with the Devil* (UK/US), *This Other Eden* (1959), *Billy Budd*, (1962), *Jason and the Argonauts* (1963), *Becket* (1964), *The Spy Who Came in from the Cold* (1965), *Torture Garden* (1967), *The Mackintosh Man* (1973). AS.

McGoohan, Patrick (*b* New York, 1928). Actor. Charismatic Anglo-Irish actor, long in the US. After an Irish childhood, he began acting in England, with experience in rep, the West End and the Old Vic, including leading Ibsen and SHAKESPEARE roles. A five-year RANK contract in 1955 resulted in several substantial roles, most memorably as one of the *Hell Drivers* (1957). Concurrently, was often starred in such TV series as *Danger Man* (1960–61, 1964–67). In 1961–62, he starred in *Life for Ruth* and *All Night Long* (a contemporary jazz-set reworking of *Othello*), both for Basil DEARDEN, and *The Quare Fellow*, a

Dublin prison drama, followed by two lightweight British DISNEY films. He then pursued a somewhat risky project, the allegorical TV series *The Prisoner* (1967–68), which he produced and occasionally directed and wrote (as 'Paddy Fitz'), as well as starring in this huge cult success. Relocating to the US in 1972, he worked extensively in film and TV, directing *Catch My Soul* (1972), as well as TV episodes. Returned to the UK to give a powerful performance as King Edward I in *Braveheart* (1995, UK/US).

OTHER BRITISH FILMS INCLUDE: *Passage Home* (1955), *Zarak* (1956), *High Tide at Noon, The Gypsy and the Gentleman* (1957), *Nor the Moon by Night* (1958), *Dr Syn Alias the Scarecrow, The Three Lives of Thomasina* (1963), *Mary Queen of Scots* (1971). Roger Philip Mellor.

McGovern, Elizabeth (*b* Evanston, Illinois, 1961). Actress. Engaging American actress, too idiosyncratic for conventional stardom, compelling in a half-dozen British films, especially in two superior period ADAPTATIONS: *The Wings of the Dove* (1997, UK/US), as the doomed girl's friend, and *The House of Mirth* (2000, UK/US), as ditto. Received AAn for bringing exactly the right sleazy style to turn-of-the-century trollop Evelyn Nesbit Thaw in *Ragtime* (1981, US).

OTHER BRITISH FILMS INCLUDE: *Broken Glass* (1996, UK/US), *Buffalo Soldiers* (2001, UK/US/Ger).

McGovern, Jimmy (*b* Liverpool, 1949). Screenwriter. Much-accoladed TV writer responsible for the likes of *Hillsborough* (1996), *The Lakes* (1997) and *Dockers* (1999), whose poor working-class background has left him with an acute understanding and sometimes ferocious sympathy for lives lived on society's edges. A lapsed but not antagonistic Catholic, he has written compassionately for the screen about lives intimately connected with the Church in *Priest* (1994) and *Liam* (2001, UK/Ger/It); *Go Now* (1996, co-sc) is a moving examination of an extrovert footballer coming to terms with a crippling illness; and the ambivalently titled *Heart* (1999) offers further reason for hoping McGovern will write more for the big screen.

MacGowran, Jack (*b* Dublin, 1918 – *d* New York, 1973). Actor. Character actor, noted for his performances in the plays of Samuel Beckett (and SHAKESPEARE and O'CASEY) and, on screen, a peerless purveyor of shifty, snivelling, cowardly types. It was as Feeney in John FORD's Irish romance, *The Quiet Man* (1952), that the Abbey-famed MacGowran came to filmgoers' notice; after that there was no stopping him, though he maintained a strong stage career in Ireland, London and New York. Often in Irish-set pieces like *Jacqueline* (1956) and *Rooney* (1958), he also twice worked memorably for POLANSKI, in *Cul-de-sac* (1966) and *Dance of the Vampires* (1967), and was in *The Exorcist* (1973, US), just before his too-early death from flu complications. His daughter, **Tara MacGowran** (*b* London, 1964), has appeared in several British films, including *Memoirs of a Survivor* (1981) and *Secret Places* (1984).

OTHER BRITISH FILMS INCLUDE: *No Resting Place* (1951), *The Gentle Gunman* (1952), *Manuela* (1957), *She Didn't Say No* (1958), *Captain Clegg* (1962), *Tom Jones* (1963), *Young Cassidy, Dr Zhivago* (UK/US) (1965), *Wonderwall* (1968), *King Lear* (1970, UK/Ger, as Fool).

McGrath, John (*b* Birkenhead, 1935 – *d* London, 2002). Screenwriter. Narrative vigour and social conscience characterised McGrath's best work, as playwright and screenwriter. Oxford-educated, he cut his teeth on 60s TV, including *Z Cars*, and was further radicalised by the political events of 1968. His play, *The Cheviot, the Stag and the Black, Black Oil* (1973), raised awareness of the exploitation of Scotland by focusing on the contemporary issue of North Sea oil. He turned to screen-writing on *Billion Dollar Brain* (1967) and on *The Bofors Gun* (1968), the film version of his own play. Out of political fashion in later decades, he nevertheless continued to work in film in his last decade, producing and co-writing *Mairi Mhor* (1994), biography of Scottish songwriter, Mary McPherson, for his own company, Freeway Films.

OTHER BRITISH FILMS: *The Reckoning* (sc), *The Virgin Soldiers* (adptn) (1969), *The Dressmaker* (1988, ex p), *Carrington* (1994, co-p).

McGrath, Joseph (*b* Glasgow, 1930). Director. On TV McGrath produced *The Goon Show* reunion (1968) and co-produced *Not Only – But Also . . .* (1965–66, 1970), winning an award as Best Comedy Producer, but by comparison his big-screen comedies are a sorry lot, though he pursued his Goonish bent in, say, *The Great McGonagall* (1974). There is mild fun to be had from *The Bliss of Mrs Blossom* (1968), virtually none from the rest, except perhaps the children's film, *Digby, the Biggest Dog in the World* (1973).

OTHER BRITISH FILMS INCLUDE: (d, sc, unless noted) *Casino Royale* (co-d), *30 Is a Dangerous Age, Cynthia* (1967), *The Magic Christian* (1969), *Secrets of a Door-to-Door Salesman* (1973), *I'm Not Feeling Myself Tonight* (1975), *Rising Damp* (1980, d).

McGrath, Leueen (*b* London, 1914 – *d* London, 1992). Actress. RADA-trained stage actress of Broadway and West End, usually in sophisticated roles; presumably only a sophisticated woman would have married (3 of 3) playwright George S. KAUFMAN. Among her handful of films, she was snobbish Clara Eynsford-Hill in *Pygmalion* (1938) and vividly recreated her stage role (1947–48) as magnate's mistress in *Edward, My Son* (1949). Married (2) Desmond DAVIS.

OTHER BRITISH FILMS: *Whom the Gods Love* (1936), *Meet Maxwell Archer* (1939), *The Saint's Vacation* (1941), *Three Cases of Murder* (1955).

McGrath, Pat (*b* 1916). Actor. Irish actor, on stage (started as dancer) before first film (*The Briggs Family*, 1940), he had a tiny role as a commando in *The Life and Death of Colonel Blimp* (1943) and was used again by Michael POWELL as the lead in the short film, *The Volunteer* (1943), for the Fleet Air Arm. Had his best role as the anti-British Irish nationalist in *The Halfway House* (1944). Also appeared in TV's *The Quatermass Experiment* (1953).

OTHER BRITISH FILMS INCLUDE: *Freedom Radio* (1940), *Odd Man Out* (1947), *Confession* (1955).

MacGreevy, Oliver (*b* Dublin, 1928). Actor. Bald-headed Irish character player, in about 20 films from the late 50s, including one role actually called 'Baldy' in the 1966 second feature, *The Christmas Tree*. Elsewhere, assorted villains, Russians (=villains) and madmen (as in *The Ruling Class*, 1971).

OTHER BRITISH FILMS INCLUDE: *The Scamp* (1957), *The Leather Boys* (1963), *The Ipcress File* (1965), *The Whisperers* (1966), *Great Catherine* (1967), *Flash Gordon* (1980).

McGregor, Ewan (*b* Crieff, Scotland, 1971). Actor. One of Scotland's most notable actors since the early 90s, McGregor, encouraged by his uncle, actor Denis LAWSON, studied theatre arts at Fife College, Kirkcaldy and drama at the Guildhall School. First major screen role was in Dennis POTTER's TV six-part series, *Lipstick on Your Collar* (1993), leading to subsequent TV work, most notably as Julien Sorel in *Scarlet and Black* (1993). His first film role was a small part in Bill FORSYTH's *Being Human* (1994), a box-office failure. Further TV roles preceded his most notable early film appearance as the sardonic journalist Alex in Danny BOYLE's *Shallow Grave*

(1994). The production team he worked with on *Shallow Grave* cast him as heroin-addict Renton in *Trainspotting* (1996), the role that established his screen persona as audacious, likeable rogue. McGregor's memorable performance in *Trainspotting*, an international box-office success, led to other major film roles in *Emma* (1996, UK/US), *Brassed Off* (1996, UK/US), in Peter GREENAWAY's *The Pillow Book* (1996, UK/Neth/Fr/Lux), *A Life Less Ordinary* (1997), *Velvet Goldmine* (1998, UK/US), *Little Voice* (1998, UK/US) and *Rogue Trader* (1999). In these, McGregor presents himself as a versatile actor who refuses to be typecast. His much-publicised antipathy to Hollywood did not prevent his accepting the role of Obi-Wan Kenobi in *Star Wars . . . The Phantom Menace* (1999, US). McGregor co-produced *Nora* (2000, UK/Ger/It/Ire), as well as playing the role of James JOYCE, and starred in Baz Luhrmann's musical *Moulin Rouge* (2001, Aust/US). Married to French film production designer Eve Mavrakis.

OTHER BRITISH FILMS: *Blue Juice* (1995), *Young Adam* (2003).

BIBLIOG: Brian Pendreigh, *Ewan McGregor*, 1998. Sarah Street.

MacGregor, Scott (*b* Edinburgh, 1914 – *d* Chichester, 1973). Production designer. Former stage designer and scenic artist who entered films as assistant to Edward CARRICK, then worked for CROWN on such films as *Children on Trial* (1946, as assistant to Carrick) and as art director on *The Cumberland Story* (1947) and *A Life in Her Hands* (1951). His work on *Fire Maidens from Outer Space* (1956) can scarcely have been his calling card but he nevertheless went on to design many HORROR and SCIENCE-FICTION films, including several stylish ones for HAMMER, as well as the odd realist drama like LOSEY's *The Criminal* (1960).

OTHER BRITISH FILMS INCLUDE: (set dec) *Five O'Clock Finish*, *Black in the Face* (1954, short), *That's an Order* (1955, short); (art d) *Out of True* (short) (1951), *The Master Plan* (1954), *Before I Wake* (1955), *Action of the Tiger* (1957), *Hello London* (1958), *Dr Blood's Coffin* (1960), *The Man Who Finally Died* (1962), *Invasion, The Frozen Dead* (1966), *Baby Love* (1967), *Taste the Blood of Dracula* (1969), *The Horror of Frankenstein* (1970), *Blood from the Mummy's Tomb, Burke & Hare* (1971), *Mutiny On the Buses* (1972), *Frankenstein and the Monster from Hell* (1973).

McGuigan, Paul (*b* Scotland, *c* 1964). Director. His debut film, *The Acid House* (1998), attested to McGuigan's power to turn the stomach and (to be charitable) fleetingly suggested a dark wit might be lurking beneath its challenging imagery. With *Gangster No. 1* (2000, UK/Ger) he made a significant advance, the unflinching violence taking on a kind of tragic poetry. Its star, Paul BETTANY, again had the lead in McGuigan's *The Reckoning* (2002), which links a priest, a murder and a band of travelling actors. A talent to watch, though not perhaps easily.

McGuire, Tucker (*b* Winchester, Virginia, 1913 – *d* London, 1988). Actress. American actress long in Britain, McGuire played supporting roles in over a dozen British films. She was Joyce HOWARD's wisecracking teacher chum in *The Night Has Eyes* (1942), played a continuing role in three short Tod SLAUGHTER thrillers in 1952, and was the good-natured, hard-bitten Mrs Brown in *A Night to Remember* (1958). In 1985, appeared in the US-made *DARYL*.

OTHER BRITISH FILMS INCLUDE: *Climbing High* (1937), *Shipyard Sally* (1940), *Black Orchid* (1952), *The Net* (1953), *The Sheriff of Fractured Jaw* (1958), *Ooh . . . You Are Awful* (1972).

McInnerny, Tim (*b* Cheadle Hulme, 1956). Actor. Tall, balding character actor who had striking appearances in several 90s films, including *Richard III* (1995), as Catesby, *Notting Hill*

(1999, UK/US), as Max, the hero's good-natured best friend, and *Rogue Trader* (1999), as an increasingly worried Baring's Bank employee. Oxford-educated, he worked in provincial theatres, including Glasgow Citizens Company, before joining the National, then the RSC, in the 80s, as well as enjoying notable TV success, including three seasons of *Blackadder* (1986, 1987, 1989), and appearing in US films, such as *101 Dalmatians* (1996).

OTHER BRITISH FILMS: *Wetherby* (1985), *Erik the Viking* (1989), *The Emperor's New Clothes* (2002, UK/Ger/It).

Mackaill, Dorothy (*b* Hull, 1903 – *d* Honolulu, 1990). Actress. Pert, light comedienne of Hollywood silents and early talkies, who came to US in 1921 as Ziegfeld chorus. Began her UK screen career with *The Face at the Window* (1920) and ended it with *Bulldog Drummond at Bay* (1937). Moved to Hawaii in 1934 after third marriage (first married Lothar MENDES) and end of Hollywood career. AS.

MacKay, Barry (*b* London, 1906 – *d* London, 1986). Actor. Innocuous leading man who played opposite Jessie MATTHEWS in *Evergreen* (1934, his debut), *Gangway* (1937) and *Sailing Along* (1938). Stage debut 1922, and made name in Drury Lane musicals such as *Rose-Marie* (1926). To US for *A Christmas Carol* (1938) and *Smuggled Cargo* (1940); WW2 service in the Canadian Navy; on British stage post-war; and supporting roles in a few 50s British films.

OTHER BRITISH FILMS INCLUDE: *The Private Life of Don Juan* (1934), *The Great Barrier* (1937), *The Pickwick Papers* (1952), *Grand National Night* (1953), *Orders Are Orders* (1954). AS.

Mackay, Fulton (*b* Paisley, Scotland, 1922 – *d* London, 1987). Actor. Probably most fondly remembered for his role as the strutting, dictatorial warder constantly up against Ronnie BARKER's superior sly wits in TV's *Porridge* (1974–77) and the SPIN-OFF FILM (1979). A former surveyor, also a playwright, he entered films in such Scottish-set items as the mining disaster film, *The Brave Don't Cry* (1952), and *Laxdale Hall* (1953), and did only a further dozen films, but he is distinctive in them, whether as the temporising newspaper magnate in *Defence of the Realm* or the voice of the Gryphon in *Dreamchild* (1985).

OTHER BRITISH FILMS INCLUDE: *The Last Moment* (1954), *A Prize of Arms* (1961), *Mystery Submarine* (1962), *Gumshoe* (1971), *Britannia Hospital* (1982), *Local Hero* (1983).

McKee, Gina (*b* Hartlepool, 1964). Actress. Tall, very attractive, intelligent player of 90s film and TV, who won a 1996 BAA for playing Mary Cox (ageing from 18 to 52) in the series, *Our Friends in the North*. On screen, she had small roles in Ken RUSSELL's *The Lair of the White Worm* (1988) and *The Rachel Papers* (1989), coming to prominence as Hugh GRANT's wheelchair-bound friend, Bella, in *Notting Hill* and, especially, as the commitment-seeking Nadia in Michael WINTERBOTTOM's *Wonderland* (1999). She can play 'ordinary' with unusual intensity and subtlety. On stage with the National Youth Theatre at age 15, she returned to the theatre after a seven-year gap in 2000 in *Five Kinds of Silence*.

OTHER BRITISH FILMS INCLUDE: *Wilt* (1989), *Naked* (1993), *Croupier* (1998, UK/Fr/Ger/Ire), *There's Only One Jimmy Grimble* (2000), *Women Talking Dirty* (2001), *The Loss of Sexual Innocence* (UK/US), *The Reckoning, The Zookeeper* (UK/Czech/Den/Neth) (2002).

McKechnie, James (*b* Glasgow, 1911 – *d* London, 1964). A leading radio actor, McKechnie was in several 40s films, most memorably as Spud in *The Life and Death of Colonel Blimp* (1943), brushing aside assumptions that 'the War starts at

midnight' and throwing Roger LIVESEY into a Turkish bath. Joined Glasgow Rep in 1931, worked regularly for the BBC in Glasgow, was with the BBC Repertory Company in Manchester in 1940, and London from 1941. Film roles included Colum McNeil in *San Demetrio–London* (1943) and an airman seeking refuge in a French internment camp in *Two Thousand Women* (1944). Familiarity with his voice made McKechnie a popular narrator for film and television, notably in *Painted Boats* (1945) and in *Madeleine* (1949), and in the 50s and 60s McKechnie was a multi-award-winning household name for radio drama.

OTHER BRITISH FILMS INCLUDE: *Caesar and Cleopatra* (1945), *The Years Between* (1946), *Bond Street, Scott of the Antarctic* (1948). Kara McKechnie.

McKellen, Sir Ian (*b* Burnley, 1939). Actor. Cambridge-educated McKellen first appeared on stage at the Belgrade, Coventry, in 1961 and has since built up a formidable reputation in plays classical (memorable *Richard II* and *Edward II* in 1970; *Hamlet* in 1971) and modern, working with the National Theatre, the RSC, in provincial theatres and on Broadway. His film debut was in *The Promise* (1969) followed by *Alfred the Great* (1969) and *A Touch of Love* (1969). Busy on stage and TV (e.g. *Ross*, 1971) during the 70s, he returned to film as D.H. LAWRENCE in *Priest of Love* (1980 – longer version, 1985), and played John Profumo in *Scandal* (1988). He created one of British screen's most compelling villains in his performance of the tyrannical King in *Richard III* (1995, UK/US). Outspokenly gay himself, he came to international attention in his Oscar-nominated roles as gay director James WHALE in *Gods and Monsters* (1998, US) and Gandalf in *Lord of the Rings* (2001, US/NZ). In the 90s, he has consciously expanded his film career and is in demand on both sides of the Atlantic. Knighted in 1991.

OTHER BRITISH FILMS INCLUDE: *Plenty* (1985, UK/US), *Thin Ice* (1994), *Restoration* (1995, UK/US), *Jack & Sarah* (UK/Fr), *Cold Comfort Farm* (TV, some cinemas) (1995), *A Bit of Scarlet* (1997), *Bent* (1997, UK/Jap/US) (1997).

BIBLIOG: Joy Leslie Gibson, *Ian McKellen*, 1986. Anne-Marie Thomas.

Mackendrick, Alexander (*b* Boston, 1912 – *d* Los Angeles, 1993). Screenwriter, director. Though others are more famous, Mackendrick has arguably been as influential as any British director of his generation; his critical status has remained high, while Terence DAVIES and Stephen FREARS are among those who testify to the inspiration both of his films and of his pioneering work as a teacher. Born in America and raised in Scotland, he moved South to work in advertising, and gained film experience in London and in post-Liberation Europe before joining EALING STUDIOS in 1946 as sketch artist and scriptwriter. The five films he directed there stand apart from the Ealing norm in their avoidance of whimsicality and their uncompromising intelligence and craftsmanship. All of them dramatise encounters between innocence and experience, whether in the Scottish outposts of *Whisky Galore!* (1949) and *The 'Maggie'* (1953), the industrial North of *The Man in the White Suit* (1951, co-written with cousin Roger MACDOUGALL), or the London of *The Ladykillers* (1955); the one non-comedy, *Mandy* (1952), is a powerful story of a deaf child's education. Between them, these films offer a penetrating analysis of a society characterised by tradition, inertia, and strongly defended vested interests; *The Ladykillers*, made shortly before the studio's closure, acts as a glorious summation of this in terms of black comedy, and, for Mackendrick, as an apt valediction before returning to America. After the brilliant *film* noir, *Sweet Smell of Success* (1957), his remaining projects were aborted or compromised, although the child protagonists of *Sammy Going South* (1963) and *A High Wind in Jamaica* (1965) are handled with characteristic sympathy. Shortly before his death he was a witty contributor to Stephen Frears's film in the centenary History of Cinema series, *Typically British* (1996).

OTHER BRITISH FILMS: (shorts) (anim, sc/storyboard) *On Parade* (1936), *What-Ho-She-Bumps, Sky Pirates* (1937), *Love on the Range* (1939), *Abu's Harvest, Abu's Dungeon, Abu and the Poisoned Well, Contraries* (co-d) (1943); (shorts, des consultant) *Handling Ships* (1945), *New Town* (1947), *Charley's Black Magic* (1949); *Nero* (1940, d); (feature) *Midnight Menace* (1937, co-orig story), *Saraband for Dead Lovers* (1948, co-sc), *The Blue Lamp* (1949, add dial, 2ud) *Dance Hall* (1950, co-sc), *The Guns of Navarone* (1961, orig d).

BIBLIOG: Charles Barr, *Ealing Studios*, 1977, 3rd edition 1999; Philip Kemp: *Lethal Innocence: the Cinema of Alexander Mackendrick*, 1991. Charles Barr.

McKenna, Siobhan (*b* Belfast, 1922 – *d* Dublin, 1986). Actress. Despite being given the meaty role of the murderous nymphomaniac (there weren't many of *those* in 40s British cinema) in Lance COMFORT's *Daughter of Darkness* (1947), McKenna never became a film star. Perhaps she was simply too unusual, in looks, voice and intensity, for the prevalent generic range. On stage from 1940, with Dublin's Abbey Theatre, 1943–46, she made her film debut in *Hungry Hill* and her London stage debut, both in 1947. She was an unlikely heroine of the South African tale, *The Adventurers* (1950); was, of course, aptly cast as Pegeen Mike in *Playboy of the Western World* (1962, UK/Ire), but the film was scarcely seen; and played Christ's mother in *King of Kings* (1961, US). Her stage career continued to flourish, and she toured in the 70s with a one-woman show, *Here Are Ladies*. Married to Denis O'DEA.

OTHER BRITISH FILMS INCLUDE: *The Lost People* (1949), *Of Human Bondage* (1964), *Doctor Zhivago* (1965, UK/US), *Memed My Hawk* (1984).

BIBLIOG: Micheál O'Aodha, *Siobhan: A Memoir of an Actress*, 1994.

McKenna, T(homas) P(atrick) (*b* Mullagh, County Cavan, Ireland, 1929). Actor. Bank clerk who became a prominent Irish character actor, on stage in Dublin, 1953, and London, 1963. For Joseph STRICK's James JOYCE screen ADAPTATIONS, he was Buck Mulligan in *Ulysses* (1967, UK/US) and Simon Dedalus in *A Portrait of the Artist as a Young Man* (1977), as well as appearing in a range of other films, many of them Irish-set, like *Young Cassidy* (1965).

OTHER BRITISH FILMS INCLUDE: *A Terrible Beauty, The Siege of Sidney Street* (1960), *The Quare Fellow* (1962), *Girl with Green Eyes* (1964), *The Charge of the Light Brigade* (1968), *Straw Dogs* (1971), *All Creatures Great and Small* (1974), *Britannia Hospital* (1982). AS.

McKenna, Virginia (*b* London, 1931). Actress. Delicately beautiful English rose (she hated the label) *par excellence*, McKenna trained at Central School, spent time with Dundee Rep and appeared in two West End plays before making her film debut in Dallas BOWER's *The Second Mrs Tanqueray* (1952). Came to filmgoers' attention with her sensitive performance as the Wren in *The Cruel Sea* (1952), becoming perhaps the most popular British female star of the 50s, with major successes in two physically arduous roles: in *A Town Like Alice* (1956), as a prisoner-of-war in Malaya, and *Carve Her Name With Pride* (1958), as Anglo-French spy Violette Szabo. She subdued her beauty in the name of REALISM and her apparent fragility worked movingly against the rigours of the roles.

With second husband Bill TRAVERS, she starred in the box-office hit, *Born Free* (1965), based on the work of gamekeeper George Adamson and wife Joy with lions in Kenya, and the following year they made *The Lions Are Free* (1967), a documentary about the lion cubs of *Born Free*. Subsequently, she and Travers established a charity called Zoo Check (later the Born Free Foundation), reflecting their concern for protecting wild life, and they appeared in several animal-oriented films, including *An Elephant Called Slowly* (1969).

She continued to work on the stage until the early 60s, with Old Vic (1954–55) and RSC (1961, 1963) seasons; appeared in international films, including *The Wreck of the Mary Deare* (1959, US) and *Waterloo* (1970, It/Russ); and has done a good deal of TV, with a striking role in *The Scold's Bridle* (1998). Returned to the screen in two cameos: in *Staggered* (1994), as a Scottish recluse, and *Sliding Doors* (1998), fleetingly as John HANNAH's mother. First husband was Denholm ELLIOTT.

OTHER BRITISH FILMS: *Father's Doing Fine* (1952), *The Oracle* (1953), *Simba, The Ship That Died of Shame* (1955), *The Barretts of Wimpole Street* (1956), *The Smallest Show on Earth* (1957), *Passionate Summer* (1958), *Two Living, One Dead* (1961), *Ring of Bright Water* (1969), *The Lion at World's End* (1971, doc), *Swallows and Amazons* (1974), *Christian the Lion* (1976), *The Disappearance* (1977, UK/Can),.

Mackenzie, David (*b* 1967). Director. After directing several short films, Mackenzie made his feature debut with *The Last Great Wilderness*, which had 2002 Edinburgh Festival screenings but was slow to find wider release. It starred his brother Alastair Mackenzie, who appeared in his brother's short film *California Sunshine* (1997), but is best known as Archie in TV's *Monarch of the Glen*, in several series round the turn of the century.

OTHER BRITISH FILMS INCLUDE: *Marcie's Dowry* (1999, short), *Young Adam* (2003).

Mackenzie, John (*b* Edinburgh, 1932). Director. Now known above all as the director of the classic gangster THRILLER, *The Long Good Friday* (1979), with its volatile mix of capitalist thugs and terrorists, Mackenzie began as production assistant to Ken LOACH and made his directorial debut with the TV drama of Glasgow-set sectarian violence, *Just Another Saturday* (1967). The latter was the first in a very productive collaboration with writer Peter McDougall in a series of well-regarded TV dramas. His first cinema film was the little-seen *One Brief Summer* (1969), but his next, *Unman, Wittering and Zigo* (1971), dealing with tensions in a boys' school has some genuinely unsettling and erotic moments. His later films have been disappointing, including *The Honorary Consul* (1983), a sexed-up, self-conscious ADAPTATION of Graham GREENE.

OTHER BRITISH FILMS INCLUDE: *The Innocent* (1984), *The Fourth Protocol* (1987), *When the Sky Falls* (2000, UK/Ire/US), *Quicksand* (2001, UK/Fr).

McKenzie, Julia (*b* Enfield, 1941). Actress. Popular stage and TV actress (and singer) who has a great flair for comedy largely ignored by films. On stage, a noted interpreter of Alan AYCKBOURN, and in TV's *Fresh Fields* (1984–86), a middle-aged suburban housewife; film roles have included *Those Glory Glory Days* (1983, TV, some cinemas), as mother to football-mad daughter, and *Shirley Valentine* (1989, UK/US), as Pauline COLLINS's friend, Gillian.

OTHER BRITISH FILMS: *Dick Deadeye – or Duty Done* (1975, voice), *The Wildcats of St Trinian's* (1980), *Vol-au-vent* (1996).

Mackenzie, Mary (*b* Burnley, Lancs, 1922 – *d* London, 1966). Actress. On stage from 1937 and in films from 1946's *Wanted for*

Murder, tall, slender Mackenzie had mainly supporting roles up to her early death, but played the plucky fashion-reporter heroine in *Cloak Without Dagger* (1955), and had funny moments as a widow taking solace in writing bad verse in *The Man Who Liked Funerals* (1958).

OTHER BRITISH FILMS INCLUDE: *Children on Trial* (1946), *The Lady with a Lamp* (1951), *The Long Memory* (1952), *Yield to the Night* (1956), *A Question of Adultery* (1958).

McKern, Leo (*b* Sydney, 1920 – *d* Bath, 2002). Actor. Rotund Australian actor long in Britain, who, after years of diligent character work, became a household name as TV's irascible, claret-toping *Rumpole of the Bailey* (1978–79/1983/1987–88/1991/1992). Settled in Britain after WW2, returning only rarely to film in Australia. Among his more than 50 British films, one recalls his excitable foreigner in *All for Mary* (1955), the wise-cracking newspaper man in *The Day the Earth Caught Fire* (1961), Thomas Cromwell in *A Man for All Seasons* (1966 – he had played the 'Common Man' on stage) and Dr Grogan in *The French Lieutenant's Woman* (1981). Rumpole, in fact, has tended to obscure the range of his achievements elsewhere, these including major roles with the Old Vic, with whom he made his London debut in 1949, the RSC and the West End, where he was Big Daddy in *Cat on a Hot Tin Roof* (1958). Married actress Jane Holland; their daughter Abigail is also an actress. Awarded Order of Australia, 1983.

OTHER BRITISH FILMS INCLUDE: *Murder in the Cathedral* (1952), *X the Unknown* (1956), *Time Without Pity* (1957), *Yesterday's Enemy* (1959), *Mr Topaze* (1961), *A Jolly Bad Fellow* (1963), *King and Country* (1964), *Help!* (1965), *Ryan's Daughter* (1970), *Candleshoe* (1977, UK/US), *The Chain* (1984), *A Foreign Field* (1993).

BIBLIOG: Autobiography, *Just Resting*, 1983.

Mackey, Percival (*b* London, 1894 – *d* London, 1950). Composer, music director. Former dentist, ventriloquist, conjuror, silent-film accompanist, WW1 soldier, leader of his own dance band in the 20s; Mackey's career as talkies composer began with the Gracie FIELDS vehicle, *This Year of Grace* (1931) and for KORDA's first British film, *Service for Ladies* (1932). Thereafter was composer and/or conductor and/or music director for many films of the 30s and 40s, most of them popular if routine programmers for BUTCHERS FILMS or BRITISH NATIONAL.

OTHER BRITISH FILMS INCLUDE: (a) *Death at Broadcasting House* (1934), *Somewhere on Leave* (1942), *Under New Management* (1946); (m d) *Honeymoon for Three* (1935, + a), *Accused* (1936), *You Will Remember* (1940), *Gert and Daisy's Weekend* (1941), *Demobbed* (1944), *The Hills of Donegal* (1947); (comp) *While Parents Sleep* (1935), *I'll Walk Beside You* (1943), *When You Come Home* (1947), *Calling Paul Temple* (1948).

McKidd, Kevin (*b* Elgin, Scotland, 1974). Actor. Fast-rising young actor of the late 1990s, curly-haired, blue-eyed blond McKidd has already a proven track record for versatility. From an impoverished working-class background, he dropped out of an engineering course to pursue acting full-time, and was first on screen as the charismatic, vicious Malky in Gillies MACKINNON's *Small Faces* (1995), and then as Tommy, the junkie who dies of AIDS, in the cult hit *Trainspotting* (1996). He is the one *not* on the famous poster. He quickly followed these successes with the critically esteemed *Regeneration* (1997, UK/Can), the hapless Johnny ('A Soft Touch') married to a slag in *The Acid House* (1998), a likeable gay furniture restorer in the very droll *Bedrooms and Hallways* (1999), a G&S singer in *Topsy-Turvy* (2000, UK/US) and a handsome, infatuated Vronsky in TV's *Anna Karenina* (2000). It is a very impressive record for so short a period.

BRITISH FILMS INCLUDE: *The Leading Man* (1996), *Dad Savage*, *Hideous Kinky* (UK/Fr), *Understanding Jane* (1998), *Dog Soldiers* (2001).

Mackie, Philip (*b* Salford, 1918 – *d* Oxford, 1985). Dramatist, screenwriter. Had a popular West End success with his neatly turned thriller, *The Whole Truth* (1955, filmed 1958), and wrote screenplays for several entries in the Edgar WALLACE SERIES of the early 60s. His first credit was for a HAMMER short, *The Right Person* (1955). Had significant TV career as producer and writer of plays and series such as *The Liars* (1966).

OTHER BRITISH FILMS INCLUDE: *The Clue of the Twisted Candle* (1960), *Number Six* (1962), *The £20,000 Kiss* (1963), *All the Way Up* (1970, UK/US), *Praying Mantis* (1982).

McKinney, Nina Mae (*b* Lancaster, South Carolina, 1913 – *d* New York, 1967). Actress. African-American actress of the 30s and 40s who appeared in three British films: *Kentucky Minstrels* (1934), in a guest role; as herself in the GPO FILM UNIT's *BBC – The Voice of Britain* (1935, doc); and, memorably, as the beautiful slave who becomes Paul ROBESON's wife in *Sanders of the River* (1935). Typically, she spent much of her Hollywood career playing maids.

MacKinnon, Allan (*b* 1912). Screenwriter. Also a novelist, MacKinnon collaborated pre-war with Roger MACDOUGALL on the highly successful comedy-thrillers, *This Man Is News* (1938) and *This Man in Paris* (1939), and on two comedies for Walter FORDE at EALING, *Let's Be Famous* and *Cheer Boys Cheer* (1939), before WW2 service with the Army (1939–45). The films he solo-authored are generally 'B' MOVIES of no special distinction, including the very feeble thriller, *The Hornet's Nest* (1955).

OTHER BRITISH FILMS INCLUDE: (co-sc) *Sleeping Car to Trieste*, *Vote for Huggett* (1948), *Traveller's Joy* (1949), *The March Hare* (1956), *On the Fiddle* (1961); (sc) *She Shall Have Murder* (1950), *Circumstantial Evidence* (1952), *The Saint's Return* (1953), *The Golden Link* (1954), *Behind the Headlines* (1956).

MacKinnon, Gillies (*b* Glasgow, 1948). Director. One of the most prolific Scottish film-makers of the 90s, MacKinnon had made a student film, *Rota* (1976, + music), for Middlesex Polytechnic before his feature debut, *Conquest of the South Pole* (1989), a Scottish Film on Four production, with Ewen SLAUGHTER. His *Small Faces* (1995), a tender and unsettling drama of teenage choices in the gang warfare of Glasgow 1968, was co-written and co-produced by brother Billy MacKinnon, who co-wrote and was assistant director on the cultish, irritating *Hideous Kinky* (1998, UK/Fr). Gillies also directed the critically acclaimed but little-seen drama of WW1 victims, *Regeneration* (1997, UK/Can). His is an unconventional talent, surprisingly capable of real warmth as he showed in the telemovie, *Last of the Blonde Bombshells* (2000), in which he so endearingly orchestrated the talents of his all-star cast. Has also worked in the US on *A Simple Twist of Fate* (1994), based on George Eliot's *Silas Marner*.

OTHER BRITISH FILMS: *Passing Glory* (1986), *The Playboys* (1992, Ire/US), *Trojan Eddie* (1996, UK/Ire).

Mackintosh, Steven (*b* Cambridge, 1967). Actor. Sombre-looking, slightly-built young actor who has made his mark on film, television and stage, coming to the fore as an obsessive surfie in *Blue Juice* (1995), as object of the attentions of *The Land Girls* (1998, UK/Fr) and as upper-class student, Winston, in *Lock, Stock and Two Smoking Barrels* (1998), after building up a very solid *cv* throughout the 90s. He was a compellingly ambiguous cop in TV's *Undercover Heart*, the enigmatic lead in the mini-series, *Our Mutual Friend* (1998), and the explosive, damaged protagonist of Antonia BIRD's *Care* (2000). Also, in 2000 he returned successfully to the stage, after nearly a decade's absence, at the Royal Court, in David HARE's *The Zinc Bed*, having made his debut aged 13 and been with the National Theatre in 1988. Married to actress **Lisa Jacobs**, who played the title role in *The Attic: the Hiding of Anne Frank* (1998).

OTHER BRITISH FILMS INCLUDE: *Prick Up Your Ears* (1987), *Memphis Belle* (1990), *London Kills Me* (1991), *Safe* (1993), *The Grotesque*, (1996), *Twelfth Night* (1996, UK/US), *House of America* (1997), *The Criminal* (UK/US), *Far from China* (2001).

McLaglen, Victor (*b* Tunbridge Wells, 1883 – *d* Newport Beach, California, 1959). Actor. Army heavyweight champion and WW1 captain with the Irish Fusiliers, who played the tough guy in British silents before going to Hollywood where he became a fixture in John FORD's movies, winning an AA/a for *The Informer* (1935) and an AAn/supp actor for *The Quiet Man* (1952). He made four further British films: *Dick Turpin* (1933, title role), *We're Going to Be Rich* (1938), opposite Gracie FIELDS in her unsuccessful bid for international stardom, *Trouble in the Glen* (1954) and, bellicose and obstreperous to the end, *Sea Fury* (1958). His son, **Andrew McLaglen** (*b* London, 1920), is a successful Hollywood director, who has made several British films, including *The Wild Geese* (1978, UK/Switz) and *North Sea Hijack* (1979). His brothers **Cyril McLaglen** (*b* London, 1899), **Kenneth McLaglen** (*b* London, 1902 – *d* London, 1979) and **Clifford McLaglen** (*b* London, 1892 – *d* Huddersfield, 1978) were all actors, and all made several British films. Clifford had supporting roles in about a dozen, including *The Chinese Bungalow* (1926) and *The Mystery of the Marie Celeste* (1935).

OTHER BRITISH FILMS: *The Glorious Adventure* (1922, UK/US), *Heartstrings* (1923), *The Passionate Adventure* (1924).

McLaren, John (*b* Keoma, Alberta, Canada, 1911). Actor. Canadian supporting player who filmed sporadically in Britain over 20 years, between playing the amiable American soldier who listens sympathetically to Eric PORTMAN's pub boastings in *Great Day* (1945) and the Brigadier in *Goldfinger* (1964). Also in US films. Married to opera singer Helen Toros.

OTHER BRITISH FILMS INCLUDES: *The Way to the Stars*, *The Man from Morocco* (1945), *No Orchids for Miss Blandish* (1948), *Poet's Pub* (1949), *The Young Lovers* (1954), *A King in New York* (1957), *The Sicilians* (1964).

McLaren, Norman (*b* Stirling, Scotland, 1914 – *d* Montreal, 1987). Animator. In 1939, McLaren, with a background in the British DOCUMENTARY movement, emigrated to the US, where he continued his innovative work as animator, and in 1941 he joined his old mentor John GRIERSON on the National Film Board of Canada. He went on to have a very distinguished career there, in charge of the Board's ANIMATION unit, and won an Oscar for his 1957 cartoon, *Neighbours*. Beside those achievements, his British career is 'prentice work. His first films were made while he was still a student at the Glasgow School of Art, and when Grierson saw his first animated film he invited him to join the GPO FILM UNIT in 1936. He made there both live-action documentaries and his first professional animated film, *Love on the Wing* (1938). Also worked with Ivor MONTAGU on *Defence of Madrid* (1936) during the Spanish Civil War, for the PROGRESSIVE FILM UNIT. Famous for further developing Len LYE's technique of drawing images directly on to filmstock.

OTHER BRITISH FILMS INCLUDE: (shorts, d unless noted) *Hand-Painted Abstractions* (anim, co-d), *Seven Till Five* (doc, + p) (1933), *Book Bargain* (doc, + p), *News for the Navy* (doc, + p), *Mony a Pickle* (anim, co-d, p) (1937), *The Obedient Flame* (1939, doc), *Around Is Around* (1951, UK/Can, anim) (1951).

McLaughlin, Gibb (*b* Sunderland, 1884 – *d* Los Angeles, 1960). Actor. On stage from 1911 and a veteran of British silent films before becoming an icon of lugubrious emaciation in dozens of talkies. His undertaker Sowerberry in LEAN's *Oliver Twist* (1948) represents merely the apogee of an enjoyably doleful career. Also, a comic monologuist and expert at disguise.

OTHER BRITISH FILMS INCLUDE: *The Road to London* (1921), *The Only Way*, *Nell Gwynne* (1926), *The Arcadians* (1927), *The W Plan* (1930), *Sally in Our Alley* (1931), *The Private Life of Henry VIII*, *Friday the Thirteenth* (1933), *Little Friend* (1934), *Broken Blossoms* (1936), *Inspector Hornleigh* (1939), *Freedom Radio* (1940), *Much Too Shy* (1942), *The Queen of Spades* (1948), *The Lavender Hill Mob* (1951), *Hobson's Choice* (1953), *The Deep Blue Sea* (1955), *Who Done It?* (1956).

MacLean, Alistair (*b* Glasgow, 1922 – *d* Munich, 1987). Author. Best-selling novelist several of whose adventure stories were successfully filmed, most spectacularly *The Guns of Navarone* (1957, filmed 1961) and *Where Eagles Dare* (1967, filmed 1968). World-wide locations and lashings of action characterise the oeuvre of the Glasgow University-educated ex-teacher, who served in the Royal Navy during WW2 (1941–46) and who also wrote biographies of T.E. LAWRENCE and Captain Cook. American ADAPTATIONS of his books include *Ice Station Zebra* (1968).

OTHER BRITISH FILMS: (adapted from novels, unless noted) *The Limping Man* (1953, co-sc), *Puppet on a Chain* (1970), *When Eight Bells Toll* (1971, + sc), *Fear Is the Key* (1972), *Caravan to Vaccares* (1974, UK/Fr), *Force 10 from Navarone* (1978), *Bear Island* (1979).

McLeod, Gordon (*b* Ivybridge, 1885 – *d* Los Angeles, 1961). Actor. Another of those extraordinarily prolific British CHARACTER ACTORS, at home as Police Inspectors, as in *Night Boat to Dublin* (1946), MPs, as in *The Winslow Boy* (1948) and doctors, as in *The House by the Lake* (1958), and he could be menacing as well as benign. Began in silent films, worked very steadily in the 30s (he is John Brown in *Victoria the Great*, 1937, and *Sixty Glorious Years*, 1938) and 40s, in films major and minor.

OTHER BRITISH FILMS INCLUDE: *A Smart Set* (1919), *The Only Way* (1926), *Death at Broadcasting House* (1934), *The Squeaker*, *The Rat* (1937), *Q Planes* (1939), *The Prime Minister*, *This Man Is Dangerous* (1941), *The First of the Few* (1942), *The Saint Meets the Tiger* (UK/US), *Yellow Canary* (1943), *He Snoops to Conquer* (1944), *Easy Money* (1948), *Floodtide* (1949), *Chance of a Lifetime* (1950), *The Million Pound Note* (1953).

MacLiammóir, Micheál (*b* London, 1890 – *d* Dublin, 1978). Actor. RN: Alfred Willmore. On stage as a child under his real name he became a celebrated actor, director and designer in Ireland, in 1928 establishing the Gate Theatre, Dublin, in association with his partner Hilton EDWARDS. Toured extensively in the 60s with his one-man show, *The Importance of Being Oscar*. Rare films include, most notably, Orson WELLES's *Othello* (1952, US/Fr), as Iago, about the filming of which he wrote *Put Money in My Purse*, 1954.

BRITISH FILMS: *Comin' Thro' the Rye* (1916), *Hamlet at Elsinore* (1951, Ire), *Tom Jones* (1963, narr), *30 Is a Dangerous Age, Cynthia* (1967), *The Importance of Being Dublin* (1974, Ire, short).

MacMillan, Kenneth (*b* Dunfermline, Scotland, 1929). Cinematographer. Came to films after working on some very prestigious TV, including the *Civilisation* series (1969) and

Hotel du Lac (1986). First feature was *A Month in the Country* (1987) and his next was its star's – Kenneth BRANAGH's – *Henry V* (1989), in which he achieved some striking effects, like the King's first silhouetted entrance, and for which he was BAA-nominated.

OTHER BRITISH FILMS: *Tree of Hands* (1988), *Circle of Friends* (1995, Ire/US), *Dancing at Lughnasa* (1998, UK/Ire/US).

McMurray, Mary (*b* Manchester, 1949). Director. After making the drama DOCUMENTARY, *A Pattern of Life* (1982), and the very promising feature, *The Assam Garden* (1985), which traces the rapprochement between a memsahib retired to southern England and her Indian neighbour, McMurray has worked entirely in TV, including several '*Inspector Wexford*' mysteries.

McNally, Kevin (*b* Birmingham, 1956). Actor. Rather sombre-looking leading and supporting actor in TV and films since the late 70s. He played the doomed diplomat in *The Berlin Affair* (1985, It/Ger), Liliane Cavani's story of *amour fou* (*amour* rarely comes more *fou* than this), but most of his best chances have been on TV as in *Thin Air* (1988).

BRITISH FILMS INCLUDE: *The Spy Who Loved Me* (1977), *The Long Good Friday* (1979), *The Bad Sister* (1983), *Cry Freedom* (1987), *Spice World* (1997), *Sliding Doors* (1998, UK/US), *Entrapment* (1999, UK/Ger/US), *Crust* (2001).

McNaught, Bob (*b* Glasgow, 1915 – *d* London, 1976). Director, associate producer. Directed only three features: the ADAPTATION of Dorothy and Campbell CHRISTIE's play, *Grand National Night* (1953); the four-in-a-lifeboat drama, *Sea Wife* (1956); and the Biblical tale, *A Story of David* (1960). The rest of his career was spent as production manager or associate producer.

OTHER BRITISH FILMS INCLUDE: (p man) *The Golden Salamander* (1949), *The Magic Box* (1951); (assoc p) *The Card* (1952), *Bobbikins* (1959), *Nine Hours to Rama* (1962).

MacNaughtan, Alan (aka MacNaughton) (*b* Bearsden, Scotland, 1920 – *d* London, 2002). Actor. Entered the industry in the early 50s, the lean, ascetic-looking MacNaughtan had a strong supporting role as Sylvia SYMS's homophobic brother in *Victim* (1961), but has had more chances on TV than in the cinema. Enjoyably sardonic as the gin-drinking master in *To Serve Them All My Days* (1980) and posh as the Head of the Secret Service in *A Very British Coup* (1988). Also US films, including *Patton* (1970).

OTHER BRITISH FILMS INCLUDE: *Bond of Fear* (1956), *The Double* (1963), *Family Life* (1971), *The Commissioner* (1997, UK/Belg/Ger/US).

McNaughton, Gus (*b* London, 1881 – *d* Castor, 1969). Actor. RN: Augustus LeClerq. With his sharp features, shrewd eyes and slicked-down hair, McNaughton's commercial traveller in *The 39 Steps* (1935) gave Robert DONAT some uneasy moments – and in several dozen other films gave audiences the pleasure of recognising a consummate character actor at work. Several times played dry foil to George FORMBY, last in *Much Too Shy* (1942), and was comic as the policeman on whom housemaid Dulcie GRAY has her eye in *A Place of One's Own* (1945). On stage from 15 and worked with Fred KARNO in pantomime; with the RFC during WW1.

OTHER BRITISH FILMS: *Comets, Murder!* (1930), *The Love Nest* (1933), *Happy, There Goes Susie* (1934), *Royal Cavalcade* (1935), *Storm in a Teacup, Keep Fit* (1937), *The Divorce of Lady X, South Riding, St Martin's Lane* (1938), *There Ain't No Justice* (1939), *South American George, Jeannie* (1941), *The Day Will Dawn* (1942), *The Shipbuilders* (1943),

Demobbed (1944), *The Trojan Brothers* (1945), *The Turners of Prospect Road* (1947).

McNaughton, Jack (*b* Mitcham, 1905 – *d* Northamptonshire, 1990). Actor. Made his first film, *They Made Me a Fugitive* (as gangster Soapy who ends up in the river), in 1947, the year in which his father, Gus MCNAUGHTON, whom he strongly resembled, made his last. Less prolific than his dad, but even so there are over 30 cab drivers (*The Young Wives' Tale*, 1951), policemen (*Rough Shoot*, 1953), soldiers (*The Camp on Blood Island*, 1957) and the like.

OTHER BRITISH FILMS INCLUDE: *The Guinea Pig* (1948), *Cardboard Cavalier* (1949), *Secret People, The Man in the White Suit* (1951), *Trent's Last Case, The Pickwick Papers* (1952), *The Million Pound Note* (1953), *Father Brown* (1954), *Lost* (1955), *Private's Progress* (1956), *The Stranglers of Bombay* (1959).

Macnee, Patrick (*b* London, 1922). Actor. Suave Steed of TV's cult series, *The Avengers* (1961–69; *New Avengers*, 1976–77), Eton-educated, Webber-Douglas-trained Macnee became a household name and face, perhaps at the cost of a more interesting film career. Post-1970, most of his work was US- or Canada-based. Before finding his debonair screen persona, he had small roles in ten British films and went to Hollywood for *Les Girls* (1957); post-*Avengers*, he made only a handful of British films in 30 years, including the BOND caper, *A View to a Kill* (1985). Most of his American work was for TV, but he plays Sir Denis Eaton-Hogg in the spoof DOCUMENTARY, *This Is Spinal Tap* (1984).

OTHER BRITISH FILMS INCLUDE: *The Fatal Night* (1948), *Seven Days to Noon* (1950), *Scrooge* (1951), *The Battle of the River Plate* (1956), *The Sea Wolves* (1980, UK/Switz/US), *Shadey* (1985).

BIBLIOG: Autobiography, *King B: A Life in the Movies*, 1993.

McNeice, Ian (*b* 1950). Actor. Short, fat, LAMDA-trained, actor, who spent four years with the RSC, and has acted on Broadway (in *Nicholas Nickleby*, as Squeers, naturally) and in Hollywood, the latter breakthrough occurring with his role of Fulton Greenwall in *Ace Ventura: When Nature Calls* (1995). Very funny on TV a florid-speaking doctor in the *Who Killed Cock Robin?* episode of *Midsomer Murders* (1997); and properly repulsive as Bernard Rice in *The Lonely Passion of Judith Hearne* (1987). Now works in both US and UK.

OTHER BRITISH FILMS INCLUDE: *Whoops Apocalypse* (1986), *Cry Freedom, Personal Services* (1987), *Valmont* (1989, UK/Fr), *Funny Bones* (UK/US), *The Englishman Who Went Up . . .* (1995), *A Life Less Ordinary* (1997), *Anazapta* (2002).

MacOwan, Norman (*b* St Andrew's, Scotland, 1877 – *d* Hastings, 1961). Actor. First film role was as Captain MacPhee who utters the opening line, 'Good health' (in Gaelic), in *Whisky Galore!* (1949), then totters home to die. In life, he lasted another dozen years and played as many more ancients, usually in Scots-set pieces like *Battle of the Sexes* (1959). On stage from 1900, and the author of several plays.

OTHER BRITISH FILMS INCLUDE: *Valley of Eagles* (1951), *Castle in the Air* (1952), *Laxdale Hall* (1953), *Footsteps in the Fog* (1955), *Tread Softly Stranger* (1958), *Kidnapped* (1960).

MacPhail, Angus (*b* London, 1903 – *d* England, 1962). Screenwriter. Throughout his 30-year career, versatile Westminster- and Cambridge-educated MacPhail worked almost always in collaboration. Now best remembered for his work at EALING, where he was story supervisor from 1939 to 1948, he entered the industry as film-title writer in 1926, had a busy time co-authoring screenplays at GAINSBOROUGH (1927–31) and was then story supervisor at GAUMONT BRITISH (1931–37). His 30s films cover the usual GENRE range of COMEDIES and THRILLERS, with some more complex assignments such as the romantic drama *The Faithful Heart* (1933) and the PRIESTLEY ADAPTATION, *The Good Companions* (1933, + p ass). At Ealing, he worked on George FORMBY and Will HAY comedies, as well as more serious fare including *Dead of Night* (1945) and *It Always Rains on Sunday* (1947). He is a key member of 40s Ealing, where his collaborators included John DIGHTON and Diana MORGAN. Also co-authored three American HITCH-COCK films, *Spellbound* (1945) *The Man Who Knew Too Much* and *The Wrong Man* (1956).

OTHER BRITISH FILMS INCLUDE: (sc) *The Wrecker* (1928), *The Return of the Rat* (1929), *Third Time Lucky* (1931); (co-sc) *A South Sea Bubble* (1928), *A Warm Corner* (1930), *Hindle Wakes*, *The Ghost Train* (1931), *Kicking the Moon Around* (1938), *Trouble Brewing* (1939), *Sailors Three* (+ co-story), *Return to Yesterday*, *Let George Do It!* (1940), *The Ghost of St Michael's*, *The Black Sheep of Whitehall* (1941, + co-story), *Went the Day Well?*, *The Next of Kin*, *The Foreman Went to France* (1942), *The Halfway House*, *Fiddlers Three*, *Champagne Charlie* (1944), *The Captive Heart* (1946), *The Loves of Joanna Godden*, *Frieda* (1947), *Whisky Galore!* (1949).

BIBLIOG: Charles Drazin, *The Finest Years: British Cinema of the 1940s*, 1998.

MacPherson, Kenneth (*b* 1903 – *d* Cetona, Italy 1971). Director, theorist. Scottish artist Macpherson was editor of the film theory journal *CLOSE UP* throughout its 1927–33 existence. His passionate commitment to the new art was further expressed in his own experimental films, made in collaboration with his wife Bryher (Annie Winifred Ellerman) and the poet H.D. (Hilda Doolittle), culminating in *Borderline* (1930), starring PAUL ROBESON. After 1933 he left films for the art world. Luke McKernan.

MacQuitty, William (*b* Belfast, 1905). Producer. Worked with a banking company in the Far East (1924–39), and, starting at age 60, has written several books drawing on his Eastern experiences, starting with *Abu Simbel* (1965). Entered films via agricultural and training DOCUMENTARIES for the government, then became associate producer for TWO CITIES, on such films as Jill CRAIGIE's *Out of Chaos* (1944, short) and *The Way We Live* (1946), also producing her fiction feature, *Blue Scar* (1949). In the 50s, he produced three films directed by Muriel BOX, beginning with *The Happy Family* (1952). As a boy, he had been taken to see the Belfast launching of the 'Titanic' in 1911; 47 years later he produced his most famous film for RANK, *A Night to Remember*, chronicling the great ship's tragic end.

OTHER BRITISH FILMS: *Street Corner* (1953), *The Beachcomber* (1954), *Above Us the Waves* (1955), *The Black Tent* (1956), *The Informers* (1963). BIBLIOG: Autobiography, *A Life to Remember*, 1991.

MacRae, Arthur (*b* London, 1908 – *d* Brighton, 1962). Playwright, screenwriter. The author of such popular theatrical fare as *Traveller's Joy* (1948, filmed 1949) and co-author of MUSICALS and revues, MacRae had a varied career in films. He acted in about half a dozen, starting with *The House Opposite* (1931) and finishing as Alabaster, disapproving secretary to Robert COOTE in *The Horse's Mouth* (1958), and he was a frequent stage actor. Most of his other credits are as co-author of COMEDY screenplays, but he also contributed to the famous DOCUMENTARY of WW2, *The True Glory* (1945).

OTHER BRITISH FILMS INCLUDE: (a) *Dusty Ermine* (1936, + co-sc), *Silver Blaze* (1937, + co-sc), *The Saint's Vacation* (1941), *The Oracle*

(1953); (co-sc, unless noted) *She Shall Have Music* (1935), *Paradise for Two* (1937), *Under Your Hat* (1940, play 1938), *Encore* (1951, sc for 'Winter Cruise').

Macrae, Duncan (*b* Glasgow, 1905 – *d* Glasgow, 1967). Actor. Scottish theatre actor, prominent on Edinburgh and Glasgow stages before becoming a popular purveyor of Scottish 'types' in British films of the 50s and 60s. Unlike cheery Gordon JACKSON, he is apt to be the 'dour Scot' type, most famously in *The Kidnappers* (1953), as the austere Nova Scotian farmer, but he is also compelling as the son who is consumed by an unrequited passion for Patricia ROC in *The Brothers* (1947).

OTHER BRITISH FILMS INCLUDE: *Whisky Galore!* (1949), *You're Only Young Twice!* (1952), *Geordie* (1955), *Rockets Galore* (1958), *The Bridal Path* (1959), *Tunes of Glory*, *Kidnapped* (1960), *Greyfriars Bobby* (1961), *Casino Royale* (1967).

McRae, Hilton (*b* Dundee, 1949). Actor. First noticed as Jeremy IRONS's watchful, on-the-make manservant in *The French Lieutenant's Woman* (1981), slight, dark McRae has made only occasional film appearances since, including the role of the slovenly Mr Price in *Mansfield Park* (1999), married to his real-life wife, Lindsay DUNCAN. Scored a stage success as dastardly villain in *My One and Only* (2001) at Chichester.

OTHER BRITISH FILMS: *Greystoke*... (1984, UK/US), *The Secret Rapture* (1993), *Voices* (1995).

McShane, Ian (*b* Blackburn, Lancs, 1942). Actor. Somewhat unruly-looking, RADA-trained leading man of all the media, McShane had probably his biggest success as the Norfolk-based antiques dealer-cum-detective in *Lovejoy* (1986, 1991–94), and he had a stage hit with the musical version of *The Witches of Eastwick* (2000). Screen career has been patchy, though he got off to a good start in the early 60s with *The Wild and the Willing* (1962), as the student educated out of his class, and as Hayley MILLS's gypsy boyfriend in *Sky West and Crooked* (1965), but there wasn't much to detain a personable young actor in British cinema of the 70s. His dark brooding looks made him an apt Heathcliff in TV's *Wuthering Heights* (1967), and in 2000 he was a wonderfully threatening crime boss in *Sexy Beast* (2001, UK/Sp/US). Married (1 of 3) actress Suzan FARMER and (3) US actress Gwen Humble.

OTHER BRITISH FILMS INCLUDE: *The Pleasure Girls* (1965), *Battle of Britain* (1969), *Villain* (1971), *Sitting Target* (1972), *Ransom* (1974), *The Fifth Musketeer* (UK/Austria) (1979), *Ordeal by Innocence* (1984).

McShane, Kitty (*b* Dublin, 1898 – *d* London, 1964). Actress. Appeared mainly with her husband and comedy partner, Arthur LUCAN, playing Kitty, the daughter of Old Mother Riley (Lucan), in all but the last in the series (*see* list for Lucan). In film after film, audiences were asked to believe that otherwise normal men wanted to make off with Kitty. This, in view of her very modest personal appeal (and even more modest singing voice), was a stretch. In real life, she and Lucan were legendarily quarrelsome and were separated at the time of his death.

McTeer, Janet (*b* Newcastle-upon-Tyne, 1961). Actress. Very tall (6'1"), highly respected actress in all the media, McTeer's career gathered great momentum in the 90s. She won a Tony as Nora in *The Doll's House* (1997), and that was daring casting considering her height; on TV she was a fiercely independent Vita Sackville-West in *Portrait of a Marriage* (1990) and, maintaining the Bloomsbury group connection, Vanessa Bell in the film, *Carrington* (1994). However, as far as film goes, it is her eye-catching work in the 1999 US-made *Tumbleweeds*, for her role (AAn) as a Southern mother on the run from botched relationships, and *Songcatcher*, as a musicologist working in the Appalachians, that she has come to filmgoers' notice. She is a risktaker who promises always to be worth watching.

OTHER BRITISH FILMS INCLUDE: *Half Moon Street* (1986, UK/US), *Hawks* (1988), *Wuthering Heights* (1992, UK/US), *Saint-Ex* (1996), *Velvet Goldmine* (1998, UK/US).

MacWilliams, Glen (*b* Saratoga, California, 1898 – *d* Seal Beach, California, 1984). Cinematographer. The very prolific MacWilliams spent the central part of his long career in Britain where, at GAUMONT–BRITISH, he lit seven of Jessie MATTHEWS' musicals, and was influential on how she – her wide eyes stressed – and the lavish mise-en-scène of her films were presented. Also lit such other major G-B productions as *King Solomon's Mines* and *The Great Barrier* (1937), as well as EALING's *The Proud Valley* (1940), before returning to Holly-wood where he received an AAn/c for HITCHCOCK's *Lifeboat* (1944) prior to drifting off into TV series.

OTHER BRITISH FILMS INCLUDE: *A Cuckoo in the Nest* (1933), *Evergreen*, (1934), *The Clairvoyant, First A Girl* (1935), *It's Love Again* (1936), *Head Over Heels, Gangway* (1937), *Sailing Along* (1938), *A Window in London* (1939).

Madden, John (*b* Portsmouth, 1949). Director. British-born director who has worked in US theatre, TV and film. He made an austerely intelligent version of *Ethan Frome* (1993, US) before becoming an international name with the charming romance, *Shakespeare in Love* (1999, UK/US), receiving AAn and BAAn for best direction. He made it both touching and funny, a fitting fable about the creation of *Twelfth Night*. Also had a success with *Mrs Brown* (1997, UK/Ire/US), which made film stars of Judi DENCH and Billy CONNOLLY, and will no doubt weather the aggrieved reviews of *Captain Corelli's Mandolin* (2001, UK/Fr/US). Obviously a gifted director of actors. His British TV includes episodes of *Inspector Morse* and *Prime Suspect*.

Madden, Peter (*b* Ipoh, Malaya, 1904 – *d* Bognor Regis, 1976). Actor. Sombre-faced character player in films from the late 40s, memorable as Tom COURTENAY's frail, ailing father in *The Loneliness of the Long Distance Runner* (1962) or as the Lama in *The Road to Hong Kong* (1961). Better chances on TV, as Patrick McGOOHAN's superior in *Danger Man* (1960–61, 1964–67) and Lestrade in *Sherlock Holmes* (1965, 1968). Also the odd US film, including *Exodus* (1960).

OTHER BRITISH FILMS INCLUDE: *Counterblast* (1948), *Tom Brown's Schooldays* (1951), *Floods of Fear* (1958), *Saturday Night and Sunday Morning* (1960), *A Kind of Loving* (1962), *From Russia with Love* (1963), *Nothing But the Best* (1964), *The Private Life of Sherlock Holmes* (1970), *Henry VIII and His Six Wives* (1972).

Maddern, Victor (*b* Ilford, 1926 – *d* London, 1993). Actor. Indefatigable exponent of proletarian steadfastness or comic opportunism in the many 50s WAR FILMS in which he played privates, corporals and the odd sergeant (as in *Cockleshell Heroes*, 1955). He is so enjoyable across a range of service roles, often seamen as in *Watch Your Stern* (1960), as skiving workmen (as in *I'm All Right Jack*, 1959), or in several of the 'CARRY ON' SERIES that one wants to see more of him, but – in the officer-dominated British cinema of the period – it was not the lot of homely-faced cockneys to carry films. Also fitted in stage and TV and worked for religious causes later in his surely crowded life.

OTHER BRITISH FILMS INCLUDE: *Morning Departure* (1950), *His Excellency* (1951), *Angels One Five* (1952), *Single-Handed, Malta Story* (1953), *The End of the Affair, Carrington VC* (1954), *The Night My Number Came Up* (1955), *Private's Progress, A Hill in Korea* (1956), *I Was Monty's Double, Dunkirk* (1958), *Sink the Bismarck!, Carry On Constable* (1960), . . . *Regardless* (1961), . . . *Spying*, . . . *Cleo* (1964), *Bunny Lake Is Missing* (1965), *Chitty Chitty Bang Bang* (1968), *Steptoe and Son* (1972), *Digby, the Biggest Dog in the World* (1973), *Freddie as F.R.O.7* (1992).

Madoc, Philip (*b* Merthyr Tydfil, 1934). Actor. Former linguist fluent in several languages, Welsh Madoc entered films and TV in the 60s, playing a range of supporting roles, like the bank manager in *Deadfall* (1968), the supplier of female bodies for the good doctor's experiments in *Dr Jekyll & Sister Hyde* (1971), and the Field Marshal in *Soft Beds, Hard Battles* (1973). Was married to TV actress **Ruth Madoc** (*b* Norwich, 1943), who also appeared in the film ADAPTATION of *Under Milk Wood* (1971).

OTHER BRITISH FILMS INCLUDE: *A High Wind in Jamaica* (1965), *The Berserk!* (1967), *A Bequest to the Nation* (1973).

magazines and journals Fan magazines were launched with great success at the very beginnings of commercial cinema. Two of the earliest and finest are highly sought after to this day – *Picturegoer* and *Picture Show*. *Picturegoer* went through a number of variant names and formats after its debut in 1913 before settling for the weekly edition for which it is best known in 1931. *Picture Show* was launched directly as a weekly in 1919 and continued like its main rival until 1960. *Picturegoer*'s main strength was its ability to draw its readers into the heart of the action – gossip columns, answering readers questions; *Picture Show* is better remembered for its give-aways, full page pictures and sometimes extraordinary competition prizes. Both were lavishly illustrated and gave the impression of having their fingers on the pulse of the industry. Decline set in during the mid-to-late 50s. *Picturegoer* attempted to revive itself by turning its attention to the world of pop music and *Picture Show* by incorporating television, but it was all to no avail.

As the two market leaders lost their way, rivals stepped in to take over the crown. Most important of these was the non-profit-making *ABC Film Review* which was launched in 1950 and continued until 1972 when it metamorphosed into *Film Review*. It is still published today, ever bland, but good to look at with extensive use of colour. A British edition of *Photoplay* was launched in 1950 with the usual mix of star portraits and stories but with the added bonus of access to the parent magazine's American archive. The still-running *Film Monthly* is a direct descendent. Another lavishly illustrated magazine but containing articles worth reading was *Films Illustrated* which ran from 1971 until 1982. These days, the appetite for gossip is satisfied by general celebrity magazines of various hues leaving little room for specialised film editions.

There has always been a call for magazines of a more serious bent, going beyond the star portraits, gossip and surveys of the latest releases. One of the earliest was CLOSE UP (1927–33), feeding off the burgeoning elitist FILM SOCIETY movement. The doyen of them all, however, was the uncompromising SEQUENCE (1946–52) whose contributors would feed directly into the halcyon years of the great survivor SIGHT AND SOUND which had launched in 1932 but found its feet in the 50s. The other key long-term upmarket magazine was the more prurient *Films and Filming* launched in 1954. In their pages could be found pioneering articles about all aspects of cinema from Britain and the rest of the world.

In their formidable wake, serious magazines have had trouble establishing themselves in Britain. One of the most notable efforts was *Movie* which brought AUTERISM to the

British market. It was launched in 1962 (still appearing intermittently) and in retrospect, with its near-contempt for British cinema, emphasises what an 'unknown cinema' it indeed was in those days. *Cinema Rising* lasted only three issues in 1972 but its range of interest from the underground to mainstream, all treated with intelligence, makes it fondly remembered. *Stills*, launched in 1980, consolidating its position when it found its feet as a multi-media magazine, was the first of note to look at film, television and video as a coherent whole. By the mid 80s it had lost its identity as it tried to become more trade-oriented. Other magazines have survived by marking out a smaller territory. *The Silent Picture*, which started in 1968, devoted itself to its subject with intelligence and originality, allocating many of its pages to a reinvestigation of British silents before decamping for the US in 1973. The most successful of these niche magazines is perhaps *Starburst*, which has been surveying the world of SCIENCE-FICTION and FANTASY cinema since 1979. Finally *Movie Collector*, starting in 1993 and surviving until 1995, was notable for its take on English-language cinema, knowledgeably discussing the new with reference to film history.

With the boom in intellectual exploration of the cinema in the wake of the turbulent 60s, as semiologists and radical theorists turned to the field, Britain produced its fair share of internationally acknowledged magazine leaders. The two best, marking the extremes of this approach, are probably *SCREEN* (1969–) and *Afterimage* (1970–). *Screen* always strove to be at the cutting edge of new criticism though prone to travel up the occasional theoretical cul-de-sac. *Afterimage* intermittently applied its take on ideology and aesthetics to the avant-garde, world cinema and political independents, to less effect as time went on.

The final magazine category is the 'trades' which provide production details and state of the industry reports. The dominant forces here were *Kine[matograph] Weekly* which ran from 1907 to 1971, in its heyday carrying wonderful full- and half-page movie advertisements; *BIOSCOPE* (1908–32), a mine of useful information, especially on its review pages; *Today's Cinema* (1935–57; 1969–71) and the current market leader *Screen International*, launched in 1975.

Today's market is dominated by general lifestyle magazines with colourful sections on cinema and free exhibition give-aways. The main exception is the runaway success of *Empire* negotiating the path between new releases in the cinema, video and DVD. On the whole, it avoids the worst pitfalls of its rivals in which content is dissipated by lack of knowledge and flashy approach. *Time Out*, a London listings magazine first seen in 1969, still carries the most influential reviews. However, for better or worse, it does not wield the power it had in the 70s when it could make or break an independent release with a capsule review, a power dissipated by a damaging strike and the emergence of credible alternatives. *Sight and Sound*, resting on past glories, struggles on, uneasily incorporating *The Monthly Film Bulletin* (1934–91), a magazine listing credits, synopses and reviews for every film released in Britain. New upmarket and semi-academic magazines still emerge with some regularity, but none have yet to make a stable impact. Richard Dacre.

Magee, Patrick (*b* Armagh, N. Ireland, 1922 – *d* London, 1982). Actor. RN: McGee. Mad-eyed Magee began as he meant to continue in *Rag Doll* (1960) as a drunken, bullying road-house proprietor, revealing already the unsettling presence he would bring to his stage roles in Beckett (who wrote *Krapp's*

Last Tape for him) and PINTER. In films, even in small roles like the Bishop in the restaurant in *The Servant* (1963), you couldn't miss him, and when he was given something to get his teeth into – repeating his stage role of De Sade in *The Marat/Sade . . .* (1966), Cornwall in *King Lear* (1970, UK/Den), the vengeful Mr Alexander in *A Clockwork Orange* (1971), or the Chevalier in *Barry Lyndon* (1975) – he was formidable indeed. First stage experience in Ireland with Anew McMaster's company, on the London stage from 1958.

OTHER BRITISH FILMS INCLUDE: *The Criminal* (1960), *The Boys* (1962), *Zulu, Seance on a Wet Afternoon* (1964), *The Skull* (1965), *The Birthday Party* (1968), *Cromwell* (1970), *Young Winston, Asylum* (1972), *And Now the Screaming Starts!* (1973), *Chariots of Fire* (1981).

Maguire, Sharon Director. With a background of the BBC and of DOCUMENTARY film-making in the 90s, Maguire made her cinema debut with the highly successful ADAPTATION of *Bridget Jones's Diary* (2001, UK/Fr/US), showing real flair and inventiveness in handling romantic COMEDY – and big pro-duction values – all at a considerable remove from her drama-DOCUMENTARY work.

Mainwaring, Bernard (*b* Ludlow, 1897 – *d* England, 1963). Director, screenwriter. Directed about a dozen minor COMEDIES and THRILLERS in the 30s, at least one of which, *Jennifer Hale* (1937, + co-sc), starring Rene RAY, was held to be above the 'QUOTA QUICKIE' level. The latter part of his career was given to directing DOCUMENTARIES about foreign places (e.g. *Wonderful Israel*, 1961) for his own production company.

OTHER BRITISH FILMS: (d, unless noted) *OK Chief* (1931), *The New Hotel* (1932, + p), *The Public Life of Henry the Ninth* (+ sc), *Old Roses* (+ p) (1935), *The Villiers Diamond* (1938); (doc) *Local Government* (1944), *Wonders of Gibraltar* (1959), *Wonderful Switzerland* (1963).

Maitland, Marne (*b* Calcutta, 1920 – *d* 1992). Actor. Beaky Anglo-Indian character player who, in the manner of British cinema, was cast indiscriminately as every kind of dusky foreigner. So, he is a Maharajah in *Father Brown* (1954), mad Arab driver in *South of Algiers* (1952), Arab spy in *I Was Monty's Double* (1958), Sheikh in *Khartoum* (1966) and Italian in *The Belly of an Architect* (1987, UK/It). Like several of British cinema's resident Germans, he kept busy for several decades as all-purpose foreigner, usually, in that way of foreigners, up to no good, running guns or drugs or simply giving the cleancut British hero a bad time.

OTHER BRITISH FILMS INCLUDE: *Cairo Road* (1950), *Outcast of the Islands* (1951), *Svengali* (1954), *The Wind Cannot Read* (1958), *The Stranglers of Bombay* (1959), *Sammy Going South* (1963), *Lord Jim* (1964), *The Reptile* (1966), *Decline and Fall . . .* (1968), *The Man with the Golden Gun* (1974), *Trail of the Pink Panther* (1982).

Makeham, Eliot (*b* London, 1882 – *d* London, 1956). Actor. Diminutive purveyor of the meek and downtrodden, Makeham racked up well over 100 credits in his quarter-century in films. Starting in 1932 as the put-upon Mills in *Rome Express* (1932), he had a few near-leads in the likes of *The Roof* and *I'm an Explosive* (1933) and he and Eve GREY are amusing as inept crooks in *The Last Journey* (1935). However, his real function in British cinema is to play clerks, chemists, hen-pecked husbands (*The Mill on the Floss*, 1937; *Daybreak*, 1948) and the like, though his sweetest moment in films may well be as the organist in *A Canterbury Tale* (1944) who provides Dennis PRICE with a transcendent moment. Married (3) actress Betty SHALE.

OTHER BRITISH FILMS INCLUDE: *Friday the Thirteenth* (1933), *Lorna Doone* (1934), *Her Last Affaire* (1935), *East Meets West* (1936), *Dark*

Journey, Storm in a Teacup (1937), *Vessel of Wrath, The Citadel* (1938), *Pastor Hall, Return to Yesterday* (1940), *The Common Touch* (1941), *They Flew Alone* (1942), *The Halfway House* (1944), *Perfect Strangers* (1945), *The Magic Bow* (1946), *Frieda* (1947), *So Evil My Love* (1948), *Forbidden* (1949), *Trio* (1950), *Scrooge* (1951), *Decameron Nights* (1952), *The Yellow Balloon* (1953), *Doctor in the House* (1954), *Sailor Beware* (1956).

Malahide, Patrick (*b* Pangbourne, 1945). Actor. RN: Duggan. Lean, austere-looking character player, adept at unsympathetic husbands, like those in *A Month in the Country* (1987) and, especially, as Reverend Casaubon in TV's *Middlemarch* (1994). After filming in the US in the mid 90s (e.g. *The Long Kiss Goodnight*, 1996), he appeared in several British films, including *Ordinary Decent Criminal* (2000, UK/Ger/Ire/US), as a sorely tried Police Commissioner, and *Billy Elliot* (2000), as daunting Principal of the Covent Garden Ballet School. Came to viewers' attention as Det. Sgt. Chisholm in *Minder* (1979–85, 1988–94), *The Singing Detective* (1986) and *The Inspector Alleyn Mysteries* (from 1993). A former stage manager, writes under name P.G. Duggan.

OTHER BRITISH FILMS INCLUDES: *Sweeney 2* (1978), *The Killing Fields, Comfort and Joy* (1984), *A Man of No Importance* (1994, UK/Ire), *The World Is Not Enough* (1999, UK/US), *Captain Corelli's Mandolin* (2001, UK/Fr/US), *The Final Curtain* (2002, UK/US).

male stars British male stars usually embody one of four broad cultural archetypes: hero, Everyman, anti-hero, and comic fool or rogue. These archetypes alter in relation to social changes, production patterns, and popular taste. Therefore, while stars may have long careers, their really significant impact is relatively short-lived.

British film stardom began circa 1910 when ambitious producers publicised films through named actors encompassing theatrical luminaries and MUSIC HALL comedians. Fred EVANS starred in many short films, 1912–22, as 'Pimple', a pantomime clown. The conventional heroic type, the 'perfectly mannered English gentlemen', was played by actors from the West End theatre including Owen NARES, Matheson LANG, the debonair, unflappable Guy NEWALL, and Stewart ROME, the first recognisable 'film star'. Henry EDWARDS had a loyal following as the quintessential Englishman, dreamy and romantic, but the most popular male star of the twenties was Ivor NOVELLO, the 'British Valentino', in a series of glamorous roles.

Notwithstanding Charles LAUGHTON's memorable Henry VIII, the 30s were dominated by Robert DONAT and Leslie HOWARD as romantic idealists. The man-about-town was the comic version, epitomised by the elegant Jack BUCHANAN, or Jack HULBERT's eager beaver, in musical comedies, and Ralph LYNN's silly-ass and Tom WALLS's worldly wise opportunist in farces. Music hall comedians – THE CRAZY GANG, Will HAY, Arthur LUCAN's Old Mother Riley – played more grotesque fools and rogues; the most popular was George FORMBY's gormless but indomitable proletarian Everyman.

During WW2, Donat, Howard, Rex HARRISON, Michael WILDING and returning Hollywood stars, Clive BROOK, David NIVEN and Laurence OLIVIER, played patriotic heroes, while comedians, including Arthur ASKEY and Tommy TRINDER, caught spies and saboteurs. Both were superseded by John MILLS' ordinary Everyman, no longer a clown, but the hero of the People's War. He was complemented by Jack WARNER's stoical, cheery paterfamilias Joe Huggett and his ordinary policeman in *The Blue Lamp* (1949). The most charismatic wartime star was James MASON, a saturnine 'wicked gentleman' in GAINSBOROUGH's bodice-rippers. Almost as popular was the athletic SWASHBUCKLER, Stewart GRANGER. After the war both Eric PORTMAN and David FARRAR starred as maladjusted, introspective anti-heroes in dark MELO-DRAMAS.

The gentlemen heroes of the 50s WAR FILMS, played by Mills, Jack HAWKINS or Richard TODD, were tough professionals, not amateurs. The most popular star, Kenneth MORE, combined 'fortitude and fun': the bantering Ambrose in *Genevieve* (1953), the indomitable Douglas Bader in *Reach for the Sky* (1956). His rival was Dirk BOGARDE, a personable Everyman in *Doctor in the House* (1954) and the new romantic yet tragic heart-throb. Norman WISDOM's Gump reworked the proletarian little man, Ronald SHINER and Alastair SIM played resourceful rogues; Alec GUINNESS, played both. The BOULTINGS' satires starred Ian CARMICHAEL as the new silly ass, TERRY-THOMAS as the cad and Peter SELLERS as the little man. Sellers developed the type as Inspector Clouseau, making him an international star.

The late 50s and 60s saw the hegemony of the anti-hero. Not pop stars, Tommy STEELE or Cliff RICHARD, always the boy-next-door, but Peter CUSHING's Baron Frankenstein and Christopher LEE's Dracula in HAMMER's Gothic horrors; Stanley BAKER's working-class tough guy; and the ANGRY YOUNG MAN, played by Laurence HARVEY, Richard BURTON, Richard HARRIS, Tom COURTENAY, Alan BATES, and Albert FINNEY who also played the uninhibited 'natural man', *Tom Jones* (1963). Michael CAINE's down-beat secret agent, Harry Palmer, and his *Alfie* (1966) were working-class Cockneys, no longer comic but smart and sexy. Scottish Sean CONNERY played the 60s' most successful hero, James BOND, combining the debonair gentleman with the muscular American tough guy. By contrast, Peter O'TOOLE's enigmatic *Lawrence of Arabia* (1962) was the successor to equivocal figures played by Trevor HOWARD and Peter FINCH.

The 70s, the decade of the television SPIN-OFF, saw the demise of the long-running 'CARRY ON' SERIES starring Kenneth CONNOR, Charles HAWTREY, Sid JAMES and Kenneth WILLIAMS, eclipsed by 'Randy Robin' ASKWITH in the 'Confessions' films. Caine, Malcolm McDOWELL and Michael YORK starred in spoof or serious international adventure films, as did Roger MOORE, who mockingly recreated James Bond as an old-style gentleman-hero.

Bob HOSKINS' memorable gangster in *The Long Good Friday* (1979, released 1981) was exceptional; the 80s revival of British cinema came through the 'HERITAGE' FILMS, making stars of a new generation of handsome, sensitive young men – Jeremy IRONS, James WILBY, Colin FIRTH, Rupert EVERETT and Kenneth BRANAGH who went on to become the 'new Olivier' – often playing sexually ambivalent gentlemen; Anthony HOPKINS was an older repressed Englishman, a type parodied by John CLEESE.

In the 90s, a new type emerged, though with echoes of Finney *et al*, a degraded working-class hero, the underclass Everyman: Robert CARLYLE in *The Full Monty* (1997), and charismatic Ewan McGREGOR's adaptable Mark Renton in *Trainspotting* (1996), which made him a popular icon. Another Celt, Pierce BROSNAN, was successful as a retro BOND, returning to the Connery mould. Hugh GRANT's diffident English charm in *Four Weddings and a Funeral* (1994) made him an international star, while Ralph FIENNES has emerged as the current romantic but troubled Englishman.

BIBLIOG: Geoffrey Macnab, *Searching for Stars: Stardom and Screen Acting in British Cinema*, 2000; Andrew Spicer, *Typical Men: The*

Representation of Masculinity in Popular British Cinema, 2000; Bruce Babington (ed), *British Stars and Stardom*, 2001. Andrew Spicer.

Malik, Art (*b* Bahawalpur, Pakistan, 1953). Actor. Pakistani actor who grew up in Britain and came to popular attention in TV in two ambitious mini-series set in the sub-continent: *The Far Pavilions* and *The Jewel in the Crown* (1984). In film, he had a small but significant role in *A Passage to India* (1984), a vivid spot as a wild-haired, Oxford-educated mojehedin leader in *The Living Daylights* (1987) and a co-starring role in the school-set *Clockwork Mice* (1995), as well as appearing in several international productions, including *Turtle Beach* (1991, Aust) and *True Lies* (1994, US). Has also pursued a busy stage career, with the Old Vic and the RSC, and continues to be in demand on TV.

OTHER BRITISH FILMS INCLUDE: *Arabian Adventure* (1979), *Underworld* (1985), *Hostage* (UK/Arg), *City of Joy* (UK/Fr) (1992), *Vicious Circle* (1998).

Malins, Geoffrey (*b* Boston, England, 1887 – *d* South Africa, 1943). Director, cinematographer. Primarily a director of short subjects (1915–28), including the *Orpheus Song Films* SERIES (1915), *Ally Sloper* series (1921), *Romances of the Prize Ring* series (1926, co-d) and *WW Jacobs Stories* series (1928). Having been a news cameraman for CLARENDON FILM COMPANY, he became noteworthy as the premier cinematographer of WW1, including famously *The Battle of the Somme* (1916), receiving the OBE for his work. His films from 1918 to 1921 feature Ena BEAUMONT, with whom he formed the production company, Garrick, in 1919.

OTHER BRITISH FILMS INCLUDE: *The Girl from Downing Street* (1918, + sc), *Patricia Brent, Spinster* (1919), *All the Winners* (1920), *Bluff* (1921), *The Recoil* (1922), *The Wonderful Wooing* (1925), *East of Singapore* (1927), *London Melody* (1930, co-d, + sc).

BIBLIOG: Autobiography, *How I Filmed the War*, 1919. AS.

Mallalieu, Aubrey (*b* Liverpool, 1873 – *d* England, 1948). Actor. It is just possible that the austere magistrate in *Twenty-One Days* (1937), the butler in *The Demi-Paradise* (1943) or the envoy in *Saraband for Dead Lovers* (1948) was once young, but to filmgoers his very name conjures up crabbed age, sometimes benign, sometimes grim, sometimes merely fussy. Usually his firmly characterful demeanour was in the service of professionals or of upper servants, in well over 100 films, not to speak of a long stage career.

OTHER BRITISH FILMS INCLUDE: *What Happened to Harkness?* (1934), *All That Glitters* (1936), *The Rat, Keep Fit* (1937), *The Stars Look Down* (1939), *Busman's Honeymoon* (1940), *Pimpernel Smith, Hatter's Castle* (1941), *The Young Mr Pitt, We'll Meet Again* (1942), *The Lamp Still Burns* (1943), *Champagne Charlie* (1944), *The Wicked Lady, Murder in Reverse* (1945), *Bedelia, Frieda* (1947), *The Winslow Boy, The Queen of Spades* (1948), dozens more.

Malleson, Miles (*b* Croydon, 1888 – *d* London, 1969). Actor, writer. Malleson was a prolific screenwriter during the 30s, in particular associated with historical subjects such as *Nell Gwyn* (1934, + a), *Tudor Rose* (1936, + a) and the hugely successful *Victoria the Great* (1937, + a). He was equally prolific as an actor. While his chinless features made him ideal casting as a bumbling or pompous fool, his intelligence and energy enabled him to endow these roles with genuine wit and vim. He is the theatre manager in Hitchcock's *The 39 Steps* (1935), the comic relief in several HAMMER horrors, and the gentleman attempting to purchase pornographic 'views' in *Peeping Tom* (1960). He is also the hangman in *Kind Hearts and Coronets* (1949) who contemplates retirement because, after hanging a duke with a silken rope, he could 'never again be content with hemp.'

OTHER BRITISH FILMS INCLUDE: (sc) *Children of Chance, The W Plan* (1930), *Sally in Our Alley, Night in Montmartre* (play) (1931), *The Water Gipsies* (1932), *Perfect Understanding* (1933, + a), *Lorna Doone, Falling in Love* (1934), *Peg of Old Drury* (1935), *Rhodes of Africa* (1936), *The Rat, Action for Slander* (1937), *Sixty Glorious Years* (1938), *Pastor Hall, The Thief of Baghdad* (1940), *They Flew Alone, Squadron Leader X, The First of the Few* (1942), *Adventures of Tartu* (1943); (a) *The Headmaster* (1921), *City of Song* (1931), *Summer Lightning* (1933), *Knight Without Armour* (1937), *The Lion Has Wings* (1939), *The Thief of Baghdad* (1940), *Major Barbara* (1941), *The First of the Few* (1942), *The Demi-Paradise* (1943), *Dead of Night* (1945), *While the Sun Shines* (1947), *The Queen of Spades* (1948), *The Man in the White Suit* (1951), *The Importance of Being Earnest* (1952), *The Captain's Paradise* (1953), *Private's Progress* (1956), *Happy is the Bride* (1957), *Dracula* (1958), *I'm All Right Jack* (1959), *The Brides of Dracula* (1960), *Murder Ahoy* (1964), *You Must Be Joking!* (1965), dozens more. Peter Hutchings.

Malo, Gina (*b* Cincinatti, 1909 – *d* New York, 1963). Actress. RN: Janet Flynn. Popular lead and second lead in twenty films of the 30s, including several operettas, such as *Goodnight Vienna* (1932), and *Jack of All Trades* (1936), in which she is a charming foil for Jack HULBERT's ever more zany schemes. A former dancer, she also had stage experience in London and New York.

OTHER BRITISH FILMS INCLUDE: *A Tight Corner* (1932), *Waltz Time, King of the Ritz* (1933), *The Private Life of Don Juan* (1934), *Where There's a Will, Windbag the Sailor* (1936), *The Door with Seven Locks* (1940).

Malone, Cavan (*b* London, 1936 – *d* Richmond, Surrey, 1982) Actor. Made his impressive debut as the contested child in *When the Bough Breaks* (1947), had several more juvenile roles and a few 'B' MOVIE parts as a young man, but his career faltered – as so often happened to CHILD ACTORS.

OTHER BRITISH FILMS INCLUDE: *Captain Boycott* (1947), *Mr Perrin and Mr Traill* (1948), *Highway to Battle* (1960), *633 Squadron* (1963), *Downfall* (1964).

Maloney, Michael (*b* Bury St Edmund's, 1957). Actor. Busy and gifted actor in all the media, Maloney entered films in a tiny role in 1980's *Richard's Things* but his career really gathered momentum at the end of the decade when he played the Dauphin-as-loose-cannon in *Henry V* (1989) and followed this by the romantic lead in the touching and popular romance, *Truly Madly Deeply* (1990). Continuing his association with Kenneth BRANAGH, he was engaging as the would-be Hamlet of a provincial production in *In the Bleak Midwinter* (1995) and a fine, forceful Laertes to Branagh's *Hamlet* (1996, UK/US), having played Rosencrantz to Mel Gibson's (1990, UK/US). Also much in demand on stage (RSC, National seasons, as well as the moderen comedy of *Mouth to Mouth*, 2001) and TV, so that having turned down 'I' in *Withnail & I* (1986) hardly seems to have hurt his career.

OTHER BRITISH FILMS INCLUDE: *Ordeal by Innocence* (1984), *Othello* (1995, UK/US).

Maltby, H(enry) F(rancis) (*b* Ceres, Cape Colony, 1880 – *d* London, 1963). Actor, screenwriter. As well as appearing in and/or (co-)writing about 100 films, usually as pompous authority figures, sometimes duplicitous, as in *Old Mother Riley, Detective* (1943), as H.G. Popplethwaite (the name tells all), often spluttering, always relishable, Maltby, with his receding chin, plump cheeks and beady eyes was scarcely off the screen for a dozen years. Sometimes, certainly, he was only briefly spotted, like one of the Covent Garden bystanders in *Pygmalion* (1938), but he was also a prolific stage actor (debut

1899), director and playwright, his filmed plays including *The Profit and the Loss* (1917) and *The Laughter of Fools* (1933).

OTHER BRITISH FILMS INCLUDE: (play) *A Temporary Gentleman* (1920), *Just My Luck* (1933); (sc) *Department Store* (1935, story), *The Howard Case* (+ play), *The Crimes of Stephen Hawke* (add dial) (1936), *Easy Riches* (1938, dial), *Something in the City* (1950, orig story); (co-sc) *The Love Nest* (1933), *Boys Will Be Girls* (1937), *Gert and Daisy's Weekend* (1941), *Rose of Tralee* (1942), *It's a Grand Life* (1953); (a) *I Spy* (1933), *Falling in Love* (1934), *Jack of All Trades* (1936), *Young and Innocent* (1937), *Owd Bob* (1938), *Under Your Hat, Return to Yesterday* (1940), *The Great Mr Handel* (1942), *A Canterbury Tale* (1944), *The Trojan Brothers* (1945).

BIBLIOG: Autobiography, *Ring Up the Curtain*, 1950.

Manahan, Sheila (*b* Dublin, 1924 – *d* Richmond, Surrey, 1988). Actress. Began her career at the Abbey Theatre, coming to London post-WW2. Played sweet second leads to such blonde hussies as Moira LISTER in *Another Shore* (1948) and Christine NORDEN in *Saints and Sinners* (1949), and had her best opportunity as the anguished scientist's daughter in *Seven Days to Noon* (1950). Also appeared in TV and on the London stage.

OTHER BRITISH FILMS INCLUDE: *Footsteps in the Fog* (1955), *Seven Waves Away* (1956), *Only Two Can Play* (1961).

Mancunian Film Corporation The only film company, complete with studio, that operated outside the south-east of England during the sound era. Established in 1934 by exhibitor/renter John E. BLAKELEY to produce films starring northern comics, the Manchester-based company initially shot its films, including George FORMBY's first two vehicles, in hired London studios. However, in 1947, Blakeley finally opened a studio in Manchester, in a converted Methodist chapel in Rusholme, where he was to produce his films until pulling out of production and selling the property to the BBC in 1953. Very much a family concern, the majority of the films were directed by Blakeley himself, with sons Tom and John Jr as production manager and cameraman respectively. Featuring the top northern comics of the day, including Norman Evans, Duggie WAKEFIELD, Nat JACKLEY, Sandy POWELL, JEWELL and Warriss, and, above all, the company's most popular star, Frank RANDLE, the films were shown almost exclusively in the north. Although Blakeley's direction may have been perfunctory at best, never venturing beyond a basic point-and-shoot style, with the comics improvising for the camera, northern audiences loved the films, and none of them lost money. Production was briefly revived in the early 60s with six mediocre London-shot thrillers.

BIBLIOG: Philip Martin Williams & David Williams, *Hooray for Jollywood: The Life of John E. Blakeley and the Mancunian Film Corporation*, 2001. John Oliver.

Mander, Kay (*b* Hull, 1915). Director, continuity 'girl'. Began her career in 1935 in CONTINUITY and became the first woman member of the ACT in 1937. During the war she directed instructional films for SHELL, Paul ROTHA Productions and REALIST FILM UNIT before setting up Basic Films with her husband Rodney Neilson BAXTER in 1945. Their first commission was the socially conscious, *Homes for the People* (1945) which looked at the appalling conditions of city, town and country dwellings from the 'ordinary' woman's viewpoint. In 1945 she won a BAA for her educational film, *La Famille Martin* (1949). She returned to continuity and worked with Truffaut, Preminger, Terence YOUNG and Ken RUSSELL, and later resumed DOCUMENTARY direction.

OTHER BRITISH FILMS INCLUDE: (d) (doc/shorts) *How to File* (1941), *Highland Doctor* (1943), *New Builders* (1944), *Mardi and the Monkey* (1953), *The New Boat* (1955), (feature) *The Kid from Canada* (1957); (cont) *The Strange World of Planet X* (1957), *Serious Charge* (1959), *The Boys* (1962), *From Russia with Love* (1963), *The Heroes of Telemark* (1965), *Country Dance* (1969), *The Little Prince* (1974, UK/US), *Tommy* (1975), *The Human Factor* (1979), *Straight to Hell* (1986, sc super). Sarah Easen.

Mander, Miles (*b* Wolverhampton, 1888 – *d* Los Angeles, 1946). Actor, director. Formerly a sheep-farmer in New Zealand, playwright, film exhibitor and WW1 aviator, the incisive, somewhat gaunt-faced Mander began in British silent films, acting as 'Luther Miles', at first reserving his real name for writing credits. Became a popular leading man in 30s cinema, in major productions such as *The Private Life of Henry VIII* and *Bitter Sweet* (1933), as well as director (and often co-screenwriter) of a number of films including the well-regarded *The First Born* (1928) and the UK/Australian co-production, *The Flying Doctor* (1937, +p). From then until his early death, he was in Hollywood playing all manner of upper-class and often duplicitous Brits; for his last few years, he was scarcely ever out of the uniform of HM services.

OTHER BRITISH FILMS INCLUDE: (a) *Once Upon a Time* (1918), *The Old Arm Chair* (1920), *Half a Truth* (1922), *The Prude's Fall* (1924), *Riding for a King* (1926), *The Fake* (1927), *Murder!* (1930), *The Lodger* (1932, co-sc), *Loyalties* (1933), *The Battle* (1934, UK/Fr); (d) *Packing Up* (1927), *The Woman Between* (+ co-sc), *Fascination* (1931), *The Morals of Marcus* (1935, + co-sc).

Mango, Alec (*b* London). Actor. In films and TV (*The Amazing Dr Clitterhouse*, 1947) from the 40s, usually playing foreigners of various kinds, such as the 'good' Arab, sole survivor of a desert dust-up, in *South of Algiers* (1952), and assorted Greeks, Italians, Spaniards, almost always of dubious intention.

OTHER BRITISH FILMS INCLUDE: *Fiddlers Three* (1944), *His Excellency* (1951), *They Who Dare* (1953), *Zarak* (1956), *Interpol, The Shiralee* (1957), *The Angry Hills* (1959), *Khartoum* (1966), *Steptoe and Son* (1972), *Gothic* (1986).

Mankiewicz, Joseph L(eo) (*b* Wilkes-Barre, Pennsylvania, 1909 – *d* Bedford Village, NY, 1993). Director, screenwriter. Though heaped with honours (including two Oscars), as he deservedly was, as one of the most truly sophisticated of Hollywood director-writers, he merits only a fleeting reference here for three British-based films: *Escape* (1948), from John GALSWORTHY's drama; *Suddenly, Last Summer* (1959), from Tennessee Williams's hothouse piece; and *Sleuth* (1972), from Anthony SHAFFER's two-hander. All play ADAPTATIONS, they show the literary leanings of Mankiewicz's talent.

Mankiewicz, Tom (*b* Los Angeles, 1942). Screenwriter. Son of Joseph MANKIEWICZ (and nephew of Herman), he co-authored three BOND adventures of the 70s, *Diamonds Are Forever* (1971), *Live and Let Die* (1973) and *The Man with the Golden Gun* (1974), and was consultant on *Superman* (1978) and *Superman II* (1980). Unlike his father, he favours action genres, in cinema and TV.

OTHER BRITISH FILMS: *The Cassandra Crossing* (1976, UK/Ger/It), *The Eagle Has Landed* (1976).

Mankowitz, Wolf (*b* London, 1924 – *d* Co. Cork, 1998). Screenwriter. Educated in East Ham and at Cambridge, a multi-talented figure who emerged in the 50s, with his TV play, *The Bespoke Overcoat* (1954), made into Jack CLAYTON's Oscar-winning SHORT FILM (1955, + sc), his novel, *A Kid for Two*

Farthings (1953), filmed by Carol REED (1954), and his satirical showbiz MUSICAL *Expresso Bongo* (1958), filmed by Val GUEST (1959, + BAA/sc). These works explored aspects of East End traditions, in semi-fantastic modes. He went on to (co-)author a wide range of films, including the jungle-set WAR FILM, *The Long and the Short and the Tall* (1960, co-sc), the SCIENCE-FICTION piece, *The Day the Earth Caught Fire* (1961, co-sc), the period spy spoof, *The Assassination Bureau* (1968, co-sc) and the chamber drama, *The Hireling* (1973). As well he maintained a high reputation as a theatrical entrepreneur, producer, playwright and manager.

OTHER BRITISH FILMS INCLUDE: (sc, unless noted) *Make Me An Offer!* (1954, novel, add dial), *The Millionairess* (1960, BAAn/sc), *Waltz of the Toreadors* (1962), *Casino Royale* (1967, co-sc), *Bloomfield* (1969, UK/Isr, + co-p), *Black Beauty* (1971, UK/Ger/Sp), *Almonds and Raisins* (1984, UK/US, doc).

Mann, Cathleen (*b* Newcastle, 1896 – *d* London, 1959). Costume designer. Trained in London (Slade) and Paris, Mann was the Marchioness of Queensberry from 1926 to 1946 and this is how she is credited for her share of the costumes for *Things to Come* (1936). This was her most famous film, but the half-dozen others for which she designed the costumes were relatively lavish 30s films. Pre-WW2, she designed posters for SHELL. An artist of distinction, her work is held in important collections, including the Victoria and Albert Museum.

OTHER BRITISH FILMS INCLUDE: *The Wandering Jew* (1933), *Evensong, Chu-Chin-Chow* (1934), *The Iron Duke* (1935), *The Three Maxims, Land Without Music* (1936).

Mann, Christopher (*b* Hull, 1903). Agent. Important actors' and authors' representative, educated at King Edward's School, Birmingham, and Birmingham University. Trained as civil engineer, he entered show business as theatre press agent before establishing his own agency in 1932 and acting for many famous stars. Once married to Greta GYNT, then, it was thought, to Eileen JOYCE, but her recent biography cast doubt on the formality of their long union.

Mann, Ned H. (*b* Redkey, Indiana, 1893 – *d* La Jolla, California, 1967). Special effects. Former roller skating professional and stage actor who became a special effects ace, working for KORDA in Britain in the latter 30s, on some of the period's most famous films – and, from Mann's point of view, some of the most demanding. These included *The Ghost Goes West* (1935), *Things to Come* and *The Man Who Could Work Miracles* (co-fx) (1936). He set up a special effects department at LONDON FILMS, where he created the Armada sequences for *Fire Over England* (1937). A lover of gadgetry, he first developed this interest in US silent films, from 1925, as a trick-photography specialist. His last work was on *Around the World in Eighty Days* (1956, US).

OTHER BRITISH FILMS INCLUDE: *The Scarlet Pimpernel* (1935), *Rembrandt, Men Are Not Gods* (1936), *Dark Journey, Knight Without Armour* (1937), *The Divorce of Lady X* (1938), *An Ideal Husband* (1947, co-fx).

Mann, Stanley (*b* Canada, 1928). Screenwriter. Began writing for British films and TV in the 50s. Mann shared an AAn for the screenplay of *The Collector* (1965, UK/US), and his other British credits include the enjoyable *Hamlet*-on-a-yacht MELODRAMA, *Woman of Straw* (1964), and – truly – *The Strange Affair* (1968), which he also co-produced.

OTHER BRITISH FILMS: (co-sc, unless noted) *Another Time, Another Place* (1958), *His and Hers* (1960), *The Mark* (1961), *A High Wind in*

Jamaica (1965), *The Naked Runner* (1967), *Theatre of Blood* (1973, co-p), *Eye of the Needle* (1981, sc).

Manners, Lady Diana (aka Diana Cooper) (*b* London, 1892 – *d* London, 1986). Actress. Eccentric socialite and legendary beauty, she was the wife of Duff Cooper, Viscount Norwich. In 1913, she appeared in a filmed dance screened for Queen Mary, who was so outraged at Manners' costume that she ordered the film destroyed. Later, she starred in *The Glorious Adventure* (1922) and *The Virgin Queen* (1923), which she described as 'an inartistic lark'. Following her film work, the actress was cast as the Madonna in Max Reinhardt's stage production, *The Miracle*, a role she played in the US until 1932. AS.

Mannheim, Lucie (*b* Berlin, 1899 – *d* Braunlage, West Germany 1976) Actress. Formerly on German stage and screen, Mannheim made a striking debut in British films as the mysterious Annabella Smith in Alfred HITCHCOCK's *The 39 Steps* (1935). Her subsequent film appearances were often memorable, but few and far between. During the war she contributed to the BBC's German-language service. Married (1941–76) to actor Marius GORING, she worked mainly in West Germany after 1945.

OTHER BRITISH FILMS INCLUDE: *East Meets West* (1936), *The Yellow Canary* (1943), *The Tawny Pipit, The True Story of Lili Marlene, Hotel Reserve* (1944), *Bunny Lake Is Missing* (1965). Tim Bergfelder.

Manvell, Roger (*b* Leicester, 1909 – *d* Boston, US, 1987). Historian. Graduate of London University, worked for the Films Division of the MOI during WW2, was appointed first Director of the BRITISH FILM ACADEMY in 1947, and was the author of many books on film. Perhaps his most influential contribution was as the author of the Pelican book, *Film* (1944), then as Executive Editor of the *Penguin Film Review* (1946–49), and co-editor of the annual publication, *The Cinema*, in the early 50s. There is a somewhat mandarin, film-as-art, anti-Hollywood strain through all this work, but it was very valuable in its time. Other books included *New Cinema in Britain* (1969) and *Theatre and Film* (1979), as well as several film biographies; also a regular broadcaster with the BBC.

Manville, Lesley (*b* Brighton, Sussex, 1956). Actress. Chameleon-like character actress whose career has been almost wholly advanced by director Mike LEIGH. She worked with him on the TV play *Grown Ups* (1980) before her role in his feature film, *High Hopes* (1988), as Laetitia, the middle-class snob, whose impatient cries of 'Chop! Chop!' as the frail Mrs Bender struggles to climb some steps, complete the characterisation beautifully. Appeared briefly, though memorably, in Leigh's celebrated feature *Secrets & Lies* (1996), as a social worker, and in *Topsy-Turvy* (2000, UK/US), was a poignant Lucy Gilbert. Has also maintained a TV career as in *The Painted Lady* (1997) opposite Helen MIRREN, and Peter MEDAK's serial *David Copperfield* (1999). Divorced from actor Gary OLDMAN.

OTHER BRITISH FILMS: *Dance with a Stranger* (1984), *High Season, Sammy and Rosie Get Laid* (1987), *Milk* (1999), *All or Nothing* (2002, UK/Fr). Melinda Hildebrandt.

Maranne, André (*b* Toulouse, France, 1926). Actor. French character actor long in Britain, who established a small niche for himself as Sergeant François Duvall, the sorely tried Dreyfus's assistant in the 'Pink Panther' films, starting with *A Shot in the Dark* (1964). Also in over two dozen other British films.

OTHER BRITISH FILMS INCLUDE: *Loser Takes All* (1956), *Harry Black* (1958), *HMS Defiant* (1962), *Thunderball* (1965), *Battle of Britain* (1969),

Return of the Pink Panther (1974), *Revenge of the Pink Panther* (1978), *The London Connection* (1979), *Trail of the Pink Panther* (1982), *Morons from Outer Space* (1985).

Marcel, Terry (*b* Oxford, 1942). Director, screenwriter. Entered the industry in the early 60s, and worked as 2nd or 3rd assistant director (e.g. on several 'Pink Panther' films), sometimes as 2nd unit director until 1977 when he co-produced *Prey*. He then directed and co-wrote several films, including the comedy-fantasy, *There Goes the Bride* (1979) and the sword-and-sorcery piece, *Hawk the Slayer* (1980). Also worked on several TV series, including *Dark Knight* (2000).

OTHER BRITISH FILMS INCLUDE: (ass d/2ud) *Khartoum* (1966), *Straw Dogs* (1971), *The Duellists* (1977), *Revenge of the Pink Panther* (1978), *Sky Bandits* (1986); (d) *Why Not Stay for Breakfast?* (1979), *Jane and the Lost City* (1987, + co-story), *The Last Seduction II* (1999, UK/US).

Marcell, Joseph (*b* St Lucia, 1948). Actor. Like many black actors in Britain, Marcell has not found roles plentiful, in spite of co-starring, with Norman BEATON as his brother-in-law, in the series, *Empire Road* (1978–79), set among Birmingham's black community. He had smallish parts in *Playing Away* (1986) and *Cry Freedom* (1987), and the US feature, *Sioux City* (1994), but most of his work has been for TV.

March, Elspeth (*b* London, 1911 – *d* Northwood, 1999). Actress. RN: Mackenzie. Sherborne-educated and Central School-trained, there was something invincibly upper-class about tall, elegant March. She made a dozen or so British films, including a miscast as Jimmy HANLEY's 'real' mum in *Boys in Brown* (1949); dignity was her strong point, even in *Carry On Again Doctor* (1969). She was a noted exponent of SHAW and an imposing figure in the National Theatre's *The Madras House* (1977–78). Married for ten years (late 30s-late 40s) to Stewart GRANGER who dominated the rest of her life after their meeting in Birmingham Rep.

OTHER BRITISH FILMS INCLUDE: *Mr Emmanuel* (1944), *His Excellency* (1951), *The Roman Spring of Mrs Stone* (1961), *Dr Crippen* (1962), *Psyche 59* (1963), *Goodbye, Mr Chips, Twinky* (1969).

Margetson, Arthur (*b* London, 1897 – *d* London, 1951). Actor. On stage from 1917, with extensive revue and musical comedy experience before embarking on films in 1930. Had substantial roles in over 20 British films, including the mother's nervous actor-boyfriend in *Little Friend* (1934), the brutal father in *Broken Blossoms* (1936), and a vain provincial actor in *Return to Yesterday* (1940). A former stockbroker's clerk, the tall, solid Margetson went to Hollywood in 1940 and plays the jumpy Chet in *Random Harvest* (1942).

OTHER BRITISH FILMS INCLUDE: *Wolves* (1930), *Lucky Girl* (lyrics), *Flat No. 9* (1932), *Royal Cavalcade, Music Hath Charms* (1935), *Juggernaut* (1936), *Smash and Grab, Action for Slander* (1937), *Me and My Pal* (1939).

Margo, George (*b* Canada – *d* Malibu, California, 2002). Actor. Stayed on in the UK post-war and played small roles in (mainly) 50s films, including *After the Ball* (1957) as US impresario, Tony Pastor, and several other Americans – as was the way with Canadians in England. Much TV, including Blackbeard the Pirate in *The Buccaneers* (1956).

OTHER BRITISH FILMS INCLUDE: *Circle of Danger* (1950), *Hell Is Sold Out* (1951), *The Red Beret* (1953), *Little Red Monkey, Lilacs in the Spring* (1954), *Joe MacBeth* (1955), *Zarak* (1956), *Windom's Way* (1957), *The Mouse That Roared* (1959), *The Adding Machine* (1969).

Margolyes, Miriam (*b* Oxford, 1941). Actress. Very bulky, very enjoyable character actress, in demand on both sides of the

Atlantic, having settled in the US in 1989. Though she had been in films since 1969's *A Nice Girl Like Me*, she really came to the fore in the 80s with strong roles in *The Good Father* (1986) and, especially, as Flora Finching in *Little Dorrit* (1987). She won a BAA (supp a) for her richly knowing portrayal of Mrs Manson Mingott in *The Age of Innocence* (1993) and more than held her own against all-conquering youth in *Romeo+Juliet* (1996), as the Nurse. She has also worked incessantly on TV (*Blackadder II*, 1986; Miss Crawley in *Vanity Fair*, 1998) and stage, winning golden opinions for her 1990s one-woman show, *Dickens' Women*, as well as doing voice-overs for such as *Babe* (1996, Aust). Awarded OBE, 2002.

OTHER BRITISH FILMS INCLUDE: *Stand Up Virgin Soldiers* (1977), *The Awakening* (1980, UK/US), *Scrubbers* (1982), *Yentl* (1983, UK/US), *Morons from Outer Space* (1985), *As You Like It* (1992), *Dreaming of Joseph Lees* (1999), *House!* (2000), *Alone, Harry Potter and the Chamber of Secrets* (UK/US), *Plots with a View* (UK/US) (2002).

Marion, Joan (*b* Launceston, Tasmania, 1908 – *d* Sheringham, 2001). Actress. RN: Nicholls. RADA-trained Australian actress on stage from 1927, in London from 1929, and on Broadway from 1935. She made about 15 films in 30s Britain, a quite forceful leading lady in such roles as a wife embittered by newspaper methods and husband's philandering in *Sensation* (1936) and the wife clearing her husband of murder in *Black Limelight* (1938). Post-war, she made only two further films and appeared as herself in a DOCUMENTARY, *I Used to Be in Pictures* (2000).

OTHER BRITISH FILMS INCLUDE: *Her Night Out* (1932), *Double Wedding* (1933), *For Valour* (1937), *Ten Days in Paris* (1939), *Trio* (1950), *Tons of Trouble* (1956).

Marion-Crawford, Howard (*b* London, 1914 – *d* London, 1969). Actor. Brisk, stocky, professional-looking character player of over 50 films, from 1935, and a popular TV 'Doctor Watson' in *The Adventures of Sherlock Holmes* (1955). Among his film oeuvre are many soldiers (*Foxhole in Cairo*, 1960), policemen (*Gideon's Day*, 1958) and doctors, including five stabs at Dr Petrie in a series of 'Fu Manchu' films in the later 60s. Made his first real film impression as Tommy in *The Hasty Heart* (1949) and was in steady demand for the rest of his life, in roles serious or comic. Married (1) RANK starlet **Junia Crawford** (*b* Northampton), who appeared in a few British films, and (2) stage actress Mary WIMBUSH.

OTHER BRITISH FILMS INCLUDE: *Brown on Resolution* (1935), *Freedom Radio* (1940), *The Rake's Progress* (1945), *Man on the Run* (1949), *Where's Charley?* (1952), *The Rainbow Jacket* (1954), *Reach for the Sky* (1956), *Virgin Island* (1958), *Carry On Regardless* (1961), *Lawrence of Arabia* (1962), *The Face of Fu Manchu* (1965), *The Brides of Fu Manchu* (1966), *The Vengeance of Fu Manchu* (1967), *The Blood of Fu Manchu, The Charge of the Light Brigade, The Castle of Fu Manchu* (UK/Ger/Sp/It) (1968).

Maritza, Sari (*b* Tientsin, China, 1910 – *d* Virgin Islands, 1987). Actress. RN: Patricia Nathan. Anglo-Austrian leading lady who took her mother's name for screen, enjoyed brief stardom during the 30s, and made a few films in Britain before heading for Hollywood. Said to have played in Hungarian films and been discovered by director Sinclair HILL for *Greek Street* (1930).

OTHER BRITISH FILMS: *Bed and Breakfast* (1930), *No Lady, Two Way Street* (1931), *The Water Gipsies, Monte Carlo Madness* (UK/Ger) (1932).

marketing Marketing is concerned with facilitating the exchange of goods and services through the creation, distribution, promotion and pricing of products (in this case, films and the cinemagoing experience) and the targeting of consumer groups. Generally, the British cinema industry has been unfavourably compared to Hollywood in the attention it has given to the key elements of the 'marketing mix'.

Ever since the Cinematograph Films Act of 1927, protectionist policies towards British cinema have been blamed for creating a climate of complacency among film producers, who have typically been content to trust their own judgement about the appeal of their product rather than engage in detailed market research. For example, British producers have mostly resisted (on financial and artistic grounds) the Hollywood practice of modifying films on the basis of test screenings. Although, in the 40s and 50s in particular, they demonstrated a successful awareness of domestic AUDIENCE TASTES, they have also been reluctant to embrace the implications of market segmentation, preferring to chase the dwindling 'family audience' rather than to tailor their products to niche markets defined by gender, age, education or race. Thus there is no British variant of the American 'blaxploitation' cycle of the 70s (although the specialist 'sexploitation' market was addressed in this period).

Before the 70s, a relatively efficient system of DISTRIBUTION, well understood by consumers and protected by 'quota' regulations, ensured a regular supply of British products. The vertical integration of Britain's 'majors', RANK and ABPC guaranteed screen space for their films, and most independent films found willing distributors and exhibitors. With the end of the STUDIO SYSTEM, the closure of single screen cinemas and the growth of the multiplex, however, British films have found theatrical EXHIBITION increasingly more difficult to achieve in the face of more aggressive American marketing.

Promotional methods developed in the silent era remained largely unchanged into the 80s. Production companies advertised their films and attempted to standardise their product images through the use of centrally issued posters and press ads, although independent exhibitors were under no obligation to use these advertisements. While production companies developed symbiotic 'product placement' and book publication arrangements with other businesses, and attempted to exert some centralised control over their product image through the issuing of 'campaign books', they relied primarily on the 'showmanship' of exhibitors and point-of-sale promotions. These ranged from hand-painted advertising hoardings and lobby displays, to elaborate 'street stunts', sometimes involving hired actors and vehicles. With the notable exceptions of EALING and HAMMER, few British producers succeeded in establishing a distinctive brand image, although the 'DOCTOR', 'CARRY ON' and 'JAMES BOND' SERIES were strong branded products, and Odeon and ABC were household names in film exhibition.

Before the 90s, TELEVISION and RADIO advertising played a very much smaller role in the promotion of films in Britain than in the US. The publicity departments of British studios and production companies concentrated on promoting stars rather than films, and on servicing the pictorial requirements of the newspaper and magazine press, supplying a flood of 'glamour' images which were the staple diet of the weekly and monthly fan publications. *Trainspotting* (1996) is often credited as one of the first British films to be promoted effectively as a branded good with multi-media tie-ins and fully-developed promotional campaign. This has supplied a template for subsequent promotions.

With the exception of limited concessionary arrangements, complimentary preview screenings and special offers during times of severe economic recession, British cinemas have steadily minimised pricing as a marketing tool. The differentiated seat pricing of the single-screen cinemas has been replaced by the unitary pricing-systems of the multiplexes. Ticket prices have never related to production costs, and the cost of admission to a low-budget British movie remains the same as that for a multi-million dollar Hollywood blockbuster. Marketing by price is more likely to be found in the distribution of films through video and DVD rental. Steve Chibnall.

Markham, David (*b* Wick, 1913 – *d* Coleman's Hatch, 1983). Actor. RN: Peter Harrison. RADA-trained stage actor, with several Old Vic seasons, and a supporting actor in British (and some international) films, mainly in the 70s, including such diverse enterprises as *Two Gentlemen Sharing* (1969), as dim impoverished gentry, *Blood from the Mummy's Tomb* and Ken LOACH's *Family Life* (1971), and *Tess* (1979), as Angel Clare's vicar father. Father of Kika MARKHAM and of Petra **Markham** (*b* Prestbury, Cheshire, 1944) who appeared in several films, including *Get Carter* (1971) as the murdered man's daughter.

OTHER BRITISH FILMS INCLUDE: *The Right Person* (1955), *A Place for Gold* (1960), *Tales from the Crypt* (1972), *Gandhi* (1982, UK/Ind).

Markham, Kika (*b* Prestbury, Cheshire, 1940). Actress. Like her father, David MARKHAM, she has worked extensively in France (e.g. Truffaut's *Anne and Muriel*, 1971), on TV (*A Very British Coup*, 1988) and on stage, where she starred with husband Corin REDGRAVE in the Coward revival, *Song at Twilight*, in 1999. Her screen career has been desultory, picking up recently with an eloquent performance of aching frustration and mangled affections in *Wonderland* (1999), following this with *Esther Khan* (UK/Fr) and *Killing Me Softly* (2002).

OTHER BRITISH FILMS: *Bunny Lake Is Missing* (1965), *Futtocks End* (1969), *Outland* (1981), *The Innocent* (1984).

Marks, Alfred (*b* London, 1921 – *d* Hillingdon, 1996). Actor. RN: Ruchel Kutchinsky. Primarily known as a stage actor, Marks appeared in about a dozen films, usually in comic roles. Starred in Vernon SEWELL's neat 'B' FILM, *Johnny, You're Wanted* (1955), as a joke novelties salesman, and as an ENSA officer caught up with WW2 spies in *Desert Mice* (1959), but mostly in supporting roles, like the General who offers his 'protection' to *Our Miss Fred* (1972). A former engineer and auctioneer, he first appeared on the London stage in 1951 and his TV included *Albert and Victoria* (1970–71) as a benign Victorian patriarch. Married to Paddie O'Neil, who appeared in three films, including *The Early Bird* (1965) as Edward CHAPMAN's plump, amorous housekeeper.

OTHER BRITISH FILMS INCLUDE: *There Was a Crooked Man* (1960), *The Frightened City* (1961), *Scream and Scream Again* (1969), *Hide and Seek* (1972), *Valentino* (1977), *Antonia and Jane* (1990).

Marks, George Harrison *see* **Harrison Marks, George**

Marks, Leo (*b* London, 1920 – *d* London, 2001). Writer. Now most famous as author of the screenplay for *Peeping Tom* (1960), much vilified at the time, now allowed masterpiece status, Marks was awarded his MBE (1946) for his WW2 work as cryptographer genius for the Special Operations Executive. Code-breaking and writing were his two ambitions, and he wrote plays, including *The Girl Who Couldn't Quite* (1947, dimly filmed in 1950), the stories on which *The Webster Boy* (1962) and *Sebastian* (1967) were based, and the poem, 'The Life that I Have', which he gave to agent Violette Szabo and which is used in the BIOPIC, *Carve Her Name With Pride* (1958, + tech adviser). The hero of the clever 'B' film, *Cloudburst* (1951, +co-sc), based on his play, is a vengeful code-breaker. His is a fascinating life – his father was a partner in the bookshop made famous by Helene Hanff's *84 Charing Cross Road* (1976, filmed 1986) – and he had success in several fields, but the strange, disturbing *Peeping Tom* has overshadowed the rest. Married (1966–2000) to Elena Gaussen.

OTHER BRITISH FILMS: (co-sc) *Guns at Batasi* (1964), *Twisted Nerve* (1968), *Soft Beds, Hard Battles* (1973).

Marks, Louis (*b* London, 1928). Producer. Notable TV producer (*Memento Mori*, 1992; *Middlemarch*, 1994, BAAn) who has made a few films, including *Poison Candy* (1988), *The Trial* (1992) and *Loving* (1995). Co-wrote the screenplay for *The Man Who Finally Died* (1962).

Marlé, Arnold (*b* Prague, 1887 – *d* London, 1970). Actor. Pre-war, he was busy in UFA films and had a long stage career. In Britain from the early 40s, he played about 20 character roles, across the usual international range: he is Dutch in *One of Our Aircraft Is Missing* (1942), German in *Mr Emmanuel* (1944), Italian in *The Glass Cage* (1955) and a Tibetan Lama in *The Abominable Snowman* (1957). Usually benign, like the Professor father of the amnesiac girl in *Portrait from Life* (1948), but could be shifty like the fence in *The Floating Dutchman* (1953).

OTHER BRITISH FILMS INCLUDE: *Men of Two Worlds* (1946), *White Cradle Inn* (1947), *The Glass Mountain* (1948), *The Little Red Monkey* (1954), *Zarak* (1956), *Operation Amsterdam* (1958), *The Snake Woman* (1961).

Marmont, Patricia (*b* Hollywood, 1921). Actress, agent. After playing minor roles in a few films, first in *Loyal Heart* (1946) in which her father, Percy MARMONT, had the lead, and some TV work (e.g. in the 'ROBIN HOOD' series), she retired from acting and became a successful agent. Married (1) Nigel GREEN and (2) Moray WATSON.

OTHER BRITISH FILMS INCLUDE: *Front Page Story* (1953), *The Crowded Day* (1954), *Fortune Is a Woman*, *No Time for Tears* (1957), *Suddenly, Last Summer* (1959).

Marmont, Percy (*b* London, 1883 – *d* Northwood, 1977). Actor. The somewhat gaunt but undeniably distinguished-looking Marmont, on stage from 1900, was a popular leading man in Hollywood silent films, returning to England in the late 20s. By the 30s he was into pipe-smoking middle age in such films as HITCHCOCK's *Rich and Strange* (1932), as the Commander who nearly turns the heroine's head, or Nova PILBEAM's Chief Constable father in *Young and Innocent* (1937). From the mid 30s, he was busy on the London stage, in major character roles in such plays as *The Philadelphia Story* (1949), as well as playing occasional film roles, including Linden TRAVERS's father in the notorious *No Orchids for Miss Blandish* (1948), his ransom spurned in favour of Slim Grissom's rough embraces. His daughter is Patricia MARMONT.

OTHER BRITISH FILMS INCLUDE: *The Warning* (1928), *The Silver King* (1929), *The Loves of Ariane* (UK/Ger), *The Written Law* (1931), *The Blind Spot* (1932), *Vanity* (1935), *Secret Agent* (1936), *Action for Slander* (1937), *Conquest of the Air* (1940), *Penn of Pennsylvania* (1941), *Loyal Heart* (1946), *Dark Secret* (1949), *The Gambler and the Lady* (1952), *The Million Pound Note* (1953), *Footsteps in the Fog* (1955), *Hostile Witness* (1968).

Marquand, Richard (*b* Cardiff, 1938 – *d* London, 1987). Director. Just as his US career seemed to be gathering momentum (*Return of the Jedi*, 1983; *Jagged Edge*, 1985), Cambridge-educated Marquand died of a heart attack. In Britain, he made a DOCUMENTARY about *Martin Luther King*

(1977) and a tightly controlled WW2 thriller, *Eye of the Needle* (1981), suggesting a real talent for creating suspense. Also directed more than 50 films for TV in Britain and the US.

OTHER BRITISH FILMS: *Men, Men, Men* (1973, short), *The Legacy* (1978).

Marriott, Moore (*b* West Drayton, 1885 – *d* London, 1949). Actor. Although he appeared in many British films, usually in straight dramatic roles (like that of the father doing for himself in *Millions Like Us*, 1943, or the murdered postman in *Green for Danger*, 1946), Marriott is now mainly remembered as a comic stooge for Will HAY and Arthur ASKEY. Usually cast as a wizened old man by the name of Jerry Harbottle (although he was only in his early fifties when he first played this part in *Windbag the Sailor*, 1936), his performances were an inspired mix of derangement and surreal humour. Especially memorable is his first appearance in the railway comedy, *Oh, Mr Porter!* (1937) when he informs a bemused Will Hay that 'the next train has left'. Often paired with fellow stooge Graham MOFFATT.

OTHER BRITISH FILMS INCLUDE: *The Grip of Iron* (1920), *Head of the Family* (1922), *The Monkey's Paw* (1923), *The Mating of Marcus* (1924), *Afraid of Love* (1925), *Every Mother's Son* (1926), *Sweeney Todd* (1928), *The Kissing Cup's Race* (1930), *Dance Pretty Lady* (1932), *Turn of the Tide* (1935), *As You Like It* (1936), *Victoria the Great, Oh, Mr Porter!* (1937), *Owd Bob, Old Bones of the River, Convict 99* (1938), *The Frozen Limits, Cheer Boys Cheer, Ask a Policeman* (1939), *Gasbags, Charley's Big-Hearted Aunt* (1940), *I Thank You, Hi, Gang!* (1941), *Back Room Boy* (1942), *Time Flies, Don't Take It to Heart* (1944), *A Place of One's Own* (1945), *The History of Mr Polly* (1948). Peter Hutchings.

Mars, Marjorie (*b* London, 1903 – *d* ?). Actress. RN: Brown. The abiding film image of Mars is as Mary Norton, plucking her eyebrows before a mirror, as she colludes with Celia JOHNSON over a 'domestic lie' in *Brief Encounter* (1945). Essentially a theatre actress, she was on the London stage from 1920, made only eight films and appeared on TV in *The Amazing Dr Clitterhouse* (1947).

OTHER BRITISH FILMS INCLUDE: *Yellow Stockings* (1928), *The Crouching Beast* (1935), *Spy of Napoleon* (1936), *Take My Life* (1947).

Marsden, Betty (*b* Liverpool, 1919 – *d* London, 1998). Actress. Exuberant actress, right at home as Terry SCOTT's wife in *Carry On Camping* (1969), Marsden was on stage from age 11, trained with Italia Conti and made her London debut in 1935, touring with ENSA during WW2. In films sporadically since 1937's *The Rat* (billed Beatrice Marsden), with fewer than 20 appearances over 50 years. Enjoyable, though, in such roles as Harry H. CORBETT's fractious wife in the excellent 'B' film, *The Big Day* (1960) or, on TV, the well-meaning bore in *Winter Sunlight* (1984).

OTHER BRITISH FILMS INCLUDE: *The Mill on the Floss* (1937), *Ships with Wings* (1941), *My Brother Jonathan* (1948), *The Young Lovers* (1954), *Carry On Regardless* (1961), *The Leather Boys* (1963), *Eyewitness* (1970), *Britannia Hospital* (1982), *The Dresser* (1983), *Little Dorrit* (1987).

Marsh, Carol (*b* Lancashire, 1929). Actress. RN: Norma Simpson. Sadly for her, waif-like Marsh was simply out of her class in *Brighton Rock* (1947), the film that should have made her a star: her locutions were too middle-class to convince as the gangster's waitress-girlfriend; and the other actors made her seem amateurish. The RANK 'COMPANY OF YOUTH' probably didn't help her much and she had roles in such stinkers as *The Romantic Age* (1949) and *Helter Skelter* (1949); had her best role as Jill ESMOND's sick daughter in *Private Information* (1952).

OTHER BRITISH FILMS INCLUDE: *Alice in Wonderland* (1949, UK/Fr/US), *Scrooge* (1951), *Dracula* (1958), *Man Accused* (1959).

Marsh, Garry (*b* St Margaret's, Surrey, 1902 – *d* London, 1981). Actor. RN: Leslie March Geraghty. How indefatigable some of these CHARACTER PLAYERS are! Marsh not only made well over 100 films from the early 30s to the late 60s, but also conducted a vigorous stage career from 1917 (London 1920) and was on TV from 1938 at least, in *The Ringer*. On-screen his bald, tall, chunky, moustachioed appearance often served caddish purposes, as in his comic bounder-foils to George FORMBY, and after WW2 service with the RAF (1939–44) he made a clumsy pass at Jean KENT's *Good-Time Girl* (1947), played the harassed Mr Brown in *Just William's Luck* (1947), several police inspectors (as in *The Voice of Merrill*, 1952) and military officers. Sometimes said to have been born at sea.

OTHER BRITISH FILMS INCLUDE: *Uneasy Virtue, Stamboul* (UK/US) (1931), *Number Seventeen* (1932), *Ask Beccles* (1933), *Gay Love* (1934), *Scrooge, Charing Cross Road* (1935), *The Vicar of Bray* (1937), *This Man Is News, Bank Holiday, Convict 99* (1938), *Trouble Brewing, This Man in Paris* (1939), *Return to Yesterday, Let George Do It!* (1940), *The Rake's Progress, Pink String and Sealing Wax, Dead of Night* (1945), *I See a Dark Stranger, The Shop at Sly Corner* (1946), *Frieda* (1947), *My Brother's Keeper* (1948), *The Lost Hours* (1952), *Aunt Clara* (1954), *Man of the Moment* (1955), *Who Done It?* (1956), *Where the Bullets Fly* (1966).

Marsh, Jean (*b* Stoke Newington, 1934). Actress. Sharp-featured former dancer and model, now a respected supporting actress of film and TV, often cast as rather severe women, like the secretary in *Frenzy* (1972). Major film work eluded her, yielding only a few memorable roles, such as murderous Miss Ballard in *Unearthly Stranger* (1963), and German spy Joanna Grey in *The Eagle Has Landed* (1976). She and Eileen ATKINS devised the highly successful costume serial *Upstairs, Downstairs* (1971–75), in which she played the no-nonsense parlourmaid Rose. They also co-wrote the period drama *The House of Eliott* (1991–94). Formerly married to Jon PERTWEE.

OTHER BRITISH FILMS INCLUDE: *The Roman Spring of Mrs Stone* (1961), *The Limbo Line* (1968), *Jane Eyre* (1970), *Adam Bede* (1991), *Monarch* (2000). Melinda Hildebrandt.

Marsh, Mae see **Americans in British silent films**

Marsh, Reginald (*b* London, 1926 – *d* Ryde, Isle of Wight, 2001). Supporting actor of the 60s and 70s, who projected an air of somewhat rumpled, intelligent decency, as in the two 'B' MOVIES he made for Ernest MORRIS, *Shadow of Past* (1963), as the heroine's kindly uncle, and *The Sicilians* (1964), as a police inspector investigating a kidnapping. He had a continuing role as 'Sir' in *The Good Life* (1975–78) and did a stint in *Coronation Street*; much theatre experience, including Stratford (1950–51) Engaged in community work for MENCAP on the Isle of Wight.

OTHER BRITISH FILMS INCLUDE: *The Ugly Duckling* (1959), *Two-Letter Alibi* (1961), *Jigsaw* (1962), *The Material Witness* (1965), *Berserk!* (1967), *Young Winston* (1972), *Sky Pirates* (1976).

Marsh, Terence (*b* London, 1931). Production designer. Winner of two shared Oscars, for *Oliver!* (1968) and *Dr Zhivago* (1965, UK/US), and nominated for two further for *Scrooge* (1970, also BAAn) and *Mary Queen of Scots* (1971), Marsh worked steadily in British films from 1955 (as draughtsman) until 1977 when he went to the US, receiving a further BAAn for *The Hunt for Red October* (1990). Of his solo British designs, he does well by such modern-set films as *Juggernaut* (1974) and the huge war film, *A Bridge Too Far* (1977, BAAn/des), but his 1975

Great Expectations prettifies Dickens.

OTHER BRITISH FILMS INCLUDE: (draughtsman) *As Long As They're Happy* (1955), *The League of Gentlemen* (1960); (co-/ass art d) *Lawrence of Arabia* (1962), *Of Human Bondage* (1964); (art d) *A Man for All Seasons* (1966), *The Looking Glass War* (1969); (des) *Perfect Friday* (1970), *Follow Me!* (1971), *A Touch of Class* (1972), *The Mackintosh Man* (1973), *Royal Flash* (1975).

Marsh-Edwards, Nadine (*b* Birmingham, 1963). Producer, editor. Came to the fore in the later 80s as producer on several of the SANKOFA Film and Video Collective for which black directors including Maureen BLACKWOOD and Isaac JULIEN made such films as *The Passion of Remembrance* (1986, p man, e) and *Young Soul Rebels* (1991). Also produced the affectionate *Bhaji on the Beach* (1993).

OTHER BRITISH FILMS INCLUDE: (p, unless noted) *Majdhar* (1984, ass e), *Looking for Langston* (1989, short), *A Family Called Abrew* (1992, doc), *Hijack Stories* (2000, UK/Fr/Ger/Zanz).

Marshall, Alan (*b* London, 1938). Producer. In the industry since the mid 50s, Marshall produced several SHORT FILMS in the early 70s before joining forces with Alan PARKER for whom he produced *Bugsy Malone* (1976) and such US films as *Fame* (1980) and *Shoot the Moon* (1982), as well as co-producing *Midnight Express* (1978). Most of his work since *Another Country* (1984) has been US-based.

OTHER BRITISH FILMS: *Our Cissy, No Hard Feelings, Footsteps* (1974, shorts), *Pink Floyd The Wall* (1982).

Marshall, Herbert (*b* London, 1890 – *d* Los Angeles, 1966). Actor. The last word in gentlemanly urbanity, with a mellifluous voice that helped make him a popular romantic leading man, a success which the loss of a leg in WW1 did nothing to impede. His main career is Hollywood-based, where sometimes the prevailing image was made nicely ambiguous as wittier and/or darker intentions intervened (see, e.g. *Trouble in Paradise*, 1932, for wit, or *The Unseen*, 1945, for velvet-smooth malevolence). In Britain, he made seven films before settling permanently in Hollywood, notably HITCHCOCK's *Murder!* (1930) and two for Victor SAVILLE, the romance, *The Faithful Heart* (1933) and the WW1 drama, *I Was a Spy*, 1933). His career continued unabated until his death and he filmed only twice more in Britain: in *Wicked As They Come* and *The Weapon* (1956). As well, he found time for a great deal of theatre and to marry five times, twice to actresses: (2) Edna BEST (1928–40) and (3) 'Boots' Mallory (1947–58). His daughter Sarah Marshall acted in several US films.

OTHER BRITISH FILMS: *Mumsie* (1927), *Dawn* (1928), *Michael and Mary, The Calendar* (1931).

Marshall, Herbert P.J. (*b* London, 1906 – *d* Cowfold, W. Sussex, 1991). Documentarist. Famous for his work in dubbing and promoting Russian films in Britain, Marshall studied film in Moscow and, on invitation from Pudovkin in 1930, worked and studied in Russian film studios. In Britain, he edited DOCUMENTARIES for John GRIERSON at the EMPIRE MARKETING BOARD from 1929; he founded the Unity Theatre in 1935 and produced for the Old Vic (1942–45); he co-wrote EALING's *The Proud Valley* (1940) and post-war he directed documentaries and the fiction feature, *Tinker* (1949, +sc, e), produced by his wife Fredda BRILLIANT. From 1952, he was director of Citizen Films, for whom he made a biography of Gandhi. An interesting, persistently left-wing figure hovering about the periphery of the British film industry for a couple of decades.

OTHER BRITISH FILMS INCLUDE: *Athletes in Training* (1948, doc, d, wrote comm), *Mr Pastry Does the Laundry*, *What's Cooking?* (1951, (d, co-p, co-sc).

Marshall, Roger (*b* Leicester, 1934). Screenwriter. Cambridge-educated Marshall entered the industry in the later 50s, and has written about a dozen British films and a great deal of TV, including episodes for such popular programmes as *The Avengers* as well as single dramas. In the early 60s, he wrote screenplays for the Edgar WALLACE second features made at MERTON PARK, and his story provided the basis for the BOULTINGS' *Twisted Nerve* (1968).
OTHER BRITISH FILMS INCLUDE: *Solo for Sparrow* (1962), *The Set-Up*, *Ricochet*, *Five to One* (1963), *Invasion*, *Theatre of Death* (co-sc) (1966), *What Became of Jack and Jill?* (1972), *And Now the Screaming Starts!* (1973).

Marshall, Zena (*b* Nairobi, 1926). Actress. RADA-trained and 'finished' at the RANK CHARM SCHOOL, Marshall was a quite chirpy, pretty brunette presence in such pieces as *Sleeping Car to Trieste* (1948), as a girl with too many hats, and, educated in France, was often in continental roles, like the Italian countess in her penultimate film, *Those Magnificent Men . . .* (1965). With supporting roles in main features or leads in 'B' MOVIES, such as *Deadly Nightshade* (1953), and without making major impact, she hung on for over 30 films, perhaps best remembered as Miss Taro in *Dr No* (1962), as well as appearing on stage and on TV from 1950. Married to Ivan FOXWELL (1992 to 2002, his death).
OTHER BRITISH FILMS INCLUDE: *Caesar and Cleopatra* (1945), *Good-Time Girl* (1947), *Miranda* (1948), *Morning Departure* (1950), *Hell Is Sold Out* (1951), *Love's a Luxury* (1952), *The Embezzler* (1954), *Let's Be Happy* (1956), *The Switch* (1963), *The Verdict* (1964).

Martelli, Angela (*b* London, 1909 – *d* Bridport, 1995). Continuity. Highly regarded CONTINUITY 'girl' whose work spanned 40 years. *A Window in London* (1939) *may* have been her first credit; record of the work of such key personnel was rarely kept carefully.
OTHER BRITISH FILMS INCLUDE: *Fame Is the Spur* (1947), *Stage Fright* (1950), *The Bridge on the River Kwai* (1957), *The Inn of the Sixth Happiness* (1958), *Sons and Lovers* (1960), *The Wrong Arm of the Law* (1962), *Of Human Bondage* (1964), *You Only Live Twice* (1967), *The Railway Children* (1971), *Frenzy* (1972), *That Lucky Touch* (1975).

Martin, Edie (*b* London, 1880 – *d* London, 1964). Actress. In 1990, Jean ANDERSON recalled that she, playing a county lady in *Lease of Life* (1954), was told one day, 'We've decided you're not going to have a dog; we're giving you Edie Martin instead'. Tiny birdlike Martin, in film after film, provided moments of pure gold, without ever having anything to do with the narrative. Thus, she is the spinster aunt who asks for tea in her room so as not to eat with 'Russians' in *The Demi-Paradise* (1943), the resident of the dreadful Brighton hotel who wonders meekly if the cross new arrivals are 'Americans' in *Genevieve* (1953), or one of Mrs Wilberforce's afternoon tea guests in *The Ladykillers* (1955). Made stage debut in 1886 as Glow-worm in *Alice in Wonderland*, and was famously Mrs Snapper in the original *Cavalcade* (1931).
OTHER BRITISH FILMS INCLUDE: *Servants All* (1936), *Under the Red Robe* (1937), *Old Mother Riley in Business* (1940), *Don't Take It to Heart* (1944), *A Place of One's Own* (1945), *Great Expectations* (1946), *Oliver Twist* (1948), *The Lavender Hill Mob*, *The Man in the White Suit* (1951), *Time Gentlemen Please!* (1952), *The End of the Road* (1954), *The Naked Truth* (1957), *Too Many Crooks* (1959), *Kidnapped* (1960).

Martin, Millicent (*b* Romford, 1934). Actress, singer. Versatile actress and singer, pert and attractive, at home as chirpy cockneys, but also with a duchess's looks and demeanour. Starred in West End musicals and revues and became nationally famous singing and performing in sketches on TV's *That Was the Week That Was* (1962–63). Underused in films, but seen to advantage in *Nothing But the Best* (1964), and in the film of the stage musical, *Stop the World I Want to Get Off* (1966) in which she played four roles. Also had her own TV shows, and performed in cabaret on both sides of the Atlantic.
OTHER BRITISH FILMS INCLUDE: *Libel* (1959), *Invasion Quartet*, *The Horsemasters* (1961), *Those Magnificent Men . . .* (1965), *Alfie* (1966). Roger Philip Mellor.

Martin-Harvey, Michael (*b* London, 1897 – *d* Great Bircham, 1975). Actor. Son of Sir John MARTIN-HARVEY, he appeared in a dozen character roles spread over two decades and just one starring role in *The Case of Charles Peace* (1949), as the eponymous Victorian criminal.
OTHER BRITISH FILMS INCLUDE: *Dark Journey* (1937), *The Drum* (1938), *Let the People Sing* (1942), *Bedelia* (1946), *The Monkey's Paw* (1948), *The Long Memory* (1952), *Happy Ever After* (1954).

Martin-Harvey, Sir John (*b* Wyvenhoe, Essex, 1863 – *d* London, 1944). Actor. A major theatrical actor-manager of his day, his greatest role was as Sidney Carton in *The Only Way* (an ADAPTATION of *A Tale of Two Cities*), which he first played on stage in 1899 and brought to the screen in 1926 in a remarkably restrained performance. Martin-Harvey also appeared on screen in *The Broken Melody* (1916), *The Breed of the Treshams* (1920, stage 1903), *The Burgomaster of Stilemonde* (1928, stage 1918), and *The Lyons Mail* (1931). AS.

Martinek, H. Oceano and **Ivy** Actors. A brother and sister team who often acted together, in fast-moving adventures, with Oceano directing. Both became stars with BRITISH AND COLONIAL, with Ivy featured in *The Exploits of Three-Fingered Kate* SERIES (1909–12); they were later together in *Big Ben* SHORTS, sometimes written by Oceano. Ivy changed her name to Ivy Montford in 1913 and retired in 1917, her brother a year earlier. Claims of being born in Spain are unsubstantiated, and Oceano is, in fact, a Portuguese name.
BRITISH FILMS INCLUDE: (Ivy as star, Oceano director) *The Butler's Revenge* (1910), *The Puritan Maid* (1911), *The Nest on the Black Cliff** (1913), *The Stolen Masterpiece** (1914), *The Clue of the Cigar Band** (1915), *The Octopus Gang* (1916). *= Oceano also acted. AS.

Martinelli, Elsa (*b* Rome, 1932). Actress. Former model and star of international films who brought an unaccustomed whiff of eroticism into British films as the object of Trevor HOWARD's passion in *Manuela* (1957). Only two further British films – *The VIPs* (1963) as a film star, and the dim thriller *Maroc 7* (1966) – in a long, not very distinguished career, of which *Hatari* (1961, US) may be the highlight.

Martins, Orlando (*b* Lagos, 1899 – *d* Lagos, 1985). Actor. On London stage from 1933, first film, *Sanders of the River* (1935); Martins got a generous share of the not-too-abundant roles for black actors in British films in the next two decades. He is the patient whose only word is 'Blossom' in the Burma military-hospital setting for *The Hasty Heart* (1949), dangerous as the witch-doctor in *Men of Two Worlds* (1946), and worried about 'the evil among my own people' as the Headman in *Simba* (1955).

OTHER BRITISH FILMS INCLUDE: *The Man from Morocco* (1945), *The End of the River*, *Good-Time Girl* (1947), *Where No Vultures Fly* (1951), *The Heart of the Matter* (1953), *West of Zanzibar* (1954), *Tarzan and the Lost Safari* (1956), *The Naked Earth* (1957), *Sapphire* (1959), *Call Me Bwana*, *Sammy Going South* (1963), *Mister Moses* (1965).

Marylebone Studio A two-stage studio, operational as a feature-producing site from the late 30s until the mid 50s, after which it was used to produce commercials, training films and TV. Post-WW2, it was owned by Henry Halsted and its output was primarily second features such as *Death in High Heels* and *Who Killed Van Loon?* (1947), including several produced there by EXCLUSIVE FILMS (e.g. *Dick Barton – Special Agent*, 1948), the latter made by contract director Alfred GOULDING.

Maschwitz, Eric (aka Holt Marvell) (*b* Birmingham, 1901 – *d* Berkshire, 1969). Screenwriter, songwriter. Repton- and Cambridge-educated, Maschwitz entered the film industry in 1933 and (co-)authored ten 30s films, including *Goodnight Vienna* (1932), from the radio play he wrote as Marvell, and sharing an AAn for the acclaimed *Goodbye, Mr Chips* (1939). After WW2 service with the Intelligence Corps (1940–45), he co-wrote *Theirs Is the Glory* (1946) and several other films, as well as continuing to write for the stage (e.g. *Love from Judy*, 1952) and a number of novels, two in collaboration with Val Gielgud. The composer of, *inter alia*, 'A Nightingale Sang in Berkeley Square', he also wrote for TV, including the serial *Little Red Monkey*, filmed in 1954, and became Head of BBC Light Entertainment in 1958. Awarded OBE, 1936. Once married to Hermione GINGOLD.

OTHER BRITISH FILMS INCLUDE: *His Lordship* (1932, co-comp, lyrics), *Death at Broadcasting House* (1934, co-author of novel), *Royal Cavalcade* (sc), *Invitation to the Waltz* (author of radio play) (1935), *King Solomon's Mines* (lyrics), *Café Colette* (co-sc) (1937), *Gaiety George* (lyrics), *Carnival* (co-sc) (1946).

Maskell, Virginia (*b* London, 1936 – *d* Stoke Mandeville, 1968). Actress. Among the somewhat anodyne ranks of 50s British would-be leading ladies, Maskell, darkly attractive, had a genuinely provocative quality, a sensuousness and emotional capacity that were refreshing. She made only nine films before committing suicide, but, as three very different kinds of wives, in *Virgin Island* (1958), *Only Two Can Play* (1961) and *Interlude* (1968), three tonally diverse films, she made a strikingly intelligent impression. Received BAAn for *Interlude* (supp a) and for *The Wild and the Willing* (1962, British a).

OTHER BRITISH FILMS: *Happy is the Bride* (1957), *The Man Upstairs* (1958), *Jet Storm* (1959), *Doctor in Love*, *Suspect* (1960).

Mason, A(rthur) E(dward) W(oodley) (*b* London, 1865 – *d* London, 1948). Author. Oxford-educated former actor who later combined politics (Liberal MP for Coventry, 1906–10) with the writing of historical adventures, romances and mystery thrillers. Nearly 30 films have been adapted from his novels, the most famous including *The Four Feathers* (1902), filmed 1915, 1929, 2001 (US) and 1921, 1939, 1955 (as *Storm over the Nile*), 1978 (UK) and *At the Villa Rose* (1916), filmed three times in Britain (1920, 1930, 1939) as was its sequel *The House of the Arrow* (1924), in 1930, 1940, 1953, both featuring his ingenious detective, Inspector Hanaud. In 1937 and 1938, KORDA made *Fire Over England* and *The Drum*, popular action films based on Mason's work.

OTHER BRITISH FILMS: (adapted from novels, unless noted) *Princess Clementina* (1911, + sc), *A Romance of Wastdale*, *The Broken Road* (co-sc), *Man and His Kingdom*, *Running Water*, *The Truants* (1922), *Slaves of Destiny* (1924), *Her Imaginary Lover* (1933, play).

Mason, Elliott (*b* Glasgow, 1896 – *d* Lingfield, 1949). Actress. Imposing character player, sometimes kindly, like restaurant-owning Frau Grumlich in *21 Days* (1937), sometimes formidable, like the German stationmistress in *The Big Blockade* (1942), comically so as the lady don in *Charley's (Big-Hearted) Aunt* (1940).

OTHER BRITISH FILMS INCLUDE: *The Ghost Goes West* (1935), *Black Limelight* (1938), *Turned Out Nice Again* (1941), *The Gentle Sex* (1943), *On Approval* (1944), *The Captive Heart* (1946).

Mason, Haddon (*b* London, 1899 – *d* London, 1966). Actor, agent. With stage background, Mason became a popular star of British silent films from the mid 20s (e.g. as the hero of *The Woman in White*, 1929), appeared in about a dozen talkies, then became an agent with Film Rights Ltd, to whose board he was elected in 1939.

OTHER BRITISH FILMS INCLUDE: *Palaver*, *Every Mother's Son* (1926), *Dawn* (1928), *French Leave* (1930), *Birds of a Feather* (1931), *The Village Squire* (1935), *Under the Red Robe* (1937).

Mason, Hal (*b* Philadelphia, 1911 – *d* Los Angeles, California, 1986). Manager, production supervisor. RN: Tinkler. Michael BALCON wrote of Mason in 1969: 'His name appeared on every film we made and deservedly so, as the whole organisation and physical control of the films came under his charge.' Before taking his position at EALING, Mason, from a family of circus troupers, had been an actor and boxer. Balcon's biography makes clear the faith he had in Mason as production supervisor, both at home and all over Europe and, especially, Africa, wherever Ealing films were set. When Ealing closed, Balcon and Mason decided to 'continue our production activities together' and worked on *The Long and the Short and the Tall* (1960, ex p) and *Sammy Going South* (1963, p), and Mason lent his expertise about filming in Africa to Carl Foreman's *Born Free* (1965, p co-ord).

OTHER BRITISH FILMS INCLUDE: (ass d) *The Avenging Hand* (1936), *The Stars Look Down* (1939), *Crimes at the Dark House* (1940), *Turned Out Nice Again* (1941); (p sup/p man) on virtually all Ealing films and *Scapegoat* (1958), *Shalako* (1968, assoc p).

Mason, Herbert (*b* Birmingham, 1891 – *d* London, 1960). Director, producer. Former actor (from 1908), awarded MC for WW1 service, a producer of stage revues in the 20s, Mason entered film industry in 1928 by presenting stage shows for the GAUMONT–BRITISH cinema circuit. After experience as production manager (e.g. on *Friday the Thirteenth*, 1933), he directed a dozen lightly enjoyable films, including *East Meets West* (1936), with George ARLISS, as a sultan yet, and the comedy-thriller, *Strange Boarders* (1938), with Tom WALLS. After directing the musical comedy, *Flight from Folly* (1945), the last film made at Warners' TEDDINGTON STUDIOS before it was bombed in 1944, he joined LONDON FILMS as an associate producer (e.g. on *Anna Karenina*, 1948), and was with MGM and FOX–BRITISH (1949–51). In the 50s he became producer for GROUP 3, at SOUTHALL STUDIOS, and also produced Lewis GILBERT's neat thriller, *Cast a Dark Shadow* (1955).

OTHER BRITISH FILMS INCLUDE: (d, unless noted) *Aunt Sally* (1933, p man), *His Lordship* (1936), *The Silent Battle* (1939), *Back Room Boy* (1942), *The Night Invader* (1943); (p) *Time Gentlemen Please!* (1952), *Background* (1953), *Child's Play*, *Conflict of Wings* (1954), *The Blue Peter*, *John and Julie* (1955).

Mason, Hilary (*b* Birmingham, 1917). Actress. Memorable as the strange, clairvoyant spinster in *Don't Look Now* (1973, UK/It), Mason has made occasional screen appearances, but has been more to the fore on TV, as in *All Passion Spent* (1986) and the series, *Love Hurts* (1992). Was married to actor **Roger Ostime**, who appeared in a few films, including *The Blue Max* (1966, as the Crown Prince).

OTHER BRITISH FILMS INCLUDE: *The Yellow Teddybears* (1963), *Absolution* (1978), *Return of the Soldier* (1982), *Afraid of the Dark* (1991, UK/Fr), *Haunted* (1995, UK/US).

Mason, James (*b* Huddersfield, 1909 – *d* Lausanne, 1984). Actor. One of the greatest of all British MALE STARS, tall, dark and saturnine Mason began as a stage actor after reading architecture at Cambridge, making his professional debut with a rep company in Croydon before being taken on by Tyrone GUTHRIE at the Old Vic in 1933 to play a useful range of roles. He entered films with 1935's newspaper thriller, *Late Extra*, and, once his film career gathered momentum, he rarely appeared on the stage again, with a 1954 season at Stratford, Ontario, as exception. He owed his film start to the legendary American, UK-based agent, Al PARKER, who 'discovered' him in 1935 and represented him till he, Parker, died, after which his widow, Margaret JOHNSTON, took over the agency and Mason.

In the 30s he made about a dozen mostly forgotten films, though given a chance to glower handsomely in, say, *The Mill on the Floss* (1937), or to be the heroine's sensitive protector in *Hatter's Castle* (1941). It was when he took a riding crop to wicked Margaret LOCKWOOD in *The Man in Grey* (1943) that he became Everywoman's favourite brute: he persecuted Phyllis CALVERT in *Fanny by Gaslight* (1944); drove Dulcie GRAY to drink and suicide in *They Were Sisters* (1945); smashed his walking stick over Ann TODD's piano-playing fingers in *The Seventh Veil* (1945); and, as a highwayman, fell in with *The Wicked Lady* (1945), Lockwood again. These skilful studies in sexy sadism made him a huge box-office draw, though, when he played the character role of the retired draper in *A Place of One's Own* (1945), his subtlest work to date, the fans were less interested. Post-war, he gave, in *Odd Man Out* (1947), what may be his greatest performance, as a wounded gunman (IRA, though not named) pursued relentlessly through the night-time city to his inevitable end. This is work of tragic stature.

At this point, Mason embarked on the American phase of his stardom, attracting a lot of chauvinistic British criticism for doing so, and for a while the received wisdom was with the *Picturegoer* scribe who wrote (1950): 'Certainly, James does not seem to be advancing his professional career in Hollywood'. An *auteurist* decade later, his work for Ophuls in *Caught* and *The Reckless Moment* (1949) and Minnelli in *Madame Bovary* (1949) would be accorded new respect. He did some fine work in Hollywood, including Rommel in *The Desert Fox* (1951), a troubled Brutus in *Julius Caesar* (1953) and the tragically doomed Norman Maine in *A Star Is Born* (1954), but it was as if he had turned his back on the easy stardom he had won in Britain in favour of becoming one of the world's best character actors.

He spent most of the 50s in US films and would continue to live in America, making sorties to Britain. He was a miraculously cast Humbert in KUBRICK's *Lolita* (1961), made witty sport of John MILLS's up-from-the-ranks colonel in *Tiara Tahiti* (1962), was compellingly vindictive in *The Pumpkin Eater* (1964), humanised a bullying patriarch in *Spring and Port Wine* (1969), gave significance to the clever, hothouse trash of *Mandingo* (1975, US), was a heart-breaking Cyril Sahib in the MERCHANT IVORY masterpiece, *Autobiography of a Princess* (1975), made sense of Dr Watson in *Murder by Decree* (1978, UK/Can), and grieved one to watch as

the decent, troubled landowner in his last British film, *The Shooting Party* (1984). Anyone who makes over 100 films is inevitably going to be associated with some rubbish; Mason's achievement is, partly, that one wouldn't think of attributing the blame to him.

He married (1) Pamela KELLINO (1941–64), journalist and semi-actress, and mother of one-time aspiring actress Portland Mason and producer Morgan Mason, and (2) Australian actress Clarissa Kaye (1971, till his death).

OTHER BRITISH FILMS: *Twice Branded, Troubled Waters, Secret of Stamboul, Prison Breaker, Blind Man's Bluff* (1936), *The High Command, Fire Over England, Catch As Catch Can, The Return of the Scarlet Pimpernel* (1937), *I Met a Murderer* (1939, + co-p, co-sc), *This Man is Dangerous* (1941), *Thunder Rock, Secret Mission, The Night Has Eyes, Alibi* (1942), *They Met in the Dark, The Bells Go Down, Candlelight in Algeria* (1943), *Hotel Reserve* (1944), *The Upturned Glass* (1947), *Pandora and the Flying Dutchman* (1950), *The Man Between* (1953), *Island in the Sun* (1957, UK/US), *A Touch of Larceny* (1959), *The Trials of Oscar Wilde* (1960), *Lord Jim* (1964), *The Blue Max, Georgy Girl, The Deadly Affair* (1966), *Stranger in the House, The London Nobody Knows* (narr) (1967), *Duffy, Mayerling* (UK/Fr), *The Sea Gull* (1968), *The Mackintosh Man* (1973), *The Marseille Contract* (UK/Fr), *11 Harrowhouse* (1974), *Great Expectations, Inside Out, The Water Babies* (UK/Pol) (1975), *Voyage of the Damned* (1976), *Cross of Iron* (1977, UK/Ger), *Murder by Decree* (UK/Can), *The Passage* (1978), *North Sea Hijack* (1979), *Evil Under the Sun* (1981), *Group Madness* (1983, doc).

BIBLIOG: Autobiography, *Before I Forget*, 1981; Kevin Sweeney, *James Mason: A Bio-Bibliography*, 1999; Peter William Evans, 'James Mason: the man between' in Bruce Babington (ed), *British Stars and Stardom*, 2001.

Mason, Margery (*b* London, 1920). Actress. Character player who has specialised on TV in wintry-faced neurotics (it's good to know she took up scuba-diving late in life), in such acclaimed series as *Talking to a Stranger* (1966) and *Family at War* (1970), as soured, disappointed mothers in both. On screen she can be spotted (she is easy to spot) as the Matron in *The Raging Moon* (1970) or a wedding guest in *Howards End* (1992), or at greater length as the nagging invalid mother in *Made* (1972). On stage from 1958.

OTHER BRITISH FILMS INCLUDE: *Charlie Bubbles* (1967), *Walk a Crooked Path* (1969), *Hennessy* (1975), *The Hawk* (1993), *Les Misérables* (1998, UK/Ger/US).

Mason, Richard (*b* Hale, Cheshire, 1919 – *d* Rome, 1997). Screenwriter. Novelist who had a brief career as a (co-) screenwriter in Britain in the latter 50s, sharing a BAAn/sc for *A Town Like Alice* (1956) and solo-authoring *Pacific Destiny* (1956). Several of his novels were filmed, including the East–West romances, *The Wind Cannot Read* (1958, + sc), and *The World of Suzie Wong* (1960). Most of the rest of his film career was spent on Australian projects.

OTHER BRITISH FILMS: *Robbery Under Arms* (1957, add scenes), *Passionate Summer* (1958).

Massey, Anna (*b* Thakeham, 1937). Actress. Red-haired daughter of Raymond MASSEY and Adrianne ALLEN and sister of Daniel MASSEY, respected and prolific actress of stage, TV and screen since the mid 50s. Made her stage debut as *The Reluctant Debutante* (1955), playing with 'nice down-to-earth determination' (Ivor Brown) and following this with a string of substantial roles over ensuing decades. Made her film debut in godfather John FORD's *Gideon's Day* (1958) and then came the female lead in the controversial *Peeping Tom* (1960), and it was clear she was not going to be a conventional film leading lady. Just over 30 she played the vinegary Miss Murdstone in *David*

Copperfield (1969), was an affectingly life-worn Mrs Linde in *The Doll's House* (1973) and a zany society mother in *Another Country* (1984). Solid supporting roles have kept coming her way, but it is at least arguable that TV has served her better, above all with the starring role in *Hotel du Lac* (1986); she seemed born to play Anita Brookner's heroine. Married (1 of 2) and divorced from Jeremy BRETT (1958–62).

OTHER BRITISH FILMS INCLUDE: *Bunny Lake Is Missing* (1965), *The Looking Glass War* (1969), *Frenzy* (1972), *The Vault of Horror* (1973), *The Chain* (1984), *The Tall Guy* (1989), *Impromptu* (1991), *Haunted, Angels and Insects* (1995, UK/US), *The Grotesque* (1996), *Driftwood* (UK/Ire), *The Slab Boys* (1997), *Déjà Vu* (1998), *Mad Cows* (1999), *Dark Blue World* (UK/Czech/Den/Ger/It), *The Importance of Being Earnest* (2002, UK/US, as Miss Prism).

Massey, Daniel (*b* London, 1933 – *d* London, 1998). Actor. Eton- and Cambridge-educated son of Raymond MASSEY and Adrienne ALLEN. With these parents and Noël COWARD for godfather, it was unlikely Massey would turn to carpentry. He actually made his debut as a child in Coward's *In Which We Serve* (1942) – and a quarter-century later won a Golden Globe award and an AAn for his skilful Coward impersonation in the Gertrude LAWRENCE biopic, *Star!* (1968, US). This was in fact his best film role, and though he made about 20 films he remained essentially a theatre actor, scoring major successes in, mainly, classical plays, including *Measure for Measure* (1983–84) for the RSC, as the Duke, and, not long before his death from Hodgkin's disease, as the German conductor, Wilhelm Furtwängler in *Taking Sides* (1995, London and Broadway). There was some notable TV, including *Intimate Contact* (1987) as an AIDS victim, but the characteristic naturalism of film seemed to constrain him (though he is droll in an early comedy like *Go to Blazes*, 1962) whereas the stage gave him full rein. Married (1) Adrienne CORRI (1961–67), (2) Penelope WILTON (1975–84) and (3) Wilton's sister, Lindy.

OTHER BRITISH FILMS INCLUDE: *Girls at Sea* (1958), *The Entertainer* (1960), *The Queen's Guards* (1961), *The Jokers* (1966), *Mary Queen of Scots* (1971), *The Incredible Sarah* (1976, UK/US), *Bad Timing* (1980), *Scandal* (1988), *In the Name of the Father* (1993, UK/Ire/US).

Massey, Raymond (*b* Toronto, 1896 – *d* Los Angeles, 1983). Actor. Tall, gaunt, Oxford-educated Massey turned his back on the family firm (Massey/Harris Agricultural Implements) and became a major actor on both sides of the Atlantic, on stage and screen, for 50 years. Now best known for his US career, which included the title role in *Abe Lincoln of Illinois* (1939), the mad and murderous Jonathan in *Arsenic and Old Lace* (1944) and James Dean's father in *East of Eden* (1955), he was also a significant presence in 30s British cinema, primarily in his work for Alexander KORDA, in such roles as the idealist hero of *Things to Come* (1936) and the wicked Prince Ghul in *The Drum* (1938). He also participated in four films for his friend Michael POWELL: as the deserter Brock in *49th Parallel* (1941); the narrator in the US version of *A Canterbury Tale* (1944); the anti-British celestial in *A Matter of Life and Death* (1946); and the Captain in *The Queen's Guards* (1961), playing father to his son, Daniel MASSEY. On stage, he played Abraham Lincoln so often it was said he wouldn't be satisfied until he was assassinated; on TV he was Dr Gillespie in the series, *Dr Kildare* (1961–66). Married (2 of 3) Adrianne ALLEN; Anna MASSEY is their daughter.

OTHER BRITISH FILMS: *High Treason* (1929), *The Speckled Band* (1931), *The Face at the Window* (1932), *The Scarlet Pimpernel* (1935), *Fire Over England, Under the Red Robe, Dreaming Lips* (1937), *Black Limelight* (1938).

BIBLIOG: Autobiographies, *When I Was Young*, 1976; *A Hundred Lives*, 1979.

Massie, Paul (*b* St Catherine, Canada, 1932). Actor. Interesting purveyor of introverted young men in his early roles – winning a BAA (Newcomer) as the American flyer under *Orders to Kill* (1958), as the boy accused of murdering his pregnant black girlfriend in *Sapphire* (1959), and a vengeful POW in *Libel* (1959) – whose career quickly ran out of steam, despite HAMMER giving him the chance to display *The Two Faces of Dr Jekyll* (1960). He was too idiosyncratic for conventional leads and at odds with the changes taking place in British cinema at the time.

OTHER BRITISH FILMS INCLUDE: *High Tide at Noon* (1957), *Raising the Wind* (1961), *The Pot Carriers* (1962).

Massine, Leonid (*b* Moscow, 1896 – *d* Borken, W. Germany, 1979). Dancer, choreographer. Trained as actor and dancer at the Imperial Theatre School, Moscow, and recruited by Diaghilev as principal dancer for the Ballets Russes, he went on to an immensely and diversely rewarding career in which films played only a small role. However, everyone remembers him as the creator/dancer of the Shoemaker in the famous ballet for *The Red Shoes* (1948). His flashing dark looks and emotional intensity made him a compelling figure in this and two other films for Michael POWELL: *The Tales of Hoffmann* (1951) and *Honeymoon* (1959), for which he also did the choreography for one of the ballet sequences. Also, a few international films.

Massingham, Richard (*b* Norfolk, 1898 – *d* Biddenden, 1953). Director, actor. Former doctor who became famous for his witty hortatory wartime SHORTS in which he encouraged people not to waste water (*The Five Inch Bather*, 1942) or advised how to avoid winter ills (*Coughs and Sneezes*, 1945). An amateur film-maker, he made two private films, *Tell Me If It Hurts* (1934) and *And So to Work* (1936), then bought an interest in and went on to become producer-in-charge of Public Relationship Films Ltd. Post-war he continued unabated to dramatise the problems of, say, austerity or toothache. The portly star of most of his own films, his persona became known as 'Mr Average Citizen'. He also acted in three features just before he died: *One Wild Oat* (1951), *Will Any Gentleman . . . ?* and *Turn the Key Softly* (1953).

OTHER BRITISH FILMS INCLUDE: (d, shorts) *Post Haste* (1934), *The Daily Round* (1937), *Come for a Stroll* (1939), *Fear and Peter Brown* (1940), *Dangers in the Dark* (1941), *Young and Healthy, Salvage* (1942), *Some Like It Rough* (1944), *Down at the Local* (1945), *Influenza* (1946), *Women Must Work* (1947), *Jet-Propelled Germs* (1948), *Handkerchief Drill* (1949), *The Cure* (1950), *He Won't Bite You* (1951), *To the Rescue* (1952).

Mass-Observation was a characteristically British approach to the rituals and practices of everyday life and 'ordinary people', founded in 1937 by Thomas Harrisson, Charles Madge and, most importantly for those interested in film in Britain, Humphrey JENNINGS, with the stated aim of creating an 'anthropology of ourselves'. In the tradition of Henry Mayhew's impressionistic social investigations of the 19th-century London poor, it can also be situated in the context of the 30s political and social debates about class, identity and nation. A national panel of volunteer writers and observers was recruited, who either kept diaries where they recorded behaviour and conversation or replied to regular open-ended questionnaires sent to them by the central team of Mass-Observers. The work focused on the public life of urban space – meetings, religious occasions, sporting and leisure activities –

and was interested in mass cultural forms, such as the cinema, and in 'the masses' themselves. However, while the project attempted to chart the experience of modernity through descriptions of 'social reality' it did so through a focus on specific individuals as representing a particular social group. Less overtly politically committed than the cinema's DOCUMENTARY MOVEMENT, Mass-Observation shared some of its allegiance to social democracy as well as its tendency to survey working-class culture from an implicitly bourgeois perspective. It continued to operate throughout WW2 and into the 50s. Its archive is housed at the University of Sussex.
BIBLIOG: Richards, Jeffrey and Sheridan, Dorothy (eds), *Mass Observation at the Movies*, 1987. Estella Tincknell.

Masters, Anthony (*b* England, 1919 – *d* France, 1990). Production designer. Shared BAA and AAn for the art direction of *2001: A Space Odyssey* (1968), but nothing else in his British career had this sort of distinction. His best UK work was probably in his recreation of the seedy London of *Expresso Bongo* (1959) and the city under environmental threat in *The Day the Earth Caught Fire* (1961). The last years of his career were mainly spent in such large-budget US films as *Buffalo Bill and the Indians* (1976) and *Dune* (1984). Was married to Heather SEARS.
OTHER BRITISH FILMS INCLUDE: (draughtsman) *Stage Fright* (1950), *Carrington VC* (1954); (art d) *The Bespoke Overcoat* (1955), *The Story of Esther Costello* (1957), *The Whole Truth*, *Corridors of Blood* (1958), *Don't Bother to Knock* (1961), *Tamahine* (1962), *The Heroes of Telemark* (1965), *That Lucky Touch* (1975, des).

Mather, Aubrey (*b* Minchinhampton, 1885 – *d* London, 1958). Actor. Bald, tubby, usually genial character player, educated at Charterhouse and Cambridge. On stage from 1905, he appeared in scores of plays (was Polonius to Leslie HOWARD's Hamlet in New York, 1936), and spent the 30s in British films before going to Hollywood, often playing butlers, vicars and valets in Brit-set pieces like *Random Harvest* (1942). Returned to England in 1951 and appeared in four further films, including *South of Algiers*, as Eric PORTMAN's superior, and as Merriman the butler in *The Importance of Being Earnest* (1952).
OTHER BRITISH FILMS INCLUDE: *Young Woodley* (1930), *Aren't We All?* (1932), *The Lash* (1934), *The Silent Passenger* (1935), *As You Like It* (1936), *Jamaica Inn* (1939).

Matheson, Hans (*b* Outer Hebrides, 1975). Actor. Discovered in a Clapham drama school, the palely personable Matheson has moved fast and had success on stage (*Mojo*, at the Royal Court), TV (as Frederick, the transvestite prostitute who dies horribly in *Branwell III* (1997), and in a string of films. The latter began with the filming of *Mojo* (1997), as the object of Harold PINTER's dubious interest; promise was confirmed with the lead as Stella's hopeless boyfriend in *Stella Does Tricks* (1996).
OTHER BRITISH FILMS: *Les Misérables* (1998, UK/Ger/US), *Still Crazy* (1998, UK/US), *Bodywork* (2000), *Deathwatch* (2002, UK/Ger).

Matheson, Murray (*b* Casterton, Australia, 1912 – *d* Los Angeles, 1985). Actor. After RAF service (1940–46), appeared in four British films before moving on to a long career as a supporting actor in US films. He had small roles in *Journey Together* (while still in the RAF), *The Way to the Stars* (1945), *School for Secrets* (1946), and bigger ones in *The Secret Tunnel* (1947), as the boy hero's father, and *The Fool and the Princess* (1948), as the Fool's pretentious friend.

Mathias, Sean (*b* Swansea, 1956). Director, actor, screenwriter. Won the Cannes Festival Young Cinema Award for

directing the concentration-camp play-made-film, *Bent* (1997, UK/US/Jap, +co-p), but has made no further film. He wrote the TV film, *The Lost Language of Cranes* (1991), and acted in several films, including *The Priest of Love* (1980), starring his then-partner, Ian MCKELLEN.

Mathieson, (James) Muir (*b* Stirling, 1911 – *d* Oxford, 1975). Musical director, conductor, composer, director. As soon as Mathieson completed his studies at the RCM, he became assistant musical director to Alexander KORDA in 1934, and was influential in attracting some of the best composers into British films of the 30s, 40s and 50s. These included BLISS for *Things to Come* (1935), Vaughan WILLIAMS for *49th Parallel* (1941), WALTON for *The First of the Few* (1942) and *Henry V* (1944), and Richard Rodney BENNETT for *Interpol* (1957). He is best known as musical director of some 500 films for LONDON FILMS and RANK. However, he also directed *Instruments of the Orchestra* (1946) and *Steps of the Ballet* (1948), and appeared on screen as one of the conductors in *The Seventh Veil* (1945). Mathieson was awarded the OBE in 1957.
OTHER BRITISH FILMS INCLUDE (m d, unless noted): *Catherine the Great*, *The Private Life of Don Juan*, *The Scarlet Pimpernel*, *Sanders of the River* (1935), *South Riding*, *The Drum* (1938), *The Four Feathers* (1939), *Conquest of the Air*, *Gaslight* (1940), *Dangerous Moonlight* (1941), *Hamlet* (1948), *A Day to Remember* (comp), *Hobson's Choice* (1953), *I Am a Camera* (1955), *The Silent Enemy* (1958), *Circus of Horrors* (1960, comp), hundreds more.
BIBLIOG: Muir Mathieson, 'Aspects of Film Music', *Tempo*, no. 9, 1944; John Huntley, *British Film Music*, 1947; Roger Manvell and John Huntley, *The Technique of Film Music*, 1957, enlarged 1975. David Burnand.

Matthews, A(lfred) E(dward) (*b* Bridlington, 1869 – *d* Bushey Heath, 1960). Actor. Supreme interpreter of the unflappably dotty upper classes on stage and screen, though by no means born to the purple: his father and uncles founded the original Christie Minstrels, his mother 'a most superior barmaid'. Began his theatrical career as a 'callboy' at the Princess Theatre, London, 1886, toured South Africa and Australia in the 80s and 90s and appeared in four *Who's Who* (1957) columns of plays over the next 60 years. Having got rid of his Yorkshire accent, he played many lords and dukes, none more famously than the Earl of Lister, who shoots rabbits from his sitting room, in *The Chiltern Hundreds* (1947–49, London and New York), his own favourite, and he recreated the role on screen (1949). This is what most filmgoers know him for, this and others like it, but his first brush with cinema occurred when he (as managing director) and a group of other famous stage actors set up the BRITISH ACTORS' FILM COMPANY at Bushey Heath and turned out a dozen features before ceasing operations in 1920 and he did virtually no further films for 20 years. There was then no stopping him and he had made over 50 by the time, as Britain's oldest working actor, he stopped at nearly 90, his timing and his way with a throwaway comic line never deserting him. Awarded OBE (1951).
OTHER BRITISH FILMS: *The Real Thing at Last*, *Wanted a Widow* (1916), *Once Upon a Time* (1918), *The Lackey and the Lady*, *Castle of Dreams* (1919), *The Iron Duke* (1935), *Men Are Not Gods* (1936), *Quiet Wedding*, *This England*, *Pimpernel Smith* (1941), *Thunder Rock*, *The Great Mr Handel* (1942), *The Life and Death of Colonel Blimp*, *The Man in Grey*, *Escape to Danger* (1943), *The Way Ahead*, *Twilight Hour*, *They Came to a City*, *Love Story* (1944), *Flight from Folly* (1945), *Piccadilly Incident* (1946), *The Ghosts of Berkeley Square*, *Just William's Luck* (1947), *William Comes to Town*, *Britannia Mews* (1948), *Whisky Galore!*, *Landfall*, *Edward, My Son* (1949), *Mr Drake's Duck* (1950), *Laughter in Paradise*, *The Magic Box*, *The Galloping Major* (1951), *I Know That My*

Redeemer Liveth, Who Goes There!, Something Money Can't Buy, Penny Princess, Made in Heaven, Castle in the Air (1952), *The Weak and the Wicked, Skid Kids, The Million Pound Note, Meet Mr Lucifer* (1953), *Aunt Clara, Happy Ever After* (1954), *Miss Tulip Stays the Night, Jumping for Joy* (1955), *Three Men in a Boat, Loser Takes All* (1956), *The Square* (short), *Doctor at Large, Carry On Admiral* (1957), *Inn for Trouble* (1959).

BIBLIOG: Autobiography, *Matty*, 1952.

Matthews, Francis (*b* York, 1927). Actor. On stage since 17, the urbane Matthews has had a sturdy stage career, often in upper-class roles, and a successful TV record, playing *Paul Temple* (1969–71) and co-starring with George COLE in *Don't Forget to Write* (1977, 1979). Made less mark in films, without being other than competent: began as an anti-British Indian in *Bhowani Junction* (1955) and as the nice young mine host of *Small Hotel* (1957); co-starred with Peter CUSHING in *The Revenge of Frankenstein* (1958); starred as the son of *A Woman Possessed* (1958); and quickly declined into supporting roles. Married (from 1963) to **Angela Browne** (*b* Walton-on-Thames, 1938 – *d* Esher, Surrey, 2001), who appeared in several films including *Press for Time* (1966).

OTHER BRITISH FILMS INCLUDE: *I Only Arsked!, Corridors of Blood* (1958), *The Hellfire Club* (1960), *Nine Hours to Rama* (1962), *The Beauty Jungle* (1964), *The Intelligence Men* (1965), *Crossplot* (1969).

Matthews, Jessie (*b* London, 1907 – *d* Eastcote, Middlesex, 1981). Actress, dancer. Gamine, graceful dancer, with a sweet, pure-toned singing voice, and waif-like sex appeal, who embodied 30s style. One of 11 children of a Soho costermonger, Matthews enjoyed dancing from an early age, and elocution lessons created her distinctive 'plummy' accent. In a chorus line at 16, she also had fleeting dancing roles in silent films. In London, 1930, she was in *Ever Green*, featuring hit song 'Dancing on the Ceiling', co-starring with Sonnie HALE (then husband of Evelyn LAYE) which led to a scandalous divorce action, Matthews cited as the 'other woman'. Her break-through film performance was as Susie Dean, dancing with airy grace and fluidity, in *The Good Companions* (1933), for Victor SAVILLE, her most sympathetic director. The dual-role film version of *Evergreen* (1934) opened at Radio City Music Hall, New York, and she was labelled 'The Dancing Divinity', although attempts to co-star her and Fred Astaire in a film never materialised. Next came the gender-swapping musical comedy *First A Girl* (1935), produced, like all of her major 30s films, by GAUMONT–BRITISH, which surrounded her with the best available talent: Americans, choreographer Buddy BRADLEY, cinematographer Glen MACWILLIAMS and song-writer Harry WOODS; art director Alfred JUNGE; and musical director Louis LEVY.

Other, weaker films were directed by HALE, and *Climbing High* (1938) was directed by Carol REED, with whom she had a brief affair, and her career at the top was over by the end of the decade. Often temperamental and unstable, she suffered from problems originating in her difficult upbringing, with many personal tragedies and nervous breakdowns, including generally loveless marriages which ended in divorce. Hale (1931–44) was her second of three husbands. Her only US film role was a cameo in the all-star fundraiser *Forever and a Day* (1943), and her song in *tom thumb* (1958) was dubbed. However, she became a celebrity again in the long-running radio soap *Mrs Dale's Diary*, and continued to work in regional theatre in the UK and abroad, including a triumphant one-woman show in Los Angeles in 1979, and was perfectly cast as

Aunt Bessie in TV's *Edward and Mrs Simpson* (1978). For most of the 30s, Matthews was the most popular female film star in England: the image of her in *Sailing Along* (1938), in a white evening gown, with a gentleman's black top hat and walking cane, performing 'Souvenir of Love' in LIME GROVE's art deco luxury sets, indelibly incarnates 30s style. Awarded OBE, 1970.

OTHER BRITISH FILMS: *The Beloved Vagabond, This England* (1923), *Straws in the Wind* (1924), *Out of the Blue* (1931), *There Goes the Bride, The Midshipmaid* (1932), *The Man from Toronto, Friday the Thirteenth* (1933), *Waltzes from Vienna* (1934), *It's Love Again* (1936), *Gangway, Head Over Heels* (1937), *Candles at Nine, Life Is Nothing Without Music* (short), *Victory Wedding* (short, d) (1944), *Making the Grade* (1947, short), *A Hundred Years Underground* (1963, short), *The Hound of the Baskervilles* (1977).

BIBLIOG: Autobiography, *Over My Shoulder*, 1974; Michael Thornton, *Jessie Matthews*, 1974. Roger Philip Mellor.

Matthews, Lester (*b* Nottingham, 1900 – *d* Los Angeles, 1975). Actor. Of his over 140 films, only the first 20-odd were British, crammed into the 1931–34 period, many of them 'QUOTA QUICKIES', though some such as *Blossom Time* (1934) had higher aspirations. After this, the tall, moustachioed, rather severe-looking actor, with wife Anne GREY, headed for Hollywood, where he played all manner of upper-class Englishmen, including indeed Charles II in *Lorna Doone* (1951). Stage (debut 1916) in UK and US.

OTHER BRITISH FILMS INCLUDE: *Gipsy Blood* (1931), *Indiscretions of Eve*, (1932), *On Secret Service* (1933), *Irish Hearts, Song at Eventide, Borrowed Clothes* (1934).

Mature, Victor (*b* Louisville, Kentucky, 1915 – *d* 1999). Actor. Mature always claimed he was no actor and that he had the reviews to prove it. This grossly underestimated his work in such films as *My Darling Clementine* (1946), but even his eight British films, including several action films for WARWICK, reveal a perfectly competent craftsman, especially in Ken Hughes's tough melodrama, *The Long Haul* (1957).

OTHER BRITISH FILMS: *Betrayed* (1954), *Safari, Zarak* (1956), *Interpol* (1957), *No Time to Die* (1958), *The Bandit of Zhobe* (1959), *Firepower* (1979).

Maturin, Eric (*b* Ninai Tawl, India, 1883 – *d* London, 1957). Actor. Tonbridge-educated character player on stage (US and UK) from 1901 who had small roles in nearly 20 films, mostly in the 30s, and three for Michael POWELL in the 40s, including a village father in *A Canterbury Tale* (1944).

OTHER BRITISH FILMS INCLUDE: *Wisp o' the Woods* (1919), *The Squeaker* (1931), *The Face at the Window* (1932), *Sanders of the River* (1935), *Contraband* (1940), *The Life and Death of Colonel Blimp* (1943), *Last Holiday* (1950).

Maude, Arthur (*b* Pontefract, 1894 – *d* ?). Director, actor. Former bank clerk and stage actor (from 1913) who became screen actor/director, and in the US experimented with colour film in the early 20s. The British films he directed from 1927 are essentially 'QUOTA QUICKIES' like *She Was Only a Village Maiden* (1934); he also played small roles in a few films, including *Call Me Mame* (1933) and *The Common Touch* (1941). Married Nancy PRICE; father of Joan MAUDE.

OTHER BRITISH FILMS INCLUDE: (d, unless noted) *Poppies of Flanders* (1927), *Watch Beverly* (1932), *The Wishbone* (1933), *Boomerang* (1934), *One Good Turn* (1951, short, + p); (a) *Head of the Family* (1933), *The Silent Battle* (1939), *Sabotage at Sea* (1942).

Maude, Cyril (*b* London, 1862 – *d* Torquay, 1951). Actor. Famous stage actor-manager (stage debut 1883), created the role of 'Grumpy', a retired criminal lawyer, in Glasgow, 1913, played it over 1,300 times and filmed it in 1930 (US). Apart from starring in two silents, he played character roles in a half-dozen British films, like the President of some fictional, vaguely Latin state in *Heat Wave* (1935), finally as an ancient admiral in *While the Sun Shines* (1947).

OTHER BRITISH FILMS: *Beauty and the Barge* (1914), *The Headmaster* (1921), *These Charming People* (1931), *Orders Is Orders*, *Counsel's Opinion* (1933), *Girls Will Be Boys* (1934).

Maude, Gillian (*b* Geneva, 1915). Actress. Stage actress who filmed occasionally, with female leads in several minor films, including *Sexton Blake and the Bearded Doctor* (1935), but finished with very small roles in the likes of *Angels One Five* (1952) and *Adultery Spanish Style* (1976, Sp). Was married to Campbell SINGER.

OTHER BRITISH FILMS INCLUDE: *Tangled Evidence* (1934), *Mistaken Identity* (1939, rel 1942), *Dick Barton – Special Agent* (1948), *Madness of the Heart* (1949), *Piccadilly Third Stop* (1960).

Maude, Joan (*b* Rickmansworth, 1908 – *d* Lewes, 1998). Actress. Graceful former dancer who, given her lineage, could scarcely have been other than a performer. Jenny Lind was a great-grandmother; Cyril MAUDE was a cousin; and her mother was the formidable Nancy PRICE. First on stage as a solo dancer in 1921, she played a wide range of roles over the next decade or so. Post-war she worked mainly in films and TV, and had some striking supporting roles: as the London official who breaks the news of the *Great Day* (1945), the Chief Recorder in *A Matter of Life and Death* and the duplicitous Sidney Vane in *Night Boat to Dublin* (1946).

OTHER BRITISH FILMS INCLUDE: *This Freedom* (1923), *Hobson's Choice* (1931), *The Wandering Jew* (1933), *Turn of the Tide* (1935), *The Lamp Still Burns* (1943), *The Rake's Progress* (1945), *Corridor of Mirrors* (1948), *Life in Her Hands* (1951).

Maude-Roxby, Roddy (*b* London, 1930). Actor. Educated at Eton and Royal College of Art, he was a painter before turning to the stage in 1951. Played mainly in comedies, musicals and revues, entering films in *The Party's Over* (1963), and was a regular in the US comedy series, *Laugh-In* (1968).

OTHER BRITISH FILMS INCLUDE: *Doctor in Clover* (1966), *The Bliss of Mrs Blossom* (1968), *Playing Away* (1986), *Number 27* (1988), *Shadowlands* (1993, UK/US).

Maugham, Robin (Lord Maugham) (*b* London, 1916 – *d* Brighton, 1981). Author. Nephew of Somerset MAUGHAM, whose short novels, *Line on Ginger* and *The Servant* have been successfully filmed, as Guy HAMILTON's *The Intruder* (1953, + co-sc) and Joseph LOSEY's 1963 masterpiece respectively.

OTHER BRITISH FILMS: *The Black Tent* (1956, story, co-sc), *The Rough and the Smooth* (1959, novel).

Maugham, W(illiam) Somerset (*b* Paris, 1874 – *d* Nice, 1965). Author. One of the most popular novelists of the 20th century, Maugham lived to see much of his work adapted to the screen (and TV), in the UK, the US and elsewhere. His well-turned narratives and strong character lines made him very suitable for ADAPTATION. The most famous silent version of his work was *Sadie Thompson* (1928, US), remade as *Rain* (1932) and *Miss Sadie Thompson* (1953). His novel, *Of Human Bondage* (1915) has also been filmed three times: 1934, 1946 (US) and 1964 (a notably troubled UK production). Other works filmed in the US include (novels) *The Razor's Edge* (1946, 1984), *The Moon and Sixpence* (1942) and *Christmas Holiday* (1944), and

(plays) *The Letter* (1929, 1940) and *Our Betters* (1933). In Britain, his best known brush with cinema was in the three PORTMANTEAU FILMS based deftly on his short stories and introduced by himself: *Quartet* (1948), *Trio* (1950) and *Encore* (1951), all stylishly acted and directed. There were two versions of the West Indies romance, *The Vessel of Wrath* (1938, and, called *The Beachcomber*, 1954), offering bravura opportunities for Charles LAUGHTON and Robert NEWTON respectively. The middle-class novelist (and dramatist) par excellence provided the source material for some equally adept middle-class cinema.

OTHER BRITISH FILMS: (films adapted from his works) *Secret Agent* (from *Ashenden*), *The Tenth Man* (from play) (1936), *Three Cases of Murder* (1955, 'Lord Mountdrago' segment, from story), *Up at the Villa* (2000, UK/US, from novel).

Maur, Meinhart (*b* Hajdu-Nanas, Hungary, 1891 – *d* London, 1964). Actor. In German films since 1919 (e.g. *Die Spinnen*, directed by Fritz Lang). In Britain since 1935, Maur appeared in small supporting roles (e.g. the restaurant keeper in *21 Days*, 1937; in POWELL AND PRESSBURGER's *The Tales Of Hoffmann*, 1951), later also on TV and radio.

OTHER BRITISH FILMS INCLUDE: *Rembrandt* (1936), *O-Kay For Sound*, *Doctor Syn* (1937), *An Englishman's Home* (1939), *Gasbags* (1940), *Jeannie* (1941), *We'll Smile Again* (1942), *It's Not Cricket*, *The Huggetts Abroad* (1949), *The Wooden Horse* (1950), *Decameron Nights* (1952), *Malaga* (1954). Tim Bergfelder.

Maureen, Mollie (*b* Ireland, 1904 – *d* London, 1987). Actress. RN: Elizabeth Mary Campfield. In *Return of the Pink Panther* (1974), she is simply listed as 'little old lady' and that is what she played in most of her ten films. She is one of the ancient aunts in the remake of *The Wicked Lady* (1983) and Queen Victoria no less in *The Private Life of Sherlock Holmes* (1970). Best known as Granny Fraser in TV's *Crossroads* (1964–70).

OTHER BRITISH FILMS INCLUDE: *The Silent Playground* (1963), *Twisted Nerve* (1968), *Callan* (1974), *The Hound of the Baskervilles* (1977), *Little Dorrit* (1987).

Maurey, Nicole (*b* Bois-Colombes, France, 1925). Actress. Auburn-haired French star, in films from 1945, notably in Robert Bresson's austere masterpiece, *Diary of a Country Priest* (1950, Fr). Her English-language debut was opposite Bing Crosby in *Little Boy Lost* (1953), and she made about a dozen British films, playing one of Rex HARRISON's 'wives' in *The Constant Husband* (1954) and Alec GUINNESS's mistress in *The Scapegoat* (1958), and co-starring with Howard KEEL in the SCIENCE-FICTION tale, *The Day of the Triffids* (1962).

OTHER BRITISH FILMS INCLUDE: *The Weapon* (1956), *The House of the Seven Hawks* (1959), *Don't Bother to Knock* (1961), *The Very Edge* (1962).

Maxsted, Jack (*b* Kingston, Surrey, 1916 – *d* Bath, 2001). Art director. After working post-war as draughtsman at GAINS-BOROUGH, Maxsted contributed to the design of some popular GENRE films in the 50s and 60s. His work on Roy Ward BAKER's atmospheric *Tiger in the Smoke* (1956), especially in the frightening underworld sequences is very impressive; he was one of several involved with *Battle of Britain* (1969).

OTHER BRITISH FILMS INCLUDE: (draughtsman) *Good-Time Girl* (1947), *Easy Money* (1948), *Encore* (1951); (ass art d) *Lancelot and Guinevere* (1962), *Kaleidoscope* (1966), *Fathom* (1967); (art d) *The Million Pound Note* (1953, co-), *The Purple Plain* (1954), *Jacqueline* (1956), *Dangerous Exile* (1957), *Rooney* (1958), *Whirlpool* (1959), *Man in the Moon* (1960), *Jason and the Argonauts* (1963, co-), *When Eight Bells Toll*, *Diamonds Are Forever* (co-) (1971), *The Deep* (1977, co, UK/US), *Warlords of Atlantis* (1978).

Maxwell, James (*b* Worcester, Massachusetts, 1929 – *d* London, 1995). Actor. Craggy American actor who trained at the Old Vic Theatre School, Bristol, and became a founder member of the Manchester Exchange Theatre. In films from 1958 (*Subway in the Sky*) in ten supporting roles, but generally had more rewarding chances on TV, in, for example, *The Hidden Truth* (1964) and a continuing role in *Raffles* (1975, 1977).

OTHER BRITISH FILMS INCLUDE: *The Damned* (1961), *Private Potter* (1962), *The Evil of Frankenstein* (1964), *Otley* (1968), *One Day in the Life of Ivan Denisovich* (1971, UK/Nor/US), *Ransom* (1974).

Maxwell, John (*b* Glasgow, 1875 – *d* Witley, 1940). Executive. Important figure in the first decade of British talkies, who started out as a solicitor in Scotland, became aware of the potential of the film industry and began to buy cinemas which, in 1928, culminated in forming the ABC cinema chain. In 1927 he set up BRITISH INTERNATIONAL PICTURES (BIP) at ELSTREE, where he produced HITCHCOCK's late silents and early talkies, including *Blackmail* (1929). Having started with big prestige silent productions, Maxwell switched to low-budget domestic productions when SOUND arrived, realising that he would have to recoup his costs at home. In the meantime, he had also turned his attention to the renting of films, and, in that connection, became chairman of the Wardour Film Company which distributed the BIP output. In 1933 he established the ASSOCIATED BRITISH Picture Corporation (ABPC) which, along with GAUMONT–BRITISH, became one of the two big cinema combines of the decade. He was very much involved in the 30s debates about quotas, and their implications for employment in the British industry, and the best possibilities for overseas DISTRIBUTION. In 1933 he made Walter MYCROFT head of production, Maxwell's name no longer appearing as Producer on individual films, though he still continued to exert major influence until Mycroft was credited as 'Director of Production' in 1935. A very shrewd businessman, he realised the importance to British exhibitors and renters of a steady supply of American films and was one of the first in Britain to understand, as Patricia Warren wrote, 'that the future lay in the formation of a combined producing/distributing/exhibiting framework with a large British studio as its foundation stone'. ABPC would answer that last need for several decades. By the end of the decade, J. Arthur RANK was making his presence felt and he quickly snapped up the new AMALGAMATED STUDIOS at Elstree in 1939, to avoid their falling to Maxwell, whom he rightly saw as major competition. Maxwell died the following year, his Elstree studios having been commandeered for the war effort. Legendarily stingy and somewhat inward-looking by comparison with, say, BALCON, KORDA and other major industry figures of the time as he was, it is still hard to overestimate his significance in the history of British film.

OTHER BRITISH FILMS: (p) *The Woman Tempted* 1926, co-p), *The Ring* (1927), *The Farmer's Wife, Champagne* (1928, ex p), *The Manxman* (ex), *Atlantic* (1929), *Elstree Calling, The Yellow Mask, Why Sailors Leave Home, Song of Soho, Murder!, The Middle Watch, The Man from Chicago, Juno and the Paycock, The Constant Husband, Kiss Me Sergeant, Compromising Daphne* (1930), *The Love Habit, The Woman Between, My Wife's Family, The Skin Game, The Shadow Between, Potiphar's Wife, Out of the Blue, Keepers of Youth, Hobson's Choice* (1931), *Rich and Strange, Old Spanish Customers, Number Seventeen, The Maid of the Mountains, Let Me Explain, Dear, Lucky Girl, The Last Coupon, Josser in the Army* (1932), *You Made Me Love You, The Song You Gave Me, Letting in the Sunshine, Leave It to Me, Facing the Music, On Secret Service* (1933).

BIBLIOG: Allen Eyles, *ABC: The First Name in Entertainment*, 1993; Patricia Warren, *Elstree: The British Hollywood*, 1983.

Maxwell, Lois (*b* Kichener, Canada, 1927). Actress. RN: Hooker. The name had to be changed, of course, and Maxwell eventually (over parental opposition) had a 40-year career, first in Britain, then Hollywood, then Italy and back to Britain where she acquired the identity and fame that would stick with her – as the coolly appraising Miss Moneypenny in 14 James BOND larks, from *Dr No* (1962) to *A View to a Kill* (1985). Most of her other British films were routine co-features, with the odd role she could get her teeth into, such as the new arrival at Freda JACKSON's 'home' for single mothers in *Women of Twilight* (1952), and KUBRICK cast her as a nurse in *Lolita* (1961); but it is Moneypenny she will be remembered for.

OTHER BRITISH FILMS INCLUDE: *Spring Song* (1946), *Corridor of Mirrors* (1948), *Lady in the Fog* (1951), *Mantrap* (1953), *From Russia with Love, The Haunting* (1963), *Goldfinger* (1964), *Thunderball* (1965), *You Only Live Twice* (1967), *Diamonds Are Forever* (1971), *Endless Night* (1972), *Live and Let Die* (1973), *The Spy Who Loved Me* (1977), *Moonraker* (UK/Fr), *Lost and Found* (1979), *For Your Eyes Only* (1981), *Octopussy* (1983).

Maxwell, Peter (*b* Vienna, 1921). Director. RN: Eugene Margitai. After directing some 'B' MOVIES in Britain, including two rather neat ones, *The Desperate Man* (1959) with William HARTNELL and *Serena* (1962) with Honor BLACKMAN, as well as episodes of such TV series as *Sir Francis Drake* (1962) and *Danger Man* (1964), Maxwell settled in Australia where he had already directed many episodes of *Whiplash* in the early 60s. Once there, he directed several feature films, including *Touch and Go* (1980, + p), and TV series.

OTHER BRITISH FILMS INCLUDE: (d, unless noted) *Three Cases of Murder* (1955, 2ud), *Blind Spot* (1958), *The Long Shadow* (1961), *Dilemma* (1962), *The Switch* (1963), *Mozambique* (1964, UK/Zanz, a).

May, Hans (*b* Vienna, 1886 – *d* Beaulieu, 1958). Composer, music director. RN: Johann Mayer. In the 1920s May composed scores for German release versions of Paramount and MGM productions. In Britain from 1934, May wrote an atmospheric and eerie soundtrack for Roy BOULTING's *Thunder Rock* (1942), but is probably best known for his rousing and melodramatic scores for GAINSBOROUGH films such as *Madonna Of The Seven Moons* (1944) and *The Wicked Lady* (1945).

OTHER BRITISH FILMS INCLUDE: (comp, unless noted) *The Flame Of Love* (1930, UK/Ger), *Let's Love And Laugh* (1931, UK/Ger), *My Song Goes Around The World* (1934), *The Lilac Domino* (1937), *The Stars Look Down* (1939), *Back Room Boy* (1942), *Two Thousand Women, Latin Quarter* (cond) (1945), *Bedelia* (1946), *Brighton Rock, Fame Is The Spur* (cond) (1947), *My Brother Jonathan* (1948), *I'll Get You for This* (1950), *Rough Shoot* (1953), *The Gypsy And The Gentleman* (1957). Tim Bergfelder.

May, Jack (*b* Henley-on-Thames, 1922 – *d* Hove, 1997). Actor. Tall, somewhat gaunt-looking stage actor (an interesting neurotic *Julius Caesar* at the Old Vic, 1958) who had intermittent supporting roles in films from the mid 40s. He is the boatman in *Brief Encounter* (1945), one of the several uncredited bits before more substantial roles a decade later, and a starring role as the murderous judge in the co-feature *Night After Night After Night* (1969). Best known as the voice of Nelson Gabriel in the BBC radio serial *The Archers*. Married to Petra DAVIES, with whom he appeared in *A Swarm in May* (1983).

OTHER BRITISH FILMS INCLUDE: *A Canterbury Tale* (1944), *No Room at the Inn* (1948), *Innocents in Paris* (1953), *The Silent Enemy* (1958), *A*

Prize of Arms (1961), *How I Won the War* (1967), *Goodbye, Mr Chips* (1969), *Trog* (1970), *The Return of the Soldier* (1982), *The Bounty, The Shooting Party* (1984), *The Doctor and the Devils* (1985).

May, Johdi (*b* US, 1975). Actress. Made her debut as a child in the anti-apartheid drama, *A World Apart* (1987). From 1994 to 1997, she was at Oxford and has had some striking roles since returning to film: she was a poignant Marty South in *The Woodlanders* (1997) and gave a fine study in repressed malice in *The House of Mirth* (2000, UK/US); played the daughter of *The Mayor of Casterbridge* (2001) on TV. Was in the US film *The Last of the Mohicans* (1992).

OTHER BRITISH FILMS: *Second Best* (UK/US), *Sister My Sister* (1994), *The Gambler* (1997, UK/Hung/Neth), *The Escapist* (2001).

Mayall, Rik (*b* Harlow, 1958). Actor. Famous for his very physical brand of TV comedy, most often in company with Adrian EDMONDSON, in such series as *The Young Ones* (1982, 1984). His films, including *Carry On Columbus* (1992), *Bring Me the Head of Mavis Davis* (1998) and the critically excoriated *Guest House Paradiso* (1999, + co-sc), have not done much for his reputation, but presumably diehard fans don't mind. In 1998, he had a very serious accident on a quad bike, from which he made a remarkable recovery.

OTHER BRITISH FILMS INCLUDE: *Eye of the Needle* (1981), *Whoops Apocalypse* (1986), *Eat the Rich* (1987), *Remember Me?* (1996), *Kevin of the North* (UK/Can) (2001).

Maybury, John (*b* London, 1958). Director. Began making short films while still at art school in the late 70s, then went on to work as costume and set designer for Derek JARMAN, as well as co-editing *The Last of England* (1987) and designing and editing the war sequences for Jarman's *War Requiem* (1989). He also directed short films and music videos (including the award-winning *Nothing Compares 2U*, on which he collaborated with Sinead O'Connor; he also directed a TV concert DOCUMENTARY called *Sinead O'Connor – The Value of Ignorance*, 1989), and exhibited as an artist during the 80s. He came to less esoteric (though hardly mainstream) audience attention with his 1998 BIOPIC of artist Francis Bacon, *Love Is the Devil* (UK/Fr/Jap), which concentrated on Bacon's destructive affair with minor East End crim, George Dyer, and avoided the clichés of the GENRE. In 2002, he directed and co-wrote *Marlowe*, one of the two biopics about Christopher Marlowe, this one depicting him as ardently heterosexual.

OTHER BRITISH FILMS INCLUDE: (d, unless noted) *The Alternative Miss World* (1980, short, a), *The Court of Miracles* (1982), *Glistening with Energy, Big Love – An Invitation to Disaster* (1984, shorts), *The Queen Is Dead* (co-d) (1986, short), *Union Jack Up* (1987, short), *Tunnel of Love* (1991, short), *Remembrance of Things Fast* (1993, + sc, ex p), *Genetron* (1996).

Mayersberg, Paul (*b* Royston, Herts, 1941). Screenwriter, director. Worked briefly in advertising before starting in films, worked as assistant to LOSEY and others, and was a founder-editor of *MOVIE* magazine and critic for *New Society*. In film, he has worked chiefly as a writer on some offbeat projects, including two for Nicolas ROEG, *The Man Who Fell to Earth* (1976) and *Eureka* (1982, UK/US), and on *Croupier* (1998, UK/Fr/Ger/Ire), rediscovered two years after its initial release. He is also the author of a provocative book about Hollywood art and commerce, *Hollywood The Haunted House* (1967).

OTHER BRITISH FILMS INCLUDE: (sc, unless noted) *The Disappearance* (1977), *Merry Christmas Mr Lawrence* (1982, UK/Jap, co-sc), *Captive* (1985, UK/Fr, + d), *Return from the River Kwai* (1988, co-sc), *The Intruder* (1999, UK/Can).

Mayflower Pictures Company set up at ELSTREE in 1937 by Charles LAUGHTON and Erich POMMER, with the support of John MAXWELL. In the event the Company made only three films at this stage: *The Vessel of Wrath* and *St Martin's Lane* (1938) and *Jamaica Inn* (1939). All starred Laughton; Pommer produced all three and directed the first, but both then left for Hollywood and the Company ceased operation. It was later taken over by Aubrey BARING (on its board from 1941) and Maxwell SETTON and produced a half-dozen or so films from the late 40s until the early 50s, including *The Spider and the Fly* (1949), *So Little Time* (1952) and *Appointment in London* (1953).

Maylam, Tony (*b* London, 1943). Director. RADA-trained Maylam directed and wrote highly regarded DOCUMENTARIES from the early 70s, winning a BAA for *White Rock* (1977, + sc), which chronicles the 1976 Winter Olympics in Innsbruck. He also directed feature films, including the pre-WW1 adventure tale, *Riddle of the Sands* (1979, + co-sc), and the US horror film, *The Burning* (1980, + story).

OTHER BRITISH FILMS INCLUDE: *Genesis – A Band in Concert* (1976, doc, + p), *Hero: The Official Film of the 1986 World Cup* (1987, doc), *Split Second* (1992).

Maynard, Bill (*b* Farnham, 1928). Actor. RN: Walter Williams. In bulky, shambling Claude Greengrass of *Heartbeat* (1992–2001), Maynard created one of TV's great originals: a chronic conman who could yet surprise with his moral exactitude, and with more than a touch of Falstaffian grandeur. Entered British films at the wrong time for a character comedian: there were four 'CARRY ON' films but the rest were mostly TV SPIN-OFFS and the dire 'Confessions of . . . ' series; as the rough-hewn Sergeant Ellis in *Adolf Hitler – My Part in His Downfall* (1972) he had perhaps his best film chance. TV was really his métier.

OTHER BRITISH FILMS INCLUDE: *Till Death Us Do Part* (1969), *Carry On Loving* (1970), *. . . Henry, . . . at Your Convenience* (1971), *. . . Matron* (1972), *Steptoe & Son Ride Again* (1973), *Man About the House* (1974), *Confessions of a Pop Performer* (1975), *. . . a Driving Instructor, It Shouldn't Happen to a Vet* (1976), *Dangerous Davies – The Last Detective* (1980).

BIBLIOG: Autobiography, *Stand Up and Be Counted*, 1997.

Mayne, Ferdy (*b* Mainz, Germany, 1916 – *d* London, 1998). Actor. RN: Ferdinand Mayer-Börckel. A supporting actor with over 150 screen credits to his name, Mayne specialised in eccentric and sinister parts, frequently of Central European origin. In British films since 1942, his best-known role was the vampire Count von Krolock in Roman POLANSKI's *The Fearless Vampire Killers* (1967).

OTHER BRITISH FILMS INCLUDE: *Old Mother Riley Overseas, The Life And Death Of Colonel Blimp, Warn That Man* (1943), *Encore* (1951), *The Divided Heart* (1954), *Blue Murder At St Trinian's* (1957), *Operation Crossbow* (1965, UK/It), *Those Magnificent Men . . .* (1965), *Barry Lyndon* (1975), *Yellowbeard* (1983). Tim Bergfelder.

Mazzei, Andrew (*b* Lancashire). Production designer. Of Italian–French parentage, Mazzei studied architecture and sculpture at Blackpool and Manchester Schools of Art. First film work was with Famous Players in the US; he also worked in Germany and Italy, before return to England in 1928. He then designed for JH PRODUCTIONS, GAUMONT–BRITISH and others before his period of greatest distinction at GAINSBOROUGH in the 40s. His designs for *Madonna of the Seven Moons* (1944) encapsulate contrasting *ideas* of Italy and moral states, and in the 50s he made several TEMPEAN second features, such as *The Frightened Man* (1952), look more expensive than they were. Colleague Maurice CARTER remembered him as 'a very quiet man and a good designer, very efficient' (1994).

OTHER BRITISH FILMS INCLUDE: (cos) *The Blarney Stone* (1933); (des) *Hindle Wakes* (1931), *Rome Express* (1932), *The Man Within* (1947); (art d) *The Flag Lieutenant* (1926), *Hindle Wakes* (1927), *High Treason* (1929), *Turn of the Tide, No Monkey Business* (1935), *The Rose of Tralee* (1942), *I'll Be Your Sweetheart* (1945), *The Magic Bow* (1946), *They Made Me a Fugitive* (1947), *This Was a Woman, The Small Voice* (1948), *The Lost Hours, Hindle Wakes* (1952).

Mead, John (aka J.F. Mead) Production designer. Worked at BIP during the 30s and was described by Edward CARRICK as having 'a real flair for film décor' (1948), his work sometimes more distinguished than the films it served, as with *The Marriage of Corbal* (1936), and his work on *Abdul the Damned* (1935, co-des), as having 'all the atmosphere of a corrupt Turkey behind it'.

OTHER BRITISH FILMS INCLUDE: (art d) *Murder!* (1930), *Hawleys of High Street* (1933), *Royal Cavalcade* (co-des) (1935), *Sensation* (1936); (des), *My Wife's Family* (1931), *Arms and the Man* (1932), *Bulldog Drummond at Bay* (1937), *Yellow Sands* (1938), *Murder In Soho* (1939).

Meadows, Shane (*b* Cheadle, 1973). Director, screenwriter. Self-taught film-maker who tells stories that relate to his youth and working-class background. Heavily influenced by the realist films of the NEW WAVE, and the contemporary REALISM of Ken LOACH and Mike LEIGH, Meadows' highly personal films render their social environment with both gravity and a sense of humour. His affection for the black and white films of the 50s is obvious in his first feature *24 7 TwentyFourSeven* (1997, + sc, a), in which directionless youthful lives are given meaning when Alan Darcy (Bob HOSKINS) teaches them boxing. The autobiographical strain in this film is sustained in *A Room for Romeo Brass* (1999, + a), which he co-scripted with childhood neighbour, Paul Fraser, again exploring issues of family and social connectedness.

OTHER BRITISH FILMS INCLUDE: *Small Time* (+ a, sc, p) (1996), *Once Upon a Time in the Midlands* (2002, d, co-sc). Melinda Hildebrandt.

Meaney, Colm (*b* Dublin, 1953). Actor. Rugged, curly-haired Irish character player now in demand for international films, after his successes in Stephen FREARS's Dublin-set *The Snapper* (1993), as the pregnant heroine's father, and *The Van* (1996, UK/Ire). He had already had some US experience in such films as *Dick Tracy* and *Die Hard 2* (1990), and was one of the guests in John HUSTON's *The Dead* (1987, UK/Ger/US).

OTHER BRITISH FILMS INCLUDE: *The Commitments* (1991, Ire/US), *Into the West* (UK/Ire/US) (1992), *War of the Buttons* (1994, UK/Fr), *The Englishman Who Went Up . . .* (1995), *The Last of the High Kings* (1996, UK/Den/Ire), *Owd Bob* (1997, UK/Can), *How Harry Became a Tree* (2001, UK/Fr/It/Ire).

Measor, Beryl (*b* Shanghai, 1908 – *d* London, 1965). Actress. RADA-trained theatre actress, on stage from 1931, starring as mother of the *Cosh Boy* (1951) and as the stoical manageress in *Separate Tables* (1954). Screen appearances were rare but vivid, as for instance sympathetic Maudie in *Odd Man Out* (1947), forbidding Nurse Brand in *The Mark of Cain* and opportunistic Mrs Spires in *Esther Waters* (1948). Married Terence DEMARNEY.

OTHER BRITISH FILMS: *Almost a Honeymoon* (1938), *English Without Tears* (1944), *Dual Alibi, While the Sun Shines* (1947).

Meckler, Nancy (*b* Long Island, NY). Director. Made an auspicious debut with *Sister My Sister* (1994), based on a true-life crime, and followed this with *Alive and Kicking* (1996),

about a dancer confronting the threat of AIDS. Married to David AUKIN.

Medak, Peter (*b* Budapest, 1937). Director. Having fled Hungary before the Russian onslaught in 1956, Medak found work in Britain as assistant/2nd unit director on several films, before making three interesting features in a row: *Negatives* (1968), a moody drama of a difficult relationship; *A Day in the Death of Joe Egg* (1970), a painful and funny version of Peter NICHOLS's play about a couple coping with a spastic child; and *The Ruling Class* (1971), a wild anarchic comedy of a lord who believes he is Christ and later Jack the Ripper. Directors have to live and the films he made over the next 20 years, mostly in the US and mostly for TV, are more or less devoid of interest; then, at the start of the 90s and back in Britain, he made *The Krays* (1990), an unsanitised BIOPIC of the East End twin gangsters, and the very moving *'Let Him Have It'* (1991), based on a true miscarriage of justice and disgracefully little seen. At best Medak's is a tough, sharp talent of which British cinema should make more use.

OTHER BRITISH FILMS INCLUDE: (ass d/2ud) *Captain Clegg* (1962), *Funeral in Berlin* (1966), *Fathom* (1967); (d) *Sporting Chance* (1976, co-d), *The Odd Job* (1978).

Medford, Paul J. (*b* London, 1967). Actor. Came to viewers' attention in *EastEnders* (1985–87) as the teenage son of Albert Square's black family, but though lively and personable never had a comparable opportunity again. In cinema, he had only small roles in obscure films (*Black Joy*, 1977; *Yesterday's Hero*, 1979) and children's SHORT FILMS (*A Horse Called Jester*, 1979; *4D Special Agents*, 1981).

MEDIA Programme Since 1991, the European Union has operated a series of programmes under the general rubric of MEDIA (derived from *Mésures pour Encourager le Développement des Industries Audiovisuelles*) intended to promote greater cross-border cooperation in film and television, and to strengthen the competitiveness of the European audiovisual industries. While MEDIA (1991–95) originally had 19 schemes addressing such issues as script development, video publishing, dubbing and subtitling and documentary, MEDIA II (1996–2000) concentrated these into the main themes of development, DISTRIBUTION and TRAINING, with additional support for cinemas regularly showing European films. MEDIA PLUS began in 2001 along similar lines, with the bulk of some 400 million euros devoted to distribution aid and the continuing aim of helping European cinema cross national frontiers and achieve larger market share in its own territories. Ian Christie.

Medina, Patricia (*b* Liverpool, 1921). Actress. Dark-haired star of a few British films of the late 30s and early 40s, with real sex appeal and style, she went to Hollywood with then-husband Richard GREENE (1941–52) and played slinky sirens in about 30 mindless adventures, usually in colour, which undoubtedly became her, but rarely filmed again in Britain. She is very attractive decoration in several WAR FILMS, but her best British film is probably the charming comedy, *Don't Take It to Heart* (1944), co-starring Greene. Married (2, 1960–94, his death) Joseph COTTEN.

OTHER BRITISH FILMS INCLUDE: *Dinner at the Ritz* (1937), *The Day Will Dawn* (1942), *They Met in the Dark* (1943), *Hotel Reserve* (1944), *Waltz Time* (1945), *The Black Knight* (1954), *The Battle of the V-1* (1958).

Medwin, Michael (*b* London, 1923). Actor, producer. Chirpy character actor who made many films post-WW2, starting with

The Root of All Evil (1947), though *Piccadilly Incident* (1946), made after, was released before it. Of cheerful countenance, he played many cockneys as well as toffs, was in fact one of the busiest all-purpose character men in the 40s and 50s and had the luck to be taken up by Alexander KORDA and Herbert WILCOX, who both gave him plenty of opportunities. Probably his best chance came with the title role in Guy HAMILTON's undervalued drama of post-war malaise, *The Intruder* (1953), in which he showed a range of response wider than he was usually allowed. He had a very successful TV career, as Corporal Springer in *The Army Game* (1957–61), and another careeer as film producer, joining forces with Albert FINNEY to form Memorial Films which produced *Charlie Bubbles* (1967), *If . . .* (1968) and others. Also had stage experience from 1940 and cites playing the lead in *Alfie* (1963–64) as his acting highlight.

OTHER BRITISH FILMS INCLUDE: (a, unless noted) *An Ideal Husband, The Courtneys of Curzon Street* (1947), *Night Beat, Trottie True* (1948), *The Queen of Spades, Boys in Brown* (1949), *Curtain Up* (1952), *The Oracle, Genevieve, Bang! You're Dead* (1953), *The Teckman Mystery* (1954), *Above Us the Waves* (1955), *Charley Moon* (1956), *Carry On Nurse* (1958), *Crooks Anonymous* (1962), *Night Must Fall* (1964), *Spring and Port Wine* (1969, p), *Scrooge* (1970, + co-sc), *O Lucky Man!* (1973, + co-p), *Britannia Hospital* (1982), *Never Say Never Again* (1983, UK/US), *Staggered* (1994), *Fanny and Elvis* (1999).

Meerson, Lazare (*b* Warsaw, 1897 – *d* London, 1938). Production designer. Studied architecture and painting in Russia, emigrating to Western Europe after the 1917 Revolution. In France from 1924, working for such directors as René Clair and Jacques Feyder, for both of whom he subsequently worked in England when sought out by Alexander KORDA. His designs were characterised by a mix of realistic and impressionistic effects. British films included the stirring romantic action drama, Feyder's *Knight Without Armour* (1937), set in 1917 Russia; the drama of rural politics, *South Riding* (1938); and the TECHNICOLOR romantic comedy, *The Divorce of Lady X* (1938); but his most famous work was probably Feyder's *La kermesse héroïque* (1935, Fr). Died young from meningitis just as he was planning to return to Paris.

OTHER BRITISH FILMS: *As You Like It* (1936), *Fire Over England, The Return of the Scarlet Pimpernel* (1937), *Break the News, The Citadel* (1938).

BIBLIOG: Catherine A. Surowiec, *Accent on Design: Four European Art Directors*, 1992.

Megahy, Francis (*b* Manchester, 1937). Director, screenwriter. With many years of TV production behind him, Megahy made a few little-seen films. Probably best known for his spoof DOCUMENTARY, *The Disappearance of Kevin Johnson* (1995, UK/US).

OTHER BRITISH FILMS INCLUDE: (d, unless noted) *Just One More Time* (1962, + sc), *Les parapluies de Belsize* (1968, story), *One Take Two* (1978), *Real Life* (1983, + sc), *Taffin* (1987).

Meheux, Phil (*b* Sidcup, 1941). Cinematographer. Trained as assistant cameraman with BBC Television (1964–65), then became a DOCUMENTARY cameraman in the 70s, especially for the series *Man Alive*. Made his name as features cinematographer on the gangster thriller, *The Long Good Friday* (1979), and has worked steadily since in British and international films, including, *GoldenEye* (1995, UK/US), directed by Martin CAMPBELL, with whom he has worked several times.

OTHER BRITISH FILMS INCLUDE: *Sweet Virgin* (1974, co-p), *Black Joy* (1977), *Scum, The Music Machine* (1979), *Who Dares Wins* (1982), *The Honorary Consul* (1983), *The Fourth Protocol* (1987), *The Trial* (1992), *Entrapment* (1999, UK/Ger/US).

Melachrino, George (*b* London, 1909 – *d* London, 1965). Composer, conductor. Dance band leader, trained to play virtually every musical instrument and musical director of Army Broadcasting during WW2, Melachrino entered films as composer and music director of *Appointment with Crime* (1946). He composed music for a dozen or so varied GENRE films in the post-war years until his untimely death (by an accident in his home), including the MELODRAMA, *The Shop at Sly Corner* and the tragic romance, *Woman to Woman* (1946).

OTHER BRITISH FILMS INCLUDE: (comp, unless noted) *Things Happen at Night* (+ m sup), *No Orchids for Miss Blandish* (1948), *Silent Dust* (m d), *Now Barabbas Was a Robber* (1949), *Eight O'Clock Walk* (1954), *The Gamma People* (1954), *Odongo* (1956).

Melandrinos, Andrea (aka Andreas Malandrinos) (*b* Greece, 1888 – *d* Surrey, 1970). Actor. Another wildly prolific 'foreigner' in the heyday for CHARACTER PLAYERS in British cinema, from the 30s through the 60s. A former MUSIC HALL comedian, fluent in six languages, he played dozens of shifty French, Italian, Spanish and, occasionally, Greek waiters (*The Sky's the Limit*, 1936; *The Teckman Mystery*, 1954), customs officials (*Her Favourite Husband*, 1950, UK/It; *The Lavender Hill Mob*, 1951), policemen, and even a gondolier (*Room for Two*, 1940); sometimes sinister, usually voluble.

OTHER BRITISH FILMS INCLUDE: *Raise the Roof* (1930), *The Lodger* (1932), *The Broken Melody* (1934), *Midshipman Easy* (1935), *Secret Agent* (1936), *Non-Stop New York* (1937), *Crook's Tour* (1940), *Flying Fortress* (1942), *Champagne Charlie* (1944), *Sleeping Car to Trieste* (1948), *The Spider and the Fly* (1949), *The Captain's Paradise* (1953), *Orders to Kill* (1958), *Help!* (1965), *The Mummy's Shroud* (1966), *Hell Boats* (1969), many more.

Melbourne-Cooper, Arthur (*b* St Albans, 1874 – *d* Cotton, Cambridgeshire, 1961). Pioneer. British film pioneer whose work is subject to dispute as to his films, their years of production and some of the claims of his family and supporters. It seems that photographer Melbourne-Cooper joined Birt ACRES as his assistant in 1892, working with him filming some of the first ACTUALITIES. In 1901, he established the Alpha Cinematograph Company in St Albans, and among his early films are *McNab's Visit to London* (1905, in which he played the title role), *The Motor Pirate* (1906), and *Matches Made in England* (1910). A pioneer of ANIMATION, he made *Animated Matches* (1908) for Bryant and May. In 1908, he opened the first custom-built cinema in the UK, the Alpha Picture Palace in St Albans. From 1925 to 1940, he produced animated ADVERTISING FILMS in Blackpool.

OTHER BRITISH FILMS INCLUDE: (d, short films) *The Village Blacksmith* (1898), *Dolly's Toys* (1901), *The Enchanted Toymaker* (1904), *The Fairy Godfather* (1906), *Dreams of Toyland* (1908), *Tales of the Ark* (1909). AS.

Melford, Austin (*b* Alverstoke, 1884 – *d* London, 1971). Screenwriter. Stage actor (London debut 1904) and playwright who, as screenwriter, almost invariably wrote in collaboration, and is now probably best remembered as one of the regular writers on George FORMBY's films before and during his EALING period. Also wrote several for Tommy TRINDER at Ealing, including *Champagne Charlie* (1944), with his frequent Ealing collaborators, John DIGHTON and Angus MACPHAIL. In the 30s he was involved with several Jack HULBERT comedies, including the droll *Jack of All Trades* (1936, co-sc) and he also co-directed (with Graham CUTTS) as well as wrote the cheerful musical comedy, *Car of Dreams* (1935). Brother of Jack MELFORD.

OTHER BRITISH FILMS: (co-sc, unless noted) *A Warm Corner* (1930, a), *Night of the Garter* (+ a), *Happy, My Song for You, Jack Ahoy!* (1934), *Seven Sinners, It's Love Again* (1936, add. dial), *The Mill on the Floss* (1937), *Thank Evans, I See Ice!* (co-dial) (1938), *A Gentleman's Gentleman* (1939), *Let George Do It!* (1940), *Turned Out Nice Again* (sc), *Ships with Wings* (1941), *When We Are Married* (co-adptn), *We'll Smile Again* (1942), *Don Chicago* (1945, sc).

Melford, Jack (*b* London, 1899 – *d* Poole, 1972). Actor. On stage age 12, in London from 1917, and films since 1931. Tall, commanding, modestly popular lead and second lead in 20 films of the 30s, including *Radio Lover* (1936), comedy co-directed by his older brother, Austin MELFORD. Had a guest singing role in *Theatre Royal* (1943), but from the 40s on was most often cast as doctors, police inspectors and other professionals, turning up as a Bishop in his last film, *Lust for a Vampire* (1970). Father of Jill MELFORD.

OTHER BRITISH FILMS INCLUDE: *The Sport of Kings* (1931), *Birds of a Feather* (1935), *Jump for Glory* (1937), *Spare a Copper* (1940), *The Rake's Progress* (1945), *The Laughing Lady* (1946), *The October Man* (1947), *My Brother Jonathan, Counterblast* (1948), *Background* (1953), *The Ladykillers* (1955), *Compelled* (1960), *A Shot in the Dark* (1964).

Melford, Jill (*b* London, 1934). Actress. Daughter of Jack MELFORD, a tall, attractive redhead, in secondary roles in 50s and 60s films, such as *Out of the Clouds* (1955) and as the young companion to Doris [Nolan] Knox in *The Servant* (1963). Trained at the Ballet Arts School, New York, on London stage in 1953 and thereafter sporadically, playing Dinsdale LANDON's love interest in *Auntie Mame* (1958–59). Still on TV in the 90s (e.g. *Taggart*, 1993). Married and divorced from John STANDING.

OTHER BRITISH FILMS INCLUDE: *Will Any Gentleman . . . ?* (1953), *The Constant Husband* (1954), *Seven Waves Away* (1956), *A Stitch in Time* (1963), *Bunny Lake Is Missing* (1965), *The Bitch* (1979), *Edge of Sanity* (1988, UK/Hung).

Melia, Joe (*b* London, 1935). Actor. Character player, often in comic roles, in films since 1959 (*Too Many Crooks, Follow a Star*), praised for his playing of the wisecracking, lonely bachelor in *Four in the Morning* (1965) and remembered as the photographer in *Oh! What a Lovely War* (1969). Also with the RSC in the early 80s and in many popular TV programmes, including *The Persuaders!*, and plays (*The School for Scandal*, 1975).

OTHER BRITISH FILMS INCLUDE: *The Intelligence Men* (1965), *Modesty Blaise* (1966), *Antony and Cleopatra* (1972), *Sweeney!* (1976), *The Odd Job* (1978), *Privates on Parade* (1982), *The Sign of Four* (1983).

Mellor, Kay (*b* Leeds, *c* 1953). Screenwriter, director. Respected, BAA-nominated writer of such TV series as *Band of Gold* (1995) and *Playing the Field* (1998), Mellor turned – with disappointing results – to big-screen directing on *Fanny and Elvis* (1999), in which her daughter **Gaynor Faye** (*b* Leeds, 1971) had a prominent role. Won her reputation with strong, regionally set dramas focussing on women's experience, and this was also true of her screenplay for *Girls' Night* (1998, UK/US).

Melly, Andrée (*b* Liverpool, 1932). Actress. Pretty brunette who made the most of a few leads and second leads in the late 50s/early 60s: she is Donald GRAY's unhappy child-wife in *The Secret Tent* (1956), the teacher-later-undead in *The Brides of Dracula* (1960), and Donald PLEASENCE's sympathetic lover in the astute 'B' MOVIE, *The Big Day* (1960). Also busy on TV in the 50s. The sister of jazz singer and media critic **George Melly** (*b* Liverpool, 1926), who wrote the screenplays for *Smashing*

Time (1967) and *Take a Girl Like You* (1970). Married to Oscar QUITAK.

OTHER BRITISH FILMS INCLUDE: *So Little Time* (1952), *The Belles of St Trinian's* (1954), *Nowhere to Go* (1958), *Beyond the Curtain* (1960), *The Horror of It All* (1964).

melodrama Strictly speaking, a 'play with music', but more commonly a popular drama of extreme emotions and situations which reached its climax in the late 19th century, boosted by the Victorian theatre's growing appetite for lavish spectacle. By the 40s, film melodrama had effectively been redefined as romance, often in period setting, and assumed to cater for an undemanding female audience. Throughout cinema history, 'melodramatic' has been a term of critical reproach – contrasted with 'realistic' – although it could be argued that most of British film drama, apart from a few episodes of self-conscious 'REALISM', should be classed as melodrama.

Early film-makers naturally borrowed from the many forms of melodrama, as in R.W. PAUL's *Buy Your Own Cherries* (1904), adapted from a popular Temperance subject already familiar as a lantern-slide narrative, or the rival versions of *The Life of Charles Peace* (1905), based on the exploits of the notorious criminal hanged in 1879. In 1913, faced with intense competition from spectacular Italian and American imports, British producers revived the melodrama repertoire, with new versions of *East Lynne*, of Henry Irving's celebrated *The Bells* and other warhorses such as *Maria Marten, The Lights of London* and *The World, The Flesh and the Devil*. Patriotic melodrama emerged during WW1, followed by attempts at modernised melodrama in the 20s, as British production struggled to remain viable, exemplified by the series of films which confirmed Ivor NOVELLO's star status, from *The Man Without Desire* (1923) to *The Rat* (1925) and *The Lodger* (1926), all variations on basic melodrama motifs.

The 30s, with a new emphasis on 'quality' and the challenge of SOUND, might have been expected to toll the death-knell of melodrama. However most of the standards were remade and the conventions of stage melodrama were knowingly observed in a series of popular vehicles starring the actor-manager Tod SLAUGHTER, whose *The Face at the Window* (1939) drew praise from Graham GREENE for its affirmation of a 'morality which has a tradition of a thousand years behind it'. If WW2 induced a wave of filmic realism, this was soon complemented by GAINSBOROUGH's run of voluptuous COSTUME ROMANCES, epitomised by *The Wicked Lady* (1945). Ambitious film-makers were not immune to this emotional imperative, which produced the sublimated surburban melodrama of LEAN's and COWARD's *Brief Encounter* (1945) as well as the exoticism of POWELL AND PRESSBURGER's Oscar-winning *Black Narcissus* (1947), while the latters' *The Red Shoes* (1948) and *The Tales of Hoffmann* (1951) could also be seen as a cultural return to the roots of melodrama in MUSIC and DANCE.

British cinema's melodramatic undercurrent erupted again in the late 50s with HAMMER's cycle of classic HORROR REMAKES – variations on Frankenstein, Dracula, Jekyll and Hyde, *The Mummy* – which achieved popular success and critical opprobrium in equal measure. Like Gainsborough, Hammer's range of subjects was not confined to the Gothic or the Victorian, but its ventures into contemporary melodrama, such as Seth HOLT's *Taste of Fear* (1961), provoked critical unease amid the 60s vogue for realism. (Likewise Hammer's 'Quatermass' SERIES has not usually been seen as melodrama, although scientific FANTASY had constituted an important strand in melodrama since the stage success of *A Message from Mars* in 1899, filmed in 1913.)

Since the 70s, a major re-evaluation of melodrama has been under way, shedding new light on the influence of stage practice on early cinema, revealing the variety of forms and traditions within the genre, and crucially, arguing against its critical dismissal. While this has placed Hollywood melodrama high on the film studies agenda, it has so far made only limited progress in changing attitudes to British cinema beyond the circumscribed GENRES of Gainsborough and Hammer. Yet the insights of melodrama scholarship, with its emphasis on self-parody, 'dream worlds' (Booth, 1965) and the equivalence of moral opposites, are equally applicable to modern gangster fantasies, ranging from *Performance* (1970) to *Lock, Stock and Two Smoking Barrels* (1998).

BIBLIOG: Michael Booth, *English Melodrama*, 1965; Sue Aspinall and Robert Murphy (eds), *Gainsborough Melodrama*, 1983; Jeffrey Richards, 'Tod Slaughter and the Cinema of Excess', in Richards (ed), *The Unknown Thirties*, 1998. Ian Christie.

Melville, Alan (*b* Berwick-on-Tweed, 1910 – *d* Brighton, 1983). Actor. Pre-war producer and scriptwriter with the BBC; after RAF service (1941–46) he became a sketch- and lyrics-writer for stage revues and the author of popular plays, of which *Castle in the Air* (1950) and *Simon and Laura* (1954) were successfully filmed in 1952 (+ co-sc) and 1955 respectively. Also had a hand in the dialogue for *Derby Day* (1952) and *All for Mary* (1955), and wrote the screenplay for *As Long As They're Happy* (1955) – not that they reflect much credit on him. He was author of the TV series, *The Very Merry Widow* (1967–69) and contributed to several others.

BIBLIOG: Autobiography, *Merely Melville*, 1971.

Melvin, Murray (*b* London, 1932). Actor. Alumnus of Joan LITTLEWOOD's Theatre Royal, Stratford, tall, frail-looking Melvin came to West End theatregoers' attention as the gentle homosexual Geoffrey in *A Taste of Honey* (1957) and to film-goers' notice when he repeated the role in the 1961 film version. While continuing to act on stage, and often with the Theatre Royal, he also became a recognisable film CHARACTER PLAYER, working several times for Ken RUSSELL, and notably as the Rev Samuel Runt in KUBRICK's *Barry Lyndon* (1975). There is often an enjoyable touch of louche, camp malice about his roles, as in his feebly authoritarian teacher in '*Let Him Have It*' (1991).

OTHER BRITISH FILMS INCLUDE: *Suspect* (1960), *Sparrows Can't Sing* (1962), *Alfie* (1966), *The Devils, The Boy Friend* (1971), *Lisztomania* (1975), *Shout at the Devil, Joseph Andrews* (1976), *Nutcracker* (1982), *Comrades* (1986), *Testimony, Little Dorrit* (1987), *The Krays* (1990), *As You Like It* (1992), *The Emperor's New Clothes* (2002, UK/Ire/It).

Melvyn, Glenn (*b* Manchester). Author, actor. Appeared in several comedies of working-class life in the 50s, including *The Love Match* (1955, + add dial), based on his own play about train drivers who race their railway engine home to get to a football match in time.

OTHER BRITISH FILMS: *The Great Game* (1953), *Ramsbottom Rides Again* (1956, + add comedy scenes), *Over the Odds* (1961).

Mendes, Lothar (*b* Berlin, 1894 – *d* London,1974). Director. Since the 20s, had a directing career in Germany, then Hollywood (e.g. *The Four Feathers*, 1929) and Britain (1933–41). Mendes' most impressive British film was the lavishly produced historical drama *Jew Süss* (1934), starring Conrad VEIDT, which was a thinly veiled parable of the rise of German fascism

and anti-Semitism. Married briefly to actress Dorothy MACKAILL.

OTHER BRITISH FILMS: *The Man Who Could Work Miracles* (1936), *Moonlight Sonata* (1937). Tim Bergfelder.

Mendleson, Anthony (*b* London, 1915 – *d* London, 1996). Costume designer. Illustrious figure, twice AA-nominated (*Young Winston*, 1972, *The Incredible Sarah*, 1976, UK/US), and BAA-winner for *Oh! What a Lovely War* (1969) and for *Young Winston* and *Alice's Adventures in Wonderland* (1972). Mendleson established himself over a wide GENRE range and not just the period jobs which tend to attract awards; he handled epic and chamber work, SHAKESPEARE and DISNEY with the same imaginative proficiency. Was for many years designer and wardrobe supervisor at EALING, responsible alike for the Victorian elegance of *Kind Hearts and Coronets* and the post-war modern of *The Blue Lamp* (1949). Studied art in France and Italy pre-war, and served in WW2 (1940–45).

OTHER BRITISH FILMS INCLUDE: (wardrobe sup) *It Always Rains on Sunday* (1947), *Saraband for Dead Lovers* (1948), *Lease of Life* (1954); (cos des) *Passport to Pimlico* (1949), *Cage of Gold* (1950), *The Lavender Hill Mob*, *Secret People* (1951), *Mandy*, *The Cruel Sea* (1952), *The Titfield Thunderbolt*, *The 'Maggie'* (1953), *The Ladykillers* (1955), *Who Done It?* (1956), *Chase a Crooked Shadow* (1957), *The Bulldog Breed* (1960), *Billy Budd* (1962), *The Mind Benders* (1963), *Thunderball* (1965), *Jane Eyre* (1970), *Macbeth* (1971), *The Ghoul* (1975), *A Bridge Too Far* (1977), *Krull* (1983).

Menges, Chris (*b* Kingstone, Herefordshire, 1940). Cinematographer, director. Major figure of 80s and 90s British cinema who won Oscars for both *The Killing Fields* (1984, + BAA), and *The Mission* (1985, + BAAn), as well as BAAn for *Local Hero* (1983) and *Michael Collins* (1996, US). Entered films via DOCUMENTARY film-making in difficult territories, and worked as camera operator on *If . . .* (1968) and in 1967 began his association with the films of Ken LOACH, drawing on Menges' documentary experience. His contrasting images of severity and tenderness are crucial to the meaning of *Kes* (1969), the film that made his and Loach's names, and his black-and-white photography for *Looks and Smiles* (1981) finds beauty without sentimentality in its deprived urban setting. He has also directed several films latterly, most notably the powerful anti-apartheid melodrama, *A World Apart* (1987, UK/Zim), and the intelligent thriller, *The Lost Son* (1999, UK/Fr/US), but his highest distinction so far has been as cameraman.

OTHER BRITISH FILMS INCLUDE: *Poor Cow* (1967, cam op), *Loving Memory* (1970, short), *Black Beauty, Gumshoe* (1971), *Bloody Kids* (1979), *Babylon* (1980), *Angel* (1982, Ire), *Comfort and Joy* (1984), *Second Best* (1994, UK/US), *The Boxer* (1998, UK/Ire/US), *Pretty Dirty Things* (2002).

Mercer, David (*b* Wakefield, Yorks, 1928 – *d* Haifa, Israel, 1980). Playwright, screenwriter. Former teacher whose TV play and screenplay formed the basis of Karel REISZ's iconoclastic film, *Morgan: A Suitable Case for Treatment* (1966). His other film work includes the screenplays for Ken LOACH's *Family Life* (1971), LOSEY's *A Doll's House* (1973), and Alain Resnais' *Providence* (1977, Fr/Switz). An abrasive, socially committed talent, nurtured in theatre and 60s television.

OTHER BRITISH FILMS: *90 in the Shade* (1964, UK/Czech), *The Sailor from Gibraltar* (1967, co-sc unc).

Merchant, Ismail *see* **Merchant Ivory Productions**

Merchant Ivory Productions James IVORY, an American director (*b* Berkeley, US, 1928), and Ismail MERCHANT, an

Indian producer (*b* Bombay, India, 1936), have made over 30 films together, several of them with British connections, from *Shakespeare Wallah* (1965), about a touring troupe of English actors in India, to *The Remains of the Day* (1993), about the relationship between a butler and a housekeeper who worked at an English country house in the 1930s. They have specialised in producing extremely tasteful quality films for the ART-HOUSE end of the market, often collaborating with the novelist/scriptwriter Ruth Prawer JHABVALA. Many of their films have been literary ADAPTATIONS, including *Quartet* (1981, UK/Fr), from a novel by Jean Rhys, *The Bostonians* (1984, UK/US) and *The Golden Bowl* (2000, UK/Fr/US), from Henry JAMES, and *The Remains of the Day*, from Kazuo Ishiguro. From the point of view of British cinema, their most important films are those adapted from E.M. FORSTER's novels, *A Room With a View* (1985), *Maurice* (1987) and *Howards End* (1992), which all impeccably recreated the England of the Edwardian middle and upper classes. *Room* and *Howards End* were substantial international successes, ensuring the on-going interest of the Hollywood majors in their specialised fare. They were also extremely influential films, both because they came to define English 'HERITAGE' CINEMA and because they convinced the major distributors that it was worth dealing with niche products that had a chance of becoming crossover mainstream successes. Critical opinion about Merchant Ivory's films has been mixed. For many, they are wonderfully refined, boast superb performances, and display production values that far supersede what might be expected from such modestly budgeted films. But others dismiss them as overly nostalgic, middlebrow and reverential, the Laura Ashley of contemporary cinema.

OTHER BRITISH FILMS: *Autobiography of a Princess* (1975), *Hullabaloo over Georgie and Bonnie's Pictures* (1978, UK/Ind), *The Europeans* (1979), *Heat and Dust* (1982), *Jefferson in Paris* (1995). Andrew Higson.

Merchant, Vivien (*b* Manchester, 1929 – *d* London, 1982). Actress. RN: Ada Thomson. Striking, idiosyncratic actress, once married to Harold PINTER, whose cryptic locutions found their perfect expression in Merchant's delivery, as in the first production of his play, *Old Times* (1971). The films she made in her sadly short life (she committed suicide) were few but choice: she is very compelling as Dirk BOGARDE's watchful wife in LOSEY's *Accident* (1967), amusing as Alec McCOWEN's distressingly gourmet-cook wife in HITCHCOCK's *Frenzy* (1972), and enigmatic (what else?) as Ruth in the film version of Pinter's *Homecoming* (1973, UK/US). Much notable theatre and TV.

OTHER BRITISH FILMS INCLUDE: *The Way Ahead* (1944, as child), *Alfie* (1966), *Alfred the Great* (1969), *The Offence* (1972), *Under Milk Wood* (1971), *The Maids* (1974, UK/Can).

Merivale, John (*b* Toronto, 1917 – *d* London, 1990). Actor. Tall, handsome stage actor who scored a hit in *The Reluctant Debutante* (1955) but made only occasional films, dying bravely in *A Night to Remember* (1958) and playing the elusive eponym in *The List of Adrian Messenger* (1963, UK/US). Companion to Vivien LEIGH in her last years, he married (1) US actress Jan Sterling (1941–48) and (2) Dinah SHERIDAN. Son of actor Philip Merivale.

OTHER BRITISH FILMS: *The Battle of the River Plate* (1956), *Circus of Horrors* (1960), *House of Mystery* (1961), *Arabesque* (1966, UK/US).

Merrall, Mary (*b* Liverpool, 1890 – *d* London, 1973). Actress. RN: Lloyd. One was so accustomed to seeing Merrall, on stage from 1907 well into her 80s, as dithery-genteel or put-upon types, that it is genuinely shocking to confront her sly harridan, Aggie, with a line in sexual innuendo, in *They Made Me a Fugitive* (1947). Perhaps taken with the pleasures of malice, she was a mischievous old dowager in *The Late Edwina Black* (1951) and a nasty mother-in-law in *Meet Me Tonight* (1952). This is not to denigrate her moving work as the defeated mother in *Love on the Dole* (1941), or the gallant old trouper of *Encore* (1951), or any other of her three dozen roles: she was an immaculate character actress whom film was too inclined to type-cast. Married (2) **Ion Swinley** (*b* 1892 – *d* 1937), who appeared in several films of the 20s and 30s, including *Bleak House* (1920) and *The Barton Mystery* (1932); (3) Franklin DYALL.

OTHER BRITISH FILMS INCLUDE: *Fatal Fingers* (1916), *Duke's Son* (1920), *Men of Steel* (1932), *Squadron Leader X* (1942), *Pink String and Sealing Wax, Dead of Night* (1945), *Nicholas Nickleby* (1947), *The Three Weird Sisters* (1948), *Badger's Green* (1949), *Trio* (1950), *The Pickwick Papers* (1952), *The Weak and the Wicked* (1953), *It's Great to Be Young!* (1956), *Campbell's Kingdom* (1957), *Spare the Rod* (1961), *Bitter Harvest* (1963), *Futtocks End* (1969).

Merrison, Clive (*b* Hertfordshire, 1945). Actor. Character player of film and TV (e.g. *A Very British Coup*, 1988) from the mid 70s, remembered as the London businessman (*ergo* unsympathetic) unhelpful to the process of *Saving Grace* (2000). Some international films, including *The English Patient* (1996).

OTHER BRITISH FILMS INCLUDE: *Henry VIII and His Six Wives* (1972), *Riddles of the Sphinx* (1977), *An Awfully Big Adventure* (1995), *Photographing Fairies* (1997), *Up at the Villa* (UK/US), *Pandaemonium* (2001).

Merritt, George (*b* London, 1890 – *d* London, 1977). Actor. On stage from 1910, he was studying theatre in Germany when WW1 broke out and was interned for four years; toured with Fred Terry's company on return, and thereafter acted in over 80 plays, as well as adapting several European plays for the English stage. In films from 1930, usually as dependable types, with many police inspectors (e.g. *No Escape*, 1934; *The Four Just Men*, 1939), as well as lower-ranking cops and the odd landlord (*Don't Take it to Heart*, 1944; *Root of All Evil*, 1947). Short and stocky, he was one of those presences one could count on – for effortless conviction – in every kind of British film in the heyday of the STUDIOS.

OTHER BRITISH FILMS INCLUDE: *The W Plan* (1930), *The Lodger* (1932), *I Was a Spy, The Ghost Camera* (1933), *Jew Süss* (1934), *Brown on Resolution* (1935), *Rembrandt* (1936), *Young and Innocent, The Return of the Scarlet Pimpernel* (1937), *They Drive By Night, Q Planes* (1939), *The Proud Valley, Gasbags* (1940), *Hatter's Castle* (1941), *The Day Will Dawn* (1942), *Escape to Danger* (1943), *A Canterbury Tale, Waterloo Road* (1944), *I'll Be Your Sweetheart* (1945), *Quiet Weekend* (1946), *Good-Time Girl* (1947), *Quartet* (1948), *Mr Drake's Duck* (1950), *The Green Scarf* (1954), *Quatermass 2* (1957), *Dracula* (1958), *What Every Woman Wants* (1962), *Cromwell* (1970), *I, Monster* (1971).

Merrow, Jane (*b* Hemel Hempstead, 1941). Actress. The 60s was probably the wrong decade for the delicately lovely Merrow in British films, but she made the most of her best opportunity: as Princess Alais in *The Lion in Winter* (1968), in which she held her own in ferocious company. Had female lead in the US/Aust period melodrama, *Adam's Woman* (1970). TV included episodes of *Hadleigh* and *Randall and Hopkirk* (1969).

OTHER BRITISH FILMS: *Don't Bother to Knock* (1961), *The Wild and the Willing* (1962), *Morgan: A Suitable Case for Treatment* (1966), *Assignment K* (1967), *Hands of the Ripper* (1971).

Merson, Billy (*b* Nottingham, 1881 – *d* London, 1947). Actor. RN: William Henry Thompson. Merson was a major star of

British MUSIC HALL, composer and singer of 'The Spaniard Who Blighted My Life', who appeared in a dozen or so films between 1915 and 1938, some of the early ones of which he wrote or were based on his sketches.

BRITISH FILMS INCLUDE: (shorts) *Billy's Spanish Love Spasm* (1915), *The Tale of a Shirt*, *The Perils of Pork Pie* (1916), *Billy the Truthful* (1917); (features) *Comets* (1930), *Bill and Coo* (1931), *Chips* (1938).

BIBLIOG: Autobiography, *Fixing the Stoof Oop*, 1926. AS.

Merton Park Studios Officially established as a company in 1937, Merton Park Studios had been used as a sound-recording and film studio producing mainly features since 1931. The STRAND FILM UNIT moved there in 1938 and Merton Park began to gain a reputation as a service studio providing sound stages, dubbing theatres, negative-cutting rooms, editing suites and a full crew of carpenters, electricians and painters for instructional, promotional and sponsored films. During the war many independent DOCUMENTARY units operated out of the studio producing government PROPAGANDA and in 1945 five of these units pooled their personnel and equipment to form the Film Producers Guild. Throughout the 40s and 50s the studio also began producing features and the Edgar LUSTGARTEN crime SHORTS. By the end of the 50s and into the mid 60s, the output of the studio was predominantly feature production and increasingly television. In 1967 the last feature was made, the thriller *Payment in Kind* (1967) and the studio closed down. Sarah Easen.

Mervyn, William (*b* Nairobi, 1912 – *d* London, 1976). Actor. RN: Pickwoad. Bald, solidly built purveyor of upper-class dignity, usually benign like the old gentleman who helps *The Railway Children* (1971) or with calm irony like the railway traveller who memorably quells some obstreperous children in one of TV's 'Saki' stories in 1966. Developed a popular persona in TV's *All Gas and Gaiters* (1967, 1969–71) as the bishop; on stage from 1934 and in films from 1947, he can be spotted as Chief Inspector Hammond in *The Blue Lamp* (1949), and appeared in several 'CARRY ON' items, usually to have his dignity punctured.

OTHER BRITISH FILMS INCLUDE: *The Loves of Joanna Godden* (1947), *That Dangerous Age* (1949), *The Long Arm* (1956), *The Battle of the Sexes* (1959), *Circus of Horrors* (1960), *Tamahine* (1962), *The Jokers* (1966), *Hot Millions* (1968), *Carry On Henry*, *The Ruling Class* (1971).

Merwin, Bannister (*b* ? – *d* London, 1922). Screenwriter. Bald, bespectacled Merwin was one of the few screenwriters of the 1910s with any reputation. Originally a magazine editor and writer, he wrote prolifically for the Edison Company from 1908 to 1913, was responsible for the first SERIAL, *What Happened to Mary?* (1912). Joined the LONDON FILM COMPANY in November 1913, organised its editorial department, and wrote a number of scripts, including *Duty*, *The Black Spot*, *The Fringe of War* (1914), and *Liberty Hall* (1915). Wife, Anne, also a writer at Edison, came to London with him.

OTHER BRITISH FILMS INCLUDE: (sc, unless noted) *Altar Chains* (1917, + d), *A Turf Conspiracy* (1918), *Her Heritage* (1919, + d), *London Pride*, *Laddie* (1920, + d), *Love at the Wheel* (1921). AS.

Merzbach, Paul (*b* Vienna, 1888 – *d* London, 1942). Director, screenwriter. RN: Peter Mersbach. In the 20s, he acquired numerous script and directing credits in Germany and Sweden, where he collaborated with Victor Sjöström. Merzbach's British films were mostly continental comedies and musicals. Screenwriter for, among others, Paul STEIN (*Mimi*, 1935, co-sc; *Gentleman Of Venture*, 1940, co-sc) and Lance COMFORT

(*Hatter's Castle*, 1941, co-sc).

OTHER BRITISH FILMS: (d, co-sc, unless noted) *Love At Second Sight* (1934), *Invitation To The Waltz* (1935), *A Star Fell From Heaven* (1936), *Hail And Farewell* (1936, co-sc). Tim Bergfelder.

Messel, Oliver (*b* London, 1904 – *d* Bridgetown, Barbados, 1978). Production designer, costume designer. Eton-educated and Slade-trained, Messel was a celebrated designer for stage, opera and ballet, as well as leaving his mark on ten films, most notably on the costumes for *The Queen of Spades* (1948). Think of Edith EVANS cocooned in fur and fabrics; or in the ponderous *Caesar and Cleopatra* (1945) the mixture of the kittenish and the regal in the dressing of Vivien LEIGH; and earlier still the flawless beauty of Merle OBERON flawlessly bedecked in *The Scarlet Pimpernel* (1935). Made CBE in 1958, his art was only tangentially at the service of the screen.

OTHER BRITISH FILMS INCLUDE: (cos, unless noted) *The Private Life of Don Juan* (1934), *The Thief of Baghdad* (1940), *Carnival* (1946), *Suddenly, Last Summer* (1959, + des).

Metzner, Ernö (*b* Szabadka, Hungary, 1892 – *d* Hollywood, 1953). Production designer. Formerly a collaborator of G.W. Pabst in Germany (e.g. *Diary Of A Lost Girl*, 1929), Metzner's British film designs in the 30s stylishly displayed both austere modernism (e.g. *The Tunnel*, 1935) and eclectic playfulness, as in the Orientalist sets of *Chu-Chin-Chow* (1934). In Hollywood, Metzner later designed René Clair's *It Happened Tomorrow* (1944).

OTHER BRITISH FILMS: *Princess Charming* (1934), *Seven Sinners* (1936), *The Robber Symphony*, *Strangers On Honeymoon* (1936), *Take My Tip* (1937). Tim Bergfelder.

Metzstein, Saul (*b* Glasgow, 1970). Director. After studying architecture and a brief spell at a US film school, Metzstein acted as production runner on *Shallow Grave* (1994) and *Trainspotting* (1996), before making his SHORT FILMS (e.g. *Santa/Claws*, 1997, + co-sc) and DOCUMENTARIES (e.g. *The Name of This Film is Dogme95*, 2000, for CHANNEL 4). His feature debut was the engaging Glasgow-filmed *Late Night Shopping* (2001), a character-driven piece about a bunch of shift-worker friends.

Meyer, H. Ernst (*b* Berlin, 1905). Composer, sound effects. In England from 1933, after training in Germany, he entered films in 1937, working with CAVALCANTI and the GPO FILM UNIT. His film scores were almost entirely for DOCUMENTARIES made for the GPO and the REALIST FILM UNIT. Committed to REALISM, he actually lived with the fishing community involved in scoring *North Sea* (1938).

OTHER BRITISH FILMS INCLUDE: (shorts, m, unless noted) *Roadways* (1937), *The Londoners* (1939), *Lambeth Walk* (1939), *A Few Ounces a Day* (1941, sd), *Newspaper Train* (1942, sd), *Work Party* (1943), *Cameramen at War* (1944).

Meyers, Jonathan Rhys *see* **Rhys Meyers, Jonathan**

MGM–British The Hollywood company, Metro–Goldwyn –Mayer (MGM), in the late 30s sought to extend its empire by turning out films from MGM's DENHAM studio, using predominantly British acting talent, though topped up with such American stars as Robert TAYLOR (*A Yank at Oxford*, 1937) and Rosalind RUSSELL (*The Citadel*, 1938). Ben Goetz, Louis B Mayer's son-in-law's brother, was appointed studio manager and Michael BALCON was production chief for a couple of unhappy years. After the triumphant success of *Goodbye, Mr Chips* (1939), followed by *Busman's Honeymoon*

(1940), the venture came to an end. However, post-war production resumed with *Edward, My Son* (1949) and in the 50s there were the box-office hits, *Ivanhoe* (1952) and the first MGM CinemaScope film, *Knights of the Round Table* (1953), as well as more modest programme films, such as *The Hour of 13* and the suspenseful *Time Bomb* (1953), all using Hollywood stars and expertise, bolstered by British actors and technical skills. Until MGM closed its British studio in 1970 and amalgamated with EMI, it turned out several productions each year from BOREHAMWOOD, including such critical and/or commercial successes as *The Adventures of Quentin Durward, Bhowani Junction* (1955), *Lust for Life* (1956), several of EALING's last films, including *Dunkirk* (1958), Margaret RUTHERFORD's four 'Miss Marple' thrillers, starting with *Murder She Said* (1961), Anthony ASQUITH's all-star last gasps, *The VIPs* (1963) and *The Yellow Rolls-Royce* (1964), Stanley KUBRICK's *Lolita* (1961) and *2001: A Space Odyssey* (1968), and – almost the end – a musical remake of one of the earliest MGM–British successes, *Goodbye, Mr Chips* (1969).

See also **Hollywood studios in Britain.**

Michael, Ralph (*b* London, 1907 – *d* Brighton, 1994). Actor. RN: Ralph Champion Shotter. Tall, patrician-seeming stage actor from 1930 (Stratford, Old Vic and popular West End successes) who had a brief burst of substantial roles at EALING in the mid 40s, notably as Googie WITHERS's weakish husband murderously obsessed by a mirror in *Dead of Night* (1945). He continued to play in character roles for another 40 years – in, for instance, *A Night to Remember* (1958), as a gambling passenger, and in *Empire of the Sun* (1987, US) – as well as a good deal of TV, including *A Murder Is Announced* (1985). Married (1) Fay COMPTON and (2) Joyce HERON.

OTHER BRITISH FILMS INCLUDE: *False Evidence* (1937), *For Those in Peril, They Came to a City* (1944), *Johnny Frenchman* (1945), *Song for Tomorrow* (1948), *The Hasty Heart* (1949), *The Sound Barrier* (1952), *The Birthday Present* (1957), *Murder Most Foul* (1964), *The Count of Monte Cristo* (1974).

Michell, Keith (*b* Adelaide, 1928). Actor. A former art teacher, Michell was auditioned by Laurence OLIVIER's Old Vic company while it was touring Australia in 1948; given a place at the Old Vic School, he made his London debut with the Young Vic in 1950. He had the looks and presence for a film leading man but his film career, apart from reprising his 1970 Emmy-winning TV role, in *Henry VIII and His Six Wives* (1972), has been largely unmemorable, though there are flashes of interest in the besotted rake of *The Gypsy and the Gentleman* (1957). A fine Mark Antony in TV's *The Spread of the Eagle* (1963). Married Jeanette STERKE; their daughter **Helena Michell** (*b* 1963), has appeared in a few British films including *Moments* (1973) and *The Deceivers* (1988), with her father.

OTHER BRITISH FILMS INCLUDE: *True as a Turtle* (1956), *Dangerous Exile* (1957), *All Night Long* (1961), *Prudence and the Pill* (1968), *The Executioner* (1970).

Michell, Roger (*b* Pretoria, 1957). Director. After Cambridge, Michell spent two years at the Royal Court Theatre, then joined the RSC in 1985, scoring successes in classic and new plays, in London and New York. In 1990 he did the BBC Drama Directors' Course, the result of which was the BAA-nominated mini-series, *The Buddha of Suburbia* (1993), followed by the BAA-winning *Persuasion* (1995). The latter, made for TV but shown in cinemas too, was perhaps the most intelligent and tender of the Jane AUSTEN ADAPTATIONS rife at the time. He brought the right lightness, with touches of real feeling, to the

wildly profitable *Notting Hill* (1999, UK, US), and then went international with *Changing Lanes* (2001). Married to TV actress Kate Buffery.

OTHER BRITISH FILMS: *My Night with Reg* (1996), *Titanic Town* (1998, UK/Ire.).

Michie, John (*b* Burma). Actor. Slight, dark actor who has become well-known for his continuing role of D.I. Robbie Ross in TV's *Taggart* (1998–2000) and appearances in series such as *Dalziel and Pascoe* (1998). Michie had his most substantial film roles to date as the priest who loses his vocation in *Monk Dawson* (1997), and as the young Englishman who tells the story of George Adamson in *To Walk with Lions* (2000, UK/Can/Kenya).

OTHER BRITISH FILMS INCLUDE: *A Passage to India* (1984, unc), *Distant Voices, Still Lives* (1988, UK/Ger), *Being Considered* (2000), *Storm* (2001, short).

Middlemass, Frank (*b* Eaglescliffe, 1919). Actor. Former army major who came to acting late in life, becoming well-known as the last Dan Archer on *The Archers* and for his work in televison productions such as *Poldark* and *As Time Goes By*. Roles opposite Bette Davis in her first made-for-television movie, *Madame Sin* (1972), and in the US feature, *The Island* (1980), may have made him wary of motion picture work. Also noted for stage work, at the National and the Royal Court, among others.

BRITISH FILMS: *Otley* (1968), *Frankenstein Must Be Destroyed* (1969), *Say Hello to Yesterday* (1970), *Barry Lyndon* (1975), *Dreamchild* (1985, voice only). AS.

Middleton, Guy (*b* Hove, 1908 – *d* Moreton-in-Marsh, 1973). Actor. RN: Middleton-Powell. Indefatigably urbane and frequently caddish, the Harrow-educated Middleton, famous for his moustache and the sexually acquisitive leer beneath it, worked (though the word doesn't really suit him) on the Stock Exchange before turning to acting. Essentially a screen actor; one can't imagine such a bounder wanting to learn a long part and perform it night after night; but what fun he was doing the thing he did better than anyone else. It was hard to take his old-school-tie villainy seriously – more cad than crim – but you wouldn't readily buy a used car from him. At his best as Rex Harrison's chum in *The Rake's Progress* (1945) or the lubricious sportsmaster in *The Happiest Days of Your Life* (1950). Also much on the West End stage in characteristic roles.

OTHER BRITISH FILMS INCLUDE: *Jimmy Boy* (1935), *A Woman Alone* (1936), *Keep Fit* (1937), *Goodbye, Mr Chips, French Without Tears* (1939), *Dangerous Moonlight* (1941), *The Demi-Paradise* (1943), *English Without Tears, The Halfway House* (1944), *The Captive Heart* (1946), *A Man About the House* (1947), *No Place for Jennifer* (1949), *Laughter in Paradise, Young Wives' Tale* (1951), *Albert RN* (1953), *The Belles of St Trinian's* (1954), *Doctor at Large* (1957), *Passionate Summer* (1958), *Waltz of the Toreadors* (1962), *Oh! What a Lovely War* (1969), *The Rise and Rise of Michael Rimmer* (1970).

Middleton, Noelle (*b* Co. Sligo, Ireland, 1926). Actress. It is somehow not surprising that this pallidly pretty 50s lead and second lead studied domestic science before stage debut at Dublin's Gate Theatre. She seemed such a nice girl, compared with flashy Yvonne DE CARLO in *Happy Ever After* or neurotic Margaret LEIGHTON in *Carrington VC* (1954), or purposeful Katharine HEPBURN in *The Iron Petticoat* (1956).

OTHER BRITISH FILMS INCLUDE: *South of Algiers* (1952), *John and Julie, You Can't Escape* (1955), *The Vicious Circle* (1957), *A Question of Suspense* (1961).

Mikell, George (*b* Tawroggen, Lithuania, 1930). Actor. In Britain from 1956, like so many fellow European émigrés before him, Mikell played a good many Germans and foreigners of every kind, in WAR FILMS such as *The One That Got Away* (1957) and *Sea of Sand* (1958), was a checkpoint guard in *The Spy Who Came In from the Cold* (1965), and was still giving the Allies a bad time as late as *The Sea Wolves* (1980, UK/Switz/US).
OTHER BRITISH FILMS INCLUDE: *Operation Bullshine* (1959), *Circle of Deception* (1960), *The Guns of Navarone* (1961), *The Victors* (1963), *Operation Crossbow* (UK/It), *Where the Spies Are* (1965), *Zeppelin* (1971), *Young Winston* (1972), *Sweeney 2* (1978).

Mikhelson, André (*b* Moscow). Actor. Another protean foreign type in two dozen British films of the 50s and 60s, playing head waiters, croupiers and untrustworthy aliens, typically cast as the suavely dangerous Hamid, official of some geographically obscure embassy in *Diplomatic Corpse* (1958).
OTHER BRITISH FILMS: *The Gambler and the Lady* (1952), *Desperate Moment* (1953), *The Divided Heart* (1954), *I Am a Camera* (1955), *Anastasia* (1956), *Dangerous Exile* (1957), *Beyond the Curtain* (1960), *Children of the Damned* (1963).

Miles, Bernard (Lord Miles) (*b* Uxbridge, 1907 – *d* Knaresborough, 1991). Actor, director. Miles sits uneasily among the knights and lords of his profession, in that he was notably down-to-earth, identified neither with the classical theatrical repertoire nor with grandiose directorial projects; he was honoured primarily for building, and then running, the new Mermaid Theatre, which opened in Blackfriars in 1959. The success of this venture owed much to goodwill earned by the quirkily likeable persona he had created over the years across a wide range of media, cinema included. Two highlights in a long career of character roles are in David LEAN films: his Petty Officer Hardy in *In Which We Serve* (1942) and his definitive Joe Gargery in *Great Expectations* (1946). To both, he brings a direct sincerity, a rich regional diction, and the ability to convey pain beneath a stoical exterior. Though few of his roles have the same depth, these qualities were repeatedly and aptly used both by Michael POWELL (e.g. *One of Our Aircraft is Missing*, 1942) and by the BOULTING brothers, for instance in the key 1940 short *Dawn Guard*, where he articulates the vision of a better post-war world, and later in *Fame is the Spur* (1947) and *The Guinea Pig* (1948). His heavy in the remake of *The Man Who Knew Too Much* (1955, US) was an effective casting against type. Miles's two films as director are attractive fables of social harmony, the RURAL COMEDY *Tawny Pipit* (1944), and the factory-set *Chance of a Lifetime* (1950), which earned brief notoriety for its challenge to the conservative booking policies of the main circuits. It was typical of his modesty to give joint credit to his editors, Charles SAUNDERS and Alan OSBISTON respectively. He was married to actress Josephine WILSON.
OTHER BRITISH FILMS: *Channel Crossing* (1933), *The Love Test* (1935), *Everything Is Thunder, Crown v Stevens, Twelve Good Men, Midnight at Madame Tussauds* (1936), *The Citadel, The Challenge, 13 Men and a Gun* (UK/It) (1938), *The Rebel Son* (UK/Fr), *The Spy in Black, The Lion Has Wings* (1939), *Band Waggon, Pastor Hall, Contraband, Freedom Radio* (1940), *Quiet Wedding, The Common Touch, Home Guard* (short) (1941), *Thunder Rock* (co-sc), *This Was Paris, The Goose Steps Out* (co-idea), *The First of the Few, The Day Will Dawn, The Big Blockade* (1942), *The New Lot* (1943, short), *Two Fathers* (1944, short), *Carnival* (1946), *Nicholas Nickleby* (1947), *Back to Zero* (1950, short), *The Magic Box* (1951), *Never Let Me Go* (1953), *Moby Dick, Zarak, Tiger in the Smoke* (1956), *Fortune Is a Woman, Saint Joan* (UK/US), *The Smallest Show on Earth* (1957), *tom thumb, The Vision of William Blake* (doc, narr) (1958), *Sapphire* (1959), *Heavens Above!* (1963), *The Specialist* (1966), *Baby Love* (1967), *Run Wild, Run Free, Lock Up Your Daughters!* (orig musical play/book) (1969), *Dangerous Game* (1975, doc, comm), *Treasure Island – The Musical* (1982, + co-adptn). Charles Barr.

Miles, Christopher (*b* London, 1939). Director. Studied at IDHEC film school in Paris and began making short films in the early 60s, winning attention with his half-hour burlesque, *The Six-Sided Triangle* (1963, AAn/short film), made with the help of the BOULTING brothers. He made an intelligent ADAPTATION of D.H. LAWRENCE's novella, *The Virgin and the Gypsy* (1970) and pursued his interest in Lawrence with the BIOPIC covering his last six years, *The Priest of Love* (1980), starring Ian McKELLEN – and with a cameo from sister Sarah MILES. He stumbled badly with *The Clandestine Marriage* (1999), actually not as bad as some reviewers suggested but unlikely to reactivate a fitful career.
OTHER BRITISH FILMS INCLUDE: (d, unless noted) + sc), *Up Jumped a Swagman* (1965), *A Time for Loving* (1971), *The Maids* (1974, UK/Can, + co-sc), *That Lucky Touch* (1975), *Daley's Decathlon* (1982, doc, + p).

Miles, Sarah (*b* Ingatestone, 1941). Actress. RADA-trained and outrageous, Miles erupted into British films as the sexy student who, in *Term of Trial* (1962), brings scandal to teacher Laurence OLIVIER, her real-life hero and off-and-on lover for many years towards the end of his life. She was equally provocative in *The Servant* (1963), luring her then-boyfriend, James FOX, to the decadence his supine nature craves; is fetching in the conventional heroine role in *Those Magnificent Men . . .* (1965); retrieved her sensual 'NEW WAVE' image in Antonioni's *Blow-Up* (1966); was Oscar-nominated for the elephantine *Ryan's Daughter* (1970), battling wind, sea and script; and went to America and got mixed up in the reporting of the suicide of David Whiting during the filming of *The Man Who Loved Cat Dancing* (1973). Her career drive seems to have declined after this, but after a few more unremarkable films she suddenly appeared, newly authoritative, in two character roles: the lascivious Alice in *White Mischief* and the WW2 mum in *Hope and Glory* (1987). She seems now to prefer writing, has published three volumes of autobiography, and has intermittently returned to the stage, playing a vivid Mary Queen of Scots in *Vivat! Vivat Regina!* (1971), by Robert BOLT, whom she married twice (1967–76 and 1987 till his death, 1995) and who directed her in *Lady Caroline Lamb* (1972, UK/It/US). Sister of Christopher MILES.
OTHER BRITISH FILMS: *The Six-Sided Triangle* (1963, short), *I Was Happy Here* (1965), *The Hireling* (1973), *Great Expectations* (1975, as Estella), *The Sailor Who Fell from Grace with the Sea* (1976), *The Big Sleep* (1978), *Priest of Love* (1980, cameo), *Venom* (1981), *Ordeal by Innocence, Steaming* (1984), *The Silent Touch* (1992, UK/Den/Pol).
BIBLIOG: Autobiographies: *A Right Royal Bastard*, 1993; *Serves Me Right*, 1996; *Bolt from the Blue*, 1996.

Milland, Ray (*b* Cymla Mountain, Wales, 1905 – *d* Torrance, California, 1986). Actor. RN: Reginald Truscott-Jones. Breezy Hollywood leading man to some of Hollywood's most famous women stars (Jean Arthur, Claudette Colbert, etc), he broke memorably with his debonair image to play an alcoholic in *The Lost Weekend* (1945) – and won an Oscar for it. He began his 55-year film career in Britain in *Piccadilly* (1929), leaving for Hollywood after a half-dozen more films, and returning only intermittently. He starred in ASQUITH's lacklustre version of the stage hit, *French Without Tears* (1939) and gave one of his best performances as a conman-artist in the minor *noir* masterpiece, *So Evil My Love* (1948), and Jacques TOURNEUR's *Circle of Danger* (1950) was a sprightly thriller that benefited by Milland's star presence. The rest are unremarkable and his main career belongs in another book.

OTHER BRITISH FILMS INCLUDE: *The Informer, The Flying Scotsman* (1929), *Orders Is Orders* (1933), *The Safecracker* (1957), *Hostile Witness* (1968, + d), *Embassy* (1972), *The House in Nightmare Park* (1973), *Gold* (1974), *Aces High* (1976), *The Uncanny* (1977), *Game for Vulture* (1979), *The Masks of Death* (1984).

BIBLIOG: Autobiography, *Wide-Eyed in Babylon*, 1976.

Millar, Adelqui (*b* Concepción, Chile, 1891 – *d* Santiago, Chile, 1956). Actor, director. RN: Adelqui Migliar Icardi. Acted as Adelqui Migliar in Dutch and Italian films, and Adelqui Millar in British, Austrian, French, Italian, Spanish, Argentinian, and Chilean films. His proud boast was that he could speak and direct in half-a-dozen languages. An exotic-looking actor, Millar appeared in films produced by Anglo Hollandia, a joint UK–Dutch concern, filming in Haarlem: *Hidden Life, As God Made Her, Fate's Plaything, John Heriot's Wife, In the Night* (1920), *The Other Person, Laughter and Tears* (+ sc) (1921), and *Circus Jim* (1922, + co-d, sc). Also appeared in the US production of *The Arab* (1924, shot in Nice), and in Michael Curtiz's Austrian-shot *Moon of Israel* (1924). In 1927, Millar co-founded WHITEHALL FILMS, and in 1928 began building a studio at BOREHAMWOOD that would later become the home of MGM–BRITISH. Before leaving Whitehall in June 1929, he directed two films for the company: *Life* (1929, + a), shot in Spain, and *The Inseparables* (1929). In 1931, he directed four Spanish-language features at the Joinville, Paris, studios of Paramount.

OTHER BRITISH FILMS: (a) *Pages of Life* (1922, + sc, p, d), *I Pagliacci* (1923), *The Apache* (1925), *London* (1926), *The Blind Ship* (1927, + p). AS.

Millar, Gavin (*b* Clydebank, Scotland, 1938). Director. Millar's most distinguished work has been for TV, including *Tinker, Tailor, Soldier, Spy* (1979), *A Murder of Quality* (1991) and *Talking Heads 2* (1998), but at least one of his intermittent films is worth noting: the strangely neglected *Dreamchild* (1985), which meshes Dennis POTTER, Coral BROWNE and Lewis Carroll in a glorious work *sui generis*.

OTHER BRITISH FILMS: (d, unless noted) *The Eye Hears, the Ear Sees* (1970, doc, a, sc), *Secrets* (1971), *The Most Dangerous Man in the World* (1988), *Funny Bones* (1995, UK/US, a), *Complicity* (2000).

Millar, Sir Ronald (*b* Reading, 1919 – *d* London, 1998). Dramatist, screenwriter. Charterhouse- and Cambridge-educated stage actor (from 1940) and popular author of such plays as *Frieda* (1946), filmed in 1947 (+ co-sc). All his meagre film work is in collaboration, at its best in *So Evil My Love* (1948). Also in Hollywood in the early 50s (*Scaramouche*, 1952; *Rose Marie*, 1954). Was speech-writer to several Conservative Prime Ministers, perhaps helping Mrs Thatcher to an undeserved reputation for wit as 'the [lady] not for turning'. Knighted 1980.

OTHER BRITISH FILMS: *We Dive at Dawn* (1943, a); (co-sc) *Train of Events* (1949), *The Miniver Story* (1950), *Never Let Me Go* (1953), *Betrayed* (1954).

Miller, Arnold Louis (*b* London, 1922). Director. Worked in the EXPLOITATION field chiefly, his titles variously exhorting viewers/voyeurs to *Take Off Your Clothes and Live!* (1962, + p, sc) or offering insights into *Primitive London* (1965, short). He did, however, have one brush with quality, as producer of *Witchfinder General* (1968), and there were also some travelogues described as 'unbearable' by David McGillivray (1992).

OTHER BRITISH FILMS INCLUDE: (short, d) *Nudist Memories* (1960), *West End Jungle* (+ sc, p), *Nudes of the World* (1961), *Under the Table*

You Must Go (1969, + co-p, sc), *House of Hookers* (1972), *The Green Desert* (1976); (d, co-p) *Skin Deep* (1981), *The English Riviera* (1984); (feature, d) *Kil 1* (+ p) (1962), *Secrets of a Windmill Girl* (1965, + p, sc), *Sex Farm* (1973, + co-p, idea); (p) *The Sorcerers, The Blood Beast Terror* (ex p) (1967).

Miller, Ben (*b* 1966). Actor. Popular TV star of the series, *Armstrong and Miller* (1997–2000, + co-sc), craggy Miller had a small role in *Plunkett & Macleane* (1999, UK/Czech) and graduated to a major one as a thieving, tattooed biker in *There's Only One Jimmy Grimble* (2000, UK/Fr).

OTHER BRITISH FILMS: *The Blind Date* (2000), *The Parole Officer, Birthday Girl* (2001).

Miller, Frank (*b* London, 1891 – *d* England, 1950). Director, art director, screenwriter. A prolific screenwriter, whose work is sometimes lurid, occasionally famous, but generally forgotten, Miller claimed that by 1928, he had written more than 200 films, including *Kipps* (1921), *The Wheels of Chance* (1922) and *The Beloved Vagabond* (1923). In 1922, he wrote more than 40 features and SHORTS, and continued writing old-fashioned scripts, such as *The Maid of the Mountains* (1932), *Bed and Breakfast* (1938), and *Trunk Crime* (1939), well into the sound era. He was also a director, and often served as his own art director on silent films.

OTHER BRITISH FILMS INCLUDE: (d, sc, unless noted) *Odd Charges, A Marked Man* (1916), *The March Hare* (1919), *Stop Press Comedies* series (1920), *Treasure Trove* (1922), *The Happy Rascals* series (1926), *Mr Nobody* (1927), *Houp-La!* (1928, d), *Lucky Girl* (1932, co-d). AS.

Miller, Hugh (*b* Berwick-on-Tweed, 1889 – *d* London, 1976). Actor. On stage from 1911 (in London 1922) and in films from 1921 (*In His Grip, The Puppet Man*), this imposing figure starred in silent films but lingered on in occasional character roles until 1962, when he played a colonel in *Lawrence of Arabia*. Was founder member of THE FILM SOCIETY in 1925.

OTHER BRITISH FILMS INCLUDE: *The Letters* (1922, short), *Bonnie Prince Charlie* (1923), *The Phantom Gambler* (1925), *The Green Pack* (1934), *I Give My Heart* (1935), *The Return of the Scarlet Pimpernel* (1937), *My Sister and I* (1948), *Before I Wake* (1955), *Behind the Mask* (1958); *Dr Zhivago* (1965, dial coach).

Miller, Joan (*b* Nelson, British Columbia, 1910 – *d* Oxford, 1988). Actress. Canadian actress first on stage in 1930, London 1934, and an early British TV celebrity as presenter of the pre-war BBC magazine programme, *Picture Page* (1936–39). Primarily a stage actress, she appeared in a few scattered films, having her best chance in *No Trees in the Street* (1958), as the working-class mother corrupted by poverty. On TV, she had a major success as the *Woman in a Dressing Gown* (1956), in the role played on screen (1957) by Yvonne MITCHELL. Married (2) Peter COTES.

OTHER BRITISH FILMS INCLUDE: *Take It from Me* (1937), *The Woman in the Hall* (1947), *Yield to the Night* (1956), *Too Young to Love* (1959), *Heavens Above!* (1963).

Miller, Sir Jonathan (*b* London, 1934). Screenwriter, director. At Cambridge, he was a member of the influential 'Beyond the Fringe' comedy team of the 60s, and he graduated as medical doctor from London's University College Hospital. On TV he presented medical programmes such as *The Body in Question* (1978), his various backgrounds converging, and was producer-director for much of the BBC's Television Shakespeare of the 80s. A stage actor from 1954 and director from 1962, he directed a memorable, Victorian-set *Merchant of Venice*, starring OLIVIER, in 1970–71. His cinema record is meagre: he acted in *One Way Pendulum* (1964) and directed the little-seen *Take a*

Girl Like You (1970) and *Monty Python Meets Beyond the Fringe* (1977, + a). Awarded CBE, 1983, knighted in 2002.

Miller, Jonny Lee (*b* Kingston-on-Thames, 1972). Actor. Charismatic leading man who reinvents himself with each role, from debut lead in cyberpunk thriller *Hackers* (1995, US), through Sick Boy in *Trainspotting* (1996), self-possessed businessman Jeffrey Byron in *Afterglow* (1997, US), and low-key, undemonstrative Edmund Bertram in *Mansfield Park* (1999, UK/US). Grandson of Bernard LEE and son of stage actor Alan Miller; began career at 17 as front-of-house staff at Theatre Royal, Drury Lane. Married to actress Angelina Jolie (1996–99). In 1997, formed production company NATURAL NYLON, with Ewan McGREGOR, Jude LAW and others.
OTHER BRITISH FILMS INCLUDE: *Regeneration* (UK/Can), *Bent* (UK/Jap/US) (1997), *Plunkett & MacLeane* (1999), *Love, Honour and Obey*, *Complicity* (2000), *The Escapist* (2001). AS.

Miller, Magda (*b* Strathblane, Scotland, 1935). Actress. A blonde blackmailer in the opening episode of *Behind the Headlines* and a mere good-time girl in *Town on Trial* (1956), but she got strangled both times. What a year. Miller did a bit of TV (e.g. episodes of *Mark Saber*) and had half a dozen other film roles, but it was finished by the end of the 50s.
OTHER BRITISH FILMS INCLUDE: *Let's Be Happy* (1956), *Man Eater*, *The Truth About Women* (1957), *The Two Faces of Dr Jekyll* (1960).

Miller, Mandy (*b* Weston-super-Mare, 1944). Actress. Child star of the 50s who was BAA-nominated for her heart-rending performance as the deaf mute protagonist of *Mandy* (1952). Touching also in the divorce drama, *Background* (1953), she had several more substantial roles, including the justifiably hysterical teenager in *The Snorkel* (1958) who can't get anyone to believe her, but did not pursue her career into adulthood.
OTHER BRITISH FILMS INCLUDE: *The Man in the White Suit* (1951), *Dance Little Lady* (1954), *Raising a Riot* (1955), *Child in the House*, *The Feminine Touch* (1956), *Kill or Cure* (1962).

Miller, Martin (*b* Kremsier, Moravia, Austria-Hungary, 1899 – *d* London, 1969). Actor. RN: Rudolf Müller. Formerly on the Austrian stage, Miller came to Britain in 1939. In British films mostly cast as a suspicious foreigner. He had a notable part as a psychiatrist in Michael POWELL's *Peeping Tom* (1960), and was a regular cast member of the perpetually running London stage production of Agatha CHRISTIE's *The Mousetrap*. Married Hannah Norbert (*b* Vienna, 1916 – *d* London, 1998) who played Peter FINCH's mother in *Sunday Bloody Sunday* (1971).
OTHER BRITISH FILMS INCLUDE: *One Of Our Aircraft Is Missing* (1942), *Squadron Leader X* (1942), *Latin Quarter* (1945), *Night Boat to Dublin* (1946), *Bond Street* (1948), *The Third Man* (1949), *Where's Charley?* (1952), *Twice Upon A Time* (1953), *The Baby and the Battleship* (1956), *Seven Thunders* (1957), *Libel*, *Expresso Bongo* (1959), *The VIPs* (1963), *Children Of The Damned* (1963), *The Yellow Rolls-Royce* (1964). Tim Bergfelder.

Miller, Max (*b* London, 1895 – *d* Brighton, 1963). Actor, comedian. RN: Thomas Henry Sargent. The 'genius of the MUSIC HALL', renowned for immaculate timing and saucy stage act, Miller served his apprenticeship in concert parties, a world evoked in *The Good Companions* (1933), in which he played the song-plugger Milbrau. Made music hall debut in 1924 as the 'cheeky chappie' with a flower-patterned suit, plus-fours and trilby hat. His impact, depending on interaction with a live audience, was blunted in films. He successfully appeared in *Educated Evans* (1936), bringing Edgar WALLACE's horse-racing tipster to life. But his real home was in the now 'Lost Empires' of the giant variety theatres, and his legacy of innuendo and seaside postcard humour was bequeathed to the 'CARRY ON' films.
OTHER BRITISH FILMS INCLUDE: *Friday the Thirteenth* (1933), *Princess Charming* (1934), *Get off My Foot* (1935), *Don't Get Me Wrong* (1937), *Thank Evans* (1938), *Hoots Mon!*, *The Good Old Days* (1939), *Asking for Trouble* (1942).
BIBLIOG: John M. East, *Max Miller: the Cheeky Chappie*, 1997. Roger Philip Mellor.

Miller, Ruby (*b* London, 1889 – *d* Chichester, 1976). Actress. Blue-eyed blonde, a RADA-trained stage actress (debut 1906) who appeared in about 20 films, mainly in the 20s and 30s, usually in secondary character roles, and was last seen in *Anna Karenina* (1948), as Countess Meskov. Also in Hollywood for *Alimony* (1924).
OTHER BRITISH FILMS INCLUDE: *Little Women* (1917), *Edge of Beyond* (1919), *The Mystery Road* (1921), *Land of Hope and Glory* (1927), *Sorrell and Son* (1933), *The Gay Old Dog* (1935), *Shadowed Eyes* (1939), *Facing the Music* (1941), *The Hundred Pound Window* (1943), *Twilight Hour* (1944).
BIBLIOG: Autobiography, *Champagne from My Slipper*, 1952.

Miller, Sam (*b* Saxmundham, 1962). Director. Trained as an actor at Arts Educational Schools Drama Department and worked for seven years as actor in theatre, television and film, including a role in *Nil by Mouth* (1997). Having made a short film, *Love's Lost Hour* (1994), he was then the originating director of the brilliant TV series *This Life* (1996), and the TV film, *King Girl* for BBC2. His first feature as director was the engaging oddball romance, *Among Giants* (1998), but *This Life* fans were disappointed by *Elephant Juice* (2000), which reunited him with screenwriter Amy MILLER and star Daniela NARDINI, and which trawled the same territory as the TV series but with less precision.

Milligan, Spike (*b* Ahmaddnagar, India, 1918 – *d* Rye, 2002). Comedian. RN: Terence Alan Milligan. Co-creator of the eccentric BBC radio programme, *The Goon Show* (1951), Milligan, son of an Irish military officer in India, served in the Royal Artillery during WW2, after which his career took off with the Goons. He and fellow Goons, Harry SECOMBE and Peter SELLERS, brought their bizarre comedy to the screen in such films as *Down Among the Z Men* (1952) and *The Case of the Mukkinese Battlehorn* (1956, short, + co-sc), but almost all of his work, film or TV, might be described as in Goonish vein. His novels – e.g. *Adolf Hitler – My Part in His Downfall* (1972, +a) and *Puckoon* (2001, +co-sc) – and play, *The Bed Sitting Room* (1969, co-author), were adapted to the screen, and he played comic supporting roles in such films as *Alice's Adventures in Wonderland* (1972), *The Hound of the Baskervilles* (1977), and such international films as *The Three Musketeers* (1973, Panama), as an unlikely husband to Raquel Welch, and *The History of the World, Part 1* (1981, US). There was also much theatre (Ben Gunn in *Treasure Island*, 1961) – he had begun in the MUSIC HALLS in the mid 30s – and TV, from the mid 50s, and in a media-versatile career he was also the author of children's books. Awarded an honorary CBE (1992) and an honorary knighthood (2000), honorary because he was an Irish citizen, and was awarded a lifetime achievement award at the 1994 British Comedy Awards, recognising him as some sort of institution.
OTHER BRITISH FILMS INCLUDE: (a, unless noted) *Penny Points to Paradise* (1951), *The Running Jumping & Standing Still Film* (short, co-idea), *Watch Your Stern*, *Suspect* (1960), *Invasion Quartet* (1961), *The*

Magic Christian (1969), *Rentadick* (1972), *Man About the House* (1974), *Monty Python's Life of Brian* (1979), *The Big Freeze* (1994).

Millington, Mary (*b* London, 1945 – *d* Walton-on-the-Hill, 1979). Actress. RN: Quilter. One of the best known exponents of the sexploitation genre, the former veterinary nurse was once known as the British Linda Lovelace. Despite psychiatric problems, run-ins with the police and general personal unhappiness, she continued filming until the year of her suicide. The films' titles speak for themselves.
BRITISH FILMS INCLUDE: *Keep It Up Downstairs, Intimate Games* (1976), *Come Play with Me* (1977), *What's Up Superdoc?, The Playbirds* (1978), *The Great Rock'n'Roll Swindle* (1979).
BIBLIOG: Julian Petley, 'There's something about Mary' in Bruce Babington (ed), *British Stars and Stardom*, 2001; Simon Sheridan, *Come Play with Me: The Life and Films of Mary Millington*, 1999.

Mills, Freddie (*b* Bournemouth, 1919 – *d* London, 1965). Actor. Former light heavyweight champion who entered films and TV in 1952, and caught some critical attention for his debut in *Emergency Call* (1952) as a boxer with a rare blood group. He also did time as presenter on TV's *Six-Five Special* (1957–58) and appeared in the film 1958 SPIN-OFF. Committed suicide.
OTHER BRITISH FILMS INCLUDE: *One Jump Ahead* (1955), *Breakaway* (1956), *Kill Me Tomorrow* (1957), *Carry On Constable* (1960), . . . *Regardless* (1961), *The Comedy Man* (1963), *Joey Boy* (1965).

Mills, Hayley (*b* London, 1946). Actress. For a brief while in the early 60s, the daughter of John MILLS and Mary Hayley Bell, and younger sister of Juliet MILLS, was one of the most famous film stars in the world. The flaxen-haired, blue-eyed charmer made her debut as the tomboy companion of a young fugitive in *Tiger Bay* (1959), starring her father, in a role originally planned for a boy, and she made an instant hit, winning a BAA as Most Promising Newcomer. DISNEY made her a world star and she won a Special Oscar (+ BAAn) for his *Pollyanna* (1960, US), and followed this with other box-office winners, including *The Parent Trap* (1961, US, as twins) and *The Moon Spinners* (1964, UK/US). She gave two further fine performances as teenagers: scared in *Whistle Down the Wind* (1961) and scarred in *The Chalk Garden* (1964). However, her virginal teenage image was wiped by her nude scene, modest as it was, in *The Family Way* (1966), a tender comedy of marriage problems, directed by Roy BOULTING to whom Mills was married from 1971–76, after which she had a long relationship with actor Leigh LAWSON (1976–84). From the mid 70s, film roles became sporadic, but she appeared in several TV shows, including the mini-series, *The Flame Trees of Thika* (1981), and scored a personal triumph on stage in 1998 in *The King and I*.
OTHER BRITISH FILMS: *So Well Remembered* (1947, as baby), *In Search of the Castaways* (1961), *The Truth About Spring* (1964), *Sky West and Crooked* (1965), *Pretty Polly, Africa – Texas Style* (1967), *Twisted Nerve* (1968), *Take a Girl Like You* (1970), *Mr Forbush and the Penguins* (1971), *Endless Night* (1972), *Deadly Strangers, What Changed Charley Farthing?* (UK/Sp) (1974), *Appointment with Death* (1988), *After Midnight* (1990, UK/Ire).

Mills, Hugh (*b c* 1913 – *d* 1971). Screenwriter. Novelist and playwright who wrote or co-wrote about a dozen screenplays, perhaps most notably for the handsome melodrama, *Blanche Fury* (1947), and shared a BAAn for *Knave of Hearts* (1954, UK/Fr, + co-dial).
OTHER BRITISH FILMS INCLUDE: (co-sc, unless noted) *The Beloved Vagabond* (1936), *Turned Out Nice Again* (1941, co-play), *The Naked Heart* and *Blackmailed* (both co-sc with Roger Vadim), *So Long at the Fair* (1950), *Prudence and the Pill* (1968, + novel).

Mills, Sir John (*b* North Elmham, Norfolk, 1908). Actor. This short, wiry former song-and-dance man became one of the most significant of all British film stars, and in his nearly 60-year career appeared in well over 100 films, as well as substantial theatre and TV performances. After training as a dancer, he was first on stage in the chorus of *The Five O'Clock Revue* (1929) and was regularly on the London stage, in revues, musicals and straight plays, throughout the 30s, as well as making about 20 films before war broke out. He is an engaging juvenile lead in such 30s pieces as *The Ghost Camera* (1933, as Ida LUPINO's brother), the chirpy musical *Car of Dreams* (1935), the love interest for Nova PILBEAM's *Tudor Rose* (1936), and the schoolboy grown into soldier in *Goodbye, Mr Chips* (1939).

But WW2 changed everything for Mills, as it did for so much connected with British cinema. The roles he played in *In Which We Serve* (1942), *We Dive at Dawn* (1943), *This Happy Breed*, *Waterloo Road* (1944) and *The Way to the Stars* (1945) defined a new kind of British film hero: he is the boy-next-door in his ordinariness, but he has also established an everyman reliability under stress; he is decent, brave and loyal; and he works enough subtle mutations on the type to avoid mere repetition. It is arguable that no British male star ever had so long and rewarding a stardom, and in predominantly British films. In the post-war era, he was a definitive Pip in *Great Expectations* (1946), emphatically a figure for a supposedly more egalitarian Britain; the tormented hero, an industrial chemist who fears he may have committed murder, in *The October Man* (1947); the archetypal British hero, *Scott of the Antarctic* (1948), who failed so bravely; and another sort of hero, the bootmaker Willie Mossop, in *Hobson's Choice* (1953). As the 50s wore on, the roles shaded subtly into character leads. He is the shabby private detective in *The End of the Affair* (1954) and the captain in *Ice Cold in Alex* (1958), pushed by exhaustion into incipient neurosis and alcoholism. The twitchy, repressed military types in *Tunes of Glory* (1960) and *Tiara Tahiti* (1962), the one headed for tragedy, the latter for the humiliations of social comedy, reveal precision as well as versatility; and he is ultimately very moving as the father in *The Family Way* (1966) who may have loved no one as much as his dead mate. Typically, he got the Oscar for a grotesque piece of facial and vocal distortion in the inflated *Ryan's Daughter* (1970) – supporting actor Oscars have always been drawn to this sort of cosmetic display – when one could nominate a dozen far less showy, more worthy contenders among his roles. Even in perfectly ordinary films like *The Vicious Circle* (1957), one never stops believing in *him*.

His later decades saw him in character cameos, in good films (e.g. *Gandhi*, 1982) and bad (e.g. *Deadly Advice*, 1994). Kenneth BRANAGH enlisted him (as whom did he not?) for *Hamlet* (1996, UK/US) to play the mute role of 'Old Norway', for whom Shakespeare had thoughtlessly failed to produce lines, and he went on appearing in TV series (e.g. *Martin Chuzzlewit*, 1994) and talk shows. Though very deaf and part-blind, he still evinced the chipper persona honed below (occasionally above) decks in those WAR FILMS half a century earlier. He tried his hand at directing and producing but he is, above all, a British film actor *par excellence*. The achievement is there in the *cv*; it has been recognised serially with CBE (1960), knighthood (1976), BAFTA Special Tribute Award (1987), and BFI

Fellowship (1995). No one could say he hadn't earned them.

Married (2) since 1941 to author Mary Hayley Bell, he is the father of actresses Hayley and Juliet MILLS.

OTHER BRITISH FILMS: (a, unless noted) *The Midshipmaid* (1932), *Britannia of Billingsgate* (1933), *Those Were the Days, The River Wolves, A Political Party, The Lash, Doctor's Orders, Blind Justice* (1934), *Royal Cavalcade, Charing Cross Road, Brown on Resolution* (1935), *The First Offence* (1936), *OHMS, The Green Cockatoo* (1937), *Happy Families* (short) (1939), *All Hands* (short), *Old Bill and Son* (1940), *Cottage to Let, The Black Sheep of Whitehall* (1941), *The Young Mr Pitt, The Goose Steps Out, The Big Blockade* (1942), *Victory Wedding* (short), *The Sky's the Limit* (doc) (1945), *Land of Promise* (doc) (1946), *So Well Remembered* (1947), *Three Days* (d, short), *The History of Mr Polly* (+ p) (1948), *Friend of the Family* (short, narr), *The Rocking Horse Winner* (+ p) (1949), *Morning Departure* (1950), *Mr Denning Drives North* (1951), *The Way to Wimbledon* (doc, narr), *The Long Memory, The Gentle Gunman* (1952), *The Colditz Story* (1954), *Escapade, Above Us the Waves* (1955), *It's Great to Be Young!, The Baby and the Battleship, Town on Trial* (1956), *I Was Monty's Double, Dunkirk* (1958), *Tiger Bay, Summer of the Seventeenth Doll* (UK/Aust) (1959), *Swiss Family Robinson* (UK/US), *The Singer Not the Song* (1960), *Flame in the Streets, The Valiant* (UK/It) (1961), *The Chalk Garden, The Truth About Spring, Operation Crossbow* (UK/It) (1965), *Sky West and Crooked* (1965, d), *The Wrong Box* (1966), *Africa – Texas Style* (1967), *Run Wild, Run Free, Oh! What a Lovely War* (1969), *Dulcima* (1971), *Young Winston, Lady Caroline Lamb* (UK/It/US) (1972), *The 'Human' Factor* (1975), *Trial by Combat* (1976), *To See Such Fun* (1977, doc), *The Big Sleep, The Thirty Nine Steps, The Quatermass Conclusion* (1978), *The Masks of Death* (1984), *When the Wind Blows* (1986, anim, voice), *The Lady and the Highwayman* (1988), *The Big Freeze* (1994), *The Grotesque* (1996), *Bean* (1997).

BIBLIOG: Autobiography, *Up in the Clouds, Gentlemen Please*, 1980.

Mills, Juliet (*b* London, 1941). Actress. Daughter of John MILLS and Mary Hayley Bell, older sister of Hayley MILLS, the sweetly blonde prettiness of Juliet Mills adorned a few 60s films before she relocated to the US and became a household name in TV's *Nanny and the Professor* (1969–71). As a child, she appeared in four of her father's films; as a young woman she played leads in such undemanding fare as *No, My Darling Daughter* (1961) and *Twice Round the Daffodils* (1962). Married (2) actor Maxwell Caulfield (1981).

OTHER BRITISH FILMS INCLUDE: *In Which We Serve* (1942), *So Well Remembered, The October Man* (1947), *The History of Mr Polly* (1948), *Nurse on Wheels* (1963), *Carry On Jack* (1964).

Mills, Reginald (*b* Suffolk, 1912 – *d* London, 1990). Editor. Haileybury- and Cambridge-educated Mills won a high reputation as editor for his work chiefly with two directors, Michael POWELL and Joseph LOSEY. He cut all Powell's films from *A Matter of Life and Death* (1946) to *The Battle of the River Plate* (1956), and was Oscar-nominated for *The Red Shoes* (1948). He contributes notably to the exquisite insertion of the flashbacks in *Black Narcissus* (1947) and Powell pays tribute to his role in creating a 'composed' film. He edited Losey's first British film, *The Sleeping Tiger* (1954), and five others including the immaculate *The Servant* (1963), where editing colludes so memorably with camera.

OTHER BRITISH FILMS INCLUDE: (e, unless noted) *The New Lot* (1943, doc), *The Small Back Room* (1948, super e), *The Elusive Pimpernel, Gone to Earth* (1950), *The Tales of Hoffmann* (1951), *Where's Charley?* (1952), *Oh, Rosalinda!!* (1955), *The Spanish Gardener* (1956), *Blind Date* (1959), *The Criminal* (1960), *The Damned* (1961), *King and Country* (1964), *Ulysses* (1967, UK/US), *Romeo and Juliet* (1968, UK/It), *The Tales of Beatrix Potter* (1971, d), *Brother Sun, Sister Moon* (1972, UK/It, super e).

Milne, A(lan) A(lexander) (*b* London, 1882 – *d* Hartfield, Sussex, 1956). Playwright. Though most famous for his children's books, Milne was also a popular playwright in his time and, apart from the US-made ADAPTATIONS of *Winnie the Pooh* (published 1926) and TV versions in several countries, he also worked on the screenplays of five British films. *Mr Pim Passes By* (1921) and *Michael and Mary* (1931) were derived from his plays, as were the US films, *The Little Adventuress* (1927) and *Where Sinners Meet* (1935), both from his *Dover Road* (1922), and *Four Days' Wonder* (1936). There were two short versions of his poem, 'The King's Breakfast' (1937, 1963). He and Adrian BRUNEL set up Minerva FILMS which made four short comedies in 1920.

OTHER BRITISH FILMS: *Twice Two, Five Pounds Reward, Bookworms, The Bump* (1920), *Birds of Prey* (1930, co-sc with Basil DEAN).

BIBLIOG: Autobiography, *It's Too Late Now*, 1939.

Milton, Billy (*b* London, 1905 – *d* Northwood, 1989). Actor. Formerly in the wine trade, Milton was on stage from 1926, popular in revue, comedy and musicals for 40 years. Appeared as lead or second lead in 20 light films of the 30s, such as *Three Men in a Boat* and *Aunt Sally* (1933), and played occasional character roles until *Sweet William* (1979). In RAF (1940–44) he toured extensively as performer and he also featured in radio serials. Brother of actor **Harry Milton** (*b* London, 1900 – *d* London), Chili BOUCHIER's first husband.

OTHER BRITISH FILMS INCLUDE: *Young Woodley* (1930), *Music Hath Charms* (1935), *Someone at the Door* (1936), *Yes Madam?* (1938), *The Key Man* (1957), *The Set-Up* (1963), *Devils of Darkness* (1964), *Monster of Terror* (1965), *Hot Millions* (1968).

BIBLIOG: Autobiography, *Milton's Paradise Mislaid*, 1976.

Milton, Ernest (*b* San Francisco, 1890 – *d* London, 1974). Actor. Distinguished American player (naturalised British subject), on stage from 1912 and with frequent Old Vic seasons. Made only a half-dozen film appearances, in supporting roles such as Robespierre in *The Scarlet Pimpernel* (1935).

OTHER BRITISH FILMS: *The Amazing Quest of Mr Ernest Bliss* (1920), *It's Love Again* (1936), *The Foreman Went to France* (1942), *Alice in Wonderland* (1949, UK/Fr/US), *Cat Girl* (1957).

Minerva Films In 1920, director Adrian BRUNEL set up this company, with actors Leslie HOWARD, C. Aubrey SMITH and Nigel PLAYFAIR, and dramatist A.A. MILNE, and with a capital of £10,000. Brunel made four short comedies from Milne's screenplays in 1920: *Twice Two, Five Pounds Reward, Bookworms, The Bump*, making use of London location shooting. The company had £28 in the bank when it was forced to close down.

BIBLIOG: Adrian Brunel, *Nice Work*, 1949.

Minghella, Anthony (*b* Isle of Wight, 1954). Director. Minghella won a BAA (1991) for his screenplay for *Truly Madly Deeply*, the first feature he directed, and there are those who would still cherish this small-scale romance more than the lavish but chilly pictorial splendours of the over-hyped *The English Patient* (1996, AA/d, BAA/film + sc), US-made with many UK personnel, or the tauter but still inflated *The Talented Mr Ripley* (1999), which brought him a director's AAn – and the BAA's David LEAN Award for Direction. That ought to be a warning for him: does he want to end up with his own version of *Doctor Zhivago* or *Ryan's Daughter*? The writing is on the wall and the wall is in some exotic location which could easily dwarf story, script and actors. He graduated from the University of Hull and wrote for radio and TV, including episodes of *EastEnders* and *Inspector Morse* in the 80s, as well as being a respected playwright. Awarded CBE, 2001.

Peter Cushing, character star, here in *The Curse of Frankenstein*.

Room at the Top (1958, d.Jack Clayton), realist drama, with Simone Signoret, Laurence Harvey.

Margaret Rutherford, character star.

Alastair Sim, character star.

Wendy Toye, director, dancer, choreographer.

Sapphire (1959, d.Basil Dearden), social problem drama.

Ted Willis (Lord Willis), screenwriter.

Earl Cameron (right), character actor, here in *A Warm December*.

Saturday Night and Sunday Morning (1960, d.Karel Reisz), realist drama, with Shirley Anne Field, Albert Finney.

A Taste of Honey (1961, d.Tony Richardson), poetic-realist drama, with Paul Danquah, Rita Tushingham.

Alan Bates, star actor.

Hattie Jacques, character comedienne.

Lawrence of Arabia (1962, d.David Lean), epic, with Peter O'Toole in the title role.

Freddie Young, cinematographer.

Lindsay Anderson, director, critic.

Sidney James, character comedian.

ABOVE **Walter Lassally**, cinematographer.

RIGHT **Dame Thora Hird**, character star.

A Hard Day's Night (1964, d.Richard Lester), pop musical, with The Beatles.

Julie Harris, costume designer.

Albert Finney, star actor.

RIGHT *Darling* (1965, d.John Schlesinger), drama, starring Julie Christie.

Accident (1967, d.Joseph Losey), drama, with Jacqueline Sassard, Dirk Bogarde.

Vanessa Redgrave, star actress, later in character roles.

ABOVE **John Barry**, composer for British and international films.

RIGHT *If...* (1968, d.Lindsay Anderson), anti-Establishment satire.

ABOVE *Women in Love* (1969, d.Ken Russell), romantic drama, with Oliver Reed, Glenda Jackson.

LEFT **Dame Maggie Smith**, star actress, later in character roles.

Performance (1970, d.Nicolas Roeg, Donald Cammell), violent thriller, with James Fox.

Ken Russell, director, first famous for TV documentaries.

Confessions of a Window Cleaner (1974, d.Val Guest), with Robin Askwith, one of a series of sex comedies.

OTHER BRITISH FILMS: *Heaven* (2002, UK/Ger, co-ex p).

Ministry of Information (MOI) and British cinema in World War 1

Government-sponsored film production during WW1 began in 1916 with the creation of the War Office Cinematograph Committee. In February 1917, with the formation of the Department of Information, headed by novelist John Buchan, the Committee was transferred to its control. T. Lennox Gilmour, described by Adrian BRUNEL as "one of the most lovable characters I have known," was liaison officer for the Department's Cinematograph Branch. In March 1918, the Department of Information became the Ministry of Information, under the chairmanship of Lord BEAVERBROOK, and with William JURY as director of the Cinematograph Department.

The MOI handled distribution of appropriate films abroad and entered production with a studio on London's Ebury Street. It sponsored D.W. Griffith's *Hearts of the World* (1918) and Herbert Brenon's *Victory and Peace* (which was completed after the close of the war and never released). Brunel claims credit for the 'film tags', two-minute PROPAGANDA SHORTS that were attached to newsreels. Cecil HEPWORTH produced a number of these highly amusing comedy situations, featuring Chrissie WHITE and Stewart ROME, just as during WW2, he produced the very similar food flashes'. AS.

Ministry of Information (MOI) and British cinema in World War 2

Film PROPAGANDA policy in Britain during WW2 was the responsibility of the Ministry of Information (MOI) whose Films Division was headed, successively, by Sir Joseph Ball (1939), Sir Kenneth Clark (1940) and Jack BEDDINGTON (1940–46). The MOI assumed control of the GPO FILM UNIT (renamed the CROWN FILM UNIT) for the production of official DOCUMENTARIES including *Target for Tonight* (1941) and *Fires Were Started* (1943). Following its experiment with *49th Parallel* (1941) it abandoned direct investment in commercial production and instead worked informally with producers in laying down guidelines for propaganda films.

BIBLIOG: James Chapman, *The British at War: Cinema, State and Propaganda, 1939–1945*, 1998; Ian McLaine, *Ministry of Morale*, 1978. James Chapman.

Minney, R(ubeigh) J(ames).

(*b* Calcutta, 1895 – *d* Hastings, Sussex, 1979). Screenwriter, producer. After reading History at King's College, London, Minney became a lecturer and broadcaster as well as inveterate traveller in exotic places. In Hollywood he co-wrote the screenplay for *Clive of India* (1935), from the play he co-wrote with W.P. LIPSCOMB, but his main function in British films was as producer of several GAINSBOROUGH melodramas, including *Madonna of the Seven Moons* (1944) and *The Wicked Lady* (1945). He came a fearful cropper with *Idol of Paris* (1948) which totally lacked the subtextual resonances of its predecessors. The only further film he produced was *The Final Test* (1953), directed by Anthony ASQUITH, whose hagiography, *Puffin Asquith*, he wrote in 1973. Active in ACT and its film-producing arm, ACT FILMS (chairman 1958–68).

OTHER BRITISH FILMS: *Dear Octopus* (1943, co-sc), *A Place of One's Own* (1945, p), *The Magic Bow* (1946, p), *Time Gentlemen Please!* (1952, novel), *Carve Her Name With Pride* (1948, biog).

Minter, George

(*b* London, 1911 – *d* London, 1966). Producer, distributor. Entered industry on the DISTRIBUTION side in 1938, founding RENOWN PICTURES CORPORATION. He moved the company, of which he became managing director, into production post-war, while continuing to distribute. The notorious *No Orchids for Miss Blandish* (1948) was the company's first production; others, on which Minter's name appeared as (co-)producer included *The Pickwick Papers* (1952) and *Our Girl Friday* (1953), both directed by Noel LANGLEY. He also operated under the names of other companies (George Minter Productions, Alderdale) for which Renown acted as distributor. His producer's career encompassed about a dozen films of the 50s.

OTHER BRITISH FILMS INCLUDE: (p, unless noted; all distributed by Renown) *Scrooge* (1951), *Grand National Night* (1953, ex p), *Dance Little Lady, Svengali* (1954), *It's a Wonderful World* (1956), *Tread Softly Stranger* (1958, ex p, co-sc), *Beat Girl, Beyond This Place* (1959, ex p).

Miramax

Leading US distribution and production company specialising in independent and foreign films. Owned by Disney since 1993, it was founded in 1982 by Harvey and Bob WEINSTEIN whose innovative and aggressive marketing strategies underpinned the company's success. An important backer of medium-budget British films since the late 80s, Miramax has been particularly effective at selling them in the US. Its credits include: *Scandal* (1988), *The Crying Game* (1992), and *Little Voice* (1998, UK/US). Stephen Guy.

Miranda, Isa

(*b* Milan, 1905 – *d* Rome, 1982). Actress. RN: Ines Isabella Sanpietro. Italian star of international films, including a couple in Hollywood, and several British ones, the most notable of which was *Summer Madness* (1955, UK/US) as the landlady of Katharine HEPBURN's pensione. Also played in the expensive, English-speaking, US-financed, Rome-based dud, *The Shoes of the Fisherman* (1968).

OTHER BRITISH FILMS: *Do You Know This Voice?* (1963), *The Yellow Rolls-Royce* (1964), *Hell Is Empty* (1967, UK/Czech).

Mirren, Helen

(*b* London, 1945). Actress. RN: Ilyena Mirnoff. Intelligent actress who can move serenely between trashy (*Caligula*, 1979, US/It) and quality (*The Madness of George III*, 1994, UK/US) roles. She showed off her body in Michael POWELL's *Age of Consent* (1969, Aust), Ken RUSSELL's *Savage Messiah* (1972) and Peter GREENAWAY's *The Cook, the Thief, His Wife & Her Lover* (1989, UK/Fr). Best known to general audiences as Jane Tennison in the *Prime Suspect* TV series (1991–96), though there have been notable film performances: in the gangster classic, *The Long Good Friday* (1979), as Morgana in *Excalibur* (1981, UK/US), as the Queen in *The Madness of King George* and as one of the mothers in *Some Mother's Son* (1996, Ire/US). Has had an extensive Hollywood career, and with her 2001 performances as Michael CAINE's widow in *Last Orders* (UK/Ger) and the housekeeper with a dark secret in her past in *Gosford Park* (UK/Ger/US, AAn/supp a), she has matured into one of Britain's great character actresses. On stage with the RSC, she proved a formidable performer as Ophelia (1970), *Miss Julie* (1971) and Lady Macbeth (1974). Married to US-based director Taylor Hackford.

OTHER BRITISH FILMS INCLUDE: *Herostratus* (1967), *Miss Julie* (1972), *O Lucky Man!* (1973), *Hamlet* (1976), *Hussy* (1979), *Cal* (1984), *Pascali's Island* (1988, UK/US), *When the Whales Came* (1989), *The Comfort of Strangers* (1990, UK/It) *Where Angels Fear to Tread* (1991), *Greenfingers* (2001, UK/US).

BIBLIOG: Amy Rennert (ed), *Helen Mirren: A Celebration*, 1995. AS.

Mitchell and Kenyon

The most significant of the regional film companies in the earliest years of British film, though the extent of that significance has only recently been made apparent. The company was formed in Blackburn by Sagar

Mitchell (*b* 1866 – *d* 1952) and James Kenyon (*b*.? – *d* 1925) in 1897; though now commonly referred to as Mitchell and Kenyon, the company's releases were known as Norden Films. Their historical reputation had been based on their surviving films recreating scenes from the Boer War and the Boxer rebellion on the hills outside Blackburn. But the discovery in the mid 90s of 800 rolls of hitherto unknown films, sealed in barrels in the basement of a shop, has revealed a considerable business with a virtually nationwide network, specialising in local films of factory gates, football matches, parades, street scenes and transport, much of it commissioned by travelling fairground showmen. The restoration, identification and historical explication of this treasure trove by the BRITISH FILM INSTITUTE and the National Fairground Archive is genuinely rewriting early British film history. Luke McKernan.

Mitchell, Charlotte (*b* Ipswich, 1926). Actress. Supporting player best remembered as comfy Mrs Tranter in *The French Lieutenant's Woman* (1981) and as Wendy CRAIG's neighbour in TV's *Not in Front of the Children*; a minor Megs JENKINS. Occasional films since 1949, usually in small roles.
OTHER BRITISH FILMS INCLUDE: *The Romantic Age* (1949), *Folly to Be Wise* (1952), *Street Corner* (1953), *Lost* (1955), *Dentist in the Chair* (1960), *Blood on Satan's Claw* (1970), *Out of the Darkness* (1985).

Mitchell, Julian (*b* Epping, 1935). Screenwriter. Oxford-educated novelist, biographer, playwright as well as screenwriter for much quality TV, including *Elizabeth R* (1971) and *Staying On* (1980), and occasional films. He adapted (BAAn) his own play, *Another Country* (1982), to the screen (1984), devised a sensitive relocation of Chekhov's *Uncle Vanya* to Wales with *August* (1996), and wittily opened *Wilde* (1997, UK/Ger/Jap/US) in the 'wild West' of the US.
OTHER BRITISH FILMS: *Arabesque* (1966, UK/US, co-sc), *Strike It Rich* (1990, UK/US, co-sc).

Mitchell, Julien (*b* Glossop, 1888 – *d* London, 1954). Actor. Hefty character player of stage and screen. First film role was as the retiring engine driver brooding over his wife's supposed infidelity in *The Last Journey* (1935); he is a formidable chief of police in *Hotel Reserve* (1944) and a benign doctor in *Bedelia* (1946), among 20 others, including *The Sea Hawk* (1940) in Hollywood.
OTHER BRITISH FILMS INCLUDE: *Educated Evans* (1936), *The Drum* (1938), *The Goose Steps Out* (1942), *The Echo Murders* (1945), *Bonnie Prince Charlie* (1948), *Chance of a Lifetime* (1950), *Hobson's Choice* (1953).

Mitchell, Leslie (*b* Edinburgh, 1905 – *d* Vancouver, 1985). Commentator. Educated at King's School, Canterbury, and in Switzerland, and on stage from 1928, Mitchell was BBC television's first male announcer, starting 1934. Famous as commentator of Fox-produced *British Movietone News* and also joined LONDON FILMS as director of publicity. He was compère of *The March of the Movies* from 1940 and later edited the book of that title. In his few films, he usually plays commentators, like the one reporting the race in *Genevieve* (1953), as himself. Much involved with commercial TV from the late 40s.
OTHER BRITISH FILMS: (a, unless noted) *Sally in Our Alley* (dancer), *Rynox* (1931), *Oxford* (1940, doc, comm), *Black Sheep of Whitehall* (1941), *Lady Godiva Rides Again* (1951), *Grand National Night* (1953), *The Heart of a Man* (1959).
BIBLIOG: Autobiography, *Leslie Mitchell Reporting*, 1980.
    See also **newsreels**.

Mitchell, Norman (*b* Sheffield, 1918 – *d* Downham Market, 2001). Actor. RN: Driver. Versatile small-part player of over 40 films and about 2,000 TV appearances, as well as 500 radio broadcasts. Made debut on TV in 1951 and in film 1954. He was the 'dray driver' in *A Challenge to Robin Hood* (1967), the policeman who arrests *Oliver!* (1968) and a 'restaurant functionary' in *Lady Caroline Lamb* (1972, UK/It/US). He did whatever he was asked and he was asked to do a great deal.
OTHER BRITISH FILMS INCLUDE: *Up to His Neck* (1954), *Beat Girl* (1959), *Carry On Cabby* (1963), . . . *Cleo*, . . . *Spying* (1964), *Bunny Lake is Missing* (1965), *Half a Sixpence* (1967, UK/US) *On the Buses* (1971), *Legend of the Werewolf* (1974), *The Pink Panther Strikes Again* (1976), *The Return of the Soldier* (1982), *Dirty Weekend* (1993), *Lighthouse* (2000).

Mitchell, Oswald (*b* London, 1890 – *d* London, 1949). Director, screenwriter. Prolific rather than distinguished, Mitchell directed five 'Old Mother Riley' COMEDIES, sometimes also writing them, and a number of forgettable MUSICALS. His post-WW2 films are minor freaks, with the exception of *No Orchids for Miss Blandish* (1948), a major scandal of the time: credited as associate producer, he took over direction when St John CLOWES fell ill.
OTHER BRITISH FILMS: (prod man/sup) *Such Is the Law* (1930), *Variety* (1935, + co-sc); (d) *Danny Boy* (1934, co-d, + co-sc, p), *Old Mother Riley in Paris* (1938, + p), *Loyal Heart* (1946), *House of Darkness* (1948,); (d, co-sc/sc), *Variety Parade* (1936), *Rose of Tralee* (1937), *Lily of Laguna* (1938), *Old Mother Riley, MP* (1939), *Sailors Don't Care* (1940), *Asking for Trouble* (1942), *The Mysterious Mr Nicholson* (1947).

Mitchell, Warren (*b* London, 1926). Actor. RADA-trained Mitchell (he'd also read chemistry at Oxford) had appeared in nearly 40 films before finding household fame as the right-wing bigot, Alf Garnett, in TV's brilliantly original sitcom, *Till Death Do Us Part* (1966–68, 1972, 1974–75). This success brought him bigger roles, there were two film SPIN-OFFS, *Till Death Us Do Part* (1969) and *The Alf Garnett Saga* (1972), but since then he has lived and worked mainly in Australia, where he has done some notable character work on stage, TV and film. In 1980, he was a much-praised Willy Loman in *Death of a Salesman* at London's National Theatre.
OTHER BRITISH FILMS INCLUDE: *The Passing Stranger* (1954), *The Trollenberg Terror* (1958), *Hell is a City* (1959), *Two Way Stretch* (1960), *We Joined the Navy* (1962), *The Sicilians, Carry on Cleo* (1964), *Help!*, *The Spy Who Came in from the Cold* (1965), *The Jokers* (1966), *The Assassination Bureau* (1968), *Innocent Bystanders* (1972), *Jabberwocky* (1977), *The Chain* (1984), *Foreign Body* (1986).

Mitchell, Yvonne (*b* London, 1925 – *d* London, 1979). Actress. RN: Yvonne Joseph. Much respected actress of stage (from 1939), films (from 1949) and TV (from 1952). Anton WALBROOK facilitated her debut in *The Queen of Spades* (1948), but in spite of being acclaimed for this she made only carefully chosen and spaced films. With her tense, dark beauty, she had an immense gift for pathos, exploited best, on film, in *The Divided Heart* (1954), winning BAA as the biological mother of the contested child, as the well-meaning but slatternly *Woman in a Dressing Gown* (1957), as the racist murderess (BAAn) in *Sapphire* (1959) – yes, there is real pathos in her lower-middle-class aspirations for her children – and as Constance Wilde in *The Trials of Oscar Wilde* (1960). On TV, she gave a much-applauded performance in *1984* (1954), and she also wrote several performed plays as well as novels and an excellent autobiography-cum-reflection on her craft, *Actress*, 1957.

OTHER BRITISH FILMS: *Children of Chance* (1949), *Turn the Key Softly* (1953), *Escapade* (1955), *Yield to the Night* (1956), *Passionate Summer* (1958), *Tiger Bay* (1959), *Conspiracy of Hearts*, *Johnny Nobody* (1960), *The Corpse* (1969), *Demons of the Mind* (1971), *The Incredible Sarah* (1976, UK/US).

Mitchum, Robert (*b* Bridgeport, Connecticut, 1917 – *d* Santa Barbara, California, 1997). Actor. Apparently sleepy and lazy, in fact wholly professional in relation to his long-established star career, Mitchum made seven films in Britain, including the leaden *Ryan's Daughter* (1970), from the tedium of which he emerged, typically, unscathed, and he repeated his Philip Marlowe turn in Michael WINNER's unsubtle remake of *The Big Sleep* (1978).

OTHER BRITISH FILMS: *The Angry Hills* (1959), *The Grass Is Greener*, *A Terrible Beauty* (1960), *Mr Moses* (1965, UK/US), *Secret Ceremony* (1968).

Modley, Albert (*b* Barnsley, Yorks, 1901 – *d* Morecambe, 1979). Actor. Popular Northern comedian from the variety halls who made three regional film farces: *Bob's Your Uncle* (1941), *Up for the Cup*, *Take Me to Paris* (1950).

Moffat, Ivan (*b* Havana, 1918– *d* Los Angeles, 2002). Screenwriter. Son of actress and poet Iris Tree, Moffat has worked mostly in the US, sharing an AAn for the screenplay of *Giant* (1956), the culmination of his work with George Stevens. Worked on wartime DOCUMENTARIES such as *Citizen's Army* (1941); later work in British films included *Bhowani Junction* (1955, UK/US, co-sc), *The Heroes of Telemark* (1965, co-sc) and *Hitler: The Last Ten Days* (1973, UK/It, English adaptation).

Moffat, Graham (*b* London 1919 – *d* Bath, 1965). Actor. The fat boy of 30s British film comedy. Usually cast as an office boy or in a similarly menial function, he managed to project a proletarian truculence rarely seen elsewhere in British cinema at this time. He could put more rebellious feeling into the word 'Oy!' than any other actor. Frequently paired with fellow stooge Moore MARRIOTT in support of Will HAY and Arthur ASKEY.

BRITISH FILMS INCLUDE: *Stormy Weather* (1935), *Windbag the Sailor* (1936), *O-Kay for Sound*, *Oh, Mr Porter!*, *Good Morning, Boys!* (1937), *Old Bones of the River*, *Convict 99* (1938), *Cheer Boys Cheer*, *Ask a Policeman* (1939), *Charley's (Big-Hearted) Aunt* (1940), *Back Room Boy* (1942), *A Canterbury Tale* (1944), *I Know Where I'm Going!* (1945), *The Second Mate* (1950), *Inn for Trouble* (1959), *80,000 Suspects* (1963). Peter Hutchings.

Moffat, John (*b* London, 1922). Actor. After a short stint as a bank clerk, tall, somewhat austere-looking Moffat took to the stage and had vast rep experience (1945–50) before his 1950 London debut, and has remained primarily a theatre actor. In occasional films since the mid 50s, in supporting roles like Square in *Tom Jones* (1963), a good deal of TV since 1953, including *Love in a Cold Climate* (1980), and specially appreciated for his Hercule Poirot on BBC radio's versions of Agatha CHRISTIE.

OTHER BRITISH FILMS INCLUDE: *Loser Takes All* (1956, unc), *The Silent Enemy* (1958), *Julius Caesar* (1970), *Murder on the Orient Express* (1974), *Galileo* (1974, UK/Can), *Britannia Hospital* (1982), *Prick Up Your Ears* (1987).

Mohner, Carl (*b* Vienna, 1921). Actor. Austrian player in occasional British films since the later 50s, he had substantial roles in *Behind the Mask* (1958), as the 'bloody foreigner' seeking appointment in a London medical practice, and starring in the ACT FILMS version of Arnold Wesker's *The Kitchen* (1961). Most of his career is in continental films,

including the great *Rififi* (1955), as Jo the Swede.

OTHER BRITISH FILMS INCLUDE: *The Camp on Blood Island* (1957), *The Key* (1958), *Sink the Bismarck!* (1960), *Assignment K* (1968), *Callan* (1974).

Mohyeddin, Zia (*b* Lyallpur [now Faisalabad, Pakistan] 1933). Actor. Educated at Punjab University and RADA-trained, Mohyeddin made his London stage debut in a leading role in *A Passage to India* (1960), repeating the role in New York (1962) and on TV (1965). Of his films, his first two – *Lawrence of Arabia* (1962) and *Sammy Going South* (1963) – gave him, arguably, his best roles, but there was some rewarding TV, including *Staying On* (1980) and *Jewel in the Crown* (1984).

OTHER BRITISH FILMS INCLUDE: *Khartoum* (1966), *The Sailor from Gibraltar* (1967), *The Assam Garden* (1985), *Partition* (1987), *Immaculate Conception* (1991).

Molina, Alfred (*b* London, 1953). Actor. Tall, bulky, formidable character player who came to the fore in the 80s, especially as one of the Russian soldiers on leave in Liverpool in *A Letter to Brezhnev* (1985) and as Joe ORTON's jealous lover/murderer in *Prick Up Your Ears* (1987), and was in much demand for international films in the 90s. Of Italian/Spanish parentage, the Guildhall-trained Molina had an RSC season before being noticed as the duplicitous guide in *Raiders of the Lost Ark* (1981). He was a stern husband who softens under the Italian sun in *Enchanted April* (1992), and he is very alarming as the despotic Iranian husband/father in *Not Without My Daughter* (1991, US); such is the potency of his persona that one always expects him to do something deranged. In such Euromesses as *Anna Karenina* (1997, US but other nations must share the blame) and the soft-centred *Chocolat* (2000, UK/US) he is one of the few to emerge untarnished. Theatre credits include a Tony-winning performance in *Art* on Broadway and several for London's National and Royal Court. Married to Jill Gascoine (*b* London, 1937), star of TV's *The Gentle Touch* (1980–84) and in a couple of minor British films.

OTHER BRITISH FILMS INCLUDE: *Because I Am King* (1980), *Water* (1985), *The Accountant* (1989), *American Friends* (1991), *The Trial* (1992), *The Steal* (1995), *Nervous Energy* (1995), *Plots with a View* (2002, UK/US).

Mollison, Clifford (*b* London, 1897 – *d* Cyprus, 1986). Actor. On stage from 1913 and a popular, breezy lead, largely in cheerful comedies until WW2 (in the Army 1940–45), on both stage and screen. He was the footballer hero with *The Lucky Number* (1933) in ASQUITH's unpretentious comedy and the poor relation lead in *Mr Cinders* (1934). His debonair style was in less demand post-war, but he played small character roles in eight more films and was active on stage for several further decades. Brother of Henry MOLLISON.

OTHER BRITISH FILMS INCLUDE: *Almost a Honeymoon* (1930), *Radio Parade of 1935* (1934), *Royal Cavalcade* (1935), *Scrooge* (1951), *The Baby and the Battleship* (1956), *The VIPs* (1963), *Oh! What a Lovely War* (1969), *That's Your Funeral* (1972), *Love Thy Neighbour* (1973).

Mollison, Henry (*b* Broughty Ferry, Scotland, 1905). Actor. Clifford MOLLISON's brother who made his stage debut in 1924 (London, 1928) and entered films in minor roles in Maurice ELVEY's *Balaclava* (1928) and Elinor GLYN's *Knowing Men* (1930). Played leads and second leads in many COMEDIES and THRILLERS of the 30s, in Hollywood (e.g. *Youth Takes a Fling*, 1938) as well as England. A prisoner-of-war for five years, post-war he played several character roles and a half-hearted romantic role in *The Loves of Joanna Godden* (1947). His first wife was actress Jane WELSH.

OTHER BRITISH FILMS INCLUDE: *Third Time Lucky* (1931), *Letting in the Sunshine* (1933), *Drake of England* (1935), *Hungry Hill* (1947), *Whisky Galore!* (1949), *The Man in the White Suit* (1951), *Front Page Story* (1953).

Mollo, Andrew (*b* London, 1940). Production designer, historian. With Kevin BROWNLOW, historian Mollo, with a thorough knowledge of the Third Reich, heroically and for financial peanuts managed to make the alarming what-if fable, *It Happened Here* (1963, co-d, co-p, co-sc, art d, hist cons). Impressive as it was, it was badly handled by distributors and the pair met similar obstacles in getting their next film seen: this was the masterly historical *Winstanley* (1975, co-d, co-p, co-sc, art d), a recreation of the failed Leveller and Digger Movements of the Civil War. Mollo, who had begun as a runner on *Saturday Night and Sunday Morning* (1960), was historical consultant on such films as *Doctor Zhivago* (1965, UK/US), *The Eagle Has Landed* (1976) and *The Pianist* (2002, UK/Fr/Ger/Pol), but most of his post-*Winstanley* career has been in production design, on films such as *Dance with a Stranger* (1984), which so vividly evokes the 50s, and on TV's 'Sharpe' series (1993–97).

OTHER BRITISH FILMS INCLUDE: *It Happened Here Again* (1976, doc, interviewee); (art d/des) *Xtro* (1982), *The Innocent* (1984), *No Surrender* (1985, UK/Can), *Pascali's Island* (1988, UK/US).

Mollo, John (*b* London, 1931). Costume designer. Twice-Oscared (*Star Wars*, 1977; *Gandhi*, 1982, + BAAn for both), Mollo emerged as a major figure in British and, indeed, international costume design in the 80s and 90s. Entered films as historical researcher/adviser on *The Charge of the Light Brigade* (1968), *The Adventures of Gerard* (1970, UK/Fr/It), *Nicholas and Alexandra* (1971, UK/US) and *Barry Lyndon* (1975). He designed the authentic-looking 18th-century garb for *Revolution* (1985, UK/Nor), did another *Star Wars* (*The Empire Strikes Back*, 1980, US) and two more for Richard ATTENBOROUGH, *Cry Freedom* (1987) and *Chaplin* (1992, UK/Fr/It/Jap/US, BAAn/cos). Also responsible for costumes on the popular TV *Hornblower* series (1998–, BAAn/TV cos).

OTHER BRITISH FILMS INCLUDE: (cos) *Alien* (1979, UK/US, BAAn/cos), *Outland* (1981), *Greystoke . . .* (1984, UK/US), *Event Horizon* (1997, UK/US).

Molloy, Mike (*b* Sydney, 1940). Cinematographer, director. Served apprenticeship on Australian documentaries and commercials, then as camera operator on two films by Nicolas ROEG (*Performance*, 1970; *Walkabout*, 1970, Aust) and two by Stanley KUBRICK (*A Clockwork Orange*, 1971; *Barry Lyndon*, 1975), before his first cinematographer credit on *James Dean – The First American Teenager* (1975, doc, co-c). Continued to work intermittently in Australia. Best work may be on *Shiner* (2000), where, in conjunction with some smart editing, he creates unsettling effects.

OTHER BRITISH FILMS INCLUDE: *Hardcore* (1977), *The Shout* (1978), *The Hit* (1984), *Link* (1985), *Scandal* (1988), *All the Little Animals* (1998), *The Fourth Angel* (2001).

Monger, Christopher (*b* Pontypridd, Wales, 1950). Director. Welsh-born Monger's most attractive film to date is the Welsh-set, post-EALING comedy, *The Man Who Went Up a Hill . . .* (1995). Cut his teeth on SHORTS in the 70s.

OTHER BRITISH FILMS INCLUDE: (shorts) *Narcissus* (1971, + co-c), *Cold Mountain* (1973); (features) *Repeater* (1979, + p, sc, e), *Crime Pays* (1986, + sc), *Just Like a Woman* (1992, + co-sc), *Girl from Rio* (2001, UK/Sp, + sc).

Monkhouse, Bob (*b* Beckenham, 1928). Actor, screenwriter. An established comic-book artist before making his radio debut in 1948, Dulwich College-educated Monkhouse was a multi-talented comic, as adroit on the page as in radio, TV and film. Also a song-writer, vocalist, TV scriptwriter and games show host (e.g. *Celebrity Squares*, 1975–79); in fact, his film work is probably the least of his achievements. He was in the first 'CARRY ON'– *Sergeant* (1968); the rest is dross, especially *She'll Have to Go* (1961).

OTHER BRITISH FILMS INCLUDE: *Secret People* (1951), *Dentist in the Chair* (1960, + add dial), *A Weekend with Lulu* (1961), *The Bliss of Mrs Blossom* (1968).

Monkman, Phyllis (*b* London, 1892 – *d* London, 1976). Actress. On stage from childhood, became a well-known musical and revue star. Occasional films from silent days (*Persian Dance*, 1913) until 1949's *Diamond City*, as Diana DORS's tough old Ma.

OTHER BRITISH FILMS INCLUDE: *Her Heritage* (1919), *On with the Dance* (1927), *Blackmail* (1929), *Everything Happens to Me* (1938), *Young Man's Fancy* (1939), *Uncensored* (1942), *Carnival* (1946).

Monlaur, Yvonne (*b* Pau, France, 1938). Actress. Attractive leading lady of a few early 60s films, including the HORROR pieces, *Circus of Horrors* and *The Brides of Dracula* (1960), in which she just misses becoming one. The rest of her career is mostly in continental, chiefly Italian, films.

OTHER BRITISH FILMS: *Inn for Trouble* (1959), *The Terror of the Tongs* (1960), *Time to Remember* (1962).

Monsarrat, Nicholas (*b* Liverpool, 1910 – *d* London, 1979). Author. Winchester- and Cambridge-educated novelist, writing from the early 30s but reaching his – as it were – high-water mark with *The Cruel Sea* (1951). This graphic account of the horrors of naval warfare made an immensely successful EALING film (1952), stressing the human more than combat action. Served in Royal Navy during WW2, rising to Lt-Commander. Other films from his novels: *The Ship That Died of Shame* (1955, story in *Three Corvettes*, 1945), a potent metaphor for post-war malaise; *The Story of Esther Costello* (1957, novel 1953), starring Joan CRAWFORD; and *Something to Hide* (1971, novel 1965).

Montagu, Ivor (*b* London 1904 – *d* Watford 1984). Producer. Much of the history of British film in the 20s and 30s could be told through a biographical account of this Cambridge-educated critic, director, editor and activist. A former zoologist and son of a titled banker, he was a communist and co-founder of THE FILM SOCIETY (1925) and the Federation of Worker's Film Societies. He was a key contributor to that era's film culture, particularly combating what was understood to be Hollywood's predominance by making available films of many countries, especially of the Soviet Union, and, Russian-speaking himself, helped secure Pudovkin and Eisenstein to lecture to Film Society members on technique. As a *CLOSE UP* contributor, translator of Pudovkin's *Film Technique*, author of *The Political Censorship of Films* (1929), and a founder member of the PROGRESSIVE FILM INSTITUTE, Montagu provided a conduit for the British appreciation of Soviet cinema. He was an influential critic of the CENSORSHIP of these films, a propounder of left-wing film culture. He also made the anti-fascist films, *Defence of Madrid* (1936), with Norman McLAREN, and *Testament of Non-Intervention* (1938), as PROPAGANDA for the Republican cause in the Spanish Civil War. In feature films, he worked in the 20s as partner with director Adrian BRUNEL, and edited films for HITCHCOCK, including *The Lodger* (1926, + titles), *Easy Virtue* and *Downhill* (1927). He later became producer or associate producer on *The Man Who Knew Too Much* (1934), *The 39 Steps* (1935) and others. Joined EALING post-war as associate producer on *Another Shore* (1948) and co-wrote *Scott of the Antarctic* (1948). A nicely individual touch: he made *Table Tennis Today* (1929), a film born out of love and significant expertise in the game.

OTHER BRITISH FILMS INCLUDE: (p, unless noted) *Blighty* (1927, story), *King of the Ritz* (1933, sc), *My Heart Is Calling, My Old Dutch* (assoc p), *Wings Over Everest* (1934, doc), *The Passing of the Third Floor Back* (1935), *Sabotage, Secret Agent* (1936), *Behind Spanish Lines, Spanish ABC* (1938, doc), *Peace and Plenty* (1939, doc), *Man – One Family* (1948, doc), *The Last Man to Hang?* (1956).

BIBLIOG: Autobiography, *The Younger Son*, 1970. Deane Williams.

Montague, Lee (*b* London, 1927). Actor. Trained at the Old Vic School, on stage from 1950 and in films from 1953's *Moulin Rouge*. Solidly authoritative, he played his share of policemen and soldiers, in 'A' films like *The Secret Partner* (1961) or *The Secret of Blood Island* (1964), as a soldier flogged for planning escape, and second features like *The Man at the Carlton Tower* (1961). Much theatre, including Shylock at the Old Vic, 1962–63, and TV, including the lead in – an oddity – a play, *Rashomon* (1960), based on the famous Japanese film.

OTHER BRITISH FILMS INCLUDE: *Another Sky* (1955), *The Silent Enemy* (1958), *Blind Date* (1959), *The Singer Not the Song* (1960), *Billy Budd* (1962), *How I Won the War* (1967), *Brother Sun, Sister Moon* (1972, UK/It), *Mahler* (1974), *Silver Dream Racer* (1980), *Lady Jane* (1985), *Madame Sousatzka* (1988), *Enigma* (2001, UK/Ger/US).

Montgomery, Bruce (*b* Chesham Bois, 1921 – *d* London, 1978). Composer, conductor. As Edmund Crispin, the Oxford-educated Montgomery wrote some witty detective stories, featuring the donnish dick, Gervase Fen, and edited influential collections of sci-fi stories. A gifted musician (and dedicated alcoholic), he turned out scores for about 30 films, mainly light comedies, including *Doctor in the House* (1954), *Carry On Sergeant* (1958) and several of their respective sequels, as well as the charming film of children in Nova Scotia, *The Kidnappers* (1953), his first feature.

OTHER BRITISH FILMS INCLUDE: (comp, unless noted) *Raising a Riot, Doctor at Sea* (1955), *Eyewitness, Checkpoint* (1956), *The Duke Wore Jeans* (1958), *Please Turn Over, Carry On Constable* (+ cond) (1960), *Raising the Wind* (+ cond, sc, story), *Carry On Regardless* (1961), *Twice Round the Daffodils* (1962).

Montgomery, Doreen (*b* Glasgow, 1913 – *d* London, 1992). Screenwriter. Now most famous as the creator of Emma Peel in TV's *The Avengers* (1965–67), Montgomery began her screen-writing career in the late 30s, when she (co-)wrote such films as *Poison Pen* (co-) and *At the Villa Rose* (1939), evincing the flair for MELODRAMA which flowered at GAINSBOROUGH in the 40s. She adapted *The Man in Grey* (1943), co-scripted *Love Story* and wrote *Fanny by Gaslight* (1944). The pickings were leaner after this, though *While I Live* (1947, co-sc) has its moments, and by the mid 50s she had gone into TV, often writing for Douglas FAIRBANKS's series.

OTHER BRITISH FILMS INCLUDE: (co-sc) *Mr Reeder in Room 13* (1938), *This Man Is Mine* (1946), *Shadow of the Eagle* (1950), *Forever My Heart, Dance Little Lady* (1954); (sc) *Lassie from Lancashire* (1938, adptn), *Bulldog Sees It Through* (1940), *Victory Wedding* (short) (1944), *One Jump Ahead* (1955), *Murder Reported* (1957).

Montgomery, Douglass (aka Kent Douglass) (*b* Brantford, Ontario, 1909 – *d* Norwalk, Connecticut, 1966). Actor.

Canadian actor who had a modest Hollywood career in the 30s, including starring roles in *Waterloo Bridge* (1931) and *Little Women* (1933, as Laurie) and who finished his film career in Britain in the 40s. His one great role is that of Johnny Hollis in *The Way to the Stars* (1945), as the US flyer who crashes his plane to avoid a village; at his best, an actor of unusual sensitivity.

OTHER BRITISH FILMS: *Five and Ten* (1931), *Everything Is Thunder, Tropical Thunder* (1936), *Woman to Woman* (1946), *Forbidden* (1949).

Monty Python Comedy group. *Monty Python's Flying Circus* (BBC1, 1969–70; 1972–74): conceived, written and performed by Graham CHAPMAN, John CLEESE, Terry GILLIAM, Eric IDLE, Terry JONES and Michael PALIN. Often cited as a defining moment in British television cult comedy, the humour provided by these surreal sketches and sight gags, lacking narrative and accompanied by Gilliam's savage cartoons, had a huge international appeal. Parodying the techniques of television itself, the sketches 'Ministry of Silly Walks', 'lumberjack song' and 'dead parrot' still remain vivid in the collective consciousness. Feature films (in a similar vein) were later produced by the team: *Monty Python and The Holy Grail* (1974, directed by Gilliam and Jones), *Monty Python's Life of Brian* (1979, directed by Jones). Some members of the Python team moved on to successful independent careers. Cleese continued acting, producing and scriptwriting, notably in the sitcom *Fawlty Towers* and the films *A Fish Called Wanda* (1988) and *Fierce Creatures* (1997, UK/US). Gilliam directed movies, including *Brazil* (1985) and *Twelve Monkeys* (1995), Jones directed further films including *Personal Services* (1987) and Palin maintained a high television profile as the presenter of travel programmes.

BIBLIOG: Robert Ross, *Monty Python Encyclopedia*, 1997. Olwen Terris.

Moody, Ron (*b* London, 1924). Actor. RN: Moodnick. Now identified with his AA-nominated performance as Fagin, a morally airbrushed version of DICKENS's villain, in *Oliver!* (1968), the London University economics graduate had already made about a dozen films. On stage from 1952, he specialised in revue, including *For Adults Only* (1958) and musicals, such as *Candide* (1959) and *Oliver!* (1960). His screen career is patchy, with only the odd memorable character spot, like the Prime Minister in *The Mouse on the Moon* (1963) and Uriah Heep in *David Copperfield* (1969). Plenty of TV (*Who's a Good Boy?*, 1966) and the US series *Nobody's Perfect* (1979), but it, like the cinema, has not fully exploited Moody's eccentric, mildly demented persona.

OTHER BRITISH FILMS INCLUDE: *Follow a Star* (1959), *Make Mine Mink* (1960), *Summer Holiday* (1962), *Murder Most Foul* (1964), *Flight of the Doves* (1971), *Legend of the Werewolf* (1974), *Dominique* (1978), *Revelation* (2002).

Moon, Keith (*b* London, 1947 – *d* London, 1978). Musician. Drummer and key member of the rock band, 'The Who', with more than a touch of ferocious, zany energy. His films, with their rock connections, all draw on the public persona. He filmed in the US (e.g. as Mae West's dress designer in *Sextette*, 1978, and the DOCUMENTARY about the group, *The Kids Are All Right*, 1978) as well as appearing in such British films as *That'll Be the Day* (1973) and *Tommy* (1975, + co-comp, drummer). Died of drug overdose, but the legend has been kept alive in clips in many TV and cinema documentaries.

OTHER BRITISH FILMS: *200 Motels* (1971), *Radio Wonderful* (1973, short), *Stardust* (1974), *Quadrophenia* (1979, co-ex p, co-comp).

Moorcroft, Judy (*b* Stockport, 1933 – *d* London, 1991). Costume designer. Best known for her period designs for *The Europeans* (1979) – and how well she distinguishes Lee REMICK from her demure cousins – and *A Passage to India* (1984), for both of which she received AAn and BAAn. However, her work on films less obviously crying out for costume awards, such as *The Killing Fields* (1984) and *Clockwise* (1985) is just as meticulous, both authentic and evocative.

OTHER BRITISH FILMS INCLUDE: *Unman, Wittering and Zigo* (1971), *Murder by Decree* (1978, UK/Can), *Quartet* (1981, UK/Fr), *Yentl* (1983, UK/US), *A Month in the Country* (1987), *The Dressmaker* (BAAn), *Without a Clue* (UK/US) (1988), *City of Joy* (1992, UK/Fr).

Moore, Dudley (*b* London, 1935 – *d* Plainfield, New Jersey, 2002). Actor, writer, composer. Diminutive (5′ 2″) comic actor with an infectious giggle, Moore studied music at Oxford during which time he met fellow comedian Peter COOK with whom he made his film acting debut in *The Wrong Box* (1966, UK), and with whom (plus famous others) he originated the revue, *Beyond the Fringe* (farewelled on TV, 1964). The duo made records together and several more films, including *Bedazzled* (1967) and the concert film, *The Secret Policeman's Ball* (1979). Moore made his solo debut in *30 Is a Dangerous Age, Cynthia* (1967), though his first film appearance was, unbilled, as a member of John DANKWORTH's band in a 'B' MOVIE, *The Third Alibi*, 1961. Now best known for his Oscar-nominated performance as *Arthur* (1981, US), but none of his subsequent US films had such success. He was a gifted jazz pianist and has recorded a number of albums and composed music for several films, including *Inadmissible Evidence* (1968). Married (1) Suzy KENDALL, (2) Tuesday Weld, two others. Awarded CBE, 2001.

OTHER BRITISH FILMS INCLUDE: *Monte Carlo or Bust!* (UK/Fr/It), *The Bed Sitting Room* (1969), *The Hound of the Baskervilles* (1977), *Santa Claus* (1985), *Blame It on the Bellboy* (1992).

BIBLIOG: Autobiography, *Off-Beat*, 1987; Barbara Paskin, *Dudley Moore: The Authorised Biography*, 1997. Anne-Marie Thomas.

Moore, Eileen (*b* London, 1932). Actress. Pretty RADA-trained actress who had some good roles in the 50s, particularly as the selfish daughter in *An Inspector Calls* (1954) and as one of the women prisoners in *A Town Like Alice* (1956). Formerly married to George COLE.

OTHER BRITISH FILMS INCLUDE: *Mr Denning Drives North* (1951), *The Happy Family* (1952), *The Good Beginning* (1953), *The Green Man* (1956), *Devil's Bait* (1959).

Moore, Eva (*b* Brighton, 1870 – *d* Maidenhead, 1955). Actress. After a long and illustrious stage career (debut 1887) in many leading roles, she became a popular character player of 30s British cinema (e.g. *Jew Süss*, 1934; *Old Iron*, 1938) but had her most memorable moments in the US gothic *The Old Dark House* (1932). Back in Hollywood in the 40s when she appeared with daughter Jill ESMOND in *The Bandits of Sherwood Forest* (1946). Married to actor-manager H.V. (Henry Vernon) Esmond (*b* Kingston, Sussex, 1869 – *d* Paris, 1922) with whom she starred in the silent film, *The Law Divine* (1920).

OTHER BRITISH FILMS INCLUDE: *Flames of Passion* (1922), *Chu Chin Chow* (1923), *Motherland* (1927), *Almost a Divorce* (1931), *I Was a Spy* (1933), *A Cup of Kindness* (1934), *Annie, Leave the Room!* (1935).

Moore, Kieron (*b* Skibereen, Co. Cork, Ireland, 1925). Actor. RN: O'Hanrahan. Without ever quite becoming the major star KORDA must have had him in mind for, tall, rugged, intense-looking Moore gave some interesting performances and hung on for about 20 years. He began well as a dangerous Italian major domo preying on English virginal innocence in *A Man About the House* and as the disturbed ex-soldier in *Mine Own Executioner* (1947), but stumbled badly as Vronsky in *Anna Karenina* (1948). Much of the rest of his work was in supporting roles (e.g. impressive as the mute accused of murder in *The Green Scarf*, 1954; the covert homosexual in *The League of Gentlemen*, 1960) or supporting films (e.g. *Recoil*, *Mantrap*, 1953). Also in occasional US films including *David and Bathsheba* (1951). Directed two DOCUMENTARIES about developing nations, *The Progress of Peoples* (1975, + narr), *The Parched Land* (1979, + narr). Married Barbara WHITE.

OTHER BRITISH FILMS INCLUDE: *The Voice Within* (1945, under real name), *Saints and Sinners* (1949), *Conflict of Wings* (1954), *The Blue Peter* (1955), *Satellite in the Sky* (1956), *The Steel Bayonet* (1957), *The Key* (1958), *The Siege of Sidney Street* (1960), *The Day of the Triffids* (1962), *Hide and Seek* (1963), *Arabesque* (1966, UK/US), *Another Island* (1985, doc, narr).

Moore, Roger (*b* London, 1927). Actor. Studied at RADA, having decided he preferred acting to painting. His first film appearance was a bit part in *Perfect Strangers* (1945, UK) and he continued to appear in bit parts until 1953 when he went to America, signed up with MGM and had secondary roles in such films as *Interrupted Melody* (1955). Back in England, in 1962 he shot to stardom as Simon Templar in TV's *The Saint* (1962–69) and in 1973 took over from Sean CONNERY in the role of James BOND in *Live and Let Die* (1973), offering here and in the films that followed a handsome but blander version of 007's famous charms. His other films have been generally routine. Married/divorced singer **Dorothy Squires** (*b* Carmarthen, Wales, 1915 – *d* Rhondda, Wales, 1998), who appeared in the 1956 film, *Stars in Your Eyes*.

OTHER BRITISH FILMS INCLUDE: *Piccadilly Incident* (1946), *Crossplot* (1969), *The Man Who Haunted Himself* (1970), *Gold* (1974), *The Man With the Golden Gun* (1974), *Shout at the Devil* (1976), *The Spy Who Loved Me* (1977), *The Wild Geese* (1978, UK/US), *Moonraker* (1979, UK/Fr), *For Your Eyes Only* (1981), *Octopussy* (1983), *A View to a Kill* (1985), *Bullseye!* (1990), *Spice World* (1997), *The Enemy* (2001, UK/Ger/Lux/US).

BIBLIOG: Roy Moseley, *Roger Moore*, 1985. Anne-Marie Thomas.

Moore, Simon (*b c* 1958). Director, screenwriter. After directing two NATIONAL FILM SCHOOL SHORTS, *Coasters* and *Sleepwalking* (1980), came to prominence for writing (and sharing a BAAn for) the powerful TV series *Traffik* (1989), and a decade later wrote the US cinema version, *Traffic* (2001). His feature debut as director was *Under Suspicion* (1991, +sc), a *noir* THRILLER good enough to make one want to see more of his work, but his only other directorial effort, *Up on the Roof* (1997, + co-sc, orig play), was scarcely seen.

Moore, Stephen (*b* London, 1937). Actor. Squeezed in among a great deal of TV, including playing the diarist's father in *The Secret Life of Adrian Mole, Aged 13¾* (1985) and Mayor Vincy in *Middlemarch* (1994), are a half-dozen character roles in such films as *Brassed Off* (1996, UK/US), enjoyable as the inevitably unsympathetic management chief checking on colliery output.

OTHER BRITISH FILMS INCLUDE: *The White Bus* (1967), *A Bridge Too Far* (1977), *Laughterhouse* (1984), *Clockwise* (1985), *Under Suspicion* (1991).

Moore, Ted (*b* Cape Province, Zanzibar, 1914 – *d* Surrey, 1987). Cinematographer. Came to England in 1930, worked in the camera department at ELSTREE, and served in the RAF FILM UNIT during WW2. Was camera operator on such popular films as *The African Queen* (1951) and *Genevieve* (1953) and then photographed a series of action films for WARWICK, starting with *A Prize of Gold*, *Cockleshell Heroes* and *The Gamma People* (1955), and in the 60s and 70s there were several BOND capers, from *Dr No* (1962) and *From Russia with Love* (1963, BAA/c) to *The Man with the Golden Gun* (1974). In between, he did hugely distinguished work on *A Man for All Seasons* (1966), bringing a look of new-made freshness to river scenes which offset the harrowing drama on the banks, and he responds to other contrasts – sunbaked New Mexico and rain-sodden Britain – in *Priest of Love* (1980).

OTHER BRITISH FILMS INCLUDE: (cam op) *Curtain Up* (1952), *Hell Below Zero* (1953), *The Black Knight* (1954); (c) *April in Portugal* (1955, short), *Odongo*, *Zarak* (1956), *Interpol* (1957), *No Time to Die* (1958), *The Trials of Oscar Wilde* (1960), *Nine Hours to Rama* (co-c) (1962), *Goldfinger* (1964), *Thunderball* (1965), *The Prime of Miss Jean Brodie* (1968), *Country Dance* (1969), *Diamonds Are Forever* (1971), *Live and Let Die* (1973), *Dominique* (1978), *Clash of the Titans* (1981).

Morahan, Christopher (*b* London, 1929). Director. Son of production designer Tom MORAHAN, made his name chiefly as a director of TV drama, going back to such early 60s series as *First Night* (1963) and *Theatre 625* (1964), for which he directed *1984* to great acclaim, and, especially, the quartet, *Talking to a Stranger* (1966). He also shared a BAA for *The Jewel in the Crown* (1984) and directed the superb mini-series, *A Dance to the Music of Time* (1997), but his cinema work has been patchy; only his first film, *Diamonds for Breakfast* (1968) and the John CLEESE comedy, *Clockwise* (1985), have been much seen. His Directors' Guild Award, 1996, was presumably on the basis of his TV work.

OTHER BRITISH FILMS INCLUDE: *All Neat in Black Stockings* (1969), *Paper Mask* (1990, + p), *Unnatural Pursuits* (1991), *Element of Doubt* (1996).

Morahan, Jim (*b* London, 1902 – *d* Sudbury, 1976). Production designer. Resident and respected EALING designer whose name appears on credits for at least 30 of the studio's films. He was assistant art director to Michael RELPH on several early films, including *My Learned Friend*, *The Bells Go Down* (1943), *The Halfway House*, *They Came to a City* (1944), and art director to Relph's production designer on the very handsome *Saraband for Dead Lovers* (1948). His chief solo work was on the films of Alexander MACKENDRICK, from *Whisky Galore!* (1949) to the tottering Victoriana of *The Ladykillers* (1955). Post-Ealing life was, as for many of its alumni, less reliably rewarding but he created a convincingly claustrophobic effect in the jungles of ELSTREE for Ealing mate Leslie NORMAN's *The Long and the Short and the Tall* (1960). Brother of Tom MORAHAN.

OTHER BRITISH FILMS INCLUDE: (art d) *Painted Boats* (1945), *Frieda* (1947), *Scott of the Antarctic* (1948, fx art d), *The Blue Lamp* (1949), *Pool of London* (1950), *The Man in the White Suit* (1951), *Mandy*, *The Cruel Sea* (1952), *The 'Maggie'* (1953), *Lease of Life* (1954), *Out of the Clouds* (1955), *The Shiralee* (1957), *Dunkirk* (1958), *A Prize of Arms* (1961), *The Mind Benders* (1963), *Witchfinder General* (1968).

Morahan, Tom (*b* London, 1906 – *d* London, 1969). Production designer. Studied architecture, sculpture and painting in London and Paris; film design drew on all three areas when he joined Vincent KORDA as draughtsman (uncredited) in 1933. His 30s credits, sometimes for 'art director', sometimes for 'settings', are all for MAYFLOWER PRODUCTIONS, comprising *Vessel of Wrath*, *St Martin's Lane* (1938) and *Jamaica Inn* (1939); and he was with EALING in the early 40s, working notably on *Went the Day Well?* and *The Next of Kin* (1942). Post-war he was involved in a mixture of lavish productions, like *Men of Two Worlds* (1946), reproducing the African jungle

at Denham, *Captain Horatio Hornblower RN* (1951, UK/US) and *Those Magnificent Men . . .* (1965, BAAn/des), and such intimate dramas as the tensely confined SCHOOL-set drama *Mr Perrin and Mr Traill* and the superbly decorative Victorian MELODRAMA, *So Evil My Love* (1948). He shared an Oscar nomination for his work on *Sons and Lovers* (1960, + assoc p), in the realist mode which he claimed was his métier. Father of Christopher MORAHAN; brother of Jim MORAHAN.

OTHER BRITISH FILMS INCLUDE: (art d/des, unless noted) *Dreaming Lips* (1937), *The Foreman Went to France* (1942), *On Approval* (1944), *Under Capricorn* (1949), *Treasure Island* (1950), *The Love Lottery* (1953), *The Rainbow Jacket* (1954), *The Night My Number Came Up* (1955, + assoc p), *The Long Arm* (1956, + assoc p), *Shake Hands with the Devil* (1959, UK/US), *Circle of Deception* (1960, p), *Play Dirty* (1968).

Moran, Nick (*b* London, 1969). Actor. Fast-rising actor of the 90s, a genuine EastEnder, a key member of the cult-bloodbath success, *Lock, Stock and Two Smoking Barrels* (1998); he's the tall one with long face, curly hair and shrewdly appraising eyes. His other British films include the truly *Rancid Aluminium* (2000) and *Another Life* (2001), a period murder piece; and he has been in such popular TV as *The Bill* (1995) and *Heartbeat* (1992–2001). Worked in Hollywood on *The Proposal* (2001). His partner is Sienna GUILLERY, with whom he appeared in the SHORT FILMS, *The Future Lasts a Long Time* (1996) and *The Rules of Engagement* (1999).

OTHER BRITISH FILMS INCLUDE: *Buddy's Song* (1990), *Miss Monday* (1998, UK/US), *Christie Malry's Own Double-Entry* (2000, released 2002, UK/Neth/Lux).

Moran, Percy (*b* Ireland, 1886 – *d* 1958). Actor, director. An athletic and virile leading man, on screen as early as 1904, Moran starred for BRITISH AND COLONIAL in the *Lt Daring* series (1911–14) and the *Dick Turpin* series (1912–13); at the end of his career, he reprised his most famous role in *Lieutenant Daring, RN and the Water Rats* (1924, + co-d). In the mid 1910s, he played a character named Lt Jack Moran in films he also directed.

OTHER BRITISH FILMS INCLUDE: (d) *London's Nighthawks* (+ a), *How Men Love Women*, *Nurse and Martyr* (+ a), *London's Enemies* (+ a) (1915), *The Redemption of His Name* (1918), *Jack, Sam and Pete* (1919, + a), *The Field of Honour* (1922, + a). AS.

More, Kenneth (*b* Gerrards Cross, 1914 – *d* London, 1982). Actor. More was one of the dominant MALE STARS of the 1950s, able to play both comic and serious roles and with a greater emotional range than has customarily been acknowledged. After being demobbed from the Royal Navy, More appeared in supporting roles that included Lieutenant Teddy Evans in *Scott of the Antarctic* (1948). Without the security of a long-term studio contract, More alternated between films and the West End stage and one of his strongest performances came in *The Deep Blue Sea* (1955), adapted from Terence RATTIGAN's 1952 play, where he repeated his theatrical success as the mal-adjusted ex-RAF pilot.

The film that launched More as a star was *Genevieve* (1953) where he played the breezy, ebullient Ambrose Claverhouse, unlucky in cars and love. More played a similar role in *Doctor in the House* (1954), another modern variation on the pre-war man-about-town, debonair, self-deprecating and warm-hearted. Other comedy roles followed in *Raising a Riot* (1955), *The Admirable Crichton* (1957), and *The Sheriff of Fractured Jaw* (1958), a spoof WESTERN. But these roles alternated with others in which he played indomitable English heroes: the disabled Battle of Britain ace Douglas Bader in *Reach for the Sky* (1956), a courageous second officer aboard the 'Titanic' in *A Night to Remember* (1958), the adventurer Richard Hannay in *The Thirty Nine Steps* (1958), defender of the Empire in *North West Frontier* (1959) and Admiralty mastermind, Captain Shepard, in *Sink the Bismarck!* (1960). More always animated his stiff-upper-lip Englishmen, through either wry self-mockery or pathos, as when Shepard weeps in relief to know his son, believed missing in action, has survived.

More's persona was so strongly associated with traditional middle-class values that his stardom could not survive the shift towards working-class iconoclasts and his career petered out in the 60s, symbolised by his performance as the struggling thespian in *The Comedy Man* (1963). He became a household name again through television, as Jolyon Forsyte in *The Forsyte Saga* (1967), which showed just how accomplished an actor he was. Second wife was actress Angela DOUGLAS.

OTHER BRITISH FILMS: *School for Secrets* (1946), *Man on the Run, Stop Press Girl, Now Barabbas Was a Robber* (1949), *Morning Departure, The Franchise Affair, Chance of a Lifetime* (1950), *The Clouded Yellow, No Highway, The Galloping Major, Appointment with Venus* (1951), *Brandy for the Parson, The Yellow Balloon, Never Let Me Go, Our Girl Friday* (1953), *Next to No Time!* (1958), *Man in the Moon* (1960), *The Greengage Summer* (1961), *We Joined the Navy, Some People* (1962), *The Mercenaries* (1967), *Oh! What a Lovely War, Battle of Britain* (1969), *Scrooge* (1970), *The Slipper and the Rose* (1976), *Leopard in the Snow* (1977).

BIBLIOG: Autobiographies, *Happy Go Lucky*, 1959; *More or Less*, 1978. Andrew Spicer.

More O'Ferrall, George *see* O'Ferrall, George More

Morecambe, Eric (*b* Morecambe, 1926 – *d* Tewkesbury, 1984), RN: Bartholomew; and, **Wise, Ernie** (*b* Leeds, 1925 – *d* Wexham, 1999), RN: Wiseman. Comedy team. Much loved duo who found enduring fame on TV, from 1961 to 1978, with Christmas Specials taking them into the 80s. In these specials, such guests as Glenda JACKSON (1972), Laurence OLIVIER (1973) and Prime Minister Harold Wilson (1978) took part. The pair made only three films – *The Intelligence Men* (1965), *That Riviera Touch* (1966) and *The Magnificent Two* (1967) – but, though these have incidental felicities, none does justice to those whose TV fans might well have called them the Magnificent Two. Short, fair, smart Ernie and tall, dark, thick Eric emerge intact from the films, but the films are not themselves worth much. They appeared as themselves in an obscure short film, *Simon Simon* (1970).

Morell, André (*b* London, 1909 – *d* London, 1978). Actor. RN: Mesritz. 'Urbane', 'civilised' and 'intelligent' are the sorts of epithets that would be commonly used to conjure up the versatile character actor who began his stage career in rep and first appeared in London in 1936. Appeared in a few films pre-war, was in the Army (1940–46), and, on return, was very productive on stage, screen and TV. His dignified bearing and cultivated voice marked him out for professional roles, including several doctors (*Trio, So Long at the Fair*, 1950) and upper-echelon police, including what is really a starring role in *Seven Days to Noon* (1950), as well as a suave criminal in the excellent co-feature, *Cash on Demand* (1961). Was married to Joan GREENWOOD.

OTHER BRITISH FILMS INCLUDE: *Many Tanks Mr Atkins* (1938), *Three Silent Men* (1940), *Unpublished Story* (1942), *Against the Wind* (1947), *Madeleine* (1949), *High Treason* (1951), *Summer Madness* (UK/US), *They Can't Hang Me* (1955), *Zarak* (1956), *The Hound of the Baskervilles* (1959), *Woman of Straw* (1964), *The Wrong Box* (1966), *The Vengeance of She* (1967), *Barry Lyndon* (1975), *The Slipper and the Rose* (1976), *The First Great Train Robbery* (1978).

Morgan, Diana (*b* Cardiff, 1910 – *d* London, 1996). Screenwriter, playwright. Studied acting at Central School and made London debut in *Cavalcade* (1931), but it is as playwright and co-author of intimate revues she is best known. In the 40s, she became virtually the only woman of the EALING creative team, collaborating on the screenplays of such diverse films as *Went the Day Well?* (1942), *The Halfway House* (1944), and *Pink String and Sealing Wax* (1945), working harmoniously with such other Ealing names as Robert HAMER and Charles CRICHTON. Post-Ealing she went to Hollywood to work on *Let's Be Happy* (1956), filmed in England, and won numerous awards for *Hand in Hand* (1960), a fable of tolerance and her last film script, though she continued to write extensively for TV, including *Emergency – Ward 10* (1957–67). She often wrote for the theatre in collaboration with husband Robert MacDERMOT.

OTHER BRITISH FILMS INCLUDE: (co-sc, unless noted) *Ships with Wings* (1941, + lyrics), *Fiddlers Three* (1944, + co-lyrics), *A Run for Your Money* (add dial), *Poet's Pub* (sc) (1949), *Dance Hall* (1950), *The Woman's Angle* (1952, adptn).

Morgan, Guy (*b* Sketty, Swansea, 1908 – *d* East Grinstead, 1964). Screenwriter, journalist. Haileybury- and Oxford-educated Morgan was film critic for the *Daily Express* (1935–40), served in the Royal Navy (1940–46), and post-war wrote, usually in collaboration, over 20 film scripts, starting with *The Captive Heart* (1946). His solo work is not very distinguished, but there are three trim co-features for Lance COMFORT: *Eight O'Clock Walk* (1954), *The Girl on the Pier* (1953) and *The Man in the Road* (1956), and *Albert RN* (1953), based on a play he co-authored, is a taut WAR FILM. Became story editor for Douglas Fairbanks Productions from 1952. In 1948 published *Red Roses Every Night: An Account of London's Cinemas Under Fire*, 1948.

OTHER BRITISH FILMS INCLUDE: (co-sc, unless noted) *Anna Karenina* (1948), *The Woman with No Name* (1950), *Hell Is Sold Out* (1951), *Never Look Back* (1952), *Love in Pawn* (1953), *The Red Dress* (1954).

Morgan, Joan (*b* Forest Hill, London, 1905). Actress, screenwriter. The 1995 version of *Little Dorrit* led to a revival of interest in the star of the 1920 version, a pretty ingenue, who enjoyed a long career as actress, screenwriter and novelist. Made her debut aged eight in a French film, that led to a contract with Joe Bamberger and her first British film, *The Cup-Final Mystery* (1914). She often played in the films of director-father Sidney MORGAN, who sent her to the US at the outbreak of WW1, where she appeared in *Sally in Our Alley* (1916) and others; to South Africa in 1922 to star in *Swallow*; and, later that year, again to the US for an abortive attempt at a Hollywood career. She became a screenwriter with *The Alley Cat* (1929, UK/Ger), using the names Joan Wentworth and Iris North. Between 1940 and 1972, she also published 15 novels.

OTHER BRITISH FILMS INCLUDE: (a) *Queenie of the Circus* (1914), *Her Greatest Performance* (1916), *Lady Noggs – Peeress* (1920), *A Lowland Cinderella* (1921), *The Shadow of Egypt* (1924), *The Woman Tempted* (1926); (sc) *The Callbox Mystery* (1932), *Chelsea Life* (1933), *Lily of Laguna* (1938), *This Was a Woman* (1948, orig play, 1944). AS.

Morgan, Sidney (*b* London, 1873 – *d* Bournemouth, 1946). Director. Morgan was a busy director of cheap, unsophisticated fare, often starring his daughter, Joan MORGAN. He had various production companies, including Renaissance Films (1915–16) and Unity Super (1916–17), but his longest-running concern was the Progress Film Co. Ltd, at SHOREHAM STUDIOS, which began production in 1913, and ended in 1922, when the studio was destroyed by fire.

BRITISH FILMS INCLUDE: *The Brass Bottle* (1914, + sc), *Our Boys* (1915, + sc), *Democracy* (1918, + sc), *Lady Noggs – Peeress* (1920), *A Lowland Cinderella* (1921), *The Lilac Sunbonnet* (1922), *The Woman Who Obeyed* (1923), *A Window in Piccadilly* (1928), *Alley Cat* (1929), *Contraband Love* (1931), *Chelsea Life* (1933), *The Minstrel Boy* (1937, + p). AS.

Morgan, Terence (*b* London, 1921). Actor. Popular leading man of the 50s. After RADA and theatre, Terence Morgan made his film debut as Laertes in Laurence OLIVIER's *Hamlet* (1948). Although handsome, he rarely played conventional romantic types as there was usually something rather duplicitous about his persona. One of his best remembered roles was as the suspicious father of *Mandy* (1952), who eventually sees the error of his ways. Morgan displayed a nice sense of comedy as a shy tax inspector in *Always a Bride* (1953), became a leading man in RENOWN films of the mid 50s, and was convincing as criminal types, as in *The Shakedown* (1959). Also filmed in Italy, and was TV's *Sir Francis Drake* (1962).

OTHER BRITISH FILMS INCLUDE: *Shadow of the Past* (1950), *Encore* (1951), *Street Corner* (1953), *Dance Little Lady*, *Svengali* (1954), *It's a Wonderful World*, *The March Hare* (1956), *The Scamp* (1957), *Tread Softly Stranger* (1958), *Piccadilly Third Stop* (1960), *The Penthouse* (1967). Roger Philip Mellor.

Moriarty, P.H. Tall, balding character player in films since the late 70s, Moriarty was first noticed as 'Razors', Bob HOSKINS's watchful right-hand man in *The Long Good Friday* (1979). He was 'Mike the Throat' in TV's *Number One* (1984) and 'Hatchet Harry' in *Lock, Stock and Two Smoking Barrels* (1998): an image was emerging. Also in the US-made *Patriot Games* (1992).

OTHER BRITISH FILMS INCLUDE: *Quadrophenia*, *Bloody Kids* (1979), *Outland* (1981), *Chaplin* (1992, UK/Fr/It/Jap/US).

Morley, Robert (*b* Semley, 1908 – *d* Reading, 1992). Actor. Morley's portly frame, double chin and perpetual look of pop-eyed surprise made him one of the screen's most recognisable performers and one of its most endearing personalities. There was often a touch of the great overgrown schoolboy about him, and his published interviews encouraged the perception that to him acting was no more than a delightful game for which one was paid. RADA-trained and on stage from 1929, he received an AAn for his film debut as the weakly foolish Louis XVI who grows in stature with adversity in *Marie Antoinette* (1938), made in the US where he had gone to star in *Oscar Wilde*, a role he would repeat in a dull film (1960). Enjoyable rather than profound, he was sought for showy character roles over five decades, but the best came early: Undershaft in *Major Barbara* (1941), almost arguing the last act into cinematic life; Katharine HEPBURN's missionary brother in *The African Queen* and the craven Almayer in *Outcast of the Islands* (1951); and the cricket-mad poet in *The Final Test* (1953); but he was good company until the end. Also co-wrote and performed in several plays, including *Edward, My Son* (1947; filmed 1949, but with Spencer TRACY in Morley's stage role), and appeared in and/or directed many more. Awarded CBE, 1957. Married Joan Buckmaster, Gladys COOPER's daughter. Sheridan Morley, critic and showbiz biographer, is their son.

OTHER BRITISH FILMS INCLUDE: *Return to Yesterday* (play), *You Will Remember* (1940), *The Young Mr Pitt*, *Partners in Crime* (short) (1942), *I Live in Grosvenor Square* (1945), *The Small Back Room* (1948), *Curtain Up* (1952), *The Story of Gilbert and Sullivan* (1953), *Beau Brummell*, *The Good Die Young* (1954), *The Doctor's Dilemma* (1958), *Libel*, *The Battle of the Sexes* (1959), *The Young Ones* (1961), *Go to Blazes* (1962), *Murder at the Gallop* (1963), *Of Human Bondage* (1964), *Those Magnificent Men . . . , Life at the Top*, *The Alphabet Murders* (1965), *Hot Millions* (1968),

Cromwell (1970), *Theatre of Blood* (1973), *The Human Factor* (1979), *Little Dorrit* (1987).

BIBLIOG: Autobiography, Robert Morley, *Responsible Gentleman*, 1966; Sheridan Morley, *Robert, My Father*, 1993.

Morrell, Penny Actress. Married to George COLE since 1964, she played about a dozen small roles in the late 50s/early 60s, including three with Norman WISDOM and, showing some comic flair, a chirpy, lower-case Dora BRYAN-type secretary in *Smokescreen* (1964).

OTHER BRITISH FILMS INCLUDE: *Brothers in Law* (1956), *Lucky Jim* (1957), *The Bulldog Breed* (1960), *Mrs Gibbons' Boys* (1962), *The Wild Affair*, *A Stitch in Time* (1963), *The Early Bird* (1965).

Morris, Aubrey (*b* Portsmouth, 1930). Actor. Supporting player of screen and TV, often in eccentric, somewhat twitchy roles. He was P.R. Deltoid in *A Clockwork Orange* (1971), the gravedigger in *The Wicker Man* (1973), and the bizarre Mr Mybug in TV's *Cold Comfort Farm* (1968). Some US films, including *Love and Death* (1975).

OTHER BRITISH FILMS: *The Quare Fellow* (1962), *The Night Caller* (1965), *The Great St Trinian's Train Robbery* (1966), *Up the Junction*, *The Magnificent Two* (1967), *Blood from the Mummy's Tomb* (1971), *Man About the House* (1974), *Lisztomania* (1975), *Night Ferry* (1976), *Lifeforce* (1985), *The Rachel Papers* (1989).

Morris, Brian (*b* Lancashire) Production designer. AA-nominated for his designs for the undervalued *Evita* (1996) and BAA-nominated for this and for *Yanks* (1979), on which he faithfully recreated provincial Britain during WW2, Morris has worked in both the US and UK. A several-times designer for Alan PARKER, but it would be unfair to blame him for the unspeakable *The Road to Wellville* (1994, US), in which the designs alone were laudable. First film experience was in early 70s SHORTS for Parker and others.

OTHER BRITISH FILMS INCLUDE: (shorts) *Day of Rest* (1970), *Footsteps, Our Cissy* (1974); (features, des/art d) *That'll Be the Day* (1973), *Stardust* (1974), *Full Circle* (1976, UK/Can), *Pink Floyd The Wall* (1982), *Another Country* (1984), *A World Apart* (1987, UK/Zimb), *The Commitments* (1991, UK/US), *Damage* (UK/Fr) (1992), *The Boxer* (1998, UK/Ire/US).

Morris, Edna (*b* Bolton, Lancs, 1906). Actress. 'You think you own the place, you young bleeder'. Thus does this robust purveyor of North Country types berate the swaggering Albert FINNEY in *Saturday Night and Sunday Morning* (1960), one of the nosey neighbours and harridan landladies she specialised in. In rep from 1935, on London stage from 1945, and on TV from 1947.

OTHER BRITISH FILMS INCLUDE: *Cure for Love* (1949), *Another Man's Poison* (1951), *Women of Twilight* (1952), *The Gypsy and the Gentleman* (1957), *Sons and Lovers* (1960), *The Idol* (1966).

Morris, Ernest (*b* London, 1915 – *d* 1987) Director. churned out second features, in an undistingushed career, and never achieved the breakthrough to major productions he wanted. What talent he had was probably wasted in efforts to capture a public mood that he may well have misinterpreted. For instance, even in 1963, titles such as *Strip Tease Murder* was unlikely to excite anyone. In fact, when he really allowed himself to deal with subjects that he knew, as in the spy thriller *Echoes of Diana* (1963), he showed a surprising sophistication. The final series of films, the *Mr Moto* comedy thrillers, with Henry Silva, lacked the sense of fun of the 30s originals and were understandably described by one commentator as 'painfully boring'. The one exception in his work as direcor is *The Tell-Tale Heart* (1960), a stylish HORROR film which hints at other possibilities. Had considerable experience as (2nd) assistant director in the 40s and early 50s.

OTHER BRITISH FILMS INCLUDE: (2nd/ass d) *The Rake's Progress* (1945), *Caravan* (1946), *Jassy* (1947), *Easy Money* (1948), *The Lost Hours* (1952), *Profile* (1954); (d) *Operation Murder* (1956), *Woman of Mystery* (1957), *On the Run* (1958), *Transatlantic* (1960), *Shadow of Fear* (1963), *The Sicilians*, *The Court Martial of Major Keller* (1964), *The Return of Mr Moto* (1965). Paul Quinn.

Morris, Flora Actress. Hepworth leading lady from 1910 to 1915, when she left to join a new company, MLB.

BRITISH FILMS INCLUDE: *A Flowergirl's Romance* (1910), *A Fool and His Money* (1911), *Oliver Twist* (1912), *Sally in Our Alley* (1913), *The Heart of Midlothian* (1914), *After Dark* (1915), *Whoso Is Without Sin* (1916). AS.

Morris, Jonathan Editor. All Morris's feature credits are on the films of Ken LOACH, from *Fatherland* (1986, UK/Fr/Ger) to *Bread and Roses* (2001, UK/Fr/Ger/It/Sp/Switz).

OTHER BRITISH FILMS: *Hidden Agenda* (1990), *Riff-Raff* (1991), *Raining Stones* (1993), *Ladybird Ladybird* (1994), *Land and Freedom* (1995, UK/Ger/Sp), *Carla's Song* (1996, UK/Ger/Sp), *My Name Is Joe* (1998, UK/Fr/Ger/It/Sp), *The Navigators* (2002).

Morris, Lana (*b* Ruislip, 1930 – *d* Windsor, 1998) Actress. RN: Pamela Matthews. One of RANK's 'young ladies' of the 40s, Morris had several good roles in post-war years, especially between 1948–50. She was a cute, attractive actress, very engaging as the saucy maid, who gave as good as she got, in *Spring in Park Lane* (1948), and as Gaiety Girl 'Bouncie Barrington', showered with jewellery by 'Stage Door Johnnies' for her looks, rather than for her talent, in *Trottie True* (1948). Apart from two Norman WISDOM films, she spent most of the 50s in supporting roles and 'B' FILMS. Later on TV as a panellist and in *The Forsyte Saga* (1967) and *Howards' Way* (1985).

OTHER BRITISH FILMS INCLUDE: *School for Secrets* (as Pamela Matthews) (1946), *The Weaker Sex* (1948), *The Chiltern Hundreds* (1949), *Morning Departure*, *Trio*, *The Woman in Question* (1950), *A Tale of Five Cities* (1951), *Trouble in Store* (1953), *Radio Cab Murder* (1954), *Man of the Moment* (1955), *No Trees in the Street* (1958), *Jet Storm* (1959), *I Start Counting* (1969). Roger Philip Mellor.

Morris, Lily (*b* London, *c* 1884 – *d* London, 1952). Actress. Celebrated MUSIC HALL star who appeared in a few MUSICAL films of the 30s, including Adrian BRUNEL's *Elstree Calling* (1930) and *Variety* (1935), but in her last film, *I Thank You* (1941), had her best chance as Lady Randall, former music-hall star who comes into her own again.

OTHER BRITISH FILMS: *Those Were the Days* (1934), *Radio Parade of 1935* (1934).

Morris, Mary (*b* Suva, Fiji, 1915 – *d* Aigle, Switz., 1988). Actress. Few British cinema actresses exhibited such strong qualities of character and intelligence. Despite noteworthy appearances as *femmes fatales* in *The Spy in Black* (1939) and *The Thief of Baghdad* (1940), leading lady status in *Pimpernel Smith* (1941), and the moral conscience to William HARTNELL in *The Agitator* (1945), British cinema unjustly neglected an actress capable of portraying independent non-stereotypical characters. However, British television recognised her talents. She played memorable roles in the BBC productions *A for Andromeda* (1961), *The Andromeda Breakthrough* (1962), Durrenmatt's *The Physicists*, Cleopatra in *The Spread of the Eagle* (1963) and a Peter Pan-costumed Number 2 in an episode of *The Prisoner* (1967). These all revealed her qualities of commanding presence and deep characterization that British cinema never fully utilised.

OTHER BRITISH FILMS INCLUDE: *Double Door* (1934), *Victoria the Great* (1937), *Prison Without Bars* (1938), *Undercover* (1943), *The Man from Morocco* (1945), *Train of Events* (1949), *High Treason* (1951). Tony Williams.

Morris, Oswald (aka 'Ossie') (*b* Ruislip, 1915). Cinematographer. One of the great British cinematographers, innovative, risk-taking and articulate about his work. Always obsessed with movies, he began as a clapper-boy (at WEMBLEY STUDIOS) in 1932, working on 'QUOTA QUICKIES', rising to camera operator on *I Met a Murderer* (1939) before being called up. Post-war, after service as a bomber pilot, he operated for, amongst others, Guy GREEN, on such notable films as *Oliver Twist* (1948, 20 years later he would shoot *Oliver!*, 1968, receiving a BAAn), before getting his first cinematographer credit on *The Golden Salamander* (1949), directed by his old mentor, Ronald NEAME. He rated Green and Neame as major influences, but in the 50s he quickly established his own parity with them, especially on the films he did with director John HUSTON, starting with *Moulin Rouge* (1953). On this, he experimented with smoke and to get the impression Huston wanted of a film that might have been made by Toulouse-Lautrec, driving TECHNICOLOR executives mad in the process. Three years later, Huston set him another challenge: that of making *Moby Dick* (1956) visually recall old etchings and whaling prints. In another vein, his grainy realist work on René Clement's *Knave of Hearts* (1954) led Tony RICHARDSON to seek him out for the NEW WAVE films, *Look Back in Anger* (1959) and *The Entertainer* (1960), to which he brought a harsh black-and-white REALISM, at least on the location-shot sequences. Almost everything he did was notable, even when the films themselves were not; for instance, he thought *Equus* (1977) was a 'terrible disappointment' but the way he lights the 'worshipping' sequences of boy with horse have a touch of real magic. Won an Oscar (+ BAAn) for *Fiddler on the Roof* (1971, US), and BAA/c for *The Pumpkin Eater* (1964), *The Hill*, *The Spy Who Came In from the Cold* (1965) in 1965, 1966 and 1967 respectively. It is a remarkable career from an unpretentious artist who never grew complacent about his art.

OTHER BRITISH FILMS INCLUDE: (cam ass) *Money for Speed* (1933); (cam op) *Green for Danger* (1946), *Captain Boycott*, *Blanche Fury* (1947), *The Passionate Friends* (1948); (c) *Cairo Road*, *Circle of Danger*, *The Adventurers* (1950), *Saturday Island*, *So Little Time*, *The Card*, *South of Algiers* (1952), *Beat the Devil* (UK/It/US) (1953), *Beau Brummell* (1954), *The Man Who Never Was* (1955), *Heaven Knows, Mr Allison* (1957, UK/US), *The Key* (1958), *Our Man in Havana* (1959), *The Guns of Navarone*, *Lolita* (1961), *Term of Trial*, *The Devil Never Sleeps*, *Come Fly with Me* (UK/US) (1962), *Of Human Bondage* (1964), *Mister Moses* (UK/US), *The Battle of the Villa Fiorita* (UK/US), *Life at the Top* (1965), *Stop the World I Want to Get Off*, *The Winter's Tale* (1966), *Great Catherine* (1967), *Goodbye, Mr Chips* (1969), *Scrooge*, *Fragment of Fear* (1970), *Sleuth*, *Lady Caroline Lamb* (UK/It/US) (1972), *The Mackintosh Man* (1973), *The Man with the Golden Gun*, *The Odessa File* (UK/Ger) (1974), *The Great Muppet Caper* (1981), *The Dark Crystal* (1982).

Morris, Phyllis (*b* London, 1894 – *d* London, 1982). Actress. Educated at Cheltenham Ladies College and with a long stage career, Morris spent 1947–52 in Hollywood, playing there, as in Britain, any number of grim-featured harridans, often uncredited, like disapproving Aunt Julia Forsyte in *The Forsyte Saga* (1949, US), and was a foolishly indulgent governess in *Mandy* (1952).

OTHER BRITISH FILMS INCLUDE: *The Girl in the Crowd* (1934), *Goodbye, Mr Chips*, *On the Night of the Fire* (1939), *I Thank You* (1941), *The Life and Death of Colonel Blimp*, *The Adventures of Tartu* (1943), *Champagne Charlie* (1944), *Top Secret* (1952), *The Embezzler* (1954).

Morris, Wolfe (*b* Portsmouth, 1925 – *d* London, 1996). Actor. Supporting player in films from 1956, often as foreigners and in several films for Val GUEST, including *The Camp on Blood Island* (1957).

OTHER BRITISH FILMS INCLUDE: *Ill Met By Moonlight* (1956), *Yesterday's Enemy* (1959), *Nine Hours to Rama* (1962), *The Best House in London* (1968), *The House That Dripped Blood* (1970), *The Mackintosh Man* (1973), *The Disappearance of Harry* (1982).

Morrissey, David (*b* Liverpool, 1964). Actor. Tall, loose-limbed Morrissey got his start with Liverpool's Everyman Youth Theatre while still in his teens, trained at RADA, and has run up an impressive roster of roles on stage (e.g. title role in the National's *Peer Gynt*), TV (a tax inspector in deep trouble in mini-series *Holding On*, 1997; the neurotic Bradley Headstone in *Our Mutual Friend*, 1998) and radio (several Shakespearean roles). His film debut was in Peter GREENAWAY's *Drowning by Numbers* (1988), and he had contrasting roles as the endlessly good-natured Kiffer in *Hilary and Jackie* (1998), the caring, exasperated brother in *Some Voices* (2000) and the Nazi officer in *Captain Corelli's Mandolin* (2001, UK/Fr/US). Has also directed the short film, *Bring Me Your Love* (2000) and the TV mini-series, *Sweet Revenge* (2001). His partner is novelist Esther Freud, who wrote *Hideous Kinky*.

OTHER BRITISH FILMS INCLUDE: *Waterland* (1992, UK/US), *Being Human* (1994), *The Commissioner* (1997, UK/Bel/Ger), *Fanny and Elvis* (1999), *Born Romantic* (2001).

Morrissey, Neil (*b* Stafford, 1962). Actor. Droll, rangy Morrissey is best known as one of TV's *Men Behaving Badly* (1993–98, 2002) and for his two-year relationship with Rachel WEISZ. In fact, as well as being one of TV's busiest actors (he was excellent as Dervla KIRWAN's tour-guide husband trying to be faithful in *Happy Birthday Shakespeare*, 2000), he is also a committed worker for the War Child charity. In films since *The Bounty* (1984), without repeating his TV success. To America for *Triggerman* (2001).

OTHER BRITISH FILMS INCLUDE: *Playing Away* (1986), *I Bought a Vampire Motorcycle* (1990), *Staggered* (1994), *Up 'n' Under* (1997), *The Match* (1999, UK/Ire/US).

Morrison, Paul (*b* London, 1944). Director. After a couple of stints as assistant director in the early 80s (*Looks and Smiles*, 1981; *Doll's Eye*, 1982), Morrison wrote and directed *Solomon and Gaenor* (1999), a drama of doomed Jew–Gentile love in Wales in the early 20th century.

Morse, Barry (*b* London, 1918). Actor. RADA-trained and in rep for several years, Morse was a pioneer of pre-war TV drama, was popular on the London stage, and entered films in the early 40s. Played the church-organist juvenile lead in *When We Are Married* (1943) and Anne CRAWFORD's farmer husband in *Daughter of Darkness* (1947), but though cast as Beau Brummell in *Mrs Fitzherbert* (1947) he was rather too serious and not quite dashing enough for major film stardom. However, he moved to Canada in the early 50s and became a fixture there in theatre, radio and TV, becoming well known in the US as Lt Gerrard in *The Fugitive* (1964–67). Occasional films, but mainly TV in the last three decades.

OTHER BRITISH FILMS INCLUDE: *The Goose Steps Out*, *Thunder Rock* (1942), *This Man Is Mine* (1946), *No Trace* (1950), *Running Scared* (1972), *Asylum* (1972), *Power Play* (1978, UK/Can).

Mortimer, Emily (*b* 1971). Actress. Oxford-educated daughter of John MORTIMER and his second wife, Mortimer has been a popular figure on TV and from the later 90s began to appear in films. She had small roles in *Elizabeth* (1998) and *Notting Hill* (1999, UK/US), as the girl Hugh GRANT found 'too perfect', made a stronger impression as Katherine in BRANAGH's *Love's Labour's Lost* (2000, UK/Fr/US) and co-starred with Robert CARLYLE and Samuel L. JACKSON in *51st State* (2001, UK/Can/US), as well as opposite Bruce Willis in *The Kid* (2000, UK). Her partner is Alessandro NIVOLA.

OTHER BRITISH FILMS INCLUDE: *Last of the High Kings* (1996, UK/Ire/Den), *Killing Joe* (1999).

Mortimer, Sir John (*b* London, 1923). Novelist, screenwriter. Educated at Harrow and Oxford, barrister-author Mortimer has had one of the most eclectically prolific careers of any British writer of the latter half of the 20th century. Most famous now as the creator of TV's irascible *Rumpole of the Bailey* (1978–79, 1983, 1987–88, 1991, 1992), he also wrote such other series as *Brideshead Revisited* (1981, BAAn/sc), one of TV's greatest *succès d'estime*, and *Paradise Postponed* (1986), as well as the autobiographical stage play, *Voyage Round My Father* (1971, with Alec GUINNESS; on TV, 1982, with Laurence OLIVIER). His cinema work has been comparatively limited: as a scriptwriter with the CROWN FILM UNIT during WW2, he worked on such films as *Children on Trial* (1946); he contributed dialogue to *Ferry to Hong Kong* (1959) and *The Innocents* (1961); two of his plays were adapted to the screen, *Lunch Hour* (1962, + sc) and *The Dock Brief* (1962); and he wrote several other screenplays over a long period, including the surprisingly sentimental *Tea with Mussolini* (1999, UK/It). Married two women called Penelope: (1) novelist **Penelope [Fletcher] Mortimer** (*b* North Wales, 1918) with whom he co-wrote the screenplay for *Bunny Lake Is Missing* (1965) and whose novel, *The Pumpkin Eater*, was filmed in 1964; (2) Penelope Glossop, mother of Emily MORTIMER. Made CBE, 1986; knighted 1998.

OTHER BRITISH FILMS: *Guns of Darkness* (1962), *The Running Man* (1963), *Maschenka* (1987, UK/Fin/Fr/Ger).

Morton, Clive (*b* London, 1904 – *d* London, 1975). Actor. Tall, dignified character player of numerous officer and other upper-class types, Morton worked for four years with the East India Dock Company before going to RADA, making his stage debut in 1926 and his first film, *The Last Coupon* in 1932. Maintained a busy stage presence for 40 years, apart from WW2 army service (1940–45) and was a frequent TV performer from 1949, but may be best remembered for his screen roles, brief as they often were: think of the courteous prison governor deeply respectful of his ducal guest in *Kind Hearts and Coronets* or, atypically down the social scale, as Sergeant Brooks in *The Blue Lamp* (1949) and another station sergeant in *The Lavender Hill Mob* (1951), or Earl Rivers in *Richard III* (1955), or any of his many Lords and Colonels. Married (1) **Joan Harben** (*b* London, 1909 – *d* London, 1953), who appeared in *The Man in the White Suit* (1951), and (2) Frances ROWE.

OTHER BRITISH FILMS INCLUDE: *The Man Who Changed His Mind* (1936), *Mine Own Executioner* (1947), *Scott of the Antarctic*, *Quartet* (1948), *Trio* (1950), *His Excellency* (1951), *Turn the Key Softly* (1953), *Carrington VC* (1954), *Seven Waves Away* (1956), *The Moonraker*, *Lucky Jim* (1957), *The Pure Hell of St Trinian's* (1960), *Lawrence of Arabia* (1962), *The Alphabet Murders* (1965), *Goodbye, Mr Chips* (1969), *Young Winston* (1972), *11 Harrowhouse* (1974).

Morton, Samantha (*b* Nottingham, 1977). Actress. Exceptionally gifted young actress on TV from age 13, compelling attention in such series as *Cracker* (1993), as a young girl sexually involved with a village priest. Came to the fore in 1997 in two diverse roles: as the spirited Sophia Western in the TV

ADAPTATION, *Tom Jones* and as the girl who spirals into promiscuity following her mother's death in *Under the Skin*; in 1999 she gave an Oscar-nominated performance as a mute woman in Woody Allen's *Sweet and Lowdown* (US); and in 2002 co-starred in Spielberg's ingenious thriller, *Minority Report*. Even in a messy piece like *Dreaming of Joseph Lees* (1999, UK/US) she registers authentic notes of dissatisfaction and longing. She has been nominated for at least a dozen notable awards and won five, for the films named above. Has a daughter by Charlie CREED-MILES, with whom she co-starred in the grimy gangster film, *The Last Yellow* (1999, UK/Ger).

OTHER BRITISH FILMS INCLUDE: *This Is the Sea* (1996, UK/Ire/US), *Pandaemonium* (2001, as Coleridge's wife), *Morvan Callar, East of Harlem* (2002).

Motley Costume designers. Famous firm (established by Sophia and Margaret Harris and Elizabeth Montgomery in the early 30s) of theatrical costume designers who have worked on several notable films, including *The Card* (1952), *The Innocents* (1961), *The Pumpkin Eater* (1964), and *The Spy Who Came in from the Cold* (1965). They have also designed costumes for TV but the stage was their true métier and there they exercised immense and – in their time – radically innovative influence.

OTHER BRITISH FILMS: *Red Wagon* (1934), *Brewster's Millions* (1935), *I Met a Murderer* (1939), *A Study in Terror* (1965).

Mottershaw, Frank (*b* 1850 – *d* Sheffield, 1932). Producer, director. Mottershaw is exemplary of individuals involved in provincial film production in the UK prior to WW1. He was a photographer with offices in Castle Street, Sheffield, in 1882, who, circa 1900, began producing short ACTUALITIES, COMEDIES, dramas and chase films with his SHEFFIELD PHOTO COMPANY. In 1902, Mottershaw built a studio in Hanover Street, Sheffield, and in 1904, he filmed the visit of King Edward VII to the city, screening his films the same evening at Sheffield's Empire Music Hall and the Royal Albert Hall. Among the films that he made up to 1909, all of them less than one-reel in length, are: *A Daring Daylight Robbery* (1903), in which a burglar is chased and apprehended; the comedy *Boys Will Be Boys* (1904); *The Eccentric Thief* (1906), a trick film with a fat policeman chasing a thin thief; the drama *The Romany's Revenge* (1907); the comedy *Banana Skins* (1908); and *The Mad Musician* (1909). AS.

Moulder Brown, John (*b* London, 1953). Actor. Promising child actor of the 60s (first film, *A Cry from the Streets*, 1958) whose most interesting roles were probably in the US–German co-productions, *Deep End* (1970), a moody study of sexual tensions set in a London municipal baths, and the Nabokov ADAPTATION, *King, Queen, Knave* (1972), both directed by Jerzy SKOLIMOWSKI.

OTHER BRITISH FILMS INCLUDE: *Night Train for Inverness* (1959), *Two Living, One Dead* (1961), *The Uncle* (1964), *Operation Third Form* (1966), *Vampire Circus* (1971), *Confessions from the David Galaxy Affair* (1979).

Mount, Peggy (*b* Southend-on-Sea, 1915 – *d* Northwood, Middx, 2001). After many years in rep (Liverpool, Dundee, etc), she stormed on to the London stage in 1955 as archetypal battleaxe, Emma Hornett, in *Sailor Beware!*, playing the role for over 1,000 performances and repeating it in the 1956 film. Her series of formidable – and funny – harridans includes Flora Ransom, vengeful scandal-sheet victim, in *The Naked Truth* (1957) and appalling Mrs Bumble in *Oliver!* (1968). On stage she played the Nurse in *Romeo and Juliet* and Mrs Hardcastle in *She Stoops to Conquer* at the Old Vic and was a virago brought low in a 1970 revival of *When We Are Married*, and was a bossy matriarch in TV's *The Larkins* (1958–60, 1963–64). Awarded OBE, 1996.

OTHER BRITISH FILMS: *The Embezzler* (1954), *Dry Rot* (1956), *Inn for Trouble* (1959), *Ladies Who Do* (1963), *One Way Pendulum* (1964).

Movie Implicitly aligning itself with the AUTEURIST imperative of much French critical writing about the cinema, the first issue of *Movie* (June 1962) provocatively introduced itself with a scathing attack on British cinema and on the contemporary critical establishment's concept of 'The Good Film'. Against *The Bridge on the River Kwai*, it posed *Hell Is for Heroes*; against 'the big subject', it posed 'the big treatment'. Over the following decade, the work of film-makers such as Minnelli, Godard, Preminger, Bergman, Hawks, HITCHCOCK, Chabrol, Penn, Bresson and Kazan took pride of place. The journal's subsequent appearances have been intermittent and its tone, critical line and polemical thrust have reflected both the changes that have taken place within British film culture since its original appearance and the particular and varied interests of its relatively stable roster of critics over the years. Its strengths have always been the admirable fluency of its writing and the analytical insights which have been on offer from longtime contributors such as Robin Wood, Victor (V.F.) Perkins, Charles Barr, Douglas Pye, Andrew Britton, Jim Hillier, Michael Walker and editor Ian Cameron. Tom Ryan.

Mowbray, Malcolm (*b* Knebworth, 1949). Director. After a considerable success with the satirical social comedy, *A Private Function* (1984, + co-story), Mowbray went to Hollywood to make two fairly obscure films, returned to Britain to direct episodes of the medieval mystery series, *Cadfael* (1994), and two features which few people have seen – *The Revenger's Comedies* (1998, UK/Fr), derived from Alan AYCKBOURN's play, and *Monsignor Renard* (1999, co-d).

OTHER BRITISH FILMS: (shorts) *Path of the Weft* (1970), *Beach Information* (1971), *Trombone* (1974).

Mower, Patrick (*b* Oxford, 1940). Actor. Off to a good start in films as the youthful victim in *The Devil Rides Out* (1967), but found his best chances on TV, especially as Cross in *Callan* (1970–72) and *Target* (1977), and from 2000 had a continuing role in *Emmerdale Farm*. Supporting roles in films of no special interest.

OTHER BRITISH FILMS INCLUDE: *Smashing Bird I Used to Know* (1969), *Cry of the Banshee* (1970), *Percy* (1971), *Carry On England* (1976), *The Asylum* (2000).

Moxey, Hugh (*b* Bristol, 1909 – *d* London, 1991). Actor. Character player on stage before entering films in the late 40s, usually in professional or military officer roles, as in *The Night My Number Came Up* (1955), as a Wing Commander, or *Time Without Pity* (1957), as the humane Prison Governor.

OTHER BRITISH FILMS INCLUDE: *Meet Simon Cherry* (1949), *The Franchise Affair* (1950), *Angels One Five* (1952), *Spaceways* (1953), *The Good Die Young* (1954), *The Dam Busters* (1955), *Brothers in Law* (1956), *The Snake Woman* (1961), *Hennessy* (1975), *The Final Conflict* (1981).

Moxey, John (aka John Llewellyn Moxey) (*b* Burlingham, 1920). Director. Entered industry as editor after WW2 service. After directing a few minor THRILLERS in the early 60s, several in the Edgar WALLACE series, as well as *Foxhole in Cairo* (1960) and *Circus of Fear* (1966), Moxey spent the rest of his prolific career in TV, adding 'Llewellyn' for his US work.

OTHER BRITISH FILMS INCLUDE: *City of the Dead* (1960), *Death Trap* (1962), *Ricochet* (1963), *Strangler's Web* (1966).

Mozart, George (*b* Great Yarmouth, 1864 – *d* London, 1947) Actor. Long a popular star of the variety stage, Mozart made a few silent film comedy SHORTS and had a burst of film-making in the 30s, including five for Lawrence HUNTINGTON and a major role with Paul ROBESON in *Song of Freedom* (1936).

OTHER BRITISH FILMS INCLUDE: *Coney As Peacemaker, Coney Gets the Glad Eye, Coney – Ragtimer* (1913, short), *George Mozart in Domestic Troubles* (1930, short), *The Public Life of Henry the Ninth* (1935), *Café Mascot* (1936), *Overcoat Sam* (1937), *Pygmalion* (3rd bystander) (1938), *The Bank Messenger Mystery* (1940).

Muggeridge, Malcolm (*b* Sanderstead, 1903 – *d* Robertsbridge, 1990). Broadcaster. Lecturer, journalist, TV reporter and interviewer and all-round sage whose life exhibited the classical paradigm of radical youth giving way to conservative age and exhibiting the curve for all to see on the small screen. A *Panorama* regular in the 50s, he had his own shows in the 60s: *Appointment with . . .* (1960–61) and *Let Me Speak* (1964–65), netting a stimulating line-up of guests, and appeared in Jonathan MILLER's famous 1966 *Alice in Wonderland*. In cinema, he played guest roles in *I'm All Right Jack* (1959) and *Heavens Above!* (1963), appeared in *Herostratus* (1967) and, as himself, in *Lenny Bruce Without Tears* (1975, US, doc).

Mulcaster, G(eorge) H. (*b* London, 1891 – *d* London, 1964). Actor. Bald character player, on stage 1910 (London 1917), and in films from 1920, sliding magisterially up and down the social scale – for example, in 1948 he was Tom WALLS's austere butler in *Spring in Park Lane* and the Duke of Newcastle in *Bonnie Prince Charlie* – and acting until the year of his death. Once married to Diana NAPIER.

OTHER BRITISH FILMS INCLUDE: *The Wife Whom God Forgot* (1920), *The Wonderful Wooing* (1925), *Inquest* (1931), *The River House Mystery* (1935), *Old Mother Riley, The £5 Man* (1937), *Night Train to Munich* (1940), *This Man Is Dangerous, Mr Proudfoot Shows a Light* (short) (1941), *Let the People Sing* (1942), *For You Alone* (1945), *The Courtneys of Curzon Street* (1947), *Under Capricorn* (1949), *Contraband – Spain* (1955), *Downfall* (1964).

Mullan, Peter (*b* Glasgow, 1959). Actor, director, screenwriter. Powerfully built Scot, briefly in celebrated films such as *Riff-Raff* (1991), *Braveheart* (1995, US) and *Trainspotting* (1996) before his break-through leading role as a recovering alcoholic in Ken LOACH's devastating *My Name is Joe* (1998), for which he was named best actor at Cannes, in a tour-de-force of stunning emotional candour. Has also worked as director and screenwriter, cutting his teeth on SHORT FILMS, *Good Day for the Bad Guys* (1995, + a), and the critically acclaimed *Fridge* (1996), before making his debut feature *Orphans* (1997). Despite distribution problems, more awards followed for this darkly comic tale (hugely successful in Mullan's native Glasgow) of siblings attempting to cope with their mother's death. Major roles since in *Miss Julie* (1999, US), in Kevin Spacey's crime film *Ordinary Decent Criminal* (2000, UK/Ger/ Ire/US), and the lead in Michael WINTERBOTTOM's *The Claim* (2001, UK/Can/Fr), as a relocated Mayor of Casterbridge.

OTHER BRITISH FILMS INCLUDE: *The Big Man* (1990), *Shallow Grave* (1994), *The Priest and the Pirate* (1995), *Bogwoman* (1996, Ire), *Caesar* (2000, ex p). Melinda Hildebrandt.

Mullard, Arthur (*b* London, 1910 – *d* London, 1995). Actor. His battered features suggest just the ex-boxer he actually was. A Cockney, he began in films as stunt double for Scots

character comedian, Archie DUNCAN. Often uncredited in his early films, he went on to more noticeable roles in the 60s, like Brassknuckles in *The Wrong Arm of the Law* (1962) and TV semi-stardom in the 70s series *Romany Jones* (1973–75) and *Yus My Dear* (1976).

OTHER BRITISH FILMS INCLUDE: *The Captive Heart* (1946), *Oliver Twist* (1948), *The Lavender Hill Mob* (1951), *The Pickwick Papers* (1952), *Rob Roy . . .* (1953), *The Ladykillers* (1955), *Moby Dick* (1956), *The Man Who Liked Funerals* (1958), *Two Way Stretch* (1960), *Crooks Anonymous* (1962), *Heavens Above!* (1963), *Casino Royale, Smashing Time* (1967), *Chitty Chitty Bang Bang* (1968), *On the Buses* (1971), *Adventures of a Plumber's Mate* (1978).

BIBLIOG: Autobiography, *Oh Yus, It's Arthur Mullard*, 1977.

Mullen, Barbara (*b* Boston, Massachusetts, 1914 – *d* London, 1979). Actress. Former dancer who became a star, albeit a character star, in TV's *Dr Finlay's Casebook* (1962–71), as she never did in films. Trained at the Webber-Douglas when she came to England and was on the London stage first in 1939, succeeding Celia JOHNSON in 1940 as Mrs de Winter in *Rebecca*. Played the title role in her first feature, *Jeannie* (1941), and, though charming, perhaps lacked star charisma. Had substantial roles in *Thunder Rock* (1942), *A Place of One's Own* and *The Trojan Brothers* (1945), but settled quickly into middle-aged character parts. Married documentarist John TAYLOR.

OTHER BRITISH FILMS INCLUDE: *Mother and Child* (1940, doc), *Welcome Mr Washington* (1944), *Corridor of Mirrors, My Sister and I* (1948), *So Little Time, The Gentle Gunman* (1952), *Innocent Sinners* (1958), *The Siege of Pinchgut* (1959).

Müller, Renate (*b* Munich, 1906 – *d* Berlin, 1937). Actress. Blonde, vivacious comedienne in European films of the late 20s and early 30s, famous for her androgynous appearance in the cross-dressing farce *Viktor und Viktoria* (1933, Ger). In Britain, she gave sparkling performances in *Sunshine Susie* (1931) and *Marry Me* (1932), both REMAKES of German productions. Despite her on screen vitality, persistent ill health brought an early end to her career, and it is alleged that she was killed by Nazis by being pushed out of a window.

BIBLIOG: R.E. Clements, *Queen of America? The Case of Renate Müller*, 1994. Tim Bergfelder.

Mullins, Peter (*b* London, 1931). Production designer. Entered films in the late 40s, and went on to be art director on dozens of TV episodes and 'B' MOVIES, helping to ensure a certain level of verisimilitude in the likes of *Smokescreen* (1964), and moving on to bigger-budget affairs like the 'Pink Panther' films. From the late 80s, after the dire *Shanghai Surprise* (1986), he worked mainly in TV.

OTHER BRITISH FILMS INCLUDE: (art d) *Transatlantic, The Clue of the New Pin* (1960), *Man Detained, Never Back Losers* (1961), *Time to Remember, Playback* (1962), *Bomb in the High Street, Accidental Death* (1963), *We Shall See, King and Country* (1964), *Dead Man's Chest* (1965), *Alfie, Company of Fools* (1966), *Pretty Polly* (1967), *Where Eagles Dare* (1968), *Zee & Co.* (1971); (des) *The Projected Man* (1966), *Puppet on a Chain* (1970), *Steptoe and Son* (1972), *Luther* (1973, UK/Can/US), *The Return of the Pink Panther* (1974), *The Pink Panther Strikes Again* (1976), *Revenge of the Pink Panther* (1978), *There Goes the Bride* (1979), *The Dogs of War* (1980), *The Holcroft Covenant* (1985).

multiple-story films *see* **portmanteau (and episodic) films**

Mulvey, Laura (*b* Oxford, 1941) and **Wollen, Peter** (*b* London, 1938). Directors, theorists. Influential experimental film-makers and film theorists. Individually, they have both authored important film texts (e.g. his structuralism-based book, *Signs and Meaning in the Cinema*, 1969; her seminal article, 'Visual Pleasure and Narrative Cinema', *Screen*, 1975, offering a feminist, psychoanalytic point of view on the workings of popular cinema); together, they have written and directed such films as *Penthislea: Queen of the Amazons* (1974, + co-p), *Riddles of the Sphinx* (1977, + co-p), and *The Bad Sister* (1983).

Mundin, Herbert (*b* St Helen's, Lancs, 1898 – *d* Van Nuys, 1939). Actor. Short, homely character player who, after a handful of early British talkies, went to Hollywood and stayed there, dying in a car crash. Played some vivid supporting roles, including the uppity servant, Bridges, in *Cavalcade* (1933) and the willing Barkis in *David Copperfield* (1935). Post-WW1 service, he had MUSIC-HALL and concert-party experience before entering films.

BRITISH FILMS INCLUDE: *Enter the Queen* (1930), *We Dine at Seven* (UK/US), *Immediate Possession, East Lynne on the Western Front* (1931).

Munro, Caroline (*b* Windsor, 1949). Actress. Provocative leading lady of the 70s, most often in HORROR films, in which she provided decorative distractions *At the Earth's Core* (1976) or from the work of *Captain Kronos: Vampire Hunter* (1972). Had a similarly hectic time in her US films, including *Maniac* (1980).

OTHER BRITISH FILMS INCLUDE: *Casino Royale* (1967), *Where's Jack?* (1969), *The Abominable Dr Phibes* (1971), *Dracula AD 1972* (1972), *The Spy Who Loved Me* (1977).

Munro, Janet (*b* Blackpool, 1934 – *d* London, 1972). Actress. RN: Horsburgh. Charming actress of the wholesome school, which ensured she was taken up by the DISNEY ORGAN-IZATION and starred in several mid 60s features, including *Darby O'Gill and the Little People* (1959, US, Irish-set) and *Third Man on the Mountain* (1959). However, there was more to her than this: she was nicely comic as a dim waitress in *Small Hotel* (1957), affecting as the provincial girl exposed to big city temptations in *Bitter Harvest* (1963) and best of all as the anguished mother in *Life for Ruth* (1962), and she seemed determined to broaden her range. The daughter of comedian Alex North, she had early rep experience, and her promising career was cut tragically short when she apparently choked to death. Married (1) Tony WRIGHT (1956–61) and (2) Ian HENDRY (1963–71).

OTHER BRITISH FILMS INCLUDE: *The Young and the Guilty, The Trollenberg Terror* (1958), *Tommy the Toreador* (1959), *The Day the Earth Caught Fire* (1961), *Hide and Seek, A Jolly Bad Fellow* (1963), *Sebastian* (1967), *Cry Wolf* (1968).

Munro, Nan (*b* Pietpotgietersurst, South Africa, 1905 – *d* London, 1992). Actress. In 1959, as Lady Carmichael in a farce called *Caught Napping*, she was wheeled across stage in a barrow, hands tied and a carrot in her mouth, maintaining her dignity the while. RADA-trained and on stage for 50 years, often touring in her native South Africa, she made only scattered film appearances, which drew on her gifts for neither comedy nor pathos, but only on her dignity, like Lady Ingram in *Jane Eyre* (1970) who needed only fleeting hauteur.

OTHER BRITISH FILMS INCLUDE: *The End of the Affair* (1954), *The Extra Day* (1956), *Offbeat* (1960), *Morgan: A Suitable Case for Treatment, The Jokers* (1966), *The Walking Stick* (1970).

Murdoch, Richard (*b* Keston, Kent, 1907 – *d* Walton Heath, 1990). Actor. Very popular radio and music-hall star, often in collaboration with Arthur ASKEY. On stage from 1927, the lanky Charterhouse- and Cambridge-educated Murdoch shone in revue and variety and, later, as pantomime dames. His screen appearances are limited and have perhaps dated badly, but he has funny moments in the creaky plotting of *Charley's (Big-Hearted) Aunt* (1940) and *The Ghost Train* (1941), though he had better material as Uncle Tom in TV's *Rumpole of the Bailey* (1978–79/1983/1987–88/1991). Often credited as 'Stinker' Murdoch.

OTHER BRITISH FILMS INCLUDE: *Over She Goes* (1937), *Band Waggon* (1940), *I Thank You* (1941), *The Golden Arrow* (1949), *The Magic Box* (1951), *Strictly Confidential* (1959), *Whoops Apocalypse* (1986).

Murphy, Brian (*b* Ventnor, 1933). Actor. Best known as the henpecked husband of the TV series, *Man About the House* (1973–76), *George and Mildred* (1976–78), and their film SPIN-OFFS, 1974 and 1980 respectively, the droopy-moustached Murphy was an alumnus of the Theatre Workshop, Stratford, making his film debut in *Sparrows Can't Sing* (1962), based on Joan LITTLEWOOD's production there.

OTHER BRITISH FILMS INCLUDE: *The Devils, The Boy Friend* (1971), *I'm Not Feeling Myself Tonight* (1975).

Murphy, Pat (*b* Dublin, 1951). Murphy has directed only three features but these have been important examples, in an Irish context, of feminist-inspired film-making. Her first feature *Maeve* (1981), co-directed with John Davies, was supported by the BFI PRODUCTION BOARD. Set in Belfast, it is her most formally experimental work and involves a questioning of male-dominated forms of Irish republicanism. The later films have been COSTUME DRAMAS that have sought to subvert conventional 'his-stories' by emphasising the role of previously marginalised women. *Anne Devlin* tells the story of a woman associated with the Irish nationalist rising of 1803 (but overshadowed by the rebel leader Robert Emmet) while *Nora* (2000, UK/Ger/Ire/It) explores the relationship between Nora Barnacle and her husband James JOYCE (played by Ewan McGREGOR whose company, NATURAL NYLON, also produced the film). John Hill.

Murray, Barbara (*b* London, 1929). Actress. Perhaps the most stylish graduate of RANK's COMPANY OF YOUTH, elegant, witty Murray came from theatrical parents and was on stage first at 13. She returned to the stage periodically, at 70 playing Miss Marple in a tour of *Murder at the Vicarage*, but her main career was in films and TV. After several minor roles, she was loaned to EALING for the female lead in the very successful comedy, *Passport to Pimlico* (1949), but she didn't subsequently get the roles that should have made her a major star. She had the second lead to the much less interesting Anne CRAWFORD in *Tony Draws a Horse* (1950), supported Bette DAVIS (and what chance had a 'nice girl' against this?) in *Another Man's Poison* (1951), was policewoman Lucy who has little to do until the last minutes of *Street Corner* (1953), and a skittish society lady patient in *Doctor at Large* (1957). On TV, she made her mark as the attractive, neglected wife in *The Plane Makers* (1963–65) and its reincarnation as *The Power Game* (1965–66), and as Madame Max in *The Pallisers* (1974). Married (1 of 2) John JUSTIN.

OTHER BRITISH FILMS INCLUDE: *Anna Karenina* (1948), *Poet's Pub, Don't Ever Leave Me, Boys in Brown* (1949), *The Dark Man* (1950), *The Frightened Man* (1952), *The Teckman Mystery* (1954), *Campbell's Kingdom* (1957), *Operation Bullshine* (1959), *A Dandy in Aspic* (1968), *Up Pompeii* (1971), *Tales from the Crypt* (1972).

Murray, Pete(r) (*b* London, 1925). Actor. Best known as TV presenter and disc jockey from such shows as *Six-Five Special* (1957–58, filmed 1958, playing himself), *Juke Box Jury* (1959) and *Top of the Pops* (1964), the fair-haired youthful Murray also appeared in a few films including *Hungry Hill* (1947), as a young lieutenant, and *My Brother Jonathan* (1948) as Michael DENISON's nephew/adopted son in the film's last scene, before becoming pop host Pete. His later films, including *Cool It Carol!* (1970), trade on his TV-honed persona.

OTHER BRITISH FILMS INCLUDE: *The Life and Death of Colonel Blimp* (1943, extra), *Caravan* (1946), *No Highway* (1951), *Peeping Tom, Escort for Hire, Transatlantic* (1960), *It's Trad, Dad!, The Cool Mikado* (1962), *Otley* (1968), *Simon Simon* (1970, short), *Radio Wonderful* (1973, short).

Murray, Ruby (*b* Belfast, 1935 – *d* Torquay, 1996). Singer. Popular Irish singer of the 50s, a big name on radio and TV, but in only two films: *A Touch of the Sun* and the school-set musical, *It's Great to Be Young!* (1956). Had a swift, alcohol-hastened decline.

Murray, Stephen (*b* Partney, 1912 – *d* London, 1983). Actor. Rather sombre, RADA-trained leading man who often played roles much older than his years, like Gladstone in *The Prime Minister* (1941), and slid prematurely into character roles. He was at his best as Nova PILBEAM's Nazi employer in *The Next of Kin* (1942) and as the magnate obsessed with the memory of his supposedly dead son (played by Nigel PATRICK, one year his junior) in *The Silent Dust* (1949); his serious mien attracted several priestly roles, like the prison chaplain in *Now Barabbas Was a Robber* (1949), and, by the time he played Dr Manette in *A Tale of Two Cities* (1958), he looked (aptly) ancient and his screen career was nearly over. Stage, from his Stratford debut in 1933, TV (from 1946) and radio (over 300 plays and 12 years of *The Navy Lark*) gave him more varied opportunities, around his WW2 service (1941–46).

OTHER BRITISH FILMS INCLUDE: *Pygmalion* (1938), *Undercover* (1943), *Master of Bankdam* (1947), *My Brother Jonathan, London Belongs to Me, For Them That Trespass* (1948), *The Magnet* (1950), *The End of the Affair* (1954), *Guilty?* (1956), *At the Stroke of Nine* (1957), *Master Spy* (1963).

Murray-Hill, Peter (*b* Bushey Heath, 1908 – *d* England, 1957). Actor. Tall, cultivated, Westminster- and Cambridge-educated supporting actor, on stage from 1933, and in a dozen late 30s/early 40s films, prior to becoming an antiquarian bookseller. Married to Phyllis CALVERT, with whom he appeared in *Madonna of the Seven Moons* (1944, as a not very convincing painter) and *They Were Sisters* (1945, as her jocular, understanding husband).

OTHER BRITISH FILMS INCLUDE: *A Yank at Oxford* (1937), *Jane Steps Out* (1938), *Poison Pen* (1939), *The Ghost Train* (1941), *Bell-Bottom George* (1944).

Murton, Lionel (*b* London, 1915). Actor. Raised and educated in Montreal, Murton was with the Canadian navy show, 'Meet the Navy', and appeared in the 1946 film version when he returned to Britain and stayed to make several dozen films, as well as appearing in all the other acting media, often as Americans of course, like the newspaper correspondent in *North West Frontier* (1959) but *unlike* club member, Mr Snodgrass, in *The Pickwick Papers* (1952). TV included *OSS* (1957–58), as Ron RANDELL's chief, and *The Dickie Henderson Show* (1960–65, 1968, 1971).

OTHER BRITISH FILMS INCLUDE: *Trouble in the Air* (1948), *The Girl Is Mine* (1950), *Raising a Riot* (1955), *Fire Down Below* (1957), *Up the Creek, Further Up the Creek* (1958), *On the Beat, Summer Holiday* (1962), *The Truth About Spring* (1964), *Doctor in Clover* (1966), *Seven Nights in Japan* (1976, UK/Fr.).

Murton, Peter Production designer. After varied experience as art director on such diverse films as *Dr Strangelove . . .* (1963),

Goldfinger (1964) and *The Lion in Winter* (1968), he became production designer on *The Ruling Class* (1971), did another BOND in his new function, *The Man with the Golden Gun* (1974), and worked on *Superman II* (1980, co-des), *Superman III* (1983), the latter perhaps more gratifying to a designer than to most personnel. Son of Walter MURTON.

OTHER BRITISH FILMS INCLUDE: (art d) *Mr Topaze* (1961), *Billy Budd* (1962), *Woman of Straw* (1964), *The Ipcress File, Thunderball* (1965), *Half a Sixpence* (1967, UK/US); (des) *Man Friday* (1975), *The Eagle Has Landed* (1976), *Death on the Nile* (1978), *The Chain* (1984).

Murton, Walter (*b* Norwich, 1892 – *d* ?). Art director. One of the best and busiest British art directors of the 20s, who slowed down in the 30s. After study at the Norwich School of Art and army service from 1914–19, Murton joined STOLL, with whom he remained until 1927. There he worked on the company's biggest films, including *The Wandering Jew, Becket* (1923), and *Boadicea* (1926), and was selected by J. Stuart BLACKTON to recreate Elizabethan England in *The Glorious Adventure* (1922). His son is Peter MURTON.

OTHER BRITISH FILMS INCLUDE: *Mr Wu* (1919), *At the Villa Rose* (1920), *The Passionate Friends, Further Adventures of Sherlock Holmes* series (1922), *Sally Bishop* (1923), *Not for Sale* (1924), *The Gold Curse* (1925), *Huntingtower* (1927), *Shooting Stars* (co-art direction), *The Guns of Loos, Zero* (1928), *Young Woodley* (1929), *A Warm Corner* (1930), *The Ghost Train* (1931), *Pot Luck* (1936), *Non-Stop New York, The Great Barrier* (1937), *Crackerjack, Climbing High* (1938), *The Man in Grey* (1943). AS.

music – classical music in British films There has been a good deal of mutual benefit between cinema and classical music. Films have exploited the unconsummated storytelling potential of classical music, especially that of the 19th century, whilst classical works have often become popular through their use in films, sometimes leading to re-releases of recordings billed as 'music from the film . . .'. Classical music, by which is meant music from the Western art music tradition, was used from the earliest days of silent cinema, when compilations of illustrative extracts would be performed by a solo pianist, a small ensemble or sometimes an orchestra.

Certain types of composer have found particular currency in the cinema, and no less so in British films. These tend to be the more melodic and less cerebral composers such as Puccini (e.g. *The Killing Fields*, 1984; *A Room with a View*, 1985), Tchaikovsky (see below) and Grieg (e.g. *The Seventh Veil*, 1945), though Bach (e.g. *A Canterbury Tale*, 1944) and Beethoven (e.g. *Moonlight Sonata*, 1937) are well represented too. Mozart's music is often used, as in *Kind Hearts and Coronets* (1949), *Sunday Bloody Sunday* (1971), *The Spy Who Loved Me* (1977), *Alien* (1979) and *Elizabeth* 1998). *The Common Touch* (1941) features Tchaikovsky's Piano Concerto No. 1, which was a popular concert piece and had already been used in the US film *The Great Lie* released a few months earlier. In both films, the music is linked with a piano-playing protagonist, hence the choice of a concerto rather than a symphonic work. This concerto proved so popular that it turned up in several more films, including a DOCUMENTARY about the wartime vicissitudes of the London Philharmonic Orchestra, *Battle for Music* (1943). It established melodic piano concertos (existing and newly composed) as a mainstay in the cinema, and not only for films about musicians. This is due to the inherent drama and contrast of a musical form that pits soloist against orchestra. By 1945 the Tchaikovsky concerto finally gave way to Rachmaninov's Piano Concerto No. 2, heard in *Brief Encounter* and *The Seventh Veil* (1945).

Whilst film-makers have continued to take a rather shallow approach to the use of classical music, there have been some notable exceptions, in particular Stanley KUBRICK. *2001: A Space Odyssey* (1968) and *A Clockwork Orange* (1971) both challenge the musical associations an audience brings with it to the cinema, rather than exploiting this prior knowledge for the sake of mere accessibility or entertainment. The music used in *2001* has attracted a good deal of interest, not least because of Kubrick's decision to shelve the original score commissioned from Alex North in favour of a diverse selection taken from the works of Johann Strauss, Richard Strauss, Khachaturian and Ligeti. These were the musical backdrops he had used during filming, in order to assist in establishing the character and pace of scenes. Significantly, Kubrick made an unlikely connection between future-space and 19th-century Romantic music. If we accept Leonard Bernstein's reading (Bazelon, p.200) of the space station scene, accompanied – as if it were a dance – by *The Blue Danube* waltz, then Kubrick revealed a kinetic anaphone that, incidentally and conveniently, returned scores for futuristic films to an orchestral form favoured by the majority of composers. In this case, music makes no attempt to locate time and place, and so stands in stark contrast with the conventional, referential approach adopted by the majority of film-makers – e.g. *The Blue Danube* waltz in *Goodbye, Mr Chips* (1939), which reminds us of nothing more than the romance of old Vienna.

The BIOPIC genre has demonstrated a continuing interest in classical performers, composers and their music, e.g. Mozart in *Whom the Gods Love* (1936), Paganini in *The Magic Bow* (1946), Tchaikovsky in *The Music Lovers* (1971) and Jacqueline Du Pré in *Hilary and Jackie* (1998).

BIBLIOG: John Huntley, *British Film Music*, 1972; Irwin Bazelon, *Knowing the Score: Notes on Film Music*, 1975; Russell Lack, *Twenty Four Frames Under: A Buried History of Film Music*, 1997. David Burnand.

music – original scores for British films

We are inclined to recall only the big tunes from the cinema, and so the most significant film music often goes unnoticed by audiences. This in no way diminishes the importance of the underscore in fulfilling a host of dramatic and narrative functions. It is the commissioned composer who is usually best placed to design the music that enters the audience's unconscious mind, since (s)he can match the timing and character of cues more effectively than a sound editor working with pre-existent music.

The pioneering period of film composition in this country coincided with the introduction of sound. Hubert BATH scored the melodrama *Kitty* (1929), which began production at ELSTREE as a silent, but was converted to a 'talking picture' in the US. Bath went on to score the first all-talking British film, HITCHCOCK's *Blackmail* (1929). The early years of film composition were understandably experimental, borrowing techniques from 19th-century programme music and the popular theatre. Given the need for a solid background in the craft of music, established composers were encouraged to become involved by music directors such as Louis LEVY at GAUMONT–BRITISH and Muir MATHIESON at LONDON FILMS. Just as Alexander KORDA believed that British cinema should have the best actors, directors and technicians, so Mathieson felt he must encourage the best composers, which he did with great success. These included Mischa SPOLIANSKY, Arthur BENJAMIN, Ralph Vaughan WILLIAMS, Arthur BLISS, Miklós RÓZSA, William WALTON, Benjamin BRITTEN, Richard ADINSELL, Malcolm ARNOLD and Richard Rodney

BENNETT. This attitude resulted in high-quality scores and performances, which Mathieson usually conducted himself. He supervised *The Private Life of Don Juan* (1934), *The Scarlet Pimpernel*, *Sanders of the River* (1935), *Things to Come* (1936), *The Four Feathers* (1939) and many more. Mathieson was music director at the CROWN FILM UNIT during the WW2, overseeing the contributions of highly regarded composers such as Vaughan Williams, who were drawn to the vernacular of film music as part of the war effort.

But attitudes in the music establishment changed after the war, especially in Britain. Despite some notable exceptions, it is clearly the perception of many composers active today in both film and concert music that there is a stigma attached to their screen work. Composers who have ignored such prejudice often give up, or become largely excluded from, the world of concert music. These include the Frenchman Georges AURIC, who scored Jack CLAYTON's *The Innocents* (1961), in which the story is told through an intriguing musical device. The tune from a music box becomes associated with the possession of the two children by their dead governess, but this link is only revealed some way into the film after the tune has been heard in a variety of diegetic and non-diegetic guises. John ADDISON was another film composer who withdrew from the world of concert music, and indeed from Britain, in later life. He was dubbed 'the composer for the ANGRY YOUNG MEN' because of his work with Tony RICHARDSON on *Look Back in Anger* (1959), *The Entertainer* (1960) and *A Taste of Honey* (1961), but he also provided a delightfully light-hearted score for Richardson's *Tom Jones* (1963). This 18th-century romp opens rather surprisingly with a prologue in silent movie style. Addison represents the contrasting periods of the plot and of the visual style with a score for the unusual combination of harpsichord and 'honky-tonk' piano. Both instruments, and their connotations, are instantly recognised by audiences, and thus support the historical juxtaposition.

One GENRE that attracted concert composers after the war was the HORROR film, allowing modernists to indulge in expressionism, atonality and even 12-tone technique on occasions. HAMMER FILMS commissioned scores from Elisabeth LUTYENS, Benjamin FRANKEL and Tristram CARY, for instance, though it was James BERNARD who best represents this film music genre, and he was primarily known as a film composer.

The developing interest in world music since the 60s has encouraged composers such as George FENTON and Richard Blackford to take a more authentic attitude to ethnic sources. In *Gandhi* (1982, UK/Ind), for instance, Fenton subtly fuses traditional Indian music with a more typically dramatic orchestral score. The same is true of historical sources, where recent films have avoided the pastiche approach used in *Tom Jones*, for instance. For *The Draughtsman's Contract* (1982) Michael NYMAN re-worked Purcell's music as a basis for his own score, partly because it is contemporary with the plot, but also because its Baroque design is admissible to a modern composer interested in systems and repetition.

What has become clear in recent years is that film scoring is now able to explore the expressive potential of the whole range of styles and media available to a contemporary composer, from tonal to atonal, and from electronic to orchestral. And there are signs that attitudes are slowly changing in the British musical establishment. Highly regarded foreign musicians such as Rosenmann, Corigliano, Takemitsu and Preisner, as well as Nyman in this country, have demonstrated that cinema does not have to be the kiss of death for a composer's career, just because of its populist and commercial associations.

BIBLIOG: John Huntley, *British Film Music*, 1972; Claudia Gorbman, *Unheard Melodies: Narrative Film Music*, 1987; Neil Brand, *Dramatic Notes: Foregrounding Music in the Dramatic Experience*, 1998. David Burnand.

music – popular music in British film Popular theme tunes and songs have been a longstanding element in the marketing of films, as far back as the so-called silent era. To an even greater extent than classical music (see above), popular music has helped to attract audiences to certain film GENRES, whilst also promoting the musical artistes themselves. By its efflorescent nature, popular music is particularly effective in establishing or referring to precise periods, locations and associated attitudes. Allan GRAY's nostalgic foxtrot, light-hearted waltz, jazz and jive cues for *The Life and Death of Colonel Blimp* (1943) track the social changes portrayed in the story, albeit from the outside, as it were. Later youth-orientated films such as *Expresso Bongo* (1959) and *A Hard Day's Night* (1964) present the musical participants and their camp followers more directly.

As with much 'found' music in film, there is a tendency for the use of popular music to be justified in the diegesis. Examples range from incidental performances by GERALDO and his Orchestra in *Limelight* (1936) and The Ivy Benson Band in *The Dummy Talks* (1943), to featured artistes such as the BEATLES in *Help!* (1965) and The SPICE GIRLS in *Spice World* (1997). Extending the definition of 'popular' to include ethnic and traditional musics, the same diegetic approaches can be found as scene-setting in *Zorba the Greek* (US/Gr) or as characterisation in *Zulu* (both 1964). In a variation on this diegetic use, 'numbers' may be introduced into a film in the manner of a musical, as in JARMAN's kitsch treatment of *The Tempest* (1979), which has Elisabeth WELCH singing 'Stormy Weather', surrounded by dancing sailors.

Alternatively, non-diegetic use of popular music can be just as effective in setting the time and place of a story. More than anything, popular music is exploited to represent the attitudes of a period. 'Swingers' are likely to be accompanied by modern jazz, for instance in *Alfie* (1966). However, such conventions can be undermined or employed ironically, e.g. the choice of Johnny DANKWORTH's music to underscore the dry-as-dust world of LOSEY's *Accident* (1967). Given its locating power, popular music can also invoke nostalgia, as in Neil JORDAN's *Mona Lisa* (1986), in which outmoded gangland 'virtues' are set against Thatcherite cynicism, and represented by the eponymous theme song, itself an outmoded reminder of a supposedly gentler past.

The association of popular music with 'unsocial behaviour made acceptable' is clearly demonstrated in the drug-infested world of *Trainspotting* (1996). This approach to popular music harks back to US movies such as *Easy Rider* (1969). The influence of another US film, *Pulp Fiction* (1994), is evident in the pop compilation soundtrack for *Lock, Stock and Two Smoking Barrels* (1998). Whilst individual items are superficially illustrative of the scenes they accompany, this selection fails to match the over-all consistency of Tarantino's mythical representation of junk-culture through popular music. Thus, *Lock, Stock and Two Smoking Barrels* relies too heavily on musical entertainment that adds nothing substantial to plot or discourse. Unfortunately, this approach is the norm, on both sides of the Atlantic, which reinforces the view that popular music is predominantly employed for MARKETING purposes, to the disadvantage of both film art and a fuller appreciation of the cinematic potential of popular and traditional musics. More thoughtful approaches can be found, nevertheless. The popular songs of *Oh! What a Lovely War* (1969) are used to emphasise the cynical side of patriotism as well as the stoicism of soldiers at the front, whilst the music in *Distant Voices Still Lives* (1988, UK/Ger) provides relief from a hard world for characters and audience alike.

BIBLIOG: David Ehrenstein & Bill Reed, *Rock on Film*, 1982; Jonathan Romney & Adrian Wootton, (eds), *Celluloid Jukebox: Popular Music and the Movies Since the 50s*, 1995. David Burnand.

music hall and British cinema Music-hall acts were a ready film subject in the early period of British cinema (at a time when the music hall itself was the prime EXHIBITION venue), the sheer novelty of movement on a screen being adequate recompense for the absence of sound. Jugglers, contortionists, magicians and comedians were all popular cinematic subjects, with notable giants of the halls, such as Dan LENO, Marie Lloyd, and Little Tich, with his big boots (although in a French-produced film), appearing before the camera. As with all novelties, however, this was relatively short-lived. While British music-hall performers Charlie CHAPLIN and Stan Laurel were to find fame and success in Hollywood, those who remained in Britain, such as George ROBEY, Ernie LOTINGA, Albert CHEVALIER and George MOZART, though appearing in films, were to remain stars of stage, not film. The loss of sound – of patter and song – was too great with regard to the majority of performers from the halls for them to achieve any lasting success in the new silent medium. A notable exception was music-hall comedian Fred EVANS, with his popular *Pimple* character, the absence of sound having limited impact on his visual slapstick.

It was not until the arrival of SOUND in the late 20s that the traditions of music hall were presented with a more viable opportunity of making a contribution to British cinema. Notable music-hall performers, such as Dick Henderson (*see* Dickie HENDERSON), Lily MORRIS and Albert WHELAN, were captured for posterity in short sound films, most notably in the DE FOREST Phonofilms of the late 20s, and in the *Pathetone Weekly* SHORTS of the 30s. In a similar vein, a spate of multi-act VARIETY features (being little more than the equivalent of shorts strung together) were to follow in the wake of *Elstree Calling* (1930), such as *Soft Lights and Sweet Music* (1936), *Variety* (1935), through to *A Ray of Sunshine* (1950).

It was in the COMEDY GENRE, however, that the music-hall tradition was to make its most resounding impact. Some of the more notable examples from the 30s and 40s of variety performers making the crossover to the screen include Gracie FIELDS and George FORMBY (the two most successful variety stage-to-screen transfers with their quintessential music-hall mixture of comedy and song), Will HAY, Max MILLER (a not too successful transition, owing to his penchant for risqué stage patter, obviously toned down for the cinema), Sid FIELD, the CRAZY GANG, Frank RANDLE, Tommy TRINDER, and, in his *Old Mother Riley* guise, Arthur LUCAN.

The music-hall milieu itself was also depicted on screen in this period with great fondness and nostalgia, the films of John BAXTER (himself an ex-music-hall performer) making a notable contribution through such heart-felt offerings as *Say It With Flowers (A Human Story)* and *Music Hall* (1934). Baxter is also of note for the number of ex-music-hall performers he employed in minor roles, and for his elevation of George CARNEY, a comedian from the halls, into a dramatic lead. *Champagne Charlie* (1944) and *I'll Be Your Sweetheart* (1945), two wartime recreations of the music-hall past, lovingly evoked the communal solidarity inherent in the original halls.

This solidarity, however, diminished in importance in post-war Britain, and with it variety. Although Randle and Lucan may have continued with their film careers through to the mid-1950s, only Norman WISDOM, with his mixture of Formby innocence and Chaplin sentiment, rose to screen stardom from the music-hall ranks. While making the occasional foray into cinema, other post-war variety performers, such as Frankie HOWERD, Jimmy EDWARDS and Max BYGRAVES, were to find their national audience largely through the new medium of television, with the latter arguably precipitating the demise of films bearing music-hall traditions, the structure of television shows providing a more natural home for the variety performer. MORECAMBE AND WISE attempted, with disastrous results, to break into film in the 60s, but this was a rarity by this period and served to act as a warning to others. If only CANNON AND BALL, stars of the execrable *The Boys in Blue* (1983), had taken heed.

BIBLIOG: Denis Gifford, *Entertainers in British Films: A Century of Showbiz in the Cinema*, 1998. John Oliver.

musicals Like the WESTERN, the film musical was virtually appropriated by Hollywood. Britain had no Busby Berkeley or Astaire and Rogers, and could rarely rival the spectacle, the pizazz or the talent displayed by the Americans, but at its best the British musical had its own parochial charm. It also had one dancing superstar, Jessie MATTHEWS, who in the 30s proved so popular that Astaire asked (unsuccessfully) for her as a partner. Matthews' best film was *Evergreen* (1934, with its great song 'Dancing on the Ceiling'), one of a string of airy, featherweight confections in which she displayed her immense buck-toothed charm and graceful, high-kicking dancing.

The two other most popular musical stars of the 30s are more typical of British cinema. Though Gracie FIELDS and George FORMBY were exceptionally talented and original performers, they also had that 'common touch' which the British public found endearing. Their musical comedies, though modest in production values, were great hits. Fields often played a working girl at war with the bosses and only occasionally, as in *The Show Goes On* (1937), would her films deal with show business. In the latter, Fields ends up starring in a lavish show (says an elderly chorus member as she makes her entrance, 'West End at last!') and has to traverse a staircase by (nervously) stepping on a succession of extended top hats. (In general, British choreographers were uneasy with the cinema, their work either too balletic or straining to be original.) The jovial, toothy Formby, like Fields, specialised in comic solos (though unlike Fields he rarely had moments of pathos or ballads to sing), and strummed his ukulele to cheeky ditties in a string of movies. British audiences also liked the laid-back unshowy tap-dancing of debonair Jack BUCHANAN, who seemed to demand vehicles more elegant than those in which he found himself, and the energetic routines of comedy duo, Jack HULBERT and Cicily COURTNEIDGE.

Some of the most likeable, least pretentious, movies were those starring Stanley LUPINO (*Cheer Up!*, 1936, *Over She Goes*, 1937, *Hold My Hand*, 1938) and *Over She Goes* includes a priceless number which Lupino, Laddie CLIFF and Syd WALKER perform shoulder-to-shoulder as the camera executes some 180-degree turns. British film-makers were happiest musically when dealing with the traditional worlds of VARIETY and MUSIC HALL, which had spawned such stars as Fields and Formby. The first British musical, *Auld Lang Syne* (1929), starred Sir Harry LAUDER – filmed as a silent, six songs were hastily synchronised with the advent of SOUND. Comedians Arthur ASKEY and Tommy TRINDER made several enjoyably unassuming musical comedies. Askey's *King Arthur Was A Gentleman* (1942) and *Miss London Ltd* (1943) benefited from the dancing of Evelyn DALL and the ballad-singing of Anne SHELTON. Trinder's films included *Sailors Three* (1940), in which he introduced Noel Gay's buoyant standard, 'All Over The Place', and *Champagne Charlie* (1944), the highlight of which was Trinder's version of the title tune, delivered on a gaslit music hall stage.

Britain's best film musical of the 40s was arguably Val GUEST's *I'll Be Your Sweetheart* (1945), with the country's most popular star Margaret LOCKWOOD (dubbed by Maudie EDWARDS) playing a music hall performer courted by rival publishers. The film's pace and flavour stood comparison to the Fox musicals of the time and dealt with a serious subject (music piracy) in lively fashion. The following year Britain produced (though with an American director) one of the biggest flops of all time, *London Town*. London itself was an important part of a series of popular films made by Herbert WILCOX starring Anna NEAGLE and Michael WILDING. Though *Piccadilly Incident* (1946) had a self-conscious production number, *The Courtneys of Curzon Street* (1947) had some beguiling songs of WW1, and *Spring in Park Lane* (1948) included a wistful romantic duet (partly in slow motion) to the tune of 'The Moment I Saw You'.

Director J. Lee THOMPSON made a game stab at rivalling Hollywood with a lavish version of *The Good Companions* (1956), which had capable choreography by Irving Davies and Paddy STONE, an engaging cast, and made imaginative use of the widescreen process. In the late 50s, as in Hollywood, musicals became a virtually extinct GENRE except for pop-star vehicles. Tommy STEELE made some modest but popular films including one based on his own life story, but the biggest hits were the Cliff RICHARD films, starting with *The Young Ones*, made in colour and featuring his group 'The Shadows'. After the mid 60s, when the BEATLES' films, *A Hard Day's Night* (1964) and *Help!* (1965), had achieved the expected success, there was little musical activity until such major international productions as *Half a Sixpence* (1967, UK/US, with Steele) and *Oliver!* (1968).The latter, splendidly directed by Carol REED, won the Best Film Oscar and again had strong echoes of Britain's MUSIC HALL past, with Lionel BART's catchy cockney numbers typified by the tavern number 'Oom Pah Pah'. It was an international hit, as was Alan PARKER's *The Commitments* (1991, UK/US), a satisfyingly old-fashioned let's-put-a-band-together tale told with brio. Tom Vallance.

Muybridge, Eadweard (*b* Kingston-upon-Thames, 1830 – *d* Kingston-upon-Thames, 1904). Pioneer. RN: Edward James Muggeridge. The founding father of the moving image. At the invitation of American railroad baron Leland Stanford, Muybridge sought to solve the age-old dilemma of whether all of a horse's legs left the ground at the same time in a gallop, something which he demonstrated through a multiple series of photographs in 1878. Muybridge developed this new art of action photography, or chronophotography, in sequential series of animals and humans in motion that have ever since haunted the imaginations of artists and scientists alike. Muybridge's work preceded motion picture films, but he was able to project silhouettes and drawings based on his images in motion through his Zoopraxiscope projector from 1879, while his work profoundly inspired the new art that then followed. Luke McKernan.

Mycroft, Walter Charles (*b* London, 1890 – *d* London, 1959). Producer. From 1922 the film critic of the *Evening Standard* and from 1925 a Council Member of the Film Society. In 1927 John MAXWELL made Mycroft Head of the Scenario Department at BRITISH INTERNATIONAL PICTURES, to select and acquire properties for the studio, but Mycroft also co-scripted several films including *Elstree Calling* (1930) and *Almost A Honeymoon* (1930). For him, character, dialogue and narrative drive were far more important than visual language – an economical, journalist's approach that appealed to tight-fisted Maxwell.

In 1933, Maxwell made Mycroft Head of Production, but not until 1935 was he allowed creative control over the company's films and the credit 'Director of Production'. Known as the 'Czar of all the Rushes', Mycroft was a benevolent but autocratic hunchback (with a voice like 'a pekinese with catarrh'), personally approving all scripts and allowing no changes during filming. Under his aegis, the studio produced a number of dramas including *The Red Wagon* (1934), several romantic MUSICALS such as *Blossom Time* (1934), numerous CRIME PICTURES including three BULLDOG DRUMMOND stories, and a string of low-budget COMEDIES starring MUSIC HALL comedians such as Leslie FULLER and Bobbie HOWES.

After Maxwell's death (1940), Mycroft produced and directed three comedies for ABPC: *Spring Meeting, My Wife's Family* and *Banana Ridge* (1941); but, when ABPC's new managing director made him redundant, he worked on two second features, co-scripting *The Phantom Shot* and directing *Comin' Thro' the Rye* (1947). His next production, *The Woman's Angle* (1952), failed at the box office and he ended his career as uncredited scenario adviser to Robert CLARK, ABPC's new Head of Production. His last credit was as scenario advisor for *Girls At Sea* (1958).

OTHER BRITISH FILMS INCLUDE: (p, unless noted) *Champagne* (adptn) (1928), *Murder!* (1930, co-adptn), *Poor Old Bill, Men Like These* (+ co-story/sc) (1931), *Sleepless Nights* (1932), *Facing the Music, The Love Nest* (1933), *Mister Cinders, Girls Will Be Boys* (1934), *Royal Cavalcade, Music Hath Charms, Mimi, Dandy Dick* (1935), *Sensation, Living Dangerously* (1936), *Aren't Men Beasts?* (1937), *Yellow Sands, Black Limelight* (1938), *Poison Pen, The Gang's All Here, The Outsider* (1939), *The House of the Arrow* (1940), *The Farmer's Wife* (1941). Vincent Porter.

Myers, Peter (*b* London, 1923). Playwright, screenwriter, lyricist. Best remembered in films for his co-authorship of screenplays and songs for the Cliff RICHARD vehicles, *The Young Ones* (1961), *Summer Holiday* (1962), and *Wonderful Life* (1964). Also contributed to a series of successful stage revues in the 50s and 60s.

OTHER BRITISH FILMS INCLUDE: (co-sc, unless noted) *The Square Ring* (co-add dial), *Meet Mr Lucifer* (1953), *Value for Money* (1955, lyrics), *Action of the Tiger* (1957), *The Snorkel* (1958), *French Dressing* (1963, + co-story).

Myers, Peter (*b*? – *d* 2000). Actor. His funniest moments came in his second film, the US-financed ADAPTATION of *The Reluctant Debutante* (1958), as the traffic-mad Guards officer. Comparable but less amusing twit types were also his lot in such films as *Bachelor of Hearts* (1958) and *The Queen's Guards* (1961).

OTHER BRITISH FILMS INCLUDE: *The Colditz Story* (1954), *Very Important Person* (1961), *The Punch and Judy Man* (1962), *The Magic Christian* (1969), *The Little Princess* (1975).

Myers, Ruth (*b* Manchester, 1940). Costume designer. Oscar-nominated for her designs for *The Addams Family* (1991, US) and *Emma* (1996, UK/US) and BAA-nominated for *Isadora* (1968) and *LA Confidential* (1997, US), four titles which testify to her versatility, Myers has worked across GENRES and, in the last two decades, mainly in the US.

OTHER BRITISH FILMS INCLUDE: *Smashing Time* (1967), *Three Into Two Won't Go* (1968), *The Virgin Soldiers* (1969), *The Ruling Class* (1971), *A Touch of Class* (1972), *That'll Be the Day, Dracula* (1973), *Stardust* (1974), *Silver Bears* (1977, UK/US), *Company Man* (2000, UK/Fr/US), *Proof of Life* (2001, UK/US), *The Four Feathers* (2003, UK/US).

Myers, Stanley (*b* Birmingham, 1930 – *d* London, 1993). Composer. Multi-award-winning composer prolific in British cinema since the mid 60s, though he'd written the song for a long-forgotten 'B' MOVIE, *Murder Reported*, in 1957. Surviving the worst excesses of the swinging 60s – *Kaleidoscope* (1966), *Otley* (1968), *Road to Saint Tropez* (1966, co-comp, short), *Two Gentlemen Sharing* (1969) – he went on to become one of the most significant and versatile British composers of the next two decades, his name appearing on diversely memorable films of the 80s, in particular. Nicolas ROEG used him regularly on such films as *Eureka* (1982, UK/US), *Insignificance* (1985) and *Castaway* (1986); he did two for Stephen FREARS, *My Beautiful Laundrette* (1985) and *Prick Up Your Ears* (1987), as well as contributing notably to the emotional quality of *Dreamchild* (1985) in its use of 30s popular music interwoven with a plangent romantic undercurrent. Became most famous for his score for *The Deer Hunter* (1978, US) and posthumously won a BAA for scoring the TV series, *Middlemarch* (1994), his last credit before his death from cancer.

OTHER BRITISH FILMS INCLUDE: (comp, cond) *Ulysses* (1967, UK/US), *A Severed Head* (1970), *Schizo* (1976), *A Portrait of the Artist as a Young Man* (1977); (comp), *The Walking Stick, The Raging Moon* (1970), *Zee & Co.* (1971), *The Wilby Conspiracy* (1974), *Conduct Unbecoming* (1975), *Yesterday's Hero* (1979, + m d), *Moonlighting* (1982), *The Honorary Consul* (1983), *The Chain* (1984), *Wish You Were Here* (BAAn), *Sammy and Rosie Get Laid* (1987), *Track 29, Paperhouse* (1988, co-comp).

mystery genre *see* **thrillers/mystery films** and **detective films**

Nn

Nabokov, Vladimir (*b* St Petersburg, 1899 – *d* Montreux, Switzerland, 1977). Author. Russian-born Cambridge-educated novelist, whose family became émigrés following the Bolshevik Revolution and who became a US citizen in 1945. Now most famous as the author of *Lolita* (1959), the scandalous account of a seedy European intellectual infatuated with a pre-adolescent American girl. It was filmed brilliantly but evasively in Britain by Stanley KUBRICK, from Nabokov's AA-nominated screenplay, (1961) and with less caution and distinction in the US in 1997, its central passion always likely to attract censorship difficulties. Other British films made from his novels include *Laughter in the Dark* (1938, English trans.), another story of erotic obsession, filmed first by Tony RICHARDSON in 1969 (UK/Fr), and allegedly about to be remade in 2000, *Maschenka* (1926, filmed 1987, UK/Fin/Fr/Ger) and *The Luzhin Defence* (2000, UK/Fr/Hung/It).

Nagy, Bill (*b* Hungary [some sources suggest Canada], 1921 – *d* London, 1973). Actor. Rugged-looking character player often seen in tough roles and perhaps best remembered as Scarff, the traveller who provides Rod Steiger with a new and problematic identity in *Across the Bridge* (1957), and as the gangster, Midnight, in *Goldfinger* (1964). Entered films in 1953 (*River Beat*), and appeared frequently on TV, as, for example, alleged anarchist Vanzetti in a 1965 '*Wednesday Play*'.
OTHER BRITISH FILMS INCLUDE: *The Brain Machine* (1954), *Joe Macbeth, Cloak Without Dagger* (1955), *High Tide at Noon* (1957), *I Was Monty's Double* (1958), *The Mouse That Roared, Bobbikins* (1959), *Transatlantic, Surprise Package* (1960), *The Girl Hunters* (1963), *Those Magnificent Men . . .* , *Where the Spies Are* (1965), *A Countess from Hong Kong* (1966), *You Only Live Twice* (1967), *The Revolutionary* (1970).

Nail, Jimmy (*b* Newcastle-upon-Tyne, 1954). Singer, actor. Rangy, beaky Geordie performer whose chief fame rests on his TV work in *Auf Wiedersehn Pet* (1983–84, 1986) and as the eponymous undercover detective, *Spender* (1991–93), and on his recording successes in the 80s. Most notable film appearances so far are as tango singer Agustin in *Evita* (1996) and as Les Wickes in *Still Crazy* (1998, UK/US).
OTHER BRITISH FILMS: *Morons from Outer Space* (1985), *Just Ask for Diamond* (UK/US), *Dream Demon* (1988).

Nair, Mira (*b* Bhubaneswar, Orissa, India, 1957). Director. Nair, educated at Delhi and Harvard Universities, began her career in DOCUMENTARY, working with Richard Leacock and D.A. Pennebaker in the US, and made her feature debut with the AA-nominated *Salaam Bombay!* (1988, UK/Fr/Ind), a sympathetic, confronting study of Bombay street life. She has since directed and co-produced and acted in *Mississippi Masala* (1991, UK/US, + a) and the feminist take on *Kama Sutra: A Tale of Love* (1996, UK/Ger/Ind/Jap, + co-sc), and in 2001 became the first woman director to win the Best Movie award at the Venice Film Festival for *Monsoon Wedding* (Fr/Ind/It/US). Now lives in New York with cinematographer husband, Mitch Epstein, who worked on *Salaam Bombay!* (co-p, des, 2uc).

Naismith, Laurence (*b* Thames Ditton, Surrey, 1908 – *d* Southport, Australia, 1992). Actor. RN: Laurence Johnson. Somewhat mournful-looking character player usually cast in benign roles; a merchant seaman before theatre debut in 1927, then with touring companies, making West End debut after WW2 service with the Royal Artillery (1939–46). He made over 70 films, starting with two for RANK's HIGHBURY STUDIOS, *A Piece of Cake* and *Trouble in the Air* (1948), and his memorable character roles include the Canon who knew the criminal as a boy in *Tiger in the Smoke* (1956), the no-good Ben Marston in *Robbery Under Arms* (1957), the *Titanic*'s doomed Captain in *A Night to Remember* (1958) and the Prince of Wales in *The Trials of Oscar Wilde* (1960), among many other Reverends, Admirals and Sirs. Much TV including the continuing role of Judge Fulton in *The Persuaders!* (1971–72). Married to actress **Christine Bocca**, who appeared in *Jigsaw* (1962), as John LE MESURIER's wife.
OTHER BRITISH FILMS INCLUDE: *Kind Hearts and Coronets, The Chiltern Hundreds* (1949), *The Happiest Days of Your Life, Pool of London* (1950), *High Treason, His Excellency* (1951), *The Long Memory, I Believe in You* (1952), *Cosh Boy, The Million Pound Note* (1953), *Carrington VC* (1954), *Richard III, The Dam Busters, The Man Who Never Was* (1955), *The Extra Day, Seven Waves Away* (1956), *I Accuse!* (1957), *Gideon's Day* (1958), *The Angry Silence, The Criminal* (1960), *Greyfriars Bobby* (1961), *We Joined the Navy, I Thank a Fool* (1962), *Jason and the Argonauts* (1963), *Deadlier Than the Male* (1966), *Scrooge* (1970), *Diamonds Are Forever* (1971), *Young Winston* (1972), *Sporting Chance* (1976).

Nalluri, Bharat (*b* Guntur, India, 1965). Director. Co-founder with producer Richard Johns of Pilgrim Films in 1993. Educated at University of Newcastle and the Northern School of Film and Television, he directed *Downtown* (1997, UK/Fr), a drama of teenage gangs in Newcastle, where he grew up from age six. Since then, he has directed the thriller *Killing Time* (1998), also Newcastle-set, the US-made *The Crow: Salvation* (2000), and *Cyclops* (2001) in CHANNEL 4's *Shocker* series, and was second-unit director on Paul ANDERSON's *Resident Evil* (2002, UK/Ger/US), a SCIENCE FICTION tale.

Napier, Alan (*b* Harborne, Birmingham, 1903 – *d* Santa Monica, California, 1988). Actor. RN: Napier-Clavering. Very tall, lean character player long in the US, after RADA training and some West End success. Appeared in about ten British films of the 30s, playing Lord Shayne in *Bitter Sweet* (1933) and Sir Hamar Ryman in *The Four Just Men* (1939), before taking his stately presence to Hollywood, where he helped to persuade audiences that films such as *Random Harvest* (1942, as the epigrammatic Julian) and *The Uninvited* (1944, as sympathetic doctor) were really set in Britain. Ended his days as butler Alfred in TV's *Batman* (1966–68).

OTHER BRITISH FILMS: *Caste* (1930), *Stamboul* (1931, UK/US), *In a Monastery Garden* (1932), *Loyalties* (1933), *Wings over Africa* (1936), *For Valour, The Wife of General Ling* (1937).

Napier, Diana (aka Mollie Ellis) (*b* Bath, 1905 – *d* Windlesham, 1982). Actress. Educated at Malvern Girls' School and in Paris, Napier was a popular stage leading lady. Perhaps in several silent films as well as a dozen 30s romances and MUSICALS, having been put under contract to LONDON FILMS by Alexander KORDA, she never became a film *star*. Married to (1) G.H. MULCASTER and (2) Richard TAUBER, appearing with the latter in the 'Viennese-style' musicals, *Heart's Desire* (1935) and *Land Without Music* (1936) and the opera film, *Pagliacci* (1936).

OTHER BRITISH FILMS INCLUDE: (silent, unconfirmed) *The Rat* (1925), *The King's Highway* (1927), *The Farmer's Wife* (1928); (sound) *Wedding Rehearsal, Her First Affaire* (1932), *Strange Evidence* (1933), *Catherine the Great, The Private Life of Don Juan* (1934), *Royal Cavalcade, Mimi* (1935), *Bait* (1949).

BIBLIOG: Autobiography, *My Heart and I*, 1959.

Napier, Russell (*b* Perth, Australia, 1910 – *d* London, 1975). Actor. Avuncular character player who found a niche in MERTON PARK's vest-pocket Scotland Yard THRILLERS. Billed at first as various policemen, he then settled as Inspector, and finally Superintendent, Duggan, playing this role over a dozen times, starting with *Person Unknown* (1956). Most of his other roles were as policemen, but he had some diversity in such films as *The Angry Silence* (1960), and, as an Admiral, in his last, *The Black Windmill* (1974). Stereotyped he was, but how redolent of a period!

OTHER BRITISH FILMS: *The End of the River* (1947), *Black Orchid* (1952), *The Saint's Return* (1953), *Thirty-Six Hours, Conflict of Wings, The Brain Machine* (1954), *The Blue Peter, A Time to Kill* (1955), *The Last Man to Hang?, The Man in the Road* (1956), *Robbery Under Arms, The Shiralee* (1957), *A Night to Remember* (1958), *The Witness, Hell Is a City* (1959), *The Last Train* (1960), *The Mark* (1961), *HMS Defiant, Mix Me a Person* (1962), *The Blood Beast Terror* (1967), *Nobody Runs Forever* (UK/US) (1968).

Nardini, Daniela (*b* Largs, Scotland, 1967). Actress. BAA-winner for her role of Anna in the brilliant BBC series *This Life* (1996–98), Nardini's anarchic, sexy neediness established her as an original, mesmeric in all she did. Television capitalised on this with strong roles in such mini-series as *Undercover Heart* (1998) and *Rough Treatment* (2000). She ought to be a major film star, but will need a tougher vehicle than *Elephant Juice* (2000), a watered-down version of *This Life*; she ought also to play Cleopatra and Antigone in one medium or other. Trained at Scottish Academy of Music and Drama and has an impressive theatre background.

OTHER BRITISH FILMS: *Flying Blind* (1997), *Hands Up* (1999, short), *Jack Brown and the Curse of the Crown* (2002).

Nares, Owen (*b* Maiden Erleigh, Berks, 1888 – *d* Brecon, Wales, 1943). Actor. RN: Ramsey. Perennial matinee idol of British stage and screen, famed for his easy charm, in films from 1913 and in theatre from 1908, who looked a little shopworn by the 30s, when he played character roles in such films as *The Private Life of Don Juan* (1934). As a silent hero, though, he had been very popular in the likes of *The Last Rose of Summer* (1920) and as the eponymous *Young Lochinvar* (1923).

OTHER BRITISH FILMS INCLUDE: *Danny Donovan, the Gentleman Cracksman* (1914), *Just a Girl* (1916), *The Sorrows of Satan* (1917), *God Bless Our Red, White and Blue* (1918), *A Temporary Gentleman* (1920), *The Sorrows of Satan* (1926), *This Marriage Business* (1927), *The Middle Watch, Loose Ends* (1930), *The Woman Between* (1931), *There Goes the Bride, Frail Women* (1932), *One Precious Year, Discord* (1933), *Royal Cavalcade, I Give My Heart* (1935), *Head Office* (1936), *The Show Goes On* (1937).

BIBLIOG: Autobiography, *Myself and Some Others*, 1925. AS.

Narizzano, Silvio (*b* Montreal, 1924). Director. His best-known film is *Georgy Girl* (1966), which, sadly, is as nearly unwatchable today as most of the flashy 'SWINGING LONDON' pieces of the 60s. He did well enough by *Loot* (1970), the film version of Joe ORTON's black farce, and the minor dedicated-slum-teacher piece, *The Class of Miss MacMichael* (1978), with Glenda JACKSON, and he had the dubious distinction of directing Tallulah Bankhead in her last film, *Fanatic* (1965), but his career drifted after the early 70s, with unremarkable international films – *Blue* (1968, US) is alone of any interest – and TV, where he did at least direct OLIVIER and Joanne Woodward in *Come Back, Little Sheba* (1978). Came to Britain after TV experience (from 1951) in Canada.

OTHER BRITISH FILMS: *Senza ragione* (1972, UK/It, + co-p).

Nascimbene, Mario (*b* Milan, 1913). Composer. Internationally famous film composer, whose scores contributed plangently to two British regional dramas, *Room at the Top* (1958) and *Sons and Lovers* (1960), and melodramatically to several exotic HAMMER adventures, including *One Million Years BC* (1966), *The Vengeance of She* (1967), *When Dinosaurs Ruled the Earth* (1969) and *Creatures the World Forgot* (1970). Much of his work was in Italian films, many not widely seen, but his eclecticism comprehended such diverse US films as *The Light in the Piazza* (1962) and *Barabbas* (1961, US/It).

OTHER BRITISH FILMS: (comp, unless noted) *Child in the House* (1956), *Subway in the Sky* (1958), *Jason and the Argonauts* (1963, m d), *Where the Spies Are* (1965, + orchestra leader), *Dr Faustus* (1967, UK/It).

Nash, Percy (*b* London, 1869 – *d* Brighton, 1958). Director. After a variety of occupations, Nash became 'stage manager' for the LONDON FILM COMPANY in 1912. He left to found the Neptune Company the following year, but quit in 1915 to make two films in Italy. In 1916, he co-founded NB Films (N=Nash, B=[Arriga]Bocchi), and co-directed its first production, *Disraeli*. When BRITISH LION was organised in 1927, Nash became its long-time production manager.

OTHER BRITISH FILMS INCLUDE: *David Garrick* (1912), *Enoch Arden* (1914), *The Little Minister* (1915), *The Flag Lieutenant, Westward Ho!* (1919), *Hobson's Choice* (1920), *The Croxley Master* (1921), *Our National Industries* series (1924). AS.

Nation, Terry (*b* Cardiff, 1930 – *d* Los Angeles, 1997). Screenwriter. Most famous as the creator of the Daleks, villains of the *Doctor Who* TV cult SCIENCE-FICTION series and the film SPIN-OFFS derived from them: *Dr Who and the Daleks* (1965) and *Daleks – Invasion Earth 2150 AD* (1966). Most of his work was in TV (including the first *Hancock's Half-Hour*, 1956, and episodes of such popular 60s series as *The Saint* and *The Baron*), latterly in the US, but he also wrote the comedy *What a Whopper!* (1961) and co-scripted two HORROR films, *And Soon the Darkness* (1970) and *The House in Nightmare Park* (1973, + co-p).

national cinema: concept, production, audience, representation This concept is used to describe a country's national output, implying a coherent culture. In the case of Britain this notion is questionable, since film production has not generally been in a position to reflect the regional, class and ethnic diversity of the British Isles. Contributing factors have been domination by Hollywood which meant that British films could never occupy more than 15% of British screentime; the geographic concentration of British film-making in the south of England; the predominantly middle-upper class background of the majority of film producers and the preferences of the British film critical establishment, which privileged quality-realist drama and DOCUMENTARY as if these were representative of 'authentic' British cinema.

Several GENRES have nevertheless been expressive of British identities and illustrate how films registered as 'British' in economic terms can represent a wide range of experiences of living in Britain. Michael BALCON's declared aim at EALING Studios was to produce 'films projecting Britain and the British character', which celebrated individuals and small communities battling against official restrictions in comedies such as *Passport to Pimlico* (1949). In the late 50s and early 60s, British 'NEW WAVE' SOCIAL PROBLEM FILMS such as *Room at the Top* (1958) and *Saturday Night and Sunday Morning* (1960) attempted to represent provincial working-class life even though they were directed by film-makers from middle-class backgrounds. Later films, including *Young Soul Rebels* (1991) and *Bhaji on the Beach* (1993), were concerned to represent the experiences of ethnic minorities in Britain. A reaction to the metropolitan bias of British film-making was evident in films including *Trainspotting* (1996) which was set in Edinburgh.

In recent years film scholars have studied the extent to which British cinema can be identified as operating in a different aesthetic mode from that of Hollywood. In the 20s Cecil HEPWORTH's films, particularly *Comin' Thro' the Rye* (1923), were noteworthy for their foregrounding of pictorialism and discourses of British 'HERITAGE' which were at odds with contemporary trends favouring classical Hollywood narrative or European modernist experiment. In subsequent decades, however, the challenge of Hollywood encouraged a degree of aesthetic symbiosis as the classical model of Hollywood production with its star system and stylistic norms was emulated around the world, usually with some degrees of national difference. In Britain J. Arthur RANK developed a STUDIO and STAR SYSTEM which dominated popular cinema in the 40s and 50s. Owing to the ascendancy of the British film critical establishment, however, the dominant conception of British national cinema remained firmly tied to documentary and films which operated in realist modes such as *In Which We Serve* (1942) and *This Happy Breed* (1944), which were interpreted as 'mirrors for England' during WW2, the period when British cinema was thought to have 'come of age'. In recent years there has been a critical re-evaluation of popular GENRES including the 'CARRY ON' SERIES, HAMMER HORROR films and GAINSBOROUGH MELODRAMAS as central to the idea of British national cinema.

BIBLIOG: Andrew Higson, *Waving the Flag*, 1995; Jeffrey Richards, *Films and British National Identity*, 1997; Sarah Street, *British National Cinema*, 1997. Sarah Street.

National Film and Television Archive (NFTVA) Founded in 1935 as part of the BRITISH FILM INSTITUTE (founded 1933), the NFTVA began life as the National Film Library, with a remit 'to preserve for posterity films of national and historical value' and to make them permanently available for research, study and public programming. Its first Curator, who remained so until his death in 1973, was Ernest LINDGREN, a major figure in the development of film archiving policies and practices. The NFL was a co-founder, in 1938, of the INTERNATIONAL FEDERATION OF FILM ARCHIVES (FIAF). In 1955, it was renamed the National Film Archive, and in 1994, it adopted its present title to reflect an equal commitment to television. It is one of the world's largest moving image archives, containing around 500,000 films and television programmes, and one of the few to have its own film laboratory, based at the J. Paul Getty Conservation Centre in Berkhamsted, Hertfordshire. It also has an extensive nitrate film store, remotely located near Gaydon, Warwickshire, and a video recording unit for the acquisition and preservation of television programmes to broadcast standard. Clyde Jeavons.

See also **archives**.

National Film and Television School (NFTS) Opened in 1971 at BEACONSFIELD STUDIOS in Buckinghamshire, its aim was to train directors, producers, cinematographers, editors, writers, animators and other personnel. It planned to move into EALING STUDIOS in the late 90s, but this plan foundered on prohibitive costs. The School originally offered a three-year full-time course, accepting about 25 students annually, permitting specialisation but also encouraging the interchange of film-making roles in practical activities. It later offered a 12–15 month course in screenwriting, and the annual intake was increased to 35. In 2001, the School moved towards a two-year diploma course, with a view to minimising the time students are out of the industry. Also in 2001, the Global Film School, a project involving the NFTS's co-operation with UCLA and the Australian Film, TV and Radio School, catering for a growing demand for practical film-making experience, and a Short Course Training Programme, were instituted. The NFTS is jointly funded by government and industry, and in 2001 Michael GRADE accepted its chairmanship. Graduates include directors Terence DAVIES, Beeban KIDRON, Lynne RAMSAY, Mark HERMON, Carine ADLER, and Eric STYLES, producer Michele CARMADA, cinematographers David TATTERSALL and Oliver STAPLETON, and screenwriter Simon MOORE.

National Film Finance Corporation (NFFC) A publicly-funded bank for film production established by Attlee's Labour Government in 1949, which was finally killed off by Thatcher's Conservative administration in 1985. In between, the NFFC made possible the production of a large number of INDEPENDENT BRITISH FILMS by advancing the more risky 'end money' to their producers, thus relieving the film distributors and the private sector banks of the most precarious element of film finance. Launched with a budget of only £5 million, £3 million of which went to support KORDA's ailing BRITISH LION, the NFFC was always precariously underfunded. In 1951, it established GROUP THREE, as part of the ill-fated Group Scheme with RANK and ABPC, which attempted to marry INDEPENDENT FILM production with industry investment. It also bankrolled a number of films that would not otherwise have been made, including *The Magic Box* (1951), the film industry's prestige contribution to the Festival of Britain. In later years, when Conservative governments refused to allow it any more public money, the NFFC began to act more like an investment bank, often taking a share of producer's profits in order to ensure that it earned enough capital to survive. It also played a major role in restructuring the finances of British Lion. The Labour Governments of the 70s tried to redirect the NFFC in a more cultural direction by appointing a film producer, rather than a lawyer or a banker, as its new Managing Director; and during the Corporation's final desperate years Channel 4 Television also loaned the corporation money for it to invest in films. Vincent Porter.

National Film Theatre The cinemathèque operated by the BRITISH FILM INSTITUTE. Soon after it opened in 1933 the BFI began showing films as part of its educational work, though these screenings were occasional and scattered. The BFI hankered after a permanent cinema, and when the Festival of Britain's Telekinema closed, the BFI took it over, opening the renamed NFT in October 1952. Technical demands and unexpected popularity led to the opening of an enlarged version in October 1957. A second, smaller screen was added in September 1970 allowing the showing of specialist films whilst popular programmes appeared in NFT1, and autumn 1988 saw the opening of a third, smaller screen as part of the Museum Of The Moving Image. NFT programmes have covered the whole range of film and television; the recent popularisation of Indian and Japanese cinema in Britain can be largely attributed to the NFT, and many personalities have visited to present and discuss their work.

BIBLIOG: Ivan Butler, *To Encourage the Art of the Film*, 1971; Deac Rossell, *Forty Years 1952–1992*, 1992; Allan Eyles (ed), *The NFT at 50. A Celebration of Fifty Years of the National Film Theatre, 1952–2002*, 2002. John Riley.

National Lottery *see* **Arts Council and Lottery**

Natural Nylon Production company founded, owned and run by Jonny LEE MILLER, Ewan McGREGOR, Jude LAW, Sadie FROST and Sean PERTWEE. The company co-produced *eXistenZ* (1999) and its plans were announced to include the £13.5m production, *Cromwell*, and *Marlowe* (2003), with Law as SHAKESPEARE. If their films prove as newsworthy as the company's founders, it should have an interesting history.

Naughton, Bill (*b* Ballyhaunis, Ireland, 1910 – *d* Isle of Man, 1992). Dramatist, screenwriter. Famous as the author of *Alfie*, the title role created on stage by John NEVILLE (1963) and, indelibly, on screen by Michael CAINE (1966). Ex-lorry driver, weaver and coalbagger Naughton was nominated for both AA and BAA for his screenplay creation of the archetypal 60s sexual adventurer. Some may have valued more his earlier play, *All in Good Time* (1963), a study in the frustrations of a young marriage and the staling of an old one, affectingly filmed by the BOULTINGS in 1966 as *The Family Way*. His 1967 play, *Spring and Port Wine* was filmed in 1969 from his screenplay, and *Alfie Darling* (1975), starring Alan PRICE, failed to emulate the success of its predecessor.

Naughton, Charles *see* **Gold, Jimmy** and **Crazy Gang, The**

Navarro, Robert (*b* Vich, Spain, 1912). Cinematographer. Came to England in 1914 and was educated at Wandsworth Technical Institute. After working as (assistant) cameraman in Portugal and Spain, he was made resident cameraman in Britain on the *March of Time* (1938–45), before turning to features post-war. Camera operator on RANK's HIGHBURY STUDIOS output in the late 40s, on such 'B' FILMS as *Penny and the Pownall Case* (1948), he then had full cinematographer credit on a handful of undistinguished films, of which *One Wild Oat* (1951) is the best known.

OTHER BRITISH FILMS INCLUDE: (cam op) *The Turners of Prospect Road* (1947), *Song for Tomorrow, Trouble in the Air* (1948); (c) *No Way Back* (1949), *She Shall Have Murder* (1950), *The Blue Parrot* (1953).

Neagle, Dame Anna (*b* London, 1904 – *d* Woking, 1986). Actress, producer. RN: Marjorie Robertson. Made stage debut as dancer in 1917, later appearing in the chorus of André Charlot's and C.B. Cochran's revues. Jack BUCHANAN encouraged her to take on a featured role in *Stand Up and Sing* (1931), and her film career developed after forming an alliance, from *Goodnight Vienna* (1932) onwards, with producer-director Herbert WILCOX. He produced and directed most of her subsequent films and they married in 1943. She appeared in other British musical films in the early 30s including *Bitter Sweet, The Little Damozel* (1933) and *Limelight* (1936), but it was her performance as Queen Victoria in the phenomenally successful historical pageant *Victoria the Great* (1937) and its sequel *Sixty Glorious Years* (1938) which cemented her prestige. These films were also popular internationally, and led to Hollywood, where she starred in *Nurse Edith Cavell* (1939) and the musicals *Irene* and *No No Nanette* (1940), and *Sunny* (1941), all produced by Wilcox for RKO. Back in England, there followed a series of high society films with Michael WILDING, starting with *Piccadilly Incident* (1946), the most successful, critically and commercially, being *Spring in Park Lane* (1948). After these films offering audiences escape from post-war austerity, Neagle then appeared as the tortured agent in WW2-occupied France, code-named *Odette* (1950). Over the years, she was particularly associated with playing strong heroines, others including *Nell Gwyn* (1934), Peg Woffington, the Irish actress in *Peg of Old Drury* (1935), Nurse Cavell, Amy Johnson in *They Flew Alone* (1942), and Florence Nightingale in *The Lady with a Lamp* (1951).

Music and glamour returned in the two films she made with Errol FLYNN, *Lilacs in the Spring* (1954) and *King's Rhapsody* (1955), middle-aged romances nourished by Ivor NOVELLO scores, but her box-office appeal faded in the mid 50s. With her husband, she produced films starring Frankie VAUGHAN, but these were out of touch with changing tastes, and lost money. To clear her husband's debts, she returned to the stage, and her legendary status created a core audience for a five-year run of *Charlie Girl* (1965–70). A leading star in British films for over 25 years from 1932, she won several awards as Britain's favourite actress and biggest female box-office draw. Awarded CBE, 1952; created DBE, 1969.

OTHER BRITISH FILMS: (a, unless noted) *The School for Scandal, The Chinese Bungalow, Should a Doctor Tell?* (1930), *The Flag Lieutenant* (1932), *The Queen's Affair* (1934), *Three Maxims* (1936), *London Melody* (1937), *The Yellow Canary* (1943), *I Live in Grosvenor Square* (1945), *The Courtneys of Curzon Street* (1947), *Elizabeth of Ladymead* (1948), *Maytime in Mayfair* (1949), *Derby Day* (1952), *My Teenage Daughter* (1956), *No Time for Tears* (1957), *Wonderful Things!* (p), *These Dangerous Years* (1957, p), *The Man Who Wouldn't Talk* (1957), *The Lady Is a Square* (+ p) (1958), *The Heart of a Man* (p) (1959).

BIBLIOG: Autobiography, *Anna Neagle says 'There's Always Tomorrow'*, 1974. Roger Philip Mellor.

Neame, Christopher (*b* Windsor, 1942). Producer. Son of Ronald NEAME, he entered the film industry in the early 60s, became a production manager for HAMMER FILMS before winning producer credit on *Emily* (1976). Has also co-produced a good deal of TV, including *The Flame Trees of Thika* (1981). Not to be confused with actor **Christopher Neame** (*b* London, 1947), who has appeared in international and a few British films, including *Dracula AD 1972* (1972) and *Licence to Kill* (1989).

OTHER BRITISH FILMS: (pr man, unless noted) *The Witches* (1966, ass d), *The Anniversary* (1967), *Blood from the Mummy's Tomb*, *On the Buses* (1971), *Our Miss Fred* (1972), *Frankenstein and the Monster from Hell* (1973), *Power Play* (1978, UK/Can, European consultant with wife Caroline Langley), *Bellman & True* (1987, co-p), *Feast of July* (1995, UK/US, co-p, sc).

Neame, Elwin (*b* Bedminster, 1886 – *d* London, 1923). Director. Pioneer photographer, who directed his wife, Ivy CLOSE, in a number of short subjects that he also wrote. They were the parents of Ronald NEAME and **Derek Neame** (*b* Esher, 1915 – *d* Italy, 1979), who co-wrote the screenplays for *The Lilac Domino* (1937) and *The Small Voice* (1948), among other films of the 30s and 40s.

OTHER BRITISH FILMS INCLUDE: *Dream Paintings* (1912), *La Cigale* (1913), *Ghosts* (1914), *The Haunting of Silas P. Gould* (1915). AS.

Neame, Ronald (*b* London, 1911). Director, cinematographer. The son of director and cinematographer Elwin NEAME, and actress Ivy CLOSE, Neame was perhaps the British cinematographer who went on to have the most successful career as a director. At ELSTREE STUDIOS from 1927 at a very lowly level, he graduated to clapper boy on HITCHCOCK's *Blackmail* (1929), and shot dozens of 'QUOTA QUICKIES' in the 30s, gradually working his way up to more prestigious numbers like the EALING romance, *Young Man's Fancy* (1939), as well as several George FORMBY comedies. His association with David LEAN began on *Major Barbara* (1941), and, after *In Which We Serve* (1942), he, Lean and Anthony HAVELOCK-ALLAN formed CINEGUILD which produced some of the top-quality films of the 40s, starting with *This Happy Breed* (1944, + co-sc), for which Neame devised an unusually muted approach to TECHNICOLOR, appropriate to the suburban setting. He was (co-)producer of *Brief Encounter* (1945, + co-sc, add ph), *Great Expectations* (1946, + co-sc) and *Oliver Twist* (1948), and had his first go as director on the smartly-paced thriller, *Take My Life* (1947). He parted company with Cineguild during the making of *The Passionate Friends* (1948), when Lean took over the direction.

Among his films as director, perhaps his best work is in the films he made starring Alec GUINNESS – *The Card* (1952), *The Horse's Mouth* (1958, + co-p) and (Neame's finest film) *Tunes of Glory* (1960) – in all of which he showed himself a very sympathetic director of actors, across a wide GENRE range. This view is also borne out by the performances he got from actresses such as Judy GARLAND, painfully convincing in *I Could Go On Singing* (1963), Edith EVANS and Deborah KERR in *The Chalk Garden* (1964) and Maggie SMITH, who won an Oscar for *The Prime of Miss Jean Brodie* (1968). But his varied experiences as screenwriter and cameraman ensured that his films were also fluent and unfussy, providing apt frameworks for his actors, in humane, beautifully crafted films. He had his biggest box-office success with the US-made *The Poseidon Adventure* (1972), a more or less absurd story of an upturned ocean liner, but in terms of dramatic interest none of his American films is as attractive as the best of his British output.

He has lived in America since the early 1970s and is now a US citizen; his son is the producer Christopher NEAME, and his grandson is Gareth Neame, a TV producer. Awarded CBE, 1996.

OTHER BRITISH FILMS INCLUDE (c) *Happy* (co-c), *Give Her a Ring*, *Girls Will Be Boys* (1934), *Music Hath Charms* (co-c), *Joy-Ride*, *Invitation to the Waltz*, *Honours Easy*, *Drake of England* (1935), *Radio Lover*, *King of the Castle*, *A Star Fell From Heaven*, *Once in a Million*, *The Improper Duchess*, *The Crimes of Stephen Hawke* (1936), *Catch as Catch Can*, *Melody Express* (doc), *Member of the Jury*, *Strange Experiment*, *Keep Fit*, *Feather Your Nest*, *Café Colette*, *Brief Ecstasy*, *Against the Tide* (1937), *Who Goes Next?*, *The Ware Case*, *Second Thoughts*, *Penny Paradise*, *It's in the Air*, *I See Ice!*, *The Gaunt Stranger* (1938), *Trouble Brewing*, *Let's Be Famous*, *The Four Just Men*, *Come on George*, *Cheer Boys Cheer* (1939), *Saloon Bar*, *Return to Yesterday*, *Let George Do It!* (1940), *One of Our Aircraft is Missing* (1942), *Blithe Spirit* (1945, + co-sc); (p) *The Magic Box* (1951); (d) *The Golden Salamander* (1949, + co-sc), *The Million Pound Note* (1953), *The Man Who Never Was* (1955), *Windom's Way* (1957), *Mister Moses* (1965, UK/US), *Prudence and the Pill* (1968), *Scrooge* (1970), *The Odessa File* (1974, UK/Ger), *Foreign Body* (1986).

BIBLIOG: Autobiography, *Straight from the Horse's Mouth*, 2002.

Nedell, Bernard (*b* New York, 1893 – *d* Los Angeles, 1972). Actor. Tall American character player, a former violinist, who had a stage career in the US and Britain, and who made about 20 British films in the 30s, including *Heat Wave* (1935, as dangerous General De Costa), before returning to a largely villainous career in Hollywood. Married to actress **Olive Blakeney**, who also appeared in a few 30s British films, including *Her Imaginary Lover* (1933), with Nedell.

OTHER BRITISH FILMS INCLUDE: *The Silver King*, *The Return of the Rat* (1929), *Shadows* (1931), *Lazybones* (1935), *The Man Who Could Work Miracles* (1936), *The Live Wire* (1937), *Oh, Boy!* (1938).

Neeson, Liam (*b* Ballymena, Northern Ireland, 1952). Actor. Husky actor who spent his teens in amateur boxing (useful training for his role in *The Big Man*, 1990), but gave it up to become a teacher, attending Queens College Belfast. He joined the Belfast Lyric Players' Theatre in 1976 and two years later moved to the Abbey Theatre, Dublin where he was discovered by John BOORMAN who cast him in *Excalibur* (1981, UK). He appeared in a number of minor roles before appearing in his first lead role in *Lamb* (1985), as a disillusioned priest. In 1993 Steven Spielberg cast him as Oskar Schindler in *Schindler's List* (1993, US) for which he received an Oscar nomination. He went on to play the title roles in *Rob Roy* (1995, US, UK-set) and *Michael Collins* (1996, US) and the tall (6'4"), commanding actor, who married Natasha RICHARDSON in 1994, is now in demand for international films. Awarded OBE, 2000.

OTHER BRITISH FILMS INCLUDE: *Nailed* (1981), *Krull* (1983), *The Bounty*, *The Innocent* (1984), *The Mission* (1985), *A Prayer for the Dying* (1987), *Under Suspicion* (1991), *Les Misérables* (1998, UK/US). Anne-Marie Thomas.

Neff, Hildegarde (*b* Ulm, Germany, 1925 – *d* Berlin, 2002). Actress. RN: Hildegard Knef. A blonde, husky-voiced, and statuesque beauty in the Marlene Dietrich mould, Neff played vamps and European women of mystery in a number of international productions of the 50s and 60s, including *Decision Before Dawn* (1951), *Diplomatic Courier* (1952), *The Snows Of Kilimanjaro* (1952!), all US-made, and Carol REED's British *The Man Between* (1953). She also starred in the Muriel BOX thriller *Subway In The Sky* (1958). Neff's second and third careers were as cabaret singer and author.

OTHER BRITISH FILMS: *Svengali* (1954), *Mozambique* (1964), *The Lost Continent* (1968). Tim Bergfelder.

Neil, Hildegarde (*b* Cape Town, 1939). Actress. Gravely beautiful South African actress who might have been expected to have a more substantial film career. While she was not quite up to the demands of Cleopatra opposite Charlton Heston in *Antony and Cleopatra* (1972, UK/Sp/Switz), her other two 1972 releases gave her excellent chances within her reach: as George Segal's wife in *A Touch of Class* and, best of all, as Michael

YORK's twin sister in *England Made Me*. Nothing of consequence since. Married to Brian BLESSED, with whom she appeared in *The Bruce* (1996).

OTHER BRITISH FILMS: *The Man Who Haunted Himself* (1970), *The Legacy* (1978), *The Mirror Crack'd* (1980), *The Seaview Knights* (1994), *Macbeth* (1997).

Neill, Roy William (*b* Dublin Harbour, Ireland, 1887 – *d* London, 1946). Director, producer, writer. RN: Roland de Gostrie. Began his long show business career as a stage actor, after working as a foreign correspondent in China, and made film directorial debut in the 1910s after working with Thomas Ince. Returned to England in the late 30s where he made films in a variety of GENRES including CRIME FILMS like *Double or Quits* (1938) and *Murder Will Out* (1939), ADVENTURES like the George ARLISS vehicle *Dr Syn* (1937), Claude HULBERT COMEDIES including *Many Tanks Mr Atkins* (1938) and *Anything to Declare?* (1939), and several notable Max MILLER comedies, *Thank Evans* (1938), *Everything Happens to Me* (1938), *The Good Old Days* (1939), and *Hoots Mon!* (1939), the latter of which he also wrote. A capable craftsman, Neill is perhaps best known for his US films at Universal in the 1940s, notably the SHERLOCK HOLMES series, with their strongly pro-British sentiments.

OTHER BRITISH FILMS: *Gypsy* (1937), *Simply Terrific, The Viper, Quiet Please* (1938), *A Gentleman's Gentleman* (1939). Stephen Shafer.

Neill, Sam (*b* Omagh, N. Ireland, 1947). Actor. Born in Ireland, raised in New Zealand where he attended Canterbury University. Now in demand for international films, tall, quietly-spoken Neill came to prominence in the Australian film revival of the 70s, especially for his role as the gentleman grazier opposite Judy DAVIS in *My Brilliant Career* (1979). Since then, without actually becoming a major film *star*, he seems never to have been out of work, whether in Australia (site of arguably his most interesting work), the US (famously in *Jurassic Park*, 1993, and *Jurassic Park III*, 2001) or Britain. He starred in *The Country Girls* (1983), the Irish-set romance derived from Edna O'BRIEN's novel, was Meryl STREEP's WW2 Resistance lover in *Plenty* (1985, US-financed, largely UK-set), and was memorably sympathetic as Streep's husband in the UK/Australian co-production, *Evil Angels* (1988). Married (1) **Lisa Harrow** (*b* Auckland, 1943) who appeared in several British films, including *It Shouldn't Happen to a Vet* (1976). Awarded OBE, 1993.

OTHER BRITISH FILMS INCLUDE: *Enigma* (1982), *Sirens* (1994, UK/Aust), *Restoration* (1995, UK/US), *Event Horizon* (1997, UK/US), *The Revenger's Comedies* (1998, UK/Fr).

Neilson, Anthony (*b* 1967). Director. Having made the critically acclaimed *The Debt Collector* (1999), which he described as a 'haggis western' – it is actually a powerful melodrama of vengeance set in Edinburgh – playwright Neilson has been slow to make his second film, but he has revealed a cinematic talent worth taking seriously.

Neilson-Terry, Dennis (*b* London, 1895 – *d* Bulawayo, Southern Rhodesia, 1932). Actor. Son of legendary stage stars, Fred Terry and Julia Neilson, tall, striking Neilson-Terry was also a well-known West End star, and made a few films before his untimely death from pneumonia. Best-known film was probably *The House of the Arrow* (1930), in which he played Inspector Hanaud. Married Mary GLYNNE; their daughter is Hazel TERRY. Brother of Phyllis NEILSON-TERRY.

OTHER BRITISH FILMS: *Masks and Faces* (UK/US), *Her Greatest Performance* (1916), *His Last Defence* (1919), *The Hundredth Chance, Desire* (1920), *77 Park Lane* (1931), *Murder at Covent Garden* (1932).

Neilson-Terry, Phyllis (*b* London, 1892 – *d* London, 1977). Actress. Distinguished stage actress, daughter of stage stars, Fred Terry and Julia Neilson, sister of Dennis NEILSON-TERRY, made London theatre debut in 1910, playing many Shakespearean and modern roles (e.g. Mrs Railton-Bell in *Separate Tables*, 1954). Repeated her stage success in/as *Trilby* (1912) in a 1922 pocket-version, and nearly 40 years later she was the object of Jimmy Porter's invective in the film version of *Look Back in Anger* (1959). Also had a singing career, and starred in the French film, *The Call of the Blood* (1919).

OTHER BRITISH FILMS: *Boadicea* (1926), *One Family* (1930), *Family Doctor* (1958), *Conspiracy of Hearts* (1960).

Nelligan, Kate (*b* London, Canada, 1951). Actress. Another 'one who got away': Canadian-born Nelligan was trained at London's Central School, made her London stage debut in 1974 and entered films the following year in LOSEY's flawed *The Romantic Englishwoman* (UK/Fr). Gave a rivetingly tense performance in *Eye of the Needle* (1981), as a lonely wife sexually drawn to a Nazi spy, after which she has filmed in the US (including the excellent kidnap drama, *Without a Trace*, 1983, and the ludicrous melodrama, *The Prince of Tides*, 1991) and Canada, where *Margaret's Museum* (1995, UK/Can) is set. Several times nominated for theatrical awards, she seems less interested in a film career and settled rather early into character roles.

OTHER BRITISH FILM: *The Count of Monte Cristo* (1974, TV, some cinemas).

Nelson, Gwen (*b* London, 1901 – *d* Long Melford, 1990). Actress. Came to films just a bit too late for the rich character pickings that should have been hers. Two mother roles – on stage, as Joan PLOWRIGHT's ignorant, scornful mum in *Roots* (1959), and on film, as Alan BATES's sympathetic but no-nonsense parent in *A Kind of Loving* (1962), who won't have him home when he walks out on his marriage – suggest eloquently what she could do. Much TV, including *Catweazle* (1970).

OTHER BRITISH FILMS INCLUDE: *The Teckman Mystery* (1954), *Tunes of Glory* (1960), *The Kitchen* (1961), *Don't Talk to Strange Men* (1962), *Stolen Hours* (1963), *Doctor Zhivago* (1965, UK/US), *The Reckoning* (1969), *Say Hello to Yesterday* (1970), *Something to Hide* (1971), *It Shouldn't Happen to a Vet* (1976), *84 Charing Cross Road* (UK/US) (1986).

Nelson, Lord (Horatio) (*b* Burnham Thorpe, Norfolk, 1758 – *d* at sea, 1805). British naval hero who has been represented in a number of films, most famously by Laurence OLIVIER in *That Hamilton Woman* (1941, US, called *Lady Hamilton* in UK) and Peter FINCH in *A Bequest to the Nation* (1973). There were also three Nelsons in British silent films: Donald CALTHROP in *Nelson* (1918), Humberstone WRIGHT in *The Romance of Lady Hamilton* (1919) and Cedric HARDWICKE in *Nelson* (1926), and Victor Varconi played him in the US silent, *The Divine Lady* (1929). Among others, Stephen HAGGARD played him in *The Young Mr Pitt* (1942) and Richard JOHNSON played the picturesquely adulterous sailor in a motley co-production, *Lady Hamilton* (1968, US/Fr/Ger/It).

Nero, Franco (*b* Palma, 1941) Actor. RN: Franceso Sparanero. Husky Italian leading man whose command of English was not quite equal to the demands of an international starring career, but who has been busy, mainly in European films for four decades. Had at least two memorable English-speaking roles: as the disruptive outsider in Christopher MILES's intelligent version of D.H. LAWRENCE's *The Virgin and the Gypsy* (1970), and as Lancelot in *Camelot* (1967, US-made, largely UK cast). In the latter he co-starred with Vanessa REDGRAVE, with whom he had a well-publicised relationship which produced a child.

OTHER BRITISH FILMS INCLUDE: *Pope Joan* (1972), *Force 10 from Navarone* (1978), *The Girl* (1987, UK/Swe), *The Innocent Sleep* (1995).

Nervo, Jimmy (*b* London, 1898 – *d* London, 1975). Actor. RN: James Holloway. *See* **Crazy Gang, The**

Nesbitt, Cathleen (*b* Cheshire, 1889 – *d* London, 1982). Actress. Celebrated beauty whose career spanned 70 years and who, after education in Belfast and France, first appeared on stage in 1910 and last in 1981 as Mrs Higgins ('Who else is old enough to play Rex HARRISON's mother?' she asked) in a touring, then Broadway, revival of *My Fair Lady*. Her illustrious stage career embraced classic and modern plays, the West End and Broadway; her film career was always secondary: though she appeared in about 35 films, most of them British, they rarely did justice to the charm and beauty which was said to have inflamed Rupert Brooke. She was a severe hospital matron in *The Lamp Still Burns* (1943), Stewart GRANGER's class-bound spinster sister in *Fanny by Gaslight* (1944) and gangster Richard BURTON's ancient mum in *Villain* (1971). She was a sweetly temporising Lady Matheson in *Separate Tables* (1958, US), repeating the role on TV, and appeared in masses of American TV, usually exuding graciousness. Married Cecil RAMAGE in 1922; separated in the early 40s. Awarded CBE, 1978.

OTHER BRITISH FILMS INCLUDE: *Canaries Sometimes Sing* (1930), *The Frightened Lady* (1932), *Falling in Love* (1934), *The Beloved Vagabond, Hearts of Humanity* (1936), *Against the Tide* (1937), *Pygmalion* (1938), *Caesar and Cleopatra* (1945), *Nicholas Nickleby, Jassy* (1947), *Madness of the Heart* (1949), *So Long at the Fair* (1950), *Promise Her Anything* (1965), *The Trygon Factor* (1966), *Full Circle* (1976, UK/Can), *Second to the Right and Straight on Until Morning* (1980).

BIBLIOG: Autobiography, *A Little Love and Good Company*, 1973.

Nesbitt, Derren (*b* London, 1932). Actor. An impressive thug in *Room at the Top* (1958), in which he beats up Laurence HARVEY, and in Vernon SEWELL's spare, chilling 'B' thrillers, *The Man in the Back Seat* and *Strongroom* (1962), Nesbitt had supporting roles in several big-budget pieces, including *The Blue Max* (1966) and *Monte Carlo or Bust!* (1969, UK/Fr/It), but never achieved the stardom he seemed to promise. In 1974, he wrote, produced and directed *The Amorous Milkman*, a drab sex farce based on his own novel. Married and divorced (1974) Anne AUBREY.

OTHER BRITISH FILMS INCLUDE: *A Night to Remember, The Silent Enemy* (1958), *In the Nick* (1959), *Sword of Sherwood Forest* (1960), *Victim* (1961), *A Matter of Choice* (co-orig story), *The Informers* (1963), *The Naked Runner* (1967), *Nobody Runs Forever* (UK/US), *Where Eagles Dare* (1968), *Burke & Hare* (1971), *Ooh . . . You Are Awful, Not Now, Darling* (1972), *Give Us Tomorrow, Playbirds* (1978), *Funny Money* (1982), *Eat the Rich* (1987), *Double X: The Name of the Game* (1992).

Nesbitt, James (*b* Broughshane, N.Ireland, 1965). Actor. Likeable purveyor of laddish types, Irish-educated, Central School-trained Nesbitt has had a rapid ascent since his debut film, *Hear My Song* (1991). He brought real sharpness of insight to the hero's randy mate in *Go Now* (1996), to a sympathetic,

frightened war correspondent in *Welcome to Sarajevo* (1997, UK/US), to a civil rights campaigner in *Bloody Sunday* (2002), and especially to Adam, the thirtyish protagonist, confronted by some difficult moral choices in TV's *Cold Feet* (1997–98, 2001).

OTHER BRITISH FILMS INCLUDE: *Jude, This Is the Sea* (UK/Ire/US), (1996), *The James Gang, The Resurrection Man* (1997), *Waking Ned* (1999, UK/Fr/US), *Women Talking Dirty, Wild About Harry, Lucky Break* (2001, UK/Ger/US).

Nettlefold, Archibald (*b* Birmingham, 1870 – *d* London, 1944). Studio Head. With money from his wealthy industrial family, Nettlefold entered show business as a theatrical producer in 1921, leasing London's Comedy Theatre. In 1926, he purchased the Hepworth studios at Walton-on-Thames, forming the only one-man financed production entity of the time, NETTLEFOLD PRODUCTIONS. He appointed W.A. Lott as production and general manager, contracted BUTCHER'S FILM SERVICE as his distributor, and began production of a series of features, beginning with *The House of Marney* (1926). Nettlefold lacked creative skills, but he did have the good sense to promote Walter FORDE as a comedian in features and to sign Mabel POULTON as his leading lady. With the coming of sound, the studio became a rental facility, but Nettlefold still continued as its head, despite losing his eyesight in 1930. AS.

Nettlefold Productions Founded by Birmingham industrialist Archibald NETTLEFOLD, this company produced modest programmers for nearly 30 years. Its first film, *The House of Marney* (1926), was directed by Cecil HEPWORTH, but after its failure direction passed to Harry HUGHES and Walter FORDE, with a batch of very SHORT FILMS made by Anson DYER. Post-war, its contract director Maclean ROGERS turned out several films featuring the detectives 'Paul Temple' and 'The Toff', and Geoffrey FAITHFULL was Nettlefold's contract cinematographer for twenty years. The company ceased production in the mid 50s.

Nettles, John (*b* St Austell, 1943). Actor. Best known as TV's eponymous offshore policeman, *Bergerac* (1981–91) and as the somewhat irritatingly superior Detective Chief Inspector Barnaby in TV's *Midsomer Murders*, Nettles has hardly touched films. His British films are: *One More Time* (1969, unc) and *All Men Are Mortal* (1995, UK/Fr/Neth).

Nettleton, John (*b* London, 1929). Actor. In TV since the mid 50s, velvet-voiced Nettleton had an intermittently recurring role, as Sir Arnold Robinson, in *Yes Minister* and *Yes Prime Minister*, during the 80s. Entered films as the jailer in *A Man for All Seasons* (1966) and has appeared in about a half-dozen films since, but his main career has been in TV, usually as toffs.

OTHER BRITISH FILMS INCLUDE: *The Last Shot You Hear* (1968), *And Soon the Darkness* (1970), *Black Beauty* (1971), *All Creatures Great and Small* (1974), *The Burning Secret* (1988), *American Friends* (1991).

Neville, John (*b* London, 1925). Actor. Celebrated theatre actor and director, artistic director of several theatres, including Nottingham Playhouse (1963–66) and the Stratford Festival, Ontario (1986–89), Neville has scarcely had time – or perhaps inclination – for a sustained film career. Educated at Willesden and Chiswick County Schools and RADA-trained, he was on stage from 1947, on TV (as Romeo) from 1957, by which time he had already established a formidable stage reputation (e.g. for his and Richard BURTON's alternating as Iago and Othello), and entered films none too auspiciously as

Bosie in the inferior BIOPIC, *Oscar Wilde* (1960). His screen persona always seemed a bit chilly, but he made it work well as SHERLOCK HOLMES in *A Study in Terror* (1965). Has also appeared in international films, including *Little Women* (1994), as Grandpa Lawrence. Awarded OBE, 1965, and appointed Honorary Professor of Drama at Nottingham University, 1967.

OTHER BRITISH FILMS INCLUDE: *Mr Topaze* (1961), *Billy Budd* (1962), *Unearthly Stranger* (1963), *The Long March* (1965), *The Adventures of Gerard* (1970, UK/It/Switz), *The Adventures of Baron Munchausen* (1988, UK/Ger/It, title role), *Swann* (UK/Can), *Dinner at Fred's* (1996), *Regeneration* (1997, UK/Can), *Sunshine* (2000, UK/Austria/Can/Ger/Hung).

Nevinson, Nancy (*b* India, 1918). Actress. Supporting player in films and TV from the mid 50s, sometimes in 'B' MOVIES such as *Night Train for Inverness* (1959) and playing several 'foreign' roles, in such films as *Very Important Person* (1961), *Foxhole in Cairo* (1960) and, as Rosanno BRAZZI's wife, in *Light in the Piazza* (1962, US).

OTHER BRITISH FILMS INCLUDE: *High Flight, Wonderful Things* (1957), *Mrs Gibbons' Boys* (1962), *Ring of Spies* (1963), *The Spy Who Came in from the Cold* (1965), *For the Love of Ada* (1972), *Symptoms* (1974), *SOS Titanic* (1979, UK/US, TV, some cinemas), *Mrs Dalloway* (1997, UK/Neth/US).

New Directors scheme A scheme instituted in 1987 by the BFI and CHANNEL 4 Television as a production fund for SHORT FILMS which, it was envisaged, would provide valuable experience for new film-makers. In the ensuing decade, 14 such had completed their first feature. It was also hoped by the BFI PRODUCTION BOARD, which had funded short films by Bill DOUGLAS, Terence DAVIES, Peter GREENAWAY and others, that the film-makers sustained by the scheme would provide distinctive if not necessarily oppositional voices in relation to the mainstream. The scheme has lower budgets and a greater concentration on writer-directors than the CHANNEL 4 eleven-minute scheme 'Short and Curlies', established at the same time. Carine ADLER is a case in point: after directing the short, *Fever*, for the scheme, she went on to make the critically acclaimed *Under the Skin* (1997), also for the BFI. Other graduates include Sandra GOLDBACHER, Gurinder CHADHA, Richard KWIETNIOWSKI, Andrew KOTTING, Patrick KEILLER, Chris NEWBY, Jim Gillespie (now filming in the US) and Lynn RAMSAY. In 1999 the scheme was abolished and the funding re-routed to the new FILM COUNCIL's 'New Cinema Fund'. Ben Gibson.

'New Wave' The key directors of the British New Wave – Lindsay ANDERSON, Tony RICHARDSON, John SCHLESINGER, Karel REISZ – all directed their first feature films between 1959 and 1963, translating to the cinema some of their generation's revolt against the complacency of the older generation and the metropolitan bourgeoisie, finding in the northern working class a vitality and toughness which the post-war cinema of EALING had not reflected. In the cinema, their immediate roots lay in the DOCUMENTARY attitude of FREE CINEMA, an attitude which owed more to the poetic impulse of Humphrey JENNINGS than to the sociological 'propaganda' (his term) of GRIERSON. They brought with them a new sense of place and observation – 'the poetry of everyday life' which they had celebrated in their critical writing in the Oxford journal *SEQUENCE*. They claimed a place in the European tradition of neorealism, a lineage also claimed at the same time by the French *Nouvelle Vague*. In the broader British culture, their roots lay in theatre and in the theatrical 'revolution' which had re-energised British culture following the success of John OSBORNE's *Look Back in Anger* at the Royal Court Theatre in 1956. Anderson and Richardson had directed at the Royal Court and were part of that generation of writers, directors and actors which swept aside the increasingly effete English theatre of country houses and the metropolitan bourgeoisie. WOODFALL, the production company most closely associated with the New Wave, was formed by Richardson, Osborne and the producer Harry SALTZMAN, with the explicit intention of exploiting the success of the Royal Court Theatre. The films associated with the New Wave are all – without exception – ADAPTATIONS of novels, stories or plays, mostly written in the mid-1950s, tracing a trajectory from *Room at the Top* (adapted from John Braine, 1958), *Look Back in Anger* (adapted from Osborne, 1959), *Saturday Night and Sunday Morning* (adapted from Alan SILLITOE, 1960), *A Taste of Honey* (adapted from Shelagh DELANEY, 1961), to *This Sporting Life* (adapted from David STOREY) and *Billy Liar* (adapted from Willis HALL) both in 1963. Somewhat symptomatically, introducing the costume drama which was to become a staple of British cinema and television, the last Woodfall production was Richardson's adaptation of Henry FIELDING's *Tom Jones* (1963), before Richardson went off to Hollywood, and Saltzman joined Cubby BROCCOLI to produce the James BOND films.

The directors were all Oxbridge men. Their identification with Northern working class men was from the outside, characteristically refracted through a romantic individualism (which they shared with the early *Nouvelle Vague*) which sought out rough, alienated heroes at odds with their society, and punished the women who trapped them into conformity. In translating the celebrated anger and vitality of the new culture to cinema they also translated some of the misogyny which fuelled it, and women did not always have much to celebrate in the anger of young men.

The British New Wave was short-lived, though Anderson claimed to be ploughing its furrow in *If . . .* (1968), *O Lucky Man!* (1973), and *Britannia Hospital* (1982). Its more immediate descendants might be traced in television rather than cinema, where the progressive drama of Denis POTTER, David MERCER, LOACH/GARNETT and others in the 60s and 70s kept a small domestic flame alive. John Caughie.

Newall, Guy (*b* Newport, Isle of Wight, 1885 – *d* London, 1937). Actor, director. A rugged-looking leading man, who made his screen debut with the LONDON FILM COMPANY in 1915, and an intelligent director, who was married to Ivy DUKE and later Dorothy BATLEY. He co-starred with Duke in about 15 mainly romantic 'society dramas', including *I Will* (1919), directing and writing several. He and Duke completed a theatrical tour in the mid 20s with his own company.

OTHER BRITISH FILMS INCLUDE: (a, unless noted) *The Heart of Sister Anne* (1915), *The Manxman* (1916), *The March Hare* (sc), *Fancy Dress, The Garden of Resurrection* (1919, + p, sc), *The Lure of Crooning Water, Duke's Son, Testimony* (d) (1920, + p, sc), *The Bigamist* (1921, + d, p, sc), *Fox Farm, Beauty and the Beast, The Persistent Lovers, Boy Woodburn, A Maid of the Silver Sea* (1922, + d, p, sc), *The Starlit Garden* (1923, + d, p, sc), *The Ghost Train* (1927), *The Marriage Bond* (1932), *Merry Comes to Town* (1937); (d) *The Rosary* (1931), *The Chinese Puzzle* (1932), *The Admiral's Secret* (1934). AS.

Newark, Derek (*b* Great Yarmouth, 1933 – *d* London, 1998). Actor. Character actor of the 60s to the 80s, best known as Det. Insp. Tucker in TV's *Barlow* (1971, 1973) and *Barlow at Large* (1974–75). Had supporting roles in films from the mid 60s, including *The Blue Max* (1966) and various policemen and military types in a dozen films.

OTHER BRITISH FILMS INCLUDE: *The Black Torment, The System* (1964), *The Little Ones* (1965), *Oh! What a Lovely War* (1969), *Fragment of Fear* (1970), *Dad's Army, Venom* (1971), *The Black Windmill* (1974), *Bellman & True* (1987).

Newbrook, Peter (*b* Chester, 1920). Producer, cinematographer. Entered film industry in 1934 at WARNER BROS' TEDDINGTON STUDIOS as assistant cameraman, joined EALING in 1939, and was with the ARMY KINEMATOGRAPH UNIT during WW2. Post-war, he worked on five films with David LEAN: as aerial unit cameraman on *The Sound Barrier* (1952), as camera operator on *Hobson's Choice* (1953), *Summer Madness* (1955, UK/US), and *The Bridge on the River Kwai* (1957), and was 2nd unit photographer on *Lawrence of Arabia* (1962). The films on which he was cinematographer and/or producer are generally less interesting, though *In the Cool of the Day* (1963) gave him some obvious pictorial scope.

OTHER BRITISH FILMS INCLUDE: (cam op, unless noted) *The New Lot* (1943, doc, 2uc), *Against the Wind* (1947, 2u cam op), *The Captain's Paradise, The Heart of the Matter* (1953); (c) *Melody Club, Third Time Lucky* (1949), *That Kind of Girl* (1963), *The Yellow Teddybears, The Black Torment* (1964), *Gonks Go Beat* (1965, + co-story); (c, co-p/p, unless noted) *The Sandwich Man, Press for Time* (1966), *Corruption* (1967), *She'll Follow You Anywhere* (p, story), *Crucible of Terror* (c, ex p), *The Asphyx* (1972, d).

Newby, Chris (*b* Leeds, 1957). Director. One of the 'graduates' of the NEW DIRECTORS SCHEME, Newby made several SHORT FILMS in the 80s and early 90s, including two for the Royal College of Art (*Feast*, 1983; *Hoy*, 1984). His debut as feature director was *Anchoress* (1993), followed by the strange, and strangely named, *Madagascar Skin* (1995), starring Bernard HILL and John HANNAH. Both were made for the BFI.

OTHER BRITISH FILMS INCLUDE: *Relax, Kiss* (1991, shorts).

Newell, Mike (*b* St Albans, 1942). Director. After a long and valuable TV apprenticeship, much of it with Granada, which he joined after Cambridge, Newell went on to become perhaps the director Britain could least afford to lose to the US – which appears to be what has happened, though he said in 1989 'I'm not happy in America'. With a string of confidently crafted films, he established himself as the mainstream director *par excellence*. *Dance with a Stranger* (1984) brought the hard bright glare of 30 years' hindsight to the socially appalling story of Ruth Ellis, the last woman to be hanged in Britain; *The Good Father* (1986) was a strongly characterised account of marital and familial tensions; *Enchanted April* (1992) is a charming fable of spiritual liberation in sun-drenched Italy, which resists the sentimentality it might have embraced; and *Four Weddings and a Funeral* (1994, BAA/d), the highest-grossing British film till then and making a star of Hugh GRANT, was so witty and engaging that it inevitably invited a sort of backlash, which fortunately had no effect whatever on its international success. However, his next film, *An Awfully Big Adventure* (1995), again starring Grant, intelligent and affectionate/abrasive as it was about provincial theatre and family secrets, was too dark for popular taste, and Newell took himself to America, where he made some interesting, low-key dramas, starting with *Donnie Brasco* (1997). His best work seems so steeped in Englishness that it seems a disservice to him as well as to the industry for him not to work the vein he obviously knows so well.

OTHER BRITISH FILMS: *The Man in the Iron Mask* (1977, TV, some cinemas), *The Awakening* (1980, UK/US), *Bad Blood* (1981, UK/NZ),

Soursweet (1988), *Into the West* (1992, UK/Ire/US), *Photographing Fairies* (1997, co-ex p), *High Fidelity* (2000, UK/US, ex p).

Newland, Mary (aka Lilian Oldland) (*b* Gloucester, 1903). Actress. Married to director and dramatist Reginald DENHAM, demurely pretty Newland starred in about 20 silents and early 30s films. The latter were mostly 'QUOTA QUICKIES', several of them directed by Denham, most notably the thriller, *Death at Broadcasting House* (1934). On stage 1924, in films from 1925 (as Oldland) in *The Secret Kingdom* and the *Bindle* series (1926); changed name for talkies.

OTHER BRITISH FILMS INCLUDE: *The Flag Lieutenant, A Daughter in Revolt* (1926), *Troublesome Wives* (1928), *To Oblige a Lady, Jealousy* (1931), *The Jewel, Ask Beccles* (1933), *Easy Money* (1934), *The Silent Passenger, The Price of Wisdom* (1935).

Newlands, Anthony (*b* London, 1924 – *d* Croydon, Surrey, 1995). Actor. Character actor busiest mainly in the 60s, often as morally suspect characters, several times in MERTON PARK's series of short THRILLERS, including *Solo for Sparrow* (1962), and with substantial roles in the HORROR films, *Circus of Fear* (1966) and *Scream and Scream Again* (1969). A regular offsider to Marius GORING in TV's *The Adventures of the Scarlet Pimpernel* (1955).

OTHER BRITISH FILMS INCLUDE: *Room at the Top* (1958), *Beyond This Place* (1959), *The Trials of Oscar Wilde, Foxhole in Cairo, Cone of Silence* (1960), *The Fourth Square* (1961), *Hysteria* (1964), *Kaleidoscope* (1966), *The Magus* (1968), *Mata Hari* (1984).

Newley, Anthony (*b* London, 1931 – *d* Jensen Beach, Florida, 1999). Actor, composer, director. Versatile character actor who became a cult figure at that critical moment when the 50s became the 60s. Whilst a tea boy at the Italia Conti stage school he was selected for a film serial and in the same year made a big impression in *Vice Versa* (1947). Playing younger than his age, he superbly portrayed the worldly-wise Artful Dodger in David LEAN's *Oliver Twist* (1948). His next break came when he was offered a contract by WARWICK FILMS, first in *Cockleshell Heroes* (1955), and becoming a familiar face in their films. It was their *Idle on Parade* (1958) that led to his next break, as one of the film's songs was a hit making Newley a pop star, and this resulted in his first musical collaboration with Leslie BRICCUSE, *Stop the World* . . . (filmed in 1966). After 1964, Newley worked increasingly in US theatre, TV and concerts. He co-wrote, directed, produced, composed and acted in *Can Hieronymus Merkin Ever Forget* . . . ? (1969), so the critics knew exactly who to blame. A critical and commercial flop, it was a Felliniesque take (with songs) on Newley's life with his then-wife (1963–71) Joan COLLINS. First married (1956–63) actress Ann LYNN.

OTHER BRITISH FILMS: (a, unless noted) *Adventures of Dusty Bates, The Little Ballerina* (1947), *Here Come the Huggetts, The Guinea Pig, Vote For Huggett* (1948), *A Boy, a Girl and a Bike, Don't Ever Leave Me* (1949), *Highly Dangerous* (1950), *Those People Next Door* (1952), *Top of the Form* (1953), *Up to his Neck* (1954), *The Blue Peter, Above us the Waves, Port Afrique* (1955), *The Battle of the River Plate, X the Unknown, The Last Man to Hang?, The Good Companions* (1956), *Fire Down Below, High Flight* (+ song), *How to Murder a Rich Uncle* (1957), *No Time to Die, The Man Inside* (1958), *The Lady is a Square, The Killers of Kilimanjaro, The Bandit of Zhobe, The Heart of a Man* (1959), *In the Nick, Jazzboat* (+ songs), *Let's Get Married* (1960), *The Small World of Sammy Lee* (1962), *Mister Quilp* (1974, + comp). Roger Philip Mellor.

Newman, Nanette (*b* Northampton, 1934). Actress. Graceful beauty who might have had a bigger star career in an earlier decade: the 60s generally favoured a rougher breed, but

Newman made the most of her opportunities, notably in the films directed by her husband, Bryan FORBES. She is a charming period heroine in *The Wrong Box* (1966) and touchingly unsentimental in his *The Raging Moon* (1970), her best role, as the girl in a wheelchair. A gift to the TECHNICOLOR cameras, she looks wonderful in the dramatically flawed *The Madwoman of Chaillot* (1969) and *International Velvet* (1978), but is also affecting as the distraught wife in the black-and-white *Seance on a Wet Afternoon* (1964). From a variety background, in films as a teenager, she returned in the mid 50s in 'B' MOVIES, including Vernon SEWELL's unsettling *House of Mystery* (1961), and became well known for TV ads for 'Fairy Liquid' – and for a well-regarded TV drama, *Jessie* (1980). Also the author of cookery books and books for children.

OTHER BRITISH FILMS INCLUDE: *Here We Come Gathering* (1945), *Personal Affair* (1953), *Faces in the Dark*, *The League of Gentlemen*, *The Rebel* (1960), *The Painted Smile* (1961), *The L-Shaped Room*, *The Wrong Arm of the Law*, *Twice Round the Daffodils* (1962), *Of Human Bondage* (1964), *The Whisperers* (1966), *Deadfall* (1968), *Oh! What a Lovely War* (1969), *Man at the Top* (1973), *Restless Natives* (1985), *The Mystery of Edwin Drood* (1993).

Newman, Widgey R(aphael) (*b* Bedford, 1900 – *d* St Albans, 1944). Director. Former film publicist (from 1921) and editor (from 1923), Newman became a prolific (co-)director of SHORTS, DOCUMENTARIES and 'QUOTA QUICKIES', the latter often made for DELTA PICTURES at Bushey studios, and almost entirely unmemorable.

BRITISH FILMS INCLUDE: (d, unless noted; f = feature) *Derby Secrets* (1925), *How I Began*, *John Henry Calling*, *Listening In* (1926, co-d), *Madalon*, *The Merchant of Venice* (1927), *A Reckless Gamble* (f) (1928), *Heroes of Mine*, *Castle Sinister* (1932, f), *Lucky Blaze* (1933, f, + sc), *The Unholy Quest* (1934, p, sc), *Pal o' Mine* (+ p, screen story), *What the Puppy Said* (1936, f), *The Inspector* (1937, + sc), *On Velvet* (1938, f, + p), *Two Smart Men*, *Henry Steps Out* (1940, f, + p), *The Parrot Goes to Sea* (doc), *Strange to Relate* (1943), *Chartered Waters* (doc), *The Four Seasons* (+ p), *Road to Yesterday* (doc) (1944).

newsreels Newsreels were a regular feature of British cinema programmes for fifty years, and in total lasted 69 years, from their inception with *Pathé's Animated Gazette* in 1910, to the quiet demise of the last of them, *British Movietone News*, in 1979. Issued twice-weekly, to match the usual change of cinema programmes, they presented a 5-to-10-minute reel of visual news that strove to be entertaining and uncontroversial. Newsreels were always exempt from the attentions of the BRITISH BOARD OF FILM CENSORS, official control only being exercised during wartime, most notably when the War Office commandeered the *Topical Budget* newsreel during WW1 and ran it as a PROPAGANDA newsreel. But in peacetime the newsreels were more than happy to side-step controversy, though in practice this meant subservience to the status quo, and for *British Movietone* in particular, strong links with the Conservative government. The newsreels reached their greatest popularity in the 30s and 40s with the arrival of the distinctive commentary voices of Leslie MITCHELL (*Movietone*), E.V.H. EMMETT (*Gaumont–British News*) and Bob Danvers WALKER (*Pathé News*), but the arrival of live television news in the 50s (initially BBC Television had shown cinema newsreels, and then produced its own *Television Newsreel*) doomed the newsreels, forever forced to be late with the news, to history. But history has become their salvation, and the newsreel libraries continue to thrive by supplying television documentaries with their rich record of the past. Luke McKernan

Newton, Robert (*b* Shaftesbury, Dorset, 1905 – *d* Los Angeles, 1956). Actor. 'He was large and rude and outrageous and lovely,' said Wendy HILLER in 1991 of her *Major Barbara* (1941) co-star, drawing attention to the wonderfully excessive quality of this famous roisterer. From an artistic family, he was on stage from 1920, though rarely as a conventional leading man. He could tear a passion to tatters, eating the scenery and other actors in his path when he was in mad-eyed mode, as he famously was as the builder of *Hatter's Castle* (1941), as flamboyant Pistol in *Henry V* (1944), in *Odd Man Out* (1947), as the artist who wants to capture fugitive James MASON on canvas, or as Bill Sykes in *Oliver Twist* (1948), unforgettably murdering Kay WALSH and hounded to his own death, and, of course, as the definitive Long John Silver in DISNEY's British-made *Treasure Island* (1950), a role he repeated on film, *Long John Silver* (1954, Aust) and TV. However, he also gave some fine performances in more subdued style: as Diana WYNYARD's country cousin in *Gaslight* (1940), suburban householder Frank Gibbons in *This Happy Breed* (1944), the harbour signalman in *Temptation Harbour* (1947), and the quietly spoken acid-bath murderer in *Obsession* (1949). It was hard to trust him as an ordinary hero, as in *The Squeaker* (1937) or *Jamaica Inn* (1939) or *Night Boat to Dublin* (1946); there was always a fear that he would sabotage the enterprise.

In the Royal Navy during WW2, he made a string of popular films in Hollywood in the 50s, including *Blackbeard the Pirate* and *Les Misérables* (1952), but there was nothing to rival his best British work. A legendally dedicated drinker, it all – life, that is – caught up with him sadly early, and he was dead at 50. His daughter, **Sally Newton** (*b* London, 1930), appeared in a couple of minor British films: *The Armchair Detective* (1951), *No Haunt for a Gentleman* (1952).

OTHER BRITISH FILMS: *Reunion* (1932), *Fire Over England*, *Dark Journey*, *Farewell Again*, *The Green Cockatoo*, *21 Days* (1937), *Vessel of Wrath*, *Yellow Sands* (1938), *Poison Pen*, *Dead Men Are Dangerous*, *Hell's Cargo* (1939), *Busman's Honeymoon*, *Channel Incident*, *Bulldog Sees It Through* (1940), *They Flew Alone* (1942), *Snowbound* (1948), *Waterfront* (1950), *Tom Brown's Schooldays* (1951), *The Beachcomber* (1954).

Newton, Thandie (*b* London, 1972). Actress. Cambridge-educated Newton was born in London, to a Zimbabwean mother and British father. Delicately beautiful, she made her film debut in the Australian youth film, *Flirting* (1991), but has been most widely seen in surely one of the most idiotic films of recent years, *Mission: Impossible 2* (2000, US/Aust). Her British films have been almost doggedly low-key, including the underrated theatrical drama, *The Leading Man* (1996); her US career began with *Interview with the Vampire* (1994) and includes the ghostly girl in *Beloved* (1998). Married to director Oliver PARKER, who wrote the TV film, *In Your Dreams* (1997), in which she starred.

OTHER BRITISH FILMS INCLUDE: *The Young Americans* (1993), *Loaded* (1994, UK/NZ), *Jefferson in Paris* (1995), *Besieged* (1998, UK/It), *It Was an Accident* (2000).

Ney, Marie (*b* London, 1895 – *d* London, 1981). Actress. On stage from 1916 in Australia, London in 1923, the rather austerely dignified Ney, convent-educated in New Zealand, made only twenty films over 30 years. She was the Spirit of Christmas Past to Seymour HICKS's *Scrooge* (1935), and perhaps most memorable as the humane prison governor in *Yield to the Night* (1956) and as an ambiguous victim of *Witchcraft* (1964). One of the legion of British stage actors who have merely dabbled in films. She did much Shakespeare at the Old Vic and toured extensively for ENSA during WW2.

OTHER BRITISH FILMS INCLUDE: *Escape* (1930), *The Wandering Jew* (1933), *Brief Ecstasy* (1937), *Jamaica Inn* (1939), *Conspirator* (1949), *Seven Days to Noon* (1950), *Simba* (1955), *The Surgeon's Knife* (1957), *West 11* (1963).

Ngakane, Lionel (*b* Pretoria, 1928). Actor. South African son of teachers, who went to Britain in 1950 to work as a journalist, and made his feature debut as the erring son, Absalom (of course), in the well-meaning but somewhat leaden drama of racial discord, *Cry, the Beloved Country* (1952). His other roles were in more conventionally exotic-set adventures and in 1966 he directed the Venice Film Festival award-winning short, *Jemima and Johnny* (+ sc), a fable of friendship between black girl and white boy.

OTHER BRITISH FILMS INCLUDE: *Dark London* (1952, short), *Duel in the Jungle* (1954), *Safari, Odongo* (1956), *Nor the Moon by Night* (1958), *The Night We Got the Bird* (1960), *The Painted Smile* (1961), *Two Gentlemen Sharing* (1969), *The Squeeze* (1977).

Niblo, Allan Producer. Following the success of *Human Traffic* (1999), critically at least, Niblo turned from Cardiff to Brixton for his next film, *SW9* (2001), and not only was it one of the few British films to be wholly privately funded but his own company, Fruit Salad, handled the distribution, because he believed too many small British films are lost through incompetent handling. He directed the virtually unseen 1997 feature, *Loop*.

Nicholas, Paul (*b* Peterborough, 1945). Actor. RN: Beuselinck. Former pop star, who starred in the stage musical *Hair* in London, 1968, and later in *Jesus Christ, Superstar* and *Grease*, and came to films in the 70s. He was in Ken RUSSELL's *Tommy* (1975) and *Lisztomania* (1975, as Wagner), but was inevitably outshone by Roger DALTREY in both. Only a few more scattered films, but he had a success with the TV series, *Just Good Friends* (1983–86) and his career continued to prosper on the musical stage.

OTHER BRITISH FILMS INCLUDE: *Blind Terror* (1971), *Stardust* (1974), *Yesterday's Hero*, *The World Is Full of Married Men* (1979), *Nutcracker* (1982), *Invitation to the Wedding* (1983).

Nicholls, Anthony (*b* Windsor, 1902 – *d* London, 1977). Actor. Tall, distinguished-looking actor who made a career of playing doctors (he tends Jeremy SPENSER in *Portrait of Clare*, 1950), lawyers (as in *Happy Ever After*, 1954), military officers (the honoured guest in *If . . .*, 1968), a gay Lord in *Victim* (1961), and even a prince in *The Dancing Years* (1950). Reliable rather than riveting, the former Slade School art student served in WW2 before making his film debut. On stage from 1936, with Stratford, Chichester, Old Vic and Broadway seasons. Married to **Faith Kent**, who played a handful of small film roles in such films as *The Pumpkin Eater* (1964) and *Half Moon Street* (1986); their daughter is Phoebe NICHOLLS.

OTHER BRITISH FILMS INCLUDE: *The Laughing Lady* (1946), *The Guinea Pig* (1948), *The Hasty Heart*, *No Place for Jennifer* (1949), *The Franchise Affair* (1950), *High Treason* (1951), *The Weak and the Wicked* (1953), *The Green Scarf*, *Make Me an Offer!* (1954), *Dunkirk* (1958), *Night of the Eagle* (1962), *Othello* (1965), *A Man for All Seasons* (1966), *Our Mother's House* (1967), *Battle of Britain* (1969), *The Man Who Haunted Himself* (1970), *O Lucky Man!* (1973).

Nicholls, Paul (*b* Bolton, Lancs, 1979). Actor. RN: Greenhalgh. *The Clandestine Marriage* (1999) received an only partially deserved critical mauling but Nicholls, as the young

architect who has contracted the titular union, emerged unscathed and created another good impression as the young soldier wounded early in the WW1 drama, *The Trench* (1999, UK/Fr). He came to films via TV where he did time in *EastEnders* (1996–97).

OTHER BRITISH FILMS INCLUDE: *Goodbye Charlie Bright* (2001).

Nicholls, Phoebe (*b* London, 1958). Actress. Vivid, dark-haired daughter of Anthony NICHOLLS and Faith Kent, she has been acting since childhood, starting as Sarah Nicholls in such films as *The Pumpkin Eater* (1964), *Our Mother's House* (1967) and *Women in Love* (1969): a good start, indeed. Since then TV has given her better chances, in, for example, *Brideshead Revisited* (1981) as idealistic Cordelia, and she was very sharp and funny as the appalling Elizabeth Elliot in *Persuasion* (1995, TV, many cinemas).

OTHER BRITISH FILMS INCLUDE: *Dr Terror's House of Terrors* (1964), *All at Sea* (1969), *The Elephant Man* (1980, US-financed, UK-made), *Ordeal by Innocence* (1984), *Maurice* (1987), *Fairytale: A True Story* (1997, UK/US).

Nichols, Dandy (*b* London, 1907 – *d* London, 1986). Actress. Now most fondly remembered as Alf Garnett's wife, the 'silly moo', in TV's *Till Death Do Us Part* (1966–68, 1972, 1974–75), as well as the SPIN-OFF films, 1969 and (*The Alf Garnett Saga*) 1972. Nichols was also a respected stage actress, in such plays as *Home* (1971), opposite GIELGUD and RICHARDSON. In films, she was one of those invaluable CHARACTER PLAYERS who vivified brief moments in dozens of films, frequently as nosy neighbours, suspicious landladies (watch her, in this function, boot out Donal Donnelly in *The Knack . . .*, 1965), housekeepers (sympathetic in *The Deep Blue Sea*, 1955), tea ladies (*O Lucky Man!*, 1973), working-class mums, charladies, barmaids – the full panoply of lower-orders character women was given its due, and more.

OTHER BRITISH FILMS INCLUDE: *Hue and Cry* (1946), *Nicholas Nickleby* (1947), *The Winslow Boy*, *The Fallen Idol*, *The History of Mr Polly* (1948), *Now Barabbas Was a Robber* (1949), *Dance Hall* (1950), *White Corridors* (1951), *The Holly and the Ivy*, *Mother Riley Meets the Vampire*, *The Happy Family*, *Women of Twilight* (1952), *Street Corner* (1953), *Mad About Men* (1954), *Lost*, *Where There's a Will* (1955), *Yield to the Night*, *Tiger in the Smoke*, *Town on Trial* (1956), *A Cry from the Streets* (1958), *Crooks Anonymous* (1962), *The Leather Boys*, *Ladies Who Do* (1963), *Act of Murder* (1964), *Help!*, *The Early Bird* (1965), *Georgy Girl* (1966), *Carry On Doctor*, *The Birthday Party* (1968), *The Bed Sitting Room* (1969), *Britannia Hospital* (1982).

Nichols, Peter (*b* Bristol, 1927). Screenwriter, dramatist. Former teacher and actor, educated at Bristol Grammar School, Nichols became one of the wittiest and most abrasive chroniclers of middle-class life and social institutions, as revealed in *A Day in the Death of Joe Egg* (1965) and *The National Health* (1969). Both of these were smartly filmed, from his own screenplays, in 1972 and 1973, respectively, retaining the anarchic elements of their antecedent texts. So, too, was the Army concert party satire, *Privates on Parade* (filmed 1982, + lyrics), and Nichols appeared in a short film about its making, *Strictly Private* (1982). Also wrote the screenplay for *Catch Us If You Can* (1965, + a) and co-wrote *Georgy Girl* (1966). His best play, *Passion Play* (1984), was given a much-praised revival in 2000.

BIBLIOG: Peter Nichols, *Diaries 1969–77*, 2000.

Nicholson, Nora (*b* Leamington, 1892 – *d* London, 1973). Actress. 'I will not stand by and hear you accuse your mother of passion', announces Nicholson to Sally Ann HOWES, in what may be a key line for historians of British cinema's depiction of love, in an inane and deservedly forgotten film, *Fools Rush In* (1949). On stage from 1912, at Stratford, she played much SHAW and Chekhov; in films, she was usually cast as dotty old ladies, not quite aware of the implications of their remarks. Even in rubbish like *The Hornet's Nest* (1955), she is fun; and she is very touching as Mrs Frith in *A Town Like Alice* (1956).

OTHER BRITISH FILMS: *Once Upon a Dream, The Blue Lagoon* (1949), *The Crowded Day* (1954), *Raising a Riot* (1955), *Sea Wife* (1956), *Light Fingers* (1957), *Law and Disorder, The Captain's Table* (1958), *The Three Lives of Thomasina* (1963), *Joey Boy* (1965), *Run a Crooked Mile* (1969), *Say Hello to Yesterday* (1970).

BIBLIOG: Autobiography, *Chameleon's Dish*, 1973.

Nicholson, William (*b* 1948). Screenwriter, dramatist. With the BBC as a documentary writer-director from 1970, Nicholson found wider acclaim with his moving account of the romance between C.S. Lewis and American poet Joy Gresham, *Shadowlands*, which has now been successful on TV (1985), stage (1989) and screen (1993, UK/US). For the latter, Nicholson's screenplay received an AAn, as did his co-authored screenplay for *Gladiator* (2000, UK/US). His humanist instincts were also revealed in *Grey Owl* (2000, UK/Can) and the little-seen drama of family identity and bonds, *Firelight* (1997, UK/US). Wholly US films include the unpopular reworking of the Arthurian legend, *First Knight* (1995). Also novelist.

Nightingale, Florence (*b* Florence, 1820 – *d* London, 1910). Organiser of the British nursing profession in Britain, foregrounding its importance through her work in the Crimean War and subsequently engaging in continuous battles with officialdom at many levels. Played on the screen several times, most famously by Anna NEAGLE as *The Lady with a Lamp* (1951), a worthy but dull film, and also by Elisabeth RISDON in *Florence Nightingale* (1915), Fay COMPTON in *Wedding Group* (1936), Joyce BLAND in *Sixty Glorious Years* (1938), and by Kay Francis in the US film, *The White Angel* (1936).

Nighy, Bill (*b* Caterham, 1949). Actor. Nighy's outstanding comic (and touching) performance as the 70s rocker attempting a comeback with his old band in *Still Crazy* (1998, UK/US) should ensure a steady career as a character player. The brilliance of his timing and control of nuance were on display in three 2001 releases, *Blow Dry* (UK/Ger/US), *The Lawless Heart*, and *Lucky Break* (UK/Ger/US), though none of these was actually built around him, as one might like. Prior to *Still Crazy*, he'd been in films since the late 70s (he was the love interest of both *Antonia and Jane*, 1990) without making a strong impression, but that may be about to change. His record on stage, including a season with the National Theatre, and on TV (he was Lord Sandwich in *Longitude*, 2000) has been impressive.

OTHER BRITISH FILMS: *Occupy!* (1976), *The Bitch* (1979), *Eye of the Needle* (1981), *Curse of the Pink Panther* (1983), *Mack the Knife* (1989, UK/Hung), *Antonia and Jane* (1990, TV, some cinemas), *Being Human* (1994), *True Blue, Alive and Kicking* (1996), *Fairytale: A True Story* (1997, UK/US), *Guest House Paradiso* (1999).

Nimmo, Derek (*b* Liverpool, 1930 – *d* London, 1999). Actor. Nimmo's reputation as silly ass supreme of the second half of the 20th century derives largely from the TV persona he perfected in such clerical series as *All Gas and Gaiters* (1967, 1969–71), as Chaplain Noote, and *Oh Brother!* (1968–70) and *Oh Father!* (1973). He was an indefatigable touring impresario,

particularly in the Far East, was a West End favourite and panellist on Radio 4's *Just a Minute*, and somehow fitted in about 15 films, including *The Amorous Prawn* (1962), in which he repeated his stage role, and *One of Our Dinosaurs is Missing* (1975, US), as an English lord. But film was the least of his attainments.

OTHER BRITISH FILMS INCLUDE: *It's Trad, Dad, Tamahine, Go to Blazes* (1962), *Heavens Above!* (1963), *A Hard Day's Night, Murder Ahoy, The Bargee, The System* (1964), *Joey Boy* (1965), *Casino Royale* (1967), *Sunstruck* (1972, UK/Aust).

Nissen, Brian (*b* London, 1927 – *d* Salisbury, 2001). Actor. On stage from 1941 and in films from childhood, as, for example, Penelope DUDLEY WARD's kid brother in *The Demi-Paradise* (1943), he was the English soldier, Court, in *Henry V* (1944) and a youthful suitor in *They Were Sisters* (1945). His acting career was patchy after that and he later became a TV writer, on such films as the US animated feature, *The Swan Princess* (1994). Married TV director, Pat Phillips.

OTHER BRITISH FILMS INCLUDE: *English Without Tears* (1944), *Badger's Green* (1949), *Richard III, The Dam Busters* (1955), *Interpol, Second Fiddle* (1957), *Night Train for Inverness* (1959), *The Fur Collar* (1962), *Ring of Spies One* (1963).

Niven, David (*b* London, 1910 – *d* Chateau d'Oex, Switz, 1983). Actor. International star of famously debonair manner, which, however, was capable of enough mutation to keep him interesting to filmgoers for 40 years. Born of a well-to-do family, he trained at the Royal Military College, Sandhurst, and followed a picturesque range of occupations after discharge from the Army and before becoming an extra in Hollywood in 1935. He looked well in a dinner-jacket, had enough polished charm to ensure his entrée to smart parties, and actually became an established, middle-rank Hollywood star before WW2. His credits then included co-starring roles in *The Charge of the Light Brigade* (1936) and *Wuthering Heights* (1939), as weak Edgar Linton, a role he hated but played intelligently.

One of the first Brits to return home and to active service when war was declared, he served as a Lt-Colonel and was twice, and not willingly, seconded to film-making in the interests of national PROPAGANDA. He was the pilot who first flies the Spitfire in *The First of the Few* (1942), and he gave one of his finest performances as Lt Jim Perry in *The Way Ahead* (1944); in the latter, he plays a garage mechanic who is commissioned and put in charge of training a bunch of raw recruits, and, as well as never striking a false note in his role, he was a crucial technical adviser to director Carol REED. Postwar, he starred for POWELL AND PRESSBURGER in the ambitious fantasy, *A Matter of Life and Death* (1946), as an airman who is shot down and over whose fate there is heavenly debate. He returned to Hollywood where he made undistinguished films for the rest of the decade, but they were as nothing compared with the awfulness of his British venture, KORDA's ill-starred *Bonnie Prince Charlie* (1948), tedious and ridiculous in equal proportions.

However, he survived and passed urbanely through about 60 further, often US films, very few of which rise above the level of pleasant time-passer. Exceptions are ASQUITH's court-martial drama, *Carrington VC* and Mario ZAMPI's very funny Irish-set comedy, *Happy Ever After* (1954); the popular, star-laden *Around the World in Eighty Days* (1956, US); *Bonjour Tristesse* (1957), in which his ageing roué is acutely observed (or neatly tailored to his persona); and above all the US-made Bournemouth-set *Separate Tables* (1958), for which he won a deserved Oscar, as an ex-Major accused of sexual misconduct. The pain behind the fake polish was moving to observe. His technique was such that he never fell below a certain competence, in whatever surroundings he found himself, and he remained a star to the end, though one might have expected his 'type' to have faded with the war. He also starred in the US caper series, *The Rogues* (1964) and several other TV dramas, and wrote two entertaining volumes of autobiography.

OTHER BRITISH FILMS: *Dinner at the Ritz* (1937), *The Elusive Pimpernel* (1950), *Happy Go Lovely*, *Appointment with Venus* (1951), *The Love Lottery* (1953), *The Silken Affair* (1956), *The Guns of Navarone*, *The Road to Hong Kong* (1961), *Guns of Darkness* (1962), *Where the Spies Are* (1965), *Eye of the Devil* (1966), *Casino Royale* (1967), *Prudence and the Pill*, *Before Winter Comes* (1968), *Vampira*, *Paper Tiger* (1974), *Candleshoe* (1977, UK/US), *Death on the Nile* (1978), *Escape to Athena* (1979), *A Nightingale Sang in Berkeley Square*, *The Sea Wolves* (1980, UK/Switz/US), *The Trail of the Pink Panther* (1982), *Better Late Than Never*, *Curse of the Pink Panther* (1983).

BIBLIOG: Autobiography, *The Moon's a Balloon*, 1971, *Bring on the Empty Horses*, 1975; Sheridan Morley, *The Dark Side of the Moon*, 1985.

Nivola, Alessandro (*b* Boston, US, 1972). Actor. Handsome Italian-American actor whose impecccable English accent in his three British films – Michael WINTERBOTTOM's *I Want You* (1998), *Mansfield Park* (1999, UK/US), as a vividly and subtly corrupt Henry Crawford, and *Love's Labour's Lost* (2000, UK/Fr/US), as the King – made his origins hard to credit. Yale-educated Nivola is now in steady demand for US films, including *Jurassic Park III* (2001).

Noble, Peter (*b* London, 1917 – *d* London, 1997). Movie columnist. Now best remembered for his indefatigable chronicling of show business affairs, information and gossip, Noble overcame a slum childhood to pursue the work that most interested him. His *British Film (and TV) Handbooks*, from the late 40s, are an invaluable resource to researchers, and he made well over 1,000 radio and TV broadcasts as well as writing columns for various publications. He had a brief career as an actor (and circus clown, wartime stretcher-bearer) on stage and screen (often in cameo roles, as in *Make Mine a Million*, 1959), but his main importance was in recording how others did it. Married (2, 1947–97, his death) to Marianne STONE.

OTHER BRITISH FILMS INCLUDE: (a, unless noted) *Variety Jubilee* (1942), *The Life and Death of Colonel Blimp*, *My Learned Friend* (song 'You Do Things to Me'), *The Bells Go Down* (1943), *Walking On Air* (1946, co-m/lyrics), *The Runaway Bus* (1953, assoc p), *To Dorothy a Son* (1954, assoc p), *Lost* (assoc p), *Fun at St Fanny's* (co-story) (1955), *The Naked Truth* (1957), *Live It Up* (1963).

BIBLIOG: Autobiography, *Reflected Glory*, 1958.

Noble, Shaun (*b* Dun Laoghaire, Ireland, 1921 – *d* London, 1999). Actor. Male starlet of RANK's COMPANY OF YOUTH whose career came to a halt after two slightly peculiar 'B' MOVIES made at HIGHBURY STUDIOS: the amnesia romance, *Song for Tomorrow* and the secret service thriller, *Penny and the Pownall Case* (1948). After some stage experience, he studied at RADA, played a bit in *Caesar and Cleopatra*, was an IRA man in *The Voice Within* (both 1945), and had one memorable role as Deborah KERR's restless Irish lover in the sublime flashback sequence of *Black Narcissus* (1947).

Nolan, Christopher (*b* London, 1970). Director. Studied literature at University College, London, and began making 16mm films while there. His first feature, after some success with SHORT FILMS, was the twisty black-and-white *Following*

(1999, + p, sc, c, ed) after which he crossed the Atlantic to make the even twistier *Memento* (2000, + sc) and the Al Pacino vehicle, *Insomnia* (2002). Britain may have lost an original talent.

Nolbandov, Sergei (*b* Moscow, 1895 – *d* Lewes, 1971). Producer, screenwriter. Perhaps the most forgotten of the wartime EALING team, Nolbandov came to England in the 20s, was associated first with Michael BALCON at GAUMONT–BRITISH. At Ealing, he worked most closely with director Penrose TENNYSON, as (associate) producer on Tennyson's three features: *There Ain't No Justice* (1939, + co-sc), *The Proud Valley*, *Convoy* (1940). Of the two he directed, *Ships with Wings* (1941, + co-sc), a paean to the Fleet Air Arm, has dated badly, and *Undercover* (1943) was dated when it first appeared, not having registered a shift in Yugoslav politics. Leaving Ealing, he worked at the MINISTRY OF INFORMATION (1943–45), and post-war, he produced RANK's DOCUMENTARY series, *This Modern Age* (1946–50), before returning to feature production in the 50s. His later features are an eclectic bunch, including the fashion-world MELODRAMA, *It Started in Paradise* (1952), the charming Nova Scotia-set parable, *The Kidnappers* (1953), both co-produced with Leslie PARKYN, and the murder drama, *Mix Me a Person* (1962).

OTHER BRITISH FILMS INCLUDE: (p, unless noted) *The Bells* (1931, co-p), *Value for Money* (1955), *She Didn't Say No* (1957), *Behind the Mask* (1958); (co-sc) *The Amateur Gentleman* (1936), *Fire Over England* (1937), *The Four Just Men* (1939).

Nonyela, Valentine (*b c* 1970). Actor. Striking young black actor who played Chris, one of the disc jockeys involved in a murder hunt in *Young Soul Rebels* (1991) and the black gang leader with a pregnant white girlfriend in *Welcome II the Terrordome* (1995). Has also appeared in such popular TV series as *The Bill* (1983) and *A Touch of Frost* (1994).

Norden, Christine (*b* Sunderland, 1924 – *d* London, 1988). Actress. RN: Mary Thornton. Touted as a blonde temptress (a rare species in British cinema), Norden had a short reign in the late 40s/early 50s in films of decreasing stature. After working as singer and actress with ENSA during WW2, she was put under contract by KORDA, given a small role as a languid socialite in *An Ideal Husband* and a better one as a seductress in *Mine Own Executioner* (1947). This was her territory: she was never going to be the girl next door but British films had little use for her type, and her most memorable moments may be as whip-cracking Cora Pearl ('In the Bois – at daybreak!' she challenges in *Idol of Paris* (1948). Her last films were in 1951 and she left for the US the following year. First married to Jack CLAYTON.

OTHER BRITISH FILMS: *Night Beat* (1948), *Saints and Sinners*, *The Interrupted Journey* (1949), *Black Widow*, *Reluctant Heroes*, *A Case for PC 49* (1951).

Norman, C.P. Production designer. RN: Norman Delaney. After studying art in Vienna, he came to England in 1919, working with his brother, scenic artist Edward Delaney, at STOLL STUDIOS and getting his first film job on *Shooting Stars* (1928). In the 30s, he worked as assistant to Vincent KORDA on such ambitious films as *The Private Life of Henry VIII* (1933), then became floor manager to LONDON FILMS when it moved production to DENHAM. His chief work as art director, as it was then designated, was on David LEAN's *This Happy Breed* (1944) and *Blithe Spirit* (1945), evoking respectively lower-middle-class suburbia and upper-class Kent, but he also helps evoke a *noir* version of London under-life in *Night and the City* (1950, UK/US).

OTHER BRITISH FILMS INCLUDE: (des) *Danny Boy* (1941), *The Gentle Sex* (1943), *The First Gentleman* (1948), *Silent Dust* (1949), *The Mudlark* (1950), *No Highway* (1951), *The Titfield Thunderbolt* (1953), *The Final Appointment* (1954).

Norman, Leslie (*b* London, 1911 – *d* London, 1993). Producer, director. Worked as editor and sound editor at WARNER BROS' TEDDINGTON STUDIOS during the 30s and joined EALING after WW2 when he was called in to re-edit *The Overlanders* (1946) so as to give the fictional story more tension. He had co-directed *Too Dangerous to Live* (1939) just before the war, which he spent with the Army's sonic warfare unit. At Ealing, where he believed he was held back by the snobbery of Michael BALCON, who preferred men with degrees, he did not get another chance to direct until 1955's ingenious thriller, *The Night My Number Came Up*, by which time Ealing's days were numbered. He worked often with director Harry WATT, especially on his Australian and African-based films. He produced such major Ealing successes as *Where No Vultures Fly* (1951, + co-sc), *Mandy* and *The Cruel Sea* (1952), and ended by directing two of its last successes: the Australian-set *The Shiralee* (1957, + co-sc), which star Peter FINCH always claimed was his favourite film, and *Dunkirk* (1958), a subdued approach to an epic subject. Post-Ealing, he directed *Summer of the Seventeenth Doll* (1959, UK/Aust, + p), a badly compromised version of a groundbreaking Australian play, and a ditto version of Willis HALL's *The Long and the Short and the Tall* (1959, filmed 1960), in which Laurence HARVEY inadequately replaced the play's star, Peter O'TOOLE. Norman suffered from throat cancer but bravely continued to work in TV, directing episodes of such series as *The Persuaders!* (1971) and *The Return of the Saint* (1978). His son is TV film reviewer, **Barry Norman** (*b* London, 1933), who was made CBE in 1998.

OTHER BRITISH FILMS: (e) *The Man From Chicago* (1930), *The Maid of the Mountains* (1932), *The Old Curiosity Shop*, *Blossom Time* (1934), *Mimi*, *Heart's Desire* (1935), *The Perfect Crime*, *Who Killed John Savage?* (1937), *The Case of the Frightened Lady* (1940), *The Prime Minister* (1941), *This Was Paris* (1942), *Nicholas Nickleby*, *Frieda* (1947), *Eureka Stockade* (1949); (assoc p) *A Run for Your Money* (1949, + co-sc), *Bitter Springs* (1950); (p) *West of Zanzibar* (1954); (d) *X the Unknown* (1956), *Spare the Rod* (1961), *Mix Me a Person* (1962), *Sporting Chance* (1976).

North, Neil (*b* Quetta, India, 1932). Actor. North played the fresh-faced young naval cadet accused of stealing a £5 note in *The Winslow Boy* (1948); 50 years later he played the First Lord of the Admiralty in the remake (1999, UK/US). It would be interesting to know what he was doing in the intervening half-century. His boyhood career finished with *Britannia Mews* (1948) and *Tom Brown's Schooldays* (1951); in 2000, he played one of the judging panel at the Royal Ballet School audition of *Billy Elliot*. Not a prolific career but a fascinating one.

Northam, Jeremy (*b* Cambridge, 1961). Actor. A BAA winner for his two 1999 releases, *An Ideal Husband* and *The Winslow Boy* (UK/US), as stuffed-shirt Sir Robert Chiltern and charismatic advocate, Sir Robert Morton, respectively, the traditionally tall, dark and handsome Northam has had a rapid rise in the 90s. From an intellectual background (both parents were Cambridge professors), he studied English at London University and drama at the Bristol Old Vic Theatre School and came to unexpected critical attention by so admirably replacing Daniel DAY-LEWIS as Hamlet at the National in September

1989 when the star suffered a nervous collapse. On-screen, he is now also in demand in the US, showing unexpected comic flair in *Happy, Texas* (1999), in which he and Steve Zahn posed as gay lovers. Round the turn of the century, he starred in succession in MERCHANT IVORY's *The Golden Bowl* (2000, UK/Fr/US) as the duplicitous Prince, in *Enigma* (2001, UK/Ger/US), and in the ADAPTATION of A.S. Byatt's teasing tale of academic excavation, *Possession* (2002, UK/US), and Robert Altman's star-stacked country house MYSTERY, *Gosford Park* (2001, UK/Ger/US) as Ivor NOVELLO.

OTHER BRITISH FILMS: *Wuthering Heights* (UK/US), *Soft Top, Hard Shoulder* (1992), *A Village Affair*, *Carrington* (UK/Fr) (1994), *Voices* (1995, UK/US), *Emma* (1996, UK/US, a watchful Knightley), *The Misadventures of Margaret* (1998, UK/Fr/US).

Northcote, Sidney Webber (*b* Glamorgan, Wales, 1897 – *d* London, 1968). Director. Director of Welsh location films for BRITISH AND COLONIAL, and also responsible for a British Western: *Through Death's Valley* (1912).

OTHER BRITISH FILMS INCLUDE: *A Tragedy of the Cornish Coast*, *A Cornish Romance*, *The Belle of Bettwys-y-Coed*, *The Pedlar of Penmaenwawr*, *The Witch of the Welsh Mountains*, *Michael Dwyer* (1912), *The King of Crime* (1914), *The Monkey's Paw* (1915). AS.

Northern Ireland and British film Geographically a part of the island of Ireland but politically a part of the UK, Northern Ireland has historically occupied a position at the margins of the British and Irish film industries. An initial burst of film-making activity occurred in the 1930s following the production of Ireland's first sound film, *The Voice of Ireland* (1932). The film starred Northern Ireland singer and actor, Richard HAYWARD, and he – along with members of the Belfast Repertory Players – subsequently appeared in a number of low-budget musical comedies: *The Luck of the Irish* (1935), *The Early Bird* (1936), *Irish and Proud of It* (1936) and *Devil's Rock* (1938). While these were all unambitious 'QUOTA QUICKIES', they proved immensely popular with local audiences and provided a rare opportunity to see Northern Ireland locations (mainly the Glens of Antrim) on screen. Belfast-born director, Brian Desmond HURST was also involved in a number of Irish-theme films at this time, including *Ourselves Alone* (1936), one of the first British films to deal with the Irish War of Independence. While the film itself is more concerned with romance than politics, it still proved sufficiently contentious to merit an unprecedented banning, under the Special Powers Act, by the Northern Ireland Home Secretary. Hurst subsequently directed a wartime documentary, *A Letter from Ulster* (1943), about the experiences of American troops stationed in Northern Ireland. This was produced by another Belfast man, William MacQUITTY, whose credits also include *A Night to Remember* (1958) about the sinking of the *Titanic*, the ill-fated liner built in Belfast.

In the 1940s, Carol REED's *Odd Man Out* (1947), a gloomy *film noir* tracing the demise of James MASON's wounded IRA man, was the first film to deal with the Northern Ireland 'troubles' since partition. It remains something of a milestone in the representation of Northern Ireland and has exerted a significant influence upon later films including Neil JORDAN's *Angel* (1982, Ire) and *The Crying Game* (1992). Subsequent films such as *The Gentle Gunman* (1952) and *Jacqueline* (1956) made occasional use of Northern Irish settings but indigenous production in Northern Ireland did not resume until the 80s when workshops funded by CHANNEL 4 were responsible for *Acceptable Levels* (1983), dealing with an English television crew filming a DOCUMENTARY in Belfast, and *Hush-A-Bye Baby* (1989), concerning a young Derry Catholic's unplanned pregnancy. Along with Pat MURPHY's earlier film *Maeve* (1981), shot in Belfast, this was a key film in bringing feminist concerns to bear upon conventional perspectives of the 'troubles'. Former BBC director and editor, Bill Miskelly also set up Aisling Films in this period and was responsible for *The End of the World Man* (1985), a children's film set in Belfast.

These developments were built upon in the 90s following the establishment of the Northern Ireland Film Council (later Commission) in 1989, the growing involvement of BBC Northern Ireland in film production, and the use – from 1995 onwards – of lottery funds to support local film-making. This activity led to a number of SHORT FILM initiatives – such as the joint BBC/NIFC scheme 'Northern Lights' which funded the Oscar-nominated *Dance Lexie Dance* (1996) – as well as an upsurge in features set, and at least partly shot, in Northern Ireland, including *Bogwoman* (1996, Ire), *Sunset Heights* (1997), *Titanic Town* (1998, UK/Fr/Ger), *Divorcing Jack* (1998, UK/Fr), *A Love Divided* (UK/Ire), *Crossmaheart, With Or Without You, The Most Fertile Man in Ireland* (1999, UK/Ire), and *Wild About Harry* (2001, UK/Ger/Ire). The historic ceasefires of 1994 also encouraged a further burst of movies about the 'troubles' which, since the renewed onset of violence in the late 1960s, had been an occasional source of interest for British cinema as in *Hennessy* (1975), *The Long Good Friday* (1979), *Cal* (1984), *A Prayer for the Dying* (1987) and *Hidden Agenda* (1990). The new cycle of films included two of the first films to focus on Loyalist paramilitaries – *Nothing Personal* (1995, UK/Ire) and *Resurrection Man* (1997) – as well as the last two of writer Terry GEORGE's loose trilogy of films begun with *In The Name of the Father* (1993, UK/Ire/US), his Hollywood-backed film about the wrongful imprisonment of the 'Guildford Four'. *Some Mother's Son* (1996, Ire/US), which he also directed, dramatises the experience of the 1981 hunger strike by Irish republicans while *The Boxer* (1998, UK/Ire/US) deals explicitly with the republican response to the 'peace process'. While such films have provided fresh, and often controversial, views of the 'troubles', the conventions of narrative features are, nevertheless, ill-equipped to deal effectively with the complexities of the Northern Ireland situation. As a result many Northern Irish films, particularly the shorts, have begun to depart from 'troubles' themes and tell different kinds of story.
BIBLIOG: Kevin Rockett, Luke Gibbons and John Hill, *Cinema and Ireland*, 1988; Martin McLoone, *Irish Film: The Emergence of a Contemporary Cinema*, 2000; John Hill, *Cinema and Northern Ireland*, 2002. John Hill.

Norton, Alex (*b* Glasgow, 1950). Actor. Scottish character player who appeared in Bill FORSYTH's early 80s Scots-based successes, *Gregory's Girl* (1980), *Local Hero* (1983) and *Comfort and Joy* (1984), played several roles (including the travelling lanternist) in Bill DOUGLAS's neglected masterpiece, *Comrades* (1986), and is the aggressive pub-landlord in Peter MULLAN's black comedy, *Orphans* (1997). He took part in CHANNEL 4's satirical Celtic celebration, *Scotch Myths* (1982); not all of his work has been set north of the border, as his role in *Little Voice* (1998, UK/US) suggests, but he was back there as a crooked detective in *Beautiful Creatures* (2001). Also in the US films, *Patriot Games* (1992) and *Braveheart* (1995), in Glasgow theatre and loads of TV.
OTHER BRITISH FILMS INCLUDE: *Hidden City* (1987), *Scandal* (1988), *Under Suspicion* (1991), *Les Misérables* (1998, UK/Ger/US), *Complicity* (2000).

Norton, Richard (Lord Grantley and Markenfield) (*b* London, 1892 – *d* London, 1954). Executive, producer. An important figure in 30s British cinema, the Oxford-educated Norton, a Captain in the Scots Guards during WW1, entered films with United Artists in 1930. He held such positions as Director of BRITISH AND DOMINIONS FILM CORPORATION, having joined its board in 1933, Executive Director of D&P Studios (1938–42), Director of PINEWOOD STUDIOS (1936) and Chairman of the British Film Production Association (1939). He was influential in restraining the expenditure of Herbert WILCOX on such films as *Nell Gwyn* (1934) and backed Paul CZINNER's productions starring his wife, Elisabeth BERGNER; in 1938, Norton, RANK and Czinner formed a small company purposely to film Bergner in *Stolen Life*, and in the same year he was one of the board of the G&S company set up to film *The Mikado* (1939), several others following, including *The Arsenal Stadium Mystery* (1939), one of the few films on which Norton actually takes a credit (as associate producer). Norton was also crucially involved in setting up the film of *Pygmalion* (1938), its producer, Gabriel PASCAL, needing all the business acumen he could muster. At the end of 1938, Norton was appointed to the board of Denham and Pinewood Studios, a company to take over from KORDA, 'leaving him free to produce', as Rachael LOW reports, and to get his chief creditor, the Prudential Assurance Co., off his back. He was also a co-founder of the Co-operative Association of Producers and Distributors, in 1938. Wherever one turns one finds evidence of Norton's astute involvement in the decade's film industry. With the ascendancy of RANK, Norton became director of many of its film-making and studio-owning companies.

Norville, Herbert (*b* London, *c* 1967). Actor. Black American who, since 1975, has occasionally worked in British films, across an eclectic GENRE range: his work includes early Mike LEIGH work for TV (e.g. the short *Probation*, 1975; *Meantime*, 1983, some cinemas), Alan PARKER's kiddie-gangster film, *Bugsy Malone* (1976), Alan CLARKE's TV and cinema film *Scum* (1977, 1979) and KUBRICK's Vietnam epic, *Full Metal Jacket* (1987).
OTHER BRITISH FILMS: *Pressure* (1975), *The Class of Miss MacMichael* (1978), *The Chain* (1984).

Norwood, Eille (*b* York, 1861 – *d* London, 1948). Actor. Norwood was the screen's first major portrayer of SHERLOCK HOLMES, presenting him as a very placid, undemonstrative hero. To Arthur Conan DOYLE, 'He has that rare quality which can only be described as glamour'. Norwood made his stage debut in 1884 and his screen debut in 1911 in *Princess Clementina*. Between 1921 and 1923, he played Sherlock Holmes in 47 films, all short subjects except for *The Hound of the Baskervilles* (1921) and *The Sign of Four* (1923). As a result of his film work, Norwood was featured on stage in *The Return of Sherlock Holmes* (1923–24). He also compiled over 2,000 crossword puzzles for *The Daily Express*.
OTHER BRITISH FILMS INCLUDE: *The Charlatan, Frailty* (1916), *The Hundredth Chance, The Tavern Knight* (1920), *A Gentleman of France* (1921). AS.

Novello, Ivor (*b* Cardiff, 1893 – *d* London, 1951). Actor. RN: David Ivor Davies. Writer, composer, manager, and playwright as well as actor, Novello was very much of his age. 'Dear Ivor,' as his fans called him, produced a string of hit musicals, starring himself, and including *Careless Rapture* (1936), *The Dancing Years* (1939), and *Perchance to Dream* (1945), all of which attracted an audience of middle-aged females. He was not a great actor on stage or screen, and his films, including *The Lodger* (1926) and *The Rat* (1925) and its sequels were successful more because of a good director than Novello's heavily made-up presence. Novello starred in the screen adaptation of Noël COWARD's *The Vortex* (1927), and it was Coward who commented rightly that 'Before a camera his face takes on a set look, his eyes become deceptively soulful, and frequently something dreadful happens to his mouth.' Novello's reputation was established with his writing of the WW1 hit, 'Keep the Home Fires Burning.' He began his screen career with a couple of films in France; was starred by D.W. Griffith in *The White Rose* (1923); appeared in Hollywood opposite Ruth Chatterton in *Once a Lady* (1931); and contributed dialogue to two 1932 Hollywood features, *But the Flesh Is Weak* and, astonishingly, *Tarzan, the Ape Man*. A number of Novello's musicals were filmed without him: *Glamorous Night* (1937), *The Dancing Years* (1950), and *King's Rhapsody* (1955). The annual awards of the Performing Rights Society are named in his honour. Jeremy NORTHAM played Novello in Robert Altman's *Gosford Park* (2001, UK/Ger/US).

OTHER BRITISH FILMS: *Carnival* (1921), *The Bohemian Girl* (1922), *Bonnie Prince Charlie*, *The Man without Desire* (1923), *The Rat* (1925, + sc), *The Triumph of the Rat* (1926), *Downhill* (1927), *The Constant Nymph*, *The South Sea Bubble* (1928), *The Return of the Rat* (1929), *Symphony in Two Flats* (1930), *The Lodger* (1932), *Sleeping Car* (1933), *I Lived with You* (sc) (1933), *Autumn Crocus* (1934), *The Rat* (1937, sc).
BIBLIOG: Richard Rose, *Perchance to Dream*, 1974; Lawrence Napper and Michael Williams, 'The curious appeal of Ivor Novello', in Bruce Babington (ed), *British Stars and Stardom*, 2001; Michael Williams, 'War-torn Dionysus: the silent passion of Ivor Novello', in Andrew Higson (ed), *Young and Innocent? The Cinema in Britain, 1896–1930*, 2002. AS.

Noy, Wilfred (*b* London, 1877 – *d* Worthing, 1948). Director. A stage actor from 1898 and on screen from 1909. Noy, uncle of Leslie HOWARD, became a director with CLARENDON in 1910, responsible for more than 70 shorts, the Clarendon Speaking Pictures SERIES (1913), the 'Didums' series (1911–13), and some features through 1917.
BRITISH FEATURE FILMS INCLUDE: (d, unless noted) *Lorna Doone* (1912), *King Charles* (1913), *Old St Paul's*, *Southern Blood* (1914), *Under the Red Robe* (1915), *The Little Breadwinner*, *The Little Damozel* (1916), *The Lost Chord*, *Home Sweet Home* (1917), *Ave Maria*, (1918), *As He Was Born* (+ sc), *Castle of Dreams*, *The Lady Clare* (1919), *The Face at the Window*, *Inheritance* (1920), *The Marriage Lines* (1921, + sc), *The Temptation of Canton Earle* (1923), *Father O' Flynn* (1935, + p), *Melody of My Heart*, *Annie Laurie* (p) (1936), *Well Done, Henry* (1937, + sc). AS.

Nunn, Sir Trevor (*b* Ipswich, 1940). Director. Nunn, the Cambridge-educated, sometimes controversial director of London's National Theatre (1997–2001), has shown little interest in the cinema. He has directed TV versions of National successes such as *Oklahoma!* (1999) but has to date made only three films specifically for the screen: *Hedda* (1975), a transfer of his stage production, starring Glenda JACKSON; *Lady Jane* (1985), a perhaps more historically authentic account of Lady Jane Grey's tragically short life than *Tudor Rose* (1936) but less moving; and an intelligent but curiously staid version of *Twelfth Night* (1996, UK/US, + sc). His reputation as a stage director is, of course, immense. Married (1) Janet SUZMAN (m.1969), (2) Imogen STUBBS (m.1994). Knighted in 2002.

Nunn-May, Ralph (*b* Birmingham). Producer. President of the National Union of Students, while at Birmingham University, 1923–24, Nunn-May was deputy director of the

Films Division of the MINISTRY OF INFORMATION during WW2, and working in this capacity he was very influential in getting *Henry V* (1944) made: '[It] would probably never have been made without him', said Dallas BOWER in 1992. Post-war he joined HIGHBURY STUDIOS and produced *Song for Tomorrow* (1948) and worked as assistant/associate producer for AQUILA FILMS on *Warning to Wantons* (1948), *Stop Press Girl* and *Floodtide* (1949), a pretty undistinguished line-up. He was production supervisor at CROWN FILM UNIT (1949–54), and at Anvil Films (housed at the old DENHAM STUDIOS) from 1954.

Nureyev, Rudolph (*b* on train near Irkutsk, Russia, 1938 – *d* Paris, 1983). Dancer. One of the 20th century's very greatest dancers, Nureyev defected to the west in 1961 and became an incomparable star of its ballet world. Film has captured him at his peak in, among others, *An Evening with the Royal Ballet* (1963), in which he unforgettably danced 'Le corsaire', and *Romeo and Juliet* (1966), co-starring his most frequent partner, Margot Fonteyn. He appeared also in a DOCUMENTARY about his life and work, *I Am a Dancer* (1972, UK/Fr) and played *Valentino* (1977), in Ken RUSSELL's flashy BIOPIC, bringing possibly more eroticism to the role than the original might have mustered. He died of AIDS complications in 1983.

Nutley, Colin (*b* 1947). Director. British director who, apart from directing some well-regarded TV, including *Going Out* (1981) and *Press Gang* (1989), has worked entirely in Swedish films, often starring Helena Bergström, as in *House of Angels* (1992).

Nye, Pat (*b* London, 1908 – *d* Richmond, Surrey, 1994). Actress. Educated at Lausanne University and trained at RADA, she made her stage debut in 1933, and was awarded OBE for her wartime service as Chief Officer with the WRNS. Post-war, she managed the Bedford Theatre, Camden Town, and acted frequently there. Made only a handful of films, starting with *Mr Perrin and Mr Traill* (1948), as school matron, and finishing *The Mirror Crack'd* (1980), as town mayoress.
OTHER BRITISH FILMS: *The Adventures of PC49* (1949), *Appointment with Venus* (1951), *Street Corner* (1953).

Nyman, Michael (*b* London, 1944). Composer. A prolific and highly respected composer, Nyman studied at London's Royal Academy of Music and at first wrote about music for journals such as *The Spectator* and *The New Statesman*. He wrote the musical scores for Peter GREENAWAY's early films, including such obscurities as *A Walk Through H*, and his career took off in 1982 with his dazzling, darting score for *The Draughtsman's Contract*; on subsequent Greenaway films critics gave the soundtrack a more than cursory listen. Nyman's technique usually involved taking simple classical pieces and expanding on them to create highly textured, emotive sounds. His work with other British directors such as Michael WINTERBOTTOM (*Wonderland*, 1999; *The Claim*, 2001, UK/Can/Fr) and Neil JORDAN (*The End of The Affair*, 1999, UK/Ger/US) has flourished as his relationship with Greenaway has declined.
OTHER BRITISH FILMS INCLUDE: *Tom Phillips* (1977), *Vertical Features Remake* (1978), *The Falls* (1980), *The Sea in Their Blood* (1983), *Making A Splash* (1984), *A Zed & Two Noughts* (1985), *The Man Who Mistook His Wife for a Hat* (1987), *Drowning by Numbers* (1988), *The Cook, the Thief, His Wife & Her Lover* (1989), *Prospero's Books* (1991), *Carrington* (1994), *Ravenous* (1999), *The Hours* (2002, UK/US). Tim Roman.

Oberon, Merle (*b* Bombay, 1911 – *d* Los Angeles, California, 1979). Actress. RN: Estelle Merle O'Brien Thompson. The career of this legendary beauty reverses the received wisdom that British cinema produced nice, 'natural' girls while Hollywood was all glamour and artificiality. With Indian mother and Irish father, she grew up poor in India, came to England in 1928 and reinvented herself as Tasmanian, deciding that the racial mix would do her career no good. Spotted by Alexander KORDA who built her up as a sort of gorgeous exotic, but gave her very little of consequence to act, she is briefly touching as Anne Boleyn, hoping her hair will be in place when her head falls, in *The Private Life of Henry VIII* (1933), and her exquisite, raven-haired beauty is aptly used in *The Scarlet Pimpernel* (1935), with whom – that is, Leslie HOWARD – she had a real-life affair, before taking Korda as first (1939–45) of four husbands. At the end of the decade Korda put her into two mild comedies, for which she had virtually no gift, but for the first time she was seen in TECHNICOLOR and that was indeed a bonus. The great pity of her British career is that her near-fatal car crash led to the shutting down of Joseph von Sternberg's production of *I, Claudius* (1937). It was made the subject of the DOCUMENTARY, *The Epic That Never Was* (1966); the surviving footage suggests that von Sternberg might have done for her what he so signally did for DIETRICH. She filmed in Britain only twice after settling in Hollywood: the ludicrous flag-waver, *The Lion Has Wings* (1939) and the dawdling romance, *24 Hours of a Woman's Life* (1952).

She went to Hollywood in the mid 30s and the films she made there, especially *These Three* (1936) and *Wuthering Heights* (1939), both directed by William Wyler, showed a new unaffectedness in her acting. She spent most of the rest of her career there, in films good and – as the case often was – bad (think of *Night in Paradise*, 1946, as a princess in love with a young man called Aesop, of fables fame). For the susceptible of a generation, though, it hardly mattered what she did (and she did George Sand in *A Song to Remember*, 1945, unforgettably); she was simply one of the world's great beauties, and stayed so for several decades.

She did some US television in the 50s, but her film career quietly tapered off. Her second husband (1945–49), ace cinematographer Lucien Ballard, made her look ravishing in some dim films; third was industrialist Bruno DePagliai; and fourth was minor actor Robert Wolders. Her strange and affecting true life story was the subject of Michael Korda's shoddy best-seller, *Queenie* (1985), made into an even shoddier mini-series (1987).

OTHER BRITISH FILMS: *The Three Passions* (1928), *The W Plan*, *Alf's Button* (1930), *Never Trouble Trouble*, *Fascination* (1931), *Service for Ladies*, *Aren't We All*, *For the Love of Mike*, *Ebb Tide*, *Wedding Rehearsal*, *Men of Tomorrow* (1932), *Strange Evidence* (1933, UK/US), *The Private Life of Don Juan*, *The Broken Melody*, *The Battle* (1934).

BIBLIOG: Charles Higham and Roy Moseley, *Merle: An Autobiography of Merle Oberon*. 1983.

O'Brien, Edna (*b* Tuamgraney, Ireland, 1932). Writer. Irish novelist and playwright (and former pharmacist), several of whose novels of wistful female longings and loneliness have been adapted to the screen. Three were sensitively directed by Desmond DAVIS: *Girl with Green Eyes* (1963) and *The Country Girls* (1983), for which O'Brien wrote the screenplays, and *I Was Happy Here* (1965). She also wrote the screenplays for *Three into Two Won't Go* (1968), *Zee & Co.* (1971), co-wrote *The Tempter* (1973, UK/It), and appeared in the DOCUMENTARY of 'SWINGING LONDON', *Tonite Let's All Make Love in London* (1967).

O'Brien, Rebecca (*b* London, 1957). Producer. Much associated with Ken LOACH's realist work, producing the BAA-nominated pair, *Land and Freedom* (1995, UK/Ger/Sp) and *My Name Is Joe* (1998), and with *Bean* (1997) as a surprising credit for her. Ironically, for left-wing film-makers, she and Loach initially ran into trouble with film unions on their first US film, *Bread and Roses* (2001, UK/US).

OTHER BRITISH FILMS INCLUDE: *Crystal Gazing* (1982, prod man), *My Beautiful Laundrette* (1985, location man), *Friendship's Death* (1987), *Hidden Agenda* (1990). Kevin Foster.

O'Brien, Richard (*b* Cheltenham, 1942). Composer, actor. Raised and educated in New Zealand, he returned to England in the late 60s and found fame in the following decade as co-writer of the cult hit, *The Rocky Horror Picture Show* (filmed 1975, + co-sc, a). Since then he has appeared mainly as actor (e.g. as the Queen's magician in *Jubilee* (1978); Lord Hampton in *Revolution*, 1985), though he composed the score for the bizarre Australian film, *The Return of Captain Invincible* (1983).

OTHER BRITISH FILMS INCLUDE: (a, unless noted) *Carry On Cowboy* (1965), *The Odd Job* (1978), *Flash Gordon* (1980), *Shock Treatment* (1981, comp, + a, co-sc, lyrics), *The Wolves of Willoughby Chase* (1989), *Spice World* (1997).

O'Bryen, W(ilfred) J(ames) ('Bill') (*b* London, 1898 – *d* Hove, 1977). Production executive. Long married to Elizabeth ALLAN and a much-decorated veteran of both World Wars, O'Bryen played several significant roles in British cinema's mid-century history. He worked in New York as manager of Curtis Brown's film and drama department before taking up such British posts as publicity and casting director at GAINSBOROUGH and production executive for BRITISH LION and LONDON FILMS. Was also Managing Director of the agency, O'Bryen, Linnit and Dunfee, and in the mid 50s, he became ditto for Television Advisory Services.

O'Callaghan, Richard (*b* London, 1945). Actor. Much on TV since the mid 60s, he has appeared in occasional films, including two 'CARRY ON' romps – . . . *Loving* (1970) and . . . *at Your Convenience* (1971, as Lewis Boggs). Had his best role as Alan BATES's about-to-be-ex-boyfriend in *Butley* (1973, UK/Can/US).

OTHER BRITISH FILMS: *The Bofors Gun* (1968), *Galileo* (1974, UK/Can).

O'Casey, Sean (*b* Dublin, 1880 – *d* Torquay, 1964). Dramatist. RN: John Casey. Controversial Irish playwright whose works, combining fierce realism and poetic intensity, have, unsurprisingly, been rarely adapted to film. HITCHCOCK, before settling to the THRILLER mode, filmed *Juno and the Paycock* (1924) in 1930, with famed O'Casey interpreter, Sara ALLGOOD, as Juno, and many long takes underlining the theatricality of the venture, which O'Casey greatly disliked; and John FORD filmed the 'Troubles' play, *The Plough and the Stars* (1936), in Hollywood. In 1965, Ford began, but became ill, and Jack CARDIFF finished, *Young Cassidy* (1965), a BIOPIC based on O'Casey's life.

O'Connolly, Jim (*b* Birmingham, 1924 – *d* Hythe, 1987). Director, screenwriter. After a decade's apprenticeship as assistant director, (co-)writer, production manager or associate producer, O'Connolly got the chance to direct and/or write a batch of modestly entertaining films, starting with two neat 'B' MOVIES, *The Hijackers* (1963, + sc), *Smokescreen* (1964, + sc), twisty crime tales making good use of actor Glynn EDWARDS and of somewhat unusual locations.

OTHER BRITISH FILMS INCLUDE: (ass d) *Trio* (1950), *The Man in the White Suit* (1951), *The Gentle Gunman, Mandy* (1952), *The Diamond* (1954); (p man) *Little Red Monkey* (1954), *Confession* (1955), *Escapement* (1957); (assoc p) *The Criminal, Konga* (1960), *The Sinister Man* (1961); (d, sc) *The Little Ones* (1965), *Crooks and Coronets* (1969, + a); (d) *Berserk!* (1967), *Vendetta for the Saint* (1969), *Mistress Pamela* (1973, + p); (p) *The Traitors* (1962, + sc, co-orig idea), *Farewell Performance* (1963, + add dial); (co-sc) *Emergency* (1962), *Shadow of Fear* (1963); (sc) *The Night Caller* (1965).

O'Connor, Derrick (*b* Dublin, *c* 1941). Actor. Somewhat lugubrious-looking supporting player in America in the 90s (e.g. in *How to Make an American Quilt*, 1995). He had some good roles in British films of the two preceding decades, including the neighbour who befriends the war-bereft Sarah MILES in *Hope and Glory* (1987), and was also in such TV series as *Fox* (1980).

OTHER BRITISH FILMS INCLUDE: *The Final Programme* (1973), *Jabberwocky* (1977), *Sweeney 2* (1978), *Bloody Kids* (1979), *Time Bandits, The Missionary* (1981), *Brazil* (1985), *Dealers* (1989).

O'Connor, Desmond (*b* London, 1900 – *d* London, 1975). Songwriter. Wrote the lyrics for many popular songs and was author of books on lyric-writing. His film career was mainly limited to BRITISH-NATIONAL MUSICALS of the early 40s, including songs for several John BAXTER films, among them the non-musical *The Common Touch* (1941) as well as the modest musicals, *Let the People Sing* and *We'll Smile Again* (1942), *Theatre Royal* (1943), and the lyrics for the title song in *Dreaming* (1944). He also wrote the lyrics for the MacLean ROGERS musical, *Heaven Is Round the Corner* (1944).

O'Connor, Frances (*b* Oxford, 1969). Actress. Very attractive, intelligent young star who came to prominence in Australian films in the latter half of the 90s, winning awards for several performances, including *Kiss or Kill* (1997). Born to professional British parents who moved to Australia when she was two years old, she was educated at Curtin University, Western Australia. Now in much demand for international films, she gave a very individual feminist interpretation of Fanny Price in *Mansfield Park* (1999, UK/US); was amusing as the passionate blue-stocking sister in *About Adam* (2001, UK/Ire); and plays witty Gwendolen in Oliver PARKER's *The Importance of Being Earnest* (2002, UK/US). In the US, she played the distraught mother in *AI: Artificial Intelligence* (2001).

O'Connor, Hazel (*b* Coventry, 1955). Actress, singer. Received a BAAn for the songs she wrote for the garish *Breaking Glass* (1980), her one serious brush with the screen, and she also played the lead, a female rock singer manipulated by a ruthless manager.

OTHER BRITISH FILMS: *Girls Come First* (1975), *Double Exposure* (1976), *Car Trouble* (1985).

O'Connor, Pat (*b* Ardmore, Ireland, 1943). Director. O'Connor's sympathetically observed, low-key scenes from Irish life, including *Cal* (1984) and *Circle of Friends* (1995, Ire/US), and the reflective, allegorically inclined *A Month in the Country* (1995), with its layered theme of restoration, have won him a reputation he hasn't quite sustained. His film version of the unaccountable stage success, *Dancing at Lughnasa* (1998, UK/Ire/US), sank tracelessly, despite Meryl STREEP's presence, and it is hard to see why anyone should have wanted to remake the 1968 weepy, *Sweet November* (2001, US). His first US film, *Stars and Bars* (1988), had some wit and style but was largely unnoticed. Trained at UCLA and Ryerson Institute, Toronto, before starting career on TV DOCUMENTARIES. Married US actress Mary Elizabeth Mastrantonio.

O'Connor, Una (*b* Belfast, 1880 – *d* New York, 1959). Actress. RN: Agnes Teresa McGlade. Minute character player who made only three British films – *Dark Red Roses* (1929), *To Oblige a Lady* (1931) and *His Brother's Keeper* (1939) – but spent the rest of her prolific career purveying lower-class British stroppiness and/or gentility in Hollywood. Her persona is aptly encapsulated by her primping her hair in refined impatience in *Random Harvest* (1942) – or moving as if on oiled casters in *The Barretts of Wimpole Street* (1934) or screaming her head off in *The Bride of Frankenstein* (1935).

O'Conor, Hugh (*b* Dublin, 1975). Actor. Studied Drama and Theatre at Trinity College Dublin, receiving a Fulbright Scholarship to study film at NYU, New York, 1998/9. On stage at Dublin's Gate Theatre (1991) and Players' Theatre (1994), and at London's Tricycle Theatre; adapted/directed Orson WELLES' *Moby Dick – Rehearsed* (1997) and his adaptation of *La Ronde*, called *Night Games*, played off-off-Broadway (2000). On-screen, he came to notice as the boy befriended by a priest in *Lamb* (1985) and young Christy Brown in *My Left Foot* (1989), survived unscathed the awfulness of *Hotel Splendide* (2000, UK/Fr) and the mush of *Chocolat* (2000, UK/US), in which his boy-priest is the one true thing.

OTHER BRITISH FILMS INCLUDE: *Rawhead Rex* (1987), *The Young Poisoner's Handbook* (1995, UK/Fr/Ger), *The Boy from Mercury* (1996, UK/Fr).

O'Conor, Joseph (*b* Dublin, 1916 – *d* London, 2001). Actor. RADA-trained and on stage from 1939, in a wide range of classic and modern plays, and with most major companies, and a playwright as well, O'Conor is nevertheless perhaps best known for playing Old Jolyon in TV's mini-series, *The Forsyte Saga* (1967). He entered films unobtrusively in 1950 in the Dublin-set *Stranger at My Door*, was an effortlessly benign Mr Brownlow in *Oliver!* (1968), and played clerical figures, for which his persona equipped him, in *Anne of the Thousand Days* (1969, Fisher) and *Tom & Viv* (1994, UK/US, Bishop of Oxford). His persona, incidentally, scarcely hinted at his declared recreations: guitar playing and judo.

OTHER BRITISH FILMS INCLUDE: *Paul Temple's Triumph* (1950), *Gorgo* (1960), *The Devil-Ship Pirates* (1963), *Crooks in Cloisters* (1964), *Doomwatch* (1972, as Vicar), *The Black Windmill* (1974), *The Dark Crystal* (1982, narr), *Elizabeth* (1998).

O'Dea, Denis (*b* Dublin, 1905 – *d* Dublin, 1978). Actor. Esteemed Abbey Theatre actor, who trained at the Theatre's School, and made his debut there in 1930, returned there frequently throughout his career and toured with the company to New York. His first films were John FORD's *The Informer* (1935) and *The Plough and the Stars* (1936); post-war, he made a further 20, including such notable British films as *Odd Man Out* (1947) and *The Fallen Idol* (1948), in both playing Police Inspectors, the sort of role to which his grave features lent conviction, and he was a robust Dr Livesey in *Treasure Island* (1950). Also in several US films, including *Captain Lightfoot* (1955). Married Siobhan McKENNA.

OTHER BRITISH FILMS INCLUDE: *The Mark of Cain* (1948), *Under Capricorn*, *Landfall* (1949), *The Long Dark Hall* (1951), *Sea Devils* (1953), *The Story of Esther Costello* (1957).

O'Dea, Jimmy (*b* Dublin, 1899 – *d* Dublin, 1965). Actor. MUSIC HALL comedian on screen from silent days, as in the Irish-made *Casey's Millions* and *Cruiskeen Lawn* (1922), but only intermittently. His best known role was as King of the leprechauns in DISNEY's *Darby O'Gill and the Little People* (1959, US).

OTHER BRITISH FILMS INCLUDE: *Jimmy Boy* (1935), *Blarney* (UK/Ire) (1938), *Let's Be Famous*, *Cheer Boys Cheer* (1939), *Dick Barton Strikes Back* (1949), *Johnny Nobody* (1960).

Odeon Cinema Chain *see* **cinemas and exhibition**

Odette, Mary (*b* Dieppe, France, 1901 – *d* India, 1987). Actress. RN: Odette Goimbault. Ethereal leading lady, with French father and English mother, whose success on stage as a child actress led to a screen career. From 1916 to 1919, she worked under her real name. Retired to India with journalist husband.

BRITISH FILMS INCLUDE: *Cynthia in the Wilderness* (1916), *Dombey and Son* (1917), *The Lady Clare* (1919), *The Wonderful Year* (1921), *She* (1925), *Emerald of the East* (1928). AS.

O'Doherty, Mignon (*b* Brisbane, 1890 – *d* London, 1961). Actress. Built on similar lines to Hattie JACQUES, she could have emulated her formidable gallery of '*CARRY ON*' battleaxes had she been born 20 years later. Her promising early roles for Victor SAVILLE in *The Faithful Heart* (1933) and *The Good Companions* (1933) were hardly followed up, but her study of an impatient woman waiting outside a telephone box in *White Corridors* (1951) typified the imprint she continued to put on even the tiniest parts. RADA-trained, on the London stage from 1913, she was in the original cast of *The Mousetrap* (1952–55).

OTHER BRITISH FILMS INCLUDE: *There Goes the Bride* (1932), *Autumn Crocus* (1934), *Dandy Dick* (1935), *Neutral Port* (1940), *Hard Steel* (1942), *The Lamp Still Burns* (1943), *Maytime in Mayfair* (1949), *The Ghost Ship* (1952), *The Whole Truth* (1958), *Never Let Go* (1960). Charles Barr.

O'Donnell, Damien (*b* Dublin, 1967). Director. After directing, writing and co-editing the SHORT FILM, *Thirty Five Aside* (1995), O'Donnell won great acclaim and several awards, including *Evening Standard* Film of the Year award for his first feature, the warm, painful intercultural comedy-drama, *East Is East* (1999). Subsequently, he co-scripted *Making Ends Meet* (1999, Ire), directed two Irish short films, *What Where?* (2000) and *Chrono-Perambulator* (2000, + sc), and the feature *Heartlands* (2001).

O'Donovan, Fred (*b* Dublin, 1889 – *d* Dublin, 1952). Actor. Supporting player of stage and screen, who directed as well as acted in several silent films, and was in some early British TV, playing the King of Hearts in a 1936 version of *Through the Looking Glass*, also producing such dramas as *Playboy of the Western World* (1946). Married Joyce Chancellor who appeared in at least one film, *Irish Hearts* (1934).

BRITISH FILMS INCLUDE: (d, a) *O'Neil of the Glen*, *The Food of Love*, *Woman's Wit* (1916), *Rafferty's Rise*, *The Eleventh Hour* (1918); (a) *A Girl of Glenbeigh* (1918), *General John Regan* (1933), *Ourselves Alone* (1936), *Young and Innocent* (1937), *Another Shore* (1948).

O'Farrell, Bernadette (*b* Birr, Ireland, 1926 – *d* Monaco, 1999). Actress. Very pretty actress who started in films – *Captain Boycott* (1947), made in Ireland by Frank LAUNDER, whom she married (1950 to 1997, his death) – then went into rep, returning to film as the nice young teacher in *The Happiest Days of Your Life* (1950). Had a half-dozen modestly effective roles in films such as *The Story of Gilbert and Sullivan* (1953) and *The Bridal Path* (1959), but real fame came as Maid Marian in TV's *The Adventures of Robin Hood* (1955–57). Retired from the screen in 1960 to raise a family, and returned only to play a small role in *The Wildcats of St Trinian's* (1980).

OTHER BRITISH FILMS: *Lady Godiva Rides Again*, *Life in Her Hands* (1951), *Lady in the Fog* (1952), *The Genie* (1953), *The Square Ring* (1953).

O'Ferrall, George More (*b* England, 1906 – *d* Spain, 1982). Director. In 1936, he became the BBC's first 'drama producer' and before WW2 service he was responsible for a dozen televersions of such well-known plays as *Journey's End* (1937) and *Cyrano de Bergerac* (1938). Post-war, he was producer-director of several televised Shakespearean plays, had varied work in films, and at last directed his first features in 1952 – the unusual, strangely muted WAR FILM, *Angels One Five*, and the heartfelt drama of family-in-polite-conflict, *The Holly and the Ivy*. Both of these films, and the two which followed, the ADAPTATION from Graham GREENE, *The Heart of the Matter* (1953) and the courtroom drama, *The Green Scarf* (1954), are marked by sensitive performances from carefully chosen casts and by sophisticated attention to detail, physical and psychological. Two years and three films later, he turned to TV and never filmed again for the cinema.

OTHER BRITISH FILMS: (ass d, unc) *Midshipman Easy* (1935), *Woman with No Name* (1950), *No Highway* (1951); (d) *Three Cases of Murder* (co-d), *The Woman for Joe* (1955), *The March Hare* (1956).

Ogilvy, Ian (*b* Woking, 1943). Actor. Handsome, 'pretty-boy' leading man, who had brief worldwide fame in title role of TV series, *The Return of the Saint* (1978–79) and leading roles in a few British films of the 60s and 70s. His most notable film was the alarming *Witchfinder General* (1968), and he did what he could with the frantic farce of *No Sex Please – We're British* (1973). As he has aged, Ogilvy has turned to character roles, concentrating on work in America, with a prominent part in *Death Becomes Her* (1992).

OTHER BRITISH FILMS INCLUDE: *The Revenge of the Blood Beast* (1966), *The Day the Fish Came Out*, *The Sorcerors* (1967), *Wuthering Heights* (1970), *And Now the Screaming Starts!* (1974). AS.

Ogle, Natalie Actress. Briefly in British films, including *Joseph Andrews* (1976), in which her Fanny Goodwill hardly stood a chance against Ann-Margaret's Lady Booby, and she played again with *Andrews* co-star, Peter FIRTH, in *The Aerodrome* (1983, TV, some cinemas). After that it was nothing but TV.

OTHER BRITISH FILMS: *The Stud* (1978).

O'Gorman, John (*b* Hove, Sussex, 1911). Make-up artist. In 1994, actress Susan HAMPSHIRE, who worked with him on *Malpertius* (1972, Belg), said of O'Gorman that he was 'a make-up artist . . . who made you feel great because he understood your face, so that you went out in front of the camera feeling and looking good'. He entered the industry with LONDON FILMS in 1939, was on WW2 service from 1940 to 1946, and returned to work for KORDA. Worked on some of the most famous faces of the day, including Ingrid BERGMAN's in *Indiscreet*, *The Inn of the Sixth Happiness* (1958) and Ursula ANDRESS's in *Dr No* (1962), *The Blue Max* (1966), *Casino Royale* (1967) and *Perfect Friday* (1970).

OTHER BRITISH FILMS INCLUDE: *Mine Own Executioner* (1947), *The Winslow Boy*, *The Fallen Idol*, *Anna Karenina* (1948), *The Franchise Affair* (1950), *Betrayed* (1954), *The Surgeon's Knife* (1957), *The Grass Is Greener* (1960), *A Hard Day's Night* (UK/US), *The Yellow Rolls-Royce* (1964), *There's a Girl in My Soup* (1970), *Endless Night* (1972), *Murder on the Orient Express* (1974), *The Fifth Musketeer* (1979, UK/Aus).

O'Hara, Gerry (aka Lawrence Britten) (*b* Boston, Lincs, 1924). Director. Entered the industry in 1941, working on DOCUMENTARY and PROPAGANDA SHORTS for Sydney BOX's VERITY FILMS. He worked at ELSTREE from 1945, before joining GAINSBOROUGH as assistant director on such films as *Quartet*, *Miranda* (1948) and *The Huggetts Abroad* (1949). In the 50s, he was involved in such distiguished films including *Richard III* (1955), but his own films as director are a motley lot, noted more for exotic locations than dramatic tension, as in the limp THRILLER, *Maroc 7* (1966), or *Amsterdam Affair* (1968). Later moved on to such (comparatively) upmarket EXPLOITATION work as *The Bitch* (1979, + sc) and *Fanny Hill* (1983).

OTHER BRITISH FILMS: (ass d) *Trio*, *The Clouded Yellow* (1950), *The Man Who Never Was* (1955), *Anastasia* (1956), *Island in the Sun* (1957), *The Key* (1958), *Our Man in Havana* (1959), *Term of Trial*, *The L-Shaped Room* (1962), *Tom Jones* (1963), *The Jigsaw Man* (1984); (d) *That Kind of Girl* (1963), *Game for Three Losers*, *The Pleasure Girls* (+sc) (1965), *The Spy's Wife* (1971, + co-sc), *The Brute* (1976, + sc), *Blind Man's Bluff*, *Leopard in the Snow* (1977), *Hot Target* (1985, sc, UK/NZ).

O'Hara, Maureen (*b* Dublin, 1920). Actress. RN: FitzSimons Archetypal gorgeous red-headed colleen who studied at the Abbey Theatre School, made her film debut in England, where she played HITCHCOCK's leading lady in *Jamaica Inn* (1939) and was then lost to Hollywood, where her looks were a gift to TECHNICOLOR. Not a great actress, but a persistently attractive one, with a gift for playing spirited women which director John FORD in particular exploited and for whom she left indelible impressions in such films as *Rio Grande* (1950) and *The Quiet Man* (1952). In her long career of about 50 films, she made only four further British films, of which only Carol REED's *Our Man in Havana* (1959) is worth noting. Married (1) George H. BROWN (producer) (1939–41), (2) director Will Price (1941–52) and (3) Brig-General Charles Blair (1968–78, his death).

OTHER BRITISH FILMS: *My Irish Molly*, *Kicking the Moon Around* (1938), *Britannia Mews* (1948), *Malaga* (1954), *The Battle of the Villa Fiorita* (1965).

O'Herlihy, Dan (*b* Wexford, Ireland, 1919). Actor. Studied architecture before turning to acting with Dublin's Gate and Abbey Theatres, and a radio announcer before entering films in 1947, as one of the feuding Brodericks in *Hungry Hill* and as one of the gang planning the robbery in *Odd Man Out*. A rugged-looking 6'3", he might have been expected to make more of a mark as a leading man, but with odd exceptions settled for strong character roles, mostly in US films, though his most notable performance was in the title role of Luis Buñuel's Mexican-made *The Adventures of Robinson Crusoe* (1954), for which he received an AAn. Appeared in only four further British films, including *The Tamarind Seed* (1974), as Sylvia SYMS's homosexual spy husband, and as Mr Browne in John HUSTON's masterpiece, *The Dead* (1987, UK/Ire/Ger). His brother, **Michael O'Herlihy** (*b* Dublin, 1928 – *d* Ireland, 1997), was a director, mainly in the US, but made *The Fighting Prince of Donegal* (1966) in the UK.

OTHER BRITISH FILMS: *That Woman Opposite* (1957), *A Terrible Beauty* (1960).

Okonedo, Sophie (*b* London, 1968). Actress. Entered films as girlfriend of the straight disc jockey in *Young Soul Rebels* (1991) and has had a couple of good roles since, but the opportunities for black actors in British films are still limited. She was attractively vivacious as Juliet AUBREY's flat-mate in *Go Now* (1996) and as the bridesmaid, cynical about the fragility of relationships, in the wedding sequence of *This Year's Love* (1999). Has also filmed in the US, as in *The Jackal* (1997), and done notable TV, including the single mum in *Never Never* (2000) and the vengeful Ellen in *Sweet Revenge* (2001).

OTHER BRITISH FILMS INCLUDE: *Mad Cows* (1999), *Peaches* (2001).

old age in British film Cinemagoing has more usually been a young person's pastime, so it is not surprising that old age has rarely figured as a key theme in British cinema. One recalls the antics of Sybil THORNDIKE, Estelle WINWOOD and Kathleen HARRISON when they escape from the old people's home in *Alive and Kicking* (1958); the haunting image of bitter old age in Martita HUNT's Miss Havisham in *Great Expectations* (1946); and cameo moments such as the old Alice Liddell (Coral BROWNE) in *Dreamchild* (1985) at last recognising and giving thanks for Lewis Carroll's gift of love to her in his stories. Perhaps the most treasurable memories are provided by performers such as Alastair SIM, Miles MALLESON, Felix AYLMER, A.E. MATTHEWS, Margaret RUTHERFORD or Esma CANNON, the kind of actors who seem never to have been young. But although British cinema has never emulated the aching poignancy of a film like *Toyko Story* (1953) on this theme, there are three films that deserve a special mention. In Alexander MACKENDRICK's *The Ladykillers* (1955), a gang of desperate criminals prove no match for the obduracy of Katie JOHNSON's Mrs Wilberforce who, living in a bygone era of her mind, in a sense nannies them all to death. As an old lady who hears voices, Dame Edith EVANS gives her greatest screen performance in Bryan FORBES's *The Whisperers* (1966), a moving study of the loneliness of old age. And in the TV movie, *Memento Mori* (1992), where the elderly are being terrorised by a mystery phone-caller saying 'Remember You Must Die', director Jack CLAYTON assembles over a thousand years' worth of acting experience in his cast, which culminates in a meeting where they are all brought together and where all the foibles of old age – deafness, incontinence, physical clumsiness – are both comically and compassionately laid bare. Contemplating the chaos after they have left, the bemused host (John WOOD) comments: 'They have a sort of stubborn gallantry with echoes of a romantic and glamorous past.' He could be commenting on a whole tradition of British screen acting. Neil Sinyard.

Oldman, Gary (b London, 1958). Actor. Formidably versatile character star who, from a difficult East End background with an alcoholic father, won a scholarship to the Rose Bruford School of Speech and Drama. After work with Glasgow's Citizens Theatre, he made his West End debut and entered films in *Remembrance* (1982). His first major break came as Sid Vicious in *Sid and Nancy* (1986), an unsettling account of the rocker's doomed relationship with Nancy Spungen. He followed this quickly with the eye-catching role of Joe ORTON in *Prick Up Your Ears* (1987), capturing the wit and charm of Orton's brief life; with *We Think the World of You* (1988), as the imprisoned object of Alan BATES's affections; with alarming football hooligan protagonist 'Bex' Bissek in Alan CLARKE's telefilm, *The Firm* (1988); and with Nicolas ROEG's obliquely compelling *Track 29* (1988), in which he plays a stranger who may be Theresa RUSSELL's son.

Since then, he has acted mainly in US films, gliding chameleon-like from Lee Harvey Oswald in *JFK* (1991), the Prince of Darkness himself in *Dracula* (1992), Beethoven in the dreadful *Immortal Beloved* (1994, UK/US), to a ruthless Republican senator in *The Contender* (2000), and having a high old time in such expensive tosh as *Air Force One* (1997) and (unrecognisable) as a victim of *Hannibal* (2001, UK/US). Back in Britain he directed the excoriating semi-autobiographical drama, *Nil by Mouth* (1997), in which the effects of alcoholic tyranny in an East End family are observed unflinchingly. At very least he extracted unforgettable performances from Ray WINSTONE, Kathy BURKE, Edna DORE, and from real-life sister Laila Morse, who also appeared in *Love, Honour and Obey* (2000). He is one of the most enjoyable CHARACTER ACTORS in contemporary film, it would be a shame if he gave up acting, but his directorial debut exhibits a talent remarkable enough to make one want to see more of it. Married/divorced (1) Leslie MANVILLE and (2) Uma THURMAN.

OTHER BRITISH FILMS: *Lost in Space* (1998, UK/US), *Plunkett & Macleane* (1999, ex p).

Oliver, Anthony (b Abersychan, Wales, 1923 – d Abersychan, 1995). Actor. On stage and TV after WW2 service (1941–46), sandy-haired Oliver played nearly 30 light supporting role in films, following his debut in *Once a Jolly Swagman* (1948). He was well-known on TV as Welsh storyteller, 'Old Dai', in the 50s. Stage work included a stint as the policeman in *The Mousetrap* (1959).

OTHER BRITISH FILMS INCLUDE: *All Over the Town* (1949), *The Crowded Yellow*, *The Magnet* (1950), *The Happy Family* (1952), *Cosh Boy*, *Street Corner* (1953), *Lost* (1955), *Checkpoint* (1956), *The Entertainer* (1960), *HMS Defiant* (1962), *It Happened Here* (1963).

Oliver, Vic (b Vienna, 1898 – d Johannesburg, 1964). Actor. RN: Viktor Oliver Samek. Stage comedian (formerly involved in banking and cloth manufacture, and as pianist) in Austria and America from the 20s, from 1932 in Britain. In the 30s and 40s he had several film roles, most notably in *I'll Be Your Sweetheart* (1945), as a songwriter subjected to 'pirates', but usually in comic parts, and he was the subject of comic strip in

Radio Fun in the 40s. He had a prolific career in radio (e.g. with Bebe DANIELS and Ben LYON in *Hi Gang!*, filmed in 1941), and TV, and also formed the British Concert Orchestra in 1945, acting as its director and conductor. Once married to actress Sarah CHURCHILL.

OTHER BRITISH FILMS INCLUDE: *Rhythm In The Air* (1936), *Who's Your Lady Friend?* (1937), *Around The Town* (1938), *Room For Two* (1940), *He Found A Star* (1941), *Give Us The Moon* (1944).

BIBLIOG: Autobiography, *Mr Show Business*, 1954. Tim Bergfelder.

Olivier, Laurence (Lord Olivier) (b Dorking, Surrey, 1907 – d Steyning, 1989). Actor, director. By any criteria, one of the very great theatre actors of the 20th century, Olivier left a substantial body of work on film, and some of it, including his Shakespearean ADAPTATIONS, rivals his theatre role-call. The biography – born to the Vicarage; the semi-impoverished childhood and the death of the beloved mother; the choir boy and budding actor at All Saints School, London; the theatre training with Elsie Fogerty at Central School; the gradual ascent in theatre and the early disdain for films – is by now so well known and documented as to need little repeating. The stage career occupies five columns of *Who's Who in the Theatre* (15th ed), and it wasn't finished then. It is hard to know what else he might have done in the theatre: there are the predictably great seasons at the Old Vic, at Stratford, at Chichester, and, amid growing controversy, the National, where he directed the inaugural production of *Hamlet* (1963); there are famous tours of Europe, including Russia, and Australasia; and there were West End and Broadway triumphs, as well.

To turn to the screen, he was a stiffly uninteresting *jeune premier* in his early British films, and Garbo famously turned him down as leading man for *Queen Christina* when he and first wife, Jill ESMOND (1930–40) were in Hollywood in the early 30s, interest being greater in Esmond. Back in England, he filmed several times without enjoying the medium, though he won some popularity for such films as *Fire Over England* (1937) and *The Divorce of Lady X* (1938), but it was William Wyler, directing him as Heathcliff in Hollywood's *Wuthering Heights* (1939), who taught him how to value film. And, apart from the SHAKESPEARE films, it is probably true to say that most of his best film performances are in US films: he is a stylish Darcy in *Pride and Prejudice* and a fine brooding DeWinter in *Rebecca* (1940), and a romantic Nelson opposite second wife (1940–60), Vivien LEIGH, in *That Hamilton Woman* (1941, US).

His beautiful film of *Henry V* (1944) is a hymn to patriotic endeavour (stripped of the play's more dubious motivations), absolutely a film for its time and one of the great popularisers of screened SHAKESPEARE. He directs this with confidence and daring and acts the eponymous warrior with the kinds of physical grace and daring that were to be hallmarks of his acting career, though it did not always transfer to the screen with the consummate ease and naturalness that it does here. His *Hamlet* (1948, d, a) owes almost as much to the contemporary *film noir* stylistics as it does to Shakespeare, but, if there are *longueurs* while the camera prowls the Elsinore corridors at the expense of the verse and some key plot elements, it still offers a telling Freudianised reading of the play, and, in its moody post-war way, is also a film of its time. *Richard III* (1955, d, a) is less innovative, perhaps more academically orthodox in its approach as a film of a famous play text, but, laden as it is with the theatre's acting great (GIELGUD is especially moving as Clarence), it cannot fail of rewards. The 1965 *Othello*, directed by Stuart BURGE, is little more than a permanent record of Olivier's much-praised performance for the National Theatre.

Among the other British films, there are some razor-sharp character studies, such as the courteous, cautious policeman called in to witness Britain's 'first' screening of a motion picture in *The Magic Box* (1951), the investigating inspector in *Bunny Lake Is Missing* (1965) and the failed teacher in *Term of Trial* (1962). It is also a treat for future generations to have on film his seedy MUSIC-HALL has-been in *The Entertainer* (1960), the theatrical version of which (1957–58) had marked his induction into the changing drama of the mid-century. His Mahdi in *Khartoum* (1966) is really outacted by the quieter, more cinematic performance of Charlton HESTON as General Gordon; this was symptomatic of how Olivier's mesmeric theatricality (and he is by no means alone in this matter in the history of British cinema) could sometimes seem too coarse for the intimacy of the cinema.

He should have stopped with *A Bridge Too Far* (1977); almost none of his dozen remaining films, mostly American, was other than an embarrassment. However, by this time he had established a record of near-unparalleled achievement on stage, screen and TV, and was so heaped with honours that nothing could have diminished him.

He and Leigh divorced, after one of the most publicised love stories of the century, and he married Joan PLOWRIGHT in 1961, starting a new family in late middle age, but the accounts of his last years do not suggest much serenity. He was knighted in 1947 and made Lord Olivier in 1970.

OTHER BRITISH FILMS: (a, unless noted) *The Temporary Widow* (UK/Ger), *Too Many Crooks* (1930), *Potiphar's Wife* (1931), *Perfect Understanding, No Funny Business* (1933), *Moscow Nights* (1935), *As You Like It* (1936), *21 Days* (1937), *Q Planes* (1939), *Conquest of the Air* (1940), *49th Parallel, Words for Battle* (doc, narr) (1941), *Malta G.C.* (1942, doc, narr), *The Volunteer, The Demi-Paradise* (1943), *This Happy Breed* (1944, narr), *Fighting Pilgrims* (1945, doc, narr), *The Drawings of Leonardo da Vinci* (doc, narr), *A Queen is Crowned* (doc, narr), *The Beggar's Opera* (+ co-p) (1953), *The Prince and the Showgirl* (1957, + d, p), *The Devil's Disciple* (1959), *Romeo and Juliet* (UK/It), *The Dance of Death* (1968), *Battle of Britain, Oh! What a Lovely War* (1969), *Three Sisters* (1970, + d), *Sleuth, Lady Caroline Lamb* (UK/It/US) (1972), *Clash of the Titans* (1981, UK/US), *The Jigsaw Man, The Bounty* (1984), *Wild Geese II* (1985), *War Requiem* (1989).

BIBLIOG: John Cottrell, *Laurence Olivier*, 1975; Anthony Holden, *Olivier*, 1988.

Olrich, April (*b* Zanzibar, 1933). Actress, dancer. Born of an English mother and American father, Olrich trained as a dancer and, after experience with the Ballets Russes, joined London's Royal Ballet, dancing principal roles. As actress, she had busy stage and TV (from 1955) careers, beside which her film career is comparatively limited. Made film debut in Michael POWELL's *The Battle of the River Plate* (1956), in which she sang as well as acted, impressing Powell with her Spanish-speaking ability. She made a further dozen or so movies, including *Macbeth* (1961), as a witch, and *The Intelligence Men* (1965), co-starring with MORECAMBE AND WISE, but seemed to favour the other media.

OTHER BRITISH FILMS INCLUDE: *Women Without Men* (1956), *Kill Me Tomorrow* (1957), *Room at the Top* (1958), *It's All Over Town* (1963), *The Skull* (1965), *Clinic Xclusive* (1971), *Hussy* (1979), *Riding High* (1980).

Olsen, Olaf (*b* Heidelberg, Germany, 1919). Actor. On stage and screen in Berlin before making British TV debut as the German prisoner in *Journey's End* (1937) and film debut as Prince Fredrick in *Sixty Glorious Years* (1938). Naturally played

his share of Nazi villains, as in *Against the Wind* (1947) and *Lilli Marlene* (1950). Much TV until 1955 when he left for the US.

OTHER BRITISH FILMS INCLUDE: *Mein Kampf – My Crimes, Sailors Three* (1940), *Tomorrow We Live, The Day Will Dawn* (1942), *Lisbon Story* (1946), *Broken Journey* (1948), *The Man in the White Suit* (1951), *Tread Softly* (1952).

Olsen, Gary (*b* London, 1957 – *d* Melbourne, 2000). Actor. The untimely death, by cancer, robbed all the acting media of a versatile character player. On stage, he played Macbeth in Liverpool (1995) and replaced Ken STOTT in the cult stage play, *Art* (1999); on TV he was PC Dave Litten in *The Bill* (1984–85) and starred as the plumber husband in the sitcom, *2 Point 4 Children* (1991–98); and on screen he had supporting roles in such films as *Turtle Diary* (1985) and *The Cook, the Thief, His Wife & Her Lover* (1989). The range of work is impressive (it includes a spell in the 70s with punk bands), even if it never quite conspired to make the bulky 6-footer a star presence.

OTHER BRITISH FILMS INCLUDE: *Bloody Kids* (1979), *Breaking Glass* (1980), *Outland* (1981), *Pink Floyd The Wall* (1982), *Loose Connections* (1983), *Underworld* (1985), *Up 'n' Under* (1997), *24 Hours in London* (2000).

Olsen, Pauline (*b* London, 1919). Actress. In films and TV from 1952, Olsen had one starring role, as the ballerina heroine of the dim romantic drama, *Star of My Night* (1954) – her presence was unequal to the conflict she is meant to have stirred up – and was scarcely heard of before or after. She worked mainly for DANZIGERS.

OTHER BRITISH FILMS INCLUDE: *The End of the Affair* (unc), *Johnny on the Spot, Calling All Cars* (1954).

O'Mara, Kate (*b* Leicester, 1939). Actress. RN: Frances Carroll. Darkly glamorous actress of few films in the later 60s/early 70s, including *The Vampire Lovers* (1970), as the governess. From the mid 70s, most of her film work has been for TV; she had roles in *Dynasty* (1986, US) and *Howards' Way* (1989–90). Her mother was stage actress Hazel Bainbridge, her sister actress **Belinda Carroll** (*b* Oxford, 1945) who appeared as Joan Winmill, Billy Graham convert, in *No Longer Alone* (1978). Married to **Jeremy Young** (*b* Liverpool, 1934), who had small roles in several British films, including *Crooks and Coronets* (1969) and *Frenzy* (1972), as well as much TV and some theatre directing.

OTHER BRITISH FILMS INCLUDE: *Great Catherine* (1967), *The Horror of Frankenstein* (1970), *The Tamarind Seed* (1974), *Feelings* (1975).

Ondra, Anny (*b* Tarnóv, Poland, 1903 – *d* Hollenstedt, West-Germany, 1987) Actress. RN: Ondrakova. Brought up in Prague, Ondra became a popular star of Czech, Austrian and German comedies in the 20s. In her British films, she proved an impressive dramatic actress, most notably in HITCHCOCK's *The Manxman* (1929) and *Blackmail* (1929). Her strong Czech accent precluded a continuation of her international career after the conversion to sound. Ondra settled in Germany in 1930, and, after marrying boxer Max Schmeling, she largely retired from the industry in the mid 30s. First married director Karl LAMAC.

OTHER BRITISH FILMS: *God's Clay* (1928), *Eileen of the Trees/Glorious Youth* (1928). Tim Bergfelder.

Ondricek, Miroslav (*b* Prague, 1933). Cinematographer. Began his career in DOCUMENTARY, then moved into features first in Czechoslovakia, working with director Milos Forman on 'New Wave' films, including *Loves of a Blonde* (1965), before coming to England. Here, he did notable work for Lindsay ANDERSON on three films: the short, *The White Bus* (1967); *If . . .* (1968), on which the combination of black-and-white and colour segments caused much speculation, though Anderson said in 1994 that colour was introduced because Ondricek had been afraid some of the interiors at Cheltenham School would be too dark in monochrome; and the Brechtian picaresque piece, *O Lucky Man!* (1973). He worked with Forman in the US on several films, including *Taking Off* (1971) and *Ragtime* (1981), and the UK/Fr co-production, *Valmont* (1989).

O'Neill, Maire (*b* Dublin, 1887 – *d* Basingstoke, 1952). Actress. RN: Maire Allgood. Small, meek-seeming character player, usually as wives or housekeepers. Often in films with Irish settings or themes, and often in the films of John BAXTER (e.g. *Love on the Dole*, 1941, as downtrodden neighbour) and Lance COMFORT (e.g. *Great Day*, 1945, in which she helped the flavour of her patriotically 'eggless' cake by adding an egg, and bridled when rebuked for 'deceit'). Sister of Sara ALLGOOD, and fellow Abbey Theatre player; married (2) Arthur SINCLAIR.
OTHER BRITISH FILMS INCLUDE: *Juno and the Paycock* (1930), *Irish Hearts, Sing As We Go!* (1934), *Peg of Old Drury* (1935), *Farewell Again, Glamorous Night* (1937), *St Martin's Lane, Mountains o' Mourne* (1938), *On the Night of the Fire, The Arsenal Stadium Mystery* (1939), *Dr O'Dowd* (1940), *Penn of Pennsylvania* (1941), *Those Kids from Town, Let the People Sing* (1942), *Murder in Reverse* (1945), *Piccadilly Incident, Gaiety George* (1946), *The Hills of Donegal* (1947), *Saints and Sinners* (1949), *The Clouded Yellow* (1950), *Scrooge* (1951), *Treasure Hunt* (1952), *The Oracle* (1953).

Onions, S(imon) D. (*b* Worcester, 1905 – *d* London, 1968). Cinematographer. Began career as a projectionist, before becoming a freelance cameraman who worked on SHORTS and DOCUMENTARIES in the 30s, including *The Saving of Bill Blewitt* (1936, co-c). Post-WW2, which he spent making training films for the RAF FILM UNIT, he sweated it out on inane FITZPATRICK travelogues and in some very 'B' FILMS, before being given a chance at more prestigious assignments. The latter included Paul CZINNER's OPERA and BALLET films, including the Fonteyn–NUREYEV *Romeo and Juliet* (1966).
OTHER BRITISH FILMS INCLUDE: (c, short) *Looking at London* (1946), *A Wee Bit of Scotland* (1949), *Murder at the Grange* (1952), *Calling All Cars* (1954, co-), *Crossroads* (1955, co-c); (c, feature) *Black Memory* (1947), *Bless 'Em All* (1948), *The Temptress* (1949), *The Six Men* (1951), *Murder at Scotland Yard* (1954), *Stars in Your Eyes* (1956), *The Devil's Pass, Night of the Demon* (fx ph) (1957), *The Royal Ballet* (1959), *The Night We Got the Bird* (1960), *Der Rosenkavalier* (1961), *Give a Dog a Bone* (1966).

Onwurah, Ngozi (*b* Nigeria, *c*1964). Director, screenwriter. Black film-maker who has directed a number of challenging SHORT FILMS, often foregrounding issues important to black women. On record as wanting African cinema to break out of its 'Art ghetto' and find an international audience, but her feature debut, *Welcome II the Terrordome* (1995, + sc), received only a muted response, despite acknowledgment of some powerful scenes.
OTHER BRITISH FILMS INCLUDE: (d, shorts) *Coffee Colored Children* (1988), *The Body Beautiful* (1991), *Flight of the Swan, Monday's Girls* (UK/Nigeria, + sc), *I Bring You Frankincense* (1996).

opera Despite never producing rivals to Verdi or Wagner, British cinema has several times celebrated national and international operatic composers. While LAUNDER and GILLIAT's *The Story of Gilbert and Sullivan* (1953) contained a mixture of fond BIOPIC and musical extracts, POWELL AND PRESSBURGER's *The Tales of Hoffmann* (1951) and *Oh, Rosalinda!!*

(1955) were more adventurous. The first film reproduced Powell's cinematic expressionistic version of Richard Wagner's 'Gesamtkunst' seen in *The Red Shoes* (1948) while the second subtly satirised Cold War politics by setting the original opera in 50s Vienna. These films were much more adventurous than Lewis Milestone's BIOPIC *Melba* (1953), starring American operatic soprano, Patrice Munsel, or Mike LEIGH's *Topsy-Turvy* (2000, UK/US). Though featuring the processes leading to the creation of Gilbert and Sullivan's *The Mikado* (itself filmed in 1938), *Topsy-Turvy*'s real achievement was in its affectionate tribute to the place of G&S in British musical theatre.

In the 30s particularly there was a series of European-set films derived from or built around opera/operetta, often starring Richard TAUBER, and including *Blossom Time* (1934), *Heart's Desire* (1935), and Karl GRUNE's *Pagliacci* (1936), and in passing, it might be noted that *Evensong* (1934), loosely based on the life of Nellie Melba, contains the only film record of the opera star, Conchita Supervia, as the rising diva. Tauber was the nearest an operatic singer came to being a British film star, though Tito Gobbi's presence in *The Glass Mountain* (1948) should also be noted. Peter BROOK's version of *The Beggar's Opera* (1953), with OLIVIER as MacHeath, had a certain vigour; Paul CZINNER's *Der Rosenkavalier* (1961) preserved a famous Salzburg performance starring Sena Jurinac; in *Aria* (1987) ten famous directors offered visual responses to ten famous arias; and films such as *Sunday Bloody Sunday* (1971) and *Onegin* (1999, UK/US) have made eloquent use of operatic music. However, despite Ken RUSSELL's mystical rock opera, *Tommy* (1975), opera has never been a popular screen genre, and has sometimes been used either parodically as in *All Over the Town* (1949) or as mere background, as in the thriller, *Take My Life* (1947). Tony Williams.

Orchard, Julian (*b* Wheatley, Oxford, 1930 – *d* London, 1979). Actor. Probably better known for his TV work than his films, Orchard was a regular in *The World of Beachcomber* (1968–69) and replaced Arthur HOWARD as Jimmy EDWARDS's dim assistant master in *Whack-O!* (1971–72). In films, he played a camp bath-salesman in *Father Came Too!* (1963), and political correctness was scarcely to be retrieved from performances in several of the 'CARRY ON' SERIES.
OTHER BRITISH FILMS INCLUDE: *Great Van Robbery* (1959), *Crooks Anonymous* (1962), *Hide and Seek* (1963), *Half a Sixpence* (UK/US), *Follow That Camel* (1967), *Carry On Doctor* (1968), *Perfect Friday* (1970), *Carry On Henry* (1971), *Bless This House* (1972), *Man About the House* (1974), *The Slipper and the Rose* (1976), *Revenge of the Pink Panther* (1978).

Orczy, Baroness (Emmuska; aka Emma Barstow) (*b* Tarna-Ors, Hungary, 1865 – *d* London, 1947). Novelist. Daughter of a noted composer and conductor, this Hungarian-born English writer famously created *The Scarlet Pimpernel* (1905), a romantic adventure of the French Revolution which has been filmed several times for the big and small screens. The best version is still the Leslie HOWARD–Merle OBERON film of 1935; the 1999 TV series, starring Richard E. GRANT, was a strangely characterless affair by comparison. Sequels to the original novel were filmed in 1937 (*The Return of the Scarlet Pimpernel*, starring Barry K. BARNES) and 1950 (*The Elusive Pimpernel*, Michael POWELL's overelaborate, under-exciting colour version starring David NIVEN), and the idea of the 'Pimpernel' and its association with Leslie Howard was exploited in the wartime thriller, *Pimpernel Smith* (1941), in which the patriot has become a professor and the enemy has moved somewhat east. In 1924, a SERIES of short mystery films was made from her stories.

OTHER BRITISH FILMS INCLUDE: (adapted from novels/stories) *Beau Brocade* (1916), *The Laughing Cavalier* (1917), *The Elusive Pimpernel* (1919), *The York Mystery* and 12 other short films (1924), *The Triumph of the Scarlet Pimpernel* (1928), *A Moorland Tragedy* (1933), *Spy of Napoleon* (1936).

O'Rourke, Brefni (*b* Dublin, 1889 – *d* 1946). Actor. Dignified character player, grey-haired and moustached, usually in professional or officer roles, such as the Coroner in *They Were Sisters* (1945) or the Brigadier in *The Next of Kin* (1942). Unusually gentle as Phyllis CALVERT's failed, sensitive father in *The Root of All Evil* (1947), he made over 30 films in five years in the earlier half of the 40s, and could be counted on to stamp brief roles with memorable authority.

OTHER BRITISH FILMS INCLUDE: *Hatter's Castle, The Black Sheep of Whitehall* (1941), *They Flew Alone, Secret Mission, The Next of Kin, Much Too Shy, The First of the Few, The Day Will Dawn* (1942), *They Met in the Dark, The Lamp Still Burns, Escape to Danger* (1943), *It Happened One Sunday, The Tawny Pipit, Don't Take It to Heart* (1944), *Perfect Strangers, They Were Sisters, The Rake's Progress, Murder in Reverse* (1945), *I See a Dark Stranger* (1946), *The Upturned Glass, Green Fingers* (1947).

Orme, Geoffrey (*b* 1904 – *d* 1978). Screenwriter. Author of nearly 30 screenplays, most of them light comedies, including four in the 'Old Mother Riley' SERIES. Much associated with the films of John BAXTER, for whose naive but true humanism Orme's screenplays provide the bases, in such films as *The Common Touch* (1941), usually working in collaboration with Barbara K. EMARY. In 1952, he joined Baxter at GROUP 3 as scenario editor, and also worked on the scripts for such films as *Devil on Horseback* (1954, add dial).

OTHER BRITISH FILMS INCLUDE: (co-sc, unless noted) *Sunshine Ahead* (1936), *What Would You Do Chums?* (1939), *Old Mother Riley's Ghosts, Old Mother Riley's Circus* (co-story) (1941), *Let the People Sing* (1942), *Theatre Royal* (1943), *Here Comes the Sun* (1945, sc), *When You Come Home* (1947), *Nothing Venture* (sc), *The Last Load* (1948), *Judgment Deferred* (1951), *Orders Are Orders, The End of the Road, Delayed Action* (sc) (1954), *The Love Match* (1955, sc), *The Heart Within* (1957, sc), *The Boy and the Bridge* (1959).

Ormond, Julia (*b* Epsom, 1965). Actress. For a brief moment in the mid 90s, there was no avoiding Ormond of the craven features. She appeared in six films in 1993–95, the first three at least part-British, including Peter GREENAWAY's daunting *The Baby of Mâcon* (1993, UK/Fr/Neth/Ger), *Nostradamus* (1994, UK/Ger) and *Captives* (1994), the romance of a prison dentist with a convicted murderer. In the US, she made three duds in a row: *Legends of the Fall* (1994), the perhaps unjustly despised *First Knight* and the ill-advised remake of *Sabrina* (both 1995). Not a real success among them, but Ormond has persisted in international films, and in 2000 the Webber-Douglas-trained actress returned to the London stage in David Hare's *My Zinc Bed*.

Ornadel, Cyril (*b* London, 1924). Composer. Responsible for the scores of a dozen movies of the late 60s and 70s, several of the HORROR/EXPLOITATION variety for director Pete WALKER, as well as for the disastrous remake of *Brief Encounter* (1974, TV, some cinemas), and for several TV mini-series, including *Edward the King* (1975). Also had a prominent recording career, and composed the music for such West End musicals as *Pickwick* (1963), winning awards for his work on several occasions.

OTHER BRITISH FILMS: (comp, unless noted) *The Limping Man* (1953, songs), *Subterfuge* (1968, UK/US, + cond), *Cool It Carol, Die Screaming, Marianne* (1970), *Not Now, Darling* (1972), *Tiffany Jones* (1973).

Orr, Buxton (*b* Glasgow, 1924 – *d* Hereford, 1997). Composer. Gave up medical training for music, studying with composer Benjamin FRANKEL. Though his non-film compositions covered a wide range, including brass band and opera, his screen scores were mostly for HORROR films of the late 50s/early 60s, including several each for directors Robert DAY and Sidney J. FURIE, and two starring Boris KARLOFF – *Grip of the Strangler* and *Corridors of Blood* (+ cond) (1958).

OTHER BRITISH FILMS INCLUDE: (comp, unless noted) *Fiend Without a Face* (1957), *Suddenly, Last Summer* (1959, co-comp, m d), *Dr Blood's Coffin* (1960), *The Eyes of Annie Jones* (1963).

Orton, J(ohn) O(verton) C. ('Jock') (*b* London, 1889 – *d c* 1943). Screenwriter. Former major in the British Army, and prolific writer of screen COMEDY throughout the 30s and early 40s, almost always in collaboration, most often with Marriott EDGAR and Val GUEST, sometimes with Frank LAUNDER or Sidney GILLIAT. He (co-)wrote films for Will HAY (several of these are classics of their kind), Arthur ASKEY and Jack HULBERT, but also worked on serious films such as *Turn of the Tide* (1935) and the SPY THRILLER, *Cottage to Let* (1941). Directed a few films in the late 20s, early 30s. Mostly associated with GAINSBOROUGH but he also worked for BRITISH INSTRUCTIONAL and BIP early in his career.

OTHER BRITISH FILMS INCLUDE: (d) *The Battles of the Coronel and Falkland Islands* (1927, ass, doc), *The Celestial City* (1929, doc), *Windjammer* (1930, doc), *Bad Companions* (1932); (sc) *Tell Me Tonight* (1932), *Just Smith* (1933), *Brown on Resolution* (1935), *Jack of All Trades* (1936), *Inspector Hornleigh on Holiday* (1939, adptn), *The Ghost Train* (1941); (co-sc) *Shooting Stars* (1928), *After the Ball* (1932), *Soldiers of the King* (1933), *Jack Ahoy!* (1934, co-story), *Bulldog Jack* (1935), *Everything is Thunder* (1936), *Non-Stop New York, Oh, Mr Porter!* (1937), *The Viper, Old Bones of the River* (1938), *The Frozen Limits, Ask a Policeman* (1939), *Band Waggon* (1940), *Hi Gang!* (1941), *Back Room Boy* (1942), *Time Flies, For Those in Peril* (1944), *Up to His Neck* (1954, co-story).

Orton, Joe (*b* Leicester, 1933 – *d* London, 1967). Dramatist. Orton's short life came to a violent end when his lover, Kenneth Halliwell, murdered him in their London home. He left behind a legacy of three major plays whose elegance seemed to unite black wit and the West End well-made play. They have been compared to Restoration drama in their calculated effects: the literal-minded films made from two of them, *Entertaining Mr Sloane* (1969) and *Loot* (1970), scarcely suggest such ancestry, despite the best efforts of distinguished casts. In 1987, Orton's life was made the subject of the BIOPIC, *Prick Up Your Ears* (based on John Lahr's biography of Orton), in which Gary OLDMAN and Alfred MOLINA memorably played Orton and Halliwell.

Orwell, George (*b* Motihari, India, 1903 – *d* London, 1950). Author. RN: Eric Blair. Eton-educated novelist, political satirist, vivid autobiographer, and one of the most astute essayists and literary critics of his time. His distrust of all political systems feeds both his most famous works, the allegorical *Animal Farm* (1945), filmed in Britain as an animated feature by HALAS AND BATCHELOR in 1951 (released 1954), and *Nineteen Eighty Four* (1949). The latter made a celebrated TV ADAPTATION in 1954, produced by Rudolph CARTIER; was indifferently filmed as *1984* (1955) with American leads, Edmond O'Brien and Jan Sterling; and more seriously if not very excitingly remade in, of course, 1984, starring Richard

BURTON. A strongly cast adaptation of *Keep the Aspidistra Flying* (1997) has been little seen.

Osborn, Andrew (*b* London, 1910 – *d* London, 1985). Actor. It was the slight, somewhat melancholy-looking Osborne's misfortune that his one bid for stardom should have been in *Idol of Paris* (1948), one of the most preposterous films ever made in Britain. For the rest, the Christ's College-educated Osborn was relegated to minor roles in 'A' films, such as *Angels One Five* (1952), and leads in 'B' MOVIES, including *Dark Interval* (1950), but even in those he was often in roles secondary to washed-up Hollywood stars like Dane Clark in *Murder by Proxy* (1955). In the 50s he became a TV producer and had much more success there, including episodes of *When the Boat Comes In* (1977). He was also producer and manager of the Richmond Theatre for four years in the early 50s.
OTHER BRITISH FILMS INCLUDE: *Who Goes Next?* (1938), *Poet's Pub* (1949), *The Woman with No Name* (1950), *The Lady with a Lamp* (1951), *Blood Orange, Three's Company* (1953).

Osborn, David (*b* 1923). Screenwriter. Educated in the US where he served in the Marine Corps, he began his British screenwriting career in the later 50s, his output including several films co-authored with his wife **Liz Charles-Williams**, with whom he co-wrote scripts for the BULLDOG DRUMMOND spoofs, *Deadlier than the Male* (1966) and *Some Girls Do* (1969), *Penny Gold* (1973) and the Swiss–Spanish co-production, *Open Season* (1974). He also wrote a good deal of TV drama and several novels.
OTHER BRITISH FILMS INCLUDE: *Chase a Crooked Shadow* (1957), *Moment of Danger* (1960), *Follow the Boys* (1963), *The Trap, Maroc 7* (1966), *Whoever Slew Auntie Roo?* (1971).

Osborne, John (*b* London, 1929 – *d* Shrewsbury, 1994). Dramatist. Never mind that the ANGRY YOUNG MEN have long since been de-fanged, and indeed characterised as reactionary homophobes in one recent account, there is no gainsaying that *Look Back in Anger* (1956) was a turning point in British theatrical history, and that Osborne and his creation, Jimmy Porter, spoke vitriolically for a generation exasperated with a class-bound Establishment. The film's (1959) radical rhetoric was compromised by Richard BURTON's star power and mellifluous tones but the next year's film version of *The Entertainer* marvellously preserves OLIVIER's performance as decaying MUSIC HALL comedian, Archie Rice. Osborne co-wrote the screenplays for both with Nigel KNEALE and solo-wrote *Tom Jones* (1963), for which he won an AA. All three were directed by Tony RICHARDSON, Osborne's former Royal Court colleague, with whom (along with Harry SALTZMAN), in the late 50s, he set up WOODFALL FILMS, which helped to bring a gust of fresh air into British cinema of the time. Other plays of Osborne's to be filmed were *Inadmissible Evidence* (1968, + sc) for Woodfall and *Luther* (1973, UK/Can/US), for an American filmed theatre series. Also acted in several films, including *Get Carter* (1971), as an effete gangland boss. Married (1) Mary URE, (2) Penelope GILLIAT, (3) Jill BENNETT, among others.
OTHER BRITISH FILMS: (a) *The Chairman's Wife* (1971, short), *Tomorrow Never Comes* (1977, UK/Can), *Flash Gordon* (1980); (co-sc) *England, My England* (1995).
BIBLIOG: Autobiographies, *A Better Class of Person*, 1981; *Almost a Gentleman*, 1991.

Oscar, Henry (*b* Hornsey, 1891 – *d* London, 1969). Actor. RN: Wale. Prolific star of stage (from 1911 at Stratford) and screen (about 75 films between 1932 and 1965), as well as frequent radio and TV performances. (He was the first actor to receive a BBC contract.) Also a theatre director, responsible for all of ENSA's dramatic entertainment (1939–45), a governor of Central School and a council member of Equity. In films, his dignified bearing and incisive features lent themselves to professional men like Justice Wills in *Oscar Wilde* or the school principal in *The Brides of Dracula* (1960), to doctors, aldermen and commanders, to counts, lords and even a king (he is James II in *Bonnie Prince Charlie*, 1948), but he is in fact more interesting when playing weaker vessels, such as the timorous Grierson in *Hatter's Castle* (1941) or Kathleen BYRON's undemanding husband in *Prelude to Fame* (1950).
OTHER BRITISH FILMS INCLUDE: *After Dark* (1932), *The Man Who Knew Too Much* (1934), *The Tunnel* (1935), *Sensation* (1936), *Fire Over England, Dark Journey* (1937), *Black Limelight* (1938), *The Four Feathers, The Saint in London, On the Night of the Fire* (1939), *Penn of Pennsylvania* (1941), *Squadron Leader X, The Day Will Dawn* (1942), *Mrs Fitzherbert* (1947), *Idol of Paris* (1948), *The Black Rose* (1950, UK/US), *Beau Brummell* (1954), *Private's Progress* (1956), *Beyond This Place* (1959), *Foxhole in Cairo* (1960).

O'Shea, Milo (*b* Dublin, 1926). Actor. Heavy-browed, tubby O'Shea had been in films off and on for over 20 years before playing his most famous role, as Leopold Bloom in Joseph STRICK's heroic adaptation of James JOYCE's *Ulysses* (1967, UK/US), a role he had previously incarnated in the BBC play, *Bloomsday* (1964). Since then, the Abbey Theatre alumnus has been an enjoyable if intermittent presence in international films, including an avuncular Friar Lawrence in ZEFFIRELLI's *Romeo and Juliet* (1968, UK/It), widower McLeavy in *Loot* (1970), and a TV series, *Me Mammy* (1969–71). But there wasn't enough scope in British cinema of the lamentable 70s and much of his subsequent work has been in US films and TV. He is very funny as the priest in the film-within-the-film in *The Purple Rose of Cairo* (1985).
OTHER BRITISH FILMS INCLUDE: *Contraband* (1940, unc), *Talk of a Million* (1951), *This Other Eden* (1959), *Mrs Gibbons' Boys* (1962), *Carry On Cabby* (1963), *The Adding Machine* (1969), *Theatre of Blood* (1973), *Percy's Progress* (1974), *The Playboys* (1992, Ire/US), *The Butcher Boy* (1997, Ire/US).

O'Shea, Tessie (*b* Cardiff, 1913 – *d* Leesburg, Florida, 1995). Actress. Popular MUSIC HALL entertainer (debut 1926), billed as 'Two-Ton Tessie' because of her size, whose screen appearances range from a starring role in *London Town* (1946), to singing 'If you were the only girl in the world' to a crowded army audience in *The Way Ahead* (1944), to little more than a background singer in *The Blue Lamp* (1949). Became an American star in 1963 with 12-minute medley of music hall songs in Noël COWARD's stage production of *The Girl Who Came to Supper*, for which she won a Tony; US stage and TV appearances followed, together with featured roles in *The Russians Are Coming, the Russians Are Coming* (1966) and *Bedknobs and Broomsticks* (1971).
OTHER BRITISH FILMS: *Holidays with Pay, Somewhere in Politics* (1948), *Tonight in Britain* (1954), *The Shiralee* (1957), *The Best House in London* (1968). AS.

Osmond, Hal (*b* London, 1919 – *d* Taunton, 1959). Actor. Small, sharp-featured supporting player, in dozens of films. He is Midge in *The Story of Robin Hood . . .* (1952), Snakey, the inept pickpocket in *Jack the Ripper* and the smaller sneak thief in *Blood of the Vampire* (both 1958), and innumerable other barmen, clerks, waiters, taxi drivers and crooks, totting up over 50 films in 20 years.

OTHER BRITISH FILMS INCLUDE: *Old Mother Riley in Paris* (1938), *Miranda*, *Quartet*, *Here Come the Huggetts* (1948), *The Spider and the Fly*, *It's Not Cricket*, *A Boy, a Girl and a Bike* (1949), *Last Holiday* (1950), *Top Secret*, *Stolen Face*, *The Brave Don't Cry* (1952), *The Net*, *The Million Pound Note*, *Three Steps to the Gallows* (1953), *Forbidden Cargo* (1954), *Value for Money*, *Tiger by the Tail* (1955), *The Last Man to Hang?* (1956), *High Flight*, *The Vicious Circle*, *The Truth About Women* (1957), *A Night to Remember*, *Tread Softly Stranger* (1958), *The Great Van Robbery* (1959).

Osmond, Lesley (*b* London). Actress. On stage in revue as well as playing supporting roles in a dozen or so films, mainly in the 40s, and including one of Vera LYNN's rare films, *We'll Meet Again* (1942), *When You Come Home* (1947) as Frank RANDLE's granddaughter, and the Sonia DRESDEL wicked-woman MELODRAMA, *This Was a Woman* (1948).
OTHER BRITISH FILMS INCLUDE: *In Which We Serve* (1942), *It's in the Bag* (1943), *The Story of Shirley Yorke*, *House of Darkness* (1948), *Let's Have a Murder* (1950), *Chelsea Story* (1951).

Ostrer, Isidore (*b* London, 1889 – *d* Surrey, 1975). Executive. RN: Ostravitch. A former stockbroker, Ostrer, along with his brothers **Mark Ostrer** (*b* London, 1892 – *d* London, 1958) and **Maurice Ostrer** (*b* London, 1896 – *d* Cannes, 1975), became financially involved with GAUMONT Co. in 1922. They were instrumental in setting up GAUMONT–BRITISH PICTURE CORPORATION and its association in 1927 with GAINS-BOROUGH FILMS, and in 1929 Isidore became chairman, with Mark as vice-chairman and Maurice as joint managing director. Having created a cinema circuit of over 350 cinemas, they set about expanding production, this leading to the reconstruction of the LIME GROVE STUDIO, SHEPHERD'S BUSH, where the major Gainsborough films of the 40s were produced. Isidore retained chairmanship of Gaumont–British until 1941. James MASON, who married Isidore OSTRER's daughter, Pamela KELLINO, considered Isidore the brains of the family, while Mark was the one who dealt with the publicity aspects of running the studios and the Gaumont–British cinemas. Maurice, however, really controlled production policy at Gainsborough during the period of its ascendancy in the 40s. He was executive producer (often credited as 'In charge of Production') on virtually all the films produced at Lime Grove from 1940 until he resigned from Gainsborough in 1946, to set up his own independent company, Premier Films, whose first film was the calamitous *Idol of Paris* (1948). (Sydney BOX then took charge of the studio.) Isidore was appointed chairman of Premier Films, but his legendary astuteness, so important behind the Gainsborough scenes, appears to have deserted him. He disappeared from the film industry shortly afterwards but the films on which his name appears constitute a significant oeuvre in British film history. There were two further, less well-known Ostrer brothers: David, who looked after European sales, and Harry, a former teacher, who was scenario editor on some of the company's films.

Ostrer, Mark *see* **Ostrer, Isidore**

Ostrer, Maurice *see* **Ostrer, Isidore**

O'Sullivan, Richard (*b* London, 1944). Actor. The mischievous-looking O'Sullivan is one of the rare CHILD ACTORS who have stayed the course into adulthood. Very busy in the 50s as a young boy, with key roles in such films as *The Stranger's Hand* (1953, UK/It), from Graham GREENE's story, and *Dangerous Exile* (1957), as boy king Louis XVII. The roles straggled on into the 70s when he became a popular TV star in

such series as *Doctor in the House* (1969–70) and its various sequels, persisting into the 80s, *Man About the House* (1973–76), plus its SPIN-OFF film (1974), and *Robin's Nest* (1977). Has also done theatre seasons, including *Boeing Boeing* (1977–78).
OTHER BRITISH FILMS INCLUDE: *The Green Scarf*, *Make Me an Offer!* (1954), *The Dark Avenger* (1955), *It's Great to Be Young!* (1956), *No Time for Tears* (1957), *Carry On Teacher* (1959), *Wonderful Life* (1964), *Au Pair Girls* (1972), *Can You Keep It Up for a Week?* (1974).

O'Sullivan, Thaddeus (*b* Dublin, 1947). Director, cinematographer. Studied at London's Royal College of Art, with an MA in film and TV studies. O'Sullivan spent 15 years as a cinematographer, on both experimental films and features such as *On the Black Hill* and *The Love Child* (1987), before directing several Irish-set features. *December Bride* (1990), a period drama of a woman who makes a difficult choice, *Nothing Personal* (1995, UK/Ire), a fiercely uncompromising account of the schism in Northern Ireland, and the more nearly mainstream *Ordinary Decent Criminal* (2000, UK/Ger/Ire/US), starring Kevin Spacey, suggest an alert, perhaps passionate talent to be watched.
OTHER BRITISH FILMS INCLUDE: (c, unless noted) *Pint of Plain* (1975, co-d, co-sc, e), *On a Paving Stone Mounted* (1978, + d, sc), *Outside In* (UK/Ger/Neth, prod team), *Our Boys* (Ire, short) (1981), *Pigs*, *Anne Devlin* (1984, Ire), *The Return* (1988).

O'Toole, Peter (*b* Connemara, 1932). Actor. Anyone who saw O'Toole on the Royal Court stage as the foul-mouthed Sgt Bamforth in *The Long and the Short and the Tall* (1959) would have confidently predicted stardom, though he was bypassed for the film version (1960). In the event, it has been an extraordinary career for the Leeds bookie's son, who began as a cub reporter, spent two years in the Royal Navy, then trained at RADA before spending several years at the Bristol Old Vic. He would return periodically to the stage, with Stratford and Old Vic seasons in the 60s and playing Professor Higgins, all flailing limbs and tweedy irascibility in *Pygmalion* (1984) and the title role in *Jeffrey Bernard is Unwell* (1989), two roles he was surely *meant* to play.

He made three modestly regarded films before bursting on the world as *Lawrence of Arabia* (1962), several others having been considered for the role. With blazing blue eyes, bleached hair and flowing white garments, he was a charismatic figure (though NOEL Coward is alleged to have said, 'If you'd been any prettier, it would have been Florence of Arabia'), winning an Oscar nomination. It was a remarkable study in obsession, catching the right balance between mystic and man of action, bringing to the role kinds of intensity and zeal that few other British actors could have done. Arguably, he never had a more challenging role but his carousing King winning the displeasure of his former comrade-in-wassail in *Becket* (1964) and another go at the same monarch, Henry II, at a later stage of his life, in *The Lion in Winter* (1968) maintained the star aura. Hardly anything after that has been as riveting: his eagerly anticipated questing hero, *Lord Jim* (1964), failed to meet expectations; he is an agreeable Chipping in the MUSICAL version of *Goodbye, Mr Chips* (1969), without dislodging Robert DONAT's image in the role; he makes an aptly bizarre figure of the Earl who believes he is Jesus in *The Ruling Class* (1971); and has a certain charm as a Hollywood legend on the drink in *My Favorite Year* (1982, US), a role which must have seemed close to the bone for the professed former alcoholic O'Toole. He made some rotten films, of which *Caligula* (1979, It/US) can serve as example; then, to one's astonishment, he picks himself up, the glamour now ravaged but still in evidence, as in his final scene in *The Last Emperor* (1987, China/It). The roistering years are apparently behind him but they took a heavy toll, though it must be said that he never stopped working. Received honorary AA in 2003 for lifetime achievement. Married (1959–79) to Siân PHILLIPS.

OTHER BRITISH FILMS: *The Savage Innocents* (UK/Fr/It/US), *The Day They Robbed the Bank of England* (1959), *Kidnapped* (1960), *The Night of the Generals* (1966, UK/Fr), *Casino Royale* (1967), *Great Catherine* (1967), *Country Dance* (1969), *Murphy's War, Under Milk Wood* (1971), *Man Friday* (1975), *Power Play* (1978), *Supergirl* (1984), *The Rainbow Thief* (1990), *Rebecca's Daughters* (1992, UK/Ger), *Fairytale: A True Story* (1997, UK/US), *The Final Curtain, Global Heresy* (2001, UK/US). BIBLIOG: Autobiographies, *Loitering with Intent: the Child*, 1992; *Loitering with Intent: The Apprentice*, 1996; Nicholas Wapshott, *Peter O'Toole: A Biography*, 1983.

Oulton, Brian (*b* Liverpool, 1908 – *d* London, 1992). Actor. Ubiquitous character player of innumerable clerkly, bureaucratic types, RADA-trained Oulton was on stage from 1928, in London and elsewhere throughout the 30s, made his film debut in *Too Many Husbands* (1938), and was in the Army, 1941–46. Post-war, he was rarely off the stage, broadcast frequently (he was 'Cyril' in the long-running children's programme, *Just William*), was in numerous TV dramas and series from 1946, including a continuing role in *Doctor at Large* (1971), and appeared in four dozen films. His film roles were mostly small but he made them memorable: he was a supercilious couturier in *Miranda* (1948), and thereafter a series of vicars, valets and government officials (usually pompous and usually overthrown); he was in four of the 'CARRY ON' series, and five of the BOULTING brothers' institutional satires; and fell embarrassing victim to a foolish cult in *Devils of Darkness* (1964). Married Peggy THORPE-BATES.

OTHER BRITISH FILMS INCLUDE: *It's Not Cricket* (1949), *Last Holiday* (1950), *Castle in the Air* (1952), *Will Any Gentleman . . . ?, The Million Pound Note* (1953), *Doctor in the House* (1954), *The Deep Blue Sea* (1955), *Private's Progress, Brothers in Law* (1956), *Happy is the Bride* (1957), *Carry On Nurse, The Thirty Nine Steps* (1958), *I'm All Right Jack* (1959), *A French Mistress, Carry On Constable, The Bulldog Breed* (1960 *The Damned* (1961), *The Iron Maiden* (1963), *The Intelligence Men* (1965), *Carry On Camping* (1969), *On the Buses* (1971), *Ooh . . . You Are Awful* (1972), *Gandhi* (1982, UK/Ind).

Oury, Gerard (*b* Paris, 1919). Actor. RN: Max-Gerald Tannenbaum. Short, sharp-featured French actor and theatre director of popular plays and, from the mid 60s of films. He also acted in over two dozen films, including a handful of British ones in the 50s: he is, for instance, the Dauphin in *The Sword and the Rose* (1953) and a police inspector in *Father Brown* (1954), but his most notable performances are in such continental films as *The Heroes Are Tired* (Fr/Ger) and *Woman of the River* (Fr/It) (1955). Made Officer of the Legion of Honour in 1985. His daughter Danièle Thompson is a screenwriter in French films.

OTHER BRITISH FILMS INCLUDE: *They Who Dare, Sea Devils, The Heart of the Matter* (1953), *House of Secrets* (1956).

Ové, Horace (*b* Belmont, Trinidad, 1939). Director, producer, screenwriter. Influential black film-maker who grew frustrated with the limits imposed on black artists in British society and has in recent years relocated to the Caribbean. Came to England to study art in 1960, and, after several DOCUMENTARIES, including *Baldwin's Nigger* (1969), made the first feature by a black British director, *Pressure* (1975), a drama of the conflict between first and second generations of a black

family living in Notting Hill, London. His other feature was *Playing Away* (1986), in which, through the metaphor of a cricket match, racial tension is tracked into the home counties. Ové claimed that his films were judged for their value as polemic not as films.

OTHER BRITISH FILMS: (doc) *The Art of the Needle* (1966), *Reggae* (1970, + p, sc), *The Mangrove Nine* (1973, + co-assoc p, stills ph), *Stretch Hunter* (1980).

Owen, Alison Producer. After acting as production co-ordinator on Peter GREENAWAY's *Drowning by Numbers* (1988, UK/Neth), she produced the oddly engaging *Hear My Song* in 1991, and worked as co-producer with WORKING TITLE on such films as *The Young Americans* (1993), *Moonlight and Valentino* (1995) and, most notably on the Oscar-nominated *Elizabeth* (1998).

OTHER BRITISH FILMS INCLUDE: *Roseanna's Grave* (1997, UK/US), *Rat* (2000, UK/US).

Owen, Alun (*b* N. Wales, 1925 – *d* New York, 1994). Dramatist, screenwriter. Former actor, with Birmingham Rep, the Old Vic, etc, and several films, including the curate nervously lunching with Bishop Patrick MAGEE in *The Servant* (1963), his last screen role. Also a playwright (e.g. the book of the musical, *Maggie May*, 1964) and author of numerous TV plays, including *No Trams to Lime Street* (1959) in the *Armchair Theatre* series, and others in such formats as *Saturday Night Theatre*, 1969–70, as well as writing screenplays for such varied films as *The Criminal* (1960) and the BEATLES romp, *A Hard Day's Night* (1964). In a productive career, though, his TV work was the most significant, and his name recalls a period when original TV drama was a burgeoning dramatic form.

OTHER BRITISH FILMS: (a) *Valley of Song* (1953), *Every Day Except Christmas* (1957, doc, narr), *In the Wake of a Stranger, Jet Storm, I'm All Right Jack* (1959).

Owen, Bill (*b* London, 1914 – *d* London, 1999). Actor. RN: William Owen Rowbotham. Diminutive, dark-haired character player, good at squaddies, spivs, jockeys, boxers – characters with a pugnacious side and strong blue-collar audience appeal. Son of a London tram driver, and a Labour Party activist from an early age, he started as a holiday camp entertainer, and for many years was an actor/sketch-writer/producer at London's Socialist Unity Theatre. Post-WW2 service, he made his feature film debut in *The Way To The Stars* (1945), and, as an ex-army spiv in *Dancing with Crime* (1947), impressed critics as a Cagney type. With a RANK contract came a change of name, his first film as Bill Owen being *When the Bough Breaks* (1947). In the 50s he starred in several EALING films directed by Basil DEARDEN: *The Square Ring* (1953), repeating his stage role, *The Rainbow Jacket* (1954), as a disgraced jockey, and *The Ship That Died of Shame* (1955), as an ex-army black marketeer; and he appeared in five early 'CARRY ON' films, after *Carry On Sergeant* (1958). There were many forgettable films after 1960, but at the end of the decade he won critical acclaim in plays at the Royal Court – *In Celebration*, directed by Lindsay ANDERSON, was filmed in 1974. He appeared in TV's *Coronation Street* and for many years in *Last of the Summer Wine* (from 1973), as the scruffy vulgarian Compo, his most famous role. Awarded MBE in 1976.

OTHER BRITISH FILMS INCLUDE: *Song of the People* (doc, short)*, *Perfect Strangers** (1945), *School for Secrets*, *Daybreak* (1946), *Easy Money, The Weaker Sex, Trottie True* (1948), *The Girl Who Couldn't Quite* (1949), *Hotel Sahara* (1951), *A Day to Remember* (1953), *Davy* (1957), *Carve Her Name With Pride, Carry On Nurse* (1958), *On the

Fiddle (1961), *Carry on Cruising* (1962), *The Secret of Blood Island* (1964), *Georgy Girl* (1966), *O Lucky Man!* (1973), *The Comeback* (1977), *Singleton's Pluck* (1984), *The Handmaid's Tale* (UK/Ger/Fr, 1990). * = as Bill Rowbotham.

BIBLIOG: Autobiography, *Summer Wine and Vintage Years: A Cluttered Life*, 1994. Roger Philip Mellor.

Owen, Cliff (*b* London, 1919 – *d* Banbury, 1993). Director. After an apprenticeship as assistant director on some early 50s films, including *The Magic Box* (1951), and as director on such TV series as *The Third Man* (1959), Owen got his chance as feature director on a neat second-feature THRILLER, *Offbeat* (1960), The films that followed, though, apart from the very funny *The Wrong Arm of the Law* (1962), which had the advantage of an excellent script, are a disappointing lot. He directed MORECAMBE AND WISE in two of their frustrating attempts at big-screen success – *That Riviera Touch* (1966) and *The Magnificent Two* (1967) – and two SPIN-OFFS from TV series, *Steptoe and Son* and *Ooh . . . You Are Awful* (from the *Dick Emery Show*) (1972). By the 80s, he was making SPONSORED SHORTS.

OTHER BRITISH FILMS INCLUDE: (ass d) *Under Capricorn* (1949), *Young Wives' Tale* (1951), *The Yellow Balloon* (1953); (d) *A Prize of Arms* (1961), *The Vengeance of She* (1967), *No Sex Please – We're British* (1973), *Health Education Council 'Walkies'* (1977, doc), *Health Education Council 'Ageing Man'* (1978, doc), *Sweetex: Lumps* (1980, doc).

Owen, Clive (*b* Coventry, 1965). Actor. Moody, tense, handsome star of many TV roles, including the opportunist *Chancer* (1990–91) and the cop going blind in *Second Sight* (1999–2000), Owen suddenly came to the notice of cinemagoers when Mike HODGES' *Croupier*, made in 1998 (UK/Fr/Ger/Ire), became an art-house hit in the US in 2000, with Owen as the author seeking inspiration and finding crime. Since then the RADA-trained actor has been in demand for international films, as well as taking his place in Robert Altman's star-packed British country-house MYSTERY, *Gosford Park* (2001, UK/Ger/US). His first film role was in Beeban KIDRON's road movie, *Vroom* (1988); he made a brooding impact in *Close My Eyes* (1991), in which he and Saskia REEVES were locked in an incestuous relationship. Also successful on stage in Patrick Marber's *Closer* (1997).

OTHER BRITISH FILMS: *Century* (1993), *The Turnaround* (1994), *Bent* (1997, UK/Jap/US), *Greenfingers* (2001).

Owen, Yvonne (*b* London, 1923 – *d* London, 1990). Actress. Pretty, vivacious and talented GAINSBOROUGH contractee of the later 40s, Owen made an excellent impression as Ann TODD's silly, bitchy friend in *The Seventh Veil* (1945) and Hazel COURT's brassy room-mate in *Holiday Camp* (1947). RADA-trained and on stage from 1941, she made thirteen films before retiring (presumably into marriage with Alan BADEL), but was too often reduced to minor bits like the maid with an ailing mum in *Silent Dust* (1949). Daughter is Sarah BADEL.

OTHER BRITISH FILMS: *The Years Between, A Girl in a Million* (1946), *My Brother's Keeper, Miranda, Portrait from Life, Quartet, Easy Money* (1948), *Marry Me* (1949), *Someone at the Door* (1950).

Owens, Patricia (*b* Golden, British Columbia, 1925 – *d* Lancaster, California. 2000). Actress. Under contract with GAINSBOROUGH from age 18 and on the London stage the following year, Owens was rushed from film to film, virtually none of which gave her anything worth doing (e.g. at 25, she was cast as one of the schoolgirls in *The Happiest Days of Your Life*, 1950). Her best chances came in US films, particularly in *No Down Payment* (1957), Martin Ritt's melodrama of married life in a Los Angeles housing development, and the cult favourite, *The Fly* (1958); most of her career from the mid 50s was spent in America. Pretty and more than competent, the Central School-trained Owens deserved more from British cinema. Retired in 1968.

OTHER BRITISH FILMS INCLUDE: *Miss London Ltd* (1943), *English Without Tears* (1944), *While the Sun Shines* (1947, unc), *Things Happen at Night* (1948), *Bait* (1949), *Ghost Ship* (1952), *House of Blackmail* (1953), *The Good Die Young* (1954), *Windfall* (1955), *Island in the Sun* (1957, UK/US), *Walk a Tightrope* (1963).

Oxley, David (*b* Wellington, Somerset, 1921 – *d* 1985). Actor. In films from 1950 (*The Elusive Pimpernel*), Oxley had perhaps two roles that are remembered: as Leigh-Fermor's chum in the Cretan escapades of *Ill Met By Moonlight* (1956), though director Michael POWELL later described the principal performances as 'atrocious', and as the viciously decadent Sir Hugo Baskerville in the opening sequence of *The Hound of the Baskervilles* (1959).

OTHER BRITISH FILMS INCLUDE: *The Elusive Pimpernel* (1950), *Svengali* (1954), *Saint Joan, Bonjour Tristesse* (1957), *Yesterday's Enemy* (1959), *Bunny Lake Is Missing, Life at the Top* (1965).

Oxley, Roy Production designer. The two features on which Oxley worked as designer, *London Belongs to Me* (1948), with its studio-set 'boarding house' for a rich mix of character actors, and EALING's *Passport to Pimlico* (1949), with its evocative use of bombsite locations, suggest a certain versatility, but his only other screen work was an obscure SHORT called *Box for One* (1953).

Oz, Frank (*b* Hereford, 1944). Director. RN: Oznowicz. Educated in California and working with Jim HENSON's Muppets from 1962, Oz rates mention here only for this connection: he is the voice of Miss Piggy and other creatures in *The Muppet Movie* (1979) and *The Great Muppet Caper* (1981, + co-p), both technically, as it were, British films. Also acted in Henson productions, *The Dark Crystal* (1982, + co-d) and *Labyrinth* (1986), and in the inventive *An American Werewolf in London* (1981, UK/US). The rest of his career, as director and actor, is in US films and TV, including playing Yoda in two recent *Star Wars* films (1999, 2002) and directing a range of unmemorable films.

Pp

Paal, Alexander (*b* Budapest, 1910 – *d* Madrid, 1972). Producer. Having entered the film industry in Europe, Paal went to America in the mid 30s and later worked there with Alexander KORDA (e.g. on *Lydia*, 1941), and, with only modest success, sought to model himself on Korda. Served as combat cameraman in WW2 (1941–45) with the US army, and came to England in 1949. He produced a handful of films there, including *A Tale of Five Cities* (1951), starring his then-wife Eva BARTOK, whom he rescued from Communist Hungary and who left him shortly after the film's release. His other British film involvement includes several enjoyable 'B' FILMS for HAMMER, such as *Cloudburst* (1951, assoc p) and three with Terence FISHER –*Stolen Face* (1952, story), *Four-Sided Triangle* and *Mantrap* (1953, co-p). From mid 50s, returned to work in European films.

OTHER BRITISH FILMS: *Three Cases of Murder* (1955, assoc p), *Countess Dracula* (1970, p, story).

Pack, Charles Lloyd *see* **Lloyd-Pack, Charles**

Pack, Roger Lloyd *see* **Lloyd-Pack, Roger**

PACT (Producers' Alliance for Cinema and Television) Founded in 1991, PACT is the trade association in the UK representing independent television, feature film, ANIMATION and new media production companies. Representing over a thousand independent production companies, it is governed by a Council elected by and from its membership. It also represents the interests of companies providing FINANCE, DISTRIBUTION, facilities and other commercial services relating to production. Although PACT engages in lobbying activities, its resources are mainly dedicated to providing a comprehensive range of production-related services for members, and to keeping members informed of business and creative opportunities available within Europe. It also negotiates terms of trade with the BBC, Channel 4 and Channel 5, and involves itself in all business matters relating to broadcasters' dealings with the independent sector. Around the turn of the century, it began to be involved with the internet, digital terrestrial and cable and satellite delivered programming.

PACT was in the news in September 2001 when some very high-profile actors supported EQUITY's claims on behalf of actors for a fairer share in film profits, initiating a fight against PACT and a round of tense negotiations. In the hope of averting a strike, PACT made some concessions about payments related to the success of a film's 'commercial exploitation' and its post-cinema life.

Paddick, Hugh (*b* Hoddesdon, 1915 – *d* London, 2000). Actor. Best known for his participation in the very popular 60s radio programme *Round the Horne*, especially for the camp duo, 'Julian and Sandy', with Kenneth WILLIAMS, involving outrageous innuendo and double-entendre. He studied originally for the Bar before taking to the stage, securing a part in the hit musical, *The Boy Friend* (1954). He went on to have a very successful theatrical career, including seasons with the National Theatre, and merely dabbled in films. The latter included two Frankie HOWERD vehicles, *Up Pompeii* and *Up the Chastity Belt* (1971).

Page, Anthony (*b* Bangalore, India, 1935). Director. Oxford-educated, trained at the Neighbourhood Playhouse, New York, he became assistant director at London's Royal Court Theatre in 1958, then its artistic director. He was a noted director of John OSBORNE's plays (including *A Patriot for Me*, 1965; *The Hotel in Amsterdam*, 1968) and his first film as director was an ADAPTATION of Osborne's *Inadmissible Evidence* (1968), an intelligent study of a human failure, which Page had also directed on stage (1964). His other cinema films are a patchy lot: only the little-seen *Alpha Beta* (1972), which chronicles a marital breakdown, has much interest, and his REMAKE of *The Lady Vanishes* (1979) is about as witless and charmless as could be conceived. He has had more success on TV, especially with BIOPICS such as *The Patricia Neal Story* (1981), for which he directed the UK sequences, and the mini-series *Middlemarch* (1994).

OTHER BRITISH FILMS: *Absolution* (1978), *Forbidden* (1984, UK/Ger/US, TV, some cinemas).

Paget-Bowman, Cicely (*b* Bedford Park, London, 1910). Actress. On stage from 1928, she served with the Volunteer Ambulance Corps and ENSA during WW2 and acted in plays ranging from SHAKESPEARE to Whitehall farce, but made only a handful of films. Her most noticeable role was as Lady Queensberry in *The Trials of Oscar Wilde* (1960), and on TV she had a good scene in an art gallery with Margaret TYZACK in *The Forsyte Saga* (1967).

OTHER BRITISH FILMS: *Conspirator* (1949), *The Miniver Story* (1950), *Isn't Life Wonderful!* (1953), *The Man Who Never Was* (1955), *Where the Spies Are* (1965), *The Trygon Factor* (1966).

Pagett, Nicola (*b* Cairo, 1945). Actress. RN: Scott. RADA-trained and very beautiful, Pagett ought to have had a more momentous career. Made her name as Elizabeth Bellamy in TV's *Upstairs, Downstairs* (1971) and did better than most as *Anna Karenina* (1977), and held her own in the star-studded 1984 stage revival of *Aren't We All?*, but films have largely passed her by. She had incisive but essentially secondary roles in *Privates on Parade* (1982) and *An Awfully Big Adventure* (1995). Some US films, including *Oliver's Story* (1978).

OTHER BRITISH FILMS INCLUDE: *The Viking Queen* (1966), *Anne of the Thousand Days* (1969), *There's a Girl in My Soup* (1970).

Pakeman, Kenneth (*b* Kingston, Surrey, 1911 – *d* Spain, 1965). Composer. With the BBC music staff from 1936 to 1947, he entered films in 1946, composing additional music for *Great Expectations* and for DOCUMENTARIES. Retired to Tarragona, Spain.

OTHER BRITISH FILMS INCLUDE: *Aircraft Carrier, Pacific Hitch-Hike* (1946), *North-East Corner, The October Man* (1947), *Beyond the Curtain* (1960).

Pal, George (*b* Cegled, Hungary, 1908 – *d* Los Angeles, 1980). Director, special effects. RN: Gyula Gyorgy Marczinczak. Celebrated director of SPECIAL EFFECTS-dominated US films such as *Destination Moon* (1950) and *War of the Worlds* (1953), Pal had worked in the cartoon department of UFA Studios, Berlin, before leaving when the Nazis came to power in 1933. His is essentially a Hollywood career, but he worked on a number of UK/Neth animated SHORTS in the later 30s, several scripted/storyboarded by Alexander MACKENDRICK. He experimented with COLOUR in *On Parade* (1936, using Gasparcolor), and other ADVERTISING FILMS also made for Horlicks, using TECHNICOLOR. In 1958, he returned to direct and produce *tom thumb*, which drew on his by now legendary special effects skills.

OTHER BRITISH FILMS: (d, shorts, animated) *Dolly Follies* (1935), *What-Ho-She-Bumps, Sky Pirates* (1937, + c), *Southsea Sweethearts* (1938), *Love on the Range* (1939, + c), *The Good Bear and the Bad Bear* (1940), *The Queen Was in the Parlour* (1941).

BIBLIOG: Gail Morgan Hickman, *The Films of George Pal*, 1977.

Palace Pictures NIK POWELL and STEVE WOOLLEY started Palace in the early 80s as a specialist video distributor and subsequently moved into film distribution and production. It became 'a studio in miniature' as one writer put it but had collapsed as a viable concern by 1992. If GOLDCREST represents 80s mainstream film culture then Palace represents its underside. Its distribution catalogues were a gallery of 80s INDEPENDENTS including John Cassavetes, the Coen brothers and John Waters from the US, Mike LEIGH and Peter GREENAWAY from Britain, together with an assortment of international ART-HOUSE names such as Fassbinder, Oshima and Bertolucci, and Sam Raimi's horror classic – *The Evil Dead* (1983). Its less experimental production record includes a number of Neil JORDAN titles, *The Company of Wolves* (1984), *Mona Lisa* (1986) and *The Crying Game* (1992), *Scandal* (1988) about the Profumo affair of the 1960s, and the ill-fated *Absolute Beginners* (1986).

BIBLIOG: Angus Finney, *The Egos Have Landed: the Rise and Fall of Palace Pictures*, 1996. Tom Ryall.

Palance, Jack (Lattimer, Penn., 1920). Actor. RN: Walter Jack Palahnuick. American tough guy, tall and craggy, who won an Oscar for his supporting role in *City Slickers* (1991) after years of the most vigorous scenery-chewing. Most of his best work was in the 50s, in films such as *Shane* (1953), as an unforgettable, black-clad villain, but he kept working in films made internationally. Over the decades, he appeared in ten British films, including the WARWICK FILMS CRIME story, *The Man Inside* (1958) and a go at *Dracula* (1973, UK/US, TV, some cinemas).

OTHER BRITISH FILMS INCLUDE: *Ten Seconds to Hell* (1958, UK/US), *Torture Garden* (1967), *Chato's Land* (1971), *Imagine* (1972), *Craze* (1973), *Hawk the Slayer* (1980).

Palin, Michael (*b* Sheffield, 1943). Actor, screenwriter. Multi-gifted Palin's career as actor and satirist dates back to his Oxford time with the Experimental Theatre Club, and he came to the fore with such 60s TV as *The Complete and Utter History of Britain* (1969). Joining the anarchic comedy satirists, the MONTY PYTHON team, he entered films via their *And Now for Something Completely Different* (1971), also acting in and co-writing the medieval romp, *Monty Python and the Holy Grail* (1974), *Life of Brian* (1979) and *The Meaning of Life* (1983, + songs). In other circumstances, he gave finely controlled comic performances as an endlessly compromised vicar in *The Missionary* (1981, + co-p, sc), as Maggie SMITH's naively honest chiropodist husband in *A Private Function* (1984), and as a stuttering crook in *A Fish Called Wanda* (1988). When not being a Python, he has been a somewhat bland TV personality in such programmes as *Around the World in 80 Days* (1989).

OTHER BRITISH FILMS: *Jabberwocky* (1977), *Time Bandits* (1981, + co-sc), *The Secret Policeman's Ball* (1979), *The Secret Policeman's Other Ball* (1982), *The Dress* (1984, short), *Brazil* (1985), *Consuming Passions* (1988, UK/US, co-play), *American Friends* (1991, + co-sc), *The Wind in the Willows* (1996), *Fierce Creatures* (1997, UK/US).

BIBLIOG: Jeremy Norvick, *Life of Michael: An Illustrated Biography of Michael Palin*, 2001.

Palk, Anna (*b* Looe, 1941 – *d* London, 1990). Actress. Beautiful lead and second lead of 60s films, including the HORROR movies *The Earth Dies Screaming* (1964) and *The Skull* (1965), and she is the new governess who arrives at the end of *The Nightcomers* (1971). Also active on stage and in such TV programmes as the gothic thriller series, *Witch Hunt* (1967). Died of cancer.

OTHER BRITISH FILMS: *Play It Cool* (1962), *The Frozen Dead* (starring), *Fahrenheit 451* (1966), *Mini Weekend* (1967), *Tower of Evil* (1972, UK/US).

Pallos, Stephen (*b* Budapest, 1902). Producer. In films from 1923, he spent 13 years with KORDA and LONDON FILMS, having met Korda in Berlin and, via Paris, going to England with him and Lajos BIRO in late 1931. Served in WW2 (1940–45) and post-war he and John STAFFORD set up Pendennis Films, which made such films as *Call of the Blood* (1948, UK/It, co-p) and *Jet Storm* (1959). There were other companies too, including Gibraltar, for which he produced *The Diamond* (1954) and *No Road Back* (1956), with minor Hollywood luminaries, and Tower, for which he executive-produced *Hotel Sahara* (1951) and *A Jolly Bad Fellow* (1963). He remained Korda's close friend but did not work for him again after 1948.

OTHER BRITISH FILMS INCLUDE: (co-p, unless noted) *Twenty Questions Murder Mystery* (1949), *The Fake* (1953, p), *Before I Wake* (1955), *No Road Back* (1956), *Sail into Danger* (1957, p), *Foxhole in Cairo* (1960), *Where the Spies Are* (1965), *Captain Nemo and the Underwater City* (1969, ex p), *To Catch a Spy* (1971, UK/Fr/US).

Palmer, Christopher (*b* London, 1946 – *d* London, 1995). Orchestrator. The main achievement of Palmer's short life (he died of an AIDS-related illness) was in the research into film music, both British and classical Hollywood. He became an honoured authority in this field, having, for instance, recovered many 'lost' scores by Miklos ROZSA. He worked with famous composers as arranger/orchestrator (e.g. with Elmer Bernstein on *Saturn 3*, 1980; with Maurice JARRE on *A Passage to India*, 1984) and composed the score for *Valmont* (1989, UK/Fr).

OTHER BRITISH FILMS INCLUDE: (orchestrator, unless noted) *The Wicked Lady* (1983, m arr), *The Bride* (1985, co-orch), *Castaway* (1986),

Track 29 (1988), *Slipstream* (1989), *Shirley Valentine* (1989, UK/US, co-orch).

Palmer, Ernest (*b* London, 1901 – *d* 1964). Cinematographer. Journeyman lenser of dozens of largely undistinguished films, Palmer entered films in the 30s at ELSTREE and did his best work for wartime EALING, on such pieces as *The Next of Kin* (1942) and *The Bells Go Down* (1943). There are a few other felicities among his six dozen credits, including Bernard VORHAUS's *The Ghost Camera* (1933), Michael POWELL's *The Edge of the World* (1937), Vernon SEWELL's FANTASY, *The Ghosts of Berkeley Square* (1947) and Daniel BIRT's gothic *The Three Weird Sisters* (1948). Competent over a wide GENRE range, he was too often mired in second-rate productions. Not to be confused with US cameraman of the same name.

OTHER BRITISH FILMS INCLUDE: *Children of Chance* (1930), *Tonight's the Night* (1932), *I Lived with You, Home Sweet Home* (1933), *Lazybones, While Parents Sleep, Birds of a Feather* (1935), *The Man Behind the Mask, Murder by Rope* (1936), *The Gang Show* (1937), *Flying Fifty-Five* (1939), *He Found a Star* (1941), *The Goose Steps Out, Go to Blazes* (1942), *For Those in Peril* (1944), *For You Alone, Waltz Time, Murder in Reverse, The Trojan Brothers* (1945), *Lisbon Story, Meet the Navy* (1946), *Uneasy Terms* (1948), *Bait* (1949), *Love's a Luxury* (1952), *It's a Grand Life* (1953), *The Heart Within, Zoo Baby* (1957), *Them Nice Americans* (1958), *The Crowning Touch* (1959).

Palmer, Geoffrey (*b* London, 1927). Actor. Palmer's good-natured bloodhound expression and wry delivery of well-written dialogue have made him a popular TV sitcom leading man, most notably opposite Wendy CRAIG in *Butterflies* (1978–83) and Judi DENCH in *As Time Goes By* (1992–2002), as the lugubrious Lionel. Former accountant, then amateur actor, he has made only about 15 films in over 40 years, though he is always distinctive, as – for instance – the British Ambassador in *The Honorary Consul* (1983) or the Queen's personal secretary in *Mrs Brown* (1997, UK/Ire/US). Forty years ago, he would have made half a dozen films every year.

OTHER BRITISH FILMS INCLUDE: *A Prize of Arms* (1961), *Ring of Spies* (1963), *O Lucky Man!* (1973), *A Zed & Two Noughts* (UK/Neth), *Clockwise* (1985), *A Fish Called Wanda, Hawks* (1988), *The Madness of King George* (1994, UK/US), *Tomorrow Never Dies* (1997, UK/US), *Rat* (2000, UK/US).

Palmer, Lilli (*b* Posen, Silesia, 1914 – *d* Los Angeles, 1986). Actress. RN: Lilli Peiser. A sophisticated presence in British and international cinema, Palmer was an actress of radiant beauty, intelligence, and warmth. In British films from 1935, she played a Western saloon girl in *The Great Barrier* (1937), and gave poignant performances in *Thunder Rock* (1942), *Beware of Pity* (1946) as the crippled heroine, and in *The Rake's Progress* (1945), acting opposite her first husband (1943–57), Rex HARRISON, as the wife who attempts suicide. After the war, she and Harrison went to Hollywood where she starred in a number of productions, including the excellent boxing melodrama, *Body and Soul* (1948). Active to the end of her life, she also wrote best-selling novels. Her two sisters, Maria Palmer (*b* Vienna, 1924 – *d* 1981), in Hollywood films, and Irene PRADOR were actresses. Second husband was Argentinian actor Carlos Thompson (*b* 1957 – *d* 1986), seen in international films.

OTHER BRITISH FILMS: *Crime Unlimited* (1935), *First Offence, Secret Agent* (1936), *Good Morning, Boys!, Sunset in Vienna* (1937), *Crackerjack* (1938), *A Girl Must Live, Blind Folly* (1939), *The Door With Seven Locks* (1940), *The Gentle Sex, English Without Tears* (1944), *The Long Dark Hall* (1951), *Conspiracy Of Hearts* (1960), *Operation Crossbow* (1965, UK/It), *Sebastian, Oedipus The King* (1967), *Nobody Runs Forever* (1968), *Night Hair Child* (1971), *The Holcroft Covenant* (1985).

BIBLIOG: Autobiography, *Change Lobsters and Dance*, 1975. Tim Bergfelder.

Paltrow, Gwyneth (*b* Los Angeles, 1972). Actress. Slender, blonde (usually) and beguiling American actress who has given some of her most attractive performances in British films and has mastered the accent to a remarkable degree. After a few minor roles, she won serious notice as wife of a policeman after a serial killer in *Se7en* (1995, US), but came to real fame with *Emma* (1996, UK/US), never losing the underlying sweetness of the presumptuously interfering heroine. Again in Britain, she did a versatile 'double turn' in the what-if romantic comedy success, *Sliding Doors* (1998, UK/US), and crowned her British achievement with an Oscar for *Shakespeare in Love* (1998, UK/US), in which her beauty and tenderness made her an appropriate inspiration for Juliet and, more crucially, Viola. US films include *Great Expectations* (1998), as a sexy take on Dickens's icy Estella.

OTHER BRITISH FILMS INCLUDE: *Jefferson in Paris* (1995), *Possession* (2002, UK/US).

Paluzzi, Luciana (*b* Rome, 1937). Actress. AKA: Paoluzzi. The lush Paluzzi, without ever being a major star, maintained her career for a quarter-century, mainly in Italian films, but with intermittent US and UK surfacings. In 1958, she played the object of sexual contention in RANK's enjoyable action tale, *Sea Fury*, and a brave Italian girl assisting Allied prisoners-of-war in WARWICK's *No Time to Die*; she had the female lead in the BOULTINGS' *Carlton-Browne of the FO* (1958) and, to her cost, resisted James BOND in *Thunderball* (1965). Had a major success in the American TV series, *Five Fingers* (1959) and was briefly (1960–62) married to US actor Brett Halsey.

OTHER BRITISH FILMS: *The One-Eyed Soldiers* (1966, UK/US/Yug), *99 Women* (UK/Ger/It/Sp), *Captain Nemo and the Underwater City* (1969).

Parallax Pictures Production company, set up in 1981 and later reconstituted; it has been responsible for Ken LOACH's films since *Riff-Raff* (1991), giving him the working base he so signally lacked in the earlier years of his career. Its producers are Sally HIBBIN, Sarah CURTIS and Rebecca O'BRIEN, its directors Loach, Les BLAIR and Chris MONGER. Along with SCALA PRODUCTIONS and GREENPOINT FILMS, it is one of the companies under the FILM CONSORTIUM, nominated for ARTS COUNCIL Lottery moneys in 1997.

Paramount–British Productions At the end of 1930, the American studio, Paramount Pictures signed a ten-year lease for a sound stage at ELSTREE from Herbert WILCOX's BRITISH AND DOMINIONS FILM CORPORATION. In July 1931, Paramount's London representative, J.C. Graham, registered its British subsidiary, Paramount–British, for the production of QUOTA QUICKIES. Specialising in literary ADAPTATIONS for the screen, Paramount–British were willing to spend more on their own productions than on films acquired from independent companies. Although the results were often disappointing, *Service for Ladies* (1932), Alexander KORDA's first British film, starring Leslie HOWARD was a success. In May 1932 Wilcox's B&D took over Paramount's quota, producing a film a month but with Paramount–British continuing to have a say in stories and casting. In 1934 Anthony HAVELOCK-ALLAN became head of production, employing many notable directors including Henry EDWARDS, Sidney MORGAN, George PEARSON and Adrian BRUNEL. When the B&D studio burned down in 1936, the Paramount quota was made by B&D at hired studios until production moved to Pinewood. Here, Paramount–

British's own production increased with directors including Harold FRENCH and John Paddy CARSTAIRS who directed the final Paramount–British film, *Incident in Shanghai* (1938). From then on Paramount–British obtained their quota from independent production companies. Paramount's post-war involvement in British cinema included funding production of such films as *So Evil My Love* (1948), *If . . .* (1968) and *The Italian Job* (1969), and it distributed many more in the US, including the Somerset MAUGHAM anthology films, *Trio* (1950) and *Encore* (1951), *Blind Date* (1959), *The Young Ones* (1961), *The Skull* (1965) and *Hitler: The Last Ten Days* (1973). Sarah Easen.

See also **Hollywood studios in Britain**.

Parély, Mila (*b* Paris, 1917). Actress. RN: Olga Perzynsky. Parély had starred in such famous French films as *La règle du jeu* (1939) and *La belle et la bête* (1946) before her two wholly unnecessary British appearances: as a possibly fake countess in *Snowbound* (1948) and the second lead in the second feature, *Blood Orange* (1953) – after the latter, she didn't film again for 36 years.

Parfitt, David (*b* Durham, 1958). Producer. Co-founder with Kenneth BRANAGH in 1987 of the Renaissance Theatre Company, Parfitt had previously been an actor, appearing mainly in TV and including *To the Lighthouse* (1983), starring Branagh. A noted West End producer of SHAKESPEARE, he was associate producer of Branagh's break-through film of *Henry V* (1989), also playing a small role. He, Branagh and business partner Stephen EVANS formed Renaissance Films which produced *Peter's Friends*, *Swan Song* (AAn/short, about John GIELGUD) (1992), *Much Ado About Nothing* (1993, UK/US), as well as Trevor NUNN's *Twelfth Night* (1996, UK/US) and *The Wings of the Dove* (1997, UK/US). He was co-producer on all of these and on *Frankenstein*, *The Madness of King George* (1994, UK/US) and *Shakespeare in Love* (1999, UK/US). In a word, much associated with the prestige arm of 90s British film-making.

Parfitt, Judy (*b* Sheffield, 1935). Actress. RADA. Compelling, somewhat sardonic looking and sounding actress who has done superb work in all the acting media. RADA-trained and on London stages from 1956, acclaimed for the title role in the Royal Court's *The Widowing of Mrs Holroyd* (1968), Gertrude in the Round House's *Hamlet* (1969), vividly repeating this role in Tony RICHARDSON's film version (1969) of this production, and witty and painfully moving in Peter NICHOLS's *Passion Play* (1984). Cinema has only rarely exploited her brilliance (three reasonably noticeable supporting roles: *Maurice*, 1987; *Diamond Skulls*, 1989; *Wilde*, 1997, UK/Ger/US/Jap), but TV has treated her better. She was Constance Lytton in the suffragette series, *Shoulder to Shoulder* (1974) and Mildred, soused in gin and malice, in *Jewel in the Crown* (1984). Married to actor **Tony Steedman** (*b* Warwickshire) who has also appeared in a few British films, including *Ascendancy* (1982) and *Mrs Dalloway* (1997, UK/Neth/US).

OTHER BRITISH FILMS: *Hide and Seek* (1963), *The Mind of Mr Soames* (1969), *Galileo* (1974, UK/Can), *Champions* (1983), *The Chain* (1984), *Loving* (1995), *Goodbye My Love, Element of Doubt* (1996).

Park, Nick (*b* Preston, 1958) Animator. Creator of the globally successful duo, Wallace and Gromit, Park was recently voted one of the five greatest animators of all time by fellow professionals. *A Grand Day Out* (1993), and the Oscar-winning *The Wrong Trousers* (1993) and *A Close Shave* (1995), all featuring the eccentric inventor and his canine companion,

have come to define English whimsy and nostalgia. *Creature Comforts* (1989), Park's first Oscar-winner, parodied DOCUMENTARY conventions and inspired a range of commercials; his penchant for caricaturing animals fully developed in the Dreamworks SKG-produced *Chicken Run* (2000, UK/US), which he co-directed with Aardman colleague, Peter Lord. Awarded CBE, 1997. Paul Wells.

Parker, Al (*b* Brooklyn, 1889 – *d* London, 1974). Director, agent. For many years an actor (allegedly at first with Douglas Fairbanks, Snr) and director in US films, then a stage producer, before coming to England in the early 30s to direct films for FOX at its WEMBLEY STUDIOS. Several of these, *Late Extra* (1935) *Troubled Waters* and *Blind Man's Bluff* (1936), starred James MASON, and, when Parker gave up directing and established an AGENCY for film and stage players, Mason became his prize client. His British films, all made at Wembley, are mainly negligible CRIME THRILLERS, but he went on to become one of the most influential agents in Britain. When his health failed, from 1965, his wife, former actress Margaret JOHNSTON, continued to run the agency which, in the 90s, still had such high-profile stars as Helen MIRREN on its books.

OTHER BRITISH FILMS INCLUDE: *After Dark, The Right to Live* (+p) (1932), *The Third Clue* (1934), *The Riverside Murder* (1935), *Strange Experiment, The £5 Man* (+ p) (1937), *Second Thoughts* (1938).

Parker, Sir Alan (*b* London, 1944). Director. Former copywriter who entered films via writing the screenplay for David PUTTNAM's tale of very young love, *SWALK* (1970), directed several SHORTS, then made *Bugsy Malone* (1976, + sc), a gangster movie in which all the roles were played by children. Came to serious fame with *Midnight Express* (1978), a nastily xenophobic account of a nice young American in a horrid Turkish prison for drug possession: repellant as some found it, it brought him a BAA and an AAn. Whatever one's views of his very variable output, he has certainly exhibited an energy uncommon in British cinema, and he has taken it to the US for the popular musical *Fame* (1980), the Viet veteran's fantasy, *Birdy* (1984) and the Southern Gothic bizarrerie of *Angel Heart* (1987), as well as the entirely appalling *The Road to Wellville* (1994). His British features have included the commercial success of *Pink Floyd the Wall* (1982), the visualisation of a pop singer's mental collapsing of fact and reality; the unexpectedly charming *The Commitments* (1991), about Dublin youth forming a soul band; the undervalued *Evita* (1996, UK/US, + co-p, co-sc); and *Angela's Ashes* (1999, Ire/US, + co-p, co-sc), which visually romanticises Irish poverty.

Parker has been an outspoken critic of various strategies involved in support for a British film industry, including the work of such bodies as the ARTS COUNCIL, BRITISH SCREEN FINANCE and the BFI PRODUCTION BOARD. In 2000, he became Chairman of the newly constituted FILM COUNCIL which was set up to reconsider the ways in which government money might be used to assist film production in this country. Knighted in 2002; some may have seen this as feeding the hand that bites them.

OTHER BRITISH FILMS: (shorts, d, sc) *No Hard Feelings* (1971), *Our Cissy, Footsteps* (1974); *Cliff Richard and the Shadows: Thank You Very Much* (1979, doc, d).

Parker, Cecil (*b* Hastings, 1897 – *d* Brighton, 1971). Actor. RN: Schwabe. One of the great CHARACTER ACTORS from their golden age, the 30s to the 60s. He could be menacing or authoritative or simply stuffy; he could draw the water of wit from the stone of the most unyielding dialogue. Listen as daughter Sheila SIM asks him in the mildewed *Dear Mr Prohack* (1949): 'Daddy, you can't lend me a hundred pounds?' 'That is so', he answers, not ceasing to set the table the while. The timing, the absorption in the role of benign but unbudgeable father, is a minute illustration of what made Parker so cherishable. On stage since 1922 and in films from 1933, he made his first real mark as 'Todhunter', the nervous would-be adulterer in *The Lady Vanishes* (1938), and twice more he and Linden TRAVERS were involved in uneasy liaisons – in *The Stars Look Down* (1939), where she is bored with him, and *Quartet* (1948), he always anxious about discovery. He could be austerely unsympathetic as in the title role of *Captain Boycott* and in *Hungry Hill* (1947); is wonderfully comic as the pained butler in *The Chiltern Hundreds* (1949) and the shifty 'Major' in *The Ladykillers* (1955); and touching as the middle-class probation officer trying to do his job in *I Believe in You* (1952). The truth is that he probably never gave a poor performance – and that there is much more variety in his work than might be supposed. Fortunately for the cinema, he came to prefer it to the stage. WW1 service left him with a neck injury which partly accounted for the courteously tilted head, and which became part of the actor's persona.

OTHER BRITISH FILMS: *The Golden Cage, A Cuckoo in the Nest* (1933), *Flat No. 3, The Silver Spoon, Princess Charming, The Office Wife, Nine Forty-Five, Little Friend, Dirty Work, The Blue Squadron* (UK/It), *Lady in Danger* (1934), *Me and Marlborough, Foreign Affaires, Crime Unlimited, Her Last Affaire* (1935), *The Man Who Changed His Mind, Jack of All Trades, Men of Yesterday, Dishonour Bright* (1936), *Dark Journey, Storm in a Teacup* (1937), *Old Iron, Housemaster, The Citadel, It Might Be You . . . !* (short) (1938), *Sons of the Sea, She Couldn't Say No, The Spider* (1939), *Under Your Hat, Two for Danger* (1940), *The Saint's Vacation, Dangerous Moonlight, Ships with Wings* (1941), *Caesar and Cleopatra* (1945), *The Magic Bow* (1946), *The Woman in the Hall* (1947), *The Weaker Sex, The First Gentleman* (1948), *Under Capricorn* (1949), *Tony Draws a Horse* (1950), *The Man in the White Suit, The Magic Box, His Excellency* (1951), *Isn't Life Wonderful!* (1953), *Father Brown, For Better, for Worse, The Constant Husband* (1954), *True as a Turtle, It's Great to Be Young!* (1956), *The Admirable Crichton, Happy is the Bride* (1957), *A Tale of Two Cities, Indiscreet, I Was Monty's Double* (1958), *The Night We Dropped a Clanger, The Navy Lark* (1959), *Swiss Family Robinson* (UK/US), *A French Mistress, Follow That Horse!, The Pure Hell of St Trinian's* (1960), *Petticoat Pirates, On the Fiddle* (1961), *Vengeance* (UK/Ger), *The Amorous Prawn* (1962), *The Iron Maiden, Heavens Above!, The Comedy Man* (1963), *Guns at Batasi, Carry On Jack* (1964), *The Amorous Adventures of Moll Flanders, A Study in Terror* (1965), *Circus of Fear* (1966), *The Magnificent Two* (1967), *Oh! What a Lovely War* (1969).

Parker, Charles E. (*b* Nova Scotia, 1910 – *d* Watford, 1977). Make-up artist. For a decade, Parker was in charge of the make-up department at MGM–BRITISH, working on such films as *Knights of the Round Table* (1953) and *Beau Brummell* (1954), subsequently working elsewhere on such major films as Ken RUSSELL's *Women in Love* (1969) and – very taxing to Parker's particular skills – *The Devils* (1971). John MILLS's squint-eyed village idiot makeup in *Ryan's Daughter* (1970) was another major challenge. Also some US films, including *Star Wars* (1977).

OTHER BRITISH FILMS INCLUDE: *The New Lot* (1943, short), *Edward, My Son, Under Capricorn* (1949), *Ivanhoe* (1952), *Moby Dick* (+ adviser re whale model), *The Barretts of Wimpole Street* (1956), *tom thumb* (1958), *Lawrence of Arabia* (1962), *Zulu* (1964), *Promise Her Anything* (1965), *The Magus* (1968), *Trog* (1970, monster design), *The Ruling Class* (1971), *Murder on the Orient Express* (1974, co-).

Parker, Clifton (*b* London, 1905 – *d* Marlow, Bucks, 1990). Composer. Spent his pre-film career as orchestral player,

entering films in 1942, going on to score the famous DOCUMENTARIES, *Western Approaches* (1944) and *Children on Trial* (1946), for the CROWN FILM UNIT. In fiction films, his versatility encompassed the melodramatic frissons of *Blanche Fury* (1947), the HORROR of *Night of the Demon* (1957), the war heroics of *Sink the Bismarck!* (1960), and much more besides.

OTHER BRITISH FILMS INCLUDE: *Yellow Canary* (1943), *Perfect Strangers, Johnny Frenchman* (1945), *The Man Within, Daughter of Darkness* (1947), *My Brother's Keeper* (1948), *The Blue Lagoon* (1949), *Treasure Island, The Wooden Horse* (1950), *The Gift Horse* (1952), *The Sword and the Rose, Single-Handed* (1953), *The Teckman Mystery* (1954), *Passage Home* (1955), *The Feminine Touch* (1956), *The Birthday Present* (1957), *Virgin Island, Sea of Sand* (1958), *The House of the Seven Hawks* (1959), *The Big Day, The Hellfire Club* (1960), *Taste of Fear* (1961), *The Informers* (1963).

Parker, Jack (*b* 1885 – *d* ?). Cinematographer. Entered films, 1908, first with CLARENDON and then with CRICKS and Martin and BRITISH INSTRUCTIONAL. Began as cinematographer on the silent film, *Boadicea* (1926), did some notably innovative work on ASQUITH's *Tell England* (1931), then settled to the usual 30s GENRES, finishing his career as camera operator on some notable EALING films of the 40s and making many DOCUMENTARIES and SHORT FILMS for GB INSTRUCTIONAL. Not to be confused with Ealing camera operator **Jack Parker**, who worked on such films as *Dead of Night* (1945) and *The Captive Heart* (1946).

OTHER BRITISH FILMS INCLUDE: (c) *The Battles of the Coronel and Falkland Islands* (1927, co-cc), *Carnival* (1931, co-c), *Dance Pretty Lady* (1932), *Meet My Sister* (1933), *Drake of England* (co-c), *Dandy Dick* (1935), *The End of the Road* (co-c), *Annie Laurie* (1936), *Old Mother Riley, Rose of Tralee* (1937), *Stepping Toes* (1938), *We'll Meet Again, The Rose of Tralee* (co-c) (1942).

Parker, Mary (*b* Bitton, 1930). Actress. Brought up in Australia by English parents, returned to England to take up a film test (directed by Basil DEARDEN) at EALING in the early 50s. Before going back to Australia in late 1956 to become a popular figure in early TV there, she had starred in England in several plays, made five feature films, including *You Lucky People* (1955), in which she co-starred with Tommy TRINDER, and appeared in several television playlets for Douglas FAIRBANKS. She did *not* marry Harold FRENCH, no matter what his obituaries said.

OTHER BRITISH FILMS: *Triple Blackmail, The Diamond Expert, Third Party Risk* (1955), *The Hostage* (1956).

Parker, Molly (*b* Vancouver, *c* 1973). Actress. Most of Parker's work has been in little-seen but in some cases well-regarded Canadian features, including *Kissed* (1996), for which she won a Genie award. The beguiling, oval-faced Parker was very affecting as the pregnant wife of a hapless husband in Michael WINTERBOTTOM's *Wonderland* (1999) and as a very different kind of wife in *Sunshine* (2000, UK/Austria/Can/Ger/Hung). Now seems to divide her very busy career between Canada and California.

OTHER BRITISH FILMS: *The Intruder, Ladies Room* (1999, UK/Can), *The War Bride* (2000, UK/Can).

Parker, Nathaniel (*b* London, 1962). Actor. Son of former British Rail Chairman, Sir Peter Parker, and brother of director Oliver PARKER, in whose *Othello* (1995, UK/US) he played the luckless Cassio, Parker worked mainly in TV in later years, including the title role in the mini-series, *Inspector Linley Mysteries* (2001). His best known film roles to date are as poet Wilfred Owen in Derek JARMAN's *War Requiem* (1989), a vivid

Laertes in ZEFFIRELLI's *Hamlet* (1990, UK/Fr/Sp/US) and as Rochester in the ADAPTATION of Jean Rhys's *Jane Eyre* prequel, *Wide Sargasso Sea* (1993, Aust). Married (1992) to **Anna Patrick** who played Emilia in *Othello* and had a small role in *An Ideal Husband* (1999, UK/US).

OTHER BRITISH FILMS: *A Village Affair* (1994).

Parker, Oliver (*b* London, 1960). Director. After making several films as an actor, including *Nuns on the Run* (1990) and, as one of five gambling addicts, *The Big Game* (1995), Parker made an impressive directorial debut with *Othello* (1995, UK/US, + sc). Impressive, that is, as a solidly intelligent, not particularly innovative version of the play; but his next literary excursion, *An Ideal Husband* (1999, UK/US, + sc), was marked by a sharp sense of its contemporary relevance and a willingness to take risks in offending WILDE purists in the interests of dis-embalming the piece. This success no doubt encouraged him to take on next *The Importance of Being Earnest* (2002, (UK/US), untouched on screen, except for TV and an unseen all-black US version (1991) since ASQUITH's seemingly definitive ADAPTATION (1952). Married to Thandie NEWTON; brother of actor Nathaniel PARKER.

OTHER BRITISH FILMS: (a) *Hellraiser* (1987), *Hellraiser II* (1988), *Shepherd on the Rock* (1995).

Parkinson, H(arry) B(roughton) (*b* Blackburn, 1884 – *d* Wallasey, 1970). Producer, director. Parkinson entered the industry in 1908 as an exhibitor, becoming a producer/director in 1920. He was noted for the series of one- and two-reel 'novelty' SHORTS he produced between 1922 and 1928, including *Tense Moments from Great Plays* (1922), *Wonderful London* (1924, SERIES), *London's Famous Cabarets, London after Dark* (series) (1925), *Across the Footlights* (1926), *Bindle* (1926), starring Tom Reynolds as the character created by Herbert Jenkins, and *Cameo Operas* (1927). Features he produced and directed include *The Law Divine* (1920), *Trapped by the Mormons* (1922) and *Married to a Mormon* (1922). As the last two titles indicate, Parkinson was attracted to the lurid and to films with publicity appeal. His most outrageous production was *The Life Story of Charles Chaplin* (1926), starring Chick Wango in the title role; as a result of legal action, the film was never released. Parkinson retired in 1930 to open a hotel. His son **Roy Parkinson** (*b* Surbiton, 1916) was a production manager, at MGM–British and other studios in the post-war decades. AS.

Parkyn, Leslie (*b* 1918 – *d* Torremolinos, 1983). Producer, executive producer. Now best remembered for his association with Julian WINTLE and their work with INDEPENDENT ARTISTS at BEACONSFIELD STUDIOS, where Parkyn joined Wintle in 1958. Previously he had worked for Production Facilities Ltd (1945–49), resigning to become associate producer on *Morning Departure* (1950). During the 50s he joined British Film Makers Ltd at PINEWOOD, forming an association with Sergei NOLBANDOV, and produced several successful films for RANK, including *The Kidnappers* (1953, co-p) and *Tiger Bay* (1959, co-p). He and Wintle followed a policy of mixing 'B' MOVIES with main features, using the former as training grounds for directors. Some of their more prestigious films, such as *This Sporting Life* (1963), bore the label 'A Wintle/Parkyn Production'. The studio ceased production in 1963 and Parkyn retired to Spain where he died.

OTHER BRITISH FILMS INCLUDE: (co-p, unless noted) *It Started in Paradise* (1952), *The Woman for Joe* (1955, p), *Tiger in the Smoke* (1956,

p), *The Big Day, Circus of Horrors* (1960), *The Man in the Back Seat, Very Important Person, House of Mystery* (1961), *Night of the Eagle, Crooks Anonymous* (1962), *Father Came Too!* (1963).

Parr-Davies, Harry (aka Harry Davies) (*b* Briton Ferry, 1914 – *d* London, 1955). Composer. Songwriter with many hits to his credit, who contributed songs to several Gracie FIELDS (for whom he was at one stage accompanist) and George FORMBY vehicles of the 30s, as well as to the romantic MELODRAMA, *Lisbon Story* (1946).

OTHER BRITISH FILMS INCLUDE: (comp, unless noted) *This Week of Grace* (1933), *Sing As We Go!* (1934, lyrics), *No Limit* (co-songs), *Look Up and Laugh* (1935), *Keep Your Seats, Please, Queen of Hearts* (1936, co-songs), *The Show Goes On* (1937, co-m/lyrics), *We're Going to be Rich, I See Ice!* (co-m/lyrics) (1938), *Sailors Three* (1940), *It Happened One Sunday* (1944), *Lilacs in the Spring* (1954).

Parrish, Robert (*b* Columbus, Georgia, 1916 – *d* Southampton, NY, 1995). Director. Capable American director and former editor and sound man (much associated with John FORD), who made some British features in the 50s and 60s. He made three proficient British action films – *Rough Shoot* (1953), *The Purple Plain* (1954), *Fire Down Below* (1957), all with US stars (Joel McCrea, Gregory PECK and Rita Hayworth, respectively) – and then, in the 60s, became involved in three jokey duds: *Casino Royale* (1967, co-d), *The Bobo* (1967) and that *echt*-60s ephemera, *Duffy* (1968). Shared an AA for editing *Body and Soul* (1948, US). His sister was actress Helen Parrish (1922–59).

OTHER BRITISH FILMS: *Doppelgänger* (1969), *A Town Called Bastard* (1971, UK/Sp), *The Marseille Contract* (1974, UK/Fr).

Parry, Gordon (*b* Liverpool, 1908 – *d* Rambouillet, France, 1981). Director. After starting as actor in the late 30s, Parry acquired experience as assistant director with GAUMONT–BRITISH, as production manager with ROCK PRODUCTIONS and, from 1940, as EALING's unit manager for PROPAGANDA film-making. After acting as 2nd unit director on *In Which We Serve* (1942) and associate producer with Anatole DE GRUNWALD on *The Demi-Paradise* (1943) and *The Way to the Stars* (1945), he was given the chance to direct two De Grunwald productions: the PORTMANTEAU comedy-drama, *Bond Street* (1948), and the earnest prison drama, *Now Barabbas Was a Robber* (1949), handling his actors and multiple story strands with workmanlike style. He wasn't able to sustain this level of production in the 50s: *Tom Brown's Schooldays* (1951) was a flat ADAPTATION of the famous tale; and *Innocents in Paris* (1953) scarcely warranted its star cast. *Woman of Twilight* (1952), another multi-stranded story, was a strongly acted drama of single mothers and baby-farming and *Front Page Story* (1953), episodes in the life of a newspaper staff, is probably his best film of the decade, with sure control over its plots and its pacing. Of his other stage adaptations, *Fast and Loose* (1954) is an inferior remake of *Cuckoo in the Nest* (1933) and *Sailor Beware* (1956) at least enshrines Peggy MOUNT's definitive stage performance. His film career just dwindled; he drifted into TV for a couple of years, then retired to Spain. Actress Natasha PARRY is his daughter.

OTHER BRITISH FILMS: (d, unless noted) *Third Time Lucky* (1949), *Golden Arrow* (1949, released 1952), *Midnight Episode* (1950), *Night Was Our Friend* (1951, p), *A Yank in Ermine* (1955), *A Touch of the Sun* (1956), *The Surgeon's Knife* (1957), *Tread Softly Stranger* (1958), *The Navy Lark, Friends and Neighbours* (1959).

Parry, Natasha (*b* London, 1930). Actress. Slender brunette beauty of the 50s who filmed only sporadically after that.

Daughter of director Gordon PARRY, she began her career as one of 'Cochran's Young Ladies', had small parts in two of her father's films – *Golden Arrow* (1949, released 1952) and *Midnight Episode* (1950) – before winning one of the starring quartet of roles in EALING's *Dance Hall* (1950). She was the wife's best friend, and one of the husband's quarries, in *Knave of Hearts* (1954, UK/Fr), the Eurasian nurse in *Windom's Way* (1957) and a youthful Lady Capulet in *Romeo and Juliet* (1968, UK/It), but her career faded out after that, and she reappeared only in rare international films. Married Peter BROOK in 1951.

OTHER BRITISH FILMS: *The Dark Man* (1950), *Crow Hollow* (1952), *The Rough and the Smooth* (1959), *The Fourth Square* (1961), *Girl in the Headlines* (1963), *Oh! What a Lovely War* (1969).

Parry, Richard (*b* Kenya, *c* 1967). Director. Parry made a substantial reputation as a news cameraman in such trouble spots as Zaire and Bosnia, before turning his attention to Brixton, a once in-the-news trouble spot nearer to home. Brixton has the title role in Parry's first feature film, *South West Nine* (2001), a drama of interlocking lives, made for producer Allan NIBLO's Fruit Salad Films.

Parsons, Nicholas (*b* Grantham, 1928). Actor. Rep experience before his West End debut in *The Hasty Heart* (1946) and his first film, *The Master of Bankdam* (1947). Became well-known on TV as the somewhat flummoxed foil to the star on *The Arthur Haynes Show* (1956–66) and as the quiz-master on *Sale of the Century* (1972–83). Film roles were mostly in comedies exploiting his easily bewildered persona, as in *Happy is the Bride* (1957), one of several films for the BOULTING brothers, as the bridegroom's brother with a daffy girlfriend. A former engineering student, he also broadcast frequently on radio with the BBC Repertory Company. Married to actress **Denise Bryer**, who provided voices in several animated films, including *Labyrinth* (1986).

OTHER BRITISH FILMS INCLUDE: *To Dorothy a Son* (1954), *Simon and Laura* (1955), *Eyewitness, Brothers in Law* (1956), *Carlton-Browne of the FO* (1958), *Too Many Crooks* (1959), *Doctor in Love* (1960), *Carry On Regardless* (1961), *Murder Ahoy, Every Day's a Holiday* (1964), *The Wrong Box* (1966), *Danger Point* (1971), *Spy Story* (1976).

BIBLIOG: Autobiography, *The Straight Man: My Life in Comedy*, 1994.

Pascal, Gabriel (*b* Arad, Transylvania, 1894 – *d* New York, 1954). Producer, director. RN: Gabor Lehöl. This Hungarian expatriate was the somewhat improbable choice of playwright George Bernard SHAW to film some of his plays. After acting on the Austrian stage and making films in Germany, he came to England in the mid 30s. Considered by some a 'con man' and a fraud, and by others a genius, Pascal captivated Shaw who, having resisted appeals from other film producers, agreed to allow him to make the celebrated film version of *Pygmalion* (1938), directed by Anthony ASQUITH and with an outstanding cast including Wendy HILLER and Leslie HOWARD (co-d). Although Pascal is credited as director of his next Shaw ADAPTATION, *Major Barbara* (1941) which also starred Hiller, some participants maintain that David LEAN shot most of the film. Pascal's lavish 1945 technicolour production of *Caesar and Cleopatra* proved an expensive failure in spite of strong performances by Vivien LEIGH and Claude RAINS. His directorial style is generally criticised as being static and stagy, but his ability to gain Shaw's trust enabled film productions of several of his better plays. Also produced *Androcles and the Lion* (1952) in Hollywood.

OTHER BRITISH FILMS: (p) *Reasonable Doubt* (1936), *Café Mascot* (1936).

BIBLIOG: Biography, Valerie Pascal, *The Disciple and his Devil* 1970; Bernard F. Dukore (ed), *Bernard Shaw and Gabriel Pascal (Selected Correspondence of Bernard Shaw)*, 1996. Stephen Shafer.

Pasco, Richard (*b* London, 1926). Actor. Sharp-featured character player, first noticed as one of Joe Lampton's Dramatic Society friends in *Room at the Top* (1958), and 40 years on he was still being incisive as Dr Jenner in *Mrs Brown* (1997, UK/Ire/US). In between, the Central School-trained actor was very busy on stage, with the Royal Court (where he played Jimmy Porter in a revival of *Look Back in Anger*, 1957), often with the Bristol Old Vic and the RSC, but made only a handful of films. Was in several of the BBC's TV Shakespeare, including Brutus in *Julius Caesar* (1979). Married (2) to Barbara LEIGH-HUNT. Awarded CBE 1977.

OTHER BRITISH FILMS: *Kill Me Tomorrow* (1957), *Yesterday's Enemy* (1959), *Sword of Sherwood Forest* (1960), *Hot Enough for June, The Gorgon* (1964), *Rasputin the Mad Monk* (1965).

Passmore, Henry (*b* London, 1905). Producer. Entered films in 1931 and worked in various capacities before being appointed managing director for HAMMER PRODUCTIONS in 1935. After WW2 naval service (1940–45), he worked with the CHILDREN'S FILM FOUNDATION, and was then appointed production manager of RANK's HIGHBURY STUDIOS where he produced such 'B' MOVIES as *Fly Away Peter* (1948). He subsequently joined ACT FILMS (1951–54) and, for his own company, produced *The Delavine Affair* (1954), directed by former Highbury colleague, Douglas PEIRCE.

OTHER BRITISH FILMS INCLUDE: (p, unless noted) *The Mystery of the Marie Celeste* (1935), *Sporting Love* (1936, assoc p), *The Last Adventurers* (1937), *Stage Frights* (1947), *Love in Waiting* (1948), *Children Galore* (1954), *Conscience Bay* (1960, co-p), *The Missing Note* (1961).

pastoral images 'Pastoral' originally meant 'pertaining to the herdsman', but its connotations have broadened to embrace various RURAL (or semi-rural) occupations, environments, and values. The pastoral world has long provided British film-makers with a subject or setting, both in the original sense (vignettes of shepherds' lives in *Owd Bob*, 1937; *The Loves of Joanna Godden*, 1947; *Far from the Madding Crowd*, 1967), and, more prolifically, in the broader, newer senses, this usage dating back to the silent days, with films such as Cecil HEPWORTH's *Comin' Thro' the Rye* (1923), which offers a nostalgically pictorial account of the rural past.

In *A Pretty British Affair* (1981), a BBC documentary on Michael POWELL, the narrator claims of the director that his 'very idea of Englishness, of Britishness' was 'incarnated in the pastoral, in the landscape, in a distant church spire, a lowing herd.' These tranquil motifs are all to be found in Powell's *A Canterbury Tale* (1944), though the main plot involves a group of village girls who become the victims of a local J.P.'s strange fetishistic practices. Threats to innocence or the imagined simplicities and harmonies of 'traditional' country life are an integral element of the pastoral mode in art, and in British film such threats derive from various sources: war and its aftermath (in *Cottage to Let*, 1941; *Went the Day Well?*, 1942; *Great Day*, 1945, *It's Not Cricket*, 1948); demonic possession (*The Village of the Damned*, 1960; *The Innocents*, 1961); crime (*Town on Trial*, 1956, *Whistle Down the Wind*, 1961); advancing technology (*Song of the Road*, 1937); meddling by city-based politicians and bureaucrats (*The Titfield Thunderbolt*, 1952), or combinations of various such factors (*Tawny Pipit*, 1944).

Forays into rural landscapes may offer characters temporary respite from the frustrations and dangers of other types of environment: metropolitan decadence (*Fanny by Gaslight*, 1944); suburban routines (*Holiday Camp*, 1947); the regimentation of a Borstal (*The Loneliness of the Long Distance Runner*, 1962); the bleakness of industrial towns (*This Sporting Life*, 1964). The almost obligatory pastoral interludes in realist cinema of the 1960s functioned as a counterpoint to and critique of the perceived monotony of urban working-class existence.

Resisting temptations to sentimentalise the rural landscape, some film-makers (notably Lance COMFORT in *Bang! You're Dead*, 1953, and *The Break*, 1962, or Ken LOACH in *Kes*, 1969) have been careful to register its austerities as well as its serenities. Other films expose the threats to harmony which emerge from social or psychological tensions within rural communities themselves (a village in *Time Gentlemen Please!*, 1952; a country house in *Blanche Fury*, 1947).

More recent pastoral images reflect a studiously disenchanted or parodic outlook (*The Ploughman's Lunch*, 1983; *Withnail & I*, 1986; *Cold Comfort Farm*, 1995; *The War Zone*, 1999, UK/It); though in general we catch only incidental glimpses of them now, except in the host of 'period' or 'HERITAGE' films, mainly adapted from literary classics. That they still have some place in modern life and postmodern consciousness is suggested by the profusion of sheep as well as spires in *Four Weddings and a Funeral* (1994, UK/US); even the thoroughly knowing American heroine momentarily contemplates a shepherdess-style bridal-gown. Ian Britain.

Patch, Wally (*b* London, 1888 – *d* London, 1970). Actor. RN: Vinnicombe. Versatile character player and comedian of over 175 British films during four decades, usually playing beefy working-class types, enlisted men, or policemen, mostly in comedies, but also in other GENRES. A MUSIC HALL performer for many years, he was almost 40 when he began playing small, memorable parts in silent features and SHORTS, and flourished in early sound features when directors like Adrian BRUNEL and Anthony ASQUITH found him a dependable presence in character roles. By 1932, he had major roles in 'QUOTA QUICKIES' like the drama, *Heroes of the Mine*, opposite Moore MARRIOTT. Sometimes starring in low-budget comedies like *Henry Steps Out* (1940), he also supported comedians like Will HAY and George FORMBY, in their more prominent comedies. Busiest in the 30s and 40s, he continued into the early 60s, finishing his performing career with several vivid TV appearances.

OTHER BRITISH FILMS INCLUDE: *High Treason* (1929), *Castle Sinister* (1932), *Britannia of Billingsgate, Don Quixote* (UK/Fr) *Tiger Bay*, (1933), *That's My Uncle* (1934), *Marry the Girl* (1935), *The Man Who Could Work Miracles* (1936), *The High Command, Missing, Believed Married* (1937), *Bank Holiday, Alf's Button Afloat* (1938), *Inspector Hornleigh, What Would You Do, Chums?* (1939), *They Came by Night, Charley's Big-Hearted Aunt* (1940), *Gert and Daisy's Weekend, Cottage to Let, The Common Touch* (1941), *The Butler's Dilemma* (1943), *Old Mother Riley at Home* (1945), *George in Civvy Street* (1946), *Calling Paul Temple* (1948), *Hammer the Toff* (1952), *Josephine and Men* (1955), *The Naked Truth* (1957), *Serena* (1962). Stephen Shafer.

Paterson, Bill (*b* Glasgow, 1945). Actor. Authoritative character player who grabbed viewers' attention as a DJ in the Scottish-set *Comfort and Joy* (1984) and has been a fixture on screens small and large ever since. On TV, he was Michael GAMBON's psychiatrist in *The Singing Detective* (1986), the equivocal Baxter in *Oliver's Travels* (1995), the humane Dr Gibson in *Wives and Daughters* (1999), and much else besides. On screen, his comfortable, homely features could be

sympathetically invoked, as in *Truly Madly Deeply* (1990), as Juliet STEVENSON's boss, comically in *The Witches* (1989, US) as Brenda BLETHYN's taxed husband, and otherwise as Ratcliffe, adherent of *Richard III* (1995). He is one of those actors who occupies a middle ground between star and character man.

OTHER BRITISH FILMS INCLUDE: *The Odd Job* (1978), *Scotch Myths* (1982), *The Ploughman's Lunch* (1983), *The Killing Fields, A Private Function* (1984), *Defence of the Realm* (1985), *Coming Up Roses* (1986), *Hidden City* (1987), *Just Ask for Diamond* (1988), *The Rachel Papers* (1989), *The Object of Beauty* (1991, UK/US), *Chaplin* (1992, UK/Fr/It/Jap/US), *Victory* (1995, UK/Fr/Ger, released 1998), *Spice World* (1977), *Hilary and Jackie* (1998), *Heart, The Match* (1999, UK/Ire/US), *Complicity* (2000), *Crush* (2001, UK/Ger).

Paterson, Neil (*b* Edinburgh, 1916). Screenwriter. Now best remembered for his AA-winning screenplay for *Room at the Top* (1958), the breakthrough ADAPTATION of John BRAINE's novel of sex and working-class aspiration. Throughout the 50s he had contributed to attractive films such as the two set in Nova Scotia, *The Kidnappers* (1953, + story) and *High Tide at Noon* (1957), but he wrote only one post-AA screenplay, *The Spiral Road* (1962, US, co-sc). All his films are notable for their humane concern for predicament and relationship. Held such positions as Director Grampian TV; committee member of Scottish Arts Council; and Governor of the BFI and the NATIONAL FILM SCHOOL.

OTHER BRITISH FILMS: (co-sc, unless noted) *Devil on Horseback* (1954), *The Woman for Joe* (1955, sc), *The Shiralee* (1957), *Innocent Sinners* (1958).

Paterson, Pat (*b* Bradford, 1911 – *d* Phoenix, Arizona, 1978). Actress. Pretty blue-eyed blonde who starred in a dozen or so minor British films of the 30s, rising to bigger things, though in a supporting role, in *Bitter Sweet* (1933), her last before leaving for Hollywood. In 1934, she starred with Spencer Tracy in the long-forgotten, *Bottoms Up*, and also married Charles Boyer, to whom she stayed married until her death and who committed suicide four days later. Apart from her last, *Idiot's Delight* (1939), her US films were as negligible as her British ones.

OTHER BRITISH FILMS INCLUDE: *The Other Woman, The Great Gay Road* (1931), *Murder on the Second Floor* (1932), *Beware of Women, The Bermondsey Kid, Head of the Family* (1933).

Pathé The French firm of Pathé Frères established an agency in Britain in 1902. It began film production in 1910 with the NEWSREEL *Pathé's Animated Gazette*. A film studio was established at Great Portland Street, and fiction films produced under the 'Britannia' brand, then through a subsidiary, Union Film Publishing Company, using the 'Big Ben' brand, with George PEARSON as house director. Fiction film production ceased with the First World War, but the newsreel flourished and in 1918 the CINEMAGAZINE *Pathé Pictorial* was launched, joined in the 20s by *Eve's Film Review*. Pathé's major business, however, was in DISTRIBUTION, where it held considerable power in the 20s, merging with First National and Provincial Cinema Theatres under John MAXWELL in 1927 to form the production–exhibition–distribution combine First National–Pathé. Feature film production began in 1927, with Graham CUTTS, Manning HAYNES and Jack RAYMOND as directors. The Pathé name was lost in 1931 when the Warner Brothers–First National company was formed, only to re-emerge in 1933 when Pathé was absorbed within Maxwell's ABPC group. ABPC used the Pathé name in a variety of forms, including Pathé Pictures, which distributed features made at the WELWYN studios.

Meanwhle the Pathé newsreel flourished, and a new cinemagazine lasted throughout the decade, *Pathetone Weekly*. It was the newsreel that maintained the Pathé name into the 40s, changing its name to *Pathé News* in 1946. After the war the distribution side of ABPC took on the name of Associated British–Pathé. In 1958 this merged with Warner Brothers to form Warner–Pathé, which then handled Warners, ABPC, Allied Artists, *Pathé News* and *Pathé Pictorial* in British cinemas. *Pathé Pictoral* ceased production in 1969, *Pathé News* the year after, but the Pathé library now contained a substantial record of the century. Ownership of ASSOCIATED BRITISH and with it the Pathé News library passed to EMI in 1969, and the newsreels were handed on to Thorn–EMI to Cannon to Weintraub, until taken on in 1995 by a newly-formed company, British–Pathé. Luke McKernan.

Pathé Pictures One of the three companies (DNA and THE FILM CONSORTIUM were the other two) which won a substantial – £33m – Lottery grant from the ARTS COUNCIL in 1998, the French-based Pathé had critical success with *Ratcatcher* and critical and some commercial success with *An Ideal Husband* (both 1999) and a stake in the very popular animated feature, *Chicken Run* (2000, UK/US). There was controversy over a French company's being singled out for Arts Council support, but its success rating at least equals that of the other two, without being in any way remarkable. Its head of production is Andrea Calderwood and the production units associated with it are: THIN MAN FILMS and Imagine Films; Allied Filmmakers and Allied Films; NFH; Sarah RADCLYFFE Productions; FRAGILE FILMS; MW Entertainment.

Patrick, Nigel (*b* London, 1913 – *d* London, 1981). Actor, director. RN: Wemyss. Authoritative leading man of stage and screen who had a sure comic touch, and excelled at cynics and suave, shallow types: spivs, men-about-town and philanderers. Active in theatre as actor and director from 1932, perfecting the then-endemic smooth 'drawing-room comedy' acting style. His film career gained momentum with a series of 'spiv' roles: in *Spring in Park Lane* (1948), a returning deserter and black marketeer in *Silent Dust* (1949), and memorably in *Noose* (1948) as Bar Gorman, with spotted bow tie and pencil-thin moustache. Also played a sponger in the 'Ways and Means' episode of *Meet Me Tonight* (1952), was a schoolmaster in *The Browning Version* (1951), and Mr Jingle in *The Pickwick Papers* (1952), and was BAA-nominated as the unflappable test pilot in *The Sound Barrier* (1952). His air of authority and military bearing were used to good effect in *League of Gentlemen* (1960), and as determined, upper-class detectives in *Sapphire* (1959) and *The Informers* (1963). He directed and starred in the black comedy *How to Murder a Rich Uncle* (1957) and the Irish-set religious allegory *Johnny Nobody* (1960), and starred in the TV series *Zero One* (1962). Married Beatrice CAMPBELL.
OTHER BRITISH FILMS: *Mrs Pym of Scotland Yard* (1939), *Uneasy Terms* (1948), *Jack of Diamonds*, *The Perfect Woman* (1949), *Morning Departure*, *Trio*, *Pandora and the Flying Dutchman* (1950), *Young Wives' Tale*, *Encore*, *Who Goes There!* (1951), *Grand National Night* (1953), *Forbidden Cargo*, *The Sea Shall Not Have Them* (1954), *All for Mary*, *A Prize of Gold* (1955), *Count Five and Die* (1957), *The Man Inside* (1958), *The Trials of Oscar Wilde* (1960), *The Virgin Soldiers*, *Battle of Britain* (1969), *The Executioner* (1970), *The Great Waltz* (US/UK), *Tales from the Crypt* (1972), *The Mackintosh Man* (1973). Roger Phillip Mellor.

Patterson, Lee (*b* Vancouver, 1929). Actor. Former publicist, based in England for most of the 50s, and busy in British films between 1956 and 60. With his dark, Brylcreemed hair, he

looked more like a 50s rock'n'roller than other 'B' FILM stars of the period, providing producers with a young virile image and a North American accent, without the expense of importing a US star. He combined small roles in first features, making his debut in *Malta Story* (1953), with starring in 'B' films from 1954 onwards, often in roles that were both tough and sympathetic, as in *Soho Incident* (1956), and he soon became particularly associated with ANGLO-AMALGAMATED crime thrillers. Since the 60s, based in the US, appearing in supporting roles in films and on television.
OTHER BRITISH FILMS INCLUDE: *The Good Die Young*, *The Passing Stranger* (1954), *Above Us the Waves* (1955), *Reach for the Sky*, *Checkpoint* (1956), *Time Lock*, *The Story of Esther Costello*, *The Flying Scot* (1957), *Jack the Ripper*, *The Spaniard's Curse*, *Cat and Mouse* (1958), *Breakout*, *Deadly Record* (1959), *Bullseye!* (1990, UK/US). Roger Philip Mellor.

Patterson, Willi Director. With experience in TV and commercials, Patterson made his feature film debut, *Don't Go Breaking My Heart* (1999), a romantic comedy which received lukewarm notices.

Paul, Fred (*b* Lausanne, Switzerland, 1880 – *d* England). Actor, director. A busy early actor from 1907 to 1936 in more than 80 films (including the lead in *East Lynne*, 1913, and, his best-known film, *Lady Windermere's Fan*, 1916); became an equally busy director of more than 50 films, beginning with *The Dop Doctor* (1915).
OTHER BRITISH FILMS INCLUDE: (d) *The Vicar of Wakefield*, *The Second Mrs Tanqueray* (1916), *Masks and Faces* (1917), *The Duchess of Seven Dials* (1920), *Brown Sugar* (1922), *The Right to Strike* (1923), *Further Mysteries of Dr Fu Manchu series* (1924), *The Last Witness* (1925), *Safety First* (1926), *The Luck of the Navy* (1927), *Thou Fool* (1928), *The Broken Melody* (1929), *Romany Love* (1931). AS.

Paul, R. Holmes see **Holmes-Paul, R**.

Paul, R(obert) W(illiam) (*b* London, 1869 – *d* London, 1943). Pioneer. A manufacturer of electrical and scientific instruments, as well as a pioneer of British film, Paul began making kinetoscopes in 1894. The following year, in association with Birt ACRES, he built a motion picture camera, a patent for which was granted on May 27, 1895. Paul exhibited his first projector, the Theatrograph, in February 1896, and on March 25 of the same year, he screened films at London's Alhambra Theatre of Varieties. Among his pioneering productions of 1896 were *The Soldier's Courtship* (sometimes referred to as the first British fiction film) and his wildly popular film of the Derby. In 1898, he opened Britain's first studio in Muswell Hill, London, and his employees included several who went on to be significant figures in the early British film industry: Walter BOOTH, G.H. CRICKS, J.H. Martin and Jack Smith among them. Paul sent a cameraman to film the Anglo-Boer War, and produced the early PROPAGANDA series *Army Life, or How Soldiers Are Made* (1900). Paul's Animatograph projector was exported the world over, and he played a considerable part in establishing a British film industry. However, his film interests were always secondary to his engineering ones, and he retired from film production in 1910. AS.

Pavey, Stanley (*b* London, 1913 – *d* 1984). Cinematographer. In films from 1929, working for various studios during the 30s, during WW2 in the ATA as Ferry Pilot until invalided out in 1943, when he became attached to EALING, first as camera operator on *My Learned Friend* (1943) and *The Halfway House* (1944), then as cinematographer. Co-founder of the BSC, he did his best work in the 40s, on *They Came to a City* (1944) and

Daughter of Darkness (1947), in which his lighting helps to create an effect of dangerous PASTORAL. Worked prolifically but with less distinction in popular GENRES until the mid 60s.
OTHER BRITISH FILMS INCLUDE: (c) *My Learned Friend* (1943), *The Halfway House* (1944); *Dreaming* (1944), *Here Comes the Sun, Dead of Night* (co-c) (1945), *The Small Voice* (1948), *The Third Man* (1949, add ph), *The Happiest Days of Your Life* (1950), *The Galloping Major* (1951), *Top Secret* (1952), *Rough Shoot* (1953), *Happy Ever After, The Belles of St Trinian's* (1954), *They Can't Hang Me* (1955), *The Man in the Road* (1956), *The Naked Truth, Hour of Decision* (1957), *Too Many Crooks, Home Is the Hero* (Ire) (1959), *Mrs Gibbon's Boys, Mystery Submarine* (1962), *Girl in the Headlines* (1963), *Just for You* (1964).

Pavlow, Muriel (*b* London, 1921). Actress. Sweet-faced, perennially youthful-looking leading lady, who had trained as an elocution teacher, first filmed as a child, in Gracie FIELDS's *Sing As We Go!* (1934) as an extra, then in *A Romance in Flanders* (1937). In fact, her screen career started three more times: she played Glynis JOHNS's stage role in *Quiet Wedding* (1941), Robert NEWTON's leading lady, a refugee in a SPY THRILLER, *Night Boat to Dublin* (1946) and then, in the early 50s she began her starring run, filming steadily throughout the decade. She was always busy on stage, at Stratford, in the West End and on Australasian tours, and in the 90s she had several vivid moments on TV, as in Jack CLAYTON's glorious *Memento Mori* (1992).

What she brought to the popular 50s films in which she had leading lady roles was a fresh, unaffected naturalness, a normality that often provided an anchor for the comic business going on around her in, say, *Doctor in the House* (1954), or the frightening events in which *Tiger in the Smoke* (1956) caught her up, and she is a properly sympathetic wife to Douglas Bader (Kenneth MORE) in *Reach for the Sky* (1956). She was married to actor Derek FARR, with whom she appeared in *The Shop at Sly Corner* (1946) and *Doctor at Large* (1957) and several times on stage.
OTHER BRITISH FILMS: *Out of True* (1951), *It Started in Paradise* (1952), *Malta Story, The Net* (1953), *Forever My Heart, Conflict of Wings* (1954), *Simon and Laura* (1955), *Eyewitness* (1956), *Rooney* (1958), *Whirlpool* (1959), *Murder She Said* (1961).

Pawle, Lennox (*b* London, 1872 – *d* Hollywood, California, 1936). Actor. Character player and comedian well known on the London stage, who made a few British silent films, including a version of *The Admirable Crichton* (1918) before going to Hollywood, where his most famous role was as the eccentric Mr Dick in George Cukor's *David Copperfield* (1935).
OTHER BRITISH FILMS: *All the Sad World Needs* (1918), *The Temptress* (1920), *The Glorious Adventure* (1922).

Payn, Graham (*b* Pietermaritzburg, Natal, 1918). Actor. South African-born actor on the British stage from 1931. Long-time companion of Noël COWARD with whom he appeared in *The Italian Job* (1969), as Keats who brings elegant prison inmate Coward the trade balance figures and the *London Illustrated News*. Also played in the drab version of Coward's *The Astonished Heart* (1950), but his main distinction was in stage musicals and revues.
OTHER BRITISH FILMS: *Love, Mirth and Melody* (1934), *Boys in Brown* (1949), *Jigsaw* (1962).

Payne, Douglas (*b* Bromley, 1875 – *d* London, 1965) Actor. A leading man in silent films and later a character actor in talkies, Payne began his career with Buffalo Bill's Wild West show before becoming an actor-manager. He played Sexton Blake in *The Further Exploits of Sexton Blake: The Mystery of the SS*

Olympic (1919) and *The Doddington Diamonds* (1922). Payne retired in 1935 but made brief stage appearances for a further ten years.
OTHER BRITISH FILMS INCLUDE: *The Adventures of Dick Turpin* (1912), *Enoch Arden* (1914), *The Little Minister* (1915), *Rodney Stone* (1920), *Old Bill 'Through the Ages'* (1924), *Red Aces* (1929), *The Flaw* (1933). AS.

Payne, Laurence (*b* London, 1919). Actor. Dark-haired, serious actor who made his film debut as the fugitive German POW in *Train of Events* (1949) and appeared in a couple of Hollywood religious epics: as Joseph in *Ben-Hur* and a disciple in *Barabbas*. Also on stage, with Stratford and Old Vic seasons. In recent years, Payne is better known as a novelist, creator of the Chief Inspector Sam Birkett, John Tibbett and Mark Savage series; his 1961 novel, *The Nose on My Face*, was filmed in 1963 as *Girl in the Headlines*. Married and divorced (1) Sheila BURRELL and (2) **Pamela Alan**, who appeared in a few British films, including *Noose for a Lady* (1952) and *Death Goes to School* (1953).
OTHER BRITISH FILMS INCLUDE: *Train of Events* (1949), *Glad Tidings* (1953), *Dangerous Exile* (1957), *The Trollenberg Terror* (1958), *The Tell-Tale Heart, The Singer Not the Song* (1960), *The Third Alibi, Crosstrap* (1961), *Vampire Circus* (1971). AS.

Paynter, Robert (*b* London, 1928). Cinematographer. In films from 1943 when he became a camera trainee with the Government Film Department. First credits were on 50s SHORT FILMS, including *The Land of Robert Burns* (1956); he shot several features (UK and US) for Michael WINNER in the late 60s/early 70s; and worked in America through most of the 80s, but was back in Britain for *When the Whales Came* (1989).
OTHER BRITISH FILMS INCLUDE: (shorts) *The Heart Is Highland* (1952, assistant), *Snowdrift at Bleath Gill* (1955), *Bernard Shaw* (1957, co-c), *Terminus* (1961, add ph), *The Bank of England at Work* (1966); (features) *Hannibal Brooks* (1968), *The Games* (1969), *Chato's Land, The Nightcomers* (1971), *The Big Sleep* (1978), *Firepower* (1979), *An American Werewolf in London* (1981, UK/US), *Superman III* (1983), *Loser Takes All* (1990, UK/US), *Get Back* (1991, doc, co-c).

Peach, L. du Garde (*b* Sheffield, 1890 – *d* ?). Screenwriter. Prolific playwright and radio writer who had about 20 screenplay credits in the 30s, for such popular films as *The Tunnel* (1935) and *Seven Sinners* (1936), not to speak of co-authoring RANK's initiation into feature film, *Turn of the Tide* (1935). Several decades later, Frank LAUNDER claimed that he and Sidney GILLIAT had to abandon most of Peach's script for *Seven Sinners*, and that his only virtue as a screenwriter was speed.
OTHER BRITISH FILMS INCLUDE: (co-sc, unless noted) *The Path of Glory* (+ radio play), *Princess Charming* (sc), *Chu-Chin-Chow, Red Ensign* (add dial) (1934), *It's a Bet, Heart's Desire, Music Hath Charms, The Case of Gabriel Perry* (1935), *Spy of Napoleon, The Man Who Changed His Mind,* (1936), *Melody and Romance* (1937), *The Great Mr Handel* (1942), *Get Cracking* (1943, + story).

Peach, Mary (*b* Durban, 1934). Actress. Blonde graduate of Central School, who entered films as the sympathetic June, Donald HOUSTON's girlfriend, in *Room at the Top* (1958), had a few leads in the 60s, including *No Love for Johnnie* (1961), opposite Peter FINCH, starred in the US war drama, *A Gathering of Eagles* (1963), and drifted into TV in the 70s (e.g. as Mae in OLIVIER's *Cat on a Hot Tin Roof*, 1976).
OTHER BRITISH FILMS INCLUDE: *The Lady Is a Square* (1958), *Follow That Horse!* (1960), *A Pair of Briefs* (1961), *Ballad in Blue* (1964), *Scrooge* (1970), *Aerodrome* (1983, TV, some cinemas).

Peacock, Trevor (*b* London, 1931). Actor. First on the London stage as a comedian at the Windmill, Peacock has had a varied career as actor, on stage, screen and TV, and as playwright, composer and lyric writer. He played major roles in the BBC's SHAKESPEARE run in the early 80s (e.g. Feste in *Twelfth Night*, 1980) but his real TV fame probably derives from playing the absurd vestryman Jim Trott ('Yes yes yes yes yes. No.') in *The Vicar of Dibley* (from 1994). Entered films in *The Barber of Stamford Hill* (1962) and has played occasional supporting roles, including the Gravedigger in ZEFFIRELLI's *Hamlet* (1990, UK/US), but film has been a minor strand in his work.

OTHER BRITISH FILMS INCLUDE: *He Who Rides a Tiger* (1965, sc), *Lady Caroline Lamb* (1972, UK/It/US), *Antonia and Jane* (1990), *The Trial* (1992), *Sunshine* (2000, UK/Austria/Can/Ger/Hung).

Pearce, Jacqueline (*b* Byfleet, 1943). Actress. RADA-trained Pearce had film bits in *Genghis Khan* (1965, US/Ger/Yug) and *The Magnificent Two* (1967), but really caught audience attention as a beauty who periodically turned into a snake creature in HAMMER's *The Reptile* (1966). After a handful of films, she went to the US to study at the Actors' Studio, returning to Britain in the early 70s and later becoming well known for her role as Supreme Commander Servalan in TV's sci-fi success, *Blake's 7* (1978–81).

OTHER BRITISH FILMS INCLUDE: *Sky West and Crooked* (1965), *The Plague of the Zombies* (1966), *White Mischief* (1987), *How to Get Ahead in Advertising* (1989), *Guru in Seven* (1998).

Pearce, Vera (*b* Broken Hill, Australia, 1896 – *d* London, 1956). Actress. Toured in pre-WW1 England before returning to Australia where she had considerable stage experience and starred in two silent films: *The Shepherd of the Southern Cross* (1914), set partly in London, and *The Martyrdom of Nurse Cavell* (1916), released months after the actual event. Back in Britain, she became a formidable character actress, especially in farce and usually in larger-than-life roles, like the temperamental diva, Gloria Spania, in *Heat Wave* (1935), Mrs Crummles in *Nicholas Nickleby* (1947) and Stanley HOLLOWAY's large, cheery wife in *One Wild Oat* (1951).

OTHER BRITISH FILMS INCLUDE: *Yes Mr Brown, Just My Luck* (1933), *Royal Cavalcade* (1935), *Please Teacher* (1937), *What a Man!, Yes Madam?* (1938), *The Men of Sherwood Forest* (1954), *The Night We Got the Bird* (1960), *Nothing Barred* (1961).

Pearl, Princess (aka Pearl Vyner-Brooke) (*b* London, 1913 – *d* 2002). Actress. RN: Elizabeth Brooke. Starred in two 30s MUSICALS with her first husband, bandleader **Harry Roy**, in his only film appearances, *Everything Is Rhythm* (1936) and *Rhythm Racketeer* (1937), and in a comedy with Claude HULBERT, *Honeymoon Merry-Go-Round* (1940). Daughter of the white British Rajah of Sarawak. Retired to US after her second marriage.

Pearson, George (*b* London, 1875 – *d* Malvern, 1973). Director. George Pearson is as much the father of British cinema as D.W. Griffith is of the American film industry. From the start of his film career with PATHÉ in 1913, Pearson worked steadfastly, creatively and honestly to transform British cinema into an art form. His background as a teacher ensured that his approach was at all times sensible and intelligent, while his Victorian upbringing added a touch of romanticism tinged with MELODRAMA to all his productions. His first important film, *A Study in Scarlet* (1914), made ambitious use of LOCATIONS, with the Cheddar Gorge standing in for the Rocky Mountains and the Southport Sands for the Salt Lake desert. With the 'Ultus' SERIES (1915–17), Pearson demonstrated a grasp of the MYSTERY film GENRE that led to a comparison with

France's Louis Feuillade. In 1918, in partnership with T.A. WELSH, Pearson founded his own company, producing and directing *The Better 'Ole* (1918), based on the stageplay and cartoons by Bruce Bairnsfather. In 1920, he directed *Nothing Else Matters*, and introduced to the screen Betty BALFOUR, whom he starred in a series of 'Squibs' comedies from 1921 to 1923. *Reveille* (1924) is a moving study of the after-effects of WW1 on a group of working-class Londoners, which James AGATE considered greater in its feeling for humanity than any of the Greek tragedies. The previous year, Pearson had directed the 'lost' *Love, Life and Laughter*, considered by many his finest achievement, though he was proudest of *The Little People* (1926). Pearson did not weather the coming of sound well, but did produce *Journey's End* (1930) in Hollywood before directing and often writing 'QUOTA QUICKIES'. He was forever the schoolteacher; in the 20s, he trained Thorold DICKINSON, Edward CARRICK and Cedric Belfrage; at the end of his career, in the 40s and 50s, he trained young film-makers from the emergent African nations, as Head of Production at the COLONIAL FILM UNIT (1942–56).

OTHER BRITISH FILMS INCLUDE: *Peg Woffington* (1912, sc), *Fair Sussex, In Dickens Land, Rambles through Hopland, Lynmouth, Where History Has Been Written, Kentish Industries, Wonderful Nights of Peter Kinema* series, *A Lighter Burden, Mr Henpeck's Dilemma, The Fool, Sentence of Death, Heroes of the Mine* (1913), *A Fishergirl's Folly, The Live Wire, Christmas Day in the Workhouse, A Son of France, Incidents in the Great European War, The Cause of the Great European War, The Life of Lord Roberts VC* (1914), *Buttons, For the Empire, A Cinema Romance, The True Story of the Lyons Mail, John Halifax, Gentleman, Ultus, the Man from the Dead* (1915), *Ultus and the Grey Lady, Ultus and the Secret of the Night, Sally Bishop* (1916), *Ultus and the Three Button Mystery, The Man Who Made the Army, Canadian Officers in the Making* (1917), *The Kiddies in the Ruins* (1918), *Pallard the Punter* (sc), *Angel Esquire* (sc), *Hughie at the Victory Derby* (1919), *Garryowen* (1920), *Mary-Find-the-Gold* (1921), *Wee McGregor's Sweetheart, Squibs Wins the Calcutta Sweep* (1922), *Squibs, MP, Squibs' Honeymoon* (1923), *Satan's Sister* (1925), *The Little People, Blinkeyes* (1926), *Huntingtower* (1927), *Love's Option* (1928), *Auld Lang Syne* (1929, assoc p), *The Third String* (1932), *A Shot in the Dark, The Pointing Finger* (1933), *River Wolves, Four Masked Men, Whispering Tongues, Open All Night* (1934), *Ace of Spades, That's My Uncle, Gentleman's Agreement, Once a Thief, Jubilee Window, Checkmate* (1935), *The Secret Voice, Shipmates o' Mine* (sc), *Wednesday's Luck, Murder by Rope, Midnight at Madame Tussauds* (1936), *Command Performance* (sc), *The Fatal Hour*(1937), *Follow Your Star* (sc), *Souvenirs, Old Soldiers, Mother of Men* (1938), *British Made* (1939, doc, short), *Land of Water, Take Cover, Rural School, A British Family in Peace and War* (1940, doc, short), *British Youth, An African in London* (1941, doc, short).

BIBLIOG: Autobiography, *Flashback*, 1957. AS.

Pearson, Lloyd (*b* Cleckheaton, 1897 – *d* London, 1966). Actor. Tubby former bank clerk who trained as an actor after WW1 service and was on the London stage with Sir Frank BENSON's company for seven years from 1920, in many classical roles. On-screen, his most characteristic roles were as somewhat pompous professional men, including Alderman Helliwell (repeating his 1938 stage role) in *When We Are Married* (1943), a nouveau riche industrialist in *Portrait of Clare* (1950), and a corrupt mayor in *Private Information* (1952).

OTHER BRITISH FILMS INCLUDE: *The Challenge* (1938), *Kipps, Banana Ridge* (1941), *The Young Mr Pitt, Uncensored* (1942), *My Learned Friend* (1943), *The Way Ahead, Time Flies* (1944), *The Three Weird Sisters, Mr Perrin and Mr Traill* (1948), *Passport to Pimlico* (1949), *Hindle Wakes* (1952), *The Good Companions* (1956), *The Angry Silence* (1960).

Pearson, Richard (*b* Monmouth, 1918). Actor. Educated at Monmouth School, Pearson was on (MUSIC-HALL) stage from

1937, did WW2 service from 1939–46, resuming his stage career and becoming a regular character player in films, usually in benign roles. He is touching as Dr Peter FINCH's worried patient (he often appeared worried) in *Sunday Bloody Sunday* (1971), as a less sympathetic doctor himself in *Macbeth* (1971), and on TV from 1947, memorable as a kindly solicitor in *Love Among the Ruins* (1975).

OTHER BRITISH FILMS INCLUDE: *The Woman in Question* (1950), *Scrooge* (1951), *Dangerous Cargo, Svengali* (1954), *Sea Fury* (1958), *Libel, The Crowning Touch* (1959), *Man in the Moon* (1960), *Guns of Darkness* (1962), *The Yellow Rolls-Royce* (1964), *How I Won the War, Charlie Bubbles* (1967), *The Strange Affair* (1968), *The Rise and Rise of Michael Rimmer* (1970), *Pope Joan* (1972), *Royal Flash* (1975), *Tess* (1979, UK/Fr), *The Mirror Crack'd* (1980), *Water* (1985).

Peck, Bob (*b* Leeds, 1945 – *d* Kingston, Surrey, 1999). Actor. Much respected for his work in all the media, Peck's untimely death from cancer robbed them of a powerful, authoritative presence, equally at home as Macbeth (Stratford, 1982–83) or the detective whose family life is threatened in TV's *Edge of Darkness* (1985), perhaps the role for which he is most widely known, or the puritanical Welsh farmer in *On the Black Hill* (1987). More actor than star, despite his easy command, his versatility was a byword. Tall, rather sombrely good-looking, he was in demand for international films, including *Jurassic Park* (1993) as game warden Muldoon, but film perhaps used him least well of the media. A graduate of the Leeds College of Art, he was a keen amateur actor before auditioning for the Royal Court and, in 1975, joining the RSC for nine years. He was married to TV actress **Jill Baker**, who appeared in the film, *Hope and Glory* (1987).

OTHER BRITISH FILMS: *Royal Flash* (1975), *Parker* (1984), *The Kitchen Toto* (1987), *Ladder of Swords* (1989), *Surviving Picasso* (1996, UK/US), *Fairytale: A True Story* (1997, UK/US), *The Canterbury Tales* (1998, UK/Russia, voice).

Peck, Gregory (*b* LaJolla, California, 1916 – *d* Los Angeles, 2003). Actor. Legendary Hollywood star, a noted, Oscar-winning purveyor of decency in *To Kill a Mockingbird* (1962, US), who made a number of notable British films, apparently winning golden opinions from all who worked with him. *Captain Horatio Hornblower RN* (1950, UK/US) was more completely within his range than Captain Ahab in *Moby Dick* (1956), but the latter was a gallant endeavour. Sterling heroes were his forte, but he handled the comedy of *The Million Pound Note* (1953) gracefully.

OTHER BRITISH FILMS: *The Purple Plain* (1954), *The Guns of Navarone* (1961), *Arabesque* (1966, UK/US), *Billy Two Hats* (1973), *The Sea Wolves* (1980, UK/Switz/US).

BIBLIOG: Gerard Molyneaux, *Gregory Peck: A Bio-Bibliography*, 1995.

Peck, Ron (*b* Surrey). Director. Gay film-maker who began by making SHORT FILMS for a production company known as Four Corners Films, for which he also made his first feature, *Nighthawks* (1978, co-d, co-p, co-sc), about a closeted gay teacher who confronts his class with the truth about his life. Much but not all of his work has dealt with related themes; he also directed a study of the work of *Edward Hopper* (1981, d, co-comp, narr). His last released film, *Strip Jack Naked* (1991, co-p, co-sc, co-c, co-e), was an autobiographically inspired account of growing up gay.

OTHER BRITISH FILMS INCLUDE: (d, unless noted) (shorts) *Bottled Garden* (1973, p), *What Can You Do with a Male Nude?* (1975, +sc), *On Allotments* (co-d, sd), *Railmen* (co-d) (1976); (features) *The Bostonians* (1984, UK/US, 2nd ass d), *Empire State* (1987, + co-sc).

Pedelty, Donovan Director, columnist. Former journalist

who would, in the 50s, become editor of the popular fan magazine, *Picturegoer*, but who, in the 30s, after some time in Hollywood, co-wrote and/or directed 20 British films, mostly 'QUOTA QUICKIES'. Of Irish descent, he seems to have favoured films with an Irish setting, including *Irish and Proud of It* (1936, + co-sc), with a teenage Dinah SHERIDAN. With Victor Greene as producer, Pedelty formed Crusade Films, and made several films partly shot in various Irish locations, some featuring singer and comedian Richard HAYWARD (e.g. *The Early Bird*, 1936, Ire) and other members of Belfast Repertory Players.

OTHER BRITISH FILMS INCLUDE: (sc/co-sc) *The Little Damozel* (1933), *Seeing Is Believing* (1934), *Brewster's Millions, City of Beautiful Nonsense* (1935), *Two on a Doorstep* (1936, story); (d, sc/co-sc) *Flame in the Heather, The Luck of the Irish* (+ co-p) (1935), *Landslide, First Night* (1937), *Murder Tomorrow, Bedtime Story* (1938), *Back Home in Ireland* (1946, doc, d).

Peel, David (*b* London, 1920 – *d* 1981). Actor. RADA-trained actor, with experience on London and New York stages, including a Stratford season (1946–47). Discharged from WW2 service in 1942, he played in several wartime films, including two for Lance COMFORT, *Squadron Leader X* (1942) and *Escape to Danger* (1943). Worked a good deal with BBC radio (1950–52) and played in a TV version of *Rope* (1953), but the stage was his main interest and his only really memorable screen role was as Martita HUNT's son in *The Brides of Dracula* (1960), unwisely freed from his chains by pretty Yvonne MONLAUR. Last film was the US comedy, *Please Stand by Me* (1972).

OTHER BRITISH FILMS: *We Dive at Dawn* (1943), *Gaiety George* (1946), *They Who Dare* (1953), *The Hands of Orlac* (1960, UK/Fr).

Peel, Eileen (*b* London, 1903 [sometimes given as 1909] – *d* London, Ontario, 1981). Actress. Elegant blonde stage actress who made occasional films over three decades from 1932 to 1961. On stage from 1924, usually in 'sophisticated' roles (= well-dressed and smoked a lot), as in *The Reluctant Debutante* (1955) or as silly Mrs Carghall in *The Elder Statesman* (1958). A few negligible film roles in the 30s were followed by a few more in later decades; stage work revealed her as more fun than a wet romance like *The White Unicorn* (1947) would have countenanced.

OTHER BRITISH FILMS INCLUDE: *The First Mrs Fraser* (1932), *Hyde Park Corner* (1935), *The Divorce of Lady X* (1938), *In Which We Serve, Talk About Jacqueline* (1942), *Lost* (1955), *The Queen's Guards* (1961).

Peers, Donald (*b* Ammanford, Wales, 1908 – *d* Brighton, 1973). Singer. Hugely popular singer, largely on the basis of one inane song ('I told each little bird . . . '), who made one unremarkable film, *Sing Along with Me* (1952) at the height of his fame, and had appeared in a forgotten wartime musical, *The Balloon Goes Up* (1942).

Peirce, Douglas (*b* Charlton, Kent, 1901 – *d* ?). Production manager. Former stage actor, in films from 1934 as assistant director at GAUMONT–BRITISH. During WW2, he served as cinema and entertainments officer (1941–43), returning to films as 1st assistant director on *Waterloo Road* (1944). He worked as 2nd unit director on several other GAINSBOROUGH films, was given a piffling HIGHBURY romantic comedy, *Love in Waiting* (1948) to direct, and thereafter, unsurprisingly, returned to production manager or associate producer on major films throughout the 50s, directing only one further film, the 'B' THRILLER, *The Delavine Affair* (1954).

OTHER BRITISH FILMS INCLUDE: *Livingstone* (1925, a); (ass d, unless noted) *The Tunnel* (1935), *Everything Is Thunder* (1936), *King Solomon's Mines, Young and Innocent, The Great Barrier* (1937), *Night Train to*

Munich, Gasbags (1940, 2ud), *Kipps* (1941), *The Young Mr Pitt* (1942), *The Wicked Lady* (2ud); (prod man, unless noted) *The Magic Bow* (1946, ass d), *Jassy* (1947), *The Calendar* (1948, assoc p), *The Clouded Yellow* (1950), *Rob Roy . . .* (1953), *Svengali* (assoc p) (1954), *The Violent Playground* (1957), *Sapphire* (1959), *Bunny Lake Is Missing* (1965), *Casino Royale* (1967).

Pelissier, Anthony (*b* London, 1912 – *d* Seaford, 1988). Director, writer. Pelissier worked as a film director for only five years, committing himself more to theatre and then TV; his films demonstrate talents that could have been more fully used. The son of actress Fay COMPTON, he had extensive stage experience as designer, writer and actor, working frequently with Noël COWARD and John MILLS. When Mills launched his own production company, he chose Pelissier to adapt and direct H.G. WELLS's *The History of Mr Polly* (1948) and D.H. LAWRENCE's *The Rocking Horse Winner* (1949), while one of his later films, *Meet Me Tonight* (1952), was a less ambitious transposition of three short Coward plays. *Meet Mr Lucifer* (1953), centred on the growth of TV, was one of EALING's less successful comedies, but it preserves a fascinating collection of material from the period of live transmission; after it, Pelissier himself abandoned cinema for the new medium, and was involved for a time with the BBC's experimental Langham Group. Among his uneven filmography, *The Rocking Horse Winner* and *Personal Affair* (1953) are notable for communicating a powerful sense of British middle-class angst and repression. Married (1) Penelope DUDLEY WARD; Tracey REED is their daughter.

OTHER BRITISH FILMS: (sc) *Over the Moon* (1939, co-), *Perfect Strangers* (1945), *Tiger in the Smoke* (1956); (d) *Night Without Stars, Encore* (co-) (1951), *The Risk Taker* (1960c, short), *Diamonds* (1967, short). Charles Barr.

Pember, Clifford Production designer. One of the first designers to graduate to art direction from architecture, he is said to have worked on D.W. Griffiths's *Way Down East* (1920, US). Designed two prestige play ADAPTATIONS, HITCHCOCK's *Easy Virtue* (1927), from Noël COWARD, and Basil DEAN's *Escape* (1930), from John GALSWORTHY; nothing of any consequence followed.

OTHER BRITISH FILMS: *The Triumph of the Scarlet Pimpernel* (1928), *Birds of Prey* (1930), *Tilly of Bloomsbury* (1931), *Looking on the Bright Side, Nine Till Six, The Sign of Four* (1932).

Pember, Ron (*b* London, 1934). Actor. Character player, educated Eastbrook Secondary Modern, Dagenham, on stage from 1949 (later often at the Mermaid Theatre) and in minor supporting film roles from *Poor Cow* (1967) to *Personal Services* (1987), often in parts designated by their function (Ferryman in *Ordeal by Innocence*, 1984) rather than a name. Plenty of TV since 1960, including episodes of *The Secret Army* (1977).

OTHER BRITISH FILMS INCLUDE: *Curse of the Crimson Altar* (1968), *Oh! What a Lovely War* (1969), *Julius Caesar* (1970), *Young Winston, Death Line* (1972), *The Land That Time Forgot* (1974), *Aces High* (1976, UK/Fr), *Murder by Decree* (1978, UK/Can), *Bullshot* (1983), *The Chain* (1984).

Pemberton, Reece (*b* Tamworth, 1914). Production designer. Stage designer since the early 50s (*Waters of the Moon*, 1951, etc), who contributed to the look of several diverse films of the 60s. The design is important in distinguishing between Alan BATES's background and his aspirations in *Nothing but the Best* (1964), both a long way from the different kinds of claustrophobic bleakness of *The Caretaker* (1963) and *Our Mother's House* (1967). Lectured in design at Bristol University, 1969–71.

OTHER BRITISH FILMS: *Time Without Pity* (1957), *Some People* (1962), *One Way Pendulum* (1964), *Arabesque* (1966, UK/US), *The Anniversary* (1967), *Diamonds for Breakfast* (1968), *Spring and Port Wine* (1969).

Pendrell, Anthony (*b* London, 1913 – *d* London, 1986). Actor. Educated at Arundel School, Pendrell was on stage from 1936 and made his film debut in MANCUNIAN's *Home Sweet Home* (1945) as the upper-class young man who falls for an evacuee. Billed as 'Tony' in his early films, he made about a further 15, often as official types, like the jury foreman in *The Man Who Wouldn't Talk* (1957). Also TV, including *Quatermass and the Pit* (1958), as a television interviewer.

OTHER BRITISH FILMS INCLUDE: *I'll Turn to You* (1946), *What a Carry On!, Blue Scar* (1949), *Shadow of the Past* (1950), *Hot Ice* (1952), *The Yellow Robe* (1955), *The Two Faces of Dr Jekyll* (1960), *Downfall* (1964).

Penhaligon, Susan (*b* Manila, Philippines, 1949). Actress. In rep and TV before making film debut in *Say Hello to Yesterday* (1970). Attractive and spirited as she was, British cinema ran out of things for her to do in the later 70s, though she had goodish roles as the young wife who wouldn't dream of saying *No Sex Please – We're British* (1973), as the vexatious Sister Felicity in *Nasty Habits* (1976), involved in an ununly affair with a young Jesuit. Since her plucky-heroine-in-grave-peril in the Australian *Patrick* (1978) she has been confined to TV, including substantial roles in *Bouquet of Barbed Wire* (1976) and *A Fine Romance* (1981).

OTHER BRITISH FILMS INCLUDE: *Private Road, Under Milk Wood* (1971), *The Land That Time Forgot* (1974), *The Uncanny, Leopard in the Snow* (1977, UK/Can).

Pennell, Nicholas (*b* Brixham, Devon, 1938 – *d* Stratford, Canada, 1995). Actor. 'Traddles' to the life in the starry but dull 1969 version of *David Copperfield*, he came to attention in TV's *The Forsyte Saga* (1967), and brought a likeable freshness to his few films, including *Battle of Britain* (1969), in which he makes his presence felt among the all-star cast of heroes.

OTHER BRITISH FILMS: *Only When I Larf, Isadora* (1968), *Mr Forbush and the Penguins* (1971).

Pennington-Richards, C.M. (*b* South Norwood, 1911). Cinematographer, director, writer. After wartime service with the CROWN FILM UNIT, notably as director of photography for Humphrey JENNINGS on *Fires were Started* (1943), Pennington-Richards was an ideal collaborator for two other Crown directors who had moved into the feature industry, Jack LEE (*The Wooden Horse*, 1950) and Pat JACKSON (*White Corridors*, 1951), giving expressive support to their project of renewing the wartime genre of DOCUMENTARY drama. When this project petered out, his career, like theirs, never regained the same momentum, though he remained active into the 60s as director and occasional scriptwriter as well as cinematographer. His directing debut with the typical GROUP THREE whimsy *The Oracle* (1953) was followed by a series of modest comedies such as the Ian CARMICHAEL vehicle *Double Bunk* (1961). Though his cinematography gave an effective *noir*ish look to thrillers like *Obsession* (1949) and *1984* (1955), his enduring claim to fame is as the common factor between the Jennings and Jackson films, two beautifully shot classics of British realist cinema.

OTHER BRITISH FILMS INCLUDE: (c, short/doc) *Canterbury Pilgrimage, William Tindale* (1937), *Fishers of Men* (1939), *Builders* (1942), *Out of Chaos* (co-c), *The Permanent Way* (1944), *Theirs is the Glory* (1946); (c, feature) *Blarney* (1938, co-, UK/Ire), *The Woman in the Hall* (1947, co-c), *Esther Waters* (1948, co-c), *Give Us This Day* (UK/US), *All Over the Town* (1949), *Tom Brown's Schooldays, Scrooge* (1951), *Something Money*

Can't Buy (1952), *Desperate Moment, Always a Bride* (1953), *Aunt Clara* (1954), *Tarzan and the Lost Safari* (1956); (d) *Hour of Decision* (1957), *Inn for Trouble* (1959), *Mystery Submarine* (1962), *Ladies Who Do* (1963), *Guns at Batasi* (1964, co-sc), *A Challenge for Robin Hood* (1967), *Sky Pirates* (1976, + sc, story). Charles Barr.

Penrose, John (*b* Southsea, Hants, 1914 – *d* London, 1983). Actor. Educated in South Africa where he studied sculpture before returning to London and RADA, winning a prize for stage design and appearing on stage first in 1936 and films in 1939 (*The Lion Has Wings*). In the Royal Navy (1940–46); postwar he and Pat NYE (who played his gang-leader Ma in the film, *The Adventures of PC 49*, 1949), purchased and ran the Bedford Theatre Camden Town. Of his dozen or so films, he is best remembered as the egregious Lionel in *Kind Hearts and Coronets* (1949), a failure in business as well as on his honeymoon. TV from 1949.

OTHER BRITISH FILMS INCLUDE: *The Spy in Black* (1939, unc), *Freedom Radio* (1940), *Adventures of Tartu* (1943), *They Made Me a Fugitive* (1947), *Corridor of Mirrors, Idol of Paris* (1948), *Secret People* (1951), *Hot Ice* (1952), *Mantrap* (1953), *Anastasia* (1956, unc).

Penry-Jones, Rupert (*b* London, 1970). Actor. Tall, blond and personable, the son of Angela HORNE and stage actor Peter Penry-Jones (*see* HORNE) has had a charmed run since the mid 90s, when he played his real-life mother's son in *Cold Comfort Farm* (1995, TV, some cinemas). He has had major stage roles, including the title role in the RSC's *Don Carlos* (2000), and starred on TV as *The Student Prince* (1997) and as one of the legal firm in *North Square* (2000). On film, he has played the brother of *Hilary and Jackie* (1998) and Bill NIGHY's drugged-out ex-rocker as a youth in *Still Crazy* (1998, UK/US), and starred with wit and flair in *Virtual Sexuality* (1999) as a computer-generated ideal for the heroine. The evidence suggests an interesting young risk-taker.

OTHER BRITISH FILMS: *Black Beauty* (1994), *Bent* (UK/Jap/US), *Food of Love* (UK/Fr) (1997), *Charlotte Gray* (2001, UK/Aust/US), *Four Feathers* (2003, UK/US).

Peploe, Clare (*b* Tanzania, 1942). Screenwriter, director. Having studied at the Sorbonne and Perugia Universities, Peploe got off to a good start in films by collaborating with, first, Antonioni on the screenplay for *Zabriskie Point* (1970, US) and Bernardo Bertolucci (whom she married) on *La Luna* (1979, It, + ass d). She subsequently directed and/or wrote several patchily released films, of which the romantic comedy, *High Season* (1987), is probably the best known. Sister of writer-director Mark PEPLOE.

OTHER BRITISH FILMS: (d, unless noted) *Couples & Robbers* (1981, + co-sc), *Rough Magic* (1995, UK/Fr), *Besieged* (1998, UK/It, co-sc, assoc p), *The Triumph of Love* (2001, UK/It, + co-sc).

Peploe, Mark (*b* Cayman Islands). Screenwriter, director. Brother of writer-director Claire PEPLOE, he has, like her, worked with Antonioni (on *The Passenger*, 1975, co-sc, story) and with his brother-in-law, Bernardo Bertolucci. His films with the latter include *The Last Emperor* (1987, UK/China, co-sc), *The Sheltering Sky* (1990, UK/It) and *Little Buddha* (1993, UK/Fr, co-sc). He co-wrote his sister's film, *High Season* (1987) and directed and wrote the psychological thriller, *Afraid of the Dark* (1991, UK/Fr), and the little seen CONRAD ADAPTATION, *Victory* (1995, UK/Fr/Ger, released 1998).

OTHER BRITISH FILMS: *The Pied Piper* (1971, co-sc), *Samson and Delilah* (1984, d, co-sc, short).

Perceval, Hugh Producer. For over 30 years, Perceval was a producer or associate producer or executive involved with many British films, his most important involvement being with Carol REED. He was associate producer of *Outcast of the Islands* (1950) in the Far East, having 'done such a splendid job with locations in Vienna on *The Third Man* (1949)', wrote Reed's biographer Nicholas Wapshott, though Perceval's budgeting for *The Man Between* (1953) came in for criticism from Alexander KORDA. During the rest of the 50s, he was associate producer on an eclectic range of films. He began his career as a screenwriter in 1931 (*These Charming People, Man of Mayfair*), then produced several films with director Reginald DENHAM for Phoenix Films, including *Death at Broadcasting House* (1934).

OTHER BRITISH FILMS INCLUDE: (p, unless noted) *After Dark* (1932, prod man), *The Jewel* (1933), *The Silent Passenger* (1935), *Secret Lives, Brief Ecstasy* (1937), *What a Man!* (1938), *Danny Boy* (1941), *Front Line Kids* (1942); (assoc p) *The Holly and the Ivy, Home at Seven, The Ringer* (1952), *The Man Who Loved Redheads* (1954), *Raising a Riot* (co-p, co-sc, co-adpt) (1955), *The Prince and the Showgirl* (1957, ex p), *Carve Her Name With Pride* (1958), *The Reckoning* (1969).

Percival, Lance (*b* Sevenoaks, 1933). Actor. Lanky, dorkish comedian who did time in *Carry On Cruising* (1962) and many other 60s romps of the *Raising the Wind* ilk (1961) and in the 70s niched into Frankie HOWERD's '*Up*' SERIES: . . . *the Chastity Belt*, . . . *Pompeii* (1971, as lubricious Captain Bilius) and . . . *the Front* (1972), supported Danny LA RUE, as Samuel Smallpiece, who makes unwelcome overtures to *Our Miss Fred* (1972), and slid into *Confessions from a Holiday Camp* (1977). It is a compendium of British low-comedy tastes over two decades. Also very busy on TV from the days of *That Was the Week That Was* (1962–63), in sharper satirical mode.

OTHER BRITISH FILMS INCLUDE: *What a Whopper!, On the Fiddle* (1961), *Twice Round the Daffodils* (1962), *The VIPs, Hide and Seek* (1963), *The Yellow Rolls-Royce* (1964), *The Big Job* (1965), *The Yellow Submarine* (1968, voice), *The Water Babies* (1975, UK/Pol, voice), *Rosie Dixon – Night Nurse* (1978).

Percy, Esmé (*b* London, 1887 – *d* Brighton, 1957). Actor. Occasionally in films from the 20s, this celebrated stage performer (debut 1904), much associated with the plays of Bernard SHAW (elected president of the Shaw Society in 1949), also appeared in 30-odd films, the last of which was the DOCUMENTARY, *Bernard Shaw* (1957). And, indeed, his most famous role on screen is probably as Karpathy, Higgins's suspicious pupil, in *Pygmalion* (1938), but he was charismatic from his first screen role as the 'half-caste' (and, by implication, homosexual) murderer in HITCHCOCK's *Murder!* (1930). Trained for stage in Brussels and Paris, allegedly in part by Sarah Bernhardt.

OTHER BRITISH FILMS INCLUDE: *The Lucky Number, Bitter Sweet* (1933), *Nell Gwyn, Lord Edgware Dies* (1934), *Abdul the Damned* (1935), *A Woman Alone, Land Without Music* (1936), *Return of the Scarlet Pimpernel, 21 Days* (1937), *Jeannie* (1941), *Dead of Night, Caesar and Cleopatra* (1945), *Lisbon Story* (1946), *The Ghosts of Berkeley Square* (1947), *Death in the Hand* (1948).

Périnal, Georges (*b* Paris, 1897 – *d* London, 1965). Cinematographer. Entered films in 1913 as assistant cameraman in Paris, winning acclaim for the films he shot for René Clair from the later 20s, including *Sous les toits de Paris* (1930), before coming to England to work for KORDA in 1933. He is responsible for the black-and-white sheen of such important LONDON FILMS productions as *The Private Life of Henry VIII* (1933) and *Things to Come* (1936), as well as of its TECHNICOLOR adventures, *The Drum* (1938) and *The Four Feathers* (1939), and the fantasy *The Thief of Baghdad* (1940). He is thus a major contributor to the prestige arm of pre-war British cinema, not to speak of the wartime glory of *The Life and Death of Colonel Blimp* (1943) and the post-war peak of *The Fallen Idol* (1948), Périnal's camera colluding with Carol REED's vision of a child's world in alarming disarray. If his 50s work is generally less distinguished, that is the fault of the films rather than his.

OTHER BRITISH FILMS: *Perfect Understanding* (co-), *The Girl from Maxim's* (1933), *Catherine the Great, The Private Life of Don Juan* (1934), *Escape Me Never, Sanders of the River* (1935), *Rembrandt* (1936), *Dark Journey, Under the Red Robe, The Squeaker* (1937), *Prison Without Bars, The Challenge* (1938), *Old Bill and Son* (1940), *Dangerous Moonlight* (1941), *The First of the Few, Our Film* (short) (1942, lighting cameraman), *It's Just the Way It Is* (short) (1943), *Perfect Strangers* (1945), *A Man About the House, An Ideal Husband* (1947), *Britannia Mews* (1948), *That Dangerous Age* (1949), *My Daughter Joy, The Mudlark, Bridge of Time* (short) (1950), *No Highway, The House in the Square* (1951), *The Man Who Loved Redheads* (1954), *Three Cases of Murder, The Woman for Joe* (1955), *Satellite in the Sky, Loser Takes All* (1956), *A King in New York, Saint Joan* (UK/US), *Bonjour Tristesse* (1957), *tom thumb* (1958), *Luna de miel* (UK/Sp), *Serious Charge, The Day They Robbed the Bank of England* (1959), *Oscar Wilde* (1960).

periodicals *see* **magazines and journals**

Perrins, Leslie (*b* Birmingham, 1902 – *d* Esher, 1962). Actor. Usually and suavely up to no good, this dark-haired, moustachioed RADA alumnus was on stage in 1922, and in SHORT FILMS from late silent days, before settling to a hectic round of smooth scoundrels in the 30s. Every now and then, a superior product, like *Tudor Rose* (1936), in which he played conniving Thomas Seymour, would emerge from the prevailing 'QUOTA QUICKIES'. By the 40s, his pace had slowed and he was the heroine's father in *Heaven Is Round the Corner* (1944) and a more or less sympathetic doctor in *The Lost Hours* (1952). On radio from 1927, notably as Chief Inspector in *PC49*.

OTHER BRITISH FILMS INCLUDE: *The Calendar, Immediate Possession* (1931), *The Pointing Finger, The Lost Chord* (1933), *The Scotland Yard Mystery, The Lash* (1934), *The Triumph of Sherlock Holmes, The Silent Passenger* (1935), *The Limping Man* (1936), *The High Command, Bulldog Drummond at Bay* (1937), *Mr Reeder in Room 13, Luck of the Navy* (1938), *I Killed the Count, The Gang's All Here* (1939), *John Smith Wakes Up* (1940), *The Prime Minister* (1941), *I'll Turn to You* (1946), *Idol of Paris* (1948), *Man on the Run* (1949), *Midnight Episode* (1950), *Grip of the Strangler* (1958).

Perry, David (*b* 1945 – *d* Bury St Edmunds, 1995). Costume designer. Perry designed costumes for a few smart 80s entertainments, of which costume pieces, *The Draughtsman's Contract* (1982, cos des co-ord) and *Lady Jane* (1985, co-cos des), were the most notable and the musical fiasco, *Absolute Beginners* (1986, co-cos des), the most lamentable.

OTHER BRITISH FILMS: *Flash Gordon* (1980, ass cos des), *Shock Treatment* (1981, cos co-ord), *Runners* (1983), *Bellman & True* (1987), *Reunion* (1989, UK/Fr/Ger).

Perry, Simon (*b* Farnham, 1943). Producer. Chairman of BRITISH SCREEN from 1991, Perry has been a significant figure in British cinema around the turn of the 20th century. A former TV and theatre producer, he entered film-making in 1974, working first as an independent and then as head of the National Film Development Fund. In 1982, he set up Umbrella Films, the company responsible for such films as Richard EYRE's *Loose Connections* (1983), Michael RADFORD's *Another Time, Another Place* (1983), *Nineteen Eighty-Four* (1984) and *White Mischief* (1987), and Gillies MACKINNON's *The Playboys* (1992, Ire/US). British Screen successes during the period of his incumbency include Mike LEIGH's *Naked* (1993) and Ken

LOACH's *Land and Freedom* (1995, UK/Ger/Sp). Awarded CBE in 1996, in acknowledgment of his efforts to boost British film production, and in 1999 he won a Special Jury Prize at the British Independent Film Awards.

OTHER BRITISH FILMS INCLUDE: *Eclipse* (1976), *Nanou, Hotel du Paradis* (1986, UK/Fr), *Rue Saint-Sulpice* (1991, UK/Fr), *Innocent Lies* (1995, UK/Fr), *House of America* (UK/Neth), *Wilde* (UK/Ger/Jap/US) (1997).

Pertwee, Jon (*b* London, 1919 – *d* New York, 1996). Actor. Sherborne-educated son of Roland, brother of Michael, and father of Sean PERTWEE, tall and tousled, he is now best known as TV's third *Dr Who* (1970–74) and from 1978 as *Worzel Gummedge*. A popular radio actor in *The Navy Lark*, following actual naval service in WW2 (1940–45), he made several dozen films without ever quite establishing himself with filmgoers as he did with his other audiences. After RADA, he was on stage from 1936, had a bit in the film, *The Four Just Men* (1939) and returned to films in the HIGHBURY STUDIOS oddities, *A Piece of Cake* and *Trouble in the Air* (1948), did a run of films for Val GUEST, was in several of the 'CARRY ON' SERIES, including the last, *Carry On Columbus* (1992, as the Duke of Costa Brava), and maintained a stage career. Married Jean MARSH.

OTHER BRITISH FILMS INCLUDE: *William Comes to Town* (1948), *Dear Mr Prohack, Miss Pilgrim's Progress* (1949), *The Body Said No!, Mr Drake's Duck* (1950), *Will Any Gentleman . . .?* (1953), *The Ugly Duckling* (1959), *Nearly a Nasty Accident* (1961), *Ladies Who Do* (1963), *Carry On Cleo* (1964), *. . . Cowboy* (1965), *. . . Screaming* (1966), *The House That Dripped Blood* (1970), *Adventures of a Private Eye* (1977), *The Boys in Blue* (1983).

Pertwee, Michael (*b* London, 1916 – *d* London, 1991). Dramatist, screenwriter. Sherborne-educated son of Roland PERTWEE, whose writing gifts he inherited, and brother of actor Jon PERTWEE, he wrote several plays, including *The Paragon* (1948, co-author with Roland, filmed as *Silent Dust*, 1949, from his screenplay), and a good deal of popular TV, including *The Grove Family* (1954–57, co-written with his father) and episodes of *The Persuaders!* (1971). He often wrote in collaboration, but his penchant as a solo screenwriter was for COMEDY, seen at his best in the late 50s pair, *The Naked Truth* (1957) and *Too Many Crooks* (1959), both directed by Mario ZAMPI and both stand up very well decades later. As a comic writer, he had the gift of giving his characters absurdities to say as if they were sanity itself. Married **Valerie French** (*b* London, 1932 – *d* New York, 1990) who appeared in several British films, including *The Constant Husband* (1954) and more in the US.

OTHER BRITISH FILMS INCLUDE: (co-sc) *Crackerjack* (1938), *Laughter in Paradise* (1951, + a), *Top Secret, Curtain Up* (1952), *Happy Ever After* (1954), *Now and Forever* (+ a), *It's a Great Day* (+ co-orig TV serial) (1955), *The Magnificent Two* (1967, + story), *Some Will – Some Won't* (1969, + co-story); (sc) *Two Thousand Women* (1944, add dial), *Against the Wind* (1947, adaptn), *The Interrupted Journey* (1949), *Night Was Our Friend* (+ a, play), *Madame Louise* (1951), *Make Mine Mink* (1960), *In the Doghouse* (1961), *The Mouse on the Moon, Ladies Who Do* (1963), *Finders Keepers* (1966), *One More Time* (1969), *Digby the Biggest Dog in the World* (1973).

Pertwee, Roland (*b* Brighton, 1885 – *d* London, 1963). Dramatist, screenwriter. Father of Michael and Jon PERTWEE and former actor on stage with H.B. Irving from 1910, he was the author of many popular stage plays, including, *Pink String and Sealing Wax* (1943, filmed 1945), often collaborating with son Michael, with whom he also co-authored TV's *The Grove Family* (1954–57), filmed from their screenplay in 1957 as *It's a Great Day*. He began work on silent films, as actor and writer, and his 30s film work embraced the usual GENRES, including THRILLERS and COMEDIES, as well as, somewhat surprisingly, *King Solomon's Mines* (1937, co-sc, dial). Later contributed to three of Leslie HOWARD's wartime films, *Pimpernel Smith* (1941, scenario, a), *The Lamp Still Burns*, *The Gentle Sex* (1943, co-sc) and to several GAINSBOROUGH MELODRAMAS, including the remarkable *Madonna of the Seven Moons* (1944).

OTHER BRITISH FILMS INCLUDE: (a) *The Second Mrs Tanqueray* (1916); (sc) *The Right Element*, *Hope* (1919), *The Last Rose of Summer* (1920, adaptn), *Packing Up* (1927, short), *Honours Easy* (1935, + play), *The Spy in Black* (scen), *Young Man's Fancy* (dial), *The Four Just Men* (dial, a) (1939), *They Were Sisters* (1945, + a), *Caravan* (1946); (co-sc) *The Bridal Chair* (1919), *Aunt Rachel* (1920), *Murder on the Second Floor*, *A Letter of Warning*, *Blind Spot* (1932), *The Ghoul* (1933), *Man of the Moment* (1935), *A Yank at Oxford*, *Non-Stop New York* (1937), *The Ware Case* (1938), *They Came by Night*, *Return to Yesterday*, *The Proud Valley* (1940), *Jeannie*, *Breach of Promise* (+ co-d) (1941), *Talk About Jacqueline* (1942, + a), *The Halfway House* (1944, co-sc contrib, a), *Diamond City* (1949), *Not Wanted on Voyage* (1957).

Pertwee, Sean (*b* London, 1965). Actor. Third generation of the theatre and film family, the son of Jon PERTWEE is a member of that in-group of late 90s actors (Jude LAW, Sadie FROST, etc) who operate NATURAL NYLON. Unfortunately, his connections involved him in deeply awful *Love, Honour and Obey* (2000), as a South London gang boss, but he seems to have recovered from this and has been in demand in the US as well as Britain, where he is based. Busy also on TV, as in *Chancer* (1990–91), *Cadfael* (1994), and *Cold Feet* (2001), and directed the SHORT FILM, *Just Another Day in London* (1996).

OTHER BRITISH FILMS INCLUDE: *Prick Up Your Ears*, (1987), *Leon the Pig Farmer* (1992), *Shopping* (1994), *Blue Juice* (1995), *ID* (UK/Ger), *Event Horizon* (UK/US) (1997), *Five Seconds to Spare* (1999), *51st State* (UK/Can/US), *Dog Soldiers* (2001).

Peters, Luan (*b* London, 1949). Actress. Sexy blonde star of the 70s who trained at the E15 Acting School and appeared in about ten films, many of them of the HORROR GENRE, starting with *Lust for a Vampire* (1970). Also much TV, including a stint in *Coronation Street*.

OTHER BRITISH FILMS INCLUDE: *Man of Violence* (1970), *Twins of Evil*, *Not Tonight Darling!* (1971), *Vampira* (1974), *The Devil's Men* (1976), *The Wildcats of St Trinian's* (1980).

Peters, Pauline (*b* Cardiff, 1896 – *d* ?). Actress. A leading lady of the 1910s who became the perfect and pretty foil to Walter FORDE in a SERIES of COMEDY SHORTS of the 20s. She emigrated to South Africa with her film executive husband George Smith.

BRITISH FILMS INCLUDE: *From Shopgirl to Duchess*, *Wild Oats* (1915), *Honour in Pawn*, *Shadows* (1915), *Home Sweet Home* (1917), *The Usurper*, *The Lady Clare* (1919), *Stop Press* comedy series, *Trent's Last Case* (1920), *The Mayor of Casterbridge* (1921), *Walter Wins a Wager*, *Walter's Trying Frolics*, (1922), *Walter's Paying Policy*, *Walter's Day Out*, *Walter Tells the Tale*, *Walter the Prodigal* (1926), *Deadlock* (1931). AS.

Petersen, Colin (*b* Kingaroy, Australia, 1946). Actor. Drummer for BEE GEES pop group who was a child actor from age seven; played the title role in *Smiley* (1956), a LONDON FILMS production largely made in Australia, and was engaging as the small boy desperate for a bicycle. He made two further films in Britain, *The Scamp* (1957), as a budding delinquent, and *A Cry from the Streets* (1958), before later taking up with the Bee Gees. After a somewhat acrimonious split with them, he returned to Australia and became a painter.

Petit, Chris (*b* Upton-upon-Severn, 1949). Director. Former critic and devotee of Wim Wenders's films, Petit has had a curious – and curiously stunted – directorial career. His first film, *Radio On* (1979, UK/Ger), a strange moody road movie (Wenders was associate producer), had a minor cult following; he made an edgy ADAPTATION of P.D. James's *An Unsuitable Job for a Woman* (1981, + sc), directed the UK/German *Flight to Berlin* (1983, + sc), and the German thriller, *Chinese Boxes* (1984). Thereafter, he has made SHORT FILMS and worked in TV, including the conventional CHRISTIE puzzle, *A Caribbean Mystery* (1989).

OTHER BRITISH FILMS: *Dream Demon* (1988, co-sc); (shorts, d) *Weather* (1992), *Surveillance*, *London Labyrinth* (1993), *Radio On Remix* (1998, + sc).

Petrie, Hay (*b* Dundee, 1895 – *d* London, 1948). Actor. On stage from 1920 and screen ten years later, Petrie was one of those indefatigable CHARACTER ACTORS who could guarantee a few minutes of pure pleasure in the silliest film (see *Laughing Lady*, 1946) and adorned many distinguished films. Think of what he does with the wretched, hectoring Pumblechook in *Great Expectations* (1946), or the clockwinder in the Embassy, oblivious to all but his trade, in *The Fallen Idol* (1948). Short and self-absorbed, he would appear, take over a scene and depart, only rarely approaching the duration of a star's role, as in *The Old Curiosity Shop* (1934), as the evil dwarf Quilp, or as the vengeance-attracting MacLaggan in *The Ghost Goes West* (1935).

OTHER BRITISH FILMS INCLUDE: *Night Birds* (UK/Ger) (1930), *Help Yourself* (1932), *The Lucky Number*, *The Private Life of Henry VIII*, *Song of the Plough* (1933), *Nell Gwyn* (1934), *Peg of Old Drury*, *Moscow Nights* (1935), *Rembrandt*, *Hearts of Humanity* (1936), *Knight Without Armour*, *21 Days* (1937), *Q Planes*, *The Four Feathers*, *Jamaica Inn*, *The Spy in Black* (1939), *Pastor Hall*, *The Thief of Baghdad* (1940), *Spellbound*, *Quiet Wedding*, *The Ghost of St Michael's*, *Cottage to Let* (1941), *They Flew Alone*, *One of Our Aircraft is Missing* (1942), *Escape to Danger* (1943), *A Canterbury Tale*, *On Approval* (1944), *Night Boat to Dublin* (1946), *The Red Shoes*, *The Guinea Pig*, *The Queen of Spades* (1948).

Pettingell, Frank (*b* Liverpool, 1891 – *d* London, 1966). Actor. As bulky and apparently relaxed as the preceding Petrie was not, Pettingell, educated at Manchester University, was similarly busy in character roles from the early 30s to the mid 60s. A former artist and journalist, he was on stage from 1910, served in WW1, and later combined films and theatre. Most of his film roles are bluff regionals, like Gracie FIELDS's Uncle Murgatroyd in *Sing As We Go!* (1934), a drunk in *The Last Journey* (1935), the deceptively alert detective in *Gaslight* (1940) and the music-hall manager in *Meet Me Tonight* (1952). On TV, however, he played Sheridan Whiteside in *The Man Who Came to Dinner* (1947).

OTHER BRITISH FILMS INCLUDE: *Hobson's Choice* (1931), *The Crooked Lady* (1932), *The Lucky Number*, *The Good Companions*, *A Cuckoo in the Nest* (1933), *The Big Splash*, *On Top of the World* (1935), *The Amateur Gentleman* (1936), *Sailing Along* (1938), *Busman's Honeymoon*, *Return to Yesterday* (1940), *This England*, *Ships with Wings*, *Kipps* (1941), *The Young Mr Pitt*, *The Goose Steps Out* (1942), *Get Cracking* (1943), *Gaiety George* (1946), *No Room at the Inn*, *Escape* (1948), *The Magic Box* (1951), *The Card* (1952), *Value for Money* (1955), *Corridors of Blood* (1958), *Term of Trial* (1962), *Becket* (1964).

Phelan, Brian (*b* Dublin, 1934). Actor. In theatre from 1953 and the author of several TV plays, Phelan had a leading role in Anthony SIMMONS's chamber drama, *Four in the Morning* (1965), and a dozen further supporting roles in the 60s.

OTHER BRITISH FILMS INCLUDE: *The Criminal* (1960), *The Kitchen* (1961), *HMS Defiant* (1962), *The Leather Boys, The Servant* (1963), *A High Wind in Jamaica* (1965), *Accident* (1967).

Pheloung, Barrington (*b* Sydney, 1954). Composer, conductor and guitarist. Australian who came to England in 1972 to study at the RCM; composes for dance, theatre, film, television, radio, CD-ROM and the concert platform. Perhaps best known for his music for TV's *Inspector Morse*, recordings of which have been awarded platinum, gold and silver discs. His film work ranges from the simple but moving chamber music for *Truly Madly Deeply* (1990), to *Nostradamus* (1994), which is characterised by references to early 16th century music and the use of period instruments within an atmospheric orchestral and choral score.

OTHER BRITISH FILMS INCLUDE: *Friendship's Death* (1987), *Shopping* (1994), *Saint-Ex* (1996), *Hilary and Jackie* (1998), *Cold Fish* (2000). David Burnand.

Phillips, Bertram Director, producer. An old-fashioned director, the managing director of Holmfirth Producing Company in 1917, whose leading lady in feature films was always Queenie THOMAS.

BRITISH FILMS: (features, d, + p from 1918) *The White Star* (1915), *The Chance of a Lifetime* (1916), *A Man the Army Made* (1917), *It's Happiness That Counts* (1918), *A Little Child Shall Lead Them* (1919), *Syncopated Picture Plays* series, *The School for Scandal* (1923), *The Gayest of the Gay* (1924); (shorts) *A Week with the King* (1917), *Arthur Roberts* (1927), *Ag and Bert* (1929). AS.

Phillips, Conrad (*b* London, 1930). Actor. Leading man in such 'B' FILMS as *Strangers' Meeting* (1957), as an overstretched doctor involved in crime, and a venturesome reporter in *The Desperate Man* (1959), Conrad generally had only supporting roles in more ambitious affairs, such as *Sons and Lovers* (1960), as Mary URE's brooding husband. However, he found fame of a kind as TV's *William Tell* (1958–59), turning up 30 years later as guest in an international co-production, *William Tell* (1989–90).

OTHER BRITISH FILMS INCLUDE: *Song for Tomorrow* (1948), *Lilli Marlene* (1950), *The Last Page, It Started in Paradise* (1952), *The Secret Tent, Zarak, Last Man to Hang?* (1956), *A Question of Adultery* (1958), *The White Trap* (1959), *Circus of Horrors* (1960), *The Secret Partner, No Love for Johnnie, Murder She Said* (1961), *Don't Talk to Strange Men* (1962), *Heavens Above!* (1963), *Who Killed the Cat?* (1966), *The Saracen* (1971).

Phillips, Gregory (*b* Hitchin, 1948). Actor. Made a striking juvenile film debut as Judy GARLAND and Dirk BOGARDE's son in *I Could Go On Singing* (1963), was one of the children in *The Pumpkin Eater* (1964) and played a few further supporting roles, but did not pursue an adult screen career. Appeared in episodes of popular TV programmes like *Dixon of Dock Green* and *Z Cars*.

OTHER BRITISH FILMS: *Who Killed the Cat?* (1966), *I Start Counting, The Virgin Soldiers* (1969), *Adolf Hitler – My Part in His Downfall* (1972).

Phillips, John (*b* Birmingham, 1914 – *d* New York, 1995). Actor. Commanding character actor, most commonly associated with high-ranking military officers or other professionals, like the Colonel in *A Prize of Arms* (1961) or the Bishop of Winchester in *Becket* (1964). He was a natural for Mr Brocklehurst in TV's *Jane Eyre* (1973) and a vivid stage presence as Alec GUINNESS's flabby brother-in-law in *The Old Country* (1978).

OTHER BRITISH FILMS INCLUDE: *Angels One Five* (1952), *Richard III* (1955), *The Shiralee, I Accuse!* (1957), *Floods of Fear* (1958), *Village of the Damned* (1960), *We Joined the Navy* (1962), *The Mouse on the Moon* (1963), *The Mummy's Shroud* (1966), *Torture Garden* (1967), *Ascendancy* (1982), *The Last of England* (1987).

Phillips, Leslie (*b* Tottenham, 1924). Actor. Debonair light comedy (latterly character) actor with a film career stretching from *Lassie from Lancashire* (1938) to *Lara Croft: Tomb Raider* (2001, US). In the period 1959–76 his image was defined in the public imagination: fair-haired, with thin moustache, rakish charm and distinctive leery laugh. From Italia Conti stage school he made his London debut in 1935, and post-WW2 service had smallish roles in British films, but it was Lt Pouter in the hit BBC-radio comedy series *The Navy Lark* in 1958 (filmed 1959) which made him a star. An expert farceur, he was very busy in British COMEDY films between 1959 and 1963 – in four CARRY ONs, and a foxy replacement for Dirk BOGARDE in three DOCTOR films. As the good taste and budget of British film comedy declined in the 70s, he was missing from films to be reborn as a character actor in the 80s, playing colonial types in two US productions *Out of Africa* (1985) and *Empire of the Sun* (1987), and perfect as Lord Astor in *Scandal* (1988). Busy since in British and US film, stage and TV, specialising in vicars, louche aristocrats and aged roués, always suggesting a rich history, and a notable Falstaff for the RSC (1997). Awarded OBE, 1998. Married (1) **Penelope Bartley**, whose only film was *The Big Chance* (1957); (2) Angela SCOULAR.

OTHER BRITISH FILMS INCLUDE: *The Citadel* (1938), *Train of Events* (1949), *Pool of London* (1950), *The Sound Barrier* (1952), *Value for Money* (1955), *Brothers in Law, The Barretts of Wimpole Street* (1956), *The Smallest Show on Earth,*(1957), *The Man Who Liked Funerals, Carry On Nurse, The Big Money* (1958), *Please Turn Over, Carry On Teacher, Inn for Trouble* (1959), *Watch Your Stern, Doctor in Love, Carry On Constable* (1960), *In the Doghouse, Very Important Person* (1961), *Crooks Anonymous, The Fast Lady* (1962), *Father Came Too!* (1963), *Doctor in Clover* (1966), *Doctor in Trouble* (1970), *Not Now, Darling* (1972), *Don't Just Lie There, Say Something* (1973), *Not Now, Comrade* (1976), *Carry On Columbus* (1992), *August* (1996), *Saving Grace* (2000). Roger Philip Mellor.

Phillips, Robin (*b* Haslemere, 1940). Actor. Trained at Bristol Old Vic, later acting and directing. Played leads in a few British films from the 60s, including the guileless Paul Pennyfeather in *Decline and Fall . . .* (1968) and an angst-ridden David Copperfield (1969), but turned to stage directing and was Artistic Director of the Stratford Festival, Canada, in the later 70s.

OTHER BRITISH FILMS: *Candidate for Murder* (1962), *Two Gentlemen Sharing* (1969), *Tales from the Crypt, Miss Julie* (co-d) (1972).

Phillips, Siân (*b* Bettws, Wales, 1934). Actress. Tall, dominant Welsh actress, of striking appearance, whose work in all the acting media has won her a high reputation, though it is arguable that her TV roles have won her most acclaim: as, for instance, Mrs Pankhurst in *Shoulder to Shoulder* (1974), the mother in *How Green Was My Valley* (1975) and the alarming Livia in *I, Claudius* (1976), in rapid succession. She began broadcasting for Welsh BBC at age 11, attended the University of Wales and trained at RADA, making her London debut in 1957, since when she has done everything from Shakespeare to *Pal Joey* (1980). Her sporadic screen career has included four films starring her then-husband (1959–79) Peter O'TOOLE: *Becket* (1964), *Goodbye, Mr Chips* (1969), co-starred in *Murphy's War* (1971) and *Under Milk Wood* (1971), as house-proud Mrs Ogmore-Pritchard, in turban and smock. With the possible exception of *House of America* (1997, UK/Neth), as an eccentric, deserted Welsh Mam, films have scarcely extended her or exploited her passionate potential, but she has made supporting roles vivid, including the refined Mrs Archer in *The Age of Innocence* (1993, US). After divorcing O'Toole, she married/divorced RADA-trained actor **Robin Sachs** (*b* London, 1951) who appeared in a few British films, including *Henry VIII and His Six Wives* (1972), as the ingratiating but doomed Culpepper, and now works in the US. Made CBE in 2000, Phillips is regarded as a Welsh national treasure.

OTHER BRITISH FILMS: *Young Cassidy* (1965), *Laughter in the Dark* (1969), *Clash of the Titans* (1981), *How Many Miles to Babylon?* (1982), *The Doctor and the Devils* (1985), *Valmont* (1989).

BIBLIOG: Autobiography, *Private Faces*, 1999.

Phillpotts, Ambrosine (*b* London, 1912 – *d* Ascot, 1980). Actress. Surveying the range of RADA-trained Phillpotts's stage work, including, say, Shakespeare with Ben Greet's company (1931–33) or Maggie in *The Man Who Came to Dinner* (1943), one realises how films merely stereotyped her as acidulous toffs, in performances she could, in later decades, have e-mailed. One remarkable exception is that of Mrs Brown in *Room at the Top* (1958), where the venom beneath the manicured surface is carefully allowed escape and the result is a critique of the sort of roles she habitually played on screen. She was never less than incisive in the bits she accepted, but she might have been much more. She was the niece of playwright Eden Phillpotts.

OTHER BRITISH FILMS INCLUDE: *This Man is Mine* (1946), *The Chiltern Hundreds* (1949), *Mr Denning Drives North* (1951), *Stolen Face, Father's Doing Fine, Angels One Five* (1952), *The Captain's Paradise* (1953), *The Truth About Women* (1957), *The Duke Wore Jeans* (1958), *Expresso Bongo* (1959), *Doctor in Love* (1960), *Raising the Wind, Carry On Regardless* (1961), *Carry On Cabby* (1963), *Life at the Top* (1965), *Ooh . . . You Are Awful* (1972), *The Wildcats of St Trinian's* (1980).

Phipps, Nicholas (*b* London, 1913 – *d* London, 1980). Actor. No film in which the ineffably upper-class, Winchester-educated Phipps appeared could be a total write-off. Tall, beaky and moustachioed, he was on stage and, according to some sources, in films from 1932, but his fame as CHARACTER ACTOR and screenwriter really postdates WW2 service with the Royal Artillery (1940–43) and subsequently ENSA. He came to attention with the screenplays for Herbert WILCOX's 'London' SERIES, including *I Live in Grosvenor Square* (1945, co-sc), *Piccadilly Incident* (1946, + scen), *The Courtneys of Curzon Street* (1947, + a), *Spring in Park Lane* (1948, + a), *Elizabeth of Ladymead* (1948, add dial, + a), and *Maytime in Mayfair* (1949, + a); and wrote several of the 'DOCTOR' films, also appearing as a Magistrate in *Doctor in the House* (1954). As actor, he honed to perfection the dinner-table or mess bore in such films as Wilcox's *Spring in Park Lane* and *The Intruder* (1953), and the 50s in particular would have been drabber without him.

OTHER BRITISH FILMS INCLUDE: (co-sc) *This Man Is Mine* (1946), *Woman Hater* (1948), *Madeleine* (1949), *The Captain's Paradise* (1953, + a), *Doctor at Sea* (1955), *The Captain's Table* (1958, + a), *No Love for Johnnie* (1961), *Doctor in Distress* (1963); (sc) *The First Gentleman* (1948), *Appointment with Venus* (1951, + a), *Doctor at Large* (1957, + a), *Doctor in Love* (1960, + a), *A Pair of Briefs* (1961, + a); (a) *Old Bill and Son* (1940), *Mad About Men* (1954), *Rockets Galore, Orders to Kill* (1958), *The Navy Lark, Don't Panic Chaps* (1959), *The Pure Hell of St Trinian's* (1960), *Summer Holiday* (1962), *Heavens Above!* (1963), *Charlie Bubbles* (1967), *Monte Carlo or Bust!* (UK/Fr/It), *Some Girls Do* (1969), *The Rise and Rise of Michael Rimmer* (1970).

Piccadilly Pictures was founded in July 1926, with C.M. WOOLF as chairman, Michael BALCON and Carlyle BLACKWELL as joint managing directors and Graham CUTTS as

contract director. It produced two films in 1926, *The Lodger*, which confirmed Alfred HITCHCOCK as a major director, and *The Triumph of the Rat*, which demonstrated that Cutts was one of the country's top film-makers. Other Piccadilly films include *Blighty, The Queen Was in the Parlour* (1927), *Beyond the Cities*, and *Bedrock* (1930). AS.

Pickard, Helena (*b* Sheffield, 1899 – *d* Henley-on-Thames, 1959). Actress. RADA-trained and on stage from 1915, Pickard played supporting roles in films over 25 years, including a victim of *The Lodger* (1944, US). She was Mrs Pepys in *Nell Gwyn* (1934) and a passenger on the ship bearing George FORMBY to Norway in *Let George Do It!* (1940), but films were incidental to a thriving stage career. As is often the lot of first spouses, she is rather summarily dismissed in former husband Cedric HARDWICKE's autobiography, *A Victorian in Orbit* (1961). Edward HARDWICKE is their son.

OTHER BRITISH FILMS INCLUDE: *Lord Richard in the Pantry* (1930), *Cupboard Love* (1931), *Music Hall* (1934), *Limelight* (1936), *Saloon Bar* (1940), *The Turners of Prospect Road* (1947), *Miss Pilgrim's Progress* (1949), *The Lady with a Lamp* (1951, as Queen Victoria), *The Love Lottery* (1953), *Doublecross* (1955).

Pickering, Donald (*b* Newcastle-upon-Tyne, 1933). Actor. Character player of upper-class demeanour, which suited him to roles such as Dolly Longstaff in TV's *The Pallisers* (1974) and, on screen, Lt-Colonel Mackenzie in *A Bridge Too Far* and Major Russell in *Zulu Dawn* (1979). Busier on TV in recent decades.

OTHER BRITISH FILMS INCLUDE: *Doctor at Large* (1957), *Nothing But the Best* (1964), *Fahrenheit 451* (1966), *A Challenge for Robin Hood* (1967), *The Breaking of Bumbo* (1970), *The Thirty Nine Steps* (1978), *Yanks* (1979), *Monk Dawson* (1997).

Pickles, Vivian (*b* London, 1931). Actress. Potent character player who came to prominence as TV's *Isadora Duncan, the Biggest Dancer in the World* (1966) for Ken RUSSELL and whose most notable work has been for TV. On-screen, she was vivid and funny as Glenda JACKSON's 'liberal' friend in *Sunday Bloody Sunday* (1971).

OTHER BRITISH FILMS: *Play Dirty* (1968), *The Looking Glass War* (1969), *Nicholas and Alexandra* (1971, UK/US), *O Lucky Man!* (1973), *Candleshoe* (1977, UK/US), *Britannia Hospital* (1982).

Pickles, Wilfred (*b* Halifax, 1904 – *d* Brighton, 1978). Actor. Esteemed North country character player, long a radio (from 1927) and TV favourite, who appeared memorably in at least two films: in *Billy Liar* (1963), as Billy's irascible dad, and *The Family Way* (1966), as sympathetic Uncle Fred. He starred in the film version (1954) of his West End stage success, *The Gay Dog* (1954), and he and Irene HANDL reprised on film (1972) their popular TV series, *For the Love of Ada* (1970–71). Awarded OBE, 1950. His niece is US-based actress Christina Pickles (*b* Yorkshire, 1935).

OTHER BRITISH FILMS: *Riding Thro' the Ridings* (1948, doc, narr), *Serious Charge* (1959).

BIBLIOG: Autobiography, *Between You and Me*, 1949.

Pickup, Ronald (*b* Oldham, 1941). Actor. Formidable character star in all the acting media, Leeds University-educated and RADA-trained Pickup was on stage from 1964 and won much praise for his playing of blighted Edmund Tyrone in Michael Blakemore's production of *Long Day's Journey into Night* (1971–72, televised in 1973). On TV, he played Shakespearean roles, including the Fool in *King Lear* (1975), a sinister Barrymore in *The Hound of the Baskervilles* (1988), and many others. He has submerged his somewhat sardonic features and tweedy demeanour in a comparable range of film roles, starting with Baron Tusenbach, his 1969 stage role, in the filmed version of *Three Sisters* (1970), the forger in *The Day of the Jackal* (1973, UK/Fr), Stravinsky in *Nijinsky* (1980, US), one of several international films, and army commander Tukhachevsky in *Testimony* (1987).

OTHER BRITISH FILMS: *Mahler* (1974), *Joseph Andrews* (1976), *The Thirty Nine Steps* (1978), *Never Say Never Again* (1983, UK/US), *The Mission* (1985), *The Fourth Protocol* (1987), *Bring Me the Head of Mavis Davis* (1998), *Breathtaking* (2000).

Picture Show *see* **magazines and journals**

Picturegoer *see* **magazines and journals**

Pierce-Roberts, Tony (*b* Birkenhead). Cinematographer. Entered films from TV in the early 80s, shooting first the idiosyncratic Jerzy SKOLIMOWSKI comedy-drama, *Moonlighting* (1982), but winning his reputation chiefly on his series of MERCHANT IVORY pieces, starting with *A Room with a View* (1985). In the latter, his differentiation of a range of outdoor lushness and interior oppressiveness in each of England and Italy was a key element in the film's accomplishment. Away from the beauties of period ADAPTATION, he contributed a powerful sense of claustrophobia in the WW1 drama *The Trench* (1999, UK/Fr). International work includes Ivory's *Mr & Mrs Bridge* (1990) and the sexual harassment thriller, *Disclosure* (1994).

OTHER BRITISH FILMS INCLUDE: *P'tang Yang Kipperbang* (1982), *A Private Function* (1984), *Howards End* (1992), *The Remains of the Day* (1993), *Haunted* (1995, UK/US), *Surviving Picasso* (1996, UK/US), *The Golden Bowl* (2000, UK/Fr/US), *Kiss Kiss (Bang Bang)* (2001), *The Importance of Being Earnest* (2002, UK/US).

Pigg, Alexandra (*b* Liverpool, 1962). Actress. RN: Sandra McKibbin. Spirited, touching and funny, Pigg made an outstanding success of her first film role as the young Liverpudlian who wrote *A Letter to Brezhnev* (1985). British cinema signally failed to capitalise on this auspicious debut, her following films making small impact, and she went into TV's *Brookside* (1982–93). And to think she changed her name to its present infelicity.

OTHER BRITISH FILMS: *Strapless* (1988), *A Chorus of Disapproval*, *Chicago Joe and the Showgirl* (1989), *Bullseye!* (1990, UK/US, cameo role), *Immortal Beloved* (1994, UK/US).

Pigott-Smith, Tim (*b* Rugby, 1946). Actor. Compelling stage actor who made his name with the RSC and subsequently did some riveting Shakespeare on TV, including Octavius Caesar in *Antony and Cleopatra* (1973) and Angelo in *Measure for Measure* (1979), as well as bringing out the coldly repressed sexual tension of Merrick in *Jewel in the Crown* (1984). He has played only supporting roles in films, none of them very interesting, with the marginal exception of Benn, the butler who marries Emma THOMPSON in *The Remains of the Day* (1993). Married **Pamela Miles**, who appeared with their son Tom in a small role in *A Fish Called Wanda* (1988).

OTHER BRITISH FILMS: *Joseph Andrews*, *Aces High* (UK/Fr) (1976), *Sweet William* (1979), *Richard's Things* (1980), *Clash of the Titans* (1981, UK/US), *Bloody Sunday* (2002).

BIBLIOG: Tim Pigott-Smith, *Out of India*, 1986.

Pike, Kelvin (*b* Roseville, NSW, 1929). Cinematographer. Trained at the Regent Street Polytechnic, London (1945–47), Pike worked as camera operator on some distinguished films, including three for KUBRICK – *Dr Strangelove . . .* (1963), *2001:*

A Space Odyssey (1968), *The Shining* (1980, UK/US) – before achieving his first cinematographer credit on *The Dresser* (1983). On this, he contributed significantly to the affectionate recreation of a now vanished kind of theatre. Since then he has worked almost entirely for TV or on such US films as *A Dry White Season* (1989) and *Betsy's Wedding* (1990).

OTHER BRITISH FILMS INCLUDE: (cam op) *A Prize of Arms* (1961), *The Nanny* (1965), *Khartoum* (1966), *Half a Sixpence* (1967, UK/US), *Valentino* (1977), *Breaking Glass* (1980), *Krull* (1983).

Pilbeam, Nova (*b* London, 1919). Actress. Exquisite teenage star of the 30s who appeared memorably for HITCHCOCK as the kidnapped child in the first version of *The Man Who Knew Too Much* (1934) and as the intrepid young heroine of the charming chase thriller, *Young and Innocent* (1937). The highpoint of her 30s career, though, was as doomed Lady Jane Grey in *Tudor Rose* (1936), in which her fresh delicacy is so cruelly betrayed by political manoeuvrings. There were several other worthwhile roles, notably as Wilfrid LAWSON's daughter in *Pastor Hall* (1940) and as the Dutch refugee in *The Next of Kin* (1942), but though she managed the transition from teenage to adult roles she was never in another major film. She said in 1990 that she had enjoyed very much playing the bitchy socialite in *Green Fingers* (1947) and she was the romantic lead in Daniel BIRT's underrated Gothic MELODRAMA, *The Three Weird Sisters* (1948), but the title roles, played by Nancy PRICE, Mary MERRALL and Mary CLARE, dominated the action. Her first husband Penrose TENNYSON was tragically killed early in WW2; she remarried in the early 50s and retired completely from acting, even from the theatre which she had always preferred. Her father was actor Arnold Pilbeam, who managed the Lyric, Hammersmith, in the 20s.

OTHER BRITISH FILMS: *Little Friend* (1934), *Cheer Boys Cheer* (1939), *Spring Meeting, Banana Ridge* (1941), *The Yellow Canary* (1943), *This Man Is Mine* (1946), *Counterblast* (1948).

Pilkington, Lorraine (*b* Dublin, 1975). Actress. Zestful, frizzy-haired young blonde star of the 90s who came to popular attention with two eye-catching roles: as the wilful clubber who gets romantically involved with John SIMM in *Human Traffic* (1999), an engagingly played mix of drugs, pop music and sex; and as the schoolteacher spikily in love with the local laird in TV's *Monarch of the Glen* (1999, 2000). She has the whiff of stardom about her but these two roles have been followed by secondary ones in *Breathtaking* and *My Kingdom* (2001). First appeared in films as a result of ducking school to take a small part in *The Miracle* (1991, UK/Ire) and made a half-dozen others, including *The Boxer* (1998, UK/Ire/US), as the bride in the wedding party sequence.

OTHER BRITISH FILMS INCLUDE: *Into the West* (1992, UK/Ire/US), *All Things Bright and Beautiful* (1994), *The Disappearance of Finbar* (UK/Fr/Ire/Swe), *The Last of the High Kings* (UK/Ger/Ire) (1996), *The Nephew* (1998, Ire).

Pinebrook Films This was a company, based at PINEWOOD, set up by Richard NORTON (later Lord Grantley) in January 1938, to help meet the unemployment crisis in the industry. The plan was for films to be made cheaply, with some personnel working on reduced salaries to be augmented later by a share of the profits. There was union criticism for this mode of production, with claims of exploited labour. However, Pinebrook scored a big success with *This Man Is News* (1938) and its sequel *This Man Is Paris* (1939), the films that launched Anthony HAVELOCK-ALLAN into main features. In 1938 Pinebrook and EALING joined forces to found the Co-operative Association of

Producers and Distributors, but in the following year, of the twelve CAPAD films made, all but one, *The Lambeth Walk*, was made at Ealing.

Pinero, Sir Arthur Wing (*b* London, 1855 – *d* London, 1934). Playwright. Popular playwright of late Victorian era, whose varied work included: ingeniously plotted farces like *The Magistrate* (1885), filmed in 1921 and, as *Those Were the Days* in 1934; realistic domestic tragedies, like his major work, *The Second Mrs Tanqueray* (1893), filmed with Sir George Alexander in 1916 and by Dallas BOWER in 1952; and the charming hymn to the theatrical life, *Trelawney of the Wells* (1898), filmed in the US in 1928, as *The Actress*, triumphantly staged in London in 1965 and as TV's 'Play of the Month' in 1971. His play on the redeeming power of love, *The Enchanted Cottage* (1922), was filmed in the US in 1924 and 1945. Eclipsed at the time by the rise of Ibsen and Shaw, Pinero seems due for another revival. Knighted 1909.

OTHER BRITISH FILMS: (adapted from his work) *Iris* (1916), *The Profligate*, *The Gay Lord Quex* (1917, also US, 1919), *His House in Order* (1928, also US, 1920), *Dandy Dick* (1935).

Pinewood Studios In late 2000, there were rumblings in the film trade press that Pinewood was to be merged with SHEPPERTON. The idea was to save on running costs and to create a single studio business which could cater to every kind of film-maker's demands, however big or small. With the Barrandov Studios in Prague, UFA Studios in Germany and the Fox Studios in Australia all competing to attract international film-makers, Pinewood faced stiffer competition than at almost any time in its history.

There are two main reasons why film producers choose one studio over another – cost and efficiency. Pinewood, built in 1936, hasn't always been the cheapest place to shoot movies. What it has consistently offered is a level of technical expertise which nowhere else could match. From POWELL AND PRESSBURGER to James BOND, from *The Red Shoes* (1948) to *The Spy Who Loved Me* (1977), many of the biggest, most flamboyant films in British cinema history have been shot at these studios.

Pinewood was built on the site of Heatherden Hall, a sumptuous Buckinghamshire country house which had once belonged to Canadian financier, Grant Morden. Methodist magnate J. Arthur RANK pooled together with Sheffield Building tycoon, Sir Charles Boot, and jute heiress Lady YULE to pay for the studio, which was constructed in under nine months. It opened in September 1936.

To begin with, business was patchy. Herbert WILCOX's company BRITISH AND DOMINION and BRITISH NATIONAL were committed to using the studio, but there were five sound stages to fill and the late 30s were not an especially robust moment in British film production history. In 1937, Rank bought Lady Yule's share in the studio and became Chairman of Pinewood. A year later, Pinewood was 'twinned' with DENHAM STUDIOS, also now under Rank's control. A special new company, Denham and Pinewood Studios Ltd was set up. Most of the film-makers working for Rank preferred making their movies at Denham. Pinewood was closed for most of WW2 (it was used by the government for storage). It was officially reopened in 1946, and for a brief period, paid host to the films made by Rank's elite cadre of film-makers, INDEPENDENT PRODUCERS LTD (IPL), David LEAN and Powell and Pressburger prominent among them.

In the 1950s, Pinewood became synonymous with the kind of cosy, unchallenging comedies that the RANK ORGANISATION

had begun to make. Both *Doctor In The House* (1954) and the Norman WISDOM vehicle, *Trouble In Store* (1953), were shot at the studio as were the later 'DOCTOR' FILMS and most of Wisdom's other movies. So was the likeable, but very gentrified comedy, *Genevieve* (1953). Outside film-makers still used the studio, but to the British public, this was the home of the Rank starlets and of all those leading men – John GREGSON, Kenneth MORE, Jack HAWKINS, Dirk BOGARDE – who dressed in tweed and flannels and smoked pipes.

Despite its stolid image, Pinewood attracted some highly inventive craftsmen. Many trained with David RAWNSLEY, who pioneered his back projection system, INDEPENDENT FRAME, at the studio in the late 1940s. Although Independent Frame was not successful in itself, its introduction helped earn Pinewood a reputation for technical excellence. The work done at Pinewood in later years on such international productions as *Batman* (1989), *Superman* (1978) and, of course, the BOND movies, suggested that British crews were indeed the best in the world.

By the 90s, the Rank Organisation had largely lost its interest in the film business. The question was not whether it would sell Pinewood but when. Eventually, in March 2000, it offloaded the studio to a consortium led by former CHANNEL 4 boss, Michael GRADE. Meanwhile, business at Pinewood went on as normal. Work had been completed in 1999 on two new 20,000 square-foot stages, to go alongside the 18 stages already in use (including the 45,000 square-foot 007 Stage). Like its mooted new partner, Shepperton, the studio was mixing and matching between big-budget Hollywood films, TV dramas and commercials. ('We do everything from the Teletubbies to James Bond,' boasted studio manager, Robin Busby.) Having survived countless crises over its 65-year history, Pinewood was still the best-known film studio in the UK, a state of affairs unlikely to change in the foreseeable future.

BIBLIOG: George Perry, *Movies from the Mansion*, 1976; Gareth Owen and Brian Burford, *The Pinewood Story*, 2000; Patricia Warren, *British Film Studios*, 2001. Geoffrey MacNab.

Pinter, Harold (*b* London, 1930). Screenwriter. Achieving widespread recognition as Britain's leading dramatist and screenwriter of the 60s, Pinter has remained an important figure in British literary culture, and latterly in dissident political circles. Only child of a Jewish Hackney tailor, he briefly attended RADA, making his debut as professional actor in 1950. Pinter's recurrent dramatic themes of time, memory, territorial control, and communication breakdown also appear in his screenplays, which include ADAPTATIONS of his plays *The Caretaker* (filmed in a Hackney house in 1964), *The Birthday Party* (1968), *The Homecoming* (1973), and *Betrayal* (1982, AAn, BAAn/adpt sc), as well as skilful reworkings of novels by Nicholas Mosley, L.P. Hartley, John Fowles and others, in which he displayed the ability to absorb their narrative ideas, yet turning them into an extension of his own world. He formed a rich creative partnership with Joseph LOSEY starting with *The Servant* (1963, + a, BAAn/sc), an adaptation of a 1949 novella which becomes classic Pinter, supplemented by Losey's rich, baroque visual textures. In the academic and sexual intrigues of *Accident* (1967, + a), every line of elliptical dialogue has a tactical purpose, and nothing is innocent of intent; *The Go-Between* (1971, BAA/sc), an exploration of youth and age, time and memory, was his final adaptation for Losey; and *The French Lieutenant's Woman* (1981, AAn/sc, BAAn/sc) was a clever reworking of a difficult novel. Pinter has regularly directed and acted in theatre, directed the film of *Butley* (1973), and appeared occasionally in minor film acting roles. Awarded CBE, 1965; BAFTA Fellowship, 1997; created CH, 2002. Married (1) Vivien MERCHANT (1956–80); (2) author Lady Antonia Fraser (1980).

OTHER BRITISH FILMS: (sc, unless noted) *The Pumpkin Eater* (1964, BAA/sc), *The Quiller Memorandum* (1966, UK/US), *Turtle Diary* (1985, + a), *The Comfort of Strangers* (1990, UK/It), *The Trial* (UK/US)(1993); (a) *The Rise and Rise of Michael Rimmer* (1970), *Mansfield Park* (2000, UK/US).

BIBLIOG: Joanne Klein, *Making Pictures: the Pinter Screenplays*, 1985; Michael Billington, *The Life and Work of Harold Pinter*, 1996; Steven H. Gale (ed), *The Films of Harold Pinter*, 2001. Roger Philip Mellor.

pioneers In 1921, at a film trade meeting, William FRIESE-GREENE died after delivering an incoherent speech on the problems of the industry. His death sparked off an industry concern about its past that led to the creation of a Cinema Veterans association in 1924, open to all those who had joined the British film industry before 1903. (Rules for admission have necessarily been revised over the years, and the organisation is now known as the Cinema and Television Veterans, and publishes the *Veteran* magazine.) Thus was pioneer status defined, and among those who joined were Robert PAUL, Charles URBAN, William Kennedy-Laurie DICKSON, Cecil HEPWORTH, Will BARKER, James WILLIAMSON, Joseph ROSENTHAL, Will DAY and Matt Raymond. In truth, there had always been an awareness of the pioneering days of the 1890s, with arguments raging in the film trade papers little more than ten years after cinema's 'invention' as to whether Friese-Greene, Thomas Edison, E.J. Marey, Eadweard MUYBRIDGE or someone else should gain the credit. British cinema's first historian, Will Day, knew many of the pioneers and did valuable work in collecting testimony and artefacts, though his uncritical championing of Friese-Greene was unfortunate. For many years the achievements of the earliest British film-makers were bound up in romantic myth, their surviving films labelled 'primitive'. More recently, particularly through the work of film historian John BARNES and his disciples, the pioneers have earned praise and intense analysis of their work, for its own sake as well as for what it allowed to follow, making so-called 'Victorian Cinema' one of the most flourishing areas in British film studies. Luke McKernan.

Piper, Frederick (*b* London, 1902 – *d* London, 1979). Actor. Former tea merchant who became one of the stalwarts of the British cinema's studio years and virtually a fixture in EALING's films of the 40s and 50s. In his protean way, he was equally convincing as the decent bosun in *San Demetrio–London* (1943), the half-cut doctor in *Pink String and Sealing Wax* (1945), the detective sergeant in *It Always Rains on Sunday* (1947), and Peggy EVANS's brutal, shiftless father in *The Blue Lamp* (1949). Ealing wasn't all, though it helped define his importance; he was under contract to RANK in the later 40s, and in a career spanning 35-odd years and 70 films he worked for most companies and in most GENRES. On TV from 1938 and in many post-war TV dramas.

OTHER BRITISH FILMS INCLUDE: *The Good Companions* (1933), *The 39 Steps* (1935), *Where There's a Will, Everything is Thunder, Sabotage* (1936), *Non-Stop New York, Young and Innocent, Oh, Mr Porter!* (1937), *Jamaica Inn* (1939), *49th Parallel* (1941), *In Which We Serve, Nine Men* (1942), *The Bells Go Down* (1943), *Fiddlers Three, Champagne Charlie* (1944), *Johnny Frenchman* (1945), *Hue and Cry* (1946), *The October Man, The Loves of Joanna Godden* (1947), *The History of Mr Polly, To the Public Danger, Penny and the Pownall Case* (1948), *Passport to Pimlico,*

It's Not Cricket (1949), *The Lavender Hill Mob* (1951), *Cosh Boy* (1953), *Lease of Life, Conflict of Wings* (1954), *Doctor at Sea* (1955), *Barnacle Bill, The Birthday Present* (1957), *Dunkirk* (1958), *The Day They Robbed the Bank of England* (1959), *Very Important Person, Only Two Can Play, What a Carve Up!* (1961), *One Way Pendulum* (1964), *He Who Rides a Tiger* (1965), *Burke & Hare* (1971).

Pithey, Wensley (*b* Cape Town, 1914 – *d* London, 1993). Actor. In England from 1947, after broadcasting experience in South Africa, where he made his stage debut aged 12. Played innumerable policemen in films as varied as *The Titfield Thunderbolt* (1953) and *Serious Charge* (1959); was grim Mr Grimwig in *Oliver!* (1968) and was several times Winston Churchill, as in TV's *Edward and Mrs Simpson* (1978).

OTHER BRITISH FILMS INCLUDE: *The Mark of Cain* (1948), *Cardboard Cavalier* (1949), *Guilt Is My Shadow* (1950), *Isn't Life Wonderful!* (1953), *Tiger in the Smoke* (1956), *Doctor at Large, Hell Drivers* (1957), *The Pure Hell of St Trinian's* (1960), *The Guilty Party, The Boys* (1962), *The Knack . . .* (1965), *White Mischief* (1987), *American Friends* (1991).

Pitt, Ingrid (*b* Treblinka, Poland, 1937/44/45?). Actress. RN: Petrovna. Polish actress whose birth is shrouded in the mists of war-torn East Europe and who eventually became a minor cult figure of British HORROR films, that traded on her voluptuous figure. She had already appeared in several international films such as *Doctor Zhivago* (1965, UK/US) shot in Spain where she lived for some years, acting with the Spanish National Theatre. In Britain, she was most famously *Countess Dracula* (1970), who bathed in the blood of her servant-girls to improve her complexion, as a wellborn woman would do.

OTHER BRITISH FILMS INCLUDE: *Where Eagles Dare* (1968), *The Vampire Lovers, The House That Dripped Blood* (1970), *The Wicker Man* (1973), *Who Dares Wins* (1982), *Parker* (1984), *Wild Geese II* (1985), *Underworld* (1985), *The Asylum* (2000).

Pitt, Peter (*b* Hendon, 1927). Editor. After apprenticeship as assistant director at RIVERSIDE STUDIOS and then in the cutting rooms, Pitt edited many TV films for Douglas FAIRBANKS, plus episodes of *The Saint, The Baron*, etc. Associated with the crisp 'B' MOVIES of Lance COMFORT, making a useful contribution to the pacy excitements of such films as *The Break* (1962), and a dozen other second features of the 50s and 60s.

OTHER BRITISH FILMS INCLUDE: *Port of Escape, The Hostage, Face in the Night* (1956), *Make Mine a Million* (1959), *Rag Doll* (1960), *The Breaking Point* (1961), *Night Without Pity* (1962), *The Haunted House of Horror* (1969), *A Warm December* (1972, UK/US), *Secrets of a Superstud* (1975).

Pitt, Ray Editor. Pitt's main film work was as editor at EALING in the early days of WW2 when he cut such COMEDIES as *Sailors Three* (1940) and *The Black Sheep of Whitehall* (1941), but was also responsible for editing the PROPAGANDA pieces, *Convoy* (1940) and *The Next of Kin* (1942). Post-war, he was limited to thick-ear CRIME films.

OTHER BRITISH FILMS INCLUDE: *Calling the Tune* (1936, co-e), *Brief Ecstasy* (1937), *Spanish ABC* (short, co-ass d), *What a Man!* (1938), *There Ain't No Justice, Come on George!* (1939), *Saloon Bar, The Proud Valley, Let George Do It!* (1940), *The Goose Steps Out* (1942), *The New Lot* (1943, doc, prod super), *A Gunman Has Escaped* (1948), *The Man in Black, Meet Simon Cherry, Dick Barton Strikes Back* (super ed) (1949).

Pizer, Larry (*b* London, 1925). Cinematographer. Began career by shooting SHORT FILMS in the 50s, including *Energy First* and *£20 a Ton* (1955) for Lindsay ANDERSON, *Blood Is Life* (1957) for director Anthony SIMMONS, for whom he subsequently worked on the features, *Four in the Morning* (1965) and *The Optimists of Nine Elms* (1973), and for Joseph LOSEY's promotional short, *First on the Road* (1960). His most distinguished work is for NEW WAVE directors – Jack CLAYTON's *Our Mother's House* (1967) and Karel REISZ's *Morgan . . .* (1966, co-c) and *Isadora* (1968), a flawed film that *looks* wonderful – and for the MERCHANT IVORY team, for whom he gave a proper freshness to *The Europeans* (1979). Since 1980, most of his work has been in the US, primarily on TV.

OTHER BRITISH FILMS INCLUDE: *The World Ten Times Over*, *The Party's Over* (1963), *All Neat in Black Stockings* (1969), *Jane Austen in Manhattan* (1980, co-c), *The Proprietor* (1996, UK/Fr/Turk/US).

Plaisetty, Rene (*b* Chicago, 1889 – *d* New York, 1955). Director. After an education in Paris, Plaisetty worked for Filma in Paris, Metro and Lubin in America and Italia Film in Italy before coming to the UK to direct four films for STOLL PICTURE PRODUCTIONS in 1921: *The Yellow Claw*, *The Four Feathers*, *The Broken Road*, and *The Knave of Diamonds*. If anything he was perhaps too innovative for British cinema, and he returned to the US. AS.

Planer, Franz (aka Frank) (*b* Karlsbad, Czechoslovakia, 1894 – *d* Los Angeles, 1963). Cinematographer. Celebrated for his collaboration with Max Ophuls, and long in Hollywood where he matchlessly shot *Letter from an Unknown Woman* (1948), as well as a lot of junk, Planer worked on a half-dozen British films of the 30s, including RANK's feature debut, *Turn of the Tide* (1935). First made his name at UFA during the 20s.

OTHER BRITISH FILMS: *Unfinished Symphony* (1934, UK/Austria/Ger), *The Divine Spark* (UK/It), *The Dictator* (1935), *The Beloved Vagabond* (1936), *The Rebel Son* (1939).

Planer, Nigel (*b* London, 1953). Actor. Better known for his TV work in such programmes as *The Young Ones* (1982), as a dim hippy, and *Nicholas Craig* (1990), as a pompous media 'personality', Planer has played occasional film roles, including Anna FRIEL's upper-class husband ('Scrap metal – made a mint') at the end of *The Land Girls* (1998, UK/Fr). Scored a stage success in Alan AYCKBOURN's *A Small Family Business* (2000), as a small family businessman out of his league.

OTHER BRITISH FILMS INCLUDE: *Brazil* (1985), *Eat the Rich* (1987), *Number 27* (1988), *Carry On Columbus* (1992), *Clockwork Mice* (1995), *The Wind in the Willows* (1996).

Plater, Alan (*b* Jarrow, 1935). Screenwriter. Though trained as an architect, Durham University-educated Plater has been a full-time writer since 1961, with distinguished credits in all the acting media. He has written many plays, including *A Little Love Besides* (1970), but is perhaps best known for his TV screenplays. After early contributions to *Z Cars*, in the 60s, he also wrote such prestige pieces as *Fortunes of War* (1987), *A Very British Coup* (1988) and *The Last of the Blonde Bombshells* (2000), a charming valentine to a bevy of actresses of a certain age. Film credits have been comparatively sparse, but in *The Virgin and the Gypsy* (1970) his screenplay laid the basis for one of the screen's most telling ADAPTATIONS of D.H. LAWRENCE.

OTHER BRITISH FILMS: *Juggernaut* (1974, add dial), *It Shouldn't Happen to a Vet* (1976), *Priest of Love* (1980), *Keep the Aspidistra Flying* (1997).

Platts-Mills, Barney (*b* England, 1944). Director. Independent film-maker who wrote and directed a few low-budget, largely improvised features, of which *Bronco Bullfrog* (1969) and *Private Road* (1971) are the best known. They are concerned with contemporary frustrations and attempts to escape constricting environments, and were made largely on location; *Bronco* was shot in six weeks in Stratford East with a mainly local cast; the later film used professionals, including some, like Bruce ROBINSON, who responded well to the director's methods, others, like Kathleen BYRON, who did not. His last feature to date, *Hero* (1982, + sc), shot in Scotland in Gaelic, is an anti-colonialist dialectic in a medieval setting. A strongly individual talent that needed more nurturing than was available.

OTHER BRITISH FILMS: *Parade* (1964, short, sd), *Love's Presentation* (1966, doc, e), *Everybody's an Actor* (1968, doc, d).

Playfair, Sir Nigel (*b* London, 1874 – *d* London, 1934). Actor. Harrow- and Oxford-educated Playfair practised as a barrister before becoming a celebrated actor-manager. He bought the Lyric Theatre, Hammersmith, in 1918 and saw its ascendancy through to the early 30s, first appeared on screen in 1911 in *Princess Clementina* and made a further seven films, in character roles, none of which unfortunately gives much sense of what made him so revered on stage.

OTHER BRITISH FILMS INCLUDE: *Lady Windermere's Fan* (1916), *Masks and Faces* (1917), *Perfect Understanding* (1933), *Little Stranger*, *The Lady Is Willing* (1934).

Pleasence, Angela (*b* Chapeltown, Yorks, *c* 1942). Actress. Busy and versatile in all the acting media, RADA-trained Pleasence made stage debut as Titania in *A Midsummer Night's Dream* (1964) for Birmingham Rep, and later played leads at the Mermaid and the National, in classics as well as modern works such as Simon Gray's *The Late Middle Classes*. On TV, she was doomed Catherine Howard in *The Six Wives of Henry VIII* (1970) and a vividly languid Lady Bertram in *Mansfield Park* (1983), and has done a great deal of radio drama. Her films are an idiosyncratic lot, including *Hitler: The Last Ten Days* (1973, UK/It), the HORROR film, *From Beyond the Grave* (1973), in which she acted with father Donald PLEASENCE, and *The Search for John Gissing* (2001, UK/US).

OTHER BRITISH FILMS INCLUDE: *Here We Go Round the Mulberry Bush* (1967), *Symptoms* (1974, starring), *A Christmas Carol* (1984), *Stealing Heaven* (1988, UK/Yug), *The Favour, the Watch and the Very Big Fish* (1991, UK/Fr).

Pleasence, Donald (*b* Worksop, 1919 – *d* Saint-Paul-de-Vence, France, 1995). Actor. Bald-headed actor with intense, staring eyes, associated with nervy, unstable characters. Briefly a railway worker, made stage debut in 1939, and returned to stage after WW2 service in RAF. Began to appear in TV drama in the 50s, including *1984* (1954), and as Prince John in *Robin Hood* (1955–57). In film character roles from 1954 (he was never going to be a handsome leading man), he was excellent as grave-robber Hare in *The Flesh and the Fiends* (1959) and in two 'B' FILM roles: a timid accountant in *The Big Day* (1960), and the weak father devoted to his pet rabbits in *The Wind of Change* (1961). He was a perfect *Dr Crippen* (1962), and, in *The Caretaker* (1963), reprised his acclaimed stage performance as the tramp Davies. In Roman POLANSKI's bizarre, darkly humorous *Cul-de-sac* (1966), he played an ineffectual husband, living in isolation on Holy Island, finally left weeping and hunched on a rock as the tide moves in. After *The Great Escape* (1962, US), he appeared in Hollywood films regularly, notably in *Halloween* (1978), the success of which made him a HORROR specialist, often in low-budget films, many of the shlocky Italian slasher variety. Excellent as saintly Reverend Harding in TV's *The Barchester Chronicles* (1982), reminding viewers he was capable of more than gore and horror. Awarded OBE, 1993. Daughter is actress Angela PLEASENCE.

OTHER BRITISH FILMS INCLUDE: *The Beachcomber* (1954), *Value for Money, 1984* (1955), *The Man in the Sky* (1956), *Barnacle Bill, Manuela* (1957), *A Tale of Two Cities, The Wind Cannot Read* (1958), *Killers of Kilimanjaro, Look Back in Anger* (1959), *Sons and Lovers*, (1960), *Spare the Rod, What a Carve Up!* (1961), *The Night of the Generals* (UK/Fr), *Eye of the Devil* (1966), *You Only Live Twice* (1967), *Kidnapped, The Pied Piper* (UK/Ger) (1971), *Tales That Witness Madness* (1973), *The Black Windmill* (1974), *The Eagle Has Landed* (1976), *Tomorrow Never Comes* (1977, UK/Can), *Dracula* (1979, US/UK), *The Monster Club* (1980). Roger Philip Mellor.

Plowright, Joan (*b* Brigg, 1929). Actress. Trained at the Old Vic Theatre School, Plowright quickly asserted herself as one of the dominant young actresses of the late 50s/early 60s. On London stage from 1954, she scored major successes at the Royal Court, and triumphed in such diverse pieces as Ionesco's *The Chairs* and *The Lesson* (1957) and *Major Barbara* (1959). She co-starred with Laurence OLIVIER, as his daughter, in *The Entertainer* (1957), repeating the role in the film version (1960), and marrying him in 1961. But, as a young woman, she had a fitful screen career, taking time to raise a family, and by the time she started appearing regularly she was too old for leads and played a series of often striking character roles. She was the mother of two disturbed young people in *Equus* (1977) and *Brimstone & Treacle* (1982), a truculent union rep in *Britannia Hospital* (1982), and starred in Peter GREENAWAY's *Drowning by Numbers* (UK/Neth) and as Jane HORROCKS's spinster aunt in *The Dressmaker* (1988). She began to appear in US films, exploiting her gift for accents in such films as *Avalon* and *I Love You to Death* (1990), but her roles increasingly encouraged grande dame mannerisms, especially in *Enchanted April* (1992), for which she received a BAAn, and she contributed to the mess of *The Scarlet Letter* (1995, US). Awarded a CBE in 1970, she has been a formidable stage actress for several decades, and it has been a shame to see her in so much screen junk in recent years – and that includes the sentimentality of *Tea with Mussolini* (1999, UK/It).

OTHER BRITISH FILMS: *Moby Dick* (1956), *Time Without Pity* (1957), *Three Sisters* (1970), *Revolution* (1985, UK/Nor), *The Summer House* (1993, TV, some cinemas), *A Pin for the Butterfly, Widow's Peak* (UK/US) (1994), *Jane Eyre* (UK/Fr/It/US), *Surviving Picasso* (UK/US) (1996), *The Assistant* (1997, UK/Can), *Tom's Midnight Garden* (1999, UK/US), *Global Heresy* (2001, UK/US).

BIBLIOG: Autobiography, *And That's Not All*, 2001.

Plumb, E(dward) Hay (*b* Norwich, 1883 – *d* Uxbridge, 1960). Actor, director. Character actor, who alternated stage with screen work, and who was sometimes billed (as a director) as Edward Hay Plumb. A busy actor with HEPWORTH from 1910, Plumb starred as the comical PC Hawkeye in shorts, beginning in 1911, that he also wrote and directed from 1912 to 1915: *PC Hawkeye Falls in Love, PC Hawkeye Goes Fishing, PC Hawkeye, Sportsman* (1912), *Hawkeye Has to Hurry, Hawkeye Meets His Match* (1913), *Hawkeye, Hall Porter* (1914), *Hawkeye, King of the Castle* (1915), etc. He was active as a director from 1912 to 1920, most famously of *Hamlet* (1913) for Hepworth; on stage only in the 20s; back to the screen in the 30s in small roles.

OTHER BRITISH FILMS INCLUDE: (d)*The Apache* (1912), *Drake's Love Story* (1913, + a), *Rhubarb and Rascals* (1914), *A Son of David* (1920); (a) *Heart of Oak* (1910), *Faust* (1911), *The Mermaid* (1912), *The Heart of Midlothian* (1914), *Orders Is Orders* (1933), *Jew Süss* (1934), *Let's Be Famous* (1939). AS.

Plummer, Christopher (*b* Toronto, 1927). Actor. RN: Arthur Christopher Orme. To his chagrin, he is probably still best known as Captain von Trapp from *The Sound of Music* (1965,

US), in spite of the dozens of international film and TV appearances since. Despite his handsome appearance, he seems to have aspired less to film stardom than to a gratifying career as an actor. On TV he was a memorably intense and intelligent *Hamlet* (1964) and he has notched up an imposing list of telemovies and series, with the junk factor inevitable among such prolificacy. His British films have included such artistic endeavours as *Oedipus the King* (1967) and (as Atahuallpa, *not* repeating his stage role of Pizarro) *The Royal Hunt of the Sun* (1967), along with more commercial projects such as *The Return of the Pink Panther* (1974) and *Murder by Decree* (1978, UK/Can), as SHERLOCK HOLMES. In an enormously busy theatrical career (debut 1952), he has frequently acted at Stratford, Ontario, as well as on Broadway and the West End, and now over 70 the work continues unabated, a recent role like that of TV anchorman Mike Wallace in *The Insider* (1999, US) reminding one of how compelling he can be. Married (1) Tammy Grimes (1956–60; their daughter **Amanda Plummer** (*b* New York, 1957), has appeared in a few British films, including *Butterfly Kiss*, 1995) and (3) Elaine TAYLOR.

OTHER BRITISH FILMS: *The Night of the Generals* (UK/Fr), *Triple Cross* (UK/Fr/Ger) (1966), *Nobody Runs Forever* (1968), *Battle of Britain, Lock Up Your Daughters!* (1969), *The Spiral Staircase, Conduct Unbecoming* (1975), *Aces High* (1976, UK/Fr), *The Disappearance* (1977, UK/Can), *International Velvet* (1978), *Hanover Street* (1979), *Ordeal by Innocence* (1984), *Souvenir* (1987), *Rock-a-Doodle* (1990, UK/Ire, voice), *Lucky Break* (2001, UK/Ger/US).

Plunkett, Patricia (*b* London, 1926). Actress. Sweet-faced, wide-eyed brunette, with a touch of melancholy, RADA-trained Plunkett scored a stage hit in *Pick-Up Girl* (1946) and entered films in 1947 as Googie WITHERS's more biddable step-daughter in *It Always Rains on Sunday*, following this with several leads, including the ingenious, if highly theatrical *Murder in Reverse* (1950). But her career ran out of steam and she played supporting roles in the rest of the decade and was seen no more after two DANZIGERS pieces in 1960: *Identity Unknown* and *Escort for Hire*.

OTHER BRITISH FILMS: *Bond Street* (1948), *For Them That Trespass* (1948), *Landfall* (1949), *Mandy* (1952), *The Crowded Day* (1954), *The Flesh Is Weak* (1957), *Dunkirk* (1958).

Plytas, Steve (*b* Istanbul, 1913 – *d* Surrey, 1997). Actor. Turkish-born Greek actor who played the characteristic 'Continental' range in British films from the late 50s: so, he is a French restaurant manager in *Passport to Shame* (1958), an East German judge in *The Spy Who Came In from the Cold* (1965), an Arabian official in *Carry On Emmannuelle* (1978) and even a Greek tycoon in *On Her Majesty's Secret Service* (1969). Also much TV, including *Robin's Nest* (1977) and *Hazell* (1978), and several international films, including *Batman* (1989, UK/US).

OTHER BRITISH FILMS INCLUDE: *A Night to Remember* (1958), *Beyond the Curtain* (1960), *Very Important Person* (1961), *The Victors* (1963), *Those Magnificent Men . . .* (1965), *Theatre of Death* (1966), *Interlude* (1968), *Oh! What a Lovely War* (1969), *Ooh . . . You Are Awful* (1972), *Revenge of the Pink Panther* (1978).

Pohlmann, Eric (*b* Vienna, 1913 – *d* Bad Reichenhall, West-Germany, 1979). Actor. Bald, heavy-weight émigré actor, in Britain since 1938, mostly in sinister roles; also in international productions, including *Lust For Life* (1956, US). He charact-eristically presented a sweaty, morally dubious persona, as in *Nor The Moon By Night* (1958), and provided the off-screen voice for the villain Blofeld in the James BOND film *From Russia With Love* (1963).

OTHER BRITISH FILMS INCLUDE: *Portrait From Life* (1948), *State Secret, Highly Dangerous, Cairo Road, Blackout* (1950), *The Clouded Yellow, Hell Is Sold Out, His Excellency* (1951), *Rob Roy . . . , The Beggar's Opera* (1953), *The Belles of St Trinian's, Forbidden Cargo* (1954), *The Adventures Of Quentin Durward* (1955, US/UK), *Reach For The Sky* (1956), *Interpol, Across The Bridge, Fire Down Below* (1957), *I Accuse!, A Tale Of Two Cities, Alive And Kicking* (1958), *Expresso Bongo* (1959), *The Singer Not The Song* (1960), *Village Of Daughters* (1962), *The Sicilians, Carry On Spying* (1964), *Those Magnificent Men . . .* (1965), *Inspector Clouseau* (US/UK 1968). Tim Bergfelder.

Polanski, Roman (*b* Paris, 1933). Director. Controversial film-maker whose work always has a dangerous edge and is characterised by a dark view of human life and relationships. This is perhaps understandable in one whose Jewish parents moved from Paris to Cracow, Poland, just in time for the Germans to invade it and who subsequently survived WW2 by the skin of his teeth. His mother died at Auschwitz and post-war he left the technical school in which his (re-married) father had entered him and attended film school. His first films after leaving Lodz Film School, the short *Two Men and a Wardrobe* (1958, + a) and the psychological thriller *Knife in the Water* (1962, + sc), won international notice; he filmed in Britain in the mid 60s (two chilling pieces – *Repulsion*, 1965; and the bizarrely set cat-and-mouse thriller, *Cul-de-sac*, 1966, both award-winners – and a misfire Dracula spoof, *Dance of the Vampires*, 1967); and he made the triumphantly chilling *Rosemary's Baby* (1968) in the US. Following the murder of his wife **Sharon Tate** (*b* Dallas, 1943 – *d* Bel Air, California, 1969), who had appeared in *Eye of the Devil* (1966) and *Dance of the Vampires*, he returned to Britain to make a notably blood-spattered *Macbeth* (1971). Following a statutory rape charge in Hollywood after making *Chinatown* (1974), he fled the US and has never returned. Along with directing and acting in stage plays in Europe, he has made several co-productions with British input: his *Tess* (1979, UK/Fr) had much to commend it but seemed short on English PASTORAL; *Bitter Moon* (1992, UK/Fr) is a steamy sex melodrama of no particular interest; but *Death and the Maiden* (1995, UK/Fr/US) is a powerful rework-ing of a play about oppression on both political and personal levels. Polanski is well-placed to grapple with such material, as he proved again with *The Pianist* (2002, UK/Fr/Ger/Pol, d, p, co-sc), for which he won the Palme d'Or at Cannes.

OTHER BRITISH FILMS: *A Day at the Beach* (1969, p, sc, rel. 1993).

BIBLIOG: Autobiography, *Roman*, 1984; Barbara Leaming, *Polanski, the Filmmaker as Voyeur*, 1982.

Poliakoff, Stephen (*b* London, 1952). Director, screenwriter. Idiosyncratic figure of stage, screen and TV, who made his name with plays focusing on the alienation of urban youth, *Hitting Town* and *City Sugar* (1975) and with *Coming in to Land* (1987), dealing with a Polish refugee in London. His TV play, *Bloody Kids* (1979), directed by Stephen FREARS, was theatrically released in 1983, as was *She's Been Away* (1989) his moving and exhilarating study of a woman loosed into the outside world after years in a mental institution. This latter starred Peggy ASHCROFT as did his brilliant TV play *Caught on a Train* (1980). Of his cinema films, *Runners* (1983), is a tense thriller and *Close My Eyes* (1991) an unprurient exploration of an incestuous passion; his Lottery-funded *Food of Love* (1996, UK/Fr, released 1999) was a critical and commercial disaster. His 2001 TV mini-series, *Perfect Strangers*, was a cleverly conceived and brilliantly acted study of family bonds and he scored a further TV success with *The Lost Prince* (2003), about the youngest son of George V.

OTHER BRITISH FILMS: *Hidden City* (1987), *Century* (1993).

police The dominant cultural image of the police in Britain up to the 50s was the stereotype of the loveable, accident-prone, comically incompetent 'bobby'. This image, deriving from the MUSIC HALL and musical comedy, inspired a tradition of films featuring top COMEDY stars: Jack HULBERT (*Jack's the Boy*, 1932), Gracie FIELDS (*Looking on the Bright Side*, 1932), Stanley HOLLOWAY (*Squibs*, 1935), Will HAY (*Ask a Policeman*, 1939), George FORMBY (*Spare a Copper*, 1940) and later Norman WISDOM (*On the Beat*, 1962) and the 'CARRY ON' team (*Carry on Constable*, 1960). The comic image was an important means of neutralising the longstanding hatred of the police among sections of the working-class and also reflected the fact that the police were themselves working-class and, like the rest of that class generally, depicted as comic until the 40s. The stars of detective work were unofficial gentleman sleuths like SHERLOCK HOLMES and Lord Peter Wimsey, who, being gentlemen, could be taken seriously.

The situation changed in 1949 with *The Blue Lamp*, the first British police procedural thriller. Its realistic account of the day-to-day life of the ordinary copper inspired a succession of semi-documentary police dramas, notably *Street Corner* (1953), a tribute to women police officers. But in the Conservative 1950s, the emphasis shifted from the man on the beat to the senior officers, with officer-and-gentleman stars cast as superintendents: John MILLS (*Tiger Bay*, 1959), David FARRAR (*Lost*, 1955), Nigel PATRICK (*Sapphire*, 1959) and Jack HAWKINS (*The Long Arm*, 1956, and *Gideon's Day*, 1958). As the British NEW WAVE emerged, there was a move towards depictions of working-class senior officers, notably in several roles from Stanley BAKER (*Violent Playground*, 1957; *Blind Date*, 1959; *Hell is a City*, 1959). This trend in turn inspired the series which dominated 60s and 70s television: *Z-Cars* and *The Sweeney*. Since the 60s, television has been the home of the police series and the cinema, with its under-thirty target audience and presumed anti-establishment attitude, has concentrated on films about criminals with the police at best peripheral to the action. Jeffrey Richards.

political films Representation of politics and politicians in British film has a long, rather uneven history. Maurice ELVEY's *The Life Story of David Lloyd George* (1918, re-discovered 1996) was the first British film to chart the life and career of a leading politician. Thorold DICKINSON's *The Prime Minister* (1941) and Carol REED's *The Young Mr Pitt* (1942), dramatised the political careers of, respectively, Benjamin Disraeli and William Pitt the Younger in BIOPIC fashion. These highly propagandist films show the two Prime Ministers as reformist leaders and honourable statesmen who put democracy, the nation and duty to its people above all. Decades later, a return to the BIOPIC in Richard ATTENBOROUGH's enjoyable but ultimately 'boys-own-adventure' version of *Young Winston* (1972) depicted the young Churchill as inspirational leader, showing courage in adversity.

Politics and politicians became the subjects of comedy in Sidney GILLIAT's *Left, Right and Centre* (1959) as Tory male and Labourite female fall in love whilst in opposition and fighting an election! Somewhat whimsical in its treatment of politics, it contrasted with the sourer (more realistic?) view of Ralph Thomas's *No Love for Johnnie* (1961), and was far removed from Peter WATKINS's *Privilege* (1967) which portrayed a totalitarian coalition government obsessed with power and control, coercing young people back to the church in order to stop them becoming concerned with politics.

If the films of earlier years had generally offered somewhat sanitised representation of politics and politicians, the 80s were to become more disturbing in tone and content, reflecting concerns about very Right-wing political ideology and practices. Richard EYRE's *The Ploughman's Lunch* (1983) began a critique of the rise of hard-line Toryism, including the 1982 party conference address of a very self-confident Prime Minister, Margaret Thatcher, which extolled the virtues of 'truth', 'patriotism', and the 'British spirit' in the aftermath of the FALKLANDS WAR. The darker side of politics and politicians was closely followed by David DURY's *Defence of the Realm* (1985). This political thriller shows government represented by shadowy, nameless characters attached to sinister governmental departments, who will conspire to keep power at whatever the cost, even murder.

The frailty of truth, and the prevalence of sleaze and sexual impropriety in political life were themes of two 1988 films: David HARE's *Paris By Night* and Michael CATON-JONES' *Scandal*. The former deals with a female Tory Euro-MP who undermines her own integrity in the face of personal problems, and the latter resurrects the 1963 John Profumo–Christine Keeler affair with its depiction of hedonistic politicians and hypocritical government. Certainly this film caused a scandal in itself when national exhibition solicited much criticism from incumbent members of parliament and the Tory press alike.

Films have become increasingly politicised and raised issues focusing, for example, upon CLASS struggle, EMPIRE and its decline, GENDER politics, UNIONISM, social inequality and race. The effect political decisions and doctrines have had upon ordinary people's lives, rather than the political characters, have been emphasised. The films of the Black Audio Film Collective and SANKOFA in the 80s and of socialist film-makers Ken LOACH and Mike LEIGH are such examples. More recently Shane MEADOWS's *24 7 TwentyFourSeven* (1997) and Jimmy McGOVERN's controversial TV movie, *Hillsborough*, are in the vanguard of this type of political film-making relying heavily upon a realist aesthetic.

Non-fictionalised films (DOCUMENTARIES and NEWSREELS) have also played a significant role. During the Spanish Civil War, the PROGRESSIVE FILM INSTITUTE, set up in 1935 to distribute feature foreign films like *Mother* (1926), produced documentaries in support of the Spanish Government. The MINISTRY OF INFORMATION embraced political film-making for propagandist purposes during WW1 and WW2. The Union of Post Office Workers (UPW) was the first trade union to use film in this way in 1924. The Workers Film Association (WFA) was heavily subsidised by the Labour Party and Trade Union Congress (TUC) and was committed to producing films with a strong left-wing political bias. From John GRIERSON's founding the British documentary film movement (1927–39), through the FREE CINEMA movement of the 50s, to John AKOMFRAH's *Handsworth Song* (1986), non-fictionalised film-making has exhibited a rich vein of politicised content and comment.

There is a distinction to be drawn between films about political lives and political issues: both have had their place in the GENRE that might be loosely designated 'political films'.

OTHER RELEVANT BRITISH FILMS INCLUDE: *Hearts of Humanity* (1936), *The Shipbuilders* (1943), *Fame is the Spur* (1947), *The Chiltern Hundreds* (1949), *The Mudlark, Chance of a Lifetime* (1950), *Kes* (1969), *Don't Just Lie There, Say Something* (1973), *Territories* (1984), *My Beautiful Laundrette* (1985), *Comrades*, (1986), *Sammy and Rosie Get*

Laid (1987), *High Hopes* (1988), *Hidden Agenda* (1990), *Damage* (1992, GB/Fr) (1992), *Naked, Raining Stones* (1993), *Land and Freedom* (UK/Ger/Sp) (1995), *Secrets & Lies* (1996), *Brassed Off* (1996, UK/US), *The Full Monty* (1997, UK/US), *My Name Is Joe* (1998). Glen Jones.

Pollock, Ellen (*b* Heidelberg, Germany, 1903 – *d* Northwood, 1997). Actress. First on stage in 1920, Pollock had an immensely long and productive theatrical career, in classic and new plays, and directing as well from the early 60s. She also appeared on TV (e.g. *The Old Men at the Zoo*, 1983) and in 40-odd films spread over 55 years. Characteristically in imperious roles, such as the Baroness in *Warning to Wantons* (1948), or as dangerous types, like the eye-rolling sadist in *So Evil, So Young* (1961), where it was clear she wouldn't let the script stand in her way.

OTHER BRITISH FILMS: *Moulin Rouge* (1928), *Piccadilly* (1929), *A Gentleman of Paris* (1931), *The First Mrs Fraser* (1932), *Channel Crossing* (1933), *Royal Cavalcade, It's a Bet* (1935), *Non-Stop New York* (1937), *Spare a Copper* (1940), *Kiss the Bride Goodbye* (1944), *The Galloping Major* (1951), *The Fake* (1953), *The Time of His Life* (1955), *The Gypsy and the Gentleman* (1957), *Finders Keepers* (1966), *The Wicked Lady* (1983).

Pollock, George (*b* Leicester, 1907). Director. After entering films in 1933 and graduating to assistant director by the end of the decade, Pollock filled this role for such prestigious names as Leslie HOWARD (*Pimpernel Smith*, 1941; *The First of the Few* (1942), David LEAN (*Blithe Spirit, Brief Encounter*, 1945; *Great Expectations* 1946, etc) and Anthony ASQUITH (*The Demi-Paradise*, 1943; *The Way to the Stars*, 1945). His chance to direct was slow in coming but brought him a measure of fame as the man who steered Margaret RUTHERFORD as Miss Marple through four Agatha CHRISTIE-based comedy-thrillers: *Murder She Said* (1961), *Murder at the Gallop* (1963), *Murder Most Foul* and *Murder Ahoy* (1964), amiable and undemanding field days for a loved character star. Also directed episodes of such TV programmes as *Gideon's Way* (1965).

OTHER BRITISH FILMS INCLUDE: (ass d) *Rhythm in the Air* (1936), *Gaslight* (1940), *Take My Life, Blanche Fury* (1947), *Oliver Twist, The Passionate Friends* (1948), *The Third Man, Madeleine* (1949), *The Woman in Question* (1950), *The Browning Version* (1951), *The Kidnappers, The Net* (1953), *Dangerous Exile* (1957); (d) *Stranger in Town* (1957), *Rooney* (1958), *Don't Panic Chaps* (1959), *Kill or Cure, Village of Daughters* (1962), *Ten Little Indians* (1965).

PolyGram films Launched in the early 1990s by Dutch music giant PolyGram, UK-based PolyGram Filmed Entertainment (PFE) was an ambitious $200m project to create a European film corporation to rival Hollywood. In 1999 the plan was derailed when it was sold by its parent company, Philips, to Seagrams, the North American drinks conglomerate and owner of Universal. PFE invested heavily in British productions, rejuvenating the industry with such hits as *Four Weddings and a Funeral* (1994), *Bean* (1997) and *Lock, Stock and Two Smoking Barrels* (1998). Stephen Guy.

Pomeroy, John (*b* 1921). Editor. In films from 1946, receiving editor's credits from the early 50s, and directing one minor film, *Dublin Nightmare* (1958), which failed to do for the Irish capital what its obvious template, *The Third Man* (1949), had done for Vienna. Pomeroy then returned to editing. Not to be confused with US producer of the same name.

OTHER BRITISH FILMS INCLUDE: *Dance Little Lady, Svengali* (1954), *It's a Wonderful World* (1956), *Carry On Admiral, Zoo Baby* (1957), *City of the Dead* (1960), *Private Potter* (1962), *Two Left Feet, The Comedy Man* (1963), *The Plank* (1967).

Pommer, Erich (*b* Hildesheim, Germany, 1889 – *d* Los Angeles, 1966). Producer. The most influential producer of early German cinema, responsible for classics such as *The Cabinet Of Dr Caligari* (1919), *Metropolis* (1927), and *The Blue Angel* (1930), he collaborated with British producer Michael BALCON in the late 20s and early 30s on several Anglo-German co-productions. Exiled from Germany, Pommer worked in Britain in the late 30s, initially for Alexander KORDA. His production venture, MAYFLOWER, with the actor Charles LAUGHTON, came to an end with *Jamaica Inn* (1939). Pommer subsequently moved to Hollywood.

OTHER BRITISH FILMS: *Fire Over England* (1937), *Farewell Again* (1937), *Vessel Of Wrath* (1938), *St Martin's Lane* (1938). Tim Bergfelder.

Poncin, Marcel (*b* France – *d* France, 1953). Actor. French character player of stage and screen, who did about 20 small 'foreign' roles, including – surprise – a high proportion of Frenchmen, in 40s and 50s British cinema, including the concierge at whose hotel the typhoid victim arrives in *So Long at the Fair* (1950).

OTHER BRITISH FILMS INCLUDE: *Johnny Frenchman* (1945), *Bedelia* (1946), *The Red Shoes, The Passionate Friends* (1948), *The Lost People, The Golden Salamander* (1949), *No Highway* (1951), *Melba, A Day to Remember* (1953).

Ponti, Carlo (*b* Magenta, Italy, *c* 1912). Producer. International film-maker, educated for the law, and famously married (twice) to Sophia LOREN, many of whose films he produced. Among the more than 120 films he has produced, most in Europe, many in the US, only a handful have British affiliations, the most significant of which are *Doctor Zhivago* (1965, UK/US) and *Blow-Up* (1966, UK/It) and the worst, the remake of *Brief Encounter* (1974, TV, some cinemas), with Signora Ponti standing in, improbably, for Celia JOHNSON.

OTHER BRITISH FILMS: *Operation Crossbow* (1965, UK/It), *Smashing Time* (1967, co-p), *Diamonds for Breakfast* (1968, co-p), *Gawain and the Green Knight* (1973, co-p), *The Cassandra Crossing* (1976, UK/Ger/It, co-p).

Ponting, Herbert George (*b* Wiltshire, 1870 – *d* London, 1935). Cinematographer. Ponting was the photographic officer on Captain Scott's last South Pole expedition, 1910–13. He wrote of his experiences in *The Great White South, or, with Scott in the Antarctic* (1921) and in 1914 received a royal command to present a film lecture on his experiences at Buckingham Palace. More than 1,000 other lectures followed, including one at the Philharmonic Hall in 1915. His footage was first released in 1911 and again in 1912 as *With Captain Scott, RN, to the South Pole*; it was also released in 1924 in feature-length form as *The Great White Silence*; and it was re-edited in 1933 as *90° South* and again, in 1936, as *The Story of Captain Scott*. AS.

Pool, Archie Actor. Black supporting player in several films of the 80s, the best known being *Playing Away* (1986), in which a black cricket team visits a home counties village. Some TV, including *Paradise Postponed* (1986).

OTHER BRITISH FILMS: *Pressure* (1975), *Babylon* (1980), *Success Is the Best Revenge* (1984, UK/Fr), *Consuming Passions* (1988, UK/US).

Pooley, Olaf (*b* Parkstone, 1916). Actor. After studying at Freiburg University and studying design and décor in Paris, he worked as assistant art director at DENHAM and PINEWOOD in the 30s, before taking to the stage as an actor in London from 1943. In films since 1948 when he had a brief moment of intensity as a scarred ex-Nazi in *Penny and the Pownall Case*, and thereafter often played foreigners, like Professor Roblettski in *Top Secret* (1952) and Zhadanov in *Anastasia* (1956). Much TV in later years, including *A Horseman Riding By* (1978).

Married stage actress/singer **Irlin Hall** (*b* Dorset) who appeared in a few British films, including *Up Pompeii* (1971) and TV's *Hadleigh* (1971).

OTHER BRITISH FILMS INCLUDE: *The Lost People* (1949), *Highly Dangerous* (1950), *The Gift Horse* (1952), *The Iron Petticoat* (1956), *Windom's Way* (1957), *The Battleaxe* (1962), *Naked Evil* (1966), *The Assassination Bureau* (1968), *The Corpse* (1969, + sc), *The Godsend* (1980, sc).

Pope, Angela (*b* Surrey, *c* 1945). Director. Pope directed two more-than-averagely interesting films in the mid 90s – *Captives* (1994), a dangerous love story, and the custody-battle drama, *Hollow Reed* (1996, UK/Ger) – but most of her other work has been for TV, some of it, like *Night Shift* (1986), starring Maureen LIPMAN, quirkily likeable.

OTHER BRITISH FILMS: *Carol's Story* (1975, doc), *Kansas in August* (1999).

Pope, Dick (*b* London, 1947). Cinematographer. Trained with Pathé Film Labs, London, in all departments, including the Optical Camera Dept and Sensitometry. After acting as camera operator from the later 70s, he became Mike LEIGH's regular cinematographer from *Life is Sweet* (1990, + cam op), equally at home in lighting the raw contemporary world of *Naked* (1993) and the theatrical warmth of the G&S ambience of *Topsy-Turvy* (2000, UK/US), and the grittier provincial theatre of Mike NEWELL's *An Awfully Big Adventure* (1995).

OTHER BRITISH FILMS INCLUDE: (c, unless noted) *Rude Boy, Inseminoid* (1980, cam op), *Nineteen Eighty-Four* (1984, 2uc), *Girl in the Picture* (1985), *The Fruit Machine* (1988), *Reflecting Skin* (1990), *Black Beauty* (1994, UK/US, co-c), *Nothing Personal* (1995, UK/Ire), *Secrets & Lies* (1996), *Career Girls, Amy Foster* (UK/Fr/US) (1997), *The Debt Collector* (1999).

Porteous, Emma (*b* Calcutta). Costume designer. Active in films since the late 60s, Porteous did her most noticed work in the 80s, on *Clash of the Titans* (1981, UK) – really no more than a lot of white sheeting for immortals and gym-slips for lesser beings – and three BOND films, *Octopussy* (1983), *A View to a Kill* (1985) and *The Living Daylights* (1987), as well as on the SCIENCE-FICTION piece, *Aliens* (1986, US), one of several international films. Married to actor **Peter Porteous**, who has had small roles in a number of British films, including *Octopussy* and *The Living Daylights*, as well as playing Petrov in TV's *Space: 1999* (1975), all with costumes designed by his wife.

OTHER BRITISH FILMS INCLUDE: *Leo the Last, Entertaining Mr Sloane* (1969), *Steptoe & Son Ride Again* (1973), *Swallows and Amazons* (1974), *Brannigan* (1975), *Force 10 from Navarone* (1978), *The Lady Vanishes* (1979), *The Dogs of War* (1980), *Nineteen Eighty-Four* (1984), *No Surrender* (1985, UK/Can), *My Life So Far* (2000, UK/US).

Porter, Eric (*b* London, 1928 – *d* London, 1995). Actor. On stage at Stratford from 1945, often in leading roles at the Old Vic and the Lyric, Hammersmith, and with several film roles under his belt, Porter nevertheless only became a household name as Soames in TV's *The Forsyte Saga* (1967). His somewhat austere features suited the repressed Soames so well that it became a real effort to accept him in other roles, impressively versatile as he was. In the event, TV and film continued to offer him better opportunities than the stage. He made his film debut as Anne Bancroft's psychiatrist in *The Pumpkin Eater* (1964) and played officers and professional men in a dozen further films, including *Antony and Cleopatra* (1972, UK/Sp/ Switz), as an acerbic Enobarbus, without repeating his popular success on TV or the prestige of his stage career.

OTHER BRITISH FILMS INCLUDE: *The Heroes of Telemark* (1965), *Kaleidoscope* (1966), *Lost Continent* (1968), *Hands of the Ripper* (1971),

The Day of the Jackal (UK/Fr), *The Belstone Fox* (1973), *Hennessy* (1975), *The Thirty Nine Steps* (1978), *Little Lord Fauntleroy* (1980).

Porter, Nyree Dawn (*b* Napier, NZ, 1940 – *d* London, 2001). Actress. Like the preceding PORTER, she came to fame in *The Forsyte Saga* (1967), after a stage career in New Zealand and some UK success in TV, including the eponymous *Madame Bovary* (1964). As Irene Forsyte, unhappy wife of Soames, she brought a delicate, rather glacial, blonde beauty and graceful bearing to the role that made her a major TV star, but she had only one more major role: that of the Contessa in TV's *The Persuaders!* (1971–72). Her pre-Forsyte films were mostly long-forgotten 'B' MOVIES; of those that followed, only *Jane Eyre* (1970), inevitably as icy Blanche Ingram, and her last, *Hilary and Jackie* (1998), as Margot Fonteyn, gave her anything worth doing, and she had more interesting work on stage. She might have been perfectly cast as Rosamond in *Middlemarch*. Awarded OBE in 1970. Her second husband (1973–87) was actor **Robin Halstead** (*b* 1950) who appeared in *Voyage of the Damned* (1976).

OTHER BRITISH FILMS INCLUDE: *Sentenced for Life* (1959), *The Man on the Carlton Tower* (1961), *Live Now, Pay Later* (1962), *Two Left Feet* (1963), *The House That Dripped Blood* (1970), *From Beyond the Grave* (1973), *The Mystery of Edwin Drood* (1993).

Portman, Eric (*b* Halifax, 1903 – *d* St Veop, 1969). Actor. Uniquely stylish actor, in British films for over 30 years. Not conventionally handsome, Eric Portman became an unlikely box-office attraction in the 40s, when audiences admired his polished, distinctive voice (both gritty and reedy) and portrayals of disturbed, complex characters. He was not really a 40s film star of the GRANGER and MASON ilk, perhaps because his persona was cold and remote, with a sinister edge. His characters (cashiered army officers, struck-off doctors, etc) often had aspects they wished to hide, or were obsessive, sucessfully tapping into Portman's persona. On stage from 1924, and in films from 1933, he finally made a big impression with critics and public as calculating Nazi U-Boat commander, Hirth, journeying across Canada to the still-neutral US, in *49th Parallel* (1941) for POWELL AND PRESSBURGER. They used him again as one of the British bomber crew in *One of Our Aircraft is Missing* (1942), and as the unconventional Kentish sage Colpepper J.P. in *A Canterbury Tale* (1944), a definitive Portman part. In the 40s, Portman's roles often fell into one of two types: blunt, straight-talking Yorkshiremen (the factory foreman in *Millions Like Us*, 1943), or obsessed, calculating murderers (*Wanted for Murder*, 1946; *Dear Murderer*, 1947). Excellent in *The Spider and the Fly* (1949), as the police chief engaged in a tense duel of wits with safecracker Guy ROLFE, he was memorable in such 50s roles as the imprisoned Colonel in *The Colditz Story* (1954), the discredited doctor in *The Deep Blue Sea* (1955), and a forthright and touching Jess Oakroyd in *The Good Companions* (1956). As starring roles became fewer, he returned to the London and New York stages with great success in *Separate Tables* (1954). In the 60s he guested in the TV series *The Prisoner* (1967), and appeared in two films for Bryan FORBES, *The Whisperers* (1966) as Edith EVANS's no-good husband, and *Deadfall* (1968), in which he gave a brave, touching performance as an ageing homosexual safecracker. Portman, fiercely protective of his private life, in later years lived quietly in remote Cornwall between assignments.

OTHER BRITISH FILMS: *The Girl from Maxim's* (1933), *Abdul the Damned, Old Roses, Maria Marten, or The Murder in the Red Barn, Hyde Park Corner* (1935), *The Cardinal, The Crimes of Stephen Hawke, Hearts*

of Humanity (1936), *Moonlight Sonata* (1937), *Squadron Leader X, Uncensored* (1942), *We Dive at Dawn, Escape to Danger* (1943), *Great Day* (1945), *Men of Two Worlds, Daybreak* (1946, released 1948), *The Mark of Cain, Corridor of Mirrors, The Blind Goddess* (1948), *Cairo Road* (1950), *The Magic Box, His Excellency* (1951), *South of Algiers* (1952), *Child in the House* (1956), *The Naked Edge* (1961), *Freud – The Secret Passion, The Man Who Finally Died* (1962), *West 11* (1963), *The Bedford Incident* (1965), *The Spy with a Cold Nose* (1966). Roger Philip Mellor.

Portman, Rachel (*b* Haslemere, 1960). Composer. Noted for her lushly romantic scoring, Portman was the first woman composer to win an AA – for *Emma* (1996, UK/US) – and, less deservedly, was nominated again for her contribution to the syrup of *Chocolat* (2000, UK/It/Ger). Studied music at Oxford and while there scored the student film, *Privileged* (1982, + m d), which starred Hugh GRANT and was seen in some cinemas. She has worked several times for directors Beeban KIDRON, both on film and TV (from *Oranges Are Not the Only Fruit*, 1990), in US and UK, and Mike LEIGH (*High Hopes*, 1988, co-comp; *Life is Sweet*, 1990). Now much in demand for major international productions, including *The Shipping News* (2001, US). Married (1995) **Uberto Pasolini**, who produced *The Full Monty* (1997, UK/US).

OTHER BRITISH FILMS INCLUDE: *The Last Day of Summer* (1984), *Antonia and Jane* (1990, TV, some cinemas), *Where Angels Fear to Tread* (1991, + orch), *Friends* (UK/Fr), *Great Moments in Aviation* (UK/US) (1993), *War of the Buttons* (UK/Fr, + orch), *Sirens* (UK/Aust, + orch) (1994), *Ratcatcher* (1999, UK/Fr), *The Emperor's New Clothes* (2002, UK/It/Ger), *Nicholas Nickleby* (2003, UK/US).

portmanteau films *see* **episodic (or portmanteau) films**

Posford, George (*b* Folkestone, 1906 – *d* Worplesdon, 1976). Composer. Cambridge-educated composer of a few – mainly 30s – scores, including *The Good Companions* (1933); he also wrote the song, 'It's a Small World' for *Hi Gang!* (1941) and contributed to the US musical, *At the Balalaika* (1939).

OTHER BRITISH FILMS INCLUDE: *Britannia of Billingsgate* (1933), *Invitation to the Waltz* (1935), *Café Colette* (1937), *Gaiety George* (1946), *Cockleshell Heroes* (1955, co-comp, + lyrics).

Posta, Adrienne (*b* London, 1948). Actress. RN: Poster. First on screen as a child in the hospital drama, *No Time for Tears* (1957), returning in the later 60s in modish pieces like *Up the Junction* and *Here We Go Round the Mulberry Bush* (1967). She was the daughter of the slatternly neighbours in *Spring and Port Wine* (1969) and other assorted sassy types, including Scrubba in *Up Pompeii* (1971) and replacing Una STUBBS as Rita in *The Alf Garnett Saga* (1972).

OTHER BRITISH FILMS INCLUDE: *To Sir, with Love* (1967), *Some Girls Do* (1969), *All the Way Up, Percy* (1971), *Three for All* (1974), *Carry On Behind* (1975), *Adventures of a Private Eye* (1977).

Postlethwaite, Pete (*b* Lancashire, 1945). Actor. Formerly a teacher, this craggy-faced CHARACTER ACTOR began his career in the theatre, training for years at Manchester's Royal Exchange, the Bristol Old Vic, the Liverpool Everyman, and the RSC. A minor player in films during the 70s and 80s, he received critical praise for his role as an abusive father who features in a series of disturbing flashbacks in Terence DAVIES' *Distant Voices Still Lives* (1988, UK/Ger). Building on this newfound status, he appeared memorably in international films such as Franco ZEFFIRELLI's *Hamlet* (1990, UK/US), the science-fiction thriller, *Alien³* (1992, US) and the romantic epic, *The Last of the Mohicans* (1992, US). Postlethwaite finally achieved stardom in his late 40s as a more endearing brand of patriarch in *In the Name of the Father* (1993, UK/Ire/US), earning an AAn/supporting actor. Subsequent roles, including the conductor of a Yorkshire colliery band in *Brassed Off* (1996, UK/US), the villainous game hunter in Spielberg's *The Lost World* (1997, US) and Rachel GRIFFITHS' love interest in *Among Giants* (1998), have confirmed his versatility.

OTHER BRITISH FILMS INCLUDE: *The Duellists* (1977), *A Private Function* (1984), *Number 27, The Dressmaker* (1988), *They Never Slept* (1990), *Waterland* (UK/US), *Split Second* (1992), *Crimetime* (1996, UK/Ger/US), *The Serpent's Kiss* (1997, UK/Fr/Ger), *When the Sky Falls* (UK/Ire/US), *Rat* (UK/US) (2000). Melinda Hildebrandt.

Potter, Dennis (*b* Forest of Dean, 1935 – *d* Ross-on-Wye, 1994). Dramatist, screenwriter. The outstanding TV playwright of the last two decades of the 20th century, with such ground-breaking series as *Pennies from Heaven* (1978) and *The Singing Detective* (1986) to his name. He took risks not merely with his subject matter (it was a long way from middle-class literary TV) but also with narrative form and style. His cinema work was less prolific but his first original screenplay, *Dreamchild* (1985), a reverie on Lewis Carroll, his Alice and his *Alice*, and on narratives of various kinds, is a minor masterpiece. He adapted his TV play, *Brimstone & Treacle* to the screen in 1982 and wrote Nicolas ROEG's *Track 29* (1988), based on his TV play *Schmoedipus*. He directed and wrote *Secret Friends* (1991), based on his novel *Ticket to Ride*, but it was little seen and regarded by some as a reworking of familiar ingredients. In fact, all his screen work (apart from *Gorky Park*, 1983, US, sc) is too esoteric for other than coterie audiences, and the peculiar rigours of TV seemed to bring out the best in him.

BIBLIOG: Humphrey Carpenter, *Dennis Potter: The Authorised Biography*, 1996.

Potter, Martin (*b* Nottingham, 1944). Actor. Potter got off to a showy start as the lead in Fellini's *Satyricon* (1969, It/Fr), but his career thereafter was disappointing; the 70s was no time for making one's way in British films. He was briefly popular as the eponymous archer in TV's *The Legend of Robin Hood* (1975), but has been scarcely seen since the 70s.

OTHER BRITISH FILMS INCLUDE: *Goodbye Gemini* (1970), *Nicholas and Alexandra* (UK/US), *All Coppers Are . . .* (1971), *Craze* (1973), *The Big Sleep* (1978).

Potter, Sally (*b* London, 1949). Director, screenwriter. Potter's background has always been divided between film and dance, and her films reveal a highly intelligent interest in the hybridity of film art. Her grasp of film history and her provocative feminism also inform her small but choice output. While training at the London School of Contemporary Dance in the 70s, she made a series of short dance films before coming to festival-audience attention with *Thriller* (1979, + p, sc, c, e, sd), 'where *La Bohème* meets *Psycho*'. She followed this by *The Gold Diggers* (1983), an affectionate critique of popular Hollywood genres filtered through a rigorous feminist ideology, and the film was an all-female enterprise.

As well as continuing to make SHORT FILMS on matters of personal interest, Potter has since directed and written three features which have brought her nearer mainstream distribution, without, however, compromising her thematic or stylistic preoccupations. *Orlando* (1992, UK/Fr/It/Neth/Russ, + comp), financially an arduously put-together co-production which made Virginia WOOLF's cross-century novel of gender politics into a visually ravishing, always stimulating experience. *The Tango Lesson* (1997, UK/Arg/Fr/Ger/Jap, + comp), in which she also acted and composed the music, enabled her to combine her twin passions for dance and film; and *The Man*

Who Cried (2000, UK/Fr/US, + story), her nearest approach to conventional narrative film, was a compelling, finally moving story of a Russian Jewish woman's flight across wartorn Europe.

OTHER BRITISH FILMS: *The Song of the Shirt* (1979, doc, musician), *Alchemy* (1983), *The London Story* (1986, short, + sc), *I Am an Ox, I Am a Horse, I Am a Man, I Am a Woman* (1988, doc).

Potts, Sarah-Jane (*b* Bradford, 1979). Actress. Young actress who made a striking impression as the teenage prostitute, Myra, in TV's *Meat* (1994), followed this with the role of the discarded white bride of a young Pakistani in *My Son the Fanatic* (1997), a secondary part in Michael WINTERBOTTOM's *Wonderland* (1999), and has since worked in the US. Also in such TV series as *Dalziel and Pascoe* (1999).

Poulton, Mabel (*b* London, 1901 – *d* London, 1994). Actress. After appearing in the stage prologue to *Broken Blossoms*, Poulton was discovered by George PEARSON and featured by him in *Nothing Else Matters* (1920). A petite and attractive blonde, Poulton never reached her full potential in British films, although she is memorable in *The Constant Nymph* (1928): 'Her Tessa frequently causes one to rub away a tear,' wrote the *New York Times*. Germaine Dulac coaxed a superb performance from Poulton in *Ame d'artiste/Heart of an Actress* (1924), and it is unfortunate that Abel Gance did not follow through on his plan to star her as Violine in *Napoléon*. A problem with alcohol and a raucous Cockney accent ruined any possibility of success in talkies.

OTHER BRITISH FILMS INCLUDE: *The Old Curiosity Shop* (1921), *Moonbeam Magic* (1924), *The Ball of Fortune* (1926), *A Daughter in Revolt* (1926), *Not Quite a Lady, Troublesome Wives* (1928), *The Return of the Rat, Taxi for Two* (1929), *Escape* (1930), *Number Please* (1931), *Crown v Stevens* (1936), *Bed and Breakfast* (1938). AS.

Powell, Anthony (*b* Chorlton-cum-Hardy, 1935). Costume designer. Working on US films since the early 80s, including *Indiana Jones and the Temple of Doom* (1984) and sequel . . . *the Last Crusade* (1989), Powell won AA for *Travels with My Aunt* (1972, UK/US) and for *Death on the Nile* (1978), and these, like *Tess* (1979, UK/Fr) and *Priest of Love* (1980), gave free reign to his flair for period design.

OTHER BRITISH FILMS INCLUDE: *The Royal Hunt of the Sun* (1969), *Nicholas and Alexandra* (1971, UK/US, 2u cos), *That Lucky Touch* (1975), *Evil Under the Sun* (1981).

Powell, Dilys (*b* Bournemouth, 1901 – *d* London, 1995). Film critic. One of the most respected film critics, Powell reviewed the week's releases for the *Sunday Times* from 1939 to 1976, then went to the weekly journal *Punch*, as well as contributing to journals such as SIGHT AND SOUND. Unlike the other 'Sunday lady', C.A. LEJEUNE, she was open to new directions in cinema, and was not constrained by the middle-class shibboleths of 'good taste' and the literary and realist parameters of quality British cinema. She was refreshingly ready to find merit in American genre films, and without being merely trendy she never seemed out of touch. She wrote with precision and elegance, always making one feel what was there in the film, not just what she thought of it, and she never lost her passion for what film could do. A regular RADIO panellist on *My Word*. Awarded CBE in 1974 and BFI Fellowship in 1983.

BIBLIOG: Christopher Cook (ed), *The Dilys Powell Film Reader*, 1992.

Powell, Eddie (*b* London, 1927 – *d* England, 2000). Stuntman, actor. Much of Powell's career was dedicated to making James

BOND, in his various incarnations, look braver and more athletic than could have been expected of mere actors. His first Bond was *From Russia with Love* (1963), his last, when he was 60, *The Living Daylights* (1987); in between were some HORROR films, including *The Devil Rides Out* (1967), in which, as he sometimes did, he also acted. Worked on some big international films, including *Batman* (1989, UK/US).

OTHER BRITISH FILMS: (stunts, unless noted) *The Mummy* (1959), *A Place to Go* (1963, fight arranger), *She* (1965, a), *Dracula – Prince of Darkness* (1965).

Powell and Pressburger. **Michael Powell** (*b* Bekesbourne, 1905 – *d* Avening, 1990) and **Emeric Pressburger** (*b* Miskolc, Hungary, 1902 – *d* Aspall, 1988). Directors, producers, screenwriters. Introduced to each other by Alexander KORDA in 1938 for *The Spy in Black*, they went on to form the most creative and flamboyant partnership in British cinema history. Taking joint credits (d, p, sc) as the ARCHERS after 1943, they produced the most experimental British feature films of WW2 and the immediate post-war years. *Contraband* (1940, Powell d, P&P sc), *49th Parallel* (1941, Powell d, Pressburger sc), *The Life and Death of Colonel Blimp* (1943), *A Canterbury Tale* (1944), *I Know Where I'm Going!* (1945), *A Matter of Life and Death* (1946), *Black Narcissus* (1947), *The Red Shoes* (1948), *The Small Back Room* (1948), *Gone to Earth* (1950, d, sc), and *The Tales of Hoffmann* (1951) explore major themes, with an offhandedness rare in British cinema. In general, Pressburger moulded the structure of the films and was the more important in both production and post- production, while Powell wrote the initial screenplay, was the floor director, and provided most of the visual inspiration. Their capriciously brilliant partnership declined in the 50s: because their work was seen as outside of British realist concerns, they could not find suitable subjects, and funding became increasingly difficult.

When they worked separately, with the exception of Powell's *Peeping Tom* (1960, d, p), which was ill-received but is now seen as one of his finest achievements, their careers floundered. They were less concerned with interpreting reality, Powell especially pouring scorn on DOCUMENTARY CINEMA, but were interested in a world constructed by imagination and by yearning.

Powell, beginning with *Two Crowded Hours* (1931) directed more than 20 second-features (or QUOTA QUICKIES) prior to working with Pressburger. Of the surviving films, only *The Fire Raisers* (1933, + co-sc) in which a corrupt insurance assessor (Leslie BANKS), moves through the flames of burning buildings 'like the devil himself', *Red Ensign* (1934, + sc), and the less distinguished *The Man Behind the Mask* (1936), hint at his interests in the primal forces of nature, earth, air, fire and water. Powell modelled his visual style on the masters of silent cinema and discovered fresh inspiration and technical challenges in the work of Walt Disney and Ludwig Berger in the sound period. After working as second unit director (although with a full-director credit) on *The Thief of Baghdad* (1940, co-d), he aspired to direct a completely pre-scored film, a formidable task before the extended use of tape-recorders and playback. He and Pressburger achieved it, in part, with *The Red Shoes* and fulfilled it, more than ten years later, with *The Tales of Hoffmann* in which actor/dancers become subservient to the music.

Pressburger's career, first in Berlin and then in Paris and England, was essentially as a scenarist, but at UFA he also received training in other departments and was ideally suited to a working partnership in which Powell was essentially preoccupied with the filming process. In a famous interview, Pressburger claimed that, unusually for a writer, 80 per cent of his ideas found their way to the screen in their films. He avoided the set when filming, but is known to have found the locations on the Island of Mull for *I Know Where I'm Going!*, to have worked closely off the set with Powell throughout productions, and to have been deeply involved in the post-production processes. Supreme delegators, they allowed their designers, Alfred JUNGE and later Hein HECKROTH, an almost free hand, never more so than in their masterpieces, *A Matter of Life and Death* and *The Tales of Hoffmann*.

Their approach was similar with actors, in whom Powell, notoriously, had little interest. It didn't prevent his achieving unforgettable imagery, especially of women. Deborah KERR's three timeless faces in *Blimp* and again in *Black Narcissus*, Pamela BROWN's in *I Know Where I'm Going!*, Kim Hunter's in *A Matter of Life and Death*, and the marionette-like Moira SHEARER of *The Red Shoes* and *Hoffmann* are emblematic of the Powell–Pressburger films. There are strong performances too from Anton WALBROOK in *The 49th Parallel*, *Blimp*, and *The Red Shoes* and Roger LIVESEY in *Blimp*, *I Know Where I'm Going!*, and *A Matter of Life and Death*, achieved less by direction than by good casting of fine actors left unconstrained. Their cinematographers, such as Erwin HILLIER during the war and Jack CARDIFF after it, were given some of Britain's most splendid locations to shoot. The beaches in *A Matter of Life and Death* and *The Small Back Room*, the downs in *Gone to Earth*, create a surreal sense of heaven on earth.

When their dramas are played out against contemporary backdrops the timelessness of their locations, even of their sets, is apparent. All the detail which would normally lock a film to a particular time and place is removed. *A Canterbury Tale* is set after the so-called Baedecker Raids on English Cathedral cities, but this can only be identified by the presence of an Emergency Water Tank in a single scene. *A Matter of Life and Death* takes place after the US enters the war, but no specific dates are given. Their films, perhaps viewed as PROPAGANDA by the MINISTRY OF INFORMATION, were consciously stripped of it by Powell and Pressburger, who stuck avidly to their own agenda.

OTHER BRITISH FILMS: (**Powell alone**, d, unless noted) *Champagne* (1928, stills ph), *A Night in London* (ed), *Blackmail* (stills ph) (1929), *Caste* (sc), *Compulsory Husband* (a, stills ph) (1930), *77 Park Lane* (sc), *Two Crowded Hours*, *My Friend the King*, *Rynox* (+ co-sc), *The Rasp*, *The Star Reporter* (+ add ph) (1931), *Hotel Splendide*, *COD*, *His Lordship*, *Born Lucky*, *Perfect Understanding* (scenario, 2ud) (1932), *The Night of the Party*, *Something Always Happens*, *The Girl in the Crowd* (1934), *Oh, Daddy!* (scenario), *Lazybones*, *The Love Test*, *The Phantom Light*, *The Price of a Song*, *Some Day* (1935), *Her Last Affaire*, *The Brown Wallet*, *Crown v Stevens* (1936), *The Edge of the World* (1937, + sc), *The Lion Has Wings* (1939, co-d), *An Airman's Letter to His Mother* (1941, short), *The Queen's Guards* (1961, + p), *Sebastian* (1967, p); (**Pressburger alone**) *The Challenge* (1938, sc), *Spy for a Day* (1940, co-sc), *Atlantic Ferry* (1941, adptn), *Squadron Leader X* (1942, story), *Wanted for Murder* (1946, co-sc), *Twice Upon a Time* (1953, d, p, sc), *Miracle in Soho* (1957, p, sc), *Behold a Pale Horse* (1964, his novel), *Operation Crossbow* (1965, UK/It, sc 'Richard Imrie' = Pressburger); (**together**, d, p, sc, unless noted) *The Silver Fleet* (p), *The Volunteer* (1943), *The End of the River* (1947, p), *The Elusive Pimpernel* (1950, d, sc), *Oh, Rosalinda!!* (1955), *The Battle of the River Plate*, *Ill Met By Moonlight* (1956), *They're a Weird Mob* (1966, UK/Aust, sc 'Richard Imrie' = Pressburger) *The Boy Who Turned Yellow* (1972, Powell d, Pressburger sc).

BIBLIOG: Michael Powell, *A Life in Movies*; 1986; *Million-Dollar Movie*, 1992; Kevin Macdonald, *Emeric Pressburger: The Life and Death of a Screenwriter*, 1994. Kevin Gough-Yates.

Powell, Nik (*b* 1950). Executive producer. Educated at Ampleforth and Sussex University, he worked first as deputy editor on the teenagers' magazine, *Student*, run in conjunction with his childhood friend Richard Branson. His middle-class background, which he later downplayed, contrasted with the working-class origins of Stephen WOOLLEY, with whom he co-founded PALACE PICTURES in 1982 as a DISTRIBUTION company, before embarking on production and scoring considerable success in both ventures. When Palace collapsed (mainly through lack of the necessary capital) in the early 90s, despite Powell's reputation as a 'brilliant businessman', and despite the world-wide success of *The Crying Game* (1992), he and Woolley recreated themselves as SCALA Productions, taking on some of Palace's unrealised projects, such as *Little Voice* (1998, UK/US), and scoring a critical success with *Last Orders* (2002, UK/Ger). In 2001 he was involved in the UK/Australian co-production, *Black and White*, starring Robert CARLYLE and filming in Adelaide.

OTHER BRITISH FILMS INCLUDE: (ex p, unless noted) *The Company of Wolves* (1984), *Absolute Beginners*, *Mona Lisa* (co-p) (1986), *Scandal* (1988), *Hardware* (UK/US), *The Big Man* (1990), *Waterland* (1992, UK/US), *Backbeat* (1994), *The Neon Bible* (1995, UK/US), *Hollow Reed* (1996, UK/Ger), *Fever Pitch*, *24 7 TwentyFourSeven* (1997), *Divorcing Jack* (1998, UK/Fr), *The Lost Son* (UK/Fr/US), *Fanny and Elvis*, *The Last Yellow* (1999, UK/Ger), *The Last September* (2000, UK/Fr/Ire), *Wild About Harry* (UK/Ger/Ire), *Christmas Carol: The Movie* (anim) (2001).

BIBLIOG: Angus Finney, *The Egos Have Landed*, 1996.

Powell, Robert (*b* Salford, Lancs, 1944). Actor. Tall, charismatic actor who has never quite become the star that might have been expected. The Manchester University-educated actor had probably his finest hour as TV's *Jesus of Nazareth* (1977), but was never less than incisive in, say, *Mahler* (1974), for Ken RUSSELL, for whom he also appeared in *Tommy* (1975), or the remakes of *The Four Feathers* and *The Thirty Nine Steps* (1978), or, perhaps best of all, in the early MERCHANT IVORY *jeu d'esprit*, *Jane Austen in Manhattan* (1980, UK/US), as the avant-garde theatrical producer locked in conflict with Anne Baxter. Since then, he has worked all over the place and done a good deal of TV, including the period spy thriller, *Hannay* (1988), as Buchan's gentleman-adventurer, and narrating DOCUMENTARIES on US television.

OTHER BRITISH FILMS INCLUDE: *The Italian Job* (1969), *Secrets* (1971), *Running Scared*, *Asylum* (1972), *The Jigsaw Man* (1984), *The Mystery of Edwin Drood* (1993).

Powell, Sandy (Albert) (*b* Rotherham, 1900 – *d* Eastbourne, 1982). Actor. MUSIC HALL comedian (debut 1907), famous for his catchphrase, 'Can you hear me, mother?' Unlike other music hall performers, Powell was always the star of his films, and, except for *The Third String* (1932) and *Cup-Tie Honeymoon* (1947), always played a character named Sandy. In films from 1931, for MANCUNIAN PICTURES.

OTHER BRITISH FILMS INCLUDE: *Sandy the Lost Policeman* (1931), *Can You Hear Me Mother?* (1935), *Leave It to Me* (1937), *I've Got a Horse* (1938), *Home from Home*, *All at Sea* (1939). AS.

Powell, Sandy (*b c* 1961). Costume designer. Distinguished designer of the 80s and 90s, Powell specialises in detailed period dress from various eras of British history, from the 16th (*Shakespeare In Love*, 1998, AA) to the 20th century (*Velvet Goldmine*, 1998, BAA). Her attention to detail and historical accuracy is evident in such varied work as *Caravaggio* (1986), *Edward II* (1991), *Orlando* (1992, UK/Fr/It/Neth/Russ), *Wittgenstein* (1993), *The Wings of the Dove* (1997, UK/US),

Hilary and Jackie (1998), and *The End of the Affair* (2000, UK/Ger/US).

OTHER BRITISH FILMS INCLUDE: *The Last of England*, *Stormy Monday* (1987), *For Queen and Country* (1988), *The Pope Must Die* (1991), *The Crying Game* (1992), *Felicia's Journey* (1999). Fiona Clark.

Power, Hartley (*b* New York, 1894 – *d* London, 1966). Actor. American-born character player long in Britain, where he first trained as an electrical engineer before making his stage debut in Belfast, 1911. Served with the French Army during WW1, toured in Australia post-war, and was thereafter constantly busy on the London stage (e.g. in *No Orchids for Miss Blandish*, 1942; *Born Yesterday*, 1947). In films from 1931 (*Down River*), often in blustering or high-powered American types, perhaps most memorably as Samuel Cunard in *Atlantic Ferry* (1941), the rival ventriloquist, Sylvester Kee, in the 'Dummy' sequence of *Dead of Night* (1945), and William HOLDEN's boss in *Roman Holiday* (1953, US). Married (2) and divorced **Betty Paul** (*b* London), who appeared in *Oliver Twist* (1948) and *Flesh and Blood* (1951).

OTHER BRITISH FILMS INCLUDE: *Yes Mr Brown* (1932), *Friday the Thirteenth* (1933), *Evergreen*, *The Camels are Coming* (1934), *Where There's a Will*, *Windbag the Sailor* (1936), *Murder Will Out* (1939), *Return to Yesterday* (1940), *Alibi* (1942), *The Way to the Stars*, *The Man from Morocco* (1945), *A Girl in a Million* (1946), *The Armchair Detective* (1951), *To Dorothy a Son* (1954), *Island in the Sun* (1957, UK/US).

Prador, Irene (*b* Vienna, 1920 – *d* Berlin, 1996). Actress. Sister of Lilli PALMER. First appeared in cabaret in Paris, then in London from 1938, on stage, radio and in cabaret, before making her film debut in a specialty act in *Let's Make a Night of It* in 1937. Her first film acting role was as the heroine's flirty maid in *No Orchids for Miss Blandish* (1947). Her film career consisted of about ten stereotypical 'foreign' roles, and she also acted and sang on TV, appearing in *Auf Wiedersehen Pet* (1983–84).

OTHER BRITISH FILMS INCLUDE: *Lilli Marlene* (1950), *Lost* (1955), *The Snorkel* (1958), *Jet Storm* (1959), *A Nice Girl Like Me* (1969), *The Last Valley* (1970), *To the Devil a Daughter* (1976, UK/Ger).

Prasad, Udayan (*b* Sevagram, India, 1953). Director. Came to Britain aged nine, and most of his work has focused on the difficulties of Asians living in Britain. For instance, his DOCUMENTARY, *A Corner of a Foreign Field* (1986), depicts two Pakistani women, long in England but still aware of racial division; and his best known film, *My Son the Fanatic* (1997), stars Om PURI as a Pakistani taxi-driver disturbed at his son's embracing his Muslim heritage instead of adapting to British life. Also directed an episode of Alan BENNETT's *Talking Heads 2* (1999).

OTHER BRITISH FILMS: *Just a Walk in the Dark* (1983, short), *They Never Slept* (1990), *Brothers in Trouble* (1995, UK/Ger), *Gabriel & Me* (2001).

Pratt, Anthony (*b* London, 1937). Production designer. Beginning his career as draughtsman in the early 60s on such films as the black-and-white beauty, *The Innocents* (1961), Pratt has gone on to design for such directors as John BOORMAN, evoking a world of medieval dream in *Excalibur* (1981, UK/US) and of war-gripped suburbia in *Hope and Glory* (1987), and Neil JORDAN, creating a more ominous sense of London in WW2 in *The End of the Affair* (2000, UK/Ger/US). He and cinematographer brother Roger PRATT are nephews of Boris KARLOFF.

OTHER BRITISH FILMS INCLUDE: (art d/des, unless noted) *Kill or Cure* (1962, draughtsman), *The Last Grenade* (1969), *Loot* (1970), *The Night Digger*, *Something to Hide* (1971), *Baxter!* (1972), *Zardoz* (1973), *Leopard in the Snow* (1977, UK/Ger), *Victor/Victoria* (1982, sketch artist), *Give My Regards to Broadway* (1984), *Santa Claus* (1985), *Paris by Night* (1988), *The Butcher Boy* (1997, Ire/US), *Grey Owl* (2000, UK/Can).

Pratt, Roger (*b* 1947). Cinematographer. Nothing if not flexible, Pratt has worked extensively for MONTY PYTHON (for whom he began as camera loader) and for Richard ATTEN-BOROUGH, and created the nightmare world of the future in *Brazil* (1985), the dark threat and glitter of Gotham City by night in *Batman* (1989, UK/US) and the subdued glow of wartime London in *The End of the Affair* (2000, UK/Ger/US). Has also done a good deal of US-based work. Brother of designer Anthony PRATT; nephew of Boris KARLOFF.

OTHER BRITISH FILMS INCLUDE: (c, unless noted) *Bleak Moments* (1971, ass c), *Jabberwocky* (1977, focus-puller), *The Dollar Bottom* (1981), *Mona Lisa* (1986), *High Hopes*, *Paris by Night* (1988), *Shadowlands* (1993, UK/US), *Mary Shelley's Frankenstein* (1994, UK/US), *Grey Owl* (1999, UK/Can), *Chocolat* (2000, UK/US).

Pravda, George (*b* Prague, 1916 – *d* London, 1985). Actor. Began career in Paris and became established as versatile character player in Melbourne in the mid 50s before moving to Britain, where he combined stage (e.g. *Variations on a Theme*, 1958), TV (*QBVII*, 1974; *I, Claudius*, 1976) and screen work. He and his wife **Hana-Maria Pravda** (*b* Prague, *c* 1923), who also appeared in several British films, including *The Man Who Cried* (2000, UK/Fr/US) and, with George, *Dracula* (1973, UK/US), were post-war refugees who found careers in Australian theatre. Pravda, a vehement anti-Nazi, naturally played his share of jackboot types in such films as *No Time to Die* (1958) and *Submarine X-1* (1968).

OTHER BRITISH FILMS INCLUDE: *Battle of the V-1* (1958), *Follow That Horse!* (1960), *Reach for Glory* (1961), *The Password Is Courage* (1962), *Hide and Seek*, *Ring of Spies* (1963), *Thunderball* (1965), *Inspector Clouseau* (1968), *Decline and Fall . . .* (1968), *Frankenstein Must Be Destroyed* (1969), *Hanover Street* (1979).

Prebble, John (*b* Edmonton, London, 1915 – *d* London, 2001). Actor, screenwriter. More noted for his TV work, which included acting as historical adviser to Peter WATKINS on *Culloden* (1964) and episodes of *Elizabeth R* (1971), than for his meagre cinema work. He co-authored *Mysterious Island* (1961) and *Sky West and Crooked* (1965), and *White Feather* (1955, US) and *Zulu* (1961, + sc) were based on his stories.

Preisner, Zbigniew (*b* Bielsko-Biala, Poland, 1955). Composer. Polish composer, prolific since the mid 80s, particularly noted for his scoring of Krzysztof Kiéslowski's films, including the *Three Colours* series (*Blue*, 1993; *White*, *Red*, 1994, Fr/Pol/Switz). His British films include *Feast of July* (1995, UK/US), *The Last September* (UK/Fr/Ire), *Dreaming of Joseph Lees* (UK/US), *Aberdeen* (2000, UK/Nor/Swe).

Pressburger, Emeric *see* **Powell and Pressburger**

Price, Alan (*b* Fairfield, Durham, 1942). Composer. Keyboard player with 'The Animals' (1963–65), Price's main work in film was in association with Lindsay ANDERSON, who used his character and songs as a kind of Brechtian commentative device in *O Lucky Man!* (1973), and he was composer on two further films for Anderson, *Britannia Hospital* (1982) and *The Whales of August* (1987). Otherwise, he acted in *Alfie Darling* (1975, + m, songs), less successful sequel to *Alfie* (1966), appeared as himself in the MUSICAL *Pop Gear* (1965) and wrote the score for the DOCUMENTARY, *The Dance Goes On* (1980).

Price, Dennis (*b* Twyford, 1915 – *d* Guernsey, 1973). Actor. RN; Dennistoun Rose-Price. Radley- and Oxford-educated, from a military background, made his stage debut in 1937, was in the Royal Artillery in WW2 (1940–42), and starred in many films without ever, paradoxically, *being* a star. Introduced to films in *A Canterbury Tale* (1944), as the sensitive young soldier, former cinema organist who realises an ambition to play in the Cathedral. Mercilessly used by GAINSBOROUGH in one unsuitable role after another (hopeless at costume heroes, better as villains such as Sir Francis in *Caravan*, 1946), he had his one great role at EALING. This was as the lynch-pin of the plot of *Kind Hearts and Coronets* (1949), where the brilliance of his contribution to the passionate but coolly satirical *comédie noire* has often been overshadowed by praise for Alec GUINNESS's octet of roles. Price's elegance, wit and sense of just-contained rage inform one of the most fully achieved roles in British film.

He was a hopeless *Bad Lord Byron* (1949), though it is hard to know who might have played that script; looked and – thanks to Ivor NOVELLO – sounded ridiculous in *The Dancing Years* (1950) and settled into smoking-jacket roles from the early 50s, though *Dear Murderer* (1947) had surely indicated that this was how it would be. He parodies himself as a vain film star in *Lady Godiva Rides Again* (1951), has a good snooty bit in *The Intruder* (1953), as a snobbish and cowardly officer, is enjoyably snooty *and* corrupt as Bertram Tracepurcel in *Private's Progress* (1956) and *I'm All Right Jack* (1959), has some telling moments as an upper-class gay in *Victim* (1961), and was the quickly disposed of drama critic in *Theatre of Blood* (1973). He soldiered on to the end, totting up over 100 credits, sometimes seeming to lift a weary eyebrow at the rubbish he found himself mired in, returned occasionally to the stage, and found a niche on TV as Jeeves in *The World of Wooster* (1965–67).

OTHER BRITISH FILMS INCLUDE: *A Place of One's Own*, *The Echo Murders* (1945), *The Magic Bow* (1946), *Hungry Hill*, *The White Unicorn*, *Master of Bankdam*, *Jassy*, *Holiday Camp*, *Good-Time Girl* (1947), *Snowbound*, *Easy Money* (1948), *The Lost People*, *Helter Skelter* (1949), *Murder Without Crime*, *The Adventurers* (1950), *The House in the Square* (1951), *Tall Headlines* (1952), *For Better, for Worse* (1954), *That Lady, Oh, Rosalinda!!* (1955), *Fortune Is a Woman*, *The Naked Truth* (1957), *Danger Within* (1958), *School for Scoundrels* (1959), *Oscar Wilde*, *Tunes of Glory*, *The Millionairess*, *The Pure Hell of St Trinian's* (1960), *No Love for Johnnie*, *What a Carve Up!* (1961), *The Wrong Arm of the Law*, *Go to Blazes*, *The Amorous Prawn*, *Tamahine* (1962), *The VIPs*, *Doctor in Distress* (1963), *Murder Most Foul*, *Wonderful Life* (1964), *A High Wind in Jamaica* (1965), *Jules Verne's Rocket to the Moon* (1967), *The Haunted House of Horror* (1969), *The Rise and Rise of Michael Rimmer* (1970), *Twins of Evil* (1971), *Alice's Adventures in Wonderland* (1972), *Horror Hospital* (1973), *Son of Dracula* (1974).

Price, Nancy (*b* Kinver, Staffs, 1880 – *d* Worthing, 1970). Actress. By many accounts (e.g. Bryan FORBES's *A Divided Life*, 1992) a daunting woman as theatrical producer and/or co-star, the indomitable Price fills over four columns in *Who's Who in the Theatre* (1957), first on London stage in 1900, and founding the People's National Theatre in 1931, presenting over 80 productions at its various London houses leading up to WW2. Appeared in a few silent films and several more in the 30s, making a powerful impression as the stoical mother in *The Stars Look Down* (1939), as thieves' den-mother in *Madonna of the Seven Moons* (1944), striking the odd feminist note which may have been close to her heart, as one of *The Three Weird Sisters* (1948) and remembered 40-odd years later as 'formid-able' by co-star Nova PILBEAM, and most imposing of all as the deaf school teacher in *Mandy* (1952). Also wrote novels and edited journals. Made CBE, 1950. Married to Charles MAUDE, mother of Joan MAUDE.

OTHER BRITISH FILMS INCLUDE: *Belphegor the Mountebank* (1921), *Comin' Thro' the Rye* (1923), *Huntingtower* (1927), *His House in Order* (1928), *The American Prisoner* (1929), *The Speckled Band* (1931), *Down Our Street* (1932), *The Crucifix* (1934), *Dead Man's Shoes* (1939), *Secret Mission* (1942), *I Know Where I'm Going!*, *I Live in Grosvenor Square* (1945), *Carnival* (1946), *Master of Bankdam* (1947), *The Naked Heart* (1950).

Price, Vincent (*b* St Louis, Missouri, 1911 – *d* Los Angeles, 1993). Actor. In films from 1938 (*Service de Luxe*, US), Price played all manner of sinister and caddish types in Hollywood (e.g. as Judith ANDERSON's kept man in *Laura*, 1944), before striking pay dirt with the HORROR GENRE. Too effete in looks and voice for a conventional hero, he took to coffins, dank moors and the occult as to the manner born, and became an adored stalwart of 60s and 70s British horrors, in the likes of *The Tomb of Ligeia* (1964), the cult classic *Witchfinder General* (1968) in the title role, *The Oblong Box* (1969) and as the Shakespearean actor seeking revenge on the Critics' Circle in *Theatre of Blood* (1973). He worked on both sides of the Atlantic until he died, turning up in Lindsay ANDERSON's affectionate farewell to film-making and to a batch of great stars, *The Whales of August* (1987, US) and the fable, *Edward Scissorhands* (1990). Much of his best work is American, but try telling that to his fans: they would have replied to third wife, Coral BROWNE's complaint that 'Vincent is [tediously] in Paris, getting some award for his services to horror', 'Rightly so'. Previously married to (1) Edith Barrett and (2) Mary Grant. Also had a stage career and became a noted art collector.

OTHER BRITISH FILMS INCLUDE: *The Masque of the Red Death* (1964, UK/US), *Scream and Scream Again* (1969), *Cry of the Banshee* (1970), *The Abominable Dr Phibes* (1971), *Dr Phibes Rises Again* (1972), *Percy's Progress, Madhouse* (1974), *The Monster Club* (1980), *House of the Long Shadows* (1982), *Bloodbath at the House of Death* (1983).

BIBLIOG: Victoria Price, *Vincent Price: A Daughter's Biography*, 1999.

Priestley, J(ohn) B(oynton) (*b* Bradford, 1894 – *d* Stratford-upon-Avon, 1984). Dramatist. Playwright, novelist, essayist and all-purpose sage, Priestley had a strong influence, and was a popular commentator, on English life over several decades in the middle of the 20th century. Characteristically, he was made Freeman of the city of Bradford, and all his major work carries a strong whiff of England's North; though a Cambridge graduate post-WW1, he seems never to have lost this primal allegiance – nor a sense of benevolent Left-leaning conscience. As far as films were concerned, there were contributions of various kinds. Several of his most famous works were filmed: the rich picaresque chronicle of a touring theatrical troupe, *The Good Companions* (1929), filmed in 1933, by Victor SAVILLE, and in 1956, by J. LEE THOMPSON; the novel, *Benighted*, filmed memorably in the US in 1932 and poorly in 1962 (UK/US) as *The Old Dark House*, and *Let the People Sing* (1939), filmed by John BAXTER in 1942; and the plays, *Dangerous Corner* (1932), filmed in the US in 1934; *Laburnum Grove* (1933), filmed by Carol REED in 1936, *When We Are Married* (1938), filmed charmingly by Lance COMFORT in 1943, *They Came to a City* (1943), filmed by Basil DEARDEN at EALING, with introductory and concluding appearances from Priestley himself (+ co-sc), and *An Inspector Calls* (1945), filmed by Guy HAMILTON in 1954. He also wrote screenplays for several films including Gracie FIELDS' populist hits, *Sing As We Go!* (1934) and *Look Up and Laugh* (1935), and *Last Holiday* (1950, + co-p), wrote the story on which *The Foreman Went to France* (1942) was based,

and appeared as himself in *Battle for Music* (1943, doc).

OTHER BRITISH FILMS INCLUDE: *We Live in Two Worlds* (1937, doc, narr), *Jamaica Inn* (1939, add dial), *Britain at Bay* (1940, doc, comm), *A Severed Head* (1970, co-play).

Priestley, Tom (*b* 1932). Editor. Associated with the work of NEW WAVE directors including Karel REISZ and Lindsay ANDERSON, whose multi-faceted works of the 60s and 70s, such as *Morgan: A Suitable Case for Treatment* (1966, BAA/e) or *O Lucky Man!* (1973, sup e), are unusually dependent on the imaginativeness of the editing. Worked several times with Michael RADFORD in the 80s.

OTHER BRITISH FILMS INCLUDE: *Whistle Down the Wind* (1961, ass e), *This Sporting Life* (ass e), *Father Came Too!* (1963), *The Skull, Repulsion* (1965, sound e), *The Marat/Sade . . .* (1966), *Our Mother's House* (1967), *Isadora* (1968), *Leo the Last* (1969), *Alpha Beta* (1972), *Voyage of the Damned* (1976), *Jubilee* (1978), *Tess* (1979, UK/Fr, co-e), *Another Time, Another Place* (1983), *Nineteen Eighty-Four* (1984), *White Mischief, The Kitchen Toto* (1987).

Priggen, Norman (*b* London, 1924). Producer. After working as assistant director and production manager at EALING in the 40s and 50s, Priggen became Joseph LOSEY's co-producer throughout his period of highest achievement in the 60s, starting with *The Servant* (1963), one of the watershed films of its period.

OTHER BRITISH FILMS INCLUDE: (ass d) *My Learned Friend* (1943), *Saraband for Dead Lovers* (1948), *The Blue Lamp, Kind Hearts and Coronets* (1949), *The Lavender Hill Mob, Secret People* (1951), *Mandy, The Cruel Sea* (1952), *The Square Ring* (1953); (p sup) *The Battle of the Sexes* (1959), *Hitler: The Last Ten Days* (1973, UK/It); (p) *The Professionals* (1960), *Payroll* (1961), *Modesty Blaise* (1966, assoc), *Tales That Witness Madness* (1973); (co-p) *King and Country* (1964), *Accident* (1967), *Boom, Secret Ceremony* (1968), *The Go-Between* (1971), *The Masks of Death* (1984).

Pringle, Bryan (*b* Glascote, 1935 – *d* London, 2002). Actor. Made a strong character impression in *Saturday Night and Sunday Morning* (1960), as Rachel ROBERTS's cuckolded husband, who arranges the beating-up of Albert FINNEY. He went on to have a steady career on stage, TV and film, one of those character players who was never out of work, though perhaps less distinctive than some. RADA-trained, he joined the Old Vic in the mid 50s and was a major stage character player from the 60s on. His films in the last two decades were rarely mainstream, but there were two for Terry GILLIAM, *Jabberwocky* (1977) and *Brazil* (1985), and he was wonderfully phlegmatic as the manservant Smith in TV's *A Dance to the Music of Time* (1997). Married actress **Anne Jameson**, who appeared in the films *A Severed Head* (1970) and *The Boy Friend* (1971).

OTHER BRITISH FILMS INCLUDE: *The Bulldog Breed* (1960), *Spare the Rod* (1961), *HMS Defiant* (1962), *French Dressing* (1963), *The Early Bird* (1965), *How I Won the War, Berserk!* (1967), *Cromwell* (1970), *The Boy Friend* (1971), *Mister Quilp* (1974), *Bullshot* (1983), *Turtle Diary* (1985), *Drowning by Numbers* (UK/US), *Consuming Passions* (UK/Neth) (1988), *American Friends* (1991), *Restoration* (UK/US), *Cruel Train* (1995), *Darkness Falls* (1998), *King's Ransom* (2000, short).

Pritchard, Hilary (*b* Isle of Man, 1942 – *d* Isle of Man, 1996). Actress. Supporting player of a few 70s films, including the sex comedies, *She'll Follow You Anywhere* (1971) and *Under the Doctor* (1976). Not a good time for character actors in British cinema, but she was also on stage (in *No Sex Please – We're British*, 1973) and TV (in several series of *Braden's Week*).

OTHER BRITISH FILMS INCLUDE: *What's Good for the Goose, Futtocks End* (1969), *All I Want Is You . . . and You . . . and You* (1974), *Adventures of a Private Eye* (1977).

Producers' Alliance for Cinema and Television *see* PACT

production design Settings in most early British films were supplied by carpenters, painters and plasterers, working to order. Only in the more prestige projects was conscious set design attempted: Cecil HEPWORTH's *Hamlet* of 1913 drew on the Arts and Craft stage scenery of Hawes Craven. By the early 20s, designers trained as architects or draughtsmen began to specialise in film production. Norman ARNOLD and Walter MURTON held sway at STOLL and elsewhere, though artistic results were held back by the studios' lack of money and ambition.

Only by the end of the 20s did British cinema begin to reflect some of the developments underway on the Continent. In 1919 in Germany the distorted sets of *The Cabinet of Dr Caligari* had shown how design could govern a film's entire mood and psychology. Production pacts with German producers in the mid 20s brought chances for British technicians to witness German methods at first hand. By the end of the decade German talent also began working in England.

The arrival of E.A. DUPONT's designer Alfred JUNGE at BRITISH INTERNATIONAL PICTURES in 1928 was significant. In the years that followed, through his own example and the training of recruits, he established a style and a working method that relied on storyboards and integrated the camera's viewpoint into the design. Significant new British names in the field included L.P. WILLIAMS and Alec VETCHINSKY, graduates of the Architectural Association; and Laurence IRVING, who had worked with Douglas Fairbanks in America.

During the 30s British film design slowly gained strength. GAUMONT–BRITISH instituted an apprentice scheme, with Junge in charge. Other German talents brought new imagination into the industry, like Oscar WERNDORFF, who designed for HITCHCOCK, and Ernö METZNER (*The Robber Symphony*, 1936). Alexander KORDA, making lavish spectacles at DENHAM, imported other continental artists. Vincent KORDA and Lazare MEERSON shaped films like *Rembrandt* (1936) and *Knight Without Armour* (1937) – films that at last allowed British art direction to expand beyond the dreary round of baronial halls, drawing rooms, and sedate nightclubs. Away from the big-budget ventures, BIP's gruelling production schedule kept inventive designers like John MEAD and Cedric DAWE busy, while 'QUOTA QUICKIE' producers gave valuable lessons in ingenuity to John BRYAN and Peter PROUD.

The onset of WW2 brought a change. In Government-sponsored DOCUMENTARIES, studio work needed to approach the REALISM of footage shot on the fighting fronts. Edward CARRICK supervised art direction at the CROWN FILM UNIT, and tirelessly promoted the craft, not least by writing the first film design textbook, *Designing for Moving Pictures* (1941), a crucial source for art directors handicapped by material shortages during the war and after.

In the 40s, the years of training for British artists finally bore fruit. John Bryan's bold design concepts and storyboarded shots stamped a distinctive romantic look upon David LEAN's Dickens adaptations, *Great Expectations* (1946) and *Oliver Twist* (1948). Junge himself found ideal adventurous partners in Michael POWELL and Emeric PRESSBURGER, earning an Oscar for *Black Narcissus* (1947). The talents of stage designer Hein HECKROTH were showcased in *The Red Shoes* (1948). Eyes widened too at the imaginative pageantry of Laurence OLIVIER's film of *Henry V* (1944), designed by Paul SHERIFF and Carmen DILLON. The output of EALING STUDIOS

followed more prosaic lines, but Michael RELPH's designs maintained high standards across a wide range, from the POW camp setting of *The Captive Heart* (1946) to the period opulence of *Saraband for Dead Lovers* (1948).

But the artistic flowering did not last. Financial problems pricked the production bubble, and encouraged RANK's promotion of INDEPENDENT FRAME, a controversial method of streamlining production promoted by art director David RAWNSLEY. In the 50s, generally, conventional product ruled and designers' flights of fancy were not required. At MGM's British base, Junge, and later Elliot SCOTT, ruled over large design staffs, busy with popular period ACTION/ADVENTURE films. John BOX built a high reputation for his work at PINEWOOD and ascended further working on international productions with Lean, including *Lawrence of Arabia* (1962) and *Doctor Zhivago* (1965, UK/US).

Films of the British NEW WAVE in the 60s tended to rely for effect more on location photography than studio sets. But a design element returned in films reflecting the swinging Sixties: Assheton GORTON's work in *Blow-Up* (1966) and the psychedelic panache of Brian EATWELL were much noticed. In a different sphere, Ken ADAM made his own mark, working with KUBRICK on *Dr Strangelove . . .* (1963), and filling James BOND films with massive, gadget-happy sets requiring every square foot of Pinewood's special 007 stage.

From the 1970s onwards the skill of British art directors and technicians in creating fantasy worlds proved a vital asset, keeping studios occupied by American productions like the *Superman* and *Star Wars* films whenever domestic projects proved hard to finance. Voyaging into the past became another profitable activity, crucial for literary ADAPTATIONS and costume dramas. For directors with more flamboyant ambitions, Christopher HOBBS's production designs became essential: he worked with Derek JARMAN (*The Last of England*, 1987), Terence DAVIES (*The Long Day Closes*, 1992), and Ken RUSSELL (*Gothic*, 1986). The baroque visual surface of Peter Greenaway's films, meanwhile, was regularly serviced by Dutch designers Ben van Os and Jan Roelfs.

By the late 90s, domestic film-making centred on cheap Lottery-funded movies where considered art direction played no part. But craft traditions are kept alive in international productions. On these Stuart CRAIG is much in demand for his skill, versatility, and visual eye, demonstrated in films as varied as *Gandhi* (1982, UK/Ind), *The Secret Garden* (1993, US), and *Harry Potter and the Sorcerer's Stone* (2001, UK/US). Tim HARVEY has also proved invaluable, giving a splash to *Hamlet* (1996, UK/US) and other Kenneth BRANAGH films. Geoff Brown.

producer–director teams Whilst a variable list of personnel can have membership of creative teams – director Anthony ASQUITH pulled off a number of critical triumphs with writer Terence RATTIGAN from *French Without Tears* (1939) to *The Yellow Rolls-Royce* (1964) and David LEAN worked several times with cinematographer Freddie YOUNG – the most constantly recurring factor in British cinema is the producer–director relationship. Such teams perhaps enabled a continuity that the stronger studio system offered in the US.

In early British cinema the differentiation of producer and director was often non-existent or unclear, the producer characteristically being a local businessman who branched into film-making. BAMFORTHS OF HOLMFIRTH originated as painters and decorators but through the owner's interests moved into film production on the verge of the 20th century.

Thus financial support and assembly of resources quickly became an entrepreneurial task. The creative process of what is now called directing may well have been undertaken by the same person. However, the increasing demand for films made it inevitable that the task of directing (even if called 'producing') became a delegated task. As companies and studios developed, producers likewise became hired hands.

KORDA (from Hungary) and RANK emerged in the 30s as driving forces of successful production teams but enduring partnerships of equals really began as WW2 loomed. John and Roy BOULTING, alternating as producer and director, made films from 1937 which were often hard-hitting (*Pastor Hall*, 1940; *Brighton Rock*, 1947) before settling mainly for comedy-dramas that frequently retained their cutting edge (*I'm All Right, Jack*, 1959; *The Family Way*, 1966). The now-legendary work of Emeric PRESSBURGER and Michael POWELL, begun with *The Spy in Black* (1939), soon developed into joint efforts as producers, directors and screenwriters. The joyously anarchic scriptwriting talents of Frank LAUNDER and Sidney GILLIAT came to fruition in *The Lady Vanishes* (1938). *Millions Like Us* (1943) was their directing debut to which they subsequently added producing, their output including the ST TRINIAN's series and several important dramas.

In the aftermath of war several lasting partnerships were founded, which may well have been in part the result of certain studios' ability to give people their head, or, in some cases, the lead came from the teams themselves. Sydney BOX (writer and producer) and wife Muriel BOX (writer, producer and, later, director) worked on films together, meeting success with *The Seventh Veil* (1945, AA/sc) and continuing up to *Rattle of a Simple Man* (1964). Sydney's sister, producer Betty BOX, branched out and, with director Ralph THOMAS, delivered many productions, most famously *Doctor in the House* (1954). From 1947 to 1968 the producer-director team of Michael RELPH and Basil DEARDEN turned out worthy, sometimes noteworthy, films such as *The Blue Lamp* (1949) and a string of socially aware dramas like *Sapphire* (1959) and *Victim* (1961). Gerald THOMAS (Ralph's younger brother) and Peter ROGERS (Betty Box's husband) finally hit the jackpot as director and producer of the 'CARRY ON' series (1959–78), which kept British cinema financially secure and are the epitome of British broad comedy. Robert S. BAKER (producer) and Monty BERMAN (director) were prolific film-makers in their day, but most people will better recall their television series like 'The Saint' than their many 50s 'B' MOVIES or *The Siege of Sidney Street* (1960).

Other pairings like Richard ATTENBOROUGH and Bryan FORBES worked for a while (*Whistle Down the Wind*, 1961; *Seance on a Wet Afternoon*, 1964). Andrew MACDONALD (producer), Danny BOYLE (director) and John HODGE (writer) make an interesting film troika (*Shallow Grave*, 1994; *Trainspotting*, 1996) though their work outside Britain (*A Life Less Ordinary*, 1997; *The Beach*, 2000, UK/US) has not received the acclaim of their native work. Overall, films nowadays tend to be one-off productions, with the production team assembled only to disperse after completion. The BOND movies are a possible exception but, though some of the personnel had long associations with the series (e.g. SALTZMAN, BROCCOLI), the feeling remains that these pictures are more a market-tested, processed product, than the work of a production team. Stephen Brown.

Progressive Film Institute Ivor MONTAGU founded the Progressive Film Institute in 1935 to distribute feature films like *Mother* (1926) and *Storm over Asia* (1928) on 35mm. Because of the impact of the Spanish Civil War, the Institute became increasingly concerned with production. The films it made about the war, like *Defence of Madrid* (1936) and *Behind Spanish Lines* (1938), were widely distributed and important in maintaining support for the Spanish Government. In 1939, Montagu directed *Peace and Plenty* (1939), a forceful attack on government policy. Its combination of formal inventiveness, humour and economy made it an excellent example of how film could be used for political purposes. Alan Lovell.

propaganda Typical of early film-makers' keenness to co-operate with authority was Robert PAUL's series *Army Life, or How Soldiers Are Made* (1900). WW1 saw the first government involvement in film production, but there was stern resistance from exhibitors to any form of propaganda in the post-war cinemas, which led to great caution from the NEWSREELS in handling politics. But various government departments became interested in promoting their activities through film, most notably Sir Stephen TALLENTS' EMPIRE MARKETING BOARD, which John GRIERSON joined in 1928. Its film arm became the GPO FILM UNIT in 1933, also under Tallents' direction. This in turn laid the foundation for the CROWN FILM UNIT's work for the MINISTRY OF INFORMATION during WW2, and thereafter for the Central Office of Information (COI) Films Division. The Crown Film Unit promoted the Labour government's plans for post-war regeneration, until it was disbanded under the Conservatives in 1951. A COLONIAL FILM UNIT was likewise created to inform and maintain links with the African colonies, ceasing production in 1955. After 1951 the COI continued to sponsor the production of public information films of all kinds, and distributed films to promote the British image abroad, a task that it continues to perform, though with television and video now the preferred media. Luke McKernan.

Proud, Peter (*b* Glasgow, 1913 – *d* London, 1989). Production designer. Educated at Dulwich College, in films from 1928, Proud worked essentially as art director, as the term was then, first at BIP, then at GAUMONT–BRITISH as assistant to Alfred JUNGE (e.g. on *Evergreen*, 1934), before acquiring solo credits at WARNER BROS' TEDDINGTON STUDIOS in 1935, often on films directed by American William BEAUDINE. These were usually routine comedies, several starring Max MILLER, and after WW2 service (1940–46) he moved somewhat upmarket, designing for LAUNDER AND GILLIAT's *Green for Danger* (1946). He co-directed one film, the lugubrious *Esther Waters* (1948, + co-p) with his 30s colleague Ian DALRYMPLE, and co-wrote *The Planter's Wife* (1952), but thereafter stuck to design, on main features (*The League of Gentlemen*, 1960) and 'B' MOVIES like *Cover Girl Killer* (1959), always competent but never greatly imaginative. Was a founder member of ACT.

OTHER BRITISH FILMS INCLUDE: (art d/des, unless noted) *Murder!* (1930, ass), *Waltzes from Vienna* (ass), *My Old Dutch*, *The Man Who Knew Too Much* (co-des) (1934), *Man of the Moment*, *Black Mask* (1935), *It's in the Bag*, *Educated Evans* (1936), *The Singing Cop* (1937), *Everything Happens to Me* (1938, co-des), *The Woman in the Hall* (1947), *Once a Jolly Swagman* (1948), *Nowhere to Go* (1958), *Desert Mice* (1959), *His and Hers* (1960), *Candidate for Murder* (1962), *It's All Over Town* (1963), *Saturday Night Out* (1964), *Fanatic* (1965, des), *Theatre of Death* (1966), *The Magnificent Six and* ½ (1967).

Proudlock, Roger (*b* 1920). Producer. Eton-educated Fleet Air Arm pilot (1941–46), who with brother **Nigel Proudlock** (*b* 1925), associate producer, formed VANDYKE PICTURES in

1947. They turned out second features until 1955, after which Roger produced for other companies and went into TV and Nigel was associate producer on SHORT FILMS and further 'B' MOVIES. *Song of Paris* (1952) is mild fun and has a strong cast; *The Second Mrs Tanqueray* (1952), again strongly cast, was probably a doomed enterprise in 1952.

OTHER BRITISH FILMS INCLUDE: (Roger, p) *The Hangman Waits* (1947), *The Six Men, Smart Alec, Four Days* (1951), *Two on the Tiles* (1951), *Black 13* (1953), *Time Is My Enemy* (1954), *They Can't Hang Me* (1955), *The Spaniard's Curse* (1957), *The Black Ice* (1958, co-sc), *Just Joe* (1960).

Provis, George (*b* ? – *d* US, 1989). Production designer. For forty years Provis worked steadily at most British STUDIOS, starting at ROCK and becoming supervising art director for GAINSBOROUGH in the later 40s, on films such as *My Brother's Keeper* (1948), his design evoking a seedy post-war England, and *Broken Journey* (1948), with its Alpine setting, and contributing to the handsome sheen of *The Late Edwina Black* (1951). For much of the 50s he worked on films for Ralph THOMAS and later moved into HORROR films, ready to try his hand at a range of GENRES.

OTHER BRITISH FILMS INCLUDE: (sup/assoc art d) *The Common Touch* (1941), *Jassy, Dear Murderer, Good-Time Girl* (1947), *The Calendar, Quartet* (1948), *Christopher Columbus, The Lost People* (1949), *The Astonished Heart* (1950); (art d) *The Man Behind the Mask, Everything is Rhythm* (1936), *We'll Meet Again* (1942), *I Didn't Do It* (1945), *The Brothers, When the Bough Breaks* (1947), *Portrait from Life* (1948), *Bad Lord Byron, A Boy, a Girl and a Bike* (1949), *Venetian Bird* (1952), *The Beachcomber* (1954), *Above Us the Waves* (1955), *The Black Tent* (1956), *The Truth About Women* (1957), *6.5 Special, Heart of a Child* (1958), *SOS Pacific, Too Young to Love* (1959), *Never Let Go* (1960), *The Painted Smile* (1961), *The Break, Night of the Prowler* (1962), *Hide and Seek, A Jolly Bad Fellow* (1963), *Witchcraft, The Earth Dies Screaming* (1964), *Joey Boy, Sands of Kalahari* (1965), *Daleks – Invasion Earth 2150 A.D* (1966), *The Oblong Box* (1969), *Cry of the Banshee* (1970), *Whoever Slew Auntie Roo?* (1971), *The Creeping Flesh* (1972), *Craze* (1973), *The Hostages* (1975), *Blind Man's Bluff* (1977).

Prowse, David (*b* Bristol, 1935). Actor. Towering – 6'7" – actor who played Darth Vader in *Star Wars* (1977) and sequels, while another actor provided the voice. Most of his career has been in HORROR films, including the Monster in *The Horror of Frankenstein* (1970) and the creature in *Frankenstein and the Monster from Hell* (1976), his physique readily conjuring up the necessary menace. Was also Christopher REEVES's trainer for the first *Superman* film (1978). Awarded CBE, 2000.

OTHER BRITISH FILMS INCLUDE: *Casino Royale* (1967), *Hammerhead* (1968), *A Clockwork Orange, Up Pompeii, Carry On Henry, Vampire Circus* (1971), *Callan* (1974), *The People That Time Forgot, Jabberwocky* (1977).

Pryce, Jonathan (*b* Holywell, N. Wales, 1947). Actor. Tall, sinewy, versatile actor whose piercing eye and incisive articulation are capable of either sinister or comic suggestion but which do not readily conduce to romantic leads. A former art student before training at RADA, he has had a distinguished stage career, playing in several musicals including *My Fair Lady* (2000), as Higgins, and his unconventional screen career gathered momentum when he played the ambitious media journalist in the 1983 state-of-the-nation piece, *The Ploughman's Lunch*. He is very droll as a hapless bureaucrat in *Brazil* (1985), the whiskery layabout Norman in *The Rachel Papers* (1989) and the epigrammatic Lytton Strachey in *Carrington* (1994, UK/Fr); is an aptly enigmatic figure as Rivière in *The Age of Innocence* (1993, US), a charismatic Juan Perón in *Evita* (1996, UK/US), and a saturnine media mogul bent on world domination (of course) in the BOND caper, *Tomorrow Never*

Dies (1997, UK/US). Into the new century, an established character star of the first magnitude, he was busier than ever, on TV as well as film and theatre.

OTHER BRITISH FILMS INCLUDE: *Voyage of the Damned* (1976), *Loophole, Breaking Glass* (1980), *The Doctor and the Devils* (1985), *Freddie as F.R.O.7* (1992, voice), *Great Moments in Aviation* (UK/US), *Shopping* (1994), *Regeneration* (1997, UK/Can), *Very Annie Mary* (2001, UK/Fr), *Bride of the Wind* (2001, UK/Ger).

Pryor, Maureen (*b* Limerick, 1923 – *d* London, 1977). Actress. RN: Maureen St John Pook. For about two minutes towards the end of *Doctor in the House* (1954), Pryor, as the mother of Dr Simon Sparrow's first delivery, injects a moment of genuine feeling into the good-natured fun. In *Doctor at Large* (1957), as a woman who fears she has cancer, she is similarly affecting, and in 1991 director Ralph THOMAS praised her 'gift of instant emotion'. She never played leads, but, with long rep and TV experience (from 1949), she was noticeable in all she did, including the mother of the child who nearly drowns in *Life for Ruth* (1962) and as Dr Ethel Smyth in TV's suffragette miniseries, *Shoulder to Shoulder* (1974).

OTHER BRITISH FILMS INCLUDE: *The Lady with a Lamp* (1951), *The Weak and the Wicked* (1953), *The Secret Place* (1957), *Heart of a Child* (1958), *Conspiracy of Hearts* (1960), *No Love for Johnnie* (1961), *The Music Lovers* (1971), *Lady Caroline Lamb* (1972, UK/It/US), *The National Health* (1973), *The Black Windmill* (1974).

Pryse, Hugh (*b* London, 1910 – *d* England, 1955). Actor. In his short life, Pryse appeared in 20 films, including minute roles under his real name, Hwfa Pryse, in *Pimpernel Smith* and *Penn of Pennsylvania* (1941). Post-war, he played character roles in both main and second features, often as authority figures, including the minister in the Gothic extravagance of *The Three Weird Sisters* (1948) and the coroner in *Marilyn* (1953), the 'B' FILM version of *The Postman Always Rings Twice*. To Hollywood to make *Botany Bay* (1953).

OTHER BRITISH FILMS INCLUDE: *School for Secrets* (1946), *Jassy* (1947), *Easy Money, Calling Paul Temple* (1948), *Dark Secret, Christopher Columbus* (1949), *The Valley of Song* (1953), *The Happiness of 3 Women* (1954), *Port of Escape* (1956).

punk films Punk rock was one of the most startling cultural outbursts since WW2. It centred upon music, inspiring more bands to form than at the height of the mid 60s beat boom. It was also important for fashion, creating a look that reversed the existing taste codes, parodying the dominant forms of young people's fashions. Cinema was not unaffected by it but there were only a handful of genuine punk films, the first being Derek JARMAN's *Jubilee* (1978). Punk's attitude had a more lasting and subtly pervasive effect, its energy and radical juxtaposition of styles and elements evident in films as diverse as *Absolute Beginners* (1986) and *Trainspotting* (1996).

British punk was born in 1976 and centred on a band called the Sex Pistols, whose entourage included manager Malcolm McLaren, clothes designer Vivienne Westwood, artist Jamie Reid and film maker Julien TEMPLE, who directed their film vehicle *The Great Rock'n'Roll Swindle*. It was released in 1980, two years after the group had disbanded and bass player Sid Vicious (subject of Alex COX's *Sid and Nancy*, 1986) had died. Despite its energy and crude wit, the film sells punk short, deeming it nothing more than a fraudster's ruse. The spirit of punk can be seen more clearly in some of the Clash's live concert footage and seemingly spontaneous moments in their film vehicle *Rude Boy* (1980), the American-made documentary *DOA* (1980), and their later documentary *Westway to the World* (1999). Kevin Donnelly.

Purcell, Noel (*b* Dublin, 1900 – *d* Dublin, 1985). Actor. Tall, bearded, gaunt and apt to be wild-eyed, this Irish scenery-chewer was in steady demand for character roles in British films for 30 years. He was obvious casting for such Irish-set dramas as *Odd Man Out*, *Captain Boycott* (1947) and comedies like *Saints and Sinners* (1949) and *Jacqueline* (1956). However, on stage from 1929, and in many classical roles with the Abbey Theatre, and in British films from 1935 (*Jimmy Boy*), the Christian Brothers-educated Dubliner was capable of a wider range as he showed in several films for John HUSTON, starting with *Moby Dick* (1956), and he became a regular in the 'DOCTOR' series of the 50s and 60s.

OTHER BRITISH FILMS INCLUDE: *Blarney* (1938, UK/Ire), *The Blue Lagoon* (1949), *No Resting Place*, *Encore* (1951), *The Pickwick Papers*, *Father's Doing Fine* (1952), *Doctor in the House*, *Svengali* (1954), *Doctor at Sea* (1955), *Rockets Galore*, *The Key*, *Rooney* (1958), *Shake Hands with the Devil* (UK/US), *Tommy the Toreador* (1959), *The Millionairess*, *Man in the Moon*, *Make Mine Mink* (1960), *The Iron Maiden*, *The Running Man* (1963), *Lord Jim* (1964), *Doctor in Clover* (1966), *Sinful Davey* (1968), *Where's Jack?* (1969), *The Mackintosh Man* (1973).

Purchase, Bruce (*b* New Zealand). Actor. Imposing, heavy-featured character player of stage, screen and TV since the mid 60s. He was the temporising Northumberland in the BBC's *Henry IV, Parts I* and *II* (1979), and his earliest film roles were in SHAKESPEARE ADAPTATIONS, *Othello* (1965) and *Macbeth* (1971). Some US films, including *Lionheart* (1987) and back in NZ for *Other Halves* (1984).

OTHER BRITISH FILMS INCLUDE: *Mary Queen of Scots* (1971), *The Optimists of Nine Elms* (1973), *The Quatermass Conclusion* (1978), *Playing Away* (1986), *Richard III* (1995), *Another Life* (2001).

Purdell, Reginald (*b* London, 1896 – *d* London, 1953). Actor, screenwriter. RN: Grasdorff. Popular stage and radio comic, Purdell became a sort of handyman in 30s British films, acting in some, co-writing a batch of WARNER BROS comedies at TEDDINGTON STUDIOS, sometimes providing additional dialogue, and even having a couple of goes at directing. He was a cheerful presence in British films for 20 years, perhaps remembered best now as one of the RAF pilots hiding out in an internment camp with *Two Thousand Women* (1944) and as blind Frank whose wife is cuckolding him with William HARTNELL in *Brighton Rock* (1947), though the 30s was his most productive time.

OTHER BRITISH FILMS INCLUDE: (dial) *Love on the Spot*, *Looking on the Bright Side* (1932); (d) *Patricia Gets Her Man*, *Don't Get Me Wrong* (co-d, + a) (1937); (co-sc) *Three Men in a Boat* (1933), *The Compulsory Wife* (1937), *The Dark Tower* (1943), *Dreaming* (1944); (a, co-sc) *Hail and Farewell* (1936), *Ship's Concert* (1937), *The Viper*, *Quiet Please*, *It's In the Blood* (1938), *Pack Up Your Troubles* (1940); (a) *The Middle Watch* (1930), *The Luck of a Sailor* (1934), *Royal Cavalcade* (1935), *Anything to Declare?* (1938), *Q Planes*, *The Middle Watch* (1939), *Busman's Honeymoon* (1940), *We Dive at Dawn* (1943), *Love Story* (1944), *London Town* (1946), *A Man About the House*, *Captain Boycott*, *Holiday Camp* (1947), *Stage Fright* (1950).

Purdom, Edmund (*b* Welwyn Garden City, 1924). Actor. Purdom had a brief flurry of Hollywood stardom, but the films in which he had leads – *The Egyptian*, *The Student Prince* (miming Mario Lanza's voice) (1954) and *The Prodigal* (1955) – have interest now only for connoisseurs of the dire. He appeared in a handful of British movies (e.g. as a vain film star in *The Beauty Jungle*, 1964), but prolonged his career in little-seen Continental films, with occasional resurfacings in English-speaking TV or film, such as *Don't Open Till Christmas* (1984), which he also directed. Married briefly

(1962–63) to Linda Christian.

OTHER BRITISH FILMS: *Moment of Danger* (1960), *The Comedy Man* (1963), *The Yellow Rolls-Royce* (1964).

Purefoy, James (*b* Taunton, 1964). Actor. Sherborne-educated and Central School-trained Purefoy has had major roles with the RSC and the National Theatre, has made high-profile TV appearances, especially as the protagonist, decent, intelligent Nick, in *A Dance to the Music of Time* (1997) and the ambitious Donald Farfrae in *The Mayor of Casterbridge* (2001), but he still needs a major cinema hit. He has been a vivid presence in such films as *Bedrooms and Hallways* (1999), *Mansfield Park* (1999, UK/US) as foolish Tom Bertram, *A Knight's Tale* (2001, US) as the Black Prince, and the generally appalling *Maybe Baby* (2000, UK/Fr) as a conceited film star – and a film star is what he seems on the verge of becoming (not necessarily conceited, one adds), especially if he gets cast as James BOND. His partner is Holly AIRD.

OTHER BRITISH FILMS INCLUDE: *Angels* (1992), *One Night Stand* (1993, short), *Feast of July* (1995, UK/US), *Lighthouse*, *The Wedding Tackle* (2000), *Women Talking Dirty* (2001), *Resident Evil* (2002, UK/Ger/US).

Puri, Om (*b* Ambala, India, 1950). Actor. Charismatic actor who studied at Punjab University and Delhi's National Drama School. With a high reputation for stage and screen work in India, he won acclaim in Britain for two parallel but contrasting Pakistani patriarchs: as the liberal father, who loves a white whore and is appalled at his Muslim fundamentalist son in *My Son the Fanatic* (1997); and as the warm-hearted but still brutal husband of a white woman in *East Is East* (2000), a woman he loves and hits, the father of children resisting his insistence on the old ways. Puri fully grasps the complexity of these characters, and of the impoverished villager in *City of Joy* (1992, UK/Fr). Since the 80s, he has been in constant demand for films in both Britain and India, plying between the two.

OTHER BRITISH FILMS: *Gandhi* (1982, UK/Ind), *In Custody* (1993), *Brothers in Trouble* (1995, UK/Ger), *The Parole Officer*, *Happy Now* (2001).

Pusey, Fred (*b* London, 1909). Production designer. In the industry from 1930, then as art director at PARAMOUNT–BRITISH and for LONDON FILMS, he first became aware of the power of the film medium while working in DOCUMENTARY FILM during WW2. Post-war, he worked for WESSEX on such productions as *Esther Waters* (1948), in which the look of the film is more arresting than its drama, and on *Prelude to Fame* (1950), which used the INDEPENDENT FRAME technique. Finished his career designing for TV, including *Jennie* (1975).

OTHER BRITISH FILMS INCLUDE: (ass/assoc art d) *Goodnight Vienna* (1932), *Things to Come* (1936), *Q Planes* (1939), *The Thief of Baghdad* (1940), *49th Parallel* (1941); (des/art d) *The Primrose Path* (1934), *Land Without Music* (1936), *Love from a Stranger* (1937), *The Challenge* (1938), *The Spy in Black* (1939), *The End of the River* (1947), *Once a Jolly Swagman* (1948), *Dear Mr Prohack*, *All Over the Town* (1949), *Tom Brown's Schooldays* (1951), *The Pickwick Papers*, *Angels One Five* (1952), *There Was a Young Lady*, (1953), *Dance Little Lady*, *Svengali* (1954).

Puttnam, David (Lord Puttnam) (*b* London, 1941). Producer. Though cast in a less extravagant mould than, say, KORDA, BALCON or RANK, Puttnam is the nearest thing to a mogul that British cinema has had in the last quarter of the 20th century. Son of an ARMY FILM UNIT cameraman, he began as photographers' agent (archetypal 60s type, David Bailey, was a client), and in the 70s he took on the producing and marketing of British films and had major successes with the musicals, *That'll Be the Day* (1973) and *Stardust* (1974) and with Alan

PARKER's tough *Midnight Express* (1978, co-p). He scored a huge hit with *Chariots of Fire* (1981) and his own company, Enigma Films, was a key contributor to some of the most critically acclaimed, if not always commercially successful films of the 80s and 90s. His 'First Love' series, for instance, included some attractive films, which gave a chance to young film-makers, but which were too parochial for international success. In 1986 he took a position as head of Columbia Pictures – and resigned a year later, having failed to turn its fortunes around or stiffen the moral fibre of its movies, and he relocated to England. GOLDCREST, with which his company had been associated, had collapsed. He has had no successes in the 90s comparable with those referred to, or with *Local Hero* (1983), *The Killing Fields* (1984) or the prestigious if not very profitable *The Mission* (1985), though he remains a force to be reckoned with in British cinema. In 1999 he produced *My Life So Far*, directed by *Chariots* colleague, Hugh HUDSON, but to much more muted effect. Awarded CBE in 1982 and life peerage in 1997, he has recently concentrated his attentions more on politics.

OTHER BRITISH FILMS: (p, unless noted) *SWALK* (1970), *The Pied Piper* (1971), *Bring It All Back Home* (1972, doc, co-p), *Swastika* (doc, co-p), *The Double-Headed Eagle* (doc, co-p), *The Final Programme* (co-ex p) (1973), *Mahler* (1974, co-ex p), *Brother Can You Spare a Dime?* (doc), *James Dean, the First American Teenager* (doc), *Lisztomania* (1975, co-p), *Bugsy Malone* (1976, ex p), *The Duellists* (1977), *P'tang Yang Kipperbang* (1982, ex p), *Cal* (co-p), *The Frog Prince* (ex p) (1984), *Mr Love, Defence of the Realm* (1985, ex p), *Memphis Belle* (1990), *Being Human* (UK/US, co-p), *War of the Buttons* (UK/Fr) (1994), *Le Confessional* (1995, UK/Can/Fr, co-p).

BIBLIOG: Andrew Yule, *David Puttnam: The Story So Far*, 1988; David Puttnam, *The Undeclared War*, 1994.

Pyne, Natasha (*b* Crawley, 1946). Actress. Leading lady and sometimes second lead in a few films of the 60s and 70s, including several of the HORROR GENRE. She was also Bianca in ZEFFIRELLI's *The Taming of the Shrew* (1966, It/US) and in the all-but-aborted *The Breaking of Bumbo* (1970), which almost no one has ever seen, and on TV was Patrick CARGILL's teenage daughter in *Father, Dear Father* (1968–73).

OTHER BRITISH FILMS: *The Devil-Ship Pirates* (1963), *The Idol, Who Killed the Cat?* (1966), *Madhouse* (1974).

Pyott, Keith (*b* London, 1902 – *d* Enfield, Middlesex, 1968). Actor. An early radio actor in Britain, Pyott came to films and TV after WW2. He was a reliable supporting player across a wide GENRE range, often as foreigners: in the Somerset MAUGHAM compendium, *Quartet* (1948, 'The Facts of Life' episode), the POW drama, *The Colditz Story* (1954), the Shakespearean ADAPTATION, *Chimes at Midnight* (1966, Sp/Switz) and the HORROR classic *The Devil Rides Out* (1967). Much TV drama since 1947, including *The Quatermass Experiment* (1953). Was married to Sheila RAYNOR.

OTHER BRITISH FILMS INCLUDE: *Call of the Blood* (1948, UK/It), *The Spider and the Fly* (1949), *Sea Devils* (1953), *Beautiful Stranger* (1954), *I Accuse!* (1957), *Operation Amsterdam* (1958), *Village of the Damned* (1960), *A Weekend with Lulu* (1962), *Masquerade* (1965).

Qq

Quarshie, Hugh (*b* Accra, Ghana, 1954). Actor. Imposing African player who played Othello with OUDS while still at Oxford and later joined the RSC, had considerable TV experience from the late 70s (e.g. *Medics*, 1992–94), and has appeared in a half-dozen or so films, starting with *The Dogs of War* (1980, UK/US) and including *Star Wars . . . The Phantom Menace* (1999, US) as Captain Panaka.
OTHER BRITISH FILMS INCLUDE: *To Walk with Lions* (2000, UK/Can/Kenya), *It Was an Accident* (2000, UK/Fr), *Conspiracy of Silence* (2003).

Quartermaine, Leon (*b* Richmond, Surrey, 1876 – *d* Salisbury, 1967). Actor. Stage actor who appeared in one silent and three talkies, notably as the melancholy Jaques in *As You Like It* (1936). Was married (2) to Fay COMPTON. His brother **Charles Quartermaine** (*b* Richmond, Surrey, 1877 – *d* Hastings, Sussex, 1958) also appeared in several British films, including *The Eleventh Commandment* (1924), co-starring Compton. Charles married (1) **Madge Titheradge** (*b* Melbourne, 1887 – *d* Fetcham, 1961), who appeared in a number of British silents, and (2) **Mary Forbes** (*see* Ralph FORBES).
OTHER BRITISH FILMS: *Settled Out of Court* (1925), *Escape Me Never*, *Dark World* (1935).

Quashie, Harry (*b* Gold Coast, West Africa, 1914). Actor. Black African actor who had supporting roles in a few films from the 30s to the 50s, when the pickings were very lean indeed. Came to England in 1932, making his stage debut in *The Miracle* (1932), and entered films in 1935, in *Sanders of the River*. War service (1940–45) was followed by tiny bits in *Caesar and Cleopatra* (1945) and *Men of Two Worlds* (1946).
OTHER BRITISH FILMS: *Song of Freedom* (1936), *Jericho, King Solomon's Mines* (1937), *Diamond City* (1949), *Hunted* (1952), *Simba* (1955), *Safari* (1956), *Passionate Summer* (1958).

Quayle, Anna (*b* London, 1936). Actress. RN: Kathleen Parke. Tall character player of film and TV, where she has probably had more varied chances than in film, including Alice in *Henry V* (1979), and where she has continued to work since films petered out in the 80s. In film, she had mainly eccentric comic cameos, like the Billingsgate woman comparing notes with Diana DORS about who does the best TV operations (Quayle prefers Ben Casey) in *The Sandwich Man* (1966) or wicked Baroness Bomburst in *Chitty Chitty Bang Bang* (1968).
OTHER BRITISH FILMS INCLUDE: *A Hard Day's Night* (1964), *Drop Dead Darling* (1966), *Up the Chastity Belt* (1971), *Three for All* (1974), *Eskimo Nell* (1974), *Adventures of a Private Eye* (1977), *Adventures of a Plumber's Mate* (1978), *Towers of Babel* (1981, short).

Quayle, Sir Anthony (*b* Ainsdale, 1913 – *d* London, 1989). Actor. Versatile, round-faced stage actor who became an unexpected film star in the 50s, appearing in a wide range of roles, excelling at authority figures, with a hint of a weakness in their nature. After Rugby and RADA, appeared regularly at the Old Vic from 1932, and, after war service with the Royal Artillery, successfully managed the Shakespeare Theatre Company at Stratford (1948–56). Although he made his film debut in 1935, and played Marcellus in OLIVIER's *Hamlet* (1948), his film career only took off after leaving Stratford, when ASSOCIATED BRITISH starred him in five films, including *Woman in a Dressing Gown* (1957), as, untypically, the dull working-class husband, tempted by pretty young work colleague, and *Ice Cold in Alex* (1958), as an ambiguous (German spy or hero?) blond-haired Afrikaner (BAAn/British Actor). From 1960 until the 80s, he combined theatre with TV and supporting character roles in British and international films such as *Lawrence of Arabia* (1962) and *Anne of the Thousand Days* (1969), as Cardinal Wolsey (AAn/supp a). Awarded CBE (1952) and knighted (1985). Married (1934–41) stage actress **Hermione Hannen** (*b* London, 1913), who appeared in one film, and (1947–89, his death) Dorothy HYSON; father of actress Jenny Quayle.
OTHER BRITISH FILMS: *Moscow Nights* (1935), *Pygmalion* (1938), *Saraband for Dead Lovers* (1948), *Oh, Rosalinda!!* (1955), *The Battle of the River Plate* (1956), *No Time for Tears, The Man Who Wouldn't Talk* (1957), *Tarzan's Greatest Adventure, Serious Charge, The Challenge* (1959), *The Guns of Navarone* (1961), *HMS Defiant* (1962), *East of Sudan* (1964), *Operation Crossbow* (UK/It), *A Study in Terror* (1965), *Before Winter Comes* (1968) *Bequest to the Nation* (1973), *The Tamarind Seed* (1974), *Great Expectations, Moses* (UK/It) (1975), *The Eagle Has Landed* (1976), *Holocaust 2000* (1977, UK/US), *Murder by Decree* (1978, UK/Can), *Buster* (1988).
BIBLIOG: Autobiography, *A Time to Speak*, 1990. Roger Philip Mellor.

Queensbury, Lady *see* **Mann, Cathleen**

Quick, Diana (*b* Dartford, 1946). Actress. Only by entering British cinema in the 70s could an actress as attractive and versatile as Quick have made so little impression in films. Now probably best known as Julia Flyte in *Brideshead Revisited* (1981), she made her film debut in *Nicholas and Alexandra* (1971, UK/US) and thereafter appeared in a series of ostentatiously unmemorable films, with the exception of Ridley SCOTT's feature debut, *The Duellists* (1977), and, perhaps, *The Leading Man* (1996). Married/divorced Kenneth CRANHAM.
OTHER BRITISH FILMS INCLUDE: *A Private Enterprise* (1974), *The Big Sleep, The Odd Job* (1978), *Ordeal by Innocence, Nineteen Nineteen* (1984), *Vroom* (1988), *Wilt* (1989), *Vigo* (1998, UK/Fr/Jap), *Saving Grace* (2000).

Quigley, Godfrey (*b* Jerusalem, 1923 – *d* Dublin, 1994). Actor. Irish character actor who appeared in a dozen or so films spread over 40 years, starting with *Saints and Sinners* (1949), and including Irish-set pieces such as *Rooney* (1958) and *The Siege of Sidney Street* (1960), and two for Stanley KUBRICK: as the prison chaplain in *A Clockwork Orange* (1971) and as Captain Grogan in *Barry Lyndon* (1975). Much TV, including the medical series, *Call Oxbridge 2000* (1961–62) and *24 Hour Call* (1963).

OTHER BRITISH FILMS INCLUDE: *The Rising of the Moon* (1957, Ire/US), *Broth of a Boy* (1959, Ire), *Nothing But the Best* (1964), *Daleks – Invasion Earth 2150 AD* (1966), *The Reckoning* (1969), *Get Carter* (1971), *Educating Rita* (1983), *All Dogs Go to Heaven* (1989, Ire, voice).

Quilley, Denis (aka Dennis) (*b* London, 1927). Actor. With Birmingham Rep from 1945 and on London stage from 1950, Quilley has remained essentially a theatre actor, with such triumphs to his credit as *Long Day's Journey into Night* (1971–72), repeating his role of Jamie Tyrone in the TV version (1973). His occasional films include two Agatha CHRISTIE ADAPTATIONS, *Murder on the Orient Express* (1974) and *Evil Under the Sun* (1981), a starring role in *Privates on Parade* (1982), and the US film, *Mr Johnson* (1990). Awarded OBE, 2001.

OTHER BRITISH FILMS INCLUDE: *Anne of the Thousand Days* (1969), *The Black Windmill* (1974), *Memed My Hawk* (1984), *Foreign Body* (1986).

Quinn, Aidan (*b* Chicago, 1959). Actor. Sensitive, handsome, largely US-based actor, of Irish parents, in international films and TV of the 80s and 90s, coming to attention as the AIDS sufferer in the telemovie *An Early Frost* (1985). He has had starring roles in such major US films as *Michael Collins* (1996), as an IRA terrorist, and made only a handful of British films, including *The Mission* (1985), as Robert De Niro's brother and romantic rival. Married to actress Elizabeth Bracco; his brother Declan Quinn is a cinematographer and another brother, Paul, is a screenwriter.

OTHER BRITISH FILMS INCLUDE: *The Playboys* (1992, Ire/US), *Frankenstein* (1994, UK/US), *Haunted* (1995, UK/US), *This Is My Father* (1998, Ire/Can, + ex p).

Quinn, Anthony (*b* Chihuahua, Mexico, 1915 – *d* Boston, 2000). Actor. Twice winner of AA/supporting actor (for *Viva Zapata!*, 1952, *Lust for Life*, 1956), the exuberant, larger-than-life and, sometimes, exhausting Quinn, appeared in over 100 international films, including eight British (co-)productions, most notably *The Guns of Navarone* (1961), as a Greek colonel, and *Lawrence of Arabia* (1962), as an Arab. He became an all-purpose exotic, and in such films as *Zorba the Greek* (1964, US/Gr) his displays of the life force in action could make inhibition seem very attractive.

OTHER BRITISH FILMS: *The Savage Innocents* (1959, UK/Fr/It/US), *A High Wind in Jamaica* (1965), *The Marseille Contract* (1974, UK/Fr), *The Passage* (1978), *The Salamander* (1980, UK/It/US), *High Risk* (1981, UK/US).

Quinn, Kave (*b* London, 1960). Designer. RN: Katharine Naylor. Studied fashion at St Martin's School of Art, London, started doing costume on films and commercials under birthname, did some retraining when she decided production design was her chief interest, and her first feature film was *Shallow Grave* (1994). Has since worked twice more for its director Danny BOYLE: on *Trainspotting* (1996) and *A Life Less Ordinary* (1997).

Quinn, Tony (*b* Naas, Ireland, 1899 – *d* London, 1967). Actor. Former clerk before taking to the stage in 1919 and having a career at the Abbey Theatre (and London from 1927), short and shuffling Quinn became a staple of British films with any kind of Irish theme or setting, as barmen or drunks, policemen or crooks, usually very briefly glimpsed as in *Non-Stop New York* (1937), as crooked Harrigan, who sets Anna LEE up with the police. Also, an expert on military history.

OTHER BRITISH FILMS INCLUDE: *Lest We Forget* (1934), *Ourselves Alone* (1936), *Danny Boy* (1941), *Unpublished Story*, *Thunder Rock* (1942), *I See a Dark Stranger* (1946), *Hungry Hill* (1947), *Saints and Sinners* (1949), *Talk of a Million*, *The Lavender Hill Mob*, *High Treason* (1951), *Treasure Hunt*, *The Gentle Gunman* (1952), *The Last Man to Hang?* (1956), *The Story of Esther Costello* (1957), *Life in Emergency Ward 10* (1958), *Hide and Seek* (1963), *Murder Ahoy* (1964), *Rotten to the Core* (1965).

Quirke, Pauline (*b* London, 1959). Actress. Popular TV star of such series as *Birds of a Feather* (from 1989) and *Maisie Raine* (1998), plump, good-humoured and wry, Quirke has appeared in a few films without making the same impression. She can be glimpsed fleetingly in such prestigious films as *The Elephant Man* (1980, UK/US), *Little Dorrit* (1987) and *Distant Voices Still Lives* (1988, UK/Ger), but it took TV to make her a household face and name.

OTHER BRITISH FILMS INCLUDE: *The Trouble with 2B* (1972), *Return of the Soldier* (1982), *Getting It Right* (1989), *Our Boy* (1997), *Arthur's Dyke* (2001).

Quitak, Oscar (*b* London, 1926). Actor. RADA-trained and on stage since 1944, with the Old Vic post-war, and in films since 1948's *The Guinea Pig*. Thereafter, he played a range of sinister and/or foreign types in the 50s, then found a better career on TV, where he played the clerk in the original TV version of *The Bespoke Overcoat* (1954) and Goebbels in *The Death of Adolf Hitler* (1973). Married Andrée MELLY.

OTHER BRITISH FILMS INCLUDE: *Cairo Road* (1950), *Hell Is Sold Out* (1951), *So Little Time* (1952), *Zarak* (1956), *The Revenge of Frankenstein*, *Operation Amsterdam* (1958), *Bloodbath at the House of Death* (1983), *Brazil* (1985).

'quota quickies' In 1927 film production in Britain, on the verge of extinction, was resuscitated by the introduction of 'quota' legislation requiring the DISTRIBUTION and screening of a percentage of British films. When drawing up the Cinematograph Films Act 1927 the British government tried to placate both a domestically strong Imperialist lobby, that argued films were an important PROPAGANDA tool in promoting British values and exports and hence Britain needed a substantial film industry, and a fiercely hostile American film lobby, with friends in high places in the American government, that argued that Britain in 1927 lacked the capacity to produce films of a professional standard. So it came up with a formula that saw the percentage of British films that had to be handled gradually rising from 7½% and 5%, for distributors and exhibitors respectively in 1928 to 20% in 1936.

The popular version of what then happened is that unsavoury British producers, out for a fast profit, churned out as cheaply as possible, mainly for American distributors, a series of excruciatingly bad films which commonly became known as quota quickies. In fact quota legislation prompted a large influx of money into film-making, and the often disappointing initial results were due more to a lack of infrastructure – both in terms of studios and experienced technicians – than funds. Yet true quota quickies (i.e. films made for a minimal cost, the £1-a-footers), while not unknown, were never the norm; however, over the years the term came to be attached to all British films made by independent producers, with the notable exception of Alexander KORDA.

Despised, dismissed and forever having to hustle new contracts, nevertheless producers such as Herbert WILCOX, Norman LOUDON, and Julius HAGEN successfully evolved a strategy which allowed them not merely to survive in an environment dominated by American companies hostile to burgeoning rival industries, but to build up their operations to the point where they could make in addition to the low-budget quota films which formed their staple output some 'quality' films. It was an exciting time in which a nascent industry attracted individuals brimming with ideals and optimism, like Bernard VORHAUS and Michael POWELL, whose enthusiasm and ingenuity allowed them occasionally to transcend the boundaries within which they had to work. Quota films provided a training ground for, Ronald NEAME, Guy GREEN and many others who in later decades became stalwarts of the British film industry.

Even before the second Cinematograph Films Act in 1938 linked quota to cost, 'quickies' proper had disappeared. In the late 20s, when the quota requirement was low, American distributors could write off the handful of films they had to commission to fulfil their statutory obligations. But by the mid 30s, with a highly skilled and well-equipped British film industry operating from studios like PINEWOOD and DENHAM, American companies could no longer argue they were unable to acquire decent British films. Also, once the percentage of British films which had to be handled reached double figures, shelving films was no longer a viable strategy. Levels of investment Americans were having to make, though puny by American standards, were nevertheless sizeable and provided an incentive to turn out quota films of a standard acceptable enough to earn a return sufficient to cover their cost.

Despite their achievements, for a variety of reasons quota films were, and continue to be, undervalued: they drew heavily on a popular culture specific to their time; the grating upper-class accents irritate; perceived as entertainment for the working class, the films lacked intellectual kudos; KORDA's genius promoted the myth that he was the only true creative force of the time; when quota legislation came up for renewal in 1938, British producers themselves underplayed their achievements to get a quality requirement incorporated into the new Act; the inaccessibility (many of these films are viewable only in archives); and the primitive technology made it difficult to achieve production values which modern audiences take for granted. Linda Wood.

Rr

Radclyffe, Sarah (*b* London, 1950). Producer. Co-founder with Tim BEVAN in 1984 of production company, WORKING TITLE, Radclyffe appeared as (co-/ex) producer on some of the most interesting films in the last two decades of the 20th century, including *My Beautiful Laundrette* (1985, co-p) and Tim ROTH's confronting directorial debut, *The War Zone* (1999, UK/It).

OTHER BRITISH FILMS INCLUDE: (p, unless noted) *The Tempest* (1979, assoc p), *Caravaggio* (1986), *Wish You Were Here, Sammy and Rosie Get Laid* (co-p), *A World Apart* (UK/Zim) (1987), *Paperhouse* (1988, co-p), *Fools of Fortune* (1989), *Les Misérables* (UK/Ger/US), *Cousin Bette* (UK/US) (1998), *There's Only One Jimmy Grimble* (2000, UK/Fr); (ex p) *Bent* (1997, UK/US/Jap), *The Lost Son* (UK/Fr/US), *Ratcatcher* (UK/Fr), *Native* (short) (1999).

Radd, Ronald (*b* Ryhope, 1924 – *d* Toronto, 1976). Actor. On the London stage from 1953 and played Doolittle in *My Fair Lady* on Broadway (1957–62); appeared in about a dozen British films, in secondary roles such as the secondhand clothes dealer plotting a jewellery heist in *Up Jumped a Swagman* (1965), showing a nice comic touch, and as Shamraev in *The Sea Gull* (1968). Theatre and TV until his untimely death from a brain haemorrhage.

OTHER BRITISH FILMS INCLUDE: *The Camp on Blood Island* (1957), *The Small World of Sammy Lee* (1962), *The Double Man* (1967), *Can Hieronymous Merkin Ever Forget . . .* (1969), *The Offence* (1972), *The Spiral Staircase* (1975).

Radford, Basil (*b* Chester, 1897 – *d* London, 1952). Actor. Hugely enjoyable character player, Radford was one of those actors who does one thing superbly well: he perfected the slightly flummoxed, unfailingly courteous, public-school, civil-servant type. He and Naunton WAYNE, as the cricketing fanatics, Charters and Caldicott, brought moments of pure joy to *The Lady Vanishes* (1938), *Night Train to Munich* (1940), and *Millions Like Us* (1943), films already enjoyable enriched further by their quintessential Englishness, played perfectly straight and leaving the audience to assess the parody level. They also appeared together memorably in such other films as *Dead of Night* (1945, in 'Golfing Story') and *Passport to Pimlico* (1949), as Whitehall chaps. Radford, on stage from 1922, was untypically touching as the family solicitor who proposes to the sister of *The Winslow Boy* (1948) and had perhaps his finest hour as Colonel Waggett driven to distraction in *Whisky Galore!* (1949). He died sadly young from a heart attack.

OTHER BRITISH FILMS: *There Goes the Bride* (1932), *A Southern Maid, Just Smith* (1933), *Dishonour Bright, Broken Blossoms* (1936), *Jump for Glory, Young and Innocent, Captain's Orders* (1937), *Climbing High, Convict 99* (1938), *Secret Journey, Jamaica Inn, Trouble Brewing, She Couldn't Say No, Lets Be Famous, Just – William, The Girl Who Forgot, The Four Just Men, Spies of the Air* (1939), *Crook's Tour, Room for Two,* *The Flying Squad, The Girl in the News* (1940), *London Scrapbook* (doc), *Unpublished Story, The Next of Kin, Flying Fortress* (1942), *Dear Octopus* (1943), *Twilight Hour* (1944), *The Way to the Stars* (1945), *A Girl in a Million, The Captive Heart* (1946), *Quartet* (1948), *Stop Press Girl, It's Not Cricket* (1949), *Chance of a Lifetime* (1950), *White Corridors, The Galloping Major* (+ story), (1951).

Radford, Michael (*b* New Delhi, 1946). Director, screenwriter. Indian-born to British father and Austrian mother, and Oxford-educated, Radford then joined the NATIONAL FILM SCHOOL, entering the industry in 1974. His first films were NFS SHORTS, including *Concerning the Surface* (1973) and *Cold Night* (1974, + e), followed by the DOCUMENTARY, *Sugar* (1976), and work for BBC television. He came to notice as feature-film director with *Another Time, Another Place* (1983), the WW2 romance between a Scottish farmer's wife and Italian prisoner-of-war. This was followed by a murky version of *Nineteen Eighty-Four* (1984) and the entertaining scandal-and-murder tale, *White Mischief* (1987), set and largely filmed in Kenya. After this film failed commercially, his career faltered, but he bounced back with a major international succes in *Il Postino* (1994, It/Fr, + sc), which dramatised the friendship between a simple Italian postman and an exiled Chilean poet and was nominated for numerous awards, including AA/Best Film/Director/Screenplay, and won BAA/Foreign Film/Direction.

OTHER BRITISH FILMS: *The Day the Fish Came Out* (1967, a), *Love Is Like a Violin* (1977, p), *B. Monkey* (1998, UK/It/US, p, co-sc).

radio and film From the short, silent ANIMATION, *A Wireless Whirl* (1926), to Chris PETIT's introspective feature film, *Radio On* (1979), radio and film in Britain appear to have coincided in an oblique and rather opaque set of historical relationships. The interplay *between* different media in British cultural history has formed neither an especial, nor an extensive focus for research. Historical scholarship has concentrated on the distinctive features associated with film, or television, the press, radio, or advertising – viewed largely as separate entities. Existing analysis of the interplay between different media tends to confirm a narrative of historical 'displacement'. In particular, television, in its ascendancy as the mass broadcast medium of the late 20th century, is held to have usurped and transformed the fortunes of both British cinema and radio in the immediate post-war decades. Within this orthodoxy, the interplay between film and radio, particularly in the important period 1930–60, has been neglected.

If, in the 30s, cinema-going in Britain became 'the essential social habit of the age' for popular entertainment – outside the home – this was in part due to advances in the recording and development of SOUND as part of the film experience. It was also in the 30s that many British households began to listen to the wireless in the home. Principally through the cultural mission of the BBC under John Reith, but also with the beginnings of some competition from Europe, radio began to provide a domestically based rival to the out-of-home attractions of the cinema. As radio sets became cheaper and the wartime importance of radio as a popular means of mobilising the war effort and morale on the 'home front' became apparent, radio listening at home became an accepted part of national household routine. Radio and cinema audiences both grew considerably during WW2 and, if British cinema began a period of decline from 1946, radio audiences enjoyed a 'golden period' of expansion and vitality well into the 50s.

From the 30s onwards, radio was used both *in* and *by* British film. The radio set has been commonly used in films to establish a sense of background mood, usually as a sign for domestic everyday life. In a number of films, the radio is used as a narrative device – usually as an authoritative relay for news relevant to the unfolding plot. *Murder!* (1930) and *Passport to Pimlico* (1949) are examples of films that make use of radio in this fashion. Radio broadcasting has also served as a significant setting in a number of films, including *Radio Parade* (1933), *Band Waggon* (1940), a spin-off from the successful radio variety series featuring Arthur Askey, *Freedom Radio* (1940), *Helter Skelter* and *The Twenty Questions Murder Mystery* (1949), and *The Voice of Merrill* (1952).

Radio was also used by British film as a resource for production. At one level, film companies were interested in radio programmes that had proved their popularity and were therefore deemed worthy of crossover to film. In the 40s and 50s a number of these spin-offs appeared often in the form of low-budget, second-feature productions concerned especially with CRIME and detection. *Send for Paul Temple* (1946), *The Adventures of PC 49* (1949), *The Man in Black* (1949), *A Case for PC 49* (1951) and *The Armchair Detective* (1951), and the three Dick Barton films, *Dick Barton – Special Agent* (1948), . . . *Strikes Back* (1949) and . . . *at Bay* (1950) were all examples of films designed to capitalise on the established popularity of BBC radio series. By the early 60s, TELEVISION superseded film in this transfer process. At another level, radio acted as a resource for film production with regard to the many stars, celebrities and personalities who, having established their initial reputation in radio, shifted into film and television. Films offered radio performers and comedians like Arthur ASKEY, Kenneth WILLIAMS, Ted RAY, Jimmy EDWARDS, Tommy HANDLEY, The Goons and many others, increased public visibility and exposure in return for their popularity. Well-known radio personalities like Leslie MITCHELL, Godfrey WINN and Richard DIMBLEBY were also featured in a number of films, as 'themselves'. The significance of radio as a medium for popular music and musical stars and their relationships to film productions should not be understated.

BIBLIOG: Asa Briggs, *Sound and Vision*, 1979; Paddy Scannell & David Cardiff, *A Social History of British Broadcasting*, 1991. Tim O'Sullivan.

Rafferty, Chips (*b* Broken Hill, Australia, 1909 – *d* Sydney, 1971). Actor. RN: John Goffage. Much-loved in his own country where he had iconic status, Rafferty came to the attention of British film-makers with his starring role in EALING's *The Overlanders* (1946), as leader of a cattle drive across Northern Australia. Ealing used his long, lean, weathered frame and laconic persona in three more films: *Eureka Stockade* (1949) and *Bitter Springs* (1950), both Australian-set, and *The Loves of Joanna Godden* (1947), set in the Romney Marshes, as farmer

Googie WITHERS's shepherd. He also appeared in Hollywood films, including *The Desert Rats* (1953), and continued to act in Australia until he died, his last performance, as a venal country-town policeman, in *Outback* (1971) possibly the finest of his career. His range was not wide, but within it he was effortlessly convincing.

OTHER BRITISH FILMS: *Bush Christmas* (1947, made in Aust. for Rank), *Operation Malaya* (1953, doc, comm), *Smiley* (1956, made in Aust. for London Films), *They're a Weird Mob* (1966, UK/Aust).

Raine, Jack (*b* London, 1898 – *d* South Laguna Beach, California, 1979). Actor. After making nearly 40 films in Britain in the 30s and 40s, Raine went first to Australia for 18 months, then to Hollywood where he played mostly Brits in such films as *Bedknobs and Broomsticks* (1971). In Britain, after leaving the Army, he was on stage from 1919 (New York from 1931), in musicals and straight plays, and entered films in the late 20s. Mainly in small roles, often as policemen though in the upper echelons, like Det-Inspector Girton breaking Jean KENT's nerve in *Good-Time Girl* (1947). Married (1) Binnie HALE and (2) **Sonia Somers** who appeared in the odd British film, including *The Belles of St Clement's* (1936). Father of Patricia RAINE.

OTHER BRITISH FILMS INCLUDE: *Piccadilly* (1929), *Harmony Heaven*, *Night Birds* (UK/Ger), *The Middle Watch* (1930), *Leap of Faith* (1931), *The Ghoul* (1933), *Little Friend* (1934), *The Clairvoyant* (1935), *Neutral Port, For Freedom* (1940), *I Didn't Do It* (1945), *Holiday Camp* (1947), *My Brother's Keeper, Quartet* (1948), *No Way Back* (1949).

Raine, Patricia (*b* London, 1926). Actress. Blue-eyed blonde, RADA-trained daughter of Jack RAINE and Binnie HALE, Raine was a pleasant minor presence in British films from 1947 (*Vice Versa*) to 1953 (*The Beggar's Opera, A Day to Remember*). Best remembered as Ann TODD's sister in *Madeleine* (1949). Married (1) Bill TRAVERS and (2) Basil HENSON (1959–90, his death).

OTHER BRITISH FILMS: *It Happened in Soho* (1948), *Helter Skelter, Fools Rush In* (1949), *Pandora and the Flying Dutchman* (1950), *Love's a Luxury* (1952).

Rains, Claude (*b* London, 1889 – *d* Laconia, New Hampshire, 1967). Actor. One of the screen's great character stars, most of whose brilliant career took place in Hollywood, where, having appeared in the British silent, *Build Thy House* (1920), he made his sensational talkie debut as *The Invisible Man* (1933). After this, his short, suave form graced many major character roles, in such films as *The Adventures of Robin Hood* (1938), as wicked Prince John, and *Now Voyager* (1942), as sympathetic shrink, Jaquith. In Britain, he starred as *The Clairvoyant* (1935), as an urbanely amused Caesar, the best thing in the ponderous *Caesar and Cleopatra* (1945), winning pity as Ann TODD's cuckolded, understanding husband in *The Passionate Friends* (1948), as *The Man Who Watched Trains Go By* (1952), and as Dryden in *Lawrence of Arabia* (1962). Son of Fred RAINS. Married relentlessly, with Isabel JEANS (1920) as first of six wives.

BIBLIOG: John T.Soister and JoAnna Wioskowski, *Claude Rains: A Comprehensive Illustrated Reference to His Work in Film, Stage, Radio, Television and Recordings*, 1999.

Rains, Fred (*b* London, 1860 – *d* London, 1945). Actor, director. Father of Claude RAINS. A character actor in sound films who began his career as a slapstick comedian in SHORTS that he directed, including the 'Jones' SERIES (1910), Rains was busy as actor from 1910 to 1936 and director from 1910 to 1924. British films as actor and director include *The Suffragette's*

Downfall (1911), *Married in Haste* (1912), *Bamboozled* (1919), and *Land of My Fathers* (1921).

OTHER BRITISH FILMS: (a) *A Welsh Singer, Sally in Our Alley* (1916), *Little Brother of God* (1922), *Mist in the Valley* (1923), *Nell Gwynne* (1926), *Victory* (1928), *Stepping Stones* (1931), *Chick* (1936). AS.

Raki, Laya (*b* Calvorde, Germany, 1927). Actress. RN: Brunhilde Marie Alma Herta Jorms. 'Exotic'-looking German-born dancer-actress Raki was cast as Polynesian, Maori and Gypsy in her three British films: *Up to His Neck, The Seekers* (1954) and *The Adventures of Quentin Durward* (1955), respectively. The rest of her films tended to use her as interchangeably exotic. Married Ron RANDELL.

Rakoff, Alvin (*b* Toronto, 1927) Director. Most of Rakoff's best work has been for TV, from, say, *Heart to Heart* (1962, in *The Largest Theatre in the World* series) to the brilliant *A Dance to the Music of Time* (1997). His cinema films, however, were either almost unseen, like *The Comedy Man* (1963), or deserved to be, like the modish rubbish of *Say Hello to Yesterday* (1970, + co-sc, co-story – so he must take the blame). There is, to be fair, at least a kind of sleazy energy in his cautionary tale, *Passport to Shame* (1958), but nothing to compare with the award-winning TV career.

OTHER BRITISH FILMS: *The Treasure of San Teresa* (1959), *Money-Go-Round* (1966), *Crossplot, Hoffman* (1969), *Death Ship* (1980, UK/Ger).

Ramage, Cecil (*b* Edinburgh, 1895 – *d* Glasgow, 1988). Actor. Scottish character player, Oxford-educated Ramage served during WW1 (1914–19), was in Parliament briefly (1923–24) representing Newcastle-on-Tyne (West), then suffered political setbacks before taking to the professional stage in 1930. Acted in about 20 films of the 30s, including *King of the Damned* (1936) as a brutal overseer of a penal colony, and several more in the 40s, finally appearing as the Crown Counsel who hears the case against Dennis PRICE in *Kind Hearts and Coronets* (1949). Also a Barrister-at-Law; married Cathleen NESBITT, separated in the early 40s.

OTHER BRITISH FILMS INCLUDE: *The Strangler* (1932), *Britannia of Billingsgate* (1933), *The Night of the Party* (1934), *Secret of Stamboul* (1936), *The Mill on the Floss* (1937), *I Live in Grosvenor Square* (1945), *Blanche Fury* (1947).

Rampling, Charlotte (*b* Sturmer, 1946). Actress. Daughter of a British NATO commander, educated in Europe and England, she started as a model, and, after drama lessons, made her film debut in 1965. Began playing slender, coolly attractive rich bitches, more recently, ruthless mature women with dark pasts and secrets to hide. Her screen image was shaped by the box-office hit *Georgy Girl* (1966) as the patronising Meredith who defies traditional conventions of marriage and motherhood, evoking the harsher side of 'SWINGING LONDON'. There were a few British films (Anne Boleyn in *Henry VIII and his Six Wives*, 1972), but since 1974 her film career has largely been in Europe, *The Night Porter* (1974, It) establishing her as an actress who was prepared to take on emotionally risky roles. Her somewhat chilly edge made her ideal for the ambitious Tory MEP in *Paris By Night* (1988), mercenary aristocrat Aunt Maude in *The Wings of the Dove* (1997, UK/US) and an excellent Miss Havisham in TV's *Great Expectations* (1999).

OTHER BRITISH FILMS: *Rotten to the Core* (1965), *The Long Duel* (1967), *Asylum* (1972), *Zardoz* (1973), *Aberdeen* (2000, UK/Nor), *The Fourth Angel* (2001). Roger Philip Mellor.

Ramsay, Lynne (*b* Glasgow, 1969). Director. A graduate of the NATIONAL FILM AND TELEVISION SCHOOL, Ramsay made

three SHORT FILMS: her graduation film, *Small Deaths* (1996, d, sc, co-c) and *Gasman* (1997, d), which both won Critics' Prizes at Cannes Film Festival in successive years; and *Kill the Day* (1997). While still at NFTS, she shot Robert BANGURA's short, *Monday* (1995). She made an impressive feature debut with *Ratcatcher* (1999), a likeable, unsettling account of childhood in Glasgow in the 70s, and followed this with *Morvan Callar* (+ co-sc), which won the Prix de la Jeunesse at the 2002 Cannes Festival. **Lynne Ramsay Jr**, who is in *Gasman*, is her niece.

Randall, Terry (*b* Cardiff) Actress. RADA-trained Randall made a memorable impression as the working-class girl who shocks Anne CRAWFORD by sleeping in her underwear in *Millions Like Us* (1943). Most of the rest was routine, though she was vivid enough as the terrified girlfriend of Teddy Courtney (Jack WATLING) in *The Courtneys of Curzon Street* (1947).

OTHER BRITISH FILMS INCLUDE: *Thursday's Child* (1943), *I'll Turn to You* (1946), *The Woman in the Hall* (1947), *School for Randle, Miss Pilgrim's Progress* (1949).

Randell, Ron (*b* Broken Hill, NSW, 1918). Actor. Randell had a long and reasonably successful career in US and international films, including a dozen or so in Britain, but it is arguable that he never surpassed his performance in the title role of *Smithy* (1946), the Australian BIOPIC based on the life of aviator Sir Charles Kingsford Smith. He was under contract to Columbia (1946–51), then played Cole Porter in *Kiss Me Kate* (1953), before coming to England where he played supporting roles in main features, such as *I Am a Camera* (1955) and *The Story of Esther Costello* (1957), and leads in 'B' MOVIES, including *The Girl on the Pier* (1953). Also did many TV playlets for *Douglas Fairbanks Presents* in Britain in the mid 50s. Married Laya RAKI.

OTHER BRITISH FILMS INCLUDE: *The Triangle* (1953), *The Final Column, A Count of Twelve* (1955), *The Hostage, Beyond Mombasa, Bermuda Affair* (1956), *Davy* (1957).

Randle, Frank (*b* Wigan, 1900 – *d* Blackpool, 1957). Actor. RN: Arthur MacEvoy. North Country comedian, immensely popular in MUSIC HALL (on stage from 1922) and on screen with working-class audiences. His fans were families who took holidays in Blackpool, where the unglamorous comedian made his home. His eccentric characters and strong Lancashire accent didn't travel south, but they didn't need to for his films, made for MANCUNIAN, to succeed. His comic persona was usually that of toothless, lecherous, often drunken reprobate, but today his films are rarely, if ever, revived even in the North where, in some areas, he was a bigger draw than George FORMBY. Though their settings were the North, his films were shot in London until 1947 when Mancunian opened its Manchester studio where Randle's last films were made. His last London-made film was *When You Come Home*, 1948, directed by John BAXTER, who was apparently not attuned to Randle's raucous style.

BRITISH FILMS: *Somewhere in England* (1940), *Somewhere in Camp, Somewhere on Leave* (1942), *Somewhere in Civvies* (1943), *Home Sweet Home* (1945), *Holidays with Pay* (1948), *Somewhere in Politics* (1948), *School for Randle* (1949), *It's a Grand Life* (1953).

BIBLIOG: Philip Martin Williams & David Williams, *Hooray for Jollywood: The Life of John E. Blakeley and the Mancunian Film Corporation*, 2001. AS.

Randolph, Elsie (*b* London, 1904 – *d* London, 1982). Actress. RN: Killick. A popular revue artist and West End stage favourite, Randolph successfully translated her comic and

musical comedy abilities into several delightful 30s films. Frequently teamed with suave musical comedy star Jack BUCHANAN in recordings and in films like *Yes Mr Brown, That's a Good Girl* (1933), *This'll Make You Whistle* (1936), and *Smash and Grab* (1937), she also worked with Sydney HOWARD in *Night of the Garter* (1933) and Gene GERARD in *Brother Alfred* (1932). She gave a delightfully quirky performance as the 'old maid' in HITCHCOCK's *Rich and Strange* (1932), and years later, she returned to play a small role in his last British production, *Frenzy* (1972), and also appeared in several British TV productions, including *Edward and Mrs Simpson* (1978).
OTHER BRITISH FILMS: *Life Goes On* (1932), *Cheer the Brave* (1951), *The Quatermass Conclusion* (1978, TV, some cinemas). Stephen Shafer.

Rank, J(oseph) Arthur (Lord Rank) (*b* Hull, 1888 – *d* Winchester, 1972). Producer. 'There's undoubtedly a certain intellectual dullness about J. Arthur Rank that seemed to permeate his character. He achieved a remarkable amount in his life: he amassed wealth; he moved in a world steeped in glamour and excitement as well as holding a very powerful position in the City; yet, in spite of it all, he managed to remain largely untouched by it.' Thus wrote Michael Wakelin in his 1996 biography of Rank. Though an admirer of Rank, even he seems perplexed by his subject's transformation from Methodist businessman to film tycoon. It is Rank's misfortune that he is so easy to parody. Compared to Alexander KORDA or to the Hollywood studio bosses with whom he did business, he was an avuncular, rather bumbling figure. His father, Joseph, a formidable Victorian capitalist who had built up a vast flour empire, had a low opinion of his prospects. 'You're a dunce at school and the only way you'll get on is in the mill,' Joe told his son.

Rank's first forays into business were far from spectacular. When his own company, Peterkins Self-Raising Flour (the very name sounds like something out of a Norman WISDOM film) collapsed, he went back to working for his father. He reached early middle-age without showing any hint that he might be the British film industry's next saviour.

Rank, like his father's flour, can fairly be said to have risen without trace. When he became involved with the Religious Film Society in the early 1930s, his aim was no more ambitious than to use cinema as a vehicle for religious education in Sunday schools and Methodist Halls. In little under a decade, though, he was the most important figure in the British film industry: by 1946, the Organisation which bore his name owned five studios (PINEWOOD and DENHAM among them), two NEWSREELS, a large number of production companies, its own DISTRIBUTION arm, its own ANIMATION department, a 'CHARM SCHOOL' for bringing on young British stars, and more than 650 cinemas. In its prime, the RANK ORGANI-SATION was a vertically integrated film company bigger than any of its Hollywood rivals.

It is easy to write off Rank's rise as the result of lucky timing and fortuitous alliances. He benefited from his pact with C.M. WOOLF, the sharpest film distributor in 30s Britain; he was in the right place at the right time and had big enough pockets to take over ODEON CINEMAS and GAUMONT–BRITISH. Critics hostile to him would doubtless say it was mere coincidence that film-makers of the quality of Michael POWELL and Emeric PRESSBURGER, David LEAN, Frank LAUNDER and Sidney GILLIAT, Ken ANNAKIN and Muriel BOX made their finest pictures under his aegis. It is instructive, though, to read what Lean and Powell said about their time as part of Rank's elite

film corps, INDEPENDENT PRODUCERS LTD. 'We can make any subject we wish, with as much money as we think that subject should have spent on it' wrote Lean (1947). 'We can cast whichever actors we choose, and we have no interference with the way the film is made . . . not one of us is bound by any form of contract. We are there because we want to be there.' Powell was similarly upbeat about the creative freedom he enjoyed at IPL in his autobiography, *A Life In Movies*, boastfully calling his time with Rank 'one of the most glorious partnerships in the history of British films'. Admittedly, Independent Producers soon collapsed, but the work that was done in the few brief years of its existence is testament to Rank's qualities as a patron. *Brief Encounter, Black Narcissus, I See a Dark Stranger, Great Expectations* and *The Red Shoes* were all made at IPL.

The film-makers, even those like Betty BOX, toiling away in under-resourced studios making modest programme-fillers while money was lavished on Lean and Powell and Pressburger at Pinewood, had a genuine affection for Rank. They called him 'Uncle Arthur'. They knew he could be prudish and purit-anical. He was accused in certain quarters of monopolistic practices and of making swollen, empty epics in an ill-fated bid to gatecrash the American market. Nevertheless, he was prepared to invest in research and marketing. He realised there were no shortcuts and that if the British film industry was to compete with Hollywood, it had to be run along the same professional lines.

In 1952, after the death of his older brother Jimmy, J. Arthur Rank went back to the family flour business. He stayed on as chairman of the Rank Organisation until 1962, but left the day-to-day running of the company to ex-accountant, John DAVIS, who was never the type to indulge the artistic whims of his producers. Rank died aged 83 in 1972. There is no denying the benevolent effect he had on British cinema of the 40s, but the company which bears his name has long since forgotten its original ideals. In hindsight, it seems half comic, half tragic, that all Rank's efforts to set the British industry on its feet should spawn nothing more than a photocopying company and a leisure conglomerate.
BIBLIOG: Alan Wood, *Mr Rank*, 1952; Geoffrey Macnab, *J. Arthur Rank and the British Film Industry*, 1993. Geoffrey Macnab.

Rank Organisation, The In the spring of 1997, Rank Film Distributors was sold to British TV company, Carlton, for £65 million. At the time, Carlton's bosses insisted they would preserve the company, whose history stretched back to 1935. They didn't keep that promise. Within months, Carlton had closed RFD down. Its main interest in acquiring Britain's oldest distribution outfit was getting hold of Rank's huge inde-pendent film library of 740 feature films.

The disappearance of RFD didn't have the impact on the industry that might have been expected. For years, it had made its money by handling US product rather than by investing in new British talent. Its parent, The Rank Organisation, had pulled out of production in 1980. 'Copier Company Quits Films,' was how the *Economist* characterised the departure. By then, movies were only a small part of what had become a huge, multinational leisure conglomerate which generated much of its profits from its stake in Xerox.

At the time of writing, The Rank Group (as it now styles itself) continues to wiggle a toe in the film industry. It retains ownership of PINEWOOD STUDIOS (built in 1936), Odeon Cinemas (which it acquired in 1941), and Deluxe Film Laboratories, but it is unrecognisable from the company that J.

Arthur RANK set up more than 60 years ago. It has diversified into pubs, casinos, holiday companies and theme parks. It still employs 40,000 people worldwide, even more than in J. Arthur Rank's heyday, but only a small proportion of those work in the film business.

In its prime, though, the Rank Organisation had been the one British film outfit with the muscle to match the Hollywood majors. At the end of WW2, it owned studios, production and distribution companies (making everything from million-dollar features to NEWSREELS, from cartoons to educational shorts) and 650 cinemas. It financed many British movies now recognised as classics: David LEAN's DICKENS ADAPTATIONS, the EALING comedies, the GAINSBOROUGH melodramas, POWELL AND PRESSBURGER's *The Red Shoes*, LAUNDER and GILLIAT's *I See a Dark Stranger*. It had a stake in UNIVERSAL and had even set up its own international sales company, Eagle–Lion Distributors Ltd.

Rank stood in many cinemagoers' eyes for the British film industry as a whole. The indelible image of Bombardier Billy WELLS (an ex-Heavyweight Champ) and his body-builder successors walloping that gong became British cinema's national symbol. The company's initiatives mirrored those of the government. Just as the Butler Education Act introduced grammar schools, so the Rank Organisation came up with the CHARM SCHOOL. At a house in Highbury, North London, various fledgling starlets (Diana DORS, Christopher LEE and Anthony STEEL among them) were put through their paces by a formidable team of hairdressers and elocution experts. The starlets were also ferried around the country to open garden fêtes. The late Olive DODDS, who used to run the Charm School, pointed out that, after the war years, 'Rank stars were giving people release from things: from poverty, from shortages: suddenly you saw all those marvellous people being very romantic, and it became very important as a release for people.'

Given that Rank was lured into cinema via the Sunday School, it's scarcely surprising that he invested in children as well as would-be stars. 'To The Odeon We Have Come/Now We Can Have Some Fun/We Are a Hundred Thousand Strong/So How Can We All Be Wrong?' ran the mantra that the kids, who turned up in their droves every Saturday morning to Gaumont Children's Clubs, used to chant. To J. Arthur's distress, they didn't always care for the moralistic newsreels and dramas that the Rank-sponsored CHILDREN'S ENTERTAINMENT FILMS outfit churned out for their benefit. Their preference was for cowboys, submarines and adventure. But at least Rank was catering for young audiences.

During the late 40s, he also poured money into research. He poached one of Disney's top directors, David HAND, to set up a British ANIMATION unit at Cookham in Kent. (Bob MONKHOUSE was among Hand's young apprentices.) He financed 'B' MOVIES at the tiny HIGHBURY STUDIOS and started a DOCUMENTARY magazine, *This Modern Age*, as a British counterpart to *The March of Time*. He even went as far as to put the US meteorologists who'd provided the allies with weather forecasts during the D-Day invasions under contract. 'It didn't save a single day's shooting,' the late Sidney GILLIAT observed of Rank's ill-fated foray into soothsaying territory.

'We shall make no "B" films, America doesn't want them,' Eagle–Lion boss, Teddy Carr, proclaimed when he was first appointed. 'We don't want American "B" films either ... while cautioning me not to waste money, Mr Rank told me that even if it cost £10 million, he was determined to establish Eagle–Lion

as a world force.' Carr's quote hints at the quixotic nature of Rank's endeavour. By instinct, J. Arthur was a canny businessman who didn't want to spend money unless he had to, but he knew the only way he could compete with the Hollywood studios was by showing he was an international player with even bigger pockets than they had.

By the late 40s, the Rank Organisation was in crisis. There had been a damaging stand-off with the Americans, who had refused to accept the Attlee Government's ad valorem tax, which entitled the British exchequer to 75% of Hollywood movies' earnings in the UK. Rank's bold production drive was faltering. He was caught in an old fix: he relied on showing Hollywood movies in his cinemas to make the money to produce British films, which, by then, nobody much wanted to see anyway in the UK, let alone the US. Under his hatchet-man accountant, John DAVIS, he therefore began the long, painful process of retrenchment. Budgets were slashed. Extravagant, high-profile film-makers like Powell and Pressburger and David Lean jumped ship for Alexander KORDA. Instead of huge epics like *The Red Shoes* (1948) or Gabriel PASCAL's *Caesar and Cleopatra* (1945), which cost more than *Gone With The Wind*, Pinewood began to make gentrified comedies. This was the era of the chap – the pipe-smoking, tweed-jacketed Kenneth MORE or Jack HAWKINS type. Admittedly, Diana Dors sported a mink bikini at the Venice Film Festival in 1955, but sex and glamour weren't much in evidence down at Pinewood: everybody was too busy making John MILLS war films to think about such matters.

After his father's death in 1952, J. Arthur Rank was too busy with the family flour business to devote much time to his film company, which was left more and more in the hands of Davis. This fearsome apparatchik ran the Rank Organisation along draconian lines. He idolised the family audience and tried to keep 'X' films out of Odeon cinemas. By the late 50s, he had begun reducing the Rank Organisation's commitment to film and diversifying into other leisure activities – ten-pin bowling alleys, dance halls, motorway service stations and even a short-lived record label. The Rank Group of today exists in his image, not that of its visionary founder.

BIBLIOG: Alan Wood, *Mr Rank*, 1952; Geoffrey Macnab, *J. Arthur Rank and the British Film Industry*, 1993. Geoffrey Macnab.

Ransome, Prunella (*b* Croydon, Surrey, 1943). Actress. Made an excellent start as a very touching Fanny Robin in *Far from the Madding Crowd* (1967) and as the female lead in *Alfred the Great* (1969), but the freckled and fetching Ransome did not maintain this momentum. There were a couple of international films, including *Man in the Wilderness* (1971), as Richard HARRIS's wife, and some TV, such as *A Horseman Riding By* (1978), but nothing apparently since then.

Raphael, Frederic (*b* Chicago, 1931). Screenwriter. American-born, Cambridge-educated novelist and screenwriter, who has contributed to some stylish screenplays in the course of a varied career. His major cinema work was on those *echt* 60s films, *Nothing But the Best* (1964, + lyrics), a cruelly witty black comedy version of *Room at the Top*, and *Darling* (1965), for which his evocation of an evanescent, superficial life-style won him an AA/sc and BAA/sc. In the 70s, he wrote a carefully faithful screenplay for the underrated *Daisy Miller* (1974) while still leaving the director room to move, and he wrote the brilliant TV series, *The Glittering Prizes* (1976). In 1999, he was back in film news again with his screenplay for the KUBRICK swansong, *Eyes Wide Shut*, and continues to work in several media.

OTHER BRITISH FILMS: *Bachelor of Hearts* (1958, co-sc), *Don't Bother to Knock* (1961, co-sc), *Two for the Road* (1966), *Far from the Madding Crowd* (1967), *A Severed Head* (1970), *Richard's Things* (1980), *The King's Mistress* (1990, UK/It/Fr, co-sc).

Rathbone, Basil (*b* Johannesburg, 1892 – *d* New York, 1967). Actor. Perhaps the screen's most famous SHERLOCK HOLMES, a role he played 14 times in Hollywood, Rathbone made his debut in British silents (1921–23) and returned to make four more British films in the 30s, including the star role in Basil DEAN's production of *Loyalties* (1933). Otherwise, his film career – especially as the best thin villain in the world (Dorothy Parker described him as 'two profiles pasted together') belongs in another book, though it is worth noting that he played an immense number of Brits, often titled, and became a leading member of the Hollywood raj.

OTHER BRITISH FILMS INCLUDE: *Innocent* (1921), *School for Scandal* (1923), *After the Ball* (1932), *Love from a Stranger* (1937).

BIBLIOG: Autobiography, *In and Out of Character*, 1967; Michael B. Druxman, *Basil Rathbone and His Films*, 1972.

Ratoff, Gregory (*b* Samara, Russia, 1897 – *d* Soleure, Switz., 1960). Director, actor. Russian émigré, who acted with the Moscow Arts Theatre, before fleeing West after the Bolshevik Revolution. Long in Hollywood where he combined acting (usually in flamboyant 'foreign' roles) and directing (most notably of *Intermezzo*, 1939), he acted in four British films of the 30s, including *Falling in Love* (1934), and directed/produced four in the post-war decades. There are two tortured romantic dramas, *That Dangerous Age* (1949) and *My Daughter Joy* (1950, + a), a *folie de grandeur* (i.e. more *folie* than *grandeur*), *Abdullah the Great* (1954, UK/Egypt, +a) and the lesser of the two almost-simultaneously released WILDE BIOPICS, *Oscar Wilde* (1960). Married (1923–49) Eugenie Leontovich.

OTHER BRITISH FILMS: (a) *Forbidden Territory* (1934), *Hello Sweetheart, 18 Minutes* (+ story) (1935).

Rattigan, Sir Terence (*b* London, 1911 – *d* Bermuda, 1977). Dramatist, screenwriter. Major figure of British theatre for about 20 years on either side of WW2, the Harrow- and Oxford-educated Rattigan wrote unashamedly – and with enormous proficiency – about and for the middle and upper classes. He and Noël COWARD held sway until the mid 50s when new trends in English theatre displaced them – temporarily, at least. Rattigan's career as screenwriter and as an adapted playwright is much associated with director Anthony ASQUITH, who brought Rattigan's first hit play, *French Without Tears* (1936) to the screen in 1939. Somewhat surprisingly, Graham GREENE praised this sunny, silly account of Englishmen acting like pickled adolescents, but there were to be much more effective Rattigan–Asquith collaborations: Rattigan co-authored the screenplay for Asquith's charming *Quiet Wedding* (1941); he wrote original screenplays for the beautiful, elegiac *The Way to the Stars* (1945, + story), *The VIPS* (1963) and its feeble all-star follow-up, *The Yellow Rolls-Royce* (1964); and Rattigan provided screenplays for several further Asquith ADAPTATIONS. The best of these are *The Winslow Boy* (1948), though David Mamet's 1999 version (UK/US) is arguably a tougher film, and *The Browning Version* (1951), which enshrines a great performance from Michael REDGRAVE, and is streets ahead of Mike FIGGIS's 1994 version, in which, however, Albert FINNEY rises admirably to the challenge of one of Rattigan's finest protagonists.

The other director with whom he was most associated was his chum, Harold FRENCH, who directed *French Without Tears* on stage, and several films from Rattigan's screenplays, including *The Day Will Dawn* (1942, co-sc), *English Without Tears* (1944) and *The Man Who Loved Redheads* (1954, from the play *Who Is Sylvia?*, 1950). David LEAN filmed *The Sound Barrier* (1952) from Rattigan's screenplay and OLIVIER directed and starred in *The Prince and the Showgirl* (1957), admittedly from one of Rattigan's feeblest plays. The point is that he attracted the top names in British cinema at the time – both directors and actors, for most of these films contain memorable acting performances, as also did Anatole LITVAK's chilly *The Deep Blue Sea* (1955, play 1952), which contains Kenneth MORE's definitive performance of the raffish, RAF-ish Freddie, and the US-made *Separate Tables* (1958, play 1954) won Oscars for David NIVEN and Wendy HILLER. Many of his plays were also adapted to TV, including *Ross* (1971), based on the life of T.E. LAWRENCE.

Much of Rattigan's dialogue has a mannered, theatrical whiff to it, but skilled direction and acting can still bring its melodramatic structures and highly wrought characters to exciting life. He might have been a 'better' playwright if he could have written openly about his homosexuality; he might have been better still if he had acknowledged the constrictions of class as a source not just of drama but of pain. However, within the bounds of constrained emotion, he can have few peers in his century. Awarded CBE, 1958, knighted 1971.

OTHER BRITISH FILMS: (co-sc, unless noted) *The Belles of St Clement's* (1936, sc), *Gypsy* (1937), *Uncensored* (1942), *Journey Together* (1945), *While the Sun Shines* (+ play), *Brighton Rock* (1947), *Bond Street* (1948, co-story), *The Final Test* (1953, sc, + TV play), *Goodbye, Mr Chips* (1969, sc), *Bequest to the Nation* (1973, sc, + play).

Rawi, Ousama (*b* Baghdad, 1939). Director, cinematographer. Edinburgh-educated Rawi worked in TV and in photographing SHORT FILMS and DOCUMENTARIES, including *A Little of What You Fancy* (1968), a history of the MUSIC HALLS, before beginning to shoot feature films with Mike HODGES's *Pulp* (1972). Married and divorced from Rita TUSHINGHAM, whom he photographed in *Rachel's Man* (1974, Israel), *The 'Human' Factor* (1975) and directed in the Ruth RENDELL ADAPTATION, *A Judgement in Stone* (1986, Can, + ex p).

OTHER BRITISH FILMS INCLUDE: (c) *The 14* (1973), *The Black Windmill*, *Gold* (1974), *Alfie Darling* (1975), *Power Play* (1978, UK/Can), *Parting Shots* (1998).

Rawle, Jeff (*b* Birmingham, 1951). Actor. Supporting actor of the 80s and 90s, much on TV where he established a droll persona as day-dreaming *Billy Liar* (1973–74) and as the hapless George in *Drop the Dead Donkey* (1990–98). Films have been less rewarding but he co-wrote the unsettling screenplay for *The Young Poisoner's Handbook* (1995, UK/Fr/Ger), and has appeared in a number of experimental SHORTS, including *Correction Please, or How We Got Into the Pictures* (1979).

OTHER BRITISH FILMS: *The Life Story of* (short), *Home Before Midnight* (1978), *Phoelix* (1979), *Rating Norman* (1980, short), *The Doctor and the Devils* (1985), *The Gift* (1990), *Who Goes There?* (2001, sc).

Rawlings, Margaret (*b* Osaka, Japan, 1906 – *d* Wendover, 1996). Actress. Distinguished, elegant, Oxford-educated stage actress who showed little interest in films, having her best film roles in the mid 50s: *Roman Holiday* (1953, US) as Audrey HEPBURN's lady-in-waiting; *Beautiful Stranger* (1954), as Stanley BAKER's wife; and *No Road Back* (1956), as a deaf-blind fence. On London stage from 1928 and in many TV programmes, including *Hamlet* in 1947.

OTHER BRITISH FILMS: *The Woman He Scorned* (1928), *Hands of the Ripper*, *Follow Me!* (1971), *The Tales of Helpmann* (1990, doc, interviewee).

Rawlings, Terence Sound editor. In films since the mid 50s, he has worked often for such diverse directors as Ken RUSSELL and Jack CLAYTON: the elegant classicism of the latter's *The Lonely Passion of Judith Hearne* (1987) presumably made claims very different from the frenzied fragmentation of the former's *Lisztomania* (1975).

OTHER BRITISH FILMS INCLUDE: (sound) *Licensed to Kill* (1965), *Our Mother's House* (1967); (sound/dubbing editor) *Rattle of a Simple Man*, *Crooks in Cloisters* (1964), *Bedazzled* (1967), *Women in Love*, *The Games* (1969), *The Music Lovers*, *The Nightcomers*, *Chato's Land* (1971), *The Duellists* (1977); (editor) *Alien* (1979, UK/US, co-e), *The Awakening* (1980), *Chariots of Fire* (1981), *Yentl* (1983, UK/US), *White of the Eye* (1986), *GoldenEye* (1995, UK/US).

Rawlinson, A(rthur) R(ichard) (*b* London, 1894 – *d* 1984). Screenwriter. Rugby and Cambridge-educated author of about 50 films since 1931. Had a distinguished WW1 career, worked as a ship repairer and coal exporter (1919–27), and began to have his plays performed in the early 30s. He worked on the screenplays of *The Man Who Knew Too Much* (1934), *King Solomon's Mines* (1937) and *Gaslight* (1940), received the OBE for his WW2 service (1939–45), and post-war was almost entirely confined to co-writing 'B' MOVIE screenplays, of no special distinction. Father of Attorney-General, Peter Rawlinson, later Baron Rawlinson of Ewell.

OTHER BRITISH FILMS INCLUDE: (co-sc) *The Third String* (1932), *Menace* (1934), *Man of the Moment* (1935), *Crackerjack*, *Strange Boarders* (1938), *This England* (1941), *The White Unicorn* (1947), *Calling Paul Temple* (1948), *Celia* (1949), *Fast and Loose* (1954), *Stock Car* (1955, + p); (sc) *The Blarney Stone*, *A Cuckoo in the Nest* (scen) (1933), *Jew Süss* (1934, + dial), *Lancashire Luck* (1937), *Teheran* (1947, adptn), *Paul Temple's Triumph* (1950), *The Broken Horseshoe* (1953), *Cloak Without Dagger* (1955, + p), *Gaolbreak* (1962); (p) *Something in the City* (1950, assoc), *There Was a Young Lady* (1953).

Rawlinson, Brian (*b* Stockport, 1931 – *d* Lyme Regis, 2000). Actor. Stocky character actor in generally routine films from the late 50s to the early 70s. He was in several 'CARRY ON' films, and in both cinema and TV versions of *Far from the Madding Crowd* (1967, 1998), though in different roles. Did a stint in *Coronation Street* (1961), as Joe Makinson, and starred in series, *Market in Honey Lane* (1967). Also on stage, starting with the Old Vic.

OTHER BRITISH FILMS INCLUDE: *Dangerous Exile* (1957), *Life in Danger* (1959), *Carry On Cruising* (1962), *Ladies Who Do*, *The Iron Maiden* (1963), *Carry On Cleo* (1964), *The Big Job* (1965), *Blind Terror* (1971).

Rawlinson, Gerald (*b* St Helen's, Lancs, 1904). Actor. In the Air Force for several years before becoming a supporting actor of the 20s and 30s, mostly in inconsequential films, *Tell England* (1931), as Lt Doon, a rare brush with distinction. Also on stage from 1931.

OTHER BRITISH FILMS INCLUDE: *The Hellcat* (1928), *The Devil's Maze* (1929), *Young Woodley* (1930), *The Old Man* (1931), *Collision* (1932), *You Made Me Love You* (1933), *Say It with Diamonds* (1935), *His Lordship Regrets* (1938).

Rawnsley, David (*b* Sevenoaks, 1909). Production designer. Invented the INDEPENDENT FRAME system – a method of preparing and shooting a film to plan – and acted as technical adviser on several films using it, including *Warning to Wantons* (1948, lumpish but tolerable), *Floodtide* (1949, competent but unexciting) and *Stop Press Girl* (1949, on many counts the

silliest film ever made). While in theory, its purpose was to accelerate the production process, it actually constricted film practice and was swiftly abandoned. Prior to his involvement with IF, he had been art director on some distinguished films, including *49th Parallel* (1941), *The Way Ahead* (1944) and *The Rake's Progress* (1945).

OTHER BRITISH FILMS INCLUDE: (art d/des, unless noted) *Out of the Blue* (1931), *Lord Camber's Ladies* (1932), *A Southern Maid* (1933), *Radio Parade of 1935*, *Blossom Time* (settings) (1934), *Royal Cavalcade* (co-), *Dance Band* (1935), *The Rat* (1937), *One of Our Aircraft is Missing*, *In Which We Serve* (1942), *I Know Where I'm Going!* (tank constructor), *They Were Sisters* (1945), *I See a Dark Stranger* (1946).

Rawsthorne, Alan (*b* Haslingden, Lancs, 1905 – *d* Cambridge, 1971). Composer. Studied at Royal Manchester College of Music (after briefly studying dentistry) and worked as a teacher and musician at Dartington Hall, composing concert hall pieces before taking up film scoring in 1937. His first work was a SHORT for the SHELL UNIT and during WW2 he composed for several DOCUMENTARIES, including the GPO FILM UNIT's *The City* (1939). He served in the Army and scored the celebrated *Burma Victory* (1945) and conducted Richard ADINSELL's score for the PROPAGANDA documentary, *The New Lot* (1943). His post-war films are eclectically interesting, including Ealing's sombre COSTUME DRAMA, *Saraband for Dead Lovers* (1948) and Albert Lewin's baroque *Pandora and the Flying Dutchman* (1950), alongside a low-key realist piece like *Lease of Life* (1954).

OTHER BRITISH FILMS INCLUDE: (features) *School for Secrets*, *The Captive Heart* (1946), *Uncle Silas* (1947), *Where No Vultures Fly* (1951), *The Cruel Sea* (1952), *The Man Who Never Was* (1955), *Floods of Fear* (1958); (doc, short) *The Dancing Fleece* (1950), *The Drawings of Leonardo da Vinci* (1953), *Messenger of the Mountains* (1963).

Ray, Andrew (*b* London, 1939). Actor. In films as a child, Ray made a strong impression as *The Mudlark* (1950) who influences Queen Victoria's decision to come out of seclusion, as the terrified young protagonist of *The Yellow Balloon* (1953) and as the son of the slatternly *Woman in a Dressing Gown* (1957). Fully adult, he was a pleasant if not very forceful presence in a few films, lacking the edge of threat needed for the lout in *Serious Charge* (1959), and worked more on TV, playing the Duke of York in *Edward and Mrs Simpson* (1978). Son of Ted RAY. Brother, **Robin Ray** (*b* London, 1934 – *d* Brighton, 1998), became a TV actor and presenter (e.g. as original chairman of *Call My Bluff*, 1965).

OTHER BRITISH FILMS INCLUDE: *A Prize of Gold*, *Escapade* (1955), *Gideon's Day*, *The Young and the Guilty* (1958), *Twice Round the Daffodils* (1962), *Great Expectations* (1975, as Herbert Pocket), *Paris by Night* (1988).

Ray, Philip (*b* London, 1898 – *d* ?). Actor. Following WW1 service in the Army and stage experience, he entered films in 1935 (*Sexton Blake and the Bearded Doctor*, *Old Roses*), and played several dozen supporting roles over the next 30 years, with a break for WW2 service (1940–45). His range included an MP in *The Winslow Boy* (1948), a tramp in *The Fake* (1953) and the clergyman on the *Carpathia* in *A Night to Remember* (1958), as well as TV from the early 50s.

OTHER BRITISH FILMS INCLUDE: *Not So Dusty* (1936), *Dark Journey* (1937), *Jamaica Inn* (1939), *Send for Paul Temple* (1946), *The October Man* (1947), *Night and the City* (1950, UK/US), *No Highway* (1951), *The Net* (1953), *The Good Die Young* (1954), *The Extra Day*, *No Road Back* (1956), *Sons and Lovers* (1960), *In the Doghouse* (1961), *The Mind Benders* (1963), *Frankenstein Created Woman* (1966).

Ray, René (*b* London, 1912 – *d* Jersey, 1993). Actress. RN: Irene Creese. Lovely, versatile performer in British films in the 30s and 40s, moving easily from COMEDIES and MUSICALS to THRILLERS. Making her debut in a small role in *High Treason* (1929), she appeared in over 40 British films over the next three decades. She scored in the early Michael POWELL musical, *Born Lucky*, (1933) as 'Mops', a waitress who becomes a stage star, she played impressive character roles in *The Passing of the Third Floor Back* (1935), *Bank Holiday* (1938) and *Housemaster* (1938), and female leads in such films as *The Green Cockatoo* (1937) and *Old Bill and Son* (1940). Returned to British films in the late 40s, after time in Hollywood (*If Winter Comes*, 1947), showing versatility as Cora, wife of a cheap crook in the *noir* thriller, *They Made Me a Criminal* (1947). She also wrote for television. Married the Earl of Middleton (1975–79).

OTHER BRITISH FILMS INCLUDE: *Young Woodley* (1930), *Dance Pretty Lady* (1932), *The King's Cup* (1933), *Tiger Bay* (1933), *Royal Cavalcade* (1935), *Crime Over London* (1936), *The Rat* (1937), *Return of the Frog, Mountains o' Mourne* (1938), *The Galloping Major* (1951), *Women of Twilight* (1952), *The Good Die Young* (1954), *The Vicious Circle* (1957). Stephen Shafer.

Ray, Ted (*b* Wigan, 1905 – *d* London, 1977). Actor. RN: Charles Olden. Violinist with a dance band before becoming a comedian, Ray toured extensively with ENSA during WW2, then had his own very popular radio show, *Ray's a Laugh*, as well as numerous TV appearances. His first film was *Radio Parade of 1935* (1934, as himself), and there was a batch of roles in the 50s, including faded MUSIC HALL star, George Pepper, in *Meet Me Tonight* (1952) and popular acting headmaster in *Carry On Teacher* (1959). However, despite his ebullient, cheery persona, he never found in films the favour he won from radio or pantomime. Father of Andrew RAY and TV presenter, Robin Ray.

OTHER BRITISH FILMS: *A Ray of Sunshine* (1950, short), *Escape by Night* (1953), *My Wife's Family* (1956), *The Crowning Touch* (1959), *Please Turn Over* (1960).

BIBLIOG: Autobiographies, *Raising the Laughs*, 1952; *My Turn Next*, 1963.

Raye, Carol (*b* London, 1923). Actress. RN: Kathleen Corkrey. Slender, gracefully attractive actress who studied dancing under Freddie CARPENTER and first appeared on stage in 1939, in Edinburgh. Made five films in the post-war years, last of which was *Green Fingers* (1947), as socialite Nova PILBEAM's rival for osteopath Robert BEATTY. Her last London stage appearance was in 1950; she then accompanied her doctor husband to Africa, the West Indies, etc, and in the mid 60s turned up on TV in Australia, where she has been ever since – on stage and screen as well.

OTHER BRITISH FILMS: *Strawberry Roan, Waltz Time* (1945), *Spring Song* (1946), *While I Live* (1947).

Raymond, Charles (*b* London, 1858 – *d* London, 1930). Director, actor. An old-fashioned director of old-fashioned films, who had acted on stage and entered the industry as an actor in 1902 and acted, on and off, through 1920. Between 1904 and 1909, Raymond directed more than 50 shorts for the WARWICK TRADING COMPANY, before moving to BRITISH AND COLONIAL. He made a number of detective dramas, including a series with Harry LORRAINE as Sexton Blake, which he also wrote: *The Mystery of the Diamond Belt* (1914), *Britain's Secret Treaty* (1914), *The Kaiser's Spies* (1914), *The Stolen Heirlooms* (1915), *The Great Cheque Fraud* (1915), *The Counterfeiters* (1915), and *The Thornton Jewel Mystery* (1915).

OTHER BRITISH FILMS INCLUDE: (d, unless noted) *Hamlet* (1912, + a), *The Great Anarchist Mystery* (1912), *The Finger of Destiny* (1914), *Betta the Gypsy* (1918), *The Great London Mystery* serial (1920, sc, a). AS.

Raymond, Cyril (*b* Rowley Regis, 1897 – *d* London, 1974). Actor. Raymond's beautifully judged portrayal of middle-class decency, as comfortable, pipe-smoking Fred, should not be under-estimated in accounting for the emotional charge of *Brief Encounter* (1945). He was not often called on for pathos; more often he played military men, like the Squadron Leader married to Dulcie GRAY in *Angels One Five* (1952), or police inspectors, as in *The Safecracker* (1957), or quiet restrained types like the husband he played on stage in *Waters of the Moon* (1951). RADA-trained, he was on stage from 1914 and in films the following year, appearing in 30-odd before RAF service (1939–45) claimed him, and a further 20 after it released him. Married (1) Iris HOEY and (2) Gillian LIND.

OTHER BRITISH FILMS INCLUDE: *Hypocrites* (1915, UK/US), *His Last Defence* (1919), *Wuthering Heights* (1920), *Moth and Rust* (1921), *Cocaine* (1922), *The Ghost Train* (1931), *Condemned to Death* (1932), *Home Sweet Home* (1933), *The Tunnel* (1935), *Thunder in the City* (1937), *Goodbye, Mr Chips, The Spy in Black, Come on George!* (1939), *Saloon Bar* (1940), *This Was a Woman, Quartet* (1948), *Rough Shoot, The Heart of the Matter* (1953), *Lease of Life* (1954), *Charley Moon* (1956), *Dunkirk* (1958), *Carry On Regardless* (1961), *Night Train to Paris* (1964).

Raymond, Gary (*b* London, 1935). Actor. From a MUSIC HALL background, Raymond won a scholarship to Gateway School, Leicester, before going to RADA. With RSC experience, the curly-haired Raymond played a few film roles in the late 50s and the 60s, but remained a stage actor. His most notable film role was as the peace-making Cliff in *Look Back in Anger* (1959); he had the lead in the much-unseen *The Playboy of the Western World* (1962, UK/Ire), and in Hollywood was Peter in *The Greatest Story Ever Told* (1965). Also TV, including series, *The Rat Patrol* (1966–67, US).

OTHER BRITISH FILMS INCLUDE: *The Moonraker* (1957), *Suddenly, Last Summer* (1959), *Jason and the Argonauts* (1963), *Red and Blue* (1967).

Raymond, Jack (*b* Winborne, 1886 – *d* London, 1953). Director. RN: Caines. Having entered films as actor in silent days (e.g. *All's Fair*, 1913, for HEPWORTH's company), he began directing in the early 20s, mainly MELODRAMAS, and had run up several dozen films, usually light COMEDIES and MYSTERIES, before WW2, better known titles including *The King of Paris* (1934), starring Cedric HARDWICKE, and *The Frog* (1937). During WW2, he produced for the War Office and the MOI, and from 1946 to 1949 he was involved in dubbing French films. His five films of the 50s are low-budget comedies: two star Northern comedian, Albert MODLEY and the other three star truculent cockney-type comic, Ronald SHINER.

OTHER BRITISH FILMS INCLUDE: (d, unless noted) *Barbara Elopes* (1921, co-d), *Second to None* (1926), *Zero* (1928), *Splinters* (1929), *Up for the Cup* (+ a), *Tilly of Bloomsbury* (UK/US, + p) (1931), *Up to the Neck, Night of the Garter, Sorrell and Son* (1933), *Come Out of the Pantry* (1935), *The Rat* (1937), *A Royal Divorce* (1938), *The Mind of Mr Reeder* (1939, + exec p), *You Will Remember* (1940), *Up for the Cup, Take Me to Paris* (1950), *Worm's Eye View, Reluctant Heroes* (1951), *Little Big Shot* (1952).

Rayner, Minnie (*b* London, 1869 – *d* London, 1941). Actress. In films from silent days (e.g. *The Pickwick Papers*, 1913, UK/US), she was in the *Bindle* series of short comedies (1926), played Mrs Hudson in several SHERLOCK HOLMES stories of the 30s, and was last seen as the sympathetic cook in *Gaslight* (1940). On stage from 1880 as a child vocalist, she had operatic and other stage experience.

OTHER BRITISH FILMS INCLUDE: *Lost and Won* (1913), *My Old Dutch* (1915), *Sunken Rocks* (1919), *The Old Curiosity Shop* (1921), *Symphony in Two Flats* (1930), *Stranglehold* (1931), *I Lived with You* (1933), *The Triumph of Sherlock Holmes*, *Barnacle Bill* (1935), *Silver Blaze* (1937), *Old Mother Riley in Society* (1940).

Raynor, Sheila (*b* London, 1908 – *d* Ipswich, 1998). Actress. Character player in occasional supporting roles since 1945, often in very small parts like those she had in *The Mark of Cain* (1948), as a prison guard, and the suspicious mother of the little Dufton girl in *Room at the Top* (1958). Also, stage and TV. Married Keith PYOTT.
OTHER BRITISH FILMS INCLUDE: *They Knew Mr Knight* (1945), *Madness of the Heart* (1949), *Lease of Life* (1954), *Value for Money* (1955), *The Violent Playground* (1957), *Monster of Terror* (1965), *A Clockwork Orange* (1971), *Madonna and Child* (from *The Terence Davies Trilogy*, 1980).

Rea, Chris (*b* Middlesborough, 1951). Actor, singer, lyricist. Popular singer and guitarist who has been involved in a handful of British films, including *La Passione* (1996, p, sc, m) and *Parting Shots* (1998, a, songs). Also (co-)scored several others, including *Black Joy* (1977), *The Krays* (1990) and *Soft Top, Hard Shoulder* (1992). His albums sold best in the late 80s/early 90s.

Rea, Stephen (*b* Belfast, 1943). Actor. Rumpled, intense-looking Irish actor who came to prominence in the 80s and 90s, particularly in films directed by compatriot Neil JORDAN. Son of a working-class Protestant family, he came to serious international attention with his role as an IRA 'volunteer' in *The Crying Game* (1992). He studied at the Abbey Theatre School and his career on stage, screen and TV got underway in the 70s. Entered films in a tiny role in the HORROR movie, *Cry of the Banshee* (1970) and had his first leading role in Jordan's *Angel* (1982), a dark THRILLER in which he plays a saxophonist with a travelling band who gets involved in murder, first as witness, later more dangerously. He brought a kind of rough-hewn charm to *Loose Connections* (1983), a romantic comedy somewhat short on charm; gave several more notable performances in Jordan's films, including *The Company of Wolves* (1984), *Michael Collins* (1996, US) and, best of all, *The End of the Affair* (2000, UK/Ger/US), in which the finely calibrated pain of his cuckolded husband arguably dominated the film. His comic gifts have been sharply exploited in his turn as a conceited fashion photographer in *Prêt-à-Porter* (1994, US) and as the keyboardist of the former rock band about to reunite in the very funny *Still Crazy* (1998, UK/US). He is now in constant demand for films made all over the place; playing Leopold Bloom in a new version of *Ulysses* (2004) may well prove his most challenging assignment so far, but his versatility is not in doubt.
OTHER BRITISH FILMS INCLUDE: *The Doctor and the Devils* (1985), *Life is Sweet* (1990), *Bad Behaviour* (1993), *Trojan Eddie* (UK/Ire), *The Last of the High Kings* (UK/Ire/Den) (1996), *A Further Gesture* (UK/Ger/Jap/Ire), *The Butcher Boy* (Ire/US) (1997).

Read, Jan (*b* Sydney, 1917). Screenwriter. Cambridge-educated Read's first screenplay was for *Helter Skelter* (1949), by any criteria one of the daftest films ever made, despite one or two moments of comic inventiveness. He retrieved reputation with his contribution to the original story for the 1949 success, *The Blue Lamp*, and the screenplay for the sober, intelligent hospital drama, *White Corridors* (1951), which he co-wrote with director Pat JACKSON. His other credits move eclectically between main and second features (the latter including the neat

thriller, *The Flying Scot*, and the oddity, *Zoo Baby*, 1957), between realist drama and FANTASY. Mostly worked in collaboration. Entered film industry in 1937, working with Paul ROTHA, and post-war, after a brief stint in the US, returned to Britain where he acted as scenario editor at GAINSBOROUGH (1947–48), story consultant for the RANK ORGANISATION (1950–52) and was British editor of *Hollywood Quarterly* (1948–54). Also, much TV work, including episodes of *Dr Finlay's Casebook*.
OTHER BRITISH FILMS: (sc/co-sc, unless noted) *Street Corner* (story), *Blood Orange* (1953), *The Secret Tent* (1956), *Grip of the Strangler* (1958), *Jason and the Argonauts* (1963), *First Men in the Moon* (1964).
BIBLIOG: Autobiography, *Young Man in Movieland*, 2003.

Reader, Ralph (*b* Crewkerne, 1903 – *d* London, 1982). Actor, choreographer. In Broadway revues of the 20s, he returned to UK in 30s, working on stage and screen as choreographer and occasional performer. Most associated with *The Gang Shows* (1932–74), featuring hordes of boy scouts often in female attire, all under the supervision of the very obviously gay Reader. There is something gloriously and politically incorrect about it all, but the Queen Mother loved it! Played minor roles in a few later British films, including *Derby Day* (1952), but his main contribution to British films was in 30s musicals. Awarded MBE, 1942; CBE, 1957.
OTHER BRITISH FILMS: (choreographer) *I Adore You* (1933), *Over the Garden Wall* (1934), *Squibs*, *First A Girl* (1935), *Limelight* (1936, + a), *The Gang Show* (1937, + co-sc, a); (a) *The Blue Squadron* (1934), *Coastal Command* (1942), *These Dangerous Years* (1957).
BIBLIOG: Autobiography, *It's Been Terrific*, 1954; *This Is the Gang Show*, 1957. AS.

realism The idea of realism is complicated and has been notoriously difficult to define. In relation to art and literature, Raymond Williams argues that the term has implied both an *attitude* and a *method*. However, if the attitude of realism has involved a commitment to the representation of 'ordinary' people and real events, the methods adopted by realism have also varied. This is because realism, no less than other forms of art, relies upon conventions that audiences accept as 'realistic'. As these conventions acquire familiarity, so they come to appear less 'realistic' and new methods of representing reality emerge. In this sense, realism is necessarily *intertextual* in character, defining itself in relation to, or against, the conventions that other works employ. This is particularly so of British cinema which, at key historical moments, has sought to differentiate itself not only from earlier British films but also from Hollywood films perceived as 'unreal' and escapist.

Although John GRIERSON, in his famous essay 'The Course of Realism'(1938), associates realism with DOCUMENTARY, it has become common critical practice to identify the conventions of realism with fiction. However, it was undoubtedly the documentary movement of the 30s that established the reputation of British cinema for realist film-making and paved the way for the coming together of documentary and narrative techniques in British films during WW2. As this suggests, there is rarely a clear-cut division between documentary and fiction film. Documentaries never simply 'document' but involve a selection and organisation of material. The documentarists of the 30s were also content to dramatise events for the camera and, in the case of Harry WATT, experimented with story-documentaries, such as *North Sea* (1938), involving the use of non-actors in scripted roles. This fusion of fiction and documentary techniques then carried over into wartime features, such as *Target for Tonight* (1941) and *Fires Were Started* (1943), as well as more mainstream dramas, such as *Millions Like Us* (1943) and *The Way Ahead* (1944). British wartime realism, in this regard, became associated with loosely-structured narratives that avoided MELODRAMA, a downplaying of the role of stars, and the adoption of various stylistic features indebted to documentary (such as location shooting).

Although elements of this tradition remained in evidence during the post-war period in the work of EALING and GROUP 3, it was the emergence of the FREE CINEMA movement and the British 'NEW WAVE' at the end of the 50s that announced a resurgence of the realist impulse in British film-making. Films such as *Room at the Top* (1958), *Saturday Night and Sunday Morning* (1960), and *A Kind of Loving* (1962) showed a commitment to the representation of the urban-industrial north of England and the lives of 'ordinary' people (especially the young working-class male) at a time of social change. These films in turn influenced the emerging aesthetic of television drama and, in *The Big Flame* (1969) and *Rank and File* (1971) in particular, the producer Tony GARNETT and director Ken LOACH successfully inflected 'New Wave' conventions in a more politicised direction. Loach's use of observational methods derived from television news and documentary, combined with an emphasis upon the social determinants of character, also led to his work being identified with 'naturalism' rather than simply 'realism' (once again indicating the difficulties in clearly defining this term).

Although realism has often been regarded as a – if not *the* – defining feature of British cinema, its critical reputation has fluctuated. Particularly, since the 70s, there has been a questioning of the merits of realism from two different camps. Leftwing critics have highlighted the political limitations of realism and have tended to prefer avant-garde or modernist works. 'Popular culture' critics, on the other hand, have stressed the aesthetic restrictions of realism and have championed FANTASY and melodrama as undervalued traditions within British film. Despite these assaults, the realist tradition of British film-making has remained remarkably resilient. Directors associated with realism, such as Loach and Mike LEIGH, produced some of their best work during the 1980s and 1990s, while young film-makers such as Shane MEADOWS (*24 7 TwentyFourSeven*, 1997) and Gary OLDMAN (*Nil by Mouth*, 1997) have demonstrated the continuing appeal of realist style. Realism has also undergone a certain revival in critical fortune, partly in response to the playfulness and depthlessness of much contemporary postmodern culture.

BIBLIOG: Andrew Higson, '"Britain's Outstanding Contribution to the Film": The Documentary-Realist Tradition', in Charles Barr (ed), *All Our Yesterdays*, 1986; John Hill, *Sex, Class and Realism: British Cinema 1956–63*, 1986; John Hill, 'From the "New Wave" to "Brit-grit": Continuity and Difference in Working-Class Realism' in J. Ashby and A. Higson (eds), *British Cinema: Past and Present*, 2000. John Hill.

Realist Film Unit One of the first independent DOCU-MENTARY units established, by Basil WRIGHT in 1937, in response to the demand for promotional films by industrial sponsors. Under the Head of Production, John TAYLOR, Realist initially produced PROPAGANDA films with a social conscience such as *The Smoke Menace* (1937) and *Children at School* (1937). During the war their prolific output comprised medical, agricultural and homefront propaganda for the government. After the war they continued making sponsored films including the medical and hygiene instructional series:

The Technique of Anaesthesia and *Your Children*. In 1956 they merged with Ken CAMERON's Anvil Films to make educational and children's feature films until the 1970s. Other Realist personnel included Stuart LEGG, Alberto CAVALCANTI, Paul ROTHA, Ruby GRIERSON, Len LYE, Frank Sainsbury, Ralph BOND and Margaret THOMSON. Sarah Easen.

Reardon, James (*b* England, 1885 – *d*?). Actor, director. Character comedian who directed a few comedy SHORTS featuring himself: *Where's the Key?* (1918), *What a Life!* (1918), *Kiss Me* (1918), *So Like Him* (1919), *To Let* (1919), *Let's Pretend* (1920), *Seeing Double* (1920, + p), and one feature in which he did not appear, *Shadow of Evil* (1922). In 1919, Reardon formed Reardon British Films and produced one feature, in which he starred, *The Glad Eye* (1920).

OTHER BRITISH FILMS INCLUDE: (a) *A Rogue in Love* (1916), *The Doubles* (1922), *Mrs May Comedies* series (1925), *Victory* (1928), *Naughty Husbands* (1930). AS.

Redgrave, Corin (*b* London, 1939). Actor. Though never a film star in the sense that his two sisters were, Redgrave has nevertheless racked up about 20 films, made in various parts of the world, while maintaining the theatrical career begun while he was at Cambridge, and doing some widely seen TV, such as the *Trial & Retribution* series (1997, 2000). He entered films in the mid 60s, played Susannah YORK's husband in *A Man for All Seasons* (1966), Steerforth in *David Copperfield* (1969) and other scattered screen roles until he established himself in the 90s as a substantial character actor, in such films as *In the Name of the Father* (1993, UK/Ire/US), *Four Weddings and a Funeral* (1994), as Andie MacDowell's dull laird-husband, *Persuasion* (1995, TV, some cinemas) as a hilariously vain Sir Walter Elliot, and *Honest* (2000), as comic gangleader Duggie. The son of Michael REDGRAVE and Rachel KEMPSON, brother of Vanessa (whose political passions he shares) and Lynn REDGRAVE, he is married to (2) Kika MARKHAM, and their daughter is Jemma REDGRAVE.

OTHER BRITISH FILMS INCLUDE: *A Study in Terror* (1965), *The Deadly Affair* (1966), *The Charge of the Light Brigade, The Magus* (1968), *When Eight Bells Toll* (1971), *Eureka* (1982, UK/US), *The Fool* (1990), *England, My England* (1995), *Enigma* (2001, UK/Ger/US).

BIBLIOG: Deirdre Redgrave (ex-wife), *To Be a Redgrave*, 1982.

Redgrave, Jemma (*b* London, 1965). Actress. LAMDA-trained daughter of Corin REDGRAVE, she has made her name on stage and as Eleanor Bramwell in TV's *Bramwell* (1995–98). Has made only a few film appearances, of which the most noticeable has been as the middle-class housewife in for some nasty shocks in *The Acid House* (1998).

OTHER BRITISH FILMS: *Dream Demon* (1988), *Howards End* (1992), *One Night Stand* (1993, short).

Redgrave, Lynn (*b* London, 1943). Actress. Trained at London's Central School, Redgrave began her career in 1963 when she appeared in *Tom Jones* (1963) followed by *Girl With Green Eyes* (1964). Her performance in the lead role in *Georgy Girl* (1966) brought stardom winning her the Golden Globe for Best Actress and the New York Film Critics Award. She appeared in a few more British films, including the underrated *The National Health* (1973), before going to live in America. In recent years she has appeared in a number of exceptional films including *Shine* (1996, UK/Aust), as pianist David Helfgott's understanding wife, and *Gods and Monsters* (1998, UK/US), as Ian MCKELLEN's devoted housekeeper, for which she received an AAn. She devised and toured with a one-woman show based around her father Michael REDGRAVE's career as actor and father. Awarded OBE, 2001. Sister of Vanessa and Corin REDGRAVE; her mother is Rachel KEMPSON.

OTHER BRITISH FILMS: *The Deadly Affair* (1966), *Smashing Time* (1967), *The Virgin Soldiers* (1969), *Sunday Lovers* (1980), *Getting It Right* (1989), *My Kingdom* (2001).

BIBLIOG: Autobiography, *This Is Living*, 1991. Anne-Marie Thomas.

Redgrave, Sir Michael (*b* Bristol, 1908 – *d* Denham, 1985). Actor. Despite a certain chilliness in his film persona, Redgrave had arguably the most sustained screen career of any of the theatrical knights of his day. He became immensely popular after his leading role as the eccentric musicologist in HITCHCOCK's *The Lady Vanishes* (1938), and gave impressive proof of his range as the idealistic son of the mining family in *The Stars Look Down* (1939), but there was always perhaps something too cerebral about his film work for easy stardom. Instead, he gave one excellent performance after another, easily sliding into character roles at an age when many stars were still bent on essaying romantic leads.

The son of actors, Roy Redgrave and Margaret SCUDAMORE, Cambridge-educated Redgrave was a schoolteacher before taking to the stage in 1934 (London 1936). His illustrious stage career involved seasons with the Old Vic (John GIELGUD's legendary company of 1937–38), Stratford and Chichester, in Shakespeare, Chekhov (a great Uncle Vanya, 1963) and many modern plays, including *The Old Boys* (1971). His theatrical *cv* occupies four columns in *Who's Who in the Theatre* (1972), and this, along with about 50 films and plentiful TV, testifies to a crowded career.

More articulate than many about the craft of acting – he was the author of two books about it – and of the relative rewards of the various media, he notched up a strikingly versatile run of screen performances. There were three fine – and notably varied – roles for director Anthony ASQUITH: as the poetic Flight-Lt who is killed in *The Way to the Stars* (1945), the failed, embittered schoolmaster in *The Browning Version* (1951), and a definitive Jack Worthing in *The Importance of Being Earnest* (1952). As well he gave brilliant studies in mounting terror as the deranged ventriloquist in *Dead of Night* (1945) and the Air Marshall caught in a nightmare in *The Night My Number Came Up* (1955), delineated movingly the rise in prestige and loss of ideals in the protagonist of *Fame Is the Spur* (1947), and, from the mid 50s, gave any number of well-wrought character studies. Of these latter, the humane, limited prison governor in *The Loneliness of the Long Distance Runner* (1962) and *The Go-Between* (1971), as ruined old man, are among the most notable. His late 40s attempt at a Hollywood star career failed, but he would from time to time appear in US films, including *The Quiet American* (1957).

Tall (6'4") and imposing, he was bumpily married (there were affairs with both men and women) to Rachel KEMPSON, and their children, Vanessa, Lynn and Corin REDGRAVE are all actors, as are his grandchildren, Joely and Natasha RICHARDSON and Jemma REDGRAVE.

OTHER BRITISH FILMS: *Secret Agent* (1936), *Climbing High* (1938), *Stolen Life, A Window in London* (1939), *Kipps, Jeannie, Atlantic Ferry* (1941), *Thunder Rock, The Big Blockade* (1942), *A Diary For Timothy* (doc, narr), *The Years Between, The Captive Heart* (1946), *The Man Within* (1947), *The Magic Box* (1951), *The Sea Shall Not Have Them, The Green Scarf* (1954), *The Dam Busters, Oh, Rosalinda!!, 1984* (1955), *Time Without Pity* (1957), *Greece the Immortal Land* (doc, voice), *Law and Disorder, Behind the Mask* (1958), *Shake Hands with the Devil* (1959, UK/US), *No, My Darling Daughter, The Innocents* (1961), *The Hill,*

Young Cassidy, The Heroes of Telemark (1965), *Palaces of a Queen* (1966, doc, narr), *Assignment K* (1967), *Battle of Britain, Goodbye, Mr Chips, Oh! What a Lovely War, Connecting Rooms, David Copperfield* (1969), *Goodbye Gemini, Nicholas And Alexandra* (UK/US) (1970), *A Christmas Carol* (1971, UK/US, anim, narr), *Rime of the Ancient Mariner* (1976).

BIBLIOG: Autobiography, *In My Mind's Eye*, 1983; Rachel Kempson, *A Family & Its Fortunes*, 1986; Corin Redgrave, *Michael Redgrave: My Father*, 1995.

Redgrave, Vanessa (*b* London, 1937). Actress. One of the great actresses of her generation, Redgrave, born into an acting dynasty (see preceding entries) and Central School-trained, gave some dazzling displays in star film roles, though her height made her difficult casting as conventional leading ladies, and then, from the 80s on, became a remarkable character actress. Her London stage debut and her first film both belong to 1958, and in both she played daughter to her real-life father, Michael REDGRAVE: on stage in *A Touch of the Sun* and on screen in a hospital drama, *Behind the Mask* (1958), old-fashioned even then. After this latter dispiriting experience she concentrated on the theatre and had a couple of dazzling Stratford seasons (in major roles, famously as Rosalind in *As You Like It*, 1961–62) before returning to the screen.

She is a key figure in the 60s revolution in British film, appearing for 'NEW WAVE' directors, Karel REISZ and Tony RICHARDSON, whom she married. For Reisz, she played an upper-class young woman married to a half-mad eccentric in *Morgan: A Suitable Case for Treatment* (1966, AAn) and made a gallant stab at the title role of legendary dancer *Isadora* (1968, AAn), though Reisz said in 1992 that he thought the film failed. For Richardson, she starred in *The Sailor from Gibraltar* (1967), the short and arty *Red and Blue* (1967), and *The Charge of the Light Brigade* (1968), as sexually willing Mrs Codrington. She worked several times in US films, notably as a glowing Guenevere in *Camelot* (1967), and in later years, as a sought-after character player, she has filmed ubiquitously. She has grown only more impressive with age, as such roles as celebrity agent Peggy Ramsay in *Prick Up Your Ears* (1987) and gentle, doomed Mrs Wilcox (AAn) in *Howards End* (1992) attest. If she never acted again, her sublime *Mrs Dalloway* (1997, UK/Neth/US) would stand as a fitting monument to the subtlety of her craft, to its informing passion, and to the beauty, only mellowed, not diminished by the years. Add to this that she has continued to do remarkable stage and TV work, winning an Emmy for *Playing for Time* (1980), controversially cast as a Jewish concentration camp victim, and has been nominated six times for Oscars, winning (Supporting Actress) as *Julia* (1977, US), and twice for BAA, and it is hard to think of anyone who can match her record.

Her marriage to Richardson ended in divorce, but produced actress daughters Joely and Natasha RICHARDSON. There were also widely publicised relationships with Franco NERO and Timothy DALTON; and her political views – pro-Palestinian; the Workers' Revolutionary Party – have also brought her to public notice.

OTHER BRITISH FILMS: *A Man for All Seasons* (cameo role), *Blow-Up* (UK/It) (1966), *Tonite Let's All Make Love in London* (1967, doc), *The Sea Gull* (1968), *Oh! What a Lovely War* (1969), *Mary Queen of Scots* (AAn), *The Devils* (1971), *Murder on the Orient Express* (1974), *Out of Season* (1975), *Agatha* (1978, UK/US), *Bear Island, Yanks* (1979), *The Bostonians* (UK/US, AAn), *Steaming* (1984), *Wetherby* (1985), *Comrades* (1986), *Consuming Passions* (1988, UK/US), *Great Moments in Aviation* (1994, UK/US), *A Month by the Lake* (1995, UK/US), *Wilde* (1997, UK/Ger/Jap/US).

BIBLIOG: Autobiography, *Vanessa Redgrave*, 1991.

Redman, Amanda (*b* Brighton, Sussex, 1959). For 20 years, Redman has been doing incisive work on TV, with the occasional film, but came to prominence in 2000 as the Lottery-winning wife in the abrasive mini-series *At Home with the Braithwaites* (2000–02) and on screen as ex-porn star wife of retired crim Ray WINSTONE in *Sexy Beast* (2001, UK/Sp/US). On TV she takes SHAKESPEARE, WILDE and sitcoms in her stride; on film, she is just finding her niche as a welcome character player in early middle age. Niece of Joyce REDMAN; was married (1984–91) to **Robert Glenister** (*b* Watford, 1960) who played Captain Harville in *Persuasion* (1995, TV, some cinemas).

OTHER BRITISH FILMS INCLUDE: *Richard's Things* (1980), *For Queen and Country* (1988), *Beck* (1997), *Mike Bassett: England Manager* (2001).

Redman, Joyce (*b* Co. Mayo, Ireland, 1918) Actress. RADA-trained Redman, on stage from 1935, with Old Vic, Stratford and National Theatre seasons, has made only five cinema films, but she won AA nominations for two: as the voracious Mrs Waters in *Tom Jones* (1963) and, repeating her stage performance, as Emilia in *Othello* (1965). Also TV, including *Victoria & Albert* (2001) as the old Queen. Amanda REDMAN is her niece.

OTHER BRITISH FILMS: *Spellbound* (1941), *One of Our Aircraft Is Missing* (1942), *Prudence and the Pill* (1968).

Redmond, Liam (*b* Limerick, Ireland, 1913 – *d* Dublin, 1989). Actor. Stalwart character player of the post-war era, who was educated at the National University of Ireland, made his Abbey Theatre debut in 1935 and stayed there for twelve years before making his first London stage appearance. His first film role was as Deborah KERR's Uncle Timothy in *I See a Dark Stranger* (1946, + add dial); he was the parish priest troubled by the heroine's sexuality in *Daughter of Darkness* (1947), the leading saboteur in *High Treason* (1951), the middle-aged seaman who goes on leave to find his fiancée has been killed, in *The Cruel Sea* (1952), and gave a further 20 carefully honed studies in the busy 50s. Several Hollywood films, including *Kid Galahad* (1962), as Father Higgins of course.

OTHER BRITISH FILMS INCLUDE: *Captain Boycott* (1947), *Saints and Sinners* (1949), *The Gentle Gunman* (1952), *Happy Ever After* (1954), *Yield to the Night, Jacqueline* (1956), *Night of the Demon* (1957), *Rooney, Alive and Kicking* (1958), *The Valiant* (1961, UK/It), *The Last Safari* (1967), *David Copperfield* (1969), *Barry Lyndon* (1975).

Redmond, Moira (*b* Bognor Regis). Actress. First on stage in 1957 and in films in 1958's *Violent Moment*. She mostly played supporting roles in films, as in *A Shot in the Dark* (1964), but was an effectively sceptical leading lady in *Pit of Darkness* (1961) and recreated her Edinburgh Festival Hermione in the filmed version of *The Winter's Tale* (1966). Post-60s, no further films but she continued on stage and TV, playing Alice Keppel in the mini-series *Edward the King* (1975). Married (2) Herbert WISE.

OTHER BRITISH FILMS INCLUDE: *Doctor in Love* (1960), *Partners in Crime* (1961), *Kill or Cure, Jigsaw* (1962), *Nightmare* (1963), *The Limbo Line* (1968).

Reece, Brian (*b* Wallasey, 1913 – *d* London, 1962). Actor. Popular light leading man of the stage from 1931, London 1938, with a break for WW2 service (1940–46), usually in musicals and comedies such as *Bless the Bride* (1947) and *Tunnel of Love* (1958). He made a half-dozen films before his sadly early death from bone disease, notably in farces such as *Fast and Loose* (1954), from Ben TRAVERS's stage hit. Also on radio as PC 49, a role he repeated in the film, *A Case for PC 49* (1951).

OTHER BRITISH FILMS: *Orders Are Orders* (1954), *Geordie* (1955), *Carry On Admiral* (1957), *Watch It, Sailor!* (1961).

Reed, Sir Carol (*b* London, 1906 – *d* London, 1976). Director. The illegitimate son of Sir Herbert Beerbohm TREE, Reed is one of the most important directors in the history of the British cinema. While still only 18 he joined Sybil THORNDIKE's company as an actor, but was soon recruited by Edgar WALLACE, who introduced him to film. After Wallace's death (1932), Reed began working for Basil DEAN, at first as a dialogue director, thereafter as second-unit director (*Autumn Crocus*, 1932), assistant director (*Java Head*, 1934, *Sing As We Go!*, 1934), and co-director (*It Happened in Paris*, 1935). He directed his first film, *Midshipman Easy* also in 1935. The characteristically cinematic qualities – such as a fondness for location work, or varied shooting angles – of Reed's mature work are already in evidence here. More striking films followed: including the Northern working-class-centred *The Stars Look Down* (1939), the neo-HITCHCOCKIAN *Night Train to Munich* (1940), and *Kipps* (1941), another study in class relations. With these and other films from this period Reed established himself as a major presence.

In the 40s he worked for the film unit of the War Office, directing a training film, *The New Lot* (1943), which was the basis for one of the finest British war films, the Eric AMBLER-scripted *The Way Ahead* (1944), a masterful study of a group of ill-assorted recruits whose initial fecklessness and cynicism eventually give way to comradeship and self-discipline in the crucible of war. Reed's focus here, and elsewhere, on male identity has sometimes led to the view that he was more at ease making male- rather than female-centred narratives. After the war he made three outstanding films in succession: *Odd Man Out* (1947), *The Fallen Idol* (1948), and *The Third Man* (1949). The former, the story of an IRA man on the run in Belfast, dramatises Reed's idea of the city as a place of loneliness and alienation, a theme further developed, through their respective London and Vienna locations, in the latter two films, both collaborations with Graham GREENE (who also worked with Reed on *Our Man in Havana*, 1958). As, also in later films like *An Outcast of the Islands* (1951) or *The Man Between* (1953), Reed surveys a trademark urban landscape devoid of mercy to lost or disorientated outsiders. The wounded gunman in *Odd Man Out* finds no haven among the fearful residents of Belfast; the butler's predicament in *The Fallen Idol* is defined by the unyielding formal architecture of his Belgravia habitat; and Harry Lime's sewer-rat instincts for survival in *The Third Man* find their reflection in the bleak images of post-war Vienna's rubble-strewn dereliction. These concerns remain a feature of Reed's films after 1956, the date from which all his work would either be made in Hollywood or else have Hollywood financial backing. The first of these productions, *Trapeze* (1956), made in Cinemascope, and starring two of Hollywood's most prominent actors of the time, Burt Lancaster and Tony Curtis, was a huge commercial success. Most of the remainder of his films, though, were only modest commercial and critical successes. The one exception was *Oliver!* (1968), which was awarded Oscars for best film and best director. In 1943 he married Diana WYNYARD (Helen in *Kipps*). Following their divorce in 1947 Reed married Penelope DUDLEY WARD (1948). Tracy REED is his stepdaughter; Oliver REED was his nephew.

OTHER BRITISH FILMS INCLUDE: (d, unless noted) *Laburnum Grove* (1936), *Talk of the Devil* (+ co-sc), *Where's Your Lady Friend?* (1937), *No Parking* (story), *Penny Paradise, Climbing High* (1938), *A Girl Must Live* (1939), *The Girl in the News, A Letter from Home* (short) (1940), *The*

Young Mr Pitt (1942), *The True Glory* (1944, UK/US, doc, co-d), *A Kid for Two Farthings* (1954), *The Key* (1957), *Our Man in Havana* (1958), *The Running Man* (1963), *Follow Me* (1971).

BIBLIOG: Robert F. Moss, *The Films of Carol Reed*, 1987; Nicholas Wapshott, *The Man Between; a Biography of Carol Reed*, 1990. Peter William Evans.

Reed, Maxwell (*b* Larne, Ireland, 1919 – *d* London, 1974). Actor. On stage from 1943, Reed, once a member of RANK's COMPANY OF YOUTH, is now forgotten except as the first husband of Joan COLLINS. However, during the 40s, his handsome looks made him a favourite of British schoolgirls. After stage experience from 1943, this former seaman appeared in a number of crime dramas playing heroes, victimised males, and villains mostly trading on his film star looks – a trait commented on in *Daybreak* (1948), in which, however, he is sombrely impressive. During the 50s his career folded and he played in American television series such as *Captain David Grief* (1956) or minor roles in *The Notorious Landlady* (1962) and *Picture Mommy Dead* (1966). Had he listened to his ex-wife and modelled his style on James MASON rather than Stewart GRANGER his film career might have been entirely different.

OTHER BRITISH FILMS INCLUDE: *The Brothers, Dear Murderer, Daughter of Darkness* (1947), *The Lost People, Madness of the Heart*, (1949) *The Clouded Yellow, The Dark Man*, (1950), *There is Another Sun* (1951), *The Square Ring* (1953), *Before I Wake* (1955).

BIBLIOG: Joan Collins, *Past Imperfect*, 1978. Tony Williams.

Reed, Michael (*b* London, 1929). Cinematographer. In films from 1945, he had experience as focus-puller (e.g. on *The Man in Black*, 1949) and clapper-loader (e.g. on *Emergency Call*, 1952) before getting full cinematographer credits in the late 50s, working initially on 'B' MOVIES, including such good ones as *Devil's Bait* (1959), which benefited from the quiet realistic look he gave it. From then on, he was essentially prolific and proficient, sometimes more as in his evocation of wintry Bath and its surrounds in *The Hireling* (1973).

OTHER BRITISH FILMS INCLUDE: (add ph) *In Search of the Castaways* (1961, UK/US), *The Three Lives of Thomasina* (1963), *The Moon Spinners* (1964, UK/US); (c) *The Ugly Duckling* (1959), *Echo of Barbara, The Big Day* (1960), *The Devil-Ship Pirates* (1963), *The Gorgon* (1964), *Dracula – Prince of Darkness, Rasputin the Mad Monk* (1965), *Guns in the Heather* (1968), *On Her Majesty's Secret Service* (1969), *The McKenzie Break* (1970), *Shout at the Devil* (1976), *Wild Geese II* (1985).

Reed, Myrtle (*b* London, *c*1930). Actress. Supporting player of about a dozen films from the early 50s, usually in small roles like that of the hotel waitress in *Cast a Dark Shadow* (1955). Quite a lot of TV, including *Dixon of Dock Green*.

OTHER BRITISH FILMS INCLUDE: *Top Secret* (1952), *Street Corner* (1953), *The Weapon* (1956), *Please Turn Over, Snowball* (1960), *A Pair of Briefs* (1961), *Bless This House* (1972), *The Slipper and the Rose* (1976).

Reed, Oliver (*b* London, 1938 – *d* Valetta, Malta, 1999). Actor. There were never many British leading men one could imagine opening a film by marching resolutely into their offices and taking an axe to their desks as an act of rebellion, as Reed did in Michael WINNER's *I'll Never Forget What's 'is Name* (1967). The charismatic hell-raising Reed managed this – and much more – with the apparently effortless aplomb that may have cost him the acclaim he often deserved. The grandson of Herbert Beerbohm TREE and nephew of Carol REED, he made, astoundingly in view of how much time his legendary bar-room brawling occupied, nearly 100 films and TV programmes. Despite his offscreen antics, co-star Glenda JACKSON said in 1994, 'What I admire in Oliver is his consummate professionalism'.

Whatever damage he was doing to himself between films – between *takes* – the moment the cameras rolled he was on the job.

Given his prolificacy, it is surprising how well how much of his work stands up. Even in early films like *The League of Gentlemen*, as a ballet dancer, and *The Angry Silence* (1960), as a factory-worker bully, one couldn't miss him. His first starring role was in *Curse of the Werewolf* (1961) and he made several further HAMMER HORROR films; he made four for Winner, when the latter was at his flashiest and zestiest; and had the good fortune to be taken up by Ken RUSSELL. This association led to the title role in TV's *The Debussy Film* (1965) and Gerald Crich in *Women in Love* (1969). His famous nude wrestling scene with Alan BATES got so much attention that it tended to obscure the fact that Reed's was one of the finest performances of the decade – any decade, really – in a British film, effacing D.H. LAWRENCE's characterisation of Gerald as blond Nordic god. Reed played with tenderness as well as intensity and gave the finally tormented character a brush with tragic stature. If this is his one indisputably great performance, there are others very much worth rescuing from the surrounding bill-payers: he is a very dangerous Bill Sikes in his uncle's *Oliver!* (1968); tackles courageously the lustful priest in *The Devils* (1971); and enters enthusiastically into the spirit of Richard LESTER's *Royal Flash* (1975) as Bismarck, as he did in Lester's *Musketeers* films (1973, 1974). He returns, after years of dross, to reclaim himself in Nicolas ROEG's *Castaway* (1986), as the man who advertises for a wife, and in 1994 he injected some camp life into Peter CHELSOM's acrid-tasting *Funny Bones* (UK/US). When all the tedious tales of trouser-dropping in public places and bullying macho competitiveness are laid to rest, these, and a few others, will attest to his real capacities.

OTHER BRITISH FILMS: *Value for Money* (1955), *The Square Peg, Life Is a Circus, Hello London, The Captain's Table* (1958), *Upstairs and Downstairs, Beat Girl* (1959), *The Two Faces of Dr Jekyll, Sword of Sherwood Forest, The Bulldog Breed, The Rebel, His and Hers* (1960), *No Love for Johnnie, Pirates of Blood River, The Damned* (1961), *Captain Clegg, Paranoiac* (1962), *The Scarlet Blade, The Party's Over* (1963), *The System* (1964), *The Brigand of Kandahar* (1965), *The Trap* (UK/Can), *The Jokers, The Shuttered Room* (1966), *Hannibal Brooks, The Assassination Bureau* (1968), *Take a Girl Like You* (1970), *The Hunting Party* (1971), *Sitting Target, The Triple Echo* (1972), *Days of Fury* (UK/It), *Blue Blood* (1973), *And Then There Were None, Mahler* (1974), *Tommy, Lisztomania, The Sellout* (UK/It) (1975), *Tomorrow Never Comes* (1977, UK/Can), *The Big Sleep* (1978), *Venom* (1981), *No Secrets* (1982, UK/Zam), *Fanny Hill . . .* (1983), *Captive* (1985, UK/Fr), *The Adventures of Baron Munchausen* (UK/Ger/It), *The Lady and the Highwayman* (1988), *The Return of the Musketeers* (1989, UK/Fr/Sp), *The Bruce* (1996), *Parting Shots* (1998), *Gladiator* (2000, UK/US).

Reed, Tracy (*b* London, 1941). Actress. Despite her distinguished antecedents – she is the daughter of Penelope DUDLEY WARD and Anthony PELISSIER, step-daughter of Carol REED – Reed had a desultory career. Her first film role, as General Turgidson's secretary in *Dr Strangelove . . .* (1963), is still the only memorable one of the 20 she made, working in the US in latter years. She is too inexpressive to make one care much about her fate as a victim of occult practices in *Devils of Darkness* (1964) and the rest are largely forgotten. Married and divorced Edward FOX.

OTHER BRITISH FILMS INCLUDE: *A Shot in the Dark* (1964), *You Must Be Joking!* (1965), *Casino Royale, Maroc 7* (1966), *Hammerhead* (1968), *SWALK* (1970), *Percy* (1971).

Rees, Angharad (*b* Cardiff, 1949). Actress. Ethereally pretty leading lady of such TV series as *Poldark* (1975–77) and as Celia in the BBC's *As You Like It* (1978), Rees has filmed only rarely, mainly in the early 70s; for example, as Gossamer Beynon in *Under Milk Wood* (1971), that rallying call to Welsh casting. Was married to Christopher CAZENOVE.

OTHER BRITISH FILMS INCLUDE: *Jane Eyre* (1970), *Hands of the Ripper* (1971), *Baffled!* (1972), *Moments* (1973), *The Wolves of Kromer* (1998).

Rees, Roger (*b* Aberystwyth, 1944). Actor. Highly regarded stage actor, notably with the RSC, for whom he starred as *Nicholas Nickleby* (1982), in a nine-hour performance subsequently televised. Slade-trained, he has shown only limited interest in film: he co-starred with Judi DENCH in *Saigon – Year of the Cat* (1983, TV, some cinemas) and played Peter Quince in *A Midsummer Night's Dream* (1999, UK/It), but most of his film work has been in the US, where he has lived since 1989 and is known as Robin Colcord in TV's *Cheers* (1989–91).

OTHER BRITISH FILMS: *A Christmas Carol* (1984).

Reeve, Ada (*b* London, 1874 – *d* London, 1966). Actress. Star of MUSIC HALL, pantomime and musical comedy (debut 1878), who lived in Australia from 1917 to 1935. Occasional screen roles as character actress, including her stage role of the charwomen in the film of *They Came to a City* (1944), and the astrology-mad old lag in *I Believe in You* (1952). Often billed as nothing more than 'old woman.'

OTHER BRITISH FILMS INCLUDE: *Meet Me at Dawn, When the Bough Breaks* (1947), *Dear Mr Prohack* (1949), *Night and the City* (1950), *Time Bomb* (1953), *Eyewitness* (1956), *The Passionate Stranger* (1956).

BIBLIOG: Autobiography, *Take It for a Fact*, 1954. AS.

Reeve, Geoffrey (*b* Tring, 1932). Producer, director. Entered films in Canada in 1956, and has directed or produced occasional films and TV series, including *The Far Pavilions* (1984), a lavish piece of TV exotica. He directed two mild action movies in the 70s – *Puppet on a Chain* (1970) and *Caravan to Vaccares* (1974) – and produced the haunting farewell to the Edwardian world, *The Shooting Party* (1984), and several films starring Michael CAINE, including *Half Moon Street* (1986, London-set, US-financed) and the brutal boxing-world drama, *Shiner* (2001). His sons, **Tom Reeve** and **James Reeve** (*b c* 1960) are also producers.

OTHER BRITISH FILMS: *The Whistle Blower* (1986, p), *Souvenir* (1987, d), *Shadow Run* (1998, p, d), *Quicksand* (2001, UK/Fr).

Reeves, Kynaston (*b* London, 1893 – *d* London, 1971). Actor. Christened Philip, he took his mother's maiden name as actor. Incisive of manner and fine-boned of feature, he brought his tall, balding, snooty authority to dozens of generals, clergymen, lords and legal men. His Lord Chief Justice in *The Winslow Boy* (1948) is typical; on TV he was formidable Mr Quelch in *Billy Bunter* (1952) and Uncle Nicholas in *The Forsyte Saga* (1967). In the Army during WW1; trained at RADA; on stage from 1920, playing a Malvolio one would like to have seen at Regent's Park in 1947.

OTHER BRITISH FILMS INCLUDE: *The Lodger* (1932), *Puppets of Fate* (1933), *Jew Süss* (1934), *Housemaster, The Citadel* (1938), *The Stars Look Down, The Outsider* (1939), *The Prime Minister* (1941), *The Young Mr Pitt* (1942), *The Rake's Progress* (1945), *Bedelia* (1946), *The Guinea Pig* (1948), *Madeleine* (1949), *The Mudlark, Trio* (1950), *Top of the Form* (1953), *Eight O'Clock Walk, The Crowded Day* (1954), *Brothers in Law* (1956), *Carlton-Browne of the FO* (1958), *School for Scoundrels* (1959), *Carry On Regardless* (1961), *Go to Blazes* (1962), *Anne of the Thousand Days* (1969), *The Private Life of Sherlock Holmes* (1970).

Reeves, Michael (*b* London, 1944 – *d* London, 1969). Director. Perhaps if he had not committed suicide (by overdose of alcohol and sedatives) at 25, Reeves might not have become a cult figure. His only British films are *Revenge of the Blood Beast* (1965, UK/It, + sc, co-p), *The Sorcerers* (1967, + co-p) and the very frightening film on which his reputation deservedly rests, *Witchfinder General* (1968, + co-sc). On the basis of this grim, unusually realistic HORROR piece, the cult is deserved.

Reeves, Saskia (*b* London, *c* 1962). Actress. Gifted and sensually attractive, Reeves, the daughter of an English father and Dutch mother, has worked on stage with the RSC and made her film debut in 1990's *December Bride*. Made a strong impression as the glamorous and worldly Antonia in *Antonia and Jane* (1990, TV, some cinemas) and as Natalie, incestuously involved with her brother in *Close My Eyes* (1991). Among the somewhat off-beat roles she has chosen since are the murderous young Miriam in *Butterfly Kiss* (1995) and the increasingly distraught Maria in *Heart* (1999). Television includes *Dune* (2000).

OTHER BRITISH FILMS: *The Bridge* (1991), *i.d.* (1995), *Different for Girls* (1996), *LA Without a Man* (1998, UK/Fin/Fr).

Reid, Alastair (*b* Edinburgh, 1939). Director. Entered the industry in 1963, directed a few features, including the EXPLOITATION piece, *Baby Love* (1967, + co-sc), turned to TV in the mid 70s, directing episodes of *Inspector Morse* (1987) and the mini-series *Nostromo* (1996), before returning to cinema with *What Rats Won't Do* (1998).

OTHER BRITISH FILMS: *The Night Digger, Something to Hide* (+ sc) (1971), *Shout at the Devil* (1976, + co-sc).

Reid, Beryl (*b* Hereford, 1920 – *d* London, 1996). Actress. Character star of the stage, which she embraced in her later teens as preferable to working in a shop, and of radio, especially as schoolgirl 'Marlene' in *Educating Archie*, and on the London stage from 1951, often in revue. She had some of the outré mischief that fuelled the two Hermiones (BADDELEY and GINGOLD) in revue, but her most famous stage role was as the vindictive but poignant lesbian soap opera queen in *The Killing of Sister George* (1965), which she transferred to the film version (1968, US). She is touching precisely because she never plays for pathos. She filmed intermittently from 1954, as Miss Wilson trying to teach *The Belles of St Trinian's*; in frilly short nightie she made the most of *Entertaining Mr Sloane* (1969), and by 1973 she was an interfering mother-in-law in *No Sex Please – We're British*. She is good company even in these inferior films, but the other media served her better including TV for which she received a BAAn for her role in *Tinker, Tailor, Soldier, Spy* (1979), a role she reprised in *Smiley's People* (1982). Awarded OBE, 1986; married (2) Derek FRANCIS.

OTHER BRITISH FILMS: *The Extra Day* (1956), *Two Way Stretch* (1960), *The Dock Brief* (1962), *Inspector Clouseau* (1968), *The Assassination Bureau* (1968), *The Beast in the Cellar* (1970), *Psychomania, Dr Phibes Rides Again, Father, Dear Father* (1972), *Joseph Andrews* (1976), *Rosie Dixon – Night Nurse, Carry On Emmannuelle* (1978), *Yellowbeard* (1983), *The Doctor and the Devils* (1985).

BIBLIOG: Autobiography, *So Much Love*, 1984.

Reid, Milton (*b* Bombay, 1917 – *d* India, *c* 1982). Actor. Former wrestler, unsurprisingly often found in tough roles, like the guard of *Dr No* (1962), and other small supporting roles calling for his bald, muscular frame, including several HORROR films (in *Berserk!*, 1967, he is simply billed as 'Strong Man').

OTHER BRITISH FILMS INCLUDE: *The Camp on Blood Island* (1957), *Blood of the Vampire* (1958), *Ferry to Hong Kong* (1959), *Captain Clegg* (1962), *Panic* (1965), *Great Catherine* (1967), *The Assassination Bureau* (1968), *Blood on Satan's Claw* (1970), *Return of the Pink Panther* (1974), *The Spy Who Loved Me, The People That Time Forgot* (1977), *Confessions of the David Galaxy Affair* (1979).

Reid, Sheila (*b* Glasgow, 1932). Actress. Scottish character player first filmed when she repeated her stage role of Bianca in *Othello* (1965) and appeared with OLIVIER again when the stage production of *Three Sisters* was filmed in 1970. Since then, sporadic supporting roles in such films as *The Winter Guest* (1998, UK/US), as one of the funeral-mad old girls, and as Timothy SPALL's pixie-ish mum in *Still Crazy* (1998, UK/US). Much TV, including *Sweeney* (1978) and *Oliver's Travels* (1995).
OTHER BRITISH FILMS INCLUDE: *The Alphabet Murders* (1965), *I Know What I Want* (1971), *The Dresser* (1983), *Brazil* (1985), *The Lonely Passion of Judith Hearne* (1987), *American Friends* (1991), *Felicia's Journey* (1999, UK/Can).

Reid, Trevor (*b* Liverpool, 1908 – *d* London, 1965). Actor. Supporting player of the 50s and 60s, often in 'B' FILMS, such as *Behind the Headlines* (1956), as a mysterious crook, made more so by the intervention of plastic surgery. On TV (e.g. *Quatermass 2*, 1955) and stage from before WW2.
OTHER BRITISH FILMS INCLUDE: *Delayed Action* (1954), *The Hornet's Nest* (1955), *Hideout* (1956), *How to Murder a Rich Uncle* (1957), *A Question of Adultery* (1958), *Bobbikins* (1959), *Dangerous Afternoon* (1961), *The Fast Lady* (1962), *Night Train to Paris* (1964).

Reisch, Walter (*b* Vienna, 1903 – *d* Los Angeles, 1983). Screenwriter. Austrian refugee from Nazism who co-wrote several British–German co-productions, and directed one British film – the romantic MELODRAMA, *Men Are Not Gods* (1936), a rare Gertrude LAWRENCE film – on his way to Hollywood, where he worked on such popular films as *Ninotchka* (1939) and *Gaslight* (1944).
OTHER BRITISH FILMS INCLUDE: (UK/Ger) *Happy Ever After* (1932, co-story), *The Only Girl* (co-story), *FP1* (co-sc) (1933); (UK) *The Song You Gave Me* (play), *Prince of Arcadia* (play) (1933), *Two Hearts in Waltz Time* (1934, co-sc), *The Divine Spark* (1935, UK/It, story).

Reissar, Jenia (*b* Tashkent, Russia, 1904 – *d* West Byfleet, 2000). Casting director. Much respected for her encyclopedic knowledge of British acting talent, Reissar joined John WOOLF's ROMULUS FILMS in 1953. She cast over 20 films for this prestigious company, including *Moulin Rouge* (1953), *Oliver!* (1968) and *The Day of the Jackal* (1973, UK/Fr), and when Woolf obtained the Anglia TV licence she worked there for him as well, casting well over 100 drama programmes, including thrillers based on the novels of P.D. James. Spirited out of Bolshevik Russia with an Irish governess, she took a secretarial course in London before becoming personal assistant to Edgar WALLACE. She 'discovered' Ingrid BERGMAN for David Selznick, whose European talent scout she was, and suggested Vivien LEIGH for Scarlett O'Hara.
OTHER BRITISH FILMS INCLUDE: *Room at the Top* (1958), *The L-Shaped Room* (1962), *Of Human Bondage* (1964), *Life at the Top* (1965), *The Odessa File* (1974, UK/Ger).

Reisz, Barney (*b* London, 1960). Producer. Apart from appearing as a child in *Les bicyclettes de Belsize* (1968), he entered films as production assistant on father Karel REISZ's US-made BIOPIC of Patsy Kline, *Sweet Dreams* (1985), came to notice as producer of the AA-nominated SHORT FILM, *It's Good to Talk* (1997), and went on to produce Phil AGLAND's sympathetic version of *The Woodlanders* (1997) and Mike FIGGIS's idiosyncratic *The Loss of Sexual Innocence* (2000, UK/US).
OTHER BRITISH FILMS: *The Tall Guy* (1989, location co-manager), *Look Me in the Eye* (1994, ass d), *Different for Girls* (1996, prod man).

Reisz, Karel (*b* Ostrava, Czechoslovakia, 1926 – *d* London, 2002). Director. 'I don't find the process very enjoyable. It's very hard to make a film', Reisz said in 1992, and this perhaps helps to explain the somewhat meagre output of one of Britain's most intelligent film-makers, who won a BAA for his first feature, *Saturday Night and Sunday Morning* (1960) but who directed only eight thereafter, three of those American. But Reisz's importance in British film history is not limited to the features he has directed.

He came to a Quaker school in England when he was 12, the rest of his Jewish family failing to survive the Holocaust, and he served with the RAF during WW2. After studying chemistry at Cambridge post-war, he taught in London and became one of the editors (with Lindsay ANDERSON and Gavin LAMBERT) of the short-lived but influential film journal, SEQUENCE. For the BRITISH FILM ACADEMY, he also wrote and compiled the landmark study, *The Technique of Film Editing* (1952), still highly regarded today; and he wrote criticism for journals such as SIGHT AND SOUND. In his function as Programme Manager of the NATIONAL FILM THEATRE, he was able in 1956 to arrange screenings of several programmes of SHORT FILMS under the umbrella heading of FREE CINEMA. These films, made by Anderson, Tony RICHARDSON and Reisz himself, among others, brought to English screens aspects of the national life largely disregarded by commercial film-making; and when their directors began to make features they brought this freshness of approach and their individuality ('films we could "sign"') to bear on working-class life as it had not been seen before.

Reisz's own contribution to this 'NEW WAVE' was the commercially and critically successful, BAA-winning *Saturday Night and Sunday Morning* (1960), with Albert FINNEY as a rebellious lathe worker, with elements of both the hero and the socially trapped. His other big success of the decade was *Morgan: A Suitable Case for Treatment* (1966, BAAn), another celebration of individualism, this time more anarchic as conveyed by protagonist David WARNER, as the film moves between farce and social satire. Reisz was dissatisfied with his other two 60s films: *Night Must Fall* (1964) which he felt 'ended up rather uncomfortably between a matinée thriller and a character study'; and *Isadora* (1968), which he 'loved making . . . but things went horribly wrong with the distribution over the editing'. Nevertheless, Vanessa REDGRAVE has some dazzling moments as the legendary dancer, and all Reisz's films have remarkable performances, including Meryl STREEP's as *The French Lieutenant's Woman* (1981, BAAn/film), Reisz's last wholly British film. He made perceptive studies of American subjects, as in *Who'll Stop the Rain?* (1978) and the Patsy Kline BIOPIC, *Sweet Dreams* (1985), but made no film after 1990, though he continued to direct for the theatre, including a highly-regarded production of *The Deep Blue Sea* (1993). Married (2) from 1963 to sensitive American actress **Betsy Blair** (*b* New York, 1923), who appeared in the British films *All Night Long* (1961) and *A Delicate Balance* (1973, UK/US).
OTHER BRITISH FILMS: (d, unless noted) *Momma Don't Allow* (1955, doc, co-d, co-sc) *Every Day Except Christmas* (1957, doc, co-p), *We Are the Lambeth Boys*, *I Want to Go to School* (co-p) (1959, doc), *This Sporting Life* (1963, p), *Everybody Wins* (1990, UK/US).
BIBLIOG: Georg Gaston, *Karel Reisz*, 1980.

religion and British film British films, from the earliest years, frequently deal with religious figures though rarely (as in GAUMONT's *The Passion Play*, 1909) portraying Jesus himself. The BRITISH BOARD OF FILM CENSORS, formed in 1912, made 'religion' its first category. Since then impersonations of Jesus,

Monty Python's Life of Brian (1979) notwithstanding, have mainly been in church films. Christ-figures (*The Passing of the Third Floor Back*, 1917, 1935) and clergy proved safer. Parsons/ priests sacrifice themselves to Nazis (*Pastor Hall*, 1940; *Went the Day Well?*, 1942); are terminally ill (Robert DONAT: *Lease of Life*, 1954), Christ-like (Peter SELLERS: *Heavens Above!*, 1963), and homosexual (Linus ROACHE: *Priest*, 1994). Thomas More is *A Man for All Seasons* (1966). Thomas of Canterbury features in *Murder in the Cathedral* (1952) and *Becket* (1964).

An interesting figure involved in the promotion of religious film was the Rev Brian Hession, who in 1938 re-edited and added a soundtrack to the silent film, *From the Manger to the Cross* (1912) and founded the Dawn Trust from his Aylesbury parish. The Trust, also working in the US on production and distribution of religious films, arranged their exhibition mainly in churches but also by means of an open-air travelling van. Its heyday was in the 30s and 40s.

A leading Methodist, J. Arthur RANK of the Religious Film Society produced *Turn of the Tide* (1935). Its director Norman WALKER said the Kingdom of God's message could only succeed in the cinema under the guise of entertainment. Rank was not averse to a 'Rita Hayworth' dimension in films (*The Wicked Lady*, 1945) he considered moral fables, nor to Sunday cinema openings, even running a 'Sunday Thought' series. His many church films include *Which Will Ye Have?* (1949), depicting Christ's passion through the eyes of Barabbas. In 1959 he founded Churches Television Centre which still produces religious (Christian) programmes for UK broadcasters. Certain Christian agencies have recently renewed their involvement in film production (e.g. *The Miracle Maker*, 2000).

The spiritual can often be discerned in mainstream cinema whether it be the Catholicism of Alfred HITCHCOCK, Graham GREENE (see the recent *The End of the Affair*, 1999, UK/Ger/ US) and Anthony MINGHELLA, David LEAN's Quaker values, or the Jewish ideals and practicalities of Michael BALCON. POWELL and (the Jewish) PRESSBURGER focus on modern pilgrimage (*A Canterbury Tale*, 1944), Heaven (*A Matter of Life and Death*, 1946) and Anglican nuns (*Black Narcissus*, 1947). Less subtly, HAMMER's repeated takes on Frankenstein and Dracula constitute a dialogue with Christian tradition. British-made Asian cinema after *East Is East* (2000) – more a clash of cultures than faiths? – may now feel encouraged to explore religious themes.

For over 50 years international church juries have given recognition to cinema's spiritual component including British contributions such as *Woman in a Dressing Gown* (1957) and several by Ken LOACH. In 1996 the Vatican itemised *Chariots of Fire* (1981) in its list of recommended films.

OTHER RELEVANT BRITISH FILMS INCLUDE: *The Wandering Jew* (1933), *Jew Süss* (1934), *Major Barbara* (1941), *The Great Mr Handel* (1942), *Brighton Rock* (1947), *Lease of Life* (1954), *The Singer Not the Song, Conspiracy of Hearts* (1960), *Whistle Down the Wind* (1961), *Sebastiane* (1976), *Gandhi* (1982, UK/Inc), *The Darkest Light* (2000).

BIBLIOG: Ivan Butler, *Religion in the Cinema*, 1969; Ronald Holloway, *Beyond the Image: Approaches to the Religious Dimension in the Cinema*, 1977. Stephen Brown.

Relph, George (*b* Cullercoats, 1888 – *d* London, 1960). Actor. Distinguished stage actor who made no more than a dozen films in over 40 years. On stage from 1905, in London from 1909, and New York from 1911, returning to Britain for WW1 service, 1916, resuming his career in everything from SHAKESPEARE to Edgar WALLACE. He appeared in a couple of British silents, but his main film roles were in EALING's

Nicholas Nickleby (1947), as Mr Bray, *I Believe in You* (1952), as an elderly out-of-touch probation officer, and *The Titfield Thunderbolt* (1953) as the train-mad Vicar. He purveyed an air of mild benevolence, streaked with eccentricity. Father of Michael RELPH and grandfather of Simon RELPH; married (2) **Mercia Swinburne**, stage actress who appeared in several films, including *Saraband for Dead Lovers* (1948).

OTHER BRITISH FILMS: *The Door That Has No Key, Candytuft, I Mean Veronica* (1921), *Too Dangerous to Live* (1939), *Give Us the Moon* (1944).

Relph, Michael (*b* Broadstone, Dorset, 1915). Production designer, producer, director. Began his career in 1932 working under Alfred JUNGE in the GAUMONT–BRITISH Art Department, joining EALING in 1942, having also designed for the stage from 1934. At Ealing he embarked on a longstanding, creative partnership with director Basil DEARDEN, sometimes sharing with Dearden the producer-director-writer credit in the manner of – if not with the same panache as – POWELL AND PRESSBURGER. Relph later described himself and Dearden as the 'workhorses' of Ealing, and certainly they turned out more films there than any of the other production teams. The films on which Relph is credited as director are not among his favourites: he never felt he had the director's temperament and also felt he only directed what Dearden didn't want to. It may be argued that Relph's greatest achievement, apart from the very considerable one of providing a congenial production climate for Dearden, was as designer, especially during his great period at Ealing in the 40s, when he was responsible for the varied production values of *They Came to a City* (1944), with its deliberately stylised sets, the realistic evocation of a prisoner-of-war camp in *The Captive Heart* (1946), the provincial chintziness under threat in *Frieda* (1947), the class-discriminatory settings in *Kind Hearts and Coronets* (1949), the DOCUMENTARY-like REALISM of *The Blue Lamp* (1949) and, above all, the AA-nominated designs for the sumptuous TECHNICOLOR period film, *Saraband for Dead Lovers* (1948). Relph and Dearden continued their successful partnership after the demise of Ealing until Dearden's death in a car crash in 1970. Relph became chairman of the BFI Production Board in 1972 and returned to film production only three more times. The son of George RELPH, he is father of Simon RELPH.

OTHER BRITISH FILMS INCLUDE: (art d) *Who Killed John Savage?* (1937), *The Bells Go Down* (1943), *The Halfway House, Champagne Charlie* (1944), *Dead of Night* (1945), *Nicholas Nickleby* (1947), *Cage of Gold* (+ des), *Pool of London* (1950); (d) *I Believe in You* (1952, co-d, + co-p, co-sc), *Davy* (1957), *Rockets Galore* (1958), *All Night Long* (1961, co-d, + co-p); (p) *The Gentle Gunman* (1952), *The Square Ring* (1953), *The Ship That Died of Shame* (1955, + co-sc), *The Smallest Show on the Earth, The Violent Playground* (1957), *Sapphire* (1959), *The League of Gentlemen* (1960), *Victim* (1961), *Life for Ruth* (1962), *The Mind Benders* (1963), *Woman of Straw* (1964, + co-sc), *The Assassination Bureau* (1968, + sc, des), *Scum* (1979, co-exec), *An Unsuitable Job for a Woman* (1981, co-p), *Heavenly Pursuits* (1986).

Relph, Simon (*b* London, 1940). Producer. After serving an apprenticeship as assistant or 2nd unit director on about 20 films (several for Ralph THOMAS) from the early 60s to the early 80s, Relph turned to producing. His name appears as (co-)producer on some key films, including *The Ploughman's Lunch* (1983, co-p, ass d) and *Comrades* (1986), but his most valuable work was as chief executive officer of BRITISH SCREEN, which, along with CHANNEL 4, 'kept the British film industry alive in the 1980s' (BFI's Film and Television Handbook, 1992). In the early 90s, he fought hard to persuade the government to extend its funding of British Screen by five years, and won a three-year extension. Behind the scenes in these ways, he exerted an important influence on low-budget British film-making for over a decade. Son of Michael RELPH, grandson of George RELPH.

OTHER BRITISH FILMS INCLUDE: (ass d/2ud) *Doctor in Distress* (1963), *Seance on a Wet Afternoon* (1964), *The High Bright Sun* (1965), *Deadlier Than the Male* (1966), *Anne of the Thousand Days* (1969), *Macbeth*, *Sunday Bloody Sunday* (1971), *A Touch of Class*, *The Triple Echo* (1972), *The Hireling*, *Zardoz* (1973), *Yanks* (1979); (p/co-p/ex p) *The Return of the Soldier* (1982), *Wetherby* (1985), *Danny, the Champion of the World* (1989), *Enchanted April* (1992), *Damage* (1992, UK/Fr), *The Secret Rapture* (1993), *Blue Juice* (1995), *The Slab Boys* (1997), *The Land Girls*, *Hideous Kinky* (1998, UK/Fr).

remakes. Remakes provide a fascinating insight into changing production practices and cultural attitudes at different moments in film history. Remakes may be subdivided into three, sometimes overlapping, categories. The first category comprises those films where the primary reference point is less an earlier film version than a well-known literary text or stage play. This applies to the numerous adaptations of SHAKESPEARE, DICKENS, and Edgar WALLACE, the most often filmed authors in British film history. Second, there are those films that explicitly attempt to copy the success of an earlier film. In this category one can place most remakes of Alfred HITCHCOCK's films: *The Lodger* (1926, 1932, 1944, 1954), *The Farmer's Wife* (1928, 1941), *The Man Who Knew Too Much* (1934, remade by Hitchcock himself in 1955, US), *The 39 Steps* (1935, 1958, 1978), and *The Lady Vanishes* (1938, 1979). Some-times remakes in this category lead to jarring anachronisms, as in the 1974 remake of *Brief Encounter* (1945), or in the 1983 remake of *The Wicked Lady* (1945). The third category includes those remakes that consciously rework an earlier film according to its new cultural and/or historical context, for example *First A Girl* (1935), a remake of the German *Viktor und Viktoria* (1933), and remade again as *Victor/Victoria* (1982), which, despite textual similarities, emerged as originals in their own right.

OTHER REMAKES FROM AND INTO BRITISH FILMS INCLUDE: *Broken Blossoms* (US/1919, 1936), *The Browning Version* (1951, 1994), *Carnival* (1921, remade as *A Double Life*, US/1947), *Chu Chin Chow* (1923, 1934), *Coming Thro' The Rye* (1916, 1923), *The Constant Nymph* (1928, 1934, US/1943), *Dreaming Lips* (Ger/1932, 1937), *Escape Me Never* (1935, US/1947), *The Four Feathers* (1921, 1929, 1939, 1955/*Storm over the Nile*, 2003, UK/US), *Gaslight* (1939, US/1943), *The Ghost Train* (1927, 1931, 1941), *Goodbye, Mr Chips* (1939, 1969), *The Good Companions* (1933, 1957), *Hindle Wakes* (1918, 1927, 1931, 1952), *Hobson's Choice* (1931, 1953), *An Ideal Husband* (1947, 1999), *The Informer* (1929, US/1935), *The Innocents* (1961, 1998), *Ivanhoe* (1913, 1952), *King Solomon's Mines* (1937, US/1950, US/1985), *Köenigsmark* (1935, remade as *Saraband for Dead Lovers*, 1948), *Lord Of The Flies* (1963, US/1990), *Night Must Fall* (US/1937, 1964), *1984* (1955, 1984), *Number Seventeen* (1928, 1932), *The Rat* (1925, 1938), *The Ringer* (1928, 1931, 1932, 1938, 1952, Ger/1964), *Rob Roy* (1953, 1995), *Rome Express* (1932, 1948/*Sleeping Car to Trieste*), *Sanders of the River* (1935, 1963), *The Scarlet Pimpernel* (1920, 1935, 1950, 1982), *She* (1916, 1925, US/1935, 1965, It/1985), *Sorrows Of Satan* (1917, US/1926), *A Stolen Life* (1939, US/1946, Mex/1946), *Sunshine Susie* (Ger/1930, 1931), *The Thief of Baghdad* (1924, 1940, It/1961, 1978), *The Tunnel* (Ger/1933, 1935), *Vice Versa* (1948, US/1988) *Village of the Damned* (1960, US/1995) *The Winslow Boy* (1948, 1999/UK/US), *The Wrecker* (1928, 1936), *A Yank At Oxford* (1937, 1984/*Oxford Blues*/US). Tim Bergfelder.

Remick, Lee (*b* Quincy, Massachusetts, 1935 – *d* Brentwood, California, 1991). Actress. Perhaps because she first brazened on to the screen as a flirty drum majorette in *A Face in the Crowd* (1957), it was thereafter always difficult to suppress the thought

that her ladylike demeanour might at any moment give way to something more sensual. She died sadly young of cancer but in her 30-year career she won respect for her prolific work on stage (*Wait Until Dark*), TV (she is too beautiful but very intelligent as Miss Gostrey in *The Ambassadors*, 1977; also starred as *Jennie: Lady Randolph Churchill*, 1975) and cinema, including the seven British films. She throws herself into the blackly comic world of Joe ORTON's *Loot* (1970) as the 'Nurse', and she is gravely charismatic as the Baroness in *The Europeans* (1979), an early MERCHANT IVORY brush with Henry JAMES.

OTHER BRITISH FILMS: *The Running Man* (1963), *A Severed Head* (1970), *A Delicate Balance* (1973, UK/Can/US), *Hennessy* (1975), *The Medusa Touch* (1978, UK/Fr).

Rendel, Robert (*b* Devon, 1901). Actor. Supporting actor who had the odd lead, as in *The Hound of the Baskervilles* (1931), in which he lent his tall, commanding presence to the first talkie SHERLOCK HOLMES. After a couple of US silents, he appeared in about two dozen British films of the 30s, almost invariably as Sirs, Lords, Admirals or Generals.

OTHER BRITISH FILMS INCLUDE: *Death at Broadcasting House* (1934), *The Crimson Circle* (1936), *Fire Over England* (1937), *The Four Feathers* (1939), *The Spy in Black*, *The Lion Has Wings* (1939), *Sailors Three* (1940).

Rendell, Ruth (*b* London, 1930). Author. Socially and psycho-logically acute exponent of crime fiction whose work has provided unending TV material, with George BAKER as her no-nonsense provincial policeman. By the big screen, she has been largely neglected, but *Tree of Hands* was filmed in Britain in 1988; there have been two ADAPTATIONS of *Judgment in Stone* (tediously filmed in Canada, 1986; alarmingly by Claude Chabrol as *La cérémonie* in 1995, Fr/Ger); and Almodovar filmed *Live Flesh* in 1997, Sp/Fr). Also writes as Barbara Vine. Appointed CBE in 1996, life peer in 1997.

Rennie, Michael (*b* Bradford, 1909 – *d* Harrogate, 1971). Actor. Tall (6'3"), handsome, Cambridge-educated actor who entered films in the 30s as stand-in to the likes of John LODER, had a run of small roles and a bigger one in *Ships With Wings* (1941), as well as acquiring rep experience along the way. Post-war he co-starred twice with Margaret LOCKWOOD at the peak of her fame, *The Wicked Lady*, *I'll Be Your Sweetheart* (1945). He played the (tubercular) rake redeemed by love in *Trio* (1950), appeared in some dreadful films like *Idol of Paris* (1948), and went to Hollywood where he was given a star's gloss and some stylish leading roles, such as Jean Valjean in *Les Misérables* (1952) and Merle OBERON's ducal husband in *Hotel* (1967). Married **Margaret McGrath** who appeared in a few British films, including *English Without Tears* (1944) and *Nowhere to Go* (1958).

OTHER BRITISH FILMS INCLUDE: *Secret Agent* (1936), *The Squeaker* (1937), *Bank Holiday* (1938), *Dangerous Moonlight*, *Pimpernel Smith*, *This Man Is Dangerous* (1941), *White Cradle Inn*, *The Root of All Evil* (1947), *Uneasy Terms* (1948), *Miss Pilgrim's Progress* (1949), *The Black Rose* (UK/US), *The Body Said No!* (1950), *The House in the Square* (1951), *Single-Handed* (1953), *Island in the Sun* (1957, UK/US), *Battle of the V-1* (1958).

Renown Pictures Distribution company founded by George MINTER in 1938, began production in 1948 with *No Orchids for Miss Blandish*.

Retford, Ella (*b* Sunderland 1885 – *d* England 1962). Actress. MUSIC HALL singer and principal boy on stage from 1900; seen as herself in *Ella Retford at Home* (1914) and *Variety Jubilee*

(1943) but generally on screen in minor character roles.

OTHER BRITISH FILMS: *Darby and Joan* (1937), *Poison Pen* (1939), *I'll Be Your Sweetheart* (1945), *Noose* (1948), *Paper Orchid* (1949), *Shadow of the Past* (1950). AS.

Revill, Clive (*b* Wellington, NZ, 1930). Actor. Educated in NZ where he began his acting career; first on London stage 1955 and to Stratford in 1956. Had a major theatrical success in *Irma La Douce* (1958) in London and New York; entered films in *Reach for the Sky* (1956), played a ghostly earl in the idiotic *The Headless Ghost* (1959), and camped it up in *Modesty Blaise* (1966) and *The Private Life of Sherlock Holmes* (1970), but films were never as rewarding to his comic potential as the stage. Also in plenty of US films and TV, without quite carving out a recognisable niche.

OTHER BRITISH FILMS FILM: *Kaleidoscope* (1966), *The Double Man*, *Fathom* (1967), *The Assassination Bureau* (1968), *The Buttercup Chain*, *A Severed Head* (1970), *The Black Windmill*, *Galileo* (UK/Can) (1974), *'Let Him Have It'* (1991).

Reville, Alma (*b* London, 1899 – *d* Los Angeles, 1982). Screenwriter. Wife of Alfred HITCHCOCK, she is thought to have been a major influence on his work. Formally listed as a story consultant in the credits of many of his films, she informally advised him on virtually all of his productions, helping him find stories and fine-tuning productions. Began career in the British film industry in the early 20s as editor's assistant and script girl, meeting her future husband at Famous Players–Lasky studio in London. They married in 1926, and though she worked on various British films such as Gracie FIELDS's first starring vehicle, *Sally in Our Alley* (1931), and with various directors like Berthold VIERTEL (*The Passing of the Third Floor Back*, 1935), and Maurice ELVEY (*The Water Gipsies*, 1932), she increasingly concentrated on her husband's productions. Hitchcock claimed she was his harshest critic, especially adept at identifying inconsistencies and flaws in his plots and he dedicated his 1979 Lifetime Achievement Award from the American Film Institute to her.

OTHER BRITISH FILMS: *The Pleasure Garden* (1925), *The Ring* (1927), *The Constant Nymph* (1928), *Murder!, Juno and the Paycock* (1930), *The Skin Game* (1931), *Rich and Strange* (1932), *Waltzes from Vienna* (1934), *The 39 Steps* (1935), *Secret Agent, Sabotage* (1936), *Young and Innocent* (1937), *The Lady Vanishes* (1938), *Jamaica Inn* (1939). Stephen Shafer.

Reynders, John (*b* London, 1888 – *d* Barnet, 1953). Composer, music director, conductor. Busy throughout the 30s, Reynders had his own orchestra which played his music for a range of travel and special interest films, such as *Father Thames* (1935) and *Happy Hampstead* (1937). As well, he worked on several early HITCHCOCK films: as conductor on *Blackmail* (1929) and *Elstree Calling* (1930, co-cond), and as music director on *Murder!* (1930) and *Rich and Strange* (1932), though his contribution seems not to have been much noted.

OTHER BRITISH FILMS INCLUDE: (comp) *The Flying Scotsman* (1929), *The Immortal Gentleman* (1935), *Elephant City, Fire Fighters* (1936, shorts), *Midnight Menace* (1937), *The First Easter* (1939, short); (m d) *The W Plan* (1930), *Dreyfus, Many Waters* (1931), *Dance Pretty Lady* (1932), *Take a Chance* (1937), *Blarney* (1938).

Reynolds, Norman (*b* London). Production designer. British designer who has made his name by working on large-scale US productions, including *Star Wars* (1977) and *Raiders of the Lost Ark* (1981, + BAA), for both of which he shared Oscars. Also nominated for sequels to these and for *The Incredible Sarah* (1976, UK/US), but his gifts are increasingly at the service of transatlantic budgets.

OTHER BRITISH FILMS: *A Warm December* (1972, UK/US, set decorator), *Phase IV* (1973, ass art d), *Mister Quilp* (1974, art d), *Superman* (1978, co-art d), *The Fifth Musketeer* (1979, UK/Austria, ass art d), *Superman II* (1980, co-art d).

Reynolds, Peter (*b* Wilmslow, 1925 – *d* Melbourne, 1975). RN: Peter Horrocks. Actor. In 1951 Reynolds starred in a forgotten 'B' film, *Smart Alec*, a title summing up many of his roles as flashy, untrustworthy types: first starred in *Guilt Is My Shadow* (1950) as a criminal on the run, and was an escaped convict again in the ludicrous *Devil Girl from Mars* (1954). The image stuck, and he regularly played post-war spivs, shifty boyfriends and blackmailers. Perhaps his roles were too unsympathetic for him to develop a following, and he made mainly second features, including BUTCHERS' *The Painted Smile* (1961), quickly released and almost immediately forgotten. Left for Australia in the 60s; his final film was the surrealistic *Private Collection* (1972, Aust). Died in a fire accident.

OTHER BRITISH FILMS INCLUDE: *The Guinea Pig* (1948), *Adam and Evelyne* (1949), *Four Days, The Magic Box* (1951), *24 Hours of a Woman's Life* (1952), *The Good Beginning* (1953), *You Can't Escape* (1955), *The Long Haul* (1957), *The Bank Raiders* (1958), *Shake Hands with the Devil* (1959, UK/US), *Spare the Rod, The Breaking Point* (1961), *West 11* (1963). Roger Philip Mellor.

Rhind-Tutt, Julian (*b* Hillingdon, 1967). Actor. Distinctive and versatile young actor, tall, reddish-haired and good at either the intensities of, say, *The Trench* (1999, UK/Fr), as the upper-class lieutenant, or the cynical wit of his roles in *Notting Hill* (1999, UK/US), as the *Time Out* journalist, and TV's *Reckless* (1997, 1998). Warwick University-educated and Central School-trained, he won an award which took him to BBC radio, then found good parts with the National Theatre, including the Duke of York in *The Madness of King George*, repeating his role in the film version (1994, UK/US). Also in US-made *The Saint* (1997).

OTHER BRITISH FILMS: *Tomorrow Never Dies* (1997, UK/US), *Les Misérables* (1998, UK/Ger/US), *Lara Croft: Tomb Raider* (2001, UK/Ger/US), *Miranda* (2002).

Rhodes, Sir Christopher (*b* Alverstoke, 1914 – *d* Blakeney, Norfolk, 1964). Actor. Very tall (6'4") stage actor and frequent BBC radio broadcaster, who was a forceful character player in nearly two dozen films in the decade before his early death. Played the self-sacrificing POW McGill in *The Colditz Story* (1954) and Marjorie Allingham's Inspector Luke in *Tiger in the Smoke* (1956) among a range of authority figures which capitalised on his dominating presence. Also in TV's *The Quatermass Experiment* (1953) and the US-made *El Cid* (1961). Third baronet, grandfather having received title from Edward VII.

OTHER BRITISH FILMS INCLUDE: *Laughing Anne* (1953), *Betrayed* (1954), *The Feminine Touch* (1956), *Dunkirk* (1958), *Shake Hands with the Devil* (UK/US), *Tiger Bay* (1959), *The Guns of Navarone* (1961), *Becket* (1964).

Rhodes, Marjorie (*b* Hull, 1897 – *d* Hove, 1979). Actress. RN: Wise. Whatever she played, there was a whiff of no-nonsense Yorkshire pudding about this great character actress. On stage with a concert party from 1920, in London from 1926, enjoying success in such forthright roles as Robert DONAT's mum, Mrs Hardacre, in *The Cure for Love* (1945), a role she repeated in his 1949 film, and the harridan Emma Hornett in *Watch It Sailor!* (+ film, both 1961). She could be tough and bossy, like the Councillor, Miss Mouncey, in *Time Gentlemen Please!* (1952), droll like the stroppy, inebriated cook in *When We Are Married*

(1943) or dizzy bigamist Suzie in *The Weak and the Wicked* (1953), or dignified like the prison wardress in *Yield to the Night* (1956). But two roles perhaps stand out. One is true-hearted Mrs Mumford, the former barmaid who'd married an Oxford graduate ('He had a lovely life. He never did a day's work – I wouldn't let him'), and who galvanises the Women's Institute, in *Great Day* (1945). The other, in a performance of extraordinary melting sympathy, is the understanding mother in *The Family Way* (1966), who brings the accumulated wisdom of her own married life to bear on helping her son to get his started; it is the jewel in the crown of a remarkable career.

OTHER BRITISH FILMS: *Poison Pen* (1939), *Love on the Dole, The Black Sheep of Whitehall* (1941), *Squadron Leader X* (1942), *When We Are Married, Theatre Royal, Old Mother Riley, Detective, The Butler's Dilemma, Escape to Danger* (1943), *It Happened One Sunday, Tawny Pipit, On Approval* (1944), *Land of Promise* (doc), *School for Secrets* (1946), *Uncle Silas, This Was a Woman, Escape* (1948), *Private Angelo* (1949), *Those People Next Door, Decameron Nights* (1952), *The Yellow Balloon, Street Corner, The Girl on the Pier* (1953), *To Dorothy a Son, Children Galore, The Case of Annie Diamond* (doc) (1954), *Footsteps in the Fog, Room in the House, Now and Forever, Lost, It's a Great Day* (1955), *It's Great to Be Young!, The Good Companions, The Passionate Stranger* (1956), *Hell Drivers, There's Always a Thursday, No Time for Tears, The Naked Truth, Just My Luck, After the Ball* (1957), *Gideon's Day, Alive and Kicking* (1958), *Over the Odds* (1961), *Those Magnificent Men . . . , I've Gotta Horse* (1965), *Mrs Brown, You've Got a Lovely Daughter* (1968), *Spring and Port Wine* (1969), *Hands of the Ripper* (1971).

Rhys, Paul (*b* Neath, 1963). Actor. Slight, dark, intense actor who has done riveting work on TV, including *Dance to the Music of Time* (1997) as the passionate idealist Charles Stringham, but has so far had relatively few chances on screen. He had small roles in *Absolute Beginners* (1986) and *Little Dorrit* (1987), a starring role in the little-seen, Welsh-set *Rebecca's Daughters* (1992, UK/Ger), played Sydney Chaplin in *Chaplin* (1992, UK/Fr/It/Jap/US), and has been in several US-made films, including *Vincent & Theo* (1990, as Theodore van Gogh) and the JACK THE RIPPER drama, *From Hell* (2001).

Rhys-Davies, John (*b* Salisbury, 1944). Actor. Educated at University of East Anglia and RADA-trained, this burly, often blusterous character player has spent most of his career on stage or TV or in US-made movies, in which he found fame as the hero's sidekick, Sallah, in *Raiders of the Lost Ark* (1981) and *Indiana Jones and the Last Crusade* (1992). Tolkien aficionados approved his casting as Gimli in the *Lord of the Rings* films (2001, 2002, 2003, NZ/US). British films have been sparse in his cv, his most memorable role being that of KGB general, Pushkin in *The Living Daylights* (1987).

OTHER BRITISH FILMS INCLUDE: *Penny Gold* (1973), *The Black Windmill* (1974), *Victor/Victoria* (1982), *Sword of the Valiant* (1983), *Wing Commander IV* (1995, UK/US).

Rhys Jones, Griff (*b* Cardiff, 1953). Actor, screenwriter. Cambridge-educated, star of the celebrated Footlights Club, cheery- and chubby-looking comic from stage and TV, where he was hugely popular in *Not the Nine O'Clock News* (1979–80, 1982), following which he and one of his co-stars, Mel SMITH, went on to their own series, *Alas Smith and Jones* (1984–87). A smattering of films includes *Morons from Outer Space* (1985, + co-sc), *Wilt* (1989), as a hapless lecturer suspected of wife-murder, and the bleak *As You Like It* (1992), as the cynical clown Touchstone.

OTHER BRITISH FILMS INCLUDE: *The Secret Policeman's Other Ball* (1982), *Staggered* (1994), *Up 'n' Under* (1997).

Rhys Meyers, Jonathan (*b* Dublin, 1977). Actor. Hovering around late 90s films like some decadent goblin, the short, dark, intense-looking Rhys Meyers had a string of telling roles without ever being in a major hit. After a troubled childhood and a tearaway adolescence, he was eventually spotted by a casting director but failed his audition for *The War of the Buttons* (1994). However, he was vividly cast as the assassin of *Michael Collins* (1996, US), caught the attention as the glam rock casualty in the unsuccessful but oddly haunting *Velvet Goldmine* (UK/US) and as the son of the house obsessed by *The Governess* (1998, UK/Fr). Has filmed internationally including a well-noticed Chiron in the baroque horror of *Titus* (2000, UK/US).

OTHER BRITISH FILMS INCLUDE: *A Man of No Importance* (1994, UK/Ire), *B. Monkey* (1998, UK/It/US), *The Loss of Sexual Innocence* (2000, UK/US), *Happy Now* (2001), *Bend It Like Beckham* (2002).

Rice, Joan (*b* Derby, 1930 – *d* Maidenhead, 1997). Actress. Pretty brunette former waitress, who enjoyed brief stardom in the 50s, in films such as *The Story of Robin Hood . . .* (1952), as Maid Marian, and played romantic leads in the war film, *The Gift Horse* (1952), and, opposite Burt Lancaster, in the adventure piece, *His Majesty O'Keefe* (1953). But she was really not arresting enough for serious stardom and her films declined in status, though were not necessarily less enjoyable than the Boy's Own titles above. Turned to real estate when she retired from acting.

OTHER BRITISH FILMS INCLUDE: *Blackmailed* (1950), *Curtain Up* (1952), *The Steel Key, A Day to Remember* (1953), *One Good Turn, The Crowded Day* (1954), *Women Without Men* (1956), *The Long Knife* (1958), *Operation Bullshine* (1959), *The Horror of Frankenstein* (1970).

Rice, Sir Tim (*b* Amersham, 1944). Lyricist. The full story of the rise and rise of Rice belongs elsewhere – indeed, he has begun to tell it himself in what seems to be Volume One of his memoirs, *Oh What a Circus* (2000) – and is inseparable from that of Andrew LLOYD WEBBER, with whom he collaborated on some of the most successful stage musicals of recent decades, including *Jesus Christ Superstar* (1970, filmed 1973, US) and *Evita* (1978). An undervalued film version of the latter was made in 1996 (UK/US, AA/Best Song), starring Madonna; otherwise, the prolific Rice's contribution to British cinema has been meagre: the lyrics for *Gumshoe* (1971), a SHORT FILM, *The Empire Blend* (1977, m arr), *Octopussy* (1983, lyrics). Knighted 1994.

Rich, Roy (*b* Plymouth, 1911 – *d* Stratford-upon-Avon, 1970). Director. Educated at Dulwich College, Rich had a background in theatre management and BBC radio, with a break for RAF service (1942–46), before making modest inroads into cinema. He was associate producer at GAINSBOROUGH, on such films as *Miranda* and *Broken Journey* (1948), and co-directed two films with Alfred ROOME: the quite resonant drama of post-war malaise, *My Brother's Keeper*, and the sometimes wildly funny *It's Not Cricket* (1949). He directed a dozen TV plays for *Douglas Fairbanks Presents* in the mid 50s and also returned to theatre managing, as well as directing a couple of minor US films. Married Brenda BRUCE (1946 till his death).

OTHER BRITISH FILMS: *Master of Laughter* (1953, short, narr), *Stranger from Venus, Diplomatic Passport* (1954).

Richard, Sir Cliff (*b* Lucknow, India, 1940). Actor. RN: Harold Webb. Singer, actor. A British pop culture phenomenon, Richard has been a celebrity since 1958, a pop icon and an enigmatic figure, a tabula rasa on to which an audience can write what it desires. His credentials as an early rock-and-roller, modelled on Elvis, lasted only from 1958 to 59; clearly his heart wasn't in it. His first film appearance was as a juvenile delinquent in *Serious Charge* (1959), followed by his celebrated performance of 'Turn Me Loose', with menacing leer, on TV's *Oh Boy!* (1959), an image soon abandoned in favour of blander pop that appealed to both teenagers and their grannies. Both *The Young Ones* (1961) and *Summer Holiday* (1962) were top UK box-office attractions of their time. The former drew on the 'Hey, guys, let's put on a show!' ethos of the Mickey Rooney and Judy Garland films such as *Babes on Broadway*, and *Summer Holiday* even had Cliff and the gang Viennese-waltzing. With his limited acting range, his films became even dumber, with diminishing box-office returns. Following his religious conversion in 1965, he appeared in *Two a Penny* (1967), which is ironic in hindsight, as a number, 'Shrine on the Second Floor', in *Expresso Bongo* (1959) had earlier satirised pop singers and religiosity. Whenever his name is invoked today it is inevitably with a heavy sense of post-modern irony; except, of course, by his ever-loyal (mainly female) fans, like the two middle-aged women reported as sleeping eight nights in a car to ensure being first in the ticket queue for his 2002 Bournemouth performance. Knighted in 1995 for charitable works.

OTHER BRITISH FILMS: *Wonderful Life* (1964), *Finders Keepers* (1966), *Take Me High* (1973).

BIBLIOG: Autobiography, *Which One's Cliff?*, 1977; Steve Turner, *Cliff Richard*, 1993. Roger Philip Mellor.

Richard, Eric (*b* Margate, 1940). Actor. Best known as integrity figure, Sgt Bob Cryer in *The Bill* (1984–2001), austere-looking Richard has also appeared in many other popular TV programmes, in a wide range of plays at leading provincial theatres (e.g. Manchester's Exchange), and a few films, including *Little Dorrit* (1987) and *The Final Conflict* (1981, US).

OTHER BRITISH FILMS: *Venom* (1981), *P'tang Yang Kipperbang* (1982), *Laughterhouse, Number One* (1984), *Prick Up Your Ears* (1987).

Richard, Wendy (*b* Middlesbrough, 1943). Actress. RN: Emerton. Perhaps Britain's favourite blonde after Diana DORS, thanks to her work as Miss Brahms in TV's *Are You Being Served?* (1973–83) and as Pauline Fowler on *EastEnders* (from 1985), Richard made her screen debut in *No Blade of Grass* (1970), and has a brilliant cameo role in her second film, *Gumshoe* (1971), exchanging verbal blows with Albert Finney in a muted accent far removed from her familiar television voice. She is also featured on the 1962 Mike SARNE hit recording of 'Come Outside'.

OTHER BRITISH FILMS: *On the Buses* (1971), *Carry On Matron* (1972), *Bless This House* (1972), *Carry on Girls* (1973). AS.

Richardson, Cliff (*b* 1905). Special effects. Entered industry in 1924 and was in charge of SPECIAL EFFECTS at EALING for several years in the 40s. In 1947, he went to work with Ned MANN and W. Percy DAY at LONDON FILMS, on films such as *Mine Own Executioner* (1947), and in the early 50s he began to freelance. His son John RICHARDSON is also a special effects director.

OTHER BRITISH FILMS INCLUDE: *Ships with Wings* (1941), *The Big Blockade* (1942), *San Demetrio–London* (1943), *They Came to a City* (1944), *Dead of Night* (1945), *Bedelia* (1946), *The Loves of Joanna Godden* (1947), *Anna Karenina* (1948), *The African Queen* (1951), *The Red Beret* (1953), *Dance Little Lady* (1954), *Fire Down Below* (1957), *Sea of Sand* (1958), *Killers of Kilimanjaro* (1959), *The Siege of Sidney Street* (1960), *Lawrence of Arabia* (1962), *The Victors* (1963), *Lord Jim* (1964), *Help!*

(1965), *Casino Royale* (1967), *Battle of Britain* (1969), *The Private Life of Sherlock Holmes* (1970), *The Day of the Jackal* (UK/Fr), *The Mackintosh Man* (1973), *Juggernaut* (1974).

Richardson, Frank A. (aka Frankland) (*b* New York, 1893 – *d* London, 1975). Director. After an apprenticeship as assistant/2nd unit director on US films of the teens, Richardson directed a batch of British (co-)productions in the early 20s and returned in the 30s to direct or produce a dozen or so light films in the GENRES of the period. He then worked for Empire Films, directing mainly advertising SHORTS before turning to modest features in the later 40s (*Amateur Night*, 1946, etc), most not much more than 30 minutes long, and loosely built around musical turns.

OTHER BRITISH FILMS INCLUDE: (d, unless noted) *The Black Tulip* (UK/Neth), *I Mean Veronica* (1921), *Peace and Quiet* (1931), *Her First Affaire* (1932), *Going Gay* (p), *For Love of You* (co-p) (1934), *The Avenging Hand* (1936), *That's the Ticket* (1940, co-sc, co-dial), *Cabaret* (1948), *I Was a Dancer, Bait* (1949, + sc).

Richardson, Ian (*b* Edinburgh, 1934). Actor. Immensely stylish actor whose line in unctuous menace in such highly regarded TV programmes as *House of Cards* (1990) and *To Play the King* (1994) brought him Best Actor BAA and BAAn respectively. The hand in the velvet glove might easily be used to push you out of a high window. Much of his best work has been on TV, the silkiness of his delivery equipping him equally for traitors like the mole who sells out in *Tinker, Tailor, Soldier, Spy* (1979) or, eponymously, *Blunt* (1985), or as a speaker of *Six Centuries of Verse* (1984). He has been sparing with screen work, making his debut in *The Marat/Sade . . .* (1966), reprising his stage role; he was a memorable SHERLOCK HOLMES in *The Hound of the Baskervilles* (1983, TV, some cinemas), a sharper-than-usual Polonius in *Rosencrantz and Guildenstern Are Dead* (1990, US) and played toffs and authority figures in another dozen or so, half of them British. Worked often with the RSC from 1960.

OTHER BRITISH FILMS INCLUDE: *A Midsummer Night's Dream* (1968, as Oberon), *The Sign of Four* (1983), *Brazil* (1985), *Cry Freedom, The Fourth Protocol* (1987), *Dirty Weekend* (1993), *The Fifth Province* (1996, UK/Ger/Ire).

Richardson, Joely (*b* London, 1965). Actress. One of the fourth generation of the Redgrave acting dynasty, Richardson, tall, willowy younger daughter of Vanessa REDGRAVE and Tony RICHARDSON, has built up an impressive list of credits, including stage work with the RSC and the Old Vic, and Connie Chatterley in Ken RUSSELL's TV mini-series, *Lady Chatterley* (1992). First filmed as an extra in her father's *The Charge of the Light Brigade* (1968) and returned as a young adult (having first tried a career as a gymnast) to play her mother as a girl in *Wetherby* (1985). Her subsequent films have mixed the critical, ART-HOUSE prestige of *Drowning by Numbers* (1988, UK/Neth) and *Sister My Sister* (1994) with big-budget jobs like *101 Dalmatians* (1996, US) and *Event Horizon* (1997, UK/US) – as well as the excruciating *Maybe Baby* (2000, UK/Fr) in which she showed that comedy is not her forté. Pretty well everything else seems to be in her range, however. In 2002, co-starred with her mother on stage in *Lady Windermere's Fan*. Married/divorced (1992–97) Tim BEVAN.

OTHER BRITISH FILMS: *Rebecca's Daughters* (1992, UK/Neth), *Anne Frank Remembered* (1995, doc), *Loch Ness* (1996), *Toy Boys* (1999, short).

Richardson, John (*b* Worthing, 1934). Actor. Husky leading man who stripped convincingly in several HAMMER epics of the mid 60s – *She* (1965), *One Million Years BC* (1966) and *The*

Vengeance of She (1967) – but subsequently spent most of his career in little-seen European EXPLOITATION films. Was married to Martine BESWICK. Not to be confused with SPECIAL EFFECTS expert John RICHARDSON.

OTHER BRITISH FILMS: *Bachelor of Hearts, Operation Amsterdam, The Thirty Nine Steps* (1958), *On a Clear Day You Can See Forever* (1970, US, partly UK-filmed).

Richardson, John (*b c* 1946). Special effects artist. Richardson has worked on some of the most popular British (and US) films since the late 60s, his range encompassing pre-history in *The People That Time Forgot* (1977), James BOND (*Octopussy*, 1983, UK) and outer space in *Aliens* (1986, US) for which he shared an AA and BAA. Most of his work in the 90s has been in US films. Son of Cliff RICHARDSON (who pioneered cinematic special effects in England in 1921).

OTHER BRITISH FILMS INCLUDE: (fx/fx super) *The Railway Children, Straw Dogs, The Devils* (1971), *Young Winston* (1972), *The Day of the Jackal* (UK/Fr), *Juggernaut, Mahler* (1974), *A Bridge Too Far* (1977), *Moonraker* (UK/Fr), *North Sea Hijack* (1979), *A View to a Kill* (1985), *The Living Daylights* (1987), *Licence to Kill* (1989), *Tomorrow Never Dies* (1997, UK/US, miniatures), *The World Is Not Enough* (1999, UK/US).

Richardson, Miranda (*b* Southport, 1958). Actress. Dominant British actress of the 80s and 90s, who trained at the Bristol Old Vic Drama School and whose range is astonishing. As platinum-blonde, vividly lipsticked Ruth Ellis in *Dance with a Stranger* (1984), she evoked the cruelty of a class and an era as well as incarnating unforgettably the doomed woman. At the opposite end of the spectrum she was the execution-mad Queen Elizabeth ('Who's Queen?' she asks rhetorically) in TV's *Blackadder* (from 1986). Is there nothing she can't do? Probably not: think of the meek wife who blossoms under the Italian sun in *Enchanted April* (1992) or the embittered wife (AAn/supp a) of a philandering politician who causes their son's death in *Damage* (1992, UK/Fr, BAA/supp a) or the alarming IRA operative, Jude, in *The Crying Game* (1992, BAAn/supp a) and the neurotic, aristocratic first Mrs T.S. Eliot (AAn/BAAn) in *Tom & Viv* (1994, UK/US). From the later 90s, she has been more often in US films, including such duds as *Sleepy Hollow* (1999), in which special effects defeated the actors, and the ill-advised remake, *Get Carter* (2002): for one who turned down *Fatal Attraction* (1987, US), they seem curious choices. Apart from *Blackadder*, her TV has included a brilliantly bitchy Pamela Flitton in *A Dance to the Music of Time* (1997).

OTHER BRITISH FILMS: *The Innocent* (1984), *Underworld* (1985), *Eat the Rich* (1987), *The Fool* (1990), *Broken Skin* (1991, short), *The Line, the Cross and the Curve, Century* (1993), *The Night and the Moment* (1994, UK/Fr/It), *Swann* (1996, UK/Can), *The Designated Mourner* (1997), *St Ives* (1998), *Chicken Run* (2000, UK/US, voice).

Richardson, Natasha (*b* London, 1963). Actress. Now a US citizen, the older daughter of Vanessa REDGRAVE and Tony RICHARDSON, like sister Joely, first appeared as a tot in father's *The Charge of the Light Brigade* (1968). She trained at Central School and quickly built up a formidable stage reputation, with work at the Old Vic, a 1985 *Three Sisters*, co-starring mother and aunt, Lynn REDGRAVE, and her Tony-winning performance as Sally Bowles in Broadway's *Cabaret* (1999). Films have been sporadic and idiosyncratic: Mary Shelley in Ken RUSSELL's maniacal *Gothic* (1986), a gentle vicar's wife in *A Month in the Country* (1987), as *Patty Hearst* (1988, UK/US), and the disquieting, Venice-set *The Comfort of Strangers* (1990, UK/It). In the US, she starred in the psychological drama, *Nell* (1994) and the remake of *The Parent Trap* (1998), and she has

done some striking TV, including *Suddenly Last Summer* (1993) and the title role in *Zelda* (1993), but the theatre has been her most rewarding medium. Married (2, 1994) Liam NEESON.

OTHER BRITISH FILMS: *Every Picture Tells a Story* (1984), *The Favour, the Watch and the Very Big Fish* (1991, UK/Fr), *Widows' Peak* (1994, UK/US), *Blow Dry* (2001, UK/Ger/US).

Richardson, Peter (*b* Newton Abbot, 1953). Director. Better known as TV director, on, for example, *Eddie Izzard: Glorious* (1997), Richardson directed (and acted in) several off-centre COMEDIES – *The Supergrass* (1985), *Eat the Rich* (1987), *The Pope Must Die* (1991) – which failed to find audiences. As an actor, he played Al Pacino playing Arthur Scargill in *The Strike* (1988) and Bart Columbus in *Carry On Columbus* (1992), and on TV he directed and wrote the bizarre *Stella Street* (1997). Perhaps a quirkish talent that will flower with the right material.

OTHER BRITISH FILMS: *The Bullshitters* (1984, a, co-sc), *Manhunt* (1992, a), *The Line, the Cross and the Curve* (1993).

Richardson, Sir Ralph (*b* Cheltenham, 1902 – *d* London, 1983). Actor. Though compared with his illustrious stage career Richardson's films probably meant considerably less to him, there are nevertheless some memorable highlights in a filmography spanning fifty years. After starting in an office job, he turned to the stage, making his professional debut in 1921; he played a wide range of Shakespearean roles, avoiding the romantic ones and pursuing the great character roles – Malvolio, Bottom, etc – as well as initiating modern roles, like the self-deluding protagonist of *Flowering Cherry* (1957–58). His film career is at once prolific and random, doing what came along for the financial rewards and perhaps 'a bit of fame', the words in which he encouraged OLIVIER to take on Hollywood's *Wuthering Heights* (1939).

There is, though, something so minutely alert, so watchful and detailed about his craft that, in some ways, film seems to suit it admirably. Never handsome, he was always going to be a limited leading man in films and his 30s films tend to the eccentric or the character lead, like 'Boss' in *Things to Come* (1936) and the barber in deep financial trouble in *On the Night of the Fire* (1939). He was in the Fleet Air Arm during WW2 (1939–44), making only a couple of PROPAGANDA FILMS, including *The Volunteer* (narr) and *The Silver Fleet* (1943, + assoc p), as a self-sacrificing Dutch patriot. Post-war, he had his ascendancy in film: as the shy boffin in *School for Secrets* (1946); the knuckle-cracking Karenin in the otherwise misfiring *Anna Karenina* (1948); the butler who becomes *The Fallen Idol* (1948), perhaps his finest screen work, full of subtle, suppressed longing and pain; the father of *The Heiress* (1949, US, AAn/supp a), gifted with a merciless irony; the humane Captain Lingard in *Outcast of the Islands* (1951); the unconsciously selfish vicar in *The Holly and the Ivy* and the more consciously demanding father in *The Sound Barrier* (1952, BAA/a). For one who had been slow to take films seriously, it is a cherishable gallery.

In the remaining 30 years, he took what came along, including those cameo roles offered to English acting knights in their twilight years in the 60s and 70s, but every so often he would remind one that he had few peers and no superiors in his particular line, that he was in fact a great original. And when he got a real part, like James Tyrone in *Long Day's Journey into Night* (1962, US), he would make clear how consummately he had mastered the medium he had been so wary of. There was TV as well, including a valuable filmed record of him and

GIELGUD in *Home* (1971) and he went on acting on the stage almost until his death. After the death of his first wife, he married Meriel FORBES. Knighted in 1947.

OTHER BRITISH FILMS: *Friday the Thirteenth, The Ghoul* (1933), *The Return of Bulldog Drummond, The King of Paris, Java Head* (1934), *Bulldog Jack* (1935), *The Man Who Could Work Miracles* (1936), *Thunder in the City* (1937), *The Divorce of Lady X, The Citadel, South Riding* (1938), *Q Planes, The Four Feathers, The Lion Has Wings* (1939), *The Day Will Dawn* (1942), *Eagles of the Fleet* (1950, doc, comm), *Home at Seven* (1952, + d), *Richard III* (1955), *Smiley, The Passionate Stranger* (1956), *Our Man in Havana* (1959), *Oscar Wilde* (1960, as Sir Edward Carson), *Woman of Straw* (1964), *Dr Zhivago* (1965, UK/US, BAAn/a), *Khartoum* (BAAn/a), *The Wrong Box* (1966, BAAn/a), *Battle of Britain, Oh! What a Lovely War, The Bed Sitting Room, The Looking Glass War* (1969), *David Copperfield* (1969, as Micawber), *Whoever Slew Auntie Roo?* (1971), *Tales from the Crypt, Lady Caroline Lamb* (UK/It/US, BAAn/supp a), *Alice's Adventures in Wonderland* (1972), *O Lucky Man!, A Doll's House* (1973), *Watership Down* (1978, voice), *Time Bandits* (1981), *Invitation to the Wedding* (1983), *Greystoke . . .* (UK/US, AAn/supp a), *Give My Regards to Broad Street* (1984).

BIBLIOG: Garry O'Connor, *Ralph Richardson: An Actor's Life*, 1985.

Richardson, Tony (*b* Shipley, 1928 – *d* Los Angeles, 1991). Director, producer, screenwriter. A catalyst for cultural change in British theatre in the staid 50s, Richardson became the most critically acclaimed British *film* director of the early 60s. After a brief time at the BBC, he became a moving force behind the English Stage Company at the Royal Court Theatre in 1956, shaking up British theatre with new plays such as John OSBORNE's *Look Back in Anger* (1956). Writing film criticism for *SIGHT AND SOUND* magazine, Richardson was also able to secure BFI support for a short film, *Momma Don't Allow*, co-directed with Karel REISZ in 1955, and screened in the FREE CINEMA programmes. His feature film career was launched with two Osborne/Royal Court ADAPTATIONS, produced by Richardson's and Osborne's WOODFALL FILMS. *Look Back in Anger* (1959, BAA Best British Film), suffered from a miscast star (Richard BURTON), but *The Entertainer* (1960) preserved on film one of Laurence OLIVIER's greatest performances. Richardson was now charting new territory for British features, following with screen adaptations of Shelagh DELANEY's *A Taste of Honey* (1961, BAA/film/sc) and Alan SILLITOE's *The Loneliness of the Long Distance Runner* (1962), both landmark films of the British NEW WAVE. The former was notable for excellent use of locations in Salford, and its loose improvisatory visual style owed much to cinematographer Walter LASSALLY: there was little sense of viewing a filmed play, and Richardson was not afraid to borrow stylistic ideas, including jump cuts and freeze frames, from the French New Wave. His next production, *Tom Jones* (1963), veered away from contemporary subjects, yet caught the 'swinging sixties' mood, proving an outstanding critical and commercial success (AA/film/d; BAA/film). Richardson had not particularly rewarding associations with European cultural giants such as Genet (*Mademoiselle*, 1965, UK/Fr), Duras (*The Sailor from Gibraltar*, 1968, + sc), and Nabokov (*Laughter in the Dark*, 1969, UK/Fr), and the costly, uneven *Charge of the Light Brigade* (1968), whose original approach to the subject lost money, ended Woodfall's bankability. Richardson also directed several US films, starting with *Sanctuary* (1961), although generally outside the Hollywood mainstream. Richardson was an excellent director of actors, and many of his films, such as *Hamlet* (1969), with Nicol WILLIAMSON, and *A Delicate Balance* (1973, UK/US/Can), starring Katharine HEPBURN, feature memorable central performances. Unlike most British directors of the 60s, he

rarely directed formula films, allowing himself the freedom to fail. The issues of REALISM and FANTASY in British cinema can fruitfully be seen in the polarities of Richardson's films of 1959–64. Married Vanessa REDGRAVE (1962–67); daughters are Natasha and Joely RICHARDSON.

OTHER BRITISH FILMS: (d, unless noted) *Saturday Night and Sunday Morning* (1960, p), *The Girl with Green Eyes* (1964, p), *Red and Blue* (1967, short), *Ned Kelly* (1970, UK/Aust, + sc), *Dead Cert* (+ sc) (1973), *Joseph Andrews* (1976, + sc).

BIBLIOG: Autobiography, *Long Distance Runner – A Memoir*, 1993; Don Radovich, *Tony Richardson: A Bio-Bibliography*, 1995; James M. Welsh and John C. Tibbetts (eds), *The Cinema of Tony Richardson: Essays and Interviews*, 1999. Roger Philip Mellor.

Richfield, Edwin (*b* London, 1921 – *d* Shrewsbury, 1990). Actor. Versatile, serious-looking supporting player of the 50s and 60s, more regularly associated with authority figures as he aged, as in *Quatermass and the Pit* (1967), as the Minister of Defence. There were all sorts of bits and pieces in 'B' FILMS, such as the café owner in *The Big Chance* and the porter in *Account Rendered* (1957), but he is most vivid in the wordless role of Sonia DRESDEL's mute brother in *The Break* (1962). Was married to Jan HOLDEN.

OTHER BRITISH FILMS INCLUDE: *Ha'penny Breeze* (1950), *The Blue Peter, The Brain Machine* (1954), *X the Unknown* (1956), *Quatermass 2* (1957), *Up the Creek, No Trees in the Street* (1958), *Inn for Trouble* (1959), *Sword of Sherwood Forest* (1960), *The Secret of Blood Island* (1964), *Champions* (1983).

Richler, Mordecai (*b* Montreal, 1931 – *d* Montreal, 2001). Screenwriter. Canadian novelist who drew on his Jewish upbringing in Montreal for his novels and spent over 20 years in England from 1954. Worked on a handful of films, including uncredited contributions to *Room at the Top* (1958), directed by close friend Jack CLAYTON, and sequel, *Life at the Top* (1965), directed by fellow Canadian, Ted KOTCHEFF, for whom he also worked on *Tiara Tahiti* (1962, add dial). Adapted his breakthrough novel, *The Apprenticeship of Duddy Kravitz* (1959) to the screen (1974, Can). Later worked in Canada until his death from cancer.

OTHER BRITISH FILMS: *Dearth of a Salesman* (co-sc), *Insomnia Is Good for You* (co-story) (1957, shorts), *No Love for Johnnie* (1961, co-sc), *The Wild and the Willing* (1962, co-sc).

Richmond, Anthony B. (Tony) (*b* London, 1942). Cinematographer. Served his apprenticeship as clapper loader on such films as *The Gorgon* (1964) and *Dr Zhivago* (1965, UK/US), having his first feature credit on Jean-Luc Godard's British-made *Sympathy for the Devil* (1968) and winning a BAA/c for Nicolas ROEG's *Don't Look Now* (1973, UK/It). He worked for Roeg several more times (*The Man Who Fell to Earth*, 1976; *Bad Timing*, 1980) and has spent most of his recent career either in TV or the US. His son **George Richmond** is also a cameraman. Not to be confused with child actor of the 50s, **Anthony Richmond**, who memorably played Jack WARNER's neglected son in *Bang! You're Dead* (1953).

OTHER BRITISH FILMS INCLUDE: (c) *Only When I Larf* (1968), *Madame Sin* (1972), *Vampira, Stardust* (1974), *The Eagle Has Landed* (1976), *Venom* (1981, co-c), *Déjà Vu* (1984, d, co-sc), *Ravenous* (1999, UK/Czech/Mex/Slov/US).

Richmond, Susan (*b* London, 1894 – *d* 1959) Actress. Well-known as drama teacher (of Stewart GRANGER, among others) and co-director of the Webber-Douglas Dramatic School (1931–41), Richmond acted on stage from 1912 and appeared in a handful of films, including *Life in Her Hands* (1951), *Crow*

Hollow (1952), *Gideon's Day* (1958) and Robert HAMER's TV version of *A Month in the Country* (1955).

Rickards, Jocelyn (*b* Melbourne, 1924). Costume designer. Australian who has worked in the British film industry since 1959. Much associated with 'NEW WAVE' directors, including Tony RICHARDSON (*Look Back in Anger*, 1959), Karel REISZ (*Morgan: A Suitable Case for Treatment*, 1966) and John SCHLESINGER (*Sunday Bloody Sunday*, 1971). Also did the historical designs for *Alfred the Great* (1969), whose director, Clive DONNER, she married. Taught costume design at University of Southern California (1979–80).

OTHER BRITISH FILMS INCLUDE: *From Russia with Love* (1963), *The Knack . . .* (1965), *Mademoiselle* (UK/Fr), *Blow-Up* (UK/It) (1966), *The Sailor from Gibraltar* (1967), *Interlude* (1968), *Ryan's Daughter* (1970).

Rickman, Alan (*b* London, 1946). Actor. The versatile Rickman, of Irish-Welsh parentage, began his stage career after RADA and scored a great success in *Les Liaisons Dangereuses*. His first film role came in 1988 when he was asked to play the villain in *Die Hard* (1988, US) and he played another memorable villain, the Sheriff of Nottingham, in *Robin Hood: Prince of Thieves* (1991, US). He has established a somewhat languid persona in films since, including *Close My Eyes* (1991), for which he won Best Actor at the 1991 Seattle International Film Festival; *Truly Madly Deeply* (1991), as the ghostly husband; *Sense and Sensibility* (1995, US/UK) as the melancholy Colonel Brandon, and *Michael Collins* (1996, US), for all of which he was BAA-nominated. Later international films included *Blow Dry* (2001, UK/Ger/US) and *The Search for John Gissing* (2001, UK/US), and he directed *Winter Guest* (1998, UK/US), a gloomy Scottish-set drama of grief and possible recovery. His TV included a marvellously unctuous Rev. Slope in the serial *Barchester Chronicles* (1982).

OTHER BRITISH FILMS: *An Awfully Big Adventure* (1995), *Play* (2000, Ire), *Harry Potter and the Sorcerer's Stone* (2001, UK/US).
BIBLIOG: Maureen Paton, *Alan Rickman*, 1996. Anne-Marie Thomas.

Ridgwell, George (*b* Woolwich, 1870 – *d* London, 1935). Director. Despite being somewhat austere in appearance, Ridgwell seems to have been a colourful character, who served 12 years with the Coldstream Guards and saw action in the Boer War, was a soloist and cornet player on the stage in both the UK and the US, and was the father of singer Audrey Ridgwell (*b* 1904 – *d* 1968). As George Ridgwell, he was an editor in the scenario department of the Vitagraph Company in Brooklyn, NY, before being appointed a director in 1915; he was active in the US, directing primarily shorts, until 1919. Ridgwell then returned to England with BRITISH AND COLONIAL, and the following year joined STOLL, where he also edited his own films and directed two SHERLOCK HOLMES SERIES: *Further Adventures of Sherlock Holmes* (1922) and *The Last Adventures of Sherlock Holmes* (1923). He ended his career as a bit player in the 30s.

OTHER BRITISH FILMS INCLUDE: *A Gamble in Lives* (1920), *The Four Just Men* (1921), *The Pointing Finger, The Crimson Circle* (1922), *Becket* (1923), *The Lily of Killarney* (1929). AS.

Ridley, Arnold (*b* Bath, 1896 – *d* London, 1984). Actor, author, director. Stage debut in 1914 was followed by WW1 service and the wounds he sustained led him to drop acting in favour of playwriting. His great success was *The Ghost Train*, filmed three times (1927, UK/Ger; 1931, 1941), an adroit mix of thrills and humour, set in a railway waiting room. Several other of his plays were adapted to the screen, including *Keepers of*

Youth (1929, filmed 1931), *Easy Money* (1947, filmed 1948), and *Beggar My Neighbour* (1952, filmed as *Meet Mr Lucifer*, 1953), and post-war he acted in several films and played Private Charles Godfrey in TV's *Dad's Army* (1968–77) and the film version (1971). Was President of Bath Rugby Football Club. Wife (2 of 3) was **Isola Strong**, who appeared in a few British films, including *The White Unicorn* (1947). Awarded OBE, 1982.

OTHER BRITISH FILMS INCLUDE: (adptd from plays) *The Wrecker* (1928, co-play), *Third Time Lucky* (1931), *The Warren Case* (1934), *Who Killed the Cat?* (1966, co-play); (a) *The Interrupted Journey* (1949), *Stolen Face* (1952), *Wings of Mystery* (1963), *Crooks in Cloisters* (1964), *Carry On Girls* (1973).

Rietti, Victor (aka Rietty) (*b* Ferrara, Italy, 1888 – *d* London, 1963). Actor. Trained in Italy, on London stage from 1922, founded the International Theatre and translated many European plays performed there. Entered films in the mid 30s and played nearly two dozen roles, including the usual multi-national assortment, across a wide class range: he is, for instance, an Italian peasant in *A Man About the House* (1947) and King Frederick of Denmark in *Mr HC Anderson* (1950). Father of Robert RIETTI.

OTHER BRITISH FILMS INCLUDE: *Jew Süss* (1934), *Juggernaut* (1936), *21 Days* (1937), *Room for Two* (1940), *The Story of Esther Costello, The Naked Truth* (1957), *Village of Daughters* (1962).

Rietty, Robert (*b* London, 1923). Actor. Son of Victor RIETTY, in films first as child, in *Emil and the Detectives* (1935, called Bobby Rietti), trained at RADA, toured with ENSA during WW2, joining the Army in 1942, and was post-war with the BBC rep company. First film as adult was *Call of the Blood* (1948), a gloomy brew of Mediterranean passions, and thereafter in small roles, including Peter FINCH's brother in *Sunday Bloody Sunday* (1971), until *Madame Sousatzka* (1988). Also author, translator, adaptor and dubber of voices for English versions of European films.

OTHER BRITISH FILMS INCLUDE: *Stock Car* (1955), *The Snorkel* (1958), *Time to Remember* (1962), *I Could Go On Singing* (1963), *The Crooked Road* (1964, UK/Yug), *On Her Majesty's Secret Service, The Italian Job* (1969), *Gulliver's Travels* (1976, voice), *Never Say Never Again* (1983, UK/US).

Rigby, Arthur (*b* London, 1900 – *d* Worthing, 1970). Actor. Stage actor who made his debut after RAF service in WW1, spending much of the 20s touring in Britain and abroad, served again in WW2, then returned to the stage. First filmed in *Q-Ships* (1928), but made only occasional appearances over the next thirty years, often as policemen, as he was, in thinning-haired middle age, in *The Blue Lamp* (1949) and in Jack WARNER's follow-up TV series, *Dixon of Dock Green* (1955–64).

OTHER BRITISH FILMS INCLUDE: (a, unless noted) *Love Lies* (1931, co-play), *You Made Me Love You, Puppets of Fate* (co-story) (1933), *The Marriage of Corbal, Cheer Up!, Hot News* (co-sc) (1936), *The Blue Parrot* (1953), *Dangerous Cargo* (1954), *The Long Arm, Behind the Headlines* (1956), *Crossroads to Crime* (1960).

Rigby, Edward (*b* Ashford, 1879 – *d* London, 1951). Actor. Resident ancient of British films for as long as can be remembered; reason suggests that he was once young, but it is hard to imagine. On stage from 1900 in Britain, America, Australia and Canada, he may have entered films as early as 1907; he is certainly in *The Blue Bird* (1910), as Bread, but his real film career begins in 1935 and in the ensuing 15 years he played 70 old codgers. He is already playing George FORMBY's grandad in *No Limit* (1935), irascibly threatening to smash George's bike if it wakes him again, and doggedly not holding with 'foreign parts' (i.e. the Isle of Man). He could be wily, shifty or cranky, but he could imbue the hero's impoverished father in *The Stars Look Down* (1939) with a touching proletarian dignity, and it is hard not to suspect a lurking benevolence beneath the crusty exterior his roles sometimes require. He had seven films released in the year before he died and the shuffling, put-upon school porter, Rainbow, in *The Happiest Days of Your Life* (1950) sums up a lot of his character appeal.

OTHER BRITISH FILMS: *The Man Who Fell by the Way* (1907), *Lorna Doone* (1934), *Windfall, Gay Old Dog* (1935), *Accused, This Green Hell, Queen of Hearts, Land Without Music, Irish for Luck, Crime Over London, The Heirloom Mystery* (1936), *Jump for Glory, Young and Innocent, Under a Cloud, The Show Goes On, Mr Smith Carries On, The Fatal Hour, A Yank at Oxford* (1937), *Yellow Sands, The Ware Case, Kicking the Moon Around, Keep Smiling* (1938), *Young Man's Fancy, There Ain't No Justice, Poison Pen, The Four Just Men* (1939), *Sailor's Don't Care, The Proud Valley, Fingers, Convoy* (1940), *Major Barbara, Penn of Pennsylvania, Kipps, The Farmer's Wife, The Common Touch* (1941), *Went the Day Well?, Salute John Citizen, Let the People Sing, Flying Fortress* (1942), *They Met in the Dark, Get Cracking* (1943), *A Canterbury Tale, Don't Take It to Heart!* (1944), *The Agitator, Perfect Strangers, Murder in Reverse, I Live in Grosvenor Square* (1945), *The Years Between, Piccadilly Incident, Quiet Weekend* (1946), *Temptation Harbour, The Loves of Joanna Godden, Green Fingers* (1947), *Daybreak, The Three Weird Sisters, Noose, It's Hard to Be Good, Easy Money* (1948), *A Run for Your Money, Don't Ever Leave Me, Christopher Columbus, All Over the Town* (1949), *The Mudlark, What the Butler Saw, Tony Draws a Horse, Into the Blue, Double Confession, Circle of Danger* (1950).

Rigby, Terence (*b* Birmingham, 1937). Actor. Solid, and solidly convincing character player first noticed as plodding PC Snow in *Softly Softly* (1966), then as Michael CAINE's cuckolded and dangerous boss in *Get Carter* (1971) and Joey in the film version of Harold PINTER's *Homecoming* (1973/UK/US). One of nature's Dr Watsons, he fulfilled this role in TV's *The Hound of the Baskervilles* (1982), he worked most on TV until the 90s when there was a steady stream of noticeable character roles, including General Bukharin in *Tomorrow Never Dies* (1997, UK/US) and the gaoler, Harrison, in the costume caper, *Plunkett & Macleane* (UK/Czech) (1999).

OTHER BRITISH FILMS INCLUDE: *Accident* (1967), *The Dogs of War* (1980), *Testimony* (1987), *Scandal* (1988), *Funny Bones* (1995, UK/US), *England, My England* (1995), *Elizabeth* (1998), *Essex Boys* (2000).

Rigg, Dame Diana (*b* Doncaster, 1938). Actress. Sophisticated dark-haired beauty of the 60s, a classically trained actress who after RADA and repertory, signed with the RSC in 1959, but found international fame as Emma Peel in second series of *The Avengers* (1965–67). The series was a tongue-in-cheek, stylish update of the William Powell–Myrna Loy movies, in which she engaged in witty repartee with Patrick MACNEE, whilst defeating a range of colourful villains. Made film debut in 1968, repeating her stage role of Helena in *A Midsummer Night's Dream* (1968). Too smart to fit comfortably into the James BOND film *On Her Majesty's Secret Service* (1969), she was better served by *In This House of Brede* (1975), and *The Hospital* (1971, US). In more recent TV films, she excels as older women, mean and obsessive as in *Mother Love* (1989, BAA/actress), and has triumphed on the London and NY stage in roles as varied as the musical *Follies* and as *Medea*, but her British cinema career is lamentably brief. Awarded CBE (1987) and DBE (1994).

OTHER BRITISH FILMS INCLUDE: *The Assassination Bureau* (1968), *Julius Caesar* (1970), *Theatre of Blood* (1973), *The Great Muppet Caper, Evil Under the Sun* (1981), *Parting Shots, The American* (1998). Roger Philip Mellor.

Rilla, Walter (*b* Neunkirchen, Germany, 1894 – *d* London, 1980). Actor. A youthful romantic lead in numerous German films of the 20s, Rilla's first contact with British cinema was in the Anglo-German co-production *The Blackguard* (1925). Rilla settled in Britain in the mid 30s, playing a diverse range of characters. In later years he was often cast as a sometimes sinister scientist, or as an elder statesman, and played his share of Nazis, including Greta GYNT's protector in *Mr Emmanuel* (1944). Rilla also wrote radio plays and directed for television. Father of director Wolf RILLA.

OTHER BRITISH FILMS INCLUDE: *The Scarlet Pimpernel* (1935), *Victoria The Great* (1937), *Sixty Glorious Years* (1938), *The Gang's All Here* (1939), *Sabotage Agent, Candlelight in Algeria* (1943), *Lisbon Story* (1946), *The Golden Salamander* (1949), *State Secret* (1950), *The Venetian Bird* (1952), *Desperate Moment* (1953), *Cairo* (1963), *Victim Five* (1964), *The Face of Fu Manchu* (1965), *Sumuru* (1967). Tim Bergfelder.

Rilla, Wolf (*b* Berlin, 1920). Director. The son of actor Walter RILLA, he directed about two dozen films from 1952 (*Noose for a Lady*) to 1974 (*Bedtime with Rosie*, + p), after which he retired to France where he runs a hotel. Had extensive experience with the BBC, both European and Home Services, before entering films, where he mixed main features, like the attractive *Pacific Destiny* (1956), with 'B' MOVIES, like *The Large Rope* (1953). There is also a thoughtful little study of old age, *The End of the Road* (1954), with a rare starring role for Finlay CURRIE, and *Village of the Damned* (1960, + co-sc) is a modest but compelling piece of SCIENCE-FICTION. Married to **Valerie Hanson**, who appeared in his film, *Stock Car* (1955).

OTHER BRITISH FILMS INCLUDE: *Glad Tidings, Marilyn* (1953, + sc), *The Black Rider* (1954), *The Blue Peter* (1955), *The Scamp* (1957, + sc), *Bachelor of Hearts* (1958), *Piccadilly Third Stop* (1960), *Watch It Sailor!* (1961), *Money-Go-Round* (1966, + co-sc).

Ringwood, Bob (*b* London). Costume designer. Now lives in Los Angeles where he works on such high-profile projects as Spielberg's *AI: Artificial Intelligence* (2001). He studied at London's Central School of Art and Design and has designed for numerous stage productions, including opera and ballet as well as straight plays. His work reveals a preference for the fantastic, as seen in his costumes for *Excalibur* (1981, UK/US, BAAn/cos), *The Draughtsman's Contract* (1982) and *Batman* (1989, US-financed, partly UK-made, BAAn), but his AA nomination was for the comparative REALISM of *Empire of the Sun* (1987, + BAA/n).

OTHER BRITISH FILMS: *Santa Claus* (1985), *Prick Up Your Ears* (1987), *Chicago Joe and the Showgirl* (1989), *American Friends* (1991).

Rintoul, David (*b* Aberdeen, 1948). Actor. RADA-trained Scottish actor, whose film work has been almost entirely for TV (he was Darcy in *Pride and Prejudice*, 1979; *Doctor Finlay*, 1993; the ship's surgeon in *Hornblower*, 2001). He starred hairily in his first film, *The Legend of the Werewolf* (1974) and was in *Scotch Myths – the Movie* (1982).

Ripper, Michael (*b* Portsmouth, 1913 – *d* London, 2000). Actor. Ripper appeared in numerous British films in the 30s but his reputation rests largely on his association with HAMMER. From the 50s onwards, he featured regularly in Hammer horror films, usually in working-class roles. His most striking performance for the company was as the downtrodden and pathetic Longbarrow in *The Mummy's Shroud* (1966). Late in his career, he became a regular on the popular BBC TV sitcom *Butterflies*.

OTHER BRITISH FILMS INCLUDE: *Busman's Holiday, The Heirloom Mystery* (1936), *Luck of the Navy* (1938), *Captain Boycott* (1947), *Oliver*

Twist (1948), *The Rocking Horse Winner* (1949), *Lady Godiva Rides Again*, *Secret People* (1951), *The Intruder* (1953), *The Rainbow Jacket*, *The Constant Husband* (1954), *Geordie* (1955), *Yield to the Night* (1956), *Woman in a Dressing Gown* (1957), *The Revenge of Frankenstein* (1958), *The Ugly Duckling*, *The Mummy* (1959), *The Brides of Dracula* (1960), *The Curse of the Werewolf*, *A Prize of Arms*, *The Pirates of Blood River* (1961), *The Phantom of the Opera* (1962), *The Devil-Ship Pirates* (1963), *The Curse of the Mummy's Tomb*, *Every Day's a Holiday* (1964), *Rasputin the Mad Monk* (1965), *The Reptile*, *The Plague of the Zombies* (1966), *Torture Garden* (1967), *Dracula Has Risen from the Grave* (1968), *Taste the Blood of Dracula* (1969), *Scars of Dracula* (1970), *Legend of the Werewolf* (1974), *No Surrender* (1985), *Revenge of Billy the Kid* (1991). Peter Hutchings.

Riscoe, Arthur (*b* Sherburn-in-Elmet, 1895 – *d* London, 1954). Actor. RN: Boorman. Yorkshire stage comic, probably best remembered for his last film role, as Chitterlow, Michael REDGRAVE's flamboyant fellow-worker in *Kipps* (1941). In several silent films in 1920 and in a half-dozen light COMEDIES in the 30s.

OTHER BRITISH FILMS INCLUDE: *Horatio's Deception*, *The Bitten Biter* (1920), *For the Love of Mike* (1932), *For Love of You* (1933), *Public Nuisance No. 1* (1936), *The Street Singer* (1937).

Risdon, Elizabeth (*b* London, 1887 – *d* Santa Monica, California, 1958). Actress. Somewhat birdlike ingenue, who became a noted character actress, often playing kindly but puritanical mothers; US stage debut 1912 and Broadway star from 1917; in British films 1913–17; from 1935 on screen in US in more than 90 films, including *Dead End* (1937) and *Random Harvest* (1942). Married director George Loane Tucker, with whom she emigrated to US in 1917, and actor Brandon Evans (1925–57).

BRITISH FILMS INCLUDE: *Maria Marten* (1913), *Midshipman Easy*, *The Christian* (1915), *The Manxman* (1916), *Smith* (1917). AS.

Ritchard, Cyril (*b* Sydney, 1897 – *d* Chicago, 1977). Actor. RN: Trimmell-Ritchard. Australian-born actor-dancer, educated at Sydney University, long in Britain. On stage in Sydney, 1917; New York, 1924; London 1925; chiefly in musicals, comedies and revues, and was a famous Captain Hook to Mary Martin's *Peter Pan* (1953–54). Very skimpy film experience over nearly 40 years, including the artist who is murdered in *Blackmail* (1929), a music hall comedian in *The Winslow Boy* (1948) and Kipps's flashy friend, Chitterlow in *Half a Sixpence* (1967, UK/US). His TV appearances were often in Christmas shows. Married stage star Madge Elliott.

OTHER BRITISH FILMS INCLUDE: *Piccadilly* (1929), *Symphony in Two Flats* (1930), *Just for a Song* (1932), *Danny Boy* (1934), *The Show Goes On* (1937), *I See Ice!* (1938).

Ritchie, Guy (*b* Hatfield, Herts, 1968). Director. Making *Lock, Stock and Two Smoking Barrels* (1998) and marrying Madonna (2000) are enough to ensure that Ritchie has one of the highest profiles in contemporary British cinema. *Lock, Stock . . .*, very violent, darkly comic, was a major success of the 90s British gangster cycle; it was nominated for numerous awards, including BAA; it spawned an often witty TV series (*Lock, Stock*, 2000); and Ritchie followed it up with *Snatch* (2000, UK/US, + sc, a), another caper film, even jokier than its famous predecessor, this time set in London's Hatton Gardens diamond-dealing centre. He has directed Madonna in the REMAKE of *Swept Away* (2002). Despite his famous sarf London locutions and referring to Madonna as the 'Missis', the truth seems to be that Ritchie's background is obdurately upper-middle-class, with a Sandhurst graduate father, a titled stepfather and an expensive boarding-school tucked away out of the sight of publicists.

OTHER BRITISH FILMS: *The Hard Case* (1995, short, d, sc), *The Mean Machine* (UK/US, p), *The Mole, Star* (short) (2001, sc).

Ritchie, June (*b* Manchester, 1939). Actress. As monstrous Thora HIRD's nice, pretty, dim daughter, inconveniently made pregnant by Alan BATES in *A Kind of Loving* (1962), Ritchie made one of the most auspicious of the many auspicious 60s debuts in British film. She established firmly the girl's limitations without losing our sympathy, and she followed this with a poignant sketch as Ian HENDRY's girlfriend, again with unlooked-for pregnancy, in *Live Now, Pay Later* (1962), but perhaps because she was equally interested in pursuing a stage career and a domestic life she never became the star one might have expected. The truth of her Ingrid, however, stands as a testimony to her subtle skills. Some TV, including *The Mallens* (1980).

OTHER BRITISH FILMS: *The Mouse on the Moon*, *The World Ten Times Over*, *This Is My Street* (1963), *The Syndicate* (1967), *Hunted* (1971).

Riverside Studios Julius HAGEN purchased the newly built studios in Hammersmith, London, in 1935 from the PDC New Ideal Film Company, for mainly 'QUOTA QUICKIES' productions, using such MUSIC-HALL artists as Sandy POWELL and Robb WILTON. After his RIVERSIDE STUDIOS went into liquidation in 1937 it was purchased by matinee idol Jack BUCHANAN. Some cartoons were made by Anson DYER featuring Stanley HOLLOWAY, but no real use of the studios was made until after the war. Then Sydney BOX made some excellent films, including *The Seventh Veil* with Ann TODD and James MASON. BUCHANAN sold to ALLIANCE FILM STUDIOS in 1948 and production continued until the early 50s, including Lewis GILBERT's *The Sea Shall Not Have Them* with Dirk BOGARDE and *Father Brown* with Alec GUINNESS. By the end of 1954 the BBC Television Film Unit was using the studios, which were no longer employed for feature film productions for outside companies.

BIBLIOG: Patricia Warren. *British Film Studios – An Illustrated History*, 2001. Patricia Warren.

Rix, Brian (Lord Rix) (*b* Cottingham, Yorkshire, 1924). Actor. One of the theatre's great actor-managers of the second half of the 20th century, Rix's name is much associated with the Whitehall and Garrick Theatres, in which he presented and starred in an amazing series of record-breaking farces. On stage from 1942, in the RAF (1944–47), he toured post-war with *Reluctant Heroes*, in 1950 bringing this into London's Whitehall where it stayed for four years, during which time he made his film bow in it (1951), repeating his stage role of the gormless Northerner, Horace. He would later reprise his role of the foolish Fred in *Dry Rot* (1954–58, film 1956) and indeed all his film roles were in farces, endlessly suggestive and radically innocent. His contribution to the mirth of nations was augmented further by TV series, including *Dial Rix* (1962–63) and its successors, as well as presenting and starring in dozens of TV plays. He has worked tirelessly for the mentally handicapped (Chairman of MENCAP), and was knighted in 1986 and made a peer in 1992. Married to Elspet GRAY since 1949.

OTHER BRITISH FILMS INCLUDE: *What Every Woman Wants*, *Up to His Neck* (1954), *Not Wanted on Voyage* (1957), *The Night We Dropped a Clanger* (1959), *The Night We Got the Bird* (1960, + co-p), *Nothing Barred* (1961, + co-p), *Don't Just Lie There, Say Something!* (1970).

BIBLIOG: Autobiography, *My Farce From My Elbow*, 1977; *Farce About Face*, 1989; *Tour de Farce*, 1992.

RKO (Radio-Keith-Orpheum) *see* Hollywood studios in Britain

Roache, Linus (*b* Burnley, 1964). Actor. Son of **William Roache** (*b* Ilkeston, 1932), star of *Coronation Street*, in which the nine-year-old Linus made his debut, and Anna CROPPER (divorced 1974), Roache made a very auspicious starring debut as the tormented gay *Priest* (1994), then took himself off on a spiritual pilgrimage to India. He had also done the TV series *Seaforth* in 1994, but it was then three years before he was on screen again, as journalist-lover-reluctant exploiter Merton Densher in the powerful ADAPTATION of *The Wings of the Dove* (1997, UK/US). Good-looking and intense, he is effortlessly convincing in such complex roles, and plays a very tormented character, the wild-haired poet Coleridge, in *Pandaemonium* (2001). Also gave acclaimed stage performances with Ralph FIENNES in *Richard II* and *Coriolanus* (2000) and was in the US film *Hart's War* (2002).

OTHER BRITISH FILMS: *Link*, *No Surrender* (1985), *Best* (2000, UK/Ire).

Robb, David (*b* London, 1947). Actor. Leading man on stage and TV from the early 70s, Robb, brought up in Edinburgh, has filmed only rarely. He was one of the officers in both *Conduct Unbecoming* (1975) and *The Four Feathers* (1978), and a doctor in the WW1 drama, *Regeneration* (1997), but has made more impact on TV, in, for example, *The Glittering Prizes* (1976), or as Lancelot in *The Legend of King Arthur* (1979). Also played Prince Charles in the execrable telemovie, *Charles & Diana: A Royal Love Story* (1982). Married to **Briony McRoberts** (*b* Welwyn Garden City, 1957), who has appeared in several British films, including *Fellow Traveller* (1989, UK/US).

OTHER BRITISH FILMS: *The Swordsman* (1974), *The Deceivers* (1988), *The World Is Not Enough* (1999, UK/US, voice).

Robbins, Richard (*b* Rockland, Massachusetts, 1940). Composer. Almost all of Robbins's work for the screen has been for the MERCHANT IVORY team. As far back as *The Europeans* (1979), he showed himself sensitively attuned to their thematic preoccupations, with a score that drew, for this elegant tale of cultural conflict, on Clara Schumann, *La Traviata*, Stephen Foster and 'Beautiful river'. He won a BAA for *A Room with a View* (1985). A graduate of New England Conservatory, he also studied in Vienna.

OTHER BRITISH FILMS INCLUDE: *Jane Austen in Manhattan* (1980, UK/US), *Quartet* (1981, UK/Fr), *Heat and Dust* (1982), *The Bostonians* (1984, UK/US), *Maurice* (1987), *Howards End* (1992), *The Remains of the Day* (1993), *Surviving Picasso* (1996, UK/US), *A Soldier's Daughter Never Cries* (1998, UK/US), *The Golden Bowl* (2000, UK/Fr/US).

Roberts, Amy (*b* London, 1949). Costume designer. BAA-winner for her designs for *An Englishman Abroad* (1983), contrasting Alan BATES's threadbare echoes of Savile Row with Coral BROWNE's furred Western luxury, Roberts has been eclectic in her choice of assignments. She dressed Prunella SCALES as the Queen, with omnipresent handbag and corgi, in TV's *A Question of Attribution* (1992), and, at some remove, the assorted drug scenes of *Traffik* (1989); on film, she has dressed the rural 20s spoof, *Cold Comfort Farm* (1995, TV, some cinemas) and the up-against-it colliers and their women in *Brassed Off* (1996, UK/US).

OTHER BRITISH FILMS INCLUDE: *Madame Sousatzka* (1988), *Close My Eyes*, *London Kills Me* (1991), *Closing Numbers* (1993), *Element of Doubt* (1996), *Station Jim* (2001).

Roberts, Andy (*b* London, 1946) Composer. Much associated with the work of Antonia BIRD, Roberts composed the score for her five-part BBC drama series, *The Men's Room* (1991), for her powerful feature debut, *Priest* (1994), her American teenage *amour fou*-cum-road movie, *Mad Love* (1995) and for the heist-gone-wrong THRILLER, *Face* (1997).

OTHER BRITISH FILMS: *Loose Connections* (1983, co-comp), *Safe* (1993, m adviser), *Going Off Big Time* (2000).

Roberts, Evelyn (*b* Reading, 1886 – *d* London, 1962). Actor. Former naval commander who served in WW1, turning to the stage in 1918, and London in 1924, in many famous and popular plays, including *Journey's End* (1929, NY). Entered films in 1928, making over a dozen before rejoining the Navy (1939–45), playing the Prince of Wales in *The Return of the Scarlet Pimpernel* (1937), and an MP in *The Winslow Boy* (1948) and the Court President in *The Green Scarf* (1954). Dignity was his thing, but Gracie FIELDS punctured it in *Sing As We Go!* (1934). Married **Daisy Cordell**, who appeared in at least one silent film, *Fine Feathers* (1915).

OTHER BRITISH FILMS INCLUDE: *Bolibar* (1928), *Say It with Music* (1932), *Sorrell and Son* (1933), *No Limit* (1935), *Keep Fit* (1937), *The Heart of the Matter* (1953), *The Man of the Moment* (1955), *A Touch of the Sun* (1956), *The Spaniard's Curse* (1957, unc).

Roberts, Ewan (*b* Edinburgh, 1914 – *d* London, 1983). Actor. RN: Thomas McEwan Hutchinson. Former tweed designer who took to the stage in 1935, served with the Royal Naval Reserve (1941–46), and made his London debut with the Old Vic's 1946–47 season. In films from *The Way We Live* (1946), he played about two dozen supporting roles, often as policemen and other (often Scottish) officials, like the customs inspector in *River Beat* (1953). Also TV, including *Colonel March of Scotland Yard* (1953–55) and a long-running stage hit, *Roar Like a Dove* (1957–59).

OTHER BRITISH FILMS INCLUDE: *London Belongs to Me* (1948), *The Man in the White Suit* (1951), *Angels One Five* (1952), *The Heart of the Matter* (1953), *The Ladykillers* (1955), *Night of the Demon* (1957), *The Three Lives of Thomasina* (1963), *Country Dance* (1969, + dial d), *The Internecine Project* (1974).

Roberts, J(ohn).H. (*b* London, 1884 – *d* London, 1961). Actor. Former shipping office clerk who made his stage debut in 1909 (London 1913), was in the Army from 1914 till 1919, made his film debut in 1920, repeating his stage role of the auctioneer in *The Skin Game*. Appeared in many popular plays and about three dozen films, usually as professional men, including many doctors, like the one who attends Valerie HOBSON in *Blanche Fury* (1947), and the Dean in *Charley's (Big-Hearted) Aunt* (1940).

OTHER BRITISH FILMS INCLUDE: *The Constant Nymph* (1928), *A Safe Affair* (+ co-p), *Alibi* (1931), *Royal Cavalcade* (1935), *Young and Innocent* (1937), *The Divorce of Lady X* (1938), *Goodbye, Mr Chips* (1939, unc), *Night Train to Munich* (1940), *Dangerous Moonlight* (1941), *Uncensored* (1942), *The Agitator* (1945), *The Ghosts of Berkeley Square* (1947), *London Belongs to Me*, *Quartet* (1948).

Roberts, Mike (*b* Woking, 1940 – *d* Bath, 2000). Camera operator. Described by director Alan PARKER, for whom he worked eight times, as 'one of the finest camera operators in the world, and probably the greatest film cameraman ever', his skills were recognised by the BAA's Michael Balcon Award for outstanding contribution to film. He also worked several times with Neil JORDAN, on *Mona Lisa* (1986) and others, and for Steven Spielberg, Roland JOFFE, Richard ATTENBOROUGH. Unknown to the public but greatly valued by film-makers for his consummate ease with everything from sprawling spectacle to human close-ups.

OTHER BRITISH FILMS INCLUDE: *The Rocky Horror Picture Show* (1975), *Priest of Love* (1980), *Britannia Hospital* (1982), *The Company of Wolves*, *The Killing Fields* (1984), *The Mission* (1985), *The Commitments* (1991, UK/US) *Shadowlands* (1993, UK/US), *Evita* (1996, UK/US), *The Butcher Boy* (1997, UK/Ire), *Notting Hill* (UK/US), *Angela's Ashes* (Ire/US) (1999), *Chocolat* (2000, UK/US).

Roberts, Nancy (*b* St Asaph, Wales, 1892 – *d* London, 1962). Actress. Stage actress who appeared in a couple of silents – *Signals in the Night* (1913), *The Devil's Profession* (1915 – doctor injects patients with madness serum) – and returned in late middle age to play a further half-dozen, including two Mothers Superior. More notable is the one who rebukes Deborah KERR for self-importance in *Black Narcissus* (1947); her *Warning to Wantons* (1948) is wasted on Anne VERNON. Famously, 'Gran' in TV's *The Grove Family* (1954–57) and the film made from it, *It's a Great Day* (1955).

OTHER BRITISH FILMS: *Prison Without Bars* (1938), *Cosh Boy* (1953), *Carry On Regardless* (1961).

Roberts, Rachel (*b* Llanelli, Wales, 1927 – *d* Los Angeles, 1980) Actress. Actress of fervour and passion, who gave forthright performances in two key films of the 60s. After a Baptist upbringing (which she rebelled against), followed by the University of Wales and RADA, she was on stage from 1951. Made her film debut in the Welsh-set comedy *Valley of Song* (1953), but was too direct and intense to fit comfortably into leading roles in 50s British films. However, these qualities led to her breakthrough BAA-winning portrayal of Brenda in Karel REISZ's *Saturday Night and Sunday Morning* (1960). Lindsay ANDERSON saw that she would be perfect as the suffering Mrs Hammond in *This Sporting Life* (1963, BAA/a and AAn). In theatre, she played at the Royal Court and was the life-enhancing tart *Maggie May* in Lionel BART's musical (1964). In films she continued to play women with lusty appetites (as in Lindsay ANDERSON's *O Lucky Man!* (1973), although the haunting Australian-made *Picnic at Hanging Rock* (1975) provided her with a different kind of role. Appeared in supporting roles in several US films after relocating to Los Angeles in the early 70s, her final British film being *Yanks* (1979, BAA/supp a). Impulsive, insecure, with self-destructive tendencies, she died from an overdose of barbiturates. Married (1) Alan DOBIE (1955–61), (2) Rex HARRISON (1962–71).

OTHER BRITISH FILMS: *The Weak and the Wicked*, *The Limping Man* (1953), *The Crowded Day* (1954), *Davy*, *The Good Companions* (1956), *Our Man in Havana* (1959), *Girl on Approval* (1961), *The Reckoning* (1969), *Baffled!* (1972, UK/US), *Alpha Beta* (1972), *Great Expectations*, *The Belstone Fox*, *Murder on the Orient Express* (1974).

BIBLIOG: Autobiography, Ed. Alexander Walker, *No Bells on Sunday*, 1984. Roger Philip Mellor.

Robertson, Iain (*b* Glasgow, 1981). Actor. Short, slight Scot who, at 13, left a poverty-stricken background to take up a scholarship with the Sylvia Young Theatre School in London. Made a striking impression as the furtive, tormented teenager in *Small Faces* (1995) and confirmed this promise in subsequent films, especially as the neophyte thug who worships Billy CONNELLY's character in *The Debt Collector* (1999).

OTHER BRITISH FILMS: *Plunkett & Macleane*, *The Match* (1999, UK/Ire/US).

Robeson, Paul (*b* Princeton, NY, 1898 – *d* Philadelphia, 1976). Singer, actor and activist. A law graduate of Columbia University, Robeson attracted large stage, film and recording audiences, through his magnificent bass voice. His fame increased following an appearance as Joe (and his recording of 'Ol' Man River') in the London production of *Show Boat* (1928), a role he reprised in NY and the 1936 Hollywood film version. Popular with British audiences, he was offered starring roles in British films, which gave him more scope than those available to black performers in Hollywood. *Sanders of the River* (1935) was a success, though Robeson later criticised the representation of Africans as savage children. *Song of Freedom* (1936) featured Robeson as a dock-worker turned concert singer, who is heir to an African tribal throne; once again the pan-African ideas voiced in this film and *Jericho* (1937) appeared merely to collude with British colonialism. Disillusioned, Robeson studied socialist and Africanist writings, and in 1938 acted at London's socialist Unity Theatre. In 1948–50, during the Cold War, his support of (and visits to) the USSR led to his passport being withdrawn. He used his celebrity to publicise a range of contentious issues (championing black minority and labour rights in the US and communism in the USSR) in an attempt to influence public opinion and promote social change. Married **Eslanda Robeson** (*b* 1921 – *d* 1965), who appeared with him in the experimental film, *Borderline* (1930), which he made for the group associated with the film theory journal, *CLOSE UP* and *Big Fella* (1937).

OTHER BRITISH FILMS: *King Solomon's Mines* (1937), *The Proud Valley* (1940).

BIBLIOG: Autobiography, *Here I Stand*, 1958.Roger Philip Mellor.

Robey, Sir George (*b* London, 1869 – *d* Saltdean, 1954). Actor. RN: George Edward Wade. On stage from 1891, after being intended for an engineering career, he was a major MUSIC HALL performer, billed as 'The Prime Minister of Mirth', whose musical monologues as captured on film seem very dated. As evidenced by his performance as Sancho Panza in G.W. Pabst's *Don Quixote* (1933), he might have been a great legitimate actor, and he is briefly memorable as Falstaff in OLIVIER's *Henry V* (1944) and as Sam Weller in *The Pickwick Papers* (1952). Awarded CBE, 1919; knighted, 1954.

OTHER BRITISH FILMS INCLUDE: *The Rats* (1900), *Good Queen Bess* (1913), *George Robey Turns Anarchist* (1914), *Blood Tells* (1916), *Doing His Bit* (1917), *Don Quixote, Harlequinade* (1923), *Safety First* (1928), *Marry Me* (1932), *Chu-Chin-Chow* (1934), *Royal Cavalcade* (1935), *Southern Roses* (1936), *A Girl Must Live* (1939), *Salute John Citizen* (1942), *They Met in the Dark* (1943), *The Trojan Brothers* (1945). AS.

BIBLIOG: Autobiography, *Looking Back on Life*, 1933; James Harding, *George Robey*, 1991.

Robin Hood The cinematic image of Robin Hood was definitively established in Hollywood by Douglas Fairbanks and Errol FLYNN. Apart from a handful of short silent films (1909, 1912, 1913), the first major British Robin Hood film was the Walt DISNEY production *The Story of Robin Hood and His Merrie Men* (1952) with Richard TODD. There was a trio of sprightly HAMMER FILMS adventures, *Men of Sherwood Forest* (1954) with Don Taylor, *Sword of Sherwood Forest* (1960) with Richard GREENE and *A Challenge for Robin Hood* (1967) with Barrie INGHAM. But the major development in the saga was the 143-episode ITV series *The Adventures of Robin Hood* (1955–59) with Richard Greene. The first major Robin Hood film for over 20 years was Richard LESTER's elegiac *Robin and Marian* (1976, UK/US) with Sean CONNERY and Audrey HEPBURN. It was, however, another television series, HTV's 26-episode *Robin of Sherwood* (1984–86), which imbued the saga with magic and mysticism. This directly influenced *Robin Hood: Prince of*

Thieves (1991), the Hollywood blockbuster with Kevin Costner that was shot in Britain. At the same time, *Robin Hood* with Patrick Bergin, made for American television but released to British cinemas, took a decidedly more realistic view of the legend.

BIBLIOG: Scott Allen Nollen, *Robin Hood: A Cinematic History of the English Outlaw and His Scottish Counterparts*, 1999. Jeffrey Richards.

Robinson, Bernard (*b* Liverpool, 1912 – *d* Surrey, 1970). Production designer. One of the most prolific art directors/ production designers in British cinema, Robinson's reputation chiefly rests on his stylish work for numerous HAMMER HORROR films of the 50s and 60s, including notably *The Hound of the Baskervilles* (1959) and *The Brides of Dracula* (1960), and very late in his career *The Devil Rides Out* and the modern SCIENCE-FICTION of *Quatermass and the Pit* (1967). On modest budgets, he created sumptuous, threatening and/or threatened worlds in such films, but he was equally adroit in suggesting a suburban bank branch in the excellent '**B**' FILM, *Cash on Demand* (1961). Educated at the Liverpool School of Art, he started in films at WARNER BROS in 1935 and during WW2 he was a camouflage designer for the Air Ministry.

OTHER BRITISH FILMS INCLUDE: (des) *While I Live* (1947), *The Curse of Frankenstein* (1957), *The Revenge of Frankenstein* (1958), *Yesterday's Enemy* (1959), *The Damned* (1961), *The Kiss of the Vampire* (1962), *The Gorgon*, *The Secret of Blood Island* (1964), *Dracula – Prince of Darkness*, *Rasputin the Mad Monk* (1965), *The Plague of the Zombies*, *The Reptile*, *The Witches* (1966); (art d) *The Case of the Frightened Lady* (1940), *The Shop at Sly Corner* (1946), *Noose* (1948), *Double Confession* (1950), *The Broken Horseshoe*, *Albert RN*, (1953), *The Good Die Young* (1954), *Escapade* (1955), *Reach for the Sky* (1956), *Quatermass 2* (1957), *Dracula*, *Carve Her Name With Pride* (1958), *The Mummy* (1959), *The Two Faces of Dr Jekyll*, *The Terror of the Tongs* (co-) (1960), *The Curse of the Werewolf* (1961, co-), *The Phantom of the Opera*, *Paranoiac* (1962, co-), *The Curse of the Mummy's Tomb* (1964), *Frankenstein Must Be Destroyed* (1969).

Robinson, Bruce (*b* London, 1946). Director, screenwriter. One of the more engaging figures round the periphery of British films in the last several decades, Robinson, born in North London but relocated to Broadstairs, Kent, aged six, came from an unhappy family background and after graduating from Central School had a decade or more of the struggling actor's life. This included Benvolio in *Romeo and Juliet* (1968), warding off ZEFFIRELLI's attentions the while, and the lead opposite Isabelle Adjani in Truffaut's *The Story of Adèle H* (1975, Fr). His two major breakthroughs came in the 80s: David PUTTNAM gave him the chance to write the BAA-winning and AA-nominated screenplay for *The Killing Fields* (1984), the widely-acclaimed drama of the tragedy of Cambodia; and in wild contrast he directed and wrote *Withnail & I* (1987), the wonderfully scabrous cult comedy about two out-of-work actors coping with rural England. Nothing he has directed since has matched its anarchic wit, and that's including several US-made films, but he returned to acting with muted éclat in the charming and funny *Still Crazy* (1998, UK/US) as the former guitarist of a reuniting 70s rock group.

OTHER BRITISH FILMS: (a, unless noted) *I Love You, I Hate You* (1968), *The Music Lovers*, *Private Road*, *Tam-Lin* (1971), *Violent Summer* (1975), *The Brute* (1976), *How to Get Ahead in Advertising* (1989, d, sc).

BIBLIOG: Alistair Owen (ed), *Smoking in Bed. Conversations with Bruce Robinson*, 2000.

Robinson, Cardew (*b* Goodmayes, 1923 – *d* Roehampton, 1992). Actor. RN: Douglas Robinson. Comic character player, popular on radio and TV, who created the prankster persona of

'Cardew the Cad', and took it into film in 1955's *Fun at St Fanny's*. Thereafter, tall, skinny Robinson played small parts in 20-odd films, including the undertaker with whose umbrella Cyril CUSACK duels in *Waltz of the Toreadors* (1962). Much TV, including *Fire Crackers* (1964–65) and *Celebrity Squares* (1978).

OTHER BRITISH FILMS INCLUDE: *Happy is the Bride* (1957), *I'm All Right Jack* (1959), *A French Mistress* (1960), *The Wrong Arm of the Law*, *Crooks Anonymous* (1962), *Father Came Too!* (1963), *Alfie* (1966), *Carry On Up the Khyber* (1968), *The Magnificent Seven Deadly Sins* (1971), *Shirley Valentine* (1989, UK/US).

Robinson, Joe (*b* South Africa, 1929). Actor. Former heavyweight wrestler who came to London in the early 50s, appearing on stage in *Wish You Were Here* (1953) and made film debut in Carol REED's *A Kid for Two Farthings* (1954), as Sam, the circus strong man who falls for Diana DORS. Appeared in nearly 20 further films, including a small part in *Diamonds Are Forever* (1971), the BOND entry about South African diamond smuggling, and several European films. Once ran a gymnasium for film and stage stars.

OTHER BRITISH FILMS INCLUDE: *The Flesh Is Weak* (1957), *Sea Fury* (1958), *The Bulldog Breed* (1960), *Carry On Regardless* (1961), *The Loneliness of the Long Distance Runner* (1962), *Doctor in Distress* (1963).

Robinson, John (*b* Liverpool, 1908 – *d* London, 1979). Actor. Urbane character player on London stage from 1935, after rep experience, in films from 1936, and engaged in war service (1940–45). His most notable film roles were as Professor Quatermass in TV's *Quatermass 2* (1955) and Sir Colenso Ridgeon whose invention of a cure for TB causes *The Doctor's Dilemma* (1958). Acted with Ingrid BERGMAN in the 1971 revival of SHAW's *Captain Brassbound's Conversion*, and on TV from 1947.

OTHER BRITISH FILMS INCLUDE: *All That Glitters* (1936), *The Lion Has Wings* (1939), *Under Your Hat* (1940), *Uneasy Terms* (1948), *Emergency Call* (1952), *The Constant Husband* (1954), *Fortune Is a Woman* (1957), *Nothing But the Night* (1972).

Robson, Dame Flora (*b* South Shields, 1902 – *d* Brighton, 1984). Actress. Immensely distinguished character star of stage and screen: too plain for leading romantic roles, she wisely settled early into middle-aged parts, playing many a dangerous spinster (as in *Poison Pen*, 1939, when she was still well short of 40), homely housekeeper (she was Nelly Dean in Hollywood's *Wuthering Heights*, 1939) or regal personage. She was, for instance, the Russian Empress Elisabeth in *Catherine the Great* (1934), Elizabeth I in *Fire Over England* (1937), and, in an extract from this, *The Lion Has Wings* (1939), and Hollywood's *The Sea Hawk* (1940). But there was much more than this to her illustrious career.

Educated at Palmer's Green High School and RADA-Bronze Medallist, she was on the London stage by 1921, acting a vast range of classical and modern characters: she did Shakespeare at the Old Vic (1933–34), the murderous Ellen Creed in *Ladies in Retirement* (1940, NY) and a harrowing Mrs Alving in *Ghosts* (1958–59). Her stage career is remarkable for the versatility of the leads she played, but her screen role-call is, unusually, almost of comparable quality. She is very moving as the careworn Mrs Ellis in *Great Day* (1945), forcing Eric PORTMAN to confront the sham of his life – and later forgiving him; is a startling Ftatateeta, 'wrinkled deep in time' indeed, as her famous mistress clearly is not, in *Caesar and Cleopatra* (1945) and even more so as the King's raddled ex-mistress in *Saraband for Dead Lovers* (1948); is touching as a spinster reclaiming a lost love in *Holiday Camp* (1947); makes an impressively unsympathetic, bossy MP in *Frieda* (1947); and her chain-smoking Miss Barker-Wise, another tough MP, in *Guns at Batasi* (1964) is a ripe, thoroughly known character. The list is so full of mesmeric stuff that it is sad to note that her last film was the inane *Clash of the Titans* (1981, UK/US), in which she plays a Stygian Witch, unrecognisable but for the distinctive voice. In Hollywood she was Oscar-nominated as Ingrid BERGMAN's mulatto servant in *Saratoga Trunk* (1945), one of her least achievements. On TV before WW2 as *Anna Christie* (1936), but she seems not to have taken the medium very seriously, contenting herself in later life with a few cameos. Created CBE in 1952, DBE in 1960; it is hard to think who might be her successor.

OTHER BRITISH FILMS: *A Gentleman of Paris* (1931), *Dance Pretty Lady* (1932), *One Precious Year* (1933), *Lest We Forget* (short), *Farewell Again* (1937), *Smith* (1939), *Two Thousand Women* (1944), *Dumb Dora Discovers Tobacco* (short), *The Years Between* (1946), *Black Narcissus*, *Good-Time Girl* (1947), *Tall Headlines* (1952), *Malta Story* (1953), *Romeo and Juliet* (1954, UK/It), *No Time for Tears, High Tide at Noon, The Gypsy and the Gentleman* (1957), *Innocent Sinners* (1958), *Murder at the Gallop* (1963), *A King's Story* (short, voice), *Those Magnificent Men . . .*, *Young Cassidy* (1965), *Cry in the Wind* (UK/Greece), *Eye of the Devil, The Shuttered Room* (1966), *Fragment of Fear, The Beast in the Cellar* (1970), *Alice's Adventures in Wonderland* (1972), *Dominique* (1978).

BIBLIOG: Kenneth Barrow, *Flora: The Life of Dame Flora Robson*, 1981.

Robson, Mark (*b* Montreal, 1913 – *d* London, 1978). Director, editor. After an apprenticeship at RKO where he edited *The Magnificent Ambersons* (1942) and edited and/or directed several of Val LEWTON's poetic HORROR films, Robson became identified with the tough school of post-war film-making, but was competent across several GENRES. He made only a half-dozen British films, of which only *The Inn of the Sixth Happiness* (1958), which enshrines Robert DONAT's last film role, is of much interest, but the others, except for the muddled *Nine Hours to Rama* (1962), at least tell their routine stories briskly.

OTHER BRITISH FILMS: *Hell Below Zero* (1953), *A Prize of Gold* (1955), *The Inspector* (1962, p), *Avalanche Express* (1979, Ire, died during post-production).

Roc, Patricia (*b* London, 1918). RN: Felicia Rose. Patricia Roc began her screen career in the late 30s with *The Gaunt Stranger* (1938) and *The Rebel Son* (1939, UK/Fr). However, wartime saw her gain prominence as one of the most popular contemporary stars of the era. After appearing in John BAXTER's *Let the People Sing* (1942), she became a 'People's War' heroine in *Millions Like Us* (1943) before featuring in GAINSBOROUGH MELO-DRAMAS. Although Roc became associated with 'nice girl' roles in *Madonna of the Seven Moons* (1944) and *The Wicked Lady* (1945), she could also do more complex, tougher females as *Love Story* (1944), *The Brothers* and *Jassy* (1947) revealed. In *The Brothers*, she combined femme fatale and 'wronged woman' characters in her performance. Roc provided a perfect complement to Margaret LOCKWOOD in Gainsborough costume melodramas. She also played herself in a cameo in *Holiday Camp* (1947) as well as performing a dual role as human and robot in the silly comedy *The Perfect Woman* (1949). Unlike LOCKWOOD's sensual performances, Roc usually represented the normal, unthreatening aspect of the attractive sincere British female stereotype in her films. Her acting potential seen in *The Brothers* was never developed. Like Phyllis CALVERT she found Hollywood wasted her talents as *Canyon Passage* (1946) and *The Man on the Eiffel Tower* (1950) both revealed. She returned to British films performing different variations of her

sincere star persona before retiring after playing 'first wife' to George SANDERS in *Bluebeard's Ten Honeymoons* (1960).

OTHER BRITISH FILMS: *A Window in London* (1939), *Three Silent Men, Gentleman of Venture, Pack Up Your Troubles, Three Silent Men* (1940), *My Wife's Family* (1941), *Suspected Person* (1942), *Two Thousand Women* (1944), *Johnny Frenchman* (1945), *When the Bough Breaks, So Well Remembered* (1947), *One Night With You* (1948), *Circle of Danger* (1950), *Something Money Can't Buy* 1952), *The Hypnotist* (1957). Tony Williams.

Rock, Crissy (*b* Liverpool, 1958). Actress. Stand-up Liverpool club comedienne Rock was chosen by Ken LOACH for the starring role of Maggie, the woman forced to surrender her children to social workers, in *Ladybird Ladybird* (1994), and she won the Berlin Festival Silver Bear award for the naked honesty of her performance. Since then, she has appeared in *Under the Skin* (1997) and in such high quality TV as *Dockers* (1999) and *Clocking Off* (2000), plus a continuing role in *Brookside* (2001-), but she ought to have films built around her.

Rock, Joe (*b* New York, 1890/1 – *d* Sherman Oaks, California, 1984). Producer. In Britain from 1930s [founder of **Rock Production Company**].

Rock Productions Named after Joe ROCK an American showman-comedian who took over the Neptune studios at ELSTREE in 1935 to make 'QUOTA QUICKIES' featuring artists like dance band leader Harry Roy. Backing came from John Henry Iles but the company was short-lived and overextended itself. Iles filed for bankruptcy. Rock's only notable achievement was the break it gave Michael POWELL who made his directorial debut for the company with *The Edge of the World*, 1937, which was shot entirely on a Scottish island. Stephen Brown.

Roddam, Franc (*b* Stockton-on-Tees, 1946). Director. Came to films via the London Film School and made several well-received TV DOCUMENTARIES, including *The Family* (1974) and *Dummy* (1977), before directing his first feature, the rock opera, *Quadrophenia* (1979, + co-sc), with a cast of future stars. Has since worked mainly in the US where his first film was *The Lords of Discipline* (1983). Married to **Carina Cooper** (*b c* 1961) who was on the crew for *Aria* (1987) for which Roddam directed and wrote a segment.

OTHER BRITISH FILMS: *Birthday* (1969, short), *The Bride* (1985).

Rodgers, Anton (*b* Wisbech, 1933). Actor. Comic character player now best known for such TV roles as Julia MACKENZIE's wry husband in *Fresh Fields* (1984–86), later relocated to France as *French Fields* (1989–91). LAMDA-trained and on the West End and other stages from his teens and later a notable lead in such plays as *Forget-Me-Not-Lane* (1971), he made a rash of films in the 60s, including two 'CARRY ON' items (. . . *Cruising*, 1962; . . . *Jack*, 1964) and starred in a lesser BOULTING brothers' caper comedy, *Rotten to the Core* (1965).

OTHER BRITISH FILMS INCLUDE: *Crash Drive* (1959), *The Spider's Web* (1960), *The Traitors* (1962), *The Iron Maiden* (1963), *Where Eagles Dare* (1968), *Scrooge* (1970), *The Day of the Jackal* (1973, UK/Fr), *The Fourth Protocol* (1987), *Impromptu* (1991).

Rodway, Geoffrey (*b* Johannesburg, 1911). Make-up artist. Educated at King Edward VI School, Retford, trained at Sheffield College of Art, Rodway entered films in 1932 at GAUMONT–BRITISH as an apprentice. After WW2 service (1941–46), he worked for various companies, including TWO CITIES, before going under contract with RANK with whom he worked throughout the 50s and 60s, inevitably making up the gang for the 'DOCTOR' films and later the 'CARRY ON' series.

OTHER BRITISH FILMS INCLUDE: *Pimpernel Smith* (1941), *Vice Versa* (1947), *The Story of Robin Hood . . .* (1952), *The Kidnappers* (1953), *The Purple Plain* (1954), *Doctor at Sea* (1955), *The Battle of the River Plate* (1956), *Carry On Sergeant*, *The Thirty Nine Steps* (1958), *Whistle Down the Wind* (1961), *The Informers* (1963), *Carry On Jack*, . . . *Cleo* (1964), *Doctor in Clover*, *Carry On Screaming* (1966), *The Sorcerers* (1967), *Carry On Doctor* (1968), . . . *Camping* (1969), . . . *Loving* (1970), . . . *Behind* (1975).

Rodway, Norman (*b* Dublin, 1929 – *d* Banbury, 2001). Actor. Rodway's East End family relocated to Dublin when he was a child and he graduated from Dublin's Trinity College, becoming first a teacher, then an academic, before turning to the theatre. Joined the RSC in 1966, winning kudos as Hotspur in *Henry IV, Pt I*, a role he also played that year in Orson WELLES's beautiful elegiac *Chimes at Midnight* (Switz, Sp), in which his strong-jawed stockiness contrasted tellingly with Keith BAXTER's morose Hal. He did masses of TV, including the star role in *Tycoon* (1978) with Jean KENT, but though there were about a dozen film roles, including co-starring with Judi DENCH in *Four in the Morning* (1965), few compared with Hotspur. Married (1 of 4) Pauline DELANEY and (2) casting director Mary SELWAY.

OTHER BRITISH FILMS INCLUDE: *This Other Eden* (1959, Ire), *Johnny Nobody* (1960), *The Webster Boy*, *The Quare Fellow* (1962), *I'll Never Forget What's 'is Name* (1967), *Who Dares Wins* (1982), *Vicious Circle* (1998), *County Kilburn* (2000).

Rodwell, Stanley (*b* London, 1902 – *d* London, 1969). Cinematographer. Worked with Anthony ASQUITH on several early films, including *Underground* (1928), *Shooting Stars* (1928, co-c), *A Cottage on Dartmoor* (1929) and *Tell England* (1931, co-c), some of the most visually ambitious films of their time, shot a few more light features in the early 30s, then went to the SHELL FILM UNIT (1934–53).

OTHER BRITISH FILMS INCLUDE: *The Battles of the Coronel and the Falkland Islands* (1927, co-c), *The Barton Mystery* (1932), *The Blarney Stone*, *One Precious Year* (1933), *Father O'Flynn* (1935).

Roeg, Nicolas (*b* London, 1928). Cinematographer, director. Nicolas Roeg once defined his cinematic credo as: 'Abandon preconceptions all ye who enter here.' His films at their best shake our perceptions about character, about cinema. In films such as *Performance* (1970, co-d Donald CAMMELL), *Walkabout* (1970, Aust), *Don't Look Now* (1973, UK/It) and *Bad Timing* (1980), he has compelled us to look at our world afresh, to question its appearances, to look beneath the surface. His films shake us up; they give us new eyes.

After national service, Roeg drifted into the film industry in the late 40s, working his way steadily up from tea-maker to clapper boy to camera operator. He worked on the second unit of such distinguished films as *The Sundowners* (1960) and *Lawrence of Arabia* (1962) and was fired from *Doctor Zhivago* (1965, UK/US) for telling David LEAN what to do with his camera. But by this time, he was amassing a considerable reputation as a great cinematographer: some of the films on which he worked – *The Masque of the Red Death* (1964), *Far from the Madding Crowd* (1967), *Petulia* (1968) – are amongst the most strikingly photographed of the decade. A particularly rewarding association was with François Truffaut on *Fahrenheit 451* (1966). Truffaut had famously commented to Hitchcock that 'British' and 'cinema' were a contradiction in terms: Roeg might have branched into film direction to prove him wrong.

Yet, if the word 'British' connoted for Truffaut something that was the opposite of good cinema (i.e. emotional constraint, tepid good taste, the prominence of the word over the image), it should be said that Roeg's films are not like that. They pulsate with desire, violence, bloodshed and death – everything in fact, that, as Billy Wilder used to say, makes life worth living. He deals with English people certainly, but he puts them in un-English settings and this leads to what one might call un-English emotions – obsession, hysteria, madness – as the characters catch a glimpse of another world. His stories are often of people adrift from their usual moral moorings and cast into a strange land without a compass: not knowing where they are, they begin to question who they are. It is a visual and narrative strategy for puncturing humanity's complacency about itself, its self-delusions.

It is not only the stories themselves: it is the way he tells them. They do not move in a logical, linear, chronological sequence – any more than our lives do. They go sideways, backwards, upwards, as Roeg revels in the 'time machine' aspect of cinema, its capacity for moving instantly through time and space, past and future. The experience can be unsettling, disorientating. *Performance* acts on us like a powerful drug; *Walkabout* is a sensual rite of passage; *Don't Look Now* blesses or curses us all with second sight; *The Man Who Fell to Earth* (1976) provides an alien vision of fallen modern man, and so on. All very disturbing, but, then, significant art seeks not to confirm what we already know: it seeks to give us new perceptions, to shed light on our dark places. Admittedly, it would be idle to pretend that Roeg's films always succeed, and after the distribution debacle of the intermittently remarkable *Eureka* (1982, UK/US), there has been a marked falling off of accomplishment. But for film makers who see cinema not simply as a narrative medium but as a stylistic and psychological adventure into the unknown, Roeg remains a hero and an inspiration. Married (1) Susan STEPHEN; (2) Theresa RUSSELL. His sister was Nicolette ROEG.

OTHER BRITISH FILMS INCLUDE: (d) *Insignificance* (1985), *Castaway* (1986), *Track 29* (1988), *The Witches* (1989), *Heart of Darkness* (1994), *Two Deaths* (1995). Neil Sinyard.

Roeg, Nicolette (*b* London, 1925 – *d* London, 1994). Actress. Of Dutch extraction, Roeg had a fine musical comedy voice and had some success on the stage (first in West End in 1947), and appeared in a few films. Sadly, they were distinctly second-rate, all but the last made for BUTCHER's. Her brother is Nicolas ROEG. Married (2) to stage actor and singer **Barry Sinclair** (*b* London, 1911), who appeared in several British films including *Half a Sixpence* (1967, UK/US).

BRITISH FILMS: *My Ain Folk* (1944), *Home Sweet Home* (1945), *Under New Management*, *I'll Turn to You* (1946), *All the Right Noises* (1969).

Roëves, Maurice (*b* Sunderland, 1937). Actor. Intense-looking lead and supporting player in films since the mid 60s, most famous for playing Stephen Dedalus in Joseph STRICK's commercially foolhardy *Ulysses* (1967, UK/US). He was one of the enlisting Smith brothers in *Oh! What a Lovely War* (1969) and still doing striking minor roles in the 90s, like the venomous drug-pusher in *The Big Man* (1990). Has had a busy TV career (in US as well as UK series) and acted and/or directed at several Edinburgh Festivals.

OTHER BRITISH FILMS INCLUDE: *The Fighting Prince of Donegal* (1966), *When Eight Bells Toll* (1971), *Young Winston* (1972), *The Eagle Has Landed* (1976), *Who Dares Wins* (1982), *Hidden Agenda* (1990), *The Acid House* (1998), *Beautiful Creatures* (2001).

Rogers, Doris (*b* Cheshire, *c* 1899). Actress. Stage actress from 1918, latterly of imposing dimensions, who played occasional supporting roles in films, including Lady Manbury-Logan-Manbury in *Maytime in Mayfair* (1949), in which she has a brief outraged scene with Michael WILDING who 'insults' her by thinking she is the manageress. Also on TV (e.g. *The Pallisers*, 1974).

OTHER BRITISH FILMS INCLUDE: *The Love Race* (1931), *Trust the Navy* (1935), *Gangway* (1937), *It's Hard to Be Good*, *Trottie True* (1948) *Madame Louise* (1951), *Life with the Lyons*, *The Lyons in Paris* (1954).

Rogers, Eric (*b* Halifax, 1920 – *d* Bucks, 1981). Composer. Rogers had his own orchestra during WW2, did uncredited work as orchestrator on *Night and the City* (1950, UK/US), but his most productive period was from the early 60s to the late 70s, and most of it was as composer-conductor for the 'CARRY ON' series, though unrelated to producer Peter ROGERS. He sometimes composed songs (e.g. for Dilys LAYE in *Carry On Spying* (1964) as well as soundtrack music, where he entered into the parodic spirit of the enterprise for nearly 20 years. His preference was clearly for the light-hearted, with a couple of more sombre entries – *Assault* (1970) and *Revenge* (1971) – and he is alleged to have transcribed the score for the stage play, *Oliver!* (1960), because its composer, Lionel BART, couldn't read or write music.

OTHER BRITISH FILMS INCLUDE: (comp, unless noted) *Meet Me Tonight* (1952, orch, cond), *Meet Mr Lucifer* (1953), *Davy* (1957, co-comp), *Dr No* (1962, cond), *Oliver!* (assoc m sup), *The Best House in London* (m d) (1968), *Toomorrow* (1970, m sup), *Carry On Girls* (1973); (comp/m d) *The Iron Maiden*, *Nurse on Wheels* (1963), *Carry On Jack*, *. . . Cleo* (1964), *. . . Cowboy* (+ a); (comp/cond) *. . . Cabby* (1963), *. . . Screaming*, *Don't Lose Your Head* (1966), *Follow That Camel* (1967), *Carry On Up the Khyber*, *. . . Doctor* (1968), *. . . Camping*, *. . . Again Doctor* (+ a) (1969), *Doctor in Trouble*, *Carry On Up the Jungle*, *. . . Loving* (1970), *. . . Matron*, *. . . Abroad*, *Bless This House* (1972), *No Sex, Please – We're British* (1973), *Carry On Emmannuelle* (1978).

Rogers, P(ercy) Maclean (*b* Croydon, 1899 – *d* Harefield, 1962). Director. One of the most prolific makers of British 'B' MOVIES, Rogers worked on nearly a hundred cheerful COMEDIES and THRILLERS all through the 30s, 40s and 50s. For many years an editor for Herbert WILCOX, he began directing with *The Third Eye* (1929), also writing (or co-writing) as he so often did. Actors like Wally PATCH and Claude HULBERT, or Hugh WILLIAMS and Dinah SHERIDAN, who went on to bigger things, the cinematographer Geoffrey FAITHFULL and art director NORMAN ARNOLD, are recurring names in his films. He worked on SERIES involving the likes of Doris and Elsie WATERS (*Gert and Daisy's Weekend*, 1941, + sc; *Gert and Daisy Clean Up*, 1942); 'Paul Temple' in *Calling Paul Temple* (1948), *Paul Temple's Triumph* (1950), *Paul Temple Returns* (1952); and the 'Toff' in *Salute the Toff*, *Hammer the Toff* (1952). All good clean fun, utterly unsophisticated but it filled the lower half of the double-bill quite painlessly. There were occasional, slightly upmarket ventures, like the musicals which failed to sell Leni LYNN to the public – *Give Me the Stars* and *Heaven Is Round the Corner* (1944) – and the romantic MELODRAMA, *Woman to Woman* (1946), but Rogers's is essentially an honourable journeyman's career.

OTHER BRITISH FILMS: (e) *Rookery Nook*, *A Warm Corner*, *The W Plan* (1930), *The Chance of a Night-Time*, *The Speckled Band* (1931); (co-sc) *The Loves of Robert Burns* (1930), *Mischief* (1931); (d, sc) *The Mayor's Nest* (1932), *Behind the Headlines* (1953, short), *Johnny on the Spot* (1954), *Not So Dusty*, *Assignment Redhead* (1956), *You Pay Your Money* (1957); (d, co-sc) *The Feathered Serpent* (1934), *Marry the Girl* (1935), *A Wife or Two*, *The Happy Family* (1936), *Farewell to Cinderella* (1937), *Garrison Follies* (1940), *Facing the Music* (1941, +p), *The Trojan Brothers* (1945), *The Story of Shirley Yorke* (1948), *Forces' Sweetheart* (1953); (d)

Up for the Derby, *Trouble*, *Summer Lightning*, *The Crime at Blossoms* (+ p) (1933), *Virginia's Husband*, *The Scoop* (+ p), *It's a Cop* (1934), *The Right Age to Marry*, *Old Faithful*, *A Little Bit of Fluff*, *The Shadow of Mike Emerald* (1935), *Twice Branded*, *A Touch of the Moon*, *To Catch a Thief*, *Nothing Like Publicity*, *Not So Dusty*, *The Heirloom Mystery*, *The Busman's Holiday*, *All That Glitters* (1936), *When the Devil Was Well*, *Strange Adventures of Mr Smith*, *Fifty-Shilling Boxer*, *Father Steps Out*, *Why Pick Me?*, *Racing Romance* (1937), *Romance à la carte*, *Paid in Error*, *Miracles Do Happen*, *Merely Mr Hawkins*, *If I Were Boss*, *His Lordship Regrets*, *Easy Riches*, *Darts Are Trumps*, *Weddings Are Wonderful*, *His Lordship Goes to Press* (1938), *Shadowed Eyes*, *Old Mother Riley Joins Up* (1939), *Front Line Kids* (1942), *Variety Jubilee*, *Somewhere in Civvies*, *I'll Walk Beside You* (1943), *Don Chicago* (1945), *Dark Secret* (1949), *Something in the City* (1950), *Old Mother Riley's Jungle Treasure*, *Madame Louise* (1951), *Down Among the Z Men* (1952), *Flannelfoot*, *Alf's Baby* (1953), *Call it Achievement*, *Calling All Cars* (1954, short), *Song of Norway* (short), *The Love Match* (p only) (1955), *The Crooked Sky* (1956, co-story only), *Not Wanted on Voyage*, *Mark of the Phoenix* (1957), *Noddy In Toyland*, *A Clean Sweep* (short) (1958), *Not a Hope in Hell*, *Just Joe* (1960).

Rogers, Paul (*b* Plympton, Devon, 1917). Actor. Famous theatre player, trained at Dartington Hall, on stage from 1938, in the Navy (1940–46), and with the Old Vic (1949–50) and for several successive seasons, playing such major roles as Falstaff. Joined the RSC in 1965 to play Max in Harold PINTER's *Homecoming*, repeating his role in the 1973 film version (UK/US). Appeared in about 20 character roles (usually in suits) in films from 1952, including the clergyman up against tropical hedonism in *The Beachcomber* (1954) and the high-principled solicitor, Hart-Jacobs, in *Life for Ruth* (1962), always making an incisive impression, as he did on TV, but the stage was his first allegiance.

OTHER BRITISH FILMS INCLUDE: *Murder in the Cathedral* (1952), *Beau Brummell*, *Svengali* (1954), *Our Man in Havana* (1959), *The Trials of Oscar Wilde* (as Frank Harris), *A Circle of Deception* (1960), *No Love for Johnnie* (1961), *Billy Budd*, *The Wild and the Willing* (1962), *Stolen Hours* (1963, UK/US), *He Who Rides a Tiger* (1965), *A Midsummer Night's Dream* (as Bottom), *Decline and Fall . . .* (1968), *The Looking Glass War* (1969), *Mister Quilp* (1974).

Rogers, Peter (*b* Rochester, 1916). Producer. Now primarily associated with the extraordinary success of the long-running 'CARRY ON' SERIES, Rogers had in fact been busy in the film industry for more than 20 years before *Carry On Sergeant* (1958) proved such a runaway hit. He began by working on RANK's Religious Films Ltd in the 30s and went from Rank to writing scripts for the BBC. Post-war, he joined GAINS-BOROUGH as script assistant to Muriel BOX and also worked as associate producer on a few of the studio's minor films. In the earlier 50s, he produced several proficient entertainments, including *You Know What Sailors Are!* (1954, + sc), *The Vicious Circle* and *Time Lock* (1957, + sc). Once 'Carry On' made its mark, it was not going to be easy for him – or director Gerald THOMAS (brother of Ralph, who worked for many years with Rogers's wife Betty BOX) – to do anything very different. They gathered a repertory team around them in front of the camera and a reliable band of craftsmen behind it and the results were there for audiences to enjoy, as they did well into the 70s, when *Carry On Emmannuelle* (1978) proved a miscalculation. Until then, Rogers had shown a clear sense of what his team could do and what sorts of targets (including sex, whatever else) the British public was willing to see lampooned in the broad brush strokes of the seaside postcard. In his retirement, he has become a successful and prolific author of thrillers with a Gothic touch.

OTHER BRITISH FILMS INCLUDE: (sc) *When the Bough Breaks* (1947), *The Gay Dog* (1954); (co-sc) *Dear Murderer, Holiday Camp* (1947), *Here Come the Huggetts* (1948); (p) *It's Not Cricket* (1949, assoc), *To Dorothy a Son* (1954, + sc), *Cat Girl* (co-), *After the Ball* (1957), *Carry On Nurse, The Duke Wore Jeans* (1958), . . . *Teacher* (1959), *Please Turn Over,* . . . *Constable* (1960), *Raising the Wind,* . . . *Regardless* (1961), . . . *Cruising, Twice Round the Daffodils* (1962), *Nurse on Wheels,* . . . *Cabby* (1963), . . . *Spying,* . . . *Jack,* . . . *Cleo* (1964), . . . *Cowboy* (1965), . . . *Screaming* (1966), . . . *Follow That Camel* (1967), . . . *Up the Khyber,* . . . *Doctor* (1968), . . . *Camping,* . . . *Again Doctor* (1969), . . . *Up the Jungle,* . . . *Loving* (1970), *Revenge* (exec), *Quest for Love* (exec), . . . *Henry,* . . . *at Your Convenience, All Coppers Are* . . . (exec) (1971), . . . *Matron,* . . . *Abroad, Bless This House* (1972), . . . *Girls* (1973), . . . *Dick* (1974), . . . *Behind* (1975), . . . *England* (1976), . . . *Columbus* (1992, exec).

Rolfe, Guy (*b* London, 1915). Actor. Immensely tall, emaciated leading man of the late 40s and 50s, who, with sad irony, had to withdraw from the role of the tubercular rake redeemed, as he would be, by the pure love of Jean SIMMONS in the 'Sanitorium' episode of *Trio* (1950), because he'd contracted TB. After considerable stage experience in Ireland and a half-dozen small roles, the former racing-car driver was first seriously noticed by filmgoers as the captain of the aircraft crashed in the Alps in *Broken Journey* (1948), and followed this with commanding roles in such films as *Portrait from Life* (1948) as an Army major and *The Spider and the Fly* (1949), perhaps his best film, in which Eric PORTMAN and he play an elegant cat-and-mouse game as, respectively, Sûreté chief and safecracker. But there were other rewarding assignments when his health returned, including a saturnine King John in MGM–British's *Ivanhoe* (1952) and the troubled Padre in Val GUEST's grim war film, *Yesterday's Enemy* (1959). Also worked in international films, including *Young Bess* (1953), as conniving Ned Seymour, and *King of Kings* (1961), as Caiaphas. Married to Jane AIRD.

OTHER BRITISH FILMS INCLUDE: *Uncle Silas, Nicholas Nickleby* (1947), *Easy Money* (1948), *Prelude to Fame, The Reluctant Widow* (1950), *Home to Danger* (1951), *Dance Little Lady* (1954), *It's Never Too Late* (1956), *Girls at Sea* (1958), *The Stranglers of Bombay* (1959), *The Alphabet Murders* (1965), *And Now the Screaming Starts!* (1973), *The Bride* (1985).

Romain, Yvonne (aka Warren; Romaine) (*b* London, 1938). Actress. RN: Warren. The slight shift in surname was perhaps useful in making this exceptionally beautiful brunette seem slightly more exotic: certainly that is how film-makers saw her, casting her as Italian (*The Baby and the Battleship*, 1956), Albanian (*Action of the Tiger*, 1957, billed as 'Warren' however) and Spanish (*The Silent Enemy*, 1958), before finding her niche in a run of HORROR films. These began with *Circus of Horrors* (1960), in which overreacher Anton DIFFRING ambitiously plans to transform her into Helen of Troy, but she is also quite fun as a possibly duplicitous widow in *Smokescreen* (1964). Long married to Leslie BRICUSSE.

OTHER BRITISH FILMS INCLUDE: *Interpol* (1957), *Seven Thunders* (1957), *Corridors of Blood* (1958), *The Curse of the Werewolf, The Frightened City* (1961), *Village of Daughters* (1962), *Devil Doll* (1963), *Double Trouble* (1966).

Rome, Stewart (*b* Newbury, 1886 – *d* Newbury, 1965). Actor. RN: Septimus Ryott. A slightly aloof and aristocratic-looking leading man, Rome, closely associated with Cecil HEPWORTH in the silent era, became a kindly character actor in talkies, making more than 150 films. He studied to be a civil engineer, but instead went on the stage. After performing in Australia, Rome returned to the UK in 1912 and joined the Hepworth Company. Hepworth renamed him Stewart Rome, and when

he left Hepworth, after WW1 service, to join Broadwest he was forced to sue to keep the name. He is memorable as the shell-shocked veteran in George PEARSON's *Reveille* (1924), but is obviously too old to remain an acceptable leading man. In 1942, Rome began appearing for RANK as Dr Goodfellow in a series of inspirational shorts, 'A Sunday Thought for the Coming Week,' roundly jeered at by audiences.

OTHER BRITISH FILMS INCLUDE: *A Throw of the Dice* (1913), *The Heart of Midlothian* (1914), *Barnaby Rudge* (1915), *Comin' Thro' the Rye* (1916), *The Cobweb* (1917), *A Daughter of Eve* (1919), *Her Son* (1920), *The Prodigal Son* (1923), *The Colleen Bawn* (1924), *The Ware Case* (1929), *Kissing Cup's Race* (1930), *Men of Yesterday* (1936), *Wings of the Morning* (1937), *One of Our Aircraft is Missing* 1942), *Jassy* (1947), *Let's Have a Murder* (1950). AS.

Romney, Edana (*b* South Africa, 1919). Actress. Trained as a dancer and on stage in Johannesburg from 1930, Romney later trained at RADA, toured with rep, and played in three insignificant films before being given a big build-up as a sort of exotic when she was starred in *Corridor of Mirrors* (1948, + co-sc). This very arty load of old cobblers failed to find an audience and Romney's cinema career was over, though she did appear in several TV plays. Was briefly married to John WOOLF.

OTHER BRITISH FILMS: *The Silence* (1939), *East of Piccadilly* (1941), *Alibi* (1942).

Romulus Films *see* **Woolf, James and Woolf, John**

Rooke, Arthur H. Actor, director. A stage actor who performed on screen (1915–18), Rooke began his directorial career co-directing with A.E. COLEBY films in which he also appeared: *A Pit-Boy's Romance, The Village Blacksmith, Holy Orders, For All Eternity* (1917), and *Thelma* (1918).

OTHER BRITISH FILMS INCLUDE (d): *The Rugged Path* (1918), *The Garden of Resurrection* (1919), *Brenda of the Barge* (1920, + sc), *A Bachelor's Baby* (1924), *The Blue Peter* (1928). AS.

Rooke, Irene (*b* Bridport, 1877 – *d* Chesham, Bucks, 1958). Actress. Well-known stage actress who appeared in several British films between 1916 (*Lady Windermere's Fan*) and 1932 (*Collision, Threads*), including *Pillars of Society* (1920), with Ellen TERRY, and *Hindle Wakes* (1927), in which she played the mother of hero, John STUART. Married to Milton ROSMER, with whom she appeared in *The Pointing Finger* (1922).

OTHER BRITISH FILMS INCLUDE: *Westward Ho!* (1919), *A Bachelor Husband* (1920), *A Romance of Wastdale* (1921), *The Loves of Mary, Queen of Scots* (1923, as Catherine de Medici), *High Treason* (1929).

Roome, Alfred (*b* London, 1908 – *d* Gerrards Cross, 1997). Editor, director. Bald, portly, genial and modest, Roome, son of the managing director of the *Daily Mirror*, was one of the most respected of British editors. His filmography amounts to a history of popular film-making in Britain, especially of changing tastes in COMEDY, from the ALDWYCH farces of the early 30s, through the sublimely anarchic Will HAY capers, the 'DOCTOR' series from 1954 and the 'CARRY ON' romps from the late 50s to the early 70s. Apart from showing himself uniquely attuned to comic editing, he also cut HITCHCOCK's classic, *The Lady Vanishes* (1938), having worked as a camera assistant on his – Britain's – first talkie, *Blackmail* (1929). It may well have been the early challenge of cutting the intransigently theatrical Tom WALLS's filmings of Aldwych to something like cinematic shape and rhythm that so well equipped him for his long professional life. During WW2 he was seconded to the MOI, editing PROPAGANDA SHORTS, such as Anthony ASQUITH's *Channel Incident* (1940), starring Peggy ASHCROFT;

post-war, he was under contract to Gainsborough, now run by Sydney BOX. At this time, he co-directed (with Roy RICH) two features – the often riotously funny *It's Not Cricket* and the unsettling *My Brother's Keeper* (1948) – but he said in 1992 that he 'wasn't too keen on dealing with actors', and went on to become associate producer for Box. He worked as editor constantly throughout the 50s and 60s, for RANK at PINEWOOD, especially for producer Betty BOX and then for her producer husband Peter ROGERS when 'Carry On' moved there. He was married for nearly 67 years to former actress Janice ADAIR.

OTHER BRITISH FILMS INCLUDE: (cutting) *Ask a Policeman* (1939), *Uncensored* (1942), *Millions Like Us* (1943), *Bees in Paradise* (1944); (assoc p) *Bad Lord Byron, A Boy, a Girl and a Bike, Christopher Columbus* (1949); (e) *Thark* (1932), *Dirty Work* (1934), *Foreign Affaires, Boys Will Be Boys, Stormy Weather* (1935), *Pot Luck* (1936), *Doctor Syn* (co-), *Oh, Mr Porter!* (1937), *Old Bones of the River* (1938), *Rush Hour* (short), *Inspector Hornleigh Goes To It* (1941), *Waterloo Road* (1944), *The Magic Bow* (1946), *Holiday Camp* (1947), *Trio* (1950), *Hotel Sahara, Encore* (1951), *Always a Bride* (1953), *The Woman for Joe* (1955), *Across the Bridge* (1957), *A Tale of Two Cities, The Thirty Nine Steps* (1958), *Conspiracy of Hearts, Doctor in Love* (1960), *No, My Darling Daughter, No Love for Johnnie* (1961), *Doctor in Distress* (1963), *Doctor in Clover* (1966), *Carry On Up the Khyber, . . . Doctor* (1968), *. . . Camping, . . . Again Doctor* (1969), *. . . Up the Jungle, . . . Loving* (1970), *. . . Henry, . . . at Your Convenience* (1971), *. . . Matron, . . . Abroad* (1972), *. . . Girls* (1973), *. . . Dick* (1974), *. . . Behind* (1975).

Roper, Brian (*b* Doncaster, 1929 – *d* 1994). Actor. Agreeably scruffy child actor who studied at the Old Vic School but, like so many, did not pursue his film career into adulthood. Came to the screen as William's mate Ginger in *Just William's Luck* (1947) and *William Comes to Town* (1948). In Hollywood he played the sturdy Dickon in *The Secret Garden* (1949).

OTHER BRITISH FILMS INCLUDE: *The Miniver Story, The Naked Heart* (1950), *The Card* (1952), *The Girl on the Pier* (1953), *The Rainbow Jacket* (1954), *The Blue Peter* (1955).

Rosay, Françoise (*b* Paris, 1891 – *d* Paris, 1974). Actress. RN: de Nalèche. Immensely distinguished French actress, on stage from 1908, originally intending to be an opera singer. In silent films from 1913, often under the guidance of husband Jacques Feyder (*b* Ixelles, Belgium, 1885 – *d* Rive-de-Prangins, Switzerland, 1948), who made *Knight Without Armour* (1937) in Britain. They were married until his death. She made only a half-dozen British films, but, silver-haired and erect, is memorable in them all – whether as the grieving mother in *The Halfway House* (1944), the dominating Electress Sophia in *Saraband for Dead Lovers* (1948) or the imperious pianist who delivers the *coup de grâce* to Dirk BOGARDE's aspirations in *Quartet* (1948). One of the most revered of French stars, she also filmed in Hollywood in the late 50s (e.g. *Interlude*, 1957).

OTHER BRITISH FILMS: *La symphonie des brigands* (1936, French-language version of UK film), *Johnny Frenchman* (1945), *The Naked Heart* (1950), *That Lady* (1955), *The Full Treatment* (1960).

BIBLIOG: Memoirs, *Le cinéma notre métier*, 1956; *La traversée d'une vie*, 1974.

Rose, Bernard (*b* 1960). Director. Graduate of the NATIONAL FILM AND TELEVISION SCHOOL, Rose has tried one GENRE after another without achieving a clear success. His ADAPTATION of *Anna Karenina* (1997), was US-financed, largely UK-cast, but of no interest to anyone, whether or not they'd read the novel; his Beethoven BIOPIC *Immortal Beloved* (1994, + sc) suffered from a tortuous flash-back narrative method; and only the wartime THRILLER, *Chicago Joe and the*

Showgirl (1989), showed moments of energy but failed to attract audiences.

OTHER BRITISH FILMS INCLUDE: (d, unless noted) *Looking at Alice* (1977, short, p, e, sc), *Smart Money* (1986), *Paperhouse* (1988), *Ivansxtc* (2000, UK/US, + c, co-sc, e).

Rose, David E. (*b* Kansas City, 1896 – *d* Phoenix, Arizona, 1992). Executive. After holding several important executive positions in the US, including director of United Artists Corporation until 1938, he became Paramount's top man in Britain until he left to form his own company Coronado. As its president, he was responsible for some moderately interesting films in Britain, usually drawing on waning Hollywood star power: he had Robert Montgomery in *Your Witness* and Ray MILLAND in *Circle of Danger* (1950), Linda Darnell in *Saturday Island* (1952), Van JOHNSON in *The End of the Affair* (1954), a mangling of Graham GREENE.

OTHER BRITISH FILMS INCLUDE: *Sea Devils* (1953, p), *Port Afrique* (1956, ex p), *The House of the Seven Hawks* (1959, p), *Dr Blood's Coffin* (1960, ex p), *Hostile Witness* (1968, p), *The File of the Golden Goose* (1969, p).

Rose, George (*b* Bicester, 1920 – *d* Puerto Rico, 1988). Actor. Former farmer and secretary, Central School-trained Rose took to acting in 1944 with the Old Vic company and became a popular character player on London and, in later life, New York stages, often in Shakespearean roles like those he played at Stratford, and famously including the Common Man in the first production of *A Man for All Seasons* (1960). In films, he often played jittery neurotics like the one in *The Night My Number Came Up* (1955), and was memorable as the drunken cook in *A Night to Remember* (1958). From the early 60s he lived in America, becoming a well-loved exponent of GILBERT & SULLIVAN and winning a Tony for the 1975 revival of *My Fair Lady*. He was murdered by thugs outside his house in the Dominican Republican.

OTHER BRITISH FILMS INCLUDE: *The Pickwick Papers* (1952), *The Square Ring* (1953), *The Good Die Young* (1954), *The Good Companions, Brothers in Law* (1956), *Barnacle Bill, The Shiralee* (1957), *A Tale of Two Cities, Jack the Ripper* (1958), *Jet Storm, The Flesh and the Fiends* (1959), *No Love for Johnnie* (1961).

Rose, Penny Costume designer. Respected designer of recent times, who has worked for Richard ATTENBOROUGH, on *Shadowlands* (1993, UK/US) in which she contrasts Debra Wingers's transatlantic dress sense, not that it is at all outré, with 50s Oxford dowdiness, and on *In Love and War* (1996, US), for Alan PARKER, notably on *Evita* (1996, UK/US), for which she was BAA-nominated, and on *The Road to Wellville* (1994, US), in which her costumes were among the few inoffensive contributions. She has moved easily between modern and period designing.

OTHER BRITISH FILMS: *Leopard in the Snow* (1977), *Quest for Fire* (1981), *Pink Floyd The Wall* (1982), *Local Hero* (1983), *Cal, Another Country* (1984), *Strapless* (1988), *The Commitments* (UK/US), *Under Suspicion* (1991), *Carrington* (1994, UK/Fr), *Entrapment* (1999, UK/Ger/US).

Rose, William (*b* Jefferson City, Montana, 1918 – *d* Jersey, CI, 1987). Screenwriter. Following WW2, during which he had crossed into Canada to enlist in the Army and was stationed in Europe, American Rose settled in Britain with his English wife, and during the 50s became one of the mainstays of British comedy writing. From the late 40s, he co-authored films which failed to take off, including *Once a Jolly Swagman* and *Esther Waters* (1948), both for WESSEX FILMS, but scored a major success with the surely perfect screenplay (AAn) for *Genevieve* (1953). Everything seems to work so effortlessly about this sunniest of comedies that it is possible to overlook the sheer wit, craftsmanship and genuine feeling in the writing on which it is all based. At EALING, where he spent the rest of his time in the UK, he worked notably for Alexander MACKENDRICK on two astringent comedies, *The 'Maggie'* (1953, BAA/n) and the shrewdly ambivalent *The Ladykillers* (1955, + story, BAA/sc, AAn/sc). Back in the US his talents seemed coarser, as in the syrupy *Guess Who's Coming to Dinner* (1967), for which he won an Oscar.

OTHER BRITISH FILMS: *My Daughter Joy, I'll Get You for This* (1950), *The Gift Horse* (1952), *Touch and Go* (1955), *Man in the Sky* (1956), *Davy* (+ story), *The Smallest Show on Earth* (1957).

Rosenberg, Max J. (b New York, 1921). Producer. Co-founder with Milton SUBOTSKY, with whom he had worked in the US on the youth musical, *Rock Rock Rock* (1956), of AMICUS FILMS. Unlike Subotsky who often (co-)wrote as well, Rosenberg kept to producing, and returned to the US in later years.

BRITISH FILMS: (co-p) *City of the Dead* (1960), *Dr Terror's House of Horrors* (1964), *Daleks – Invasion Earth 2150 AD, The Psychopath, The Deadly Bees* (1966), *The Terrornauts, Torture Garden* (1967), *The Birthday Party* (1968), *A Touch of Love, Scream and Scream Again* (1969), *The House That Dripped Blood* (1970), *Tales from the Crypt, Asylum, The Vault of Horror* (1973), *From Beyond the Grave* (1973), *The Beast Must Die* (1974), *At the Earth's Core* (1976, co-ex p).

Rosenthal, Jack (b Manchester, 1931). Screenwriter. Notable TV writer, whose work includes a reputed 150 episodes of *Coronation Street* as well as many TV plays. He has also written a half-dozen British films, including two which began on TV but were shown in some cinemas – two sweet-tempered films about school children and their passions, *P'tang Yang Kipperbang* (1982) and *Those Glory Glory Days* (1983, sc e). Also co-wrote with Barbra Streisand her UK/US co-production, *Yentl* (1983) and the funny, perceptive comedy about house-moving, *The Chain* (1984). Married (since 1973) to Maureen LIPMAN.

OTHER BRITISH FILMS: *The Lovers!* (1972, sc for orig TV series), *The Lucky Star* (1980, adptn, dial), *Captain Jack* (1998, sc).

Rosenthal, Joseph (b London, 1864 – d London, 1946), Cinematographer. Rosenthal has rightly been praised by historian Stephen Bottomore as the man who helped invent the NEWSREEL (though he is more accurately described as a war, travel and ACTUALITY cameraman) and Rachael LOW indeed describes him as the first professional war cameraman. A photographer who worked for Charles URBAN's Trading Company for several years, and became a cinematographer for the WARWICK TRADING COMPANY in 1898, Rosenthal travelled the world, filming the Boer War, the Boxer Rebellion and the Russo-Japanese War. He left Warwick, for which his sister Alice also worked, in 1907, and the following year formed his own company, Rosie Film, in Croydon, which lasted until 1913 and primarily produced comedies. Rosenthal continued to film newsreels through the 30s, and his son, Joe Rosenthal Jr, was also a cinematographer.

BIBLIOG: Stephen Bottomore, 'Joseph Rosenthal: The Most Glorious Profession', *Sight and Sound*, 1983. AS.

Rosher, Charles (b London, 1885 – d Lisbon, 1974). Cinematographer. A major American cinematographer, active through mid 50s, closely associated with Mary Pickford in silent era. Received, along with Karl Struss, the first Cinematography Oscar for *Sunrise* (1927). Lent his talents to a handful of British films with major directors such as E.A. DUPONT, Alexander KORDA and Elinor GLYN.

BRITISH FILMS: *The Vagabond Queen, Atlantic* (1929), *Knowing Men, The Price of Things, Two Worlds* (1930), *Men Are Not Gods* (1936). AS.

Rosmer, Milton (b Southport, 1882 – d Chesham, 1971). Actor, Director. RN: Arthur Milton Lunt. A major stage actor, who made his debut in 1889 and was busy also as a manager and director through the 50s, Rosmer was director of the Stratford-upon-Avon Memorial Theatre, 1943–44. On-screen he was an ageing leading man in silent films who became a character actor with the coming of sound. Rosmer also directed a number of interesting films including *Cash on Delivery* (1927), *Balaclava* (1928, co-d, co-sc), *PC Josser, Dreyfus* (co-d), *Many Waters* (1931), *After the Ball* (1932), *Channel Crossing* (1933), *The Secret of the Loch* (1934), *The Guv'nor* (1935), *Everything is Thunder* (1936), *The Great Barrier* (1937, co-d, co-sc), *The Challenge* (1938, co-d, co-sc). Married to actress Irene ROOKE.

OTHER BRITISH FILMS INCLUDE: (a) *The Mystery of the Hansom Cab* (1915), *Lady Windermere's Fan* (1916), *Little Women* (1917), *The Diamond Necklace* (1920), *A Romance of Wastdale* (1921), *The Passionate Friends* (1922), *The Woman Juror* (1926), *High Treason* (1929), *The Phantom Light* (1935), *Silent Barriers* (1937), *South Riding* (1938), *Goodbye, Mr Chips, The Stars Look Down* (1939), *Hatter's Castle* (1941), *Daybreak* (1946, rel. 1948), *Frieda, Fame Is the Spur* (1947), *The Small Back Room* (1948). AS.

Ross, Benjamin (b London, 1964). Director. There was such an engaging sense of escalating black comedy and freewheeling satire about Ross's first feature, *Young Poisoner's Handbook* (1995, + co-sc), that it is disappointing to note since then only the TV movie, *RKO 281* (1999), based on the making of *Citizen Kane*, and the war drama, *Who Goes There?* (2001), starring Jamie BELL. Ross's seems like a talent to nurture. Studied at Columbia Film School and also directed the SHORT FILM, *My Little Eye* (1992).

Ross, Hector (b Southport, 1914 – d London, 1980). Actor. After rep experience and WW2 service (1940–46), Ross first appeared on London stage and TV in 1946 and entered films shortly after. Played the nice young man who nearly loses Anne CRAWFORD to a post-war spiv type in *Night Beat* (1948) and the sinister 'contact' of a foreign power in *Deadly Nightshade* (1953). Spent four years in the mid 50s acting and producing in Australia. Was married to June Sylvaine (*see* Vernon SYLVAINE).

OTHER BRITISH FILMS INCLUDE: *Bonnie Prince Charlie* (1948), *Happy Go Lovely* (1951), *The Steel Key* (1953), *The Fur Collar* (1962), *Ring of Spies* (1963).

Ross, Lee (b c 1971). Actor. Busy actor of the 90s who played Samantha MORTON's brashly sexual lover who can't compete with her *Dreaming of Joseph Lees* (1999) and who had a drunk scene with Ewan McGREGOR in *Rogue Trader* (1999). He had a good small role as Claire RUSHBROOK's scaffolder boyfriend in *Secrets & Lies* (1996) and was Spalding in *The English Patient* (1996, UK/US); otherwise, he has been in too many little-seen films for the good of his career, which fortunately has also included some excellent TV, such as *Dockers* (1999).

OTHER BRITISH FILMS INCLUDE: *Buddy's Song* (1990), *The Guilty* (1993), *The Hurting, i.d.* (1995), *Metroland* (UK/Fr/Sp), *Vigo* (1998, UK/Fr/Jap), *Secret Society* (2000, UK/Ger).

Rossington, Norman (b Liverpool, 1928 – d Manchester, 1999). Actor. Ubiquitous character player who began work as messenger on the Liverpool docks, stumbled into amateur drama and then trained at the Bristol Old Vic School, starting his professional career on the Bristol stage. On-screen from the mid 50s, often as army rankers, but more famous for his TV role as Private 'Cupcake' Cook in *The Army Game* (1957–61) and the film SPIN-OFF, *I Only Arsked!* (1958). Short and smudge-featured, gifted at accents, he played numerous working-class sidekicks, one of the most notable being as Albert FINNEY's mate in *Saturday Night and Sunday Morning* (1960), and he is engaging as the BEATLES' hard-pressed manager in *A Hard Day's Night* (1964) and Robin PHILLIPS's randy chum in *Two Gentlemen Sharing* (1969). From the early 70s he worked more in TV but had the odd cinema role until the early 90s as in *The Krays* (1990) and *'Let Him Have It'* (1991). His many stage roles included Touchstone in *As You Like It* (1961) at Stratford.

OTHER BRITISH FILMS INCLUDE: *Keep It Clean* (1955), *A Night to Remember, Carry On Sergeant, . . . Nurse* (1958), *The League of Gentlemen, Crooks Anonymous, Lawrence of Arabia* (1962), *Nurse on Wheels, The Comedy Man* (1963), *Those Magnificent Men . . .* (1965), *The Wrong Box* (1966), *The Charge of the Light Brigade* (1968), *The Rise and Rise of Michael Rimmer* (1970), *Young Winston* (1972), *Joseph Andrews* (1976), *Rhubarb, Rhubarb* (1980).

Rossiter, Leonard (*b* Liverpool, 1926 – *d* London, 1984). Actor. Originally a stage actor, his film career began in the early 60s, spanned a quarter century and included 24 films. Early supporting roles in films such as *A Kind of Loving* (1962), *This Sporting Life* (1963, as a snide reporter) and *Billy Liar* (1963, as Billy's narky colleague) established him as a kind of manic petty tyrant, a type of role he returned to frequently in subsequent performances. He was also memorably cast as Captain Quin in Stanley Kubrick's *Barry Lyndon* (1975). In the 70s he became one of the best known TV actors in Britain: his film performance as tyrannical landlord Rupert Rigsby in *Rising Damp* (1980) arose out of the comedy series of the same name. On stage from the late 50s, he gave an award-winning performance in the title role of *The Resistible Rise of Arturo Ui* (1968–69). Married (1) **Josephine Tewson** (*b* London, 1939) who appeared in several films including *Wilt* (1989) and (2) **Gillian Raine** (*b* Colombo) who had a major role in the unreleased film, *The Last of the Long-Haired Boys* (1968).

OTHER BRITISH FILMS INCLUDE: *A Jolly Bad Fellow* (1963), *Hotel Paradiso* (UK/Fr), *The Wrong Box, The Witches, The Whisperers* (1966), *Oliver!, 2001: A Space Odyssey, Deadfall, Otley* (1968), *The Pink Panther Strikes Again, Voyage of the Damned* (1976), *Britannia Hospital* (1982), *Water* (1985).

BIBLIOG: Robert Tanitch, *Leonard Rossiter*, 1985. Simon Caterson.

Rosson, Harold (*b* New York, 1895 – *d* Palm Beach, Florida, 1988). Cinematographer. Illustrious Hollywood cameraman imported to Britain in the 30s by Alexander KORDA. At very least, he made Merle OBERON look absolutely stunning in the lustrous black-and-white sheen of *The Scarlet Pimpernel* (1935). His remarkable US career lasted until 1967.

OTHER BRITISH FILMS INCLUDE: *The Ghost Goes West* (1935), *As You Like It, The Man Who Could Work Miracles* (1936), *A Yank at Oxford* (1937).

Roth, Tim (*b* London, 1961). Actor, director. The stubbly pinch-faced Roth, who first wished to be a sculptor and trained at Camberwell School of Art, can be one of the most alarming people in films and US director Quentin Tarantino has exploited his dangerous persona in *Reservoir Dogs* (1992) and *Pulp Fiction* (1994). Exposure in such films, both widely

popular *and* cultish, has made Roth a very bankable actor. His career is now essentially an international one, but his early appearances were in such well-regarded British films as Stephen FREARS's *The Hit* (1984), for which he received a BAAn, as a hitman-in-the-making, *A World Apart* (1987, UK/Zim) and *The Cook, the Thief, His Wife & Her Lover* (1989, UK/Fr). But his most significant British work is as director of *The War Zone* (1999, UK/It), a devastating account of a family ripped apart by incest. It is a hard film to watch but its unswerving honesty repays the effort, and it has won awards at several film festivals. Since then, he has filmed all over the place and, even in the failed US comedy, *Lucky Numbers* (2000), he is mesmerisingly watchable as a dodgy barman. Won a BAA (and AAn) for his performance in *Rob Roy* (1995).

OTHER BRITISH FILMS INCLUDE: *Meantime* (1983, TV, some cinemas), *Backsliding* (1991, UK/Aust), *Captives* (1994), *The Million Dollar Hotel* (UK/Ger/US), *Vatel* (UK/Fr) (2000), *Bread and Roses* (UK/Fr/Ger/It/Sp/Switz), *Invincible* (UK/Ger/US) (2001).

Rotha, Paul (*b* London, 1907 – *d* Wallingford, 1984). Producer, director. RN: Paul Thompson. A socialist documentarist, Rotha was not only a crucial figure in the British documentary movement but also a film theorist, critic and historian. He came to prominence in 1930 with his book *The Film Till Now*, the first English-language history of the cinema. Trained at the Slade School of Art, he entered the industry as an assistant art director at BRITISH INTERNATIONAL PICTURES. In 1931, Rotha met John GRIERSON and worked for him at the EMPIRE MARKETING BOARD. However, Rotha's independent, maverick nature, which was to characterise his later role in the DOCUMENTARY movement, led to his dismissal. Through Jack BEDDINGTON of Shell-Mex BP, Rotha directed his first film *Contact* (1933) and went on to make sponsored films at GAUMONT–BRITISH INSTRUCTIONAL. *Shipyard* (1935), one of the first documentaries with a strong social conscience, illustrates his socio-political film-making style as opposed to the more realist tradition of Grierson. In 1935 Rotha joined STRAND FILMS as a producer and helped found Associated Realist Film Producers. He formed Paul Rotha Productions in 1941 producing numerous films for the civilian war effort and Britain's post-war reconstruction. Rotha's socialism is evident in *World of Plenty* (1943), *Land of Promise* (1946), *The World is Rich* (1947) and *World Without End* (1953) of which the latter two won BAAs. *World of Plenty* and *The World is Rich* investigate world hunger while *Land of Promise* advocates a planned economy for post-war Britain. *World Without End* highlights the economic and social issues of undeveloped nations. From 1953 to 1955 Rotha was Head of the BBC Documentary Department, where he commissioned a series on world problems, *The World is Ours*. As well as television, Rotha ventured in to feature film production. He had previously written several unrealised scripts but during the 50s and 60s he directed three films: *No Resting Place* (1951) and *The Silent Raid* (1963) drew on his documentary background but *Cat and Mouse* (1958) was a commercial suspense thriller. In the 70s, he returned to writing, revising several of his earlier publications as well as continuing to influence film culture in general with his writings on film history, theory and practice.

OTHER BRITISH FILMS INCLUDE: (doc) (d) *Rising Tide* (1934), *The Face of Britain* (1935), *Peace of Britain* (1936), *New Worlds for Old* (1938), *The Fourth Estate* (1940), *Total War in Britain* (1945), *A City Speaks* (1946), *The Life of Adolf Hitler* (1961); (p) *Cover to Cover* (1936), *Today We Live* (1937), *Children of the City* (1944), *Worker and Warfront* cinemagazine (1942–46), *The Centre* (1947).

BIBLIOG: Duncan Petrie and Robert Kruger (eds), *A Paul Rotha Reader*, 2000. Sarah Easen.

Rotherhithe Studios Two disused warehouses in Rotherhithe have provided the home for Sands Films, the company set up by director Christine EDZARD and her producer husband Richard GOODWIN. They moved in to the site in 1975, produced several SHORTS and then embarked on the wildly – and triumphantly – ambitious six-hour production of *Little Dorrit* (1987). They have gone on to produce several further features, including an interesting if bleak *As You Like It* (1992) at Rotherhithe which also accommodates independent productions and has a very large stock of scenery and costumes.

Rotheroe, Dom Director. Rotheroe, graduate of Westminster University's film course, had made a number of SHORT FILMS and politically engaged DOCUMENTARIES, including the notable CHANNEL 4-backed *A Sarajevo Diary* (1993), which had wide festival exposure, before turning to his first feature, *My Brother Tom* (2001). This is a stylistically ambitious treatment of teenage *amour fou*, with a strong sense of hovering darkness.

OTHER BRITISH FILMS INCLUDE: (doc) *Shadows on the Street, Blockade* (1996), *The Coconut Revolution, Mission Rescue* (1999).

Rothwell, Talbot (*b* Bromley, Kent, 1916 – *d* Worthing, Sussex, 1981). Screenwriter. A mainstay of the 'CARRY ON' team for many years, Rothwell wrote some of the SERIES' funniest screenplays. Producer Peter ROGERS said of him, in 1992, that, unlike fellow-screenwriter Norman HUDIS, he 'didn't write with heart at all; he was against all that. He used to write crazy gags . . . and marvellous one-liners' [and excruciating puns], and stayed almost until the end. After WW2 service, he worked as a playwright, wrote for the CRAZY GANG and for RADIO comics including Terry-THOMAS, and had considerable experience as a screenwriter before joining the 'Carry On' team. Also wrote for such TV series as *Up Pompeii* and *The Army Game*. Awarded OBE in 1977.

OTHER BRITISH FILMS INCLUDE: *Is Your Honeymoon Really Necessary?* (1953), *The Crowded Day* (1954), *Stars in Your Eyes* (1956), *Three Spare Wives* (1962, play), *Carry On Cabby* (1963), . . . *Spying* (co–), . . . *Jack,* . . *Cleo* (1964), . . . *Cowboy, Three Hats for Lisa, The Big Job* (1965), *Carry On Screaming* (1966), . . . *Up the Khyber,* . . . *Doctor* (1968), . . . *Camping,* . . . *Again Doctor* (1969), . . . *Up the Jungle,* . . . *Loving* (1970), *Up Pompeii* (orig idea/TV series), *Carry On Henry,* . . . *at Your Convenience* (1971), . . . *Matron,* . . . *Abroad* (1972), . . . *Girls* (1973), . . . *Dick* (1974).

Rousselot, Philippe (*b* Briey, France, 1945). Cinematographer. Award-winning French cameraman who has shot some distinguished British films, including John BOORMAN's *Hope and Glory* (1987), for which he won the BSC Award, as well as receiving AA and BAA nominations. He won an AA for *A River Runs Through It* (1992, US) and a BAA and BSC award for the dark, suggestively lit *Interview with the Vampire* (1994, US), and he worked again for Boorman on *The Tailor of Panama* (2001, Ire/US). His French credits include the lushly shot period piece, *La reine Margot* (1994) and he directed the UK/ French/German co-production, *The Serpent's Kiss* (1997).

OTHER BRITISH FILMS: *Dream One* (1984, UK/Fr), *The Emerald Forest* (1985), *The Miracle* (1991, UK/Ire), *Mary Reilly* (1996, UK/US).

Routledge, Patricia (*b* Birkenhead, 1929). Actress. Before becoming a household name and face as indefatigable social climber Hyacinth Bucket (pronounced 'Bouquet' and famous for 'candlelight suppers') in TV's *Keeping Up Appearances* (1990–95) and later as the housewife-sleuth in *Hetty*

Wainthropp Investigates (from 1996), Routledge had appeared in a few British films without making the impression she should have. Educated at Liverpool University and trained at the Bristol Old Vic School, she had minor roles in such films as *To Sir, with Love* (1967) and *Lock Up Your Daughters!* (1969), but stage (from 1952, London 1954, including Lady Bracknell, 1999) and TV knew much better how to use her emphatic persona. Watching her in Alan BENNETT's *Talking Heads* (1988, 1998) is to be aware of a very considerable actress at work. Awarded OBE in 1993.

OTHER BRITISH FILMS INCLUDE: *Pretty Polly* (1967), *The Bliss of Mrs Blossom* (1968), *Girl Stroke Boy* (1971), *Keep Off the Grass* (1984, short).

Rover (*b* ? – *d* Walton-on-Thames, 1914). Actor. RN: Blair. The leading player in Cecil HEPWORTH's *Rescued by Rover* (1905) never gained the international star status of JEAN, THE VITAGRAPH DOG, but he was, as *The Bioscope* noted at his passing, 'the first animal to play an independent part in a cinematograph film'. He was the hero of many productions, including *Rover Takes a Call* (1905), intended as a curtain call to *Rescued by Rover, The Dog Outwits the Kidnapper* (1908), *The Shepherd's Dog* (1909), and *Rover the Peacemaker* (1911). AS.

Rowden, W(alter) C(ourtenay) Director, screenwriter. A former screenwriter who became a director, primarily of shorts, for H.B. PARKINSON.

BRITISH FILMS INCLUDE: (sc) *Westward Ho!* (1919), *Pillars of Society, Rodney Stone* (1920), *Hard Cash* (1921), *Simple Simon* (1922); (d) *Daniel Deronda* (+ sc), *Eileen Alannah, Sally in Our Alley* (1922), *Vanity Fair, Master Song Scenas* series (1922). AS.

Rowe, Ashley (*b* 1959). Cinematographer. In films since the mid 80s, Rowe has done some very distinctive work in such disparate films as Shane MEADOWS's black-and-white fable of youthful alienation in Nottingham, *24 7 TwentyFourSeven*, and the lush evocation of HARDY's Wessex in *The Woodlanders* (1997), the fond, acidly nostalgic *Still Crazy* (1998, UK/US), and the Dublin-set romantic comedy *When Brendan Met Trudy* (2001, UK/Ire). These are all notably good-looking films, thanks partly to Rowe's lighting.

OTHER BRITISH FILMS INCLUDE: *One Full Moon* (1991), *A Man of No Importance* (UK/Ire), *Sister My Sister, Widows' Peak* (UK/US) (1994), *The Governess* (UK/Fr), *B. Monkey* (UK/It/US), *Bedrooms and Hallways* (1999), *A Room for Romeo Brass* (1999, UK/Can), *Mad About Mambo* (UK/Can/US), *Beautiful Mistake* (2000).

Rowe, Frances (Fanny) (*b* Preston, Lancs, 1913 – *d* London, 1988). Actress. Webber-Douglas-trained stage actress, on stage from 1936 and in films from 1944 when she repeated her stage role in EALING's version of *They Came to a City*, as Philippa, who finds the courage to leave her domineering mother. Many TV appearances, including a continuing role in *Fresh Fields* (1984–86), as Julia MACKENZIE's mother. Was married to Clive MORTON.

OTHER BRITISH FILMS INCLUDE: *Never Look Back* (1952), *Street Corner* (1953), *The Teckman Mystery, Aunt Clara* (1954), *The Moonraker, The Birthday Present* (1957), *Jane Eyre* (1970, unc), *Lady Caroline Lamb* (1972, UK/It/US).

Rowlands, Patsy (*b* London, 1934). Actress. Guildhall-trained and on stage from 1951, spending several years at London's Players' Theatre, and entering films in 1961. She was a quite vivid presence in such key 60s films as *A Kind of Loving* (1962) as the heroine's tenacious girlfriend, was in eight 'CARRY ON' films and was landlady of Tess's penultimate resting-place in *Tess* (1979, UK/Fr). Plenty of TV, including hapless neighbour

Betty in *Bless This House* (1971–76) and colourful Lottie Grady in *When We Are Married* (1987).

OTHER BRITISH FILMS INCLUDE: *On the Fiddle* (1961), *Vengeance* (1962, UK/Ger), *Tom Jones, A Stitch in Time* (1963), *Carry On Again Doctor* (1969), . . . *Loving* (1970), *Please, Sir!, Carry On Henry* (1971), . . . *Matron, Alice's Adventures in Wonderland* (1972), *Carry On Girls* (1973), . . . *Behind* (1975), *Joseph Andrews* (1976), *Little Lord Fauntleroy* (1980), *Crimestrike* (1990).

Rowson, Leslie (*b* Manchester, 1903). Cinematographer. Entered film industry in 1926 in Hollywood as assistant with United Artists, then other companies before making his UK debut with *The Crimson Circle* (1929, UK/Ger). Busy with GAINSBOROUGH throughout the first half of the 30s, on such films as *The Ringer* (1931), and *Jack's the Boy* (1932). After WW2 service in RAF (1940–46), he joined EALING, working as camera operator on such films as *Hue and Cry* (1946) and *The Loves of Joanna Godden* (1947, 2uc).

OTHER BRITISH FILMS INCLUDE: *The Ghost Train* (1931), *Lord Babs, Wedding Rehearsal* (1932), *The Fire Raisers* (1933), *Road House, The Red Ensign* (1934), *The Iron Duke* (exterior ph), *Her Last Affaire* (1935), *Just William's Luck* (1947, co-c), *Things Happen at Night* (1948).

Rowson, Simon (*b* Manchester, 1877 – *d* London, 1950) Executive. A noted physicist, mathematician and statistician who joined IDEAL FILM COMPANY in 1911 and was in charge of production from 1915. He produced Maurice ELVEY's *The Life Story of Lloyd George* in 1918, withdrawn before it could be released, under political pressure, and thought lost until its recent rediscovery and release (to acclaim) in 1996. He also became a director of GAUMONT–BRITISH, with which Ideal merged in 1927, of Denman Picture Houses Ltd, and a member of the Joint Trade Committee on British Films from 1926. As statistician he compiled valuable information about British cinemagoing habits and he became adviser to the Board of Trade on films policy, including the formation of a 'Film Institute' which was the precursor of the BFI, founded in 1933. He was producing films well into the 30s, for the reformulated New Ideal Company, including *Can You Hear Me Mother?* and *Her Last Affaire* (1935). His brother Harry (*b* 1875 – *d* 1951) was a fellow executive at Ideal.

Royal Air Force Film Production Unit. This operated from 1941 until disbanded in 1945. It sprang from the Air Ministry's desire to create a clear record of the RAF's work as well as a means of PROPAGANDA for home and abroad. Once under way, it provided useful footage, compiled from hundreds of operational flights, for its own films and those made in collaboration with others, as with the ARMY FILM AND PHOTOGRAPHIC UNIT. Training and briefing films were also made by RAFFPU. The output grew so large from its base at PINEWOOD STUDIOS that a new film processing laboratory had to be built. Recurring elements in its films are the teamwork, the ordinariness of some of the tasks being performed, and the social mix, matters not always realised in other organisations' depiction of life in the RAF. Gender roles are likewise challenged. In *The Big Pack*, 1944 the Air Transport Auxiliary pilot is a woman flying in foggy conditions in a Hawker Hurricane that has gone wrong. Cast and crew, recruited from the ranks, included several established film-makers including editor Derek TWIST and director-to-be Jack CLAYTON. By using active service people the FPU was able to obtain shots in the course of other duties that took them into situations of great risk and in the line of fire, thus leading to a number being killed, injured or made prisoners of war. Much of FPU's output

found its way into the cinemas' NEWSREELS. By the time *Journey Together* (1945), scripted by Terence RATTIGAN, was ready the war was over but such was the quality that it gained a commercial release. It concerned the Flying Training Command, at home and abroad, following the career of Richard ATTENBOROUGH as a new aircraftman. There is a maturity about the FPU's work, largely unknown to today's audiences, that would repay a visit. Stephen Brown.

Royal Film Performance The idea of a honouring the film industry through a Royal Film Performance equal in status to the Royal Variety Performance, was first conceived in 1939 but delayed by the war until 1 November 1946 when *A Matter of Life and Death* was screened. Held every year, it is the most prestigious of royal premieres, attended by senior members of the royal family, a host of stars and worthies from the film industry. Great pains are taken to ensure a memorable event – in the early days including an elaborate star-studded stage show – whose proceeds go to the Cinema and Television Benevolent Fund.

The film chosen should not display a 'gratuitous amount of violence, bad language or sex'; a scene was deleted from the one 'X' film chosen, *The Prime of Miss Jean Brodie* (1969). No crime or horror film has ever been selected, but almost always films set safely in the past, especially costume dramas. Occasionally even these can generate controversy. *Beau Brummell* (1954) was judged offensive in depicting the royal family's direct ancestors as mad or weak. But the real debate has been whether the Royal Film Performance should be an advert for British films, especially those celebrating the national character – *Scott of the Antarctic* (1948) or *Chariots of Fire* (1981) – or good publicity for American blockbusters such as *Titanic* (1997). As the last native film chosen was *True Blue* in 1996, it would seem that the Royal Film Performance is no longer a celebration of British cinema.

OTHER BRITISH FILMS CHOSEN: *The Mudlark* (1950), *Where No Vultures Fly* (1951), *Rob Roy* . . . (1953), *The Battle of the River Plate* (1956), *The Horse's Mouth* (1958), *Sammy Going South* (1963), *Born Free* (1965), *Romeo and Juliet* (1968), *Anne of the Thousand Days* (1969), *Mary Queen of Scots* (1971), *The Slipper and the Rose* (1976), *Evil Under the Sun* (1981), *The Dresser* (1983), *A Passage to India* (1985), *84 Charing Cross Road* (1986), *Madame Sousatzka* (1988), *Chaplin* (1992).

BIBLIOG: Andrew Spicer, 'Fit for a King? The Royal Film Performance', *Journal of Popular British Cinema* 6, 2003. Andrew Spicer.

royalty There is an H.M. Bateman cartoon in which two capitalists, the real powers in British life, decide to let the royal family live: 'after all', one admits, 'they are the finest cinema performers that we possess'. Learning to perform before the cameras became an essential part of British royal public life as soon as film was invented. With the NEWSREELS, royalty became part of the public's weekly cinema diet, and royal approval similarly became important to British cinema, from the first film show before royalty (proudly given by Birt ACRES, on 21 July 1896), to the annual ROYAL FILM PERFORMANCES, which started in 1946 with POWELL AND PRESSBURGER's *A Matter of Life and Death*. Royalty as fictional subject matter began with Will BARKER's pageant-like life of Victoria, *Sixty Years a Queen* (1913), its obsequious approach being inherited by Herbert WILCOX's *Victoria the Great* (1937) and *Sixty Glorious Years* (1938), starring Anna NEAGLE. A more playful attitude could then only be contemplated for distant history, as in *The Private Life of Henry VIII* (1933), with Charles LAUGHTON's rumbustious title performance casting its shadow over all subsequent interpretations, from *The Sword* *and the Rose* (1953, James Robertson JUSTICE), to *Henry VIII and his Six Wives* (1972, Keith MICHELL, who previously played him in the rather better TV series *The Six Wives of Henry VIII*, 1970), to the downmarket delights of *Carry on Henry* (1971, Sidney JAMES); the appalling Prince Regent depicted by Peter GRAVES (*Mrs Fitzherbert*, 1947) and Peter USTINOV (*Beau Brummell*, a cheeky choice for Royal Command Performance of 1954); and the witty sparring of Peter O'TOOLE and Katharine HEPBURN as Henry II and Eleanor of Aquitaine in *The Lion in Winter* (1968). The monarch now given greatest due is Elizabeth I, being nobly portrayed by Flora ROBSON (*Fire Over England*, 1937), Glenda JACKSON (the TV series *Elizabeth R*, 1971, and the film *Mary Queen of Scots*, 1971) and Cate BLANCHETT (*Elizabeth*, 1998), though Queen Victoria was given a more human face by Judi DENCH in *Mrs Brown* (1997, UK/Ire/US). For present royalty, the passing of time and deference has seen **Jeanette Charles**, a Queen Elizabeth II-lookalike, enjoy a long career in film (e.g. *Steppin' Out*, 1979) and television with facetious cameos, and *The Madness of King George* (1994, UK/US), with Nigel HAWTHORNE as the hapless George III and Rupert EVERETT as the Prince Regent, used the past as a metaphor for a modern institution a film could now only portray as absurd. Luke McKernan.

Roza, Lita (*b* Liverpool, 1926). Singer. Popular singer and recording star of the early 50s who frequently dubbed the singing voices of movie stars and appeared on screen in *Cast a Dark Shadow* (1955) and *My Way Home* (1978), in both cases singing rather than acting. With Ted Heath's band for five years; extensive radio and TV, including *Sheep's Clothing* (1957) and variety shows.

Rozsa, Miklos (*b* Budapest, 1907 – *d* Los Angeles, California, US, 1995) Composer. A skilled violinist and prize-winning composer from his early childhood, Rozsa admired the music of Bartok and Kodaly while studying in Leipzig and Paris in the 20s and early 30s. A successful concert hall career well underway, he began as a film composer when **Jacques Feyder** (*see* Françoise ROSAY) was impressed by Rozsa's music for a ballet performed in London in the mid 30s, and arranged for him to score his Korda-produced *Knight Without Armour* (1937), earning Rozsa significant praise. After similar success scoring *Thunder in the City* (1937), he was hired by Korda and scored several of his films, before following him to Hollywood to finish *The Thief of Baghdad* (1940). Rozsa remained in America, becoming one of the cinema's most celebrated composers and serving as a professor at the University of Southern California.
OTHER BRITISH FILMS: *The Squeaker* (1937), *The Green Cockatoo* (1937), *The Divorce of Lady X, The Drum* (1938), *The Four Feathers, The Spy in Black, Ten Days in Paris, On the Night of the Fire* (1939).
BIBLIOG: Autobiography, *Double Life: A Precarious Autobiography of Success and Survival*, 1989. Stephen Shafer.

Ruby, Thelma (*b* Leeds, 1925). Actress. Educated in Leeds, Dublin and New York, Ruby was on TV from 1951 and films sporadically from the mid 50s, meanwhile making her name in stage roles from 1945, ranging from revue to Goneril in *King Lear* (1970). She is George COLE's squabbling wife in *Where There's a Will* (1955) and games mistress along Joyce GRENFELL lines in *The Man Who Liked Funerals* (1958), but she mostly had small roles. On TV in the nostalgically cast *The Last of the Blonde Bombshells* (2000).
OTHER BRITISH FILMS INCLUDE: *Johnny, You're Wanted* (1955), *Room at the Top* (1958), *Invasion Quartet* (1961), *The Sellout* (1975, UK/It), *Leon the Pig Farmer* (1992).

Ruddock, John (*b* Lima, Peru, 1897 – *d* Guildford, 1981). Actor. Character player of 40s and 50s who came to the screen after a long stage career. Served in the Army in WW1, then studied at the Royal Academy of Music before making his stage debut in 1922, and subsequently played several seasons at Stratford and the Old Vic. Made film debut in *Lancashire Luck* (1937) and thereafter lent his tall, somewhat gaunt frame and features to two dozen roles, usually as professional types, like the benign police doctor in *The Fallen Idol* (1948). He is the less ancient of the two Chelsea Pensioners who act as a chorus in *The Way Ahead* (1944); international films include *Lust for Life* (1956).
OTHER BRITISH FILMS INCLUDE: *Escape to Danger* (1943), *Strawberry Roan, Pink String and Sealing Wax* (1945), *Wanted for Murder, Laughing Lady* (1946), *Frieda* (1947), *Under Capricorn* (1949), *Ivanhoe, Secret People* (1951), *Lawrence of Arabia* (1962), *Chitty Chitty Bang Bang* (1968).

Runacre, Jenny (*b* Cape Town, 1943). Actress. Striking South African actress whose most noticeable roles were in the 70s, including Stephen DWOSKIN's *Dynamo* (1972), exploring the perceptions of strip-club girls, Queen Elizabeth in Derek JARMAN's *Jubilee* (1978), and, more commercially intended, 'Mrs Todhunter'(the old Linden TRAVERS role) in the dire remake of *The Lady Vanishes* (1979). Not much since.
OTHER BRITISH FILMS INCLUDE: *Goodbye, Mr Chips* (1969), *The Creeping Flesh* (1972), *The Mackintosh Man* (1973), *Son of Dracula* (1974), *Joseph Andrews* (1976), *The Duellists* (1977), *Hussy* (1979), *Shadey* (1985), *Restoration* (1995, UK/US).

rural life Although images of an English country garden often colour memories of this depiction, British cinema often displays an ambivalent, rather than positive, image of this icon. Every idyllic image appearing on the screen tends to have its dark equivalent of a *Cold Comfort Farm*. In Arthur Conan DOYLE's 'The Copper Beeches', SHERLOCK HOLMES warns Dr Watson about praising a supposedly peaceful countryside which is often more violent than the city. Despite the two versions Cecil HEPWORTH made of *Comin' Thro' the Rye* (1916, 1923) which championed the HERITAGE and landscape imagery still prevalent today, we must remember that the baby's kidnapper in *Rescued by Rover* (1905) came from the countryside.

Although never incarnating Karl Marx's definition of the 'idiocy of rural life', British cinema did depict its darker aspects. Both *This England* (1941) and *Went the Day Well?* (1942) depict rural inhabitants using violence against anyone threatening the sleepy *status quo* whether independent female or German invaders. In *Carnival* (1946), Michael WILDING arrives too late to save Sally GRAY from a grim rural fate personified by Bernard MILES and his vindictive mother, and in *Bang! You're Dead* (1953) the rural scene is messy with post-war leavings.

The negative imagery relating to rural life still continues today. In 1995, John SCHLESINGER directed a new version of Stella Gibbons' 1932 satire, *Cold Comfort Farm*, in which orphaned aspiring novelist Kate BECKINSALE discovers her country cousins to be a sloppy, ill-mannered bunch of neurotic misfits. Paul MORRISON's *Solomon and Gaenor* (1999) depicts the romantic relationship between an orthodox Jew and fundamentalist chapel girl on the lines of 'Abe's Irish Rose meets How Green is my Valley'. Unfortunately, by desiring to relate the values of 1911 to the present day, the film anachronistically plunges both lovers immediately into the haystack and loses sight of alternative cultural imagery which would contradict the quick union between them. While Sharon MAGUIRE's *Bridget Jones's Diary* (2001, UK/Fr/US) may satirize rural heritage values in certain scenes, Jamie THRAVES's *The Low-Down* (2001) contains a brief scene showing the countryside to be a place of savage values.

However, films such as *Song of the Road* (1937), *Tawny Pipit* (1944), *Conflict of Wings* (1954) and *The Woodlanders* (1997), despite threats to serenity, present more positive images, suggesting some capacity for rewarding rural living. Tony Williams.

See also **pastoral images**; **village life**.

Rush, Geoffrey (*b* Toowoomba, Queensland, 1952). Actor. Rush began as an amateur actor in Brisbane before attending drama school in Paris in the 60s, after which he returned to Australia and won a high reputation as a theatre actor. He had small roles in 80s films, repeated his stage Aguecheek in *Twelfth Night* (1987), and suddenly, or so it seemed, became an international star in *Shine* (1996, UK/Aust), winning both AA and BAA (among other awards) for his performance as the manic pianist, David Helfgott. Since then, he has been in incessant demand everywhere: his British films (often co-productions) have cast him as Javert in *Les Misérables* (UK/Ger/US), a malevolent Walsingham in *Elizabeth* and a very funny Henslowe (Rush has an antic streak which films have rarely exploited) in *Shakespeare in Love* (UK/US) (all 1998), the Marquis de Sade in the US-financed UK-filmed *Quills* (2000) and the title role in John BOORMAN's *The Tailor of Panama* (2001, Ire/US). One of the great character stars to emerge round the turn of the century. Married to actress **Jane Menalaus** (*b* London, 1959) who appeared with him in *Quills* and on stage.

Rushbrook, Claire (*b* Hitchin, 1971). Actress. Boldly idiosyncratic performer who has specialised in sour-faced, carping, usually working-class characters. This proclivity made Rushbrook a prime candidate to play Roxanne in Mike LEIGH's *Secrets & Lies* (1996). She holds nothing back in this difficult role of a cheerless and foul-mouthed young woman who screws her face up into an ugly mask of anger and resentment. Rushbrook re-trod this path, though a little more sympathetically, as Samantha MORTON's nagging, yet caring sister in Carine ADLER's *Under the Skin* (1997). After a subtle performance in the otherwise gaudy *Spice World* (1997), she returned to what she does best as the ostentatiously repugnant Lady Estelle in *Plunkett & Macleane* (1999, UK/Czech). OTHER BRITISH FILMS: *Shiner* (2001). Melinda Hildebrandt.

Rushton, William (aka Willie) (*b* London, 1937 – *d* London, 1996). Actor. One of the founders of that archetypal 60s satirical organ, *Private Eye*, and, equally 60s, one of the original panel for TV's satirical *That Was the Week That Was* (1962–63), Shrewsbury-educated Russell also pursued a minor career as an actor, usually in comedies such as *Those Magnificent Men . . .* (1965) and *Keep It Up Downstairs* (1976). His sharpness in the other media is scarcely reflected in his film work. OTHER BRITISH FILMS INCLUDE: *It's All Over the Town* (1963), *Nothing But the Best* (1964), *The Best House in London* (1968), *Monte Carlo or Bust!* (1969, UK/Fr/It), *Flight of the Doves* (1971), *Adventures of a Private Eye* (1977), *Consuming Passions* (1988, UK/US).

Russell, Billy (*b* Aston, Birmingham, 1893 – *d* London, 1971). Actor. RN: Adam George Brown. MUSIC HALL comedian and tumbler who appeared in a few films spread over 30 years. Alleged to have taught Charles LAUGHTON how to fall down a chute in *Hobson's Choice* (1953).

BRITISH FILMS INCLUDE: *Take Off That Hat* (1938), *For Freedom* (1940), *The Galloping Major* (1951), *Negatives* (1968), *Leo the Last* (1969).

Russell, Catherine (*b* London, 1966) Actress. RN: Smith. Busier on stage, both in London and elsewhere, and TV (co-starring in *Chandler and Co.*, 1994–95) than on screen. The very attractive, Central School-trained Russell has played supporting roles in a few films, most of them (e.g. crematorium cleaner in *Shooting Fish*, 1997) produced by husband Richard HOLMES. Daughter of TV actor **Nicholas Smith** (*b* Banstead, 1934), hapless manager in *Are You Being Served?* (1973–83) and in minor roles in several films, including *Baxter!* (1972). OTHER BRITISH FILMS INCLUDE: *Soft Top, Hard Shoulder* (1992), *Solitaire for 2*, *Clockwork Mice* (1995).

Russell, Ken (*b* Southampton, 1927). Director. The *enfant terrible* of British film came to cinema only after training for the Navy, doing some time in the RAF during WW2, and then going in for ballet before making a few amateur films during the 50s. Whatever misgivings anyone might have about his work, it offers an important riposte to the oft-made claim that British cinema was always too verbal – not when Russell got to work on it. And yet, despite the notoriety of the Oliver REED–Alan BATES nude wrestling scene in *Women in Love* (1969), the really audacious thing about Russell's ADAPTATION of D.H. LAWRENCE was perhaps the extraordinary amount of *talk*, of Lawrence's dialectic, he contrived to retain and to render cinematic. This remains not merely the finest screen version of Lawrence but a remarkable British film as well: it is passionate, sensual, intelligent and visually daring, and his direction deserved its AAn and BAAn.

This would not have been so surprising to those who had followed his preceding career in TV. He credited Huw Weldon with 'educating' him and he made about 20 DOCUMENTARIES for Weldon's arts programme, *Monitor* (1958–65), of which Russell's iconoclastic biographical studies are probably now the best remembered. His *Prokofiev* (1961), *Elgar* (1962), *Bartok* (1964), *The Debussy Film* (1965) starring Oliver Reed (all for *Monitor*); the study of dancer *Isadora Duncan* (1966); and, for *Omnibus* (1967), the haunting *Song of Summer* (1968), an episode in the life of Delius, described new parameters for the BIOPIC genre and remain a high point of British TV.

His feature debut is the largely forgotten but sometimes funny *French Dressing* (1963), set in a damp seaside resort, and he contributed a proficient entry in the Harry Palmer SERIES, *Billion Dollar Brain* (1967). But it was *Women in Love* that made it impossible to ignore him as a film-maker, much as a farrago like *The Music Lovers* (1971) might have made one try to. This wildly flashy, often disgusting go at Tchaikovsky's troubled life alerted one to the wilder shores of Russell's art: *The Devils* (1971, + p, co-sc), a heady brew of lust, religious obsession, sacrilege, masturbation, whirling visuals and shrieking sound, was a sore test for those who valued Russell's flamboyant intervention in British cinema; *The Boy Friend* (1971, + p, sc), sledgehammers to death a sweet-tempered stage musical; and *Lisztomania* (1975, + sc, co-lyrics) is an almost unwatchably fragmented and puerile fantasy on the composer's life, the sort of gimmicky enterprise that makes 'cinematic' a dirty word. However, between the last two named, there are real compensations in *Savage Messiah* (1972, + p), four years in the life of painter Gaudier, in *Mahler* (1974, + sc), a further composer biopic but more in the mode of his TV work than of *The Music Lovers*; in the rock OPERA *Tommy* (1975, + co-p, sc, a); and even in the florid, sensationalised *Valentino* (1977, + a, co-sc), with Rudolf

NUREYEV bringing to the title role an eroticism which was at least appropriate to the Valentino myth.

Since then, Russell has worked often in the US, where *Altered States* (1980) had fair success as a sort of updated Jekyll and Hyde; has acted on film (*The Russia House*, 1990) and TV (*The Secret Life of Sir Arnold Bax*, 1992, as Bax, + d, sc); and has had a couple more brushes with Lawrence. But *The Rainbow* (1989) and TV's *Lady Chatterley* (1992) are disappointingly tame renderings from a man who once made the old sexual warrior seem of such contemporary importance. *Whore* (1991, US, + sc, a) was his last much-noticed work, but he goes on working unabated and may yet have a shock or two for filmgoers. In 2000 he claimed his new interest was in minimalist film-making, like his short film *Lion's Mouth* (2000, + p, e, sc), made in his garden. His first of three wives was costume designer Shirley RUSSELL (1956–78).

OTHER BRITISH FILMS: (d, unless noted) (shorts) *Knights on Bikes* (1956) *Peepshow, Amelia and the Angel, Lourdes* (1958), *McBryde and Coquhoun: Two Scottish Painters* (1959), *A House in Bayswater* (1960); (features) *Gothic* (1986, + a), *Aria* (1987, co-d, co-sc), *The Lair of the White Worm* (1988, + p, sc), *The Fall of the House of Usher* (2001, + sc, e).

BIBLIOG: Joseph Gomez, *Ken Russell*, 1976; Autobiography, *A British Picture*, 1989.

Russell, Kennedy (*b* London, 1883 – *d* Radlett, Herts, 1954). Composer, music director. Worked busily in British films for just over a decade, mostly at BRITISH NATIONAL, and mostly for John BAXTER, making his contribution to the naive PASTORALISM of *Song of the Road* (1937) and to the Victorian charm of *When We Are Married* (1943), produced by Baxter, directed by Lance COMFORT. Often conducted as well as contributed to scores.

OTHER BRITISH FILMS INCLUDE: (comp, unless noted) *Hearts of Humanity* (1936), *Talking Feet* (1937, + md), *What Would You Do Chums?* (1939), *Crook's Tour* (1940, + songs) *Old Mother Riley's Circus* (+ cond), *The Common Touch* (+ m d), *Old Mother Riley's Ghosts* (1941), *We'll Smile Again* (songs), *Salute John Citizen* (1942), *Old Mother Riley, Detective* (m d), *The Shipbuilders* (+ m d) (1943), *Heaven Is Round the Corner* (1944, songs), *Here Comes the Sun* (1945, + m d), *Nothing Venture* (1948, + m d), *Judgment Deferred* (1951, + m d).

Russell, Shirley (*b* London, 1935 – *d* Richmond, Surrey, 2002). Costume designer. RN: Kingdom. Highly regarded designer from the early 60s when she began work on her then-husband (1956–78) Ken RUSSELL's feature debut, *French Dressing* (1963) and his TV BIOPICS, including *Song of Summer* (1968). She received AAn and BAAn for her sartorial evocation of the 20s in *Women in Love* (1969), and further nominations for meticulous period designs for *Agatha* (1978, UK/US, AAn, BAAn), and, for two wartime fashion reconstructions, won a BAA for *Yanks* (1979) and received BAAn for *Hope and Glory* (1987). Maintaining her reputation for period work, she distinguished exactly between Saffron BURROWS' 40s glamour and Kate WINSLET's dowdiness in *Enigma* (2001, UK/Ger/US), not to forget between nerdy Dougray SCOTT, all baggy tweeds, and Jeremy NORTHAM's well-cut three-piecers. A major figure in her field. Son Jamie Russell (*b* 1962) is a TV producer.

OTHER BRITISH FILMS: *Billion Dollar Brain* (1967), *The Music Lovers, The Devils, The Boy Friend* (1971), *Savage Messiah* (1972), *Mahler* (1974), *Inserts, Tommy, Lisztomania* (1975), *Valentino* (1977), *Lady Chatterley's Lover* (1981, UK/It), *The Return of the Soldier* (1982), *Greystoke . . .* (1984, UK/US), *The Bride* (1985).

Russell, Theresa (*b* San Diego, California, 1957). Actress. Not without reason, *Empire* magazine chose her as one of the 100 sexiest stars ever; she came in at No. 58 and might have been expected higher on the list than that in view of the sensuality she displayed in such films as husband Nicolas ROEG's *Insignificance* (1985), as a Monroe-type actress, or as the murderous Catharine in *Black Widow* (1987, US). A photographer's model from age 12, she studied acting at the Lee Strasberg Institute, and entered films in 1976 (*The Last Tycoon*, US). Her main films have been made for Roeg, including such unsettling art-house pieces as *Bad Timing* (1980), *Eureka* (1982, UK/US), *Track 29* (1988, UK, US-set) and *Cold Heaven* (1991, US). Compelling actress as she is, she made something of namesake Ken RUSSELL's *Whore* (1991), but the 90s were not kind to her; only the witty Florida *noir* of *Wild Things* (1998, US) properly exploited her provocative talents.

OTHER BRITISH FILMS: *Aria* (1987), *Being Human* (1994), *The Grotesque* (1996), *The Proposition* (1997).

Russell, William (*b* Sunderland, 1924). Actor. RN: Russell Enoch. After national service in the RAF and Oxford, Russell, acting under his real name until 1955, went into rep, then to the Bristol Old Vic and the London stage. Made film debut in *The Gift Horse* (1952), played secondary roles, except for the ill-fated *Intimate Relations* (1953) – the very title should have warned him of its incompatibility with 50s British cinema. He is an agreeable leading man in the lively 'B' film, *The Big Chance* (1957), but TV gave him better chances to be a dashing hero in the likes of *The Adventures of Sir Lancelot* (1956–57) and as Ian Chesterton in *Dr Who* (1963–65). Married (1953) French actress **Balbina**, who played small roles, including a staff member in *The Belles of St Trinian's* (1954).

OTHER BRITISH FILMS INCLUDE: *They Who Dare* (1953), *One Good Turn, The Gay Dog* (1954), *Above Us the Waves* (1955), *The Share Out* (1962), *Superman* (1978), *Mark Gertler: Fragments of a Biography* (1981, doc).

Russell, Willy (*b* Whiston, Lancs, 1941) Dramatist, composer, screenwriter. Former hairdresser who became a popular playwright two of whose long-running successes, *Educating Rita* and *Shirley Valentine*, he adapted to the screen in 1983 and 1989 respectively. Both deal with women finding their own voices and learning not to submit to stereotyped expectations; the former received AAn and BAAn, the latter BAAn; Julie WALTERS was BAA-nominated for *Educating Rita* and Pauline COLLINS was AA-nominated for her star role in *Shirley Valentine* (UK/US). His musical, *Blood Brothers*, has been running continuously in London since 1983.

OTHER BRITISH FILMS: *Mr Love* (1985, comp), *Dancin' Thru the Dark* (1990, sc, comp).

Rutherford, Dame Margaret (*b* London, 1892 – *d* Chalfont St Peter, 1972). Actress. Much-loved English comic character actress, her quiddity summed up in *The Demi-Paradise* (1943) where Penelope DUDLEY WARD tries to explain her to OLIVIER's Russian visitor and ends up just laughing helplessly 'Well, you've seen her for yourself!' Her dumpling shape typically tented in capacious blouses, skirts, and capes, often of clashing patterns that lent oddity to their determined sensibleness, she played a succession of indomitable spinster enthusiasts and determinedly sexless, often authoritarian, eccentrics, both middle-class and aristocratic, as well as pursuing a notable stage career. Originally a teacher of elocution, which left its mark on the highly developed comic instrument of her voice. In films from 1936, in 1945 she played the first of her great roles (which she had also performed on stage), the clairvoyant Madame Arcati in *Blithe Spirit*. She was unflappable as Nurse Carey, undisturbed that Glynis JOHNS was a mermaid, in *Miranda* (1948), academically absorbed as Professor Hatton-Jones proving Pimlico to be Burgundy in *Passport to Pimlico* (1949), and inimitable as that distant daughter of Miss Buss and Miss Beale, Miss Whitchurch, headmistress of St Swithin's, locked in conflict with Alastair SIM, in *The Happiest Days of Your Life* (1950). She was Miss Prism in *The Importance of Being Earnest* (1952), a petshop owner versed in animal languages in *An Alligator Named Daisy* (1955), and quite properly part of those self-conscious celebrations of British cinema, *The Magic Box* (1951) and *The Smallest Show on Earth* (1957). Surviving into the age of satire, she played Ian CARMICHAEL's aunt in *I'm All Right Jack* (1959) and then attained a more foregrounded stardom as a robust serial inflection of Agatha CHRISTIE's Miss Marple, beginning with *Murder She Said* (1961). Orson WELLES made ART-HOUSE tribute by casting her as Mistress Quickly in *Chimes at Midnight* (1966, Sp/Switz), the year she was made DBE, and after she had won the Best Supporting Actress Oscar in *The VIPs* (1963). Long married to Stringer DAVIS.

OTHER BRITISH FILMS: *Dusty Ermine, Talk of the Devil* (1936), *Beauty and the Barge, Missing, Believed Married, Catch As Catch Can, Big Fella* (1937), *Quiet Wedding, Spring Meeting* (1941), *The Yellow Canary* (1943), *English Without Tears* (1944), *Meet Me at Dawn, While the Sun Shines* (1947), *Her Favourite Husband* (1950), *Curtain Up, Castle in the Air, Miss Robin Hood* (1952), *Innocents in Paris, Trouble in Store* (1953), *The Runaway Bus, Mad About Men, Aunt Clara* (1954), *Just My Luck* (1957), *On the Double* (1961), *Murder at the Gallop, Murder Ahoy, The Mouse on the Moon* (1963), *Murder Most Foul* (1964), *The Alphabet Murders* (1965), *A Countess from Hong Kong* (1966), *To See Such Fun* (1977, compilation).

BIBLIOG: Dawn Langley Simmons, *Margaret Rutherford: A Blithe Spirit*, 1983. Bruce Babington.

Ryan, Kathleen (*b* Dublin, 1922 – *d* Dublin, 1985). Actress. Lovely, redheaded Irish actress, wife of a Limerick doctor, she had had only limited but well-regarded stage experience when Carol REED cast her as the girlfriend of the wounded IRA gunman in *Odd Man Out* (1947). She made a very poignant impression and followed this with leads in LAUNDER AND GILLIAT's *Captain Boycott* (1947), the lugubrious *Esther Waters* (1948), in the title role, and the grim Depression- and Brooklyn-set *Give Us This Day* (1949, UK/US) as the hero's mistress. There were a couple of US films, including the powerful *The Sound and the Fury* (1950), but she never really recovered momentum after being associated with the archdud, *Christopher Columbus* (1949), and her career fizzled out sadly during the 50s.

OTHER BRITISH FILMS: *Prelude to Fame* (1950), *Laxdale Hall, The Yellow Balloon* (1953), *Jacqueline* (1956), *Sail Into Danger* (1957).

Ryan, Madge (*b* Townsville, Queensland, 1919 – *d* London, 1994). Actress. On stage in Australia from 1945, she originated the part of the reluctant Pearl in *Summer of the Seventeenth Doll* in 1956 and went with the production to London in 1957, to New York 1958. She became a respected actress on London stages, playing *Mother Courage* (1965) at the Old Vic, and entered films in 1959 (*Upstairs and Downstairs, Witness in the Dark*), was an amusing American tourist in *Tiara Tahiti* (1962), a bizarre Aunt Mary in *The Strange Affair* (1968), and Ronnie CORBETT's mum in TV's *Now Look Here!* (1971–73).

OTHER BRITISH FILMS INCLUDE: *Hand in Hand* (1960), *Summer Holiday* (1962), *Doctor in Distress* (1963), *I Start Counting* (1969), *A Clockwork Orange* (1971), *Frenzy* (1972), *The Lady Vanishes* (1979), *Splitting Heirs* (1993).

Ryecart, Patrick (*b* Leamington Spa, 1952). Actor. Most of Ryecart's work has been on TV, where he played Romeo in the *BBC Television Shakespeare* (1978) and the very confused Captain in the comedy series, *The High Life* (1995). Has also starred on stage, but film work has been sparse.

BRITISH FILMS: *A Bridge Too Far* (1977), *Silver Dream Racer* (1980), *Twenty-One* (1991), *Parting Shots* (1998).

Rylance, Mark (*b* Ashford, Kent, 1960). Actor. Artistic director of Globe Theatre and RSC leading man, RADA-trained Rylance has worked mainly in the theatre, but he came to (art-house) filmgoers' attention in no uncertain terms in *Intimacy* (2001, UK/Fr), in which he was required to engage in sexual activity of a candour not usually found in mainstream cinema. His few films have yielded two other striking roles: shipwrecked Ferdinand in *Prospero's Books* (1991, UK/Fr/It/Neth) and the dedicated naturalist in *Angels and Insects* (1995, UK/US).

OTHER BRITISH FILMS: *Loving* (1995), *The Institute Benjamenta* (1995).

Sabrina (*b* Cheshire, 1935). Actress. RN: Norma Sykes. Blondely bulbous non-actress, first on TV as a dumb blonde in Arthur ASKEY's *Before Your Very Eyes* (1954), made a few film 'appearances' in the 50s, mainly in sex-symbol cameo roles, like that in *Blue Murder at St Trinian's* (1957), then turned up in US films such as *The House of the Black Death* (1965).
OTHER BRITISH FILMS: *Stock Car* (1955), *Ramsbottom Rides Again* (1956), *Just My Luck* (1957), *Make Mine a Million* (1959).

Sabu (*b* Karapur, India, 1924 – *d* Los Angeles, 1963). Actor. RN: Sabu Dastagir. A stable boy in his native India, he was discovered by DOCUMENTARY film-maker Robert FLAHERTY who cast him in *Elephant Boy* (1937). His youthful likeability resulted in his being cast in Korda's *The Drum* (1938) and, most notably, in *The Thief of Baghdad* (1940). To Hollywood in the early 40s, appearing in Korda's ADAPTATION of Kipling's *Jungle Book* (1942), he then worked at Universal in Technicolor Maria Montez vehicles and in various adventure films in the US and elsewhere over the next two decades. He made a notable appearance as the Young Prince in the celebrated POWELL AND PRESSBURGER production of *Black Narcissus* (1947) and also appeared in *The End of the River* (1947), which was produced by THE ARCHERS. His tragically early death of a heart attack occurred shortly after he completed his first film at the Disney studios. Stephen Shafer.

Sachs, Andrew (*b* Berlin, 1930). Actor. The uptight father in TV's *Jack of Hearts* (1999) was barely recognizable as Manuel ('He's from Barcelona'), the hapless waiter in the classic sitcom, *Fawlty Towers* (1975, 1979). He had been in films sporadically from 1959 (*The Night We Dropped a Clanger*), before becoming a household face, but TV has remained his chief medium.
OTHER BRITISH FILMS INCLUDE: *Nothing Barred* (1961), *Hitler: The Last Ten Days* (1973), *Frightmare* (1974), *Are You Being Served?* (1977), *Revenge of the Pink Panther* (1978), *Consuming Passions* (1988), *The Mystery of Edwin Drood* (1993).

Sachs, Leonard (*b* Roodeport, Transvaal, South Africa, 1909 – *d* London, 1990). Actor. Educated in South Africa, Sachs came to England in 1929, was on the London stage in the same year, founded the Players' Theatre in 1936. Entered films in *Stamboul Train* (1936), served in the Army (1941–44) and then resumed production at the Players'. Played supporting roles in about 30 films – the Sheriff of Nottingham in *The Men of Sherwood Forest* (1954), the sinister Conrad in *Pit of Darkness* (1961) – and did some prestige TV, including *The Glittering Prizes* (1976), but was most famous as the Chairman of the MUSIC HALL series, *The Good Old Days* (1953–83). Married (1947–90) to Eleanor SUMMERFIELD, father of **Robin Sachs** (*see* Siân PHILLIPS).

OTHER BRITISH FILMS INCLUDE: *State Secret* (1950), *Malaga* (1954), *The Gamma People* (1955), *Odongo* (1956), *Man from Tangier, The Man Who Wouldn't Talk* (1957), *Oscar Wilde, Beyond the Curtain* (1960), *Taste of Fear* (1961), *Stranglehold, Number Six* (1962), *Thunderball* (1965).

St Helier, Ivy (*b* St.Helier, Jersey, 1886 – *d* London, 1971). Actress. RN: Aitchinson. On stage from 1910, she entered films by reprising her stage role in the film version of *Bitter Sweet* (1933), and had two memorable roles in 40s films: as the Princess's lady-in-waiting in *Henry V* (1944) and good-time Connie in *London Belongs to Me* (1948).
OTHER BRITISH FILMS: *The Singing Cop* (1937), *The Gold Express* (1955).

St John, Betta (*b* Hawthorne, California, 1929). Actress. RN: Betty Striedler. Dancer and actress on Broadway from her teens in *Carousel* and on London stage in *South Pacific* before making film debut in the US in *Dream Wife* (1953), following this with a further half-dozen roles. Back in UK from the mid 50s, working for Douglas FAIRBANKS and the DANZIGERS, as well as the lead in the Nova Scotian-set drama, *High Tide at Noon* (1957).
OTHER BRITISH FILMS INCLUDE: *Alias John Preston* (1955), *Tarzan and the Lost Safari* (1956), *The Snorkel, Corridors of Blood* (1958), *Tarzan the Magnificent* (1960).

St John, Earl (*b* Baton Rouge, Louisiana, 1892 – *d* Torremolinos, Spain, 1968). Executive producer. After long experience in the film industry in America (US and Mexico) and Britain, as distributor and exhibitor, running the Paramount circuit in Britain before WW2 and culminating as assistant to the managing director of Odeon Cinemas, St John went to work for the RANK ORGANISATION in 1947. He acted first as production adviser, then as joint-managing director of TWO CITIES FILMS, and finally as executive producer of Rank's production arm at PINEWOOD, where he was familiarly known as 'Studio Boss'. Allegedly a former fair barker, St John is remembered for his semi-roughneck approach, but he presided over more than 130 films for Rank, including such huge successes as *Genevieve* (1953), the 'DOCTOR' SERIES, the Norman WISDOM comedies, and the 'Titanic' drama, *A Night to Remember* (1948). His name appears on virtually every film deriving from Pinewood in the 50s and early 60s, so there is no point listing them here; the full extent of his influence (e.g. in relation to that of John DAVIS) needs to be further researched.

St John, Jill (*b* Los Angeles, 1940). Actress. Reputedly highly intelligent, the ravishing, red-haired St John was not often asked to draw heavily on this attribute in her largely US-based career, during which she played romantic leads in comedies and thrillers, and had her best moments as Rosemary Hoyt in

Tender Is the Night (1962). In her handful of British films, she played second fiddle to Vivien LEIGH in *The Roman Spring of Mrs Stone* (1961) and was one of the most memorable BOND girls, in *Diamonds Are Forever* (1971). Married (1) Lance Reventlow, (2) singer Jack Jones, (3) Robert Wagner.

OTHER BRITISH FILMS: *The Liquidator* (1965), *Sitting Target* (1972), *Something to Believe In* (1998, UK/Ger).

St Paul, Stuart Director, stunt co-ordinator. Best known as stunt co-ordinator on a wide range of films, including *Superman II* (1980) and several BOND adventures, as well as 'quieter' affairs like *Howards End* (1992), St Paul also directed several films, including the ADAPTATION of a Thomas Hardy story, *The Scarlet Tunic* (1997, + co-sc), and has worked on such big-budget US films shot in Britain as *Batman* (1989, at PINEWOOD) and *Robin Hood: Prince of Thieves* (1991, at SHEPPERTON). Also, much TV, including *GBH* (1991).

OTHER BRITISH FILMS: (stunts, unless noted) *Breaking Glass* (1980), *Britannia Hospital* (1982), *Octopussy, Never Say Never Again* (UK/US) (1983), *A View to a Kill, Revolution* (UK/Nor) (1985), *Hope and Glory* (1987), *Lair of the White Worm* (1988), *Wild West* (1992), *Small Faces* (1995), *An American Werewolf in Paris* (1997, + 2ud), *Hideous Kinky* (1998, UK/Fr), *The Criminal* (2001, UK/US).

'St Trinian's' series It was probably the success of their sublimely funny school comedy, *The Happiest Days of Your Life* (1950) that inspired Frank LAUNDER and Sidney GILLIAT to film *The Belles of St Trinian's* (1954). Based on Ronald SEARLE's cartoons featuring an anarchic girls' public school, it reunited many of the cast from the previous film. They turned in beautifully judged performances, notably Alastair SIM as the serenely complacent headmistress (and as her seedy brother Clarence), Joyce GRENFELL as a gawky undercover police-woman and George COLE as a cockney spiv. The box-office success of the film ensured that there would be four sequels, each less funny than its predecessor as the law of diminishing returns set in: *Blue Murder at St Trinian's* (1957), *The Pure Hell of St Trinian's* (1960), *The Great St Trinian's Train Robbery* (1966) and *The Wildcats of St Trinian's* (1980). Jeffrey Richards.

Sakamoto, Ryuichi (*b* Tokyo, 1952). Composer. A huge star in Japan, Sakamoto has made a successful cultural crossover to Western-style music. His ability to fuse classical music with global beats has brought fame in popular music circles, particularly through his collaborations with former 'Japan' lead singer, David Sylvian. With Sylvian providing vocals, Sakamoto entered Western consciousness with a ground-breaking original score for *Merry Christmas Mr Lawrence* (1982, + a), winning AA and BAA. Sakamoto and collaborator David Byrne (of 'Talking Heads' fame) won AA for the score of *The Last Emperor* (1987); and he wrote subtler, creeping work for *Love is the Devil* (1998, UK/Fr/Jap), BIOPIC of the artist, Francis Bacon. Sakamoto's contributions to English-language films are sparing but memorable.

OTHER BRITISH FILMS: *The Sheltering Sky* (1990, UK/It), *Gohatto* (1999, UK/Jap/Fr). Tim Roman.

Salew, John (*b* Portsmouth, Hants, 1902 – *d* London, 1961). Actor. Distinctive, bald and beady-eyed character player of dozens of films in the 40s and 50s, usually in middle-class pro-fessional, often faintly pompous types. He can be easily spotted arguing the supremacy of air power in a pub in *The Way Ahead* (1944), or as a county husband whose wife cannot 'afford' to divorce him in *Bedelia* (1946), or as a stuffy solicitor succumb-ing to the life force at the end of *Alive and Kicking* (1958).

OTHER BRITISH FILMS INCLUDE: *The Silent Battle* (1939), *Pastor Hall, The Thief of Baghdad* (1940), *Atlantic Ferry* (1941), *One of Our Aircraft is Missing, The Young Mr Pitt, Squadron Leader X* (1942), *We Dive at Dawn, Millions Like Us* (1943), *Tawny Pipit, Don't Take It to Heart!* (1944), *The Rake's Progress, Murder in Reverse* (1945), *I See a Dark Stranger, Wanted for Murder* (1946), *Temptation Harbour, Uncle Silas, The October Man, It Always Rains on Sunday* (1947), *London Belongs to Me, Quartet* (1948), *Kind Hearts and Coronets, The Blue Lamp* (1949), *The Lavender Hill Mob, Hotel Sahara* (1951), *Father Brown* (1954), *The Good Companions* (1956), *Night of the Demon* (1957), *Left, Right and Centre* (1959).

Sallis, Crispian Production designer. In his function as set decorator, Sallis shared AA nominations for *Aliens* (1986, US), *Driving Miss Daisy* (1989, US) and *Gladiator* (2000, UK/US). His production design credits have included two for Michael WINNER (*Dirty Weekend*, 1993; *Parting Shots*, 1998) and two enterprising low-budget features: Shane MEADOWS' *A Room for Romeo Brass* (1999), and *Borstal Boy* (2000, UK/Ire), an ADAPTATION from Brendan Behan. Son of Peter SALLIS.

OTHER BRITISH FILMS INCLUDE: (set decorator, unless noted) *The Return of the Soldier* (1982), *Octopussy* (1983), *A View to a Kill* (1985), *Buster* (1988), *The Browning Version* (1994), *Event Horizon* (1997, UK/US), *Hannibal* (2001, UK/US).

Sallis, Peter (*b* Twickenham, 1921). Actor. Probably best known now as Clegg in TV's long-running *Last of the Summer Wine* (from 1973), Sallis had been playing subdued, faintly diffident-seeming supporting roles since 1954 when he played the grocer in *Child's Play* and thereafter a typical run of doctors, solicitors and officials. He was heard as Wallace in the 'Wallace and Gromit' ANIMATED FILMS, *A Grand Day Out, The Wrong Trousers* (1993), *A Close Shave* (1995) and *Tortoise vs Hare* (2002). Stage work included the original London pro-duction of *Cabaret*. His son is Crispian SALLIS.

OTHER BRITISH FILMS INCLUDE: *Anastasia* (1956), *The Doctor's Dilemma* (1958), *Saturday Night and Sunday Morning* (1960), *The Curse of the Werewolf* (1961), *The VIPs* (1963), *Charlie Bubbles* (1967), *Inadmissible Evidence* (1968), *Scream and Scream Again, The Reckoning* (1969), *Wuthering Heights* (1970), *Full Circle* (UK/Can), *The Incredible Sarah* (UK/US) (1976),.

Salmon, Colin (*b* London, *c* 1965). Actor. After a charismatic display as the black Sergeant who has an affair with Helen MIRREN in TV's *Prime Suspect 2* (1992) and the lead in *Frantz Fanon: Black Skin White Mask* (1996), Isaac JULIEN's too-little-seen semi-DOCUMENTARY on the life of Frantz Fanon, black intellectual and revolutionary, Salmon created the recurring role of Robinson, M's Chief of Staff in the BOND movies, *Tomorrow Never Dies* (1997, UK/US) and *The World Is Not Enough* (1999, UK/US).

OTHER BRITISH FILMS INCLUDE: *Captives* (1994), *The Wisdom of Crocodiles* (1998), *Fanny and Elvis* (1999), *Mind Games* (2000), *My Kingdom, Resident Evil* (2002, UK/Ger/US).

Saltzman, Harry (*b* St John, Canada, 1915 – *d* Paris, 1994). Producer. Saltzman was partner in one of the most financially successful film-producing enterprises: the worldwide success of the James BOND FILMS. After experience managing a New York theatre and in television, he started in British films as deal-fixer, bringing Bob HOPE and Katharine HEPBURN over for *The Iron Petticoat* (1956), receiving a co-producer credit. Saltzman then entered an unlikely alliance with the ANGRY YOUNG MEN of the Royal Court Theatre, when he formed WOODFALL films with Tony RICHARDSON and John OSBORNE, negotiating the deals for *Look Back in Anger* (1959). He co-produced two more Woodfall films, including the successful *Saturday Night and Sunday Morning* (1960), but split with them, apparently over the casting of *A Taste of Honey*. However, he acquired the rights for $50,000 to the Bond novels (except *Thunderball* and *Casino Royale*), and formed EON Productions with Albert R. BROCCOLI in 1962. The phenomenal success of their first, *Dr No* (1962), starring Sean CONNERY, meant Saltzman could forget kitchen-sink realism. He launched a successful parallel spy SERIES with Len DEIGHTON's downbeat Harry Palmer (Michael CAINE) in *The Ipcress File* (1965). He dissolved his partnership with Broccoli in the mid 70s after eight Bond films, and his share of the Bond franchise was bought out by UNITED ARTISTS. He was partner in several European ventures, most notably Orson WELLES's *Chimes at Midnight* (1966, Sp/Switz), but it is for Bond that he will be remembered.

OTHER BRITISH FILMS (co-prod, unless shown): *The Entertainer* (1960), *From Russia with Love* (1962), *Call Me Bwana* (1963), *Goldfinger* (1964), *Funeral in Berlin* (1966), *You Only Live Twice*, *Billion Dollar Brain* (p) (1967), *Play Dirty* (p), *Battle of Britain* (1969), *On Her Majesty's Secret Service* (1969), *Toomorrow* (1970), *Diamonds Are Forever* (1971), *Live and Let Die* (1973), *The Man with the Golden Gun* (1974). Roger Philip Mellor.

Salzedo, Leonard (*b* London, 1921 – *d* Leighton Buzzard, 2000). Composer. Apart from the score for HAMMER success, *The Revenge of Frankenstein* (1958), Salzedo's film career was largely limited to 'B' MOVIES of the mid 50s, though he did get to score the oddity, *Sea Wife* (1956).

OTHER BRITISH FILMS INCLUDE: *The Stranger Came Home*, *Mask of Dust* (1954), *Before I Wake* (1955), *Women Without Men* (1956), *The Steel Bayonet* (1957).

Samson, Ivan (*b* Brighton, 1894 – *d* London, 1963). Actor. On stage from 1914, and after WW1 service (1915–19) returned to a busy stage career in London, New York and elsewhere, entering films in 1920 (*Twice Two, Nance*). Played Lord Dudley in *The Loves of Mary, Queen of Scots* (1923), but his film work is mainly in dignified supporting roles, like that of Captain Flower in *The Winslow Boy* (1948). He was a regular BBC broadcaster from 1926 and on TV from 1936, in a production of *Hassan*.

OTHER BRITISH FILMS INCLUDE: *The Fake* (1927), *White Ensign* (1934), *Royal Cavalcade* (1935), *Stepping Toes* (1938), *The Great Mr Handel* (1942), *Waltz Time* (1945), *The Browning Version* (1951), *Innocents in Paris* (1953), *Libel* (1959).

Samuelson, G(eorge) B(erthold) (*b* Southport, 1889 – *d* Great Barr, 1947). Producer. The most colourful personality of British silent films, G.B. Samuelson was a rotund, jovial producer responsible for some of the most lavish and the most controversial of features, ranging from his first, *Sixty Years a Queen* (1913) through an adaptation of Marie Stopes' *Married Love* (1923) to the Betty BLYTHE vehicle, *She* (1925). Samuelson entered the industry in Southport as Britain's first film renter in 1910, encouraged by his mother, Bertha (1854–1918), a refugee from the 1870s Eastern European pogroms, and moved to Birmingham the following year, setting up business premises there in 1912. In 1914, he acquired WORTON HALL, ISLE-WORTH, Middlesex, as his studio, hired George PEARSON as his first director and founded the Samuelson Film Manufacturing Company Ltd, with its first production being *A Study in Scarlet* (1914). He was the first British producer to take a company to Hollywood, making six films there in a four-month period during 1919–20. The British film industry declined in the 20s and in 1924 Samuelson sold Worton Hall. Brother Julian Wylie (*b* 1875 – *d* 1934) was the eminent pantomime producer, and

sons David, Sydney, Michael and Anthony (*b* London, 1929) formed a very important audio-visual equipment rental organisation. **David Samuelson** (*b* London, 1924) became a noted NEWSREEL cameraman for *British Movietone News*. **Michael Samuelson** (*b* London, 1931 – *d* London, 1998) also produced several DOCUMENTARIES, including *Winter Rock* (1976, UK/US) and his daughter is actress Emma Samms, who has worked in the US since 1980. Sydney SAMUELSON's sons, Marc and Peter SAMUELSON are also in the industry.

OTHER BRITISH FILMS INCLUDE: (p, unless noted) *The Great European War* (1914), *John Halifax, Gentleman*, *Adventures of Deadwood Dick* series (1915), *Milestones* (1916), *Little Women* (+ co-d) (1917), *Hindle Wakes*, *The Admirable Crichton* (+ d) (1918), *Convict 99* (+ co-d), *Quinneys*, *Damaged Goods* (1919), *The Husband Hunter*, *The Last Rose of Summer*, *Love in the Wilderness*, *David and Jonathan* (co-d) (1920), *The Ugly Duckling*, *The Winning Goal* (+ d), *Mr Pim Passes By* (1921), *The Magistrate*, *The Game of Life* (+ co-d), *Tilly of Bloomsbury*, *The Faithful Heart* (1922), *A Royal Divorce*, *Should a Doctor Tell?* (+ co-d) (1923), *Afterglow* (+ co-d), *This England* (+ co-d) (1924), *Who Is the Man?* (1925), *Milestone Melodies* series (+ co-d, sc), *Twisted Tales* series (+ co-d, sc), *If Youth But Knew* (1926), *For Valour* (+ d, story, sc), *Yesterday and Today* (+ d, story, sc) (1928), *The Valley of Ghosts* (d), *Spanish Eyes* (d) (1930), *The Other Woman* (+ d, co-sc) (1931), *Jealousy* (+ d, co-sc), *Collision* (+ d, co-sc), *Threads* (+ d, co-sc) (1932), *Matinee Idol* (ass d) (1933), *Spotting* series (d, sc), *The Crucifix* (d, co-story, sc) (1934), *Castles in the Air* (filmed 1922, released 1935). AS.

Samuelson, Marc (*b* London, 1961). Producer. Son of Sir Sydney SAMUELSON, he has been active as producer in British films since the mid 90s, co-producing with his largely US-based brother Peter SAMUELSON two literary BIOPICS, *Tom & Viv* (1994, UK/US, BAAn/film) and *Wilde* (1997, UK/Jap/Ger/US), among several others. As well, they have co-produced US films, including *Arlington Road* (1999), for their company, Samuelson Productions, which also produces DOCUMENTARIES for CHANNEL 4.

OTHER BRITISH FILMS INCLUDE: (co-p, unless noted) *White Mischief* (1987, p assoc), *This Is the Sea* (1996, UK/Ire/US, co-ex p), *The Commissioner* (1997, UK/Belg/Ger/US), *Gabriel & Me* (2001).

Samuelson, Peter (*b* London, 1951). Producer. Cambridge-educated Samuelson began as production assistant and worked on several US films as production manager and later as producer in the 70s and 80s, and from the mid 90s he and brother Marc SAMUELSON produced a dozen films in the UK (starting with *Tom & Viv*, 1994, UK/US, BAAn/film) and the US (e.g. *Arlington Road*, 1999) for their family company, Samuelson Productions. He has been honoured for his work in the US as founder-president of Starbright Pediatric Network, which creates educational and leisure materials for seriously ill children. Son of Sir Sydney SAMUELSON.

OTHER BRITISH FILMS INCLUDE: (co-p, unless noted) *The Return of the Pink Panther* (1974, a, p man), *Playmaker* (1994, UK/US), *The Commissioner* (1997, UK/Belg/Ger/US), *Guest House Paradiso* (1999, co-ex p), *Gabriel & Me* (2001).

Samuelson, Sir Sydney (*b* London, 1925). Director. A knighthood in 1995 is only one of the many honours that have marked his contribution to British film. He entered the film industry in 1939 as rewind boy at a Lancing cinema, then worked as projectionist (1939–42), did RAF service (1943–47), was camera operator, cameraman on DOCUMENTARIES covering a wide range of subjects filmed in many countries – from *Oil in Pakistan* (1956, + d) to *Prince Charles Backstage at Covent Garden* (1979) – and on a children's SERIAL, *The Carringford Mystery* (1958); and he is now Chairman of the Samuelson

Group of film and TV production servicing companies, having founded Samuelson Film Services in 1954. It is perhaps true to say that his real, and, by every account, genuinely benign, influence on British cinema has been in the behind-scenes roles he has played. He was, for instance, Chairman of BAFTA Council (1973–75) and of its Board of Management from 1976; in 1985 he won its Michael BALCON Award for 'Outstanding British Contribution to Cinema; he was a Governor of the BRITISH SOCIETY OF CINEMATOGRAPHERS (1969–79) and its Vice-President (1975–6); was President of the CINEMA AND TELEVISION VETERANS (1980–81); and served as the first British Film Commissioner (1991–97). In 1978 he was made CBE, and, in 1997, a Fellow of the BRITISH FILM INSTITUTE. As well he has had sustained involvement with many charitable organisations, some but not all connected with the industry. His first and third sons are film-makers Peter SAMUELSON and Marc SAMUELSON; his second, Jonathan, is an accountant.

OTHER BRITISH FILMS INCLUDE: (c, unless noted) *Smallpox* (1950), *Lone Flight*, *Changing Face of Europe* (cam op) (1951), *Brandy for the Parson* (ass c) (1952), *Missing Persons* (1953), *The Secret of the Forest* (1955), *The Sui Gas Pipeline* (1956), *The Way Ahead*, *Time We Woke Up!*, *Yorkshire Imperial on Thames* (1957), *Gateway to Adventure* (1958), *The Electronic Computer in Commerce*, *Passport Brittany* (d) (1959), *Design for Living* (1960), *Sam Spiegel in a Discussion with Ludovic Kennedy* (1961), *Filmharmonic '75* (1975), *Filmharmonic '76* (1976), *G'Olé* (1982, cam op).

Sanders, George (*b* St Petersburg, Russia, 1906 – *d* Barcelona, 1972). Actor. Sanders's suicide note informed the world that he was leaving it because he was 'bored'. This seems sadly ironic when one considers how much fun he gave filmgoers of several decades as they watched him being suavely vile to a range of stars – and consequently often getting his comeuppance rather than 'the girl'. Hollywood made him a sort of character star, memorably in such films as *The Picture of Dorian Gray* (1945), as Lord Henry Wotton, and *All About Eve* (1950), for which he won an Oscar as a cynical theatre critic. He started in British films in the mid 30s, went to Hollywood in 1936, and thereafter returned only intermittently and rarely to best effect, though he was a finely sneering De Bois-Guilbert in *Ivanhoe* (1952) and, nostalgically, murdered several 40s leading ladies (Jean KENT, Patricia ROC and Greta GYNT) in *Bluebeard's Ten Honeymoons* (1960). His family fled the Russian Revolution; he was educated in Britain; his brother was Tom CONWAY; and he married serially, wives including (2) Zsa Zsa Gabor (1949–57) and (4) Benita HUME (1959–67, her death).

OTHER BRITISH FILMS INCLUDE: *Things to Come, The Man Who Could Work Miracles* (1936), *The Saint in London* (1939), *The Stranger Came Home* (1954, novel), *The Whole Truth* (1958), *A Touch of Larceny* (1959), *Village of the Damned, The Rebel, Cone of Silence* (1960), *Operation Snatch* (1962), *A Shot in the Dark* (1964), *The Quiller Memorandum* (1966, UK/US), *The Best House in London* (1968), *Psychomania, Endless Night* (1972).

BIBLIOG: Autobiography, *Memoirs of a Professional Cad*, 1960; Richard Vanderbeets, *An Exhausted Life*, 1991.

Sanderson, Challis N. (*b* 18? – *d* 19?). Director. A former film editor and assistant director (with STOLL), who also worked as a costumier and location manager. Associated with H.B. PARKINSON in the early 20s.

BRITISH FILMS INCLUDE: *Three Men in a Boat, The Law Divine* (1920, co-d), *The Scarlet Letter, The Bride of Lammermoor, The Masked Rider* (1922), *John Henry Calling* series (1926, co-d), *Scraggs* (1930, + sc), *The King of Whales* (1934), *Cock o' the North* (1935, co-d), *Stars on Parade* (1936, co-d, p). AS.

Sands, Julian (*b* Otley, Yorkshire, 1958). Actor. Handsome, Central School-trained actor who came to filmgoers' notice as troubled George Emerson in *A Room with a View* (1985) and whose subsequent career has been mainly conducted in the US, and in some very idiosyncratically chosen British films, such as *Gothic* (1986), in which he played the poet Shelley, and *Impromptu* (1991), as Franz Liszt. For director Mike FIGGIS, he played a Latvian pimp in *Leaving Las Vegas* (1995, US) and had the lead (more or less) in Figgis's strange, fascinating *The Loss of Sexual Innocence* (2000, UK/US).

OTHER BRITISH FILMS INCLUDE: *Privates on Parade* (1982), *The Killing Fields* (1984), *The Doctor and the Devils* (1985), *The Naked Lunch* (1992, UK/Can), *The Browning Version* (1994), *Never Ever* (1996, UK/US), *Hotel* (2001, UK/It).

Sands, Leslie (*b* Bradford, Yorkshire, 1921 – *d* Chepstow, 2001). Actor. Heavy-featured character player, best known for such TV roles as the eponymous *Cluff* (1964), the Yorkshire detective, and Robin's father in *A Man About the House* (1973). Of his film roles, the most notable is that of the opportunistic reporter in *Life for Ruth* (1962). Educated at Leeds University, on stage from childhood, first in London 1946, and the author of a number of plays, one of which (*Deadlock*) became the film *Another Man's Poison* (1951).

OTHER BRITISH FILMS INCLUDE: *The Clue of the New Pin* (1960), *The Deadly Affair* (1966), *Danger Route* (1967), *One More Time* (1969), *Escape from the Dark* (1976).

Sangster, Jimmy (*b* N.Wales, 1924). Screenwriter. Entered films in the later 40s, and after considerable experience as assistant or second-unit director, on such idiotic but entertaining 'B' MOVIES as *The Man in Black* (1949), or as production manager on the likes of *Break in the Circle* (1955), he settled to screenwriting for HAMMER. He turned out scripts for such notable HORROR films as *The Curse of Frankenstein* (1957), *Dracula, The Revenge of Frankenstein* (1958), and *The Brides of Dracula* (1960), as well as such SCIENCE-FICTION pieces as *The Trollenberg Terror* (1958), and a couple of MELODRAMAS for Bette DAVIS, *The Nanny* (1965, + p) and *The Anniversary* (1967, + p).

OTHER BRITISH FILMS INCLUDE: (ass d) *Celia* (1949), *Room to Let* (1950), *Black Widow, Cloudburst* (1951), *The Last Page* (1952), *The Saint's Return, Spaceways* (1953), *The House Across the Lake* (1954); (p man) *Mask of Dust* (1954), *X the Unknown* (1956, + story, sc); (sc) *A Man on the Beach* (1955, short), *Jack the Ripper* (1958), *The Mummy* (1959), *The Criminal* (story), *The Terror of the Tongs* (1960), *Paranoiac* (1962), *The Devil-Ship Pirates* (1963), *Hysteria* (1964, + p); (co-sc) *The Snorkel* (1958), *The Siege of Sidney Street* (+ a), *The Hellfire Club* (+ story) (1960), *Crescendo* (1969), *Whoever Slew Auntie Roo?* (1971, + co-p); (d) *The Horror of Frankenstein* (+ p, co-sc), *Lust for a Vampire* (1970), *Fear of the Night* (1972, + p, co-sc).

BIBLIOG: Autobiography, *Do You Want It Good or Tuesday?*, 1997.

Sankofa This pioneering black Film and Video Collective, partly financed by CHANNEL 4, was established in 1984, with film-maker and artist Isaac JULIEN as one of its founder members. It has produced some notable work dealing with black experience, including Julien's award-winning drama-documentary, *Looking for Langston* (1989), based on the life of Harlem poet Langston Hughes, and Maureen BLACKWOOD and Julien's *The Passion of Remembrance* (1986). Sankofa's films are crucially concerned with matters of race, GENDER and CLASS. The company's name refers to a bird with its head turned backwards, a symbol perhaps of the film-makers' concern with reclaiming the past.

'Sapper' (*b* 1888 – *d* 1937). Author. RN: H.C. McNeile. *See* **Bulldog Drummond**

Sargent, Herbert (*b* Plumstead, Kent, 1873 – *d* ?). Author, screenwriter. Co-originator with Con WEST of the popular 'Josser' character, played by Ernie LOTINGA in several 30s COMEDIES, beginning with *Acci-dental Treatment* (1929), based on the Sargent–West play, *The Mousetrap*. Instead of quitting while ahead, Sargent also co-wrote the idiotic 1958 musical, *Hello London*.

OTHER BRITISH FILMS INCLUDE: (co-sc, unless noted) *PC Josser* (1931), *Josser Joins the Navy, Josser in the Army* (co-story) (1932), *My Old Duchess* (1933), *Josser on the Farm* (1934), *Smith's Wives* (1935), *One Good Turn, Love Up the Pole* (1936, co-story).

Sarne, Michael (*b* London, 1939). Actor, director. Modish 60s 'personality' and singer, who directed, wrote and starred in *Myra Breckinridge* (1970), a film described by *Time* as being 'about as funny as a child molester'. It would have taken a much more securely established career than Sarne's to withstand this nadir of camp rubbish: before it, he had had his best role in Basil DEARDEN's *A Place to Go* (1963), and had directed and written the SHORT FILM *Road to Saint Tropez* (1966, + p, co-m) and the worst of the 'SWINGING LONDON' films (one can scarcely be more severe), *Joanna* (1968). Since then, intermittent appearances; directed *The Punk* (1993), revised as *The Punk and the Princess* (1994).

OTHER BRITISH FILMS INCLUDE: (a, unless noted) *On the Fiddle* (1961), *Every Day's a Holiday* (1964), *Intimidade* (1975, UK/Brazil, d, sc), *Moonlighting* (1982), *Success Is the Best Revenge* (1984, UK/Fr), *Glastonbury the Movie* (1995, doc, co-d, co-c).

Sasdy, Peter (*b* Budapest, 1933). Director. Most prominently associated with HAMMER HORROR, this Hungarian director, in the British industry from 1958, began in TV, including episodes of *Callan* (1967) and a graceful, intelligent version of Henry JAMES's *The Spoils of Poynton* (1971). Actually there were only three Hammer films, but they are memorable: *Taste the Blood of Dracula* (1969), *Countess Dracula* (1970, + co-story), and *Hands of the Ripper* (1971), described by Phil Hardy as 'arguably the last masterpiece produced by Hammer'. Post-1970, he has worked mainly on TV (including the series, *Hammer House of Horror*, 1980) and he directed the US feature, *The Lonely Lady* (1982), starring Pia Zadora, and was lucky to survive that.

OTHER BRITISH FILMS: *Journey into Darkness* (1968, co-d), *Nothing But the Night, Doomwatch* (1972), *I Don't Want to Be Born* (1975), *Welcome to Blood City* (1977, UK/Can).

Saunders, Charles (*b* London, 1904 – *d* Denham, Bucks, 1997). Director, editor. Bedales-educated Saunders had over a decade's experience as editor before becoming a prolific director of often enjoyable 'B' MOVIES. Entered the industry in 1927 and acted as assistant director and editor with various companies, including two stints with GAUMONT–BRITISH. The turning point for him occurred when he joined TWO CITIES as editor, and co-directed the charming PASTORAL, *Tawny Pipit* (1944, + co-sc), with Bernard MILES, who acknowledged the importance of Saunders' cutting skills. The three dozen 'B' FILMS he directed benefit from his editor's background: they include pacy THRILLERS like *One Jump Ahead* (1955) and the more socially ambitious *Jungle Street* (1961), as well as the domestic comedy-drama, *There's Always a Thursday* (1957), which has the advantage of well-seasoned stars in Charles VICTOR and Frances DAY. His career came to a halt when exhibition patterns changed and the supporting

feature was no more; while it lasted, he made more than his share of good ones.

OTHER BRITISH FILMS INCLUDE: (e) *The Guv'nor* (1935), *Everything is Thunder* (1936), *The Gaunt Stranger* (1938), *Young Man's Fancy* (1939), *Return to Yesterday* (1940), *The Gentle Sex* (1943); (d) *No Exit* (1930, + p, sc), *Trouble in the Air, Fly Away Peter* (1948), *Dark Interval* (1950), *One Wild Oat* (1951), *Black Orchid* (1952), *Love in Pawn* (1953), *Meet Mr Callaghan* (1954), *The Hornet's Nest* (1955), *Find the Lady* (1956), *The End of the Line* (1957), *Naked Fury* (1959), *Dangerous Afternoon* (1961), *Danger by My Side* (1962).

Saunders, Jennifer (*b* Sleaford, Lincs, 1958). Actress. Surely one of the funniest women in the English-speaking world, Saunders originally trained as a drama teacher at Central School, where she met future comedy partner, Dawn FRENCH. Her greatest successes have been on TV where her name is indissolubly linked with French's in a series of wide-ranging satirical comedy revues, and with the hugely successful series, *Absolutely Fabulous* (1992, 1993, 2001), in which she played a neurotic public relations harridan, endlessly guzzling 'Bolly' with Joanna LUMLEY's drug-dimmed fashion editor. She has been too idiosyncratic for a career in British films and her half-dozen roles scarcely hint at her comic genius; her cameo in *In the Bleak Midwinter* (1995) is perhaps the nearest approach to opportunity films have given her. Married to Adrian EDMONDSON since 1985.

OTHER BRITISH FILMS: *The Supergrass* (1985), *Eat the Rich* (1987), *Prince Cinders* (1993), *Spice World* (1997, guest role), *Fanny and Elvis* (1999).

Savident, John (*b* Guernsey, Channel Islands, 1938). Actor. Bluff, balding character player often seen in somewhat pompous, usually professional roles from the late 60s, including doctors in *Remains of the Day* (1993) and *Loch Ness* (1996). Much TV, including a stint in *Coronation Street* from 1994, as Fred Elliott, winning a British Soap Award for this.

OTHER BRITISH FILMS INCLUDE: *Inadmissible Evidence* (1968), *Battle of Britain* (1969), *The Raging Moon* (1970), *A Clockwork Orange* (1971), *Butley* (1973, UK/Can/US), *Galileo* (1974, UK/Can), *Trial by Combat* (1976), *Seal Island* (1977), *Gandhi* (1982, UK/Ind), *The Wicked Lady* (1983), *Impromptu* (1991), *Tom & Viv* (1994, UK/US), *Othello* (1995, UK/US).

Saville, Phillip (*b* London, 1930). Actor, director. Before beginning to direct in the mid 60s, RADA-trained Saville had appeared in about a dozen films, most memorably as the philandering Ben Jones who is killed (or is he?) in the pre-credits sequence of *Bang! You're Dead* (1953). He was under contract to RANK in the late 40s and appeared in two HIGHBURY STUDIOS idiocies, *A Piece of Cake* and *Penny and the Pownall Case* (1948), as well as having stage experience. In the mid 50s he became a TV producer, joining the ABC Manchester studios in 1956, and much of his work since has been for TV, very notably including a *Hamlet* (1964) filmed at Elsinore, the famed Mersey-side black comedy series, *Boys from the Black Stuff* (1982) and *The Lives and Loves of a She-Devil* (1990). His sporadic film-directing career has included a workmanlike *Oedipus the King* (1967, + co-adptn), *The Fruit Machine* (1988), a thriller about a gangland murder witnessed by two teenage gays, and the TV-made *Those Glory Glory Days* (1983), an endearing account of football-mad teenagers which had some cinema showings.

OTHER BRITISH FILMS INCLUDE: (a) *The Straw Man* (1953), *Contraband – Spain* (1955), *Three Crooked Men* (1958), *An Honourable Murder* (1960); (d) *Stop the World I Want to Get Off* (1966), *The Best*

House in London (1968), *Secrets* (1971, + story), *Shadey* (1985), *Angels* (1992), *Metroland* (1997, UK/Fr/Sp).

Saville, Victor (*b* Birmingham, 1897 – *d* London, 1979). Director, producer, screenwriter. RN: Salberg. Son of a Birmingham art dealer, Saville's expectations of a law career were interrupted by WWI during which he was severely wounded at the Battle of Loos. Returning to Birmingham, he was employed by a film distributor and managed a small cinema in Coventry before going to work in the Features and Newsreel Department at PATHÉ in London. With Michael BALCON forming Victory Films and supervising several DOCUMENTARIES, they produced a successful movie ADAPTATION of Michael Morton's *Woman to Woman* (1923), written by Alfred HITCHCOCK. The failure of two subsequent releases led to Saville's move to GAUMONT–BRITISH where, as producer, he teamed successfully with director Maurice ELVEY. After his directing debut, a silent adaptation of the stage musical *The Arcadians* (1927), Saville launched Burlington Films, and, with studios located at British International, directed *Tesha* (1928) and an adaptation of Warwick Deeping's *Kitty* (1929), begun as a silent, but completed as a part-talkie. During this period, he also contributed to the writing of several of the films he supervised.

After directing the successful SPY MELODRAMA, *The W Plan* (1930), with Madeleine CARROLL, Saville rejoined Balcon as a director at GAINSBOROUGH. Over the next six years, with Balcon as producer, Saville directed 16 films, including some of Britain's finest 30s productions and establishing him as one of Britain's premier directors. They consisted of a wide variety of GENRES, including a sound REMAKE of the regional drama, *Hindle Wakes* (1931), two attractive romances, *Michael and Mary* (1931) and *The Faithful Heart* (1933), HISTORICAL pieces like *Me and Marlborough* (1935) starring Cicely COURTNEIDGE with Tom WALLS as the Duke, the Wellington BIOPIC, *The Iron Duke* (1935), starring George ARLISS, and the true war story, *I Was a Spy*, voted Best British film of 1933. His all-star productions of J.B. PRIESTLEY's novel, *The Good Companions* (1933) and the intriguing disaster story, *Friday the Thirteenth* (1933), also were well received.

But the stylish MUSICALS he directed were probably his most memorable films during this period. They included the highly successful *Sunshine Susie* (1931) with Renate MULLER singing the international hit 'Today I feel so happy', the Jack HULBERT vehicle, *Love on Wheels* (1932), Evelyn LAYE's *Evensong* (1934), and especially the Jessie MATTHEWS films: *Evergreen* (1934) with music by Rodgers and Hart, *First A Girl* (1935) remade nearly 50 years later as *Victor/Victoria*, and *It's Love Again* (1936). Forming his own production company, Saville, over the next two years, directed three of his best films: another SPY FILM, *Dark Journey* (1937) with Vivien LEIGH and Conrad VEIDT; the Capra-esque comedy, *Storm in a Teacup* (1937) with Leigh and Rex HARRISON; and the excellent regional drama *South Riding* (1938), based on Winifred Holtby's novel. With many of these films gaining attention in Hollywood, Saville agreed to a contract with MGM to produce. His first two productions made in England for the studio were the celebrated films *The Citadel* (1938) and *Goodbye, Mr Chips* (1939). When the war caused MGM to close their English studios, Saville moved to Hollywood where he produced films for several years. In 1943 he helped coordinate the Anglo-American production, *Forever and a Day* with numerous British stars to raise money for war charities.

In 1949, he returned to Britain for MGM to direct Elizabeth Taylor in her first adult role, the spy melodrama, *Conspirator*. Following the lavish production of *Kim* (1950), he completed his MGM career with the British-made, *Calling Bulldog Drummond* (1951). His career wound down with several Mickey Spillane thrillers in the mid 50s, a Warners' religious spectacular, and two British dramas in the early 1960s. He was a complete professional, truly one of the most important British directors and producers to emerge from the 20s and 30s, showing ability in many genres and demonstrating knowledge of all areas of film-making and distribution.

OTHER BRITISH FILMS: (p) *The White Shadow* (1923), *The Prude's Fall* (1924), *Mademoiselle from Armentières* (1926), *Hindle Wakes* (1927), *Roses of Picardy* (1927), *The Glad Eye* (1927), *The Flight Commander* (1928), *Action for Slander* (1937), *The Greengage Summer* (1961), *Mix Me a Person* (1962); (d) *Woman to Woman* (1929), *A Warm Corner* (1930), *The Sport of Kings* (1930), *The Dictator* (1935), *Twenty-Four Hours of a Woman's Life* (1952).

BIBLIOG: Cyril Rollins and Robert J. Wareing, *Victor Saville*, 1972; Roy Moseley, *Evergreen: Victor Saville in his Own Words*, 2000. Stephen Shafer.

Sawalha, Nadim (*b* Jordan, 1935). Actor. Busy supporting player, who migrated to England in the 60s, in films and TV since the early 70s, in a range of 'Eastern' roles, including two BOND films, *The Spy Who Loved Me* (1977) and *The Living Daylights* (1987). Also in such international films as *Ishtar* (1987, US) and the US-financed, UK-set *The Avengers* (1998), and with a continuing role as Dr Hamada in *Dangerfield* (1995–98). Father of Julia SAWALHA.

OTHER BRITISH FILMS INCLUDE: *A Touch of Class* (1972), *Gold, Return of the Pink Panther, Callan, Vampira* (1974), *Sweeney!* (1976), *Are You Being Served?* (1977), *The Awakening* (1980, UK/US), *Pascali's Island* (1988, UK/US), *The Hawk* (1993).

Sawalha, Julia (*b* London, 1968). Actress. Most famous for her endearing role of Saffy, the severe, ultra-sensible, bespectacled daughter of outrageously self-absorbed hedonist, Edina Monsoon, in TV's cult hit, *Absolutely Fabulous* (1992, 1993, 2001), throwing serious doubt on the idea of genetic imprinting. She was, contrastingly, a brilliantly self-absorbed, hedonistic Lydia in the BBC's wildly popular *Pride and Prejudice* (1995). On TV first in *Press Gang* (1989–93), opposite her then-boyfriend, Dexter FLETCHER, she has had only a spotty cinema career, the highlights being the provincial actress playing Ophelia in *In the Bleak Midwinter* (1995) and *Chicken Run* (2000, UK/US), in which she provided the voice of Ginger. A potentially major talent awaiting a commensurate film career. Daughter of Nadim SAWALHA and sister of actress Nadia Sawalha (*b* London, 1967), who has appeared mainly on TV.

OTHER BRITISH FILMS: *Buddy's Song* (1990), *The Wind in the Willows* (1996), *The Final Curtain* (2002, UK/US).

Sayle, Alexei (*b* Liverpool, 1952). Actor. Major TV comic since the early 80s, portly, balding Sayle has merely grazed the common of cinema, compared to his TV appearances in the likes of the unscrupulous landlord of *The Young Ones* (1982, 1984) or in *Stuff* (1988) or any of the numerous guest stints or *The All New Alexei Sayle Show* (1994). In cinema, he was the Sultan in *Indiana Jones and the Last Crusade* (1989, US) and Achmed in the last and least of the 'CARRY ON' SERIES, *Carry On Columbus* (1992), but it is not for these that he was awarded an Honorary Professorship by Thames Valley University (1995). Has also published a novel, *Barcelona Pirates*.

OTHER BRITISH FILMS INCLUDE: *The Secret Policeman's Other Ball* (1982), *The Bride*, *The Supergrass* (1985), *Whoops Apocalypse* (1986), *The Love Child* (1987), *Swing* (1999).

Scacchi, Greta (*b* Milan, 1960). Actress. RN: Gracco. Daughter of Italian father and English mother, raised in Milan, then moved to London and, in 1975, to Australia, the gorgeous Scacchi trained at the Old Vic Theatre School and entered films in the early 80s. Even dressed, which was not always the case, she commanded attention in such films as MERCHANT IVORY's *Heat and Dust* (1982) as the memsahib who strays, in *White Mischief* (1987), as another faithless colonial wife, in *The Browning Version* (1994), faithless again, as the wife of dessicated teacher Albert FINNEY, and, against what had come to seem type, as understanding Mrs Weston in *Emma* (1996, UK/US), not to speak of playing Gale Sondergaard, great actress but no beauty, in *One of the Hollywood Ten* (2000, UK/Sp). But apart from such British-based work, she has made films in Germany, Australia (winning an AFI award for *Looking for Alibrandi*, 2000) and the US (seductive as ever in *Presumed Innocent*, 1990). She had a four-year relationship with her *Salt on Our Skin* (1992, Can/Fr/Ger) co-star, Vincent D'Onofrio, by whom she has a daughter.

OTHER BRITISH FILMS INCLUDE: *Defence of the Realm* (1985), *Jefferson in Paris* (1995), *The Serpent's Kiss* (1997, UK/Fr/Ger), *The Red Violin* (UK/Can/It), *Love and Rage* (Ger/Ire) (1998), *Cotton Mary* (UK/Fr/US), *Ladies' Room* (UK/Can) (1999).

Scaife, Ted (*b* London, 1912 – *d* Chichester, 1994). Cinematographer. With GAINSBOROUGH sound department from 1939, then with Technicolour Ltd for seven years (1940–47), Scaife worked as camera operator or as 2nd unit cameraman on such notable films as *Black Narcissus* (1947, cam op) and *Pandora and the Flying Dutchman* (1950, 2uc), before receiving his first cinematographer credits. These were on modest black-and-white films, but in *The Holly and the Ivy* (1952) he contributes to the contrasts of Yule warmth and the sense of emotional chill, and his lighting is essential to the frissons of *Night of the Demon* and the sunniness of *Happy is the Bride* (1957). In general, though, his work is functional rather than inspired, but always equal to the occasion.

OTHER BRITISH FILMS INCLUDE: (cam op) *The Life and Death of Colonel Blimp* (1943), *Caesar and Cleopatra* (1945), *The Third Man* (1949), *State Secret* (1950); (2uc) *The African Queen* (1951); (c) *Home at Seven* (1952), *Melba*, *The Intruder* (1953), *An Inspector Calls*, *A Kid for Two Farthings* (1954), *Storm over the Nile* (1955), *The Birthday Present* (1957), *The Boy and the Bridge* (1959), *Please Turn Over*, *Carry On Constable* (1960), *All Night Long* (1961), *The Truth About Spring* (1964), *Young Cassidy* (1965), *Khartoum* (1966), *Play Dirty* (1968), *Sitting Target* (1972).

Scala, Gia (*b* Liverpool, 1934 – *d* Los Angeles, 1972). Actress. RN: Giovanna Scoglio. Daughter of Irish mother and Italian father, raised in Rome and in the US from 17, brunette beauty Scala worked steadily in the 50s without becoming a top star, and died young from an accidental overdose of drugs. Three of her best roles were in British films: *The Two-Headed Spy* (1958), *The Angry Hills* (1959), and *The Guns of Navarone* (1961).

Scala Productions This company's previous incarnation was PALACE PRODUCTIONS founded in 1983 by Nik POWELL and Stephen WOOLLEY, their first feature being *The Company of Wolves*, 1984, directed by Neil JORDAN with whom they have frequently been associated. They moved into some American-based production after *Mona Lisa* (1986). *The Crying Game* (1992) won the Producer's Guild of America's 'Producer of the

Year' award for Woolley, and was nominated for six Oscars, including Best Picture, Jordan winning for Original Screenplay. *Backbeat* (1994), *The Neon Bible* (1995, UK/US) and *Fever Pitch* (1997) all reached certain sections of audience, as did the praiseworthy Scala–BBC FILMS co-production *24 7 TwentyFourSeven* (1997). The Scarborough-set *Little Voice* (1998, UK/US) found appreciative audiences, and this concentration on British-based subjects paid off with *Last Orders* (2002, UK/Ger), an excellent assembly piece starring Michael CAINE, Bob HOSKINS, Tom COURTENAY, Helen MIRREN, David HEMMINGS and Ray WINSTONE. Scala also ventured into ANIMATION with *Christmas Carol: The Movie* (2001) employing the voices of Kate WINSLET and others, and a raft of new titles in production in 2000 included one based in Mississippi. Stephen Brown.

Scales, Prunella (*b* Sutton Abinger, Surrey, 1932). Actress. RN: Illingworth. So firmly is Scales now established in the public mind with Sybil Fawlty, barking out orders to husband John CLEESE or placating outraged guests in *Fawlty Towers* (1975, 1979) that it is easy to forget how much else she has done. Trained at London's Old Vic School and on stage from 1951, in plays classic and modern, she entered films in 1953 (*Laxdale Hall*), played one of Charles LAUGHTON's less stroppy daughters in *Hobson's Choice* (1953), and can be glimpsed in the Council Office in *Room at the Top* (1958). But she didn't make much impression in films until the late 80s, when she played the protagonist's friend in *The Lonely Passion of Judith Hearne* (1987) and began to appear in noticeable supporting roles in such films as *Howards End* (1992), *An Awfully Big Adventure* (1995) and *An Ideal Husband* (1998, UK/US). Films simply failed to give her the chances she had elsewhere, as in TV's *A Question of Attribution* (1992), in which she does an exquisitely lethal job as the Queen. Married since 1963 to Timothy WEST and mother of Samuel WEST. Awarded CBE 1992.

OTHER BRITISH FILMS INCLUDE: *Waltz of the Toreadors* (1962), *Escape from the Dark* (1976), *The Hound of the Baskervilles* (1977), *The Wicked Lady* (1983), *A Chorus of Disapproval* (1989), *Second Best* (1994), *Stiff Upper Lips* (1996, UK/Ind), *Mad Cows* (1999), *Station Jim* (2001, as Queen Victoria).

Schach, Max (*b* Zenta, Hungary, 1886 – *d* London, 1957). Producer. A prolific producer in Germany, Schach ventured into Anglo-German co-productions in the late 1920s. He emigrated to Britain in 1934 and founded several companies (Trafalgar, Capital, Cecil, and Grafton), specialising in lavish costume dramas (e.g. *Köenigsmark*, 1935, co-p, and *The Marriage of Corbal*, 1936), and operettas (e.g. *Land Without Music*, 1936), often with a substantial artistic input from other émigrés. Dependent on extensive loans, Schach's productivity but meagre box-office success precipitated a financial collapse in 1937 which was felt throughout the industry, and for which Schach was blamed. He subsequently retired from the film-making business altogether.

OTHER BRITISH FILMS INCLUDE: *Abdul The Damned* (1935), *Moscow Nights* (1935, co-p), *Pagliacci*, *Southern Roses* (co-p) (1936), *Jericho* (co-p), *Love From A Stranger* (1937), *Second Best Bed* (1938). Tim Bergfelder.

Schell, Catherine (aka Catherina von Schell) (*b* Budapest, 1944). Actress. RN: Szell. In European films from the mid 60s, Schell had a few leads in British films (e.g. *Amsterdam Affair*, 1968; *Moon Zero Two*, 1969) before settling into supporting 'foreign' roles. Also active on TV, as in *Space: 1999* (1975–77).

OTHER BRITISH FILMS INCLUDE: *Traitor's Gate* (1965), *On Her Majesty's Secret Service* (1969), *Madame Sin* (1972), *The Black Windmill*,

Return of the Pink Panther, Callan (1974), *The Island of Adventure* (1982), *On the Black Hill* (1987).

Schell, Maria (*b* Vienna, 1926). Actress. Rather too intense Austrian star of international films, on screen first aged 16, and sporadically in British films from 1949, when she starred in the lugubrious *The Angel with the Trumpet* (1949), the English-speaking version of a German-language saga. It didn't do her much good and though she was affecting as the first Mrs Friese-Greene, who dies of poverty, in *The Magic Box* (1951), it was not successful, and the wartime romance, *So Little Time* (1952), co-starring Marius GORING, was too low-key to fix her in the public mind. She went to the US in the later 50s, to co-star in *The Brothers Karamazov* (1958) and *The Hanging Tree* (1959), but she remained respected, especially for such continental films as *Gervaise* (1956, Fr), rather than widely popular and later returned in character roles. Sister of Maximilian SCHELL.

OTHER BRITISH FILMS INCLUDE: *The Heart of the Matter* (1953), *The Mark* (1961), *The Odessa File* (1974, UK/Ger), *Voyage of the Damned* (1976), *Superman* (1978), *Nineteen Nineteen* (1984).

Schell, Maximilian (*b* Vienna, 1930). Actor. Oscar-winner for *Judgment at Nuremberg* (1961), Schell, younger brother of Maria SCHELL, has won a reputation as an intelligent, ambitious actor on the international scene, on both stage and screen, apparently uninterested in capitalising on his good looks to become a conventional leading man. In a prolific career, he has made a handful of British films, including *The Odessa File* (1974, UK/Ger), with sister Maria, and *A Bridge Too Far* (1977), as a German general. Also Oscar-nominated for his lead in *The Man in the Glass Booth* (1975, US) and supporting role in *Julia* (1977, US), and much praised for his DOCUMENTARY, *Marlene* (1984), based on the legendary Dietrich.

OTHER BRITISH FILMS: *Return from the Ashes* (1965), *The Deadly Affair* (1966), *Pope Joan* (1972), *Cross of Iron* (1977).

Schepisi, Fred (*b* Melbourne, 1939). Director. Schepisi came to prominence in the Australian film revival of the 70s and most of his later work has been in the US, but he warrants mention here chiefly for his 2002 success, *Last Orders* (UK/Ger), with its notable cast playing so harmoniously together, strengthening his reputation as a fine director of actors. His *Plenty* (1985) is US-financed, partly UK-filmed and with largely UK cast; *Evil Angels* (1988), based on a celebrated trial, is a UK/Australian co-production; and he completed the direction of *Fierce Creatures* (1997, UK/US).

Schiaparelli, Elsa (*b* Rome, 1896 – *d* Paris, 1973). Costume designer. Italian designer, with couture houses in London and Paris, who worked as a film scriptwriter in the US before returning to Paris in 1920. She designed the costumes, usually in collaboration (e.g. with Norman HARTNELL on *Little Friend*, 1934; *Brewster's Millions*, 1935), for several British films of the 30s and Zsa Zsa Gabor's gowns for *Moulin Rouge* (1953). 'Shocking pink' was her invention and, indeed, she liked to shock.

OTHER BRITISH FILMS: *A Gentleman of Paris* (1931, co-cos), *The Tunnel* (1935, co-cos), *The Beloved Vagabond, King of the Damned* (1936), *Jump for Glory* (1937, co-cos), *Pygmalion* (1938, co-cos).

Schifrin, Lalo (Boris) (*b* Buenos Aires, 1932). Composer. After studying classical music and jazz in Paris and forming his own jazz band in Argentina, Schifrin became one of the world's most prolific film composers, receiving a half-dozen Oscar nominations, including that for the British film, *Voyage of the Damned* (1976). Most of his work is US-based, but there is a handful of British films, including the very popular *The Eagle Has Landed* (1976). Famous for the theme of the TV series *Mission: Impossible* which the 1996 film reused, and also a composer of concert works.

OTHER BRITISH FILMS: *The Liquidator* (1965, + cond), *Escape to Athena* (1979), *Loophole* (1980), *The Fourth Protocol* (1987), *Return to the River Kwai* (1988).

Schiller, Frederick (*b* Vienna, 1901 – *d* Wellingborough, Northants, 1994). Actor. Austrian actor who studied under Max Reinhardt and had much stage experience in Vienna. Served with the British Army in WW2 and naturally played many Nazi swine in such WAR FILMS as *Albert RN* (1953) and *The Colditz Story* (1954). However, his 'foreign-ness' is used to comic effect in *Small Hotel* (1957) and he is comparatively benign in *The Trollenberg Terror* (1958).

OTHER BRITISH FILMS INCLUDE: *Mr Emmanuel* (1944), *The Captive Heart* (1946), *Counterblast* (1948), *Secret People* (1951), *Oh, Rosalinda!!* (1955), *Who Done It?* (1956), *Operation Amsterdam* (1958), *Sammy Going South* (1963), *Barry Lyndon* (1975), *Quincy's Quest* (1979).

Schlesinger, John (*b* London, 1926). Director. Began directing features when the British NEW WAVE was well underway. After Uppingham School, WW2 army service and Oxford (where he made student films), he began acting in repertory from 1950, playing occasional bit parts in British films, as well as working as assistant director on TV series, including *The Four Just Men* (1957–8), and directing short topical and arts features for *Tonight* and *Monitor* (1958–61), winning an Edinburgh Festival prize for *The Innocent Eye* (1959). A commission from BRITISH TRANSPORT FILMS led to *Terminus* (1961) (BAA, Best Short Film); this and his BBC work attracted the attention of producer Joseph JANNI. His first feature, the warmly human, unpretentious *A Kind of Loving* (1962, BAA/film) has excellent use of Lancashire industrial town locations and background detail, but displays also a touch of misogyny, with women depicted as shallow consumers and marriage as a female trap. *Billy Liar* (1963, BAA/d/film) confused audiences expecting farce rather than tragi-comedy. With its uneasy blend of realism and laboured Walter Mitty-type fantasy sequences, it is a mid point between the New Wave and 'SWINGING LONDON', tantalisingly a train ride away, which Billy cannot bring himself to make. The international success, *Darling* (1965, + co-sc, AAn/d, BAA/British Film), with its superficial borrowings, heavy-handed messages, and its presentation of effete 60s media types, is as vacuous as its characters. Even the director now regards it as an embarrassment. *Far from the Madding Crowd* (1967) has pictorial beauties (cinematography by Nicholas ROEG) and bravura sequences but is long, slow and dramatially uninvolving. *Midnight Cowboy* (1969, AA/d, BAA/d/film), a British outsider's take on the underside of New York life, was a critically acclaimed international hit. The unconventional, compassionate triangular love story *Sunday Bloody Sunday* (1971, BAA/d/film, AAn/d) is Schlesinger's best and most personal film (exploring gay relationships and Jewish identity in fashionable Hampstead), much superior to the bland WW2 romance *Yanks* (1979, BAAn/d). Two of his finest films have been for BBC television from Alan BENNETT screenplays: *An Englishman Abroad* (1983) and *A Question of Attribution* (1992). Their light touch and keen sense of observation led him to be styled 'the Lubitsch of British espionage'. Latterly he has directed impersonal US films, notably in the thriller genre, combined with more intimate British films, such as the high-camp 30s literary satire *Cold Comfort Farm* (1995,

TV, some cinemas), as well as directing for the RSC and the National, and opera at Covent Garden. Awarded CBE, 1970 and BAFTA Fellowship, 1996.

OTHER BRITISH FILMS (a) *Horror* (1946, short), *Black Legend* (1948, short) (1948), *The Starfish* (1950, doc, + co-d), *Single-Handed* (1953), *The Divided Heart* (1954), *Oh, Rosalinda!!* (1955), *The Battle of the River Plate, Sunday in the Park* (s, doc), *Brothers in Law, The Last Man to Hang?* (1956), *Stormy Crossing, Seven Thunders,* (1957); (d) *Israel* (1967, short), *Visions of Eight* (1973), *Madame Sousatzka* (1988), *The Innocent* (1993, UK/Ger).

BIBLIOG: Nancy J. Brooker, *John Schlesinger: a Guide to References and Resources,* 1978: Gene D Phillips, *John Schlesinger,* 1981. Roger Philip Mellor.

Schneer, Charles H. (*b* Norfolk, Virginia, 1920). Producer. American-born producer who spent the latter half of his career making FANTASY and action films in Britain, as well as the UK/US co-production, the MUSICAL, *Half a Sixpence* (1967). With SPECIAL EFFECTS genius Ray HARRYHAUSEN, he had a big success with *Jason and the Argonauts* (1963), but sadly their last collaboration, *Clash of the Titans* (1981, UK/US), was a lamentably feeble affair.

OTHER BRITISH FILMS INCLUDE: (p, unless noted) *The Three Worlds of Gulliver* (1960, UK/US/Sp), *Mysterious Island* (1961), *The Siege of the Saxons* (1963, co-p), *East of Sudan* (1964, ex p), *The Executioner* (1970), *Sinbad and the Eye of the Tiger* (1977, co-p).

Schneider, Romy (*b* Vienna, 1938 – *d* Paris, 1982). Actress. RN: Rosemarie Albach-Retty. Born to a theatrical family and a youthful success in a series about European royalty, the very attractive Schneider had an international fling from the early 60s, including a handful of British films, none of which showed her at her best: *The Victors* (1963), *Triple Cross* (1966, UK/Fr/Ger), *Otley* (1968), *My Lover, My Son, Bloomfield* (UK/Israel) (1969). A difficult personal life included the tragic accidental death of her son, and some believed her own death was by suicide.

Schofield, Johnnie (*b* London, 1889 – *d* London, 1961). Actor. Indefatigable character player who made nearly 100 films in 20 years, working for most companies, in films major and minor, and in virtually every GENRE. He appeared in several for John BAXTER in the 30s, lectured on the Lewis gun in *The Way Ahead* (1944), was a chirpy presence in *The Way to the Stars* (1945), and his irrepressible, chunky persona enlivened such '**B**' MOVIES as *Three Steps to the Gallows* and *Scarlet Web* (1954) with fleeting moments of veracity. In 1943 he had his only starring role: as the stage manager in the MUSICAL, *Down Melody Lane.*

OTHER BRITISH FILMS INCLUDE: *Hawleys of High Street* (1933), *The Outcast* (1934), *A Real Bloke* (1935), *Song of Freedom* (1936), *Talking Feet* (1937), *The Spy in Black* (1939), *Contraband* (1940), *Went the Day Well?, The Next of Kin* (1942), *The Bells Go Down* (1943), *Waterloo Road, Tawny Pipit* (1944), *The Shop at Sly Corner* (1946), *While I Live* (1947), *Mr Perrin and Mr Traill* (1948), *Train of Events* (1949), *White Corridors* (1951), *The Voice of Merrill* (1952), *The Net* (1953), *Carrington VC* (1954).

schools and schooldays British society is famously obsessed with schools, a reflection perhaps of those other supposed national preoccupations: tradition, CLASS, and sex – or the lack of it. Such issues certainly find a convenient focal point in the microcosm of the school community. It is not surprising, then, that films with a school setting should be legion.

Stephen FREARS's historical DOCUMENTARY on the nation's cinema, *Typically British* (1996), appropriately begins with scenes from *Goodbye, Mr Chips* (1939), which chronicles the life of a teacher at an independent boarding school for upper- and

middle-class boys: the classic English 'public school'. Although – or because – these institutions have catered for a small, mainly privileged minority, they have proved a particular source of fascination for British film-makers and audiences. An ADAPTATION of *Tom Brown's Schooldays,* the classic public-school novel, dates back to 1916; there was a remake in 1951. Frears's parade of 'typically British' films continues with *Boys Will Be Boys* (1935), *The Housemaster* (1938), *If . . .* (1968) and, in a subsequent segment, *The Happiest Days of Your Life* (1950): all dealing with public schools – boys', girls', or both – though the first of these (itself the first of a popular series, starring the comic, Will HAY) sends up a dodgy version of the species. Among this sample, only *If . . .* broaches any concerted criticism of the traditional public school (not uninfected by a certain grim nostalgia on the part of its public-school-educated director, Lindsay ANDERSON).

Frears's sample, however, is not fully representative. While there has been a continuous stream of nostalgic and/or critical treatments of the public school (including *Take My Life* and *Vice Versa,* 1947; *The Guinea Pig* and *Mr Perrin and Mr Traill,* 1948; *The Browning Version,* 1951, remade 1994 ; *Escapade,* 1955; the *St Trinian's* series, 1954–80; *A French Mistress,* 1960; a musical remake of *Goodbye, Mr Chips,* 1969; *Unman, Wittering and Zigo,* 1971; *I'll Never Forget What's 'is Name,* 1967; *Another Country,* 1984; *Clockwise,* 1985), it is a stream which has begun to thin, and which has never been completely dominant. Many other sorts of educational establishment, at all levels of social class or age, have provided fertile settings for drama, comedy, and contemporary social observation: kindergartens (*Bunny Lake is Missing,* 1965); 'prep schools' (segments in *Portrait of Clare,* 1950 and *Decline and Fall . . . ,* 1968); tough inner-city secondary schools (*Carry on Teacher,* 1959; *Term of Trial,* 1962; *To Sir, with Love,* 1967); grammar schools or 'comprehensives' in more genteel-seeming surroundings (*A Personal Affair,* 1953; *P'tang Yang Kipperbang,* 1982; *Get Real,* 1999); a Scottish private day school for girls (*The Prime of Miss Jean Brodie,* 1968); a mixed-race school in Jamaica on the eve of British withdrawal (*Passionate Summer,* 1958); language schools (*French Without Tears,* 1939); borstals (*Boys in Brown,* 1949; *The Loneliness of the Long Distance Runner,* 1963); finishing schools (*The Romantic Age,* 1949); and UNIVERSITIES (traditional 'Oxbridge' in *Bachelor of Hearts,* 1958, *Accident,* 1967, *Chariots of Fire,* 1981; newer-style provincial in *Lucky Jim,* 1957). Ian Britain.

Schreyeck, Elaine (*b* London, 1924). Continuity. Entered industry in 1941 and was with EALING from 1942 to 1946, winning a reputation as a respected 'continuity girl', on such films as *Dead of Night* (1945). From 1946, she freelanced, working with such major US directors as Fred ZINNEMANN (on *The Sundowners,* 1960, US/Aust) and Billy Wilder (on *The Private Life of Sherlock Holmes,* 1970), as well as such British directors as Herbert WILCOX, Ronald NEAME, Lance COMFORT, Robert HAMER, Guy HAMILTON and Lewis GILBERT. Worked on six BOND films, retiring in 1986. Also had 'script supervisor' credits on several films.

OTHER BRITISH FILMS INCLUDE: (cont) *For Those in Peril, They Came to a City* (1944), *Bedelia* (1946), *Temptation Harbour, Daughter of Darkness* (1947), *Maytime in Mayfair* (1949), *Seagulls Over Sorrento* (1954), *Gideon's Day* (1958), *Suddenly, Last Summer* (1959), *The Private Life of Sherlock Holmes* (1970), *Diamonds Are Forever* (1971), *England Made Me* (1972, UK/Yug), *Sleuth, Live and Let Die* (1973), *The Man with the Golden Gun* (1974), *Superman* (1978, sup), *Moonraker* (1979, UK/Fr), *The Mirror Crack'd* (1980), *For Your Eyes Only, Evil Under the Sun* (1981); (sc super) *The Cure for Love* (1949), *Hope and Glory* (1987).

Schüfftan, Eugen (*b* Breslau, Silesia 1893 – *d* New York, 1977). Cinematographer. One of the greatest cinematographers, and an influential innovator in the area of special effects and depth of field. For Fritz Lang's *Metropolis* (Ger 1927) Schüfftan employed miniature models and mirrors to create the optical illusion of real sets, a patented device which was used worldwide as the 'Schüfftan process' (HITCHCOCK first used it in *Blackmail*, 1929) until it was replaced by 'matte' shots. Schüfftan achieved his most accomplished work in France in the 30s (e.g. *Quai des Brumes*, 1938). His British assignments during the same period included the visually striking expressionist fairy-tale *The Robber Symphony* (1936). From 1940, Schüfftan only slowly re-established himself in Hollywood, and worked mainly in France after the war. He won an AA for *The Hustler* (1961).

OTHER BRITISH FILMS: *Madame Pompadour* (1928, tech adviser), *Number Seventeen* (1928, UK/Ger, tech adviser), *The Mistress Of Atlantis* (1932, UK/Fr/Ger), *Irish Hearts* (1934, co-c), *The Invader* (1936), *Children Of The Fog* (1937). Tim Bergfelder.

Schüfftan process *see* **Schüfftan, Eugen**

Schulz, Franz (*b* Prague, 1897 – *d* Muralto, Switz, 1971). Screenwriter. Finished his career in Hollywood in the 40s and early 50s as Franz Spencer, having been responsible for the story and/or screenplay of a number of light GAINSBOROUGH films and UK/German co-productions in the 30s. His play provided the basis for *Sunshine Susie* (1931), starring the delightful German star, Renate MULLER; Anthony ASQUITH's *The Lucky Number* (1933) was based on his story; and he co-authored the original scenario for *Two Hearts in Waltz Time* (1934) and the popular 'Viennese' romance, *Blossom Time* (1934).

OTHER BRITISH FILMS INCLUDE: *Two Worlds* (1930, UK/Ger, co-sc), *Monte Carlo Madness* (UK/Ger, co-sc), *Love on Wheels* (co-story) (1932), *Sleeping Car* (1933).

Schuster, Harold D. (*b* Cherokee, Iowa, 1902 – *d* Westlake Village, California, 1986). Director. Former editor and prolific director of largely routine Hollywood GENRE films, Schuster made three films in Britain in the 30s, including the first TECHNICOLOR feature film produced in Britain, the popular romance of horse-racing and GYPSY life, *Wings of the Morning* (1937).

OTHER BRITISH FILMS: *Dinner at the Ritz* (1937), *Queer Cargo* (1938).

Schwarz, Hanns (*b* Vienna, 1888 – *d* Hollywood, 1945). Director. RN: Ignatz Schwartz. Contract director at Germany's UFA studios since 1925, specialising in romantic comedies. Director of the first German sound film *Melodie des Herzens* (1929). In the 30s, his career took him to France, Britain, and Hollywood, where he settled in 1939. During the war, he worked for the American secret service.

BRITISH FILMS: *The Prince of Arcadia* (1933), *The Return of the Scarlet Pimpernel* (1938). Tim Bergfelder.

Schwartz, Stefan Director, screenwriter. Schwartz and producer Richard HOLMES run a production company known as the Gruber Brothers, which had a success with the comic caper film, *Shooting Fish* (1997). Prior to his directing debut in 1992 (*The Lake*, short, + co-sc; *Soft Top, Hard Shoulder*), he had acted on TV, as in *Portrait of a Marriage* (1990).

OTHER BRITISH FILMS: *The Abduction Club* (2001).

science fiction and British cinema Until the 50s British science fiction films were comparatively rare. Some early trick films, such as Walter BOOTH's *The Airship Destroyer* (1909), *The Aerial Submarine* (1910) and *The Aerial Anarchists* (1911), drew on the GENRE to reflect genuine fears of invasion and war in the skies, while a handful of SF–FANTASY films were produced in the 20s and 30s (*The Fugitive Futurist* (1924), *High Treason* (1929), *Once in a New Moon* (1935), *The Tunnel* (1935) and *The Man Who Changed His Mind* (1936). Of these by far the most important was *Things to Come* (1936), a one-off prestige project written by H.G. WELLS. Although grandiose, naive and talky, *Things to Come* still impresses by the frigid utopianism of its set design, faith in scientific progress and scenes, eerily prophetic of the Blitz, of London under aerial bombardment.

Commercial failure, however, ensured that it was not till the 50s, when SF took off in the United States, that British studios would experiment again with the genre. HAMMER's *Four-Sided Triangle* (1953) and *Spaceways* (1953); *Stranger from Venus* (1954), a remake of *The Day the Earth Stood Still* (1951); *Devil Girl from Mars* (1954) and *Fire Maidens from Outer Space* (1956) – such titles are characteristic of early British SF, unabashed EXPLOITATION films either closely imitative of American successes or adapted from radio and television productions.

Hammer's *The Quatermass Experiment* (1955), taken from Nigel KNEALE's TV series, laid down the blueprint for the high proportion of British SF films in which a cross-section of social types fend off symbolic incursions of Otherness and modernity. Although a significant handful of films were SPIN-OFFS from children's television series such as *Doctor Who* and *Thunderbirds*, most reworked *Quatermass*'s combination of gruesome horror and paranoid invasion narrative. American films of the period, such as *Invasion of the Body Snatchers* (1955), are convulsed with fears of Communist subversion. British ones, however, focus on interior threats to fragile postwar consensus: the enemy within could be the Establishment, taken over by aliens in *Quatermass 2* (1957); precocious youth in *Children of the Damned* (1963); or even women, in *The Night Caller* (1965). Often the films rework motifs from WW2 and especially the Blitz, to explore the survival, after Suez and the end of EMPIRE, of wartime myths of British 'spirit', social cohesion and strength of character.

Although Stanley Kubrick's *2001: A Space Odyssey* (1968) is without doubt the greatest SF film made in Britain, its resources and ambitions went well beyond most of its British counterparts. Celebration of space travel, too, distanced it from British concerns. Although in the 50s some British SF films such as *Spaceways* and *Satellite in the Sky* (1956) casually assumed that Britain would lead the space race, these fantasies of a real life Dan Dare quickly evaporated. Not surprisingly, since the 60s British space flight movies have been rather uncommon, and with very few exceptions (*Spaceflight IC-1*, 1965; *Journey to the Far Side of the Sun*, 1969; *Moon Zero Two*, 1969) tend to be either nostalgic ADAPTATIONS of Victorian novels (*First Men in the Moon*, 1964) or comedies mocking the very idea of Brits making it into space (*Morons from Outer Space*, 1985), *A Grand Day Out*, 1993).

The 70s saw some interesting oddities among the SF-horror output of the waning exploitation market: John BOORMAN's Jungian dystopia *Zardoz* (1973), the Michael Moorcock adaptation, *The Final Programme* (1973), Nicolas ROEG's *The Man who Fell to Earth* (1976). Since then, however, Britain's main contribution to SF has been as a base for international co-productions such as *Superman* (1978), *Alien* (1979, UK/US) and *Event Horizon* (1997, UK/US), which, it is uncontroversial to remark, lack any distinctively 'British' themes.

Till recently critical interest in British SF cinema has been limited to isolated films with AUTEURIST interest (*2001, Zardoz, The Damned, The Man Who Fell to Earth, Alien, Brazil*). The consensus remains that, the films being so often hampered by low budgets and pressure to imitate American models, the most innovative British screen SF is actually to be found in the quirky absurdism of TV fantasy: *Doctor Who, The Prisoner, The Avengers, Quatermass.*

BIBLIO: I.Q. Hunter (ed), *British Science Fiction Cinema*, 1999. I.Q. Hunter.

Scofield, Paul (*b* Hurstpierpoint, 1922). Actor. Celebrated stage star who looks and seems almost too remorselessly intelligent for conventional film stardom. On stage while still at school in Brighton, then professionally in London from 1940, he has played most of the great Shakespearean roles (including Hamlet, by invitation, in the USSR, 1955), with many Stratford seasons, and, in the 70s, at the National Theatre, starring in *Volpone* (1977–78) and *Othello* (1980), as well as many modern plays. His preference for the stage has limited his film work, but even there he has been much honoured: he won AA and BAA for Best Actor for repeating his London (1961) and Broadway (1962) stage role of Sir Thomas More in *A Man for All Seasons* (1966), capturing brilliantly the scholarliness, humanity and unassailable integrity of the man; nearly 30 years later he was AA- and BAA-nominated as Best Supporting Actor for his role as the literary mandarin in *Quiz Show* (1994, US), and a BAA for ditto in *The Crucible* (1997, US). It is not the kind of film career to attract much multiplex attention, most often focusing on such literary enterprises as: *Bartleby* (1970), from Herman Melville's novella; the bleakly magisterial *King Lear* (1970, UK/Ger); *A Delicate Balance* (1973, UK/Can/US), a sort of 'concert' performance of Edward Albee's talkfest; Kenneth BRANAGH's *Henry V* (1989), as the careworn King of France; and ZEFFIRELLI's *Hamlet* (1990, UK/US), as the Ghost. One can almost imagine film-makers wondering if what they have to offer is worthy of his attention, though he is, by all accounts, a modest man who declined a knighthood, but was later distinguished by being appointed to the prestigious Order of the Companions of Honour in 2001. Married stage actress Joy Parker (*b* London, 1924) in 1943.

Scotland and British film The early consolidation of the British film industry in and around LONDON had major implications for film-making in Scotland. The dominant cinematic representations of Scotland were consequently an external and romanticised view inspired by the novels of Walter SCOTT and R.L. STEVENSON, resulting in films like *Rob Roy* (1922), *Bonnie Prince Charlie* (1923) and *Young Lochinvar* (1923). The Jacobite romance continued to be influential, particularly after the advent of colour which considerably enhanced the exotic spectacle of tartanry and highland scenery in the 1948 version of *Bonnie Prince Charlie, Rob Roy . . .* (1953) and *The Master of Ballantrae* (1953). The construction of Scotland as a remote 'other' world, far removed from the realities of modern existence, also informs a number of diverse films from *Edge of the World* (1937) and *I Know Where I'm Going!* (1945) to *The Brothers* (1947) and *Whisky Galore!* (1949). In this way Scotland functioned as a fantasy space in which the desires and anxieties of the British cinema audience could be played out. An alternative urban vision of Scotland was constructed by a number of films set against the backdrop of shipbuilding, including *Red Ensign* (1934), *Shipyard Sally* (1939), *The Shipbuilders* (1943) and *Floodtide* (1949). In addition

to shipbuilding's being depicted as a patriotic endeavour uniting bosses and workers, the films also explore the idea of community, a theme also canvassed in *The Brave Don't Cry* (1952), which recounts a famous mining disaster.

While a number of Scots including John GRIERSON, John MAXWELL, Alexander MACKENDRICK and Sean CONNERY made major contributions to the British cinema it was not until the 70s that the Scottish feature film became a possibility, pioneered by the work of writer-directors Bill DOUGLAS and Bill FORSYTH. With films like *Gregory's Girl* (1980) and *Local Hero* (1983), Forsyth was also a leading figure in the short-lived 'renaissance' in British cinema during the early 80s. The advent of CHANNEL 4 created new opportunities for INDEPENDENT FILM-MAKERS in Scotland who had been nurtured in the world of SPONSORED DOCUMENTARY and a small but significant number of features began to appear in the 80s including *Another Time, Another Place* (1983), *Heavenly Pursuits* (1986), *Venus Peter* (1989) and *Silent Scream* (1990), the latter two produced by the BFI. The Scottish Film Production Fund, was established in 1982 and by the 1990s this had grown into a significant source of development finance. When production money also became available from the Glasgow Film Fund and the Scottish Arts Council Lottery, a separate Scottish film industry finally became a possibility.

The profile of Scottish cinema was given a major boost in the 1990s with a number of high profile successes including *Shallow Grave* (1994), *Trainspotting* (1996) and Hollywood epics like *Rob Roy* (1995) and the Oscar-winning *Braveheart* (1995). Since then the momentum has been sustained by acclaimed films like *My Name is Joe* (1998, UK/Fr/Ger/It/Sp), *Orphans* and *Ratcatcher* (UK/Fr) (1999), and with film production reaching record levels in the year a new devolved parliament was convened in Edinburgh, the future of the new Scottish cinema looked bright.

BIBLIOG: Colin McArthur (ed), *Scotch Reels*, 1982; Janet McBain, *Scotland in Silent Cinema*, 1998; Duncan Petrie, *Screening Scotland*, 2000. Duncan Petrie.

Scott, Allan (*b* Elgin, Scotland, 1940). Screenwriter, producer. RN: Shiach. Former chairman of Macallan whisky distillery, Scott entered films in the early 70s, starting as co-writer of such films as *The Man Who Had Power over Women* (1970) and *Don't Look Now* (1973, UK/It). He later acted as (co-/ex) producer on such Scottish-set films as *Shallow Grave* (1994) and *The Match* (1999, UK/Ire/US), receiving a shared BAAn for *Regeneration* (1997, + sc), set in the Scottish psychiatric hospital to which WW1 poet, Siegfried Sassoon is sent for treatment. Wrote several films for Nicolas ROEG, including *Castaway* (1986) and *The Witches* (1989, US). Made Chairman of the Scottish Film Council in 1992.

OTHER BRITISH FILMS INCLUDE: (co-sc) *The Spiral Staircase* (1975), *Joseph Andrews* (1976), *The Awakening* (1980, UK/US); (p, co-/ex p) *Taffin* (1987, UK/US), *Two Deaths* (1995, + sc), *True Blue* (1996), *The Fourth Angel* (2001, UK/Can), *Darkness Falling* (2002, UK/Can).

Scott, Ann Producer. Along with several other significant producers, Scott came under the umbrella of the FILM CONSORTIUM, the biggest of the Lottery-funded franchises set up in 1997 by the ARTS COUNCIL. She had co-produced the state-of-the-nation piece, *The Ploughman's Lunch* (1983) with Simon RELPH for their GREENPOINT FILMS, which had a popular success with *Enchanted April* (1992) but bombed with *Hideous Kinky* (1998, UK/Fr). Married to Jack SHEPHERD.

OTHER BRITISH FILMS INCLUDE: *Laughterhouse* (1984), *The Good Father* (1986), *Tree of Hands* (1988), *Swann* (1996, UK/Can, co-p).

Scott, Avis (*b* London, 1927). Actress. RN: Scutt. Quite striking brunette whose down-to-earth quality was best seen in the MELODRAMA, *Waterfront* (1950), as Richard BURTON's loyal girlfriend, contrasted with flighty sister, Susan SHAW. Played with Noël COWARD in the 1947 revival of *Present Laughter* and worked extensively in TV when her screen career cut out in the mid 50s (e.g. on the panel of *I've Got a Secret*, 1956).
OTHER BRITISH FILMS INCLUDE: *Millions Like Us* (1943), *Brief Encounter* (1945), *Fame Is the Spur* (1947), *To Have and to Hold* (1951), *It Started in Paradise, Emergency Call* (1952), *Five Days* (1954), *Storm over the Nile* (1955).

Scott, Dougray (*b* St Andrew's, Scotland, 1965) Actor. RN: Stephen Scott. Tall, sardonic-looking young Scottish actor, very busy from the late 90s. After a small role in *Princess Caraboo* (1994, US), he appeared in Keith ALLEN's black comedy, *Twin Town* (1997), set in Wales, played Robert Graves in *Regeneration* (1997, UK/Can), made a mark as the villain in *Mission: Impossible 2* (2000, US/Aust), providing a relief from John Woo's pyrotechnics and Tom Cruise's teeth, and starred as the mathematical genius in *Enigma* (2001, UK/Ger/Neth/US). Also in demand in US films (e.g. *Ever After*, 1998) and TV, and scored a stage success in *To the Green Fields Beyond* (2000).
OTHER BRITISH FILMS: *Love in Paris* (UK/Fr/US), *Faeries* (voice), *This Year's Love, Gregory's Two Girls* (1999).

Scott, Elliot (*b* London, 1915 – *d* Hillingdon, 1993). Production designer. Began his nearly 50-year career as draughtsman on two ARCHERS' films, *A Canterbury Tale* (1944), *Black Narcissus* (1947), and finished as designer for Spielberg in Hollywood on *Indiana Jones and the Last Crusade* (1989) and *Hook* (1991), receiving an AAn for *Who Framed Roger Rabbit* (1988). In between, a wide GENRE range of British films, including COMEDY (*Lucky Jim*, 1957), SCIENCE-FICTION (*Children of the Damned*, 1963), and an Agatha CHRISTIE MYSTERY (*Evil Under the Sun*, 1981).
OTHER BRITISH FILMS INCLUDE: (draughtsman) *Edward, My Son* (1949); (art d) *Final Column, The Yellow Robe* (1955), *Safari* (1956), *I Accuse!* (1957), *tom thumb* (1958), *A Touch of Larceny* (1959), *Gorgo* (1960), *Invasion Quartet* (1961), *Nine Hours to Rama* (1962), *The Yellow Rolls-Royce* (1964, English sequences), *No Blade of Grass* (1970), *A Doll's House* (1973); (des) *The Scapegoat* (1958), *The Haunting* (1963), *Pope Joan* (1972), *Mister Quilp* (1974), *The Pirates of Penzance* (1982), *Labyrinth* (1986).

Scott, Gregory (*b* Sandy, 1879 – *d*?). Actor. Scott was a prolific leading man on stage and on screen from 1914 to 1926, but he made little impact.
BRITISH FILMS INCLUDE: *She Stoops to Conquer, Enoch Arden* (1914), *The Little Minister* (1915), *The Black Knight* (1916), *The Ware Case* (1917), *Trent's Last Case* (1920), *The Happy Rascals* (series of five shorts, 1926). AS.

Scott, Jake (*b* 1965). Director. Son of director Ridley SCOTT, he came to film via music videos, including Oasis's *Morning Glory* and R.E.M.'s award-winning *Everybody Hurts*. His first feature, *Plunkett & Macleane* (1999, UK/Czech), was not much liked but had a certain cheeky charm. Was 'visual co-ordinator' on *Dealers* (1989).

Scott, Janette (*b* Morecambe, 1938). Actress. Daughter of actress Thora HIRD, Scott appeared as a child extra in her mother's films. Made first major impression as a child in the weepie *No Place for Jennifer* (1949), and, throughout the 50s, was promoted as a rising star. Under contract to ASSOCIATED

BRITISH, she starred in *Now and Forever* (1955), and, as Susie Dean, singing and dancing in a delightful MUSICAL remake of *The Good Companions* (1956). *Happy is the Bride* (1957) was her first of several comedies co-starring Ian CARMICHAEL; she appeared in two HAMMER films, *The Old Dark House* and *Paranoiac* (1962); and *The Beauty Jungle* (1964) gave her the central role in the best and last of her British films. By the 60s, 'NEW WAVE' British actresses (e.g. Rita TUSHINGHAM) had arrived, and Scott's appeal seemed nostalgic rather than contemporary. Married (2 of 3) Mel Tormé (1966–77).
OTHER BRITISH FILMS INCLUDE: *Went the Day Well?* (1942), *Two Thousand Women* (1944), *Conspirator* (1949), *The Galloping Major, No Highway* (1951), *Background* (1953), *The Lady Is a Square, The Devil's Disciple, School for Scoundrels* (1959), *The Day of the Triffids* (1962), *Siege of the Saxons* (1963).
BIBLIOG: Autobiography, *Act One*, 1953. Roger Philip Mellor.

Scott, John (aka Patrick John Scott) (*b* Bristol, 1930). Composer. Active in British film music since 1965 (*A Study in Terror*), often conducting as well as composing. Favouring no particular GENRE, he has composed even-handedly for SHAKESPEARE (*Antony and Cleopatra*, 1972, UK/Sp/Switz), *Doctor in Clover* (1966, + cond), and the elegiac *The Shooting Party* (1984, + cond). Has also worked on US films, including *Lionheart* (1990) and composed many TV themes.
OTHER BRITISH FILMS INCLUDE: (comp) *Jules Verne's Rocket to the Moon* (1967), *Billy Two Hats* (1973), *Symptoms* (1974), *The People That Time Forgot* (1977), *Experience Preferred . . . But Not Essential* (1982), *Black Rainbow* (1989); (comp/cond) *The Long Duel* (1967), *Amsterdam Affair* (1968), *Crooks and Coronets* (1969), *Trog* (1970), *Girl Stroke Boy* (1971), *England Made Me* (1972, UK/Yug), *Hennessy* (1975), *Greystoke . . .* (1984, UK/US), *The Whistle Blower* (1986), *The Scarlet Tunic* (1997).

Scott, Margaretta (*b* London, 1912). Actress. Gravely beautiful, dark-haired and distinctive actress who made about 30 films but whose first allegiance remained the stage, where, having made her debut in 1929, she was still performing in 1995. RADA-trained, she played several seasons at Stratford and the Open Air, Regent's Park, and toured with ENSA during WW2 in *Quiet Wedding*, having appeared in the film version in 1941. She is memorable in almost all her films, whether as Ralph RICHARDSON's doxy in *Things to Come* (1936), the heroine of the strange drama, *The Man from Morocco* (1945), the Prince Regent's mistress (she did mistresses very well, often with a dangerous edge to them) in *The First Gentleman* (1948), Dona Lucia in *Where's Charley?* (1952) or the mischief-making mother-in-law in *A Woman Possessed* (1958). Best of all, though, was her sensual, cold-hearted, entirely believable Alicia in *Fanny by Gaslight* (1944), a performance strikingly stylish and truthful. Also, a long and illustrious TV career, starting before WW2 and including *Elizabeth R* (1971, as Catherine de Medici) and *All Creatures Great and Small* (from 1978, as benign aristocrat, Mrs Pumphrey). Was married to John WOOLDRIDGE; daughter is Susan WOOLDRIDGE, son is theatre director Hugh Wooldridge.
OTHER BRITISH FILMS INCLUDE: *Dirty Work* (1934), *Peg of Old Drury* (1935), *The Return of the Scarlet Pimpernel, Action for Slander* (1937), *The Girl in the News* (1940), *Atlantic Ferry* (1941), *Mrs Fitzherbert* (1947), *Idol of Paris, Counterblast* (1948), *Landfall* (1949), *Town on Trial* (1956), *The Scamp* (1957), *An Honourable Murder* (1960), *Percy* (1971).

Scott, Peter Graham (*b* East Sheen, 1923). Director, producer. A minor feature film director who was primarily active in television as a major TV director/producer from 1953. His television work as a director includes *Our Marie* (1953) and

Memory of October (1964); TV work as producer includes *The Citadel* (1960), *The Onedin Line* (1970–73), *Kidnapped* (1978), and *The Canterville Ghost* (1986). Scott began as child actor in 1937; he can be seen as a pageboy in *Young and Innocent* (1937). After WW2, he became a film editor, with his first feature *Brighton Rock* (1947), and began directing features in 1948 with *Panic at Madame Tussaud's*. Among his features are two very nifty 'B' MOVIES, *Devil's Bait* (1959) and *The Big Day* (1960) and the sunny comedy *Father Came Too!* (1963). Scott was elected a Fellow of the Royal Television Society in 1959 and honoured with its Sir Ambrose Fleming Award for 'Outstanding Service to Television' in 1984.

OTHER BRITISH FILMS INCLUDE: (e) *The Perfect Woman* (1949), *Landfall* (1949), *The Shadow of the Eagle* (1950); (d) *Sudan Dispute* (1947, p), *Sing Along with Me* (1952), *Escape Route* (1952, co-d), *Captain Clegg* (1962), *The Pot Carriers* (1962), *Bitter Harvest* (1963), *The Cracksman* (1963), *Subterfuge* (1968).

BIBLIOG: Autobiography, *British Television: An Insider's History*, 2000. AS.

Scott, Sir Ridley (*b* South Shields, 1939). Director. After study at the Royal College of Art, Scott worked as a set designer for BBC TV and obtained wide experience as a director of hundreds of TV COMMERCIALS before getting his chance to direct his first feature, *The Duellists* (1977), a highly intelligent, visually arresting ADAPTATION of Joseph CONRAD's novella of the Napoleonic Wars. This won critical acclaim (including a Cannes 'Best First Work' award) but it was his second feature, the SCIENCE-FICTION classic, *Alien* (1979, UK/US), that established him at the box-office, with its genuinely scary aura and stunning design: Scott's initial training had not been wasted. He spent the next decade or so in the US, making the troubled (and troubling) *Blade Runner* (1982, + p), a relative failure then, now, in the 'director's cut' version, seen as a dark masterpiece, and the exhilarating feminist rampage of *Thelma & Louise* (1991, + p), AA- and BAA-nominated. His contribution to the Columbus quingentenary, *1492: Conquest of Paradise* (1992, UK/Fr/Sp, + co-p), was a dire return to British film-making; he co-produced the REMAKE of *The Browning Version* (1994); there are three further UK/US co-productions, of which the stirring, sweeping, AA-winning and BAA-nominated *Gladiator* (2000, + co-p) is alone notable; and he produced Benjamin ROSS's smart TV movie, *RKO 281* (1999), based on the making of *Citizen Kane*. In 1994, he received BAFTA's Michael Balcon Award. His is now only marginally a British career. His brother, **Tony Scott** (*b* Newcastle, 1944), has made only two short films in Britain, including a version of Henry JAMES's *The Author of Beltraffio* (1974), and some popular US films, notably *Top Gun* (1986). Their production company is Scott Free Films and in 1995 they headed a consortium which bought SHEPPERTON STUDIOS. Ridley's son is Jake SCOTT. Knighted, 2003.

OTHER BRITISH FILMS: *Boy and Bicycle* (1965, short, d, p, sc), *GI Jane* (1997, UK/US, d, co-p), *Hannibal* (2001, UK/US, d, co-p).

Scott, Terry (*b* Watford, Herts, 1927 – *d* Godalming, 1994). Actor. Chunky, popular comic of films and TV from the late 50s, often thick, sometimes raucous, sometimes on the make, Scott had trained to be an accountant. On TV, he became famous for two main series: *Hugh and I* (1962–67), as the conniving son of Hugh LLOYD's landlady, and co-starring with June WHITFIELD in *Happy Ever After* (1974–78) and its follow-up, *Terry and June* (1979–87). On-screen, he is best known for starring in seven 'CARRY ON' romps, notably as the hen-

pecked husband in *Carry On Camping* (1969) and as the profoundly inept Cardinal Wolsey in *Carry On Henry* (1971). On stage, he was best known as naughty schoolboy and pantomime dame.

OTHER BRITISH FILMS INCLUDE: *Blue Murder at St Trinian's* (1957), *Carry On Sergeant* (1958), *Too Many Crooks, I'm All Right Jack* (1959), *The Night We Got the Bird* (1960), *A Pair of Briefs* (1961), *Father Came Too!* (1963), *Murder Most Foul* (1964), *Doctor in Clover, The Great St Trinian's Train Robbery* (1966), *Carry On Up the Khyber* (1968), . . . *Up the Jungle*, . . . *Loving* (1970), . . . *Matron* (1972), *The Pantomime Dame* (1982, doc).

Scott, Sir Walter (*b* Edinburgh, 1771 – *d* Abbotsford, Scotland, 1832). Author. Famous chronicler of romantic period adventures, less frequently adapted to the big screen than one might have expected. There were a half-dozen or so silent adaptations, including two British versions of *Rob Roy* (1911 and 1922), re-filmed in Britain by DISNEY in 1953 with Richard TODD as the eponymous hero, and in 1995 there was a US-financed, UK-filmed version with Liam NEESON. Two handsome MGM–BRITISH productions appeared in the 50s, both starring Robert TAYLOR: *Ivanhoe* (1952) and *The Adventures of Quentin Durward* (1955). Both these novels were also made into British TV series, *Quentin Durward* (1971) and *Ivanhoe* (1982, 1997), and, surprisingly perhaps, they were both adapted to Russian cinema in the 80s. *The Bride of Lammermoor* has turned up in various guises (sometimes via Donizetti's opera, *Lucia di Lammermoor*), including a US silent (1909), a British silent short (1922), various European TV versions, and Don BOYD's *Lucia* (1998), about a small opera company setting up a production of the opera.

OTHER BRITISH FILMS: (based on Scott's works) *The Black Knight* (1954, from poem), *The Lady of the Lake* (1995, anim, short, from poem).

Scott Thomas, Kristin (*b* Redruth, 1960). Actress. Somewhat austerely beautiful star who came to prominence in the 90s in British and international films. She was especially impressive (winning BAA/supp a) as the apparently icy Fiona, in *Four Weddings and a Funeral* (1994), nursing a secret passion for Hugh GRANT, whose wife she had played in POLANSKI's *Bitter Moon* (1992, UK/Fr). For *The English Patient* (1996), she was AA- and BAA-nominated for her performance as aristocratic Katherine engaged in a passionate affair. Educated at Cheltenham Ladies College, trained as a drama teacher at Central School, which rejected her as a drama student, she went to live in Paris where she did her drama training and, speaking fluent French, worked in a few films. She played in several big-budget Hollywood films, including *Mission: Impossible* (1996), co-starred with Robert Redford in *The Horse Whisperer* (1998) and Harrison Ford in *Random Hearts* (1999), generally winning more recognition than the films did, and in Britain she was one of the fabulous all-star cast of Robert Altman's country-house MYSTERY, *Gosford Park* (2001, UK/Ger/US). In an earlier decade, she would have been a great 'Other Woman'. Her sister is **Serena Scott Thomas** (*b* 1962), who starred in TV's *Harnessing Peacocks* (1992) and appeared in the films *'Let Him Have It'* (1991) and *The World Is Not Enough* (1999, UK/US).

OTHER BRITISH FILMS INCLUDE: *A Handful of Dust* (1987), *Richard III* (1995), *Angels and Insects* (1995, UK/US), *The Revengers' Comedies* (1998, UK/Fr), *Up at the Villa* (2000, UK/US).

Scoular, Angela (*b* London, 1945). Actress. Supporting actress of films of the 60s and 70s, including such disposables as *Here We Go Round the Mulberry Bush* (1967) and *Doctor in*

Trouble (1970), the latter co-starring her husband, Leslie PHILLIPS. TV gave her more rewarding assignments, including a go at Cathy in the 1967 mini-series version of *Wuthering Heights*. Niece of Margaret JOHNSTON.

OTHER BRITISH FILMS INCLUDE: *Casino Royale* (1967), *A Countess from Hong Kong* (1966), *On Her Majesty's Secret Service* (1969), *Adventures of a Private Eye* (1977).

Screen is the British film journal which assumed the dominant position in film studies throughout the 70s and continues one of the most influential internationally. Published by The Society for Education in Film and Television (SEFT), with assistance from the BRITISH FILM INSTITUTE, *Screen* introduced English speaking readers to post-1968 theory from France. Rejecting an aesthetic or art-for-art's-sake approach, the new direction in theory held that film, and film criticism, was fundamentally political. *Screen* published articles on four interrelated areas: semiotics, structuralism, Marxism and psychoanalytic theory. SEFT also brought out *Screen Education* which focused more directly on the relationship between theory, popular culture and teaching. *Screen* also galvanised debates in its publication of articles on feminist film theory. In 1975 *Screen* published what is undeniably the most influential article of the period – Laura MULVEY's 'Visual Pleasure and Narrative Cinema'.

It has been argued that 70s *Screen* adopted a monolithic position towards theory but, more accurately, *Screen* published different contributions and perspectives on the same THEORETICAL DEBATES. With the late 70s critique of Althusser's notion of subjectivity and interpellation, *Screen* eventually abandoned its attempt to establish a unified theory of the screen-spectator relationship. Since the 80s, it has continued to pioneer new debates, specifically in the areas of postmodernism, masculinity, gay and lesbian spectatorship, race and postcolonial cinema. Barbara Creed.

Scudamore, Margaret (*b* Portsmouth, 1884 – *d* London, 1958). Actress. Stage actress from 1898, London from 1903, mother of Michael REDGRAVE, she was in a few films from 1932 (*Arms and the Man*). Her most vivid film roles are both for Michael POWELL: as Eric PORTMAN's mother in *A Canterbury Tale* (1944) and as Deborah KERR's grandmother in the beautiful flashback sequence in *Black Narcissus* (1947).

OTHER BRITISH FILMS: *Melody and Romance*, *Beauty and the Barge*, *Double Alibi* (1937), *My Wife's Family* (1941).

Seacombe, Dorothy (*b* Bolton, Lancs, 1905). Actress. Taken when six to Australia where she was educated and made her stage debut, she returned to England in the mid 20s. Played light comedy roles on stage and made her film debut in supporting roles in the silent *Blinkeyes* and *The Flag Lieutenant* (1926), and had leading roles in a few talkies, including the romantic comedy, *Lord Richard in the Pantry* (1930).

OTHER BRITISH FILMS INCLUDE: *The Third Eye* (1929), *The Yellow Mask* (1930), *The Ware Case* (1938).

Seager, Chris (*b* Leicester, 1949). Cinematographer. Nominated for BAA/c for his work on the two mini-series, *Frenchman's Creek* (1998) and *Lorna Doone* (2000), Seager has shot a half-dozen features, including the gay activist piece *Stonewall* (1995) and the football-centred comedy, *Fever Pitch* (1997).

OTHER BRITISH FILMS INCLUDE: *Skallagrigg* (1994), *Cold Comfort Farm* (1995, TV, some cinemas), *Beautiful Thing* (1996), *Alive and Kicking* (1996).

Seagrove, Jenny (*b* Kuala Lumpur, 1958). Actress. In 2000, Seagrove courageously and with remarkable success played on stage the role of Laura Jesson, so indelibly associated with Celia JOHNSON, in a version of *Brief Encounter*. It was enough to make one wonder why screen has made so little use of her gentle beauty; her best role was as the pretty oceanographer in one of her earliest films, *Local Hero* (1983). She has appeared in several films, including *A Chorus of Disapproval* (1989) for Michael WINNER with whom she had a long relationship, and had a leading role in the TV mini-series, *The Woman in White* (1978) and *A Woman of Substance* (1983).

OTHER BRITISH FILMS INCLUDE: *Moonlighting* (1982), *To Hell and Back Before Breakfast* (1985, short), *Bullseye!* (1990, UK/US), *Zoe* (2001).

Seal, Elizabeth (*b* Genoa, 1933). Actress. Trained as dancer at the Royal Academy of Dancing, on stage in London from 1951, she scored an immense hit as *Irma La Douce* (1958), taking the musical to Broadway in 1960 and winning a Tony for her performance. Dark-haired and sexy, she is given an 'Introducing' credit on the excellent 1956 THRILLER, *Town on Trial*, as a rebellious girl who becomes a murderer's victim, but she had already been glimpsed in *Radio Cab Murder* (1954) – and hardly ever filmed again. Was a charming Avonia Bunn in TV's *Trelawney of the Wells* (1971).

OTHER BRITISH FILMS: *Cone of Silence* (1960), *Vampire Circus* (1971), *Mack the Knife* (1989, UK/Hung).

Searle, Francis A. (*b* London, 1909 – *b* London, 2002). Director. Also, literally, carried out every other job in the film industry that he was anxious to enter from an early age. Directed some of the very best small films of the 50s and 60s and used, in the process, many of the character actors of the day. This should not disguise the quality of the work which he produced on small budgets and with minimal resources. His *Cloudburst* (1951) produced acting of high order from its imported American star, Robert Preston. Is rightly proud of his pioneering location work, in various country houses, owned by EXCLUSIVE FILMS, with whom he had a long association. Formed his own company Bayford films in the 60s. At a late 90s retrospective of his work, *The Man in Black* (1949), produced applause for its early and excellent use of FILM NOIR techniques.

OTHER BRITISH FILMS INCLUDE: (d, unless noted) (shorts) *War Without End* (1936, doc), *Airwoman, Hospital Nurse, Coal Front* (1941, doc), *An English Oilfield* (1942, doc), *Music with Max Jaffa* (1958), *Miss MacTaggart Won't Lie Down* (1966, + p), *It all Goes to Show* (1970, + story), *A Couple of Beauties* (1972, + p); (features) *A Girl in a Million*, (1946), *Celia* (1949, + sc), *The Lady Craved Excitement* (+ sc), *Someone at the Door* (1950), *Love's a Luxury* (1952), *Whispering Smith Hits London* (1952), *Final Appointment* (p), *A Yank in Ermine* (assoc p) (1954), *One Way Out* (1955), *The Gelignite Gang* (1956), *Diplomatic Corpse* (1958, p), *Emergency* (+p), *Night of the Prowler* (1962), *The Marked One* (1963). Paul Quinn.

Searle, Ronald (*b* Cambridge, 1920). Cartoonist. Painter and author as well, Searle is the celebrated creator of the monstrous schoolgirls of ST TRINIAN's, whose exploits were the subject of five popular but decreasingly funny films, starting with *The Belles of St Trinian's* (1954), with credits designed by Searle. Studied at Cambridge School of Art, was a prisoner-of-war for over three years, and later designed animated films such as *The King's Breakfast* (1963) and *Dick Deadeye – or Duty Done* (1975), as well as the animated sequences for *Those Magnificent Men . . .* (1965) and its follow-up, *Monte Carlo or Bust!* (1969, UK/Fr/It). Was theatrical cartoonist for *Punch* (1956–61).

OTHER BRITISH FILMS: *On the Twelfth Day* (1955, short, des, cos), *Blue Murder at St Trinian's* (1957), *The Pure Hell of St Trinian's* (1960), *The Great St Trinian's Train Robbery* (1966), *The Wildcats of St Trinian's* (1980).

Sears, Ann (*b* London, 1933). Actress. Played the nurse who captures William HOLDEN's passing fancy in *The Bridge on the River Kwai* (1957) and co-starred in Paul ROTHA's ART-HOUSE piece, *Cat and Mouse* (1958), but otherwise spent her brief career in 'B' MOVIES like the inane *She Always Gets Their Man* (1962). Sister of Heather SEARS.

OTHER BRITISH FILMS: *Lady of Vengeance* (1957), *Crash Drive* (1959), *The Unstoppable Man* (1960), *Man Detained* (1961), *The Lamp in Assassin Mews* (1962).

Sears, Heather (*b* London, 1935 – *d* Hichley Wood, 1994). Actress. In all the writing about the deserved importance of *Room at the Top* (1958) in British cinema, Sears probably gets less than her due. However, the middle-class sweetness and prissiness of her Susan Brown is, in its way, as significant to the film's meaning as Simone SIGNORET's wonderful Alice. Sears, under contract to the WOOLF brothers, won a BAA for the title role of the stirring MELODRAMA, *The Story of Esther Costello* (1957), and played the female lead in the last EALING film, *The Siege of Pinchgut* (1959) and neurotic Miriam Lievers in *Sons and Lovers* (1960), but the 60s favoured other types. Last seen as Biddy in the 1975 colour version of *Great Expectations*. Was married to Anthony MASTERS. Sister of Ann SEARS.

OTHER BRITISH FILMS: *Touch and Go* (1955), *Dry Rot* (1956), *The Phantom of the Opera* (1962), *Saturday Night Out, Black Torment* (1964).

Secombe, Sir Harry (*b* Swansea, Wales, 1921 – *d* Guildford, Surrey, 2001). Actor. Much loved former member of the BBC's RADIO comedy programme, *The Goon Show* (1951–60), the tubby Secombe served with the Welsh Territorials during WW2. He had also worked as a clerk before taking to the Windmill stage in 1946 and going on to become a national treasure as singer (he had a classical tenor voice) and comedian, famously in the title role of *Pickwick* (1963, NY 1965). He became a great TV favourite, with his own show in 1968, later as presenter of *Highway* (1983–93), a Sunday talk and song show. His film career was sporadic: after several minor films, including *Down Among the Z Men* (1952), a muffed attempt to transfer the Goons' humour to the screen, he starred in the uninspired EALING musical, *Davy* (1957), was a memorable, if somewhat too jovial Bumble in *Oliver!* (1968), and was agreeable as an English teacher in outback Australia in *Sunstruck* (1972, UK/Aust). But his real fame, recognised by a CBE in 1963 and a knighthood in 1981, lay elsewhere, and included his untiring work for charities. His son, **Andrew Secombe** (*b* Mumbles Head, Wales, 1953), has acted in several British films, including *Adventures of a Taxi Driver* and *I Don't Want To Be Born* (1975).

OTHER BRITISH FILMS INCLUDE: *Helter Skelter* (1949), *Penny Points to Paradise* (1951), *Svengali* (1954), *Jet Storm* (1959), *The Bed Sitting Room* (1969), *Doctor in Trouble* (1970), *The Magnificent Seven Deadly Sins* (1971).

Seely, Tim (*b* 1935). Actor. Pleasant young lead and supporting player of a few films from the late 50s, including *Please Turn Over* (1960), as boyfriend of imaginative teenager Julia LOCKWOOD, thereafter seen mainly on TV. In the US film, *Mutiny on the Bounty* (1962).

OTHER BRITISH FILMS INCLUDE: *Sally's Irish Rogue* (1958, Ire), *Agatha* (1978, UK/US), *P'Tang Yang Kipperbang* (1982), *A Shocking Accident* (1982), *Laughterhouse* (1984), *Plenty* (1985, UK/US).

Sefton, Ernest (*b* London, 1883 – *d* London, 1954). Actor. Appeared in about 40 character roles in the 30s and earlier 40s, mostly in very small roles, like that of the film publicity man in *Britannia of Billingsgate* (1933), which starred his real-life sister, Violet LORAINE.

OTHER BRITISH FILMS INCLUDE: *Old Spanish Customers* (1932), *The Bermondsey Kid* (1933), *No Limit, Hello Sweetheart* (1935), *Broken Blossoms* (1936), *The Great Barrier* (1937), *I See Ice!* (1938), *Old Mother Riley's Circus* (1941), *Here Comes the Sun* (1945), *The Grand Escapade* (1946).

Seiber, Matyas (*b* Budapest, 1905 – *d* South Africa, 1960). Composer. Hungarian who had studied at Budapest's Royal Academy of Music and moved to England in 1935, working as choral conductor and composer. Specialised in ANIMATED and SHORT FILMS with the HALAS–BATCHELOR British cartoon unit. Also scored a few straight dramas of the 50s, including Michael ANDERSON's entertaining MELODRAMA, *Chase a Crooked Shadow* (1957), whose tension was heightened by Seiber's work.

OTHER BRITISH FILMS: (animated shorts) *Little Paper People* (1936, marionette film), *Coupon Hearers* (1943), *Abu Zeid Builds a Dam, The Big Top* (1944), *Old Wives' Tale* (1946), *New Town* (1947), *As Old as the Hills* (1950), *The Figurehead* (1952), *The Christmas Visitor* (1959); (features) *The Fake* (1953), *Animal Farm* (anim), *The Diamond* (1954), *A Town Like Alice* (1956), *Robbery Under Arms* (1957, + cond).

Sekacs, Ilona (*b* Blackpool, 1948). Composer. Active since the mid 80s, Sekacz has worked chiefly in TV but contributed contrasting scores to two late 90s films: the harsh, contemporary *Under the Skin* (1997) and the graceful evocation of earlier decades, *Mrs Dalloway* (1997, UK/Neth/US), directed by Marleen Gorris for whom Sekacz also scored *Antonia* (1995, UK/Belg/Neth). TV scores include the gothicised *Northanger Abbey* (1986).

OTHER BRITISH FILMS: *A Pin for the Butterfly* (1994, UK/Czech), *Solomon and Gaenor* (1999).

Sekka, Johnny (*b* Dakar, Senegal, 1939). Actor. Given the meagre opportunities open to black actors in 60s British films, Sekka was lucky to land the key role of Sylvia SYMS's boyfriend in *Flame in the Streets* (1961), a strident but still powerful study in racism. He was obvious casting for such African-set enterprises as *East of Sudan* (1964), *Khartoum* (1966), *The Last Safari* (1967); he went to the US in the 70s but found only minor and often stereotypical supporting roles. Had continuing role in US TV series *Babylon 5: The Gathering* (1993).

OTHER BRITISH FILMS INCLUDE: *The Wild and the Willing* (1962), *Woman of Straw* (1964), *Doctors Wear Scarlet* (1970), *A Warm December* (1972).

Selby, Nicholas (*b* London, 1925). Actor. Character player, chiefly on TV, usually in upper-class, indeed aristocratic, roles, including Sir Walter Raleigh in *Elizabeth R* (1971) and Lord Billsborough in *House of Cards* (1990), and in a few films, including *A Midsummer Night's Dream* (1968), as Egeus, and *Macbeth* (1971) as King Duncan.

OTHER BRITISH FILMS: *Mata Hari* (1984), *The Madness of King George* (1994, UK/US), *The Affair* (1995, UK/US), *Stiff Upper Lips* (1996, UK/Ind).

Selby, Tony (*b* London, 1938). Actor. After training at the Italia Conti Stage School, first on stage as adult in 1956, having entered films in *An Alligator Named Daisy* (1955), curly-headed Selby played supporting roles in a dozen films, while pursuing a busy stage and TV career. His TV included *Get Some In* (1975) as Corporal Marsh and episodes of *Love Hurts* (1992), and he had several theatre seasons at the Royal Court.

OTHER BRITISH FILMS INCLUDE: *The Queen's Guards* (1961), *Alfie* (1966), *Press for Time* (1966), *Poor Cow* (1967), *Witchfinder General*, *Before Winter Comes* (1968), *Villain* (1971), *Adolf Hitler – My Part in His Downfall* (1972), *Loop* (1997).

Selfe, Ray (*b* Croydon, 1932 – *d* 2001). Director, editor. Described by writer David McGillivray as 'a household name' in 'the skid row film community', Selfe entered the EXPLOITATION film industry in 1970 with *Sweet and Sexy* (p, c) and thereafter variously acted in, directed, produced, wrote and edited sex titillation films and ran several cinemas dedicated to their exhibition. Later in career, made several compilation films outside his usual GENRE.

OTHER BRITISH FILMS INCLUDE: *Look at Love* (1971, d, short), *White Cargo* (1973, d, co-sc, story), *The Hot Girls* (1974, short, a, co-c), *Over-Exposed* (1977, short, co-p, e), *Can I Come Too?* (1979, d, a), *Don't Open Til Christmas* (1984, e), *The Young Duke: Wayne Before Stagecoach* (1989, doc, d).

Sellars, Elizabeth (*b* Glasgow, 1923). Actress. RADA-trained and with rep and ENSA experience, Sellars interestingly combined the demure with a suggestion of steel, in a way which should have brought her more demanding roles. The stage, with Stratford seasons, and taking over the title role in *The Prime of Miss Jean Brodie* (1967), and TV, as in *Winter Sunlight* (1984), playing a middle-aged wife who quits a selfish husband, probably gave her better opportunities than films did, but she made the most of what was going. Made her debut as flighty Judy in *Floodtide* (1949), losing Gordon JACKSON to refined Rona ANDERSON; was nicely passionate and tough-minded as a former Resistance member in *Cloudburst* (1951), and aptly sluttish as Dirk BOGARDE's faithless wife in *Hunted* (1952) and Peter FINCH's ditto in *The Shiralee* (1957); and properly tense and ambivalent in *The Long Memory* (1952) as the woman married to the detective who has sent her previous lover to prison. Played supporting roles in several big US films, including *The Barefoot Contessa* (1954) and *55 Days at Peking* (1962), in both of which, unsurprisingly, attention was focused on Ava GARDNER.

OTHER BRITISH FILMS INCLUDE: *Madeleine* (1949), *Guilt Is My Shadow* (1950), *The Gentle Gunman* (1952), *Forbidden Cargo* (1954), *The Man in the Sky* (1956), *Law and Disorder* (1958), *Never Let Go* (1960), *The Chalk Garden* (1964), *The Hireling* (1973).

Sellers, Peter (*b* Southsea, 1925 – *d* London, 1980). Actor. Sellers, born into a touring theatrical family, became a 'drummer, pianist and general funnyman' for RAF Gang Shows during the war. After demobilisation, he worked on RADIO as an impressionist, exhibiting the extraordinary vocal inventiveness that became one of his trademarks and was a cornerstone of radio's highly popular *The Goon Show* (1951–60). Sellers made two Goon Show spin-off films, *Down Among the Z Men* (1952) and *The Case of the Mukkinese Battlehorn* (1956). His other 50s film parts were bewilderingly varied: timorous Teddy Boy in *The Ladykillers* (1955), fly Petty Officer in *Up the Creek* (1958), aged, obfuscating Scottish accountant in *The Battle of the Sexes* (1959), or Brummie villain in *Never Let Go* (1960), complemented by multiple roles in *The Naked Truth* (1957) and *The Mouse That Roared* (1959).

The role that confirmed his acting ability was Fred Kite, the Communist shop steward in *I'm All Right Jack* (1959), where his brilliant performance captured both the vanity and poignancy of this ideologue and intellectual *manqué*. It was this mixture of sharp observation and pathos that characterised Sellers' ordinary men with aspirations: the provincial librarian in *Only Two Can Play* (1961), the idealistic vicar in *Heavens Above!* (1963). These qualities infused his most popular achievement, Inspector Clouseau, in five films beginning with *The Pink Panther* (1963) through to *Revenge of the Pink Panther* (1978). In Clouseau, Sellers combined his vocal ingenuity and skill as a slapstick comedian, yet always retained an essential humanity through the inspector's indefatigable dignity in the face of a hostile universe. His other performance which endures in the memory was the triple role in *Dr Strangelove . . .* (1963), as the well-meaning US President, unflappable RAF group-captain and the nightmarish Dr Strangelove himself, the government's adviser on nuclear warfare, who is unable to control his own body, the black gloved hand always trying to make a Nazi salute, expressing an ineradicable desire to dominate and destroy.

Always restless, insecure and self-critical, Sellers sought to play romantic roles as in *The Bobo* (1967) or *Hoffman* (1969), but was always more successful in parts that sent up his own vanities and pretensions, as with the TV presenter and narcissistic lothario in *There's a Girl in My Soup* (1970). Sellers' career meandered in the 70s; only his role as the humble gardener turned guru in *Being There* (1979, US) showed the range of his talent. Was married to actresses Britt EKLAND (2) and Lynne FREDERICK (4).

OTHER BRITISH FILMS: *Penny Points to Paradise* (1951), *Orders Are Orders* (1954), *John and Julie* (1955), *The Smallest Show on Earth* (1957), *tom thumb*, *Carlton-Browne of the FO* (1958), *The Running, Jumping and Standing Still Film* (1959), *Two Way Stretch*, *The Millionairess* (1960), *Mr Topaze* (1961), *Waltz of the Toreadors*, *The Wrong Arm of the Law*, *The Dock Brief* (1962), *A Shot in the Dark* (1964), *The Wrong Box* (1966), *Casino Royale* (1967), *The Magic Christian* (1969), *Soft Beds, Hard Battles*, *Ghost in the Noonday Sun*, *The Blockhouse* (1973), *The Return of the Pink Panther*, *The Great McGonagall* (1974), *The Pink Panther Strikes Again* (1976), *Trail of the Pink Panther* (1982, compiled from unused material).

BIBLIOG: Alexander Walker, *Peter Sellers*, 1981; Michael Starr, *Peter Sellers: A Film History*, 1991. Andrew Spicer.

Selten, Morton (*b* Marlborough, 1860 – *d* London, 1939). Actor. RN: Stubbs. On stage from 1881, this famous theatrical figure (alleged illegitimate son of Edward VII) made a couple of silent films (*Branded*, 1920; *Somebody's Darling*, 1925) but took to films seriously in the 30s, appearing in two dozen roles as lords (*The Divorce of Lady X*, 1938), kings (*His Majesty and Co.*, 1935), judges (*Action for Slander*, 1937), and other imposing figures. On stage for 50 years, much of the time spent in the US, before becoming a revered character player, often in films for Alexander KORDA.

OTHER BRITISH FILMS: *The Shadow Between* (1931), *Service for Ladies*, *Wedding Rehearsal* (1932), *The Love Wager*, *Falling for You* (1933), *How's Chances?* (1934), *The Ghost Goes West*, *Ten Minute Alibi*, *Once in a New Moon*, *Dark World*, *Annie, Leave the Room!*, *Moscow Nights* (1935), *Two's Company*, *Fire Over England*, *Juggernaut*, *In the Soup*, *A Yank at Oxford* (1937), *Young Man's Fancy*, *Shipyard Sally* (1939), *The Thief of Baghdad* (1940).

Selway, Mary (*b* Norwich, 1936). Casting director. Described by Richard E. GRANT, whom she cast as Withnail, as 'instantly reassuring and near-maternal' when he presented himself for *Withnail & I* (1986), is one of the most respected and prolific of her profession in the last three decades of the 20th century. And prepared to take a chance: not everyone would have thought of Sarah MILES as a suburban mum, for *Hope and Glory* (1987).

She has also cast many major international films, including *Out of Africa* (1985) and *The Russia House* (1990). Her skills were recognised by BAFTA's 2001 Michael Balcon Award. Married/divorced Norman RODWAY.

OTHER BRITISH FILMS INCLUDE: (co/casting) *SWALK* (1970), *Royal Flash* (1975), *Alien* (1979, UK/US), *Castaway*, *Gothic* (1986), *White Mischief*, *A Prayer for the Dying*, *Stormy Monday* (1987), *Paris by Night*, (1988), *Emma* (1996, UK/US), *Fairytale: A True Story* (1997) *The Clandestine Marriage*, *Notting Hill* (UK/US), *Onegin* (1999, UK/US), *Maybe Baby* (2000, UK/Fr), *Enigma* (2001, UK/Ger/Neth/US), *Gosford Park* (2001, UK/Ger/US).

Sequence For a journal which appeared only 14 times in five years (1947–52), *Sequence* has a remarkably firm niche in the history of British film culture, and, entirely amateur as it was, in the sense that no one ever got paid for it, it remains amazingly fresh and readable. Established at Oxford where it grew out of the Film Society magazine, *Sequence One* was edited by Lindsay ANDERSON and others; *Sequence Two* set the format; and *Sequence Three* moved to London where Gavin LAMBERT joined its editorial team, until he left to edit *SIGHT AND SOUND*, and Karel REISZ, a contributor, co-edited the last issue. The journal was committed to cinema as an art form and was drawn to those it considered film artists, including John FORD, but it was prepared to find art and excitement in unexpected places, such as an MGM musical or a minor *FILM NOIR* piece like *Criss Cross* (1948). In its concern for standards, no one rode easy on an auteurist reputation, but it is arguable that its stance, pre- and indeed anti-theory, anticipated the AUTEUR flurry at the end of the 50s. It also ran an engaging feature titled 'People we like' in which Diana DORS once figured. Generally, though, it gave British cinema a hard time.

serials Multi-episode action/adventure films, remembered with nostalgic affection for the exploits of lantern-jawed heroes pitted against the machinations of master criminals, otherworldly or otherwise, defined by their format of weekly two-reel chapters which concluded with a moment of 'cliffhanging' tension, sometimes literally, in order to entice the audience back the following week. Primarily a US phenomenon, few examples were to emerge from the British film industry. Although a number of British films were marketed as serials, particularly in the 1910s and 20s, these are more correctly classified as SERIES. *The Adventures of Deadwood Dick* (1915), for example, which was publicised as Britain's first serial, actually consisted of episodes which were 'complete in themselves and distinct' (a commonly used phrase at the time in relation to other film series or 'serials'), and did not have one over-all story divided into chapters. Other possible contenders from this period for classification as serials include *Till Our Ship Comes In* (1919), marketed as the first comedy serial, *The Mystery of Dr Fu Manchu* (1923), and its sequel *The Further Mysteries of Dr Fu Manchu* (1924), *Dr Sin Fang* (1928), another Oriental villain with world domination on his mind, and *The Adventures of Dick Turpin* (1933). While they all bear witness to a thread of narrative continuity traceable between the episodes, they are, nevertheless, closer to being series than serials, owing to the episodes having individual, self- contained stories minus the presence of a defining climactic moment leading directly into the following chapter's opening scene.

The first British films to be influenced by a serial format actually looked to France for inspiration, with George PEARSON's seven Louis Feuillade-inspired feature-length 'Ultus' films. Like their continental counterparts the films were not issued weekly but over a period of time, in this case between 1915 and 1917. The first 'conventional' serial appears to have been the eight-chapter *Boy Scouts Be Prepared* (1917), in which the youthful heroes of the title foil the nefarious exploits of a gang of spies during WW1. The only other British silent serial, *The Great London Mystery* (1920), yet another claimant in its publicity for the title of first British serial, saw magician David DEVANT heroically defeat, over twelve chapters, the criminal gang of oriental mastermind Ching Fu, yet another villain struck from the Oriental mould.

The 'golden era' of the Hollywood sound serial was also marked by a paucity of British entries. *Lloyd of the CID* appeared in 1931, a twelve-chapter serial which saw police inspector Jack Lloyd outwit another master criminal by the name of 'The Panther', but even this was produced, directed and co-written by an American serial practitioner, Henry MacRae. Other than *Dick Barton – Special Agent* in 1948 (also released as a feature) the British serial scene was moribund, with the exception of four serials produced specifically for children's cinema clubs between 1946 and 1950 by RANK and John BAXTER. *The Adventures of Dick Barton* (1955) and *Adventures with the Lyons* (1957) were two serials re-edited from earlier feature films and are arguably not the genuine article.

The aforementioned children's serials actually showed the way forward. As the US serial was riding into the sunset owing to the rise of television (the last being produced in 1956), the British serial paradoxically began to flourish, at least comparatively, courtesy of the CHILDREN'S FILM FOUNDATION. Beginning in 1956, 28 serials were to be commissioned by the CFF for children's Saturday morning shows. Role model children were to the fore in these films, as they outwitted bumbling crooks in an Enid Blytonesque world. Indeed two of the serials, *Five on a Treasure Island* (1957) and *Five Have a Mystery to Solve* (1964), were based on Blyton stories. Animal adventures and comedies were also a popular staple. Despite the competition of television, the last CFF serial was released as late as 1976.

BIBLIOG: Alex Marlow-Mann, 'British Series and Serials in the Silent Era', in Andrew Higson (ed), *Young and Innocent? The Cinema in Britain, 1896–1930*, 2002. John Oliver.

series The term refers to groups of films that largely share the same cast of characters and actors in the lead roles, or may be linked by a shared theme. Unlike SERIALS, which have one over-all story divided into chapters, the films within a series contain stories that are complete in themselves. It was through such films that the stable of larger-than-life heroes and villains that generally populated US serials was offered by the British film industry to the cinemagoers of the 1910s and 20s. Indeed, many series were actually issued in weekly episodes, as per the serial format. The exploits of master criminals Three-Fingered Kate (1909–12) and Dr Brian Pellie (1910–13) were early entries in the series field. The other side of the criminal coin came in the form of dashing naval heroes Lieutenant Rose (1910–15) and Lieutenant Daring (1911–14). Among other characters to appear within series in the period was SHERLOCK HOLMES, portrayed by Georges Treville in a 1912 series, to be followed by Eille NORWOOD in three series produced between 1921 and 1923. CRIME being a popular subject, the series format was to find homes for other detective masterminds, including Dorcas Dene, Detective (1919), Inscrutable Drew, Investigator (1926) and Sexton Blake (1928), while the mastermind of the criminal variety was catered for by Harry Agar LYONS in two Fu Manchu series in 1923 and 1924, followed by Dr Sin Fang in 1928. COMEDY also flourished, with the knockabout humour of Fred EVANS' Charley Smiler and Pimple characters and Reggie Switz's Winky, being just three examples among many, finding a ready audience, although there was also room for more gentle humour, notably Betty BALFOUR in the four *Squibs* films produced between 1921 and 1923. These two genres of crime and comedy were to remain the mainstays of the few series to emerge over the ensuing decades.

Film series, principally of the weekly variety, had quickly dwindled with the onset of sound, although some staple character types continued to make appearances, albeit in short-lived pseudo-series of only a few films each, such as those featuring Arthur WONTNER's Sherlock Holmes, George CURZON's Sexton Blake, John BENTLEY's Paul Temple, and Don STANNARD's Dick Barton. None of these, however, were series in the US vein, such as The Lone Wolf or Boston Blackie, to name but two examples, which were planned as long-running series from the outset in order to fill the lower half of double bills. The British variety merely capitalised on a successful first film, but, having done so, still failed to enjoy the longevity of their US counterparts. The British cinema rarely took full advantage of a winning formula. One would dearly have loved to see more than the meagre two and three entries produced, respectively, for the *This Man . . .* and *Inspector Hornleigh* strands. Those British films that actually came closest to the Hollywood model were the three series of crime mysteries produced at MERTON PARK STUDIOS in the 50s and 60s: *Scotland Yard* (1953–61), *Scales of Justice* (1962–67), both introduced and narrated by Edgar LUSTGARTEN, and a series of murder yarns based on the stories of Edgar WALLACE produced between 1960 and 1964.

Nevertheless, it was the capitalising on the success of one film that generally led the way in the development of film series in British cinema, and remained so well after the Hollywood variety had fallen victim to the rise of television. Notable examples from the post-war period include the HUGGETT family series produced between 1947 and 1949; the 'DOCTOR' ADAPTATIONS from 1954 to 1970; the 'St TRINIAN's' films of LAUNDER AND GILLIAT between 1954 and 1980; the 'CARRY ON' films, the longest-running series of them all, beginning in 1958, the bawdy humour of which was later superseded by the lamentable crudity of another series, the *Confessions of . . .* films, unleashed between 1974 and 1977; HAMMER's colourful revivification of Count Dracula, Baron Frankenstein and the Mummy from the late 50s and into the 70s; and the most influential British series of them all, and sole survivor in the field, James BOND, beginning with *Dr No* in 1962.

BIBLIOG: Alex Marlow-Mann, 'British Series and Serials in the Silent Era', in Andrew Higson (ed), *Young and Innocent? The Cinema in Britain, 1896–1930*, 2002. John Oliver.

Serkis, Andy (*b* 1964) Actor. Rising actor in films from the early 90s and in the theatre and TV before this. Came to notice as the yuppy coke-head in Mike LEIGH's *Career Girls* (1997), Gilbert's choreographer in Leigh's *Topsy-Turvy* (2000), and drug-dealer Fitz in *Stella Does Tricks* (1996), but better known as the voice of Gollum in *Lord of the Rings* (2001/02/03, US/NZ). A memorable Bill Sikes in the 1999 TV mini-series of *Oliver Twist*.

OTHER BRITISH FILMS INCLUDE: *Grushko* (1993), *The Near Room* (1995), *Mojo*, *Loop* (1997), *Among Giants* (1998), *Pandaemonium*, *Shiner* (2001), *Deathwatch* (UK/Ger), *The Escapist*, *24 Hour Party People* (2002).

Serra, Eduardo (*b* Lisbon, 1943). Cinematographer. Deservedly won a BAA and received an AA (among other awards) for his work on *The Wings of the Dove* (1997, UK/US), in which his lighting of the contrasts of English and Venetian mise-en-scène contributed significantly to the film's meaning. Most of his work has been in French films but his British films include the darkly masterly *Jude* (1996).

OTHER BRITISH FILMS: *Map of the Human Heart* (1992, UK/Aust/Can/Fr), *Funny Bones* (1995, UK/US), *The Disappearance of Finbar* (1996, UK/Fr/Ire/Swe).

Sessions, John (*b* Largs, Scotland, 1953). Actor. Character player much seen on TV as a teller of 'Tall Tales' (1991, 1994) and as a range of characters including Al Pacino in the bizarre cult series, *Stella Street* (1997). In films from 1982, and an eclectic bunch they make, including two brushes with SHAKESPEARE (*Henry V*, 1989; *A Midsummer Night's Dream*, 1999, UK/It) and a semi-brush in BRANAGH's *In the Bleak Midwinter* (1995), in which he played an actor playing Queen Gertrude in a provincial *Hamlet*. A PhD from Toronto's MacMaster University, he trained at RADA.

OTHER BRITISH FILMS INCLUDE: *The Bounty* (1984), *Castaway* (1986), *The Pope Must Die* (1991, UK/US), *Freddie as F.R.O.7* (1992, voice), *The Scarlet Tunic* (1997), *Cousin Bette* (1998, UK/US), *High Heels and Low Lifes* (2001, UK/US).

Seth, Roshan (*b* Patnar Bihar, India, 1942). Actor. Indian character player of theatre (e.g. in David HARE's *A Map of the World*, with which he toured in the early 80s), TV, including notably *The Buddha of Suburbia* (1993), as the hero's hypocritical father, as well as a dozen or so films. He was memorable as Nehru in *Gandhi* (1982, UK/Ind) and as Papa in *My Beautiful Laundrette* (1985), has been a key figure in BRITISH-ASIAN FILM-MAKING. Trained at LAMDA, he had considerable rep experience and toured in Peter BROOK's *A Midsummer Night's Dream* (1971).

OTHER BRITISH FILMS INCLUDE: *Juggernaut* (1974), *A Passage to India* (1984), *Little Dorrit* (1987), *Mississippi Masala* (UK/US), *London Kills Me* (1991), *Solitaire for 2* (1995), *South West 9* (2001).

Seton, Sir Bruce (*b* Simla, India, 1909 – *d* London, 1969). Actor. Despite his real-life aristocratic credentials – he became 11th Baronet of Abercorn in 1963 on death of his brother – Seton is probably best remembered, among his screen roles, as the likeable Sergeant Odd, wooing Joan GREENWOOD in *Whisky Galore!* (1949). In fact, in his over 70 movies he played up and down the social scale: he is simply a 'henchman' in *The Green Cockatoo* (1937), but is Lord Wolverbury, grown-up son to Margaret JOHNSTON in *Portrait of Clare* (1950), all sorts of servicemen and policeman, including Det. Insp. Fabian in a couple of films before finding household fame in the TV series, *Fabian of the Yard* (1954–56). He had an impressive quiet competence that elicited confidence. On stage prior to film debut; WW2 service 1939–45. Married (1) Tamara DESNI (1937–40), (2) Antoinette CELLIER (1940 to his death).

OTHER BRITISH FILMS INCLUDE: *Flame in the Heather* (1935), *Jack of All Trades* (1936), *Love from a Stranger* (1937), *The Middle Watch* (1939), *Return to Yesterday* (1940), *Bonnie Prince Charlie*, *Scott of the Antarctic* (1948), *The Blue Lamp* (1949), *Seven Days to Noon* (1950), *White Corridors*, *High Treason* (1951), *The Cruel Sea* (1952), *Eight O'Clock Walk* (1953), *Man of the Moment* (1955), *West of Suez* (1957), *The Thirty Nine Steps* (1958), *Make Mine a Million* (1959), *The League of Gentlemen* (1960), *Dr Syn Alias the Scarecrow* (1963).

Seton, Joan (*b* London, 1926). Actress. Stage player who made her debut in *Quiet Weekend* (1941) and appeared in a few films, notably as the hero's nice girlfriend in the Grand Guignol THRILLER, *Latin Quarter* (1945) and in TV plays from the mid 50s, including *The Romantic Young Lady* (1956).
OTHER BRITISH FILMS: *Lisbon Story, Meet Me at Dawn* (1947), *The Monkey's Paw* (1948), *A Case for PC 49* (1951).

Setton, Maxwell (*b* Cairo, 1909). Producer. Educated at London University and the Sorbonne, Paris, the former barrister held directorships in several film companies, including MAYFLOWER, and was producer of some enjoyable 50s entertainments, including two for director John GUILLERMIN: the gripping THRILLER, *Town on Trial* (1956) and the more-than-usually-interesting WAR FILM, *I Was Monty's Double* (1958).
OTHER BRITISH FILMS INCLUDE: (p/co-p) *The Spider and the Fly* (1949), *Cairo Road* (1950), *So Little Time, South of Algiers* (1952), *Appointment in London* (1953), *Footsteps in the Fog* (1955), *Wicked As They Come* (1956), *The Long Haul* (1957), *Beyond This Place* (1959).

Sewell, B(rian) C. (*b* Lowestoft, 1910). Music recordist. Spent most of his career at GAINSBOROUGH's LIME GROVE studios which he joined in 1939, after first working in the sound departments at BRITISH AND DOMINION, ELSTREE (1929–35), then at PINEWOOD. Responsible for sound on the Gainsborough MELODRAMAS from *The Man in Grey* (1943) on, staying put when Sydney BOX took over in mid-decade.
OTHER BRITISH FILMS INCLUDE: (sound sup) *Gasbags, Night Train to Munich* (1940), *Cottage to Let* (1941), *Uncensored* (1942), *Millions Like Us* (1943), *Waterloo Road, Madonna of the Seven Moons, Love Story, Fanny by Gaslight* (1944), *I'll Be Your Sweetheart, The Wicked Lady, They Were Sisters, The Rake's Progress* (1945), *The Magic Bow, Caravan, Beware of Pity* (1946), *Jassy, Dear Murderer* (1947), *My Brother's Keeper* (1948), *It's Not Cricket* (1949); (sound d) *Good-Time Girl* (1947), *The Calendar, Quartet, Miranda, Easy Money* (1948), *A Boy, a Girl and a Bike, Christopher Columbus* (1949).

Sewell, George (*b* England, 1924). Actor. Forceful character actor probably better known for his TV roles in such series as *Spindoe* (1968), as a vengeful detective, or as Superintendent Cottam in *The Detectives* (1993), than for his dozen or so scattered film roles, starting with *Sparrows Can't Sing* (1962).
OTHER BRITISH FILMS INCLUDE: *This Sporting Life, The Informers* (1963), *Kaleidoscope* (1966), *The Vengeance of She* (1967), *The Haunted House of Horror* (1969), *Get Carter* (1971), *Barry Lyndon* (1975).

Sewell, Rufus (*b* London, 1967). Actor. Half-Welsh, half-Australian, Sewell, of the brooding dark looks, has spent so much time standing around smouldering in films that one wishes someone would cast him as Heathcliff and have done with it. Central School-trained, he had some stage success (including the lead in Tom STOPPARD's *Arcadia* and a well-received Macbeth in 1999) as well as appearing in some high-profile films and TV during the 90s. Made film debut as Patsy KENSIT's junkie lover in *Twenty-One* (1991, UK/US), played the supposedly sex-crazed Seth who really wants a movie career in *Cold Comfort Farm* (1995, TV, some cinemas), was a strikingly forceful Fortinbras in BRANAGH's *Hamlet* (1996, UK/US) and gave his most fully developed performance as the faithful Giles in *The Woodlanders* (1997). Keeps seeming on the verge of international stardom, then turns up in a secondary role, as in *A Knight's Tale* (2001), upstaged by both Heath Ledger and Paul BETTANY. On TV, a natural for rebellious romantic, Will Ladislaw, in *Middlemarch* (1994).

OTHER BRITISH FILMS INCLUDE: *Dirty Weekend* (1993), *A Man of No Importance* (UK/Ire), *Carrington* (UK/Fr) (1994), *Victory* (1995, UK/Fr/Ger, released 1998), *Light in the Sky* (2002).

Sewell, Vernon (*b* London, 1903 – *d* Durban, 2001). Director. Marlborough-educated Sewell began in films as camera operator on Castleton KNIGHT's *Kissing Cup's Race* (1930) and directed his first film, *The Medium* (1934), from a screenplay by Michael POWELL who later described him as 'the most competent man I have ever known'. Sewell acted as technical assistant on *The Edge of the World* (1937) and Powell produced Sewell's first major directorial assignment, *The Silver Fleet* (1943, + co-sc), a popular wartime drama set in Holland. He made about 30 further films, many of them 'B' MOVIES, though often with a touch of visual flair and a quite unsettling edge to them: for example, both *The Man in the Back Seat* and *The House of Mystery* (1961, + sc) excite a sharp intake of breath at their unexpected endings. More ambitiously, he made: the long-missed Grand Guignol piece, *Latin Quarter* (1945, + sc), on which he worked productively with cinematographer Gunther KRAMPF; a FANTASY with some genuine wit in *The Ghosts of Berkeley Square* (1947); and the remarkably taut *Strongroom* (1962), which combines a tense THRILLER plot with an admirably shot and acted human drama involving bank employees caught in a vault over a weekend. Again, the ending is far from reassuring. It may well be true that Sewell was at least as interested in sailing his yacht (he was still doing this into his 90s) as in film-making, but his unpretentious oeuvre is almost always worth watching. Long married to Joan CAROL.
OTHER BRITISH FILMS: (d unless noted) *Men Against the Sea* (1936, doc), *A Test for Love, Breakers Ahead* (1937), *What Men Live By* (1938, co-d, + sc), *The World Owes Me a Living* (+ co-sc) (1945), *Uneasy Terms* (1948), *The Jack of Diamonds* (1949, + a, p), *The Trek of Mashomba* (doc), *The Dark Light, Black Widow* (1951), *Ghost Ship* (1952, + p, sc), *The Floating Dutchman* (+ sc), *Counterspy* (1953), *Dangerous Voyage* (+ story), *Radio Cab Murder* (+ sc, co-story) (1954), *Johnny, You're Wanted, Where There's a Will* (1955), *Soho Incident, Home and Away* (+ co-sc) (1956), *Rogue's Yarn* (1957, + a, co-sc), *Battle of the V-1* (1958), *Wrong Number* (1959), *Urge to Kill* (1960), *The Wind of Change* (1961), *Strictly for the Birds, A Matter of Choice* (1963, co-story), *Some May Live, The Blood Beast Terror* (1967), *Curse of the Crimson Altar* (1968), *Burke & Hare* (1971).

sex and sexuality British puritanism, towards images of sex and nudity, is evident in early cinema. The American film *A Fool There Was* (1916), was unclassified because of Theda BARA's portrayal of a 'vamp', and the British drama *Five Nights* (1915) was banned in parts of England, because of a localised belief that it was sensualist. British productions moralised sexuality in the PROPAGANDA film, which peaked in the years after WW1. These social problem films dealt with issues of purity and dangerous sexuality: venereal disease in *Whatsoever a Man Soweth* (1919), and rape, prostitution, and syphilis in *Damaged Goods* (1919).

The depiction of miscegenation was a concern, the American film *The Bitter Tea of General Yen* (1932) banned by local censors in British colonies. An inter-racial marriage had been permitted in the British film *Li-Hang the Cruel* (1921), but the union was shown to be forced and unsustainable. In *Jew Süss* (1934), Jews and gentiles are forbidden from having sexual relations, an anti-semitism topic relevant during the film's production and release, at a time of growing Nazi oppression.

A different type of British historical drama, the GAINSBOROUGH MELODRAMAS, was popular with female audiences during WW2 and immediately after. With flamboyant costumes emphasising sexual difference, films such as *The Man in Grey* (1943) and *The Wicked Lady* (1945) showed repressed sexuality, female desire, and forbidden love.

Screen depictions of sex and sexuality in British cinema underwent radical change in the 50s, though the subjects remained strongly regulated by the BRITISH BOARD OF FILM CENSORS and local authorities, under the shadow of laws regarding obscenity and indecency. Such have been the prohibitions that the history of this cinema has become a series of certificated sexual firsts: the first film to show pubic hair (*Blow-Up*, 1966), the first film to depict full frontal nudity (the Swedish production *Hugs and Kisses*, 1967), the first erect penis (*WR – Mysteries of the Organism*, 1971, Ger/Yug), and the first theatrically distributed film to depict fellatio (*Intimacy*, 2001, UK/Fr).

The introduction of the 'Adults Only' 'X' CERTIFICATE in January 1951 was designed to allow films to exhibit material that would otherwise have been censored. This could be observed in the social realist 'kitchen sink' school of films – *Room at the Top* (1958), *Saturday Night and Sunday Morning* (1960), *A Taste of Honey* (1961) – and the SOCIAL PROBLEM FILMS – *Women of the Twilight* (1952), *Sapphire* (1959), *Victim* (1961) – which dealt frankly with adult themes, including miscegenation, abortion, homosexuality.

In the 50s, 'adult' films were emerging from the American EXPLOITATION circuits and, more significantly, from continental Europe. The British-made sex feature can be traced to mid 50s America, where the burlesque film was being replaced by the nudist picture, of which the naturist film was an early form. The imitative style of the first British naturist film *Nudist Paradise* (1958), inspired a series of productions that included *Naked as Nature Intended* (1961), *My Bare Lady* (1962), and *Take off Your Clothes and Live* (1962). The pseudo-DOCUMENTARY style of these productions, and the sex exposé (*West End Jungle*, 1961, *London in the Raw*, 1964) and the sex education film (*Love Variations*, 1969) allowed the film's intentions to appear honourable. Only after 1964 were films permitted to make reference to sex in their titles; previously, with naturism and nudity, suggestion was made by words such as 'sun' and 'bare'.

British sexploitation developed as a GENRE in the 60s, as restrictions were relaxed and attitudes changed in an increasingly liberal society. The most distinctive and dominant form of British sexploitation was the sex comedy – films such as *Au Pair Girls* (1972), and *Can You Keep it Up For a Week?* (1974) – where, within the limits established by film censorship, COMEDY allowed for the mediation of sex and smutty humour and sexual innuendo thrived. The more mainstream examples of such cinema are the 'CARRY ON' films; comedy and sex also merged for the social dramas *Personal Services* and *Wish You Were Here* (1987).

British sexploitation is 'soft core' in that it shows only simulated sex. A British definition of 'hard core' – actual sexual penetration – has been seen in British films only in those versions made for the foreign market – Martin CAMPBELL's *The Sex Thief* (1973), released in the United States as *Her Family Jewels* and *Handful of Diamonds* – or in short blue movies produced mainly by John LINDSAY in the 70s, and shown in private clubs. His early 8mm films sometimes featured Mary MILLINGTON, the closest Britain had to a porn star. Today, the video classification 'R18' allows for greater sexual explicitness in pornography, though the popular porn actor, Omar, and the film-maker Steve Perry (aka Ben Dover) still produce harder

versions of their films for the overseas market.

Other British films which suggest trends in the changing representation of sexuality include *Peeping Tom* (1960), *Saturday Night Out* (1964), *The Pleasure Girls* (1965), *Alfie* (1966), *Here We Go Round the Mulberry Bush* (1967), *Ooh . . . You are Awful* (1972), *Carry on Emmannuelle* (1978), *Mona Lisa* (1986), *Scandal* (1988), *The Pleasure Principle* (1991).

BIBLIOG: John Trevelyan, *What the Censor Saw*, 1973; Ian Conrich, 'Forgotten cinema: the British style of sexploitation', *Journal of Popular British Cinema* 1, 1998; Julian Petley, 'The censor and the state: Or why *Horny Catbabe* matters', *Journal of Popular British Cinema* 3, 2000. Ian Conrich.

See also **exploitation films** and **gender representation**.

Seyler, Athene (*b* London, 1889 – *d* London, 1990). Actress. The fact that she lived so long has tended to obscure the range of Seyler's achievements, though this should not have led *The Times* obituary (13/9/1990) to the wild inaccuracy of referring to the 'almost 20 films' she made when in fact there were over 60. Certainly her stage career was pre-eminent: RADA-trained, she made her debut in 1909 and excelled at comedy, whether Shakespearean, Restoration or Wildean, and at just on 70 starred in *Breath of Spring* (1958) which she subsequently filmed as *Make Mine Mink* (1960), as leader of a gang of genteel fur-thieves, stealing for charity. In films from 1921 as Rachel Wardle in *The Adventures of Mr Pickwick* (she was Miss Witherfield in the 1952 version, *The Pickwick Papers*); she is very funny as Desmond TESTER's aunt in *Non-Stop New York* (1937), as further aunts in *Quiet Wedding* (1941) and its 1957 REMAKE, *Happy is the Bride*, and as Sybil THORNDIKE's partner-in-crime in *The Weak and the Wicked* (1953). She could, however, be serious with equal facility, as she showed on stage in, say, *The Corn Is Green* (1939), or on screen as the sympathetic prison visitor in *Yield to the Night* (1956). Married (2 of 2) to Nicholas HANNEN, after a famously long-running romance. Elected President of RADA Council in 1950, the first ex-pupil to become so. Co-author with Stephen HAGGARD of *The Craft of Comedy*, 1944, republished and launched to an enthusiastic audience on her 101st birthday. Made CBE 1959.

OTHER BRITISH FILMS INCLUDE: *This Freedom* (1923), *The Perfect Lady* (1931), *Blossom Time* (1934), *Scrooge, Moscow Nights* (1935), *Sensation, It's Love Again* (1936), *The Mill on the Floss* (1937), *The Citadel* (1938), *The Saint in London, Young Man's Fancy* (1939), *Dear Octopus* (1943), *Nicholas Nickleby* (1947), *The Queen of Spades* (1948), *The Franchise Affair* (1950), *Young Wives' Tale, Secret People* (1951), *For Better, for Worse* (1954), *Night of the Demon* (1957), *A Tale of Two Cities, The Inn of the Sixth Happiness* (1958), *A French Mistress* (1960), *I Thank a Fool* (1962), *Nurse on Wheels* (1963).

Seymour, Jane (*b* Hillingdon, 1951). Actress. RN: Joyce Frankenberg. After making her stage debut with the London Festival Ballet, Seymour turned to acting, played a BOND girl in *Live and Let Die* (1973) and the female lead in the REMAKE of *The Four Feathers* (1978), but most of her career is in US films and TV. The latter includes her long-running role as Dr Michaela Quinn in *Dr Quinn, Medicine Woman* (from 1992), as a frontier medico; it was hard to take her – or it – seriously after seeing what Jennifer SAUNDERS made of it, but it apparently made her a fortune. Married (2 of 4) Geoffrey PALMER and (4) US director James Keach. Awarded OBE, 2002.

OTHER BRITISH FILMS: *Oh! What a Lovely War* (1969), *Marlowe* (1970, short), *Young Winston* (1972), *Sinbad and the Eye of the Tiger* (1977).

Seyrig, Delphine (*b* Beirut, Lebanon, 1932 – *d* Paris, 1990). Actress. Beautiful, elegant French actress who came to international attention with her roles for Alain Resnais in the art-house triumphs, *L'année dernière à Marienbad* (1961, Fr/It) and *Muriel* (1963, Fr/It). In a few British films, she worked notably with Joseph LOSEY in *Accident* (1967), as Dirk BOGARDE's old flame, and in *A Doll's House* (1973, UK/Fr), in which she and Edward FOX made something very fine of their scenes together. On British TV, she was a stylish Mme de Vionnet in *The Ambassadors* (1977).

OTHER BRITISH FILMS: *The Day of the Jackal* (1973, UK/Fr), *The Black Windmill* (1974).

Shaffer, Anthony (*b* Liverpool, 1926 – *d* London, 2001). Dramatist, screenwriter. Twin brother of equally celebrated playwright, Peter SHAFFER, Anthony Shaffer's name, despite his other achievements, inevitably evokes his famously twisty, two-hander, *Sleuth* (1970), triumphant on Broadway as well as in London, and in 1972 turned into a successful film, from his own screenplay. A former barrister, Cambridge-educated Shaffer also wrote screenplays for HITCHCOCK's return to England, *Frenzy* (1972), for the very unsettling HORROR piece, *The Wicker Man* (1973), and the Agatha CHRISTIE ADAPT-ATIONS, enjoyably star-studded *Death on the Nile* (1978) and *Evil Under the Sun* (1981) and abysmal *Appointment with Death* (1988, co-sc). His second wife was Diane CILENTO (1985 till his death). He and his brother wrote novels together under the name Peter Anthony.

OTHER BRITISH FILMS: *Mr Forbush and the Penguins* (1971), *Murder on the Orient Express* (1974, co-sc unc), *Absolution* (1978).

Shaffer, Peter (*b* Liverpool, 1926). Dramatist, screenwriter. Twin brother of Anthony SHAFFER, and also educated at St Paul's School, London, and Cambridge, Shaffer had a West End hit with his first play, *Five Finger Exercise* (1958), a domestic drama subsequently and appallingly filmed in Hollywood (1962). Most famous now for that other drama of tormented family relations, *Equus* (1973, AAn/BAAn/sc), filmed in 1977 (+ sc) in ways that diminished its flexibility about time and place, and for his examination of the genius of Mozart and the jealousy of Salieri in *Amadeus* (1980, AA/BAAn/sc), flashily but popularly filmed in 1984 (US). In fact, his theatre work has been invariably more dextrously exciting than the films made from it – see *The Royal Hunt of the Sun* (1964, filmed 1969) and *The Private Ear* and *The Public Eye*, the 1962 double-bill filmed as, respectively, *The Pad and How to Use It* (1966, US) and *Follow Me!* (1971, + sc). Wrote novels with brother under name of Peter Anthony.

Shakespeare and British silent film It is not surprising that there are more than 400 references to Shakespeare, his plays and characters in the NATIONAL FILM AND TELEVISION ARCHIVE. No one writer has been more appealing for screen ADAPTATION and no one individual has figured more prominently in the history of fictional film-making.

The first Shakespearean film was also the first filmed record of a Shakespearean production: Herbert Beerbohm TREE's *King John* in September 1899, produced by the BRITISH MUTO-SCOPE & BIOGRAPHY COMPANY. It was the precursor of upwards of 200 silent screen adaptations from Shakespeare, both serious and comic. There was hardly a year between 1899 and 1928 that Shakespeare was not represented on film and some years – 1908, 1910, 1911, and 1913 – saw more than a dozen films based on plays of the Bard.

Following in the footsteps of Tree, Sarah Bernhardt filmed *Hamlet* in 1900, Godfrey TEARLE starred in *Romeo and Juliet* (1908), Johnston FORBES-ROBERTSON was *Hamlet* (1913), Sir Frank and Lady Constance BENSON starred in 1911 in *Julius Caesar*, *Macbeth*, *The Taming of the Shrew* and *Richard III*, Matheson LANG played *The Merchant of Venice* (1916), and Asta Nielsen was *Hamlet* (1920). In the US, the Vitagraph Company was the foremost producer of Shakespeare adaptations, with numerous versions of the major plays in the 1910s.

In the UK, *The Tempest* was filmed by Charles URBAN in 1905 and by CLARENDON in 1908, with the former consisting only of the shipwreck scene. W.G. BARKER filmed *Henry VIII* in 1911, starring Herbert Beerbohm TREE, and *Hamlet* in 1912, Eric Williams filmed *Hamlet* in 1914 (complete with a primitive sound system) and W.P. KELLINO in comic form in 1915. Costumier Willie Clarkson starred as himself in a comic 1915 version of *Romeo and Juliet* and in the same year BRITISH AND COLONIAL produced a 'sound' scene from *The Taming of the Shrew*. A two- reel version of *The Taming of the Shrew* and a three-reel *Falstaff the Tavern Knight* were part of the 1923 series, *Gems of Literature*. Similar to *A Double Life* some 26 years later, *Carnival* (1921) has a plot revolving around an actor (Matheson LANG) who nearly strangles his wife (Hilda BAYLEY) playing Desdemona during a performance of *Othello*.

Slapstick comedian Pimple parodied both *Hamlet* and *A Midsummer Night's Dream* in 1916. Cartoonist Anson DYER produced Shakespearean burlesques of which those of *Hamlet* in *Oh Phelia* (1919) and *Othello* (1920) survive. The American fixation with all things new was ridiculed by the BRITISH ACTORS' FILM COMPANY in *The Real Thing at Last* (1916), in which an American producer (Edmund GWENN) attempts to modernise *Macbeth*.

British And Colonial attempted to present *The Life of Shakespeare* in 1914, with Albert WARD in the title role and Sybil Hare as Ann Hathaway. Kineto filmed *Shakespeare Land* (1910), and along similar lines, Cecil HEPWORTH filmed *Stratford-on-Avon* (1925) and H.B. PARKINSON filmed *Shakespeare's Country* (1926). As Robert Hamilton Ball, quoting the Bard, wrote, Shakespeare in silent films has 'a strange eventful history'. Perhaps the strangeness is that while British silent cinema did manage to capture some of the great actors of the day in their most famous Shakespearean roles, it failed to produce one film ADAPTATION of any greatness, and in terms of sheer quantity of numbers was easily overwhelmed by efforts from the Continent (more than 100 titles) and the US.

OTHER RELEVANT BRITISH FILMS INCLUDE: *Hubert and Arthur* (1914, from *King John*), *England's Warrior King* (1915, from *Henry V*), *Love in a Wood* (1916, from *As You Like it*), *The Merchant of Venice*, *Othello*, *Romeo and Juliet*, *The Taming of the Shrew* (1920, burlesques).

BIBLIOG: Robert Hamilton Ball, *Shakespeare on Silent Film: A Strange Eventful History*, 1968, Luke McKernan and Owen Terris, *Walking Shadows: Shakespeare in the National Film and Television Archive*, 1994; Roberta E. Pearson, 'Shakespeare's Country: The National Poet, English Identity and British Silent Cinema', in Andrew Higson (ed), *Young and Innocent? The Cinema in Britain, 1896–1930*, 2002. AS.

Shakespeare and British sound film Filmed Shakespeare began in Britain, and the world, in September 1899. The film was scenes from Herbert BEERBOHM TREE's forthcoming production of *King John* at Her Majesty's Theatre, London. In 1999 Kenneth BRANAGH's musical version of *Love Labour's Lost* (UK/Fr/US) was in post-production. In the intervening century, many silent film directors, OLIVIER in his propa-gandist *Henry V* (1944) and regarded by many as the first 'proper' Shakespeare film, Peter HALL's expressionist and neorealist *A Midsummer Night's Dream* (1968) and Peter BROOK's existentialist *King Lear* (1970, UK/Den) have continued the rich tradition of British films which have attempted to capture the essence of Shakespeare on camera.

Critical debate has revealed two broad approaches to filming Shakespeare. Should a film director try to recreate a stage performance? Tony RICHARDSON's bitter *Hamlet* (1969) and Adrian NOBLE's *A Midsummer Night's Dream* (1996) were both inspired by a specific production. Or should a director, believing that Shakespeare's language is essentially theatrical, embodying its own stage direction, throw away the text and try to capture cinematically the spirit of the universal themes of life and death conveyed in the camera's own language?

BRANAGH's full-length and star-studded *Hamlet* (1996, UK/US) offers a conventional and resolutely illustrative interpretation of the text. JARMAN's ART-HOUSE *The Tempest* (1979) by contrast remains faithful to the spirit of the play wrenched out of the context of historic academic textual debate. Richard LONCRAINE's *Richard III* (1995), abandoning the profitless debate as to whether film or theatre wins in the end as an art form, delivers a much-cut text but what remains is faithful, and the urban sets compelling.

Are there problems inherent in filming Shakespeare different from those in filming, say, Restoration comedy or Tom STOPPARD? Shakespeare certainly holds his own in the multiplexes; filming his work has been sponsored by the NATIONAL LOTTERY; he is taught in the national curriculum. And Shakespeare remains synonymous with quality product – the epitome of classic period drama best filmed, so international reputation has it, by the British.

OTHER BRITISH FILMS INCLUDE: *Hamlet* (1948), *Romeo and Juliet* (1954, UK/It), *Othello* (1965), *Romeo and Juliet* (1966, ballet film), *Romeo and Juliet* (1968, UK/It), *Macbeth* (1971), *Hamlet* (1976), *Hamlet* (1990, UK/US), *As You Like It* (1992), *Much Ado About Nothing* (1993, UK/US), *A Midsummer Night's Dream* (1999, UK/It).

BIBLIOG: Roger Manvell, *Shakespeare and the Film*, 1971; Kenneth S. Rothwell, *Shakespeare on screen: an International Filmography and Videography*, 1990. Olwen Terris.

Shale, Betty (*b* London). Actress. Educated in France, on stage aged 17, blue-eyed blonde Shale made about ten usually light films from the early 30s, several times appearing with husband Eliot MAKEHAM, as in the *noir* melodrama, *Night and the City* (1950, UK/US).

OTHER BRITISH FILMS INCLUDE: *Yellow Stockings* (1928), *The Water Gipsies* (1932), *Trouble* (1933), *Evergreen* (1934), *Full Circle* (1935), *Royal Eagle* (1936), *Full Speed Ahead* (1939), *The Loves of Joanna Godden* (1947), *Green Grow the Rushes* (1951), *Miracle in Soho* (1957).

Shaps, Cyril (*b* London, 1923). Actor. In films and TV from the late 50s, short, slight character player Shaps was still working steadily as he neared 80 in such films as *The End of the Affair* (2000, UK/Ger/US), as a sympathetic waiter, and as the father of *The Lost Son* (1999, UK/Fr/US), having played nationals of various kinds in several dozen films from *Miracle in Soho* and *Interpol* (1957) and such TV series as *Never Mind the Quality, Feel the Width* (1967–68) as Rabbi Levi. Especially adept at accents.

OTHER BRITISH FILMS INCLUDE: *The Silent Enemy* (1958), *SOS Pacific* (1959), *Never Let Go* (1960), *Up Jumped a Swagman* (1965), *To Sir, with Love* (1967), *11 Harrowhouse*, *The Odessa File* (UK/Ger) (1974), *The Spy Who Loved Me* (1977), *The Madness of King George* (1994, UK/US, as Pepys), *The Governess* (1998, UK/Fr), *The Clandestine Marriage* (1999), *The Man Who Cried* (2000, UK/Fr/US).

Sharif, Omar (*b* Alexandria, Egypt, 1932). Actor. RN: Michel Shalhoub. From a wealthy Lebanese–Egyptian family, Sharif, after a brief spell in the family lumber business, took to acting and, already established in Egyptian films, made a spellbinding debut on the international scene when he rode out of the mirage and into film history in *Lawrence of Arabia* (1962), as Sherif Ali Ibn El Karish. How much his impact was due to director David LEAN and ace cinematographer Freddie YOUNG must be debatable: Lean used him again in and as *Dr Zhivago* (1965, UK/US), but he wasn't really interesting enough to keep its longueurs at bay; and, handsome as he was, he was not a very compelling romantic lead in such films as *Funny Girl* (1968, US), where, admittedly, he had powerhouse competition from Barbra Streisand in her film debut, or the REMAKE of *Mayerling* (1968, UK/Fr), as doomed Rudolf, and in *The Tamarind Seed* (1974) his suave charms seemed passé. By this time, his alternative career as a world-class bridge-player may have been consuming more of his attention, though he continued to appear in the odd film (*The Parole Officer*, 2001) and rather more TV. Was formerly married to Egyptian actress Faten Hamama.

OTHER BRITISH FILMS: *The Yellow Rolls-Royce* (1964), *The Night of the Generals* (1966, UK/Fr), *The Last Valley* (1970), *Juggernaut* (1974), *The Pink Panther Strikes Again* (1976), *Green Ice* (1981), *The Rainbow Thief* (1990).

Sharp, Anthony (*b* London, 1915 – *d* London, 1984). Actor. Maybe best known now as Penelope KEITH's Brigadier uncle in TV's *To the Manor Born* (1979), former insurance policy draughtsman and LAMDA graduate Sharp was on stage before WW2, served in the Royal Artillery (1940–46), and made his film debut in *Teheran* (1947). Thereafter, in occasional films (e.g. as the Minister in *A Clockwork Orange*, 1971; Lord Ambrose in the 1983 BOND, *Never Say Never Again*) and remained a busy stage actor and director, often of plays on tour in the UK and abroad, and was the author of several plays.

OTHER BRITISH FILMS INCLUDE: *The Sword and the Rose* (1953), *Left, Right and Centre* (1959), *Doctor in Clover* (1966), *Hot Millions* (1968), *No Blade of Grass*, (1970), *I Want What I Want* (1971), *Percy's Progress* (1974), *Barry Lyndon* (1975).

Sharp, Don (*b* Hobart, Australia, 1922). Director, screenwriter. An actor from childhood in Australia, Sharp came to Britain in the late 40s as actor, appearing in the good-natured *Ha'penny Breeze* (1950), which he also co-wrote and co-produced. He brought a similar freshness to *The Blue Peter* (1955, ass d), based on his story and co-screenplay, a story of naval cadets and a nerve-shattered war veteran sorting each other out. He did some second unit work on *Those Magnificent Men . . .* (1965) but director Ken ANNAKIN, while praising his direction of 'the flights in formation', wrote (2001) that 'he had no real eye for comedy'; perhaps not, because his real forté proved to be in the HORROR genre where he turned out some stylishly atmospheric pieces, including *Witchcraft* (1964). However, there are some genial moments in *Jules Verne's Rocket to the Moon* (1967) and in 1978 he keeps the pace up in a couple of REMAKES: *The Four Feathers* and (much better than Ralph THOMAS's 1958 version) *The Thirty Nine Steps*. Married actress **Mary Steele** (*b* London) who co-starred in his 1958 film *The Golden Disc* (+ co-sc), and appeared in a good deal of TV in the 50s.

OTHER BRITISH FILMS INCLUDE: (d, unless noted) *The Cruel Sea* (1952, a), *Appointment in London* (a), *Background* (co-sc) (1953), *The Adventures of Hal 5* (1958, + sc), *The Professionals*, *Linda* (1960), *The Fast Lady* (2ud), *Kiss of the Vampire* (1962), *It's All Happening* (1963), *Curse* of the Fly, *Rasputin the Mad Monk* (1965), *Our Man in Marrakesh, The Brides of Fu Manchu* (1966), *Puppet on a Chain* (1970, 2ud), *Psychomania* (1972), *Callan* (1974), *Hennessy* (1975), *Bear Island* (1979, UK/Can, + co-sc), *Guardian of the Abyss* (1985).

Sharp, Lesley (*b* Liverpool, 1964). Actress. Self-effacing actress who has consistently given performances of warmth and emotional truth. Mike LEIGH used these qualities to great effect in his celebrated film *Naked* (1993), where, as Johnny's (David THEWLIS) old girlfriend Louise, Sharp provided a small ray of light in an otherwise bleak world. She was notable once again as the anguished mother confronted with incest in *Priest* (1994), and as the loving wife of the overweight Dave (Mark ADDY) in the hit *The Full Monty* (1997, US/UK), for which she was nominated for BAA (supp a). Has also worked well on TV, especially as the benevolent Trudy in the Jimmy McGOVERN-scripted series *Clocking Off* (2000), and was wonderfully cast against type as the terrifying Mrs Joe in *Great Expectations* (1999).

OTHER BRITISH FILMS INCLUDE: *Rita, Sue and Bob Too* (1986), *The Love Child* (1987), *The Rachel Papers* (1989), *Close My Eyes* (1991), *Syrup* (1993, short). Melinda Hildebrandt.

Sharp-Bolster, Anita (aka Anita Bolster) (*b* Kanturk, Co. Cork, 1895 – *d* North Miami, Florida 1985). Actress. Wonderful old hatchet-face of two dozen Hollywood films of the 40s, often British-set, like *Kitty* (1945). She returned to England (she had long been on stage and made some earlier films there) for *The Perfect Woman* (1949) and stayed to make another 20, often playing homely old crones, and very funny as Lady Hunter in *The Man Who Liked Funerals* (1958), who, reading proofs of her late military husband's memoirs, asks the publisher, 'Tell me Mr Hurd, do many people read?' On the London stage as no-nonsense maid to Beatrice LILLIE's *Auntie Mame* (1958) and on TV in several playlets in the *Douglas Fairbanks Presents* series in the 50s.

OTHER BRITISH FILMS INCLUDE: *Would You Believe It?* (1929), *Lassie from Lancashire* (1938), *Talk of a Million* (1951), *The Final Test* (1953), *The Reluctant Bride, Raising a Riot* (1955), *Alive and Kicking* (1958), *School for Scoundrels* (1959), *Payroll* (1961), *Promise Her Anything* (1965), *Craze* (1973), *Jabberwocky* (1977).

Sharpe, Edith (*b* London, 1894 – *d* Los Angeles, 1968). Actress. On stage from 1919 and toured with major companies (e.g. Matheson LANG's) in the 20s, often in leading Shakespearean roles. Appeared in nearly 20 films from 1935, including several for the BOULTING brothers, among them *The Guinea Pig* (1948), as the Headmaster's patient wife and *Happy is the Bride* (1957), as the bride's harassed mother, and part of a fine team in the excellent 'B' MOVIE, *Cash on Demand* (1961), as one of bank manager Peter CUSHING's staff.

OTHER BRITISH FILMS INCLUDE: *Music Hath Charms* (1935), *Broken Blossoms* (1936), *When the Bough Breaks* (1947), *Landfall, No Place for Jennifer* (1949), *Cloudburst* (1951), *Brothers in Law* (1956), *A French Mistress* (1960), *The Devil Never Sleeps* (1962).

Shaughnessy, Alfred (*b* 1915). Director, writer, producer. After an EALING apprenticeship, it was predictable that Eton- and Sandhurst-educated Shaughnessy should then work with GROUP THREE, for instance as writer/producer of the gentle Scottish comedy *Laxdale Hall*, but his subsequent film career was startlingly diverse: he directed an early contribution to the horror cycle in *Cat Girl* (1957) and a film version of the TV pop-music show *6.5 Special* (1958), and wrote for Norman WISDOM (*Just My Luck*, 1957) and, later, for the EXPLOITATION king Pete WALKER. This diversity contrasts with the rewarding

continuity he enjoyed in TV, notably as permanent script editor of the series *Upstairs, Downstairs* (1971–75), 15 of whose 68 episodes he wrote himself, and whose consensus values can be linked to those of Ealing and Group Three. Though this series will rightly be his memorial, the eerily sexy qualities of *Cat Girl* suggest that he could have gone in intriguingly different directions. Married to Jean LODGE; his son **David Shaughnessy** is a TV actor.

OTHER BRITISH FILMS INCLUDE: (p) *Room in the House* (1955, + sc), *Heart of a Child* (1958), *Lunch Hour* (1962); (d) *Suspended Alibi* (1956), *The Impersonator* (1961, + co-sc); (co-sc) *Follow That Horse!* (1960), *Crescendo* (1969); (sc) *High Terrace, A Touch of the Sun* (1956), *Light Fingers* (1957), *Tiffany Jones* (1973).

BIBLIOG: Autobiography, *Both Ends of the Candle*, 1978. Charles Barr.

Shaw and British film Foreseeing from the first LUMIÈRE productions the momentous impact of cinema as a social leveller and a purveyor of social and political ideologies, Shaw remained an avid cinema-goer and film critic to the end of his days declaring 'the cinema is going to be the mind of England'. Shaw's conviction that a good film is a filmed play gave directors of his works many problems and much of the critical debate surrounding Shaw and cinema confronts the problem of Shaw's forcefulness in denying cinema's unique art form and propelling it towards the perfection of theatre. Never at ease with silent film (believing that only the spoken word distinguishes great literary works from tawdry MELODRAMA) he found sympathy with producer Gabriel PASCAL and director Anthony ASQUITH. In *Pygmalion* (1938) and *The Doctor's Dilemma* (1958) Shaw found film-makers who matched the rhythm of his words with a corresponding visual flow; what Asquith called 'an indissoluble marriage of words and pictures', and supported Shaw's belief in the central role of the screenwriter. *Major Barbara* (1941), ostensibly directed by Pascal but in fact largely by David LEAN, was well-regarded without quite repeating the success of *Pygmalion*, but *Caesar and Cleopatra* (1945), the end of Pascal's attempts to bring Shaw to British screens, was a costly and lavish failure. Among US versions of Shaw, *Androcles and the Lion* (1952) is now all but forgotten, but *My Fair Lady* (1964), based on the stage musical version of *Pygmalion*, won several Oscars, including Best Actor for Rex HARRISON's definitive Higgins. There have also been TV ADAPTATIONS starting with *How He Lied to Her Husband* (1937), starring Greer GARSON.

OTHER BRITISH FILMS: (adapted from Shaw's plays) *How he Lied to her Husband* (1931), *Arms and the Man* (1932), *Saint Joan* (1957, UK/US), *The Doctor's Dilemma* (1958), *The Devil's Disciple, The Millionairess* (1960), *Great Catherine* (1967). Olwen Terris.

Shaw, Alexander (*b* London, 1910). Producer, director. Having worked on early films for the EMPIRE MARKETING BOARD, Shaw joined the GPO FILM UNIT in 1934. Subsequently worked as director or producer at the STRAND FILM COMPANY from 1936 to 1947, often in association with director John ELDRIDGE, and, between 1940 and 1942, also worked at the CROWN FILM UNIT, BRITISH TRANSPORT FILMS and the MINISTRY OF INFORMATION. Between 1948 and 1970, acted as an adviser on audio-visual aids for the third world for Unesco. Influential films include *The Future's in the Air* (1937), for British Transport, with commentary written by Graham GREENE, and *Men of Africa* (1940), which was one of Strand's most important films. Directed *Soldier, Sailor* (1944), a semi-documentary, featuring actors such as Rosamund JOHN, and produced Humphrey JENNINGS' *The Cumberland Story* (1947).

He was also significant in his promotion of DOCUMENTARY film production worldwide through his work at Unesco.
OTHER BRITISH FILMS INCLUDE: (d, unless noted) *Cable Ship* (1933, co-d), *The Children's Story* (1938), *Oxford* (1940, p), *Tank Patrol* (p), *Penicillin* (1941), *New Towns for Old* (1942, p), *French Town* (1945), *Instruments of the Orchestra* (1946). Ian Aitken.

Shaw, Anthony (*b* London, 1897 – *d* England, 1980). Actor. Character player almost invariably associated with officer/official types, like the English major at the *Hotel Reserve* (1944), usually in small roles. On London stage from 1928, and toured as Stanhope in *Journey's End* (1929).
OTHER BRITISH FILMS INCLUDE: *Educated Evans* (1936), *This Man in Paris* (1939), *This Man Is Dangerous* (1941), *Unpublished Story, They Flew Alone* (1942), *Escape to Danger* (1943), *The Long Dark Hall* (1951), *Top Secret* (1952), *Appointment in London* (1953), *The Dam Busters* (1955), *How to Murder a Rich Uncle* (1957).

Shaw, Denis (*b* London, 1921 – *d* London, 1971). Actor. Hefty character player, more often than not up to no good, his thickset features tending to rule out hero roles. Hence, one finds him brutishly leading the rabble in pursuit of a dumb, innocent bystander in *Jack the Ripper* (1958). In TV from the late 30s, later in such series as *Robin Hood*, prior to his untimely death from a heart attack.
OTHER BRITISH FILMS INCLUDE: *The Long Memory* (1952), *The Colditz Story* (1954), *Who Done It?* (1956), *The Flesh is Weak* (1957), *A Woman Possessed* (1958), *The Mummy* (1959), *The Night We Got the Bird* (1960), *The Curse of the Werewolf* (1961), *The Viking Queen* (1966), *The File of the Golden Goose* (1969).

Shaw, Fiona (*b* Cork, Ireland, 1958). Actress. Distinguished stage actress, graduate of Cork University College and winner of RADA's Bancroft Gold Medal, who has worked extensively for the RSC, the National and the Old Vic, Dublin's Abbey Theatre and on Broadway, winning numerous awards for her work, an honorary doctorate from the University of Dublin, and an Hon. CBE in 2001. She has played many major Shakespearean roles, none more controversial than that of Richard II. Came to filmgoers' attention as Dr Eileen Cole in *My Left Foot* (1989), and as the gawky headmistress in the inane *Three Men and a Little Lady* (1990, US), played the endearing Mrs Croft in *Persuasion* (1995, TV, some cinemas) with endearing warmth, and provided some needed grit in *Harry Potter and the Philosopher's Stone* (2001, UK/US) as nasty Aunt Petunia. A fiercely distinctive, risk-taking actress of whom the screen should, in general, make better use.
OTHER BRITISH FILMS: *London Kills Me* (1991), *Maria's Child* (1993), *Jane Eyre* (1996, UK/Fr/It/US), *The Butcher Boy* (1997, Ire/US), *The Last September* (UK/Ire/Fr), *Mind Games* (2000), *The Triumph of Love* (2001, UK/US), *Harry Potter and the Chamber of Secrets* (2002, UK/US).

Shaw, Harold (*b* Bromsville, Tennessee, 1878 – *d* Los Angeles, 1926). Director. Shaw was a prominent director in Britain as a result of his being appointed 'general stage director' of the LONDON FILM COMPANY in June 1913. He had earlier been an actor with the Edison Company (1908–13) and a director with IMP in the US. Shaw remained with London until 1916 and returned again to direct its films in 1920. In 1916, he went to South Africa, with his first film there being the epic production, *De Voortrekkers/Winning a Continent* (1916), and, in 1918, formed the Harold Shaw Producing Company; also in South Africa, he married actress Edna FLUGRATH in 1917. Shaw directed three minor films in the US for Metro (1923–24). His early death was the result of an motor accident.

BRITISH FILMS INCLUDE: (for London Film Company) *The House of Temperley* (1913), *Her Children, Duty, Child o' My Heart, England's Menace, Trilby* (1914), *The Two Roads* (1915), *The Last Challenge* (1916), *True Tilda* (1920); (other British films) *The Land of Mystery* (1920, + p), *Kipps, A Dear Fool, The Woman of His Dreams, General John Regan, False Evidence* (1921), *The Wheels of Chance* (1922). AS.

Shaw, Martin (*b* Birmingham, 1945). Actor. Very popular TV actor who won an international following for his role as the former policeman turned undercover agent in *The Professionals* (1977–83) and a respected stage star who scored a major success as Lord Goring (modelling himself on Wilde) in *An Ideal Husband* (1992, London, subsequently NY, winning a Tony Award). Only a handful of film roles, starting with Banquo in POLANSKI's *Macbeth* (1971). A suavely villainous Chauvelin in the 1999 series, *The Scarlet Pimpernel*. Son **Joe Shaw** (*b* 1973) has appeared mainly on TV.
OTHER BRITISH FILMS INCLUDE: *The Golden Voyage of Sinbad* (1973), *The Hound of the Baskervilles* (1983), *The Most Dangerous Man in the World* (1988), *Ladder of Swords* (1989).

Shaw, Maxwell (*b* London, 1929 – *d* London, 1985). Actor. RN: Jacques. Tall supporting player of TV and films from the late 50s when he appeared in such WARWICK action films as *The Man Inside* and *No Time to Die* (1958) and the TV series, *Who, Me?* (1959). Trained first as artist before turning to acting, gaining experience with Joan LITTLEWOOD's company in the 50s. For health reasons, turned to teaching drama in his last decade.
OTHER BRITISH FILMS INCLUDE: *The Criminal* (1960), *In Search of the Castaways* (1961), *Dr No* (1962), *The Oblong Box* (1969), *Mister Quilp* (1974).

Shaw, Robert (*b* Westhoughton, 1927 – *d* Tourmakeady, Ireland, 1978). Actor and writer. RADA-trained, he earned a reputation for playing menacing, violent characters, notably as steely-eyed killer Grant in *From Russia with Love* (1963), a type he returned to frequently throughout his career, both in Britain and America. He showed versatility in playing historical characters, receiving an AAn (Supporting Actor) as Henry VIII in *A Man for All Seasons* (1966). Other striking roles included Lord Randolph Churchill in *Young Winston* (1972) and appearances in ADAPTATIONS of two Harold PINTER plays, *The Birthday Party* (1968) and *The Caretaker* (1963), though he may now be most famous for his role as Quint in *Jaws* (1975, US). Also wrote the successful play, *The Man in the Glass Booth*, filmed in 1975 (US). His novel, *The Hiding Place*, was filmed as *Situation Hopeless – But Not Serious* in 1965. Married (2) Mary URE.
OTHER BRITISH FILMS: *The Lavender Hill Mob* (1951), *Doublecross, The Dam Busters* (1955), *A Hill in Korea* (1956), *Man from Tangier* (1957), *Sea Fury* (1958), *Libel* (1959), *The Valiant* (1961, UK/It), *Tomorrow at Ten* (1962), *The Cracksman* (1963), *Battle of Britain, The Royal Hunt of the Sun* (1969), *Figures In A Landscape* (1970), *A Town Called Bastard* (1971, UK/Sp), *The Hireling, The Golden Voyage of Sinbad* (1973), *The Deep* (1977, UK/US), *Force 10 from Navarone* (1978), *Avalanche Express* (1979, Ire). Matthew Caterson.

Shaw, Sebastian (*b* Holt, Norfolk, 1905 – *d* Brighton, 1994). Actor. On stage from 1914, he trained at RADA and made his London debut as an adult in 1925, appearing in a wide range of modern and classic plays. Popular as urbanely handsome leading man in about 20 films of the 30s, including *Men Are Not Gods* (1936), as an Othello-playing actor who gets carried away with the role, and as *The Squeaker* (1937). After WW2 service (1940–46), he played a few character roles, including that of composer Michael DENISON's bearded lyricist friend in *The Glass Mountain* (1948), the doctor in Kevin BROWNLOW and Andrew MOLLO's *It Happened Here* (1963) and Anakin Skywalker in *Return of the Jedi* (1983, US).

OTHER BRITISH FILMS INCLUDE: *Caste* (1930), *A Taxi to Paradise* (1933), *Badger's Green* (1934), *Brewster's Millions*, *Birds of a Feather* (1935), *Tomorrow We Live* (1936), *The Spy in Black* (1939), *Bulldog Sees It Through* (1940), *East of Piccadilly* (1941), *Journey Together* (1945), *Landfall* (1949), *Laxdale Hall* (1953), *High Season* (1987).

Shaw, Susan (*b* West Norwood, 1929 – *d* Middlesex, 1978). Actress. RN: Patsy Sloots. Wan blonde graduate of Sydney BOX's COMPANY OF YOUTH, an attractive enough heroine in, say, *It's Not Cricket* (1949) or *Pool of London* (1950) but more interesting as more contentious types. A former typist, in films from mid teens, she had vivid character roles in *It Always Rains on Sunday* (1947), as Googie WITHERS's flighty stepdaughter, in *The Woman in Question* (1950), as Jean KENT's self-centred sister, and in *The Intruder* (1953), as Michael MEDWIN's faithless girlfriend. Her career then dwindled into 'B' MOVIES, including, it must be said, *Fire Maidens from Outer Space* (1956), but she deserved better. There was a suggestive vulnerability, a hint of moral as well as physical fragility about her that differentiated her from the English rose stereotype. Married (1) Albert LIEVEN (1949–53) and (2) Bonar COLLEANO (1954–58). It is alleged that she never recovered fully from Colleano's death in a road accident and thereafter fought a drink problem for the rest of her life. Their son **Mark Colleano** (*b* London, 1955) is an actor whose films include *The Horsemen* (1970, US) and *Lady Chatterley's Lover* (1981).

OTHER BRITISH FILMS INCLUDE: *Walking on Air* (1946), *Holiday Camp* (1947), *To the Public Danger*, *London Belongs to Me*, *Quartet* (1948), *Train of Events* (1949), *Waterfront* (1950), *Wide Boy* (1952), *Small Town Story*, *The Large Rope* (1953), *The Good Die Young* (1954), *The Diplomatic Corpse*, *Carry On Nurse* (1958), *The Big Day* (1960), *Stranglehold* (1962).

Shearer, Moira (*b* Dunfermline, Scotland, 1926). Dancer, actress. RN: King. Few stars have so secure a grasp of popular esteem on the basis of so few films as red-haired Shearer does. Michael POWELL finally wore down the resistance of the prima ballerina to play Vicky Page in the famously successful BALLET film, *The Red Shoes* (1948), of which she said in 1994 'there never was a ballet company anywhere which was like that' and thought Vicky's 'conflict' and its suicidal resolution was absurd. However, it made her a *film star*, a role that never meant much to her, and she made two more appearances for Powell, with whom she had a difficult professional relationship: *The Tales of Hoffmann* (1951), in which she danced three roles; and the notorious *Peeping Tom* (1960), in which she (replacing Natasha PARRY) did a banal little dance for the film's murderer. Her most attractive film work is as the variants on the 'Sylvia' character in *The Man Who Loved Redheads* (1954), in which she showed a feeling for comedy unglimpsed in her other films. Made one Hollywood film appearance, in an episode of *The Story of Three Loves* (1953), but missed the lead in *Hans Christian Andersen* by falling pregnant. Married to author Sir Ludovic Kennedy from 1950, she has occasionally acted on stage but made no film since the French *Black Tights* (1960).

Shearmur, Edward (*b* London, 1966). Composer. Classically trained Shearmur nevertheless cut his film-scoring teeth on such US action fare as the *Die Hard* trilogy, working under Hollywood composer Michael KAMEN. In Britain he ran up some interesting credits in the 90s, including additional music

for the harrowing '*Let Him Have It*' (1991) and the magisterial ADAPTATION of Henry JAMES, *The Wings of the Dove* (1997, UK/US, + cond), in which his score significantly intensified the sense of dark passions at work, seeing his job as to 'bring [the film's] conflict out and play the psychological drama that exists beneath the surface'. Very busy on US films around the turn of the century, he has also collaborated as keyboard player with such pop artists as Annie Lennox and Pink Floyd.

OTHER BRITISH FILMS INCLUDE: *The Adventures of Baron Munchausen* (1988, UK/Ger/It), *The Leading Man*, *Remember Me?* (1996), *The Butcher Boy* (Ire/US, cond), *Girls' Night* (UK/US), *The Governess* (UK/Fr) (1998), *The Count of Monte Cristo* (2002, UK/US).

Sheen, Michael (*b* Newport, Wales, 1969). Actor. Much admired and award-winning, RADA-trained stage actor who has appeared in a few films since the mid 90s, including *Othello* (1995, UK/US), as Lodovico, in at the death in Cyprus, and *Wilde* (1997, UK/Ger/Jap/US), as his friend and seducer, Robbie Ross. On TV since the 1993 ADAPTATION of Barbara Vine's *Gallowglass*. Has daughter by longtime partner, Kate BECKINSALE.

OTHER BRITISH FILMS: *Mary Reilly* (1996, UK/US), *Heartlands* (2001).

Sheen, Ruth (*b* London, 1952). Actress. Probably best known for her continuing role as the austere but compassionate Nurse Ethel Carr in TV's *Bramwell* (1995–98), Sheen, trained at the E15 Theatre School, really came to notice for her role as the good-hearted Shirley in Mike LEIGH's *High Hopes* (1988). Plain and toothy, she projects an effortless sympathy in whatever she does, but there is also obvious comic flair, as seen in *The Young Poisoner's Handbook* (1995).

OTHER BRITISH FILMS: *Little Dorrit* (1987), *Different for Girls* (1996), *Secrets & Lies* (1996), *Virtual Sexuality* (1999), *All or Nothing* (2002, UK/Fr).

Sheffield Photo Company Pioneering film company run by Frank MOTTERSHAW, who extended his Sheffield photographic business to include the cinematograph in 1900. Initially producing ACTUALITIES, production became more ambitious when his son Frank S. returned from a period working with Robert PAUL. Multi-scene works such as *A Daring Daylight Robbery*, *Robbery of the Mail Coach* (1903), and *The Life of Charles Peace* (1905) brought together editing techniques with the thrill of re-enacted crime. These titles were hugely popular in Britain, and are generally accepted to have influenced Edison's *The Great Train Robbery* and by extension the emerging American genres of the CRIME film and the WESTERN. Frank S. Mottershaw also undertook a trip to Serbia in 1904 to film the coronation of King Peter. The Sheffield Photo Company ceased film production in the 1910s, but continued as a film business into the 1920s, and the Mottershaw family continued in film into the 1960s. Luke McKernan.

Shell Film Unit After a report by John GRIERSON in 1933, Edgar ANSTEY became producer for the Unit the following year. Its first film was *Airport*, made by Roy Lockwood. Much of the early output concentrated on carefully explaining potentially complicated technical subject matter. A companion *Shell Cinemagazine* (1938–52) was intermittently published. During the war years the Unit was put at the disposal of government departments before re-emerging with several notable productions including *Powered Flight* (1953). The quality of the Unit's films owed much to the personnel recruited. Arthur ELTON, who produced several of these, had a background in feature films as well as documentaries. Bert Haanstra, also associated with Jacques Tati, made in 1955 one of Shell's best nature films, *The Rival World*. Since 1990, the organisation has been called the Shell Film and Video Unit. Stephen Brown.

Shelley, Barbara (*b* London, 1933). Actress. RN: Kowin. Brunette beauty and former model, Shelley had a tiny role in Hammer's *Mantrap* (1953), then made her next half-dozen films in Italy before returning to England to become Hammer's Queen of horror, from the late 50s, though her first venture in the genre, *Cat Girl* (1957) was for another company and she also made other kinds of film. Her major horror films include *Village of the Damned* (1960), derived from John Wyndham's alarming novel, *Dracula – Prince of Darkness* and *Rasputin the Mad Monk* (1965); she is the only woman in the (ridiculous) war film, *The Secret of Blood Island* (1964) and is quite compelling as a blind man's faithless wife in *Blind Corner* (1963). Also, plenty of TV, including *The Troubleshooters* (1970–72).

OTHER BRITISH FILMS INCLUDE: *The Camp on Blood Island* (1957), *Blood of the Vampire* (1958), *Bobbikins* (1959), *The Shadow of the Cat* (1961), *Death Trap, Stranglehold* (1962), *The Gorgon* (1964), *Quatermass and the Pit* (1967), *Ghost Story* (1974).

Shelley, Carole (*b* London, 1939). Actress. RADA-trained, part-time milliner, Shelley was first on the London stage as a child, then regularly from 1955. When she played gushing Gwen Pigeon on Broadway in *The Odd Couple* (1965) and repeated this role hilariously (along with 'sister' Monica Evans) in the film (1968), she was lost to British films. Before crossing the Atlantic, she had appeared in a handful, including two in the 'Carry On' series, . . . *Regardless* (1961) and . . . *Cabby* (1963).

OTHER BRITISH FILMS: *It's Great to Be Young!* (1956), *No, My Darling Daughter* (1961), *The Cool Mikado* (1962).

Shelley, Norman (*b* London, 1903 – *d* London, 1980). Actor. Allegedly the 'voice' for recordings of some of Winston Churchill's famous WW2 speeches, the rotund Shelley, Colonel Danby in radio's *The Archers*, educated at Merchant Taylor's School, London, was on stage from 1919 and in films from 1930 (*Thread o' Scarlet*). Main film career from the 40s, when his voice is recognisable as Wendy Hiller's magnate fiancé in *I Know Where I'm Going!* (1945) and his substantial form as Dora Bryan's jittery boyfriend in *The Blue Lamp* (1949) and as one of the managers in *The Angry Silence* (1960). TV series include *The Pallisers* (1974) and *I, Claudius* (1976).

OTHER BRITISH FILMS INCLUDE: *Down River* (1931), *The River Wolves* (1934), *Went the Day Well?* (1942), *They Came to a City* (1944), *I See a Dark Stranger* (1946), *Daughter of Darkness* (1947), *Vote for Huggett* (1948), *Her Favourite Husband* (1950), *Private Information* (1952), *Very Important Person* (1961), *A Place to Go* (1963), *Otley* (1968), *Oh! What a Lovely War* (1969).

Shelton, Anne (*b* London, 1923 – *d* Herstmonceux, 1994). Actress. RN: Patricia Sibley. Very popular blonde vocalist, especially in wartime, when she did weekly radio broadcasts. Once a singer with Ambrose's orchestra, she made only a few films, including three modest musical comedies with Arthur Askey: *King Arthur Was a Gentleman* (1942), *Miss London Ltd* (1943), and *Bees in Paradise* (1944). She can be heard, conjuring up 1943, with 'You'll never know' on the soundtrack of *Enigma* (2001, UK/Ger/Neth/US).

OTHER BRITISH FILMS: *Jeannie* (1941), *Come Dance with Me* (1950).

Shelton, Joy (*b* London, 1922 – *d* Richmond, Surrey, 2000). Actress. RADA-trained actress on stage from 1938 and frequently in radio plays. Her gentle-mannered 'ordinary' girls made her modestly popular in such films as *Millions Like Us*

(1943) and, as John Mills's wife led astray by spiv Stewart Granger, in *Waterloo Road* (1944). In the sturdy 'B' movie, *Impulse* (1955), she is especially effective as a somewhat complacent small-town wife. Had her own TV programme, *Home with Joy Shelton*, in the mid 50s. Married Sydney Tafler.

OTHER BRITISH FILMS INCLUDE: *Bees in Paradise* (1944), *Send for Paul Temple* (1946), *Uneasy Terms, No Room at the Inn* (1948), *Once a Sinner* (1950), *A Case for PC 49* (1951), *Emergency Call* (1952), *Park Plaza 605* (1953), *The Greengage Summer* (1961), *HMS Defiant* (1962).

Shenson, Walter (*b* San Francisco, 1919 – Los Angeles, 2000). Producer. Stanford University-educated Shenson worked in Hollywood from 1941, on promotional shorts, and came to Britain in the mid 50s, spending two years in charge of publicity for Columbia's European productions. Branching out as an independent producer, he scored successes with the comedies, *The Mouse That Roared* (1959, ex p) and *The Mouse on the Moon* (1963), but his real acumen was shown in his faith in the Beatles as a lasting phenomenon and he produced both *A Hard Day's Night* (1964) and *Help!* (1965). Both cashed in hugely on the popularity of the Fab Four who showed engaging cinematic potential. He made several more films in Britain without repeating this success and in 1973 returned to the US, where his films included *Reuben, Reuben* (1983).

OTHER BRITISH FILMS: *A Matter of Who* (1961, co-p), *Don't Raise the Bridge, Lower the River, 30 Is a Dangerous Age, Cynthia* (1967), *Welcome to the Club* (1970, + d), *Digby the Biggest Dog in the World* (1973).

Shenton, William Cinematographer. Shot about 20 silent and early talkie features, often for Maurice Elvey at Gaumont–British (he and Jack Cox shot *Hindle Wakes*, 1927), as well as the famous documentary, *BBC – The Voice of Britain* (1935, co-c).

OTHER BRITISH FILMS: (c, unless noted) *A Woman of No Importance* (1921, a), *We Women, Somebody's Dancing, Settled Out of Court, The Happy Ending* (1925), *The Woman Juror, London Love, The Greater War, Cash on Delivery, Mademoiselle from Armentières* (1926), *Roses of Picardy* (1927, co-c), *The Triumph of the Scarlet Pimpernel* (1928), *Thread o' Scarlet, Bed and Breakfast* (1930), *Third Time Lucky, The Hound of the Baskervilles* (co-c) (1931), *The Temperance Fete* (1932).

Shepherd, Elizabeth (*b* London, 1936). Actress. Blonde supporting player of the 60s, as, for example, William Sylvester's endlessly understanding secretary in *Blind Corner* (1963), but she had the lead opposite Vincent Price in the horror film, *The Tomb of Ligeia* (1964). Most of her post-60s work was either for TV or in the US.

OTHER BRITISH FILMS: *The Queen's Guards* (1961), *What Every Woman Wants* (1962), *Hell Boats* (1969), *Invitation to the Wedding* (1983).

Shepherd, Horace (*b* Richmond, Surrey, 1892 – *d* London, 1960). Composer, music director. Shepherd's career looks too diverse to be convincing, sometimes acting as director, producer and writer as well as filling his music-related functions. As composer, his wild scoring behind the opening sequences of *Hatter's Castle* (1941) suggests a melodramatic flair he might have developed with profit. Most of his subsequent work is in short films, often on musical subjects, and made for his own company, Inspiration Pictures Ltd; the exploitation feature, *Nudist Paradise* (1958), is an anomaly.

OTHER BRITISH FILMS INCLUDE: (m arr) *The Beggar Student* (1931), *Isles of Beauty – Ireland* (1935, short); (comp) *Hearts of Oak* (1933); (d, feature) *The Music Maker* (1936, + sc, co-p), *The Flamingo Affair* (1948, + p); (d, short) *Love on Leave* (1940), *Swingonometry* (1943), *Westminster Abbey* (1945), *Making the Grade* (1947), *A Ray of Sunshine* (+ p),

A Crazy Day with Max Wall (1950), *Beautiful Bedfordshire* (1956), *The Story of Regent Street* (1962, + p, comp).

Shepherd, Jack (*b* Leeds, 1940). Actor. Very popular for such TV series as *Wycliffe* (1994–95), as the Cornish-based detective, Shepherd has also directed plays at the Shakespeare Globe Theatre. Entered films in 1969, and, among his occasional appearances since, his broken-loser father in Michael WINTERBOTTOM's *Wonderland* (1999) is an achingly poignant character study. Trained for the stage at London's Drama Centre. Married to Ann SCOTT.

OTHER BRITISH FILMS INCLUDE: *The Virgin Soldiers, The Bed Sitting Room* (1969), *The Last Valley* (1970), *Something to Hide* (1971), *Angry Earth* (1989), *Crimestrike, The Big Man* (1990), *The Scarlet Tunic* (1997), *The Martins, Charlotte Gray* (UK/Aust/US) (2001).

Shepherd, Jean (aka Shepheard) (*b* Lancashire). Actress. Character player who appeared in about a dozen films of the 40s, including two versions of English film PASTORAL, *A Canterbury Tale* (1944) and *Great Day* (1945), and, most notably, in a very touching performance as the hero's careworn mother in *Fame Is the Spur* (1947).

OTHER BRITISH FILMS INCLUDE: *Inquest* (1939), *Thunder Rock* (1942), *Mr Emmanuel* (1944), *The White Unicorn* (1947), *No Place for Jennifer* (1949), *Stage Fright* (1950), *Mandy* (1952).

Shepherd's Bush Studios (aka Lime Grove Studios) In 1898 the BROMHEAD brothers formed the GAUMONT company UK, distributing films made by Léon Gaumont in France. Film production followed in 1912 at Shepherd's Bush and in 1915 they acquired additional premises. In 1922, GAUMONT–BRITISH became a solely British company and expanded again in 1926 with financial backing from the OSTRER brothers and Maurice ELVEY as head of production. Inexpensive 'QUOTA QUICKIES' were made but the coming of SOUND, plus the absorption of GAINSBOROUGH PICTURES into the Gaumont group made for more successful films such as *Evergreen* and HITCHCOCK's *The 39 Steps*. American films, however, affected Gaumont's output and by 1937 closure was imminent. RANK offered a rescue package, absorbing the company and leaving some film-making at Gaumont's ISLINGTON STUDIO. But at the outbreak of war (1939) this studio was considered unsafe and production was transferred to Shepherd's Bush with Maurice OSTRER and Edward BLACK in charge of production. A period of popular GAINSBOROUGH romances followed with Phyllis CALVERT, Stewart GRANGER, Jean KENT, Margaret LOCKWOOD, James MASON, and Patricia ROC. In 1946, when Sydney and Muriel BOX took over production, the RANK empire was in difficulties and Shepherd's Bush Studios were eventually sold to BBC Television in 1949.

BIBLIOG: Patricia Warren. *British Film Studios – An Illustrated History,* 2001. Patricia Warren.

Shepley, Michael (*b* Plymouth, 1907 – *d* London, 1961). Actor. RN: Shepley-Smith. Immensely enjoyable purveyor of blustery buffoons, sometimes choleric (like Major Watson in *Home at Seven,* 1952), sometimes merely well-meaning and bumble-footed (like the golf-mad husband in *Quiet Wedding,* 1941), and sometimes with a hint of pathos (like Christine NORDEN's obtuse husband in *Mine Own Executioner,* 1947). His filmography is rife with Colonels and the like. Westminster- and Oxford-educated, on stage from 1927; famously played Beecham the butler in *The Chiltern Hundreds* (1947–48). Died shortly after starring in *The Amorous Prawn* on stage in Australia.

OTHER BRITISH FILMS INCLUDE: *Black Coffee* (1931), *Lord Edgware Dies* (1934), *Housemaster* (1938), *The Great Mr Handel* (1942), *The Demi-Paradise* (1943), *Henry V* (1944), *I Live in Grosvenor Square* (1945), *Nicholas Nickleby* (1947), *Elizabeth of Ladymead* (1948), *Secret People* (1951), *Happy Ever After* (1954), *Dry Rot* (1956), *Gideon's Day* (1958), *Don't Bother to Knock* (1961).

Sheppard, Morgan (aka W[illiam] Morgan Sheppard) (*b* London). Actor. Educated in Ireland, trained at RADA, Sheppard spent twelve years with the RSC, entering films in 1962 in Vernon SEWELL's excellent 'B' MOVIE, *Strongroom,* as the criminal who is killed in a road accident. Also in the film versions of two of Peter BROOK's stage transfers: *The Marat/ Sade . . .* (1966), having played his role on Broadway, and *Tell Me Lies* (1967), a documentary-style feature about the Vietnam war. From the mid 80s, most of his film work was on TV or in the US.

OTHER BRITISH FILMS INCLUDE: *The Duellists* (1977), *The Sea Wolves* (1980, UK/Switz/US), *Nutcracker* (1982), *The Doctor and the Devils, Lady Jane* (1985), *Cry Freedom* (1987).

Shepperton Studios Businessman Norman LOUDON purchased an estate at Shepperton and founded the SOUND CITY FILM PRODUCING & RECORDING STUDIOS in 1932. By the end of that year the company had registered five productions, three SHORTS for MGM and two features. The studios beckoned young enthusiastic directors and producers including Ralph INCE, John Paddy CARSTAIRS and John BAXTER who made realistic dramas and COMEDIES of the 30s and 40s including *Song Of The Plough* (1933), which pointed to the 'NEW WAVE' school of the 50s and 60s. In April 1946 BRITISH LION headed by Alexander KORDA acquired a controlling interest in Sound City (Films) Ltd, and British Lion Films Ltd took over from British Lion in 1955, with practical film-makers, including Roy and John BOULTING, LAUNDER and GILLIAT. In 1972 Barclay Securities headed by John Bentley, acquired the studios and, between 1970 and the 1990s, Richard ATTENBOROUGH made some of his finest films there, including *Gandhi* (1982, UK/Ind) and *Shadowlands* (1993, UK/US). Other Shepperton classics include *An Ideal Husband* (1947), *Room At The Top* (1958), *Becket* (1964), *The Madness Of King George* (1994, UK/US) and *Four Weddings And A Funeral* (1994). In 1984 Lee International purchased SHEPPERTON which was sold in 1995 to a consortium led by British film directors Ridley and Tony SCOTT.

BIBLIOG: Patricia Warren, *British Film Studios – An Illustrated History,* 2001. Patricia Warren.

Sher, Sir Antony (*b* Cape Town, South Africa, 1949). Actor. Famously versatile stage star, a now-legendary, spidery Richard III (1986), Sher served briefly in the South African Defence Force before coming to England, where he trained at the Webber-Douglas School. His film roles have been sporadic but always arresting, including the cliché-spouting psychiatrist, Ziegler, in *The Young Poisoner's Handbook* (1995, UK/Fr/Ger), Disraeli in *Mrs Brown* (1997, UK/Ire/Us) and Dr Moth, confidant to *Shakespeare in Love* (1998, UK/US). He has also published several novels, volumes of autobiography and on acting. TV work has included the obnoxious academic Howard Kirk in the witty mini-series, *The History Man* (1981). Openly gay, he lives with director Gregory Doran. Knighted in 2000.

OTHER BRITISH FILMS: *Yanks* (1979), *Superman II* (1980), *Shadey* (1985), *Erik the Viking* (1989), *Genghis Cohn* (1993), *The Wind in the Willows* (1996).

BIBLIOG: Autobiography, *Beside Myself,* 2001.

Sheridan, Dinah (*b* London, 1920). Actress. RN: Mec. On stage at 12, while still studying at the Italia Conti School, and in films three years later in *Irish and Proud of It* (1936), Sheridan had only a few years as a top star and yet, if she had done nothing other than *Genevieve* (1953), her place in filmgoers' affections would be secure. In that sunniest of films, her performance as the increasingly exasperated wife is a model of comic timing, naturalistic charm and unexpected sexiness. She served a long apprenticeship in the later 30s (she is a dancer in *As You Like It*, 1936); did the obligatory stint as George FORMBY's leading lady (*Get Cracking*, 1943); co-starred with first husband Jimmy HANLEY in *For You Alone* and *29 Acacia Avenue* (1945), a film RANK found too daring to distribute, and in *The Huggetts Abroad* (1949), replacing Jane HYLTON at the last minute; and starred in a couple of neat little TEMPEAN THRILLERS, *No Trace* and *Blackout* (1950). But those last two titles might have summed up her career if the planned (but to this day undisclosed) leading lady for EALING's *Where No Vultures Fly* (1951) hadn't dropped out. As the gamekeeper's wife, she had the only female role in the Royal Command Film and received much wider notice than ever before. In short order, she then played: the second female lead in David LEAN's *The Sound Barrier* (1952), bringing a needed warmth to that somewhat chilly enterprise; the WAAF who falls in love with Dirk BOGARDE in *Appointment in London* (1953), a role intended by writer John WOOLDRIDGE for wife Margaretta SCOTT, then pregnant; Sullivan's girlfriend in *The Story of Gilbert and Sullivan* (1953); and then came *Genevieve*, whose producers had originally wanted Claire BLOOM. Following its success, she married again, to John DAVIS, Rank's managing director, and did not act again until this marriage was over. She starred charmingly in *The Railway Children* (1971), returned to the stage on several occasions, and had a continuing role in the TV series, *Don't Wait Up* (1983). Married (3) actor John MERIVALE. Mother of Jenny HANLEY.

OTHER BRITISH FILMS: *Landslide, Father Steps Out, Behind Your Back* (1937), *Merely Mr Hawkins* (1938), *Full Speed Ahead* (1939), *Salute John Citizen* (1942), *Murder in Reverse* (1945), *The Hills of Donegal* (1947), *The Story of Shirley Yorke, Calling Paul Temple* (1948), *Dark Secret* (1949), *Paul Temple's Triumph* (1950), *The Mirror Crack'd* (1980), *The 13th Reunion* (1981, unreleased).

Sheridan, Jim (*b* Dublin, 1949). Director, screenwriter. Since the international success of *My Left Foot* (1989), which received AAn and BAAn for Best Director and Screenplay and won Oscars for stars, Daniel DAY-LEWIS and Brenda FRICKER, Sheridan, formerly a successful stage director and playwright, has been a major force in British and Irish cinema. *My Left Foot* was an emotionally charged BIOPIC, celebrating the artistic and literary achievements of cerebral palsy victim, Christy Brown, and Sheridan confirmed the impression that he is a superb director of actors with two further films starring Day-Lewis: *In the Name of the Father* (1993, UK/Ire), in which he and Pete POSTLETHWAITE are a very affecting son-and-father team, at the centre of the 'Guildford four' frame-up; and *The Boxer* (1998, UK/Ire/US, + co-p, co-sc), a drama of the redemption of an ex-IRA prisoner. He also directed the often rambunctious Richard HARRIS to brilliant effect in *The Field* (1990, UK/Ire, + sc); and co-wrote and co-produced the grimly effective drama of the 1981 Northern Ireland prison hunger strike, *Some Mother's Son* (1996, Ire/US). His own company, Hell's Kitchen, has been a partner in all his films since *Agnes Browne* (1999, Ire/US, p). Daughter **Kristen Sheridan** directed *Disco Pigs*, 2001.

OTHER BRITISH FILMS: *Into the West* (1992, UK/Ire/US, sc), *Borstal Boy* (UK/Ire, ex p), *On the Edge* (co-p) (2000), *Bloody Sunday* (co-ex p), *East of Harlem* (d, sc) (2002).

Sheridan, Paul (*b* Paris, 1897 – *d* 1973). Casting director, actor. Educated in Paris and Oxford, made his stage debut in 1920 and entered films in 1932, both in Paris. After playing French supporting roles in about 30 British films, including *Two Thousand Women* (1944) and *Man from Morocco* (1945), as military officers, he became a casting director in the mid 50s, working for several companies, including David E. ROSE's Coronado Films.

OTHER BRITISH FILMS: (a) *It Happened in Paris* (1935), *The Rat* (1937), *This Man in Paris* (1939), *My Brother Jonathan* (1948), *Penny Princess* (1952), *Wicked as They Come* (1956); (casting d) *Cockleshell Heroes* (1955), *Seven Waves Away* (1956), *The Bridal Path* (1959), *Only Two Can Play* (1961).

Sherie, Fenn Screenwriter. Co-wrote about ten light COMEDIES and THRILLERS in the 30s, almost always in collaboration with Ingram D'Abbes (*b* Enfield, Middlesex). Both playwrights, they have the minor distinction of co-authoring the screenplay of James MASON's first film, *Late Extra* (1935). Sherie's solo effort was *The Silver King* (1929), a late silent.

OTHER BRITISH FILMS INCLUDE: (co-sc, unless noted) *Blue Smoke* (1935, co-story), *Song of Freedom* (+ adptn), *Sporting Love* (1936), *Leave It to Me, Big Fella* (1937), *I've Got a Horse* (1938).

Sheriff, Paul (*b* Moscow, *c* 1904 – *d* London, 1960). Production designer. RN: Paul Schouvaloff. A former mining engineer who came to Britain in the late 30s, working first as assistant to André ANDREJEW on *The Dictator* (1935), then to Lazare MEERSON when he came to work at DENHAM. Unlike fellow expatriates, Sheriff, Oxford-educated, was fluent in English. He became art director at TWO CITIES in 1939, working on *French Without Tears* (1939) for Anthony ASQUITH, with whom he was often associated. He and Carmen DILLON shared an AAn (art d) for *Henry V* (1944), on which his use of the medieval manuscripts effects was so striking, and he won an AA for the imaginative evocation of *fin-de-siècle* Paris in *Moulin Rouge* (1953). For Harold FRENCH's charming comedy, *The Man Who Loved Redheads* (1954), he skilfully registered the three distinct periods of the film's narrative. Also designed for the stage during the 40s, including Michael REDGRAVE's *Macbeth* (1947).

OTHER BRITISH FILMS INCLUDE: *Freedom Radio* (1940), *Quiet Wedding* (1941), *The First of the Few* (1942), *The Gentle Sex, The Demi-Paradise* (1943, sup), *Henry V* (1944), *The Way to the Stars* (1945, sup), *Hamlet* (1948, fx), *Adam and Evelyne* (1949), *The Captain's Paradise* (1953), *Aunt Clara* (1954), *Tarzan and the Lost Safari* (1956), *Chase a Crooked Shadow* (1957), *The Doctor's Dilemma* (1958), *The Grass is Greener* (1960).

Sherlock Holmes in silent films Arthur Conan DOYLE's Victorian detective made his screen debut in *Sherlock Holmes Baffled* (1900, US), and there were more than 60 Holmes silent films produced in the US and Europe. Holmes, portrayed by a Frenchman, Georges Tréville, made his first British appearance in a series of eight shorts, produced by the ECLAIR COMPANY in 1912 and filmed at Bexhill-on-Sea: *The Speckled Band, The Reigate Squires, The Beryl Coronet, The Adventures of the Copper Beeches, A Mystery of Boscombe Vale, The Stolen Papers, Silver Blaze,* and *The Musgrave Ritual*.

The first feature-length version of a Holmes story was *A Study in Scarlet* (1914, published 1887), directed by George

PEARSON for producer G.B. SAMUELSON. A non-professional, an accountant named James Bragington, played Holmes. Samuelson followed this with *The Valley of Fear* (1916), directed by Alexander BUTLER, and with H.A. Saintsbury as Holmes. Britain's last Holmes of the silent era, and one of his greatest delineators, was Eille NORWOOD, who starred in three SERIES for STOLL: *Adventures of Sherlock Holmes* (1921), consisting of 15 SHORTS and the feature-length *The Hound of the Baskervilles*, all directed by Maurice ELVEY; *Further Adventures of Sherlock Holmes* (1922), consisting of 15 shorts, directed by George RIDGWELL; and *The Last Adventures of Sherlock Holmes* (1923), consisting of 15 shorts, directed by Ridgwell, and the feature-length *The Sign of Four*, directed by Elvey. Arthur Cullin played Dr Watson in the last; Herbert Wills in the others. Norwood played Holmes on the cinema screen more than any other actor, and was praised by Conan Doyle for 'his wonderful impersonation of Holmes', and starred in the West End in *The Return of Sherlock Holmes* (1923), again with Conan Doyle's approval.

BIBLIOG: Michael Pointer, *The Public Life of Sherlock Holmes*, 1975. AS.

Sherlock Holmes in sound films Every generation has produced its definitive Sherlock Holmes in the movies. Although Raymond MASSEY played a youthful and updated Holmes in *The Speckled Band* (1931) and Robert RENDEL, a middle-aged and uncharismatic Holmes in *The Hound of the Baskervilles* (1931), the 30s belonged to Arthur WONTNER as a mature and reflective Holmes in *The Sleeping Cardinal* (1931), *The Sign of Four* (1932), *The Missing Rembrandt* (1932), *The Triumph of Sherlock Holmes* (1935) and *Silver Blaze* (1937). The 40s produced Basil RATHBONE's Hollywood Holmes. But Peter CUSHING successfully took on the role in HAMMER's *Hound of the Baskervilles* (1959), followed by a BBC TV Holmes series in 1968 and a telefilm, *The Masks of Death*, in 1984. Sherlock Holmes encountered JACK THE RIPPER in *A Study of Terror* (1965), with an effective John NEVILLE, and Sigmund Freud in *The Seven-Per-Cent Solution* (1976, US) with an ineffective Nicol WILLIAMSON. Robert STEPHENS was a memorable Holmes in Billy Wilder's mellow late masterpiece *The Private Life of Sherlock Holmes* (1970). But the latest, definitive Holmes has been Jeremy BRETT in 41 episodes of a Granada TV series which ran from 1984 to 1994.

BIBLIOG: Chris Steinbrunner and Norman Michaels, *The Films of Sherlock Holmes*, 1978. Jeffrey Richards.

Sherriff, R(obert) C(edric) (*b* Kingston-on-Thames, 1896 – *d* Kingston-on-Thames, 1975). Author, screenwriter. Oxford-educated playwright and novelist, most famous as the author of the classic WW1 trenches drama, *Journey's End* (1928), filmed in Hollywood (1930, UK/US) and over 40 years later provided the basis for *Aces High* (1976, UK/Fr), as well as being televised in 1937, 1983 and 1988. Others of his plays to be filmed were *Badger's Green* (1930, filmed 1934, 1949), *Windfall* (1933, filmed 1935) and *Home at Seven* (1950, filmed 1952). As well he wrote a number of screenplays for both British and US films, the latter including *That Hamilton Woman* (1941). In Britain he wrote the suspenseful nightmare drama, *The Night My Number Came Up* (1955, BAAn/sc), collaborating on several other famous films, including *Goodbye, Mr Chips* (1939), for which he shared an AAn.

OTHER BRITISH FILMS: (co-sc, unless noted) *The Four Feathers* (1939), *Odd Man Out* (1947), *Quartet* (1948, sc), *Trio* (1950), *No Highway* (1951), *The Dam Busters* (1955, BAAn/sc), *Storm over the Nile* (1955).

Sherrin, Ned (*b* Low Ham, 1931). Actor, producer. Former barrister who became a TV producer and 'personality', and produced such influential programmes as *That Was the Week That Was* (1962–63), *Not So Much a Programme, More a Way of Life* (1964–65) and *BBC3* (1965–66) before turning to film production in the late 60s. His film credits are mainly on moderately funny comedies, including the TV SPIN-OFF *The Alf Garnett Saga* (1972), and he made an urbanely portly appearance as Addison in Sally POTTER's *Orlando* (1992, UK/Fr/It/Neth/Russ). Also the co-author (with Caryl Brahms) of several stage plays, including *No Bed for Bacon* (1959). Awarded CBE, 1997.

OTHER BRITISH FILMS INCLUDE: (p) *The Virgin Soldiers*, *Every Home Should Have One* (1969); (co-p) *Up the Chastity Belt*, *Girl Stroke Boy* (1971), *Up the Front* (1972), *The National Health* (1973).

Sherwin, David (*b* Oxford, 1942). Screenwriter. Tonbridge- and (briefly) Oxford-educated Sherwin is famous for three screenplays he wrote for Lindsay ANDERSON: *If . . .* (1968, BAAn/sc), *O Lucky Man!* (1973, + co-p) and *Britannia Hospital* (1982), films whose stature grows with the years and which evolved from a very creative, often rancorous association. *If . . .* grew out of *Crusaders*, an earlier screenplay Sherwin had written with former school-fellow, John Howlett. Sherwin has written brilliantly about all of this and more in *Going Mad in Hollywood . . . And Life with Lindsay Anderson* (1996).

Sherwood, Lydia (*b* London, 1906 – *d* London, 1989). Actress. RN: Lily Shavelson. RADA-trained, on stage from 1925, playing many Shakespearean roles at Stratford and elsewhere. In films from 1932 (*Yellow Stockings*), particularly impressive as Nova PILBEAM's self-centred mother in *Little Friend* (1934), as good-time Lottie Grady in *When We Are Married* (1943) and briefly vivid as the older woman 'keeping' Bryan FORBES in *The League of Gentlemen* (1960).

OTHER BRITISH FILMS INCLUDE: *Don Quixote* (1933, UK/Fr), *King of Paris* (1934), *The Four Just Men* (1939), *Theatre Royal* (1943), *Romeo and Juliet* (1954, UK/It, as Lady Capulet), *Darling* (1965, unc).

Sheybal, Vladek (*b* Zgierz, Poland, 1923 – *d* London, 1992). Actor. Hollow-cheeked character player who had appeared (as Wladyslaw Sheybal) in the Polish classic, *Kanal* (1957), and after coming to England became a TV director as well as playing in about two dozen films. He appeared several times for Ken RUSSELL, starting with TV's *The Debussy Film* (1965), but perhaps most memorably as the watchful, sardonic Loerke in *Women in Love* (1969). Otherwise, foreigners of all nations, in the usual ecumenical way of British cinema.

OTHER BRITISH FILMS INCLUDE: *Dr No* (1962), *Billion Dollar Brain* (1967), *Deadfall* (1968), *Leo the Last* (1969), *Puppet on a Chain* (1970), *The Boy Friend* (1971), *The Lady Vanishes* (1979), *Funny Money* (1982), *The Jigsaw Man* (1984), *Loser Takes All* (1990, UK/US).

Shine, Bill (aka Billy Shine) (*b* London, 1911 – *d* London, 1997). Actor. Long-faced and luxuriantly moustachioed character player of about 90 films, Shine was the son of stage actor Wilfred SHINE. On stage from 1917, in London from 1928, and in films from 1929, usually in affable cameo roles, often as upper-class twits, but, really, doing whatever came along, whether it was Fred the journalist's photographer in *The Winslow Boy* (1948), the Duke of Chiddingford in *There Was a Young Lady* (1953) or the landlord in *Burke & Hare* (1971). Latterly, popular on TV as Inventor Black in *Supergran* (1985–87).

OTHER BRITISH FILMS INCLUDE: *The Flying Scotsman* (1929), *The Man from Toronto* (1933), *The Scarlet Pimpernel, Late Extra* (1935), *Sensation* (1936), *Young and Innocent* (1937), *Over the Moon* (1939), *Let George Do It!* (1940), *Champagne Charlie* (1944), *The Red Shoes* (1948), *The Chiltern Hundreds* (1949), *Scarlet Thread* (1951), *Knave of Hearts* (UK/Fr), *Happy Ever After* (1954), *Richard III, The Deep Blue Sea* (1955), *Jack the Ripper* (1958), *Libel* (1959), *Double Bunk* (1961), *Not Tonight Darling!* (1971), *The Jigsaw Man* (1984).

Shine, Wilfred (*b* Manchester, 1863 – *d* Kingston, Surrey, 1939). Actor. Of Irish descent, on stage from 1879, in a vast range of roles from panto to Shakespeare and in many countries, and in about a dozen films, starting in such silents as *The Burgomaster of Stilemonde* (1928) and *The Manxman* (1929) and finishing with *Over the Moon* (1939) in the year he died. Father of Bill SHINE.

OTHER BRITISH FILMS: *Lily of Killarney* (1929), *The Last Hour, Cross Roads* (1930), *The Hound of the Baskervilles* (1931), *Marooned* (1933).

Shiner, Ronald (*b* London, 1903 – *d* London, 1966). Actor. This former Mountie was a Cockney with aggressively beaky nose (allegedly insured with Lloyds of London for a large sum), eyes narrowed in calculation or suspicion, as often as not haranguing those under his thumb, but for (audience) laughs rather than threat. Shiner had been in dozens of films playing shysters of every hue from 1934 (*My Old Dutch, Doctor's Orders*) and on stage since 1928 (London 1929), before striking it rich as a Cockney spiv in a play called *Worm's Eye View*, which he finally steered into the Whitehall Theatre in 1945. It ran until 1950. From then on, he was a highly popular comic figure in such service pieces as *Seagulls over Sorrento* (1950–54) and, on screen, *Worm's Eye View* and (as a barking sergeant) *Reluctant Heroes* (1951). Never remotely subtle, he was nevertheless very funny and a huge box-office draw in the early 50s, giving one of his most engaging performances in *Aunt Clara* (1954), as an old reprobate's fly valet who helps Margaret RUTHERFORD manage the old man's dubious legacy. He remade Will HAY's *Good Morning Boys* (1937) as *Top of the Form* (1953), but lacked Hay's subtle seediness and as the decade wore on he was replaced as British cinema's favourite comic by Norman WISDOM. Crude in his effects as he often was, and rough and ready as most of his films were, Shiner was mercifully free from the sentimentality which always hovers around Wisdom's capers, and he seems never to have had any illusions about his capacities.

OTHER BRITISH FILMS INCLUDE: *Royal Cavalcade* (1935), *Dinner at the Ritz* (1937), *They Drive By Night* (1939), *Let George Do It!* (1940), *Unpublished Story, Those Kids from Town* (1942), *Miss London Ltd, Get Cracking* (1943), *I Live in Grosvenor Square* (1945), *Little Big Shot* (1952), *Innocents in Paris, Laughing Anne* (1953), *Up to His Neck* (1954), *See How They Run, Keep It Clean* (1955), *Dry Rot* (1956), *Carry On Admiral* (1957), *Girls at Sea* (1958), *Operation Bullshine, The Navy Lark* (1959), *The Night We Got the Bird* (1960).

Shingler, Helen (*b* London, 1919). Actress. Trained for ballet and, at the Webber-Douglas, for the stage, Shingler had considerable rep and touring experience (including the lead in *No Orchids for Miss Blandish*, on tour, 1942–43) before entering films in 1946. She had the lead in the picturesque but pedestrian *The Silver Darlings* and was the affected city girl not enjoying a *Quiet Weekend* (1946), but subsequent roles gave her limited opportunities. On TV, she quickly became prominent in the late 40s drama, and played the wife of *Maigret* (1960–63).

OTHER BRITISH FILMS INCLUDE: *The Lady with a Lamp, Judgment Deferred* (1951), *Love's a Luxury* (1952), *Laughing Anne, Background* (1953), *Family Doctor* (1958).

Shingleton, Wilfrid (*b* London, 1914 – *d* 1983). Production designer. Shingleton shared with John BRYAN an AA for the black-and-white designs of *Great Expectations* (1946), and 20 years later received a BAA for his art direction of *The Blue Max* (1966) and BAAn for *Heat and Dust* (1982), his last film. His prolific career dates back to EALING in 1932 when he became assistant to Edward CARRICK, taking over as the studio's designer when Carrick left in 1938. He worked as Admiralty camouflage officer during WW2 (1941–44), then joined CINEGUILD. Very busy throughout the 50s and 60s, credited variously as art director or production designer, on films for John HUSTON, David LEAN, Carol REED, Ronald NEAME and many others, across a wide genre range, embracing the ambiguous chiaroscuro of Jack CLAYTON's *The Innocents* (1961) and the Technicolored evocation of London and the theatre world in *I Could Go On Singing* (1963).

OTHER BRITISH FILMS: (art d) *Keep Fit* (1937), *Penny Paradise* (1938), *Young Man's Fancy, There Ain't No Justice* (1939), *The Proud Valley, Let George Do It!, Convoy* (1940), *The Ghost of St Michael's* (1941), *Take My Life, Blanche Fury* (1947), *The Cure for Love* (1949), *State Secret* (1950), *The African Queen* (1951), *Hobson's Choice* (1953), *A Kid for Two Farthings, Carrington VC* (1954), *Fortune Is a Woman* (1957, co-), *Tunes of Glory* (1960); (des) *Bonnie Prince Charlie* (1948), *The Key, I Was Monty's Double* (1958), *Waltz of the Toreadors, Term of Trial* (1962), *Stolen Hours* (1963, UK/US), *The Best House in London* (1968), *Macbeth* (1971), *Voyage of the Damned* (1976), *Eye of the Needle* (1981).

Shivas, Mark Producer. Oxford-educated Shivas worked at various times for the *New York Times*, for Granada and BBC TV from the late 60s, making his name with *The Six Wives of Henry VIII* (1970, nominated for three Emmys), then going on to produce a good deal of classy TV, such as *The Glittering Prizes* (1976). He produced such 80s films as *Moonlighting* (1982) and *A Private Function* (1984); then, as head of BBC Films, he was influential as executive producer on such popular films of the 90s as *Truly Madly Deeply* (1990) and *Enchanted April* (1992), as well as Michael WINTERBOTTOM's bleak masterworks, *Jude* (1996) and *The Claim* (2001, UK/Can/Fr). Founded Perpetual Motion Pictures 1997.

OTHER BRITISH FILMS INCLUDE: (ex p, unless noted) *Bad Blood* (1981, UK/NZ), *The Trial* (1992), *The Snapper, Priest* (1994), *An Awfully Big Adventure, Small Faces* (1995), *The Van* (1996), *Regeneration* (1997, UK/Can), *The Revengers' Comedies, Hideous Kinky* (1998, UK/Fr), *East Is East* (2000, consultant).

Shonteff, Lindsay (aka Michael Elam) (*b* Toronto, 1935). Director. Shonteff has been directing and sometimes producing films since the 60s, mostly THRILLERS (e.g. *Night After Night After Night*, 1969), sometimes with an element of parody, as in *Licensed to Love and Kill* (1979, + assoc p). None, however, has brought him much attention.

OTHER BRITISH FILMS INCLUDE: *Devil Doll* (1963), *Licensed to Kill* (1965, + co-sc), *Clegg* (1969), *Permissive* (1970), *The Yes Girls* (1971, + p, sc), *The Swordsman* (1974, + co-p), *Harry and the Hookers* (1975), *Spy Story* (1976, + p), *How Sleep the Brave* (1981), *Number One Gun* (1990).

Shore, Simon (*b* London, *c* 1959). Director. After attracting some notice for his RCA-made SHORT FILMS, *La Boule*, which won a BAA/short, and *Monsieur Mickey* (1986), Shore co-directed *The English Wife* (1995) with David HAYMAN, and won several festival awards for his first solo feature, *Get Real* (1999), a gentle and sometimes funny account of growing up gay in middle-class Basingstoke.

Shoreham Studio Founded in 1913 as the home of the Sunny South and Sealight Film Company, this studio turned out some popular films, including *The Jockey* (1914), based on and starring, Will Evans, one of the Company's founders. Other films made there included *Lady Noggs – Peeress* (1920), starring Joan MORGAN and directed and written by her father Sidney MORGAN, whose Progress Film Company used the studio until 1922, when it was destroyed by fire.

BIBLIOG: Neb Walters, *Bungalow Town: Theatre & Film Colony*, 1985.

short films. The Film Act of 1960 defined the British theatrically released short film as anything less than 33.3 minutes long. Today, with the short's sustained omniformity – and formats including 16mm, 35mm, analogue and digital video – length is no longer an issue. In a 1967 report by Derrick Knight and Vincent Porter, short films were broadly divided into four categories – theatrical, non-theatrical and non-sponsored (such as amateur film-making and art college production), television films, and the factual film. The latter is subdivided into films SPONSORED by industry (those DOCU-MENTARIES made for SHELL, Dunlop and ICI); Government films (films from the MINISTRY OF INFORMATION, and Central Office of Information); the educational film (aimed at schools and developing nations); and scientific and research films. Theatrically released shorts include experimental film, CINEMAGAZINES (such as the PATHÉ Pictorials) and news programmes, live action drama, and ANIMATION. Pop promos, and commercials must also be included; now the most visible forms of the short film, these are the new training grounds for many feature film-makers such as Ridley SCOTT, Tony Kaye, Jonathan GLAZER, and Lynne RAMSAY. Much ANIMATION and live action short film drama is financially supported – by the BRITISH FILM INSTITUTE until recently, CHANNEL 4, or SC4 – but cinema no longer exhibits a full supporting programme, leaving television and film festivals, often presenting short film packages comparable to the length of a feature film, to provide the main audience. AA-winning British short films have included the following: for Best Documentary Short Subject *Thursday's Children* (1954), *Giuseppina* (1959), *Dylan Thomas* (1961); for Best Live Action Short Subject *The Bespoke Overcoat* (1956), *Wild Wings* (1965), *Franz Kafka's It's A Wonderful Life* (1993); and for Best Animated Short Film *Great* (1974, Bob Godfrey), *Manipulation* (1991), *The Wrong Trousers* (1993, Nick Park), *Bob's Birthday* (1994), and *A Close Shave* (1995, Nick Park). Other well-known titles include such wartime shorts as *Miss Grant Goes to the Door* (1940), *Channel Incident* (1940), and *Mr Proudfoot Shows a Light* (1941), and a decade later, *The Stranger Left No Card* (1952).

BIBLIOG: Robert Dunbar (ed), *10 Years of British Short Films Abroad*, 1976; Bob Geoghegan (ed), *The Short Film index*, 1993; Derrick Knight and Vincent Porter, *A Long Look at Short Films: An ACTT Report on the Short Entertainment and Factual Film*, 1967. Ian Conrich.

Shotter, Winifred (*b* London, 1904 – *d* Montreux, Switz, 1996). Actress. Pretty and popular stage star, who made her London debut at 14 (playing a boy) and was from 1926 notably associated with the ALDWYCH FARCES, often repeating her stage roles in the film versions of the 30s, starting with *Rookery Nook* (1930). Briefly and unhappily in Hollywood (for *Petticoat Fever*, 1936), she made only four further films, including the attractive Coronation-set comedy, *John and Julie* (1955), but was still appearing on stage, looking very young and slim, in the 1959 farce, *Caught Napping*. Was a TV announcer for the BBC in the 50s.

OTHER BRITISH FILMS: *On Approval* (1930), *Plunder*, *Mischief*, *The Chance of a Night-Time* (1931), *A Night like This*, *The Love Contract* (1932), *Up to the Neck*, *Summer Lightning*, *Just My Luck*, *Night of the Garter* (1933), *Lilies of the Field* (1934), *The Rocks of Valpré*, *D'Ye Ken John Peel?*, *Marry the Girl* (1935), *His Lordship Regrets* (1938), *Candles at Nine* (1944), *The Body Said No!* (1950).

Shrapnel, John (*b* Birmingham, 1942). Actor. Very substantial character player in all the acting media, Shrapnel was a memorable Creon in a rare TV brush with the Greek classics, in *Oedipus the King*, *Oedipus at Colonus* and *Antigone* (1984), and an enjoyably vile Lord Steyne in TV's *Vanity Fair* (1987). On the big screen, he was very droll as a harassed PR man in *Notting Hill* (1999, UK/US) and, in contrasting vein, he was Gaius in *Gladiator* (2000, UK/US). TV has generally offered him the choicest morsels.

OTHER BRITISH FILMS INCLUDE: *Nicholas and Alexandra* (1971, UK/US), *Pope Joan* (1972), *Hennessy* (1975), *Testimony* (1987), *Two Deaths, England, My England* (1995), *Alone* (2002).

Shurey, Dinah. Director, producer. A flamboyant character, Shurey had served with the French Red Cross in WW1, organised Lena Ashwell's 'Concerts at the Front' and been business manager to H.V. Esmond (*see* Eva MOORE) before entering film production as the founder of Britannia Films in 1924. For Britannia, she produced *Second to None* (1926), which gave Desmond DICKINSON his first assignment as lighting cameraman, produced and directed *Carry On!* (1927) and *The Last Post* (1929, + sc). In 1929, she founded Showman Films, but the company failed and Shurey was declared bankrupt in 1934. AS.

Shute, Nevil (*b* Ealing, 1899 – *d* Melbourne, 1960). Author. RN: Norway. Popular Oxford-educated middlebrow novelist and former aeronautical engineer, several of whose novels were filmed. Most famous was *On the Beach* (1959, US/Aust); British ADAPTATIONS include *No Highway* (1948, filmed 1951), a tense drama based on a scientist's fear of metal fatigue in aircraft, and *A Town Like Alice* (1949, filmed 1956; Aust mini-series 1981), a harrowing account of women surviving a wartime trek in Malaya. Other British versions of his novels are *The Lonely Road* (1936) and *Landfall* (1949).

Siddons, Harold (*b* Belfast, 1922). Actor. Supporting player on screen and TV in the 50s, during which he appeared in about two dozen films, usually in small roles like that of gormless motorcycle cop, offsider to Geoffrey KEEN, in *Genevieve* (1953).

OTHER BRITISH FILMS INCLUDE: *Angels One Five* (1952), *They Who Dare*, *Appointment in London* (1953), *Conflict of Wings* (1954), *The Dam Busters* (1955), *The Baby and the Battleship* (1956), *A Night to Remember*, *Dunkirk* (1958), *The Wrong Arm of the Law* (1962).

Sight and Sound The first edition of this journal of record was Spring 1932 (called *The Quarterly Review of Modern Aids*), an adjunct to the British Institute for Adult Education. Under the newly-formed BRITISH FILM INSTITUTE the magazine became in 1934 *Sight and Sound, A Review of Modern Aids to Learning*. Despite this aspiration *Sight and Sound* has long concentrated much of its space on films which make no such educational assertions. It has battled to retain an editorial stance that is independent of the British Film Institute and, indeed, British cinema. This has meant being criticised by native film-makers as well as the BFI. *Sight and Sound* currently receives no sub-sidies other than sharing a building with the BFI. The magazine's internationalism, encouragement of ART-HOUSE features, and even-handed engagement with cinematic debates has on occasions led to an Olympian tone. A high standard of prestigious film writers has been maintained over the journal's lifetime and in 1965 it won (under the editorship of Penelope HOUSTON) the Plaquette Leone di S. Marco at the Venice Film Book Exhibition. Since 1952, *Sight and Sound*'s Ten Best Films list compiled each decade from critics' choices is eagerly awaited. In 1991 *Sight and Sound* became a monthly (as it had been 1949–51) when it amalgamated with *The Monthly Film Bulletin*. Under the editorship of Nick James (from 1997), *Sight and Sound* has largely eschewed esoteric stances, working at the interface between film fans, the industry and academia. Stephen Brown.

Signoret, Simone (*b* Wiesbaden, Germany, 1921 – *d* Autheuil-Anthouillet, France, 1985). Actress. RN: Kaminker. Of French parents, raised in Paris and in England from early in WW2, the wonderful Signoret, sexy, womanly, shrewd as she always seemed, made about five dozen films, but regrettably only a handful of these were British. Regrettably for British cinema, that is, because her great French roles, in the likes of *Casque d'or* (1951) and *Les diaboliques* (1955), are there testifying to her unique talents. However, she would belong in this book if she had done no other than play Alice Aisgill, the French woman unhappily married and stranded in a north of England town in *Room at the Top* (1958): the pain of sexual longing and the unforced poignancy of her rejection by Laurence HARVEY feed into one of the great performances in British cinema, wholly deserving its AA and BAA. She was also memorable as Laurence OLIVIER's wife in *Term of Trial* (1962), taunting him for being gutless, but then all she did, in whatever country, was apt to be memorable. Married (1) Yves Allegret and (2) Yves Montand.
OTHER BRITISH FILMS: *Against the Wind* (1947), *The Deadly Affair* (1966), *The Sea Gull* (1968).
BIBLIOG: Autobiography, *Nostalgia Isn't What it Used to Be*, 1976; Catherine David, *Simone Signoret*, 1992.

Sillitoe, Alan (*b* Nottingham, 1928). Screenwriter. Novelist, poet, playwright and occasional screenwriter. Sillitoe's disaffected working-class heroes, particularly Arthur Seaton of *Saturday Night and Sunday Morning* (1960) (BAAn/sc), closely aligned him with the ANGRY YOUNG MEN. Yet Sillitoe is also the chronicler of a changing post-war world where the working classes face an unappetising choice between drudgery, degradation and despair or the materialist blandishments of deadening suburban affluence. His work for the screen was always as elegiac as it was polemical, owing more to Richard Hoggart than Jimmy Porter.
OTHER BRITISH FILMS: *The Loneliness of the Long Distance Runner* (1962), *The Ragman's Daughter* (1972). Kevin Foster.

Silva, Simone (*b* Cairo, 1928 – *d* London, 1957). Actress. RN: DeBouillard. Of French parentage, Silva appeared in French films before becoming a starlet in about a dozen 50s British films, mostly purveying a stereotyped version of 'exotic' sex appeal. She was a devious belly-dancer in *South of Algiers* (1952), and a nightclub singer in Francis SEARLE's modestly entertaining 'B' MOVIE, *The Gelignite Gang* (1956), rendering 'Soho Mambo'. Had an unproductive time in Hollywood in 1954–55.
OTHER BRITISH FILMS INCLUDE: *Secret People* (1951), *Desperate Moment*, *Street of Shadows* (1953), *Duel in the Jungle* (1954), *Third Party Risk* (1955).

Silver, Christine (*b* London, 1883 – *d* London, 1960). Actress. Like so many British players, Silver had a very long stage career, starting in 1902 and lasting almost until her death, and made

only occasional films, usually in gentle or twittery roles. Thus she was the landlady to (possibly) JACK THE RIPPER in *Room to Let* (1950) and, with Nora NICHOLSON, one of a pair of fly old ladies in *The Hornet's Nest* (1955), her last. Also in a few minor silent films, and starred as *The Little Welsh Girl* (1920).
OTHER BRITISH FILMS INCLUDE: *The Pleydell Mystery* (1916), *Judge Not* (1920), *Dead Men Tell No Tales* (1938), *Heaven Is Round the Corner* (1944), *Mystery Junction* (1951), *Whispering Smith Hits London* (1952).

Silverstone, Ben (*b* London, 1979). Actor. Educated at St Paul's School, London, and Cambridge, Silverstone made his debut as donor of *The Browning Version* (1994), directed by family friend Mike FIGGIS, and appeared very briefly as young Humbert in the remake of *Lolita* (1997, US), but made his strongest impression as the Basingstoke schoolboy coming to terms with his sexuality in *Get Real* (1999), making the anxieties real indeed. Also on stage (e.g. the lead in *The Age of Consent*, 2001, at the Edinburgh Festival) and TV (in *Shackleton*, 2001).

Sim, Alastair (*b* Edinburgh, 1900 – *d* London, 1976). Actor. Memorable character player of faded Anglo-Scottish gentility, whimsically put-upon countenance, and sepulchral, sometimes minatory, laugh. On stage first in 1930 (a bit part in Robeson's *Othello*), he was in films from 1935. By the mid 40s he was a (slightly decaying) national institution. The American sociologists Wolfenstein and Leites (circa 1950) noted the prominent place of father figures in British as opposed to American cinema. Sim proved their point. A never-youthful character, he attained star status through portraying eccentric authority: doctors (*Waterloo Road*, 1944; *The Doctor's Dilemma*, 1959); schoolteachers (*The Happiest Days of Your Life*, 1950; *The Belles of St Trinian's*, 1954, in drag); gentlemen of the cloth (*Folly To Be Wise*, 1952); policemen (*Green For Danger*, 1946); lairds and lords (*Geordie*, 1955, UK/Ind; *Left, Right and Centre*, 1959). Where the sociologists went astray was in missing the ambivalence of which Sim was the paradigm – authority figure, yes, but often shadily duplicitous, often a manipulator of official rhetoric, his sexless bachelor persona containing strains of sexual ambiguity, his jolliness a latent vampirism. In the first half of *Cottage to Let* (1941) he seemed, convincingly, to be a Nazi agent, and in *The Green Man* (1956) he was a chortling assassin. And he was certainly unsettling as the spectral Poole in *An Inspector Calls* (1954). Sim was above all associated with LAUNDER AND GILLIAT for whom he made many films from 1939 to 1959, most unforgettably *The Happiest Days of Your Life*, as the Headmaster of Nutbourne pitted against Margaret RUTHERFORD's obdurate Headmistress, a role that is a microcosm of his talents, of a mode of British comedy, and of the post-war decline of the upper-middle-class hegemony which he embodied so antically. Awarded CBE, 1953.
OTHER BRITISH FILMS: *Riverside Murder*, *The Case of Gabriel Perry*, *A Fire Has Been Arranged*, *Private Secretary*, *Late Extra* (1935), *Troubled Waters*, *Wedding Group*, *The Big Noise*, *The Man in the Mirror*, *Keep Your Seats, Please*, *The Mysterious Mr Davis*, *She Knew What She Wanted* (1936), *Strange Experiment*, *Clothes and the Woman*, *Gangway*, *The Squeaker*, *Romance in Flanders*, *Melody and Romance* (1937), *Sailing Along*, *The Terror*, *Alf's Button Afloat*, *This Man is News*, *Climbing High* (1938), *Inspector Hornleigh*, *This Man in Paris*, *Inspector Hornleigh on Holiday* (1939), *Law and Disorder* (1940), *Cottage to Let*, *Inspector Hornleigh Goes to It* (1941), *Let the People Sing* (1942), *Journey Together* (1945), *Hue and Cry*, *Captain Boycott* (1947), *London Belongs to Me* (1948), *Stage Fright* (1950), *Scrooge* (1951), *Innocents in Paris* (1953), *Escapade* (1955), *Blue Murder at St Trinian's* (1957), *School for*

Edward Fox, character actor, here in *The Day of the Jackal*.

Howards End (1992, d.James Ivory), drama, with Samuel West, Helena Bonham Carter.

LEFT *The Cook, the Thief, His Wife and Her Lover* (1989, d.Peter Greenaway), satire, with Helen Mirren, Michael Gambon.

BELOW LEFT **Ricky Tomlinson**, character actor, here in *Riff-Raff*.

BELOW **Ewan McGregor**, star actor, here in *Shallow Grave*.

ABOVE *Four Weddings and a Funeral* (1994, d.Mike Newell), romantic comedy, with Simon Callow, John Hannah, Charlotte Coleman.

ABOVE LEFT *Secrets & Lies* (1996, d.Mike Leigh), comedy-drama, with Timothy Spall.

LEFT **Emma Thompson**, leading actress, here in *The Remains of the Day*.

BELOW **Jim Broadbent**, character star, here in *Life Is Sweet*.

Trainspotting (1996, d.Danny Boyle), black comedy, with Robert Carlyle, Ewan McGregor.

My Name Is Joe (1998, d.Ken Loach), realist drama, with Peter Mullan.

East Is East (1999, d.Damien O'Donnell), comedy-drama, with Linda Bassett, Om Puri.

Helena Bonham Carter, star actress, here in *The Wings of the Dove*.

Wonderland (1999, d.Michael Winterbottom), realist drama, with Gina McKee, Jack Shepherd.

Ralph Fiennes, star actor, here in *Onegin*.

Brenda Blethyn, character star.

Dame Judi Dench, star actress, here in *Shakespeare in Love*.

Kenneth Branagh, actor, director.

for her second husband, director Richard BROOKS (1960 to 1997, divorce). She returned to film in Britain in 1955, as a scheming housemaid in the enjoyable Victorian melodrama, *Footsteps in the Fog* (1955), opposite Granger, and was Susan Brown, grown bitchy with the years, in *Life at the Top* (1965), but most of her work since 1951 has been in the US and/or on TV. In 1989, she played Miss Havisham in the mini-series *Great Expectations*; the poignancy she evoked was not wholly to do with the role. Awarded OBE, 2003.

OTHER BRITISH FILMS: *Mr Emmanuel, Meet Sexton Blake, Kiss the Bride Goodbye, Sports Day* (short) (1944), *Hungry Hill, The Woman in the Hall* (1947), *Trio* (1950), *Footsteps in the Fog* (1955), *The Grass Is Greener* (1960), *Say Hello to Yesterday* (1970), *Dominique* (1978), *Going Undercover* (1988).

Simon, Charles (*b* Wolverhampton, 1909 – *d* Harrow, 2002). Actor. Still performing into his 90s, Simon was one of Britain's oldest working actors, busy on TV (e.g. *Happy Birthday Shakespeare*, 2000), stage (he had seasons with the National and the RSC) and screen, the latter increasing with age. He was Gilbert's father in *Topsy-Turvy* (2000, UK/US), Lord Carnivore in *102 Dalmatians* (2000), and during 2000 appeared in the TV programme, *Starstruck: Holding On*, one of a number of actors explaining why they kept on working – and how it felt when they weren't. At 91, he could scarcely have been more chipper. Probably best known for playing Dr Dale in the BBC radio serial, *The Dales* (1963–69).

OTHER BRITISH FILMS INCLUDE: *The Darwin Adventure* (1971), *Little Dorrit* (1987), *American Friends* (1991), *Shadowlands* (1993, UK/US), *Stiff Upper Lips* (1996, UK/Ind), *Whatever Happened to Harold Smith?* (2000), *The Final Curtain* (2002).

Simpson, Alan (*b* London, 1929). Screenwriter. Most famous for his collaboration with Ray GALTON, in co-creating such TV successes as *Hancock's Half-Hour* (1956–60), and HANCOCK's film *The Rebel* (1960) and *Steptoe and Son* (1972, filmed 1972, sequel *Steptoe & Son Ride Again*, 1973), and they collaborated on the screenplays of several witty films, including *The Wrong Arm of the Law* (1962) and *Loot* (1970).

OTHER BRITISH FILMS: *The Siege of Sidney Street* (1960, a); (co-sc) *The Bargee* (1964), *The Spy with a Cold Nose* (1966), *Up the Chastity Belt, The Magnificent Seven Deadly Sins* (1971), *Le Petomane* (1979, short).

See also **Galton, Ray**.

Simpson, Peggy (*b* Leeds, 1913 – *d* London, 1994). Actress. Studied with Italia Conti and on stage from 1929, with a busy theatrical and minor film career. She had small roles in *Sunshine Susie* (1931) and as Godfrey TEARLE's maid in *The 39 Steps* (1935), and played the title role of the mermaid in the TV version of *Miranda* (1949).

OTHER BRITISH FILMS INCLUDE: *Sleeping Car* (1933), *Fighting Stock, Temptation* (UK/Fr) (1935), *Everything Is Thunder, Jack of All Trades* (1936), *Young and Innocent* (1937), *No Kidding* (1960).

Sims, Joan (*b* Laindon, 1930 – *d* London, 2001). Actress. Fondly remembered above all as one of the most durable members of the 'CARRY ON' team, Sims was also a RADA-trained theatre actress. Her performing debut was on the Laindon railway platform, where her father was stationmaster and she would entertain waiting travellers; her London stage debut was in 1952 and she had a success as Athene SEYLER's no-nonsense maid in *Breath of Spring* (1958). In films from 1953, she caught cinemagoers' amused attention as the austere nurse 'Rigor Mortis' in *A Doctor in the House* (1954), was in a couple more 'DOCTOR' films (typically plump, sexually predatory and alarming to Dirk BOGARDE), and was an invariably welcome

RANK supporting regular in the likes of *Upstairs and Downstairs* (1959). Her 'CARRY ON' roles included suspicious wives of many kinds, most famously perhaps as a nagging Calpurnia in *Carry On Cleo* (1964) and as Lady Joan Ruff-Diamond, constantly on the *qui vive* for the peccadilloes of husband Sidney JAMES in *Carry On Up the Khyber* (1968), and, for contrast, a glamorous (well, more or less) Belle Armitage in *Carry On Cowboy* (1965). In her last years, from 1994, she had a continuing role in TV's *As Time Goes By*, as Geoffrey PALMER's lively stepmother; and there were rich character studies too: in *Waters of the Moon* (1983), as a cheerful vulgarian in a genteel private hotel; surprisingly affecting, as one of a lesbian pair with Paola DIONOSOTTI in *A Murder Is Announced* (1985); and finally in *The Last of the Blonde Bombshells* (2000). When she died, it was sad to read of a lonely life, lived largely alone in a rented flat.

OTHER BRITISH FILMS INCLUDE: *Will Any Gentleman . . . ?, Trouble in Store, The Square Ring* (1953), *The Young Lovers, The Belles of St Trinian's* (1954), *Doctor at Sea* (1955), *Stars in Your Eyes, Dry Rot, The Silken Affair* (1956), *No Time for Tears, The Naked Truth, Just My Luck, Davy, Carry On Admiral* (1957), *Carry On Nurse, Passport to Shame, The Captain's Table, Life in Emergency Ward 10* (1958), *Carry On Teacher* (1959), *. . . Constable* (1960), *No, My Darling Daughter,* (1961), *Twice Round the Daffodils* (1962), *Nurse on Wheels* (1963), *Doctor in Clover, Carry On Screaming, Don't Lose Your Head* (1966), *Follow That Camel* (1967), *Carry On Up the Khyber, . . . Doctor* (1968), *. . . Camping, . . . Again Doctor* (1969), *Doctor in Trouble, Carry On Up the Jungle, . . . Loving* (1970), *. . . Henry, . . . at Your Convenience* (1971), *. . . Matron, . . . Abroad, The Alf Garnett Saga* (1972), *Carry On Girls* (1973), *. . . Dick* (1974), *. . . Behind* (1975), *. . . England* (1976), *. . . Emmannuelle* (1978), *The Fool* (1990).

Sinclair, Andrew (*b* Oxford, 1935). Director. Novelist who directed some little-seen films, including *The Breaking of Bumbo* (1970), based on his own novel about an old Etonian Guards officer coming to grief. Kevin BROWNLOW and Andrew MOLLO were signed to direct but sacked before shooting began, and the whole enterprise remains pretty mysterious, never receiving serious cinema showings. His ADAPTATION of *Under Milk Wood* (1971) misguidedly transfers a theatrical, highly verbal fantasy to the unforgiving realism of cinema and viewers of the other films he directed may well be countable on the fingers of a damaged hand. Wrote a demystifying biography of Sam SPIEGEL (1987) and a more conventional one of John FORD (1979).

OTHER BRITISH FILMS: *Before Winter Comes* (1968, sc), *The Seaweed Children* (1973, add dial, co-p), *Blue Blood* (1973, d, sc), *Tuxedo Warrior* (1982, d).

Sinclair, Arthur (*b* Dublin, 1883 – *d* Belfast, 1951). Actor. RN: McDonnell. Irish character player, who appeared as father to singer Evelyn LAYE in *Evensong* (1934), wanting her to marry and settle down, and to Anna LEE, in *King Solomon's Mines* (1937), going off greedily after treasure and leaving her to her own resources. Finished his film career as a feuding patriarch in *Hungry Hill* (1947). Married Maire O'NEILL.

OTHER BRITISH FILMS: *M'Blimey* (1931), *Wild Boy, Sing As We Go!* (1934), *Peg of Old Drury* (1935), *The Show Goes On* (1937), *Welcome Mr Washington* (1944).

Sinclair, Hugh (*b* London, 1903 – *d* Slapton, 1962). Actor. Charterhouse-educated and RADA-trained leading man (on stage from 1922) who played enjoyably suave types in nearly two dozen films, suggesting the kind of moral unreliability that went inevitably with a smoking jacket. A woman never knew where she was with him, but selfish Anne CRAWFORD met her match in him in *They Were Sisters* (1945) and plucky Dinah SHERIDAN nearly pays for her devotion with her life in *No Trace* (1950). Repeated his stage role of Sebastian in the film of *Escape Me Never* (1935), and was good casting as Simon Templar in *The Saint's Vacation* (1941) and *The Saint Meets the Tiger* (1943, UK/US), as, of course, he was on stage as Elyot in *Private Lives* (1945). He was nicely treacherous in *Circle of Danger* (1950), but his kind of caddishness was on the way out in the 50s. TV from 1951; married (1 of 2) Valerie TAYLOR.

OTHER BRITISH FILMS INCLUDE: *The Marriage of Corbal* (1936), *A Girl Must Live*, *The Four Just Men* (1939), *Alibi* (1942), *Flight from Folly* (1945), *Corridor of Mirrors*, *Trottie True* (1948), *The Rocking Horse Winner* (1949), *Judgement Deferred* (1951), *The Second Mrs Tanqueray* (1952), *Mantrap* (1953).

Sinclair, Peter (*b* Kirkintilloch, Scotland, 1900 – *d* London, 1994). Actor. Character player of Scots types on stage and screen, who entered films as Anton WALBROOK's loyal Scots colleague in *The Man from Morocco* (1945), was the gillie, a rare authentic note in the synthetic tartanry of *Trouble in the Glen* (1954), and a crook who changes sides in the lively 'B' MOVIE, *One Jump Ahead* (1955). Best known for playing the grandfather of *The Clitheroe Kid* on BBC radio (1958–72).

OTHER BRITISH FILMS INCLUDE: *Escape by Night* (1953), *Cross Channel*, *No Smoking* (1955), *Let's Be Happy* (1956), *Zoo Baby* (1957), *On the Fiddle* (1961), *Invasion* (1966).

Sinden, Sir Donald (*b* Plymouth, 1923). Actor. Jovial, sometimes bombastic leading man, noted for his rich, plummy voice, one of the RANK ORGANISATION's leading contract stars 1954–58, particularly in light comedy roles. On stage since 1941, with Stratford and Bristol Old Vic seasons, he made his film debut in 1948, but his film career only took off in 1953, when he appeared as Lt Lockhart, Jack HAWKINS' second in command, in EALING's superb naval drama *The Cruel Sea* (1952), probably his finest film role. This led to a Rank contract and the phenomenally successful *Doctor in the House* (1954), in which Kenneth MORE and duffel-coated Sinden regularly failed their finals, spending most of their time chasing pretty nurses. In 1956, he had a rare role as a ruthless robber, murdering a cinema manager (ODEON, of course) and ruthlessly trying to eliminate the only *Eyewitness* (1956). More typically, he was a songwriter who finds himself landed with *An Alligator Named Daisy* (1955), in which his comic timing was seen to good effect, and as hero in the underrated atmospheric thriller *Tiger in the Smoke* (1956). Following non-renewal of his Rank contract in 1958 (affected like many others by British NEW WAVE acting styles), he threw himself wholeheartedly into the theatre, joining the RSC in 1963, receiving great acclaim in Shakespeare and other classical roles. Since the 60s, he has appeared in occasional films, in character roles in telemovies (e.g. *The Canterville Ghost*, 1997), and starred in such series as *Two's Company* (1975–9). Awarded CBE, 1979, and knighted, 1997. Father of actors Jeremy SINDEN and Marc Sinden (*b* London, 1954), who has appeared in several films, including *The Wicked Lady* (1983) and *The Brylcreem Boys* (1996).

OTHER BRITISH FILMS: *Portrait from Life* (1948), *Mogambo* (US/UK), *A Day to Remember* (1953), *You Know What Sailors Are*, *The Beachcomber*, *Simba*, *Mad About Men* (1954), *Above Us the Waves*, *Josephine and Men* (1955), *The Black Tent* (1956), *Doctor at Large* (1957), *The Captain's Table*, *Rockets Galore* (1958), *Operation Bullshine* (1959), *The Siege of Sidney Street*, *Your Money or Your Wife* (1960), *Mix Me a Person*, *Twice Round the Daffodils* (1962), *Decline and Fall . . .* (1968), *Villain* (1971), *Rentadick*, *Father, Dear Father* (1972), *The Day of the Jackal* (UK/Fr),

The National Health (1973), *That Lucky Touch* (1975), *The Children* (UK/Ger) (1990).

BIBLIOG: Autobiography, *A Touch of the Memoirs*, 1982; *Laughter in the Second Act*, 1985. Roger Philip Mellor.

Sinden, Jeremy (*b* London, 1950 – *d* London, 1996). Actor. Supporting player of stage and TV (e.g. *Brideshead Revisited*, 1981), who made his film debut in the original *Star Wars* (1977, US) and appeared in about ten other films. His roles were often small but noticeable, like the President of the GILBERT AND SULLIVAN Society in *Chariots of Fire* (1981) and the *Telegraph* reporter who comes to the anguished parents for a 'response' in '*Let Him Have It*' (1991). Died sadly young of cancer.

OTHER BRITISH FILMS INCLUDE: *Rosie Dixon – Night Nurse* (1978), *Ascendancy* (1982), *Madame Sousatzka* (1988), *The Innocent* (1993, UK/Ger).

Singer, Campbell (*b* London, 1909 – *d* London, 1977). Actor. Raised in South Africa were he made his stage debut in 1928, before returning to England in 1931 and appearing on the London stage in 1935, entering films in *Premiere* (1938). After WW2 service with the Royal Artillery (1940–46), he returned to stage and screen. Over the next 15 years, his long, thin face, with disciplined moustache and thinning hair, was seen over the uniform of several dozen policeman, like the Station Sergeant in *The Blue Lamp* (1949) or *The Ringer* (1952), though he was several times promoted to Inspector, as in *Home at Seven* (1952), in which he repeated his stage role. One of his most popular stage roles was as Inspector Lord in the long-running *The Spider's Web* (1954–56). Also co-authored a number of plays, including the excellent boardroom drama, *Any Other Business?* (1958). Was married to Gillian MAUDE.

OTHER BRITISH FILMS INCLUDE: *Take My Life* (1947), *Dick Barton at Bay*, *Pool of London* (1950), *The Quiet Woman* (1951), *The Happy Family* (1952), *The Titfield Thunderbolt*, *The Intruder* (1953), *No Trees in the Street* (1958), *The Trials of Oscar Wilde* (1960), *The Fast Lady* (1962).

Singer, John (aka Johnny Singer) (*b* Hastings, 1923 – *d* Tunbridge Wells, 1987). Actor. Popular child actor of the 30s, making nearly 20 films in the decade, including *This Green Hell* (1936), as son of Edward RIGBY. He appeared in several MANCUNIAN FILMS in the 40s, including *Somewhere in England* (1940), as well as in such classier products as *In Which We Serve* (1942) and *The Cruel Sea* (1952), but the roles grew smaller as he matured; his career may have lost momentum when he was in the armed forces (1942–47) and he returned as a rather overage juvenile in *Fly Away Peter* (1948).

OTHER BRITISH FILMS INCLUDE: *King of the Ritz* (1933), *My Heart Is Calling* (1934), *Dandy Dick* (1935), *Not So Dusty* (1936), *Somewhere in Camp* (1942), *School for Randle* (1949), *The Dark Man* (1950), *The Brave Don't Cry* (1952), *Betrayed* (1954), *Further Up the Creek* (1958).

Singuineau, Frank (*b* Port of Spain, Trinidad, 1913 – *d* London, 1992). Actor. West Indian character player who scored a better than average number of the limited roles available to black actors in 50s and 60s Britain, starting in such African-set adventures as *Simba* and *Storm over the Nile* (1955) and including most vividly Anne BANCROFT's enigmatic visitor, the 'King of Israel', in *The Pumpkin Eater* (1964). Also some TV, including an episode of *Emergency – Ward 10* (1961).

OTHER BRITISH FILMS INCLUDE: *Safari* (1956), *The Mummy* (1959), *Night of the Eagle* (1962), *Seance on a Wet Afternoon* (1964), *The Wrong Box* (1966), *Follow That Camel* (1967), *Hot Millions* (1968), *Baxter!* (1972), *O Lucky Man!* (1973), *Pressure* (1975), *Biggles* (1986).

Sinyor, Gary   (*b* Manchester, 1962). Director. Sinyor made his feature debut on the low-budget British-Jewish comedy, *Leon the Pig Farmer* (1992), co-directing and co-producing with Vadim JEAN and also collaborating on the screenplay. The film had only a minor cultish success; since then he has directed *Solitaire for 2* (1995, + sc) and the strongly cast but little seen MERCHANT IVORY spoof, *Stiff Upper Lips* (1996, UK/Ind, + co-p, co-sc).

Siodmak, Curt   (*b* Dresden, Germany, 1902 – *d* Three Rivers, California, 2000). Screenwriter, novelist. Brother of director Robert Siodmak, he started as a journalist and author of science-fiction and horror novels. Siodmak's screenwriting career in 30s Britain included his futuristic, but imaginable visions for *FP1* (UK/Ger 1933, adapted from his 1930 novel), and *The Tunnel* (1935); and work on the aborted *I, Claudius* (1937). In Hollywood from 1937, he became a prolific writer for Universal (e.g. *The Wolf Man*, 1941). His novel 'Donovan's Brain' (1942) was filmed four times, including *Vengeance* (UK/Ger 1962). Elements of two of his later novels were, uncredited, used in the James BOND film *Moonraker* (UK/Fr, 1978).
OTHER BRITISH FILMS: *Girls Will Be Boys, It's a Bet* (1935, co-sc), *I Give My Heart* (1935, co-sc), *Non-Stop New York* (1937, co-sc), *Sherlock Holmes And The Deadly Necklace* (1962, UK/Fr/Ger, sc).
BIBLIOG: *Even A Man Who Is Pure In His Heart*, 1997, republished 2001 as *Wolf Man's Maker*. Tim Bergfelder.

Sistrom, William   (*b* Lincolnshire, 1884 – *d* California, 1972). Producer. Sistrom's early experience was in Hollywood, first with Carl Laemmle and then as producer for RKO, which sent him back to England in 1939 to supervise RKO–BRITISH films, including the Simon Templar THRILLERS, *The Saint in London* (1939), *The Saint's Vacation* (1941) and *The Saint Meets the Tiger* (1943, UK/US), and the hugely successful wartime romance, *Dangerous Moonlight* (1941). He later moved to TWO CITIES where he produced the touching drama of Jewish persecution in Nazi Germany in *Mr Emmanuel* (1944).
OTHER BRITISH FILMS: *Meet Maxwell Archer* (1939), *Escape to Danger* (1943), *Hungry Hill* (1947), *Woman Hater* (1948), *Adam and Evelyne* (1949).

Skinner, Claire   (*b* Watford, Herts, 1965). Actress. LAMDA-trained Skinner's sculpted features and versatility have been on view in such varied films as Mike LEIGH's *Life is Sweet* (1990), as the plumber sister of Jane HORROCKS, and *Naked* (1993) and as the heroine's rival in *Bridget Jones's Diary* (2001, UK/Fr/US). Also to the fore in such TV programmes as *Dance to the Music of Time* (1997) and as Clive OWEN's sidekick, in the know about his looming blindness, in the series *Second Sight* (1999–2000). Played Desdemona to Michael GAMBON's *Othello* in Alan AYCKBOURN's production at Scarborough.

Skolimowski, Jerzy   (*b* Lodz, Poland, 1938). Director. A graduate of Warsaw University and Lodz Film School, along with Roman POLANSKI, whose *Knife in the Water* (1962) he co-wrote, Skolimowski has made some idiosyncratic films in Western Europe. His best received British film was *Moonlighting* (1982, + p, co-sc), a compelling piece set in London at the time of the proclamation of martial law in Poland, 1981. His first Western film was the lavish co-production, *The Adventures of Gerard* (1970, UK/It/Switz, + co-sc); the US/German co-production, *Deep End* (1970), set in a London swimming baths, and with a British cast, was an atmospheric account of youthful sexuality; and *The Shout* (1978, + co-sc), from Robert Graves's novel, though it found some genuine

menace in the English countryside, was too bizarre for most filmgoers. Skolimowski managed to transfer his talents to the West, and his films have a very distinctive, un-British flavour. Round the turn of the century he acted in several US films, including *Mars Attacks!* (1996).
OTHER BRITISH FILMS: *Success Is the Best Revenge* (1984, UK/Fr, + p, sc), *Ferdydurke* (1992, UK/Fr/Pol, + co-sc).

Skutezky, Victor   (*b* Brno, Czech, 1893 – *d* ?). Producer. After experience in Continental films, starting in Berlin, 1922, Skutezky was active in British films from the mid 40s to the later 50s, his more notable films including Lance COMFORT's sombre masterwork, *Temptation Harbour* (1947, + co-sc), and several of J. Lee THOMPSON's early films – *Murder Without Crime* (1950), *The Yellow Balloon* and *The Weak and the Wicked* (1953), all for ASSOCIATED BRITISH.
OTHER BRITISH FILMS INCLUDE: *It Happened One Sunday* (1944), *Quiet Weekend* (1946, co-sc), *Landfall* (1949), *Young Wives' Tale* (1951), *It's Great to Be Young!* (1956), *Alive and Kicking* (1958).

Slaney, Ivor   (*b* Birmingham, 1921 – *d* 1998). Composer. Busiest in the 50s when he scored nearly 20 'B' MOVIES, of which the most notable is probably Ken HUGHES's *The House Across the Lake* (1954), in which his moody music, starting behind the credits, contributes tellingly to the film's *noir* agenda. Worked on several pre-HORROR HAMMER films; some TV work, too, including music director on *Sir Francis Drake* (1961–62).
OTHER BRITISH FILMS INCLUDE: (comp, unless noted) *Lady in the Fog* (1952), *Spaceways* (+ m d), *The Flanagan Boy* (1953), *Five Days* (1954), *The Reluctant Bride* (1955), *Sail into Danger* (1957), *Sally's Irish Rogue* (1958, Ire), *A King's Story* (1965, doc, + m d), *Bachelor of Arts* (1969, short), *Terror* (1978), *Death Ship* (1980).

Slater, John   (*b* London, 1916 – *d* London, 1975). Actor. Indispensable Cockney character player in British films for over 25 years. Educated at St Clement Dane's Grammar School, he was on stage from childhood (1924) and on the London stage from 1942, with seasons at Stratford (1949) and the Whitehall (*Dry Rot*, 1954). His homely, furrowed features made him a natural for such roles as the fishmonger keen on Jane HYLTON in *Passport to Pimlico* (1949), and he played character leads in minor films such as Vernon SEWELL's entertaining *Johnny, You're Wanted* (1955), as a lorry driver who rounds up a dope gang, but it is the supporting roles in bigger films that stay in the mind. There was a mixture of crooks and police, and on TV he became a regular in *Z Cars* (1967–72). Also narrated the *Mining Review* DOCUMENTARY SHORTS in the post-war years. Prolific as he was, he was hindered by bouts of ill-health and an air crash injury in 1946.
OTHER BRITISH FILMS INCLUDE: *Pimpernel Smith, Love on the Dole* (1941), *Our Film* (short), *Went the Day Well?* (1942), *We Dive at Dawn, Millions Like Us* (1943), *For Those in Peril* (1944), *A Canterbury Tale, Murder in Reverse, I Live in Grosvenor Square, The Seventh Veil* (1945), *It Always Rains on Sunday, Against the Wind* (1947), *Passport to Pimlico* (1949), *Prelude to Fame* (1950), *The Long Memory* (1952), *The Million Pound Note, The Flanagan Boy* (1953), *The Devil's Pass* (1957), *The Night We Got the Bird* (1960), *A Place to Go* (1963), *The Yellow Hat* (1966).

Slater, Montagu   (*b* Bootle, 1902 – *d* London, 1956). Screenwriter. Also a playwright, novelist and critic, Slater entered the film industry in 1942 as script editor for the MINISTRY OF INFORMATION, and wrote or co-wrote several films in the late 40s and 50s. He worked on several occasions with GROUP 3, on *The Brave Don't Cry* (1952), the moving mining disaster film directed by his then-son-in-law, Philip LEACOCK, the Uganda-set *Man of Africa* (1953), and the racing drama, *Devil on Horseback* (1954, co-sc). The dirttrack-racing drama, *Once a Jolly Swagman* (1948), was based on his novel, and he wrote commentaries for two BRITISH TRANSPORT FILMS productions: *Berth 24* (1950), *Journey into History* (1952). Also worked as dramatic critic for *Reynolds News* in the latter 40s.

Slaughter, Tod (*b* Newcastle-upon-Tyne, 1885 – *d* Derby, 1956). Actor. Beginning his acting career at 20, Norman Carter Slaughter, known as Tod, was an original, touring in the provinces on stage for decades, usually as villain in Victorian MELODRAMAS, before starting a film career in similar roles in period HORROR films usually produced by George KING in the mid 30s. He continued for the next 15 years in such films as *Maria Marten, or The Murder in the Red Barn* (1935), *Sweeney Todd, The Demon Barber of Fleet Street* (1936), *Crimes at the Dark House* (1940), and *The Curse of the Wraydons* (1946) with a heavily theatrical but very entertaining, if hammy, style of acting. Plots typically centred on the rescue of maidens threatened by Slaughter's evil and greedy villains. Finished his film career with some TV work as a master criminal in the early 50s.

OTHER BRITISH FILMS INCLUDE: *The Crimes of Stephen Hawke* (1936), *Song of the Road, The Ticket of Leave Man, It's Never Too Late to Mend, Darby and Joan* (1937), *Sexton Blake and the Hooded Terror* (1938), *The Face at the Window* (1939), *The Greed of William Hart* (1948), *Murder at Scotland Yard* (1954).

BIBLIOG: Jeffrey Richards, 'Tod Slaughter and the Cinema of Excess', in Richards (ed), *The Unknown 1930s*, 1998. Stephen Shafer.

Sloan, John R. (*b* 1912 – *d* Ayrshire, 2001). Producer. Entered films in 1932, obtaining very varied experience with BIP, then working for WARNER BROS, first in Hollywood, then at TEDDINGTON STUDIOS, until war service (1939–46). Post-war, he worked as associate producer or co-producer for ALLIANCE, on such films as *Just William's Luck* (1947) and *The Brass Monkey* (1948). In the 50s he formed a production company with Maxwell SETTON, called Marksman, for which they produced *Beautiful Stranger* (1954) and *Keep It Clean* (1955), and he also produced middle-level films for other companies, such as Coronado (*Sea Devils*, 1952) and Copa (*Seven Waves Away*, 1956).

OTHER BRITISH FILMS INCLUDE: (p, unless noted) *Paper Orchid* (1949, co-p), *Cairo Road* (assoc p), *Circle of Danger* (co-p) (1950), *Port Afrique* (1956), *Killers of Kilimanjaro* (1959), *The Running Man* (1963, assoc p), *To Sir, with Love* (1967, ex p), *Dad's Army* (1971), *The Odessa File* (1974, UK/Ger), *Force 10 from Navarone* (1978, co-p).

Sloane, Olive (*b* London, 1896 – *d* London, 1963). Actress. Began performing as Baby Pearl, aged eight, then in MUSIC HALLS, before making her London stage debut in 1912. She made a half-dozen silents before settling seriously into films in 1933 and generally working enjoyable permutations on that hardy character standby, the good-hearted blonde floozie in nearly 50 films. A sort of senior, slightly more genteel Dora BRYAN, often showing a sturdy streak of working-class commonsense, as she does in her best role – that of Goldie, who, sceptic as she is, tries to comfort the deranged Barry JONES in *Seven Days to Noon* (1950), for the BOULTINGS who often used her – but she is fun, too, in smaller roles, such as prison inmate Nellie, getting herself ready, in flashback, for a day's theft in *The Weak and the Wicked* (1953).

OTHER BRITISH FILMS INCLUDE: *Greatheart* (1921), *Money Isn't Everything* (1925), *The Good Companions* (1933), *Alibi Inn* (1935), *Café Colette* (1937), *Make It Three* (1938), *Inquest* (1939), *The Tower of Terror*

(1941), *Thunder Rock, Those Kids from Town* (1942), *They Knew Mr Knight* (1945), *The Guinea Pig* (1948), *Under Capricorn* (1949), *Curtain Up* (1952), *A Prize of Gold* (1955), *Brothers in Law* (1956), *Wrong Number* (1959), *Heavens Above!* (1963).

Slocombe, Douglas (*b* London, 1913). Cinematographer. One of the most distinguished, versatile and prolific of British cameramen, former journalist and stills photographer Slocombe intially worked for the MINISTRY OF INFORMATION shooting NEWSREELS and PROPAGANDA films during WW2, filming the invasions of Holland and Poland. During the 40s and 50s he worked almost exclusively at EALING, becoming its chief cameraman. He lit with equal dexterity and dramatic flair the realist urban contemporary drama of *It Always Rains on Sunday* and the PASTORAL beauty of *The Loves of Joanna Godden* (1947), the lavish COSTUME ROMANCE of *Saraband for Dead Lovers* (1948), Ealing's first brush with TECHNICOLOR, and the exquisite Victoriana of *Kind Hearts and Coronets* (1949), as visually delectable as it is literately witty. He experimented boldly with contrasts of light and shade, in both colour and black-and-white, and when Ealing closed he found rewards in freelancing.

His contribution to the subtly changing mood of Joseph LOSEY's *The Servant* (1963), much of it confined to a single elegant terrace house, is immense, winning him a deserved BAA and a BSC award, and in the 60s he came to terms with CinemaScope on such productions as *The Lion in Winter* (1968). He was involved in some inferior films (e.g. the remake of *The Lady Vanishes*, 1979) but his work ensured they at least looked better than they deserved, and their GENRE range suggested that nothing was outside his capacities. In the last decade of his career he worked on such international films as *Julia* (1977) and Steven Spielberg's 'Indiana Jones' trilogy. Three times Oscar-nominated (*Travels with My Aunt*, 1973; *Julia*, 1977; *Raiders of the Lost Ark*, 1981, all US), he won further BAAs for *The Great Gatsby* (1974, US) and *Julia*, he also won in 1995 a Lifetime Achievement Award from the BSC, of which he was a founder, as well as five of its annual awards.

OTHER BRITISH FILMS: *Went the Day Well?* (reporting camera), *Big Blockade* (1942), *Champagne Charlie* (cam op), *For Those in Peril* (outdoors) (1944), *Painted Boats, Dead of Night* (co-c, + lighting) (1945), *The Captive Heart, Hue and Cry* (1946), *Another Shore* (1948), *A Run for your Money, Whisky Galore!* (2uph) (1949), *Dance Hall, Cage of Gold* (1950), *The Man in the White Suit, The Lavender Hill Mob, His Excellency* (1951), *Mandy* (1952), *The Titfield Thunderbolt, The Love Lottery* (1953), *Lease of Life* (1954), *Touch and Go* (1955), *Sailor Beware, The Man in the Sky* (1956), *Barnacle Bill, The Smallest Show on Earth, Davy* (1957), *Tread Softly Stranger* (1958), *Circus of Horrors, The Boy Who Stole a Million* (1960), *The Mark, The Young Ones, Taste of Fear* (1961), *The L-Shaped Room* (1962), *The Third Secret, Guns at Batasi* (1964), *A High Wind in Jamaica, Promise Her Anything* (1965), *The Blue Max* (1966), *Dance of the Vampires, Fathom, Robbery* (1967), *Boom* (+ lighting cameraman), *The Italian Job* (1969), *The Buttercup Chain* (1970), *The Music Lovers, Murphy's War* (1971), *The Marseille Contract* (UK/Fr), *The Maids* (UK/Can), *That Lucky Touch, Hedda, The Bawdy Adventures of Tom Jones* (1975), *The Sailor Who Fell from Grace with the Sea, Nasty Habits* (1976), *Lost and Found* (1979), *The Pirates of Penzance* (1982), *Never Say Never Again* (1983, UK/US), *Water, Lady Jane* (1985).

BIBLIOG: Duncan Petrie, *The British Cinematographer*, 1996.

Smart, Patsy (*b* Chingford, 1918 – *d* Northwood, Middlesex, 1996). Actress. Small-part character player in all the media, probably best remembered now as Lady Marjorie's maid, who, unlike her mistress, survives the 'Titanic' in TV's *Upstairs, Downstairs* (1971–73). Born to play such Dickensian creations as Mrs Wopsle in *Great Expectations* (1975) and Miss LaCreevy in

TV's *Nicholas Nickleby* (1977), and popped up regularly in bits like Malcolm McDowell's northern mum in *The Raging Moon* (1970) and a distraught old lady in *Elephant Man* (1980, UK/US).

OTHER BRITISH FILMS INCLUDE: *The Flying Scot* (1957), *Sons and Lovers*, *The Tell-Tale Heart* (1960), *Never Mention Murder* (1964), *Leo the Last* (1969), *Steptoe and Son* (1972), *O Lucky Man!* (1973), *The Hound of the Baskervilles* (1977), *Tess* (1979, UK/Fr), *The Wildcats of St Trinian's* (1980), *The Chain* (1984).

Smart, Ralph (*b* London, 1908 – *d* Spain, 2001). Director, screenwriter. Former cutter with BIP from 1927, Smart worked chiefly (often in collaboration) on screenplays during the early 30s, including seven 'QUOTA QUICKIES' for Michael POWELL, starting with *The Star Reporter* (1931). Later in the decade, he also directed several SHORT FILMS and DOCUMENTARIES for Publicity Films, made at MERTON PARK STUDIOS, including *Workaday* (1937), which explored the lives of Bournville's factory workers. Of Australian parents, he was sent to Australia in 1940 to direct PROPAGANDA films for the Australian Air Force and the Department of Information, stayed on to produce the EALING cattle-drive epic, *The Overlanders* (1946), and to direct the charming children's film, *Bush Christmas* (1947, + p, sc) for RANK's CHILDREN'S ENTERTAINMENT (later FILM FOUNDATION). He returned to direct the Ealing outback adventure, *Bitter Springs* (1950, + story), less successful but sympathetic in its view of racial problems. The remaining British films he directed are generally a modest lot, but they also offer modest pleasures. His 'Facts of Life' segment of *Quartet* (1948) retains MAUGHAM's wit; *A Boy, a Girl and a Bike* (1949) makes refreshing use of its Yorkshire LOCATIONS and a cycling club; and a minor comedy about a team of likeable frauds, *Always a Bride* (1953), is surprisingly and consistently funny. After that, he spent the rest of his career in TV, directing episodes of such popular programmes as *Robin Hood* (1955) and *Danger Man* (1960, 1964).

OTHER BRITISH FILMS INCLUDE: (sc/co-sc, unless noted) *A Cottage on Dartmoor* (1929, cont), *The Woodpigeon Patrol* (1930, short, + co-d), *Born Lucky* (1932), *The Phantom Light* (1935), *Alf's Button Afloat* (1938), *Convict 99* (1938), *Charlie's Big-Hearted Aunt* (1940), *Where No Vultures Fly* (1951); (d, unless noted) (shorts) *Sweet Success* (1936), *For Dealers Only* (1937), *The Green* (1938); (features) *Never Take No for an Answer* (1951, co-d, co-sc), *Curtain Up* (1952).

Smedley-Aston, Brian (*b* Edgware, 1955). Editor. Marlborough-educated son of producer E.M. SMEDLEY-ASTON, he entered films in the 60s as editor on films like the three he did for director Desmond DAVIS: *Girl with Green Eyes* (1963), *The Uncle* (1964) and *I Was Happy Here* (1965). Also worked on several films for Tony RICHARDSON, including the US-made *The Loved One* (1965), and on that key film of its time, *Performance* (1970, co-e). His films as producer are largely devoid of interest.

OTHER BRITISH FILMS INCLUDE: (p, unless noted) *Vampyres* (1974), *Exposé* (1975), *Hardcore* (1977), *The Music Machine* (1979, + e), *The Wildcats of St Trinian's* (1980, assoc p), *Memed My Hawk* (1984, co-p);(e) *Tom Jones* (1963, ass e), *The Shuttered Room*, *The Sailor from Gibraltar*, *Sebastian* (1967), *The Strange Affair* (1968), *Girl Stroke Boy* (1971), *Intimate with a Stranger* (1994), *Let's Stick Together* (1996, UK/Ire).

Smedley-Aston, E(dward) M(ichael) (*b* Birmingham, 1912). Producer. Marlborough-educated, he entered films in 1932 as runner (a contribution difficult to assess in the final product) at BIP, graduated to assistant director at LIME GROVE and

SOUND CITY in the mid 30s, on popular films such as *OHMS* (1937) and (at MGM–BRITISH) *Goodbye, Mr Chips* (1939), before WW2 service with the RAF (1939–45). Post-war, he was production manager for INDEPENDENT PRODUCERS, working for LAUNDER AND GILLIAT on *Captain Boycott* (1947) and *The Blue Lagoon* (1949), and as associate producer on their *The Happiest Days of Your Life* (1950). As a fully-fledged producer or co-producer, he made some enjoyable comedies, including *Two Way Stretch* (1960) and *The Wrong Arm of the Law* (1962, co-p).

OTHER BRITISH FILMS INCLUDE: (ass d) *Drake of England* (1935), *Once in a Million* (1936), *Double Exposures*, *Riding High* (1937), *Sexton Blake and the Hooded Terror* (1938); (p man) *The Chinese Bungalow* (1940), *The Spider and the Fly* (1947); (p) *The Extra Day* (1956), *Life Is a Circus* (1958), *Offbeat* (1960), *Theatre of Death* (1966), *Ooh . . . You Are Awful* (1972), *The Wildcats of St Trinian's* (1980).

Smethurst, Jack (*b* Collyhurst, Manchester, 1932). Actor. Supporting player most popular on TV as Leslie Pollitt in the TV series, *For the Love of Ada* (1970–71) and, elevated to the lead, as racial bigot Eddie Booth in *Love Thy Neighbour* (1972–76). He repeated these roles in the TV SPIN-OFFS, in 1972 and 1973 respectively; other film roles mainly insignificant. Played Johnny Webb in *Coronation Street* (1980–83).

OTHER BRITISH FILMS INCLUDE: *Carry On Sergeant* (1958), *On the Fiddle* (1961), *A Kind of Loving* (1962), *The Main Chance* (1964), *Night After Night After Night* (1969), *Please, Sir!* (1971), *Chariots of Fire* (1981), *La Passione* (1996).

Smith, Brian (*b* London, 1912). Director. Former commercial artist and DOCUMENTARY film-maker who began producing 16mm educational films in 1934. Served with the ARMY FILM UNIT (1941–42), and then directed a series of documentaries for REALIST FILM UNIT. He was in charge of production here from 1947 to 1955, when he was appointed Unesco Visual Aids adviser to the Cambodian Government. Not to be confused with the following.

Smith, Brian (*b* Nottingham, 1933). Actor. In films from his teens, most memorably as the well-intentioned donor of *The Browning Version* (1951), he played supporting roles in a few films as a young man, including one of the sons in *The Barretts of Wimpole Street* (1956).

OTHER BRITISH FILMS INCLUDE: *Captain Boycott* (1947), *No Place for Jennifer* (1949), *Glad Tidings* (1953), *Betrayed* (1954), *It's Great to Be Young!*, *Yangtse Incident* (1956), *Gideon's Day* (1958), *Rivals* (1963), *The 14* (1973).

Smith, Sir C(harles) Aubrey (*b* London, 1863 – *d* Los Angeles 1948). Actor. Hair and moustache roughly pomaded with essence of Imperial Gentleman, Smith, ramrod-lean, with authoritarian jaw and jutting eyebrows, played Hollywood variations on an English archetype for over 30 years. He really did captain England at cricket (1889) was a former stockbroker, then actor on London and New York stages, was in American films from 1915, only leaving Hollywood for occasional British screen appearances such as the General in *The Four Feathers* (1939) whose habit of recreating bloody battles at the dining table anticipated General D'Ascoyne's in *Kind Hearts and Coronets* (1949). In Hollywood, he was the eternal Colonel in *Wee Willie Winkie* (1937) and others and was memorable in *Queen Christina* (1934) and, never more so, in *Love Me Tonight* (1932) where, kicking over the traces, and in his pyjamas, he sang 'Mimi'.

OTHER BRITISH FILMS: *Castles in Spain* (1920), *The Bohemian Girl* (1922), *The Bird of Prey* (1930), *Transatlantic Tunnel* (1935), *Sixty Glorious Years* (1938), *An Ideal Husband* (1947). Bruce Babington.

Smith, Constance (*b* Aronachursa, Co. Limerick, 1928). Actress. Sensually attractive brunette who had a minor career in British films and a more rewarding time in Hollywood, where she went in 1951, preceding her then-husband Bryan FORBES (1951–55). Their marriage collapsed soon after his arrival in 1951, but she had a contract with 20th Century–Fox and co-starred in such films as *Red Skies of Montana* and *Lure of the Wilderness* (1952). Before going to the US, she had appeared in small roles in about ten films, mainly as part of her RANK contract. She sang in *Brighton Rock* (1947) but got her best acting chances in *The Mudlark* and the JACK THE RIPPER thriller, *Room to Let* (1950). When she returned, she brought a convincing Hollywood gloss to her *femme fatale* role in TEMPEAN's neat *film noir, Impulse* (1955). Her later films were mainly Italian costume pieces.

OTHER BRITISH FILMS INCLUDE: *Jassy* (1947), *Now Barabbas Was a Robber, The Calendar* (1948), *I'll Get You for This* (1950), *Tiger by the Tail* (1955).

Smith, Cyril (*b* Peterhead, Scotland, 1892 – *d* London, 1963). Actor. RN: Bruce-Smith. Wildly prolific supporting player, on stage from 1900 (much in the US), and, according to *Who's Who in the Theatre* (1957), in over 500 films from 1908 (*The Great Fire of London*). That sounds exaggerated, but he was certainly in at least 100, including *The Good Companions* (1933), as Leonard Oakroyd, *Friday the Thirteenth* (1933), as the bus driver, *When We Are Married* (1943), as the reporter sniffing a story, and so on and on, climaxing his 50-year career by repeating on film his 1955 stage role of the henpecked husband, Henry Hornett, in *Sailor Beware!* (1956) and its sequel *Watch It Sailor!* (1961). This role suited admirably his characteristically rather downtrodden look in later years.

OTHER BRITISH FILMS INCLUDE: *Old St Paul's* (1914), *A Broken Contract* (1920), *The Mayor's Nest* (1932), *Waltzes from Vienna* (1934), *Brown on Resolution* (1935), *Pot Luck* (1936), *Storm in a Teacup* (1937), *The Challenge* (1938), *They Flew Alone* (1942), *One Exciting Night* (1944), *Appointment with Crime, School for Secrets* (1946), *They Made Me a Fugitive, Daughter of Darkness* (1947), *Escape* (1948), *The Rocking Horse Winner* (1949), *The Dark Man* (1950), *No Highway* (1951), *The Lost Hours, Women of Twilight* (1952), *Wheel of Fate* (1953), *Svengali* (1954), *Value for Money* (1955), *On the Fiddle* (1961), *She Knows Y'Know* (1962).

Smith, F(rank) Percy (*b* 1880 – *d* London, 1945). Cinematographer. A former clerk with the Board of Education, Smith was a major pioneer in the use of cinematography for scientific purposes He entered the film industry with Charles URBAN in 1908, filming nature and zoological films. In 1910, Smith filmed *Birth of a Flower*, using slow motion photography, which was released the following year as a KINEMACOLOR subject: at the same time he also made *Gladioli* and *The Story of the Wasp*, and opened his own studio at Southgate. He was a prominent figure in the production of the *Secrets of Nature* SERIES throughout the 20s and 30s, and in 1938, he co-produced with Mary FIELD *The Tough 'Un*, a film about dandelions, shown at the New York World's Fair. The co-author of *Secrets of Nature* (1934) and *Cinebiology* (1941), Smith was responsible for more than 200 films. AS.

Smith, G(eorge) A(lbert) (*b* London, 1864 – *d* Brighton, 1959). Pioneer. An astronomer, magic lanternist, and former stage hypnotist, associated with the Society for Psychical Research, Smith first became interested in cinematography in 1896. The following year he converted part of his Hove estate, St Anne's Well and Gardens, into a film laboratory. Also in 1897, Smith began making short comedies, such as *The Miller and the Sweep*, ACTUALITIES, and a record of *Queen Victoria's Diamond Jubilee Procession*. In 1898, Smith began to specialize in trick films, such as *Santa Claus* and *Cinderella*. *Grandma's Reading Glass, As Seen Through a Telescope, Let Me Dream Again* and *The House That Jack Built* are all titles from 1900 where Smith demonstrated through close-ups, subjective viewpoints and superimpositions some of the imaginative possibilities of cinema. He also developed a successful film-processing business, and in 1898, he joined the WARWICK TRADING COMPANY, continuing to produce films as well as process them to 1903, when he turned his attentions to invention. In 1906, Smith took out a patent for colour cinematography, KINEMACOLOR, which he demonstrated in 1908 before the Royal Society of Arts, and which was to be exploited by Charles URBAN, from whom Smith parted in a dispute over the patent rights in 1914. Smith's long life ended with acclaim from a generation of post-war film historians, and a guest appearance at the opening of the NATIONAL FILM THEATRE in 1952 alongside Gina Lollobrigida, Akira Kurosawa and John FORD. AS.

Smith, Herbert (*b* London, 1901 – *d* Margate, 1986). Producer, director. Smith, who entered films with G.B. SAMUELSON, worked as assistant director before becoming a busy director and/or producer for BRITISH LION across a typical range of 30s programme films: MUSICALS, COMEDIES and THRILLERS. On joining TWO CITIES, he worked on such higher-prestige films as *The Demi-Paradise* (1943, prod man), *The Tawny Pipit* (assoc p), *Mr Emmanuel* (1944, p), and finished his career producing such lively youth-orientated entertainments as *6.5 Special* (1958), and *Too Young to Love* (1959). His brother was S(amuel) W(oolf) **Smith**, managing director of British Lion on its founding in 1927, but described by Rachael Low as a 'producer of too little vision' to carry out its plans for popularising Edgar WALLACE's work on film. Herbert Smith became production supervisor there at the end of 1932. Not to be confused with art director of same name.

OTHER BRITISH FILMS: (d) *The Ringer* (1931, ass), *Night Mail* (1935, + p), *They Didn't Know* (1936, + p), *Calling All Stars* (1937), *I've Got a Horse* (1938, + p), *All at Sea* (1939, + p); (p, unless noted) *This Is the Life* (1933), *Flat No. 3* (1934), *Marry the Girl, Charing Cross Road, The Case of Gabriel Perry* (1935), *The Interrupted Honeymoon, The Happy Family* (1936), *Fine Feathers* (1937), *They Were Not Divided* (1950), *The Tommy Steele Story* (1957).

Smith, Herbert Art director. BAA-nominated for his stark evocation of wartime rigours in *The Hill* (1965), Smith began as draughtsman (on such films as *Against the Wind*, 1947) and designed some 'B' MOVIES in the 50s before moving on to bigger-budget affairs in the 60s, starting with *The Roman Spring of Mrs Stone* (1961). Not to be confused with producer of same name.

OTHER BRITISH FILMS INCLUDE: *The End of the Line, A Date with Disaster* (1957), *A Woman Possessed* (1958), *Jason and the Argonauts* (co-art d), *The Running Man* (ass art d) (1963), *Wonderful Life* (1964), *Dutchman* (1966), *Shalako, The Dance of Death* (1968), *Catlow* (1971), *Paper Tiger* (1974, des), *Game for Vulture* (1979).

Smith, Keith (*b* Liverpool, 1926). Actor. Former LAMDA fencing instructor, in films from the late 50s (he is one of the skiving card-players in *I'm All Right Jack*, 1959), the often-moustachioed Smith had small roles in the 60s and 70s. Much TV: e.g. *Q5* (1969), and as Mr Wheeler in *The Beiderbecke Affair* (1984), and its follow-ups.

OTHER BRITISH FILMS INCLUDE: *The Naked Truth* (1957), *The Ugly Duckling* (1959), *The Criminal* (1960), *Dangerous Afternoon* (1961), *Ricochet* (1963), *The Bliss of Mrs Blossom* (1968), *The Magnificent Seven Deadly Sins* (1971), *What's Up Nurse?* (1977), *Splitting Heirs* (1993).

Smith, Liz (*b* Scunthorpe, 1925). Actress. Came into films just as one might have supposed the great days of British CHARACTER ACTORS were past, after years of other occupations, including, apparently, saleswoman. Since appearing in Mike LEIGH's *Bleak Moments* (1971), she has become an increasingly noticeable presence in a diversity of films, including: the post-war-austerity comedy, *A Private Function* (1984), as Maggie SMITH's dim mother (BAA/supp actress); the strange, erotically charged *Apartment Zero* (1988), in which she replaced the ailing Beryl REID as Dora BRYAN's ailing sister; and *The Cook, the Thief, His Wife & Her Lover* (1989, UK/Fr), as Grace who manages to avoid Spica's contumely. On TV, she has twice played Peg Sliderskew in *Nicholas Nickleby* (1977, 2000), the crone Sally in *Oliver Twist* (1999) – she is made for DICKENS – and is irresistibly funny as Nana in *The Royle Family* (1998–2000), tonelessly droning on about how she never drinks, except . . .

OTHER BRITISH FILMS INCLUDE: *It Shouldn't Happen to a Vet* (1976), *Agatha* (1978, UK/US), *The Monster Club* (1980), *The French Lieutenant's Woman* (1981), *Britannia Hospital* (1982), *Curse of the Pink Panther* (1983), *Little Dorrit* (1987), *We Think the World of You* (1988), *Haunted* (1995, UK/US), *Secrets & Lies* (1996), *Keep the Aspidistra Flying* (1997), *The Revengers' Comedies* (1998, UK/Fr), *Tom's Midnight Garden* (1999, UK/US).

Smith, Madeleine (*b* Hartsfield). Actress. Supporting player of film and TV, busiest in the 70s and several times in the HORROR GENRE, including *Taste the Blood of Dracula* (1969) and *The Vampire Lovers* (1970), as well as the witty horror spoof, *Theatre of Blood* (1973). Also showed her versatility in a couple of Frankie HOWERD's cod-lubricious pieces – *Up Pompeii* (1971) and *Up the Front* (1972). Was married to the late David BUCK.

OTHER BRITISH FILMS INCLUDE: *Come Back Peter* (1969), *The Magnificent Seven Deadly Sins* (1971), *The Devil's Widow* (1971), *Carry On Matron*, *The Amazing Mr Blunden* (1972), *Live and Let Die, Take Me High* (1973), *Percy's Progress, Galileo* (UK/Can) (1974), *The Passionate Pilgrim* (1984, short).

Smith, Dame Maggie (*b* Ilford, 1934). Actress. The entry on this actress could well be taken up with a recital of the nominations and awards she has received solely for her work in films, let alone her extraordinary stage and TV records. Perhaps the most delectable comedienne of her generation, she went on to exhibit an almost unlimited range. Educated at Oxford High School for Girls and trained at Oxford Playhouse School, she was first on stage with OUDS in 1952, on Broadway in 1956, and in London from 1957. Said to have played a tiny role in the 1956 film, *Child in the House*, she made a vivid impact (and was BAA-nominated) as the society-girl heroine who gets caught up in crime in the late EALING thriller, *Nowhere to Go* (1958), at the same time winning critical acclaim on stage for *The Stepmother*. She had seasons with the Old Vic and the National, in classical roles including Desdemona to OLIVIER's *Othello* (1964), winning her first AA nomination for repeating the role in the film version (1965), but she triumphed equally in revue and modern comedy, like *Lettice and Lovage* (1989).

On-screen, her versatility encompasses the selfless, devoted secretary in *The VIPs* (1963), the indolent, mischievous Philpott in *The Pumpkin Eater* (1964), the zealous and misguided teacher in *The Prime of Miss Jean Brodie* (1968, AA and BAA),

the music hall star whose song lures young men to the doom of WW1 in *Oh! What a Lovely War* (1969), Bette DAVIS's brusque companion who can't stand 'heat and heathens' in *Death on the Nile* (1978), bringing individuality to Agatha CHRISTIE's cut-outs in this and *Evil Under the Sun* (1981), the upwardly aspiring wife of Michael PALIN's gentle chiropodist in *A Private Function* (1984), the heartrending protagonist of *The Lonely Passion of Judith Hearne* (1987), tippling her way into unloved middle-age, and the cruelly severe Duchess of York in *Richard III* (1995). On TV, she repeated her magical stage Beatrice in *Much Ado About Nothing* (1972), was irresistibly malicious as the vicar's dissatisfied wife in an episode of Alan BENNETT's *Talking Heads* (1988) and led the star line-up in Jack CLAYTON's immaculate swansong, *Memento Mori* (1992). Against this honour-roll, it must be said that some directors have let her indulge mannerisms at the expense of rounding out a character, so that she is unexpectedly tiresome in *Washington Square* (1997, US) or the sentimental *Tea with Mussolini* (1999, UK/It), a study in one-note hauteur; but such lapses are few compared to the compensating glories. It will be a shame if she becomes known to filmgoers chiefly as Harry Potter's form mistress – 'Jean Brodie with a witch's hat' as she said. She has been very successful in the US, including *California Suite* (1978, AA/supp a), but remains, somehow, obdurately British, growing only sharper and wryer with age.

Married (1) Robert STEPHENS (1967–74) and (2) Beverley CROSS. Mother of actors Toby STEPHENS and **Chris Larkin** (*b* London, 1967) who has appeared in several British films including *Jane Eyre* (1996, UK/Fr/It/US) and *Tea with Mussolini* (1999).

OTHER BRITISH FILMS: *Go to Blazes* (1962), *Young Cassidy* (1965), *Hot Millions* (1968), *Clash of the Titans, Quartet* (UK/Fr), *The Missionary* (1981), *Better Late Than Never* (1983), *A Room with a View* (1985), *The Last September* (2000, UK/Fr/Ire), *Harry Potter and the Philosopher's Stone* (UK/US), *Gosford Park* (UK/Ger/US, AAn/supp a) (2001), *Harry Potter and the Chamber of Secrets* (2002, UK/US).

Smith, Mel (*b* London, 1952). Actor, director. Smudge-featured, Oxford-educated comedian who is probably much better known for such TV programmes as *Not the Nine O'Clock News* (1979–80, 1982) and *Alas Smith and Jones* (1984–87), both co-starring Griff RHYS-JONES, than for his sporadic film appearances. However, he was an apt Toby Belch in Trevor NUNN's undervalued film of *Twelfth Night* (1996, UK/US), and he has directed several films, including the wildly successful *Bean* (1997) with old TV co-star, Rowan ATKINSON, and, for FRAGILE FILMS, the second production at the revived EALING STUDIOS, *High Heels and Low Lifes* (2001, UK/US).

OTHER BRITISH FILMS INCLUDE: *Bloody Kids* (1979), *Babylon* (1980), *Bullshot, Slayground* (1983), *Restless Natives, Morons from Outer Space* (+ co-sc with co-star Rhys-Jones) (1985), *The Tall Guy, Wilt* (1989).

Smith, Ray (*b* Trealaw, Wales, 1936 – *d* Cardiff, 1991). Actor. Best known for TV roles as abrasive Chief Superintendent Spikings in TV's *Dempsey and Makepeace* (1985–86), Smith entered films in 1961 as one of three young men celebrating in a club in *The Painted Smile* (1961) and played drunken Mr Waldo in *Under Milk Wood* (1971).

OTHER BRITISH FILMS INCLUDE: *Candidate for Murder* (1962), *Tomorrow at Ten* (1962), *Made* (1972), *The Sailor's Return* (1978).

Snell, Anthony (*b* Tunbridge Wells, 1922 – *d* London, 1997). Actor. After distinguished WW2 service as a fighter pilot (dubbed 'The man they could not kill'), Snell appeared in supporting roles in a half-dozen or so British films of the 50s, starting with *Cry, the Beloved Country* and *The Sound Barrier* (1952), as well as some TV.

OTHER BRITISH FILMS: *The Cruel Sea* (1952), *The Story of Gilbert and Sullivan, The Heart of the Matter* (1953), *Three Cornered Fate* (1955), *Hour of Decision* (1957).

Snowden, Alec C(rawford) (*b* Keighley, 1901). Studio manager, producer. Entered films in 1919, as assistant director at STOLL studios, had experience in theatre management in New Zealand, and returned to Britain in 1913 and worked for many companies, as business or production manager. He joined MERTON PARK STUDIOS as studio manager in the late 40s, and later became a director of the company, overseeing production of its half-hour 'Scotland Yard' SERIES, narrated by Edgar LUSTGARTEN, as well as several enjoyable 'B' MOVIES, including Ken HUGHES's *The Brain Machine* (1954) and *Confession* (1955) and Montgomery TULLY's *Escapement* (1957).

OTHER BRITISH FILMS INCLUDE: *The Drayton Case* (1953), *Little Red Monkey* (1954), *Dial 999, Timeslip* (1955), *Wall of Death* (1956), *Man in the Shadow* (1957), *The Strange Awakening* (1958), *This Other Eden, Broth of a Boy* (1959, Ire), *Over the Odds* (1961).

social problem films An important strand of British film culture has been its emphasis upon the social utility of film. The 'father' of the British DOCUMENTARY movement John GRIERSON stressed the educative and propagandistic value of film and, during WW2, both film documentary and drama were mobilised in support of the war effort. The belief that fiction film could play a beneficial social role carried over into peacetime via a series of films that subsequently became identified as 'social problem' films. These were films that sought to 'sugar the pill' of social didacticism through the use of narrative and generic conventions derived from the 'entertainment' film. As such, the social problem film constituted something of a generic hybrid, typically combining elements of social REALISM (contemporary subject-matter, 'ordinary' people, a degree of location shooting) with plot and character elements drawn from popular GENRES such as the crime film (as in *Sapphire*, 1959) and the family MELODRAMA (as in *Victim*, 1961). However, while the use of mainstream narrative conventions permitted the films to reach a popular audience, they also compromised their ability to explore fully the *social* dimensions of their problems by typically converting them into individual psychological dramas.

A concern to dramatise contemporary social conditions was becoming apparent in a number of pre-war films such as Pen TENNYSON's *There Ain't No Justice* (1939), set in a working-class community, and Carol REED's *The Stars Look Down* (1939), dealing with a mining disaster. The social problem cycle was, however, primarily a post-war phenomenon and gathered particular momentum in the 50s. As such, the films were responding to the economic and social changes of the time: the refashioning of old social relations and the building of a new social consensus, the development of the welfare state, changing gender and sexual roles, and legal reforms in relation to private moral conduct. The 'problem' of youth, or juvenile delinquency, inspired the greatest number of films, which included *I Believe in You* (1952), *Cosh Boy* (1953), *My Teenage Daughter* (1956), *Violent Playground* (1957), *The Young and the Guilty* , *No Trees in the Street* (1958), *Serious Charge* (1959), *Spare the Rod* (1961), *The Wild and the Willing* (1962), *The Party's Over* (1963) and *A Place to Go* (1963). Other major topics included 'race relations' (*Sapphire*; *Flame in the Streets*, 1961; *The Wind of Change*, 1961), capital punishment (*Yield to the Night*, 1956), prostitution (*The Flesh is Weak*, 1957; *Passport to Shame*, 1958), and homosexuality (*Victim*, 1961). While some of the later films (such as *Beat Girl*, 1959, and *That Kind of Girl*, 1963) displayed an 'exploitative' impulse in the way that they sought to capitalise on topical social issues for sensational or prurient ends, the predominant attitude of the cycle was liberal paternalism. A range of mainstream directors, including Lewis GILBERT, J LEE THOMPSON and Roy Ward BAKER, contributed to the cycle, but the producer-director team of Michael RELPH and Basil DEARDEN was responsible for the greatest number of such films, as well as some of the most durable. Films such as *Sapphire* and *Victim* have continued to attract critical attention and illustrate well how social problem films are often riven by internal tensions resulting from a clash between the films' ostensible projects of liberal reform and the release of 'excessive' energies and desires that the dramatisation of problems entails. While the reformist (and paternalist) attitudes of the films were in line with the period to which they belonged, they became subject to strain in the more radical era of the late 60s and early 70s. Coinciding with a decline in the economic viability of British films aimed primarily at the home market, the British social problem film had virtually disappeared by the end of the 60s while the strain of social consciousness apparent in British cinema re-emerged in different formats.

BIBLIOG: Richard Dyer, '*Victim*: Hermeneutic Project', *Film Form*, Vol. 1 No. 2, 1977; John Hill, *Sex, Class and Realism: British Cinema 1956–63*, 1986; Marcia Landy, *British Genres*, 1991. John Hill.

Sofaer, Abraham (*b* Rangoon, 1896 – *d* Los Angeles, 1988). Actor. Burmese former schoolmaster, on stage from 1921, toured in over 100 Shakespearean roles, made London debut in 1925, and was a famous Disraeli to Helen HAYES's *Victoria Regina* (1936–38), playing Disraeli again in the screen comedy, *The Ghosts of Berkeley Square* (1947). His somewhat gaunt features lent themselves easily and equally to the sinister (he played his share of untrustworthy foreigners, like Ali in *Crook's Tour*, 1940) or the austerely benign (as in *Rembrandt*, 1936, as the doctor friend). Prominent British roles included the heavenly judge in *A Matter of Life and Death* (1946) and another judge in *Pandora and the Flying Dutchman* (1950). Spent his last twenty years mainly in US films, playing Joseph of Arimathaea in *The Greatest Story Ever Told* (1965). In TV from 1939.

OTHER BRITISH FILMS INCLUDE: *Stamboul* (1931), *The Flying Squad* (1932), *The Wandering Jew, Ask Beccles* (1933), *Nell Gwyn* (1934), *Things to Come* (1936), *Freedom Radio* (1940), *Dual Alibi* (1947), *Christopher Columbus* (1949), *Cairo Road* (1950), *His Majesty O'Keefe* (1953), *Out of the Clouds* (1955).

Softley, Iain (*b* England, 1958). Director, producer, screenwriter. After the cult hit, *Backbeat* (1994, d, co-sc), a BAA-nominated fictionalised account of the BEATLES' early years, Cambridge-educated Softley directed a modest US thriller, *Hackers* (1995), before turning out one of the finest ADAPTATIONS of Henry JAMES's intransigently interior novels. *The Wings of the Dove* (1997, UK/US) was magisterial in its ruthless shearing away of what belonged utterly to the literary, making the mise-en-scène work fiercely hard to dramatise the conflicts at the novel's core, and focusing attention on its central trio of dying heiress and desperate lovers. Then there was nothing for four years until the US-made *K-PAX* (2001).

Soldati, Mario (*b* Turin, 1906 – *d* Tellaro, Liguria, Italy, 1999). Director, screenwriter. Multi-talented (also novelist, non-fiction writer and actor), Soldati squeezes into this book for two films only: a boisterous Anglo-Italian comedy, *Her Favourite Husband* (1950, UK/It), with Jean KENT married to the meek lookalike of an Italian gangster; and *The Stranger's Hand* (1953, UK/It), based on a Venice-set story by Graham GREENE. Greene, a friend of Soldati's, co-produced the film. Soldati also directed the battle scenes for *War and Peace* (1956, UK/It).

Solon, Ewen (*b* Auckland, NZ, 1917 – *d* Addlestone, 1985). Actor. Somewhat stern-looking actor who played numerous police inspectors, military officers and so on in first features like *The Dam Busters* (1955) and 'B' MOVIES like *Account Rendered* (1957), before finding household fame as Lucas, assistant to TV's *Maigret* (1960–63). Thereafter, his film career tapered off and it finished in such dross as *Nutcracker* (1982) and *The Wicked Lady* (1983).
OTHER BRITISH FILMS INCLUDE: *London Belongs to Me* (1948), *Highly Dangerous* (1950), *Assassin for Hire* (1951), *The Card*, *Hunted* (1952), *The Sword and the Rose*, *Rob Roy . . .* (1953), *The End of the Road* (1954), *Yangtse Incident* (1956), *Robbery Under Arms*, *There's Always a Thursday* (1957), *Jack the Ripper* (1958), *The Hound of the Baskervilles* (1959), *The Curse of the Werewolf* (1961), *Infamous Conduct* (1966, short), *The Biggest Bank Robbery* (1980).

Somers, Julian (*b* London, 1906 – *d* London, 1976). Actor. Sturdy character player, busiest in the 50s, memorable as Dirk BOGARDE's farmer brother in *Hunted* (1952), putting respectability before family ties, and finally playing one of HARDY's yokels in *Far from the Madding Crowd* (1967).
OTHER BRITISH FILMS INCLUDE: *A Royal Divorce* (1938), *Men of Rochdale* (1944), *Caravan* (1946), *Blue Scar* (1949), *The Long Memory* (1952), *Three Steps to the Gallows* (1953), *The Battle of the River Plate* (1956), *The One That Got Away* (1957), *A Night to Remember*, *Room at the Top* (1958).

Somlo, Josef (*b* Papá, Hungary, 1884 – *d* Locarno, Switzerland, 1973). Producer. A continental European producer with many international connections, Somlo and his business partner Hermann Fellner (*b* 1878 – *d* 1936) were close associates of Michael BALCON in the late 20s and early 30s, internally referred to as Balcon's 'Polish Corridor'. Somlo permanently settled in London in 1933, having been involved in European films from 1908. From the late 30s to 1958 he worked for a succession of British companies, including LONDON FILMS in the 30s and, as late as 1954, with *The Man Who Loved Redheads*, but later mostly affiliated to the RANK ORGANISATION.
OTHER BRITISH FILMS INCLUDE: *Number Seventeen* (1928), *Tell Me Tonight* (1932), *Action For Slander*, *Dark Journey* (1937), *South Riding* (1938), *On the Night of the Fire*, *The Arsenal Stadium Mystery* (1939), *Alibi* (1942), *Uncle Silas* (1947), *Trottie True* (1948), *Madness Of The Heart* (1949) *The Teckman Mystery* (1954), *Behind The Mask* (1958). Tim Bergfelder.

Sommer, Elke (*b* Berlin, 1940). Actress. RN: Schletz. Sommer's screen image – as sexpot – scarcely hints at her educated background, and her prolific career, lasting over 40 years, has rarely had English-speaking film roles that required much in the way of intelligence. After appearing in a dozen or so German films, she made her British debut in the farce, *Don't Bother to Knock* (1961), had a more conspicuous role in the star-laden war epic, *The Victors* (1963) and the female lead in *A Shot in the Dark* (1964), and declined into *Percy* (1971). Also filmed in the US (e.g. *The Oscar*, 1966) and did much TV, especially on talk shows. Married to writer Joe Hyams.

OTHER BRITISH FILMS INCLUDE: *Deadlier than the Male* (1966), *Zeppelin* (1971), *And Then There Were None* (1974), *Carry On Behind* (1975), *The Biggest Bank Robbery* (1980).

Sopel, Anne (*b* 1961). Editor. Worked as assistant editor on such high-profile films of the 80s as *Local Hero* (1983) and *A Passage to India* (1984) and edited a couple of SHORTS, *My Little Eye* and *Breathing* (1992), before getting her first feature as editor, the smart black comedy, *The Young Poisoner's Handbook* (1995).
OTHER BRITISH FILMS: (e) *Sweet Angel Mine*, *Food of Love* (UK/Fr) (1995), *Crush* (2001, UK/Ger).

Soskin, Paul (*b* Kerch, South Russia, 1905 – *d* London, 1975). Producer. Trained as architect, Soskin entered films as art director (in 1932, he became art director of British European Film Corporation), then as editor for BRITISH AND DOMINION FILMS. His own company was variously called Soskin Productions (*Two's Company*, 1936) and Conqueror Productions (*Quiet Wedding*, 1941), co-produced with PARAMOUNT. Also produced for other companies, including RANK (*All for Mary*, 1955, + co-sc). Perhaps a frustrated director, he allegedly tried to take over the direction of *Waterfront* (1950, + co-sc).
OTHER BRITISH FILMS INCLUDE: *While Parents Sleep* (1935), *The Day Will Dawn* (1942), *The Weaker Sex* (1948, + co-sc), *High Treason* (1951), *Happy is the Bride* (1957), *Law and Disorder* (1958).

sound The history of sound in British cinema naturally forms part of the larger international picture, especially in relation to US developments. For instance, between 1900 and 1911, successful efforts to synchronise gramaphone and phonograph records to the cinematograph were made by Léon Gaumont in France, Oska Messter in Germany, Thomas Edison in America – and Cecil HEPWORTH in Britain. The most significant achievement between 1900 and 1914 was that of Frenchman Eugene Lauste (1857–1935), who produced sound and picture on a single film at his workshop in Brixton, London. War and amplification problems halted developments in Britain. During the 1920s Stanley Watkins (1888–1975) and George Groves (1901–76), British engineers, working for the Bell Telephone Laboratories, played an important part in the development of Vitaphone, the sound-on-disc system used by Warner Bros. for *The Jazz Singer* (1927, US), generally recognised as the start of 'talking pictures'.

In Britain, H. Grindell Mathews and Arthur Kingston successfully recorded sound on film using a variable area system, but lack of financial backing prevented its commercial development. Sound-on-film developments were more successful in the US: Lee DeForest's Phonofilm, Theodore Case's Movietone and Charles Hoxie's RCA Photophone systems were all imported into Britain. As early as 1923 British Phonofilms using DeForest's sound-on-film system produced a number of variety shorts in a small studio in Clapham. Alfred HITCHCOCK's *Blackmail* (1929), Britain's first talkie, was recorded on RCA Photophone. Western Electric replaced the Movietone AEO light system with a light valve developed by E.C. Wente of Bell Telephone Laboratories, and Western Electric and RCA became the two major recording and reproduction systems.

In 1932, Vitaphone Sound System, manufactured by the Marconi Wireless Co., was installed at SOUND CITY studios; and the British Acoustic Sound System was installed at SHEPHERD'S BUSH studios. By 1935, EALING, ELSTREE, TEDDINGTON and TWICKENHAM studios were equipped with

RCA Photophone system, and in 1936 DENHAM and PINEWOOD studios opened using Western Electric system. Denham used portable channels; Pinewood had sound control rooms on each stage. During the 30s, improvements, such as ground-noise reduction systems, occurred, but nothing during WW2.

Post-war, studios re-equipped with American equipment. MGM opened a new studio at BOREHAMWOOD, with Alfred WATKINS as Head of Sound, while John Cox, Cyril Crowhurst and Harold King filled this role at SHEPPERTON, Pinewood and ABPC Elstree. In 1951, the Leevers Rich Synchro-Pulse portable magnetic tape recorder was introduced, with separate pulse track for camera synchronisation, and magnetic recording adopted as the main system for production and post-production recording. In 1965, Ray Dolby opened Clapham Laboratory to develop a magnetic noise reduction system, Ioan Allen joining the company to adapt the system to film sound. *Callan* (1974), was the first film with Dolby Sound. Dolby Stereo (1974), Dolby Spectral (1986), SR Digital (1991) and Surround Ex (1999) followed. The early 1990s saw the adoption of digital sound recording, replacing the use of analogue magnetic. By 2000, over 900 UK cinemas were equipped for digital sound.

British Oscar-winners for sound include: John COX, *The Sound Barrier* (1952), *Lawrence of Arabia* (1962), *Oliver!* (1968); Simon KAYE, *Gandhi* (1982, UK/Ind); and Peter HANDFORD, *Out of Africa* (1985, UK/US). John Aldred and Bob Allen.

Sound City Film Production & Recording Company
Sound City Studios were built at SHEPPERTON in the early 30s, by Norman LOUDON for the purpose of producing the then-popular 'flicker' books, designed to give an illusion of sportsmen in motion. Having bought the 60-acre site, Loudon founded the Sound City Film Production & Recording Company in 1932 to begin film production. The Studio's country-house, lake-and-parkland setting attracted the attention of other film-makers as well, including John BAXTER and George KING, and thus the productive history of Shepperton Studios was established, starting with 'QUOTA QUICKIES' and moving on to more ambitious productions in other hands. In 1936, Sound City was reorganised and Sound City Distributors was formed, with John Baxter and John BARTER as its joint chairmen, but by the end of the 30s it had ceased to operate as a production company, and in 1946 LONDON FILMS acquired its studios.

Southall Studios
There is a confusing set of other organisations – Cromwell, Metropolitan, Britone, Kingsway, ALLIANCE – all associated with this converted hangar in Gladstone Road in West London. G. B. SAMUELSON established a 7,500-square-foot stage there in 1924. 'QUOTA QUICKIES' were made soon thereafter and some notable people, including Will HAY, used the studio. There was a fire in 1937. After WW2, Sydney BOX took a long lease, and in 1951 John GRIERSON was appointed Joint Executive Producer of GROUP THREE at Southall Studios. Films made there include *Dancing With Crime* (1947), starring Richard ATTENBOROUGH, and *Time Gentlemen Please!* (1952), directed by Lewis GILBERT. By 1954 films were making way for television productions there, till the building was partly demolished, the rest becoming a warehouse. Stephen Brown.

Southwark Studios
Former dog biscuit factory converted to film production, with four sound stages, in 1984, for both feature film-making (e.g. *Personal Services*, *Prick Up Your Ears*, 1987), as well as TV programmes and commercials.

Spall, Timothy (*b* London, 1957). Actor. Proof that the great tradition of British CHARACTER ACTORS is alive and well, Spall has given one memorable performance after another since the early 90s, often associated with Mike LEIGH, with whom he first worked on stage and TV. Think of the drunken, incompetent bistro-owner in *Life is Sweet* (1990), Brenda BLETHYN's photographer brother in *Secrets & Lies* (1996), and the temperamental D'Oyly Carte singer (BAAn) in *Topsy-Turvy* (2000, UK/US); but think equally of his hapless Rosencrantz in BRANAGH's *Hamlet* (1996, UK/US) or Don Armado in *Love's Labour's Lost* (2000, UK/Fr/US); or the ex-rock drummer in *Still Crazy* (1998, UK/US); or perhaps best of all the cuckolded husband in *Intimacy* (2001, UK/Fr), who can be pushed just so far. He is even enjoyable as the *nouveau riche* Sterling in *The Clandestine Marriage* (1999); *any* film will be more entertaining for boasting his plump-featured presence in its cast. Awarded OBE, 2000.
OTHER BRITISH FILMS INCLUDE: *Quadrophenia* (1979), *The Missionary* (1981), *The Bride* (1985), *Gothic* (1986), *Dream Demon* (1988), *1871*, *The Sheltering Sky* (1990), *The Wisdom of Crocodiles* (1998), *Vatel*, *Chicken Run* (UK/US, voice) (2000), *Lucky Break* (2001, UK/Ger/US), *All or Nothing* (2002, UK/Fr).

Speaight, Robert (*b* St Margaret-at-Cliffe, 1904 – *d* Tonbridge, 1976). Actor, author. Haileybury College- and Oxford-educated actor, who created the role of Thomas Becket in T.S. Eliot's *Murder in the Cathedral* (1935), and who filmed hardly at all. His dignified demeanour cast him as the priest in *Madonna of the Seven Moons* (1944) and the Cardinal in *The Magic Bow* (1946). Awarded CBE, 1958.
OTHER BRITISH FILMS: (doc, short, narr) *The Sword of the Spirit* (1942), *The Visitation* (1947), *The Vision of William Blake* (1958).

Spear, Bernard (*b* London, 1919 – *d* 2003). Actor. More often on TV (e.g. as Morris in the Manchester-set soap, *Albion Market*, 1985–86) than in the cinema, this supporting actor entered films in the mid 60s, in *Daleks – Invasion Earth 2150 AD* (1966). Often in Jewish roles, in such films as *Yentl* (1983, UK/US) and *The Man Who Cried* (2000, UK/Fr/US). Played Sancho Panza in the London production of *Man of La Mancha* (1968).
OTHER BRITISH FILMS INCLUDE: *Drop Dead Darling* (1966), *Bedazzled* (1967), *Chitty Chitty Bang Bang* (1968), *Hide and Seek* (1972), *Wombling Free* (1977), *Not Quite Jerusalem* (1984).

Spear, Eric (*b* Croydon, Surrey, 1908 – *d* Southampton, 1966). Composer. In films from 1931, he was busiest in the 50s churning out scores for 'B' MOVIES, including several for Vernon SEWELL (e.g. *Ghost Ship*, 1952; *Meet Mr Callaghan*, 1954), but his best was his highly atmospheric work for Lance COMFORT's *Bang! You're Dead* (1953). Also a BBC producer and a composer for such TV series as *Coronation Street* and *The Grove Family*.
OTHER BRITISH FILMS INCLUDE: (comp, unless noted) *City of Beautiful Nonsense* (1935, m d, m numbers), *No Way Back* (1949), *She Shall Have Murder* (1950), *The Floating Dutchman* (m d), *Street of Shadows*, *Counterspy* (1953), *Diplomatic Passport*, *Stranger from Venus* (1954), *A Touch of the Sun* (1956), *The Big Chance* (1957), *Stranglehold* (1962, + m d), *The Switch* (1963, + m d), *The Vulture* (1966, UK/Can/US).

special effects The use of special effects technologies to simulate spectacular visual impossibilities, or to circumvent impracticalities of location shooting, is principally the domain of the studio-based Hollywood film industry, which is unique in world cinema for the high proportion of its budgets devoted to the production of visual effects. Although British studios such as ELSTREE and PINEWOOD have been used to shoot principal photography on such Hollywood blockbusters as the *Star Wars* trilogy, *Batman* (1989), and the 'Indiana Jones' films, most of the post-production visual effects were added at American effects houses, primarily George Lucas's California-based Industrial Light and Magic. The James BOND film franchise represents Britain's most prominent attempt to compete with Hollywood in terms of spectacle – explosive action and foregrounded special effects are recurring motifs of the SERIES. Before the establishment of powerful STUDIO SYSTEMS, some of the earliest British film-makers, including Cecil HEPWORTH and R.W. PAUL, were producing trick films. The use of stop-motion substitutions, double exposures and model ANIMATION in early shorts such as *Explosion of a Motor Car* (1900) and *The '?' Motorist* (1906) laid the groundwork for the future conventions of trick photography, and acted as counterpoint to the ACTUALITIES recorded by the LUMIÈRE Bros. Paul, in partnership with Walter R. BOOTH, is known for shooting some beautiful exterior views, but some of his finest illusory achievements, amongst them *Cheese Mites* (1901), were recorded in a studio purpose-built to allow the production of special effects. He had clearly recognised the importance of this new art form. Producer Alexander KORDA's devotion to producing spectacular work to rival the output of the major American studios compelled him to incorporate lavish sets and special effects in films including *Things to Come* (1936) and *The Thief of Baghdad* (1940). Michael POWELL also made optical effects a central part of the visual design of *A Matter of Life and Death* (1946), *Black Narcissus* (1947) and *The Red Shoes* (1948). David RAWNSLEY's attempts to combine sophisticated back-projection techniques and mobile sets for RANK Film Research Department's INDEPENDENT FRAME represent an early exploration of the possibilities of virtual studio spaces, exploiting technologies which had previously been reserved for special effects shots in order to reduce costly, lengthy shooting schedules. Most of the later work of American Ray HARRYHAUSEN, arguably the greatest practitioner of stop-motion animation in cinema history and a protégé of Willis O'Brien, was for British productions, most notably *Jason and the Argonauts* (1963) and *The Golden Voyage of Sinbad* (1973). His primary skill lies in his ability to imbue models of mythical creatures with distinctive characteristics and movements. Gifted matte artist Les BOWIE supervised composite shots for *Superman* (Richard Donner, 1978), but previously had lent his services to over 40 films, many of them HAMMER productions such as Terence FISHER's *The Curse of the Werewolf* (1961) and Peter SYKES's *To the Devil a Daughter* (1976, UK/Ger). The formation, in 1997, of Mill Film, a London-based special effects facility which can count Ridley SCOTT's *Gladiator* (2000, UK/US) among its achievements, was one of the most promising of recent developments. Dan North.

Spector, Maude (*b* Barnet, 1916 – *d* 1995). Casting director. Began film career as assistant to Irene HOWARD, working on TWO CITIES films, before becoming casting director to RKO–BRITISH and then for RANK at DENHAM in 1947. Since then she has worked for many companies, including DISNEY–BRITISH, and on a wide range of films encompassing *Lawrence of Arabia* (1962) and several BOND adventures, acquiring a doyenne's reputation in her field. Also, as freelance, she cast such international films as *The Omen* (1976), and *The Razor's Edge* (1984), in which she won only qualified approval

for updating Tyrone POWER with Bill Murray.
OTHER BRITISH FILMS INCLUDE: *So Well Remembered* (1947), *Scrooge* (1951), *Svengali* (1954), *In Search of the Castaways* (1961, UK/US), *The Three Lives of Thomasina* (1963), *The Moon Spinners* (1964, UK/US), *Cul-de-sac, The Night of the Generals* (UK/Fr) (1966), *Casino Royale, Bedazzled* (1967), *Country Dance* (1969), *The Last Valley* (1970), *Nicholas and Alexandra* (1971, UK/US), *The Man with the Golden Gun* (1974), *The Spy Who Loved Me, Valentino* (1977), *The Big Sleep* (1978), *For Your Eyes Only* (1981), *The Shooting Party* (1984), *The Whistle Blower* (1986), *Souvenir* (1987).

Speed, Lancelot (*b* 1860 – *d* 1931). Animator. A book and magazine illustrator, Speed became Britain's first major film cartoonist when he went to work for the Neptune Company in 1914, producing 'lightning sketches' in 1914 and 1915 for the 'Bully Boy' series. Later, he animated a series of WW1 PROPAGANDA SHORTS: *Tank Pranks, The U Tube* (1917), *Tommy Atkins, Old Father William, Britain's Effort,* and *Britain's Honour* (1918). In 1921–22, he was responsible for *The Wonderful Adventures of Pip, Squeak and Wilfred* series, 26 one-reel shorts based on the *Daily Mirror* cartoon strip. AS.

Speer, Hugo (*b* Harrogate, 1968). Actor. Famous as the 'lunchbox' stripper in the international success, *The Full Monty* (1997, UK/US), the rugged Speer went on to star in *Swing* (1999), as an ex-prisoner desperate to start a swing band, and *An Angel for May* (2002). Son of a Jockey Club official and a Scottish writer, whose divorce caused him a troubled adolescence, he began training with the Arts Educational drama school at age 21 and landed a small role in *Bhaji on the Beach* (1993) and some TV. As to the latter, he was excellent in the lead in two superior mini-series, *Hearts and Bones* (2000) and *Do or Die* (2001, UK/Aust).

Speight, Johnny (*b* London, 1920 – *d* Chorleywood, 1998). Screenwriter. Former milkman, most famous as the creator of arch-bigot – and major comic invention – Alf Garnett, controversial protagonist of TV's *Till Death Do Us Part* (1966–68), which revealed a brilliantly sharp ear for various kinds of vernacular cliché and vituperation, and which spawned two SPIN-OFF movies, *Till Death Us Do Part* (1969) and *The Alf Garnett Saga* (1972, + a). Other TV successes included *The Arthur Haynes Show* (1956–66) and *The Lady Is a Tramp* (1983–84), but film contributions were sparse.
OTHER BRITISH FILMS: *French Dressing* (1963, add d), *Privilege* (1967, novel), *Rhubarb* (1969, short, a), *The Secret Policeman's Third Ball* (1987, co-sc).

Spence, Richard (*b* Doncaster, 1957). Director. Active in TV from the 80s, Oxford-educated Spence was a trainee producer with the BBC (1981–82) and directed the movies *Skallagrigg* (1994), a BBC FILMS production focussing on a cerebral palsy sufferer, and *Different for Girls* (1996), centred on a reunion of two schoolfriends, one of whom has had a sex-change operation. Has also filmed in the US (e.g. the sci-fi thriller, *New World Disorder*, 1999), but most of his work has been for TV, including the drama, *Thacker* (1992).

Spencer, Marian (*b* London, 1905). Actress. Former dancing and elocution teacher who studied at RADA and the RCM, making her stage debut in 1929 (London 1933), playing several roles with GIELGUD's company, 1944–45, and entering films in 1936 as the wife of *David Livingstone*. She was the gentle-mannered one of the three wives in *When We Are Married* (1943) and brought her elegant bearing to about 20 other films, starring as the possessive mother in *Intimate Relations* (1953), the doomed British version of Cocteau's *Les parents terribles*. Some TV, including the benignly interfering Lady Russell in *Persuasion* (1971).

OTHER BRITISH FILMS INCLUDE: *The Captain's Table* (1936), *Auld Lang Syne* (1937), *Spellbound* (1941), *Dangerous Moonlight* (1941), *Let the People Sing* (1942), *The Demi-Paradise* (1943), *Bond Street* (1948), *The Secret* (1955), *Corridors of Blood* (1958), *The World of Suzie Wong* (1960), *Seance on a Wet Afternoon* (1964).

Spencer, Norman (*b* London, 1914). Associate producer, screenwriter. In the film industry from the mid 30s, filling various roles, including assistant director, production manager and others. Much associated with the films of David LEAN, whose production manager he became when he joined CINEGUILD in 1944. He shared a BAAn for the screenplay (with Lean and Wynyard Browne) for *Hobson's Choice* (1953, + assoc p) and was in charge of the Moroccan shooting for *Lawrence of Arabia* (1962).

OTHER BRITISH FILMS INCLUDE: (prod man, unless noted) *Unpublished Story* (1942), *The Demi-Paradise* (1943, 2 ass d), *The Way Ahead* (1944), *Blithe Spirit* (unit man), *The Rake's Progress* (1945), *Great Expectations* (1946), *Take My Life*, *Blanche Fury* (1947), *Oliver Twist*, *The Passionate Friends* (1948), *Madeleine* (1949); (assoc p) *The Sound Barrier* (1952), *Summer Madness* (1955, UK/US), *Cry Freedom* (1987, co-p).

Spenser, Jeremy (*b* Ceylon, 1937). Actor. Dark-haired, somewhat sulky-looking child star from the late 40s, whose career tailed off in adulthood. Had some good juvenile roles, including Vivien LEIGH's son in *Anna Karenina* (1948), Dennis PRICE as a child in *Kind Hearts and Coronets* (1949) and John JUSTIN ditto in *The Man Who Loved Redheads* (1954), Margaret JOHNSTON's spoilt son in *Portrait of Clare* (1950), and the musical prodigy in *Prelude to Fame* (1950). Survived as a teenager, as in *The Prince and the Showgirl*, repeating his stage role of the young king, and the MUSICAL, *Wonderful Things* (1957), but his career was over by the mid 60s, having lasted longer than that of many child notables.

OTHER BRITISH FILMS INCLUDE: *The Spider and the Fly* (1949), *The Planter's Wife* (1952), *Background* (1953), *Devil on Horseback* (1954), *Escapade* (1955), *It's Great to Be Young!* (1956), *Ferry to Hong Kong* (1959), *King and Country* (1964), *Operation Crossbow* (1965, UK/It), *Fahrenheit 451* (1966).

Sperber, Milo (*b* Vienna, 1911 – *d* London, 1992). Actor. Had numerous theatre engagements in Salzburg and Vienna before emigrating to Britain in 1939. Continued mainly as a stage actor (e.g. with the Old Vic), with occasional film appearances, often in European-set films such as *Mr Emmanuel* (1944). Also TV, including *The History Man* (1981) and episodes of *Are You Being Served?*.

OTHER BRITISH FILMS INCLUDE: *Thunder Rock* (1942), *The End Of The River* (1947), *Golden Arrow* (1949), *Foreign Intrigue* (1956), *Bluebeard's Ten Honeymoons* (1960), *The Victors* (US/UK 1963), *Operation Crossbow* (1965, UK/It), *Billion Dollar Brain* (1967), *Voyage Of The Damned* (1976), *Providence* (1977). Tim Bergfelder.

Spice Girls, The Pop group. Very popular five-girl vocal group of the 90s, whose real names are Geri Halliwell (Ginger Spice), Melanie Brown (Scary Spice), Victoria Adams (Posh Spice), Melanie Clinton (Sporty Spice) and Emma Bunton (Baby Spice). Merely being chartbusters and sexy media icons doesn't mean they are interesting, and their flashy, sometimes funny, first film venture, *Spice World* (1997), in which a number of people who should have known better appear as guest artistes, does not offer conclusive evidence. An appraisal of their musical gifts belongs elsewhere.

Spiegel, Sam (aka Sam P. Eagle) (*b* Jaroslau, Poland, 1901 – *d* Ile-Saint-Martin, Antilles, 1985). Producer. After spending time in Palestine, as a Zionist Pioneer, Spiegel, who kept reinventing his own past, (as Eagle) spent time in Hollywood. He lacked serious educational qualifications but was gifted with languages and had a passion for the theatre as well as for film. He became MGM's story adviser, and returned to Europe in 1929 to head Universal's organisation in Berlin, producing foreign-language versions of US films. Fleeing Berlin in 1933, the Jewish Spiegel made films in Vienna and Paris, returned to Hollywood where he produced several films, including *We Were Strangers* (1949) for director John HUSTON, for whom he would make his first British film, the much-loved hit, *The African Queen* (1951). For the rest of his career he worked on both sides of the Atlantic, producing *On the Waterfront* (1954) in the US and two of David LEAN's biggest successes, *The Bridge on the River Kwai* (1957) and *Lawrence of Arabia* (1962), all three of which won Best Picture Oscars. The mogul's cigar-chomping flamboyance concealed a considerable intelligence, and a substantial body of films, often lavish but also the minimalist *Betrayal* (1982), are a monument to his flair and shrewdness. Won Irving Thalberg Memorial Award 1964, and BAFTA Fellowship, 1984.

OTHER BRITISH FILMS: *Melba* (1953), *Suddenly, Last Summer* (1959), *The Night of the Generals* (1966, UK/Fr), *Nicholas and Alexandra* (1971, UK/US).

BIBLIOG: Andrew Sinclair, *Spiegel: The Man Behind the Pictures*, 1987.

Spiers, Bob Director. Several times nominated for BAA, for Best TV Comedy Series, for his work on *Absolutely Fabulous*, and winning in 1992, as he did for *Fawlty Towers* (1975, 1979), Spiers has yet to make a comparable mark in film. He is probably responsible for what wit surffaces in *Spice World* (1997), his feature debut. In the early 2000s, he was filming in Australia.

OTHER BRITISH FILMS: *Kevin of the North* (2001, UK/Ger).

Spikings, Barry (*b* Boston, Lincs, 1939) Producer. Entered industry in 1963 and became joint manager of BRITISH LION, for which he produced *Conduct Unbecoming* (1975) and *The Man Who Fell to Earth* (1976). Won Best Film Oscar for co-producing *The Deer Hunter* (1978) for EMI of which he was Managing Director, and has since worked in the US.

Spinetti, Victor (*b* Cwm, Wales, 1933). Actor. Son of Italian father and Welsh mother, educated at Monmouth School and Cardiff College of Music and Drama, Spinetti was on stage from 1953 (London, 1956), and was much associated with the Theatre Workshop, Stratford East. Entered films in the early 60s, noticeably in the BEATLES films, *A Hard Day's Night* (1964, as the understandably neurotic TV director) and *Help!* (1965, as a crazy scientist), and co-adapted and directed for the stage John Lennon's book, *In His Own Write*, 1968. Has continued to film sporadically in the UK (he was, of course, in *Under Milk Wood*, 1971) and elsewhere (e.g. *The Taming of the Shrew*, 1967, US/It), and to work on stage and TV, where he was one of the team involved in *That Was the Week That Was* (1962–63).

OTHER BRITISH FILMS INCLUDE: *Sparrows Can't Sing* (1962), *The Wild Affair* (1963), *Becket* (1964), *Can Hieronymous Merkin Ever Forget . . .* (1969), *Digby the Biggest Dog in the World* (1973), *Return of the Pink Panther* (1974), *Voyage of the Damned* (1976), *Hardcore* (1977), *The Krays* (1990), *Julie and the Cadillacs* (1999).

spin-offs from television *see* **television-to-cinema spin-offs**

Spoliansky, Mischa (*b* Bialystok, Russia, 1898 – *d* London, 1985). Composer. In the 20s a highly celebrated composer for cabarets and musical revues in Berlin and Paris, Spoliansky came to Britain in 1933, initially working for Alexander KORDA. A writer of popular yet sophisticated songs, Spoliansky was often better at creating memorable melodies in his films than at devising cohesive scores. In HITCHCOCK's *Stage Fright* (1950) he wrote songs for Dietrich, whom he had discovered for a Berlin revue in the late 20s, and composed 'Goodbye Trouble', sung by John MILLS in *The History of Mr Polly* (1948). Also worked on international productions, including *Saint Joan* (1957, UK/US).

OTHER BRITISH FILMS INCLUDE: *The Private Life Of Don Juan* (1934), *My Song For You* (1934), *Evensong* (1934), *Sanders of the River* (1935), *The Ghost Goes West* (1935), *The Man Who Could Work Miracles* (1936), *King Solomon's Mines* (1937), *Over the Moon* (1939), *Jeannie* (1941), *Mr Emmanuel* (1944), *The Man From Morocco* (1945), *Wanted For Murder* (1946), *Temptation Harbour* (1947), *Idol Of Paris* (1948), *Adam And Evelyne* (1949), *The Happiest Days Of Your Life* (1950), *Happy Go Lovely* (1951), *Turn The Key Softly* (1953), *Duel In The Jungle* (1954), *North West Frontier* (1959), *The Battle of the Villa Fiorita* (1965), *The Best House in London* (1968). Tim Bergfelder.

sponsored films Sponsorship has played an important part in British cinema since the very beginning. While, strictly speaking, the term 'sponsorship' implies funding something that is of no direct benefit to the funder, the term has always been used rather more loosely with regard to the cinema. The earliest examples of sponsorship were ADVERTISING FILMS, followed, in the 1910s, by the idea of renters themselves funding the production of films they thought their audiences would like, particularly versions of West End stage successes. During WW1, the government employed established film-makers to produce PROPAGANDA films. The War Office Cinematograph Committee took over what was renamed the *War Office Official Topical Budget*, later *Pictorial News (Official)* from 1917, a NEWSREEL, while also putting money – unusually – into a feature film, D.W. Griffith's *Hearts of the World* (1918). By the 20s, ministries, local authorities, charities and religious groups had all recognised the value of cinema as a means of promoting their own causes. Sponsorship for public service matters reached its heyday in the 30s when companies such as the British Commercial Gas Association financed films like *Housing Problems* (1935). During WW2, the government's own CROWN FILM UNIT was only one of the many companies employed by the MINISTRY OF INFORMATION for propaganda purposes.

In the post-war period, industrial sponsors, led by the many oil companies, came to the fore. The Iraq Petroleum Company, for example, sponsored films like the FILM CENTRE's *Rivers of Time* (1957), a history of the Mesopotamian civilisations. The BRITISH FILM INSTITUTE's Experimental Film Fund, later renamed the BFI PRODUCTION BOARD, was set up in 1951 to provide money and resources for young film-makers unable to find funding elsewhere. At the same time, the Ford Motor Company was persuaded to finance a few films from the FREE CINEMA movement.

Though public screenings of non-fiction and SHORT FILMS generally have become rarer in more recent years, the non-theatrical market continues to flourish. Central and local governments, and charities remain major sponsors. Management training films have become a huge growth area, many funded by official organisations like the Department of Employment, and others by NGOs such as the Institute of Personnel Management. Financing of fiction films has increased as both the BBC and, in particular, CHANNEL 4 Television have funded films for cinema distribution as well as for television transmission, while Channel 4 has also become a major sponsor or commissioning company for animated and experimental films. Elaine Burrows.

sport Despite its important role within 20th-century British culture, sport has not been nearly as prominent in British films as in Hollywood ones. British sporting dramas have been a less attractive prospect for the international market, not just because others may not know the rules of our games – this doesn't stop baseball and American football films being made and exported – but because our sporting activities don't easily translate into the elemental terms of intense struggle and confrontation that inform melodramas like *Raging Bull* (1980), *The Mean Machine* (1974), and *Pride of the Yankees* (1942).Two rare exceptions to this pattern are Lindsay ANDERSON's *This Sporting Life* (1963), set in the hard Northern milieu of Rugby League in which the author, David STOREY, had played as a professional, and *Chariots of Fire*, whose international success culminated at the Oscars ceremony of 1981 (Best Film, Screenplay, Score). *Chariots of Fire* puts its track-racing into a brilliantly seductive context, offering a rich 'HERITAGE' iconography of landscapes and old buildings, a climactic Anglo-American encounter at the Paris Olympics of 1924, and above all a pair of heroes whose twin task is to run faster and to negotiate the complexities of the British CLASS system.

Perhaps one reason for the consistent failure to produce a successful drama about Soccer, the 'world game', is that none of these three contexts is easily available. Even in 1939, the centring of *The Arsenal Stadium Mystery* on a match between professional and amateur sides seemed tame and anachronistic. Despite recurring efforts such as *Best* (UK/Ire), *There's Only One Jimmy Grimble* (UK/Fr), and *Purely Belter* (all 2000), football has still not produced much in the way of interest.

In contrast, the strong heritage and class associations of cricket have made it an attractive subject, touched on frequently in short scenes or in dialogue; yet it has never formed the central theme of a successful film. The most sustained attempt is *The Final Test* (1953), timed to exploit the strong public interest surrounding the series against Australia in Coronation year, and featuring a number of then-current England players, including the captain, Len Hutton; but their acting, like that of the authentic footballers of *The Arsenal Stadium Mystery* and its successors, is stilted, and the action into which the film incorporates them is similarly unconvincing. The cricketing public is represented by Robert MORLEY, as an eccentric poet, and by Richard WATTIS, a silly-ass upper-class figure in the mould of Basil RADFORD and Naunton WAYNE. The memorable cameos of that pair in *The Lady Vanishes* (1938), as bachelors indifferent to the menace of fascism and concerned only to get back to England for the Test match, had created a strong cluster of comic or reactionary associations around the game that were hard to shake off, whether viewed indulgently, as by most film-makers, or scathingly, as by POWELL AND PRESSBURGER in *A Matter of Life and Death* (1946).

The treatment of cricket in British cinema remains more consistent and substantial than that of other sports, and two immigrant directors have handled it in particularly vigorous ways. Horace OVE's *Playing Away* (1986) uses a match between an English village and a team of London-based West Indians as a potent metaphor for cultural tensions and changes. The brief but intense cricket scenes in *Accident* (1967) and, especially, *The Go-Between* (1971) are shaped by an eloquent combination of the cricketing expertise of screenwriter Harold PINTER, Joseph LOSEY's handling of space and movement, and their shared fascination with the class system. *The Go-Between*'s titanic encounter, in a beautiful rural setting, between the opposing styles of Edward FOX, as Lord Trimingham, and Alan BATES, as the bucolic servant Burgess, stands as a reminder of the potency of sport, even very British sport, as drama of an intensity that could sustain a whole film. *Chariots of Fire* need not, as a sport-centred international success, continue to stand alone indefinitely.

OTHER RELEVANT BRITISH FILMS INCLUDE: *The Ring* (1927, boxing), *No Limit* (1935, TT racing), *There Ain't No Justice* (boxing), *Come On George!* (horse-racing) (1939), *Dead of Night* (1945, golf), *Once a Jolly Swagman* (1948, speedway racing), *A Boy, a Girl and a Bike* (1949, cycling), *Genevieve* (vintage car-racing), *The Square Ring* (boxing) (1953), *The Rainbow Jacket* (1954, horse-racing), *Geordie* (1955, hammer-throwing), *Just My Luck* (1957, horse-racing), *School for Scoundrels* (1959, tennis), *The Green Helmet* (1961, motor-racing), *The Loneliness of the Long Distance Runner* (1962, running), *The Games* (1969, marathon), *Champions* (1983, horse-racing), *Number One, Billy the Kid and the Green Baize Vampire* (1984, snooker), *Blue Juice* (1995, surfing). Charles Barr.

Spriggs, Elizabeth (*b* Buxton, 1929). Actress. Came late to stage stardom as an unforgettable Beatrice in the RSC's *Much Ado About Nothing* (1971), and settled thereafter into a series of notable character studies in all the acting media. On TV, she won great acclaim as South London matriarch Connie in *Fox* (1980), as Mrs Cadwallader in *Middlemarch* (1994) and many others. On-screen she has lent her bulk and comic gifts to the likes of *Sense and Sensibility* (1995, UK/US) as good-hearted vulgar Mrs Jennings and, in different vein, as the snobbish Mrs Roberts in *Paradise Road* (1997, US/Aust), and she was the fat lady in *Harry Potter and the Philosopher's Stone* (2001, UK/US), though it didn't give her much to do.

OTHER BRITISH FILMS INCLUDE: *Work Is a Four Letter Word* (1967), *Three Into Two Won't Go* (1968), *Richard's Things* (1980), *Lady Chatterley's Lover, An Unsuitable Job for a Woman* (1981), *Parker* (1984), *Impromptu* (1991), *The Secret Agent* (1996, UK/US).

Sproxton, David *see* **Aardman Animation**

spy films 'They're just a bunch of seedy, squalid bastards, little men, like me: drunkards, queers, hen-pecked husbands, civil servants playing cowboys and Indians to brighten their rotten little lives!' Richard BURTON's embittered definition of his profession comes towards the end of Martin Ritt's magnificent film version of John Le Carre's *The Spy Who Came In From the Cold* (1965), the ultimate demystification of spying as an honourable pursuit. It was bucking the trend of a decade which, through the amorous adventurism of Sean CONNERY's James BOND and Michael CAINE's Harry Palmer, had given a real allure to the art of deception on behalf of Her Majesty's Secret Service. Framing this glamorous portrait were, on the one side, Carol REED's *Our Man in Havana* (1959), his stolid but intermittently amusing version of Graham GREENE's marvellous satire of so-called British Intelligence; and on the other, Michael ANDERSON's *The Quiller Memorandum* (1966, UK/US), where Harold PINTER's screenplay subjects spying to ironic, circumspect scrutiny. The best spy films have been those that have combined a suspenseful tale with a mature commentary on ideological positions and democratic values: one thinks of HITCHCOCK's 30s thrillers and also two remarkable

films from Thorold DICKINSON, *The Next of Kin* (1942) and *Secret People* (1951). For a droller perspective, there is Alan Bennett's drama about the Russian exile of super-traitor, Kim Philby in John SCHLESINGER's *An Englishman Abroad* (1983). Neil Sinyard.

Squire, Anthony (*b* London, 1914 – *d* London, 2000). Screenwriter, director. Eton-educated son of poet, Sir John Squire (1884–1958), he was essentially a second unit director, on, among others, a couple of BOND films (*Casino Royale*, 1967; *On Her Majesty's Secret Service*, 1969), and he directed the location sequences for *The Heart of the Matter* (1953). He directed a few minor films, including the GROUP 3 SPY THRILLER, *Doublecross* (1955), which he also co-wrote, and produced the WAR FILM, *A Hill in Korea* (1956). For TV, he directed episodes of *William Tell* (1958) and wrote for *The Saint* (1962). Was pilot with RAF (1940–44) and with the RAF FILM UNIT (1944–45), and postwar formed Anglo-Scottish Pictures, based at SHEPPERTON, to make DOCUMENTARIES. Once married to actress Shelagh FRASER.

OTHER BRITISH FILMS INCLUDE: (doc, short) *Increase the Harvest* (1946, d), *Young Housewife* (1947, p), *New York* (1972, d); (features) (2ud/ ass d, unless noted) *The Sound Barrier* (1952), *The Intruder* (1953, addit scenes), *Macbeth* (1961, tech d), *The Blue Max* (1966), *Candleshoe* (1977, UK/US), *The Eye of the Needle* (1981), *Sword of the Valiant* (1983).

Squire, Julia (*b* Thursley, 1926). Costume designer. Trained at Central London School of Art, Squire entered the industry as uncredited assistant on *London Town* (1946), but went on to less ill-starred ventures, sometimes billed as 'costume designer' (as on *Gone to Earth*, 1950), sometimes as 'costume supervisor' (as on *Hobson's Choice*, 1953). Her designs for Moira SHEARER in *The Man Who Loved Redheads* (1954), across three characters and half a century, attested to her versatility and her capacity to make costume signify character, class and period.

OTHER BRITISH FILMS INCLUDE: (cos super) *Under Capricorn* (1949), *Moulin Rouge* (1953); (cos des/dress des) *The Magic Box* (1951), *Women of Twilight* (1952), *The Captain's Paradise* (1953), *Father Brown, The End of the Affair* (Deborah KERR's costumes), *An Inspector Calls* (1954), *The Feminine Touch* (1956), *Beyond This Place* (1959).

Squire, Ronald (*b* Tiverton, 1886 – *d* London, 1958). Actor. RN: Squirl. Son of British army colonel, as one would have guessed, Wellington College-educated Squire was for several decades one of the finest purveyors of dinner-jacketed comedy on the London stage, in a line that included Gerald DU MAURIER and Rex HARRISON. In retrospect, he seems like an actor who did one thing supremely well – that is, drawing-room comedy – but he also played SHAW, BARRIE and MAUGHAM with ineffable ease. His three dozen films celebrate the persona which grows more avuncular as he ages, sometimes imbued with an enjoyable caddishness, as in his gossip columnist, 'Mary Jane', in *It Started in Paradise* (1952), or the confidence trickster in *Always a Bride* (1953), and he played Stewart GRANGER's valet in *Woman Hater* (1948) without surrendering his inbuilt superiority. However, he is probably best remembered for films such as *While the Sun Shines* (1947), repeating his stage role of the irascible Duke, and for his clubmen in *The Million Pound Note* (1953) and *Around the World in Eighty Days* (1956), but his finest performance may be as the boy's uncle, concerned at first, then glinting with opportunism in *The Rocking Horse Winner* (1949). There is probably no place for his like in contemporary British cinema (unless one could imagine MERCHANT IVORY with a sense of humour), and it is the poorer for that.

OTHER BRITISH FILMS INCLUDE: *Whoso Is Without Sin* (1916), *The Wild Boy* (1934), *Dusty Ermine* (1936), *Action for Slander* (1937), *Freedom Radio* (1940), *The Flemish Farm* (1943), *Don't Take It to Heart!* (1944), *Journey Together* (1945), *The First Gentleman* (1948), *No Highway*, *Encore* (1951), *Laxdale Hall* (1953), *The Man Who Loved Redheads* (1954, unc), *Footsteps in the Fog*, *Raising a Riot* (1955), *Sea Wife* (1956), *Island in the Sun* (1957, UK/US), *The Inn of the Sixth Happiness* (1958).

Squire, William (*b* Neath, Wales, 1916 – *d* London, 1989). Actor. Rugged character player only occasionally in films. Formerly a bell-founder, he trained at RADA, made stage debut at the Old Vic in 1945, played many Shakespearean roles, there and at Stratford, often acting with friend and compatriot, Richard BURTON, with whom he also appeared in the films, *Anne of the Thousand Days* (1969), as Thomas More to Burton's *Henry VIII*, and *Where Eagles Dare* (1968). TV work included *Black Arrow* (1972–75) and episodes of *Callan*, as departmental head, 'Hunter' (1970–72).
OTHER BRITISH FILMS INCLUDE: *The Man Who Never Was* (1955), *The Battle of the River Plate* (1956), *Dunkirk* (1958), *The Thirty Nine Steps* (1978), *Testimony* (1987).

Stafford, Brendan J(ames) (*b* Dublin, 1915 – *d* Hampshire, 1991). Cinematographer. Also director. Pre-war, he photographed SHORT FILMS for the Irish Tourist Board, GB INSTRUCTIONAL and other companies, and, post-war, children's films for RANK. Most of his post-war career involved shooting 'B' FILMS, but he contributed notably to the oddly unsettling effect of Lance COMFORT's *Bang! You're Dead* (1953), and directed a couple of minor features, including *The Armchair Detective* (1951). Also shot numerous TV programmes, including Douglas FAIRBANKS's series in the 50s, and worked increasingly for TV after 1960, lighting episodes in such popular series as *Danger Man* and *The Prisoner*. A busy if not especially distinguished career.
OTHER BRITISH FILMS INCLUDE: (short, d, c) *Foolsmate* (1940, Ire), *A Nation Once Again* (1946), *Our Country* (1948, Ire), *Proud Canvas* (1949), *Portrait of Dublin* (1952, Ire), *Forest Pony* (1972); (short, d) *Hermione's Hamburger Heaven* (1950), *Crystal Clear* (1959, Ire); (feature, c) *Fortune Lane* (1947), *Journey for Jeremy* (1949, lighting), *Paul Temple's Triumph* (1950), *Circumstantial Evidence* (1952), *The Genie* (1953), *Eight O'Clock Walk*, *The Red Dress* (1954), *One Jump Ahead* (1955), *Find the Lady* (1956), *There's Always a Thursday* (1957), *Witness in the Dark* (1959), *And Women Shall Weep* (1960), *The Masks of Death* (1984).

Stafford, John (*b* London, 1893 – *d* London, 1966). Producer. RN: Smith. After Hollywood experience, returned to Britain in 1927 as independent producer. Set up John Stafford Productions in the early 30s, sometimes sharing production company credit with a partner such as STOLL, sometimes the credit reading Premier–Stafford Production. In the latter 40s, he formed Pendennis Films, with Stephen PALLOS, first making *Teheran* (1947). He is associated chiefly with three directors: Victor HANBURY, who directed a dozen films for him in the 30s, and with whom he co-directed *No Funny Business* (1933) and *Dick Turpin* (1933); Ladislao VAJDA, who directed several 30s Stafford Productions, including the exotically-set *Wings Over Africa* (1936) and *The Wife of General Ling* (1937), and two later romances with Phyllis CALVERT, *The Golden Madonna* (1949) and *Woman with No Name* (1950), and Ken ANNAKIN, for whom he produced his last four films. These bigger-budget affairs included *The Planter's Wife* (1952), *Across the Bridge* (1957) and *Nor the Moon by Night* (1958), made for RANK.

OTHER BRITISH FILMS INCLUDE: (producer unless noted) *The Inseparables* (1929, co-d), *Where Is This Lady?* (1932, + co-sc), *There Goes Susie* (+co-d), *Spring in the Air* (1934), *Admirals All* (1935), *Beloved Imposter*, *Second Bureau* (1936), *Tomorrow We Live* (assoc p), *The First of the Few* (co-p) (1942), *Candlelight in Algeria* (1943), *Call of the Blood* (1948), *The Stranger's Hand* (1953), *Loser Takes All* (1956).

Stainton, Philip (*b* Kings Norton, 1908 – *d* London, 1961). Actor. Portly character player who appeared in two dozen films between 1948 and 1955 (*Cast a Dark Shadow*, as Dirk BOGARDE's vulgar chum). On stage from 1922, toured with Fred Terry in 1927, made London debut in 1928, and served with the Police Reserve during WW2, this latter no doubt equipping him for the many policemen (like PC Spiller in *Passport to Pimlico*, 1949, and the Sergeant in *The Ladykillers*, 1955) he played in the ensuing decade.
OTHER BRITISH FILMS INCLUDE: *Night Beat* (1948), *Poet's Pub*, *The Blue Lagoon* (1949), *White Corridors* (1951), *Made in Heaven*, *Angels One Five* (1952), *Innocents in Paris*, *Hobson's Choice* (1953), *Up to His Neck* (1954), *John and Julie* (1955), *Moby Dick*, *Who Done It?* (1956).

Stallich, Jan (*b* Prague, 1907 – *d* Prague, 1973). Cinematographer. Czech who worked briefly in Britain during the mid 30s, several times on films involving European settings and personnel, including *Whom the Gods Love* (1936), the Mozart BIOPIC. Famously shot *Extase* (1932, Austria/Czech), starring the nude Hedy Lamarr.
OTHER BRITISH FILMS INCLUDE: *The Silent Passenger* (1935), *The Lonely Road*, *Guilty Melody* (UK/Fr) (1936), *Moonlight Sonata*, *The Show Goes On*, *21 Days* (1937), *Hell Is Empty* (1967, UK/Czech, co-c).

Stamp, Terence (*b* London, 1938). Actor. Confidently working-class and proud of his cockney origins (the son of a Thames tug master), Stamp was one of a new generation of stars with fresh attitudes who found favour in the 60s. And with his soulful, intense looks, ladies found him irresistible, and he soon became associated with a 'swinging 60s' lifestyle, with celebrity girlfriends. After Webber-Douglas training and (brief) theatre experience, he impressed as the angelic, ill-fated young seaman *Billy Budd* (1962, AAn/supp a, BAAn/newcomer). His brooding looks made him ideal for portraying enigmatic, other-worldly characters, such as *The Collector* (1965, UK/US), an unbalanced recluse who kidnaps art student Samantha EGGAR. Resplendent in soldier's uniform, he was a dashing Sergeant Troy in *Far from the Madding Crowd* (1967), impressing Julie CHRISTIE with his sabre display. Bored by the trappings of fame, he spent much of the 70s exploring alternative lifestyles in India, occasionally returning to Europe to appear in continental films. Notable later roles include Prince Lubovedsky in Peter BROOK's *Meetings with Remarkable Men* (1978), and the haunted ex-con in *The Hit* (1984), one of his finest performances. He has appeared in supporting roles in many US films since 1984, and impressed as Bernadette in *The Adventures of Priscilla, Queen of the Desert* (Aust, 1994), a cult international success. In recent years Stamp has appeared in many films though surprisingly few in Britain, but was unquestionably an icon of 60s British cinema.
OTHER BRITISH FILMS: *Term of Trial* (1962), *Modesty Blaise* (1966), *Poor Cow* (1967), *The Mind of Mr Soames* (1969), *Superman* (1978), *Superman II* (1980), *The Company of Wolves* (1984), *Link* (1985), *Revelation* (2002).
BIBLIOG: Autobiographies: *Stamp Album*, 1987; *Coming Attractions*, 1988; *Double Feature*, 1989. Roger Philip Mellor.

Stamp-Taylor, Enid (*b* Whitley Bay, 1904 – *d* London, 1946). Actress. Former beauty-contest winner and blonde leading lady of the 30s, usually in minor films, but spirited and attractive in such roles as John STUART's romantic interest in *Talking Feet* (1937), and a characterful 'other woman' to Gracie FIELDS in *Queen of Hearts* (1936). Died sadly young after a fall, just as she was finding her true métier as a character actress: while scarcely old enough to play Michael WILDING's mother in *The Farmer's Wife* (1941), she is very vivid as Robert NEWTON's barmaid mistress in *Hatter's Castle* (1941) and as the worldly Lady Kingsclere in *The Wicked Lady* (1945). On stage as a dancer from 1922, she appeared in several late silent films from 1927 (*Land of Hope and Glory*).

OTHER BRITISH FILMS INCLUDE: *Easy Virtue* (1927), *Yellow Stockings, Cocktails* (1928), *Meet My Sister* (1933), *Gay Love* (1934), *While Parents Sleep, Radio Pirates,* (1935), *House Broken* (1936), *Action for Slander* (1937), *Stepping Toes, Climbing High* (1938), *The Lambeth Walk* (1939), *Spring Meeting, South American George* (1941), *Alibi* (1942), *Caravan* (1946).

Stander, Lionel (*b* Bronx, New York, 1908 – *d* Los Angeles, 1994). Actor. Gravel-voiced American comic actor, often seen as gangster, who became a sort of European cult figure, having lost his Hollywood career in the wake of the McCarthy witch-hunt trials. Among his British films, the most famous is POLANSKI's black COMEDY, *Cul-de-Sac* (1966), as a wounded gangster who terrorises the occupants of an isolated castle.

OTHER BRITISH FILMS: *Promise Her Anything* (1965), *A Dandy in Aspic* (1968), *Treasure Island* (1972, UK/Fr/Ger/Sp, as Billy Bones), *Pulp* (1972), *The Cassandra Crossing* (1976, UK/Ger/It).

Standing, John (*b* London, 1934). Actor. RN: Leon. A hereditary baronet, the son of actress Kay HAMMOND, grandson of Sir Guy Standing, he does courtesy almost more convincingly than anyone in films, rivalled only by Edward FOX. Glimpsed early as the languid young aristocratic student making fun of class in *The Wild and the Willing* (1962), he was one of Sandy Dennis's boyfriends in *A Touch of Love* (1969) and matured gracefully into character roles, including the understanding husband of *Mrs Dalloway* (1997, UK/Neth/US) and Peter Baring under threat from *Rogue Trader* (1999). On TV, he provided the necessary calm centre for the interlocking lives performing *A Dance to the Music of Time* (1997). Has also appeared in US films, including *The Man Who Knew Too Little* (1997). Married (1) Jill MELFORD and (2) Sarah Forbes.

OTHER BRITISH FILMS INCLUDE: *A Pair of Briefs* (1961), *The Iron Maiden* (1963), *The Psychopath* (1966), *Torture Garden* (1967), *Zee & Co.* (1971), *The Eagle Has Landed* (1976), *The Sea Wolves* (1980, UK/Switz/US), *Privates on Parade* (1982), *Chaplin* (1992, UK/Fr/It/Jap/US), *8½ Women* (1999, UK/Ger/Lux/Neth).

Stanelli (*b* Dublin, 1894 – *d* Datchett, 1961). Radio personality. RN: Edward deGroot. Popular on RADIO in the 30s, violinist-comedian Stanelli appeared in a few, mostly revue-style films, including the SHORT, *The Fiddle Fanatics* (1931) and *Radio Parade* (1933), both with radio partner Edgar, and *Radio Parade of 1935* (1934, with his 'Hornchestra'). He starred in and provided the music for *It Happened to Jane* (1949), and had guest roles in a few others.

OTHER BRITISH FILMS INCLUDE: *Greek Street* (1930), *British Lion Varieties* (series, No. 1), *Hearts of Humanity* (1936), *Give Me the Stars* (1944), *Dear Mr Prohack* (1949).

Stanley, Phyllis (*b* Hitchin, 1914). Actress. Sassy blonde of stage musical comedies, who enlivened a dozen or so British films before going to Hollywood in 1951 for *Thunder on the Hill* and staying there. Worked her way up the cast of WARNER BROS' British-made 'QUOTA QUICKIES' in the 30s; had a couple of good roles at EALING, as the hero's increasingly desperate sister in *There Ain't No Justice* (1939) and the dancer/spy in *The Next of Kin* (1942), but rarely had more than second lead status.

OTHER BRITISH FILMS INCLUDE: *Too Many Millions* (1934), *Hello, Sweetheart* (1935), *Command Performance* (1937), *St Martin's Lane* (1938), *Jeannie* (1941), *We'll Smile Again* (1942), *One Exciting Night* (1944), *Good-Time Girl* (1947), *Look Before You Love* (1948), *That Dangerous Age* (1949).

Stanmore, Frank (*b* London, 1877 – *d* England, 1943). Actor. It is difficult to believe but this plump, jovial character actor was once slim and, on stage (debut 1898), he played the Artful Dodger in *Oliver Twist* in a number of West End productions between 1905 and 1915. He was in more than 80 films, 1912–36, at his best for director George PEARSON in *Squibs, MP, Squibs' Honeymoon* (1923), *Reveille* (1924), *Satan's Sister* (1925), *The Little People* and *Blinkeyes* (1926).

OTHER BRITISH FILMS INCLUDE: *For the Empire* (1914), *The Christian* (1915), *The Manxman* (1916), *London Pride* (1920), *Master and Man* (1929), *The Great Gay Road* (1931), *Don Quixote* (1933), *The Amazing Quest of Ernest Bliss* (1936, UK/US). AS.

Stannard, Don (*b* Westcliffe-on-Sea, 1916 – *d* Cookham Dean, 1949). Actor. Strapping young actor, RADA-trained, who was just making a name for himself as hero of the 'Dick Barton' films (*Dick Barton – Special Agent*, 1948; . . . *Strikes Back*, 1949; . . . *at Bay*, 1950) when he was killed in a car crash. He had small roles in major mid 40s films and starred in some lesser ones, but it was the hearty thick-ear THRILLERS that were his real break. He had an MGM contract pre-war but doesn't seem actually to have made any films in Hollywood, and returned to England to serve in the Royal Navy during WW2.

OTHER BRITISH FILMS: *Caesar and Cleopatra, They Were Sisters, Pink String and Sealing Wax* (1945), *I'll Turn to You* (1946), *Death in High Heels* (1947), *The Temptress* (1949).

Stannard, Eliot (*b* 1888 – *d* London 1944). Screenwriter. Between 1914 and 1929, Stannard scripted over a hundred silent films. In a succession of articles around 1920, he showed that he was alive to the possibilities of the medium at a time of rapid change, and was, in the wake of D.W. Griffith, moving from a simple 'cut and slash' approach to literary ADAPTATION towards more sophisticated models of construction involving cross-cutting and metonymy. After early collaborations with Maurice ELVEY and A.V. BRAMBLE, he began in 1925 an intensive association with a promising new director; the nine silent films that resulted, on seven of which Stannard has sole scenario credit, are at the same time brilliant realisations of the constructional models he had been articulating, and the start of a successful career for Alfred HITCHCOCK. Only Hitchcock's notorious lack of generosity to collaborators, combined with the myopia of a dominant film culture that has shown little interest either in writers or in early British cinema, can explain the obliteration of Stannard, whose career did not survive the conversion to sound, from the critical literature.

BRITISH FILMS INCLUDE: *The Lodger* (1926), *The Manxman* (1929).

BIBLIOG: Eliot Stannard, *Writing Screen Plays*, 1920; Charles Barr, 'Writing Screen Plays: Stannard and Hitchcock', in Andrew Higson (ed), *Young and Innocent? The Cinema in Britain, 1896–1930,* 2002. Charles Barr.

Stapleton, Oliver (*b* London, 1948). Cinematographer. Educated at the University of Capetown and a graduate of the NATIONAL FILM AND TELEVISION SCHOOL (1980), Stapleton has been much associated with the films of director Stephen FREARS, from *My Beautiful Laundrette* (1985), working with him in the US (e.g. on *Accidental Hero*, 1992). He has also worked on films for Julien TEMPLE, and though *Absolute Beginners* (1986) is widely regarded as a disaster Stapleton's lighting of its hard, bright world is exemplary. He was shooting SHORT FILMS while still a student, also worked on the comedy revue film, *The Secret Policeman's Other Ball* (1982), and has shot such high-profile US films as *State and Main* (2000) and *The Shipping News* (2001).

OTHER BRITISH FILMS INCLUDE: (c/co-c) (shorts) *The Wardrobe* (1979), *The Boldon Lad, Sam Sherry* (1980), *Poets Against the Bomb* (1981); (features) *Restless Natives* (1985), *Prick Up Your Ears, Sammy and Rosie Get Laid, Aria* (segment) (1987), *'Let Him Have It'* (1991), *The Snapper* (1993), *Restoration* (1995, UK/US), *The Van* (1996, UK/Ire), *A Midsummer Night's Dream* (1999, UK/It).

Stark, Graham (*b* Wallasey, 1922). Actor. Comic supporting player of dozens of British films, usually in small roles but, also, usually memorable, like his waiter in *Victor/Victoria* (1982) and in several 'Clouseau' films as Peter SELLERS' off-sider, or as Humphrey whose homely virtues are made to look nerdish in the shadow of Michael CAINE's *Alfie* (1966). Also, much radio and television; a friend of Sellers', he appeared in the Goons' attempts to transfer their RADIO humour to the screen in *Down Among the Z Men* (1952) and *The Running Jumping & Standing Still Film* (1960, short).

OTHER BRITISH FILMS INCLUDE: *Emergency Call* (1952), *Flannelfoot* (1953), *Inn for Trouble* (1959), *Sink the Bismarck!* (1960), *Only Two Can Play, A Pair of Briefs* (1961), *The Wrong Arm of the Law* (1962), *The Mouse on the Moon* (1963), *Becket, A Shot in the Dark* (1964), *Those Magnificent Men . . .* (1965), *The Wrong Box* (1966), *The Magic Christian* (1969), *Magnificent Seven Deadly Sins* (1971, d, p, co-sc), *Hide and Seek* (1972), *Return of the Pink Panther* (1974), *Scrooge* (1975), *Revenge of the Pink Panther* (1978), *The Sea Wolves* (1980, UK/Switz/US), *Victor/Victoria, Trail of the Pink Panther* (1982), *Superman III* (1983), *Moonacre* (1995, UK/Czech).

BIBLIOG: Autobiography, *Stark Naked*, 2002.

Starr, Ringo *see* **Beatles, The**

star system in Britain It is a moot point whether there ever really has been a star system in British cinema. British producers started putting actors under contract at around the same time as their American counterparts. By 1910–11, the names of Cecil HEPWORTH's contract players (Gladys SYLVANI and Chrissie WHITE among them) were appearing regularly in the trade press. Throughout the silent era, 'stars' from stage and music hall (Sir Johnston FORBES-ROBERTSON, Sir Herbert TREE, George ROBEY, Billy MERSON) were lured in front of the cameras. In the 20s, Ivor NOVELLO was briefly touted as Britain's answer to Valentino and such homely, home-grown actresses as Betty BALFOUR, Alma TAYLOR and Mabel POULTON were held in enormous affection by British fans, but studios and publicists were not prepared (or not able) to invest in promoting new talent in the same brash way as their Hollywood rivals.

Each decade, there was a new attempt at establishing a star system. Alexander KORDA in the 30s established his own repertory company at London Films, putting the likes of Merle OBERON, Wendy BARRIE, John LODER, Emlyn WILLIAMS and Robert DONAT under contract. He also helped Charles LAUGHTON to become the first British actor to win an Oscar (for *The Private Life of Henry VIII*, 1933.) Dancing divinity Jessie MATTHEWS, her career nurtured along by director Victor SAVILLE, Anna NEAGLE, promoted by Svengali-like Herbert WILCOX, and Gracie FIELDS and George FORMBY all became major stars in the years leading up to WW2.

Edward BLACK and Maurice OSTRER at GAINSBOROUGH in the 40s made a thoroughgoing attempt at creating their own stable of stars: Margaret LOCKWOOD, Phyllis CALVERT, Stewart GRANGER, Eric PORTMAN, Patricia ROC, James MASON, John MILLS and Jean KENT were all groomed for celebrity. They featured in advertising campaigns, the actresses wore gowns designed by famous fashion houses, and they made personal appearances. Nevertheless, *Picturegoer*, the best-selling British fan magazine first published in 1921, continued to feature more Hollywood than British stars.

Sydney BOX set up the COMPANY OF YOUTH at RIVERSIDE STUDIOS at the end of the WW2. His intention was to offer youngsters a screen acting apprenticeship, but, when he was hired by RANK in 1947 to run Gainsborough, the Company of Youth quickly mutated into the Charm School (the name was coined by journalists.) Anthony STEEL, Christopher LEE, Pete MURRAY and Diana DORS are among the more celebrated graduates from this unusual academy, but many sceptics argued that the real idea behind the Charm School was to unearth as many pretty girls as possible to introduce a little glamour into austerity-era Britain. Few of its charges went on to have substantial movie careers.

The RANK ORGANISATION, like the Hollywood studios it was trying to emulate, had its own contract system. As late as the mid 50s, it had over 50 artistes under contract. This was the decade of the 'chap,' the leading man in tweed jacket and slacks portrayed by publicists as if he was a country squire. (The likes of Kenneth MORE, John GREGSON and – a little uncomfortably – Dirk BOGARDE, were made to fit this mould.) As the 50s wore on, and Rank and ASSCCIATED-BRITISH made cutbacks, stars' contracts were not renewed. British films were still being made in considerable quantity and new British actors were continuing to emerge, but the rules had changed. There was a new emphasis on internationalism as Britain paid court to runaway American productions. Stars emerged even more regularly than before. From Julie CHRISTIE to Ewan McGREGOR, from Michael CAINE to Jude LAW, any number of new British faces became as well known as their Hollywood counterparts, but the difference now was that they were as likely to be attached to individual producers or to have their careers managed by AGENTS as to be tied to big studios. The star system – such as it existed – was coming to an end.

BIBLIOG: John Russell Taylor and John Kobal, *Portraits of the British Cinema*, 1985; Geoffrey Macnab, *Searching for Stars*, 2000. Geoffrey Macnab.

Stassino, Paul (*b* Limassol, Cyprus – *d* 1983). Actor. Memorable as Palazzi, who undergoes plastic surgery and whose greed does for him in *Thunderball* (1965), the dark-haired Greek actor played assorted Europeans – sometimes even Greeks, as in *A Boy Is Ten Feet Tall* (1963) – in British films from the mid 50s. In comic mode, he was an Italian crim in *The Man Who Liked Funerals* (1958 – 'To Nick, a good son and a fine gangster, Love Ma' reads one of the floral tributes at his demise) – and Le Pirate, a French desperado, in *That Riviera Touch* (1966). Also a popular multinational support in such TV programmes as *Danger Man* (1961) and *The Avengers* (1962).

OTHER BRITISH FILMS INCLUDE: *Ill Met By Moonlight* (1956), *Ice Cold in Alex* (1958), *The Bandit of Zhobe, Tiger Bay, The Stranglers of Bombay* (1959), *The Secret Partner, The Roman Spring of Mrs Stone* (1961), *Stolen Hours* (UK/US), *The Long Ships* (UK/Yug) (1963), *The High Bright Sun* (1965), *The Private Life of Sherlock Holmes* (1970), *Escape to Athena* (1979).

Statham, Jason (*b* England, 1972). Actor. Statham got the part of the balding thug, Bacon, in *Lock, Stock and Two Smoking Barrels* (1998) by conning director Guy RITCHIE about his previous experience, and Ritchie cast him again, as Turkish, in the yet more complicated heist piece, *Snatch* (2000). He simply went from film to film around the turn of the century, on both sides of the Atlantic.

OTHER BRITISH FILM: *The Mean Machine* (2001, UK/US).

Staunton, Imelda (*b* 1958). Actress. Marvellously droll stage and screen actress who has made a career out of being a homely semi-neurotic. In *Antonia and Jane* (1990), she is of course the plain one whose boyfriend is only aroused if she reads *Wuthering Heights* to him, whereas Antonia is effortlessly glamorous and successful. In *Peter's Friends* (1992) she can't enjoy a weekend away without constantly phoning the babysitter. In *Sense and Sensibility* (1995, UK/US), she is very funny as the imbecilic Mrs Palmer and in *Twelfth Night* (1996, UK/US) she is the scheming Maria. On stage, often with the RSC and the National, her range has been much broader, encompassing comedy, drama and musicals, winning several awards (e.g. in *Into the Woods*, 1991). Her many TV credits have included *The Singing Detective* (1986), in which her husband, Jim CARTER, also appeared.

OTHER BRITISH FILMS: *Comrades* (1986), *Much Ado about Nothing* (1993, UK/US), *Deadly Advice* (1994), *Shakespeare in Love* (1999, UK/US).

Steadman, Alison (*b* Liverpool, 1946). Actress. Very gifted, in drama or comedy, trained at East 15 Acting School, former secretary Steadman made her stage debut in 1968 and has worked at London's National Theatre (in *The Rise and Fall of Little Voice*), the RSC and the Old Vic. Repeated her acclaimed stage role in former husband Mike LEIGH's *Abigail's Party* on TV (1977) when Leigh was trying to break into film, and appeared memorably in several of his cinema films: in *Life is Sweet* (1990), as the wife of a family stretched to survive, and brief but vivid bits in *Secrets & Lies* (1996) and *Topsy-Turvy* (2000, UK/US). She made her feature debut as the teacher in *P'tang Yang Kipperbang* (1982), was wife to John CLEESE's increasingly distraught headmaster in *Clockwise* (1985) and the domineering wife of *Wilt* (1989) who is suspected of murdering her. On TV since the 60s, she was in several of Leigh's tele-movies, had a dual role in *The Singing Detective* (1986) and, just once, overacted shrilly as Mrs Bennett in *Pride and Prejudice* (1995). Awarded OBE, 2000.

OTHER BRITISH FILMS INCLUDE: *Champions* (1983), *A Private Function* (1984), *Stormy Monday* (1987), *Shirley Valentine* (1989, UK/US), *Blame It on the Bellboy* (1992), *Happy Now* (2001).

Steafel, Susan (aka Staefel) (*b* Johannesburg, 1939). Actress. South African supporting actress in British films and TV since the mid 60s. She is the journalist to whom James DONALD talks about 'one of the most remarkable finds ever made' in an early sequence of *Quatermass and the Pit* (1967) and her TV includes *The Frost Report* (1966) and *The World of Beachcomber* (1968). Film roles thinned out after the 70s. Married and divorced from Harry H. CORBETT.

OTHER BRITISH FILMS INCLUDE: *Daleks – Invasion Earth 2150 AD* (1966), *Baby Love* (1967), *Otley* (1968), *Goodbye, Mr Chips*, (1969), *SWALK* (1970), *Percy*, *Catch Me a Spy* (UK/Fr/US) (1971), *Are You Being Served?* (1977), *Bloodbath at the House of Death* (1983), *Parting Shots* (1998).

Stears, John (*b* Uxbridge, 1934 – *d* Los Angeles, 1999). Special effects artist. Best known for his work on the BOND movies,

Spears won an Oscar for his contribution to *Thunderball* (1965). He orchestrated major effects sequences such as the Aston Martin chase (complete with ejector seat) in *Goldfinger* (1964) and devised minor but eye-catching felicities like the poisoned spikes in Rosa Kleb's boots in *From Russia with Love* (1963). He also designed the amphibious flying car in *Chitty Chitty Bang Bang* (1968) and shared an Oscar for *Star Wars* (1977, US), claiming to dislike films in which special effects dominated. Trained at Harrow College of Art, he joined the RANK ORGANISATION in 1955, devising model aircraft and ships for such films as *Reach for the Sky* (1956) and *A Night to Remember* (1958). Finished his career in the US.

OTHER BRITISH FILMS INCLUDE: *Sink the Bismarck!* (1960), *You Only Live Twice* (1967), *On Her Majesty's Secret Service* (1969), *Toomorrow* (1970), *The Pied Piper* (1971), *Sitting Target* (1972), *Theatre of Blood*, *O Lucky Man!* (1973), *That Lucky Touch* (1975), *The Thief of Baghdad* (1978, UK/Fr), *The Awakening* (1980, UK/US), *Outland* (1981), *The Bounty* (1984).

Steel, Anthony (*b* London, 1920 – *d* London, 2001). Actor. One of the more successful products of the RANK 'CHARM SCHOOL', Cambridge-educated Steel graduated from small supporting roles to stardom with *The Wooden Horse* (1950) where his muscular physique contrasted with the pigeon chests of his fellow POWs. Dubbed the 'Wooden Dish', this tall, hand-some and athletic ex-Grenadier Guardsman was one of the few 50s British male stars who could play effectively in ACTION ADVENTURE FILMS, both WAR FILMS – *Albert RN* (1953), and *The Black Tent* (1956), his most romantic role – and 'EMPIRE' films, including *Where No Vultures Fly* (1951), his most popular film, and its sequel, *West of Zanzibar* (1954), where he played a game park warden, saving African wildlife from poachers. *Storm over the Nile* (1955), Alexander KORDA's attempt to remake *The Four Feathers* in CinemaScope, was unsuccessful, and Steel's fame in the late 50s came from being Anita EKBERG's husband. Their marriage, and his hopes of Hollywood stardom, lasted only three years. After this point his career plummeted through the depths of Italian and German 'B' features before hitting bottom with British porn films such as *Let's Get Laid* (1977), a sad end for an actor born a generation too late.

OTHER BRITISH FILMS: *Saraband for Dead Lovers*, *Portrait from Life*, *A Piece of Cake*, *Trottie True* (1948), *Poet's Pub*, *Marry Me*, *Helter Skelter*, *Don't Ever Leave Me*, *The Chiltern Hundreds*, *The Blue Lamp* (1949), *The Mudlark* (1950), *Laughter in Paradise* (1951), *Another Man's Poison*, *The Planter's Wife*, *Something Money Can't Buy*, *Emergency Call* (1952), *The Master of Ballantrae*, *Malta Story* (1953), *The Sea Shall Not Have Them* (1954), *Passage Home*, *Out of the Clouds* (1955), *Checkpoint* (1956), *Harry Black*, *A Question of Adultery* (1958), *Honeymoon* (1959), *The Switch*, *A Matter of Choice* (1963), *Hell Is Empty* (1967), *Hardcore* (1977), *The World Is Full of Married Men* (1979), *The Monster Club*, *The Mirror Crack'd* (1980). Andrew Spicer.

Steele, Barbara (*b* Liverpool, 1937). Actress. Tall, willowy, sensual Steele had to go to Italy to become an international cult figure for the terrible things she did and had done to her in dozens of HORROR films. Trained as a painter and sculptor, she was sidetracked into the theatre where she worked in rep, made her TV debut in *Dial 999* (1938) and her first film was *Bachelor of Hearts* (1958), and she also had small roles in *Upstairs and Downstairs* (1959) and *Your Money or Your Wife* (1960), but it was Mario Bava's *La Maschera del demonia* (1960, It) and Roger Corman's *The Pit and the Pendulum* (1961, US), with Vincent PRICE, which determined the way her career would go, to the gratification of horror fans everywhere. Was married to notable US screenwriter James Poe.

OTHER BRITISH FILMS: *Revenge of the Blood Beast* (1965, UK/It), *Curse of the Crimson Altar* (1968).

Steele, Tommy (*b* London, 1936). Actor, singer. RN: Thomas Hicks. A diminutive light-haired cockney with a genial grin and guitar appears on a nightclub stage in the forgotten 'B' film *Kill Me Tomorrow* (1957) and performs 'Rock with the Cave Man' – the ignominious beginning of rock music in British movies. In 1956, Hicks had met Lionel BART and Mike Pratt, two songwriter-performers, and they formed a skiffle group 'The Cavemen', who began playing in Soho coffee bars, and caused a sensation. Record and film offers soon appeared. Semi-autobiographical, *The Tommy Steele Story* (1957) was hurriedly filmed to cash in on the new phenomenon. He was a hit as Kipps in the stage musical *Half A Sixpence* (London 1963, NY 1965), and in the UK/US film version (1967). This led to starring roles in Hollywood musicals *The Happiest Millionaire* (1967) and *Finian's Rainbow* (1968). Since the 70s, exclusively on stage. Always too eager to please an audience to be a convincing rocker, he is a born entertainer with an ebullient extrovert personality. Awarded OBE in 1979.

OTHER BRITISH FILMS: *The Duke Wore Jeans* (1958), *Tommy the Toreador* (1959), *Light Up the Sky* (1960), *It's All Happening* (1963), *Where's Jack?* (1969). Roger Philip Mellor.

Steiger, Rod (*b* Westhampton, NY, 1925– *d* Los Angeles, 2002). Actor. One of the most celebrated exponents of the New York Actors' Studio's 'Method' technique, the hefty Steiger had a 50-year career embracing all the acting media and several continents. Sometimes overpowering company under the camera's close scrutiny, but his best work rivets the attention with its intensity and lived-in conviction. Of his handful of British films, the first, *Across the Bridge* (1957), a tense ADAPTATION of Graham GREENE, contains one of his most restrained performances, and, in Peter HALL's drama of sexual mores, *Three into Two Won't Go* (1968), Steiger co-starred with his then-wife (1959–69) Claire BLOOM. Won AA as the racial bigot in *In the Heat of the Night* (1967, US).

OTHER BRITISH FILMS: *The Mark* (1961), *Dr Zhivago* (1965, UK/US), *Hennessy* (1975), *American Gothic* (1987), *That Summer of White Roses* (1989, UK/Yug).

Stein, Paul L(udwig) (*b* Vienna, 1892 – *d* London, 1951). Director. Directing career at UFA from 1920; from 1926 fifteen films in Hollywood. Stein moved to Britain in 1932, specialising in romantic comedies, operettas and MUSICALS (often starring Richard TAUBER, who introduced 'Pedro the Fisherman' in *Lisbon Story*, 1946), though he also made several taut 'B' THRILLERS (*The Saint Meets The Tiger*, 1943; *Counterblast*, 1948). In the 40s he mostly worked for BRITISH NATIONAL, which gave him some uphill work with Anne ZIEGLER and Webster BOOTH in the leaden musicals, *Waltz Time* (1945) and *The Laughing Lady* (1946).

OTHER BRITISH FILMS INCLUDE: *Lily Christine* (1932), *Red Wagon* (1934), *Blossom Time* (1934), *Mimi* (1935), *Faithful* (1936), *Café Colette* (1937), *Black Limelight* (1938), *Poison Pen, The Outsider* (1939), *Talk About Jacqueline* (1942), *Twilight Hour* (1944), *The Twenty Questions Murder Mystery* (1950). Tim Bergfelder.

Stellman, Martin (*b* 1943). Director. Oddly truncated career, the highspot of which is the taut screenplay for the POLITICAL THRILLER, *Defence of the Realm* (1985), which skilfully meshes private pecadilloes and public dangers. His feature debut as director, *For Queen and Country* (1988, UK/US, co-sc), on the other hand, makes a mess of both its personal drama and the political resonances.

OTHER BRITISH FILMS: (co-sc) *Quadrophenia* (1979), *Babylon* (1980), (d) *Cheap Perfume* (1980, short).

Stepanek, Karel (*b* Brünn, Moravia, 1899 – *d* Los Angeles, 1981). Actor. Gaunt, dark, and Slavic-looking supporting player of numerous British, European, and Hollywood productions. On stage in Europe from 1920, London 1941, he had played in several dozen Continental films before making his first British appearances in a series of SPY THRILLERS. Frequently typecast as Nazi or as Eastern European spy; for example, as the Gestapo officer in *The Cafptive Heart* (1946); may also be glimpsed as one of the actors in the theatre scene in *The Third Man* (1949). Once married to **Wanda Rotha** (*see* Whiley MANNING).

OTHER BRITISH FILMS INCLUDE: *Secret Mission* (1942), *Our Film* (1942, short), *Escape To Danger, They Met In The Dark* (1943), *Counterblast, The Fallen Idol, Broken Journey* (1948), *Conspirator, Give Us This Day* (1949), *Cairo Road, State Secret* (1950), *Our Man In Havana* (1959), *Sink the Bismarck!* (1960), *Operation Crossbow* (1965, UK/It). Tim Bergfelder.

Stephen, Susan (*b* London, 1931 – *d* Sussex, 2000). Actress. Mid 50s star with pretty 'English Rose' complexion, short wavy hair, middle-class looks and manner, in limited range of roles. RADA-trained, she entered films with *His Excellency* (1951), donned WRAF uniform for WARWICK's *The Red Beret* (1953), was Dirk BOGARDE's young bride in the comedy *For Better, for Worse* (1954), starred in RANK's *Value for Money* (1955), in the latter, vying with Diana DORS for the affections of stingy Yorkshire businessman John GREGSON. Image-bound, she was perfect as Denholm ELLIOTT's young colonial wife in *Pacific Destiny* (1956). Three starring roles for the DANZIGERS ended her film career rather ignominiously. Married to Nicolas ROEG (1957–77) and actor Lawrence Ward.

OTHER BRITISH FILMS INCLUDE: *Father's Doing Fine* (1952), *The House Across the Lake, Golden Ivory* (1954), *It's Never Too Late, The Barretts of Wimpole Street* (1956), *Carry On Nurse* (1958), *Three Spare Wives* (1962). Roger Philip Mellor.

Stephens, Ann (*b* London, 1931). Actress. Child player who had a good run in the 40s, starting as Noël COWARD's daughter in *In Which We Serve* (1942), and having rewarding opportunities as the young *Fanny by Gaslight* (1944), as Anne CRAWFORD's unwanted daughter in *They Were Sisters* (1945), and, best of all, the mendacious Betty in *The Franchise Affair* (1950). Like so many child actors, she drifted out of films in adulthood.

OTHER BRITISH FILMS INCLUDE: *Dear Octopus* (1943), *The Upturned Glass* (1947), *No Room at the Inn* (1948), *Your Witness* (1950), *The Good Beginning* (1953), *Doublecross* (1955), *Intent to Kill* (1958).

Stephens, Martin (*b* London, 1949). Actor. Child player who later gave up acting and became an architect, but not before giving at least one remarkable performance – as the child driven to his death by who knows what demons in *The Innocents* (1961). Had a few other good roles, notably as Glynis JOHNS's son in the wet romance, *Another Time, Another Place* (1958), and as George SANDERS's son in the alarming SCI-FI movie, *Village of the Damned* (1960).

OTHER BRITISH FILMS INCLUDE: *The Divided Heart* (1954), *Passionate Summer, Harry Black* (1958), *The Witness* (1959), *The Battle of the Villa Fiorita* (1965, UK/US), *The Witches* (1966).

Stephens, Sir Robert (*b* Bristol, 1931 – *d* London, 1995). Actor. Films never quite corralled the wayward, lankily raffish persona of Stephens, though there are several remarkable performances that leave one wishing there were more. Trained at the Northern Theatre School, Bradford, he was on the

London stage from 1956, as a member of the Royal Court's English Stage Company. He had immense success with the National Theatre in the 60s, notably as Benedick to then-wife Maggie SMITH's Beatrice (1965), becoming an associate director of the National in 1969. The wonder is that he fitted in as many films as he did. His caddish fancy man in *A Taste of Honey* (1961) resonates with some infinitesimally minor public school and a lifetime of conning impressionable women; caddish again, he is one of Smith's swains in *The Prime of Miss Jean Brodie* (1968); he is a finely flamboyant Pistol in BRANAGH's *Henry V* (1989); and he gives his one sublime screen performance in the title role in *The Private Life of Sherlock Holmes* (1970). Here, all his physical attributes and the other sorts of baggage (battered, romantic) he carries with him, never quite right for conventional film leading man roles, are pressed into service by a great director, Billy WILDER, working from a screenplay which meshes comedy, pathos, romance and mystery to perfection. Actors Toby STEPHENS and Chris Larkins (*see* Maggie SMITH) are his sons.

OTHER BRITISH FILMS: *Circle of Deception* (1960), *The Queen's Guards* (1961), *Lunch Hour, The Inspector, The Small World of Sammy Lee* (1962), *Morgan: A Suitable Case for Treatment* (1966), *Romeo and Juliet* (1968, UK/It), *The Asphyx* (1972), *Luther* (1973, UK/Can/US), *The Duellists* (1977), *The Shout* (1978), *Comrades* (1986), *High Season, Testimony* (1987), *The Fruit Machine, American Roulette* (1988), *The Children* (1990, UK/Ger), *The Pope Must Die* (UK/US), *Afraid of the Dark* (UK/Fr), *Ferdydurke* (UK/Fr/Pol/US) (1991), *Chaplin* (1992, UK/Fr/It/Jap/US), *The Secret Rapture, Century* (1993), *England, My England* (1995).

Stephens, Toby (*b* London, 1969). Actor. Given his lineage (son of Robert STEPHENS and Maggie SMITH), it is not surprising that Stephens should seem like one of the most extravagantly promising actors of his generation. Entering the theatre as a stagehand at Chichester, he went on to give a mesmeric (and award-winning) account of *Coriolanus* for the RSC in 1995, commanding the stage in a way that made his stocky person seem ten feet tall and imbuing this complex role with full measure of passion and rage. On TV he has done choice work as the dogged, decent Gilbert in *The Tenant of Wildfell Hall* (1996) and in Stephen POLIAKOFF's acclaimed *Perfect Strangers* (2001). Entered films in *Orlando* (1992, UK/Fr/It/Neth/Russ), was a notably human Orsino in Trevor NUNN's *Twelfth Night* (1996, UK/US) and very moving as loyal, doomed Lensky in *Onegin* (1999, UK/US). Has appeared in US films several times since then, including a co-starring role in *Possession* (2002, UK/US), from A.S. Byatt's literary tease.

OTHER BRITISH FILMS INCLUDE: *Photographing Fairies* (1997), *Cousin Bette* (1998, UK/US), *The Announcement* (2000, UK/US), *Die Another Day* (2002, UK/US).

Stephenson, James (*b* Yorkshire, 1889 – *d* Pacific Palisades, California, 1941). Actor. After unremarkable roles in largely forgotten British films, mostly for producer Irving ASHER at WARNER BROS–BRITISH, he went to Hollywood where Warners gave him better parts in thirty films, notably *The Old Maid* (1939) and *The Letter* (1940), before his untimely death following a heart attack. Gravely elegant, he became a minor star; his only starring role in England was away from Warners, as a gentleman crook in John ARGYLE's *Dangerous Fingers* (1938).

OTHER BRITISH FILMS INCLUDE: *Transatlantic Trouble, The Perfect Crime, Mr Satan* (1937), *It's in the Blood, The Dark Stairway* (1938).

Stephenson, Pamela (*b* Auckland, NZ, 1950). Actress. Married since 1989 to Billy CONNOLLY by whom she has three children, lively blonde Stephenson made her name in such British TV as *Not the Nine O'Clock News* (1979–80, 1982), has made a handful of British films since *Stand Up Virgin Soldiers* (1977) and the revue film, *The Secret Policeman's Other Ball* (1982), as well as a couple in Australia. Now a practising psychologist, she has retired from acting. First married TV actor **Nicholas Ball** (*b* Leamington, 1946), of TV's 'Hazell' series (1978–79) and a couple of British films, including *Lifeforce* (1985) and *Croupier* (1998, UK/Fr/Ger/Ire).

OTHER BRITISH FILMS: *The Comeback* (1977), *Superman III* (1983), *Bloodbath at the House of Death, Scandalous* (1983).

Sterke, Jeannette (*b* Prague, 1934). Actress. Educated in France before settling in England and enrolling at RADA. The auburn-haired Sterke acted with the Old Vic, worked in radio and TV (Anne Boleyn in *The White Falcon*, 1956), and made her film debut in the only female role in *The Prisoner* (1955). Appeared in such international films as *Lust for Life* (1956) and *The Nun's Story* (1959), and a handful of British films, without becoming a star, though she was Norman WISDOM's leading lady in *A Stitch in Time* (1963). Long married to Keith MICHELL, with whom she starred in *Moments* (1973).

OTHER BRITISH FILMS: *Final Column* (1955), *The Safecracker* (1957), *Live Now, Pay Later* (1962), *The Double* (1963).

Sterling, Joseph (*b* 1916). Director, editor. Former commercial artist in films as assistant director, then in the cutting-room, from 1936; served as cameraman with the ARMY FILM UNIT from 1940, and post-war acted chiefly as editor, though he also directed two 1955 films: the Goons' SHORT, *The Case of the Mukkinese Battlehorn* and a 'B' MOVIE espionage tale, *Cloak and Dagger*. He is credited as editor on *Whisky Galore!* (1949) but in fact Charles CRICHTON took over to reassemble the footage. After this, he edited chiefly second features in the 50s.

OTHER BRITISH FILMS INCLUDE: (e) *Green Fingers, The Ghosts of Berkeley Square* (1947), *The Weaker Sex* (1948), *There Was a Young Lady* (1953), *Orders Are Orders* (1954), *The Love Match* (1955).

Sterndale-Bennett, Joan (*b* London, 1914 – *d* Hayling Island, 1996). Actress. Supporting player of stage and screen. She had a dozen or so small roles between Anthony ASQUITH's MOI SHORT, *Rush Hour* (1941), about British workers at rush hours, and *All at Sea* (1969), was Delia, one of the two giggling girls on the beach early in *Brighton Rock* (1947), a WAAF in *Angels One Five* (1952), and Queen Victoria in *Jules Verne's Rocket to the Moon* (1967).

OTHER BRITISH FILMS INCLUDE: (a, unless noted) *Love, Life and Laughter* (1934, co-story), *We Dive at Dawn* (1943), *Tawny Pipit* (1944), *Poet's Pub* (1949), *Bow Bells* (1954), *The Spider's Web* (1960), *Don't Bother to Knock* (1961), *Decline and Fall . . .* (1968).

Stevens, C(harles) C(yril) (*b* Andover, 1907 – *d* Sutton Green, 1974). Music recordist. Associated with two AA nominations for sound recording, for *Goodbye, Mr Chips* (1939) and *One of Our Aircraft is Missing* (1942), Stevens entered films in 1930 in Paris, involved in the post-synchronising of foreign versions of US films. At PINEWOOD from 1932 to 1937 and became chief production mixer at DENHAM STUDIOS from 1937. Responsible for the sound recording of many notable British films, including some of Michael POWELL's major achievements.

OTHER BRITISH FILMS INCLUDE: *The Citadel* (1938), *Contraband* (1940), *49th Parallel* (1941), *In Which We Serve* (1942), *The Life and Death of Colonel Blimp* (1943), *The Way Ahead, A Canterbury Tale* (1944), *I Know Where I'm Going!* (1945), *A Matter of Life and Death* (1946), *Trio* (1950), *The Long Memory* (1952), *Genevieve* (1953), *Simon and Laura* (1955), *The One That Got Away* (1957), *Carve Her Name With Pride* (1958), *Peeping Tom* (1960), *Victim* (1961), *Tiara Tahiti* (1962), *Carry On Spying* (1964), *The Early Bird* (1965), *Pretty Polly* (1967).

Stevens, Dorinda (*b* Southampton, 1932). Actress. Blonde supporting player of about 20 films from the early 50s to the mid 60s, mainly in small roles, some of them quite eye-catching, an unfortunate epithet considering what happens to her in the opening sequence of *Horrors of the Black Museum* (1959) when she looks through a pair of spiked binoculars. She is also the spirited one of a pair of music hall girls dining privately with lascivious toffs in *Jack the Ripper* (1958).
OTHER BRITISH FILMS INCLUDES: *It Started in Paradise* (1952), *The Golden Link* (1954), *Confession* (1955), *The Shakedown* (1959), *Make Mine Mink, Carry On Constable* (1960), *Raising the Wind* (1961), *Night Without Pity* (1962), *Carry On Jack* (1964).

Stevens, Ronnie (*b* London, 1925). Actor. Attended Camberwell School of Art prior to war service in the RAF (1943–47), making his stage debut in 1948 (London, 1953), establishing himself as a revue artiste, and a straight actor who played Shakespearean clowns as well as pantomime dames. Had small roles in about 40 films, from 1952 (*Top Secret, Made in Heaven*), including light comedies of the 'DOCTOR' SERIES and a 'CARRY ON' (*Cruising*, 1962), and was still playing cameos in the 90s, such as the Albert Hall judge in the finale to *Brassed Off* (1996, UK/US). Much TV, including revue in Australia's *The Mavis Branston Show* (1966) and *Twelfth Night* (1980).
OTHER BRITISH FILMS INCLUDE: *The Embezzler* (1954), *Value for Money* (1955), *Danger Within* (1958), *I'm All Right Jack* (1959), *Doctor in Love, Dentist in the Chair* (1960), *It's Trad, Dad!, On the Beat* (1962), *Those Magnificent Men . . .* (1965), *Smashing Time* (1967), *Goodbye, Mr Chips* (1969), *Morons from Outer Space* (1985), *Killing Dad* (1989), *Blame It on the Bellboy* (1992).

Stevenson, Juliet (*b* Kelvedon, 1956). Actress. RN: Juliette Stevens. Highly regarded stage actress who went straight from RADA to the RSC, doing a series of Shakespearean heroines, including a brilliant Isabella in *Measure for Measure* (1983–84), as well as some striking modern plays such as *Death and the Maiden*. Best known to filmgoers for her poignant performance as the woman coming to terms with grief and new love in the popular romance, *Truly Madly Deeply* (1990), but has had no comparable starring opportunity since, though she was properly grating as the egregious Mrs Elton in *Emma* (1996, UK/US).
OTHER BRITISH FILMS INCLUDE: *Drowning by Numbers* (1988, UK/Neth), *The Trial* (1992), *The Secret Rapture* (1993), *The Search for John Gissing* (2001, UK/US), *The One and Only, Bend It like Beckham* (UK/Ger/US) (2002), *Nicholas Nickleby* (2003, UK/US).

Stevenson, Robert (*b* Buxton, 1905 – *d* Santa Barbara, California, 1986). Director, screenwriter. Working for the DISNEY ORGANISATION in the US from 1957, Stevenson became one of the most successful directors in the world in box-office terms, but it would not be too eccentric to prefer his 30s British GENRE films, made largely for GAINSBOROUGH. Certainly he is better known now as the purveyor of such glossy, award-winning, ersatz Englishry as *Mary Poppins* (1964) and *Bedknobs and Broomsticks* (1971), than for such intelligent entertainments as his last two films before going to Hollywood

to take up an unproductive contract with David O. Selznick: the vivacious, surprisingly abrasive cross-class romantic comedy, *Young Man's Fancy* (1939, + story) and that sweet-tempered but uncloying valentine to provincial theatre, *Return to Yesterday* (1940, + co-sc), both starring his then-wife, Anna LEE.

Cambridge-educated in the mechanical sciences and psychology, he caught the attention of Michael BALCON, then heading Gainsborough, and finished his British career with Balcon at EALING. He started as a writer, on several films for Victor SAVILLE, including *The Faithful Heart* (1933), and other major directors at the studio. The films he directed reveal him as the British genre director *par excellence* of the period. Apart from the romantic comedies mentioned, he made his name with the poignant HISTORICAL DRAMA, *Tudor Rose* (1936), with Nova PILBEAM as Lady Jane Grey; and also directed the SCIENCE-FICTION tale, *The Man Who Changed His Mind* (1936), the African ADVENTURE, *King Solomon's Mines* (1937), the nifty THRILLER, *Non-Stop New York* (1937), all starring Lee, and the drama of RURAL LIFE, *Owd Bob* (1938). It is a diverse and pleasing line-up, its very diversity perhaps working against Stevenson's receiving full credit for his unobtrusive craftsmanship. He made only two further British films after 1940: a respectable version of *Kidnapped* (1960), with Peter FINCH, and the Disney co-production, *In Search of the Castaways* (1961). He ended by having a nearly 50-year career, and it would be a pity to overlook the black-and-white pleasures that came out of pre-war suburban London.
OTHER BRITISH FILMS: (co-sc, unless noted) *Greek Street* (1930), *Sunshine Susie, Michael and Mary, The Calendar, The Ringer* (1931), *Love on Wheels, Lord Babs, Happy Ever After* (1932), *The Only Girl, FPI, Early to Bed, Falling For You* (+ d) (1933), *Little Friend* (assoc p), *The Battle* (UK/Fr), *The Camels are Coming* (assoc p) (1934), *Windbag the Sailor* (1936, co-story), (d) *Jack of All Trades* (1936, co-d), *The Ware Case* (1938).
BIBLIOG: Brian McFarlane, 'Jack of All Trades: Robert Stevenson', in Jeffrey Richards (ed), *The Unknown 1930s*, 1998.

Stevenson, Robert Louis (*b* Edinburgh, 1850 – *d* Vailima, Samoa, 1894). Author. *Dr Jekyll and Mr Hyde* (1886), one of modern literature's most famous studies of man's nature torn between its higher and lower impulses, was first filmed in the US in 1908, marking the start of the cinema's passion for the works of the Scottish former engineer and lawyer who became one of the most popular of all Victorian novelists. About 90 films and TV series have been made, in many languages, from such famous works as *Jekyll and Hyde* (most distinguished is still Rouben Mamoulian's 1931 US version), *Treasure Island* (1883), combining south-coast smuggling and South Seas romance, and the Scottish adventures, *Kidnapped* (1886) and *The Master of Ballantrae* (1889). All these have been filmed in Britain, though less prolifically than elsewhere. *Jekyll and Hyde* was filmed silently as *The Duality of Man* (1910), and later as *The Two Faces of Dr Jekyll* (1960), *I, Monster* and *Dr Jekyll & Sister Hyde* (1971), DISNEY made *Treasure Island* in 1950, and a UK/US version appeared in 1999; *Kidnapped*, several times adapted in the US, was filmed in Britain in 1960 (with Peter FINCH) and 1971 (with Michael CAINE), *The Master of Ballantrae* (1953), starred an ageing Errol FLYNN; *The Wrong Box* (1966) brought an all-star cast to bear on a black comedy; and *St Ives*, posthumously completed by Arthur Quiller-Couch, was filmed in 1998. Further mutations and TV versions are too numerous to list here. Generally, it is true to say that Stevenson's more serious purposes have been neglected in favour of his more obviously crowd-pleasing elements.

Steward, Ernest (*b* London, 1914 – *d* 1990). Cinematographer. After doing second unit work on such films as *Great Expectations* (1946), *The Card* (1952) and *The Malta Story* (1953), Steward settled down to a long journeyman career with RANK, working often with director Ralph THOMAS, and became the permanent cameraman for the 'CARRY ON' SERIES, making them look more expensive than they were.

OTHER BRITISH FILMS INCLUDE: (cam op) *Take My Life* (1947), *London Belongs to Me* (1948), (c) *Venetian Bird* (1952), *Trouble in Store* (1953), *Doctor in the House* (1954), *Simon and Laura* (1955), *A Tale of Two Cities* (1958), *Conspiracy of Hearts* (1960), *House of Mystery*, *No Love for Johnnie* (1961), *The Wrong Arm of the Law* (1962), *The High Bright Sun* (1965), *Circus of Fear* (1966), *The Magnificent Two* (1967), *Carry On Up the Khyber* (1968), . . . *Camping*, . . . *Again Doctor* (1969), *Doctor in Trouble, Carry On Up the Jungle*, . . . *Loving* (1970), . . . *at Your Convenience* (1971), *Ooh . . . You Are Awful* (1972), *Callan* (1974), *Hennessy* (1975), *The Wildcats of St Trinian's* (1980).

Stewart, Alexandra (*b* Montreal, 1939). Actress. Most of Paris-trained Stewart's career has been in European films, where she became briefly the darling of new 60s cinema, in such films as *Le feu follet* (1963, Fr/It), *Mickey One* (1965, US) and *The Bride Wore Black* (1967, Fr/It), but attractive and intelligent as she was she never became an international star. Her British films are a motley lot, including *Maroc 7* (1966) as a gun-toting beauty named Michele, and *Only When I Larf* (1968), as one of a series of confidence tricksters.

OTHER BRITISH FILMS INCLUDE: *Tarzan the Magnificent* (1960), *Zeppelin* (1971), *The Uncanny* (1977, UK/Can), *Chanel Solitaire* (1981, UK/Fr).

Stewart, Athole (*b* London, 1879 – *d* Leighton Buzzard, 1940). Actor. Supporting player of three dozen 30s films, after a distinguished stage career dating back to 1901. On-screen, seen mostly as upper-class, often titled, characters, like Michael REDGRAVE's devious Uncle Reggie in *Climbing High* (1938) or the benign Duke in *Old Mother Riley in Society* (1940), and played Dr Watson in *The Speckled Band* (1931).

OTHER BRITISH FILMS INCLUDE: *To What Red Hell* (1929), *The Faithful Heart* (1933), *The Constant Nymph* (1933), *The Path of Glory* (1934), *The Clairvoyant* (1935), *Dusty Ermine* (1936), *Doctor Syn* (1937), *The Spy in Black*, *Poison Pen* (1939), *They Came by Night* (1940).

Stewart, Donald (*b* Philadelphia, 1910 – *d* Chertsey, 1966). Actor. RN: Wintermute. American light actor and singer, trained for opera but sidetracked into musical comedy in the 30s. Made a few British films, with modest leads in *One Exciting Night* (1944), with Vera LYNN, and *Welcome Mr Washington* (1944), as a US soldier wooing the lady of the manor. Rare supporting roles thereafter as he pursued stage career. Married to Renée HOUSTON.

OTHER BRITISH FILMS INCLUDE: *Fine Feathers* (1937), *The Peterville Diamond*, *Flying Fortress* (1942), *I'll Get You for This* (1950), *The Reluctant Bride* (1955), *The Sheriff of Fractured Jaw* (1958).

BIBLIOG: Renée Houston, *Don't Fence Me In*, 1974.

Stewart, Eve (*b* London, 1961). Production designer. Studied theatre design at London's Central School of Art, won a scholarship to work in a theatre, worked as a theatre designer for eight years, then gained an MA in Interior Architecture. After two films as art director with Mike LEIGH was then asked to design. Her work on *Topsy-Turvy* (2000, UK/US) is a key element in the film's loving recreation of the world of Victorian theatre, and she has been busy ever since.

OTHER BRITISH FILMS INCLUDE: (art d) *Naked* (1993), *Secrets & Lies* (1996); (prod des) *Career Girls* (1997), *Sorted* (UK/US), *Saving Grace* (2000), *The Hole* (2001, UK/Fr).

Stewart, Ewan (*b* Edinburgh, 1957). Actor. Son of Scottish folk singer, Andy Stewart, did a lot of TV (from the late 70s), some theatre, and had small roles in about ten films including *Rob Roy* (1995, UK/US) before making a striking impression in *Stella Does Tricks* (1996), as Stella's standup comic dad, whose crotch she sets alight in reprisal for past abuse and neglect. Not a big role, but a significant one – more so than playing a First Officer in *Titanic* (1997, US). Married to **Claire Byam Shaw** who played Lady Elgin in TV's *Lord Elgin and Some Stones of No Value* (1985).

OTHER BRITISH FILMS INCLUDE: *Who Dares Wins* (1982), *Not Quite Jerusalem* (1984), *Resurrected* (1989), *The Closer You Get* (2000), *Football* (2001).

Stewart, Hugh (*b* Cornwall, 1910) Producer. Cambridge-educated Stewart edited many films at GAUMONT–BRITISH and DENHAM in the 30s, including such famous titles as *The Man Who Knew Too Much* (1934), *South Riding* (1938) and *The Spy in Black* (1939); that is, for Britain's most prominent directors of the time (HITCHCOCK, SAVILLE, POWELL). After a distinguished WW2 career, including the co-direction (with Roy BOULTING) of the famous DOCUMENTARY, *Tunisian Victory* (1944, + co-p), for the ARMY FILM UNIT, he turned to production at TWO CITIES, with the charming period musical, *Trottie True* (1948). His main producing career involved the most popular film comedian of his day, Norman WISDOM, for whom he produced ten films, starting with *Man of the Moment* (1955), and of whom he said in 1992 'he does represent something uncrushable'. He was less successful with MORECAMBE AND WISE, household gods who never really embraced the big screen, though there are felicities in all three of their films, produced by Stewart. In his 80s, the very active Stewart was lecturing in a nearby polytechnic, having retired from the industry after producing three children's films in the early 70s.

OTHER BRITISH FILMS INCLUDE: (e) *Charing Cross Road* (1935), *Dark Journey* (1937), *Q Planes* (1939), *49th Parallel* (1941, assoc), *Troopship* (1942, d, doc); (p) *The Long Memory* (1952), *Up in the World* (1956), *Just My Luck* (1957), *Innocent Sinners* (1958), *Follow a Star* (1959), *On the Beat* (1962), *A Stitch in Time* (1963), *The Intelligence Men* (1965), *That Riviera Touch* (1966), *The Magnificent Two* (1967), *All at Sea* (1969), *Mr Horatio Knibbles* (1971), *Anoop and the Elephant* (1972), *The Flying Sorcerer* (1974).

Stewart, Jack (*b* Larkhall, Scotland, 1913 – *d* London, 1966). Actor. Scottish character player in films from 1949, often in settings north of the border, like his first film *The Gorbals Story* (1949), *The Brave Don't Cry* (1952) and *The 'Maggie'* (1953). Also a quietly authoritative police inspector in David EADY's sympathetic 'B' FILM, *The Heart Within* (1957) and a wry, intelligent Sergeant in Vernon SEWELL's excellent *Strongroom* (1992). On BBC television from the early 50s.

OTHER BRITISH FILMS INCLUDE: *Morning Departure* (1950), *Hunted* (1952), *The Kidnappers* (1953), *Trouble in the Glen* (1954), *Johnny, You're Wanted* (1955), *The Spanish Gardener* (1956), *Devil's Bait* (1959), *Snowball*, *Kidnapped* (1960), *The Frightened City* (1961), *Tom Jones* (1963).

Stewart, Patrick (*b* Mirfield, England, 1940*)* Actor, producer, director. Bald-headed actor with a honeyed growl. Studied at the Bristol Old Vic Theatre School in 1957 and joined the Royal Shakespeare Company in 1966. Stewart made his film debut in *Hennessy* (1975) after spending many years on stage and appearing in a number of television productions including a guest role in *Sesame Street* in 1969. Best known for his portrayal of Captain Jean-Luc Picard in TV's *Star Trek: The Next Generation*.

OTHER BRITISH FILMS INCLUDE: *Hedda* (1975), *Wild Geese II, Lady Jane* (1985), *Dad Savage* (1998). Anne-Marie Thomas.

Stewart, Sophie (*b* Crieff, Scotland, 1908 – *d* Cupar, Scotland, 1977). Actress. Sweet-faced stage star, who originally trained for ballet, abandoned this as result of an accident, then studied at RADA, making her stage debut in 1925 (London, 1929). Very popular, especially for the lead in *Marigold* (1927–30), which she filmed in 1938, and 30 years later she played the heroine's mother in the musical version (1958–59). Was an attractive leading lady in 30s films, including several for LONDON FILMS, notably *Things to Come, The Man Who Could Work Miracles* (1936) and *The Return of the Scarlet Pimpernel* (1937). In Hollywood, for *Nurse Edith Cavell* (1939) and *My Son, My Son* (1940), post-war she took character roles in a further seven films, and toured extensively in Australia, first as the unhappy wife in *Edward My Son* (1949–50), having married Australian actor Ellis IRVING.

OTHER BRITISH FILMS INCLUDE: *Her Last Affaire* (1935), *As You Like It* (1936), *Under the Red Robe* (1937), *The Lamp Still Burns* (1943), *Strawberry Roan* (1945), *Uncle Silas* (1947), *Made in Heaven* (1952), *Devil Girl from Mars* (1954), *No Time for Tears* (1957).

Sting (*b* Wallsend, 1951). Singer, actor. RN: Gordon Sumner. Achieved massive fame fronting the post-punk trio, 'The Police'. An intelligent and charismatic leader, he had his first screen role as a punk in the quintessential mod film *Quadrophenia* (1979). He distinguished himself as the unnerving Martin Taylor in the Dennis POTTER-written *Brimstone & Treacle* (1982), but his film work has generally tended towards cult status; a minor role as respectable barman JD in *Lock, Stock and Two Smoking Barrels* (1998) was his most populist film work to date. Married (1) Frances TOMELTY (1976–82) and (2) Trudie Styler, who appeared in *The Grotesque* (1996).

OTHER BRITISH FILMS INCLUDE: *Radio On* (1979, UK/Ger), *Urgh! A Music War* (1981, doc), *The Secret Policeman's Other Ball* (1982), *Plenty, The Bride* (1985, UK/US), *Stormy Monday* (1987, UK/US), *Twentieth Century Blues: The Songs of Noël Coward* (1998, doc).

BIBLIOG: Christopher Sandford, *Sting: Demolition Man*, 1998. Tim Roman.

Stirling, Pamela (*b* London, 1920). Actress. Supporting actress, mainly in 40s and 50s films, she also appeared in several French films, starting – unbilled – in *La Marseillaise* (1938), and several times playing French characters in British films, as in *Candlelight in Algeria* (1943) and *Madness of the Heart* (1949), and 'foreigner' Eric POHLMANN's hysterical wife in *Nor the Moon by Night* (1958).

OTHER BRITISH FILMS INCLUDE: *The Echo Murders* (1945), *Teheran* (1947), *The Lost People* (1949), *The Divided Heart* (1954), *The Safecracker* (1957), *Return from the Ashes* (1965).

Stock, Nigel (*b* Malta, 1919 – *d* London, 1986). Actor. Stocky, indeed, seems the word for this reliable RADA-trained character player who rose in the cinematic military ranks as he aged but was very convincing early on in prole roles, like the gang member Cubit in *Brighton Rock* (1947), Patricia PLUNKETT's decent boyfriend in *It Always Rains on Sunday* (1947), and Googie WITHERS' cuckolded, then murdered husband in *Derby Day* (1952). Was on stage from 1931, as child, TV (from 1949, with the lead in *Boys in Brown*) and screen (from 1937, in *Lancashire Luck*, though there may have been earlier uncredited appearances). Never a star in films, but always a welcome addition to the cast, whether as thug (*Eyewitness*, 1956) or dignitary (*Cromwell*, 1970), bestowing effortless verisimilitude on whatever he did. Was married to

stage actress **Sonia Williams** (*b* Richmond, Surrey, 1926), who also appeared in TV and the film *Out of True* (1951).

OTHER BRITISH FILMS INCLUDE: *Luck of the Navy* (1938), *Goodbye, Mr Chips* (1939), *The Malta Story* (1953), *Aunt Clara* (1954), *The Dam Busters, The Night My Number Came Up* (1955), *Never Let Go* (1960), *Victim* (1961), *Nothing But the Best* (1964), *The Night of the Generals* (1966, UK/Fr), *The Lion in Winter* (1968), *The Mirror Crack'd* (1980).

Stockfeld, Betty (*b* Sydney, 1905 – *d* London, 1966). Actress. Australian-born, educated in Britain and Paris, blonde Stockfeld was on stage from 1924, and became a popular star in light dramas and comedies. Made film debut in 1931 and was busy in both British and French films throughout the 30s, tapering off somewhat from the early 40s but still continuing to act in both languages. She played Maurice Chevalier's leading lady in *Beloved Vagabond* (1936, made in bilingual versions), moving into character roles by the end of the decade. Her last British films were the dim little morality, *The Girl Who Couldn't Quite* (1949), repeating her stage role, and *True as a Turtle* (1956), as wife to titled yacht-owner.

OTHER BRITISH FILMS INCLUDE: *77 Park Lane* (1931), *Money for Nothing* (1932), *King of the Ritz* (1933), *Brides to Be, The Battle* (UK/Fr) (1934), *Dishonour Bright* (1936), *I See Ice!* (1938), *Flying Fortress* (1942), *Guilty?* (1956, UK/Fr).

Stoddard, Malcolm (*b* Epsom, 1948) Actor. Former farrier, then trained at the Old Vic Theatre School, a leading man on TV, in such series as *The Voyage of Charles Darwin* (1978), in the title role, and *Emmerdale Farm* (1998), as Lord Thornfield, Stoddard has filmed only rarely, playing Captain Smollet in the 1999 version of *Treasure Island* (UK/US).

OTHER BRITISH FILMS: *Luther* (1973, UK/Can/US), *The Godsend* (1980), *Tree of Hands* (1988).

Stoker, Bram (*b* Clontarf, Ireland, 1847 – *d* London, 1912). Author. There was more to Stoker than the creation of Dracula, the Transylvanian vampire, but the mythology that has grown up around this has all but eclipsed his other writing and his long partnership (1878–1905) with actor Sir Henry Irving in running the Lyceum Theatre, London, out of which he wrote *Personal Reminiscences of Henry Irving* (1906). Among the famous screen versions of *Dracula* (1897) are: *Nosferatu* (1922, Ger), Tod Browning's *Dracula* (1931, US), starring Bela Lugosi, and HAMMER's *Dracula* (1958), starring horrorcrats Peter CUSHING and Christopher LEE. Hammer mined the Dracula and Frankenstein phenomena to great financial effect over the next couple of decades, offering such permutations as *Dracula, Prince of Darkness* (1965), *Dracula Has Risen from the Grave* (1968), *Taste the Blood of Dracula* (1969), *Countess Dracula* (1970), *The Scars of Dracula* (1970), all starring Lee, *Dracula* (1973, UK/US), starring Jack PALANCE, and there was a black version, *Blacula* (1972, US). As well, his novel *The Jewel of Seven Stars* (1903) has been filmed twice in Britain: as *Blood from the Mummy's Tomb* (1971) and *The Awakening* (1980, UK/US); and *The Lair of the White Worm* (1925) was filmed by Ken RUSSELL in 1988.

BIBLIOG: H.Ludlam, *A Biography of Dracula*, 1962.

Stoker, H(ew) G(ordon) (*b* Dublin, 1885 – *d* London, 1966). Actor, dramatist. Former naval commander who served in both World Wars and made his stage debut in 1920. Played a variety of professional and/or titled chaps in both theatre and film, as well as authoring several plays. On screen from 1933, as captain of the steamer making the *Channel Crossing* and in 1937 as the airship captain flying *Non-Stop to New York*.

OTHER BRITISH FILMS INCLUDE: *One Precious Year* (1933), *Forever England* (1935), *Pot Luck* (1936), *Crackerjack* (1938), *Call of the Blood* (UK/It), *Woman Hater* (1948), *The Reluctant Widow* (1950), *Where's Charley?* (1952).

Stoll, John (*b* London, 1913). Production designer. Shared AA with John Box for the design of *Lawrence of Arabia* (1962), confirming his position as one of Britain's top designers. Entering films as assistant in 1946 and billed as art director during the 50s, he worked on numerous 'B' MOVIES, as well as the odd main feature, like Lewis GILBERT's nicely taut THRILLER, *Cast a Dark Shadow* (1955). Moving into bigger-budget territory at the end of the decade, he helped make another Gilbert feature, *Ferry to Hong Kong* (1959) look better than it was, and post-*Lawrence* he designed such varied fare as the Malayan ACTION/ADVENTURE *The 7th Dawn* (1964, UK/US), William Wyler's chamber piece, *The Collector* (1965, UK/US), the HISTORICAL FILM, *Cromwell* (1970), and the FANTASY, *The Golden Voyage of Sinbad* (1973). His long association with Gilbert continued until his last film, *Shirley Valentine* (1989, UK/US).

OTHER BRITISH FILMS INCLUDE: (art d) *River Beat, The Large Rope* (1953), *The Sleeping Tiger, The Black Rider* (1954), *Johnny, You're Wanted, Room in the House* (1955), *Face in the Night* (1956), *That Woman Opposite, The Flesh is Weak* (1957), *A Cry from the Streets* (1958), *The Greengage Summer* (1961), *The Running Man, Psyche 59* (1963), *How I Won the War* (1967), *The Beast Must Die* (1974); (des) *A Terrible Beauty* (1960), *Hannibal Brooks* (1968), *Living Free* (1972), *Seven Nights in Japan* (1976, UK/Fr), *Firepower* (1979), *Not Quite Jerusalem* (1984).

Stoll, Sir Oswald *see* **Stoll Picture Productions**

Stoll Picture Productions A major British theatrical impresario, Sir Oswald Stoll (*b* Melbourne, Australia, 1866 – *d* London, 1942), knighted in 1919, took over the London Coliseum in 1904 and quickly gained a controlling interest in theatres throughout Britain. In April 1918, he founded the Stoll film company as both a distributor and producer (its first film was *Comradeship*, 1919, directed by Maurice ELVEY), and the company was to remain a major player in British cinema until the 1930s. The Stoll company's silent output included more than two dozen directed by Elvey from 1919 to 1924, among them such titles as *The Hound of the Baskervilles* (1921), starring Eille NORWOOD, and *The Passionate Friends* (1922), starring Milton ROSMER. In 1920, it acquired a converted aeroplane factory at CRICKLEWOOD as its studio, ownership of which Stoll retained until 1938. In the 30s, the studio, which had been slow to adopt sound, was mainly used by independent producers and mainly for SHORT FILMS, but late in the decade it was used by BUTCHER's to make *Old Mother Riley* (1937) and John BAXTER made several films there from the mid 30s. Stoll himself, a cold and formal individual, was, however, an enthusiastic supporter of the British film industry, if never a creative producer in the American mould. AS.

Stone, John (*b* Cardiff, 1924). Actor. After WW2 service in the RAF, he appeared on stage, joined the BBC Repertory Company and entered films all in 1945. Following some small roles, he had a good part as Ursula JEANS's steady soldier son, later killed, in *The Weaker Sex* (1948), was in the TV series, *The Quatermass Experiment* (1953) and *Quatermass 2* (1955), and later played the submarine captain in the BOND caper, *You Only Live Twice* (1967).

OTHER BRITISH FILMS INCLUDE: *Johnny Frenchman, Night Boat to Dublin* (1945), *Holiday Camp* (1947), *Bad Lord Byron* (1949), *Operation Murder* (1956), *Moment of Indiscretion* (1958), *The Frightened City* (1961), *Deadlier Than the Male* (1966), *Assault* (1970).

Stone, Lew (*b* London, 1898 – *d* London, 1969). Composer, music director. Dance-band leader who appeared in a few 30s films, sometimes with his band (e.g. in *The Street Singer*, 1937), and sometimes composed, as for *Under Your Hat* (1940, + m d).

OTHER BRITISH FILMS INCLUDE: *The Mayor's Nest* (m arr, m d), *The Flag Lieutenant* (m d), *It's a King* (co-m) (1932), *Bitter Sweet* (m d), *The King's Cup* (+ band) (1933), *Appointment with Crime* (1946, a).

Stone, Marianne (aka Mary Stone) (*b* London, 1923) Actress. A remarkably prolific Stone has possibly appeared in more British films in the post-war period than any other performer, usually in very small roles (and sometimes uncredited). An attractive but unobtrusive presence in a range of thrillers, comedies, horrors and science-fiction films, her most memorable role is probably the non-speaking one of Vivian Darkbloom, the mysterious woman glimpsed dancing with Peter SELLERS in Stanley Kubrick's *Lolita* (1961). Married Peter NOBLE.

OTHER BRITISH FILMS INCLUDE: *Brighton Rock* (1947), *Escape Dangerous, Marry Me* (1949), *Seven Days to Noon* (1950), *The Magic Box* (1951), *Angels One Five* (1952), *Spaceways, The Net, A Day to Remember* (1953), *Mad About Men, You Know What Sailors Are, The Good Die Young, 36 Hours, The Brain Machine* (1954), *Lost, Simon and Laura, The Quatermass Experiment, Barbados Quest* (1955), *Person Unknown, Passport to Treason, Yield to the Night* (1956), *Just My Luck, Woman in a Dressing Gown, Hell Drivers, Quatermass 2* (1957), *Carry On Nurse, No Trees in the Street, The Golden Disc, Jack the Ripper, A Night to Remember* (1958), *I'm All Right Jack, The Man Who Liked Funerals, Tiger Bay* (1959), *The Big Day, Never Let Go, The Angry Silence* (1960), *The Frightened City, Watch it, Sailor!, Double Bunk* (1961), *Two and Two Make Six, The Fast Lady, The Night of the Prowler, The Wild and the Willing, Paranoiac* (1962), *Return to Sender, Heavens Above!, Echo of Diana, The Hijackers, Ladies Who Do, The Marked One* (1963), *The Beauty Jungle, Carry On Jack, Witchcraft, The Curse of the Mummy's Tomb, Act of Murder, We Shall See, Devils of Darkness, Nothing but the Best* (1964), *Traitor's Gate, Hysteria, The Night Caller, You Must Be Joking!, Catch Us If You Can* (1965), *Strangler's Web, Carry On Screaming, The Wrong Box, Carry On Don't Lose Your Head, A Countess from Hong Kong* (1966), *The Long Duel, To Sir, with Love, Berserk!* (1967), *Carry on Doctor* (1968), *All the Right Noises, Oh! What a Lovely War* (1969), *Doctor in Trouble, The Firechasers, Scrooge, The Raging Moon, Countess Dracula, Assault* (1970), *Carry On at Your Convenience, Danny Jones, Mr Forbush and the Penguins, Whoever Slew Auntie Roo?, All Coppers Are . . .* (1971), *Bless This House, Carry On Matron, Tower of Evil, The Creeping Flesh, The Love Ban, The Cherry Picker* (1972), *Carry On Girls, Craze, Penny Gold, The Vault of Horror, Mistress Pamela* (1973), *Carry On Dick, Confessions of a Window Cleaner, Percy's Progress* (1974), *Carry On Behind, That Lucky Touch, I'm Not Feeling Myself Tonight* (1975), *Confessions from a Holiday Camp* (1977), *The Class of Miss MacMichael, Sammy's Super T-Shirt, What's Up Superdoc* (1978), *The Human Factor* (1979), *Funny Money* (1982), *Déjà Vu* (1984), *Terry on the Fence* (1985). Peter Hutchings.

Stone, Paddy (*b* Winnipeg, 1924 – *d* Winnipeg, 1986). Choreographer, dancer. Paddy Stone's witty and skilful dance routines (often with **Irving Davies**, *b* Barry, Wales – *d* London, 2002) enlivened several mid 50s British films. Featured male dancers were rare in British cinema, and his 'Where There's You' routine in *The Good Companions* (1956) reveals that he certainly had the talent. After dance training in Canada, he appeared in NY and (with Davies) in the West End in *Annie Get Your Gun* (1947). They were jointly featured in three films, with Stone as dancer and choreographer: *As Long as They're Happy, Value for Money* (1955), and *The Good Companions*, the latter including a 12-minute dance highlight, 'Around the World', devised by Stone. Davies also featured in the 'Ring Around the Rosy' episode of Gene Kelly's *Invitation to the Dance* (filmed 1952, released 1954), Throughout the 60s, they regularly choreographed for stage variety and TV specials.

OTHER BRITISH FILMS: *6.5 Special* (1958), *Great Catherine* (chor only) (1968), *Scrooge* (1970), *Victor/Victoria* (1982). Roger Philip Mellor.

Stone, Philip (*b* Leeds, 1924). Actor. Urbane, bald character player, several times used by Stanley KUBRICK (*A Clockwork Orange*, 1971; *Barry Lyndon*, 1975; and most vividly as caretaker/butler/murderer Delbert Grady in *The Shining*, UK, 1980). Had a series of roles in Lindsay ANDERSON's picaresque fable, *O Lucky Man!* (1973), a continuing role in the TV series, *Justice* (1972–74) starring Margaret LOCKWOOD, and was the Bishop in Peter GREENAWAY's confronting oddity, *The Baby of Mâcon* (1993, UK/Fr/Ger/Neth). Played Captain Blumburtt in *Indiana Jones and the Temple of Doom* (1984, US).

OTHER BRITISH FILMS INCLUDE: *Unearthly Stranger* (1963), *Thunderball* (1965), *Where Eagles Dare* (1968), *Two Gentlemen Sharing* (1969), *Fragment of Fear, Carry On Loving* (1970), *Voyage of the Damned* (1976), *Flash Gordon* (1980), *Green Ice* (1981).

Stoppard, Sir Tom (*b* Zlín, Czech, 1937). Dramatist, screenwriter. RN: Straussler. His association with film predates his much more prolific career as a playwright: in the 50s he became film and theatre critic for two provincial English newspapers. His original screenplay of *Brazil* (1985), co-authored by Terry GILLIAM and Charles McKeown, was Oscar-nominated. Subsequently he adapted *Empire of the Sun* (1987), *The Russia House* (1990, UK/US) and *Billy Bathgate* (1991, US). In 1990 he directed his own ADAPTATION of his first and best-known play *Rosencrantz and Guildenstern Are Dead* (US) and in 1999 shared an Oscar for best original screenplay for the witty and touching *Shakespeare in Love* (UK/US).

OTHER BRITISH FILMS: *The Romantic Englishwoman* (1975, UK/Fr), *The Human Factor* (1979, UK/US).

BIBLIOG: Katherine E. Kelly, *The Cambridge Companion to Tom Stoppard*, 2001. Simon Caterson.

Storey, David (*b* Wakefield, 1933). Screenwriter. Novelist (winner of the 1976 Booker Prize), playwright and poet as well as screenwriter. Storey's *This Sporting Life* (1963) and its raging-bull protagonist, Arthur Machin, may have established him among the ANGRY YOUNG MEN but the isolated men at the centre of his novels, drama and film work, fired into self-improvement by the school of hard labour and the hard knocks it gave them, are forever tearing at the scenery of middle-class respectability in pursuit of a lost authenticity, both collective and personal. The poet laureate of Rugby League? Television projects included: *Home* (1971) and *Early Days* (1982).

OTHER BRITISH FILMS: *In Celebration* (1974). Kevin Foster.

Storm, Lesley (*b* Maud, Aberdeenshire, 1898 – *d* London, 1975). Dramatist, screenwriter. RN: Mabel Cowie. Educated at Aberdeen University, former journalist Storm was a popular playwright, of the 40s especially and three of her plays were successfully adapted to the screen: *Great Day* (1945, filmed same year, + co-sc) is a perceptive study of VILLAGE LIFE; *The Day's Mischief* (1951), filmed in 1953 as *Personal Affair*, whose screenplay she wrote, makes sturdy MELODRAMA of a schoolgirl's infatuation with her teacher; and *Tony Draws a Horse* (1939, filmed 1950, not to her screenplay). She also worked on several other screenplays, usually in collaboration (e.g. on *The Golden Salamander*, 1949, with author Victor CANNING and director Ronald NEAME). Her play, *Heart of a City* (1942), was filmed in Hollywood as *Tonight and Every Night* (1944).

OTHER BRITISH FILMS INCLUDE: (co-sc, unless noted) *Discipline* (1935, story), *East of Piccadilly, Banana Ridge* (1941), *Unpublished Story* (1942), *Flight from Folly* (1945), *White Cradle Inn* (1947), *The Spanish Gardener* (1956).

Stott, Ken (*b* Edinburgh, 1955). Actor. Of Scottish father and Sicilian mother, Stott came to theatregoers' attention in the original cast of *Art* (1996) with Albert FINNEY and Tom COURTENAY. Previously worked with the Traverse Theatre, Edinburgh, and the RSC, notably as the bellicose Douglas in *Henry IV, Pt I*, he did some notable TV, including *The Singing Detective* (1986) and *Dockers* (1999). In films since 1989 (*For Queen and Country*), he made a real mark in 1999 with two accounts of ill-controlled ferocity: as the class-angry, obsessive thief-taker in *Plunkett & Macleane* and, especially, as the relentless cop determined to make *The Debt Collector* pay his debts. It is a brilliant study in repressed sexuality and rage, announcing a major new character star in the stocky, pugnacious Stott.

OTHER BRITISH FILMS: *Franz Kafka's It's a Wonderful Life* (1993, short), *Being Human, Shallow Grave* (1994), *Saint-Ex* (1996), *Fever Pitch, The Boxer* (UK/Ire/US) (1997), *Vicious Circle* (1998).

Stow, Percy (*b* Islington, London – *d* Torquay). Director. Responsible for more than 250 shorts for CLARENDON, of which he was co-founder, between 1904 and 1915, including the *Lt Rose* SERIES. Previously associated with HEPWORTH from 1901–03, where he specialised in trick films. AS.

Stradling Snr, Harry (*b* New Jersey, 1901 – *d* Los Angeles, 1970). Cinematographer. British-born cameraman whose hugely prolific, Oscar-winning career was spent almost entirely in the US, except for a batch of quality films shot in Britain in the later 30s. He had worked in France during the early 30s and came to Britain with director Jacques Feyder when Alexander KORDA invited the latter to direct *Knight Without Armour* (1937). *Dark Journey* (1937), *South Riding* and *Pygmalion* (1938) are among the best – and best-looking – films of the time, in their elegant black-and-white images, and, in two of Korda's early TECHNICOLOR films, *The Divorce of Lady X* (1938) and *Over the Moon* (1939), he gave modest subjects a handsome, though scarcely naturalistic gloss. Back in the US, he received 13 AA nominations and twice won: for *The Picture of Dorian Gray* (1945) and *My Fair Lady* (1964). His son, Harry Stradling Jr, was also a famous Hollywood cameraman.

OTHER BRITISH FILMS: *Action for Slander* (1937), *The Citadel* (1938), *Q Planes, Jamaica Inn, The Lion Has Wings* (co-c) (1939).

Strand Film Company Established as a feature film company in 1928 by Julius HAGEN, documentarists Donald TAYLOR and Ralph KEENE took the company over in 1935. With Paul ROTHA and Stuart LEGG they began to produce social DOCUMENTARIES such as *Here is the Land* (1937) and *Today We Live* (1937) as well as commercially sponsored and travel films. The success of six educational zoology films, made in 1938 with the assistance of Julian Huxley, led to the creation of Strand Film Zoological Productions and a move to larger premises at MERTON PARK STUDIOS. In 1942, Strand became part of BRITISH NATIONAL, contributing substantially to the wartime PROPAGANDA effort, specialising in instructional films. Postwar, Strand's DOCUMENTARY output declined, as it was absorbed into BRITISH NATIONAL. Other film-makers associated with Strand include Ralph BOND, Ruby and Marion GRIERSON, Alexander SHAW and John ELDRIDGE. Sarah Easen.

Strassner, Joe (*b* 1887 – *d* New York, 1965). Costume designer. Strassner left Berlin for Hollywood in 1923, coming to Britain in 1934, where he worked mostly for GAUMONT–BRITISH. Credits included such high-profile productions as *Escape Me Never* (1935), *Tudor Rose* (1936) and several HITCHCOCK films: *The 39 Steps* (1935), *The Secret Agent* (1936) and *Sabotage* (1936). His last credit, on *He Found a Star* (1941), was shared with Norman HARTNELL.

OTHER BRITISH FILMS INCLUDE: *The Clairvoyant*, *The Tunnel* (co-des) (1935), *Stormy Weather*, *Rhodes of Africa*, *As You Like It* (co-des) (1936), *Under Your Hat* (1940).

Stratton, John (*b* Clitheroe, 1925). Actor. On stage from 1943, in the Royal Navy 1944–47, made his London debut in 1948 and ten years later was in the original cast of *The Birthday Party*. Had an uncredited bit in *The Small Back Room* (1948) but came to filmgoers' notice as faithless Dora BRYAN's fancy man in *The Cure for Love* (1949) and as the nervous young officer, Ferraby, in *The Cruel Sea* (1952). His film career petered out in the 60s, but there were some notable TV appearances, including *Trinity Tales* (1975), Alan PLATER's updating of Chaucer, and the lead in Plater's dramatisation of *The Good Companions* (1980).

OTHER BRITISH FILMS INCLUDE: *Seven Days to Noon* (1950), *The Happy Family* (1952), *Seven Waves Away* (1956), *The Challenge* (1959), *The Love Pill* (1971), *Frankenstein and the Monster from Hell* (1973).

Streep, Meryl (*b* Summit, New Jersey, 1949). Actress. Dominant US star of the 80s and 90s who sneaks in here for her immaculate impersonations of Englishwomen in *The French Lieutenant's Woman* (1981), in two roles, and in the US-backed, UK-set *Plenty* (1985), as a woman for whom peacetime Britain has lacked the challenges of war; and as the eldest of the Irish sisters in *Dancing at Lughnasa* (1998, UK/US). She is brilliant with accents as she also showed in playing Lindy Chamberlin in *Evil Angels* (1988, UK/Aust).

Stretton, George (aka Dudgeon-Stretton) (*b* Cranbrook, 1901 – *d* Amersham, 1955). Cinematographer. Cambridge-educated former naval commander who entered films in 1931 at the new SOUND CITY STUDIOS, shooting the films of John BAXTER, Ivar CAMPBELL and others, and later in the decade working for BRITISH LION. During WW2, he served as director of naval photography; he co-photographed the DOCUMENTARY *Theirs is the Glory* (1946); and was involved in the development of the short-lived INDEPENDENT FRAME technique, pioneered by RANK in the later 40s. He shot the first film made on this system, the children's adventure, *Under the Frozen Falls* (1948) and four of the adult features.

OTHER BRITISH FILMS INCLUDE: *Watch Beverly* (1932), *Song of the Plough* (1933), *Lest We Forget*, *Menace* (1934), *Honeymoon for Three* (1935), *The Happy Family* (1936), *Calling All Stars* (1937), *I've Got a Horse* (1938), *The Mind of Mr Reeder* (1939), *Warning to Wantons* (1948), *Poet's Pub*, *Floodtide* (1949), *Prelude to Fame*, *Blackmailed* (1950).

Stribling, Melissa (*b* Gourock, Scotland, 1929 – *d* Watford, 1992). Actress. Blue-eyed blonde who entered films as cutting-room assistant at EALING before RADA training and rep experience. In films from 1946 (*The First Gentleman*), she had mainly small roles during the 50s, like the party guest aboard the *Ghost Ship* (1952), but moved up the cast to play Mina, in danger of being vampirised by *Dracula* (1958). Also appeared in several films directed by her husband, Basil DEARDEN, including *League of Gentlemen* (1960), in which she exchanged saucy dialogue with Nigel PATRICK.

OTHER BRITISH FILMS INCLUDE: *Decameron Nights* (1952), *Thought to Kill* (1953), *Out of the Clouds* (1955), *The Safecracker* (1957), *The Secret Partner* (1961), *Road to Saint Tropez* (1966, short), *Only When I Larf* (1968), *Paris by Night* (1988).

Strick, Joseph (*b* Pittsburgh, 1923). Director. A film-maker who sets about bringing James JOYCE to the screen is likely to be more than usually enterprising – even, perhaps, foolhardy. However, Strick made a brave stab at the daunting monolith of *Ulysses* (1967, UK/US), well served by Milo O'SHEA as Bloom and Barbara JEFFORD as Molly, and his version of *A Portrait of the Artist as a Young Man* (1977), on easier but still treacherous ground, dealt uncompromisingly with the sustained dialectic of the book's final section, rather skimming the more obviously filmable earlier sections. He produced two British films – *Ring of Bright Water* (1969) and *The Darwin Adventure* (1971) – with American director Jack Couffer, with whom he had worked in the US, where he conducted the rest of his idiosyncratic career. Won AA for his DOCUMENTARY, *Interviews with My Lai Veterans* (1970, US) and BAA for *The Savage Eye* (1960, US).

Stride, John (*b* London, 1936). Actor. Found instant audience favour as Judi DENCH's Romeo in the Old Vic's 1960 production, but the RADA-trained Stride, who has had a rewarding stage career, especially in Shakespeare, has merely dabbled with film. He had the male lead as the nice young pub handyman who fails to save the heroine from big-city corruption in *Bitter Harvest* (1963) and was Ross in POLANSKI's *Macbeth* (1971). Otherwise, TV has treated him better, as with the lead in the legal series *The Main Chance* (1969–75) and *Henry VIII* (1979).

OTHER BRITISH FILMS: *Sink the Bismarck!* (1960), *Something to Hide* (1971), *Juggernaut* (1974), *Brannigan* (1975), *A Bridge Too Far* (1977).

Strong, Mark (*b* London, 1963). Actor. RN: Marco Salussolia. Forceful, balding actor, of Italian father and Austrian mother, who somewhat suggests a British Ed Harris in looks and style, Strong initially studied law but dropped it in favour of the Old Vic Theatre School. Came to attention in the 90s: on stage with the National and the RSC, and with Kevin Spacey in *The Iceman Cometh* at the Almeida (1998); on TV, as Tosker Cox in *Our Friends in the North* (1996), an austere Mr Knightley to Kate BECKINSALE's *Emma* (1996), an engagingly philandering Oblonsky in *Anna Karenina* (2000); and in films, as Colin FIRTH's best pal in *Fever Pitch* (1997), the disappointing *Elephant Juice* (2000), and then in one film after another, including the big-budget US film, *To End All Wars* (2002). He has a screen style that compels attention by seeming to do very little – as many a star before him has done.

OTHER BRITISH FILMS INCLUDE: *Century* (1993), *Captives* (1994), *Sunshine* (2000, UK/Austria/Can/Ger/Hung), *The Martins* (2001).

Strong, Percy (*d* London, 1896 – *d* Kent, 1939). Cinematographer. A former laboratory assistant for W.G. BARKER, to whom he was related, Strong became a leading British cameraman of the 20s, first with STOLL and then for George PEARSON; also worked in France with Abel Gance, Louis Mercanton and others.

BRITISH FILMS INCLUDE: *The Flame* (1920), *Frailty* (1921), *The River of Stars* (1921), *Squibs, MP* (1923), *Reveille* (1924), *The Secret Kingdom* (1925), *Cinders* (1926), *A Sister to Assist 'Er* (1927), *Palais de Danse* (1928), *A Sister to Assist 'Er*, *The Great Game* (1930), *The Happy Ending* (1931), *After the Ball* (1932), *Soldiers of the King* (1933, co-c), *The Girl in the Flat* (1934). AS.

Stross, Raymond (*b* Leeds, 1916 – *d* Los Angeles, 1988). Producer. Stross, who entered films in 1933, in the sound department, became known from the 50s as a producer of sensationalist dramas, often dealing with cutting-edge sexual attitudes. Hence, *The Flesh Is Weak* (1957) focuses on prostitution, *A Question of Adultery* (1958) on artificial insemination, *The Mark* (1961) on child molestation, *The Leather Boys* (1963) and *The Fox* (1968, US) on homosexual relationships, and *I Know What I Want* (1971) on transsexualism, the last two starring Anne HEYWOOD, whom he married in 1960. These films, sometimes surprisingly low-key in treating their then-potentially explosive themes, were a contrast to the anodyne comedies he produced in the mid 50s, including *An Alligator Named Daisy* (1955). He had his own production company from the early 50s.

OTHER BRITISH FILMS: (d) *The Show's the Thing* (1936), *The Reverse Be My Lot* (1938); (p) *Hell Is Sold Out* (1951), *The Man Who Watched Trains Go By, Tall Headlines* (1952), *Rough Shoot, Star of India* (UK/It) (1953), *As Long As They're Happy, Jumping for Joy* (1955), *A Touch of the Sun* (1956), *The Angry Hills* (1959), *A Terrible Beauty* (1960), *Vengeance* (UK/Ger), *The Very Edge* (+ story) (1962), *90 in the Shade* (1964, UK/Czech).

Stroud, Pauline (*b* London). Actress. Stroud's career in films is as sad as that of Marjorie Clark, the beauty queen winner she played in her debut film *Lady Godiva Rides Again* (1951). Though she is the centre of the action, virtually everyone else in the film overshadows her, and she is saved from a squalid end by John McCALLUM. Stroud never had such a key role again, made only three further films and disappeared, perhaps back into rep.

OTHER BRITISH FILMS: *Alf's Baby* (1953), *Passport to Shame* (1958), *Life in Emergency Ward 10* (1958).

Strueby, Katherine (*b* London, 1905 – *d* 1988). Screenwriter. Worked on the screenplays for 15 or so British films, after some Hollywood experience, from the 30s to the 50s, including a batch of four for director George KING in the 40s: the WAR FILM, *Tomorrow We Live* (1942); the MUSICAL BIOPIC *Gaiety George* (1946), the CRIME THRILLER, *The Shop at Sly Corner* (1946), adapted from the stage success; and the romantic MELODRAMA, *Forbidden* (1949). Among her first credits is the motor-racing tale, *Death Drives Through* (1935), which she co-wrote with Gordon WELLESLEY, whom she married.

OTHER BRITISH FILMS INCLUDE: (sc/co-sc) *It Happened in Paris* (1935), *Café Colette, The High Command* (1937), *Special Edition* (1938), *The First of the Few* (co-story), *Candlelight in Algeria* (1943), *They Were Sisters* (adptn), *Flight From Folly* (1945) *Eight O'Clock Walk* (1954).

Strummer, Joe (*b* Ankara, Turkey, 1952 – *d* Broomfield Somerset, 2002). Composer, actor. RN: John Mellor. Former lead singer and guitarist with punk band, 'The Clash', Strummer is the son of a British diplomat, but maintained his bad boy cred by being jailed several times in the 70s before the group developed its social conscience. Film work was mainly in concert films or mock-documentaries, and not much of it was British, but he provided music for *Rude Boy* (1980, +a) and *Sid and Nancy* (1986).

OTHER BRITISH FILMS: (a) *The Punk Rock Movie* (1978, doc), *Straight to Hell* (1986), *I Hired a Contract Killer* (1990, UK/Fin/Ger/Swe).

Stuart, Aimée (*b* Glasgow, 1885 – *d* Brighton, 1981). Screenwriter, dramatist. RN: McHardy. Well-known popular playwright of such pieces as *Jeannie* (1941, co-written with husband Philip Stuart), filmed in 1942 with Barbara MULLEN, and the MUSICAL *Let's Be Happy* (1956), starring Vera-Ellen. She contributed additional dialogue to *The Gentle Sex* (1943), *Fanny by Gaslight* (1944) and *The Wicked Lady* (1945). She and

her husband co-wrote the screenplay for *Borrowed Clothes* (1934), from their play, and *Nine Till Six* (1932) was adapted from their 1930 play.

Stuart, Binkie (*b* Kilmarnock, Scotland, 1932 – *d* Reading, 2001). Juvenile entertainer. RN: Fiona Stewart. British producers tried to emulate Shirley Temple's success by promoting the irrepressible singing and dancing Stuart (whose talents were no match for Temple's) in eight 'QUOTA QUICKIES' between 1936 and 1938, mainly produced by John ARGYLE and released by BUTCHERS. They are generally simple-minded Victorian tearjerkers (orphan Binkie placed with cruel adults), oversentimental or 'heart-warming' according to taste, but popular in the UK regions and, because *Rose of Tralee* (1937) and *My Irish Molly* (1938, with Maureen O'HARA) were set in Ireland, amongst the US Irish community. Also in *Moonlight Sonata* (1937) with the concert pianist Jan Paderewski (*see* Marie TEMPEST), and with George FORMBY in *Keep your Seats, Please* (1936), as 'Fiona Stuart'.

OTHER BRITISH FILMS: *Little Miss Somebody, Our Fighting Navy, Splinters in the Air* (1937), *Little Dolly Daydream* (1938). Roger Philip Mellor.

Stuart, John (*b* Edinburgh, 1898 – *d* London, 1979). Actor. RN: John Croall. An amiable leading man in silent films and 30s talkies who became a reliable character actor in later years in a career that lasted from 1920 through 1978 and included more than 150 titles. Appropriately, he ended his career as it began, with a silent role, as one of the Krypton elders in *Superman* (1978). Memorable films include Hitchcock's first feature, *The Pleasure Garden* (1925, UK/Ger) as well as the director's *Number Seventeen* (1932), one of the first talkies, *Kitty* (1929), and Brigitte Helm's lover in the English-language version of G.W. Pabst's *Atlantide* (1933). He could even bring sincerity to the thankless role of Kitty McSHANE's boyfriend in *Old Mother Riley in Society* (1940) and *Old Mother Riley's Ghosts* (1941). Married (2) Muriel ANGELUS (3) acting and voice teacher Barbara Francis, mother of his son, theatrical biographer Jonathan Croall.

OTHER BRITISH FILMS INCLUDE: *Her Son* (1920, and first), *School for Scandal* (1923), *Hindle Wakes* (1927), *Atlantic* (1929), *The Hound of the Baskervilles* (1931), *The Wandering Jew* (1933), *Bella Donna* (1934), *Abdul the Damned* (1935), *Penn of Pennsylvania* (1941), *Madonna of the Seven Moons* (1944), *Men of Sherwood Forest* (1954), *The Mummy* (1959), *Sink the Bismark!* (1960), *Young Winston* (1972).

BIBLIOG: Autobiography, *Caught in the Act*, 1971. AS.

Stuart, Josephine (*b* Watford, 1926). Actress. Best remembered as the unwed mother of *Oliver Twist* (1948), staggering pregnantly against a lowering sky, then dying poignantly in the opening scenes of David LEAN's definitive ADAPTATION, Stuart made about ten films without ever again having anything so striking to do. On stage from 1944, she made her film debut in *Silver Darlings* (1946), and was in TV's *Destiny of a Spy* (1969).

OTHER BRITISH FILMS INCLUDE: *The Loves of Joanna Godden* (1947), *My Brother Jonathan* (1948), *The Weak and the Wicked* (1953), *No Time for Tears* (1957), *Night Train for Inverness* (1959).

Stuart, Madge (*b* 1897 – *d*?). Actress. Unlike most silent screen leading ladies, Madge Stuart made her stage debut (1918) *after* she had made a name for herself in films. A planned US career in the mid 20s came to nothing.

BRITISH FILMS INCLUDE: *Flames* (1917), *Nature's Gentleman* (1918), *The Elusive Pimpernel* (1919), *The Amateur Gentleman* (1920), *Innocent* (1921), *The Passionate Friends, Fortune's Fool* (1922), *She Stoops to*

Conquer, Beloved Vagabond (1923), *Women and Diamonds* (1924), *The Only Way* (1925), *Kenilworth Castle and Amy Robsart* (1926). AS.

Stuart, Nicholas (*b* Montreal, 1910). Actor. Educated at McGill University, Stuart entered films in Hollywood in 1930, came to England in 1938 and appeared in about 15 character roles, often as military officers like those he played in *Secret Mission* (1942) and *We Joined the Navy* (1962). Also played the 'King Duncan' role in *Joe Macbeth* (1955) and Lt-Gen Omar Bradley in the US war epic, *The Longest Day* (1962).

OTHER BRITISH FILMS INCLUDE: *The Gentle Sex* (1943), *Time Flies* (1944), *Night Beat* (1948), *The Love Lottery* (1953), *The Divided Heart* (1954), *The Night My Number Came Up* (1955), *High Tide at Noon* (1957), *The Adding Machine* (1969).

Stubbs, Imogen (*b* Rothbury, 1961). Actress. A much respected stage actress, of serene, faintly secret beauty, Stubbs has made about a dozen films, starting with *Privileged* (1982), while she (and co-star Hugh GRANT) were still at Oxford. Westminster- and Oxford-educated and RADA-trained, she quickly achieved success, especially as Desdemona in *Othello* produced by Trevor NUNN whom she married in 1994. Her major screen role was as a convincingly gender-ambiguous Viola in Nunn's *Twelfth Night* (1996, UK/US), but she also did a very funny turn as sly, finger-crooking-genteel Lucy Steele in *Sense and Sensibility* (1995, UK/US), while working through a hefty stage and TV agenda.

OTHER BRITISH FILMS INCLUDE: *Nanou* (1986, UK/Fr), *A Summer Story* (1987), *Erik the Viking* (1989), *Jack & Sarah* (1995, UK/Fr).

Stubbs, Una (*b* Welwyn Garden City, 1937). Actress. Best known as bigot Alf Garnett's daughter Rita in TV's *Till Death Do Us Part* (1966–68, 1972, 1974–75) and the SPIN-OFF film in 1968, and for her co-starring role with Jon PERTWEE in TV's *Worzel Gummidge* (1979–81, 1987, 1989), small perky brunette Stubbs had second leads in two Cliff RICHARD vehicles, *Summer Holiday* (1962) and *Wonderful Life* (1964), early in her career, but not much else. Married and divorced (1) Peter GILMORE and (2) Nicky HENSON.

OTHER BRITISH FILMS INCLUDE: *West 11* (1963), *The Bargee* (1964), *Three Hats for Lisa* (1965), *Mister Ten Per Cent* (1967), *Penny Gold* (1973), *The Water Babies* (1975, UK/Pol).

studios It is a common refrain, echoed again and again by politicians and producers, that 'British technicians are the best in the world'. Anybody who quibbles with this assessment is referred immediately to the BOND movies, Batman and Superman, all shot at PINEWOOD STUDIOS, to *Star Wars* (shot at ELSTREE) and countless other big-budget Hollywood movies that have been made as runaway productions at SHEPPERTON or Elstree because the facilities are so good. *Band of Brothers* (2001), the $100m WW2 mini-series produced by Steven Spielberg for HBO, was shot in a specially converted British aerospace factory in Hatfield while WARNER BROS made the $35m *Harry Potter and the Philosopher's Stone* (2001, UK/US) in LEAVESDEN, the ex-Rolls Royce factory converted into studios in the mid 90s.

There is a paradox here. By citing their success in attracting US productions, the British are tacitly acknowledging that there is no longer a British 'studio system' as such. There certainly used to be one. How can you tell? Mention the name of any British studio in its heyday and a particular style of film-making will spring to mind.

The most important British studio of the silent era, WALTON-ON-THAMES, had a very clear identity. It was here

that the pioneering producer Cecil HEPWORTH made a series of wholesome films, many of them romantic melodramas, celebrating (or so Hepworth claimed) 'all that is beautiful and interesting in England'.

In the early talkie era, British studios were self-consciously modelled on their Hollywood counterparts, with stars signed up to seven-year contracts, and separate story and publicity departments established. DENHAM, where KORDA set up shop in the mid 30s, had seven sound stages, restaurants, theatres, hairdressing centres and even its own labs. Pinewood, opened in 1936, was even grander.

Just as Warner Bros during the Depression specialised in gangster pics and escapist musicals and MGM under Irving Thalberg was renowned for fashioning luxurious star vehicles, certain British studios likewise became known for specializing in specific genres. In the 40s, GAINSBOROUGH was known for its COSTUME MELODRAMAS, EALING was celebrated for its character-driven COMEDIES (films, as studio boss Michael BALCON put it, 'projecting Britain and the British character') and BRAY in Berkshire became home to the HAMMER HORROR pictures.

If there is no longer a studio system as such in the UK, it is largely because there is no continuity of production. Fewer movies are made. Instead of a centralised system, films are now packaged by producers, financiers and agents on a one-off basis. Although companies will set up offices at the studios where they are shooting, they don't own the studios, and rarely stay for longer than it takes to complete a particular film.

There have been various faltering attempts to revive British studios' identities. In 1995, Shepperton was taken over by a consortium led by the SCOTT brothers, Ridley and Tony, two of the most commercially successful British directors of their generation. In the summer of 2000, FRAGILE FILMS, the outfit behind such comedies as *Kevin And Perry Go Large* (2000, UK/US) and *Lucky Break* (2001, UK/Ger/US), acquired Ealing and announced plans to shoot a series of films in the vein of the comedies that had made the Ealing name famous. Michael GRADE, the ex-CHANNEL 4 boss, was equally bullish about his plans for Pinewood, of which he became Chairman in early 2000.

All the patriotic chest-thumping that has gone on in recent years can't hide the fact that the studio system in Britain is dead. The reason for its demise is obvious: there are no longer any vertically-integrated film-making outfits with the resources or the expertise to make films along factory lines. The one major consolation is that Britain's technicians remain as good as ever. Geoffrey Macnab

Sturridge, Charles (*b* London, 1951). Director. Winner of BAAs for such classy TV programmes as *Brideshead Revisited* (1981) and *Longitude* (2000), Sturridge has made only a few films, but they bear the same literary sheen and costly production values. However, *A Handful of Dust* (1987, +cosc) and *Where Angels Fear to Tread* (1991, + co-sc) are respectable, if not really exciting versions of their precursor novels; and 2001–2 saw him up to his eyes in Arctic snow for TV's *Shackleton* and an ADAPTATION of J.M. Coetzee's *Disgrace*.

OTHER BRITISH FILMS: *If . . .* (1968, a), *Runners* (1983, d), *Aria* (1987, co-d, co-sc), *Fairytale: A True Story* (1997, UK/US).

Styles, Edwin (*b* London, 1899 – *d* London, 1960). Actor. Former stock broker, then popular light leading man and later character player on London, New York and Australian stages, he made his debut with a concert party in 1920 and London debut in 1930. After a few insignificant 30s film roles, he reappeared as Stewart GRANGER's posh chum in *Adam and Evelyne* (1949), was widowed Anna NEAGLE's even posher friend in *Derby Day* (1952) and, eccentrically, a magician called Bamboula befriended by Donald WOLFIT in *Isn't Life Wonderful!* (1953).

OTHER BRITISH FILMS INCLUDE: *Road House* (1934), *The £5 Man* (1937), *The Lady with a Lamp* (1951), *Top Secret* (1952), *The Weak and the Wicked* (1953), *For Better, for Worse* (1954), *The Dam Busters* (1955), *The Full Treatment* (1960).

Styles, Eric (*b* Neath, Wales, 1967). Director. Award-winning TV director, a graduate of the NATIONAL FILM AND TELEVISION SCHOOL (1991), whose first two feature films could scarcely have been more contrasted: the haunting love story, *The Dreaming of Joseph Lees* (1999, UK/US) and the film version of Noël COWARD's brittle comedy, *Relative Values* (2000, UK/US). He worked for most of the 90s with BBC Cardiff, directing both drama and DOCUMENTARY.

Subotsky, Milton (*b* New York, 1921 – *d* London, 1991). Producer. After WW2 experience, Subotsky began his career in US television, produced the youth musical *Rock Rock Rock* (1956, + co-sc) before moving to England in 1960. He (with partner Max ROSENBERG) launched AMICUS PRODUCTIONS with the MUSICAL, *It's Trad, Dad!* (1962), but came into his own with films in the HORROR (e.g. *The Skull*, 1965, + sc), or SCIENCE-FICTION (e.g. *Dr Who and the Daleks*, 1965, + sc) modes, though the company occasionally produced other kinds of film, including a very non-commercial version of PINTER's *The Birthday Party* (1968). TV included *The Martian Chronicles* (1979).

OTHER BRITISH FILMS INCLUDE: (co-p unless noted) *City of the Dead* (1960, + story), *Dr Terror's House of Horrors* (1964, + sc), *Daleks – Invasion Earth 2150 AD* (+ sc), *The Psychopath*, *The Deadly Bees* (1966), *Torture Garden*, *They Came From Beyond Space* (+ sc), (1967), *Scream and Scream Again* (1969), *Tales from the Crypt* (+ sc), *Asylum* (1972), *The Vault of Horror* (UK/US, + sc), *Tales That Witness Madness*, *From Beyond the Grave* (1973), *The Beast Must Die* (1974), *Dominique* (1978), *The Monster Club* (1980, p).

Suchet, David (*b* London, 1946). Actor. TV actor who has made a name as Agatha CHRISTIE's Belgian sleuth, *Poirot* (1989–93, 1995), and in various Christie telemovies, including two in 2001) and as the inept handyman in *Blott on the Landscape* (1985). He has appeared in cinemas only rarely, but had a major role as Napoleon in *Sabotage!* (2000, UK/Fr/Sp). Awarded OBE, 2002.

OTHER BRITISH FILMS: *The Missionary* (1981), *Greystoke . . .* (1984, UK/US), *A World Apart* (1987, UK/Zim), *When the Whales Came* (1989).

Suedo, Julie (*b* London, 1902 – *d* Wembley, 1978). Actress. Small, dark speciality solo dancer, popular in London theatre and cabaret, on stage from 1918 and in films from 1920. Most of her films are now forgotten; those that are not, such as *Nell Gwyn* (1934), are not remembered for her tiny contributions to them. Married **Stanley Grant**, who photographed a few minor 30s films and contributed to special photographic effects on a few major post-war films, including *A Matter of Life and Death* (1946) and *Oliver Twist* (1948).

OTHER BRITISH FILMS INCLUDE: *The Queen of Hearts* (1923), *The Rat* (1925), *The Triumph of the Rat* (1926), *The Vortex* (1927), *A Window in Piccadilly*, (1928), *The Woman from China* (1930), *Love's Old Sweet Song* (1933), *Queen of Hearts* (1936), *Our Fighting Navy* (1937), *The Villiers Diamond* (1938), *Dark Eyes of London* (1939), *Saloon Bar* (1940), *Kiss the Bride Goodbye* (1944).

Sugarman, Sara (*b* Rhyl, Wales, 1962). Director. Entered films as actress in 1983 as one of the football-mad girls in *Those Glory Glory Days* (TV, some cinemas); was in several other films before receiving a BAAn for her SHORT FILM, *Anthrakitis* (1998). She recovered from the disaster of her first feature, *Mad Cows* (1999, + co-sc), to write and direct *Very Annie Mary* (2001, UK/Fr), a touching romance set in the Rhondda Valley. Was married to David THEWLIS.

Sullivan, Francis L(oftus) (*b* London, 1903 – *d* New York, 1956). Actor. On stage from 1921, in films from 1933, imposing six-footer Sullivan was possibly the best fat actor in British cinema. Most often menacing, as in innumerable 30s THRILLERS, such as *Non-Stop New York* (1937), he is best remembered for his embodiment of two great DICKENS grotesques: the hand-washing Jaggers in *Great Expectations* (1934 in Hollywood, 1946 for David LEAN in Britain) and Bumble the beadle in Lean's *Oliver Twist* (1948), smarm giving way to a quick cuff. He was an outspoken mining unionist in *The Citadel* (1938) and a sort of hero in *The Four Just Men* (1939), but once he hit his stride, in, perhaps, *Pimpernel Smith* (1941, as General von Graum), it was hard to trust him again. After repelling his barely faithful wife, Googie WITHERS, as club-owner Phil Nosseross in *Night and the City* (1950, UK/US), he took his bulk to Hollywood for good – or ill, as was mostly the case – playing in such highly coloured tosh as *Sangaree* (1953) and *The Prodigal* (1955). Won a Tony for stage role in *Witness for the Prosecution* (1955).

OTHER BRITISH FILMS: *The Missing Rembrandt*, *When London Sleeps*, *The Chinese Puzzle* (1932), *The Right to Live*, *The Stickpin*, *FP1* (UK/Ger), *The Wandering Jew*, *Called Back*, *The Fire Raisers* (1933), *The Return of Bulldog Drummond*, *What Happened Then?*, *Red Wagon*, *Princess Charming*, *Jew Süss*, *Chu-Chin-Chow* (1934), *Her Last Affaire* (1935), *Spy of Napoleon*, *A Woman Alone*, *The Limping Man*, *The Interrupted Honeymoon* (1936), *Dinner at the Ritz*, *Fine Feathers*, *Action for Slander*, *21 Days* (1937), *The Ware Case*, *The Drum*, *Kate Plus Ten*, *The Gables Mystery*, *Climbing High* (1938), *Young Man's Fancy* (1939), *Lady from Lisbon*, *The Foreman Went to France*, *The Day Will Dawn* (1942), *The Butler's Dilemma* (1943), *Fiddlers Three* (1944), *Caesar and Cleopatra* (1945), *The Laughing Lady* (1946), *The Man Within*, *Take My Life* (1947), *The Winslow Boy*, *Broken Journey* (1948), *Christopher Columbus* (1949).

Sullivan, Tim (*b* Germany). Director, screenwriter. Came to films via TV, including *Thatcher – The Final Days*, and co-wrote screenplays for Charles STURRIDGE's *A Handful of Dust* (1987) and *Where Angels Fear to Tread* (1991), before directing his first feature, *Jack & Sarah* (1995, UK/Fr, + sc). This mildly engaging sentimental comedy ought to have been followed by something tougher, but he has concentrated on writing since.

Summerfield, Eleanor (*b* London, 1921 – *d* London, 2001). Actress. A bright and sassy performer, both in supporting roles in major films – including *Mandy* (1952) and *Lost* (1955) – and leading roles in support features – notably four for Terence FISHER, *The Last Page* (1952), *Final Appointment* (1954), *Face the Music* (1954) and *Murder by Proxy* (1955). While not conventionally beautiful, Summerfield brought an energy to the screen that made her seem more attractive than some of the more conventional British leading ladies of the 50s. Married Leonard SACHS.

OTHER BRITISH FILMS INCLUDE: *Take My Life* (1947), *London Belongs to Me* (1948), *Man on the Run*, *All Over Town* (1949), *Laughter in Paradise* (1951), *Top Secret* (1952), *Isn't Life Wonderful!*, *Street Corner* (1953), *It's Great to Be Young!*, *No Road Back* (1956), *A Cry from the Streets* (1958), *Don't Bother to Knock*, *Spare the Rod* (1961), *On the Beat*

(1962), *The Running Man* (1963), *The Watcher in the Woods* (1982). Peter Hutchings.

Summers, Jeremy (*b* St Albans, 1931). Director. Son of Walter SUMMERS, he began as assistant director at ABPC in the 50s (e.g. on *The Weak and the Wicked*, 1956), directed about a dozen minor features, then found his niche in TV, where he has directed episodes of many popular programmes, including *Danger Man* (1964) and *Shoestring* (1979).

OTHER BRITISH FILMS INCLUDE: (d, unless noted) *The Moonraker* (1957, ass d), *Depth Charge* (1960, + sc), *The Punch and Judy* (1962), *Crooks in Cloisters* (1964), *San Ferry Ann* (1965), *Five Golden Dragons* (1967), *One Hour to Zero* (1976), *Sammy's Super T-Shirt* (1978).

Summers, Walter (*b* Barnstaple, 1896 – *d* England, 1973). Director, screenwriter. Summers was on active duty in WW1 from 1914 to 1918 and also served with the Territorial Unit in India in 1920, winning the MC, the DCM and the MM. It was that war service which dominated his work on screen; with films such as *Ypres* (1925), *Mons* (1926), *Nelson* (1926), all of which he both wrote and directed, stressing the bravery of the British military. He served with R.C. SHERIFF, and, as Sheriff utilised his war experiences in *Journey's End*, Summers used those same experiences to great effect in *The Lost Patrol* (1929) and *Suspense* (1930), both of which he wrote and directed. After work in the theatre as a property maker and call-boy, Summers joined the LONDON FILM COMPANY as assistant director to George Loane TUCKER in 1914. After the war, he was again an assistant director, for Cecil HEPWORTH, before joining G.B. SAMUELSON as screenwriter in 1922, making his debut as a director in 1923 with *I Pagliacci* and *Afterglow*, both of which he also wrote. Summers was at the height of his career from 1925 to 1929 with BRITISH INSTRUCTIONAL. Son is Jeremy SUMMERS.

OTHER BRITISH FILMS: *The Faithful Heart*, *If Four Walls Told*, *Castles in the Air* (1922), *A Royal Divorce*, *Should a Doctor Tell* (1923, co-sc), *She* (1925), *The Mutiny of the Elsinore* (1937, co-sc), *Black Limelight* (1938, co-sc); (d, sc) *Who Is the Man?* (1924), *The Perfect Crime* (1925), *Bolibar* (1928), *Chamber of Horrors* (1929), *Raise the Roof* (1930, co-sc), *Men Like These* (1931, co-sc), *Timbuctoo* (1933, co-d), *The Return of Bulldog Drummond* (1934), *The Limping Man* (1936), *Dark Eyes of London* (1939, co-sc); (d) *The Battles of the Coronel and Falkland Islands* (1927), *Ourselves Alone* (1936, co-d), *Premiere* (1938), *At the Villa Rose* (1939). AS.

Sumner, David (*b* Mitcham, 1933). Actor. Educated at Sutton Grammar School, RADA-trained Sumner made a very striking start in films as the nervous neophyte criminal in Lance COMFORT's superior 'B' MOVIE, *Touch of Death* (1962), but rarely had a comparably good role again in films, though he starred in Montgomery TULLY's *Out of the Fog* (1962). However, he worked very steadily in the theatre – for the National, the RSC, the Royal Court – and in TV, starring as Pat Sullavan in the legal series, *The Sullavan Brothers* (1964–65).

OTHER BRITISH FILMS: *The Wild and the Willing* (1962), *The Wild Affair* (1963), *The Long Duel* (1967), *Submarine X-1* (1968), *Monique* (1969).

Sumner, Geoffrey (*b* Ilfracombe, 1908 – *d* Alderney, 1959). Actor. Amusing 'silly ass' bumbler and expostulator, round-faced, moustachioed Sumner was educated at Clifton College, entered films at ABPC's ELSTREE studios in the late 30s, served with the directorate of Army Kinematography during WW2, and returned to make a couple of dozen films usually in COMEDY mode. An ex-conman in *Always a Bride* (1953), asked what he's been doing these last three years, he replies concisely, 'Three years'. Fun in films, he was famous on TV as the idiot

Major Upshott-Bagley of *The Army Game* (1957–61), repeating his role in the SPIN-OFF film, *I Only Arsked!* (1958).

OTHER BRITISH FILMS INCLUDE: *Premiere* (1938), *She Couldn't Say No* (1939), *While the Sun Shines* (1947), *Traveller's Joy* (1949), *The Dark Man* (1950), *Top Secret* (1952), *Doctor in the House* (1954), *The Silken Affair* (1956), *Hazard* (1959, p, co-d), *Cul-de-sac* (1966), *There Goes the Bride* (1979).

surrealism A European artistic movement of the 20s and 30s that had great impact on continental cinema but never took root in Britain. Even so, in common with their counterparts in Hollywood, several British directors incorporated surrealist touches into their work, especially for dream sequences, hallucinations and other flights of fancy. The most direct use was made by Alfred HITCHCOCK in *Spellbound* (1945, US), which contains a dream sequence devised by Salvador Dali, and several of Hitchcock's American films have features that may be thought to have surrealist features. (It has been suggested that Brian Desmond HURST's *The Tell-Tale Heart*, 1934, has surrealist touches which pre-figure the Hitchcock–Dali sequence.) Michael POWELL is perhaps the next most obvious example: the dipsomanic hallucination in *The Small Back Room* (1948) is one well-known example, but other Powell films such as *A Canterbury Tale* (1944) and *Black Narcissus* (1947) also have a surrealist atmosphere. A more experimental approach to surrealism was adopted by Humphrey JENNINGS and Len LYE. Jennings, a former surrealist painter, was closely associated with the British Surrealists and a member of the organising committee of the International Surrealist Exhibition in London, 1936, and if his films would generally be characterised as 'poetic' rather than 'surrealist', there are certainly touches of the latter in their unexpected juxtapositions of imagery. Surrealism features more explicitly in the work of Len LYE, most notably *When the Pie Was Opened* (1941) and the wartime training film *Kill or Be Killed* (1943). Lye's approach was built upon in America by Norman McLAREN. Later generations of film-makers such as Ken RUSSELL and Nicolas ROEG drew on surrealist imagery as part of the freewheeling abstraction of their time. Still later, Neil JORDAN's *The Company of Wolves* (1984) displays distinctly surrealist features, though by this time, as Peter GREENAWAY has observed, surrealism had become such a familiar part of popular culture it was difficult to quarantine: 'Walking up and down London's Picadilly, you'll see thousands of images which owe their origin to surrealist painting'. Simon Caterson.

Suschitzky, Peter (*b* London, 1940). Cinematographer. Much associated with, and a major contributor to the shock tactics of, the films of Canadian film-maker David Cronenberg, for whom he has shot such co-productions as *Naked Lunch* (1991, UK/Can) and the SCIENCE-FICTION piece, *eXistenZ* (1999, UK/Fr/Can), as well as the controversial Canadian *Crash* (1996). Entered films in the 60s, working on such non-mainstream fare as *It Happened Here* (1963), the youth revolt movie *Privilege* (1967), and Tony RICHARDSON's revisionist *The Charge of the Light Brigade* (1968, 2uc), on a few more conventional jobs, like *Henry VIII and His Six Wives* (1972), and two brushes with Ken RUSSELL, at his flashiest in *Lisztomania* (1975) and receiving BAAn/c for *Valentino* (1977); then the very big time with *The Empire Strikes Back* (1980, US). Since then, he has worked internationally, most often in Canada and the US. Son of Wolfgang SUSCHITZKY.

OTHER BRITISH FILMS: *Road to Saint Tropez* (short), *The Christmas Tree* (1966), *Giacometti* (co-c, short), *Charlie Bubbles* (1967), *A Midsummer*

Night's Dream (1968), *A Touch of Love, Lock Up Your Daughters!, Leo the Last* (1969), *Figures in a Landscape, SWALK* (1970), *The Pied Piper* (1971), *That'll Be the Day* (1973), *All Creatures Great and Small* (1974), *The Rocky Horror Picture Show* (1975), *Krull* (1983), *Immortal Beloved* (1994, UK/US), *The Man in the Iron Mask* (1998, UK/US).

Suschitzky, Wolfgang (*b* Vienna, 1912) Cinematographer. Came to England in 1934 after training in photography in Vienna, worked in various capacities before becoming camera-man for Paul ROTHA, first on his DOCUMENTARIES such as *Life Begins Again* (1942) and *Hello! West Indies* (1943, co-c), later on his features, contributing a notable visual eloquence to the picaresque melodrama of *No Resting Place* (1951). His subsequent credits are eclectic indeed, embracing the art-house daring of *Ulysses* (1967, UK/US, BAAn/c), the animal films, *Ring of Bright Water* (1969) and *Living Free* (1972) (Rotha had found him 'a gifted photographer, especially of animals and children'), and the harsh gangster classic, *Get Carter* (1971), whose bleak images of northern life stay in the mind. Father of Peter SUSCHITZKY.

OTHER BRITISH FILMS INCLUDE: *The Oracle* (1953), *The Bespoke Overcoat* (1955), *Cat & Mouse* (1958), *The Small World of Sammy Lee* (1962), *The Vengeance of She* (1967), *Les bicyclettes de Belsize* (1968, short), *Something to Hide* (1971), *Theatre of Blood, Moments* (1973), *The Chain* (1984).

Sutherland, Donald (*b* St John, Canada, 1934). Actor. Very tall (6'4"), gloomy-looking but charismatic international star whose career got off to an unexceptional start in British films of the 60s, though 'unexceptional' hardly does justice to the swinging awfulness of *Joanna* (1968). Fortunately for Suther-land, *M*A*S*H* (1970, US) beckoned and he became a sort of 70s icon, and deservedly so for work in such films as *Klute* (1971, US), the genuinely strange and famously erotic *Don't Look Now* (1973, UK/It), *1900*, Fellini's *Casanova* (1976, It) and *The First Great Train Robbery* (1978). He has gone on filming relentlessly and wherever the work is to be found; this has not often been in Britain, and not much of it has been remarkable, but his watchful intensity has always been worth the viewer's atten-tion, whether in a conventional wartime thriller like *Eye of the Needle* (1981), the elephantine *Revolution* (1985, UK/Nor), the sophisticated filmed theatre of *Six Degrees of Separation* (1993), or junk like *Ordeal by Innocence* (1984). Father of actor Kiefer Sutherland.

OTHER BRITISH FILMS: *The World Ten Times Over* (1963), *Dr Terror's House of Horrors* (1964), *Fanatic, The Bedford Incident, Promise Her Anything* (1965), *The Dirty Dozen* (UK/US), *The Billion Dollar Brain, Oedipus the King, Sebastian* (1967), *Interlude* (1968), *The Eagle Has Landed* (1976), *The Disappearance* (1977), *Murder by Decree* (1978), *Bear Island* (1979, UK/Can), *Virus* (1999, UK/Fr/Ger/Jap/US).

Sutherland, Duncan (*b* Glasgow, 1905). Production designer. Among his almost 50 films, on which he is usually credited as 'art director', those he made at EALING in the 40s represent the peak of Sutherland's career. There, he moved easily between the grey wartime realism of *San Demetrio–London* (1943), the decorative expressiveness of the studio's Victorian Brighton in *Pink String and Sealing Wax* (1945), and the *noir* blending of these two modes in *It Always Rains on Sunday* (1947). Trained as architect at the Glasgow School of Architecture, he then took to the stage as actor, before becoming art department assistant at BIP's ELSTREE studio. After slogging his way through largely unremembered 30s GENRE pieces, he led into Ealing via such distinctively atmospheric films as *Gaslight* (1940), in which his sets superbly evoke a sinister, dusty corner of Victorian London

suburbia, the strange and evocative lighthouse setting for *Thunder Rock* and the expressionist effects of *The Night Has Eyes* (1942). Post-Ealing, there is a steady drift into 'B' MOVIES, some of them, like the bank-set *Strongroom* (1962), worth more than passing attention, but it still looks like the decline of a major talent – or one that could no longer find the sorts of vehicles it needed.

OTHER BRITISH FILMS INCLUDE: (art d, unless noted) *After Office Hours*, (1932), *No Funny Business* (1933), *Those Were the Days* (1934), *Dandy Dick* (1935), *The Dark Eyes of London* (1939), *Pimpernel Smith* (1941, settings), *Nine Men* (1942), *Undercover* (1943), *For Those in Peril, Fiddlers Three* (1944), *Johnny Frenchman* (1945), *Bedelia* (1946), *The Loves of Joanna Godden* (1947), *The History of Mr Polly* (1948), *Obsession* (1949), *Last Holiday* (1950), *Night Was Our Friend* (1951), *Intimate Relations* (1953), *Home and Away* (1956), *Zoo Baby* (1957), *The Trollenberg Terror* (1958), *The Bandit of Zhobe* (1959), *Jungle Street* (1961), *Emergency* (1962), *The Hi-Jackers* (1963), *The Vulture* (1966, UK/Can/US).

Sutro, John R. (*b* London, 1903 – *d* Monte Carlo, 1985). Producer. Rugby- and Cambridge-educated son of a playwright, and keenly interested in film, it was he who brought Michael POWELL and the MOI together to make the Canadian-set wartime drama, *49th Parallel* (1941), on which he acted as co-producer and production manager and the film was made jointly for his company Ortus (his name backwards) and the MOI. Also co-produced *The Way Ahead* (1944) and produced *Men of Two Worlds* (1946), both for TWO CITIES. All three were more than usually taxing productions. Sutro's sub-sequent career tapered off in lame UK/Italian co-productions like *Her Favourite Husband* (1950); then, in the 60s, he translated POLANSKI's original screenplays for *Cul-de-sac* (1966) and *Dance of the Vampires* (1967).

OTHER BRITISH FILMS: (co-p, unless noted) *Carnival* (1946), *The Glass Mountain* (1948, ex p), *Children of Chance* (1949, UK/It), *Honeymoon Deferred* (UK/It), *Cheer the Brave* (1951).

Sutton, Dudley (*b* East Molesey, 1933). Actor. Curly-haired, knowing-looking supporting player in films for over 40 years, making a real impression as the young hoodlum in *The Boys* (1962) and the biker who finally, and bleakly, reveals his homosexual feelings for his friend in *The Leather Boys* (1963). He never became a star but was enjoyably scruffy company across a range of roles, including the continuing role of Tinker, none-too-scrupulous chum of TV's *Lovejoy* (1986, 1991–92, 1993–94), and turned up in 2001 in *This Filthy Earth*, Andrew KÖTTING's drama of rural hardship, playing an old man. His work encompassed ART-HOUSE fare like *Orlando* (1992, UK/Fr/It/Neth/Russ) as well as such crowd-pleasers as *The Pink Panther Strikes Again* (1976), playing for menace or mirth as required.

OTHER BRITISH FILMS INCLUDE: *Go to Blazes* (1962), *Rotten to the Core* (1965), *The Walking Stick* (1970), *The Devils* (1971), *Madame Sin* (1972), *Great Expectations* (1975), *Valentino* (1977), *The Big Sleep* (1978), *George and Mildred* (1980), *Trail of the Pink Panther, Brimstone & Treacle* (1982), *Lamb* (1985), *The Rainbow* (1989), *Edward II* (1991), *Up at the Villa* (2000, UK/US).

Suzman, Janet (*b* Johannesburg, 1939). Actress. The failure of the somewhat stately HISTORICAL piece, *Nicholas and Alexandra* (1971, UK/US), to find large popular audiences probably cost Suzman her chance for big-time international stardom. Equally, though, she probably didn't care too much: she was already, and has continued, a highly respected stage actress, LAMDA-trained and with a formidable RSC record from 1962. This daughter of anti-apartheid activists has done distinctive work in several other films, including *A Day in the Death of Joe Egg* (1970), as the mother of the spastic child, the difficult, demanding Frieda Lawrence in *Priest of Love* (1980), and *The Draughtsman's Contract* (1982), as the ambiguous lady of the manor. On TV, she repeated her acclaimed stage role in *Antony and Cleopatra* (1974) and co-starred in *The Singing Detective* (1986). Married and divorced Trevor NUNN.

OTHER BRITISH FILMS: *The Black Windmill* (1974), *Voyage of the Damned* (1976), *Nuns on the Run* (1990), *Leon the Pig Farmer* (1992).

Swanson, Maureen (*b* Glasgow, 1932). Actress. Trained for the ballet and on stage at Sadlers Wells and as dancer in *Carousel* at Drury Lane, the tiny, attractive brunette had a brief career in the 50s before retiring to marry into the aristocracy. She made her film debut as a dancer in *Moulin Rouge* (1953); is a charming Elaine of Astolat in *Knights of the Round Table* (1953), convincingly harrowed in *A Town Like Alice* (1956), an appealing leading lady for Norman WISDOM in *Up in the World* (1956); and a moderately Spanish Maria in *The Spanish Gardener* (1956).

OTHER BRITISH FILMS INCLUDE: *Valley of Song* (1953), *Orders Are Orders* (1954), *Jacqueline* (1956), *Robbery Under Arms* (1957), *The Malpas Mystery* (1960).

swashbucklers The swashbuckler was a GENRE essentially created by Douglas Fairbanks Snr in Hollywood in the 1920s. At its best, it was an exhilarating excursion into pure style, a heady blend of beauty, grace, colour and acrobatic action. British cinema produced almost no swashbucklers until the 50s and then it was as a result of the desire of Hollywood companies to utilize 'frozen funds' (income which they were legally debarred from removing from Britain). MGM produced a splendid trio of films starring Robert TAYLOR (*Ivanhoe*, 1952, *Knights of the Round Table* 1953, *The Adventures of Quentin Durward*, 1955) and DISNEY contributed an engaging trio starring Richard TODD (*The Story of Robin Hood* . . . , 1952; *Rob Roy* . . . , 1953; *The Sword and the Rose*, 1953). Swashbuckling superstar Errol FLYNN himself came to Britain to star in *The Master of Ballantrae* (1953) and *The Dark Avenger* (US: *The Warriors*) (1955) and Cornel Wilde directed and starred in a notable late entry, *Lancelot and Guinevere* (1962). British companies followed suit with stylish 'A' features, *Dangerous Exile* (1957) and *The Moonraker* (1957). Otherwise, the native British swashbucklers tended to be lower-budget offerings from companies primarily associated with horror films. HAMMER produced a ROBIN HOOD trilogy along with *The Pirates of Blood River* (1961), *The Scarlet Blade* (1963) and *Devil-Ship Pirates* (1963); and Robert S. BAKER and Monty BERMAN, *The Hellfire Club*, *Fury at Smuggler's Bay* and *Treasure of Monte Cristo* (all 1960). The swashbuckling revivals in the 70s and 90s, while often using British actors, were mostly shot in France and Spain. Jeffrey Richards.

Sweeney, Birdy (aka Birdie) (*b* Dungannon, Ireland, 1931 – *d* Dublin, 1999). Actor. Christened Edmund, he took his professional name from his mimicry skills, spent much of his life as a touring comic, and found fame at the end of his life as the straggle-haired but ingenious farmer Eamon Byrne in four seasons of TV's *Ballykissangel* (1996–99). Was in several films for Neil JORDAN, was mutely memorable as a lugubrious lift attendant in *Divorcing Jack* (1998, UK/Fr), and scored a success on the Belfast stage in 1997 in *Playboy of the Western World*.

OTHER BRITISH FILMS INCLUDE: *The Crying Game* (1992), *The Snapper* (1993), *Everybody's Gone* (1995), *The Butcher Boy* (Ire/US), *Downtime* (UK/Fr) (1997), *Angela's Ashes* (1999, Ire/US).

Sweeney, Steve Actor. Distinctively gravel-voiced, usually dishevelled-looking character player of the 90s, lucky enough to have good roles in two key films: as Danny in *Nil by Mouth* (1997) and Plank in *Lock, Stock and Two Smoking Barrels* (1998).

OTHER BRITISH FILMS INCLUDE: *Staggered* (1994), *i.d.* (1995, UK/Ger), *Face* (1997), *Beautiful People* (1999), *Silent Cry* (2002).

Sweet, Sheila (aka Carole Mowlam) (*b* Coventry, 1927). Actress. RADA-trained and on stage from 1953, she is best known as Pat, daughter of *The Grove Family* (1954–57), a role she repeated in the screen SPIN-OFF, *It's a Great Day* (1955), and as George COLE's girlfriend in TV's *A Life of Bliss* (1960–61). Married and divorced William SYLVESTER.

OTHER BRITISH FILMS INCLUDE: *Three's Company* (1953), *Conflict of Wings* (1954), *Man of the Moment* (1955), *Life in Emergency Ward 10* (1958).

Swift, Clive (*b* Liverpool, 1936). Actor. Cambridge-educated, gingery-haired character player who had been giving intelligent performances for years, on the professional stage from 1959 (he was with the RSC for eight years), wonderfully venal as Councillor Huggins in TV's *South Riding* (1974) and craven Bishop Proudie in *The Barchester Chronicles* (1982), before becoming a household face, at least, as Hyacinth Bucket's long-suffering husband in the series *Keeping Up Appearances* (1990–95). Occasional films included *A Passage to India* (1984), as Anglo-Indian Major Callendar. Married and divorced novelist Margaret Drabble. Brother of actor David SWIFT.

OTHER BRITISH FILMS INCLUDE: *Catch Us If You Can* (1965), *A Midsummer Night's Dream* (1968), *Frenzy*, *The National Health*, *Man at the Top* (1973), *Praying Mantis* (1982), *Memed My Hawk* (1984).

Swift, David (*b* Liverpool, 1933). Actor. Most often on TV where he played the dissolute, irascible anchor-man Henry in the series *Drop the Dead Donkey* (1990–98), Swift has played supporting roles in occasional films from the early 70s, including Jack's father in *Jack & Sarah* (1995, UK/Fr). Brother of Clive SWIFT.

OTHER BRITISH FILMS INCLUDE: *The Day of the Jackal* (1973, UK/Fr), *The Internecine Project* (1974), *The Black Panther* (1977), *We Think the World of You* (1988), *Secret Friends* (1991).

Swinburne, Nora (*b* Bath, 1902 – *d* London, 2000). Actress. RN: Elinore Johnson. RADA-trained leading lady on stage from 1914, in London from 1916, and on screen from 1920. Graceful, elegant, sympathetic, she was a popular stage leading lady, usually in light comedies and dramas, scoring major successes in *Watch on the Rhine* (1943) and *The Years Between* (1945–46). She was in about 60 films, but was a curiously unexciting leading lady in such 30s melodramas as *Potiphar's Wife* (1931), in which she co-starred with and tried to seduce Laurence OLIVIER. Character roles used her better in films: for GAINSBOROUGH she was Mrs Fitzherbert to Raymond LOVELL's Prince Regent in *The Man in Grey* (1943), Phyllis CALVERT's mother who had loved-not-wisely-but-too-well (there was a lot of that about) in *Fanny by Gaslight* (1944), and, best of all, was true and touching in/as 'The Colonel's Lady' in *Quartet* (1948). She married three actors: (1) **Edward Ashley** (*b* Australia, 1904 – *d* San Diego, California, 2000), who made a few insignificant British films in the 30s, including *The Villiers Diamond* (1938) before leaving to spend the rest of his career in Hollywood; (2) Francis LISTER; and (3) Esmond KNIGHT (1946–87, his death), with whom she appeared in Jean Renoir's *The River* (1951) and in *Anne of the Thousand Days* (1969), in which she brought an apt sharpness to her brief scene.

OTHER BRITISH FILMS INCLUDE: *Saved from the Sea, Branded* (1920), *Hornet's Nest* (1923), *A Girl of London* (1925), *One Colombo Night* (1926), *These Charming People* (1931), *Perfect Understanding* (1933), *Lend Me Your Husband* (1935), *Dinner at the Ritz* (1937), *The Citadel* (1938), *The Farmer's Wife* (1941), *Dear Octopus* (1943), *Jassy, Good-Time Girl* (1947), *The Blind Goddess* (1948), *Christopher Columbus* (1949), *My Daughter Joy* (1950), *The End of the Affair* (1954), *Third Man on the Mountain* (1959), *Interlude* (1968), *Up the Chastity Belt* (1971).

'swinging London' films These films emerged from a short-lived period roughly between 1965 and 1970. Although the films themselves are fairly diverse, they are unified by a common temperament and the premise that LONDON was the centre of the world for modernity, fashion, music and the emergent ideas of the burgeoning youth culture, not least open sexuality. In 1966, American *Time* magazine coined the term 'swinging London', and there is an undoubted travelogue dimension to these films, which is little surprising seeing that they were driven by the influx of Hollywood production interests and investment in British film production at the time.

Richard Lester's *The Knack . . .* (1965) was full of energetic camera tricks and had a big impact, but Michelangelo Antonioni's *Blow-Up* (1966, UK/It) was probably the archetypal 'Swinging London' film, although it also can be seen as a critique. A similar play of celebration and critique can been seen in *Alfie* (1966), *Georgy Girl* (1966) and the musical *Smashing Time* (1967). These films certainly comprise one of the boldest periods in British film production, and, although they may appear mannered to more recent tastes, are astounding in their a wide range of both visual and musical techniques, amounting to a technical bravura arguably unmatched in British cinema history. Kevin Donnelly.

Swinton, Tilda (*b* London, 1961). Actress. Formidably gifted actress who has carved out an international reputation as a risk-taker, a one-off, resolutely eschewing conventional leading lady roles. Cambridge-educated, she worked with the Traverse Theatre, Edinburgh, and the RSC before entering films in the mid 80s, embarking on a rewarding association with director Derek JARMAN, for whom she appeared notably in *Caravaggio* (1986), *The Last of England* (1987) and, as the spurned Queen Isabella, in his revisionist *Edward II* (1991). There is a unique *glamour* about the red-headed Swinton, a glamour that is not cosmetically derived but comes from the genuine whiff of the exotic she gives off, nowhere better seen than as the gender- and time-traversing *Orlando* (1992, UK/Fr/It/Neth/Russ) in Sally POTTER's daring ADAPTATION of Virginia WOOLF's novel. But she was just as distinctive as bitchy Muriel, part of Francis Bacon's circle in *Love Is the Devil* (1998, UK/Fr/Jap), was terribly poignant in Tim ROTH's excoriating family drama, *The War Zone* (1999, UK/It), relaxed the tension somewhat in the more mainstream drama of *The Beach* (2000, UK/US), and won universal acclaim as the housewife protecting her son from the law in *The Deep End* (2001, US). Her work persistently and intelligently explores aspects of women's experience of a kind and at a level of intensity unusual in commercial cinema.
OTHER BRITISH FILMS INCLUDE: *Friendship's Death, Aria* (1987), *Degrees of Blindness* (1988), *War Requiem, Melancholia* (UK/Ger) (1989), *Man to Man* (1992), *Wittgenstein* (as Lady Ottoline Morrell), *Blue* (voice), *Remembrance of Things Fast* (1993), *The Dilapidated Dwelling* (2000, doc, voice), *Young Adam* (2003).

Syal, Meera (*b* Wolverhampton, 1963). Actress. Significantly smart, attractive, witty figure in Asian–British film, TV, radio and theatre since the later 80s, Syal co-wrote the story on which the very engaging *Bhaji on the Beach* (1993) was based. She entered films as Rani in *Sammy and Rosie Get Laid* (1987), was a teacher in *Beautiful Thing* (1996), and a regular in *Goodness Gracious Me*, the popular TV comedy of British-Asian life. Has appeared at the Old Vic, the Royal Court and elsewhere, in plays as diverse as *Peer Gynt* and *The Vagina Monologues*; also a comic author. Awarded OBE, 1997.
OTHER BRITISH FILMS INCLUDE: *Flight* (1996), *The Sixth Happiness* (1997), *Girls' Night* (1998, UK/US), *Anita and Me* (2002, sc, from her novel).

Sydney, Basil (*b* St Osyth, 1885 – *d* London, 1968). Actor. RN: Nugent. Commanding character actor who made two American silents, *Romance* (1920), starring his first wife, Doris Keane, and *Red Hot Romance* (1922), turned down a long-term contract, and did not film again until 1932 (*The Midshipmaid*). He moved easily between charm and menace, occasionally in more or less conventional leading-man roles, as in the rural comedy, *The Farmer's Wife* (1941), but was better used as smooth-spoken villains, like those in *Went the Day Well?* (1942) as one of the disguised German Officers (the one whose German chocolate bar alerts Harry FOWLER's suspicions) infiltrating an English village, or in *Jassy* (1947), as suavely swinish Nick Helmar, or especially as that 'adulterate beast', Claudius, in OLIVIER's *Hamlet* (1948), in which his look of handsome, middle-aged, slightly furtive distinction brilliantly serves the role's demands. There are interesting studies in the 50s, including the benevolent but inevitably paternalistic Crawford in *Simba* (1955) and Lawyer Hawkins in the generally drab ADAPTATION of SHAW's *The Devil's Disciple* (1959). A noted stage exponent of Shaw, he also played Rufio in Gabriel PASCAL's costly *Caesar and Cleopatra* (1945). Son of a theatrical manager, he was on stage from 1909, busy in both the US and Britain. Married (2) Mary ELLIS (3) Joyce HOWARD.
OTHER BRITISH FILMS: *The Third Clue, Dirty Work* (1934), *White Lilac, The Tunnel, The Riverside Murder* (1935), *The Amateur Gentleman, Accused, Rhodes of Africa, Crime Over London, Blind Man's Bluff, Talk of the Devil* (1936), *Shadowed Eyes, The Four Just Men* (1939), *Spring Meeting, Ships with Wings, The Black Sheep of Whitehall* (1941), *The Next of Kin, Big Blockade* (1942), *The Man Within, Meet Me at Dawn* (1947), *The Angel with the Trumpet* (1949), *Treasure Island* (1950), *The Magic Box* (1951), *Ivanhoe* (1952), *Star of India* (UK/It), *Hell Below Zero, Three's Company* (1953), *The Dam Busters* (1955), *Sea Wife* (1956), *Island in the Sun* (1957, UK/US), *A Question of Adultery* (1958), *A Story of David, The 3 Worlds of Gulliver* (UK/Sp/US), *The Hand of Orlac* (UK/Fr) (1960).

Sydney, Derek (*b* London, 1920 – *d* San Marcos, California, 2000). Actor. RADA-trained Londoner, Sydney played a surprising number of foreigners in British films of the 50s and 60s, in main features like *The Constant Husband* (1954), as one of Nicole MAUREY's excitable Italian family, and 'B' MOVIES like *Man from Tangier* (1957), as Darracq, whom we distrust even before he syringes the heroine in a marketplace because we've seen him sitting about decadently in a silk dressing-gown. On stage and TV as well, especially in the 50s.
OTHER BRITISH FILMS INCLUDE: *Captain Horatio Hornblower RN* (1950, UK/US), *A Kid for Two Farthings* (1954), *The Woman for Joe* (1955), *Seven Waves Away* (1956), *The Trollenberg Terror* (1958), *Make Mine Mink* (1960), *Carry On Spying* (1964), *Carry On Up the Khyber* (1968).

Sykes, Eric (*b* Oldham, Lancs, 1923). Actor, screenwriter, director. Dark-haired, lanky comedy actor and scriptwriter with mournful looks and rather doleful voice. Famous for his radio and TV work, and his later wordless shorts, *The Plank* (1967) and *Rhubarb* (1969). Son of a cotton-mill worker, after

WW2 service in RAF, he was a gag writer for BBC radio comedy shows (*Educating Archie*), making his film debut as a private soldier in the GROUP 3 comedy *Orders Are Orders* (1954, + co-sc), and other cameos followed. Starred with Hattie JACQUES in the long-running sitcom *Sykes* (BBC, 1960–80), and in three films – *Invasion Quartet*, *Village of Daughters* (1962) and *Kill or Cure* (1962), was the deadpan manservant to bounder TERRY-THOMAS in the lavish international all-star comedies *Those Magnificent Men . . .* (1965) and *Monte Carlo or Bust!* (1969, UK/Fr/It), and was the sinister gardener in *The Others* (2001, US/Sp). Awarded OBE, 1986.

OTHER BRITISH FILMS INCLUDE: *Charlie Moon* (1956), *Tommy the Toreador* (1959), *Heavens Above!* (1963), *Very Important Person, One Way Pendulum* (1964), *Rotten to the Core* (1965), *The Spy with a Cold Nose* (1966), *Shalako* (1968), *The Alf Garnett Saga* (1972), *Theatre of Blood* (1973), *The Big Freeze* (UK/Fin, d, sc), *Splitting Heirs* (1993). Roger Philip Mellor.

Sykes, Peter (*b* Melbourne, 1939). Director. Late recruit to HAMMER to whose HORROR cycle he contributed two minor, intermittently scary pieces – *Demons of the Mind* (1971) and *To the Devil a Daughter* (1976, UK/Ger) – before making the US feature on the life of *Jesus* (1979). Before going in for horror, he was executive producer on Peter BROOKS' semi-documentary about the Vietnam War, *Tell Me Lies* (1967) and was production assistant on the oddity, *Herostratus* (1967).

OTHER BRITISH FILMS: *The Committee* (1968), *Venom* (1971), *The House in Nightmare Park* (1973), *The Blues Band* (1981).

Sylvaine, Vernon (*b* Manchester, 1897 – *d* Angmering, 1957). Screenwriter, playwright. Author of popular light comedies and farces, several of which were filmed, including *As Long As They're Happy* (1955), a dopey swipe at pop music which not even J. Lee THOMPSON could salvage. The out-and-out farces fare slightly better but not much; they include *Women Aren't Angels* (1942, + co-sc) and *One Wild Oat* (1951, + co-sc), and they benefit from the presence of such expert farceurs as Robertson HARE. Daughter **June Sylvaine** appeared in the latter and in the thriller *The Marked One* (1963).

Sylvani, Gladys (*b* London, 1885 – *d* Alexandria, Virginia, 1953). Actress. HEPWORTH's leading lady, whose leading men were either Hay PLUMB or Alec WORCESTER, Sylvani was one of the first British actresses to be promoted as a star and claimed to be the first to receive a term contract. In 1912, *The Bioscope* hailed her as 'the most popular of all English picture actresses'. She retired at the height of her fame and moved to the US in 1939.

BRITISH FILMS: *Heart of a Fishergirl* (1910), *The Three Lovers, Harry the Footballer, Mother's Boy, A Sprained Ankle, A Double Deception, Till Death Us Do Part, Twin Roses, The Torn Letter, Jim of the Mounted Police, Wealthy Brother John, The Greatest of These, Rachel's Sin, All's Right with the World, The Stolen Letters* (1911), *The Editor and the Millionaire, A Fisherman's Love Story, A Girl Alone, Our Bessie, The Deception, The Traitress of Parton's Court, The Bachelor's Ward, Love Wins in the End, At the Eleventh Hour, Love in a Laundry, Pamela's Party, Jimmy Lester, Convict and Gentleman, Church and Stage, Jasmine, Her Only Son, A Woman's Wit* (1912), *Fisherman's Luck* (1913). AS.

Sylvester, William (*b* Oakland, California, 1922 – *b* Sacramento, California, 1995). Actor. Dark-haired actor (on US stage from 1941), at RADA from 1946, and remained in UK for over 20 years, often cast for his soft-spoken US accent. Best remembered for Dr Heywood Floyd in *2001: A Space Odyssey* (1968), he made his film debut in the Brooklyn-set drama *Give Us This Day* (1949, UK/US), followed by a plausible villain role

in *The Yellow Balloon* (1953). His sometimes superior 50s 'B' FILMS included *House of Blackmail* (1953) and *Dublin Nightmare* (1958), interspersed with higher-budget films: he was a gambler in the Nova Scotia-set drama *High Tide at Noon* (1957), a murderer on the run in *Whirlpool* (1959), an MI5 agent in *Offbeat* (1960) and a blind composer with a faithless wife in *Blind Corner* (1963). Stardom eluded him, except on TV in *The Gemini Man*. Married (1) Sheila SWEET and (2) Veronica HURST (1954–70).

OTHER BRITISH FILMS: *Appointment in London, Albert RN* (1953), *Portrait of Alison* (1955), *Gorgo* (1960), *Devils of Darkness* (1964), *The Hand of Night* (1966), *The Syndicate* (1967). Roger Philip Mellor.

Sylvestre, Cleo (*b* Hitchin, 1945). Actress. Daughter of Trinidadian RAF Flight Sergeant and Yorkshire tap-dancer mother, she began as a child dancer, entered films in the CHILDREN'S FILM FOUNDATION's production of *Johnny on the Run* (1953), worked with the Negro Theatre Workshop, and made her TV debut in the mid 60s, appearing in such realist dramas as *Up the Junction* and *Cathy Come Home* (1966), both for Ken LOACH. She had supporting roles in films such as *Smashing Bird I Used to Know* (1969) and *Sammy and Rosie Get Laid* (1987), and was one of the first British-born black actresses to find herself used in film roles that reflected her own experience.

OTHER BRITISH FILMS INCLUDE: *Till Death Us Do Part* (1969), *Trog* (1970), *The Alf Garnett Saga* (1972), *The Love Child* (1987), *The Attendant* (1993, short).

Symons, Annie Costume designer. Symons's wit as a costume designer is seen in the attire of Tom HOLLANDER's outrageous gay in *Bedrooms and Hallways* (1999) – he's 'in danger from the fashion police' – and her decking out of the Lake poets and their set in *Pandaemonium* (2001), but she has also contributed to the tough REALISM of *Stella Does Tricks* (1996) and the sub-EALING whimsy of *Saving Grace* (2000).

OTHER BRITISH FILMS INCLUDE: *Kiss* (1991, short), *Anchoress* (1993, Uk/Belg), *Madagascar Skin* (1995), *Love Is the Devil* (1998, UK/Fr/Jap, + a), *Step Into My World* (2003, UK/US).

Syms, Sylvia (*b* London, 1934). Actress. Not many pretty young stars develop into satisfying CHARACTER ACTORS, but Syms, in the later 50s the freshest new face in British films, has doggedly held on to her career in all the acting media. Watch a perfectly unexceptional Ruth RENDELL mystery, *The Master of the Moor* (1994), come alive for a few minutes when Syms suddenly appears as a long-missing mother and you see what character playing means: in her maturity, she can suggest all the appropriate resonances that give the role a sense of a past. She credits Herbert WILCOX with launching and nurturing her film career; he co-starred her with wife Anna NEAGLE in *My Teenage Daughter* (1956), a genteel version of the rebellious youth syndrome so popular then. She signed a contract with ASSOCIATED BRITISH, which she later regretted, but it netted her some good roles, including two for J. Lee THOMPSON: *Woman in a Dressing Gown* (1957), playing the 'other woman' with feeling and dignity, and *Ice Cold in Alex* (1958), as the Army nurse engaged on a perilous journey. For other companies, she brought strength and humanity to the roles of the bigot's daughter in love with a black man in *Flame in the Streets* and the anguished wife of the gay barrister in *Victim* (1961), a role turned down by several other actresses, and was sharp and funny as Laurence HARVEY's strip-tease girlfriend in the MUSICAL, *Expresso Bongo* (1959). In other words, she had some of the best chances going for a young actress at the time. She stayed busy in the 60s but the roles grew less rewarding. She was bitchy second lead to crisply dull Julie ANDREWS in *The Tamarind Seed* (1974), and this perhaps marks the start of her later career as a character actress. Not that the screen has offered her much, but she made the most of the headmistress in *Shirley Valentine* (1989, UK/US) and the bride's waspish mother in *Staggered* (1994). TV and the stage (moving as the mother in the Noël COWARD resuscitation, *Post-Mortem*, in 1992) have kept her in sight; in the 90s, on both stage and screen she played Mrs Thatcher: in TV's *Thatcher – The Final Days* and in the Tricycle Theatre's *Half the Picture*. Her daughter is Beatie EDNEY.

OTHER BRITISH FILMS: *No Time for Tears, The Moonraker, The Birthday Present* (1957), *No Trees in the Street, Bachelor of Hearts* (1958), *Ferry to Hong Kong* (1959), *Conspiracy of Hearts, The World of Suzie Wong* (1960), *The Quare Fellow, The Punch and Judy Man* (1962), *The World Ten Times Over* (1963), *East of Sudan* (1964), *Operation Crossbow* (UK/It), *The Big Job* (1965), *Danger Route, The Fiction Makers* (1967), *Hostile Witness* (1968), *Run Wild, Run Free* (1969), *Asylum* (1972), *Give Us Tomorrow* (1978), *There Goes the Bride* (1979), *Absolute Beginners* (1986), *A Chorus of Disapproval* (1989), *Dirty Weekend* (1993), *Food of Love* (1996, UK/Fr), *The House of Angelo* (1997).

Tt

20th Century–Fox *See* **Fox–British Pictures; Wembley Studios; Hollywood studios in Britain**

Tabori, George (*b* Budapest, 1914). Screenwriter. Novelist and playwright Tabori worked on several British screenplays, including the Cold War romance, *The Young Lovers* (1954, co-sc, story, BAA/sc), *The Journey* (1959, US-financed, many UK personnel), and LOSEY's baroque *Secret Ceremony* (1968). *Leo the Last* (1969), John BOORMAN's race-relations comedy, was based on Tabori's play and *My Mother's Courage* (1995, UK/Austria/Ger) on his novel. Married and divorced Viveca Lindfors; father of US actor Kristoffer Tabori.

Tabori, Paul (*b* Budapest, 1908 – *d* London, 1974). Novelist, screenwriter. Educated in Hungary, Switzerland and Berlin, he came to England in 1937, and worked as film critic for the *Daily Mail* and, inevitably, a stint for KORDA (1943–48) as contract writer, though nothing much seems to have come from this latter. Also wrote the screenplays for 20 mainly minor films, some of them quite enjoyable, like the pre-HORROR HAMMER pieces for Terence FISHER, including *Mantrap* (1953, co-sc, adptn), and the PORTMANTEAU film, *Gilbert Harding Speaking of Murder* (1953, sc, episode), directed by Paul DICKSON for whom he also wrote the lugubrious love story, *Star of My Night* (1954). From the mid 50s, he threw in his lot with the DANZIGERS, and cut his coat, as it were . . . . Also wrote a great many TV playlets, some forming part of cinema features, others for US television.
OTHER BRITISH FILMS: (co-sc, unless noted) *Valley of Eagles* (1951), *Four-Sided Triangle* (+ adptn), *Spaceways* (1953), *Alias John Preston* (1955), *The Malpas Mystery* (1960), *Strip Tease Murder* (sc), *Beware of the Dog* (6-episode serial) (1963).

Tafler, Sydney (*b* London, 1916 – *d* London, 1979). Actor. In the post-war decade, Tafler could have menaced for England, with the broad, bland, smooth-faced suggestion of endless corruptibility he brought to dozens of blackmarketeers, Cockney spivs, nightclub owners fronting dodgy enterprises, and other slickly dressed low-lifes. There were a couple of policemen (e.g. *Cockleshell Heroes*, 1955), but they weren't fooling anyone, and there was a real effort of audience adjustment required when he played, say, an RAF officer in *Reach for the Sky* (1956). RADA-trained and on London stage from 1936 (Old Vic season, 1944–46), his range was actually larger than the above suggests – see his 'Madame Rita' in *A Kid for Two Farthings* (1954) and Nat in the film of *The Birthday Party* (1968) – but the 50s shyster image clings to him. On TV from 1947, he was sidekick to Sid JAMES in *Citizen James* (1960–62). Long married to Joy SHELTON.

OTHER BRITISH FILMS INCLUDE: *Cottage to Let* (1941), *It Always Rains on Sunday* (1947), *Passport to Pimlico* (1949), *Once a Sinner* (1950), *Assassin for Hire*, *Secret People* (1951), *Time Gentlemen Please!* (1952), *The Floating Dutchman*, *Johnny on the Run* (1953), *Fire Maidens From Outer Space* (1956), *Interpol* (1957), *Carve Her Name With Pride* (1958) *The Bulldog Breed* (1960), *Carry On Regardless* (1961), *Alfie* (1966), *The Spy Who Loved Me* (1977).

Tait, Margaret (*b* Kirkwall, Orkney, 1918 – Firth, Orkney, 1999). Director. Trained as doctor (she was Edinburgh-educated), also a painter and poet, Tait, in the 50s, turned her attention to INDEPENDENT FILM-MAKING. She was fascinated by what film could capture that eluded the eye (the opening of a flower, for instance) and by the power of editing. She took time off to train in Rome (1950–52) and subsequently set up workshop in Edinburgh, where she stayed until her final move back to Orkney in 1974. One of her best-known SHORT FILMS is *Hugh MacDiarmid: A Portrait* (1964); she made only one feature film, *Blue Black Permanent* (1992, + sc), which won critical acclaim for its originality even if it was not widely seen.
OTHER BRITISH FILMS INCLUDE: (shorts, d, unless noted) *One Is One* (1951), *Calypso* (1955), *Rose Street* (1958, co-d), *Palindrome* (1964), *Splashing* (1966), *He's Back* (+ sc), *Eightsome* (1970), *Aerial* (1974, co-d).

Tallents, Sir Stephen (*b* 1884 – *d* 1958). Educated at Harrow and Oxford, the son of a barrister, Tallents worked for the Ministries of Munitions and of Food during WW1. Between 1919 and 1920, he was Chief British Delegate for Relief and Supply of Poland, between 1920 and 1922, British Commissioner for Baltic Provinces. From 1922 to 1926, he was private secretary to the Lord-Lieutenant of Ireland, then, 1926–33, Secretary to the EMPIRE MARKETING BOARD. Here, he helped found the BRITISH DOCUMENTARY FILM MOVEMENT, by his employment of John GRIERSON and the setting up of the Film Unit, which Tallents took with him as Public Relations Officer at the GPO (1933–35) when the EMB was disbanded. He was familiar with the importance of public relations and therefore supported Grierson, and was in full accord with Grierson's ideas about using PROPAGANDA to ensure public unity, making it a condition of his employment at the GPO that Grierson and others should also transfer. He was Controller Public Relations, BBC (1935–40) and worked for the BBC Overseas Service (1940–41). Between 1943 and 1949 he worked for the Ministry of Town and Country Planning, and, in 1949, was appointed first President and Fellow of the Institute of Public Relations. Without Tallents the documentary film movement might not have come into being. Knighted in 1932.
BIBLIOG: Autobiography, *Man and Boy*, 1943.

Tamiroff, Akim (*b* Baku, Russia, 1899 – *d* Palm Springs, California, 1972). Actor. Very prolific and compelling supporting actor in nearly 130 international films, increasingly European in origin in his last years, but his is essentially a Hollywood career, in which he naturally played foreigners of every hue, most famously perhaps as *The General* [who] *Died at Dawn* (1936) and Pablo in *For Whom the Bell Tolls* (1944), both Oscar-nominated. His earthy, sweaty humanity, which could be screen-channelled into comedy or threat, found its way into about ten British films, none of them his best, but he is at least an amusing President of Agraria in the mildly funny *You Know What Sailors Are!* (1954) and is one of the White Russians exploiting *Anastasia* (1956). Worked several times with Orson WELLES, including *Confidential Report* (1955, UK/Sp/Switz).

OTHER BRITISH FILMS INCLUDE: *They Who Dare* (1953), *Yangtse Incident* (1956), *Lord Jim* (1964), *Hotel Paradiso* (1966, UK/Fr), *Great Catherine* (1967).

Tandy, Jessica (*b* London, 1909 – *d* Easton, Connecticut, 1994). Actress. British-born character star of US films, Oscared for *Driving Miss Daisy* (1989) and nominated for *Fried Green Tomatoes* (1991). She appeared in two minor British films, *The Indiscretions of Eve* (1932) and *Murder in the Family* (1938) but became a respected stage actress (trained at Ben Greet Academy of Acting) in Britain and America, where she finally began to take films seriously in the mid 40s. After the breakup of her first marriage to Jack HAWKINS, she worked almost entirely in the US, winning a Tony for her Blanche in *A Streetcar Named Desire* (1947–49). Married Hume CRONYN (1942), and they often acted together. She made only three further British films: *Butley* (1973, UK/Can/US), *The Bostonians* (1984, UK/US) and *Camilla* (1994, UK/Can). Daughter is Tandy Cronyn (*b* Los Angeles, 1945) who has appeared in a few films, including the British *Praise Marx and Pass the Ammunition* (1968).

Tani, Yoko (*b* Paris, 1932 – *d* Paris, 1999) Actress. RN: Itani. Attractive but histrionically limited Japanese actress in international films, including a British handful, of which *The Wind Cannot Read* (1958), as Dirk BOGARDE's doomed love interest, gave her most prominence. Following the cinema's undiscriminating line on ethnic/racial difference, she was an Eskimo in Nicholas Ray's *The Savage Innocents* (1959, UK/Fr/It/US).

OTHER BRITISH FILMS: *Piccadilly Third Stop* (1960), *The Partner* (1963), *Invasion* (1966).

Tanner, Peter (*b* Tilford, 1914 – *d* Stoke Poges, 2002) Editor. Westminster-educated, Tanner entered film industry in the early 30s, eventually becoming editor for FOX–BRITISH at WEMBLEY STUDIOS. After a brief stint with Fox in the US, he returned to Britain and joined Sydney BOX at VERITY FILMS, where he edited DOCUMENTARIES during WW2. His period of chief distinction came later at EALING, cutting such classics as *Kind Hearts and Coronets* (1949), where editorial control matches precision of word and image. (A pity he couldn't have evoked such skills to shake up that postcard movie, *A Month by the Lake*, 1995, UK/US.) Post-Ealing, he edited across a wide GENRE range, from horrorfests like *And Now the Screaming Starts!* (1973) to gentle chamber works like *Stevie* (1978), as well as working on such TV programmes as *The Avengers*.

OTHER BRITISH FILMS INCLUDE: *Double Alibi* (1937), *Out of Chaos* (1944, short), *Five Towns* (1947, short), *Scott of the Antarctic* (1948), *The Blue Lamp* (1949), *Secret People* (1951), *The Cruel Sea* (1952), *The 'Maggie'* (1953), *Lease of Life* (1954), *The Man in the Sky* (1956), *Tamahine* (1962), *A Jolly Bad Fellow* (1963), *The Best House in London* (1968), *Asylum* (1972), *Hedda* (1975), *Nasty Habits* (1976), *The Monster*

Club (1980), *Turtle Diary* (1985), *Without a Clue* (1988), *Widow's Peak* (1994, UK/US).

Tanner, Tony (*b* 1932). Actor. Stage player, especially in revue, who made a few films in the 60s, including the allegorically named protagonist, Littlechap, in the film version of the Anthony NEWLEY-Leslie BRICUSSE stage musical, *Stop the World I Want to Get Off* (1966), but the cinema never took much heed of him.

OTHER BRITISH FILMS: *Strictly for the Birds* (1963), *A Home of Your Own* (1964), *The Pleasure Girls* (1965), *The Sandwich Man* (1966).

Tannura, Phil (*b* New York, 1897 – *d* Beverly Hills, California, 1973). Cinematographer. Prominent US cinematographer who began his career as boy actor in New York with the Edison Company, where he learned to use a camera. Brought to the UK by PARAMOUNT in early 30s, he liked the British so well that he stayed until WW2, working on major features, and happiest under contract to Tom WALLS, shooting popular, if somewhat visually uninspired, film versions of ALDWYCH FARCES, including *A Cup of Kindness* and *Dirty Work* (1934).

OTHER BRITISH FILMS INCLUDE: *Men of Tomorrow* (1932), *Channel Crossing* (1933), *Lady in Danger* (1934), *Fighting Stock, Moscow Nights* (1935), *Love from a Stranger* (1937), *Stolen Life* (1939). AS.

Tapley, Colin (*b* Dunedin, NZ, 1911 – *d* Cirencester, Wilts, 1995). Actor. After winning a Paramount talent contest, Tapley went to the UK, then spent time in Hollywood in the 30s, usually playing British types, like William Dobbin in *Becky Sharp* (1935). When he returned to England in 1951, he played about 30 titled chaps, police inspectors and other professionals, mainly in the 'B' FILMS of such exponents as Ernest MORRIS and Godfrey GRAYSON, and Francis SEARLE, for whom Tapley is the investigating officer in *Cloudburst* (1951), his first British film, and the doctor in *Emergency* (1962), two superior examples. His firm, dignified presence ensured a touch of verity at the edges of such films. Also in a trickle of main features, including *The Dam Busters* (1955).

OTHER BRITISH FILMS INCLUDE: *Angels One Five* (1952), *Barbados Quest* (1955), *The Safecracker* (1957), *An Honourable Murder* (1960), *Strongroom* (1962), *Shadow of Fear* (1963).

Tate, Harry (*b* Scotland, 1872 – *d* London, 1940). Actor. RN: Ronald Hutchinson. MUSIC HALL comedian famous for his 'Motoring' sketch and an influential force in the comedy of W.C. Fields. On-screen as himself in *Harry Tate Grimaces* (1899), *Harry Tate Impersonations* (1899), *Motoring* (1927), *Royal Cavalcade* (1935), *Soft Lights and Sweet Music* (1936), and *Variety Parade* (1936), and in other films as a character comedian. Killed in an air raid. Son **Harry Tate Jr** (*b* 1902) was also on screen in two features, *Variety Parade* (1936) and *It Happened in Leicester Square* (1949).

OTHER BRITISH FILMS INCLUDE: *Her First Affaire* (1932), *I Spy* (1933), *Happy* (1934), *Look Up and Laugh, Midshipman Easy* (1935), *Keep Your Seats, Please* (1936), *Wings of the Morning, Storm in a Teacup* (1937). AS.

Tate, Reginald (*b* Garforth, 1896 – *d* London, 1955). Actor. Gentlemanly, incisive purveyor of well-bred professionalism, as in Phyllis CALVERT's doctor in *Madonna of the Seven Moons* or the Company Commanding Officer in *The Way Ahead* (1944), he could also bring a convincing hint of threat to his persona as he does in *The Man from Morocco* (1945), as the man Margaretta SCOTT marries in the interests of patriotism. Served in WW1 and WW2; was on stage from 1922 and suaved his way into films in *Whispering Tongues* and *Tangled Evidence*

(1934); had possibly his finest hour as the eponymous Professor of TV's *The Quatermass Experiment* (1953).

OTHER BRITISH FILMS INCLUDE: *The Phantom Light* (1935), *The Man Behind the Mask* (1936), *Dark Journey* (1937), *Poison Pen* (1939), *The Next of Kin* (1942), *The Life and Death of Colonel Blimp* (1943), *Uncle Silas*, *So Well Remembered* (1947), *Secret People* (1951), *King's Rhapsody* (1955).

Tattersall, David (*b* Barrow-in-Furness, 1960). Cinematographer. Educated at Goldsmiths College, London, and trained at the NATIONAL FILM AND TELEVISION SCHOOL, where he shot several SHORT FILMS, one of which, *King's Christmas* (1986) was BAA-nominated. Though involved in such big-time affairs as *Star Wars . . . The Phantom Menace* (1999) and *Star Wars . . . Attack of the Clones* (2002), his work on the small scale, *Whatever Happened to Harold Smith?* (2000), evoking 70s Sheffield and punk with tenderness and precision, suggested a more personal talent.

OTHER BRITISH FILMS INCLUDE: *Moonlight Resurrection*, *Metropolis Apocalypse* (1988, short), *The Bridge* (1991), *The Wind in the Willows* (1996), *Soldier* (1998, UK/US), *Die Another Day* (2002).

Tattersall, Gale (*b* Wirral, 1948). Cinematographer. London Film School graduate who came to attention for his work on two films for Bill DOUGLAS: his images complemented the austerity of Douglas's 1973 autobiographical *My Ain Folk* (he had done some work on its 1972 predecessor, *My Childhood*); and, in the masterly *Comrades* (1986), they ensured that the lighting contrasts between rain-sodden Dorset and the harshness of outback colonial Australia significantly contributed to meaning. In the 70s, he worked as camera operator on four Australian films, as well as several in Britain; apart from *The Commitments* (1991, UK/US), he spent the 90s on US projects such as *Pushing Tin* (1999).

OTHER BRITISH FILMS INCLUDE: (cam op) *Sweet William* (1979), *The Emerald Forest*, *Link* (1985);(c) *Aria* (1987, segment), *Vroom* (1988).

Tauber, Richard (*b* Linz, Austria 1891 – *d* London, 1948). Actor, singer. Legendary operatic tenor on the European and international stage in the 20s, Tauber made his film debut in Germany in 1929. In the 30s he appeared in a number of tailor-made British star vehicles, showcasing his singing talents, although his range as an actor was rather limited. In the pedestrian post-war MUSICAL, *Lisbon Story* (1946), he enthralled his legion of fans by singing 'Pedro the Fisherman'. Tauber became a British citizen in 1940. Married to Diana NAPIER, who appeared with him in the musical romances, *Heart's Desire* (1935) and *Land Without Music* (1936), and the opera film, *Pagliacci* (1936).

OTHER BRITISH FILMS: *Blossom Time* (1934), *Pagliacci* (1936), *Waltz Time* (1945), *Lisbon Story* (1946).

BIBLIOG: Diana Napier Tauber, *Richard Tauber*, 1949; *My Heart and I*, 1959. Tim Bergfelder.

Taylor, Alma (*b* London, 1895 – *d* London, 1974). Actress. Alma Taylor spent virtually her entire silent career, beginning in 1907, with producer Cecil HEPWORTH, co-starring with Chrissie WHITE in the 'Tilly Girl' series (1910–15) as well as 75 or more short subjects. She was the obvious favourite of the producer, who was proud that she never used make-up in any of his films, and Taylor, in return, was Hepworth's most loyal performer, starring in his last film, *The House of Marney* (1926). She starred in only three non-Hepworth films: *The Shadow of Egypt* (1924), *Quinneys* (1927) and *Two Little Drummer Boys* (1928). In 1924, she was named by the *Daily News*, along with Betty BALFOUR, as Britain's top star. With the coming of

sound, the actress played minor, matronly roles, in a handful of films, including *Bachelor's Baby* (1932), *Things Are Looking Up* (1935), *Lilacs in the Spring* (1954), and *Blue Murder at St Trinian's* (1957).

OTHER BRITISH FILMS INCLUDE: *Trelawney of the Wells*, *Comin' Thro' the Rye* (1916), *Sheba* (1919), *Alf's Button* (1920), *Tansy* (1921), *Mist in the Valley* (1923), *Comin' Thro' the Rye* (1923). AS.

Taylor, Donald (*b* London, 1911 – *d* 1966). Director, producer. Oxford-educated Taylor worked as a producer and director at the EMPIRE MARKETING BOARD FILM UNIT until 1935. He then founded the STRAND FILM COMPANY, the first of the independent units within the DOCUMENTARY MOVEMENT, and worked there until 1943. Along with John GRIERSON, Edgar ANSTEY and Arthur ELTON, he also established the Associated Realist Film Producers' Association in 1935. Between 1943 and 1945 he worked as a producer at Gryphon Films, and, from 1946 to 1949, at the CROWN FILM UNIT. From 1949 he worked as a freelance director and producer in England and the US, directing his last film, *Night of the Full Moon*, in 1954. Among the many films he produced, the most important is probably Alexander SHAW's *These Children Are Safe* (1940). Committed suicide in 1966.

OTHER BRITISH FILMS INCLUDE: (doc) *Lancashire at Work* (1933), *Conquest of the Air*, *Spring Comes to England* (1934), *Lancashire, Home of Industry*, *The Order of the Bath*, *Taking the Plunge*, *Citizens of the Future*, *Private Life of Mister Therm*, *Sixpenny Telegrams*, *So This is Lancashire* (1935), *Of All the Gay Places* (1937), *African Skyway* (1940), *Home Guard*, *Flax* (1944), *Ruth* (1948), *The Straw Man* (1953). Ian Aitken.

Taylor, Elaine (*b* Hemel Hempstead, 1943). Actress. Insulted by an eye-patched Bette DAVIS ('I find body odour offensive') is perhaps not the most attractive souvenir of a screen career. However, though Taylor had a half-dozen other roles none offered anything as memorable as these moments in the tasteless *The Anniversary* (1967). On TV, she was utterly charming as *Trelawney of the Wells* (1971), PINERO offering her better chances than her screenwriters. She is Susannah YORK's chum in *Lock Up Your Daughters!* (1969), co-starrring Christopher PLUMMER whom she married in 1970.

OTHER BRITISH FILMS INCLUDE: *Half a Sixpence* (1967, UK/US), *Diamonds for Breakfast* (1968), *The Games* (1969), *Love Potion* (1987, co-p).

Taylor, Dame Elizabeth (*b* London, 1932). Actress. One of the most celebrated stars in film history, not just for – or even primarily for – her talents, though these are not negligible, but for her astonishing beauty when young and her equally astonishing capacity to stay in the headlines for several decades. Few private lives have been lived so publicly: her career as an actress, begun enchantingly as a child, scarcely rivalled those as serial bride (eight times at last count, including twice to Richard BURTON, involving a decade-long media circus), diamond collectress, and survivor of life-threatening illnesses. Most of her film career, embracing *National Velvet* (1944) and *Cleopatra* (1963), belongs to Hollywood. Her family moved there when she was ten, and her ravishing looks, which lasted well into the early 60s, along with her steadily improving histrionic capacities, ensured a run of films which took her from childhood to adult stardom, picking up Oscars on the way for *Butterfield 8* (1960) and, deservedly, *Who's Afraid of Virginia Woolf?* (1966). Her British film roles include Rebecca in *Ivanhoe* (1952), the lobotomised Catherine in *Suddenly, Last Summer* (1959), the leads in two of LOSEY's least successful films, *Boom* and *Secret Ceremony* (1968), and a film star – what else? – in the Agatha CHRISTIE MYSTERY, *The Mirror Crack'd* (1980). Other husbands included (2) Michael WILDING, (3) producer Mike Todd, (4) actor/singer Eddie Fisher. Made a Dame (the title seemed apt) in 2000, but, above all, a survivor.

OTHER BRITISH FILMS: *Conspirator* (1949), *Beau Brummell* (1954), *The VIPs* (1963), *Doctor Faustus* (1967, as Helen of Troy), *Anne of the Thousand Days* (1969, unc), *Zee & Co., Under Milk Wood* (1971), *Night Watch* (1973).

BIBLIOG: Kitty Kelly, *Elizabeth Taylor: The Last Star*, 1981; Alexander Walker, *Elizabeth*, 1991.

Taylor, Ernest (*b* London, 1913). Make-up artist. If he had done no more than help to create the eight different d'Ascoynes played by Alec GUINNESS in *Kind Hearts and Coronets* (1949), Taylor would have earned his place in the story. As it was, in films from 1933, working in the ABPC makeup department at ELSTREE, he became director of makeup at EALING after finishing RAF service (1939–43), working on some of the studio's most notable films. In contrasting modes, he ensures Joan GREENWOOD looks charmingly natural in *Whisky Galore!* (1949) and Flora ROBSON bitterly raddled in *Saraband for Dead Lovers* (1948).

OTHER BRITISH FILMS INCLUDE: *Pink String and Sealing Wax* (1945), *Nicholas Nickleby, It Always Rains on Sunday* (1947), *Scott of the Antarctic* (1948), *Passport to Pimlico, The Blue Lamp* (1949), *The Lavender Hill Mob* (transforming Guinness again), *The Man in the White Suit* (1951), *Mandy* (1952), *Moon Zero Two* (1969).

Taylor, Gilbert (*b* Bushey Heath, 1914). Cinematographer. In the industry from 1929 as assistant in the GAUMONT–BRITISH camera department, Taylor came into his own after his RAF service. Worked as camera operator for the BOULTINGS on *Fame is the Spur* and *Brighton Rock* (1947), then as director of photography on three films for the brothers: *The Guinea Pig* (1948), and the contemporary THRILLERS, *Seven Days to Noon* (1950) and *High Treason* (1951), in which he began to develop his realistic use of black-and-white film. Less concerned with aesthetic beauty than with dramatic veracity, he honed his technique further on the dramas he made for J. Lee THOMPSON, notably *Yield to the Night* (1956), *Woman in a Dressing Gown* (1957) and *Ice Cold in Alex* (1958) – and on the BEATLES' debut film, *A Hard Day's Night* (1964). His achievements in black-and-white were recognised in his BAA nominations for the POLANSKI films, *Repulsion* (1965) and the visually remarkable *Cul-de-sac* (1966). He also worked with Stanley KUBRICK, but with apparently less satisfaction.

OTHER BRITISH FILMS INCLUDE: (cam ass) *Third Time Lucky* (1931), *Turn of the Tide* (1935); (cam op) *School for Secrets* (1946), (c) *The Weak and the Wicked, Single-Handed, Front Page Story* (1953), *The Dam Busters* (1955, fx ph), *The Good Companions* (1956), *No Trees in the Street* (1958), *Dr Strangelove . . .* (1963), *Theatre of Death* (1966), *2001: A Space Odyssey* (1968, add ph), *Macbeth* (1971), *Frenzy* (1972), *Flash Gordon* (1980), *Venom* (1981).

BIBLIOG: Duncan Petrie, *British Cinematographers*, 1996.

Taylor, Jill (*b* Van Nuys, California, 1951). Costume designer. Most prominently associated with the sartorial authenticity, in relation to such matters as class and temperament, of such contemporary-set British films of the 90s as *Priest* (1994), *The Full Monty* (1997, UK/US), *This Year's Love* (1999) and *Last Orders* (2002, UK/Ger), Taylor has also shown herself equal to the period challenge of TV's *The Mill on the Floss* (1997), for which she was BAA-nominated.

OTHER BRITISH FILMS INCLUDE: *Safe* (1993), *Face* (1997), *Sliding Doors* (1998, UK/US), *Purely Belter* (2000), *Born Romantic, Crush* (UK/Ger) (2001).

Taylor, John (*b* London, 1914 – *d* 1992). Director. Joined the EMB FILM UNIT in 1930, at the age of sixteen, one of John GRIERSON's first appointees. Produced and directed there, and at the GPO FILM UNIT, until 1936, then at the STRAND FILM COMPANY between 1936 and 1938. From 1937 to 1947, he was head of production of the REALIST FILM UNIT, overseeing such groundbreaking social and political films as *The Smoke Menace* (1937) and *Advance Democracy* (1938). Worked as a producer at the CROWN FILM UNIT between 1946 and 1948, at the COLONIAL FILM UNIT (1948–50), and then as a freelance director up till 1964, making his last film, *Wild Wings*, that year. Other influential films included *Scotland Today* (1938) and *The Londoners* (1939). Married Barbara MULLEN.

OTHER BRITISH FILMS INCLUDE: (d, doc) *The Future is in the Air, Watch and Ward in the Air, Air Outpost* (1937, co-d), *The Dawn of Iran* (1938), *Island People* (co-d), *Letter from Aldershot* (1940), *Goodbye Yesterday* (1941), *Journey Into History* (1952, co-d), *Holiday* (1957), *River of Life* (1960). Ian Aitken.

Taylor, Marjorie Actress. Leading lady of a dozen or so films in the later 30s, most often associated with the directors Maclean ROGERS (e.g. *Racing Romance*, 1937) and George KING, for whom she co-starred with Tod SLAUGHTER in several rip-roaring MELODRAMAS, including *The Crimes of Stephen Hawke* (1936), as the innocent adoptive daughter of the eponymous criminal, and *The Face at the Window* (1939).

OTHER BRITISH FILMS INCLUDE: *The Heirloom Mystery* (1936), *Easy Riches* (1938), *Three Silent Men* (1940).

Taylor, Peter (*b* Portsmouth, 1922 – *d* Rome, 1977). Editor. Oscar-winner for cutting *The Bridge on the River Kwai* (1957), Taylor worked on several occasions for director David LEAN, before Lean's final elephantiasis set in, when some zippier editing might have warded off *longueurs*. He also worked on 'B' FILMS such as the neatly structured *The Big Day* (1960), but his most important later achievement is in the editing of *This Sporting Life* (1963), in which narrative and editing are mutually dependent. Married to Italian editor Franca Silvi.

OTHER BRITISH FILMS INCLUDE: *The Third Man* (1949, assembly cutter), *Thought to Kill* (1953), *For Better, for Worse* (1954), *The Man Who Never Was* (1955), *Sea Wife* (1956), *Honeymoon* (1959, UK/Sp), *Waltz of the Toreadors* (1962), *One Way Pendulum* (1964), *Monte Carlo or Bust!* (1969, UK/Fr/It).

Taylor, Robert (*b* Filley, Nebraska, 1911 – *d* Santa Monica, California, 1969). Actor. RN: Spangler Arlington Brugh. A name to be changed if ever there was one; under his bland new name the handsome if not especially dynamic or versatile Taylor remained a popular star for 30 years. In his pre-war British film, MGM's *A Yank at Oxford* (1937), he does the brash-American-mellowed-by-Old-World-traditions act engagingly enough. He made only seven of his roughly 80 films in Britain, but they contain some of his most attractive work, especially the three COSTUME DRAMAS he did for MGM–BRITISH in the 50s: *Ivanhoe* (1952), *Knights of the Round Table* (1953) and *The Adventures of Quentin Durward* (1955), all enjoyably rousing entertainments, made just before his decline set in. This was signalled, as was often the case, by a round with WARWICK FILMS. Married to actresses Barbara Stanwyck and Ursula Thiess.

OTHER BRITISH FILMS: *Conspirator* (1949), *The House of the Seven Hawks, The Killers of Kilimanjaro* (1959).

Taylor, Rod (*b* Sydney, 1929). Actor. Virile, outdoorsy type who started his acting career in Australian radio and the odd film but went to Hollywood in the mid 50s and gradually acquired a modest international reputation – and equipped himself vocally for acting characters from either side of the Atlantic. Among his handful of British films, only *Young Cassidy* (1965), loosely based on the early life of Sean O'CASEY, is of much – and not *very* much – interest, though he is agreeable enough in ASQUITH's all-star *The VIPs* (1963) as a self-made tycoon baled out by his adoring secretary, Maggie SMITH.

OTHER BRITISH FILMS INCLUDE: *The Liquidator* (1965), *Nobody Runs Forever* (1968, UK/US, as Australian detective), *The Man Who Had Power Over Women* (1970).

Taylor, Ronnie (*b* London, 1924). Cinematographer. Shared AA and BAAn for his work on *Gandhi* (1982, UK/Ind), having begun as a focus-puller with GAINSBOROUGH during WW2, working as camera operator on conventional GENRE pieces like *The Baby and the Battleship* (1956) and then on such NEW WAVE films as *Room at the Top* (1958) and *Morgan: A Suitable Case for Treatment* (1966). Made his feature debut as cinematographer on *Tommy* (1975), having operated several times for Ken RUSSELL, though this experience did not deter him from several times working for Richard ATTENBOROUGH, at the other end of the stylistic spectrum.

OTHER BRITISH FILMS INCLUDE: (focus-puller) *Millions Like Us* (1943), *Two Thousand Women* (1944); (cam op) *Lost* (1955), *The Battle of the Sexes* (1959), *The Innocents* (1961), *The Whisperers, The Wrong Box* (1966), *The Devils* (1971), *Young Winston, Savage Messiah* (1972), *Barry Lyndon* (1975), *Valentino* (1977); (c) *Two and Two Make Six* (co-c), *The War Lover* (co-aerial ph) (1962), *Ballad in Blue* (1964), *The Hound of the Baskervilles, Champions* (1983), *Cry Freedom* (1987), *The Rainbow Thief* (1990), *The Steal* (1995).

Taylor, Valerie (*b* London, 1902 – *d* London, 1988). Actress. Interesting, rather angular-looking stage leading lady, RADA-trained, in West End by 1924 and New York by 1929, Taylor had a varied theatrical career, with modern and classic plays well mixed. On-screen only very rarely, including *Berkeley Square* (1933) in Hollywood, but she is at least once wholly memorable: as the Vicar's daughter who shoots the treasonous squire (Leslie BANKS) in *Went the Day Well?* (1942). Her performance is so well-judged as to make one wish there had been much more. Co-author of the excellent THRILLER, *Take My Life* (1947). Married (1 of 2) Hugh SINCLAIR.

OTHER BRITISH FILMS INCLUDE: *Designing Women* (1934), *Macbeth, What a Carve Up!* (1961), *Repulsion* (1965), *Baffled!* (1972).

Tcherina, Ludmilla (*b* Paris, 1924). Actress. RN: Monique Tchemerzine. Beautiful and vivacious brunette, of Franco-Russian parentage, a former prima ballerina with the Monte Carlo ballet, who made about 15 international films over two decades. She appeared in four for Michael POWELL, with whom, in film terms, she is indissolubly associated: as Irina, against whom Moira SHEARER will be pitted, in *The Red Shoes* (1948), the courtesan Giulietta in *The Tales of Hoffmann* (1951), in the title role of *Oh, Rosalinda!!* (1955) and, last and least, *Honeymoon* (1959, UK/Sp).

Tearle, Sir Godfrey (*b* New York City, 1884 – *d* London, 1953). Actor. American-born stage star, imposingly dignified, whether benign (like the senior bomber-crew member in *One of Our Aircraft Is Missing*, 1942) or menacing (like the professor with a missing finger in *The 39 Steps*, 1935). Most interesting, though, is his perceptive study of benignity atrophied into self-

absorption as the grandfather of *Mandy* (1952). On stage from 1893 and in films from 1908, as Romeo, he played leads in a dozen or more silents such as *Queen's Evidence* (1919), easing into character roles in the 30s. Twice married, he finally lived with Jill BENNETT until his death, and she has written movingly about their life together. Brother **Malcolm Tearle** (*b* 1888 – *d* London, 1935) was in the British film, *Her Reputation* (1931) and half-brother **Conway Tearle** (*b* New York, 1878 – *d* Los Angeles, 1938, RN: Frederick Levy) appeared in about 90 films (1914–36), only one of them British: *Captivation* (1931). Knighted 1951.

OTHER BRITISH FILMS INCLUDE: *The Real Thing at Last* (1916), *Nobody's Child, A Sinless Sinner, Fancy Dress* (1919), *Salome of the Tenements* (1925), *One Colombo Night, If Youth But Knew* (1926), *Infatuation* (1930), *These Charming People, The Shadow Between* (1931), *Puppets of Fate* (1933), *The Last Journey* (1935), *Tomorrow We Live, East Meets West* (1936), *Tomorrow We Live* (1942), *Undercover, The Lamp Still Burns* (1943), *The Rake's Progress* (1945), *Private Angelo* (1949), *White Corridors* (1951), *I Believe in You, Decameron Nights* (1952), *The Titfield Thunderbolt* (1953).

Technicolor in British film The first British feature to be photographed in three-COLOUR Technicolor – the cinema's first commercially successful three-colour process – was *Wings of the Morning* (1937), produced two years after the first such US venture, *Becky Sharp*. In contrast to Hollywood, however – and because of the high cost of filming in Technicolor and its technical demands – a British Technicolor film remained a relatively rare event, right up to the introduction of the cheaper, faster Eastmancolor stock in the early 50s. Apart from a few animated SHORTS (such as Anthony Gross's wonderful *Foxhunt*, 1936), Technicolor output was virtually confined to films produced by Alexander KORDA's LONDON FILMS (e.g. *The Divorce of Lady X, The Four Feathers*, 1939; *The Thief of Baghdad*, 1940), the POWELL AND PRESSBURGER collaborations (*The Life and Death of Colonel Blimp*, 1943; *A Matter of Life and Death*, 1946; *Black Narcissus*, 1947; *The Red Shoes*, 1948; *Gone to Earth*, 1950; *The Tales of Hoffmann*, 1951), a couple of wartime films directed by David LEAN for TWO CITIES (*This Happy Breed*, 1944; *Blithe Spirit*, 1945), and some later RANK productions (such as *Blanche Fury*, 1947; *Scott of the Antarctic*, 1948). Even GAINSBOROUGH PICTURES, famous for its racy COSTUME MELODRAMAS, managed only one in Technicolor, *Jassy* (1947). A remarkable achievement on Rank's part, however, was to photograph the 1948 London Olympic games (*The XIVth Olympiad – The Glory of Sport*) in Technicolor – the first live-action feature DOCUMENTARY to use cumbersome Technicolor cameras. (The scarcity of Technicolor cameras in British studios was highlighted by the fact that their deployment for the Olympics held up production on another Rank Technicolor feature, *The Blue Lagoon*, for several weeks.)

Unfairly, as it turns out, British Technicolor films acquired a reputation for being dull and muted compared with their vividly-coloured Hollywood counterparts: this was due partly to the shortcomings of the British laboratories at the time (Michael Powell, among others, has attested to this) and partly to the unique survival of poorly-graded prints which (because they were so costly) were put into distribution instead of being discarded. Laboratory technicians called these, disparagingly, 'North of Watford' prints. Thankfully, a sustained programme of restoration work on Britain's Technicolor heritage carried out by the NATIONAL FILM AND TELEVISION ARCHIVE (NFTVA) since the mid 80s has helped to put the record straight by revealing the dazzling and often subtle colours captured by such accomplished pioneer cinematographers as Jack CARDIFF, whose mastery of Technicolor is manifest in the restored versions of such films as *Western Approaches* (1944), *A Matter of Life and Death*, *Black Narcissus*, *The Red Shoes* and *The Magic Box* (1951). Although long obsolete, original Technicolor is still revered, not only for its visual richness but also because of its innate stability – unlike the first Eastmancolor stocks, which were subject to swift and rampant fading and, despite improvements, remain vulnerable.

BIBLIOG: John Huntley, *British Technicolor Films*, 1948; Duncan Petrie, *British Cinematographers*, 1996. Clyde Jeavons.

Teddington Studios *see* **Warner Bros/Warner Bros–First National; Hollywood studios in Britain**

Tee, Elsa Actress. Acting from childhood, Tee interspersed her stage appearances with a few films, mostly in small roles except for *Here Comes the Sun* (1945), in which she has the female lead (not that that is worth much) to FLANAGAN and ALLEN.

OTHER BRITISH FILMS INCLUDE: *Heaven Is Round the Corner*, *Twilight Hour* (1944), *Flight from Folly* (1945), *Death in High Heels* (1947), *Calling Paul Temple* (1948), *School for Randle* (1949).

television commercials and feature film directors Although directors such as Dick LESTER, John SCHLESINGER and Mai ZETTERLING, to name but three, worked in commercials in their early directorial careers in the late 50s/early 60s, those more closely associated with having emerged from the commercials arena embarked on feature film careers in the late 70s/early 80s. Alan PARKER (Hamlet cigar ads), Ridley SCOTT (Hovis boy and bicycle ad), Tony SCOTT (Hovis boy and policeman ad), Hugh HUDSON (Courage bitter 'Gertcha' ad) and Adrian LYNE (Polo mints ads) all enjoyed, to a greater or lesser extent, success in features.

This did not, as some anticipated, lead to a wave of film-makers following in their wake, although more recent British directors with a commercials background have included Tony KAYE, with *American History X* (1998), Jake SCOTT, son of Ridley, with *Plunkett & Macleane* (1999), Barry SKOLNICK, with *Mean Machine* (2001, UK/US), Guy RITCHIE, with *Snatch* (2000, UK/US) and Jonathan GLAZER, who progressed from the Guinness 'Surfing' ad to *Sexy Beast* (2001, UK/Sp/US). John Oliver.

See also **television and film** and **advertising films**.

television and film Following the televising of the Coronation of Queen Elizabeth II in 1953, the advent of commercial TV in 1955, and the extension of TV reception across virtually the whole of the UK in the late 50s, a rapid growth in TV audiences occurred. Although part of a more general shift in patterns of consumption and leisure within Britain, the rise of TV was commonly perceived by the British film industry as responsible for the decline in cinema audiences. While a few pre-war films such as *High Treason* (1929) had offered predictive glimpses of television, such 50s films as *Meet Mr Lucifer* (1953) and *Simon and Laura* (1955) mocked the new medium; and the FILM INDUSTRY DEFENCE ORGANISATION (FIDO) was established in 1958 to try to block the appearance of British films on TV. Given TV's huge appetite for film, and the additional source of revenue it provided, FIDO's strategy foundered on the rocks of commercial reality and, in 1964, the Cinematograph Exhibitors' Association (CEA) abandoned its general opposition to TV transmission of films in favour of time-limited bans. Since then TV (along with video) has become the major

site for viewing films of all kinds, more British films now watched by more people on TV than at the cinema. Since the 90s the growth of satellite, cable and digital television services has also been driven by the development of specialist film (as well as sport) channels, particularly those offered by Rupert Murdoch's Sky (launched in 1989). The content of these, however, has been overwhelmingly Hollywood rather than British films.

Television's relationship with film has altered in other ways. TV has historically been seen as a medium distinct from film but use of film has always been a part of television activity. Initially, film was used to record – or telecine –TV broadcasts for future use (as in the case of the BBC's coverage of the Coronation). Independent TV companies were also alert to the export potential of programmes with the result that series such as ABC's *The Adventures of Robin Hood* (1955–59) were shot quickly on film (in this case at the NETTLEFOLD Studios). During the 60s, there was also a move towards shooting single dramas on film, making use of lightweight 16mm cameras previously employed in news. This trend was particularly identified with Tony GARNETT and Ken LOACH's work for the BBC's 'Wednesday Play' series (1964–70), which included the groundbreaking *Cathy Come Home* (1966), shot mostly on film, and *The Big Flame* (1969), filmed entirely on LOCATION. The popularity of shooting TV drama on film continued into the 70s when, at a time of decline for the British film industry, TV nurtured the careers of directors such as Stephen FREARS and Mike LEIGH. It became a common claim that 'British cinema was alive and well on television'.

However, while TV plays were shot on film they were not exhibited in cinemas (although the idea of showing *Cathy Come Home* in cinemas was explored following the controversy surrounding its broadcast). The turning-point in this regard was the launch, in 1982, of the UK's fourth terrestrial channel, CHANNEL 4, a public-service broadcaster funded by advertising which follows a 'publishing' model of commissioning rather than producing in-house. Inspired by the example of German and Italian television, Channel 4 – via its Drama Department (responsible for Film on Four) and its Department for Independent Film and Video (supporting more politically radical and formally experimental work) – embarked upon a policy of providing finance for feature films for cinema release prior to TV transmission. The channel also reached agreement with the CEA on reduction in the time-scale in which this could happen. At a time when private and public finance for British film was scarce, the Channel provided the film industry with an important lifeline and was involved in many of the most successful and/or critically acclaimed films of the 80s and 90s, including *The Ploughman's Lunch* (1983), *My Beautiful Laundrette* (1985), *Distant Voices Still Lives* (1988, UK/Ger), *The Crying Game* (1992), and *Trainspotting* (1996). In doing so, the channel has encouraged a relatively new direction in British cinema, involving a fusion of the formal interests of 'ART CINEMA' with the socio-political concerns of public-service television.

Although Channel 4 made money on only a minority of its productions, the cultural prestige and international profile it derived from support for film production encouraged others to follow suit, particularly in the late 80s when ITV companies such as Thames Television (*A Month in the Country*, 1987), Central Television (*Sid and Nancy*, 1986; *Wish You Were Here*, 1987) and Granada (*Strapless*, 1988; *My Left Foot*, 1989) were all engaged in film production. The BBC also invested in films for theatrical release such as *Truly Madly Deeply* (1990), *Edward II* and *Enchanted April* (1992), subsequently establishing BBC FILMS which, *inter alia*, has backed *Mrs Brown* (1997, UK/Ire/US), *Wonderland* (1999), *Ratcatcher* (1999), *Billy Elliot* (2000) and *The Last Resort* (2001). In the late 90s, Channel 4 restructured its operations, establishing FilmFour Ltd as a subsidiary company and launching a FilmFour pay-TV channel, with a shift towards more commercial projects and bigger budgets (as in the case of *Charlotte Gray*, 2002, UK/Aust/US), although FilmFour Lab, launched in 1999, had a remit to support more experimental, low-budget work. Despite recurring criticisms that TV-supported films are not 'proper' cinema, TV companies, particularly Channel 4, have been crucial to the maintenance of British cinema since the 80s and, despite increase in alternative sources of funding (e.g. Lottery funds), have been key players in the British film industry. July 2002, however, saw the slashing of Channel 4's budget for film production, and the demise of FilmFour.

BIBLIOG: John Hill and Martin McLoone (eds), *Big Picture, Small Screen: The Relations Between Film and Television*, 1996; Christopher Williams, 'The Social Art Cinema: a Moment in the History of British Film and Television Culture' in Williams (ed), *Cinema: the Beginnings and the Future*, 1996. John Hill.

television-to-cinema spin-offs Television was used as a source for cinema as early as 1953 whenTerence RATTIGAN's written-for-television play *The Final Test* (1951, as part of BBC's Television Festival Drama) was co-opted for the big screen (1953), featuring a new cast. Various other plays and serials subsequently made the transition, notably the works of Francis DURBRIDGE (e.g. the 1952 serial *The Broken Horseshoe* became a feature in 1953) and Nigel KNEALE (the *Quatermass* serials). In 1955 a continuing programme – the BBC soap opera *The Grove Family* – was made into a feature film, *It's A Great Day*, with the original TV cast reprising their roles. Others followed spasmodically (notably the Granada sitcom *The Army Game* which inspired 1958's *I Only Arsked!*) but it wasn't until the late 60s and 70s that the practice became a phenomenon with virtually all TV's top-rated sitcoms and some dramas sporting screen versions (including *Till Death Us Do Part*, *Steptoe and Son*, *The Likely Lads*, *Man About the House*, *Rising Damp*, *Porridge*, *Please, Sir!*, *Doomwatch*, *Callan*, and *The Sweeney*). HAMMER FILMS was a major player in this arena and scored a jackpot with the feature version of *On The Buses* (1971), the most successful British film of its year. The practice fell out of favour by the end of the 70s although there was the odd exception such as *Bean* (1997), drawing successfully on Rowan ATKINSON's TV character, and subsequently feature-length episodes of popular shows would air as seasonal specials. A Hollywood fad using nostalgic TV programmes as a source for film material (e.g. *Mission: Impossible*, *Charlie's Angels*, etc) is a completely different project although UK shows (*The Saint*, *The Avengers*) have featured in the mix. Dick Fiddy.

Tempean Films Tempean Films was a production company founded by Robert S. BAKER and Monty BERMAN. Baker and Berman mainly acted as co-producers, but Berman was also cinematographer on most Tempean productions and Baker an occasional writer and director. Between 1948 and 1958 there were twenty-four Tempean features, mostly 'B' FILMS. That seventeen of these productions were CRIME FILMS is indicative of the forces at play in the market for second features in post-war British cinema. Their signature film, therefore, was the low-budget thriller, making use of locations and *noir*

influences, with an eye on the bottom line, but with an ambition for quality underlined by their classical name and Greek-columned logo. Their first crime film, *No Trace* (1950), a murder thriller, was written and directed by John GILLING, who had creative credit on a further eleven Tempean crime films. Typical British second feature leads included Patrick HOLT and Dermot WALSH, in *13 East Street* (1952) and *The Frightened Man*, respectively, but American leading men, such as Jeff Morrow in *Hour of Decision* and Alex Nicol in *Stranger in Town* (both 1957), were frequently used to achieve wider distribution.

Tempean's first two productions, *A Date with a Dream* (1948) and *Melody Club* (1949), were COMEDIES starring Terry-THOMAS, but only three more comedies were made, *Love in Pawn* (1953), *The Reluctant Bride* (1955), and *No Smoking* (1955), about a clash between a village chemist and the tobacco industry. Tempean's last two films were starkly contrasting one-offs in terms of the company's production history, but also very representative of 50s cinema. *Sea of Sand* (1958) was a first feature that characteristically referenced WW2 as a battle against nature as well as the enemy, whilst *The Trollenberg Terror* (1958) was a SCIENCE FICTION-Horror 'B' film with a Cold War alien-invasion narrative.

BIBLIOG: Brian McFarlane, 'Value for Money: Baker and Berman and Tempean Films', in Ian McKillop and Neil Sinyard (eds), *British Cinema in the 1950s*, 2002. Andrew Clay.

Tempest, Dame Marie (*b* London, 1864 – *d* London, 1942). Actress. RN: Etherington. Legendary stage star who appeared in screen versions of excerpts from her stage productions in 1900 – *San Toy*, *English Nell* – and starred in the US film, *Mrs Plum's Pudding* (1915). She never really took to film and appeared only twice more: opposite pianist-composer Ignacy Paderewski (*b* Kurilowka, Poland, 1860 – *d* New York, 1941), as himself in his one film role, in *Moonlight Sonata* (1937), reissued with 40 minutes cut under the title, *The Charmer* (1943); and, in the best record of her work on film, *Yellow Sands* (1938), as a characterful old lady in a Cornish village. Also trained as an singer, she was famed for the wit, grace and technical skill she brought to such roles as Judith Bliss in *Hay Fever* (1925). Awarded DBE, 1937.

Temple, Julien (*b* London, 1953) Director. Cambridge-educated graduate of the NATIONAL FILM SCHOOL whose rackety film career has certainly attracted its share of opprobrium, but who can never be described as dull. Came to notice with *The Great Rock'n'Roll Swindle*, his famous and exhilarating 1979 DOCUMENTARY account, of the punk group, the Sex Pistols, mixing ANIMATION with live action and newsfilm. He revisited the group 20 years later in *The Filth and the Fury* (2001), in which he debunks some of the myths of the culture charted in the earlier film. In between were such diverse enterprises as the Amnesty revue films, *The Secret Policeman's Other Ball* (1982), the dud MUSICAL, *Absolute Beginners* (1986), which all but finished the GOLDCREST company, and an episode of the OPERA smorgasbord on film, *Aria* (1987, + co-sc). There were some forgettable US films, including *Earth Girls Are Easy* (1988); *Vigo* (1998, UK/Fr/Jap, + co-sc), a sort of BIOPIC of the famous French director who had been Temple's inspiration, was a little-seen disaster; but it is hard not to admire the cheek of someone who thinks there's a mainstream film in the lives of the Lake Poets, on show in *Pandaemonium* (2001).

OTHER BRITISH FILMS: (d, unless noted) *The Tunnyng of Elinor Rummying* (1976, short, m), *Punk Can Take It* (1979, short), *Mantrap* (1983, + sc), *The Secret Policeman's Private Parts* (1984, + a).

Templeman, Harcourt Producer. Former silent-screen director and writer and co-director of a couple of early talkies, including *Money Means Nothing* (1932) with Herbert WILCOX, Templeman produced seven minor films for Grosvenor Sound Films (1935–38). These were all directed by Sinclair HILL; all lost money; and they ended the careers of both men.

OTHER BRITISH FILMS INCLUDE: (d, sc, unless noted) *The White Lie* (d), *The Impatient Patient* (1925), *The King's Highway* (1927, co-sc), *City of Song* (assoc d), *The Bells* (1931, co-d); (p) *Hyde Park Corner* (1935), *The Cardinal* (1936), *Command Performance* (1937), *Follow Your Star* (1938).

Temple-Smith, John (*b* London). Producer, writer. One of the unsung heroes of the British film industry, particularly for services to the British 'B' FILM. As a producer at SHEPPERTON, he worked on some of the best small films of the 1950s in collaboration with Peter Graham SCOTT, including *The Big Chance* (1957). But it was his energy and ability to conjure up a set and cast at incredibly low cost that is still spoken of with awe. If he never made it to the very top he was, nevertheless, one of the men who kept alive an industry for longer than it may have deserved.

OTHER BRITISH FILMS INCLUDE: (p, unless noted) *Girl on the Pier* (1953), *Profile* (1954), *One Way Out* (1955, + sc), *Find the Lady* (1956), *Account Rendered* (1957), *Captain Clegg* (1962), *The Viking Queen* (1966, + sc). Paul Quinn.

Tennant, Victoria (*b* London, 1950). Actress. Central School-trained, in films from 1971 (*The Ragman's Daughter*), Tennant exhibited great beauty but didn't get much chance to do serious acting. Went to the US in the 80s, achieved some success particularly on such TV mini-series as *The Winds of War* (1983), married and divorced Steve Martin, with whom she appeared in *All of Me* (1984) and *LA Story* (1991). She is the daughter of agent Cecil Tennant, and ballerina **Irina Baranova** (*b* Petrograd, Russia, 1919), who appeared in the EALING film, *Train of Events* (1949) and was the ballet mistress for *Nijinsky* (1980, UK/US).

OTHER BRITISH FILMS: *Hussy* (1979), *The Dogs of War* (1980, UK/US), *Inseminoid* (1980), *The Holcroft Covenant* (1985).

Tennyson, Penrose (*b* London, 1912 – *d* 1941). Director, screenwriter. Oxford-educated descendant of the poet Tennyson, he left school to pursue a career in film, working for Michael BALCON. He assisted HITCHCOCK on *The Man Who Knew Too Much* (1934) and *The 39 Steps* (1935) and King Vidor on *The Citadel* (1938). After directing his first feature, *There Ain't No Justice* (1939) and completing the Paul ROBESON mining film *The Proud Valley* (1940), which he also co-wrote, he directed the highly praised Ealing film, *Convoy* (1940), for which, as a member of the Royal Navy Volunteer Reserve, he was given leave to direct and for which he had prepared by spending time aboard HMS Valorous. Apparently on the verge of an outstanding career, while preparing to make navy training films, he was killed in a plane crash, cutting short the career of one of the most promising young directors in British film. Married to Nova PILBEAM.

BIBLIOG: C.T. Atkinson, *Penrose Tennyson*, 1943. Stephen Shafer.

Tenser, Tony (*b* 1920). Executive producer. Described by David McGillivray (1992) as 'the Irving Thalberg of the EXPLOITATION movie', Tenser had for more than a decade a sure sense of certain lucrative corners of the marketplace. He began with nudist films like *Naked as Nature Intended* (1961), co-producing with partner Michael KLINGER, for their company Compton-Cameo, which also produced POLANSKI's *Repulsion* (1965) and *Cul-de-sac* (1966). When the company was sold in 1967, Tenser formed his own (later called TIGON) and favoured the HORROR mode, producing some important examples of the GENRE such as *Witchfinder General* (1968), as well as non-horror works like the TELEVISION-TO-FILM SPIN-OFF, *For the Love of Ada* (1972).

OTHER BRITISH FILMS INCLUDE: (ex p, unless noted) *The Black Torment* (1964, co-p), *The Sorcerers* (co-p), *The Blood Beast Terror* (1967), *Curse of the Crimson Altar*, *Love in Our Time* (p) (1968), *The Haunted House of Horror* (1969), *Blood on Satan's Claw* (1970), *The Creeping Flesh*, *Miss Julie* (1972), *Frightmare* (1974).

Terraine, Molly Teacher. Former actress and drama teacher with such illustrious schools as the Webber-Douglas and RADA, and producer with the Connaught Theatre, Worthing, Terraine became director of RANK's COMPANY OF YOUTH, rather cruelly dubbed the Charm School. This was intended to give fledgling actors training and perhaps place them in small roles, but it and Terraine became objects of derision. Diana DORS (1982) described her as 'a dreadful harridan of a woman who struck fear and terror into everyone', and, although she was an acknowledged elocutionist, her teaching methods in other areas seemed more related to deportment than acting. She played small roles in a couple of films: *The Toilers* (1919) and *Twice Upon a Time* (1953), and was alleged to have 'worked on' (capacity unspecified) *Richard III* and *Oh, Rosalinda!!* (1955).

Terriss, Ellaline (*b* Stanley, Falkland Islands, 1871 – *d* London, 1971). Actress. Daughter of famous stage actor William Terriss, who was assassinated outside the stage door of London's Adelphi Theatre, the tiny (5'1") Terriss made her stage debut with Beerbohm TREE in 1888 and appeared in SHORT FILMS in 1907. She appeared with a cast of theatrical luminaries, in *Masks and Faces* (1917). Married to Seymour HICKS, with whom she appeared in the films, *David Garrick* (1913), *Always Tell Your Wife* (1923), *Blighty* (1927) and *Glamour* (1931); she was wife to George ARLISS as *The Iron Duke* (1935).

OTHER BRITISH FILMS INCLUDE: *Atlantic* (1929), *Royal Cavalcade* (1935), *The Four Just Men* (1939).

BIBLIOG: Seymour Hicks, *Me and My Missus*, 1939.

Terry, Dame Ellen (*b* Coventry, 1848 – *d* Tenterden, 1928). Actress. Legendary actress of the British theatre (stage debut 1856), Terry evinced some interest in the motion picture; in 1897, she appeared for G.A. SMITH in *Miss Ellen Terry at Home* and in 1925, she was one of the founding members of THE FILM SOCIETY. She appeared in five feature films, none of which reputedly did her justice: *Her Greatest Performance* (1916), *Victory and Peace* (1918), *Pillars of Society* (1920), *The Bohemian Girl* (1922), *Potter's Clay* (1922). Her third husband was actor James CAREW. Made DBE in 1925. AS.

Terry, Harry (*b* London, 1887 – *d* ?). Actor. Tall supporting player of stage and screen who made his theatrical debut in 1900 and his film debut allegedly in 1909, but whose period of liveliest screen activity was in the 30s. Had small roles for HITCHCOCK in *The Ring* (1927) and *The Manxman* (1929) and in *The Scarlet Pimpernel* (1935), and finished his career in the abysmal *The Laughing Lady* (1946) as a watchman.

OTHER BRITISH FILMS INCLUDE: *Cocktails* (1928), *Piccadilly*, *The Return of the Rat* (1929), *Reunion* (1932), *The Broken Melody* (1934), *The*

Penny Pool (1937), *Young Man's Fancy* (1939), *Old Mother Riley, Detective* (1943), *Here Comes the Sun* (1945).

Terry, Hazel (*b* London, 1918 – *d* London, 1974). Actress. The daughter of Mary GLYNNE and Dennis NEILSON-TERRY, and the cousin of John GIELGUD for whom she played Ophelia (1944), on stage from 1935. Entered films the same year, starred in three minor pieces, was reduced to fleeting support in *Sweet Devil* (1938), and was seen no more in films until she played two character roles in the 60s, when she was an 'orgy' guest in a big hat in *The Servant* (1963). Married (1) Geoffrey KEEN.

OTHER BRITISH FILMS: *The Marriage of Corbal* (1936), *Our Fighting Navy, Missing, Believed Married* (1937), *Kill or Cure* (1962).

Terry, Nigel (*b* Bristol, 1945). Actor. Imposing stage actor, with much RSC, National and other experience, who has filmed only sparingly since making an impressive debut as Prince John in *The Lion in Winter* (1968). He was King Arthur in John BOORMAN's glowing medieval recreation, *Excalibur* (1981, UK/US), then did five films for Derek JARMAN, including playing the eponymous *Caravaggio* (1986) and providing an off-screen voice in *Blue* (1993). Astutely cast as the intense Mr Boldwood in TV's *Far from the Madding Crowd* (1998).

OTHER BRITISH FILMS INCLUDE: *The Last of England* (1987), *War Requiem* (1989), *Edward II* (1991).

Terry-Lewis, Mabel (*b* London, 1872 – *d* London, 1957). Actress. Daughter of famous stage players Arthur Lewis and Kate Terry, and niece of Ellen TERRY, she came to films in middle age and played about a dozen character roles, the last of which was as the overbearing mother of Frances ROWE in PRIESTLEY's visionary allegory, *They Came to a City* (1944).

OTHER BRITISH FILMS INCLUDE: *Love Maggie* (1921), *Caste* (1930), *The Scarlet Pimpernel* (1935), *The Squeaker* (1937), *Jamaica Inn* (1939), *The Adventures of Tartu* (1943).

Terry-Thomas (*b* London, 1911 – *d* Godalming, 1990). Actor. RN: Thomas Terry Hoar-Stevens. A jobbing cabaret artiste before wartime work in the 'Stars in Battledress' troupe made his name, post-war he appeared in variety and on radio and TV as a stand-up comedian and impressionist, playing himself in early films such as *Helter Skelter* (1949) where he performed his famous 'Technical hitch' sketch. It was the BOULTINGS who encouraged Terry-Thomas to develop a screen persona, as the blustering Major Hitchcock in *Private's Progress* (1956) and its sequel *I'm All Right Jack* (1959), whose exasperated harangue, 'You're an absolute shower!' became a national catch-phrase. In *Carlton-Browne of the FO* (1958) he was the quintessential upper-class 'silly-ass', a sad relic of a vanished world. In *Blue Murder at St Trinian's, The Naked Truth* (1957), *Too Many Crooks* and *School for Scoundrels* (1959) that famous gap-toothed smile, military moustache, dandified attire and rich, fruity voice with its 'Oh, good show' banter, made him the definitive post-war cad or rotter, constantly scheming to avoid his creditors or ensnare some hapless heiress. American audiences also enjoyed his caricatured upper-class Englishman and he appeared in several Hollywood films in the 60s and co-productions such as *Those Magnificent Men . . .* (1965). Terry-Thomas's career was curtailed when he contracted Parkinson's disease in 1971, reducing him to occasional appearances, as in *The Bawdy Adventures of Tom Jones* (1975).

OTHER BRITISH FILMS INCLUDE: *It's Love Again* (1936, extra), *A Date with a Dream, The Brass Monkey* (1948), *Melody Club* (1949), *The Green Man, Brothers in Law* (1956), *Lucky Jim* (1957), *Happy is the Bride* (1957), *tom thumb* (1958), *Make Mine Mink, That's Odd* (short) (1960), *A Matter of Who* (1961), *Kill or Cure, Operation Snatch* (1962), *The Mouse*

on the Moon, *The Wild Affair* (1963), *You Must Be Joking!* (1965), *Our Man in Marrakesh, The Sandwich Man* (1966), *Jules Verne's Rocket to the Moon, Don't Raise the Bridge, Lower the River* (1967), *Arthur? Arthur!* (1969, unrel), *The Abominable Dr Phibes* (1971), *Dr Phibes Rides Again, The Cherry Picker, The Special London Bridge Special* (cameo role) (1972), *The Vault of Horror* (1973, UK/US), *Side by Side, Spanish Fly* (UK/Sp) (1975), *The Hound of the Baskervilles* (1977).

BIBLIOG: Autobiographies, *Filling the Gap*, 1959; *Terry-Thomas Tells Tales*, 1990, with Terry Daum; Robert Ross, *The Complete Terry-Thomas*, 2002. Andrew Spicer.

Tester, Desmond (*b* Ealing, London, 1919 – *d* Sydney, 2002). Actor. The busiest and most versatile boy star in the 30s, working for HITCHCOCK and Carol REED, Tester declared himself a conscientious objector in relation to WW2 and his career lost its momentum. Trained for the stage, he got his first job from the fearsome Nancy PRICE, who a decade later played his hard-pressed mother in *The Stars Look Down* (1939). He is probably best remembered now as the boy carrying a bomb on a London bus in *Sabotage* (1936), saying in 1996 that he objected to the dog's being inserted into the scene to milk sympathy. He is also vivid as the sickly boy-king in *Tudor Rose* (1936) and the musical prodigy in the comedy-thriller, *Non-Stop New York* (1937), both for Robert STEVENSON. In the 50s, his career in the doldrums, he went to Australia where he settled in Sydney, worked in theatre, in a long-running children's TV programme and in several films.

OTHER BRITISH FILMS: *Midshipman Easy, Late Extra* (1935), *The Beloved Vagabond* (1936), *The Drum* (1938), *An Englishman's Home* (1939), *The Turners of Prospect Road* (1947), *Barry McKenzie Holds His Own* (1974).

Te Wiata, Inia (*b* Otaki, NZ, 1915 – *d* London, 1971). Actor. Imposing Maori opera singer who played an enlightened chieftan who helps Jack HAWKINS in the colonial adventure, *The Seekers* (1954), and played four more exotic roles in British films, including the King of Tawaki in the Norman WISDOM vehicle, *Man of the Moment* (1955).

OTHER BRITISH FILMS: *Pacific Destiny* (1956), *Sands of the Desert* (1960), *In Search of the Castaways* (1961, UK/US).

Thatcher, Heather (*b* London, 1896 – *d* Northwood, Middx, 1987). Actress. Watching Thatcher as dithery Lady Buckering, mother of a brood of improbably diverse daughters, in *Father's Doing Fine* (1952), is to realise how intransigently her style as a leading lady belongs to pre-war Britain. In fact, she began as an EXTRA in films in 1916, was on stage the same year and starred in mostly forgotten plays, wore a monocle (even, it is said, when playing tennis), made 17 mostly minor films in Britain, went to Hollywood and played (1937–44) many a blue-blooded English lady, none bluer than Aunt Pat in *Beau Geste* (1939), toured with ENSA during WW2, and returned to British films in character roles in 1948. In her highly artificial style, she is indeed amusing company in the likes of *Trottie True* (1948) and as George COLE's awesome mother-in-law in *Will Any Gentleman . . . ?* (1953).

OTHER BRITISH FILMS INCLUDE: *The Key of the World* (1918), *The First Men in the Moon* (1919), *The Plaything* (1929), *A Warm Corner* (1930), *Loyalties* (1933), *The Dictator* (1935), *Anna Karenina* (1948), *Dear Mr Prohack* (1949), *Encore* (1951), *The Hour of 13* (1952), *The Deep Blue Sea* (1955).

Thatcher, Torin (*b* Bombay, 1905 – *d* Newbury Park, California, 1981). Actor. This former schoolteacher was the sort of Englishman, adequately handsome, well-built, immaculately well-spoken, who has always been in demand for Hollywood villains. RADA-trained, on the London stage from 1927, like Basil SYDNEY whom he somewhat resembles, he was Claudius in *Hamlet* (at Elsinore, in fact, 1937), and was well established in British films before army service (1940–45). One never quite trusted him as an unambiguous hero, and it is no surprise to find him a U-boat commander in *Let George Do It!* or an SS man in *Gasbags* (1940). Post-war, he is an urbanely caddish Bentley Drummle in *Great Expectations* (1946) and a humane policeman in *The Fallen Idol* (1948), and after several more character parts took off for Hollywood where he played a range of suave villains and officers, usually of British extraction.

OTHER BRITISH FILMS INCLUDE: *Red Wagon* (1934), *Sabotage* (1936), *Young and Innocent* (1937), *The Spy in Black* (1939), *Night Train to Munich*, *Contraband* (1940), *The Next of Kin* (1942), *I See a Dark Stranger* (1946), *The Man Within, Jassy* (1947), *The Black Rose* (1950, UK/US).

Thatcherism and film Margaret Thatcher's premiership (1979–90) saw Britain riven with deep divisions, unsurprisingly reflected in contemporary films. The main plank of Thatcherism was individualistic free enterprise, paradoxically backed by populist morality and conformity (to 'Victorian values'), leaving many disenfranchised. Opposed to state subsidy, it reduced even the little help that the film industry had been receiving and, in the early 80s, production was at an all-time low. From this it would be easy to imagine all the films of the time as opposing Thatcherism, but this was not the case. While HERITAGE films (later perfected by MERCHANT IVORY), albeit ambivalently, echoed Thatcherism's nostalgia, open protests rose against the government's social policy and the homophobia, racism, social divisiveness, philistinism and greed that was tacitly encouraged. The BRITISH FILM INSTITUTE, BRITISH SCREEN, CHANNEL 4, and others supported a wide range of directors including Peter GREENAWAY, Derek JARMAN, Mike LEIGH and Ken LOACH as well as members of ethnic minorites and animators. There were also attempts at the mainstream from companies including CANNON, GOLDCREST, HANDMADE, PALACE, POLYGRAM and VIRGIN. While it would be simplistic to argue that British cinema flourished under Thatcherite adversity, new creative voices did emerge and the variety of styles and subjects covered reflected the tumult of the period.

BIBLIOG: Lester Friedman (ed), *British Cinema and Thatcherism*, 1993. John Riley.

Thaw, John (*b* Manchester, 1942 – *d* Luckington, Wilts, 2002). Actor. Widely admired for his irascible Inspector Jack Regan ('Get yer trousers on, you're nicked', he would bark) in TV's *The Sweeney* (1975–76, 1978; film SPIN-OFFS, 1976 and 1978), then recklessly adored as Oxford-based opera-loving *Inspector Morse* (1987–92) – was there a middle-aged woman anywhere who did not feel she could fill the lonely spaces in his life? As a result, the working-class, RADA-trained Thaw, on stage from 1960, had scarcely time to develop a film career. However, apart from the spin-offs, there were about ten screen outings for his precociously white thatch and no-nonsense tone, perhaps given most to do as Glenda JACKSON's husband in the sexual harassment drama, *Business as Usual* (1987). He also worked twice for friend Richard ATTENBOROUGH: in *Cry Freedom* (1987) – he was BAA-nominated for playing a member of the South African secret police – and *Chaplin* (1992, UK/Fr/It/Jap/US), as Fred KARNO. Married (2) Sheila HANCOCK (1973–2002).

OTHER BRITISH FILMS INCLUDE: *The Loneliness of the Long Distance Runner* (1962), *Dead Man's Chest* (1965), *The Bofors Gun, Praise Marx and Pass the Ammunition* (1968), *Dr Phibes Rises Again* (1972), *Monsignor Renard* (1999).

theatre and film British cinema and British theatre have always closely combined, firstly for simple reasons of geography. Whereas in America Broadway and Hollywood were separated by a continent, in Britain theatres and cinema studios were almost all centred around London, and actors moved readily from one to the other, frequently acting before the cameras by day before turning to the stage in the evening. This proximity went hand-in-hand with a cultural belief in the superiority of the theatrical tradition, and a trust in the products of that tradition that has seen British cinema viewed, a little too glibly, as being theatrically based. Certainly there have been notable theatrical high spots in British film history that reflect the Shakespearean tradition, from Beerbohm TREE's brief appearance in *King John* (1899), to Johnston FORBES-ROBERTSON in *Hamlet* (1913) and Laurence OLIVIER's five Shakespearean films, of which *Richard III* (1955) alone boasted four theatrical knights (Olivier, GIELGUD, RICHARDSON, HARDWICKE). The playwrights Noël COWARD, Terence RATTIGAN, J.B. PRIESTLEY and Bernard SHAW all contributed, directly or indirectly, to a significant number of British cinema's greatest achievements, and Anthony ASQUITH's *The Importance of Being Earnest* (1952) was perhaps the quintessential British theatrical film, down to the curtains that open and close the film. Another theatrical tradition deep-rooted in British film is that of MUSIC HALL and VARIETY, from comic SHORTS around 1900 starring Dan LENO through to such stars of the halls as George FORMBY, Gracie FIELDS, Will HAY, the CRAZY GANG and Frank RANDLE. The ALDWYCH FARCES of the 30s transferred Ben TRAVERS's comedies lock, stock and barrel to the screen, a tactic followed with equally limited cinematic invention but rather less wit and subtlety by the Brian RIX Whitehall farces of the 50s and 60s. Theatre supplied not only plays and actors, but directors such as Basil DEAN, Basil DEARDEN, Henry CASS, Albert DE COURVILLE, Harold FRENCH and Tony RICHARDSON. The latter's presence is a reminder of the influence of the theatre on the British cinema's NEW WAVE: *Look Back in Anger* (1959), *The Entertainer* (1960) and *A Taste of Honey* (1961). John OSBORNE moved into film production with Richardson and WOODFALL FILMS, while Harold PINTER crossed confidently between theatre and film, enjoying a notable collaboration with Joseph LOSEY (*The Servant*, 1963; *Accident*, 1967; *The Go-Between*, 1971), though films based directly on his plays have been less successful (e.g. *The Caretaker*, 1963). In the 70s and 80s individual theatrical hits continued to receive their honorary embalming in film, with often flat results (Ronald HARWOOD's *The Dresser*, 1983; Peter NICHOLS' *Privates on Parade*, 1982), but the vigorous popular appeal of Willy RUSSELL's *Educating Rita* (1983) and *Shirley Valentine* (1989, UK/US) shone through Lewis GILBERT's leaden directorial non-technique. In recent years British films have had less need of the theatrical inheritance, and actors training for their profession have more need of learning how to respond to the intimate needs of the camera than of knowing how to project their voices to the back of an auditorium. Nevertheless, the success of Kenneth BRANAGH in his productions of *Henry V* (1989), *Much Ado About Nothing* (1993, UK/US) and *Hamlet* (1996, UK/US), and repeated awards showered on Judi DENCH, indicate that the allure of the more established theatrical traditions remains strong in some quarters. However, there has also been a surprising tale of success for the cream of British stage directors in film since the 1990s. Whereas the previous generation of Peter HALL (*Two into Three Won't Go*, 1968), Trevor NUNN (*Hedda*, 1975) and Richard EYRE (*Laughterhouse*, 1984) largely failed to make the successful cross-over into film, the young guns of British theatre, Nicholas HYTNER (*The Madness of King George*, 1994, UK/US), Sam MENDES (*American Beauty*, 1999, US) and Stephen DALDRY (*Billy Elliot*, 2000) have brought an innovative approach to some individual projects. The successes of these, the heartening revival in the fortunes of Mike LEIGH, with his background in experimental theatre, and Anthony MINGHELLA's crossover from playwright to skilful film director indicate that British theatrical talent no longer brings just prestige to British film, but a refreshing vision that has ensured some of the best in British film in recent years.

BIBLIOG: Geoff Brown, '"Sister of the Stage": British Film and British Theatre', in Charles Barr (ed), *All Our Yesterdays*, 1986. Luke McKernan.

Theodorakis, Mikis (*b* Chios, Greece, 1925). Composer. Educated in Athens and Paris, and a staunch patriot and supporter of left-wing causes, Theodorakis suffered exile and imprisonment for his beliefs, finally returning to Greece and his musical career in 1974. Above all, despite the variety of his work, which embraces symphonies and operas, he is known for the score of *Zorba the Greek* (1964), with its famous theme which contributed so much to the popularity of the film. He worked again for *Zorba* director Michael Cacoyannis on *The Day the Fish Came Out* (1967, UK/Gr), and several times for Michael POWELL (*Ill Met By Moonlight*, 1956; *Honeymoon*, 1959; *They're a Weird Mob*, 1966, UK/Aust), but *Zorba* overshadowed everything else in his film career. He was the subject of a 1974 British DOCUMENTARY, *Mikis Theodorakis: A Profile of Greekness*. 1974

OTHER BRITISH FILMS: *The Barefoot Battalion* (1953, UK/US), *Faces in the Dark* (1960, co-m), *The Shadow of the Cat* (1961), *Greece of Christian Greeks* (1971, doc).

theoretical debates Film theory in the UK has always been strongly influenced by ideas from continental Europe, and especially from France. For example, *Movie*, which first appeared in 1962, clearly owed a considerable debt to the 'AUTEUR' theorists of *Cahiers du Cinéma*, whilst Peter WOLLEN's seminal *Signs and Meaning in the Cinema* (1969), was one of the first film books published in English to introduce readers to structuralism and semiotics. Two years later, SCREEN, house journal of the Society for Education in Film and Television (SEFT), which had hitherto concerned itself with the practical aspects of film teaching, underwent a complete transformation to become the main conduit for post-1968 French theories, not simply into film studies but into the wider intellectual life of the UK, and thence to North America and Australia. What became known as 'Screen theory' combined (not always comfortably) structuralism, semiotics, feminism, Lacanian psychoanalysis, Althusserian marxism and various forms of post-structuralism, and, as well as publishing translations of key texts by the likes of Christian Metz and Raymond Bellour, the journal also became a key site for indigenous theorists such as Stephen Heath, Claire Johnston, Colin MacCabe, Laura MULVEY, Paul Willemen and Peter Wollen. *Screen* also attempted to bridge the traditional divide between film theory and practice by playing a key role as a forum for debate amongst British independent and avant-garde filmmakers, especially those grouped in the Independent Film-

makers Association (IFA). Nor were its efforts to create an entirely new constituency and re-define the terms of serious debate about film in Britain limited to the written word, since a crucial part of *Screen's* activity lay in organising weekend schools and involving itself in the retrospectives and special events which so distinguished the Edinburgh Film Festival under Lynda Myles. Bizarrely, however, the new *Screen's* early interest in structuralism, ironically tagged by Gilbert Adair 'a bulbous green reptilian H.R. Giger-designed alien erupting from the pudgy soft belly of British film criticism', managed to ignite a full-blown anti-intellectual witch-hunt by the mainstream media. This was joined, sadly, by the likes of Paul ROTHA, Alexander Walker, Kevin BROWNLOW, Lindsay ANDERSON and Kenneth TYNAN, and reached some kind of nadir when in 1974 BBC film critic Barry Norman 'reviewed' the publication marking the Edinburgh Film Festival retrospective of Raoul WALSH by hurling it across the studio floor in the course of his *Film Night* programme. The attack also spread to take in the BRITISH FILM INSTITUTE, which made an annual grant to SEFT and whose education department included various members of the *Screen* board, and which found itself very publicly accused, in effect, of spreading subversive, left-wing, and, worst of all, foreign, propaganda. This ludicrous nonsense, crass even by the standards of British philistinism and insularity, eventually died down, and what can now be perceived very clearly is the extent to which *Screen*, along with other journals such as *Framework* and *Afterimage*, played a crucial role in endowing the study of film with the academic respectability necessary to establish it as a discipline within higher education. Thus yesterday's intellectual heresies become today's academic orthodoxies.

BIBLIOG: Gilbert Adair, 'The Critical Faculty', *Sight and Sound*, Autumn 1982; Colin MacArthur, *Dialectic!*, 1982; Colin MacCabe, *Theoretical Essays*, 1985. Julian Petley.

Thesiger, Ernest (*b* London, 1879 – *d* London, 1961). Actor. The cadaverous ancient of, say, *Laughter in Paradise* or *The Man in the White Suit* (1951), which is no doubt how he is remembered by film buffs, was in earlier decades a famous eccentric in London's literary and social circles. Impeccably descended and Marlborough-educated, he delighted in shocking (there are tales of his wearing pearls next the skin, of his displaying his legs in pale moleskin shorts, of taking his needlework with him to the trenches in 1915), and even going on the stage, as he did professionally in 1909 with Sir George Alexander, was a rebellious act. His stage credits ran to four columns in *Who's Who in the Theatre* (1957) and he appeared in nearly 60 films. In the US, he was the memorably waspish, epicene host of *The Old Dark House* (1932) and mad scientist Dr Pretorius in *The Bride of Frankenstein* (1935). His British credits are full of slyly conceived cameos of prissiness, pedantry and esoteric professionalism: he is the Duc de Berri in *Henry V* (1944), the hand-writing expert in *The Winslow Boy* (1948) and the undertaker in *Scrooge* (1951), putting his mark on the film in the few minutes which were often all he had to work with.

OTHER BRITISH FILMS INCLUDE: *The Real Thing at Last* (1916), *Nelson, The Life Story of David Lloyd George* (unreleased until 1996) (1918), *The Adventures of Mr Pickwick* (1921), *Number 13* (1922), *Weekend Wives* (1928), *The Vagabond Queen* (1929), *The Ghoul* (1933), *The Night of the Party* (1934), *They Drive by Night* (1939), *The Lamp Still Burns* (1943), *Don't Take It to Heart!* (1944), *A Place of One's Own* (1945), *Beware of Pity* (1946), *Quartet* (1948), *Last Holiday* (1950), *The Million Pound Note* (1953), *Father Brown* (1954), *The Adventures of Quentin Durward* (1955),

The Horse's Mouth (1958), *Sons and Lovers* (1960), *The Roman Spring of Mrs Stone* (1961).

BIBLIOG: Autobiography, *Practically True*, 1927; *Adventures in Embroidery*, 1945.

Thewlis, David (*b* Blackpool, 1963). Actor. RN: Wheeler. Versatile and compelling young actor who, initially favouring a career in pop music, came to London with his band 'Door 66', but turned to acting as student at the Guildhall School. Played a few small roles on TV and film, including the lover of the anorexic played by Jane HORROCKS in Mike LEIGH's *Life is Sweet* (1990), then electrified filmgoers in Leigh's 1993 film, *Naked*, in which his misogynistic, twisted Johnny is as deeply disturbing a character as is to be found in recent British cinema. It won him several awards, including that of the New York Critics, and announced the arrival of an edgy, major talent. Not everything since has measured up to this promise; certainly not the role of the poet Verlaine in the wildly mis-conceived *Total Eclipse* (1995, UK/Belg/Fr) or the US-made remake of *The Island of Dr Moreau* (1996), but in 2000 he was on dazzling form as the urbane gangster who undergoes a sort of redemption before returning to the 'outside' several decades later in *Gangster No. 1*, perhaps the most substantial of the British gangster cycle of the late 90s. In 1995, he directed the SHORT FILM, *Hello, Hello, Hello* (1995). Formerly married to director Sara SUGARMAN, his partner is now Anna FRIEL.

OTHER BRITISH FILMS INCLUDE: *Little Dorrit* (1987), *Vroom* (1988), *Resurrected* (1989), *Afraid of the Dark* (1991, UK/Fr), *Damage* (UK/Fr), *The Trial* (1992), *Black Beauty* (1994, UK/US), *Restoration* (1995, UK/US), *Seven Years in Tibet* (1997, UK/US), *Divorcing Jack* (1998, UK/Fr), *Whatever Happened to Harold Smith?* (2000), *Goodbye Charlie Bright* (2001).

Thin Man Films Company formed by Mike LEIGH and Simon Channing-Williams, who had acted as co-producer on Leigh's *High Hopes* (1988), after which they set up Thin Man to pro-duce Leigh's films exclusively. Named for their corpulent shapes.

Thomas, Dylan (*b* Swansea, 1914 – *d* New York, 1953). Screenwriter. Almost as famous for his heroic benders as for his writing, Thomas was not only a poet (famously of 'Fern Hill' and 'Do not go gentle into that goodnight'), but also a radio playwright (his *Under Milk Wood*, 1954, was filmed starrily if not very successfully in 1971), a short story writer (as in *Portrait of the Artist as a Young Dog*, 1940) and, less well known, a screenwriter. In this latter capacity, he wrote screenplays or commentaries for eight wartime SHORT DOCUMENTARY films directed by John ELDRIDGE for various companies, including STRAND and VERITY. He also co-authored two films for that unsung melodramatist, Daniel BIRT: *The Three Weird Sisters* (1948), a sometimes splendidly flamboyant piece, co-written with Birt's wife Louise; and *No Room at the Inn* (1948), about the wartime victimisation of evacuees, co-written with Ivan FOXWELL. Other films based on his writings include two directed by Welshman Karl FRANCIS – *The Mouse and the Woman* (1980) and *Rebecca's Daughters* (1992, UK/Ger) – and *Return Journey* (1990, UK/Neth), directed by Anthony HOPKINS, but largely unseen. Ronald HARWOOD reworked an earlier Thomas screenplay for the HORROR film, *The Doctor and the Devils* (1985).

Thomas, Gerald (*b* Hull, 1920 – *d* Beaconsfield, 1993). Director. Once he embarked on the 'CARRY ON' phenomenon, that was virtually that for Thomas. The younger brother of Ralph THOMAS, he directed the whole series from its successful inception with *Carry On Sergeant* (1958), with Peter ROGERS as producer and a whole entourage. Entered the industry in 1946, in the cutting rooms first, working on several of his brother's early films, including *Appointment with Venus* (1951), before directing his first film, *Circus Friends* (1956). Apart from his 'Carry On' career, he directed two tautly proficient THRILLERS, *The Vicious Circle* and *Time Lock* (1957) and the diverting COMEDY, *Please Turn Over* (1960). After that, it was 'Carry On' in fact or in all but name.

OTHER BRITISH FILMS: (e) *Twenty Questions Murder Mystery* (1949), *Tony Draws a Horse* (1950), *I'm a Stranger, Venetian Bird* (1952), *The Sword and the Rose, A Day to Remember* (1953), *Mad About Men, Doctor in the House* (1954), *Above Us the Waves* (1955); (d) *The Passionate Stranger* (assoc p), *Chain of Events* (1957), *The Duke Wore Jeans, The Solitary Child, Carry On Nurse* (1958), . . . *Teacher* (1959), . . . *Constable, Watch Your Stern, No Kidding* (1960), . . . *Regardless, Raising the Wind* (1961), . . . *Cruising, Twice Round the Daffodils* (1962), . . . *Cabby, The Iron Maiden, Nurse on Wheels* (1963), . . . *Spying,* . . . *Jack,* . . . *Cleo* (1964), . . . *Cowboy, The Big Job* (1965), . . . *Screaming* (+ voice), *Don't Lose Your Head* (1966), *Follow That Camel* (1967), . . . *Up the Khyber,* . . . *Doctor* (1968), . . . *Camping,* . . . *Again, Doctor* (1969), . . . *Up the Jungle,* . . . *Loving* (1970), . . . *Henry,* . . . *at Your Convenience* (1971), . . . *Matron,* . . . *Abroad, Bless This House* (1972), . . . *Girls* (1973), . . . *Dick* (1974), . . . *Behind* (1975, + voice), . . . *England* (1976), *That's Carry On* (1977, doc), . . . *Emmannuelle* (1978), *The Second Victory* (1986, + p), . . . *Columbus* (1992).

Thomas, Jameson (*b* London, 1888 – *d* Sierra Madre, California, 1939). Actor. Began his screen career with *Chu Chin Chow* (1923), his moustache making his look either dashing or sleazy. He went to the US when his wife contracted TB, from which *he* later died; and he made more than 40 US films from 1930, memorable as fortune-hunting playboy whom Claudette Colbert marries in *It Happened One Night* (1934).

OTHER BRITISH FILMS INCLUDE: *Pearl of the South Seas, Roses of Picardy* (1927), *The Farmer's Wife* (1928), *Piccadilly* (1929). AS.

Thomas, Jeremy (*b* London, 1949). Producer. Influential figure in British film who entered the industry in the late 60s, began in the cutting-room, with editor's credit on the DOCUMENTARY, *Brother Can You Spare a Dime?* (1975), and went on to produce some very daring films in the quarter-century following his first, *The Shout* (1978), made for his own Recorded Picture Co. He (and his company) produced challenging films for Nicolas ROEG (*Bad Timing*, 1980; *Eureka*, 1982, UK/US; *Insignificance*, 1985), Nagisa Oshima (*Merry Christmas Mr Lawrence* (1982, UK/Jap), and, most famously, for Bernardo Bertolucci, including *The Last Emperor* (1987, It/China), *The Sheltering Sky* (1990, UK/It), *Little Buddha* (1993, UK/Fr) and *Stealing Beauty* (1996, UK/It/Fr). Add to these Stephen FREARS's *The Hit* (1984), Peter MEDAK's painfully moving *'Let Him Have It'* (1991, ex p) and the more recent *Sexy Beast* (2001, UK/Sp/US), perhaps destined to be a sort of classic of the gangster GENRE, it will be seen that few producers have racked up such a set of credentials in the last two decades. In 1998, he directed his first film, *All the Little Animals* (1998, + p), but it was not successful enough to tempt him to repeat the experience quickly. Was also Chairman of the BFI (1993–97), and received BFI Fellowship in 1998. Son of Ralph THOMAS, nephew of Gerald THOMAS.

OTHER BRITISH FILMS: (p/ex p) *The Great Rock'n'Roll Swindle* (1979, doc, co-ex), *Everybody Wins* (1990, UK/US), *The Naked Lunch* (1992, UK/Can), *A Hundred and One Nights* (UK/Fr, co-p), *Victory* (UK/Fr/Ger) (1995, released 1998), *Der Unhold* (UK/Fr/Ger), *Blood and Wine* (UK/US) (1996), *Gohatto* (1999, UK/Fr/Jap), *The Triumph of Love, Heaven and Hell* (2001, UK/It), *Young Adam* (2003).

Thomas, Madoline (*b* Abergavenny, Wales, 1890 – *d* Weston-super-Mare, 1989). Actress. RN: Mary Price. Welsh supporting player of stage and screen who appeared in a dozen or so films, as kindly mums (*Painted Boats*, 1945), housekeepers (*Ghost Ship*, 1952) and grannies (the Welsh-set *Blue Scar*, 1949; the neat 'B' MOVIE, *Suspended Alibi*, 1956).

OTHER BRITISH FILMS INCLUDE: *The Last Days of Dolwyn* (1949), *No Trace* (1950), *Valley of Song, The Square Ring* (1953), *Second Fiddle* (1957), *Burke & Hare* (1971).

Thomas, Queenie (*b* Cardiff, 1898 – *d* Sunningdale, 1977). Actress. Leading lady of the 1910s and 20s, usually starring in Bertram PHILLIPS productions. She retired in 1919, but returned in 1922, initially starring in two SERIES of SHORTS, *Rainbow Comedies* (1922) and *Syncopated Picture Plays* (1923), both for Phillips.

OTHER BRITISH FILMS INCLUDE: *John Halifax, Gentleman* (1915), *The White Star* (1915), *Frills* (1916), *A Man the Army Made* (1917), *Meg o' the Woods* (1918), *A Little Child Shall Lead Them* (1919), *Trousers* (1920), *School for Scandal* (1923), *Her Redemption* (1924), *Safety First* (1926), *Warned Off* (1928). AS.

Thomas, Rachel (*b* Alltwen, Wales, 1905 – *d* Cardiff, 1995). Actress. Strong-featured Welsh character player who made about ten films spread over 30 years, most of them in Welsh-set dramas like *The Proud Valley* (1940), *Blue Scar* (1949), *Valley of Song* (1953) and finally in *Under Milk Wood* (1971) as Mary Ann Sailors. She was also Mrs Morgan in Paul DICKSON's celebrated SHORT FILM, *David* (1951). On TV, she was the mother in an early ADAPTATION of *How Green Was My Valley* (1960). Awarded OBE, 1968; BAFTA Cymru Lifetime Achievement Award, 1991.

OTHER BRITISH FILMS INCLUDE: *Undercover* (1943), *The Halfway House* (1944), *The Captive Heart* (1946), *Tiger Bay* (1959), *Sky West and Crooked* (1965).

Thomas, Ralph (*b* Hull, 1915 – *d* London, 2001). Director. In 1990, Thomas described himself as 'a sort of journeyman director . . . generally happy to make anything I felt to be half-way respectable'. There is an element of truth in this self-appraisal: he did whatever came his way at PINEWOOD for over 20 years: it is unduly modest, though, in relation to the very real achievements of about 40 features, some of which go well beyond the 'journeyman' tag. With his producer for virtually all that time, Betty BOX, he turned out some very proficient entertainments, across a wide GENRE range (THRILLERS, COMEDIES, ADVENTURES, etc), and was never guilty of pretension.

Educated at Middlesex University College, he entered the industry as a clapper-boy at SOUND CITY studios, worked as camera assistant and editor at BRITISH LION, served in WW2 (1940–44), then joined the RANK ORGANISATION in 1946 to work in the trailer-making department, experience he later found useful in the matter of economical storytelling. His first few films as director, including the idiotic *Helter Skelter* (1949), were feeble comedies made at GAINSBOROUGH STUDIOS, but he hit his stride with the tautly crafted thriller, *The Clouded Yellow* (1950), which mixed chase, espionage, romance and post-war malaise to compelling effect. In 1954, he orchestrated the talents of some very bright young rising stars, led by Dirk BOGARDE and Kenneth MORE, through Nicholas PHIPPS's cleverly constructed screenplay, to score a major commercial success with *Doctor in the House*. It ran to six sequels, several of which maintained a pleasing standard of comic invention, and Thomas revealed a flair for naturalistic comedy, which sadly found some unworthy vehicles later in his career, notably the

penis-transplant comedy, *Percy* (1971), and its sequel, *Percy's Progress* (1974). His adventures set in the picturesque locations favoured by producer Box, are generally dull, *Campbell's Kingdom* (1957), for instance, foundering on Bogarde's incapacity to play a convincing action hero, and the spy spoofs of the 60s are mildly amusing in their perfunctory way. His major achievement was undoubtedly *No Love for Johnnie* (1961), a perceptive, properly sceptical drama of political life, which resists the sweetener of a happy ending and elicits a finely shaded performance from Peter FINCH.

If Thomas lacks the visual flair or tough organising intelligence of some of the big names of the industry, he nevertheless managed for several decades to give the public what it wanted – and did it well enough for the public not to be ashamed of wanting it. His brother was director Gerald THOMAS; his son is producer Jeremy THOMAS.

OTHER BRITISH FILMS: (as director unless noted) *Second Bureau* (1936, e), *Once Upon a Dream, Traveller's Joy* (1949), *Appointment with Venus* (1951), *Venetian Bird* (1952), *The Dog and the Diamonds, A Day to Remember* (1953), *Mad About Men* (1954), *Doctor at Sea, Above Us the Waves* (1955), *The Iron Petticoat, Checkpoint* (1956), *Doctor at Large* (1957), *A Tale of Two Cities, The Wind Cannot Read, The Thirty Nine Steps* (1958), *Upstairs and Downstairs* (1959), *Conspiracy of Hearts, Doctor in Love* (1960), *No, My Darling Daughter, A Pair of Briefs* (1961), *The Wild and the Willing* (1962), *Doctor in Distress* (1963), *Hot Enough for June* (1964), *The High Bright Sun* (1965), *Doctor in Clover, Deadlier Than the Male* (1966), *Nobody Runs Forever* (1968, UK/US), *Some Girls Do* (1969), *Doctor in Trouble* (1970), *Quest for Love* (1971), *It's a 2¢ 6≤ Above the Ground World* (1973, + co-p), *The Biggest Bank Robbery* (1980), *Pop Pirates* (1984, p).

Thomas, Trevor (*b* Jamaica). Actor. Thomas got off to a good start in *Black Joy* (1977) with the role of the naive Benjamin who arrives in London from Guyana and is targeted by a couple of conmen. In the 20-odd years that followed, he did not find film work easy to come by for black actors: he had small roles in *International Velvet* (1978) and *Inseminoid* (1980), and a bigger one in the cricket-and-race drama, *Playing Away* (1986); and there was some TV, including the series *London Bridge* (1995).

OTHER BRITISH FILMS INCLUDE: *Yesterday's Hero* (1979), *Underworld* (1985), *The Nine Lives of Thomas Katx* (2000, UK/Ger).

Thompson, David Producer, executive producer. A very busy figure in 90s British cinema, in his capacity of Head of BBC FILMS, as a result of which his name appears as executive producer on such important and/or successful films as *Wonderland* (1999), *Billy Elliot* (2000) and *Iris* (2002, UK/US), as well, of course, as on such duds as *Maybe Baby* (UK/Fr) and *Love, Honour and Obey* (2000). Entered the industry as a TV producer in 1979, sharing BAAs for *Shadowlands* (1985) and *Safe* (1993); and was executive producer on the acclaimed TV drama, *Perfect Strangers* (2001).

OTHER BRITISH FILMS INCLUDE: *Captives* (1994), *Go Now* (1996), *24 7 TwentyFourSeven* (1997), *Among Giants, St Ives* (1998), *A Room for Romeo Brass* (UK/Can), *Mansfield Park* (1999, UK/US), *About Adam* (UK/Ire), *The Last Resort, Liam* (UK/Ger/It), *Born Romantic* (2001), *The Claim* (UK/Can/Fr), *I Capture the Castle* (2002).

Thompson, Derek (*b* Belfast, 1948). Actor. Character player who performed as a child with his twin sister; now best known for his long-running stint (from 1986 on) as Charlie Fairhead in the TV soap, *Casualty*. Among his few film roles, his most notable was as Bob HOSKINS's right-hand man, Jeff, who comes to a nasty end, in the gangster THRILLER, *The Long Good Friday* (1979). His wife is TV actress, Dee Sadler.

OTHER BRITISH FILMS INCLUDE: *Gonks Go Beat* (1965, unc), *Yanks* (1979), *Breaking Glass* (1980), *Wild Geese II* (1985), *Resurrection Man* (1997).

Thompson, Emma (*b* London, 1959). Actress, screenwriter. Multi-award-winning star who came to international prominence in the 90s. As the daughter of stage and TV director Eric Thompson, and actress Phyllida LAW, her career was foreshadowed, and at Cambridge she performed with the Footlights Club, meeting actors such as Hugh LAURIE and Stephen FRY, with whom she would play in the witty, indulgent 1992 comedy of former university chums reuniting, *Peter's Friends*. The director (and other star) of that film was Kenneth BRANAGH, the most influential figure in her career for some years after they first worked together in the highly regarded mini-series, *The Fortunes of War* (1987).

Branagh, whom she married and divorced, directed and co-starred with her in a TV version of *Look Back in Anger* (1989), cast her as Princess Katherine in his very popular film of *Henry V* (1989), their real-life romance and their film co-starrings elevating them to theatrical-darlings status. They were also together in the absurd, but not unenjoyable US thriller *Dead Again* (1991) and made a delightfully sparring Beatrice and Benedict in *Much Ado About Nothing* (1993, UK/US), both directed by Branagh, after which their partnership began to unravel. But not her career: she won an Oscar for her eloquent playing of Margaret Schlegel in MERCHANT IVORY's *Howards End* (1992) and was nominated for their *Remains of the Day* and as the crusading solicitor in *In the Name of the Father* (1993, UK/Ire/US), and was much admired for her playing of Bloomsbury group artist, *Carrington* (1994, UK/Fr). She won a further Oscar for her screenplay for *Sense and Sensibility* (1995, UK/US), in which she also gave an affecting account of Elinor Dashwood, whose 'sense' does not preclude the play of passionate feeling. Nothing could save the self-pitying heroine of *The Winter Guest* (1998, UK/US) from being tedious company: one could never have supposed such a judgement likely in the case of clever, handsome, witty Thompson, who has claimed she wants to stop acting. Now living with Greg WISE, Willoughby in *Sense and Sensibility*. Sister of Sophie THOMPSON.

OTHER BRITISH FILMS: *The Tall Guy* (1989), *Impromptu* (1991), *Primary Colors* (1998, UK/Fr/Ger/Jap/US), *Maybe Baby* (2000, UK/Fr), *Love Actually* (2003).

Thompson, J(ohn) Lee (*b* Bristol, 1914 – *d* Vancouver Island, 2002). Director, producer, screenwriter. One of the few British directors to establish a Hollywood career before the 70s, Lee Thompson began as a playwright, joining ABPC as a screenwriter in the mid 30s. In 1950 he was given the opportunity to film his successful play, *Murder Without Crime* (1950), and, over the next decade, directed a string of critically-acclaimed pictures for ABPC, RANK, and the independent production company he formed with Ted WILLIS and Frank GODWIN. A highly versatile director working in a wide range of GENRES, he showed particular flair for the socially-concerned THRILLER and for eliciting surprisingly intense performances from his actors, notably Diana DORS in the harrowing death-cell drama, *Yield to the Night* (1956), and newcomer Hayley MILLS in *Tiger Bay* (1959). Extraordinary ensemble acting and taut direction also characterised his two major commercial successes of the period, the classic WAR FILM *Ice Cold in Alex* (1958), and the award-winning *Woman in a Dressing Gown* (1957). Received five BAA best picture nominations during a 'purple patch' between 1954 and 1959, and, when he demonstrated his ability

to handle large-scale action-adventures with *North West Frontier* (1959) and received an AAn for *The Guns of Navarone* (1961), he was readily accepted by Hollywood.

Although perhaps none of his subsequent 24 American films quite fulfilled the promise of his first, *Cape Fear* (1962), he remained in demand as a director until the age of 75, periodically returning to Britain to make more personal films like *Country Dance* (1969). A strong advocate of a humanitarian agenda in film-making and a public critic of the BBFC, Lee Thompson's major contribution to British cinema was to combine a facility for visual suspense with a willingness to explore the tensions of moral decision-making. Married (2 of 3) to Joan HENRY.

OTHER BRITISH FILMS: *The Price of Folly* (1937, play), *The Middle Watch* (1939, co-sc), *East of Piccadilly* (1941, co-sc), *No Place for Jennifer* (1949, sc) *The Yellow Balloon*, *The Weak and the Wicked* (1953), *For Better, For Worse* (1954), *As Long As They're Happy*, *An Alligator named Daisy* (1955), *The Good Companions* (1956), *No Trees in the Street* (1958), *Return from the Ashes* (1965), *Eye of the Devil* (1966), *Before Winter Comes* (1968), *The Most Dangerous Man in the World* (1969), *The Passage* (1978).

BIBLIOG: Steve Chibnall, *J. Lee Thompson*, 2000. Steve Chibnall.

Thompson, Sophie (*b* London, 1962). Actress. Revue may be the natural milieu for the brilliantly funny Thompson, encapsulating character – bizarre, merely eccentric or possessed – in a matter of moments. Her range is narrower than that of sister Emma THOMPSON, but within it she never puts a foot wrong: think of Lydia, rapacious bride to David HAIG in *Four Weddings and a Funeral* (1994), of whingeing, hypochondriac Mary Musgrove in *Persuasion* (1995), of prattling Miss Bates in *Emma* (1996, UK/US), and of plain and plain-spoken Moxie in *Relative Values* (2000, UK/US). On stage, she has done high-profile work in the classics and modern plays, and been in TV since the mid 80s: film cameos may be icing on the cake to her but they are undeniably toothsome. Married to Richard Lumsden, who played slick Robert Ferrars in *Sense and Sensibility* (1995, UK/US).

OTHER BRITISH FILMS: *The Missionary* (1981), *Twenty-One* (1991, UK/US), *Dancing at Lughnasa* (1998, UK/Ire/US), *Gosford Park* (2001, UK/Ger/US).

Thomson, Alex (*b* London, 1929). Cinematographer. In films from 1946, first as clapper loader, then camera operator on some key films of the 60s, and 2nd unit cameraman on *Lawrence of Arabia* (1962). His features as cinematographer range from flashy 'SWINGING LONDON' pieces to Kenneth BRANAGH's *Hamlet* (1996, UK/US) and the pretty but vacuous *Love's Labour's Lost* (2000, UK/Fr/US).

OTHER BRITISH FILMS INCLUDE: (clapper loader) *The Perfect Woman* (1949); (cam op) *Dr Crippen* (1962), *The Caretaker* (1963), *The System* (1964), *Fahrenheit 451* (1966), *Superman* (1978, add ph); (c) *Band of Thieves* (1962), *The Strange Affair* (1968), *Alfred the Great* (1969), *Fear Is the Key*, *Dr Phibes Rises Again* (1972), *The Class of Miss MacMichael* (1978), *Eureka* (1982, UK/US), *Bullshot* (1983), *Electric Dreams* (1984, UK/US), *Track 29* (1988), *The Rachel Papers* (1989), *Black Beauty* (1994, UK/US).

Thomson, John (aka Patrick-Thomson) Actor. Best known for his sympathetic, detailed performance as chubby, decent Pete Gifford in TV's *Cold Feet*, which had several successful seasons in the late 90s, Thomson has also appeared in many other 90s TV programmes and about ten films. His best screen role to date may be as the pub landlord in *Up 'n' Under* (1997).

OTHER BRITISH FILMS: *The Young Poisoner's Handbook*, *Dangerous Lady* (1995), *The Man Who Knew Too Little* (1997, UK/Ger/US), *The Girl* with *Brains in Her Feet* (1997), *Born Romantic, Dog Eat Dog, Redemption Road* (2001), *24 Hour Party People* (2002).

Thomson, Margaret (*b* Australia, 1910) Instructional/ educational director. Settled in England from New Zealand in 1934. With a background in zoology she began work for Bruce WOOLFE at GAUMONT–BRITISH INSTRUCTIONAL. By 1938 she found work through the DOCUMENTARY movement at SHELL, STRAND FILM UNIT and with Marion GRIERSON. Until 1948 she worked for the REALIST FILM UNIT directing and producing films for the 'Dig for Victory' campaign, *The Technique of Anaesthesia* SERIES and the *Your Children* series. After a short spell with the CROWN FILM UNIT, Thomson made *Child's Play* (1954), a feature film for the state film company, GROUP 3. She returned to non-fiction production, making instructional, promotional and industrial films until she retired in 1977. Sarah Easen.

Thorburn, June (*b* 1931, Kashmir, 1931 – *d* Fernhurst, 1967). Actress. Former skating champion, with 'English rose' looks, Thorburn, briefly at the RANK CHARM SCHOOL, followed by repertory, made her debut in *The Pickwick Papers* (1952). She was delightful on a yachting honeymoon with John GREGSON in *True as a Turtle* (1956), was the Forest Queen in *tom thumb* (1958), and starred in the Richard TODD comedy *Don't Bother to Knock* (1961). Her untutored beauty also made her ideally suited to the Irish-set *Rooney* (1958) and *Broth of a Boy* (1959, Ire), as well as the romantic interest in *The Three Worlds of Gulliver* (1960, UK/Sp/US) and *The Scarlet Blade* (1963); there were also 'B' FILMS including *Transatlantic* (1960). She died in a plane crash.
OTHER BRITISH FILMS INCLUDE: *The Cruel Sea* (1952), *Delayed Action, Children Galore* (1954), *Touch and Go, The Hornet's Nest* (1955), *Escort for Hire* (1960), *Master Spy* (1963). Roger Philip Mellor.

Thorndike, Russell (*b* Rochester, Kent, 1885 – *d* London, 1972). Actor. Award-winning chorister before acting training at Ben Greet's Academy, on stage from 1904 (London 1905), with many seasons at the Old Vic and the Open Air Theatre, Regent's Park. Appeared in about 20 films, from 1922 (*Tense Moments from Great Plays*), was *Macbeth* (1922) and *Scrooge* (1923), and finally appeared in small character roles, including those in OLIVIER's SHAKESPEARE films: *Henry V* (1944), *Hamlet* (1948, as the 'churlish priest') and *Richard III* (1955). Also famous as the author of the series of *Dr Syn* tales of the smuggling parson, filmed several times (1937, 1962 as *Captain Clegg*, 1963). Brother of Dame Sybil THORNDIKE.
OTHER BRITISH FILMS INCLUDE: *The School for Scandal, The Bells* (1923), *Miriam Rozella* (1924), *A Shot in the Dark* (1933), *Fame* (1936), *Fiddlers Three* (1944), *Caesar and Cleopatra* (1945).

Thorndike, Dame Sybil (*b* Gainsborough, 1882 – *d* London, 1976). Actress. Most majestic of the great British theatre ladies, whose successes embraced virtually all the challenging classical roles for women (Medea, Lady Macbeth, etc) and who, in 1924, stamped SHAW's *St Joan* indelibly with her own kind of moral power. Trained at Ben Greet's Academy, on stage from 1904, an indomitable touring player as well as a mainstay of the Old Vic for decades, she dealt only sparingly – but memorably and sometimes ambitiously – with the cinema. She 'gave' some of her famous stage roles in the silent anthology, *Tense Moments from Great Plays* (1922) and was a famous Edith Cavell in *Dawn* (1928); she was Belle CRYSTALL's grim old mum in *Hindle Wakes* (1931), Nova PILBEAM's warm-hearted nurse in *Tudor Rose* (1936), the Salvation Army General in *Major Barbara*

(1941), and the vile old harridan, Mrs Squeers, in *Nicholas Nickleby* (1947). She brought a breath of life to *The Prince and the Showgirl* (1957) as the Dowager Queen, and was last seen as the Nurse in the definitive Chichester production of *Uncle Vanya*, filmed for TV in 1963, released in 1977. She seems almost a force of nature, very nearly too 'large' for the screen, so that it is a matter for thanks that some sense of her formidable gifts have been marshalled to its scrutiny. Married to Sir Lewis CASSON, with whom in her later decades she gave many poetry recitals. Heaped with honours, including DBE, 1931.
OTHER BRITISH FILMS: *Bleak House* (1920), *Moth and Rust* (1921), *Tense Moments with Great Authors, Lady Macbeth, Nancy* (1922), *To What End Hell* (1929), *A Gentleman of Paris* (1931), *Britannia Mews* (1948), *Stage Fright, Gone to Earth* (1950), *The Magic Box, The Lady with a Lamp* (1951), *The Weak and the Wicked, Melba* (1953), *Bernard Shaw* (1957, doc), *Alive and Kicking* (1958), *Shake Hands with the Devil* (UK/US), *Jet Storm* (1959), *Hand in Hand* (1960).
BIBLIOG: Sheridan Morley, *Sybil Thorndike*, 1977.

Thorne, Angela (*b* Karachi, 1939). Actress. Famous on TV as Penelope KEITH's dim friend Marjorie in *To the Manor Born* (1979–81) and the snobbish mother-in-law in *Three Up, Two Down* (1985–89), as well as for her stage appearance as Mrs Thatcher. Films have been few and the roles small, best being that of Mrs Hawk-Monitor in *Cold Comfort Farm* (1995, TV, some cinemas), as mother to her real-life son, Rupert PENRY-JONES. Married to actor **Peter Penry-Jones** (*b* Cardiff, 1938), who appeared in the film version of the National Theatre's production of *The Dance of Death* (1968) and *Superman IV* (1987, US).
OTHER BRITISH FILMS INCLUDE: *Oh! What a Lovely War* (1969), *North Sea Hijack* (1979), *The Human Factor* (1979, UK/US), *Bullshot* (1983).

Thorne, Ken (*b* 1926). Composer. Latterly most of Thorne's work has been in the US or for TV, but he was busy in British films in the 60s and 70s, his versatility best seen in his several scores for Richard LESTER, on such films as *Help!* (1965, m d), *A Funny Thing Happened on the Way to the Forum* (1966, UK/US, shared AA), *Juggernaut* (1974), *Royal Flash* (1975) and *The Ritz* (1976, + arr, cond).
OTHER BRITISH FILMS INCLUDE: (comp) *The Clouded Crystal* (1948), *She Knows Y'Know* (1962), *Inspector Clouseau* (1968), *The Bed Sitting Room* (1969), *Superman III* (1983); (comp/cond) *The Touchables, Sinful Davey* (+ m d) (1968), *The Magic Christian* (1969, + m d), *Hannie Caulder* (1971), *Superman II* (1980), *Green Ice* (1981, cond, orch).

Thornton, Cecil V. (*b* London). Sound recordist. After WW1 service, City of London School-educated Thornton studied electrical engineering, worked with the BBC and entered films in 1929, doing uncredited work on *Blackmail*. Subsequently worked at BEACONSFIELD, TEDDINGTON and ELSTREE STUDIOS, particularly busy during the 30s and 40s, and especially for BRITISH NATIONAL, finishing his career in 50s 'B' MOVIES.
OTHER BRITISH FILMS INCLUDE: (sd) *Murder!* (1930), *My Wife's Family* (1931), *No Funny Business, Radio Parade of 1935* (1934), *Invitation to the Waltz* (1935), *Kicking the Moon Around* (1938), *Tomorrow We Live* (1942), *One Exciting Night* (1944); (sd recording) *Juno and the Paycock* (1930), *Gypsy Melody* (1936), *The Saint in London* (1939), *Atlantic Ferry* (1941), *Candlelight in Algeria* (1943), *Mr Emmanuel* (1944), *Lisbon Story, Appointment with Crime* (1946), *My Brother Jonathan* (1948), *The Hasty Heart* (1949), *Happy Go Lovely* (1951), *Valley of Song* (1953), *Delayed Action* (1954).

Thornton, F. Martin Director, actor. On-screen as actor from 1909, American-born Thornton turned to direction in 1912, filming many of the short dramas produced by Charles URBAN in KINEMACOLOR, together with two features, *The World, the Flesh and the Devil* (1914) and *Little Lord Fauntleroy* (1914). In 1916, he became a director with the WINDSOR FILM COMPANY at its studio in Catford; he was with HARMA (1917–19) and STOLL (1919–22).

OTHER BRITISH FEATURE FILMS INCLUDE: (d) *Jane Shore* (1915, co-d), *Diana and Destiny* (1916), *The Happy Warrior* (1917), *The Splendid Conrad* (1918), *The Great Imposter* (1918), *The Power of Right* (1919), *The Iron Stair* (1920, + sc), *My Lord Conceit* (1921, + sc), *Lamp in the Desert* (1922), *The Romany* (1923), *Women and Diamonds* (1924), *Mutiny* (1925). AS.

Thornton, Frank (*b* London, 1921). Actor. RN: Ball. Sniffy, prissily moustached 'Captain' Peacock, floorwalker at Grace Bros in TV's *Are You Being Served?* (1973–83) and its SPIN-OFF film, was a natural for Robert Altman's all-Brit lineup in *Gosford Park* (2001, UK/Ger/US), as a butler; surely Peacock's father had been in service? In fact, Thornton had had a respectable stage career and small roles in several dozen films before the politically incorrect sitcom made him a sitting-room fixture. He began in such 50s 'B' MOVIES as *Radio Cab Murder* (1954) and *Stock Car, Cloak Without Dagger* (1955), before TV rescued him.

OTHER BRITISH FILMS INCLUDE: *The Tell-Tale Heart* (1960), *Victim* (1961), *It's Trad, Dad!, The Dock Brief* (1962), *The Early Bird* (1965), *Carry On Screaming* (1966), *The Bed Sitting Room* (1969), *The Private Life of Sherlock Holmes* (1970), *Up the Chastity Belt* (1971), *That's Your Funeral, Bless This House* (1972), *Steptoe & Son Ride Again* (1973), *Vampira* (1974), *Are You Being Served?* (1977).

Thornton, James (*b* Bradford, 1966). Actor. Was plucked from LAMDA for the role of the rapist in TV's dark mini-series, *The Lakes* (1997), and then co-starred in Sam MILLER's pylon-painting drama, *Among Giants* (1998), as Pete POSTLETH-WAITE's randy offsider, jealous of his relationship with Rachel GRIFFITHS. His next two films were less successful – the oddly likeable but widely *un*liked *Plunkett & Macleane* and, for Miller again, the widely unseen *Elephant Juice* (2000). He was a hulking, endearing Ham Peggotty in TV's *David Copperfield* (1999).

Thorpe, George (*b* Croydon, Surrey, 1891 – *d* Maidenhead, 1961). Actor. Ex-farmer who took to acting after WW1 service (1914–19), made stage debut in 1920 and became a popular leading man in London and New York. Perhaps appeared in unconfirmed silent films, later reappeared as dignified, balding character actor in *Unpublished Story* (1942), and made a further dozen, usually as sturdy middle-class husbands or fathers, like those he played in two very different rurally-set films: *Quiet Weekend* (1946), repeating the stage role he had played over 1,000 times, and *Daughter of Darkness* (1947).

OTHER BRITISH FILMS INCLUDE: *Yellow Canary, The Demi-Paradise* (1943), *Portrait from Life, Quartet* (1948), *Morning Departure* (1950), *Father's Doing Fine* (1952), *The Rainbow Jacket* (1954).

Thorpe, Richard (*b* Hutchinson, Kansas, 1896 – *d* Palm Springs, California, 1991). Director. RN: Rollo Smolt Thorpe. Archetypal Hollywood studio director who did whatever came his way – and an enormous amount did. He acquired a reputation for efficiency, and much of what he did was no more than efficient, but in 1937 he made a rich melodramatic meal of *Night Must Fall* (1937) and directed some lively entertainments in virtually every GENRE in the 40s at MGM. His relevance here lies in the stirring COSTUME ADVENTURES he made for MGM–BRITISH in the 50s: *Ivanhoe* (1952), *Knights of the Round Table* (1953) and *The Adventures of Quentin Durward* (1955). All are curiously and attractively different from their Hollywood counterparts, perhaps are marginally more reflective. Thorpe also directed two proficient British action films, *The House of the Seven Hawks* and *The Killers of Kilimanjaro* (1959). No one is likely to make auteurist claims for Thorpe but his kind of studio know-how is as unlikely as his prolificacy to be found again.

Thorpe-Bates, Peggy (*b* London, 1914 – *d* London, 1989). Actress. RN: Bates. Famously 'She-who-must-be-obeyed', wife Hilda to *Rumpole of the Bailey* (1978–83), RADA-trained Thorpe-Bates, daughter of musical comedy star Thorpe Bates, had made her debut at Stratford in 1934, worked for many provincial reps and was a member of the BBC Repertory Company (1956–57). She appeared in a few films, playing Sandy Dennis's mother in *A Touch of Love* (1969), but when Hilda hove into view her goose was cooked. A Council member of Actors' Equity from 1956 to 1962. Married Brian OULTON.

OTHER BRITISH FILMS: *Peeping Tom* (1960), *In the Doghouse* (1961), *Georgy Girl* (1966), *Mosquito Squadron* (1968), *Galileo* (1974, UK/Can).

Thorpe Davie, Cedric (*b* London, 1913 – *d* Dalry, 1983). Composer. Former master of Music at St Andrew's University, Scotland, he scored several dramas at GAINSBOROUGH STUDIOS in the later 40s, starting with the Skye fishing-family tragedy, *The Brothers* (1947). Several of his later films reflected this Scottish interest: *Rob Roy . . .* (1953), *Rockets Galore* (1958), *The Bridal Path* (1959) and *Kidnapped* (1960).

OTHER BRITISH FILMS INCLUDE: *Snowbound* (1948), *Bad Lord Byron* (1949), *You're Only Young Twice!* (1952), *The Dark Avenger* (1955), *The Green Man* (1956), *A Terrible Beauty* (1960).

Thraves, Jamie (*b* Romford, Essex, 1969). Director. Trained at the Royal College of Art, Thraves came to attention as a maker of pop videos and promos, and of SHORT FILMS which did well at festivals. His first feature, *The Low-Down* (2001), was a critically well-received, naturalistically observed study of young people in unresolved relationships.

OTHER BRITISH FILMS: (shorts) *Scratch* (1991), *The Take Out* (1993), *The Hackney Downs* (1994).

Threlfall, David (*b* Manchester, 1953). Actor. First came to attention on stage as Smike in *The Life and Adventures of Nicholas Nickleby*, and since then primarily on TV where he made an excellent impression as opportunist Leslie Titmuss in John MORTIMER's *Paradise Postponed* (1986) and *Titmuss Regained* (1991) and uncannily suggested Prince Charles in *Diana: Her True Story* (1993). Threlfall has filmed very rarely: in *Scum* (1979), *When the Whales Came* (1989), *The Lake* (1992, short), *The Summer House* (1993, TV, some cinemas) as an unbeguiling bridegroom, and in the international productions, *The Russia House* (1990, UK/US) and *Patriot Games* (1992, US).

thrillers/mystery films: 'I aim to give the public good healthy mental shake-ups,' said Alfred HITCHCOCK, whose 30s English films such as *The 39 Steps* (1935) and *The Lady Vanishes* (1938) set the standard by which subsequent British thrillers were to be judged. What distinguished the thriller from the whodunnit, Hitchcock believed, was the intensity of emotional involvement: it provided not a puzzle to be solved but a form that dealt with murderous passions, underworld morality and the eruptions of chaos into normality that shattered complacent notions of civilisation. In the 40s, the British thriller often undercut post-war optimism and trailed *film noir*ish shadows across tales of evil, betrayal and social disillusionment: one thinks of such 1947 films as the BOULTINGS' *Brighton Rock*, Robert HAMER's *It Always Rains on Sunday* and CAVALCANTI's *They Made Me a Fugitive*.There was also the extraordinary trio of films on which Carol REED's reputation principally rests, *Odd Man Out* (1947), *The Fallen Idol* (1948) and *The Third Man* (1949), which use the thriller to comment on existential loneliness, the conflict between innocence and experience, and the amorality of the post-war world. In the 50s, the team of Michael RELPH and Basil DEARDEN was particularly successful in marrying the excitement of MELODRAMA with mature observations of social issues – racial prejudice in *Sapphire* (1959), homophobia in *Victim* (1961).The 70s was a particularly rich period for British thrillers, perhaps reflecting a post-60s disillusionment with a stagnant decade: Mike HODGES's *Get Carter* (1971), Nicolas ROEG's *Don't Look Now* (1973, UK/It), Richard LESTER's *Juggernaut* (1974), and John MACKENZIE's *The Long Good Friday* (1979). They provide a summation of the best qualities of the British thriller: gangster grittiness, social criticism, cinematic flair and the sensuality of suspense: but mention should also be made of the cycle of gangster thrillers begun in the late 90s. These included *Lock, Stock and Two Smoking Barrels* (1998), *Snatch* (UK/US) and *Gangster No. 1* (UK/Ger/Ire) (2000), and *Sexy Beast* (2001, UK/Sp/US), all more graphically violent than their predecessors. Neil Sinyard.

See also **crime films** and **detective films**.

Tickle, Frank (*b* London, 1893 – *d* London, 1955). Actor. Former bank manager who appeared in about 20 supporting roles, such as the Governor of ill-fated Harfleur in *Henry V* (1944), spread over so many years.

OTHER BRITISH FILMS INCLUDE: *Two on a Doorstep* (1936), *The Lion Has Wings* (1939), *Atlantic Ferry* (1941), *Fiddlers Three* (1944), *The Winslow Boy* (1948), *Children of Chance* (1949), *It Started in Paradise* (1952), *The Adventures of Quentin Durward* (1955).

Tiernan, Andrew (*b* Birmingham, 1965). Actor. On stage in the Donmar Warehouse production of *A Lie of the Mind* as a hunting fanatic, and TV's *Prime Suspect* (1991, 1992) as DC Rosper, Tiernan has had supporting roles in about 15 films of the 90s, notably as Piers Gaveston, favourite of *Edward II* (1991) and, more in multiplex mode, *Lock, Stock and Two Smoking Barrels* (1998) – and the US-made *Interview with the Vampire* (1994).

OTHER BRITISH FILMS INCLUDE: *Dead Cat* (1989), *The Trial* (1992), *Safe* (1993), *Two Deaths* (1995), *Face* (1997), *The Criminal* (2001, UK/US), *Mr In-Between* (2001).

Tierney, Malcolm Actor. Heavily set actor much on TV as police superintendents, in, for example, *Dalziel and Pascoe* (1998–99), a constant target for Warren CLARKE's iconoclasm, as well as several years of Tommy McArdle in *Brookside* (1983–87). Tierney has imposed his authority on character roles in a few films, including *Braveheart* (1995, UK/US) and *Shiner* (2001), but TV has offered more.

OTHER BRITISH FILMS INCLUDE: *All Neat in Black Stockings* (1969), *Family Life* (1971), *McVicar* (1980), *Little Dorrit* (1987), *In the Name of the Father* (1993, UK/Ire/US), *A Life for a Life* (1998).

Tigon Production company formed in 1966 by the enterprising Tony TENSER. It made some superior HORROR films, including *The Sorcerers* (1967), starring Boris KARLOFF, and the critical and cult favourite, *Witchfinder General* (1968). It also made the comedy, *The Magnificent Seven Deadly Sins* (1971), the conventional ADAPTATION of *Black Beauty* (1971) and the

TELEVISION-TO-FILM SPIN-OFF, *For the Love of Ada* (1972). Tenser reputedly resigned in 1972 because he disliked graphic violence.

OTHER BRITISH FILMS INCLUDE: *The Blood Beast Terror* (1967), *Curse of the Crimson Altar* (1968), *Blood on Satan's Claw* (1970), *Doomwatch*, *The Creeping Flesh* (1972).

Till, Eric (*b* London, 1929). Director. Before going to Canada in the later 70s, Till directed three proficient British films: the caper comedy, *Hot Millions* (1968), with Peter USTINOV and Maggie SMITH, the romantic melodrama, *The Walking Stick* (1970), and *It Shouldn't Happen to a Vet* (1976), based on James Herriot's characters. The rest is almost wholly Canada and TV.

Till, Stewart (*b* Rochford, Essex, 1951). Producer. Formerly President of Polygram Filmed Entertainment which he joined when it was set up in 1992, then holding a similar role with the London-based activities of UNIVERSAL PICTURES, Stewart has been an influential figure in film DISTRIBUTION and production since the early 90s. Like Alan PARKER (Till is his Deputy Chairman on the FILM COUNCIL), he began in advertising, and has a strong sense of the need to *sell* films. He has been associated with the distribution of such successes as *Four Weddings and a Funeral* (1994), but was also co-executive producer on the darker, less obviously box-office titles, *Jude* (1996), *I Want You* (1998) and *Wonderland* (1999), three masterly films directed by Michael WINTERBOTTOM, which must have taxed Till's commercial instincts. Awarded CBE, 2000.

Tilvern, Alan (*b* London, 1919). Actor. In films from the mid 40s, and about 30 supporting roles since, as well as TV drama and stage work (including the courtroom drama, *The Trial of Mary Dugan*, 1958), Tilvern has been a reliable and versatile presence, playing foreigners of various kinds, such as Carlos, a very untrustworthy 'butler' in *Chase a Crooked Shadow* (1957) and a German captain in the services comedy, *Desert Mice* (1959).

OTHER BRITISH FILMS INCLUDE: *The Small Voice* (1948), *Night and the City* (UK/US), *Cairo Road* (1950), *The Master Plan* (1954), *The Bespoke Overcoat* (1956), *A Tale of Two Cities* (1958), *The Siege of Pinchgut* (1959), *Shadow of Fear* (1963), *Khartoum*, *The Frozen Dead* (1966), *Percy's Progress* (1974), *Superman* (1978), *1919* (1984).

Timothy, Christopher (*b* Bala, Wales, 1940). Actor. Made his name as nice young James Herriot, the Yorkshire vet, in TV's *All Creatures Great and Small* (1978–90) and became so identified with the role that other pickings, as he suggested in a TV programme in 2000, were apt to be lean. He had played a half-dozen small film roles before this but was passed over in favour of Simon WARD and John ALDERTON in the two SPIN-OFF films of the series.

OTHER BRITISH FILMS INCLUDE: *Othello* (1965), *Alfred the Great*, *Spring and Port Wine* (1969), *Up the Chastity Belt* (1971), *Eskimo Nell* (1974).

Tingwell, Charles ('Bud') (*b* Sydney, 1923). Actor. After WW2 service, Tingwell secured several important roles in the not-very-plentiful cinema of post-war Australia, had a supporting role in the US-made *The Desert Rats* (1953), went to England to complete a small role in EALING's *The Shiralee* (1957) – and stayed for 16 years. During that time he became popular as surgeon Alan Dawson in TV's *Emergency-Ward 10* (1957–67), and in the SPIN-OFF FILM. He also landed a dozen film roles, including that of Inspector Craddock whose patience is tried by Margaret RUTHERFORD in four 'Miss Marple' MYSTERIES.

Since returning to Australia in the early 70s, he has become one of the most prolific and respected actors on the local scene.

OTHER BRITISH FILMS INCLUDE: *Bitter Springs* (1950, UK/Aust), *Smiley* (1956, UK/Aust), *Bobbikins* (1959), *Cone of Silence* (1960), *Murder She Said* (1961), *Murder at the Gallop* (1963), *Murder Most Foul, Murder Ahoy* (1964), *Nobody Runs Forever* (1968, UK/US), *Evil Angels* (1988, UK/Aust).

Tobias, Oliver (*b* Zurich, 1947). Actor. RN; Tobias Oliver Freitag. Intense, dark-haired leading man of international films from 1970, including a sprinkling of British-made jobs like *The Stud* (1978), as a nightclub owner with whom Joan COLLINS has her way, and the REMAKE of *The Wicked Lady* (1983), as Faye Dunaway's one true love. Co-starred with Charlotte RAMPLING in an Italian version of *'Tis Pity She's a Whore* (1971).

OTHER BRITISH FILMS INCLUDE: *The Biggest Bank Robbery* (1980), *The Brylcreem Boys* (1996), *Grizzly Falls* (1999), *Don't Look Back!* (2001).

Todd, Ann (*b* Hartford, Cheshire, 1909 – *d* London, 1993). Actress. When James MASON brought his cane down on her hands as she sat at the piano in that ripe but irresistible load of old tosh, *The Seventh Veil* (1945), Ann Todd acquired the stardom that 15 years of largely nondescript film roles had failed to deliver. The film was a heady mixture of psychiatry, (popular) classical music and charismatic leading performances and it was just what audiences wanted at the end of WW2. Unfortunately, Todd never again had such a box-office hit.

Trained at Central School to be a drama teacher, she switched to acting after her first taste of it, and in the interstices of her film career she acquired a respectable, if not actually dazzling, stage career, during which she played the murderess *Lottie Dundas* (1943) and Lady Macbeth (1954–55). Of her pre-*Veil* film roles, only neurotic Madge Carne in *South Riding* (1938) and Robert DONAT's wartime romantic dalliance in *Perfect Strangers* (1945) are worth noting. Post-*Veil*, she went to Hollywood where she played Gregory PECK's wife in one of HITCHCOCK's most leaden films, *The Paradine Case* (1947), an experience she always overrated. Back in England, she gave what may be her finest performance in the superb PARAMOUNT–BRITISH Victorian MELODRAMA, *So Evil My Love* (1948), as the missionary's widow who returns to England, and lets down her hair, literally and figuratively, to her very great cost. Her chiselled blonde beauty, with its conflicting suggestions of propriety and sensuality, brilliantly caught by Max GREENE's lustrous camera, was never more skilfully used, and she rose to poignant heights at its conclusion. David LEAN became her third husband and directed her in three films before they separated in 1954: *The Passionate Friends* (1948), an upmarket, unmoving re-telling of a *Brief Encounter*-style triangle; *Madeleine* (1949), in which again her ambiguous beauty was cleverly exploited; and *The Sound Barrier* (1952, BAAn/a), in which she played second fiddle to men and aeroplanes.

As her career petered out in the 60s, she took to making DOCUMENTARIES in exotic places, like Nepal in *Thunder in Heaven* (1964), but they were never widely shown. She continued to act on stage occasionally, as in *The Vortex* (1965); she had been in the first British TV serial, *Ann and Harold* (1938) and she made TV appearances in both the US and the UK in later years. Her first husband was Victor Malcolm, brother of famed TV presenter Mary Malcolm, and her second was **Nigel Tangye** who acted as technical adviser on *Things to Come* (1936) and *Conquest of the Air* (1940). Her brother was **Harold**

Brooke (*b* London, 1910, RN: Todd), who wrote plays and several screenplays with wife Kay Bannerman.

OTHER BRITISH FILMS: (a) *These Charming People, Keepers of Youth, The Ghost Train* (1931), *The Water Gipsies* (1932), *The Return of Bulldog Drummond* (1934), *Things to Come* (1936), *The Squeaker, Action for Slander* (1937), *Poison Pen* (1939), *Ships with Wings* (1940), *Danny Boy* (1941), *Gaiety George* (1946), *The Green Scarf* (1954), *Time Without Pity* (1957), *Taste of Fear* (1961), *90 in the Shade* (1964, UK/Czech), *The Fiend* (1971), *The Human Factor* (1979, UK/US), *The McGuffin* (1985); (d, doc) *Thunder of the Gods* (1966), *Thunder of the Kings* (1967), *Thunder of Silence* (1975).

BIBLIOG: Autobiography, *The Eighth Veil*, 1980.

Todd, Bob (*b* Faversham, 1921 – *d* Sussex, 1992). Actor. Entered films in 1961 and played about two dozen supporting roles over the following two decades, not exactly prime time for British CHARACTER ACTORS, and he had to make do with the likes of *Mutiny on the Buses* (1972), *The Ups and Downs of a Handyman* (1975) and *Confessions of a Pop Performer* (1975). The bald-headed comedian was better known for his TV work with Tony HANCOCK (*Hancock's*, 1967) and Benny HILL through much of the 60s.

OTHER BRITISH FILMS INCLUDE: *Postman's Knock* (1961), *Hot Millions* (1968), *Bachelor of Arts* (1969), *The Scars of Dracula* (1970), *That's Your Funeral, Adolf Hitler – My Part in His Downfall* (1972), *Superman III* (1983), *The Return of the Musketeers* (1989, UK/Fr/Sp).

Todd, Richard (*b* Dublin, 1919). Actor. RN: Palethorpe-Todd. As ASSOCIATED BRITISH PICTURE CORPORATION's leading man, Richard Todd starred in a variety of GENRES, starting as an unjustly convicted criminal in *For Them That Trespass* (1948). He established his reputation, on both sides of the Atlantic, in *The Hasty Heart* (1949), for his moving, Oscar-nominated performance as an insecure, incurably ill Scotsman in a Burmese military hospital, his misanthropy gradually overcome by the kindness of his fellow inmates. ABPC loaned him to DISNEY for three swashbucklers, *The Story of Robin Hood . . .* (1952), *The Sword and the Rose* (1953) and *Rob Roy . . .* (1953), which cemented his reputation without establishing a clear persona. This came with his best remembered role, as Guy Gibson in *The Dam Busters* (1955), where he epitomised the derring-do of the British officer. Todd played the same character type in *The Yangtse Incident* (1956), but he fought hard in the late 50s against his stereotyping as the stiff-upper-lipped hero, playing a worm-turning cosmetics salesman in *Never Let Go* (1960). He was a womanising travel agent in *Don't Bother to Knock* (1961) which he co-produced, but his turn to COMEDY was unsuccessful. Like all the 50s male stars, Todd struggled to find effective roles in 60s films, often playing roles as high-ranking officers, overshadowed by American leads, as in *Operation Crossbow* (1965, UK/It). He resumed his stage career and was also regularly seen on television. Awarded OBE, 1993.

OTHER BRITISH FILMS: *Interrupted Journey* (1949), *Stage Fright, Portrait of Clare* (1950), *Flesh and Blood* (1951), *Venetian Bird, Elstree Story, 24 Hours of a Woman's Life* (1952), *Chase a Crooked Shadow, The Naked Earth, St Joan* (UK/US) (1957), *Intent to Kill, Danger Within* (1958), *The Long and the Short and the Tall* (1960), *The Hellions* (1961, UK/S Af), *The Very Edge, The Boys* (1962), *Death Drums Along the River* (1963, UK/Ger/Zanz), *Coast of Skeletons* (1964), *The Battle of the Villa Fiorita* (1965), *Subterfuge* (1968), *Asylum* (1972), *Number One of the Secret Service* (1977), *The Big Sleep* (1978), *Home Before Midnight* (1978), *House Of The Long Shadows* (1982).

BIBLIOG: Autobiographies: *Caught in the Act*, 1986; *In Camera*, 1989. Andrew Spicer.

Toeplitz, Ludovico (*b* Genoa, Italy, 1893 – *d* 1958). Producer. RN: Toeplitz de Grand Rey. Huge, film-loving son of an Italian banker, he helped KORDA to finance *The Private Life of Henry VIII* (1933) and was, for a brief while, Korda's business partner. In 1934. he formed his own company, Toeplitz Productions, for which he produced two handsome romances, *The Dictator* (1935), with Madeleine CARROLL and Clive BROOK brought back from Hollywood, and *The Beloved Vagabond* (1936), with Maurice CHEVALIER. However, neither production was financially successful and Toeplitz produced no more. Assisted Mario ZAMPI in forming TWO CITIES FILMS (Rome and London were the 'two'), returned to Italy during WW2 and to England post-war, but his only subsequent film was *Children of Chance* (1949).

Toibin, Niall (*b* Cork, Ireland, 1929). Actor. Rumpled, grizzled Irish character player in films from the 60s, often in Irish-set pieces like *Ryan's Daughter* (1970), *Tristan and Isolde* (1979), *The Country Girls* (1983) and *Far and Away* (1992, Ire/US). TV includes *Stay Lucky* (1989–91) and *Ballykissangel* (1996), as Father MacAnally.
OTHER BRITISH FILMS INCLUDE: *Guns in the Heather* (1968), *Flight of the Doves* (1971), *Fools of Fortune* (1989), *The Pope Must Die* (1991, UK/US), *Rat* (2000, UK/US).

Tomelty, Frances (*b* Belfast, *c* 1950). Actress. Daughter of Joseph TOMELTY, she has made about ten films, starting with a tiny role in *The Romantic Englishwoman* (1975, UK/Fr), and has become a reliable character player on film and TV. Had sharp supporting roles as Hugh O'CONOR's mother in *Lamb* (1985), Mrs Carter, dark and intense in her dealings with *Monk Dawson* (1997), and as Lucy's mother in the quirky TV sitcom, *Lucy Sullivan Is Getting Married* (1999). Married to STING (1976–82).
OTHER BRITISH FILMS INCLUDE: *The Medusa Touch* (1978, UK/Fr), *Bullshot* (1983), *Bellman & True* (1987), *The Field* (1990, UK/Ire).

Tomelty, Joseph (*b* Portoferry, Ireland, 1911 – *d* Belfast, 1995). Actor. As well as being a playwright and stage actor, white-haired Tomelty appeared in about 30 films, usually as endearing types like Will Sparks in *The Sound Barrier* (1952), and benign professionals, like the doctors in Irish-set *The Gentle Gunman* (1952) and Kenya-set *Simba* (1955). Benignity did not, however, preclude wiliness, which was on display in *Happy Ever After* (1954), out for David NIVEN's blood, or even the confidence trickery he and Nora NICHOLSON were up to in *Upstairs and Downstairs* (1959). Father of Frances TOMELTY.
OTHER BRITISH FILMS INCLUDE: *Odd Man Out* (1947, + Irish adviser), *The Oracle*, *Hobson's Choice*, *Front Page Story* (1953), *The Young Lovers*, *A Kid for Two Farthings* (1954), *John and Julie*, *Timeslip* (1955), *Moby Dick* (1956), *A Night to Remember* (1958), *Lancelot and Guinevere* (1962).

Tomlinson, David (*b* Henley-on-Thames, 1917 – *d* Mursley, 2000). Actor. Amiable light comedy actor with lugubrious features, popular on stage and in British films from 1948 to 1960, often as endearing upper-class fools, often flustered and bewildered, sometimes providing a light touch in serious films such as *The Wooden Horse* (1950). After Tonbridge School and (briefly) the Grenadier Guards, he made his West End debut in 1938, and was spotted by Anthony ASQUITH while touring in *Quiet Wedding* and cast in the 1941 film. After RAF service in WW2, he continued in supporting roles, becoming busy in the late 40s, when he featured more prominently in such GAINSBOROUGH films as *Broken Journey* (1948), *My Brother's Keeper* (1948), and the popular mermaid comedy *Miranda*

(1948). In another popular success, *The Chiltern Hundreds* (1949), he starred as a twittish Viscount who unsuccessfully stands for both Tory and Labour as an election candidate. In the 50s, he starred on the West End stage in *The Little Hut* for three years. His reputation for playing genial upper-class twits continued with the infantile Humpy in *All for Mary* (1955), 'J' in *Three Men in a Boat* (1956), and Lt Fairweather in *Up the Creek* and *Further Up the Creek* (both 1958). A sighting of Tomlinson on stage by Walt Disney led to his his best remembered role, the prosperous Edwardian father in *Mary Poppins* (US, 1964), resulting in other US and British children's films, such as *Bedknobs and Broomsticks* (US, 1971) and *Wombling Free* (1977).
OTHER BRITISH FILMS INCLUDE: *Name, Rank and Number* (1940, short), *Pimpernel Smith* (1941), *The Way to the Stars*, *Journey Together* (1945), *School for Secrets* (1946), *Master of Bankdam*, *Fame Is the Spur* (1947), *Here Come the Huggetts*, *Sleeping Car to Trieste*, *Warning to Wantons*, *Vote for Huggett* (1948), *So Long at the Fair* (1950), *Hotel Sahara* (1951), *Made in Heaven* (1952), *Is Your Honeymoon Really Necessary?* (1953), *Carry On Admiral* (1957), *Tom Jones* (1963), *The Truth About Spring* (1964), *The Water Babies* (1975), *Dominique* (1978).
BIBLIOG: Autobiography, *Luckier Than Most*, 1990. Roger Philip Mellor.

Tomlinson, Ricky (*b* Bispham, 1940). Actor. If he had done nothing more than play Mancunian householder Jim Royle, slumped in a chair in front of the telly, dishing out orders and (more or less) mild abuse in TV's brilliantly observed, award-winning *The Royle Family* (1998–2000, BAAn/a), sniggering to himself with self-indulgent delight, indolent and sharp, Tomlinson's fame would be assured. However, the former shop steward who once went to prison for his principles, has offered other evidence for being considered one of the major British actors of the turn of the century: he was heart-breaking as the father determined to get a communion dress for his daughter in Ken LOACH's *Raining Stones* (1993); had some much-noticed TV in *Cracker* (1994–96), replacing Christopher ECCLESTON's character, in *Dockers* (1999), as a scab, and in *Clocking Off* (2000), as a driver on the take; and he had the title role in the spoof DOCUMENTARY *Mike Bassett: England Manager* (2001). Whether he likes it or not, and he almost certainly wouldn't, rumpled, bearded, homely Tomlinson is a national treasure. This status was indicated by his being offered a six-figure fee for his autobiography in 2002, though only a five-figure one to pose naked; the discrepancy is understandable.
OTHER BRITISH FILMS: *Riff-Raff* (1991), *Butterfly Kiss* (1995), *Bob's Weekend* (1996), *Preaching to the Perverted*, *Mojo* (1997), *Nasty Neighbours* (2000), *Lounge Act* (2000, anim, short, voice), *The 51st State* (UK/Can/US), *Al's Lads* (2001), *Once Upon a Time in the Midlands* (2002).

Tompkinson, Stephen (*b* Stockton-on-Tees, 1965). Actor. Central School-trained, hulking (6'4") Tompkinson may now be best known for playing Father Peter in the soft-centred Oirish sitcom, *Ballykissangel* (1996–99). If so, this is a pity, since, though most of his work has been for TV, his major performance is surely as the out-of-work, out-of-luck miner in *Brassed Off* (1996, UK/US). This has moments of real pain that suggest depths hardly touched on his more prolific TV career, which included a nicely sharp sketch of an opportunistic reporter in *Drop the Dead Donkey* (1990–98) and *Lucky Jim* (2002). Theatre has included a stint in that actors' delight, *Art* (2000).
OTHER BRITISH FILMS: *Hotel Splendide* (2000, UK/Fr), *Tabloid* (2001).

Toms, Carl (*b* Kirkby-in-Ashfield, 1927 – *d* Broxbourne, 1999). Costume designer. Celebrated production designer for all the major stage companies (National, RSC, Old Vic, Royal Court), especially favoured by Tom STOPPARD, Toms also designed costumes for occasional films, mostly for HAMMER FILMS and most famously Raquel WELCH's prehistoric bikini for *One Million Years BC* (1966). Trained at the Royal College of Art and the Old Vic School, he greatly preferred stage work, though he also designed the film production of *The Winter's Tale* (1966). Awarded OBE, 1969.

OTHER BRITISH FILMS INCLUDE: *She* (1965), *The Quiller Memorandum* (UK/US), *Slave Girls* (1966), *Lost Continent* (1968), *When Dinosaurs Ruled the Earth* (1969).

Toone, Geoffrey (*b* Dublin, 1910). Actor. Charterhouse- and Cambridge-educated Irish leading man of stage and screen, on stage from 1931 and in British films since the late 30s. In the Royal Artillery from 1939 to 1942, he was invalided out, resuming his stage career in 1943, not returning to films until 1951. Among his best remembered film roles are those of Claire BLOOM's brother in *The Man Between* (1953) and the gentlemanly Englishman from Anna's past in *The King and I* (1956, US); on stage he was often at the Old Vic but also played Bea LILLIE's gallant Beau in *Auntie Mame* (1958–59). Also in Hollywood and much on TV.

OTHER BRITISH FILMS INCLUDE: *Queer Cargo* (1938), *Poison Pen* (1939), *Hell Is Sold Out* (1951), *The Great Game* (1953), *The Entertainer*, *The Terror of the Tongs* (1960), *Dr Crippen* (1962), *Dr Who and the Daleks* (1965).

Topical Film Company Producers of the *Topical Budget* NEWSREEL, one of the major British newsreels of the silent era, first issued in September 1911. In 1917 the company was taken over by the War Office and the newsreel turned into a PROPAGANDA reel under the title *War Office Official Topical Budget*, later *Pictorial News (Official)*. Both the footage and the copyright are now owned by the BRITISH FILM INSTITUTE, except for the years 1917–18 which are owned by the Imperial War Museum. In 1925, Adrian BRUNEL produced a parody of *Topical Budget* titled *A Typical Budget*. The newsreel ceased production in March 1931, but the company continued as Brent Laboratories until 1986.

BIBLIOG: Luke McKernan, *Topical Budget: The Great British News Film*, 1992. AS.

Torrens, Pip (*b* Bromley, Kent, 1960) Actor. Sturdy character actor, Cambridge- educated and trained at Drama Studio, London, has worked extensively in TV, including *To Play The King* (1994) and *Longitude* (2000), theatre, including *Absolute Hell* (1995) at the National Theatre, and radio. In films, he was noticeable as Nick Leeson's dour superior in *Rogue Trader* (1999) and has played in such international films as *Patriot Games* (1992) and *To End All Wars* (2002).

OTHER BRITISH FILMS INCLUDE: *Lady Jane* (1985), *Little Dorrit* (1987), *The Object of Beauty* (1991, UK/US), *The Remains of the Day* (1993), *Tomorrow Never Dies* (1997, UK/US).

Tottenham, Merle (*b* Quetta, India, 1901 – *d* Bexhill, 1958). Actress. Supporting player of stage and screen, who originated the servant Annie in *Cavalcade* (1931) and went to Hollywood to reprise her role in the film version (1933) and played several other parts there, including the maid in *Night Must Fall* (1937). When she returned to England in 1938, she played secondary roles in such big films as *This Happy Breed* (1944), once again in domestic service.

OTHER BRITISH FILMS INCLUDE: *Immediate Possession* (1931), *Here's George* (1932), *Night Club Queen* (1934), *Bank Holiday* (1938), *Poison Pen, A Girl Must Live, Goodbye, Mr Chips* (1939), *Headline* (1943),

Caravan (1946), *The Weaker Sex, My Brother Jonathan* (1948), *Room to Let, The Woman in Question* (1950).

Tovey, Roberta (*b* London, 1953). Actress. Had several good roles as a child, but, like so many, failed to have an adult acting career. She was Richard TODD's daughter in *Never Let Go* (1960), the boathouse keeper's daughter used as a hostage in *Touch of Death* (1962) and one of the endangered children on a ship seized by pirates in *A High Wind in Jamaica* (1965). In TV's *Not in Front of the Children* (1967–69), she was one of the latter.

OTHER BRITISH FILMS: *The Piper's Tune* (1961), *Runaway Railway, Dr Who and the Daleks* (1965), *Daleks – Invasion Earth 2150 AD, Operation Third Form* (1966).

Tourneur, Jacques (*b* Paris, 1904 – *d* Bergerac, France, 1977). Director. French-born son of director Maurice Tourneur, he is now best known for his HORROR films, both in the US and, especially, for the British-made *Night of the Demon* (1957), but he also worked with imagination and verve in a range of GENRES. His other two British films attest to this: *Circle of Danger* (1950), a lively, sophisticated THRILLER, and *City under the Sea* (1965, UK/US), a colourful adventure FANTASY. But *Demon* is a real chiller, among his best work, with the flair for suggesting rather than showing horror that he brought to his classics for Val Lewton, including *I Walked with a Zombie* (1943, US).

Towb, Harry (*b* Larne, Ireland, 1925). Actor. Supporting actor who most often appeared in COMEDY roles in the 60s and 70s. Made a quite striking debut as Jane HYLTON's no-good fugitive husband in the enterprising 'B' FILM, *The Quiet Woman* (1951) and was often a vivid, sometimes aggressive, presence, whether as thug or doctor. Also, on the London stage from 1950 and Broadway from 1966, and much TV, including *The Army Game* (1959) as Private Dooley. Continued to appear in TV and occasional films into the 90s. Married to Diana Hoddinott (*b* Somerset, 1945), who appeared in *Girl Stroke Boy* (1971) and *The Man Who Cried* (2000, UK/Fr/US).

OTHER BRITISH FILMS INCLUDE: *The Gift Horse* (1952), *The Sleeping Tiger* (1954), *A Prize of Gold* (1955), *The End of the Line* (1957), *All Night Long* (1961), *The Blue Max* (1966), *The Bliss of Mrs Blossom* (1968), *Carry On at Your Convenience* (1971), *Barry Lyndon* (1975), *Lamb* (1985).

Towers, Harry Alan (aka Peter Welbeck) (*b* London, 1920). Producer, screenwriter. Prolific film-maker from the early 60s who most often wrote screenplays under the Welbeck name, and whose work tends to favour the HORROR and THRILLER mode, as evinced in such titles as *Circus of Fear* (1966) and *Night of the Blood Monster* (1969, UK/Ger/It/Sp) and three versions of Agatha CHRISTIE's *Ten Little Niggers* (1939): *Ten Little Indians* (1965, p, sc), *And Then There Were None* (1974, p, sc) and *Ten Little Indians* (1989, US). Much of his work has been in Europe and the US.

OTHER BRITISH FILMS INCLUDE: (sc) *Secret Cities: Berlin* (1961, short), *The Girl From Rio* (1968, co-sc); (p) *Black Beauty* (1971, co-p), *Fanny Hill* (1983, exec p), *Edge of Sanity* (co-p, UK/Hun) (1988), *She* (2001, exec p, UK/Can/Bul/It); (p, sc/story) *Death Drums Along the River* (1963, UK/Ger/Zanz), *Mozambique* (1964), *24 Hours to Kill, The Face of Fu Manchu* (1965), *The Brides of Fu Manchu* (1966), *The Vengeance of Fu Manchu, Five Golden Dragons* (1967), *Castle of Fu Manchu* (1968), *Bullet to Beijing* (1995, UK/Can/CIS), *High Adventure* (2001).

Townley, Toke (*b* Essex, 1912 – *d* Leeds, 1984). Actor. Eccentric-looking character player with high forehead, bald top surrounded by white aureole of hair, noticeable in a wide range of films from the early 50s on. He can be spotted as the harassed stage manager in the 'Red Peppers' segment of *Meet Me Tonight* and dim servant Willy in the dim *Treasure Hunt* (1952), as the shop assistant selling John MILLS a lock and key in *The Chalk Garden* (1964), and in three films for Lewis GILBERT.

OTHER BRITISH FILMS INCLUDE: *Lady Godiva Rides Again* (1951), *The Runaway Bus, Bang! You're Dead* (1953), *The Quatermass Experiment, Doctor at Sea* (1955), *Three Men in a Boat* (1956), *The Admirable Crichton, Barnacle Bill* (1957), *A Cry from the Streets* (1958), *Libel* (1959), *The Fast Lady* (1962), *The Scars of Dracula* (1970).

Townsend, Stuart (*b* Howth, Co. Dublin, 1973). Actor. Versatile, handsome young actor who gained rapid ascendancy in the 90s. Trained at Dublin's Gaiety School of Acting, he made his film debut in *Trojan Eddie* (1996), with Richard HARRIS, showed comedy flair as the shy conman in *Shooting Fish* (1997), and used his sexiness to dangerous effect on Samantha MORTON's flailing character in *Under My Skin* (1997), to seduce Gina McKEE with no thought of the pain he causes in *Wonderland* (1999) and to be all things to at least three women in *About Adam* (2001, UK/US). Being sacked from *Lord of the Rings* (2001), in which he was to play Aragorn, may have slowed his progress – but probably not for long, and he subsequently followed Tom Cruise's fangprints as the vampire Lestat, in *The Queen of the Damned* (2002, US).

OTHER BRITISH FILMS: *Summertime* (1996, short), *Resurrection Man* (1997), *Simon Magus* (2000, UK/Ger/It).

Toye, Wendy (*b* London, 1917). Director. Had it not been so fiendishly difficult in the film industry of her time for women to get a foothold as directors, it would not be necessary to make so much of Toye's features. They are agreeable enough COMEDIES, with perhaps a mildly feminist slant in *All for Mary* and *Raising a Riot* (1955) or THRILLERS, like the modestly suspenseful *The Teckman Mystery* (1954), and the film that launched her directorial career, the famous SHORT, *The Stranger Left No Card* (1952), which won an award at the Cannes Festival, and which is probably her best work. The wonder is that she got the chance to make them at all in the male chauvinist preserve of the film industry of the 50s. It would have been good to see her working on tougher projects but it is important to be grateful for what she did with what she got: she always shows a strong sense of character, encouraging her casts to make bricks from what looks suspiciously like straw, and she kept the narratives moving as if their piffling plots mattered. Toye, a trained dancer and choreographer, exercised both skills in several films, including *I'll Be Your Sweetheart* (1945) and *Piccadilly Incident* (1946). Also had an extensive stage career as dancer, actress, choreographer and director of ballet, musical comedy and straight plays.

OTHER BRITISH FILMS: (choreog) *Pagliacci, Southern Roses* (1936), *South American George* (1941); (d) *Three Cases of Murder* ('The Picture' segment), *On the Twelfth Day* (short, + a), *True as a Turtle* (1956), *We Joined the Navy* (1962), *The King's Breakfast* (1963, short).

Tracy, Arthur (*b* Kamenetz-Podolsk, Ukraine, 1900 – *d* New York, 1997). Actor. RN: Abraham Alter Tratserofski. Prominent RADIO singer, billed as 'The Street Singer', and with theme song of 'Marta', who was immensely popular in the UK on screen and in MUSIC HALL from 1935 to 1941. Use of his poignant rendering of 'Pennies from Heaven' in 1981 US film of same name led to a small role in *Crossing Delancey* (1988) and US stage tour in *Social Security*.

BRITISH FILMS: *Flirtation* (1935), *Limelight* (1936), *The Street Singer, Command Performance* (1937), *Follow Your Star* (1938). AS.

Trafalgar Film Productions Company founded by Max SCHACH in January 1936, intending to make big-budget productions at DENHAM for distribution by United Artists. However, in the event only three films were made: *Pagliacci*, a costly and lavish commercial disaster, starring Richard TAUBER; *Dreaming Lips*, starring Elisabeth BERGNER, an expensive novelette; and, the most successful, *Love from a Stranger* (all 1936), a THRILLER with Hollywood stars, Ann Harding and Basil RATHBONE.

Train, Jack (*b* Plymouth, 1902 – *d* London, 1966). Actor. Became well-known on the Tommy HANDLEY radio programme, and joined Handley in the film version of *ITMA* (*It's That Man Again*) (1943), and appeared in several other films, usually in comedy roles in the 40s, including the HIGHBURY co-feature, *Colonel Bogey* (1948), in which he provided the ghost's voice.

OTHER BRITISH FILMS INCLUDE: *The Nursemaid Who Disappeared* (1939), *King Arthur Was a Gentleman* (1942), *Miss London Ltd* (1943), *Gaiety George* (1946), *Twenty Questions Murder Mystery* (1949).

BIBLIOG: Autobiography, *Up and Down the Line*, 1956.

training Until the 60s, technical crafts training in the British film industry was largely 'on the job', working alongside a more experienced mentor in one of the studios, just as cinematographer Jack CARDIFF trained with Freddie YOUNG at GAUMONT BRITISH studios in the 1930s (Young himself had started at the studio as a 15 year old lab assistant in 1917). Film directors, often honed their craft on 'QUOTA QUICKIES' (Michael POWELL), were former assistant directors (George POLLOCK), editors (David LEAN), cinematographers (Freddie FRANCIS), scriptwriters (J. Lee THOMPSON), or came from the THEATRE (Harold FRENCH), DOCUMENTARY SHORTS (Harry WATT, Lindsay ANDERSON), or 50s TELEVISION (Julian AYMES). The stability of employment found in film studios of the 30s and 40s made this system possible, and it only really began to fall apart in the 60s, as studios abandoned continuity of production and discarded their permanent technical staff and contract directors.

In 1967, the Labour government published the Lloyd Report, which recommended expanding formal training provision in technical skills for the UK film and television industries. This led to the foundation of the NATIONAL FILM AND TELEVISION SCHOOL in 1971, occupying the former Beaconsfield film studios, and with substantial financial support from the Department of Education and the film/television industries. NFTS alumni include directors Nick BROOMFIELD, Bill FORSYTH, Michael RADFORD, Terence DAVIES and Beeban KIDRON. *The London Film School* has gone through several name changes since its origins as 'The London School of Film Technique' in 1957 (also known as 'The London International Film School', 1974–2001), and its alumni include directors Mike LEIGH and Franc RODDAM. Both of these dedicated film schools offer two year full-time film-making programmes, as well as short courses. Since the 80s there has been an expansion in media studies courses of varying quality and usefulness at UK universities and art colleges, some with a substantial practical element, but with the older universities providing less emphasis on the practical skills needed for employment in the industry.

Skillset is now the British film industry's first port of call for anyone interested in a career in film. The BUFVC's database describes it as 'the national training organisation for broadcast, film, video and interactive media. It proves general and practical advice for both professionals already working in

British film and TV and young people looking to join the industry. It is supported by PACT, the Film Council and the terrestrial television networks.'

BIBLIOG: Lavinia Orton (ed), *Media Courses UK 2002* (published annually). Roger Philip Mellor.

trains *see* **travel and transport**

transvestism in British film *see* **drag appearances**

Trauner, Alexander (*b* Budapest, 1906 – *d* Omonville-la-Petite, France, 1993). Production designer. Celebrated international designer who trained in Paris under Lazare MEERSON and whose oeuvre is located chiefly in France and the US, but whose British work includes the exquisitely subtle, decorative designs for *The Private Life of Sherlock Holmes* (1970).

OTHER BRITISH FILMS: *The Night of the Generals* (1966, UK/Fr), *The Rainbow Thief* (1990).

travel and transport Transport and moving pictures were made for each other. In *Lt Daring and the Plans of the Minefield* (1913) the hero travels by bicycle, motorbike, car, aeroplane and train as he chases the villainess – in just 15 minutes! Actuality footage includes the 1925 *Centenary Celebrations of the Stockton and Darlington Railway* and the building of crack locomotives of the day. Features such as Geza von BOLVARY's *The Wrecker* (1928) often included a spectacular train crash (filmed here on the Basingstoke-Alton line, also the setting for Marcel VARNEL's 1937 *Oh! Mr Porter*). Walter FORDE's *Rome Express* (1932) is a splendid thriller set almost entirely on a Paris–Rome train; and Bernard VORHAUS's 'QUOTA QUICKIE', *The Last Journey* (1935), shot on the GWR, and the pioneering GPO FILM UNIT DOCUMENTARY *Night Mail* (1936) are other 30s highlights. The 40s are distinguished by films featuring war-time transport: a German U-boat in Michael POWELL's *49th Parallel* (1941) and in Pat JACKSON's DOCUMENTARY *Western Approaches* (1944), Spitfire aircraft in Leslie HOWARD's *First of the Few* (1942), and women truck convoy drivers of the ATS in *The Gentle Sex* (1943). The BRITISH TRANSPORT FILMS unit produced documentaries such as *Elizabethan Express* (1954), *Ocean Terminal* (1952) and John SCHLESINGER's *Terminus* (1961). Fifties films include Roy Ward BAKER's 'Titanic' film, *A Night to Remember* (1958), David LEAN's *A Bridge on the River Kwai* (1957) set on the Burma-Siam railway, Henry CORNELIUS's *Genevieve* (1953) about a vintage car, and Cy ENDFIELD's *Hell Drivers* (1957), about fierce competition among lorry-drivers. The 60s brought Peter YATES's *Summer Holiday* (1962) set aboard a London bus, Ken ANNAKIN's star-laden romps, *Those Magnificent Men . . .* (1965) and *Those Daring Young Men . . .* (1969), and Peter COLLINSON's *The Italian Job* (1969) which featured the British Mini. Lionel JEFFRIES' *The Railway Children* (1971) signalled the way forward to the many HERITAGE and literary films painstakingly recreating their period using original transport, including *Murder on The Orient Express* (1974). The trend for putting TV hits onto the big screen provided Harry BOOTH's *On the Buses* (1971).

OTHER RELEVANT BRITISH FILMS INCLUDE: *The Flying Scotsman* (1929), *Seven Sinners* (1936), *The 39 Steps* (1935), *The Lady Vanishes* (1938), *Painted Boats* (1945), *Sleeping Car to Trieste* (1948), *Train of Events* (1949), *The Titfield Thunderbolt* (1952), *The Gold Express* (1955), *The Flying Scot* (1957), *Death on the Nile* (1978), *The Long Good Friday* (1979), *Bhaji on the Beach* (1993).

BIBLIOG: John Huntley, *Railways in the Cinema*, 1969. Andrew Youdell.

Travers, Alfred (*b* Istanbul, 1906). Director. Having worked with Paul CZINNER in Europe, he came to England in the 30s, worked with the BRITISH COUNCIL and the MOI during WW2, and joined BRITISH NATIONAL post-war. He directed *Meet the Navy* (1946), based on a musical show performed by the Canadian Navy, and the THRILLER, *Dual Alibi* (1947, + co-sc), starring Herbert LOM in a dual role. He co-directed *Don Giovanni* (1954), based on a Salzburg performance, with Czinner, and acted as his technical director on *The Royal Ballet* (1959). The rest are long-forgotten 'B' MOVIES.

OTHER BRITISH FILMS INCLUDE: (shorts) *Men of Tomorrow* (1942), *Their Invisible Inheritance, Beyond the Pylons* (1945); (features) *The Stranger Came* (1949, + co-sc), *Alive on Saturday* (1957), *Men of Tomorrow* (1958), *One for the Pot* (1968, + p).

Travers, Ben (*b* London, 1886 – *d* London, 1980). Author. Famous author of theatrical farces, many of which, after their successful staging at London's ALDWYCH, were transferred to the screen, in many cases with members of the original cast, including Tom WALLS, who often directed the screen versions. Filmed titles include *Rookery Nook* (1930), *Plunder* (1931) and *Fighting Stock* (1935). He also collaborated on the screenplays of other films, including, surprisingly, the Gothic MELODRAMA, *Uncle Silas* (1947). Educated at Charterhouse, he had an unparalleled run of successes in the theatre and the film ADAPTATIONS were also popular in their time, depending as they did on such stand-bys of farce as henpecked husbands, sexual peccadilloes averted in the nick of time, compromising situations and complications of inheritance.

OTHER BRITISH FILMS: (editor/titles, uncr) *A Little Bit of Fluff* (1928); (play) *Mischief, The Chance of a Night-Time* (1931), *Second Best Bed* (1938); (sc) *Up to the Neck, Just My Luck* (1933), *Foreign Affairs* (1935), *Pot Luck, Dishonour Bright* (1936), *For Valour* (1937), *Old Iron* (1938); (co-sc) *So This Is London* (1939); (co-sc, play) *A Night Like This* (1932), *Banana Ridge* (1941), *Fast and Loose* (1954); (sc, play) *Thark* (1932), *Turkey Time, A Cuckoo in the Nest* (adptn/dial, + play) (1933), *Dirty Work, A Cup of Kindness, Lady in Danger* (1934), *Stormy Weather* (1935).

BIBLIOG: Autobiography, *Vale of Laughter*, 1957.

Travers, Bill (*b* Newcastle-upon-Tyne, 1922 – *d* Dorking, 1994). Actor. RN: William Lindon-Travers. After small roles in ten films, the handsome, strapping (6'4") Travers was noticed as Benvolio in *Romeo and Juliet* (1954, UK/It) and then became a star as the weakling-turned-Olympic-hero in *Geordie* (1955). His gangling, good-natured persona perfectly suited this role, as it did the guileless Hebridean mistaken for all sorts of unlikely wrongdoers in the prettily set and punningly titled *The Bridal Path* (1959). In the meantime, Travers, who had resumed an acting career after war service, had married Virginia McKENNA, with whom he appeared in several films, starting with *The Barretts of Wimpole Street* (1956), in which he was none too suitably cast as Robert Browning. They co-starred effectively as the young couple determined to make a go of a run-down old cinema in *The Smallest Show on Earth* (1957), made the most together of a West Indian *Passionate Summer* (1958), then had a major hit with *Born Free* (1965). This film, made on location in Africa, stimulated their interest in animal welfare and together they formed companies dedicated to promoting this aim. As well, several of their subsequent films reflect this concern: *The Lions are Free* (1967), *Ring of Bright Water* (+ co-sc), and *An Elephant Called Slowly* (+ co-p, co-sc) (1969). His sister was Linden TRAVERS.

OTHER BRITISH FILMS: *The Wooden Horse, Trio* (1950), *The Browning Version* (1951), *The Story of Robin Hood . . .* , *The Planter's Wife, Hindle Wakes* (1952), *The Genie, Mantrap, Street of Shadows, The Square Ring,*

Counterspy (1953), *Romeo and Juliet* (1954, UK/It), *Footsteps in the Fog* (1955), *Gorgo* (1960), *Two Living, One Dead* (UK/Swe), *The Green Helmet, Invasion Quartet* (1961), *A Midsummer Night's Dream* (1968), *The Lion at World's End* (1971, + co-d, co-p, co-sc, narr), *The Belstone Fox* (1973), *Death Trap* (1975, co-d, doc), *Christian the Lion* (1976, + co-d, co-sc, co-p), *The Young Visiters* (1984, exec p).

Travers, Linden (*b* Houghton-le-Spring, 1914 – *d* St Ives, 2001). Actress. RN: Florence Lindon-Travers. Gorgeously beautiful, dark auburn-haired Linden Travers ought to have been a major star, not merely because of her looks but because of the effortless sensuality and style she brought to largely undeserving material. Totally free from the debilitating gentility that hampered so many aspiring young actresses of her day, she ought to have had a career to rival Googie WITHERS'. An actress from childhood, she had experience in rep before entering films in the mid 30s, attracting the critical attention of Graham GREENE no less for her performance in *Brief Ecstasy* (1937). She played the increasingly fed-up mistress of a pusillanimous Cecil PARKER in *The Lady Vanishes* (1938), and was twice more involved with Parker – as his dissatisfied wife in *The Stars Look Down* (1939) and his tactful mistress in 'The Colonel's Lady' episode of *Quartet* (1948). The film that should at last have clinched her stardom was *No Orchids for Miss Blandish* (1948), in which she is far more attractive than the role or the much-excoriated film warrant. She had the bad luck to follow this critical disaster with two much more pretentious disasters: *Christopher Columbus* and *Bad Lord Byron* (1949), and shortly afterwards walked away from an industry that never knew how to value her and made a new life for herself as an artist and a psychologist. Sister of Bill TRAVERS, aunt of Penelope WILTON, and mother-in-law of ace portrait photographer Cornell LUCAS.

OTHER BRITISH FILMS INCLUDE: *Wednesday's Luck* (1936), *The Last Adventurers, Double Alibi* (1937), *Bank Holiday, The Terror* (1938), *Inspector Hornleigh on Holiday* (1939), *South American George, The Ghost Train* (1941), *The Missing Million* (1942), *Beware of Pity* (1946), *Jassy* (1947), *Don't Ever Leave Me* (1949), *The Schemer* (1956, short).

Tree, David (*b* London, 1915). Actor. RN: David Parsons. Tree's promising career was cut short when he lost an arm in WW2 (1939–45). Prior to that, he had made over a dozen films, mostly for KORDA's LONDON FILMS, including *The Drum* (1938) and *Over the Moon* (1939). However, he may be better remembered as nice, gormless Freddy Eynsford-Hill in Anthony ASQUITH's *Pygmalion* (1938) and as Anna LEE's young man in the charming romance *Return to Yesterday* (1940). Post-war, he filmed only once: as the schoolmaster in *Don't Look Now* (1973, UK/It).

OTHER BRITISH FILMS INCLUDE: *Knight Without Armour, The Return of the Scarlet Pimpernel* (1937), *Q Planes, Goodbye, Mr Chips, French Without Tears* (1939), *Major Barbara* (1941).

Tree, Sir Herbert Beerbohm (*b* London, 1853 – *d* London, 1917). Actor. One of the great actor-managers of the Victorian and Edwardian eras, Tree was most closely associated with Her Majesty's Theatre, London, which he reopened in 1897. He starred in an ambitious 1911 film ADAPTATION of *Henry VIII*, based on a stage production at the theatre, and was also brought to Hollywood by D.W. Griffith in 1916 to play the title role in *Macbeth*.

OTHER BRITISH FILMS: *King John* (1899), *Trilby* (1914). AS.

Tree, Lady (*b* London, 1857 – *d* London, 1937). Actress. RN: Helen Maude Holt. Celebrated stage actress, the wife of Sir Herbert Beerbohm TREE, she finished her career in several LONDON FILMS productions, her best remembered role being that of the Nurse to the King's children in *The Private Life of Henry VIII* (1933), licensed to address the King with a freedom allowed no one else. On stage from 1883, she had appeared in the silent films, *Still Waters Run Deep* (1916) and *Little Dorrit* (1920). Her daughter **Viola Tree** (*b* London, 1884 – *d* London, 1938), on stage from 1904, appeared in several films, including *Unmarried* (1920), *Heart's Desire* (1935) and finally *Pygmalion* (1938), as Perfide, the social reporter at the Embassy ball.

OTHER BRITISH FILMS: *Such Is the Law* (1930), *Wedding Rehearsal* (1932), *The Girl from Maxim's, Early to Bed, Her Imaginary Lover* (1933), *The Man Who Could Work Miracles* (1936).

Trevelyan, John (*b* London, 1903 – *d* London, 1985). Censor. Famously liberal, and liberalising, film censor who presided over the BRITISH BOARD OF FILM CENSORS during an important transitional period which coincided with major shifts in what the public regarded as acceptable in matters of sexuality and violence particularly. Trevelyan, who combined a genuine open-mindedness with a real love of film, began as a part-time film examiner in 1951 and was personally in charge of the BBFC as Secretary for 13 years (1958–71) when watershed British films such as *Room at the Top* (1958) and *Women in Love* (1969) revealed an enlightened CENSORSHIP at work.

BIBLIOG: Memoir, *What the Censor Saw*, 1973.

Treves, Frederick (*b* Cliftonville, 1925). Actor. Dignified character player, specialising in military officers, doctors, titled chaps of various kinds, Treves was in films from 1953 (*The Wheel of Fate*), but became much better known as Colonel Layton in TV's *The Jewel in the Crown* (1984). After this, he was seen more frequently in films (he played the Austro-Hungarian emperor in *Sunshine* (2000, UK/Austria/Can/Ger/Hung), though TV gave him better opportunities, as in *A Dance to the Music of Time* (1997).

OTHER BRITISH FILMS INCLUDE: *The High Terrace, The Long Arm* (1956), *One Hour to Zero* (1976), *Sweeney 2* (1978), *The Elephant Man* (1980, UK/US), *Defence of the Realm* (1985), *Paper Mask, The Fool* (1990), *Afraid of the Dark* (1991, UK/Fr), *Mad Dogs and Englishmen* (1994).

Trevor, Austin (*b* Belfast, 1897 – *d* London, 1978). Actor. RN: Schilsky. Imposing character player who specialised in professional types, often of a sinister cast. On stage in the US from 1915, then in the Army until 1919, the Swiss-educated Trevor joined the Stratford company in 1920, building up a formidable theatre *cv*. In films from 1930, he won a modest following as the first screen incarnation of Agatha CHRISTIE's Hercule Poirot in *Black Coffee, Alibi* (1931) and *Lord Edgware Dies* (1934). He was also an unpleasant café owner in *A Night in Montmartre* (1931), an anarchist instructing Oscar HOMOLKA in *Sabotage* (1936), the Headmaster urging Robert DONAT to retire in *Goodbye, Mr Chips* (1939), the Duke opposing his son's wish to marry a MUSIC HALL girl in *Champagne Charlie* (1944) and various high-ranking policemen in *So Long at the Fair* (1950) and *The Horrors of the Black Museum* (1959).

OTHER BRITISH FILMS INCLUDE: *At the Villa Rose, Escape* (1930), *Death at Broadcasting House* (1934), *Royal Cavalcade, The Silent Passenger* (1935), *Rembrandt* (1936), *Dark Journey* (1937), *Night Train to Munich* (1940), *The Young Mr Pitt* (1942), *The New Lot* (1943, short), *The Red Shoes* (1948), *Father Brown* (1954), *Seven Waves Away* (1956), *Carlton-Browne of the FO* (1958), *The Day the Earth Caught Fire* (1961), *The Alphabet Murders* (1965).

Trimble, Larry (*b* Robbinston, Maine, 1885 – *d* Los Angeles, 1954). Director. A prominent director with the US Vitagraph

Company from 1908 to 1913, Trimble came to the UK in 1912 to direct comedian John Bunny in four shorts, including *The Pickwick Papers* (1913). He returned the following year with actress Florence TURNER and his dog, JEAN, and remained with Turner's company until August 1915, when he returned to the US, where he remade one of his British features, *My Old Dutch*, in 1926.

OTHER BRITISH FILMS INCLUDE: *Rose of Surrey* (1913), *The Awakening of Nan, Shopgirls* (1914), *My Old Dutch, Caste, Far from the Madding Crowd* (1915), *Sally in Our Alley, Grim Justice* (1916). AS.

Trinder, Tommy (*b* London, 1909 – *d* Chertsey, 1989). Actor. Saucy cockney comedian from the variety stage with pork pie hat, leery grin (catchphrase 'You Lucky People!'), and long chin, like a proletarian Jack HULBERT. Apeared as boy singer in MUSIC HALL in 1922, by 1926 was a stand-up comedian, and starring in the West End, making his film debut in 1938 in routine farces until signed by EALING. After *Sailors Three* (1940) a knockabout comedy, he played a cheerful British tommy in occupied France helping Clifford EVANS in *The Foreman Went to France* (1942), and in *The Bells Go Down* (1943) he was in the Auxiliary Fire Service, dying bravely in a failed rescue attempt. Starred regularly in variety at the Palladium (1942–44), and returned to film comedy with *Fiddlers Three* (1944); had his best role as the Victorian entertainer George Leybourne, known as *Champagne Charlie* (1944), and his final Ealing role in the Australian venture *Bitter Springs* (1950). He compered TV's *Sunday Night at the London Palladium* (1955–57), starred in (+co-wrote) a rusty army farce, its title borrowing his catchphrase, *You Lucky People* (1955, + co-sc). He continued on screen, radio and stage into the 1970s. Awarded CBE, 1975.

OTHER BRITISH FILMS: *Almost a Honeymoon, Save a Little Sunshine* (1938), *She Couldn't Say No, Laugh It Off* (1939), *Eating Out with Tommy* (short) (1941), *Make Mine a Million* (1959), *The Damned* (1961), *The Beauty Jungle* (1964), *Under the Table You Must Go* (short) (1969). Roger Philip Mellor.

Tronson, Robert (*b* Chilmark, 1924). Director. Tronson came into film after directing many TV plays for Associated Rediffusion, directed about ten minor films, and went back to TV where he directed episodes of such popular series as *Rumpole of the Bailey* (1978) and *Hetty Wainthropp Investigates* (from 1996). Most of his films were run-of-the-mill MERTON PARK second-feature THRILLERS, but *Ring of Spies* (1963), based on the actual case of the Lonsdale-Kroger spy ring, is more ambitious in budget, length and casting, with a screenplay by Frank LAUNDER and Peter BARNES, and a DOCUMENTARY flavour in the rounding up of the subversives.

OTHER BRITISH FILMS INCLUDE: *The Man on the Carlton Tower* (1961), *Number Six, The Traitors* (1962), *On the Run* (1963), *All in Good Time* (1964, short), *Against the Tide* (1965).

Troughton, David (*b* London, 1950). Actor. A critically acclaimed Bolingbroke in the RSC's *Henry IV, Parts I* and *II* (2000), good enough to make one reviewer write: 'from the moment you see him . . . , you know that Shakespeare did not botch his title.' He has also done some brilliant TV, like the dull, nice vet in *Norman Conquests* (1978) and the hapless Martin in *Underworld* (1997); sadly, this very eloquent actor has hardly touched the cinema, but was part of *The Chain* (1984), Jack GOLD's comedy of house-moving and the deadly sins. Son of Patrick TROUGHTON, and brother of TV actor **Michael Troughton** (*b* London, 1955), who had a small role in *Enigma* (2001, UK/US).

OTHER BRITISH FILMS INCLUDE: *Give Us This Day* (1982), *Dance with a Stranger* (1984), *The Canterbury Tales* (1998, UK/Russ).

Troughton, Patrick (*b* London, 1920 – *d* Columbus, Georgia, 1987). Actor. After stage training in both London and New York, the somewhat severe-looking Troughton did WW2 service with the Royal Navy (1940–45), going into rep when demobbed. On TV from 1947 and in films the following year, as the Player King in OLIVIER's *Hamlet* and as a shepherd in *Escape*. However, though he continued to play small roles in films (Olivier cast him again in *Richard III*, 1955, as Tyrrell), it was TV that made him a household name, especially as the second *Dr Who* (1966–69). There was other rewarding TV, too, including the lead, as Quilp, in *The Old Curiosity Shop* (1962) and *A Family at War* (1970). Father of David TROUGHTON and Michael Troughton.

OTHER BRITISH FILMS INCLUDE: *Treasure Island, Chance of a Lifetime* (1950), *White Corridors* (1951), *The Moonraker* (1957), *The Phantom of the Opera* (1962), *Jason and the Argonauts* (1963), *The Viking Queen* (1966), *The Scars of Dracula* (1970), *Frankenstein and the Monster from Hell* (1973), *A Hitch in Time* (1978).

Trouncer, Cecil (*b* Southport, 1898 – *d* London, 1953). Actor. Forceful character player with resonant voice, mostly on stage, but in ten strong supporting film roles. Most memorable was the reactionary Head of House who resists the social engineering at work in *The Guinea Pig* (1948), though he is also amusing as Dr Barsmith, Exmoor resort entrepreneur in *Isn't Life Wonderful!* (1953).

OTHER BRITISH FILMS INCLUDE: *Pygmalion* (1938), *While the Sun Shines* (1947), *Saraband for Dead Lovers* (1948), *The Lady with a Lamp* (1951), *The Weak and the Wicked* (1953).

Trubshawe, Michael (*b* Chichester, 1905 – *d* England, 1985). Actor. Extravagantly moustachioed former regular army officer, probably at least as famous for being David NIVEN's army buddy, whose name was mentioned in every Niven film after 1938, as for any of the numerous character cameos in which he appeared. (He returned the favour by playing a character called Niven in *Those Magnificent Men . . .*, 1965.) In his 40-odd films, he usually played military types, often hearty, sometimes irascible, starting with Major Bushey Noble in *They Were Not Divided* (1950), but he also did upper-class civilians like the Ambassador in *The Lavender Hill Mob* (1951).

OTHER BRITISH FILMS INCLUDE: *Dance Hall* (1950), *The Card* (1952), *The Titfield Thunderbolt* (1953), *Private's Progress* (1956), *Gideon's Day* (1958), *The Guns of Navarone* (1961), *A Hard Day's Night* (1964), *Bedazzled* (1967), *The Magic Christian* (1969).

Truman, Michael (*b* Bristol, 1916 – *d* Newbury, Berks, 1974). Director. London University-educated Truman entered the industry in 1934, working at such studios as STOLL and DENHAM, in capacities including assistant director and editor, before WW2 service (1939–44). Post-war, he worked at EALING, first as editor on some very notable 40s films, then produced several 50s films, including *The Titfield Thunderbolt* and *The 'Maggie'* (1953), and directed the somewhat lacklustre comedy of family conflicts, *Touch and Go* (1955). Of the few other films he directed, *Go to Blazes* (1962), though made for ABPC, has some nicely comic bits of invention and character that recall Truman's Ealing background.

OTHER BRITISH FILMS INCLUDE: (e) *Stepping Toes* (1938), *Pink String and Sealing Wax* (1945), *Bedelia* (1946), *The Loves of Joanna Godden, It Always Rains on Sunday* (1947), *Saraband for Dead Lovers* (1948), *Passport to Pimlico* (1949); (d) *The Bridge* (1954), *Girl in the Headlines*

(1963), *Daylight Robbery* (1964); (p) *The Lavender Hill Mob* (assoc), *The Divided Heart* (1954), *Cry Wolf* (1968).

Truman, Ralph (*b* London, 1900 – *d* Ipswich, 1977). Actor. Commanding character actor who could move effortlessly between the eloquent chivalry of the Herald, Montjoy, in *Henry V* (1944), the sinister Monks of *Oliver Twist* and the cynical schoolmaster of *Mr Perrin and Mr Traill* (1948), and the brusque police inspector of *The Interrupted Journey* (1949). Also in international films, including *Quo Vadis* (1951) and *The Man Who Knew Too Much* (1955), Truman studied at the Royal College of Music before becoming a regular radio performer from 1925, making several thousand broadcasts. His 30s films are mainly 'QUOTA QUICKIES', but when he found himself with more chance, as with the role of Giordano, in charge of the Italian alpine expedition, in *The Challenge* (1938), it was clear that he took to the screen with real authority. Married radio actress Ellis Powell.

OTHER BRITISH FILMS INCLUDE: *The Bells* (1931), *The Silent Passenger*, *Late Extra* (1935), *East Meets West* (1936), *South Riding* (1938), *Sabotage at Sea* (1942), *Beware of Pity*, *Woman to Woman* (1946), *The Man Within*, *Mrs Fitzherbert* (1947), *Eureka Stockade* (1949), *Treasure Island* (1950), *Beau Brummell* (1954), *The Night My Number Came Up* (1955), *The Good Companions* (1956), *Lady Caroline Lamb* (1972, UK/It/US).

Truman-Taylor, Totti (*b* London, 1915). Actress. After considerable stage experience, made her film debut in *The Woman in the Hall* (1947) and subsequently played over 20 character roles, mostly small but sometimes fvivid, like the silly, twittery Miss Ribden-White in *Eight O'Clock Walk* (1954). One oddity in her credits: in 1955 she went to Paris to appear in Preston Sturges' swansong, *Les carnets de Major Thompson*. Also, much TV, some of it spent as a semi-regular of *Hancock's Half-Hour* (1956).

OTHER BRITISH FILMS INCLUDE: *The Million Pound Note* (1953), *A Woman Possessed* (1958), *There Was a Crooked Man* (1960), *Crooks Anonymous* (1962), *The Wrong Box* (1966), *A Nice Girl Like Me* (1969).

Trumper, John (*b* Plymouth, 1923). Editor. Winchester-educated Trumper worked in DOCUMENTARIES such as John ELDRIDGE's *Waverley Steps* (1948), before beginning to edit features. His first features were the GROUP 3 films, *The Brave Don't Cry* and *Brandy for the Parson* (1952), and he subsequently worked on a mixture of 'A' films such as *The Italian Job* (1969) and *Get Carter* (1971) and 'B' FILMS on which his cutting sharpened the impact of, say, the wordless first twelve minutes of *The Flying Scot* (1957), of Vernon SEWELL's admirable *Strongroom* (1962), and the suspense of Lance COMFORT's *Tomorrow at Ten* (1962).

OTHER BRITISH FILMS INCLUDE: *Three Dawns to Sydney* (1948), *The Kidnappers* (1953), *Pacific Destiny* (1956), *Time Lock* (1957), *Danger Within* (1958), *Devil's Bait* (1959), *House of Mystery* (1961), *Touch of Death*, *Crooks Anonymous* (1962), *Blind Corner* (1963), *Circus of Fear* (1966), *Privilege*, *Up the Junction* (1967), *The Long Day's Dying* (1968), *Entertaining Mr Sloane* (1969), *And Then There Were None* (1974), *Alfie Darling* (1975), *Boyfriends* (1996).

Trytel, W(illiam) L. (*b* 1894 – *d* ?). Music director, composer. Trained at the Royal College of Music, Tryel was music director on several dozen, largely nondescript films of the 30s, though the music certainly beefs up the drama in Bernard VORHAUS's *The Last Journey* (1935). Historian Rachael LOW described some of his work at TWICKENHAM as 'a rambling and endless accompaniment, churning on regardless of changes of shot, sequence or mood' (1985). Also headed a company providing ready-made music for SHORT FILMS.

OTHER BRITISH FILMS INCLUDE: (m/m d) *Hindle Wakes* (1931), *Squibs* (1935), *Juggernaut* (1936), *The Angelus* (1937); (p) *A Sister to Assist 'Er* (1948); (m d) *The Outsider* (1931), *The Lodger* (1932), *Broken Blossoms*, *Dusty Ermine* (1936), *Undercover Girl* (1958); (m) *Scrooge* (1935), *Dead Men Tell No Tales* (1938), *Murder at the Grange* (1952), *The Adventure of Hal 5* (1958).

Tuchner, Michael (*b* Berlin, 1934). Director. After four features in the early 70s, none very successful, including the unlovely gangster THRILLER, *Villain* (1971), and the MUSICAL, *Mister Quilp* (1974), derived from DICKENS's *The Old Curiosity Shop*, Tuchner spent most of the rest of his career in US television. He returned in 1989 to make the film version of Tom Sharpe's *Wilt*. Educated at Manchester Grammar School, he joined the BBC as a TV editor in 1958.

OTHER BRITISH FILMS: (d) *Music!* (1971, BAAn/doc), *Fear Is the Key* (1972), *The Likely Lads* (1976).

Tucker, Anand (*b* Bangkok, 1963). Director. A graduate of Harrow Film School, Tucker worked on the BBC arts programme, *The Late Show*, won a BAA for best documentary for his TV film, *A Vampire's Life* (1993), about the life of gothic novelist Anne Rice, then made the little-seen *Saint-Ex* (1996, + p), inspired by the life of aviator and author, Antoine de Saint-Exupéry. His first major feature was another BIOPIC, *Hilary and Jackie* (1998), a skilfully constructed, BAA-nominated account of the short, difficult life of cellist Jacqueline du Pré and the rivalry and love between her and her sister Hilary. He and producer Andy Paterson and screenwriter Frank COTTRELL-BOYCE own the production company, Archer Street Ltd.

Tucker, George Loane (*b* Chicago, 1872 – *d* Los Angeles, 1921). Director. Tucker's first American feature, *Traffic in Souls* (1913), established him as a major directorial force; his last, *The Miracle Man* (1919) further enhanced his career and established Lon Chaney as a major Hollywood star. Kenneth Macgowan writing in *Motion Picture Classic* in 1919 praised him as 'A man who, in supervision, editing and directing, stands squarely in the forefront of photoplay art'. Tucker's first wife died in childbirth in 1904, at which point he changed careers from railroad clerk to actor, becoming a director with the IMP Company in 1910. He came to England as one of the two directors with the LONDON FILM COMPANY, bringing with him the leading lady from *Traffic in Souls*, Jane Gail. She was to be his leading lady in *The Third String*, *She Stoops to Conquer*, *The Black Spot*, *The Difficult Way*, *England Expects*, *On His Majesty's Service*, *Called Back*, *The Fringe of War* (1914), *1914*, *The Middleman*, *The Prisoner of Zenda*, and *Rupert of Hentzau* (1915). These and Tucker's other British films were described by *The Bioscope* as 'thoroughly English in tastes and sympathies'. Tucker returned to the US in 1917, taking some of his British films with him; he made five more films in America prior to his death. In the UK, Tucker married Elizabeth RISDON.

OTHER BRITISH FILMS INCLUDE: *The Cage* (1914), *The Sons of Satan*, *An Odd Freak* (1915), *Arsene Lupin*, *The Man Without a Soul*, *The Manxman*, *A Mother's Influence* (1916). AS.

Tucker, Joe (*b* 1967). Director. After acting in several notable films from the mid 90s, including two for Mike LEIGH, *Secrets & Lies* (1996), and, as the sleazy Adrian in *Career Girls* (1997), Tucker made a controversial debut as director with *Lava* (2002), which he also wrote and acted in. Filmed in an unpicturesque Notting Hill, it was variously greeted as a wickedly black comedy, making the most of its limited budget, and as a tasteless addition to the British gangster cycle.

OTHER BRITISH FILMS: (a) *Captives* (1994), *Under the Skin* (1997).

Tufano, Brian (*b* 1939) Cinematographer. Tufano entered the film industry at age 12 as a page boy at LIME GROVE STUDIOS. After a long apprenticeship with the BBC where he worked with such about-to-be-influential film-makers as Ken LOACH, Mike LEIGH and Stephen FREARS in the 60s and 70s, he spent time in the US working on commercials and also on such films as *Blade Runner* (1982). Returning to England in the early 90s, he became associated with some of the most successful films of the resurgent British cinema, starting with two for Danny BOYLE: *Shallow Grave* (1994) and *Trainspotting* (1996), films that enjoyed cult status on a very commercial basis. Eschewing equally the gritty, hand-held look of the urban REALISM strand or the high pictorial gloss of HERITAGE film-making, he has found a way to combine the realist with an element of poetic commentary in such films as *Billy Elliot* (2000), *Late Night Shopping* (2001, UK/Ger) and *Last Orders* (2002, UK/Ger).

OTHER BRITISH FILMS: *The Waterloo Bridge Handicap* (1978, short), *Quadrophenia* (1979), *Riding High* (1980), *Windprints* (1990, UK/Zim), *True Blue, Element of Doubt* (1996), *The Life of Stuff, A Life Less Ordinary* (1997), *What Rats Won't Do* (1998), *Virtual Sexuality, Women Talking Dirty* (1999), *East Is East* (2000), *Alien Love Triangle* (2001), *Once Upon a Time in the Midlands* (2002).

BIBLIOG: Saul Metzein, 'Grit and polish', *Sight and Sound*, May 2001.

Tully, Montgomery (*b* Dublin, 1904 – *d* London, 1988). Director, screenwriter. Educated at the University of London, Montgomery Tully began his film career as a director of DOCUMENTARIES in 1929, but by the mid 40s he was making feature films, often CRIME and suspense films. Tully has been underrated as a director, and his best films, including *Murder in Reverse* (1945), *Dial 999* (1955), *The Glass Cage* (1955), *Man in the Shadow* (1957), are skilfully crafted examples of modest-budget British film-making. Perhaps Tully's finest film is *Escapement* (1957), one of five he directed in that year, which deals with mind-control in a clinic in the south of France. As well as crime films, he also directed the COSTUME ROMANCE, *Mrs Fitzherbert* (1947), and wrote screenplays for two MUSICALS, *Waltz Time* (1945) and *Lisbon Story* (1946), both directed by Paul STEIN. Tully also directed a great deal of work for TV, including numerous episodes of *The Edgar Wallace Theatre* at MERTON PARK STUDIOS.

OTHER BRITISH FILMS INCLUDE: *Boys in Brown* (1949), *The Diamond, Thirty-Six Hours* (1954), *Night Crossing, The Hypnotist* (1957), *I Only Asked!* (1958), *The Third Alibi* (1961), *Out of the Fog, She Knows Y'Know* (1962), *Master Spy* (1963), *Battle Beneath the Earth* (1967).

BIBLIOG: Wheeler Winston Dixon, 'The Marginalised Vision of Montgomery Tully', in *Classic Images* 224 and 225 (February, March 1994). Wheeler Winston Dixon.

Turleigh, Veronica (*b* Newtowncunningham, Ireland, 1903 – *d* London, 1971). Actress. RN: Turley. Distinguished, RADA-trained theatre actress on London stage from 1925, who made only three films, but was memorable in two of them: *The Card* (1952), as Alec GUINNESS's working-class mum who profits by his social mobility; and culture vulture Lady Beeder, who succumbs to Guinness's flattery in *The Horse's Mouth* (1958). Also in *King Arthur Was a Gentleman* (1942).

Turnbull, John (*b* Dunar, Scotland, 1880 – *d* London, 1956). Actor. Burly Scottish character player who made nearly 80 films between 1931, when he appeared in seven releases, and his last, *The Happiest Days of Your Life* (1950), as a member of

Alastair SIM's staff. On stage from 1901, he also directed plays and produced for ENSA during WW2. His filmography includes numerous police inspectors – he was too authoritative for lower ranks – and dignitaries of various kinds, one of whom, briefly glimpsed, is the artist Holbein having a go at Charles LAUGHTON in *The Private Life of Henry VIII* (1933).

OTHER BRITISH FILMS INCLUDE: *77 Park Lane* (1931), *Ask Beccles* (1933), *Badger's Green* (1934), *The Scarlet Pimpernel* (1935), *Tudor Rose* (1936), *Song of the Road* (1937), *Inspector Hornleigh on Holiday* (1939), *Return to Yesterday* (1940), *Shipbuilders* (1943), *Fanny by Gaslight* (1944), *A Place of One's Own* (1945), *Daybreak* (1948).

Turner, Anna (*b* Rio de Janeiro, 1918). Actress. Character player who made some sharp impressions in 15 or so cameo roles from the early 50s, including the woman being treated for anxiety neurosis near the end of *Lost* (1955) and a wife nagging to get to the cinema on time when her key-maker husband is needed for more urgent matters in the excellent THRILLER, *Strongroom* (1962). Also briefly glimpsed early on in *Empire of the Sun* (1987).

OTHER BRITISH FILMS INCLUDE: *Emergency Call* (1952), *The Floating Dutchman* (1953), *Eyewitness* (1956), *Urge to Kill* (1960), *The Silent Playground* (1963), *Bedazzled* (1967).

Turner, Florence (*b* New York, 1887 – *d* Los Angeles, 1946). Producer, actress. Turner is, arguably, America's first film star, making her debut with the Vitagraph Company in 1907. When she left the company in 1913, she decided to produce films in England, bringing with her director Larry TRIMBLE and JEAN, THE VITAGRAPH DOG. Her company was located at the Cecil HEPWORTH studios at Walton-on-Thames, and the films she made in the UK owe more to the slow Hepworth style of film-making than to sophisticated American production standards. Turner made more than 25 films in England, including *My Old Dutch* (1915), *Far from the Madding Crowd* (1915), *A Welsh Singer* (1915), and *East Is East* (1916). The films were released in the US and proved relatively successful. In 1916, Turner returned to America, but was back in the UK in 1921, remaining until 1924. Her later career was a steady decline from featured roles to bit parts to extra work.

OTHER BRITISH FILMS: *The Rose of Surrey, Jean's Evidence, The Younger Sister, The Lucky Stone, The Harper Mystery* (1913), *Creatures of Habit, Flotilla the Flirt, Daisy Doodad's Dial, Polly's Progress, One Thing After Another, Snobs, Florence Turner Impersonates Film Favourites, The Murdock Trial, For Her People, Through the Valley of Shadows, Shepherd Lassie of Argyle, Shopgirls* (1914), *As Ye Repent, Alone in London, Lost and Won, Doorsteps* (1915), *Grim Justice* (1916), *The Ugly Duckling* (1921), *The Old Wives' Tale* (1921), *The Little Mother, Was She Justified?, Lights o' London, The Street Tumblers* (1922), *The Hornet's Nest, Sally Bishop* (1923), *The Boatswain's Mate, Film Favourites, Women and Diamonds* (1924). AS.

Turner, George (*b* Findon Manor, 1902 – *d* London, 1968). Actor. Played supporting roles in the 20s and 30s and later became a makeup artist. Also made several films in the US, including *A Yank in Dutch* (1942).

BRITISH FILMS INCLUDE: *The English Rose* (1920), *Running Water* (1922), *Early Birds* (1923), *The Diamond Man* (1924), *Q-Ships* (1928), *White Cargo* (1929), *Britannia of Billingsgate* (1933), *Café Mascot* (1936), *Twin Faces* (1937), *Two Smart Men* (1940).

Turner, Lana (*b* Wallace, Idaho, 1920 – *d* Los Angeles, 1995). Actress. The very personification of the star system, Turner, a glamorous blonde presence in about 60 films, could sometimes be coaxed into giving respectable performances by directors like Vincente Minnelli and Douglas Sirk. Her rare brushes with

British cinema offered no such mentors and are incidental to a career remarkable in its kind, meshed with a private life remarkable in *its* kind.

BRITISH FILMS: *Betrayed, The Flame and the Flesh* (1954, UK/US), *Another Time, Another Place* (1958), *Persecution* (1974).

Turner, Simon Fisher (aka Simon Fisher-Turner; Simon Turner) (*b* Dover, 1954). Composer. Former child TV actor and recording artist who came to attention in films through his work for Derek JARMAN on such films as *Caravaggio* (1986, + a), *The Last of England* (1987), *Edward II* (1991). Later work included the 'sleeper' *Croupier* (1998, re-released 2000, UK/Fr/Ger/Ire), and *My Kingdom* (2001, UK/It), Don BOYD's Manchester-set re-working of *King Lear*, and he was credited with 'sound design' on *Gangster No. 1* (2000), but he is not usually found in the mainstream. TV scoring includes the enjoyable melodramatics of *Reckless* (1998).

OTHER BRITISH FILMS INCLUDE: *The Big Sleep* (1978, a), *Melancholia* (1989, UK/Ger), *The Garden* (1990), *No Head for Heights* (short), *Elenya* (UK/Ger) (1992), *Blue* (1993), *Loaded* (1994, UK/NZ).

Turner, Tim (*b* Bexley, 1924). Actor. Reliable 'B' MOVIE leading man of the 50s in such programmers as *Police Dog* (1955) and several of Republic's '*Case of . . .*' SERIES, he also had supporting roles in popular main features such as *The Dam Busters* (1955) and *A Night to Remember* (1958), and provided the voice for *The Invisible Man* (1958) on TV.

OTHER BRITISH FILMS INCLUDE: *Top Secret, The Gift Horse* (1952), *The Case of the Black Falcon, . . . the Soho Red, The Red Beret* (1953), *A Town Like Alice* (1956), *Dunkirk* (1958), *Jackpot* (1960).

Turpin, Gerry (*b* London, 1925 – *d* Gloucestershire, 1997). Cinematographer. Entered films during WW2 and had a long apprenticeship as focus-puller and camera operator before embarking on his own career as cinematographer. His varied output includes several films for each of Michael POWELL (*Peeping Tom*, 1960, cam op; *The Queen's Guards*, 1961), Bryan FORBES and Richard ATTENBOROUGH. To his credit are the contrasting achievements of the oppressive greyness of *Seance on a Wet Afternoon* (1964), the decorative Technicolor Victoriana of *The Wrong Box* (1966 – star Nanette NEWMAN thought he 'was wonderful at lighting women') and the tragic lyricism of the wide last shots of *Oh! What a Lovely War* (1969, BAA/c).

OTHER BRITISH FILMS INCLUDE: (cam op) *Rough Shoot* (1953), *Too Many Crooks* (1959), *Night of the Eagle* (1962); (c) *The Whisperers* (BAA/c), *Dutchman, Morgan: A Suitable Case for Treatment* (1966), *Deadfall* (1968), *Young Winston* (1972), *The Doctor and the Devils* (1985).

Tushingham, Rita (*b* Liverpool, 1942). Actress. A pharmacist's daughter, in convent school plays, followed by a professional debut at Liverpool Playhouse in 1960, she became the first significant female face of the British 'NEW WAVE'. Not conventionally pretty, with dark cropped hair, large soulful eyes and 'ugly duckling' looks, she was perfect for gauche, fey young women and offbeat roles, and especially for Tony RICHARDSON's *A Taste of Honey* (1961). Her untutored, truthful debut performance (BAA/newcomer) as Jo impressed audiences and critics alike, with its craving for affection, zany sense of humour and Lancashire fortitude. As the young wife in the 'married-but-gay' biker drama *The Leather Boys* (1963), she won the NY Film Critics Award; the Irish-set romance, *Girl with Green Eyes* (1963) used her shy, awkward persona to great effect (BAAn); and in *Doctor Zhivago* (1965, UK/US) she appeared briefly as a confused, fragile orphan. She was another naive young women up from the provinces in the self-consciously modish comedy *The Knack . . .* (1965), and she was a young hippy who journeys to India to meet *The Guru* (1969), a sceptical look at 60s counter-culture. Made a new career in films in North America, Europe and Israel, including *Judgement in Stone* (Canada/US) (1986), directed by her former husband Ousama RAWI. She reappeared in British films again after *An Awfully Big Adventure* (1995).

OTHER BRITISH FILMS: *A Place to Go* (1963), *The Trap* (UK/Canada) (1966), *Smashing Time* (1967), *Diamonds for Breakfast* (1968), *The Bed Sitting Room* (1969), *Straight on Till Morning* (1972), *The 'Human' Factor* (1975), *The Boy from Mercury* (1996, UK/Ireland) (1996), *Under the Skin* (1997), *Swing, Out of Depth* (1999). Roger Philip Mellor.

Tutin, Dame Dorothy (*b* London, 1931 – *d* Midhurst, 2001). Actress. A very versatile stage actress whose film work only hints at the depth and range of her talent. RADA-trained, she was on the London stage from 1949, had several seasons with the Old Vic, was a touching Viola in Stratford's 1958 *Twelfth Night*, a properly dazzling Sally Bowles in *I Am a Camera* (1954 – she turned down the film role), and the silent ruthless wife in PINTER's *Old Times* (1971). The cinema couldn't – or didn't – compete and Tutin said in 1994 that she would have liked to film more, but felt she hadn't the right looks for the screen. This seems hardly likely: she is an enchanting Cecily (BAAn) in *The Importance of Being Earnest* (1952) and pretty as a picture, but this was followed by two lacklustre ADAPTATIONS: *The Beggar's Opera* (1953) as Polly Peachum to OLIVIER's MacHeath and *A Tale of Two Cities* (1958), as Lucy Manette, requested for the role by Dirk BOGARDE. But the screen failed to exploit her elfin beauty and gifts for comedy and pathos, until she was middle-aged, when she was a touching Queen Henrietta Maria in *Cromwell* (1970), vividly obsessive as Sophie Brzeska in *Savage Messiah* (1972), her favourite film role, for which she composed her own song, and her Lady Minnie beautifully complements James MASON's elegiac quality in *The Shooting Party* (1984). There was some excellent TV, including *South Riding* (1974) and, as a monstrous mother, *Jake's Progress* (1995). Awarded CBE, 1967, and DBE, 2000. Married Derek WARING.

OTHER BRITISH FILMS: *Great Moments in Aviation* (1994, UK/US), *Alive and Kicking* (1996).

TVC (Television Cartoons) Established in 1957 as an English outpost for UPA (United Productions of America), but financial difficulties led to the withdrawal of American funding, and the proposed closure of the studio. Its director, Canadian, George Dunning, sought English-based financial backing, with ex-Associated Rediffusion business manager, John Coates, and continued production, predominantly in commercials. Approached by King Features to produce a TV series, *The Beatles*, TVC enjoyed Stateside success, which prompted the feature production, *The Yellow Submarine* (1968). Heinz Edelmann's distinctive designs, popular Beatles songs, and state-of-the-art psychedelic sequences combined to make the film a milestone in ANIMATION history, although it failed to influence the field long-term, and only enjoyed limited critical and popular success. Though contributing to other features like *The Lion, the Witch and the Wardrobe* (1978) and *Heavy Metal* (1981), TVC specialised in ADAPTATIONS of the work of Raymond Briggs, beginning with *The Snowman* (1982), making the feature, *When the Wind Blows* (1986), and enjoyed success with their television series, *The Tales of Beatrix Potter*, initially envisaged as a feature. Paul Wells.

Twickenham Studios One of the UK's oldest surviving studios, the Twickenham site was bought in 1912 by Dr Ralph JUPP who formed the LONDON FILM COMPANY to produce stylish films for the American market, his first being *The House Of Temperley*. He also employed legendary actors such as Sir Herbert TREE and American producers Harold M. SHAW and George Loane TUCKER. Financial and health problems caused him to sell in 1920 to the ALLIANCE COMPANY; 'big on ideas, short on experience', it collapsed in 1922. From 1923 to 1928 the studios were leased to various companies then Julius HAGEN founded the Twickenham Film Studios Ltd, with actor Henry EDWARDS and director Leslie HISCOTT. For the period he made a suprising number of films attracting good actors and directors including Michael POWELL. Financial problems resulted in the sale of the studios in 1937 to Studio Holdings Ltd, until 1938. The studios were bombed during WW2, then were used for mainly TV productions until Guido COEN developed the studio's international profile, attracting the producers of such films as *Saturday Night And Sunday Morning* (1960), *A Hard Day's Night* (1964), *Reds* (1981, US) and *Shirley Valentine* (1989, UK/US). A tiny studio with a long established reputation for filming, television, commercials and post production facilities.
BIBLIOG: Patricia Warren, *British Film Studios – An Illustrated History*, 2001. Patricia Warren.

Twiggy (*b* London, 1949). Actress. RN: Lesley Hornby. Whippet-thin 60s icon, former fashion model Twiggy went on to have a respectable acting career when the 60s stopped swinging. Made her film debut as Polly in Ken RUSSELL's over-elaborate, under-imagined *The Boy Friend* (1971) and had her best role as the prostitute Jenny in *The Doctor and the Devils* (1985), bringing some dignity and pathos to the part. Did a well-regarded Eliza in a TV version of *Pygmalion* (1981), has had some success as a recording artist, and has filmed in the US. Married (2) Leigh LAWSON.
OTHER BRITISH FILMS: *There Goes the Bride* (1979), *Madame Sousatzka* (1988), *Woundings* (1998).
BIBLIOG: Autobiography, *Twiggy*, 1975.

Twist, Derek (*b* London, 1905 – *d* Chelmsford, 1979). Director. Former producer with the RAF FILM UNIT (1940), Rugby- and Cambridge-educated Twist had been an editor at GAINSBOROUGH before WW2, which he spent in the RAF (1940–45), where he was head of the RAF FILM UNIT. Postwar, he joined INDEPENDENT PRODUCERS and directed the minor ARCHERS production (he had worked several times with Michael POWELL), *End of the River* (1947), an Amazon-set drama starring SABU. There were several other modestly attractive films, including *All Over the Town* (1949), with its theme of post-war adjustment in a seaside town, for WESSEX FILMS, and *Green Grow the Rushes* (1951, + co-sc), a Kentish marshland-set comedy on sub-EALING lines, for ACT FILMS. Also wrote and directed many TV playlets for Douglas FAIRBANKS Jr. Married Vida HOPE.
OTHER BRITISH FILMS INCLUDE: (e, unless noted) *Sunshine Susie* (1931, co-sc), *After the Ball* (1932), *The Fire Raisers* (1933), *Princess Charming* (1934), *The 39 Steps, The Phantom Light* (1935), *The Edge of the World* (1937), *They Drive by Night* (1939), *Old Bill and Son* (1940, co-sc), *Once a Jolly Swagman* (1948, assoc p), *Angels One Five* (1952, co-p, sc), *Police Dog* (1955, d), *Family Doctor* (1958, d, sc, co-adptn).

Two Cities dating from 1937 Two Cities was initially envisaged as a production company operating in the two cities of London and Rome which gave the company its name. Its first significant film was *French Without Tears* (1939) produced by MARIO ZAMPI but the company is most closely associated with 'the golden age of British cinema' – the 1940s – and with big-budget 'prestige' picture-making for the Rank Organization. The flamboyant driving force of the company was the Italian-born FILIPPO DEL GIUDICE and despite his brief internment during the war along with Zampi, Two Cities produced a number of 'quintessentially English' film classics including the most popular British film from the wartime period – *In Which We Serve* (1942). Other Two Cities films such as *This Happy Breed* (1944), *The Way Ahead* (1944), *Henry V* (1944), and *The Way to the Stars* (1945) form the backbone of the 'quality' cinema much favoured by critics of the day and contributed significantly to the high critical reputation acquired by the British cinema of the time. In the mid 40s Two Cities became part of the RANK ORGANIZATION producing key films such as *Odd Man Out* (1947) and *Hamlet* (1947) towards the end of the decade. Tom Ryall.

Tyler, Grant (*b* London, 1929). Actor. Photographic model as small child and on the stage from 1943, this actor had only one memorable film role: as Larry Tallent who falls victim to the *Daughter of Darkness* (1947), his youthful freshness giving poignancy to the role. A handful of other supporting roles, some stage and TV, then he disappeared from view.
OTHER BRITISH FILMS: *The Common Touch, Danny Boy* (1941), *Eureka Stockade* (1949), *Quatermass and the Pit* (1967).

Tyler, Liv (*b* Portland, Maine, 1977). Actress. Sumptuously beautiful actress in US films from her teens; she has appeared to striking effect in a few British films, starring in Bertolucci's *Stealing Beauty* (1996, UK/Fr/It), very moving as Tatiana, tragically in love with *Onegin* (1999, UK/US), and entering into the spirit of *Plunkett & Macleane* (1999, UK). Scored a comedy success with *One Night at McCool's* (2001, US) and is in all the *Lord of the Rings* films (2001, 2002, 2003, NZ/US).

Tynan, Kenneth (*b* Birmingham, 1927 – *d* Santa Monica, California, 1980). Critic. The most influential theatre critic of the 50s and 60s and briefly (1961–62) film reviewer for *The Observer*, Cambridge-educated Tynan later became literary consultant to the National Theatre. His only direct connection with film was as co-author of two screenplays: for the bleak, neo-*noir* EALING swansong, *Nowhere to Go* (1958) and for POLANSKI's controversial *Macbeth* (1971), on which he was also 'artistic adviser'. His idiosyncratic, opinionated film criticism was not of the same order as his in-depth appraisals of theatrical giants and trends.

Tyson, Cathy (*b* Liverpool, 1965). Actress. Trained at Liverpool's Everyman Theatre and the RSC, this striking actress made a stunning debut as Simone, the elegant and mysterious black prostitute in Neil JORDAN's acclaimed *Mona Lisa* (1986). Her assured performance received a BAAn and a Golden Globe (supporting actress). Significant film work failed to follow and subsequent minor roles, such as those in *Business as Usual* (1987) and *Priest* (1994), indicate that it is lack of opportunity rather than ability that has stalled her film career. In the excellent TV series *Band of Gold* (1995), Tyson revisited the world of prostitution with the dignity and composure one associates with her. She is the niece of American actress Cicely Tyson.
OTHER BRITISH FILMS: *Turbulence* (1990), *Out of the Blue* (1991), *Angels* (1992). Melinda Hildebrandt.

Tyzack, Margaret (*b* London, 1931) Actress. Wonderfully eloquent of voice and able to suggest depth of feeling in a glance or gesture, Tyzack ought to have been a major film character actress, but stage has been her first allegiance. However, the RADA-trained actress first came to popular attention in TV's *The Forsyte Saga* (1967) as Soames's sister Winifred, restrained and affecting, then won a BAA for her TV role as Queen Anne in *The First Churchills* (1969). On the London stage from 1959, she played Elizabeth I in *Vivat! Vivat Regina!* (1971) and many other leading roles. Film roles were disappointingly few but she made her presence felt for KUBRICK in *2001: A Space Odyssey* (1968) and *A Clockwork Orange* (1971). Awarded OBE in 1970.

OTHER BRITISH FILMS INCLUDE: *Passport to Shame* (1958), *Ring of Spies* (1963), *The Whisperers* (1966), *A Touch of Love* (1969), *The Quatermass Conclusion* (1978), *Mr Love* (1985), *Prick Up Your Ears* (1987), *Mrs Dalloway* (1997, UK/Neth/US).

Tzelniker, Meier (*b* Bessarabia, 1894 – *d* 1982). Actor. Jewish character actor who toured Europe and the US with his own company before settling in 1928 in England where he became well-known in the Yiddish theatre. Entered films in 1944 as Greta GYNT's father in *Mr Emmanuel* and thereafter appeared in about 20 films, usually in small but telling roles, like those of Isadore Strauss, *Titanic* passenger in *A Night to Remember* (1958) and Soho entrepreneur Mayer in *Expresso Bongo* (1959).

OTHER BRITISH FILMS INCLUDE: *It Always Rains on Sunday* (1947), *Last Holiday* (1950), *Make Me An Offer!* (1954), *The Woman for Joe* (1955), *The Long Haul* (1957), *Jungle Street* (1961), *The Sorcerers* (1967).

Uu

UFA and British film culture The German 'Universum Film Aktiengesellschaft', founded in 1917, and comprising a large studio complex in Neubabelsberg near Berlin, became one of the most important international film companies of the 20s and 30s, producing the impressive artistic and technical achievements of directors such as Ernst Lubitsch, Fritz Lang, and F.W. Murnau, while also maintaining a strong line of popular entertainment. From the mid 20s, UFA's most powerful producer Erich POMMER established contacts and co-production agreements with British producers such as Michael BALCON, and companies such as BIP. In exchange for access to the British market, UFA offered technical expertise and training opportunities for British technicians. Co-productions included *Congress Dances* (1931) and *FP1* (1933). The mutually beneficial exchange came to an end after 1933, when UFA came under the control of the Nazis, and many of UFA's personnel fled to Britain and Hollywood (see also **Europeans in British Film**). UFA's monopoly in German cinema was dismantled by the Allies after the war. Tim Bergfelder.

Ullman, Tracey (*b* Slough, 1954). Actress. Ullman has done everything except British films: she has succeeded on stage, as a recording artist, had her own TV show and appeared in US films such as *Small Time Crooks* (2000). She squeezes into this book for her very engaging and funny turn as Meryl STREEP's chum in *Plenty* (1985, US-financed but partly filmed in UK). Other British films are *The Young Visiters* and *Give My Regards to Broad Street* (1984).

Underdown, Edward (*b* London, 1908 – *d* Kingsclere, Hants, 1989). Actor. Former steeplechase jockey, Eton-educated Underdown was on stage from 1932, made a few 30s films to little effect, and did WW2 service from 1939 to 1945. Post-war, he had a better run of films, with co-starring roles in *Woman with No Name* and *They Were Not Divided* (his best role) (1950) and *The Voice of Merrill* (1952), as Valerie HOBSON's lover, but he was in truth a rather dull leading man, too restrained to suggest passion, not quite authoritative enough to make a serious mark as purveyor of upper-class professionals in the character roles that became his lot from the mid 50s.

OTHER BRITISH FILMS INCLUDE: *The Warren Case* (1934), *Wings of the Morning* (1937), *Inspector Hornleigh* (1939), *The Woman in the Hall* (1947), *Man on the Run* (1949), *The Dark Man* (1950), *Beat the Devil* (UK/It/US), *Recoil* (1953), *The Rainbow Jacket* (1954), *The Camp on Blood Island* (1957), *The Day the Earth Caught Fire* (1961), *Dr Crippen* (1962), *Woman of Straw* (1964), *Thunderball* (1965), *Khartoum* (1966), *The Last Valley* (1970), *The Abdication* (1974), *Tarka the Otter* (1978).

unemployment The British economy has experienced two periods of protracted unemployment since the advent of sound cinema in the late 1920s. The Great Depression of the 30s was so profound as to question the efficacy of industrial capitalism, although flirtations with extremist politics evident among sections of society were effectively kept off British cinema screens by the censors. Instead, audiences were offered the role model of popular star Gracie FIELDS, who promoted cheery stoicism in the face of adversity in films like *Sing As We Go!* (1934). Equally innocuous was the sentimentality of film-maker John BAXTER, whose *Doss House* (1933) at least detailed the milieu of privation. More significant was Baxter's *Love on the Dole* (1941), a biting examination of the social impact of unemployment, only acceptable to the censors following the outbreak of WW2.

The full-employment of WW2 lasted until the 70s. The second major period of unemployment followed the radical monetarist restructuring of the economy in the 80s and several significant films treated the harsh realities of its economic dislocation. Social realist film-makers like Ken LOACH were persistent critics of THATCHERISM, and in *Raining Stones* (1993) he produced a sensitive examination of the masculine dilemmas experienced by the unemployed. In fact, emasculation was a constant feature of such British films dealing with unemployment: in the politically strident manner of *Business as Usual* (1987), wherein the lower-paid female spouse assumes the role of breadwinner, leaving her former shop-steward husband to child-care duties; or in popular COMEDIES, notably *The Full Monty* (1997, UK/US), which humorously explore the shifting GENDER alignments thrown up in the devastated working-class communities of the industrial north. While managing to entertain the general audience to considerable effect, such films did not avoid the tragedies of social reality, or, in the case of *Brassed Off* (1996, UK/US), a passionate rebuttal of the government's uncaring industrial policy. Other films dealing with unemployment include: *Something Always Happens* (1934), *Look Up and Laugh* (1935), *Tomorrow We Live* (1936), *The Proud Valley* (1940), *Rita, Sue and Bob Too* (1986), *Vroom* (1988).

BIBLIOG: Jeffrey Richards, *The Age of the Dream Palace*, 1984; S.C. Shafer, *British Popular Films 1929–1939*, 1997; John Hill, *British Cinema in the Eighties*, 1999. Alan Burton.

Union Jack Film Co. Ltd Operational from 1913 to 1920, it had studios in a former gas works on Tuileries Street, Hackney. In 1914, it co-produced *The World, the Flesh and the Devil*, based on a popular play by Laurence Cowen, in KINEMACOLOR. AS.

unionism Representation of trade unions, its organisation and labour relations in British films was, until the mid 80s, rather negative. This jaundiced image and portrayal can be seen in films such as King VIDOR's *The Citadel* (1938), in which a doctor battles against corrupt union officials in a Welsh mining village, through to Carol REED's *The Stars Look Down* (1939), in which union officials are barely distinguishable from management and the union is somewhat totalitarian in its organisation. Alexander MACKENDRICK's highly satirical *The Man in the White Suit* (1951) shows management and unions colluding to preserve their own interests whilst Roy BOULTING's *I'm All Right Jack* (1959) again satirises the arrogant, politically-driven shop steward dictating to a bloody-minded workforce that operates in a unionised factory. In 1960 Guy GREEN's *The Angry Silence*, in the same vein as *I'm All Right Jack* but without the satire, attempted to show the dynamic tensions between individual and the 'closed shop' working environment which results in representations of workers as a thuggish mob sheepishly following orders given by Communist shop stewards.

If trade unions and labour relations were often vilified in dramatic fashion, they became the subject of farce and comedy in films such as Peter HALL's *Work is a Four Letter Word* (1967), Gerald THOMAS's *Carry on at your Convenience* (1971) and Frank LAUNDER's *The Wildcats of St Trinian's* (1980).

However, a significantly more positive and sympathetic representation of the union movement occurred in the mid 80s, conveyed against the back-drop of anti-union Thatcherite dogma and policies. Bill DOUGLAS's *Comrades* (1986) charts the fight taken up by the Tolpuddle Martyrs for better pay and working conditions in the 1830's whilst Lezli-An BARRETT's *Business as Usual* (1987) portrays union officials and fellow workers as very supportive of a sexually harassed female employee. The representation of unionism in British film has, over the last decade or so, taken a different approach from those earlier films cited above. In some respects films such as Loach's *Riff-Raff* (1991), Mark HERMAN's *Brassed Off* (1996, UK/US) and, for TV, Jimmy McGOVERN's *Dockers* (1999) have explored the difficulties and consequences for the workforce after de-unionisation.

OTHER RELEVANT BRITISH FILMS INCLUDE: *Red Ensign, Sing As We Go!* (1934), *A Real Bloke, On Top of the World* (1935), *Love on the Dole, The Common Touch* (1941), *Hard Steel* (1942), *The Shipbuilders, Millions Like Us* (1943), *My Ain Folk, This Happy Breed* (1944), *Chance of a Lifetime* (1950), *High Treason* (1951), *Flame in the Streets* (1961), *The Strike* (1988). Glen Jones.

United Artists United Artists has played an important role in the British cinema from the 30s onwards. In 1932 the company signed contracts with BRITISH AND DOMINIONS for quality 'QUOTA QUICKIES' which would also be marketable in the US and also became involved in financing Alexander KORDA's *The Private Life of Henry VIII* (1933). Following its spectacular success, Korda was signed on a 16-picture contract, became a partner in the company, and was also involved in a number of failed attempts to buy it, including one with member-owner Samuel Goldwyn which would have turned United Artists into a British-financed company. United Artists also bought a half-share in the ODEON cinema group, although control remained in British hands with Oscar DEUTSCH. In addition, J. Arthur RANK was interested in acquiring a share in the company during the 40s though this came to nothing. During the 60s, United Artists, along with other US majors, was heavily involved in the financing of British production. In the post-war period the company released a number of British films – *The Red Shoes*, EALING comedies – in the US under the banner of 'art cinema' – and this strategy was continued in the 60s when the company struck a multiple-picture deal with WOODFALL FILMS after their financing of the enormously successful *Tom*

Jones (1963). However, apart from *Women in Love* (1969), the films were not particularly successful and United Artists enjoyed greater success with their sponsorship of the BEATLES films, and truly spectacular success in conjunction with Cubby BROCCOLI and Harry SALTZMAN and the phenomenon of the James BOND picture cycle. Tom Ryall.

See also **Hollywood studios in Britain**.

Universal This studio became caught up in the various manoeuvres leading to the formation of the RANK ORGANISATION in the early 40s and was an important factor in its rise to prominence. Universal had established its position in the American film industry as a producer of genre pictures – most notably the classic horror films, *Dracula* (1931) and *Frankenstein* (1931) – but had gone into receivership in 1933 and was taken over by a New York banking firm in 1936. The Rank group, in a reversal of the normal process whereby US firms bought into British companies, was involved in the take-over, acquiring a 25 per cent interest in the company. This was a move of singular importance which gave the Rank interests the DISTRIBUTION rights to Universal's films in Britain, the first time that a British company had acquired rights for the output of a major Hollywood company. In the 40s, Rank was to supply Universal with 'quality' films such as OLIVIER's *Hamlet* (1948) for US release alongside the studio's generic output of Abbott and Costello comedies, crime films and melodramas. During the 60s, along with the other major American companies, Universal financed a number of British films, including CHAPLIN's *A Countess from Hong Kong* (1966), Truffaut's *Fahrenheit 451* (1966), and LOSEY's *Boom* and *Secret Ceremony* (1968). Despite an impressive array of stars, including Marlon Brando, Albert FINNEY, Elizabeth TAYLOR, Vanessa REDGRAVE and Richard BURTON, and important experienced film-makers in Chaplin, Losey and Karel REISZ, the programme of thirteen features failed to make a significant impression at the box-office. Tom Ryall.

See also **Hollywood studios in Britain**.

universities These institutions do not figure as commonly as SCHOOLS in British cinema, and the represented range is even more narrowly confined. There is certainly no genre comparable to the US campus movie. Early examples of university-set films, such as *A Yank at Oxford* (1937) or *Charley's (Big-Hearted) Aunt* (1940), established a focus on Oxford, the oldest of the English universities, that has not diminished even in recent times: witness *Dreamchild* (1985), *Shadowlands* (1993, UK/US), *Iris* (2002, UK/US). The only substantial competition in this respect has come from the second oldest university, Cambridge, which has provided settings (wholly or partly) for romantic comedies of varying weights – *Bachelor of Hearts* (1958); *I'll Never Forget What's 'is Name* (1967) – or that portentous reassertion of trueBrit values, *Chariots of Fire* (1981). This preoccupation with traditional universities might reflect the disproportionate number of British film-makers who were students there; though outsiders to these places, such as the makers of Oxford-set *Accident* (1967), director Joseph LOSEY and screenwriter Harold PINTER, have also shown a keen appreciation of the visual and dramatic possibilities of historic buildings in beguiling, semi-rural landscapes.

The focus has occasionally shifted to branches of London University, as in the earliest of the *Doctor* . . . film SERIES, and *Butley* (1973, UK/Can/US), or to newer provincial universities, as with *Lucky Jim* (1957), *The Wild and the Willing* (1962), and *Educating Rita* (1983). The process of educating, however, has only rarely provided the main subject matter or narrative basis for university-set films; the interest of their settings would seem to be mainly in the opportunities these provide for examining the social and emotional entanglements of a range of more or less quirky character-types. Ian Britain.

Unsworth, Geoffrey (*b* Leigh, Lancs, 1914 – *d* Brittany, 1978). Cinematographer. Winner of two Oscars (*Cabaret*, 1972, US; *Tess*, 1979, UK/Fr, shared) and five BAAs, including those for *2001: A Space Odyssey* (1968), Unsworth entered films in his teens, spending five years at GAUMONT–BRITISH (1932–37). He then joined TECHNICOLOR where he worked as assistant or operator on a number of notable British colour films, including *The Drum* (1938), *The Life and Death of Colonel Blimp* (1943), *A Matter of Life and Death* (1946). After his first feature, the dire MUSICAL, *The Laughing Lady* (1946), he worked on the GAINSBOROUGH MELODRAMAS, *The Man Within* and *Jassy* (1947), his sombre use of colour oddly making these seem less 'colourful' than their black-and-white predecessors; and he had a similarly inclined collaborator in Guy GREEN on the handsomely subdued *Blanche Fury* (1947). Working with RANK at PINEWOOD in the 50s, he shot exotically set ADVENTURES, such as *The Seekers* (1954), glossy COMEDIES like *Value for Money* (1955), moody black-and-white THRILLERS like *Tiger in the Smoke* (1956), in which he makes the first half-hour genuinely scary in its evocation of a foggy underworld, and *Hell Drivers* (1957), toughly redolent of midlands quarries and lorries, and contributed to the DOCUMENTARY-like observational plainness of *A Night to Remember* (1958). Subsequently, he was drawn to large-scale affairs like *Becket* (1964), *Cromwell* (1970), *A Bridge Too Far* (1977) and *Superman* (1978), on the one hand, and filmed theatre, such as *Othello* (1965) and *The Dance of Death* (1968), on the other. He died in Brittany while filming *Tess*. Awarded OBE, 1976. His wife, **Maggie Unsworth**, collaborated on the screenplay of *Half a Sixpence* (1967, UK/US), which he shot, and also worked as a continuity person.

OTHER BRITISH FILMS INCLUDE: (cam op) *The Four Feathers* (1939), *The Thief of Baghdad* (1940), *The Great Mr Handel* (1942); (c) *The People's Land* (1943, doc), *Scott of the Antarctic* (1948), *The Blue Lagoon*, *The Spider and the Fly* (1949), *Trio*, *The Clouded Yellow* (1950), *Where No Vultures Fly* (1951), *The Planter's Wife* (1952), *The Million Pound Note* (1953), *The Purple Plain* (1954), *Simba*, *Passage Home* (1955), *A Town Like Alice*, *Jacqueline* (1956), *Dangerous Exile* (1957), *North West Frontier* (1959), *Don't Bother to Knock* (1961), *Tamahine* (1962), *An Evening with the Royal Ballet* (1963), *The Reckoning* (1969), *Unman, Wittering and Zigo* (1971), *Baxter!* (1972), *Zardoz* (1973), *Murder on the Orient Express*, *Return of the Pink Panther* (1974), *Royal Flash* (1975), *The First Great Train Robbery* (+ a) (1978).

Unwin, Stanley (*b* Pretoria, 1911 – *d* Daventry, 2002) Comedian of the 40s famous for his crazy gibberish, giving a surreal, Pythonesque ring to the most harmless storytelling. He joined the BBC as a sound engineer in 1940 and later had his own very popular show and appeared on TV, eventually with his own series, *Unwin Time*. His sense of nonsense, pitched somewhere between Edward Lear and James JOYCE, was on show in a half-dozen films, including *Press for Time* (1966), with Norman WISDOM, one of his fans.

OTHER BRITISH FILMS: *Fun at St Fanny's* (1955), *Inn for Trouble* (1959), *Carry On Regardless* (1961), *Chitty Chitty Bang Bang* (1968).

BIBLIOG: Autobiography, *Deep Joy*, 1984.

Urban, Charles (*b* Cincinnati, Ohio, 1867 – *d* Brighton, 1942). Pioneer. Never was a man more better named than Charles Urban, for he was the very model of urbanity, depicted in a 1912 *Vanity Fair* cartoon as the essence of the well-dressed English gentleman. He was an American, but his contribution to British cinema was considerable. Urban came to the UK in August 1897 as manager of the London office of Maguire & Baucus, Edison's agents. He brought with him his 'invention' (really the work of engineer Walter Isaacs), the Bioscope projector, which made his name. In May 1898, Urban reorganised Maguire & Baucus as the WARWICK TRADING COMPANY and distributed films from the LUMIÈRE Brothers, Georges Méliès and G.A. SMITH, as well as embarking on production, with Cecil HEPWORTH as his first cameraman. In 1903, he founded his own company, the Charles Urban Trading Company, and as proof of his motto, 'We put the world before you,' he sent cameramen around the world to shoot ACTUALITY subjects and scientific and educational films, among them F. Ormiston-Smith, H.M. Lomas, Jack Avery and Joseph ROSENTHAL. Urban was a strong advocate for the educational use of films, and in 1904 first introduced 'Urbanora' educational programmes London's Alhambra Theatre, with cinemicroscopic films by F. Martin Duncan, who was followed as Urban's favourite scientific film-maker by Percy SMITH. On 5 May 1908, he opened Urbanora House, the first film business located on WARDOUR STREET, complete with its own laboratory and studio. Exploiting G.A. Smith's invention of KINEMACOLOR, Urban formed the Natural Color Kinematograph Company in 1909. Urban also formed the Kineto company and the Eclipse company in France, but Kinemacolor became his great passion, and his films of the Delhi Durbar ceremonies in 1911 his greatest triumph. He worked for British PROPAGANDA outfits during WW1, producing the DOCUMENTARY feature *Britain Prepared* (1915) and editing *The Battle of the Somme* (1916), and from 1916 he relocated to America where he was responsible for the promotion of British propaganda films. After the war he turned to the production of educational films in America, but his plans were overambitious and led to his financial collapse in 1925. Urban was unique as a promoter of British cinema, one of the few in the industry who understood the American market, and he was the major figure in British films before the War. He became a British citizen in 1907. The Charles Urban Collection of papers is housed at the Science Museum in South Kensington, London. AS.

Urban, Stuart (*b* Newport, Isle of Wight, 1958). Director. Urban had a SHORT FILM, *The Virus of War* (1972), screened at the Cannes Film Festival when he was 13, later made his name on TV as director-writer of *An Ungentlemanly Act* (1992), with its FALKLANDS WAR setting, and the acclaimed mini-series, *Our Friends in the North* (1996). His first feature films were *Preaching to the Perverted* (1997, + co-p, sc) and *Revelation* (2002, + p, sc), a none-too-well-received fantasy on religious themes.

Ure, Gudrun *see* **Gudrun, Ann**

Ure, Mary (*b* Glasgow, 1933 – *d* London, 1975). Actress. Tragic victim of accidental death, fragile-looking blonde Ure was essentially a stage actress. Trained at Central School, she was on the London stage from 1954, starring in *Time Remembered*, but her real fame derives from playing verbally lashed, middle-class Alison in *Look Back in Anger* (1956), the watershed play by her first husband John OSBORNE, and she repeated the role in the film version in 1959. There was perhaps something too coolly astringent about her persona for conventional film stardom: she was an unremarkable heroine in the imperial drama, *Storm over the Nile* (1955), the remake of *The Four Feathers*, and in the Malayan-set political melodrama, *Windom's Way* (1957), but brought some necessary sensuality to the role of Clara in *Sons and Lovers* (1960). She also filmed several times with second husband Robert SHAW, including the US-financed *Custer of the West* (1967).

OTHER BRITISH FILMS: *The Mind Benders* (1963), *Where Eagles Dare* (1968).

Urquhart, Molly (*b* Glasgow, 1906 – *d* Glasgow, 1977). Actress. Former Civil Servant and amateur actress who made her professional debut in 1934 (London in 1945), often playing in Scottish-set dramas. In films from 1949 (*Floodtide*), the cosy, plump Urquhart played Margaret JOHNSTON's faithful servant in *Portrait of Clare* (1950), the mother of *Geordie* (1955), and, in two neat 'B' MOVIES for director Peter Graham SCOTT, a landlady with an eye to getting her money in *Devil's Bait* (1959) and a fawning secretary in *The Big Day* (1960). Worked three times for Fred ZINNEMANN, finally in *Julia* (1977).

OTHER BRITISH FILMS INCLUDE: *Happy Go Lovely* (1951), *Hunted*, *You're Only Young Twice!* (1952), *Yield to the Night* (1956), *Behold a Pale Horse* (1964, UK/US), *A Man for All Seasons* (1966), *The Black Windmill* (1974).

Urquhart, Robert (*b* Ullapool, Scotland, 1922 – *d* London, 1995). Actor. After spending WW2 with the Merchant Service (1939–46), Urquhart made his stage debut, trained at RADA and was on the London stage from 1951 and in films the following year. Mostly played decent, slightly dull young heroes, like Frank in *Isn't Life Wonderful!* (1953) and the brave, non-mercenary brother in *Golden Ivory* (1954), but was a likeably good-humoured Gawain in *Knights of the Round Table* (1953) and an amusingly jocular undercover detective in *The Break* (1962). Unexciting as he often seemed, he went on working in film and TV until the 90s, last seen in the Ruth RENDELL mystery, *Master of the Moor* (1994). Married and divorced Zena WALKER.

OTHER BRITISH FILMS INCLUDE: *Tread Softly* (1952), *The House of the Arrow* (1953), *Happy Ever After* (1954), *Yangtse Incident* (1956), *The Curse of Frankenstein* (1957), *Dunkirk* (1958), *Foxhole in Cairo* (1960), *Murder at the Gallop* (1963), *The Syndicate* (1967), *The Looking Glass War*, *Country Dance* (1969), *P'Tang Yang Kipperbang* (1982), *Playing Away* (1986), *Testimony* (1987).

Ustinov, Sir Peter (*b* London, 1921). Actor, director, author. If English-born Ustinov, of Russian parentage, seems to have been around for ever, this is only because he has. He was only 17 when he made his stage debut, 19 when he appeared in his first films, and in his early 20s when Private Ustinov was legendarily meeting with Captain Carol REED, Colonel David NIVEN and Lieutenant Eric AMBLER at the Ritz to prepare the screenplay for *The Way Ahead* (1944), in which he also played the North African café owner (he didn't look English enough for anything else). Post-war he directed three quirkily likeable films: *School for Secrets* (1946, + p, co-sc), *Vice-Versa* (1947, co-d, co-p, sc) and *Private Angelo* (1949, co-d, co-p, co-sc). He then did some notable acting turns, including his protean hotelier in *Hotel Sahara* (1951), the Prince of Wales ('Who's your fat friend?') in *Beau Brummell* (1954), several Hollywood roles including Nero (AAn/supp a) in *Quo Vadis?* (1951), and the circus master in Max Ophuls' glorious *Lola Montès* (1955, Fr). He directed, produced, co-wrote and starred in a cleanly intelligent version of Melville's *Billy Budd* (1962), making one wish he'd persevered as director, but, if there is something of the Renaissance man about Ustinov (he is also a playwright, autobiographer, raconteur of one-man show proportions), there may also be something of the dilettante, as if he can't quite settle to anything because of all the conflicting claims on his darting imagination. The problem is that he does them all well. Film is probably lucky to have had as much of his attention as it has had: he was a memorably pompous Poirot in *Death on the Nile* (1978) and *Evil Under the Sun* (1981) and the Oscars twice rewarded his personality displays: in 1960 for *Spartacus* and 1964 for *Topkapi* (both US). Awarded CBE 1975, knighted 1990. Married (2) Suzanne CLOUTIER; their daughter is **Pavla Ustinov** (*b* Santa Monica, California, 1954), who has appeared in several films, including *The Thief of Baghdad* (1978), with her father.

OTHER BRITISH FILMS: (a, unless noted) *Mein Kampf, My Crimes*, *Hullo Fame* (1940), *One of Our Aircraft Is Missing, Let the People Sing*, *The Goose Steps Out* (1942), *The New Lot* (1943, short, + co-sc), *The True Glory* (1945, UK/US, doc, co-sc), *Odette* (1950), *The Magic Box* (1951), *The Legend of Good Beasts* (1956, short, narr), *School for Scoundrels* (1959, co-sc), *Peaches* (1964, anim, narr), *Hot Millions* (1968, + co-sc), *Tarka the Otter* (1978, narr), *The Great Muppet Caper* (1981), *Stiff Upper Lips* (1996).

BIBLIOG: Autobiography, *Dear Me*, 1977.

Uzzaman, Badi (*b* Phulpur, Azamgarh, India, 1939). Actor. Indian actor, educated in Pakistan, who has appeared steadily in British TV and films since the mid 80s. His TV appearances have included episodes in such programmes as *A Touch of Frost* (1996) and *Casualty* (1998), as well as the excellent mini-series, *The Buddha of Suburbia* (1993). Has appeared in about a dozen films, starting with *My Beautiful Laundrette* (1985), playing Uncle in the charming *Bhaji on the Beach* (1993), and the shopkeeper in one of the few sane moments in the idiotic *Kevin & Perry Go Large* (2000, UK/US). In 2001, he appeared on stage in a revival of Max Frisch's *Andorra*, as the carpenter.

OTHER BRITISH FILMS INCLUDE: *Cry Freedom, Sammy and Rosie Get Laid, Personal Services* (1987), *Immaculate Conception* (1991), *My Son the Fanatic* (1997), *Mad Cows* (1999), *The Baby Juice Express* (2001).

V v

Vajda, Ladislao (*b* Budapest, *c* 1905 – *d* Barcelona, 1965). Director. Prolific Hungarian director who worked on a few British films, several in the 30s including *The Wife of General Ling* (1937), and three more in the late 40s, none of any significance, though Phyllis CALVERT claimed that *The Golden Madonna* (1949) was cut in such a way that it ended by making no sense. Few would disagree. Vajda's real significance belongs elsewhere; for example, as co-writer of *Kameradschaft* (1931, Fr/Ger).

OTHER BRITISH FILMS INCLUDE: *Where Is This Lady?* (1932, co-d, co-sc), *Wings over Africa* (1936, d), *The Woman with No Name* (1950, d, co-sc).

Valenska, Paula (*b* Prague, 1922). Actress. Vivacious blonde Czech actress who enlivened two British films, both directed by Gordon PARRY, in the late 40s: the PORTMANTEAU drama, *Bond Street* (1948), in which she accounted for the light relief; and *Golden Arrow*, released in 1952, but made three years earlier, a fantasy in which a Frenchman, American and Englishman daydream about a girl they have met on a train. She was never heard of again in films.

Valentine, Anthony (*b* Blackburn, Lancs, 1939). Actor. Former child actor, in films since *No Way Back* (1949) according to some sources, certainly in *The Girl on the Pier* (1953), as the crime-mad son of Chief Inspector Charles VICTOR, and on TV was one of *The Children of the New Forest* (1955). In fact, most of his adult career has been spent on TV: among many others, he had a semi-regular role as supercilious offsider to *Callan* (1969–72); was gentleman-cracksman, *Raffles* (1977); and played Baron de Belleme in *Robin of Sherwood* (1984–85). One of his more substantial screen roles was as Nastassia KINSKI's protector in *To the Devil a Daughter* (1976, UK/Ger). Married **Susan Skipper**, who appeared in a few films including *Sweeney!* (1976) and *Wish You Were Here* (1987).

OTHER BRITISH FILMS INCLUDE: *The Brain Machine* (1954), *The Damned* (1961), *Escape to Athena* (1979), *The Monster Club* (1980), *Jefferson in Paris* (1995).

Valentine, Val (*b* London, 1898 – *d* Brighton, 1971). Screenwriter. RN: Thomas Pechey. Valentine, also a playwright, was a very prolific screenwriter from 1929 (*Alf's Carpet*) to 1961 (*Left, Right and Centre*), specialising in COMEDY but not limited to it, as his successes in the realist vein with *Waterloo Road* (1944) or the THRILLER, *The Ringer* (1952) suggest. However, he is probably best remembered for work (usually in collaboration) for such comics as the CRAZY GANG (*Gasbags*, 1940), George FORMBY (*Come on George!*, 1939, + co-story), and several in the 'ST TRINIAN'S' SERIES. He also provided the stories for two Gracie FIELDS films, *Keep Smiling* (1938) and *Shipyard Sally* (1939), as well as for the superbly crafted LAUNDER AND GILLIAT drama, *The Rake's Progress* (1945). His career might well repay further investigation.

OTHER BRITISH FILMS INCLUDE: (sc) *Why Sailors Leave Home, Elstree Calling* (1930), *Pyjamas Preferred* (1932, + d), *The Balloon Goes Up* (1942, UK/Fr), *Up with the Lark* (1943), *The Weaker Sex* (add scenes), *This Was a Woman* (1948), *Old Mother Riley's Jungle Treasure* (1951), *Time Gentlemen Please!* (adptn), *Miss Robin Hood* (1952), *Fortune Is a Woman* (1957, adptn); (co-sc) *The Vagabond Queen* (1929), *The Love Habit, My Wife's Family* (1931), *Rich and Strange* (1932), *Captain Bill* (1935), *Feather Your Nest, The High Command* (co-dial), *Café Colette* (1937), *We Dive at Dawn* (1943, + co-story), *I'll Be Your Sweetheart* (1945), *Lady Godiva Rides Again* (1951), *The Belles of St Trinian's, The Constant Husband* (1954), *See How They Run* (1955), *The Pure Hell of St Trinian's* (1960); (story) *Song of Soho* (1930), *Forbidden* (1949), *A Weekend with Lulu* (1961, co-story).

Valk, Frederick (*b* Hamburg, 1895 – *d* London, 1956). Actor. Born in Germany but of Czech parents, this portly supporting player was often cast as a figure of pompous authority and abusive power. On stage from boyhood, he had a distinguished theatrical career in Europe and Britain, playing an acclaimed Othello, Macbeth and other Shakespearean roles. In numerous British films from 1939, memorable as the psychiatrist in *Dead Of Night* (1945), as the Elector of Hanover in *Saraband for Dead Lovers* (1948), and as the humane Kommandant in *The Colditz Story* (1954).

OTHER BRITISH FILMS INCLUDE: *Traitor Spy* (1939), *Night Train To Munich* (1940), *Dangerous Moonlight* (1941), *The Young Mr Pitt* (1942), *Thunder Rock* (1942), *Hotel Reserve* (1944), *Latin Quarter* (1945), *The Magic Box, Outcast Of The Islands* (1951), *Top Secret* (1952), *Never Let Me Go* (1953), *I Am A Camera* (1955), *Zarak* (1956). Tim Bergfelder.

Valli, Alida (*b* Pola, Italy, 1921). Actress. RN: Altenberger. Famously beautiful Italian star of international films, including a late 40s brush with Hollywood (e.g. *The Paradine Case*, 1947), Valli, as she was known, belongs in this book above all for her unforgettable Anna Schmidt in *The Third Man* (1949), and especially for her final walk straight past Joseph COTTEN – and into screen history. Of her three other British films, *The Stranger's Hand* (1953, Uk/It) reunited her with Graham GREENE and Trevor HOWARD; *The Cassandra Crossing* (1976, UK/Ger/It) is a lifeless disaster movie; and *A Month by the Lake* (1995, UK/US) is tedious beyond words. But Anna Schmidt is imperishable.

Vanbrugh, Dame Irene (*b* Exeter, 1872 – *d* London, 1949). Actress. RN: Barnes. Stage actress of fabled charm, who in later life was a forceful presence in about a dozen films mainly in the 30s, when she played princesses in *Catherine the Great* (1934) and *Girls Will Be Boys* (1934) and a duchess in *Knight Without Armour* (1937). She was exceptionally hearty in her last film role in *I Live in Grosvenor Square* (1945), doing her bit for Anglo-

American relations. Married (1901) Irish producer/actor **Dion Boucicault Jr** (*b* New York, 1859 – *d* Hurley, Bucks, 1929), in whose productions she often appeared and who was in the film *Masks and Faces* (1917), in which Irene played Peg Woffington. Made DBE 1941. Sister was **Violet Vanbrugh** (*b* Exeter, 1967 – *d* London, 1942), who appeared in several British films, including *Henry VIII* (1911), as the Ambassadress in *Pygmalion* (1938), finally in *Young Man's Fancy* (1939).

OTHER BRITISH FILMS: *The Real Thing at Last* (1916), *The Gay Lord Quex* (1917), *Head of the Family* (1933), *Youthful Folly*, *The Way of Youth* (1934), *Escape Me Never* (1935), *Wings of the Morning* (1937), *I Want to Be an Actress* (1943, short), *It Happened One Sunday* (1944).

Vance, Dennis (*b* Birkenhead, 1924 – *d* London, 1983). Actor. After WW2 service with the Fleet Air Arm and experience with the BBC, Vance joined Sydney BOX's COMPANY OF YOUTH, from which he was cast in a couple of HIGHBURY second features, *Trouble in the Air* and *Penny and the Pownall Case* (1948). He appeared in about ten films without making much impression – he is Charles Wright in *Scott of the Antarctic* (1948), Richard GREENE's loyal aide in *Shadow of the Eagle* (1950) – and turned to TV where he directed (and sometimes produced) episodes of such popular shows as *The Scarlet Pimpernel* (1955), *The Avengers* (1961) and *Van der Valk* (1972), and became Senior Drama Producer with ABC Television.

OTHER BRITISH FILMS INCLUDE: *Hungry Hill* (1947), *Hamlet* (1948), *Landfall* (1949), *Stage Fright* (1950), *Sing Along with Me* (1952, co-sc).

Vance, Leigh (*b* Harrogate, 1922 – *d* Los Angeles, 1994). Screenwriter, producer. Involved with TV production and scriptwriting from the early 50s, Vance (co-)wrote about a dozen modestly energetic features and co-features, starting with *The Flesh Is Weak* (1957), a Raymond STROSS 'exposé' of London vice, and including *The Frightened City* (1961, + co-p, co-story), a THRILLER of London gang warfare, and Don Siegel's British SPY drama, *The Black Windmill* (1974).

OTHER BRITISH FILMS INCLUDE: (sc/co-sc) *Heart of a Child* (1958), *Witness in the Dark* (1959), *And Women Shall Weep* (1960), *Dr Crippen* (1962), *It's All Happening* (1963), *Crossplot* (1969).

Vandeleur, Iris (*b* 1901). Actress. Supporting player busiest in films in the early 40s, when she played tough old birds in such 1941 films as *Love on the Dole* (as Ma Nattle, doing well out of pawn commissions) and *Gert and Daisy's Weekend* (as belligerent Ma Butler). In 1947, she was one of the Irish harpies driving the heroine out of the village in *Daughter of Darkness*, and she was Mrs Hudson in the 1951 TV *Sherlock Holmes* series.

OTHER BRITISH FILMS INCLUDE: *Old Mother Riley's Circus*, *The Common Touch* (1941), *The Rose of Tralee* (1942), *Home Sweet Home* (1945), *Good-Time Girl* (1947), *Emergency Call* (1952), *The Love Match* (1955), *Trouble with Eve* (1959).

Van Enger, Charles (*b* Port Jervis, NY, 1890 – *d* Los Angeles, 1980). Cinematographer. Prolific US cameraman from silent days, who shot about 20 British films in the 30s, mostly for GAINSBOROUGH, including *I Was a Spy* and *Friday the Thirteenth* (1933), both for Victor SAVILLE. Back in the US he worked solidly for Universal during the 40s, but not on films of visual – or any other – distinction. His brother, **Willard Van Enger** (*b* New York, 1901 – *d* Los Angeles, 1947) was also a cinematographer and shot a couple of British films: *Murder on the Second Floor* (1932) and *Going Straight* (1933), both for WARNERS–BRITISH.

OTHER BRITISH FILMS INCLUDE: *Help Yourself* (1932), *Aunt Sally* (1933), *My Song for You* (UK/Ger), *Forbidden Territory* (1934), *Me and*

Marlborough, *Boys Will Be Boys*, *The Case of Gabriel Perry* (1935), *Jack of All Trades* (1936).

Vandyke Picture Corporation Ltd Minor company set up in 1947, by Nigel and Roger PROUDLOCK.

Van Eyck, Peter (*b* Steinwehr, Pommerania, 1911 – *d* Männedorf, Switzerland, 1969). Actor. RN: Götz von Eick. Tall, ice-blond, and projecting a cool, brutish charm, van Eyck epitomised the Germanic stereotype, both in heroic and villainous parts. In America from the early 30s, he appeared in several Hollywood films from 1943 to 1945, inevitably playing Nazis in such wartime films as *Edge of Darkness* and *The Moon Is Down* (1943). Back in Europe after the war, he starred in numerous French, German and British films; among the latter, memorable performances as an ambiguously sinister villain in *The Snorkel* (1958) and in Seth HOLT's desert MELODRAMA *Station Six Sahara* (1963).

OTHER BRITISH FILMS: *Single-Handed* (1953), *Foxhole In Cairo* (1960), *The Devil's Agent*, *Vengeance* (1962), *The Spy Who Came In From The Cold* (1965), *Shalako* (1968). Tim Bergfelder.

Van Eyssen, John (*b* Fauresmith, South Africa, 1922 – *d* London, 1995). Actor, executive. Came to England following WW2, trained as actor at Central School and subsequently joined the RSC. In films from 1949 (*The Angel with the Trumpet*), he moved between 'B' MOVIES like *Account Rendered* (1957), as an artist who is Ursula HOWELLS' 'tame protégé', and main features like *Dracula* (1958), as Jonathan Harker, and those he did for the BOULTINGS and for Joseph LOSEY. He left acting in the early 60s, became first a literary agent with London Management, then worked for COLUMBIA-UK, becoming its managing director (1967–73) and promoting production of such successful films as *Born Free* (1965). He finished his career as an independent producer in the US.

OTHER BRITISH FILMS INCLUDE: *Four-Sided Triangle* (1953), *Cockleshell Heroes* (1955), *Brothers in Law* (1956), *Quatermass 2, The One That Got Away* (1957), *Carry On Nurse, Carlton-Browne of the FO* (1958), *I'm All Right Jack, Blind Date* (1959), *The Criminal* (1960).

Vangelis (*b* Valos, Greece, 1943). Composer. RN: Evangelos Papathanassiou. Most famous for his lushly stirring, Oscar-winning score for *Chariots of Fire* (1981), Vangelis has worked in the US, notably on *Blade Runner* (1982), for which he received BAAn, and in France, Italy and Germany. There were only three other British scores: *The Bounty* (1984, + cond), *Bitter Moon* (1992, UK/Fr), *1492: Conquest of Paradise* (1992, UK/Fr/Sp). He has become well-known for his inventive use of electronic music.

Van Gyseghen, André (*b* London, 1906 – *d* London, 1979). Actor. Formerly in music-publishing, RADA-trained stage actor and producer, on London stage from 1928, Van Gyseghen appeared in occasional films from 1944, usually in small roles such as Harold WARRENDER's valet-of-all-work in *Warning to Wantons* (1948). Main work was on stage; on TV, he had a continuing role in *Maigret* (1959–63). Married to stage actress Jean Forbes-Robertson.

OTHER BRITISH FILMS INCLUDE: *Candles at Nine* (1944), *The Limping Man* (1953), *Face in the Night* (1956), *The House of the Seven Hawks* (1959), *Rotten to the Core* (1965), *Cromwell* (1970), *The Pied Piper* (1971).

Van Loewen, Jan (*b* Berlin, 1901 – *d* Switzerland, 1987). Actor. RN: Lowenstein. Former opera singer who first filmed in Italy in 1928 and came to England in 1938, playing more or less stereotyped foreigners in a dozen films, starting with *The Life and Death of Colonel Blimp* (1943).

OTHER BRITISH FILMS INCLUDE: *The Adventures of Tartu* (1943), *Heaven Is Round the Corner, English Without Tears* (1944), *Flight from Folly, The Rake's Progress* (1945), *The Shop at Sly Corner* (1946), *Broken Journey* (1948).

Vanna, Nina (*b* St Petersburg, 1901 – *d* ?). Actress. An ingenue, this Russian-born actress appeared in a surprising number of very English roles, including the lead in *Lady Jane Grey; or, The Court of Intrigue* (1923), Alice in *Scrooge* (1923), and Lady Teazle in *The School for Scandal* (1923). She was married to British exhibitor/producer Eric Hakim.

OTHER BRITISH FILMS INCLUDE: *Lucrezia Borgia, Guy Fawkes* (1923), *The Money Habit* (1924), *We Women* (1925), *The Woman Tempted* (1926), *Triumph of the Rat* (1927), *The Show Goes On* (1937). AS.

Vansittart, Rupert (*b* Cranleigh, 1958). Actor. Lolling back with a whisky bottle in a post-wedding blur in *Four Weddings and a Funeral* (1994), Vansittart boorishly confides: 'I couldn't see any point in going to university. If you work in the money market, what use are the novels of Wordsworth going to be?' It is all over in a couple of minutes, but the Charterhouse-educated, Central School-trained actor notably makes every moment count. He was Lord Bottoms in *Braveheart* (1995, US), and, even in the unspeakable *Kevin & Perry Go Large* (2000), one remembers his severe bank manager. On TV he had excellent cameos as a barking officer in *A Dance to the Music of Time* (1997) and the unsmiling headmaster in *Take a Girl Like You* (2000). Also busy on stage and radio; in the great tradition of British CHARACTER ACTORS.

OTHER BRITISH FILMS INCLUDE: *Half Moon Street* (1986, UK/US), *Eat the Rich* (1987), *Buster* (1988), *The Remains of the Day* (1993), *The Perfect Blue, Monk Dawson* (1997), *Eviction* (1999, Ire).

Van Straalen, Dien Costume designer. Much associated with the films of Peter GREENAWAY, first as wardrobe mistress, from *A Zed & Two Noughts* (1985, UK/Neth) and latterly as costume designer, on *Drowning by Numbers* (1988, UK/Neth), *The Baby of Mâcon* (1993, UK/Fr/Ger/Neth) and *The Pillow Book* (1996, UK/Fr/Lux/Neth), though in the latter it was skin rather than fabrics which dominated the scene. Resolutely ART-HOUSE, it seems, she also designed for Sally POTTER's *Orlando* (1992, UK/Fr/It/Neth/Russ), a challenge in terms of time and place ranges, and *The Gambler* (1997, UK/Hung/Neth).

Van Thal, Dennis (*b* London, 1909 – *d* Northwood, Middx). Casting director. Of Dutch parents, educated at University College, London, Van Thal became one of the most influential figures in 20th-century British stage and screen. After beginning as musical director for André Charlot's revues in the 20s, he entered the film industry in the 30s as casting director for KORDA's DENHAM STUDIOS, returning there when demobbed from the Royal Navy in 1946. He also acted as associate producer on several films, including *Dear Mr Prohack* (1949) for WESSEX, and, for Michael BALCON, *Barnacle Bill* (1957), *Dunkirk* and *The Scapegoat* (1958). However, his main importance was as agent, when he and Joy Diamond set up London Management in 1959. His long experience in casting, his nose for talent, and his background in both theatre and film, enabled the pair to establish an agency which handled such top talent as actors Dirk BOGARDE and Alec GUINNESS, director Fred ZINNEMANN and cinematographer Oswald MORRIS.

Varden, Norma (*b* London, 1898 – *d* Santa Barbara, California, 1989). Actress. For what seemed – nay, *were* – decades,

Varden would pop up in Hollywood films, as often as not vivifying some dim, English-set film with a lively display of hoity-toity Britishness. She slid up and down the social scale: she could be convincingly aristocratic (like Lady Beekman in *Gentlemen Prefer Blondes*, 1953) or touchingly homely (like Emily French in *Witness for the Prosecution*, 1957) or absurd and frightened (like the society woman nearly strangled in *Strangers on a Train*, 1951). So, Hollywood's gain . . . She was a piano-playing child prodigy before turning to acting and she became one of the regular repertory of ALDWYCH FARCE performers from 1929 to 1933, reprising several of her roles in these in the 30s film versions, including *A Night Like This* (1932) and *Foreign Affaires* (1935). With her long face, tall figure and commanding presence, she was also a wonderful foil for Will HAY on several occasions, including *Boys Will Be Boys* (1935) and *Where There's a Will* (1936). Then she upped and went to Hollywood and never came back, not to work at any rate, and British cinema lost a great character comedienne.

OTHER BRITISH FILMS: *Turkey Time* (1933), *Happy, Evergreen* (1934), *The Iron Duke, Music Hath Charms, Get Off My Foot, The Student's Romance, Stormy Weather* (1935), *Windbag the Sailor, East Meets West, The Amazing Quest of Ernest Bliss* (UK/US) (1936), *Fire Over England, Wanted, The Strange Adventures of Mr Smith, Rhythm Racketeer, Make-Up, The Lilac Domino* (1937), *You're the Doctor, Everything Happens to Me* (1938), *Shipyard Sally, Home from Home* (1939).

variety films Films which showcase a series of acts, these had their origin in the music hall and variety shows on stage. As a format, it already existed on the radio, with films like *Elstree Calling* (1930), *On the Air* (1934) and *Radio Parade of 1935* (1934), adding visuals to the sort of show that was popular on the BBC. In the 30s, variety films were common, with Herbert SMITH directing *On the Air* (1934), *Soft Lights and Sweet Music* (1936), *Calling All Stars* (1937) and *Around the Town* (1938). Music performances were usually central. BUTCHER's *Music Hall Parade* (1939) featured Billy Cotton and his Band, while *In Town Tonight* (1935) included Val Rosing's band and *Saturday Night Revue* (1937), featuring Billy Reid and his Band and the John Reynders Orchestra. Essentially, variety films should be seen as an industrial phenomenon, comprising programme-fillers and 'B' MOVIES. Other variety showcases included *Hello London* (1958), and the short-lived pop music revue film such as *It's Trad, Dad!* (1961) and *Pop Gear* (1965). The advent and expansion of TELEVISION as a mass medium simply siphoned the constituents of this type of cinema on to TV. Kevin Donnelly.

Varley, Beatrice (*b* Manchester, 1896 – *d* London, 1969). Actress. Archetypal careworn drudge of mid-century British cinema, Varley in fact had a range wider than that suggests. Certainly, she is very touching in such roles as Robert NEWTON's bullied wife in *Hatter's Castle* (1941), Jack WARNER's downtrodden wife, neglected in favour of his younger mistress, in *My Brother's Keeper* (1948), and Laurence HARVEY's aunt, worried about his selling out for 'brass', in *Room at the Top* (1958). But, in her long filmography, there are other rich character pickings: she is Martin MILLER's terrified wife in *Squadron Leader X* (1942), the pregnant girl's mean-spirited aunt in *Holiday Camp* (1947), and shocks with the vindictiveness of Mrs Cash in *Tiger in the Smoke* (1956). On stage long before entering films and in TV from 1947, she made nearly 70 film appearances in 25 years, a guarantee of tough, insightful purchase on even perfunctorily written roles.

OTHER BRITISH FILMS: *Young and Innocent, Spring Handicap* (1937), *Poison Pen* (1939), *Rush Hour* (short), *South American George, Kipps*

(1941), *Talk About Jacqueline*, *Secret Mission* (1942), *We Dive at Dawn*, *Millions Like Us*, *The Man in Grey*, *I'll Walk Beside You*, *The Bells Go Down*, *A Welcome to Britain* (short), *Men of Rochdale* (doc) (1943), *Victory Wedding* (short), *Welcome Mr Washington*, *Waterloo Road*, *Love Story*, *Bees in Paradise* (1944), *The Agitator*, *The Wicked Lady*, *Johnny Frenchman*, *Great Day*, *The Seventh Veil* (1945), *Bedelia*, *Send for Paul Temple* (1946), *The Upturned Glass*, *So Well Remembered*, *Master of Bankdam*, *Jassy*, *The Little Ballerina*, *Good-Time Girl* (1947), *No Room at the Inn*, *My Brother Jonathan* (1948), *Adam and Evelyne*, *Marry Me* (1949), *Gone to Earth*, *She Shall Have Murder*, *Paul Temple's Triumph* (1950), *Out of True* (1951), *Hindle Wakes* (1952), *Melba*, *Death Goes to School*, *Bang! You're Dead* (1953), *Tony*, *The Black Rider* (1954), *Tiger in the Smoke*, *The Feminine Touch*, *The Good Companions*, *Sea Wife* (1956), *Hell Drivers*, *The Surgeon's Knife* (1957), *Bachelor of Hearts* (1958), *The Rough and the Smooth*, *The Horrors of the Black Museum*, *Hazard* (short) (1959), *Identity Unknown*, *Echo of Barbara* (1960), *Night Without Pity* (1962).

Varnel, Marcel (*b* Paris, 1894 – *d* London, 1947). Director, producer. RN: Le Bozec. Director of some of Britain's funniest comedies of the 30s and 40s most frequently at GAINSBOROUGH STUDIOS, Varnel began his career as a stage actor in France. He began film-directing in Hollywood in the early 30s before his move to Britain in 1934 where he was to achieve his greatest successes in his professional handling of COMEDIES, with a diverse group of veteran performers, many of whom were experienced MUSIC HALL personalities. After several early efforts, including his participation in the joint directing of the celebratory film, *Royal Cavalcade* (1935), Varnel gained attention with his direction of such comedies and MUSICALS as *Girls will be Boys* (1934), *No Monkey Business*, *Dance Band* (1935), and *All In* (1936). The first of his four films with the 'CRAZY GANG' was *O-Kay for Sound* (1937), followed by *Alf's Button Afloat* (1938), *The Frozen Limits* (1939), and *Gasbags* (1940), which he co-directed with Walter FORDE. Varnel's ability to balance the involvement of the three teams of comics made him an ideal choreographer for the wacky and chaotic silliness of these popular films.

Although he directed no less than nine of George FORMBY's films, of somewhat diminishing popularity, beginning with *Let George Do It!* (1940) and including *Turned Out Nice Again*, *South American George* (1941), *Much Too Shy* (1942), *Get Cracking* (1943), *Bell-Bottom George*, *He Snoops to Conquer* (1944), *I Didn't Do It* (1945), and *George in Civvy Street* (1946), and also directed three Arthur ASKEY features, *Band Waggon* (1940), *I Thank You* (1941), and *King Arthur Was a Gentleman* (1942), it was his earlier direction of eight Will HAY comedies that constituted his most celebrated work. The classic *Oh, Mr Porter!* (1937), is regarded as one of the greatest of all film comedies. The other seven, *Good Morning, Boys!* (1937), *Old Bones of the River*, *Hey! Hey! USA!*, *Convict 99* (1938), *Where's That Fire?*, *Ask a Policeman* (1939), and *The Ghost of St Michael's* (1941) continued to display the same excellent comic pacing that characterised Varnel's work, and their success, especially in the North of England, was continuous. Serving as producer in some of his later films, Varnel died in a motor accident, bringing an outstanding career to a tragically early end.

OTHER BRITISH FILMS: (d) *Freedom of the Seas* (1934), *I Give My Heart* (1935), *Public Nuisance No. 1* (1936), *Neutral Port* (1940), *The Net*, *Hi Gang!* (1941), *This Man is Mine* (1946). Stephen Shafer.

Varnel, Max (*b* Paris, 1925 – *d* Sydney, 1996). Director. Son of Marcel VARNEL, he entered films in the late 40s as 2nd or 3rd assistant director, working on such films as *Dear Mr Prohack* (1949) and *The Woman in Question* (1950), then moved up the ladder to become assistant director on several WARWICK

FILMS productions, such as *Interpol* and *How to Murder a Rich Uncle* (1957), before getting the chance to direct his own films. When he did, he was pretty much limited to 'B' MOVIES, though some of them, like *A Woman Possessed* (1958), starring Margaretta SCOTT, and *Return of a Stranger* (1962), were rather good, and his touch was sure for the modest material he worked on. He moved to Australia in the 60s and directed episodes of such series as *The Young Doctors* (1977–82) and *Neighbours* (1986–89).

OTHER BRITISH FILMS INCLUDE: (ass d) *The Magic Box* (1951), *The Card* (1952), *Rough Shoot* (1953), *Father Brown* (1954), *Cockleshell Heroes* (1955); (d) *Moment of Indiscretion* (1958), *Web of Suspicion* (1959), *A Taste of Money* (1960), *A Question of Suspense*, *The Silent Invasion* (1961), *The Rivals* (1963).

Varney, Arthur (aka Varney-Serrao) (*d* 1960). Director, producer. RN: Amerigo Serrao. American director who used several pseudonyms and made some nondescript early talkies, mainly for Paramount Film Service in Britain, under the company title of Starcraft Films, made at TWICKENHAM, and mainly from screenplays by Brock WILLIAMS. Once married to US silent film director, Nell Shipman.

BRITISH FILMS: (d, unless noted) *Enter the Queen* (1930), *The Wrong Mr Perkins*, *The Eternal Feminine* (+ p, a, co-sc), *Almost a Divorce* (+ story) (1931).

Varney, Reg (*b* London, 1922). Actor. After long experience in variety and radio, homely Cockney comedian Varney found his true niche in TV: first, as Reg, cutter of Fenner's Fashions, in *The Rag Trade* (1961–63); then, reunited with Peter JONES (Fenner) in *Beggar My Neighbour* (1967–68); and especially as Stan Butler in *On the Buses* (1969–73). This was low comedy – and hugely popular – and Varney reprised his role in the TELEVISION-TO-FILM SPIN-OFFS, *On the Buses* (1971), *Mutiny on the Buses* (1972) and *Holiday on the Buses* (1973). Nothing else he did was as popular and his career faltered after the 70s.

OTHER BRITISH FILMS INCLUDE: *Miss Robin Hood* (1952), *Joey Boy* (1965), *The Great St Trinian's Train Robbery* (1966), *Go for a Take* (1972).

Vaughan, Frankie (*b* Liverpool, 1928 – *d* High Wycombe, 1999). Actor. RN: Frank Abelson. Started entertaining with Al Jolson impressions, and singing with provincial dance bands. Introduced to films in *Ramsbottom Rides Again* (1956), Vaughan was then taken up by Herbert WILCOX and Anna NEAGLE, in an attempt to win a youth audience for their films, and was cast as a gang leader (who, of course, reforms) in *These Dangerous Years* (1957). After several more Wilcox films, Vaughan was invited to Hollywood for *Let's Make Love* (1960) with Marilyn Monroe, famously turning down her invitation to do just that. Although filming in the early rock'n'roll years, Vaughan did not have the rocker's required lean and hungry look, and was at least 10 years too old. Rather, he projected solid masculinity (in the Victor MATURE mould) and attacked his songs at full throttle. A great showman, he contined to appear in variety until his ill health in the 90s. Awarded OBE (1965) and CBE (1997) for charitable work.

OTHER BRITISH FILMS: *Wonderful Things* (1957), *The Lady Is a Square* (1958), *The Heart of a Man* (1959), *It's All over Town* (1963). Roger Philip Mellor.

Vaughan, Gwyneth (*b* Pontarddulais, Wales, 1926). Actress. RN: Lloyd. Dark-haired Welsh actress who studied at the London School of Economics, then had repertory experience. Appeared in a few films in the late 40s, getting her best roles in the last two: *Blue Scar* (1949), as a miner's ambitious daughter, and *Ha'penny Breeze* (1950), a Suffolk-set yachting tale.

OTHER BRITISH FILMS: *Things Happen at Night, The Brass Monkey* (1948), *Melody Club, The Man from Yesterday, The Interrupted Journey* (1949).

Vaughan, Matthew (*b* 1970). Producer. Stowe-educated production associate of Guy RITCHIE was in part responsible for the visceral black-comedy-gangster success, *Lock, Stock and Two Smoking Barrels* (1998), and its follow-up, the less wildly hip but still smartly comic punch-in-the-face, *Snatch* (2000). OTHER BRITISH FILMS: *The Innocent Sleep* (1995), *Mean Machine* (2001).

Vaughan, Norman (*b* Liverpool, 1923 – *d* London, 2002). Presenter, actor. Television host on such programmes as *Saturday Night at the Palladium* in the late 50s and the game show *The Golden Shot* in the 70s, Vaughan appeared in several films usually in guest roles like the TV comic in *Twinky* (1969). OTHER BRITISH FILMS: *You Must Be Joking!* (1965), *Doctor in Clover* (1966), *Bachelor of Arts* (1969), *Come Play with Me* (1977), *Hear My Song* (1991).

Vaughan, Peter (*b* Wem, 1923). Actor. RN: Ohm. Character actor with stage experience, good at police inspectors, Soviet agents and other assorted heavies, and, latterly, literary characters in TV ADAPTATIONS (e.g, *Our Mutual Friend*, 1998). With heavy jaw and small deep-set eyes, he has a face you remember, and his bulky frame can suggest menace, as well as solid dependability. Made his film debut in 1959, remaining in small parts, except for starring as a quirky insurance investigator in the 'B' MOVIE *Smokescreen* (1964). Usually cast as villains, he had some good supporting roles in late 60s, including a German thug in *A Twist of Sand* (1968), Sgt. Walker in *The Bofors Gun* (1968), heavies in *The Man Outside* (1967) and *The Naked Runner* (1967), and, in different mode, Anthony HOPKINS' father in *The Remains of the Day* (1993). Married (1 of 2) Billie WHITELAW.
OTHER BRITISH FILMS INCLUDE: *Sapphire* (1959), *Village of the Damned* (1960), *I Thank a Fool* (1962), *The Victors* (1963), *Fanatic* (1965), *Hammerhead* (1968), *Alfred the Great* (1969), *Straw Dogs* (1971), *Savage Messiah* (1972), *The Mackintosh Man* (1973), *11 Harrowhouse* (1974), *Valentino* (1977), *The French Lieutenant's Woman, Time Bandits* (1981), *Brazil* (1985), *The Secret Agent* (UK/US), *The Crucible* (UK/US) (1996), *Face* (1997), *An Ideal Husband* (1999, UK/US), *Kiss Kiss (Bang Bang)* (2000). Roger Philip Mellor.

Vaughan Williams, Ralph (*b* Down Ampney, 1872 – *d* London, 1958). English composer and conductor, and the central figure in the renaissance of British serious music in the 20th century. Educated at Charterhouse and Cambridge, he studied at the RCM, and later in Paris with Ravel. Muir MATHIESON invited him to write the first of his eleven film scores, *49th Parallel* (1941), which coincided with the start of the British government's wartime policy to use cinema to rouse the nation's spirits. He was pre-eminent among the many big names of concert music who were keen to get involved in this populist cause at such a decisive stage in the conflict, especially where this involved DOCUMENTARY or semi-documentary approaches to the subjects of war, sacrifice and noble effort. Vaughan Williams' film scores tend to ignore narrative and visual detail, but intensify the drama with through-composed music, which was sometimes written before filming had begun. This was the case with *Scott of the Antarctic* (1948), of which Ernest IRVING said (1948), '[it is] the function of music to bring to the screen the hidden and spiritual illustration into which the camera . . . is unable to peer'. Appointed OM, 1935.

OTHER BRITISH FILMS INCLUDE: *Coastal Command* (1942, doc), *The People's Land* (doc), *The Flemish Farm* (1943), *Stricken Peninsula* (1945, doc), *The Loves of Joanna Godden* (1947), *Dim Little Island* (1948, short, + voice), *Bitter Springs* (1950), *The England of Elizabeth* (1955, doc), *The Vision of William Blake* (1958, short).
BIBLIOG: 'Vaughan Williams, the cinema and England', in Jeffrey Richards, *Films and British National Identity*, 1997; D. James: *Scott of the Antarctic, the Film and its Production*, 1948; R. Vaughan Williams: 'Film Music', *The RCM Magazine*, 1944, Vol XL, No. 1. David Burnand.

Veidt, Conrad (*b* Berlin, 1893 – *d* Los Angeles, 1943). Actor. From the murderous somnambulist in the German classic *The Cabinet of Dr Caligari* (1919) to SS Major Strasser in Hollywood's *Casablanca* (1943), Veidt was the iconic embodiment of Expressionist acting, conveying an aura of menace and sexual deviance with his gaunt and feline demeanour and piercing eyes. During the 30s he was one of the few émigré actors to achieve star status in Britain, where his film roles covered an impressive range of characters, from the persecuted Jew in *Jew Süss* (1934), to the Christ-like stranger of *The Passing of the Third Floor Back* (1935), and from the ambiguous German U-boat Commander in *The Spy in Black* (1939) to the flamboyant villain Jaffar in *The Thief of Baghdad* (1940). From 1940 until his death from a heart attack Veidt worked exclusively in Hollywood.
OTHER BRITISH FILMS: *Rome Express* (1932), *The Wandering Jew* (1933), *I Was A Spy* (1933), *King Of The Damned* (1935), *Dark Journey, Under The Red Robe* (1937), *Contraband* (1940).
BIBLIOG: Sue Harper, '"Thinking Forward and Up": The British Films of Conrad Veidt', in Jeffrey Richards (ed), *The Unknown 1930s*, 1998. Tim Bergfelder.

Veness, Amy (*b* Aldeburgh, 1876 – *d* Saltdean, 1960). Actress. Watch Amy Veness spitefully pull out the wireless plug in *A Boy, a Girl and a Bike* (1949), or give Alison LEGGATT, into Higher Thought, a hard time in *This Happy Breed* (1944) and one is aware of the inexhaustible riches of British character playing. She could be equally convincing in sympathetic roles, like Phyllis CALVERT's protective maid, Tessa, in *Madonna of the Seven Moons* (1944) or Mrs Bedwin in *Oliver Twist* (1948) or the grandmother of Dr Dirk BOGARDE's first delivery in *Doctor in the House* (1954), but it is the harridan touch that makes her so memorable. Think of roles like those of the bed-ridden dowager who makes life hell for Valerie HOBSON in *Blanche Fury* (1947), or Jean KENT's old hag of a landlady in *Good-Time Girl* (1947) or, very fleetingly, the battle-axe objecting to smoking in the train in *Portrait of Clare* (1950). She was on stage for many years, in the US as well as Britain, before entering films in 1931.
OTHER BRITISH FILMS: *My Wife's Family, Hobson's Choice* (1931), *Tonight's the Night, Self-Made Lady, Pyjamas Preferred, Murder on the Second Floor, Money for Nothing, The Marriage Bond, Let Me Explain, Dear, Flat No. 9* (1932), *Their Night Out, A Southern Maid, The Love Nest, Hawleys of High Street* (1933), *The Old Curiosity Shop, Lorna Doone* (1934), *Brewster's Millions, Royal Cavalcade, Play Up the Band, Joy-Ride, Drake of England* (1935), *The Beloved Vagabond, Windbag the Sailor, Skylarks, King of Hearts, Crime Over London* (1936), *Did I Betray?* (UK/Ger), *The Show Goes On, Our Island Nation* (doc), *The Mill on the Floss, Aren't Men Beasts?, The Angelus* (1937), *Yellow Sands, Thistledown* (1938), *Just – William, Flying Fifty-Five* (1939), *John Smith Wakes Up* (1940), *The Saint Meets the Tiger* (UK/US), *Millions Like Us, The Man in Grey* (1943), *Fanny by Gaslight, Don't Take It to Heart!* (1944), *The World Owes Me a Living, Don Chicago* (1945), *Carnival* (1946), *Master of Bankdam, The Turners of Prospect Road* (1947), *My Brother's Keeper, Here Come the Huggetts, Vote for Huggett* (1948), *The Huggetts Abroad, Madeleine* (1949), *The Astonished Heart, The Woman with No Name, Chance of a Lifetime, Captain Horatio Hornblower RN* (UK/US) (1950),

Tom Brown's Schooldays, The Magic Box (1951), *Angels One Five* (1952), *The Woman for Joe* (1955).

Ventham, Wanda (*b* Brighton, 1938). Actress. Blonde Central School-trained player, much on TV, who appeared in such popular programmes as *The Avengers* (1965) and *Doctor Who* (1967, 1977, 1987), co-starred with Ian HENDRY in *The Lotus Eaters* (1971–73), and had a continuing role in *Hetty Wainthropp Investigates* (from 1996). Has made a dozen or so films, including *Carry On Cleo* (1964) and *Carry On Up the Khyber* (1968), as well as the HORROR films, *The Blood Beast Terror* and *Dr Kronos: Vampire Hunter* (1967).
OTHER BRITISH FILMS INCLUDE: *My Teenage Daughter* (1956), *We Joined the Navy* (1962), *The Knack . . . , The Big Job* (1965), *The Spy with a Cold Nose* (1966), *Mister Ten Per Cent* (1967).

Ventimiglia, Baron (*b* Catania, Sicily, 1888 – *d* 1973). Cinematographer. Grandson of a Governor of Sicily, Giovanni Ventimiglia always billed himself as Baron in a career embracing the shooting of HITCHCOCK's first three films, *The Pleasure Garden* (UK/Ger), *The Mountain Eagle* (UK/Ger) and *The Lodger* (1926). His work on the last helped establish the director as a major figure in British cinema, and also introduced German expressionism to this country. Giovanni emigrated to the US at the age of 23, becoming a press photographer for Associated Press and the Newark (New Jersey) *Sunday Times*. On his return to Italy, he became a cinematographer, working with various companies and also co-photographing the US production, *Toilers of the Sea* (1923), shot in Italy.
OTHER BRITISH FILMS INCLUDE: *The Money Habit* (1924), *A Woman in Pawn* (1927), *The Physician* (UK/Ger), *Smashing Through* (1928), *Downstream* (1929). AS.

Verity Films began trading in 1940 under the overall command of Sydney BOX, making short films at MERTON PARK for the war effort. Within a couple of years there was a stream of units turning out DOCUMENTARIES. Titles included the *Cooking Hints* series for the Ministry of Food. Verity employed some noteworthy personnel, including Ken ANNAKIN who made his mark there; after the war, Box gave him his chance to direct feature films. With the coming of peacetime, Verity made various public service films. Box left in 1946 to concentrate on full-length films. Always a versatile operator, he had started making features alongside the PROPAGANDA films whilst still running Verity, which became one of the companies associated with the Film Producers Guild Ltd. Stephen Brown.

Verne, Jules (*b* Nantes, France, 1828 – *d* Amiens, France, 1905). Author. Only an undistinguished handful of the many movies made from Verne's imaginative fantasies have been even partly British: *Mysterious Island, In Search of the Castaways* (UK/US) (1961), *Jules Verne's Rocket to the Moon* (1967), *The Southern Star* (1968, UK/Fr), *Captain Nemo and the Underwater City* (1969). Hollywood, on the other hand, made adventures as rousing as *20,000 Leagues Under the Sea* (1954) and as charming as *Journey to the Centre of the Earth* (1959), among others.
BIBLIOG: Thomas C. Renzi, *Jules Verne on Film*, 1998.

Verney, Guy (*b* London, 1915 – *d* London, 1970). Actor. Had his most noticeable film role first: that of Sam, the fiery socialist tamed by marriage in *This Happy Breed* (1944). Further film roles were small, but he has a memorable bit as Grandpa in *Fame Is the Spur* (1947), recalling in flashback how his girlfriend was killed in the Peterloo Massacre. On stage from childhood,

he also directed and sometimes produced episodes of such TV programmes as *The Avengers* (1961) and *Callan* (1967). Married (1) **Joan Verney** (*b* Hastings, 1921), who appeared in a few British films, including *A Matter of Life and Death* (1946) and (2) Margaret ANDERSON.
OTHER BRITISH FILMS INCLUDE: *Anna Karenina* (1948), *Train of Events* (1949), *Cage of Gold* (1950), *The Floating Dutchman* (1953), *The Battle of the River Plate* (1956).

Verno, Jerry (*b* London, 1894 – *d* London, 1975). Actor. Chipper Cockney actor with MUSIC HALL background, first as boy vocalist, then in variety; after WW1 service (1914–19), made London regular stage debut in 1925; in Shakespeare, pantomime, musicals and modern plays, notably as Banjo in *The Man Who Came to Dinner* (1941). In films from 1931, very busy in the 30s and memorable as one of the commercial travellers in *The 39 Steps* (1935). Later in very small character roles, like Alf the bookmaker in *The Belles of St Trinian's* (1954).
OTHER BRITISH FILMS INCLUDE: *Two Crowded Hours* (1931), *There Goes the Bride* (1932), *Royal Cavalcade* (1935), *Sensation, Pagliacci, Broken Blossoms* (1936), *Non-Stop New York, Young and Innocent* (1937), *St Martin's Lane, Queer Cargo* (1938), *The Chinese Bungalow* (1940), *The Common Touch* (1941), *The Red Shoes* (1948), *Dear Mr Prohack* (1949), *After the Ball* (1957), *A Place to Go* (1963), *The Plague of the Zombies* (1966).

Vernon, Anne (*b* Saint-Denis, France, 1925). Actress. RN: Edith Antoinette Vignaud. Beautiful star of about 40 international films, including the glorious *Les parapluies de Cherbourg* (1964), and in five British films starting with the leaden *Warning to Wantons* (1948), which didn't deserve her perky freshness. Starred in four early 50s films, of which *Time Bomb* (1953), as Glenn Ford's worried wife, gave her the best chance. A former fashion designer and later actress with La Comédie Française.
OTHER BRITISH FILMS: *A Tale of Five Cities* (1951), *Song of Paris* (1952), *The Love Lottery* (1953).

Vernon, Dorothy (*b c* 1894 – *d* Surrey, 1952) Actress. Not to be confused with prolific US actress of the same name, this Vernon appeared in supporting roles in a dozen or so 30s films, including Roy BOULTING's first, *The Landlady* (1938), and her last was in a bit role in Boulting's *Seven Days to Noon* (1950). Married/divorced John WOOLF.
OTHER BRITISH FILMS: *Cleaning Up* (1933), *A Political Party* (1934), *All at Sea, Father O'Flynn* (1935), *Find the Lady* (1936), *Old Mother Riley* (1937), *A Sister to Assist 'Er* (1938), *The Great Mr Handel* (1942), *Good-Time Girl* (1947).

Vernon, Richard (*b* Reading, 1925 – *d* London, 1997). Actor. Central School-trained character player of several dozen British films, some prestige TV, including *The Duchess of Duke Street* (1976), and, from 1950, a stage career that included *Any Other Business?* (1958) and, memorably, as a dour man from MI5 in *A Pack of Lies* (1983–84). He projected a faintly weary upper-class persona that equipped him well for the dessicated aristocrat he played in *The Servant* (1963), but he was just as convincing as harassed civil servants and as the bank employee under Peter CUSHING's iron regime in *Cash on Demand* (1961). His impeccable comic timing was glimpsed in his railway-carriage vignette with the BEATLES in *A Hard Day's Night* (1964), and he was last seen the year before his death as an aged professor in *Loch Ness* (1996).
OTHER BRITISH FILMS INCLUDE: *Conquest of the Air* (1940), *Stop Press Girl* (1949), *Indiscreet* (1958), *Village of the Damned* (1960), *We Joined the Navy* (1962), *Goldfinger, The Yellow Rolls-Royce* (1964), *The Intelligence Men, The Early Bird* (1965), *The Satanic Rites of Dracula* (1974), *The*

Human Factor (1979), *Gandhi* (1982, UK/Ind), *Lady Jane* (1985), *A Month in the Country* (1987).

Versois, Odile (*b* Paris, 1930 – *d* Paris, 1980). Actress. RN: Katiana de Poliakoff-Baidarov. Exquisite French star and former ballerina, who as a child performed with the Corps de Ballet of the Paris Opera. Among her 30-odd films are a half-dozen British features, most notable of which is Anthony ASQUITH's tragic Cold War romance, *The Young Lovers* (1954), in which she and David KNIGHT played the title roles, divided by the Iron Curtain. She was wasted in her other British films, including Robert HAMER's flavourless romantic comedy, *To Paris with Love* (1954) and the absurd innocent-lured-into-vice drama, *Passport to Shame* (1958). Returned to French films and died sadly young of cancer. Sister of actress **Marina Vlady** (*b* Paris, 1937), who appeared in many European films and the UK/Fr co-production, *The Thief of Baghdad* (1978).

OTHER BRITISH FILMS: *Into the Blue* (1950), *A Day to Remember* (1953), *Checkpoint* (1956).

Vertes, Marcel (*b* Budapest, 1895 – *d* Paris, 1961). Costume designer, production designer. French designer who worked on *The Thief of Baghdad* (1940), in which the costumes played their role in evoking a world of oriental fantasy. He also won an Oscar for the costumes for *Moulin Rouge* (1953) and shared one with Paul SHERIFF for its art direction, both working powerfully to recreate an idea of *fin-de-siècle* Paris.

OTHER BRITISH FILM: *The Merry Monarch* (1933, des, cos).

Vetchinsky, Alexander (aka Alex) (*b* London, 1904 – *d* Hove, 1980). Production designer. One of the legendary designers of British cinema, Vetchinsky (often billed by surname only) was a trained architect who, after a short period in an architect's office, joined GAINSBOROUGH as an assistant and by the early 30s was already designing major films in the studio's output. According to his assistant Maurice CARTER in 1994, 'he never made a sketch'; in fact, a few of his sketches do survive, but he seems to have had an extraordinary perception of what could be built and how it could be shot. Among his earlier films, *Tudor Rose* (1936) creates the kind of décor that can be seen as threatening to the young protagonist; the Will HAY comedy classic, *Oh, Mr Porter!* (1937), brilliantly evokes the dusty rural railway station; and for HITCHCOCK's *The Lady Vanishes* (1938) he contrived to suggest a much larger railway station and international train in the tiny ISLINGTON STUDIOS. Among his post-war films, the design and the camerawork in *The October Man* (1947) help to articulate the growing panic of the film's hero and the oppressively heavy sets for *The Mark of Cain* (1948) out-act the principals and give the film its major distinction. He went on working until the mid 70s, on a very wide GENRE range: he evoked the terrifying claustrophobia of the doomed submarine in *Morning Departure* (1950), recreated Malayan jungles at PINEWOOD for *A Town like Alice* (1956), helped make several in the 'CARRY ON' SERIES look more expensive than they were, gave *Life for Ruth* (1962) a convincing air of seaside town and court, and received a BAAn for *Rotten to the Core* (1965). But among 100-odd titles, there is plenty to choose from.

OTHER BRITISH FILMS INCLUDE: (des) *Sunshine Susie* (1931), *The Faithful Heart* (1933), *Boys Will Be Boys, Stormy Weather* (1935), *Convict 99* (1938), *Where's That Fire?* (1939), *The Lamp Still Burns* (1943), *Beware of Pity* (1946), *Hungry Hill* (1947); (art d) *Lord Babs* (1932), *The Lucky Number, Friday the Thirteenth, Falling for You, Aunt Sally* (1933), *The Phantom Light, Foreign Affaires* (1935), *Jack of All Trades, The Man Who Changed His Mind, Windbag the Sailor* (1936), *Doctor Syn* (1937), *O-Kay*

for Sound, Good Morning, Boys! (1937), *Old Bones of the River* (1938), *Shipyard Sally* (1939), *Gasbags, Night Train to Munich* (1940), *Cottage to Let* (1941), *The Young Mr Pitt, Uncensored* (1942), *Waterloo Road, Tawny Pipit* (1944), *Escape* (1948), *Madness of the Heart, Give Us This Day* (1949), *High Treason* (1951), *Hunted, The Long Memory* (1952), *Trouble in Store* (1953), *The Colditz Story* (1954), *Value for Money* (1955), *Ill Met By Moonlight* (1956), *A Night to Remember* (1958), *Carry On Teacher, North West Frontier* (1959), *The Singer Not the Song* (1960), *Flame in the Streets, Victim* (1961), *Tiara Tahiti* (1962), *A Study in Terror* (1965), *The Long Duel* (1967), *Carry On Up the Khyber* (1968), *David Copperfield* (1969), *Kidnapped* (1971), *Gold* (1974, co-des).

Victor, Charles (*b* Southport, Lancs, 1896 – *d* London, 1965). Actor. It has been said that Victor was a marvellous Doolittle in *My Fair Lady* (US, 1957) and he had played the role in *Pygmalion* (1951, 1953); it is perhaps true to say that films never gave him quite such a rewarding role, but in the well over 100 he appeared in, he virtually never struck a false note. On stage for many years before entering films, Victor, who came from a theatrical family, was a member of Sir Barry Jackson's Birmingham Rep from 1928 to 1938, when he finally turned to films, and subsequently rarely appeared on stage but became a pillar of British film CHARACTER ACTING for the next 20 years. Whether in comedy or drama, he imbued his work with an effortless conviction and humanity: he came to attention as Andreas in *49th Parallel* (1941); had an amusing bit in a pub in *When We Are Married* (1943), was in the framing sequence of *The Rake's Progress* (1945), suggested a lifetime of shoddy carnivals in *Temptation Harbour* (1947), was dangerously in love with Jean KENT in *The Woman in Question* (1950) in a major role, was – unusually for him – a middle-class husband in *Made in Heaven* (1952), and played the usual string of policemen at various levels of their profession. Though socially more mobile than some CHARACTER ACTORS, he was essentially one of nature's bosuns. He also brought the distinction of serious character studies to three 'B' MOVIE leads: *The Frightened Man* (1952), *The Embezzler* (1954) and *There's Always a Thursday* (1957). Actors like Victor are one of the reasons these second features are often better than they deserve.

OTHER BRITISH FILMS: *Hell's Cargo* (1939), *Dr O'Dowd, Old Mother Riley in Business, Old Mother Riley in Society, Laugh It Off, Contraband, You Will Remember* (1940), *East of Piccadilly, Major Barbara, This England, Ships with Wings, He Found a Star, Breach of Promise, Atlantic Ferry* (1941), *They Flew Alone, Those Kids from Town, Squadron Leader X, The Peterville Diamond, The Next of Kin, The Missing Million, Lady from Lisbon, The Foreman Went to France* (1942), *The Silver Fleet, The Saint Meets the Tiger* (UK/US), *Undercover, They Met in the Dark, San Demetrio–London, Rhythm Serenade, My Learned Friend, The Bells Go Down, Escape to Danger* (1943), *It Happened One Sunday, Soldier, Sailor* (1944), *Caesar and Cleopatra, The Way to the Stars, I Live in Grosvenor Square, The Man from Morocco* (1945), *This Man Is Mine, The Magic Bow, Gaiety George, Woman to Woman* (1946), *While the Sun Shines, While I Live, Meet Me at Dawn, Green Fingers* (1947), *Broken Journey, The Calendar, Vote for Huggett* (1948), *Landfall, Fools Rush In, The Cure for Love* (1949), *The Elusive Pimpernel, Waterfront* (1950), *The Magic Box, The Galloping Major, Calling Bulldog Drummond, Encore* (1951), *Those People Next Door, Something Money Can't Buy, The Ringer* (1952), *The Saint's Return, Street Corner, Appointment in London, Meet Mr Lucifer, The Girl on the Pier, The Love Lottery* (1953), *Fast and Loose, The Rainbow Jacket, For Better, for Worse* (1954), *Value for Money, Police Dog, Now and Forever, Dial 999, An Alligator Named Daisy* (1955), *Tiger in the Smoke, Home and Away, Eyewitness, The Extra Day, Charley Moon* (1956), *The Prince and the Showgirl, After the Ball* (1957).

Victor, Henry (*b* London, 1892 – *d* Hollywood, 1945). Actor. A star of silent films, Victor became a character actor with the coming of sound, giving splendid performances as Hercules the Strongman in *Freaks* (1932) and a sinister German in *Confessions of a Nazi Spy* (1939). A German education and a subsequent German accent may have hurt his chances in British films, but was no hindrance in a Hollywood career that began in 1925.

BRITISH FILMS INCLUDE: *Revolution* (1914), *She, The Picture of Dorian Gray* (1916), *Call of the Sea* (1919), *The Colleen Bawn, Slaves of Destiny* (1924), *Luck of the Navy* (1927), *The Scotland Yard Mystery* (1934), *Fine Feathers* (1937), *Conquest of the Air* (1940). AS.

Vidgeon, Robin (*b* London, 1939). Cinematographer. After experience as focus-puller, camera operator, assistant and 2nd unit cameraman, starting with *The L-Shaped Room* (1962), Vidgeon had his first credit as cinematographer with *Hellraiser* (1987), shot two films for Christine EDZARD (*The Fool*, 1990; *As You Like It*, 1992, to which he gave a bleakly non-pastoral look), and the Welsh-set version of *Uncle Vanya*, Anthony HOPKINS's melancholy *August* (1996). Also, a great deal of TV, including *The Secret Life of Sir Arnold Bax* (1992).

OTHER BRITISH FILMS: (c) *Hellbound: Hellraiser II* (1988), *Dead on Time* (1999, short).

Vierny, Sacha (*b* Bois-le-Roi, France, 1919 – *d* Paris, 2001). Cinematographer. Frenchman who has worked numerous times with Peter GREENAWAY, who has described him as 'my most important collaborator', giving a miraculous opulence and depth to these relatively low-budget ART-HOUSE triumphs. The colour coding of *The Cook, the Thief, His Wife & Her Lover* (1989) is brilliantly conceived and executed.

OTHER BRITISH FILMS INCLUDE: *A Zed & Two Noughts* (1985, UK/Neth), *The Belly of an Architect* (1987, UK/It), *Drowning by Numbers* (1988, UK/Neth), *Prospero's Books* (1991, UK/Fr/It/Neth), *The Baby of Mâcon* (1993, UK/Fr/Ger/Neth), *The Pillow Book* (1996, UK/Fr/Lux/Neth), *8 ½ Women* (1999, UK/Ger/Lux/Neth), *The Man Who Cried* (2000, UK/Fr/US).

Viertel, Berthold (*b* Vienna, 1885 – *d* Vienna, 1953). Director. An urbane intellectual, Viertel contributed to Austrian literature, theatre, and cinema before moving to Hollywood in the late 20s. Viertel's films for GAUMONT–BRITISH in the mid 30s include at least one minor masterpiece, the subtle domestic drama *Little Friend* (1934), featuring an astonishing performance by the young Nova PILBEAM. Viertel's other British films were *The Passing of The Third Floor Back* (1935), a flawed but fascinating blend of magical parable and documentary realism, and *Rhodes of Africa* (1936), a ponderous colonialist drama, after which he concentrated on stage direction for the rest of his life. Viertel's experiences in the British film industry were documented by Christopher ISHERWOOD in his roman-à-clef *Prater Violet* (1946). Viertel's son, screenwriter Peter Viertel, married Deborah KERR.

BIBLIOG: 'Berthold Viertel at Gaumont–British', in Jeffrey Richards (ed), *The Unknown 1930s*, 1998. Tim Bergfelder.

village life The village has enjoyed a distinctive status in British mythology and literature. Themes of the society in microcosm, combined with a vision of traditional Englishness, have often tempted British film-makers, though the portrayal of village life, especially in the 30s, was too often just a snobbish fantasy. *Once in a New Moon* (1935), where a stereotypical English village is transported to the Moon (it is not in the least bit the fun that it sounds to be), is typical; *Tawny Pipit* (1944), where village life is upset by a pair of the rare birds nesting, is insufferably quaint, but does at least boast the memorable scene where the villagers gather to sing the 'Internationale'. The more interesting films have been those that have exposed the underlying tensions. None does this better than *Poison Pen* (1939), where Flora ROBSON's anonymous hate letters start to tear the community apart. *Great Day* (1945) has the troubled Eric PORTMAN bringing clouds to the village preparing for a visit from Eleanor Roosevelt. Portman again is the village JP with odd tendencies in *A Canterbury Tale* (1944). But the most distinctive films have been those in which the village represents society under threat, having to fight back. The cosy villagers in CAVALCANTI's *Went the Day Well?* (1942) arm themselves to fight off the German invaders; the village in *Village of the Damned* (1960) has to repel aliens in the form of its own children. An unpleasant reversal of the theme comes in Sam Peckinpah's *Straw Dogs* (1971), where the drunken villagers become the villains, bent on assaulting the American outsider and his wife. Luke McKernan.

See also **pastoral images** and **rural life**.

Villiers, James (*b* London, 1933 – *d* Arundel, 1998). Actor. Supporting actor from the late 50s who excelled in snooty upper-class condescension, like that he offered loftily to Alan BATES in *Nothing But the Best* (1964) or, as a supercilious decorator, to Stanley BAXTER in *Father Came Too!* (1963), but had a more sympathetic role as the accused boy's counsel in *'Let Him Have It'* (1991). Educated at Wellington College and RADA-trained, he joined the Old Vic in 1955 and was on TV from 1960, with prominent roles in *House of Cards* (1990) and *A Dance to the Music of Time* (1997).

OTHER BRITISH FILMS INCLUDE: *Carry On Sergeant* (1958), *The Damned* (1961), *Murder at the Gallop* (1963), *King and Country* (1964), *The Nanny, You Must Be Joking!, Repulsion, The Alphabet Murders* (1965), *The Wrong Box* (1966), *Half a Sixpence* (1967, UK/US), *The Touchables, Otley* (1968), *A Nice Girl Like Me* (1969), *The Ruling Class* (1971), *Joseph Andrews* (1976), *For Your Eyes Only* (1981), *Scandal* (1988), *The Tichborne Claimant* (1998).

Villiers, Kenneth (*b* Colombo, 1912 – *d* Surrey, 1992). Actor, producer, director. Had experience as actor in Berlin with UFA from 1929, played supporting roles in a few British films from the mid 30s, served in WW2 (1940–45), and made only one further film, *Against the Wind* (1947). He is the venturesome Maurice Passworthy in the final scenes of *Things to Come* (1936), but other roles are insignificant. Joined the short-lived company, International Motion Pictures, in the late 40s.

OTHER BRITISH FILMS: *White Ensign* (1934), *Mr Cohen Takes a Walk* (1935), *They Didn't Know, Broken Blossoms* (1936), *A Yank at Oxford* (1937).

Villiers, Mavis (*b* Sydney, 1911 – *d* London, 1976). Actress. Cheerful, latterly enjoyably blowsy blonde in British films from the late 30s, after a Hollywood debut as a child in *Little Lord Fauntleroy* (1921), usually as showy types – or Americans, like the women she played in *Suddenly, Last Summer* (1959) and *No Sex, Please – We're British* (1973) – but probably most vivid as pub habitué in *Victim* (1961).

OTHER BRITISH FILMS INCLUDE: *King of the Castle* (1936), *Double Alibi* (1937), *Gasbags* (1940), *Went the Day Well?* (1942), *One Exciting Night* (1944), *Corridor of Mirrors* (1948), *Pool of London* (1950), *A Touch of Larceny* (1959), *The Roman Spring of Mrs Stone* (1961), *The Haunting* (1963), *Promise Her Anything* (1965), *Baxter!* (1972).

Villis, Marjorie (*b* London, 1894 – *d* London, 1981). Actress. A forceful leading lady who tried unsuccessfully for a career on screen or stage in the US. E. Temple Thurston encouraged her to enter films, and she made her debut in the adaptation of his play *Traffic* (1915). Villis was primarily a leading lady to James

KNIGHT in such HARMA productions as *A Romany Lass* (1918), *The Man Who Forgot* (1919), *Brenda of the Barge* (1920), *Love in the Welsh Hills* (1921), *No. 7 Brick Row* (1922). Also appeared as extra in 30s films.

OTHER BRITISH FILMS: *The Cobbler* (1915), *Sally Bishop* (1916), *The Rugged Path* (1918), *The Starting Point* (1919), *The Farmer's Wife* (1928, unc). AS.

Vincent, Robbie (*b* England, 1895 – *d* Blackpool, 1966). Actor. Northern MUSIC HALL comic who played Private Enoch in all four films he made. The first three were rough-and-ready but, in the North, immensely popular Frank RANDLE vehicles, *Somewhere in England* (1940), *Somewhere on Leave* (1942) and *Somewhere in Camp* (1942). The character had been created for the radio show, *Happidrome*, which the BBC broadcast for seven years and which was filmed in 1943.

Vines, Margaret (*b* Lourenço Marques, Mozambique, 1910 – *d* East Grinstead, 1997). Actress. RADA-trained stage actress who appeared in a few 30s films, including *Open All Night* (1934) in which she co-starred with Frank VOSPER, was in TV from 1938 (*The Breadwinner*), reappeared fleetingly in *Saraband for Dead Lovers* (1948), and then was gone. Married (2) **Denis Gordon** (*b* London, 1925) who appeared in *Daughter of Darkness* (1947).

OTHER BRITISH FILMS: *Frail Women* (1932), *The Vicar of Bray* (1937).

Vincze, Ernest (*b* Budapest, 1942). Cinematographer. Active in film since the mid 60s, Vincze has won awards for his TV SHORTS and DOCUMENTARIES. However, his film work, though sporadic, has had its aesthetic highlights. Was there ever a better-looking black-and-white historical film than *Winstanley* (1975), with Vincze's images both ravishing in themselves and evocative of the extraordinary rigours of the lives represented? And he bathed two early MERCHANT IVORY gems – *Roseland* (1977, US) and *Jane Austen in Manhattan* (1980, UK/US) – in just the right glow of affection and truth. His TV has included such mini-series as *A Very British Coup* (1988) and *The Camomile Lawn* (1992).

OTHER BRITISH FILMS INCLUDE: *Men, Men, Men* (1973, short), *Sound of the City of London 1964–73* (doc), *Sweet Virgin* (1974), *The Secret Policeman's Ball* (1979), *Scrubbers* (1982), *Biggles* (1986), *Shanghai Surprise* (1986), *Business as Usual* (1987, UK).

violence Although British cinema has tended to be characterised by moderation and restraint, this has more to do with strict CENSORSHIP than with anything intrinsic to the national character. When denied the pleasures of watching public executions at the end of the 19th century, the English people turned to grizzly theatrical melodramas and newspapers which revelled in gory details of violent crimes. Vestiges of this sensibility can be traced in the cycle of low-budget MELO-DRAMAS starring Tod SLAUGHTER such as *The Crimes of Stephen Hawke* (1936) and *The Ticket of Leave Man* (1937).

After WW2, censorship eased to allow the depiction of violence in more contemporary films such as *Brighton Rock* (1947) and *Good-Time Girl* (1947) where gangsters threaten their girlfriends with bottles of vitriol. An 'X' CERTIFICATE was introduced in 1951 to allow sophisticated continental films like Max Ophuls' *La Ronde* to be shown uncut to adult audiences. The most significant beneficiaries, however, were those companies, like HAMMER, which revitalised the HORROR FILM with graphic depictions of amputations, blood-sucking and torture.

By the end of the 60s violence had broken out of the confines of the horror genre to affect the rest of British cinema. In *The Strange Affair* (1968) gangsters drill holes in the cheeks of a young policeman; in *Villain* (1971) they razor-slash a croupier and leave him dripping blood from his high-rise flat window; but the combined violent effect of *Straw Dogs*, *The Devils* and *A Clockwork Orange* (1971) led to a backlash. Retrenchment – periodically punctuated by violent horror and CRIME films – lasted until the mid 90s, when young British film-makers attempted to emulate Quentin Tarantino's success with *Reservoir Dogs* and *Pulp Fiction*. Their cycle of British gangster films had a callously casual attitude to violence, which in the case of the better films such as *Gangster No. 1* and *Essex Boys* (2000) is integral to the story and heightens the emotional impact. But in too many of these films violence is used to flesh out weak plots and talentless direction. With the exception of Guy RITCHIE's *Lock, Stock and Two Smoking Barrels* (1997) and *Snatch* (2000), they were critically disparaged and performed poorly at the box-office.

It would be wrong to assume there was anything incompatible between British cinema and violence, but as far as the critics and the international box-office is concerned, it is better suited to the decorous period antics of *An Ideal Husband* (1999, UK/US) and *Tea with Mussolini* (1999, UK/It). Robert Murphy.

Virgin Films began producing features in 1971 though probably not until *Nineteen Eighty-Four* (1984) did the company's name impinge on the general public's awareness. This was due, in part, to a heated argument over which music to use. *Absolute Beginners* (1986) also got much publicity but was not well-received. Of subsequent productions the American-based *sex, lies and videotape* (1989) is the only one likely to remain critically popular, not least because it was the directorial debut of Steven Soderburgh. In subsequent years the Virgin Group's concern with films has been concentrated on its video and soundtrack interests. Stephen Brown.

Vitali, Leon (*b* Leamington Spa, 1948). Actor, production assistant. Vitali auditioned successfully for the part of Lord Bullingdon in Stanley KUBRICK's *Barry Lyndon* (1975) and thereafter was involved as production assistant (including work on scripting and video release) on all Kubrick's subsequent films, acting again in *Eyes Wide Shut* (1999, UK/US).

OTHER BRITISH FILMS: (prod ass, unless noted) *Super Bitch* (1973, UK/It, a), *The Shining* (1980, UK/US), *Full Metal Jacket* (1987).

Von Sydow, Max (*b* Lund, Sweden, 1929). Actor. Renowned Swedish star, and latterly character player of dozens of international films, who trained at Stockholm's Royal Dramatic Theatre School, and came to fame as a member of the great repertory company of director Ingmar Bergman, whose films so engrossed ART-HOUSE audiences of the 50s and 60s. His tall, gaunt frame and blond, ascetic features were completely attuned to the director's Nordic intensities in such masterworks as *The Seventh Seal* (1957). Hollywood grabbed him for Jesus (obvious casting) in the lumbering *The Greatest Story Ever Told* (1965); he made a smattering of British films of no special distinction including a go at BOND villain, Blofeld, in *Never Say Never Again* (1983, UK/US). Only *The Quiller Memorandum* (1966, UK/US), a Berlin-set SPY THRILLER, with script by Harold PINTER, is of much interest.

OTHER BRITISH FILMS INCLUDE: *Embassy* (1972), *Voyage of the Damned* (1976), *March or Die* (1977), *The Silent Touch* (1992, UK/Den/Pol).

Vorhaus, Bernard (*b* New York, 1904 – *d* London, 2000). Director, producer, writer. The film world's small but select pantheon of 'lost' directors could well be headed by Vorhaus. Only inadequate, largely erroneous entries about him can be found in the standard reference texts. Yet, Vorhaus's career spanned screenwriting in 20s Hollywood, directing in England during the 30s and back in the United States in the 40s, where he made such entertaining films as *The Affairs of Jimmy Valentine* (1942) and *The Spiritualist* (1948), plus two tailenders in Europe following his unhappy BLACKLISTING during the HUAC witchhunts. But the 13 features that he made in England contain undeniable evidence of ambition and intricacy, with an innate understanding of camera and editing techniques more distinctive than most of his better known contemporaries; *Crime on the Hill* (1933), *The Ghost Camera* (1933) and *The Last Journey* (1935) are remarkable movies by any standard. In the 1980s, David LEAN, who had edited two of Vorhaus's features in the 30s, attested to his influence, helping to launch a process of rediscovery.

OTHER BRITISH FEATURES: *On Thin Ice, Money for Speed* (1933), *Night Club Queen, The Broken Melody, Blind Justice* (1934), *Street Song, Ten Minute Alibi, Dark World* (1935), *Broken Blossoms* (assoc prod), *Dusty Ermine* (1936), *Cotton Queen* (1937).

BIBLIOG: Autobiography, *Saved from Oblivion*, 2000; Patrick McGilligan and Paul Buhle, *Tender Comrades*, 1997; Geoff Brown, 'Money for Speed: The British Films of Bernard Vorhaus', in Jeffrey Richards (ed), *The Unknown 1930s*, 1998. David Meeker.

Vosper, Frank (*b* London, 1899 – *d* at sea, registered in Sussex, 1937). Actor, playwright. Now best remembered for his famous lady-in-danger theatrical thriller, *Love from a Stranger*, filmed several times, including the 1937 British version with Hollywood stars, Ann Harding and Basil RATHBONE, and an early British TV version with Edna BEST and Henry OSCAR. Another of his plays, *Murder on the 2nd Floor*, was filmed in 1932 and he co-wrote the script for *No Funny Business* (1933). As actor, he could, as J.C. Trewin wrote (1951), 'encompass the suave and the devilish' and his broad but enjoyable playing

across this range is on view in about 15 British films, including HITCHCOCK's *The Man Who Knew Too Much* (1934), as the sinister cracksman, Ramon, and the musical, *Heart's Desire* (1935).

OTHER BRITISH FILMS: *The Woman Juror, Blinkeyes* (1926), *The Last Post* (1929), *Rome Express* (1932), *Strange Evidence, Dick Turpin* (1933), *Waltzes from Vienna, Open All Night* (starring role), *Jew Süss, Blind Justice, Red Ensign* (1934), *Royal Cavalcade, Königsmark* (1935), *Spy of Napoleon, Secret of Stamboul* (1936).

Vyner, Margaret (*b* Armidale, Australia, 1915 – *d* Reading, 1993). Actress. Beautiful actress (and former artist's model) who had modest leads and second leads in the 30s, in such films as *Sensation* (1936), as newspaperman John LODGE's long-suffering fiancée, and *Climbing High* (1938), as scheming Lady Constance. Roles became smaller in the 40s (e.g. wounded Stewart GRANGER's girlfriend in *The Lamp Still Burns*, 1943) and mere glimpses by the time she played Nigel PATRICK's rich wife in *Encore* (1951). However, her serious career as a playwright was getting under way, and she and husband Hugh WILLIAMS turned out several charming light comedies, of which *The Grass Is Greener* (1959) is best known. Simon WILLIAMS is their son.

OTHER BRITISH FILMS INCLUDE: *The Flying Doctor* (UK/Aust), *Cavalier of the Streets* (1937), *This Man Is Dangerous* (1941), *Mr Emmanuel, Give Me the Stars* (1944), *Something Money Can't Buy* (1952).

Vyvyan, Jack (*b c*1900). Actor. Busy small-part actor of the 30s and 40s, characteristically cast as policeman (*Sheepdog of the Hills*, 1941) or mechanic (*The Rake's Progress*, 1945) or court usher (*The White Unicorn*, 1947), often uncredited.

OTHER BRITISH FILMS INCLUDE: *That's My Wife* (1933), *The Howard Case* (1936), *Young and Innocent* (1937), *This Man Is News, I See Ice!, Dead Men Tell No Tales* (1938), *Home from Home* (1939), *Millions Like Us, Get Cracking, Dear Octopus* (1943), *He Snoops to Conquer* (1944), *My Sister and I* (1948), *The Interrupted Journey* (1949), *The Reluctant Widow* (1950)

Waddell, Justine (*b* Johannesburg, 1976). Actress. Unconventionally beautiful, with frizzy hair and large eyes, Cambridge-educated Waddell had a rapid ascent as star of several TV literary serials in the late 90s, winning particular acclaim as Estella in an intelligent reworking of *Great Expectations* and Molly in *Wives and Daughters* (1999). Much has been made of her period roles, as though she were to inherit Helena BONHAM CARTER's mantle, but, after playing wilful Julia Bertram in *Mansfield Park* (2000, UK/US) on the big screen, she went into modern-day romance, *The One and Only* (2002). Made her film debut in the dire *Anna Karenina* (1997, US); scored a stage success as Nina in *The Seagull* (2000), for the RSC.
OTHER BRITISH FILMS INCLUDE: *The Misadventures of Margaret* (1998, UK/Fr/US).

Waddington, Patrick (*b* York, 1901 – *d* York, 1987). Actor. Oxford-educated theatre actor, on the professional stage from 1924 (London 1925). Played over 1,000 performances as Colonel Pickering in a 1964 tour of *My Fair Lady*. Made only about 15 films over 30 years, usually as upper-class types, like the complacent Sir Richard in *A Night to Remember* (1958), but also very funny in a demented theatre scene in *It's Not Cricket* (1949), as a sub-Coward actor called Valentine Christmas. With the RAF during WW2, and administrator of the Actors' Orphanage Fund (1952–56). Much radio and TV.
OTHER BRITISH FILMS INCLUDE: *If Youth But Knew* (1926), *Loyalties* (1933), *Journey Together* (1945), *Gaiety George* (1946), *The Clouded Crystal* (1948), *The Wooden Horse* (1950), *The Moonraker* (1957), *Family Doctor* (1958).

Waddington, Steven (*b* Leeds, 1968). Actor. Tall, blond, leading actor since the early 90s, when he played the title role in Derek JARMAN's polemical version of *Edward II* (1991) and very touching as big, dumb, devoted Stevie who hardly knows what's going on in Antonia BIRD's *Face* (1997). Also US films, including *Sleepy Hollow* (1999).
OTHER BRITISH FILMS INCLUDE: *1492: Conquest of Paradise* (1992, UK/Fr/Sp), *Carrington* (1994, UK/Fr), *The Hole* (UK/Fr), *The Parole Officer* (2001).

Wadham, Julian (*b* Norfolk, 1958). Actor. Dark, incisive of feature and voice, Ampleforth-educated Wadham has so far made stronger impressions in such TV series as *Kavanagh QC* (1998) and *Middlemarch* (1994), than in film. However, he has made the most of supporting roles such as Pitt in *The Madness of King George* (1994, UK/US) and Madox in *The English Patient* (1996, UK/US). Theatre work includes seasons with the National and the Royal Court.
OTHER BRITISH FILMS INCLUDE: *Maurice* (1987), *The Secret Agent* (1996, UK/US), *Keep the Aspidistra Flying* (1997), *High Heels and Low Lifes* (UK/US), *Gypsy Woman* (2002).

Wager, Anthony (*b* London, 1932). Actor. When the convict Magwitch loomed up from the off-screen space in *Great Expectations* (1946), contemporary audiences gasped in shock as he grabbed the terrified young Pip. This was Wager's most memorable moment in film and he played the child with edge and sensitivity. He had a few other good juvenile roles, as in *Fame Is the Spur* (1947), and he held on longer than most CHILD ACTORS, but still, as he matured, the film pickings were lean, and he seemed less distinctive. There was some TV and theatre, but little has been heard of him since the 60s, except the odd film or TV role in Australia, where he and other former child star, Desmond TESTER, co-starred on stage in *Sailor Beware!* in 1956.
OTHER BRITISH FILMS INCLUDE: *The Secret Tunnel, Hungry Hill* (1947), *Above Us the Waves* (1955), *The Captain's Table* (1958), *Two Left Feet, The Hi-jackers* (1963), *The Night Caller* (1965).

Wagstaffe, Elsie (*b* London, 1899 – *d* ?). Actress. Educated at Roedean and Cheltenham and trained at London Guildhall School of Music, Wagstaffe specialised in homely mothers, aunts (memorably, Hayley MILLS's kind Auntie Dorothy in *Whistle Down the Wind*, 1961), and landladies (Van JOHNSON's in *The End of the Affair*, 1954). About 20 films interspersed with stage and TV work.
OTHER BRITISH FILMS INCLUDE: *April Fools* (1936), *The Show Goes On* (1937), *The Balloon Goes Up* (1942), *The Dark Tower* (1943), *Welcome Mr Washington* (1944), *Appointment with Crime* (1946), *My Brother Jonathan* (1948), *The Golden Link* (1954), *Barnacle Bill* (1957), *Saturday Night and Sunday Morning* (1960), *Heavens Above!* (1963), *Frankenstein and the Monster from Hell* (1973).

Wainwright, Richard (*b* Chicago, 1895 – *d* ?). Producer. Wainwright and his father were associated with DISTRIBUTION and EXHIBITION in England, before becoming involved with the production side – on Anatole LITVAK's *Sleeping Car* (1933, assoc p). Wainwright made several films at SOUND CITY, of a standard clear of the 'QUOTA QUICKIE' slur. For distribution by UNIVERSAL, they included the Jack HULBERT vehicle, *Kate Plus Ten* (1938). Post-war, he produced only one further film, *Madness of the Heart* (1949) for TWO CITIES, having been in the US for the preceding ten years.
OTHER BRITISH FILMS INCLUDE: *Forbidden Territory* (1934), *Emil and the Detectives* (1935), *Secret of Stamboul* (1936, co-p, co-sc), *School for Husbands* (1937).

Waite, Trevor Editor. Waite's distinction has come from his association with the films of Michael WINTERBOTTOM, all of which he has edited since *Butterfly Kiss* (1995), and the controlled pacing of which owes a good deal to Waite's skills. Won a BAA/e for Winterbottom's *Go Now* (1996). He also worked on Tim ROTH's stunning, anguished debut as director,

The War Zone (1999, UK/It) and Shane MEADOWS's *Once Upon a Time in the Midlands* (2002). Prior to his film career, edited numerous BBC TV documentaries.

OTHER BRITISH FILMS: *Life After Life* (1995), *Jude* (1996), *Welcome to Sarajevo* (1997, UK/US), *I Want You* (1998), *Wonderland, With or Without You* (1999), *The Claim* (2001, UK/Can/Fr), *24 Hour Party People* (2002).

Wakefield, Duggie (*b* Sheffield, 1899 – *d* Brighton, 1951). Actor. Popular Northern comic whose most prominent role was as farm hand Sam Gates mistaken for a famous German spy in Mario ZAMPI's *Spy for a Day* (1940). He also co-starred twice with Gracie FIELDS: in *This Week of Grace* (1933) and *Look Up and Laugh* (1935). Married Fields's sister Edie Stansfield.

OTHER BRITISH FILMS: *Crook's Tour* (1933, UK/US), *The Penny Pool* (1937), *Calling All Crooks* (1938).

Wakefield, Gilbert (*b* Sandgate, 1892 – *d* London, 1963). Screenwriter. Scenarist with LONDON FILMS, responsible for several screenplays of the 30s, including the Merle OBERON vehicle, *The Divorce of Lady X* (1938), previously filmed with Binnie BARNES as *Counsel's Opinion* (1933), and based on Wakefield's play of that name. Harrow- and Oxford-educated, he was called to the Bar in 1919, and began his playwright's career in 1923. Married Isabel JEANS.

OTHER BRITISH FILMS INCLUDE: *Aren't We All?*, *Lord Camber's Ladies* (1932, co-sc), *Room for Two* (1940, play).

Wakefield, Hugh (*b* Wanstead, 1888 – *d* London, 1971). Actor. On the London stage aged 10 and thereafter busily so for the next five decades, often in West End successes, like *While the Sun Shines* (1944), in which he took over from Ronald SQUIRE and played for two years. He made about 25 films in the 30s, usually in upper-class roles, like those opposite Gertrude LAWRENCE in *Aren't We All?* (1932) or Yvonne ARNAUD in *The Improper Duchess* (1936). After WW2 service with the RAF (1940–44), he returned in supporting roles, including sceptical Dr Bradman in *Blithe Spirit* (1945).

OTHER BRITISH FILMS INCLUDE: *The Sport of Kings* (1931), *King of the Ritz* (1933), *The Man Who Knew Too Much* (1934), *No Monkey Business* (1935), *The Street Singer* (1937), *Journey Together* (1945), *One Night with You* (1948), *No Highway* (1951), *Love's a Luxury* (1952, + co-sc).

Wakefield, Oliver (*b* Durban, 1909 – *d* Rye, NY, 1956). Actor. Came to England where he trained at RADA, and worked as comedian with the BBC before entering films in the 30s. He appeared in secondary roles in a handful of light films, including *Shipyard Sally* (1939) with Gracie FIELDS and *The Peterville Diamond* (1942). Served with the RAF (1941–46) and post-war toured in variety.

OTHER BRITISH FILMS: *There Was a Young Man, French Leave* (1937), *George and Margaret* (1940), *Let the People Sing* (1942).

Wakeman, Rick (*b* London, 1949). Composer. Keyboard player, member of the folk-rock band The Strawbs, and, later, the progressive-rock band Yes, as well as solo recording artist, Wakeman trained at the RCM with a view to becoming a concert pianist, but preferred popular venues. Has scored an eclectic batch of films, including *Lisztomania* (1975, + a), *Creepshow 2* (1987, US) and the Len DEIGHTON-based THRILLER, *Bullet to Beijing* (1995, UK/Can/CIS).

OTHER BRITISH FILMS INCLUDE: *White Rock* (1976, UK/US, doc), *G'Olé!* (1982, doc), *Alone* (2002, a).

Walbrook, Anton (*b* Vienna, Austria 1896 – *d* Garatshausen, West Germany, 1967). Actor. RN: Adolf Wohlbrück.

Walbrook's screen acting combined melancholic irony and old-worldly charm, chilling arrogance and tragic pathos. A dark, handsome and suave dandy, Walbrook was a romantic lead in German films before emigrating in 1936. His first major British success was as Prince Albert, opposite Anna NEAGLE as *Victoria The Great* (1937). Best remembered for his roles in several POWELL AND PRESSBURGER films, particularly as Prussian Theo in *The Life And Death Of Colonel Blimp* (1943) and Svengali-like ballet impresario Lermontov in *The Red Shoes* (1948). Other memorable performances included the sadistic husband in *Gaslight* (1940), and the romantic hero of *Dangerous Moonlight* (1941). Post-war, Walbrook also appeared in German and French films, most notably in Max Ophuls' *La Ronde* (1950) and *Lola Montès* (1955), and in the British-made *Saint Joan* (1957, UK/US) and *I Accuse!* (1957). Also on the London stage from 1939 in *Design for Living* and co-starred with Ethel Merman in *Call Me Madam* (1952).

OTHER BRITISH FILMS: *The Rat* (1937), *Sixty Glorious Years* (1938), *49th Parallel* (1941), *The Man from Morocco* (1945), *The Queen Of Spades* (1949), *Oh, Rosalinda!!* (1955). Tim Bergfelder.

Waldock, Denis (*b* Cambridge, 1911). Screenwriter. Perse School- and Cambridge-educated Waldock entered films in the 30s, collaborating on *Dance Band, Mimi* (1935), etc. During WW2, he worked as scriptwriter with the BBC European Service, and subsequently returned to writing plays and to co-authoring such screenplays as *Miranda* and *Trottie True* (1948).

OTHER BRITISH FILMS INCLUDE: (co-sc) *At the Villa Rose* (1939), *The Flying Squad* (1940), *Marry Me* (1949, with Lewis GILBERT), *Fun at St Fanny's* (1955, co-story).

Wales and British cinema Two British cinema pioneers lived and worked in Wales. **Arthur Cheetham** (*b* 1864 – *d* 1936), an entrepeneur based in Rhyl and Aberystwyth, made ACTUALITY FILMS from 1898 including *Children Playing on the Beach at Rhyl* and *Mailboat Munster Arriving at Holyhead from Dublin*. William HAGGAR, a south-Wales based travelling showman, cast his family in dramas (34 documented titles, most distributed by GAUMONT), including accomplished GENRE works, such as chase films (e.g. *A Desperate Poaching Affray*, 1903; *The Life of Charles Peace*, 1905), and the comic *Mirthful Mary* SERIES.

Wales's landscape has long attracted outside film-makers, from the makers of American Biograph's coloured *Conway Castle* phantom train-ride (1898), to creators of many MELODRAMAS of the 1910s and 20s, including *A Welsh Singer* (1915), based on Welsh writer Allen Raine's novel, with Henry EDWARDS directing and co-starring with Florence TURNER.

From the late 30s Welsh themes – especially the southern mining valleys' hallmark combination of hardship and comradeship – fascinated audiences in such features as *The Citadel* (1938), *The Proud Valley* (1940), *How Green Was My Valley* (1941, US), and *The Corn is Green* (1945, US). Such British films as Emlyn WILLIAMS's *The Last Days of Dolwyn* (1949), Jill CRAIGIE's *Blue Scar* (1949) and Paul DICKSON's *David* (1951), went beyond stereotype to highlight real indigenous concerns. 'Coal and comradeship' also engaged social documentarists of the 30s and 40s, as exemplified by Ralph BOND's *Today We Live*, Donald ALEXANDER's *Eastern Valley* (1937) and Humphrey JENNINGS's *Silent Village* (1943), which recreates in Cwmgiedd the story of Nazi-crushed Lidice, Czechoslovakia.

The first Welsh post-war film-maker to reach British audiences was Jack HOWELLS (1913–90). Working for Donald

Alexander before joining Associated British Pathé and later HTV, he found his distinct, witty voice in films such as *The Peaceful Years* (1948) and *Scrapbook for 1933* (1949). Prolific and evocative in style, Howells is best known for *Dylan Thomas* (1961, AA/doc), narrated by Richard BURTON. In the mid 70s director Karl FRANCIS (*b* 1942), launched a Welsh brand of 'gritty realism'. Fracture in community and family/industrial relationships is central to his early work: e.g. *Above Us the Earth* (1977), *The Mouse and the Woman* (1980), and in such later features for S4C (Wales's fourth television channel) as *The Happy Alcoholic* (1984), *Boy Soldier* (1986). Truth and authenticity are again pursued in *One of the Hollywood Ten* (2000), which reveals the impact of the McCarthy witch-hunt on Hollywood director Herbert Biberman.

S4C (launched 1982), brought unprecedented opportunities for Welsh-language film-making, pioneered in 1935 but largely unsupported for decades. Directors such as Stephen Bayly (*Coming Up Roses* 1986), Endaf EMLYN (*One Full Moon* 1991), Paul Turner (*Hedd Wyn*, 1992, AAn), are all award-winners who have gained cinema distribution outside Wales. Lottery finance has aided significant productions for general release, e.g. *House of America* (1997), *Human Traffic* (1999), *Very Annie Mary* (2001, UK/Fr). The oeuvre of director Chris MONGER, apprenticed in Cardiff in the 70s, is expanding in Hollywood following the success of *The Englishman Who Went Up . . .* (1995).

ANIMATION from Wales reached British cinema screens as early as 1925, when cartoon canine *Jerry the Tyke* was created for PATHÉ by Cardiff projectionist Sid Griffiths. From the 80s there has been an astonishing revival, with award-winners such as the Cartwn Cymru and Siriol teams, the Oscar-nominated Joanna Quinn (*Famous Fred*, (1997) and many other talents contributing to successes such as the feature-length, Disney-distributed *The Miracle Maker* (2000, S4C).

Individual Welsh artists have left their mark on international cinema since the early 20th century. Gareth Hughes, Ivor NOVELLO, Richard Burton, Stanley BAKER, Emlyn Williams, Meredith EDWARDS, Hugh GRIFFITH, Kenneth GRIFFITH and Anthony HOPKINS have all made lasting contributions. Their legacy is upheld by a new wave of international actors, including Ioan GRUFFUDD, Rhys IFANS, Matthew RHYS, and Catherine ZETA-JONES.

The story of Wales in British cinema continues to emerge thanks to film historians and organisations, including the National Screen and Sound Archive of Wales, which in 1996 restored the 'lost' government-suppressed BIOPIC, *The Life Story of David Lloyd George* (1918), thus progressing the rediscovery of cinema history.

BIBLIOG: David Berry, *Wales and Cinema – the First Hundred Years*, 1994. Iola Baines.

Walken, Christopher (*b* Astoria, NY, 1943). Actor. Intense, glassy-eyed Walken has had a prolific, highly individual career since coming to attention in the 70s, notably in *The Deer Hunter* (1978) for which he received an AA and BAAn (supp a). Most of his work is US-based, but he has appeared in a few British films, of which the moody Venice-set *The Comfort of Strangers* (1990, UK/It) is most notable, especially for his resonant suggestions of corrupt possibilities; his BOND villain in *A View to a Kill* (1985) also suits the dangerous element of his persona.

OTHER BRITISH FILMS: *The Dogs of War* (1980), *A Business Affair* (1994, UK/Fr/Ger/Sp), *The Opportunists* (2000, UK/US), *Plots with a View* (2002, UK/US).

Walker, Fiona (*b* London, 1943). Actress. Walker's work has been mainly on TV, some of it very notable, like *I, Claudius* (1976), as Agrippina, and the three *Norman Conquests* plays (1978). Films have been rare, but she was a touching Liddy in *Far from the Madding Crowd* (1967).

OTHER BRITISH FILMS INCLUDE: *The Asphyx* (1972), *Century* (1993).

Walker, Martin (*b* Harrow, 1901 – *d* London, 1955). Actor. On stage (London and New York) from 1917 and in supporting roles in films from 1931 (*The Flying Fool*) until 1954 (*The Belles of St Trinian's*). Most active in films of the 30s, when he appeared in several major productions, such as *Sanders of the River* (1935), playing Sanders' temporary replacement who is killed and dies without a whimper.

OTHER BRITISH FILMS: *The Flying Fool* (1931), *Help Yourself* (1932), *Mimi* (1935), *Sensation* (1936), *The Drum* (1938), *The Outsider* (1939), *Love on the Dole* (1941), *The Night Invader* (1943), *The Woman in the Hall* (1947), *Black 13* (1953).

Walker, Norman (*b* Bolton, Lancashire, 1892 – *d* ?). Director. Former actor and Captain in WW1, Walker is probably now best remembered as the director of J. Arthur RANK's initial foray into film production, the fishing village romance, *The Turn of the Tide* (1935). The whiff of moral earnestness about this perhaps endeared him to Rank, and much of his subsequent work was of an improving nature, including *The Great Mr Handel* (1942) and the glum homily, *They Knew Mr Knight* (1945, + co-p, co-sc). He was one of the three founders of GHW Productions, which made films on religious and morally uplifting themes, often for non-theatrical DISTRIBUTION.

OTHER BRITISH FILMS INCLUDE: (d, unless noted) *The Flag Lieutenant* (ass p), *Oxford Bags* (+ sc, p) (1926), *Blighty* (1927, ass d), *Uneasy Virtue* (1931, + sc), *Dangerous Ground* (1934), *The First Easter* (1939), *The Man at the Gate* (1941), *Hard Steel* (1942), *The Way Ahead* (1944, co-p), *John Wesley* (1953), *The Shield of Faith* (1956), *Walking on Water* (1968, + p, short).

Walker, Peter (aka Pete) (*b* Brighton, 1939) Producer, director, screenwriter, actor and exhibitor. Best known as a maker of mischievous HORROR movies, Peter Walker directed 16 films between 1967 and 1983, producing and financing all but one. After a childhood in orphanages, foster homes and Catholic schools, Walker made and distributed 8mm 'glamour' films before expanding into feature-length sex COMEDIES and THRILLERS including *School for Sex* (1968) and *Man of Violence* (1970). Experimented with 3-D in *Four Dimensions of Greta* (1972), but eventually found his métier as low-budget *auteur* with a series of gloomy, gruesomely effective horror films. Beginning with the *The Flesh and Blood Show* (1972) and including the paranoid chillers *House of Whipcord* (1974), *Frightmare* (1974) and *House of Mortal Sin* (1975), these studies of madness, obsession and violence established Walker as the most significant contributor to British horror cinema between the fall of HAMMER and the arrival of **Clive Barker** (*b* Liverpool, 1952), who directed the first two *Hellraiser* (1987, 1988) films in Britain. Disillusioned with the film business after making the Gothic parody, *House Of The Long Shadows* (1982), Walker turned to property-dealing and the EXHIBITION side of cinema. Steve Chibnall.

Walker, Polly (*b* Warrington, Cheshire, 1966). Actress. Vivid, dark-haired actress who made a strong impression as one of the four women seeking liberation in sunny Italy in *Enchanted April* (1992). She has filmed regularly since then, though her roles in the two ADAPTATIONS, *Emma* (1996, UK/US) and *The Woodlanders* (1997) were so truncated that their function in their respective novels was unclear. She was TV's *Lorna Doone* (1990) and had another go at Hardy in *The Mayor of Casterbridge* (2001); some international filming included *Patriot Games* (1992, US).

OTHER BRITISH FILMS INCLUDE: *The Trial* (1992), *Restoration* (1995, UK/US), *The Gambler* (1997, UK/Hung/Neth), *8½ Women* (1999, UK/Ger/Lux/Neth).

Walker, Robert C. Danvers (*b c* 1906 – *d c* 1989) Bob Danvers Walker was an Australian who worked as an announcer for Radio Normandy in the 30s, before becoming a BBC announcer and a commentator for the PATHÉ NEWSREEL during the war. Briefly promoted in 1946 to news editor, Walker returned to commentary for the newsreel and remained with it into the 60s, his authoritative tones becoming one of the most familiar voices in British cinemas, and now, thanks to the reuse of newsreels in historical DOCUMENTARIES, an instant vocal emblem of Britain's past. Luke McKernan.

Walker, Rudolph (*b* Trinidad, 1939). Actor. West Indian actor in supporting roles in British films and TV since the 60s. Prominent in such TV programmes as *Love Thy Neighbour* (1972–76), as Jack SMETHURST's easy-going neighbour, and *Empire Road* (1978–79), Britain's first black-conceived and -written series. Film roles, apart from the SPIN-OFF *Love Thy Neighbour* (1973) have been small, like the driver in '*Let Him Have It*' (1991).

OTHER BRITISH FILMS INCLUDE: *The Witches* (1966), *10 Rillington Place* (1970), *Man About the House* (1974), *Bhaji on the Beach* (1993), *The House of Angelo* (1997).

Walker, Syd (*b* Salford, 1886 – *d* Hove, 1945). Actor. RN: Kirkman. Stage comic monologuist who appeared in about ten films in the 30s, including John BAXTER's sentimental tale, *What Would You Do Chums?* (1939), the title of which was Walker's own RADIO catch-phrase.

OTHER BRITISH FILMS INCLUDE: *Old Bill 'Through the Ages'* (1924), *The Gift of Gab* (1934), *Over She Goes* (1937), *Oh, Boy!* (1938), *The Gang's All Here* (1939).

Walker, Zena (*b* Birmingham, 1934). Actress. Intelligent, incisive stage actress, RADA-trained, who played Juliet at Stratford in 1954, and also did some striking modern roles, as in *Passion Play* (1984). Film work has been sparing, but several times memorable: she was the anguished mother in the tense '*B*' FILM, *Emergency* (1962), Sammy's aunt in Cape Town in *Sammy Going South* (1963), wife to Richard HARRIS's *Cromwell* (1970), and '*Her Ladyship*' in *The Dresser* (1983). Much TV since 1951, including *Albert and Victoria* (1970–71) and as wife of *Man at the Top* (1970–72). Married/divorced (1) Robert URQUHART, (2) Julian HOLLOWAY.

OTHER BRITISH FILMS INCLUDE: *Snowball* (1960), *The Hellions* (1961, UK/S Af), *The Traitors* (1962), *Girl in the Headlines* (1963), *The Reckoning* (1969), *The Likely Lads* (1976).

Wall, Max (*b* London, 1908 – *d* London, 1990). Actor. RN: Lorimer. On stage from age 14, in London theatre from 1925, and thereafter in variety, revues, pantomimes as well as straight plays, with RAF service 1941–43. Rare film appearances, most often in comedy roles, including King Bruno the Questionable in *Jabberwocky* (1977) and a less-than-sinister Barrymore in the 1977 spoof version of *The Hound of the Baskervilles*.

OTHER BRITISH FILMS INCLUDE: *On the Air* (1934), *Save a Little Sunshine* (1938), *Chitty Chitty Bang Bang* (1968), *Max Wall: Funny Man*

(1975), *Hanover Street* (1979), *Little Dorrit* (1987), *We Think the World of You* (1988), *Loser Takes All* (1990, UK/US).

Wallace, Bryan (aka Bryan Edgar Wallace) (*b* 1904 – *d* 1971). Screenwriter. Son of Edgar WALLACE, he worked on a dozen or so 30s screenplays, including several based on his father's works: *The Flying Squad* (1932 – also acted in the 1929 version), *The Frightened Lady* (1932, co-sc), *Strangers on Honeymoon* (1936, co-sc), *The Squeaker* (1937, co-sc). Was assistant director on the Michael POWELL films, *The Fire Raisers* (1933) and *The Night of the Party* (1934).

OTHER BRITISH FILMS INCLUDE: (co-sc, unless noted) *Whiteface* (1932), *Orders Is Orders* (1933, ass d), *My Old Dutch* (1934), *The Clairvoyant* (1935), *OHMS* (1937), *Inspector Hornleigh* (1939).

Wallace, Edgar (*b* London, 1875 – *d* Los Angeles, 1932). Author, screenwriter. Incredibly prolific novelist and play-wright, whose works inspired an extraordinary number of films. Raised by a fish-porter, the orphaned Wallace left school in 1887, and later enlisted in the Army. After his 1899 discharge, he became a journalist, and began writing fiction, typically about spies, crime, and detectives. His first novel, *The Four Just Men* (1905), was twice filmed in Britain (1921, 1939), and inspired a late 50s British TV series. His vast popularity led to many other screen ADAPTATIONS, beginning with *The Man Who Bought London* (filmed 1916). For instance, his imperialist stories, notably *Sanders of the River* (1911), resulted in Zoltán KORDA's 1935 film, remade as *Death Drums Along the River* (1963); and one of his recurring characters, investigator J.G. Reeder, appeared in four films: *Red Aces* (1929, + sc), which Wallace directed, *Mr Reeder in Room 13* (1938), *The Mind of Mr Reeder*, and *The Missing People* (1939).

Wallace's extravagant lifestyle and costly fascination with horse-racing created a persistent need for money and probably motivated his furious writing pace: by 1932, he had written approximately 175 books and 24 plays. His works often were filmed several times: for example, novels, *The Crimson Circle* (1922, 1936) and *The Flying Squad* (1929, 1932, 1940), and plays, *The Case of the Frightened Lady* (1932; 1940, + co-sc), and *The Calendar* (1931, 1948); and another play, *The Ringer* was filmed three times (1928, 1931, 1953). By the late 20s Wallace had become involved in film-making, directing *The Squeaker* (1931), remade in 1937, and writing screenplays, including 1931's *The Hound of the Baskervilles*. His success took him to Hollywood where several of his stories had been adapted to film; he was to assist in the writing of *King Kong*, but died before contributing much. His continuing popularity led to a string of highly popular German films, several English TV series, and a SERIES of short THRILLERS shot at MERTON PARK in the early 60s adapted from his works. His son was Bryan Edgar WALLACE.

OTHER BRITISH FILMS INCLUDE: (works adapted, unless noted) *Pallard the Punter* (1919), *The Valley of Ghosts* (1928, + sc), *The Yellow Mask* (1930), *The Jewel* (1933), *The Feathered Serpent* (1934), *The Clairvoyant* (co-sc), *The Lad* (1935), *The Frog* (1937), *The Terror* (1938), *Dark Eyes of London* (1939), *The Door With Seven Locks* (1940), *Marriage Of Convenience* (1960), *Attempt to Kill* (1961), *Accidental Death* (1963), many more.

BIBLIOG: Margaret Lane, *Edgar Wallace: The Biography of a Phenomenon*, 1938. Stephen Shafer.

Wallace, Hedger (*b* Winchester, ? – *d* 2000). Actor. As well as being the author of several plays, Wallace appeared in supporting roles in films and TV from the later 50s, most often in HORROR films, including *Gorgo* (1960), *The Creeping Flesh*

(1972), *The Doctor and the Devils* (1985), usually in small roles and often as doctors of various kinds.

OTHER BRITISH FILMS INCLUDE: *Action of the Tiger* (1957), *Gideon's Day* (1958), *I'm All Right Jack* (1959), *The Girl on the Boat* (1962), *Sammy Going South* (1963), *Children of the Damned, A Hard Day's Night* (1964), *The Oblong Box* (1969), *Tales from the Crypt* (1972), *Ooh . . . You Are Awful* (1972), *Aces High* (1976, UK/Fr).

Wallace, Nellie (*b* Glasgow, 1870 – *d* London, 1948). Actress. Scottish stage performer, who appeared in a handful of light film entertainments, starting in the silent *Golden Pippin Girl* (1920), as a servant who wins a beauty contest. She was a great MUSIC HALL performer, and subsequently in 30s revue and pantomime.

OTHER BRITISH FILMS: *The Wishbone* (1933), *Radio Parade of 1935* (1934), *Variety* (1935), *Boys Will Be Girls* (1937), *Cavalcade of the Stars* (1938, short).

Waller, Anthony (*b* Beirut, Lebanon, 1959). Director, producer. Of British parentage, Waller is a NATIONAL FILM SCHOOL graduate with a background as prolific maker of commercials. His first feature was the well-received, Moscow-set thriller *Mute Witness* (1995, UK/Ger/Russ, + p, co-sc), with Alec GUINNESS as mystery guest star, followed by *An American Werewolf in Paris* (1997, UK/Lux/Neth, + ex p, co-sc, cam op). OTHER BRITISH FILMS: *When the Rain Stops* (1981, short for NFTS), *The Guilty* (2000, UK/Can/US).

Waller, David (*b* Street, Somerset, 1920 – *d* London, 1997). Actor. On stage from 1937, with Old Vic and RSC seasons in which he played many Shakespearean roles, Waller has also done some notable TV, including *Edward and Mrs Simpson* (1981), as Stanley Baldwin, and as Inspector Jowett in the series *Cribb* (1980–81). Films have been sparse: first in DOCUMENTARIES, he then appeared three times for Peter HALL, in *Work Is a Four Letter Word* (1967), *Perfect Friday* (1970) and the SHORT FILM, *Landscape* (1976) with Peggy ASHCROFT.

OTHER BRITISH FILM: *Lady Jane* (1985).

Waller, Tom (*b* Hull, 1975) Director, producer, editor. Waller's directorial debut, *Monk Dawson* (1997), about a priest who loses his vocation, was rigorous enough in character delineation for his next film, the Irish-set *Eviction* (1999, Ire), to be awaited with some interest but it has been scarcely seen. In 2002, he produced the Thai-set backpacker's romance, *Butterfly Man*.

Wallis, Shani (*b* London, 1933). Actress. Popular stage musical comedy star (e.g. as *Irma La Douce*, 1960) who made a few films, most notably as a poignant Nancy in *Oliver!* (1968), impressing as both singer and actress.

OTHER BRITISH FILMS: *Ramsbottom Rides Again, The Extra Day* (1956), *A King in New York* (1957), *The Pebble and the Penguin* (1995, narr).

Walls, Tom (*b* Kingsthorpe, 1883 – *d* Edwell, 1949). Director, actor. Actor, director. On stage from his early 20s, after trying horse racing and police work, Walls made a late but successful start in films in the early sound era. Herbert WILCOX, transferring to the screen the popular formulaic ALDWYCH FARCES, typically by Ben TRAVERS or Frederick LONSDALE, which Walls had starred in and produced in the 20s, assigned Walls to direct the films. Beginning with *Rookery Nook* (1930) and continuing well into the mid 30s, Walls directed and acted in a string of Aldwych ADAPTATIONS and other COMEDIES, with his roles usually those of 'black sheep' playing off Lynn's 'silly asses' and Hare's hen-pecked husbands. Wall's directing

style may have been stagey and unimaginative, particularly early on, but the films were profitable and successful. He let the farcical situations, with ensemble performances, embarrassing comic misunderstandings, sexual innuendos, and typical confusion, develop naturally from the clever screenplays, often by W.P. LIPSCOMB and Travers himself. Walls directed and appeared in 16 films written by Travers or based on his plays, and three written by Lonsdale, as well as *Leap Year* (1932) and *The Blarney Stone* (1933) without his Aldwych colleagues. He also directed but did not appear in such films as *Tons of Money* (1931) and Travers's *Dirty Work* (1934), and co-starred with Cicely COURTNEIDGE in *Me and Marlborough* (1935) as the Duke. Once his directing career waned, in the late 30s and 40s Walls showed his versatility as a character actor, appearing in roughly a dozen British films, from war stories and dramas to mysteries and musical comedy. Son **Tom Walls Jr** (*b* St Albans, Herts, 1912 – *d* Sutton, Surrey, 1992) also appeared in several films, including *Maytime in Mayfair* (1949), with his father.

OTHER BRITISH FILMS: (p) *Tons of Money* (1924); (d, a) *Canaries Sometimes Sing, On Approval* (1930), *Plunder* (1931), *Thark, A Night Like This* (1932), *Turkey Time, A Cuckoo in the Nest, Just Smith* (1933), *Lady in Danger, A Cup of Kindness* (1934), *Foreign Affaires, Fighting Stock, Stormy Weather* (1935), *Pot Luck, Dishonour Bright* (1936), *For Valour* (1937), *Second Best Bed, Old Iron* (1938); (a only) *Crackerjack, Strange Boarders* (1938), *Undercover, They Met in the Dark* (1943), *Love Story, The Halfway House* (1944), *Johnny Frenchman* (1945), *This Man is Mine* (1946), *While I Live, Master of Bankdam* (1947), *Spring in Park Lane* (1948), *Interrupted Journey* (1949). Stephen Shafer.

Walsh, Dermot (*b* Dublin, 1924 – *d* Tunbridge Wells, 2002). Actor. Walsh's career as a leading man started strongly with good performances in *Jassy* (1947), *Hungry Hill* (1947) and *The Mark of Cain* (1948). However, his most striking appearance in the 40s was in *To the Public Danger* (1948), a short film directed by Terence FISHER at HIGHBURY. Here Walsh played Captain Cole, a vicious and drunken bully, with a psychological intensity rarely seen in British films of this period (or since, for that matter). Walsh never again had the opportunity to play such a challenging role. However, he did provide some effective performances in numerous 1950s support features and in the early 1960s starred in the television series *Richard the Lionheart*. His first wife was Hazel COURT (1949–63).

OTHER BRITISH FILMS INCLUDE: *Bedelia* (1946), *My Sister and I* (1948), *Torment* (1949), *The Frightened Man, Ghost Ship* (1952), *The Floating Dutchman, Counterspy* (1953), *The Hideout* (1956), *At the Stroke of Nine* (1957), *Sea Fury* (1958), *The Flesh and the Fiends, The Bandit of Zhobe* (1959), *The Tell-Tale Heart* (1960), *The Breaking Point* (1961), *Emergency* (1962), *The Wicked Lady* (1983). Peter Hutchings.

Walsh, Kay (*b* London, 1914). Actress. Pretty, resourceful blonde lead of a dozen or so 30s comedies, the former revue dancer (she had danced from childhood) went on to become one of the most respected character leads in British films. She co-starred twice with George FORMBY (*Keep Fit*, 1937; *I See Ice!*, 1938) as well as working with other less well remembered comics, but really hit her stride in the two films she made in the early 40s for then-husband David LEAN: *In Which We Serve* (1942), which Noël COWARD co-directed, and *This Happy Breed* (1944), from Coward's play. To both roles – as John MILLS's wife and as rebellious Queenie respectively – she brought warmth and sympathetic understanding. Widely read herself, she introduced Lean to DICKENS and collaborated on the screenplay of his benchmark ADAPTATION of *Great Expectations* (1946) and was a very poignant Nancy in Lean's *Oliver Twist* (1948).

She moved into character roles rather young but some of these were rewarding leads: the housekeeper in *Last Holiday* (1950); the music hall partner in the 'Red Peppers' segment of *Meet Me Tonight* (1952); the tireless and tiring spinster enjoying a 'Winter Cruise' in *Encore* (1951), one of her most detailed studies; the vicar's exhausted and tempted wife in *Lease of Life* (1954); and pub landlord Coker in *The Horse's Mouth* (1958), for which she was BAA-nominated. All these roles are reinforced by an effortless humanity and social exactness. The parts were smaller from the 60s on, but she could still imbue, say, Aunt Cissie in *The Virgin and the Gypsy* (1970) with the authentic flash of vituperative life. Her US films included *Young Bess* (1953).

OTHER BRITISH FILMS: *Get Your Man* (1934), *Smith's Wives*, *The Luck of the Irish* (1935), *Secret of Stamboul*, *If I Were Rich*, *All That Glitters* (1936), *The Last Adventurers* (1937), *Meet Mr Penny* (1938), *Sons of the Sea*, *The Mind of Mr Reeder*, *The Middle Watch*, *All at Sea*, *The Missing People* (1939), *The Second Mr Bush*, *The Chinese Bungalow* (1940), *The October Man*, *Vice Versa* (1947), *Stage Fright*, *The Magnet* (1950), *The Magic Box* (1951), *Hunted* (1952), *Gilbert Harding Speaking of Murder* (1953), *The Rainbow Jacket* (1954), *Now and Forever*, *Cast a Dark Shadow* (1955), *Tunes of Glory* (1960), *Greyfriars Bobby*, *Reach for Glory* (1961), *Lunch Hour*, *The L-Shaped Room* (1962), *Dr Syn Alias the Scarecrow*, *80,000 Suspects* (1963), *The Beauty Jungle* (1964), *A Study in Terror*, *He Who Rides a Tiger* (1965), *The Witches* (1966), *Taste of Excitement* (1968), *Connecting Rooms* (1969), *Scrooge* (1970), *The Ruling Class* (1971).

Walsh, Percy (*b* Luton, 1888 – *d* London, 1952). Actor. Prolific small-part character player of over 50 films of the 30s and 40s, often as military officers and other dignitaries, like the Prison Governors he played in *Boys Will Be Boys* (1935) and *The Four Just Men* (1939), and he is the bookseller who realises the hero's aspirations in *Fame Is the Spur* (1947). Often in support of comics such as Will HAY and George FORMBY.

OTHER BRITISH FILMS INCLUDE: *The Wrong Mr Perkins* (1931), *Jew Süss* (1934), *Me and Marlborough* (1935), *King of the Damned* (1936), *Oh, Mr Porter!* (1937), *Pastor Hall* (1940), *Mr Proudfoot Shows a Light* (short), *Pimpernel Smith* (1941), *Adventures of Tartu* (1943), *I Live in Grosvenor Square* (1945), *The Courtneys of Curzon Square* (1947), *The Guinea Pig* (1948), *Train of Events* (1949), *Dick Barton at Bay* (1950).

Walsh, Raoul (*b* New York, 1887 – *d* Los Angeles, 1980). Director. Revered American action director who made a handful of British films, none of them up to the standard of his very best US work which is altogether faster, more vigorous and intelligent. However, *OHMS* (1937) is a moderately exciting tale of military adventure and *Captain Horatio Hornblower RN* (1950, UK/US) is handsome enough.

OTHER BRITISH FILMS: *Jump for Glory* (1937), *Sea Devils* (1953), *The Sheriff of Fractured Jaw* (1958).

Walter, Ernest (*b* Cardiff, 1919 – *d* Harrow, 1999). Editor. Former accountant who made his name as a member of the ARMY FILM AND PHOTO UNIT responsible for shooting the Normandy landings in June 1944. When demobbed, he turned to editing, first at MGM–BRITISH on *The Adventures of Quentin Durward* (1955). His career was cut short by a stroke but he taught at the NATIONAL FILM SCHOOL and wrote a book on editing.

OTHER BRITISH FILMS INCLUDE: *Beyond Mombasa* (1956), *The Inn of the Sixth Happiness* (1958), *Beyond This Place* (1959), *Murder She Said* (1961), *The Haunting*, *Children of the Damned* (1963), *Eye of the Devil* (1966), *The Private Life of Sherlock Holmes*, *10 Rillington Place* (1970), *The Wilby Conspiracy* (1974).

Walter, Harriet (*b* London, 1951). Actress. Highly regarded stage actress who has worked for all the major companies and in 2001 starred in the West End in *The Royal Family*. Came to popular attention as Harriet Vane, donnish partner of Lord Peter Wimsey, in TV's 1987 series from Dorothy Sayers's novels. Film roles have been intermittent but choice: as Anthony HOPKINS's ex-wife in *The Good Father* (1986), snobbish Fanny Dashwood in *Sense and Sensibility* (1995, UK/US), Simon CALLOW's wife (they run consciousness-raising sessions in their trendy home) in *Bedrooms and Hallways* (1999). Never a film leading lady, she may yet be a major screen character actress. Niece of Christopher LEE. Awarded CBE, 2000.

OTHER BRITISH FILMS INCLUDE: *The French Lieutenant's Woman* (1981, scenes cut), *Turtle Diary* (1985), *The Leading Man* (1996), *Keep the Aspidistra Flying* (1997), *The Governess* (1998, UK/Fr), *Onegin* (1999, UK/US).

Walter-Ellis, Desmond (*b* London, 1914). Actor. Tall beaky purveyor of 'silly-ass' roles, such as Willy Oughton-Formby in *Carry On Admiral* (1957), Sherborne-educated Walter-Ellis was on stage from 1932, early on in Shakespeare, then mainly in modern comedy. WW2 service in the Army (1940–45); film debut as Peter GRAVES's shady associate in *Maytime in Mayfair* (1949); and a great deal of TV from 1946.

OTHER BRITISH FILMS INCLUDE: *A Run for Your Money* (1949), *Penny Princess* (1952), *The Hellfire Club* (1960), *The Great St Trinian's Train Robbery* (1966), *The Rise and Rise of Michael Rimmer* (1970).

Walters, Julie (*b* Birmingham, 1950). Actress. Former nurse, the Manchester Poly-educated Walters came to the screen in 1983 with éclat when she reprised her triumphant stage role as the working-class wife who takes to university study in *Educating Rita*, receiving a BAA and AAn. The tough, gutsy humanity she brought to the part, and which she would bring to other roles such as the anguished Kate Keller in the National Theatre's acclaimed revival of *All My Sons* (2000) and on screen as the chain-smoking ballet teacher who spots the potential of *Billy Elliot* (2000, BAA/supp a; AAn), established her as a major actress. Fans of the TV comedy series of the 80s in which she partnered Victoria WOOD may have wondered if they were watching the same performer. By now, however, it is clear that she will tackle almost anything, from Lady Macbeth to the outrageous old trollop she played in TV's *Dinnerladies* (1998), from businesslike 'madam' in *Personal Services* (1987), to the train robber's expatriated wife longing for England in *Buster* (1988), the domineering Madame Danzard in *Sister My Sister* (1994) and the fiercely loyal friend in *Girls' Night* (1998, UK/US). Awarded OBE, 2000.

OTHER BRITISH FILMS: *Occupy!* (1976), *Film No 1* (short), *She'll Be Wearing Pink Pyjamas* (1984), *Dreamchild* (voice), *Car Trouble* (1985), *Prick Up Your Ears* (1987), *Mack the Knife* (UK/Hung), *Killing Dad* (1989), *Just Like a Woman* (1992), *Intimate Relations* (1996), *Titanic Town* (1998, UK/Ger/Fr), *All Forgotten* (2000, UK/US), *Harry Potter and the Philosopher's Stone* (2001, UK/US), *Before You Go* (2002).

Walters, Thorley (*b* Teigngrace, Devonshire, 1913 – *d* London, 1991). Actor. Square-faced character actor with dark, trimmed moustache, best remembered for comedy roles in the 50s, good at army officer types, bungling civil servants and ineffectual agents of authority. A 1933 Old Vic season was followed by repertory, and appearances in several 'QUOTA QUICKIES,' but his first sizeable film role was in *Waltz Time* (1945). In West End revue and musical comedy for the next decade; recalled to films by Roy BOULTING for *Josephine and Men* (1955), he became a regular supporting player in BRITISH LION films (1955–68), notably in *Blue Murder at St Trinian's*

(1957) and, for the Boulting brothers, *Private's Progress* (1956) and *Carlton-Browne of the FO* (1958), as Terry-THOMAS's gung-ho military aide. His only starring role was in the minor comedy *Second Fiddle* (1957); also featured in HAMMER films, including *The Phantom of the Opera* (1962) and *Dracula – Prince of Darkness* (1965); and played numerous TV roles, memorably as Tufty in *Tinker, Tailor, Soldier, Spy* (1979).

OTHER BRITISH FILMS INCLUDE: *The Love Test* (1935), *Secret Journey* (1939), *Medal for the General* (1944), *They Were Sisters* (1945), *Who Done It?* (1956), *Happy is the Bride*, *The Birthday Present* (1957), *Don't Panic Chaps* (1959), *Two Way Stretch*, *Suspect*, *A French Mistress* (1960), *Heavens Above!* (1963), *The Earth Dies Screaming* (1964), *The Wrong Box*, *The Family Way* (1966), *Twisted Nerve* (1968), *Frankenstein Must Be Destroyed* (1969), *Bartleby* (1970), *Young Winston* (1972), *The People That Time Forgot* (1977), *The Wildcats of St Trinian's* (1980). Roger Philip Mellor.

Walthamstow studios Although there were several studios in the Walthamstow area, there were two main film companies in operation based at Hoe Street and Wood Street respectively. Hoe Street was the home of the BRITISH AND COLONIAL KINEMATOGRAPH COMPANY (1913–24) and the studio, an ex-skating rink, could hold 20 sets at a time. Directors included Maurice ELVEY and Ernest and Ethyle BATLEY. By the end of WWI, output had declined dramatically. New management failed to revive production with imported American actors and directors and after a period of hiring out the studio in the early 20s B and C went into receivership in June 1924. Built in 1914 by Cunard Films, the studio at 245 Wood Street was purchased by Broadwest in 1916 to produce such films as *The Merchant of Venice* (1916) starring Matheson LANG. When Broadwest was dissolved in 1921 the studio was leased for five years to the makers of SHORT FILMS until British Filmcraft acquired it in August 1926. They made a series of shorts and four features (1926–28) before folding in 1930 and the Wood Street studio was closed. Sarah Easen.

Walton, Herbert C. (*b* 1879 – *d* London, 1955). Actor. After a long stage career (debut 1897) and radio experience, Walton came to films in the mid 40s and made about 20 appearances in the years till his death, mainly in small roles like that of the gardener in *The Weak and the Wicked* (1953).

OTHER BRITISH FILMS INCLUDE: *Appointment with Fear* (1946, shorts, series), *Take My Life* (1947), *Britannia Mews* (1948), *Mr Denning Drives North* (1951), *I Believe in You*, *The Cruel Sea* (1952), *Time Bomb*, *Hobson's Choice* (1953), *The End of the Road* (1954).

Walton, Tony (*b* Walton-on-Thames, 1934). Costume designer, production designer. Formerly married to Julie ANDREWS (1959–69), whose costumes he designed for *Mary Poppins* (1964, AAn), Walton has had a distinguished stage career as designer and director, and since the late 70s has worked chiefly in the US. His British work, involving both production and costume design, a dual function that made him very influential in the look of the films, included three for Sidney LUMET: *The Sea Gull* (1968), *Murder on the Orient Express* (1974, AAn/cos; BAAn/cos/des), a very elegant evocation of between-wars, and *Equus* (1977). He can hardly be held responsible for the way the design swamped the innocent gaiety of Sandy Wilson's *The Boy Friend* (1971) in Ken RUSSELL's ADAPTATION. Shared AA/des for *All That Jazz* (1979); entered TV with design for *The Julie Andrews Show* (1959).

OTHER BRITISH FILMS: *Fahrenheit 451* (1966, des, cos, prod man), *Petulia* (1968, des, cos).

Walton, Sir William (*b* Oldham, 1902 – *d* Ischia, 1983). Composer. Walton, composer of orchestral, chamber, choral and dramatic works, including over a dozen film scores, was born into a poor but musical family. In 1912 he became a chorister at Christ Church Cathedral, Oxford, and began to compose from an early age. Whilst Walton often claimed to be largely self-taught, he did receive a thorough musical training at Oxford University. Mixing in the artistic circle of the Sitwells, he met Stravinsky, Gershwin and other influential figures whilst still in his 20s. Always concerned for his financial position in the early years, Walton scored his first film, *Escape Me Never* (1935), for a fee of £350. As with many composers of his generation, the war effort offered him fruitful opportunities to score patriotic films, notably OLIVIER's *Henry V* (1944). This film was significant in establishing the reputation of British cinema on both sides of the Atlantic. As a film for Britain in wartime, it provided encouragement and comfort at home. To its wider audience, it was about HERITAGE, and the gravitas that a theatrical tradition can bring to cinema. Walton's score is an integral part of this multiple effect, and clearly demonstrates the composer's broader musical inclinations, in which tonality, orchestration and musical structure are inherently dramatic tools.

His attention to dramatic detail and pacing put him at the forefront of 'serious' composers willing and able to work in cinema, and many of his film scores were adapted as orchestral concert suites. Then, after a flurry of activity in the 40s, Walton's return to film scoring, with *Battle of Britain* (1969), did not find favour at United Artists. All of his music, except the 'Battle in the Air' cue, was replaced by Ron GOODWIN's last-minute score, thus setting a seal on the golden age of British film music in a symphonic tradition. However, there were plans in 2002, supported by MGM and United Artists, to reinstate all of Walton's cues in a new cut of the film.

OTHER BRITISH FILMS: *As You Like It* (1936), *Dreaming Lips* (1937), *Stolen Life* (1939), *Major Barbara* (1941), *Next of Kin* (1942), *The Foreman Went to France* (1942), *The First of the Few* (1942), *Went the Day Well?* (1942), *Hamlet* (1948), *Richard III* (1955), *Three Sisters* (1969). David Burnand.

Walton-on-Thames studios In 1899, 25-year-old film pioneer and inventor Cecil HEPWORTH built a small outdoor stage in his garden at Walton. Four years later, he constructed one of the first covered studios in Britain and by 1905 had expanded this to include two large studios, a workshop and viewing theatre as well as separate areas for film processing and printing. By 1906, Hepworth was producing over 200 films a year. Several years of hardship followed, not helped by a fire at the studio, but in the 1910s Hepworth was again a force in the British film industry. His studio became home to Britain's first wave of authentic film stars, in particular Alma TAYLOR and Stuart ROME, as well as several independent companies, most notably Turner Films, the company of former American film star and 'Vitagraph Girl', Florence TURNER, and Elwin NEAME's Ivy CLOSE Films. Despite depletion of studio workers during WWI, Hepworth made PROPAGANDA SHORTS and continued to rent the studio to other companies. Post-war, studio operations increased. Hepworth purchased another property and decided to float his company to raise capital to build a six-stage studio. The stock sold poorly and even the release of *Comin' Thro' the Rye* (1923) could not save him. The company was wound up in June 1924. In 1926, theatrical producer Archibald NETTLEFOLD bought the studios, renaming it

NETTLEFOLD STUDIOS. SOUND equipment was installed in 1930 and the studio was hired out to independent production companies. During WW2, the government requisitioned the studios and part of the Vickers-Armstrong aircraft factory was moved there. Throughout the 50s the studios were once again hired to independent producers. However in the late 50s many smaller studios, of which Nettlefold was one, fell victim to the declining market for low- and medium-budget films. The studios were closed and demolished in 1961. Sarah Easen.

Walturdaw Company Ltd Formally registered in 1904 as a public company, it was founded by J.D. Walker, E.G. Turner and J.H.J. Dawson, who began renting films as early as 1897 and are generally acknowledged as Britain's first distributors. Walturdaw is also credited with originating the concept of formal release dates for films. Primarily a distributor, the company began limited production as early as July 1905, and as late as 1919, it produced three features. It ceased DISTRIBUTION in 1924 but continued as a support company for cinemas with the Walturdaw Cinema Supply Co. Ltd. AS.

Wanamaker, Sam (*b* Chicago, 1919 – *d* London, 1993). Actor, director. American who spent chunks of his career in Britain and was awarded an honorary CBE in 1993 for his tireless work in the restoration of Shakespeare's Globe Theatre. On stage in the US before WW2 service, he first appeared in British film as the Italian migrant in *Give Us This Day* (1949), Brooklyn-set but filmed in the UK by fellow BLACKLIST victim, Edward DMYTRYK, and on the London stage in 1952 (*Winter Journey*). For the rest of his life, he worked on stage (director as well as actor), screen and TV in both countries. He made nearly 20 further British film appearances, between Eileen MOORE's lawyer fiancé in *Mr Denning Drives North* (1951) and the all-star Agatha CHRISTIE entertainment, *Death on the Nile* (1978), always a persuasively authoritative presence. Daughter is Zoë WANAMAKER.

OTHER BRITISH FILMS INCLUDE: *The Battle of the Sexes* (1959, narr), *The Criminal* (1960), *Those Magnificent Men . . . , The Spy Who Came In from the Cold* (1965), *Danger Route* (1967), *The Executioner* (1970), *Catlow* (1971), *The Sellout* (1975), *Voyage of the Damned* (1976).

Wanamaker, Zoë (*b* New York City, 1949). Actress. Brought up in Britain when father Sam WANAMAKER fell foul of the McCarthy persecutions in the US, she has had an impressive career on stage and TV: the range includes Greek tragedy, the sitcom, *Love Hurts* (1992–94), co-starring Adam FAITH, and a wonderfully bad-tempered Audrey in *A Dance to the Music of Time* (1997). Pert and watchful, she is too idiosyncratic for conventional leading-lady roles, but has made the most of the character parts films have sought her for, including Ada Leverson in *Wilde* (1997, UK/Ger/Jap/US) and Madam Xiomara Hooch in *Harry Potter and the Philosopher's Stone* (2001, UK/US). Married Gawn GRAINGER in 1994.

OTHER BRITISH FILMS INCLUDE: *The Raggedy Rawney* (1988), *The Countess Alice* (1992), *The English Wife* (1995), *Amy Foster* (1997, UK/Fr/US).

war films WORLD WAR 1 was treated directly on few occasions in British feature films at the time, as compared with the proliferation of wartime subjects during WW2. Exceptions included *The Better 'ole* (1918) and the unreleased *Victory and Peace* (1918), and the 20s and 30s saw such productions as *Mademoiselle from Armentières* (1927), Anthony ASQUITH's *Tell England* (1931) and Victor SAVILLE's *I Was a Spy* (1933). Later, the Korean war appears to have provided the material for

just a single film, *A Hill in Korea* (1956) and the FALKLANDS WAR only a significant handful, but WW2 represented for many years a prevalent theme in British cinema. During the war itself, substantial numbers of films treated the conflict, though apart from DOCUMENTARY features such as *Desert Victory* (1943) and occasional high-profile works like the naval saga *In Which We Serve* (1942) or the Army's riposte to this success, *The Way Ahead* (1944), their emphasis tended to be on espionage and resistance or on the home front, rather than on military action. Such notable films as *The Life and Death of Colonel Blimp* and *Millions Like Us* (1943) and *Great Day* (1945) fall into such categories.

But within a few years of the war's end, retrospective accounts of wartime events came to form what during the 50s was arguably British cinema's dominant GENRE. Some of the numerous sub-divisions within the genre included: dramatised reconstructions of significant actions – *The Dam Busters* (1955), *Battle of the River Plate* (1956), *Dunkirk* (1958); fictional tributes to different branches of the armed services – *They Were Not Divided* (1950, the Brigade of Guards), *Appointment in London* (1953, RAF Bomber Command), *The Sea Shall Not Have Them* (1954, air-sea rescue operations); ADAPTATIONS of successful novels – *The Cruel Sea* (1952), *A Town Like Alice* (1956); BIOPICS on heroic individuals – *Reach for the Sky* (1956, Douglas Bader), *Carve Her Name With Pride* (1958, Violette Szabo); and prisoner-of-war escape stories – *The Wooden Horse* (1950), *Albert RN* (1953), *The Colditz Story* (1954).

The retrospective association of these films tends to be with the 'stiff upper lip' and a spirit of unquestioning devotion to duty; and, while the tragic implications of warfare are not avoided, it is true that these films generally rely on an external observation of character and situation. As a result, however sincere the makers' intentions, the films – with one or two exceptions, notably *The Cruel Sea* – lack the capacity to penetrate very far into the tensions and anxieties of the experiences they are describing. Virtually all the industry's principal actors, writers and directors were at this time associated with the war GENRE to some degree, but the player most readily identified with it is probably Jack HAWKINS, while the director most prolific in treating war subjects was Lewis GILBERT. The prevailing style of the films is that of low-key REALISM, though studio-based rather than utilising any explicitly DOCUMENTARY approach, and the great majority were shot in black-and-white. A contrast is afforded by the productions of the American-backed WARWICK FILMS – *The Red Beret* (1953), *Cockleshell Heroes* (1955) – which were shot in colour and in a more showmanlike mode.

In the late 50s a small number of 'anti-war' films made their appearance, perhaps partly in response to the international acclaim visited on *The Bridge on the River Kwai* (1957). These modestly scaled films included *Orders to Kill* (1958), with a French resistance background, and *Yesterday's Enemy* (1959) and *The Long and the Short and the Tall* (1960), both set, like *Kwai*, in the Far East. Rather than adopting a pacifist stance, they aspire to be exercises in lethal irony, attempting to deploy shock tactics over such matters as the shooting of prisoners. It may be noted that, about the same time, ostensibly mainstream war films like *Sea of Sand* (1958) incorporated a more jaundiced view of the conflict than their predecessors. This undertone later developed into the strenuous cynicism of such technically British productions as *The Dirty Dozen* (1967, UK/US) and *Play Dirty* (1968).

More generally during the 60s, as the war became a more

distant prospect and the vogue for blockbusters and international co-production (foreshadowed by *Kwai*) set in, British-made war films tended, in the wake of the success of *The Longest Day* (1962), to assume the format of ostensible historical reconstruction, whether in the guise of ADVENTURE stories – *Operation Crossbow* (1965, UK/It), *The Heroes of Telemark* (1965) – or of spectacle – the rather anaemic *Battle of Britain* (1969). A little later, *A Bridge Too Far* (1977), directed by Richard ATTENBOROUGH with a star-filled cast, dramatised the ill-fated battle of Arnhem, and sought self-consciously both to assume epic status and in its latter stages to memorialise a Wilfred Owen-like sense of war's 'pity'. The degree of its achievement is debatable, but its lack of successors means that it effectively constituted a valediction to the British WW2 movie. Tim Pulleine.

See also **World War I and British film**; **Falklands War and British film**.

Warbeck, David (*b* Christchurch, NZ, 1941 – *d* London, 1997). Actor. RN: Michell. RADA-trained Warbeck made his debut as Robin Hood in *Wolfshead: The Legend of Robin Hood* (1969), then spent most of the rest of his film career in HORROR films, most of them made in Europe. The comedy thriller, *The Sex Thief* (1973), is an exception among his films. Also appeared in US films, including *Lassiter* (1983).
OTHER BRITISH FILMS INCLUDE: *Trog* (1970), *Twins of Evil* (1971), *Craze* (1973), *Sudden Fury* (1997), *Razor Blade Smile* (1998).

Warbeck, Stephen Composer. Former actor and prolific composer for the theatre (much associated with the RSC), Warbeck turned to film scoring in the 90s, establishing an enviable reputation in such critically and commercially acclaimed films as *Mrs Brown* (1997, UK/Ire/US), *Shakespeare in Love* (1998, UK/US) and *Billy Elliot* (2000). His versatility was further demonstrated by scores for two powerful but less widely seen, darker pieces: *Sister My Sister* (1994) and *Heart* (1999), as well as for all the TV *Prime Suspect* series from 1991.
OTHER BRITISH FILMS INCLUDE: *Skallagrigg* (1994), *Element of Doubt* (1996), *My Son the Fanatic* (1997), *Fanny and Elvis* (1999), *Quills* (2000, UK/US), *Captain Corelli's Mandolin* (UK/Fr/US), *Very Annie Mary* (UK/Fr), *Gabriel & Me* (2001), *Charlotte Gray* (2001, UK/Aust/US).

Ward, Albert (*b* 1870 – *d* London, 1956). Actor, director, screenwriter. After a long stage career, Ward entered the industry as an actor with HEPWORTH. As a director he was associated with British Empire for his first seven films and with G.B. SAMUELSON for his last eight.
BRITISH FILMS INCLUDE: (d) *When Woman Hates*, *The Phantom Picture* (1916, + sc), *Queen of My Heart* (1917), *A Member of Tattersall's* (1919, + sc), *The Last Rose of Summer*, *Nance* (1920), *Mr Pim Passes By* (1921, + sc), *Stable Companions* (1922). AS.

Ward, David (*b* Bolton, Lancs, 1916). Actor. With pre-war stage experience and invalided out of the armed forces in 1941, Ward, not to be confused with the US actor of the same name, appeared in supporting roles in about a dozen British films of the 40s. He can be glimpsed struggling with a large fish in *Hotel Reserve* (1944).
OTHER BRITISH FILMS INCLUDE: *One of Our Aircraft Is Missing* (1942), *Adventures of Tartu* (1943), *The Rake's Progress* (1945), *Beware of Pity* (1946), *Blanche Fury* (1947), *Murder in the Cathedral* (1952).

Ward, Mackenzie (*b* Eastbourne, 1903). Actor. On stage aged 15, London from 1925 and New York from 1926, he first appeared in films in Hollywood, including *Lucky in Love* (1929). In British films from the mid 30s, he was Touchstone in

Paul CZINNER's *As You Like It* (1936) and played supporting roles, like that of the photographer in *A Run for Your Money* (1949), in about 20 further films. In much TV drama from 1946, including a spruce Jack Favell in *Rebecca* (1947). Brother of Ronald WARD.
OTHER BRITISH FILMS INCLUDE: *While Parents Sleep* (1935), *Over the Moon* (1939), *Kipps* (1941), *Caesar and Cleopatra* (1945), *Carnival* (1946), *The Happiest Days of Your Life* (1950), *Laughter in Paradise*, (1951), *The Two Faces of Dr Jekyll* (1960).

Ward, Michael (*b* Carnmenellis, Cornwall, 1909 – *d* London, 1997). Actor. First noticed as the prissy ornithologist who is surprisingly met by a pretty girl after travelling on the *Sleeping Car to Trieste* (1948), Central School-trained Ward played variations on a camp persona in over 60 films. The roles were usually small but always noticeable, as skinny, crinkle-haired Ward offered fastidious support to comedians including Norman WISDOM, first in *Trouble in Store* (1953), and Frankie HOWERD, first in *Jumping for Joy* (1955), in five for the BOULTING brothers and in five 'CARRY ON' capers. Only rarely, as in TEMPEAN's *The Frightened Man* (1952), as a clearly knowledgeable antiques dealer, was he given a chance to develop a more rounded character. Of whatever he did, though, as sniffy salesmen, mincing photographers, fops of every hue, he made a series of irresistibly entertaining cameos. He was also a regular guest on TV programmes, including *The Morecambe and Wise Show*.
OTHER BRITISH FILMS INCLUDE: *An Ideal Husband* (1947), *Trottie True* (1948), *Seven Days to Noon*, *No Trace* (1950), *Tom Brown's Schooldays* (1951), *Tread Softly*, *Song of Paris*, *13 East Street* (1952), *Street Corner* (1953), *Man of the Moment*, *Lost* (1955), *Private's Progress*, *Up in the World* (1956), *Just My Luck* (1957), *Carlton-Browne of the FO* (1958), *Doctor in Love* (1960), *Carry On Regardless*, *A Pair of Briefs* (1961), *Father Came Too!* (1963), *Carry On Cleo* (1964), *Don't Lose Your Head* (1966), *Frankenstein and the Monster from Hell* (1973), *Revenge of the Pink Panther* (1978).

Ward, Nick (*b* Geelong, Australia, 1962). Director, screenwriter. Cambridge-educated Ward has written, produced and directed two little-seen features: *Dakota Road* (1992), an examination of a Norfolk farming community, and the psychological thriller, *Look Me in the Eye* (1994, + ed).

Ward, Penelope Dudley *see* **Dudley Ward, Penelope**

Ward, Polly (*b* Mitcham, 1908 – *d* Reading/Woking, Berks, 1987). Actress. RN: Byno Poluski. From a famous acting family, she began career as a chorus girl, then joined the Co-Optimists company, and appeared in nearly 20 films, mainly in the 30s, and mainly light COMEDIES or MUSICALS. She co-starred once with Max MILLER (*Thank Evans*, 1938) and twice with George FORMBY (*Feather Your Nest*, 1937; *It's in the Air*, 1938), and her lively manner and even livelier dancing made her popular.
OTHER BRITISH FILMS INCLUDE: *This Marriage Business* (1927), *His Lordship* (1932), *It's a Bet* (1935), *Annie Laurie* (1936), *St Martin's Lane* (1938), *Women Aren't Angels* (1942).

Ward, Ronald (*b* Eastbourne, Sussex, 1901 – *d* London, 1978). Actor. After brief stint in insurance broker's office, Ward was on stage from his later teens, touring in Australasia in 1918 (he was there again in 1924) and returning to the London stage in 1920. Like brother, Mackenzie WARD, he played Jack Favell in *Rebecca*, but on stage (1940), and appeared in nearly 30 films, starting with *Alibi* (1931), usually in small roles. Repeated his 1950 stage role of worldly Cayley Drummle in *The Second Mrs Tanqueray* in Dallas BOWER's little-seen 1952 film. Was married (2 of 2) to **Betty Baskcomb** (*b* London, 1914), who appeared in a few British films, including *It Always Rains on Sunday* (1947).

OTHER BRITISH FILMS INCLUDE: *Partners Please* (1932), *Girls Will Be Boys* (1934), *The Passing of the Third Floor Back* (1935), *East Meets West* (1936), *St Martin's Lane* (1938), *Goodbye, Mr Chips* (1939), *Escape to Danger* (1943), *Green for Danger* (1946), *My Daughter Joy* (1950), *Aunt Clara* (1954), *Lost* (1955).

Ward, Simon (*b* London, 1940). Actor. Leading man of the 70s, who had and took some showy chances in such films as *Young Winston* (1972), *The Three Musketeers* (1973, Panama) and *Aces High* (1976, UK/Fr), as, respectively, Churchill, the Duke of Buckingham (also in *The Four Musketeers*, 1974, Panama/Spain), and the young officer in the remake of *Journey's End*. Since the 70s, he has worked chiefly in TV. Father of Sophie WARD.

OTHER BRITISH FILMS INCLUDE: *If . . .* (1968), *Frankenstein Must Be Destroyed, I Start Counting* (1969), *Quest for Love* (1971), *Hitler: The Last Ten Days* (1973, UK/It), *All Creatures Great and Small* (1974), *Dominique* (1978), *The Monster Club* (1980), *Wuthering Heights* (UK/US), *Double X: The Name of the Game* (1992).

Ward, Sophie (*b* London, 1965). Actress. Daughter of Simon WARD, she was in films as a child – in *Full Circle* (UK/Can) and *The 'Copter Kids* (1976) – and returned to features in *A Shocking Accident* in 1982. She has filmed in both the US (e.g. *Young Sherlock Holmes*, 1985) and Britain, without quite establishing herself as a star. Her marriage to her lesbian partner in 2000 brought her a deal of publicity, more perhaps than her film work has.

OTHER BRITISH FILMS INCLUDE: *Aria* (1987), *Little Dorrit* (1987), *A Summer Story* (1987), *Wuthering Heights* (1992, UK/US), *A Village Affair* (1994), *Dead in the Water* (2001).

Ward, Warwick (*b* St Ives, 1891 – *d* Welwyn Garden City, 1967). Actor. A suave, debonair leading man, Ward was multi-talented. On-screen (1919–33), he was featured in the US-made *Madame Sans-Gêne* (1925), and starred in a number of German films, including *Variety* (1925 – the *New York Times* described his performance as 'brilliant') and the English-language versions of *Ariane* (1931) and *FP1 Does Not Answer* (1933). In 1935, he made his home in Welwyn Garden City and became general manager of the studios there. Later produced and co-scripted *The Man from Morocco* (1945), *Quiet Weekend* (1946) and *The Dancing Years* (1950), and produced *My Brother Jonathan* (1948).

OTHER BRITISH FILMS INCLUDE: *The Silver Lining* (1919), *Wuthering Heights* (1920), *Bulldog Drummond* (1923), *The White Sheik* (1928), *Stamboul* (1931), *Life Goes On* (1932). AS.

Wardour Street It was Charles URBAN who first located his film business in Wardour Street, when he built Urbanora House (the building still bears the name) in 1908. This street in London's Soho continues to act as a generic term for today's more scattered film production, DISTRIBUTION and EXHIBITION businesses. A few companies still have offices there. The convergence on Soho had already begun before the onset of the WWI, with companies like Pathé attracted by the large-sized terraced houses in which to house filmstock and the links to theatreland and railway. It used to be invoked satirically as the scene of soulless wheeling and dealing having no regard for the artistic aspects of film-making. The street gave its name to Wardour Films, a renting company built up in the 1910s by John MAXWELL.

BIBLIOG: 'Chapter 7: Wardour Street' in Ernest Betts, *The Film Business: A History of British Cinema 1896–1972*, 1973.

Wareing, Lesley (*b* London, 1913 – *d* Swalecliffe, 1988). Actress. RADA-trained and on stage from childhood (London from 1930) and in ten films of the 30s, mainly for BIP, including the female lead opposite Sir Seymour HICKS in *It's You I Want* (1936).

OTHER BRITISH FILMS INCLUDE: *Men Like These* (1931), *The Iron Duke, Fighting Stock* (1935), *Bedtime Story* (1938), *The Mind of Mr Reeder, The Outsider* (1939).

Waring, Barbara (*b* Kent, 1912). Actress. Stage actress who appeared in supporting roles in a few films of the 30s and 40s, including spoilsport Joan as a member of *The Gentle Sex* (1943).

OTHER BRITISH FILMS INCLUDE: *The Girl in the Crowd* (1934), *In Which We Serve* (1942), *Heaven Is Around the Corner, A Canterbury Tale* (1944), *Hungry Hill* (1947).

Waring, Derek (*b* London, 1930). Actor. RN: Derek Aylward. Best known for his work on TV, including the lead in *Moody and Pegg* (1974–75), he also had supporting roles in several British films, starting with *Barnacle Bill* (1957). Married to Dorothy TUTIN (1963–2001, her death). Also theatre and radio experience.

OTHER BRITISH FILMS INCLUDE: *I Accuse!* (1957), *Dunkirk* (1958), *Battle of Britain* (1969), *Hitler: The Last Ten Days* (1973).

Warner Brothers–First National–British In June 1931, Warner Brothers bought TEDDINGTON STUDIOS from Henry EDWARDS and in August registered a British subsidiary, Warner Brothers–First National, to make 'QUOTA QUICKIES' there. Run with the efficiency of a mini-Hollywood studio, Warners released over forty short CRIME FILMS or MELO-DRAMAS during their first two years. Michael POWELL directed a number of quota films for the company, as did George KING and Maurice ELVEY; Frank LAUNDER and Sidney GILLIAT wrote screenplays; and Errol FLYNN starred in *Murder at Monte Carlo* (1935), which resulted in his Hollywood contract. In 1935, fewer films were produced but with higher production values such as *Man of the Moment* (1935) starring Douglas FAIRBANKS JR. In 1936 Warners enlarged the studios, brought in more directors and made more expensive films, including Arthur WOODS' excellent proto-*noir*, *They Drive By Night* (1939). Warners continued to make short feature films throughout WW2 until the studio was bombed in 1944. It was rebuilt in 1948 but by then Warners had invested heavily in the ASSOCIATED BRITISH PICTURE CORPORATION and production moved to ELSTREE. In 1955 the studios were sold to a television production company. Sarah Easen.

See also **Hollywood studios in Britain**.

Warner, David (*b* Manchester, 1941). Actor. RADA-trained ex-bookseller who came to prominence in the 60s as a young Hamlet with the RSC (1965) and, after a couple of supporting roles in films, as *Morgan: A Suitable Case for Treatment* (1966), an eccentric, possibly insane protagonist, and a key figure of the new British cinema of the decade. Tall, rangy and without the conventional looks of a film leading man, he filmed steadily throughout the 60s and 70s. He was a memorable figure as mean-spirited Blifil in *Tom Jones* (1963), Konstantin in *The Sea Gull* and Lysander in *A Midsummer Night's Dream* (1968), and the village idiot in *Straw Dogs* (1971). He is too severe and brusque as Torvald in LOSEY's *A Doll's House* (1973, UK/Fr) to make one believe Nora would ever have married him, and he settled into character roles, often menacing like JACK THE

RIPPER in *Time After Time* (1979, US), shortly after, his British films sparsely scattered among masses of TV (e.g. *The Choir*, 1995) and international films, including *Titanic* (1997). He made news in 2002 when, after 30 years, he returned to the stage in *Feast of Snails* (2002).

OTHER BRITISH FILMS: *We Joined the Navy* (1962), *The King's Breakfast* (short) (1963), *A King's Story* (1965, voice), *The Deadly Affair* (1966), *Work Is a Four Letter Word* (1967), *The Bofors Gun* (1968), *Perfect Friday* (1970), *From Beyond the Grave* (1973), *Little Malcolm . . .* , *Mister Quilp* (1974), *Cross of Iron* (UK/Ger), *Age of Innocence* (UK/Can), *The Disappearance* (UK/Can), *Silver Bears* (UK/US) (1977), *The Thirty Nine Steps* (1978), *The French Lieutenant's Woman* (1981), *The Company of Wolves*, *A Christmas Carol* (1984), *The Leading Man* (1996), *Superstition* (2001, UK/Neth/Lux).

Warner, Deborah (*b* 1959). Director. Acclaimed theatre director, with the RSC from 1987, followed by experience with the National and Dublin's Abbey Theatre and with directing opera, Warner made her feature film debut with *The Last September* (2000, UK/Fr/It), from Elizabeth Bowen's novel and a cross between Chekhov and the last days of the Raj, and set in Ireland, 1920. Has also directed for TV and a US short, *The Waste Land* (1995).

Warner, Jack (*b* Bromley, 1896 – *d* London, 1981). RN: Horace John Waters. Actor. Avuncular character actor, usually in sympathetic roles, who represented the average, decent 'man on the Clapham omnibus', who became a film star of the Clement Attlee era (1945–51), often playing policemen and honest, dependable working-class fathers, and British audiences could easily identify with his aspirations. He also had a nice line in film villains, who were all the more shocking because of his image. Warner was in the Royal Flying Corps in WW1, and from the 20s in variety as a comedian, delivering comic monologues – his sisters were variety performers Elsie and Doris WATERS. His film debut was in a variety theatre mystery, *The Dummy Talks* (1943), and he soon became an EALING regular, with good roles in *Hue and Cry* (1946), as leader of a gang of crooks, and in *Against the Wind* (1947), as the traitor shot dead by the French resistance heroine. One of his best villains was as a hardened escaped convict chained to young George COLE in *My Brother's Keeper* (1948).

But he will always be remembered for two roles. First was London bus driver Joe Huggett, representative of the steady, reliable working man, on a family holiday at *Holiday Camp* (1947), in which Warner and Kathleen HARRISON, described by one critic as 'South London's answer to Ma and Pa Kettle', captured the spirit of post-war Labour Britain – 'making do' and generally promoting the wartime egalitarian spirit in peacetime. Three more HUGGETT FILMS followed, as well as a longrunning 50s radio series on the BBC Light programme, all presenting an idealised version of working-class family life. Second, in *The Blue Lamp* (1949), Warner played the fatally heroic PC George Dixon, a character so popular that he was revived by Ted WILLIS for BBC television in *Dixon of Dock Green* (1955–76). It presented a reassuring, nostalgic world where young thugs see the error of their ways after a homily from fatherly PC Dixon, who matured into the oldest serving constable in the country. In *The Ladykillers* (1955), he was at the police station desk again, reassuring little old Katie JOHNSON. But for most of the 50s, he was in supporting roles, often in domestic settings, as in *Home and Away* (1956), which repeated the Huggett formula. His last starring role (following TV popularity as Dixon) was as the police inspector in *Jigsaw* (1962).

Awarded OBE, 1965.

OTHER BRITISH FILMS: *The Captive Heart* (1946), *It Always Rains on Sunday, Dear Murderer* (1947), *Easy Money, Here Come the Huggetts, Vote for Huggett* (1948), *Train of Events, The Huggetts Abroad, Boys in Brown* (1949), *Talk of a Million, Valley of Eagles, Scrooge* (1951), *Emergency Call, Meet Me Tonight, Those People Next Door* (1952), *Albert RN, The Final Test, The Square Ring, Bang! You're Dead* (1953), *Forbidden Cargo* (1954), *The Quatermass Experiment, Now and Forever* (1955), *Carve Her Name With Pride* (1958), *Dominique* (1978).

BIBLIOG: Jack Warner, *Jack of All Trades: An Autobiography*, 1975. Roger Philip Mellor.

Warner, John (*b* George, South Africa, 1924 – *d* Canterbury, 2001). Actor. In supporting roles since *The Cruel Sea* (1952), on stage and TV. Made his name as the youthful singing lead in the charming stage musical, *Salad Days* (1954) which ran for five years.

OTHER BRITISH FILMS INCLUDE: *The Captain's Table* (1958), *Isadora* (1968), *Sunday Bloody Sunday* (1971), *Sweet Virgin* (1974), *Little Dorrit* (1987), *Without a Clue* (1988, UK/US).

Warren, Betty (*b* Fareham, 1907 – *d* Yeovil, 1990). Actress. RN: Babette Hilda Hogan. On stage from childhood and in London from 1925, Warren was a warm, engaging presence in a few films, mainly in the 40s. Her best film roles are for EALING, as MUSIC HALL star, Bessie Bellwood, in *Champagne Charlie* (1944) and as storekeeper Stanley HOLLOWAY's wife in *Passport to Pimlico* (1949), in which her good-humoured, down-to-earth presence make a serious contribution to the tone of the films. In *Secret Mission* (1942), on the other hand, she seems more like the mother than the wife of cockney Michael WILDING. Her stage roles were mainly in musicals.

OTHER BRITISH FILMS: *The Farmer's Wife* (1941), *Variety Jubilee* (1943), *They Met in the Dark* (1943), *The Magic Bow* (1946), *So Long at the Fair* (1950), *Tread Softly Stranger* (1958).

Warren, C(harles) Denier (*b* Chicago, Illinois, 1889 – *d* Torquay, 1971). Actor. American-born actor long in Britain, he came from a family of variety performers and was on stage from 1897, had a stint in music-publishing in Paris, and returned to the London stage in 1912, thereafter appearing in Shakespeare, Shaw, panto and musical comedy – as well as about 80 films. Busiest in film in the 30s, appearing in about 50 films, in substantial supporting roles, like those of Colonel D'Alvarez in *Heat Wave* (1935) and the Minister of Education in *Good Morning, Boys!* (1937), often in support of comedians, including George FORMBY and Arthur LUCAN, and still active in the 60s, when he played a hotel assistant manager in *Lolita* (1961). Frequently cast as bibulous Americans despite his long residence in Britain, his chubby, balding presence was a fixture in British films for a decade.

OTHER BRITISH FILMS INCLUDE: *Let Me Explain, Dear* (1932), *Counsel's Opinion* (1933), *The Clairvoyant, Be Careful, A Fire Has Been Arranged, Charing Cross Road, Birds of a Feather* (1935), *The Beloved Vagabond, It's In the Bag* (1936), *Who Killed John Savage?, Keep Fit* (1937), *The Divorce of Lady X, Strange Boarders, Old Mother Riley in Paris* (1938), *Trouble Brewing* (1939), *The Shipbuilders* (1943), *Twilight Hour* (1944), *Night and the City* (UK/US) (1950), *Is Your Honeymoon Really Necessary?* (1953), *Bluebeard's Ten Honeymoons* (1960), *The Adding Machine* (1969).

Warren, Kenneth J. (*b* Parramatta, Australia, 1929 – *d* Effingham, 1973). Actor. Came to Britain with the breakthrough Australian play, *The Summer of the Seventeenth Doll* (1959), and stayed to appear in several dozen films, mostly in tough parts, with the usual quota of policemen who gained authority from his burly, balding presence. Also played his share of thugs in the likes of *The Criminal* (1960) and *The Frightened City* (1961) and did time in several HORROR movies, including one of his last, *The Creeping Flesh* (1972).

OTHER BRITISH FILMS INCLUDE: *I Was Monty's Double* (1958), *The Siege of Pinchgut* (1959), *Doctor Blood's Coffin* (1960), *On the Fiddle* (1961), *Life for Ruth* (1962), *A High Wind in Jamaica* (1965), *Leo the Last* (1969), *The Revolutionary* (1970), *Demons of the Mind* (1971).

Warrender, Harold (*b* London, 1903 – *d* Gerrards Cross, 1953). Actor. Imposingly tall, dignified lead and second lead of 20-odd films from the early 30s to the early 50s. He became more interesting in middle age, playing for instance the rakish count in *Warning to Wantons* (1948), the philosophical Wilson in *Scott of the Antarctic* (1948) and an unscrupulous ivory hunter in *Where No Vultures Fly* (1951). Went on stage directly from Cambridge, served in the Royal Navy (1940–45), and was an early Peter Wimsey on TV in *Busman's Honeymoon* (1940).

OTHER BRITISH FILMS INCLUDE: *I Spy* (1933), *Lazybones, Mimi* (1935), *Convoy, Contraband* (1940), *Under the Frozen Falls* (1948), *Conspirator* (1949), *Pandora and the Flying Dutchman* (1950), *Ivanhoe* (1952), *Intimate Relations* (1953).

Warrington, Kenneth Actor. Supporting player of the 30s and 40s, with a long stage career. From Norma VARDEN's untrustworthy shipping-line partner in *Windbag the Sailor* (1936) to Major Wrigley in the once-controversial 'flapper' sequence of *Elizabeth of Ladymead* (1948), he appeared in about 15 films.

OTHER BRITISH FILMS INCLUDE: *Strange Cargo* (1936), *The Spy in Black* (1939), *Old Mother Riley at Home* (1945), *Appointment with Crime* (1946), *The Courtneys of Curzon Street* (1947), *Bonnie Prince Charlie* (1948).

wartime newsreel and documentary film-making British officials are traditionally cautious in their attitude to front-line filming because of concerns about security and the effects on domestic morale of images of death or disaster. Lord Kitchener's ban at the outbreak of the Great War has been echoed by efforts to control the media in more recent conflicts. Acknowledgement of the public's 'right to know' and appetite for images has, however, always obliged the authorities to permit some coverage. In 1915, the War Office appointed its first 'official cinematographers' and later took over a newsreel – TOPICAL BUDGET – as an outlet for their film. In WW2, specially trained cameramen of the ARMY FILM UNIT and RAF FILM PRODUCTION UNIT, and NEWSREEL cameramen accredited as war correspondents, filmed combat and other scenes, restricted only by the limitations of their cameras. After military censorship, their material was released to the newsreels and edited into records of the war in progress – a tradition established in 1916 with the world's first feature-length battle DOCUMENTARY, *The Battle of the Somme*, and continued a generation later with such films as the Academy Award-winners *Desert Victory* (1943) and *The True Glory* (1945). While these films include scenes specially shot for the camera, such material is exceptional. Cameramen identified closely with the units they accompanied and the cause for which they fought, and knew what was appropriate to film. In WW2, 25 AFU cameramen were killed in action, and others were severely wounded. Roger Smither.

See also **documentary film in Britain**.

Warwick Films Warwick Films, the partnership between the abrasive Irving ALLEN and the more emollient Albert 'Cubby' BROCCOLI, was formed in 1952. Allen, an editor and latterly

director in Hollywood, and Broccoli, a go-between for the Famous Artists Agency, decided to go into partnership based on a good knowledge of the industry and a shrewd judgement that independent production was a cost-effective option if based in Britain where overheads were considerably lower and where successful films benefited from the EADY LEVY. Warwick's launch film was *The Red Beret* (1953), starring Alan Ladd, also the lead in *Hell Below Zero* (1953) and *The Black Knight* (1954). These three films characterise Warwick's oeuvre, with variations on the male ACTION-ADVENTURE formula, be it war, contemporary THRILLER or COSTUME DRAMA. The casting of a Hollywood lead was also part of the Warwick package, as was the use of colour, spectacle and exotic locations. Warwick was the first independent company to shoot in CinemaScope, beginning with *Cockleshell Heroes* (1955), another WAR FILM. Warwick's films were carefully tailored to an international market – its deal with COLUMBIA ensured world-wide distribution – with straightforward plots that required frequent displays of taciturn male strength and courage, and a strong romantic interest. This simple formula, energetically pursued, in three years made Warwick the largest and most successful independent production company in Europe.

Though lauded in the trade press, Warwick's films were consistently attacked by the critics as cuckoos in the nest. Indeed, British actors are cast in supporting roles or as villains, including Roland CULVER's braggart aristocrat in *Safari* (1956), a typical jungle adventure starring Victor MATURE. Mature also starred as a tribal chieftain in *Zarak* (1956) and *The Bandit of Zhobe* (1959), more than a match for the dull-witted British officers who oppose him.

Warwick experienced a dip in fortune after the expensive failure of *Fire Down Below* (1957), which Allen judged 'too arty', trimmed its operations and also produced several more modestly budgeted films, including *Odongo* (1956), scripted and cast in five weeks in order to be shot using the same locations as *Safari*. Warwick's final film, Ken HUGHES's *The Trials of Oscar Wilde* (1960), is perhaps the best, a serious BIOPIC with Peter FINCH giving one of his best performances as WILDE. But by then Broccoli and Allen had gone their separate ways: Allen clung to the shards of the Warwick formula with *The Long Ships* (1963) and Broccoli entered into another, more lasting and lucrative partnership, with Harry SALTZMAN as EON Films, the home of James BOND.

Though its films were formulaic and often two-dimensional, Warwick's international action pictures can now be seen to presage the type of film that was to dominate the screens in the following two decades.

BIBLIOG: Cubby Broccoli (with Donald Zec), *When the Snow Melts: The Autobiography of Cubby Broccoli*, 1998. Andrew Spicer.

Warwick, John (*b* Bellengen River, Australia, 1905 – *d* Sydney, 1972). Actor. RN: Beattle. Warwick's career was bookended by Australian films in the 30s, including quite high-profile features such as *The Silence of Dean Maitland* (1935), and again in the early 70s. In between, he brought his stern features to bear on many crooks and policemen (mostly the latter as he aged) in about 50 British films, both main features like *Street Corner* (1953) and 'B' MOVIES like *The Desperate Man* (1959), playing police inspectors in both.

OTHER BRITISH FILMS: *Find the Lady* (1936), *A Yank at Oxford, 21 Days* (1937), *This Man is News* (1938), *The Saint's Vacation* (1941), *The Day Will Dawn* (1942), *Woman to Woman* (1946), *Dancing with Crime* (1947), *The Franchise Affair* (1950), *The Lavender Hill Mob* (1951),

Trouble in Store, Bang! You're Dead (1953), *Up to His Neck* (1954), *The Long Arm* (1956), *Just My Luck* (1957), *The Square Peg, Law and Disorder* (1958), *Go to Blazes* (1962).

Warwick, Richard (*b* Longfield, 1945 – *d* London, 1997). Actor. RN: Winter. Good-looking juvenile who developed into a rugged character actor. His first screen role as gay schoolboy Wallace in *If . . .* (1968) paved the way for a career dominated by gay roles – notably Justin in Derek JARMAN's *Sebastiane* (1976) and TV's *The Lost Language of Cranes* (1991) – and work for gay directors, such as Franco ZEFFIRELLI: *Romeo and Juliet* (1968, UK/It), *Hamlet* (1990) and *Jane Eyre* (1996, UK/Fr/It/US). Starring in Andrew SINCLAIR's *The Breaking of Bumbo* (1970) failed to make him a star, but he was outstanding in a TV production of *The Vortex* (1971). Not to be confused with American actor of same name. Died of AIDS.

OTHER BRITISH FILMS: *The Bed Sitting Room* (1969), *Nicholas and Alexandra* (1971, UK/US), *International Velvet* (1978), *The Tempest* (1979), *White Hunter, Black Heart* (1990). AS.

Warwick Trading Company Founded by American Charles URBAN in 1898 out of the Edison agency Maguire & Baucus, and named after Warwick Court in London, where its offices were located. Warwick was a major early distributor of films from the LUMIÈRE Brothers, Georges Méliès, James WILLIAMSON and G.A. SMITH, and a producer of ACTUALITY and travel films from around the world, taken by Joseph ROSENTHAL, Edgar M. Hyman, Sydney Goldman, Jack Avery, and others. Of considerable importance to the young British film industry, Warwick lost influence on Urban's departure in 1903, but regained some of its authority when Will BARKER took over as manager in 1906. Warwick was subsequently purchased by Cherry KEARTON, but ceased trading in 1915. AS.

Washbourne, Mona (*b* Birmingham, 1903 – *d* London, 1988). Actress. Washbourne was a trained pianist long before becoming one of British screen's great CHARACTER PLAYERS. She was in concert parties from 1924 and on the London stage from 1937; she played the gushing journalist more interested in curtains than justice in *The Winslow Boy* (1946), reprising this role as her entrée to films (1948). She never looked back and appeared in about 50, often in small vivid cameos, but when given the scope showed what she could do. Think of Dirk BOGARDE's doting, older wife, murdered for her money, in *Cast a Dark Shadow* (1955), of the hero's homely mother and her sophisticated fantasy counterpart in *Billy Liar* (1963), of firm-minded Mrs Pearce in *My Fair Lady* (1964, US), or of the rich old harridan in danger from Albert FINNEY in *Night Must Fall* (1964), a film which failed but in which she made something tough, poignant and real of her character. She simply got better with age, as the chamber piece, *Stevie* (1978), attests: she makes of Stevie Smith's 'lion aunt of Hull' one of the most memorable figures in 70s British film. As well, there was a good deal of TV, including a transfer of her 1970 stage success in David Storey's *Home* (1971). Married Basil DIGNAM.

OTHER BRITISH FILMS: *Once Upon a Dream, Maytime in Mayfair* (1949), *Double Confession, Dark Interval* (1950), *The Gambler and the Lady* (1952), *Johnny on the Run, The Million Pound Note* (1953), *Child's Play, To Dorothy a Son, Star of My Night, Doctor in the House, Adventure in the Hopfields* (1954), *The Yellow Robe, Lost, John and Julie, A Count of Twelve, Alias John Preston* (1955), *Yield to the Night, Loser Takes All, It's Great to Be Young!, Circus Friends, The Good Companions* (1956), *Stranger in Town, Son of a Stranger* (1957), *A Cry from the Streets* (1958), *The Brides of Dracula* (1960), *Ferry Cross the Mersey, One Way Pendulum* (1964), *The Collector* (1965, UK/US), *Casino Royale, Two a Penny* (1967), *Mrs Brown, You've Got a Lovely Daughter, If . . .* (1968), *The Bed Sitting*

Room, The Games (1969), *Fragment of Fear* (1970), *What Became of Jack and Jill?* (1972), *O Lucky Man!* (1973), *Mister Quilp* (1974), *The London Connection* (1979).

Washington, Denzel (*b* Mount Vernon, NY, 1954). Actor. Charismatic US star, twice-Oscared (1989, 2002) and nominated four more times, Washington has appeared only three times in British films, but to striking effect in *Cry Freedom* (1987), receiving an AAn for playing anti-apartheid activist Steve Biko. Also in *For Queen and Country* (1988, UK/US), a film spoiled in post-production, and in the co-production *Mississippi Masala* (1991, UK/US).

Wason, Wendy (*b* South Africa, 1973). Actress. Educated at Glasgow University, trained at the London Method Studio, she had a juicy role as a cocaine dealer who sets out to break up a marriage in *The Truth Game* (2001).

OTHER BRITISH FILMS: *Magic Moments* (1997), *Club Le Monde* (2002).

Waterhouse, Keith (*b* Hunslet, 1929). Screenwriter. Humorist, columnist, playwright and novelist, Waterhouse's bittersweet satires of the bleakness of north country life and the fragile sanctuary of the imagination, laid the foundations for a career as a much- loved polemicist, whose blunt forthrightness rarely impeded the subtlety of his social commentary. His credits are mostly shared with Willis HALL, with whom he created the blueprints for several key films of the NEW WAVE of the early 60s, including *A Kind of Loving* (1962) and *Billy Liar* (1963, based on his novel and stage play; a TV series followed, 1973–74), for both of which they were BAA-nominated. Both evoke northern life, but not without their share of well-grounded comedy. Also wrote a great deal of TV, including the series, *Queenie's Castle* (1970–72) and *Budgie* (1971–72), with Hall, and the telemovie, *Charlie Muffin* (1983).

OTHER BRITISH FILMS INCLUDE: (co-sc) *Whistle Down the Wind* (1961, BAAn/sc), *The Valiant* (1961), *West 11* (1963), *Man in the Middle* (1963), *Pretty Polly* 1967, *Lock Up Your Daughters!* (1969). Kevin Foster.

Waterman, Dennis (*b* London, 1948). Actor. Former boy actor, who starred in two highly successful TV series, and occasional films from 1959. His adult roles often reflected his Clapham background – street-wise, living by his wits – although trained at Corona Stage School to be polite. Made adult debut as a working-class malcontent cruising Battersea in his VW van in *Up the Junction* (1967), but became famous as bellicose assistant to John THAW's Jack Regan, in *The Sweeney* (TV, 1974–78), and was in two SPIN-OFF movies – *Sweeney!* (1976) and *Sweeney 2* (1978). This was followed by the equally popular *Minder* (1979–89), an inspired partnership with George COLE, and he was at his best as second-fiddle in these series. Also on stage, he acted with the RSC and played in musicals, including the National's *My Fair Lady* (2000). Married/divorced Rula LENSKA.

OTHER BRITISH FILMS INCLUDE: *Snowball* (1960), *Crooks Anonymous* (1962), *My Lover, My Son* (US/UK), *The Scars of Dracula* (1970), *Fright* (1971), *The Belstone Fox* (1973).

BIBLIOG: Dennis Waterman (with Jill Arlon), *Reminder*, 2000. Roger Philip Mellor.

Waters, Doris (*b* London, 1904 – *d* London, 1978) and **Elsie** (*b* London, 1894 – *d* Steyning, 1990). Actresses. Fondly regarded MUSIC HALL and RADIO stars who appeared in two VARIETY films, *Radio Parade* (1933) and *It's in the Bag* (1943), and in two rough-and-ready, demotically conceived wartime comedies, *Gert and Daisy's Weekend* (1941) and *Gert and Daisy Clean Up*

(1942), as the resourceful Cockney pair of the titles. Had a short-lived TV series, *Gert and Daisy* (1959). Sisters of Jack WARNER.

Waters, Russell (*b* Glasgow, 1908 – *d* 1982). Actor. Educated at Glasgow University, Waters, on stage from 1932, began his film career in the 30s, appearing in DOCUMENTARIES for Richard MASSINGHAM, including *Tell Me If It Hurts* (1934, doc) and *Daily Round* (1937, doc). After WW2 service, he returned to films, playing about six dozen clerks, teachers and police officers. Perhaps because he almost always played variations on a mild persona, typically exhibited as a Ministry man in *The Happiest Days of Your Life* (1950), he is less well remembered than other equally prolific CHARACTER ACTORS, such as fellow Scot, Wylie WATSON. Always on hand for Scottish-set numbers like *The 'Maggie'* (1953). Son is John Waters, star of Australian films.

OTHER BRITISH FILMS INCLUDE: *And So to Work* (1936, short), *Let George Do It!* (1940), *The Woman in the Hall* (1947), *Obsession* (1949), *State Secret, The Wooden Horse* (1950), *Lady Godiva Rides Again* (1951), *The Brave Don't Cry* (1952), *Street Corner* (1953), *The Young Lovers* (1954), *The Man in the Sky* (1956), *A Night to Remember, The Key* (1958), *Heavens Above!* (1963), *The Heroes of Telemark* (1965), *The Devil Rides Out* (1967), *Kidnapped* (1971), *The Wicker Man* (1973).

Waterston, Sam (*b* Cambridge, Massachusetts, 1940). Actor. Much-respected actor rather than a star, Waterston has projected a quietly alert, morally rigorous persona in a wide range of films, most of them of anything but British origin. However, he was AA- and BAA-nominated for his role as the journalist with a conscience, at large in *The Killing Fields* (1984), and was very striking as Indian White Bull in *Eagle's Wing* (1978).

OTHER BRITISH FILMS: *Three* (1969), *Sweet William* (1979), *The Proprieter* (1996, UK/Fr/Turk/US).

Watford, Gwen (*b* London, 1927 – *d* London, 1994). Actress. Character player who latterly specialised in rather hearty matrons like Miss Marple's friend Dolly Bantry in the TV series, including *The Mirror Crack'd* (1992). On London stage from 1945 and in films from 1949, perhaps buried alive in *The Fall of the House of Usher*, she had the lead in the child-molestation drama, *Never Take Sweets from a Stranger* (1960), and played Penelope WILTON's mother in *Cry Freedom* (1987), but was mostly on stage, both in London and in rep, and on TV. Married Richard BEBB.

OTHER BRITISH FILMS INCLUDE: *The Very Edge* (1962), *Taste the Blood of Dracula* (1969), *The Ghoul* (1975).

Watkin, David (*b* Margate, 1925). Cinematographer. AA-winner for *Out of Africa* (1985) and BAA-nominated eight times for both US (e.g. *Catch-22*, 1970) and UK films (e.g. *Chariots of Fire*, 1981), Watkin came to the fore in the 60s as cinematographer for Richard LESTER and Ken RUSSELL, and has been busy ever since. As one watches the staid pictorialism of *Tea with Mussolini* (1999, UK/It), it is hard to remember the black-and-white vivacity of *The Knack . . .* (1965) or the elegiac period glow of *Robin and Marian* (1976).

OTHER BRITISH FILMS INCLUDE: *Men on the Mend* (1956, co-c, doc), *The Six-Sided Triangle* (1963), *Help!* (1965), *How I Won the War* (1967), *The Charge of the Light Brigade* (1968), *The Bed Sitting Room* (1969), *The Devils, The Boy Friend* (1971), *The Homecoming* (UK/US), *A Delicate Balance* (UK/Can/US) (1973), *Joseph Andrews* (1976), *Yentl* (1983, UK/US), *Memphis Belle* (1990), *Jane Eyre* (1996, UK/It/Fr/US), *All Forgotten* (2000, UK/US).

Watkins, A(lfred) W(ilfred) (*b* Kidderminster, 1895 – *d* Stoke Poges, 1970). Music recordist. In the industry from 1928, he became sound director for LONDON FILMS from its incorporation in 1932, one of only three Britishers in charge of his department there, and stayed at DENHAM until 1947, his name appearing on some of the most prestigious films ever made in England. He then became recording director for MGM–BRITISH films, supervising the sound of such films as *Knights of the Round Table* (1953), for which he was AA-nominated, as he also was for *Goodbye, Mr Chips* (1939) and *Libel* (1959). His prolificacy was rivalled only by certain British character players.

OTHER BRITISH FILMS INCLUDE: (sd/sd d/recording d/recording super) *The Sport of Kings* (1931), *The Private Life of Henry VIII* (1933), *Catherine the Great* (1934), *The Scarlet Pimpernel, Sanders of the River, The Ghost Goes West* (1935), *Things to Come, Rembrandt* (1936), *Knight Without Armour, Fire Over England* (1937), *The Drum, South Riding, The Citadel* (1938), *The Four Feathers* (1939), *Contraband, The Thief of Baghdad* (1940), *49th Parallel* (1941), *One of Our Aircraft is Missing* (1942), *The Gentle Sex* (1943), *Perfect Strangers* (1945), *Edward, My Son* (1949), *The Miniver Story* (1950), *Ivanhoe* (1952), *Beau Brummell* (1954), *The Adventures of Quentin Durward* (1955), *tom thumb* (1958), *Village of the Damned* (1960), *I Thank a Fool* (1962), *Murder at the Gallop* (1963), *The Chalk Garden* (1964), *The Hill* (1965), *2001: A Space Odyssey* (1968).

Watkins, Arthur (aka Watkyn, Arthur) (*b* Aberystwyth, 1907 – *d* London, 1965). Dramatist, censor. A former civil servant on the staff of the Home Office (1941–47), Watkins joined the Board of Film Censors in 1948 and was its second secretary until 1957. Described by John TREVELYAN, the next-but-one incumbent, as 'a remarkably brilliant man who in his nine years of office revolutionised the Board' (1973), paving the way for Trevelyan's still more far-reaching reforms of British CENSORSHIP. Watkins made a point of visiting the film studios to gain a better working knowledge of the medium of his concern. Tonbridge- and Oxford-educated, he was also (as Watkyn) the author of plays for radio and stage; two staged in 1952, *For Better, for Worse* and *The Moonraker* were filmed in, respectively, 1954 and 1957.

Watkins, Peter (*b* Norbiton, 1935). Director. Few film careers have been as dramatic as that of Peter Watkins. Recruited from the amateur cine-world in the early 60s, he directed two seminal films for BBC TV which made striking use of a vérité DOCUMENTARY style to reconstruct factual events in power-fully dramatic ways. Yet whilst *Culloden* (1964) – re-enacting the famous Scottish battle – was heaped with critical praise, *The War Game* (1966) – Watkins's carefully researched prediction of the horrors of nuclear war – was sensationally banned from TV for 20 years, despite winning a 1967 Oscar (Best DOCUMENTARY Feature). Disgusted at what he saw as complicity with Government in banning the film, Watkins resigned from the BBC and in 1968 quit Britain for good. Since then, he has carved out perhaps the most internationalist career of any British film-maker, living and working, often under great difficulty, as politically radical director and media theorist in cultures as diverse as the US, Scandinavia, Australasia and Lithuania. Key international films include *Punishment Park* (1971, US), *Edvard Munch* (1973, Nor/Swe), *The Journey* (1988, Swe/Can). In 1999, Watkins directed a long-planned recon-struction of the 1871 Paris Commune, collaborating with over 200 French citizens as amateur actors. *La Commune de Paris* (1999) was screened at the 2000 London Film Festival – a belated return from the cold, perhaps, for British film-making's most challenging and uncompromising 'exile'.

OTHER BRITISH FILMS: (shorts) *The* Web (1956), *The Diary of an Unknown Soldier* (1959), *Dust Fever* (1961); (feature) *Privilege* (1967). John Cook.

Watling, Jack (*b* Chingford, 1923 – *d* Chelmsford, 2001). Actor. Perennially youthful-looking actor, often conveying an air of good-natured ineffectuality as he did in the role of the frivolous older brother of *The Winslow Boy* or the young tennis player who ignores his father's advice in the 'Facts of Life' episode of *Quartet* (both 1948). On stage from 1935, he had his favourite role in Terence RATTIGAN's *Flare Path* (1942), then did RAF service in WW2 (1943–46), starring in the RAF FILM UNIT feature, *Journey Together* (1945). He starred in such '**B**' FILMS as *Private Information* (1952), but was generally better served with solid supporting roles in main features, usually cast as one of nature's second lieutenants, but once or twice allowed to suggest something more reprehensible, like the feckless playboy doctor in *White Corridors* (1951) or Tony BRITTON's untrustworthy chum in *The Birthday Present* (1957). Also, a good deal of TV, including *The Power Game* (1965–66) and *The Pathfinders* (1972–73); on stage, he was always going to mature into, not Higgins but Pickering, as he did in the 1984 revival of *Pygmalion*. Was married to **Patricia Hicks**, who appeared in a couple of British films in the later 40s; three of his children, Dilys, Deborah and Giles, are actors.

OTHER BRITISH FILMS INCLUDE: *Sixty Glorious Years* (1938), *We Dive at Dawn*, *The Demi-Paradise* (1943), *The Courtneys of Curzon Street* (1947), *Under Capricorn* (1949), *Father's Doing Fine* (1952), *Meet Mr Lucifer* (1953), *The Sea Shall Not Have Them*, *Dangerous Cargo* (1954), *Windfall* (1955), *The Admirable Crichton* (1957), *A Night to Remember* (1958), *Sink the Bismarck!* (1960), *Mary Had a Little . . .* (1961), *Flat Two* (1962), *The Nanny* (1965), *Follow Me!* (1971), *11 Harrowhouse* (1974).

Watson, Cavan (aka Caven) (*b* Glasgow, 1903 – *d* Northolt, 1953). Actor. Scots character player of friendly mien who was on the stage for many years before playing supporting roles in about 15 films, starting with *Goodbye, Mr Chips* (1939). During WW2, he was in several MOI films, including *Welcome to Britain* (1943).

OTHER BRITISH FILMS INCLUDE: *In Which We Serve* (1942), *The Shipbuilders*, *San Demetrio–London* (1943), *The Way to the Stars* (1945), *Wanted for Murder* (1946), *The October Man* (1947), *Bonnie Prince Charlie* (1948), *The Sword and the Rose* (1953).

Watson, Emily (*b* London, 1967). Actress. Strikingly talented star of films since the mid 90s when she was AA- and BAA-nominated for her debut role as the sexually obsessed heroine of Lars von Trier's *Breaking the Waves* (1996, Den/Fr/Neth/Nor/Swe), and followed this with equally eye-catching work in *The Boxer* (1998, UK/Ire/US) and, especially, as gifted, wayward Jacqueline du Pré (again AAn, BAAn) in *Hilary and Jackie* (1998). Her unconventional, rather grave beauty made her an ideal Maggie Tulliver in the telemovie of *The Mill on the Floss* (1997) and she fashioned an enigmatically real character of the head housemaid in *Gosford Park* (2001, UK/Ger/US). In the artificiality of *Angela's Ashes* (1999, UK/US), she strikes no false note as the much-tried, poverty-stricken mother, and has filmed several times in the US. Trained at the Drama Studio, has acted with the RSC and the National Theatre. Married to actor **Jack Waters**, who appeared in *The Boxer*.

OTHER BRITISH FILMS: *Metroland* (1997, UK/Fr/Sp), *The Luzhin Defence* (2000, UK/Fr), *In Search of the Assassin* (2001).

Watson, Jack (*b* Thorney, 1915 – *d* Bath, 1999). Actor. 'Craggy' and 'rugged' are probably the two epithets most used to describe tall, burly character player Watson, born to theatrical parents. First appeared on stage at 16 with his father and in TV from 1938, was in the Royal Navy during WW2, and made his film debut in *Captain Horatio Hornblower RN* (1950, UK/US). Did masses of TV, notably as adulterer Bill Gregory in *Coronation Street* over 20 years (1962–84), with some gaps along the way, and in *Edge of Darkness* (1985). In the cinema, he was first noticed as the investigating police inspector in *Peeping Tom* (1960), was one of Richard HARRIS's football mates in *This Sporting Life* (1963) and stroppy POW Jock McGrath in *The Hill* (1965). Most often in action films, including such US titles as *Tobruk* (1967), he invested whatever he did with effortless authority.

OTHER BRITISH FILMS INCLUDE: *Konga* (1960), *The Queen's Guards* (1961), *On the Beat* (1962), *The Gorgon* (1964), *The Idol* (1966), *The Strange Affair* (1968), *The McKenzie Break* (1970), *Kidnapped* (1971), *From Beyond the Grave* (1973), *Juggernaut* (1974), *Brannigan* (1975), *Schizo* (1976), *The Wild Geese* (1978, UK/Switz), *North Sea Hijack* (1979).

Watson, Moray (*b* Sunningdale, 1928). Actor. Like father-in-law Percy MARMONT, Watson plays the typical English gentleman, and has been a busy actor on stage since 1955 and given some memorable television performances in *The Quatermass Experiment* (1953), *Compact* (1962–63) and *Rumpole of the Bailey* (1978–79). Film work has been sporadic, but does include *The Grass Is Greener* (1961), in which he reprises his 1958 stage role. Married Patricia MARMONT.

OTHER BRITISH FILMS INCLUDE: *Find the Lady* (1956), *The Valiant* (1961), *Operation Crossbow* (1965, UK/It), *The Sea Wolves* (1980, UK/Switz/US), *Still Crazy Like a Fox* (1987). AS.

Watson, Tom (*b* Auchinleck, Scotland – *d* St Andrews, Scotland, 2001). Actor. Long established TV actor (he was Supt. Murray in *Killer*, 1983, the lead-in to *Taggart*), Watson stepped up film appearances in the 90s, mainly in Scottish-set items like *The Big Man* (1990) and *The Slab Boys* (1997).

OTHER BRITISH FILMS INCLUDE: *Fahrenheit 451* (1966), *Nosey Dobson* (1976), *Another Time, Another Place* (1983), *Silent Scream* (1990), *Go Now*, *The Winter Guest* (UK/US) (1998), *The Emperor's New Clothes* (2002, UK/Ger/It).

Watson, Wylie (*b* Scotland, 1889 – *d* Scotland, 1966). Actor. RN: John Wylie Robertson. A versatile supporting player, Watson is best remembered for a performance from near the beginning of his film career, that of Mr Memory in Alfred HITCHCOCK's *The 39 Steps* (1935). Here he managed to invest a small role with considerable pathos, so that, when a dying Mr Memory finally recites the secret plans he has been hired to memorize and then asks 'Am I right, sir?', it is a genuinely moving moment. Later roles were less distinctive, but his repentant thief in *Tawny Pipit* (1944) and his down-at-heel gangster in *Brighton Rock* (1947) are worthy of mention.

OTHER BRITISH FILMS INCLUDE: *For the Love of Mike* (1932), *Road House* (1934), *Black Mask* (1935), *Queer Cargo, Yes Madam?* (1938), *Jamaica Inn* (1939), *Pack Up Your Troubles* (1940), *Danny Boy* (1941), *The Lamp Still Burns* (1943), *Waterloo Road* (1944), *Murder in Reverse*, *The World Owes Me a Living*, *The Trojan Brothers* (1945), *Fame Is the Spur*, *Temptation Harbour* (1947), *London Belongs to Me* (1948), *Whisky Galore!* (1949), *Morning Departure* (1950), *Happy Go Lovely* (1951), *The Sundowners* (1960). Peter Hutchings.

Watt, Harry (*b* Edinburgh, 1906 – *d* Amersham, 1987). Director. Worked as director and producer at the EMB, GPO and CROWN FILM UNITS between 1931 and 1942 and was director and script supervisor at EALING STUDIOS, 1942–45. Between 1945 and 1948, he made two films for Ealing in Australia – *The Overlanders* (1946), *Eureka Stockade* (1949).

Was a producer with Granada TV, 1955–56, and from 1956 to 1959 worked again at Ealing as director. Alongside Alberto CAVALCANTI, Watt was responsible for developing the documentary-drama genre of film-making within the DOCUMENTARY FILM MOVEMENT. The key film in this respect was *North Sea* (1938, for GPO), in which Watt and Cavalcanti introduced characterisation and dramatic development into the documentary film. Watt benefited greatly from his association with Cavalcanti and Humphrey JENNINGS; however, his abilities were always circumscribed, and, at Ealing, Michael BALCON marginalised him, sending him off to Australia for extensive periods of time. Most influential documentaries were *North Sea* (1938), *The First Days* (1939), *London Can Take It!* (1940), *Target for Tonight* (1941).

OTHER BRITISH FILMS: (features) *Nine Men* (1942), *Where No Vultures Fly* (1951), *West of Zanzibar* (1954), *The Siege of Pinchgut* (1959).

BIBLIOG: Autobiography, *Don't Look at the Camera*, 1974. Ian Aitken.

Wattis, Richard (*b* Wednesbury, 1912 – *d* London, 1975). Actor. Character player almost always in comedy cameos, with occasional straighter army officer types. On stage from 1935, in *A Yank at Oxford* (1937, unc), from the late 40s, with his round spectacles, owlish look and thinning bald patch, he became a familiar film face expressing horror or outrage, in distinctive superior manner. Playing variations on the same role over a range of toffs and supercilious authority figures, including prep school masters, and prudish/camp rural vicars, he usually had only one brief scene to make an impression, presenting the audience with instantly recognisable, sharply drawn characterisation. In *The Happiest Days of Your Life* (1950) he was a school master in Alastair SIM's boys' preparatory school, and in *The Belles of St Trinian's* (1954) was a stressed education ministry official trying to cope with horrendous schoolgirls. He seemed to pop up in every other British film of the 50s, and cinema audiences tittered with delight every time he appeared on screen.

OTHER BRITISH FILMS INCLUDE: *The Chiltern Hundreds* (1949), *The Clouded Yellow* (1950), *Lady Godiva Rides Again* (1951), *The Importance of Being Earnest*, *Top Secret* (1952), *The Final Test*, *Background*, *Hobson's Choice* (1953), *Doctor in the House*, *Lease of Life* (1954), *See How They Run*, *An Alligator Named Daisy*, *Simon and Laura*, *The Man Who Never Was* (1955), *It's a Wonderful World*, *The Iron Petticoat*, *The Green Man* (1956), *The Prince and the Showgirl*, *Blue Murder at St Trinian's* (1957), *The Captain's Table* (1958), *Left, Right and Centre*, *Follow a Star*, *Libel* (1959), *Follow That Horse!* (1960), *Very Important Person* (1961), *The VIPs* (1963), *Carry On Spying* (1964), *Up Jumped a Swagman*, *Bunny Lake Is Missing*, *The Alphabet Murders* (1965), *The Great St Trinian's Train Robbery* (1966), *Chitty Chitty Bang Bang* (1968), *Monte Carlo or Bust!* (1969, UK/Fr/It), *That's Your Funeral* (1972), *Confessions of a Window Cleaner* (1974). Roger Philip Mellor.

Watts, Dodo (*b* London, 1910 – *d* Teddington, Middlesex, 1990). Actress. Tiny (5′) lead and second lead of about a dozen early sound films, including Walter SUMMERS' well-regarded CRIME THRILLER, *The Man from Chicago* (1930), and, after a long recess, returned as the young widow who finally gets her man in *Sing Along with Me* (1952), the film which failed to launch the screen career of singer Donald PEERS. On stage from age eight, and later played in many theatrical melodramas.

OTHER BRITISH FILMS INCLUDE: *Confessions* (1925), *Auld Lang Syne* (1929), *Almost a Honeymoon* (1930), *Uneasy Virtue* (1931), *Little Fella*, *Impromptu* (1932), *Dora* (1933).

Watts, Gwendolyn Actress. After an amusing film debut as the noisy fiancé of *Billy Liar* (1963), Watts had small roles in a few further films, including three 'CARRY ON' romps, without ever again having such a good comic part.

OTHER BRITISH FILMS INCLUDE: *Fanatic* (1965), *The Wrong Box* (1966), *Carry On Doctor* (1968), . . . *Again Doctor*, *The Games* (1969), *Carry On Matron* (1972).

Watts, Queenie (*b* London, 1923 – *d* London, 1980). Actress. Better known for her TV appearances in series such as *Romany Jones* (1973–75) and its follow-up, *Yus, My Dear* (1976) than for her appearances in films. She had supporting roles in about a dozen films, chiefly comedies like *Steptoe and Son* (1972), and played working-class characters in such dramas as *Poor Cow* (1967). An East End pub landlord and blues singer, she was the subject of *Portrait of Queenie* (1964), a short feature in which, in flashback, she sings to entertain customers.

OTHER BRITISH FILMS INCLUDE: *Sparrows Can't Sing* (1962), *Alfie* (1966), *Up the Junction* (1967), *All Coppers Are . . .* (1971), *Holiday on the Buses*, *Keep It Up, Jack!* (1973), *Schizo* (1976), *Come Play with Me* (1977).

Watts, Stephen (*b* Glasgow, 1910). Author, critic. Maintained a very long career as film critic, starting with *The Bulletin*, Glasgow (1928–32), followed by the London-based *Film Weekly* (1932–24), the *Sunday Express* (1934–39 and 1945–49, with a break for WW2 service), and was London film correspondent for the *New York Times* (1949–59). Author and playwright as well, he was President of the Critics' Circle (1953–54) and Council member for many more years. Also acted as technical adviser on *I Was Monty's Double* (1958). Was married to Margaret FURSE.

Watts, Tom Director. Minor director of a dozen minor films between 1915 and 1920, twice also writing the screenplays: *The Autocrat* and *Father O'Flynn* (1919).

BRITISH FILMS INCLUDE: *The Angel of the Ward*, *Somewhere in France* (1915), *Abide with Me* (1916), *The Call of the Pipes* (1917), *The Toilers* (1919), *A Cigarette Maker's Romance* (1920). AS.

Waugh, Evelyn (*b* London, 1903 – *d* Combe Florey, 1966). Author. Immaculate stylist and penetrating satirist of social England, Waugh has not been much sought after by film-makers. There were prestige-laden TV versions of *Brideshead Revisited* (1948, mini-series 1981), to cavil over which was, in some circles, like swearing in church, *Scoop* (telefilm, 1987), and the intelligently disenchanted *Sword of Honour* (1952–61, mini-series 2001). On screen, Tony RICHARDSON turned the wickedly astute look at US burial habits, *The Loved One* (1948, film 1965, US), into a film with 'something to offend everyone', an advertising tag that proved all too true, including critics and audiences; *Decline and Fall* (1928), one of the wittiest novels of its century, was much coarsened on its way to the screen, a process signalled in its filmed title, *Decline and Fall of a Bird Watcher* (1968); and *A Handful of Dust* (1934, film 1987), truer to Waugh, just wasn't very interesting. Waugh also made satirical amateur films with friends during the 20s, including *The Scarlet Woman*, in which he appeared with Elsa LANCHESTER, and, like many other writers, was briefly (1936–37) contracted to KORDA – to write the script for the unfilmed *Lovelies from America*.

Waxman, Harry (*b* London, 1912 – *d* Chichester, 1984). Cinematographer. In films aged 14 as dark-room assistant, he worked as camera assistant at several studios during the 30s, including MERTON PARK (1934–39) before joining Sydney BOX at RIVERSIDE. Served with the RAF FILM UNIT during WW2 and shot *Journey Together* (1945) for John BOULTING at the Unit. Post-war he worked again for the Boulting brothers, contributing the *noir* sheen to *Brighton Rock* (1947), reinforced the brooding atmosphere of EALING's *The Long Memory* (1952) and the mounting panic of Val GUEST's SCIENCE-FICTION classic, *The Day the Earth Caught Fire* (1961), and, in colour, won a BAA for the evocation of lower-middle-class and black ghetto life in late 50s London in *Sapphire* (1959) and helped to make *The Wicker Man* (1973) one of the most unsettling British films. There is plenty of dross in his long filmography but his reputation was not at risk as a result.

OTHER BRITISH FILMS INCLUDE: *Happy in the Morning* (1938, doc), *Fame is the Spur* (1947, assoc), *To the Public Danger, Trottie True* (1948), *Waterfront, They Were Not Divided* (1950), *The Gift Horse* (1952), *Father Brown, The Sleeping Tiger* (1954), *Lost* (1955), *The Baby and the Battleship* (1956), *Robbery Under Arms* (1957), *Swiss Family Robinson* (UK/US), *Man in the Moon* (1960), *The Roman Spring of Mrs Stone* (1961), *Lancelot and Guinevere* (1962), *She, The Nanny* (1965), *Khartoum* (2uph), *The Family Way* (1966), *The Anniversary* (1967), *Twisted Nerve* (1968), *There's a Girl in My Soup* (1970), *Mr Forbush and the Penguins* (1971), *Endless Night* (1972), *Vampyres* (1974), *The Pink Panther Strikes Again* (1976), *A Bridge Too Far* (1977, 2uc), *Flash Gordon* (1980, add ph).

Way, Ann (*b* Wiveliscombe, 1915). Actress. Tiny character player who appeared in about 20 films from 1954 (*The Belles of St Trinian's*), played further schoolmistresses in *The Prime of Miss Jean Brodie* (1968) and *Twinky* (1969), but was perhaps most memorable as the wife of twitchy colonel, Alan CUTHBERTSON, in an episode of *Fawlty Towers*, constantly trying to emerge under his elbow.

OTHER BRITISH FILMS INCLUDE: *Carry On Loving* (1970), *Hands of the Ripper* (1971), *Jabberwocky* (1977), *The Dresser, Bullshot* (1983), *Brazil, Clockwise* (1985), *The Dawning* (1988), *Anchoress* (1993).

Way, Eileen (*b* New Malden, 1911 – *d* Canterbury, 1994). Actress. Supporting player of the 50s and 60s, in main features such as *Knave of Hearts* (1954) and 'B' MOVIES such as *Blood Orange* (1953), usually in small roles. In later years, much more often on TV (e.g. in *Paradise Postponed*, 1986).

OTHER BRITISH FILMS INCLUDE: *Cheer the Brave* (1951), *The Stranger Left No Card* (1952), *Street of Shadows* (1953), *The Singer Not the Song* (1960), *Village of Daughters* (1962), *The Bargee* (1964), *Drop Dead Darling* (1966), *Memed My Hawk* (1984), *Queen of Hearts* (1989).

Wayne, Naunton (*b* Llanwonno, S. Wales, 1900 – *d* Surbiton, 1970). Actor. RN: Davies. Superb purveyor of civil service aplomb just behind which comic confusions and anxieties are held at bay, and one of a famous pair with Basil RADFORD. The two played quintessential middle-class Englishmen, Charters and Caldicott, created by LAUNDER AND GILLIAT and first seen in *The Lady Vanishes* (1938) where they can contemplate nothing more serious than not getting back to England for the cricket. This pair proved so successful that they appeared in three further films: *Crook's Tour, Night Train to Munich* (1940) and *Millions Like Us* (1943). Also appeared together in different roles in several other films, including *Quartet* (1948), *Passport to Pimlico* (as Whitehall men), *It's Not Cricket* (as incompetent real estate partners) (1949). Radford died in 1952 and Wayne never again had such richly comic material, but he did impeccably what turned up, even rubbish like *Treasure Hunt* (1952), in which he played a sub-EALING version of the outsider succumbing to old-world eccentricities. Educated at Clifton College and on stage from 1920, in concert parties for ten years before debut on London stage where he typically played dapper West End leading men, with a gift for comic timing.

OTHER BRITISH FILMS: *The First Mrs Fraser* (1932), *Going Gay, For Love of You* (1933), *A Girl Must Live* (1939), *The Next of Kin* (1942), *Dead of Night* (1945), *A Girl in a Million* (1946), *Obsession, Stop Press Girl* (1949),

Trio, Highly Dangerous, Double Confession, Circle of Danger (1950), *The Happy Family, Tall Headlines* (1952), *The Titfield Thunderbolt* (1953), *You Know What Sailors Are!* (1954), *Operation Bullshine* (1959), *Nothing Barred, Double Bunk* (1961).

Webb, Alan (*b* York, 1906 – *d* Chichester, 1982). Actor. Former naval officer on stage from 1924, much associated with the plays of Noël COWARD (he was also in the dreadful film of *The Astonished Heart*, 1950), as well as a good deal of SHAKESPEARE and SHAW. Served in the Army during WW2, returning to the stage in *Blithe Spirit* (1945). Increasingly gaunt and ascetic-looking in later life, he gave a run of fine film performances in the 60s, playing Peter FINCH's father in *The Pumpkin Eater* (1964), a very touching Justice Shallow in *Chimes at Midnight* (1966, Sp/Switz), 'Dadda' in *Entertaining Mr Sloane* (1969), Oliver REED's humane father in *Women in Love* (1969) and an eloquent Gloucester to Paul SCOFIELD's *King Lear* (1970, UK/Den).

OTHER BRITISH FILMS INCLUDE: *West of Zanzibar, Lease of Life* (1954), *The Scapegoat* (1958), *The Third Secret* (1964), *Interlude* (1968), *The Duellists* (1977), *The First Great Train Robbery* (1978).

Webb, Rita (*b* London, 1904 – *d* London, 1981). Actress. With portly figure and mop of flaming red hair, Rita Webb was never destined for movie stardom, but carved her niche as admired comedy actress and scene-stealing bit player. She ran away from home at 14 to become a chorus girl and, in the late 40s, began working as an extra, recognisable in films like *Moulin Rouge* (1953) and *Suddenly, Last Summer* (1959). By the mid 60s she began making regular appearances as cockney charladies, landladies, shopkeepers, market stall holders and nosy neighbours in films like *The Young Ones* (1961), *Sparrows Can't Sing* (1962) and *To Sir, with Love* (1967). In 1971 she gave a memorable performance as a rough and ready Maid Marian to Hugh PADDICK's camp Robin Hood in the comedy *Up the Chastity Belt*. In 1977 she told a journalist, 'They don't hire me for my good looks. If they did, I'd bleedin' well starve!'

OTHER BRITISH FILMS INCLUDE: *The Boy and the Bridge* (1959), *The Bay of Saint Michel* (1963), *Percy* (1971), *The Hound of the Baskervilles* (1977), *Venom* (1981). Stephen Bourne.

Webster, Ben (*b* London, 1864 – *d* Los Angeles, 1947). Actor. Originally trained for the Bar, Webster became a distinguished stage actor, before appearing regularly in silent films from the mid 1910s, including *The Vicar of Wakefield* (1916) and Fred PAUL's ambitiously cast *Masks and Faces* (1917). He also co-starred with Ivor NOVELLO in HITCHCOCK's *Downhill* (1927) and appeared in a half-dozen talkies before going to Hollywood with wife Dame May WHITTY. They appeared as husband and wife in his last film, *Lassie Come Home* (1943). Their daughter was stage actress and director, Margaret Webster.

OTHER BRITISH FILMS INCLUDE: *His Daughter's Dilemma* (1916), *The Profligate, The Gay Lord Quex* (1917), *Nobody's Child* (1919), *Miriam Rozella* (1924), *The Only Way* (1926), *Threads* (1932), *Perfect Understanding* (1933), *The Old Curiosity Shop* (1934), *Drake of England* (1935), *Conquest of the Air* (1940).

Webster, Joy (*b* Birmingham, 1934). Actress. Archetypal 50s starlet (signalled typically by *Picturegoer* cover), introduced as the bridesmaid Daphne in *Sailor Beware* (1956), in which she gave a caricature impression of sexiness, and played a handful of other unmemorable roles, like the strip-club ticketseller in *Jungle Street* (1961). Also TV from 1955.

OTHER BRITISH FILMS INCLUDE: *Womaneater, Second Fiddle* (1957), *Stormy Crossing* (1958), *Curse of the Werewolf* (1961).

Webster, Paul (*b c* 1952). Producer, executive producer. Head of films at CHANNEL 4 since 1997, Webster began producing in the mid 80s, having been a successful distributor, coming to the fore with promoting *The Evil Dead* (1983). His somewhat anarchic talents found a rackety home with PALACE FILMS; he was production co-ordinator on *A Letter to Brezhnev* (1985); and he moved out of DISTRIBUTION and into production in the later 80s, on *Dream Demon* (1988) and *The Tall Guy* (1989), before spending several years on US productions such as *Bob Roberts* (1992, ex p). Appointed vice-president of MIRAMAX in 1995, then chief executive of FilmFour, and since then has had a hand in such interestingly offbeat projects as *Little Voice* (1998, UK/US), *Late Night Shopping* (UK/Ger) and *My Brother Tom* (2001), as well as the bigger-scale *Charlotte Gray* (2001, UK/Aust/US).

OTHER BRITISH FILMS INCLUDE: *My Life So Far* (2000, UK/US), *Jump Tomorrow* (UK/US), *Crush* (UK/Ger), *Lucky Break* (UK/Ger/US) (2001), *Buffalo Soldiers* (UK/Ger/US), *Miranda, Once Upon a Time in the Midlands* (2002).

Weeks, Stephen (*b* Grimsby, 1948). Director. In films from the mid 60s making SHORTS, ADVERTISING FILMS and DOCUMENTARIES, Weeks made the short WW1 drama, *1917* (1968, + sc), before directing four further features. These were two HORROR films, *I, Monster* (1971) and *Ghost Story* (1974, + p, co-sc/story), made after the HAMMER vein had been worked out, and two Arthurian pieces, *Gawain and the Green Knight* (1973, + co-sc) and, another, more ambitious go at the Green Knight legend, *Sword of the Valiant* (1983, + co-sc). Some TV but no further cinema films.

Weiland, Paul (*b* Stoke Newington, 1953). Director. Co-directed (with Mel SMITH) the phenomenally successful *Bean* (1997), but otherwise Weiland's work has been mainly for TV. He directed the BAA-nominated SHORT FILM, *Keep Off the Grass* (1984, + co-sc) and directed the Italian-set *Roseanna's Grave* (1997, UK/US), and shared a BAAn for TV's *Blackadder Back and Forth* (1999).

Weinstein, Harvey (*b* Buffalo, NY, *c* 1952) and **Weinstein, Bob** (*b c* 1954). Executive producers. Together they founded MIRAMAX FILMS in 1979, having success with such medium-budget films as *Scandal* (1988), promoting such films profitably in the US, before selling the company to Disney in 1993, while retaining creative and financial autonomy. The company name continued to appear on such high-profile productions as Robert Altman's *Prêt-à-Porter* (1994, US) and *Emma* (1996, UK/US) and they shared AA and BAA for *Shakespeare in Love* (1999, UK/US) and the Special Jury Prize of the British Independent Film Awards, 2001. They have acquired a reputation as brilliant salesmen and shrewd entrepreneurs, their names associated with such diversely successful features as *Iris* (UK/US) and *Lord of the Rings: The Fellowship of the Ring* (NZ/US) (2001). Most often working together, they founded Excalibur Films in 1995.

OTHER BRITISH FILMS INCLUDE: (both) *Deep End* (1985), *Loser Takes All* (1990, UK/US), *Rage in Harlem, The Pope Must Die* (1991), *A Month by the Lake* (UK/US), *The Englishman Who Went Up . . .* (1995), *Jane Eyre* (UK/Fr/It/US), *The English Patient* (1996, UK/US), *The Wings of the Dove* (1997, UK/US), *Velvet Goldmine, Little Voice, Playing by Heart* (1998, UK/US), *My Life So Far, Mansfield Park* (UK/US), *Love's Labour's Lost* (UK/Fr/US), *Chocolat* (UK/US) (2000), *About Adam* (UK/Ire), *Heartlands* (2001); (Harvey) *Heaven* (2002, UK/Ger/It).

Weir, Molly (*b* Glasgow, 1920). Actress. As a radio actress, the tiny Weir was associated with such long-running favourites as

ITMA (as Tottie) and *Life with the Lyons*, reprising her role of Aggie in the 1954 film version and its sequel, *The Lyons in Paris* (1954). She was very busy on TV, in both commercials and home-centred programmes, but made only about two dozen films in 50 years, and mostly in small roles as landlady (*John and Julie*, 1955) or maid (*Hands of the Ripper*, 1971) and, by 1978, Grannie in *The Selkie*, and in such Scottish-set entertainments as *Let's Be Happy* (1956) and *The Bridal Path* (1959).

OTHER BRITISH FILMS INCLUDE: *Two Thousand Women* (1944), *Floodtide* (1949), *Flesh and Blood* (1951), *Value for Money* (1955), *Carry On Regardless* (1961), *The Prime of Miss Jean Brodie* (1968), *Scrooge* (1970), *Up for the Cup* (1971, short), *Bless This House* (1972), *Captain Jack* (1998).

Weisz, Rachel (*b* London, 1970). Actress. Perhaps it is the dark brown eyes, the knowing alertness she brings to her characters; perhaps it's the no-nonsense aura she carries with her; perhaps it's simply a case of her striking beauty. But Weisz has a potent screen persona which lends a sharp intelligence to those she plays, ensuring that they're always *there*, even when not the centre of the camera's attention. Soon after leaving Cambridge she won the 1994 Drama Critics' Outstanding Newcomer Award for her stage performance in *Design for Living*, and, since, has contributed significantly to films as various as Bertolucci's *Stealing Beauty* (1996, UK/Fr/It), Michael WINTERBOTTOM's *I Want You* (1998), Istvan Szabo's *Sunshine* (2000, UK/Austria/Can/Ger/Hung) and *The Mummy* (1999) and its unfortunate sequel (2001).

OTHER BRITISH FILMS INCLUDE: *Death Machine* (1995), *Swept from the Sea* (UK/Fr /US), *Bent* (UK/Jap/US) (1997), *The Land Girls* (1998, UK/Fr), *Beautiful Creatures, Enemy at the Gates* (2001, UK/Ger/Ire/US), *About a Boy* (2002, UK/Fr/Ger/US). Tom Ryan.

Welch, Elisabeth (*b* New York, 1904). Actress. Great African-American entertainer who settled in London in the 30s and became a celebrated singer for café society and an established star of film, radio and television. In 1923, she introduced the 'Charleston' in *Runnin' Wild*. Ten years later, she came to London to star on stage in Cole Porter's *Nymph Errant* (1933). After her film debut in *Death at Broadcasting House* (1934), Welch was generally found in cameo roles on screen, simply singing one song in films such as *Soft Lights and Sweet Music* (1936), *Around the Town* (1938), *Alibi* (1942), and *This Was Paris* (1942), but unlike her Hollywood counterparts she always projected a glamorous image and sang with white bands. She is memorable as Paul ROBESON's leading lady in *Song of Freedom* (1936) and *Big Fella* (1937) and in the CAVALCANTI sequence from *Dead of Night* (1945). In 1933, Welch introduced 'Stormy Weather' to British audiences; in 1979, she sang it for Derek JARMAN in *The Tempest*. She was subject of a 1987 documentary, *Keeping Love Alive*.

OTHER BRITISH FILMS: *Calling All Stars* (1937), *Over the Moon* (1939), *Fiddlers Three* (1944), *Coco and the Bean, Coco and the Angler* (1946, anim, voice), *Our Man in Havana* (1959), *Girl Stroke Boy* (1971), *Revenge of the Pink Panther* (1978), *Arabian Adventure* (1979). AS.

Welch, Raquel (*b* Chicago, 1940). Actress. RN: Teresa Jo Tejada. Famously sexy American star in films from the mid 60s, Welch has made a handful of British films, including *One Million Years BC* (1996), in which she wore a sort of prehistoric bikini, and, aptly, as Lilian Lust in *Bedazzled* (1967), about her presence in which one (female) reviewer wrote, 'bless her well-protected heart'. A limited actress at best, she has, however, hung on gamely and was vivid and funny in *Legally Blonde* (2001, US).

OTHER BRITISH FILMS: *Fathom* (1967), *The Magic Christian* (1969), *Hannie Caulder* (1971).

Welchman, Harry (*b* Barnstaple, 1886 – *d* Penzance, 1966). Actor. On London stage from 1906, often in musical comedies such as *The Desert Song* (1927), Welchman made a few silent films from the mid 1910s and returned in the 30s in such MUSICALS as *The Maid of the Mountains* (1932) as a somewhat middle-aged bandit hero. Later settled into character roles like that of the judge whose wife dies during a trial in *Eight O'Clock Walk* (1954).

OTHER BRITISH FILMS INCLUDE: *Mr Lyndon at Liberty* (1915), *A Princess of the Blood* (1916), *The House on the Marsh* (1920), *A Southern Maid* (1933), *The Last Waltz* (1936, UK/Fr), *The Common Touch* (1941), *The Life and Death of Colonel Blimp, The Gentle Sex* (1943), *Lisbon Story* (1946), *Green Fingers* (1947), *Mad About Men* (1954), *Three Cases of Murder* (1955).

Welland, Colin (*b* Liverpool, 1934). Screenwriter, actor. RN: Williams. Notoriously waving his Oscar for the screenplay of *Chariots of Fire* (1981) aloft, he announced 'The British are coming!'. In the ensuing years, it must often have seemed as if they – and Welland – had lost their way. Nothing in his subsequent career, much on TV, has matched *Chariot*'s eloquent, nostalgic hymn to British achievement: there were the South African-set *A Dry White Season* (1989, US) and *The War of the Buttons* (1994, UK/Fr), but neither found audiences. He has always maintained an acting career as well, but, again, his first film role, as the sympathetic English teacher in *Kes* (1969) remains his best. On TV, he was in *Z Cars* (1963–65) and *Bramwell* (1998).

OTHER BRITISH FILMS: (a) *Villain, Straw Dogs* (1971), *Sweeney!* (1976); (co-sc) *Yanks* (1979).

Welland, James (*b* Haslemere, 1961). Cinematographer. Active in British film and TV from the early 90s, versatile Welland, trained at the Royal College of Art, shot Derek JARMAN's *Wittgenstein* (1993) and the Irish-set political drama, *Divorcing Jack* (1998, UK/Fr) as well as the TV mini-series *Aristocrats* (1999) and the nostalgically 1950s-set *Take a Girl Like You* (2000), meeting admirably their very different visual needs.

OTHER BRITISH FILMS: *Caught Looking* (1992), *3 Steps to Heaven* (1995), *Beautiful Creatures* (2001), *The Last Minute* (2001, UK/US), *Plots with a View* (2002, UK/US).

Welles, Orson (*b* Kenosha, Wisconsin, 1915 – *d* Los Angeles, California, 1985). Actor, director, screenwriter. When someone wins an Honorary Oscar, as Welles did in 1971, it is usually because the Academy has hitherto overlooked major achievement. True, it nominated both *Citizen Kane* (1941) and *The Magnificent Ambersons* (1942) as Best Pictures, but the only AA he ever won was the shared one for the *Kane* screenplay. The full story of Welles's magnificent, flawed, wayward career of course belongs elsewhere, but he would have merited inclusion here if he had done nothing else in British films than play that charming, witty, lethal murderer Harry Lime in *The Third Man* (1949). He only enters the film two-thirds of the way through but then picks it up and runs with it. He is properly imposing as Manderson in *Trent's Last Case* (1952) but could hardly have expected Herbert WILCOX would know what to do with him (and that includes putting him in a kilt for *Trouble in the Glen*, 1954), but from his other British films only *Moby Dick* (1956), as Father Mapple, and *A Man for All Seasons* (1966), as a Wolsey who needed no padding, are really worth noting. None comes within striking distance of his sublime Falstaff in *Chimes*

at Midnight (1966, Sp/Switz, with many British cast members), which he also wrote and directed in the most rigorous circumstances. He tended to make any film he was in a Welles film, and most were probably better for that.

OTHER BRITISH FILMS: *Three Cases of Murder* (1955), *Ferry to Hong Kong* (1959), *The VIPs* (1963), *The Finest Hours* (1964, narr), *A King's Story* (1965, narr), *Casino Royale, The Sailor from Gibraltar, I'll Never Forget What's 'is Name, Oedipus the King* (1967), *The Southern Star* (1968, UK/Fr), *Treasure Island* (1972, UK/Fr/Ger/Sp), *Paradise Garden* (1974, doc, reading poems), *And Then There Were None* (1974), *Voyage of the Damned* (1976), *The Muppet Movie* (1979), *Where Is Parsifal?* (1983), *Almonds and Raisins* (1983, UK/US). ·

BIBLIOG: Barbara Leaming, *Orson Welles*, 1985.

Wellesley, Gordon Wong (*b* Sydney, 1906). Director, producer, screenwriter. Though he shares director-screenwriter credit with Vernon SEWELL on the successful WAR FILM, *The Silver Fleet* (1943), for ARCHERS, it does not appear that he had much to do with the final product, according not only to Sewell's 1994 recollections but also to Michael POWELL who wrote unequivocally 'Vernon Sewell directed the film. We got him out of the Navy to do it' (1986). Wellesley had some DOCUMENTARY experience with the Malay Government (1929–30) and in Hollywood (on the screenplay for *Shanghai Madness*, 1933), but was back in England the same year at ATP, collaborating on screenplays such as *Sing As We Go!* (1934) and *Lorna Doone* (1934). He wrote the original story (AAn) for *Night Train to Munich* (1940), co-wrote several wartime films, including *Freedom Radio* (1940) and *Mr Emmanuel* (1944), and post-war was Head of the Scenario Department for INDEPENDENT PRODUCERS at PINEWOOD. At the end of the decade he produced a couple of films at GAINSBOROUGH (*The Lost People*, 1949; *The Reluctant Widow*, 1950, co-sc), and thereafter, with the exception of directing the short, *Trouble with Junia* (1967), worked as screenwriter. Married Katherine STRUEBY.

OTHER BRITISH FILMS INCLUDE: (co-sc) *The Right to Live* (1933), *Java Head* (1934), *Laburnum Grove* (1936), *Sailors Three* (1940), *Atlantic Ferry* (1941), *Flying Fortress* (1942), *The Shipbuilders* (1943), *The March Hare* (1956), *The Malpas Mystery* (1960); (sc/scen super/e) *Look Up and Laugh, No Limit* (1935), *Queen of Hearts* (1936), *Dead Man's Evidence* (1962); (sc) *Death Drives Through* (1935), *The Green Scarf* (1954), *Visa to Canton* (1960); (p) *The High Command* (1937); (d) *Rhythm Serenade* (1943).

Wells, 'Bombardier' Billy (*b* London, 1889 – *d* London, 1967). Actor. Longest-reigning British heavyweight boxing champion (1911–19), who was featured in a handful of silent films and played 'bit' parts in talkies – and famously was the first to bang the gong at the start of RANK movies.

BRITISH FILMS INCLUDE: *Kent the Fighting Man* (1916), *The Great Game* (1918), *The Silver Lining* (1919), *The Game Chicken* (1926), *The Ring* (1927), *Find the Lady* (1936), *Old Mother Riley, Detective* (1943), *The Beggar's Opera* (1953). AS.

Wells, Frank (*b* Sandgate, 1903 – *d* Welwyn, 1982). Production designer, producer, screenwriter. Cambridge-educated younger son of H.G. WELLS, he was active in 30s British cinema as designer, acting as assistant designer on the ADAPTATION of his father's *[The Shape of] Things to Come* (1936) and, also for KORDA, *Fire Over England* (1937). In 1928, he adapted three of his father's stories – *Bluebottles, The Tonic* and *Daydreams* – into short films, all starring Elsa LANCHESTER and the first and last Charles LAUGHTON as well. Post-war, he worked in DOCUMENTARY and educational films with GB INSTRUCTIONAL, producing and writing a few minor films, mostly for children, in the 50s and 60s.

OTHER BRITISH FILMS INCLUDE: (des) *The Rasp*, *The Star Reporter* (1931); (art d) *The Celestial City* (1929), *His Lordship* (1932), *Dinner at the Ritz*, *Under the Red Robe* (ass) (1937); (p) *Proud Canvas* (1949, assoc), *The Clue of the Missing Ape* (1953, + co-story), *Five on a Treasure Island* (1957); (story) *The Piper's Tune*, *The Missing Note* (1961), *Seventy Deadly Pills* (1963), *Escape from the Sea* (1968).

Wells, H(erbert) G(eorge) (*b* Bromley, Kent, 1866 – *d* London, 1946). Author. Former draper's apprentice (like his famous hero Kipps) and teacher, Wells became a prolific author across a wide genre range. Famous for socially conscious satirical comedies like *Kipps* (1905, filmed 1921, with George K. ARTHUR, and 1941, starring Michael REDGRAVE; made into stage musical *Half a Sixpence*, filmed 1967 (UK/US), starring Tommy STEELE) and *The History of Mr Polly* (1910, filmed 1948, with John MILLS), he was equally renowned for his SCIENCE-FICTION works. These included, above all, *The Shape of Things to Come* (1933, filmed by Alexander KORDA, 1936, as *Things to Come*), still, for all its overwrought didacticism, a milestone in British sci-fi cinema. Other such works filmed were *The Invisible Man* (1897, first filmed 1933, US), *The Island of Dr Moreau* (1896, first filmed 1933, US, as *Island of Lost Souls*) and *The Time Machine* (1960, 2002, US), the FANTASY, *The Man Who Could Work Miracles* (1936), from a short story Wells expanded into a screenplay for Korda's LONDON FILMS. His somewhat turgid romantic triangle tale, *The Passionate Friends* (1913), was filmed by Maurice ELVEY in 1922 and David LEAN, as a vehicle for wife Ann TODD, in 1948. There is a great deal more of Wells transferred to the screen, most of it non-British in production. Wells, in his time regarded as avant-garde in his thinking in political and sexual matters, may now seem seriously dated, but there is no denying how attractive he has been to film and TV producers, this association going back as far as GAUMONT's version of *The First Men in the Moon* (1901, filmed 1919) – and, indeed, to 1895 when R.W. PAUL invited him to make a film journey (essentially a proto-phantom ride) inspired by *The Time Machine*.

OTHER BRITISH FILMS: (orig story) *The Wheels of Chance* (1922), *The Tonic*, *H.G. Wells Comedies*, *Daydreams*, *Bluebottles* (1928), *The Magic Shop* (1983, short); (a) *BBC – The Voice of Britain* (1935, doc); (screen story) *Dead of Night* (1945); (novel) *First Men in the Moon* (1964).
BIBLIOG: Alan Wykes, *H.G. Wells in the Cinema*, 1977.

Wells, Ingeborg (*b* Wollstyn, Poland, 1917). Actress. RN: Von Kusserow. Petite Polish-born actress who was a dancer as a child, worked in German films of the 30s and 40s, and, under English name, made about a dozen British films in the 50s. Most of these are 'B' MOVIES like *House of Blackmail* (1953) and *Double Exposure* (1954), usually as second lead, but she had small roles in bigger features like *Captain Horatio Hornblower RN* (1950), as Virginia Mayo's maid, and *Across the Bridge* (1957), as wife of wanted but dead killer.
OTHER BRITISH FILMS INCLUDE: *One Wild Oat*, *Secret People* (1951), *Women of Twilight* (1952), *Child's Play* (1954), *Port of Escape* (1956).

Welsh, Irvine (*b* Edinburgh, 1957). Author, actor, screenwriter. Grew up on an Edinburgh housing estate, did many jobs in Edinburgh and London, graduating MBA from Edinburgh University. His novel, *Trainspotting* (1993), vigorously and explicitly engaged with youthful clubbing, sexuality and drug-taking, was filmed with immense popular and critical success in 1996, and his collection of scabrous short stories, *The Acid House* (1994) was filmed in 1998, from his own screenplay, with some dark wit and unusually repulsive imagery. He appeared in both and featured also in the TV DOCUMENTARY, *Dockers* (1999).

Welsh, Jane (*b* Bristol, 1905 – *d* London, 2001). Actress. RN: Louise Tudor-Jones. Graceful theatre star, on stage from 1923 (London 1924), usually in modern plays. Best remembered perhaps for two mother roles: on stage as Mrs Darling in *Peter Pan* every Christmas from 1947 to 1952, and on screen as long-suffering mother of scapegrace William in two post-war ADAPTATIONS of Richmal CROMPTON's children's books, *Just William's Luck* (1947) and *William Comes to Town* (1948). These were preceded by a dozen films in the 30s and followed by a few more character roles before retirement in the 60s. Married (1 of 2) and divorced Henry MOLLISON.
OTHER BRITISH FILMS INCLUDE: *Two Crowded Hours* (1931), *The Chinese Puzzle* (1932), *Spring in the Air* (1934), *Annie, Leave the Room!* (1935), *Bell-Bottom George* (1944), *The Second Mate* (1950), *Mantrap* (1953), *Little Red Monkey* (1954), *Another Time, Another Place* (1958).

Welsh, John (*b* Wexford, Ireland, 1904 – *d* London, 1985). Actor. Tall, thin and austere-looking character player, familiar to televiewers as Uncle James in *The Forsyte Saga* (1967) and as Merriman in *The Duchess of Duke Street* (1976) and from many other series. Brought his gaunt and balding presence to well over 60 films, from the mid 50s, usually as dignified professionals, including brigadiers, bishops and admirals, the Mayor, briefly glimpsed in *Room at the Top* (1958), and sometimes in the interests of comedy as in *Lucky Jim* (1957), as the university principal. Much theatre, including Gate Theatre, Dublin, and RSC.
OTHER BRITISH FILMS INCLUDE: *Isn't Life Wonderful!* (1953), *An Inspector Calls* (1954), *The Man Who Never Was* (1955), *The Birthday Present* (1957), *The Revenge of Frankenstein* (1958), *Operation Bullshine* (1959), *The Trials of Oscar Wilde* (1960), *The Mark* (1961), *Go to Blazes* (1962), *Rasputin the Mad Monk* (1965), *Cromwell* (1970), *The Thirty Nine Steps* (1978).

Welsh, T(homas) A(rthur) (*b* Scotland, 1880 – *d* Scotland, 1950). Executive. Welsh was an assistant to A.C. BROMHEAD when GAUMONT first opened offices in London in September 1898, and remained with the company as its secretary and general manager until 1919. It was Welsh who persuaded George PEARSON to join Gaumont as a director, and who, in 1918, partnered Pearson in the formation of the production entity, Welsh–Pearson Ltd. He was its chairman and managing director, a position he continued to hold when the company was reorganised as Welsh–Pearson–Elder Films Ltd in 1928. Welsh's last production, in association with Michael BALCON, was *The Good Companions* (1933). AS.

Welwyn Studios These Hertfordshire studios opened in 1928 and were the home of BRITISH INSTRUCTIONAL FILMS, founded by H(Harry). Bruce WOOLFE. The attraction of locating studios in Welwyn Garden City was that it was only 25 minutes by train from London, land and houses were cheaper, and the air was cleaner. At the time the structure had a larger roof span than any other studio in Europe. One end of the building was removable for the shooting of outdoor/indoor scenes. Anthony ASQUITH's *A Cottage on Dartmoor* (1929) was its first sound film (music only, with the exception of an additional talking scene produced in Germany) but with enlargement of its facilities more ambitious projects were possible. One such film was *I Was A Spy* (1933) which starred Madeleine CARROLL, Herbert MARSHALL and Conrad VEIDT. A huge replica of a Belgian town square was built, foreign steam trains and trams were imported and it boasted a large cast of cavalry. After it was taken over by BRITISH INTERNATIONAL PICTURES (BIP) various production companies filmed at

Welwyn as well as BIP making its own supporting features. *The Dark Eyes of London* (1939), starring Bela Lugosi, was made there and was the first British-made film to earn an H (for Horrific) certificate. British stars continued to work at Welwyn in the post-war years: *I Live in Grosvenor Square* (1945) starred Anna NEAGLE, Rex HARRISON and Robert MORLEY; and *Quiet Weekend* (1946) was also filmed there. Stephen Brown.

Wembley National Studios These studios were the remnant of plans to turn the 1924 Wembley Exhibition into national studios. Quick to assess the future importance of sound, the studio adopted the Phonofilm system and in 1927 the company became British Talking Pictures. A subsidiary was called British Sound Film Productions. A range of shorts and feature length films were made there. Under FOX–BRITISH, this included 'QUOTA QUICKIES'. In the post-war period there were various attempts to revive the studio's fortunes. Stephen Brown.

Wenham, Jane (*b* Southampton, 1927). Actress. RN: Figgins. Central School-trained, Wenham was on stage from 1945 at the Old Vic and did a lot of prestige TV, including the Shakespearean *The Spread of the Eagle* (1963) and *Testament of Youth* (1979), as Vera Brittain's mother, but she did almost no film. Considering how touchingly vulnerable she was in her first film as the victimised girl in *An Inspector Calls* (1954), this is matter for regret. Married/divorced Albert FINNEY.
OTHER BRITISH FILMS: *Make Me an Offer!*, *The Teckman Mystery* (1954).

Werndorff, Oscar F. (Friedrich) (*b* Vienna, 1887 – *v*London, 1938). Production designer. Werndorff designed a number of Anglo-German co-productions in the late 20s, among them *The Queen Was In The Parlour* (1927), *The Ghost Train* (1927), *The Gallant Hussar* (1928), *The Wrecker* (1928), and *Number Seventeen* (1928). In Britain from 1930 he quickly established himself as a sought-after craftsman, specialising in stylish yet functional sets. Werndorff co-directed (with Harcourt TEMPLEMAN) one film, *The Bells* (1931), a brooding historical drama photographed by Günther KRAMPF and Eric CROSS in the Scottish Highlands.
OTHER BRITISH FILMS INCLUDE: *City of Song* (1931), *The First Mrs Fraser* (1932), *Waltzes From Vienna* (1934), *Fighting Stock*, *The 39 Steps*, *First A Girl*, *The Passing Of The Third Floor Back* (1935), *East Meets West*, *King Of The Damned*, *Secret Agent*, *Rhodes Of Africa*, *Sabotage* (1936), *Keep Smiling*, *The Gaunt Stranger*, *The Ware Case* (1938) *Let's Be Famous* (1939). Tim Bergfelder.

Werner, Oskar (*b* Vienna, 1922 – *d* Marbourg, Germany, 1984). Actor. RN: Boschliessmayer. Renowned star of European stage, the intense, fair-haired Werner filmed only occasionally including a half-dozen British films, but the three he made in the 60s all gave him good opportunities. They were as the clever, ambitious Fiedler in *The Spy Who Came In from the Cold* (1965), the book-burning Montag in François Truffaut's *Fahrenheit 451* (1966) and the celebrated conductor tempted into an affair in *Interlude* (1968), but his best known film is Truffaut's *nouvelle vague* romance, *Jules et Jim* (1961, Fr).
OTHER BRITISH FILMS: *The Angel with the Trumpet* (1949), *The Wonder Kid* (1951), *Voyage of the Damned* (1976).

Weske, Brian (*b* London, 1932 – *d* London, 2001). Actor. In films as a tot, in the documentary, *Health of a Nation* (1935), Weske returned as a child player in the 40s, notably playing Hugh BURDEN's character as a child in *Fame Is the Spur* (1947) and William's chum Henry in *Just William's Luck* (1947) and *William Comes to Town* (1948). He hung on longer than most

CHILD ACTORS, was in some popular TV, including *Dixon of Dock Green* (1955) and about 20 adult roles in the later 50s and the 60s, mostly in small roles. His father was actor **Victor Weske**, who appeared in a few British films, including *The Bells Go Down* (1943).
OTHER BRITISH FILMS INCLUDE: *Medal for the General* (1944), *Perfect Strangers* (1945), *Woman to Woman* (1946), *Night and the City* (1950, UK/US), *Orders Are Orders* (1954), *I Was Monty's Double* (1958), *Operation Bullshine* (1959), *On the Fiddle* (1961), *The Boys* (1962), *Panic* (1965), *A Hole Lot of Trouble* (1969).

Wessex Films Production company formed by Ian DALRYMPLE, set up in the later 40s as one of RANK's INDEPENDENT PRODUCERS. It never acquired the prestige of the similarly placed companies, CINEGUILD, THE ARCHERS or INDIVIDUAL PICTURES, but its films are not without interest. Jack LEE was its chief contract director, responsible for its first production, *The Woman in the Hall* (1947), the dirt-track racing drama, *Once a Jolly Swagman* (1948), starring Dirk BOGARDE, and the company's single great critical and commercial success, *The Wooden Horse* (1950), one of the best prisoner-of-war stories. In the 50s and 60s, Wessex turned out a mixture of DOCUMENTARIES and feature films, the former including *Bank of England* (1960) and the latter, the WAR FILM, *A Hill in Korea* (1956), a rare British film dealing with a 'neglected' war. Dalrymple himself directed the turgid romance, *Esther Waters* (1948) and contributed to the screenplay of several Wessex films, and other associates included producer Derek TWIST, who actually directed *All Over the Town* (1949) and cinematographers H.E. FOWLE and C. PENNINGTON-RICHARDS, both, like LEE, formerly with the CROWN FILM UNIT. Its final films were two SHORTS released in 1967: *Library*, a documentary, and *Jacqueline*, a fiction short about a young girl.

West, Con (*b* London, 1891 – *d* 19?). Screenwriter. Wrote prolifically for COMEDY films of the 30s and 40s, working for GAINSBOROUGH, BIP, BUTCHER's and other companies. His credits include four of the Ernie LOTINGA 'Josser' SERIES, starting with *PC Josser* (1931), providing story or screenplay, and *Old Mother Riley* (1937) and seven of its follow-ups. Several times associated with the films of John BAXTER from 1935, his taste for demotic comedy finding a niche with Baxter's naive but true humanity. Entered the industry in 1923 as a writer of subtitles for GAUMONT and his first talkie screenplay was for the Lotinga SHORT FILM, *The Raw Recruit* (1928). Also wrote for the stage, including plays (first 1913) and revue sketches for the CRAZY GANG and the musical biography, *The Fred Karno Story* (1950), having adapted some of KARNO's material to the screen (e.g. *Bad Companions*, 1932).
OTHER BRITISH FILMS INCLUDE: (co-sc, unless noted) *Up for the Cup* (1931), *Josser Joins the Navy*, *Josser in the Army* (co-story) (1932), *My Old Duchess* (1933), *Josser on the Farm* (1934), *Birds of a Feather* (1935), *Variety Parade*, *Sunshine Ahead* (1936), *Why Pick on Me?* (co-story) (1937), *Old Mother Riley in Paris* (sc, story), *Miracles Do Happen* (1938), *What Would You Do, Chums?* (1939), *Old Mother Riley's Ghosts* (1941), *Somewhere in Civvies*, *It's in the Bag* (1943, sc), *Old Mother Riley's New Venture* (1949), *Up for the Cup*, *Old Mother Riley, Headmistress* (1950).

West, Dominic (*b* Sheffield, 1969). Actor. Educated at Trinity College, Dublin, and Guildhall-trained West has worked in the theatre (including the Old Vic, winning an award for *The Seagull*, 1997) and TV (including episodes of *A Touch of Frost*, 1992), as well as a dozen films since his feature debut as Richmond in *Richard III* (1995). He had the romantic lead in

Diana & Me (1996, UK/Aust) and was one of the squabbling lovers in *A Midsummer Night's Dream* (1999, UK/It), since when he has worked in international films such as *Star Wars . . . The Phantom Menace* (1999). Starred in the mysteriously unseen drama of academe, *E=MC2* (1995).

OTHER BRITISH FILMS INCLUDE: *Surviving Picasso* (UK/US), *True Blue* (1996), *The Gambler* (UK/Hung/Neth), *Spice World* (1997).

West, Jake (*b* 1972). Director. West produced, wrote and edited as well as directed *Razor Blade Smile* (1998), a vampire thriller, but subsequently merely co-edited the campy, semi-porn, convent-set *Sacred Flesh* (2000).

West, Lockwood (*b* Birkenhead, 1905 – *d* Brighton, 1989). Actor. RN: Harry West. Educated at St Paul's School, London, and formerly employed by Doncaster Collieries Association, he turned to acting in 1926, made his London debut in 1931, and brought his balding, benign astuteness to films in the late 40s, after WW2 service with Police War Reserve (1940–45). Usually in small roles, but sometimes quite vivid like those of the complacent solicitor who doesn't want to help a hapless Tony BRITTON in *The Birthday Present* (1957), the police inspector at the end of *Strongroom* (1962), and the elderly actor (which he was), Thornton, in *The Dresser* (1983). TV included an episode of *Lord Peter Wimsey* (1972). Father of Timothy WEST, grandfather of Sam WEST.

OTHER BRITISH FILMS INCLUDE: *Song for Tomorrow* (1948), *Edward, My Son*, *No Place for Jennifer* (1949), *High Treason* (1951), *Single-Handed*, *The Oracle* (1953), *Private's Progress* (1956), *Tunes of Glory* (1960), *The Leather Boys* (1963), *Up the Junction*, *Bedazzled* (1967), *Jane Eyre* (1970), *The Satanic Rites of Dracula* (1974), *The Shooting Party* (1984).

West, Samuel (*b* London, 1966). Actor. Oxford-educated West had a rapid rise in the 90s in all the acting media. In *Stiff Upper Lips* (1996) and his brief film-within-a-film role in *Notting Hill* (1999, UK/US), he parodied the period pieces in which he had made his name, notably *Howards End* (1992), as the unfortunate class-riven Leonard Bast (AAn/supp a), *Carrington* (1994, UK/Fr), *Persuasion* (1995), as the charming, duplicitous Mr Elliot, and *Jane Eyre* (1996, UK/Fr/It/US), as the zealot St John Rivers. He played the poet Southey in *Pandaemonium* (2001, UK/US) and an early lover of Iris Murdoch in *Iris* (2002, UK/US), while also pursuing a stage career, enjoying critical acclaim as Prince Hal to the Falstaff of father Timothy WEST in *Henry IV, Part I* and as *Richard II* and *Hamlet* for the RSC. Also, much TV, including *Longitude* (2000), and his eloquent voice has made him in much demand for radio and voice-overs. Mother is Prunella SCALES.

OTHER BRITISH FILMS INCLUDE: *Reunion* (1989, UK/Fr/Ger), *A Feast at Midnight* (1994), *Complicity* (2000), *Bread and Roses* (UK/Fr/Ger/It/Sp/Switz) (2001).

West, Timothy (*b* Bradford, Yorks, 1934). Actor. Dominant character star of British stage and TV who has done some striking work in films but not on the same scale as in the other media. Educated at Regent Street Polytechnic, he was a recording engineer before making his stage debut in 1956 (London, 1959), since when he has appeared with all the major acting companies, in many classic roles, including Lear, Shylock and Falstaff, as well as such modern pieces as the revival of PINTER's *The Birthday Party* (1999). His burly figure and no-nonsense looks have made him natural casting on TV for such roles as Bounderby in *Hard Times* (1977), Churchill in *Churchill and the Generals* (1979) and bullying Albert Parker in

When We Are Married (1987). By comparison with all this distinction and prolificacy, his film work has been sporadic, starting with *The Deadly Affair* (1966), including an excellent Brack in *Hedda* (1975) and an authoritative few minutes in *Iris* (2002, UK/US), playing in middle age the role played as a young man by his son Sam WEST. Married to Prunella SCALES since 1963. Awarded CBE, 1984.

OTHER BRITISH FILMS INCLUDES: *Twisted Nerve* (1968), *The Looking Glass War* (1969), *The Day of the Jackal* (UK/Fr), *Hitler: The Last Ten Days* (UK/It) (1973), *Joseph Andrews* (1976), *The Thirty Nine Steps*, *Agatha* (UK/US) (1978), *Cry Freedom* (1987), *Consuming Passions* (1988, UK/US), *Villa des roses* (2002, UK/Belg/Lux/Neth).

West, Walter (*b* London, 1881 – *d* ?). Producer, director. West founded his own company, Broadwest, in 1914, with a studio at ESHER, where his first film was *The Woman Who Did* (1915), and later at WALTHAMSTOW; the company ended its existence in 1923, and, in 1927, West formed a second company, QTS. He directed many films, usually starring Violet HOPSON.

OTHER BRITISH FILMS INCLUDE: (for Broadwest) *The Merchant of Venice* (1916), *The Ware Case* (1917), *The Perfect Lover* (1921), *In the Blood* (1923), *The Great Turf Mystery* (1924); (other) *Trainer and Temptress* (1925, + sc), *Maria Marten*, *Warned Off* (1928), *Hundred to One* (1932), *Bed and Breakfast* (1938), *We Do Believe in Ghosts* (1947, + p). AS.

Westbrook, John (*b* Teignmouth, 1922 – *d* London, 1989). Actor. RN: Westbrook-Stevens. In rep from 1939, then in the RAF (1943–46), Westbrook made his London debut in 1946 and had an interesting stage career that included performances of *Comus* (1953) at Ludlow Castle and a tour of the US as *Coriolanus* (1961). His intermittent films included two for Roger Corman, *The Masque of the Red Death* (UK/US) and *The Tomb of Ligeia* (1964), but he is best remembered in films as vile, swaggering Jack Wales in *Room at the Top* (1958). Also busy with radio and poetry recitals.

OTHER BRITISH FILMS INCLUDE: *There Is Another Sun* (1951), *Foxhole in Cairo* (1960), *A Prize of Arms* (1961), *North Sea Hijack* (1979), *The Dress* (1984, short).

Westerby, Robert (*b* London, 1909 – *d* Los Angeles, 1968). Screenwriter. Former novelist, political essayist and journalist, Westerby entered films in the late 40s, his first solo screenplay being that for the GAINSBOROUGH air crash drama, *Broken Journey* (1948). His novels formed the basis for the screenplays of *The Small Voice* (1948) and *Soho Incident* (1956), and *The Spider and the Fly* (1949) and *Cairo Road* (1950) were adapted from his stories. Proficient across a GENRE range (WAR FILMS, ADVENTURE, THRILLERS), he worked several times for the DISNEY ORGANISATION in the last decade of his life.

OTHER BRITISH FILMS INCLUDE: *The White Unicorn* (1947, co-sc), *Woman Hater* (co-sc), *Don't Ever Leave Me* (1949), *Prelude to Fame* (1950), *South of Algiers* (1952), *The Square Ring* (1953), *Wicked as They Come*, *Town on Trial* (1956, co-sc), *Sea of Sand* (1958), *Cone of Silence* (1960), *Greyfriars Bobby* (1961), *The Legend of Young Dick Turpin* (1965), *The Fighting Prince of Donegal* (1966).

Westerns In a filmography produced for the NATIONAL FILM THEATRE, Luke McKernan lists no fewer than forty British Westerns made between 1900 and 1915. At least two have survived. HEPWORTH's *The Squatter's Daughter* (1906), in which a girl is captured by Indians, was reputedly shot on Putney Common. The action is authentic, the scenery less so. *The Scapegrace* (1913), produced by CRICKS and Martin, depicts the adventures of an Englishman in the Yukon goldrush. Since then, British Westerns have mostly been parodies, including the CRAZY GANG in *The Frozen Limits* (1939), Arthur ASKEY in *Ramsbottom Rides Again* (1956) and *Carry On Cowboy* (1965), with Sid JAMES as the Rumpo Kid. Stories set in the EMPIRE in the 19th century such as the Australian trail-driving saga *The Overlanders* (1946) or *Diamond City* (1949), set in the South African goldfields, are Westerns in all but location. There are also Westerns proper which technically qualify as British productions, though they often involve American personnel or locations; examples are Raoul WALSH's *The Sheriff of Fractured Jaw* (1958), shot at PINEWOOD with Kenneth MORE, Edward DMYTRYK's *Shalako* (1968), with Sean CONNERY, Michael WINNER's *Chato's Land* (1971), *Eagle's Wing* (1978), directed for RANK by the Briton Anthony HARVEY, and *Painted Angels* (1998) financed by BRITISH SCREEN and directed by Jon Sanders. Michael WINTERBOTTOM's California goldrush saga *The Claim* (2001, UK/Can/Fr), starring PETER MULLAN, is a distinguished recent addition. Edward Buscombe.

Weston, Charles H. (*b* ? – *d* New York, 1919). Director. After directing shorts in the US, 1912–13, Weston came to the UK to direct *The Battle of Waterloo* (1913) for BRITISH AND COLONIAL, boasting thousands of extras. With Arthur FINN, he formed the Weston–Finn Company (later the Regent Company) the following year, with a studio in Bayswater, and again directed a spectacle, *The Seventh Day* (1914), with 3,000 extras. A Charles H. Weston committed suicide in New York in 1919 and is believed to be the director.
BRITISH FILMS INCLUDE: *Through the Clouds* (1913, + sc), *A Mother in Exile, The Master Spy, The Road to Calais, Self-Accused* (+ sc) (1914), *Vice and Virtue* (+ sc), *Pimple's The Case of Johnny Walker, The Vengeance of Nana* (1915). AS.

Weston, David (*b* 1938). Actor. Serviceable player, mainly in the 60s, when he had substantial supporting roles in such films as *Becket* (1964) and *The Heroes of Telemark* (1965), was Janette SCOTT's dull, predictable boyfriend whom she ditches for the delusive bright lights of *The Beauty Jungle* (1964). He was the brave young Gino in *The Masque of the Red Death* (1964) and starred for DISNEY in *The Legend of Young Dick Turpin* (1965). Also on stage with RSC and a good deal of TV, in popular series such as *Softly Softly* (1973).
OTHER BRITISH FILMS INCLUDE: *The Mind Benders, Doctor in Distress* (1963), *Witchcraft* (1964), *The Winter's Tale* (1966), *Quest for Love* (1971).

Weston, Ken (*b* London, 1947 – *d* London, 2001). Sound recordist. Served apprenticeship in SHORT FILMS and as boom operator on major features, including two for Alan PARKER (*Bugsy Malone*, 1976; *Midnight Express*,1978), and latterly busy as award-winning recordist and mixer in British and international films, including *Evita* (1996, AAn/sd), *Gladiator* (2000, UK/US, AA/sd) and *Pearl Harbor* (2001, UK), as well as smaller-scale titles like *Jack & Sarah* (1995, UK/Fr).
OTHER BRITISH FILMS INCLUDE: (co-sd, short) *Our Cissy, No Hard Feelings, Footsteps* (1974); (sd rec) *Another Country, Dance with a Stranger* (1984), *The Doctor and the Devils* (1985), *Business as Usual* (1987), *Buster* (1988), *Under Suspicion* (1991), *Haunted* (1995, UK/US); (prod/sd mixer) *The Run of the Country* (Ire/US) (1995), *Angela's Ashes* (Ire/US) (1999), *Breathtaking* (2000), *My Life So Far* (UK/US), *Shiner* (2001).

Weston, Leslie Actor. Small-part player of over two dozen films of the 40s and 50s, often in roles merely designated by their function, like jailer in *The Constant Husband* (1954) and publican in *High Flight* (1957), and in a neat character study of a gossipy private hotel resident in *The Embezzler* (1954).
OTHER BRITISH FILMS INCLUDE: *Glamour Girl* (1938), *We Dive at Dawn* (1943), *Send for Paul Temple* (1946), *Corridor of Mirrors, Sleeping*

Car to Trieste (1948), *Last Holiday* (1950), *Derby Day, Folly to Be Wise* (1952), *Above Us the Waves* (1955), *The Green Man* (1956), *Manuela* (1957), *The House of the Seven Hawks* (1959).

Weston, R.P. Screenwriter, lyricist. Most often in collaboration, usually with Bert Lee, sometimes with Jack Marks, Weston made contributions to the screenplay or lyrics of about 20 light entertainments of the 30s, often for BRITISH AND DOMINIONS and for BIP, and often for comedian Sydney HOWARD, in such films as *Up for the Cup* (1931) and *Splinters in the Navy* (1931).
OTHER BRITISH FILMS INCLUDE: (co-sc, unless noted) *The Black Hand Gang* (1930, co-play), *Out of the Blue, No Lady* (1931), *The Flag Lieutenant* (co-lyrics), *It's a King* (1932), *Up for the Derby* (1933), *Girls Please!* (1934), *Where's George?, Squibs* (co-monologue) (1935), *Fame* (1936), *Splinters in the Air, O-Kay for Sound* (co-songs) (1937), *Yes Madam?* (1938, co-lyrics).

Wetherell, M(armaduke) A(rundel) (*b* Leeds, 1886 – *d* Johannesburg, South Africa, 1939). Actor, director. A flamboyant character, who was on stage from 1902 and boasted of his exploits as a big game hunter, Wetherell directed at least two films in South Africa, *The Buried City* (1921) and *The Vulture's Prey* (1922). He played the title roles, directed and wrote *Livingstone* (1925), filmed in Africa, and *Robinson Crusoe* (1927), filmed in Tobago. In 1994, it was revealed that Wetherell was responsible for creating and photographing the much-vaunted 1934 appearance of the Loch Ness Monster.
OTHER BRITISH FILMS INCLUDE: (a) *Man and His Kingdom* (1922), *Darkness* (1923), *Women and Diamonds* (1924); (d) *Adventure* (1925), *The Somme* (1927), *Victory* (1928), *Hearts of Oak* (1933). AS.

Wetherell, Virginia (aka Weatherall) (*b* Farnham, Surrey, 1943). Actress. Supporting player with stage experience in films from the 60s, several times in EXPLOITATION pieces such as two for Pete WALKER, *The Big Switch* (1968) and *Man of Violence* (1970), in which she had female leads. Later in small character roles and in TV's *Minder on the Orient Express* (1985). Married to Ralph BATES (1973–91, his death), and she later managed a cancer fund run in his name.
OTHER BRITISH FILMS INCLUDE: *Ricochet* (1963), *Alfie* (1966), *Curse of the Crimson Altar* (1968), *A Clockwork Orange, Demons of the Mind* (1971), *Disciple of Death* (1972), *Real Life* (1983), *Love Is the Devil* (1998, UK/Fr/Jap).

Whale, James (*b* Dudley, Worcestor, 1896 – *d* Los Angeles, 1957). Director. Best known for his stylish 30s Universal horror films made in Hollywood, Whale began his versatile movie career by directing a filmed version of his British staging of R.C. Sherriff's *Journey's End* (1930), which was produced by George PEARSON, though filmed in Hollywood. Whale was heavily involved with the London theatre world in the 20s, and, when his directing career began to flourish in Hollywood, he invariably cast his movies with English performers he had known in the West End.
BIBLIOG: James Curtis, *James Whale: A New World of Gods and Monsters*, 1998. Stephen Shafer.

Whalley, Joanne (aka Whalley-Kilmer) (*b* Salford, 1964). Actress. Lost to the British cinema from circa 1990 when she went to Hollywood, and married American star, Val Kilmer (1988–96), hence her name change. Came to film through TELEVISION, creating many a frisson as Nurse Mills in Dennis POTTER's TV series *The Singing Detective* (1986). Her short British film career was most notable for her playing of a part to die for, Christine Keeler, in *Scandal* (1988), the call girl romanticised into the vulnerable sensual fulcrum of swinging, boundary-eroding '60s London. It was a key part in a key British film. Her subsequent, mostly American films have never touched such heights; they include *A Good Man in Africa* (1994), and in TV series the iconic figures of Scarlett O'Hara in *Scarlett* (1994) and Jackie Kennedy in *Jackie Bouvier Kennedy Onassis* (2000).

OTHER BRITISH FILMS: *Pink Floyd The Wall* (1982), *No Surrender* (1985), *Dance with a Stranger* (1984), *The Good Father* (1986). Bruce Babington.

Whatham, Claude Director. Most of Whatham's work has been for TV, including episodes of *Elizabeth R* (1971) and *Disraeli* (1978). His cinema films include the two rock-inspired musicals, *That'll Be the Day* (1973), which had the benefit of then-popular David ESSEX, and *Buddy's Song* (1990), starring Roger DALTREY in middle age, and, in other mode, the Yorkshire-set *All Creatures Great and Small* (1974), derived from James Herriot's accounts of a provincial vet's life between wars, and the quite clever thriller, *Hoodwink* (1981, Aust). A modestly likeable talent.

OTHER BRITISH FILMS: *Swallows and Amazons* (1974), *Sweet William* (1979), *Murder Elite* (1985).

Whately, Kevin (*b* Newcastle-upon-Tyne, 1951). Actor. Best known as TV's Sergeant Lewis, devoted and long-suffering offsider to John THAW's *Inspector Morse* (1987–92) and rural doctor in *Peak Practice* (1993–94). His few films have not given him comparable chances, though he had a noticeable supporting role as Hardy in *The English Patient* (1996, UK/US) and was interestingly cast against nice-guy type as a bullying teacher in *Purely Belter* (2000).

OTHER BRITISH FILMS INCLUDE: *The Return of the Soldier* (1982), *Skallagrigg* (1994), *Paranoid* (2000), *Silent Cry* (2002).

Wheatley, Alan (*b* Thames Ditton, 1907 – *d* London, 1991). Actor. Though perhaps best remembered as the Sheriff of Nottingham in TV's *The Adventures of Robin Hood* (1955–59), he was in fact a stylish character actor with a range of memorable credits. A former industrial psychologist, on stage from 1928 (London 1930), he appeared in the film, *The Conquest of the Air* (1940), was principal announcer and newsreader for the BBC's European Service during WW2, and returned to films post-war. He could be devious like the crooked traveller on the *Sleeping Car to Trieste* (1948), suavely corrupt like the financier in *Delayed Action* (1954), smoothly patronising like the police inspector in *Tomorrow at Ten* (1962), but is most vivid as gaunt, hunted Hale in the opening sequences of *Brighton Rock* (1947), setting the sad, seedy, brutal tone for the whole film. On TV from mid 40s, starring in *Rope* (1950) and regularly on stage until the 70s.

OTHER BRITISH FILMS INCLUDE: *The Rake's Progress* (1945), *Appointment with Crime* (1946), *Jassy* (1947), *It's Not Cricket* (1949), *Home to Danger* (1951), *The Pickwick Papers* (1952), *The House Across the Lake* (1954), *The Duke Wore Jeans* (1958), *The Shadow of the Cat* (1961), *A Jolly Bad Fellow* (1963).

Wheatley, Dennis (*b* London, 1897 – *d* 1977). Author. Popular novelist whose work combines historical fiction and fascination with satanic rites. Those which have been filmed include most notably the HAMMER classic, *The Devil Rides Out* (1967). He co-wrote the screenplay for *An Englishman's Home* (1939) and appeared in a SHORT FILM, *Spotlight on Bestsellers* (1951, doc), discussing his work.

OTHER BRITISH FILMS INCLUDE: (adapted from his novels) *Secret of Stamboul* (1936, from *The Eunuch of Stamboul*), *The Lost Continent* (1968, from *Uncharted Seas*), *To the Devil a Daughter* (1976, UK/Ger).

Wheddon, Horace (*b* London, *c* 1891 – *d* 1958). Cinematographer. Rather unkindly described by Rachael LOW as a 'lowly' cameramen at ELSTREE in the 30s, Wheddon worked on about 15 silent films, for such companies as STOLL and IDEAL, and including Walter SUMMERS's reconstruction of the WW1 battle of *Mons* (1926). He made about the same number of talkies, mostly for BIP (often for SUMMERS), mostly in collaboration, and mostly on 'QUOTA QUICKIES'. Exceptions to the latter were *Dreyfus* (1931) and *Royal Cavalcade* (1935), both shared credits. Was with the Army Kinematograph Service during WW2.

OTHER BRITISH FILMS INCLUDE: (c/co-c) *Mr Gilfil's Love Story* (1920), *Sybil* (1921), *This Freedom* (1923), *The Conspirators*, *The Drum* (1924), *The Fake* (1927), *Remembrance* (1928), *The Squeaker*, *Hobson's Choice* (1931), *Brother Alfred* (1932), *Music Hath Charms*, *RAF* (doc) (1935), *Cotton Queen* (1937).

Whelan, Albert (*b* Melbourne, 1875 – *d* London, 1961). Actor. RN: Waxman. MUSIC HALL star, billed as 'The Australian Entertainer', first to use a signature tune, noted for his debonair appearance and his whistling. Appears as himself in *An Intimate Interlude* (1928), *Stars on Parade* (1936) and *Mad about Money* (1938), but generally nothing more than a minor character player on screen.

OTHER BRITISH FILMS INCLUDE: *OK Chief* (1931), *Anything Might Happen* (1934), *Dance Band* (1935), *Educated Evans* (1936), *Action for Slander* (1937), *Candlelight in Algeria* (1943), *English without Tears* (1944), *Keep It Clean* (1955). AS.

Whelan, Tim (*b* Cannelton, Indiana, 1893 – *d* Los Angeles, 1957). Director. In films as writer from silent days, Whelan did virtually all his best work in Britain in the 30s, returning to the US to make routine musicals such as *Higher and Higher* (1944), notable only for Frank Sinatra's acting debut. In Britain, he worked on cheerful GAINSBOROUGH COMEDIES, starring Cicely COURTNEIDGE (*Aunt Sally*, 1933, + story), Jack HULBERT (*The Camels are Coming*, 1934) and the very snappy comedy-thriller, *Smash and Grab* (1937). For KORDA's LONDON FILMS, his work included the Merle OBERON romantic comedy, *The Divorce of Lady X* (1938) and a share – it is unclear how much; the action sequences, according to Karol Kulik (1975) – of the direction of *The Thief of Baghdad* (1940). He made a workmanlike ADAPTATION of *The Mill on the Floss* (1937, + co-sc) and post-war he came back to give Sonia DRESDEL her head in *This Was a Woman* (1948), a MELODRAMA worth reappraisal. Began as an actor, and later gag writer to Harold Lloyd, probably his most noteworthy work in the US, he showed himself in Britain an engaging minor talent.

OTHER BRITISH FILMS: *Adam's Apple* (+ co-sc), *When Knights Were Bold* (1929), *It's a Boy!* (1933), *Two's Company* (1936, + co-sc), *Farewell Again*, *Action for Slander* (1937), *St Martin's Lane* (1938), *Q Planes*, *Ten Days in Paris* (1939).

Whicker, Alan (*b* Cairo, 1925). Actor. Doyen of TV interviewers in the earlier days of the medium, he became popular on the BBC's *Tonight* (1957–65), then became a national institution with *Whicker's World*, a globe-trotting series of interviews in exotic locations. His connection with cinema is minimal: he appeared as himself in *The Angry Silence* (1960), covering the wildcat strike; played a TV commentator in *The Magic Christian* (1969); and was himself again in *Whatever Happened to Harold Smith?* (2000).

Whiley, Manning (*b* London, 1915 – *d* 1975). Actor. Dark, saturnine actor who starred in a very early BOULTING brothers' film, *Trunk Crime* (1939), as a vengeful student, but thereafter quickly found his true métier as supporting villain. During WW2, his busiest period, he was apt to be cast as Nazi swine, like the SS trooper in *Freedom Radio* (1940), or smooth villains like the one in *The Shop at Sly Corner* (1946). Married **Wanda Rotha** (*b* Vienna, 1917 – *d* London, 1982), who appeared in a few films, including the British *Mrs Fitzherbert* (1947).

OTHER BRITISH FILMS INCLUDE: *The Four Just Men* (1939), *Pastor Hall*, *Saloon Bar*, *Gasbags*, *Contraband* (1940), *Mr Proudfoot Shows a Light* (short), *Pimpernel Smith* (1941), *Big Blockade* (1942), *Meet Sexton Blake* (1944), *The Seventh Veil* (1945), *Uncle Silas*, *Teheran* (1947), *Children of Chance* (1949), *Little Big Shot* (1952).

Whitby, Gwynne (aka Gwen) (*b* Leamington Spa, 1903 – *d* London, 1984). Actress. Popular stage actress, in London, Stratford, New York and on many tours, she made only a few films. She repeated her stage role (1941–44) as Marcia, the long-suffering golf widow, in *Quiet Weekend* (1946) and was a no-nonsense policewoman in *The Blue Lamp* (1949). Married and divorced Hugh WILLIAMS.

OTHER BRITISH FILMS INCLUDE: *Mine Own Executioner* (1947), *Britannia Mews* (1948), *I Believe in You* (1952), *Time Without Pity* (1957).

White, Alan (*b* Sydney, 1925). Actor. After one Australian film, *Into the Straight* (1949) and some stage experience, in 1954 White followed friend Peter FINCH to London, immediately got the lead in ITV's first play, *Mid-Level*, made his West End debut in 1955 and had a tiny role in OLIVIER's *Richard III* (1955). Won a contract with ABPC on the strength of playing the stage lead in *Doctor in the House*, and was cast as bantering young doctor in the soppy *No Time for Tears* (1957). Nothing much worth noting followed but he was the policeman investigating *A Lady Mislaid* (1958), opposite Phyllis CALVERT.

OTHER BRITISH FILMS INCLUDE: *Girls at Sea* (1958), *Seven Keys* (1962), *Girl in the Headlines* (1963), *The Most Dangerous Man in the World* (1969).

White, Barbara (*b* Sheerness, 1925). Actress. Perhaps marriage to Keiron MOORE led to the retirement from the screen of the enchantingly pretty and endearing White. Her handful of performances have retained their unaffected freshness: she is the daughter Miranda who wins her love away from sophisticated competition in *Quiet Weekend* (1946), repeating her stage role (1944); a Wrens' uniform becomes her in *While the Sun Shines* (1947) as she deals with three suitors; and she is touchingly anxious as the wife of the war-damaged hero (Moore) in *Mine Own Executioner* (1947).

OTHER BRITISH FILMS: *It Happened One Sunday* (1944), *The Voice Within* (1945), *This Was a Woman* (1948).

White, Carol (*b* London, 1943 – *d* Miami, Florida, 1991). Actress. Former child actress, who in the 60s played working-class girls, with blonde bouffant hairdo and air of sensuality, fatally attracted to criminal types. Whilst at Corona Stage school she starred in two children's films, *Circus Friends* (1956) and *Web of Suspicion* (1959), and later in two superior 'B' FILMS: as *Linda* (1960), who falls for a young criminal, and Jean, married to one in *The Man In the Back Seat* (1961). But she became famous for two TV plays directed by Ken LOACH: *Up the Junction* (1965), and notably as a homeless single mother in the harsher, angrier *Cathy Come Home* (1966). Also starred in Loach's determinedly sordid low life drama *Poor Cow* (1967), and as the runaway gold-digger *Dulcima* (1971), lusted after by

miserly farmer John MILLS, but her British film career was in decline. She appeared in US movies from 1965, but few of any quality. Died of drug overdose.

OTHER BRITISH FILMS INCLUDE: *Carry On Teacher*, *Beat Girl* (1959), *Never Let Go* (1960), *A Matter of Who* (1961), *Village of Daughters*, *The Boys* (1962), *Ladies Who Do* (1963), *I'll Never Forget What's 'is Name* (1967), *The Fixer* (US/UK) (1968), *The Man Who Had Power Over Women* (1970), *Made* (1972), *The Squeeze* (1977), *Nutcracker* (1982, UK/US).

BIBLIOG: Carol White with Clifford Thurlow, *Carol Comes Home*, 1982. Roger Philip Mellor.

White, Chrissie (*b* London, 1894 – *d* Chobham, 1989). Actress. RN: Ada Constance White. An athletic leading lady, with a sense of humour, who formed a romantic partnership with fellow actor and director Henry EDWARDS, and married him in November 1922. Chrissie White joined HEPWORTH in 1908 as a child actress co-starring with Alma TAYLOR in the 'Tilly the Tomboy' SERIES (beginning in 1910), and making more than 150 films for the producer, the majority of them short subjects. She retired in 1924 after starring in *The World of Wonderful Reality* for Hepworth and her husband, but returned briefly to play opposite her husband in *The Call of the Sea* (1930) and *General John Regan* (1933). The couple also toured together on stage in 1930 in *The Flag Lieutenant*.

OTHER BRITISH FILMS INCLUDE: (features) *Barnaby Rudge* (1915), *Comin' Thro' the Rye* (1916), *Dick Carson Wins Through* (1917), *The City of Beautiful Nonsense* (1919), *The Amazing Quest of Mr Ernest Bliss* (1920), *Wild Heather* (1921), *Tit for Tat* (1922), *Lily of the Valley* (1923), *The Naked Man* (1923). AS.

White, Leonard (*b* Newhaven, 1916). Actor. Entered films in *The Silver Darlings* (1946) and had about ten supporting roles in the 50s, including the usual quota of policemen, like the detective he played in *The Dark Man* (1950). Also in *Martin Luther* (1953, US/Ger).

OTHER BRITISH FILMS INCLUDE: *Hunted*, *Circumstantial Evidence* (1952), *The Large Rope*, *River Beat* (1953), *Passage Home*, *Lost* (1955), *Violent Moment* (1958).

White, Onna (*b* Nova Scotia). Choreographer. White's exhilarating Oscar-winning choreography for her only British film, *Oliver!* (1968), may not have been in the best interests of DICKENS's dark vision of Victorian London, but it was certainly in the interests of making *Oliver!* one of the best British musicals ever. For the rest, she has frequently created dazzling dance sequences on New York and London stages, and in such US films as *The Music Man* (stage 1957, screen 1962).

White, Sheila (*b* London, 1947). Actress. Began career as child, but there was nothing much for a sweet-faced singer and dancer to do in British films by the time she was grown up. She was Bet in *Oliver!* (1968), and, in the 70s, was reduced to appearing in four of the lamentable *Confessions of . . .* series (. . . *a Window Cleaner*, 1974; . . . *a Pop Performer*, 1975, etc.). She was finished with films by 1980's *Silver Dream Racer*.

OTHER BRITISH FILMS INCLUDE: *Here We Go Round the Mulberry Bush* (1967), *Villain* (1971), *Alfie Darling* (1975).

White, Valerie (*b* Simon's Town, South Africa, 1915 – *d* London, 1975). Actress. Educated in England and trained under Elsie Fogarty, White, a former commercial artist, made her London debut in 1939; first on Broadway in *The Winslow Boy*, 1947. She made only a few films, but is vivid as the estranged wife of Richard BIRD in *The Halfway House* (1944) and the villainess in *Hue and Cry* (1946), tied up by the schoolboy gang as they seek information. On TV, she re-played her stage role as *Frieda* (1947). Married (1 of 2) Albert LIEVEN.

OTHER BRITISH FILMS INCLUDE: *My Learned Friend* (1943), *The Blue Parrot* (1953), *Women Without Men* (1956), *The Battle of the V-1* (1958), *Travels with My Heart* (1972).

White, Wilfrid Hyde *see* Hyde-White, Wilfrid

Whitehall Studios Situated near Elstree Station, this studio was built for £35,000 in 1929 at the instigation of Adelqui MILLAR, as Managing Director, who had founded the production company, Whitehall Films, in 1927, and who directed two films in the new studios before departing. However, despite the installation of sound equipment, used to give soundtracks to films made elsewhere, the company collapsed and the studio was in receivership late in 1929. The studios were subsequently used by other companies: in 1934 work began on *Things to Come* at what was now called the Consolidated Studio; and in 1935 Julius HAGEN bought the studio as a base for his company, JH Productions, but its fortunes were short-lived.

Whitehead, Jack (*b* London, 1900 – *d* Chicago, 1989). Special effects, cinematographer. In films from age 15, then became a projectionist, served in WW1, worked in various photography-related jobs, including stills photographer for several studios, before joining GAUMONT–BRITISH in 1932 in the SPECIAL EFFECTS department. There he contributed to such famous films as *Rome Express* (1932) and *The 39 Steps* (1935), working several times with their respective directors, Walter FORDE and Alfred HITCHCOCK, and was with GAINSBOROUGH FILMS until becoming director of special effects for TWO CITIES in the mid 40s. His credits are wide-ranging – they embrace *Hamlet* (1948) and *Devil Girl from Mars* (1954) – and he did uncredited work on many films, including additional photography on *Mogambo* (1953, UK/US).

OTHER BRITISH FILMS INCLUDE: (special effects, unless noted) *The Tunnel* (1935), *Young and Innocent* (1937), *Goodbye, Mr Chips* (1939), *Busman's Honeymoon* (1940), *Millions Like Us* (1943), *Time Flies* (1944), *A Matter of Life and Death* (1946, back projection), *Master of Bankdam* (1947), *Tarzan's Peril* (1951, US, African footage), *Two Before Zero* (1962, c).

Whitelaw, Billie (*b* Coventry, 1932). Actress. Distinguished stage actress, acclaimed for performances in Samuel Beckett plays, who almost became a film star in the 60s. With rather harsh features, she excels at playing strongwilled, embittered women who have been through the mill, tigerish or tough/straight-talking as occasion requires. A child radio actor from age 11, she made her theatre debut in 1950, entering films in 1953. She won a BAA/Newcomer for the bookie's wife in *Hell Is a City* (1960), was a security guard's vengeful widow in *Payroll* (1961), and the landlady who fatally tries to seduce Hywel BENNETT in *Twisted Nerve* (1968, BAA/Supp Actress). Two of her best roles were with Albert FINNEY: as his estranged wife in *Charlie Bubbles* (1968, BAA/Supporting Actress, 1969) and as the sister-in-law in *Gumshoe* (1971); also memorable as Violet, devoted mum of *The Krays* (1990). Since 1980, there have been many TV roles. Once married to Peter VAUGHAN. Awarded CBE, 1991.

OTHER BRITISH FILMS INCLUDE: *The Fake* (1953), *Small Hotel* (1957), *Carve Her Name With Pride* (1958), *No Love for Johnnie* (1961), *Leo the Last* (1969), *Frenzy* (1972), *Night Watch* (1973), *The Chain* (1984), *Maurice* (1987), *The Dressmaker* (1988), *The Lost Son* (1999, UK/Fr).

BIBLIOG: Autobiography, *Who, He?*, 1996. Roger Philip Mellor.

Whiteley, Jon (*b* Monymusk, Scotland, 1945). Actor. Appealingly natural child actor of the 50s who made his mark as Dirk BOGARDE's companion on the run in *Hunted* (1952), as one of *The Kidnappers* (1953), for which he won an honorary AA, and, again befriended by Bogarde as *The Spanish Gardener* (1956). Also in the US-made *Moonfleet* (1955) and the small boy who finds *The Weapon* (1956), then was seen no more.

Whitfield, June (*b* London, 1925). Actress. Much-loved character comedian who has outlasted most of the male stars (ASKEY, HOWERD, etc.) she supported in her over-50-year career, and, if they don't ease up on the Bolly, she may well outlast the famous females – Joanna LUMLEY and Jennifer SAUNDERS – she has been so brilliantly supporting in *Absolutely Fabulous* (1992, 1993, 2001). Her fame goes back to the early 50s RADIO show, *Take It from Here*; she was a regular on *Hancock's Half Hour* (1956) and *Hancock's* (1967), and co-starred with Terry SCOTT in the series *Happy Ever After* (1974–78) and its mutation into *Terry and June* (1979–87). All this, and theatre too, means there hasn't been much time for film: the dozen or so she did make included four 'CARRY ON' capers (. . . *Nurse*, 1958; . . . *Abroad*, 1972; . . . *Girls*, 1973; . . . *Columbus*, 1992, as Queen Isabella) and a brief, serious role as Aunt Drusilla in *Jude* (1996). Had a stage success in 2002 revival of *Bedroom Farce*. Mother of actress **Suzy Aitchinson**, who appeared in *Bloody New Year* (1987). Awarded CBE, 1998.

OTHER BRITISH FILMS INCLUDE: *Friends and Neighbours* (1959), *Double Bunk* (1961, voice), *The Spy with a Cold Nose* (1966), *Bless This House* (1972), *Romance with a Double Bass* (1974, short), *Not Now, Comrade* (1976), *Faeries* (1999, voice).

BIBLIOG: Autobiography, *. . . and June Whitfield*, 2000.

Whiting, Leonard (*b* London, 1950). Actor. Whiting had played only one small role at age 15 in *The Legend of Young Dick Turpin* (1965) when he was given a great chance: he was chosen for Romeo in ZEFFIRELLI's ground-breaking, youth-centred *Romeo and Juliet* (1968, UK/It). He made the most of his youthful appeal (purists complained in vain that the verse suffered), but never again had such scope. There are a couple of international films, including his last, *Rachel's Man* (1974), made in Israel and co-starring Mickey ROONEY, and the abysmal homegrown novelette, *Say Hello to Yesterday* (1970).

OTHER BRITISH FILMS: *The Royal Hunt of the Sun* (1969), *Frankenstein: The True Story* (1973, TV, some cinemas).

Whiting, Margaret (*b* Chicago, 1924). Actress. Very popular singer of the late 40s and the 50s ('It might as well be spring', etc.), Whiting made a handful of British films, including the THRILLER, *The Informers* (1963), co-starring Nigel PATRICK. TV includes *Shroud for a Nightingale* (1984). Sister is US-based actress Barbara Whiting and their father was composer Richard Whiting who contributed music and lyrics to 30s American films.

OTHER BRITISH FILMS: *The Password Is Courage* (1962), *Mister Quilp* (1974), *Sinbad and the Eye of the Tiger* (1977).

Whitling, Townsend (*b* Oxford, 1875 – *d* London, 1952). Actor. Long on stage before venturing into films in the 30s and lending his dignified presence to ten small roles, culminating in *Blanche Fury* (1947), as the butler Banks, but by then his voice had failed and Maurice DENHAM filled in vocally.

OTHER BRITISH FILMS INCLUDE: *The Chinese Puzzle* (1932), *The Secret of the Loch* (1934), *Take a Chance* (1937), *Contraband* (1940), *The First of the Few, Tomorrow We Live* (1942).

Whitman, Stuart (*b* San Francisco, 1926). Actor. Rugged American actor who played in dozens of international films and TV programmes after his 1951 debut, but never became a major star. He made only five British films, but two of them are among his best known: *The Mark* (1961), as the sex offender struggling to put his past behind him, brought him an AAn; and *Those Magnificent Men . . .* (1965) brought him the girl (Sarah MILES) – and world-wide exposure in a popular film.

OTHER BRITISH FILMS: *Sands of the Kalahari* (1965), *Shatter* (1974, UK/Hong Kong), *The Monster Club* (1980).

Whitrow, Benjamin (*b* Oxford, 1937). Actor. Stage and TV actor who has played small roles in about a dozen films, including *Clockwise* (1985), as one of the conferring head-masters, and an Oxford academic in *The Saint* (1997, UK/US). The benevolent-looking, moustachioed Whitrow won critical acclaim for his playing of the rural justice in the RSC's *Henry IV, Pt II* (2001), and, among his many TV roles, that of Mr Bennett in *Pride and Prejudice* (1995) is probably best known, though he is really too benign for the cruel things he is given to say; he is also recalled as blameless Squire Allworthy in *Tom Jones* (1997).

OTHER BRITISH FILMS INCLUDE: *Quadrophenia* (1979), *A Shocking Accident*, *Brimstone & Treacle* (1982), *Personal Services*, *On the Black Hill* (1987), *Hawks* (1988), *Damage* (UK/Fr), *Chaplin* (UK/Fr/It/Jap/US) (1992), *Restoration* (1995, UK/US), *Chicken Run* (2000, UK/US, voice, anim).

Whitsun-Jones, Paul (*b* Newport, Wales, 1923 – *d* London, 1974). Actor. Plump character player in nearly three dozen films from the mid 50s to the early 70s, usually in small roles, like the man in the pub near the end of *Room at the Top* (1958), with slightly more to do as Dusty Miller, the mess president in *Tunes of Glory* (1960), and as the police sergeant whose eye Jekyll avoids by changing sex in *Dr Jekyll & Sister Hyde* (1971). Portly Porthos in TV's *The Three Musketeers* (1954) and the milliner boss of *Wild, Wild Women* (1969).

OTHER BRITISH FILMS INCLUDE: *The Diamond*, *The Constant Husband* (1954), *The Moonraker* (1957), *Wrong Number* (1959), *There Was a Crooked Man* (1960), *Doctor in Distress* (1963), *The Masque of the Red Death* (1964), *Life at the Top* (1965), *The Magnificent Seven Deadly Sins* (1971), *Keep It Up, Jack!* (1973).

Whittaker, Ian (*b* London, 1928). Actor, art director. Supporting player of the 50s and 60s who began in teenage roles such as that of Alfie Collins, led astray by James KENNEY's *Cosh Boy* (1953), and biffed by mum, Hermione BADDELEY for his pains. Went on to play many a services ranker, as in *The Silent Enemy* (1958) and *On the Fiddle* (1961). He changed career in the mid 60s, becoming an art director. He shared Oscar (with Luciana ARRIGHI) for the class- and temperament-discriminating designs for *Howards End* (1992), and shared three further nominations: for *Alien* (1979), *Remains of the Day* (1993) and *Anna and the King* (1999), the latter two again with Arrighi. Began as set decorator in the mid 60s, had full art director credits on *Downhill Racer* (1969, US) and worked in various capacities on Ken RUSSELL's *The Devils* (1971, set dec), *Mahler* (1974, art d), *The Rainbow* (1989, art d) and others. Has worked internationally in more recent decades.

OTHER BRITISH FILMS INCLUDE: (a) *The Sea Shall Not Have Them* (1954), *Reach for the Sky* (1956), *The Steel Bayonet* (1957), *The Revenge of Frankenstein*, *I Was Monty's Double*, *Carry On Sergeant* (1958), *Sink the Bismarck!* (1960), *Carry On Regardless* (1961), *Dr Crippen* (1962), *The Secret of Blood Island* (1964); (set dec) *Catch Us If You Can* (1965), *Our Mother's House* (1967), *Lock Up Your Daughters!* (1969), *The Music Lovers* (1971), *The Boy Friend* (+ m d), *Savage Messiah* (1972),

Juggernaut, *Akenfield* (co-art d) (1974), *Lisztomania*, *Tommy* (1975), *Joseph Andrews* (1976), *Valentino* (1977), *The Tempest* (art d), *The Missionary* (1981), *The Return of the Soldier* (1982, art d), *Highlander* (1986), *Without a Clue* (UK/US), *Madame Sousatzka* (art d) (1988), *Sense and Sensibility* (UK/US), *Victory* (UK/Fr/Ger) (1995 released 1998), *A Midsummer Night's Dream* (1999, UK/It).

Whittingham, Jack (*b* Scarborough, 1910 – *d* Valetta, Malta, 1972). Screenwriter. Charterhouse-and Oxford-educated, he began his career as film reviewer for the *Morning Post* (1936–37), making his screenwriting debut with the witty and exciting *Q Planes* (1939, co-story) before WW2 service (1939–42) intervened. After an unpromising association with director Paul STEIN on several stodgy romances, some with, but not alleviated by, music (just think of *The Laughing Lady*, 1946), he hit his stride at EALING in the 50s, on such contrasting films as the MELODRAMA, *Cage of Gold*, and the low-key realist *Pool of London* (1950). Perhaps his most interesting later film, though, was Pat JACKSON's taut cautionary tale, *The Birthday Present* (1957, + p), for which, along with *The Divided Heart* (1954) he was BAA-nominated, but *Thunderball* (1965, orig story) was no doubt more profitable.

OTHER BRITISH FILMS: (sc/co-sc) *Escape to Danger* (1943), *Kiss the Bride Goodbye* (1944), *Waltz Time* (1945), *Green Fingers* (1947), *Counterblast* (1948), *The Dancing Years* (1950), *Hunted*, *Mandy*, *I Believe in You* (1952), *The Prince and the Pauper* (1962), *Never Say Never Again* (1983, UK/US, orig story).

Whitty, Dame May (*b* Liverpool, 1865 – *d* Hollywood, California, 1948). Actress. Pillar of Britishness as she was in several dozen Hollywood films between 1915 and 1948, notably as the harridan Mrs Bramson in *Night Must Fall* (1937) and Lady Beldon pushed into democracy in *Mrs Miniver* (1942), she scarcely ever filmed in Britain. There were three silents, an unbilled dowager with George FORMBY in *Keep Your Seats, Please* (1936), a warm-hearted theatrical in *Return to Yesterday* (1940) – and the role that made her famous in films. This is Miss Froy in *The Lady Vanishes* (1938) and, short, dumpy and authoritative, she is exactly cosy and sharp enough to make this key role unforgettable. Married Ben WEBSTER. Awarded DBE in 1918 for wartime services.

Wicking, Christopher (*b* London, 1943). Screenwriter. Educated at St Martin's School of Art, he has worked chiefly in the HORROR mode, mainly for AIP and then HAMMER. He began work as technician with the BBC and also wrote for various film journals, including *Cahiers du Cinéma* before getting his first credit (for 'additional dialogue') on the script for *The Oblong Box* (1969), followed by screenplay credit for *Scream and Scream Again* (1969). Interested in unconventional narrative structures, he showed as Julian Petley wrote (1998), 'an ability at once to work within generic frameworks and to make them work for him'. When he moved out of the horror GENRE, he must have found the results – *Lady Chatterley's Lover* (1981, co-sc) and *Absolute Beginners* (1986, co-sc) – less rewarding.

OTHER BRITISH FILMS: *Cry of the Banshee* (1970, co-sc), *Blood from the Mummy's Tomb*, *Venom* (co-sc), *Demons of the Mind* (co-story, sc) (1971), *To the Devil a Daughter* (1976, UK/Ger, sc), *Dream Demon* (1988, co-sc), *The Dive* (1989, UK/Nor, sc consultant).

Widmark, Richard (*b* Sunrise, Minnesota, 1914). Actor. Durable American star much acclaimed in his first film, *Kiss of Death* (1947), as a maniacally cackling killer. Starting with the excellent *film noir*, *Night and the City* (1950), as racketeer Harry Fabian, he made about a dozen British films, his professionalism spoken of with respect by those who worked with him. Most at home in THRILLERS of various kinds, like *The Bedford Incident* (1965), he made a brave stab at playing the Dauphin in a drab *St Joan* (1957, UK/US).

OTHER BRITISH FILMS: *A Prize of Gold* (1955), *The Secret Ways* (1961, UK/US), *The Long Ships* (1963, UK/Yug), *Murder on the Orient Express* (1974), *The Sellout* (1975, UK/It), *To the Devil a Daughter* (1976, UK/Ger), *Bear Island* (1979, UK/Can), *Who Dares Wins* (1982).

Wiggins, Les Sound recordist. Shared BAA sound awards for *Jesus Christ Superstar* (1973, US), *Bugsy Malone* (1976), *A Bridge Too Far* (1977) and *Fame* (1980, US). Entered the industry towards the end of the studio years, in time to be involved with some conventional GENRE fare, and continued to find plenty of work after the system had collapsed. Worked internationally from the early 70s, on such major films as *Fiddler on the Roof* (1971, US).

OTHER BRITISH FILMS INCLUDE: (sd) *Just My Luck* (1957), *The Horsemasters* (1961), *Nurse on Wheels* (1963), *That Riviera Touch* (1966); (sd re-rec) *England Made Me* (1972, UK/Yug), *Theatre of Blood* (1973), *Juggernaut* (1974); (sd e) *Carve Her Name With Pride* (1958), *Carry On Teacher* (1959), *Victim* (1961), *Life for Ruth* (1962), *The Tomb of Ligeia* (1964), *Zeppelin* (1971), *The Black Windmill* (1974), *Brannigan* (1975), *The Dogs of War* (1980), *Privates on Parade* (1982), *Greystoke . . .* (1984, UK/US), *Shopping* (1994), *A Month by the Lake* (1995, UK/US).

Wight, Peter (*b* Worthing, Sussex, 1950). Actor. Oxford-educated, Wight began acting with OUDS, has since done much theatre in the US and UK and a great deal of TV, including *Our Mutual Friend* (1998), as Mr Wilfer, and Antonia BIRD's *Care* (2000). On-screen, he is a recognizably solid, greying character player, remembered as the security guard harangued by David THEWLIS in *Naked* (1993), for Mike LEIGH for whom he also appeared in *Meantime* (1983, TV) and *Secrets & Lies* (1996), and the police inspector whose passion for boxing comes between him and his duty in *Shiner* (2001).

OTHER BRITISH FILMS INCLUDE: *The Bitch* (1979), *Personal Services* (1987), *The Blind Date* (2000), *Lucky Break* (2001, UK/Ger/US).

Wilby, James (*b* Rangoon, Burma, 1958). Actor. Good-looking blond leading man who found a niche as upper-class types in such films as *A Room with a View* (1985) and eponymously in *Maurice* (1987), the 'type' being critiqued in his role as the Hon Freddie Nesbitt in *Gosford Park* (2001, UK/Ger/US), as the adulterous aristocrat who has married for money and been displeased to find there wasn't as much of it as he'd thought. He first appeared with Hugh GRANT in the Oxford-based student-made film, *Privileged* (1982), was one of the young men mocking Dodgson at the picnic in *Dreamchild* (1985), starred as the hapless Tony in *A Handful of Dust* (1987) and played tormented poet Sassoon in the fine but little-seen *Regeneration* (1997, UK/Can). Also stage and TV, the latter including *Lady Chatterley* (1992) as Sir Clifford.

OTHER BRITISH FILMS INCLUDE: *A Summer Story* (1987), *Howards End* (1992), *Tom's Midnight Garden* (UK/US), *Cotton Mary* (UK/Fr/US), *Jump Tomorrow* (2001, UK/US).

Wilcox, Herbert (*b* Cork, Ireland/London?, 1892 – *d* London, 1977). Producer, director, screenwriter. One of the most significant figures in British film, Wilcox, who himself (in 1967) acknowledged confusion about his birthplace, had been a journalist before his WWI service. Using his wartime earnings, Wilcox began as a film distributor in 1919, which experience, he later claimed, helped him become an astute judge of public taste. In 1922, he combined with Graham CUTTS to form a production company to make his first film *The Wonderful Story*, increasing the marketability of subsequent releases by importing well-known overseas talent like Mae Marsh, Dorothy Gish, Will Rogers, and Werner Krauss for his films.

His directing career began when he obtained the film rights to the long-running stage musical, *Chu Chin Chow* (1923), which he also produced and adapted for the screen. With even some limited experimentation in synchronous sound, it was his first of many MUSICAL ADAPTATIONS, including even a silent rendering of the Gershwin musical *Tiptoes* (1928). With considerable directing success in lush productions in the mid 20s like *Decameron Nights* (1924, UK/Ger) and in HISTORICAL DRAMAS like *Nell Gwynne* (1926, + sc), *Madame Pompadour* and *Dawn* (+ p, co-sc) (1928), with Sybil THORNDIKE as Edith Cavell, Wilcox helped found ELSTREE STUDIOS. By the end of the decade, he was head of production for BRITISH AND DOMINIONS PRODUCTIONS and a significant figure in the industry. At the outset of the SOUND era, as a producer, Wilcox again displayed an understanding of British filmgoing tastes when he signed comic Sydney HOWARD for the first sound film to be made at B&D; the success of *Splinters* (1929) led to a string of popular Howard comedies produced by Wilcox over the next eight years. He also produced a string of successful ALDWYCH FARCES in the early 30s, beginning with *Rookery Nook* (1930), said to have returned over ten times its cost in box-office receipts.

Wilcox also played a significant role in developing the careers of Jack BUCHANAN and Anna NEAGLE (whom Wilcox would marry in 1943). The extraordinarily successful musical *Goodnight Vienna* (1932), which Wilcox produced and directed, launched a string of successes for both performers. Invariably following a familiar but bankable formula, Wilcox then produced Buchanan COMEDIES for the next five years in some of the debonair performer's most memorable films, including *Yes Mr Brown* (1933, + d) and *This'll Make You Whistle* (1936, + d). As producer, he continued to supervise such GENRES as dramas like *Sorrell and Son* (1933), *The King of Paris* (1934), and *Escape Me Never* (1935), MYSTERIES like *The Frog* (1937) and *The Return of the Frog* (1938), CRIME FILMS like *The Rat* (1937), WAR FILMS like *Our Fighting Navy* (1937), and historical dramas like *A Royal Divorce* (1938).

But as director, Wilcox concentrated most attention on Neagle's career, directing all but two of her subsequent films over the next 27 years, including musicals like *The Little Damozel* (1933, + p) and Noël COWARD's *Bitter Sweet* (1933, + p, sc) and historical films like *Nell Gwyn* (1934, + p), *Peg of Old Drury* (1935, + p), and much later, *The Lady with a Lamp* (1951, + p). He directed and produced her greatest successes, two episodic BIOPICS, nostalgically depicting the life of Queen Victoria, *Victoria the Great* (1937) and the fully TECHNICOLOR production, *Sixty Glorious Years* (1938). After making several films in Hollywood to a more mixed reception, Wilcox and Neagle returned to England, where he paired her with Michael WILDING in a series of very popular post-war dramas, escapist comedies, and musicals, including such films as *Piccadilly Incident* (1946), *The Courtneys of Curzon Street* (1947), *Spring in Park Lane* (1948), and *Maytime in Mayfair* (1949) (all d, p). His later films, including two with an ageing Errol FLYNN, were not as successful, and in the 60s, he declared bankruptcy. His best films were patriotic productions with historical topics or musical comedies and romances with a light touch. Certainly from the 20s through the 40s, Wilcox demonstrated an unerring sense of what the British public wanted and proved himself to be one of the industry's great showmen.

OTHER SELECTED BRITISH FILMS: (d, p, unless noted) *Southern Love* (1924, + sc), *The Only Way* (+ sc), *London* (d) (1926), *Mumsie* (1927), *The Woman in White* (+ co-sc), *The Bondman* (1929, d), *The Loves of Robert Burns* (1930, d), *The Chance of a Night-Time* (co-d, p), *Carnival* (1931), *Money Means Nothing* (co-d, p), *The Blue Danube* (1932), *Yes Mr Brown*, *The King's Cup* (1933, co-d, p), *The Queen's Affair* (1934), *Three Maxims* (UK/Fr), *Limelight* (1936), *London Melody* (1937), *They Flew Alone* (1942), *Yellow Canary* (1943), *I Live in Grosvenor Square* (1945), *Elizabeth of Ladymead* (1948), *Into the Blue* (d), *Odette* (1950), *Trent's Last Case*, *Derby Day* (1952), *Laughing Anne* (1953), *Trouble in the Glen*, *Lilacs in the Spring* (1954), *King's Rhapsody* (1955), *My Teenage Daughter* (1956), *These Dangerous Years* (d), *Wonderful Things* (d), *The Man Who Wouldn't Talk* (1957), *The Lady is Square* (1958), *The Heart of a Man* (1959, d); (p, unless noted) *Flames of Passion* (+sc), *The Wonderful Story* (1922), *Wolves*, *On Approval*, *Canaries Sometimes Sing* (1930), *Up for the Cup*, *Tons of Money* (+ co-sc), *The Speckled Band*, *Plunder*, *Mischief*, *Almost a Divorce* (1931), *Thark*, *Say It with Music*, *The Mayor's Nest*, *A Night Like This*, *The Love Contract*, *Life Goes On*, *Leap Year*, *The Flag Lieutenant*, *It's a King*, *The Barton Mystery* (1932), *The Blarney Stone*, *Up to the Neck*, *Up for the Derby*, *Trouble*, *That's a Good Girl*, *Summer Lightning*, *Purse Strings*, *One Precious Year*, *Night of the Garter*, *Mixed Doubles*, *Lord of the Manor*, *Just My Luck*, *General John Regan*, *Discord* (1933), *Lucky Loser*, *Lilies of the Field*, *It's a Cop* (+ sc), *Girls Please!*, *Faces* (1934), *Brewster's Millions*, *Where's George?*, *Come Out of the Pantry* (1935), *Millions*, *Fame* (1936), *Sunset in Vienna*, *The Gang Show*, *The Rat*, *Splinters in the Air* (1937), *No Parking*, *Blondes for Danger*, *A Royal Divorce* (1938), *The Beggar's Opera* (1953), *Yangtse Incident* (1956), *The Navy Lark* (1959).

BIBLIOG: (autobiography) *Twenty-Five Thousand Sunsets*, 1967. Stephen Shafer.

Wilcox, John (*b* Stoke-on-Trent, 1913 – *d* Torbay, 1979). Cinematographer. After a long apprenticeship, having entered the industry in 1930, at BRITISH AND DOMINIONS STUDIOS, Wilcox was camera operator during the 30s, often uncredited, especially on Herbert WILCOX films such as *Peg of Old Drury* (1935), though not to be confused with Herbert Wilcox's son John who was a production manager. After WW2 service (1939–45) with the Fleet Air Arm and the Army Kinematograph Service, for which he shot the dramatised DOCUMENTARY, *The New Lot* (1943), he worked on a number of prestigious films as 2uc, including *The Third Man* (1949) and *State Secret* (1950). From the early 50s to the late 70s, he shot about four dozen films, as varied as the highly atmospheric *Outcast of the Islands* (1951), the decorative period piece, *Waltz of the Toreadors* (1962), and the HORROR films with which he finished his career, including *The Ghoul* (1975), *The Hound of the Baskervilles* (1977).

OTHER BRITISH FILMS: (cam op) *The Winslow Boy* (1948); (add ph) *The Sound Barrier* (1952, aerial unit ph), *The Guns of Navarone* (1961), *The Moon Spinners* (1964, UK/US), *The Eagle Has Landed* (1976, 2uc); (c) *Mr Denning Drives North*, *Who Goes There!* (1951), *The Red Beret*, *Hell Below Zero* (1953), *Cockleshell Heroes* (1955), *Carve Her Name With Pride*, *Harry Black* (1958), *The Mouse That Roared*, *Expresso Bongo* (1959), *Only Two Can Play* (1961), *Some People*, *Summer Holiday* (1962), *Hysteria* (1964), *The Skull* (1965), *The Psychopath* (1966), *Where's Jack?* (1969), *Steptoe and Son* (1972), *Craze* (1973), *Legend of the Werewolf* (1974).

Wilcoxon, Henry (*b* Antilles, Dominica, 1905 – *d* Los Angeles, 1984). Actor. Tall, somewhat stately leading man of British 30s films such as *A Woman Alone* (1936), who went to the US to appear on stage and stayed to become a usually dignified character actor. He played British roles in such films as *That Hamilton Woman* (1941), as Captain Hardy, and *Mrs Miniver* (1942), as the Vicar, a role he repeated in his only post-war British film, *The Miniver Story* (1950). Became a production associate for Cecil B. DeMille, in several of whose films he

appeared. Formerly married to actress Joan Woodbury.

OTHER BRITISH FILMS INCLUDE: *Two Way Street*, *The Perfect Lady* (1931), *The Flying Squad* (1932), *Taxi to Paradise* (1933), *Princess Charming* (1934), *Jericho* (1937).

BIBLIOG: *Lionheart in Hollywood: The Autobiography of Henry Wilcoxon*, 1991.

Wild, Jack (*b* Royton, 1952). Actor. Wild had been in the 10-part children's serial, *Danny the Dragon* (1966), before getting a career-making chance as the Artful Dodger in Carol REED's award-winning *Oliver!* (1968). He received AAn and BAAn for his wonderfully vivacious, impudent display, and had several reasonably solid follow-up roles in such films as the US-made *Pufnstuf* (1970) and two British films that reunited him with *Oliver!* co-stars: *SWALK* (1970), a tale of youthful friendship, with Mark ('Oliver') LESTER, and *Flight of the Doves* (1971), in which he was pursued across Ireland by Ron ('Fagin') MOODY. By the 80s, it petered out; by his own admission unable to cope with the trappings of celebrity, in 2000 he warned the young star of *Harry Potter* to beware of fame.

OTHER BRITISH FILMS: *The Pied Piper* (1971), *The 14* (1973), *Keep It Up Downstairs* (1976), *Alice* (1981, UK/Belg/Pol), *Basil* (1998).

Wilde, Colette Actress. Supporting player of the 50s and 60s, most noticeable as the young woman disfigured in the opening sequence of *Circus of Horrors* (1960), and briefly glimpsed when she and her husband (played by Ronald HINES) show interest in buying the *House of Mystery* (1961).

OTHER BRITISH FILMS INCLUDE: *The House of the Arrow* (1953), *Three Cases of Murder* (1955), *The Secret Partner* (1961), *The Day of the Triffids* (1962), *Maroc 7* (1966).

Wilde, Marty (*b* London, 1939). Actor. RN: Reginald Smith. Pop singer with rock groups, mainly in the 60s, who appeared in a few films but never took off as a film star. First film presented him as a vain celebrity (in company with Jackie LANE) who goes to pieces in *Jet Storm* (1959, + lyrics), but in his last he had only a minor role in the MUSICAL *Stardust* (1974), starring David ESSEX.

OTHER BRITISH FILMS: *The Hellions* (1961, UK/SAf), *What a Crazy World* (1963).

Wilde, Oscar (*b* Dublin, 1854 – *d* Paris, 1900). Writer. RN: Oscar Fingal O'Flahertie Wills. There have been well over 100 film and television versions of Wilde's plays and stories, most of them made elsewhere than in Britain. However, ASQUITH's 1952 version of *The Importance of Being Earnest*, with cast to die for, headed by Edith EVANS's magisterial Lady Bracknell, remains a high point. It was re-filmed in 2002 (UK/US) by Oliver PARKER who had had a solid success with *An Ideal Husband* (1999, UK/US), and there had been a rival production of the latter in 1998 by **William P. Cartlidge** (*b* 1945), a first-time director. Alexander KORDA filmed *An Ideal Husband* in 1947, with Paulette Goddard imported to play the dangerous Mrs Cheveley, just as Parker imported Julianne Moore in 1999. There were British silent versions of *Lady Windermere's Fan* (1916) and *A Woman of No Importance* (1921), but though these – indeed all four of the famous plays – are always being revived on stage and TV, and attract major acting talents, they have not since been filmed in Britain. In the US, there was a fine *Lady Windermere's Fan* (1925), directed by Ernst Lubitsch, and a feebly updated one by Otto Preminger (*The Fan*) in 1949, and in 1945 maverick director Albert Lewin made a wonderfully ornate and atmospheric version of *The Picture of Dorian Gray* (there was a British silent version in 1916), with an urbane

George SANDERS standing in for Wilde. However, the definitive portrayal of Wilde himself may well be Stephen FRY's in *Wilde* (1997, UK/Ger/Jap/US), though there were also competing BIOPICS in 1960 starring, respectively, Robert MORLEY (*Oscar Wilde*) and Peter FINCH (*The Trials of Oscar Wilde*). Given the high degree of verbal and general cultural competence Wilde's work might seem to require for full enjoyment, it is perhaps surprising how much attention he has had from film-makers.

OTHER BRITISH FILMS: (adapted from his works) *Man of Rope* (1961, short, from poem), *Black and Silver* (1981, story), *Salome's Last Dance* (1988, play), *Dorian* 2001, UK/Can).

Wilding, Michael (*b* Westcliff-on-Sea, 1912 – *d* London, 1979). Actor. After working as an extra and supporting player in the 30s, Wilding established a reputation in wartime as fly Cockney – *Sailors Three* (1940) and *Secret Mission* (1942) – or well-bred young man, in *In Which We Serve* (1942) and *Dear Octopus* (1943). RATTIGAN's *English Without Tears* (1944) revealed that Wilding's forté was light comedy. Stardom came when he replaced Rex HARRISON as Anna NEAGLE's partner in Herbert WILCOX's 'London' series. Wilding's height, bearing and wistful good looks lent themselves to portraying self-sacrificing aristocrats in *Piccadilly Incident* (1946) and *The Courtneys of Curzon Street* (1947). When the series switched to romantic comedy with *Spring in Park Lane* (1948) and *Maytime in Mayfair* (1949), he was a charming, affable man-about-town, able to overcome any obstacle in an easy-going manner and revealing a lithe elegance and grace of movement in the 'dream-dance' sequences.

Wilding's persona was indelibly associated with this anti-austerity fantasy of old-world charm and his stardom faded in the 50s despite his marriage to Elizabeth TAYLOR (1952–57). He appeared in both US and UK films but in rather dull roles, as in *Zarak* (1956), where he was a stiff-necked English officer opposite Victor MATURE as a charismatic rebel chieftain. He retired from acting in the 60s, becoming a theatrical agent with only the occasional appearance, including *Lady Caroline Lamb* (1972, UK/It/US). Was also married to (1) Kay Young (*b* London, 1915), who appeared in a few films, including *In Which We Serve* (1942) and *Woman to Woman* (1946), (3) agent Susan Nell and (4) Margaret LEIGHTON.

OTHER BRITISH FILMS: *There Ain't No Justice* (1939), *Tilly of Bloomsbury, Sailors Don't Care, Convoy* (1940), *Spring Meeting, Ships with Wings, Kipps, The Farmer's Wife, Cottage to Let* (1941), *The Big Blockade* (1942), *Undercover* (1943), *Carnival* (1946), *An Ideal Husband* (1947), *Under Capricorn* (1949), *Stage Fright, Into the Blue* (1950), *The Lady with a Lamp* (1951), *Trent's Last Case, Derby Day* (1952), *Danger Within* (1959), *The World of Suzie Wong* (1960), *The Naked Edge* (1961), *Waterloo* (1970).

BIBLIOG: Autobiography: *Apple Sauce: The Story of My Life* (with Pamela Wilcox, 1982). Andrew Spicer.

Wilhelm, Wolfgang (*b* Stettin, Germany, 1906 – *d* ?) Screenwriter. Spent the years 1928–33 at UFA's script department in Berlin. In the 30s and 40s, he wrote numerous screenplays for British films, including Leslie HOWARD's wartime THRILLER, *Pimpernel Smith* (1941), Roy BOULTING's allegorical *Thunder Rock* (1942) and Frank LAUNDER's SPY piece, *I See a Dark Stranger* (1946). Wilhelm also wrote the original script for the Hollywood production *A Dispatch From Reuters* (1940).

OTHER BRITISH FILMS INCLUDE: *There Goes the Bride* (original story, 1932), *Brewster's Millions* (1935), *Farewell Again* (1937), *The Silent Battle* (1939), *Freedom Radio* (1940, co-sc), *Squadron Leader X* (1942), *Escape To Danger* (1943), *Great Day* (1945), *The End Of The River* (1947),

Captain Boycott (1947), *Secret People* (1951), *Don't Blame the Stork* (1953). Tim Bergfelder.

Wilkinson, J(oseph) Brooke (*b* 1870 – *d* London, 1948). Was Secretary of the British Board of Film Censors (BBFC) from 1913 until his death. During this period he served under five BBFC Presidents, but he was the real power behind the scenes and, in effect, the founding father of British film CENSORSHIP. He viewed his task at the BBFC as to save the film industry from public controversy, to which end he adopted flexibly conservative censorship policies towards the screen depiction of, for example, contemporary international affairs, religion, sex and violence. A staunch upholder of late Victorian and Edwardian establishment political and social values, he at times steered the BBFC into a secret, closer relationship with government departments than was perhaps appropriate in a parliamentary democracy. Nevertheless, it was due to him more than to any other single individual that the BBFC became a permanent feature of the British film (and latterly video) scene. James Robertson.

Wilkinson, Marc (*b* Paris, 1929). Composer. Former harpsichordist and lecturer, Wilkinson has scored an eclectic batch of films since the late 60s, when he conducted his own score for *If . . .* (1968), making its contribution to the film's satiric intentions. Other contrasting assignments included the HORROR film, *Blood on Satan's Claw* (1970), Ken LOACH's rigorous *Family Life* (1971) and the British WESTERN, *Eagle's Wing* (1978, + cond). Has also worked extensively for TV, including Loach's *Days of Hope* (1975), and theatre, composing for the RSC, the National and others.

OTHER BRITISH FILMS: (comp, unless noted) *The Royal Hunt of the Sun* (1969), *The Triple Echo* (1972) *The Hireling* (1973, + cond), *The Quatermass Conclusion* (1978, + cond), *Looks and Smiles* (1981, co-comp), *Enigma* (1982, co-comp), *Coming Through* (1985).

Wilkinson, Tom (*b* Leeds, Yorkshire, 1948). Actor. Though he had been, in his own words (2000), 'a moderately successful actor for 25 years', it was being part of that ensemble in *The Full Monty* (1997, UK/US), that made Wilkinson such a hot property around the turn of the century. He'd had earlier successes on stage (as, for example, T.S. Eliot in *Tom & Viv*, 1984, and as King Lear, 1993, both at the Royal Court) and on TV (in entertaining rubbish like *First Among Equals*, 1986, and as Pecksniff in *Martin Chuzzlewit*, 1994). He'd had telling character roles in such films as *In the Name of the Father* (1993, UK/Ire/US), *Priest* (1994, as an indulgent one) and *Sense and Sensibility* (1995, as dying Mr Dashwood), but the success of *Monty*, in which he played the middle-class manager, gave him new status and he filmed incessantly after that. He was the choleric, obsessive Marquess of Queensberry in *Wilde* (1997, UK/Ger/Jap/US), the sexually tempted employer of *The Governess* (1998, UK/Fr), very funny (BAAn/supp a) as the theatrical entrepreneur who fancies himself as actor in *Shakespeare in Love* (1999, UK/US), and, in the US domestic tragedy, *In the Bedroom* (2001), unbearably moving as the bereaved father, receiving AAn and BAAn. University of Kent-educated Wilkinson had become a major character star, with a remarkable gift – one among several – for conveying inner pain. Married to **Diana Hardcastle**, who was in Mike FIGGIS's *The House* (1984).

OTHER BRITISH FILMS: *Parker* (1984), *Wetherby* (1985), *Paper Mask* (1990), *The Prince of Jutland* (UK/Den/Fr/Ger), *A Business Affair* (UK/Fr/Ger/Sp), *All Things Bright and Beautiful* (1994), *Jilting Joe*

(1997), *Essex Boys* (2000), *Another Life* (2001), *The Importance of Being Earnest* (UK/US), *Before You Go* (2002).

Willard, Edmund (*b* Brighton, 1884 – *d* Kingston-upon-Thames, 1956). Actor. Character player, often as villains, in two dozen-odd 30s films, many for LONDON FILMS, including *The Scarlet Pimpernel* (1935) and *Rembrandt* (1936), in small roles, and resurfacing comically as Cromwell in *Cardboard Cavalier* (1949). On stage from 1900 (New York); in London from 1903, and solidly there 1943–49, including *Arsenic and Old Lace*.

OTHER BRITISH FILMS INCLUDE: *A Window in Piccadilly* (1928), *Rynox* (1931), *The Private Life of Don Juan* (1934), *The Iron Duke, Moscow Nights* (1935), *King of the Damned* (1936), *Dark Journey, Smash and Grab* (1937), *The Stars Look Down* (1939), *Pastor Hall* (1940), *Atlantic Ferry* (1941), *The Young Mr Pitt* (1942), *Helter Skelter* (1949).

Willcox, Toyah (*b* Birmingham, 1958). Actress, singer. Diminutive rock star who has maintained an acting career in theatre (she played the title role in *Carrington* at Chichester and Sally Bowles in *Cabaret* in the West End), television (often in guest roles as herself, on, say, *French and Saunders*, 1988, in her own series, *Toyah!*, 1997), as well as a few films. Of the latter, her best known are the two she did for Derek JARMAN: *Jubilee* (1978) and, as Miranda, *The Tempest* (1979). Married to musician Robert Fripp.

OTHER BRITISH FILMS INCLUDE: *The Quatermass Conclusion* (1978), *Quadrophenia* (1979), *Midnight Breaks* (1988), *Anchoress* (1993, UK/Belg), *Julie and the Cadillacs* (1999).

Williams, Ben (*b* Macon, Mississippi, 1889 – *d* ?). Actor. Very prolific character player: from the mid 30s, after long stage career, until the late 50s he appeared on either side of the law in about 70 films, in main features (he is a detective in *Women of Twilight*, 1952) and 'B' MOVIES (he is a taxi driver in *Whispering Smith Hits London*, 1952), and dozens of other minor functionaries, often uncredited in the haphazard way of earlier decades.

OTHER BRITISH FILMS INCLUDE: *Sexton Blake and the Mademoiselle* (1935), *False Evidence* (1937), *The Stars Look Down, Mrs Pym of Scotland Yard* (1939), *The Proud Valley* (1940), *Love on the Dole, The Common Touch, Pimpernel Smith* (1941), *Get Cracking, The Demi-Paradise* (1943), *Waterloo Road* (1944), *Murder in Reverse* (1945), *Dual Alibi* (1947), *Quartet, The Calendar* (1948), *Prelude to Fame* (1950), *No Highway, Scarlet Thread* (1951), *There Was a Young Lady* (1953), *Storm over the Nile, The Love Match, The Gold Express* (1955), *Caught in the Net* (1960).

Williams, Billie (*b* London, 1895 – *d* Morden, 1951). Cinematographer. Now probably more famous as the father of Billy WILLIAMS, he photographed many films from the 30s to the early 50s. In the industry from 1910, working in various capacities, and a free-lance cameraman from 1919, he spent WW2 shooting DOCUMENTARIES and training films. Post-war, worked in Kenya with the COLONIAL FILM UNIT, and several times with James ANDERSON, on for instance the latter's *Echo of Applause: An Excursion into Motion Pictures* (1946, doc, co-c).

OTHER BRITISH FILMS INCLUDE: *Schweik's New Adventures* (1943), *All the King's Horses, Punch and Judy* (1947, short), *Here Today – Gone Tomorrow* (1952), *Model Girl* (1954, doc, short), *Tickle the Palate* (1955, doc, short).

Williams, Billy (*b* Walthamstow, 1929). Cinematographer. Oscar-sharer for *Gandhi* (1982, UK/Ind), he began his career during the 40s working as assistant to his father Billie WILLIAMS on NEWSREELS and DOCUMENTARY films for the Admiralty, Air Force and COLONIAL FILM UNIT. Through work in TV commercials, he came to know such feature

directors as Ken RUSSELL and in 1969 he received an AAn for the evocative period imagery he brought to Russell's *Women in Love*. Here, as in *Sunday Bloody Sunday* (1971), contrasts in lighting were used subtly to establish and foreground contrasts in lifestyles and temperaments, or, in *Dreamchild* (1985) 'reality' and 'fantasy', Oxford and New York. Has also worked extensively in the US and received AAn and BSCn for the luminous pastoral of *On Golden Pond* (1981).

OTHER BRITISH FILMS INCLUDE: *Five Guineas a Week* (1956), *San Ferry Ann* (1965), *Red and Blue, Billion Dollar Brain* (1967), *Magus* (1968), *Two Gentlemen Sharing* (1969), *Zee & Co.* (1971), *Voyage of the Damned* (1976), *Eagle's Wing* (1978), *Saturn 3* (1980), *Ordeal by Innocence* (1984), *The Rainbow* (1989), *Driftwood* (1997, UK/Ire).

Williams, Bransby (*b* London, 1870 – *d* London, 1961). Actor. RN: Bransby William Pharez. Former clerk and MUSIC HALL star, famous for his Dickens character studies, who filmed sporadically over several decades, and is now most associated with the good-hearted humanism of John BAXTER. He had the lead in Baxter's picaresque PASTORAL, *Song of the Road* (1937), as a transport worker who refuses to acknowledge that motor vans have replaced horses. He had an endearing approach which kept the worst excesses of sentimentality at bay. Father of Eric Bransby WILLIAMS.

OTHER BRITISH FILMS INCLUDE: *Hard Times* (1915), *The Greatest Wish in the World, Adam Bede* (title role) (1918), *The Adventures of Mr Pickwick* (1921), *Scrooge* (1928, title role), *Hearts of Humanity* (1936), *The Common Touch* (1941), *Those Kids from Town* (1942), *The Trojan Brothers* (1945), *Judgment Deferred* (1951).

BIBLIOG: Autobiography. *By Himself*, 1954.

Williams, Brock (*b* Truro, 1894 – *d* Richmond, Surrey, 1968). Screenwriter. Wildly prolific screenwriter over three decades from 1930. Most of his 30s films are 'QUOTA QUICKIES', his aspirations rising as the decade wore on, and in the 40s, when he was scenario editor at GAINSBOROUGH, he wrote the charming ghost story, *A Place of One's Own* (1944). He directed as well as wrote *The Root of All Evil* (1947), a sort of English *Mildred Pierce*, starring Phyllis CALVERT, but without the melodramatic power of the Warners classic. Later on, he was mostly busy with 'B' MOVIES, of which *Rag Doll* (1960) and *Naked Fury* (1959) have a certain vernacular energy.

OTHER BRITISH FILMS INCLUDE: (co-sc) *Chin Chin Chinaman, Black Coffee* (1931), *Her First Affaire* (1932), *The Life of the Party* (1934, co-play), *Fair Exchange* (1936), *The Singing Cop* (1937), *Q Planes* (co-story), *The Midas Touch* (1939), *Contraband* (co-scen) (1940), *The Prime Minister* (1941), *Flying Fortress* (1942, + story) (1942), *The Dark Tower, The Night Invader* (1943), *Dancing with Crime* (1947), *The Time of His Life* (1955, co-story), *Operation Cupid* (1959); (sc) *Almost a Divorce* (1931), *Head of the Family* (1933), *The Girl in the Crowd* (1934), *Crown v Stevens, It's in the Bag* (1936), *You Live and Learn, Wanted* (+ play) (1937), *Love Story* (scen e), *Madonna of the Seven Moons* (sc e) (1944), *They Were Sisters* (1945, scen e), *Tony Draws a Horse* (1950), *Isn't Life Wonderful!* (+ novel), *Meet Mr Malcolm* (1953), *The Gilded Cage* (1955), *Stormy Crossing* (1958), *The Gentle Trap* (1960).

Williams, Brook (*b* London, 1938). Actor. Character player who began to appear in very small roles in the early 60s, like that of a reporter in *The VIPs* (1963), moving somewhat up the cast for, say, the Sergeant in *Where Eagles Dare* (1968), but remaining essentially a supporting actor. Appeared in several films for maverick Tony PALMER: *Testimony* (1987), *The Children* (1990, UK/Ger), *England, My England* (1995). Son of Emlyn WILLIAMS.

OTHER BRITISH FILMS INCLUDE: *Hot Enough for June* (1964), *The Heroes of Telemark* (1965), *The Jokers* (1966), *Anne of the Thousand Days*

(1969), *The Raging Moon* (1970), *Villain* (1971), *The Wild Geese* (UK/Switz), *Absolution* (1978), *North Sea Hijack* (1979), *Pascali's Island* (1988, UK/US).

Williams, Cedric (*b* Birkenhead, 1913 – *d* Aylesbury, 1999). Cinematographer. In the industry in various assistant capacities from the early 30s, Williams began shooting features in the later 40s. He worked mostly in 'B' MOVIES, but one of his first films, Mario ZAMPI's *The Fatal Night* (1948), has acquired a minor cult reputation as being genuinely scary, and several other rightly unpretentious pieces, like Francis SEARLE's absurd but watchable *The Man in Black* (1949) and *The Gelignite Gang* (1956), benefit from his modest efforts to make them look as if they cost more than they did. Also collaborated on a couple of DOCUMENTARIES – *The Road to Canterbury* (1952) and *The Story of Regent Street* (1962), but it is essentially a minor career.

OTHER BRITISH FILMS: *Comin' Thro' the Rye* (1947), *Third Time Lucky*, *The Adventures of PC 49*, *Dick Barton Strikes Back* (1949), *Room to Let* (1950), *The Fake* (1953), *It's a Great Day*, *The Flaw* (1955), *Blue Horizons* (1957), *Breath of Life* (1963).

Williams, Charles (*b* London, 1893 – *d* Worthing, 1978). Composer, music director. Williams's fame now rests almost wholly on his pseudo-classical composition, 'The Dream of Olwen', for the 1947 MELODRAMA, *While I Live*, which was reissued under the title of its hugely popular theme tune. He studied at the Royal Academy of Music, was a conductor for the BBC, and had dealings with cinema since composing accompaniments for silent films. With GAUMONT–BRITISH during the 30s, he conducted and/or composed for FOX, ASSOCIATED BRITISH and BRITISH NATIONAL, during the 40s, scored *Kipps* (1941) and *The Young Mr Pitt* (1942) for Carol REED, and finished his film career as music director on ASQUITH's *The Doctor's Dilemma* (1958).

OTHER BRITISH FILMS INCLUDE: (comp, unless noted) *Blackmail* (1929, co-comp), *The 39 Steps* (1935, co-comp), *The Night Has Eyes* (1942), *Warn That Man*, *The Life and Death of Colonel Blimp* (m d/cond), *English Without Tears* (m d/cond), *It Happened One Sunday* (1944), *The Man from Morocco*, *The Way to the Stars* (1945, cond), *Quiet Weekend* (1946), *Noose* (1948), *The House of the Arrow* (1953, m d), *You Can't Escape* (1955).

Williams, D(avid) J(ohn) (*b c* 1868 – *d* Bushey, 1949) Actor. Very busy character player of the 30s, in small, often uncredited roles throughout the decade and up to 1942, often in major films, but the inadequate cast lists of the period mean that, while his curmudgeonly features may be familiar, only the most dedicated buffs will know his name. He directed one silent, *The Shuttle of Life* and acted in another, *Inheritance* (both 1920), then took to films seriously in 1933.

OTHER BRITISH FILMS INCLUDE: *The Pointing Finger* (1933), *My Song for You* (UK/Ger), *The Lash* (1934), *The Clairvoyant*, *Scrooge* (1935), *The Man Who Changed His Mind* (1936), *Wings of the Morning*, *Elephant Boy* (1937), *Stolen Life* (1939), *Pastor Hall* (1940), *The Ghost Train* (1941), *Tomorrow We Live*, *The Great Mr Handel* (1942).

Williams, Derick (aka Derrick; Derek) (*b* Nottingham, 1906 – *d* ?). Cinematographer, producer. Educated at Nottingham University, Williams was assistant cameraman to Jack COX at BIP on HITCHCOCK's *Blackmail* (1929) and *Juno and the Paycock* (1930), was at GAINSBOROUGH, where he shot ASQUITH's *The Lucky Number* (1933), and went to Australia as cameraman on *Flying Doctor* (1937, UK/Aust). He subsequently worked for EALING (*The Ghost of St Michael's*, 1941) and TWO CITIES, collaborating on *In Which We Serve* (1942), *The Way*

Ahead (1944) and as director of photography on *The Way to the Stars* (1945). In the 60s, he produced several children's films (for his own company), directed by Pat JACKSON. It is perhaps too scattered a career for real distinction, but he was involved at some key moments of British film-making.

OTHER BRITISH FILMS INCLUDE: (c, unless noted) *Inspector Hornleigh* (1939), *The Flemish Farm* (fx), *The Gentle Sex* (visual effects) (1943), *Beware of Pity* (1946), *White Cradle Inn* (1947), *My Brother Jonathan* (1948), *Don't Talk to Strange Men* (1962), *Seventy Deadly Pills* (1963, p), *On the Run* (1969, p).

Williams, Emlyn (*b* Mostyn, Wales, 1905 – *d* London, 1987). Actor, screenwriter. The brilliant son of a greengrocer and tavern keeper, Williams emerged from a poor Welsh mining community, receiving a scholarship to Oxford, where he began writing and performing in plays with OUDS. On New York stage at 22, London stage in 1928, and on screen from 1932, when recreating his stage role as a homicidal maniac in *The Frightened Lady* earned him recognition among filmgoers and began a tendency for him to be cast as men ultimately revealed as criminals. He co-wrote the screenplays for Victor SAVILLE's *Friday the Thirteenth* (1933), in which he played shyster Blake, and *Evergreen* (1934), and contributed dialogue to *The Divine Spark* (1935, UK/It) and HITCHCOCK's *The Man Who Knew Too Much* (1934). Had other memorable film appearances in Saville's *Evensong*, Maurice ELVEY's *Road House* and *My Song for You* (1934), Adrian BRUNEL's *City of Beautiful Nonsense* (1935), and John BRAHM's remake of *Broken Blossoms* (1936), for which Williams helped write the screenplay, and was to have played Caligula in von Sternberg's ill-fated *I, Claudius* (1937).

A prolific playwright, Williams achieved his greatest fame with his chilling play *Night Must Fall* (1935) and his autobiographical *The Corn Was Green* (1938), both subsequently filmed in America (1937 and 1945 respectively); the former also was re-made in Britain in 1964. When not on stage, he played in a variety of British films, giving strong performances in the CRIME FILMS, *Dead Men Tell No Tales* (1938) and *They Drive by Night* (1939), and Carol REED's *The Stars Look Down* (1939) and *Girl in the News* (1940), and the seducer Dennis in *Hatter's Castle* (1941), excelling as somewhat devious characters. After his vivid depiction of Snobby Price in Gabriel PASCAL's production of *Major Barbara* (1941), Williams wrote and starred in the patriotic *This England* the same year. Long a stage director, in 1949 he wrote and starred in the only film he directed, the flawed but interesting Welsh tale, *The Last Days of Dolwyn*, in which Richard BURTON made his film debut. After making several films in the early 50s for Hollywood companies, he returned to the English stage, appearing occasionally in striking character roles, like the suave abortionist of *The L-Shaped Room* (1962), in films and television. Until his death he toured extensively in his one-man show as Charles DICKENS. Awarded CBE, 1962. Son is Brock WILLIAMS.

OTHER BRITISH FILMS: *Sally Bishop*, *Men of Tomorrow* (1932), *The Iron Duke*, *The Dictator* (1935), *The Citadel* (+ dial), *Night Alone* (1938), *Jamaica Inn* (1939), *You Will Remember*, *Mr Borland Thinks Again* (short) (1940), *The Magic Box*, *Another Man's Poison* (1951), *Ivanhoe* (1952), *The Deep Blue Sea* (1955), *I Accuse*, *Time Without Pity* (1957), *Beyond this Place* (1959), *Eye of the Devil* (1966), *The Walking Stick*, *David Copperfield* (1969).

BIBLIOG: Autobiographies, *George*, 1961 and *Emlyn*, 1973; James Harding, *Emlyn Williams: A Life*, 2002. Stephen Shafer.

Williams, Eric (*b* Sunningdale, 1906 – *d* ?). Music recordist. Educated at London Polytechnic, Williams initially joined BIP, then moved on to EALING in 1933, becoming its chief sound recordist and technical supervisor, his name appearing on virtually every film made there over the next dozen years, as well as on several for other studios. He was then succeeded by Stephen DALBY and appointed Ealing's general manager in Australia. Awarded the MBE in 1946.

BRITISH FILMS INCLUDE: (sd rec) *The Secret of the Loch* (1934), *Whom the Gods Love* (UK/Ger), *I See Ice!* (1938); (rec/sd sup) *The Gaunt Stranger* (1938), *Cheer Boys Cheer* (1939), *Sailors Three*, *Convoy* (1940), *The Goose Steps Out*, *Went the Day Well?* (1942), *San Demetrio–London* (1943), *The Halfway House*, *For Those in Peril* (1944), *Pink String and Sealing Wax*, *Dead of Night* (1945), *The Captive Heart*, *Hue and Cry* (1946); (sd) *The Dictator* (1935), *The Ware Case* (1938), *Trouble Brewing*, *Young Man's Fancy* (1939), *The Proud Valley* (1940), *Big Blockade* (1942), *Johnny Frenchman* (1945), *Nicholas Nickleby* (1947).

Williams, Eric Bransby (*b* London, 1900 – *d* 1994). Actor. The son of Bransby WILLIAMS had a career as a leading man in the 1920s, including a major role in HITCHCOCK's version of COWARD's *Easy Virtue* (1927), and also appeared in a couple of 1927 Australian films: *Hound of the Deep* and *Jungle Woman*.

OTHER BRITISH FILMS INCLUDE: *After Dark*, *The Sins Ye Do* (1924), *Confessions*, *The Wonderful Wooing* (1925), *The Hellcat*, *Troublesome Wives* (1928), *Little Miss London* (1929), *The Wonderful Story* (1932). AS.

Williams, Harcourt (*b* Croydon, 1880 – *d* London, 1957). Actor. On stage from 1898 in Belfast, in London 1900, in *Henry V*, in OLIVIER's film of which he made his screen debut surprisingly late in 1944, playing a feeble Charles VI of France, a role he has first played on stage in 1914 and again in 1937 at the Old Vic, where from 1929 to 1934 he produced over 50 plays. A revered stage actor and RADA teacher, he reprised another stage role, that of seedy lawyer Prewitt, in the film ADAPTATION of *Brighton Rock* (1947), and did 20 more memorable character studies in the ensuing decade. He was the benign ducal father-in-law of *Trottie True* and the Player King in OLIVIER's *Hamlet* (1948), and James DONALD's elderly doctor father in *Cage of Gold* (1950), finishing his illustrious career in *Around the World in Eighty Days* (1956, US). Heaps of TV from 1946.

OTHER BRITISH FILMS INCLUDE: *Vice Versa* (1947), *No Room at the Inn* (1948), *Third Time Lucky*, *Under Capricorn*, *The Lost People* (1949), *Your Witness* (1950), *The Magic Box*, *The Late Edwina Black* (1951), *Time Bomb* (1953), *The Adventures of Quentin Durward* (1955).

Williams, Heathcote (*b* Helsby, 1941). Actor. RN: John Heathcote-Williams. Played Prospero in Derek JARMAN's visually arresting, verbally traditional *The Tempest* (1979), but since then has had only supporting roles in film. Also a poet, he has appeared in international films, including *Looking for Richard* (1996, US).

OTHER BRITISH FILMS INCLUDE: *Night Shift* (1986), *Wish You Were Here*, *Little Dorrit*, *Stormy Monday* (1987), *Slipstream* (1989), *Orlando* (1992, UK/Fr/It/Neth/Russ), *The Steal*, *Blue Juice* (1995), *The Tango Lesson* (1997, UK/Arg/Fr/Ger/Jap/US), *Cousin Bette* (1998, UK/US), *Honest* (2000), *Hotel* (UK/It), *Revelation* (2002).

Williams, Hugh (*b* Bexhill-on-Sea, 1904 – *d* London, 1969). Actor. Handsome, urbane stage leading man who appeared in over 50 films following his debut in *Charley's Aunt* (1930) in the US where he was appearing on stage in *Journey's End*. Haileybury-educated and RADA-trained, he was an archetypal West End star, first on the London stage in 1922, usually in upper-class roles in modern plays. He had some good roles in 30s British cinema, including the caddish Gerald in *The Last Journey* (1935), Linden TRAVERS's lover in *Brief Ecstasy* (1937)

and Margaret LOCKWOOD's boyfriend in *Bank Holiday* (1938). However, neither these nor further Hollywood roles, such as Steerforth in *David Copperfield* (1935) and the drunken Hindley in *Wuthering Heights* (1939), quite established him as a film *star*. The films he fitted in while doing WW2 service (1939–45) tended to be ensemble pieces like *Ships with Wings* (1941) and *One of Our Aircraft Is Missing* (1942); in post-war cinema his kind of leading man began to look a little obsolete and he settled into character roles, such as the avuncular Richard in *The Holly and the Ivy* (1952) and Jack HAWKINS's golfing chum in *The Intruder* (1953). He had, in any case, started another career as playwright, co-authoring such agreeable light comedies as *The Grass Is Greener* (1958) with second wife, Margaret VYNER. Their son is Simon WILLIAMS. His first wife was Gwynne WHITBY.

OTHER BRITISH FILMS INCLUDE: *Night in Montmatre* (1931), *Rome Express*, *Insult* (1932), *Her Last Affaire* (1935), *The Amateur Gentleman*, *The Happy Family* (1936), *Gypsy* (1937), *Premiere*, *The Dark Stairway* (1938), *Dark Eyes of London* (1939), *Talk About Jacqueline*, *The Day Will Dawn* (1942), *A Girl in a Million* (1946), *An Ideal Husband*, *Take My Life* (1947), *Elizabeth of Ladymead*, *The Blind Goddess* (1948), *The Gift Horse* (1952), *Twice Upon a Time* (1953), *Star of My Night* (1954), *Khartoum* (1966), *Doctor Faustus* (1967, UK/It).

Williams, J(ames) B(ailiff). (*b* Workington, 1904 – *d* London, 1965). Screenwriter. Directed and co-produced two early talkies, *White Cargo* (1929, + sc) and *The Chinese Bungalow* (1930, co-d, + co-sc), thereafter acting in *The Mystery of the Marie Celeste* (1935) and (co-)authoring a half-dozen screenplays. His solo work notably included an ADAPTATION of A.J. CRONIN's novel, *The Stars Look Down* (1939), and he shared the credit with Sidney GILLIAT for *London Belongs to Me* (1948), though Gilliat felt the overcrowded story line of the original novel defeated them. Some experience in writing for post-war DOCUMENTARY film-making.

OTHER BRITISH FILMS INCLUDE: *Owd Bob* (1938); (co-sc) *Neutral Port* (1940), *We Dive at Dawn* (1943, + story), *A Man About the House* (1947).

Williams, Kenneth (*b* London, 1926 – *d* London, 1988). Actor. Vitriolic, nostril-flaring, hypochondriac actor whose catch-phrases included 'Stop messing about!' and 'Oh, get on with it!' Former lithographic draughtsman, Williams began his career in rep (1948) before he began working on radio appearing from 1954 on *Hancock's Half Hour* where he gained popularity for the comical voices he could produce. He appeared uncredited in his first film *Trent's Last Case* (1952) but in 1958, cast as James Bailey in *Carry on Sergeant* (1958), he began to make a name for himself appearing alongside actors such as Sid JAMES, Hattie JACQUES and Eric BARKER in 26 'CARRY ON' films over a 20-year period. His wildly camp persona often added a teasing note of sexual ambiguity to his most apparently innocent remarks. After these films ceased production, Williams continued to appear regularly on radio as a panellist on *Just A Minute*. He also became a regular on the chat-show circuit especially after the publication of his autobiography *Just Williams* (1985).

OTHER BRITISH FILMS: *Innocents in Paris*, *Valley of Song*, *The Beggar's Opera* (1953), *The Seekers* (1954), *Carry On Nurse* (1958), . . . *Teacher*, *Tommy the Toreador* (1959), *Make Mine Mink*, *Carry On Constable*, *His and Hers* (1960), *Raising the Wind*, *Carry On Regardless* (1961), . . . *Cruising*, *Love Me, Love Me, Love Me* (narr, anim short), *Twice Round the Daffodils* (1962), *Carry On Spying*, . . . *Jack*, . . . *Cleo* (1964), . . . *Cowboy* (1965), . . . *Screaming*, *Don't Lose Your Head* (1966), *Follow That Camel* (1967), *Carry On Up the Khyber*, . . . *Doctor* (1968), . . . *Camping*, . . . *Again Doctor* (1969), . . . *Loving* (1970), . . . *Henry*, . . . *at Your*

Convenience (1971), . . . *Matron*, . . . *Abroad* (1972), . . . *Dick* (1974), . . . *Behind* (1975), *That's Carry On*, *The Hound of the Baskervilles* (1977), *Carry On Emmannuelle* (1978).

BIBLIOG: Russell Davies (ed), *The Kenneth Williams Diaries*, 1993. Anne-Marie Thomas.

Williams, Lawrence Paul (*b* Slough, 1905 – *d* Oxfordshire, 1996). Production designer. A trained architect who entered the film industry in 1928 at STOLL STUDIOS and went on to become Herbert WILCOX's art director on most of his 30s films made for BRITISH AND DOMINION, including *Nell Gwyn* (1934) and *Victoria the Great* (1937), and several Jack BUCHANAN vehicles, including *This'll Make You Whistle* (1936). He went to Hollywood with Wilcox and worked on such Wilcox-NEAGLE films as *Irene* (1940). With the RAF during WW2, he achieved perhaps his highest distinction with his post-war design for *Brief Encounter* (1945), colluding with Robert KRASKER's expressionist black-and-white photography greatly to heighten the intensity of the drama. Accompanying him to Hollywood in 1939 was his wife, Queenie LEONARD (1936–47). He retired in 1949.

OTHER BRITISH FILMS INCLUDE: *The Chance of a Night-Time* (1931), *A Night Like This* (1932), *Bitter Sweet*, *Summer Lightning* (1933), *Peg of Old Drury*, *While Parents Sleep* (1935), *Limelight* (1936), *A Yank at Oxford* (1937), *Sixty Glorious Years* (1938), *So Well Remembered* (1947).

Williams, Michael (*b* Manchester, 1935 – *d* Outwood, 2001). Actor. Versatile player in all the acting media, Williams, of Irish descent, trained at RADA and began his professional career on stage in 1959, joining the RSC in 1963 and staying for 14 years. The stage seems to have been his first allegiance, and he scored notable successes over 40 years, one of his last being the one-man performance of John Aubrey's *Brief Lives* (1998). He acted several times with his wife of 30 years, Judi DENCH: among others, on stage in *A Pack of Lies* (1983); in the popular TV sitcom, *A Fine Romance* (1981–84); and, on screen, in *Tea with Mussolini* (1999, UK/It). Williams had a wry, faintly rumpled manner that could be used for comedy, as in snooker-loving Ted Jeavons in TV's *Dance to the Music of Time* (1997), or for serious dramatic purposes, as Williams in Kenneth BRANAGH's *Henry V* (1989). Shortly before his death, he played Watson in a radio adaptation of the SHERLOCK HOLMES stories. He is the father of actress **Finty Williams** (*see* Judi DENCH). Appointed Knight of St Gregory by the Catholic Church.

OTHER BRITISH FILMS: *The Marat/Sade* . . . (1966), *Tell Me Lies* (1967), *Eagle in a Cage* (1970), *Dead Cert* (1974), *Enigma* (1982, UK/Fr), *Educating Rita* (1983).

Williams, Olivia (*b* London, 1968). Actress. Cambridge-educated daughter of two barristers, Williams had about ten roles in rapid succession from the turn of the century. She played Jane Fairfax in the TV version of *Emma* (1996), was chosen by Kevin Costner to co-star with him in *The Postman* (1998), and has worked on both sides of the Atlantic since. Her unquestioned beauty is underpinned by a talent honed with the RSC and though her films have not been notably successful she has emerged unscathed: *A Knight's Tale* (US) and *Lucky Break* (UK/Ger/US), both 2001, gave her nicely contrasted chances.

OTHER BRITISH FILMS INCLUDE: *Born Romantic* (2001), *The Heart of Me*, *Cromwell & Fairfax* (2002).

Williams, Ralph Vaughan *see* **Vaughan Williams, Ralph**

Williams, Randall (*b* Liverpool, 1846 – *d* Grimsby, 1898). Pioneer. Williams was a fairground showman, billed as 'the King of Showmen', who converted his 'ghost show' attraction to a film presentation, which he presented for the first time at the World's Fair Exhibition at Islington's Royal Agricultural Hall in December 1896. He was the first to bring films, in the form of bioscope shows, to fairgrounds, beginning with Kings Lynn, Hull and Sheffield in 1897. After his death his son-in-law Richard Monte and his brother James Monte continued to tour with the bioscope show until it was destroyed by fire at Thirsk in 1913. Richard Monte adopted the name of Randall Williams and is sometimes confused with his father-in-law.

BIBLIOG: Vanessa Toulmin, *Randall Williams: King of Showmen*, 1998. AS.

Williams, Richard (*b* Toronto, 1933). Animator. Having initially worked with George Dunning – later the director of *Yellow Submarine* (1968) – in Montreal, Williams moved to London in 1955 to embrace the advertisements boom prompted by emerging commercial television. Work on these films funded more personal projects like *The Little Island* (1958), a cynical allegory about the worst kinds of Truth, Beauty and Goodness, and the more humane and passionate *Love Me, Love Me, Love Me* (1962), which ultimately led to Williams making the titles and insert ANIMATION for *The Charge of the Light Brigade* (1968), drawing heavily on the British caricaturial tradition epitomised in the work of Gilray and Rowlandson. Deeply influenced by the work of the 'Golden Era' DISNEY veterans, Williams sought to bring the Disney finesse to his Oscar-winning *A Christmas Carol* (1971), and later, the ill-fated *Raggedy Ann & Andy* (1976), but especially to his most personal project, *The Thief and the Cobbler* (2000), in the making over 20 years and ultimately released in a studio-determined re-cut form, which did not reflect his *auteurist* imperatives. Most renowned for his extraordinary work on *Who Framed Roger Rabbit* (1988), Williams is one of the true masters of animation, who has never fully gained the recognition he deserves.

OTHER BRITISH FILMS INCLUDE: *Story of the Motor car Engine* (1958); *A Lecture on Man* (1962). Paul Wells.

Williams, Simon (*b* Windsor, 1946). Actor. The son of Hugh WILLIAMS and Margaret VYNER, Simon Williams has had better opportunities on TV, notably as the son of the house of Bellamy in the series, *Upstairs, Downstairs*, in which his traditionally tall, dark and handsome looks, allied to an upper-class bearing, were aptly used and at least in part critiqued. He had small roles in such 60s junk as *Joanna* and *The Touchables* (1968), and fared somewhat better in the 70s, in such films as *The Incredible Sarah* (1976, UK/US), *The Prisoner of Zenda* (1979, US) and *No Longer Alone* (1978), made for the Billy Graham Organisation, and starring **Belinda Carroll**, whom he married and divorced and who also appeared in the British film, *Yellow Dog* (1973). His second wife is Lucy Fleming (*see* Celia JOHNSON).

OTHER BRITISH FILMS INCLUDE: *Blood on Satan's Claw* (1970), *Three for All* (1974), *The Uncanny* (UK/Can), *Jabberwocky* (1977), *The Odd Job* (1978).

Williamson, Cecil H(ugh) (*b* Paignton, 1909 – *d* North Devon, 1999). Director. In films from silent days, at STOLL STUDIOS, Williamson worked variously as editor, screenwriter and producer as well as director of SHORT FILMS, DOCUMENTARIES and a few fairly obscure 'B' MOVIES, first of which was *Held in Trust* (1948, d, p, sc, c). War service with Royal Signals until 1946, after which he formed his own company, Do-U-Know (DUK) Pictures.

OTHER BRITISH FILMS INCLUDE: (e) *Troubled Waters* (1936), *The Mill on the Floss* (1937), *Three Silent Men* (1941), *Mistaken Identity* (1942); (short films/doc, d unless noted) *Prisoners of the Tower* (1946), *The Gods Can Laugh* (1948, + sc, c), *The Clown* (+ c), *Trophy Island* (+ sc, c) (1950), *Silent World* (1953); (features) *Hangman's Wharf* (1949, + p, c, sc), *Soho Conspiracy* (1950, + co-sc), *Action Stations* (1958, + co-p, s).

Williamson, James (*b* Pathhead, Fife, 1855 – *d* Richmond, Surrey, 1933). Pioneer. Williamson was the first Britisher to use and understand the technique of film editing for dramatic effect with such films as *Attack on a China Mission* (1900), filmed in his backyard, and *Fire* (1901). A Brighton and Hove-based pioneer, Williamson was the owner of a chemist's shop, who began filming and exhibiting shorts in 1898. Most were comedies, such as *Washing the Sweep* and the *Two Naughty Boys* series, featuring his sons, Tom and Stuart, or ACTUALITIES, such as *Children Bathing on Hove Beach* and *Sussex County Cricketers* (all 1898). According to historian John BARNES, his agent Prestwich lists 39 Williamson films in its 1898 catalogue. In 1907, Williamson opened a London office, in Cecil Court, as Williamson's Kinematographic Company Ltd; he continued in film production through 1909, but eventually abandoned it in favour of the manufacture of film equipment. BIBLIOG: Martin Sopocy, *James Williamson: Studies and Documents of a Pioneer of the Film Narrative*, 1998. AS.

Williamson, Lambert (aka W.L. Williamson) (*b* England, 1907). Composer, conductor. The Marlborough- and Leeds University-educated Williamson entered films on Michael POWELL's *The Edge of the World* (1937), on which he supervised orchestrations. He scored DOCUMENTARIES during WW2, feature films in the post-war years, then a rash of '**B**' MOVIES in the 50s, and finished his career as conductor or music director on such upmarket ventures as *Room at the Top* (1958) and *The Innocents* (1961). Perhaps his most distinguished work as composer was for Paul DICKSON's famous documentary, *The Undefeated* (1950); was music director for ROMULUS FILMS in the 50s.

OTHER BRITISH FILMS INCLUDE: (comp) *The End of the River, Good-Time Girl* (1947), *Woman Hater* (1948), *Cardboard Cavalier* (1949), *They Were Not Divided* (1950), *Cosh Boy* (1953), *To Dorothy a Son* (1954); (m d) *Beat the Devil* (1953, UK/It/US), *The Story of Esther Costello* (1957), *Term of Trial* (1962), *A Countess from Hong Kong* (1966, + cond, m arr); (comp/m d) *The Case of Express Delivery, . . . Gracie Budd, . . . Soho Red, . . . the Black Falcon, . . . the Bogus Count, . . . the Studio Payroll* (1953), *Forbidden Cargo* (1954), *Track the Man Down* (1955); (cond) *A Matter of Life and Death* (1946, ass), *Romeo and Juliet* (1954, UK/It), *Bonjour Tristesse* (1957); (comp/cond) *Cross Channel* (1955), *This Other Eden* (1959, Ire), *Sons and Lovers* (1960).

Williamson, Malcolm (*b* Sydney, 1931 – *d* Cambridge, 2003). Composer. Australian-born composer who scored several British films in the 60s and 70s, mostly in the HORROR GENRE, making a significant contribution to the stylish atmospherics of *The Brides of Dracula* (1960). Appointed CBE in 1976.

OTHER BRITISH FILMS: *Crescendo* (1969), *The Horror of Frankenstein* (1970), *Nothing But the Night* (1972), *Watership Down* (1978).

Williamson, Nicol (*b* Hamilton, Scotland, 1938). Actor. Charismatic purveyor of raw, truculent emotion, Williamson has remained actor rather than film star. Began his career with Dundee Rep in 1960, London 1961, repeating two of his most famous stage roles on screen: Bill Maitland in John OSBORNE's *Inadmissible Evidence* (1964–65, film 1968) and his memorably abrasive, anguished Hamlet, filmed 1969, by Tony RICHARDSON from his own stage production at London's Roundhouse,

where the film was shot. His may still be the most invincibly intelligent screen account of this most challenging role, and his edgy intelligence was also on display in his performance in *The Reckoning* (1969), as a businessman caught between two worlds. He was an aggressive, genial Little John in Richard LESTER's beautiful elegy to *Robin and Marian* (1976, UK/US) and an eye-catching Merlin in *Excalibur* (1981, US), but since then his films have been patchy, often US-made, like *Black Widow* (1987). Some notable TV has included the title role in *Lord Mountbatten: The Last Viceroy* (1986) and he had a major stage success with his 1994 one-man show, *Jack* (Barrymore, that is). Married/divorced Jill **Townsend** (*b* Los Angeles, 1945), who appeared in several British films, including *Alfie Darling* (1975).

OTHER BRITISH FILMS: *The Six-Sided Triangle* (1963), *Of Human Bondage* (1964), *The Bofors Gun* (1968), *Laughter in the Dark* (1969, UK/Fr), *The Wilby Conspiracy* (1974), *The Human Factor* (1979, UK/US), *Venom* (1981), *The Hour of the Pig* (1993, UK/Fr), *The Wind in the Willows* (1996).

Williamson, W.K. Screenwriter. Wrote a series of screenplays based on famous lives and filmed by American James A. FITZPATRICK in Britain in the later 30s. Eclectically chosen hagiographical subjects include *David Livingstone* (1936), starring Percy MARMONT, Robert Burns (*Auld Lang Syne*, 1937) and *Georges Bizet, Composer of Carmen* (1938).

OTHER BRITISH FILMS: *The Last Rose of Summer* (Lord Byron), *The Bells of St Mary's* (1937), *The Life of Chopin, A Dream of Love* (Liszt) (1938).

Willis, Ted (Lord Willis) (*b* Tottenham, 1914 – *d* Chiselhurst, 1992). Screenwriter. Along with the Norman WISDOM japery, Willis (inadvertently?) chronicled the changing face of urban Britain from the late 40s to the early 60s, tracing the emerging social fault lines of the times most notably in *Flame in the Streets* (1961), his study of a mixed-race relationship and its disruptive consequences. After his association with the Left-wing Unity Theatre ended, he turned to screenwriting in the later 40s, collaborated on *The Blue Lamp* (1949), and resuscitated the murdered PC George Dixon (Jack WARNER) for a very long-running TV series, *Dixon of Dock Green* (1955–76). He made a real contribution to the sympathetic representation of working-class life in the post-war decades. Made life peer in 1963.

OTHER BRITISH FILMS INCLUDE: *Good-Time Girl, Holiday Camp* (1947), *A Boy, a Girl and a Bike, The Huggetts Abroad* (1949), *The Undefeated* (1950, doc), *The Wallet* (1952), *Trouble in Store, Top of the Form* (1953), *One Good Turn, Up to His Neck* (1954), *It's Great to be Young* (1956), *Woman in a Dressing Gown* (1957), *No Trees in the Street, The Young and the Guilty* (1958), *Bitter Harvest* (1963). Kevin Foster.

Willman, Noel (*b* Londonderry, N. Ireland, 1918 – *d* New York, 1988). Actor. Stage actor and director, trained at London Theatre Studio, he received a Tony for directing *A Man for All Seasons* (1960, London; 1961, NY). Lent his somewhat austere persona to about 20 films: he is the Mexican police chief questioning Rod STEIGER in *Across the Bridge* (1957), the interrogator who gets his face slapped by Virginia McKENNA in *Carve Her Name With Pride* (1958), and the watchful prison governor in *The Criminal* (1960) – and a hardly florid enough Lord Byron in *Beau Brummell* (1954). A sharp rather than endearing character presence.

OTHER BRITISH FILMS INCLUDE: *The Pickwick Papers* (1952), *Malta Story* (1953), *Seven Waves Away* (1956), *Never Let Go* (1960), *Two Living, One Dead* (1961, UK/Swe), *Kiss of the Vampire* (1962), *Doctor Zhivago*

(1965, UK/US), *The Vengeance of She* (1967), *The Odessa File* (1974, UK/Ger).

Willoughby, Lewis (*b* London, 1876 – *d* Clearwater, Florida, 1968). Actor. After a brief career as a leading man in silent films and director of *Wisp o' the Woods* (1919), Willoughby settled down as the second and subservient husband of eccentric, feminist diva Olga Petrova, starring in her 1923 play *Hurricane*. OTHER BRITISH FILMS: *Colonel Newcome* (1920), *Bluff* (1921), *The Scarlet Lady*, *Trapped by the Mormons*, *Shifting Sands* (1922). AS.

Wills, Brember (*b* Reading, 1883 – *d* England, 1948). Actor. RN: Le Couteur. Distinguished character player on stage from 1905, Wills made only a few films, most famous of which was the US-made *The Old Dark House* (1932), in which he played ancient Saul Femm. OTHER BRITISH FILMS: *Carnival* (1931), *The Unfinished Symphony* (1934, UK/Austria/Ger), *The Scarlet Pimpernel* (1935), *What Happened to Harkness?* (1934, title role).

Wills, Drusilla (*b* London, 1884 – *d* London, 1951). Actress. Stage character player from 1902, Wills appeared in a couple of silents, then had small roles in about 20 talkies, including a jury member in HITCHCOCK's *Murder!* (1930), a housewife agog at the prospect of an Italian film director in the neighbourhood in *Britannia of Billingsgate* (1933), and finally Edith EVANS's aged servant in *The Queen of Spades* (1948). OTHER BRITISH FILMS INCLUDE: *Old Wives' Tale* (1921), *What the Butler Saw* (1924), *The Happy Ending* (1925), *To What Red Hell* (1929), *The Lodger* (1932), *Night Club Queen* (1934), *Squibs* (1935), *The High Command* (1937), *Yellow Sands* (1938), *A Girl Must Live* (1939), *The Man in Grey* (1943), *Champagne Charlie* (1944), *Johnny Frenchman* (1945), *Nicholas Nickleby* (1947).

Wills, J. Elder (*b* London, 1900 – *d* ?). Art director, director. Wills had an unusual career, beginning and ending as an art director, but graduating to director in the mid 30s, on *Tiger Bay* (1933), *Song of Freedom* (1936), *Everything in Life* (1936), *Sporting Love* (1936), *Big Fella* (1937). A scenic artist at Drury Lane, he entered the industry in 1927 with BRITISH INTERNATIONAL PICTURES, remaining there through 1929. In 1948, he wrote *Against the Wind*, based on his wartime experiences, and was also appointed a production designer and producer for RANK, producing *They Were Not Divided* (1950); from 1952 to 1955, he was art director on various HAMMER films, including *Spaceways* (1953), *Men of Sherwood Forest* (1954) and *The Quatermass Experiment* (1955); and he ended his career in the late 50s with Rank Screen Services. OTHER BRITISH FILMS INCLUDE: (art d) *Poppies of Flanders* (1927), *Adam's Apple*, *Tommy Atkins* (1928), *The Informer* (1929, ass art d) (1929), *The Lure* (1933), *Sing as We Go!* (1934), *Look Up and Laugh*, *No Limit* (1935), *Queen of Hearts* (1936). AS.

Wilmer, Douglas (*b* London, 1920). Actor. Educated at King's School, Canterbury, and RADA-trained, Wilmer trained for architecture before making his stage debut in 1945 (London, 1946). Had Old Vic and RSC seasons, and played Claudius to Ian MCKELLEN's Hamlet (1970–71). Sporadic film appearances over 30 years, from *Men of Sherwood Forest* (1954) and *Richard III* (1955), and including the icy, unctuous headmaster in *Unman, Wittering and Zigo* (1971) and Holmes in the US-made *Sherlock Holmes' Smarter Brother* (1975). Also a notable TV Holmes in the 60s. OTHER BRITISH FILMS INCLUDE: *The Right Person* (1955), *The Battle of the River Plate* (1956), *Macbeth* (1961), *Jason and the Argonauts* (1963), *Khartoum* (1966), *The Vengeance of Fu Manchu* (1967), *The Reckoning*

(1969), *Cromwell* (1970), *Antony and Cleopatra* (1972), *The Incredible Sarah* (1976, UK/US), *Octopussy* (1983).

Wilshin, Sunday (*b* London, 1905 – *d* Broomfield, 1991). Actress. RN: Mary Aline Wilshin. Blue-eyed blonde lead and second lead of a dozen or so 30s films, after which she was heard of no more. On stage from childhood; many of her films are long forgotten, but she starred as the guilty adventuress in *Collision* (1932). OTHER BRITISH FILMS INCLUDE: *Hutch Stirs 'em Up* (1923), *An Obvious Situation* (1930), *Michael and Mary* (1931), *Dance Pretty Lady* (1932), *As Good as New* (1933), *Some Day* (1935), *First Night* (1937).

Wilson, Donald (*b* Dunblane, Scotland, 1910 – *d* Gloucestershire, 2002). Producer. Former journalist and cartoonist, trained at Glasgow School of Art, Wilson entered films as scriptwriter with BIP, under Walter MYCROFT, in the early 30s, sometimes working unbilled as assistant director. After gruelling WW2 service (1939–45), he was one of the pioneers of the INDEPENDENT FRAME technique, producing several films made on this system, including *Under the Frozen Falls* (1948) and *Prelude to Fame* (1950). He directed and wrote as well as produced the somewhat heavy-handed romantic comedy, *Warning to Wantons* (1948) on the IF system; this was made for AQUILA PRODUCTIONS, a company he formed with Frederick WILSON and IF's inventor David RAWNSLEY. Later went into TV, and as head of serials at the BBC was responsible for the groundbreaking success of *The Forsyte Saga* (1967), which he produced and co-wrote. OTHER BRITISH FILMS INCLUDE: (ass d) *Mimi*, *Dandy Dick* (1935), *Land Without Music* (1936), *Jericho* (1937), *Goodbye, Mr Chips* (1939); (p) *Stop Press Girl*, *Poet's Pub*, *Floodtide* (1949), *Miss Robin Hood* (1952); *Three Cases of Murder* (1955, segment).

Wilson, Frank (*b* Norfolk, 1873 – *d* London, 1951). Actor, director. A former stage actor who became a prolific director from 1908 to 1917 at HEPWORTH, where he also acted, 1907–08. Wilson directed many shorts in the 'Mr Mugwump' SERIES (1910–11), the 'Tilly' series (1912–15) and 'The Exploits of Tubby' series (1916). Later he worked for producer Walter WEST. OTHER BRITISH FILMS INCLUDE: (d) *The Snare*, *The Woman Wins* (1918), *The Irresistible Flapper* (1919), *With All Her Heart* (1920), *The White Hope* (1922); (sc) *The Mystery of Dr Fu Manchu* series (1923). AS.

Wilson, Frederick (*b* London, 1912 – *d* London, 1964). Director. Earliest film experience (from 1928) was in the cutting room, getting his first credits as editor in the mid 30s and returning to editing after brief period as director for AQUILA FILMS, which he formed with David RAWNSLEY (whose INDEPENDENT FRAME technique the company used) and Donald WILSON (no relation). The films he directed are the mildly agreeable features, *Poets' Pub* and *Floodtide* (+ sc) (1949), and DOCUMENTARY, *The Dancing Fleece* (1950, + p, doc), which he made for the CROWN FILM UNIT, for whom he produced several semi-documentaries in the early 50s. OTHER BRITISH FILMS INCLUDE: (e, unless noted) *Come Out of the Pantry* (1935), *Break the News* (1938), *Spellbound* (1941), *The Lamp Still Burns* (1943), *Don't Take It to Heart!* (1944), *While the Sun Shines* (1947), *Festival in London* (p, doc), *Life in Her Hands* (assoc p), *Out of True* (p) (1951), *The Young Lovers* (1954), *The Prisoner*, *All for Mary* (1955), *The Iron Petticoat* (1956), *Campbell's Kingdom* (1957), *The Captain's Table* (1958), *North West Frontier* (1959), *Reach for Glory* (1961), *Lancelot and Guinevere* (1962), *Rattle of a Simple Man*, *The Third Secret* (1964),

Arabesque, The Quiller Memorandum (1966, UK/US), *The Nightcomers* (sup), *Chato's Land* (1971), *The Big Sleep* (1978, sup).

Wilson, Ian (*b* London, 1902 – *d* Exeter, 1987). Actor. Small actor in small roles in numerous British films, particularly for the BOULTING brothers (from *Seven Days to Noon*, 1950). Often cast as a bespectacled, put-upon little man, his most substantial performance was, paradoxically, his most atypical, as the murderous dwarf in Terence FISHER's *The Phantom of the Opera* (1962).

OTHER BRITISH FILMS INCLUDE: *A Master of Craft* (1922), *The Cavern Spider* (1924), *A Mercenary Motive* (1925), *Splinters in the Navy* (1931), *The Broken Rosary, The Unholy Quest* (1934), *Birds of a Feather* (1935), *Trottie True* (1948), *The Lady Craved Excitement* (1950), *The Floating Dutchman* (1953), *The Good Companions, Brothers in Law* (1956), *Happy is the Bride* (1957), *I'm All Right Jack* (1959), *Suspect, Two Way Stretch* (1960), *Carry On Regardless* (1961), *The Day of the Triffids* (1962), *Heavens Above!* (1963), *Carry On Cleo* (1964), *Rotten to the Core, Help!* (1965), *The Wicker Man* (1973). Peter Hutchings.

Wilson, Ian (*b* London, 1939). Cinematographer. Busy from the late 60s on low-budget independent films, this London Film School graduate hit his stride in 70s HORROR films such as *Fright* (1971) and *The Quatermass Conclusion* (1978), as well as a couple of broadly funny Frankie HOWERD vehicles, *Up the Chastity Belt* and *Up Pompeii* (1971). In more ambitious fare from the late 80s, he colluded with the minimalistic design to create a menacing effect in *Edward II* (1991), achieved a contrastingly sundrenched glow in *Emma* (1996, UK/US) and was in charge of the second unit on *Little Voice* (1998, UK/US) in north coastal Scarborough.

OTHER BRITISH FILMS INCLUDE: *Gala Day* (1963, short), *Tell Me Lies* (1967), *Bartleby* (1970), *Girl Stroke Boy* (1971), *The House in Nightmare Park* (1973), *Three for All* (1974), *Privates on Parade* (1982), *Wish You Were Here* (1987), *Dream Demon* (1988), *The Big Man* (1990), *Dakota Road* (1992), *Backbeat* (1994), *A Midsummer Night's Dream* (1996), *Swing* (1999).

Wilson, James (aka Jimmy) Cinematographer. In a career ranging over nearly four decades, Wilson racked up well over 100 credits. In film laboratories from 1918, he became assistant cameraman in 1924, with credit on such an upmarket production as *The Constant Nymph* (1928). There are several discernible phases in his career: in the early 30s he was mainly at BIP, often shooting films directed by Walter SUMMERS, such as *What Happened Then?* (1934); he became John BAXTER's regular cameraman from 1938, and his most distinguished work is probably in lighting the studio-set *Love on the Dole* (1941) and Lance COMFORT's lovingly recreated Victoriana, *When We Are Married* (1943), produced by Baxter; he stayed with BRITISH NATIONAL until 1948 (*No Room at the Inn* and *Counterblast*); did a batch of broad COMEDIES for Jack RAYMOND in the early 50s, including *Reluctant Heroes* (1951); then went into 'B' MOVIES for the rest of his career. This latter phase included work for the DANZIGERS and, in the 60s, for MERTON PARK where he photographed several of Alan BRIDGES's superior co-features, including *Act of Murder* (1964) and *Invasion* (1966).

OTHER BRITISH FILMS INCLUDE: *Taxi for Two* (1929), *Potiphar's Wife* (1931), *Timbuctoo* (1933), *The Secret of the Loch* (1934), *The Luck of the Irish* (1935), *Wife of General Ling* (1937), *What Would You Do Chums?* (1939), *Crook's Tour* (1940), *The Common Touch* (1941), *Those Kids from Town, Salute John Citizen* (1942), *The Shipbuilders, Old Mother Riley, Detective* (1943), *Heaven Is Round the Corner* (1944), *Strawberry Roan* (1945), *Appointment with Crime, Woman to Woman* (1946), *Dual Alibi, Mrs Fitzherbert* (1947), *Take Me to Paris* (1950), *Worm's Eye View* (1951),

Little Big Shot (1952), *Diplomatic Passport* (1954), *Satellite in the Sky* (1956), *A Woman of Mystery* (1957), *A Woman Possessed* (1958), *Date at Midnight* (1959), *An Honourable Murder, The Tell-Tale Heart* (1960), *Incident at Midnight* (1963), *Company of Fools* (1966).

Wilson, Josephine (*b* Bramley, Leeds, 1904 – *d* London, 1990). Actress. Already a respected stage actress when she met and married Bernard MILES, Wilson made only a few films but was a firm presence in them. She was, for instance, the ambiguous Madame Kummer in *The Lady Vanishes* (1938), the understanding Mary Jarrow in *Quiet Weekend* (1946) and the secretary flexible enough to see that the workers have a point in Miles's *Chance of a Lifetime* (1950).

OTHER BRITISH FILMS INCLUDE: *The Citadel, South Riding* (1938), *Those Kids from Town, Uncensored* (1942), *We Dive at Dawn* (1943), *The End of the Affair* (1954).

Wilson, Lambert (*b* Neuilly-sur-Seine, France, 1956). Actor. French-born star of international films, including several British/European co-productions. First was a tiny role in *Chanel Solitaire* (1981, UK/Fr), but the next was a co-starring part in Peter GREENAWAY's *The Belly of an Architect* (1987, UK/It), after a dozen French and US films. Continues to act ubiquitously, and was a striking Racine in *Marquise* (1997). He is the son of actor-director Georges Wilson.

OTHER BRITISH FILMS INCLUDE: *Strangers* (1991), *Jefferson in Paris* (1995), *The Leading Man* (1996), *The Last September* (2000, UK/Fr/Ire), *Far From China* (2001).

Wilson, Maurice J. (*b* London, 1892 – *d* London, 1978). Producer, director. Built HIGHBURY STUDIOS in 1937 and leased it out to companies other than his own, GRAND NATIONAL PRODUCTIONS, founded in 1938. Post-war he directed two modest films for GN – *The Voice Within* (1945) and *The Turners of Prospect Road* (1947) – and Highbury became the centre for RANK's short-lived 'B' MOVIE venture. In the 50s and 60s, he produced and often co-wrote a dozen 'B' films, some of which, like *The Third Alibi* (1961, + co-sc), are quite zippy examples of their kind, and GN continued as a distributor.

OTHER BRITISH FILMS INCLUDE: (p, unless noted) *Infatuation* (1930), *Sam Small Leaves Town* (1937), *What Do We Do Now?* (1945); (p, co-sc, unless noted), *A Tale of Five Cities* (1951), *Guilty?* (1956, UK/Fr, sc), *Jackpot* (1960), *She Knows Y'Know, Out of the Fog* (p) (1962), *Master Spy* (1963), *Every Day's a Holiday* (1964, co-p), *Who Killed the Cat?* (1966).

Wilson, Rex (*b c* 1873 – *d* London, 1951). Director, screenwriter. Creator of some major British silent films, Wilson began his directorial career with the WINDSOR Company in 1916, and was associated from 1918 to 1921 with G.B. SAMUELSON: *Tinker, Tailor, Soldier, Sailor, White and Blue* (1918), *In Bondage, Sweethearts, Some Artist, Quinneys, Mrs Thompson* (1919), *Tilly of Bloomsbury* (1921), and others.

OTHER BRITISH FILMS INCLUDE: *Tom Brown's Schooldays* (1916, + sc), *The Life of Lord Kitchener* (1917, + sc), *Lead, Kindly Light* (1918), *Unmarried* (1920, p), *St Elmo* (1923, p, sc). AS.

Wilson, Richard (*b* Greenock, Scotland, 1936). Actor. RADA-trained character player who became a household name as terminal curmudgeon and resentful retiree Victor Meldrew in TV's long-running sitcom, *One Foot in the Grave*, from 1990, winning two BAAs and nominated for two more. His rare film appearances have been largely unmemorable, with the marginal exception of *A Passage to India* (1984) in which he played Anglo-Indian administrator Turton. Awarded OBE, 1994.

OTHER BRITISH FILMS INCLUDE: *Junket 89* (1970), *The Trouble with 2B* (1972), *Foreign Body, Whoops Apocalypse* (1986), *Prick Up Your Ears* (1987), *Carry On Columbus* (1992), *Women Talking Dirty* (2001).

Wilson, Stuart (*b* Guilford, 1946). Actor. Exactly the kind of British actor in demand for cad roles in US films, memorably so as philandering Julius Beaufort in *The Age of Innocence* (1993). The dark, suave Wilson really came to attention first on TV, as Vronsky in *Anna Karenina* (1977), and as caddish Jimmy Clarke in *Jewel in the Crown* (1984) and most of his films have been American. His best British film role has been as the husband of vengeful Paulina in POLANSKI's *Death and the Maiden* (1995, UK/Fr/US).

OTHER BRITISH FILMS: *Dulcima* (1971), *Wetherby* (1985), *The Luzhin Defence* (2000, UK/Fr).

Wilson, T-Bone Actor. Has been more seen on TV (e.g. *Prime Suspect 2*, 1992) than cinema, but had roles in two early films dealing with black experience in Britain: *Pressure* (1975) and *Black Joy* (1977). Also in *Babylon* (1980).

Wilton, Ann Actress. RADA-trained actress who made her stage debut in Ireland and first filmed in the silent version of *The Flag Lieutenant* (1926) as a child. Had about a dozen small supporting roles, mainly in the 40s, and most memorably as Margaretta SCOTT's 'French' maid who lapses into Cockney in *Fanny by Gaslight* (1944).

OTHER BRITISH FILMS INCLUDE: *First Night* (1937), *Dead Men Tell No Tales* (1938), *The Man in Grey* (1943), *The Tawny Pipit* (1944), *The Way to the Stars* (1945), *School for Secrets* (1946), *The October Man* (1947), *The Miniver Story* (1950), *Richard III* (1955).

Wilton, Penelope (*b* Scarborough, 1946). Actress. Very versatile player in all the acting media, the long-faced, slightly solemn-looking Wilton has probably been underused by the cinema, but how vividly her occasional roles stay in the mind, from Jeremy IRONS's wife in the present-day sequences of *The French Lieutenant's Woman* (1981) to Janet Stone, friend of *Iris* (2002, UK/US), her face eloquent with the pain of a last parting. On stage, she was a rapturously received Hester in Karel REISZ's production of *The Deep Blue Sea* (1993), reprising the role on TV, where she had also made an indelible impression in comedy, as Annie in the drollery of Alan AYCKBOURN's *Norman Conquests* (1978). Married (1) Daniel MASSEY (1975–84) and (2) Ian HOLM (1991–2001).

OTHER BRITISH FILMS INCLUDE: *Joseph Andrews* (1976), *Laughterhouse* (1984), *Clockwise* (1985), *Cry Freedom* (1987), *Blame It on the Bellboy* (1992), *Carrington* (1994, UK/Fr), *The Borrowers* (1997), *Tom's Midnight Garden* (1999, UK/US).

Wilton, Robb (*b* Liverpool, *c*1881 – *d* London, 1957). Actor. First on screen in a comedy sketch, *The Fire Brigade* (1928), Wilton made nearly 20 films in the 30s, several of them MUSICALS, including *Stars on Parade* (1936), the Cicely COURTNEIDGE farce, *Take My Tip* (1937), and *Break the News* (1938). Also in the *Pathetone Parade* revue SERIES (1936, 1939, 1940, 1941, 1942) and several other VARIETY films.

OTHER BRITISH FILMS INCLUDE: *The Secret of the Loch* (1934), *The Silent Passenger, Look Up and Laugh* (1935), *The Interrupted Honeymoon* (1936), *Fine Feathers* (1937), *The Gang's All Here* (1939), *Pictorial Revue of 1943* (1943), *Pathé Radio Music Hall* (1945), *The Love Match* (1955).

Wimbush, Mary (*b* 1924). Actress. Stage actress (acidly witty as Alan BATES's colleague in *Butley*, 1971), who has also been much on TV (a continuing role as Aunt Agatha in *Jeeves and Wooster* in 1990) but in only three films. However, she received a BAAn as the mother of the Smith family in *Oh! What a Lovely War* (1969), showing feeling for both the reality of the role and the artifice of the treatment. Other films were *Fragment of Fear* (1970) and *Vampire Circus* (1971).

Wimperis, Arthur (*b* London, 1874 – *d* Maidenhead, 1953). Screenwriter. Award-winning Wimperis, educated at University College, London, worked as newspaper artist after Boer War and WWI service. He contributed to numerous 30s British films, most often directed by Alexander or Zoltán KORDA, including *Wedding Rehearsal, Men of Tomorrow* (1932), *Cash* (1933), *The Drum* (1938), *The Four Feathers* (1939), and notably, the award-winning *The Private Life of Henry VIII* (1933). He also worked in a variety of other GENRES – ADVENTURES, THRILLERS, COMEDIES and MUSICALS – for such prominent directors as Victor SAVILLE (*Dark Journey*, 1937), Paul CZINNER (*Catherine the Great*, 1934), and Brian Desmond HURST (*Prison Without Bars*, 1938). He collaborated with numerous well-known screenwriters, including R.C. SHERRIFF (*The Four Feathers*), but most frequently worked with Lajos BIRO. In the 40s, he went to Hollywood and achieved notable success at MGM, particularly with screenplays for *Mrs Miniver* (1942, AA/sc) and *Random Harvest* (1942).

OTHER BRITISH FILMS INCLUDE: *Harmony Heaven* (1929), *A Warm Corner* (1930), *Brewster's Millions* (1935), *Counsel's Opinion* (1933), *The Scarlet Pimpernel* (1935), *Knight Without Armour* (1937), *The Divorce of Lady X* (1938), , *Over the Moon, Q Planes* (1939). Stephen Shafer.

Windsor, Barbara (*b* London, 1937). Actress. RN: Barbara Deeks. Comedy actress with a cheeky smile and blonde beehive hairdo, in the Diana DORS tradition, but more comic caricature than sex symbol, whose film roles had names like Goldie Locks, and Miss Hope Springs. Whilst at the Aida FOSTER Stage School, she appeared on stage in the West End chorus of *Love From Judy*, and later worked as film extra, singer in West End nightclubs, and scantily-clad film magazine pin-up of late 50s. Her break came in the East End musical *Fings Ain't Wot They Used T'Be* (1959) and Joan LITTLEWOOD's play and 1962 film *Sparrows Can't Sing* (BAAn as Best British Actress). She appeared in nine 'CARRY ON' films, mainly as the comic foil for Sid JAMES, famously managing to lose her bikini top in *Carry on Camping* (1969). With a history of colourful relationships, she latterly brought credibility to the role of pub landlady in the soap *EastEnders* (1994–), a role which extended her career.

OTHER BRITISH FILMS INCLUDE: *The Belles of St Trinian's* (1954), *Lost* (1955), *Too Hot to Handle* (1960), *On the Fiddle* (1961), *Death Trap* (1962), *Carry On Spying, A Study in Terror* (1965), *Carry on Doctor Chitty Chitty Bang Bang* (1968), *Carry On Again Doctor* (1969), . . . *Henry* (1970), *The Boy Friend* (1971), *Not Now, Darling, Carry On Abroad,* . . . *Matron* (1972), . . . *Girls* (1973), . . . *Dick* (1974), *Comrades* (1986).

BIBLIOG: Barbara Windsor, *All Of Me: My Extraordinary Life*, 2000. Roger Philip Mellor.

Windsor, Frank (*b* Walsall, 1927). Actor. Popular TV star of the groundbreaking police series, *Z Cars* (1962–65, 1978) and its spin-off, *Softly, Softly* (1966–70), as Det. Sgt. John Watt, offsider to the abrasive Barlow, as well as appearing in dozens of other series into the late 90s, Windsor made only a few films. However, several of these were quite vivid: he is the dentist under whose anaesthetic Richard HARRIS recalls incidents from *This Sporting Life* (1963), the husband of the 'liberal' household in *Sunday Bloody Sunday* (1971) and Glass the gamekeeper in *The Shooting Party* (1984). On stage before starting TV career.

OTHER BRITISH FILMS INCLUDE: *Spring and Port Wine* (1969), *Barry McKenzie Holds His Own* (1974), *The Plank* (1979), *The London Connection* (1979), *Revolution* (1985, UK/Nor).

Windsor Studio Situated at Catford, South London, it was constructed in 1914 by an Italian distributor, the Marquis Serra, who founded the Windsor Film Company in the same year. The Company produced about 15 films between 1915 and 1920, several of them directed by Arrigo Bocchi and written by and starring Kenelm FOSS. Rachael Low describes such films as *Not Guilty* and *Fettered* (1919) as 'sophisticated melodrama with a leaning towards sex and sensation', of 'sufficiently high standard' to be sought by important renters. After legal problems, the studios were sold to Walter WEST's company Broadwest; the company ceased operation but the studios remained in use until 1921.

Winn, Godfrey (*b* King's Norton, 1906 – *d* Lewes, 1971). Screenwriter, actor. After a brief career as a stage juvenile lead from the mid 20s, Winn, also a champion junior tennis player, and later bridge ace, turned to writing. He became a famous, waspish columnist from the 40s on, joining the *Daily Sketch* in 1956, though his gifts as a writer were open to question. He contributed to the screenplay for *Holiday Camp* (1947), along with several others, and appeared as a disc jockey in *Billy Liar* (1963), parodying his own RADIO fame as compère of *Housewives' Choice*.

OTHER BRITISH FILMS: *Blighty* (1927), *Eyewitness* (1956), *Very Important Person* (1961), *The Bargee* (1964), *The Great St Trinian's Train Robbery* (1966), *Up the Chastity Belt* (1971, as 'Archbishop of all England').

Winner, Michael (*b* London, 1935). Director, screenwriter. Educated at a Quaker school and at Cambridge where he read law, Winner was writing a show business gossip column for a Kensington paper at 14, gaining access to the studios and the stars with the kind of relentless cheek and energy that kept him filming solidly for over 30 years. Critical opinion on his work has rarely been kind, certainly not since the 60s when he managed to tap into the *zeitgeist* with such films as *The System* (1964), *The Jokers* (1966, + story) and *I'll Never Forget What's 'is Name* (1967, + p). These films, aimed at an international youthful audience and all starring Oliver REED, established Winner as having a certain Hollywood-style narrative flair, and he became a bankable director on US films, first with the WESTERN *Lawman* (1971), with *Scorpio* (1973), both starring Burt LANCASTER, and the films he made with Charles Bronson, *The Mechanic* (1972) and *Death Wish* (1974) and its sequels (1982, 1985). He believed fervently in star power, paid all-star casts to adorn his films (even when the films were as slack as his REMAKE of *The Big Sleep*, 1978, or *Parting Shots*, 1998), ran his own company, surrounded himself with behind-camera personnel he was used to, and for several decades proved adept at judging what the market wanted.

He took some risks. He filmed a prequel to Henry JAMES's *The Turn of the Screw* as a sexy vehicle for Marlon Brando, *The Nightcomers* (1971, + p, ed) and failed at the box-office, as he did with his ADAPTATION of Alan AYCKBOURN's play, *A Chorus of Disapproval* (1989, + co-sc, ed), despite an excellent cast and an affectionate evocation of an amateur drama company in Scarborough. It became a critical cliché to give him a bad time, which is what some but by no means all of his films deserved. He has been a famously outspoken critic of aspects of the British film industry, and he has maintained a public profile as gourmet food writer ('Winner's Dinners') and commentator on a range of topics. Had a long relationship with Jenny SEAGROVE.

OTHER BRITISH FILMS: (d, short) *The Square* (1957), *Danger, Women at Work* (1959), *Young Entry* (+ sc), *It's Magic* (1960), *Haunted England* (+ p), *Girls, Girls, Girls, Behave Yourself* (1961), *Dead Heat* (1962, assoc p only); (d, feature) *Man With a Gun* (1958, sc only), *Climb Up the Wall* (+ co-sc), *Shoot to Kill* (+ sc), *Old Mac* (+ assoc p) (1960), *Out of the Shadow* (+ assoc p, sc), *Some Like It Cool* (1961), *Play It Cool, The Cool Mikado* (+ sc) (1962), *West 11* (1963), *You Must Be Joking!* (1965, + co-story), *Hannibal Brooks* (+ p, co-story), *The Games* (1969), *Chato's Land, The Nightcomers* (1971, + e, p), *Firepower* (1979, + e, p, co-story), *The Wicked Lady* (1983), + e, co-sc), *Claudia* (1985, co-sc, co-p, add scenes e/d), *Dirty Weekend* (1993, + e, co-p, sc); (a) *Calliope* (short), *Decadence* (1993), *Shelf Life* (2000, short).

BIBLIOG: Bill Harding, *The Films of Michael Winner*, 1978.

Winnington, Richard (*b* London, 1904 – *d* London, 1953). Critic. One of the most respected reviewers of his day, his selected writings (edited by Paul ROTHA) retain a freshness and discerning wit that make them a valuable record of a decade of cinema. He was *News Chronicle* critic from 1943 till his early death, and his sometimes lethal words (he writes of the 'mossy ineptitude' of *Bonnie Prince Charlie*, 1948) were complemented by his merciless caricatures. Less flippant than C.A. Lejeune and not perhaps as solidly intellectual as Dilys POWELL, he more nearly resembles the American James Agee in his rigorous, demanding love of the cinema.

BIBLIOG: Winnington, *Drawn and Quartered*, 1948c; Paul Rotha (ed), *Richard Winnington: Film Criticism and Caricatures, 1943–53*, 1975.

Winslet, Kate (*b* Reading, 1975). Actress. Vivacious Winslet, from a theatrical family, has much in common with her screen characters. Just as she purposefully throws herself into her performances, her gallery of forthright young women give their all to make things happen. Many turn out to be lost souls: the deeply troubled Juliet in *Heavenly Creatures* (1994, Aust/NZ), the doomed Ophelia in Kenneth BRANAGH's *Hamlet* (1996, UK/US), the long-suffering Sue in *Jude* (1996), the feisty Madeleine in *Quills* (2000, UK/US), even the adventurous young Iris Murdoch (AAn, BAAn) in *Iris* (2002, UK/US). Others eventually rise above the storm: the determined Marianne (BAA, AAn) in *Sense and Sensibility* (1995, UK/US), the spirited Rose (AAn) in *Titanic* (1997, US), the part that made the actress internationally famous, the determined Ruth in *Holy Smoke!* (1999), the restless Julia in *Hideous Kinky* (1998, UK/Fr). But they're all single-minded in pursuit of their dreams, whether valiantly struggling against the constraints of circumstances or simply trying to survive.

OTHER BRITISH FILMS: *Faeries* (1999, anim, voice), *Therese Raquin* (+ ex p), *Enigma* (UK/Ger/US), *Christmas Carol: The Movie* (UK/Ger, voice) (2001). Tom Ryan.

Winston, Bruce (*b* Liverpool, 1879 – *d* at sea, bound for New York, 1946). Actor. On the MUSIC HALL stage (famous for 'fat' parts) from 1912, Winston played supporting roles in two dozen films, mainly in the 30s, including the judge in the final scene of CAVALCANTI's famous GPO FILM UNIT short, *Pett and Pott* (1934) and the director of the clinic endowed by heiress Merle OBERON in *Over the Moon* (1939). Was also a designer of theatrical costumes.

OTHER BRITISH FILMS INCLUDE: *Queen's Evidence* (1919), *The Temptress* (1920), *Alf's Button* (1930), *The Private Life of Don Juan, My Song for You* (UK/US) (1934), *The Man Who Could Work Miracles, The Last Waltz* (UK/Fr) (1936), *The Arsenal Stadium Mystery* (1939), *The Thief of Baghdad* (1940), *The Young Mr Pitt* (1942), *Latin Quarter* (1945), *Caravan* (1946).

Winstone, Ray (*b* London, 1957). Actor. Former amateur boxer of some renown with a flair for playing vividly menacing Cockney hard men. Thick-set and physically imposing, Winstone studied drama at the Corona School without much success and decided to quit acting altogether when he was cast by director Alan CLARKE in the BBC TV's *Scum* (1979). Unfortunately, its harsh content caused it to be shelved for two years before being released theatrically. Winstone toiled throughout the 80s with minor film and television work before gaining attention for his violent role in Ken LOACH's *Ladybird Ladybird* (1994). His international reputation was confirmed when Gary OLDMAN and Tim ROTH cast him as unforgettably abusive patriarchs in their respective directorial debuts, *Nil by Mouth* (1997, BAFTAn/a) and *The War Zone* (1999, UK/It). These attracted a variety of offers, including roles in Antonia BIRD's crime thriller, *Face* (1997), the romantic comedy *Martha, Meet Frank, Daniel and Laurence* (1998), and the excellent television series *Births, Marriages and Deaths* (1999). In 2000, Winstone co-starred with Jude Law, Jonny Lee MILLER and Sadie FROST in the hip but failed gangster film *Love, Honour and Obey* and was brilliant in *Sexy Beast* (UK/Sp/US) as the oiled, sun-bronzed ex-crim lured back to rainy England for one last job. To US for *Ripley's Game* (2002).

OTHER BRITISH FILMS: *Quadrophenia, That Summer!* (1979), *Tank Malling* (1988), *Woundings, Final Cut, The Sea Change* (UK/Sp), *Darkness Falls* (1998), *Fanny and Elvis, Five Seconds to Spare* (1999), *There's Only One Jimmy Grimble* (2000, UK/Fr), *The Martins* (2001), *Last Orders* (UK/Ger) (2002). Melinda Hildebrandt.

Winter, Donovan (*b* London, 1933). Director, screenwriter. After acting in a few 50s films, Winter turned to directing. Described by David McGillivray as an 'amiable eccentric', he started with a trim enough 'B' MOVIE, *The Trunk* (1960), then worked mainly in the EXPLOITATION mode, often writing as well as directing on such films as *Escort Girls* (1974, + p, e) and *Deadly Females* (1976, + p, e). It is auteurism of a kind.

OTHER BRITISH FILMS INCLUDE: (a) *The Galloping Major* (1951), *Time Gentlemen Please!* (1952), *Moulin Rouge, Appointment in London* (1953); (d, short) *The Awakening Hour* (1957, + a, p, sc), *Honeymoon in Broadland* (1959), *Swing Aboard the Mary* (+ p), *Honeymoon Abroad* (1965), *Sunday in the Park* (1970, + p, sc, e); (d, sc, feature) *World Without Shame* (1961, + lyrics), *Come Back Peter* (1969, + p, e), *Give Us Tomorrow* (1978, + p, story).

Winter, Vincent (*b* Aberdeen, 1947 – *d* Chertsey, 1998). Actor. Began as a child actor in the acclaimed fable, *The Kidnappers* (1953), for which he and co-star Jon WHITELEY won miniature Oscars, and for which he was discovered by children's coach Margaret THOMSON. He had several more good roles as a child, including the taut thriller, *Time Lock* (1957) and the DISNEY feature, *Almost Angels* (1962, Austria/US), then went to work in the technical side of film-making, eventually becoming production manager on big-budget films such as *Superman II* (1980), *For Your Eyes Only* (1981) and BRANAGH's *Henry V* (1989). Died of heart failure.

OTHER BRITISH FILMS INCLUDE: (a) *The Dark Avenger* (1955), *Beyond This Place, The Bridal Path* (1959), *Greyfriars Bobby* (1961), *The Three Loves of Thomasina, The Horse Without a Head* (1963); (ass d) *Juggernaut* (1974), *Royal Flash* (1975), *The Hound of the Baskervilles, Are You Being Served?* (1977), *Superman, The Stud* (1978), *The Dark Crystal* (1982); (prod man) *Superman III* (1983), *Santa Claus* (1985), *Under Suspicion* (1991, co-p), *Restoration* (1995, UK/US), *The Wind in the Willows* (1996, sup).

Winterbottom, Michael (*b* Blackburn, 1961) Director, producer. Arguably the most impressive of all the British film-makers to emerge during the 90s, Oxford-educated Winterbottom, who entered films via TV DOCUMENTARIES, is also one of the most adventurous. His films are cast in a heavily-stylised REALISM, which sometimes inclines towards an edgy SURREALISM. Persistently dealing with people living on the edge, they are also unblinking in their directness. The daring *Jude* (1996), an uncompromising ADAPTATION of a Thomas HARDY novel, rubs against the genteel grain generated by the other literary adaptations of its time. The confronting *Welcome to Sarajevo* (1997, UK/US) boldly grafts a domestic MELO-DRAMA on to a contemporaneous war story. The criss-crossing narrative lines of the humanist masterwork, *Wonderland* (1999), gradually come together in a compelling portrait of troubled parents and lost children searching for a glimmer of hope. Producer Andrew EATON (with whom he formed Revolution Films in 1993), writer Frank COTTRELL-BOYCE and editor Trevor WAITE are but three of the regular collaborators associated with his films.

OTHER BRITISH FILMS: *Love Lies Bleeding* (1994), *Butterfly Kiss* (1995), *I Want You* (1998), *With or Without You* (1999), *The Claim* (2001, UK/Can/Fr/US), *24 Hour Party People* (2002). Tom Ryan.

Winters, Shelley (*b* East St Louis, Illinois, 1922). Actress. RN: Shirley Schrift. Durable blonde Hollywood star and latterly character player, in films from 1943 and an AA winner for her role in Guy GREEN's *A Patch of Blue* (1965). She has made a smattering of films in Britain since first appearing there in *To Dorothy a Son* (1954): was very fine as vulgar, touching Charlotte in KUBRICK's *Lolita* (1961), worldly as Ruby who is not about to be victimised by *Alfie* (1966) and, 30 years later, as Nicole KIDMAN's aunt in *The Portrait of a Lady* (1996, UK/US). The pleasures of Winters in full cry are not to be taken lightly. Married (2) Vittorio Gassman (1952–54), (3) Anthony Franciosa (1957–60).

OTHER BRITISH FILMS: *I Am a Camera* (1955), *Arthur? Arthur!* (1969), *Whoever Slew Auntie Roo?* (1971), *That Lucky Touch* (1975), *Fanny Hill* (1983), *Déjà Vu* (1984).

Wintle, Julian (*b* Liverpool, 1913 – *d* Brighton, 1980). Editor, producer. Despite precarious health, deriving from haemophilia, Wintle led a very busy life in British cinema. After being in the first batch of students trained in the industry at the Polytechnic School of Kinematography in 1932, he started as an editor in the mid 30s, joining the BBC in 1940, the Producers' Guild in 1942, making films for the services and the Central Office of Information, and TWO CITIES FILMS in 1949. The first film he personally produced was the seaside THRILLER, *The Dark Man* (1950), for his PINEWOOD-based company INDEPENDENT ARTISTS; then, in 1958, he took Leslie PARKYN on as a partner and they produced an interesting mixture of risky main features, such as *This Sporting Life* (1963) and more modest programme films, alternating distribution between RANK and ANGLO-AMALGAMATED. There is a distinction to be drawn between films 'Produced by Julian Wintle and Leslie Parkyn' (listed below) and 'A Wintle-Parkyn Production', when the producer credit is assigned to someone else. His wife, Anne Francis, has written a revealing account of Wintle's life and work: *Julian Wintle: A Memoir* (1984).

OTHER BRITISH FILMS INCLUDE: (e) *Wings over Africa* (1936), *We of the West Riding* (short), *29, Acacia Avenue* (1945); (p) *Assassin for Hire* (1951), *Hunted* (1952), *Passage Home* (1955), *The One That Got Away, High Tide at Noon* (1957), *Breakout* (1959), *The Firechasers* (1970); (co-p) *You Know What Sailors Are!* (1954), *House of Secrets* (1956), *Tiger Bay* (1959), *The Big Day, Snowball, The Malpas Mystery, Circus of Horrors* (1960), *The Man in the Back Seat, House of Mystery* (1961), *Night of the*

Eagle (co-ex), *Crooks Anonymous*, *The Fast Lady* (1962), *Father Came Too!* (1963), *Madame Sin* (1972, TV, some cinemas).

Winwood, Estelle (*b* Lee, 1883 – *d* Los Angeles, 1984). Actress. RN: Goodwin. A slight, birdlike lady with a large, irascible personality, noted for her longevity, her outrageous comments on life and her friendship with Tallulah Bankhead. On stage at age of five, and Broadway debut in 1916, she made only two British films, her first, *The House of Trent* (1933) and *Alive and Kicking* (1955), but a familiar, eccentric character actress in Hollywood productions from the 50s, particularly the salacious old lady in *The Producers* (1967). AS.

Wisdom, Sir Norman. (*b* London, 1915) Actor. The dominant clown of British post-war cinema, Wisdom brought his comic character, the Gump, developed through stage and television, to the cinema with immediate success in *Trouble in Store* (1953) for which he won a BAFTA as Most Promising Newcomer. His little man against the world was portrayed with robust, physical slapstick in a series of films produced by the RANK ORGANISATION peaking commercially with *A Stitch in Time* (1963). He made two films independently in order to extend his range, one of which, *There Was a Crooked Man* (1960) is amongst his finest, but the cinema public craved only the Gump. Wisdom's popularity extended well beyond Britain – reaching the Iron Curtain countries and Iran. However, it was his musical-comedy debut on Broadway that bought him to the attention of Hollywood where he made *The Night They Raided Minsky's* (1968). In 1981 Wisdom made *Going Gently* for television, a non-comic role as a dying cancer patient.
OTHER BRITISH FILMS: *A Date with a Dream* (1948), *One Good Turn* (1954), *Man of the Moment* (1955), *Up In the World* (1956), *Just My Luck* (1957), *The Square Peg* (1958), *Follow a Star* (1959), *The Bulldog Breed*, *The Girl on The Boat*, *On the Beat* (1962), *The Early Bird* (1965), *The Sandwich Man*, *Press For Time* (1966), *What's Good for the Goose* (1969), *Double X* (1991).
BIBLIOG: Richard Dacre, *Trouble in Store*,1991; Norman Wisdom, *Don't Laugh At Me*, 1992. Richard Dacre.

Wise, Ernie *see* **Morecambe, Eric and Wise, Ernie**

Wise, Greg (*b* Newcastle, 1966). Actor. Graduating from Glasgow's Royal Scottish Academy of Music and Drama in 1991, Wise made his mark in 1995: in TV's *The Buccaneers*, from minor Edith Wharton; and in cinemas in MERCHANT IVORY's *Feast of July* (UK/US), in which Ben CHAPLIN pummels him to death with a stone, and notably as Kate WINSLET's faithless lover in *Sense and Sensibility* (UK/US). His partner is Winslet's on screen sister, Emma THOMPSON, with whom he has a child, and with whom he appeared in the US *noir* semi-spoof, *Judas Kiss* (1998). In the disastrous *Mad Cows* (1999), he fared better back in costume in TV's *Madame Bovary* (2000).

Wise, Herbert (*b* Vienna, 1924). Director. RN: Weisz. Highly regarded TV director (*The Norman Conquests*, 1978; episodes of *Inspector Morse*, *A Touch of Frost*, etc.), Wise has directed only two cinema films: *To Have and to Hold* (1963), a 'B' MOVIE in the Edgar WALLACE SERIES, and *The Lovers!* (1972), SPIN-OFF from the TV series. Married Moira REDMOND. Daughter is actress Susannah Wise.

Wiseman, Debbie (aka Debra) (*b* London, 1963). Composer, conductor, pianist. A graduate of the Guildhall School of Music and Drama, Wiseman composes concert and electro-acoustic music, but is primarily known for her TV and film music, especially her work with director BRIAN GILBERT. Her strengths are in writing descriptive and dramatic music, which often provide an additional emotional subtext, for instance in *Tom & Viv* (1994) and *Haunted* (1995). Her melodic skills have also produced many memorable themes and signature tunes.
OTHER BRITISH FILMS INCLUDE: *Wilde* (1997, UK/Ger/Jap/US), *Tom's Midnight Garden* (1999), *Lighthouse* (2000), *The Guilty* (UK/Can/US), *Randall's Flat* (2001). David Burnand.

Withers, Googie (*b* Karachi, 1917). Actress. RN: Georgette Lizette Withers. Just 73 years after her London debut in 1929, the great Googie Withers was starring in London's West End, in *Lady Windermere's Fan*. In between those dates, she created as indelible an impression as any actress ever has in British films, as well as working extensively on stage and TV. She began as a dancer and had little formal theatrical training, and this may help to account for the absolute ease with which she commanded the *screen* – she had not acquired a battery of stage technique she needed to suppress. She had minor roles in about 30 mostly minor films from the mid 30s, but she was lucky enough to be in four of Michael POWELL's 'QUOTA QUICKIES', starting with her debut in *The Girl in the Crowd* (1934) – and he was lucky to have her. Even then, she stood out from the artifice around her, with a wit and boldness, an intelligent sensuality which would make her virtually unique in British films of the period. She also has a small part for HITCHCOCK in the charming opening sequences of *The Lady Vanishes* (1938) and is Robert NEWTON's girlfriend in *Busman's Honeymoon* (1940), but the best was yet to be.

It was Powell who gave her her first two serious dramatic roles in films, playing Dutch patriots (her mother was in fact part-Dutch) in both *One of Our Aircraft Is Missing* (1942) and *The Silver Fleet* (1943); she reprised her stage lead in EALING's film version of the J.B. PRIESTLEY play, *They Came to a City* (1944); more than held her own with Clive BROOK, Roland CULVER and the incomparable Beatrice LILLIE in the high comedy of *On Approval* (1944); and seized centre screen with *Pink String and Sealing Wax* (1945), as a Victorian pub landlady with murder on her mind. There was no other contemporary actress who so persistently created women of purpose, whether ruthless as in *Night and the City* (1950, UK/US) or selfless like Dr Sophie Dean in *White Corridors* (1951), or who could have so convincingly run a sheep farm as she does in *The Loves of Joanna Godden* (1947). Perhaps best of all was the complex, flawed Rose in *It Always Rains on Sunday* (1947), who, having made her domestic bed, ends by gratefully lying in it, having watched the destructive effects of passion. Virtually everything she did from 1942 is worth discussing. Mid 50s British cinema was no place for a lady, and she accompanied her husband John McCALLUM, with whom she often co-starred, to Australia and they spent the next 50 years commuting between the stages of the two countries. She made several films in Australia and did some notable TV in Britain, starring for several seasons as the Prison Governor in *Within These Walls* (1973–75) and joining a luminous cast in *Ending Up* (1989). Awarded CBE in 2001 – and not a moment too soon.
OTHER BRITISH FILMS: *The Love Test, All at Sea, Windfall, Dark World, Her Last Affaire* (1935), *Crown v Stevens, Accused, She Knew What She Wanted, King of Hearts, Crime Over London* (1936), *Pearls Bring Tears, Paradise for Two, Action for Slander* (1937), *You're the Doctor, Strange Boarders, Paid in Error, Kate Plus Ten, If I Were Boss, Convict 99* (1938), *Trouble Brewing, She Couldn't Say No, Murder In Soho, The Gang's All Here, Dead Men Are Dangerous* (1939), *Bulldog Sees It Through* (1940), *Jeannie* (1941), *Back Room Boy* (1942), *Dead of Night* (1945), *Once Upon a Dream, Traveller's Joy* (1949), *Lady Godiva Rides Again, The Magic Box*

(1951), *Derby Day* (1952), *Devil on Horseback* (1954), *Port of Escape* (1956), *Shine* (1996, UK/Aus).
BIBLIOG: John McCallum, *My Life with Googie*, 1979.

Withers, Margaret (*b* Worcestershire). Actress. Specialist in vinegary spinster types like the teacher who gave Ann TODD a bad time in *The Seventh Veil* (1945), berated Valerie HOBSON in *Blanche Fury* (1947), and was Walter FITZGERALD's possessive sister in *Great Day* (1945), suggesting an incestuous repression that poisons her dealings with others. She was untypically genial as Eliot MAKEHAM's wife in *Daybreak* (1946, released 1948), slyly comic as a woman reading 'Crime' magazine on *The Flying Scot* (1957), wintry again in *Ferry to Hong Kong* (1959). A gifted actress with a long stage career, she made small roles count on screen, where she was seven times directed by Compton BENNETT.
OTHER BRITISH FILMS INCLUDE: *Car of Dreams* (1935), *The Demi-Paradise* (1943), *Don't Take It to Heart!* (1944), *The Upturned Glass* (1947), *Quartet* (1948), *That Dangerous Age, It's Not Cricket* (1949), *It Started in Paradise* (1952), *Conflict of Wings* (1954), *That Woman Opposite* (1957), *How to Undress in Public Without Undue Embarrassment* (1965).

Withers, Margery (*b* Patagonia, 1905 – *d* Pinner, 1999). Actress. With a background that included posts as librarian to the former King Mañuel of Portugal and, during WW2, in the press office of the British Embassy in Lisbon, followed by over 20 years in the BBC's European service, for which she was awarded MBE, she didn't take up professional acting until 1960. She then acted until her death, doing a good deal of TV, memorable as Granny Barnacle in *Memento Mori* (1992), and appeared in a few films, mainly in the 90s, the last being *Onegin* (1999, UK/US), as Nanya.
OTHER BRITISH FILMS: *Arthur? Arthur!* (1969), *Staggered* (1994), *Secrets & Lies* (1996), *Amy Foster* (1997, UK/Fr/US).

Witty, John (*b* Bristol, 1915 – *d* Bristol, 1990). Actor. Oxford-educated leading man on stage from 1936, who made his debut in *Champagne Charlie* (1944). He was 'the pigfood man' who is really the boss's son in a film as inane as it sounds, *Love in Waiting* (1948), a likeable lead in two minor THRILLERS, *Hangman's Wharf* (1949) and *Soho Conspiracy* (1950), then slipped to supporting roles in both main features like *Captain Horatio Hornblower RN* (1950, UK/US) and 'B' FILMS like *Moment of Indiscretion* (1958). In TV from 1946, and, in demand for poetry-reading and narration, he had vast radio experience.
OTHER BRITISH FILMS INCLUDE: *Christopher Columbus* (1949), *Hell Below Zero, John Wesley* (1953), *A Prize of Gold* (1955), *Alive on Saturday* (1957), *The Frightened City* (1961).

Wodehouse, Sir P(elham) G(renville) (*b* Guildford, 1891 – *d* Southampton, NY, 1975). Author, screenwriter. Published 97 books under his own name as well as collaborating on the lyrics and scenarios of stage plays and musicals, but diverse as his gifts were he became best known and loved for his creation of Jeeves, Bertie Wooster and Blandings Castle. Lived in the US after WW2 because, politically inept, he had while interned in Germany made some humorous radio broadcasts and this was viewed by some in Britain as treason. His work was mainly filmed in Hollywood where his lyrics for 'Bill' were also heard in the various versions of *Showboat*. In Britain, TV made him famous all over again, with such series as *The World of Wooster* (1965–67) and *Blandings Castle* (1967) derived from his works. In Britain, a SERIES of six SHORTS was made from his golfing stories in 1924, by STOLL PICTURE PRODUCTIONS, starting

with *The Clicking of Cuthbert*; two of his co-authored plays were filmed as *Brother Alfred* (1932) and *Leave It to Me* (1933); and two of his novels were filmed as *Summer Lightning* (1933) and *The Girl on the Boat* (1962). That he was finally forgiven in Britain was signified by his being knighted just before his death.
BIBLIOG: Frances Donaldson, *P.G. Wodehouse*, 1982.

Wolf, Rita (*b* Calcutta, 1960). Actress. RN: Ghose. Indian actress in film and TV from the mid 80s. She had the lead in *Majdhar* (1984), as a young Pakistani woman deserted in London by her husband, and made a strong impression in *My Beautiful Laundrette* (1985) as the independent-minded Tania who is marginalised by men straight and gay. She had a stint in *Coronation Street* (1990), as Flick Khan. In the US, she was in Spike Lee's *Girl 6* (1996).
OTHER BRITISH FILMS INCLUDE: *The Chain* (1984), *Slipstream* (1989), *Wild Justice* (1994).

Wolfe, Digby (*b* London, 1925). Actor. Trained as scenic designer, Wolfe made his stage debut as both actor and designer in 1944. An affable leading man, he first filmed in *The Weaker Sex* (1948) as Lana MORRIS's cheery naval brother, Benjie, and had the juvenile lead in the film version of the popular services comedy, *Worm's Eye View* (1951). In 1956 he had his own TV show, *Wolfe at the Door*; also had some success in cabaret.
OTHER BRITISH FILMS INCLUDE: *The Guinea Pig* (1948), *Adam and Evelyne* (1949), *Little Big Shot* (1952), *For Better, for Worse* (1954), *Bond of Fear* (1956, story), *The Big Money* (1958).

Wolfit, Sir Donald (*b* Newark-on-Trent, 1902 – *d* London, 1968). Actor. The last of the great barnstorming actor-managers who did just enough on film for subsequent generations to see why he was once revered. On stage from 1920, then toured with Fred Terry (1922–23) before his London debut as *The Wandering Jew* (1924). He had major seasons with the Old Vic and Stratford, formed his own Shakespearean touring company in 1937 and was awarded CBE (1950) and ultimately knighted (1957) for his indefatigable morale-boosting performances during WW2, especially during the Battle of Britain. His wartime experiences and his larger-than-life persona were the subject 40 years later of Ronald HARWOOD's play (1980) and the film derived from it, *The Dresser* (1983).

In films from 1934, he is already striking as villainous Camberley in *The Silent Passenger* (1935), bringing real excitement to the climax of a modest THRILLER. His main film career belongs to the 50s and 60s, while he still maintained the rigours of theatrical touring. He was Sergeant Buzfuz in *The Pickwick Papers* (1952), a properly charismatic *Svengali* (1954) to Hildegarde NEFF's Trilby, acted up an eye-rolling storm in several minor HORROR films, and gave his finest film performance – both subtle and full-blooded – as Mr Brown in *Room at the Top* (1958), and its sequel, *Life at the Top* (1965). Here, his self-made man, doting on his daughter, determined her seducer will marry her, parrying his wife's patrician snobberies, is a fully rounded figure, drawn from life. Much of the time he was asked to do less detailed character-drawing on screen, but he is never less than mesmeric. Married (3) stage actress Rosalind Iden (*b* Prestwich, Lancs) with whom he often performed.
OTHER BRITISH FILMS: *Death at Broadcasting House* (1934), *Sexton Blake and the Bearded Doctor, Late Extra, Hyde Park Corner, Drake of England, Checkmate* (1935), *Calling the Tune* (1936), *The Ringer* (1952), *Isn't Life Wonderful!* (1953), *A Prize of Gold, A Man on the Beach* (1955),

Satellite in the Sky, Guilty? (UK/Fr), *The Man in the Road* (1956), *The Traitor, I Accuse!* (1957), *Blood of the Vampire* (1958), *The Angry Hills, The House of the Seven Hawks, The Rough and the Smooth* (1959), *The Hands of Orlac* (1960, UK/Fr), *The Mark* (1961), *Lawrence of Arabia, Dr Crippen* (1962), *Becket, 90 in the Shade* (1964), *The Sandwich Man* (1966), *The Charge of the Light Brigade, Decline and Fall . . .* (1968).

BIBLIOG: Autobiography, *First Interval*, 1955; Ronald Harwood, *The Knight Has Been Unruly*, 1971.

Wollen, Peter *see* Mulvey, Laura

women film-makers of the silent era On 16 March 1930, THE FILM SOCIETY devoted a programme to women directors, including two from British cinema, Mary FIELD and Dinah SHUREY. There were several others who might have participated. As early as the 1890s, Laura Bayley, the wife of G.A. SMITH was active in her husband's pioneering production company. Another Brighton-based female producer was Nell Emerald, whose niece was Ida LUPINO. Occasional women film-makers who embodied the adventuring British spirit were Stella Court Treatt, who filmed her husband's African expedition, *Cape to Cairo* and later in 1929, *The Stampede*, about the wanderings of the Habbania tribe in the Sudan; Jessica Borthwick, who filmed the 1913 Balkan War; Rosita Forbes, responsible for the travel film *Red Sea to Blue Nile* (1926); and Mrs Aubrey Le Blond, who made travel films in Switzerland in 1900. In 1919, Mary Marsh Allen produced and starred in *Forgive Us Our Trespasses*, and Edith Mellor produced, co-directed and wrote the melodrama, *The Laundry Girl*. Other women directors of this period included Ethyle BATLEY, Jakidawdra Melford and Frances E. Grant.

However, most women involved in film production at this time, apart from actresses, were scenarists and scriptwriters. Among these, some of the most significant were Lydia Hayward (who wrote for LUCOCQUE, GAUMONT and STOLL), Blanche MacIntosh (HEPWORTH's leading scenarist), Alicia Ramsey (Gaumont and Stoll) and Gladys, Marchioness of Townsend, who provided scenarios of a kind for CLARENDON. Other names of interest are Abby Meehan, producer and editor of the proto-CINEMAGAZINE *Kinemacolor Fashion Gazette* (1913), pioneering scientific film-maker Mrs D.H. Scott, and Ada Aline Urban, co-director of the Natural Color Kinematograph Company with her husband, Charles URBAN.

BIBLIOG. Katherine Newey, 'Women and early British film', in Linda Fitzsimmons and Sarah Street, *Moving Performance*, 2000. AS.

women film-makers in British sound cinema Despite sexism, women have made important and pioneering contributions as film-makers. British women film-makers include Marion GRIERSON, who helped pioneer the British DOCUMENTARY, and Joy BATCHELOR, with John HALAS, pioneered the full-length animated film, their stunning work, *Animal Farm* (1954), a fine example of this form, their Halas–Batchelor Productions the largest post-war ANIMATION house in Britain. The *Secrets of Nature* SERIES (1933–43), regarded as one of the first 'nature films', was directed by Mary FIELD, who is also notable for creation of the Children's Entertainment Division of the RANK ORGANISATION. Wendy TOYE, Jill CRAIGIE, and Muriel BOX were notably active film-makers in the 40s and 50s. Toye directed a series of well-crafted *film noirs* and mysteries, including *The Teckman Mystery* (1954); Craigie specialised in documentary, including *To Be a Woman* (1951), notable for its feminist subject matter, and also directed the fiction film, *The Blue Scar* (1949), concerning a mining family. Muriel Box had a very successful and long career as a writer and director,

mainly at GAINSBOROUGH FILMS, where her sister-in-law, Betty Box (1915–99), was a powerful and talented producer. *The Beachcomber* (1954) is probably Muriel Box's best-known film. Opportunities behind the camera were better for women in the 70s, when many women directed documentaries and experimental films. Perhaps the most frequently revived film of the period is *Riddles of the Sphinx* (1977), by film theorists Laura MULVEY and Peter WOLLEN. This film took up the feminist avant-garde aesthetic agenda expounded in Mulvey's famous essay, 'Visual Pleasure in the Narrative Cinema', (1975), which introduced the idea of male spectatorship and the objectifying 'male gaze'. Around this time *Circles*, a feminist distribution collective, was formed in response to the FEMINIST MOVEMENT.

In the 80s, several women film-makers of colour began actively organising and film-making. Pratibha Parmar (*b* 1960), for example, made groundbreaking films such as *Sari Red* (1988). Her films centre on such issues as homosexuality, the treatment of British South Asians, and other social issues. Gurinder CHADHA, another British Indian woman film-maker, also began making documentaries in the eighties. Later, Chadha directed the brilliant feminist feature, *Bhaji on the Beach* (1993), a witty look at nine Asian women who take off on a road trip and enjoy a voyage of self-discovery. Maureen BLACKWOOD, a black woman film-maker, helped found SANKOFA, a black film collective. Her *Passion of Remembrance* (1986) was co-directed with Isaac JULIEN. Another black British woman film-maker of note, Ngozi ONWURAH, also began directing films from a black perspective, including *And Still I Rise* (1993), a documentary inspired by Maya Angelou.

Dancer and film-maker Sally POTTER, who became very well known after the international success of her brilliantly cinematic ADAPTATION of Virginia Woolf's *Orlando* (1992, UK/Fr/It/Neth/Russ), began her career in the politically aware 70s. Her early work is celebrated for representing women through female gaze and feminist aesthetic. *Thriller* (1979) is a fascinating and engaging early Potter film; an avant-garde feminist murder mystery of sorts. In *The Gold Diggers* (1983), Potter deconstructed the conventions of the classical Hollywood musical, displaying her feminism in her selection of an all-female crew. She returned to a dance-themed film, with *The Tango Lesson* (1997, UK/Arg/Fr/Ger/Jap), a film about a director (played by Potter) who becomes involved with a dancer who is to star in her film. British women film-makers continue to break new ground as they find new opportunities behind the camera as producers and directors.

OTHER BRITISH FILMS DIRECTED BY WOMEN FILM-MAKERS INCLUDE: *The Stranger Left No Card* (1952), *Raising a Riot* (1955) (Toye); *Out of Chaos* (1944), *The Way We Live* (1946) (Craigie); *This was England* (1935), *I Married a Stranger* (1944) (Field); *The Truth about Women* (1957), *Rattle of a Simple Man* (1964) (Box); *Home Away from Home* (1994, Blackwood), *The Body Beautiful* (1991, Onwurah), *Warrior Marks* (1993, Paramour).

BIBLIOG: Muriel Box, *Odd Woman Out*, 1974; Pam Cook and Philip Dodd, *Women in Film: A Sight and Sound Reader*, 1993; Gwendolyn Foster, *Women Film-makers of the African and Asian Diaspora*, 1997. Gwendolyn Foster.

Wong, Anna May (*b* Los Angeles, 1905 – *d* Los Angeles, 1961). Actress. RN: Luong Liu Tsong. Delicately beautiful Chinese-American actress, a star in Hollywood from the silent days, who occasionally appeared in British films. The first of the latter was E.A. DUPONT's *Piccadilly* (1929, filmed as silent, sound added), an expressionist-influenced CRIME THRILLER, and she starred in the film version of the long-running stage musical, *Chu-Chin-Chow* (1934).

OTHER BRITISH FILMS: *The Flame of Love* (UK/Ger), *Elstree Calling* (1930), *Tiger Bay* (1933), *Java Head* (1934), *The Savage Innocents* (1959, UK/Fr/It/US), *Just Joe* (1960).

Wontner, Arthur (*b* London, 1875 – *d* London, 1960). Actor. Probably best known for his cerebral and highly regarded portrayals of SHERLOCK HOLMES in five British films in the 30s, Wontner appeared in character roles in numerous British films from the 20s into the 50s. On stage from 1897, he entered films in 1916, appearing in a silent version of *Lady Windermere's Fan*. First played Holmes in *The Sleeping Cardinal* (1931), and, though Wontner was in his mid fifties, many Sherlockians and even the widow of Conan Doyle thought him perfect in the role. He made four further Holmes films, *The Missing Rembrandt, The Sign of Four* (1932), *The Triumph of Sherlock Holmes* (1935), and *Silver Blaze* (1937), appeared in Walter FORDE's *Condemned to Death* (1932), an apparently lost film, and other 30s productions, often playing judges or other legal officials. With small roles in the 40s and 50s, he continued in films and television.

OTHER BRITISH FILMS INCLUDE: *Bonnie Prince Charlie* (1923), *The Diamond Man* (1924), *A Gentleman of Paris* (1931), *Dishonour Bright* (1936), *Thunder in the City, Storm in the Teacup* (1937), *The Life and Death of Colonel Blimp* (1943), *Blanche Fury* (1947), *The Elusive Pimpernel* (1950), *Sea Devils, Genevieve* (1953). Stephen Shafer.

Wood, Charles (*b* Guernsey, Channel Islands, 1932). Screenwriter. Though much associated with the swinging 60s, Wood has contrived to maintain a career that includes the distinction of the BAA-nominated screenplay for *Iris* (2002, UK/US), in which his mobility in time and place stop the film from being merely the depressing account of a major figure's collapse. His co-authored screenplay for *Help!* and the dauntingly with-it *The Knack . . .* (+ a) (1965) made his name, though it is now hard to see why, but two modishly anti-war pieces of the period, *How I Won the War* (1967) and *The Charge of the Light Brigade* (1968) wear their age with more dignity. There was also a lot of TV, including the monumental mini-series, *Wagner* (1983), and the 'Sharpe' series of the 90s.

OTHER BRITISH FILMS: *The Long Day's Dying* (1968), *The Bed-Sitting Room* (1969, adptn).

Wood, David (*b* Sutton, Surrey, 1944). Actor. Oxford-educated, with OUDS acting experience, he made his film debut as Malcolm McDOWELL's 2iC in *If . . .* (1968), spraying the crowd with his Sten gun in the film's last scene. He never again had such a showy role; he supported McDowell again in *Aces High* (1976, UK/Fr) and gradually disappeared from film view. On London stage from 1964, and later a notable writer of children's plays.

OTHER BRITISH FILMS: *Tales That Witness Madness* (1973), *North Sea Hijack* (1979), *Sweet William* (1979).

Wood, John (*b* Derbyshire, *c* 1930). Actor. Oxford-educated, OUDS president, stocky, intelligent-looking Wood had considerable experience with the Old Vic, and played in several minor films of the 50s and 60s without becoming a film name. However, in the 90s he became a character player to reckon with, doing subtle work in such films as *Shadowlands* (1993, UK/US), as a don, *Richard III* (1995), as King Edward, and *An Ideal Husband* (1999, UK/US), though it is arguable that his most memorable performance on film is as the sympathetic police inspector in Jack CLAYTON's beautiful telemovie,

Memento Mori (1992). Has also filmed in US, as, for example, the chauffeur-father of *Sabrina* (1995). On stage, he was riveting as *The Master Builder* for the RSC in 1989.

OTHER BRITISH FILMS INCLUDE: *A Stolen Face* (1952), *Sea Wife* (1956), *The Challenge* (1959), *Invasion Quartet* (1961), *The Mouse on the Moon* (1963), *One More Time* (1969), *Lady Jane* (1985), *Orlando* (1992, UK/Fr/It/Neth/Russ), *The Young Americans* (1993), *The Madness of King George* (UK/US), *Jane Eyre* (1996, UK/Fr/It/US), *Metroland* (UK/Fr/Sp), *The Gambler* (UK/Neth/Hun) (1997), *The Revengers' Comedies* (1998, UK/Fr), *Chocolat* (2000, UK/US).

Wood, Victoria (*b* Prestwich, 1953). Actress. Her serious fame is as a TV comedian, with many of her own comedy shows, some in collaboration with Julie WALTERS. Awarded the first Eric Morecambe Award from Comic Heritage 1995, and won and nominated for many other awards. Educated at Birmingham University, pleasant-looking Wood has barely touched films: she had spots in *The Secret Policeman's Other Ball* (1982) and played the tea lady in *The Wind in the Willows* (1996), but the well-deserved OBE (1997) was for her warmhearted, sharp-witted TV comedy. Married (1980) actor Geoffrey Durham, who has appeared in a couple of British films, including *Wish You Were Here* (1987).

OTHER BRITISH FILMS: *The Pantomime Dame* (1982, doc), *Bred and Born* (1983).

Woodbridge, George (*b* Exeter, 1907 – *d* London, 1973). Actor. A burly presence in several HAMMER horror films, Woodbridge proved ideal stereotypical casting for pub landlord – in *Dracula* (1958) and *Dracula – Prince of Darkness* (1965) – and for dim-witted Police Sergeant – *The Mummy* (1959). Woodbridge's physical bulk limited the parts he was offered, but he did get to play a rare villainous role as the sadistic caretaker in *The Revenge of Frankenstein* (1958). Somewhat unexpectedly given his horror credentials, in the latter part of his career he became a children's television presenter with the series *Inigo Pipkin*. On London stage from 1928, in both classical and modern plays.

OTHER BRITISH FILMS INCLUDE: *Tower of Terror, The Black Sheep of Whitehall* (1941), *Green for Danger, I See a Dark Stranger* (1946), *Blanche Fury, The October Man, Temptation Harbour* (1947), *The Fallen Idol, The Queen of Spades* (1948), *Silent Dust*, (1949), *Cloudburst* (1951), *The Flanagan Boy* (1953), *An Inspector Calls* (1954), *Richard III, Passage Home* (1955), *Jack the Ripper* (1958), *Two Way Stretch* (1960), *The Curse of the Werewolf, What a Carve Up!* (1961), *Heavens Above!* (1963), *The Reptile* (1966), *Where's Jack?, Bachelor of Arts* (1969), *Take a Girl Like You* (1970), *Up Pompeii* (1971), *Doomwatch* (1972). Peter Hutchings.

Woodfall Films Harry SALTZMAN, on the basis of having produced his first film, *The Iron Petticoat*, was in a position to found Woodfall Productions in 1958 with playwright John OSBORNE and director Tony RICHARDSON. Saltzman's involvement was short-lived. He acquired for $1,000 an option on Ian FLEMING's James BOND novels and began developing these with Cubby BROCCOLI. In some ways Woodfall was a natural progression of the FREE CINEMA movement, with which Richardson was involved at the time. Several early films were of Osborne stage plays (*Look Back in Anger*, 1959; *The Entertainer*, 1960), proving that good films, showing British life as it is, could be made cheaply. The company skilfully drew on and often developed directorial talents such as Karel REISZ (*Saturday Night and Sunday Morning*, 1960), though soon came co-productions such as with BRYANSTON FILMS and UNITED ARTISTS. Several of their directors helped to describe and re-define the 60s: Desmond DAVIS (*Girl with Green Eyes*, 1963); Richard LESTER (*The Knack . . .*, 1965); Lindsay ANDERSON

(*The White Bus*, 1967). Its most successful film was *Tom Jones* (1963) which majored on sexual abandonment. More often, Woodfall productions were characterised by black-and-white realistic photography and starring working-class people caught up in harsh surroundings. Its spiritual heir is Ken LOACH whose film *Kes* (1969) was made for Woodfall. Stephen Brown.

Woods, Arthur (*b* West Derby, 1904 – *d* Emsworth, 1944). Director. As with Penrose TENNYSON, WW2 robbed British cinema of one of its most promising directorial talents when Woods was killed in an air crash. He had more films to his credit than Tennyson when he died, most of them in the THRILLER and COMEDY categories that account for much 30s British film-making. He turned his back on Cambridge and a family shipping business in 1924 to go into the film industry, became an editor with GB INSTRUCTIONAL in 1926 and from 1929 directed its 'Secrets of Nature' SERIES, before getting his chance with features in 1933, starting with a shared credit with prolific Walter SUMMERS on *Timbuctoo* (1933). He also co-wrote screenplays as well, those filmed including *A Southern Maid* and *The Pride of the Force* (1933). He moved from BIP to WARNER–BRITISH in the mid 30s and his first film there, *Where's Sally?* (1936), was well received, and Graham GREENE wrote of his best known film, *They Drive by Night* (1939), that it 'is a murder-story set against the authentic background of dance palaces, public houses, seedy Soho clubs, and the huge wet expanse of the Great North Road', praising it because 'the settings for the first time in an English low-life story are not romanticised'. Time alone would have told whether this promise would be fulfilled but his last film, *Busman's Honeymoon* (1940) brings to its mystery story a wit and charm that is certainly not there in Dorothy Sayers' snobbish original.

OTHER BRITISH FILMS: (d, unless noted) *The Marquis of Bolibar* (1928, art d), *The Lost Patrol* (1929, a), *A Cottage on Dartmoor* (art d), *Stark Nature* (+ p) (1930), *Tell England* (1931, art d), *Dual Control* (1932, ass d, short), *On Secret Service* (+ co-sc), *I Spy* (co-sc) (1933), *Happy* (co-sc), *Red Wagon* (co-sc), *Radio Parade of 1935*, *Give Her a Ring* (1934), *Drake of England*, *Music Hath Charms* (co-d) (1935), *Once in a Million*, *Irish for Luck* (+ co-sc) (1936), *You Live and Learn*, *The Windmill*, *Mayfair Melody*, *Don't Get Me Wrong*, *The Compulsory Wife*, *The Singing Cop*, *Mr Satan* (1937), *Thistledown*, *The Return of Carol Deane*, *Glamour Girl*, *The Dark Stairway*, *Dangerous Medicine* (1938), *The Nursemaid Who Disappeared*, *Confidential Lady* (1939).

Woods, Aubrey (*b* London, 1928). Actor. Supporting actor of rather eccentric roles who made his film debut as the ill-treated Smike in *Nicholas Nickleby* (1947), was camply droll on stage as the hero's chum in *Valmouth* (1958–59), filmed *Willy Wonka & the Chocolate Factory* (1971) in the US, supported Frankie HOWERD in *Up the Chastity Belt* and *Up Pompeii* (1971) and was the canting old Joseph in *Wuthering Heights* (1970). Also a good deal of TV, including a spell in the tardis as Controller in *Doctor Who* (1963), but over-all it's, though busy, not quite as productive a career as one might have expected.

OTHER BRITISH FILMS INCLUDE: *The Greed of William Hart*, *The Queen of Spades* (1948), *Father Brown* (1954), *School for Scoundrels* (1959), *Spare the Rod* (1961), *San Ferry Ann* (1965), *Loot* (1970), *The Abominable Dr Phibes* (1971), *That Lucky Touch* (1975).

Woods, Harry (*b* N.Chelmsford, Massachusetts, 1896 – *d* Phoenix, Arizona, 1970). Songwriter. US songwriter with tough image (drinker, fighter) whose ditties cheered the Depression years. At GAUMONT–BRITISH in the mid 30s he wrote songs for Jessie MATTHEWS – e.g. 'Over My Shoulder' (*Evergreen*, 1934); 'I Nearly Let Love Go Slipping Through My

Fingers' (*It's Love Again*, 1936) – Arthur TRACY ('Whistling Waltz', *Limelight*, 1936), Violet LORAINE, Jack HULBERT and Cicely COURTNEIDGE. Some of his work can be heard on the CD, 'The Songs of Harry Woods'.

OTHER BRITISH FILMS: *Aunt Sally* (1933), *Road House*, *Jack Ahoy!* (1934). Roger Philip Mellor.

Woodthorpe, Peter (*b* York, 1931). Actor. Cambridge-educated Woodthorpe began acting there with the Marlowe Society, made professional debut as Estragon in *Waiting for Godot* (1955) and had several RSC seasons. On TV since 1955, in films since *Father Came Too!* (1963), he was noticed as the mesmerist who reactivates the monster in *The Evil of Frankenstein* (1964), and played supporting roles in about ten more films, including the US-made *Eleni* (1985). TV includes *Inspector Morse* episodes and other popular programmes.

OTHER BRITISH FILMS INCLUDE: *Hysteria* (1964), *The Blue Max* (1966), *The Charge of the Light Brigade* (1968), *The Mirror Crack'd* (1980), *Testimony* (1987), *The Madness of King George* (1994, UK/US), *England, My England* (1995), *Jane Eyre* (1996, UK/Fr/It/US).

Woodvine, John (*b* South Shields, 1929). Actor. RADA-trained actor who joined the Old Vic in 1954 and in the mid 80s was a great Falstaff for Michael Bogdanov's company. Craggy, silver-haired Woodvine probably made his first impact as Detective Chief Superintendent Kingdom in TV's *New Scotland Yard* (1972–74) and he has done an enormous amount of TV, in popular series like *The Avengers* and drama like *The Life and Adventures of Nicholas Nickleby* (1982) as scheming Uncle Ralph. Screen appearances have been limited but his distinctive looks ensure that he is noticed, even in small roles like the one he had in *Young Winston* (1972) and he was an imposing Captain Croft in *Persuasion* (1995, TV, many cinemas).

OTHER BRITISH FILMS: *The Walking Stick* (1970), *The Devils* (1971), *An American Werewolf in London* (1981), *The Trial*, *Leon the Pig Farmer* (1992).

Woodward, Edward (*b* Croydon, Surrey, 1930). Actor, singer, producer. A fine actor with a splendid singing voice, RADA-trained and on stage from 1946 (rep until 1954), he made his film debut in *Where There's a Will* (1955), repeating his stage role (1954). In 1967 he was cast as David Callan in the television series *A Magnum for Schneider* (1967) later retitled *Callan* and filmed as such (1974). In this role Woodward demonstrated his ability to express controlled rage which occasionally explodes, and his stoic demeanour has seen him cast in similar roles since. Most memorable as repressed Sergeant Howie in the chilling (oc)cult thriller *The Wicker Man* (1973) and gallant Harry Morant in *Breaker Morant* (1980, Aust), he appeared more recently in *The House of Angelo* (1997) and on TV in *Gulliver's Travels* (1996). He has recorded a number of albums over the years, including *Edwardian Woodward*. Married (2) Michele DOTRICE (1987). Father of Timothy WOODWARD.

OTHER BRITISH FILMS INCLUDE: *Inn for Trouble* (1959), *Becket* (1964), *The File of the Golden Goose* (1969), *Sitting Target* (1972), *Young Winston* (1972), *Charley One-Eye* (1973), *Three for All* (1974), *Stand Up Virgin Soldiers* (1977), *The Appointment* (1981), *Champions* (1983), *Deadly Advice* (1994). Anne-Marie Thomas.

Woodward, Timothy (*b* London, 1953). Actor. Came to attention in the late 70s, for the starring role of early fighter pilot, Alan Farmer, in TV's *Wings* (1977–78) and as Lee REMICK's light-hearted young brother who surrenders to the charms of his New England cousins in *The Europeans* (1979).

More often on TV than on cinema screens since, he had good supporting roles in several films: as one of the clients for *Personal Services* (1987), in *Some Mother's Son* (1996, Ire/US) and *B. Monkey* (1998). Son of Edward WOODWARD.

OTHER BRITISH FILMS INCLUDE: *Galileo* (1974, UK/Can), *Closing Numbers* (1993), *The James Gang* (1997), *K-19: The Widowmaker* (2002, UK/US).

Woof, Emily (*b* Newcastle, 1970). Actress. Woof's star rose rapidly in the late 90s, from her supporting role as Robert CARLYLE's ex-wife in *The Full Monty* (1997, UK/US), to the lead in the undervalued version of HARDY's *The Woodlanders* (1997), to Catherine McCORMACK's lesbian lover in *This Year's Love* (1999) and then Dorothy Wordsworth in *Pandaemonium* (2001, UK/US). Cambridge-educated Woof has a wistful, slightly melancholy beauty which makes her ideal for the unhappily placed young women she has mostly played, including Nancy in TV's bold ADAPTATION of *Oliver Twist* (1999).

OTHER BRITISH FILMS: *Photographing Fairies* (1997), *Velvet Goldmine* (UK/US), *Fast Food* (1998), *Silent Cry* (2002).

Wooland, Norman (*b* Dusseldorf, Germany, 1910 – *d* Staplehurst, 1989). Actor. Wooland had established a reputation in pre-war repertory, but his admired Horatio in OLIVIER's *Hamlet* (1948) boosted his fledgling film career, and he starred in *All Over the Town* (1949) as a campaigning journalist. But he was never distinctive enough to elevate himself above the ranks of other well-spoken, patrician actors and he became marooned in supporting roles: the decent-but-dull suitor in *Madeleine* (1949), the prospective stepfather in *My Teenage Daughter* (1956), or pipe-smoking police inspectors in *No Road Back* (1956) and *The Flesh Is Weak* (1957). He could always find roles in costume drama, stretching from King Richard in *Ivanhoe* (1952) through *Richard III* (1955) to *The Fall of the Roman Empire* (1964, US) and *The Fighting Prince of Donegal* (1966), where his height, broad shoulders and resonant diction were definite assets. After this point, he appeared mainly in television series.

OTHER BRITISH FILMS INCLUDE: *£5 Man*, *The Gap* (1937), *This England* (1941), *Look Before You Love*, *Escape* (1948), *The Angel with the Trumpet* (1949), *Background* (1953), *Romeo and Juliet* (UK/It), *The Master Plan* (1954), *Guilty?* (UK/Fr), *The Rough and the Smooth* (1959), *An Honourable Murder* (1960), *The Guns of Navarone* (1961), *Life for Ruth* (1962), *International Velvet* (1978).

BIBLIOG: 'This Man Wooland!', *Picturegoer* 9 April 1949. Andrew Spicer.

Wooldridge, John (*b* Barnstaple, 1911 – *d* Waterford, 1958). Composer. Highly decorated war hero (DFM, DFC) of the RAF, entered films in 1946, scoring the BOULTING brothers' *Fame is the Spur* (1947). He composed a further dozen film scores, notably for *Edward, My Son* (1949), *The Woman in Question* (1950, + cond) and two which, with their RAF-based stories, must have had special resonance for him: *Angels One Five* (1952) and *Appointment in London* (+ cond) (1953), also co-authoring the screenplay for the latter. He composed for orchestra and organ, as well as for the screen. He was married to Margaretta SCOTT; their children are Susan WOOLDRIDGE and theatre impresario Hugh Wooldridge.

OTHER BRITISH FILMS: *The Guinea Pig* (1948), *Conspirator* (+ m d), *Torment* (1949), *Blackmailed* (1950), *The Last Man to Hang?* (1956), *Soapbox Derby* (1957), *Family Doctor* (+ m d), *Count Five and Die* (1957).

Wooldridge, Susan (*b* London). Actress. Eloquent of face and voice, the daughter of John WOOLDRIDGE and Margaretta SCOTT, has done compelling work in all the acting media. She made her film debut as a student in *Butley* (1973, UK/Can/US),

won a BAA for her supporting role as good-time Molly who deserts her nice husband in *Hope and Glory* (1987), and had solid secondary parts in *Afraid of the Dark* (1991, UK/Fr) and *Just Like a Woman* (1992). However, she has had work that stretched her more on TV, in, for example, *The Jewel in the Crown* (1984, receiving BAAn/a) and the black comedy thriller series, *Underworld* (1997), and on stage starred in PINTER's critically acclaimed *Celebration* (2001).

OTHER BRITISH FILMS INCLUDE: *The Shout* (1978), *How to Get Ahead in Advertising* (1989), *The Hummingbird Tree* (1992).

Woolf, C(harles) M(oss) (*b* London, ? – *d* 1942). Producer, distributor. Began in the business as a partner in the distribution company, W&F Film Service, of which he rose to be managing director. He was a very influential figure in 30s British cinema: he was with GAUMONT–BRITISH early in the decade as joint managing director with the OSTRER brothers, and on the board of GAINSBOROUGH, associated with but not at first controlled by G-B. He had originally backed Michael BALCON's entry to film production and in 1969 Balcon wrote of Woolf as 'an extraordinary man . . . regarded generally with a mixture of awe and affection', with 'awe' often in the ascendant, his suggestions usually being regarded as commands. Woolf had run G-B's DISTRIBUTION through W&F, before splitting with the Ostrers in 1935 and forming GENERAL FILM DISTRIBUTORS (GFD), with the backing of J.Arthur RANK and the assurance of films to sell by producer Max SCHACH. However, in 1936 GFD was wholly taken over by the General Cinema Finance Corporation, which allied it closely with the US company UNIVERSAL. GFD had become part of Rank's growing empire by the early 40s. His sons were the producers James and John WOOLF.

Woolf, James (*b* London, 1919 – *d* Los Angeles, 1966), and, **Woolf, Sir John** (*b* London, 1913 – *d* London, 1999). Producers. The Eton-educated sons of C.M. WOOLF, they became powerful figures in 50s and 60s British film, largely through their production company, Romulus Films. They formed Romulus to produce their own films following their experience with their DISTRIBUTION company, Independent Film Distributors (formed 1949). They had invested in films which they would then distribute but which had lost money, and their notion with Romulus was to break out of what they saw as the parochialism of British films and to make a series of UK/US co-productions, films that would sell in America. They had two hits in *The African Queen* (1951) and *Moulin Rouge* (1953), both directed by John HUSTON and with US stars; they then did a series of smaller, more English films in the 50s, with exceptions like *I Am a Camera* (1955), with US stars Julie HARRIS and Shelley WINTERS, and *The Story of Esther Costello* (1957), with US director David Miller and star, Joan Crawford. In 1955 they had allowed young assistant producer Jack CLAYTON to direct the Oscar-winning SHORT FILM, *The Bespoke Overcoat*, and in 1958 they gave him his chance to direct a feature: it was *Room at the Top*, which proved to be a landmark film, ushering in a NEW WAVE of working-class REALISM which revitalised British cinema. It was the first time they had put their names on a film and they won a BAA for it.

The brothers rarely took credits on their films, but it seems to have been generally felt that John was the financial brain and James took more interest in the creative side. Whatever the disposition of abilities, they were a major force in bringing a Hollywood style of showmanship to the domestic industry. Their efforts were frequently rewarded with AA and BAA nominations for the actors and others associated with them. They had a strong sense of what would succeed with the public, with James miscalculating only on *Of Human Bondage* (1964) which he personally produced for Seven Arts.

James died in Hollywood, where he had produced *King Rat* (1965), over 30 years before John who went on to have several further enormous successes. John won a Best Picture AA with *Oliver!* (1968), the most lavish MUSICAL made in England until then; and *The Day of the Jackal* (1973, UK/Fr) and *The Odessa File* (1974, UK/Ger), both derived from popular novels by Frederick FORSYTH and both carrying on Woolf's old Romulus-based tradition of importing international talents. In 1958 he co-founded Anglia Television and by the time he retired in 1988 he had produced over 100 episodes of his most successful series, *Tales of the Unexpected*. He married (1) Dorothy VERNON, (2) Edana ROMNEY and (3) Anne Saville, daughter of Victor SAVILLE. He was knighted in 1975.

OTHER BRITISH FILMS INCLUDE: (p/co-p, for Romulus) *Innocents in Paris*, *Beat the Devil* (1953, UK/It/US), *Carrington VC*, *The Good Die Young* (1954), *Dry Rot*, *Sailor Beware*, *Three Men in a Boat* (1956), *The Silent Enemy* (1958), *Term of Trial*, *The L-Shaped Room* (1962); (p, James only, for Romulus) *The Pumpkin Eater* (1964), *Life at the Top* (1965).

Woolfe, H(arry) Bruce (*b* London, 1888 – *d* Brighton, 1965). Producer, director. One of the more intelligent contributors to British silent cinema, Woolfe encouraged other intellectuals to join the industry as his company, BRITISH INSTRUCTIONAL FILMS, gained a wide reputation for its DOCUMENTARY and nature subjects. Woolfe joined the industry in 1910 and by 1912 was a salesman for Ruffell's. After service in the Army (1914–19), he purchased half an army hut at ELSTREE and created British Instructional Films. Later, in 1925, he founded New Era, as a distributor, with C.L. Buckle and E. Gordon Craig. When STOLL took over British Instructional in 1924, Woolfe remained as its head and also became a producer for Stoll, responsible for the first six films of Anthony ASQUITH: *Shooting Stars* (1928), *Underground* (1928), *The Runaway Princess* (1929), *A Cottage on Dartmoor* (1929), *Tell England* (1931), and *Dance, Pretty Lady* (1931). British Instructional became a public company in 1927, with Woolfe as its managing director, but he resigned in 1933 when the company was taken over by BRITISH INTERNATIONAL PICTURES. He established GAUMONT–BRITISH INSTRUCTIONAL, producing more than 300 classroom films in the 30s; during WW2, he produced training films for the military, followed by children's entertainment films, and, from 1949 to 1952, DOCUMENTARIES for Science Films Ltd.

OTHER BRITISH FILMS INCLUDE: (p) *The Battle of Jutland* (1921), *Armageddon* (1923, + d), *Zeebrugge* (1924, + co-d), *Sons of the Sea* (1925, + d), *Mons*, *Boadicea* (1926), *The Battles of the Coronel and Falkland Islands* (1927), *Windjammer* (1930). AS.

Woolley, Stephen (*b* London, 1956). Producer. Co-founder of PALACE PRODUCTIONS, and SCALA PRODUCTIONS with Nik POWELL, short, pony-tailed, working-class Woolley was one half of perhaps the most dynamic duo in British films from the mid 80s. His passion for the movies from childhood led him first to selling tickets at the Islington 'Screen on the Green', then to writing for trendy entertainment guide, *Time Out*, before being hired first by The Other Cinema, a left-wing collective short on marketing energy, then with the Scala cinema as programme director. In 1982 he and Powell founded Palace Pictures, as first a DISTRIBUTION company for video; they then went into production and scored some major

successes during the years up to 1992, the year of their international, BAA-winning hit, *The Crying Game* (1992). After the collapse of Palace, he and POWELL reformed ranks as Scala Productions and had success with such films as *Little Voice* (1998, UK/US) and *succès d'estime* with *24 7 TwentyFourSeven* (1997). In 1999, he co-produced *The End of the Affair* (UK/Ger/US) for his own company and in 2000 executive-produced the football flick, *Purely Belter* (2000). Tenacity has paid off for Woolley.

OTHER BRITISH FILMS INCLUDE: (co-ex p/co-p, unless noted) *The Company of Wolves* (1984), *Absolute Beginners*, *Mona Lisa* (1986), *The Courier* (1987), *Scandal* (1988), *Hardware* (UK/US, ex p), *The Big Man* (p) (1990), *The Miracle* (UK/Ire, p), *The Pope Must Die* (UK/US, p) (1991), *Waterland* (1992, UK/US, ex p), *Backbeat* (1994), *The Neon Bible* (1995), *Hollow Reed* (1996, UK/Ger), *Fever Pitch*, *The Butcher Boy* (Ire/US), *Downtime* (1997, UK/Fr), *Divorcing Jack* (UK/Fr), *B. Monkey* (UK/It/US) (1998), *The Lost Son* (UK/Fr/US), *History Is Made at Night* (UK/Fr/Ger/Fin) (1999), *The Last September* (UK/Fr/Ire) (2000).

Worcester, Alec (*b* Brockley, 1887 – *d* Isles of Scilly, 1952). Actor. Worcester was married to one of HEPWORTH's leading ladies, Violet HOPSON, and starred in more than fifty SHORTS for the producer, made between 1912 and 1914, together with four feature films: *Kissing Cup*, *Shadows of a Great City*, *The Cloister and the Hearth* (1913), and *Justice* (1914). AS.

Wordsworth, Richard (*b* Halesowen Rectory, 1915 – *d* Kendal, 1993). Actor. Cambridge-educated great-great-grandson of poet William Wordsworth, around whose life he built, and toured extensively with, a one-man show, *The Bliss of Solitude* (1969–70). His main career was on the stage (from 1938); he played seasons with the Old Vic, the RSC and the Mermaid, where he starred in the opening play, *Lock Up Your Daughters* (1959). He had only a minor role in the film version (strenuously naughty and dull, 1969) and his major claim to film fame is as the astronaut turning into a vegetable in HAMMER's *The Quatermass Experiment* (1955), achieving both horror and pathos. TV included *The Regiment* (1972–73); also in the US film *Song of Norway* (1970) as Hans Christian Anderson.

OTHER BRITISH FILMS: *Time Without Pity*, *The Camp on Blood Island* (1957), *The Revenge of Frankenstein* (1958), *The Curse of the Werewolf* (1961).

Worker, Adrian (*b* Kempston, 1916). Producer. Entered films in the finance department at LIME GROVE in 1943, before turning to production, first with RANK's Production Facilities Ltd, then as production supervisor of HIGHBURY STUDIOS. In this capacity, he had responsibility for that strange little collection of 'B' MOVIES made there in 1948, mostly as production manager. As a free-lance production manager, he worked several times with Val GUEST (e.g. on *Mr Drake's Duck*, 1950) and for TEMPEAN (e.g. *Steel Key*, 1953), then became production supervisor at WARWICK FILMS. Career largely over by end of the decade.

OTHER BRITISH FILMS INCLUDE: (p man/super, unless noted) *A Piece of Cake*, *My Song for You*, *Love in Waiting*, *To the Public Danger*, *Colonel Bogey* (1948), *The Body Said No!* (1950), *Another Man's Poison* (1951), *The Voice of Merrill* (1952), *The Black Knight* (1954), *Safari*, *Beyond Mombasa* (1956, co-p), *Action of the Tiger*, *The Naked Earth* (p) (1957), *Intent to Kill* (p), *Danger Within* (assoc p), (1958), *I'm All Right Jack* (1959), *Fern the Red Deer* (1976, p).

Workers' Film and Photo League Later known as The Film and Photo League, this was one of a number of independent film organisations that were formed in the 30s to use the cinema in support of left-wing politics. The League's main purpose was film production. Almost all of the films made under its auspices were NEWSREELS or DOCUMENTARIES although it did have some aspirations to make fiction films. Its most successful film was *Jubilee*, a lively agit-prop account of the royal celebrations of 1935. In the late 30s the League worked closely with the Left Book Club. Alan Lovell.

Working Title Films Sarah RADCLYFFE (later working independently), Tim BEVAN (born in New Zealand) and Eric FELLNER were highly successful in creating popular, British-based films of international appeal with this company. Its first film, Stephen FREARS' *My Beautiful Laundrette* (1985), led to an AAn/sc for Hanif KUREISHI and an acting one for Daniel DAY-LEWIS. More recently it has successfully produced *Four Weddings and a Funeral* (1994), *Bean* (1997), *Elizabeth* (1998), *Notting Hill* (1999, UK/US), *Bridget Jones's Diary* (2001, UK/Fr/US), *About A Boy* (2002, UK/Fr/Ger/US). Actor Hugh GRANT and writer Richard CURTIS have been party to several of these films. A key element in the company's working methods has been its attention to MARKETING, striking deals with American and European companies, thus ensuring world-wide DISTRIBUTION for its products. A frequent observation of the company's methods is the inordinate amount of time spent on developing scripts and extensively working on re-writes. Despite its access to high finance, Working Title is also committed to low-budget films with new writers. Such was the case with *Billy Elliot* (2000). Stephen Brown.

Workshop Movement The Workshop Movement developed from the activities of late 60s film groups like **Cinema Action** in London and **AMBER** in Newcastle (both formed 1968). The term 'workshop' was adopted in the 70s for a unit which, in principle, produces, distributes and exhibits film or video, is managed collectively, operates egalitarian working practices, and nurtures long-term relationships with subjects and audiences. During the 70s and 80s workshops campaigned through the Independent Film-Makers' Association (IFA 1974–90) and National Organization Of Workshops (NOW, formed 1984) The ACTT Workshop Declaration (1984) brought union recognition for workshop practice and provided a basis for CHANNEL 4 funding. Numbers of workshops increased up to the late 80s and declined through the 90s when collective enterprise fell out of favour with funding organisations. Margaret Dickinson.

World Film News Launched in 1936, this journal was committed to the documentary-realist aesthetic, and was a key organ of the DOCUMENTARY FILM MOVEMENT. It was critical of 30s British cinema's preoccupation with what it saw to be artificial, irrelevant GENRE entertainments at the expense of addressing matters of pressing contemporary importance, though, in holding such views, it was somewhat out of line with what the general cinema-going public was looking for. Under the editorship of Marion GRIERSON, it attacked British film CENSORSHIP, the financial dealings of the commercial film industry and other controversial matters, until it ceased publication in 1938. According to Paul ROTHA (1973), though it was 'the best of its kind in the world' it foundered on professional inexperience in running a journal, and 'I am afraid that it was [John] GRIERSON's own fault'.

World War I and British film This was a watershed time for indigenous films. The war efforts; a shortage of celluloid due to it containing material needed for munitions; the rise of Hollywood as a key supplier of films: all led to a serious change in British cinema's fortunes. An estimated weekly audience of 20 million were watching films despite many others soldiering abroad and the recent introduction of Entertainment Tax. What they were seeing of British origin included *The Prisoner of Zenda* (1915) and Cecil HEPWORTH's *Comin' Thro' the Rye* (1916). SHORTS continued to be made, including such popular fare as both the 'Pimple' and the 'Tilly' SERIES.

The subject of the war itself tended to come in films made abroad – e.g. *Shoulder Arms*, Charlie CHAPLIN's film about life in the trenches. This was partly because the public were kept ill-informed about conditions at the front until 1916 when PROPAGANDA films were released. Among these was *Battle of the Somme* which drew large audiences and used a good deal of factual material though what is seen includes staged events among the DOCUMENTARY footage. The MINISTRY OF INFORMATION, which handled distrbution of appropriate films abroad, entered production with a studio in Ebury Street, London. It sponsored D.W. Griffith's *Hearts of the World* (1918) and Herbert Brenon's *Victory and Peace* (which was completed after the close of the war and never rleased). Feature films about WWI, not always of British origin, began being made in the aftermath of hostilities; *Alf's Button* (1920), *Journey's End* (1930, UK/US), and *All Quiet on the Western Front* (1930, US) being among the best known, and important later titles include *Dark Journey* (1937), *King and Country* (1964), and *Oh! What a Lovely War* (1969), derived from Joan LITTLEWOOD's end-of-pier anti-war stage musical. WWI continues to this day to fascinate movie-makers as subject matter, as films such as *Regeneration* (1997, UK/Can) and *The Trench* (1999, UK/Fr) attest. Stephen Brown.

See also **war films; Ministry of Information (MOI) and British cinema in World War I**.

World War 2 and British film *see* **war films; wartime newsreels and propaganda; Ministry of Information (MOI) and British cinema in World War 2; documentary film-making**

Worth, Brian (*b* London, 1914 – *d* 1978). Actor. The conventionally tall, dark and handsome Worth was just getting himself established in such films as *The Arsenal Stadium Mystery* (1939), as Greta GYNT's footballer boyfriend, when WW2 service (1941–46) intervened. Demobbed, he returned first to the stage and re-entered films in the foolish 1948 comedy, *One Night with You*, and was in steady, unremarkable demand throughout the 50s, sometimes in supporting roles in main features, such as *An Inspector Calls* (1954), as the daughter's fiancé who has misused the dead girl, sometimes in leads in 'B' FILMS, like the REMAKE of *Hindle Wakes* (1952).

OTHER BRITISH FILMS INCLUDE: *The Lion Has Wings* (1939), *Pastor Hall* (1940), *Cardboard Cavalier* (1949), *Last Holiday* (1950), *Scrooge, The Man in the White Suit* (1951), *It Started in Paradise, Father's Doing Fine* (1952), *Windfall* (1955), *The Battle of the River Plate, Ill Met By Moonlight* (1956), *The Square Peg* (1958), *Peeping Tom, Moment of Danger* (1960), *On Her Majesty's Secret Service* (1969), *The Boy Who Turned Yellow* (1972).

Worth, Irene (*b* Fairbury, Nebraska, 1916 – *d* New York, 2002). Actress. RN: Harriet Abrams. Celebrated stage star of two continents, to whom filming was no more than a sideline. Her most indelible film image is that of the Resistance worker issuing *Orders to Kill* (1958) the wrong man. First appeared in films in two dreadful 1948 British comedies, *One Night with You* and *Another Shore*, a flimsy whimsy from EALING, by whom she was better served as the friendly policewoman in Thorold DICKINSON's drama of anarchists in London, *Secret People* (1951). She is a searing Goneril to Paul SCOFIELD's *King Lear* (1970, UK/Den), and in the US she had an eccentric role in *Deathtrap* (1982), but she remains above all one of the *plus grandes dames* of the stage, as anyone who saw her as *Mary Stuart* (1958) would attest.

OTHER BRITISH FILMS: *The Scapegoat* (1958), *Nicholas and Alexandra* (1971, UK/US), *Forbidden* (1984, UK/Ger/US), *Onegin* (1999, UK/US).

Worton Hall studio *see* Isleworth Studios

Wray, Fay (*b* Alberta, Canada, 1907). Actress. Legendary star of *King Kong* (1933), who is infinitely better as Erich von Stroheim's leading lady in *The Wedding March* (1928). On screen 1925–58, with brief British career in mid 30s. She hated being directed by Walter FORDE in *Bulldog Jack* (1935), but liked Maurice ELVEY's direction of *The Clairvoyant* (1935), and was happy as Jack BUCHANAN's leading lady in *Come Out of the Pantry* (1935) and *When Knights Were Bold* (1936). AS.

Wrede, Caspar (*b* Varberg, Finland, 1929 – *d* Helsinki, 1998). Director. Finnish film-maker who directed four films in Britain, most famous of which is the decently austere ADAPTATION of Alexander Solzhenitsyn's *One Day in the Life of Ivan Denisovich* (1971, UK/Nor/US), starring Tom COURTENAY, with whom he had also worked in *Private Potter* (1962). Also a notable stage director. Married/divorced Dilys HAMLETT.

OTHER BRITISH FILMS: *The Barber of Stamford Hill* (1962), *Ransom* (1974).

Wright, Basil (*b* Sutton, Surrey, 1907 – *d* London, 1987). Director. Sherborne- and Cambridge-educated, Wright joined the EMB FILM UNIT in 1929. Between 1929 and 1936 he produced and directed films for the EMB and GPO FILM UNIT before leaving to establish the REALIST FILM UNIT. He stayed at Realist until 1945, when he was appointed as a film producer within the CROWN FILM UNIT. However, he stayed at Crown for only a year, before founding the International Realist company. He produced and directed films there until 1960. Wright was one of John GRIERSON's first appointees to the DOCUMENTARY FILM MOVEMENT, and one of his closest associates. Wright's finest film is undoubtedly *The Song of Ceylon* (1934), one of the best British documentaries ever made. However, his later film-making failed to equal this early achievement. He published *The Use of the Film* (1948) and *The Long View* (1974).

OTHER BRITISH FILMS INCLUDE: (doc) (p, unless noted) *The Fairy of the Phone, Rainbow Dance* (co-p) (1936), *Modern Orphans of the Storm* (co-p, + co-d), *The League at Work* (UK/IA) (1937), *The Londoners* (1939, assoc), *Men of Africa* (1940), *Mobile Canteen, The Green Girdle* (1941), *The Harvest Shall Come, Battle for Freedom* (1942), *A Diary for Timothy, Children on Trial* (1946), *The Drawings of Leonardo da Vinci, World Without End* (+ co-d, co-scen) (1953), *Greek Sculpture* (1959, co-p, + co-d); (d, unless noted) *O'er Hill and Dale* (1932), *Liner Cruising South* (1933), *Pett and Pott* (1934, assoc), *Night Mail* (1936, co-d, + co-e, co-p, co-sc), *Children at School* (1937), *Postal Special* (1939), *This Was Japan* (1945), *The Stained Glass at Fairford* (1956, + p), *Greece the Immortal Land* (1958, + co-p), *A Place for Gold* (1960, + p). Ian Aitken.

Wright, Haidee (*b* London, 1868 – *d* London, 1943). Actress. From a family of actors, she played supporting roles in about 15 films, starting in silent days when she played the title role in *Aunt Rachel* (1920). Had a major role with Godfrey TEARLE in

Tomorrow We Live (1936); the rest of her sound film roles were small. Her brother Huntley Wright (*b* London, 1869 – *d* Bangor, Wales, 1941) made several 30s films, including *The Only Girl* (1933, UK/Ger), and her sister was Marie WRIGHT, with whom she several times appeared.

OTHER BRITISH FILMS INCLUDE: *Faith* (1919), *The Winning Goal* (1920), *The Old Country, Demos* (1921), *Paddy the Next Best Thing* (1923) *The Sea Urchin* (1926), *The Blarney Stone* (1933), *Jew Süss* (1934), *The Citadel* (1938).

Wright, Hugh E. (*b* Cannes, France, 1879 – *d* Windsor, 1940). Actor. A popular purveyor of the Cockney character even in silent films. Began career under direction of George PEARSON in *The Better 'Ole* and *The Kiddies in the Ruins* (1918), and at his best as bookie father of Betty BALFOUR in 'Squibs' SERIES (1921–23). Father of Tony WRIGHT.

OTHER BRITISH FILMS INCLUDE: *Garryowen* (1920), *The Old Curiosity Shop* (1921), *Auld Lang Syne* (1929), *The Good Companions* (1933), *Scrooge* (1935), *Royal Eagle* (1936). AS.

Wright, Humberston (*b* London, 1885 – *d* ?). Actor. On stage from 1897 and some sources suggest he was in films from 1907, but the earliest confirmed seems to be *Trapped by the London Sharks* (1916). Thereafter, he was in great demand through the rest of the silent period and into the 30s, often in dignified roles, including 'Dr Petrie' in over 20 SHORT FILMS of 1923–24, and frequently in the films of Maurice ELVEY, including *Hindle Wakes* (1927) as the heroine's father and *In a Monastery Garden* (1932) as an abbot.

OTHER BRITISH FILMS INCLUDE: *Thelma* (1918), *The Rocks of Valpre* (1919), *The English Rose* (1920), *The Peacemaker* (1922), *The Sign of Four, Aaron's Rod, Sally Bishop* (1923), *Slaves of Destiny, The Green Mist* (1924), *A Dear Liar* (1925), *The Flag Lieutenant, London Love* (1926), *Roses of Picardy* (1927), *What Money Can Buy, Sailors Don't Care* (1928), *High Treason* (1929), *Thread o'Scarlet, Alf's Button* (1930), *Down River* (1931), *Commissionaire* (1933), *Strictly Illegal* (1935), *Young and Innocent* (1937), *Escape Dangerous* (1949).

Wright, Marie (*b* Dover, 1862 – *d* London, 1949). Actress. Sister of Huntley and Haidee WRIGHT, she had a long stage career before entering films in the silent era, including Graham CUTTS's *Paddy the Next Best Thing* (1923) and *The Sea Urchin* (1926), in both appearing with Haidee. It is probably unfair that the abiding image one now has of her is as the old woman being strangled by Anton WALBROOK in the opening sequence of *Gaslight* (1940), her penultimate film.

OTHER BRITISH FILMS INCLUDE: *God Bless Our Red, White and Blue* (1918), *Quinneys* (1919), *Testimony* (1920), *Bluebottles* (1928), *Murder!* (1930), *Black Coffee* (1931), *Love's Old Sweet Song* (1933), *A Cup of Kindness* (1934), *Victoria the Great* (1937), *Sixty Glorious Years, Strange Boarders, The Landlady* (1938), *Black Eyes* (1939), *False Rapture* (1941).

Wright, Tony (*b* London, 1925 – *d* London, 1986). Actor. Light-haired actor, briefly in starring roles in the 50s playing men of action, portrayed by fan magazines as the 'beefcake boy' of British films. With limited acting range (too lightweight for villains), he had a laid-back charm, but was rarely given roles to display it. After navy service, and, reputedly, whaling in the Antarctic, was on stage from 1946. Made film debut as the boxer in HAMMER's *The Flanagan Boy* (1953), travelled to France to play private eye Slim Callaghan in 1954, then was offered a contract by RANK (1955–57), keen to promote its films in French markets. Cast as villain in search of hidden loot in the atmospheric THRILLER *Tiger in the Smoke* (1956), he was not really sinister enough, but brought a lighter touch to his role as an escaped POW in *Seven Thunders* (1957). Into 'B' FILMS by 1958, and soon declined into cameos in third-rate EXPLOITATION films. Son of Hugh E. WRIGHT; married Janet MUNRO (1956–61).

OTHER BRITISH FILMS INCLUDE: *Jumping for Joy* (1955), *Jacqueline* (1956) *The Spaniard's Curse* (1957), *The Rough and the Smooth* (1959), *Faces in the Dark* (1960), *Attempt to Kill* (1961), *The Liquidator* (1965), *Clinic Xclusive, All Coppers Are . . .* (1971), *The Creeping Flesh* (1972), *Can I Come Too?* (1979). Roger Philip Mellor.

Wyer, Reginald (*b* London, 1901 – *d* Bognor Regis, 1970). Cinematographer. Wyer had wide experience in many aspects of cinematography, from 1918, before assuming solo responsibility for a feature film – Sydney BOX's *The Seventh Veil* (1945). He worked with Box on DOCUMENTARIES at VERITY Films (and at the MINISTRY OF INFORMATION during WW2), and was at GAINSBOROUGH throughout the Box regime in the latter half of the 40s, when at least *The Upturned Glass* (1947) and *Daybreak* (1946, rel 1948) owe some of their dark impact to Wyer's black-and-white images, even if the HUGGETTS, say, might have been photographed by anyone. He was at PINEWOOD in the mid 50s when blandness was pervasive, but there are sharper visual pleasures in *Across the Bridge* (1957) and in Vernon SEWELL's minor but oddly chilling *The Man in the Back Seat* (1961). In COLOUR, he discriminates well between the hero's everyday world and the sinister world of the occult in *Devils of Darkness* (1964).

OTHER BRITISH FILMS INCLUDE: (c, unless noted) *The Unholy Quest* (1934, co-p), *Men of Rochdale* (1944, co-sc), *The Years Between, A Girl in a Million* (1946), *The White Unicorn* (1947), *Here Come the Huggetts, Quartet* (co-c) (1948), *Diamond City* (1949), *So Long at the Fair* (1950), *Tread Softly* (1952), *Spaceways, Personal Affair* (1953), *The Beachcomber* (1954), *The Prisoner, All for Mary* (1955), *True as a Turtle, Eyewitness* (1956), *Sea Fury* (1958), *Carry On Teacher* (1959), *The Kitchen* (1961), *Night of the Eagle* (1962), *A Place to Go, Father Came Too!* (1963), *Rattle of a Simple Man* (1964), *Island of Terror* (1966), *Night of the Big Heat* (1967).

Wymark, Patrick (*b* Grimsby, 1920 – *d* Melbourne, 1970). Actor. RN: Cheeseman. Imposing character player, on stage from 1951, well remembered for the ruthless tycoon, Wilder, in TV's *The Plane Makers* (1963–65) and, especially, its reincarnation as *The Power Game* (1965–66). Otherwise, most famous for his vocal impersonations of CHURCHILL in Jack LEVIEN's compilation films, *The Finest Hours* (1964) and *A King's Story* (1965), going visual as the leader in *Operation Crossbow* (1965, UK/It). Elsewhere, there is a series of striking supporting roles, including Cromwell in *Witchfinder General* (1968) and Strafford in *Cromwell* (1970). Early death following heart attack.

OTHER BRITISH FILMS INCLUDE: *The League of Gentlemen, The Criminal* (1960), *A Woman's Privilege, Children of the Damned* (1963), *The Other World of Winston Churchill* (doc, voice), *The Secret of Blood Island* (1964), *Repulsion* (1965), *The Psychopath* (1966), *Where Eagles Dare* (1968), *Battle of Britain* (1969).

Wyndham, Bray Producer. Responsible for a half-dozen 30s features, some made for his own production company, including two MELODRAMAS with 'exotic' stars: *Matinee Idol* (1933), starring Camilla HORN, and *Tiger Bay* (1933), with Anna May WONG.

Wyndham, Dennis (*b* Natal, SA, 1887 – *d* ?). Actor. After a few silent films, including the lead in *Lorna Doone* (1920), and the *Twisted Tales* (1926) SERIES, former mounted policeman and miner, Wyndham became a busy character actor in the 30s and early 40s, while maintaining a stage career (London debut, 1911). He was villainous Don Silvio, foiled (improbably) by

Midshipman Easy (1935), and tangled several times with Will HAY (e.g. in *Oh, Mr Porter!*, 1937), 'Old Mother Riley', and George FORMBY (e.g. *Bell-Bottom George*, 1944). Wife acted as Poppy WYNDHAM.

OTHER BRITISH FILMS INCLUDE: *The Informer* (1929), *Juno and the Paycock* (1930), *The Man They Couldn't Arrest* (1931), *The Face at the Window* (1932), *Money Mad* (1934), *The Immortal Gentleman* (1935), *Windbag the Sailor, Sensation* (1936), *Convict 99* (1938), *Old Mother Riley MP, The Arsenal Stadium Mystery* (1939), *Neutral Port* (1940), *Love on the Dole, The Common Touch, Old Mother Riley's Ghosts* (1941), *Battle for Music* (1943, doc), *I Didn't Do It* (1945), *Dancing with Crime* (1947), *For Better, for Worse* (1954), *Ramsbottom Rides Again* (1956).

Wyndham, Joan (*b* London, 1911). Actress. Brunette star of stage from 1929; made her film debut in the US opposite Francis X. Bushman in *Call of the Circus* (1930). Trained at the Royal Academy of Music, London, she returned to England in 1930 and appeared in ten films, most notably as Clifford MOLLISON's new girlfriend in *The Lucky Number* (1933), in which, despite an accent at odds with the character's class, she is very charming. Where did she go after 1936?

OTHER BRITISH FILMS INCLUDE: *Dr Josser KC, Up for the Cup* (1931), *High Society* (1932), *Loyalties, Love's Old Sweet Song* (1933), *The Gay Old Dog* (1935), *Juggernaut* (1936).

Wyndham, John (*b* Birmingham, 1903 – *d* London, 1969). Author. RN: Harris. Wrote very popular SCIENCE-FICTION (a term he disliked) in the 50s, after apprenticeship in US pulp fiction in the 30s, including private eye stories. His best known novels represent alien forces invading everyday life, and those that have been filmed in Britain include *Village of the Damned* (1960, from *The Midwich Cuckoos*, 1957), *The Day of the Triffids* (1962, novel 1951) and *Quest for Love* (1971, from his story, *Random Quest*).

Wyndham, Poppy (*b* Simla, India, 1901 – *d* on transatlantic flight, 1928). Actor. Minor aristocrat (*b* Hon. Elsie Mackay) who enjoyed equally minor career as leading lady. Married (1) Lionel Atwill; (2) Dennis WYNDHAM.

OTHER BRITISH FILMS INCLUDE: *Snow in the Desert* (1919), *A Son of David, The Tidal Wave, The Town of Crooked Ways* (1920). AS.

Wyndham, Robert Actor. Former flyer who was under contract to EALING in the mid 40s, who had his best role in his debut, as Sqr Ldr Leverett in the air-sea rescue drama, *For Those in Peril* (1944). For the rest, supporting roles like that of the man passed over by Jane BARRETT because she's fallen for Derek BOND in *The Captive Heart* (1946), but he's not a POW, so he doesn't get much screen time.

OTHER BRITISH FILMS INCLUDE: *Fiddlers Three, Champagne Charlie* (1944), *Dead of Night* (1945), *School for Secrets* (1946), *Against the Wind* (1947).

Wyndham-Lewis, D(ominic) B(evan) (*b* 1894 – *d* Alicante, Spain, 1969). Screenwriter. Credited as co-author with Charles BENNETT of the story for HITCHCOCK's *The Man Who Knew Too Much* (1934). Bennett later played down Wyndham-Lewis's contribution, though it is restated on the 1956 US REMAKE. Also a journalist and essayist, he (co-) authored other 30s screenplays, including several for Grosvenor Sound Films, directed by Sinclair HILL, and 'usually of poor quality' according to Rachael LOW.

OTHER BRITISH FILMS INCLUDE: (co-sc, unless noted) *Three Men in a Boat* (1933), *Hyde Park Corner* (1935, sc), *The Gay Adventure* (sc), *Chick, The Cardinal* (sc) (1936), *Take a Chance* (1937).

Wyngarde, Peter (*b* Marseilles, 1927). Actor. RN: Cyril Goldbert. Of Anglo-French parentage and four years of his childhood spent in a concentration camp in Shanghai, the long-faced, quizzical-looking Wyngarde tried law and advertising before turning to acting. He had considerable success on stage (with Vivien LEIGH in *Duel of Angels*, 1958–59) and on TV (especially as raffish author and playboy, Jason King, in the series *Department S*, 1969, and the follow-up simply called *Jason King*, 1971–72), but made only a few films. He is, however, memorable in two of them: as the alarming Quint in *The Innocents* (1961) and as the academic whose rationalism takes an occult beating in *Night of the Eagle* (1962).

OTHER BRITISH FILMS: *The Siege of Sidney Street* (1960), *Flash Gordon* (1980), *Tank Malling* (1988).

Wynne, Bert (*b* Croydon, 1889 – *d* Somerset, 1971). Director, actor. Journeyman actor who began his film career as an extra in 1908. Among the features in which he appeared are *The Shulamite*, *The Christian* (1915), *The Manxman* (1916), *Tom Jones* (1917), *The Wages of Sin* (1918), and *Splendid Folly* (1919). As late as the 60s, Wynne was directing TV commercials.

OTHER BRITISH FILMS INCLUDE: (d) *The Manchester Man* (1920), *Handy Andy*, *Stormflower*, *Dick's Fairy*, *Little Meg's Children*, *Jessica's First Prayer* (1921), *The Call of the East* (1922, + sc), *God's Prodigal* (1923), *Remembrance* (1928), *A Safe Affair* (1931), *A Night of Magic* (1944). AS.

Wynter, Dana (*b* London, 1930). Actress. RN: Dagmar Spencer-Marcus Wynter. After a few small parts in such films as *Lady Godiva Rides Again* and *White Corridors* (1951, both as Dagmar Wynter), South African-raised Wynter went to the US in the mid 50s and became a minor Fox star. Her most interesting US film was not in the plushy Fox jobs but the scary Allied Artists' SCIENCE-FICTION classic, *Invasion of the Body Snatchers* (1955). She made only two further British films: *Shake Hands with the Devil* (1959, UK/US), caught up in the Dublin 'troubles' of 1921, and *Sink the Bismarck!* (1960), as Kenneth MORE's romantic interest. Gravely beautiful and intelligent, but not quite charismatic enough for stardom.

OTHER BRITISH FILMS: (as Dagmar Wynter) *The Woman's Angle*, *It Started in Paradise* (1952), *Colonel March Investigates*, *Knights of the Round Table* (1953).

Wynyard, Diana (*b* London, 1906 – *d* London, 1964). Actress. RN: Dorothy Cox. Beautiful, ladylike and subtly sexy, Wynyard was on stage from 1925, and, though she made some notable films, she remained essentially a theatre star, famous on both sides of the Atlantic, first appearing on Broadway in 1932. She starred mainly in modern plays, including *Design for Living* (1939) and *Watch on the Rhine* (1942), but had a major Stratford season (1948–49), playing Lady Macbeth and Desdemona, among others. Her earliest films were made in Hollywood, where she appeared with the Barrymores (John, Ethel and Lionel) in *Rasputin and the Empress* and starred in the film version of Noël COWARD's famous flag-waver, *Cavalcade* (1933), for which she received an AAn as the courageous and dignified heroine. She did not film in Britain until the end of the decade, when she was miscast but interesting as the extravagant wife of a small-time barber in the grim drama, *On the Night of the Fire* (1939). She was very touching as the imperilled wife in Thorold DICKINSON's fine film version of *Gaslight* (1940) and as Mrs Disraeli in his *The Prime Minister* (1941), and her elegant beauty served well the role of Helen, unobtainable object of the affections of *Kipps* (1941), directed by Carol REED, whom she married the following year and divorced in 1947. Post-war, she made only four further films, all British and all in not very interesting character roles, the pick being the priggish Lady Chiltern in *An Ideal Husband* (1947), who learns not to expect too much. Awarded CBE, 1953.

OTHER BRITISH FILMS: *Freedom Radio* (1940), *Tom Brown's Schooldays* (1951), *The Feminine Touch* (1956), *Island in the Sun* (1957, UK/US).

'X' Certificate This CENSORSHIP classification was introduced in January 1951 by the British Board of Film Censors, to designate 'a single category of films . . . from which children should be excluded'. It was to embrace those films previously classed as 'H' (=Horror) as well as films on obviously adult themes, such as *Yield to the Night* (1956), with its plea for the abolition of capital punishment. While the category included many films in EXPLOITATION modes, it also permitted a new frankness in the treatment of sexual matters in such serious films as *Room at the Top* (1958), and represented an important step in the liberalisation of film censorship.

Yy

Yarde, Margaret (*b* Dartmouth, 1878 – *d* London, 1944). Actress. Trained for opera under Marchesi Pavesi, and on London stage from 1907, Yarde appeared in a few silent films, starting as Madame de Stael no less in *Madame Recamier; or, The Prince of Virtue* (1923) and playing The Vengeance in *The Only Way* (1926), adapted from *A Tale of Two Cities*. Hit her film stride in the 30s, playing character roles, up and down the social scale, in about 40 films, with landladies (*Trouble in Store*, 1934) and titled ladies (*Gypsy Melody*, 1936), usually on the formidable side.

OTHER BRITISH FILMS:, *The Lady in Furs, The Painted Lady* (1925), *Night Birds* (1930, UK/Ger), *Third Time Lucky* (1931), *The Man from Toronto, The Good Companions* (1933), *Sing As We Go!* (1934), *Scrooge, Squibs* (1935), *Queen of Hearts, No Escape* (1936), *Prison Without Bars* (1938), *French Without Tears* (1939), *George and Margaret* (1940), *Tomorrow We Live* (1942), *Thursday's Child* (1943), *Two Fathers* (1944, short).

Yates, Marjorie (*b* Birmingham, 1941). Actress. Usually a supporting player, especially busy on TV in such programmes as *A Very British Coup* (1988), Yates had leading roles on stage in David STOREY's *Stages* (1992) and on screen as the mother in the second of Terence DAVIES's semi-autobiographical elegies to time past, *The Long Day Closes* (1992).

OTHER BRITISH FILMS INCLUDE: *The Optimists of Nine Elms* (1973), *The Legend of the Werewolf* (1974), *Priest of Love* (1980), *Wetherby* (1985).

Yates, Pauline (*b* St Helen's, Lancs). Actress. Much better known for her TV work, especially as Leonard ROSSITER's understanding wife in *The Fall and Rise of Reginald Perrin* (1976–79) and for *Keep It in the Family* (1980–83), than her intermittent screen appearances. She had leads in a couple of 'B' MOVIES, including *Identity Unknown* (1960) for DANZIGERS, but is probably better remembered as Dirk BOGARDE's cheated-on wife in *Darling* (1965). Married Donald CHURCHILL.

OTHER BRITISH FILMS INCLUDE: *Never Mention Murder* (1964), *The Four Feathers* (1978), *She'll Be Wearing Pink Pyjamas* (1984).

Yates, Peter (*b* Aldershot, 1929). Director. Britisher who developed a Hollywood career, working with top stars in commercially successful projects. After Charterhouse and RADA, Yates worked as actor, stage manager and director at the Royal Court. Entered films as dubbing assistant, rising to assistant director on *The Guns of Navarone* and *A Taste of Honey* (1961), and combining this with directing TV episodes for *Danger Man* and *The Saint*. His feature debut was Cliff RICHARD's *Summer Holiday* (1962): such pop musicals, disdained by established directors, provided opportunities for a younger generation (see also WINNER, BOORMAN, LESTER). His next film, the surreal suburban comedy *One Way Pendulum* (1964), based on N.F. Simpson's play, harks back to his Royal Court years (with Jonathan MILLER memorably teaching his 'speak your weight' machines to perform the 'Hallelujah Chorus'). A former professional racing driver, he staged a thrilling car chase for *Robbery* (1967), so impressing Steve McQueen that Yates was offered his first Hollywood film, *Bullitt* (1968), and many other successful films followed. Returned to England for another highly regarded theatrical subject, *The Dresser* (1983, AAn/film/d and BAAn/film/d).

OTHER BRITISH FILMS: (ass d) *Cover Girl Killer* (1959), *Sons and Lovers* (1960), *The Roman Spring of Mrs Stone* (1961); (d) *Murphy's War* (1971), *Krull* (1983), *The Run of the Country* (1995, UK/Ireland). Roger Philip Mellor.

Yeldham, Peter (*b* Gladstone, New South Wales, 1927). Screenwriter. The first ten years of Yeldham's career were spent in writing screenplays for British films, starting with the undeservedly neglected *The Comedy Man* (1963), followed by more conventional ADVENTURES and THRILLERS, including *Mozambique* (1964, UK/S Af) and *The Liquidator* (1965). He wrote Michael POWELL's Australian-set *The Age of Consent* (1969) and spent his later career mainly in Australian TV.

OTHER BRITISH FILMS INCLUDE: *24 Hours to Kill, Ten Little Indians* (co-sc) (1965), *Our Man in Marrakesh* (1966), *The Long Duel* (1967).

York, Derek (*b* London, 1927 – *d* Poole, 1994). Editor. After making a SHORT FILM about post-war problems, *Smith, Our Friend* (1946, + co-d, co-p, sc, e), starring Bryan FORBES, York and his co-p/co-d friend, cinematographer Walter LASSALLY, made another short film, *Saturday Night* (1950), again with Forbes. He then settled to editing, at first on SHORT FILMS, such as Lindsay ANDERSON's *Three Installations* (1951), then on features including Forbes's *Seance on a Wet Afternoon* (1964).

OTHER BRITISH FILMS INCLUDE: *The Winslow Boy* (1948, co-ed), *Royal Heritage* (1952, doc), *A High Wind in Jamaica, Life at the Top* (1965), *Inadmissible Evidence* (1968), *Son of Dracula* (1974).

York, Michael (*b* Fulmer, 1942). Actor. First acted with the National Youth Theatre before joining OUDS while at Oxford, graduating in 1964. His blonde, blue-eyed boyish looks and plummy accent incarnated a traditionally English public-school manliness, which Joseph LOSEY exploited in York's first screen role as the doomed aristocrat William in *Accident* (1967). Then, as Tybalt in Franco ZEFFIRELLI's innovative *Romeo and Juliet* (1968, UK/US), he demonstrated a sinewy athleticism rare amongst English actors. He used this quality to great effect as Viking chieftain Guthrum in *Alfred the Great* (1969), and D'Artagnan in *The Three Musketeers* (1973, Panama) and sequel *The Four Musketeers* (1974, Panama/Sp). Although York continued to play derring-do heroes in *The Last Remake of Beau Geste* (1977, US) and as the quintessentially English

Charles Carruthers in *The Riddle of the Sands* (1979), he also performed convincing variations on the introspective, bored, dissipated or disillusioned Englishman in *Justine* (1969), *England Made Me, Cabaret* (US) (1972) and *Conduct Unbecoming* (1975). In the 80s and 90s, played supporting or cameo roles and became familiar to younger audiences as Basil Exposition in the 'Austin Powers' films (1997, 1999).

OTHER BRITISH FILMS: *Smashing Time* (1967), *The Strange Affair* (1968), *The Guru* (1969), *Zeppelin* (1971), *Seven Nights in Japan* (1976, UK/Fr), *Success Is the Best Revenge* (1984), *Borstal Boy* (2000).
BIBLIOG: Autobiography, *Travelling Player*, 1991. Andrew Spicer.

York, Susannah (*b* London, 1942). RN: Fletcher. Actress. Luminous leading lady of the 60s, fair-haired with dreamy blue eyes, she started in conventional ingenue roles, but hinted at inner depths and an independent spirit, and she played several offbeat, psychologically complex characters. Raised in rural Scotland, trained at RADA, followed by rep and TV plays, she made her film debut in *Tunes of Glory* (1960), the first of three films from James KENNAWAY screenplays (the others: *Battle of Britain* and *Country Dance*, 1969). She co-starred in Norman WISDOM's best (and least seen) comedy *There Was a Crooked Man* (1960), but *The Greengage Summer* (1961) provided her first substantial role as Jos, a schoolgirl gradually realizing the power that her radiant sexuality gives her over men. With peaches-and-cream complexion, she was a cameraman's dream as the object of Albert FINNEY's affections in the megahit *Tom Jones* (1963), which made her an international star. She was a profoundly disturbed patient in *Freud* (1962, US), and touching as Thomas More's daughter in *A Man for All Seasons* (1966). There were also 60s 'dolly bird' roles in 'SWINGING LONDON' capers – as a trendy Hampstead boutique owner in *Kaleidoscope* (1966) and a cute code breaker in *Sebastian* (1967). In the bitchy *The Killing of Sister George* (US, 1968) she played neurotic nymphet Alice 'Childie' McNaught, the immature doll-clutching lover of Beryl REID. A favourite film of the actress, perhaps because of its Scottishness (though mostly filmed in Ireland) is the neglected *Country Dance* (1969) starring Peter O'TOOLE as a mentally disturbed Scottish landowner who harbours incestuous yearnings for York. She was a flapper in *They Shoot Horses, Don't They?* (US, 1969) (BAA/supp a; AAn), and gave a superb performance as Cathryn, a possibly schizophrenic author of children's books, in the enigmatic thriller *Images* (Ire/US). Since the 60s she has divided her time between ART-HOUSE – *The Maids* (1974), *The Shout* (1978) and *Melancholia* (1989, UK/Ger) – and more commercial fare, such as playing the Kryptonian mother of *Superman* (1978, UK/US). Also active in theatre and TV, she wrote the screenplay for *Falling in Love Again* (1980, US), and several popular children's books. Married/divorced (1960–76) actor Michael Wells.

OTHER BRITISH FILMS: *The Seventh Dawn, Scene Nun, Take One** (1964), *Sands of the Kalahari, Scruggs** (1965), *Duffy* (1968), *Lock Up Your Daughters!, Oh! What a Lovely War* (1969), *Jane Eyre* (1970), *Zee and Co.* (1971), *Dunhallow Home** (Ireland, 1973), *Gold* (1974), *Conduct Unbecoming, That Lucky Touch* (1975), *The Long Shot* (1978), *The Awakening* (UK/US), *Superman II* (1980), *Loophole, Late Flowering Love** (1981), *Yellowbeard* (1983, UK/US), *Daemon* (1985), *A Summer Story, Just Ask for Diamond, American Roulette* (UK/Aust) (1988), *The Higher Mortals* (1993), *Romance and Rejection* (1996), *Loop* (1997).
* = shorts. Roger Philip Mellor.

Yorke, Doris (*d* London, 1996). Actress. When short and dumpy Yorke, with earrings a-jangle, hints darkly to the police about what 'goes on' upstairs in her artist lodger's rooms in *Account Rendered* (1957), she encapsulates a whole mini-tradition of British character women, landladies and chars, deeply suspicious of the behaviour of their social betters. She is also the cinema cashier on the night of the hold-up in *The Blue Lamp* (1949) but her real milieu is the shabby lodging-house.

OTHER BRITISH FILMS INCLUDE: *Train of Events* (1949), *The Franchise Affair* (1950), *The Gentle Gunman* (1952), *Glad Tidings* (1953), *The Green Man* (1956), *The Big Chance* (1957), *The Desperate Man* (1959).

Young, Arthur (*b* Bristol, 1898 – *d* London, 1959). Actor. Stern-faced character player, RADA-trained and on stage from 1914, touring extensively before London debut in 1925. In films from mid 30s, with a bit in *Lorna Doone* (1934) and Gladstone in *Victoria the Great* (1937), settling into severity in the 40s in such roles as Hubert GREGG's ruthless businessman father in *The Root of All Evil* (1947) and war-profiteer opponent of *My Brother Jonathan* (1948). He did Gladstone again (he could never have suggested Disraeli) in *The Lady with a Lamp* (1951) and was the self-righteous father in *An Inspector Calls* (1954).

OTHER BRITISH FILMS INCLUDE: *No Limit* (1935), *Wedding Group* (1936), *21 Days* (1937), *San Demetrio–London* (1943), *Two Fathers* (1944, short), *Twenty Questions Murder Mystery* (1949), *Isn't Life Wonderful!* (1953), *No Smoking* (1955), *The Gelignite Gang* (1956).

Young, Dan (*b* 1899 – *d* London, 1970). Actor. Enormously popular in Northern MUSIC HALLS where he was billed as the 'Dude Comedian', with monocle, cane, trim moustache and phoney upper-class accent, he toured in the 40s with his own revue, *Young Ideas*. Almost his entire film career is in films directed by John E. BLAKELEY for the MANCUNIAN FILM CORPORATION, starting with *Off the Dole* (1935), starring George FORMBY, and, as Private Young in a series of wartime comedies starring Frank RANDLE. The first of these knockabout entertainments was *Somewhere in England* (1940), and he was still playing Private Young in his last film, *It's a Grand Life* (1953).

OTHER BRITISH FILMS INCLUDE: *The New Hotel* (1932), *Somewhere on Leave, Somewhere in Camp* (1942), *Demobbed* (1944), *Under New Management* (1946), *School for Randle* (1949), *Over the Garden Wall* (1950).

Young, Frederick A. (Freddie) (*b* London, 1902 – *d* London, 1998). Cinematographer. Young entered films in the silent era, and the primacy of the visual image stayed with him. In 1917 he was taken on at SHEPHERD'S BUSH, his first credit as assistant cameraman on *Rob Roy* (1922). By 1928 he was chief cameraman, and in 1929 Herbert WILCOX, largely ignorant of the technical aspects of film craft, placed Young under contract to his company BRITISH AND DOMINIONS, leading to his first solo credit in 1930. Any visual flair in Wilcox's films of the 30s was largely due to Young's inventiveness and technical skill; his first use of TECHNICOLOR was in one reel of Wilcox's *Victoria the Great* (1937). During WW2, he was chief cameraman in the ARMY FILM UNIT, working on army training films. From 1948, he was under contract to MGM–British, receiving his first AAn for the Technicolored *Ivanhoe* (1952) and revealing his mastery of black-and-white in the night train sequences in *Time Bomb* (1953). In 1958, he made *Solomon and Sheba* (US), his first 70mm film, becoming a master of the new format.

Aged 60, Young won his first AA (and other awards) for the majestic desert landscapes of *Lawrence of Arabia* (1962), which features one of the greatest shots in cinema, the three-minute mirage sequence in which a figure slowly emerges from the desert haze. Had further BAA nominations for *The Seventh Dawn* (1964), and *Lord Jim* (1964), and won another AA for *Doctor Zhivago* (1965, UK/US), in which he created the illusion of a Russian winter in Spanish locations. In *The Deadly Affair* (1966, BAAn/c), he devised the technical innovation of pre-exposing COLOUR film (pre-fogging) to mute the colours, altering the look of colour photography to suit the subject. The spectacular Irish sea storm (taking months to film in arduous conditions) was a standout sequence in *Ryan's Daughter* (1970), bringing him another AA and BAAn, and his final AAn was for capturing the opulence of *Nicholas and Alexandra* (1971, UK/US). Combining a painstaking perfectionism with practicality, he was particularly useful to directors less knowledgeable about what the camera and lenses could do. Awarded OBE (1970), BAFTA Fellowship (1972) and International Award, American Society of Cinematographers (1993).

OTHER BRITISH FILMS (c, unless noted): *The Flag Lieutenant* (1926, co-c), *Victory* (1928, co-c), *The W Plan* (co-c), *Canaries Sometimes Sing, On Approval* (1930), *Carnival* (co-c), *Almost a Divorce* (co-c), *The Speckled Band, The Chance of a Night-Time, Up for the Cup, Plunder, Mischief, Tons of Money* (1931), *The Blue Danube, The Little Damozel, A Night Like This, Goodnight Vienna, The Love Contract, The Mayor's Nest, Thark, Leap Year, It's a King* (1932), *Just My Luck, The King's Cup, Yes Mr Brown, Up for the Derby, Night of the Garter, Summer Lightning, That's a Good Girl, Trouble* (1933), *Nell Gwyn, The Queen's Affair, Girls Please!, The King of Paris* (1934), *Come Out of the Pantry, Escape Me Never, Peg of Old Drury* (1935), *Three Maxims, Two's Company, Fame, This'll Make You Whistle, Millions, When Knights Were Bold* (1936), *The Rat, London Melody, The Frog, Sunset in Vienna* (1937), *Sixty Glorious Years, Blondes For Danger, A Royal Divorce* (1938), *Goodbye, Mr Chips* (1939), *Contraband, Busman's Honeymoon* (1940), *49th Parallel, They Flew Alone* (1941), *The Young Mr Pitt* (1942), *Caesar and Cleopatra* (1945), *Bedelia* (1946), *So Well Remembered, While I Live* (1947), *Escape, The Winslow Boy* (1948), *Edward, My Son, Conspirator* (1949), *Treasure Island* (1950), *Calling Bulldog Drummond* (1951), *Knights of the Round Table* (1953), *Invitation to the Dance* (1954, UK/US), *Bhowani Junction* (1955), *Beyond Mombasa, The Barretts of Wimpole Street* (1956), *I Accuse!, Island in the Sun* (1957), *Gideon's Day, The Inn of the Sixth Happiness, Indiscreet* (1958), *Gorgo* (1960), *Hand in Hand, The Greengage Summer* (1961), *Rotten to the Core* (1965), *You Only Live Twice* (1967), *Sinful Davey* (1968), *Battle of Britain* (1969), *The Asphyx* (1972), *Luther* (1973), *The Tamarind Seed* (1974), *Permission to Kill* (UK/Austria) (1975), *Stevie* (1978), *Richard's Things* (1980), *Invitation to the Wedding* (US/UK), *Sword of the Valiant* (1983).

BIBLIOG: Freddie Young (with Peter Busby), *Seventy Light Years*, 1999. Roger Phillip Mellor.

Young, Hal (*b* Croydon, Surrey, 1889 – *d* Elstree, 1970). Cinematographer. In 1919, when Famous Players–Lasky decided to establish a British studio on Poole Street, Islington, it brought over a prominent member of its US camera crew, Young, to photograph the company's first two British productions: *The Call of Youth* and *The Great Day* (1920), directed by American Hugh Ford. Young also shot two other films at Poole Street, *Appearances* and *Beside the Bonnie Briar Bush* (both 1921), directed by Donald CRISP. Worked in Britain in the 20s and early 30s, providing fluid camerawork, very modernistic in style, for the films of Graham Cutts: *The Prude's Fall, The Rat* (1925), *The Sea Urchin* and *The Triumph of the Rat* (1926).

OTHER BRITISH FILMS INCLUDE: *Fox Farm* (1922), *The Rolling Road, Somehow Good* (1927), *Suspense* (1930, co-c), *Many Waters* (1931, co-c), *Broken Blossoms* (1936, co-c). AS.

Young, Harold (*b* Portland, Oregon, 1897 – *d* Los Angeles, 1970). Director, editor. Young should have stayed in Britain where he worked as editor for KORDA on a run of prestige LONDON FILMS productions, starting with *Service for Ladies* (1932) and including *The Private Life of Henry VIII* (1933), and where he directed the one distinguished film of his long career. This was the swift and charming *The Scarlet Pimpernel* (1935),

with Leslie HOWARD and Merle OBERON entering into the spirit of the enterprise. He had been an editor in US films from the mid 20s and when he returned there from England he directed 30 odd low-budget, utterly routine films, including such titles as *Hi, Buddy* (1943) and *Jungle Captive* (1945).

OTHER BRITISH FILMS: (e) *Wedding Rehearsal* (1932), *It's a Boy!, The Girl from Maxim's, Counsel's Opinion* (1933), *Catherine the Great, The Private Life of Don Juan, Too Many Millions* (1934).

Young, Joan (*b* Newcastle-on-Tyne, 1903 – *d* London, 1984). Actress. RN: Wragge. Plump grump of over two dozen films, working her housekeeperly way through some very well-known films of the 40s and 50s. For instance, in 1948 alone she is the daily help at the Embassy in *The Fallen Idol*, the housekeeper in the tense household of *The Small Voice*, the cook in *Things Happen at Night*, Mervyn JOHNS's overbearing wife in *Easy Money*, a midwife attending 'titled births' in *The First Gentleman*, and Jean KENT's mum warning against the stage life in *Trottie True*. The stamina of these players! Young, born to MUSIC-HALL performers, was also on stage from 1918, in variety, then worked solidly on radio (famous for the series, *Navy Mixture*), returning to the stage in 1944.

OTHER BRITISH FILMS INCLUDE: *Victoria the Great* (1937), *Strawberry Roan* (1945), *School for Secrets* (1946), *Good-Time Girl* (1947), *Cardboard Cavalier* (1949), *Time Gentlemen Please!* (1952), *Child's Play* (1954), *All for Mary* (1955), *The Admirable Crichton* (1957), *Suddenly, Last Summer* (1959), *Carry On Constable* (1960), *The Last Shot You Hear* (1968), *Blood from the Mummy's Tomb* (1971).

Young, John (*b* Edinburgh, 1916 – Glasgow, 1996). Actor. Character player frequently in films set at least partly in his native Scotland, notably in *The Way Home* (1978), the third part of Bill DOUGLAS's great autobiographical trilogy, and as Ian CHARLESON's minister father in *Chariots of Fire* (1981). Had comedy success in *Monty Python and the Holy Grail* (1974) in several roles, and was taken up by the PYTHON gang. Played Ramsay MacDonald in TV's *Days of Hope* (1975). Son is actor Paul YOUNG.

OTHER BRITISH FILMS INCLUDE: *Depth Charge* (1960), *Ring of Bright Water* (1969), *The Wicker Man* (1973), *Black Jack, Monty Python's Life of Brian* (1979), *Black Angel* (1980), *Time Bandits* (1981).

Young, Paul (*b* Edinburgh, 1944). Actor. Son of actor John YOUNG, he first appeared on screen playing *Geordie* (1955) as a child, and like his father he has often been in Scottish-set films. These include the WW2 romance, *Another Time, Another Place* (1983), the WW1 hospital-set drama, *Regeneration* (1997, UK/Can) and *My Life So Far* (2000, UK/US), based on the early life of Sir Denis FORMAN, playing doctors in the latter two. Has also filmed internationally, including *Mad Max* (1979, Aust) and *A Change of Seasons* (1980, US). TV has included *My Fragile Heart* (2000).

OTHER BRITISH FILMS INCLUDE: *Submarine X–1* (1968), *Chato's Land* (1971), *Girl in the Picture* (1985), *Ashes* (1990), *Complicity* (2000).

Young, Raymond (*b* London, 1918). Actor. Entered films as Jean SIMMONS's youthful admirer who loses out of course to Stewart GRANGER in *Adam and Evelyne* (1949), and played supporting roles in nearly 20 films over the next few decades, including *The Beauty Jungle* (1964), as one of the judges, and several of the EXPLOITATION mode. Also much TV, in such mini-series as *Poldark* (1975) and *Nicholas Nickleby* (1977).

OTHER BRITISH FILMS INCLUDE: *Midnight Episode* (1950), *Venetian Bird* (1952), *Destination Death* (1956), *The Silent Enemy* (1958), *Goldfinger* (1964), *Drop Dead Darling* (1966), *The Love Box* (1972), *The Superstud* (1975), *Deadly Females* (1976), *The Thirty Nine Steps* (1978).

Young, Robert (*b* Cheltenham, 1933). Director. Former actor, LAMDA-trained, who has worked a great deal in TV and on DOCUMENTARIES and commercials, but whose feature films have been rare. His first was *Vampire Circus* (1971) and his best known, *Fierce Creatures* (1997, UK/US), finished by Fred SCHEPISI, suffered by comparison with *A Fish Called Wanda* (1988), wrongly advertised as equal rather than sequel. Shared a BAAn for the hard-hitting TV series, *GBH* (1991).

OTHER BRITISH FILMS INCLUDE: *Keep It Up Downstairs* (1976), *The World Is Full of Married Men* (1979), *Splitting Heirs* (1993), *Captain Jack* (1998).

Young, Roland (*b* London, 1887 – *d* New York, 1953). Actor. Famous Hollywood character player, usually purveying benign befuddlement as in *Topper* (1937), but also a marvellously obsequious Uriah Heep in *David Copperfield* (1935), and at least once very moving, in his scenes with Gladys COOPER in *Forever and a Day* (1943). RADA-trained, on the London stage from 1908, on Broadway in 1912, and in US films from 1922 as Watson to John Barrymore's *Sherlock Holmes*, he became an irresistible character presence in US films, sadly making only six in his native Britain. He was with KORDA several times in the 30s, notably as *The Man Who Could Work Miracles* (1936) and as Commander Good in *King Solomon's Mines* (1937). Post-war, he returned only once: as the bride's harassed father in *Bond Street* (1948).

OTHER BRITISH FILMS: *Wedding Rehearsal* (1932), *Gypsy* (1937), *Sailing Along* (1938).

Young, Terence (*b* Shanghai, China, 1915 – *d* Cannes, France, 1994). Director, screenwriter. There may be a slim volume in Cambridge-educated Young's varied career in films, though the researcher would have to be ready to sit through some flavourless, WARWICK-dominated 50s fustian, like *The Red Beret* (1953) and *Zarak* (1956). He entered films as a scriptwriter at ELSTREE in 1936, his first credit being for the very dark *On the Night of the Fire* (1939), and if he wrote only one sentence of the sublime *On Approval* (1944) this should be remembered to his credit. He began to direct after WW2 service (1940–46), and it says something for his tenacity that he survived the bizarre pretensions of *Corridor of Mirrors* (1948) and the inanities of *One Night with You* and *Woman Hater* (1948). Surely more experienced directors had turned these down. But he managed to make the rather stiff-upper-lip WAR FILM, *They Were Not Divided* (1950, + sc) moving in spite of itself and *That Lady* (1955) is a strangely compelling, if over-stately, period piece. What Warwick and those other 50s ADVENTURES such as *Storm over the Nile* (1955) and *Action of the Tiger* (1957) gave him was a facility in handling ACTION, which stood him in good stead when he became the first and perhaps the best of the BOND directors, on *Dr No* (1962), *From Russia with Love* (1963, + cameo appearance) and *Thunderball* (1965). For the rest, *Serious Charge* (1959), with its theme of homosexual assault allegation, holds up better than might have been supposed; *Wait Until Dark* (1967, US) has some genuinely alarming moments; and Ava GARDNER and James MASON ensure that the REMAKE of *Mayerling* (1968, UK/Fr, + sc) has some romantic charge. After that, he worked all over the place to little effect.

OTHER BRITISH FILMS: (d, unless noted) *Dangerous Moonlight* (1941, story, sc), *Hungry Hill* (1947, co-sc), *Bad Lord Byron* (1949, co-sc), *Valley of Eagles* (1951, + sc), *Tall Headlines* (1952), *Safari*, *Zarak* (1956), *No Time to Die* (1958, + co-sc), *Too Hot to Handle* (1960), *The Amorous Adventures of Moll Flanders* (1965), *Triple Cross* (1966, UK/Ger/US), *Where Is Parsifal?* (1983, ex p), *The Jigsaw Man* (1984).

Young, Tony (*b* Tynemouth, 1921 – *d* Chatham, Kent, 1966). Director. Began film career in the GAINSBOROUGH editing department in 1945, and was a freelance cameraman until he got his first directorial chance on *Penny Points to Paradise* (1951), whose only interest today is for the early glimpse it gives of Goons, Peter SELLERS *et al.* His other films were 'B' FILMS, mainly THRILLERS, with the slightly upmarket exception of *Port of Escape* (1956, + co-sc), which at least had the benefit of Googie WITHERS and John McCALLUM, and was lively enough though hardly an adequate British swansong for its stars.

OTHER BRITISH FILMS INCLUDE: (d, unless noted) *My Death Is a Mockery* (1952), *Hands of Destiny* (1954, + p), *Hidden Homicide* (1958, + co-sc), *The Runaway*, *Delayed Flight* (co-d) (1964).

youth films The search by youth for its place in society has provided a constant source of drama, even as its treatment by film-makers has evolved and changed. However, it needs to be noted that not all films dealing with youthful aspirations and problems are necessarily 'youth films' as the term is now used: the idea of the 'youth film' as a GENRE is a post-war – perhaps even 60s – phenomenon. The child's wide-eyed naiveté in *Great Expectations* (1946) and *Oliver Twist* (1948) leads to the misguided adulation of adults in *The Fallen Idol* (1948), a confused view of the adult world in *Hue and Cry* (1946) and *Whistle Down The Wind* (1961) and the death of childhood innocence in *Lord of The Flies* (1963). The 50s saw the rise of teenage hoodlums in such films as *Cosh Boy* (1953) and *Violent Playground* (1957), whereas the hedonistic 60s unveiled new sexual freedom, in such films as *A Taste of Honey* (1961), *The Knack . . .* (1965) and *Here We Go Around The Mulberry Bush* (1968), and self-gratification in *Darling* (1965). The search for idealised love has continued in *Letter To Brezhnev* (1985), *My Beautiful Laundrette* (1985), *Martha, Meet Frank, Daniel and Laurence* (1998) and *Bedrooms And Hallways* (1998). *Look Back In Anger* (1959) and *A Kind of Loving* (1962) addressed the issues of disaffection and dysfunctional lives of young people in an indifferent society, themes essayed by Ken LOACH in *Cathy Come Home* (1966), *Kes* (1969), *Ladybird Ladybird* (1994); by Mike LEIGH in *Naked* (1993) and *Career Girls* (1997), Shane MEADOWS in *24 7* (1997) and *A Room for Romeo Brass* (1999), and Carine ADLER (*Under the Skin* (1997). Social rebellion and delinquency challenge the status quo in *The Guinea Pig* (1948) and *If . . .* (1968), a film very popular with young audiences, and vicious acts are matched by vicious punishment in *The Blue Lamp* (1949), *A Clockwork Orange* (1971) and *Small Faces* (1995), while more recent issues of youthful nihilism and drug culture are explored in *Trainspotting* (1996) and *Human Traffic* (1999). Matthew Caterson.

Yule, Lady (*b c* 1875 – *d* Bricket Wood, 1950). Widow of Sir Charles Yule, jute multimillionaire, she joined J. Arthur RANK and John CORFIELD in forming BRITISH NATIONAL FILMS in 1934. Her passion in life was racehorses, though she did share Rank's religious outlook, and, while her interest in film was minimal, she was happy to be one of the backers for Rank's first feature film, *The Turn of the Tide* (1935), made at ELSTREE. Shortly after, she and Rank became major shareholders in the new PINEWOOD STUDIOS, but she sold out to Rank in 1937, bought out his interest in British National and ran it with Corfield. During WW2, she acquired the Rock Studios, renaming them British National, and a string of modestly popular films was made there until the company was wound up in 1948. There is about her the charm of privileged eccentricity enjoying its privileges – and happily proving useful to the British film industry the while.

Zz

Zampi, Mario (*b* Rome, 1903 – *d* London, 1963). Producer, director. After a brief career as an actor in Italy, Zampi moved to England, working throughout the 1930s as an editor at WARNER–BRITISH. In 1937 he formed TWO CITIES with Filippo DEL GIUDICE, producing two inventive and amusing comedies *French Without Tears* (1939), and *Spy for a Day* (1940) that he also directed. Both Zampi and Del Giudice were interned as enemy aliens, Zampi for the duration of hostilities. Zampi resuscitated his career after the war, producing and directing three low-budget THRILLERS distributed by Columbia, and the more ambitious crime drama *Third Time Lucky* (1949).

As one of a growing number of independent producers, Zampi found his *métier* in a return to COMEDY, beginning with *Laughter in Paradise* – a lively farce in which ALASTAIR SIM is outstanding as one of four relatives who have to perform acts foreign to their natures in order to inherit a fortune that never materialises – the top-grossing film of 1951. *Top Secret* (1952) followed, a Cold War comedy-thriller specially written for GEORGE COLE and *Happy Ever After* (1954) with DAVID NIVEN as a bullying squire. All three were intelligently scripted by Michael PERTWEE and Jack DAVIES, and distributed by ABPC. After the sentimental cross-class romance *Now and Forever* (1955), Zampi resumed comedy with *The Naked Truth* (1957) memorable for Peter SELLERS' multiple roles, *Too Many Crooks* (1959) in which Terry-THOMAS again plays a mercenary dandy, and *Bottoms Up* (1959) starring Jimmy EDWARDS, a SPIN-OFF from the television series *Whack-O!* The best of Zampi's films are unpretentious and often very funny comedies that combine high farce expertly played by accomplished actors with an indulgent satire on human greed and national obsessions, the subject of his neglected final film, *Five Golden Hours* (1961). His son **Guilio Zampi** (*b* London, 1923) edited several of his father's early films and acted as associate producer on them all from 1954.

OTHER BRITISH FILMS: *13 Men and a Gun* (1938), *Freedom Radio* (1940), *The Phantom Shot* (1947), *The Fatal Night* (1948), *Shadow of the Past* (1950), *Come Dance with Me* (1950). Andrew Spicer.

Zeffirelli, Franco (*b* Florence, Italy, 1923). Director. RN: Gian Franco Corsi. Italian stage director who took seriously to film directing, after 2nd unit work in the 50s, in the mid 60s and made his English-speaking debut with his boisterous ADAPTATION of *The Taming of the Shrew* (1967, + p, sc), starring Elizabeth TAYLOR and Richard BURTON at the height of their popularity. But this was outshone by his hugely successful *Romeo and Juliet* (1968, UK/It), which was perhaps the first filmed SHAKESPEARE to enjoy a widespread youth audience, chiming with the spirit of youthful rebellion that the

very date now conjures up. With its headlong approach to narrative, pausing only to give a genuinely lyrical and erotic weight to the love scenes, he broke new ground in the filming of Shakespeare.

Since then, he directed Mel Gibson in *Hamlet* (1990, UK/US) with curiously unexciting results, despite a cast of trusted British actors supporting the action hero, and *Tea with Mussolini* (1999, UK/It), a sentimentalised version of his own illegitimate childhood, with a cast of distinguished British and American actresses encouraged to indulge themselves. It is a long time since he did anything rigorous on film, and certainly his US films, including *The Champ* (1979) and *Endless Love* (1981), are difficult to endure. Much of the rest of his time has been spent in directing OPERA films in Italian, and he has directed opera at Covent Garden.

OTHER BRITISH FILMS: *Brother Sun, Sister Moon* (1968, UK/It, + co-sc), *Franco Zeffirelli: A Florentine Artist* (1973, doc, participant), *Jesus of Nazareth* (1977, UK/It, TV and cinemas, co-sc), *Jane Eyre* (1996, UK/Fr/It/US, + co-sc).

Zelnik, Frederic (*b* Czernowitz, Austria-Hungary, 1885 – *d* London, 1950). Director, producer. Director of numerous box-office hits in Germany from 1915. In the 20s he was producer for German subsidiaries of First National and Fox, then turned director again in Britain in the 30s, specialising in continental-style romantic dramas and comedies. After some films in the Netherlands in the late 30s, in the early 40s he was producer for BRITISH NATIONAL.

OTHER BRITISH FILMS INCLUDE: (d) *Happy* (+ p), *Mister Cinders* (1934), *Southern Roses* (1936), *The Lilac Domino* (1937); (p), *I Killed The Count* (1939), *The Stars Look Down* (1939, prod super), *Heaven Is Round the Corner*, *Give Me The Stars* (1944), *The Glass Mountain* (1948, co-p), *Hell Is Sold Out* (1951). Tim Bergfelder.

Zeta Jones, Catherine (*b* Swansea, 1969). Actress. The 'Zeta', her grandmother's Christian name, was a cunning addition: she *sounds* like a film star, and increasingly that is how she looks. Dark and sensual, her clothes seemingly laminated around her, she is married to Michael Douglas, and has embraced Hollywood as fervently (if with a nice touch of knowingness) as it has her. First noticed in TV's *The Darling Buds of May* (1991), made several films which failed to take off, then took herself off to LA to star in *The Phantom* (1996). It wasn't much good either, but it got her known, and she co-starred with Sean CONNERY in *Entrapment* (1999, UK/Ger/US), filmed mainly at PINEWOOD, and that was a major commercial success, since when she has gone from one US film to another. AA 2003 for best supporting actress for her part in *Chicago*.

OTHER BRITISH FILMS: *Out of the Blue* (1991), *Splitting Heirs* (1993), *Blue Juice* (1995), *High Fidelity* (2000, UK/US).

Zetterling, Mai (*b* Västerås, Sweden, 1925 – *d* London, 1994). Actress. After an impoverished childhood and training at the Royal Dramatic Theatre School, Stockholm, she made film and stage debuts in her mid teens. Her starring role in *Frenzy* (1944) brought her to the attention of British film-makers and she came to England to play *Frieda* (1947), Basil DEARDEN's version of the stage play about the problems of an RAF officer's German bride in dealing with post-war prejudice in his home town. RANK put her under contract but didn't find anything very rewarding for the fragile-looking blonde to do: she had fair chances in two displaced-persons dramas, *Portrait from Life* (1948) and *The Lost People* (1949), looked decorative as Jack WATLING's seducer in *Quartet* (1948), but could do nothing – no one could have – with *Bad Lord Byron* and *The Romantic Age* (1949). She co-starred with Hollywood's Richard WIDMARK in *A Prize of Gold* (1955) and Tyrone Power in *Seven Waves Away* (1956), and, *in* Hollywood, with Danny Kaye in *Knock on Wood* (1954). But, of the rest, only the Welsh-set COMEDY *Only Two Can Play* (1961), as the object of Peter SELLERS's illicit passion, gave her anything worthwhile during her starring career. As a character player, she was better served by the grandmother role in the US-made *The Witches* (1989) and by Ken LOACH's *Hidden Agenda* (1990), but by then she was more interested in directing, scoring a considerable success with the Swedish *Night Games* (1966) and *Scrubbers* (1982, + co-sc), for HANDMADE, about young female offenders sent to Borstal. Her other directorial work was made elsewhere than Britain. Married/divorced (1) Tutte (Samuel) LEMKOW and (2) writer **David Hughes**, with whom she co-wrote the screenplay of the SHORT FILM *The War Game* (1962) she directed.

OTHER BRITISH FILMS: (a) *Blackmailed* (1950), *Hell Is Sold Out* (1951), *The Ringer*, *Tall Headlines* (1952), *Desperate Moment* (1953), *Dance Little Lady* (1954), *The Truth About Women* (1957), *Jet Storm* (1959), *Piccadilly Third Stop*, *Faces in the Dark*, *Offbeat* (1960), *The Man Who Finally Died*, *The Main Attraction* (1962), *The Bay of Saint Michel* (1963).

BIBLIOG: Autobiography, *All Those Tomorrows*, 1985.

Ziegler, Anne (*b* Liverpool, 1909). Actress, singer. RN: Irene Eastwood. In films from 1934. Well-known on the operatic and musical comedy stage and on RADIO, Ziegler and husband Webster BOOTH made two more or less deplorable films for BRITISH NATIONAL in the mid 40s: *Waltz Time* (1945) and *The Laughing Lady* (1946), and provided one of the variety turns in MANCUNIAN's *Demobbed* (1944). They were heard on the soundtrack of *Uncle Lord Pete* (1962), made in South Africa, whither they emigrated when their vogue was past.

Ziemann, Sonja (*b* Eichenwald, Germany, 1926). Actress. Most of Ziemann's prolific career of over 50 films was conducted in her native Germany. Made her English-speaking debut as the disruptively sexy Hungarian maid in the mild COMEDY of marital manners, *Made in Heaven* (1952), and subsequently co-starred with Terry-THOMAS in *A Matter of WHO* (1961) and with Tony WRIGHT in the 'B' MOVIE *Journey into Nowhere* (1963, UK/Ger/SAf).

Zimmer, Hans (*b* Frankfurt, Germany, *c* 1957). Composer. Hugely productive Zimmer is famous for his use of computer-synthesised soundtracks, for the combining of modern technologies with traditional orchestral music. Came to Britain in the early 80s, collaborating with Stanley MYERS on the score of *Moonlighting* (1982) and thereafter they worked together on some of the most interesting British films of the 80s, including Nicolas ROEG's *Insignificance* (1985) and Stephen FREARS's *My Beautiful Laundrette* (1985) and *Prick Up Your Ears* (1987). Hollywood inevitably beckoned and he has worked solo on such high-profile films as *Rain Man* (1988), *Driving Miss Daisy* (1989) and *Thelma & Louise* (1991), AA-nominated on a half-dozen occasions and winning for *The Lion King* (1994).

OTHER BRITISH FILMS INCLUDE: *Success Is the Best Revenge* (1984, UK/Fr), *Castaway* (1986), *A World Apart* (1987, UK/Zimb), *Paperhouse*, *The Fruit Machine* (1988), *Diamond Skulls* (1989), *The Borrowers* (1997).

Zinkeisen, Doris (*b* Kilcreggan, Scotland, 1898 – *d* 1991). Costume designer. Painter as well as designer of theatrical and film costume, Zinkeisen did most of her film work for Herbert WILCOX productions from 1923 to 1938. This included what he described (1967) as 'an outrageously daring diaphanous dress' for Anna NEAGLE in *The Little Damozel* (1933), and Neagle herself wrote (1974) of the 'lovely dresses' Zinkeisen designed for *Bitter Sweet* (1933). In Hollywood, she designed costumes for *Showboat* (1936). Her paintings were exhibited in London and Paris; wrote *Designing for the Stage* (1938).

OTHER BRITISH FILMS: (cos des, unless noted) *Carnival* (1931, des), *Goodnight Vienna* (1932), *Nell Gwyn* (dresses), *Queen's Affair* (1934), *Peg of Old Drury* (1935), *Victoria the Great* (1937, des), *Sixty Glorious Years* (1938, co-cos des).

Zinnemann, Fred (*b* Vienna, 1907 – *d* London, 1997). Celebrated, much AA- and BAA-nominated Hollywood director who had an enormous *succès d'estime* with *A Man for All Seasons* (1966), which won AA for film and director and BAA as best British film and best film from any source. He gave fresh dramatic life to the issues of Robert BOLT's play and displayed a fine sense of British period. *The Day of the Jackal* (1973, UK/Fr, + p), also BAA-nominated, is a skilful divertissement based on Frederick FORSYTH's thriller, and several other of his films, technically US, have strong British input, including cast and technicians on *The Nun's Story* (1959), *The Sundowners* (1960, Aust/US), and *Five Days One Summer* (1982, UK/US, + p). One of the most successful European directors to find an English-speaking career.

Zucco, George (*b* Manchester, 1886 – *d* Los Angeles, 1960). Actor. On stage from 1908 in Canada, returning to England in the 20s. After a dozen or so films in the 30s, including *The Midshipmaid* (1932), as Lord Dore, and *The Man Who Could Work Miracles* (1936), as a butler, Zucco took off for Hollywood and menaced his way through a further seven dozen films, occasionally as British toffs, as in *The Black Swan* (1942), but more often as international obsessives of every hue. It is not surprising he found professional life more interesting in the US, becoming a cult mad-scientist figure, which playing a couple of priests (*Desire Me*, 1947; *The First Legion*, 1951) did nothing to dispel.

OTHER BRITISH FILMS INCLUDE: *Dreyfus* (1931), *There Goes the Bride* (1932), *The Good Companions* (1933), *Road House*, *The Lady Is Willing*, *Autumn Crocus* (1934), *Abdul the Damned* (1935).

AWARDS

This list of award-winning British films and recipients is arranged by year of ceremony. Only ceremonies with British winners are listed.

'British winners' include:

- people born in the UK
- people born elsewhere who acquired UK citizenship
- non-British people associated with films made (or partly made) in the UK
- British people associated with US-made films.

Academy Award Winners

First ceremony 16 May 1929, covering films released 1927–28. The awards ceremony is currently held annually in March, covering films released in the US in the previous year.

1929 STATUETTE: Charles Chaplin, *The Circus* (US)

1930 (3 April) (covers 1928–29)
ĐIRECTOR: Frank Lloyd, *The Divine Lady* (US)

1930 (5 Nov) (covers 1929–30)
ACTOR: George Arliss, *Disraeli* (US)

1934 (covers 1932–33)
ACTOR: Charles Laughton, *The Private Life of Henry VIII*
DIRECTOR: Frank Lloyd, *Cavalcade* (US)
ART DIRECTION: William S. Darling, *Cavalcade* (US)

1936 ACTOR: Victor McLaglen, *The Informer* (US)
SHORT (NOVELTY): *Wings Over Everest* (Educational Films. Directors: Ivor Montagu, Geoffrey Barkas)

1939 SCREENPLAY: Ian Dalrymple, Cecil Lewis, W.P. Lipscomb (adapted from George Bernard Shaw), *Pygmalion*

1940 ACTOR: Robert Donat, *Goodbye, Mr Chips*
ACTRESS: Vivien Leigh, *Gone With the Wind* (US)

1941 CINEMATOGRAPHY (COLOUR): Georges Perinal, *The Thief of Baghdad*
ART DIRECTION (COLOUR): Vincent Korda, *The Thief of Baghdad*
SPECIAL EFFECTS: Lawrence Butler and Jack Whitney, *The Thief of Baghdad*
SPECIAL AWARD: Bob Hope

1942 SUPPORTING ACTOR: Donald Crisp, *How Green Was My Valley* (US)
ACTRESS: Joan Fontaine, *Suspicion* (US)
SOUND RECORDING: Jack Whitney, *That Hamilton Woman* (US)

SPECIAL AWARD: Ministry of Information, for the documentary *Target for Tonight*

1943 ACTRESS: Greer Garson, *Mrs Miniver* (US)
SCREENPLAY (ORIGINAL): Emeric Pressburger, *49th Parallel*
SPECIAL AWARD: Noël Coward for *In Which We Serve*

1944 DOCUMENTARY FEATURE: *Desert Victory* (Ministry of Information/Army Film Unit. Director: David MacDonald)
ART DIRECTION (B/W): William S. Darling, *The Song of Bernadette* (US)

1945 HONORARY AWARD: Bob Hope

1946 ACTOR: Ray Milland, *The Lost Weekend* (US)
CINEMATOGRAPHY (B/W): Harry Stradling, *The Picture of Dorian Gray* (US)
DOCUMENTARY FEATURE: *The True Glory* (UK/US) (Ministry of Information/US Office of War Information. Directors: Carol Reed, Garson Kanin)

1947 ORIGINAL STORY: Clemence Dane, *Perfect Strangers*
SCREENPLAY (ORIGINAL): Muriel and Sydney Box, *The Seventh Veil*
SPECIAL EFFECTS: Thomas Howard, *Blithe Spirit*
SPECIAL AWARD: Laurence Olivier for *Henry V*
ACTRESS: Olivia De Havilland, *To Each His Own* (US)
ART DIRECTION (B/W): William S. Darling, *Anna and the King of Siam* (US)

1948 ACTOR: Ronald Colman, *A Double Life* (US)
SUPPORTING ACTOR: Edmund Gwenn, *Miracle on 34th Street* (US)
CINEMATOGRAPHY (B/W): Guy Green, *Great Expectations*
ART DIRECTION/ SET DECORATION (B/W): John Bryan/Wilfred Shingleton, *Great Expectations*
CINEMATOGRAPHY (COLOUR): Jack Cardiff, *Black Narcissus*
ART DIRECTION/ SET DECORATION (COLOUR): Alfred Junge, *Black Narcissus*

1949 FILM: *Hamlet* (Two Cities–Rank. Producer: Laurence Olivier)
OTHER AWARDS FOR THIS FILM:
ACTOR: Laurence Olivier
ART DIRECTION/ SET DECORATION (B/W): Roger K. Furse/Carmen Dillon
COSTUME DESIGN (B/W): Roger K. Furse
ART DIRECTION/ SET DECORATION (COLOUR): Hein Heckroth, Arthur Lawson, *The Red Shoes*
MUSIC SCORING: Brian Easdale, *The Red Shoes*

1950 DOCUMENTARY FEATURE: *Daybreak in Udi* (British Information Services/Crown Film Unit. Director: Terry Bishop)
ACTRESS: Olivia De Havilland, *The Heiress* (US)

1951 CINEMATOGRAPHY (B/W): Robert Krasker, *The Third Man*

1952 ACTOR: Humphrey Bogart, *The African Queen*
ACTRESS: Vivien Leigh, *A Streetcar Named Desire* (US)
SCREENPLAY (STORY): Paul Dehn, James Bernard, *Seven Days to Noon*

1953 SCREENPLAY (ORIGINAL): T.E.B. Clarke, *The Lavender Hill Mob*
ART DIRECTION/SET DECORATION (COLOUR): Paul Sheriff, Marcel Vertes, *Moulin Rouge*
COSTUME DESIGN (COLOUR): Marcel Vertes, *Moulin Rouge*
SOUND RECORDING: London Films sound department, *The Sound Barrier*
HONORARY AWARD: Bob Hope

1954 ACTRESS: Audrey Hepburn, *Roman Holiday* (US)

1955 DOCUMENTARY (SHORT): *Thursday's Children* (Morse Films/British Information Services. Directors: Lindsay Anderson, Guy Brenton)
MINIATURE STATUETTES (FOR OUTSTANDING JUVENILE PERFORMANCES): Jon Whiteley and Vincent Winter, *The Kidnappers*

1957 SHORT (TWO REEL): *The Bespoke Overcoat* (Romulus Films. Producer/Director: Jack Clayton)

1958 FILM: *The Bridge on the River Kwai* (Horizon Films, Columbia. Producer: Sam Speigel)
OTHER AWARDS FOR THIS FILM:
ACTOR: Alec Guinness
DIRECTOR: David Lean
SCREENPLAY (ADAPTED): Pierre Boulle, Carl Foreman, Michael Wilson
CINEMATOGRAPHY: Jack Hildyard
FILM EDITING: Peter Taylor
MUSIC SCORING: Malcolm Arnold

1959 ACTOR: David Niven, *Separate Tables* (US)
SUPPORTING ACTRESS: Wendy Hiller, *Separate Tables* (US)
SPECIAL EFFECTS: Thomas (Tom) Howard, *tom thumb*
COSTUME DESIGN: Cecil Beaton, *Gigi* (US)

1960 ACTRESS: Simone Signoret, *Room at the Top*
SCREENPLAY (ADAPTED): Neil Paterson, *Room at the Top*
SUPPORTING ACTOR: Hugh Griffith, *Ben-Hur* (US)
COSTUME DESIGN (COLOUR): Elizabeth Haffenden, *Ben-Hur*
JEAN HERSHOLT HUMANITARIAN AWARD: Bob Hope

1961 ACTRESS: Elizabeth Taylor, *Butterfield 8* (US)
SUPPORTING ACTOR: Peter Ustinov, *Spartacus* (US)
CINEMATOGRAPHY (B/W): Freddie Francis, *Sons and Lovers*
MINIATURE STATUETTE (FOR OUTSTANDING JUVENILE PERFORMANCE): Hayley Mills, *Pollyanna* (US)
DOCUMENTARY (SHORT SUBJECT): *Giuseppina* (British Petroleum Films. Producer/Director: James Hill)

1962 SPECIAL EFFECTS: Bill Warrington, Vivian C. Greenham, *The Guns of Navarone*

1963 FILM: *Lawrence of Arabia* (Horizon Films, Columbia. PRODUCER: Sam Speigel)

OTHER AWARDS FOR THIS FILM:
DIRECTOR: David Lean
CINEMATOGRAPHY (COLOUR): Freddie Young
MUSIC SCORE (ORIGINAL): Maurice Jarre
ART DECORATION (COLOUR): John Box, John Stoll (SET DECORATION: Dario Simoni)
SOUND: John Cox, Shepperton Studios sound department
FILM EDITING: Anne Coates
DOCUMENTARY (SHORT SUBJECT): *Dylan Thomas* (TWW. Producer, Jack Howells)

1964 FILM: *Tom Jones* (Woodfall Films/United Artists. Producer: Tony Richardson)
OTHER AWARDS FOR THIS FILM:
DIRECTOR: Tony Richardson
SCREENPLAY (ADAPTED): John Osborne
MUSIC SCORE (ORIGINAL): John Addison
SUPPORTING ACTRESS: Margaret Rutherford, *The VIPs*

1965 ACTOR: Rex Harrison, *My Fair Lady* (US)
CINEMATOGRAPHY (COLOUR): Harry Stradling, *My Fair Lady* (US)
COSTUME DESIGN (COLOUR): Cecil Beaton, *My Fair Lady* (US)
ART DECORATION (COLOUR): Cecil Beaton, *My Fair Lady* (US)
ACTRESS: Julie Andrews, *Mary Poppins* (US)
SUPPORTING ACTOR: Peter Ustinov, *Topkapi* (US)
CINEMATOGRAPHY (B/W): Walter Lassally, *Zorba the Greek*
SCREENPLAY (ADAPTED): Edward Anhalt, *Becket*
SOUND EFFECTS: Norman Wanstall, *Goldfinger*

1966 SCREENPLAY (ADAPTED): Robert Bolt, *Doctor Zhivago* (UK/US)
CINEMATOGRAPHY (COLOUR): Freddie Young, *Doctor Zhivago*
ART DECORATION (COLOUR): John Box, Terry Marsh (SET DECORATION: Dario Simoni), *Doctor Zhivago*
COSTUME DESIGN (COLOUR): Phyllis Dalton, *Doctor Zhivago*
MUSIC SCORE (ORIGINAL): Maurice Jarre, *Doctor Zhivago*
ACTRESS: Julie Christie, *Darling*
SCREENPLAY (ORIGINAL): Frederic Raphael, *Darling*
COSTUME DESIGN (B/W): Julie Harris, *Darling*
SPECIAL VISUAL EFFECTS: John Stears, *Thunderball*
SPECIAL AWARD (GOLD MEDAL): Bob Hope

1967 FILM: *A Man For All Seasons* (Highland Films, Columbia. Producer: Fred Zinnemann)
OTHER AWARDS FOR THIS FILM:
ACTOR: Paul Scofield
DIRECTOR: Fred Zinnemann
SCREENPLAY (ADAPTED): Robert Bolt
CINEMATOGRAPHY (COLOUR): Ted Moore
COSTUME DESIGN (COLOUR): Elizabeth Haffenden, Joan Bridge
ACTRESS: Elizabeth Taylor, *Who's Afraid of Virginia Woolf?* (US)
MUSIC (SONG): John Barry(m) and Don Black(l) for 'Born Free', *Born Free*
MUSIC SCORE (ORIGINAL): John Barry, *Born Free*
MUSIC SCORING (ADAPTED): Ken Thorne, *A Funny Thing Happened on the Way to the Forum*
SOUND EFFECTS: Gordon Daniel, *Grand Prix* (US)

SHORT FILM: *Wild Wings* (British Transport Films.
Producer: Edgar Anstey)
DOCUMENTARY FEATURE: *The War Game* (BBC TV.
Producer: Peter Watkins)

1968 SOUND EFFECTS: John Poyner, *The Dirty Dozen* (UK/US)
MUSIC (SONG): Leslie Bricusse (m/l) for 'Talk to the
Animals', *Doctor Doolittle* (US)
IRVING G. THALBERG MEMORIAL AWARD: Alfred Hitchcock

1969 FILM: *Oliver!* (Romulus Films, Columbia. Producer:
John Woolf)
OTHER AWARDS FOR THIS FILM:
DIRECTOR: Carol Reed
ART DIRECTION: John Box, Terence Marsh (SET
DECORATION: Vernon Dixon, Ken Muggleston)
SOUND: Shepperton Studios sound department
MUSIC SCORING (ADAPTED): John Green
STATUETTE FOR CHOREOGRAPHY: Onna White
ACTRESS: Katharine Hepburn, *A Lion in Winter*
SCREENPLAY (ADAPTED): James Goldman, *A Lion in
Winter*
MUSIC SCORE (ORIGINAL): John Barry, *A Lion in Winter*
CINEMATOGRAPHY: Pasqualino De Santis, *Romeo and
Juliet* (UK/It)
COSTUME DESIGN: Danilo Donati, *Romeo and Juliet*
SPECIAL EFFECTS: Stanley Kubrick, *2001: A Space Odyssey*
SCIENTIFIC/TECHNICAL STATUETTE: Charles D. Staffell
(Rank Organization) for a reflex background projection
system for composite cinematography

1970 ACTRESS: Maggie Smith, *The Prime of Miss Jean Brodie*
DIRECTOR: John Schlesinger, *Midnight Cowboy* (US)
COSTUME DESIGN: Margaret Furse, *Anne of the Thousand
Days*
HONORARY STATUETTE: Cary Grant

1971 ACTRESS: Glenda Jackson, *Women in Love*
SUPPORTING ACTOR: John Mills, *Ryan's Daughter*
CINEMATOGRAPHY: Freddie Young, *Ryan's Daughter*
COSTUME DESIGN: Nino Novarese, *Cromwell*
MUSIC (ORIGINAL SONG SCORE): The Beatles, *Let It Be*

1972 ART DIRECTION: John Box, Ernest Archer, Jack Maxsted,
Gil Parrondo (SET DECORATION: Vernon Dixon),
Nicholas and Alexandra (UK/US)
COSTUME DESIGN: Yvonne Blake, Antonio Castillo,
Nicholas and Alexandra
CINEMATOGRAPHY: Oswald Morris, *Fiddler on the Roof*
(US)
SOUND: Gordon K. McCullum and David Hildyard,
Fiddler on the Roof
MUSIC SCORING (ADAPTED): John Williams, *Fiddler on the
Roof*
DOCUMENTARY (SHORT): *Sentinels of Silence* (US)
(Producer: Robert Amram)
HONORARY AWARD: Charles Chaplin

1973 CINEMATOGRAPHY: Geoffrey Unsworth, *Cabaret*
SOUND: Robert Knudson, David Hildyard, *Cabaret*
MUSIC (ORIGINAL SCORE): Charles Chaplin, *Limelight*
(US, 1952) (belated award)
COSTUME DESIGN: Anthony Powell, *Travels with my Aunt*
SHORT FILM (ANIMATION): *A Christmas Carol* (US)
(ABC TV. Director: Richard Williams)

1974 ACTRESS: Glenda Jackson, *A Touch of Class*

1975 SUPPORTING ACTRESS: Ingrid Bergman, *Murder on the
Orient Express*
SPECIAL ACHIEVEMENT FOR VISUAL EFFECTS: Albert
Whitlock, *Earthquake* (US)

1976 CINEMATOGRAPHY: John Alcott, *Barry Lyndon*
ART DECORATION: Ken Adam, Roy Walker (SET
DECORATION: Vernon Dixon), *Barry Lyndon*
COSTUME DESIGN: Britt Soderlund, Milena Canonero,
Barry Lyndon
MUSIC SCORING (ADAPTED): Leonard Rosenman, *Barry
Lyndon*
SPECIAL ACHIEVEMENT FOR VISUAL EFFECTS: Albert
Whitlock, *The Hindenburg* (US)
SHORT FILM (ANIMATION): *Great* (Bob Godfrey Movie
Emporium/British Lion. Producer: Bob Godfrey)

1977 ACTOR: Peter Finch, *Network* (US)
MUSIC SCORE (ORIGINAL): Jerry Goldsmith, *The Omen*
(UK/US)

1978 ART DIRECTION: Norman Reynolds, John Barry, Leslie
Dilley (SET DECORATION: Roger Christian), *Star Wars*
(UK/US, made at Elstree)
COSTUME DESIGN: John Mollo, *Star Wars*
SOUND: Don Macdougall, Bob Minkler, Derek Ball, Ray
West, *Star Wars*
FILM EDITING: Marcia Lucas and Richard Chew, *Star
Wars*
VISUAL EFFECTS: Grant McCune, John Stears, John
Dykstra, Richard Edlund, Robert Blalack, *Star Wars*
MUSIC SCORE (ORIGINAL): John Williams, *Star Wars*
SPECIAL ACHIEVEMENT AWARD FOR SOUND EFFECTS
CREATIONS: Benjamin Burtt Jr, *Star Wars*
SUPPORTING ACTRESS: Vanessa Redgrave, *Julia* (UK/US)

1979 SUPPORTING ACTRESS: Maggie Smith, *California Suite*
(US)
SCREENPLAY (ADAPTED): Oliver Stone, *Midnight Express*
MUSIC (ORIGINAL SCORE): Giorgio Moroder, *Midnight
Express*
COSTUME DESIGN: Anthony Powell, *Death on the Nile*
SPECIAL ACHIEVEMENT AWARD FOR VISUAL EFFECTS: Les
Bowie, Colin Chilvers, Denys Coop, Roy Field, Derek
Meddings, Zoran Perisic, *Superman*
HONORARY AWARD: Laurence Olivier

1980 ART DIRECTION: Tony Walton, Philip Rosenberg (SET
DECORATION: Edward Stewart, Gary Brink), *All That Jazz*
(US)
VISUAL EFFECTS: H.R. Giger, Carlo Rambaldi, Brian
Johnson, Nick Allder, Denys Ayling, *Alien*
HONORARY AWARD: Alec Guinness

1981 CINEMATOGRAPHY: Geoffrey Unsworth, Ghislain
Cloquet, *Tess* (UK/Fr)
ART DIRECTION/SET DECORATION: Jack Stephens, Pierre
Guffroy, *Tess*
COSTUME DESIGN: Anthony Powell, *Tess*
SOUND: Peter Sutton, Bill Varney, Greg Landaker, Steve
Maslow, *The Empire Strikes Back*
SPECIAL ACHIEVEMENT AWARD FOR VISUAL EFFECTS: Brian
Johnson, Richard Edlund, Dennis Muren, Bruce
Nicholson, *The Empire Strikes Back*
SHORT (LIVE ACTION): *The Dollar Bottom* (Rocking Horse
Films. Producer: Lloyd Phillips/Director: Roger
Christian)

SCIENTIFIC AND ENGINEERING AWARD: David W. Samuelson (and others) of Samuelson Film Service Ltd for the engineering and development of the Louma Camera Crane and remote control system for film production

1982   FILM: *Chariots of Fire* (Enigma Films/Allied Stars. Producer: David Puttnam)
OTHER AWARDS FOR THIS FILM:
SCREENPLAY (ORIGINAL): Colin Welland
COSTUME DESIGN: Milena Canonero
MUSIC (ORIGINAL SCORE): Vangelis
SUPPORTING ACTOR: John Gielgud, *Arthur* (US)
ART DIRECTION: Norman Reynolds, Leslie Dilley (SET DECORATION: Michael Ford), *Raiders of the Lost Ark* (US)
SOUND: Roy Charman, Bill Varney, Steve Maslow, Gregg Landaker, *Raiders of the Lost Ark*
SPECIAL ACHIEVEMENT AWARD FOR SOUND EFFECTS EDITING: Ben Burtt and Richard L. Anderson, *Raiders of the Lost Ark*
FILM EDITING: Michael Kahn, *Raiders of the Lost Ark*
VISUAL EFFECTS: Kit West, Joe Johnston, Richard Edlund, Bruce Nicholson, *Raiders of the Lost Ark*
MAKE-UP: Rick Baker, *An American Werewolf in London*
SCIENTIFIC AND ENGINEERING AWARD: Peter D. Parks, Oxford Scientific Films, for the development of the OSF microcosmic zoom device for microscopic photography
IRVING G. THALBERG MEMORIAL AWARD: Albert R. Broccoli

1983   FILM: *Gandhi* (UK/Ind) (Goldcrest/Indo-British Int. Film Investors/National Film Dev. Corp. of India/Columbia. Producer: Richard Attenborough)
OTHER AWARDS FOR THIS FILM:
ACTOR: Ben Kingsley
DIRECTOR: Richard Attenborough
SCREENPLAY (ORIGINAL): John Briley
CINEMATOGRAPHY: Billy Williams, Ronnie Taylor
ART DIRECTION: Stuart Craig, Bob Laing (SET DECORATION: Michael Seirton)
COSTUME DESIGN: John Mollo, Bhanu Athaiya
FILM EDITING: John Bloom
ORIGINAL SONG SCORE ADAPTED: Leslie Bricusse, Henry Mancini, *Victor Victoria*
SHORT (LIVE ACTION): *A Shocking Accident* (Flamingo Pictures. Producer: Christine Oestreicher/Director: James Scott)
SCIENTIFIC AND ENGINEERING AWARD: Colin F. Mossman and Rank Laboratories for the engineering and implementation of a 4,000-metre printing system for film laboratories

1984   ORIGINAL SONG SCORE: Michel Legrand (m), Alan and Marilyn Bergman(l), *Yentl* (UK/US)
SPECIAL ACHIEVEMENT AWARD FOR VISUAL EFFECTS: Ken Ralston, Dennis Muren, Phil Tippett, Richard Edlund, *Return of the Jedi*
SCIENTIFIC AND ENGINEERING AWARD: Gerald L. Turpin, Lightflex International Ltd. for the design, engineering and development of an on-camera device providing contrast control, sourceless fill light and special effects for motion picture photography

1985   SUPPORTING ACTRESS: Peggy Ashcroft, *A Passage to India*
MUSIC (ORIGINAL SCORE): Maurice Jarre, *A Passage to India*
CINEMATOGRAPHY: Chris Menges, *The Killing Fields*

EDITING: Jim Clark, *The Killing Fields*
SCREENPLAY (ADAPTED): Peter Shaffer, *Amadeus* (US)
VISUAL EFFECTS: George Gibbs, Dennis Muren, Lorne Peterson, Michael McAlister, *Indiana Jones and the Temple of Doom* (US)

1986   FILM: *Out of Africa* (UK/US) (Universal. Producer: Sydney Pollack)
OTHER AWARDS FOR THIS FILM:
DIRECTOR: Sydney Pollack
CINEMATOGRAPHY: David Watkin
ART DIRECTION: Stephen Grimes (SET DECORATION: Josie MacAvin)
SOUND: Peter Handford, Chris Jenkins, Gary Alexander, Larry Stensvold
MUSIC (ORIGINAL SCORE): John Barry

1987   SUPPORTING ACTOR: Michael Caine, *Hannah and Her Sisters* (US)
SCREENPLAY (ADAPTED): Ruth Prawer Jhabvala, *A Room with a View*
ART DIRECTION: Brian Ackland-Snow and Gianni Quaranta (SET DECORATION: Brian Saregar and Elio Altramura), *A Room with a View*
COSTUME DESIGN: Jenny Beavan and John Bright, *A Room with a View*
CINEMATOGRAPHY: Chris Menges, *The Mission*
VISUAL EFFECTS: John Richardson, Stan Winston, Suzanne Benson, Robert Skotak, *Aliens*
SOUND EFFECTS EDITING: Don Sharpe, *Aliens*
SOUND: Simon Kaye, *Platoon* (US)
DOCUMENTARY (SHORT): *Women – For America, For the World* (US) (Educational Film and Video Project. Producer: Vivienne Verdon-Roe)
TECHNICAL ACHIEVEMENT AWARD: Lee Electric (Lighting) Ltd for the design and development of an electronic, flicker-free discharge lamp control system
TECHNICAL ACHIEVEMENT AWARD: Peter D. Parks, Oxford Scientific Films for the development of a live aero-compositor for special effects photography
TECHNICAL ACHIEVEMENT AWARD: David W. Samuelson and William B. Pollard

1988   FILM: *The Last Emperor* (UK/It/US) (Hemdale/Recorded Pictures Company/Screenframe Ltd/Soprofilms/TAO Film/Yanco/AAA Productions. Producer: Jeremy Thomas)
OTHER AWARDS FOR THIS FILM:
DIRECTOR: Bernardo Bertolucci
SCREENPLAY (ADAPTED): Mark Peploe, Bernardo Bertolucci
CINEMATOGRAPHY: Vittorio Storaro
ART DIRECTION: Ferdinando Scarfiotti (SET DECORATION: Bruno Cesari, Osvaldo Desideri)
EDITING: Gabriella Cristiani
MUSIC (ORIGINAL SCORE): David Byrne, Ryuichi Sakamoto, Cong Su
COSTUME DESIGN: James Acheson
SOUND: Ivan Sharrock, Bill Rowe
SUPPORTING ACTOR: Sean Connery, *The Untouchables* (US)

1989   SCREENPLAY (ADAPTED): Christopher Hampton, *Dangerous Liaisons* (US)
COSTUME DESIGN: James Acheson, *Dangerous Liaisons*
ART DIRECTION/SET DECORATION: Stuart Craig, Gérard James, *Dangerous Liaisons*

SUPPORTING ACTOR: Kevin Kline, *A Fish Called Wanda*
CINEMATOGRAPHY: Peter Biziou, *Mississippi Burning* (US)
VISUAL EFFECTS: Richard Williams, *Who Framed Roger Rabbit?* (US)
SPECIAL ACHIEVEMENT AWARD FOR ANIMATION: Richard Williams, *Who Framed Roger Rabbit?*

1990 ACTOR: Daniel Day-Lewis, *My Left Foot*
ACTRESS: Jessica Tandy, *Driving Miss Daisy* (US)
SUPPORTING ACTRESS: Brenda Fricker, *My Left Foot*
COSTUME DESIGN: Phyllis Dalton, *Henry V*
CINEMATOGRAPHY: Freddie Francis, *Glory* (US)
ART DIRECTION: Anton Furst, Peter Young, *Batman* (UK/US)
SHORT (LIVE ACTION): *Work Experience* (North Inch Productions. Producer/Director: James Hendrie)

1991 ACTOR: Jeremy Irons, *Reversal of Fortune* (US)
MUSIC (ORIGINAL SCORE): John Barry, *Dances with Wolves* (US)
SHORT (ANIMATION): *Creature Comforts* (Aardman Animations/Channel Four Films. Producers: Sara Mullock, Alan Gardner/ Director: Nick Park)

1992 ACTOR: Anthony Hopkins, *Silence of the Lambs* (US)
SHORT (ANIMATION): *Manipulation* (BFI/Tandem Films. Director: Daniel Greaves)

1993 ACTRESS: Emma Thompson, *Howards End*
ART DIRECTION: Ian Whittaker (SET DECORATION: Luciana Arrighi), *Howards End*
SCREENPLAY (ADAPTED): Ruth Prawer Jhabvala, *Howard's End*
SCREENPLAY (ORIGINAL): Neil Jordan, *The Crying Game*
SOUND: Simon Kaye, *The Last of the Mohicans* (US)
MUSIC (ORIGINAL SONG): Tim Rice for 'A Whole New World', *Aladdin* (US)
JEAN HERSHOLT HUMANITARIAN AWARD: Elizabeth Taylor, Audrey Hepburn (Joint Winners)

1994 SHORT (ANIMATION): *The Wrong Trousers* (Aardman Animations. Director: Nick Park)
HONORARY AWARD: Deborah Kerr

1995 ART DIRECTION: Ken Adam and Carolyn Scott, *The Madness of King George* (UK/US)
MUSIC (ORIGINAL SONG): Elton John (m) and Tim Rice (l) for 'Can You Feel the Love Tonight', *The Lion King* (US)
SHORT (LIVE ACTION): *Franz Kafka's 'It's a Wonderful Life'* (BBC/ Conundrum Films. Producers: Peter Capaldi and Ruth Kenley-Letts)
SHORT (ANIMATION): *Bob's Birthday* (UK/Can) (Channel Four Films/National Film Board of Canada/Snowden Fine Animation. Producers/Directors: Alison Snowden and David Fine)

1996 FILM: *Braveheart* (UK/US) (20th Century–Fox/B.H. Finance C.V./Icon Ent. Int./Paramount/Ladd Co. Producers: Mel Gibson, Alan Ladd Jr, Bruce Davey)
OTHER AWARDS FOR THIS FILM:
DIRECTOR: Mel Gibson
CINEMATOGRAPHY: John Toll
SOUND EFFECTS EDITING: Lon Bender, Per Hallberg
MAKEUP: Peter Frampton, Lois Burwell, Paul Pattison
SCREENPLAY (ADAPTED): Emma Thompson, *Sense and Sensibility* (UK/US)

COSTUME DESIGN: James Acheson, *Restoration* (UK/US)
ART DIRECTION/SET DECORATION: Eugenio Zanetti, *Restoration*
DOCUMENTARY FEATURE: *Anne Frank Remembered* (Jon Blair Film Co/BBC. Director: Jon Blair)
SHORT (ANIMATION): *A Close Shave* (Aardman Animations/BBC. Producers: Michael Rose, Carla Shelley. Director: Nick Park)

1997 FILM: *The English Patient* (UK/US) (J&M Entertainment/Miramax Films/Tiger Moth Productions. Producer: Saul Zaentz)
OTHER AWARDS FOR THIS FILM:
DIRECTOR: Anthony Minghella
SUPPORTING ACTRESS: Juliette Binoche
CINEMATOGRAPHY: John Seale
COSTUME DESIGN: Ann Roth
SOUND: Walter Murch, Mark Berger, David Parker, Christopher Newman
FILM EDITING: Walter Murch
MUSIC: Gabriel Yared
ART DIRECTION: Stuart Craig and Stephanie McMillan
MUSIC (ORIGINAL SCORE): Rachel Portman, *Emma* (UK/US)
MUSIC (ORIGINAL SONG): Andrew Lloyd Webber (m) and Tim Rice (l) for 'You Must Love Me', *Evita* (UK/US)

1998 MUSIC (ORIGINAL SCORE): Anne Dudley, *The Full Monty* (UK/US)
ART DIRECTION: Michael Ford (SET DECORATION: Peter Lamont), *Titanic* (US)

1999 FILM: *Shakespeare in Love* (UK/US) (Bedford Falls Productions/Miramax/Universal. Producers: David Parfitt, Donna Gigliotti, Harvey Weinstein, Edward Zwick, Marc Norman)
OTHER AWARDS FOR THIS FILM:
ACTRESS: Gwyneth Paltrow
SUPPORTING ACTRESS: Judi Dench
SCREENPLAY (ORIGINAL): Tom Stoppard, Marc Norman
ART DIRECTION: Martin Childs, Jill Quertier
COSTUME DESIGN: Sandy Powell
MUSIC (ORIGINAL SCORE): Stephen Warbeck
SCREENPLAY (ADAPTED): Bill Condon, *Gods and Monsters* (UK/US)
MAKEUP: Jenny Shircore, *Elizabeth*
SOUND: Andy Nelson, *Saving Private Ryan* (US)

2000 DIRECTOR: Sam Mendes, *American Beauty* (US)
SUPPORTING ACTOR: Michael Caine, *The Cider House Rules* (US)
ART DIRECTION: Rick Heinrichs (SET DECORATION: Peter Young), *Sleepy Hollow* (US/Ger)
COSTUME DESIGN: Lindy Hemming, *Topsy-Turvy* (UK/US)
MAKE-UP: Christine Blundell and Trefor Proud, *Topsy-Turvy*
MUSIC (ORIGINAL SONG): Phil Collins for 'You'll Be In My Heart', *Tarzan* (US)
DOCUMENTARY FEATURE: *One Day in September* (Arthur Cohn/Passion Pictures. Producers: Kevin Macdonald, Arthur Cohn)

2001 COSTUME DESIGN: Janty Yates, *Gladiator* (UK/US)
HONORARY AWARD: Jack Cardiff

2002 SUPPORTING ACTOR: Jim Broadbent, *Iris* (UK/US)
SCREENPLAY (ORIGINAL): Julian Fellowes, *Gosford Park* (UK/US)
MAKEUP: Peter Owen, *The Lord of the Rings: The Fellowship of the Ring* (US/NZ)
SOUND: Chris Munro, *Black Hawk Down* (US)

2003 SUPPORTING ACTRESS: Catherine Zeta Jones, *Chicago* (US)
FILM EDITING: Martin Walsh, *Chicago* (US)
SCREENPLAY (ADAPTED): Ronald Harwood, *The Pianist* (UK/Ger/Pol)
SOUND: Mike Hopkins, *The Lord of the Rings: The Two Towers* (US/NZ)
HONORARY AWARD: Peter O'Toole

British Academy Award (BAFTA) Winners

Started as the awards of the *British Film Academy*, the first awards ceremony being held in 1948, for films premiered in the UK during the previous year. In 1976, renamed the *British Academy of Film and Television Arts* (BAFTA). For winning films, the name of director is in brackets.

1948 BRITISH FILM: *Odd Man Out* (p/d: Carol Reed) (Two Cities–Rank)
SPECIAL AWARD: *The World Is Rich* (Paul Rotha)

1949 Film: *Hamlet* (p/d: Laurence Olivier) (Two Cities–Rank)
BRITISH FILM: *The Fallen Idol* (Carol Reed) (London Films. Prod: Carol Reed, David O. Selznick)
SPECIAL AWARD: *Atomic Physics* (aka: *The Atomic Theory*) (Derek Mayne)

1950 BRITISH FILM: *The Third Man* (Carol Reed) (London Films. Prod: Carol Reed, Alexander Korda, David O. Selznick)
DOCUMENTARY: *Daybreak in Udi* (Terry Bishop) (Crown Film Unit)

1951 BRITISH FILM: *The Blue Lamp* (Basil Dearden) (Ealing. Prod: Michael Relph)
DOCUMENTARY: *The Undefeated* (Paul Dickson)
SPECIAL AWARD: *This Modern Age: The True Face of Japan* (Rank. Prod: Sergei Nolbandov)

1952 BRITISH FILM: *The Lavender Hill Mob* (Charles Crichton) (Ealing. Prod: Michael Truman)

1953 FILM: *The Sound Barrier* (p/d: David Lean) (London Films)
BRITISH FILM: *The Sound Barrier*
ACTOR: Ralph Richardson, *The Sound Barrier*
ACTRESS: Vivien Leigh, *A Streetcar Named Desire* (US)
NEWCOMER: Claire Bloom, *Limelight* (US)
UN AWARD: *Cry, the Beloved Country* (Zoltan Korda)
SPECIAL AWARD: *Animated Genesis* (Joan and Peter Foldes)

1954 BRITISH FILM: *Genevieve* (p/d: Henry Cornelius) (Sirius/Rank)
ACTOR: John Gielgud, *Julius Caesar* (US)
ACTRESS: Audrey Hepburn, *Roman Holiday* (US)
NEWCOMER: Norman Wisdom, *Trouble in Store*
DOCUMENTARY: *The Conquest of Everest* (Thomas Stobart)
CERTIFICATE OF MERIT: *A Queen Is Crowned*, and to

Thomas Stobart, for his work as director/cameraman on the film of the 1953 Everest expedition, *The Conquest of Everest*.
UN AWARD: *World Without End* (Basil Wright, Paul Rotha)

1955 BRITISH FILM: *Hobson's Choice* (p/d: David Lean) (London Films)
ACTRESS: Yvonne Mitchell, *The Divided Heart*
FOREIGN ACTRESS: Cornell Borchers, *The Divided Heart*
UN AWARD: *The Divided Heart*
ACTOR: Kenneth More, *Doctor in the House*
SCREENPLAY: Robin Estridge, George Tabori, *The Young Lovers*
NEWCOMER: David Kossoff, *The Young Lovers*

1956 FILM: *Richard III* (p/d: Laurence Olivier) (London Films)
BRITISH FILM: *Richard III*
BRITISH ACTOR: Laurence Olivier, *Richard III*
BRITISH ACTRESS: Katie Johnson, *The Ladykillers*
SCREENPLAY: William Rose, *The Ladykillers*
NEWCOMER: Paul Scofield, *That Lady*
SPECIAL AWARD: *The Bespoke Overcoat* (Jack Clayton)

1957 BRITISH FILM: *Reach for the Sky* (Lewis Gilbert) (Pinnacle/Rank. Prod: Daniel M. Angel)
ACTOR: Peter Finch, *A Town Like Alice*
ACTRESS: Virginia McKenna, *A Town Like Alice*
SCREENPLAY: Nigel Balchin, *The Man Who Never Was*

1958 FILM: *The Bridge on the River Kwai* (David Lean) (Horizon Films/Columbia. Prod: Sam Speigel)
OTHER AWARDS FOR THIS FILM:
BRITISH FILM ACTOR: Alec Guinness
SCREENPLAY: Pierre Boulle
ACTRESS: Heather Sears, *The Story of Esther Costello*
NEWCOMER: Eric Barker, *Brothers in Law*
DOCUMENTARY: *Journey Into Spring* (Ralph Keene) (British Transport Films. Prod: Edgar Anstey)

1959 FILM: *Room at the Top* (Jack Clayton) (Remus Films. Prod: John and James Woolf)
OTHER AWARD FOR THIS FILM:
BRITISH FILM FOREIGN ACTRESS: Simone Signoret
ACTOR: Trevor Howard, *The Key*
ACTRESS: Irene Worth, *Orders to Kill*
NEWCOMER: Paul Massie, *Orders to Kill*
SCREENPLAY: Paul Dehn, *Orders to Kill*
ANIMATED FILM: *The Little Island* (Richard Williams)
SPECIAL AWARD: Children's Film Foundation

1960 BRITISH FILM: *Sapphire* (Basil Dearden) (Artna/Rank. Prod: Michael Relph)
ACTOR: Peter Sellers, *I'm All Right Jack*
SCREENPLAY: John Boulting, Frank Harvey, Alan Hackney, *I'm All Right Jack*
ACTRESS: Audrey Hepburn, *The Nun's Story* (US)
NEWCOMER: Hayley Mills, *Tiger Bay*
BEST SPECIALISED FILM: *This Is the BBC* (Richard Cawston)

1961 BRITISH FILM: *Saturday Night and Sunday Morning* (Karel Reisz) (Woodfall Films. Prod: Harry Saltzman, Tony Richardson)
OTHER AWARDS FOR THIS FILM:
ACTRESS: Rachel Roberts

NEWCOMER: Albert Finney
ACTOR: Peter Finch, *The Trials of Oscar Wilde*
SCREENPLAY: Bryan Forbes, *The Angry Silence*
SHORT: *High Journey* (Peter Baylis)
SPECIALISED FILM: *Dispute* (Fred Moore)

1962 BRITISH FILM: *A Taste of Honey* (p/d: Tony Richardson) (Woodfall Films)
OTHER AWARDS FOR THIS FILM:
ACTRESS: Dora Bryan
NEWCOMER: Rita Tushingham
SCREENPLAY: Shelagh Delaney, Tony Richardson
SCREENPLAY (SHARED AWARD): Val Guest, Wolf Mankowitz, *The Day the Earth Caught Fire*
ACTOR: Peter Finch, *No Love for Johnnie*
SHORT: *Terminus* (John Schlesinger) (British Transport Films)
UN AWARD WINNER: *Let My People Go* (John Krish)

1963 FILM: *Lawrence of Arabia* (David Lean) (Horizon Films/Columbia. Prod: Sam Speigel)
OTHER AWARDS FOR THIS FILM:
BRITISH FILM
ACTOR: Peter O'Toole
SCREENPLAY: Robert Bolt
ACTRESS: Leslie Caron, *The L-Shaped Room*
NEWCOMER: Tom Courtenay, *The Loneliness of the Long Distance Runner*
ANIMATED FILM: *The Apple* (George Dunning)
UN AWARD: *Reach for Glory* (Philip Leacock)

1964 FILM: *Tom Jones* (p/d: Tony Richardson) (Woodfall Films)
OTHER AWARDS FOR THIS FILM:
BRITISH FILM
SCREENPLAY: John Osborne
ACTOR: Dirk Bogarde, *The Servant*
NEWCOMER: James Fox, *The Servant*
CINEMATOGRAPHY: (B/W) Douglas Slocombe, *The Servant* (COLOUR) Ted Moore, *From Russia with Love*
ACTRESS: Rachel Roberts, *This Sporting Life*
ANIMATED FILM: *Automania 2000* (John Halas) (Halas and Batchelor)

1965 FILM: *Dr. Strangelove or: How I Learned to Stop Worrying and Love the Bomb* (p/d: Stanley Kubrick) (Columbia)
OTHER AWARDS FOR THIS FILM:
BRITISH FILM
UN AWARD
PRODUCTION DESIGN (B/W): Ken Adam
PRODUCTION DESIGN (COLOUR): John Bryan, *Becket*
COSTUME (COLOUR): Margaret Furse, *Becket*
CINEMATOGRAPHY: (B/W) Oswald Morris, *The Pumpkin Eater* (COLOUR) Geoffrey Unsworth, *Becket*
FOREIGN ACTRESS: Anne Bancroft, *The Pumpkin Eater*
SCREENPLAY: Harold Pinter, *The Pumpkin Eater*
BRITISH COSTUME (B/W): Motley, *The Pumpkin Eater*
ACTOR: Richard Attenborough, *Seance on a Wet Afternoon* and *Guns at Batasi*
ACTRESS: Audrey Hepburn, *Charade* (US)
NEWCOMER: Julie Andrews, *Mary Poppins* (US)
SPECIALISED FILM: *Driving Technique – Passenger Trains* (British Transport Films)

1966 BRITISH FILM: *The Ipcress File* (Sidney J. Furie) (Rank/Steven/Lowndes. Prod: Harry Saltzman)

OTHER AWARDS FOR THIS FILM:
CINEMATOGRAPHY (COLOUR): Otto Heller
PRODUCTION DESIGN (COLOUR): Ken Adam
ACTOR: Dirk Bogarde, *Darling*
ACTRESS: Julie Christie, *Darling*
SCREENPLAY: Frederic Raphael, *Darling*
PRODUCTION DESIGN (B/W): Ray Simm, *Darling*
CINEMATOGRAPHY (B/W): Oswald Morris, *The Hill*
NEWCOMER: Judi Dench, *Four in the Morning*
COSTUME (COLOUR): Osbert Lancaster; Dinah Greet, *Those Magnificent Men in Their Flying Machines*
SHORT: *Rig Move* (Don Higgins)
ANIMATED FILM: *Do Be Careful Boys* (Vera Linnecar, Nancy Hanna, Keith Learner) (Biographic Cartoon Films)
SPECIALISED FILM: *I Do – And I Understand* (Derek Williams)

1967 BRITISH FILM: *The Spy Who Came in from the Cold* (p/d: Martin Ritt) (Salem/Paramount)
OTHER AWARDS FOR THIS FILM:
CINEMATOGRAPHY (B/W): Oswald Morris
PRODUCTION DESIGN (B/W): Tambi Larsen
ACTOR: Richard Burton, *The Spy Who Came in from the Cold* and *Who's Afraid of Virginia Woolf?* (US)
ACTRESS: Elizabeth Taylor, *Who's Afraid of Virginia Woolf?*
CINEMATOGRAPHY (COLOUR): Christopher Challis, *Arabesque* (UK/US)
PRODUCTION DESIGN (COLOUR): Wilfred Shingleton, *The Blue Max*
SCREENPLAY: David Mercer, *Morgan: A Suitable Case for Treatment*
FILM EDITING: Tom Priestley, *Morgan: A Suitable Case for Treatment*
COSTUME (COLOUR): Julie Harris, *The Wrong Box*
NEWCOMER: Vivien Merchant, *Alfie*
SPECIALISED FILM: *Exploring Chemistry* (Robert Parker)
FLAHERTY DOCUMENTARY AWARD: *Goal! The World Cup* (Abidine Dino; Ross Devenish)
SHORT: *The War Game* (Peter Watkins) (BBC TV)
UN AWARD: *The War Game*

1968 FILM: *A Man for All Seasons* (p/d: Fred Zinnemann. Highland Films, Columbia)
OTHER AWARDS FOR THIS FILM:
BRITISH FILM
ACTOR: Paul Scofield
SCREENPLAY: Robert Bolt
PRODUCTION DESIGN: John Box
COSTUME (COLOUR): Elizabeth Haffenden, Joan Bridge
CINEMATOGRAPHY (COLOUR): Ted Moore
CINEMATOGRAPHY (B/W): Gerry Turpin, *The Whisperers*
ACTRESS: Edith Evans, *The Whisperers*
COSTUME (B/W): Jocelyn Rickards, *Mademoiselle* (UK/Fr)
SHORT: *Indus Waters* (Derek Williams)

1969 SUPPORTING ACTOR: Ian Holm, *The Bofors Gun*
SUPPORTING ACTRESS: Billie Whitelaw, *Twisted Nerve* and *Charlie Bubbles*
CINEMATOGRAPHY: Geoffrey Unsworth, *2001: A Space Odyssey*
PRODUCTION DESIGN: Tony Masters, Harry Lange, Ernie Archer, *2001: A Space Odyssey*
SOUND: Winston Ryder, *2001: A Space Odyssey*

MUSIC: John Barry, *The Lion in Winter*

ANTHONY ASQUITH AWARD FOR FILM MUSIC: John Barry, *The Lion in Winter*

SPECIALISED FILM: *The Threat in the Water* (Richard Bigham)

FLAHERTY DOCUMENTARY AWARD: *In Need of Special Care: Camphill Rudolph Steiner School, Aberdeen* (Jonathan Stedall)

1970 DIRECTOR: John Schlesinger, *Midnight Cowboy* (US)

ACTRESS: Maggie Smith, *The Prime of Miss Jean Brodie*

SUPPORTING ACTRESS: Celia Johnson, *The Prime of Miss Jean Brodie*

SUPPORTING ACTOR: Laurence Olivier, *Oh! What a Lovely War*

CINEMATOGRAPHY: Gerry Turpin, *Oh! What a Lovely War*

PRODUCTION DESIGN: Don Ashton, *Oh! What a Lovely War*

COSTUME DESIGN: Anthony Mendleson, *Oh! What a Lovely War*

SOUND: Don Challis, Simon Kaye, *Oh! What a Lovely War*

UN AWARD: *Oh! What a Lovely War* (Richard Attenborough)

SHORT: *Picture to Post* (Sarah Erulkar)

SPECIALISED FILM: *Let There Be Light* (Peter de Normanville)

1971 SUPPORTING ACTRESS: Susannah York, *They Shoot Horses, Don't They?* (US)

SUPPORTING ACTOR: Colin Welland, *Kes*

NEWCOMER: David Bradley, *Kes*

SHORT: *The Shadow of Progress* (Derek Williams)

ANIMATED FILM: *Henry Nine 'til Five* (Bob Godfrey)

1972 FILM: *Sunday Bloody Sunday* (John Schlesinger) (Vectia/United Artists. Prod: Joseph Janni)

OTHER AWARDS FOR THIS FILM:

DIRECTOR: John Schlesinger

ACTOR: Peter Finch

ACTRESS: Glenda Jackson

FILM EDITING: Richard Marden

SUPPORTING ACTOR: Edward Fox, *The Go-Between*

SUPPORTING ACTRESS: Margaret Leighton, *The Go-Between*

NEWCOMER: Dominic Guard, *The Go-Between*

SCREENPLAY: Harold Pinter, *The Go-Between*

SHORT: *Alaska: The Great Land* (Derek Williams)

SPECIALISED FILM: *The Savage Voyage* (Eric Marquis)

1973 SOUND: David Hildyard, Robert Knudson, Arthur Piantadosi, *Cabaret*

CINEMATOGRAPHY: Geoffrey Unsworth, *Cabaret; Alice's Adventures in Wonderland*

COSTUME DESIGN: Anthony Mendleson, *Alice's Adventures in Wonderland; Macbeth; Young Winston*

JOHN GRIERSON AWARD: *Memorial* (James Allen)

SPECIALISED FILM: *Cutting Oils and Fluids* (British Petroleum Films)

1974 SUPPORTING ACTOR: Arthur Lowe, *O Lucky Man!*

MUSIC: Alan Price, *O Lucky Man!*

ANTHONY ASQUITH AWARD FOR FILM MUSIC: Alan Price, *O Lucky Man!*

NEWCOMER: Peter Egan, *The Hireling*

PRODUCTION DESIGN: Natasha Kroll, *The Hireling*

COSTUME DESIGN: Phyllis Dalton, *The Hireling*

CINEMATOGRAPHY: Anthony Richmond, *Don't Look Now*

(UK/It)

SOUND: Les Wiggins, Gordon K. McCallum, Keith Grant, *Jesus Christ Superstar* (US)

FILM EDITING: Ralph Kemplen, *The Day of the Jackal* (UK/Fr)

JOHN GRIERSON AWARD: *Caring for History*

SPECIALISED FILM: *A Man's World*

1975 SUPPORTING ACTOR: John Gielgud, *Murder on the Orient Express*

SUPPORTING ACTRESS: Ingrid Bergman, *Murder on the Orient Express*

MUSIC: Richard Rodney Bennett, *Murder on the Orient Express*

ANTHONY ASQUITH AWARD FOR FILM MUSIC: Richard Rodney Bennett, *Murder on the Orient Express*

CINEMATOGRAPHY: Douglas Slocombe, *The Great Gatsby* (US)

PRODUCTION DESIGN: John Box, *The Great Gatsby*

NEWCOMER: Georgina Hale, *Mahler*

JOHN GRIERSON AWARD: *Location North Sea*

SPECIALISED FILM: *Monet in London* (David Thompson) (Arts Council)

1976 DIRECTOR: Stanley Kubrick, *Barry Lyndon*

CINEMATOGRAPHY: John Alcott, *Barry Lyndon*

PRODUCTION DESIGN: John Box, *Rollerball* (US)

ANIMATED FILM: *Great* (Bob Godfrey)

JOHN GRIERSON AWARD: *Sea Area Forties* (John Armstrong) (British Petroleum Films)

1977 SUPPORTING ACTRESS: Jodie Foster, *Bugsy Malone*

NEWCOMER: Jodie Foster, *Bugsy Malone* and *Taxi Driver* (US)

SCREENPLAY: Alan Parker, *Bugsy Malone*

PRODUCTION DESIGN: Geoffrey Kirkland, *Bugsy Malone*

SOUND: Les Wiggins, Clive Winter, Ken Barker, *Bugsy Malone*

FACTUAL FILM: *The End of the Road* (John Armstrong)

SPECIALISED FILM: *Hydraulics* (Anthony Searle)

1978 ACTOR: Peter Finch, *Network* (US)

SUPPORTING ACTOR: Edward Fox, *A Bridge Too Far*

CINEMATOGRAPHY: Geoffrey Unsworth, *A Bridge Too Far*

MUSIC: John Addison, *A Bridge Too Far*

ANTHONY ASQUITH AWARD FOR FILM MUSIC: John Addison, *A Bridge Too Far*

SOUND: Peter Horrocks, Gerry Humphreys, Simon Kaye, Robin O'Donoghue, Les Wiggins, *A Bridge Too Far*

SUPPORTING ACTRESS: Jenny Agutter, *Equus*

FACTUAL FILM: *The Living City* (Phillip De Normanville, Sarah Erulkar)

1979 FILM: *Julia* (UK/US, Fred Zinnemann) (20th Century-Fox. Prod: Julien Derode)

OTHER AWARDS FOR THIS FILM:

ACTRESS: Jane Fonda

SCREENPLAY: Alvin Sargent

CINEMATOGRAPHY: Douglas Slocombe

DIRECTOR: Alan Parker, *Midnight Express*

SUPPORTING ACTOR: John Hurt, *Midnight Express*

FILM EDITING: Gerry Hambling, *Midnight Express*

MUSIC: John Williams, *Star Wars*

ANTHONY ASQUITH AWARD FOR FILM MUSIC: John Williams, *Star Wars* (US)

SOUND: Sam Shaw, Robert R. Rutledge, Gordon

Davidson, Gene Corso, Derek Ball, Don MacDougall, Bob Minkler, Ray West, Michael Minkler, Les Fresholtz, Richard Portman, Ben Burtt, *Star Wars*
COSTUME DESIGN: Anthony Powell, *Death on the Nile*
NEWCOMER: Christopher Reeve, *Superman*
MICHAEL BALCON AWARD: Les Bowie, Colin Chilvers, Denys N. Coop, Roy Field, Derek Meddings, Zoran Perisic, Wally Veevers
SHORT FACTUAL FILM: *Hokusai: An Animated Sketchbook* (Tony White) (Arts Council)
SPECIALISED FILM: *Twenty Times More Likely* (Robert Young)
FLAHERTY DOCUMENTARY AWARD: *The Silent Witness* (David W. Wolfe) (Screenpro Films)

1980 SUPPORTING ACTRESS: Rachel Roberts, *Yanks*
COSTUME DESIGN: Shirley Russell, *Yanks*
PRODUCTION DESIGN: Michael Seymour, *Alien* (UK/US)
SOUND: Derrick Leather, Jim Shields, Bill Rowe, *Alien*
SHORT: *Butch Minds the Baby* (Peter Webb)
MICHAEL BALCON AWARD: Children's Film Foundation

1981 FILM: *The Elephant Man* (UK/US) (David Lynch) (Brooksfilms/EMI. Prod: Stuart Cornfield)
OTHER AWARDS FOR THIS FILM:
ACTOR: John Hurt
PRODUCTION DESIGN: Stuart Craig
MUSIC: John Williams, *The Empire Strikes Back* (US)
SOUND: Les Wiggins, *Fame* (US)
SHORT: *Sredni vashtar* (Andrew Birkin) (Laurentic Film Productions)

1982 FILM: *Chariots of Fire* (Hugh Hudson) (Enigma Films/Allied Stars. Prod: David Puttnam)
OTHER AWARDS FOR THIS FILM:
SUPPORTING ACTOR: Ian Holm
COSTUME DESIGN: Milena Canonero
ACTRESS: Meryl Streep, *The French Lieutenant's Woman*
MUSIC: Carl Davis, *The French Lieutenant's Woman*
ANTHONY ASQUITH AWARD FOR FILM MUSIC: Carl Davis, *The French Lieutenant's Woman*
SOUND: Don Sharp, Ivan Sharrock, Bill Rowe, *The French Lieutenant's Woman*
SCREENPLAY: Bill Forsyth, *Gregory's Girl*
CINEMATOGRAPHY: Geoffrey Unsworth, Ghislain Cloquet, *Tess* (UK/Fr)
PRODUCTION DESIGN: Norman Reynolds, *Raiders of the Lost Ark* (US)
SHORT: *Recluse* (Bob Bentley)
FLAHERTY DOCUMENTARY AWARD: *Soldier Girls* (Nick Broomfield, Joan Churchill)
MICHAEL BALCON AWARD: David Puttnam

1983 FILM: *Gandhi* (UK/Ind) (p/d: Richard Attenborough) (Goldcrest/Indo-British International Film Investors/National Film Development Corporation of India/Columbia)
OTHER AWARDS FOR THIS FILM:
DIRECTOR: Richard Attenborough
ACTOR: Ben Kingsley
NEWCOMER: Ben Kingsley
SUPPORTING ACTRESS (SHARED AWARD): Rohini Hattangadi
SUPPORTING ACTRESS (SHARED AWARD): Maureen Stapleton, *Reds* (US/UK)

SUPPORTING ACTOR: Jack Nicholson, *Reds*
PRODUCTION DESIGN: Lawrence G. Paull, *Blade Runner* (US)
COSTUME DESIGN: Charles Knode, Michael Kaplan, *Blade Runner*
SOUND: James Guthrie, Eddy Joseph, Clive Winter, Graham V. Hartstone, Nicolas Le Messurier, *Pink Floyd The Wall*
ORIGINAL SONG: Roger Waters, for 'Another Brick in the Wall', *Pink Floyd The Wall*
ANIMATED FILM: *Dreamland Express* (David Anderson) (BFI Films)
SHORT: *The Privilege* (Ian Knox)
MICHAEL BALCON AWARD: Arthur Wooster

1984 FILM: *Educating Rita* (p/d: Lewis Gilbert) (Acorn/Rank)
OTHER AWARDS FOR THIS FILM:
ACTOR: Michael Caine
ACTRESS: Julie Walters
DIRECTOR: Bill Forsyth, *Local Hero*
SUPPORTING ACTOR: Denholm Elliott, *Trading Places* (US)
NEWCOMER: Phyllis Logan, *Another Time, Another Place*
ADAPTED SCREENPLAY: Ruth Prawer Jhabvala, *Heat and Dust*
MUSIC: Ryuichi Sakamoto, *Merry Christmas, Mr Lawrence* (UK/Japan)
SPECIAL VISUAL EFFECTS: Richard Edlund, Dennis Muren, Ken Ralston, Kit West, *Star Wars: Episode VI – Return of the Jedi* (US)
SHORT ANIMATED FILM: *Henry's Cat* (Bob Godfrey)
SHORT: *Goodie-Two-Shoes* (Ian Emes) (Timeless Films)
MICHAEL BALCON AWARD: Colin Young

1985 FILM: *The Killing Fields* (Roland Joffe) (Goldcrest/Enigma. Prod: David Puttnam)
OTHER AWARDS FOR THIS FILM:
ACTOR: Haing S. Ngor
NEWCOMER: Haing S. Ngor
ADAPTED SCREENPLAY: Bruce Robinson
CINEMATOGRAPHY: Chris Menges
PRODUCTION DESIGN: Roy Walker
SOUND: Ian Fuller, Clive Winter, Bill Rowe
EDITING: Jim Clark
ACTRESS: Maggie Smith, *A Private Function*
SUPPORTING ACTOR: Denholm Elliott, *A Private Function*
SUPPORTING ACTRESS: Liz Smith, *A Private Function*
SPECIAL VISUAL EFFECTS: Dennis Muren, George Gibbs, Michael J. McAlister, Lorne Peterson, *Indiana Jones and the Temple of Doom* (US)
MAKE-UP: Paul Engelen, Peter Frampton, Rick Baker, Joan Hills, *Greystoke: The Legend of Tarzan, Lord of the Apes* (UK/US)
SHORT: *The Dress* (Eva Sereny)

1986 ACTRESS: Peggy Ashcroft, *A Passage to India*
SUPPORTING ACTOR: Denholm Elliott, *Defence of the Realm*
SPECIAL VISUAL EFFECTS: George Gibbs, Richard Conway, *Brazil*
PRODUCTION DESIGN: Norman Garwood, *Brazil*
SHORT: *Careless Talk* (Noella Smith)
MICHAEL BALCON AWARD: Sydney Samuelson

1987 FILM: *A Room with a View* (James Ivory) (Channel Four Films/Curzon/Enigma/Goldcrest/Merchant Ivory

Productions. Prod: Ismail Merchant)

OTHER AWARDS FOR THIS FILM:
ACTRESS: Maggie Smith
SUPPORTING ACTRESS: Judi Dench
PRODUCTION DESIGN: Gianni Quaranta, Brian Ackland-Snow
ACTOR: Bob Hoskins, *Mona Lisa*
ADAPTED SCREENPLAY: Kurt Luedtke, *Out of Africa* (UK/US)
CINEMATOGRAPHY: David Watkin, *Out of Africa*
SOUND: Tom McCarthy Jr, Peter Handford, Chris Jenkins, *Out of Africa*
SUPPORTING ACTOR: Ray McAnally, *The Mission*
EDITING: Jim Clark, *The Mission*
MUSIC: Ennio Morricone, *The Mission*
SPECIAL VISUAL EFFECTS: Robert Skotak, Brian Johnson, John Richardson, Stan Winston, *Aliens* (US)
SHORT: *La Boule* (Simon Shore)

1988 ACTOR: Sean Connery, *The Name of the Rose* (Fr/It/Ger)
ACTRESS: Anne Bancroft, *84 Charing Cross Road* (UK/US)
SUPPORTING ACTRESS: Susan Wooldridge, *Hope and Glory*
ORIGINAL SCREENPLAY: David Leland, *Wish You Were Here*
SOUND: Jonathan Bates, Simon Kaye, Gerry Humphreys, *Cry Freedom*
MICHAEL BALCON AWARD: Monty Python Team

1989 FILM: *The Last Emperor* (UK/It/US) (Bernardo Bertolucci) (Hemdale/Recorded Pictures Company/Screenframe Ltd/Soprofilms/TAO Film/Yanco/AAA Productions. Prod: Jeremy Thomas)
OTHER AWARDS FOR THIS FILM:
COSTUME DESIGN: James Acheson
MAKE-UP: Fabrizio Sforza
ACTOR: John Cleese, *A Fish Called Wanda*
SUPPORTING ACTOR: Michael Palin, *A Fish Called Wanda*
ACTRESS: Maggie Smith, *The Lonely Passion of Judith Hearne*
SUPPORTING ACTRESS: Judi Dench, *A Handful of Dust*
CINEMATOGRAPHY: Allen Daviau, *Empire of the Sun* (UK/US)
MUSIC: John Williams, *Empire of the Sun*
SOUND: Charles L. Campbell, Louis L. Edemann, Robert Knudson, Tony Dawe, *Empire of the Sun*
SPECIAL EFFECTS: George Gibbs, Richard Williams, Ken Ralston, Ed Jones *Who Framed Roger Rabbit* (US)
ORIGINAL SCREENPLAY: Shawn Slovo, *A World Apart* (UK/Zimb)
ANIMATED FILM: *The Hill Farm* (Mark Baker)
MICHAEL BALCON AWARD: Charles Crichton

1990 DIRECTOR: Kenneth Branagh, *Henry V*
ACTOR: Daniel Day-Lewis, *My Left Foot*
SUPPORTING ACTOR: Ray McAnally, *My Left Foot*
ADAPTED SCREENPLAY: Christopher Hampton, *Dangerous Liaisons* (US)
ACTRESS: Pauline Collins, *Shirley Valentine* (UK/US)
CINEMATOGRAPHY: Peter Biziou, *Mississippi Burning* (US)
EDITING: Gerry Hambling, *Mississippi Burning*
PRODUCTION DESIGN: Dante Ferretti, *The Adventures of Baron Munchausen* (UK/ Ger/It)
COSTUME DESIGN: Gabriella Pescucci, *The Adventures of Baron Munchausen*
MAKE UP: Maggie Weston, Fabrizio Sforza, Pam Meager,

The Adventures of Baron Munchausen
SHORT: *The Candy Show* (Peter Hewitt, David Freeman, Damian Jones)
ANIMATED FILM: *Wallace & Gromit: A Grand Day Out* (Nick Park)
MICHAEL BALCON AWARD: Lewis Gilbert

1991 ACTRESS: Jessica Tandy, *Driving Miss Daisy* (US)
CINEMATOGRAPHY: Vittorio Storaro, *The Sheltering Sky* (UK/It)
SHORT: *Say Good-bye* (John Roberts) (Prod: Michele Camarda)
MICHAEL BALCON AWARD: Jeremy Thomas

1992 FILM: *The Commitments* (Alan Parker) (Beacon Communications/First Film Co./Dirty Hands Productions/Sovereign Pictures. Prod: Roger Randall-Cutler, Lynda Myles)
OTHER AWARDS FOR THIS FILM:
DIRECTOR: Alan Parker
ADAPTED SCREENPLAY: Dick Clement, Ian La Frenais, Roddy Doyle
EDITING: Gerry Hambling
ACTOR: Anthony Hopkins, *The Silence of the Lambs* (US)
SUPPORTING ACTOR: Alan Rickman, *Robin Hood: Prince of Thieves* (US)
SUPPORTING ACTRESS: Kate Nelligan, *Frankie and Johnnie* (US)
ORIGINAL SCREENPLAY: Anthony Minghella, *Truly Madly Deeply*
SHORT: *The Harmfulness of Tobacco* (Nick Hamm) (Prod: Barry Palin)
ANIMATED FILM: *Balloon* (Ken Lidster) (National Film and Television School)
MICHAEL BALCON AWARD: Derek Jarman

1993 FILM: *Howards End* (James Ivory) (Merchant Ivory Productions/Nippon Herald Films/Channel Four. Prod: Ismail Merchant)
OTHER AWARD FOR THIS FILM:
ACTRESS: Emma Thompson
ACTOR: Robert Downey Jr, *Chaplin* (UK/Fr/It/Jap/US)
SUPPORTING ACTRESS: Miranda Richardson, *Damage* (UK/Fr)
MAKE-UP: Peter Robb-King, *The Last of the Mohicans* (US)
ANIMATED FILM: *Daumier's Law* (Geoff Dunbar) (Grandslamm Partnership. Prod: Ginger Gibbons)
MICHAEL BALCON AWARD: Kenneth Branagh
Alexander Korda Award for Best British Film: *The Crying Game* (Neil Jordan) (Palace Pictures. Prod: Stephen Woolley)

1994 BRITISH FILM: *Shadowlands* (UK/US) (Richard Attenborough) (Shadowlands Productions/Price Ent. Prod: Richard Attenborough, Brian Eastman)
OTHER AWARDS FOR THIS FILM:
ACTOR: Anthony Hopkins
ALEXANDER KORDA AWARD FOR BEST BRITISH FILM
SUPPORTING ACTOR: Ralph Fiennes, *Schindler's List* (US)
SUPPORTING ACTRESS: Miriam Margolyes, *The Age of Innocence* (US)
PRODUCTION DESIGN: Andrew McAlpine, *The Piano* (Aust/Fr)
MAKE-UP: Morag Ross, *Orlando* (UK/Fr/It/Neth/Russ)
SHORT: *Franz Kafka's It's a Wonderful Life* (Peter

Capaldi) (BBC/Conundrum Films. Prod: Ruth Kenley-Letts)

ANIMATED FILM: *The Wrong Trousers* (Nick Park) (Aardman Animations. Prod: Christopher Moll, Nick Park)

MICHAEL BALCON AWARD: Ken Loach

SPECIAL AWARDS: Phyllis Dalton, Richard Attenborough, Thora Hird

1995 FILM: *Four Weddings and a Funeral* (Mike Newell) (Working Title Films/Channel Four. Prod: Duncan Kenworthy)

OTHER AWARDS FOR THIS FILM:

DIRECTOR: Mike Newell

ACTOR: Hugh Grant

SUPPORTING ACTRESS: Kristin Scott Thomas

DAVID LEAN AWARD FOR DIRECTION: Mike Newell

BRITISH FILM: *Shallow Grave* (Danny Boyle) (Channel Four/Figment Films/Noel Gay Motion Picture Co. Prod: Allan Scott, Andrew MacDonald)

ALEXANDER KORDA AWARD FOR BEST BRITISH FILM: *Shallow Grave*

CINEMATOGRAPHY: Philippe Rousselot, *Interview with the Vampire* (UK/US)

PRODUCTION DESIGN: Dante Ferretti, *Interview with the Vampire*

MUSIC: Don Was, *Backbeat*

ANTHONY ASQUITH AWARD FOR FILM MUSIC: Don Was, *Backbeat*

ANIMATED FILM: *The Big Story* (Tim Watts, David Stoten) (Screwball Films)

SHORT: *Zinky Boys Go Underground* (UK/USSR) (Paul Tickell)(BBC/BFI/Lara Globus Int./ Screen Two. Prod: Tatiana Kennedy)

MICHAEL BALCON AWARD: Ridley Scott, Tony Scott

1996 FILM: *Sense and Sensibility* (UK/US, Ang Lee) (Columbia Pictures/Tristar/Mirage. Prod: Sydney Pollack, Lindsay Doran, Geoff Stier, Laurie Borg, James Schamus)

OTHER AWARDS FOR THIS FILM:

ACTRESS: Emma Thompson

SUPPORTING ACTRESS: Kate Winslet

BRITISH FILM: *The Madness of King George* (UK/US, Nicholas Hytner) (Channel Four/Close Call Films/Mad George Films/Samuel Goldwyn Co. Prod: Stephen Evans, David Parfitt, Mark Cooper)

ACTOR: Nigel Hawthorne, *The Madness of King George*

MAKE-UP/HAIR: Lisa Westcott, *The Madness of King George*

ALEXANDER KORDA AWARD FOR BEST BRITISH FILM: *The Madness of King George*

DIRECTOR: Michael Radford, *The Postman/Il Postino* (Belg/Fr/It)

DAVID LEAN AWARD FOR DIRECTION: Michael Radford, *The Postman/Il Postino*

ANTHONY ASQUITH AWARD FOR FILM MUSIC: Luis Enríquez Bacalov, *The Postman/Il Postino*

SUPPORTING ACTOR: Tim Roth, *Rob Roy* (UK/US)

ADAPTED SCREENPLAY: John Hodge, *Trainspotting*

CINEMATOGRAPHY: John Toll, *Braveheart* (UK/US)

COSTUME DESIGN: Charles Knode, *Braveheart*

SOUND: Per Hallberg, Lon Bender, Brian Simmons, Andy Nelson, Scott Millan, Anna Behlmer, *Braveheart*

SHORT: *It's Not Unusual* (Kfir Yefet) (Prod: Asmaa

Pirzada, Margaret Matheson)

ANIMATED FILM: *A Close Shave* (Nick Park) (Aardman Animations/BBC. Prod: Carla Shelley, Michael Rose, Peter Lord, Colin Rose, David Sproxton)

MICHAEL BALCON AWARD: Mike Leigh

1997 FILM: *The English Patient* (UK/US, Anthony Minghella) (J&M Entertainment/Miramax Films/Tiger Moth Productions. Prod: Saul Zaentz)

OTHER AWARDS FOR THIS FILM:

SUPPORTING ACTRESS: Juliette Binoche

ADAPTED SCREENPLAY: Anthony Minghella

CINEMATOGRAPHY: John Seale

EDITING: Walter Murch

MUSIC: Gabriel Yared

ANTHONY ASQUITH AWARD FOR FILM MUSIC: Gabriel Yared

BRITISH FILM: *Secrets & Lies* (Mike Leigh) (Channel Four/CiBy 2000/Thin Man Films. Prod: Simon Channing-Williams)

ACTRESS: Brenda Blethyn, *Secrets & Lies*

ORIGINAL SCREENPLAY: Mike Leigh, *Secrets & Lies*

ALEXANDER KORDA AWARD FOR BEST BRITISH FILM: *Secrets & Lies*

SUPPORTING ACTOR: Paul Scofield, *The Crucible* (US)

PRODUCTION DESIGN: Tony Burrough, *Richard III*

COSTUME DESIGN: Shuna Harwood, *Richard III*

PRODUCTION DESIGN: Tony Burrough, *Richard III*

MICHAEL BALCON AWARD: Channel Four Films

ACADEMY FELLOWSHIP: Julie Christie

1998 FILM: *The Full Monty* (UK/US, Peter Cattaneo) (Channel Four/Fox Searchlight Pictures/Redwave Films. Prod: Uberto Pasolini, Paul Bucknor, Polly Leys, Lesley Stewart)

OTHER AWARDS FOR THIS FILM:

ACTOR: Robert Carlyle

SUPPORTING ACTOR: Tom Wilkinson

AUDIENCE AWARD

BRITISH FILM: *Nil by Mouth* (Gary Oldman) (Se8 Group/Seaside Prods. Prod: Luc Bresson, Gary Oldman)

ALEXANDER KORDA AWARD FOR BEST BRITISH FILM: *Nil by Mouth*

ORIGINAL SCREENPLAY: Gary Oldman, *Nil by Mouth*

ACTRESS: Judi Dench, *Mrs Brown* (UK/Ire/US)

COSTUME DESIGN: Deirdre Clancy, *Mrs. Brown*

CINEMATOGRAPHY: Eduardo Serra, *The Wings of the Dove* (UK/US)

MAKE-UP/HAIR: Sallie Jaye, Jan Archibald, *The Wings of the Dove*

ANIMATED SHORT: *Stage Fright* (Steve Box) (Prod: Helen Nabarro, Michael Rose)

SHORT: *The Deadness of Dad* (Mandy Sprague, Philippa Cousins, Stephen Volk)

MICHAEL BALCON AWARD: Mike Roberts

ACADEMY FELLOWSHIP: Sean Connery

1999 FILM: *Shakespeare in Love* (UK/US, John Madden) (Bedford Falls Productions/Miramax/Universal. Prod: David Parfitt, Donna Gigliotti, Harvey Weinstein, Edward Zwick, Marc Norman)

OTHER AWARDS FOR THIS FILM:

SUPPORTING ACTOR: Geoffrey Rush

SUPPORTING ACTRESS: Judi Dench

EDITING: David Gamble

BRITISH FILM: *Elizabeth* (Shekhar Kapur) (Channel Four/Polygram/Working Title Films. Prod: Tim Bevan, Eric Fellner, Alison Owen, Debra Hayward, Mary Richards, Liza Chasin)
OTHER AWARDS FOR THIS FILM:
ACTRESS: Cate Blanchett
CINEMATOGRAPHY: Remi Adefarasin
MUSIC: David Hirschfelder
ANTHONY ASQUITH AWARD FOR FILM MUSIC: David Hirschfelder
MAKE-UP/HAIR: Jenny Shircore
ALEXANDER KORDA AWARD FOR BEST BRITISH FILM
AUDIENCE AWARD: *Lock, Stock and Two Smoking Barrels* (Guy Ritchie)
COSTUME DESIGN: Sandy Powell, *Velvet Goldmine* (UK/US)
ANIMATED SHORT: *The Canterbury Tales* (UK/USSR) (Jonathan Myerson) (Prod: Christopher Grace)
SHORT: *Home* (Morag McKinnon, Colin McLaren, Douglas Buck) (Prod: Hannah Lewis)
ACADEMY FELLOWSHIP: Elizabeth Taylor

2000 FILM: *American Beauty* (US, Sam Mendes) (DreamWorks SKG-Jinks/Cohen Co. Prod: Alan Ball)
EDITING: Tariq Anwar, Christopher Greenbury, *American Beauty*
ALEXANDER KORDA AWARD FOR BEST BRITISH FILM: *East is East* (Damien O'Donnell) (BBC/Channel 4/Assassin Films. Prod: Alan J. Wands, Leslee Udwin, Shellie Smith)
SUPPORTING ACTOR: Jude Law, *The Talented Mr Ripley* (US)
SUPPORTING ACTRESS: Maggie Smith, *Tea with Mussolini* (UK/It)
ADAPTED SCREENPLAY: Neil Jordan, *The End of the Affair* (UK/Ger/US)
AUDIENCE AWARD: *Notting Hill* (UK/US, Roger Michell)
PRODUCTION DESIGN: Rick Heinrichs, *Sleepy Hollow* (US/Ger)
COSTUME: Colleen Atwood, *Sleepy Hollow*
MAKE-UP/HAIR: Christine Blundell, *Topsy-Turvy* (UK/US)
NEWCOMER: Richard Kwietniowksi, *Love and Death on Long Island* (UK/Can)
ANIMATED SHORT: *The Man with the Beautiful Eyes* (Jonathan Hodgson) (Prod: Jonathan Bairstow)
SHORT: *Who's My Favourite Girl?* (Adrian McDowall) (Prod: Joern Utkilen, Kara Johnston, Adrian McDowall)
MICHAEL BALCON AWARD: Joyce Herlihy
ACADEMY FELLOWSHIPS: Michael Caine, Stanley Kubrick

2001 ACTOR: Jamie Bell, *Billy Elliot*
SUPPORTING ACTRESS: Julie Walters, *Billy Elliot*
ALEXANDER KORDA AWARD FOR BEST BRITISH FILM: *Billy Elliot* (Stephen Daldry) (BBC/Tiger Aspect/Working Title. Prod: Greg Brenman, Jonathan Finn)
NEWCOMER: Paul Pavlikovsky, *Last Resort*
SHORT FILM: *Shadowscan* (Tinge Krishnan) (Prod: Gary Holding, Justine Leahy)
ANIMATED FILM: *Father and Daughter* (Michael Dudok de Wit) (UK/Neth.) (Cloudrunner Ltd/CineTe Filmproductie BV. Prod: Claire Jennings, Willem Thijssen)

MICHAEL BALCON AWARD: Mary Selway
ACADEMY FELLOWSHIPS: Albert Finney, John Thaw

2002 ALEXANDER KORDA AWARD FOR BEST BRITISH FILM: *Gosford Park* (UK/Ger/US) (Robert Altman) (Film Council/Capitol Films/Chicagofilms/Medusa/Sandcastle 5/USA Films. Prod: Robert Altman/Bob Balaban/David Levy)
COSTUME DESIGN: Jenny Beavan, *Gosford Park*
ACTRESS: Judi Dench, *Iris* (UK/US)
SUPPORTING ACTOR: Jim Broadbent, *Moulin Rouge* (Aust/US)
CARL FOREMAN AWARD FOR NEWCOMERS TO BRITISH FILM: Joel Hopkins, Nicola Usborne, *Jump Tomorrow*
CINEMATOGRAPHY: Roger Deakins, *The Man Who Wasn't There* (US/UK)
SHORT: *About a Girl* (Brian Percival)
SHORT (ANIMATION): *Dog* (Suzie Templeton)
MICHAEL BALCON AWARD: Vic Armstrong
ACADEMY FELLOWSHIP: Merchant Ivory Productions (Ismail Merchant, James Ivory, Ruth Prawer Jhabvala)
SPECIAL AWARD: Eon Productions (for James Bond films)

2003 FILM: *The Pianist* (Roman Polanski) (UK/Fr/Ger/Pol) (R.P. Productions–Heritage films–Studio Babelsberg–Runteam. Producers: Roman Polanski, Robert Benmussa, Alain Sarde)
OTHER AWARD FOR THS FILM:
DAVID LEAN FOR DIRECTION
ALEXANDER KORDA AWARD FOR BEST BRITISH FILM: *The Warrior* (Producer: Bertrand Faivre)
BEST ACTRESS: Nicole Kidman, *The Hours* (UK/US)
BEST SUPPORTING ACTRESS: Catherine Zeta-Jones, *Chicago* (US)
CARL FOREMAN AWARD FOR NEWCOMER TO BRITISH FILM: Asif Kapadia (director/co-author)
ANTHONY ASQUITH AWARD FOR FILM MUSIC: Philip Glass, *The Hours* (UK/US)
MICHAEL BALCON AWARD (contribution to British cinema): David Tamblin, Michael Stevenson

Cannes Film Festival Awards

First competition was held in 1946 (the 1939 festival was abandoned), and no competitions were held in 1948, 1950 and 1968. Special Jury Prize added 1951, Golden Palm/Palme d'Or (for best film) in 1955, and Golden Camera/Camera d'Or (for best first feature) in 1979.

1946 GRAND PRIZE: *Brief Encounter* (David Lean) (Cineguild/Rank. Prod: Anthony Havelock-Allan, Ronald Neame) (shared award)
ACTOR: Ray Milland, *The Lost Weekend* (US)

1949 GRAND PRIZE: *The Third Man* (Carol Reed) (London Films. Prod: Carol Reed, Alexander Korda, David O. Selznick)

1951 PRIZE FOR SUPERIOR TECHNIQUE: *The Tales of Hoffman* (Michael Powell, Emeric Pressburger)
SPECIAL JURY PRIZE FOR ORIGINALITY/LYRICAL FILM ADAPTED: *The Tales of Hoffman*
ACTOR: Michael Redgrave, *The Browning Version*
SCREENPLAY: Terence Rattigan, *The Browning Version*

1952 SHORT (COLOUR): *Animated Genesis* (Joan and Peter Foldes)

1953 SHORT (FICTION): *The Stranger Left No Card* (Wendy Toye) (Meteor/British Lion. Prod: George K. Arthur)

1954 SPECIAL JURY PRIZE: *Knave of Hearts* (UK/Fr) (René Clement) (Transcontinental/Associated British. Prod: Paul Graetz)
SHORT (FANTASY/POETIC FILM): *The Pleasure Garden* (James Broughton)

1959 ACTRESS: Simone Signoret, *Room at the Top*
PRIZE FOR SUPERIOR TECHNIQUE: *Luna de Miel* (UK title: *Honeymoon*) (Sp/UK) (Michael Powell)

1962 ACTRESS: Rita Tushingham, *A Taste of Honey* (shared award)
ACTOR: Murray Melvin, *A Taste of Honey* (shared award)
ACTOR: Ralph Richardson, *Long Day's Journey into Night* (US) (shared award)

1963 INTERNATIONAL CRITICS PRIZE: *This Sporting Life* (Lindsay Anderson) (Independent Artists. Prod: Karel Reisz)
ACTOR: Richard Harris, *This Sporting Life*

1964 ACTRESS: Anne Bancroft, *The Pumpkin Eater* (shared award)

1965 GOLDEN PALM: *The Knack . . . And How to Get It* (Richard Lester) (Woodfall Films. Prod: Oscar Lewenstein)
TECHNICAL GRAND PRIZE, SPECIAL MENTION: *The Knack . . . And How to Get It*
ACTRESS: Samantha Eggar, *The Collector* (UK/US)
ACTOR: Terence Stamp, *The Collector*
SCREENPLAY: Ray Rigby, *The Hill*

1966 ACTRESS: Vanessa Redgrave, *Morgan: A Suitable Case for Treatment*
SPECIAL JURY PRIZE: *Alfie* (Lewis Gilbert)

1967 GOLDEN PALM: *Blow-Up* (UK/It, Michelangelo Antonioni) (Bridge Films/MGM. Prod: Carlo Ponti)
SPECIAL JURY PRIZE: *Accident* (Joseph Losey) (London Independent Producers. Prod: Joseph Losey, Norman Priggen)

1969 GOLDEN PALM: *If . . .* (Lindsay Anderson) (Memorial Enterprises. Prod: Lindsay Anderson, Michael Medwin)
ACTRESS: Vanessa Redgrave, *Isadora*

1970 DIRECTOR: *Leo the Last* (John Boorman)

1971 GOLDEN PALM: *The Go-Between* (Joseph Losey) (World Film Services/MGM-EMI. Prod: John Heyman, Norman Priggen)

1972 ACTRESS: Susannah York, *Images* (US/Eire)

1973 GOLDEN PALM: *The Hireling* (Alan Bridges) (Champion Films/World Film Services/Columbia. Prod: Ben Arbeid) (shared award)

1974 TECHNICAL GRAND PRIZE: *Mahler* (Ken Russell)

1975 GOLDEN PALM (SHORT): *Lautrec* (Geoff Dunbar) (Arts Council/Curzon Films/Dragon Productions)

1976 SHORT (JURY PRIZE): *Nightlife* (Robin Lehman) (Opus Films) (shared award)

1977 BEST FIRST FILM (JURY PRIZE): *The Duellists* (Ridley Scott) (Scott Free/National Film Finance Corporation. Prod: David Puttnam)

1978 SPECIAL JURY PRIZE: *The Shout* (Jerzy Skolimowski) (Recorded Picture Company. Prod: Jeremy Thomas) (shared award)

1979 FIPRESCI AWARD (OUT OF COMPETITION): *Black Jack* (Ken Loach) (shared award)

1980 GOLDEN PALM (SHORT): *Seaside Woman* (Oscar Grillo)

1981 ACTRESS: Isabelle Adjani, *Quartet* (UK/Fr)
SUPPORTING ACTOR: Ian Holm, *Chariots of Fire*
ECUMENICAL JURY PRIZE (SPECIAL MENTION): *Chariots of Fire* (Hugh Hudson) and *Looks and Smiles* (Ken Loach) (shared award)
CONTEMPORARY CINEMA PRIZE: *Looks and Smiles* (Ken Loach) (shared award)
ARTISTIC CONTRIBUTION TO THE POETICS OF CINEMA: *Excalibur* (UK/US) (John Boorman)

1982 SCREENPLAY: Jerzy Skolimowski, *Moonlighting*

1983 GRAND JURY PRIZE: *Monty Python – The Meaning of Life* (Terry Jones) (Celandine/Monty Python Partnership/Universal. Prod: John Goldstone)

1984 ACTRESS: Helen Mirren, *Cal* (UK/Ire)
BEST ARTISTIC CONTRIBUTION (CINEMATOGRAPHY): Peter Biziou, *Another Country*

1985 GRAND JURY PRIZE: *Birdy* (US) (Alan Parker) (Tri-Star. Prod: Alan Marshall)
TECHNICAL PRIZE: *Insignificance* (Nicolas Roeg)
CONTEMPORARY (YOUNG CINEMA) AWARD: *Dance with a Stranger* (Mike Newell)

1986 GOLDEN PALM: *The Mission* (Roland Joffe) (Enigma/Goldcrest/Kingsmere Productions/Fernando Ghia. Prod: David Puttnam)
TECHNICAL PRIZE: *The Mission*
ACTOR: Bob Hoskins, *Mona Lisa*

1987 BEST ARTISTIC CONTRIBUTION: Stanley Myers (music), *Prick Up Your Ears*
FIPRESCI AWARD: *Wish You Were Here* (David Leland) (shared award)

1988 GRAND JURY PRIZE: *A World Apart* (UK/Zimb) (Chris Menges) (British Screen/Palace Pictures/Working Title/Atlantic Ent. Prod: Sarah Radclyffe)
ACTRESS: Barbara Hershey, *A World Apart* (shared award)
ACTRESS: Jodhi May, *A World Apart* (shared award)
ACTRESS: Linda Mvusi, *A World Apart* (shared award)
ECUMENICAL JURY PRIZE: *A World Apart*
Best Artistic Contribution: *Drowning By Numbers* (Peter Greenaway)
GOLDEN CAMERA: *Salaam Bombay!* (UK/Fr/Ind) (Mira Nair)
FIPRESCI AWARD: *Distant Voices, Still Lives* (UK/Ger) (Terence Davies) (shared award)

1990 JURY PRIZE: *Hidden Agenda* (Ken Loach) (Initial Films. Prod: John Daly, Derek Gibson)
ECUMENICAL JURY PRIZE (SPECIAL MENTION): *Hidden Agenda* (shared award)

1991 FIPRESCI AWARD: *Riff-Raff* (Ken Loach) (shared award)

1992 45TH ANNIVERSARY PRIZE: *Howards End* (James Ivory)

1993 ACTOR: David Thewlis, *Naked*
DIRECTOR: Mike Leigh, *Naked*

JURY PRIZE: *Raining Stones* (Ken Loach) (Channel 4/Parallax Pictures. Prod: Sally Hibbin)

1994 SHORT FILM (SECOND PRIZE, SPECIAL MENTION): *Syrup* (Dir: Paul Unwin) (prod: Anita Overland, Nick Vivian. Channel Four/First Choice)

1995 SPECIAL JURY PRIZE: *Carrington* (Christopher Hampton) (UK/Fr) (Cinea/Dora Productions/Freeway/Polygram. Prod: John McGrath, Ronald Shedlo)
DIRECTOR: Christopher Hampton, *Carrington*
SCREENPLAY: Christopher Hampton, *Carrington*
ACTOR: Jonathan Pryce, *Carrington*
ACTRESS: Helen Mirren, *The Madness of King George* (UK/US)
ECUMENICAL JURY PRIZE: *Land and Freedom* (Ken Loach)
FIPRESCI AWARD: *Land and Freedom* (UK/Sp/Ger) (shared award)
PUBLIC PRIZE: *Someone Else's America* (UK/Fr/Ger) (Goran Paskaljevic)

1996 GOLDEN PALM: *Secrets & Lies* (Mike Leigh) (Channel Four/Ciby 2000/Thin Man Films. Prod: Simon Channing-Williams)
ACTRESS: Brenda Blethyn, *Secrets & Lies*

ECUMENICAL JURY PRIZE: *Secrets & Lies*
SPECIAL JURY PRIZE: *Crash* (David Cronenberg) (Can/Fr/UK) (Alliance Communications/Movie Network/Telefilm Canada. Prod: Jeremy Thomas, Chris Auty)
SHORT (JURY PRIZE): *Small Deaths* (Lynne Ramsay)

1997 ACTRESS: Kathy Burke, *Nil By Mouth*
CONTEMPORARY (YOUNG CINEMA) AWARD: Sean Mathias, *Bent*
GOLDEN PALM (SHORT): *Is it the Design on the Wrappper?* (Tessa Sheridan. Sankofa Films)

1998 ACTOR: Peter Mullan, *My Name is Joe*
BEST ARTISTIC CONTRIBUTION: Todd Haynes, *Velvet Goldmine* (UK/US)
DIRECTOR: John Boorman, *The General* (UK/US)
SHORT (JURY FIRST PRIZE): *Gasman* (Lynne Ramsay)
SHORT (JURY PRIZE): *Horseshoe* (David Lodge)

2001 SHORT (SPECIAL JURY PRIZE): *Daddy's Girl* (Irvine Allan) (prod: Carolyne Sinclair Kidd) (shared award)

2002 BEST SCREENPLAY: Paul Laverty, *Sweet Sixteen* (Ken Loach)
PRIX DE LA JEUNESSE: Lynne Ramsay, *Morvan Callar*

SOME TITLE CHANGES

Britain *to* America

The Admirable Crichton	*Paradise Lagoon*
Albert RN	*Break for Freedom*
The Amorous Prawn	*The Playgirl and the War Minister*
Appointment with Venus	*Island Rescue*
Atlantic Ferry	*Sons of the Sea*
Background	*Edge of Divorce*
Bank Holiday	*Three on a Weekend*
Barnacle Bill	*All at Sea*
The Battle of the River Plate	*Pursuit of the Graf Spee*
Battle of the V–1	*Missiles from Hell*
Beat Girl	*Wild for Kicks*
Before I Wake	*Shadow of Fear*
Beyond This Place	*Web of Evidence/PO Box 303*
Blind Date	*Chance Meeting*
Brighton Rock	*Young Scarface*
Britannia Mews	*The Forbidden Street*
Captain Clegg	*Night Creatures*
The Card	*The Promoter*
Carlton-Browne of the FO	*Man in a Cocked Hat*
Carrington VC	*Court Martial*
Cone of Silence	*Trouble in the Sky*
Confidential Report	*Mr Arkadin*
Conflict of Wings	*Fuss Over Feathers*
Contraband	*Blackout*
Cosh Boy	*The Slasher*
Cottage to Let	*Bombsight Stolen*
Country Dance	*Brotherly Love*
The Courtneys of Curzon Street	*The Courtney Affair*
Danger Within	*Breakout*
The Dark Avenger	*The Warriors*
The Day Will Dawn	*The Avengers*
Dear Octopus	*The Randolph Family*
The Demi-Paradise	*Adventure for Two*
Derby Day	*Four Against Fate*
The Devil Rides Out	*The Devil's Bride*
The Drum	*Drums*
The Elusive Pimpernel	*The Fighting Pimpernel*
English Without Tears	*Her Man Gilbey*
Family Life	*Wednesday's Child*
Fanny by Gaslight	*Man of Evil*
Father Brown	*The Detective*
The First of the Few	*Spitfire*

The Flesh and the Fiends	*Mania*
The Foreman Went to France	*Somewhere in France*
Fortune Is a Woman	*She Played with Fire*
49th Parallel	*The Invaders*
Freedom Radio	*A Voice in the Night*
Gaiety George	*Showtime*
Gaslight	*Angel Street*
Geordie	*Wee Geordie*
Gideon's Day	*Gideon of Scotland Yard*
The Gift Horse	*Glory at Sea*
Girl in the Headlines	*The Model Murder Case*
Gone to Earth	*The Wild Heart*
Grand National Night	*Wicked Wife*
The Guinea Pig	*The Outsider*
Happy Ever After	*Tonight's the Night*
The Happy Family	*Mr Lord Says No*
Her Favourite Husband	*The Taming of Dorothy*
The High Bright Sun	*McGuire Go Home*
Highly Dangerous	*Time Running Out*
Hot Enough for June	*Agent 8¾*
House of Secrets	*Triple Deception*
Hunted	*The Stranger in Between*
I Live in Grosvenor Square	*A Yank in London*
I See a Dark Stranger	*The Adventuress*
Ice Cold in Alex	*Desert Attack*
I'll Get You for This	*Lucky Nick Cain*
Ill Met By Moonlight	*Night Ambush*
Isadora	*The Loves of Isadora*
The Kidnappers	*The Little Kidnappers*
Knave of Hearts	*Lover Boy*
Lady Godiva Rides Again	*Beauty Queen*
The Last Days of Dolwyn	*Woman of Dolwyn*
The Late Edwina Black	*Obsessed*
Latin Quarter	*Frenzy*
Laxdale Hall	*Scotch on the Rocks*
Life for Ruth	*Walk in the Shadow*
Light Up the Sky	*Skywatch*
Lilacs in the Spring	*Let's Make Up*
London Belongs to Me	*Dulcimer Street*
London Town	*My Heart Goes Crazy*
The Long, the Short and the Tall	*Jungle Fighters*
Love Story	*A Lady Surrenders*

The 'Maggie'	*High and Dry*
The Man Who Watched Trains Go By	*Paris Express*
The Man Within	*The Smugglers*
Mandy	*The Crash of Silence*
Manuela	*Stowaway Girl*
A Matter of Life and Death	*Stairway to Heaven*
Men of Two Worlds	*Witch Doctor*
Midshipman Easy	*Men of the Sea*
The Million Pound Note	*Man with a Million*
Morning Departure	*Operation Disaster*
My Teenage Daughter	*Teenage Bad Girl*
The Naked Truth	*Your Past is Showing*
The Net	*Project M7*
The Night Has Eyes	*Terror House*
Night of the Eagle	*Burn Witch Burn*
Nobody Lives Forever	*The High Commissioner*
Nor the Moon by Night	*Elephant Gun*
North West Frontier	*Flame over India*
Odd Man Out	*Gang War*
Once a Jolly Swagman	*Maniacs on Wheels*
The Passionate Friends	*One Woman's Story*
The Passionate Stranger	*A Novel Affair*
Penn of Pennsylvania	*The Courageous Mr Penn*
Perfect Strangers	*Vacation from Marriage*
Pimpernel Smith	*Mister V*
The Planter's Wife	*Outpost in Malaya*
Pretty Polly	*A Matter of Innocence*
Q Planes	*Clouds over Europe*
Quatermass and the Pit	*Five Million Years to Earth*
The Quatermass Experiment	*The Creeping Unknown*
Quatermass 2	*Enemy from Space*
The Raging Moon	*Long Ago Tomorrow*
The Rake's Progress	*Notorious Gentleman*
Rockets Galore	*Mad Little Island*
The Romantic Age	*Naughty Arlette*
Rough Shoot	*Shoot First*
Sailor Beware	*Panic in the Parlor*
St Martin's Lane	*The Sidewalks of London*
Saraband for Dead Lovers	*Saraband*
Sea of Sand	*Desert Patrol*
Seagulls Over Sorrento	*Crest of the Wave*
The Seekers	*Land of Fury*
Seven Waves Away	*Abandon Ship*
The Ship That Died of Shame	*P.T. Raiders*
The Shop at Sly Corner	*The Code of Scotland Yard*
The Siege of Pinchgut	*Four Desperate Men*
Singlehanded	*Sailor of the King*
Sixty Glorious Years	*Queen of Destiny*
Sky West and Crooked	*Gypsy Girl*

The Small Back Room	*Hour of Glory*
The Smallest Show on Earth	*Big Time Operators*
The Small Voice	*Hideout*
Soft Beds, Hard Battles	*Undercover Hero*
The Sound Barrier	*Breaking the Sound Barrier*
South of Algiers	*The Golden Mask*
The Spy in Black	*U-Boat 29*
The Squeaker	*Murder on Diamond Row*
The Story of Esther Costello	*The Golden Virgin*
Street Corner	*Both Sides of the Law*
Summer of the Seventeenth Doll	*Season of Passion*
The Tall Headlines	*The Frightened Bride*
Taste of Fear	*Scream of Fear*
Tell England	*The Battle of Gallipoli*
These Dangerous Years	*Dangerous Youth*
They Flew Alone	*Wings and the Woman*
They Made Me a Fugitive	*I Became a Criminal*
Tom Brown's Schooldays	*Adventures at Rugby*
Top Secret	*Mr Potts Goes to Moscow*
A Town Like Alice	*The Rape of Malaya*
The Trials of Oscar Wilde	*The Man with the Green Carnation*
Trottie True	*The Gay Lady*
Tudor Rose	*Nine Days a Queen*
24 Hours in a Woman's Life	*Affair in Monte Carlo*
Uncle Silas	*The Inheritance*
Venetian Bird	*The Assassin*
The Voice of Merrill	*Murder Will Out*
Waterfront	*Waterfront Women*
The Way Ahead	*Immortal Battalion*
The Way to the Stars	*Johnny in the Clouds*
The Weak and the Wicked	*Young and Willing*
Went the Day Well?	*48 Hours*
Where No Vultures Fly	*Ivory Hunter*
Whisky Galore	*Tight Little Island*
White Cradle Inn	*High Fury*
The White Unicorn	*Bad Sister*
Who Goes There?	*The Passionate Sentry*
Witchfinder General	*The Conqueror Worm*
The Woman in Question	*Five Angles on Murder*
Women of Twilight	*Twilight Women*
The Woman with No Name	*Her Panelled Door*
Yangtse Incident	*Battle Hell*
Yield to the Night	*Blonde Sinner*
Young and Innocent	*The Girl Was Young*
The Young Lovers	*Chance Meeting*
Zee & Co.	*X, Y and Zee*

SELECT BIBLIOGRAPHY

NB This bibliography contains only books, not journal articles. Very detailed bibliographies are to be found in the texts marked with asterisks* below.

General histories and references

(For further reference works, see 'Sources' section of **Introduction**.)

ADAIR, G. and RODDICK, N. *A Night at the Pictures: Ten Decades of British Film*. Bromley, 1985.

ARMES, R. *A Critical History of British Cinema*. London, 1978.

*ASHBY, J. and HIGSON, A. (eds) *British Cinema, Past and Present*. London, 2000.

BARR, C (ed.) *All Our Yesterdays: 90 years of British Cinema*. London, 1986.

BERRY, D. *Wales and Cinema: The First Hundred Years*. Cardiff, 1994.

BETTS, E. *The Film Business: A History of British Cinema 1896–1972*. London, 1973.

BETTS, E. *Inside Pictures*. London, 1960.

BOURNE, S. *Black in the British Frame: Black People in British Film and Television 1896–1996*. London, 1998.

BRUCE, D. *Scotland the Movie*. Edinburgh, 1996.

BURROWS, E. *et al. The British Source Book: BFI Archive Viewing Copies and Library Materials*, 1995.

BURTON, A. *The People's Cinema: Film and the Co-operative Movement*. London, 1994.

BUTLER, I. *Cinema in Britain: An Illustrated Survey*. London, 1973.

CAUGHIE, J. and ROCKETT, K. *The Companion to British and Irish Cinema*. London, 1996.

COOK, P. *Fashioning the Nation: Costume and Identity in British Cinema*. London, 1996.

CROSS, R. *The Big Book of British Cinema*. London, 1984.

*CURRAN, J. and PORTER, V. (eds.) *British Cinema History*. London, 1983.

DICK, E. (ed.) *From Limelight to Satellite: A Scottish Film Book*. London, 1990.

DIXON, W. W. (ed.) *Re-viewing British Cinema 1900–1992*. Albany, NY, 1994.

GIFFORD, D. *The British Film Catalogue. Volume 1: Fiction Film 1895–1994; Volume 2: Non-Fiction Film 1895–1994*, London, 2001.

GIFFORD, D. *The Illustrated Who's Who in British Films*, London, 1978.

HARPER, S. *Women in British Cinema: Mad, Bad and Dangerous to Know*. London, 2000.

HIGSON, A. *Waving the Flag. Constructing a National Cinema in Britain*. Oxford, 1996.

HIGSON, A. (ed.) *Dissolving Views: Key Writings on British Cinema*. London, 1996.

HILL, J. and McLOONE, M. (eds) *Border Crossing: Film in Ireland, Britain and Europe*. Belfast, 1994.

McARTHUR, C. (ed.) *Scotch Reels: Scotland in Cinema and Television*. London, 1982.

MAYER, J.P. *British Cinemas and their Audiences*. London, 1948.

MERCER, K. (ed.) *Black Film, British Cinema*. London, 1988.

MURPHY, R. *The British Cinema Book*, London, 2001.

OAKLEY, C. *Where We Came In: The Story of the British Cinematograph Industry*. London, 1964.

PALMER, S. *British Film Actors' Credits, 1895–1987*. Jefferson, North Carolina, 1988.

PARK, J. *British Cinema: The Lights that Failed*. London, 1990.

The Penguin Film Review West Drayton, later Harmondsworth, 1946–49.

PERRY, G. *The Great British Picture Show*. London, 1974.

PETRIE, D. *Screening Scotland*. London, 2000.

ROCKETT, K. *et al. Cinema and Ireland*. London, 1987.

RICHARDS, J. *Films and British National Identity*. 1997.

RYALL, T. *Britain and the American Cinema*. London, 2001.

SELLAR, M. *Best of British*. London, 1987.

SLIDE, A. *50 Classic British Films 1932–82*. New York, 1985.

SPICER, A. *Typical Men: The Representation of Masculinity in Popular British Cinema*. London, 2001.

STAPLES, T. *All Pals Together: The Story of Children's Cinema*. London, 1994.

STEAD, P. *Film and the Working Class: The Feature Film in British And American Society*. London, 1989.

STREET, S. *British National Cinema*. London, 1997.

TAYLOR, J. R. and KOBAL, J. *Portraits of the British Cinema*, London, 1985.

VERMILYE, J. *The Great British Films*. Secaucus, NJ: Citadel, 1978.

WARREN, P. *British Cinema in Pictures: The British Film Collection*. London, 1993.

Particular periods

ALDGATE, A. and RICHARDS, J. *Britain Can Take It: The British Cinema in the Second World War*. Oxford, 1986.

ALLON, Y. *et al* (eds) *Contemporary British and Irish Film Directors*. London, 2001.

AUTY, M. and RODDICK, N. *British Cinema Now*, 1985.

BARNES, J. *The Beginnings of Cinema in England 1894–1901.* (5 vols) Exeter, 1996–98.

BOURNE, S. *Brief Encounters: Lesbians and Gays in British Cinema 1930–1971.* London, 1996.

BRITISH FILM INSTITUTE. *BFI Film and Television Handbook.* London, annually from 1983.

CHANAN, C. *The Dream That Kicks.* London, 1980.

CHAPMAN, J. *The British Cinema at War: Cinema, State and Propaganda, 1939–1945.* London, 1998.

COULTASS, C. *Images for Battle: British Film and the Second World War, 1939–1945.* London, 1989.

DRAZIN, C. *The Finest Years: British Cinema of the 1940s.* London, 1998.

DURGNAT, R. *A Mirror for England: British Movies from Austerity to Affluence.* London, 1970.

FIELD, M. *The Story of the Children's Entertainment Film Movement in Great Britain 1943–1950.* London, 1952.

FORMAN, D. *Films 1945–1950.* London, 1951.

FRIEDMAN, L. (ed.) *British Cinema and Thatcherism: Fires Were Started.* London, 1993.

GLEDHILL, C. and SWANSON, G. (eds) *Nationalising Femininity: Culture, Sexuality and British Cinema in the Second World War.* Manchester, 1996.

HIGSON, A. (ed.) *Young and Innocent? The Cinema in Britain 1896–1930.* Exeter, 2002.

HOGENKAMP, B. *Deadly Parallels: Film and the Left in Britain.* London, 1997.

HILL, J. *Sex, Class and Realism: British Cinema 1956–63.* London, 1986.

HILL, J. *British Cinema in the 1980s: Issues and Themes.* Oxford, 1999.

HUNTLEY, J. *British Technicolor Films.* London, 1949.

HURD, G. (ed.) *National Fictions: World War Two in British Films and Television.* London, 1984.

JONES, S.G. *The British Labour Movement and Film, 1918–1939.* London, 1987.

LANT, A. *Blackout: Reinventing Women for Wartime British Cinema.* Princeton, 1991.

LOW, R. *The History of the British Film* (7 vols): Vol 1 *1896–1906* (1948), Vol 2 *1906–1914* (1949), Vol 3 *1914–18* (1950), Vol 4 *1918–29* (1971), Vol 5 *Documentary and Educational Films of the 1930s* (1979), Vol 6 *Films of Comment and Persuasion* (1979), Vol 7 *Filmmaking in 1930s Britain* (1985). London.

McGILLIVRAY, D. *Doing Rude Things: The History of the British Sex Film 1957–1981.* London, 1992.

MACPHERSON, D. *Traditions of Independence: British Cinema in the Thirties.* London, 1980.

MORGAN, G. *Red Roses Every Night: An Account of London's Cinemas Under Fire.* London, 1948.

MURPHY, R. *British Cinema and the Second World War.* London, 2000.

MURPHY, R. (ed.) *British Cinema of the 90s.* London, 2000.

MURPHY, R. *Realism and Tinsel: Cinema and Society in Britain 1939–1948.* London, 1989.

MURPHY, R. *Sixties British Cinema.* London, 1992.

PARK, J. *Learning to Dream: The New British Cinema.* 1984.

PETRIE, D. *Creativity and Constraint: Contemporary British Cinema.* London, 1990.

QUINLAN, D. *British Sound Films: The Studio Years.* London, 1984.

RICHARDS, J. and ALDGATE, A. *Best of British: Cinema and Society 1930–1970.* Oxford, 1983.

RICHARDS, J. *The Age of the Dream Palace: Cinema and Society in Britain 1929–39.* London, 1984.

RICHARDS, J. *The Unknown 1930s: An Alternative History of the British Cinema 1929–39.* London, 1998.

RICHARDS, J. and SHERIDAN, D. (eds) *Mass-Observation at the Movies.* London, 1987.

SEDGWICK, J. *Popular Filmgoing in 1930s Britain: A Choice of Pleasures.* Exeter, 2000.

SHAFER, S. *British Popular Films 1929–39: The Cinema of Reassurance,* London, 1997.

SINYARD, N. and MCKILLOP, I. (eds) *British Cinema in the 50s.* Manchester, 2003.

TAYLOR, P. (ed.) *Britain and the Cinema in the Second World War.* London, 1974.

WALKER, A. *Hollywood England: British Cinema in the Sixties.* London, 1986.

WALKER, A. *National Heroes: British Cinema in the Seventies and Eighties.* London, 1985.

WILLIAMS, T. *Structures of Desire: British Cinema 1939–1955.* Albany, NY, 2000.

Film-makers

(See individual entries for memoirs, biographies and autobiographies; some critical monographs may be repeated here, but essentially biographical works are not.)

AITKEN, I. *Alberto Cavalcanti: Realism, Surrealism and National Cinemas.* Trowbridge, 2000.

BABINGTON, B. *British Stars and Stardom.* Manchester, 2001.

BABINGTON, B. (ed.) *Launder and Gilliat.* Manchester, 2001.

BARR, C. *English Hitchcock,* Moffat, 1999.

BROWN, G. *Launder and Gilliat,* London, 1977.

BROWN, G. *Walter Forde.* London, 1977.

BROWN, G., with Tony Aldgate, *The Common Touch – The Films of John Baxter.* London, 1989.

BROWN, G. and KARDISH, L. *Michael Balcon: the Pursuit of British Cinema.* New York, 1984.

BURTON, A. *et al* (eds) *Liberal Directions: Basil Dearden and Postwar British Film Culture.* Trowbridge, 1997.

BURTON, A. *et al* (eds) *The Family Way: The Boulting Brothers and British Film Culture.* Trowbridge, 1997.

CARRICK, E. *Art and Design in the British Film.* London, 1948

CHIBNALL, S. *J. Lee Thompson.* Manchester, 2001.

CHRISTIE, I. *Powell, Pressburger and Others.* London, 1978.

CHRISTIE, I. *Arrows of Desire: The Films of Michael Powell and Emeric Pressburger.* London, 1994.

COVENEY, M. *The World According to Mike Leigh.* London, 1996.

DICK, E. *et al* (eds) *Bill Douglas: A Lanternist's Account.* London, 1993.

DIXON, W.W. *The Films of Freddie Francis.* Metuchen, NJ/London, 1991.

GOUGH-YATES, K. *Michael Powell in Collaboration with Emeric Pressburger.* London, 1971.

GRANT, I. *Cameramen at War.* Cambridge, 1980.

HACKER, J. and PRICE, D. *Take Ten: Contemporary British Film Directors.* Oxford, 1991.

HANKE, K. *Ken Russell's Films.* Metuchen, NJ/London, 1984.

HUNTLEY, J. *British Film Music.* London, 1972.

HUTCHINGS, P. *Terence Fisher.* Manchester, 2002.

JOHNSON, L. and JONES, G. (eds) *Talking Pictures: Interviews with Contemporary British Film-makers*. London, 1997.

KEMP, P. *Lethal Innocence: The Cinema of Alexander Mackendrick*. London, 1991.

LAWRENCE, A. *The Films of Peter Greenaway*. Cambridge, 1997.

MACNAB, G. *J. Arthur Rank and the British Film Industry*. London, 1992.

MACNAB, G. *Searching for Stars: Stardom and Screen Acting in British Cinema*. London, 2000.

McFARLANE, B. *An Autobiography of British Cinema*. London, 1997.

McFARLANE, B. *Sixty Voices: Celebrities Recall the Golden Age of British Cinema*. London, 1992.

McFARLANE, B. *Lance Comfort*. Manchester, 1999.

McKNIGHT, G. (ed.) *Agent of Challenge and Defiance: The Films of Ken Loach*. Trowbridge, 1997.

NOBLE, P. (ed.) *British Screen Stars*. London, 1946.

PETRIE, D. *The British Cinematographer*. London, 1996.

PETRIE, D. *Inside Stories: Diaries of British Film-makers at Work*. London, 1996.

PETTIGREW, T. *British Character Actors: Great Names and Memorable Moments*. London, 1982.

RICHARDS, J. *Thorold Dickinson and the British Cinema*. London, 1997.

RYALL, T. *Alfred Hitchcock and the British Cinema*. London, 1986.

SILVER, A. and URSINI, J. *David Lean and His Films*. London, 1974.

SINYARD, N. *The Films of Richard Lester*. Beckenham, 1985.

SINYARD, N. *Jack Clayton*. Manchester, 2000.

SUROWIEC, C. *Accent on Design: Four European Art Directors*. London, 1992.

WILDE, J. *British and Irish Cinematography Credits*. 2001.

YULE, A. *Enigma: David Puttnam, the Story So Far*. London, 1989.

Studios and production companies

BARR, C. *Ealing Studios*. London, 1993 (revised edition).

COOK, P. (ed.) *Gainsborough Pictures*. London, 1997.

EBERTS, J. and ILOTT, T. *My Indecision Is Final*. London, 1990.

EYLES, A. *et al* (eds) *The House of Horror: The Story of Hammer Films*. London, 1973.

FALK, Q. *The Golden Gong: Fifty Years of the Rank Organisation*. London, 1987.

FINNEY, A. *The Egos Have Landed: The Rise and Fall of Palace Pictures*. London, 1996.

LUKINS, J. *The Fantasy Factory: Lime Grove Studios, London 1915–1991*. London, 1996.

MEIKLE, D. *A History of Horrors: The Rise and Fall of the House of Hammer*. Lanham, MD/London, 1996.

OWEN, G. and BURFORD, B. *The Pinewood Story*. Richmond, Surrey, 2000.

PERRY, G. *Forever Ealing*. Fakenham, 1981.

PERRY, G. *Movies from the Mansion: A History of Pinewood Studios*. London, 1976.

STOCKHAM, M. *The Korda Collection: Alexander Korda's Film Classics*. London, 1992.

THREADGALL, D. *Shepperton Studios: An Independent View*. London, 1994.

WARREN, P. *British Film Studios: An Illustrated History*. London, 2001 (revised edition).

WARREN, P. *Elstree: The British Hollywood*. London, 1983.

WILLIAMS, P.M. and WILLIAMS, D.L. *Hooray for Jollywood: The Life of John E. Blakeley & The Mancunian Film Corporation*. London, 2001.

WILSON, D. (ed.) *Projecting Britain: Ealing Film Posters*. London, 1982.

Genre

ASPINALL, S. and MURPHY, R. *Gainsborough Melodrama*. London, 1983.

BENNETT, T. and WOOLLACOTT, J. *Bond and Beyond: The Political Career of a Popular Hero*. Basingstoke, 1987.

BURTON, A. and PETLEY, J. (eds) *Journal of Popular British Cinema: No. 1 Genre and British Cinema*. Trowbridge, 1998.

CHAPMAN, J. *Licence to Thrill: A Cultural History of the James Bond Films*. London, 1999.

CHIBNALL, S. and MURPHY, R. *British Crime Cinema*. London, 1999.

DONNELLY, K.J. *Pop Music in British Cinema: A Chronicle*. London, 2001.

GERAGHTY, C. *British Cinema in the Fifties: Gender, Genre and The 'New Look'*. London, 2000.

HARPER, S. *Picturing the Past: The Rise and Fall of the British Costume Film*. London, 1994.

HUNTER, I.Q. *British Science Fiction Cinema*. London, 1999.

HUTCHINGS, P. *Hammer and Beyond: The British Horror Film*. Manchester, 1973.

LANDY, M. *British Genres: Cinema and Society, 1930–1960*. Princeton, 1991.

LAY, S. *British Social Realism*. London, 2002.

PIRIE, D. *A Heritage of Horror: The English Gothic Cinema 1946–1972*. London, 1973.

RIGBY, J. *English Gothic*. London, 2000.

ROSS, R. *The Carry On Companion*. London, 1996.

SUTTON, D. *A Chorus of Raspberries: British Film Comedy 1929–1939*. Exeter, 2000.

THOMPSON, J.O. *Monty Python: Complete and Utter Theory of the Grotesque*. London, 1982.

Industry, exhibition, legislation and regulation

ALDGATE, A. *Censorship and the Permissive Society: British Cinema and Theatre 1955–1965*. Oxford, 1995.

ATWELL, D. *Cathedrals of the Movies: A History of the British Cinemas and Their Audiences*. London, 1980.

BRITISH FILM ACADEMY. *The Film Industry in Great Britain: Some Facts and Figures*. London, *c* 1950.

DICKINSON, M. and STREET, S. *Cinema and State: The Film Industry and the British Government 1927–84*. London, 1985.

DOCHERTY, D. *et al*. *The Last Picture Show? Britain's Changing Film Audiences*. London, 1987.

EYLES, A. *ABC, The First Name in Entertainment*. London, 1993.

EYLES, A. *Gaumont British Cinemas*. London, 1996.

EYLES, A. *Odeon Cinemas 1: Oscar Deutsch Entertains Our Nation*. London, 2001.

HIGSON, A. and MALTBY, R. (eds.) *'Film Europe' and 'Film America': Cinema, Commerce and Cultural Exchange, 1920–1939.* Exeter, 1999.

JARVIE, I. *Hollywood's Overseas Campaign: The North Atlantic Movie Trade, 1920–1950.* Cambridge, 1992.

KELLY, T. *et al. A Competitive Cinema.* London, 1966.

MANVELL, R. *A Seat at the Cinema.* London, 1951.

MATHEWS, T.D. *Censored.* London, 1994.

MINNEY, R.J. *Talking of Films.* London, 1947.

POLITICAL AND ECONOMIC PLANNING *The British Film Industry.* London, 1952.

POLITICAL AND ECONOMIC PLANNING *The British Film Industry 1958.* London, 1958.

PORTER, V. *On Cinema.* London, 1985.

PUTTNAM, D. *The Undeclared War: The Struggle for Control of the World's Film Industry.* London, 1997.

ROBERTSON, J.C. *The British Board of Film Censors, 1896–1956.* London, 1895.

ROBERTSON, J.C. *The Hidden Cinema: British Film Censorship in Action, 1913–1972.* London, 1989.

SLIDE, A. *Banned in the USA: British Films in the United States and Their Censorship, 1933–60.* London, 1998.

SPRAOS, J. *The Decline of the Cinema: An Economist's Report.* London, 1962.

STREET, S. *British Cinema in Documents.* London, 2000.

STREET, S. *Transatlantic Crossings: British Feature Films in the USA.* London, 2002.

TREVELYAN, J. *What the Censor Saw.* London, 1973.

Individual films

ANDERSON, L. *Making a Film: The Story of 'Secret People'.* London, 1952.

BILBOW, M. *To the Devil a Daughter – The Facts About a Feature Film.* Ultimo, NSW, 1978.

BROWNLOW, K. *How It Happened Here.* London, 1968.

BUSCOMBE, E. *Making 'Legend of the Werewolf'.* London, 1976.

COLLIER, J.W. *A Film in the Making: 'It Always Rains on Sunday'.* London, 1947.

DEANS, M. *Meeting at the Sphinx: Caesar and Cleopatra.* London, 1946.

DRAZIN, C. *In Search of 'The Third Man'.* London, 1999.

DYER, R. *Brief Encounter.* London, 1993.

FRAYLING, C. *Things to Come.* London, 1995.

GEDULD, H.M. *Filmguide to Henry V.* Bloomington, 1973.

GILES, J. *The Crying Game.* London, 1997.

HOUSTON, P. *Went the Day Well?* London, 1992.

JAMES, D. *'Scott of the Antarctic': The Film and Its Production.* London, 1948.

KENT, H. *Single Bed for Three: A 'Lawrence of Arabia' Notebook.* London, 1963.

RYALL, T. *Blackmail.* London, 1993.

SANDERSON, M. *Don't Look Now.* London, 1997.

VAUGHAN, D. *Odd Man Out.* London, 1995.

WOOD, R. *The Wings of the Dove.* London, 2000.

Collections of British critics

AGATE, J. *Around Cinemas.* (2 vols) London, 1946, 1948.

ANSTEY, E. *et al. Shots in the Dark.* London, 1951.

COOK, C. (ed.) *The Dilys Powell Film Reader.* Oxford, 1992.

GREENE, G. *The Pleasure-Dome: The Collected Film Criticism 1935–40.* London, 1972.

HARDY, F. (ed.) *Grierson on the Movies.* London, 1981.

LEJEUNE, A. (ed.) *The C.A. Lejeune Film Reader.* Manchester, 1991.

LEJEUNE, C.A. *Chestnuts in Her Lap 1936–1947.* London, 1947.

PARKINSON, D. (ed.) *The Graham Greene Film Reader: Mornings in the Dark.* Manchester, 1993.

POWELL, D. *The Golden Screen: Fifty Years of Films.* London, 1989.

ROTHA, P. *Rotha on the Film: A Selection of Writings about the Cinema.* London, 1958.

ROTHA, P. (ed.) *Richard Winnington: Film Criticism and Caricatures 1943–53.* London, 1975.

WINNINGTON, R. *Drawn and Quartered: A Selection of Weekly Film Reviews and Drawings.* London, *c* 1948.

Documentary and non-fiction film

AITKEN, I. *Film and Reform: John Grierson and the Documentary Film Movement.* London, 1990.

AITKEN, I. (ed.) *The Documentary Movement: An Anthology.* Edinburgh, 1998.

ALDGATE, A. *Cinema and History: British Newsreels and the Spanish Civil War.* London, 1979.

BALLANTYNE, J. *Researcher's Guide to British Newsreels* (3 vols). London, 1983, 1988, 1993.

HARDY, F. (ed.) *Grierson on Documentary.* London, 1966.

Informational Film and Television Yearbook. London, from 1947.

LOVELL, A. and HILLIER, J. *Studies in Documentary.* London, 1972.

LOW, R. *The History of the British Film: Documentary and Educational Films of the 1930s.* London, 1979.

McKERNAN, L. *Topical Budget: The Great British News Film.* London, 1992.

ROTHA, P. *Documentary Diary: An Informal History of the British Documentary Film, 1928–1939.* London, 1973.

SUSSEX, E. *The Rise and Fall of British Documentary: The Story of the Film Movement Founded by John Grierson.* London, 1975.

THORPE, F. and PRONAY, N. *British Official Films in the Second World War: a Descriptive Catalogue.* Oxford, 1980.

Art cinema and independent cinema.

CURTISS, D. and DUSINBERRE, D. (eds) *A Perspective on English Avant-Garde Film.* London, 1978.

KNIGHT, D. and PORTER, V. *A Long Look at Short Films.* London, 1967.

LOVELL, A. (ed.) *British Film Institute Production Board.* London, 1976.

O'PRAY, M. (ed.) *The British Avant-Garde Film, 1926–1995: An Anthology of Writings.* London, 1996.

RANK ORGANISATION. *No Case for Compulsion.* London, 1967.

REES, A.L. *A History of Experimental Film and Video.* London, 1999.

STONEMAN, R. and THOMPSON, H. (ed.) *The New Social Function of Cinema: Catalogue of British Film Institute Productions 1979/80.* London, 1981.

PICTURE CREDITS

The editors and publisher acknowledge with thanks the following organisations for permission to use the illustrations contained in this encyclopedia. Every effort has been made to trace copyright owners for the use of illustrations. If any errors or omissions have accidentally occurred, they will be corrected in subsequent editions if notification is sent to the publisher.

Comin' Thro' the Rye – Max Fleischer Studio; *The Rat* – Gainsborough Pictures; *The Private Life of Henry VIII* – London Film Productions/Carlton; *The Last Journey* – Twickenham Film Studios Productions/BBC; *Tudor Rose* – Gainsborough Pictures/Carlton; *First a Girl* – Gaumont British Picture Corporation/Carlton; *South Riding* – London Film Productions; *Keep Smiling* – Twentieth Century Production Ltd/20th Century Fox; *The Four Feathers* – London Film Productions/Carlton; *The First of the Few* – © British Aviation Pictures; *The Way to the Stars* – Two Cities Films/Carlton; *Fame is the Spur* – Two Cities Films/Rank UK/Pathé; *Temptation Harbour* – Associated British Picture Corporation; *Blanche Fury* – Cineguild/Independent Producers; *Black Narcissus* – © Independent Producers/Carlton; *The Fallen Idol* – London Film Productions/British Lion; *Trottie True* – Two Cities Films/Carlton; *Passport to Pimlico* – Ealing Studios/Canal +; *Gone to Earth* – © London Film Productions/Pearson's; *The Happiest Days of Your Life* – Individual Pictures/British Lion Film Corporation/Canal+; *The Wooden Horse* – London Film Productions/Wessex Film Productions/British Lion Film Corporation/Canal+; *Genevieve* – © Sirius Productions/Carlton; *Ice Cold in Alex* – Associated British Picture Corporation/Canal+; *A Night to Remember* – Rank Organisation Film Productions/Carlton; *Carry On Sergeant* – © Anglo Amalgamated Film Distributors/Canal+; *The Curse of Frankenstein* – Hammer Film Productions/Clarion/Warners; *Room at the Top* – Remus Films-Continental/Lion International Films UK; *Sapphire* – Artna Films/Carlton; *A Warm December* – Verdon Productions/First Artists Productions; *Saturday Night and Sunday Morning* – Woodfall Film Productions/MGM; *A Taste of Honey* – Woodfall Film Productions/MGM; *Lawrence of Arabia* – © Horizon Pictures,

Columbia; *A Hard Day's Night* – Proscenium Film Ltd; *Darling* – Vic Film Ltd/Appia Films/Canal+; *Accident* – Royal Avenue Chelsea Productions/Canal+; *if . . .* – Memorial Enterprises/Paramount Pictures Corporation/UIP; *Women in Love* – Brandywine Productions/Warners; *Performance* – Warner Bros/Goodtimes Enterprises; *Confessions of A Window Cleaner* – Swiftdown Productions/ Columbia UK Ltd; *The Day of the Jackal* – Warwick Film Productions/Universal Productions France; *Murder on the Orient Express* – © EMI Film Distributors/Canal+; *Chariots of Fire* – Enigma Productions/Twentieth Century-Fox Film Corporation/Allied Stars; *Gandhi* – Indo-British Films/International Film Investors/Goldcrest Films International/National Film Development Corporation; *My Beautiful Laundrette* – Working Title Films/SAF Productions/Channel Four; *A Letter to Brezhnev* – Yeardream/Film Four International/Palace Productions; *Distant Voices, Still Lives* – Channel Four/British Film Institute Production/Zweites deutsches fernsehen; *Howards End* – FilmFour International; *The Cook, the Thief, His Wife and Her Lover* – Allarts Enterprises/Erato Films/Films Inc./Elsevier-Vendex Film Beheer; *Riff-Raff* – © Channel Four; *Shallow Grave* – Channel Four/Figment Films; *Four Weddings and a Funeral* – Working Title Films/Channel Four/Universal; *Secrets & Lies* – CiBy 2000/Thin Man Films/Channel Four Films; *The Remains of the Day* – Merchant Ivory Productions Ltd; *Life is Sweet* – Thin Man Films/Film Four International/British Screen; *Trainspotting* – Channel Four Films/Figment Films/Noel Gay Motion Picture Company; *My Name is Joe* – Parallax (Joe) Ltd/Road Movies Vierte Produktionen GmbH; *East is East* – © Film Four Ltd; *Wonderland* – © Polygram Films (UK) Ltd; *Room with a View* – Merchant Ivory Productions Ltd/Goldcrest/Universal; *Onegin* – © Onegin Productions Limited; *Shakespeare in Love* – © Miramax Films/© Universal Pictures; *Billy Elliot* – © Tiger Aspect, Arts Council of England, BBC, Universal; *Elizabeth* – © Polygram Filmed Entertainment, Inc; *About a Boy* – © Tribeca/Working Title Films/KALIMA Productions GmbH and Co. KG/Universal/StudioCanal.